# BOOKS FOR COLLEGE LIBRARIES

# BOOKS
# FOR COLLEGE
# LIBRARIES

A CORE COLLECTION OF 50,000 TITLES

*Third edition*

A project of the Association of College and Research Libraries

Volume 5

Psychology · Science · Technology · Bibliography

American Library Association
*Chicago and London 1988*

Preliminary pages composed by Impressions, Inc.,
    in Times Roman on a Penta-driven
    Autologic APS-$\mu$5
    Phototypesetting system

Text pages composed by Logidec, Inc., in Times Roman on an
    APS-5 digital typesetter

Printed on 50 lb. Glatfelter B-16, a pH neutral stock,
    and bound in Roxite B-grade cloth by
    Edwards Brothers.

The paper used in this publication meets the minimum
requirements of American National Standard for Information
Sciences—Permanence of Paper for Printed Library Materials,
ANSI Z39.48-1984.

**Library of Congress Cataloging-in-Publication Data**

Books for college libraries.

"A project of the Association of College and Research
Libraries."

Contents: v. 1.  Humanities—v. 2.  Language
and literature—v. 3.  History—[etc.]
1.  Libraries, University and college—Book
lists.  2.  Bibliography—Best books.  I.  Association of
College and Research Libraries.
Z1039.C65B67  1988      025.2'1877      88-16714
ISBN 0-8389-3357-2 (v. 1)
ISBN 0-8389-3356-4 (v. 2)
ISBN 0-8389-3355-6 (v. 3)
ISBN 0-8389-3354-8 (v. 4)
ISBN 0-8389-3358-0 (v. 5)
ISBN 0-8389-3359-9 (v. 6)

Copyright © 1988 by the American Library Association.
All rights reserved except those which may be granted by
Sections 107 and 108 of the Copyright Revision Act of 1976.
Printed in the United States of America.

# BOOKS FOR COLLEGE LIBRARIES

# Volumes 1–6    Contents

# Volume 5   Contents

# Contents

# Introduction

Books for College Libraries (BCL3) presents a third recommended core collection for undergraduate libraries in full awareness of the tensions and paradoxes implicit in such list making. There is the pull between ideals of excellence and sufficient coverage of all subjects. There is the balance to be weighed among subjects. There are the rival temptations to identify the basic with the time tested and to equate the important with the new. There is the risk of ranking with the obsolete the merely temporary victims of scholarly fashion. There is the certainty that new definitive works will be published just as the selection closes.

That BCL3 exists supposes some resolution of these problems. A final paradox remains: BCL3 can fully succeed only by failing. It would be disastrous should the collection it suggests serve perfectly to ratify the finished work of the book selection in any library. Some inclusions and some omissions should displease everyone; for on-going professional questioning and the search for individual library answers remain as basic to collection development as basic book lists.

In overall plan and appearance, BCL3 is much the same as BCL2 (1975). The division into five volumes takes the same liberties with Library of Congress classification to provide coherent subject groups and volumes similar in size. Individual entries contain the same elements of full cataloging and classification information; and within volumes, entries are arranged in exact call number order.

BCL3 also exists as a database to allow further development of formats alternative to print. An electronic tape version will be made available. Since BCL2, online catalogs and reference databases have become familiar library tools. The provision of BCL3 in searchable form is thus important; and it may add possible uses of the list within larger libraries—easy identification of key titles in very large online catalogs, for instance.

## HISTORY

The first bibliography to bear this title was published in 1967 as a replacement for Charles B. Shaw's *List of Books for College Libraries* (1931). The origin of BCL1 was in the University of California's New Campuses Program (1961–1964), which also made use of other compilations such as the published catalog of Harvard's Lamont Library (1953) and the shelflist of the undergraduate library of the University of Michigan. The 1963 cut-off date for BCL1 titles deliberately coincided with the 1964 beginning of *Choice*, whose current reviews for academic libraries were foreseen as a complementary, on-going revision and supplement. Such a role proved impossible, however, even for so comprehensive a journal as *Choice* with its 6,600 reviews a year and its retrospective evaluation of perhaps another 1,000 titles in topical monthly bibliographic essays. Periodic reassessments that could include categories of material not usually reviewed by *Choice* (revisions, fiction, works published abroad, for instance) seemed still an essential aid in college library collection development. BCL2 appeared in 1975; work on BCL3 began in late 1985.

## SIZE AND SCOPE: STANDARDS, LIBRARIES AND BOOK LISTS

The number of books of which college libraries need potentially to be aware continues its relentless growth. In the years from the Shaw list to BCL1, total annual United States book output averaged slightly more than 11,500 volumes. Between the cut-off dates for BCL1 and BCL2, that figure (revised to show titles, a lesser number) was just under 32,000. Since the 1973 BCL2 cut-off, the annual average has been 41,000.[1] Given such increase, the task of book selectors would be challenging enough, even had the growth of buildings and book budgets characteristic of the late 1960s and early 1970s continued. By the time BCL2 was published, however, the rate of academic library book acquisitions had begun to fall. This downward trend continues, and it makes careful title selection ever more vital, especially for the small library.[2]

When BCL1 was published, the already outdated 1959 standards for college libraries called for a minimum undergraduate collection of only 50,000 titles; BCL1 recommended 53,400. BCL2 and the 1975 revision of those standards appeared in the same year. The new standards set out a formula whose add-on stipulations plus a starting figure of 85,000 raised basic requirements for even very small institutions to 100,000. The 1970 proposal for BCL2 called for a list of 40,000 titles. The thinking behind this lower figure may be explained by a published study of 1977 library

[1]*Bowker Annual of Library & Book Trade Information.* New York: Bowker. 26th ed., 1981; 32nd ed., 1987.

[2]"Three Years of Change in College and University Libraries, Prepared by the National Center for Education Statistics, Washington, D.C." *College & Research Libraries News* 45 (July/August 1984): 359–361.

statistics against the 1975 standards. This analysis found that 52 percent of all undergraduate libraries still reported fewer than 100,000 volumes and that 55 percent of private undergraduate libraries held even fewer than the "starter" figure of 85,000.[3] A very brief basic list might thus serve rather than intimidate the many libraries still far below standard.

The college library standards were revised again in 1985, just as work on BCL3 began.[4] The same formula (Standard 2.2, Formula A) was recommended. Applying it to a very small hypothetical college of 100 faculty and 1,000 students pursuing majors in only 10 fields of study yields a basic book requirement of 104,000 volumes. BCL3 suggests about half that number, hoping again to pause somewhere between usefulness and utopia. Very recent figures show that the average book expenditures for academic libraries in 26 U.S. states fall below the figure that would be necessary to meet the median annual growth rate of our hypothetical library, also set by the 1985 standards.[5]

In scope, the focus of BCL3 remains the traditionally book-using disciplines. Contributors were asked to keep in mind an imaginary college or small university that concentrates on the customary liberal arts and sciences curriculum but also offers work at the undergraduate level in business, computer science, engineering, and the health sciences. The proportions of the broad subject groupings by volume have remained roughly constant through the three BCL editions. (See Table 1.) There have been steady decreases in the humanities and literature allocations, however, very slightly offset by increased use of single-entry "complete works" citations that include large numbers of titles.

These changes have come about despite editorial quotas candidly designed to minimize them. Sharp

[3]Ray L. Carpenter, "College Libraries: A Comparative Analysis in Terms of the ACRL Standards," *College and Research Libraries* 42 (January 1981): 7–18.

[4]"Standards for College Libraries, 1986, Prepared by the College Library Standards Committee, Jacquelyn M. Morris, chair," *College & Research Libraries News* 47 (March 1986): 189–200.

[5]*Bowker Annual of Library & Book Trade Information.* 32nd ed. New York: Bowker, 1987. The preceding calculation by the BCL editor is based on figures given in the *Bowker Annual* using the formula in the standards cited in note 4.

difficulties confront both BCL editors and librarians juggling hopes for lasting value, necessities for current coverage, and the certainties of obsolescence. Some of the growth in Volume 5 is attributable to a marked increase in its bibliography component, which serves all subjects; but it may be well to repeat, with reference both to Volume 4 and to Volume 5, a statement from my BCL2 introduction that "Perhaps only those works already sufficiently outdated to be ranked as history may safely be included in a 'basic' collection." Despite their increases, both volumes remain brief in comparison with the volume of publication.

As to those titles constituting the rest of the minimal 104,000 requirement but not named in BCL3, much of any collection must respond uniquely to the demands of individual and current curricula. But some, it is to be hoped, will continue to consist of those works, especially belles lettres, not subject to cumulation and replacement by current scholarship. These are often difficult to continue to justify in lists which though "basic" cannot remain immune to shifts in academic enthusiasms.

Across these proportionate subject representations, the focus remains the undergraduate user of the undergraduate library. Both are protean concepts, but they permit some limitation, for instance almost wholly to works in English except for dictionaries and editions chosen to support foreign-language study. With the exception of some of the more basic surveys among "annual reviews" and some serial reference works, the limitation is not only to print but, further, to monographs. There is a need for college-level model collections of periodicals and of nonprint material, but this project does not address it. Still further to define the print universe, BCL3 contributors were asked not to recommend classroom texts unless exceptional, especially for their bibliographies. Volumes of previously published works are seldom listed except for literary anthologies which, together with their indexes, received special consideration in this edition. In-print availability was not considered an important factor.

## CONTRIBUTORS AND WORKING MATERIALS

BCL3 was from the beginning designed as a two-stage selection process and there were two distinct sets

**Table 1. Distribution of Titles by Volume. (In percentages.)**

| Volumes & Subjects | BCL1 | BCL2 | BCL3 |
|---|---|---|---|
| v. 1 (Humanities) | 16.4 | 15.1 | 13.6 |
| v. 2 (Language & Literature) | 32.2 | 30.0 | 28.4 |
| v. 3 (History) | 18.7 | 19.7 | 18.8 |
| v. 4 (Social Sciences) | 20.8 | 21.2 | 22.2 |
| v. 5 (Psychology, Science, Technology, Bibliography) | 11.9 | 14.0 | 17.0 |

of contributors. The first-round team numbered more than 400 college faculty members and about 50 academic reference librarians who made the reference selections. The second group consisted of 64 academic librarian referees, picked for their combination of subject specialization and collection development skills. The librarian referees were asked to review broader subject areas than their faculty counterparts with the intent of adding a wider perspective to help assure the overall coverage and balance to the collection.

Virtually all of the first-round contributors and about half of the second-round referees are *Choice* reviewers. They were selected for excellence, needed subject coverage, altruism (all served unpaid), and availability at the crucial time. (A few sabbaticals were much regretted in the BCL office.) Contributors were not selected with statistical games in mind, but it is an interesting if incidental function of the nature of the *Choice* reviewer pool that they prove a nationally representative lot. They come from 265 institutions in 44 states. The 10 states with the most academic institutions provide 8 of the 10 largest contributor groups. Institutions are divided between public, including federal (145) and private (120), with a mix of small and large from each sector. There are 10 representatives of 2-year campuses. There are 134 women. There are 15 Canadian and 2 British contributors.

As working materials, the round-one contributors received pages from BCL2 (latest titles 1973) and selected *Choice* review cards (1972 through 1985). Approximately 60,000 of some 85,000 reviews published in those years were distributed. Contributors were asked to assign one of four rankings to each title; they were also urged to recommend any other titles they felt essential to undergraduate work in their fields. Many did so. Assignments, some of which overlapped, ranged from 25 to 600 titles.

Preparation of 450 packets of working lists involved the fascinating task of reconciling various assumptions about the organization of knowledge. It was necessary to "deconstruct" and rearrange the LC-classed BCL2 and the subject organization of *Choice* to match the convictions of academics as to just what constituted the definitions and boundaries of their subjects.

## COMPILATION AND REVIEW

Working list packets came back displaying varying neatness, erudition, zeal, and attention to editorial instructions and deadlines. A very few were reassigned; most were extremely well done and miraculously on time. All titles rated "essential" (and some lesser ratings, depending on subject coverage and the rigor of contributor selectivity) were requested, by LC card number if possible, from the Utlas database. (Utlas, the Canadian bibliographic utility, had previously been

selected as the vendor to house the BCL3 database while the collection was being compiled.)

As lists came in and major blocks of LC classification were judged to be reasonably complete, Utlas was asked to produce provisional catalogs in LC class order, showing complete catalog records. These catalogs, after review by the editor, were divided among the second-round referees, whose assignments typically included the work of several first-round contributors. Referees were asked to assess overall quality and suitability of the selections, coverage of the various aspects of a field, and compliance with numerical quotas. The editor's review included the making and insertion of page headings and further observations of (and occasional interventions in) rival views of knowledge as the academic visions of round one were once more refracted through the prism, the worldview of LC classification. A second set of provisional catalogs, reviewed by the editor's assistant, incorporated referee suggestions and the page headings for a final check before typesetting.

## PRESENTATION: HEADINGS, ENTRIES, AND ARRANGEMENT

Page headings are phrased to outline LC classification, to gloss the sometimes very miscellaneous contents of the sections they head, and to indicate the method of arrangement of some special sequences. The printed BCL3 entries contain conventionally complete cataloging and classification information, but not every element of a full LC MARC record. Among notes, only the general (MARC tag 500) are printed; cross-reference and authority information tagged in the 800s is omitted. Those entries for items retained from BCL2 in exactly the same version carry a special symbol, a heavy dot (.) preceding the item number. Entries are sequentially numbered within each volume. The cataloging in some of the entries made by contributors to the Utlas database is less full than the original LC cataloging; some entries vary in other ways.

Database response to titles requested for the collection displayed significant changes since the compilation of BCL2. During that project, both LC MARC and electronic cataloging and bibliographic utilities were new. Nearly two-thirds of BCL2 entries had to be converted especially for that project. BCL3 is in some ways the victim of the success of such cataloging enterprises. There are now many versions of catalog records, especially for pre-1968 titles. These offer varying degrees of adoption of AACR2 and equally various and often unsignalled states of adherence to LC classification, to say nothing of the range of simple cataloging and typing skills. It is therefore impossible to repeat here the certainties of the BCL2 Introduction about the use of LC cataloging and classification, although preference was certainly for LC records. Call numbers completed or assigned by BCL are identified with "x" as the final character, but there are numbers not so flagged that are not LC assignments. BCL3 is designed as a book selection guide, however, not as an exemplar of either cataloging or classification.

Arrangement has been stated to be by LC call number; but some catalog records carry more than one number, some sections of LC classification are being redeveloped, and some allow alternate treatments. BCL3's editor, therefore, had decisions to make. In all volumes, the existence of new LC sequences is signposted with cross-references. Individual subject classification of titles published in series was preferred to numerical gatherings within series. For Volume 2, alternate national literature numbers were selected or created in preference to PZ3 and PZ4 for fiction. Works by and about individual Canadian, Caribbean, African, South Asian, and Australasian authors writing in English have been pulled from the PR4000–6076 sequence and united with the general historical and critical material on those literatures in the PR9000s. Volume 5 displays the decision to keep most subject bibliography in class Z.

## INDEXES

The computer-made Author Index lists personal and institutional names of writers, editors, compilers, translators, sponsoring bodies, and others identified in the numbered "tracings" that bear roman numerals at the ends of entries. The Title Index, also machine generated, lists both uniform and title page titles from the printed entries, including nondistinctive titles and adding variant titles if traced. Because of the use of many "complete works" entries, many famous and highly recommended titles, especially novels, are absent from this index though present by implication in the list. References in the Author and Title indexes are to the sequential numbers, within volume, as-

signed to each entry. The Subject Index is a handmade guide to classification. It has its own brief explanatory introduction.

## LACUNAE, ERRORS AND REVISIONS

The virtual absence of serials and the exclusion of formats other than print have been noted under Size and Scope. Additionally, although undergraduate study ranges ever wider, student information needs outside fairly "academic" disciplines and some traditional sporting activities are not fulfilled here; users are referred to college bookstores and recommended lists for public libraries for titles in many craft, technical, and recreational subjects.

Errors of cataloging and questionable classifications will, as it has been stated, be noted. They are present in the database used and though many were corrected, others as surely remain. Reports of errors, expressions of opinion about favorite titles missing and abhorrences present, and general suggestions for future revisions are sincerely sought. They may be addressed to: Editor, Books for College Libraries, c/o *Choice*, 100 Riverview Center, Middletown, CT 06457–3467.

With the breakup of BCL1 into the individual volumes of BCL2, separate revision in an on-going project was predicted. That did not happen, and it would offer some difficulties in indexing and the handling of subjects split among volumes. It is a challenge to assemble the mix of organization to command the seemingly more and more specialized contributors required, the technology to facilitate presentation, and the finance to enable the whole. But it is to be hoped that the even greater challenges college libraries face in collection development will continue to find *Choice* and its reviewers, ACRL, and ALA ready with the help future circumstances require.

VIRGINIA CLARK, *Editor*

# Acknowledgments

Without the contributors and referees of the many subject lists, BCL3 would not exist. They are named in the appropriate volumes and identified by academic or other professional institution and by subject field. To enable the calling together of this team, however, and the presentation of its work took vision, planning, determination, and much help from many groups and individuals.

Both the users and the editorial staff of BCL3 owe thanks to the staff and two successive Executive Directors of the Association of College and Research Libraries (ACRL). Julie Virgo and JoAn S. Segal convened a preliminary investigative committee and commissioned a request for proposal (RFP) that established the first outline of the project for the revised edition. Patricia Sabosik, newly appointed Editor and Publisher of *Choice*, encompassed in her initial plans for the magazine the BCL project. Her response to ACRL's RFP involved the *Choice* staff in the editorial work and the Canadian bibliographic utility Utlas in the technical construction of the database. The staffs of *Choice* and BCL3 are grateful to ACRL for accepting this proposal and to Publishing Services of the American Library Association for co-funding the project with ACRL. Patricia Sabosik served as Project Manager. Liaison with ALA Books was Managing Editor Helen Cline.

An editorial advisory committee, chaired by Richard D. Johnson, SUNY College at Oneonta, was selected to allow the BCL3 Editor to draw advice from representatives of academic libraries of different types, sizes, and locales. Stephen L. Gerhardt, Cerritos College; Michael Haeuser, Gustavus Adolphus College; Barbara M. Hirsh, formerly Marist College; Thomas Kirk, Berea College; Craig S. Likness, Trinity University; and Mary K. Sellen, Spring Valley College, served the project well. Special thanks are due Richard D. Johnson and Craig S. Likness, each of whom also contributed subject lists, and Michael Haeuser, who spent several days as a volunteer in the BCL office and served as committee secretary.

The BCL project was housed in space in the *Choice* office and enjoyed a unique member/guest relationship that involved virtually every member of the *Choice* staff in some work for BCL. The subject editors—Robert Balay, Claire C. Dudley, Ronald H. Epp, Francine Graf, Helen MacLam, and Kenneth McLintock—suggested from their reviewer lists most of the BCL contributors and several referees. Claire C. Dudley and Helen MacLam served as referees; Claire C. Dudley

and Francine Graf gave much other valuable help. Library Technical Assistant Nancy Sbona, Systems Manager Lisa Gross, Office Assistant Mary Brooks, and Administrative Assistant Lucille Calarco deserve special mention for extraordinary assistance.

In addition to using the bibliographic and personnel resources of *Choice*, the Editor of BCL relied for vital support on the collections, equipment, and staffs of five very gracious institutions. Particular thanks go to the libraries of Kenyon College, Wesleyan University, and the Library Association, London, for use of behind-the-scenes cataloging and classification tools in addition to reference sources publicly available; to Trinity University, San Antonio, for tapes of BCL2; and to Trinity College, Hartford, for outstanding help from George R. Graf on preliminary aspects of the project in addition to those for which he is named in the contributor lists.

For work without regard for office hours or job description the Editor would particularly like to thank Judith Douville. She edited the science sections of Volume 5 in addition to assisting the Editor with some parts of Volume 4. She coordinated the corrections to the BCL3 computer file and reviewed the final page proofs. Her enthusiasm and dedication were vital in bringing the project to completion.

BCL3 secretary Anna Barron worked throughout the project. Special thanks are also owed to short-term staff members Alison Johnson and Virginia Carrington.

## CONTRIBUTORS

Title selection for BCL3 reflects three types of expert opinion: from scholars teaching in the field, from reference librarians, and from special referees chosen for their combination of subject and collection-development knowledge. Names appear in the approximate order of contributions in the volume, but Library of Congress classification will have scattered many titles selected by those named here into other sections of the list. The topical labels try to suggest both the depth of specialization required of some contributors and the broad knowledge and responsibility demanded of others; but no list such as this can do more than hint at the nature and amount of work for which these contributors are most gratefully thanked.

PSYCHOLOGY: Linda M. C. Abbott, California School of Professional Psychology; Irving H. Balow, University of California, Riverside; Norman Bell, University of Toronto; Irvin L. Child, Yale University; Peter L. Derks, College of William and Mary; Richard K. Eyman, University of California, Riverside; Karen Hartlep, California State University, Bakersfield; Sharon Herzberger, Trinity College, Conn.; Bernard Kaplan, Clark University; E. D. Lawson, SUNY College at Fredonia; Aldora Lee, formerly Washington State University; Robert Shilkret, Mt. Holyoke College; Francine Smolucha, Moraine Valley Community College; Robert B. Wallace, University of Hartford. *Reference*: Kris Salomon, Oakland University. *Referee*: Raymond G. McInnis, Western Washington University.

SCIENCE: *General & History & Philosophy*: Joseph W. Dauben, Herbert H. Lehman College, CUNY; Franklin Potter, University of California, Irvine. *Reference*: Robert W. Mautner, University of Arizona. *Referees*: Nadine George, Kenyon College; David Goodman, Princeton University.

MATHEMATICS & STATISTICS: R. Bharath, Northern Michigan University; David V. Feldman, University of New Hampshire; Francis Giesbrecht, North Carolina State University. *Reference & Referee*: Cathy C. Greene, Massachusetts Institute of Technology.

COMPUTER & INFORMATION SCIENCE: John Beidler, University of Scranton; John Y. Cheung, University of Oklahoma; Michael Henle, Oberlin College; Thomas L. Naps, Lawrence University; Robert J. Wernick, San Francisco State University. *Reference*: Julia Gelfand, University of California, Irvine.

ASTRONOMY & PHYSICS: Heinrich K. Eichhorn, University of Florida; Herman Erlichson, College of Staten Island, CUNY; Thornton Page, NASA Johnson Space Center; Harvey S. Picker, Trinity College, Conn.; Howard C. Roberts, University of Illinois, emeritus; Kenneth L. Schick, Union College; Hla Shwe, East Stroudsburg University; Peter D. Skiff, Bard College; Robert L. Stearns, Vassar College. *Referee*: Alice Lefler Primack, University of Florida.

CHEMISTRY: Curt W. Beck, Vassar College; L. W. Fine, Columbia University; Albert Fry, Wesleyan University; Harold Goldwhite, California State University, Los Angeles; Kenneth L. Marsi, California State University, Long Beach; Reuben Rudman, Adelphi University. *Biochemistry*: Lawrence C. Davis, Kansas State University. *Reference & Referee*: David Goodman, Princeton University.

EARTH SCIENCES & METEOROLOGY: Clarence J. Casella, Northern Illinois University; M. Ira Dubins, SUNY College at Oneonta; Frank T. Manheim, U.S. Geological Survey; Carl Mendelson, Beloit College; Arthur N. Palmer, SUNY College at Oneonta; William C. Peters, University of Arizona; Allen E. Staver, Northern Illinois University. *Reference*: Cathy C. Greene, Massachusetts Institute of Technology. *Referees*: Marie Dvorzak, University of Wisconsin–Madison; Mary L. Larsgaard, Colorado School of Mines.

BIOLOGICAL SCIENCES: David Bardack, University of Illinois at Chicago; Robert J. Doyle, University of Windsor; John R. Jungck, Beloit College; David W. Kitchen, Humboldt State University; John C. Kricher, Wheaton College, Mass.; Paul E. Lutz, University of North Carolina at Greensboro; Lee A. Meserve, Bowling Green State University; Richard L. Ridenhour, Humboldt State University; Dennison A. Smith, Oberlin College; Robert L. Smith, West Virginia University; Donald M. Tuttle, University of Arizona; Francis W. Yow, Kenyon College. *Reference & Referee*: Richard J. Dionne, Yale University.

BOTANY: Raymond C. Poincelot, Fairfield University. *Reference*: Richard J. Dionne, Yale University. *Referee*: Arlene Luchsinger, University of Georgia.

MEDICAL SCIENCES: Jane H. Barnsteiner, University of Pennsylvania; Ada Romaine Davis, formerly Georgetown University; Clarice Louise Dietrich, Onondaga Community College; Garabed Eknoyan, Baylor College of Medicine; Thomas A. Frank, Pennsylvania State University; Thomas P. Gariepy, Stonehill College; D. R. Shanklin, University of Chicago; Joyce E. Thompson, University of Pennsylvania; Suzanne Van Ort, University of Arizona. *Nutrition & Cookery*: Christine Bulson, SUNY College at Oneonta; Julie Miller Jones, College of St. Catherine. *Reference*: James W. Galloway, Texas Woman's University. *Referees*: Norma Kobzina, University of California, Berkeley (Nutrition); Pamela Johnson Ploeger, Dartmouth College.

AGRICULTURAL SCIENCES: Franklin E. Boteler, West Virginia University; Donald L. Hauxwell, Humboldt State University; Herbert W. Ockerman, Ohio State University; Morton Rothstein, University of California, Davis.

TECHNOLOGY & ENGINEERING: *Industrial*: R. Bharath, Northern Michigan University; William C. Struning, Seton Hall University. *Civil, Environmental, & Structural*: Larry Canter, University of Oklahoma; R. P. Khera, New Jersey Institute of Technology; William C. Schnobrich, University of Illinois at Urbana-Champaign; Donald B. Stafford, Clemson University. *Transportation*: see Economics, v. 4. *General & Mechanical*: Lawrence L. Ambs, University of Massachusetts at Amherst; Abdul Aziz, Gonzaga University; John F. Carney III, Vanderbilt University; Mark Levinson, University of Maine at Orono; Joseph P. Neville, Wentworth Institute of Technology; Alvin M. Strauss, Vanderbilt University. *Energy, Electrical, & Electronic*: Ohannes Eknoyan, Texas A & M University; T. J. Jones, formerly Trinity University; Sol Lapatine, College of Staten Island, CUNY; G. R. Peirce, University of Illinois at Urbana-Champaign, emeritus; Martin S. Roden, California State University, Los Angeles; Leonard A. Wenzel, Lehigh University. *Mining*: see Earth Sciences. *Chemical*: Ron Darby, Texas A & M University; Leonard A. Wenzel, Lehigh University. *Reference*: Robert J. Havlik, University of Notre Dame.

*Referee*: Sandra Sandor Kerbel, University of Pittsburgh.

PHOTOGRAPHY: Glenn Arnold, Columbia University; John Bloom, Academy of Art College, San Francisco; Peter C. Bunnell, Princeton University; Carl Chiarenza, University of Rochester. *Reference & Referee*: Claire C. Dudley, *Choice Magazine*.

MILITARY & NAVAL HISTORY: see v. 3

BIBLIOGRAPHY & LIBRARY SCIENCE: John Bidwell, University of California, Los Angeles; Thomas L. Bonn, SUNY College at Cortland; D. W. Krummel, University of Illinois at Urbana-Champaign; Patricia Stenstrom, University of Illinois at Urbana-Champaign.

# BF    Psychology

**Psychological abstracts.** **5.1**
v. 1- Jan. 1927-. [Washington, etc., American Psychological Association] v. 26 cm. Monthly. I. Hunter, Walter Samuel, 1889-1954, ed. II. American Psychological Association.
BF1.P65    150/.5    *LC* 29-23479

## BF20–28 CONGRESSES. COLLECTIONS

**Wann, T. W., ed.** • **5.2**
Behaviorism and phenomenology: contrasting bases for modern psychology / contributors: Sigmund Koch [and others. — Chicago]: Published for William Marsh Rice University by the University of Chicago Press [1964] xi, 190 p.; 24 cm. (Rice University semicentennial publications) 1. Psychology — Congresses. I. Rice University. II. T.
BF20.W28    150.19    *LC* 64-12257

**Kaplan, Bernard.** • **5.3**
Perspectives in psychological theory: essays in honor of Heinz Werner / edited by Bernard Kaplan and Seymour Wapner. — New York: International Universities Press, [1960]. 384 p.: ill. 1. Werner, Heinz, 1890- 2. Psychology — Collections. I. Wapner, Seymour, 1917- II. T.
BF21.K28

**Marx, Melvin Herman. ed.** • **5.4**
[Psychological theory] Theories in contemporary psychology. New York, Macmillan [1963] xi, 628 p. illus. 24 cm. First published in 1951 under title: Psychological theory. 1. Psychology — Addresses, essays, lectures. I. T.
BF21.M45 1963    150.82    *LC* 63-15264

**New horizons in psychology.** **5.5**
1- 1966-. [Middlesex, Eng., Baltimore] Penguin Books. illus. 18-20 cm. Triennial. 1966 issued as Pelican book, A775; 1972- as Penguin education. I. Foss, Brian M. 1921- ed. II. Dodwell, Peter C. 1930- ed.
BF21.N4x    *LC* sn 83-5254

**Skinner, B. F. (Burrhus Frederic), 1904-.** • **5.6**
Cumulative record: a selection of papers / [by] B. F. Skinner. — 3d ed. New York: Appleton-Century-Crofts [1972] xi, 604 p.: ill.; 24 cm. (Century psychology series) 1. Psychology — Addresses, essays, lectures. 2. Human behavior I. T.
BF21.S5 1972    150/.8    *LC* 72-78259

**Tolman, Edward Chace, 1886-.** • **5.7**
Behavior and psychological man: essays in motivation and learning / by Edward Chace Tolman. — Berkeley: University of California Press, 1958. 269 p.: ill. 1. Psychology — Addresses, essays, lectures. I. T.
BF21.T65 1958    *LC* 58-14906

**Tutorial essays in psychology: a guide to recent advances /** **5.8**
edited by N. S. Sutherland.
Hillsdale, N.J.: L. Erlbaum Associates; New York: distributed by the Halsted Press, 1979-. v. (vii, 161 p.): ill.; 24 cm. 1. Psychology — Collected works. I. Sutherland, N. S. (Norman Stuart)
BF21.T87    150/.8    *LC* 78-31703    *ISBN* 047026652X

**Jung, C. G. (Carl Gustav), 1875-1961.** **5.9**
Collected works. Editors: Herbert Read, Michael Fordham and Gerhard Adler. [New York] Pantheon Books, 1953-1968. 20 v. in 21. illus. 24 cm. (Bollingen series. 20) 1. Psychology — Collected works. I. T. II. Series.
BF23.J76    *LC* 52-8757

**Annual review of psychology.** **5.10**
v. 1- 1950-. Stanford, Calif., Annual Reviews. v. 23 cm. Annual. 1. Psychology — Periodicals. I. Stone, Calvin Perry, 1892-1954, ed.
BF30.A56    150.58    *LC* 50-13143

## BF31 DICTIONARIES

**Encyclopedia of psychology / editors, H.J. Eysenck, W. Arnold,** **5.11**
**and R. Meili.**
Unabridged ed. — New York: Continuum, 1982, c1972. xviii, 1187 p.; 24 cm. 'Originally published in 1972 in three volumes'—T.p. verso. 1. Psychology — Dictionaries. I. Eysenck, H. J. (Hans Jurgen), 1916- II. Arnold, Wilhelm, 1911- III. Meili, Richard.
BF31.E52 1982    150/.3/21 19    *LC* 82-8001    *ISBN* 0826400973

**Encyclopedia of psychology / Raymond J. Corsini, editor;** **5.12**
**Bonnie D. Ozaki, assistant editor.**
New York: Wiley, c1984. 4 v.: ill.; 29 cm. 'A Wiley-Interscience publication.' Includes indexes. 1. Psychology — Dictionaries. I. Corsini, Raymond J. II. Ozaki, Bonnie D. (Bonnie Davis)
BF31.E52 1984    150/.3/21 19    *LC* 83-16814    *ISBN* 047186594X

**The Encyclopedic dictionary of psychology / edited by Rom** **5.13**
**Harré and Roger Lamb; editorial board, R.D. Attenborough ...**
**[et al.].**
1st MIT Press ed. — Cambridge, Mass.: MIT Press, 1983. 718 p.: ill.; 27 cm. 1. Psychology — Dictionaries. I. Harré, Rom. II. Lamb, Roger.
BF31.E555 1983    150/.3/21 19    *LC* 83-920    *ISBN* 0262081350

**English, Horace Bidwell, 1892-.** • **5.14**
A comprehensive dictionary of psychological and psychoanalytical terms: a guide to usage / by Horace B. English and Ava Champney English. — New York: McKay [1964, c1958] xiv, 594 p.: diagrs.; 22 cm. 1. Psychology — Dictionaries. 2. Psychoanalysis — Dictionaries. I. English, Ava Champney, joint author. II. T. III. Title: Psychological and psychoanalytical terms. IV. Title: Psychoanalytical terms.
BF31.E58 1964    *LC* 64-2463

**Goldenson, Robert M.** • **5.15**
The encyclopedia of human behavior; psychology, psychiatry, and mental health [by] Robert M. Goldenson. — [1st ed.]. — Garden City, N.Y.: Doubleday, 1970. 2 v. (xxviii, 1472 p.): illus. (part col.); 25 cm. 1. Psychology — Dictionaries. 2. Psychiatry — Dictionaries. I. T.
BF31.G6    150/.3    *LC* 68-18077

**Wolman, Benjamin B.** **5.16**
Dictionary of behavioral science, compiled and edited by Benjamin B. Wolman. In collaboration with Gerhard Adler [and others]. — New York: Van Nostrand Reinhold Co., [1973] ix, 478 p.: illus.; 26 cm. 1. Psychology — Dictionaries. I. T.
BF31.W64    150/.3    *LC* 73-748    *ISBN* 0442295669

## BF38–67 THEORY. METHODOLOGY

**Allport, Gordon W. (Gordon Willard), 1897-1967.** • **5.17**
Becoming; basic considerations for a psychology of personality. New Haven, Yale University Press, 1955. 106 p. 22 cm. (The Terry lectures) 1. Psychology I. T.
BF38.A38    137    *LC* 55-5975

**Boden, Margaret A.** **5.18**
Minds and mechanisms: philosophical psychology and computational models / Margaret A. Boden. — Ithaca, N.Y.: Cornell University Press, 1981. 311 p.: ill.; 23 cm. 1. Boden, Margaret A — Bibliography. 2. Artificial intelligence 3. Psychology — Philosophy I. T.
BF38.B57 1981    150/.1 19    *LC* 81-66652    *ISBN* 0801414318

**Broadbent, Donald Eric.** • **5.19**
Perception and communication. — New York: Pergamon Press, 1958. 338 p.: ill.; 22 cm. 1. Information theory in psychology 2. Attention 3. Hearing I. T.
BF38.B685    150.151    *LC* 58-11832

**Eacker, Jay N.**                                                          **5.20**
Problems of metaphysics and psychology / Jay N. Eacker. — Chicago: Nelson-Hall, c1983. xii, 289 p.; 23 cm. Includes index. 1. Psychology — Philosophy I. T.
BF38.E128 1983        150/.1 19        *LC* 82-8053        *ISBN* 088229685X

**Eacker, Jay N.**                                                          **5.21**
Problems of philosophy and psychology / Jay N. Eacker. — Chicago: Nelson-Hall, [1975] xi, 201 p.; 23 cm. Includes index. 1. Psychology — Philosophy I. T.
BF38.E13        150/.1        *LC* 75-17548        *ISBN* 0882292021

**Explaining human behavior: consciousness, human action, and**        **5.22**
**social structure / Paul F. Secord, editor.**
Beverly Hills: Sage Publications, c1982. 320 p.: ill.; 23 cm. 1. Psychology — Philosophy — Addresses, essays, lectures. 2. Consciousness — Addresses, essays, lectures. 3. Social psychology — Philosophy — Addresses, essays, lectures. 4. Social structure — Psychological aspects — Addresses, essays, lectures. I. Secord, Paul F.
BF38.E87 1982        302/.12 19        *LC* 82-868        *ISBN* 0803918224

**Flanagan, Owen J.**                                                      **5.23**
The science of the mind / Owen J. Flanagan, Jr. — Cambridge, Mass.: MIT Press, c1984. xii, 336 p.; 24 cm. 'A Bradford book.' Includes indexes. 1. Psychology — Philosophy I. T.
BF38.F58 1984        150/.1 19        *LC* 83-26770        *ISBN* 0262060906

**Fodor, Jerry A.**                                                    ● **5.24**
Psychological explanation; an introduction to the philosophy of psychology [by] Jerry A. Fodor. — New York: Random House, [1968] xxi, 165 p.; 21 cm. — (A Random House Study in problems of philosophy) (Studies in philosophy.) 1. Psychology — Philosophy I. T.
BF38.F6        150/.1        *LC* 67-20628

**Garner, Wendell R.**                                                 ● **5.25**
Uncertainty and structure as psychological concepts / Wendell R. Garner. — New York: Wiley, 1962. ix, 369 p.: ill.; 24 cm. 1. Psychology — Methodology 2. Information theory I. T.
BF38.G3        *LC* 62-10919

**Gregory, R. L. (Richard Langton).**                                      **5.26**
Mind in science: a history of explanations in psychology and physics / Richard L. Gregory. — Cambridge [Cambridgeshire]: Cambridge University Press, 1981. xi, 641 p.: ill.; 24 cm. Includes index. 1. Psychology — Philosophy 2. Science — Philosophy 3. Physics — Philosophy 4. Psychology — History. 5. Science — History 6. Science and psychology I. T.
BF38.G67        153/.01 19        *LC* 81-7732        *ISBN* 0521243076

**Malcolm, Norman, 1911-.**                                            ● **5.27**
Problems of mind: Descartes to Wittgenstein. — New York: Harper & Row, [1971] xi, 103 p.; 21 cm. — (Harper essays in philosophy) (Harper torchbooks) 1. Descartes, René, 1596-1650. 2. Wittgenstein, Ludwig, 1889-1951. 3. Psychology 4. Dualism I. T.
BF38.M347        128/.2        *LC* 70-146796

**Marx, Melvin Herman.**                                                   **5.28**
Systems and theories in psychology / Melvin H. Marx, W.A. Cronan-Hillix. — 4th ed. — New York: McGraw-Hill, c1987. p. cm. (McGraw-Hill series in psychology.) Includes index. 1. Psychology — Philosophy I. Cronan-Hillix, W. A. (William Allen), 1927- II. T. III. Series.
BF38.M38 1987        150.19 19        *LC* 86-15167        *ISBN* 0070406804

**May, Gerald G.**                                                         **5.29**
Will and spirit: a contemplative psychology / Gerald G. May. — 1st ed. — San Francisco: Harper & Row, c1982. viii, 360 p.; 24 cm. 1. Psychology — Philosophy 2. Psychology and religion 3. Will — Psychological aspects. 4. Spiritual life 5. Christian life I. T.
BF38.M388 1982        150.19 19        *LC* 82-47751        *ISBN* 0060655348

**Neel, Ann, 1927-.**                                                      **5.30**
Theories of psychology: a handbook / Ann Neel. — Rev. and enl. ed. — Cambridge, Mass.: Schenkman Pub. Co.; New York: distributed solely by Halsted Press, c1977. 699 p.; 23 cm. 1. Psychology — Philosophy — Handbooks, manuals, etc. 2. Psychology — History — Handbooks, manuals, etc. I. T.
BF38.N38 1977        150/.19/09        *LC* 76-39778        *ISBN* 0470989688.
*ISBN* 0470989696 pbk

**Psychology: a study of a science / edited by Sigmund Koch.**         ● **5.31**
New York; Toronto: McGraw-Hill, 1959-. v.: ill. 1. Psychology I. Koch, Sigmund. ed.
BF38.P8        150.82        *LC* 57-14691/L

**Sarason, Seymour Bernard, 1919-.**                                       **5.32**
Psychology misdirected / Seymour B. Sarason. — New York: Free Press; London: Collier Macmillan Pub., c1981. xiii, 192 p.; 24 cm. Includes index.

1. Psychology — Philosophy 2. Psychology — Social aspects. 3. Psychology — United States — History. I. T.
BF38.S227        150.1 19        *LC* 80-69283        *ISBN* 0029281008

**Wilkes, K. V.**                                                          **5.33**
Physicalism / by K. V. Wilkes. — Atlantic Highlands, N.J.: Humanities Press, 1978. 142 p.; 19 cm. — (Studies in philosophical psychology.) Portions based on the author's thesis, Princeton, 1974. Includes index. 1. Psychology — Philosophy 2. Mind and body I. T. II. Series.
BF38.W74        150/.19/2        *LC* 77-28169        *ISBN* 0391007416

**Cummins, Robert.**                                                       **5.34**
The nature of psychological explanation / Robert Cummins. — Cambridge, Mass.: MIT Press, c1983. x, 219 p.: ill.; 24 cm. 'A Bradford book.' Includes index. 1. Psychology — Philosophy 2. Hermeneutics 3. Cognition I. T.
BF38.5.C85 1983        150/.1 19        *LC* 82-20895        *ISBN* 0262030942

**Miller, George Armitage, 1920-.**                                    ● **5.35**
Plans and the structure of behavior [by] George A. Miller, Eugene Galanter [and] Karl H. Pribram. — New York: Holt, [1960] 226 p.: illus.; 24 cm. 1. Psychology — Methodology 2. Human behavior I. T.
BF38.5.M5        150.18        *LC* 60-7982

**Runyan, William McKinley.**                                              **5.36**
Life histories and psychobiography: explorations in theory and method / William McKinley Runyan. — New York: Oxford University Press, 1982. xiii, 288 p. Includes index. 1. Case method 2. Psychology — Methodology 3. Psychohistory 4. Personality 5. Biography (as a literary form) I. T.
BF38.5.R86        155 19        *LC* 82-6458        *ISBN* 019503189X

**Sidowski, Joseph B., 1925- ed.**                                     ● **5.37**
Experimental methods and instrumentation in psychology, edited by Joseph B. Sidowski. — New York: McGraw-Hill, [1966] ix, 803 p.: illus.; 26 cm. — (McGraw-Hill series in psychology) 1. Psychology — Methodology I. T.
BF38.5.S52        150.18        *LC* 65-23210

# BF39 Statistical Methods

**Bock, Richard Darrell, 1927-.**                                      ● **5.38**
The measurement and prediction of judgment and choice [by] R. Darrell Bock [and] Lyle V. Jones. — San Francisco: Holden-Day, [1968] 370 p.: illus.; 24 cm. — (Holden-Day series in psychology) 1. Thurstone, Louis Leon, 1887-1955. 2. Scale analysis (Psychology) 3. Psychometrics I. Jones, Lyle V. joint author. II. T.
BF39.B67        150/.1/82        *LC* 66-17897

**Cattell, Raymond B. (Raymond Bernard), 1905-.**                          **5.39**
The scientific use of factor analysis in behavioral and life sciences / Raymond B. Cattell. — New York: Plenum Press, c1978. xxii, 618 p.: ill.; 24 cm. Includes indexes. 1. Factor analysis 2. Psychometrics I. T.
BF39.C33        519.5/3        *LC* 77-10695        *ISBN* 0306309394

**Contemporary developments in mathematical psychology. Edited**           **5.40**
**by David H. Krantz [and others].**
San Francisco: W. H. Freeman, [1974] 2 v.: illus.; 25 cm. 1. Human behavior — Mathematical models 2. Psychometrics I. Krantz, David H., 1938- ed.
BF39.C59        150/.1/84        *LC* 73-21887        *ISBN* 0716708485

**Coombs, Clyde Hamilton, 1912-.**                                     ● **5.41**
Mathematical psychology; an elementary introduction [by] Clyde H. Coombs, Robyn M. Dawes [and] Amos Tversky. — Englewood Cliffs, N.J.: Prentice-Hall, [1970] xi, 419 p.: illus.; 25 cm. — (Prentice-Hall series in mathematical psychology) 1. Psychology — Mathematical models 2. Psychometrics I. Dawes, Robyn M., 1936- joint author. II. Tversky, Amos. joint author. III. T.
BF39.C62        150/.1/51        *LC* 73-101580        *ISBN* 0135621577

**Coombs, Clyde Hamilton, 1912-.**                                     ● **5.42**
A theory of data / Clyde H. Coombs. — New York: Wiley, c1964. xviii, 585 p. 1. Psychometrics 2. Psychology — Mathematical models I. T.
BF39.C639        *LC* 63-20629

**Coombs, Clyde Hamilton, 1912-.**                                     ● **5.43**
A theory of psychological scaling. — [Ann Arbor]: Engineering Research Institute, University of Michigan, 1951 [i.e. 1952] 94 p.: ill. — (University of Michigan. Engineering Research Institute. Bulletin; no. 34) I. T.
BF39.C64

**Cronbach, Lee J. (Lee Joseph), 1916-.**                              ● **5.44**
Psychological tests and personnel decisions [by] Lee J. Cronbach [and] Goldine C. Gleser. [2d ed.] Urbana, University of Illinois Press, 1965. viii, 347 p. illus.

24 cm. 1. Psychological tests 2. Decision-making I. Gleser, Goldine C. joint author. II. T.
BF39.C7 1965    151.26    *LC* 64-18667

**Edwards, Allen Louis.**    **5.45**
Experimental design in psychological research / Allen L. Edwards. — 5th ed. — New York: Harper & Row, c1985. xxiii, 584 p.; 24 cm. Includes indexes. 1. Experimental design 2. Psychometrics 3. Psychology — Research I. T.
BF39.E3 1985    150/.724 19    *LC* 84-12785    *ISBN* 0060418737

**Edwards, Allen Louis.**    • **5.46**
Techniques of attitude scale construction. — New York: Appleton-Century-Crofts, [c1957] 256 p.: illus.; 22 cm. — (Century psychology series) 1. Psychometrics 2. Attitude (Psychology) — Testing I. T.
BF39.E33    151.25    *LC* 56-11542

**Guilford, J. P. (Joy Paul), 1897-.**    • **5.47**
Psychometric methods. 2d ed. New York: McGraw-Hill, 1954. 597 p.: ill.; 24 cm. (McGraw-Hill series in psychology) 1. Psychometrics I. T.
BF39.G8 1954    152.8    *LC* 53-12430

**Lewis, Don, 1901-.**    • **5.48**
Quantitative methods in psychology. — New York: McGraw-Hill, 1960. 558 p.: ill. (McGraw-Hill series in psychology.) Includes bibliography. 1. Psychology 2. Mathematics I. T. II. Series.
BF39.L4 1960

**Lindquist, Everet Franklin.**    • **5.49**
Design and analyusis of experiments in psychology and education. — Boston: Houghton Mifflin, 1953. 398p.,illus. 1. Psychology — Methodology I. T.
BF39.L5    150.72    *LC* 53-9156

**Luce, R. Duncan (Robert Duncan) ed.**    • **5.50**
Developments in mathematical psychology, information, learning, and tracking: A study of the Behavioral Models Project, Bureau of Applied Social Research, Columbia University / with contributions by R. Duncan Luce, Robert R. Bush [and] J. C. R. Licklider. — Glencoe, Ill.: Free Press, [1960] 294p.: ill. 1. Human behavior — Mathematical models I. T.
BF39.L78    *LC* 58-6488

**Luce, R. Duncan (Robert Duncan) ed.**    • **5.51**
Handbook of mathematical psychology, edited by R. Duncan Luce, Robert R. Bush [and] Eugene Galanter. New York, Wiley [1963-65] 3 v. illus. 24 cm. 1. Psychology — Mathematical models 2. Psychometrics I. Bush, Robert R. joint ed. II. Galanter, Eugene. joint ed. III. T.
BF39.L79 1963    150.151    *LC* 63-9428

**Luce, R. Duncan (Robert Duncan)**    • **5.52**
Individual choice behavior: a theoretical analysis / R. Duncan Luce. — New York: Wiley, 1959. xii, 153 p.; 24 cm. Includes index. 1. Psychometrics 2. Choice (Psychology) I. T.
BF39.L8    153.8/3    *LC* 59-9346

**Luce, R. Duncan (Robert Duncan)**    • **5.53**
Readings in mathematical psychology / edited by R. Duncan Luce, Robert R. Bush, Eugene Galanter. — New York: Wiley, 1963-1965. 2 v.: ill.; 25 cm. 'Designed as source materials to accompany the [editors'] ... Handbook of mathematical psychology.' 1. Psychology — Mathematical models 2. Psychometrics I. Bush, Robert R. II. Galanter, Eugene. III. T.
BF39.L83    *LC* 63-14066

**Restle, Frank.**    • **5.54**
Introduction to mathematical psychology [by] Frank Restle [and] James G. Greeno. — Reading, Mass.: Addison-Wesley, [1970] xii, 371 p.: illus.; 24 cm. — (Addison-Wesley series in behavioral science) 1. Psychology — Mathematical models 2. Psychometrics I. Greeno, James G. joint author. II. T. III. Title: Mathematical psychology.
BF39.R38    152/.01/8    *LC* 77-100880

**Schiffman, Susan S.**    **5.55**
Introduction to multidimensional scaling: theory, methods, and applications / Susan S. Schiffman, M. Lance Reynolds, Forrest W. Young; with contributions by J. Douglas Carroll ... [et al.]; with a foreword by Joseph B. Kruskal. — New York: Academic Press, 1981. xvi, 413 p.: ill.; 24 cm. 1. Multidimensional scaling 2. Multidimensional scaling — Computer programs. 3. Psychometrics 4. Social sciences — Methodology I. Reynolds, M. Lance. II. Young, Forrest W. III. T.
BF39.S33    001.4/226 19    *LC* 81-10842    *ISBN* 0126243506

**Thurstone, Louis Leon, 1887-1955.**    • **5.56**
The measurement of values. — [Chicago]: University of Chicago Press, [1959]. 322 p.: ill. Selections from the author's papers previously published in various periodicals. 1. Psychometrics 2. Attitude (Psychology) I. T.
BF39.T49

**Thurstone, Louis Leon, 1887-1955.**    • **5.57**
Multiple–factor analysis: a development and expansion of The vectors of mind / by L. L. Thurstone. — Chicago: University of Chicago Press, 1947. xix, 535 p.: ill., diagrs.; 23 cm. 1. Factor analysis 2. Psychological tests 3. Psychology — Methodology I. T.
BF39.T53    *LC* 47-2981

**Torgerson, Warren S.**    • **5.58**
Theory and methods of scaling. New York, Wiley [1958] 460 p. illus. 24 cm. 1. Psychometrics I. T.
BF39.T6    152.83    *LC* 58-10812

**Tyler, Leona Elizabeth, 1906-.**    **5.59**
Tests and measurements / Leona E. Tyler, W. Bruce Walsh. — 3d ed. — Englewood Cliffs, N.J.: Prentice-Hall, c1979. xii, 144 p.: ill.; 24 cm. — (Foundations of modern psychology series) Includes index. 1. Psychological tests 2. Psychometrics I. Walsh, W. Bruce, 1936- joint author. II. T.
BF39.T9 1979    150/.28    *LC* 78-23772    *ISBN* 0139118594

**Green, Bert F.**    • **5.60**
Digital computers in research: an introduction for behavioral and social scientists. — New York: McGraw-Hill [1963] 333 p.: ill.; 24 cm. (Lincoln Laboratory publications) 1. Psychology — Data processing 2. Electronic digital computers — Programming I. T.
BF39.5.G7    510.7834    *LC* 62-21790

**Reynolds, James H., 1930-.**    **5.61**
Computing in psychology: an introduction to programming methods and concepts / James H. Reynolds. — Englewood Cliffs, N.J.: Prentice-Hall, 1987. xii, 354 p.: ill.; 23 cm. Includes indexes. 1. Psychology — Data processing 2. Programming (Electronic computers) I. T.
BF39.5.R49 1987    150/.28/5526 19    *LC* 86-593    *ISBN* 0131658123

# BF41–80 Special Aspects. Research

**Madden, Edward H.**    • **5.62**
Philosophical problems of psychology. — New York, Odyssey Press [1962] 149 p. 21 cm. Includes bibliography. 1. Psychology 2. Philosophy I. T.
BF41.M18    150.1    *LC* 62-20548

**May, Rollo. ed.**    **5.63**
Existential psychology. — 2d ed. — New York: Random House, [1969] ix, 117 p.; 19 cm. — (Studies in psychology, PP19) 1. Existential psychology I. T.
BF41.M3 1969    150.19/2    *LC* 70-79689

**Broadbent, Donald Eric.**    **5.64**
In defence of empirical psychology [by] Donald E. Broadbent. London, Methuen, 1973. ix, 222 p. illus. 23 cm. Distributed in the USA by Harper & Row Publishers. 'Contains the 1971 William James Lectures at Harvard.... In addition there are reprints of four shorter lectures....' 1. Psychology — Research I. T.
BF76.5.B76 1973    150/.7/24    *LC* 73-331257    *ISBN* 041676780X

**Cole, Michael, 1938-.**    **5.65**
Comparative studies of how people think: an introduction / Michael Cole and Barbara Means. — Cambridge, Mass.: Harvard University Press, 1981. 208 p.; 22 cm. Includes index. 1. Psychology — Research — Cross-cultural studies. 2. Thought and thinking — Cross-cultural studies. I. Means, Barbara, 1949- joint author. II. T.
BF76.5.C63    153/.072 19    *LC* 80-23825    *ISBN* 0674152603

**Lewin, Miriam, 1931-.**    **5.66**
Understanding psychological research: the student researcher's handbook / Miriam Lewin. — New York: Wiley, c1979. xi, 452 p.: ill.; 24 cm. Includes index. 1. Psychology — Research 2. Experimental design 3. Psychology — Methodology 4. Psychometrics I. T.
BF76.5.L47    150/.7/2    *LC* 78-27842    *ISBN* 0471658375

**Rosenthal, Robert, 1933-.**    **5.67**
Experimenter effects in behavioral research / Robert Rosenthal. — Enl. ed. — New York: Irvington Pubishers, c1980. 1 v. (The Century psychology series) 1. Psychology — Research — Effect of experimenters on I. T.
BF76.5.R63 1980    150/.724 19    *LC* 80-22119    *ISBN* 0829004033

**Publication manual of the American Psychological Association.**    **5.68**
3rd ed. — Washington, D.C.: The Association, c1983. 208 p.; 26 cm. Rev. ed. of: Publication manual. 2nd ed. 1974. Includes index. 1. Communication in

psychology 2. Psychology — Authorship. I. American Psychological Association. II. Publication manual.
BF76.7.P83 1983      808/.02 19      LC 83-2521      ISBN 0912704578

**Graduate study in psychology and associated fields.**      **5.69**
1983-      . — Washington, D.C.: American Psychological Association, c1983-. v.; 22 cm. Annual. 1. Psychology — Study and teaching (Graduate) — United States — Directories. 2. Psychology — Study and teaching (Graduate) — Canada — Directories. I. American Psychological Association.
BF77.G73      150/.7/1173 19      LC 84-641215

---

# BF81–109 HISTORY. BIOGRAPHY

**Brett, George Sidney, 1879-1944.**      • **5.70**
Brett's History of psychology. Edited and abridged by R. S. Peters. [2d rev. ed.] Cambridge, Mass., M.I.T. Press [1965] 778 p. 21 cm. (The M.I.T. paperback series, MIT24) 1. Psychology — History. 2. Philosophy, Ancient 3. Psychology, Patristic I. Peters, R. S. (Richard Stanley), 1919- ed. II. T. III. Title: History of psychology.
BF81.B7 1965      150.9      LC 65-15931

**Diamond, Solomon, 1906- comp.**      **5.71**
The roots of psychology; a sourcebook in the history of ideas. — New York: Basic Books, [1974] xvii, 781 p.: illus.; 25 cm. Contributions translated from various languages. 1. Psychology — History — Addresses, essays, lectures. I. T.
BF81.D5      BF81 D5.      150/.9      LC 72-76919      ISBN 0465067409

**Henle, Mary, 1913-.**      **5.72**
Historical conceptions of psychology. Edited by Mary Henle, Julian Jaynes [and] John J. Sullivan. — New York: Springer, [1973] xii, 323 p.: port.; 24 cm. 1. Psychology — History. I. Jaynes, Julian, joint comp. II. Sullivan, John J., 1919- joint comp. III. T.
BF81.H38      150/.19/09      LC 73-80600      ISBN 082611430X

**MacLeod, Robert Brodie, 1907-1972.**      **5.73**
The persistent problems of psychology / by Robert B. MacLeod. — Pittsburgh: Duquesne University Press; Atlantic Highlands, [N.J.]: distributed by Humanities Press, [1975] x, 207 p.; 23 cm. 'An unfinished book ... a table of contents of the intended volume is included.' 1. Psychology — History. I. T.
BF81.M28 1975      150/.9      LC 75-15635      ISBN 0391003933

**Murphy, Gardner, 1895-.**      • **5.74**
Psychological thought from Pythagoras to Freud; an informal introduction. — [1st ed.]. — New York: Harcourt, Brace & World, [1968] ix, 211 p.; 21 cm. (An original Harbinger book) Originated as a series of lectures delivered in 1966-67 at the Menninger School of Psychiatry, Topeka, Kans. 1. Psychology — History. I. T.
BF81.M8      150.19      LC 68-25371

**Murphy, Gardner, 1895- comp.**      • **5.75**
Western psychology; from the Greeks to William James, edited by Gardner Murphy and Lois B. Murphy. — New York: Basic Books, [1969] x, 296 p.; 24 cm. 1. Psychology — History. I. Murphy, Lois Barclay, 1902- joint comp. II. T.
BF81.M82      128/.3/091821      LC 72-78454

**Watson, Robert Irving, 1909-.**      **5.76**
The great psychologists / Robert I. Watson, Sr. — 4th ed. — Philadelphia: Lippincott, c1978. xiv, 645 p.; 23 cm. 1. Psychology — History. I. T.
BF81.W35 1978      150/.92/2      LC 77-12990      ISBN 0397473753

**Boring, Edwin Garrigues, 1886-1968.**      • **5.77**
A history of experimental psychology. 2d ed. — New York: Appleton-Century-Crofts, [1950] xxi, 777 p.: illus., port., map (on lining papers); 25 cm. — (The Century psychology series) 1. Psychology, Experimental — History. I. T.
BF95.B6 1950      150.72      LC 50-7893

**Heidbreder, Edna Francis, 1890-.**      • **5.78**
Seven psychologies / by Edna Heidbreder. — Student's edition. — New York: Appleton-Century-Crofts, 1933. viii, 450 p.; 20cm. — (Century psychology series) Includes index. 1. Psychology — History. I. T. II. Series.
BF95.H4 1933      150.19      LC 33-13339

**Murphy, Gardner, 1895-.**      **5.79**
Historical introduction to modern psychology / [by] Gardner Murphy [and] Joseph K. Kovach. — 3d ed. — New York: Harcourt Brace Jovanovich, [1972] xiv, 526 p.; 25 cm. 1. Psychology — History. 2. Psychology I. Kovach, Joseph K., joint author. II. T.
BF95.M8 1972      150/.9      LC 72-185804      ISBN 0155362453

**Stevens, Gwendolyn.**      **5.80**
The women of psychology / by Gwendolyn Stevens and Sheldon Gardner. — Cambridge, Mass.: Schenkman Pub. Co., 1982. 2 v.: ports.; 21 cm. 1. Psychology — History. 2. Women psychologists 3. Psychology — United States — History. I. Gardner, Sheldon. II. T.
BF95.S73 1982      150/.88042 19      LC 81-14394      ISBN 0870734431

**Basic writings in the history of psychology / [compiled by]**      **5.81**
**Robert I. Watson, Sr.**
New York: Oxford University Press, 1979. xviii, 420 p.: ill.; 24 cm. 1. Psychology — History — Addresses, essays, lectures. 2. Psychology — Early works to 1850 — Addresses, essays, lectures. I. Watson, Robert Irving, 1909-
BF98.B23      150/.8      LC 78-7274      ISBN 0195024435

**Robinson, Daniel N., 1937-.**      **5.82**
Toward a science of human nature: essays on the psychologies of Mill, Hegel, Wundt, and James / Daniel N. Robinson. — New York: Columbia University Press, 1982. xiii, 258 p.; 22 cm. 1. Mill, John Stuart, 1806-1873. 2. Hegel, Georg Wilhelm Friedrich, 1770-1831. 3. Wundt, Wilhelm Max, 1832-1920. 4. James, William, 1842-1910. 5. Psychology — History — 19th century. I. T.
BF103.R62      150/.92/2 19      LC 81-38458      ISBN 0231051743

**Wolman, Benjamin B.**      • **5.83**
Historical roots of contemporary psychology, edited by Benjamin B. Wolman. — New York: Harper & Row, [1968] viii, 376 p.; 24 cm. 1. Psychology — History — Addresses, essays, lectures. I. T.
BF103.W6      150      LC 68-10810

**Fernald, L. Dodge (Lloyd Dodge), 1929-.**      **5.84**
The Hans legacy: a story of science / Dodge Fernald; illustrated by James Edwards. — Hillsdale, N.J.: L. Erlbaum Associates, 1984. v, 241 p.: ill., maps; 24 cm. Maps on lining papers. Includes index. 1. Freud, Sigmund, 1856-1939. Analyse der Phobie eines fünfjährigen Knaben 2. Psychology — Methodology 3. Clever Hans (Horse) 4. Psychology — History. 5. Behaviorism (Psychology) 6. Psychoanalysis I. T.
BF105.F47 1984      150/.9 19      LC 83-11539      ISBN 0898593018

**Guthrie, Robert V.**      **5.85**
Even the rat was white: a historical view of psychology / Robert V. Guthrie. — New York: Harper & Row, c1976. xii, 224 p.: ill.; 24 cm. Includes index. 1. Psychology — History. 2. Afro-American psychologists 3. Ethnopsychology — History. 4. Anthropometry — History. 5. Blacks — Psychology. I. T.
BF105.G87      155.8      LC 75-26520      ISBN 006042561X

**A History of psychology in autobiography.**      **5.86**
v. 1- 1930-. Englewood Cliffs, N.J. [etc.] Prentice-Hall [etc.] v. ill. 24 cm. (v. 1-4: The International university series in psychology) (v. 5-6: The Century psychology series) (v. 7- : A Series of books in psychology) 1. Psychology — History — Collected works. 2. Psychologists — Biography — Collected works.
BF105.H5      150/.92/2 B      LC 30-20129

**Kozulin, Alex.**      **5.87**
Psychology in Utopia: toward a social history of Soviet psychology / Alex Kozulin. — Cambridge, Mass.: MIT Press, c1984. xi, 179 p.: ill.; 24 cm. 1. Psychology — Soviet Union — History. 2. Psychology — Soviet Union — Philosophy. 3. Psychology — Social aspects — Soviet Union. I. T.
BF108.S65 K68 1984      150/.947 19      LC 83-22264      ISBN 0262110873

**Meyer, Donald B.**      **5.88**
The positive thinkers: a study of the American quest for health, wealth and personal power from Mary Baker Eddy to Norman Vincent Peale. — Garden City, N.Y.: Doubleday, c1965. 358p. 1. Psychology — History — United States 2. Psychology, Applied — History 3. Success 4. Spiritual healing I. T.
BF108.U5M4      LC 65-12056

**Roback, A. A. (Abraham Aaron), 1890-1965.**      • **5.89**
History of American psychology [by] A.A. Roback. New, rev. ed. New York, Collier Books [1964] 575 p. 18 cm. 'CS13.' 1. Psychology — United States — History. I. T.
BF108.U5 R6 1964      150.973      LC 64-16138

---

# BF109 Biography

**Krawiec, T. S. (Theophile Stanley), 1913-.**      **5.90**
The psychologists. Edited by T. S. Krawiec. New York, Oxford University Press, 1972-. v. illus. 22 cm. 1. Krawiec, T. S. (Theophile Stanley), 1913- 2. Psychologists I. T.
BF109.A1 K7      150/.92/2      LC 78-188293

Models of achievement: reflections of eminent women in                 5.91
psychology / edited by Agnes N. O'Connell and Nancy Felipe
Russo.
New York: Columbia University Press, 1983. xiii, 338 p.: ports.; 24 cm.
1. Women psychologists — United States — Biography. 2. Psychology —
United States — History — 20th century. 3. Sex discrimination in psychology
— United States. I. O'Connell, Agnes N. II. Russo, Nancy Felipe, 1943-
BF109.A1 M6 1983      150/.88042 19      LC 82-23583      *ISBN*
0231053126

Nordby, Vernon J.                                                      5.92
A guide to psychologists and their concepts [by] Vernon J. Nordby and Calvin
S. Hall. — San Francisco: W. H. Freeman; trade distributor: Scribner, New
York, [1974] 187 p.: ports.; 24 cm. — (A Series of books in psychology)
1. Psychologists — Biography. 2. Psychology I. Hall, Calvin S. (Calvin
Springer), 1909- II. T.
BF109.A1 N67      150/.92/2 B      LC 74-11165      ISBN 0716707608

Zusne, Leonard, 1924-.                                                 5.93
Biographical dictionary of psychology / Leonard Zusne. — Westport, Conn.:
Greenwood Press, 1984. xxi, 563 p.; 25 cm. Rev. ed. of: Names in the history of
psychology. 1975. 1. Psychologists — Biography. 2. Psychology — History.
I. Zusne, Leonard, 1924- Names in the history of psychology. II. T.
BF109.A1 Z85 1984      150/.92/2 B 19      LC 83-18326      *ISBN*
0313240272

Boring, Edwin Garrigues, 1886-1968.                                 • 5.94
Psychologist at large: an autobiography and selected essays. — New York:
Basic Books, [1961] 371 p.: ill. (Contemporary men of science.)
1. Psychologists, American — Correspondence, reminiscences, etc.
2. Psychology — Addresses, essays, lectures. I. T. II. Series.
BF109.B65 A3

Bruner, Jerome S. (Jerome Seymour)                                    5.95
In search of mind: essays in autobiography / Jerome Bruner. — 1st ed. — New
York: Harper & Row, c1983. xii, 306 p.; 25 cm. — (Alfred P. Sloan Foundation
series.) Includes index. 1. Bruner, Jerome S. (Jerome Seymour)
2. Psychologists — United States — Biography. I. T. II. Series.
BF109.B78 A35 1983      153/.092/4 B 19      LC 83-47526      *ISBN*
0060151919

Evans, Richard Isadore, 1922-.                                      • 5.96
Dialogue with Erik Erikson, by Richard I. Evans. [1st ed.] New York, Harper &
Row [1967] xvi, 142 p. 22 cm. (His Dialogues with notable contributors to
personality theory, v. 3) 1. Erikson, Erik H. (Erik Homburger), 1902-
2. Psychoanalysis I. Erikson, Erik H. (Erik Homburger), 1902- II. T.
BF109.E7 E9      150.19/5      LC 67-13707

Stevens, Richard.                                                     5.97
Erik Erikson, an introduction / Richard Stevens. — New York: St. Martin's
Press, 1983. 148 p.; 24 cm. 1. Erikson, Erik H. (Erik Homburger), 1902-
2. Psychoanalysis 3. Psychoanalysis — Social aspects. I. T.
BF109.E7 S73 1983      150.19/5/0924 19      LC 83-3256      *ISBN*
0312258127

Jung, C. G. (Carl Gustav), 1875-1961.                              • 5.98
Memories, dreams, reflections. Recorded and edited by Aniela Jaffé. Translated
from the German by Richard and Clara Winston. New York, Pantheon Books
[1963] 398 p. illus. 24 cm. I. T.
BF109.J8 A33      921      LC 62-14264

Evans, Richard Isadore, 1922-.                                        5.99
Konrad Lorenz: the man and his ideas / Richard I. Evans. — 1st ed. — New
York: Harcourt Brace Jovanovich, [1975] xviii, 302 p.; 22 cm. Includes index.
1. Lorenz, Konrad, 1903- 2. Psychology — Addresses, essays, lectures.
I. Lorenz, Konrad, 1903- II. T.
BF109.L67 E93      156/.092/4 19      LC 75-9581      ISBN 0151472858

Luriia, A. R. (Aleksandr Romanovich), 1902-.                         5.100
The making of mind: a personal account of Soviet psychology / A. R. Luria;
Michael Cole and Sheila Cole, eds.; introd. and epilogue by Michael Cole. —
Cambridge, Mass.: Harvard University Press, 1979. 234 p.: ill.; 24 cm.
1. Luriia, A. R. (Aleksandr Romanovich), 1902- 2. Psychologists — Soviet
Union — Biography. 3. Psychology — Soviet Union. I. Cole, Michael, 1938-
II. Cole, Sheila. III. T.
BF109.L87 A35      153/.092/4      LC 79-15203      ISBN 0674543262

Evans, Richard Isadore, 1922-.                                       5.101
Carl Rogers: the man and his ideas / Richard I. Evans. — 1st ed. — New York:
Dutton, 1975. lxxxviii, 195 p.; 22 cm. — (His Dialogues with notable
contributors to personality theory; v. 8) Includes index. 1. Rogers, Carl R.
(Carl Ransom), 1902- 2. Psychologists — United States — Biography.
3. Client-centered psychotherapy.
BF109.R63 E9 1975      150/.19/5      LC 74-23270      ISBN 052507645X

Evans, Richard Isadore, 1922-.                                     • 5.102
B. F. Skinner: the man and his ideas / [by] Richard I. Evans. — [1st ed.] New
York: Dutton, 1968. xiv, 140 p.; 19 cm. (His Dialogues with notable
contributors to personality theory, v. 4) 1. Skinner, B. F. (Burrhus Frederic),
1904- 2. Psychologists — United States — Biography. 3. Personality I. T.
BF109.S55 E9      150/.924      LC 68-28886

# BF110–149 GENERAL WORKS.
## TREATISES

Broad, C. D. (Charlie Dunbar), 1887-1971.                          • 5.103
Mind and its place in nature / by C. D. Broad. — London: K. Paul, Trench,
Trubner, 1925. 674 p.: ill. — (International library of psychology, philosophy,
and scientific method.) (Tarner lectures. 1923) 'Tarner lectures delivered in
Trinity college, Cambridge, 1923.' 1. Psychology 2. Knowledge, Theory of
3. Consciousness 4. Subconsciousness 5. Immortality I. T. II. Series.
III. Series: Tarner lectures. 1923
BF121 B8      LC 25-17638      ISBN 0710030347

Gleitman, Henry.                                                     5.104
Psychology / Henry Gleitman. — 1st ed. — New York: Norton, c1981. xxii,
745, 93 p.: ill.; 26 cm. 1. Psychology I. T.
BF121.G58 1981      150 19      LC 80-21380      ISBN 0393951022

Goodman, George J. W.                                                5.105
Powers of mind / Adam Smith [i.e. G. J. W. Goodman]. — 1st ed. — New
York: Random House, [1975] xi, 418 p.; 22 cm. 1. Psychology I. T.
BF121.G65      150      LC 75-10310      ISBN 0394498321

Helson, Harry, 1898- ed.                                           • 5.106
Contemporary approaches to psychology / edited by Harry Helson and
William Bevan in association with Jack A. Adams [and others]. — Princeton,
N.J.: Van Nostrand, [1967] xii, 596 p.: ill.; 25 cm. — (The University series in
psychology) 'Successor to [the first editor's] Theoretical foundations of
psychology (1951)' 1. Psychology I. Bevan, William, 1922- joint ed. II. T.
BF121.H42      150      LC 67-6959

Hilgard, Ernest Ropiequet, 1904-.                                  • 5.107
Introduction to psychology [by] Ernest R. Hilgard, Richard C. Atkinson [and]
Rita L. Atkinson. — 5th ed. — New York: Harcourt Brace Jovanovich, [1971]
xv, 640 p.: illus. (part col.); 25 cm. 1. Psychology I. Atkinson, Richard C. joint
author. II. Atkinson, Rita L. joint author. III. T.
BF121.H5 1971      150      LC 72-141606      ISBN 0155436473

James, William, 1842-1910.                                          5.108
The principles of psychology / William James; [Frederick H. Burkhardt,
general editor; Fredson Bowers, textual editor; Ignas K. Skrupskelis, associate
editor]. — Cambridge, Mass.: Harvard University Press, 1981. 3 v. (lxviii,
1740 p.); 24 cm. — (The Works of William James) Vol. 3: Notes appendixes,
apparatus, general index. 1. Psychology I. Burkhardt, Frederick, 1912-
II. Bowers, Fredson Thayer. III. Skrupskelis, Ignas K., 1938- IV. T.
BF121.J2 1981      150 19      LC 81-4194      ISBN 0674705599

Wilshire, Bruce.                                                    • 5.109
William James and phenomenology; a study of The principles of psychology. —
Bloomington: Indiana University Press, [1968] xi, 251 p.; 25 cm. 1. James,
William, 1842-1910. The principles of psychology. I. T.
BF121.J3 W5 1968      150.19/2      LC 68-27358

Werner, Heinz, 1890-.                                              • 5.110
Comparative psychology of mental development. With a foreword by Gordon
W. Allport. Rev. ed. New York, International Universities Press, 1957, [c1948]
xii, 564 p. illus. 22 cm. Translation by E. B. Garside of Einführung in die
Entwicklungs-psychologie. 1. Psychology I. T.
BF 123 W493      LC A 58-3272

Wundt, Wilhelm Max, 1832-1920.                                     • 5.111
Outlines of psychology. Translated, with the cooperation of the author, by
Charles Hubbard Judd. Leipzig, W. Engelmann, New York, G. E. Stechert,
1897. — St. Clair Shores, Mich.: Scholarly Press, [1969?] xviii, 342 p.; 22 cm.
1. Psychology I. Judd, Charles Hubbard, 1873-1946, tr. II. T.
BF123.W93 1969      150      LC 70-7682      ISBN 0403000386

Young, Paul Thomas, 1892-.                                         • 5.112
Motivation and emotion: a survey of the determinants of human and animal
activity. — New York: Wiley, [1961] 648 p.: illus.; 24 cm. 1. Psychology
2. Psychology, Comparative 3. Motivation (Psychology) 4. Emotions I. T.
BF131.Y58      159.4      LC 61-11495

## BF149 Addresses. Essays. Lectures

**Bertalanffy, Ludwig von, 1901-1972.** • **5.113**
Robots, men, and minds: psychology in the modern world. — New York: G. Braziller, [1967] x, 150 p.; 22 cm. 'Based upon the Heinz Werner inaugural lectures presented by the author at Clark University, January 13 and 14, 1966.' 1. Psychology — Addresses, essays, lectures. 2. Science — Addresses, essays, lectures. I. T.
BF149.B4     150     *LC* 67-27524

**A Century of psychology as science** / edited by Sigmund Koch, **5.114**
David E. Leary.
New York: McGraw-Hill, c1985. xi, 990 p.: ill.; 25 cm. 1. Psychology — Addresses, essays, lectures. 2. Psychology — History — Addresses, essays, lectures. I. Koch, Sigmund. II. Leary, David E.
BF149.C36 1985     150/.9 19     *LC* 83-9836     *ISBN* 0070352496

**Goodman, Paul, 1911-1972.** **5.115**
Nature heals = Natura sanat non medicus: the psychological essays of Paul Goodman / edited by Taylor Stoehr. — 1st ed. — New York: Free Life Editions, 1977. xxiv, 259 p.; 22 cm. — (His Weapons that do not weigh one down) 1. Psychology — Addresses, essays, lectures. 2. Psychoanalysis — Addresses, essays, lectures. 3. Psychology, Pathological — Addresses, essays, lectures. I. Stoehr, Taylor, 1931- II. T. III. Title: Natura sanat non medicus. IV. Series.
BF149.G66 1977     150/.19/5     *LC* 77-71941     *ISBN* 0914156187

**McClelland, David Clarence.** • **5.116**
The roots of consciousness / by David C. McClelland. — Princeton, N. J.,: Van Nostrand, [1964]. –. v, 219 p.: ill.; 18 cm. — (An Insight book; 21) 1. Psychology — Addresses, essays, lectures. I. T.
BF149.M2     150.82     *LC* 64-9683

**Masterson, Jenny (Gove) pseud.** • **5.117**
Letters from Jenny / edited and interpreted by Gordon W. Allport. — New York: Harcourt, Brace & World [1965] xii, 223 p.: ill., facsim., ports.; 21 cm. (An Original harbinger book) Originally published in the Journal of abnormal and social psychology, v. 41, no. 3-4. 1. Mental illness — Case studies. I. Allport, Gordon W. (Gordon Willard), 1897-1967. ed. II. T.
BF149.M35     132.6     *LC* 65-18327

**Murray, Henry Alexander, 1893-.** **5.118**
Endeavors in psychology: selections from the personology of Henry A. Murray / edited by Edwin S. Shneidman. — 1st ed. — New York: Harper & Row, c1981. vi, 641 p.; 24 cm. Includes index. 1. Psychology — Addresses, essays, lectures. 2. Personality — Addresses, essays, lectures. I. Shneidman, Edwin S. II. T.
BF149.M864 1981     150 19     *LC* 80-7598     *ISBN* 0060140399

**Psychology and extrasensory perception** / edited and with an **5.119**
introd. by Raymond Van Over.
New York; Scarborough, Ont.: New American Library, c1972. 416 p. — (A Mentor book) 1. Psychology — Addresses, essays, lectures 2. Psychical research — Addresses, essays, lectures 3. Extrasensory perception — Addresses, essays, lectures I. Van Over, Raymond.
BF149 P795     *LC* 72-88856

**Thorndike, Edward L. (Edward Lee), 1874-1949.** • **5.120**
Selected writings from a connectionist's psychology. New York, Greenwood Press [1969, c1949] vii, 370 p. port. 23 cm. (The Century psychology series) 1. Psychology — Addresses, essays, lectures. I. T.
BF149.T48 1969     150/.8     *LC* 76-94621     *ISBN* 0837125707

**Vanderplas, James M.** • **5.121**
Controversial issues in psychology / James M. Vanderplas. — Boston: Houghton Mifflin, 1966. x, 438 p. 1. Psychology — Addresses, essays, lectures. I. T.
BF149.V26     150     *LC* 66-7511

## BF150–171 MIND AND BODY

**Langer, Susanne Katherina Knauth, 1895-.** **5.122**
Mind: an essay on human feeling / [by] Susanne K. Langer. — Baltimore: Johns Hopkins Press, 1967-1982. 3 v.: ill.; 24 cm. 1. Mind and body 2. Senses and sensation 3. Aesthetics I. T.
BF161.L28     152.4/4     *LC* 66-26686     *ISBN* 0801814286

**Sayre, Kenneth M., 1928-.** **5.123**
Cybernetics and the philosophy of mind / Kenneth M. Sayre. Atlantic Highlands, N.J.: Humanities Press, 1976. xiii, 265 p.; 23 cm. (International library of philosophy and scientific method.) Includes index. 1. Mind and body 2. Cybernetics I. T. II. Series.
BF161.S23 1976     001.53     *LC* 76-4930     *ISBN* 0391005944

**Searle, John R.** **5.124**
Minds, brains, and science / John Searle. — Cambridge, Mass.: Harvard University Press, 1985 [c1984] 107 p.; 22 cm. (The 1984 Reith lectures) Includes index. 1. Mind and body 2. Brain 3. Thought and thinking I. T.
BF161.S352 1984     128/.2 19     *LC* 84-25260     *ISBN* 0674576314

**Miller, Jonathan, 1934-.** **5.125**
States of mind / Jonathan Miller. — New York: Pantheon, c1983. 316 p.: ill.; 24 cm. Includes index. 1. Psychology — Addresses, essays, lectures. 2. Scientists — Interviews. I. T.
BF171.M54 1983     150 19     *LC* 82-48953     *ISBN* 0394530144

## BF173–175 PSYCHOANALYSIS

**Abraham, Karl, 1877-1925.** • **5.126**
[Selections. English.] Selected papers of Karl Abraham, M.D. / with an introductory memoir by Ernest Jones; translated by Douglas Bryan and Alix Strachey. — New York: Brunner/Mazel, [1979] c1927. 527 p.: port.; 23 cm. (The Brunner/Mazel classics in psychoanalysis; no. 3) On spine: Selected papers on psycho-analysis. Reprint of the ed. published by Hogarth Press and the Institute of Psycho-analysis, London as no. 13 of the International psycho-analytical library. Includes index. 1. Psychoanalysis I. Jones, Ernest, 1879-1958. II. T. III. Title: Selected papers on psycho-analysis.
BF173.A3 1979     150/.19/52     *LC* 79-11443     *ISBN* 0876302061

**Adler, Alfred, 1870-1937.** • **5.127**
The individual psychology of Alfred Adler: a systematic presentation in selections from his writings / edited and annotated by Heinz L. Ansbacher and Rowena R. Ansbacher. — [1st ed.]. — New York: Basic Books, [1956] xxiii, 503 p.: port., diagrs.; 25 cm. 1. Psychoanalysis I. T.
BF173.A47     131.3463     *LC* 55-6679

**Adler, Alfred, 1870-1937.** **5.128**
Superiority and social interest: a collection of later writings / Alfred Adler; edited by Heinz L. Ansbacher and Rowena R. Ansbacher; with a biographical essay by Carl Furtmüller and Adler bibliography. — 3d rev. ed. — New York: Norton, 1979. xix, 438 p.; 19 cm. 1. Saller, Alfred, 1870-1937. 2. Psychoanalysis 3. Psychoanalysts — Austria — Biography. I. Ansbacher, Heinz Ludwig, 1904- II. Ansbacher, Rowena R. III. T.
BF173.A548 1979     150/.19/5308     *LC* 78-27620     *ISBN* 0393009106

**Arlow, Jacob A.** **5.129**
Psychoanalytic concepts and the structural theory. New York, International Universities Press [1964] xii, 201 p. 23 cm. 1. Psychoanalysis I. Brenner, Charles, 1913- joint author. II. T.
BF173.A688     *LC* 64-16190

**Brill, A. A. (Abraham Arden), 1874-1948.** • **5.130**
Basic principles of psychoanalysis, with an introd. by Philip R. Lehrman. [1st ed.] Garden City, N.Y., Doubleday, 1949. xv, 298 p. 22 cm. A new ed. of Fundamental conceptions of psychoanalysis, rev. and rewritten by the author; editing completed by Philip R. Lehrman. 1. Psychoanalysis I. Lehrman, Philip Raphael, 1895- II. T.
BF173.B82 1949     *LC* 49-7285

**Eagle, Morris N.** **5.131**
Recent developments in psychoanalysis: a critical evaluation / Morris N. Eagle. — New York: McGraw-Hill, c1984. xi, 259 p.; 24 cm. Includes index. 1. Psychoanalysis 2. Interpersonal relations 3. Self I. T.
BF173.E16 1984     150.19/5 19     *LC* 83-23887     *ISBN* 0070185972

Erdelyi, Matthew Hugh. **5.132**
Psychoanalysis: Freud's cognitive psychology / Matthew Hugh Erdelyi. — New York: W.H. Freeman, c1985. xv, 303 p.: ill.; 24 cm. (Series of books in psychology.) Includes indexes. 1. Freud, Sigmund, 1856-1939. 2. Psychoanalysis 3. Psychotherapy I. T. II. Series.
BF173.E646 1985    150.19/52 19    LC 84-6056    ISBN 0716716178

## BF173 Freud, Sigmund

**Freud, Sigmund, 1856-1939.** • **5.133**
[Selections. English. 1938] The basic writings of Sigmund Freud; translated and edited, with an introduction, by Dr. A. A. Brill. New York, The Modern library [c1938] vi, 1001 p. diagrs. 21 cm. (The Modern library of the world's best books) 'First Modern library edition, 1938.' 1. Psychoanalysis I. Brill, A. A. (Abraham Arden), 1874-1948. ed. and tr. II. T.
BF173.F625    131.3462 159.964262    LC 38-27462

**Freud, Sigmund, 1856-1939.** • **5.134**
The standard edition of the complete psychological works of Sigmund Freud / translated from the German under the general editorship of James Strachey, in collaboration with Anna Freud, assisted by Alix Strachey and Alan Tyson. — London: Hogarth Press, 1953-1974. 24 v.: ill., ports. Vol. 24, indexes and bibliographies compiled by A. Richards. 1. Psychoanalysis I. Strachey, James. II. Freud, Anna, 1895- III. Richards, Angela. IV. T.
BF173.F6253    150/.19/52    LC a 53-7988

**Freud, Sigmund, 1856-1939.** • **5.135**
[Abriss der Psychoanalyse. English] An outline of psycho-analysis. Translated and newly edited by James Strachey. New York, W. W. Norton [1970, c1969] xi, 75 p. 21 cm. Translation of Abriss der Psychoanalyse. 1. Psychoanalysis I. Strachey, James. ed. II. T.
BF173.F62913 1970    150.19/52    LC 72-108329    ISBN 039301083X

**Freud, Sigmund, 1856-1939.** • **5.136**
[Aus den Aufäugen der Psychoanalyse. English] The origins of psycho-analysis; letters to Wilhelm Fliess, drafts and notes, 1887–1902. Edited by Marie Bonaparte, Anna Freud [and] Ernst Kris; authorized translation by Eric Mosbacher and James Strachey. Introd. by Ernst Kris. [1st ed.] New York, Basic Books [1954] xi, 486 p. diagrs. 24 cm. 1. Psychoanalysis I. Fliess, Wilhelm, 1858-1928. II. T.
BF173.F62943    131.3462    LC 54-8148

**Freud, Sigmund, 1856-1939.** • **5.137**
The case of Dora and other papers / translations by Joan Riviere [and others] — New York: Norton [c1952] vi, 243 p. I. T.
BF173.F6296

**Freud, Sigmund, 1856-1939.** • **5.138**
The ego and the id. Newly translated from the German and edited by James Strachey. [1st American ed.] New York, Norton [1961, c1960] 88 p.; 22 cm. 1. Psychoanalysis I. T.
BF173.F645 1961    131.341    LC 61-5935

**Freud, Sigmund, 1856-1939.** • **5.139**
[Jenseits des Lustprinzips. English] Beyond the pleasure principle. Translated and newly edited by James Strachey. Introd. by Gregory Zilboorg. New York, Liveright [1970, c1961] xx, 68 p. 21 cm. Translation of Jenseits des Lust-Prinzips. 1. Pleasure principle. 2. Psychoanalysis I. Strachery, James, ed. II. T.
BF173.F65 1970    150.19/52    LC 70-114388

**Freud, Sigmund, 1856-1939.** **5.140**
The essentials of psycho-analysis / Sigmund Freud; selected, with an introduction and commentaries, by Anna Freud; translated from the German by James Strachey. — London: Hogarth and the Institute of Psycho-Analysis, 1986. x, 597 p.; 23 cm. (International psycho-analytical library. no.116) Includes index. 1. Freud, Sigmund, 1856-1939. 2. Psychoanalysis I. Freud, Anna, 1895- II. Institute of Psycho-analysis (London, England) III. T. IV. Series.
BF173.F657    150.19/52 19    ISBN 0701207205

**Freud, Sigmund, 1856-1939.** • **5.141**
[Selections. English. 1959] Collected papers / authorized translation under the supervision of Joan Riviere. — [1st American ed.] New York: Basic Books [1959] 5 v.: ill.; 22 cm. (The International psycho-analytical library; no. 7-10, 37) Vols. 1-4 are a translation, rearranged in cooperation with the author, of Sammlung kleiner Schriften zur Neurosenlehre. Vol. 3: Authorized translation by Alix and James Strachey; v. 5 edited by James Strachey. 1. Psychoanalysis I. Riviere, Joan, 1883- II. Strachey, James. III. T.
BF173.F673    150/.19/5208    LC 59-8642

**Freud, Sigmund, 1856-1939.** • **5.142**
The origin and development of psychoanalysis / Sigmund Freud; introd. by Eliseo Vivas. — South Bend, Indiana: Gateway Editions, 1955. 59 p.; 18 cm. — (Gateway edition) 1. Psychoanalysis I. T.
BF173.F6784    LC 55-4350

**Freud, Sigmund, 1856-1939.** • **5.143**
[Unbehagen in der Kultur. English] Civilization and its discontents / newly translated from the German and edited by James Strachey. — [1st American ed.] New York: W. W. Norton [1962, c1961] 109 p.; 22 cm. Translation of Das Unbehagen in der Kultur. 1. Psychoanalysis and culture 2. Civilization I. T.
BF173.F682 1962    131    LC 61-11340

**Freud, Sigmund, 1856-1939.** • **5.144**
[Vorlesungen zur Einführung in die Psychoanalyse. English] The complete introductory lectures on psychoanalysis. Translated and edited by James Strachey. New York, W. W. Norton [1966] 690 p. 25 cm. 1. Psychoanalysis I. Freud, Sigmund, 1856-1939. Vorlesungen zur Einführung in die Psychoanalyse. Neue Folge. English. 1966. II. Strachey, James. ed. and tr. III. T.
BF173.F7 1966    150.1952    LC 66-16766

**Freud, Sigmund, 1856-1939.** **5.145**
Group psychology and the analysis of the ego / authorized translation by James Strachey. — New York: Liveright Pub. Corp.,c1951. 134 p. — (The International psychoanalytical library) 1. Psychoanalysis 2. Social psychology I. T. II. Series.
BF173.F713 1951

**Freud, Sigmund, 1856-1939.** • **5.146**
[Zur Psychopathologie des Alltagslebens. English] The psychopathology of everyday life. Translated from the German by Alan Tyson. Edited with an introd. and additional notes by James Strachey. New York, Norton [1966, c1965] xiii, 310 p. 21 cm. 1. Psychoanalysis 2. Memory 3. Repression (Psychology) 4. Association of ideas 5. Mental illness I. Strachey, James. ed. II. T.
BF173.F825    157    LC 65-21619

**Freud, Sigmund, 1856-1939.** **5.147**
[Correspondence. English. Selections] The complete letters of Sigmund Freud to Wilhelm Fliess, 1887–1904 / translated and edited by Jeffrey Moussaieff Masson. — Cambridge, Mass.: Belknap Press of Harvard University Press, 1985. xv, 505 p., [20] p. of plates: ill., ports.; 24 cm. Includes index. 1. Freud, Sigmund, 1856-1939 — Correspondence. 2. Fliess, Wilhelm, 1858-1928. 3. Psychoanalysts — Correspondence. 4. Psychoanalysis I. Masson, J. Moussaieff (Jeffrey Moussaieff), 1941- II. Fliess, Wilhelm, 1858-1928. III. T.
BF173.F85 A4 1985    150.19/52 19    LC 84-24516    ISBN 0674154207

**Freud, Sigmund, 1856-1939.** • **5.148**
Psychoanalysis and faith; the letters of Sigmund Freud and Oskar Pfister. Edited by Heinrich Meng and Ernst L. Freud. Translated by Eric Mosbacher. New York, Basic Books [1964, c1963] 152 p. 22 cm. Bibliographical footnotes. 1. Psychoanalysis 2. Psychiatry and religion I. Pfister, Oskar, 1873-1956. II. T.
BF173.F85A443    131.3462    LC 63-22668

## Biography. Criticism

**Bettelheim, Bruno.** **5.149**
Freud and man's soul / Bruno Bettelheim. — 1st ed. — New York: A.A. Knopf: Distributed by Random House, 1983, c1982. xi, 111 p.; 22 cm. 1. Freud, Sigmund, 1856-1939. 2. Psychoanalysis 3. Psychoanalysis — Translating. 4. Soul — Psychological aspects. I. T.
BF173.F85 B46 1983    150.19/52 19    LC 82-47809    ISBN 0394524810

**Brown, J. A. C. (James Alexander Campbell), 1911-1964.** • **5.150**
Freud and the post–Freudians. London, Cassell [1963, c1961] viii, 227 p. 21 cm. 1. Freud, Sigmund, 1856-1939. I. T.
BF173.F85 B76 1963    LC 63-25081

**Fine, Reuben, 1914-.** • **5.151**
Freud: a critical re-evaluation of his theories. — New York: D. McKay Co., [1962] 307 p.; 22 cm. 1. Freud, Sigmund, 1856-1939. I. T.
BF173.F85 F5    131.3462    LC 62-18462

**Fisher, Seymour.** • **5.152**
The scientific credibility of Freud's theories and therapy / Seymour Fisher & Roger P. Greenberg. — New York: Basic Books, c1977. x, 502 p.; 24 cm. Includes indexes. 1. Freud, Sigmund, 1856-1939 — Criticism and interpretation. 2. Psychoanalysis I. Greenberg, Roger P. joint author. II. T.
BF173.F85 F55    150/.19/52    LC 76-30453    ISBN 0465073859

**Freud and his patients / edited by Mark Kanzer and Jules Glenn.**    **5.153**
New York: Aronson, c1980. viii, 452 p. — (Downstate Psychoanalytic Institute twenty-fifth anniversary series. v. 2) 1. Freud, Sigmund, 1856-1939. 2. Psychoanalysis — Case and studies I. Glenn, Jules, 1921- II. Kanzer, Mark, 1908- III. Freud, Sigmund, 1856-1939. IV. Series.
BF173F85 F736    *ISBN* 0876683677

**Hall, Calvin S. (Calvin Springer), 1909-.**    **• 5.154**
A primer of Freudian psychology. — [1st ed.]. — Cleveland: World Pub. Co., [1954] 137 p.; 21 cm. 1. Freud, Sigmund, 1856-1939. 2. Psychology 3. Personality I. T.
BF173.F85 H32    131.3462    *LC* 54-10357

**Jones, Ernest, 1879-1958.**    **• 5.155**
The life and work of Sigmund Freud. — [1st ed.]. — New York: Basic Books, [1953-57] 3 v.: illus., ports.; 24 cm. 1. Freud, Sigmund, 1856-1939. I. T.
BF173.F85 J6    926.1 921.36    *LC* 53-8700

**Rieff, Philip, 1922-.**    **• 5.156**
Freud, the mind of the moralist / by Philip Rieff. — New York: Viking Press, c1959. — xvi, 397 p.; 22 cm. 1. Freud, Sigmund, 1856-1939. I. T.
BF173.F85 R48 1959    *LC* 59-5646

## BF173 F–M

**Evans, Richard Isadore, 1922-.**    **• 5.157**
Dialogue with Erich Fromm, by Richard I. Evans. — [1st ed.]. — New York: Harper & Row, [1966] xix, 136 p.; 22 cm. — (His Dialogues with notable contributors to personality theory, v. 2) 1. Fromm, Erich, 1900- 2. Psychologists — United States — Biography. 3. Personality I. T.
BF173.F89 E9    150.1957    *LC* 66-13939

**Greenberg, Jay R., 1942-.**    **5.158**
Object relations in psychoanalytic theory / Jay R. Greenberg and Stephen A. Mitchell. — Cambridge, Mass.: Harvard University Press, 1983. x, 437 p.; 25 cm. Includes index. 1. Psychoanalysis 2. Object relations (Psychoanalysis) I. Mitchell, Stephen A., 1946- II. T.
BF173.G714 1983    150.19/5 19    *LC* 83-8580    *ISBN* 0674629752

**Grünbaum, Adolf.**    **5.159**
The foundations of psychoanalysis: a philosophical critique / Adolf Grünbaum. — Berkeley: University of California Press, 1984. xiv, 310 p.; 23 cm. (Pittsburgh series in philosophy and history of science.) Includes indexes. 1. Freud, Sigmund, 1856-1939. 2. Psychoanalysis — Philosophy. I. T. II. Series.
BF173.G76 1984    150.19/52 19    *LC* 83-9264    *ISBN* 0520050169

**Hartmann, Heinz, 1894-.**    **5.160**
Essays on ego psychology: selected problems in psychoanalytic theory. — New York: International Universities Press [1964] xv, 492 p.; 25 cm. 1. Psychoanalysis — Addresses, essays, lectures. I. T.
BF173.H397    *LC* 64-14655

**Heider, Fritz, 1896-.**    **• 5.161**
On perception, event structure, and psychological environment: selected papers / by Fritz Heider. — New York: International Universities Press, 1959. xi, 123 p.:bill.; 23 cm. — (Psychological issues; v.1, no.3, Monograph 3.) 1. Perception I. T.
BF173.H432    *LC* 60-1572

**Holt, Robert R. comp.**    **5.162**
Motives and thought; psychoanalytic essays in honor of David Rapaport, edited by Robert R. Holt. — New York: International Universities Press, [1967] v, 413 p.: port.; 23 cm. — (Psychological issues, v. 5 no. 2-3. Monograph 18/19) 1. Motivation (Psychology) — Addresses, essays, lectures. 2. Cognition — Addresses, essays, lectures. 3. Psychoanalysis — Addresses, essays, lectures. I. Rapaport, David. II. T. III. Series.
BF173.H735    150.19/5    *LC* 67-20615

**Horney, Karen, 1885-1952.**    **• 5.163**
New ways in psychoanalysis / Karen Horney. — New York: W.W. Norton, 1939. 313 p. 1. Psychoanalysis I. T.
BF173.H762 1939    *LC* 39-5922

**Horney, Karen, 1885-1952.**    **• 5.164**
Self–analysis [by] Karen Horney, M. D. — New York: W. W. Norton & company, inc., [1942] 309 p.; 22 cm. 'First edition.' 1. Psychoanalysis I. T.
BF173.H7625    131.342    *LC* 42-6940

**Jung, C. G. (Carl Gustav), 1875-1961.**    **5.165**
[Selections. English. 1983] The essential Jung / selected and introduced by Anthony Storr. — Princeton, N.J.: Princeton University Press, c1983. 447 p.:

ill.; 22 cm. Includes index. 1. Psychoanalysis — Addresses, essays, lectures. I. Storr, Anthony. II. T.
BF173.J6623 1983    150.19/54 19    *LC* 82-61441    *ISBN* 0691024553

**Jung, C. G. (Carl Gustav), 1875-1961.**    **• 5.166**
Basic writings / edited with an introd. by Violet Staub de Laszlo. — New York: Modern Library [1959] xxiii, 552 p.; 19 cm. (The Modern library of the world's best books [300]) 1. Psychoanalysis I. T.
BF173.J67    131.3464    *LC* 59-5910

**Jung, C. G. (Carl Gustav), 1875-1961.**    **5.167**
Modern man in search of a soul. [Translated by W. S. Dell and Cary F. Baynes] New York, Harcourt, Brace [1950?] ix, 282 p. 22 cm. 'With one exception, all the essays which make up this volume have been delivered as lectures. The German texts of four of them have been brought out in separate publications and the others are to be found in a volume [Seelenprobleme der Gegenwart] together with several other essays which have already appeared in English.' 1. Psychoanalysis 2. Therapeutics, Suggestive I. T.
BF173.J74 1950    131.3464    *LC* 50-4826

**Jung, C. G. (Carl Gustav), 1875-1961.**    **• 5.168**
The portable Jung. Edited, with an introd., by Joseph Campbell. Translated by R. F. C. Hull. New York, Viking Press [1971] xlii, 659 p. 19 cm. (Viking portable library 70) 1. Psychoanalysis I. Campbell, Joseph, 1904- ed. II. T.
BF173.J743 1971    150.19/54/08    *LC* 78-157974    *ISBN* 0670410624 *ISBN* 0670010707

**Evans, Richard Isadore, 1922-.**    **5.169**
Jung on elementary psychology: a discussion between C. G. Jung and Richard I. Evans / Richard I. Evans. — 1st ed. — New York: Dutton, 1976. xi, 242 p.; 19 cm. Rev. and expanded ed. of the work published in 1964 under title: Conversations with Carl Jung and reactions from Ernest Jones. Includes both an edited version and the complete transcripts of 4 one-hour discussions between Jung and Evans, Aug. 5-8, 1957. The Jones material is omitted from this ed. Includes index. 1. Jung, C. G. (Carl Gustav), 1875-1961. 2. Psychoanalysis. I. Jung, C. G. (Carl Gustav), 1875-1961. II. T.
BF173.J85 E9 1976    150/.19/54    *LC* 75-29196    *ISBN* 0525474153

**Klein, George Stuart, 1917-.**    **5.170**
Psychoanalytic theory: an exploration of essentials / George S. Klein. — New York: International Universities Press, [1976] x, 330 p.; 24 cm. Includes index. 1. Psychoanalysis I. T.
BF173.K47    150/.19/5    *LC* 75-18508    *ISBN* 0823650596

**Klein, Melanie.**    **5.171**
Love, guilt, and reparation & other works, 1921–1945 / Melanie Klein; with an introd. by R. E. Money–Kyrle. — [New York]: Delacorte Press/S. Lawrence, c1975. xi, 468 p.: ill.; 24 cm. (Her The writings of Melanie Klein) Includes index. 1. Psychoanalysis — Addresses, essays, lectures. 2. Personality in children — Addresses, essays, lectures. 3. Child analysis — Addresses, essays, lectures. I. T. II. Series.
BF173.K4825 1975    150/.19/52    *LC* 77-351135    *ISBN* 0440050219

**Segal, Hanna.**    **5.172**
Introduction to the work of Melanie Klein. — New enl. ed. — New York: Basic Books, [1974, c1973] x, 144 p.; 22 cm. 1. Klein, Melanie. 2. Psychoanalysis I. T.
BF173.K49 S4 1974    150/.19/50924    *LC* 73-91077    *ISBN* 0465035817

**Lasswell, Harold Dwight, 1902-.**    **• 5.173**
Psychopathology and politics. A new ed. with after thoughts by the author.— New ed.— New York: Viking Press, [1960] 319p. (Compass books; C71) 1. Psychoanalysis 2. Political science I. T.
BF173 L24 1960    *LC* 60-16208

**Marcuse, Herbert, 1898-.**    **• 5.174**
Eros and civilization: a philosophical inquiry into Freud. — Boston: Beacon Press, [1955] xii, 227 p.: diagr.; 22 cm. — (Humanitas; Beacon studies in humanities) 1. Freud, Sigmund, 1856-1939. 2. Social psychology 3. Civilization 4. Psychoanalysis I. T.
BF173.M3566    131.3462    *LC* 55-10920

**Menninger, Karl Augustus, 1893-.**    **• 5.175**
The human mind [by] Karl A. Menninger. 3rd ed., corr., enl. & rewritten. New York, A. A. Knopf, 1945. xvii, 517, xiv p., 1 l., diagrs. 24 cm. 1. Psychoanalysis 2. Psychology, Pathological 3. Mental health 4. Personality, Disorders of I. T.
BF173.M36 1945    132    *LC* 45-3595

**Mullahy, Patrick, 1912-.**    **• 5.176**
Oedipus: myth and complex; a review of psychoanalytic theory. Introd. [by] Erich Fromm. [1st ed.] New York, Hermitage Press, 1948. xix, 538 p. 22 cm. 'The Oedipus trilogy by Sophocles: Oedipus Rex, Antigone, Oedipus at

Colonus': p. [339]-506. Bibliography: p. 532-538. 1. Oedipus. 2. Psychoanalysis I. Sophocles. II. T.
BF173.M82      131.34123      LC 49-530 *

**Munroe, Ruth Learned, 1903-.**                                    • **5.177**
Schools of psychoanalytic thought: an exposition, critique, and attempt at integration. — [New York]: Dryden Press [1955] 670 p.; 26 cm. (The Dryden Press publications in interpersonal relations) 1. Psychoanalysis I. T. II. Series.
BF173.M825      LC 55-14811

## BF173 N–Z

**New York University Institute of Philosophy. 2d, 1958.**          • **5.178**
Psychoanalysis: scientific method and philosophy; a symposium. New York, Grove Press [1960, c1959] xiii, 370 p. 20 cm. 1. Psychoanalysis — Addresses, essays, lectures. I. Hook, Sidney, 1902- ed. II. T.
BF173.N44 1958a      LC 60-50526

**Perls, Frederick S.**                                              • **5.179**
Ego, hunger, and aggression; the beginning of gestalt therapy, by F. S. Perls. — New York: Random House, [1969] 273 p.: illus.; 22 cm. 1. Freud, Sigmund, 1856-1939. 2. Ego (Psychology) 3. Gestalt therapy I. T.
BF173.P46 1969      150.19/82      LC 68-28547

**Psychology versus metapsychology: psychoanalytic essays in          5.180
memory of George S. Klein / edited by Merton M. Gill and
Philip S. Holzman.**
New York: International Universities Press, c1976. 376 p.: port.; 24 cm. (Psychological issues. v. 9, no. 4, monograph 36) 1. Psychoanalysis — Addresses, essays, lectures. I. Klein, George Stuart, 1917-1971. II. Gill, Merton Max, 1914- III. Holzman, Philip S., 1922- IV. Series.
BF173.P777      150/.19/5      LC 75-23354      ISBN 0823655865

**Pumpian-Mindlin, Eugene, 1908-1976, ed.**                          • **5.181**
Psychoanalysis as science; the Hixon lectures on the scientific status of psychoanalysis, [by] Ernest R. Hilgard, Lawrence S. Kubie [and] E. Pumpian-Mindlin. Edited by E. Pumpian-Mindlin. — Westport, Conn.: Greenwood Press, [1970, c1952] x, 174 p.: illus.; 24 cm. 'Delivered at the California Institute of Technology, Department of Biology, Pasadena, California, March-May 1950, under the sponsorship of the Hixon Fund Committee.' 1. Psychoanalysis I. Hilgard, Ernest Ropiequet, 1904- II. Kubie, Lawrence Schlesinger, 1896- III. California Institute of Technology, Pasadena. Hixon Fund. IV. T.
BF173.P78 1970      150.19/5      LC 70-106692      ISBN 0837133653

**Menaker, Esther.**                                                  **5.182**
Otto Rank, a rediscovered legacy / Esther Menaker. — New York: Columbia University Press, 1982. xvii, 166 p.; 24 cm. Includes index. 1. Rank, Otto, 1884-1939. 2. Freud, Sigmund, 1856-1939. 3. Psychoanalysis I. T.
BF173.R36 M46      150.19/5/0924 19      LC 81-15489      ISBN 0231051166

**Rapaport, David.**                                                  **5.183**
Collected papers/ Edited by Merton M. Gill.— New York: Basic books, [1967] x, 943 p. port. 1. Psychoanalysis — Collected works I. T.
BF173 R3615

**Rapaport, David.**                                                  • **5.184**
The structure of psychoanalytic theory: a systematizing attempt / David Rapaport. — New York: International Universities Press, 1960. 158 p.; 23 cm. — (Psychological issues. v.2, no.2. Monograph 6.) 1. Psychoanalysis I. T. II. Series.
BF173.R362      LC 60-2852

**Reich, Wilhelm, 1897-1957.**                                        • **5.185**
[Charakteranalyse. English] Character–analysis; tr. by Theodore P. Wolfe. 3d, enl. ed. New York, Orgone Institute Press, 1949. xxvi, 516 p. diagrs. 24 cm. Translation of Charakteranalyse, and of Psychischer Kontakt und vegetative Strömung. To these have been added two articles: The expressive language of the living in orgone therapy, and The schizophrenic split. 1. Psychoanalysis 2. Sex (Psychology) I. T.
BF173.R372 1949      131.34      LC 49-5130

**Reik, Theodor, 1888-1969.**                                        • **5.186**
Listening with the third ear; the inner experience of a psychoanalyst. New York, Grove Press [1956, c1948] 514 p. illus. 21 cm. (Evergreen book. E-34) 1. Psychoanalysis I. T. II. Series.
BF173.R4x      LC 56-8438

**Rorschach, Hermann, 1884-1922.**                                   • **5.187**
Psychodiagnostics; a diagnostic test based on perception, including Rorschach's paper: The application of the form interpretation test (published posthumously by Emil Oberholzer) Translation and English ed. by Paul Lemkau and Bernard Kronenberg. Editor, W. Morgenthaler. — 3d ed., rev. and enl. — Berne: Huber,

[c1942-. 238 p. and portfolio of plates plates. I. Oberholzer, Emil, 1883- II. Lemkau, Paul, 1909- III. Morgenthaler, Walter, 1882- IV. T.
BF173.R623      LC 48-36909

**Schafer, Roy.**                                                     • **5.188**
Psychoanalytic interpretation in Rorschach testing: theory and application / Roy Schafer. — New York: Grune & Stratton, c1954. xiv, 446 p. — (Monograph series / Austen Riggs Foundation; no. 3) Includes indexes. 1. Psychoanalysis 2. Rorschach test I. T.
BF173.R63 S3      LC 54-9030      ISBN 0808904043

**Sarbin, Theodore R.**                                              • **5.189**
Studies in behavior pathology: the experimental approach to the psychology of the abnormal / Edited by Theodore R. Sarbin. New York: Holt, Rinehart and Winston, c1961. 341 p. ill. 1. Psychology, Pathological 2. Psychiatry I. T. II. Title: Behavior pathology
BF173.S326      BF173.S23.      132      LC 61-14604

**Schafer, Roy.**                                                     **5.190**
A new language for psychoanalysis / Roy Schafer. — New Haven: Yale University Press, 1976. xii, 394 p.; 25 cm. Includes index. 1. Psychoanalysis I. T.
BF173.S3278      150/.19/5      LC 75-18185      ISBN 0300018940

**White, Robert Winthrop.**                                           **5.191**
Ego and reality in psychoanalytic theory; a proposal regarding independent ego energies. — New York: International Universities Press, c1963. iv, 210 p.; 23 cm. — (Psychological issues, v. 3, no. 3. Monograph 11) 1. Ego (Psychology) I. T. II. Series.
BF173.W443      LC 63-19631

# BF175 Special Aspects

**Abraham, Karl, 1877-1925.**                                        • **5.192**
On character and libido development: six essays / edited with an introd. by Bertram D. Lewin; translated by Douglas Bryan and Alix Strachey. — New York: W.W. Norton, 1966. 206 p. (The Norton library, N316) 1. Psychoanalysis — Addresses, essays, lectures. 2. Sex (Psychology) — Addresses, essays, lectures. I. Lewin, Bertram David, 1896- II. T.
BF175.A25

**Brown, Norman Oliver, 1913-.**                                     • **5.193**
Love's body, by Norman O. Brown. — New York: Random House, [1966] 276 p.; 22 cm. 1. Psychoanalysis I. T.
BF175.B72      150.195      LC 66-11979

**Edelson, Marshall.**                                                **5.194**
Hypothesis and evidence in psychoanalysis / Marshall Edelson. — Chicago: University of Chicago Press, c1984. xiv, 179 p.; 22 cm. Includes index. 1. Psychoanalysis 2. Psychoanalysis — Research. I. T.
BF175.E29 1984      616.89/17 19      LC 83-9281      ISBN 0226184323

**Edinger, Edward F.**                                                **5.195**
Ego and archetype; individuation and the religious function of the psyche, by Edward F. Edinger. — New York: Published by Putnam for the C. G. Jung Foundation for Analytical Psychology [1972] xv, 304 p.: illus. (part col.); 24 cm. 1. Psychoanalysis and religion 2. Ego (Psychology) 3. Archetype (Psychology) I. Jung Foundation for Analytical Psychology, New York. II. T.
BF175.E3 1972      150/.19/54      LC 75-188717

**Erikson, Erik H. (Erik Homburger), 1902-.**                        • **5.196**
Identity and the life cycle; selected papers, with a historical introd. by David Rapaport. New York, International Universities Press, 1959. 171 p. illus. 23 cm. (Psychological issues. v. 1, no. 1. Monograph 1) 1. Ego (Psychology) 2. Life cycle, Human 3. Identity (Psychology) I. T. II. Title: Life cycle. III. Series.
BF175.E7      131.34      LC 60-1937

**Hartmann, Heinz, 1894-1970.**                                      • **5.197**
Ego psychology and the problem of adaptation / Heinz Hartmann; translated by David Rapaport. — New York: International Universities Press, [1958]. xi, 121 p. — (Journal of the American Psychoanalytic Association. Monograph series; no. 1) 1. Psychoanalysis I. T.
BF175.H373      LC 58-13783

**Hillman, James.**                                                   **5.198**
Archetypal psychology: a brief account: together with a complete checklist of works / by James Hillman. — Dallas, Tex.: Spring Publications, 1983. 88 p.; 23 cm. Originally published in translation in Enciclopedia del novecento, vol. 5,

under title: Psicologia archetipica. 1981. 1. Archetype (Psychology) 2. Psychoanalysis I. T.
BF175.H458 1983    150.19/54 19    LC 82-19663    *ISBN* 0882143212

**Loevinger, Jane.**    **5.199**
Ego development: [conceptions and theories] / Jane Loevinger, with the assistance of Augusto Blasi. 1st ed. — San Francisco: Jossey-Bass Publishers, 1976. xx, 504 p.: ill.; 24 cm. (Jossey-Bass behavioral science series) Includes indexes. 1. Ego (Psychology) 2. Developmental psychology I. Blasi, Augusto, joint author. II. T.
BF175.L63    155.2/5    LC 75-44880    *ISBN* 0875892752

**Essential papers on object relations** / Peter Buckley, editor.    **5.200**
New York: New York University Press, 1986. xxv, 477 p.; 24 cm. (Essential papers in psychoanalysis.) 1. Object relations (Psychoanalysis) — Addresses, essays, lectures. 2. Psychoanalysis — History — Addresses, essays, lectures. I. Buckley, Peter, 1943- II. Series.
BF175.5.O24 E87 1986    150.19/5 19    LC 85-13882    *ISBN* 0814710794

# BF176 PSYCHOLOGICAL TESTS AND TESTING

**Anastasi, Anne, 1908-.**    **5.201**
Psychological testing / Anne Anastasi. — 5th ed. — New York: Macmillan; London: Collier Macmillan, c1982. xiii, 784 p.: ill.; 24 cm. Includes indexes. 1. Psychological tests I. T.
BF176.A5 1982    150/.28/7 19    LC 81-6018    *ISBN* 0023029609

**Cronbach, Lee J. (Lee Joseph), 1916-.**    **5.202**
Essentials of psychological testing / Lee J. Cronbach. — 4th ed. — New York, N.Y.: Harper & Row, c1984. xx, 630 p.: ill.; 25 cm. Includes indexes. 1. Psychological tests I. T.
BF176.C76 1984    150/.28/7 19    LC 83-22613    *ISBN* 0060414197

**Tests: a comprehensive reference for assessments in psychology,**    **5.203**
**education, and business** / Richard C. Sweetland, Daniel J. Keyser, editors; William A. O'Connor, associate editor; Sam Pirnazar, contributing consultant.
Library ed., 1st ed. — Kansas City: Test Corp. of America, 1983. lxxii, 890 p.; 24 cm. Includes indexes. 1. Psychological tests 2. Educational tests and measurements 3. Occupational aptitude tests I. Sweetland, Richard C., 1931- II. Keyser, Daniel J., 1935-
BF176.T43 1983    153.9/3 19    LC 83-5074    *ISBN* 0961128607

# BF180–205 EXPERIMENTAL PSYCHOLOGY

**The First century of experimental psychology** / edited by Eliot    **5.204**
**Hearst.**
Hillsdale, N.J.: L. Erlbaum Associates; New York: distributed by Halsted Press Division, Wiley, 1979. xxiii, 693 p.: ill.; 24 cm. 1. Psychology, Experimental — History. I. Hearst, Eliot Sanford, 1932-
BF181.F5    150/.7/24    LC 79-16970    *ISBN* 0470268158

**Hebb, D. O. (Donald Olding)**    • **5.205**
The organization of behavior: a neuropsychological theory. — New York: Wiley, 1949. xix, 335 p.: diagrs.; 22 cm. (A Wiley book in clinical psychology) 1. Neuropsychology I. T.
BF181.H4    131    LC 49-50182

**Lashley, Karl Spencer, 1890-1958.**    • **5.206**
The neuropsychology of Lashley; selected papers, edited by Frank A. Beach [and others]. New York, McGraw-Hill, 1960. 564 p. illus. 22 cm. (McGraw-Hill series in psychology.) 1. Neuropsychology I. T. II. Series.
BF181.L28    131    LC 59-15059

**Luriia, A. R. (Aleksandr Romanovich), 1902-.**    • **5.207**
The nature of human conflicts; or, Emotion, conflict and will; an objective study of disorganisation and control of human behaviour / by A. R. Luria. Translated from the Russian and edited by W. Horsley Gantt. With a foreword by Adolf Meyer. 1st Evergreen ed. New York, Grove Press, 1960, c1932. 431 p. ill., 21

cm. (Evergreen, E-256) 1. Psychophysiology 2. Psychology, Pathological I. T.
BF181.L8 1960    LC 60-11108

**McGuigan, F. J. (Frank J.), 1924-.**    **5.208**
Experimental psychology: methods of research / F.J. McGuigan. — 4th ed. — Englewood Cliffs, N.J.: Prentice-Hall, c1983. xv, 381 p.: ill.; 25 cm. Includes index. 1. Psychology, Experimental 2. Psychology — Research 3. Experimental design I. T.
BF181.M24 1983    150/.724 19    LC 82-15130    *ISBN* 0132951886

**Stevens, S. S. (Stanley Smith), 1906-1973, ed.**    • **5.209**
Handbook of experimental psychology. New York, Wiley, 1951. xi, 1436 p. illus. 24 cm. (A Wiley publication in psychology) 1. Psychophysiology I. T.
BF181.S8    150.72    LC 51-11046

**Thinès, Georges, 1923-.**    **5.210**
Phenomenology and the science of behaviour: an historical and epistemological approach / Georges Thinès. — London; Boston: G. Allen & Unwin, 1977. 174 p.; 24 cm. — (Advances in psychology series) Includes indexes. 1. Psychology, Experimental 2. Phenomenological psychology 3. Psychology — Philosophy I. T.
BF181.T45    150/.19/2    LC 77-375761    *ISBN* 0041210182

**Underwood, Benton J., 1915-.**    • **5.211**
Experimental psychology [by] Benton J. Underwood. — 2d ed. — New York: Appleton-Century-Crofts, [1966] ix, 678 p.: illus.; 25 cm. — (The Century psychology series) 1. Psychology, Experimental I. T.
BF181.U5 1966    152    LC 66-17260

**Woodworth, Robert Sessions, 1869-1962.**    **5.212**
Experimental psychology. — Rev. ed. [by] Robert S. Woodworth [and] Harold Schlosberg. — New York: Holt, [1954] 948 p.: illus.; 24 cm. 1. Psychology, Experimental I. Schlosberg, Harold, 1904- joint author. II. T.
BF181.W6 1954    150.72    LC 52-13912

**Verhave, Thom, 1929-.**    • **5.213**
The experimental analysis of behavior: selected readings / Thom Verhave. — New York: Appleton-Century-Crofts, 1966. ix, 533 p.: ill. 24 cm. — (The Century psychology series) 1. Psychology — Addresses, essays, lectures. I. T.
BF191.V43    152.08    LC 65-26734

# BF199 Behaviorism

**Berlyne, D. E.**    • **5.214**
Conflict, arousal, and curiosity. — New York: McGraw-Hill, 1960. 350 p.: illus.; 24 cm. — (McGraw-Hill series in psychology) 1. Human behavior I. T. II. Title: Arousal and curiosity.
BF199.B38    150.1943    LC 60-8017

**Bindra, Dalbir.**    • **5.215**
Motivation: a systematic reinterpretation / Dalbir Bindra. — New York: Ronald Press Co., c1959. vii, 361 p.: ill. 1. Motivation (Psychology) I. T.
BF199.B5    LC 59-6101

**Essays in neobehaviorism; a memorial volume to Kenneth W.**    • **5.216**
**Spence.** Edited by Howard H. Kendler [and] Janet T. Spence.
New York: Appleton-Century-Crofts, [1971] xii, 345 p.: illus.; 25 cm. — (Century psychology series) 1. Behaviorism (Psychology) I. Spence, Kenneth Wartenbee, 1907-1967. II. Kendler, Howard Harvard, 1919- ed. III. Spence, Janet Taylor. ed.
BF199.E86    150.19/434    LC 79-163704    *ISBN* 0390503401

**Hull, Clark Leonard.**    • **5.217**
Behavior system: an introduction to behavior theory concerning the individual organism. — New Haven: Yale University Press, 1952. 372 p.: ill.; 25 cm. (Science editions) 1. Psychophysiology 2. Psychology, Comparative 3. Animal intelligence I. T. II. Series.
BF199.H74 1952    LC 52-9267

**Hull, Clark Leonard, 1884-1952.**    • **5.218**
Essentials of behavior. — New Haven: Published for the Institute of Human Relations by Yale University Press, [c1951]. 145 p. 1. Psychophysiology I. T.
BF199.H75

**Hull, Clark Leonard, 1884-1952.**    • **5.219**
Principles of behavior; an introduction to behavior theory. New York, Appleton-Century-Crofts, 1966, c1943. x, 422 p. illus., diagrs. 22 cm. (The Century psychology series.) 1. Behaviorism (Psychology) I. T. II. Series.
BF199.H77    LC 66-28615

**Tolman, Edward Chace, 1886-1959.**    • **5.220**
Purposive behaviour in animals and men / by Edward Chace Tolman. — New York: Appleton-Century-Crofts, c1967. xx, 463 p.: ill. — (The Century psychology series) 1. Psychology 2. Behaviorism (Psychology) 3. Animal intelligence 4. Psychology, Comparative I. T.
BF199.T6 1967a

**Watson, John Broadus, 1878-1958.**    • **5.221**
Behaviorism. — [Rev. ed. — Chicago] University of Chicago Press [1958, c1930] 308 p. illus. 21 cm. — (Phoenix books, P23) 1. Behaviorism (Psychology) I. T.
BF199.W3 1958     150.1943     LC 58-14680

**Zuriff, G. E. (Gerald E.)**    **5.222**
Behaviorism: a conceptual reconstruction / G.E. Zuriff. — New York: Columbia University Press, 1985. xiii, 369 p.; 24 cm. Includes index. 1. Behaviorism (Psychology) 2. Behaviorism (Psychology) — Philosophy. 3. Behaviorism (Psychology) — History. I. T.
BF199.Z88 1985     150.19/43 19     LC 84-12657     ISBN 0231059124

**Evans, Jean, 1912-.**    • **5.223**
Three men; an experiment in the biography of emotion. Introd. by Gordon W. Allport. [1st ed.] New York, Knopf, 1954. 297 p. 22 cm. 1. Psychology, Pathological — Case studies. I. T.
BF200.E8     616.8     LC 54-12188

**Lashley, Karl Spencer, 1890-1958.**    • **5.224**
Brain mechanisms and intelligence: a quantitative study of injuries to the brain. — New York: Hafner Pub. Co., 1964. xiv, 186 p.: ill., diagrs.; 24 cm. (Behavior research fund monographs.) 1. Brain damage 2. Neuropsychology 3. Psychology, Comparative 4. Brain — Localization of functions I. T. II. Series.
BF200.L3 1964     131     LC 63-18172

# BF203 Gestalt Psychology

**Ellis, Willis Davis.**    • **5.225**
A source book of Gestalt psychology / prepared by Willis D. Ellis; with an introd. by K. Koffka. — New York: Humanities Press, [1967] xiv, 403 p.: ill.; 23 cm. 'A series of abstracts or summaries of thirty-four articles and one book, published in Germany between 1915 and 1929.' 1. Gestalt psychology — Addresses, essays, lectures. I. T.
BF203.E48 1967     150.19/82/08     LC 66-25161

**Köhler, Wolfgang, 1887-1967.**    • **5.226**
Gestalt psychology; an introduction to new concepts in modern psychology. — New York: Liveright, [1970, c1947] 369 p.: illus.; 21 cm. 1. Gestalt psychology I. T.
BF203.K6 1970     150.19/82     LC 72-114375

**Koffka, Kurt, 1886-1941.**    • **5.227**
Principles of gestalt psychology / by K. Koffka. — London: K. Paul, Trench, Trubner & co., ltd.; New York: Harcourt, Brace and company, 1935. xi, 720 p.: ill. (incl. music) diagrs.; 22 cm. 1. Gestalt psychology I. T.
BF203.K64 1935a     LC 35-13955

**Wertheimer, Max, 1880-1943.**    • **5.228**
Productive thinking. — Enl. ed., edited by Michael Wertheimer. — New York: Harper, [1959] 302 p.: illus.; 22 cm. 1. Gestalt psychology 2. Thought and thinking I. T.
BF203.W45 1959     153.6     LC 59-15141

# BF204 Humanistic Psychology

**Child, Irvin Long, 1915-.**    **5.229**
Humanistic psychology and the research tradition: their several virtues / [by] Irvin L. Child. — New York: Wiley, [1973] vi, 213 p.; 23 cm. 1. Humanistic psychology 2. Psychology, Experimental I. T.
BF204.C48     150     LC 72-6595     ISBN 0471155705

**Humanistic psychology: new frontiers / edited by Dorothy D. Nevill.**    **5.230**
New York: Gardner Press: distributed by Halsted Press, c1977. xii, 230 p.; 24 cm. 1. Humanistic psychology I. Nevill, Dorothy D.
BF204.H87     150/.19/2     LC 77-23369     ISBN 0470991658

**Mahrer, Alvin R.**    **5.231**
Experiencing: a humanistic theory of psychology and psychiatry / by Alvin R. Mahrer. — New York: Brunner/Mazel, c1978. 884 p.: ill.; 24 cm. Includes indexes. 1. Humanistic psychology 2. Developmental psychology 3. Experiential psychotherapy 4. Humanistic psychotherapy I. T.
BF204.M34     150/.19/2     LC 77-27269     ISBN 087630160X

# BF207–209 PSYCHOTROPIC DRUGS

**Carlton, Peter Lynn, 1931-.**    **5.232**
A primer of behavioral pharmacology: concepts and principles in the behavioral analysis of drug action / Peter L. Carlton. — New York: W.H. Freeman, c1983. 301 p.: ill.; 24 cm. — (Series of books in psychology.) Includes index. 1. Psychopharmacology — Research 2. Behavioral assessment I. T. II. Series.
BF207.C28 1983     615/.78 19     LC 83-9083     ISBN 0716714515

**Masters, Robert E. L.**    **5.233**
The varieties of psychedelic experience, by R. E. L. Masters and Jean Houston,. — [1st ed.]. — New York: Holt, Rinehart and Winston, [1966] 326 p.; 24 cm. 1. Hallucinogenic drugs I. Houston, Jean. joint author. II. T.
BF207.M3     154     LC 66-13202

**Abel, Ernest L., 1943-.**    **5.234**
Marihuana, the first twelve thousand years / Ernest L. Abel. — New York: Plenum Press, c1980. xi, 289 p.; 24 cm. Includes index. 1. Marihuana — History. 2. Marihuana I. T.
BF209.C3 A23     615/.7827     LC 80-15606     ISBN 0306404966

# BF231–299 SENSATION

**Blackwell, Harold Richard, 1921-.**    • **5.235**
Psychophysical thresholds: experimental studies of methods of measurement. — [Ann Arbor]: Engineering Research Institute, Univ. of Michigan, 1953. viii, 227 p.: diagrs.; 23 cm. (University of Michigan, Engneering Research Institute. Bulletin; no. 36) Project NR 142-106, Contract N5 ori-116. Task Order V. between the University of Michigan and the Office of Naval Research, U. S. Navy. I. Michigan. University Engineering Research Institute. II. T.
BF233.B55

**Boring, Edwin Garrigues, 1886-1968.**    • **5.236**
Sensation and perception in the history of experimental psychology / by Edwin G. Boring. — New York; London: D. Appleton-Century company, incorporated, [1942] xv, 644 p.: incl. ill., tables, diagrs., front. (port.); 23 cm. — (The Century psychology series; R. M. Elliott, editor) Diagram on lining-papers. '[Bibliographical] notes' at end of each chapter except the last. 1. Senses and sensation 2. Perception 3. Psychology — Hist. I. T.
BF233.B6     152     LC 42-11837

**Coren, Stanley.**    **5.237**
Sensation and perception / Stanley Coren, Clare Porac, Lawrence M. Ward. — 2nd ed. — Orlando: Academic Press, c1984. x, 606 p., [4] p. of plates: ill. (some col.); 25 cm. Cover title: Sensation & perception. Includes indexes. 1. Senses and sensation 2. Perception I. Porac, Clare. II. Ward, Lawrence M. III. T. IV. Title: Sensation & perception.
BF233.C59 1984     153.7 19     LC 83-73183     ISBN 0121885550

**Geldard, Frank Arthur.**    • **5.238**
The human senses. — New York: Wiley, [1953] 365 p.: illus.; 24 cm. — (A Wiley publication in psychology) 1. Senses and sensation I. T.
BF233.G43     152     LC 52-13881

**Gibson, James Jerome, 1904-.**    • **5.239**
The senses considered as perceptual systems [by] James J. Gibson. — Boston: Houghton Mifflin, [1966] xiv, 335 p.: illus.; 24 cm. 1. Perception 2. Senses and sensation I. T.
BF233.G5     152.1     LC 66-7132

**Marks, Lawrence E.**    **5.240**
The unity of the senses: interrelations among the modalities / Lawrence E. Marks. — New York: Academic Press, 1978. xi, 289 p.: ill.; 24 cm. — (Academic Press series in cognition and perception) Includes indexes. 1. Senses and sensation 2. Intersensory effects 3. Poetry — Psychological aspects. 4. Music — Psychological aspects. I. T.
BF233.M27     152.1     LC 77-25625     ISBN 0124729606

**Perkins, Moreland, 1927-.**                                        **5.241**
Sensing the world / Moreland Perkins. — Indianapolis, Ind.: Hackett Pub. Co., c1984 [1983] x, 352 p.; 22 cm. '575'—On spine. 1. Senses and sensation 2. Consciousness I. T.
BF233.P43 1983          153.7 19          *LC* 83-10825          *ISBN* 0915145758

**Fechner, Gustav Theodor, 1801-1887.**                              • **5.242**
Elements of psychophysics. Translated by Helmut E. Adler. Edited by Davis H. Howes [and] Edwin G. Boring, with an introd. by Edwin G. Boring. — New York, Holt, Rinehart and Winston [1966-. v. port. 22 cm. — (A Henry Holt edition in psychology) 'A short bibliography of Fechner's books': v. 1, p. xxvi. Bibliographical footnotes. 1. Psychophysiology I. Adler, Helmut E. tr. II. Howes, Davis H., ed. III. Boring, Edwin Garrigues, 1886-1968. ed. IV. T.
BF237.F3313          152          *LC* 65-12802

**Green, David Marvin, 1932-.**                                      • **5.243**
Signal detection theory and psychophysics [by] David M. Green [and] John A. Swets. — New York: Wiley, [1966] xi, 455 p.: illus.; 24 cm. 1. Signal detection (Psychology) I. Swets, John Arthur, 1928- joint author. II. T.
BF237.G7          152.1          *LC* 66-21059

**Marks, Lawrence E.**                                               **5.244**
Sensory processes: the new psychophysics [by] Lawrence E. Marks. — New York: Academic Press, 1974. x, 334 p.: illus.; 24 cm. 1. Senses and sensation 2. Psychometrics I. T.
BF237.M33          152.1          *LC* 73-2070          *ISBN* 0124729509

**Dember, William N. (William Norton), 1928-.**                      • **5.245**
Visual perception: the nineteenth century/ William N. Dember.— New York: Wiley, [1964] xii, 222 p.: ill.— (Perspectives in psychology) 1. Visual perception I. T.
BF241.D4          *LC* 64-25895

**Gregory, R. L. (Richard Langton).**                                **5.246**
Illusion in nature and art / edited by R. L. Gregory and E. H. Gombrich; with contributions by Colin Blakemore ... [et al.]. — New York: Scribner, c1973. 288 p.: ill. (some col.); 25 cm. 1. Optical illusions 2. Visual perception I. Gombrich, E. H. (Ernst Hans), 1909- II. Blakemore, Colin. III. T.
BF241.G728 1973b          152.1/48          *LC* 73-21146          *ISBN* 068413800X

**Haber, Ralph Norman.**                                             **5.247**
The psychology of visual perception / Ralph Norman Haber, Maurice Hershenson. — 2d ed. — New York: Holt, Rinehart and Winston, c1980. ix, 431 p., [2] leaves of plates: ill.; 24 cm. Includes indexes. 1. Visual perception I. Hershenson, Maurice. joint author. II. T.
BF241.H27 1980          152.1/4          *LC* 80-12544          *ISBN* 0030202760

**Kaufman, Lloyd.**                                                  **5.248**
Sight and mind; an introduction to visual perception. — New York: Oxford University Press, 1974. xvi, 580 p.: illus.; 24 cm. Stereo viewer inserted in pocket. 1. Visual perception I. T.
BF241.K38          152.1/4          *LC* 73-90350          *ISBN* 0195017633

**Kennedy, John Miller, 1942-.**                                     **5.249**
A psychology of picture perception [by] John M. Kennedy. [1st ed.] San Francisco, Jossey-Bass, 1974. xiii, 174 p. illus. 24 cm. (The Jossey-Bass behavioral science series) 1. Picture perception I. T.
BF241.K44 1974          152.1/423          *LC* 72-5892          *ISBN* 0875892043

**Rock, Irvin.**                                                     • **5.250**
The nature of perceptual adaptation. — New York: Basic Books, [1966] x, 289 p.: illus.; 25 cm. 1. Vision 2. Adaptability (Psychology) I. T.
BF241.R6          152.14          *LC* 66-26218

**Moore, Brian C. J.**                                               **5.251**
Introduction to the psychology of hearing / Brian C. J. Moore. Baltimore: University Park Press, c1977. 310 p.; 22 cm. Includes index. 1. Auditory perception 2. Hearing I. T.
BF251.M66 1977          152.1/5          *LC* 76-30756          *ISBN* 0839109962

**Mueller, Conrad George, 1920-.**                                   • **5.252**
Sensory psychology / [by] Conrad G. Mueller. — Englewood Cliffs, N.J.: Prentice-Hall, [1965] viii, 120 p.: ill.; 24 cm. — (Foundations of modern psychology series) 1. Senses and sensation I. T.
BF292.M8          152          *LC* 65-13814

**Rock, Irvin.**                                                     **5.253**
Orientation and form. — New York: Academic Press, 1973. ix, 165 p.: ill.; 24 cm. 1. Form perception 2. Orientation (Psychology) I. T.
BF293.R63 1973          152.1/423          *LC* 72-13618          *ISBN* 0125912501

**Bartenieff, Irmgard.**                                             **5.254**
Body movement: coping with the environment / by Irmgard Bartenieff with Dori Lewis. — New York: Gordon and Breach Science Publishers, c1980 (1983 printing) xiv, 289 p.: ill.; 26 cm. Includes index. 1. Movement, Psychology of

2. Motor ability 3. Dance therapy 4. Physical therapy 5. Movement, Psychology of — Cross-cultural studies. I. Lewis, Dori. II. T.
BF295.B32 1980          152.3 19          *LC* 80-7454          *ISBN* 0677055005

**Motor control: issues and trends / edited by George E.**           **5.255**
**Stelmach.**
New York: Academic Press, 1976. x, 232 p.: ill.; 24 cm. 1. Motor learning I. Stelmach, George E.
BF295.M66          152.3/34          *LC* 75-37675          *ISBN* 0126659508

# BF309–499 CONSCIOUSNESS. COGNITION. PERCEPTION

**Allport, Floyd Henry, 1890-.**                                     • **5.256**
Theories of perception and the concept of structure: a review and critical analysis with an introduction to a dynamic–structural theory of behavior. — New York: Wiley, [1955] 709 p.: ill.; 24 cm. 1. Perception I. T.
BF311.A5          152.7          *LC* 55-6130

**Alternate states of consciousness / edited by Norman E.**          **5.257**
**Zinberg.**
New York: Free Press, c1977. x, 294 p.: ill.; 25 cm. Includes index. 1. Consciousness I. Zinberg, Norman Earl, 1921-
BF311.A52          154          *LC* 76-46722          *ISBN* 0029357705

**Boring, Edwin Garrigues, 1886-1968.**                              • **5.258**
The physical dimensions of consciousness / by Edwin G. Boring. — New York: Dover, 1963. xviii, 251 p.: ill. 1. Consciousness 2. Psychophysiology I. T.
BF311.B6 1963          *LC* 63-17900

**Bruner, Jerome S. (Jerome Seymour)**                               **5.259**
Beyond the information given; studies in the psychology of knowing [by] Jerome S. Bruner. Selected, edited, and introduced by Jeremy M. Anglin. Contributors with Jerome S. Bruner to papers in this volume: George Austin [and others. 1st ed.]. — New York: Norton, [1973] xxiv, 502 p.: illus.; 24 cm. 1. Perception 2. Thought and thinking 3. Education 4. Cognition in children I. T.
BF311.B77 1973          153.7          *LC* 72-13402          *ISBN* 0393010953

**Carterette, Edward C.**                                            **5.260**
Historical and philosophical roots of perception / edited by Edward C. Carterette and Morton P. Friedman. — New York: Academic Press, 1974. xix, 431 p.: ill.; 24 cm. (Handbook of perception, v. 1) 1. Perception I. Friedman, Morton P. joint author. II. T.
BF311.C29          153.7          *LC* 73-21837          *ISBN* 012161901X

**Cohen, Gillian.**                                                  **5.261**
The psychology of cognition / Gillian Cohen. — London; New York: Academic Press, 1977. ix, 241 p.: ill.; 24 cm. 1. Cognition 2. Thought and thinking 3. Psycholinguistics 4. Digital computer simulation 5. Left and right (Psychology) I. T.
BF311.C5548          153.4          *LC* 77-81382          *ISBN* 0121787508

**Das, J. P. (Jagannath Prasad)**                                    **5.262**
Simultaneous and successive cognitive processes / J. P. Das, John R. Kirby, Ronald F. Jarman, with a chapter by James P. Cummins. — New York: Academic Press, 1979. xii, 247 p.; ill.; 24 cm. (Educational phychology) Includes index. 1. Cognition 2. Cognition in children I. Kirby, John R. joint author. II. Jarman, Ronald F. joint author. III. T. IV. Series.
BF311.D34          153.4          *LC* 78-20039          *ISBN* 0122031504

**Fodor, Jerry A.**                                                  **5.263**
The modularity of mind: an essay on faculty psychology / Jerry A. Fodor. — Cambridge, Mass.: MIT Press, c1983. 145 p.; 21 cm. 'A Bradford book.' 1. Cognition I. T.
BF311.F5615 1983          153 19          *LC* 82-24892          *ISBN* 0262060841

**Gibson, Eleanor Jack.**                                            • **5.264**
Principles of perceptual learning and development [by] Eleanor J. Gibson. — New York: Appleton-Century-Crofts, [1969] viii, 537 p.: illus.; 25 cm. — (Century psychology series) 1. Perception 2. Perceptual learning I. T.
BF311.G48          152.1          *LC* 72-77536          *ISBN* 0390361453

**Handbook of learning and cognitive processes / edited by W. K.**   **5.265**
**Estes.**
Hillsdale, N.J.: L. Erlbaum Associates; New York: distributed by the Halsted Press Division of Wiley, 1975-1978. 6 v.: ill.; 24 cm. 1. Cognition 2. Learning, Psychology of I. Estes, William Kaye.
BF311.H334          153 19          *LC* 75-20113          *ISBN* 0470245859

**Handbook of perception and human performance / editors,**    **5.266**
**Kenneth R. Boff, Lloyd Kaufman, James P. Thomas.**
New York: Wiley, c1986. 2 v.: ill.; 29 cm. Also published in special ed. with different foreword for limited distribution to the U.S. Dept. of Defense. 'A Wiley-Interscience publication.' 1. Perception 2. Cognition 3. Human information processing 4. Performance I. Boff, Kenneth R. II. Kaufman, Lloyd. III. Thomas, James P. (James Peringer), 1932-
BF311.H3345    153.7 19    *LC* 85-20375    *ISBN* 0471885444

**Hunt, Morton M., 1920-.**    **5.267**
The universe within: a new science explores the human mind / by Morton Hunt. — New York: Simon and Schuster, c1982. 415 p.: ill.; 24 cm. Includes index. 1. Cognition 2. Thought and thinking I. T.
BF311.H82 1982    153 19    *LC* 81-13611    *ISBN* 0671252585

**Jackson, Frank, 1943-.**    **5.268**
Perception: a representative theory / Frank Jackson. Cambridge [Eng.]; New York: Cambridge University Press, 1977. 180 p.; 23 cm. Includes index. 1. Perception I. T.
BF311.J23    153.7    *LC* 76-30316    *ISBN* 0521215501

**Jaynes, Julian.**    **5.269**
The origin of consciousness in the breakdown of the bicameral mind / Julian Jaynes. Boston: Houghton Mifflin, 1977, c1976. 467 p.: ill.; 25 cm. 1. Consciousness 2. Consciousness — History. I. T.
BF311.J36    128/.2    *LC* 76-28748    *ISBN* 0395207290

**Keen, Ernest, 1937-.**    **5.270**
Psychology and the new consciousness. — Monterey, Calif.: Brooks/Cole Pub. Co., [1972] vii, 152 p.; 23 cm. — (Contemporary psychology series) 1. Freud, Sigmund, 1856-1939. 2. Consciousness 3. Phenomenological psychology 4. Ontology 5. Political psychology I. T.
BF311.K35    154    *LC* 72-77605    *ISBN* 0818500727

**Klein, David Ballin, 1897-.**    **5.271**
The concept of consciousness: a survey / David Ballin Klein. — Lincoln: University of Nebraska Press, c1984. x, 250 p.; 24 cm. 1. Consciousness I. T.
BF311.K625 1984    154 19    *LC* 83-5851    *ISBN* 0803227078

**Kreitler, Hans.**    **5.272**
Cognitive orientation and behavior / Hans Kreitler, Shulamith Kreitler. New York: Springer Pub. Co., c1976. xv, 447 p.; 24 cm. Includes index. 1. Cognition 2. Orientation (Psychology) 3. Psychology I. Kreitler, Shulamith, joint author. II. T.
BF311.K696    153.4    *LC* 76-20597    *ISBN* 0826120504

**Luriia, A. R. (Aleksandr Romanovich), 1902-.**    **5.273**
Language and cognition / Alexander R. Luria; edited by James V. Wertsch. — Washington: V. H. Winston; New York: Wiley, c1982. vii, 264 p.; 24 cm. 1. Cognition 2. Psycholinguistics I. Wertsch, James V. II. T.
BF 311 L945 E5 1982    BF311L945 E5 1982.    *LC* 81-70188    *ISBN* 0471093025

**Mandler, George.**    **5.274**
Mind and emotion / George Mandler. — New York: Wiley, [1975] xvi, 280 p.; 23 cm. Includes indexes. 1. Cognition 2. Emotions 3. Human information processing I. T.
BF311.M23    153 19    *LC* 75-15727    *ISBN* 047156690X

**The Meeting of the ways: explorations in East/West psychology**    **5.275**
**/ edited by John Welwood.**
1st ed. — New York: Schocken Books, 1979. xvi, 240 p.; 21 cm. Includes index. 1. Consciousness — Addresses, essays, lectures. 2. Meditation — Addresses, essays, lectures. 3. Identity (Psychology) — Addresses, essays, lectures. 4. Psychology — Asia — Addresses, essays, lectures. I. Welwood, John, 1943-
BF311.M437    158/.9 19    *LC* 78-26509    *ISBN* 0805237089

**The Metaphors of consciousness / edited by Ronald S. Valle**    **5.276**
**and Rolf Von Eckartsberg.**
New York: Plenum Press, c1981. xxii, 521 p.: ill.; 24 cm. 1. Consciousness 2. Knowledge, Theory of I. Valle, Ronald S. II. Von Eckartsberg, Rolf, 1932-
BF311.M449    150/.1 19    *LC* 80-24803    *ISBN* 0306405202

**Neisser, Ulric.**    **5.277**
Cognition and reality: principles and implications of cognitive psychology / Ulric Neisser. San Francisco: W. H. Freeman, c1976. xiii, 230 p.: ill.; 22 cm. Includes indexes. 1. Cognition I. T.
BF311.N43    153.4    *LC* 76-24813    *ISBN* 0716704781

**Neisser, Ulric.**    • **5.278**
Cognitive psychology. — New York: Appleton-Century-Crofts, [1967] xi, 351 p.: ill.; 24 cm. — (The Century psychology series) 1. Cognition I. T.
BF311.N44    153.4    *LC* 67-27727

**Noddings, Nel.**    **5.279**
Awakening the inner eye: intuition in education / Nel Noddings, Paul J. Shore. — New York: Teachers College, Columbia University, 1984. xv, 236 p.; 23 cm. Includes index. 1. Intuition (Psychology) 2. Educational psychology I. Shore, Paul J., 1956- II. T.
BF311.N63 1984    153.4/4 19    *LC* 83-18057    *ISBN* 0807727512

**Organization and representation in perception / edited by Jacob**    **5.280**
**Beck.**
Hillsdale, N.J.: L. Erlbaum Associates, 1982. xii, 387 p.: ill.; 24 cm. 'Based on a conference on 'Processes of perceptual organization and representation' held in Abano, Italy, in June 1979'—Introd. 1. Perception — Congresses. 2. Gestalt psychology — Congresses. 3. Human information processing — Congresses. I. Beck, Jacob.
BF311.O67 1982    153.7 19    *LC* 82-7463    *ISBN* 0898591759

**Ornstein, Robert Evans.**    **5.281**
The psychology of consciousness [by] Robert E. Ornstein. — San Francisco: W. H. Freeman, [1972] xii, 247 p.: illus.; 23 cm. — (A Series of books in psychology) 1. Consciousness I. T.
BF311.O75    153    *LC* 72-4432    *ISBN* 0670581984

**The Pathology and psychology of cognition / edited by Andrew**    **5.282**
**Burton.**
London; New York: Methuen, 1982. x, 306 p.: ill.; 22 cm. — (Psychology in progress.) 1. Cognition 2. Cognition disorders 3. Human information processing I. Burton, Andrew. II. Series.
BF311.P315 1982    153 19    *LC* 82-12526    *ISBN* 0416308104

**Pennycuick, John.**    **5.283**
In contact with the physical world. — London: Allen and Unwin; New York: Humanities P., 1972 [1971] 3-150 p.;: map.; 23 cm. — (Muirhead library of philosophy) 1. Perception I. T.
BF311.P345    121    *LC* 76-867245    *ISBN* 0041210158

**Piaget, Jean, 1896-.**    **5.284**
[Réussir et comprendre. English] Success and understanding / Jean Piaget, collaborators M. Amann ... [et al.]; translated by Arnold J. Pomerans. — Cambridge, Mass.: Harvard University Press, 1978. vi, 236 p.; 24 cm. Translation of Réussir et comprendre. 1. Cognition I. T.
BF311.P51913    153.4    *LC* 78-16435    *ISBN* 0674853873

**Boden, Margaret A.**    **5.285**
Jean Piaget / Margaret A. Boden. — New York: Viking Press, 1980, c1979. xii, 176 p.; 22 cm. — (Modern masters) Includes index. 1. Piaget, Jean, 1896-2. Cognition 3. Cognition in children 4. Knowledge, Theory of I. T.
BF311.P523 B62    155.4/13/0924 B    *LC* 79-24259    *ISBN* 0670406325

**Posner, Michael I.**    **5.286**
Cognition: an introduction / [by] Michael I. Posner. — Glenview, Ill.: Scott, Foresman, 1974 (c1973) 208 p.: ill.; 24 cm. — (Scott, Foresman basic psychological concepts series) 1. Cognition I. T.
BF311.P64    153.4    *LC* 73-91228    *ISBN* 0673078604

**Rock, Irvin.**    **5.287**
The logic of perception / Irvin Rock. — Cambridge, Mass.: MIT Press, c1983. xiii, 365 p.: ill.; 24 cm. 'A Bradford book.' Includes index. 1. Perception 2. Thought and thinking I. T.
BF311.R555 1983    153.7 19    *LC* 82-24911    *ISBN* 0262181096

**Rundle, Bede.**    **5.288**
Perception, sensation and verification. — Oxford: Clarendon Press, 1972. ix, 256 p.; 23 cm. 1. Perception 2. Senses and sensation 3. Cognition I. T.
BF311.R86    121    *LC* 72-191915    *ISBN* 0198243901

**Schank, Roger C., 1946-.**    **5.289**
Scripts, plans, goals, and understanding: an inquiry into human knowledge structures / Roger C. Schank, Robert P. Abelson. — Hillsdale, N.J.: L. Erlbaum Associates; New York: distributed by the Halsted Press Division of John Wiley and Sons, 1977. 248 p.; 24 cm. — (The Artificial intelligence series) Includes indexes. 1. Cognition 2. Artificial intelligence 3. Psycholinguistics 4. Psychology — Mathematical models 5. Digital computer simulation I. Abelson, Robert P. joint author. II. T.
BF311.S378    153.4    *LC* 76-51963    *ISBN* 0470990333

**Tart, Charles T., 1937- comp.**    **5.290**
Altered states of consciousness: a book of readings / Charles T. Tart, editor. — New York: Wiley, [1969] 575 p.; 23 cm. 1. Consciousness — Addresses, essays, lectures. I. T.
BF311.T28    154    *LC* 69-16040

**Vygotskiĭ, L. S. (Lev Semenovich), 1896-1934.**    **5.291**
Mind in society: the development of higher psychological processes / L. S. Vygotsky; edited by Michael Cole ... [et al.]. — Cambridge: Harvard University

Press, 1978. xi, 159 p.: ill.; 24 cm. Includes index. 1. Cognition 2. Cognition in children I. Cole, Michael, 1938- II. T.
BF311.V93 1978     155.4/13     *LC* 77-26023     *ISBN* 0674576284

**Weimer, Walter B.**            **5.292**
Cognition and the symbolic processes, edited by Walter B. Weimer and David S. Palermo. — Hillsdale, N.J.: Lawrence Erlbaum Associates; distributed by Halsted Press Division, Wiley, New York, 1975 (c1974). xii, 450 p.: ill.; 24 cm. 1. Cognition I. Palermo, David Stuart, 1929- joint author. II. T.
BF311.W374     153.4     *LC* 74-13834     *ISBN* 0470925507

**Wilber, Ken.**            **5.293**
No boundary, Eastern and Western approaches to personal growth / Ken Wilber. — Los Angeles: Center Publications, [1979] 160 p.; 23 cm. — (Whole mind series.) 1. Consciousness 2. Self-perception 3. Psychology — Philosophy 4. East and West I. T. II. Series.
BF311.W577     158/.1     *LC* 79-20124     *ISBN* 0916820114

# BF318–319.5 Learning. Conditioned Response

**Bugelski, B. R. (Bergen Richard), 1913-.**        **5.294**
Principles of learning and memory / B. R. Bugelski. — New York: Praeger, 1979. xvii, 419 p.: ill.; 25 cm. Includes index. 1. Learning, Psychology of 2. Memory I. T.
BF318.B83     153.1     *LC* 78-19760     *ISBN* 0030465966

**Bower, Gordon H.**            **5.295**
Theories of learning / Gordon H. Bower, Ernest R. Hilgard. — 5th ed. — Englewood Cliffs, N.J.: Prentice-Hall, c1981. vii, 647 p.: ill.; 24 cm. — (The Century psychology series) Authors' names in reverse order in 3d and 4th eds. Includes index. 1. Learning, Psychology of I. Hilgard, Ernest Ropiequet, 1904- joint author. II. T.
BF318.H55 1981     153.1/5 19     *LC* 80-19396     *ISBN* 0139144323

**Hintzman, Douglas L.**            **5.296**
The psychology of learning and memory / Douglas L. Hintzman. — San Francisco: W. H. Freeman, c1978. xvi, 456 p.: ill.; 24 cm. — (A Series of books in psychology) Includes indexes. 1. Learning, Psychology of 2. Memory I. T.
BF318.H56     153.1     *LC* 77-16295     *ISBN* 0716700352

**Leahey, Thomas Hardy.**            **5.297**
Human learning / Thomas Hardy Leahey, Richard Jackson Harris. — Englewood Cliffs, N.J.: Prentice-Hall, c1985. xii, 448 p.: ill.; 24 cm. Includes index. 1. Learning, Psychology of 2. Learning — Physiological aspects 3. Human behavior 4. Cognition I. Harris, Richard Jackson. II. T.
BF318.L37 1985     153.1 19     *LC* 84-13381     *ISBN* 0134451643

**Rosenthal, Ted L.**            **5.298**
Social learning and cognition / Ted L. Rosenthal, Barry J. Zimmerman. — New York: Academic Press, 1978. xiv, 338 p.; 24 cm. Includes indexes. 1. Social learning 2. Cognition in children 3. Socialization I. Zimmerman, Barry J. joint author. II. T.
BF318.R67     155.4/13     *LC* 78-4549     *ISBN* 0125967500

**Ferster, Charles B., 1922-.**        • **5.299**
Schedules of reinforcement / by C. B. Ferster and B. F. Skinner. — Englewood Cliffs, N.J.: Prentice-Hall, c1957. 741 p.: bill. (The Century psychology series) 1. Reinforcement (Psychology) I. Skinner, B. F. (Burrhus Frederic), 1904- II. T.
BF319.F4

**Hilgard, Ernest Ropiequet, 1904-.**        • **5.300**
[Conditioning and learning] Hilgard and Marquis' Conditioning and learning. Rev. by Gregory A. Kimble. 2d ed. New York, Appleton-Century-Crofts [1961] 590 p. illus. 25 cm. (The Century psychology series) 1. Conditioned response 2. Reflexes 3. Learning, Psychology of I. Marquis, Donald George, joint author. II. T. III. Title: Conditioning and learning.
BF319.H5 1961     158.423     *LC* 61-5440

**Honig, Werner K. ed.**        • **5.301**
Operant behavior: areas of research and application / edited by Werner K. Honig. — New York: Appleton-Century-Crofts, [1966] xi, 865 p.: ill.; 24 cm. — (The Century psychology series) 1. Operant behavior — Addresses, essays, lectures. I. T.
BF319.H58     152     *LC* 66-11455

**Lawrence, Douglas H.**        • **5.302**
Deterrents and reinforcement: the psychology of insufficient reward / [by] Douglas H. Lawrence and Leon Festinger. — Stanford, Calif.: Stanford University Press, 1962. 180 p.: ill.; 24 cm. (Stanford studies in psychology, 2) Includes bibliography. 1. Reinforcement (Psychology) 2. Learning, Psychology of I. Festinger, Leon, 1919- joint author. II. T.
BF319.L3     154.44     *LC* 62-8664

**Logan, Frank Anderson.**        • **5.303**
Incentive: how the conditions of reinforcement affect the performance of rats / Frank A. Logan. — New Haven: Yale University Press, 1960. -. xv, 288 p.: diagrs., tables; 25 cm. — 1. Reinforcement (Psychology) I. T.
BF319.L58     159     *LC* 60-7825

**Classical conditioning: a symposium / edited by William F.**        • **5.304**
**Prokasy.**
New York: Appleton-Century-Crofts, 1965. ix, 421 p.: ill. — (Century psychology series.) 'Sponsored by Grant GB-275 to the editor from the National Science Foundation.' 1. Conditioned response — Addresses,essays,lectures. I. Prokasy, William F. (William Frederick), 1930-
BF319.P74     158.423     *LC* 65-16466

**Spence, Kenneth Wartenbee, 1907-1967.**        • **5.305**
Behavior theory and conditioning / by Kenneth W. Spence. — New York: Yale University Press, c1956. vii, 262 p.: graphs; 22 cm. (Yale University Mrs. Hepsa Ely Silliman memorial lectures) Includes indexes. 1. Conditioned response I. T.
BF319.S66 1978     153     *LC* 56-9491

**Reynolds, George Stanley, 1936-.**        **5.306**
A primer of operant conditioning / G. S. Reynolds. — Rev. ed. — Glenview, Ill.: Scott, Foresman, [1975] xiv, 155 p.: ill.; 24 cm. 1. Operant conditioning I. T.
BF319.5.O6 R48 1975     153.1/5     *LC* 74-12788     *ISBN* 0673079643

**Williams, Jon L.**        **5.307**
Operant learning; procedures for changing behavior [by] Jon L. Williams. — Monterey, Calif.: Brooks/Cole Pub. Co., [1973] 248 p.: illus.; 24 cm. 1. Operant conditioning I. T.
BF319.5.O6 W54     153.1/52     *LC* 72-91088     *ISBN* 0818500581

**The Effects of punishment on human behavior / edited by Saul**        **5.308**
**Axelrod, Jack Apsche; contributors, Saul Axelrod ... [et al.].**
New York: Academic Press, 1983. xii, 356 p.: ill.; 24 cm. 1. Punishment (Psychology) — Addresses, essays, lectures. 2. Aversion therapy — Addresses, essays, lectures. I. Axelrod, Saul. II. Apsche, Jack.
BF319.5.P8 E34 1983     155.4 19     *LC* 82-13892     *ISBN* 0120687402

# BF321–323 Attention. Apperception

**Kahneman, Daniel, 1934-.**        **5.309**
Attention and effort. — Englewood Cliffs, N.J.: Prentice-Hall, [1973] x, 246 p.: ill.; 24 cm. — (Prentice-Hall series in experimental psychology) 1. Attention I. T.
BF321.K26     153.7/33     *LC* 73-3375     *ISBN* 0130505188

**Underwood, Geoffrey.**        **5.310**
Attention and Memory / by Geoffrey Underwood. Oxford; New York: Pergamon Press, c1976. viii, 280 p.: ill.; 21 cm. (Pergamon international library of science, technology, engineering, and social studies) Includes indexes. 1. Attention 2. Memory I. T.
BF321.U5 1976     153.1/2     *LC* 75-17614     *ISBN* 0080196152

**Sherwood, Michael.**        **5.311**
The logic of explanation in psychoanalysis. New York, Academic Press, 1969. x, 276 p. 24 cm. 1. Psychoanalysis 2. Psychoanalysis — Case studies. I. T.
BF323.E8 S5     150     *LC* 68-28897

**Ziff, Paul, 1920-.**        **5.312**
Understanding understanding. — Ithaca [N.Y.]: Cornell University Press, [1972] viii, 146 p.; 22 cm. 1. Comprehension 2. Psycholinguistics I. T.
BF325.Z53     410/.1     *LC* 72-4573     *ISBN* 0801407443

## BF335–353 Nature and Nurture. Environment

**Festinger, Leon, 1919-.**                                                    • **5.313**
A theory of cognitive dissonance. Evanston, Ill.: Row, Peterson [1957] 291 p.: ill.; 22 cm. Rev. and enl. German translation published in 1978 under title: Theorie der kognitiven Dissonanz. 1. Cognitive dissonance I. T. II. Title: Dissonance.
BF335.F4      137.33      LC 57-11351

**Lewontin, Richard C., 1929-.**                                              **5.314**
Not in our genes: biology, ideology, and human nature / R.C. Lewontin, Steven Rose, and Leon J. Kamin. — 1st ed. — New York: Pantheon Books, c1984. xi, 322 p.; 25 cm. 1. Nature and nurture — Political aspects. 2. Determinism (Philosophy) — Political aspects. 3. Behavior genetics — Political aspects. 4. Psychology — Methodology — Political aspects. 5. Psychiatry — Methodology — Political aspects. 6. United States — Social policy I. Rose, Steven Peter Russell, 1938- II. Kamin, Leon J. III. T.
BF341.L49 1984      304.5 19      LC 83-43145      ISBN 0394508173

**Barker, Roger Garlock, 1903-.**                                             • **5.315**
Ecological psychology; concepts and methods for studying the environment of human behavior [by] Roger G. Barker. — Stanford, Calif.: Stanford University Press, 1968. vi, 242 p.: illus.; 24 cm. Reports the results of research at the Midwest Psychological Field Station, University of Kansas. 1. Environmental psychology 2. Psychology I. Kansas. University. Midwest Psychological Field Station. II. T.
BF353.B3      155.9      LC 68-21287

**Human behavior and environment: advances in theory and**                    **5.316**
**research / edited by Irwin Altman and Joachim F. Wohlwill.**
New York: Plenum Press, 1981. 285 p.: ill., map; 24 cm. 1. Environmental psychology I. Altman, Irwin. II. Everett, Peter B. (Peter Ben), 1943- III. Wohlwill, Joachim F. IV. Title: Children and the environment. V. Title: Environment and culture. VI. Title: Transportation and behavior. VII. Title: Behavior and the natural environment. VIII. Title: Elderly people and the environment. IX. Title: Home environments.
BF353.H85      301.31      LC 76-382942      ISBN 0306407736

## BF360–395 Association and Reproduction of Ideas. Mental Imagery

**Hannay, Alastair.**                                                          **5.317**
Mental images: a defence. — London, Allen and Unwin; New York, Humanities P., 1973 [c1971] 3-264 p. 23 cm. — (Muirhead library of philosophy). 1. Imagery (Psychology) I. T. II. Series.
BF367.H3 1971      128/.2      LC 72-182115      ISBN 0041000307

**Imagery / edited by Ned Block.**                                            **5.318**
Cambridge, Mass.; London: MIT Press, c1981. 261 p.: ill.; 24 cm. — (A Bradford book) 1. Imagery (Psychology) I. Block, Ned.
BF367.I453      153.3 18      153.3/2 19      LC 81-24732      ISBN 0262021684

**Kosslyn, Stephen Michael, 1948-.**                                          **5.319**
Ghosts in the mind's machine: creating and using images in the brain / Stephen Michael Kosslyn. — 1st ed. — New York: Norton, c1983. xv, 249 p.: ill.; 22 cm. Includes index. 1. Imagery (Psychology) — Physiological aspects. 2. Brain I. T.
BF367.K66 1983      153.3/2 19      LC 82-19038      ISBN 0393952576

**Kosslyn, Stephen Michael, 1948-.**                                          **5.320**
Image and mind / Stephen Michael Kosslyn. — Cambridge, Mass.: Harvard University Press, 1980. xv, 500 p.: ill.; 24 cm. Includes index. 1. Visualization 2. Imagery (Psychology) 3. Memory I. T.
BF367.K67      153.3/2      LC 80-10329      ISBN 0674443659

**Shepard, Roger N.**                                                         **5.321**
Mental images and their transformations / Roger N. Shepard, Lynn A. Cooper, with chapters coauthored by J.E. Farrell ... [et al.]. — Cambridge, Mass.: MIT Press, c1982. viii, 364 p.: ill.; 24 cm. 'A Bradford book.' Includes indexes. 1. Imagery (Psychology) 2. Thought and thinking I. Cooper, Lynn A. II. T.
BF367.S55 1982      153.3/2 19      LC 81-14276      ISBN 0262192004

## BF370–385 MEMORY. ATTITUDE

**Baddeley, Alan D., 1934-.**                                                 **5.322**
The psychology of memory / Alan D. Baddeley. New York: Basic Books, c1976. xvii, 430 p.: ill.; 24 cm. (Basic topics in cognition series) Includes index. 1. Memory I. T.
BF371.B23      153.1/2      LC 75-36769      ISBN 0465067360

**Bartlett, Frederic Charles, Sir, 1887-1969.**                               • **5.323**
Remembering: a study in experimental and social psychology / by Sir Frederic C. Bartlett. — London: Cambridge U.P., 1967. x, 317 p.: ill., 2 plates, maps, diagrs.; 21 cm. 1. Recollection (Psychology) 2. Recognition (Psychology) I. T.
BF371.B26 1967      152      LC 68-75898      ISBN 0521094410

**Comparative perspectives on the development of memory /**                   **5.324**
**edited by Robert Kail, Norman E. Spear.**
Hillsdale, N.J.: L. Erlbaum Associates, 1984. x, 374 p.: ill.; 24 cm. Based on a conference held at Purdue University, May 19-21, 1982. 1. Memory — Congresses. 2. Memory in children — Congresses. 3. Psychology, Comparative — Congresses. I. Kail, Robert V. II. Spear, Norman E.
BF371.C717 1984      156/.312 19      LC 83-20507      ISBN 0898593174

**Crowder, Robert George.**                                                   **5.324a**
Principles of learning and memory / [by] Robert G. Crowder. Hillsdale: Erlbaum; New York; London [etc.]: Distributed by Wiley, 1976. xv, 523 p.: ill.; 24 cm. (The experimental psychology series) Index. 1. Memory 2. Learning, Psychology of I. T. II. Series.
BF371.C8x LB1051      153.1/2 153.1/5      LC 76-7336      ISBN 0470150270

**Eysenck, Michael W.**                                                       **5.325**
Human memory: theory, research, and individual differences / by Michael W. Eysenck. — Oxford; New York: Pergamon Press, c1977. x, 366 p.: graphs; 22 cm. — (International series in experimental psychology; v. 22) Includes indexes. 1. Memory I. T.
BF371.E95 1977      153.1/2      LC 77-358      ISBN 0080204058

**Human memory and amnesia / edited by Laird S. Cermak.**                     **5.326**
Hillsdale, N.J.: L. Erlbaum Associates, 1982. x, 388 p.: ill.; 24 cm. 1. Memory 2. Memory, Disorders of 3. Amnesia I. Cermak, Laird S.
BF371.H757 1982      616.85/232 19      LC 80-39586      ISBN 0898590957

**Klatzky, Roberta L.**                                                       **5.327**
Memory and awareness: an information-processing perspective / Roberta L. Klatzky. — New York: W.H. Freeman, c1984. vii, 155 p.: ill.; 24 cm. — (Series of books in psychology.) Includes index. 1. Memory 2. Awareness 3. Human information processing I. T. II. Series.
BF371.K533 1984      153.1/2 19      LC 84-4017      ISBN 0716715996

**Loftus, Geoffrey R.**                                                       **5.328**
Human memory: the processing of information / Geoffrey R. Loftus, Elizabeth F. Loftus. — Hillsdale, N.J.: L. Erlbaum Associates; New York: distributed by the Halsted Press Division of John Wiley, 1976. xii, 179 p.: ill.; 23 cm. Includes indexes. 1. Memory 2. Human information processing I. Loftus, Elizabeth F., 1944- joint author. II. T.
BF371.L64      153.1/2      LC 75-20266      ISBN 0470543361

**Malcolm, Norman, 1911-.**                                                   **5.330**
Memory and mind / Norman Malcolm. — Ithaca, N.Y.: Cornell University Press, 1977. 277 p.; 22 cm. 1. Memory I. T.
BF371.M339      153.1/2      LC 78-17889      ISBN 0801410185

**Memory organization and structure / edited by C. Richard Puff.**           **5.331**
New York: Academic Press, c1979. xv, 411 p.: ill.; 24 cm. 1. Memory I. Puff, C. Richard.
BF371.M46      153.1/2      LC 79-21039      ISBN 0125667507

**Murdock, Bennet Bronson.**                                                  **5.332**
Human memory: theory and data / by Bennet B. Murdock, Jr. — Potomac, Md.: Lawrence Erlbaum Associates; distributed by Halsted Press Division, Wiley, New York, 1974. x, 362 p.: ill.; 23 cm. — (The Experimental psychology series) 1. Memory I. T. II. Series.
BF371.M77      153.1/2      LC 74-888      ISBN 0470625252

**Norman, Donald A.**                                                         **5.333**
Learning and memory / Donald A. Norman. — San Francisco: W.H. Freeman, c1982. xi, 129 p.: ill.; 24 cm. Includes index. 1. Memory 2. Artificial intelligence 3. Learning, Psychology of I. T.
BF371.N568 1982      153.1 19      LC 82-7441      ISBN 0716712997

**Piaget, Jean, 1896-.**                                                      **5.334**
[Mémoire et intelligence. English] Memory and intelligence / [by] Jean Piaget and Bärbel Inhelder; in collaboration with Hermine Sinclair-De Zwart;

translated from the French by Arnold. J. Pomerans. — New York: Basic Books, 1974 (c1973) xii, 414 p.: ill.; 25 cm. 1. Memory I. Inhelder, Bärbel. joint author. II. T.
BF371.P5513 1973b    153.1    *LC* 72-89197    *ISBN* 046504445X

**Richardson, John T. E.**      5.335
Mental imagery and human memory / John T. E. Richardson. — New York: St. Martin's Press, 1980. x, 178 p.; 24 cm. Includes indexes. 1. Memory 2. Imagery (Psychology) I. T.
BF371.R525 1980    153.1/32    *LC* 79-26849    *ISBN* 0312529759

**The structure of human memory** / edited by Charles N. Cofer.    5.336
San Francisco: W. H. Freeman, c1976. 213 p.: ill.; 24 cm. — (A Series of books in psychology) 'Papers presented at a symposium ... held under the joint sponsorship of the Section on Psychology (J) and the Section on Information and Communication (T) on January 29, 1975, at the annual meeting of the American Association for the Advancement of Science.' 1. Memory — Congresses. I. Cofer, Charles Norval. II. American Association for the Advancement of Science. Section on Psychology III. American Association for the Advancement of Science. Section on Information and Communication.
BF371.S84    153.1/2    *LC* 76-2581    *ISBN* 0716707055

**Tulving, Endel.**      5.337
Elements of episodic memory / Endel Tulving. — Oxford [Oxfordshire]: Clarendon Press; New York: Oxford University Press, 1983. xi, 351 p.: ill.; 24 cm. — (Oxford psychology series. no. 2) Includes indexes. 1. Memory 2. Recollection (Psychology) I. T. II. Series.
BF371.T84 1983    153.1 19    *LC* 82-8241    *ISBN* 0198521022

**Underwood, Benton J., 1915-.**      5.338
Temporal codes for memories: issues and problems / Benton J. Underwood. — Hillsdale, N.J.: L. Erlbaum Associates; New York: distributed by Halsted Press, 1977. vi, 158 p.: ill.; 24 cm. — (John M. MacEachran memorial lecture series. 1976) Includes index. 1. Memory 2. Human information processing 3. Time — Psychological aspects. I. T. II. Series.
BF371.U5    153.1/2    *LC* 77-1954    *ISBN* 0470991151

**Luriia, A. R. (Aleksandr Romanovich), 1902-.**      • 5.339
[Malen'kaia knizhka o bol'shoĭ pamiati. English] The mind of a mnemonist; a little book about a vast memory [by] A. R. Luria. Translated from the Russian by Lynn Solotaroff. With a foreword by Jerome S. Bruner. New York, Basic Books [1968] xi, 160 p. illus. 21 cm. Translation of Malen'kaia knizhka o bol'shoĭ pamiati. 1. Memory, Disorders of — Case studies. 2. Memory I. T.
BF376.L813    153.1/2 19    *LC* 68-15918

**Rokeach, Milton.**      • 5.340
The open and closed mind: investigations into the nature of belief systems and personality systems / in collaboration with Richard Bonier [and others]. — New York: Basic Books [1960] xv, 447 p.: diagrs., tables; 25 cm. 1. Attitude (Psychology) 2. Dogmatism I. T.
BF378.A75 R57    157.5    *LC* 60-5888

**Shaw, Marvin E.**      5.341
Scales for the measurement of attitudes [by] Marvin E. Shaw [and] Jack M. Wright. — New York: McGraw-Hill, [1967] xxii, 604 p.; 23 cm. — (McGraw-Hill series in psychology) 1. Attitude (Psychology) — Testing I. Wright, Jack Mason, 1931- joint author. II. T.
BF378.A75 S45    152.4/52    *LC* 66-22791

# BF408–426 Creative Processes. Imagination

**Arieti, Silvano.**      5.342
Creativity: the magic synthesis / Silvano Arieti. — New York: Basic Books, c1976. xv, 448 p.: ill.; 24 cm. Includes indexes. 1. Creative ability I. T.
BF408.A64    153.3/5    *LC* 75-36374    *ISBN* 0465014437

**Axelrod, Charles David.**      5.343
Studies in intellectual breakthrough: Freud, Simmel, Buber / Charles David Axelrod. — Amherst: University of Massachusetts Press, 1979. 93 p.; 24 cm. Includes index. 1. Freud, Sigmund, 1856-1939. 2. Simmel, Georg, 1858-1918. 3. Buber, Martin, 1878-1965. 4. Creative thinking 5. Originality I. T.
BF408.A93    153.3/5/0926 B    *LC* 78-53177    *ISBN* 0870232568

**Koestler, Arthur, 1905-.**      5.344
The act of creation / Arthur Koestler. — 2nd Danube ed. [i.e. 1st ed. reprinted]. — London: Hutchinson, 1976. 4-751 p.: ill.; 21 cm. — (The Danube edition) Includes book 2, Habit and originality, omitted in 1st Danube ed. Includes

index. 1. Creative thinking 2. Creation (Literary, artistic, etc.) 3. Creative ability I. T.
BF408.K6 1976    153.3/5    *LC* 78-310679    *ISBN* 0091282705

**May, Rollo.**      5.345
The courage to create / Rollo May. — 1st ed. — New York: Norton, [1975] 143 p.; 21 cm. 1. Creation (Literary, artistic, etc.) I. T.
BF408.M33 1975    153.3/5    *LC* 75-23055    *ISBN* 0393011194

**Perkins, D. N., 1942-.**      5.346
The mind's best work / D.N. Perkins. — Cambridge, Mass.: Harvard University Press, 1981. ix, 314 p.; 24 cm. Includes index. 1. Creation (Literary, artistic, etc.) 2. Creative ability I. T.
BF408.P387    153.3/5 19    *LC* 81-4223    *ISBN* 0674576276

**Rugg, Harold Ordway, 1886-1960.**      5.347
Imagination / with a foreword and editorial comments by Kenneth D. Benne. — [1st ed.] New York: Harper & Row [1963] 361 p.; 22 cm. 1. Creation (Literary, artistic, etc.) 2. Imagination I. T.
BF408.R76    155.3    *LC* 63-8008

**Taylor, Irving A.**      5.348
Perspectives in creativity / edited by Irving A. Taylor, J. W. Getzels. — Chicago: Aldine Pub. Co., 1975. xiv, 353 p.: ill. 1. Creation (Literary, artistic, etc.) — Addresses, essays, lectures. 2. Creative ability — Addresses, essays, lectures. I. Getzels, Jacob W. II. T.
BF408.T3    BF408 T3.    *ISBN* 0202251217

**Warnock, Mary.**      5.349
Imagination / Mary Warnock. — Berkeley: University of California Press, c1976. 213 p.; 23 cm. 1. Imagination I. T.
BF408.W28 1976    153.3    *LC* 75-22663    *ISBN* 0520031156

# BF431–433 Intelligence. Mental Ability. Tests and Testing

**Brody, Erness Bright.**      5.350
Intelligence: nature, determinants, and consequences / Erness Bright Brody, Nathan Brody. New York: Academic Press, 1976. x, 241 p.: ill.; 24 cm. (Educational psychology) Includes index. 1. Intellect 2. Intelligence tests 3. Nature and nurture I. Brody, Nathan. joint author. II. T.
BF431.B6844    153.9    *LC* 76-39781    *ISBN* 0121342506

**Eysenck, H. J. (Hans Jurgen), 1916-.**      5.351
[Intelligence controversy] The intelligence controversy / H. J. Eysenck versus Leon Kamin. — New York: Wiley, 1981. 192 p.: ill.; 23 cm. 'Published in Great Britain as Intelligence: the battle for the mind.' 'A Wiley-Interscience publication.' Includes index. 1. Intellect 2. Intelligence tests 3. Nature and nurture 4. Twins — Psychology I. Kamin, Leon J. joint author. II. T.
BF431.E945    153.9 19    *LC* 80-28571    *ISBN* 0471088846

**Gardner, Howard.**      5.352
Frames of mind: the theory of multiple intelligences / Howard Gardner. — New York: Basic Books, c1983. xiii, 440 p.; 25 cm. 1. Intellect I. T.
BF431.G244 1983    153 19    *LC* 83-70765    *ISBN* 0465025080

**Gould, Stephen Jay.**      5.353
The mismeasure of man / by Stephen Jay Gould. — 1st ed. — New York: Norton, c1981. 352 p.: ill.; 22 cm. Includes index. 1. Intelligence tests — History. 2. Ability — Testing — History. 3. Personality tests — History. 4. Craniometry — History. I. T.
BF431.G68 1981    153.9/3 19    *LC* 81-38430    *ISBN* 0393014894

**Guilford, J. P. (Joy Paul), 1897-.**      • 5.354
The nature of human intelligence [by] J. P. Guilford. New York, McGraw-Hill [1967] 538 p. illus. 23 cm. (McGraw-Hill series in psychology) 1. Intellect I. T.
BF431.G835    153    *LC* 67-11207

**Handbook of human intelligence** / edited by Robert J. Sternberg.    5.355
Cambridge [Cambridgeshire]; New York: Cambridge University Press, 1982. xii, 1031 p.: ill.; 24 cm. 1. Intellect 2. Intellect — Research. I. Sternberg, Robert J.
BF431.H3186 1982    153.9 19    *LC* 82-1160    *ISBN* 0521228700

**How and how much can intelligence be increased** / edited by    5.356
Douglas K. Detterman, Robert J. Sternberg.
Norwood, N.J.: Ablex Pub. Corp., c1982. viii, 241 p.; 24 cm. 1. Intellect 2. Cognition 3. Success I. Detterman, Douglas K. II. Sternberg, Robert J.
BF431.H63 1982    153.9 19    *LC* 82-1787    *ISBN* 0893911178

**Jensen, Arthur Robert.**     **5.357**
Genetics and education [by] Arthur R. Jensen. — [1st U.S. ed.]. — New York: Harper & Row, [c1972] vii, 379 p.: illus.; 22 cm. 1. Academic achievement 2. Intellect — Genetic aspects 3. Human genetics I. T.
BF431.J395 1972     370.15/2     *LC* 72-86636     *ISBN* 0060121920

**Kamin, Leon J.**     **5.358**
The science and politics of I.Q., by Leon J. Kamin. — Potomac, Md.: L. Erlbaum Associates; distributed by Halsted Press, New York, 1974. vii, 183 p.: illus.; 24 cm. — (Complex human behavior) 1. Intellect — Social aspects. 2. Intelligence tests 3. Nature and nurture I. T.
BF431.K3646     153.9/3     *LC* 74-13883     *ISBN* 0470455748

**Lord, Frederic M., 1912-.**     • **5.359**
Statistical theories of mental test scores [by] Frederic M. Lord and Melvin R. Novick. With contributions by Allan Birnbaum. — Reading, Mass.: Addison-Wesley Pub. Co., [1968] xvii, 568 p.: illus.; 24 cm. — (The Addison-Wesley series in behavioral science: quantitative methods) 1. Intelligence tests 2. Psychometrics I. Novick, Melvin R., joint author. II. T.
BF431.L59     153.9/3     *LC* 68-11394

**The nature of intelligence / edited by Lauren B. Resnick.**     **5.360**
Hillsdale, N.J.: Lawrence Erlbaum Associates; New York: distributed by Halsted Press Division of J. Wiley, 1976. x, 364 p.: ill.; 24 cm. Based on papers presented at a conference held March 1974 at the Learning Research and Development Center, University of Pittsburgh. 1. Intellect — Congresses. I. Resnick, Lauren B. II. University of Pittsburgh. Learning Research and Development Center.
BF431.N38     153.9     *LC* 75-37871     *ISBN* 0470013842

**Piaget, Jean, 1896-.**     • **5.361**
[Psychologie de l'intelligence. English] The psychology of intelligence. [Translated from the French by Malcolm Piercy and D. E. Berlyne] London, Routledge & Paul [1950] viii, 182 p. 23 cm. (International library of psychology, philosophy, and scientific method.) 1. Intellect I. T. II. Series.
BF431.P48272     151     *LC* 51-991

**Premack, David.**     **5.362**
Intelligence in ape and man / David Premack. — Hillsdale, N.J.: L. Erlbaum Associates; New York: distributed by Halsted Press, 1976. xiii, 370 p.: ill.; 24 cm. Includes indexes. 1. Intellect 2. Animal intelligence 3. Psycholinguistics 4. Animal communication 5. Chimpanzees — Psychology. I. T.
BF431.P683     156/.3/9     *LC* 76-26570     *ISBN* 0470989092

**Sagan, Carl, 1934-.**     **5.363**
Broca's brain: reflections on the romance of science / Carl Sagan. — 1st ed. — New York: Random House, c1979. xv, 347 p.; 24 cm. Includes index. 1. Broca, Paul, 1824-1880. 2. Intellect 3. Brain 4. Space sciences I. T.
BF431.S19     128/.2     *LC* 78-21810     *ISBN* 0394501691

**Sagan, Carl, 1934-.**     **5.364**
The dragons of Eden: speculations on the evolution of human intelligence / Carl Sagan. 1st ed. — New York: Random House, c1977. 263 p.: ill.; 24 cm. Includes index. 1. Intellect 2. Brain 3. Genetic psychology I. T.
BF431.S2     153     *LC* 76-53472     *ISBN* 0394410459

**Super, Donald Edwin, 1910-.**     • **5.365**
Appraising vocational fitness by means of psychological tests [by] Donald E. Super [and] John O. Crites. — Rev. ed. — New York: Harper, [1962] 688 p.: illus.; 25 cm. 1. Ability testing I. Crites, John Orr. joint author. II. T.
BF431.S873 1962     151.223     *LC* 61-7929

**Talent and society: new perspectives in the identification of talent / David C. McClelland.**     • **5.366**
Princeton, N.J.: Van Nostrand, 1958. vii, 275 p. 1. Ability 2. Gifted children I. McClelland, David Clarence.
BF431.T2     270

**Wechsler, David, 1896-.**     • **5.367**
The range of human capacities. 2d ed. Baltimore, Williams & Wilkins, 1952. 190 p. illus. 24 cm. 1. Ability 2. Variation (Biology) 3. Psychophysiology 4. Mental tests. I. T. II. Title: Human capacities.
BF431.W37 1952     151     *LC* 52-3462

**Jensen, Arthur Robert.**     **5.368**
Bias in mental testing / Arthur R. Jensen. — New York: Free Press, c1980. xiii, 786 p.: ill.; 26 cm. Includes indexes. 1. Intelligence tests 2. Educational tests and measurements 3. Psychological tests for minorities 4. Test bias I. T.
BF432.A1 J46     153.9/3     *LC* 79-7583     *ISBN* 0029164303

**Grover, Sonja C.**     **5.369**
The cognitive basis of the intellect: a response to Jensen's 'Bias in mental testing' / Sonja C. Grover. — Washington, D.C.: University Press of America, c1981. ix, 138 p.; 23 cm. 1. Jensen, Arthur Robert. Bias in mental testing.

2. Intelligence tests 3. Intellect 4. Cognition 5. Psychological tests for minorities I. Jensen, Arthur Robert. Bias in mental testing. II. T.
BF432.A1 J4634     153.9/3 19     *LC* 81-40303     *ISBN* 0819117412

**Loehlin, John C.**     **5.370**
Race differences in intelligence / John C. Loehlin, Gardner Lindzey, J. N. Spuhler. — San Francisco: W. H. Freeman, [1975] xii, 380 p.: ill.; 24 cm. — (A Series of books in psychology) 'Prepared under the auspices of the Social Science Research Council's Committee on Biological Bases of Social Behavior.' Includes indexes. 1. Intelligence levels — United States. 2. Race 3. Ethnic groups 4. Nature and nurture I. Lindzey, Gardner. joint author. II. Spuhler, James N., joint author. III. Social Science Research Council. Committee on Biological Bases of Social Behavior. IV. T.
BF432.A1 L6     155.8/2     *LC* 75-1081     *ISBN* 0716707543. *ISBN* 0716707535 pbk

**Scarr, Sandra.**     **5.371**
Race, social class, and individual differences in I.Q. / Sandra Scarr; commentaries by Leon J. Kamin, Arthur R. Jensen. — Hillsdale, N.J.: Lawrence Erlbaum Associates, 1981. xii, 545 p.: ill.; 24 cm. 1. Intelligence levels — Social aspects. 2. Race 3. Social classes 4. Variability (Psychometrics) 5. Ethnopsychology 6. Nature and nurture I. T.
BF432.A1 S3     153.9/2 19     *LC* 80-29591     *ISBN* 0898590558

**Eysenck, H. J. (Hans Jurgen), 1916-.**     **5.372**
[IQ argument] Race, intelligence and education [by] H. J. Eysenck. London, Temple Smith, Ltd [for] 'New Society', 1971. 160 p.; illus. 22 cm. (Towards a new society) American ed. (New York, Library Press) published under title: The IQ argument. 1. Afro-Americans — Intelligence levels 2. Afro-Americans — Education 3. Intelligence tests I. T.
BF432.N5 E9 1971b     153.9/2     *LC* 77-859796     *ISBN* 0851170102

**Flynn, James Robert, 1934-.**     **5.373**
Race, IQ, and Jensen / James R. Flynn. — London; Boston: Routledge & Kegan Paul, 1980. 313 p.; 22 cm. 1. Jensen, Arthur Robert. 2. Blacks — Intelligence levels 3. Intelligence tests 4. Intellect I. T.
BF432.N5 F59     155.8/2 19     *LC* 80-49972     *ISBN* 0710006519

## BF441–463 Judgment. Reasoning. Thinking. Psychology of Language and Meaning

**Davis, Gary A., 1938-.**     **5.374**
Psychology of problem solving: theory and practice [by] Gary A. Davis. — New York: Basic Books, [1973] xii, 206 p.: illus.; 22 cm. — (Basic topics in cognition series) 1. Problem solving I. T.
BF441.D35     158     *LC* 72-92795     *ISBN* 0465067387

**Induction: processes of inference, learning, and discovery / John H. Holland ... [et al.].**     **5.375**
Cambridge, Mass.: MIT Press, c1986. xvi, 385 p.: ill.; 24 cm. — (Computational models of cognition and perception.) Includes index. 1. Induction (Logic) 2. Artificial intelligence 3. Inference 4. Learning, Psychology of 5. Machine learning 6. Memory I. Holland, John H. (John Henry), 1929- II. Series.
BF441.I53 1986     153 19     *LC* 86-2811     *ISBN* 0262081601

**Janis, Irving Lester, 1918-.**     **5.376**
Decision making: a psychological analysis of conflict, choice, and commitment / Irving L. Janis, Leon Mann. — New York: Free Press, c1977. xx, 488 p.: ill.; 25 cm. Includes indexes. 1. Decision-making 2. Conflict (Psychology) 3. Stress (Psychology) 4. Commitment (Psychology) I. Mann, Leon, joint author. II. T.
BF441.J3     153.8/3     *LC* 76-19643     *ISBN* 0029161606

**Restle, Frank.**     • **5.377**
Psychology of judgement and choice: a theoretical essay. — New York: Wiley, 1961. 235 p.: ill.; 24 cm. 1. Judgement. 2. Choice (Psychology) I. T.
BF441.R43     *LC* 61-15409

**Bartlett, Frederic Charles, Sir, 1887-1969.**     • **5.378**
Thinking: an experimental and social study / Sir Frederic Bartlett. — New York: Basic Books, 1958. 203 p.: ill. 1. Thought and thinking I. T.
BF455.B33 1958     *LC* 58-8916

**Berlyne, D. E.**     • **5.379**
Structure and direction in thinking [by] D. E. Berlyne. — New York: Wiley, [1965] xi, 378 p.: illus.; 24 cm. 1. Thought and thinking I. T.
BF455.B37     153     *LC* 65-12720

**Blanshard, Brand, 1892-1987.**     **5.380**
The nature of thought. New York, Humanities Press, 1964. 2 v. 23 cm.
1. Thought and thinking 2. Knowledge, Theory of 3. Necessity (Philosophy)
4. Truth 5. Meaning (Psychology) I. T.
BF455.B48 1964     LC 64-23938

**Brown, Roger William, 1925- comp.**     • **5.381**
Psycholinguistics: selected papers / by Roger Brown; with Albert Gilman [and others]. — New York: Free Press, [1970] xviii, 392 p.: ill.; 21 cm.
1. Psycholinguistics 2. Language acquisition I. T.
BF455.B73 1970     401.9     LC 73-95296

**Bruner, Jerome S. (Jerome Seymour)**     **5.382**
A study of thinking / Jerome S. Bruner, Jacqueline J. Goodnow, George A. Austin; with a new preface by Jerome S. Bruner and Jacqueline J. Goodnow; appendix on language by Roger W. Brown. — New Brunswick, N.J., U.S.A.: Transaction Books, c1986. xx, 330 p.: ill.; 23 cm. — (Social science classics series.) Reprint. Originally published: New York: Wiley, 1956. Includes indexes. 1. Thought and thinking I. Goodnow, Jacqueline J. II. Austin, George A. III. T. IV. Series.
BF455.B75 1986     153.4/2 19     LC 86-1913     ISBN 0887386563

**Duncker, Karl, 1903-.**     • **5.383**
[Zur Psychologie des produktiven Denkens. English] On problem–solving. Translated by Lynne S. Lees. Westport, Conn., Greenwood Press [1972] ix, 113 p. illus. 26 cm. At head of title: Psychological monographs. Translation of Zur Psychologie des produktiven Denkens. Reprint of the 1945 ed., which was issued as v. 58, no. 5, whole no. 270 of Psychological monographs series.
1. Problem solving I. T.
BF455.D815 1972     153     LC 73-138621     ISBN 0837157331

**Evans, Jonathan St. B. T., 1948-.**     **5.384**
The psychology of deductive reasoning / Jonathan St. B.T. Evans. — London; Boston: Routledge & Kegan Paul, 1982. 277 p.; 23 cm. — (International library of psychology.) Includes indexes. 1. Thought and thinking 2. Logic 3. Reasoning (Psychology) I. T. II. Series.
BF455.E93 1982     153.4/33 19     LC 81-13991     ISBN 0710009232

**Mandler, Jean Matter. ed.**     • **5.385**
Thinking: from association to Gestalt [by] Jean Matter Mandler and George Mandler. New York, Wiley [1964] x, 300 p. illus. 22 cm. (Perspectives in psychology) Bibliographical footnotes. 1. Thought and thinking 2. Association of ideas I. Mandler, George. joint ed. II. T.
BF455.M3     153     LC 64-23852

**Miller, George Armitage, 1920-.**     **5.386**
Language and perception / George A. Miller, Philip N. Johnson–Laird. — Cambridge, Mass.: Belknap Press of Harvard University Press, 1976. viii, 760 p.: ill.; 25 cm. Includes indexes. 1. Psycholinguistics 2. Perception I. Johnson-Laird, P. N. (Philip Nicholas), 1936- joint author. II. T.
BF455.M59     153     LC 75-30605     ISBN 0674509471

**Norman, Donald A.**     **5.387**
Memory and attention: an introduction to human information processing / Donald A. Norman. — 2d ed. — New York: Wiley, c1976. xiii, 262 p.: ill.; 23 cm. (Series in psychology) Includes indexes. 1. Human information processing 2. Memory 3. Attention I. T.
BF455.N66 1976     153.1/2     LC 76-236     ISBN 0471651362

**Radford, John.**     **5.388**
Thinking: its nature and development [by] John Radford and Andrew Burton. London, New York, Wiley, 1974. [7],440 p. illus. 24 cm. Includes index.
1. Thought and thinking I. Burton, Andrew. joint author. II. T.
BF455.R2     153.4/2     LC 73-8197     ISBN 0471704768 ISBN 047170475X

**Reed, Stephen K.**     **5.389**
Psychological processes in pattern recognition / [by] Stephen K. Reed. — New York: Academic Press, 1973. xvi, 244 p.: ill.; 24 cm. (Academic Press series in cognition and perception) 1. Human information processing 2. Pattern perception I. T.
BF455.R34     152.1/423     LC 72-13620     ISBN 0125853505

**Ryle, Gilbert, 1900-1976.**     **5.390**
On thinking / Gilbert Ryle; edited by Konstantin Kolenda; with an introd. by G. J. Warnock. — Totowa, N.J.: Rowman and Littlefield, 1979. xv, 136 p.; 23 cm. Includes index. 1. Thought and thinking I. Kolenda, Konstantin. II. T.
BF455.R94 1979     153.4/2     LC 79-16519     ISBN 0847662039

**Simon, Herbert Alexander, 1916-.**     **5.391**
Models of thought / Herbert A. Simon. — New Haven: Yale University Press, 1979. xviii, 524 p.: ill.; 26 cm. 1. Human information processing 2. Thought and thinking I. T.
BF455.S525     153.4     LC 78-31744     ISBN 0300023472

**Skinner, B. F. (Burrhus Frederic), 1904-.**     • **5.392**
Verbal behavior. New York: Appleton-Century-Crofts [1957] 478 p.; 25 cm. (The Century psychology series) 1. Verbal behavior I. T.
BF455.S53     158.83     LC 57-11446

**Strategies of information processing / edited by Geoffrey Underwood.**     **5.393**
London; New York: Academic Press, 1978. x, 455 p.: ill.; 24 cm. 1. Human information processing 2. Cognition I. Underwood, Geoffrey.
BF455.S74     153.4     LC 77-93215     ISBN 0127089500

**Vinacke, William Edgar, 1917-.**     **5.394**
The psychology of thinking [by] W. Edgar Vinacke. — 2d ed. — New York: McGraw-Hill, [1974] xvi, 616 p.: illus.; 23 cm. — (McGraw-Hill series in psychology) 1. Thought and thinking I. T.
BF455.V47 1974     153     LC 73-15756     ISBN 0070674868

**Gibson, Eleanor Jack.**     **5.395**
The Psychology of reading [by] Eleanor J. Gibson and Harry Levin. — Cambridge, Mass.: MIT Press, [1975] xii, 630 p.: illus.; 23 cm. 1. Reading, Psychology of I. Levin, Harry, 1925- joint author. II. T.
BF456.R2 G46     418     LC 74-9810     ISBN 0262070634

**Goodman, Kenneth S.**     **5.396**
Language and literacy: the selected writings of Kenneth S. Goodman / edited and introduced by Frederick V. Gollasch. — London; Boston: Routledge & Kegan Paul, 1982. 356 p.; 22 cm. 1. Reading, Psychology of 2. Psycholinguistics I. T.
BF456.R2 G63     153.6 19     LC 81-11848     ISBN 0710008759

**Interactive processes in reading / edited by Alan M. Lesgold, Charles A. Perfetti.**     **5.397**
Hillsdale, N.J.: Lawrence Erlbaum Associates, 1981. xi, 420 p.: ill. Proceedings of a conference held at the Learning Research and Development Center, University of Pittsburgh, in Sept. 1979. 1. Reading, Psychology of I. Lesgold, Alan M. II. Perfetti, Charles A.
BF456.R2 I54     BF456R2 I54.     428.4/01/9 19     LC 80-21048
    ISBN 0898590795

**Sperber, Dan.**     **5.398**
[Symbolisme en général. English] Rethinking symbolism / Dan Sperber; translated [from the French] by Alice L. Morton. — Cambridge; New York: Cambridge University Press, 1975. xiii, 153 p.; 23 cm. — (Cambridge studies in social anthropology 0068-6794) Translation of Le symbolisme en général. 1. Symbolism (Psychology) I. T.
BF458.S7213     153.2     LC 76-361918     ISBN 0521208343. ISBN 0521099676 pbk

**Werner, Heinz, 1890-.**     **5.399**
Symbol formation: an organismic–developmental approach to language and the expression of thought / [by] Heinz Werner and Bernard Kaplan. — New York: Wiley [1963] xiii, 530 p.: diagrs., tables; 24 cm. Bibliography: p. 505-517. 1. Symbolism I. Kaplan, Bernard, joint author. II. T.
BF458.W4     153.65     LC 63-20643

**Snider, James G., 1928- comp.**     **5.400**
Semantic differential technique; a sourcebook. Edited by James G. Snider and Charles E. Osgood. — Chicago: Aldine Pub. Co., [1969] xiii, 681 p.: illus.; 26 cm. 1. Semantic differential technique I. Osgood, Charles Egerton. joint comp. II. T.
BF463.M4 S55     155.28/4     LC 68-19874

# BF467–475 Time. Space. Causality

**Michotte, Albert Edouard, 1881-.**     • **5.401**
The Perception of causality / A. Michotte; ttranslated by T. R. Miles and Elaine Miles. — New York: Basic Books, 1963. xxii, 424 p.: ill. Translation of: La perception de la causalité. 1. Causation I. T.
BF467.M513 1963a

**Cottle, Thomas J.**     **5.402**
The present of things future; explorations of time in human experience [by] Thomas J. Cottle and Stephen L. Klineberg. New York: Free Press, [1974] xiii, 290 p.; 21 cm. 1. Time — Psychological aspects. I. Klineberg, Stephen L., 1940- II. T.
BF468.C6     153.7/53     LC 73-5292     ISBN 0029068207

**Fraisse, Paul.**     • **5.403**
The psychology of time / translated by Jennifer Leith. — New York: Harper & Row, [1963] 343 p. 1. Time perception I. T.
BF468.F683

**Hall, Edward Twitchell, 1914-.**     **5.404**
Handbook for proxemic research / by Edward T. Hall. — Washington: Society for the Anthropology of Visual Communication, c1974. iii, 124 p.: ill.; 28 cm. — (Studies in the anthropology of visual communication) 1. Personal space — Testing. 2. Psychology — Research 3. Ethnopsychology I. Society for the Anthropology of Visual Communication. II. T. III. Series.
BF469.H29     301.11     *LC* 75-322330

**Hall, Edward Twitchell, 1914-.**     **5.405**
The hidden dimension [by] Edward T. Hall. — [1st ed.]. — Garden City, N.Y.: Doubleday, 1966. xii, 201 p.: illus.; 25 cm. 1. Space perception 2. Space and time I. T.
BF469.H3     301.3     *LC* 66-11173

**Olson, David R.**     **5.406**
Spatial cognition: the structure and development of mental representations of spatial relations / David R. Olson and Ellen Bialystok. — Hillsdale, N.J.: L. Erlbaum Associates, 1983. xii, 277 p.: ill.; 24 cm. — (Child psychology.) Includes indexes. 1. Space perception I. Bialystok, Ellen. II. T. III. Series.
BF469.O45 1983     153.7/52 19     *LC* 83-5605     *ISBN* 0898592526

# BF481 Work

**Job stress and burnout: research, theory, and intervention**     **5.407**
**perspectives** / edited by Whiton Stewart Paine.
Beverly Hills: Sage Publications, c1982. 296 p.: ill.; 22 cm. — (Sage focus editions; 54) Includes index. 1. Burn out (Psychology) 2. Job stress I. Paine, Whiton Stewart.
BF481.J55 1982     158.7 19     *LC* 82-7339     *ISBN* 0803918488

**Neff, Walter Scott, 1910-.**     **5.408**
Work and human behavior / Walter S. Neff. — 2d ed. — Chicago: Aldine Pub. Co., 1977. xii, 332 p.; 24 cm. Includes indexes. 1. Work — Psychological aspects 2. Labor and laboring classes — Mental health. I. T.
BF481.N34 1977     158.7     *LC* 77-71250     *ISBN* 0202260844

**Pines, Ayala M.**     **5.409**
Burnout: from tedium to personal growth / Ayala M. Pines and Elliot Aronson with Ditsa Kafry. — New York: Free Press, c1981. ix, 229 p.; 24 cm. Includes index. 1. Work — Psychological aspects 2. Burn out (Psychology) I. Aronson, Elliot. II. Kafry, Ditsa. III. T.
BF481.P63 1981     158.7     *LC* 80-755     *ISBN* 0029253500

# BF501–593 Motivation. Feeling. Emotion

**Brenner, Charles, 1913-.**     **5.410**
The mind in conflict / by Charles Brenner. — New York: International Universities Press, c1982. 266 p.; 24 cm. Includes indexes. 1. Conflict (Psychology) 2. Psychoanalysis 3. Psychology, Pathological I. T.
BF503.B73 1982     150.19/5 19     *LC* 82-21391     *ISBN* 0823633659

**The Emotions, by Carl Georg Lange and William James.**     • **5.411**
New York: Hafner Pub. Co., 1967. 135 p.; 24 cm. Reprint of the 1922 ed. The emotions, by Lange, translated by I. A. Haupt from Kurella's German version of Om sindsbevaegelser; with a reprinting of James' What is an emotion? and his chapter on 'The emotions' from the Principles of psychology. 1. Emotions I. Lange, Carl Georg, 1834-1900. The emotions. II. James, William, 1842-1910.
BF531.E5 1967     152.4     *LC* 67-20562

**Human emotions** / [edited] by Carroll E. Izard.     **5.412**
New York: Plenum Press, c1977. xvi, 495 p.: ill.; 24 cm. (Emotions, personality, and psychotherapy.) Includes indexes. 1. Emotions I. Izard, Carroll E. (Carroll Ellis), 1923- II. Series.
BF531.H78     152.4     *LC* 77-1989     *ISBN* 0306309866

**Laing, Ronald David.**     **5.413**
The voice of experience / R.D. Laing. — 1st American ed. — New York: Pantheon Books, c1982. 178, [2] p.; 22 cm. 1. Experience 2. Emotions 3. Expression 4. Autonomy (Psychology) 5. Psychiatry — Methodology I. T.
BF531.L28 1982     152.4 19     *LC* 81-47199     *ISBN* 0394515528

**Tomkins, Silvan Solomon, 1911-.**     • **5.414**
Affect, cognition, and personality: empirical studies / edited by Silvan S. Tomkins, Carroll E. Izard. New York: Springer Pub. Co., 1965. vii, 464 p.: ill.; 24 cm. 'Expanded version of a symposium ... held at the 1964 meeting of the American Psychological Association.' Errata slip inserted. 1. Emotions I. Izard, Carroll E. II. American Psychological Association. III. T.
BF531.T57     *LC* 65-17489

**Explaining emotions** / edited by Amélie Oksenberg Rorty.     **5.415**
Berkeley: University of California Press, 1980. vi, 543 p.; 22 cm. — (Topics in philosophy; 5) 1. Emotions I. Rorty, Amélie.
BF561.E95     152.4     *LC* 78-62859     *ISBN* 0520037758

**Solomon, Robert C.**     **5.416**
The passions / Robert C. Solomon. 1st ed. — Garden City, N.Y.: Anchor Press/Doubleday, 1976. xxv, 448 p.; 22 cm. 1. Emotions 2. Life 3. Existentialism I. T.
BF561.S64     152.4     *LC* 74-33691     *ISBN* 0385097409

# BF575 Special Forms of Emotion, A–Z

**Aggression in global perspective** / edited by Arnold P.     **5.417**
**Goldstein, Marshall H. Segall.**
New York: Pergamon Press, c1983. viii, 496 p.: ill.; 27 cm. — (Pergamon general psychology series. 115) 1. Aggressiveness (Psychology) — Cross-cultural studies I. Goldstein, Arnold P. II. Segall, Marshall H. III. Series.
BF575.A3 A52 1983     302.5/4 19     *LC* 82-10131     *ISBN* 0080263461

**Aggression, theoretical and empirical reviews** / edited by     **5.418**
**Russell G. Geen, Edward I. Donnerstein.**
New York: Academic Press, 1983-. v. < 2 >: ill.; 24 cm. 1. Aggressiveness (Psychology) 2. Violence I. Geen, Russell G., 1932- II. Donnerstein, Edward I.
BF575.A3 A525 1983     155.2/32 19     *LC* 82-24348     *ISBN* 012278801X

**Berkowitz, Leonard, 1926-.**     • **5.419**
Aggression: a social psychological analysis. — New York: McGraw-Hill, [1962] 361 p.: illus.; 24 cm. — (McGraw-Hill series in psychology) 1. Aggressiveness (Psychology) I. T.
BF575.A3 B4     157.3     *LC* 62-12479

**Buss, Arnold H., 1924-.**     • **5.420**
The psychology of aggression. New York, Wiley [1961] 307 p. 24 cm. 1. Aggressiveness (Psychology) I. T.
BF575.A3 B8     157.3     *LC* 61-15395

**Eibl-Eibesfeldt, Irenäus.**     **5.421**
[Krieg und Frieden aus der Sicht der Verhaltensforschung. English] The biology of peace and war: men, animals, and aggression / Irenäus Eibl-Eibesfeldt; translated from the German by Eric Mosbacher. — New York: Viking Press, 1979. viii, 294 p.: ill.; 24 cm. Translation of Krieg und Frieden aus der Sicht der Verhaltensforschung. Includes index. 1. Aggressiveness (Psychology) 2. Psychology, Comparative 3. War — Psychological aspects I. T.
BF575.A3 E313 1979     301.6/3     *LC* 77-26617     *ISBN* 0670167096

**Hornstein, Harvey A., 1938-.**     **5.422**
Cruelty and kindness: a new look at aggression and altruism / Harvey A. Hornstein. — Englewood Cliffs, N.J.: Prentice-Hall, c1976. vi, 154 p.; 21 cm. (The Patterns of social behavior series) (A Spectrum book) 1. Aggressiveness (Psychology) 2. Cruelty 3. Altrism. 4. Kindness I. T.
BF575.A3 H67     152.4     *LC* 76-6911     *ISBN* 0131949284

**Montagu, Ashley, 1905- comp.**     **5.423**
Man and aggression / ed. by Ashley Montagu; contributors: S. A. Barnett [and others]. — 2d ed. New York: Oxford University Press, 1973. xix, 278 p.; 22 cm. 1. Ardrey, Robert. Territorial imperative. 2. Lorenz, Konrad, 1903- Sogenannte Böse. 3. Aggressiveness (Psychology) I. T.
BF575.A3 M6 1973     155.2/32 19     *LC* 72-91012     *ISBN* 0195016815

**Scott, John Paul, 1909-.**     **5.424**
Aggression / John Paul Scott. — 2d ed., rev. and expanded. — Chicago: University of Chicago Press, 1975. xiii, 233 p.; 22 cm. — (The Scientist's library) Includes indexes. 1. Aggressiveness (Psychology) 2. Aggressive behavior in animals I. T.
BF575.A3 S37 1975     152.5/2     *LC* 75-14423     *ISBN* 0226742946

**Stepansky, Paul E.**     **5.425**
A history of aggression in Freud / Paul E. Stepansky. New York: International Universities Press, c1977. ix, 201 p.; 24 cm. (Psychological issues. v. 10, no. 3: Monograph; 39) Includes index. 1. Freud, Sigmund, 1856-1939. 2. Aggressiveness (Psychology) 3. Psychoanalysis I. T. II. Series.
BF575.A3 S76     152.5/2     *LC* 76-53907     *ISBN* 0823623262

**Tavris, Carol.**     **5.426**
Anger, the misunderstood emotion / Carol Tavris. — New York: Simon and Schuster, c1982. 302 p.; 23 cm. Includes index. 1. Anger I. T.
BF575.A5 T38 1982     152.4 19     *LC* 82-10610     *ISBN* 0671250949

**Anxiety: current trends in theory and research. Edited by**     **5.427**
**Charles D. Spielberger. Contributors: Ernest S. Barratt [and others]**
New York, Academic Press, 1972. 2 v. (xiv, 510 p.) illus. 24 cm. Consists of papers and discussion presented at a symposium sponsored by Florida State University and held in Tallahassee in Mar. and Apr. 1970. 1. Anxiety — Congresses. I. Spielberger, Charles Donald, 1927- ed. II. Barratt, Ernest S. III. Florida State University.
BF575.A6 A58     616.8/522/07     *LC* 70-182630     *ISBN* 0126574014

**Gaudry, Eric.**     **5.428**
Anxiety and educational achievement [by] Eric Gaudry [and] Charles D. Spielberger. — Sydney; New York: J. Wiley & Sons Australasia, [1971] viii, 174 p.: illus.; 25 cm. 1. Anxiety 2. Academic achievement I. Spielberger, Charles Donald, 1927- joint author. II. T.
BF575.A6 G35     152.4/34     *LC* 76-171907     *ISBN* 0471292893

**Izard, Carroll E. (Carroll Ellis), 1923-.**     **5.429**
Patterns of emotions; a new analysis of anxiety and depression [by] Carroll E. Izard. With chapters coauthored by Edmund S. Bartlett [and] Alan G. Marshall. New York, Academic Press, 1972. xii, 301 p. 24 cm. 1. Anxiety 2. Depression, Mental 3. Emotions I. T.
BF575.A6 I9     616.8/522     *LC* 72-82657     *ISBN* 012377750X

**May, Rollo.**     **5.430**
The meaning of anxiety / by Rollo May. — Rev. ed. — New York: Norton, c1977. xx, 425 p.; 22 cm. Includes index. 1. Anxiety I. T.
BF575.A6 M35 1977     152.4/34     *LC* 77-1359     *ISBN* 0393011364

**Doi, Takeo.**     **5.431**
The anatomy of dependence / Takeo Doi; translated by John Bester. — Tokyo: Kodansha International Ltd.; New York: Distributed by Harper & Row, 1981, c1973. 180 p. On cover: The key analysis of Japanese behavior. 1. National characteristics, Japanese 2. Ethnopsychology I. T.
BF575D34D6413     155.84956     *ISBN* 0870114948

**Ulanov, Ann Belford.**     **5.432**
Cinderella and her sisters: the envied and the envying / by Ann and Barry Ulanov. — 1st ed. — Philadelphia: Westminster Press, c1983. 186 p.; 21 cm. 1. Envy I. Ulanov, Barry. II. T.
BF575.E65 U4 1983     152.4 19     *LC* 83-10463     *ISBN* 0664244823

**Duck, Steve.**     **5.433**
Friends, for life: the psychology of close relationships / Steve Duck. — New York: St. Martin's Press, 1983. 181 p.; 22 cm. Includes index. 1. Friendship 2. Intimacy (Psychology) I. T.
BF575.F66 D83 1983     158/.25 19     *LC* 82-25081     *ISBN* 0312305648

**Bowlby, John.**     • **5.434**
Attachment and loss. New York: Basic Books, [1969-. v.; 24 cm. 1. Maternal deprivation 2. Grief in children 3. Bereavement in children 4. Attachment behavior in children 5. Separation anxiety in children 6. Psychology, Pathological I. T.
BF575.G7 B68 1969b     155.4/18 19     *LC* 70-78464

**Caine, Lynn.**     **5.435**
Widow. — New York: Morrow, 1974. 222 p.; 21 cm. 1. Caine, Lynn. 2. Bereavement — Psychological aspects 3. Widows — Biography. I. T.
BF575.G7 C34     155.9/37     *LC* 73-23124     *ISBN* 0688028500

**Handbook of humor research / edited by Paul E. McGhee and**     **5.436**
**Jeffrey H. Goldstein.**
New York: Springer-Verlag, c1983. 2 v.: ill.; 25 cm. 1. Wit and humor — Psychological aspects — Addresses, essays, lectures. 2. Wit and humor — Social aspects — Addresses, essays, lectures. 3. Wit and humor — Research — Addresses, essays, lectures. I. McGhee, Paul E. II. Goldstein, Jeffrey H.
BF575.L3 H36 1983     152.4 19     *LC* 83-6675     *ISBN* 0387908528

**Ziv, Avner.**     **5.437**
Personality and sense of humor / Avner Ziv. — New York: Springer Pub. Co., c1984. xiii, 189 p.: ill.; 24 cm. Includes index. 1. Wit and humor — Psychological aspects. 2. Personality I. T.
BF575.L3 Z58 1984     152.4 19     *LC* 84-1372     *ISBN* 082614540X

**The Anatomy of loneliness / edited by Joseph Hartog, J. Ralph**     **5.438**
**Audy, and Yehudi A. Cohen.**
New York: International Universities Press, c1980. xiv, 617 p.; 24 cm. 1. Loneliness — Addresses, essays, lectures. I. Hartog, Joseph. II. Audy, J. Ralph. III. Cohen, Yehudi A.
BF575.L7 A68     158/.2     *LC* 79-53591     *ISBN* 0823601463

**Loneliness: a sourcebook of current theory, research, and**     **5.439**
**therapy / edited by Letitia Anne Peplau, Daniel Perlman.**
New York: Wiley, c1982. xvii, 430 p.; 24 cm. — (Wiley series on personality processes. 0195-4008) 'A Wiley-Interscience publication.' Includes indexes. 1. Loneliness I. Peplau, Letitia Anne. II. Perlman, Daniel. III. Series.
BF575.L7 L66 1982     152.4 19     *LC* 81-16272     *ISBN* 0471080284

**Alberoni, Francesco.**     **5.440**
[Innamoramento e amore. English] Falling in love / Francesco Alberoni; translated from the Italian by Lawrence Venuti. — 1st American ed. — New York: Random House, c1983. 166 p.; 22 cm. Translation of: Innamoramento e amore. 1. Love 2. Change (Psychology) 3. Social change I. T.
BF575.L8 A413 1983     306.7/3 19     *LC* 83-42757     *ISBN* 0394530071

**On love and loving / Kenneth S. Pope and associates.**     **5.441**
1st ed. — San Francisco, Calif.: Jossey-Bass, c1980. xix, 377 p.; 24 cm. — (The Jossey-Bass social and behavioral science series) Includes index. 1. Love — Psychological aspects. I. Pope, Kenneth S.
BF575.L8 O48     152.4 19     *LC* 80-8012     *ISBN* 0875894798

**Tennov, Dorothy.**     **5.442**
Love and limerence: the experience of being in love / Dorothy Tennov. — New York: Stein and Day, 1979. xi, 324 p.; 24 cm. Includes index. 1. Love I. T.
BF575.L8 T46     152.4     *LC* 77-20117     *ISBN* 0812823281

**Davis, Fred, 1925-.**     **5.443**
Yearning for yesterday: a sociology of nostalgia / [Fred Davis]. — New York: Free Press, c1979. 146 p. Includes index. 1. Nostalgia 2. Personality 3. Arts — Psychological aspects. 4. United States — Popular culture I. T.
BF575.N6 D38 1979     301.1     *LC* 78-19838     *ISBN* 0029069505

**Allport, Gordon W. (Gordon Willard), 1897-1967.**     **5.444**
The nature of prejudice / Gordon W. Allport; introd. by Kenneth Clark, foreword by Thomas Pettigrew. — Unabridged, 25th anniversary ed. — Reading, Mass.: Addison-Wesley Pub. Co., [1979], c1954. xxxii, 537 p.: ill.; 22 cm. 1. Prejudices and antipathies. I. T.
BF575.P9 A38 1979     301.45/1/042     *LC* 79-112200     *ISBN* 0201001780

**Wurmser, Leon.**     **5.445**
The mask of shame / Léon Wurmser. — Baltimore: Johns Hopkins University Press, c1981. xiii, 345 p.; 24 cm. 1. Shame 2. Psychoanalysis 3. Psychotherapy I. T.
BF575.S45 W87     152.4 19     *LC* 81-964     *ISBN* 080182527X

**Cooper, Cary L.**     **5.446**
The stress check: coping with the stresses of life and work / Cary L. Cooper. — Englewood Cliffs, N.J.: Prentice Hall, c1981. x, 211 p.: ill.; 20 cm. — (A Spectrum book) Includes index. 1. Stress (Psychology) 2. Personality 3. Family 4. Work — Psychological aspects I. T.
BF575.S75 C65     158 19     *LC* 80-20796     *ISBN* 0138526400

**Handbook of stress: theoretical and clinical aspects / edited by**     **5.447**
**Leo Goldberger and Shlomo Breznitz.**
New York: Free Press; London: Collier Macmillan, c1982. xxi, 804 p.: ill.; 26 cm. 1. Stress (Psychology) 2. Stress (Physiology) I. Goldberger, Leo. II. Breznitz, Shelomo.
BF575.S75 H35 1982     155.9 19     *LC* 82-8448     *ISBN* 0029120306

**Janis, Irving Lester, 1918-.**     **5.448**
Stress, attitudes, and decisions: selected papers / Irving L. Janis. — New York, N.Y.: Praeger Publishers, 1982. xii, 352 p.: ill., port.; 25 cm. — (Centennial psychology series.) 1. Stress (Psychology) — Addresses, essays, lectures. 2. Attitude change — Addresses, essays, lectures. 3. Decision-making — Addresses, essays, lectures. I. T. II. Series.
BF575.S75 J33 1982     150 19     *LC* 82-9007     *ISBN* 0030590361

# BF608–635 WILL. VOLITION. CHOICE

**Harré, Rom.**                                                                **5.449**
Motives and mechanisms: an introduction to the psychology of action / Rom Harré, David Clarke, and Nicola de Carlo. — London; New York: Methuen, 1985. x, 161 p.: ill.; 23 cm. Includes indexes. 1. Intentionalism 2. Motivation (Psychology) I. Clarke, David D. II. De Carlo, Nicola. III. T.
BF619.5.H37 1985        150/.1 19        LC 84-22730        ISBN 0416362303

**Langer, Ellen J., 1947-.**                                                  **5.450**
The psychology of control / Ellen J. Langer; foreword by Irving L. Janis; collaborators, Robert P. Abelson ... [et al.]. — Beverly Hills: Sage Publications, c1983. 311 p.: ill.; 23 cm. 1. Control (Psychology) I. Abelson, Robert P. II. T.
BF632.5.L36 1983        153.8/3 19        LC 83-11224        ISBN 080391962X

**Lifton, Robert Jay.**                                                     • **5.451**
Thought reform and the psychology of totalism: a study of 'brainwashing' in China / Robert Jay Lifton. — 1st ed. — New York: Norton, 1961. x, 510 p. 1. Brainwashing I. T.
BF633.L5        131.333        LC 61-5934

# BF636–637 APPLIED PSYCHOLOGY

**Heider, Fritz, 1896-.**                                                   • **5.452**
The psychology of interpersonal relations. — New York: Wiley, [1958] 322 p.: illus.; 24 cm. 1. Interpersonal relations I. T.
BF636.H383        150.13        LC 58-10801

**Sullivan, Harry Stack, 1892-1949.**                                       • **5.453**
The interpersonal theory of psychiatry; edited by Helen Swick Perry and Mary Ladd Gawel, with an introd. by Mabel Blake Cohen. — [1st ed.]. — New York: Norton, [1953] xviii, 393 p.; 22 cm. 1. Interpersonal relations 2. Psychiatry I. T.
BF636.S77        616.89*        LC 53-9402

# BF637 Special Topics, A–Z

**Helping people change: a textbook of methods / edited by**                   **5.454**
**Frederick H. Kanfer, Arnold P. Goldstein.**
3rd ed. — New York: Pergamon Press, c1986. x, 490 p.; 24 cm. — (Pergamon general psychology series. 52) 1. Behavior modification 2. Personality I. Kanfer, Frederick H., 1925- II. Goldstein, Arnold P. III. Series.
BF637.B4 H45 1986        158 19        LC 85-6267        ISBN 0080316018

**Mahoney, Michael J.**                                                       **5.455**
Cognition and behavior modification [by] Michael J. Mahoney. — Cambridge, Mass.: Ballinger Pub. Co., [1974] xv, 351 p.: illus.; 24 cm. 1. Behavior modification 2. Cognition I. T.
BF637.B4 M32        153.8/5        LC 74-13019        ISBN 0884105008

**Progress in behavior modification.**                                        **5.456**
Vol. 1 (1975) -        . — New York: Academic Press, 1975-        . — Irregular. 1. Behavior modification — Periodicals. I. Hersen, Michel. II. Eisler, Richard M. III. Miller, Peter M.
BF637.B4 P76        BF637.B4 P66.        LC 75-646720

**Sherman, A. Robert.**                                                       **5.457**
Behavior modification: theory and practice [by] A. Robert Sherman. — Monterey, Calif.: Brooks/Cole Pub. Co., [1973] 183 p.; 23 cm. 1. Behavior modification 2. Behavior therapy I. T.
BF637.B4 S57        616.8/914        LC 72-85941        ISBN 0818500662

**Willis, Jerry.**                                                            **5.458**
Great experiments in behavior modification / abstracted by Jerry Willis and Donna Giles; under the general editorship of B. R. Bugelski. — Indianapolis: Hackett Pub. Co., c1976. xviii, 288 p.: ill.; 24 cm. — (Great experiments in psychology series) Consists of abstracts of 116 articles. Includes indexes.

1. Behavior modification — Abstracts. I. Giles, Donna, 1949- II. T. III. Series.
BF637.B4 W54        361/.06        LC 76-7365        ISBN 0915144204. ISBN 0915144190 pbk

**Ferguson, Marilyn.**                                                        **5.459**
The Aquarian conspiracy: personal and social transformation in the 1980s / by Marilyn Ferguson; foreword by Max Lerner. — 1st ed. — Los Angeles: J. P. Tarcher; New York: distributed by St. Martin's Press, c1980. 448 p.; 25 cm. Includes indexes. 1. Change (Psychology) 2. Social change I. T.
BF637.C4 F47 1980        303.4        LC 79-91722        ISBN 0312904185

**Birdwhistell, Ray L., 1918-.**                                            • **5.460**
Kinesics and context; essays on body motion communication / [by] Ray L. Birdwhistell. — Philadelphia: University of Pennsylvania Press, [1970] xiv, 338 p.: illus.; 24 cm. — (University of Pennsylvania publications in conduct and communication; [no. 2]) 1. Nonverbal communication I. T.
BF637.C45 B57        153        LC 77-122379        ISBN 0812276051

**Handbook of methods in nonverbal behavior research / edited**                **5.461**
**by Klaus R. Scherer and Paul Ekman.**
Cambridge [Cambridgeshire]; New York: Cambridge University Press; Paris: Editions de la Maison des Sciences de l'Homme, 1982. xiii, 593 p.: ill.; 25 cm. — (Studies in emotion and social interaction.) 1. Nonverbal communication (Psychology) — Research. 2. Psychology — Research — Methodology. I. Scherer, Klaus Rainer. II. Ekman, Paul. III. Series.
BF637.C45 H29 1982        BF637C45 H29 1982.        152.3/84 19        LC 81-9940        ISBN 0521236142

**Key, Mary Ritchie.**                                                        **5.462**
Paralanguage and kinesics: (nonverbal communication), with a bibliography / by Mary Ritchie Key. Metuchen, N.J.: Scarecrow Press, 1975. 246 p.; 22 cm. Includes index. 1. Nonverbal communication (Psychology) I. T.
BF637.C45 K48        153        LC 74-30217        ISBN 0810807890

**Knapp, Mark L.**                                                          • **5.463**
Nonverbal communication in human interaction [by] Mark L. Knapp. — New York: Holt, Rinehart and Winston, [1972] viii, 213 p.: illus.; 23 cm. 1. Nonverbal communication I. T.
BF637.C45 K57        153        LC 74-187114        ISBN 0030858623

**Miller, George Armitage, 1920-.**                                         • **5.464**
The psychology of communication; seven essays [by] George A. Miller. — New York: Basic Books, [1967] vii, 197 p.; 22 cm. 1. Communication — Psychological aspects — Addresses, essays, lectures. I. T.
BF637.C45 M5        001.5/01/9        LC 67-17390

**Non-verbal communication; edited by R. A. Hinde.**                         • **5.465**
Cambridge [Eng.]: University Press, 1972. xiii, 441 p.: illus.; 24 cm. Papers by members of the Royal Society Study Group on Non-Verbal Communication. 1. Nonverbal communication (Psychology) I. Hinde, Robert A. ed. II. Royal Society of London. Study Group on Non-Verbal Communication.
BF637.C45 N65        153        LC 75-171675        ISBN 0521083702

**Combs, Arthur Wright.**                                                     **5.466**
Helping relationships; basic concepts for the helping professions [by] Arthur W. Combs, Donald L. Avila [and] William W. Purkey. Boston, Allyn and Bacon [1971] vii, 360 p. 22 cm. 1. Counseling 2. Helping behavior I. Avila, Donald L. joint author. II. Purkey, William Watson. joint author. III. T.
BF637.C6 C48        158/.3 19        LC 78-144036

**Cross-cultural counseling and psychotherapy / edited by**                    **5.467**
**Anthony J. Marsella, Paul B. Pedersen.**
New York: Pergamon Press, c1981. xii, 358 p.; 24 cm. — (Pergamon general psychology series; v. 93) Based on a conference held in Honolulu in June 1979 and sponsored by the Culture Learning Institute of the East-West Center. 1. Counseling — Cross-cultural studies — Congresses. 2. Psychotherapy — Cross-cultural studies — Congresses. I. Marsella, Anthony J. II. Pedersen, Paul, 1936- III. East-West Center. Culture Learning Institute.
BF637.C6 C73 1981        616.89/14        LC 80-18472        ISBN 0080255450

**Gibson, Robert L. (Robert Lewis), 1927-.**                                  **5.468**
Introduction to counseling and guidance / Robert L. Gibson, Marianne H. Mitchell. — 2nd ed. — New York: Macmillan; London: Collier Macmillan, c1986. xv, 499 p.: ill.; 27 cm. Rev. ed.: Introduction to guidance. c1981. 1. Counseling I. Mitchell, Marianne. II. Gibson, Robert L. (Robert Lewis), 1927- Introduction to guidance. III. T.
BF637.C6 G48 1986        158/.3 19        LC 85-8809        ISBN 0023418001

**Handbook of cross-cultural counseling and therapy / edited by**             **5.469**
**Paul Pedersen.**
Westport, Conn.: Greenwood Press, 1985. xiv, 353 p.; 24 cm. 1. Cross-cultural counseling 2. Psychotherapy — Cross-cultural studies 3. Minorities — Counseling of. I. Pedersen, Paul, 1936-
BF637.C6 H317        158/.3 19        LC 84-12832        ISBN 0313239142

**Sue, Derald Wing.** 5.470
Counseling the culturally different: theory and practice / Derald W. Sue, with chapter contributions by Edwin H. Richardson, Rene A. Ruiz, Elsie J. Smith. — New York: Wiley, c1981. xvi, 303 p.; 24 cm. — (Wiley series in counseling and human development) 'A Wiley-Interscience publication.' Errata sheet inserted. 1. Cross-cultural counseling I. T.
BF637.C6 S85 158/.3 19 LC 80-24516 ISBN 0471042188

**Snyder, C. R.** 5.471
Excuses: masquerades in search of grace / C.R. Snyder, Raymond L. Higgins, Rita J. Stucky. — New York: Wiley, c1983. xxii, 327 p.: ill.; 24 cm. — (Wiley series on personality processes. 0195-4008) 'A Wiley-Interscience publication.' 1. Excuses — Psychological aspects. I. Higgins, Raymond L. II. Stucky, Rita J. III. T. IV. Series.
BF637.E95 S68 1983 158 19 LC 83-6615 ISBN 0471877026

**Lasswell, Harold Dwight, 1902-.** • 5.472
Power and personality. [1st ed.] New York: W. W. Norton [1948] 262 p.; 21 cm. (New York Academy of Medicine. Thomas William Salmon Memorial lectures) 1. Leadership 2. Psychology, Applied I. T.
BF637.L4 L35 LC 48-7325

**Fisher, Roger, 1922-.** 5.473
Getting to yes: negotiating agreement without giving in / Roger Fisher and William Ury; with Bruce Patton, editor. — Boston: Houghton Mifflin, 1981. xiii, 163 p.; 22 cm. 1. Negotiation I. Ury, William. II. T.
BF637.N4 F57 158/.5 19 LC 81-6515 ISBN 0395317576

**Personality and persuasibility, by Irving L. Janis [and others]** • 5.474
New Haven, Yale University Press, 1959. xiv, 333 p. diagrs., tables. 23 cm. (Yale studies in attitude and communication. v. 2) 1. Persuasion (Psychology) 2. Personality 3. Change (Psychology) I. Janis, Irving Lester, 1918- II. Series.
BF637.P4 P4 155.2/32 19 LC 59-7284

**Urquhart, John, 1934-.** 5.475
Risk watch: the odds of life / John Urquhart and Klaus Heilmann. — New York, N.Y.: Facts on File, 1984. xviii, 214 p.; 24 cm. 'Revised English language version of Keine Angst vor der Angst ... published March 1983 by Kindler Verlag, Munich'—Verso t.p. Includes index. 1. Risk-taking (Psychology) 2. Fear 3. Technological innovations 4. Civilization, Modern — 1950- I. Heilmann, Klaus. II. T.
BF637.R57 U77 1985 153.4 19 LC 84-4046 ISBN 0816000786

**Parker, Gail Thain, 1943-.** 5.476
Mind cure in New England; from the Civil War to World War I, by Gail Thain Parker. — Hanover, N.H.: University Press of New England, 1973. xi, 197 p.: illus.; 24 cm. 1. New Thought I. T.
BF639.P13 615/.851 LC 72-92704 ISBN 0874510732

# BF660–666 COMPARATIVE PSYCHOLOGY. ANIMAL AND HUMAN PSYCHOLOGY

**Harlow, Harry Frederick, 1905-.** 5.477
The human model: primate perspectives / Harry F. Harlow and Clara Mears. — Washington: V. H. Winston; New York: Wiley, 1979. viii, 312 p.: ill.; 24 cm. 'Distributed solely by Halsted Press.' Includes index. 1. Psychology, Comparative 2. Primates — Behavior I. Mears, Clara. joint author. II. T.
BF671.H37 156 LC 78-27597 ISBN 0470266422

**Kuo, Zing-Yang, 1898-1970.** 5.478
The dynamics of behavior development: an epigenetic view / Zing–Yang Kuo. New enl. ed. / prepared by Gilbert Gottlieb. — New York: Plenum Press, c1976. xlii, 237 p.: ports; 24 cm. 1. Psychology, Comparative 2. Genetic psychology I. Gottlieb, Gilbert, 1929- II. T.
BF671.K74 1976 156 LC 76-27831 ISBN 0306309769

**Passingham, R. E., 1943-.** 5.479
The human primate / R.E. Passingham. — Oxford; San Francisco: W.H. Freeman, c1982. xii, 390 p.: ill.; 25 cm. Includes indexes. 1. Psychology, Comparative 2. Primates — Behavior 3. Human behavior I. T.
BF671.P4 1982 156 19 LC 81-5474 ISBN 071671356X

**Schneirla, T. C. (Theodore Christian), 1902-1968.** 5.480
Selected writings of T. C. Schneirla. Edited by Lester R. Aronson [and others]. — San Francisco: W. H. Freeman, [1972] xiv, 1032 p.: illus.; 25 cm. 1. Psychology, Comparative I. T.
BF671.S35 156/.08 LC 71-135632 ISBN 0716709309

# BF683 Motivation

**Boden, Margaret A.** 5.481
Purposive explanation in psychology / [by] Margaret A. Boden. — Cambridge, Mass.: Harvard University Press, 1972. 408 p.; 25 cm. 1. Goal (Psychology) I. T.
BF683.B58 153.8 LC 73-169858 ISBN 0674739027

**Bolles, Robert C.** 5.482
Theory of motivation / Robert C. Bolles. — 2d ed. — New York: Harper & Row, [1975] viii, 568 p.: graphs; 25 cm. (Harper's experimental psychology series) Includes indexes. 1. Motivation (Psychology) I. T.
BF683.B6 1975 156/.2/5 LC 74-28083 ISBN 006040793X

# BF692 Sexual Behavior

**Bernard, Jessie Shirley, 1903-.** • 5.483
The sex game [by] Jessie Bernard. — Englewood, Cliffs, N.J.: Prentice-Hall, [1968] ix, 372 p.; 24 cm. 1. Sex (Psychology) 2. Communication — Psychological aspects I. T.
BF692.B4 155.3 LC 68-13219

**Gay, Peter, 1923-.** 5.484
Education of the senses: Victoria to Freud / Peter Gay. New York: Oxford University Press, 1984. 534, [32] p. of plates : ill.; 24 cm. (The Bourgeois experience; v.1) Includes index. 1. Sex (Psychology) — Social aspects — Europe, Western — History — 19th century. 2. Sex (Psychology) — Social aspects — United States — History — 19th century. 3. Middle classes — Europe, Western — History — 19th century. 4. Middle classes — United States — History — 19th century. I. T. II. Series.
BF692.G36 1984 LC 83-8187 ISBN 0195033523

**Higgins, Loretta Pierfedeici.** 5.485
Human sexuality across the life span: implications for nursing practice / Loretta P. Higgins, Joellen W. Hawkins with Ronna E. Krozy ... [et al.]. — Monterey, Calif.: Wadsworth Health Sciences Division, c1984. xiii, 322 p.: ill.; 24 cm. 1. Sex (Psychology) 2. Sex (Biology) 3. Life cycle, Human 4. Human reproduction 5. Psychosexual disorders 6. Sick — Psychology 7. Nursing I. Hawkins, Joellen Watson. II. T.
BF692.H54 1984 612/.6/024613 19 LC 84-2379 ISBN 0534032257

**Maccoby, Eleanor E., 1917- ed.** • 5.486
The development of sex differences / edited by Eleanor E. Maccoby; with contributions by Roy G. D'Andrade [and others]. — Stanford, Calif.: Stanford University Press, 1966. 351 p.: ill.; 24 cm. (Stanford studies in psychology, 5) Papers based on the discussions of a work group that met at Stanford University, 1962, 1963, 1964, sponsored by the Committee on Socialization and Social Structure of the Social Science Research Council. 1. Sex differences (Psychology) — Addresses, essays, lectures. I. D'Andrade, Roy G. II. Stanford University. III. Social Science Research Council. Committee on Socialization and Social Structure. IV. T. V. Series.
BF692.M27 155.3308 LC 66-22984

**Maccoby, Eleanor E., 1917-.** 5.487
The psychology of sex differences / Eleanor Emmons Maccoby and Carol Nagy Jacklin. — Stanford, Calif.: Stanford University Press, 1974. xiii, 634 p.; 25 cm. Includes index. 1. Sex differences (Psychology) 2. Sex differences (Psychology) — Bibliography. I. Jacklin, Carol Nagy, joint author. II. T.
BF692.M274 155.3/3 LC 73-94488 ISBN 0804708592

**Mahoney, E. R. (E. Richard)** 5.488
Human sexuality / E.R. Mahoney. — New York: McGraw-Hill, c1983. xxvii, 642 p.: ill.; 24 cm. Includes indexes. 1. Sex (Psychology) 2. Sex (Biology) 3. Sex — Social aspects. I. T.
BF692.M278 1983 306.7 19 LC 82-12708 ISBN 0070396507

**Zillmann, Dolf.** 5.489
Connections between sex and aggression / Dolf Zillmann. — Hillsdale, N.J.: Lawrence Erlbaum Associates, 1984. x, 258 p.; 24 cm. Includes indexes. 1. Sex (Psychology) 2. Sex (Biology) 3. Aggressiveness (Psychology) I. T.
BF692.Z54 1984 155.3 19 LC 83-20633 ISBN 0898593336

**Human sexuality: a comparative and developmental perspective**    **5.490**
/ **Herant A. Katchadourian, editor.**
Berkeley: University of California Press, c1979. vi, 358 p.; 23 cm. 1. Sex role
2. Identity (Psychology) 3. Sex (Psychology) I. Katchadourian, Herant A.
BF692.2.H85    155.3    *LC* 77-93458    *ISBN* 0520036549

**Money, John, 1921-.**    **5.491**
Sexual signatures: on being a man or a woman / John Money, Patricia Tucker.
— 1st ed. — Boston: Little, Brown, [1975] 250 p.: ill.; 21 cm. Includes index.
1. Sex role 2. Sex determination, Genetic 3. Sexual deviation I. Tucker,
Patricia, joint author. II. T.
BF692.2.M66    155.3/3    *LC* 74-26632    *ISBN* 0316578266

**Spence, Janet Taylor.**    **5.492**
Masculinity & femininity: their psychological dimensions, correlates, and
antecedents / by Janet T. Spence & Robert L. Helmreich. — Austin: University
of Texas Press, c1978. xi, 297 p.; 24 cm. Includes indexes. 1. Femininity
(Psychology) 2. Masculinity (Psychology) I. Helmreich, Robert, joint author.
II. T.
BF692.2.S68    155.33    *LC* 77-10693    *ISBN* 029276443X

# BF697 Individuality

**The Category of the person: anthropology, philosophy, history /**    **5.493**
**edited by Michael Carrithers, Steven Collins, Steven Lukes.**
Cambridge [Cambridgeshire]; New York: Cambridge University Press, 1985.
viii, 309 p.; 24 cm. Includes index. 1. Mauss, Marcel, 1872-1950 — Addresses,
essays, lectures. 2. Self — Addresses, essays, lectures. 3. Self — Cross-cultural
studies — Addresses, essays, lectures. 4. Individualism — Addresses, essays,
lectures. 5. Individualism — Cross-cultural studies — Addresses, essays,
lectures. I. Carrithers, Michael. II. Collins, Steven, 1951- III. Lukes, Steven.
BF697.C288 1985    302.5/4 19    *LC* 84-23288    *ISBN* 0521259096

**Fisher, Seymour.**    **5.494**
Body consciousness: you are what you feel. — Englewood Cliffs, N.J.: Prentice-
Hall, [1973] xiv, 176 p.; 22 cm. — (A Spectrum book) 1. Body image I. T.
BF697.F484    155.2    *LC* 73-163    *ISBN* 013078527X

**Harré, Rom.**    **5.495**
Personal being: a theory for individual psychology / Rom Harré. —
Cambridge, Mass.: Harvard University Press, 1984. x, 299 p.; 24 cm.
Continues: Social being. 1. Identity (Psychology) 2. Individuality 3. Self I. T.
BF697.H374 1984    155.2 19    *LC* 83-12838    *ISBN* 0674663136

**Kohut, Heinz.**    **5.496**
The restoration of the self / Heinz Kohut. New York: International
Universities Press, c1977. xxii, 345 p.; 23 cm. Includes index. 1. Self
2. Psychoanalysis I. T.
BF697.K65    616.8/5    *LC* 76-45545    *ISBN* 0823658104

**Rosenberg, Morris.**    **5.497**
Conceiving the self / Morris Rosenberg. — New York: Basic Books, c1979. xvi,
319 p.; 24 cm. Includes index. 1. Self-perception 2. Self-respect 3. Self-
perception in children 4. Defense mechanisms (Psychology) I. T.
BF697.R657    155.2    *LC* 78-19813    *ISBN* 046501352X

**Tyler, Leona Elizabeth, 1906-.**    **5.498**
Individuality: human possibilities and personal choice in the psychological
development of men and women / Leona E. Tyler. — 1st ed. — San Francisco:
Jossey-Bass Publishers, 1978. xvi, 274 p.: diagrs.; 24 cm. — (The Jossey-Bass
series in social and behavioral science & in higher education) Includes index.
1. Individuality 2. Personality 3. Developmental psychology I. T.
BF697.T793    155.2    *LC* 78-50897    *ISBN* 0875893651

**Waterman, Alan S.**    **5.499**
The psychology of individualism / Alan S. Waterman. — New York: Praeger,
1984. xv, 359 p.; 24 cm. Includes indexes. 1. Individuality 2. Personality
3. Individualism — Psychological aspects. I. T.
BF697.W325 1984    155.2 19    *LC* 84-11712    *ISBN* 003060477X

**Whyte, William Hollingsworth.**    • **5.500**
The organization man. — New York: Simon and Schuster, 1956. 429 p.: illus.;
22 cm. 1. Individuality 2. Loyalty I. T.
BF697.W47    301.15    *LC* 56-9926

**Wylie, Ruth C.**    **5.501**
The self-concept, by Ruth C. Wylie. Rev. ed. Lincoln, University of Nebraska
Press [1974-79] 2 v. 24 cm. 1. Self-perception 2. Self-perception —
Bibliography. 3. Psychology — Research I. T.
BF697.W92 1974    155.2    *LC* 72-97165    *ISBN* 0803208308

# BF698 PERSONALITY

**Allport, Gordon W. (Gordon Willard), 1897-1967.**    • **5.502**
The nature of personality: selected papers / by Gordon W. Allport. —
Cambridge, Mass.: Addison-Wesley Press, 1950. vii, 220 p.: illus.; 22 cm.
1. Personality — Addresses, essays, lectures. I. T.
BF698.A38 1950    155.2    *LC* 51-9059

**Allport, Gordon W. (Gordon Willard), 1897-1967.**    • **5.503**
Pattern and growth in personality. New York: Holt, Rinehart and Winston
[1961] 593 p.: ill.; 24 cm. 'Although in one sense this volume is a revision of ...
[the author's] Personality: a psychological interpretation (1937), in another
sense it is wholly new.' 1. Personality 2. Characters and characteristics I. T.
BF698.A39    137    *LC* 61-15283

**Allport, Gordon W. (Gordon Willard), 1897-1967.**    • **5.504**
Personality: a psychological interpretation / Gordon W. Allport. — New York:
Holt, c1937. xiv, 588 p.: ill. 1. Personality 2. Characters and characteristics
I. T.
BF698.A4    *LC* 37-25297

**Allport, Gordon W. (Gordon Willard), 1897-1967.**    • **5.505**
Personality and social encounter: selected essays. — Boston: Beacon Press
[1960] 386 p.; 21 cm. 1. Personality — Addresses, essays, lectures. I. T.
BF698.A42    137    *LC* 60-14675

**Borgatta, Edgar F., 1924-.**    **5.506**
Handbook of personality theory and research, edited by Edgar F. Borgatta and
William W. Lambert. — Chicago: Rand McNally, [1968] xiv, 1232 p.: illus.; 25
cm. 1. Personality — Addresses, essays, lectures. I. Lambert, William Wilson,
1919- joint author. II. T.
BF698.B623    155.2    *LC* 67-14685

**Case workbook in personality / [editors] Robert W. White,**    **5.507**
**Margaret M. Riggs, Doris C. Gilbert.**
Prospect Heights, Ill.: Waveland Press, 1982, c1976. vii, 259 p.; 24 cm. —
1. Personality — Case studies. 2. Adjustment (Psychology) — Case studies.
I. White, Robert Winthrop. II. Riggs, Margaret M. III. Gilbert, Doris C.
BF698.C26 1982    *ISBN* 0917974808

**Cattell, Raymond B. (Raymond Bernard), 1905-.**    **5.508**
The structure of personality in its environment / Raymond B. Cattell. — New
York: Springer Pub. Co., c1979. xxiv, 421 p.: ill.; 24 cm. (His Personality and
learning theory; vol. 1) Includes indexes. 1. Personality I. T.
BF698.C323 vol. 1    155.2 s 155.2    *LC* 79-593    *ISBN* 0826121209

**Cattell, Raymond B. (Raymond Bernard), 1905-.**    **5.509**
The scientific analysis of personality and motivation / R. B. Cattell and P.
Kline. — New York: Academic Press, 1977. xii, 385 p.: ill.; 24 cm. (Personality
and psychopathology; 17) Edition of 1966 published under title: The scientific
analysis of personality. Includes indexes. 1. Personality I. Kline, Paul. joint
author. II. T.
BF698.C36 1977    155.2    *LC* 77-71812    *ISBN* 012164250X

**Coan, Richard W.**    **5.510**
The optimal personality; an empirical and theoretical analysis [by] Richard W.
Coan. — New York: Columbia University Press, 1974. x, 242 p.; 23 cm.
1. Personality I. T.
BF698.C545 1974    155.2    *LC* 74-11498    *ISBN* 0231038070

**The Course of life: psychoanalytic contributions toward**    **5.511**
**understanding personality development / Stanley I. Greenspan**
**and George H. Pollock, editors.**
Adelphi, Md. (2340 University Blvd., East, Adelphi, Md. 20783): Mental
Health Study Center, Division of Mental Health Service Programs, National
Institute of Mental Health, U.S. Dept. of Health and Human Services, Public
Health Service, Alcohol, Drug Abuse, and Mental Health Administration;
Washington, D.C.: For sale by the Supt. of Docs., 1980-1981. 3 v.: ill.; 24 cm. —
(DHHS publication. no. (ADM) 80-786, 80-999, 81-1000) S/N
017-024-01026-0 (v. 1) S/N 017-024-01027-8 (v. 2) S/N 017-024-01062-6(v. 3)
Item 507-B-5. 1. Personality 2. Psychoanalysis 3. Developmental psychology
I. Greenspan, Stanley I. II. Pollock, George H. III. National Institute of
Mental Health (U.S.). Mental Health Study Center. IV. Series.
BF698.C68    155 19    *LC* 79-600150

**Current personality theories / edited by Raymond J. Corsini.**    **5.512**
Itasca, Ill.: F. E. Peacock Publishers, c1977. xiv, 465 p.: ill.; 25 cm.
1. Personality I. Corsini, Raymond J.
BF698.C84    155.2    *LC* 76-41995

**Evans, Richard Isadore, 1922-.**    **5.513**
Gordon Allport, the man and his ideas [by] Richard I. Evans. [1st ed.] New York, Dutton [1971] xiii, 157 p. 21 cm. 1. Allport, Gordon W. (Gordon Willard), 1897-1967. 2. Psychologists — United States — Biography. 3. Personality. I. Allport, Gordon W. (Gordon Willard), 1897-1967. II. T.
BF698.E84     155.2/0924     *LC* 74-125908     *ISBN* 0525116028

**Eysenck, H. J. (Hans Jurgen), 1916-.**    **5.514**
Personality and individual differences: a natural science approach / Hans J. Eysenck and Michael W. Eysenck. — New York: Plenum Press, c1985. xviii, 424 p.: ill.; 24 cm. (Perspectives on individual differences.) Includes indexes. 1. Personality 2. Individuality I. Eysenck, Michael W. II. T. III. Series.
BF698.E948 1985     155.2 19     *LC* 84-24851     *ISBN* 0306418444

**Eysenck, H. J. (Hans Jurgen), 1916-.**    • **5.515**
The structure of human personality [by] H. J. Eysenck. — London: Methuen, [1970] viii, 476 p.: illus.; 21 cm. — (Methuen's manuals of modern psychology) Distributed in the U.S.A. by Barnes and Noble. 1. Personality I. T.
BF698.E97 1970     155.2/64     *LC* 70-494620     *ISBN* 0416180302

**Eysenck, H. J. (Hans Jurgen), 1916-.**    • **5.516**
The scientific study of personality. — London: Routledge & K. Paul, 1952. xiii, 320 p.: ill. 1. Personality I. T.
BF698.E97 S4     *LC* 52-3338

**Feffer, Melvin.**    **5.517**
The structure of Freudian thought: the problem of immutability and discontinuity in developmental theory / by Melvin Feffer. — New York: International Universities Press, c1982. ix, 298 p.; 23 cm. Includes index. 1. Freud, Sigmund, 1856-1939. 2. Personality 3. Developmental psychology I. T.
BF698.F354 1982     150.19/52 19     *LC* 81-23610     *ISBN* 0823661857

**Franz, Marie-Luise von, 1915-.**    **5.518**
Puer aeternus / Marie–Louise von Franz. — 2nd ed. — Santa Monica, CA: Sigo Press, c1981. 292, [3] p.: ill.; 23 cm. Rev. ed. of: The problem of the puer aeternus. 1st ed. c1970. 1. Jung, C. G. (Carl Gustav), 1875-1961. 2. Saint-Exupéry, Antoine de, 1900-1944. Petit prince. 3. Personality 4. Psychology, Pathological I. T.
BF698.F7155 1981     155.2/32 19     *LC* 80-28090     *ISBN* 0938434039

**Hall, Calvin S. (Calvin Springer), 1909-.**    **5.519**
Theories of personality / Calvin S. Hall, Gardner Lindzey. — 3d ed. — New York: Wiley, c1978. xvi, 725 p.: ill.; 25 cm. 1. Personality I. Lindzey, Gardner. joint author. II. T.
BF698.H33 1978     155.2     *LC* 77-26692     *ISBN* 0471342270

**Handbook of modern personality theory / edited by Raymond B. Cattell, Ralph Mason Dreger.**    **5.520**
Washington: Hemisphere Pub. Corp.; New York: Wiley: distributed solely by Halsted Press, c1977. xi, 804 p.: ill.; 24 cm. (The Series in clinical and community psychology) Includes index. 1. Personality I. Cattell, Raymond B. (Raymond Bernard), 1905- II. Dreger, Ralph Mason.
BF698.H334     155.2     *LC* 76-22764     *ISBN* 047015201X

**Jourard, Sidney M.**    • **5.521**
Self–disclosure: an experimental analysis of the transparent self / [by] Sidney M. Jourard. — New York: Wiley-Interscience, [1971] xiii, 248 p.: ill.; 23 cm. 1. Self-disclosure I. T.
BF698.J636 1971     155.28     *LC* 72-146590     *ISBN* 0471451509

**Kelly, George Alexander, 1905-1967.**    • **5.522**
The psychology of personal constructs. — [1st ed.]. — New York, Norton [1955] 2 v. (1218 p.) illus. 22 cm. 1. Personality 2. Psychiatry 3. Psychotherapy I. T.
BF698.K38     137     *LC* 55-2090 rev

**Lecky, Prescott, 1892-1941.**    • **5.523**
Self–consistency: a theory of personality / by Prescott Lecky; edited and interpreted by Frederick C. Thorne. — [Hamden, Conn.]: Shoe String Press, 1961, c1951. v, 275 p. 1. Personality I. T.
BF698.L377     155.2/8     *LC* 61-4940

**Lewin, Kurt, 1890-1947.**    • **5.524**
A dynamic theory of personality: selected papers / translated by Donald K. Adams and Karl E. Zener. — New York: McGraw-Hill [1959, c1935] 286 p.: ill.; 21 cm. — (McGraw-Hill paperback series, 37451) Includes bibliography. 1. Psychophysiology 2. Personality 3. Gestalt psychology I. T.
BF698.L4 1959     137     *LC* 59-65223

**Lundberg, Margaret J.**    **5.525**
The incomplete adult; social class constraints on personality development [by] Margaret J. Lundberg. — Westport, Conn.: Greenwood Press, [1974] xv, 245 p.; 21 cm. — (Contributions in sociology, no. 15) 1. Personality 2. Social classes 3. Socialization I. T.
BF698.L8     155.2/34     *LC* 74-67     *ISBN* 0837173620

**Maddi, Salvatore R.**    **5.526**
Humanism in personology: Allport, Maslow, and Murray [by] Salvatore R. Maddi [and] Paul T. Costa. Chicago, AldineAtherton [1972] xviii, 200 p. 22 cm. (Perspectives on personality) 1. Allport, Gordon W. (Gordon Willard), 1897-1967. 2. Maslow, Abraham H. (Abraham Harold) 3. Murray, Henry Alexander, 1893- 4. Humanistic psychology I. Costa, Paul T. joint author. II. T.
BF698.M2367     155.2     *LC* 72-169516     *ISBN* 020225089X *ISBN* 0202250903

**Maddi, Salvatore R.**    **5.527**
Personality theories: a comparative analysis / Salvatore R. Maddi. — 4th ed. — Homewood, Ill.: Dorsey Press, 1980. xi, 772 p.; 24 cm. — (The Dorsey series in psychology) Includes index. 1. Personality I. T.
BF698.M237 1980     155.2     *LC* 79-55221     *ISBN* 0256022992

**Maslow, Abraham H. (Abraham Harold)**    • **5.528**
The farther reaches of human nature [by] Abraham H. Maslow. — New York: Viking Press, [1971] xxi, 423 p.; 25 cm. — (An Esalen book) 1. Personality I. T.
BF698.M336     155.2     *LC* 75-158417     *ISBN* 0670308536

**Maslow, Abraham H. (Abraham Harold)**    • **5.529**
Toward a psychology of being [by] Abraham H. Maslow. — 2d ed. — Princeton, N.J.: Van Nostrand, [1968] xvi, 240 p.; 19 cm. — (Van Nostrand insight books, 5) 1. Personality 2. Motivation (Psychology) 3. Humanistic psychology I. T.
BF698.M338 1968     155.2/5     *LC* 68-30757

**Murphy, Gardner, 1895-.**    • **5.530**
Personality: a biosocial approach to origins and structure. — New York: Basic Books [1966] xiv, 999 p.: ill.; 24 cm. Bibliography: p. 947-968. 1. Personality I. T.
BF698.M87 1966     155.2     *LC* 66-19958

**Parsons, Talcott, 1902-.**    • **5.531**
Social structure and personality. — [New York]: Free Press of Glencoe, [1964] 376 p.: diagr.; 22 cm. 1. Socialization 2. Personality and culture I. T.
BF698.P256     137.33     *LC* 64-11218

**Personality: basic aspects and current research / edited by Ervin Staub.**    **5.532**
Englewood Cliffs, N.J.: Prentice-Hall, c1980. xiv, 386 p.; 24 cm. 1. Personality I. Staub, Ervin.
BF698.P373     155.2     *LC* 79-19169     *ISBN* 0136579329

**Rychlak, Joseph F.**    **5.533**
A philosophy of science for personality theory / Joseph F. Rychlak. — 2d ed. — Malabar, Fla.: Krieger Pub. Co., 1981. xxi, 560 p.; 24 cm. Includes index. 1. Personality — Philosophy. 2. Psychology — Philosophy 3. Psychology — Methodology I. T.
BF698.R95 1981     155.2     *LC* 80-15614     *ISBN* 0882758896

**Schultz, Duane P.**    **5.534**
Theories of personality / Duane Schultz. — 3rd ed. — Monterey, Calif.: Brooks/Cole Pub. Co., c1986. xvii, 478 p.: ill.; 25 cm. Includes index. 1. Personality I. T.
BF698.S36 1986     155.2 19     *LC* 85-21361     *ISBN* 0534055443

**Sherif, Muzafer, 1905-.**    **5.535**
The psychology of ego–involvements: social attitudes & identifications / by Muzafer Sherif and Hadley Cantril. New York: J. Wiley, 1947. viii, 525 p. — (Wiley publications in psychology) 1. Self 2. Social psychology I. Cantril, Hadley, 1906-1969. II. T.
BF698.S515     *LC* 47-3913

**White, Robert Winthrop.**    **5.536**
Lives in progress: a study of the natural growth of personality / Robert W. White. — 3d ed. — New York: Holt, Rinehart and Winston, [1975] xii, 387 p.; 21 cm. Includes index. 1. Personality — Case studies. 2. Genetic psychology — Case studies. I. T.
BF698.W46 1975     155.2     *LC* 74-20758     *ISBN* 0030894034

**Witkin, Herman A.**    • **5.537**
Personality through perception; an experimental and clinical study [by] H. A. Witkin [and others]. — Westport, Conn.: Greenwood Press, [1972, c1954] xxvi, 571 p.: illus.; 23 cm. Original ed. issued in series: Harper's psychological series. 1. Personality 2. Personality tests 3. Perception I. T.
BF698.W53 1972     155.28     *LC* 74-138194     *ISBN* 0837152763

## BF698.4–698.8 Personality Assessment and Testing

**Kline, Paul.**      5.538
Personality: measurement and theory / Paul Kline. — New York: St. Martin's Press, 1983. 174 p.; 23 cm. Includes index. 1. Personality assessment 2. Personality tests 3. Personality I. T.
BF698.4.K56 1983b    155.2/8 19    *LC* 83-13798    *ISBN* 0312602308

**Wiggins, Jerry S.**      5.539
Personality and prediction: principles of personality assessment / Jerry S. Wiggins. — Reading [Mass.]: Addison-Wesley Pub. Co., 1973. xii, 656, I-35 p.: ill.; 25 cm. — (Addison-Wesley series in psychology.) Includes indexes. 1. Personality assessment I. T. II. Series.
BF698.4.W53 1973    155.2/8    *LC* 74-156590    *ISBN* 0201086425

**Buros, Oscar Krisen, 1905-.**      • 5.540
Personality tests and reviews; including an index to The mental measurements yearbooks. Edited by Oscar Krisen Buros. Highland Park, N.J., Gryphon Press [1970] xxxi, 1659 p. 1. Personality tests 2. Personality tests — Bibliography. I. Buros, Oscar Krisen, 1905- The mental measurements yearbook. II. T.
BF698.5.B87    *LC* 74-13192    *ISBN* 910674108

**Chun, Ki-Taek.**      5.541
Measures for psychological assessment: a guide to 3,000 original sources and their applications / Ki–Taek Chun, Sidney Cobb, John R. P. French, Jr.; with a foreword by E. Lowell Kelly. — Ann Arbor, Mich.: Survey Research Center, Institute for Social Research, 1975. xxiv, 664 p.; 27 cm. Includes indexes. 1. Personality tests — Directories. 2. Mental tests — Directories. I. Cobb, Sidney, 1916- joint author. II. French, John R. P. joint author. III. T.
BF698.5.C45    016.1552/8    *LC* 74-620127    *ISBN* 0879441682

**Lake, Dale G.**      5.542
Measuring human behavior; tools for the assessment of social functioning [by] Dale G. Lake, Matthew B. Miles [and] Ralph B. Earle, Jr. — New York: Teachers College Press, [1973] xviii, 422 p.; 23 cm. 1. Personality tests 2. Behavioral assessment I. Miles, Matthew B. joint author. II. Earle, Ralph B., joint author. III. T.
BF698.5.L34    155.2/8    *LC* 72-82083

**Murstein, Bernard I. ed.**      • 5.543
Handbook of projective techniques / edited by Bernard I. Murstein. — New York: Basic Books, [1965] xxiv, 934 p.: ill.; 25 cm. 1. Projective techniques I. T.
BF698.7.M87    155.284    *LC* 65-21190

**Zubin, Joseph, 1900-.**      • 5.544
An experimental approach to projective techniques. New York Wiley [1965] 645p. 1. Projective techniques I. Eron, Leonard D. jt. author II. Schumer, Florence. jt. author III. T.
BF698.7 Z8

**Bellak, Leopold, 1916-.**      5.545
The thematic apperception test, the children's apperception test, and the senior apperception technique in clinical use / Leopold Bellak. — 4th ed. / revised with the collaboration of David M. Abrams. — Orlando: Grune & Stratton, c1986. xxiv, 392 p.: ill.; 27 cm. Cover title: The T.A.T., C.A.T., and S.A.T. in clinical use. Includes index. 1. Thematic apperception test 2. Children's apperception test 3. Senior apperception technique I. Abrams, David M. II. T. III. Title: T.A.T., C.A.T., and S.A.T. in clinical use. IV. Title: TAT, CAT, and SAT in clinical use.
BF698.8.T5 B42 1986    155.2/844 19    *LC* 86-4763    *ISBN* 080891815X

## BF698.9 Special Topics

**Eysenck, H. J. (Hans Jurgen), 1916-.**      • 5.546
The biological basis of personality, by H. J. Eysenck. Springfield, Ill., Thomas [1967] xvii, 399 p. illus. 24 cm. (American lecture series, publication no. 689. A monograph in the Bannerstone division of American lectures in living chemistry) 1. Personality I. T.
BF698.9.B5 E9    155.2    *LC* 67-18338

**Skinner, B. F. (Burrhus Frederic), 1904-.**      • 5.547
Beyond freedom and dignity [by] B. F. Skinner. [1st ed.] New York, Knopf, 1971. 225 p. 22 cm. 1. Personality and culture 2. Conditioned response 3. Control (Psychology) I. T.
BF698.9.C8 S57    150.19/434    *LC* 75-98652    *ISBN* 0394425553

## BF699–724.85 GENETIC PSYCHOLOGY. DEVELOPMENTAL PSYCHOLOGY

**Piaget, Jean, 1896-.**      5.548
[Comportement moteur de l'evolution. English] Behavior and evolution / Jean Piaget; translated from the French by Donald Nicholson–Smith. — 1st American ed. — New York: Pantheon Books, c1978. xxvi, 165 p.; 22 cm. Translation of Le comportment moteur de l'evolution. 1. Genetic psychology 2. Movement, Psychology of I. T.
BF702.P49313 1978    155.7    *LC* 77-88762    *ISBN* 0394418107

**Emotions, cognition, and behavior / edited by Carroll E. Izard,**      5.549
**Jerome Kagan, and Robert B. Zajonc.**
Cambridge [Cambridgeshire]; New York: Cambridge University Press, 1984. x, 620 p.: ill.; 25 cm. 'Based, in part, on workshops sponsored by the Committee on Social and Affective Development During Childhood, of the Social Science Research Council.' 1. Developmental psychology 2. Emotions 3. Cognition 4. Emotions in children 5. Cognition in children I. Izard, Carroll E. (Carroll Ellis), 1923- II. Kagan, Jerome. III. Zajonc, Robert B. (Robert Boleslaw), 1923-
BF713.E47 1984    153.4 19    *LC* 83-7765    *ISBN* 0521256011

**Handbook of developmental psychology / Benjamin B. Wolman,**      5.550
**editor; George Stricker, associate editor.**
Englewood Cliffs, N.J.: Prentice-Hall, c1982. xv, 960 p.; 29 cm. 1. Developmental psychology I. Wolman, Benjamin B. II. Stricker, George.
BF713.H363 1982    155 19    *LC* 81-13830    *ISBN* 0133725995

**Kegan, Robert.**      5.551
The evolving self: problem and process in human development / Robert Kegan. — Cambridge, Mass.: Harvard University Press, 1982. xi, 318 p.: ill.; 25 cm. Includes index. 1. Piaget, Jean, 1896- 2. Developmental psychology 3. Personality change 4. Self 5. Meaning (Psychology) 6. Psychotherapy I. T.
BF713.K44 1982    155.2/5 19    *LC* 81-6759    *ISBN* 0674272307

**Lerner, Richard M.**      5.552
Concepts and theories of human development / Richard M. Lerner. — 2nd ed. — New York: Random House, c1986. xviii, 522 p.: ill.; 25 cm. Includes indexes. 1. Developmental psychology I. T.
BF713.L47 1986    155 19    *LC* 85-28127    *ISBN* 0394352106

**Herron, R. E.**      5.553
Child's play / [by] R. E. Herron [and] Brian Sutton–Smith. — New York: Wiley, [1971] xii, 386 p.: ill.; 24 cm. 1. Play — Psychological aspects — Addresses, essays, lectures. I. Sutton-Smith, Brian. joint author. II. T.
BF717.H396    155.41/8    *LC* 73-136714    *ISBN* 0471373303

**Bower, T. G. R., 1941-.**      5.554
Development in infancy / T.G.R. Bower. — 2nd ed. — San Francisco: W.H. Freeman, c1982. x, 304 p.: ill.; 24 cm. — (Series of books in psychology.) Includes index. 1. Infant psychology 2. Cognition in children I. T. II. Series.
BF719.B68 1982    155.4/22 19    *LC* 81-12544    *ISBN* 0716713012

**Handbook of infant development / edited by Joy Doniger**      5.555
**Osofsky.**
2nd ed. — New York: Wiley, c1987. xix, 1391 p.: ill.; 26 cm. — (Wiley series on personality processes.) 'Wiley-Interscience publication.' 1. Infant psychology 2. Infants — Development I. Osofsky, Joy D. II. Series.
BF719.H36 1987    155.4/22 19    *LC* 86-28906    *ISBN* 0471885657

**Lichtenberg, Joseph D.**      5.556
Psychoanalysis and infant research / Joseph D. Lichtenberg. — Hillsdale, N.J.: Analytic Press, 1983. xii, 262 p.; 24 cm. — (Psychoanalytic inquiry book series. v. 2) Includes indexes. 1. Infant psychology 2. Self 3. Psychoanalysis I. T. II. Series.
BF719.L52 1983    155.4/22 19    *LC* 83-2842    *ISBN* 0881630020

**Stern, Daniel N.**      5.557
The interpersonal world of the infant: a view from psychoanalysis and developmental psychology / Daniel N. Stern. — New York: Basic Books,

c1985. x, 304 p.; 24 cm. Includes index. 1. Infant psychology 2. Psychoanalysis 3. Developmental psychology I. T.
BF719.S75 1985     155.4/22 19     *LC* 85-47553     *ISBN* 0465034039

**Kaye, Kenneth.** • 5.558
The mental and social life of babies: how parents create persons / Kenneth Kaye. — Chicago: University of Chicago Press, 1982. x, 289 p.; 24 cm. Includes index. 1. Infant psychology 2. Child development 3. Parent and child 4. Parenting — Psychological aspects. I. T.
BF720.P37 K39 1982     155.4/22 19     *LC* 82-6965     *ISBN* 0226428478

# BF721–723 Child Psychology

**Baldwin, Alfred Lee, 1914-.** • 5.559
Theories of child development [by] Alfred L. Baldwin. — New York: Wiley, [1966, c1967] xii, 618 p.: illus., ports.; 24 cm. 1. Child study. I. T.
BF721.B148     155.4     *LC* 66-26733

**Bijou, Sidney William, 1908-.** 5.560
Child development: the basic stage of early childhood / by Sidney W. Bijou. — Englewood Cliffs, N.J.: Prentice-Hall, c1976. xiii, 210 p.; 20 cm. (The Century psychology series) 1. Child psychology I. T.
BF721.B4242     155.4/23     *LC* 75-40137     *ISBN* 0131304194

**Carmichael, Leonard, 1898-.** • 5.561
[Manual of child psychology] Carmichael's manual of child psychology / Paul H. Mussen, editor. — 3d ed. New York: Wiley [1970]-. v. 1- 26 cm. Rev. ed. published as Handbook of child psychology / Paul H. Mussen, editor — 4th ed. — ... <1983- > 1. Child psychology I. Mussen, Paul Henry. ed. II. T.
BF721.C213     155.4     *LC* 69-16127     *ISBN* 0471626953

**Clarke, Ann M. (Ann Margaret).** 5.562
Early experience: myth and evidence / [edited by] Ann M. Clarke and A. D. B. Clarke. — New York: The Free Press, 1977,c1976. xiv, 314 p.: ill.; 23 cm. Includes indexes. 1. Child psychology 2. Personality change I. Clarke, A. D. B. (Alan Douglas Benson) II. T.
BF721.E18 1977     155.4     *LC* 76-21992

**Elkind, David, 1931-.** 5.563
The child and society: essays in applied child development / David Elkind. — New York: Oxford University Press, 1979. xii, 304 p.; 22 cm. 1. Child psychology 2. Socialization 3. Cognition in children I. T.
BF721.E35     155.4/18     *LC* 78-2758     *ISBN* 0195023714

**Freud, Anna, 1895-.** • 5.564
[Works. English. 1967] The writings of Anna Freud. — New York: International Universities Press, 1967- <c1981 >. v. <1-5, 7-8 >; 23 cm. Vol. 1 published in 1974. Vol. 2 has copyright date 1966. 1. Child psychology — Collected works. 2. Child analysis — Collected works. 3. Psychoanalysis — Collected works. I. Burlingham, Dorothy. II. T.
BF721.F692     618.92/89 19     *LC* 67-9514     *ISBN* 0823668703

**Gesell, Arnold, 1880-1961.** • 5.565
Child development: an introduction to the study of human growth / by Arnold Gesell [and] Frances L. Ilg, in collaboration with Louise B. Ames, Janet Learned [and] Glenna E. Bullis. — New York: Harper [1949] 2 v. in 1: ill.; 25 cm. Each vol. previously published separately. 1. Child psychology I. Ilg, Frances Lillian, 1902- joint author. II. T.
BF721.G477     136.7     *LC* 49-50170

**Handbook of cross–cultural human development / edited by** 5.566
**Ruth H. Munroe, Robert L. Munroe, Beatrice B. Whiting.**
New York: Garland STPM Press, c1981. xiv, 888 p.: ill.; 24 cm. — (Garland anthropology and human development series.) 1. Child psychology 2. Child psychology — Cross-cultural studies I. Munroe, Ruth H. II. Munroe, Robert L. III. Whiting, Beatrice Blyth. IV. Series.
BF721.H243     155.8     *LC* 79-12028     *ISBN* 0824070453

**Inhelder, Bärbel.** • 5.567
[De la logique de l'enfant à la logique de l'adolescent. English] The growth of logical thinking from childhood to adolescence; an essay on the construction of formal operational structures [by] Bärbel Inhelder and Jean Piaget. Translated by Anne Parsons and Stanley Milgram. [New York] Basic Books [1958] 356 p. illus. 22 cm. 1. Child study. 2. Logic 3. Cognition in children I. Piaget, Jean, 1896- joint author. II. T.
BF721.I473     136.7354     *LC* 58-6439

**Kagan, Jerome.** 5.568
The nature of the child / Jerome Kagan. — New York: Basic Books, c1984. xvii, 309 p.; 25 cm. Includes index. 1. Child psychology I. T.
BF721.K158 1984     155.4 19     *LC* 83-45263     *ISBN* 0465048501

**Luriia, A. R. (Aleksandr Romanovich), 1902-.** 5.569
The selected writings of A. R. Luria / edited with an introd. by Michael Cole. — White Plains, N.Y.: M. E. Sharpe, 1979 (c1978). xxii, 351 p.: ill.; 24 cm. 1. Child psychology — Addresses, essays, lectures. 2. Neuropsychology — Addresses, essays, lectures. I. Cole, Michael, 1938- II. T.
BF721.L82     155.4 19     *LC* 78-64342     *ISBN* 0873321278

**Maier, Henry William.** • 5.570
Three theories of child development: the contributions of Erik H. Erikson, Jean Piaget, and Robert R. Sears, and their applications [by] Henry W. Maier. Rev. ed. New York, Harper & Row [1969] ix, 342 p. ports. 22 cm. 1. Erikson, Erik H. (Erik Homburger), 1902- 2. Piaget, Jean, 1896- 3. Sears, Robert Richardson, 1908- 4. Child psychology I. T.
BF721.M196 1969     155.41/0922     *LC* 69-14983

**Piaget, Jean, 1896-.** • 5.571
[Causalité physique chez l'enfant] The child's conception of physical causality, by Jean Piaget. London, K. Paul, Trench, Trubner & co. ltd.; New York, Harcourt, Brace & company, 1930. viii, 309 p. illus. 23 cm. (International library of psychology, philosophy, and scientific method.) 'Translated by Marjorie Gabain.' 1. Child psychology I. T. II. Title: Physical causality, The child's conception of. III. Title: Causality, physical, The child's conception of. IV. Series.
BF721.P43     136.72     *LC* 30-17187

**Piaget, Jean, 1896-.** • 5.572
Play, dreams, and imitation in childhood / translated by C. Gattegno and F.M. Hodgson. — London: Heinemann, 1951. 296 p. 1. Child psychology 2. Imitation 3. Play 4. Symbolism I. T.
BF721.P452 1951     *LC* 52-3385

**Piaget, Jean, 1896-.** • 5.573
[Naissance de l'intelligence chez l'enfant. English] The origins of intelligence in children; translated by Margaret Cook. New York, International Universities Press [c1952] 419 p. 23 cm. 1. Child psychology 2. Intellect I. T.
BF721.P473     136.72     *LC* 52-14807

**Piaget, Jean, 1896-.** • 5.574
[Psychologie de l'enfant. English] The psychology of the child / [by] Jean Piaget and Bärbel Inhelder; translated from the French by Helen Weaver. — New York: Basic Books [1969] xiv, 173 p.; 22 cm. Translation of La psychologie de l'enfant. 1. Child psychology I. Inhelder, Bärbel. joint author. II. T.
BF721.P4813     155.4     *LC* 73-78449

**Piaget, Jean, 1896-.** • 5.575
[Représentation du monde chez l'enfant. English] The child's conception of the world, by Jean Piaget. London, K. Paul, Trench, Trubner & co., ltd.; New York, Harcourt, Brace and company, 1929. ix, 397 p. illus. 23 cm. (International library of psychology, philosophy, and scientific method.) 'Translated by Joan and Andrew Tomlinson.' 1. Child study. 2. Imagery (Psychology) in children — Congresses. 3. Drawing ability in children — Congresses. 4. Earth in art — Congresses. I. Tomlinson, Joan, tr. II. Tomlinson, Andrew, tr. III. T. IV. Series.
BF721.P5     *LC* 29-5717

**Rabin, Albert I. ed.** • 5.576
Projective techniques with children / edited by Albert I. Rabin and Mary R. Haworth. — New York: Grune & Stratton, [1960] 392 p.: ill.; 26 cm. 1. Projective techniques 2. Child study. I. Haworth, Mary (Robbins) 1911- joint editor. II. T.
BF721.R273     137.84     *LC* 60-7253

**Singer, Robert D., 1931-.** • 5.577
Psychological development in children [by] Robert D. Singer [and] Anne Singer. — Philadelphia: Saunders, 1969. xv, 437 p.: illus.; 25 cm. — (Saunders books in psychology) 1. Child study. I. Singer, Anne, joint author. II. T.
BF721.S536     155.4     *LC* 73-81828

**Spock, Benjamin, 1903-.** • 5.578
Dr. Spock talks with mothers: growth and guidance / by Benjamin Spock. — Boston: Houghton Mifflin, 1961. 306 p.; 23 cm. 1. Child psychology 2. Juvenile delinquency I. T.
BF721.S577 1961     136.7     *LC* 61-13338

**Wallach, Michael A.** • 5.579
Modes of thinking in young children; a study of the creativity–intelligence distinction [by] Michael A. Wallach and Nathan Kogan. New York, Holt, Rinehart and Winston [1965] viii, 357 p. illus. 24 cm. 1. Cognition in children 2. Creative ability in children 3. Children — Intelligence levels. 4. Personality

in children 5. Personality and cognition 6. Educational psychology I. Kogan, Nathan. joint author. II. T.
BF721.W23    155.413    *LC* 65-21085

**Yale University. Clinic of Child Development.**    **5.580**
The first five years of life; a guide to the study of the pre–school child. [9th ed.] New York, Harper [c1940] xiii, 393 p. illus. 24 cm. Bibliography: p. 369-376. 1. Child study. 2. Psychophysiology 3. Learning, Psychology of I. Gesell, Arnold, 1880-1961. II. T.
BF721.Y3 1940a    136.7352    *LC* 51-48838

**Bronfenbrenner, Urie, 1917-.**    **5.581**
The ecology of human development: experiments by nature and design / Urie Bronfenbrenner. — Cambridge, Mass.: Harvard University Press, 1979. xv, 330 p.; 24 cm. Includes index. 1. Child psychology — Research. I. T.
BF722.B76    155.4    *LC* 78-27232    *ISBN* 0674224566

**Johnson, Orval G., 1917-.**    **5.582**
Tests and measurements in child development: a handbook [by] Orval G. Johnson [and] James W. Bommarito. [1st ed.] San Francisco Jossey-Bass 1971. 518p. (Jossey-Bass behavioral science series) 1. Child study — Methodology 2. Personality tests I. Bommarito, James W., 1922-, jt. author II. T.
BF722 J64

**Johnson, Orval G., 1917-.**    **5.583**
Tests and measurements in child development: handbook II / Orval G. Johnson. 1st ed. — San Francisco: Jossey-Bass Publishers, 1976. 2 v. (xii, 1327 p.); 27 cm. (The Jossey-Bass behavioral science series) 1. Psychological tests for children I. T.
BF722.J643    155.4/1    *LC* 76-11890    *ISBN* 0875892787

## BF723 SPECIAL TOPICS, A–Z

**Fowler, William, 1921-.**    **5.584**
Potentials of childhood / William Fowler. — Lexington, Mass.: Lexington Books, 1983. 472 p.; 23 cm. 1. Ability in children 2. Cognition in children 3. Learning 4. Education, Preschool I. T.
BF723.A25 F68 1983    155.4 19    *LC* 80-8839    *ISBN* 0669043877

**Growing up to be violent: a longitudinal study of the development of aggression / Monroe M. Lefkowitz ... [et al.].**    **5.585**
New York: Pergamon Press, c1977. ix, 236 p.: ill.; 24 cm. — (Pergamon general psychology series; 66) Includes indexes. 1. Aggressiveness (Child psychology) 2. Aggressiveness (Psychology) 3. Longitudinal method I. Lefkowitz, Monroe M., 1922-
BF723.A35 G76 1976    155.4/18    *LC* 75-44349    *ISBN* 0080195156

**Sarason, Seymour Bernard, 1919-.**    **• 5.586**
Anxiety in elementary school children; a report of research [by] Seymour B. Sarason [and others]. — New York: Wiley, [1960] viii, 351 p.: illus.; 24 cm. 1. Anxiety in children I. T.
BF723.A5 S36    136.741512    *LC* 60-10297

**Toman, Walter.**    **5.587**
Family constellation: its effects on personality and social behavior / Walter Toman. 3rd ed. — New York: Springer Pub. Co., c1976. ix, 333 p.; 22 cm. Includes indexes. 1. Birth order I. T.
BF723.B5 T6 1976    155.44/3    *LC* 76-368119    *ISBN* 0826104940

**Piaget, Jean, 1896-.**    **5.588**
[Genèse de l'idée de hasard chez l'enfant. English] The origin of the idea of chance in children [by] Jean Piaget and Bärbel Inhelder. Translated by Lowell Leake, Jr., Paul Burrell, and Harold D. Fishbein. New York, Norton [1975] xx, 251 p. illus. 21 cm. Translation of La genèse de l'idée de hasard chez l'enfant. 1. Chance 2. Cognition in children I. Inhelder, Bärbel. joint author. II. T.
BF723.C4 P513    155.4/13    *LC* 74-11040    *ISBN* 0393011135

**Piaget and education / edited by Jeanette McCarthy Gallagher and J. A. Easley, Jr.**    **5.589**
New York: Plenum Press, c1978. xix, 294 p.; 24 cm. — (Knowledge and development; v. 2) 1. Piaget, Jean, 1896- 2. Cognition in children 3. Education — Philosophy I. Gallagher, Jeanette McCarthy, 1932- II. Easley, J. A. III. Series.
BF723.C5 BF311.K6385 vol. 2    153.4 s 370.15/2    *LC* 79-103886

**Bryant, Peter, 1937-.**    **5.590**
Perception and understanding in young children: an experimental approach / [by] Peter Bryant. — New York: Basic Books [1974] viii, 195 p.: ill.; 21 cm. 1. Cognition in children I. T.
BF723.C5 B74 1974b    155.4/13    *LC* 73-92722    *ISBN* 0465054889

**Evans, Richard Isadore, 1922-.**    **5.591**
Jean Piaget, the man and his ideas [by] Richard I. Evans. Translated by Eleanor Duckworth. [1st ed.] New York, E. P. Dutton, 1973. lxi, 189 p. 21 cm. (His Dialogues with notable contributors to personality theory, v. 7) Includes Piaget's developmental model and comparisons with Skinner, Freud, and Erikson, by R.I. Evans, W.J. Krossner, and H.J. Ginsburg; and Jean Piaget, and autobiography, and list of his major published works. 1. Piaget, Jean, 1896- 2. Psychologists — Switzerland — Biography. 3. Cognition in children 4. Psychology I. Piaget, Jean, 1896- II. T.
BF723.C5 E9    155.4/13/0924 19    *LC* 73-79550    *ISBN* 0525136606    *ISBN* 0525473602

**Flavell, John H.**    **5.592**
Cognitive development / John H. Flavell. — 2nd ed. — Englewood Cliffs, N.J.: Prentice-Hall, c1985. xi, 338 p.: ill., port.; 24 cm. Includes indexes. 1. Cognition in children I. T.
BF723.C5 F62 1985    155.4/13 19    *LC* 84-15046    *ISBN* 0131397915

**Piaget, Jean, 1896-.**    **5.593**
The essential Piaget / edited by Howard E. Gruber and J. Jacques Vonèche. — New York: Basic Books, 1978 (c1977). xlii, 881 p.: ill.; 25 cm. Includes index. 1. Cognition in children — Collected works. 2. Knowledge, Theory of — Collected works. 3. Biology — Collected works. I. Gruber, Howard E. II. Vonèche, Jacques. III. T.
BF723.C5 P494    155.4/13/08    *LC* 76-9337    *ISBN* 0465020585

**Piaget, Jean, 1896-.**    **• 5.594**
Genetic epistemology. Translated by Eleanor Duckworth. New York, Columbia University Press, 1970. 84 p. 22 cm. (Woodbridge lectures delivered at Columbia University in October of 1968, no. 8) 1. Cognition in children 2. Thought and thinking I. T.
BF723.C5 P5    155.41/3    *LC* 74-100665    *ISBN* 0231033869

**The Psychology of discipline / edited by Darwin Dorr, Melvin Zax, Jack W. Bonner, III.**    **5.595**
New York, N.Y.: International Universities Press, c1983. xv, 263 p.: ill.; 22 cm. 1. Discipline of children — Psychological aspects. I. Dorr, Darwin, 1940- II. Zax, Melvin. III. Bonner, Jack W., 1940-
BF723.D54 P79 1983    649/.64 19    *LC* 81-20775    *ISBN* 0823655814

**Piaget, Jean, 1896-.**    **• 5.596**
[Représentation de l'espace chez l'enfant. English] The child's conception of space, by Jean Piaget and Bärbel Inhelder. Translated from the French by F. J. Langdon & J. L. Lunzer. New York, W. W. Norton [1967] xii, 490 p. illus. 20 cm. (The Norton library, no. 408) Translation of La représentation de l'espace chez l'enfant. 1. Space perception in children 2. Drawing ability in children 3. Imagery (Psychology) in children I. Inhelder, Bärbel. joint author. II. T.
BF723.D7 P513 1967    155.4    *LC* 67-5864

**Getzels, Jacob W.**    **• 5.597**
Creativity and intelligence: explorations with gifted students / by Jacob W. Getzels and Philip W. Jackson. — London; New York: Wiley, [1962] 293 p.: ill.; 23 cm. 1. Gifted children 2. Creation (Literary, artistic, etc.) I. Jackson, Philip W. (Philip Wesley), 1928- joint author. II. T.
BF723.G5 G4    136.765    *LC* 62-10828

**McGhee, Paul E.**    **5.598**
Humor, its origin and development / Paul E. McGhee; illustrated by Edie Pistolesi. — San Francisco: W. H. Freeman, c1979. xi, 251 p.: ill.; 24 cm. (A Series of books in psychology) 1. Humor in children 2. Wit and humor — Psychological aspects. I. T.
BF723.H85 M32    152.4    *LC* 79-15401    *ISBN* 0716710951

**Hauser, Stuart T.**    **• 5.599**
Black and white identity formation; studies in the psychosocial development of lower socioeconomic class adolescent boys [by] Stuart T. Hauser. New York, Wiley-Interscience [1971] xv, 160 p. 23 cm. (Wiley series on psychological disorders) 1. Identity (Psychology) 2. Socially handicapped children — Attitudes 3. Afro-Americans — Psychology 4. Teenage boys I. T.
BF723.I56 H38 1971    155.5    *LC* 77-138910    *ISBN* 047136150X

**Brackbill, Yvonne.**    **• 5.600**
Infancy and early childhood: a handbook and guide to human development / edited by Yvonne Brackbill. — New York: Free Press [1967] x, 523 p.: ill.; 24 cm. Includes bibliographies. 1. Infants I. T.
BF723.I6B63 1967    155.4    *LC* 67-17171

**Gesell, Arnold, 1880-1961.**    **• 5.601**
The embryology of behavior; the beginnings of the human mind, by Arnold Gesell ... in collaboration with Catherine S. Amatruda ... — New York, London, Harper & brothers [1945] xix p., 1 l., 289 p. incl. front., illus., plates, diagrs. (1 col.) 23.5 cm. 'First edition.' 'Selected references': p. 271-276.

1. Infants 2. Child psychology I. Amatruda, Catherine (Strunk) 1903- joint author. II. T.
BF723.I6G39        136.735        *LC* 45-435

**Gesell, Arnold, 1880-1961.**                                                    • **5.602**
Infant development: the embryology of early human behavior. — [1st ed.] New York: Harper [1952] xi, 108 p.: ill.; 25 cm. 1. Infants 2. Child study. I. T. II. Title: The embryology of early human behavior.
BF723.I6 G42        136.7352        *LC* 51-11915

**Mahler, Margaret S.**                                                          **5.603**
The psychological birth of the human infant: symbiosis and individuation / Margaret S. Mahler, Fred Pine, Anni Bergman. — New York: Basic Books, [1975] xii, 308 p.: ill.; 25 cm. Includes indexes. 1. Infant psychology 2. Symbiosis (Psychology) 3. Separation-individuation I. Pine, Fred, 1931- II. Bergman, Anni, 1919- III. T.
BF723.I6 M33        155.4/22        *LC* 74-77255        *ISBN* 0465066593

**Tavistock Seminar on Mother-Infant Interaction.**                              **5.604**
Determinants of infant behaviour [I–IV]: proceedings of a Tavistock study group on mother–infant interaction held in the house of the CIBA Foundation, London, September, 1959 / edited by B. M. Foss; with a foreword by John Bowlby. — London: Methuen, 1961-1969. 4 v.: ill.; 22 cm. Convened by the Tavistock Child Development Research Unit, Tavistock Institute of Human Relations, and held at the house of the CIBA Foundation, London, in Sept. 1959, 1961, 1963, and 1969. Vols. 1 and 3 contain the proceedings of the Tavistock Study Group on Mother-Infant Interaction. Vol. 4 has subtitle: Based on the proceedings of the Fourth Tavistock Study Group on Mother-Infant Interaction. 1. Mother and child I. Foss, Brian M. II. Tavistock Child Development Research Unit. III. Ciba Foundation. IV. T.
BF723.I6 T3 1959        *LC* 62-2053        *ISBN* 0416647103

**Thomas, Alexander.**                                                           • **5.605**
Behavioral individuality in early childhood / Alexander Thomas et al. New York: New York University P., 1963. xii, 135 p.; 25 cm. 1. Infants 2. Personality I. T.
BF723I6 T5        *LC* 63-18666

**Perspectives on the development of memory and cognition /**                    **5.606**
**edited by Robert V. Kail, Jr., John W. Hagen.**
Hillsdale, N.J.: L. Erlbaum Associates; New York: distributed by the Halsted Press Division of J. Wiley, 1977. xiii, 498 p.; 24 cm. 1. Memory in children 2. Cognition in children I. Kail, Robert V. II. Hagen, John W.
BF723.M4 P47        155.4/13        *LC* 77-23942        *ISBN* 0470992735

**Kohlberg, Lawrence, 1927-.**                                                   **5.607**
Essays on moral development / Lawrence Kohlberg. — 1st ed. — San Francisco: Harper & Row, 1981-. 3 v.; 20 cm. Includes bibliographies and index. 1. Moral development 2. Justice (Philosophy) I. T. II. Title: The philosophy of moral development. III. Title: The psychology of moral development. IV. Title: Education and moral development.
BF 723.M54 K62        *LC* 80-8902        *ISBN* 0060647604

**Moral development, moral education, and Kohlberg: basic issues**               **5.608**
**in philosophy, psychology, religion, and education / edited by**
**Brenda Munsey.**
Birmingham, Ala.: Religious Education Press, c1980. viii, 478 p.; 23 cm. 1. Kohlberg, Lawrence, 1927- 2. Moral development 3. Moral education I. Munsey, Brenda.
BF723.M54 M684        370.11/4 19        *LC* 80-50        *ISBN* 0891350209

**Developing talent in young people / Benjamin S. Bloom, editor;**              **5.609**
**contributors, Lauren A. Sosniak ... [et al.].**
1st ed. — New York: Ballantine Books, 1985. x, 557 p.; 22 cm. 1. Achievement motivation in children 2. Achievement motivation 3. Performance in children 4. Performance 5. Genius 6. Gifted children 7. Talented students I. Bloom, Benjamin Samuel, 1913- II. Sosniak, Lauren A.
BF723.M56 D48 1985        155.4/13 19        *LC* 84-90809        *ISBN* 0345319516

**Piaget, Jean, 1896-.**                                                         • **5.610**
[Genèse du nombre chez l'enfant. English] The child's conception of number. [Translated by C. Gattegno and F. M. Hodgson] London, Routledge & Paul [1952] ix, 248 p. 22 cm. (International library of psychology, philosophy, and scientific method.) Translation of La genèse du nombre chez l'enfant. 1. Child study. 2. Number concept I. T. II. Series.
BF723.N8 P53        136.745101        *LC* 52-4983

**Biller, Henry B.**                                                             • **5.611**
Father, child, and sex role; paternal determinants of personality development [by] Henry B. Biller. — Lexington, Mass.: Heath Lexington Books, [1971] xi, 193 p.; 23 cm. 1. Father and child 2. Sex role I. T.
BF723.P25 B53        155.9/2/4        *LC* 74-145580

**Biller, Henry B.**                                                             **5.612**
Paternal deprivation: family, school, sexuality, and society / [by] Henry B. Biller. — Lexington, Mass.: Lexington Books, [1974] xi, 226 p.; 23 cm. 1. Paternal deprivation 2. Father and child 3. Sex role in children 4. Sex role I. T.
BF723.P33 B54        155.9/2/4        *LC* 74-928        *ISBN* 0669916943

**Brown, Alan R., comp.**                                                        • **5.613**
Prejudice in children / edited by Alan R. Brown. — Springfield, Ill.: C. C. Thomas, [1972] x, 214 p.; 24 cm. 1. Prejudices in children I. T.
BF723.P75 B76        301.45/1042        *LC* 73-169874        *ISBN* 039802247X

**Clark, Kenneth Bancroft, 1914-.**                                              • **5.614**
Prejudice and your child. 2d ed., enl. Boston, Beacon Press [1963] 247 p. 21 cm. (A Beacon paperback) 1. Race awareness in children 2. Prejudices in children — United States. 3. Self-perception in children — United States. 4. Racism — United States. 5. Prejudices — United States. 6. Segregation in education — United States 7. United States — Race relations I. T.
BF723.R3 C5 1963        157.3        *LC* 63-9467

**Coopersmith, Stanley, 1926-.**                                                 • **5.615**
The antecedents of self–esteem. San Francisco, W. H. Freeman [1967] ix, 283 p. 25 cm. (A Series of books in behavioral science) 1. Self-respect in children I. T.
BF723.S3 C6        155.41/8        *LC* 67-21126

**Bank, Stephen P., 1941-.**                                                     **5.616**
The sibling bond / Stephen P. Bank, Michael D. Kahn. — New York: Basic Books, c1982. xiii, 363 p.; 24 cm. Includes index. 1. Brothers and sisters 2. Developmental psychology I. Kahn, Michael D., 1936- II. T.
BF723.S43 B36 1982        155.9/24 19        *LC* 81-68401        *ISBN* 0465078184

**Stress in childhood / edited by James H. Humphrey.**                           **5.617**
New York: AMS Press, c1983. xii, 327 p.: ill.; 24 cm. (AMS studies in modern society: political and social issues; no. 17) 1. Stress in children I. Humphrey, James Harry, 1911-
BF723.S75 S78 1984        155.4 19        *LC* 83-45028        *ISBN* 0404616240

**Watson, Peter.**                                                               **5.618**
Twins: an uncanny relationship? / Peter Watson. — New York: Viking Press, 1982, c1981. 207 p.; 22 cm. 1. Twins — Psychology 2. Nature and nurture 3. Coincidence I. T.
BF723.T9 W37        155.2/34 19        *LC* 81-51909        *ISBN* 0670736023

**Vurpillot, Éliane.**                                                           **5.619**
[Monde visuel du jeune enfant. English] The visual world of the child / Eliane Vurpillot; foreword by Jerome Bruner; pref. by Paul Fraisse; translated from the French by W. E. C. Gillham. — New York: International Universities Press, c1976. 372 p.: ill.; 24 cm. Translation of Le monde visuel du jeune enfant. Includes index. 1. Visual perception 2. Cognition in children 3. Child psychology I. T.
BF723.V5 V8713        155.4/13        *LC* 75-790        *ISBN* 0823667499

# BF724–724.85 Adolescence. Adulthood. Old Age

**Female adolescent development / edited by Max Sugar.**                          **5.620**
New York: Brunner/Mazel, c1979. xvii, 362 p.: ill.; 24 cm. 1. Adolescent psychology 2. Women — Psychology I. Sugar, Max, 1925-
BF724.F435        155.5/33        *LC* 78-31743        *ISBN* 0876301928

**Handbook of adolescent psychology / edited by Joseph Adelson.**                **5.621**
New York: Wiley, c1980. xiv, 624 p.: ill.; 26 cm. (Wiley series on personality processes) 'A Wiley-Interscience publication.' 1. Adolescent psychology — Addresses, essays, lectures. I. Adelson, Joseph.
BF724.H33 1980        155.5        *LC* 79-21927        *ISBN* 0471037931

**Peel, Edwin Arthur.**                                                          **5.622**
The nature of adolescent judgment / [by] E. A. Peel. — New York: Wiley-Interscience, 1972 (c1971) 184 p.: ill.; 23 cm. 1. Judgment 2. Adolescent psychology I. T.
BF724.3.J8 P4 1971b        155.5        *LC* 76-177951        *ISBN* 0471677159

**Kimmel, Douglas C.**                                                           **5.623**
Adulthood and aging; an interdisciplinary, developmental view [by] Douglas C. Kimmel. — New York: Wiley, [1974] ix, 484 p.: illus.; 23 cm. 1. Adulthood 2. Aging I. T.
BF724.5.K55        155.6        *LC* 73-13557        *ISBN* 0471477001

Handbook of the psychology of aging / editors, James E.    **5.624**
Birren, K. Warner Schaie, with the assistance of associate
editors Vern Bengtson, Lissy Jarvik. Timothy Salthouse.
2nd ed. — New York: Van Nostrand Reinhold, c1985. xvii, 931 p.: ill.; 27 cm.
(Handbooks of aging.) 1. Aging — Psychological aspects I. Birren, James E.
II. Schaie, K. Warner (Klaus Warner), 1928- III. Title: Psychology of aging.
IV. Series.
BF724.55.A35 H36 1985      155.67 19      LC 84-25598      ISBN
0442214014

The Seasons of a man's life / by Daniel J. Levinson ... [et al.].    **5.625**
1st ed. — New York: Knopf, c1978. xiv, 363 p.; 25 cm. 1. Middle age —
Psychological aspects 2. Men — Psychology I. Levinson, Daniel J.
BF724.6.S42 1978      155.6/32      LC 77-20978      ISBN 039440694X

Williams, Richard Hay, 1912-.    **• 5.626**
Lives through the years: styles of life and successful aging / by Richard H.
Williams and Claudine G. Wirths. — New York: Atherton, 1965. xiii, 298 p.;
24 cm. 1. Aging I. Wirths, Claudine G. II. T.
BF724.8.W5      155.67      LC 65-28139

# BF755–839 Psychology of Nations. Psychology of Special Subjects

Putney, Snell.    **5.627**
Normal neurosis: the adjusted American / [by] Snell Putney and Gail J. Putney.
— [1st ed.]. — New York: Harper & Row, [1964] xii, 210 p.; 22 cm. 1. National
characteristics, American 2. Neuroses I. Putney, Gail J. joint author. II. T.
BF755.A5 P8      917.3      LC 64-12678

Riesman, David, 1909-.    **• 5.628**
The lonely crowd: a study of the changing American character / by David
Riesman in collaboration with Reuel Denney and Nathan Glazer. — New
Haven: Yale University Press, 1950. xvii, 386 p.; 24 cm. — (Studies in national
policy, 3) 1. National characteristics, American 2. Ethnopsychology I. T.
BF755.A5 R5      136.4973      LC 50-9967

Pruyser, Paul W., 1916-.    **5.629**
Between belief and unbelief [by] Paul W. Pruyser. — [1st ed.]. — New York:
Harper & Row, [1974] xvii, 301 p.; 22 cm. 1. Belief and doubt I. T.
BF773.P78 1974      121      LC 73-18686      ISBN 0060667001

Stich, Stephen P.    **5.630**
From folk psychology to cognitive science: the case against belief / Stephen P.
Stich. — Cambridge, Mass.: MIT Press, c1983. xii, 266 p.; 23 cm. 'A Bradford
book.' Includes index. 1. Belief and doubt 2. Psychology — Philosophy
3. Cognition I. T.
BF773.S75 1983      153/.01 19      LC 82-25883      ISBN 0262192152

Klinger, Eric, 1933-.    **5.631**
Meaning & void: inner experience and the incentives in people's lives / Eric
Klinger. — Minneapolis: University of Minnesota Press, c1977. xiv, 412 p.; 24
cm. Includes indexes. 1. Meaning (Psychology) 2. Incentive (Psychology)
3. Alienation (Social psychology) I. T.
BF778.K56 1977      155.2      LC 77-81425      ISBN 0816608113

Wittgenstein, Ludwig, 1889-1951.    **5.632**
[Bemerkungen über die Farben. English and German] Remarks on colour /
Ludwig Wittgenstein; edited by G. E. M. Anscombe; translated by Linda L.
McAlister and Margarete Schättle. — Berkeley: University of California Press,
c1977. 63, 63 p.; 23 cm. Added t.p.: Bemerkungen über die Farben. English and
German. Opposite pages numbered in duplicate. 1. Color — Psychological
aspects I. Anscombe, G. E. M. (Gertrude Elizabeth Margaret) II. T.
III. Title: Bemerkungen über die Farben.
BF789.C7 W513      110      LC 76-40595      ISBN 0520033353

Kübler-Ross, Elisabeth.    **• 5.633**
On death and dying. — [New York]: Macmillan, [1969] viii, 260 p.; 22 cm.
1. Death — Psychological aspects I. T.
BF789.D4 K8      155.9/3      LC 69-11789

Thomas, Alexander, 1914-.    **5.634**
Temperament and development / Alexander Thomas and Stella Chess. New
York: Brunner/Mazel, c1977. xv, 270 p.; 24 cm. 1. Temperament
2. Developmental psychology I. Chess, Stella. joint author. II. T.
BF798.T47      618.9/28/9071      LC 76-49428      ISBN 0876301391

Riesman, David, 1909-.    **• 5.635**
Faces in the crowd: individual studies in character and politics / by David
Riesman in collaboration with Nathan Glazer. — New Haven: Yale University
Press, 1952. xii, 751 p.; 25 cm. (Studies in national policy, 4) 1. Personality and
culture 2. National characteristics, American I. T.
BF818.R5      136.4973      LC 52-5357

# BF1001–1389 PSYCHIC RESEARCH. PSYCHOLOGY OF THE UNCONSCIOUS

Mauskopf, Seymour H.    **5.636**
The elusive science: origins of experimental psychical research / Seymour H.
Mauskopf and Michael R. McVaugh; afterword by J. B. and L. E. Rhine. —
Baltimore: Johns Hopkins University Press, 1981 (c1980). xvi, 368 p.: ill.; 24
cm. 1. Psychical research — History. I. McVaugh, Michael R. joint author.
II. T.
BF1028.M38      133.8/01/5      LC 80-7991      ISBN 0801823315

The Basic experiments in parapsychology / compiled and edited    **5.637**
by K. Ramakrishna Rao.
Jefferson, N.C.: McFarland, c1984. viii, 264 p.: ill.; 24 cm. Includes index.
1. Psychical research — Addresses, essays, lectures. I. Ramakrishna Rao, K.
BF1029.B37 1984      133.8/072 19      LC 83-42883      ISBN 0899500846

Broad, C. D. (Charlie Dunbar), 1887-1971.    **• 5.638**
Lectures on psychical research / incorporating the Perrott lectures given in
Cambridge University in 1959 and 1960. — New York: Humanities Press,
[1962] 450 p.: ill.; 23 cm. (International library of philosophy and scientific
method) 1. Psychical research I. T.
BF1031.B745

Foundations of parapsychology: exploring the boundaries of    **5.639**
human capability / foreword by T.X. Barber; [contributors]
Hoyt L. Edge ... [et al.].
Boston; London: Routledge & Kegan Paul, 1986. xvi, 432 p., [8] p. of plates: ill.,
ports.; 24 cm. Includes index. 1. Psychical research I. Edge, Hoyt L.
BF1031.F6x      133 19      LC 85-20486      ISBN 0710202261

Handbook of parapsychology / Benjamin B. Wolman, editor;    **5.640**
Laura A. Dale, Gertrude R. Schmeidler, Montague Ullman,
associate editors.
New York: Van Nostrand Reinhold, [1977] xxi, 967 p., [7] leaves of plates: ill.;
24 cm. Includes indexes. 1. Psychical research — Addresses, essays, lectures.
I. Wolman, Benjamin B.
BF1031.H254      133      LC 77-8336      ISBN 0442295766

LeShan, Lawrence L., 1920-.    **5.641**
The medium, the mystic, and the physicist: toward a general theory of the
paranormal / by Lawrence LeShan. — New York: Viking Press, [1974] xix,
299 p.; 22 cm. — (An Esalen book) 1. Psychical research I. T.
BF1031.L43 1974      133.8      LC 73-8147      ISBN 0670465666

Murphy, Gardner, 1895-.    **• 5.642**
Challenge of psychical research: a primer of parapsychology / by Gardner
Murphy; with the collaboration of Laura A. Dale. — [1st ed.]. — New York:
Harper [1961] 297 p.: ill.; 20 cm. — (World perspectives, v. 26) Includes
bibliography. 1. Psychical research I. T.
BF1031.M78      133.07      LC 61-6180

Myers, Frederic William Henry, 1843-1901.    **• 5.643**
Human personality and its survival of bodily death. Edited by Susy Smith. —
New Hyde Park, N. Y., University Books [1961] 416 p. illus. 24 cm.
1. Personality 2. Immortality 3. Psychical research I. T.
BF1031.M85 1961      133.07      LC 61-9319

Psychic exploration: a challenge for science / Edgar D. Mitchell    **5.644**
... [et al.]; edited by John White.
New York: Putnam, [1974] 708 p., [4] leaves of plates: ill., graphs; 24 cm.
1. Psychical research — Addresses, essays, lectures. 2. Psychical research —
United States — Addresses, essays, lectures. I. Mitchell, Edgar D. II. White,
John Warren, 1939-
BF1031.P79 1974      133.8      LC 73-93737      ISBN 0399113428

Rhine, J. B. (Joseph Banks), 1895-1980.    **• 5.645**
Extra-sensory perception, by J. B. Rhine. With a foreword by William
McDougall and an introd. by Walter Franklin Prince. Boston, B. Humphries
[1964] xlviii, 240 p. illus., ports. 22 cm. Bibliography: p. xlvi—xlviii.
Bibliographical footnotes. 1. Extrasensory perception I. T.
BF1031.R37 1964      133.81      LC 64-21051

**Rhine, Louisa E., 1891-.** 5.646
The invisible picture: a study of psychic experiences / Louisa E. Rhine. — Jefferson, N.C.: McFarland, 1981. viii, 267 p.; 24 cm. 1. Psychical research I. T.
BF1031.R39    133.8    *LC* 80-10545    *ISBN* 0899500153

**Chauvin, Rémy.** 5.647
[Parapsychologie. English] Parapsychology: when the irrational rejoins science / by Rémy Chauvin; translated by Katharine M. Banham. — Jefferson, N.C.: McFarland, c1985. xi, 164 p.; 23 cm. Translation of: La parapsychologie. Includes index. 1. Psychical research I. T.
BF1032.C4813 1985    133 19    *LC* 84-43225    *ISBN* 0899501451

**McClenon, James.** 5.648
Deviant science: the case of parapsychology / James McClenon. — Philadelphia: University of Pennsylvania Press, c1984. xiii, 282 p.: ill.; 23 cm. Includes index. 1. Psychical research I. T.
BF1040.M326 1984    133.8 19    *LC* 83-14680    *ISBN* 0812211782

**Zusne, Leonard, 1924-.** 5.649
Anomalistic psychology: a study of extraordinary phenomena of behavior and experience / Leonard Zusne, Warren H. Jones. — Hillsdale, N.J.: Erlbaum Associates, 1982. xiii, 498 p.: ill.; 24 cm. Includes index. 1. Psychical research — Psychological aspects. 2. Occultism — Psychological aspects. 3. Supernatural — Psychological aspects. I. Jones, Warren H. joint author. II. T.
BF1040.Z87 1982    133.8/01/5    *LC* 80-17345    *ISBN* 089859068X

**Science and the paranormal: probing the existence of the** 5.650
**supernatural / edited by George O. Abell and Barry Singer.**
New York: Scribner, c1981. xi, 414 p.: ill. 1. Psychical research — Addresses, essays, lectures. 2. Occultism — Addresses, essays, lectures. 3. Science — Addresses, essays, lectures. I. Abell, George O. (George Ogden), 1927-1983. II. Singer, Barry.
BF1045.S33 S38    133.8/01/5 19    *LC* 81-26839    *ISBN* 0684166550

# BF1068–1389 Sleep. Dreaming. Hypnotism. Spiritualism

**Foulkes, William David, 1935-.** • 5.651
The psychology of sleep / [by] David Foulkes. — New York: Scribner, [1966] xii, 265 p.: ill.; 25 cm. 1. Sleep I. T.
BF1071.F73    154.6    *LC* 66-15978

**Freud, Sigmund, 1856-1939.** • 5.652
[Traumdeutung. English] The interpretation of dreams; translated by A. A. Brill. New York, Modern Library [1950] 477 p. 19 cm. (The Modern library of the world's best books, 96) 1. Dreams 2. Psychoanalysis I. T.
BF1078.F72 1950    135.383    *LC* 50-6784

**Fromm, Erich, 1900-.** • 5.653
The forgotten language: an introduction to the understanding of dreams, fairy tales, and myths. — New York: Rinehart [1951] 263 p.; 22 cm. 1. Dreams 2. Psychoanalysis 3. Symbolism (Psychology) I. T.
BF1078.F84    135.38    *LC* 51-13653

**Handbook of dreams: research, theories, and applications /** 5.654
**edited by Benjamin B. Wolman, consulting editors, Montague**
**Ullman, Wilse B. Webb.**
New York: Van Nostrand Reinhold, c1979. x, 447 p.: ill.; 24 cm. 1. Dreams — Addresses, essays, lectures. I. Wolman, Benjamin B.
BF1078.H28    154.6/34    *LC* 79-653    *ISBN* 0442295928

**O'Flaherty, Wendy Doniger.** 5.655
Dreams, illusion, and other realities / Wendy Doniger O'Flaherty. — Chicago: University of Chicago Press, 1984. xvi, 361 p.: ill.; 24 cm. Includes tales from the 'Yogavāsistha.' Includes indexes. 1. Yogavāsistharāmāyana. 2. Dreams 3. Mythology, Indic 4. Yoga — Early works to 1800. I. Yogavāsistharāmāya.na II. T.
BF1078.O45 1984    111 19    *LC* 83-17944    *ISBN* 0226618544

**Ullman, Montague.** 5.656
Dream telepathy / [by] Montague Ullman, Stanley Krippner, with Alan Vaughan. — New York: Macmillan [1973] xiii, 300 p.: ill.; 22 cm. 1. Dreams 2. Telepathy I. Krippner, Stanley, 1932- joint author. II. Vaughan, Alan. joint author. III. T.
BF1091.U43    133.8    *LC* 72-91264

**Hartmann, Ernest.** 5.657
The nightmare: the psychology and biology of terrifying dreams / Ernest Hartmann. — New York: Basic Books, c1984. viii, 294 p.: ill.; 22 cm. Includes index. 1. Nightmares — Psychological aspects. 2. Nightmares — Physiological aspects. I. T.
BF1099.N53 H37 1984    154.6/32 19    *LC* 83-46070    *ISBN* 046505109X

**Bowers, Kenneth S.** 5.658
Hypnosis for the seriously curious / Kenneth S. Bowers. — Monterey, Calif.: Brooks/Cole Pub. Co., c1976. ix, 176 p.: graphs; 23 cm. (Contemporary psychology series) Includes indexes. 1. Hypnotism I. T.
BF1141.B68 1976    154.7    *LC* 75-31448    *ISBN* 0818501812

**Fromm, Erika.** 5.659
Hypnosis: developments in research and new perspectives / edited by Erika Fromm, Ronald E. Shor. — New and rev. 2d ed. — New York: Aldine Pub. Co., 1979. xv, 793 p.: ill.; 25 cm. Includes indexes. 1. Hypnotism — Addresses, essays, lectures. I. Shor, Ronald E. II. T.
BF1141.F93 1979    154.7    *LC* 79-89279    *ISBN* 0202260852

**Fornell, Earl Wesley.** 5.660
The unhappy medium: spiritualism and the life of Margaret Fox / drawings by Howell Collins. — Austin: University of Texas Press [1964] x, 204 p.: ill., ports.; 24 cm. 1. Fox family 2. Spiritualism I. T.
BF1283.F7 F6    *LC* 64-10317

**Lund, David H.** 5.661
Death and consciousness / by David H. Lund. — Jefferson, N.C.: McFarland, c1985. x, 194 p.; 23 cm. Includes index. 1. Future life 2. Consciousness 3. Spiritualism I. T.
BF1311.F8 L8 1985    133.9/01/3 19    *LC* 84-43211    *ISBN* 0899501400

**Blackmore, Susan J., 1951-.** 5.662
Beyond the body: an investigation of out–of–the–body experiences / Susan J. Blackmore. — London: Heinemann, 1984, c1982. xv, 271 p., [16] p. of plates: ill.; 23 cm. 'Published on behalf of the Society for Psychical Research.' Includes index. 1. Astral projection I. Society for Psychical Research (London, England) II. T.
BF1389.A7 B53 1982    133.9 19    *LC* 82-222062    *ISBN* 0434074705

# BF1405–1999 OCCULT SCIENCES

**The Satan trap: dangers of the occult / edited by Martin Ebon.** 5.663
1st ed. — Garden City, N.Y.: Doubleday, 1976. xii, 276 p.; 21 cm. 1. Occultism — Addresses, essays, lectures. 2. Psychical research — Addresses, essays, lectures. I. Ebon, Martin.
BF1411.S34    133    *LC* 75-14816    *ISBN* 0385079419

**Smith, Richard Furnald.** 5.664
Prelude to science: an exploration of magic and divination / by Richard Furnald Smith; drawings Anne Corrough. — New York: Scribner, [1975] viii, 129 p.: ill.; 24 cm. 1. Occultism I. T.
BF1411.S656    133    *LC* 75-17959    *ISBN* 0684143704

**Wilson, Colin, 1931-.** 5.665
The occult: a history. — [1st American ed.] — New York: Random House [c1971] 601 p.: ill., ports. 1. Occultism — history. 2. Occultism I. T.
BF1411.W53 1973    *LC* 76-159389    *ISBN* 0394465555 10.00

**Yeats, W. B. (William Butler), 1865-1939.** 5.666
[Vision] A critical edition of Yeats's A vision (1925) / edited by George Mills Harper and Walter Kelly Hood. — London: Macmillan (dist. by Humanities), 1980 (C1978). l, xxiii, 256, 108 p.: ill.; 23 cm. Reprint of 1st ed., which was privately printed for subscribers only by T. W. Laurie, London, 1925. Includes indexes. 1. Occultism I. Harper, George Mills. II. Hood, Walter Kelly. III. T. IV. Title: Vision.
BF1411.Y4    828/.807 19    *LC* 79-303970    *ISBN* 0333212991

**Dodds, Eric Robertson, 1893-.** • 5.667
The Greeks and the irrational / by E. R. Dodds. — Berkeley: University of California Press, 1951. ix, 327 p. (Sather classical lectures. v. 25) 1. Occultism — History. 2. Greece — Civilization I. T. II. Series.
BF1421.D6 1951

**Shumaker, Wayne.**     5.668
The occult sciences in the Renaissance; a study in intellectual patterns.
Berkeley, University of California Press [1972] xix, 284 p. illus. 26 cm.
1. Occultism — History. I. T.
BF1429.S58     133/.09/024     *LC* 70-153552     *ISBN* 0520020219

**Yates, Frances Amelia.**     5.669
The occult philosophy in the Elizabethan age / Frances A. Yates. — London;
Boston: Routledge & K. Paul, 1979. x, 217 p., [8] leaves of plates: ill.; 23 cm.
1. Occultism — England — History. 2. Occultism — Europe — History.
3. Cabala — England — History. 4. Cabala — Europe — History. I. T.
BF1434.G7 Y37     133/.094     *LC* 79-40827     *ISBN* 071000320X

**Gauld, Alan.**     5.670
Poltergeists / Alan Gauld and A. D. Cornell. — London; Boston: Routledge &
Kegan Paul, 1979. xii, 406 p., [4] leaves of plates: ill.; 23 cm. Includes indexes.
1. Poltergeists — Case studies. I. Cornell, A. D. joint author. II. T.
BF1483.G38     133.1/4     *LC* 79-321311     *ISBN* 0710001851

**Huxley, Aldous, 1894-1963.**     • 5.671
The devils of Loudun. London: Chatto & Windus, 1970. [8], 376 p., 2 plates: 2
ill., 2 facsims., 3 ports.; 21 cm. (His collected works) 1. Grandier, Urbain,
1590-1634. 2. Loudun, France. Ursuline convent. 3. Demoniac possession —
France — Louden. I. T.
BF1517.F5 H8 1970     133.4/26/094463     *LC* 72-180236     *ISBN*
0701107952

**Marwick, Max, comp.**     • 5.672
Witchcraft and sorcery; selected readings, edited by Max Marwick. —
[Harmondsworth, Eng.; Baltimore, Md.]: Penguin Books, [1970] 416 p.; 18 cm.
— (Penguin modern sociology readings) 1. Witchcraft — Collections. I. T.
BF1563.M3 1970     133.4/08     *LC* 70-18967     *ISBN* 0140801553

**Starhawk.**     5.673
The spiral dance: a rebirth of the ancient religion of the great goddess /
Starhawk. — 1st ed. — San Francisco: Harper & Row, c1979. vi, 218 p.; 24 cm.
1. Witchcraft I. T.
BF1566.S77 1979     299     *LC* 79-1775     *ISBN* 0060675357

**Russell, Jeffrey Burton.**     5.674
Witchcraft in the Middle Ages. — Ithaca, N.Y.: Cornell University Press,
[1972] ix, 394 p.; 23 cm. 1. Witchcraft — History. I. T.
BF1569.R88 1972     914/.03/1     *LC* 72-37755     *ISBN* 0801406978

**Gardner, Gerald Brosseau, 1884-.**     5.675
Witchcraft today; introduction by Margaret Murray. — London: Jarrolds,
1968. 192 p.; 21 cm. 1. Witchcraft I. T.
BF1571.G3 1968     133.4     *LC* 68-92606     *ISBN* 0090478118

**Starhawk.**     5.676
Dreaming the dark: magic, sex, & politics / Starhawk. — Boston: Beacon Press,
c1982. xvi, 242 p.: ill.; 22 cm. 1. Witchcraft 2. Sex and religion. 3. Religion
and politics 4. Women and religion I. T.
BF1572.S4 S7 1982     299 19     *LC* 81-70485     *ISBN* 0807010006

**Adler, Margot.**     5.677
Drawing down the Moon: witches, Druids, goddess–worshippers, and other
pagans in America today / Margot Adler. — New York: Viking Press, 1979. xi,
455 p., [4] leaves of plates: ill.; 25 cm. 1. Witchcraft — United States. 2. Cults
— United States 3. Women and religion I. T.
BF1573.A34 1979     299 19     *LC* 79-12023     *ISBN* 0670283428

**Demos, John.**     5.678
Entertaining Satan: witchcraft and the culture of early New England / John
Putnam Demos. — New York: Oxford University Press, 1982. xiv, 543 p.; 24
cm. 1. Witchcraft — New England 2. New England — Social life and customs
I. T.
BF1576.D42 1982     974/.02 19     *LC* 81-22463     *ISBN* 0195031318

**Mappen, Marc.**     5.679
Witches & historians: interpretations of Salem / edited by Marc Mappen. —
Huntington, N.Y.: R. E. Krieger Pub. Co., 1980. v, 120 p.; 23 cm. (The
American problem studies) 1. Witchcraft — Massachusetts — Salem —
Addresses, essays, lectures. 2. Salem (Mass.) — History — Addresses, essays,
lectures. I. T.
BF1576.M34     974.4/5     *LC* 78-2579     *ISBN* 0882756532

**Monter, E. William.**     5.680
Witchcraft in France and Switzerland: the borderlands during the Reformation
/ E. William Monter. — Ithaca, N.Y.: Cornell University Press, 1976. 232 p.:
ill.; 23 cm. Includes index. 1. Witchcraft — Jura Mountain region. I. T.
BF1582.M6     272/.8/09445     *LC* 75-31449     *ISBN* 0801409632

**Cohn, Norman Rufus Colin.**     5.681
Europe's inner demons: an enquiry inspired by the great witch–hunt / Norman
Cohn. — New York: Basic Books, [1975] xvi, 302 p., [4] leaves of plates: ill.; 24
cm. (The Columbus Centre series) 1. Witchcraft — Europe. 2. Demonology
I. T.
BF1584.E9 C63     940.1/7     *LC* 74-79498     *ISBN* 046502131X

**Kieckhefer, Richard.**     5.682
European witch trials: their foundations in popular and learned culture,
1300–1500 / Richard Kieckhefer. — Berkeley: University of California Press,
1976. x, 181 p.; 23 cm. 1. Trials (Witchcraft) — Europe. I. T.
BF1584.E9K5x     345/.4/0288     *LC* 74-29807     *ISBN* 0520029674

**Peters, Edward, 1936-.**     5.683
The magician, the witch, and the law / Edward Peters. — [Philadelphia]:
University of Pennsylvania Press, 1978. xviii, 218 p.; 24 cm. — (Middle Ages.)
1. Magic — History. 2. Witchcraft — History. I. T. II. Series.
BF1593.P42     133.4/094     *LC* 78-51341     *ISBN* 0812277465

**Mauss, Marcel, 1872-1950.**     5.684
A general theory of magic / translated from the French by Robert Brain. —
London; Boston: Routledge and K. Paul, 1972. [5], 148 p.; 23 cm. 1. Magic
I. T.
BF1611.M38 1972     301.2/1     *LC* 72-169466     *ISBN* 0810073380

**Hopper, Vincent Foster, 1906-.**     5.685
Medieval number symbolism: its sources, meaning, and influence on thought
and expression / by Vincent Foster Hopper. — New York: Columbia
University Press, 1938. xii, 241 p. — (Columbia University studies in English
and comparative literature; no. 132) Issued also as thesis (PH. D.) Columbia
university. 1. Symbolism of numbers 2. Mysticism — Middle ages, 600-1500.
I. T. II. Series.
BF1623.P9 H53 1938a     *LC* 39-1970

**Garin, Eugenio, 1909-.**     5.686
[Zodiaco della vita. English] Astrology in the Renaissance: the zodiac of life /
Eugenio Garin; translated by Carolyn Jackson and June Allen; translation
revised in conjunction with the author by Clare Robertson. — London; Boston:
Routledge & Kegan Paul, 1983. xiv, 144 p.; 23 cm. Translation of: Lo zodiaco
della vita. 1. Astrology — History 2. Renaissance I. T.
BF1676.G3713 1983     133.5 19     *LC* 82-13188     *ISBN* 0710092598

**Ficino, Marsilio, 1433-1499.**     5.687
[De triplici vita. English] The book of life / Marsilio Ficino; a translation by
Charles Boer of Liber de vita (or De vita triplici). — 1st ed. — Irving, Tex.:
Spring Publications, 1980. xix, 217 p.; 23 cm. Includes index. 1. Astrology —
Early works to 1800. 2. Medicine, Medieval I. T.
BF1680.F5513     615.8/99 19     *LC* 81-128012     *ISBN* 0882142127

**Festinger, Leon, 1919-.**     • 5.688
When prophecy fails / by Leon Festinger, Henry W. Riecken and Stanley
Schachter. — Minneapolis: University of Minnesota Press [1956] vii, 256 p.; 23
cm. 1. Prophecies (Occultism) I. T.
BF1809.F4     133.3     *LC* 56-11611

# Q General Science

## Q1–113 SOCIETIES. COLLECTED WORKS

**McClellan, James E. (James Edward), 1946-.** **5.689**
Science reorganized: scientific societies in the eighteenth century / James E. McClellan III. — New York: Columbia University Press, 1985. xxix, 413 p.: ill., maps; 24 cm. Includes index. 1. Science — Societies, etc. — History. 2. Learned institutions and societies — History. I. T.
Q10.M38 1985    506 19    LC 84-22993    ISBN 0231059965

**World guide to scientific associations = Internationales** **5.690**
**Verzeichnis wissenschaftlicher Verbände und Gesellschaften /**
**[edited by Michael Zils and Willi Gorzny].**
3rd ed. — München; New York: Saur; Detroit, Mich.: Distributed by Gale Research Co., 1982. 619 p.; 30 cm. — (Handbook of international documentation and information; v. 13 = Handbuch der internationalen Dokumentation und Information; Bd. 13) Distributor from label on t.p. Rev. ed. of: World guide to scientific associations and learned societies. 2nd ed. 1978. 1. Science — Societies, etc. — Directories. 2. Learned institutions and societies — Directories. I. Zils, Michael. II. Gorzny, Willi. III. Title: Internationales Verzeichnis wissenschaftlicher Verbande und Gesellschaften. IV. Title: World guide to scientific associations and learned societies.
Q10.W67 1982    506/.01 19    LC 82-199881    ISBN 3598205171

**Hellman, Geoffrey Theodore, 1907-.** • **5.691**
The Smithsonian octopus on the Mall, by Geoffrey T. Hellman. — [1st ed.]. — Philadelphia: Lippincott, [1967] 224 p.; 22 cm. 1. Smithsonian Institution. I. T.
Q11.S8 H4    506/.1/753    LC 67-20172

**Oehser, Paul Henry, 1904-.** **5.692**
The Smithsonian Institution / Paul H. Oehser; Louise Heskett, research associate; foreword by S. Dillon Ripley. — 2nd ed., rev. and expanded. — Boulder, Colo.: Westview Press, 1983. xiv, 223 p., [2] p. of plates: ill.; 24 cm. — (Westview library of federal departments, agencies, and systems.) Includes index. 1. Smithsonian Institution. I. Heskett, Louise. II. T. III. Series.
Q11.S8 O39 1983    069/.09753 19    LC 83-7026    ISBN 0865313008

**Morrell, Jack.** **5.693**
Gentlemen of science: early years of the British Association for the Advancement of Science / Jack Morrell & Arnold Thackray. — Oxford: Clarendon Press; New York: Oxford University Press, 1981. xxiii, 592 p., [16] p. of plates: ill.; 24 cm. Includes indexes. 1. British Association for the Advancement of Science — History. I. Thackray, Arnold, 1939- II. T.
Q41.B85 M67 1981    506/.041 19    LC 81-201474    ISBN 0198581637

**Caroe, G. M.** **5.694**
The Royal Institution: an informal history / Gwendy Caroe, with a final chapter by Alban Caroe. — London: J. Murray, 1985. xi, 180 p., [12] p. of plates: ill., ports.; 24 cm. Includes index. 1. Royal Institution of Great Britain — History. I. T.
Q41.C27 1985    506/.041 19    LC 86-140414    ISBN 0719542456

**Hall, Marie Boas, 1919-.** **5.695**
All scientists now: the Royal Society in the nineteenth century / Marie Boas Hall. — Cambridge [Cambridgeshire]; New York: Cambridge University Press, 1984. xii, 261 p.: ports.; 24 cm. Includes index. 1. Royal Society (Great Britain) — History. 2. Science — Great Britain — History. I. T.
Q41.L85 H35 1984    506/.041 19    LC 84-7705    ISBN 0521267463

**Hunter, Michael Cyril William.** **5.696**
The Royal Society and its fellows, 1660–1700: the morphology of an early scientific institution / Michael Hunter. — Chalfont St. Giles, Bucks, England: British Society for the History of Science, 1982. 270 p.; 21 cm. — (BSHS monographs. 4) 1. Royal Society (Great Britain) — History. 2. Scientists — Great Britain — Registers. I. T. II. Series.
Q41.L85 H95 1982    506/.041 19    LC 83-209776    ISBN 0906450039

**Purver, Margery.** • **5.697**
The Royal Society: concept and creation. With an introd. by H. R. Trevor-Roper. Cambridge, M.I.T. Press [1967] xvii, 246 p. illus., ports. 23 cm. 1. Royal Society (Great Britain) I. T.
Q41.L86 P86 1967a    506/.2/421    LC 66-25631

**Hahn, Roger, 1932-.** **5.698**
The anatomy of a scientific institution: the Paris Academy of Sciences, 1666–1803. Berkeley, University of California Press, 1971. xiv, 433 p. illus. 24 cm. 1. Académie des sciences (France) I. T.
Q46.A15 H33    506/.2/44    LC 70-130795    ISBN 0520018184

**The Realm of science / David Rosenberg, director; Stanley B.** **5.699**
**Brown, editor–in–chief.**
Louisville, Ky.: Touchstone Pub. Co. [1972] 21 v.: ill.; 27 cm. 1. Science — Collected works I. Rosenberg, David, 1914- II. Brown, Stanley Barber, 1919- ed.
Q111.R38    508/.1    LC 76-157124

**Gibbs, J. Willard (Josiah Willard), 1839-1903.** • **5.700**
[Works. 1961] Scientific papers. New York: Dover Publications [1961] 2 v.: ill.; 22 cm. 'An unabridged and unaltered republication of the first edition ... originally published ... in 1906.' 1. Science — Collected works 2. Thermodynamics 3. Statistical mechanics I. T.
Q113.G44 1961    508.1    LC 61-1262

**Henry, Joseph, 1797-1878.** **5.701**
The papers of Joseph Henry. Editor: Nathan Reingold. Assistant editors: Stuart Pierson and Arthur P. Molella with the assistance of James M. Hobbins and John R. Kerwood. Washington, Smithsonian Institution Press, distributed by Braziller, New York, 1972- < 1985 >. v. < 1-2, 4-5 > illus. 27 cm. 1. Henry, Joseph, 1797-1878. 2. Smithsonian Institution — History — Sources — Collected works 3. Science — Collected works 4. Science — United States — History — Sources — Collected works. 5. Physicists — United States — Biography — Collected works. I. Reingold, Nathan, 1927- ed. II. T.
Q113.H43    537/.092/4    LC 72-2005    ISBN 0874741238

**Priestley, Joseph.** **5.702**
Joseph Priestley: selections from his writings / edited by Ira V. Brown. — See full entry at AC7.P68 I. T.

## Q121–123 DICTIONARIES. ENCYCLOPEDIAS

**McGraw–Hill encyclopedia of science & technology: an** **5.703**
**international reference work in twenty volumes including an**
**index.**
6th ed. — New York: McGraw-Hill, c1987. p. cm. 1. Science — Dictionaries 2. Technology — Dictionaries I. Title: McGraw-Hill encyclopedia of science and technology. II. Title: Encyclopedia of science & technology. III. Title: Encyclopedia of science and technology.
Q121.M3 1987    503/.21 19    LC 86-27422    ISBN 0070792925

**McGraw–Hill yearbook of science and technology.** • **5.704**
1962-. [New York, McGraw-Hill Book Co.] v. ill. 26 cm. Annual. 1. Science — Yearbooks. 2. Technology — Yearbooks. I. McGraw-Hill encyclopedia of science and technology.
Q121.M312    505 19    LC 62-12028

**Van Nostrand's scientific encyclopedia / Douglas M. Considine,** **5.705**
**editor; Glenn D. Considine, managing editor.**
6th ed. — New York: Van Nostrand Reinhold, c1983. xiv, 3067 p.: ill.; 30 cm. 1. Science — Dictionaries 2. Engineering — Dictionaries. I. Considine, Douglas Maxwell. II. Title: Scientific encyclopedia.
Q121.V3 1983    503/.21 19    LC 82-4936    ISBN 0442251610

**De Vries, Louis, 1885-.** **5.706**
German–English science dictionary / Louis De Vries; updated and expanded by Leon Jacolev, with the assistance of Phyllis L. Bolton. — 4th ed. — New York: McGraw-Hill, c1978. xxxviii, 628 p.; 21 cm. Third ed. published in 1959 under title: German-English science dictionary for students in chemistry, physics, biology, agriculture, and related sciences. 1. Science — Dictionaries —

German. 2. German language — Dictionaries — English. I. Jacolev, Leon. II. Bolton, Phyllis L. III. T.
Q123.D4 1978      503    *LC* 78-6465      *ISBN* 0070166021

**Dorian, A. F. (Angelo Francis), 1908-.**                              **5.707**
Dictionary of science and technology: German–English / compiled and arranged by A.F. Dorian. — 2nd rev. ed. — Amsterdam; New York: Elsevier Scientific, 1981. 1119 p.; 25 cm. English and German. Added t.p. in German: Handwörterbuch der Naturwissenschaft und Technik. Cover title: Dorian's Dictionary of science and technology. 1. Science — Dictionaries — German. 2. Technology — Dictionaries — German. 3. German language — Dictionaries — English. I. T. II. Title: Handwörterbuch der Naturwissenschaft und Technik. III. Title: Dorian's Dictionary of science and technology.
Q123.D673 1981      503/.31 19      *LC* 81-208536      *ISBN* 0444419977

**Harrap's French and English science dictionary / editorial team:**      **5.708**
**Peter Collin ... [et al.]; consultant editor D.E. Hathway.**
London: Harrap, 1985. ix, 320, 302 p.; 24 cm. 1. Science — Dictionaries — French. 2. French language — Dictionaries — English. I. Collin, P. H. II. Hathway, D. E. (David Ernest), 1919- III. Title: French and English science dictionary.
Q123.H265      503/.41 19      *ISBN* 0245540725

**McGraw–Hill dictionary of scientific and technical terms /**      **5.709**
**Sybil P. Parker, editor in chief.**
3rd ed. — New York: McGraw-Hill Book Co., c1984. xv, 1781, 65 p.: ill.; 29 cm. 1. Science — Dictionaries 2. Technology — Dictionaries I. Parker, Sybil P.
Q123.M34 1984      503/.21 19      *LC* 83-11302      *ISBN* 0070452695

**Uvarov, E. B. (Eugene Boris), 1910-.**                              **5.710**
The Penguin dictionary of science / E. B. Uvarov and D. R. Chapman. — Rev. for the 5th ed. / by Alan Isaacs and E. B. Uvarov. — New York: Schocken Books, 1980. 488 p., 20 cm. 1. Science — Dictionaries I. Chapman, D. R. (Dennis Raymond), 1926- joint author. II. Isaacs, Alan, 1925- III. T.
Q123.U8 1980      503    *LC* 79-22035

**Zimmerman, Mikhail.**                                              **5.711**
Russian–English translators' dictionary: a guide to scientific and technical usage / Mikhail Zimmerman. — 2nd ed. — Chichester [West Sussex]; New York: Wiley, c1984. 544 p.; 24 cm. 'A Wiley-Interscience publication.' 1. Science — Dictionaries — Russian. 2. Russian language — Dictionaries — English. I. T.
Q123.Z55 1984      503/.9171 19      *LC* 83-10229      *ISBN* 0471902187

## Q124.6–127 HISTORY

**Schlagel, Richard H., 1925-.**                                    **5.712**
From myth to the modern mind: a study of the origins and growth of scientific thought / Richard H. Schlagel. — New York: P. Lang, c1985. 1 v.; 23 cm. (American university studies. Series V, Philosophy; vol. 12-) 1. Science, Ancient 2. Science — Philosophy — History. I. T.
Q124.95.S35 1985      509/.3 19      *LC* 84-23361      *ISBN* 0820402192

**Science in the Middle Ages / edited by David C. Lindberg.**      **5.713**
Chicago: University of Chicago Press, 1978. xv, 549 p.: ill.; 24 cm. — (Chicago history of science and medicine.) Includes index. 1. Science, Medieval I. Lindberg, David C. II. Series.
Q124.97.S35      509/.02      *LC* 78-5367      *ISBN* 0226482324

# Q125 Modern

## Q125 A–F

**Born, Max, 1882-1970.**                                          • **5.714**
My life & my views / introd. by I. Bernard Cohen. — New York: Scribner, [1968] 216 p.; 22 cm. Part II (p. 63-206) is a translation of Von der Verantwortung des Naturwissenschaftlers. 1. Science and civilization 2. Physics — Philosophy I. T.
Q125.B629      501    *LC* 68-12510

**Butterfield, Herbert, Sir, 1900-.**                              • **5.715**
The origins of modern science: 1300–1800. — [Rev. ed.]. — New York: Macmillan, 1957. 242 p.; 22 cm. 1. Science — History 2. Science — Philosophy I. T.
Q125.B97 1957a      509

**Clagett, Marshall, 1916-.**                                        **5.716**
Greek science in antiquity. New York, Abelard-Schuman [1955] 217 p. illus. 25 cm. 1. Science, Ancient I. T.
Q125.C49      509.3      *LC* 55-11905

**Cohen, I. Bernard, 1914-.**                                        **5.717**
From Leonardo to Lavoisier, 1450–1800 / I. Bernard Cohen. — New York: Scribner, c1980. xiii, 298 p.: ill.; 28 cm. — (Album of science.) Includes index. 1. Science — History I. T. II. Series.
Q125.C54      509/.03      *LC* 80-15542      *ISBN* 0684153777

**Cohen, I. Bernard, 1914-.**                                        **5.718**
Revolution in science / I. Bernard Cohen. — Cambridge, Mass.: Belknap Press of Harvard University Press, 1985. xx, 711 p., [1] leaf of plates: ill. (some col.); 24 cm. Includes index. 1. Science — History I. T.
Q125.C542 1985      509 19      *LC* 84-12916      *ISBN* 0674767772

**Conant, James Bryant, 1893-1978 ed.**                            • **5.719**
Harvard case histories in experimental science / [by] James Bryant Conant, general editor [and others]. — Cambridge: Harvard University Press, 1957. 2 v. (xvi, 639 p.): ill., diagrs.; 24 cm. Each case published also separately under its respective title in the Harvard case histories in experimental science series. 1. Science — History 2. Science — Experiments I. T.
Q125.C57      507.2      *LC* 57-12843

**Crombie, A. C. (Alistair Cameron), 1915-.**                        **5.720**
Medieval and early modern science. — [2d ed.]. — Cambridge, Mass.: Harvard University Press, 1963 [c1961] 2 v.: ill., diagrs.; 19 cm. First published in London in 1952 under title: Augustine to Galileo; the history of science, A.D. 400-1650. 1. Science — History I. T.
Q125.C68 1963      509      *LC* 63-19150

**Crowther, J. G. (James Gerald), 1899-.**                          • **5.721**
The social relations of science / [by] J. G. Crowther. — Revised ed. London: Cresset P., 1967. xi, 474 p.: 2 diagrs.; 22 1/2 cm. 1. Science — History 2. Civilization I. T.
Q125.C74 1967      301.2/4      *LC* 67-78365

**Dampier, William Cecil Dampier, Sir, 1867-1952.**                  • **5.722**
A history of science and its relations with philosophy & religion. 4th ed. reprinted with a postscript by I. Bernard Cohen. London, Cambridge U.P., 1966. xxvii, 544 p. illus., tables, diagrs. 23 cm. 1. Science — History 2. Philosophy I. T.
Q125.D17 1966      509      *LC* 66-70313

**De Santillana, Giorgio, 1902-.**                                    **5.723**
The origins of scientific thought: from Anaximander to Proclus, 600 B.C. to 300 A.D. — [Chicago]: University of Chicago Press [1961] 320 p.: diagrs.; 23 cm. (The History of scientific thought, v. 1) 1. Science, Ancient I. T.
Q125.D34      509.3      *LC* 61-17073

**Dictionary of the history of science / edited by W.F. Bynum,**      **5.724**
**E.J. Browne, Roy Porter.**
Princeton, N.J.: Princeton University Press, c1981. 494 p.: ill.; 24 cm. 1. Science — History I. Bynum, W. F. (William F.), 1943- II. Browne, E. J. (E. Janet), 1950- III. Porter, Roy, 1946-
Q125.D45      509 19      *LC* 81-47116      *ISBN* 0691082871

**Dijksterhuis, E. J. (Eduard Jan), 1892-1965.**                      **5.725**
[Mechanisering van het wereldbeeld. English] The mechanization of the world picture: Pythagoras to Newton / by E.J. Dijksterhuis; translated by C. Dikshoorn; foreword by D.J. Struik. — Princeton, N.J.: Princeton University Press, 1986. p. cm. Translation of: De mechanisering van het werelbeeld. Reprint. Originally published: Oxford: Clarendon Press, 1961. Includes index. 1. Science — History 2. Science — Philosophy — History. 3. Philosophy, Ancient I. T.
Q125.D512 1986      509 19      *LC* 85-43374      *ISBN* 0691084033

**Farrington, Benjamin, 1891-.**                                      **5.726**
Science and politics in the ancient world / by Benjamin Farrington. — 2d. ed. — New York: Barnes & Noble, 1966. 243 p.; 22 cm. I. T.
Q125.F24 1966      509.3      *LC* 66-5242

**Forbes, R. J. (Robert James), 1900-.**                            • **5.727**
A history of science and technology / [by] R.J. Forbes and E.J. Dijksterhuis. Baltimore: Penguin Books, [1963] 2 v.: ill.; 18 cm. (Pelican books) 1. Science — History 2. Technology — History. I. Dijksterhuis, E. J. (Eduard Jan), 1892-1965. II. T.
Q125.F594      509      *LC* 63-2088

## Q125 G–J

**Gibson, William Carleton.** • **5.728**
Young endeavour: contributions to science by medical students of the past four centuries / with a foreword by Henry Dale. — Springfield, Ill.: Thomas [1958] 292 p.: ill.; 24 cm. 1. Science — History 2. Medicine — History I. T.
Q125.G48 1958  610.903  *LC* 58-8419

**Gillispie, Charles Coulston.** **5.729**
The edge of objectivity: an essay in the history of scientific ideas. — Princeton, N.J.: Princeton University Press, 1960. 562 p.: ill.; 23 cm. 1. Science — History 2. Science — Philosophy I. T.
Q125.G49  509  *LC* 60-5748

**Gjertsen, Derek.** **5.730**
The classics of science: a study of twelve enduring scientific works / Derek Gjertsen. — New York: Lilian Barber Press, 1984. iii, 374 p.: ill.; 25 cm. Includes index. 1. Science — History — Sources. I. T.
Q125.G54 1984  509 19  *LC* 83-27539  *ISBN* 0936508094

**Grant, Edward, 1926-.** **5.731**
Physical science in the Middle Ages. — New York: Wiley, [1971] xi, 128 p.: illus.; 22 cm. — (Wiley history of science series) 1. Science — History I. T.
Q125.G76  500.2/09/02  *LC* 70-151727  *ISBN* 0471322547

**Hall, A. Rupert (Alfred Rupert), 1920-.** **5.732**
The revolution in science, 1500–1750 / A. Rupert Hall. — 3rd ed. — London; New York: Longman, 1983. viii, 373 p.; 23 cm. Revision of: The scientific revolution, 1500-1800. 2nd ed. 1962. 1. Science — History 2. Science — Methodology 3. Science — Philosophy I. Hall, A. Rupert (Alfred Rupert), 1920- The scientific revolution, 1500-1800. 2nd ed. II. T.
Q125.H28 1983  509/.03 19  *LC* 82-8978  *ISBN* 0582491339

**Hall, Marie Boas, 1919-.** **5.733**
The scientific renaissance, 1450–1630 / Marie Boas. — New York: Harper & Brothers, 1962. 380 p.: ill. — (The Rise of modern science; 2) 1. Science, Medieval I. T.
Q125.H295  *LC* 62-8615  *ISBN* 0061305839

**Hankins, Thomas L.** **5.734**
Science and the Enlightenment / Thomas L. Hankins. — Cambridge; New York: Cambridge University Press, 1985. viii, 216 p.: ill.; 22 cm. (Cambridge history of science.) Includes index. 1. Science — History I. T. II. Series.
Q125.H355 1985  509 19  *LC* 84-16988  *ISBN* 0521243491

**Holton, Gerald James.** **5.735**
Thematic origins of scientific thought; Kepler to Einstein [by] Gerald Holton. — Cambridge, Mass.: Harvard University Press, 1973. 495 p.: illus.; 24 cm. 1. Science — History 2. Science — Philosophy 3. Physics — History. 4. Physics — Philosophy I. T.
Q125.H722  509  *LC* 72-88126  *ISBN* 0674877454

**Information sources in the history of science and medicine /** **5.736**
editors, Pietro Corsi, Paul Weindling.
London; Boston: Butterworth Scientific, 1983. xvi, 531 p.: ill.; 22 cm. (Butterworths guides to information sources.) Includes index. 1. Science — History — Information services. 2. Medicine — History — Information services. I. Corsi, Pietro. II. Weindling, Paul. III. Title: History of science and medicine. IV. Series.
Q125.I46 1983  509 19  *LC* 86-135026  *ISBN* 0408107642

**Institute for the History of Science, University of Wisconsin,** • **5.737**
**1957.**
Critical problems in the history of science: proceedings / edited by Marshall Clagett. — Madison: University of Wisconsin Press, 1959. xiv, 555 p.: chart, diagrs.; 25 cm. 1. Science — History — Collected works. I. Clagett, Marshall, 1916- ed. II. T.
Q125.I5 1957  509  *LC* 59-5304

**Jeans, James Hopwood, Sir, 1877-1946.** • **5.738**
The growth of physical science. [2d ed.]. Cambridge [Eng.]: Univeristy Press, 1951. x, 364 p.: ill.; 20 cm. 1. Science — History 2. Physics — History. I. T.
Q125.J4 1951  509  *LC* 51-10028

**Jeffries, Theodore W.** **5.739**
Science in civilization [by] Theodore W. Jeffries. — Dubuque, Iowa: Kendall/ Hunt Pub. Co., [1971] xi, 249 p.: illus.; 28 cm. 1. Science and civilization I. T.
Q125.J43  301.2/43  *LC* 78-169973  *ISBN* 0840304943

## Q125 K–R

**Knight, David M.** **5.740**
Sources for the history of science, 1660–1914 / by David Knight. — Ithaca, N.Y.: Cornell University Press, 1975. 223 p.; 23 cm. (The Sources of history, studies in the uses of historical evidence) 1. Science — History — Sources. I. T.
Q125.K57  509  *LC* 74-19776  *ISBN* 0801409411

**Laudan, Larry.** **5.741**
Progress and its problems: toward a theory of scientific growth / Larry Laudan. Berkeley: University of California Press, c1977. x, 257 p.; 24 cm. Includes index. 1. Science — History 2. Science — Philosophy I. T.
Q125.L34  501  *LC* 76-24586  *ISBN* 0520033302

**Marks, John.** **5.742**
Science and the making of the modern world / John Marks. — London; Exeter, N.H.: Heinemann, 1983. xiii, 507 p.: ill.; 24 cm. Includes index. 1. Science — History I. T.
Q125.M334 1983  509 19  *LC* 83-212054  *ISBN* 0435547801

**Menard, Henry W. (Henry William), 1920-1986.** **5.743**
Science: growth and change / [by] Henry W. Menard. — Cambridge, Mass.: Harvard University Press, 1971. xii, 215 p.: ill.; 25 cm. 1. Science — History 2. Scientific literature I. T.
Q125.M437  509  *LC* 77-156138  *ISBN* 0674792807

**Natural order: historical studies of scientific culture / edited by** **5.744**
**Barry Barnes and Steven Shapin.**
Beverly Hills, Calif.: Sage Publications, c1979. 255 p.; 22 cm. — (Sage focus editions.) 1. Science — History I. Barnes, Barry. II. Shapin, Steven. III. Title: Scientific culture. IV. Series.
Q125.N36  509  *LC* 78-19650  *ISBN* 0803909586

**Newman, James Roy, 1907-1966.** • **5.745**
Science and sensibility. New York: Simon and Schuster, 1961. 2 v.: ill.; 23 cm. 1. Science — History 2. Scientists 3. Philosophers I. T.
Q125.N48  509  *LC* 61-12869

**Bronfenbrenner, Martha Ornstein, 1879-1915.** **5.746**
The rôle of scientific societies in the seventeenth century, by Martha Ornstein. 3rd ed. — Chicago,Ill., The University of Chicago press [1938] 4 p.l., vii-xviii, 308 p. xiv pl. (incl. 2 port., facsims.) 23 cm. (The history of medicine series, issued under the auspices of the Library of the New York academy of medicine. no. 6) 'Privately printed, 1913 ... Published May 1928. Third edition May 1938.' 'In reprinting this study the editor has endeavored not to alter the text as printed in 1913.'—Editor's note, signed: Alfred E. Cohn. 1. Scientific societies — History. 2. Science — History I. Cohn, Alfred E. (Alfred Einstein), 1879-1957. ed. II. T.
Q125.O8 1938  506.2  *LC* 38-16977

**The Reception of unconventional science / edited by Seymour** **5.747**
**H. Mauskopf.**
Boulder, Colo.: Published by Westview Press for the American Association for the Advancement of Science, 1979. x, 137 p.; 24 cm. — (AAAS selected symposium; 25) 1. Science — History I. Mauskopf, Seymour H.
Q125.R357 1979  509/.04  *LC* 78-19735  *ISBN* 0891582975

**Reid, Robert William.** • **5.748**
Tongues of conscience: weapons research and the scientists' dilemma / [by] R. W. Reid. — New York: Walker, [1969] 351 p.; 24 cm. 1. Science — Social aspects 2. Science and ethics I. T.
Q125.R38 1969b  174/.9/6234072  *LC* 70-86964

**Ronan, Colin A.** **5.749**
Science, its history and development among the world's cultures / by Colin A. Ronan. — New York, NY: Facts on File, 1982. 543 p.: ill. Includes index. 1. Science — History I. T.
Q125.R7426 1983  509 19  *LC* 82-12176  *ISBN* 0871967456

## Q125 S–Z

**Science policies of industrial nations: case studies of the United** **5.750**
**States, Soviet Union, United Kingdom, France, Japan, and**
**Sweden / edited by T. Dixon Long, Christopher Wright.**
New York: Praeger, 1975. xiii, 232 p.; 25 cm. (Praeger special studies in international politics and government) Includes index. 1. Science and state 2. Technology and state I. Long, Theodore Dixon, 1933- II. Wright, Christopher, 1926-
Q125.S183  338.4/7/5  *LC* 74-13616  *ISBN* 0275056007

**Sarton, George, 1884-1956.** • **5.751**
A guide to the history of science: a first guide for the study of the history of science, with introductory essays on science and tradition. — Waltham, Mass.: Chronica Botanica Co., 1952. xvii, 316 p.: ill.; 24 cm. At head of title: Horus. Classified and annotated. 1. Science — History 2. Science — History — Bibliography. I. T.
Q125.S24  509  *LC* 52-10902

**Sarton, George, 1884-1956.**                                    • **5.752**
A history of science. — Cambridge: Harvard University Press, 1952-59. 2 v.: illus., maps, facsims.; 25 cm. No more published. 1. Science — History 2. Science, Ancient 3. Civilization, Ancient I. T.
Q125.S246      509/.01      *LC* 52-5041

**Sarton, George, 1884-1956.**                                    • **5.753**
The life of science: essays in the history of civilization / introd. by Conway Zirkle. — Bloomington: Indiana University Press [1960] 197 p.; 20 cm. (A Midland book, MB-27) 1. Science — History 2. Civilization I. T.
Q125.S323 1960      504      *LC* 60-50082

**Schroeer, Dietrich.**                                    **5.754**
Physics and its fifth dimension: society. — Reading, Mass.: Addison-Wesley Pub. Co., [1972] xvi, 378 p.: illus.; 22 cm. — (Addison-Wesley series in physics) 1. Science and state I. T.
Q125.S425      301.24/3      *LC* 75-184158

**Science in America, a documentary history, 1900–1939 / edited,**      **5.755**
**selected, and with an introduction by Nathan Reingold and Ida**
**H. Reingold.**
Chicago: University of Chicago Press, c1981. xii, 490 p.; 24 cm. — (Chicago history of science and medicine.) 1. Science — History 2. Science — United States — History. I. Reingold, Nathan, 1927- II. Reingold, Ida H. III. Series.
Q125.S43433      500 19      *LC* 81-2584      *ISBN* 0226709469

**Singer, Charles Joseph, 1876-1960.**                                    • **5.756**
From magic to science: essays on the scientific twilight. — New York: Dover Publications, [1958] 253 p.: ill.; 21 cm. 1. Gildas, 516?-570? 2. Hildegard, Saint, 1098-1179. 3. Science — History 4. Medicine — History 5. Medicine, Magic, mystic, and spagiric I. T.
Q125.S55 1958      509      *LC* 58-11284

**Singer, Charles Joseph, 1876-1960.**                                    • **5.757**
A short history of scientific ideas to 1900. Oxford: Clarendon Press, 1959. xviii, 525 p.: ill., maps, diagrs.; 23 cm. 'Based on ... A short history of science ... published in 1941.' 1. Science — History 2. Science — Philosophy I. T. II. Title: Scientific ideas to 1900.
Q125.S583      509      *LC* 59-4952

**Singer, Charles Joseph, 1876-1960. ed.**                                    **5.758**
Studies in the history and methods of science / edited by Charles Singer. — Oxford: Clarendon press, 1917-21. 2 v.: col. fronts., ill., plates (part. col.) ports., facsims. (part col.); 29 cm. 1. Science — History 2. Medicine — History I. T.
Q125.S6      *LC* 18-17504

**Taton, René. ed.**                                    **5.759**
[Histoire generale des sciences. English] History of science / translated by A. J. Pomerans. — New York: Basic Books, 1964-. v. : ill., ports.; 25 cm. Translation of Histoire générale des sciences. 1. Science — History I. T.
Q125.T233      509      *LC* 63-21689

**Thorndike, Lynn, 1882-1965.**                                    • **5.760**
A history of magic and experimental science / by Lynn Thorndike. — New York: Columbia University Press, 1934-1958. 8 v.; 23 cm. Vols. 3-6 published as History of Science Society publications, new ser., 4. 1. Science — History 2. Magic — History. I. T.
Q125.T52      *ISBN* 0231087942

**Wightman, W. P. D. (William Persehouse Delisle)**                                    • **5.761**
The growth of scientific ideas. Edinburgh: Oliver and Boyd, 1950. xii, 495 p.: ill., maps (on lining papers); 23 cm. 1. Science — History I. T.
Q125.W66      509      *LC* 50-14497

**Winter, Henry James Jacques.**                                    • **5.762**
Eastern science: an outline of its scope and contribution. — [1st ed.]. London: J. Murray [1952] vii, 114 p.; 18 cm. (The Wisdom of the East series) 1. Science — Asia — History. 2. Science — Philosophy — History. 3. Civilization, Ancient I. T.
Q125.W794      509.3      *LC* 52-10111

# Q125.1–126.8 Special Periods.
# Special Topics

**Murdoch, John Emery, 1927-.**                                    **5.763**
Antiquity and the Middle Ages / John E. Murdoch. — New York: Scribner, c1984. xii, 403 p.: ill.; 28 cm. (Album of science.) Includes index. 1. Scientific illustration — History. 2. Science, Ancient 3. Science, Medieval I. T. II. Series.
Q125.1.M8x      509/.01 19      *LC* 84-1400      *ISBN* 068415496X

**Debus, Allen G.**                                    **5.764**
Man and nature in the Renaissance / Allen G. Debus. — Cambridge; New York: Cambridge University Press, 1978. x, 159 p.; 22 cm. — (Cambridge history of science) Includes index. 1. Science, Renaissance 2. Science — Philosophy 3. Man 4. Nature I. T.
Q125.2.D4      509/.024      *LC* 77-91085      *ISBN* 0521219728

**Goldstein, Thomas.**                                    **5.765**
Dawn of modern science: from the Arabs to Leonardo da Vinci / Thomas Goldstein. — Boston: Houghton Mifflin, 1980. xvii, 297 p.: ill.; 24 cm. Includes indexes. 1. Science, Renaissance I. T.
Q125.2.G64      509/.024      *LC* 79-23753      *ISBN* 0395262984

**Williams, L. Pearce (Leslie Pearce), 1927-.**                                    **5.766**
The nineteenth century / L. Pearce Williams. — New York: Scribner, c1978. xiv, 413 p.: ill.; 28 cm. (Album of science.) (Scribner pictorial reference library) Includes index. 1. Science — History — Pictorial works. I. T. II. Series.
Q125.6.W54      509/.034 19      *LC* 77-3907      *ISBN* 0684150476

**Needham, Joseph, 1900-.**                                    **5.767**
Moulds of understanding: a pattern of natural philosophy / Joseph Needham; edited and introduced by Gary Werskey. New York: St. Martin's Press, 1976. 320 p.; 23 cm. 1. Science — History — Addresses, essays, lectures. 2. Science — Social aspects — Addresses, essays, lectures. I. T.
Q126.8.N44 1976      301.24/3/08      *LC* 75-37252

**Problems of scientific revolution: progress and obstacles to**      **5.768**
**progress in the sciences / edited by Rom Harré.**
Oxford: Clarendon Press, 1975. vi, 104 p., [1] leaf of plates: ill.; 22 cm. (Herbert Spencer lectures. 1973) 1. Science — History — Addresses, essays, lectures. 2. Science — Philosophy — Addresses, essays, lectures. I. Harré, Rom. II. Series.
Q126.8.P76      501      *LC* 75-327470

# Q127 By Country, A–Z

**Doern, G. Bruce.**                                    **5.769**
Science and politics in Canada [by] G. Bruce Doern. — Montreal: McGill-Queen's University Press, 1972. xiv, 238 p.: illus.; 24 cm. 1. Science and state — Canada. I. T.
Q127.C2 D64      354/.71/00855      *LC* 79-180255      *ISBN* 0773501088

**Ancient China's technology and science / compiled by the**      **5.770**
**Institute of the History of Natural Sciences, Chinese Academy**
**of Sciences.**
1st ed. — Beijing: Foreign Languages Press: Distributed by China Publications Centre, 1983. 632 p., [8] p. of plates: ill.; 21 cm. (China knowledge series.) Colophon in Chinese. Includes index. 1. Science — China — History. 2. Technology — China — History. I. Chung-kuo k'o hsüeh yüan. Tzu jan k'o hsüeh shih yen chiu so. II. Series.
Q127.C5 A74 1983      509.31 19      *LC* 83-222110      *ISBN* 083511001X

**Needham, Joseph, 1900-.**                                    • **5.771**
The grand titration: science and society in East and West. — Toronto: University of Toronto Press, [1969] 350 p.: ill.; 22 cm. 1. Science and civilization 2. Science — China — History. I. T.
Q127.C5 N42 1969b      301.2/4      *LC* 76-483302      *ISBN* 0802016367

**Needham, Joseph, 1900-.**                                    **5.772**
Science in traditional China: a comparative perspective / Joseph Needham. — Cambridge, Mass.: Harvard University Press, 1981. x, 134 p.: ill.; 24 cm. 1. Science — China — History. I. T.
Q127.C5 N46 1981      509.51 19      *LC* 81-6962      *ISBN* 0674794389

**Sigurdson, Jon.**                                    **5.773**
Technology and science in the People's Republic of China: an introduction / by Jon Sigurdson. — 1st ed. — Oxford; New York: Pergamon Press, 1980. vii, 169 p.: ill.; 26 cm. — (Pergamon international library of science, technology, engineering, and social studies) Includes index. 1. Science — China. 2. Technology — China. I. T.
Q127.C5 S56 1979      509/.51      *LC* 79-40575      *ISBN* 008024288X

**Tang, Tong B.**                                    **5.774**
Science and technology in China / Tong B. Tang. — London: Longman; Detroit, Mich.: Distributed by Gale Research, 1984. x, 269 p.: map; 24 cm. (Longman guide to world science and technology.) 3) Distributor from label mounted on t.p. Includes index. 1. Science — China. 2. Science and state — China. 3. Technology — China. 4. Technology and state — China. 5. Research — China. I. T. II. Series.
Q127.C5 T36 1984      509/.51 19      *LC* 84-132986      *ISBN* 0582900565

**Gillispie, Charles Coulston.**      **5.775**
Science and policy in France at the end of the old regime / Charles Coulston Gillispie. — Princeton, N.J.: Princeton University Press, 1981 (c1980). xii, 601 p.; 25 cm. Includes index. 1. Science — France — History. 2. Science and state — France. I. T.
Q127.F8 G53     509.44 19     LC 80-7521     ISBN 0691082332

**Cannon, Susan Faye.**      **5.776**
Science in culture: the early Victorian period / Susan Faye Cannon. — Kent, Eng.: Dawson; New York: Science History Publications, 1978. xii, 296 p.; 24 cm. Includes index. 1. Science — England — History. 2. Physics — England — History. I. T.
Q127.G4 C36 1978     509/.42     LC 77-26004     ISBN 0882021729

**Crowther, J. G. (James Gerald), 1899-.**      • **5.777**
Founders of British science: John Wilkins, Robert Boyle, John Ray, Christopher Wren, Robert Hooke, Isaac Newton. — London: Cresset Press, 1960. 296 p.: ill.; 23 cm. 1. Science — History — Great Britain. 2. Scientists — Great Britain. I. T.
Q127.G4 C77     509.42     LC 60-51868

**Hunter, Michael Cyril William.**      **5.778**
Science and society in restoration England / Michael Hunter. — Cambridge [Cambridgeshire]; New York: Cambridge University Press, 1981. xii, 233 p.; 23 cm. Includes index. 1. Science — England — History. 2. Science — Social aspects — England — History. I. T.
Q127.G4 H85     509.41 19     LC 80-41071     ISBN 0521228662

**Taylor, James, Sir, 1902-.**      **5.779**
The scientific community. London, Oxford University Press, 1973. viii, 79 p. 22 cm. (Science and engineering policy series) Includes index. 1. Science — Great Britain — History. 2. Technology — Great Britain — History. 3. Scientific societies — Great Britain. I. T.
Q127.G4 T39     509/.42     LC 73-172913     ISBN 0198583141

**Webster, Charles, 1936-.**      **5.780**
The great instauration: science, medicine and reform, 1626–1660 / Charles Webster. — New York: Holmes & Meier Publishers, 1976. xvi, 630 p.; 26 cm. Includes index. 1. Science — England — History — 17th century. 2. Medicine — England — History — 17th century. 3. Great Britain — History — Puritan Revolution, 1642-1660 I. T.
Q127.G4 W4 1976     509/.42     LC 76-4550     ISBN 0841902674

**Farrington, Benjamin, 1891-.**      • **5.781**
Greek science: its meaning for us. Baltimore: Penguin Books, [1961] 320 p.: ill.; 18 cm. — (Pelican books A142.) 1. Science — Greece — History. I. T.
Q127.G7 F3 1961     509.38     LC 61-66344

**Lloyd, G. E. R. (Geoffrey Ernest Richard), 1933-.**      **5.782**
Early Greek science: Thales to Aristotle [by] G. E. R. Lloyd. New York, Norton [1971, c1970] 156 p. illus., 1 map. 21 cm. (Ancient culture and society) 1. Science — Greece — History. I. T.
Q127.G7 L57 1971     509/.38     LC 77-128041     ISBN 0393043401

**Lloyd, G. E. R. (Geoffrey Ernest Richard), 1933-.**      **5.783**
Greek science after Aristotle [by] G. E. R. Lloyd. London, Chatto and Windus, 1973. xiv, 189 p. illus., map. 21 cm. (Ancient culture and society) 1. Science — Greece — History. 2. Technology — Greece — History. I. T.
Q127.G7 L58 1973b     509/.38     LC 73-156100     ISBN 070111889X
ISBN 0701119063

**Sardar, Ziauddin.**      **5.784**
Science, technology, and development in the Muslim world / Ziauddin Sardar. — Atlantic Highlands, N.J.: Humanities Press, c1977. 215 p.; 23 cm. Includes index. 1. Science — Islamic countries. 2. Technology — Islamic countries. 3. Research — Islamic countries. 4. Islam and science I. T.
Q127.I74 S27 1977     509/.17/671     LC 77-12756     ISBN 0391007718

**Sardar, Ziauddin.**      **5.785**
Science and technology in the Middle East: a guide to issues, organizations, and institutions / Ziauddin Sardar. — London; New York: Longman; Detroit, Mich., USA: Distributed exclusively in the USA and Canada by Gale Research Co., 1982. x, 324 p., [1] leaf of plates: ill.; 24 cm. — (Longman guide to world science and technology. 1) Includes indexes. 1. Science — Near East — Handbooks, manuals, etc. 2. Technology — Near East — Handbooks, manuals, etc. I. T. II. Series.
Q127.N15 S27 1982     338.956 19     LC 82-203337     ISBN 0582900522

**Graham, Loren R.**      **5.786**
Science and philosophy in the Soviet Union [by] Loren R. Graham. [1st ed.] New York, Knopf, 1972. xii, 584, xvi p. 25 cm. 1. Science — Soviet Union — History. 2. Dialectical materialism I. T.
Q127.R9 G72 1972     509/.47     LC 77-136313     ISBN 039444387X

**Vucinich, Alexander, 1914-.**      • **5.787**
Science in Russian culture. Stanford, Calif., Stanford University Press, 1963-. v. 24 cm. 1. Science — History — Soviet Union. I. T.
Q127.R9 V8     509.47     LC 63-19238

# Q127.U6 UNITED STATES

**Baxter, James Phinney, 1893-.**      • **5.788**
Scientists against time. Cambridge, Mass.: M.I.T. Press [1968] xxi, 473 p.: ill., maps, ports.; 21 cm. Reprint of the 1946 ed. 1. United States. Office of Scientific Research and Development. 2. Science — United States — History. 3. Scientists — United States I. T.
Q127.U6 B3 1968     623/.072/073     LC 68-25373

**Daniels, George H.**      • **5.789**
Science in American society; a social history [by] George H. Daniels. — [1st ed.]. — New York: Knopf, 1971. xii, 390, x p.; 25 cm. 1. Science — United States — History. 2. Science and civilization I. T.
Q127.U6 D33     301.2/43/0973     LC 79-118708     ISBN 0394443861

**Dickson, David, 1947-.**      **5.790**
The new politics of science / David Dickson. — 1st American ed. — New York: Pantheon Books, c1984. 404 p.; 24 cm. Includes index. 1. Science and state 2. Science — Social aspects 3. Technology and state 4. Technology — Social aspects I. T.
Q127.U6 D53 1984     306/.45 19     LC 83-19408     ISBN 0394524047

**Greene, John C.**      **5.791**
American science in the age of Jefferson / John C. Greene. — 1st ed. — Ames: Iowa State University Press, 1984. xiv, 484 p., [2] leaves of plates: ill. (some col.); 24 cm. 1. Jefferson, Thomas, 1743-1826. 2. Science — United States — History. I. T.
Q127.U6 G69 1984     509.73 19     LC 83-8513     ISBN 081380101X

**Historical writing on American science: perspectives and prospects** / edited by Sally Gregory Kohlstedt and Margaret W. Rossiter.      **5.792**
Baltimore, Md.: Johns Hopkins University Press, 1986. p. cm. Reprint. Originally published: Philadelphia, PA: History of Science Society, 1985. Originally published in series: Osiris. Includes index. 1. Science — United States — History. I. Kohlstedt, Sally Gregory, 1943- II. Rossiter, Margaret W.
Q127.U6 H54 1986     509/.73 19     LC 86-20890     ISBN 0801834384

**Jaffe, Bernard, 1896-.**      • **5.793**
Men of science in America: the story of American science told through the lives and achievements of twenty outstanding men from earliest colonial times to the present day. — Rev. ed. — New York: Simon and Schuster, 1958. 715 p.: ill.; 22 cm. 1. Scientists — United States 2. Science — United States — History. I. T.
Q127.U6 J27 1958     509/.2/2     LC 58-59443

**Katz, James Everett.**      **5.794**
Presidential politics and science policy / James Everett Katz; foreword by Irving Louis Horowitz. — New York: Praeger, 1978. xix, 292 p.; 25 cm. Includes index. 1. Science and state — United States. 2. Technology and state — United States 3. Research — United States 4. Presidents — United States 5. Executive power — United States I. T.
Q127.U6 K37     509/.73     LC 77-14024     ISBN 0030409411

**Lambright, W. Henry, 1939-.**      **5.795**
Presidential management of science and technology: the Johnson presidency / by W. Henry Lambright. — 1st ed. — Austin: University of Texas Press, 1985. xii, 224 p.; 24 cm. (An Administrative history of the Johnson presidency series) Includes index. 1. Johnson, Lyndon B. (Lyndon Baines), 1908-1973. 2. Science and state — United States — History. 3. Technology and state — United States — History. 4. United States — Politics and government — 1963-1969 I. T.
Q127.U6 L29 1985     338.97306 19     LC 84-28420     ISBN 0292764944

**Rosenberg, Charles E.**      **5.796**
No other gods: on science and American social thought / Charles E. Rosenberg. — Baltimore: Johns Hopkins University Press, c1976. xiii, 273 p.; 24 cm. Includes index. 1. Science — United States — History. 2. Science — Social aspects — United States. 3. United States — Social conditions — 1865-1918 I. T.
Q127.U6 R618     301.24/3/0973     LC 75-36942     ISBN 0801817110

**Struik, Dirk Jan, 1894-.**      • **5.797**
Yankee science in the making. New rev. ed. New York: Collier Books [1962] 544 p.; 18 cm. 1. Science — United States — History. I. T.
Q127.U6 S8 1962     509.73     LC 62-12299

**Trenn, Thaddeus J.**                                                          **5.798**
America's golden bough: the science advisory intertwist / Thaddeus J. Trenn. — Cambridge, Mass.: Oelgeschlager, Gunn & Hain, c1983. xxviii, 307 p.: ill.; 24 cm. Includes index. 1. Science and state — United States. I. T.
Q127.U6 T73 1983        338.4/75/0973 19        *LC* 82-18873        *ISBN* 0899461603

**Wiesner, Jerome B. (Jerome Bert), 1915-.**                              • **5.799**
Where science and politics meet / by Jerome B. Wiesner. — New York: McGraw-Hill [1965] viii, 302 p.; 21 cm. 1. Science and state — United States. I. T.
Q127.U6 W5        509.73        *LC* 65-16157

**Wilson, John T. (John Todd), 1914-.**                                       **5.800**
Academic science, higher education, and the federal government, 1950–1983 / John T. Wilson. — Chicago: University of Chicago Press, 1983. ix, 116 p.; 22 cm. 'This essay was originally prepared as part of the seminar 'Higher Education and the Federal Government,' Department of Education, University of Chicago, spring quarter, 1983'—T.p. verso. 1. Science and state — United States — History. 2. Higher education and state — United States — History. I. T.
Q127.U6 W534 1983        353.0085/5/09 19        *LC* 83-17964        *ISBN* 0226900517

# Q130–143 Biography

**Climbing the ladder: an update on the status of doctoral women**       **5.801**
**scientists and engineers / Committee on the Education and**
**Employment of Women in Science and Engineering, Office of**
**Scientific and Engineering Personnel, National Research**
**Council.**
Washington, D.C.: National Academy Press, 1983. 106 p. in various pagings: ill.; 28 cm. 1. Women scientists — United States. 2. Women engineers — United States. 3. Women in science — United States. 4. Women in engineering — United States. 5. Doctor of philosophy degree — United States. 6. Universities and colleges — United States — Graduate work of women. I. National Research Council (U.S.). Committee on the Education and Employment of Women in Science and Engineering.
Q130.C54 1983        331.4/815/0973 19        *LC* 83-60184        *ISBN* 0309033411

**Merchant, Carolyn.**                                                         **5.802**
The death of nature: women, ecology, and the scientific revolution / Carolyn Merchant. — 1st ed. — San Francisco: Harper & Row, c1980. xx, 348 p.: ill.; 22 cm. 1. Women in science — Social aspects. 2. Philosophy of nature 3. Human ecology I. T.
Q130.M47 1980        301.31        *LC* 79-1766        *ISBN* 0062505718

**Rossiter, Margaret W.**                                                      **5.803**
Women scientists in America: struggles and strategies to 1940 / Margaret W. Rossiter. — Baltimore: Johns Hopkins University Press, c1982. xviii, 439 p.: ill.; 24 cm. Includes index. 1. Women scientists — United States. 2. Women in science — United States. I. T.
Q130.R68 1982        331.4/815/0973 19        *LC* 81-20902        *ISBN* 0801824435

**Women and minorities in science: strategies for increasing**            **5.804**
**participation / edited by Sheila M. Humphreys.**
Boulder, Colo.: Published by Westview Press for the American Association for the Advancement of Science, 1982. xvi, 218 p.: ill.; 24 cm. (AAAS selected symposium. 66) 'Based on a symposium ... held at the 1980 AAAS national annual meeting in San Francisco, California, January 3-8'—Copr. p. 1. Women in science — United States — Addresses, essays, lectures. 2. Minorities in science — United States — Addresses, essays, lectures. I. Humphreys, Sheila M. II. American Association for the Advancement of Science. III. Series.
Q130.W65        509 19        *LC* 81-19843        *ISBN* 0865313172

**Women in scientific and engineering professions / edited by**           **5.805**
**Violet B. Haas and Carolyn C. Perrucci, with the assistance of**
**Jean E. Brenchley ... [et al.].**
Ann Arbor: University of Michigan Press, c1984. viii, 246 p.: ill.; 23 cm. — (Women and culture series.) Papers originally presented as part of a national Conference on Women in the Professions: Science, Social Science, Engineering, which was held at Purdue University, Mar. 20-21, 1981. 1. Women in science — Congresses. 2. Women in engineering — Congresses. 3. Women scientists — Congresses. 4. Women engineers — Congresses. I. Haas, Violet B., 1921- II. Perrucci, Carolyn Cummings. III. Series.
Q130.W66 1984        305.4 19        *LC* 83-23575        *ISBN* 0472080423

**American men & women of science: physical and biological**              **5.806**
**sciences / edited by Jaques Cattell Press.**
16th ed. — New York: R.R. Bowker, 1986. — 8 v.; 29 cm. 1. Scientists — United States — Biography — Directories. 2. Scientists — Canada — Biography — Directories. 3. Scholars — United States — Biography — Directories. 4. Scholars — Canada — Biography — Directories. I. Cattell, Jaques, 1904-1960. II. Title: American men and women of science.
Q141.A427 1986        *ISBN* 0835222217

**Asimov, Isaac, 1920-.**                                                     **5.807**
Asimov's biographical encyclopedia of science and technology: the lives and achievements of 1510 great scientists from ancient times to the present chronologically arranged / by Isaac Asimov. — 2nd rev. ed. — Garden City, N.Y.: Doubleday, 1982. xxxv, 941 p., [24] p. of plates: ill.; 24 cm. Includes index. 1. Scientists — Biography I. T. II. Title: Biographical encyclopedia of science and technology.
Q141.A74 1982        509/.2/2 B 19        *LC* 81-47861        *ISBN* 0385177712

**Dictionary of scientific biography / Charles Coulston Gillispie,**      **5.808**
**editor in chief.**
New York: Scribner, 1981, c1980. 16 v. in 8; 29 cm. 'Published under the auspices of the American Council of Learned Societies.' 1. Scientists — Biography I. Gillispie, Charles Coulston. II. American Council of Learned Societies.
Q141.D5 1981        509/.2/2 B 19        *LC* 80-27830        *ISBN* 0684169622

**Elliott, Clark A.**                                                         **5.809**
Biographical dictionary of American science: the seventeenth through the nineteenth centuries / Clark A. Elliott; consultant editors, Sally Gregory Kohlstedt ... [et. al.]. — Westport, Conn.: Greenwood Press, 1979. xvii, 360 p.; 29 cm. 'A retrospective companion to American men of science.' 1. Scientists — United States — Biography. I. American men of science. II. T.
Q141.E37        509/.2/2 B        *LC* 78-4292        *ISBN* 0313204195

**McGraw–Hill modern scientists and engineers.**                         **5.810**
New York: McGraw-Hill, c1980. 3 v.: ill.; 29 cm. Edition of 1966-1968 published under title: McGraw-Hill modern men of science. 1. Scientists — Biography 2. Engineers — Biography. I. McGraw-Hill Book Company. II. McGraw-Hill modern men of science. III. Title: Modern scientists and engineers.
Q141.M15 1980        509/.22 19        *LC* 79-24383        *ISBN* 0070452660

**National Academy of Sciences (U.S.)**                                   • **5.811**
Biographical memoirs. v. 1-. Washington, National Academy of Sciences, 1877-. v. ports. 24 cm. 1. Scientists — United States I. T.
Q141.N2        *LC* 05-26629

**Ogilvie, Marilyn Bailey.**                                                 **5.812**
Women in science: antiquity through the nineteenth century: a biographical dictionary with annotated bibliography / Marilyn Bailey Ogilvie. — Cambridge, Mass.: MIT Press, c1986. xi, 254 p.; 27 cm. Includes index. 1. Women scientists — Biography. 2. Women in science — Bibliography. 3. Science — Bibliography I. T.
Q141.O34 1986        509.2/2 B 19        *LC* 86-7507        *ISBN* 026215031X

**A Passion to know: 20 profiles in science / Allen L. Hammond,**         **5.813**
**editor.**
New York: Scribner, c1984. xii, 240 p., [1] leaf of plates: ports.; 24 cm. Includes index. 1. Scientists — Biography 2. Science — History I. Hammond, Allen L.
Q141.P374 1984        509.2/2 B 19        *LC* 84-16145        *ISBN* 0684182092

**Pelletier, Paul A., 1944-.**                                               **5.814**
Prominent scientists: an index to collective biographies / edited by Paul A. Pelletier. — New York: Neal-Schuman, c1980. xxviii, 311 p.; 26 cm. 1. Scientists — Biography — Indexes. I. T.
Q141.P398        509/.2/2 B 19        *LC* 80-23224        *ISBN* 0918212413

**Roe, Anne, 1904-.**                                                        • **5.815**
The making of a scientist. New York: Dodd, Mead [1953] 244 p.; 22 cm. 1. Scientists I. T.
Q141.R52        506.9        *LC* 53-8405

**World who's who in science: a biographical dictionary of notable**      • **5.816**
**scientists from antiquity to the present. Editor: Allen G. Debus.**
**Associate editors: Ronald S. Calinger [and] Edward J. Collins.**
**Managing editor: Stephen J. Kennedy.**
1st ed. — Chicago: Marquis-Who's Who, inc., [1968] xvi, 1855 p.; 28 cm. — (Marquis biographical library) 1. Scientists — Biography — Directories. I. Debus, Allen G. ed. II. Marquis Who's Who, Inc.
Q141.W7        509/.22        *LC* 68-56149        *ISBN* 0837910013

# Q143 Individual Biography

**Ore, Øystein, 1899-1968.**　　　　　　　　　• **5.817**
Cardano: the gambling scholar / by Øystein Ore; with a translation from the Latin of Cardano's Book on games of chance by Sidney Henry Gould. — New York: Dover Publications, 1965, c1953. xiv, 249 p.: ill., ports. Includes index. 1. Cardano, Girolamo, 1501-1576. 2. Gambling I. Cardano, Girolamo, 1501-1576. Liber de ludo aleae. English. 1953 II. T.
Q143.C3.O7 1965　　*LC* 65-17670

**Gillmor, C. Stewart, 1938-.**　　　　　　　　　**5.818**
Coulomb and the evolution of physics and engineering in eighteenth–century France [by] C. Stewart Gillmor. Princeton, N.J., Princeton University Press, 1971 [i.e. 1972, c1971] xvii, 328 p. illus. 25 cm. 1. Coulomb, C. A. (Charles Augustin), 1736-1806. 2. Physics — France — History — 18th century. 3. Engineering — France — History. I. T.
Q143.C65 G55　　　530/.0924 B　　*LC* 79-155006　　*ISBN* 069108095X

**Shirley, John William, 1908-.**　　　　　　　　　**5.819**
Thomas Harriot, a biography / by John W. Shirley. — Oxford [Oxfordshire]: Clarendon Press; New York: Oxford University Press, 1983. xii, 508 p.; 22 cm. Includes index. 1. Hariot, Thomas, 1560-1621. 2. Scientists — Great Britain — Biography. 3. Science — Great Britain — History — Sources. I. T.
Q143.H36 S46 1983　　510/.92/4 B 19　　*LC* 83-3961　　*ISBN* 0198229011

**De Terra, Helmut, 1900-.**　　　　　　　　　• **5.820**
Humboldt: the life and times of Alexander von Humboldt, 1769–1859. — [1st ed.]. New York: Knopf, 1955. xii, 386, ix p.: ill., ports., maps; 22 cm. 1. Humboldt, Alexander von, 1769-1859. I. T.
Q143.H9 D4　　925　　*LC* 55-5606

**Killian, James Rhyne, 1904-.**　　　　　　　　　**5.821**
Sputnik, scientists, and Eisenhower: a memoir of the first special assistant to the President for science and technology / James R. Killian, Jr. — Cambridge, Mass.: MIT Press, c1977. xix, 315 p.: ill.; 24 cm. Includes index. 1. Killian, James Rhyne, 1904- 2. Eisenhower, Dwight D. (Dwight David), 1890-1969. 3. Technology and state — United States 4. Science and state — United States. 5. United States — History — Sources I. T.
Q143.K42 A37　　353.008/55/0924　　*LC* 77-21560　　*ISBN* 0262110660

**Hart, Ivor Blashka, 1889-.**　　　　　　　　　• **5.822**
The mechanical investigations of Leonardo da Vinci. With a foreword by Ernest A. Moody. — [2d ed.]. — Berkeley: University of California Press, 1963. 240 p.: ill.; 21 cm. 1. Leonardo, da Vinci, 1452-1519. 2. Aeronautics 3. Flight 4. Mechanics — History I. T.
Q143.L5H3 1963　　620.1　　*LC* 63-2320

**Zammattio, Carlo.**　　　　　　　　　**5.823**
Leonardo the scientist / Carlo Zammattio, Augusto Marinoni, Anna Maria Brizio. — New York: McGraw-Hill, 1980. 192 p.: ill. (some col.); 21 cm. Essays originally published in The unknown Leonardo, edited by Ladislao Reti, with additional illustrations. 1. Leonardo, da Vinci, 1452-1519. 2. Scientists — Italy — Biography. I. Marinoni, Augusto. joint author. II. Brizio, Anna Maria. joint author. III. Reti, Ladislao. Unknown Leonardo IV. T.
Q143.L5 Z28 1980b　　509/.2/4　　*LC* 80-10622　　*ISBN* 0070727236

**Dubos, René J. (René Jules), 1901-.**　　　　　　　　　• **5.824**
Louis Pasteur: free lance of science / by Rene J. Dubos. — 1st ed. — Boston: Little, Brown, 1950. — xii, 418 p., [7] leaves of plates: ports. Includes index. 1. Pasteur, Louis, 1822-1895. I. T.
Q143.P2 D78　　591.23/22/0924　　*LC* 50-5543

**Stegner, Wallace Earle, 1909-.**　　　　　　　　　• **5.825**
Beyong the hundredth meridian: John Wesley Powell and the second opening of the West / with an introd. by Bernard De Voto. — Boston: Houghton, Mifflin, 1954. xxiii, 438 p.: ill., maps; 22 cm. 1. Powell, John Wesley, 1834-1902. 2. West (U.S.) — History — 1848-1950 I. T.
Q143.P8 S8　　925　　*LC* 53-9245

**Brown, Sanborn Conner, 1913-.**　　　　　　　　　**5.826**
Benjamin Thompson, Count Rumford / Sanborn C. Brown. — Cambridge, Mass.: MIT Press, c1979. xii, 361 p.: ill.; 24 cm. 1. Rumford, Benjamin, Graf von, 1753-1814. 2. Scientists — Great Britain — Biography. I. T.
Q143.R8 B69　　530/.092/4 B　　*LC* 79-9110　　*ISBN* 0262021382

# Q145 DIRECTORIES

**Scientific and technical organizations and agencies directory.**　　**5.827**
1st ed.-　　. — Detroit, Mich.: Gale Research Co., c1985-. v.; 29 cm. Issued in parts. Supplements issued between editions. 1. Science — United States — Societies, etc. — Directories. 2. Engineering — United States — Societies, etc. — Directories. 3. Technology — United States — Societies, etc. — Directories. 4. United States — Executve departments — Directories. I. Young, Margaret Labash. II. Gale Research Company.
Q145.S35　　506/.073 19　　*LC* 86-641378

# Q147–149 SCIENCE AS A PROFESSION

**Ben-David, Joseph.**　　　　　　　　　**5.828**
The scientist's role in society: a comparative study: with a new introduction / Joseph Ben-David. — Chicago: University of Chicago Press, 1984. xxvi, 209 p.: ill.; 23 cm. Reprint. Originally published: Englewood Cliffs, N.J.: Prentice-Hall, c1971. 1. Scientists 2. Science and civilization I. T.
Q147.B45 1984　　303.4/83 19　　*LC* 84-2758　　*ISBN* 0226042219

**Connolly, Terry.**　　　　　　　　　**5.829**
Scientists, engineers, and organizations / Terry Connolly. — Monterey, Calif.: Brooks/Cole Engineering Division, c1983. xii, 388 p.: ill.; 24 cm. Includes indexes. 1. Science — Vocational guidance 2. Engineering — Vocational guidance 3. Organizational behavior I. T.
Q147.C57 1983　　650.1/0245 19　　*LC* 82-22703　　*ISBN* 0534014097

**Klaw, Spencer, 1920-.**　　　　　　　　　• **5.830**
The new brahmins; scientific life in America. New York, Morrow, 1968. 315 p. 22 cm. 1. Scientists — United States 2. Science — Vocational guidance — United States. I. T.
Q147.K55　　502/.3　　*LC* 68-31960

**Zuckerman, Harriet.**　　　　　　　　　**5.831**
Scientific elite: Nobel laureates in the United States / Harriet Zuckerman. — New York: Free Press, c1977. xv, 335 p.: ill.; 24 cm. Includes index. 1. Scientists — United States 2. Nobel prizes 3. Science — Social aspects — United States. 4. Scientists — United States — Biography. I. T.
Q149.U5 Z8　　507/.2073　　*LC* 76-26444　　*ISBN* 0029357608

# Q151–157 SCIENCE: EARLY WORKS TO 1800

**Aristotle.**　　　　　　　　　**5.832**
[De generatione et corruptione. English] Aristotle's De generatione et corruptione / translated with notes by C.J.F. Williams. — Oxford; New York: Oxford University Press, 1982. xvi, 239 p.; 21 cm. — (Clarendon Aristotle series) Translation of: De generatione et corruptione. Includes index. 1. Aristotle. De generatione et corruptione. I. Williams, Christopher John Fards. II. T. III. Title: De generatione et corruptione. IV. Series.
Q151.A613 1982　　500 19　　*LC* 81-21727　　*ISBN* 0198720629

**Aristotle.**　　　　　　　　　• **5.833**
[Physics. Book 1-2. English] Aristotle's Physics: Books 1 & 2 / translated [from the Greek]; with introduction and notes by W. Charlton. — Oxford: Clarendon P., 1970. xvii, 151 p.; 21 cm. (Clarendon Aristotle series) 1. Science, Ancient 2. Physics — Early works to 1800. I. Charlton, W., tr. II. T. III. Title: Physics.
Q151.A72 1970　　501　　*LC* 70-503838　　*ISBN* 0198720254

**Aristotle.**　　　　　　　　　**5.834**
[Physics. Book 3-4. English] Aristotle's Physics, books III and IV / translated with notes by Edward Hussey. — Oxford [Oxfordshire]: Clarendon Press; New York: Oxford University Press, 1983. xlix, 226 p.; 21 cm. — (Clarendon

Aristotle series.) Translation of: Physics. Includes indexes. 1. Science, Ancient 2. Physics — Early works to 1800. I. Hussey, Edward. II. T. III. Series.
Q151.A7913 1983      500.2 19      *LC* 82-18996      *ISBN* 0198720688

**Descartes, René, 1596-1650.**                                      **5.835**
[Monde. English & French] Le monde, ou, Traité de la lumière / René Descartes; translation and introduction by Michael Sean Mahoney. — New York: Abaris Books, 1979. xxvi, 224 p.: ill.; 24 cm. — (Janus series. 2) English and French. Spine title: The world. 1. Science — Early works to 1800 2. Science — History — Sources. I. T. II. Title: Monde. III. Title: World. IV. Series.
Q155.D43513 1979      500 19      *LC* 77-86236      *ISBN* 0913870358

---

# Q158–163 Science: General Works, 1801–

---

**The Encyclopaedia of ignorance: everything you ever wanted to**      **5.836**
**know about the unknown** / edited by Ronald Duncan and
**Miranda Weston–Smith.**
Oxford [Eng.]; New York: Pergamon Press, 1977. x, 443 p.: ill. 1. Science I. Duncan, Ronald Frederick Henry, 1914- II. Weston-Smith, Miranda.
Q158.5.E53      500      *ISBN* 0080212387

**Harrington, John Wilbur, 1918-.**                                  **5.837**
Discovering science / John W. Harrington; [cover photo. by James Scherer]. — Boston: Houghton Mifflin, c1981. xvi, 184 p.: ill.; 24 cm. 1. Science I. T.
Q160.2.H37      500 19      *LC* 80-80721      *ISBN* 0395255279

**Gamow, George, 1904-1968.**                                      • **5.838**
One, two, three ... infinity: facts & speculations of science / illustrated by the author. — [Explorer books ed., newly rev. by the author]. — New York: Viking Press, [1961] 340 p.: ill.; 20 cm. — (Viking explorer books, X21) 1. Science I. T.
Q162.G23 1961      500      *LC* 61-3926

**Goswami, Amit.**                                                  **5.839**
The cosmic dancers: exploring the physics of science fiction / by Amit Goswami, with Maggie Goswami. — 1st ed. — New York: Harper & Row, c1983. xi, 292 p.: ill.; 25 cm. Includes index. 1. Science — Popular works. 2. Physics — Popular works. 3. Science fiction — History and criticism I. Goswami, Maggie. II. T.
Q162.G67 1983      809.3/876 19      *LC* 82-48118      *ISBN* 0060150831

**Weisskopf, Victor Frederick, 1908-.**                              **5.840**
Knowledge and wonder, the natural world as man knows it / Victor F. Weisskopf. — 2d ed. — Cambridge, Mass.: MIT Press, 1979. xi, 290 p.: ill.; 21 cm. Includes index. 1. Science — Popular works. I. T.
Q162.W4 1979      500      *LC* 79-19148      *ISBN* 0262230984

---

# Q171–173 Addresses. Essays. Lectures

---

**Bernstein, Jeremy, 1929-.**                                        **5.841**
A comprehensible world: on modern science and its origins. — New York: Random House, [1967] xii, 269 p.; 22 cm. 'Articles ... appeared originally in the New Yorker.' 1. Science — Addresses, essays, lectures. I. T.
Q171.B5373      501      *LC* 67-12740

**Bronowski, Jacob, 1908-1974.**                                    • **5.842**
Science and human values. — Rev. ed. with a new dialogue, The abacus and the rose, by J. Bronowski. — New York: Harper & Row, [1965] xiv, 119 p.: illus.; 21 cm. 'The three essays which make up Science and human values were first given as lectures at the Massachusetts Institute of Technology on 26 February, 5 March and 19 March 1953.' The dialogue was originally broadcast by the BBC Third programme in 1962. 1. Science — Addresses, essays, lectures. I. T. II. Title: The abacus and the rose.
Q171.B8785 1965      508.1      *LC* 65-1816

**Conant, James Bryant, 1893-1978.**                                • **5.843**
Modern science and modern man. New York: Columbia University Press, 1952. 111 p.; 21 cm. (Bampton lectures in America, no. 5) 1. Science — Addresses, essays, lectures. 2. Science — Philosophy I. T.
Q171.C76225 1952      504      *LC* 52-14147

**Dubos, René J. (René Jules), 1901-.**                              **5.844**
The dreams of reason; science and utopias. New York, Columbia University Press, 1961. xii, 167 p. illus., ports. 23 cm. (The George B. Pegram lectures) 1. Science — Addresses, essays, lectures. I. T. II. Title: Science and utopias. III. Series.
Q171.D73      508.1      *LC* 61-11753

**Haldane, J. B. S. (John Burdon Sanderson), 1892-1964.**           • **5.845**
What is life? London, L. Drummond [1949] x, 261 p. 20 cm. 1. Science — Addresses, essays, lectures. 2. Biology — Addresses, essays, lectures. I. T.
Q171.H1565 1949      *LC* 50-55610

**Huxley, Thomas Henry, 1825-1895.**                                **5.846**
Autobiography and essays / by Thomas Henry Huxley; ed. by Brander Matthews. — New York: Kraus Reprint, 1969. 276 p.: 1 portr. — (Living literature series) 1. Science — Addresses, essays, lectures I. Matthews, Brander, 1852-1929. II. T.
Q171.H914 1969      *LC* 20-195

**Medawar, P. B. (Peter Brian), 1915-.**                            **5.847**
The hope of progress: a scientist looks at problems in philosophy, leterature and science / [by] Peter B. Medawar. — [1st ed. in U.S.A.] Garden City, N.Y.: Anchor Press [1973, c1972] 145 p.; 18 cm. 1. Science — Addresses, essays, lectures. I. T.
Q171.M45 1973      508/.1      *LC* 73-81423      *ISBN* 0385076150

**Oppenheimer, J. Robert.**                                         • **5.848**
Science and the common understanding. New York: Simon and Schuster, 1954. 120 p. (Reith lectures. 1953.) 1. Science — Addresses, essays, lectures. I. T. II. Series.
Q171.O6      504      *LC* 54-8650

**Polanyi, Michael, 1891-.**                                        • **5.849**
Science, faith and society. — [Chicago]: University of Chicago Press, [1964] 96 p.; 21 cm. 1. Science — Addresses, essays, lectures. I. T.
Q171.P77 1964      508.1      *LC* 64-22254

**Price, Derek J. de Solla (Derek John de Solla), 1922-1983.**      • **5.850**
Little science, big science / Derek J. de Solla Price. — New York: Columbia University Press, 1963. xv, 119 p.: ill. — (George B. Pegram lectures; 1962) 1. Science — Addresses, essays, lectures. 2. Scientists I. T.
Q171.P9464      *LC* 63-10524      *ISBN* 0231085621

**Price, Derek John de Solla.**                                     • **5.851**
Science since Babylon. — New Haven: Yale University Press, 1961. 149 p.: illus.; 22 cm. 1. Science 2. Science — History I. T.
Q171.P9465      509      *LC* 61-10186

**Shapley, Harlow, 1885-1972.**                                     • **5.852**
Readings in the physical sciences / edited by Harlow Shapley, Helen Wright [and] Samuel Rapport. — New York: Appleton-Century-Crofts, [1948] xiii, 502 p.: ill. 1. Science — Addresses, essays, lectures. I. Wright, Helen, 1914- II. Rapport, Samuel Berder, 1903- III. T.
Q171.S5823      504      *LC* 48-8683

**Weizsäcker, Carl Friedrich, Freiherr von, 1912-.**                • **5.853**
The relevance of science: creation and cosmogony / [by] C. F. Weizsäcker. — New York: Harper, [c1964]. 192 p. — (Gifford lectures. 1959-60) 1. Science — Addresses, essays, lectures. I. T. II. Series.
Q171.W42 1964      508.1

**Whitehead, Alfred North, 1861-1947.**                             • **5.854**
Science and the modern world. Lowell lectures, 1925, by Alfred North Whitehead. — New York: The Macmillan company, 1948, c1925. xii, 304 p.; 23 cm. 1. Science — Addresses, essays, lectures. I. Lowell institute lectures, 1925. II. T.
Q171.W55 1948      504

**Science, technology, and economic development: a historical and**      **5.855**
**comparative study** / edited by William Beranek, Jr., Gustav
**Ranis.**
New York: Praeger Publishers, 1978. xv, 347 p.: ill.; 25 cm. 'Papers ... presented on October 11, 1976, at the NAS Bicentennial Symposium.' 1. Science 2. Technology 3. Economic development I. Beranek, William, 1946- II. Ranis, Gustav. III. National Academy of Sciences (U.S.)
Q172.S33      500      *LC* 78-5660      *ISBN* 0030418011

**Teller, Edward, 1908-.**                                          **5.856**
The pursuit of simplicity / Edward Teller. — Malibu, Calif.: Pepperdine University Press, c1980. 173 p.: ill.; 23 cm. Based on 5 lectures given at Pepperdine University in 1978-1979. Includes index. 1. Science I. T.
Q172.T44      500 19      *LC* 80-82499      *ISBN* 0932612024

**Broad, William, 1951-.** **5.857**
Betrayers of the truth / by William Broad and Nicholas Wade. — New York: Simon and Schuster, 1982. 256 p.; 22 cm. 1. Fraud in science I. Wade, Nicholas. II. T.
Q172.5.F7 B76    507/.24 19    *LC* 82-10583    *ISBN* 0671447696

**Rosen, Joe.** **5.858**
Symmetry discovered: concepts and applications in nature and science / Joe Rosen. — Cambridge; New York: Cambridge University Press, 1975. xi, 138 p.: ill.; 24 cm. Includes index. 1. Symmetry I. T.
Q172.5.S95 R67    500    *LC* 75-6006    *ISBN* 0521206952

**Rosen, Joe.** **5.859**
A symmetry primer for scientists / Joe Rosen. — New York: Wiley, c1983. xi, 192 p.: ill.; 24 cm. 'A Wiley-Interscience publication.' Includes index. 1. Symmetry 2. Groups, Theory of I. T.
Q172.5.S95 R674 1983    500 19    *LC* 82-10876    *ISBN* 0471876720

# Q174–175 Philosophy. Methodology

**Krige, John.** **5.860**
Science, revolution, and discontinuity / John Krige. — Brighton, Sussex, Eng.: Harvester Press; Atlantic Highlands, N.J.: Humanities Press, 1980. 231 p.; 23 cm. Based on the author's thesis, University of Sussex, 1978. Includes index. 1. Science — Philosophy — History. 2. Science — History I. T.
Q174.8.K74 1980    501 19    *LC* 80-39643    *ISBN* 0391020943

# Q175 General

## Q175 A–B

**Achinstein, Peter.** • **5.861**
Concepts of science: a philosophical analysis / Peter Achinstein. — Baltimore: Johns Hopkins Press, c1968. xiii, 266 p. 1. Science — Methodology I. T.
Q175.A26    510.018    *LC* 68-15451

**Ackermann, Robert John, 1933-.** **5.862**
Data, instruments, and theory: a dialectical approach to understanding science / Robert John Ackermann. — Princeton, N.J.: Princeton University Press, c1985. xii, 216 p.; 25 cm. Includes index. 1. Science — Philosophy 2. Science — Social aspects 3. Logic I. T. II. Title: Dialectical approach to understanding science.
Q175.A269 1985    501 19    *LC* 84-15938    *ISBN* 0691072965

**Ackoff, Russell L.** • **5.863**
Scientific method: optimizing applied research decisions / Russell L. Ackoff, with the collaboration of Shiv K. Gupta and J. Sayer Minas. — New York: Wiley, 1962. xii, 464 p.: ill. 1. Operations research 2. Methodology 3. Decision-making I. T.
Q175.A28    501.8    *LC* 62-10914

**Bergmann, Gustav, 1906-.** • **5.864**
Philosophy of science. ∠ Madison,: University of Wisconsin Press, 1958. 181 p. 1. Science — Philosophy 2. Logic 3. Psychology I. T.
Q175.B466    *LC* 57-5237

**Blake, Ralph M.** • **5.865**
Theories of scientific method; the Renaissance through the nineteenth century. Seattle: University of Washington Press, 1960. 346 p. 1. Science — Methodology 2. Science — Philosophy I. T.
Q175.B58    501.8    *LC* 60-8577

**Braithwaite, R. B. (Richard Bevan)** • **5.866**
Scientific explanation: a study of the function of theory, probability and law in science / based upon the Tarner lectures, 1946. — Cambridge [Eng.]: University Press, 1953. xi, 375 p.: diagrs.; 23 cm. 1. Science — Methodology I. Tarner lectures, 1946. II. T.
Q175.B7845    501.8    *LC* 53-9489

**Brillouin, Léon, 1889-.** • **5.867**
Science and information theory / Leon Brillouin. — 2d ed. — New York: Academic Press, 1962. 351 p.: illus.; 24 cm. 1. Information theory I. T.
Q175.B786 1962    519.7    *LC* 62-1909

**Brody, Baruch A. comp.** **5.868**
Science: men, methods, goals: a reader: methods of physical science / edited by Boruch A. Brody [and] Nicholas Capaldi. — New York: W. A. Benjamin, 1968. viii, 343 p.; 24 cm. 1. Science — Philosophy I. Capaldi, Nicholas. joint comp. II. T.
Q175.B7914    501    *LC* 68-29930

**Bronowski, Jacob, 1908-1974.** **5.869**
The ascent of man [by] J. Bronowski. — [1st American ed.]. — Boston: Little, Brown, [1974, c1973] 448 p.: illus.; 26 cm. 1. Science — Philosophy 2. Science — History 3. Man I. T.
Q175.B7918 1974    501    *LC* 73-20446    *ISBN* 0316109304

**Bronowski, Jacob, 1908-1974.** • **5.870**
The common sense of science / by J. Bronowski. — Cambridge, Mass.: Harvard University Press, 1953. — 154 p.; 21 cm. — Includes index. 1. Science — Philosophy I. T.
Q175.Q79216    *LC* 53-9924

**Bunge, Mario Augusto.** • **5.871**
Intuition and science. Englewood Cliffs, N.J., Prentice-Hall [1962] x, 142 p. 21 cm. (A Spectrum book, S-22) 1. Intuition 2. Science — Philosophy I. T.
Q175.B823    143    *LC* 62-7451/L

## Q175 C–G

**Capra, Fritjof.** **5.872**
The turning point: science, society, and the rising culture / Fritjof Capra. — New York: Simon and Schuster, c1982. 464 p.: ill.; 24 cm. Includes index. 1. Science — Philosophy 2. Physics — Philosophy 3. Science — Social aspects I. T.
Q175.C246 1982    501 19    *LC* 81-16584    *ISBN* 067124423X

**Chalmers, A. F. (Alan Francis), 1939-.** **5.873**
What is this thing called science?: an assessment of the nature and status of science and its methods / A.F. Chalmers. — 2nd ed. — St. Lucia, Qld.: University of Queensland Press, 1982. xix, 179 p.: ill.; 22 cm. Includes index. 1. Science — Philosophy I. T.
Q175.C446 1982    501 19    *LC* 82-220485    *ISBN* 0702218316

**Churchman, C. West (Charles West), 1913-.** • **5.874**
Introduction to operations research [by] C. West Churchman, Russell L. Ackoff [and] E. Leonard Arnoff, in collaboration with Leslie C. Edie [and others] New York, Wiley [1957] 645 p. illus. 24 cm. 1. Operations research 2. Research, Industrial I. T.
Q175.C478    658.072    *LC* 57-5907

**Clarke, Desmond M.** **5.875**
Descartes' philosophy of science / Desmond M. Clarke. — University Park, Pa.: Pennsylvania State University Press, 1982. xii, 249 p.; 23 cm. — (Studies in intellectual history.) 1. Descartes, René, 1596-1650. 2. Science — Philosophy I. T. II. Series.
Q175.C58 1982    *LC* 82-82082    *ISBN* 0271003251

**Conant, James Bryant, 1893-1978.** • **5.876**
Science and common sense. — New Haven: Yale University Press, 1951. xii, 371 p.: ill.; 21 cm. Bibliography: p. 355-357. 1. Science — Methodology 2. Science — Experiments I. T.
Q175.C64    507.2    *LC* 51-1078

**Cox, D. R. (David Roxbee)** **5.877**
Planning of experiments. New York, Wiley [1958] 308 p. illus. 24 cm. (A Wiley publication in applied statistics) 1. Experimental design I. T.
Q175.C8    311.2    *LC* 58-13457

**Dingle, Herbert, 1890-.** • **5.878**
The scientific adventure; essays in the history and philosophy of science. New York, Philosophical Library [1953] 372 p. illus. 23 cm. 1. Science — History 2. Science — Philosophy I. T.
Q175.D635 1953    *LC* 53-8041

**Eddington, Arthur Stanley, Sir, 1882-1944.** • **5.879**
The nature of the physical world, by A.S. Eddington. — New York, The Macmillan company, Cambridge, Eng., University press, 1929. xvii p., 2 l., 361 p. diagrs. 23 cm. — (Gifford lectures. 1927.) 1. Science — Philosophy 2. Physics — Philosophy I. T. II. Title: The physical world, The nature of. III. Series.
Q175.E3 1929    *LC* 29-15261

**Eigen, M. (Manfred), 1927-.** **5.880**
[Spiel. English] Laws of the game: how the principles of nature govern chance / by Manfred Eigen and Ruthild Winkler; translated by Robert and Rita Kimber. — 1st American ed. — New York: Knopf: Distributed by Random House,

1981. xiv, 347 p.: ill. (some col.); 22 cm. Translation of Das Spiel. 1. Science — Philosophy 2. Chance 3. Reality I. Winkler, Ruthild, 1941- II. T.
Q175.E3713 1981   123/.3 19   *LC* 79-3494   *ISBN* 0394418069

**Faust, David, 1952-.** **5.881**
The limits of scientific reasoning / David Faust; foreword by Paul E. Meehl. — Minneapolis: University of Minnesota Press, c1984. xxvii, 198 p.; 24 cm. Includes index. 1. Science — Philosophy 2. Reasoning 3. Judgment (Logic) I. T.
Q175.F269 1984   501 19   *LC* 84-5172   *ISBN* 0816613567

**Readings in the philosophy of science / Herbert Feigl and May** • **5.882**
**Brodbeck, editors.**
New York: Appleton-Century-Crofts, c1953. 811 p.: ill. 'On the notion of cause, with applications to the free-will problem / Bertrand Russell': p. 387-407. 1. Science — Philosophy I. Feigl, Herbert. II. Brodbeck, May. III. Russell, Bertrand, 1872-1970.
Q175.F38   501   *LC* 53-6438/L

**Feyerabend, Paul K., 1924-.** **5.883**
Against method: outline of an anarchistic theory of knowledge / Paul Feyerabend. — Atlantic Highlands, N.J.: Humanities Press, [1975] c1974. 339 p.: ill.; 22 cm. 1. Science — Philosophy 2. Methodology 3. Rationalism I. T.
Q175.F42 1975   501   *LC* 75-2149   *ISBN* 039100381X

**Foundations of scientific method: the nineteenth century. Edited** **5.884**
**by Ronald N. Giere and Richard S. Westfall.**
Bloomington: Indiana University Press, [1973] ix, 306 p.; 22 cm. Papers presented at a conference held in Bloomington, Nov. 26-29, 1970, to celebrate the 10th anniversary of the founding of the Dept. of History and Philosophy of Science at Indiana University. 1. Science — Methodology — Congresses. 2. Science — Philosophy — Congresses. 3. Science — History — Congresses. I. Giere, Ronald N. ed. II. Westfall, Richard S. ed. III. Indiana. University. Dept. of History and Philosophy of Science.
Q175.F72 1973   501   *LC* 72-79910   *ISBN* 0253324009

**Frank, Philipp, 1884-1966.** • **5.885**
Philosophy of science: the link between science and philosophy. — Englewood Cliffs, N. J.: Prentice-Hall, 1957. 394 p.: ill. 1. Science — Philosophy I. T.
Q175.F782   *LC* 57-6980

**Glass, Bentley, 1906-.** • **5.886**
Science and ethical values / by Bentley Glass. Chapel Hill: University of North Carolina Press [1965] ix, 101 p.; 23 cm. (John Calvin McNair lectures.) 1. Science — Philosophy — Addresses, essays, lectures. 2. Ethics — Addresses, essays, lectures. I. T. II. Series.
Q175.G58   174/.9574 19   *LC* 65-25599

## Q175 H

**Harré, Rom.** **5.887**
An Introduction to the logic of the sciences. — London: Macmillan; New York: St. Martin's Press, 1960. viii, 180 p. . diagrs. , 23 cm. 1. Science — Philosophy I. T. II. Title: The Logic of the sciences.
Q175.H17   *LC* 61-2770

**Hacking, Ian.** **5.888**
Representing and intervening: introductory topics in the philosophy of natural science / Ian Hacking. — Cambridge [Cambridgeshire]; New York: Cambridge University Press, 1983. xv, 287 p.; 23 cm. 1. Science — Philosophy I. T.
Q175.H2 1983   501 19   *LC* 83-5132   *ISBN* 0521238293

**Hanson, Norwood Russell.** • **5.889**
Patterns of discovery: an inquiry into the conceptual foundations of science / by Norwood Russell Hanson. — Cambridge [Eng.]: University Press, 1958. ix, 240 p.: ill. 1. Science — Philosophy I. T.
Q175.H27

**Hanson, Norwood Russell.** • **5.890**
Perception and discovery; an introduction to scientific inquiry. Edited by Willard C. Humphreys. — San Francisco: Freeman, Cooper, [1970, c1969] x, 435 p.: illus.; 24 cm. 1. Science — Philosophy 2. Science — Methodology 3. Perception I. T.
Q175.H274   501   *LC* 75-95161   *ISBN* 0877355096

**Harré, Rom.** **5.891**
An introduction to the logic of the sciences / Rom Harré. — 2nd ed. — New York: St. Martin's Press, 1983. ix, 182 p.: ill.; 23 cm. Includes indexes. 1. Science — Philosophy I. T.
Q175.H3255 1983   501 19   *LC* 82-42709   *ISBN* 0312429118

**Harré, Rom.** • **5.892**
Matter & method / [by] R. Harré. — London: Macmillan; New York: St. Martin's Press, 1965, c1964. 124 p. 1. Science — Philosophy 2. Science — History I. T.
Q175 H326

**Harré, Rom.** • **5.893**
Scientific thought 1900–1960: a selective survey; edited by R. Harré. Oxford, Clarendon P., 1969. viii, 277 p. 8 plates, illus. 25 cm. 1. Science — Methodology — Addresses, essays, lectures. 2. Science — Philosophy — Addresses, essays, lectures. I. T.
Q175.H327   509/.04   *LC* 74-409990   *ISBN* 0198581254

**Heisenberg, Werner, 1901-1976.** • **5.894**
[Naturbild der heutigen Physik. English] The physicist's conception of nature. Translated from the German by Arnold J. Pomerans. Westport, Conn., Greenwood Press [1970, c1958] 192 p. 23 cm. Translation of Das Naturbild der heutigen Physik. 1. Science — Philosophy I. T.
Q175.H393 1970   501   *LC* 72-90526   *ISBN* 0837131073

**Hesse, Mary B.** **5.895**
Revolutions and reconstructions in the philosophy of science / Mary Hesse. — Bloomington: Indiana Univerity Press, c1980. xxvi, 271 p.; 22 cm. 1. Science — Philosophy 2. Science — History I. T.
Q175.H4317   501   *LC* 80-7819   *ISBN* 0253333814

**Hempel, Carl Gustav, 1905-.** • **5.896**
Aspects of scientific explanation: and other essays in the philosophy of science / Carl G. Hempel. — New York: Free Press, 1965. ix, 505 p.; 24 cm. 1. Science — Philosophy I. T.
Q175.H4834   501   *LC* 65-15441

**Horwich, Paul.** **5.897**
Probability and evidence / Paul Horwich. — Cambridge [Cambridgeshire]; New York: Cambridge University Press, 1982. vii, 146 p.: ill.; 23 cm. — (Cambridge studies in philosophy.) Includes index. 1. Science — Philosophy 2. Probabilities 3. Evidence I. T. II. Series.
Q175.H797 1982   501 19   *LC* 81-18144   *ISBN* 0521237580

**Hübner, Kurt, 1921-.** **5.898**
[Kritik der wissenschaftlichen Vernunft. English] Critique of scientific reason / Kurt Hübner; translated by Paul R. Dixon, Jr., & Hollis M. Dixon. — Chicago: University of Chicago Press, c1983. xii, 283 p.; 24 cm. Translation of: Kritik der wissenschaftlichen Vernunft. 1. Science — Philosophy 2. Quantum theory 3. Technology — Philosophy I. T.
Q175.H891513 1983   501 19   *LC* 82-23690   *ISBN* 0226357082

**Hutten, Ernest H. (Ernest Hirschlaff), 1908-.** • **5.899**
The origins of science: an inquiry into the foundations of Western thought. — London: Allen and Unwin [1962] 241 p.; 23 cm. 1. Science — Philosophy 2. Science — History I. T.
Q175.H96   501   *LC* 63-2658

## Q175 I–L

**International Colloquium in the Philosophy of Science (1965:** • **5.900**
**Bedford College)**
Criticism and the growth of knowledge; edited by Imre Lakatos [and] Alan Musgrave. Cambridge [Eng.] University Press, 1970. viii, 282 p. 23 cm. (International Teleconference Symposium (1984: Sydney, N.S.W., etc.) Proceedings, v. 4) 1. Science — Philosophy — Congresses. I. Lakatos, Imre. ed. II. Musgrave, Alan. ed. III. T. IV. Series.
Q175.I514 1965   501   *LC* 78-105496   *ISBN* 0521078261

**International encyclopedia of unified science / edited by Otto** • **5.901**
**Neurath, Rudolf Carnap [and] Charles Morris.**
[Combined ed.] Chicago: University of Chicago Press, c1955-. v.: ill. — 1. Science — Philosophy 2. Science — Collected works 3. Semantics I. Neurath, Otto, 1882-1945.
Q175.I58

**Jeffreys, Harold, Sir, 1891-.** **5.902**
Scientific inference. — 3d ed. — Cambridge [Eng.]: Cambridge University Press, 1973. viii, 273 p.; 22 cm. 1. Science — Methodology 2. Science — Philosophy I. T.
Q175.J35 1973   501/.8   *LC* 71-179159   *ISBN* 0521084466

**Jevons, William Stanley, 1835-1882.** • **5.903**
The principles of science: a treatise on logic and scientific method / with a new introd. by Ernest Nagel. — New York: Dover Publications, [1958] 786 p.: ill. 1. Logic 2. Science — Methodology I. T.
Q175.J4 1958

**Joravsky, David.** • **5.904**
Soviet Marxism and natural science, 1917–1932. New York: Columbia U.P., 1961. 433 p. (Studies of the Russian Institute, Columbia University) 1. Science — Philosophy 2. Dialectical materialism 3. Science — Soviet Union — History. I. T.
Q175 J64 1961    530.1    *LC* 60-14070

**Jordon, Pascual, 1902-.** • **5.905**
Science and the course of history / by Pasual Jordon; translated by Ralph Manheim. — New Haven: Yale University Press, 1955. 139 p. 1. Science — Philosophy 2. Science and civilization I. T.
Q175J66    *LC* 55-10255

**Keller, Evelyn Fox, 1936-.** **5.906**
Reflections on gender and science / Evelyn Fox Keller. — New Haven: Yale University Press, c1985. viii, 193 p.; 22 cm. Includes index. 1. Science — Philosophy 2. Women in science 3. Science — History I. T.
Q175.K28 1985    501 19    *LC* 84-17327    *ISBN* 0300032919

**Kemeny, John G.** • **5.907**
A philosopher looks at science. — Princeton, N.J.: Van Nostrand, [1959] 273 p.: illus.; 24 cm. 1. Science — Philosophy I. T.
Q175.K3    501    *LC* 59-8064

**Kuhn, Thomas S.** • **5.908**
The structure of scientific revolutions / Thomas S. Kuhn. — 2nd ed. enl. — Chicago: University of Chicago Press, c1970. xii, 210 p. 'Also issued as Vol. II, No. 2, of the International encyclopedia of unified science.' 1. Science — Philosophy 2. Science — History I. T.
Q175.K95    501    *LC* 79-107472    *ISBN* 0226458040

**Kuhn, Thomas S.** **5.909**
The essential tension: selected studies in scientific tradition and change / Thomas S. Kuhn. — Chicago: University of Chicago Press, 1977. xxiii, 366 p.; 23 cm. 1. Science — Philosophy — Collected works. 2. Science — History — Collected works. I. T.
Q175.K954    501    *LC* 77-78069    *ISBN* 0226458059

**Levi, Isaac, 1930-.** • **5.910**
Gambling with truth; an essay on induction and the aims of science. — New York: Knopf, 1967. xiv, 246, v p.; 22 cm. — (Borzoi books in the philosophy of science) 1. Science — Methodology I. T.
Q175.L445    501/.8    *LC* 67-10712

## Q175 M–P

**Madden, Edward H.** • **5.911**
The structure of scientific thought: an introduction to philosophy of science. — Boston: Houghton Mifflin, 1960. 381 p.: ill. 1. Science — Philosophy I. T.
Q175.M24    *LC* 60-16020

**Medawar, P. B. (Peter Brian), 1915-.** **5.912**
The limits of science / P.B. Medawar. — 1st ed. — New York: Harper & Row, c1984. — xiii, 108 p.: ill.; 22 cm. 'A Cornelia & Michael Bessie book.' Includes index. 1. Science — Philosophy I. T.
Q175.M433 1984    501 19    *LC* 83-48841    *ISBN* 0060390360

**Morgenbesser, Sidney, 1921- ed.** • **5.913**
Philosophy of science today, edited by Sidney Morgenbesser. New York, Basic Books [1967] xvi, 208 p. 1. Science — Philosophy — Addresses, essays, lectures I. T.
Q175 M657    *LC* 67-17391

**Moravcsik, Michael J.** **5.914**
How to grow science / Michael J. Moravcsik. — New York: Universe Books, 1980. 206 p.; 22 cm. 'A Publishers creative book.' Includes index. 1. Science — Philosophy I. T.
Q175.M79    501    *LC* 80-17469    *ISBN* 0876633440

**Morris, Richard, 1939-.** **5.915**
Dismantling the universe: the nature of scientific discovery / Richard Morris. — New York: Simon and Schuster, c1983. 224 p.; 23 cm. Includes index. 1. Science — Methodology 2. Creative ability in science I. T.
Q175.M869 1983    501 19    *LC* 83-11324    *ISBN* 0671452398

**Nagel, Ernest, 1901-.** • **5.916**
Sovereign reason, and other studies in the philosophy of science / Ernest Nagel. — Glencoe, Ill.: Free Press, c1954. 315 p. 1. Science — Philosophy I. T.
Q175.N2    *LC* 54-10668

**Nagel, Ernest, 1901-.** • **5.917**
The structure of science; problems in the logic of scientific explanation. — New York: Harcourt, Brace & World, [1961] 618 p.; 22 cm. 1. Science — Philosophy I. T.
Q175.N22    501    *LC* 60-15504

**Pap, Arthur, 1921-1959.** • **5.918**
An introduction to the philosophy of science / with an epilogue by Brand Blanshard. — [New York]: Free Press of Glencoe [1962] 444 p.; 24 cm. 1. Science — Philosophy I. T. II. Title: Philosophy of science.
Q175.P337    501    *LC* 61-10901

**Pearson, Karl 1857-1936.** • **5.919**
The grammar of science. New York: Meridian Books, [1957] 394 p.: ill.; 21 cm. (The Meridian library; ML7) 1. Science — Philosophy 2. Evolution 3. Classification of sciences I. T.
Q175 P36 1937

**Planck, Max, 1858-1947.** • **5.920**
Where is science going? / by Max Planck; prologue by Albert Einstein; translation and biographical note by James Murphy. — New York: W.W. Norton, 1932. 221 p. 1. Science — Philosophy 2. Physics — Philosophy 3. Causation 4. Free will and determinism I. T.
Q175.P57 1932a

**Poincaré, Henri, 1854-1912.** • **5.921**
The foundations of science / by H. Poincaré; authorized translation by George Bruce Halsted; with a special preface by Poincaré and an introd. by Josiah Royce. — Lancaster, Pa.: Science Press, 1946. xi, 553 p.; 25 cm. — (Science and education; v.1) 1. Science — Philosophy 2. Science — Methodology 3. Mathematics — Philosophy I. Halsted, George Bruce, 1853-1922. II. T.
Q175.P8 1946    *LC* 47-1921

**Polanyi, Michael, 1891-.** • **5.922**
Personal knowledge: towards a post–critical philosophy / by Michael Polanyi. — Chicago: University of Chicago Press, [c1958] xiv, 428 p. — (Gifford lectures. 1951-52) 1. Science — Philosophy 2. Knowledge, Theory of I. T. II. Series.
Q175.P82    501    *LC* 58-5162

**Popper, Karl Raimund, Sir, 1902-.** • **5.923**
[Logik der Forschung. English] The logic of scientific discovery. New York, Basic Books [1959] 479 p. illus., facsim. 25 cm. Translation of Logik der Forschung. 1. Science — Methodology I. T.
Q175.P863    501.8    *LC* 59-8371

**Popper, Karl Raimund, Sir, 1902-.** **5.924**
Realism and the aim of science / Karl R. Popper. — Totowa, N.J.: Rowman and Littlefield, 1983. xxxix, 420 p.; 24 cm. — (The Postscript to The logic of scientific discovery / as edited by W.W. Bartley, III) 1. Science — Philosophy I. Bartley, William Warren, 1934- II. T.
Q175.P8643 1983    501 19    *LC* 82-501    *ISBN* 0847670155

**Prigogine, I. (Ilya)** **5.925**
Order out of chaos: man's new dialogue with nature / by Ilya Prigogine and Isabelle Stengers; foreword by Alvin Toffler. — 1st ed. — Boulder, CO: New Science Library: Distributed by Random House, 1984. xxxi, 349 p.; 24 cm. Based on the authors' La nouvelle alliance. 1. Science — Philosophy 2. Physics — Philosophy I. Stengers, Isabelle. II. Prigogine, I. (Ilya) Nouvelle alliance. III. T.
Q175.P8822 1984    501 19    *LC* 84-8415    *ISBN* 0877733023

## Q175 R–T

**Rescher, Nicholas.** **5.926**
Peirce's philosophy of science: critical studies in his theory of induction and scientific method / Nicholas Rescher. — Notre Dame: University of Notre Dame Press, c1978. x, 125 p.: ill.; 21 cm. Includes indexes. 1. Peirce, Charles S. (Charles Sanders), 1839-1914. 2. Science — Philosophy 3. Science — Methodology I. T.
Q175.R39333    501    *LC* 77-82479    *ISBN* 0268015260

**Reichenbach, Hans, 1891-1953.** • **5.927**
Modern philosophy of science; selected essays translated and edited by Maria Reichenbach. Foreword by Rudolf Carnap. London, Routledge & Paul; New York, Humanities Press [1959] ix, 214 p. 1. Science — Philosophy I. T.
Q175.R4x    *LC* a 60-2289

**Russell, Bertrand, 1872-1970.** • **5.928**
The impact of science on society / Bertrand Russell. — New York: Simon and Schuster, 1953 (i.e. 1952). 114 p. 1. Science — Philosophy I. T.
Q175.R86 1952a    504    *LC* 52-14878

**Salk, Jonas, 1914-.** **5.929**
Anatomy of reality: merging of intuition and reason / Jonas Salk. — New York: Columbia University Press, 1982. xxvii, 127 p.: ill.; 24 cm. — (Convergence) 1. Science — Philosophy 2. Reality 3. Intuition 4. Reason I. T.
Q175.S2326 1983    128 19    *LC* 82-17828    *ISBN* 0231053282

**Salmon, Wesley C.**    • 5.930
The foundations of scientific inference [by] Wesley C. Salmon. — [Pittsburgh]: University of Pittsburgh Press, [1967] 157 p.: illus.; 21 cm. — (Pitt paperback, 28) 'Based upon five lectures in the philosophy of science series at the University of Pittsburgh ... March 1963 ... -October 1965.' 1. Science — Philosophy I. T.
Q175.S234     501     LC 67-21649

**Salmon, Wesley C.**    5.931
Scientific explanation and the causal structure of the world / Wesley C. Salmon. — Princeton, N.J.: Princeton University Press, c1984. xiv, 305 p.; 24 cm. Includes index. 1. Science — Philosophy 2. Science — Methodology I. T.
Q175.S23415 1984     501 19     LC 84-42562     ISBN 0691072930

**Scheffler, Israel.**    • 5.932
The anatomy of inquiry: philosophical studies in the theory of science / Israel Scheffler. — New York: Knopf, 1963. xii, 332, v p. — (Borzoi books in the philosophy of science) 1. Science — Philosophy 2. Science — Methodology I. T.
Q175.S33     LC 63-11049

**Schlegel, Richard, 1913-.**    5.933
Inquiry into science: its domain and limits / [by] Richard Schlegel; illus. by Al Nagy. — [1st ed.] — Garden City, N.Y.: Doubleday, 1972. x, 108 p.: ill.; 22 cm. (Science study series.) 1. Science — Methodology I. T. II. Series.
Q175.S3526     500     LC 74-144295

**Simon, Herbert Alexander, 1916-.**    5.934
The sciences of the artificial / Herbert A. Simon. — 2d ed., rev. and enl. — Cambridge, Mass.: MIT Press, c1981. xiii, 247 p.: ill.; 20 cm. 1. Science — Philosophy I. T.
Q175.S564 1981     501 19     LC 80-28273     ISBN 0262191938

**Sindermann, Carl J.**    5.935
Winning the games scientists play / Carl J. Sindermann. — New York: Plenum Press, c1982. xii, 290 p.: ill.; 22 cm. Includes index. 1. Science — Methodology 2. Scientists I. T.
Q175.S569 1982     306/.45 19     LC 82-12225     ISBN 0306410753

**Toulmin, Stephen Edelston.**    • 5.936
Foresight and understanding: an enquiry into the aims of science / Stephen Toulmin; foreword by Jacques Barzun. — Bloomington: Indiana University Press, [1961]. — 115 p.; 21 cm. — 1. Science — Philosophy — Addresses, essays, lectures. I. T.
Q175.T64 1963     501     LC 61-13719

**Toulmin, Stephen Edelston.**    • 5.937
The philosophy of science: an introduction / by Stephen Toulmin. — London: Hutchinson's University Library. c1953. viii, 176 p.: ill. — (Hutchinson's University Library: Philosophy) 1. Science — Philosophy I. T.
Q175.T65     LC 53-1625

## Q175 U–Z

**Van Fraassen, Bastiaan C., 1941-.**    5.938
The scientific image / Bas C. van Fraassen. — Oxford: Clarendon Press; New York: Oxford University Press, 1980. xi, 235 p.: ill.; 23 cm. — (Clarendon library of logic and philosophy) 1. Science — Philosophy I. T.
Q175.V335 1980     501     LC 79-42793     ISBN 019824424X

**Waddington, C. H. (Conrad Hal), 1905-1975.**    • 5.939
The scientific attitude / by C. H. Waddington. — Harmondsworth, Middlesex: Penguin Books, 1941. 128 p.: ill., port. — (Pelican books; A84) 1. Science — Philosophy I. T.
Q175.W25     301.2     LC 42-11349

**Wartofsky, Marx W.**    • 5.940
Conceptual foundations of scientific thought: an introduction to the philosophy of science / Marx W. Wartofsky. — New York: Macmillan, c1968. xii, 560 p.: ill. 1. Science — Philosophy I. T.
Q175.W28     501     LC 67-15542

**Weizsäcker, Carl Friedrich, von, Freiherr.**    • 5.941
The history of nature / C.F. von Weizsäcker. — Chicago: University of Chicago Press, 1949. — vi, 191 p. Phoenix books. 1. Science — Philosophy I. T.
Q175.W5117     504     LC 49-10907

**Whewell, William, 1794-1866.**    • 5.942
The philosophy of the inductive sciences, founded upon their history. A facsim. of the 2d ed., London, 1847, with a new introd. by John Herivel. — New York: Johnson Reprint Corp., 1967 [c1966] 2 v.; 22 cm. — (The Sources of science, no. 41) 'Inductive table of optics': fold. table inserted. 1. Science — Philosophy I. T.
Q175.W55 1967     501     LC 66-26484

**Whitehead, Alfred North, 1861-1947.**    • 5.943
The interpretation of science: selected essays / edited, with an introd., by A.H. Johnson. — Indianapolis: Bobbs-Merrill [1961] 274 p.; 21 cm. (The Library of liberal arts, no. 117) 1. Science — Philosophy I. T.
Q175.W575     501     LC 60-16699

**Whitehead, Alfred North, 1861-1947.**    • 5.944
The Concept of nature: Tarner lectures delivered in Trinity College, November, 1919 / by A. N. Whitehead. — Cambridge: The University press, 1920. viii, 202 p.; 22 cm. — (Tarner lectures. 1919.) A companion volume to the author's 'An enquiry concerning the principles of natural knowledge.' cf. Pref. 1. Nature 2. Science — Philosophy 3. Knowledge, Theory of I. T. II. Series.
Q175.W58     LC 21-6777

**Whitehead, Alfred North, 1861-1947.**    • 5.945
Essays in science and philosophy. — New York: Greenwood Press, 1968 [c1947] vi, 348 p.; 24 cm. 1. Science — Addresses, essays, lectures. 2. Philosophy — Addresses, essays, lectures. 3. Education — Addresses, essays, lectures. I. T.
Q175.W62 1968     082     LC 68-21332

**Whitehead, Alfred North, 1861-1947.**    • 5.946
Nature and life. — New York: Greenwood Press, [1968, c1934] 46 p.; 23 cm. 1. Science — Philosophy 2. Philosophy of nature I. T.
Q175.W63 1968     501     LC 69-14150

**Whittaker, E. T. (Edmund Taylor), 1873-1956.**    • 5.947
From Euclid to Eddington: a study of conceptions of the external world. — Cambridge, Eng.: University Press, 1949. ix, 212 p.; 23 cm. (Tarner lectures. 1947.) 1. Science — Philosophy I. T. II. Series.
Q175.W6513     LC 49-9939

**Wiener, Norbert, 1894-1964.**    • 5.948
Cybernetics; or, Control and communication in the animal and the machine. — 2d ed. — New York: M.I.T. Press, 1961. 212 p.: illus.; 24 cm. 1. Cybernetics I. T.
Q175.W6516 1961     006     LC 61-13034

**Wiener, Norbert, 1894-1964.**    • 5.949
The human use of human beings; cybernetics and society. Boston: Houghton Mifflin, 1954. 188 p.; 21 cm. 1. Cybernetics 2. Science — Social aspects I. T.
Q175.W6517 1954a     501     LC 54-3471

**Ziman, J. M. (John M.), 1925-.**    5.950
Reliable knowledge: an exploration of the grounds for belief in science / John Ziman. — Cambridge [Eng.]; New York: Cambridge University Press, 1979 (c1978). ix, 197 p.: ill.; 24 cm. 1. Science — Philosophy I. T.
Q175.Z55     501     LC 78-3792     ISBN 0521220874

**Zuckerman, Solly Zuckerman, Baron, 1904-.**    • 5.951
Scientists and war: the impact of science on military and civil affairs. — [1st U.S. ed.] New York: Harper & Row [1967] xiv, 177 p.; 22 cm. 1. Science 2. Science and civilization I. T.
Q175.Z83 1967     501     LC 67-11333

# Q175.3 Addresses, Essays, Lectures

**Bernstein, Jeremy, 1929-.**    5.952
Science observed: essays out of my mind / Jeremy Bernstein. — New York: Basic Books, c1982. vii, 376 p.; 22 cm. Includes index. 1. Minsky, Marvin Lee, 1927- — Addresses, essays, lectures. 2. Science — Philosophy — Addresses, essays, lectures. 3. Artificial intelligence — Addresses, essays, lectures. I. T.
Q175.3.B476     501 19     LC 81-68404     ISBN 0465073409

**Laudan, Larry.**    5.953
Science and hypothesis: historical essays on scientific methodology / Larry Laudan. — Dordrecht, Holland; Boston, U.S.A.: D. Reidel; Hingham, MA: Sold and distributed in the U.S.A. and Canada by Kluwer Boston Inc., c1981. x, 258 p.; 23 cm. — (University of Western Ontario series in philosophy of science. v. 19) 1. Science — Methodology — Addresses, essays, lectures. I. T. II. Series.
Q175.3.L38     502/.8 19     LC 81-15423     ISBN 9027713154

**Paradigms and revolutions: appraisals and applications of**    5.954
**Thomas Kuhn's philosophy of science / edited by Gary Gutting.**
Notre Dame: University of Notre Dame Press, c1980. viii, 339 p.; 24 cm. Includes index. 1. Kuhn, Thomas S — Addresses, essays, lectures. 2. Science — Philosophy — Addresses, essays, lectures. I. Gutting, Gary.
Q175.3.P37     501 19     LC 80-20745     ISBN 0268015422

# Q175.4–175.55 Social Aspects

**The Social implications of the scientific and technological**                 **5.955**
**revolution: a Unesco symposium.**
Paris: Unesco, 1981. xvi, 392 p.: ill.; 25 cm. Contributions to an international conference held on Sept. 6-10, 1976 in Prague, and organized jointly by Unesco and the Czechoslovak Academy of Sciences in co-operation with the Czechoslovak Commission for Unesco. Includes indexes. 1. Science — Social aspects — Congresses. 2. Technology — Social aspects — Congresses. 3. Science and state — Congresses. 4. Technology and state — Congresses. I. Unesco. II. Československá akademie věd. III. Československá komise pro spolupráci s Unesco.
Q175.4.S6      303.4/83 19      LC 81-169437      ISBN 9231016644

**Brannigan, Augustine, 1949-.**                                             **5.956**
The social basis of scientific discoveries / Augustine Brannigan. — Cambridge [Eng.]; New York: Cambridge University Press, 1981. xi, 212 p.: 24 cm. Includes index. 1. Science — Social aspects I. T.
Q175.5.B73      501 19      LC 81-6129      ISBN 0521236959

**Graham, Loren R.**                                                          **5.957**
Between science and values / Loren R. Graham. — New York: Columbia University Press, 1981. x, 449 p.; 24 cm. Includes index. 1. Science — Social aspects 2. Science — History 3. Science — Philosophy I. T.
Q175.5.G72      303.4/83 19      LC 81-4436      ISBN 0231051921

**A guide to the culture of science, technology, and medicine /**             **5.958**
**general editor, Paul T. Durbin, area editors, Jerome R. Ravetz**
**... [et al.].**
New York: Free Press, c1980. xl, 723 p.; 26 cm. 1. Science 2. Technology 3. Social medicine I. Durbin, Paul T.
Q175.5.G84      303.4/83 19      LC 79-7582      ISBN 0029078202

**Haas, Ernst B.**                                                            **5.959**
Scientists and world order: the uses of technical knowledge in international organizations / Ernst B. Haas, Mary Pat Williams, and Don Babai. — Berkeley: University of California Press, 1978 (c1977). x, 368 p.; 25 cm. 1. Science — Social aspects 2. Technology — Social aspects 3. Science — Philosophy I. Williams, Mary Pat. joint author. II. Babai, Don. joint author. III. T. IV. Title: International organizations.
Q175.5.H33      301.24/3      LC 76-47981      ISBN 0520033418

**Jevons, F. R. (Frederick Raphael), 1929-.**                                 **5.960**
Science observed: science as a social and intellectual activity / [by] F. R. Jevons. — London: Allen & Unwin, 1974 (c1973) 186 p.; 23 cm. 1. Science — Social aspects I. T.
Q175.5.J48      301.5      LC 73-173011      ISBN 0045020019 ISBN 0045020027

**Lowrance, William W., 1943-.**                                              **5.961**
Modern science and human values / William W. Lowrance. — New York: Oxford University Press, 1985. xiv, 250 p.; 25 cm. Includes index. 1. Science — Social aspects 2. Technology — Social aspects 3. Humanities I. T.
Q175.5.L68 1985      303.4/83 19      LC 84-29609      ISBN 0195036050

**Science, technology, and society: a cross–disciplinary perspective**        **5.962**
**/ edited by Ina Spiegel–Rösing and Derek de Solla Price; under**
**the aegis of the International Council for Science Policy**
**Studies.**
London; Beverly Hills, Calif.: SAGE Publications, c1977. 607 p.; 24 cm. 1. Science — Social aspects 2. Technology — Social aspects I. Spiegel-Rösing, Ina-Susanne. II. Price, Derek J. de Solla (Derek John de Solla), 1922-1983. III. International Council for Science Policy Studies.
Q175.5.S373      500      LC 76-55928      ISBN 0803998589

**Ziman, J. M. (John M.), 1925-.**                                            **5.963**
The force of knowledge: the scientific dimension of society / John Ziman. — Cambridge; New York: Cambridge University Press, 1976. ix, 374 p.: ill.; 25 cm. Includes bibliographical references and index. 1. Science — Social aspects I. T.
Q175.5.Z54      301.24/3      LC 75-23529      ISBN 0521206499. ISBN 052109917X pbk

**Easlea, Brian.**                                                            **5.964**
Witch hunting, magic, and the new philosophy: an introduction to debates of the scientific revolution, 1450–1750 / Brian Easlea. — Brighton, Sussex: Harvester Press; Atlantic Highlands, N.J.: Humanities Press, 1980. xii, 283 p.: ill.; 24 cm. — (Harvester studies in philosophy.) 1. Science — Social aspects —

Europe. 2. Science — Europe — History. 3. Science — Philosophy — History. I. T. II. Series.
Q175.52.E85 E2      303.4/83/094 19      LC 81-119864      ISBN 039101806X

**Victorian science and Victorian values: literary perspectives /**          **5.965**
**edited by James Paradis and Thomas Postlewait.**
New York, N.Y.: New York Academy of Sciences, 1981. xiii, 362 p.: ill.; 24 cm. — (Annals of the New York Academy of Sciences; v. 360) 1. Science — Social aspects — England — Addresses, essays, lectures. 2. Literature and science — Addresses, essays, lectures. I. Paradis, James G., 1942- II. Postlewait, Thomas.
Q175.52.G7V5x Q11.N5 vol. 360      500 s 304.4/83 19      LC 80-29513

**Lubrano, Linda L.**                                                         **5.966**
Soviet sociology of science / Linda L. Lubrano. — Columbus, Ohio: American Association for the Advancement of Slavic Studies, 1976. 102 p.; 23 cm. 1. Science — Social aspects — Russia. I. T.
Q175.52.R9 L8      301.5      LC 77-155982

**Cole, Jonathan R.**                                                         **5.967**
Social stratification in science / Jonathan R. Cole & Stephen Cole. — Chicago: University of Chicago Press, 1973. xiv, 283 p.; 24 cm. 1. Science — Social aspects — United States. I. Cole, Stephen, 1941- joint author. II. T.
Q175.52.U5 C65      301.4      LC 73-78166      ISBN 0226113388

**Cole, Leonard A., 1933-.**                                                  **5.968**
Politics and the restraint of science / Leonard A. Cole. — Totowa, N.J.: Rowman & Allanheld, 1983. xii, 187 p.: forms; 22 cm. 1. Science — Social aspects — United States. 2. Science — Political aspects — United States. 3. Science and state — United States. I. T.
Q175.52.U5 C653 1983      500 19      LC 83-2992      ISBN 0865981256

**Ziman, J. M. (John M.), 1925-.**                                           **5.969**
Puzzles, problems and enigmas: occasional pieces on the human aspects of science / John Ziman. — Cambridge: Cambridge University Press, 1981. ix, 373 p.: ill. 1. Science — Social aspects — Addresses, essays, lectures I. T.
Q175.55.Z56      LC 80-42112      ISBN 0521236592

# Q179 Terminology

**Nybakken, Oscar Edward, 1904-.**                                            **5.970**
Greek and Latin in scientific terminology. — Ames: Iowa State College Press, [1959] 321 p.; 23 cm. 1. Science — Terminology 2. English language — Foreign elements — Latin. 3. English language — Foreign elements — Greek. 4. English language — Word formation I. T.
Q179.N9      501.4      LC 59-5992

# Q179.9–225.5 Research. Study and Teaching. Tables

# Q179.98 Directories

**Government research directory.**                                            **5.971**
3rd ed.-      . — Detroit, Mich.: Gale Research Co., c1985-. v.; 29 cm. Supplements issued between editions. 1. Research — United States — Directories. 2. Research institutes — United States — Directories. I. Gale Research Company.
Q179.98.G68      001.4/025/73 19      LC 85-647549

# Q180 General Works. History

**Beveridge, W. I. B. (William Ian Beardmore), 1908-.**                    **• 5.972**
The art of scientific investigation. [Rev. ed.] New York, Norton [1957] 178 p. illus. 22 cm. Continued by the author's Seeds of discovery. 1. Research I. T.
Q180.A1 B48 1957      507.2      LC 57-14582

**Zuckerman, Solly** Zuckerman, Baron, 1904-. **5.973**
Beyond the ivory tower: the frontiers of public and private science. — New York: Taplinger Pub. Co., [1971, c1970] ix, 244 p.: ill.; 23 cm. 1. Research 2. Science — Philosophy I. T.
Q180.A1 Z85 1971　301.2/43　　LC 72-137412　　ISBN 0800807332

**Science in contemporary China** / edited by Leo A. Orleans, **5.974**
with the assistance of Caroline Davidson.
Stanford, Calif.: Stanford University Press, 1980. xxxii, 599 p.: ill.; 25 cm. 1. Research — China. 2. Science and state — China. 3. Science — China — History. I. Orleans, Leo A. II. Davidson, Caroline.
Q180.C6 S33　509/.51 19　　LC 79-65178　　ISBN 0804710783

**Irvine, John.** **5.975**
Foresight in science: picking the winners / John Irvine and Ben R. Martin. — London; Dover, N.H.: F. Pinter, 1984. xiv, 166 p.: ill.; 24 cm. 1. Research — Great Britain. 2. Science and state — Great Britain. 3. Research — Forecasting. 4. Technological forecasting I. Martin, Ben R. II. T.
Q180.G7 I78 1984　338.941 19　　LC 84-42926　　ISBN 086187496X

**Geiger, Roger L., 1943-.** **5.976**
To advance knowledge: the growth of American research universities, 1900–1940 / Roger L. Geiger. — New York: Oxford University Press, 1986. x, 325 p.; 25 cm. Includes index. 1. Research institutes — United States — History. 2. Science — United States — History. 3. Universities and colleges — United States I. T.
Q180.U5 G34 1986　001.4/0973 19　　LC 85-30971　　ISBN 0195038037

**Nelkin, Dorothy.** **5.977**
Science as intellectual property: who controls research? / Dorothy Nelkin. — New York: Macmillan, c1984. ix, 130 p.; 22 cm. (AAAS series on issues in science and technology.) Includes index. 1. Research — United States 2. Science and state — United States. 3. Communication in science — United States. 4. Confidential communications — United States. I. T. II. Series.
Q180.U5 N37 1984　001.4 19　　LC 83-3805　　ISBN 0029490804

## Q180.55 Special Topics. Methodology

**Drew, Clifford J., 1943-.** **5.978**
Introduction to designing and conducting research / Clifford J. Drew. — 2d ed. — St. Louis: Mosby, 1980. xi, 356 p.: ill.; 24 cm. First ed. published in 1976 under title: Introduction to designing research and evaluation. 1. Research — Methodology. I. T.
Q180.55.M4 D73 1980　001.4/2　　LC 79-25403　　ISBN 0801614600

**Leedy, Paul D.** **5.979**
Practical research: planning and design / Paul D. Leedy. — 3rd ed. — New York: Macmillan, c1985. xi, 313 p.: ill.; 28 cm. 1. Research — Methodology. I. T.
Q180.55.M4 L43 1985　001.4/2 19　　LC 84-731　　ISBN 0023692200

**Stock, Molly.** **5.980**
A practical guide to graduate research / Molly Stock. — New York: McGraw-Hill, c1985. viii, 168 p.: ill.; 20 cm. Includes index. 1. Research — Methodology. 2. Universities and colleges — Graduate work I. T.
Q180.55.M4 S86 1985　001.4 19　　LC 84-7927　　ISBN 0070615837

**Weimer, Walter B.** **5.981**
Notes on the methodology of scientific research / Walter B. Weimer. — Hillsdale, N.J.: L. Erlbaum Associates; New York: distributed by the Halsted Press Division of Wiley, 1979. xiii, 257 p.; 24 cm. Includes indexes. 1. Research — Methodology. 2. Science — Philosophy 3. Knowledge, Theory of I. T.
Q180.55.M4 W44　507/.2 19　　LC 78-31093　　ISBN 0470266503

## Q181–199 Study and Teaching. Tables

**Comber, L. C.** **5.982**
Science education in nineteen countries; an empirical study [by] L. C. Comber and John P. Keeves. With a foreword by Torsten Husén. — New York: Wiley, [1973] 403 p.: illus.; 22 cm. — (International studies in evaluation, 1) 'A Halsted Press book.' 1. Science — Study and teaching (Secondary) 2. Scientific surveys I. Keeves, John P. joint author. II. T. III. Series.
Q181.C548　507/.12　　LC 73-8048　　ISBN 0470166827

**Conant, James Bryant, 189-.** • **5.983**
On understanding science: an historical approach / by James B. Conant; with a new foreword by the author. — [New York]: New American Library, 1951. 144 p.: ill.; 18 cm. — (Mentor book; M68) 1. Science — Study and teaching 2. Science — History 3. Science — Philosophy I. T.
Q181.C56 1951　　LC 51-8972

**Education in the 80's—science** / Mary Budd Rowe, editor; **5.984**
classroom teacher consultant, Wilbert S. Higuchi.
Washington, D.C.: National Education Association, c1982. 172 p.: ill.; 23 cm. — (Education in the 80's.) 1. Science — Study and teaching I. Rowe, Mary Budd. II. Series.
Q181.E46 1982　507/.1 19　　LC 81-18865　　ISBN 0810631628

**Harré, Rom.** **5.985**
Great scientific experiments: twenty experiments that changed our view of the world / Rom Harré. — Oxford [Oxfordshire]; New York: Oxford University Press, 1983, c1981. viii, 216 p., [4] p. of plates: ill.; 20 cm. — (Oxford paperbacks) Includes index. 1. Science — Methodology — Case studies. 2. Science — Experiments — Philosophy. 3. Science — History — Sources. 4. Scientists — Biography I. T.
Q182.3.H37 1983　507/.2 19　　LC 82-19035　　ISBN 0192860364

**John, J. A.** **5.986**
Experiments, design, and analysis. — 2nd ed. / [by] J. A. John and M. H. Quenouille. — London: Griffin, 1977. 296 p.: ill.; 25 cm. First ed. by M. H. Quenouille alone published in 1953 under title: The design and analysis of experiment. Includes index. 1. Science — Experiments 2. Mathematical statistics I. Quenouille, M. H. joint author. II. T.
Q182.3.J64 1977　001.4/24　　LC 78-314211　　ISBN 0852642229

**Collette, Alfred T.** **5.987**
Science instruction in the middle and secondary schools / Alfred T. Collette, Eugene L. Chiappetta. — St. Louis: Times Mirror/Mosby College Pub., 1984. xvi, 565, 42, 13 p.: ill.; 25 cm. 1. Science — Study and teaching (Secondary) — United States. I. Chiappetta, Eugene L. II. T.
Q183.3.A1 C637 1984　507/.1273 19　　LC 83-12126　　ISBN 0801610958

**Nelkin, Dorothy.** **5.988**
Science textbook controversies and the politics of equal time / Dorothy Nelkin. Cambridge, Mass.: MIT Press, c1977. xi, 174 p.; 24 cm. Includes index. 1. Science — Study and teaching — United States 2. Science — Text-books. I. T.
Q183.3.A1 N44　507/.1073　　LC 76-58459　　ISBN 0262140276

**Skolnick, Joan.** **5.989**
How to encourage girls in math & science: strategies for parents and educators / Joan Skolnick, Carol Langbort, Lucille Day. — Englewood Cliffs, N.J.: Prentice-Hall, c1982. xi, 192 p.: ill.; 24 cm. 'A Spectrum book.' 1. Science — Study and teaching — United States 2. Mathematics — Study and teaching — United States 3. Women — Education — United States. I. Langbort, Carol. II. Day, Lucille. III. T.
Q183.3.A1 S56 1982　507/.1073 19　　LC 82-390　　ISBN 0134056701

**Kahn, Brian.** **5.990**
Computers in science: using computers for learning and teaching / Brian Kahn. — Cambridge [Cambridgeshire]; New York: Cambridge University Press, 1985. 130 p.: ill.; 21 cm. (Cambridge science education series.) 1. Science — Data processing 2. Science — Study and teaching — Data processing. 3. Computers I. T. II. Series.
Q183.9.K34 1985　507 19　　LC 84-17048　　ISBN 0521278074

**Daumas, Maurice.** **5.991**
[Instruments scientifiques aux XVIIe et XVIIIe siècles. English] Scientific instruments of the seventeenth and eighteenth centuries. Translated and edited by Mary Holbrook. New York, Praeger Publishers [1972] 361 p. illus. 26 cm. Translation of Les instruments scientifiques aux XVIIe et XVIIIe siècles. 1. Scientific apparatus and instruments I. T.
Q185.D3513　502/.8　　LC 77-112019

**National Research Council (U.S.)** • **5.992**
International critical tables of numerical data, physics, chemistry and technology: prepared under the auspices of the International Research Council and the National Academy of Sciences / by the National Research Council of the United States of America; editor-in-chief Edward W. Washburn, associate editors Clarence J. West [et al.]. — 1st ed. — New York: Published for the National Research Council by the McGraw-Hill, 1926-1930. 7 v.: ill. 1. Science — Tables, etc. I. Washburn, Edward Wight, 1881- II. West, Clarence Jay, 1886- III. International Council of Scientific Unions. IV. National Academy of Sciences (U.S.) V. T.
Q199.N32　　LC 26-10495

**Grogan, Denis Joseph.** **5.993**
Science and technology: an introduction to the literature / Denis Grogan. — 4th ed. — London: C. Bingley, 1982. 400 p.; 23 cm. 1. Scientific literature

2. Technical literature 3. Reference books — Science. 4. Reference books — Technology. I. T.
Q225.5.G76 1982    507 19    *LC* 82-182696    *ISBN* 0851573150

## Q295 SYSTEM THEORY

**Iberall, Arthur S.**    5.994
Toward a general science of viable systems [by] Arthur S. Iberall. — New York: McGraw-Hill, [1971, c1972] xvi, 414 p.: illus.; 23 cm. 1. System theory I. T.
Q295.I24    501    *LC* 77-128790    *ISBN* 0070316724

**Vemuri, V.**    5.995
Modeling of complex systems: an introduction / V. Vemuri. — New York: Academic Press, 1978. xvi, 448 p.: ill.; 24 cm. — (Operations research and industrial engineering) 1. System theory I. T. II. Title: Complex systems.
Q295.V45    003    *LC* 77-77246    *ISBN* 0127165509

**Weinberg, Gerald M.**    5.996
An introduction to general systems thinking / Gerald M. Weinberg. — New York: Wiley, [1975] xxi, 279 p.: ill.; 23 cm. (Wiley series on systems engineering and analysis) 'A Wiley-Interscience publication.' 1. System theory I. T.
Q295.W44 1975    003    *LC* 74-26689    *ISBN* 0471925632

## Q310–360 CYBERNETICS. ARTIFICIAL INTELLIGENCE. INFORMATION THEORY

## Q310 Cybernetics

**Arbib, Michael A.**    5.997
The metaphorical brain; an introduction to cybernetics as artifical intelligence and brain theory [by] Michael A. Arbib. Illustrated by Auro Lecci. — New York: Wiley-Interscience, [1972] xii, 243 p.: illus.; 26 cm. 1. Cybernetics 2. Artificial intelligence 3. Neuropsychology I. T.
Q310.A72    001.53/5    *LC* 72-2490    *ISBN* 0471032492

**Hassenstein, Bernhard.**    5.998
Information and control in the living organism: an elementary introduction. — London: Chapman and Hall, 1972 (c1971). viii, 159 p.: illus.; 22 cm. Rev. translation of the 3d German ed., published under title: Biologische Kybernetic. Distributed in the U.S.A. by Barnes & Noble. 1. Cybernetics 2. Information theory in biology I. T.
Q310.H3713    612/.022    *LC* 72-176190    *ISBN* 0412106906

## Q334–336 Artificial Intelligence

**The AI business: the commercial uses of artificial intelligence /**    5.999
**edited by Patrick H. Winston, Karen A. Prendergast.**
Cambridge, Mass.: MIT Press, c1984. 324 p.: ill.; 24 cm. Includes index. 1. Artificial intelligence — Congresses. 2. Robots, Industrial — Congresses. 3. Expert systems (Computer science) — Congresses. I. Winston, Patrick Henry. II. Prendergast, Karen A. III. Title: A.I. business.
Q334.A45 1984    338.4/700153/5 19    *LC* 83-25572    *ISBN* 0262231174

**Hunt, V. Daniel.**    5.1000
Artificial intelligence & expert systems sourcebook / V. Daniel Hunt. — New York: Chapman & Hall, 1986. xi, 315 p.: ill.; 25 cm. — (Chapman and Hall advanced industrial technology series.) 1. Artificial intelligence — Dictionaries. 2. Expert systems (Computer science) — Dictionaries. I. T. II. Title: Artificial intelligence and expert systems sourcebook. III. Series.
Q334.6.H86 1986    006.3/03/21 19    *LC* 86-210815    *ISBN* 0412012111

**Aleksander, Igor.**    5.1001
Designing intelligent systems: an introduction / Igor Aleksander. — New York: UNIPUB, c1984. 166 p.: ill.; 23 cm. Includes index. 1. Artificial intelligence 2. Mathematical models 3. Robotics 4. System theory I. T.
Q335.A442 1984    001.53/5 19    *LC* 84-40552    *ISBN* 0890590435

**Applications in artificial intelligence / edited by Stephen J.**    5.1002
**Andriole.**
Princeton, N.J.: Petrocelli Books, c1985. xxiv, 528 p.: ill.; 24 cm. 1. Artificial intelligence I. Andriole, Stephen J.
Q335.A67 1985    001.53/5 19    *LC* 84-26450    *ISBN* 0894332198

**Artificial intelligence, an MIT perspective / edited by Patrick**    5.1003
**Henry Winston and Richard Henry Brown.**
Cambridge, Mass.: MIT Press, c1979. 2 v.: ill.; 24 cm. — (MIT Press series in artificial intelligence.) 1. Artificial intelligence I. Winston, Patrick Henry. II. Brown, Richard Henry. III. Series.
Q335.A7865    001.53/5    *LC* 78-26640    *ISBN* 0262230968

**Bellman, Richard Ernest, 1920-.**    5.1004
An introduction to artificial intelligence: can computers think? / Richard Bellman. — San Francisco: Boyd & Fraser Pub. Co., c1978. x, 146 p.: ill.; 23 cm. 1. Artificial intelligence 2. Computers I. T.
Q335.B43    001.53/5    *LC* 78-9474    *ISBN* 0878350667

**Boden, Margaret A.**    5.1005
Artificial intelligence and natural man / Margaret A. Boden. — New York: Basic Books, c1977. ix, 537 p.; 24 cm. Includes indexes. 1. Artificial intelligence 2. Thought and thinking I. T.
Q335.B56    001.53/5    *LC* 76-8117    *ISBN* 0465004504

**Charniak, Eugene.**    5.1006
Introduction to artificial intelligence / Eugene Charniak, Drew McDermott. — Reading, Mass.: Addison-Wesley, c1985. xvii, 701 p.: ill.; 24 cm. Includes index. 1. Artificial intelligence I. McDermott, Drew V. II. T.
Q335.C483 1985    001.53/5 19    *LC* 84-14542    *ISBN* 0201119455

**Computational models of discourse / edited by Michael Brady**    5.1007
**and Robert C. Berwick; contributors, James Allen ... [et al.].**
Cambridge, Mass.: MIT Press, c1983. xxiii, 403 p.: ill.; 24 cm. — (MIT Press series in artificial intelligence.) Includes index. 1. Artificial intelligence 2. Linguistics — Data processing 3. Speech processing systems I. Brady, Michael, 1945- II. Berwick, Robert C. III. Allen, James. IV. Series.
Q335.C56 1983    001.53/5 19    *LC* 82-20402    *ISBN* 0262021838

**Dreyfus, Hubert L.**    5.1008
What computers can't do; a critique of artificial reason, by Hubert L. Dreyfus. — [1st ed.]. — New York: Harper & Row, [1972] xxxv, 259 p.; 22 cm. 1. Artificial intelligence I. T.
Q335.D74 1972    001.53/5    *LC* 67-22524    *ISBN* 0060110821

**Shapiro, Stuart Charles.**    5.1009
Encyclopedia of artificial intelligence / Stuart C. Shapiro, editor in chief, David Eckroth, managing editor. — New York: Wiley, 1987. 2 v. 'A Wiley-Interscience publication.' 1. Artificial intelligence — Dictionaries. I. Eckroth, David. II. T.
Q335.E53 1987    006.3/03/21 19    *LC* 86-26739    *ISBN* 0471807486

**The Handbook of artificial intelligence / edited by Avron Barr**    5.1010
**and Edward A. Feigenbaum.**
Stanford, Calif.: HeirisTech Press, c1981-. v. < 1 >: ill.; 24 cm. Includes index. 1. Artificial intelligence I. Barr, Avron, 1949- II. Feigenbaum, Edward A.
Q335.H36    001.53/5 19    *LC* 80-28621    *ISBN* 0865760047

**McCorduck, Pamela, 1940-.**    5.1011
Machines who think: a personal inquiry into the history and prospects of artificial intelligence / Pamela McCorduck. — San Francisco: W. H. Freeman, c1979. xiv, 375 p.: ports.; 24 cm. Includes index. 1. Artificial intelligence — History. I. T.
Q335.M23    001.53/9/09    *LC* 79-13809    *ISBN* 0716710722

**Machine intelligence.**    5.1012
Chichester [West Sussex]: New York: Halsted Press. v.: ill.; 26 cm. Annual. Began in 1967; ceased with 10, in 1982. Description based on vol. 9. 1. Artificial intelligence — Collected works. I. Machine Intelligence Workshop. Proceedings. II. International Machine Intelligence Workshop.
Q335.M27    001.5/35    *LC* 67-13648

**Michie, Donald.**    5.1013
The knowledge machine: artificial intelligence and the future of man / Donald Michie and Rory Johnston. — 1st ed. — New York: W. Morrow, c1985. 300 p.: ill.; 22 cm. Includes index. 1. Artificial intelligence 2. Computers — Social aspects. 3. Technology — Social aspects I. Johnston, Rory. II. T.
Q335.M468 1985    303.4/834 19    *LC* 84-29582    *ISBN* 0688032672

**Nilsson, Nils J., 1933-.** **5.1014**
Principles of artificial intelligence / Nils J. Nilsson. — Palo Alto, Calif.: Tioga Pub. Co., c1980. xv, 476 p.: ill.; 24 cm. Includes indexes. 1. Artificial intelligence I. T.
Q335.N515      001.53/5      LC 79-67584      ISBN 0935382011

**Robot vision / edited by Alan Pugh.** **5.1015**
[Kempston]: IFS (Publications); Berlin; New York: Springer, 1983. xi, 356 p.: ill.; 24 cm. — (International trends in manufacturing technology.) 1. Information display systems industry 2. Robots, Industrial 3. Artificial intelligence 4. Automata. I. Pugh, A. (Alan) II. Series.
Q335.R62 1983      ISBN 0903608324

**Turner, Raymond, 1947-.** **5.1016**
Logics for artificial intelligence / Raymond Turner. — Chichester: E. Horwood; New York: Halsted Press, 1984. 121 p.: ill.; 25 cm. (Ellis Horwood series in artificial intelligence.) 1. Artificial intelligence 2. Logic, Symbolic and mathematical I. T. II. Series.
Q335.T87 1984      001.53/5 19      LC 84-19810      ISBN 0470201231

**Winston, Patrick Henry.** **5.1017**
Artificial intelligence / Patrick Henry Winston. — 2nd ed. — Reading, Mass.: Addison-Wesley, c1984. xv, 527 p.: ill.; 24 cm. — (Addison-Wesley series in computer science.) Includes index. 1. Artificial intelligence I. T. II. Series.
Q335.W56 1984      001.53/5 19      LC 83-19691      ISBN 0201082594

**Feigenbaum, Edward A. ed.** • **5.1018**
Computers and thought / a collection of articles by Armer [and others]; edited by Edward A. Feigenbaum & Julian Feldman. — New York: McGraw-Hill, [c1963] xiv, 535 p.: ill.; 24 cm. 1. Artificial intelligence — Addresses, essays, lectures. 2. Digital computer simulation — Addresses, essays, lectures. I. Feldman, Julian. joint ed. II. T.
Q335.5.F4      006      LC 63-17596

**Charniak, Eugene.** **5.1019**
Artificial intelligence programming / Eugene Charniak, Christopher K. Riesbeck, Drew V. McDermott. — Hillsdale, N.J.: L. Erlbaum Associates;

New York: distributed by the Halsted Press Division, Wiley, 1980. xii, 323 p.; 24 cm. Includes indexes. 1. Artificial intelligence — Data processing 2. LISP (Computer program language) I. Riesbeck, Christopher K. joint author. II. McDermott, Drew V. joint author. III. T.
Q336.C48 1980      001.53/5/0285542      LC 79-22120      ISBN 0898590043

**Inside computer understanding: five programs plus miniatures /** **5.1020**
**edited by Roger C. Schank and Christopher K. Riesbeck.**
New Haven, Ct.: Yale University, Computer Science Dept., c1981. xii, 386 p.: ill.; 24 cm. Includes indexes. 1. Artificial intelligence 2. Programming (Electronic computers) I. Schank, Roger C., 1946- II. Riesbeck, Christopher K.
Q336.I55 1981      001.64/2      LC 80-18314      ISBN 089859071X

# Q360 Information Theory

**Abramson, Norman.** • **5.1021**
Information theory and coding. — New York: McGraw-Hill, c1963. xvi, 201 p.: ill. — (McGraw-Hill electronic sciences series.) 1. Information theory I. T. II. Series.
Q360.A2      519.7      LC 63-16192

**Campbell, Jeremy, 1931-.** **5.1022**
Grammatical man: information, entropy, language, and life / by Jeremy Campbell. — New York: Simon and Schuster, c1982. 319 p.; 22 cm. 1. Information theory I. T.
Q360.C33 1982      001.53/9 19      LC 82-3272      ISBN 0671440616

# QA Mathematics

## QA1–99 REFERENCE. GENERAL WORKS

**Frege, Gottlob, 1848-1925.** 5.1023
[Kleine Schriften. English. Selections] Collected papers on mathematics, logic, and philosophy / Gottlob Frege; edited by Brian McGuinness; translated by Max Black ... [et al.]. — Oxford, UK; New York, NY, USA: B. Blackwell, 1984. viii, 412 p.: ill.; 24 cm. Translation of most of the papers which appeared in: Kleine Schriften. 1. Mathematics — Collected works. I. McGuinness, Brian. II. T.
QA3.F732513 1984    510 19    *LC* 84-12490    *ISBN* 0631127283

**Newman, James Roy, 1907-1966. ed.** • 5.1024
The world of mathematics; a small library of the literature of mathematics from A'h–mosé the scribe to Albert Einstein, presented with commentaries and notes by James R. Newman. — New York: Simon and Schuster, 1956. 4 v. (xviii, 2535 p.): illus.; 23 cm. 1. Mathematics — Collected works. I. T.
QA3.N48    510.82    *LC* 55-10060

## QA5 Dictionaries

**James, Glenn, 1882- ed.** 5.1025
Mathematics dictionary / James [and] James; contributors, Armen A. Alchian ... [et al.]; translators, J. George Adashko ... [et al.]. — 4th ed. — New York: Van Nostrand Reinhold Co., c1976. vii, 509 p.: ill.; 24 cm. Index in French, German, Russian, and Spanish. 1. Mathematics — Dictionaries — Polyglot. 2. Dictionaries, Polyglot I. James, Robert C. (Robert Clarke) joint author. II. Alchian, Armen Albert, 1914- III. T.
QA5.J32 1976    510/.3    *LC* 76-233    *ISBN* 0442240910

**Nihon Sūgakkai.** 5.1026
[Iwanami sūgaku jiten. English] Encyclopedic dictionary of mathematics / by the Mathematical Society of Japan; edited by Shōkichi Iyanaga and Yukiyosi Kawada; translation reviewed by Kenneth O. May. — Cambridge, Mass.: MIT Press, c1977. 2 v. (xiv, 1750 p.): ill.; 30 cm. Translation of Iwanami sūgaku ziten (i.e. jiten) 1. Mathematics — Dictionaries I. Iyanaga, Shōkichi, 1906- II. Kawada, Yukiyosi, 1916- III. T.
QA5.N513    510/.3    *LC* 77-1129    *ISBN* 0262090163

**Russian–English dictionary of the mathematical sciences. By** • 5.1027
**A.J. Lohwater with the collaboration of S.H. Gould, under the joint auspices of the National Academy of Sciences of the USA, the Academy of Sciences of the USSR [and] the American Mathematical Society.**
Providence, American Mathematical Society, 1961. xiii, 267 p. 24 cm. 'Publication of the English-Russian half ... [was] undertaken by the Soviet Academy of Sciences [under the title: Anglo-russkiĭ slovar' matematicheskikh terminov] 1. Mathematics — Dictionaries — Russian. 2. Russian language — Dictionaries — English. I. Lohwater, A. J. II. National Academy of Sciences (U.S.) III. American Mathematical Society. IV. Matematicheskiĭ institut im. V.A. Steklova. Anglo-russkiĭ slovar' matematicheskikh terminov
QA5. R8    510.3    *LC* 61-15685

## QA7 Essays. Lectures

**Hardy, Godfrey Harold, 1877-1947.** • 5.1028
A mathematician's apology, by G. H. Hardy. [1st ed.] reprinted with a foreword by C. P. Snow. London, Cambridge U.P., 1967. 153 p. 19 cm. 1. Mathematics — Addresses, essays, lectures. I. Snow, C. P. (Charles Percy), 1905- II. T.
QA7.H3 1967    510    *LC* 67-21958

**Lang, Serge, 1927-.** 5.1029
The beauty of doing mathematics: three public dialogues / Serge Lang. — New York: Springer-Verlag, c1985. vii, 127 p.: ill.; 24 cm. 'Originally, they were published in the Revue du Palais de la découverte [in French]'—Pref. 1. Mathematics — Addresses, essays, lectures. I. T.
QA7.L28 1985    510 19    *LC* 85-13838    *ISBN* 0387961496

**Mathematics: people, problems, results / edited by Douglas M.** 5.1030
**Campbell and John C. Higgins.**
Belmont, Calif.: Wadsworth International, c1984. 3 v.: ill.; 24 cm. 1. Mathematics — Addresses, essays, lectures. I. Campbell, Douglas M., 1943- II. Higgins, John C., 1935-
QA7.M34466 1984    510 19    *LC* 83-17039    *ISBN* 0534028799

**Mathematics tomorrow / edited by Lynn Arthur Steen.** 5.1031
New York: Springer-Verlag, c1981. vi, 250 p.: ill.; 24 cm. 1. Mathematics — Addresses, essays, lectures. I. Steen, Lynn Arthur, 1941-
QA7.M3448    510 19    *LC* 81-370    *ISBN* 0387905642

## QA8–8.7 Philosophy

**Davis, Philip J., 1923-.** 5.1032
The mathematical experience / Philip J. Davis, Reuben Hersh; with an introd. by Gian–Carlo Rota. — Boston: Birkhäuser, 1981 (c1980). xix, 440 p.: ill.; 24 cm. Includes index. 1. Mathematics — Philosophy 2. Mathematics — History. 3. Mathematics — Study and teaching I. Hersh, Reuben, 1927- joint author. II. T.
QA8.4.D37    510    *LC* 80-17910    *ISBN* 376433018X

**Lakatos, Imre.** 5.1033
Proofs and refutations: the logic of mathematical discovery / by Imre Lakatos; edited by John Worrall and Elie Zahar. — Cambridge; New York: Cambridge University Press, 1976. xii, 174 p.; 23 cm. Includes indexes. 1. Mathematics — Philosophy 2. Logic, Symbolic and mathematical I. T.
QA8.4.L34    511/.3    *LC* 75-32478    *ISBN* 052121078X

**Pottage, John, 1924-.** 5.1034
Geometrical investigations: illustrating the art of discovery in the mathematical field / John Pottage; foreword by Stillman Drake. — Reading, Mass.: Addison-Wesley, 1983. xxi, 480 p.: ill.; 25 cm. Includes index. 1. Mathematics — Philosophy 2. Mathematics — History. I. T.
QA8.4.P67 1983    510/.1 19    *LC* 82-11357    *ISBN* 0201057336

**Wittgenstein, Ludwig, 1889-1951.** 5.1035
[Bemerkungen über die Grundlagen der Matematik. English] Remarks on the foundations of mathematics / by Ludwig Wittgenstein; edited by G. H. von Wright, R. Rhees, G. E. M. Anscombe; translated by G. E. M. Anscombe. — Rev. ed. — Cambridge, Mass.: MIT Press, 1978. 444 p.: ill.; 23 cm. Translation of Bemerkungen über die Grundlagen der Mathematik. Includes index. 1. Mathematics — Philosophy I. Wright, G. H. von (Georg Henrik von), 1916- II. Rhees, Rush. III. Anscombe, G. E. M. (Gertrude Elizabeth Margaret) IV. T.
QA8.4.W5613 1978b    510/.1    *LC* 78-59781    *ISBN* 0262230801

## QA9–10.3 Mathematical Logic

(see also: BC131-135)

**Anderson, Alan Ross.** 5.1036
Entailment: the logic of relevance and necessity, vol. I / by Alan Ross Anderson, Nuel D. Belnap, Jr.; with contributions by J. Michael Dunn ... [et al.]. — Princeton, N.J.: Princeton University Press, c1975. 1 v.; 25 cm. Includes indexes. 1. Entailment (Logic) I. Belnap, Nuel D., 1930- joint author. II. T.
QA9.A634 1975    511/.3    *LC* 72-14016    *ISBN* 0691071926

**Carnap, Rudolf, 1891-1970.** • 5.1037
Foundations of logic and mathematics / by Rudolf Carnap. — Chicago: University of Chicago Press, 1939. iv, 71 p. — (International encyclopedia of

unified science. Foundations of the unity of science; v.1, no. 3) Includes index. 1. Logic, Symbolic and mathematical 2. Mathematics — Philosophy I. T.
QA9.C3x      LC 40-3146

**Chang, Chin-Liang, 1937-.**                                                            **5.1038**
Symbolic logic and mechanical theorem proving [by] Chin–liang Chang [and] Richard Char–tung Lee. New York, Academic Press [1973] xiii, 331 p. illus. 24 cm. (Computer science and applied mathematics) 1. Logic, Symbolic and mathematical 2. Automatic theorem proving 3. Artificial intelligence I. Lee, Richard Char-tung, 1939- joint author. II. T.
QA9.C483      511'.3      LC 72-88358

**Enderton, Herbert B.**                                                                 **5.1039**
A mathematical introduction to logic [by] Herbert B. Enderton. — New York: Academic Press, [1972] xiii, 295 p.: illus.; 24 cm. 1. Logic, Symbolic and mathematical I. T.
QA9.E54 1972      511'.3      LC 78-182659      ISBN 0122384504

**Frege, Gottlob, 1848-1925.**                                                       • **5.1040**
The foundations of arithmetic; a logico–mathematical enquiry into the concept of number. English translation by J. L. Austin. — 2d ed. — Evanston, Ill.: Northwestern University Press, 1968 [c1959] xii, xii [superscript e], xi, xi [superscript e], 119, 119 [superscript e]; 23 cm. German and English on opposite pages, numbered in duplicate. Reprint of the 1953 ed. 1. Number concept 2. Arithmetic — Foundations I. T.
QA9.F7514 1968      512/.81      LC 68-8996

**Greenstein, Carol Horn.**                                                              **5.1041**
Dictionary of logical terms and symbols / Carol Horn Greenstein. — New York: Van Nostrand Reinhold, c1978. xiii, 188 p.: ill.; 24 cm. 1. Logic, Symbolic and mathematical — Dictionaries. I. T.
QA9.G698      511'.3/03      LC 77-17513      ISBN 0442228341

**Hadamard, Jacques, 1865-1963.**                                                    • **5.1042**
An essay on the psychology of invention in the mathematical field / by Jacques Hadamard. — New York: Dover publications, 1954, c1945. 145 p.; 22 cm. 'An unabridged and unaltered reprint of the first edition.' 1. Mathematics — Philosophy 2. Psychology 3. Inventions I. T. II. Title: The psychology of invention in the mathematical field.
QA9.H25 1954      QA9.H25.      LC 54-4731

**Hintikka, Jaakko, 1929- comp.**                                                    • **5.1043**
The philosophy of mathematics. Edited by Jaako Hintikka. London, Oxford U.P., 1969. [5], 186 p. illus. 21 cm. (Oxford readings in philosophy) 1. Mathematics — Philosophy — Addresses, essays, lectures. I. T.
QA9.H53      510/.01      LC 71-441791      ISBN 0198750110

**Kleene, Stephen Cole, 1909-.**                                                     • **5.1044**
Introduction to metamathematics / by Stephen Cole Kleene. — Amsterdam: North-Holland Pub., 1952. x, 550 p.; 23 cm. — 1. Metamathematics I. T.
QA9.K6 1952      510.1

**Manin, IU. I.**                                                                        **5.1045**
A course in mathematical logic / Y. I. Manin; translated from the Russian by Neal Koblitz. — New York: Springer Verlag, c1977. xiii, 286 p.; 25 cm. — (Graduate texts in mathematics. 53) Includes index. 1. Logic, Symbolic and mathematical I. T. II. Series.
QA9.M29613      511'.3      LC 77-1838      ISBN 0387902430

**Mendelson, Elliott.**                                                                  **5.1046**
Introduction to mathematical logic / Elliott Mendelson. — 2d ed. — New York: Van Nostrand, c1979. viii, 328 p.; 24 cm. Includes index. 1. Logic, Symbolic and mathematical I. T.
QA9.M4 1979      511'.3      LC 78-65959      ISBN 0442253079

**Nagel, Ernest, 1901-.**                                                            • **5.1047**
Gödel's proof, by Ernest Nagel and James R. Newman. — [New York]: New York University Press, 1958. 118 p.: illus.; 21 cm. 1. Gödel's theorem I. Newman, James Roy, 1907-1966. joint author. II. T.
QA9.N3      510.1      LC 58-5610

**Polya, George, 1887-.**                                                            • **5.1048**
Mathematics and plausible reasoning. — Princeton, N.J.: Princeton University Press, 1954. 2 v.: diagrs., tables.; 25 cm. 1. Mathematics — Philosophy 2. Logic, Symbolic and mathematical I. T.
QA9.P57      510.1      LC 53-6388

**Russell, Bertrand, 1872-1970.**                                                    • **5.1049**
Introduction to mathematical philosophy. London, G. Allen and Unwin [1970] xii, 208 p. 23 cm. (The Muirhead library of philosophy) 'First published in 1919 ... thirteenth impression, 1970.' 1. Mathematics — Philosophy I. T. II. Title: Mathematical philosophy.
QA9.R8 1970      510/.1      LC 79-25179      ISBN 0045100209

**Tarski, Alfred.**                                                                  • **5.1050**
Introduction to logic and to the methodology of deductive sciences. 3d ed.rev. New York: Oxford U.P., 1965. 252p. (Galaxy book; GB133.) "Partially modified and extended editon of the author's On mathematical logic and deductive method, which appeared first in 1936 in Polish and then in 1937 in an exact German translation (under the title: Einführung in die mathematische Logik und in die Methodologie der Mathematik)" 1. Mathematics — Philosophy 2. Arithmetic — Foundations I. T.
QA9.T28 1965      510.1      LC 65-3257

**Weyl, Hermann, 1885-1955.**                                                        • **5.1051**
[Philosophie der mathematik und naturwissenschaft. English] Philosophy of mathematics and natural science. Rev. and augm. English ed., based on a translation of Olaf Helmer. Princeton, Princeton University Press, 1949. x, 311 p. diagrs. 24 cm. 1. Mathematics — Philosophy 2. Science — Philosophy I. T.
QA9.W412 1949      510.1      LC 49-9797

**What is mathematical logic? / J. N. Crossley...[et al.].**                             **5.1052**
London: Oxford University Press, 1972. 82 p.: ill.; 21 cm. — (Oxford paperbacks university series; 60) 1. Logic, Symbolic and mathematical I. Crossley, John N.
QA9.W47      511.3      LC 73-154003      ISBN 0198850875

**Hindley, J. Roger.**                                                                   **5.1053**
Introduction to combinators and [lambda]–calculus / J. Roger Hindley, Jonathan P. Seldin. — Cambridge [Cambridgeshire]; New York: Cambridge University Press, 1986. 360 p.: ill.; 24 cm. — (London Mathematical Society student texts. 1) Includes index. 1. Combinatory logic 2. Lambda calculus I. Seldin, J. P. II. T. III. Series.
QA9.5.H56 1986      511/.6 19      LC 85-29908      ISBN 0521268966

**Rogers, H. (Hartley), 1926-.**                                                         **5.1054**
Theory of recursive functions and effective computability / Hartley Rogers, Jr. — 1st MIT Press pbk. ed. — Cambridge, Mass.: MIT Press, 1987. xxi, 482 p.; 23 cm. Includes indexes. 1. Recursive functions 2. Computable functions I. T.
QA9.615.R64 1987      511.3 19      LC 86-33764      ISBN 0262680521

**Chang, Chen Chung, 1927-.**                                                            **5.1055**
Model theory / C. C. Chang and H. J. Keisler. — 2d ed. — Amsterdam; New York: North-Holland Pub. Co.; New York: distributed by Elsevier North-Holland, 1977, c1973. xii, 554 p.; 23 cm. Includes indexes. 1. Model theory I. Keisler, H. Jerome. joint author. II. T.
QA9.7.C45 1977      511/.8      LC 77-374871      ISBN 0720406927

**Hofstadter, Douglas R., 1945-.**                                                       **5.1056**
Gödel, Escher, Bach: an eternal golden braid / Douglas R. Hofstadter. — New York: Basic Books, c1979. xxi, 777 p.: ill.; 24 cm. Includes index. 1. Bach, Johann Sebastian, 1685-1750. 2. Escher, M. C. (Maurits Cornelis), 1898-1972. 3. Gödel, Kurt. 4. Metamathematics 5. Symmetry 6. Artificial intelligence I. T.
QA9.8.H63      510/.1      LC 78-19943      ISBN 0465026850

**Johnstone, P. T.**                                                                     **5.1057**
Stone spaces / Peter T. Johnstone. — Cambridge [Cambridgeshire]; New York: Cambridge University Press, 1983. xxi, 370 p.: ill.; 24 cm. (Cambridge studies in advanced mathematics. 3) Includes indexes. 1. Algebra, Boolean 2. Representations of algebras 3. Topology 4. Algebra 5. Functional analysis I. T. II. Series.
QA10.3.J63 1983      511.3/24 19

# QA11–20 Study and Teaching

**Higgins, Jon L.**                                                                      **5.1058**
Mathematics teaching and learning [by] Jon L. Higgins. — Worthington, Ohio: C. A. Jones Pub. Co., [1973] viii, 228 p.: illus.; 24 cm. — (International series in education) 1. Mathematics — Study and teaching 2. Learning, Psychology of I. T.
QA11.H48      510/.7      LC 70-184675      ISBN 0839600135

**Polya, George, 1887-.**                                                            • **5.1059**
How to solve it; a new aspect of mathematical method. — 2d ed. — Garden City, N.Y.: Doubleday, 1957. 253 p.; 18 cm. — (Doubleday anchor books, A93) 1. Mathematics — Study and teaching 2. Mathematics — Problems, exercises, etc. I. T. II. Title: Mathematical method.
QA11.P6 1957      510.7      LC 57-5794

**Resnick, Lauren B.**                                                                   **5.1060**
The psychology of mathematics for instruction / Lauren B. Resnick, Wendy W. Ford. — Hillsdale, N.J.: L. Erlbaum Associates, 1981. vi, 266 p.: ill.; 24 cm.

1. Mathematics — Study and teaching — Psychological aspects I. Ford, Wendy W. joint author. II. T.
QA11.R47     370.15/6 19     *LC* 80-29106     *ISBN* 0898590299

**Tobias, Sheila.**        **5.1061**
Overcoming math anxiety / Sheila Tobias. — 1st ed. — New York: Norton, c1978. 278 p.: ill.; 22 cm. 1. Mathematics — Study and teaching — Psychological aspects I. T.
QA11.T67 1978     510/.7     *LC* 78-17583     *ISBN* 0393064395

**Brush, Lorelei R., 1946-.**        **5.1062**
Encouraging girls in mathematics: the problem and the solution / Lorelei R. Brush, with the assistance of Cynthia Char, Nancy Irwin. Glen Takata. Nancy Irwin. — Cambridge, Mass.: Abt Books, c1980. xv, 163 p.: ill.; 24 cm. Includes index. 1. Mathematics — Study and teaching (Secondary) — United States — Psychological aspects. 2. Teenage girls — Education — United States. 3. Mathematics — Study and teaching (Secondary) — New England — Longitudinal studies. I. T.
QA13.B78     510/.7/12     *LC* 79-55774     *ISBN* 0890115427

**Kline, Morris, 1908-.**        **5.1063**
Why Johnny can't add: the failure of the new math. — New York: St. Martin's Press, [1973] 173 p.: illus.; 22 cm. 1. Mathematics — Study and teaching — United States I. T.
QA13.K62     372.7/3/044     *LC* 72-80894

**Papert, Seymour.**        **5.1064**
Mindstorms: children, computers, and powerful ideas / Seymour Papert. — New York: Basic Books, c1980. viii, 230 p.: ill.; 24 cm. 1. Mathematics — Computer-assisted instruction. 2. Computer-assisted instruction I. T.
QA20.C65 P36 1980     372.7     *LC* 79-5200     *ISBN* 0465046274

**Solomon, Cynthia.**        **5.1065**
Computer environments for children: a reflection on theories of learning and education / Cynthia Solomon. — Cambridge, Mass.: MIT Press, c1986. viii, 183 p.: ill.; 24 cm. Originally presented as the author's thesis (doctoral—Harvard Univesity, 1985). Includes index. 1. Mathematics — Computer-assisted instruction. 2. Computer-assisted instruction 3. Mathematics — Study and teaching (Elementary) I. T.
QA20.C65 S64 1986     372.13/9445 19     *LC* 86-3018     *ISBN* 0262192497

# QA21–29 History. Biography

## QA21 GENERAL

**Bochner, S. (Salomon), 1899-.**        **• 5.1066**
The role of mathematics in the rise of science. Princeton, N.J., Princeton University Press, 1966. x, 386 p. 22 cm. 1. Mathematics — History. 2. Science — History I. T.
QA21.B6     510.09     *LC* 66-10550

**Boyer, Carl B. (Carl Benjamin), 1906-.**        **• 5.1067**
A history of mathematics [by] Carl B. Boyer. New York, Wiley [1968] xv, 717 p. illus., ports. 23 cm. 1. Mathematics — History. I. T.
QA21.B767     510/.09     *LC* 68-16506

**Cajori, Florian, 1859-1930.**        **• 5.1068**
A history of mathematical notations, by Florian Cajori. — Chicago, Ill.: The Open court publishing company, [1928-29] 2 v.: illus. (incl. facsims.); 24 cm. 1. Mathematical notation 2. Mathematics — History. 3. Numerals I. T. II. Title: Notations in elementary mathematics.
QA21.C135 1928     510.148     *LC* 28-24355

**Coolidge, Julian Lowell, 1873-1954.**        **• 5.1069**
A history of geometrical methods / by Julian Lowell Coolidge. — New York: Dover publications 1963. — xviii, 451 p.: ill.; 22 cm. 1. Geometry — History. I. T. II. Title: Geometrical methods.
QA21.C65 1963     *LC* 63-3529

**From the calculus to set theory, 1630–1910: an introductory**        **5.1070**
history / edited by I. Grattan–Guinness; with chapters by H. J. M. Bos ... [et al.].
London: Duckworth, 1980. 306 p.: ill.; 24 cm. Includes indexes. 1. Mathematics — History. I. Grattan-Guinness, I. II. Bos, H. J. M.
QA21.F77     510/.9/03 19     *LC* 80-489901     *ISBN* 0715612956

**Kline, Morris, 1908-.**        **5.1071**
Mathematical thought from ancient to modern times. — New York: Oxford University Press, 1972. xvii, 1238 p.: illus.; 24 cm. 1. Mathematics — History. I. T.
QA21.K516     510/.9     *LC* 77-170263     *ISBN* 0195014960

**Kline, Morris, 1908-.**        **• 5.1072**
Mathematics and the physical world. — New York: Crowell, [1959] 482 p.; 23 cm. 1. Mathematics — History. 2. Science — History I. T.
QA21.K517     510.9     *LC* 59-5252

**Lanczos, Cornelius, 1893-.**        **• 5.1073**
Space through the ages; The evolution of geometrical ideas from Pythagoras to Hilbert and Einstein. — London; New York: Academic Press, 1970. x, 320 p.: illus.; 24 cm. 1. Geometry — History. I. T.
QA21.L28     513/.09     *LC* 77-107936     *ISBN* 0124358500

**Smith, David Eugene, 1860-1944.**        **• 5.1074**
History of mathematics ... by David Eugene Smith. Boston, New York [etc.] Ginn and company [c1923-25] 2 v. illus. (incl. ports., facsims.) 22 cm. 1. Mathematics — History. I. T.
QA21.S6     *LC* 23-17980

**Struik, Dirk Jan, 1894-.**        **• 5.1075**
A concise history of mathematics, by Dirk J. Struik. — 3d rev. ed. — New York: Dover Publications, [1967] x, 195 p.: illus., facsims., ports.; 22 cm. 1. Mathematics — History. I. T.
QA21.S87 1967     510/.09     *LC* 66-28622

**Struik, Dirk Jan, 1894- comp.**        **• 5.1076**
A source book in mathematics, 1200–1800, edited by D. J. Struik. — Cambridge, Mass.: Harvard University Press, 1969. xiv, 427 p.: illus.; 24 cm. — (Source books in the history of the sciences.) 1. Mathematics — Early works to 1800. I. T. II. Series.
QA21.S88     510/.08     *LC* 68-21986

**Wilder, Raymond Louis, 1896-.**        **5.1077**
Mathematics as a cultural system / by Raymond L. Wilder. — 1st ed. — Oxford; New York: Pergamon Press, c1981. xii, 182 p.; 22 cm. — (Foundations and philosophy of science and technology series) Includes index. 1. Mathematics — History. 2. Mathematics — Social aspects. I. T. II. Series.
QA21.W368 1981     303.4/83 19     *LC* 80-41255     *ISBN* 0080257968

## QA22–27 BY PERIOD OR COUNTRY

**Heath, Thomas Little, Sir, 1861-1940.**        **• 5.1078**
A manual of Greek mathematics, by Sir Thomas L. Heath ... Oxford, The Clarendon Press, 1931. xvi, 552 p. diagrs. 20 cm. In substance the same as the author's History of Greek Mathematics (Oxford, 1921) cf. Pref. 1. Mathematics, Greek 2. Mathematics — History. I. T.
QA22.H42     *LC* 31-16397

**Neugebauer, O. (Otto), 1899-.**        **• 5.1079**
The exact sciences in antiquity. 2d ed. Providence, Brown University Press, 1957. xvi, 240 p. illus. 24 cm. 1. Mathematics, Ancient 2. Astronomy, Ancient I. T.
QA22.N36 1957     510.93     *LC* 57-12342

**Waerden, B. L. van der (Bartel Leendert), 1903-.**        **5.1080**
Science awakening / English translation by Arnold Dresden; with additions of the author; with contributions by Peter Huber. — New York: Oxford University Press, 1961-1974. 2 v.: ill., plates, ports., map, diagrs., tables; 26 cm. Vol. 1 is a rev. translation of Ontwakende wetenschap. Vol. 2 has subtitle The birth of astronomy, which is a rev. translation of Die Anfänge der astronomie. Erratum slip inserted. 1. Mathematics, Egyptian 2. Mathematics, Babylonian 3. Mathematics, Greek 4. Astronomy, Assyro-Babylonian I. T.
QA22.W33     510/.93     *LC* a 54-7774

**Daffā', 'Alī 'Abd Allāh.**        **5.1081**
The Muslim contribution to mathematics / Ali Abdullah Al–Daffa'. Atlantic Highlands, N.J.: Humanities Press, c1977. 121 p.: ill.; 23 cm. Includes index. 1. Mathematics, Arabic I. T.
QA23.D33 1977     510/.917/4927     *LC* 77-3521     *ISBN* 0391007149

**Mikami, Yoshio.**        **5.1082**
The development of mathematics in China and Japan / by Yoshio Mikami. — 2d ed. — New York: Chelsea Pub. Co., 1974. x, 389 p.: ill.; 21 cm. 1. Mathematics, Chinese 2. Mathematics, Japanese I. T.
QA27.C5 M5 1974     *ISBN* 0828401497

**Gillings, Richard J.**    5.1083
Mathematics in the time of the Pharaohs [by] Richard J. Gillings. — Cambridge, Mass.: MIT Press, [1972] x, 286 p.: illus.; 26 cm. 1. Mathematics, Egyptian I. T.
QA27.E3 G52    512/.1/0932    *LC* 74-137469    *ISBN* 0262070456

**Dubbey, John Michael, 1934-.**    5.1084
The mathematical work of Charles Babbage / J. M. Dubbey. — Cambridge, [Eng.]: Cambridge University Press, 1978. viii, 235 p.: ill.; 23 cm. 1. Babbage, Charles, 1791-1871. 2. Mathematics — Great Britain — History. 3. Computers — History. I. T.
QA27.G7 D8    519.4/092/4    *LC* 77-71409    *ISBN* 0521216494

**Sarasvati Amma, T. A.**    5.1085
Geometry in ancient and medieval India / T. A. Sarasvati Amma. — 1st ed. — Delhi: Motilal Banarsidass, 1979. xi, 280 p.: ill.; 23 cm. Includes quotations in Prakrit or Sanskrit. Originally presented as the author's thesis, Ranchi University. Includes index. 1. Geometry — India — History. I. T.
QA27.I4 S29 1979    516/.00934    *LC* 79-902588    *ISBN* 0896840204

## QA28 BIOGRAPHY, COLLECTIVE

**Bell, Eric Temple, 1883-1960.**    • 5.1086
Men of mathematics, by E. T. Bell. — New York: Simon and Schuster, 1937. xxi, 592 p., 1 l.: front., ports., diagrs.; 25 cm. 1. Mathematicians 2. Mathematics — History. I. T.
QA28.B4    925.1    *LC* 37-27177

**Black mathematicians and their works / edited by Virginia K. Newell ... [et al.].**    5.1087
Ardmore, Pa.: Dorrance, c1980. xvi, 327 p.: ill.; 27 cm. 1. Afro-American mathematicians 2. Mathematics — Addresses, essays, lectures. I. Newell, Virginia K.
QA28.B58    510    *LC* 78-72929    *ISBN* 0805925562

**Heims, Steve J.**    5.1088
John Von Neumann and Norbert Wiener: from mathematics to the technologies of life and death / Steve J. Heims. — Cambridge, Mass.: MIT Press, c1980. xviii, 547 p.: ill.; 24 cm. 1. Von Neumann, John, 1903-1957. 2. Wiener, Norbert, 1894-1964. 3. Mathematicians — United States — Biography. I. T.
QA28.H44    510/.92/2 B    *LC* 80-16185    *ISBN* 0262081059

**Osen, Lynn M.**    5.1089
Women in mathematics [by] Lynn M. Osen. — Cambridge, Mass.: MIT Press, [1974] xii, 185 p.: ports.; 21 cm. 1. Women mathematicians — Biography. I. T.
QA28.O83 1974    510/.92/2 B    *LC* 73-19506    *ISBN* 026215014X

**Perl, Teri.**    5.1090
Math equals: biographies of women mathematicians + related activities / Teri Perl. — Menlo Park, Calif.: Addison-Wesley Pub. Co., c1978. v, 250 p.: ill.; 24 cm. — (Addison-Wesley innovative series) 1. Women mathematicians — Biography. I. T.
QA28.P47    510/.92/2 B    *LC* 78-110110    *ISBN* 0201057093

## QA29 BIOGRAPHY, INDIVIDUAL, A–Z

**Mahoney, Michael Sean.**    5.1091
The mathematical career of Pierre de Fermat (1601–1665). — Princeton, N.J.: Princeton University Press, [1973] xviii, 419 p.: illus.; 25 cm. An expansion and revision of the author's thesis, Princeton University. 1. Fermat, Pierre de, 1601-1665. I. T.
QA29.F45 M33 1973    510/.92/4 B    *LC* 72-733    *ISBN* 0691081190

**Grattan-Guinness, I.**    5.1092
Joseph Fourier, 1768–1830; a survey of his life and work, based on a critical edition of his monograph on the propagation of heat, presented to the Institut de France in 1807 [by] I. Grattan–Guinness, in collaboration with J. R. Ravetz. — Cambridge: MIT Press, [1972] x, 516 p.: illus.; 27 cm. Includes Fourier's original unpublished text of 1807 with title: Théorie de la propagation de la chaleur dans les solides. The first separately published version appeared in 1822 under title: Théorie analytique de la chaleur. 1. Fourier, Jean Baptiste Joseph, baron, 1768-1830. 2. Heat I. Fourier, Jean Baptiste Joseph, baron, 1768-1830. Théorie analytique de la chaleur. 1972. II. T.
QA29.F68 G7    510/.924 B    *LC* 76-128538    *ISBN* 0262070413

**Bühler, W. K. (Walter Kaufmann), 1944-.**    5.1093
Gauss: a biographical study / W.K. Bühler. — Berlin; New York: Springer-Verlag, c1981. viii, 208 p.: ill.; 24 cm. Includes index. 1. Gauss, Carl Friedrich, 1777-1855. 2. Mathematicians — Germany — Biography. I. T.
QA29.G3 B83    510/.92/4 B 19    *LC* 80-29515

**Hankins, Thomas L.**    5.1094
Sir William Rowan Hamilton / Thomas L. Hankins. — Baltimore: Johns Hopkins University Press, c1980. xxi, 474 p.: ill.; 24 cm. Includes index. 1. Hamilton, William Rowan, Sir, 1805-1865. 2. Mathematicians — Ireland — Biography. I. T.
QA29.H2 H36    510/.92/4 B    *LC* 80-10627    *ISBN* 0801822033

**Reid, Constance.**    5.1095
Hilbert. With an appreciation of Hilbert's mathematical work by Hermann Weyl. — Berlin; New York: Springer-Verlag, 1970. xi, 290 p.: illus., ports.; 25 cm. 1. Hilbert, David, 1862-1943. I. Weyl, Hermann, 1885-1955. II. T.
QA29.H5 R4    510/.0924 B    *LC* 76-97989

**Koblitz, Ann Hibner.**    5.1096
A convergence of lives: Sofia Kovalevskaia, scientist, writer, revolutionary / Ann Hibner Koblitz. — Boston: Birkhäuser, 1984 (c1983). xx, 305 p., [11] p. of plates: ill.; 25 cm. Includes index. 1. Kovalevskaia, S. V. (Sof'ia Vasil'evna), 1850-1891. 2. Mathematicians — Soviet Union — Biography. I. T.
QA29.K67 K6    510/.92/4 B 19    *LC* 83-17233    *ISBN* 0817631623

**Emmy Noether: a tribute to her life and work / editors, James W. Brewer, Martha K. Smith.**    5.1097
New York: M. Dekker, c1981. x, 180 p.; 24 cm. — (Monographs and textbooks in pure and applied mathematics. v. 69) 1. Noether, Emmy, 1882-1935. 2. Mathematicians — Germany — Biography. 3. Algebra — Addresses, essays, lectures. I. Noether, Emmy, 1882-1935. II. Brewer, James W., 1942- III. Smith, Martha K., 1944- IV. Series.
QA29.N6 E47    510/.92/4 B 19    *LC* 81-15203    *ISBN* 0824715500

**Hodges, Andrew.**    5.1098
Alan Turing: the enigma / Andrew Hodges. — New York: Simon and Schuster, 1983. 587 p., [8] p. of plates: ill., ports.; 24 cm. 1. Turing, Alan Mathison, 1912-1954. 2. Mathematicians — Great Britain — Biography. I. T.
QA29.T8 H63 1983    510/.92/4 B 19    *LC* 83-19149    *ISBN* 0671492071

**Ulam, Stanislaw M.**    5.1099
Adventures of a mathematician / S. M. Ulam. — New York: Scribner, c1976. xi, 317 p., [11] leaves of plates: ill.; 24 cm. Includes index. 1. Ulam, Stanislaw M. I. T.
QA29.U4 A33    510/.92/4 B    *LC* 75-20133    *ISBN* 0684143917

**Wiener, Norbert, 1894-1964.**    • 5.1100
I am a mathematician, the later life of a prodigy; an autobiographical account of the mature years and career of Norbert Wiener as a continuation of the account of his childhood in Ex–prodigy. — [1st ed.]. — Garden City, N.Y.: Doubleday, 1956. 380 p.; 22 cm. — 1. Wiener, Norbert, 1894-1964. I. T.
QA29.W497 A35    925.1    *LC* 56-5598

**Wiener, Norbert, 1894-1964.**    • 5.1101
Ex–prodigy: my childhood and youth / by Norbert Wiener. — Cambridge, Mass.: M. I. T. Press, 1964, c1953. 309 p. I. T.
QA29.W6x    925.1    *LC* 64-22203

# QA31–41 Mathematics: General Works

### QA31–35 Early to 1800

**Euclid.**    • 5.1102
[Elements English] The thirteen books of Euclid's Elements, translated from the text of Heiberg, with introd. and commentary by Sir Thomas L. Heath. 2d ed., rev. with additions. New York, Dover Publications [1956] 3 v. facsim., diagrs. 22 cm. 'An unabridged and unaltered republication of the second edition [published in 1926]' 1. Mathematics, Greek 2. Geometry — Early works to 1800 I. Heath, Thomas Little, Sir, 1861-1940. ed. and tr. II. T.
QA31.E875 1956    513    *LC* 56-4336

**Newton, Isaac, Sir, 1642-1727.**    • 5.1103
The mathematical works of Isaac Newton / assembled by D. T. Whiteside . — New York: Johnson Reprint Corp., 1964. 2 v. 1. Mathematics — Early works to 1800. 2. Mathematics — Collected works. I. Whiteside, Derek Thomas, ed. II. T.
QA35.N5649    510/.8    *LC* 64-17026

## QA36–39 1801–

**Handbook of applicable mathematics** / chief editor, Walter **5.1104**
Ledermann.
Chichester; New York: J. Wiley, 1984. 2 v., 985 p.: ill.; 26 cm. 'A Wiley-
Interscience publication.' 1. Mathematics — 1961- I. Ledermann, Walter,
1911-
QA36.H36      510      LC 79-42724      ISBN 0471278211

**Courant, Richard, 1888-1972.** • **5.1105**
What is mathematics? An elementary approach to ideas and methods, by
Richard Courant and Herbert Robbins. London, New York [etc.] Oxford
university press [c1948] 3 p. l., v-xix, 521 p. illus., diagrs. 24 cm. 'Suggestions
for further reading': p. 511-514. 1. Mathematics I. Robbins, Herbert. joint
author. II. T.
QA37.C675      510      LC 41-25632

**Dieudonné, Jean Alexandre, 1906-.** **5.1106**
[Panorama des mathématiques pures. English] A panorama of pure
mathematics, as seen by N. Bourbaki / Jean Dieudonné; translated by I.G.
Macdonald. — New York: Academic Press, 1982. x, 289 p.; 24 cm. — (Pure
and applied mathematics; 97) Translation of: Panorama des mathématiques
pures. Includes index. 1. Mathematics — 1961- I. T.
QA37.2.D5 QA3.P8 vol. 97      510 19      LC 80-2330      ISBN
0122155602

**Gårding, Lars, 1919-.** **5.1107**
Encounter with mathematics / Lars Gårding. — New York: Springer-Verlag,
1977. ix, 270 p.: ill.; 24 cm. 1. Mathematics — 1961- I. T.
QA37.2.G28      510      LC 76-54765      ISBN 0387902295

**Jaeger, J. C. (John Conrad), 1907-.** **5.1108**
An introduction to applied mathematics, by J. C. Jaeger and A. M. Starfield. —
2nd ed. — Oxford: Clarendon Press, 1974. xii, 504 p.; 22 cm. 1. Mathematics
— 1961- I. Starfield, A. M. joint author. II. T.
QA37.2.J3 1974      515/.14      LC 74-165469      ISBN 0198531516

**Modules in applied mathematics** / [edited by William F. Lucas]. **5.1109**
New York: Springer-Verlag, c1983. 4 v.: ill.; 25 cm. 1. Mathematics — 1961-
2. Mathematical models I. Lucas, William F., 1933-
QA37.2.M6 1983      510 19      LC 82-10439      0387907246

**Strang, Gilbert.** **5.1110**
Introduction to applied mathematics / Gilbert Strang. — Wellesley, Mass.:
Wellesley-Cambridge Press c1986. ix, 758 p.: ill.; 25 cm. Includes index.
1. Mathematics — 1961- I. T.
QA37.2.S87 1986      510 19      LC 84-52450      ISBN 0961408804

**Klein, Felix, 1849-1925.** • **5.1111**
Elementary mathematics from an advanced standpoint: arithmetic, algebra,
analysis. tr. from the 3d German ed. by E. R. Hedrick and C. A. Noble. With
125 figures. New York, Dover Publications, 1945. ix, 274 p. illus., diagrs. 23 cm.
A translation of v. 1 of the author's three-volume work Elementar-mathematik
vom höheren Standpunkt. 1. Mathematics I. Hedrick, Earle Raymond,
1876-1943, tr. II. Noble, C. A. (Charles Albert), b. 1867. joint tr. III. T.
QA39.K55      510      LC A 48-5461 *

**Herstein, I. N.** **5.1112**
Matters mathematical [by] I. N. Herstein [and] I. Kaplansky. — New York:
Harper & Row, [1974] viii, 246 p.: illus.; 25 cm. 1. Mathematics — 1961-
I. Kaplansky, Irving, 1917- joint author. II. T.
QA39.2.H48      510      LC 74-3755      ISBN 0060428031

**Malkevitch, Joseph, 1942-.** **5.1113**
Graphs, models, and finite mathematics / Joseph Malkevitch, Walter Meyer. —
Englewood Cliffs, N.J.: Prentice-Hall, c1974. x, 515 p.: ill.; 24 cm.
1. Mathematics — 1961- 2. Graph theory 3. Mathematical models I. Meyer,
Walter J. (Walter Joseph), 1943- II. T.
QA39.2.M335 1973      510      LC 73-7580      ISBN 0133634655

## QA40–41 HANDBOOKS. FORMULAS

**Handbook of applied mathematics: selected results and methods** **5.1114**
/ edited by Carl E. Pearson.
2nd ed. — New York: Van Nostrand Reinhold Co., c1983. xiii, 1307 p.: ill.; 24
cm. 1. Mathematics — Handbooks, manuals, etc. I. Pearson, Carl E. II. Title:
Applied mathematics.
QA40.H34 1983      510/.2/02 19      LC 82-20223      ISBN 0442238665

**Korn, Granino Arthur, 1922-.** • **5.1115**
Mathematical handbook for scientists and engineers: definitions, theorems, and
formulas for reference and review / [by] Granino A. Korn [and] Theresa M.
Korn. — 2d, enl. and rev. ed. New York: McGraw-Hill [c1968] xvii, 1130 p.:

ill.; 23 cm. (McGraw-Hill handbooks) 1. Mathematics — Handbooks,
manuals, etc. I. Korn, Theresa M. joint author. II. T.
QA40.K598 1968      510/.02/02      LC 67-16304

**The VNR concise encyclopedia of mathematics** / W. Gellert ... **5.1116**
[et al.], editors; K. A. Hirsch, H. Reichardt, scientific advisors.
1st American ed. — New York: Van Nostrand Reinhold Co., 1977, c1975.
760 p., [28] leaves of plates: ill.; 24 cm. First published under title: Mathematics
at a glance. Includes indexes. 1. Mathematics — Handbooks, manuals, etc.
I. Gellert, Walter. II. Van Nostrand Reinhold Company.
QA40.V18 1977      510/.2/02      LC 76-14575      ISBN 0442226462

**Use of mathematical literature** / editor, A. R. Dorling. **5.1117**
London; Boston: Butterworths, 1977. xii, 260 p.; 23 cm. — (Information
sources for research and development) 1. Mathematical literature
2. Mathematics — Bibliography I. Dorling, Alison Rosemary.
QA41.7.U83      016.51      LC 77-30014      ISBN 0408709138

# QA43 Problems. Solutions

**Guy, Richard K.** **5.1118**
Unsolved problems in number theory / Richard K. Guy. — New York:
Springer-Verlag, c1981. xviii, 161 p.: ill.; 24 cm. — (Problem books in
mathematics.) (Unsolved problems in intuitive mathematics; v. 1) 1. Numbers,
Theory of — Problems, exercises, etc. I. T. II. Series.
QA43.G88 vol. 1 QA141      510/.76 s 512/.7/076 19      LC 81-14551
      ISBN 0387905936

**Larson, Loren C., 1937-.** **5.1119**
Problem–solving through problems / Loren C. Larson. — New York: Springer-
Verlag, c1983. xi, 332 p.: ill.; 25 cm. (Problem books in mathematics.)
1. Mathematics — Problems, exercises, etc. 2. Problem solving I. T.
II. Series.
QA43.L37 1983      510 19      LC 82-19493      ISBN 038790803X

**Polya, George, 1887-.** • **5.1120**
Mathematical discovery; on understanding, learning, and teaching problem
solving. — New York: Wiley, [1962-65] 2 v.: illus.; 24 cm. 1. Mathematics —
Problems, exercises, etc. 2. Problem solving I. T.
QA43.P62      510.76      LC 62-8784

**The Scottish book: mathematical problems from the Scottish** **5.1121**
Cafe / edited by R. Daniel Mauldin.
Boston: Birkhäuser, 1981. xiii, 268 p.: ill.; 25 cm. Includes selected papers from
the Scottish Book Conference, held at North Texas State University in May
1979. 1. Mathematics — Problems, exercises, etc. I. Mauldin, R. Daniel, 1943-
II. Scottish Book Conference (1979: North Texas State University)
QA43.S39      510/.76 19      LC 81-9934      ISBN 3764330457

**Steinhaus, Hugo, 1887-1972.** • **5.1122**
[Sto zadań. English] One hundred problems in elementary mathematics. With a
foreword by Martin Gardner. New York, Basic Books [1964] 174 p. diagrs. 22
cm. Translation of Sto zadań. English version is a revised ed., translated by Mr.
Bharucha-Reid. 1. Mathematics — Problems, exercises, etc. I. T.
QA43.S783      510.76      LC 63-22780

# QA47–59 Tables

**Abramowitz, Milton, 1915-1958. ed.** • **5.1123**
Handbook of mathematical functions, with formulas, graphs, and mathematical
tables, edited by Milton Abramowitz and Irene A. Stegun. New York, Dover
Publications [1965] xiv, 1046 p. illus. 27 cm. 'Unaltered, unabridged
republication of #55, National Bureau of Standards, Applied mathematics
series (1964) corrected edition.'—p. [iv] of cover. 1. Functions 2. Mathematics
— Tables. I. Stegun, Irene A. joint ed. II. T.
QA47.A34 1965      517.5083      LC 65-12253

**Fletcher, A. (Alan), 1903-.** **5.1124**
An index of mathematical tables. 2d ed., by A. Fletcher and others]. Reading,
Mass.: fro Scientific Computing Service [by] Addison-Wesley Pub. Co., 1962. 2
v. (xi, 994 p.); 26 cm. (Addison-Wesley international series) 1. Mathematics —
Tables — Indexes. I. T.
QA47.F55 1962      510.83      LC 62-13521

CRC standard mathematical tables / editor of mathematics and **5.1125**
statistics, William H. Beyer.
27th ed. — Boca Raton, Fla.: CRC Press, c1984. 613 p.: ill.; 23 cm.
1. Mathematics — Tables. I. Beyer, William H, 1930-. II. Chemical Rubber
Company. III. Title: Standard mathematical tables
QA47.S4 1984          510          *LC* 30-4052          *ISBN* 0849306272

# QA75–76.95 Calculating Machines. Electronic Computers. Computer Science

**Babbage, Charles, 1791-1871.**          ● **5.1126**
Charles Babbage and his calculating engines; selected writings by Charles
Babbage and others. Edited with an introd. by Philip Morrison and Emily
Morrison. New York, Dover Publications [1961] 400 p. illus. 21 cm.
1. Calculators 2. Scientists — Correspondence. I. T.
QA75.B28          510.78          *LC* 61-19855

## QA76–76.27 General Works

**Raphael, Bertram.**          **5.1127**
The thinking computer: mind inside matter / Bertram Raphael. — San
Francisco: W. H. Freeman, c1976. xiii, 322 p.: ill.; 24 cm. (A Series of books in
psychology) 1. Computers 2. Problem solving — Data processing 3. Artificial
intelligence I. T.
QA76.R268          001.6/4          *LC* 75-30839          *ISBN* 0716707225

**Tomeski, Edward Alexander.**          **5.1128**
People–oriented computer systems: the computer in transition / Edward
Alexander Tomeski and Harold Lazarus, Konrad Sadek. — Rev. ed. —
Malabar, Fla.: R.E. Krieger Pub. Co., 1983. xx, 347 p.: ill.; 24 cm. 1. Electronic
data processing 2. Computers I. Lazarus, Harold. II. Sadek, Konrad. III. T.
QA76.T58 1983          001.64 19          *LC* 81-14304          *ISBN* 0898743850

**Von Neumann, John, 1903-1957.**          ● **5.1129**
The computer and the brain. — New Haven: Yale University Press, 1958. 82 p.;
21 cm. — (Mrs. Hepsa Ely Silliman memorial lectures) 1. Computers
2. Cybernetics 3. Nervous system I. T.
QA76.V6          510.78          *LC* 58-6542

**Warnier, Jean Dominique.**          **5.1130**
[Homme face a l'intelligence artificielle. English] Computers and human
intelligence / Jean–Dominique Warnier. — Englewood Cliffs, N.J.: Prentice-
Hall, c1986. xv, 141 p.; 24 cm. Translation of: L'homme face a l'intelligence
artificielle. 'A Reston book.' Includes index. 1. Computers 2. Computers and
civilization 3. Artificial intelligence I. T.
QA76.W24313 1986          006.3 19          *LC* 85-21483          *ISBN* 0835909654

**Warnier, Jean Dominique.**          **5.1131**
[Pratique de la construction d'un ensemble de données. English] Logical
construction of systems / Jean Dominique Warnier. — New York: Van
Nostrand Reinhold, c1981. xi, 179 p.; 25 cm. Translation of Pratique de la
construction d'un ensemble de données. Includes index. 1. Electronic data
processing 2. Data base management I. T.
QA76.W24513          001.64 19          *LC* 80-19363          *ISBN* 0442225563

**Weizenbaum, Joseph.**          **5.1132**
Computer power and human reason: from judgment to calculation / Joseph
Weizenbaum. San Francisco: W. H. Freeman, c1976. xii, 300 p.: ill.; 24 cm.
1. Computers 2. Computers and civilization 3. Programming (Electronic
computers) I. T.
QA76.W44          001.6/4          *LC* 75-19305          *ISBN* 0716704641

## QA76.15–.17 Dictionaries. Encyclopedias. Handbooks. History

**Edmunds, Robert A.**          **5.1133**
The Prentice–Hall standard glossary of computer terminology / Robert A.
Edmunds. — Englewood Cliffs, N.J.: Prentice-Hall, Business and Professional
Division, c1985. xv, 489 p.: ill.; 29 cm. 1. Electronic data processing —

Dictionaries. 2. Computers — Dictionaries. I. T. II. Title: Standard glossary
of computer terminology.
QA76.15.E185 1985          001.64/03/21 19          *LC* 84-4765          *ISBN*
0136982344

**Encyclopedia of computer science and engineering / Anthony** **5.1134**
**Ralston, editor; Edwin D. Reilly, Jr., associate editor.**
2nd ed. — New York: Van Nostrand Reinhold Co., c1983. xxix, 1664 p.: ill.; 25
cm. Rev. ed. of: Encyclopedia of computer science. 1st ed. c1976. 1. Computers
— Dictionaries. 2. Electronic data processing — Dictionaries. 3. Information
science — Dictionaries. I. Ralston, Anthony. II. Reilly, Edwin D.
QA76.15.E48 1983          001.64/0321 19          *LC* 82-2700          *ISBN*
0442244967

**Gordon, M. (Michael)**          **5.1135**
Dictionary of new information technology acronyms / M. Gordon, A.
Singleton, C. Rickards. — London: K. Page; Detroit: Gale Research Co., 1984.
217 p.; 25 cm. 1. Electronic data processing — Acronyms. 2. Information
science — Acronyms. I. Singleton, Alan. II. Rickards, C. (Clarence) III. T.
QA76.15.G67 1984          004/.0148 19          *LC* 83-216153          *ISBN*
0810343096

**Complete multilingual dictionary of computer terminology:** **5.1136**
**English, French, Italian, Spanish, Portuguese / compiled by**
**Georges Nania.**
Lincolnwood, Ill.: Passport Books, c1984. 916 p.; 24 cm. Includes indexes.
1. Electronic data processing — Dictionaries — Polyglot. 2. Computers —
Dictionaries — Polyglot. 3. Dictionaries, Polyglot I. Nania, Georges.
QA76.15.N37 1984          001.64/03 19          *LC* 84-150057          *ISBN*
0844291080

**Rosenberg, Jerry Martin.**          **5.1137**
Dictionary of computers, information processing, and telecommunications /
Jerry M. Rosenberg. — 2nd ed. — New York: Wiley, c1987. xv, 734 p.; 25 cm.
Includes glossary of terms in English, Spanish, and French. Rev. ed. of:
Dictionary of computers, data processing, and telecommunications. c1984.
1. Computers — Dictionaries. 2. Electronic data processing — Dictionaries.
3. Telecommunication — Dictionaries. I. Rosenberg, Jerry Martin.
Dictionary of computers, data processing, and telecommunications. II. T.
III. Title: Computers, information processing & telecommunications.
QA76.15.R67 1987          004/.03/21 19          *LC* 87-10407          *ISBN*
0471855596

**Sippl, Charles J.**          **5.1138**
Computer dictionary / Charles J. Sippl. — 4th ed. — Indianapolis, Ind.,
U.S.A.: H.W. Sams, c1985. xii, 562 p.: ill.; 25 cm. 1. Computers —
Dictionaries. 2. Electronic data processing — Dictionaries. I. T.
QA76.15.S5 1985          004/.03/21 19          *LC* 84-51436          *ISBN* 0672222051

**Shurkin, Joel N., 1938-.**          **5.1139**
Engines of the mind: a history of the computer / Joel Shurkin. — New
York: Norton, c1984. 352 p.: ill.; 22 cm. Includes index. 1. Computers —
History. I. T.
QA76.17.S49 1984          001.64/09 19          *LC* 83-11433          *ISBN* 0393018040

## QA76.24–.27 Lectures. Study and Teaching

**Advanced microprocessors / edited by Amar Gupta, Hoo–min** **5.1140**
**D. Toong.**
New York, NY: IEEE Press, c1983. viii, 359 p.: ill.; 29 cm. — (IEEE Press
selected reprint series) 'Prepared under the sponsorship of the IEEE Computer
Society.' 1. Microprocessors — Addresses, essays, lectures. I. Gupta, Amar.
II. Toong, Hoo-min D. III. IEEE Computer Society.
QA76.24.A34 1983          001.64 19          *LC* 83-6092          *ISBN* 0879421673

## QA76.5–.54 Digital Computers, A–J

**Alexandridis, Nikitas A., 1943-.**          **5.1141**
Microprocessor system design concepts / Nikitas A. Alexandridis. —
Rockville, MD: Computer Science Press, c1984. xvi, 623 p.: ill.; 24 cm.
1. Microprocessors 2. Computer architecture 3. Computer engineering I. T.
QA76.5.A369 1984          621.3819/58 19          *LC* 82-18189          *ISBN*
0914894668

**Brinch Hansen, Per, 1938-.**     **5.1142**
Operating system principles. — Englewood Cliffs, N.J.: Prentice-Hall, [1973] xviii, 366 p.: illus.; 25 cm. — (Prentice-Hall series in automatic computation) 1. Operating systems (Computers) 2. Computer programming management I. T.
QA76.5.B76     001.6/44/04     LC 73-491     ISBN 0136378439

**Ceruzzi, Paul E.**     **5.1143**
Reckoners: the prehistory of the digital computer, from relays to the stored program concept, 1935–1945 / Paul E. Ceruzzi. — Westport, Conn.: Greenwood Press, 1983. xii, 181 p.: ill.; 25 cm. — (Contributions to the study of computer science. 0734-757X; no. 1) Includes index. 1. Electronic digital computers — History. I. T. II. Series.
QA76.5.C4164 1983     621.3819/58/09 19     LC 82-20980     ISBN 0313233829

**Davis, Thomas W., 1946-.**     **5.1144**
Experimentation with microprocessor applications / Thomas W. Davis. — Reston, Va.: Reston Pub. Co., c1981. viii, 237 p.: ill.; 24 cm. Includes index. 1. Microprocessors — Laboratory manuals. I. T.
QA76.5.D295     001.64/04/028 19     LC 80-24272     ISBN 0835918122

**The Handbook of computers and computing / edited by Arthur**     **5.1145**
**H. Seidman, Ivan Flores.**
New York, N.Y.: Van Nostrand Reinhold Co., c1984. xiii, 874 p.: ill.; 25 cm. 1. Electronic digital computers — Handbooks, manuals, etc. 2. Programming (Electronic computers) — Handbooks, manuals, etc. 3. Programming languages (Electronic computers) — Handbooks, manuals, etc. I. Seidman, Arthur H. II. Flores, Ivan.
QA76.5.H3544 1984     001.64 19     LC 83-16942     ISBN 0442231210

## QA76.5 K–R

**Katzan, Harry.**     **5.1146**
Introduction to computer science / Harry Katzan, Jr. — New York: Petrocelli/Charter Publishers, 1975. xii, 500 p.: ill.; 24 cm. 1. Electronic digital computers 2. Electronic data processing I. T.
QA76.5.K374 1975     001.6/4     LC 75-5751     ISBN 0884053091

**Khambata, Adi J.**     **5.1147**
Microprocessors/microcomputers: architecture, software, and systems / Adi J. Khambata. — New York: Wiley, c1982. xxiii, 577 p.: ill.; 24 cm. Includes index. 1. Microprocessors 2. Microcomputers 3. Computer software I. T.
QA76.5.K43 1982     001.64/04 19     LC 81-11360     ISBN 0471064904

**Kobayashi, Hisashi.**     **5.1148**
Modeling and analysis: an introduction to system performance evaluation methodology / Hisashi Kobayashi. — 'Corrected ed., 1981.' Reading, Mass.: Addison-Wesley Pub. Co., 1981, c1978. xvii, 446 p.: graphs; 25 cm. (The Systems programming series) 1. Electronic digital computers — Evaluation I. T. II. Title: System performance evaluation methodology.
QA76.5.K578 1981     001.6/4     LC 77-73946     ISBN 0201144573

**Krutz, Ronald L., 1938-.**     **5.1149**
Microprocessors and logic design / Ronald L. Krutz. — New York: Wiley, c1980. xvi, 467 p.: ill.; 24 cm. 1. Microprocessors 2. Logic design I. T.
QA76.5.K77     001.6/4/04     LC 79-17874     ISBN 0471020834

**Logsdon, Tom, 1937-.**     **5.1150**
Computers today and tomorrow: the microcomputer explosion / Tom Logsdon. — Rockville, Md.: Computer Science Press, c1985. xiii, 361 p.: col. ill.; 24 cm. Includes index. 1. Microcomputers 2. Computers — Social aspects. I. T.
QA76.5.L612 1985     004 19     LC 84-19999     ISBN 0881750263

**Rooney, Victor M.**     **5.1151**
Microprocessors and microcomputers / Victor M. Rooney, Amin R. Ismail. — New York: Macmillan; London: Collier Macmillan, c1984. xi, 468 p.: ill.; 25 cm. Includes index. 1. Microprocessors 2. Microcomputers I. Ismail, Amin R. II. T.
QA76.5.R526 1984     001.64 19     LC 83-11254     ISBN 0024034509

## QA76.5 S–Z

**Short, Kenneth L.**     **5.1152**
Microprocessors and programmed logic / Kenneth L. Short. — 2nd ed. — Englewood Cliffs, NJ: Prentice-Hall, c1987. xvii, 619 p.: ill.; 25 cm. 1. Microprocessors I. T.
QA76.5.S496 1987     004.165 19     LC 86-25385     ISBN 0135806062

**Single–chip microcomputers / edited by Paul F. Lister.**     **5.1153**
New York: McGraw-Hill, c1984. viii, 231 p.: ill.; 24 cm. 1. Microcomputers 2. Microprocessors I. Lister, Paul F. II. Title: Single-chip micro-computers.
QA76.5.S5538 1984     001.64 19     LC 84-19444     ISBN 0070380309

**Thurber, Kenneth J.**     **5.1154**
Large scale computer architecture: parallel and associative processors / Kenneth J. Thurber. Rochelle Park, N.J.: Hayden Book Co., c1976. 324 p.; 24 cm. 1. Electronic digital computers 2. Parallel processing (Electronic computers) 3. Associative storage I. T.
QA76.5.T538     001.6/44/04     LC 76-10610     ISBN 081045775X

**Tutorial supercomputers: design and applications / [edited by]**     **5.1155**
**Kai Hwang.**
Silver Spring, MD: IEEE Computer Society Press; Los Angeles, CA: Order from IEEE Computer Society, c1984. viii, 640 p.: ill.; 28 cm. 'IEEE catalog number EH0219-6.' 1. Supercomputers I. Hwang, Kai.
QA76.5.T88 1984     001.64 19     LC 84-81316     ISBN 0818605812

**Van Young, Sayre.**     **5.1156**
MicroSource: where to find answers to questions about microcomputers / Sayre Van Young. — Littleton, Colo.: Libraries Unlimited, 1986. xii, 220 p.; 28 cm. Includes indexes. 1. Microcomputers — Miscellanea. I. T.
QA76.5.V28 1986     004.16 19     LC 85-23862     ISBN 087287527X

## QA76.54 REAL TIME DATA PROCESSING

**Martin, James, 1933-.**     **5.1157**
Design of man–computer dialogues. — Englewood Cliffs, N.J.: Prentice-Hall, [1973] xiii, 559 p.: illus.; 25 cm. — (Prentice-Hall series in automatic computation) 1. Real-time data processing 2. Man-machine systems I. T.
QA76.54.M36     001.6/44/04     LC 72-7868     ISBN 0132012510

## QA76.6 Programming, A–B

**Abelson, Harold.**     **5.1158**
Structure and interpretation of computer programs / Harold Abelson and Gerald Jay Sussman, with Julie Sussman; foreword by Alan J. Perlis. — Cambridge, Mass.: MIT Press; New York: McGraw-Hill, c1985. xx, 542 p.: ill.; 24 cm. — (MIT electrical engineering and computer science series.) Includes index. 1. Electronic digital computers — Programming 2. LISP (Computer program language) I. Sussman, Gerald Jay. II. Sussman, Julie. III. T. IV. Series.
QA76.6.A255 1985     001.64/2 19     LC 84-9688     ISBN 0262010771

**Aho, Alfred V.**     **5.1159**
The design and analysis of computer algorithms / Alfred V. Aho, John E. Hopcroft, Jeffrey D. Ullman. — Reading, Mass.: Addison-Wesley Pub. Co., [1974] x, 470 p.: ill.; 24 cm. (Addison-Wesley series in computer science and information processing) Includes index. 1. Electronic digital computers — Programming 2. Algorithms I. Hopcroft, John E., 1939- joint author. II. Ullman, Jeffrey D., 1942- joint author. III. T.
QA76.6.A36     001.6/42     LC 74-3995     ISBN 0201000296

**Baase, Sara.**     **5.1160**
Computer algorithms: introduction to design and analysis / Sara Baase. — Reading, Mass.: Addison-Wesley Pub. Co., c1978. xvii, 286 p.: ill.; 25 cm. — (Addison-Wesley series in computer science) Includes index. 1. Electronic digital computers — Programming 2. Algorithms I. T.
QA76.6.B25     519.4     LC 77-81197     ISBN 0201003279

**Beizer, Boris, 1934-.**     **5.1161**
Software system testing and quality assurance / Boris Beizer. — New York: Van Nostrand Reinhold, c1984. xxii, 358 p.: ill.; 24 cm. (Van Nostrand Reinhold electrical/computer science and engineering series.) Includes index. 1. Computer software — Testing. 2. Computer software — Reliability. I. T. II. Series.
QA76.6.B4328 1984     001.64/25 19     LC 83-10458     ISBN 0442213069

**Berztiss, A. T.**     **5.1162**
Data structures: theory and practice / A. T. Berztiss. — 2d ed. — New York: Academic Press, [1975] xv, 586 p.: ill.; 24 cm. (Computer science and applied mathematics) Includes index. 1. Data structures (Computer science) 2. Electronic digital computers — Programming I. T.
QA76.6.B475 1975     001.6/42     LC 74-17977     ISBN 012093552X

**Binder, Robert, 1950-.**    5.1163
Application debugging: an MVS abend handbook for COBOL, Assembly, PL/I, and FORTRAN programmers / Robert Binder. — Englewood Cliffs, N.J.: Prentice-Hall, c1985. xi, 366 p.: ill.; 24 cm. (Prentice-Hall software series.) Includes index. 1. Debugging in computer science 2. MVS (Computer system) 3. COBOL (Computer program language) 4. Assembler language (Computer program language) 5. PL/I (Computer program language) 6. FORTRAN (Computer program language) I. T. II. Series.
QA76.6.B56 1985    001.64/2 19    *LC* 84-15987    *ISBN* 0130393487

**Birns, Peter M.**    5.1164
UNIX for people: a modular guide to the UNIX operating system: visual editing, document preparation, & other resources / Peter M. Birns, Patrick B. Brown, John C. C. Muster. — Englewood Cliffs, N.J.: Prentice-Hall, c1985. xiii, 528 p., [5] leaves of plates: ill.; 25 cm. 1. UNIX (Computer operating system) I. Brown, Patrick B. II. Muster, John C. C. III. T. IV. Title: U.N.I.X. for people.
QA76.6.B5725 1985    001.64/2 19    *LC* 84-10678    *ISBN* 0139374590

**Boehm, Barry W.**    5.1165
Software engineering economics / Barry W. Boehm. — Englewood Cliffs, N.J.: Prentice-Hall, c1981. xxvii, 767 p.: ill.; 25 cm. (Prentice-Hall advances in computing science and technology series.) Includes indexes. 1. Electronic digital computers — Programming — Economic aspects. 2. Electronic digital computers — Programming — Economic aspects — Case studies. I. T. II. Series.
QA76.6.B618    001.64/25/0681 19    *LC* 81-13889    *ISBN* 0138221227

## QA76.6 C–F

**Calingaert, Peter.**    5.1166
Operating system elements: a user perspective / Peter Calingaert. — Englewood Cliffs, N.J.: Prentice-Hall, c1982. xv, 240 p.: ill.; 24 cm. — (Prentice-Hall software series.) Includes index. 1. Operating systems (Computers) I. T. II. Series.
QA76.6.C338    001.64/25 19    *LC* 81-10617    *ISBN* 0136374212

**Chorafas, Dimitris N.**    5.1167
The software handbook / Dimitris N. Chorafas. — Princeton, N.J.: Petrocelli Books, c1984. x, 461 p.: ill.; 25 cm. Includes index. 1. Computer programming management — Handbooks, manuals, etc. 2. Computer software — Handbooks, manuals, etc. I. T.
QA76.6.C4555 1984    001.64/2/068 19    *LC* 84-1169    *ISBN* 0894332481

**Classics in software engineering / edited by Edward Nash**    5.1168
**Yourdon.**
New York: Yourdon Press, c1979. xi, 424 p.: ill.; 26 cm. 1. Electronic digital computers — Programming — Addresses, essays, lectures. I. Yourdon, Edward.
QA76.6.C54    001.64/2    *LC* 79-63449    *ISBN* 0917072146

**Coffman, E. G. (Edward Grady), 1934-.**    5.1169
Operating systems theory [by] Edward G. Coffman, Jr. [and] Peter J. Denning. — Englewood Cliffs, N.J.: Prentice-Hall, [1973] xvi, 331 p.: illus.; 24 cm. — (Prentice-Hall series in automatic computation) 2. Algorithms I. Denning, Peter J., 1942- joint author. II. T.
QA76.6.C62    001.6/42    *LC* 73-18    *ISBN* 0136378684

**Dahl, Ole-Johan, 1931-.**    5.1170
Structured programming, [by] O.–J. Dahl, E. W. Dijkstra [and] C. A. R. Hoare. London, New York, Academic Press, 1972. viii, 220 p. illus. 24 cm. (A.P.I.C. studies in data processing, no. 8) 1. Structured programming I. Dijkstra, Edsger Wybe. joint author. II. Hoare, C. A. R. (Charles Antony Richard), 1934- joint author. III. T.
QA76.6.D33    001.6/42    *LC* 72-84452    *ISBN* 0122005503

**Deitel, Harvey M., 1945-.**    5.1171
An introduction to operating systems / Harvey M. Deitel. — Rev. 1st ed. — Reading, Mass.: Addison-Wesley Pub. Co., c1984. xxviii, 673 p.: ill.; 25 cm. 1. Operating systems (Computers) I. T.
QA76.6.D44 1984    001.64/25 19    *LC* 83-7153    *ISBN* 0201145014

**DeMarco, Tom.**    5.1172
Controlling software projects: management, measurement & estimation / Tom DeMarco; foreword by Barry W. Boehm. — New York, NY: Yourdon Press, c1982. xii, 284 p.: ill.; 26 cm. Includes index. 1. Computer programming management I. T.
QA76.6.D453 1982    001.64/2/068 19    *LC* 82-51100    *ISBN* 0917072324

**Dijkstra, Edsger Wybe.**    5.1173
A discipline of programming / Edsger W. Dijkstra. — Englewood Cliffs, N.J.: Prentice-Hall, c1976. xvii, 217 p.; 24 cm. (Prentice-Hall series in automatic computation) 1. Electronic digital computers — Programming I. T.
QA76.6.D54    001.6/42    *LC* 75-40478    *ISBN* 013215871X

**Foster, Caxton C., 1929-.**    5.1174
Content addressable parallel processors / Caxton C. Foster. — New York: Van Nostrand Reinhold, c1976. xiii, 233 p.: ill.; 25 cm. (Computer science series) Includes index. 1. Parallel processing (Electronic computers) I. T.
QA76.6.F67 1976    001.6/4    *LC* 75-31922    *ISBN* 0442224338

**Fundamental structures of computer science / Wm. A. Wulf ...**    5.1175
**[et al.].**
Reading, Mass.: Addison-Wesley, c1981. xviii, 621 p.: ill.; 24 cm. Includes index. 1. Electronic digital computers — Programming 2. Data structures (Computer science) I. Wulf, William Allan.
QA76.6.F86    001.6/42    *LC* 79-12374    *ISBN* 0201087251

## QA76.6 G–J

**Garey, Michael R.**    5.1176
Computers and intractability: a guide to the theory of NP–completeness / Michael R. Garey, David S. Johnson. — San Francisco: W. H. Freeman, c1979. x, 338 p.: ill.; 24 cm. — (A Series of books in the mathematical sciences) Includes indexes. 1. Electronic digital computers — Programming 2. Algorithms 3. Computational complexity I. Johnson, David S., 1945- joint author. II. T. III. Title: NP-completeness.
QA76.6.G35    519.4    *LC* 78-12361    *ISBN* 0716710447. *ISBN* 0716710455 pbk

**Gonnet, G. H. (Gaston H.)**    5.1177
Handbook of algorithms and data structures / G.H. Gonnet. — London; Reading, Mass.: Addison-Wesley Pub. Co., c1984. xi, 286 p.: ill.; 24 cm. — (International computer science series.) 'Coded in Pascal and C'—Cover. Includes index. 1. Electronic digital computers — Programming 2. Algorithms 3. Data structures (Computer science) I. T. II. Series.
QA76.6.G636 1984    001.64/2 19    *LC* 83-27301    *ISBN* 020114218X

**Goodman, Seymour E.**    5.1178
Introduction to the design and analysis of algorithms / S. E. Goodman, S. T. Hedetniemi. New York: McGraw-Hill, c1977. xi, 371 p.: ill.; 25 cm. (McGraw-Hill computer science series) Includes index. 1. Electronic digital computers — Programming 2. Algorithms I. Hedetniemi, S. T., joint author. II. T.
QA76.6.G66    511/.8    *LC* 76-43363    *ISBN* 0070237530

**Handbook of software engineering / edited by C.R. Vick, C.V.**    5.1179
**Ramamoorthy.**
New York: Van Nostrand Reinhold Co., c1984. xxxiii, 683 p.: ill.; 26 cm. — (Van Nostrand Reinhold electrical/computer science and engineering series.) 1. Electronic digital computers — Programming — Handbooks, manuals, etc. I. Vick, Charles R. (Charles Ralph) II. Ramamoorthy, C. V. (Chittoor V.), 1926- III. Title: Software engineering. IV. Series.
QA76.6.H3335 1984    001.64/25 19    *LC* 82-24784    *ISBN* 0442262515

**Henderson, Peter, 1944-.**    5.1180
Functional programming: application and implementation / Peter Henderson. — Englewood Cliffs, N.J.: Prentice-Hall International, c1980. xi, 355 p.: ill.; 24 cm. Includes index. 1. Electronic digital computers — Programming 2. Functional programming languages I. T.
QA76.6.H46    001.6/42    *LC* 79-16840    *ISBN* 0133315797

**Hoare, C. A. R. (Charles Antony Richard), 1934-.**    5.1181
Communicating sequential processes / C.A.R. Hoare. — Englewood Cliffs, N.J.: Prentice/Hall International, c1985. viii, 256 p.: ill.; 24 cm. (Prentice-Hall International series in computer science.) Includes index. 1. Electronic digital computers — Programming 2. Parallel processing (Electronic computers) I. T. II. Series.
QA76.6.H57 1985    005 19    *LC* 84-22324    *ISBN* 0131532715

**Hogger, Christopher John.**    5.1182
Introduction to logic programming / Christopher John Hogger. — London; Orlando: Academic Press, 1984. xii, 278 p.: ill.; 24 cm. — (APIC studies in data processing; no. 21) Includes index. 1. Logic programming I. T.
QA76.6.H624 1984    001.64/2 19    *LC* 84-14533    *ISBN* 0123520908

## QA76.6 K–O

**Kernighan, Brian W.** 5.1183
The elements of programming style / Brian W. Kernighan, P. J. Plauger. — 2d ed. — New York: McGraw-Hill, c1978. xii, 168 p.; 23 cm. Includes index. 1. Electronic digital computers — Programming I. Plauger, P. J., 1944- joint author. II. T.
QA76.6.K47 1978   001.6/42   LC 78-3498   ISBN 0070342075

**Kernighan, Brian W.** 5.1184
The UNIX programming environment / Brian W. Kernighan, Rob Pike. — Englewood Cliffs, N.J.: Prentice-Hall, c1984. x, 357 p.: ill.; 25 cm. — (Prentice-Hall software series.) Includes index. 1. UNIX (Computer operating system) 2. Electronic digital computers — Programming I. Pike, Rob. II. T. III. Title: U.N.I.X. programming environment. IV. Series.
QA76.6.K495 1984   001.64/25 19   LC 83-62851   ISBN 0139376992

**Knuth, Donald Ervin, 1938-.** 5.1185
The art of computer programming [by] Donald E. Knuth. — 2d ed. — Reading, Mass.: Addison-Wesley Pub. Co., [c1973- <c1981>. v. <1-3>: illus.; 25 cm. — (Addison-Wesley series in computer science and information processing) Includes indexes. Vol. 3 is 1st ed. 1. Electronic digital computers — Programming I. T. II. Title: Fundamental algorithms. III. Title: Seminumerical algorithms. IV. Title: Sorting and searching.
QA76.6.K64   001.6/42   LC 73-1830   ISBN 0201038099

**Kruse, Robert Leroy, 1941-.** 5.1186
Data structures and program design / Robert L. Kruse. — Englewood Cliffs, N.J.: Prentice-Hall, c1984. xxi, 486 p.: ill.; 25 cm. — (Prentice-Hall software series.) 1. Electronic digital computers — Programming 2. Data structures (Computer science) 3. Pascal (Computer program language) I. T. II. Series.
QA76.6.K77 1984   001.64/2 19   LC 83-13839   ISBN 0131962531

**Lewis, T. G. (Theodore Gyle), 1941-.** 5.1187
Software engineering: analysis and verification / T.G. Lewis. — Reston, Va.: Reston Pub. Co., c1982. x, 470 p.: ill.; 25 cm. 1. Electronic digital computers — Programming 2. Computer software — Verification I. T.
QA76.6.L477 1982   001.64/2 19   LC 81-22637   ISBN 083597023X

**Lorin, Harold.** 5.1188
Operating systems / Harold Lorin, Harvey M. Deitel. — Reading, Mass.: Addison Wesley, c1981. xxi, 378 p.: ill.; 24 cm. — (The Systems programming series) Includes index. 1. Operating systems (Computers) I. Deitel, Harvey M., 1945- joint author. II. T.
QA76.6.L639   001.64/.25   LC 80-10625   ISBN 0201144646

**McGowan, Clement L., 1942-.** 5.1189
Top–down structured programming techniques / Clement L. McGowan, John R. Kelly. — 1st ed. — New York: Petrocelli/Charter, 1975. vi, 288 p.: ill.; 24 cm. Includes index. 1. Electronic digital computers — Programming I. Kelly, John R., 1944- joint author. II. T.
QA76.6.M318 1975   001.6/42   LC 74-30427   ISBN 0884053040

**Manna, Zohar.** 5.1190
Mathematical theory of computation. — New York: McGraw-Hill, [1974] x, 448 p.: illus.; 24 cm. — (McGraw-Hill computer science series) 1. Electronic digital computers — Programming 2. Debugging in computer science I. T.
QA76.6.M356   001.6/425   LC 73-12753   ISBN 0070399107

**Birnes, William J.** 5.1191
McGraw–Hill personal computer programming encyclopedia: languages and operating systems / William J. Birnes, editor. — New York: McGraw-Hill, c1985. xiii, 696 p.: ill. Includes index. 1. Microcomputers — Programming 2. Programming languages (Electronic computers) 3. Operating systems (Computers) I. McGraw-Hill Book Company. II. T.
QA76.6.M414 1985   001.64/2 19   LC 85-135   ISBN 0070053898

## QA76.6 P–Z

**Peters, Lawrence J.** 5.1192
Software design: methods & techniques / Lawrence J. Peters; foreword by L.A. Belady. — New York, N.Y.: Yourdon Press, c1981. xiv, 234 p.: ill.; 26 cm. 1. Electronic digital computers — Programming I. T.
QA76.6.P473   001.64/25 19   LC 80-50609   ISBN 0917072197

**Peterson, James Lyle.** 5.1193
Operating system concepts / James L. Peterson, Abraham Silberschatz. — 2nd ed. — Reading, Mass.: Addison-Wesley, 1985. xiv, 625 p.: ill.; 25 cm. Includes index. 1. Operating systems (Computers) I. Silberschatz, Abraham. II. T.
QA76.6.P475 1985   001.64/2 19   LC 84-21637   ISBN 0201060892

**Rus, Teodor.** 5.1194
Data structures and operating systems / Teodor Rus. — Bucuresṭi: Editura Academiei; New York: Wiley, 1979. xi, 364 p.: ill; 25 cm. — (Wiley series in computing) Updated translation of Structuri de date sʲi sisteme operative. 'A Wiley-Interscience publication.' 1. Operating systems (Computers) 2. Data structures (Computer science) 3. Multics (Electronic computer system) I. T.
QA76.6.R8613 1979   001.6/4   LC 77-3262   ISBN 0471995177

**Sedgewick, Robert, 1946-.** 5.1195
Algorithms / Robert Sedgewick. — Reading, Mass.: Addison-Wesley, c1983. viii, 551 p.; ill.; 25 cm. — (Addison-Wesley series in computer science.) 1. Algorithms I. T. II. Series.
QA76.6.S435 1983   519.4 19   LC 82-11672   ISBN 0201066726

**Shneiderman, Ben.** 5.1196
Software psychology: human factors in computer and information systems / Ben Shneiderman. — Cambridge, Mass.: Winthrop Publishers, c1980. xv, 320 p.: ill.; 24 cm. — (Winthrop computer systems series.) Includes indexes. 1. Electronic digital computers — Programming — Psychological aspects. I. T. II. Series.
QA76.6.S543   001.6/4/019   LC 79-17627   ISBN 0876268165

**Skees, William D., 1939-.** 5.1197
Computer software for data communications / William D. Skees; [illustrator, John Foster]. — Belmont, Calif.: Lifetime Learning Publications, c1981. xi, 163 p.: ill.; 24 cm. 1. Electronic digital computers — Programming 2. Computer networks I. T.
QA76.6.S597   001.64/2 19   LC 80-24266   ISBN 0534979793

**Structured concurrent programming with operating systems** 5.1198
**applications** / R. C. Holt ... [et al.].
Reading, Mass.: Addison-Wesley Pub. Co., c1978. 262 p.: ill.; 23 cm. — (Addison-Wesley series in computer science) Includes index. 1. Structured programming 2. Parallel processing (Electronic computers) 3. Operating systems (Computers) I. Holt, R. C. (Richard C.), 1941-
QA76.6.S84   001.6/42   LC 77-90124   ISBN 0201029375

**Tanenbaum, Andrew S., 1944-.** 5.1199
Structured computer organization / Andrew S. Tanenbaum. — 2nd ed. — Englewood Cliffs, N.J.: Prentice-Hall, c1984. xiii, 465 p.: ill.; 25 cm. Includes index. 1. Electronic digital computers — Programming I. T.
QA76.6.T38 1984   001.64/2 19   LC 83-2916   ISBN 0138544891

**Ullman, Jeffrey D., 1942-.** 5.1200
Fundamental concepts of programming systems / Jeffrey D. Ullman. — Reading, Mass.: Addison-Wesley Pub. Co., c1976. ix, 328 p.: ill.; 25 cm. — (Addison-Wesley series in computer science and information processing) 1. Electronic digital computers — Programming 2. Programming languages (Electronic computers) I. T.
QA76.6.U44   001.6/42   LC 75-374   ISBN 0201076543

**Van Tassel, Dennie, 1939-.** 5.1201
Program style, design, efficiency, debugging, and testing / Dennie Van Tassel. — 2d ed. — Englewood Cliffs, N.J.: Prentice-Hall, c1978. ix, 323 p.: ill.; 24 cm. 1. Electronic digital computers — Programming 2. Debugging in computer science 3. Computer programs — Testing I. T.
QA76.6.V37 1978   001.6/42   LC 78-9078   ISBN 0137299478

**Wand, Mitchell.** 5.1202
Induction, recursion, and programming / Mitchell Wand. — New York: North Holland, c1980. xii, 202 p.; 24 cm. Includes index. 1. Electronic digital computers — Programming 2. Induction (Mathematics) 3. Recursion theory I. T.
QA76.6.W34   001.6/42   LC 79-25360   ISBN 0444003223

**Weinberg, Gerald M.** • 5.1203
The psychology of computer programming / [by] Gerald M. Weinberg. — New York: Van Nostrand Reinhold, [1971] xv, 288 p.; 24 cm. (Computer science series) 1. Electronic digital computers — Programming — Psychological aspects. I. T.
QA76.6.W45   001.6/42/019   LC 72-165813

**Wirth, Niklaus.** 5.1204
Algorithms + data structures=programs / Niklaus Wirth. — Englewood Cliffs, N.J.: Prentice-Hall, c1976. xvii, 366 p.: ill.; 24 cm. (Prentice-Hall series in automatic computation.) 1. Electronic digital computers — Programming 2. Data structures (Computer science) 3. Algorithms I. T.
QA76.6.W56   001.6/42   LC 75-11599   ISBN 0130224189

# QA76.7–.76 Programming Languages

**Horowitz, Ellis.**                                                    **5.1205**
Fundamentals of programming languages / Ellis Horowitz. — 2nd ed. — Rockville, MD: Computer Science Press, c1984. xv, 446 p.: ill.; 24 cm. Includes index. 1. Programming languages (Electronic computers) I. T.
QA76.7.H67 1984      001.64/24 19      *LC* 83-15369      *ISBN* 0881750042

**Pagan, Frank G.**                                                    **5.1206**
Formal specification of programming languages: a panoramic primer / Frank G. Pagan. — Englewood Cliffs, N.J.: Prentice-Hall, c1981. x, 245 p.; 24 cm. — (Prentice-Hall software series.) Includes index. 1. Programming languages (Electronic computers) — Syntax 2. Programming languages (Electronic computers) — Semantics I. T. II. Series.
QA76.7.P33      001.64/24 19      *LC* 80-23516      *ISBN* 0133290522

## QA76.73 INDIVIDUAL LANGUAGES, A–E

**Katzan, Harry.**                                                  • **5.1207**
APL programming and computer techniques [by] Harry Katzan, Jr. New York, Van Nostrand Reinhold [1970] xiii, 329 p. illus. 24 cm. (Computer science series) 1. APL (Computer program language) 2. Electronic digital computers — Programming I. T.
QA76.73.A27 K38 1970      651.8      *LC* 72-122671

**Buhr, R. J. A.**                                                    **5.1208**
System design with Ada / R.J.A. Buhr. — Englewood Cliffs, N.J.: Prentice-Hall, c1984. xv, 256 p.: ill.; 25 cm. — (Prentice-Hall software series.) Includes index. 1. Ada (Computer program language) 2. System design I. T. II. Series.
QA76.73.A35 B83 1984      001.64/2 19      *LC* 83-13673      *ISBN* 0138816239

**Gehani, Narain, 1947-.**                                            **5.1209**
Ada: concurrent programming / Narain Gehani. — Englewood Cliffs, N.J.: Prentice-Hall, c1984. 261 p.: ill.; 24 cm. — (Prentice-Hall software series.) Includes index. 1. Ada (Computer program language) 2. Parallel programming (Computer science) I. T. II. Series.
QA76.73.A35 G433 1984      001.64/24 19      *LC* 84-4      *ISBN* 0130040118

**Kemeny, John G.**                                                   **5.1210**
True BASIC reference manual / John G. Kemeny, Thomas E. Kurtz, Brig Elliott. — Reading, Mass.; Don Mills, Ont.: Addison-Wesley, c1985. xix, 331 p.: ill. Includes index. 1. BASIC (Computer program language) I. Kemeny, John G. II. Kurtz, Thomas E. III. Elliott, Brig. IV. T.
QA76.73.B3 K4 1985      *ISBN* 0201157012

**Harbison, Samuel P.**                                               **5.1211**
C, a reference manual / Samuel P. Harbison, Guy L. Steele, Jr. — Englewood Cliffs, N.J.: Prentice-Hall, c1984. x, 352 p.; 25 cm. 1. C (Computer language) I. Steele, Guy. II. T.
QA76.73.C15 H38 1984      001.64/24      *LC* 84-6909      *ISBN* 0131100165

**Kernighan, Brian W.**                                               **5.1212**
The C programming language / Brian W. Kernighan, Dennis M. Ritchie. — Englewood Cliffs, N.J.: Prentice-Hall, c1978. x, 228 p.; 24 cm. — (Prentice-Hall software series.) Includes index. 1. C (Computer program language) I. Ritchie, Dennis M., 1941- joint author. II. T. III. Series.
QA76.73.C15 K47      001.6/424      *LC* 77-28983      *ISBN* 0131101633

**Grauer, Robert T., 1945-.**                                         **5.1213**
Structured COBOL programming / Robert T. Grauer. — Englewood Cliffs, N.J.: Prentice-Hall, c1985. xvi, 479 p.: ill.; 28 cm. Includes index. 1. COBOL (Computer program language) 2. Structured programming I. T.
QA76.73.C25 G7373 1985      001.64/24 19      *LC* 84-26358      *ISBN* 0138542171

**Spence, J. Wayne.**                                                 **5.1214**
COBOL for the 80's / J. Wayne Spence. — 2nd ed. — St. Paul: West Pub. Co., c1985. xx, 883 p.: ill.; 25 cm. Includes index. 1. COBOL (Computer program language) I. T.
QA76.73.C25 S657 1985      001.64/24 19      *LC* 85-639      *ISBN* 0314853030

## QA76.73 F–O

**Brodie, Leo.**                                                      **5.1215**
Thinking FORTH: a language and philosophy for solving problems / Leo Brodie. — Englewood Cliffs, N.J.: Prentice-Hall, c1984. xiv, 300 p.: ill.; 24 cm. 'A Spectrum book.' Includes index. 1. FORTH (Computer program language) I. T.
QA76.73.F24 B763 1984      001.64/24 19      *LC* 84-8362      *ISBN* 0139175768

**Metcalf, Michael.**                                                 **5.1216**
Effective FORTRAN 77 / Michael Metcalf. — Oxford [Oxfordshire]: Clarendon Press; New York: Oxford University Press, 1985. xii, 231 p.: ill.; 24 cm. (Oxford science publications) Includes index. 1. FORTRAN (Computer program language) I. T.
QA76.73.F25 M478 1985      001.64/24 19      *LC* 84-28522      *ISBN* 0198537093

**Steele, Guy.**                                                      **5.1217**
COMMON LISP: the language / Guy L. Steele, Jr., with contributions by Scott E. Fahlman ... [et al.]. — Burlington, MA: Digital Press, c1984. xii, 465 p.; 24 cm. Includes index. 1. LISP (Computer program language) I. T. II. Title: COMMON L.I.S.P.
QA76.73.L23 S73 1984      001.64/24 19      *LC* 84-7681      *ISBN* 093237641X

**Winston, Patrick Henry.**                                           **5.1218**
LISP / Patrick Henry Winston, Berthold Klaus Paul Horn. — 2nd ed. — Reading, Mass.: Addison-Wesley, c1984. xii, 434 p.: ill.; 23 cm. Includes indexes. 1. LISP (Computer program language) I. Horn, Berthold. II. T. III. Title: L.I.S.P.
QA76.73.L23 W56 1984      001.64/24 19      *LC* 84-9328      *ISBN* 0201083728

**Clark, K. L. (Keith L.)**                                           **5.1219**
Micro–PROLOG: programming in logic / K.L. Clark and F.G. McCabe; with contributions by M.H. van Emden ... [et al.]. — Englewood Cliffs, N.J.: Prentice/Hall International, c1984. xi, 401 p.: ill.; 23 cm. Includes index. 1. Micro-PROLOG (Computer program language) I. McCabe, F. G. (Frank G.), 1953- II. T.
QA76.73.M5 C55 1984      001.64/2 19      *LC* 83-16066      *ISBN* 013581264X

**Beidler, John, 1941-.**                                             **5.1220**
Modula–2 / John Beidler, Paul Jackowitz. — Boston: PWS Engineering and Computer Science, c1986. xv, 347 p.: ill.; 24 cm. Includes index. 1. Modula-2 (Computer program language) I. Jackowitz, Paul, 1955- II. T. III. Title: Modula-two.
QA76.73.M63 B45 1986      001.64/24 19      *LC* 85-6298      *ISBN* 0871509121

## QA76.73 P–Z

**Cooper, Doug.**                                                     **5.1221**
Oh! Pascal! / by Doug Cooper and Michael Clancy. — 2nd ed. — New York: W.W. Norton, c1985. xxxi, 607 p.: ill.; 24 cm. Includes indexes. 1. Pascal (Computer program language) I. Clancy, Michael, 1950- II. T.
QA76.73.P2 C677 1985      005.13/3 19      *LC* 85-179352      *ISBN* 0393954455

**Jensen, Kathleen, 1949-.**                                          **5.1222**
Pascal user manual and report / Kathleen Jensen, Niklaus Wirth. — 3rd ed. / prepared by Andrew B. Mickel, James F. Miner. — New York: Springer-Verlag, c1985. xvi, 266 p.: ill.; 24 cm. 'Revised for the ISO Pascal standard.' Includes index. 1. Pascal (Computer program language) I. Wirth, Niklaus. II. Mickel, Andrew B. III. Miner, James F. IV. T.
QA76.73.P2 J46 1985      001.64/24 19      *LC* 84-10615      *ISBN* 0387960481

**Rohl, J. S. (Jeffrey Soden), 1938-.**                               **5.1223**
Recursion via Pascal / J.S. Rohl. — Cambridge [Cambridgeshire]; New York: Cambridge University Press, 1984. x, 191 p.: ill.; 24 cm. — (Cambridge computer science texts; 19) Includes index. 1. Pascal (Computer program language) 2. Electronic digital computers — Programming 3. Recursion theory I. T.
QA76.73.P2 R634 1984      001.64/2 19      *LC* 83-26335      *ISBN* 0521263298

**Clarke, Gordon R.**                                                 **5.1224**
Practical PL/I / Gordon R. Clarke, Sue Green, Peter Teague. — Cambridge [Cambridgeshire]; New York: Published by Cambridge University Press on behalf the British Computer Society, 1985. ix, 217 p.; 23 cm. (The British Computer Society monographs in informatics) 'British Computer Society, PL/I

Specialist Group.' 1. PL/I (Computer program language) I. Green, Sue.
II. Teague, Peter. III. British Computer Society. PL/I Specialist Group.
IV. T.
QA76.73.P25 C54 1985     005.13/3 19     *LC* 85-24359     *ISBN*
0521317681

**Clocksin, W. F. (William F.), 1955-.**          5.1225
Programming in Prolog / W.F. Clocksin, C.S. Mellish. — 2nd ed. — Berlin;
New York: Springer-Verlag, 1985. p. cm. 1. Prolog (Computer program
language) I. Mellish, C. S. (Christopher S.), 1954- II. T.
QA76.73.P76 C57 1985     001.64 /24 19     *LC* 84-26706     *ISBN*
0387150110

## QA76.76 SPECIAL TOPICS

**Aho, Alfred V.**          5.1226
Compilers, principles, techniques, and tools / Alfred V. Aho, Ravi Sethi, Jeffrey
D. Ullman. — Reading, Mass.: Addison-Wesley Pub. Co., c1986. x, 796 p.: ill.;
24 cm. Includes index. 1. Compilers (Computer programs) I. Sethi, Ravi.
II. Ullman, Jeffrey D., 1942- III. T.
QA76.76.C65 A37 1986     005.4/53 19     *LC* 85-15647     *ISBN*
0201100886

# QA76.8 Special Computers and Systems

**Triebel, Walter A.**          5.1227
16–bit microprocessors: architecture, software, and interface techniques /
Walter A. Triebel, Avtar Singh. — Englewood Cliffs, N.J.: Prentice-Hall,
c1985. viii, 392 p.: ill.; 25 cm. Includes index. 1. Intel 8086 (Microprocessor)
2. Motorola 68000 (Microprocessor) 3. Microcomputers I. Singh, Avtar,
1947- II. T. III. Title: Sixteen-bit microprocessors.
QA76.8.I292 T75 1985     001.64 19     *LC* 84-13472     *ISBN*
0138114072

# QA76.9 Other Topics, A–Z

## QA76.9 A–C

**Computer structures: principles and examples / [edited by]**          5.1228
**Daniel P. Siewiorek, C. Gordon Bell, Allen Newell.**
New York: McGraw-Hill, c1982. xvi, 926 p.: ill.; 25 cm. — (McGraw-Hill
computer science series) Includes index. 1. Computer architecture —
Addresses, essays, lectures. I. Siewiorek, Daniel P. II. Bell, C. Gordon.
III. Newell, Allen.
QA76.9.A73 C65     621.3819/5 19     *LC* 80-27926     *ISBN* 0070573026

**Mano, M. Morris, 1927-.**          5.1229
Computer system architecture / M. Morris Mano. — 2nd ed. — Englewood
Cliffs, N.J.: Prentice-Hall, c1982. xii, 531 p.: ill.; 25 cm. 1. Computer
architecture I. T.
QA76.9.A73 M36 1982     621.3819/52 001.64 19     *LC* 81-15799
    *ISBN* 0131666118

**Tomek, Ivan.**          5.1230
Introduction to computer organization / Ivan Tomek. — Rockville, Md.:
Computer Science Press, c1981. xii, 456 p.: ill.; 24 cm. — (Digital system design
series.) Includes index. 1. Computer architecture I. T. II. Series.
QA76.9.A73 T65     621.3819/52 19     *LC* 80-24238     *ISBN*
0914894080

**Boyer, Robert S.**          5.1231
A computational logic / Robert S. Boyer and J. Strother Moore. — New York:
Academic Press, c1979. xiv, 397 p.; 24 cm. — (ACM monograph series)
Includes index. 1. Automatic theorem proving I. Moore, J. Strother, 1947-
joint author. II. T.
QA76.9.A96 B68     519.4     *LC* 79-51693     *ISBN* 0121229505

**The Computer age: a twenty–year view / edited by Michael L.**          5.1232
**Dertouzos and Joel Moses.**
Cambridge, Mass.: MIT Press, c1979. xvi, 491 p.: ill.; 24 cm. — (MIT
bicentennial studies) 1. Computers and civilization I. Dertouzos, Michael L.
II. Moses, Joel.
QA76.9.C66 C63     301.24/3     *LC* 79-13070     *ISBN* 0262040557

## QA76.9 D

**Advanced database machine architecture / David K. Hsiao,**          5.1233
**editor.**
Englewood Cliffs, N.J.: Prentice-Hall, c1983. xxii, 394 p.: ill.; 24 cm. 1. Data
base management 2. Computer architecture I. Hsiao, David K., 1933-
QA76.9.D3 A343 1983     001.64 19     *LC* 83-11032     *ISBN*
0130112623

**Bray, Olin H.**          5.1234
Data base computers / Olin H. Bray, Harvey A. Freeman. — Lexington, Mass.:
Lexington Books, c1979. xi, 179 p.: ill.; 24 cm. — (Lexington Books series in
computer science.) Includes index. 1. Data base management 2. Electronic
digital computers I. Freeman, Harvey A. joint author. II. T. III. Series.
QA76.9.D3 B7     001.6/4     *LC* 78-24765     *ISBN* 0669028347

**Date, C. J.**          5.1235
An introduction to database systems / C.J. Date. — 4th ed. — Reading, Mass.:
Addison-Wesley Pub. Co., c1986-. v. < 1 >: ill.; 25 cm. (Addison-Wesley
systems programming series.) 1. Data base management I. T. Series.
QA76.9.D3 D37 1986     001.64 19     *LC* 85-1422     *ISBN* 0201142015

**Freeman, Donald E.**          5.1236
I/O design: data management in operating systems / Donald E. Freeman,
Olney R. Perry. Rochelle Park, N.J.: Hayden Book Co., c1977. 374 p.: ill.; 24
cm. Includes index. 1. Data base management 2. Operating systems
(Computers) I. Perry, Olney R., joint author. II. T.
QA76.9.D3 F73     001.6/44     *LC* 76-54767     *ISBN* 081045789X

**Kroenke, David.**          5.1237
Database processing: fundamentals, design, implementation / David M.
Kroenke. — 2nd ed. — Chicago: Science Research Associates, c1983. xiv,
607 p.: ill.; 24 cm. Includes index. 1. Data base management I. T.
QA76.9.D3 K76 1983     001.6/442 19     *LC* 82-10676     *ISBN*
0574213201

**Ullman, Jeffrey D., 1942-.**          5.1238
Principles of database systems / Jeffrey D. Ullman. — Potomac, Md.:
Computer Science Press, c1980. 379 p.: ill.; 24 cm. — (Computer software
engineering series.) Includes index. 1. Data base management I. T. II. Title:
Database systems. III. Series.
QA76.9.D3 U44     001.6/4     *LC* 79-20071     *ISBN* 0914894137

**Held, Gilbert, 1943-.**          5.1239
Data compression: techniques and applications: hardware and software
considerations / Gilbert Held. — Chichester [West Sussex]; New York: Wiley,
c1983. xii, 126 p.: ill.; 24 \cm. 'A Wiley Heyden publication.' Includes index.
1. Data compression (Computer science) I. T.
QA76.9.D33 H44 1983     001.64/2 19     *LC* 82-23783     *ISBN*
047126248X

**Aho, Alfred V.**          5.1240
Data structures and algorithms / Alfred V. Aho, John E. Hopcroft, Jeffrey D.
Ullman. — Reading, Mass.: Addison-Wesley, 1985. xi, 427 p.: ill.; 25 cm. —
(Addison-Wesley series in computer science and information processing.)
Includes index. Reprinted with corrections March, 1985. 1. Data structures
(Computer science) 2. Algorithms I. Hopcroft, John E., 1939- II. Ullman,
Jeffrey D., 1942- III. T. IV. Series.
QA76.9.D35 A38 1985     001.64 19

**Horowitz, Ellis.**          5.1241
Fundamentals of data structures in Pascal / Ellis Horowitz, Sartaj Sahni. —
2nd ed. — Rockville, Md.: Computer Science Press, c1987. xiv, 542 p.: ill.; 24
cm. 1. Data structures (Computer science) 2. Pascal (Computer program
language) I. Sahni, Sartaj. II. T. III. Title: Data structures in Pascal.
QA76.9.D35 H67 1987     005.7/3 19     *LC* 86-13679     *ISBN*
0881751650

**Standish, Thomas A., 1941-.**          5.1242
Data structure techniques / Thomas A. Standish. — Reading, MA: Addison-
Wesley, c1980. xvi, 447 p.: ill.; 24 cm. — (Addison-Wesley series in computer
science) Includes index. 1. Data structures (Computer science) I. T.
QA76.9.D35 S73     001.6/42     *LC* 78-67454     *ISBN* 0201072564

**Tarjan, Robert E. (Robert Endre), 1948-.**          5.1243
Data structures and network algorithms / Robert Endre Tarjan. —
Philadelphia, Pa.: Society for Industrial and Applied Mathematics, 1983. vii,
131 p.: ill.; 25 cm. — (CBMS-NSF regional conference series in applied

mathematics; 44) 1. Data structures (Computer science) 2. Algorithms. 3. Trees (Graph theory) I. T. II. Series.
QA76.9.D35 T37 1983    001.64/2 19    *LC* 83-61374    *ISBN* 0898711878

**Distributed computing / edited by Fred B. Chambers, David A.**    **5.1244**
**Duce, Gillian P. Jones.**
London; Orlando: Academic Press, 1984. xii, 327 p. — (A.P.I.C. studies in data processing; v. 20) 1. Electronic data processing — Distributed processing I. Chambers, Fred B. II. Duce, David A. III. Jones, Gillian P.
QA76.9.D5 D49 1984    001.64 19    *LC* 84-18467    *ISBN* 0121673502

### QA76.9 E–M

**Ferrari, Domenico, 1940-.**    **5.1245**
Computer systems performance evaluation / Domenico Ferrari. — Englewood Cliffs, N.J.: Prentice-Hall, c1978. xxi, 554 p.: ill.; 25 cm. Includes index. 1. Electronic digital computers — Evaluation I. T.
QA76.9.E94 F47    621.3819/58    *LC* 77-15096    *ISBN* 0131651269

**Building expert systems / edited by Frederick Hayes–Roth,**    **5.1246**
**Donald A. Waterman, Douglas B. Lenat.**
Reading, Mass.: Addison-Wesley Pub. Co., 1983. xvi, 444 p.: ill.; 24 cm. — (Teknowledge series in knowledge engineering. v. 1) Includes indexes. 1. Expert systems (Computer science) 2. System design I. Hayes-Roth, Frederick. II. Waterman, D. A. (Donald Arthur), 1936- III. Lenat, Douglas B. IV. Series.
QA76.9.E96 B84 1983    001.64/2 19    *LC* 82-24511    *ISBN* 0201106868

**Rule–based expert systems: the MYCIN experiments of the**    **5.1247**
**Stanford Heuristic Programming Project / edited by Bruce G.**
**Buchanan, Edward H. Shortliffe.**
Reading, Mass.: Addison-Wesley, c1984. xix, 748 p.: ill.; 24 cm. — (The Addison-Wesley series in artificial intelligence) Includes indexes. 1. Expert systems (Computer science) 2. MYCIN (Computer system) I. Buchanan, Bruce G. II. Shortliffe, Edward Hance. III. Series.
QA76.9.E96 R84 1984    001.53/5 19    *LC* 83-15822    *ISBN* 0201101726

**Cooke, D. J. (Derek John), 1947-.**    **5.1248**
Computer mathematics / D.J. Cooke and H.E. Bez. — Cambridge [Cambridgeshire]; New York: Cambridge University Press, 1984. xii, 394 p.: ill.; 24 cm. — (Cambridge computer science texts. 18) Includes index. 1. Electronic data processing — Mathematics I. Bez, H. E. II. T. III. Series.
QA76.9.M35 C66 1984    519.4 19    *LC* 83-7588    *ISBN* 0521253411

### QA76.9 P–Z

**Brod, Craig.**    **5.1249**
Technostress: the human cost of the computer revolution / Craig Brod. — Reading, Mass.: Addison-Wesley, 1984. xiii, 242 p.; 24 cm. Includes index. 1. Electronic digital computers — Psychological aspects. 2. Stress (Psychology) I. T. II. Title: Techno stress.
QA76.9.P75 B76 1984    001.64 19    *LC* 83-25866    *ISBN* 0201112116

**Oborne, David J.**    **5.1250**
Computers at work: a behavioural approach / David J. Oborne. — Chichester; New York: Wiley, c1985. xv, 420 p.: ill.; 24 cm. (Wiley series in psychology and productivity at work.) Includes indexes. 1. Computers — Psychological aspects. I. T. II. Series.
QA76.9.P75 O26 1985    001.64/01/9 19    *LC* 84-17335    *ISBN* 0471904104

**Rafiquzzaman, Mohamed.**    **5.1251**
Microprocessors and microcomputer development systems: designing microprocessor-based systems / Mohamed Rafiquzzaman. — New York: Harper & Row, c1984. xv, 679 p.: ill.; 25 cm. Includes index. 1. System design 2. Microprocessors 3. Microcomputers I. T.
QA76.9.S88 R33 1984    001.64 19    *LC* 83-12626    *ISBN* 0060453125

**Shooman, Martin L.**    **5.1252**
Software engineering: design, reliability, and management / Martin L. Shooman. — New York: McGraw-Hill, c1983. xx, 683 p.: ill.; 25 cm. (McGraw-Hill computer science series.) Includes indexes. 1. System design 2. Computer software — Reliability. 3. Computer programming management I. T. II. Series.
QA76.9.S88 S56 1983    001.64/25 19    *LC* 82-9943    *ISBN* 0070570213

## QA76.95 Problem Solving by Computer

**Bundy, Alan.**    **5.1253**
The computer modelling of mathematical reasoning / Alan Bundy. — London; New York: Academic Press, 1983. xiv, 322 p.: ill.; 23 cm. Includes index. 1. Mathematics — Data processing 2. Logic, Symbolic and mathematical 3. Automatic theorem proving I. T.
QA76.95.B86 1983    511.3 19    *LC* 82-72881    *ISBN* 0121412520

## QA93–99 Mathematical Recreations

**Jacobs, Harold R.**    **5.1254**
Mathematics, a human endeavor: a book for those who think they don't like the subject / Harold R. Jacobs. — 2nd ed. — San Francisco: W.H. Freeman, c1982. xiii, 649 p.: ill. (some col.); 26 cm. 1. Mathematics — Popular works. I. T.
QA93.J33 1982    510 19    *LC* 81-17499    *ISBN* 0716713268

**Steinhaus, Hugo, 1887-1972.**    • **5.1255**
[Kalejdoskop matematyczny. English] Mathematical snapshots [by] H. Steinhaus. 3d American ed., rev. and enl. New York, Oxford University Press, 1969. 311 p. illus. 22 cm. Translation of Kalejdoskop matematyczny. 1. Mathematics — Popular works. 2. Mathematical recreations I. T.
QA93.S713 1969    510    *LC* 68-56181

**Berlekamp, Elwyn R.**    **5.1256**
Winning ways, for your mathematical plays / Elwyn R. Berlekamp, John H. Conway, Richard K. Guy. — London; New York: Academic Press, 1982. 2 v., 850 p. 1. Mathematical recreations I. Conway, John Horton. II. Guy, Richard K. III. T.
QA95.B446 1982    793.7/4 19    *LC* 81-66678    *ISBN* 0120911507

**Carroll, Lewis, 1832-1898.**    • **5.1257**
Mathematical recreations of Lewis Carroll [pseud.]. — New York: Dover Publications, [1958] 2 v.: illus.; 21 cm. 1. Mathematical recreations 2. Logic, Symbolic and mathematical I. T. II. Title: Symbolic logic. III. Title: The game of logic.
QA95.D6    793.74    *LC* 58-14299

**Gardner, Martin, 1914-.**    **5.1258**
Aha! Gotcha: paradoxes to puzzle and delight / Martin Gardner. — San Francisco: W.H. Freeman, c1982. vii, 164 p.: ill.; 24 cm. 1. Mathematical recreations 2. Paradox I. T.
QA95.G24    793.7/4 19    *LC* 81-19543    *ISBN* 0716714140

**Ogilvy, Charles Stanley, 1913-.**    • **5.1259**
Tomorrow's math; unsolved problems for the amateur [by] C. Stanley Ogilvy. — 2d ed. — New York: Oxford University Press, 1972. 198 p.: illus.; 21 cm. 1. Mathematical recreations 2. Mathematics — Problems, exercises, etc. I. T.
QA95.O34 1972    510/.76    *LC* 77-173328    *ISBN* 0195015088

**Rademacher, Hans, 1892-1969.**    • **5.1260**
The enjoyment of mathematics; selections from mathematics for the amateur, by Hans Rademacher and Otto Toeplitz. Translated by Herbert Zuckerman. — Princeton: Princeton University Press, 1957. 204 p.: illus.; 25 cm. 'A translation from Von Zahlen und Figuren ... Chapters 15 and 28 by Herbert Zuckerman have been added to the English language edition.' 1. Mathematical recreations I. Toeplitz, Otto, 1881-1940. joint author. II. T.
QA95.R313    510.4    *LC* 57-627

## QA101–145 ARITHMETIC

**Adams, Sam, 1916-.**    **5.1261**
Teaching mathematics: with emphasis on the diagnostic approach / Sam Adams, Leslie Ellis, B. F. Beeson. — New York: Harper & Row, c1977. vi, 259 p.: ill.; 24 cm. 1. Mathematics — Study and teaching (Elementary) I. Ellis, Leslie, joint author. II. Beeson, B. F., joint author. III. T.
QA135.5.A3    372.7    *LC* 77-8652    *ISBN* 0060401648

**Copeland, Richard W.**      **5.1262**
How children learn mathematics: teaching implications of Piaget's research / Richard W. Copeland. — 4th ed. — New York: Macmillan; London: Collier Macmillan, c1984. viii, 449 p.: ill.; 24 cm. 1. Mathematics — Study and teaching (Elementary) I. T.
QA135.5.C5957 1984     372.7 19     *LC* 82-25867     *ISBN* 0023247703

**Gelman, Rochel.**      **5.1263**
The child's understanding of number / Rochel Gelman and C. R. Gallistel. — Cambridge, Mass.: Harvard University Press, 1978. xiii, 260 p.: ill.; 24 cm. 1. Number concept I. Gallistel, C. R., 1941- joint author. II. T.
QA141.15.G44     372.7/2/044     *LC* 78-5124     *ISBN* 0674116364

**Ifrah, Georges.**      **5.1264**
[Histoire universelle des chiffres. English] From one to zero: a universal history of numbers / Georges Ifrah; translated by Lowell Bair. — New York: Viking, 1985. xvi, 503 p.: ill.; 25 cm. Translation of: Histoire universelle des chiffres. 1. Numeration — History. 2. Numerals — History. I. T.
QA141.2.I3613 1985     513/.5 19     *LC* 83-40648     *ISBN* 0670373958

**Menninger, Karl W., 1898-.**      • **5.1265**
[Zahlwort und Ziffer. English] Number words and number symbols; a cultural history of numbers [by] Karl Menninger. Translated by Paul Broneer from the rev. German ed. Cambridge, Mass., M.I.T. Press [1969] xiii, 480 p. illus., facsims., maps. 26 cm. Translation of Zahlwort und Ziffer. 1. Numerals — History 2. Numeration — History 3. Abacus — History. I. T.
QA141.2.M4513     511/.1     *LC* 68-20048     *ISBN* 0262130400

# QA150–297 ALGEBRA

**Waerden, B. L. van der (Bartel Leendert van der), 1903-.**      **5.1266**
Geometry and algebra in ancient civilizations / B.L. van der Waerden. — Berlin; New York: Springer-Verlag, 1983. xii, 223 p.: ill.; 25 cm. 1. Algebra — History. I. T.
QA151.W34 1983     512/.009 19     *LC* 83-501     *ISBN* 0387121595

**Lang, Serge, 1927-.**      • **5.1267**
Algebra. Reading, Mass., Addison-Wesley Pub. Co. [1965] xvii, 508 p. illus. 24 cm. (Addison-Wesley series in mathematics.) 1. Algebra I. T. II. Series.
QA154.L35     512.8     *LC* 65-23677

**Jacobson, Nathan, 1910-.**      • **5.1268**
Basic algebra / Nathan Jacobson. — 2nd ed. — New York: W.H. Freeman, c1985. 2 v.: ill.; 24 cm. 1. Algebra I. T.
QA154.2.J32 1985     512.9 19     *LC* 84-25836     *ISBN* 0716714809

**Herstein, I. N.**      • **5.1269**
Topics in algebra / I.N. Herstein. — Waltham, Mass.: Blaisdell Pub. Co., c1964. viii, 342 p.; 24 cm. — (A Blaisdell book in the pure and applied sciences) 1. Algebra I. T.
QA155.H4     512.8     *LC* 63-17982

**Hungerford, Thomas W.**      **5.1270**
Algebra / Thomas W. Hungerford. — New York: Springer-Verlag, 1980,[c1974] xxiii, 502 p.; 25 cm. — (Graduate texts in mathematics. 73) 1. Algebra I. T. II. Series.
QA155.H83 1974b     512

**Waerden, B. L. van der (Bartel Leendert), 1903-.**      • **5.1271**
[Moderne Algebra. English] Algebra [by] B. L. van der Waerden. In part based on lectures by E. Artin and E. Noether. Translated by Fred Blum and John R. Schulenberger. New York, Ungar [1970] 2 v. illus. 25 cm. Translation of Moderne algebra. Vol. 1 is translated from the 7th ed.; vol. 2 from the 5th ed. 1. Algebra, Abstract I. Artin, Emil, 1898-1962. II. Noether, Emmy, 1882-1935. III. T.
QA155.W323     512/.8     *LC* 71-107030     *ISBN* 0804449481

**Mac Lane, Saunders, 1909-.**      **5.1272**
Algebra / Saunders Mac Lane, Garrett Birkhoff. — 2d ed. — New York: Macmillan, c1979. xv, 586 p.: ill.; 24 cm. 1. Algebra, Abstract I. Birkhoff, Garrett, 1911- joint author. II. T.
QA162.M33 1979     512/.02     *LC* 78-6946     *ISBN* 0023743107

# QA164–165 Combinatorial Analysis

**Aigner, Martin, 1942-.**      **5.1273**
Combinatorial theory / Martin Aigner. — New York: Springer Verlag, 1979. viii, 483 p.: ill.; 25 cm. — (Grundlehren der mathematischen Wissenschaften. 234) Includes index. 1. Combinatorial analysis I. T. II. Series.
QA164.A36     511/.6     *LC* 79-1011     *ISBN* 0387903763

**Bogart, Kenneth P.**      **5.1274**
Introductory combinatorics / Kenneth P. Bogart. — Boston: Pitman, c1983. xii, 388 p.: ill.; 25 cm. 1. Combinatorial analysis 2. Electronic data processing — Mathematics I. T.
QA164.B63 1983     511/.6 19     *LC* 82-22392     *ISBN* 0273019236

**Foulds, L. R., 1948-.**      **5.1275**
Combinatorial optimization for undergraduates / L.R. Foulds. — New York: Springer-Verlag, c1984. xii, 227 p.: ill.; 25 cm. — (Undergraduate texts in mathematics.) Includes index. 1. Combinatorial optimization I. T. II. Series.
QA164.F68 1984     519 19     *LC* 84-5381     *ISBN* 038790977X

**Nijenhuis, Albert.**      **5.1276**
Combinatorial algorithms for computers and calculators / Albert Nijenhuis and Herbert S. Wilf. — 2d ed. — New York: Academic Press, 1978. xv, 302 p.: ill.; 24 cm. — (Computer science and applied mathematics) First ed. published in 1975 under title: Combinatorial algorithms. Includes index. 1. Combinatorial analysis — Computer programs. 2. Algorithms I. Wilf, Herbert S., 1931- joint author. II. T.
QA164.N54 1978     511/.6/0285425     *LC* 78-213     *ISBN* 0125192606

**Reingold, Edward M., 1945-.**      **5.1277**
Combinatorial algorithms: theory and practice / Edward M. Reingold, Jurg Nievergelt, Narsingh Deo. — Englewood Cliffs, N.J.: Prentice-Hall, c1977. xii, 433 p.: ill.; 25 cm. 1. Combinatorial analysis — Data processing I. Nievergelt, Jurg. joint author. II. Deo, Narsingh, 1936- joint author. III. T.
QA164.R43     511/.6     *LC* 76-46474     *ISBN* 013152447X

**The Traveling salesman problem: a guided tour of combinatorial optimization / edited by E.L. Lawler ... [et al.].**      **5.1278**
Chichester [West Sussex]; New York: Wiley, c1985. x, 465 p.: ill.; 25 cm. (Wiley-Interscience series in discrete mathematics.) 'A Wiley-Interscience publication.' Includes index. 1. Combinatorial optimization 2. Traveling-salesman problem I. Lawler, Eugene L. II. Series.
QA164.T73 1985     511/.6 19     *LC* 85-3158     *ISBN* 0471904139

**Tucker, Alan, 1943 July 6-.**      **5.1279**
Applied combinatorics / Alan Tucker. — 2nd ed. — New York: Wiley, c1984. xi, 447 p.: ill.; 25 cm. Includes index. 1. Combinatorial analysis 2. Graph theory I. T.
QA164.T83 1984     511/.6 19     *LC* 84-7393     *ISBN* 0471863718

**Goulden, I. P.**      **5.1280**
Combinatorial enumeration / I.P. Goulden and D.M. Jackson; with a foreword by Gian–Carb Rota. — New York: Wiley, c1983. xxiv, 569 p.: ill.; 24 cm. — (Wiley-Interscience series in discrete mathematics. 0277-2698) 'A Wiley-Interscience publication.' 1. Combinatorial enumeration problems I. Jackson, D. M. II. T. III. Series.
QA164.8.G68 1983     511/.62 19     *LC* 82-20101     *ISBN* 0471866547

**Andrews, George E., 1938-.**      **5.1281**
The theory of partitions / George E. Andrews. — Reading, Mass.: Addison-Wesley Pub. Co., Advanced Book Program, 1976. xiv, 255 p.: ill.; 24 cm. (Encyclopedia of mathematics and its applications; v. 2: Section, Number theory) 1. Partitions (Mathematics) 2. Numbers, Theory of I. T.
QA165.A58     512/.73     *LC* 76-41770     *ISBN* 0201135019

**Dénes, József.**      **5.1282**
Latin squares and their applications / by J. Dénes, A. D. Keedwell. — New York: Academic Press, 1974. 547 p.: ill.; 24 cm. Includes index. 1. Magic squares I. Keedwell, A. D., joint author. II. T.
QA165.D42 1974b     512.9/25     *LC* 73-19244     *ISBN* 012209350X

# QA166–169 Graph Theory. Homological Algebra

**Capobianco, Michael.**                                                                    **5.1283**
Examples and counterexamples in graph theory / Michael Capobianco, John C. Molluzzo; foreword by Gary Chartrand. — New York: North-Holland—New York, c1978. xii, 259 p.: ill.; 24 cm. Includes index. 1. Graph theory I. Molluzzo, John C. joint author. II. T.
QA166.C36     511/.5 19     LC 77-26857     ISBN 0444002553

**Gondran, Michel.**                                                                        **5.1284**
[Graphes et algorithmes. English] Graphs and algorithms / Michel Gondran and Michel Minoux; translated by Steven Vajda. — Chichester [West Sussex]; New York: Wiley, c1984. xix, 650 p.: ill.; 25 cm. — (Wiley-Interscience series in discrete mathematics.) Translation of: Graphes et algorithmes. 'A Wiley-Interscience publication.' 1. Graph theory — Data processing 2. Algorithms I. Minoux, Michel. II. T. III. Series.
QA166.G6513 1984     511/.5 19     LC 82-1975     ISBN 0471103748

**Graham, Ronald L., 1935-.**                                                               **5.1285**
Ramsey theory / Ronald L. Graham, Bruce L. Rothschild, Joel H. Spencer. — New York: Wiley, c1980. ix, 174 p.: ill.; 24 cm. — (Wiley-Interscience series in discrete mathematics.) 'A Wiley-Interscience publication.' 1. Ramsey theory I. Rothschild, Bruce L., 1941- joint author. II. Spencer, Joel H. joint author. III. T. IV. Series.
QA166.G68     511/.6     LC 80-14110     ISBN 0471059978

**Harary, Frank.**                                                                          **5.1286**
Graphical enumeration [by] Frank Harary [and] Edgar M. Palmer. — New York: Academic Press, 1973. xiv, 271 p.: illus.; 24 cm. 1. Graph theory 2. Combinatorial enumeration problems I. Palmer, Edgar M. joint author. II. T.
QA166.H38     511/.5     LC 72-82653     ISBN 0123242452

**Tucker, Alan, 1943 July 6-.**                                                             **5.1287**
Applied combinatorics / Alan Tucker. — New York: Wiley, c1980. ix, 385 p.: ill.; 24 cm. 1. Combinatorial analysis 2. Graph theory I. T.
QA166.T78     511/.6 19     LC 79-22339     ISBN 047104766X

**Welsh, D. J. A.**                                                                         **5.1288**
Matroid theory / D. J. A. Welsh. London; New York: Academic Press, 1976. xi, 433 p.: diagrs.; 24 cm. (L.M.S. monographs; 8) Includes indexes. 1. Matroids I. T.
QA166.6.W44     511/.6     LC 76-10493     ISBN 012744050X

**Mac Lane, Saunders, 1909-.**                                                              **5.1289**
Categories for the working mathematician [by] S. MacLane. New York, Springer-Verlag 1972 (c1971) ix, 262 p. 25 cm. (Graduate texts in mathematics. 5) 1. Categories (Mathematics) I. T. II. Series.
QA169.M33     512/.55     LC 78-166080     ISBN 0387900357 ISBN 0387900365

**Rotman, Joseph J., 1934-.**                                                               **5.1290**
An introduction to homological algebra / Joseph J. Rotman. — New York: Academic Press, 1979. xi, 376 p.: ill.; 23 cm. (Pure and applied mathematics, a series of monographs and textbooks; 85) Includes index. 1. Algebra, Homological. I. T.
QA169.R6x QA3.P8 vol. 85     512/.55     LC 78-20001     ISBN 0125992505

**Silvester, John R.**                                                                      **5.1291**
Introduction to algebraic K–theory / John R. Silvester. — London: Methuen, 1981. xi, 255 p.; 23 cm. — (Chapman and Hall mathematics series.) Includes index. 1. K-theory I. T. II. Series.
QA169.S54 1981     512/.55 19

# QA171–188 Theory of Groups. Linear Algebras

## QA171 A–L

**Artin, Emil, 1898-1962.**                                                            • **5.1292**
Galois theory: lectures delivered at the University of Notre Dame / by Emil Artin; edited and supplemented with a section on applications by Arthur N. Milgram. — 2d ed., with additions and revisions. — Notre Dame, Ind.: University of Notre Dame, 1944. 82 p.; 24 cm. — (Notre Dame mathematical lectures. no. 2) 1. Galois theory I. Milgram, Arthur N. (Arthur Norton), 1912- II. T. III. Series.
QA171.A75 1944     LC 44-26795

**Benson, C. T. (Clark T.)**                                                           • **5.1293**
Finite reflection groups [by] C. T. Benson [and] L. C. Grove. Tarrytown-on-Hudson, N.Y., Bogden & Quigley [1971] viii, 110 p. illus. 24 cm. 1. Finite groups 2. Transformations (Mathematics) I. Grove, Larry C. joint author. II. T.
QA171.B43     512/.2     LC 74-150337     ISBN 0800500016

**Feit, Walter, 1930-.**                                                                    **5.1294**
Characters of finite groups. — New York: W. A. Benjamin, 1967. viii, 186 p.; 24 cm. — (Mathematics lecture notes) 1. Finite groups 2. Representations of groups 3. Characters of groups I. T.
QA171.F35     512/.86     LC 67-20769

**Fuchs, László.**                                                                          **5.1295**
Partially ordered algebraic systems. Oxford, New York, Pergamon Press, 1963. ix, 229 p. 22 cm. (International series of monographs on pure and applied mathematics, v. 28) 1. Groups, Theory of 2. Fields, Algebraic I. T.
QA171.F82 1963     512.86     LC 62-10262

**Fuchs, László.**                                                                          **5.1296**
Infinite Abelian groups. — New York: Academic Press, 1970-73. 2 v.: illus.; 24 cm. — (Pure and applied mathematics (Academic Press) v. 36) 1. Abelian groups I. T. II. Series.
QA171.F8x     510/.8 s 512/.2     LC 78-97479     ISBN 0122696018

**Gorenstein, Daniel.**                                                                     **5.1297**
Finite simple groups: an introduction to their classification / Daniel Gorenstein. — New York: Plenum Press, c1982. x, 333 p.; 24 cm. — (The University series in mathematics) Includes index. 1. Finite simple groups I. T.
QA171.G6417 1982     512/.2 19     LC 81-23414     ISBN 0306407795

**Hall, Marshall, 1910-.**                                                             • **5.1298**
The theory of groups. — New York: Macmillan, [1959] 434 p.; 22 cm. 1. Groups, Theory of I. T.
QA171.H27     512.86     LC 59-5035

**Kaplansky, Irving, 1917-.**                                                               **5.1299**
Infinite Abelian groups. — Rev. ed. — Ann Arbor: University of Michigan Press, [1969] vii, 95 p.; 23 cm. 1. Abelian groups I. T.
QA171.K35 1969     512/.86     LC 69-15839

**Keown, R.**                                                                               **5.1300**
An introduction to group representation theory / R. Keown. — New York: Academic Press, 1975. xi, 331 p.: diagrs.; 24 cm. (Mathematics in science and engineering. v. 116) Includes index. 1. Finite groups 2. Representations of groups I. T. II. Series.
QA171.K417     512/.2     LC 74-27783     ISBN 0124042503

**Kurosh, A G.**                                                                       • **5.1301**
The theory of groups / translated from the Russian and edited by K. A. Hirsch. — 2d English ed. — New York: Chelsea Pub. Co., 1960. 2 v. 1. Groups, Theory of I. T.
QA171.K983 1960     LC 60-8965

## QA171 M–Z

**Mackey, George Whitelaw, 1916-.**                                                         **5.1302**
Unitary group representations in physics, probability, and number theory / George W. Mackey. — Reading, Mass.: Benjamin/Cummings Pub. Co., 1978. xiv, 402 p.: ill.; 24 cm. — (Mathematics lecture notes series; 55) 1. Unitary

groups 2. Representations of groups 3. Mathematical physics 4. Probabilities 5. Numbers, Theory of I. T.
QA171.M173　　512/.2　　LC 78-23563　　ISBN 0805367020. ISBN 0805367039 pbk

**Montgomery, Deane, 1909-.**　　　　　　　　　　5.1303
Topological transformation groups [by] Deane Montgomery [and] Leo Zippin. New York, Interscience Publishers [1955] 282 p. 24 cm. (Interscience tracts in pure and applied mathematics. 1) 1. Groups, Theory of 2. Topology 3. Transformations (Mathematics) I. Zippin, Leo, joint author. II. T.
QA171.M84　　512.86　　LC 55-12711

**Rotman, Joseph J., 1934-.**　　　　　　　　　　5.1304
The theory of groups; an introduction [by] Joseph J. Rotman. — 2d ed. — Boston: Allyn and Bacon, [1973] ix, 342 p.; 24 cm. — (Allyn and Bacon series in advanced mathematics) 1. Groups, Theory of I. T.
QA171.R67 1973　　512/.22　　LC 72-91980

**Suzuki, Michio.**　　　　　　　　　　5.1305
[Gunron. English] Group theory / Michio Suzuki. — Berlin; New York: Springer-Verlag, c1982-c1986. 2 v.: ill.; 25 cm. (Grundlehren der mathematischen Wissenschaften. 247-248) Translation of: Gunron. Includes index. 1. Groups, Theory of I. T. II. Series.
QA171.S7913 1982　　512/.22 19　　LC 81-9159　　ISBN 0387109153

**Weinstein, Michael, 1945-.**　　　　　　　　　　5.1306
Examples of groups / Michael Weinstein. Passaic, NJ: Polygonal Pub. House, c1977. x, 307 p.: ill.; 24 cm. Includes indexes. 1. Groups, Theory of I. T.
QA171.W39　　512/.22　　LC 76-51379

**Weiss, Edwin.**　　　　　　　　　　5.1307
Cohomology of groups. New York, Academic Press, 1969. x, 274 p. illus. 24 cm. (Pure and applied mathematics; a series of monographs and textbooks; v. 34) 1. Class field theory 2. Groups, Theory of 3. Homology theory I. T.
QA171.W4x　　512/.89　　LC 78-84239

**Weyl, Hermann, 1885-1955.**　　　　　　　　• 5.1308
The theory of groups and quantum mechanics / by Hermann Weyl; translated from the second (revised) German edition by H.P. Robertson. — London: Methuen, [1931] xxii, 422 p.: ill.; 20 cm. Translation of Gruppentheorie und quantenmechanik. 1. Groups, Theory of 2. Quantum theory I. T.
QA171.W54　　512.86　　LC 32-2928

## QA171.5 Lattice Theory

**Birkhoff, Garrett, 1911-.**　　　　　　　　　　5.1309
Lattice theory. [3d. ed.] Providence, American Mathematical Society [1967] vi, 418 p. illus. 26 cm. (American Mathematical Society. Colloquium publications, v. 25) 1. Lattice theory I. T.
QA171.5.B5x　　512/.865　　LC 66-23707

**Grätzer, George, 1936-.**　　　　　　　　　　5.1310
Lattice theory; first concepts and distributive lattices. — San Francisco: W. H. Freeman, [1971] xv, 212 p.: illus.; 24 cm. — (A Series of books in mathematics) 1. Lattice theory 2. Lattices, Distributive I. T.
QA171.5.G73　　512/.7　　LC 75-151136　　ISBN 0716704420

## QA184–188 Linear Algebras. Matrices

**Greub, Werner Hildbert, 1925-.**　　　　　　　　5.1311
[Lineare Algebra. English] Linear algebra [by] Werner Greub. 4th ed. New York, Springer-Verlag, 1976. xvi, 451 p. 24 cm. (Graduate texts in mathematics. v. 23) 1. Algebras, Linear I. T. II. Series.
QA184.G7313 1975　　512/.5　　LC 75-19560　　ISBN 0387901108

**Nomizu, Katsumi, 1924-.**　　　　　　　　　　5.1312
Fundamentals of linear algebra / Katsumi Nomizu. — 2d ed. — New York: Chelsea Pub. Co., [1979, c1977] x, 325 p.: ill.; 24 cm. Includes index. 1. Algebras, Linear I. T.
QA184.N65　　512/.5　　LC 77-7468　　ISBN 0828402760

**Minc, Henryk, 1919-.**　　　　　　　　　　5.1313
Permanents / Henryk Minc; with a foreword by Marvin Marcus. — Cambridge: Cambridge University Press, 1984. xxiii, 205 p.: ill.; 24 cm. (Encyclopedia of mathematics and its applications. v.6) 1. Permanents (Matrices) I. T. II. Series.
QA188.M56　　512.9/43 19　　LC 85-121118　　ISBN 0521302269

# QA211–224 Theory of Equations

**Cheney, E. W. (Elliott Ward), 1929-.**　　　　　　5.1314
Introduction to approximation theory / E.W. Cheney. — 2nd ed. — New York, N.Y.: Chelsea Pub. Co., c1982. x, 259 p.: ill.; 24 cm. Includes index. 1. Approximation theory I. T.
QA221.C47 1982　　511/.4 19　　LC 81-67708　　ISBN 0828403171

**Powell, M. J. D. (Michael James David), 1936-.**　　5.1315
Approximation theory and methods / M. J. D. Powell. — Cambridge [Eng.]; New York: Cambridge University Press, 1981. x, 339 p.: grapgs; 24 cm. Includes index. 1. Approximation theory I. T.
QA221.P65　　511/.4 19　　LC 80-40880　　ISBN 0521224721

**Schumaker, Larry L., 1939-.**　　　　　　　　　5.1316
Spline functions: basic theory / Larry L. Schumaker. — New York: Wiley, c1981. xiv, 553 p.; ill.; 24 cm. — (Pure and applied mathematics 0079-8185) 'A Wiley-Interscience publication.' Includes index. 1. Spline theory I. T.
QA224.S33　　511/.42　　LC 80-14448　　ISBN 0471764752

# QA241–247.5 Theory of Numbers

## QA241 General Works, A–H

**Algebraic number theory.** Proceedings of an instructional　　5.1317
conference organized by the London Mathematical Society (a NATO advanced study institute) with the support of the International Mathematical Union. Edited by J. W. S. Cassels and A. Fröhlich.
London, New York, Academic Press, 1967. xviii, 366 p. 23 cm. 1. Algebraic number theory I. Cassels, J. W. S. (John William Scott) ed. II. Fröhlich, A. (Albrecht), 1916- ed. III. London Mathematical Society. IV. International Mathematical Union.
QA241.A42 1967b　　512/.81　　LC 68-92648

**Apostol, Tom M.**　　　　　　　　　　5.1318
Modular functions and Dirichlet series in number theory / Tom M. Apostol. New York: Springer-Verlag, 1976. x, 198 p.: ill.; 24 cm. (Graduate texts in mathematics. 41) The second of two works evolved from a course (Mathematics 160) offered at the California Institute of Technology, continuing the subject matter of the author's Introduction to analytic number theory. Includes index. 1. Numbers, Theory of 2. Functions, Elliptic 3. Functions, Modular 4. Series, Dirichlet I. T. II. Series.
QA241.A62　　512/.73　　LC 76-10236　　ISBN 038790185X

**Borevich, Z. I. (Zenon Ivanovich)**　　　　　　　5.1319
Number theory / by Z. I. Borevich and I. R. Shafarevich; translated by Newcomb Greenleaf for Scripta Technica, translators, New York. — New York: Academic Press, [1966] x, 435 p. — (Pure and applied mathematics (Academic Press) 20) 1. Numbers, Theory of I. Shafarevich, I. R. (Igor' Rostislavovich), 1923- II. T. III. Series.
QA241.B6x　　512.81　　LC 65-28624

**Conway, John Horton.**　　　　　　　　　　5.1320
On numbers and games / J. H. Conway. London; New York: Academic Press, 1976. ix, 238 p.: ill.; 24 cm. (L.M.S. monographs; no. 6) Includes index. 1. Numbers, Theory of 2. Game theory I. T.
QA241.C69　　519.3　　LC 75-19626　　ISBN 0121863506

**Davenport, Harold, 1907-.**　　　　　　　　　5.1321
Multiplicative number theory / Harold Davenport. — 2d ed. / rev. by Hugh L. Montgomery. — New York: Springer-Verlag, c1980. xiii, 177 p.; 24 cm. — (Graduate texts in mathematics. 74) Includes index. 1. Numbers, Theory of 2. Numbers, Prime I. Montgomery, Hugh L. II. T. III. Series.
QA241.D32 1980　　512/.7 19　　LC 80-26329

**Dickson, Leonard E. (Leonard Eugene), 1874-.**　　• 5.1322
History of the theory of numbers ... by Leonard Eugene Dickson ... Washington, Carnegie Institution of Washington, 1919-1923. 3 v. 27 cm. (Carnegie Institution of Washington publication. no. 256, vol. I-III) 1. Numbers, Theory of 2. Mathematics — History. I. T. II. Series.
QA241.D5　　LC 19-7579

**Edwards, Harold M.**      **5.1323**
Riemann's zeta function [by] H. M. Edwards. New York, Academic Press, 1974. xiii, 315 p. 24 cm. (Pure and applied mathematics; a series of monographs and textbooks; 58) 1. Numbers, Theory of 2. Functions, Zeta I. T.
QA241.E3 QA3.P8 vol. 58     510/.8 s 512/.73     *LC* 73-794     *ISBN* 0122327500

**Hardy, Godfrey Harold, 1877-1947.**      • **5.1324**
An introduction to the theory of numbers, by G. H. Hardy and E. M. Wright. — 4th ed. — Oxford, Clarendon Press, 1960. xvi, 421 p. diagrs. 24 cm. Bibliography: p. [414]-415. 1. Numbers, Theory of I. Wright, Edward Maitland, 1906- joint author. II. T.
QA241.H28x     *LC* A 63-574

**Honsberger, Ross, 1929-.**      **5.1325**
Mathematical gems / by Ross Honsberger. — [Washington]: Mathematical Association of America, < c1976 >. v. < 2 > : ill.; 23 cm. (The Dolciani mathematical expositions; < no. 2 > ) 1. Numbers, Theory of 2. Combinatorial analysis 3. Geometry I. T.
QA241.H63     512/.7     *LC* 76-15927     *ISBN* 0883853000

## QA241 I–Z

**Ireland, Kenneth F.**      **5.1326**
A classical introduction to modern number theory / Kenneth Ireland, Michael Rosen. — New York: Springer-Verlag, [1982] xiii, 341 p.; 25 cm. — (Graduate texts in mathematics; 84) Includes index. 1. Numbers, Theory of. I. Rosen, Michael I. II. T. III. Series.
QA241.I667 1982     512/.7 19     *LC* 81-23265     *ISBN* 0387906258

**Ireland, Kenneth F.**      **5.1327**
Elements of number theory; including an introduction to equations over finite fields [by] Kenneth Ireland [and] Michael I. Rosen. Tarrytown-on-Hudson, N.Y., Bogden & Quigley [1972] vi, 169 p. 24 cm. 1. Numbers, Theory of 2. Finite fields (Algebra) I. Rosen, Michael I. joint author. II. T.
QA241.I67     512/.7     *LC* 73-170778     *ISBN* 0800500253

**Koblitz, Neal, 1948-.**      **5.1328**
p–adic numbers, p–adic analysis, and zeta–functions / Neal Koblitz. — 2nd ed. — New York: Springer-Verlag, c1984. xii, 150 p.: ill.; 25 cm. — (Graduate texts in mathematics. 58) Includes index. 1. p-adic numbers 2. p-adic analysis 3. Functions, Zeta I. T. II. Series.
QA241.K674 1984     512/.74 19     *LC* 84-5503     *ISBN* 0387960171

**Landau, Edmund, 1877-1938.**      • **5.1329**
Elementary number theory, by Edmund Landau. Translated by Jacob E. Goodman. With exercises by Paul T. Bateman and Eugene E. Kohlbecker. [2d ed.] New York, Chelsea Pub. Co. [1966] 256 p. 24 cm. 1. Numbers, Theory of I. T.
QA241.L243 1966     *LC* 66-2147

**Mahler, Kurt.**      **5.1330**
p–adic numbers and their functions / Kurt Mahler. — 2d ed. — Cambridge [Eng.]; New York: Cambridge University Press, 1981. x, 320 p.; 23 cm. — (Cambridge tracts in mathematics. 76) First published in 1973 under title: Introduction to p-adic numbers and their functions. Includes index. 1. p-adic numbers 2. Numerical functions I. T. II. Series.
QA241.M22 1981     512/.74     *LC* 79-20103     *ISBN* 0521231027

**Rademacher, Hans, 1892-1969.**      • **5.1331**
Lectures on elementary number theory. — New York: Blaisdell Pub. Co., [1964] ix, 146 p.: illus.; 24 cm. — (A Blaisdell book in the pure and applied sciences. Introduction to higher mathematics) 1. Numbers, Theory of I. T.
QA241.R22     512.81     *LC* 64-10050

**Schroeder, M. R. (Manfred Robert), 1926-.**      **5.1332**
Number theory in science and communication: with applications in cryptography, physics, biology, digital information, and computing / M.R. Schroeder. — Berlin; New York: Springer-Verlag, 1984. xvi, 324 p.: ill.; 24 cm. — (Springer series in information sciences. 7) 1. Numbers, Theory of I. T. II. Series.
QA241.S318 1984     512/.7 19     *LC* 83-20454     *ISBN* 0387121641

**Weil, André, 1906-.**      **5.1333**
Number theory: an approach through history from Hammurapi to Legendre / Andre Weil. — Boston: Birkhäuser, c1984. xxi, 375 p.: ill.; 23 cm. Includes index. 1. Numbers, Theory of — History. I. T.
QA241.W3418 1984     512/.7/09 19     *LC* 83-11857     *ISBN* 0817631410

## QA242–246 SPECIAL FORMS AND SPECIAL FUNCTIONS

**Mordell, L. J. (Louis Joel), 1888-.**      **5.1334**
Diophantine equations [by] L. J. Mordell. London, New York, Academic P., 1969. x, 312 p. 23 1/2 cm. (Pure and applied mathematics; a series of monographs and textbooks; v. 30) 1. Diophantine analysis I. T.
QA242.M6x     512/.74     *LC* 68-9112

**Lam, T. Y. (Tsit-Yuen), 1942-.**      **5.1335**
The algebraic theory of quadratic forms [by] T. Y. Lam. Reading, Mass., W. A. Benjamin, 1973. xi, 344 p. 24 cm. (Mathematics lecture note series) 1. Forms, Quadratic 2. Fields, Algebraic I. T.
QA243.L25     512.9/44     *LC* 72-11103     *ISBN* 0805356643 *ISBN* 0805356651

**Rankin, Robert A. (Robert Alexander), 1915-.**      **5.1336**
Modular forms and functions / Robert A. Rankin. — Cambridge, [Eng.]; New York: Cambridge University Press, 1977. xiii, 384 p.; 24 cm. Includes indexes. 1. Forms, Modular 2. Functions, Modular I. T.
QA243.R36     512.9/44     *LC* 76-11089     *ISBN* 052121212X

**Serre, Jean Pierre.**      **5.1337**
[Cours d'arithmétique. English] A course in arithmetic [by] J.–P. Serre. New York, Springer-Verlag [1973] viii, 115 p. illus. 25 cm. (Graduate texts in mathematics. 7) Translation of Cours d'arithmétique. 1. Forms, Quadratic 2. Analytic functions I. T. II. Series.
QA243.S4713     512.9/44     *LC* 70-190089     *ISBN* 0387900403 *ISBN* 0387900411

**Ribenboim, Paulo.**      **5.1338**
13 lectures on Fermat's last theorem / Paulo Ribenboim. — New York: Springer-Verlag, c1979. xvi, 302 p.: port.; 24 cm. 1. Fermat's last theorem I. T.
QA244.R5     512/.74     *LC* 79-14874     *ISBN* 0387904328

**Titchmarsh, E. C. (Edward Charles), 1899-.**      **5.1339**
The theory of the Riemann zeta–function / by E.C. Titchmarsh. — 2nd ed. / revised by D.R. Heath-Brown. — Oxford [Oxfordshire]: Clarendon Press; New York: Oxford University Press, 1986. x, 412 p.; 24 cm. — (Oxford science publications.) 1. Functions, Zeta I. Heath-Brown, D. R. II. T. III. Series.
QA246.T44 1986     512/.73 19     *LC* 86-12520     *ISBN* 0198533691

## QA247–247.5 ALGEBRAIC FIELDS. ALGEBRAIC NUMBERS

**Cohn, Harvey.**      **5.1340**
A classical invitation to algebraic numbers and class fields / Harvey Cohn. — New York: Springer-Verlag, c1978. xiii, 328 p.: ill.; 24 cm. 'With two appendices by Olga Taussky: 'Artin's 1932 Göttingen lectures on class field theory' and 'Connections between algebraic number theory and integral matrices.'' 1. Algebraic number theory 2. Class field theory I. T.
QA247.C63     512/.74     *LC* 78-13785     *ISBN* 0387903453

**Goldstein, Larry Joel.**      • **5.1341**
Analytic number theory. — Englewood Cliffs, N.J.: Prentice-Hall, [1971] xv, 282 p.; 24 cm. 1. Algebraic number theory I. T.
QA247.G67     512/.73     *LC* 77-140688     *ISBN* 0130348430

**McCoy, Neal Henry, 1905-.**      • **5.1342**
Rings and ideals / by Neal H. McCoy. — [Buffalo]: Mathematical Assn. of America, [1948] xii, 216 p. — (Carus mathematical monographs. no. 8) 1. Fields, Algebraic 2. Algebra, Abstract I. T. II. Series.
QA247.M2     *LC* 48-23679

**Serre, Jean Pierre.**      **5.1343**
[Corps locaux. English] Local fields / Jean–Pierre Serre; translated from the French by Marvin Jay Greenberg. — New York: Springer-Verlag, c1979. 241 p.; 24 cm. (Graduate texts in mathematics. 67) Translation of: Corps locaux. Includes index. 1. Homology theory 2. Local fields (Algebra) I. T. II. Series.
QA247.S4613     512/.74     *LC* 79-12643     *ISBN* 0387904247

**Washington, Lawrence C.**      **5.1344**
Introduction to cyclotomic fields / Lawrence C. Washington. — New York: Springer-Verlag, c1982. xi, 389 p.; 25 cm. — (Graduate texts in mathematics. 83) Includes index. 1. Fields, Algebraic 2. Cyclotomy I. T. II. Series.
QA247.W35 1982     512/.3 19     *LC* 82-755     *ISBN* 0387906223

**Ritt, Joseph Fels, 1893-1951.**      **5.1345**
Differential algebra. — New York: Dover Publications, [1966, c1950] viii, 184 p.; 24 cm. An unabridged and unaltered republication of the work

originally published by the American Mathematical Society in 1950 as vol. 33 of the Society's Colloquium publications. 1. Algebra, Differential I. T.
QA247.4.R5 1966    517.38    *LC* 66-23746

**Baker, Alan, 1939-.**       **5.1346**
Transcendental number theory / Alan Baker. — London; New York: Cambridge University Press, 1975. x, 147 p.; 24 cm. 'Original papers': p. 130-144. Includes index. 1. Numbers, Transcendental 2. Numbers, Transcendental — Bibliography. I. T.
QA247.5.B24    512/.73    *LC* 74-82591    *ISBN* 0521204615

# QA248–248.3 Aggregates. Set Theory

**Dauben, Joseph Warren, 1944-.**      **5.1347**
Georg Cantor: his mathematics and philosophy of the infinite / Joseph Warren Dauben. — Cambridge, Mass.: Harvard University Press, 1979 (c1978). ix, 404 p.; 24 cm. Includes index. 1. Cantor, Georg, 1845-1918. 2. Set theory — History. 3. Numbers, Transfinite — History. 4. Infinite I. T.
QA248.D27    512/.7    *LC* 77-23435    *ISBN* 0674348710

**Devlin, Keith J.**       **5.1348**
Fundamentals of contemporary set theory / Keith J. Devlin. — New York: Springer-Verlag, c1979. viii, 182 p.; 24 cm. — (Universitext) Includes index. 1. Set theory I. T.
QA248.D38    511/.3    *LC* 79-17759    *ISBN* 0387904417

**Drake, Frank R.**       **5.1349**
Set theory: an introduction to large cardinals / Frank R. Drake. — Amsterdam: North-Holland Pub. Co.; New York: American Elsevier Pub. Co., 1974. xii, 351 p.; 23 cm. (Studies in logic and the foundations of mathematics. v. 76) Includes index. 1. Set theory 2. Numbers, Cardinal I. T. II. Series.
QA248.D73    512/.72    *LC* 75-305311    *ISBN* 0444105352

**Halmos, Paul Richard, 1914-.**     • **5.1350**
Naive set theory. — Princeton, N.J.: Van Nostrand, [1960] 104 p.; 24 cm. — (The University series in undergraduate mathematics) 1. Set theory 2. Arithmetic — Foundations I. T.
QA248.H26    512.817    *LC* 60-11059

**Jech, Thomas J.**       **5.1351**
The axiom of choice [by] Thomas J. Jech. — Amsterdam: North-Holland Pub. Co.; New York: American Elsevier Pub. Co., 1973. xi, 202 p.; 23 cm. — (Studies in logic and the foundations of mathematics. v. 75) 1. Axiom of choice I. T. II. Series.
QA248.J4 1973    511/.3    *LC* 73-75535    *ISBN* 0444104844

**Jech, Thomas J.**       **5.1352**
Set theory / Thomas Jech. — New York: Academic Press, 1978. xi, 621 p.: ill.; 24 cm. (Pure and applied mathematics, a series of monographs and textbooks; 79) Includes index. 1. Set theory I. T.
QA248.J4x    510/.8 s 511/.3    *LC* 77-11214    *ISBN* 0123819504

**Kuratowski, Kazimierz, 1896-.**     **5.1353**
[Teoria mnogości. English] Set theory: with an introduction to descriptive set theory / K. Kuratowski and A. Mostowski. — 2d completely rev. ed. — Amsterdam: North-Holland Pub. Co.; New York: distributor, Elsevier/North-Holland, 1976. xiv, 514 p.; 23 cm. — (Studies in logic and the foundations of mathematics. v. 86) Translation of Teoria mnogości. Includes index. 1. Set theory 2. Descriptive set theory I. Mostowski, Andrzej. joint author. II. T. III. Series.
QA248.K7683 1976    511/.3    *LC* 74-83731    *ISBN* 0720404703

**Moore, Gregory H.**       **5.1354**
Zermelo's axiom of choice: its origins, development, and influence / Gregory H. Moore. — New York: Springer-Verlag, c1982. xiv, 410 p.: ill.; 25 cm. — (Studies in the history of mathematics and physical sciences. 8) Includes indexes. 1. Zermelo, Ernst, 1871- 2. Axiom of choice I. T. II. Series.
QA248.M59 1982    511.3 19    *LC* 82-10429    *ISBN* 0387906703

**Moschovakis, Yiannis N.**      **5.1355**
Descriptive set theory / Yiannis N. Moschovakis. — Amsterdam; New York: North-Holland Pub. Co.; New York: Sole distributors for the U.S.A. and Canada, Elsevier-North Holland, c1980. xii, 637 p.: ill.; 23 cm. — (Studies in logic and the foundations of mathematics. v. 100) Includes indexes. 1. Descriptive set theory I. T. II. Series.
QA248.M66    511/.3    *LC* 79-11792    *ISBN* 0444853057

# QA251–265 Universal Algebra. Linear Algebra

## QA251–251.5 UNIVERSAL ALGEBRA. RINGS

**Anton, Howard.**       **5.1356**
Elementary linear algebra. — New York: Wiley, [1973] xii, 296, A29, I4 p.; 23 cm. 1. Algebras, Linear I. T.
QA251.A57    512/.5    *LC* 72-5511    *ISBN* 0471032476

**Artin, Emil, 1898-1962.**     • **5.1357**
Geometric algebra. — New York: Interscience Publishers, [1957] 214 p.; 24 cm. — (Interscience tracts in pure and applied mathematics, no. 3) 1. Algebras, Linear 2. Geometry, Projective I. T.
QA251.A7    516    *LC* 57-6109

**Atiyah, Michael Francis, 1929-.**     **5.1358**
Introduction to commutative algebra [by] M. F. Atiyah [and] I. G. Macdonald. Reading, Mass., Addison-Wesley Pub. Co. [1969] viii, 128 p. 25 cm. (Addison-Wesley series in mathematics) 1. Commutative algebra 2. Rings (Algebra) 3. Commutative rings I. Macdonald, I. G. (Ian Grant) joint author. II. T.
QA251.A8    512/.815    *LC* 72-79530

**Cohn, P. M. (Paul Moritz)**      **5.1359**
Universal algebra / P. M. Cohn. — Rev. ed. — Dordrecht; Boston: D. Reidel Pub. Co.; Hingham, MA: Sold and distributed in the U.S.A. and Canada by Kluwer Boston, c1981. xv, 412 p.; 23 cm. (Mathematics and its applications; v. 6) Includes index. 1. Algebra, Universal I. T.
QA251.C55 1981    512 19    *LC* 80-29568    *ISBN* 9027712131

**Auslander, Maurice.**       **5.1360**
Groups, rings, modules [by] Maurice Auslander [and] David A. Buchsbaum. — New York: Harper & Row, [1974] x, 470 p.: illus.; 25 cm. — (Harper's series in modern mathematics) 1. Commutative rings 2. Modules (Algebra) 3. Groups, Theory of I. Buchsbaum, David Alvin, joint author. II. T.
QA251.3.A93    512/.4    *LC* 73-13199    *ISBN* 006040387X

**Matsumura, Hideyuki, 1930-.**     **5.1361**
Commutative algebra / Hideyuki Matsumura. — 2d ed. — Reading, Mass.: Benjamin/Cummings Pub. Co., 1980. xv, 313 p.; 24 cm. — (Mathematics lecture note series; 56) Includes indexes. 1. Commutative algebra I. T.
QA251.3.M37 1980    512/.24    *LC* 80-11958    *ISBN* 0805370269

**Zariski, Oscar, 1899-.**      **5.1362**
Commutative algebra / Oscar Zariski, Pierre Samuel, with the cooperation of I. S. Cohen. New York: Springer-Verlag, [1975-1976] c1958-c1960. 2 v.; 25 cm. (Graduate texts in mathematics. 28-29.) Reprint of the ed. published by Van Nostrand, Princeton, N.J., in series: The University series in higher mathematics. Includes indexes. 1. Commutative algebra I. Samuel, Pierre, 1921- joint author. II. Cohen, Irvin Sol, 1917- joint author. III. T. IV. Series.
QA251.3.Z37 1975    512/.24    *LC* 75-17751    *ISBN* 0387900896

**Abian, Alexander, 1925-.**      **5.1363**
Linear associative algebras. — New York: Pergamon Press, [1971] vii, 166 p.; 24 cm. 1. Associative algebras 2. Algebras, Linear I. T.
QA251.5.A5 1971    512/.24    *LC* 74-130799    *ISBN* 0080165648

## QA261–265 VECTOR CALCULUS. MATRICES. LINEAR PROGRAMMING

**Halmos, Paul R. (Paul Richard), 1916-.**    • **5.1364**
Finite-dimensional vector spaces. — 2d ed. — Princeton, N.J.: Van Nostrand, [1958] 200 p.; 24 cm. — (The University series in undergraduate mathematics) Includes index. 1. Vector spaces 2. Transformations (Mathematics) I. T.
QA261.H33 1958    512.86    *LC* 58-8446

**Schey, Harry Moritz, 1930-.**     **5.1365**
Div, grad, curl, and all that; an informal text on vector calculus [by] H. M. Schey. — [1st ed.]. — New York: Norton, [1973] x, 163 p.: illus.; 24 cm. 1. Vector analysis I. T.
QA261.S318 1973    515/.63    *LC* 72-13436    *ISBN* 0393093670

**Gantmakher, F. R. (Feliks Ruvimovich)**    • **5.1366**
[Teoriia matrits. English] The theory of matrices, by F.R. Gantmacher. [Translation by K.A. Hirsch]. New York, Chelsea Pub. Co. [1959] 2 v. 24 cm. 1. Matrices I. T.
QA263.G353    512.896    *LC* 59-11779

**Nemhauser, George L.**    **5.1367**
Introduction to dynamic programming [by] George L. Nemhauser. — New York: Wiley, [1966] xiii, 256 p.: illus.; 24 cm. — (Series in decision and control) 1. Dynamic programming I. T. II. Title: Dynamic programming.
QA264.N4    519.92    *LC* 66-21046

**Dantzig, George Bernard, 1914-.**    **5.1368**
Linear programming and extensions. — Princeton, N.J.: Princeton University Press, 1963. xvi, 625 p.: maps, diagrs.; 25 cm. — ([A Rand Corporation research study]) 1. Linear programming 2. Mathematical models I. T.
QA265.D3 1963    519.92    *LC* 62-10891

# QA266–268 Machine Theory

**Bruck, Richard Hubert.**    **5.1369**
A survey of binary systems. — 3rd print., corr. — Berlin; New York: Springer, 1971. viii, 186 p.; 24 cm. — (Ergebnisse der Mathematik und ihrer Grenzgebiete. Bd. 20) 1. Algebra, Abstract 2. Groups, Theory of 3. Binary system (Mathematics) I. T. II. Series.
QA266.B7 1971    512/.74    *LC* 79-143906    *ISBN* 0387034978

**Denning, Peter J., 1942-.**    **5.1370**
Machines, languages, and computation / Peter J. Denning, Jack B. Dennis, Joseph E. Qualitz. — Englewood Cliffs, N.J.: Prentice-Hall, c1978. xxii, 601 p.: ill.; 24 cm. Includes indexes. 1. Machine theory 2. Formal languages I. Dennis, Jack B. (Jack Bonnell) joint author. II. Qualitz, Joseph E., 1948- joint author. III. T.
QA267.D45    621.3819/52    *LC* 77-18128    *ISBN* 0135422582

**Hopcroft, John E., 1939-.**    **5.1371**
Introduction to automata theory, languages, and computation / John E. Hopcroft, Jeffrey D. Ullman. — Reading, Mass.: Addison-Wesley, c1979. x, 418 p.: ill.; 24 cm. — (Addison-Wesley series in computer science) Includes index. 1. Machine theory 2. Formal languages 3. Computational complexity I. Ullman, Jeffrey D., 1942- joint author. II. T.
QA267.H56    629.8/312    *LC* 78-67950    *ISBN* 020102988X

**Lewis, Harry R.**    **5.1372**
Elements of the theory of computation / Harry R. Lewis, Christos H. Papadimitriou. — Englewood Cliffs, N.J.: Prentice-Hall, c1981. xiv, 466 p.: ill.; 24 cm. — (Prentice-Hall software series.) 1. Machine theory 2. Formal languages 3. Computational complexity 4. Logic, Symbolic and mathematical I. Papadimitriou, Christos H. joint author. II. T. III. Series.
QA267.L49    511 19    *LC* 80-21293

**Harrison, Michael A.**    **5.1373**
Introduction to formal language theory / Michael A. Harrison. — Reading, Mass.: Addison-Wesley Pub. Co., c1978. xiv, 594 p.: ill.; 25 cm. — (Addison-Wesley series in computer science) Includes index. 1. Formal languages I. T.
QA267.3.H37    001.54    *LC* 77-81196    *ISBN* 0201029553

**Preston, Kendall, 1927-.**    **5.1374**
Modern cellular automata: theory and applications / Kendall Preston, Jr. and Michael J.B. Duff. — New York: Plenum Press, c1984. xviii, 340 p.: ill.; 26 cm. (Advanced applications in pattern recognition.) Includes indexes. 1. Cellular automata I. Duff, M. J. B. II. T. III. Series.
QA267.5.C45 P74 1984    001.64 19    *LC* 84-11672    *ISBN* 0306417375

**Hamming, R. W. (Richard Wesley), 1915-.**    **5.1375**
Coding and information theory / R. W. Hamming. — Englewood Cliffs, N.J.: Prentice-Hall, c1980. xii, 239 p.: ill.; 24 cm. Includes index. 1. Coding theory 2. Information theory I. T.
QA268.H35 1980    519.4    *LC* 79-15159    *ISBN* 0131391399

**MacWilliams, Florence Jessie, 1917-.**    **5.1376**
The theory of error correcting codes / F. J. MacWilliams, N. J. A. Sloane. — Amsterdam; New York: North-Holland Pub. Co.; New York: sole distributors for the U.S.A. and Canada, Elsevier/North-Holland, 1977. 2 v. (xv, 762 p.): ill.; 23 cm. — (North-Holland mathematical library; v. 16) Includes index. 1. Error-correcting codes (Information theory) I. Sloane, N. J. A. (Neil James Alexander), 1939- joint author. II. T.
QA268.M31    519.4    *LC* 76-41296    *ISBN* 0444850090

# QA269–271 Game Theory

**Blackwell, David Harold, 1919-.**    • **5.1377**
Theory of games and statistical decisions [by] David Blackwell [and] M. A. Girshick. — New York: Wiley, [1954] 355 p.: illus.; 24 cm. — (Wiley publications in statistics) 1. Game theory 2. Mathematical statistics I. Girshick, Meyer A., joint author. II. T.
QA269.B5    519    *LC* 54-7259

**Davis, Morton D., 1930-.**    **5.1378**
Game theory: a nontechnical introduction / Morton D. Davis. — Rev. ed. — New York: Basic Books, c1983. xix, 252 p.: ill.; 21 cm. — (Harper colophon books; CN5107) Includes index. 1. Game theory I. T.
QA269.D38 1983    519.3 19    *LC* 83-70771    *ISBN* 0465026281

**Rapoport, Anatol, 1911-.**    **5.1379**
The 2 X 2 game / by Anatol Rapoport, Melvin J. Guyer, and David G. Gordon. Ann Arbor: University of Michigan Press, c1976. x, 461 p.: ill.; 24 cm. Includes indexes. 1. Game theory I. Guyer, Melvin. joint author. II. Gordon, David G., joint author. III. T.
QA269.R36 1976    519.3    *LC* 74-25947    *ISBN* 0472087428

**Von Neumann, John, 1903-1957.**    • **5.1380**
Theory of games and economic behavior, by John Von Neumann and Oskar Morgenstern. — [3d ed.]. — Princeton: Princeton University Press, 1953 [c1944] 641 p.: illus.; 25 cm. 1. Game theory 2. Economics, Mathematical I. Morgenstern, Oskar, 1902- joint author. II. T.
QA269.V65 1953    330.182    *LC* 53-4426

# QA273–273.4 Probabilities

**Feller, William, 1906-.**    • **5.1381**
An introduction to probability theory and its applications. 3d ed. New York: Wiley [1967, c1968-. v.    : ill.; 24 cm. (Wiley series in probability and mathematical statistics) 1. Probabilities I. T.
QA273.F3713    519/.1    *LC* 68-11708

**Itō, Kiyoshi, 1915-.**    **5.1382**
[Kakuritsuron. 1-4-shō. English] Introduction to probability theory / Kiyosi Itô. — Cambridge [Cambridgeshire]; New York: Cambridge University Press, 1984. ix, 213 p.; 24 cm. Translation of: Kakuritsuron. 1-4-shō. Includes index. 1. Probabilities I. T.
QA273.I822513 1984    519.2 19    *LC* 83-23187    *ISBN* 0521264189

**Kalbfleisch, J. G.**    **5.1383**
Probability and statistical inference / J. G. Kalbfleisch. — New York: Springer-Verlag, 1979. 2 v.: ill. (Universitext) Includes index. 1. Probabilities 2. Mathematical statistics I. T.
QA273.K27 1979    519.2    *LC* 79-22910    *ISBN* 0387904581

**Carnap, Rudolf, 1891-1970.**    **5.1384**
Studies in inductive logic and probability. Rudolf Carnap and Richard C. Jeffrey, editors. — Berkeley: University of California Press, 1980. 305 p. Vol. 2: R. C. Jeffrey, editor. 1. Probabilities 2. Induction (Mathematics) I. Jeffrey, Richard C. II. T.
QA273.4.C37    519.2 19    *LC* 77-136025    *ISBN* 0520038266

# QA274 Stochastic Processes

**Çinlar, E. (Erhan), 1941-.**    **5.1385**
Introduction to stochastic processes. Englewood Cliffs, N.J.: Prentice-Hall, [c1975] 402p. 1. Stochastic processes I. T.
QA274.C56    *LC* 74-5256    *ISBN* 0134980891

# QA276–295 Mathematical Statistics

## QA276 General Works, A–J

**Cramér, Harald, 1893-.**                                                **• 5.1386**
Mathematical methods of statistics, by Harald Cramér ... Princeton, Princeton university press, 1946. xvi, 575 p. incl. tables, diagrs. 23.5 cm. ([Princeton mathematical series ... 9]) 'First published in Sweden, Uppsala, 1945, by Almqvist & Wiksells.' 'List of references': p. 561-570. 1. Mathematical statistics I. T.
QA276.C72      *LC* A 46-5922

**Freund, John E.**                                                       **5.1387**
Mathematical statistics / John E. Freund, Ronald E. Walpole. — 4th ed. — Englewood Cliffs, N.J.: Prentice-Hall, c1987. p. cm. 1. Mathematical statistics I. Walpole, Ronald E. II. T.
QA276.F692 1987      519.5 19      *LC* 86-21249      *ISBN* 0135620759

**Hoel, Paul Gerhard, 1905-.**                                            **5.1388**
Introduction to mathematical statistics / Paul G. Hoel. — 5th ed. — New York: Wiley, c1984. x, 435 p.: ill.; 24 cm. — (Wiley publication in mathematical statistics.) (Wiley series in probability and mathematical statistics) Includes index. 1. Mathematical statistics I. T. II. Series.
QA276.H57 1984      519.5 19      *LC* 83-19818      *ISBN* 0471890456

**Hogg, Robert V.**                                                       **5.1389**
Introduction to mathematical statistics / Robert V. Hogg, Allen T. Craig. — 4th ed. — New York: Macmillan, c1978. x, 438 p.: ill.; 24 cm. Includes index. 1. Mathematical statistics I. Craig, Allen Thornton, 1905- joint author. II. T.
QA276.H59 1978      519      *LC* 77-2884      *ISBN* 0023557109

## QA276 K–Z

**Kendall, Maurice G. (Maurice George), 1907-.**                          **5.1390**
The advanced theory of statistics, by Maurice G. Kendall and Alan Stuart. — 3rd ed. — London: Griffin, 1969-. v.    : illus.; 26 cm. 1. Mathematical statistics I. Stuart, Alan, 1922- joint author. II. T.
QA276.K4262      519      *LC* 78-467813      *ISBN* 0852641419

**Kendall, Maurice G. (Maurice George), 1907-.**                          **5.1391**
Multivariate analysis / Sir Maurice Kendall. — 2nd ed. New York: Macmillan, 1980. 210 p.: ill.; 24 cm. Rewritten version of A course in multivariate analysis. - 1. Mathematical statistics I. T. II. Title: A course in multivariate analysis
QA276.K434 1980      *LC* 75-9882

**Li, Jerome C. R. (Jerome Ching-ren), 1914-.**                           **• 5.1392**
Statistical inference [by] Jerome C. R. Li. Ann Arbor, Mich., Distributed by Edwards Bros. [1964] 2 v. illus. 24 cm. 'Volume I is the revised edition of Introduction to statistical inference, which was published in 1957, and volume II is a new work.' 1. Mathematical statistics I. T.
QA276.L52      519.5 19      *LC* 64-11805

**Meyer, Stuart L., 1937-.**                                              **5.1393**
Data analysis for scientists and engineers [by] Stuart L. Meyer. — New York: Wiley, [1975] 513 p.: illus.; 26 cm. 1. Mathematical statistics 2. Probabilities I. T.
QA276.M437      519.2      *LC* 74-8873      *ISBN* 0471599956

**Mood, Alexander McFarlane, 1913-.**                                     **• 5.1394**
Introduction to the theory of statistics / [by] Alexander M. Mood, Franklin A. Graybill [and] Duane C. Boes. — 3d ed. — New York: McGraw-Hill, [1973] xvi, 564 p.: ill.; 24 cm. (McGraw-Hill series in probability and statistics) 1. Mathematical statistics I. Graybill, Franklin A. joint author. II. Boes, Duane C., joint author. III. T.
QA276.M67 1974      519.5      *LC* 73-292      *ISBN* 0070428646

## QA276.12 Descriptive Statistics

**Dixon, Wilfrid Joseph, 1915-.**                                         **5.1395**
Introduction to statistical analysis / Wilfrid J. Dixon, Frank J. Massey, Jr. — 4th ed. — New York: McGraw-Hill, c1983. xv, 678 p.: ill.; 24 cm. Includes index. 1. Statistics I. Massey, Frank Jones. II. T.
QA276.12.D58 1983      519.5 19      *LC* 81-19313      *ISBN* 0070170738

**The Fascination of statistics / edited by Richard J. Brook ... [et     5.1396
al.].**
New York: Dekker, c1986. xi, 433 p.: ill.; 24 cm. (Popular statistics. 4) Includes index. 1. Statistics I. Brook, Richard J. II. Series.
QA276.12.F37 1986      519.5 19      *LC* 85-29171      *ISBN* 0824773292

**Ferguson, George Andrew.**                                              **5.1397**
Statistical analysis in psychology and education / George A. Ferguson. — 5th ed. — New York: McGraw-Hill, c1981. x, 549 p.: ill.; 25 cm. — (McGraw-Hill series in psychology) Includes index. 1. Statistics 2. Psychometrics 3. Educational statistics I. T.
QA276.12.F45 1981      519.5 19      *LC* 80-19584      *ISBN* 0070204829

**Snedecor, George Waddel, 1881-.**                                       **5.1398**
Statistical methods / George W. Snedecor, William G. Cochran. — 7th ed. — Ames, Iowa: Iowa State University Press, c1980. xvi, 507 p.: ill.; 24 cm. 1. Statistics I. Cochran, William Gemmell, 1909- joint author. II. T.
QA276.12.S59 1980      519.5      *LC* 80-14582      *ISBN* 0813815606

## QA276.14–276.4 Dictionaries. Tables. Graphic Methods

**Encyclopedia of statistical sciences / editors–in–chief, Samuel        5.1399
Kotz, Norman L. Johnson; associate editor, Campbell B. Read.**
New York: Wiley, c1982. 6 v.: ill.; 26 cm. 'A Wiley-Interscience publication.' 1. Mathematical statistics — Dictionaries. 2. Statistics — Dictionaries. I. Kotz, Samuel. II. Johnson, Norman Lloyd. III. Read, Campbell B.
QA276.14.E5 1982      519.5/03/21 19      *LC* 81-10353      *ISBN* 0471055468

**Kendall, Maurice G. (Maurice George), 1907-.**                          **5.1400**
A dictionary of statistical terms / prepared for the International Statistical Institute by Sir Maurice G. Kendall & William R. Buckland. — 4th ed., rev. and enl. — London; New York: Published for the International Statistical Institute by Longman, 1982. 213 p.; 25 cm. 1. Statistics — Dictionaries. I. Buckland, William R. II. International Statistical Institute. III. T.
QA276.14.K46 1982      001.4/22/0321 19      *LC* 81-11829      *ISBN* 0582470080

**Beyer, William H., comp.**                                              **• 5.1401**
CRC handbook of tables for probability and statistics / editor: William H. Beyer. — 2d ed. Cleveland: Chemical Rubber Co. [1968] xiv, 642 p.; 28 cm. 1. Mathematical statistics — Tables. 2. Probabilities — Tables. I. Chemical Rubber Company. II. T. III. Title: Handbook of tables for probability and statistics.
QA276.25.B48 1968      519/.0212      *LC* 68-5038

**Graphical methods for data analysis / John M. Chambers ... [et         5.1402
al.].**
Belmont, Calif.: Wadsworth International Group; Boston: Duxbury Press, c1983. xiv, 395 p.; 24 cm. — (Wadsworth statistics/probability series.) Includes index. 1. Statistics — Graphic methods — Congresses. 2. Computer graphics — Congresses. I. Chambers, John M. II. Series.
QA276.3.G73 1983      001.4/22 19      *LC* 83-3660      *ISBN* 053498052X

**Schmid, Calvin Fisher, 1901-.**                                         **5.1403**
Statistical graphics: design principles and practices / Calvin F. Schmid. — New York: Wiley, c1983. x, 212 p.: ill.; 28 cm. 'A Wiley-Interscience publication.' 1. Statistics — Graphic methods I. T.
QA276.3.S35 1983      001.4/226 19      *LC* 82-19971      *ISBN* 0471875252

## QA276.6 Sampling

**Cochran, William Gemmell, 1909-.**                                      **5.1404**
Sampling techniques / William G. Cochran. — 3d ed. — New York: Wiley, c1977. xvi, 428 p.: ill.; 24 cm. (Wiley series in probability and mathematical statistics) (A Wiley publication in applied statistics) Includes indexes. 1. Sampling (Statistics) I. T.
QA276.6.C6 1977      001.4/222      *LC* 77-728      *ISBN* 047116240X

## ✓QA278 MULTIVARIATE ANALYSIS

**Agresti, Alan.**                                                   **5.1405**
Analysis of ordinal categorical data / Alan Agresti. — New York: Wiley, 1984.
ix, 287 p.; 24 cm. (Wiley series in probability and mathematical statistics.
Applied probability and statistics.) Includes index. 1. Multivariate analysis
I. T. II. Series.
QA278.A35 1984       519.5/35 19       *LC* 83-23535       *ISBN* 0471890553

**Finn, Jeremy D.**                                                  **5.1406**
A general model for multivariate analysis [by] Jeremy D. Finn. — New York:
Holt, Rinehart and Winston, [1974] xiii, 407, 166, 410-423 p.: ill.; 24 cm. —
(International series in decision processes) 1. Multivariate analysis 2. Analysis
of variance I. T.
QA278.F56       519.5/3       *LC* 74-8629       *ISBN* 003083239X

**Green, Paul E.**                                                   **5.1407**
Analyzing multivariate data / Paul E. Green; with contributions by J. Douglas
Carroll. — Hinsdale, Ill.: Dryden Press, c1978. xvi, 519 p.: ill.; 25 cm. Includes
index. 1. Multivariate analysis I. Carroll, J. Douglas. II. T.
QA278.G72       519.5/3       *LC* 77-81241       *ISBN* 003020786X

**Johnson, Richard Arnold.**                                         **5.1408**
Applied multivariate statistical analysis / Richard A. Johnson, Dean W.
Wichern. — Englewood Cliffs, N.J.: Prentice-Hall, c1982. xiii, 594 p.: ill.; 25
cm. 1. Multivariate analysis I. Wichern, Dean W. II. T.
QA278.J63 1982       519.5/35 19       *LC* 81-19894       *ISBN* 013041400X

## ✓ QA278.2–279.5 REGRESSION ANALYSIS.
## ANALYSIS OF VARIANCE

**Bartlett, M. S. (Maurice Stevenson)**                              **5.1409**
The statistical analysis of spatial pattern / M. S. Bartlett. — London: Chapman
and Hall; New York: Wiley, 1976 (c1975). ix, 90 p.: graphs; 23 cm.
(Monographs on applied probability and statistics) 'A Halsted Press book.'
Includes index. 1. Spatial analysis (Statistics) I. T.
QA278.2.B37       519.5/3       *LC* 75-31673       *ISBN* 0470054670

**Weisberg, Sanford, 1947-.**                                        **5.1410**
Applied linear regression / Sanford Weisberg. — New York: Wiley, c1980. xii,
283 p.: ill.; 24 cm. — (Wiley series in probability and mathematical statistics)
Includes index. 1. Regression analysis I. T.
QA278.2.W44       519.5/36       *LC* 80-10378       *ISBN* 0471044199

**Hollander, Myles.**                                                **5.1411**
Nonparametric statistical methods / [by] Myles Hollander [and] Douglas A.
Wolfe. — New York: Wiley, [1973] xviii, 503 p.: ill.; 24 cm. — (Wiley series in
probability and mathematical statistics) (A Wiley publication in applied
statistics) 1. Nonparametric statistics I. Wolfe, Douglas A. joint author. II. T.
QA278.8.H65       519.5/3       *LC* 72-11960       *ISBN* 047140635X

**Milliken, George A., 1943-.**                                      **5.1412**
Analysis of messy data / George A. Milliken, Dallas E. Johnson. — Belmont,
Calif.: Lifetime Learning Publications, 1984. 473 p.: ill. Includes index.
1. Analysis of variance 2. Experimental design 3. Sampling (Statistics)
I. Johnson, Dallas E., 1938- II. T.
QA279.M48 1984       519.5/352 19       *LC* 84-839       *ISBN* 053402713X

**Myers, Jerome L.**                                                 **5.1413**
Fundamentals of experimental design / Jerome L. Myers. — 3d ed. — Boston:
Allyn and Bacon, c1979. xii, 524 p.: ill.; 25 cm. & Appendix tables.
1. Experimental design 2. Psychometrics I. T.
QA279.M93 1979       001.4/34       *LC* 78-12815       *ISBN* 0205064205

**Winkler, Robert L.**                                               **5.1414**
An introduction to Bayesian inference and decision [by] Robert L. Winkler. —
New York: Holt, Rinehart and Winston, [1972] xi, 563 p.: illus.; 24 cm. —
(Series in quantitative methods for decision making) 1. Bayesian statistical
decision theory I. T.
QA279.5.W55       519.5/4       *LC* 70-166109       *ISBN* 0030813271

## QA280–295 SERIES. INEQUALITIES

**Box, George E. P.**                                                **5.1415**
Time series analysis: forecasting and control / George E. P. Box and Gwilym
M. Jenkins. — Rev. ed. — San Francisco: Holden-Day, c1976. xxi, 575 p.: ill.;
24 cm. — (Holden-Day series in time series analysis and digital processing)
1. Time-series analysis 2. Prediction theory 3. Transfer functions

4. Feedback control systems — Mathematical models. I. Jenkins, Gwilym M.,
joint author. II. T.
QA280.B67 1976       629.8/312 19       *LC* 76-8713       *ISBN* 0816211043

**Sloane, Neil James Alexander, 1939-.**                             **5.1416**
A handbook of integer sequences / [by] N. J. A. Sloane. — New York:
Academic Press, 1973. xiii, 206 p.: ill.; 24 cm. 1. Sequences (Mathematics)
2. Numbers, Natural I. T.
QA292.S58       515/.242       *LC* 72-82647       *ISBN* 012648550X

**Beckenbach, Edwin F.**                                             **5.1417**
Inequalities by Edwin F. Beckenbach and Richard Bellman. Berlin, Springer,
1961. 198 p. 24 cm. (Ergebnisse der Mathematik und ihrer Grenzgebiete, n.F.,
Heft 30. Reihe: Reelle Funktionen) 1. Inequalities (Mathematics)
2. Mathematical analysis I. Bellman, Richard Ernest, 1920- joint author.
II. T.
QA295.B37       *LC* 62-4593

**Hardy, Godfrey Harold, 1877-1947.**                                **5.1418**
Divergent series. Oxford, Clarendon Press, 1949. xvi, 396 p. 25 cm. 1. Series,
Divergent I. T.
QA295.H29       *LC* 49-5496

**Kazarinoff, Nicholas D.**                                          **5.1419**
Analytic inequalities. New York, Holt, Rinehart and Winston [1961] 89 p. illus.
25 cm. 1. Inequalities (Mathematics) I. T.
QA295.K34       517       *LC* 61-6544

**Khinchin, Aleksandr IAkovlevich, 1894-1959.**                      **5.1420**
[TSepnye drobi. English] Continued fractions. [Translated from the Russian by
Scripta Technica, inc. English translation edited by Herbert Eagle. 3d ed.].
Chicago, University of Chicago Press [1964] xi, 95 p. 21 cm. 1. Fractions,
Continued I. T.
QA295.K513 1964       517.21       *LC* 64-15819

**Kinderlehrer, David.**                                             **5.1421**
An introduction to variational inequalities and their applications / David
Kinderlehrer, Guido Stampacchia. — New York: Academic Press, 1980. xiv,
313 p.; 24 cm. (Pure and applied mathematics, a series of monographs and
textbooks; 88) Includes index. 1. Variational inequalities (Mathematics)
I. Stampacchia, Guido. joint author. II. T.
QA295.K5x       510/.8 s 512.9/7 19       *LC* 79-52793       *ISBN*
0124073506

**Knopp, Konrad.**                                                 **• 5.1422**
Theory and application of infinite series. 2d ed. London: Blackie, 1951. 563 p.
bibl. Translated from the 2d German ed. and rev. in accordance with the 4th. by
R.C.H. Young. 1. Series, Infinite I. T.
QA295 K74 1951       512.4       *LC* 51-7902

**Korovkin, P. P. (Pavel Petrovich)**                                **5.1423**
[Narravenstva. English] Inequalities. Translated from the Russian by Halina
Moss. Translation editor: Ian N. Sneddon. Oxford, New York, Pergamon
Press, 1961. 60 p. illus. 23 cm. (Popular lectures in mathematics series, v. 6)
1. Inequalities (Mathematics) I. T.
QA295.K813 1961       *LC* 61-11526

**Polya, George, 1887-.**                                           **5.1424**
Isoperimetric inequalities in mathematical physics / by G. Polya and G. Szegö.
— Princeton: Princeton University Press, 1951. xvi, 279 p. –. (Annals of
mathematics studies. 27) 1. Inequalities (Mathematics) 2. Mathematical
physics I. Szegő, Gábor, 1895- joint author II. T. III. Series.
QA295.P6       530.151       *LC* 51-6244

## ✓ QA297–299.82 Numerical Analysis

**Atkinson, Kendall E.**                                             **5.1425**
An introduction to numerical analysis / Kendall E. Atkinson. — New York:
Wiley, c1978. xiii, 587 p.: ill.; 24 cm. 1. Numerical analysis I. T.
QA297.A84       519.4       *LC* 78-6706       *ISBN* 0471029859

**Hamming, R. W. (Richard Wesley), 1915-.**                         **• 5.1426**
Introduction to applied numerical analysis [by] Richard W. Hamming. New
York, McGraw-Hill [c1971] x, 331 p. illus. 23 cm. (McGraw-Hill computer
science series) 1. Numerical analysis — Data processing I. T.
QA297.H275       517/.6       *LC* 78-127970       *ISBN* 0070258899

**Ortega, James M., 1932-.**     **5.1427**
Numerical analysis; a second course [by] James M. Ortega. — New York: Academic Press, [1972] xiii, 201 p.: illus.; 24 cm. — (Computer science and applied mathematics) 1. Numerical analysis I. T.
QA297.O78     519.4     *LC* 75-182669     *ISBN* 0125285604

**Todd, John, 1911-.**     **5.1428**
Basic numerical mathematics / by John Todd. — Basel: Birkhäuser Verlag, 1977-1979. 2 v.: ill.; 25 cm. — (International series of numerical mathematics. v. 14, 22) 1. Numerical analysis — Collected works. 2. Numerical analysis — Data processing — Collected works I. T. II. Series.
QA297.T58 1977     519.4     *LC* 78-312462     *ISBN* 3764307293

**Vandergraft, James S.**     **5.1429**
Introduction to numerical computations / James S. Vandergraft. — 2nd ed. — New York: Academic Press, 1983. xiv, 372 p.: ill.; 24 cm. — (Computer science and applied mathematics.) Includes index. 1. Numerical analysis I. T. II. Series.
QA297.V28 1983     519.4 19     *LC* 82-16252     *ISBN* 0127113568

**Murray, J. D. (James Dickson)**     **5.1430**
Asymptotic analysis / J.D. Murray. — [Springer ed.]. — New York: Springer-Verlag, c1984. vi, 164 p.: ill.; 25 cm. — (Applied mathematical sciences; v. 48) An earlier version of this book was published by Clarendon Press, Oxford in 1974. Includes index. 1. Approximation theory 2. Asymptotic expansions 3. Integrals 4. Differential equations — Numerical solutions I. T.
QA297.5.M8     510 s 515/.24 19     *LC* 83-20426     *ISBN* 0387909370

**Watson, G. A.**     **5.1431**
Approximation theory and numerical methods / G. A. Watson. — Chichester; New York: J. Wiley, c1980. x, 229 p.: ill.; 24 cm. 'A Wiley-Interscience publication.' Includes index. 1. Approximation theory 2. Numerical analysis I. T.
QA297.5.W37     511/.42     *LC* 79-42725     *ISBN* 0471277061

**Davis, Philip J., 1923-.**     **5.1432**
Methods of numerical integration [by] Philip J. Davis [and] Philip Rabinowitz. — New York: Academic Press, 1975. xii, 459 p.; 24 cm. — (Computer science and applied mathematics) 1. Numerical integration I. Rabinowitz, Philip. joint author. II. T.
QA299.3.D28     515/.624     *LC* 73-18976     *ISBN* 0122063503

**Bishop, Errett, 1928-1983.**     **5.1433**
Constructive analysis / Errett Bishop, Douglas Bridges. — Berlin; New York: Springer-Verlag, c1985. xii, 477 p.; 24 cm. (Grundlehren der mathematischen Wissenschaften. 279) An outgrowth of: Foundations of constructive analysis / Errett Bishop. [1967] Includes index. 1. Mathematical analysis — Foundations I. Bridges, D. S. (Douglas S.), 1945- II. Bishop, Errett, 1928-1983. Foundations of constructive analysis. III. T. IV. Series.
QA299.8.B57 1985     515 19     *LC* 85-2828     *ISBN* 0387150668

**Stroyan, K. D.**     **5.1434**
Introduction to the theory of infinitesimals / K. D. Stroyan in collaboration with W. A. J. Luxemburg. — New York: Academic Press, 1976. xiii, 326 p.: ill.; 24 cm. (Pure and applied mathematics, a series of monographs and textbooks; 72.) Includes index. 1. Mathematical analysis, Nonstandard I. Luxemburg, W. A. J., 1929- joint author. II. T. III. Title: Infinitesimals.
QA299.82.S8x     510/.8 s 515/.33     *LC* 76-14344     *ISBN* 0126741506

# QA300–433 MATHEMATICAL ANALYSIS

## QA300 General Works. Treatises

**Apostol, Tom M.**     • **5.1435**
Calculus [by] Tom M. Apostol. 2d ed. Waltham, Mass., Blaisdell Pub. Co. [1967-69] 2 v. illus. 27 cm. (Blaisdell book in pure and applied mathematics.) 1. Mathematical analysis 2. Calculus I. T. II. Series.
QA300.A572     517     *LC* 67-14605

**Bartle, Robert Gardner, 1927-.**     **5.1436**
The elements of real analysis / Robert G. Bartle. — 2d ed. — New York: Wiley, c1976. xv, 480 p.: ill.; 24 cm. Includes index. 1. Mathematical analysis I. T.
QA300.B29 1976     515/.8     *LC* 75-15979     *ISBN* 047105464X

**Birkhoff, Garrett, 1911- comp.**     **5.1437**
A source book in classical analysis. Edited by Garrett Birkhoff with the assistance of Uta Merzbach. — Cambridge: Harvard University Press, 1973. xii, 470 p.; 26 cm. — (Source books in the history of the sciences.) 1. Mathematical analysis — Addresses, essays, lectures. 2. Mathematical analysis — History — Sources. I. T. II. Series.
QA300.B54     515/.08     *LC* 72-85144     *ISBN* 0674822455

**Cooke, Roger.**     **5.1438**
The mathematics of Sonya Kovalevskaya / Roger Cooke. — New York: Springer-Verlag, c1984. xiii, 234 p.; 25 cm. Includes index. 1. Kovalevskaia, S. V. (Sof'ia Vasil'evna), 1850-1891. 2. Mathematical analysis — History. 3. Mathematicians — Soviet Union — Biography. I. T.
QA300.C65 1984     515/.09 19     *LC* 84-10599

**Dieudonné, Jean Alexandre, 1906-.**     • **5.1439**
Foundations of modern analysis / [by] J. Dieudonné. — New York: Academic Press, 1969- . –. v.; 24 cm. — (Pure and applied mathematics (Academic Press) 10) Vols. 2- have title: Treatise on analysis. - Vol. 1, 'an enlarged and corrected printing' of the author's Foundations of modern analysis, published in 1960. - 1. Mathematical analysis I. T. II. Title: Treatise on analysis. III. Series.
QA300.D5x     510/.8 s 515     *LC* 73-10084     *ISBN* 0122155033

**Franklin, Philip, 1898-.**     • **5.1440**
A treatise on advanced calculus; including those parts of the theory of functions of real and complex variables which form the logical basis of the infinitesimal analysis and its applications to geometry and physics. — New York, Dover Publications [1964, c1940] xii, 595 p. illus. 22 cm. Bibliography: p. 585-586. 1. Calculus 2. Functions I. T.
QA300.F7 1964     517     *LC* 64-21659

**Gelbaum, Bernard R.**     • **5.1441**
Counterexamples in analysis [by] Bernard R. Gelbaum [and] John M.H. Olmsted. San Francisco, Holden-Day, 1964. xxiv, 194 p. illus. 24 cm. (The Mathesis series) 1. Mathematical analysis I. Olmsted, John Meigs Hubbell, 1911- joint author. II. T.
QA300.G4     517.5     *LC* 64-21715

**Lang, Serge, 1927-.**     **5.1442**
Undergraduate analysis / Serge Lang. — New York: Springer-Verlag, c1983. xiii, 545 p.: ill.; 24 cm. — (Undergraduate texts in mathematics) Rev. ed. of: Analysis I. 1968. Includes index. 1. Mathematical analysis. I. Lang, Serge, 1927- Analysis I. II. T. III. Series.
QA300.L27 1983     515 19     *LC* 83-659     *ISBN* 0387908005

**Lang, Serge, 1927-.**     • **5.1443**
Analysis II. — Reading, Mass.: Addison-Wesley Pub. Co., [1969] xi, 476 p.: illus.; 24 cm. — (Addison-Wesley series in mathematics) 1. Mathematical analysis I. T.
QA300.L273     517     *LC* 69-16750

**Rudin, Walter, 1921-.**     • **5.1444**
Principles of mathematical analysis. — 2d ed. — New York: McGraw-Hill, [1964] ix, 270 p.: diagrs.; 23 cm. — (International series in pure and applied mathematics) 1. Mathematical analysis I. T.
QA300.R8 1964     517     *LC* 63-21479

**Rudin, Walter, 1921-.**     **5.1445**
Real and complex analysis / Walter Rudin. — 3rd ed. — New York: McGraw-Hill, c1987. xiv, 416 p.; 24 cm. Cover title: Real & complex analysis. Includes index. 1. Mathematical analysis I. T. II. Title: Real & complex analysis.
QA300.R82 1987     515 19     *LC* 86-7     *ISBN* 0070542341

**Stromberg, Karl Robert, 1931-.**     **5.1446**
Introduction to classical real analysis / Karl R. Stromberg. — Belmont, Calif.: Wadsworth International Group, c1981. ix, 575 p.; 24 cm. Includes index. 1. Mathematical analysis I. T.
QA300.S89     515 19     *LC* 80-26939     *ISBN* 0534980120

## QA303–316 Calculus

**Boyer, Carl B. (Carl Benjamin), 1906-.**     • **5.1447**
The history of the calculus and its conceptual development: (The concepts of the calculus) / by Carl B. Boyer; with a foreword by Richard Courant. — [New York]: Dover publication, [1959] 346 p.: ill. First published in 1949 under title The concepts of the calculus, a critical and historical discussion of the derivative and the integral. 1. Mathematics — History. 2. Calculus 3. Mathematics — Philosophy I. T. II. Title: The concepts of calculus.
QA303.B65     *LC* A60-3661     *ISBN* 0486605094

**Buck, R. Creighton (Robert Creighton), 1920-.**      • **5.1448**
Advanced calculus [by] R. Creighton Buck with the collaboration of Ellen F. Buck. — 2d ed. — New York: McGraw-Hill, [1965] xiii, 527 p.: illus.; 23 cm. — (International series in pure and applied mathematics) 1. Calculus 2. Mathematical analysis I. Buck, Ellen F., joint author. II. T.
QA303.B917 1965      517      LC 64-18399

**Clark, Colin Whitcomb, 1931-.**      **5.1449**
The theoretical side of calculus. [by] Colin Clark. Belmont, Calif., Wadsworth Pub. Co. [1972] xv, 240 p. illus. 24 cm. Second ed. published in 1981 as: Introduction to mathematical analysis. 1. Calculus I. T.
QA303.C58      515      LC 72-75511      ISBN 0534001041

**Courant, Richard, 1888-1972.**      • **5.1450**
Introduction to calculus and analysis [by] Richard Courant and Fritz John. — New York: Interscience Publishers, [1965-74] 2 v.: illus.; 24 cm. Based on the first author's Vorlesungen über Differential- und Intergralrechnung. Vol. 2 published by Wiley. 'A Wiley-Interscience publication.' 1. Calculus 2. Mathematical analysis I. John, Fritz, 1910- joint author. II. Courant, Richard, 1888-1972. Vorlesungen über Differential- und Integralrechnung. III. T.
QA303.C838      515      LC 65-16403      ISBN 0471178624

**Edwards, C. H. (Charles Henry), 1937-.**      **5.1451**
The historical development of the calculus / C. H. Edwards, Jr. — New York: Springer-Verlag, c1979. xii, 351 p.: ill.; 25 cm. 1. Calculus — History. I. T.
QA303.E224      515/.09      LC 79-15461      ISBN 0387904360

**Grabiner, Judith V.**      **5.1452**
The origins of Cauchy's rigorous calculus / Judith V. Grabiner. — Cambridge, Mass.: MIT Press, c1981. 252 p.; 24 cm. Includes index. 1. Cauchy, Augustin Louis, baron, 1789-1857. 2. Calculus — History. I. T.
QA303.G74      515.09 19      LC 80-28969      ISBN 0262070790

**Hardy, Godfrey Harold, 1877-1947.**      **5.1453**
Inequalities / by G. H. Hardy, J. E. Littlewood, G. Pólya. — 2nd ed. — Cambridge, [Eng.]: Cambridge University Press, 1952. xii, 324 p.: diagrs.; 23 cm. 1. Calculus I. T.
QA303.H25 1952      517      LC 52-10789      ISBN 0521052608

**Hardy, G. H.**      • **5.1454**
A course of pure mathematics. 10th ed. Cambridge, University Press, 1955. 509 p. 23 cm. 1. Functions 2. Calculus I. T.
QA 303 H26 C 1955

**Nickerson, H. K. (Helen Kelsall), 1918-.**      • **5.1455**
Advanced calculus, by H.K. Nickerson, D.C. Spencer, and N.E. Steenrod. Princeton, N.J., Van Nostrand [1959] ix, 540 p. 28 cm. 'These notes were prepared for the honors course in advanced calculus, Mathematics 303-304, Princeton University.' 1. Calculus 2. Vector analysis I. T.
QA303.N64      516.83      LC 59-4467

**Oldham, Keith B.**      **5.1456**
The fractional calculus; theory and applications of differentiation and integration to arbitrary order [by] Keith B. Oldham [and] Jerome Spanier. — New York: Academic Press, 1974. xiii, 234 p.: illus.; 24 cm. — (Mathematics in science and engineering. v. 111) 1. Calculus I. Spanier, Jerome, 1930- joint author. II. T. III. Series.
QA303.O34      515      LC 73-5304      ISBN 0125255500

# QA308–313 CALCULUS. MEASURE THEORY. ERGODIC THEORY

**Ritt, Joseph Fels, 1893-.**      **5.1457**
Integration in finite terms: Liouville's theory of elementary methods. — New York: Columbia Univ. Press, 1948. vii, 100 p. 1. Liouville, Joseph, 1809-1882. 2. Calculus, Integral I. T.
QA308.R5 1948      LC 48-2225

**Dwight, Herbert Bristol, b. 1885.**      **5.1458**
Tables of integrals and other mathematical data. 4th ed. New York, Macmillan [1961] 336 p. illus. 22 cm. 1. Integrals I. T.
QA310.D8 1961      517.39      LC 61-6419

**Oxtoby, John C.**      **5.1459**
Measure and category: a survey of the analogies between topological and measure spaces / John C. Oxtoby. — 2d ed. — New York: Springer-Verlag, c1980. ix, 106 p.; 24 cm. — (Graduate texts in mathematics; 2) Includes index. 1. Measure theory. 2. Topological spaces. 3. Categories (Mathematics) 4. Spaces of measure. I. T. II. Series.
QA312.O9 1980      515.4/2      LC 80-15770      ISBN 0387905081

**Weir, Alan J.**      **5.1460**
Lebesgue integration and measure [by] Alan J. Weir. — Cambridge [Eng.]: University Press, 1973. xii, 281 p.; 24 cm. Continued by General integration and measure. 1. Integrals, Generalized 2. Measure theory I. T.
QA312.W4      515/.42      LC 72-83584      ISBN 0521087287

**Halmos, Paul R. (Paul Richard), 1916-.**      **5.1461**
Ergodic theory. — [Chicago]: Dept. of Mathematics, University of Chicago, [1955] v, 112 leaves; 28 cm. 'Math. 373 A, Summer 1955.' 1. Statistical mechanics I. T.
QA313.H3x      LC a 59-69

**Ornstein, Donald, 1934-.**      **5.1462**
Ergodic theory, randomness, and dynamical systems / by Donald S. Ornstein. — New Haven: Yale University Press, 1974. vii, 141 p.; 23 cm. (Yale mathematical monographs; 5) (James K. Whittemore lectures in mathematics given at Yale University) 1. Ergodic theory. 2. Transformations (Mathematics) 3. Isomorphisms (Mathematics) 4. Stochastic processes. I. T. II. Series.
QA313.O76      515/.42      LC 73-90903      ISBN 0300017456

**Parry, William, 1934-.**      **5.1463**
Classification problems in ergodic theory / William Parry and Selim Tuncel. — Cambridge [Cambridgeshire]; New York: Cambridge University Press, 1982. 101 p.: ill.; 23 cm. — (London Mathematical Society lecture note series. 0076-0552; 67) Includes index. 1. Ergodic theory 2. Isomorphisms (Mathematics) I. Tuncel, Selim. II. T. III. Series.
QA313.P368 1982      515.4/2 19      LC 82-4350      ISBN 0521287944

**Walters, Peter, 1943-.**      **5.1464**
An introduction to ergodic theory / Peter Walters; with 8 illustrations. — New York: Springer-Verlag, c1982. ix, 250 p.; 24 cm. — (Graduate texts in mathematics. 79) Previously published as: Ergodic theory. 1975. Includes index. 1. Ergodic theory I. T. II. Series.
QA313.W34 1982      515.4/2 19      LC 81-9319      ISBN 0387905995

# QA315–316 CALCULUS OF VARIATIONS

**Bliss, Gilbert Ames, 1876-1951.**      • **5.1465**
Calculus of variations / by Gilbert Ames Bliss. — La Salle, Ill.: Pub. for the Mathematical Association of America by the Open Court Publishing Company, 1944. xiii, 189 p: ill. — (Carus mathematical monographs. [1]) 1. Calculus of variations I. T. II. Series.
QA315.B5      515.64      LC 25-10087

**Carathéodory, Constantin, 1873-1950.**      **5.1466**
[Variationsrechnung und partielle Differentialgleichungen erster Ordnung. English] Calculus of variations and partial differential equations of the first order / C. Carathéodory; translated by Robert B. Dean; Julius J. Brandstatter, translating editor. — 2nd (rev.) English ed. — New York, N.Y.: Chelsea Pub. Co., 1982. xix, 402 p.: ill.; 24 cm. Translation of: Variationsrechnung und partielle Differentialgleichungen erster Ordnung. Includes index. 1. Calculus of variations 2. Differential equations, Partial I. T.
QA315.C2733 1982      515/.64 19      LC 81-71519      ISBN 082840318X

**Gel'fand, I. M. (Izrail' Moiseevich).**      • **5.1467**
Calculus of variations / [by] I. M. Gelfand [and] S. V. Fomin. — Rev. English ed. Translated and edited by Richard A. Silverman. — Englewood Cliffs, N.J., Prentice-Hall [1963] vii, 232 p.: diagrs.; 24 cm. — (Selected Russian publications in the mathematical sciences) 1. Calculus of variations I. Fomin, S. V. (Sergeĭ Vasil'evich) joint author. II. T.
QA315.G417      517.4      LC 63-18806

**Goldstine, Herman Heine, 1913-.**      **5.1468**
A history of the calculus of variations from the 17th through the 19th century / Herman H. Goldstine. — New York: Springer-Verlag, c1980. xviii, 410 p.: ill.; 25 cm. — (Studies in the history of mathematics and physical sciences. 5) Includes index. 1. Calculus of variations — History. I. T. II. Series.
QA315.G58      515/.64/0903      LC 80-16228      ISBN 0387905219

**Morse, Marston, 1892-.**      **5.1469**
The calculus of variations in the large / by Marston Morse. — New York: The American mathematical society, 1934. ix, 368 p. — (American mathematical society. Colloquium publications; v.18) 'The research of the writer has been oriented by a conception of what might be termed macro-analysis.'—Foreword. 1. Calculus of variations I. T.
QA315.M6      LC 34-40909      ISBN 0821810189

**Cesari, Lamberto.**      **5.1470**
Optimization–theory and applications: problems with ordinary differential equations / Lamberto Cesari. — New York: Springer-Verlag, c1983. xiv, 542 p.: ill.; 24 cm. — (Applications of mathematics. 17) Includes index.

1. Calculus of variations 2. Mathematical optimization 3. Differential equations I. T. II. Series.
QA316.C47 1983    515/.64 19    *LC* 82-5776    *ISBN* 0387906762

# QA320–326 Functional Analysis

**Kreyszig, Erwin.**    **5.1471**
Introductory functional analysis with applications / Erwin Kreyszig. — New York: Wiley, 1978 (c1977). xiv, 688 p.: ill.; 24 cm. Includes index. 1. Functional analysis I. T.
QA320.K74    515/.7    *LC* 77-2560    *ISBN* 0471507318

**Rudin, Walter, 1921-.**    **5.1472**
Functional analysis. — New York: McGraw-Hill, [1973] xiii, 397 p.; 24 cm. — (McGraw-Hill series in higher mathematics) 1. Functional analysis I. T.
QA320.R83    515/.7    *LC* 71-39686    *ISBN* 0070542252

**Sawyer, W. W. (Walter Warwick), 1911-.**    **5.1473**
A first look at numerical functional analysis / W. W. Sawyer. — Oxford: Clarendon Press, 1978. xi, 186 p.: ill.; 23 cm. (Oxford applied mathematics and computing science series) Includes index. 1. Functional analysis 2. Numerical analysis I. T.
QA320.S25    519.4    *LC* 77-30689    *ISBN* 0198596286

**Shilov, G. E. (Georgiĭ Evgen'evich)**    **5.1474**
Elementary functional analysis [by] Georgi E. Shilov. Rev. English ed. translated and edited by Richard A. Silverman. Cambridge, Mass., MIT Press [1974] vi, 334 p. illus. 23 cm. (His Mathematical analysis, v. 2) Rev. translation of pt. 3 of Matematicheskiĭ analiz, funktsii odnovo peremennovo. 1. Functional analysis I. Silverman, Richard A. ed. II. T.
QA320.S6x QA300.S455 vol. 2    515/.7    *LC* 73-21882    *ISBN* 0262191229

**Yoshida, Kôsaku, 1909-.**    **5.1475**
Functional analysis / Kôsaku Yosida. — 6th ed. — Berlin; New York: Springer-Verlag, 1980. xii, 500 p.; 24 cm. (Grundlehren der mathematischen Wissenschaften; 123) Includes index. 1. Functional analysis I. T.
QA320.Y6 1980    515.7    *LC* 80-18567    *ISBN* 0387102108

**Grothendieck, A. (Alexandre)**    **5.1476**
[Espaces vectoriels topologiques. English] Topological vector spaces [by] A. Grothendieck. Translated from the French by Orlando Chaljub. — New York: Gordon and Breach, [1975] x, 245 p.; 24 cm. — (Notes on mathematics and its applications) Translation of Espaces vectoriels topologiques. 1. Linear topological spaces I. T.
QA322.G7613 1975    QA322 G7613 1975.    515/.73

**Luxemburg, W. A. J., 1929-.**    **5.1477**
Riesz spaces [by] W. A. J. Luxemburg and A. C. Zaanen. London, North-Holland Pub. Co.; New York, American Elsevier Pub. Co., 1971-<83 >. v. <1-2 > 23 cm. (North-Holland mathematical library) 1. Riesz spaces I. Zaanen, Adriaan Cornelis, 1913- joint author. II. T.
QA322.L89    515/.73    *LC* 72-184996    *ISBN* 0444101292

**Takesaki, Masamichi, 1933-.**    **5.1478**
Theory of operator algebras I / Masamichi Takesaki. — New York: Springer-Verlag, c1979. vii, 415 p.; 24 cm. Includes indexes. 1. Operator algebras I. T.
QA326.T34    512/.55    *LC* 79-13655    *ISBN* 0387903917

**Wermer, John.**    **5.1479**
Banach algebras and several complex variables / John Wermer. — 2d ed. — New York: Springer-Verlag, 1976. ix, 161 p.; 25 cm. (Graduate texts in mathematics. 35) Includes index. 1. Banach algebras 2. Functions of several complex variables I. T. II. Series.
QA326.W47 1976    512/.55    *LC* 75-34306    *ISBN* 0387901604

# QA329 Operator Theory

**Douglas, Ronald G.**    **5.1480**
Banach algebra techniques in operator theory [by] Ronald G. Douglas. New York, Academic Press, 1972. xvi, 216 p. 24 cm. (Pure and applied mathematics; a series of monographs and textbooks; v. 49) 1. Operator theory 2. Banach algebras 3. Hilbert space I. T.
QA329.D6    510/.8 s 515/.72    *LC* 78-187253    *ISBN* 0122213505

**Gohberg, I. (Israel), 1928-.**    **5.1481**
Basic operator theory / Israel Gohberg, Seymour Goldberg; edited by I. Gohberg. — Boston; Basel: Birkhäuser, 1981. xiii, 285 p.; 24 cm. Includes index. 1. Operator theory I. Goldberg, Seymour, 1928- joint author. II. T.
QA329.G64    515.7/24 19    *LC* 80-25882    *ISBN* 3764330287

**Dunford, Nelson.**    **5.1482**
Linear operators [by] Nelson Dunford and Jacob T. Schwartz. With the assistance of William G. Bade and Robert G. Bartle. New York, Interscience Publishers, 1958-71. 3 v. (xiv, 2592 p.) 24 cm. (Pure and applied mathematics, v. 7) 1. Linear operators I. Schwartz, Jacob T. joint author. II. T.
QA329.2.D85    512/.5    *LC* 57-10545    *ISBN* 0471226394

# QA331–360 Theory of Functions

**Ahlfors, Lars Valerian, 1907-.**    **5.1483**
Complex analysis: an introduction to the theory of analytic functions of one complex variable / Lars V. Ahlfors. — 3d ed. — New York: McGraw-Hill, c1979. xiv, 331 p.: ill.; 24 cm. — (International series in pure and applied mathematics) Includes index. 1. Analytic functions I. T.
QA331.A45 1979    515/.93    *LC* 78-17078    *ISBN* 0070006571

**Hörmander, Lars.**    **• 5.1484**
An introduction to complex analysis in several variables. Princeton, N.J., Van Nostrand [1966] x, 208 p. 24 cm. (University series in higher mathematics.) 1. Functions of several complex variables 2. Differential equations, Partial 3. Analytic functions I. T. II. Series.
QA331.H64    517.8    *LC* 66-2809

**Kolmogorov, A. N. (Andreĭ Nikolaevich), 1903-.**    **• 5.1485**
[Elementy teorii funktsiĭ i funktsional'nogo analiza. English] Elements of the theory of functions and functional analysis, by A.N. Kolmogorov and S.V. Fomin. Translated from the 1st Russian ed. by Leo F. Boron. Rochester, N.Y., Graylock Press, 1957- v. illus. 24 cm. Vol. 2, translated by Hyman Kamel and Horace Komm, published in Albany. 1. Functions of real variables 2. Functional analysis I. Fomin, S. V. (Sergeĭ Vasil'evich) joint author. II. T.
QA331.K733    517.5    *LC* 57-4134

**Koosis, Paul.**    **5.1486**
Introduction to Hp spaces, with an appendix on Wolff's proof of the corona theorem / Paul Koosis. — Cambridge [Eng.]; New York: Cambridge University Press, 1980. xv, 376 p.: ill.; 23 cm. (London Mathematical Society lecture note series; 40) 1. Hardy spaces I. T.
QA331.K739    515.7/3 19    *LC* 80-65175    *ISBN* 0521231590

**Luecking, D. H. (Daniel H.)**    **5.1487**
Complex analysis: a functional analysis approach / D.H. Luecking, L.A. Rubel. — New York: Springer-Verlag, c1984. vi, 176 p.: ill.; 24 cm. (Universitext) 1. Functions of complex variables 2. Functional analysis I. Rubel, Lee A. II. T.
QA331.L818 1984    515.9 19    *LC* 84-5354    *ISBN* 0387909931

**Mackey, George Whitelaw, 1916-.**    **5.1488**
Lectures on the theory of functions of a complex variable, by George W. Mackey. — Princeton, N.J.: Van Nostrand, [c1967] iv, 266 p.: illus.; 21 cm. — (Van Nostrand mathematical studies, 9) 1. Functions of complex variables I. T. II. Title: The theory of functions of a complex variable.
QA331.M26    517/.8    *LC* 68-20907

**Marsden, Jerrold E.**    **5.1489**
Basic complex analysis [by] Jerrold E. Marsden, with the assistance of Michael Buchner, Michael Hoffman [and] Clifford Risk. — San Francisco: W. H. Freeman, [1973] x, 472 p.: illus.; 24 cm. 1. Functions of complex variables I. T.
QA331.M378    515/.9    *LC* 72-89894    *ISBN* 071670451X

**Spanier, Jerome, 1930-.**    **5.1490**
An atlas of functions / Jerome Spanier, Keith B. Oldham. — Washington: Hemisphere Pub. Corp., c1987. 700 p.: ill. (some col.); 29 cm. Includes indexes. 1. Functions I. Oldham, Keith B. II. T.
QA331.S685 1987    515 19    *LC* 86-18294    *ISBN* 0891165738

**Roberts, A. Wayne (Arthur Wayne), 1934-.**    **5.1491**
Convex functions [by] A. Wayne Roberts [and] Dale E. Varberg. New York: Academic Press, 1973. xx, 300 p. illus. 24 cm. (Pure and applied mathematics; a series of monographs and textbooks; 57) 1. Convex functions I. Varberg, Dale E. joint author. II. T.
QA331.5.R6 QA3.P8 vol. 57    515/.88    *LC* 72-12186    *ISBN* 0125897405

**Royden, H. L.**    • 5.1492
Real analysis [by] H. L. Royden. — 2d ed. — New York: Macmillan, [1968] xii, 349 p.; 24 cm. 1. Functions of real variables 2. Functional analysis 3. Measure theory I. T.
QA331.5.R6 1968    517/.52    LC 68-10518

## QA333–343 RIEMANNIAN SURFACES. ELLIPTIC FUNCTIONS

**Ahlfors, Lars Valerian, 1907-.**    5.1493
Riemann surfaces, by Lars V. Ahlfors and Leo Sario. Princeton, N.J., Princeton University Press, 1960. 382 p. illus. 24 cm. (Princeton mathematical series, 26) 1. Riemann surfaces 2. Topology I. Sario, Leo. joint author. II. T.
QA333.A43    517.81    LC 59-11074

**Beardon, Alan F.**    5.1494
A primer on Riemann surfaces / A.F. Beardon. — Cambridge [Cambridgeshire]; New York: Cambridge University Press, 1984. x, 188 p.: ill.; 23 cm. (London Mathematical Society lecture note series. 78) Includes index. 1. Riemann surfaces I. T. II. Series.
QA333.B43 1984    515/.223 19    LC 82-4439    ISBN 0521271045

**Farkas, Hershel M.**    5.1495
Riemann surfaces / by H. M. Farkas, I. Kra. — New York: Springer-Verlag, c1980. x, 337 p.: ill.; 24 cm. — (Graduate texts in mathematics. 71) Includes index. 1. Riemann surfaces I. Kra, Irwin. joint author. II. T. III. Series.
QA333.F37    515/.223    LC 79-24385    ISBN 0387904654

**Weyl, Hermann, 1885-1955.**    5.1496
The concept of a Riemann surface. Translated from the German by Gerald R. Maclane. — 3d ed., 1955. — Reading, Mass., Addison-Wesley Pub. Co. [1964,c1955] x, 191 p. illus. 24 cm. — (ADIWES international series in mathematics) 1. Riemann surfaces I. T.
QA333.W413 1964    517.81    LC 64-14329

**Lang, Serge, 1927-.**    5.1497
Elliptic functions. — Reading, Mass.: Addison-Wesley Pub. Co., Advanced Book Program, 1973. xii, 326 p.; 24 cm. 1. Functions, Elliptic I. T.
QA343.L35    515/.983    LC 72-1767    ISBN 0201041626

## QA351–355 SPECIAL TOPICS

**Shimura, Gorō, 1930-.**    5.1498
Introduction to the arithmetic theory of automorphic functions. [Tokyo] Iwanami Shoten [Princeton, N.J.] Princeton University Press, 1971. xiii, 267 p. 27 cm. (Kanō memorial lectures, 1) (Publications of the Mathematical Society of Japan, 11) 1. Functions, Automorphic I. T. II. Series.
QA351.S49    515/.9    LC 74-153844

**Tsuji, Masatsugu, 1894-1960.**    5.1499
Potential theory in modern function theory. — [2d ed.]. — New York: Chelsea Pub. Co., [c1975] x, 590 p.: illus.; 21 cm. 1. Potential, Theory of 2. Harmonic functions 3. Conformal mapping I. T.
QA355.T77 1975    515/.7    LC 74-4297    ISBN 0828402817

# QA371–387 Differential Equations

**Aubin, Jean Pierre.**    5.1500
Differential inclusions: set–valued maps and viability theory / Jean–Pierre Aubin, Arrigo Cellina. — Berlin; New York: Springer-Verlag, 1984. xiii, 342 p.: ill.; 24 cm. (Grundlehren der mathematischen Wissenschaften. 264) Includes index. 1. Differential inclusions 2. Set-valued maps 3. Feedback control systems I. Cellina, Arrigo, 1941- II. T. III. Title: Viability theory. IV. Series.
QA371.A93 1984    515/.5 19    LC 84-1327    ISBN 0387131051

**Boyce, William E.**    5.1501
Elementary differential equations and boundary value problems / William E. Boyce, Richard C. DiPrima. — 4th ed. — New York: Wiley, c1986. xvi, 654, [49] p.: ill.; 25 cm. 1. Differential equations 2. Boundary value problems I. DiPrima, Richard C. II. T.
QA371.B773 1986    515.3/5 19    LC 85-20244    ISBN 0471078956

**Brand, Louis, 1885-.**    5.1502
Differential and difference equations. — New York: Wiley, [1966] xvi, 698 p.: illus.; 24 cm. 1. Differential equations 2. Difference equations I. T.
QA371.B79    517.38    LC 66-17645

**Golomb, Michael, 1909-.**    • 5.1503
Elements of ordinary differential equations [by] Michael Golomb [and] Merrill Shanks. 2d ed. New York, McGraw-Hill [c1965] xi, 410 p. illus. 23 cm. (International series in pure and applied mathematics.) 1. Differential equations I. Shanks, Merrill E., 1911- joint author. II. T. III. Series.
QA371.G6 1965    517.38    LC 63-23387

**Lefschetz, Solomon, 1884-1972.**    5.1504
Differential equations: geometric theory / Solomon Lefschetz. — 2d ed. — New York: Dover Publications, 1977. x, 390 p.: ill.; 21 cm. 'Unabridged republication of the second (1963) edition of the work originally published by Interscience Publishers in 1957 as volume VI of the Interscience pure and applied mathematics series.' Includes index. 1. Differential equations 2. Topology I. T.
QA371.L36 1977    515/.35    LC 76-53978    ISBN 0486634639

**Nayfeh, Ali Hasan, 1933-.**    5.1505
Introduction to perturbation techniques / Ali Hasan Nayfeh. — New York: Wiley, c1981. xiv, 519 p.: ill.; 24 cm. 'A Wiley-Interscience publication.' Includes index. 1. Differential equations — Numerical solutions 2. Equations — Numerical solutions 3. Perturbation (Mathematics) I. T.
QA371.N32    515.3/5    LC 80-15233    ISBN 0471080330

**Nemytskiĭ, Viktor Vladimirovich, 1900-.**    5.1506
Qualitative theory of differential equations / by V. V. Nemytskii and V. V. Stepanov. — Princeton, N. J.: Princeton University Press, 1960. 523 p.: ill. — (Princeton mathematical series; 22) 1. Differential equations 2. Dynamics I. Stepanov, V. V. (Viacheslav Vasil'evich), 1889-1950. II. T.
QA371.N413    517.38    LC 60-12240    ISBN 0691080208

**Rainville, Earl David, 1907-.**    5.1507
Elementary differential equations / Earl D. Rainville, Phillip E. Bedient. — 6th ed. — New York: Macmillan; London: Collier Macmillan, c1981. xiv, 529 p.: ill.; 24 cm. Includes index. 1. Differential equations I. Bedient, Phillip Edward, 1922- joint author. II. T.
QA371.R29 1981    515.3/5    LC 80-12849    ISBN 0023977701

**Rainville, Earl David, 1907-.**    5.1508
Intermediate differential equations. 2d ed. New York, Macmillan [1964] xi, 307 p. diagrs. 24 cm. First ed. published in 1943 under title: Intermediate course in differential equations. 1. Differential equations I. T.
QA371.R3 1964    517.38    LC 64-10581

**Ritt, Joseph Fels, 1893-.**    5.1509
Differential equations from the algebraic standpoint / by Joseph Fels Ritt. — New York: American Mathematical Society, 1932. x, 172 p. — (Colloquium publications (American Mathematical Society) 14) 1. Differential equations I. T. II. Series.
QA371.R45    LC 32-35201

## QA372 ORDINARY DIFFERENTIAL EQUATIONS

**Arnol'd, V. I. (Vladimir Igorevich), 1937-.**    5.1510
[Dopolnitel'nye glavy teorii obyknovennykh differentsial'nykh uravnenii. English] Geometrical methods in the theory of ordinary differential equations / V.I. Arnold; translated by Joseph Szücs; English translation edited by Mark Levi. — New York: Springer-Verlag, c1983. x, 334 p.: ill.; 25 cm. — (Grundlehren der mathematischen Wissenschaften. 250) Translation of: Dopolnitel'nye glavy teorii obyknovennykh differentsial'nykh uravnenii. 1. Differential equations I. Levi, Mark, 1951- II. T. III. Series.
QA372.A6913 1983    515.3/52 19    LC 82-5464    ISBN 0387906819

**Birkhoff, Garrett, 1911-.**    5.1511
Ordinary differential equations / Garrett Birkhoff, Gian–Carlo Rota. — 3d ed. — New York: Wiley, c1978. xi, 342 p.: ill.; 24 cm. Includes index. 1. Differential equations. I. Rota, Gian Carlo, 1932- joint author. II. T.
QA372.B58 1978    515/.352    LC 78-8304    ISBN 047107411X

**Gear, C. William (Charles William), 1935-.**    5.1512
Numerical initial value problems in ordinary differential equations [by] C. William Gear. Englewood Cliffs, N.J., Prentice-Hall [1971] xvii, 253 p. illus. 24 cm. (Prentice-Hall series in automatic computation) 1. Differential equations — Data processing 2. Numerical integration — Data processing I. T.
QA372.G4    515/.352    LC 75-152448    ISBN 0136266061

**Hille, Einar, 1894-.**     **5.1513**
Lectures on ordinary differential equations. — Reading, Mass.: Addison-Wesley Pub. Co., [1968, c1969] xi, 723 p.: illus.; 24 cm. — (Addison-Wesley series in mathematics) 1. Differential equations I. T.
QA372.H55    517/.382    *LC* 69-14427

**Hille, Einar, 1894-.**     **5.1514**
Ordinary differential equations in the complex domain / Einar Hille. — New York: Wiley, c1976. xi, 484 p.: ill.; 24 cm. (Pure and applied mathematics) 'A Wiley-Interscience publication.' Includes index. 1. Differential equations 2. Functions of complex variables I. T.
QA372.H56    515/.352    *LC* 75-44231    *ISBN* 0471399647

**Hirsch, Morris W., 1933-.**     **5.1515**
Differential equations, dynamical systems, and linear algebra [by] Morris W. Hirsch and Stephen Smale. New York, Academic Press [1974] xi, 358 p. illus. 25 cm. (Pure and applied mathematics; a series of monographs and textbooks; v. 60) 1. Differential equations 2. Algebras, Linear I. Smale, Stephen, 1930- joint author. II. T.
QA372.H5x    510/.8 s 515/.35    *LC* 73-18951    *ISBN* 0123495504

**Hurewicz, Witold, 1904-1956.**     **5.1516**
Lectures on ordinary differential equations. [Cambridge] Technology Press of the Massachusetts Institute of Technology [1958] 122 p. illus. 24 cm. (Technology Press books in science and engineering.) First published in 1943 under title: Ordinary differential equations in the real domain with emphasis on geometric methods. 1. Differential equations I. T. II. Series.
QA372.H93 1958    517.38    *LC* 58-7901

**IAkubovich, V. A. (Vladimir Andreevich)**     **5.1517**
[Lineĭnye differentsial'nye uravneniia s periodicheskimi koėffitsientami i ikh prilozheniia] Linear differential equations with periodic coefficients / V. A. Yakubovich and V. M. Starzhinskii; translated from Russian by D. Louvish. — New York: Wiley, [1975] 2 v. (xii, 839 p.): ill.; 25 cm. Translation of Lineĭnye differentsial'nye uravneniia s periodicheskimi koėffitsientami i ikh prilozheniia. 'A Halsted Press book.' Includes index. 1. Differential equations, Linear I. Starzhinskiĭ, V. M. (Viacheslav Mikhaĭlovich) joint author. II. T.
QA372.I213    515/.35    *LC* 75-4982    *ISBN* 0470969539

**Jordan, D. W. (Dominic William)**     **5.1518**
Nonlinear ordinary differential equations / D.W. Jordan and P. Smith. — 2nd ed. — Oxford [Oxfordshire]; New York: Oxford University Press, 1986. p. cm. (Oxford applied mathematics and computing science series.) Includes index. 1. Differential equations, Nonlinear I. Smith, Peter, 1935- II. T. III. Series.
QA372.J648 1986    515.3/52 19    *LC* 86-18000    *ISBN* 019859657X

**Lapidus, Leon.**     **5.1519**
Numerical solution of ordinary differential equations [by] Leon Lapidus and John H. Seinfeld. — New York: Academic Press, 1971. xii, 299 p.; 24 cm. — (Mathematics in science and engineering. v. 74) 1. Differential equations — Numerical solutions I. Seinfeld, John H. joint author. II. T. III. Series.
QA372.L27    515/.352    *LC* 73-127689

**Mickens, Ronald E., 1943-.**     **5.1520**
An introduction to nonlinear oscillations / Ronald E. Mickens. — Cambridge [Eng.]; New York: Cambridge University Press, 1981. xiv, 224 p.: ill.; 24 cm. Includes index. 1. Differential equations, Nonlinear — Numerical solutions 2. Approximation theory 3. Nonlinear oscillations I. T.
QA372.M615    515.3/55    *LC* 80-13169    0521222089

**Olver, Peter J.**     **5.1521**
Applications of Lie groups to differential equations / Peter J. Olver. — New York: Springer-Verlag, c1986. xxvi, 497 p.: 10 ill.; 25 cm. (Graduate texts in mathematics. 107) Includes indexes. 1. Differential equations 2. Lie groups I. T. II. Series.
QA372.O55 1986    515.3/5 19    *LC* 85-17318    *ISBN* 0387962506

**Shampine, Lawrence F.**     **5.1522**
Computer solution of ordinary differential equations: the initial value problem / L. F. Shampine, M. K. Gordon. — San Francisco: W. H. Freeman, [1975] x, 318 p.: ill.; 25 cm. Includes index. 1. Differential equations — Numerical solutions — Data processing 2. Initial value problems — Numerical solutions — Data processing I. Gordon, M. K. (Marilyn Kay) joint author. II. T.
QA372.S416    515/.352/02854    *LC* 74-23246    *ISBN* 0716704617

## QA373–377 DIFFERENTIAL–DIFFERENCE EQUATIONS. PARTIAL DIFFERENTIALS

**Temam, Roger.**     **5.1523**
Navier–Stokes equations: theory and numerical analysis / Roger Temam. — Rev. ed. — Amsterdam; Oxford: North-Holland; New York: Sole distributors for the U.S.A. and Canada, Elsevier Science, c1984. xii, 526 p.; 23 cm. —

(Studies in mathematics and its applications; v.2) Includes index. 1. Navier-Stokes equations I. T.
QA373.T4x    515.3/52 19    *ISBN* 0444875581

**Ames, William F.**     **5.1524**
Numerical methods for partial differential equations / William F. Ames. 2d ed. — New York: Academic Press, 1977. xiv, 365 p.: ill.; 24 cm. (Computer science and applied mathematics) 1. Differential equations, Partial — Numerical solutions I. T.
QA374.A46 1977    515/.353    *LC* 77-5786    *ISBN* 0120567601

**Trèves, François, 1930-.**     **5.1525**
Linear partial differential equations with constant coefficients; existence, approximation, and regularity of solutions. — New York: Gordon and Breach, [1966] x, 534 p.; 24 cm. — (Mathematics and its applications, v. 6) 1. Differential equations, Partial I. T.
QA374.T69    517/.383    *LC* 65-24873

**Tyn Myint U.**     **5.1526**
Partial differential equations of mathematical physics / Tyn Myint–U. — 2d ed. — New York: North Holland, c1980. xiii, 380 p.: ill.; 24 cm. Includes index. 1. Differential equations, Partial I. T.
QA374.T94 1980    515.3/53 19    *LC* 79-19310    *ISBN* 0444003525

**Bers, Lipman.**     **5.1527**
Partial differential equations / by Lipman Bers, Fritz John [and] Martin Schechter. — New York: Amer. Math. Soc., 1966. 343p. 1. Differential equations, Partial I. John, Fritz, 1910- II. Schechter, Martin. jt. author III. T.
QA377 B47

**Ciarlet, Philippe G.**     **5.1528**
The finite element method for elliptic problems / Philippe G. Ciarlet. — Amsterdam; New York: North-Holland Pub. Co.; New York: sole distributors for the U.S.A. and Canada, Elsevier North-Holland, 1978. xvii, 530 p.: ill.; 23 cm. — (Studies in mathematics and its applications. v. 4) 1. Differential equations, Elliptic — Numerical solutions 2. Boundary value problems — Numerical solutions 3. Finite element method I. T. II. Series.
QA377.C53    515/.353    *LC* 77-24477    *ISBN* 0444850287

**Copson, E. T. (Edward Thomas), 1901-.**     **5.1529**
Partial differential equations / E. T. Copson. — Cambridge; New York: Cambridge University Press, 1975. vii, 280 p.; 24 cm. Includes index. 1. Differential equations, Partial I. T.
QA377.C77    515/.353    *LC* 74-12965    *ISBN* 0521205832

**Hörmander, Lars.**     **5.1530**
The analysis of linear partial differential operators / Lars Hörmander. — Berlin; New York: Springer-Verlag, 1983-c1985. 4 v.; 24 cm. (Grundlehren der mathematischen Wissenschaften. 256-257, 274-275) Expanded version of the author's 1 vol. work: Linear partial differential operators. 1. Differential equations, Partial 2. Partial differential operators I. T. II. Series.
QA377.H578 1983    515.7/242 19    *LC* 83-616

**Zauderer, Erich.**     **5.1531**
Partial differential equations of applied mathematics / Erich Zauderer. — New York: Wiley, c1983. xiii, 779 p.: ill.; 24 cm. — (Pure and applied mathematics, 0079-8185) 'A Wiley-Interscience publication.' Includes index. 1. Differential equations, Partial I. T.
QA377.Z38 1983    515.3/53 19    *LC* 82-21855    *ISBN* 0471875171

## QA379–387 BOUNDARY PROBLEMS. INVARIANTS. TOPOLOGICAL GROUPS

**Hanna, J. Ray.**     **5.1532**
Fourier series and integrals of boundary value problems / J. Ray Hanna. — New York: Wiley, c1982. xi, 271 p.: ill.; 25 cm. — (Pure and applied mathematics, 0079-8185) 'A Wiley-Interscience publication.' Includes index. 1. Boundary value problems 2. Fourier series I. T. II. Series.
QA379.H36    515.3/5 19    *LC* 81-16063    *ISBN* 0471081299

**Oden, J. Tinsley (John Tinsley), 1936-.**     **5.1533**
An introduction to the mathematical theory of finite elements / J. T. Oden, J. N. Reddy. — New York: Wiley, c1976. xii, 429 p.: ill.; 24 cm. (Pure and applied mathematics) 'A Wiley-Interscience publication.' 1. Boundary value problems — Numerical solutions 2. Differential equations, Elliptic — Numerical solutions 3. Approximation theory 4. Finite element method I. Reddy, J. N. (Junuthula Narasimha), 1945- joint author. II. T.
QA379.O3    515/.353    *LC* 76-6953    *ISBN* 047165261X

**Stakgold, Ivar.**     **5.1534**
Green's functions and boundary value problems / Ivar Stakgold. — New York: Wiley, c1979. xv, 638 p.: ill.; 24 cm. — (Pure and applied mathematics) 'A

Wiley-Interscience publication.' 1. Boundary value problems 2. Green's functions 3. Mathematical physics I. T.
QA379.S72    515/.35    *LC* 78-27259    *ISBN* 0471819670

**Flanders, Harley.**      • **5.1535**
Differential forms, with applications to the physical sciences. New York, Academic Press, 1963. xiii, 203 p. diagrs. 24 cm. (Mathematics in science and engineering. v. 11) 1. Differential forms 2. Mathematical physics I. T. II. Series.
QA381.F56    516.7    *LC* 63-20569

**Armacost, D. L. (David L.), 1944-.**      **5.1536**
The structure of locally compact abelian groups / D.L. Armacost. — New York: M. Dekker, c1981. vii, 154 p.; 24 cm. — (Monographs and textbooks in pure and applied mathematics. 68) Includes index. 1. Locally compact Abelian groups I. T. II. Series.
QA387.A75    512/.2 19    *LC* 81-12527    *ISBN* 0824715071

**Gilmore, Robert, 1941-.**      **5.1537**
Lie groups, Lie algebras, and some of their applications. — New York: Wiley, [1974] xx, 587 p.; illus.; 23 cm. 'A Wiley-Interscience publication.' 1. Lie groups 2. Lie algebras I. T.
QA387.G54    512/.55    *LC* 73-10030    *ISBN* 0471301795

**Robert, Alain.**      **5.1538**
Introduction to the representation theory of compact and locally compact groups / Alain Robert. — Cambridge [Cambridgeshire]; New York: Cambridge University Press, 1983. viii, 205 p.: ill.; 23 cm. — (London Mathematical Society lecture note series. 80) Includes index. 1. Compact groups 2. Locally compact groups 3. Representations of groups I. T. II. Series.
QA387.R62 1983    512/.2 19    *LC* 82-19730    *ISBN* 0521289750

**Warner, Garth, 1940-.**      **5.1539**
Harmonic analysis on semi–simple Lie groups. Berlin, New York, Springer-Verlag, 1972. 2 v. 24 cm. (Grundlehren der mathematischen Wissenschaften in Einzeldarstellungen mit besonderer Berücksichtigung der Anwendungsgebiete. Bd. 188-189) 1. Semisimple Lie groups 2. Representations of groups 3. Harmonic analysis I. T. II. Series.
QA387.W37    512/.55    *LC* 70-160590    *ISBN* 0387054685

# QA401–427 Mathematical Physics. Engineering Mathematics

## QA401 GENERAL WORKS

**Courant, Richard, 1888-1972.**      • **5.1540**
[Methoden der mathematischen physik. English] Methods of mathematical physics, by R. Courant and D. Hilbert. 1st English ed., translated and rev. from the German original. New York, Interscience Publishers, 1953-62. 2 v. illus. 24 cm. 1. Mathematical physics I. Hilbert, David, 1862-1943. joint author. II. T.
QA401.C724    530.151    *LC* 53-7164

**Kreyszig, Erwin.**      **5.1541**
Advanced engineering mathematics / Erwin Kreyszig. — 5th ed. — New York: Wiley, c1983. xvii, 988, [92] p.: ill.; 26 cm. 1. Mathematical physics 2. Engineering mathematics I. T.
QA401.K7 1983    510/.2462 19    *LC* 82-15988    *ISBN* 0471862517

**Whittaker, E. T. (Edmund Taylor), 1873-1956.**      **5.1542**
A course of modern analysis; an introduction to the general theory of infinite processes and of analytic functions; with an account of the principal transcendental functions / by E.T. Whittaker...and G.N. Watson...— 4th ed., reprinted. –. Cambridge England: the University press, 1940. 5 p. l., [3]-608 p.: diagrs.; 27 cm. 1. Series, Infinite 2. Functions 3. Harmonic analysis I. Watson, G. N. (George Neville), 1886- joint author. II. T.
QA 401.W62 1963    *LC* 41-5650

**Zadeh, Lotfi Asker.**      **5.1543**
Linear system theory; the state space approach [by] Lotfi A. Zadeh & Charles A. Desoer. New York, McGraw-Hill [1963] xxi, 628 p. diagrs. 23 cm. (McGraw-Hill series in system science.) 1. System analysis 2. State-space methods 3. Linear systems I. Desoer, Charles A. II. T. III. Series.
QA401.Z32    517    *LC* 63-14581

# QA402–402.5 SYSTEM ANALYSIS. CONTROL THEORY. OPTIMIZATION. PROGRAMMING

**Luenberger, David G., 1937-.**      **5.1544**
Introduction to dynamic systems: theory, models, and applications / David G. Luenberger. — New York: Wiley, c1979. xiv, 446 p.: ill.; 24 cm. Includes index. 1. System analysis 2. Differential equations 3. Control theory I. T. II. Title: Dynamic systems.
QA402.L84    003    *LC* 78-12366    *ISBN* 0471025941

**Weinberg, Gerald M.**      **5.1545**
On the design of stable systems / Gerald M. Weinberg, Daniela Weinberg; illustrated by Sally Cox. — New York: Wiley, c1979. xvi, 353 p.: ill.; 24 cm. — (Wiley series on systems engineering and analysis) 'A companion volume to An introduction to general systems thinking by Gerald M. Weinberg.' 'A Wiley-Interscience publication.' Includes indexes. 1. System analysis I. Weinberg, Daniela. joint author. II. T.
QA402.W43    003    *LC* 79-13926    *ISBN* 0471047228

**Ruymgaart, P. A. (Peter Arnold), 1925-.**      **5.1546**
Mathematics of Kalman–Bucy filtering / P.A. Ruymgaart, T.T. Soong. — Berlin; New York: Springer-Verlag, 1985. x, 170 p.: ill.; 24 cm. (Springer series in information sciences. v. 14) 1. Kalman filtering 2. Probabilities 3. Calculus 4. Hilbert space I. Soong, T. T. II. T. III. Series.
QA402.3.R89 1985    519.2 19    *LC* 84-20293    *ISBN* 0387135081

**Adby, P. R.**      **5.1547**
Introduction to optimization methods / [by] P. R. Adby and M. A. H. Dempster. — London: Chapman and Hall; New York: Halsted Press, [1974] x, 204 p.: ill.; 22 cm. (Chapman and Hall mathematics series) 1. Mathematical optimization I. Dempster, M. A. H. (Michael Alan Howarth), 1938- joint author. II. T.
QA402.5.A4    515    *LC* 74-4109    *ISBN* 047000830X

**Bradley, Stephen P., 1941-.**      **5.1548**
Applied mathematical programming / Stephen P. Bradley, Arnoldo C. Hax, Thomas L. Magnanti. Reading, Mass.: Addison-Wesley Pub. Co., c1977. xvi, 716, [19] p.: ill.; 25 cm. 1. Programming (Mathematics) I. Hax, Arnoldo C. joint author. II. Magnanti, Thomas L., joint author. III. T.
QA402.5.B7    519.7    *LC* 76-10426    *ISBN* 020100464X

**Gill, Philip E.**      **5.1549**
Practical optimization / Philip E. Gill, Walter Murray, Margaret H. Wright. — London; New York: Academic Press, 1981. xvi, 401 p.: ill.; 25 cm. Includes index. 1. Mathematical optimization I. Murray, Walter. II. Wright, Margaret H. III. T.
QA402.5.G54 1981    515 19    *LC* 81-66366    *ISBN* 0122839528

**Papadimitriou, Christos H.**      **5.1550**
Combinatorial optimization: algorithms and complexity / Christos H. Papadimitriou, Kenneth Steiglitz. — Englewood Cliffs, N.J.: Prentice Hall, c1982. xvi, 496 p.: ill.; 24 cm. 1. Mathematical optimization 2. Combinatorial optimization 3. Computational complexity I. Steiglitz, Kenneth, 1939- II. T.
QA402.5.P37    519 19    *LC* 81-5866    *ISBN* 0131524623

**Scales, L. E.**      **5.1551**
Introduction to non–linear optimization / L.E. Scales. — New York: Springer-Verlag, c1985. xi, 243 p.: ill.; 24 cm. Includes index. 1. Mathematical optimization 2. Maxima and minima I. T.
QA402.5.S33 1985    519 19    *LC* 84-10553    *ISBN* 0387912525

# QA403–404.5 HARMONIC ANALYSIS. FOURIER ANALYSIS AND FUNCTIONS. ORTHOGONAL SERIES AND FUNCTIONS

**Hewitt, Edwin, 1920-.**      **5.1552**
Abstract harmonic analysis / Edwin Hewitt, Kenneth A. Ross. — 2d ed. — Berlin; New York: Springer-Verlag, 1979-. v.; 25 cm. (Grundlehren der mathematischen Wissenschaften; 115) Includes indexes. 1. Harmonic analysis I. Ross, Kenneth A. joint author. II. T.
QA403.H4 1979    515/.2433    *LC* 79-13097    *ISBN* 0387094342

**Katznelson, Yitzhak.**      **5.1553**
An introduction to harmonic analysis. — New York: Wiley, [1968] xiv, 264 p.; 23 cm. 1. Harmonic analysis I. T. II. Title: Harmonic analysis.
QA403.K3    517/.355    *LC* 68-18581

**Nussbaumer, Henri J., 1931-.**      **5.1554**
Fast Fourier transform and convolution algorithms / Henri J. Nussbaumer. —
2nd corr. and updated ed. — Berlin; New York: Springer-Verlag, 1982. xii,
276 p.: ill.; 24 cm. — (Springer series in information sciences. 2) 1. Fourier
transformations — Data processing. 2. Convolutions (Mathematics) — Data
processing. 3. Digital filters (Mathematics) I. T. II. Series.
QA403.5.N87 1982     515.7/23 19     *LC* 82-10650     *ISBN*
038711825X

**Amerio, Luigi.**      **5.1555**
Almost–periodic functions and functional equations [by] Luigi Amerio and
Giovanni Prouse. — New York: Van Nostrand Reinhold, [1970, c1971] viii,
184 p.; 24 cm. — (The University series in higher mathematics) 1. Almost
periodic functions 2. Functional equations 3. Banach spaces I. Prouse,
Giovanni, joint author. II. T.
QA404.A46     515/.98     *LC* 72-112713

**Edwards, R. E. (Robert E.), 1926-.**      **5.1556**
Fourier series, a modern introduction / R. E. Edwards. — 2d ed. — New York:
Springer-Verlag, 1979-. v.; 25 cm. — (Graduate texts in mathematics. 64-)
Includes index. 1. Fourier series I. T. II. Series.
QA404.E25 1979     515/.2433     *LC* 79-11932     *ISBN* 0387904123

**Titchmarsh, E. C. (Edward Charles), 1899-.**      **5.1557**
Introduction to the theory of Fourier integrals, by E. C. Titchmarsh ... — 3rd
ed. — [S.l]: Chilsen Publ., 1986. 394 p. 25 cm. 'First published 1937.'
1. Fourier's series. I. T.
QA404.T5     517.35     *LC* 86-70932

**Zygmund, Antoni, 1900-.**      **5.1558**
Trigonometric series [by] A. Zygmund. — London: Cambridge U.P., 1968. 2 v.
in 1.; 27 cm. First ed. published in 1935 under title: Trigonometrical series.
1. Fourier series I. T.
QA404.Z9 1968     517/.355     *LC* 77-385642     *ISBN* 0521074770

**Rivlin, Theodore J., 1926-.**      **5.1559**
The Chebyshev polynomials [by] Theodore J. Rivlin. — New York: Wiley,
[1974] vi, 186 p.: illus.; 23 cm. — (Pure and applied mathematics) 'A Wiley-
Interscience publication.' 1. Chebyshev polynomials I. T.
QA404.5.R58 1974     515/.55     *LC* 74-10876     *ISBN* 047172470X

**Szegő, Gábor, 1895-.**      **5.1560**
Orthogonal polynomials / by Gabor Szegő. — 4th ed. — Providence: American
Mathematical Society, 1939 i.e. 1975. xiii, 432 p.; 26 cm. (Colloquium
publications - American Mathematical Society; v. 23) 1. Orthogonal
polynomials I. T.
QA404.5.S9 1975     515/.55     *LC* 77-476087     *ISBN* 0821810235

# QA431 Difference Equations. Functional Equations. Integral Equations

**Hochstadt, Harry.**      **5.1561**
Integral equations. — New York: Wiley, [1973] viii, 282 p.; 23 cm. — (Pure and
applied mathematics) 'A Wiley-Interscience publication.' 1. Integral equations
I. T.
QA431.H73     515/.45     *LC* 73-4230     *ISBN* 047140165X

**Jerri, Abdul J., 1932-.**      **5.1562**
Introduction to integral equations with applications / Abdul J. Jerri. — New
York: Dekker, c1985. x, 254 p.: ill.; 24 cm. (Monographs and textbooks in pure
and applied mathematics; 93) Includes index. 1. Integral equations —
Numerical solutions I. T.
QA431.J47 1985     515.4/5 19     *LC* 84-28628     *ISBN* 0824772938

# QA432 Operational Calculus

**Erdélyi, Arthur.**      • **5.1563**
Operational calculus and generalized functions. New York, Holt, Rinehart and
Winston [1962] 103 p. 24 cm. (Athena series) 1. Calculus, Operational I. T.
QA432.E67     517.7     *LC* 61-13029

# QA440–699 GEOMETRY

# QA445–447 General Works

**Coxeter, H. S. M. (Harold Scott Macdonald), 1907-.**      • **5.1564**
Introduction to geometry. New York, Wiley [1961] 443 p. illus. 25 cm.
1. Geometry I. T.
QA445.C67     513     *LC* 61-11175

**Moise, Edwin E.**      **5.1565**
Elementary geometry from an advanced standpoint [by] Edwin E. Moise. — 2d
ed. — Reading, Mass.: [Addison-Wesley Pub. Co., 1974] xv, 425 p.: illus.; 25
cm. 1. Geometry I. T.
QA445.M58 1974     *LC* 73-2347     *ISBN* 0201047934

**Mandelbrot, Benoit B.**      **5.1566**
The fractal geometry of nature / Benoit B. Mandelbrot. — San Francisco: W.H.
Freeman, c1982. 460 p., [1] leaf of plates: ill. (some col.); 24 cm. Rev. ed. of:
Fractals. c1977. Includes indexes. 1. Geometry. 2. Mathematical models.
3. Stochastic processes. 4. Fractals. I. T.
QA447.M357 1982     516/.15 19     *LC* 81-15085     *ISBN* 0716711869

**Mandelbrot, Benoit B.**      **5.1567**
[Objets fractals. English] Fractals: form, chance, and dimension / Benoit B.
Mandelbrot. — San Francisco: W. H. Freeman, c1977. xvi, 365 p.: ill.; 24 cm.
Translation of Les objets fractals. Includes index. 1. Geometry
2. Mathematical models 3. Stochastic processes 4. Fractals I. T.
QA447.M3613     516/.15     *LC* 76-57947     *ISBN* 0716704730. *ISBN*
0716704749 pbk

# QA451–497 Elementary Geometry

**Klein, Felix, 1849-1925.**      • **5.1568**
[Vorträge über ausgewählte fragen der elementargeometrie. English] Famous
problems of elementary geometry: the duplication of the cube, the trisection of
an angle, the quadrature of the circle. Translation by Wooster Woodruff Beman
and David Eugene Smith. 2d ed. rev. and enl. with notes by Raymond Clare
Archibald. New York, Dover Publications [1956] xi, 92 p. illus. 21 cm. 'S298.'
Translation of Vorträge über ausgewahlte Fragen der Elementargeometrie.
'Unabridged and unaltered republication of the second revised edition ...
enlarged ... by Raymond Clare Archibald [1930]' 1. Geometry — Problems,
Famous I. Archibald, Raymond Clare, 1875-1957. ed. II. T.
QA466.K64 1956     513.92     *LC* 63-6120

**Seidenberg, A. (Abraham), 1916-.**      • **5.1569**
Lectures in projective geometry. Princeton, N.J., Van Nostrand [1962] 230 p.
illus. 24 cm. (University series in undergraduate mathematics). 1. Geometry,
Projective 2. Geometry, Analytic I. T. II. Title: Projective geometry.
III. Series.
QA471.S42     516.57     *LC* 62-1569

**Stevenson, Frederick W.**      **5.1570**
Projective planes [by] Frederick W. Stevenson. — San Francisco: W. H.
Freeman, [1972] x, 416 p.: illus.; 24 cm. — (A Series of books in mathematics)
1. Projective planes I. T.
QA471.S86     516/.5     *LC* 72-156824     *ISBN* 0716704439

**Veblen, Oswald, 1880-1960.**      • **5.1571**
Projective geometry, by Oswald Veblen and John Wesley Young. Boston, New
York, Ginn and Company [1910-18] 2 v. diagrs. 24 cm. 1. Geometry,
Projective I. Young, John Wesley, 1879-1932. II. T.
QA471.V4     *LC* 10-22268

## QA481–497 SPECIAL TOPICS IN PLANE GEOMETRY

**Kazarinoff, Nicholas D.**                                    **5.1572**
Geometric inequalities. — [New York]: Random House, [1961] 132 p.: illus.; 23 cm. — (New mathematical library. 4) 1. Geometry, Plane 2. Inequalities (Mathematics) I. T. II. Series.
QA481.K35          513.1          LC 61-6229

**Lockwood, E. H. (Edward Harrington)**                                    **5.1573**
A book of curves. Cambridge [Eng.] University Press, 1961. xi, 198 p. mounted illus., diagrs. 26 cm. 1. Curves, Plane I. T.
QA483.L62          513.1          LC 61-65797

**Boltianskiĭ, V. G. (Vladimir Grigor'evich), 1925-.**                                    **5.1574**
[Tret'ia problema Gil'berta. English] Hilbert's third problem / Vladimir G. Boltianskii; translated by Richard A. Silverman and introduced by Albert B. J. Novikoff. — Washington: Winston; New York: distributed solely by Halsted Press, 1978. x, 228 p.: ill.; 23 cm. — (Scripta series in mathematics) Translation of: Tret'ia problema Gil'berta. Includes index. 1. Hilbert, David, 1862-1943. 2. Tetrahedra I. T. II. Series.
QA491.B6213          516/.23          LC 77-19011          ISBN 0470262893

**Frey, Alexander H.**                                    **5.1575**
Handbook of cubik math / by Alexander H. Frey, Jr., and David Singmaster. — Hillside, N.J.: Enslow Publishers, c1982. viii, 193 p.: ill.; 23 cm. Includes index. 1. Rubik's Cube 2. Groups, Theory of I. Singmaster, David. II. T.
QA491.F73 1982          512/.22 19          LC 81-12525          ISBN 0894900587

## QA551–608 Analytic Geometry. Algebraic Geometry

**Dieudonné, Jean Alexandre, 1906-.**                                    **5.1576**
[Cours de géométre algébrique. English] History of algebraic geometry: an outline of the history and development of algebraic geometry / Jean Dieudonne; translated by Judith Sally. — Monterey, Calif.: Wadsworth Advanced Books & Software, c1985. xii, 186 p.: ill.; 25 cm. (Wadsworth mathematics series.) Translation of: Cours de géométre algébrique, v. 1. Includes indexes. 1. Geometry, Algebraic — History. I. T. II. Series.
QA564.D513 1985          516.3/5 19          LC 84-17213          ISBN 0534037232

**Griffiths, Phillip, 1938-.**                                    **5.1577**
Principles of algebraic geometry / Phillip Griffiths and Joseph Harris. — New York: Wiley, c1978. xii, 813 p.: ill.; 24 cm. — (Pure and applied mathematics) 'A Wiley-Interscience publication.' 1. Geometry, Algebraic I. Harris, Joseph, 1951- joint author. II. T.
QA564.G64 1978          516/.35          LC 78-6993          ISBN 0471327921

**Lang, Serge, 1927-.**                                    **5.1578**
Diophantine geometry. New York, Interscience Publishers [1962] 170 p. 24 cm. (Interscience tracts in pure and applied mathematics, no. 11) 1. Geometry, Algebraic 2. Diophantine analysis I. T.
QA564.L29          516          LC 62-16309

**Thomas, A. D. (Alan David), 1946-.**                                    **5.1579**
Zeta-functions: an introduction to algebraic geometry / A. D. Thomas. — London; San Francisco: Pitman, c1977. vii, 230 p.; 25 cm. (Research notes in mathematics. 12) Includes index. 1. Geometry, Algebraic 2. Functions, Zeta I. T. II. Series.
QA564.T45          516/.35          LC 76-57938          ISBN 0273010387

**Walker, Robert John, 1909-.**                                    • **5.1580**
Algebraic curves. — Princeton: Princeton University Press, 1950. x, 201 p.: ill. — (Princeton mathematical series. 13) 1. Geometry, Algebraic 2. Curves, Algebraic I. T. II. Series.
QA564.W35          LC 50-5732

**Clemens, C. Herbert (Charles Herbert), 1939-.**                                    **5.1581**
A scrapbook of complex curve theory / C. Herbert Clemens. — New York: Plenum Press, c1980. ix, 186 p.: ill.; 24 cm. (The University series in mathematics) Includes index. 1. Curves, Algebraic 2. Functions, Theta 3. Jacobi varieties I. T.
QA565.C55          516.3/5 19          LC 80-20214          ISBN 0306405369

**Fulton, William, 1939-.**                                    **5.1582**
Algebraic curves; an introduction to algebraic geometry. Notes written with the collaboration of Richard Weiss. — [2d print. with corrections]. — Reading, Mass.: W. A. Benjamin, 1969 [i.e. 1974] xiii, 226 p.; 24 cm. — (Mathematics lecture note series) 1. Curves, Algebraic I. Weiss, Richard, 1948- II. T.
QA565.F97 1974          512/.33          LC 74-170911          ISBN 0805330806

**Koblitz, Neal, 1948-.**                                    **5.1583**
Introduction to elliptic curves and modular forms / Neal Koblitz. — New York: Springer-Verlag, c1984. viii, 248 p.: ill.; 25 cm. — (Graduate texts in mathematics. 97) Includes index. 1. Curves, Elliptic 2. Forms, Modular 3. Numbers, Theory of I. T. II. Series.
QA567.K63 1984          516.3/5 19          LC 84-10517          ISBN 0387960295

## QA601–608 TRANSFORMATIONS

**Fejes Tóth, L.**                                    **5.1584**
Regular figures, by L. Fejes Tóth. New York, Macmillan, 1964. xi, 339 p. illus. (part. col.) 23 cm. (International series of monographs on pure and applied mathematics, v. 48) 'A Pergamon Press book.' Part of illustrative matter in pocket. 1. Symmetry 2. Transformations (Mathematics) 3. Topology 4. Decoration and ornament I. T.
QA601.F38          516.5          LC 63-10121

# QA611–614.9 Topology

## QA611 GENERAL WORKS, A–H

**Bennett, H. R.**                                    **5.1585**
A selective survey of axiom–sensitive results in general topology / by H. R. Bennett and T. G. McLaughlin; with an appendix by T.G. McLaughlin and R. C. Woodcock. — [Lubbock: Texas Tech University, 1976?] iv, 114 p. — (Mathematics series/Texas Tech University; no. 12) Errata sheet tippes in. 1. Topology 2. Topology I. McLaughlin, T. G. II. Woodcock, R. C. III. T.
QA611.B36

**Christenson, Charles O.**                                    **5.1586**
Aspects of topology / Charles O. Christenson and William L. Voxman. New York: M. Dekker, c1977. xi, 517 p.: ill.; 24 cm. (Pure and applied mathematics; 39) Includes index. 1. Topology I. Voxman, William L. joint author. II. T.
QA611.C436          514          LC 75-40764          ISBN 0824763319

**Gillman, Leonard.**                                    **5.1587**
Rings of continuous functions, by Leonard Gillman and Meyer Jerison. Princeton, N.J., Van Nostrand [1960] 300 p. 24 cm. (University series in higher mathematics.) 1. Function spaces 2. Functions, Continuous 3. Rings (Algebra) 4. Ideals (Algebra) I. Jerison, Meyer, 1922- joint author. II. T. III. Series.
QA611.G5          512.815          LC 60-14787

**Greenberg, Marvin J.**                                    **5.1588**
Lectures on algebraic topology [by] Marvin J. Greenberg. — New York: W. A. Benjamin, 1967. x, 235 p.: illus.; 24 cm. — (Mathematics lecture notes) 1. Algebraic topology I. T. II. Title: Algebraic topology.
QA611.G65          513/.83          LC 66-30015

**Gottschalk, Walter Helbig, 1918-.**                                    **5.1589**
Topological dynamics/ by Walter Helbig Gottschalk and Gustav Arnold Hedlund. — Providence: American Mathematical Society, 1955. vii, 151 p. — (American Mathematical Society. Colloquium publications; v. 36) 1. Topology 2. Dynamics I. Hedlund, Gustav Arnold, 1904- II. T.
QA611.G6x          LC 55-12710

**Halmos, Paul Richard, 1914-.**                                    • **5.1590**
Measure theory. — New York, Van Nostrand, 1950. xi, 304 p. 24 cm. — (The University series in higher mathematics) Bibliography: p. 293-296. 1. Topology I. T.
QA611.H25          513.83          LC 50-5811

**Hu, S. T. (Sze-Tsen), 1914-.**                                    **5.1591**
Homology theory; a first course in algebraic topology. San Francisco, Holden-Day, 1966. 247 p. 24 cm. (Holden-Day series in mathematics.) 1. Homology theory I. T. II. Series.
QA611.H792          512.8          LC 66-23035

**Hu, S. T. (Sze-Tsen), 1914-.**     **5.1592**
Homotopy theory / [by] Sze–tsen Hu. — New York: Academic Press, 1959.
xiii, 347 p. — (Pure and applied mathematics (Academic Press) 8)
1. Homotopy theory I. T. II. Series.
QA611.H7x     *LC* 59-11526

## QA611 J–Z

**James, I. M. (Ioan Mackenzie), 1928-.**     **5.1593**
General topology and homotopy theory / I.M. James. — New York: Springer-
Verlag, c1984. 248 p.: ill.; 25 cm. 1. Topology I. T.
QA611.J33 1984     514 19     *LC* 84-5435     *ISBN* 0387909702

**Lefschetz, Solomon, 1884-1972.**     **5.1594**
Applications of algebraic topology: graphs and networks: the Picard–Lefschetz
theory and Feynman integrals / S. Lefschetz. — New York: Springer-Verlag,
1975. viii, 189 p.: ill.; 26 cm. — (Applied mathematical sciences; v. 16) Includes
indexes. 1. Algebraic topology 2. Graph theory 3. Electric networks
4. Feynman integrals I. T.
QA611.L4x     510/.8 s 514/.2     *LC* 75-6924     *ISBN* 038790137X

**Milnor, John Willard, 1931-.**     **5.1595**
Morse theory. Based on lecture notes by M. Spivak and R. Wells. Princeton,
N.J., Princeton University Press, 1963. 153 p. illus. 24 cm. (Annals of
mathematics studies, no. 51) 1. Homotopy theory 2. Geometry, Differential
I. T.
QA611.M55     513.8     *LC* 63-13729

**Nagami, Keiō, 1925-.**     **5.1596**
Dimension theory. With an appendix by Yukihiro Kodama. New York,
Academic Press, 1970. xi, 256 p. 24 cm. (Pure and applied mathematics; a series
of monographs and textbooks; v. 37) 1. Dimension theory (Topology)
2. Metric spaces I. T.
QA611.N3x     513/.83     *LC* 73-107576

**Pontriagin, L. S. (Lev Semenovich), 1908-.**     • **5.1597**
[Nepreryvnye gruppy. English] Topological groups [by] L.S. Pontryagin.
Translated from the Russian by Arlen Brown. 2d ed. New York, Gordon and
Breach [1966] xv, 543 p. 24 cm. (Russian monographs and texts on advanced
mathematics and physics.) 1. Topological groups I. T. II. Series.
QA611.P62 1966     513.83     *LC* 65-16828

**Seifert, H. (Herbert), 1907-.**     **5.1598**
[Lehrbuch der Topologie. English.] Seifert and Threlfall, A textbook of
topology / H. Seifert and W. Threlfall; translated by Michael A. Goldman, and
Seifert, Topology of 3–dimensional fibered spaces / H. Seifert; translated by
Wolfgang Heil; edited by Joan S. Birman and Julian Eisner. — New York:
Academic Press, 1980. xvi, 437 p.: ill.; 24 cm. (Pure and applied mathematics, a
series of monographs and textbooks; 89) Translation of Lehrbuch der
Topologie, and of an article from Acta mathematica, v. 60, p. 147-288, with the
title 'Topologie dreidimensionaler gefaserler Räume.' Includes index.
1. Topology I. Threlfall, W. (William), 1888- joint author. II. Birman, Joan
S., 1927- III. Eisner, Julian. IV. Seifert, H. (Herbert), 1907- Topologie
dreidimensionaler gefaserter Räume. English. 1980. V. T. VI. Title: Textbook
of topology.
QA611.S4 QA3.P8 vol. 89     510 s 514     *LC* 79-28163     *ISBN*
0126348502

**Simmons, George Finlay, 1925-.**     • **5.1599**
Introduction to topology and modern analysis. — New York: McGraw-Hill,
[1963] 372 p.: illus.; 24 cm. — (International series in pure and applied
mathematics) 1. Topology 2. Mathematical analysis I. T.
QA611.S49     513.83     *LC* 62-15149

**Singer, I. M. (Isadore Manuel), 1924-.**     **5.1600**
Lecture notes on elementary topology and geometry [by] I.M. Singer and John
A. Thorpe. [Glenview, Ill.] Scott, Foresman [1967] 214 p. illus. 25 cm.
1. Topology 2. Algebraic topology 3. Geometry, Differential I. Thorpe, John
A. joint author. II. T.
QA611.S498     513/.83     *LC* 67-17218

**Stillwell, John.**     **5.1601**
Classical topology and combinatorial group theory / John Stillwell. — New
York: Springer-Verlag, c1980. xii, 301 p.: ill.; 25 cm. — (Graduate texts in
mathematics. 72) Includes index. 1. Topology 2. Combinatorial group theory
I. T. II. Series.
QA611.S84     514     *LC* 80-16326     *ISBN* 0387905162

**Willard, Stephen, 1941-.**     **5.1602**
General topology. — Reading, Mass.: Addison-Wesley Pub. Co., [1970] xii,
369 p.: illus.; 25 cm. — (Addison-Wesley series in mathematics) 1. Topology
I. T.
QA611.W55     513/.83     *LC* 74-100890

## QA611.3–611.5 Topological Dynamics

**Steen, Lynn Arthur, 1941-.**     **5.1603**
Counterexamples in topology / Lynn Arthur Steen, J. Arthur Seebach, Jr. — 2d
ed. — New York: Springer-Verlag, c1978. xi, 244 p.: ill.; 24 cm. Includes index.
1. Topological spaces I. Seebach, J. Arthur, joint author. II. T.
QA611.3.S74 1978     514/.3     *LC* 78-1623     *ISBN* 0387903127

**Brown, James Russell, 1932-.**     **5.1604**
Ergodic theory and topological dynamics / James R. Brown. — New York:
Academic Press, 1976. x, 190 p.; 24 cm. (Pure and applied mathematics, a series
of monographs and textbooks; 70) Includes index. 1. Topological dynamics
2. Ergodic theory I. T.
QA611.5.B7x     510/.8 s 515/.42     *LC* 75-40607     *ISBN* 0121371506

**Kornfel'd, I. P. (Isaak Pavlovich)**     **5.1605**
[Ergodicheskaia teoriia. English] Ergodic theory / I.P. Cornfeld, S.V. Fomin,
Ya.G. Sinai. — New York: Springer-Verlag, c1982. x, 486 p.; 25 cm. —
(Grundlehren der mathematischen Wissenschaften. 245) Includes index.
1. Ergodic theory 2. Differentiable dynamical systems I. Fomin, S. V. (Sergeĭ
Vasil'evich) II. Sinaĭ, IAkov Grigor'evich, 1935- III. T. IV. Series.
QA611.5.F65 1982     515.4/2 19     *LC* 81-5355     *ISBN* 0387905804

**Hájek, Otomar.**     **5.1606**
Dynamical systems in the plane. London, New York, Academic P., 1968. viii,
235 p. 25 cm. 1. Differential equations 2. Topological dynamics I. T.
QA611.5.H35     510     *LC* 67-28007

## QA612–612.8 Algebraic Topology. Knots. Spectral Sequences

**Giblin, P. J.**     **5.1607**
Graphs, surfaces, and homology: an introduction to algebraic topology / P.J.
Giblin. — 2nd ed. — London; New York: Chapman and Hall, 1981. xvii,
329 p.: ill.; 22 cm. — (Chapman and Hall mathematics series.) 1. Algebraic
topology I. T. II. Series.
QA612.G5 1981     514/.2 19     *LC* 81-12267     *ISBN* 0412239000

**Lloyd, Noel Glynne, 1946-.**     **5.1608**
Degree theory / N. G. Lloyd. — Cambridge; New York: Cambridge University
Press, 1978. x, 172 p.; 23 cm. — (Cambridge tracts in mathematics. 73)
Includes index. 1. Degree, Algebraic 2. Differential equations — Numerical
solutions 3. Functional analysis I. T. II. Series.
QA612.L57     515/.7     *LC* 77-3205     *ISBN* 0521216141

**Massey, William S.**     **5.1609**
Algebraic topology, an introduction / William S. Massey. — 4th corrected
printing. — New York: Springer-Verlag, [1977] c1967. xxi, 261 p.: graphs; 25
cm. — (Graduate texts in mathematics. 56) 1. Algebraic topology I. T.
II. Series.
QA612.M37 1977     514/.2     *LC* 77-22206     *ISBN* 0387902716

**Spanier, Edwin Henry, 1921-.**     **5.1610**
Algebraic topology / Edwin H. Spanier. — 1st corr. Springer ed. — New York:
Springer-Verlag, [1981?], c1966. xiv, 528 p.; 24 cm. Includes index.
1. Algebraic topology I. T.
QA612.S6 1981     514/.2 19     *LC* 81-18415     *ISBN* 0387906460

**Kauffman, Louis H., 1945-.**     **5.1611**
On knots / by Louis H. Kauffman. — Princeton, N.J.: Princeton University
Press, 1987. xv, 480 p.: ill.; 25 cm. — (Annals of mathematics studies; no. 115)
1. Knot theory. I. T. II. Series.
QA612.2.K38 1987     514/.224 19     *LC* 87-3195     *ISBN* 0691084343

**Rolfsen, Dale.**     **5.1612**
Knots and links / Dale Rolfsen. Berkeley, CA: Publish or Perish, c1976. 439 p.:
ill.; 26 cm. (Mathematics lecture series; 7) Includes index. 1. Knot theory
2. Link theory I. T.
QA612.2.R65     514/.224     *LC* 76-15514     *ISBN* 0914098160

**Weeks, Jeffrey R., 1956-.**     **5.1613**
The shape of space: how to visualize surfaces and three–dimensional manifolds
/ Jeffrey R. Weeks. — New York: M. Dekker, c1985. x, 324 p.: ill.; 24 cm.
(Monographs and textbooks in pure and applied mathematics. 96) Includes
index. 1. Three-manifolds (Topology) 2. Surfaces I. T. II. Series.
QA612.2.W44 1985     514.3 19     *LC* 85-10394     *ISBN* 082477437X

**McCleary, John.**　　　　　　　　　　　　　　**5.1614**
User's guide to spectral sequences / John McCleary. — Wilmington, Del.: Publish or Perish, c1985. xiii, 423 p.: ill. — (Mathematics lecture series; 12) 1. Spectral sequences (Mathematics) 2. Algebraic topology I. T. II. Series.
QA612.8 M33 1985　　　*LC* 85-63230　　　*ISBN* 0914098217

## QA613–614.8 Manifolds. Differential Topology. Global Analysis. Catastrophes

**Bott, Raoul, 1924-.**　　　　　　　　　　　　**5.1615**
Differential forms in algebraic topology / Raoul Bott, Loring W. Tu. — New York: Springer-Verlag, c1982. xiv, 331 p.: ill.; 25 cm. — (Graduate texts in mathematics. 82) Includes index. 1. Differential topology 2. Algebraic topology 3. Differential forms I. Tu, Loring W. II. T. III. Series.
QA613.6.B67 1982　　　514/.72 19　　　*LC* 81-9172　　　*ISBN* 0387906134

**Guillemin, V., 1937-.**　　　　　　　　　　　**5.1616**
Differential topology [by] Victor Guillemin [and] Alan Pollack. — Englewood Cliffs, N.J.: Prentice-Hall, [1974] xvi, 222 p.: illus.; 24 cm. 1. Differential topology I. Pollack, Alan, joint author. II. T.
QA613.6.G84　　　514/.7　　　*LC* 74-4115　　　*ISBN* 0132126052

**Lu, Yung-Chen, 1938-.**　　　　　　　　　　**5.1617**
Singularity theory and an introduction to catastrophe theory / Yung-chen Lu. New York: Springer-Verlag, c1976. xii, 199 p.: ill.; 24 cm. (Universitext) Includes index. 1. Differentiable mappings 2. Singularities (Mathematics) 3. Catastrophes (Mathematics) I. T.
QA613.64.L8　　　514/.7　　　*LC* 76-48307　　　*ISBN* 038790221X

**Palis Júnior, Jacob.**　　　　　　　　　　　**5.1618**
Geometric theory of dynamical systems: an introduction / Jacob Palis, Jr., Welington de Melo; translated by A.K. Manning. — New York: Springer-Verlag, 1982. xii, 198 p.: ill.; 24 cm. Includes index. 1. Global analysis (Mathematics) 2. Differentiable dynamical systems I. Melo, Welington de. II. T.
QA614.P2813　　　514/.74 19　　　*LC* 81-23332　　　*ISBN* 0387906681

**Smale, Stephen, 1930-.**　　　　　　　　　　**5.1619**
The mathematics of time: essays on dynamical systems, economic processes, and related topics / Steve Smale. — New York: Springer-Verlag, c1980. vi, 151 p.: ill.; 23 cm. 1. Global analysis (Mathematics) — Addresses, essays, lectures. 2. Economics, Mathematical — Addresses, essays, lectures. I. T.
QA614.S6　　　514/.74 19　　　*LC* 80-20827

**Boothby, William M. (William Munger), 1918-.**　　　　**5.1620**
An introduction to differentiable manifolds and Riemannian geometry / William M. Boothby. — New York: Academic Press, 1975. xiv, 424 p.: ill.; 24 cm. (Pure and applied mathematics, a series of monographs and textbooks; 63) Includes index. 1. Differentiable manifolds 2. Riemannian manifolds I. T.
QA614.3.B6 QA3.P8 vol. 63　　　516/.36　　　*LC* 73-18967　　　*ISBN* 0121160505

**Crowell, Richard H.**　　　　　　　　　　• **5.1621**
Introduction to knot theory, by Richard H. Crowell and Ralph H. Fox. Boston, Ginn [1963] 182 p. illus. 24 cm. (Introductions to higher mathematics.) 1. Knot theory I. Fox, Ralph H. (Ralph Hartzler), 1913- joint author. II. T. III. Series.
QA614.5.K6 C74　　　513.8　　　*LC* 62-8920

**Poston, T.**　　　　　　　　　　　　　　**5.1622**
Catastrophe theory and its applications / Tim Poston and Ian Stewart. — London; San Francisco: Pitman, 1978. xviii, 491 p.: ill.; 26 cm. — (Surveys and reference works in mathematics. 2) Includes index. 1. Catastrophes (Mathematics) I. Stewart, Ian. joint author. II. T. III. Series.
QA614.58.P66　　　514/.7　　　*LC* 77-19029　　　*ISBN* 0273010298

**Collet, Pierre, 1948-.**　　　　　　　　　　**5.1623**
Iterated maps on the interval as dynamical systems / Pierre Collet, Jean–Pierre Eckmann. — Basel; Boston: Birkhäuser, c1980. vii, 248 p.: ill.; 24 cm. — (Progress in physics; 1) Includes index. 1. Differentiable dynamical systems 2. Mappings (Mathematics) I. Eckmann, Jean Pierre. joint author. II. T.
QA614.8.C64 1980　　　003 19　　　*LC* 80-20751　　　*ISBN* 3764330260

**Devaney, Robert L., 1948-.**　　　　　　　　**5.1624**
An introduction to chaotic dynamical systems / Robert L. Devaney. — Menlo Park, Calif.: Benjamin/Cummings, c1986. xii, 320 p.: ill.; 25 cm. Includes index. 1. Differentiable dynamical systems 2. Chaotic behavior in systems I. T.
QA614.8.D48 1986　　　515.3/52 19　　　*LC* 85-15801　　　*ISBN* 0805316019

**Irwin, M. C. (Michael Charles), 1934-.**　　　　**5.1625**
Smooth dynamical systems / M. C. Irwin. — London; New York: Academic Press, 1980. x, 259 p.: ill.; 24 cm. (Pure and applied mathematics a series of monographs and textbooks; 94) Includes index. 1. Differentiable dynamical systems I. T.
QA614.8.I7x　　　510 s 515/.35　　　*LC* 80-40031　　　*ISBN* 0123744504

**Percival, Ian, 1931-.**　　　　　　　　　　**5.1626**
Introduction to dynamics / Ian Percival, Derek Richards. — Cambridge; New York: Cambridge University Press, 1983 (c1982). 228 p.: ill.; 24 cm. Includes index. 1. Differentiable dynamical systems 2. Hamiltonian systems I. Richards, Derek. II. T.
QA614.8.P47 1983　　　515.3/5 19　　　*LC* 81-15514　　　*ISBN* 0521236800

## QA641–680 Differential Geometry

**Carmo, Manfredo Perdigão do.**　　　　　　　**5.1627**
Differential geometry of curves and surfaces / Manfredo P. do Carmo. — Englewood Cliffs, N.J.: Prentice-Hall, c1976. viii, 503 p.: ill.; 24 cm. 'A free translation, with additional material, of a book and a set of notes, both published originally in Portuguese.' 1. Geometry, Differential 2. Curves 3. Surfaces I. T.
QA641.C33　　　516/.36　　　*LC* 75-22094　　　*ISBN* 0132125897

**Kobayashi, Shoshichi, 1932-.**　　　　　　　**5.1628**
Foundations of differential geometry [by] Shoshichi Kobayashi and Katsumi Nomizu. New York, Interscience Publishers, 1963-69. 2 v. 24 cm. (Interscience tracts in pure and applied mathematics, no. 15, v. 1-2) 1. Geometry, Differential 2. Topology I. Nomizu, Katsumi, 1924- joint author. II. T.
QA641.K6　　　516.7　　　*LC* 63-19209

**Spivak, Michael.**　　　　　　　　　　　　**5.1629**
A comprehensive introduction to differential geometry / Michael Spivak. — 2d ed. — Berkeley: Publish or Perish, inc., 1979. 5 v.: ill.; 24 cm. 1. Geometry, Differential I. T. II. Title: Differential geometry.
QA641.S59 1979　　　516/.36　　　*LC* 78-71771　　　*ISBN* 0914098837

**Sternberg, Shlomo.**　　　　　　　　　　　**5.1630**
Lectures on differential geometry / Shlomo Sternberg. — 2nd ed. — New York, N.Y.: Chelsea Pub. Co., c1983. xi, 442 p.: ill.; 24 cm. Title on spine: Differential geometry. 1. Geometry, Differential I. T. II. Title: Differential geometry.
QA641.S66 1983　　　516.3/6 19　　　*LC* 81-71141　　　*ISBN* 0828403163

**Bruce, J. W. (James William), 1952-.**　　　　**5.1631**
Curves and singularities: a geometrical introduction to singularity theory / J.W. Bruce and P.J. Giblin. Cambridge [Cambridgeshire]; New York: Cambridge University Press, 1985, c1984. xii, 222 p.: ill.; 24 cm. 1. Singularities (Mathematics) 2. Curves I. Giblin, P. J. II. T.
QA649.B74 1985　　　516.3/6 19　　　*LC* 83-14456　　　*ISBN* 0521249457

## QA681 Foundations of Geometry

**Hilbert, David.**　　　　　　　　　　　　　**5.1632**
Foundations of geometry / David Hilbert; translated by Leo Unger from the German ed. — 10th ed. rev. and enl./ Paul Bernays. — La Salle, Ill.: Open Court, 1971. ix, 226 p.: ill. 1. Geometry — Foundations I. Bernays, Paul. II. T.
QA681.H58x

**Pogorelov, A. V. (Alekseĭ Vasil'evich), 1919-.**　　　**5.1633**
[Chetvertaia problema Gil'berta. English.] Hilbert's fourth problem / Aleksei Vasil'evich Pogorelov; translated by Richard A. Silverman; edited by Irwin Kra, in cooperation with Eugene Zaustinskiy. — Washington: V. H. Winston; New York: distributed solely by Halsted Press, 1979. vi, 97 p.; 23 cm. (Scripta series in mathematics) Translation of Chetvertaia problema Gil'berta. Includes index. 1. Geometry — Foundations I. Kra, Irwin. II. Zaustinskiy, Eugene. III. T. IV. Series.
QA681.P5913　　　516/.1　　　*LC* 79-14508　　　*ISBN* 0470267356

## QA685 Non–Euclidean Geometry

**Coxeter, H. S. M. (Harold Scott Macdonald), 1907-.**                    **5.1634**
Non–Euclidean geometry / by H.S.M. Coxeter. — 5th ed. — Toronto:
University of Toronto Press, 1965, c1957. xv, 309 p.: ill. — (Mathematical
expositions. no. 2) Includes index. 1. Geometry, Non-Euclidean I. T.
II. Series.
QA685.C78 1965      513.8

**Hilbert, David, 1862-1943.**                                        • **5.1635**
[Anschauliche Geometrie. English. 1952] Geometry and the imagination, by D.
Hilbert and S. Cohn–Vóssen; translated by P. Nemenyi. New York, Chelsea
Pub. Co., 1952. 357 p. illus. 24 cm. Translation of Anschauliche Geometrie.
1. Geometry, Non-Euclidean I. T.
QA685.H515      513      LC 52-2894

## QA691–699 Hyperspace. Fourth Dimension

**Coxeter, H. S. M. (Harold Scott Macdonald), 1907-.**                    **5.1636**
Regular complex polytopes / H. S. M. Coxeter. — London: Cambridge
University Press, 1974. x, 185 p.: ill.; 26 x 28 cm. Includes index. 1. Polytopes.
I. T.
QA691.C66      516/.182      LC 73-75855      ISBN 052120125X

**Halmos, Paul Richard, 1914-.**                                      • **5.1637**
Introduction to Hilbert space and the theory of spectral multiplicity / by Paul
R. Halmos. — New York: Chelsea, 1951. 114 p.; 24 cm. 1. Hyperspace I. T.
II. Title: Spectral multiplicity.
QA691.H34      LC 51-7033

**Abbott, Edwin Abbott, 1838-1926.**                                  • **5.1638**
Flatland; a romance of many dimensions, with illus. by the author, a square
(Edwin A. Abbott) With introd. by William Garnett. 5th ed., rev. New York,
Barnes & Noble [1963] 108 p. illus. 21 cm. (University paperbacks 45)
1. Fourth dimension I. T.
QA699.A13 1963      530.1/1 19      LC 63-12454      ISBN 0064800059

**Dewdney, A. K.**                                                      **5.1639**
The planiverse: computer contact with a two–dimensional world / A.K.
Dewdney. — New York: Poseidon Press, c1984. 267 p.: ill.; 24 cm.
1. Hyperspace I. T. II. Title: Two-dimensional world.
QA699.D48 1984      530.8 19      LC 83-24799      ISBN 0671463632

## QA801–939 ANALYTIC MECHANICS

## QA801–807 History. General Works

**Newton, Isaac, Sir, 1642-1727.**                                      **5.1640**
[Principia] Philosophiae naturalis principia mathematica. 3d ed. (1726), with
variant readings, assembled and edited by Alexandre Koyré and I. Bernard
Cohen, with the assistance of Anne Whitman. [Cambridge, Mass.] Harvard
University Press, 1972. 2 v. (xl, 916 p.) illus. 29 cm. The work is better known
under title: Principia. 'The history and purpose of the edition are explained at
length in the companion volume, Introduction to Newton's Principia [by I. B.
Cohen] published simultaneously with these two text volumes.' Latin text, with
editorial matter in English. 1. Mechanics — Early works to 1800.
2. Mechanics, Celestial — Early works to 1800. I. Koyré, Alexandre,
1892-1964. ed. II. Cohen, I. Bernard, 1914- ed. III. T.
QA803.A2 1972      531      LC 75-78515      ISBN 0674664752

**Cohen, I. Bernard, 1914-.**                                          • **5.1641**
Introduction to Newton's 'Principia' [by] I. Bernard Cohen. — Cambridge
[Eng.]: University Press, 1971. xxviii, 380 p.: facsims.; 29 cm. 1. Newton, Isaac,
Sir, 1642-1727. Principia 2. Mechanics — Early works to 1800. I. T.
QA803.C64      531      LC 76-75429

**Burghes, David N.**                                                  **5.1642**
Modern introduction to classical mechanics & control / David N. Burghes,
Angela M. Downs. — Chichester, Eng.: E. Horwood; New York: Halsted
Press, 1975. 320 p.: ill.; 24 cm. (Mathematics & its applications) Includes index.
1. Mechanics 2. Mathematics — 1961- I. Downs, Angela M., joint author.
II. T.
QA805.B94 1975      531/.01/51      LC 75-16463      ISBN 0470123621

**Goldstein, Herbert, 1922-.**                                        • **5.1643**
Classical mechanics. — Cambridge, Mass.: Addison-Wesley Press, 1950. xii,
399 p.: diagrs.; 24 cm. 1. Mechanics, Analytic I. T.
QA805.G6      531      LC 50-7669

**Lanczos, Cornelius, 1893-.**                                          **5.1644**
The variational principles of mechanics / by Cornelius Lanczos. — 4th ed. —
New York: Dover Publications, 1986, c1970. xxix, 418 p.: ill.; 22 cm. (Dover
books on physics and chemistry.) Reprint. Originally published: Toronto:
University of Toronto Press, c1970. (Mathematical expositions; no. 4). Includes
index. 1. Mechanics, Analytic 2. Variational principles I. T. II. Series.
QA805.L278 1986      531/.01/51 19      LC 85-29168      ISBN
0486650677

**Landau, L. D. (Lev Davidovich), 1908-1968.**                          **5.1645**
[Mekhanika. English] Mechanics / by L. D. Landau and E. M. Lifshitz;
translated from the Russian by J. B. Sykes and J. S. Bell. — 3d ed. — Oxford;
New York: Pergamon Press, 1976. xxvii, 169 p.: ill.; 25 cm. (Course of
theoretical physics; v. 1) Translation of Mekhanika. 'Lev Davidovich Landau
(1908-1968)' by E. M. Lifshitz: p. 1. Mechanics, Analytic I. Lifshits, E. M.
(Evgeniĭ Mikhaĭlovich) joint author. II. T.
QA805.L283 1976      531/.01/515      LC 76-18997      ISBN 0080210228

**Fowles, Grant R.**                                                    **5.1646**
Analytical mechanics / Grant R. Fowles. — 4th ed. — Philadelphia: Saunders
College Pub., c1986. ix, 342 p.: ill.; 25 cm. (Saunders golden sunburst series)
Includes index. 1. Mechanics, Analytic I. T.
QA807.F65 1986      531/.01/515 19      LC 85-8180      ISBN 0030041244

**Fung, Y. C. (Yuan-cheng), 1919-.**                                  • **5.1647**
Foundations of solid mechanics/ Y. C. Fung. — Englewood Cliffs, N. J.:
Prentice-Hall, [1965] xiv, 525 p.: ill. — (Prentice-Hall international series in
dynamics) 1. Mechanics, Analytic 2. Elasticity I. T.
QA807.F85      531.017      LC 65-18496

**Osgood, William F. (William Fogg), 1864-1943.**                        **5.1648**
Mechanics. New York: Macmillan, c1937. 495 p. 1. Mechanics, Analytic I. T.
QA807.O8      LC 37-13039

## QA808–808.5 Special Aspects

**Malvern, Lawrence E., 1916-.**                                        **5.1649**
Introduction to the mechanics of a continuous medium [by] Lawrence E.
Malvern. — Englewood Cliffs, N.J.: Prentice-Hall, [1969] xii, 713 p.: illus.; 24
cm. — (Prentice-Hall series in engineering of the physical sciences)
1. Continuum mechanics I. T.
QA808.2.M3      531      LC 69-13712      ISBN 0134876032

**Sard, R. D., 1915-.**                                                  **5.1650**
Relativistic mechanics: special relativity and classical particle dynamics / [by]
R. D. Sard. — New York: W. A. Benjamin, 1970. xxi, 376 p.: ill.; 24 cm.
(Lecture notes and supplements in physics) 1. Relativistic mechanics
2. Dynamics of a particle 3. Special relativity (Physics) I. T.
QA808.5.S26      530.11      LC 74-80665      ISBN 080538491X

## QA821–842 Statics. Kinematics

**Lamb, Horace, Sir, 1849-1934.**                                      • **5.1651**
Statics, including hydrostatics and the elements of the theory of elasticity. 3d
ed. Cambridge, Eng.: Cambridge U.P. 1960. 357p.illus. 1. Statics
2. Hydrostatics 3. Elasticity I. T.
QA821.L3 1960      CIVENG531.2L218.3      LC 61-2165

**MacMillan, William Duncan, 1871-1948.**                    **5.1652**
The theory of the potential / by William Duncan MacMillan. — New York: Dover Publications, 1958. — xii, 469 p.: ill.; 21 cm. — (MacMillan's Theoretical mechanics) 'Unabridged and unaltered republication of the first edition.' Includes index. 1. Potential, Theory of I. T.
QA825.M3 1958      LC 58-59865

# QA845–871 Dynamics. Oscillations

**Abraham, Ralph.**                    **5.1653**
Dynamics—the geometry of behavior / by Ralph H. Abraham and Christopher D. Shaw. — Santa Cruz, Calif.: Aerial Press, [1982]- < [c1985] >. v. < 1-3 >: ill. (some col.); 25 cm. (The Visual mathematics library. Vismath books; v. 1- < 3 >) 1. Dynamics I. Shaw, Christopher D. II. T.
QA845.A26 1982      531/.11 19      LC 81-71616      ISBN 0942344014

**Arnol'd, V. I. (Vladimir Igorevich), 1937-.**                    **5.1654**
[Problèmes ergodiques de la mécanique classique. English] Ergodic problems of classical mechanics [by] V. I. Arnold and A. Avez. New York, Benjamin, 1968. ix, 286 p. illus. 24 cm. (The Mathematical physics monograph series) Translation of Problèmes ergodiques de la mécanique classique. 1. Dynamics 2. Ergodic theory I. Avez, A. (André) joint author. II. T.
QA845.A713      531      LC 68-19936

**Timoshenko, Stephen, 1878-1972.**                    **5.1655**
Advanced dynamics / by S. Timoshenko and D.H. Young. — New York; Toronto: McGraw-Hill 1948. xii, 400 p.: ill.; 24 cm. 1. Dynamics I. Young, Donovan Harold, 1904- II. T.
QA845.T5      531.3      LC 48-28240

**Webster, Arthur Gordon, 1863-1923.**                    **• 5.1656**
The dynamics of particles and of rigid plastic, and fluid bodies; being lectures on mathematical physics. 2d ed. New York, Dover Publications [1959] 588 p. illus. 21 cm. 'An unabridged and unaltered republication of the second edition.' 1. Dynamics 2. Potential, Theory of 3. Strains and stresses 4. Hydrodynamics I. T.
QA845.W38 1959      531.36      LC 59-10914

**Whittaker, E. T. (Edmund Taylor), 1873-1956.**                    **• 5.1657**
A treatise on the analytical dynamics of particles and rigid bodies: with an introduction to the problem of three bodies / by E. T. Whittaker. — 4th ed. — London: Cambridge University Press, [1937] xiv, 456 p.: ill. 1. Dynamics 2. Three-body problem 3. Orbits I. T.
QA845.W62 1937

**Mann, Ronald A.**                    **5.1658**
The classical dynamics of particles: Galilean and Lorentz relativity [by] Ronald A. Mann. — New York: Academic Press, 1974. x, 299 p.: illus.; 24 cm. 1. Dynamics of a particle 2. Relativity (Physics) 3. Groups, Theory of I. T.
QA852.M36      531/.163      LC 73-18937      ISBN 0124692508

**Andronov, A. A. (Aleksandr Aleksandrovich), 1901-1952.**                    **• 5.1659**
[Teoriia kolebaniĭ. English] Theory of oscillators / by A.A. Andronov, A.A. Vitt, and S.E. Khaidin; translated from the Russian by F. Immirzi; the translation edited and abridged by W. Fishwick. — Oxford; New York: Pergamon Press [U.S.A. ed. distributed by Addison-Wesley Pub. Co., Reading, Mass., 1966] xxxii, 815 p.: ill.; 23 cm. (International series of monographs in physics, v. 4) 1. Oscillations I. Vitt, A. A. (Aleksandr Adol'fovich), d. 1937. joint author. II. Khaĭkin, S. É. (Semen Émmanuilovich) joint author. III. T.
QA871.A52 1966      531.3201      LC 66-3922

# QA901–930 Fluid Mechanics. Fluid Dynamics

**Anderson, Dale A. (Dale Arden), 1936-.**                    **5.1660**
Computational fluid mechanics and heat transfer / Dale A. Anderson, John C. Tannehill, Richard H. Pletcher. — Washington: Hemisphere Pub. Corp.; New York: McGraw-Hill, c1984. xii, 599 p.: ill.; 25 cm. — (Series in computational methods in mechanics and thermal sciences.) Includes index. 1. Fluid mechanics 2. Heat — Transmission I. Tannehill, John C. II. Pletcher, Richard H. III. T. IV. Series.
QA901.A53 1984      532 19      LC 83-18614      ISBN 0070503281

**Landau, L. D. (Lev Davidovich), 1908-1968.**                    **• 5.1661**
[Mekhanika sploshnykh sred. English] Fluid mechanics, by L.D. Landau and E.M. Lifshitz. Translated from the Russian by J.B. Sykes and W.H. Reid. London, Pergamon Press; Reading, Mass., Addison-Wesley Pub. Co., 1959. 536 p. illus. 24 cm. (Their Course of theoretical physics, v. 6) The A-W series in advanced physics. Translation of [Mekhanika sploshnykh sred] 1. Fluid mechanics I. Lifshits, E. M. (Evgeniĭ Mikhaĭlovich) joint author. II. T.
QA901.L283      532      LC 59-10525

**Batchelor, G. K. (George Keith)**                    **• 5.1662**
An introduction to fluid dynamics / by G. K. Batchelor. — Cambridge: U.P., 1967. xviii, 615 p.: 24 plates, diagrs.; 24 cm. 1. Fluid dynamics I. T.
QA911.B33      532/.05      LC 67-21953

**Chandrasekhar, S. (Subrahmanyan), 1910-.**                    **5.1663**
Hydrodynamic and hydromagnetic stability / by S. Chandrasekhar. — Dover ed. — New York: Dover Publications, 1981, c1961. xix, 652 p., [13] leaves of plates: ill.; 21 cm. Reprint. Originally published: Oxford: Oxford University Press, 1961. (International series of monographs on physics) Includes index. 1. Hydrodynamics 2. Magnetohydrodynamics I. T.
QA911.C42 1981      532/.5 19      LC 80-69678      ISBN 048664071X

**Monin, A. S. (Andreĭ Sergeevich), 1921-.**                    **5.1664**
[Statisticheskaia gidromekhanika. English] Statistical fluid mechanics; mechanics of turbulence [by] A. S. Monin and A. M. Yaglom. Edited by John L. Lumley. English ed. updated, augmented and rev. by the authors. Cambridge, Mass.: MIT Press, 1971. 769 p. Translation of Statisticheskaia gidromekhanika. 1. Hydrodynamics 2. Fluid mechanics 3. Turbulence I. IAglom, A. M. joint author. II. T.
QA911.M6313      532/.0527      LC 70-110232      ISBN 0262130629

**Cebeci, Tuncer.**                    **5.1665**
Analysis of turbulent boundary layers [by] Tuncer Cebeci and A. M. O. Smith. New York, Academic Press, 1974. xvii, 404 p. illus. 24 cm. (Applied mathematics and mechanics, 15) 1. Turbulent boundary layer I. Smith, Apollo Milton Olin, joint author. II. T.
QA913.C4      532/.052      LC 73-18985      ISBN 0121646505

**Tennekes, H.**                    **5.1666**
A first course in turbulence / [by] H. Tennekes and J. L. Lumley. — Cambridge, Mass.: MIT Press [1972] xii, 300 p.: ill.; 24 cm. 1. Turbulence 2. Dimensional analysis I. Lumley, John L. (John Leask), 1930- joint author. II. T.
QA913.T44      532/.0527      LC 77-165072      ISBN 0262200198

**Theoretical approaches to turbulence / edited by D.L. Dwoyer,**                    **5.1667**
**M.Y. Hussaini, R.G. Voigt.**
New York: Springer-Verlag, c1985. xii, 373 p.: ill.; 24 cm. (Applied mathematical sciences; v. 58) 1. Turbulence — Addresses, essays, lectures. I. Dwoyer, Douglas L. II. Hussaini, M. Yousuff. III. Voigt, Robert G.
QA1.A647 vol. 58 QA913.T4x      510 s 532/.0527 19      LC 85-14765
ISBN 0387961917

**Clift, R. (Roland)**                    **5.1668**
Bubbles, drops, and particles / R. Clift, J. R. Grace, and M. E. Weber. — New York: Academic Press, 1978. xiii, 380 p.: ill.; 24 cm. 1. Multiphase flow 2. Particles 3. Drops 4. Bubbles 5. Heat — Transmission 6. Mass transfer I. Grace, John R. joint author. II. Weber, Martin E. joint author. III. T.
QA922.C56      532/.052      LC 77-6592      ISBN 012176950X

**Bhatnagar, P. L., 1912-.**                    **5.1669**
Nonlinear waves in one-dimensional dispersive systems / by P. L. Bhatnagar. — Oxford: Clarendon Press; New York: Oxford University Press, 1980 (c1978). xii, 142 p.: ill.; 25 cm. — (Oxford mathematical monographs) 1. Nonlinear waves I. T.
QA927.B48      531/.1133      LC 79-40272      ISBN 0198535317

**Drazin, P. G.**                    **5.1670**
Solitons / P.G. Drazin. — Cambridge [Cambridgeshire]; New York: Cambridge University Press, 1983. viii, 136 p.: ill.; 23 cm. — (London Mathematical Society lecture note series; 85) Includes indexes. 1. Solitons. I. T. II. Series.
QA927.D69 1983      532/.0593 19      LC 83-7170      ISBN 0521274222

# QA931–939 Elasticity. Plasticity

**Landau, L. D. (Lev Davidovich), 1908-1968.**                    **5.1671**
[Teoriia uprugosti. English] Theory of elasticity / by L.D. Landau and E.M. Lifshitz; translated from the Russian by J.B. Sykes and W.H. Reid. — 3rd English ed. revised and enlarged by E.M. Lifshitz, A.M. Kosevich, and L.P. Pitaevskii. — Oxford; New York: Pergamon Press, 1986. p. cm. (Course of

theoretical physics; v. 7) Translation of: Teoriia uprugosti. Includes index. 1. Elasticity 2. Elastic solids I. Lifshits, E. M. (Evgeniĭ Mikhaĭlovich) II. Kosevich, Arnol'd Markovich. III. Pitaevskiĭ, L. P. (Lev Petrovich) IV. T.
QA931. L283 1986     531/.38 19     *LC* 86-2450     *ISBN* 0080339174

**Pearson, Carl E.**             **5.1672**
Theoretical elasticity. Cambridge, Harvard University Press, 1959. 218 p. illus. 22 cm. (Harvard monographs in applied science, no. 6) 1. Elasticity I. T.
QA931.P38     531.38     *LC* 59-9283

**Timoshenko, Stephen, 1878-1972.**     • **5.1673**
Theory of elasticity / [by] S. P. Timoshenko [and] J. N. Goodier. — 3d ed. New York: McGraw-Hill [1969, c1970] xxiv, 567 p.: ill.; 23 cm. (Engineering societies monographs.) 1. Elasticity 2. Strains and stresses 3. Strength of materials I. Goodier, J. N. (James Norman), 1905- joint author. II. T. III. Series.
QA931.T55 1970     531/.3823     *LC* 69-13617

**Timoshenko, Stephen, 1878-1972.**     • **5.1674**
Theory of plates and shells [by] S. Timoshenko [and] S. Woinowsky–Krieger. — 2d ed. — New York: McGraw-Hill, 1959. 580 p.: illus.; 24 cm. — (Engineering societies monographs) 1. Elastic plates and shells I. Woinowsky-Krieger, S., joint author. II. T.
QA931.T56 1959     620.11282     *LC* 58-59675

# QB Astronomy

## QB1–136 Reference. General Works

**Shapley, Harlow, 1885-1972. ed.** • **5.1675**
Source book in astronomy, 1900–1950. — Cambridge: Harvard University Press, 1960. xv, 423 p.: illus., diagrs., tables.; 24 cm. — (Source books in the history of the sciences.) 'Identification and sources': p. [411]-417. 1. Astronomy — Collected works. I. T. II. Series.
QB3.S52    520.82    LC 60-13294

**Sky catalogue 2000.0 / edited by Alan Hirshfeld and Roger W.** **5.1676**
**Sinnott.**
Cambridge [Cambridgeshire]; New York: Cambridge University Press; Cambridge, Mass.: Sky Pub. Corp., 1982-1985. 2 v.: ill.; 31 cm. 1. Stars — Catalogs I. Hirshfeld, Alan. II. Sinnott, Roger W.
QB6.S54    523.8/908 19    LC 81-17975    ISBN 0521247101

**Smithsonian Astrophysical Observatory.** • **5.1677**
Star catalog: positions and proper motions of 258,997 stars for the epoch and equinox of 1950.0 / Smithsonian Astrophysical Observatory. — Washington: Smithsonian Institution: for sale by the Superintendent of Documents, U.S. Govt. Print. Off., 1974. 4 v.: ill. — (Publication (Smithsonian Institution). 4652) "Sources for the catalog": v. 1, p. xx-xxiv. 1. Stars — Catalogs I. T. II. Series.
QB6 S57    QB6 S57.    523.8908    LC 65-62534

**The Astronomical almanac for the year ...** **5.1678**
Washington: Issued by the Nautical Almanac Office, United States Naval Observatory by direction of the Secretary of the Navy and under the authority of Congress: For sale by the Supt. of Docs., U.S. G.P.O.; London: For sale by Her Majesty's Stationery Office. v.: ill.; 27 cm. Annual. Began with 1981. 1982. Description based on: 1982. 1. Nautical almanacs — Periodicals. 2. Ephemerides — Periodicals. I. United States Naval Observatory. Nautical Almanac Office. II. Great Britain. Nautical Almanac Office. III. Science Research Council (Great Britain)
QB8.U6 A77    528    LC gp 82-3295

**Apparent places of fundamental stars.** **5.1679**
1941-    . — London: H.M.S.O., 1940-. v: tables; 27 cm. Annual. Published: Heidelberg: Astronomisches Rechen-Institut, <1985-> 1. Stars — Ephemerides — Periodicals. I. Great Britain. Admiralty. II. Astronomisches Rechen-Institut, Heidelberg. III. International Astronomical Union. IV. Great Britain. Nautical Almanac Office.
QB9.I5    LC sn 85-22783

**The Facts on File dictionary of astronomy / edited by Valerie** **5.1680**
**Illingworth.**
2nd ed. — New York, N.Y.: Facts on File, 1985. 437 p.: ill.; 24 cm. 1. Astronomy — Dictionaries. I. Illingworth, Valerie. II. Facts on File, Inc.
QB14.F3 1985 ·    520/.3/21 19    LC 85-20409    ISBN 0816013578

**Hopkins, Jeanne.** **5.1681**
Glossary of astronomy and astrophysics / Jeanne Hopkins; foreword by S. Chandrasekhar. — 2nd ed., rev. and enl. — Chicago: University of Chicago Press, 1980. ix, 196 p.; 24 cm. 'Published under the auspices of the Astrophysical journal'—verso t.p. 1. Astronomy — Dictionaries. 2. Astrophysics — Dictionaries. I. Astrophysical journal. II. T.
QB14.H69 1980    520/.32/1 19    LC 80-5226    ISBN 0226351718

**Weigert, Alfred, 1927-.** **5.1682**
Concise encyclopedia of astronomy / A. Weigert and H. Zimmermann; translated by J. Home Dickson. — 2d English ed. / rev. by H. Zimmermann. — London: A. Hilger, 1976, c1975. 532 p., 8 leaves of plates: ill., maps (5 folded in pocket), graphs. Translation of: ABC der Astronomie, 3d ed. 1. Astronomy — Dictionaries. I. Zimmermann, Helmut. II. T.
QB14.W413 1976    520/.3    ISBN 0852740999

## QB15–36 History. Biography

**Christianson, Gale E.** **5.1683**
This wild abyss: the story of the men who made modern astronomy / Gale E. Christianson. — New York: Free Press, c1978. xvii, 461 p., [8] leaves of plates: ill.; 25 cm. Includes index. 1. Astronomy — History. I. T.
QB15.C44    520/.9    LC 77-81428    ISBN 0029053803

**Dreyer, John Louis Emil, 1852-1926.** • **5.1684**
A history of astronomy from Thales to Kepler / by J. L. E. Dreyer. — 2nd. ed. / revised with a foreword by W. H. Stahl. — New York: Dover Publications, c1953. x, 430 p.: ill. 1. Astronomy — History. 2. Solar system I. T.
QB15.D77    520.9    LC 53-12387

**Moore, Patrick.** **5.1685**
Patrick Moore's History of astronomy. — 6th rev. ed. — London: Macdonald, 1983. 327 p.: ill. (some col.); 29 cm. Rev. ed. of: The story of astronomy. 4th rev. ed. 1972. Includes index. 1. Astronomy — History. 2. Astronomy — Popular works. I. Moore, Patrick. The story of astronomy. II. T. III. Title: History of astronomy.
QB15.M63 1983    520/.9 19    LC 84-118017    ISBN 0356086070

**Van Helden, Albert.** **5.1686**
Measuring the universe: cosmic dimensions from Aristarchus to Halley / Albert van Helden. — Chicago: University of Chicago Press, 1985. viii, 203 p.: ill.; 24 cm. Includes index. 1. Astronomy — History. 2. Cosmological distances I. T.
QB15.V33 1985    523.1 19    LC 84-16397    ISBN 0226848817

**Archaeoastronomy and the roots of science / edited by E.C.** **5.1687**
**Krupp.**
Boulder, Colo.: Published by Westview Press for the American Association for the Advancement of Science, 1984. xii, 336 p.: ill.; 24 cm. — (AAAS selected symposium. 71) 'Based on a symposium that was held at the 1980 AAAS National Annual Meeting in San Francisco, California, January 3-8 ... sponsored by AAAS Sections D (Astronomy) and H (Anthropology)'—T.p. verso. 1. Astronomy, Prehistoric I. Krupp, E. C. (Edwin C.), 1944- II. American Association for the Advancement of Science. Section D—Astronomy. III. American Association for the Advancement of Science. Section H—Anthropology. IV. Series.
QB16.A73 1984    520/.93 19    LC 83-50763    ISBN 0865314063

**Hadingham, Evan.** **5.1688**
Early man and the cosmos / Evan Hadingham. — New York: Walker and Co., 1984. x, 271 p.: ill.; 27 cm. Includes index. 1. Astronomy, Ancient 2. Astronomy, Prehistoric I. T.
QB16.H3 1984    520/.93 19    LC 83-42727    ISBN 0802707459

**Trefil, James S., 1938-.** **5.1689**
Space, time, infinity: the Smithsonian views the universe / James S. Trefil; introductory essays by Kenneth L. Franklin. — 1st ed. — New York: Pantheon books; Washington: Smithsonian Books, c1985. 255 p.: ill. (some col.); 26 cm. Includes index. 1. Astronomy — History. 2. Cosmology — History. I. Franklin, Kenneth L. II. Smithsonian Institution. III. T.
QB32.T74 1985    520 19    LC 85-42940    ISBN 0394548434

**The Biographical dictionary of scientists. Astronomers / general** **5.1690**
**editor, David Abbott.**
New York: P. Bedrick Books, 1984. 204 p.: ill.; 26 cm. Includes index. 1. Astronomers — Biography. I. Abbott, David, 1937- II. Title: Astronomers.
QB35.B56 1984    520/.92/4 B 19    LC 84-9236    ISBN 0911745807

**Drake, Stillman.** **5.1691**
Galileo / by Stillman Drake. — 1st American ed. — New York: Hill and Wang, 1981 (c1980) vii, 200 p.; 20 cm. — (Past masters) 1. Galilei, Galileo, 1564-1642. I. T.
QB36.G2    LC 80-84162    ISBN 0809014165

**De Santillana, Giorgio, 1902-.** • **5.1692**
The crime of Galileo. — [Chicago]: University of Chicago Press, [1955] xx, 338 p.: ports., diagrs.; 24 cm. 1. Galilei, Galileo, 1564-1642. I. T.
QB36.G2 D4 1955    925.2    LC 55-7400

**Koyré, Alexandre, 1892-1964.**　　**5.1693**
[Études galiléennes. English] Galileo studies / Alexandre Koyré; translated from the French by John Mepham. — Atlantic Highlands, N.J.: Humanities Press, 1978. 278 p.: ill.; 24 cm. — (European philosophy and the human sciences) Translation of Études galiléennes. 1. Galilei, Galileo, 1564-1642. 2. Descartes, René, 1596-1650. 3. Dynamics 4. Science — Philosophy I. T.
QB36.G2 K6813 1978　　509/.2/4　　*LC* 77-18003　　*ISBN* 0391007602

**Newton, Robert R.**　　**5.1694**
The crime of Claudius Ptolemy / Robert R. Newton. — Baltimore: Johns Hopkins University Press, c1977. xiv, 411 p.: ill.; 24 cm. Includes index. 1. Ptolemy, fl. 2nd cent. 2. Astronomers — Greece — Biography. I. T.
QB36.P83 N47　　520/.92/4　　*LC* 77-4211　　*ISBN* 0801819903

**Kuhn, Thomas S.**　　**• 5.1695**
The Copernican revolution: planetary astronomy in the development of Western thought. — Cambridge: Harvard University Press, 1957. xviii, 297 p.: charts, diagrs.; 25 cm. 1. Copernicus, Nicolaus, 1473-1543. De revolutionibus orbium coelestium. 2. Cosmology. I. T.
QB41.C815 K8　　523.2　　*LC* 57-7612

**Kepler, Johannes, 1571-1630.**　　**• 5.1696**
Somnium; the dream, or posthumous work on lunar astronomy. Translated with a commentary by Edward Rosen. Madison, University of Wisconsin Press, 1967. xxiii, 255 p.: ill., ports. 24 cm. Includes index. 1. Astronomy — Early works to 1800. I. Rosen, Edward, 1906- II. T. III. Title: The dream.
QB41.K4213　　523.3　　*LC* 65-20639

# QB42–55 Astronomy: General Works, 1701–

**Lambert, Johann Heinrich, 1728-1777.**　　**5.1697**
[Cosmologische Briefe über die Einrichtung des Weltbaues. English] Cosmological letters on the arrangement of the world–edifice / J. H. Lambert; translated with an introd. and notes by Stanley L. Jaki. — 1st ed. — New York: Science History Publications, 1976. 245 p.: facsim.; 24 cm. Translation of Cosmologische Briefe über die Einrichtung des Weltbaues. Includes index. 1. Cosmology — Early works to 1800. I. T.
QB42.L25 1976　　523.1　　*LC* 75-31623　　*ISBN* 0882020420

**Gamow, George, 1904-1968.**　　**• 5.1698**
The birth and death of the sun: stellar evolution and subatomic energy / by George Gamow; illustrated by the author. — New York: The Viking press, 1949, c1945. xvi, 245 p.: ill. 1. Sun 2. Stars 3. Atoms I. T.
QB43.G19　　　　*LC* 50-2196

**The Cambridge encyclopaedia of astronomy / editor–in–chief,**　　**5.1699**
Simon Mitton; foreword by Sir Martin Ryle.
New York: Crown Publishers, 1977. 481 p.: ill.; 27 cm. Includes index. 1. Astronomy I. Mitton, Simon, 1946-
QB43.2.C35　　520　　*LC* 77-2766　　*ISBN* 0517528061

**Field, George B., 1929-.**　　**5.1700**
The invisible universe: probing the frontiers of astrophysics / by George B. Field and Eric J. Chaisson; astronomical images and descriptions by Thomas P. Stephenson. — Boston: Birkhäuser, c1985. xiv, 195 p.: ill. (some col.); 25 cm. Includes index. 1. Astronomy 2. Radio astronomy 3. Astrophysics I. Chaisson, Eric. II. Stephenson, Thomas P. III. T.
QB43.2.F54 1985　　520 19　　*LC* 84-24621　　*ISBN* 0817632352

**Henbest, Nigel.**　　**5.1701**
The new astronomy / Nigel Henbest, Michael Marten. — Cambridge [Cambridgeshire]; New York: Cambridge University Press, 1983. 240 p.: ill. (some col.); 29 cm. Includes index. 1. Astronomy I. Marten, Michael. II. T.
QB43.2.H463 1983　　520 19　　*LC* 83-7716　　*ISBN* 0521256836

**Hoyle, Fred, Sir.**　　**5.1702**
Astronomy and cosmology: a modern course / Fred Hoyle. — San Francisco: W. H. Freeman, [1975] xiv, 711 p., [8] leaves of plates: ill.; 24 cm. 1. Astronomy 2. Cosmology I. T.
QB43.2.H69　　520　　*LC* 74-28441　　*ISBN* 0716703513

**Kaufmann, William J.**　　**5.1703**
Universe / William J. Kaufmann, III. — New York: W.H. Freeman, c1985. xvi, 594 p.: ill. (some col.); 27 cm. 1. Astronomy 2. Cosmology I. T.
QB43.2.K38 1985　　523 19　　*LC* 84-13830　　*ISBN* 0716716739

**National Research Council (U.S.). Astronomy Survey**　　**5.1704**
Committee.
Astronomy and astrophysics for the 1980's / Astronomy Survey Committee, Assembly of Mathematical and Physical Sciences, National Research Council. — Washington, D.C.: National Academy Press, 1982. 189 p.: ill.; 23 cm. Includes index. 1. Astronomy 2. Astrophysics I. T.
QB43.2.N38 1982　　520 19　　*LC* 82-8014　　*ISBN* 0309032490

**Pasachoff, Jay M.**　　**5.1705**
University astronomy / Jay M. Pasachoff, Marc L. Kutner. — Philadelphia: Saunders, 1978. xvii, 763 p.: ill. — (Saunders golden sunburst series) 1. Astronomy I. Kutner, Marc Leslie. joint author. II. T.
QB43.2.P36　　QB43.2 P36.　　520　　*LC* 77-11347

**Shu, Frank H.**　　**5.1706**
The physical universe: an introduction to astronomy / Frank H. Shu. — Mill Valley, Calif.: University Science Books, c1982. xi, 584 p., [16] p. of plates: ill. (some col.); 29 cm. — (Series of books in astronomy.) Includes index. 1. Astronomy I. T. II. Series.
QB43.2.S54 1982　　523 19　　*LC* 81-51271　　*ISBN* 0935702059

**The State of the universe / edited by Geoffrey Bath.**　　**5.1707**
Oxford: Clarendon Press; New York: Oxford University Press, 1980. vii, 199 p., [4] leaves of plates: ill.; 25 cm. (Wolfson College lectures; 1979) 1. Astronomy I. Bath, Geoffrey.
QB43.2.S73　　521 19　　*LC* 79-41393　　*ISBN* 0198575491

**Moore, Patrick.**　　**• 5.1708**
Suns, myths, and men. — New York: Norton, [1969, c1968] 236 p.: ill.; 22 cm. — (The Amateur astronomer's library) 1. Astronomy I. T.
QB44.M56 1969　　523　　*LC* 79-1749

**Pickering, James S. (James Sayre)**　　**5.1709**
1001 questions answered about astronomy / by James S. Pickering. — Fully rev. and brought up to date / by Patrick Moore. — New York: Dodd, Mead & Co., 1976. ix, 420 p., [8] leaves of plates: ill. Includes index. 1. Astronomy 2. Questions and answers — Astronomy. I. Moore, Patrick. II. T.
QB44.P63 1976　　520　　*LC* 75-4045　　*ISBN* 0396071848

**Sky & telescope.**　　**• 5.1710**
Wanderers in the sky; the motions of planets and space probes. Edited by Thornton Page & Lou Williams Page. — New York: Macmillan Co., [1965] xiv, 338 p.: illus.; 23 cm. — (Sky and telescope library of astronomy, v. 1) 1. Astronomy — Popular works. 2. Astronautics in astronomy I. Page, Thornton. ed. II. Page, Lou Williams. ed. III. T.
QB44.S5734　　523　　*LC* 65-12722

**Alter, Dinsmore, 1888-1968.**　　**5.1711**
Pictorial astronomy / Dinsmore Alter, Clarence H. Cleminshaw, John G. Phillips. — 5th rev. ed. — New York: Harper & Row, c1983. 374 p.: ill.; 28 cm. Includes index. 1. Astronomy — Popular works. I. Cleminshaw, Clarence H. (Clarence Higbee), 1902- II. Phillips, John G. (John Gardner), 1917- III. T.
QB44.2.A45 1983　　523 19　　*LC* 81-47878　　*ISBN* 0061810193

**Asimov, Isaac, 1920-.**　　**5.1712**
The universe: from flat earth to black holes—and beyond / Isaac Asimov. — 3d ed., rev. — New York: Walker, c1980. 321 p., [8] leaves of plates: ill.; 25 cm. Includes index. 1. Astronomy — Popular works. I. T.
QB44.2.A84 1980　　523 19　　*LC* 79-48052　　*ISBN* 080270655X

**Ditfurth, Hoimar von.**　　**5.1713**
[Kinder des Weltalls. English] Children of the universe; the tale of our existence. Translated from the German by Jan van Heurck. [1st ed.] New York, Atheneum, 1974. viii, 301 p. illus. 25 cm. Translation of Kinder des Weltalls. 1. Astronomy — Popular works. I. T.
QB44.2.D5513 1974　　520　　*LC* 73-91629　　*ISBN* 0689105886

**Gribbin, John R.**　　**5.1714**
Genesis: the origins of man and the universe / John Gribbin. — New York: Delacorte Press/Eleanor Friede, c1981. xvi, 360 p.: ill.; 24 cm. Includes index. 1. Astronomy 2. Life — Origin I. T.
QB44.2.G753　　577 19　　*LC* 80-24267　　*ISBN* 0440028329

**Jastrow, Robert, 1925-.**　　**5.1715**
Red giants and white dwarfs / Robert Jastrow. — New ed. — New York: W. W. Norton, c1979. 275 p.: ill.; 24 cm. Includes index. 1. Astronomy — Popular works. 2. Life — Origin I. T.
QB44.2.J36 1979　　523.1/2 19　　*LC* 80-130433　　*ISBN* 0393850021

**Moore, Patrick.**　　**5.1716**
The new atlas of the universe / Patrick Moore. — New York: Crown, c1984. 271 p.: ill. (some col.); p. cm. Rev. ed. of: The concise atlas of the universe. Completely rev. 1974. Includes index. 1. Astronomy — Popular works. I. Moore, Patrick. Concise atlas of the universe. II. T.
QB44.2.M66 1984　　523 19　　*LC* 84-4246　　*ISBN* 051755500X

**Abell, George O. (George Ogden), 1927-1983.**    **5.1717**
Exploration of the universe / George O. Abell, David Morrison, Sidney C. Wolff. — 5th ed. — Philadelphia: Saunders College Pub., 1987. 1 v. (Saunders golden sunburst series) Includes index. 1. Astronomy I. Morrison, David, 1940- II. Wolff, Sidney C. III. T.
QB45.A16 1987    520 19    *LC* 86-26045    *ISBN* 0030051436

**Gaposchkin, Cecilia Helena Payne, 1900-.**    **• 5.1718**
Introduction to astronomy [by] Cecilia Payne–Gaposchkin [and] Katherine Haramundanis. — 2d ed. — Englewood Cliffs, N.J.: Prentice-Hall, [1970] x, 610 p.: illus.; 24 cm. 1. Astronomy I. Haramundanis, Katherine, 1937- joint author. II. T.
QB45.G3 1970    520    *LC* 70-95752    *ISBN* 0134781074

**Jones, Aubrey.**    **5.1719**
Mathematical astronomy with a pocket calculator / Aubrey Jones. — New York: Wiley, 1979 (c1978) 254 p.: ill.; 23 cm. 'A Halsted Press book.' Includes index. 1. Astronomy — Mathematics 2. Calculators I. T.
QB47.J66 1978    522/.028/54    *LC* 78-12075    *ISBN* 0470265523

**Kaufmann, William J.**    **5.1720**
The cosmic frontiers of general relativity / William J. Kaufmann, III. Boston: Little, Brown, c1977. x, 306 p.: ill.; 24 cm. Includes index. 1. Astronomy 2. General relativity (Physics) I. T.
QB47.K38    521    *LC* 76-46800

**Ashbrook, Joseph, d. 1980.**    **5.1721**
The astronomical scrapbook: skywatchers, pioneers, and seekers in astronomy / Joseph Ashbrook; edited by Leif J. Robinson; introduction by Owen Gingerich. — Cambridge [Cambridgeshire]; New York: Cambridge University Press; Cambridge, Mass.: Sky Pub. Corp., 1984. xii, 468 p.: ill.; 24 cm. Includes index. 1. Astronomy — Addresses, essays, lectures. I. Robinson, Leif J. II. T.
QB51.A77 1984    520 19    *LC* 84-12036    *ISBN* 0521300452

**A Source book in astronomy and astrophysics, 1900–1975 /**    **5.1722**
**edited by Kenneth R. Lang and Owen Gingerich.**
Cambridge, Mass.: Harvard University Press, 1979. xx, 922 p.: ill.; 29 cm. — (Source books in the history of the sciences.) 1. Astronomy — Addresses, essays, lectures. 2. Astrophysics — Addresses, essays, lectures. I. Lang, Kenneth R. II. Gingerich, Owen. III. Series.
QB51.S67    520/.8    *LC* 78-9463    *ISBN* 0674822005

**Space science and astronomy: escape from earth / edited by**    **5.1723**
**Thornton Page and Lou Williams Page.**
New York: Macmillan, c1976. xvii, 467 p.: ill.; 24 cm. (The Macmillan Sky and telescope library of astronomy; v. 9) 'Articles that first appeared in ... Sky and telescope.' Includes index. 1. Astronomy — Addresses, essays, lectures. 2. Astronautics — Addresses, essays, lectures. I. Page, Thornton. II. Page, Lou Williams. III. Sky & telescope.
QB51.S68    520/.8    *LC* 76-5879    *ISBN* 0025943103

**Microcomputers in astronomy / Russell M. Genet, editor; Anna**    **5.1724**
**M. Genet, assistant editor.**
Fairborn, Ohio: Fairborn Observatory, c1983. 253 p.: ill.; 22 cm. 1. Astronomy — Data processing 2. Microcomputers I. Genet, Russell. II. Genet, Anna M.
QB51.3.E43 M525 1983    522/.2/0285416 19    *LC* 85-182774    *ISBN* 0911351035

**Baugher, Joseph F.**    **5.1725**
On civilized stars: the search for intelligent life in outer space / Joseph F. Baugher. — Englewood Cliffs, N.J.: Prentice-Hall, c1985. xi, 260 p.: ill.; 23 cm. (Frontiers of science.) 'A Spectrum book.' Includes index. 1. Life on other planets I. T. Series.
QB54.B38 1985    574.999 19    *LC* 84-18374    *ISBN* 0136344119

**Extraterrestrials–where are they? / edited by Michael H. Hart**    **5.1726**
**and Ben Zuckerman.**
New York: Pergamon Press, c1982. ix, 182 p.: ill.; 24 cm. 1. Life on other planets — Congresses. 2. Life — Origin — Congresses. I. Hart, Michael H. II. Zuckerman, Ben, 1943-
QB54.E95 1982    574.999 19    *LC* 81-1876    *ISBN* 0080263429

**Goldsmith, Donald.**    **5.1727**
The search for life in the universe / Donald Goldsmith, Tobias Owen. — Menlo Park, Calif.: Benjamin/Cummings Pub. Co., c1980. xi, 434 p.: ill.; 24 cm. 1. Life on other planets 2. Astronomy I. Owen, Tobias C. joint author. II. T.
QB54.G58    574.999    *LC* 79-18653    *ISBN* 0805333258

**Life in the universe / John Billingham, editor.**    **5.1728**
1st MIT Press ed. — Cambridge, Mass.: MIT Press, 1982 (c1981). xix, 461 p.: ill.; 26 cm. Proceedings of the Conference on Life in the Universe, held at NASA Ames Research Center, June 19-20, 1979. 1. Life on other planets — Congresses. I. Billingham, John. II. Ames Research Center. III. Conference on Life in the Universe (1979: Ames Research Center)
QB54.L483    574.999 19    *LC* 81-15626    *ISBN* 0262520621

**Sagan, Carl, 1934-.**    **5.1729**
The cosmic connection: an extraterrestrial perspective / produced by Jerome Agel. — [1st ed.]. — Garden City, N.Y.: Anchor Press, 1973. xiii, 274 p.: ill.; 22 cm. 1. Life on other planets 2. Life — Origin I. T.
QB54.S24    523    *LC* 73-81117    *ISBN* 0385004575

# QB63–68 Guides. Atlases

**Howard, Neale E.**    **5.1730**
The telescope handbook and star atlas / by Neale E. Howard. — Updated ed. — New York: Crowell, [1975] ix, 226 p.: ill.; 29 cm. Includes index. 1. Astronomy — Observers' manuals I. T.
QB63.H68 1975    523/.002/02    *LC* 75-6601    *ISBN* 0690006861

**Liller, William, 1927-.**    **5.1731**
The Cambridge astronomy guide: a practical introduction to astronomy / William Liller and Ben Mayer. — Cambridge [Cambridgeshire]; New York: Cambridge University Press, 1985. 176 p.: ill. (some col.); 24 cm. Includes index. 1. Astronomy — Amateurs' manuals. I. Mayer, Ben. II. T.
QB63.L55 1985    523 19    *LC* 85-16582    *ISBN* 0521257786

**Burnham, Robert.**    **5.1732**
[Celestial handbook] Burnham's celestial handbook: an observer's guide to the Universe beyond the solar system / Robert Burnham, Jr. — Rev. and enl. ed. — New York: Dover Publications, 1978. 3 v. (2138 p.): ill.; 24 cm. Includes indexes. 1. Astronomy — Observers' manuals I. T. II. Title: Celestial handbook.
QB64.B85 1978    523.8/9    *LC* 77-82888    *ISBN* 048623567X

**Evans, David Stanley.**    **• 5.1733**
Observation in modern astronomy [by] David S. Evans. — New York: American Elsevier Pub. Co., 1968. xiv, 273 p.: illus.; 26 cm. 1. Astronomy — Observers' manuals I. T.
QB64.E86x    522    *LC* 67-20394

**Menzel, Donald Howard, 1901-.**    **5.1734**
A field guide to the stars and planets / Donald H. Menzel and Jay M. Pasachoff; with monthly sky maps and atlas charts by Wil Tirion. — 2nd ed., completely rev. and enl. — Boston: Houghton Mifflin, 1983. x, 473 p.: ill. (some col.); 20 cm. — (Peterson field guide series.) Includes index. 1. Astronomy — Observers' manuals I. Pasachoff, Jay M. II. T. III. Series.
QB64.M4 1983    523 19    *LC* 83-8392    *ISBN* 039534641X

**Muirden, James.**    **5.1735**
The amateur astronomer's handbook / James Muirden. — 3rd ed. — New York: Harper & Row, c1983. 472 p.: ill.; 24 cm. Includes index. 1. Astronomy — Observers' manuals I. T.
QB64.M85 1983    520 19    *LC* 81-48044    *ISBN* 0061816221

**Robinson, J. Hedley.**    **5.1736**
Astronomy data book / J. Hedley Robinson and James Muirden. — 2d ed. — New York: Wiley, c1979. 272 p., [1] fold. leaf of plates: ill.; 23 cm. 'A Halsted book.' Includes index. 1. Astronomy — Observers' manuals I. Muirden, James. joint author. II. T.
QB64.R58 1979    523    *LC* 78-21698    *ISBN* 0470265949

**Bečvář, Antonín, 1901-.**    **5.1737**
Atlas coeli 1950.0. [4. vyd.]. Praha: Nakl. Československé akademie věd, 1962. [4] p., 16 col. charts; 42 x 59 cm. Transparent sheet with locating and measuring device inserted. 1. Stars — Atlases I. T.
QB65.B38 1962    *LC* 64-28084

**Dixon, Robert S.**    **5.1738**
A master list of nonstellar optical astronomical objects / compiled by Robert S. Dixon and George Sonneborn. — [Columbus]: Ohio State University Press, c1980. 835 p.; 29 cm. 1. Astronomy — Catalogs. I. Sonneborn, George. joint author. II. T.
QB65.D56    523    *LC* 79-27627    *ISBN* 0814202500

**Grand atlas de l'astronomie. English.**    **5.1739**
The Cambridge atlas of astronomy / edited by Jean Audouze and Guy Israel. — Cambridge [Cambridgeshire]; New York: Cambridge University Press, c1985. 432 p.: ill. (some col.); 37 cm. Translation of: Le Grand atlas de l'astronomie. Includes index. 1. Astronomy — Charts, diagrams, etc. I. Audouze, Jean. II. Israël, Guy. III. T. IV. Title: Atlas of astronomy.
QB65.G6813 1985    523 19    *LC* 84-73453    *ISBN* 0521263697

**Norton, Arthur P. (Arthur Philip)**    **5.1740**
[Star atlas and reference handbook (epoch 1950.0)] Norton's star atlas and reference handbook (Epoch 1950.0) / by Arthur P. Norton. — 17th ed. / the reference handbook and lists of interesting objects revised and rewritten by

Christopher R. Kitchin ... [et al.]; edited by Gilbert E. Satterthwaite in consultation with Patrick Moore & Robert G. Inglis. — Edinburgh: Gall and Inglis, 1978. viii, 116, [36] p., [2] leaves of plates: ill., charts (chiefly col.); 29 cm. Includes indexes. 1. Astronomy — Observers' manuals I. Kitchin, C. R. (Christopher R.) II. Satterthwaite, Gilbert Elliott. III. Moore, Patrick. IV. Inglis, R. M. G. V. T. VI. Title: Star atlas and reference handbook (Epoch 1950.0)
QB65.N7 1978     523     *LC* 78-325890     *ISBN* 0852489005

**Smithsonian Astrophysical Observatory.**       **5.1741**
Smithsonian Astrophysical Observatory star atlas of reference stars and nonstellar objects / prepared by the staff; foreword by Joseph Ashbrook. — Cambridge, Mass.: MIT Press [1969] 1 case (ix, 13 p., 2 charts, 152 plates); 38 cm. Title on case: Star atlas of reference stars and nonstellar objects. On plates: SAO star chart—1967; equinox and epoch 1950.0; FK4 system; scale 6'.95/mm. Projections: Stereographic polar, Lambert conic, or Mercator. Includes an overlay 'Interpolation reseaux.' Companion vol. to the observatory's Star catalog, published in 1966. 1. Stars — Atlases I. T. II. Title: Star atlas of reference stars and nonstellar objects.
QB65.S65     523.89/03     *LC* 75-84659     *ISBN* 0262190613

**Snyder, George Sergeant.**       **5.1742**
Maps of the heavens / by George Sergeant Snyder. — 1st ed. — New York: Abbeville Press, c1984. 144 p.: ill. (some col.); 39 cm. 1. Astronomy — Charts, diagrams, etc. I. T.
QB65.S95 1984     523/.0022/2 19     *LC* 84-6478     *ISBN* 0896594564

**Tirion, Wil.**       **5.1743**
Sky atlas 2000.0: 26 star charts, covering both hemispheres / Wil Tirion. — Deluxe ed. — Cambridge, Mass.: Cambridge University Press: Sky Pub. Corp., 1981. [2] folded p., 26 folded leaves: 26 maps; 41 cm. Transparent overlay of projection grinds laid in. Includes index to constellations and index maps to charts. Includes index. 1. Stars — Atlases I. T.
QB65.T54 1981     523.8/9 19     *LC* 81-52999     *ISBN* 0933346336

**Warner, Deborah Jean.**       **5.1744**
The sky explored: celestial cartography, 1500–1800 / Deborah J. Warner. — New York: A. R. Liss, c1979. xvii, 293 p.: ill.; 29 cm. Includes index. 1. Stars — Atlases — History. 2. Stars — Catalogs — History. 3. Cartography — History I. T.
QB65.W36     523.8/9     *LC* 78-24737     *ISBN* 0845117009

# QB81–88 Observatories. Astronomical Instruments. Telescopes

**Marx, Siegfried, 1934-.**       **5.1745**
[Sternwarten der Welt. English] Observatories of the world / Siegfried Marx, Werner Pfau; [translated from the German by C.S.V. Salt; edited and revised by Simon Mitton]. — New York: Van Nostrand Reinhold, 1982. 199 p.: ill. (some col.); 23 cm. Translation of: Sternwarten der Welt. Includes index. 1. Astronomical observatories I. Pfau, Werner. II. Mitton, Simon, 1946- III. T.
QB81.M3913 1982     522/.1 19     *LC* 81-70024     *ISBN* 0442262701

**Hiltner, William Albert, 1914- ed.**       • **5.1746**
Astronomical techniques. Chicago: University Press [1962] xxi, 635 p.: ill., diagrs., tables; 25 cm. (Stars and stellar systems; compendium of astronomy and astrophysics, v. 2) 1. Astronomical instruments I. T.
QB86.H5     520.78     *LC* 62-9113

**IAU Colloquium. (67th: 1981: Zelenchukskaia, R.S.F.S.R.)**       **5.1747**
Instrumentation for astronomy with large optical telescopes: proceedings of IAU Colloquium no. 67, held at Zelenchukskaya, U.S.S.R., 8–10 September, 1981 / edited by Colin M. Humphries. — Dordrecht, Holland; Boston, U.S.A.: D. Reidel Pub. Co.; Hingham, MA: Sold and distributed in the U.S.A. and Canada by Kluwer Boston, c1982. xvii, 321 p.: ill.; 25 cm. — (Astrophysics and space science library; v. 92) 1. Astronomical instruments — Congresses. 2. Telescope — Congresses. I. Humphries, Colin M. (Colin Michael), 1938- II. T. III. Series.
QB86.I57 1982     522/.2 19     *LC* 81-23374

**Kuiper, Gerard Peter, 1905- ed.**       • **5.1748**
Telescopes, edited by Gerard P. Kuiper and Barbara M. Middlehurst. [Chicago] University of Chicago Press [1961, c1960] xv, 255 p.: illus., diagrs., tables. 25 cm. (Stars and stellar systems; compendium of astronomy and astrophysics, 1) 1. Telescope 2. Astronomical observatories I. Middlehurst, Barbara M. ed. II. T.
QB88.K8     522.2     *LC* 60-14356

**Muirden, James.**       **5.1749**
How to use an astronomical telescope: a beginner's guide to observing the cosmos / by James Muirden. — New York: Linden Press/Simon & Schuster, 1985. 397 p.: ill.; 25 cm. Includes index. 1. Telescope — Amateurs' manuals. I. T.
QB88.M85 1985     522/.2 19     *LC* 84-21777     *ISBN* 0671477447

**Sky & telescope.**       • **5.1750**
Telescopes; how to make them and use them. Edited by Thornton Page & Lou Williams Page. — New York: Macmillan, [1966] xiv, 338 p.: illus., ports.; 27 cm. — (The Macmillan sky and telescope library of astronomy, v. 4) 1. Telescope I. Page, Thornton. ed. II. Page, Lou Williams. ed. III. T.
QB88.S62     522.2     *LC* 66-22532

**Astronomy from space: Sputnik to space telescope / edited by**       **5.1751**
**James Cornell and Paul Gorenstein.**
Cambridge, Mass.: MIT Press, c1983. viii, 248 p.: ill.; 24 cm. 1. Space astronomy I. Cornell, James. II. Gorenstein, Paul.
QB136.A79 1983     522 19     *LC* 83-9349     *ISBN* 0262030977

# QB140–341 PRACTICAL AND SPHERICAL ASTRONOMY. TIME. GRAVITY

**Brown, R. Hanbury (Robert Hanbury)**       **5.1752**
Man and the stars / Hanbury Brown. — Oxford; New York: Oxford University Press, 1978. ix, 185 p.: ill.; 26 cm. Includes indexes. 1. Astronomy, Spherical and practical I. T.
QB145.B75     522     *LC* 78-40237     *ISBN* 0198510012

**Mueller, Ivan Istran, 1930-.**       • **5.1753**
Spherical and practical astronomy: as applied to geodesy / [by] Ivan I. Mueller. With a contribution by Heinrich Eichhorn. — New York: F. Ungar Pub. Co. [1969] xxx, 615 p.: ill., maps; 24 cm. 1. Astronomy, Spherical and practical I. T.
QB145.M8     526/.6     *LC* 68-31453     *ISBN* 0804446679

**Taff, Laurence G., 1947-.**       **5.1754**
Computational spherical astronomy / Laurence G. Taff. — New York: Wiley, c1981. x, 233 p.: ill.; 24 cm. 'A Wiley-Interscience publication.' Includes index. 1. Astronomy, Spherical and practical — Mathematics. I. T.
QB149.T33     522     *LC* 80-18834     *ISBN* 047106257X

**The Enigma of time / compiled and introduced by P.T.**       **5.1755**
**Landsberg.**
Bristol: A. Hilger, c1982. xii, 248 p.: ill.; 24 cm. 1. Time I. Landsberg, Peter Theodore.
QB209.E54 1982     529 19     *LC* 82-195438     *ISBN* 0852745451

**Fraser, J. T. (Julius Thomas), 1923-.**       **5.1756**
The genesis and evolution of time: a critique of interpretation in physics / J.T. Fraser. — Amherst: University of Massachusetts Press, 1982. 205 p.; 23 cm. 1. Time 2. Relativity (Physics) 3. Thermodynamics 4. Life — Origin I. T.
QB209.F7 1982     529 19     *LC* 82-8622     *ISBN* 087023370X

**Whitrow, G. J.**       **5.1757**
The natural philosophy of time / by G. J. Whitrow. — 2d ed. — Oxford: Clarendon Press; New York: Oxford University Press, 1980. ix, 399 p.; 24 cm. 1. Time I. T.
QB209.W45 1980     529     *LC* 79-41145     *ISBN* 0198582129

**Howse, Derek.**       **5.1758**
Greenwich time and the discovery of the longitude / Derek Howse. — Oxford; New York: Oxford University Press, 1980. xviii, 254 p.: ill.; 22 cm. Includes index. 1. Royal Greenwich Observatory — History. 2. Longitude 3. Time — Systems and standards I. T.
QB223.H75     529/.7     *LC* 79-40052     *ISBN* 0192159488

**Narlikar, Jayant Vishnu, 1938-.**       **5.1759**
The lighter side of gravity / Jayant V. Narlikar. — San Francisco: W.H. Freeman, c1982. viii, 194 p.: ill.; 23 cm. Includes index. 1. Gravity I. T.
QB331.N37 1982     521/.1 19     *LC* 81-19496     *ISBN* 0716713446

**Tsuboi, Chūji, 1902-.**       **5.1760**
[Jūryoku. English] Gravity / Chuji Tsuboi. — London; Boston: G. Allen & Unwin, 1983. xiv, 254 p.: ill.; 25 cm. Translation of: Jūryoku. 1979. Includes indexes. 1. Gravity I. T.
QB331.T7313 1983     531/.14 19     *LC* 82-11543     *ISBN* 0045510733

**Bullen, K. E. (Keith Edward), 1906-.**     **5.1761**
The Earth's density [by] K. E. Bullen. — London: Chapman and Hall; New York: Wiley, [1975] xiii, 420 p.: illus.; 25 cm. 'A Halsted Press book.'
1. Seismology 2. Earth — Density I. T.
QB341.B93 1975     551.1     *LC* 74-19282     *ISBN* 0470120606

**Davies, P. C. W.**     **5.1762**
The search for gravity waves / P. C. W. Davies. — Cambridge [Eng.]; New York: Cambridge University Press, 1980. viii, 144 p.: ill.; 22 cm. 1. Gravity waves I. T.
QB341.D38     521.1     *LC* 79-42616     *ISBN* 0521231973

# QB351–421 THEORETICAL ASTRONOMY. CELESTIAL MECHANICS. SATELLITES

**Hagihara, Yūsuke, 1897-.**     **5.1763**
Celestial mechanics. — Cambridge, Mass.: MIT Press, [1970- <76>. v. <1,2,3,5> in. <5>: illus.; 24 cm. Revision of the work originally published beginning in 1947 under title: Tentai rikigaku no kiso. Vol. 5 published by the Japan Society for the Promotion of Science. 1. Mechanics, Celestial I. T.
QB351.H26     521     *LC* 74-95280     *ISBN* 0262080370

**Sterne, Theodore E.**     • **5.1764**
An introduction to celestial mechanics. New York, Interscience Publishers, 1960. 206 p. illus. 21 cm. (Interscience tracts on physics and astronomy. 9)
1. Mechanics, Celestial I. T. II. Series.
QB351.S75     521.1     *LC* 60-16549

**Taff, Laurence G., 1947-.**     **5.1765**
Celestial mechanics: a computational guide for the practitioner / Laurence G. Taff. — New York: Wiley, c1985. xx, 520 p.: ill.; 24 cm. 'A Wiley-Interscience publication.' Includes index. 1. Mechanics, Celestial 2. Gravitation 3. Artificial satellites — Orbits — Measurement. 4. Perturbation (Mathematics) I. T.
QB351.T34 1985     521/.1 19     *LC* 84-20989     *ISBN* 0471893161

**Satellites of Jupiter / edited by David Morrison, with the assistance of Mildred Shapley Matthews; with 47 collaborating authors.**     **5.1766**
Tucson, Ariz.: University of Arizona Press, c1982. x, 972 p.: ill. (some col.); 24 cm. (Space science series.) 1. Satellites — Jupiter. I. Morrison, David, 1940- II. Matthews, Mildred Shapley. III. Series.
QB404.S34 1982     523.9/85 19     *LC* 81-13050     *ISBN* 0816507627

# QB450–480 COSMOCHEMISTRY. ASTROPHYSICS. RADIO ASTRONOMY

**Tayler, R. J. (Roger John)**     **5.1767**
The origin of the chemical elements / [by] R. J. Tayler. — New York: Springer-Verlag, 1972. ix, 169 p.: ill.; 22 cm. — (The Wykeham science series, 23)
1. Cosmochemistry I. T.
QB450.T38     523.01     *LC* 72-193715     *ISBN* 0851092802

**Allen, C. W. (Clabon Walter)**     **5.1768**
Astrophysical quantities / by C.W. Allen. — 3rd ed. 1973, Repr. with corrections 1976. — London: Athelone Press; [Atlantic Highlands] N.J.: [Distributor for] U.S.A. and Canada, Humanities Press, c1976 (1983 printing) x, 310 p.: graphs; 24 cm. 1. Astrophysics — Tables. I. T.
QB461.A564 1983     523.01/0212 19     *LC* 85-6138

**Frontiers of astrophysics / Eugene H. Avrett, editor.**     **5.1769**
Cambridge: Harvard University Press, 1976. vi, 554 p.: ill.; 25 cm.
1. Astrophysics I. Avrett, Eugene H., 1933-
QB461.F79     523.01     *LC* 76-10135     *ISBN* 0674326598. *ISBN* 0674326601 pbk

**Harwit, Martin, 1931-.**     **5.1770**
Astrophysical concepts. — New York: Wiley, [1973] xiv, 561 p.: illus.; 23 cm.
1. Astrophysics I. T.
QB461.H37     523.01     *LC* 73-3135     *ISBN* 0471358207

**Kitchin, C. R. (Christopher R.)**     **5.1771**
Astrophysical techniques / C.R. Kitchin. — Bristol: A. Hilger, c1984. xiv, 438 p.: ill.; 24 cm. Includes index. 1. Astrophysics — Technique. 2. Astronomy — Technique. 3. Astronomical instruments 4. Imaging systems in astronomy I. T.
QB461.K57 1984     523.01 19     *LC* 84-670169     *ISBN* 0852744617

**Lang, Kenneth R.**     **5.1772**
Astrophysical formulae: a compendium for the physicist and astrophysicist / Kenneth R. Lang. — 2d corrected and enl. ed. — Berlin; New York: Springer-Verlag, 1980. xxix, 783 p.: ill.; 25 cm. Includes indexes. 1. Astrophysics — Formulae I. T.
QB461.L36 1980     523.01/02/12     *LC* 80-12918     *ISBN* 0387066055

**Nebulae and interstellar matter / edited by Barbara M. Middlehurst and Lawrence H. Aller.**     • **5.1773**
Chicago: University of Chicago Press [1968] xxii, 835 p.: ill.; 24 cm. (Stars and stellar systems; compendium of astronomy and astrophysics, 7)
1. Astrophysics — Addresses, essays, lectures. 2. Interstellar matter — Addresses, essays, lectures. 3. Nebulae — Addresses, essays, lectures. I. Middlehurst, Barbara M. ed. II. Aller, Lawrence H. (Lawrence Hugh), 1913- ed.
QB461.N4     523.1/135     *LC* 66-13879

**Rose, William K., 1935-.**     **5.1774**
Astrophysics / [by] William K. Rose. — New York: Holt, Rinehart and Winston, [1973] xi, 287 p.: ill.; 24 cm. 1. Astrophysics I. T.
QB461.R58     523.01     *LC* 72-89470     *ISBN* 0030791553

**Pacholczyk, A. G., 1935-.**     • **5.1775**
Radio astrophysics; nonthermal processes in galactic and extragalactic sources [by] A. G. Pacholczyk. — San Francisco: W. H. Freeman, [1970] xxi, 269 p.: illus.; 24 cm. — (A Series of books in astronomy and astrophysics) 1. Radio astrophysics I. T.
QB462.5.P25     523.01/3     *LC* 70-95657     *ISBN* 0716703297

**The Early years of radio astronomy: reflections fifty years after Jansky's discovery / edited by W.T. Sullivan III.**     **5.1776**
Cambridge [Cambridgeshire]; New York: Cambridge University Press, 1984. ix, 421 p.: ill.; 24 cm. 1. Radio astronomy — History. I. Sullivan, Woodruff Turner.
QB475.A25 E37 1984     522/.682 19     *LC* 83-23227     *ISBN* 052125485X

**Classics in radio astronomy / selection and commentary by Woodruff Turner Sullivan, III.**     **5.1777**
Dordrecht, Holland; Boston, U.S.A.: Reidel Pub. Co.; Hingham, MA: Sold and distributed in the U.S.A. and Canada by Kluwer Boston, c1982. xxiv, 348 p.: ill.; 23 cm. — (Studies in the history of modern science. v. 10) Includes indexes.
1. Radio astronomy I. Sullivan, Woodruff Turner. II. Series.
QB475.C55 1982     522/.682 19     *LC* 81-23476     *ISBN* 9027713561

**Kraus, John Daniel, 1910-.**     • **5.1778**
Radio astronomy [by] John D. Kraus. With a chapter on radio–telescope receivers, by Martti E. Tiuri. — New York: McGraw-Hill, [1966] x, 481 p.: illus.; 23 cm. 1. Radio astronomy I. T.
QB475.K7     523.016     *LC* 65-28593

**The Physics of pulsars. Edited by Allen M. Lenchek.**     **5.1779**
New York: Gordon and Breach, [c1972] ix, 173 p.: illus.; 24 cm. — (Topics in astrophysics and space physics) Contains mainly a series of lectures given at the University of Maryland in the fall of 1969. 1. Pulsars — Addresses, essays, lectures. I. Lenchek, Allen M., ed.
QB475.P47 1972     523     *LC* 76-150793     *ISBN* 0677142900

**Rohlfs, K. (Kristen), 1930-.**     **5.1780**
Tools of radio astronomy / Kristen Rohlfs. — Berlin; New York: Springer-Verlag, c1986. xii, 319 p.: ill.; 25 cm. — (Astronomy and astrophysics library.) Includes index. 1. Radio astronomy 2. Radio astronomy — Instruments. I. T. II. Series.
QB475.R63 1986     522/.682 19     *LC* 86-1802     *ISBN* 0387161880

**Ronan, Colin A.**     **5.1781**
Invisible astronomy [by] Colin A. Ronan. — Philadelphia: Lippincott, 1972. xvi, 173 p.: illus.; 23 cm. 1. Radio astronomy 2. Nuclear astrophysics 3. Stars — Spectra I. T.
QB475.R65 1972     522/.682     *LC* 78-165154     *ISBN* 0397006497

**Hey, J. S.**     **5.1782**
The radio universe / by J.S. Hey. — 3rd ed. — Oxford [Oxfordshire]; New York: Pergamon Press, 1983. viii, 246 p.: ill.; 24 cm. — (Pergamon international library of science, technology, engineering, and social studies.) Includes index. 1. Radio astronomy — Popular works. I. T. II. Series.
QB477.H47 1983     522/.682 19     *LC* 82-18982     *ISBN* 008029152X

**Smith, F. Graham (Francis Graham), 1923-.** • 5.1783
Radio astronomy / [by] F. Graham Smith; text figures drawn by Ronald Dickens. — Harmondsworth: Penguin, [1960] 264 p.: ill.; 19 cm. — (Pelican books, A479) 1. Radio astronomy I. T.
QB477.S6 1960       523.016       LC 61-2535

**Lovell, Bernard, Sir, 1913-.** 5.1784
The Jodrell Bank telescopes / Bernard Lovell. — Oxford [Oxfordshire]; New York: Oxford University Press, c1985. xvi, 292 p.: ill.; 25 cm. 1. Nuffield Radio Astronomy Laboratories, Jodrell Bank. 2. Astronomical observatories — England — Decision making. I. T.
QB479.G72 N85 1985       522/.19427/16 19       LC 84-14837       ISBN 0198581785

# QB500–903 DESCRIPTIVE ASTRONOMY

## QB500–701 Universe. Space. Solar System

**Papagiannis, Michael D., 1932-.** 5.1785
Space physics and space astronomy [by] Michael D. Papagiannis. New York, Gordon and Breach Science Publishers [1972] xiv, 293 p. illus. 24 cm. 1. Space sciences 2. Space astronomy I. T.
QB500.P27       500.5       LC 72-179021       ISBN 0677040008

**The World in space: a survey of space activities and issues /** 5.1786
**prepared for UNISPACE 82; United Nations; Ralph Chipman, editor.**
Englewood Cliffs, N.J.: Prentice-Hall, c1982. xiv, 689 p.: ill.; 24 cm. Rev. background papers prepared for the Second United Nations Conference on the Exploration and Peaceful Uses of Outer Space, to be held Aug. 9-21, 1982 in Vienna, Austria. 1. Space sciences 2. Astronautics 3. Outer space — Exploration I. Chipman, Ralph. II. United Nations. III. United Nations Conference on the Exploration and Peaceful Uses of Outer Space. (2nd: 1982: Vienna, Austria)
QB500.W67 1982       333.7/0999 19       LC 82-3794       ISBN 0139677453

**Hartmann, William K.** 5.1787
Moons and planets; an introduction to planetary science [by] William K. Hartmann. — Tarrytown-on-Hudson, N.Y.: Bogden & Quigley, [1972] xi, 404 p.: illus.; 25 cm. 1. Solar system I. T.
QB501.H37       523.2       LC 70-170777       ISBN 0800500326

**Man and cosmos: nine Guggenheim lectures on the solar system** 5.1788
**/ sponsored by the Smithsonian Institution; edited by James Cornell and E. Nelson Hayes; with an introd. by Thornton Page.**
1st ed. — New York: Norton, [1975] 191 p.: ill.; 24 cm. 'A Smithsonian special publication.' 1. Solar system — Addresses, essays, lectures. I. Cornell, James. II. Hayes, Eugene Nelson, 1920- III. Smithsonian Institution.
QB501.M35 1975       523.2       LC 75-6687       ISBN 0393064026

**Moore, Patrick.** 5.1789
Atlas of the solar system / Patrick Moore & Garry Hunt. — Chicago: Rand McNally, 1983. 464 p.: ill. (some col.); 29 cm. 'Published in association with the Royal Astronomical Society.' Includes index. 1. Solar system — Handbooks, manuals, etc. I. Hunt, Garry E. II. Royal Astronomical Society. III. T.
QB501.M687 1983       523.2 19       LC 83-61018       ISBN 0528811223

**The New solar system / edited by J. Kelly Beatty, Brian** 5.1790
**O'Leary, Andrew Chaikin; introduction by Carl Sagan.**
2nd ed. — Cambridge, Mass.: Sky Pub. Corp.; Cambridge [Cambridgeshire]; New York: Cambridge University Press, 1982. 240 p.: ill. (some col.); 29 cm. Includes index. 1. Solar system I. Beatty, J. Kelly. II. O'Leary, Brian, 1940- III. Chaikin, Andrew, 1956-
QB501.N47 1982       523.2 19       LC 82-4396       ISBN 0521249880

**Sky & telescope.** • 5.1791
The origin of the solar system: genesis of the sun and planets, and life on other worlds / edited by Thornton Page & Lou Williams Page. — New York: Macmillan, [1966] xiv, 336 p.: ill.; 23 cm. — (Sky and telescope library of astronomy, v. 3) Articles originally published in slightly different form in Sky and telescope and its predecessors the Sky and the Telescope. 1. Solar system I. Page, Thornton. ed. II. Page, Lou Williams. ed. III. T.
QB501.S56       523.2       LC 66-15028

**Gamow, George, 1904-1968.** • 5.1792
A star called the sun. — New York: Viking Press, [1964] xiii, 208 p.: illus. (part col.) ports.; 22 cm. 1. Sun I. T.
QB521.G26       523.7       LC 64-13594

**Nicolson, Iain.** 5.1793
The sun / Iain Nicolson; foreword by Archie E. Roy. — New York: Published in association with the Royal Astronomical Society [by] Rand McNally, c1982. 96 p.: ill. (some col.); 29 cm. — (Rand McNally library of astronomical atlases for amateur and professional observers.) Includes index. 1. Sun I. Royal Astronomical Society. II. T. III. Series.
QB521.N53 1982       523.7 19       LC 80-53882       ISBN 0528815407

**Mitton, Simon, 1946-.** 5.1794
Daytime star, the story of our sun / Simon Mitton. — New York: Scribner, c1981. xv, 191 p.: ill.; 22 cm. Includes index. 1. Sun — Popular works. I. T.
QB521.4.M57       523.7 19       LC 81-669       ISBN 0684168405

**Zirin, Harold.** • 5.1795
The solar atmosphere. — Waltham, Mass.: Blaisdell Pub. Co., [1966] ix, 501 p.: ill.; 23 cm. — (A Blaisdell book in the pure and applied sciences) 1. Solar atmosphere I. T.
QB528.Z5       523.7       LC 65-21458

**Newton, Robert R.** 5.1796
Medieval chronicles and the rotation of the earth [by] Robert R. Newton. — Baltimore: Johns Hopkins University Press, [1972] xvii, 825 p.; 23 cm. 1. Eclipses, Solar 2. Astronomy, Medieval I. T.
QB542.N57       523.7/8/0902       LC 78-39780       ISBN 0801814022

**Cadogan, Peter H.** 5.1797
The moon: our sister planet / Peter H. Cadogan. — Cambridge [Eng.]; New York: Cambridge University Press, 1981. viii, 391 p.: ill.; 26 cm. Includes index. 1. Moon I. T.
QB581.C32       523.3 19       LC 80-41564       ISBN 0521236843

**Newton, Robert R.** 5.1798
The moon's acceleration and its physical origins / Robert R. Newton. — Baltimore: Johns Hopkins University Press, c1979-c1984. 2 v.; 24 cm. Includes indexes. 1. Moon — Observations. 2. Acceleration (Mechanics) — Observations. 3. Moon — Origin I. T.
QB581.N54       523.3/3       LC 78-20529       ISBN 0801822165

## QB600–701 PLANETS

**Jackson, Joseph Hollister.** 5.1799
Pictorial guide to the planets / Joseph H. Jackson & John H. Baumert. — 3d ed. — New York: Harper & Row, c1981. viii, 246 p., [2] leaves of plates: ill.; 29 cm. Includes index. 1. Planets I. Baumert, John H. joint author. II. T.
QB601.J3 1981       523.4 19       LC 80-7897       ISBN 0060148691

**Jaki, Stanley L.** 5.1800
Planets and planetarians: a history of theories of the origin of planetary systems / Stanley L. Jaki. — New York: Wiley, [1977] vi, 266 p., [14] leaves of plates: ill.; 25 cm. 'A Halsted Press book.' 1. Planets 2. Planets, Theory of 3. Astronomy — History. 4. Life on other planets I. T.
QB601.J34       521/.54/09 19       LC 77-4200       ISBN 0470991496

**Whipple, Fred Lawrence, 1906-.** 5.1801
Orbiting the sun: planets and satellites of the solar system / Fred L. Whipple. — Cambridge, Mass.: Harvard University Press, 1981. x, 338 p., [4] p. of plates: ill.; 24 cm. (The Harvard books on astronomy) 'A new and enlarged edition of Earth, moon, and planets.' Includes index. 1. Planets 2. Earth 3. Moon I. T.
QB601.W6 1981       523.2 19       LC 80-19581       ISBN 0674641256

**Williams, Iwan Prys.** 5.1802
The origin of the planets / I. P. Williams. Bristol: A. Hilger, 1975. vi, 108 p.; 26 cm. (Monographs on astronomical subjects) Includes indexes. 1. Planets — Origin I. T.
QB602.9.W54       521/.54       LC 76-376248       ISBN 0852742584

**Chamberlain, Joseph W. (Joseph Wyan), 1928-.** 5.1803
Theory of planetary atmospheres: an introduction to their physics and chemistry / Joseph W. Chamberlain; in collaboration with Donald M. Hunten. — 2nd ed. — Orlando: Academic Press, 1987. xiv, 481 p.: ill.; 24 cm. — (International geophysics series. v. 36) 1. Planets — Atmospheres I. Hunten, Donald M. II. T. III. Series.
QB603.A85 C48 1987       551.5/0999/2 19       LC 86-10850       ISBN 0121672514

**Glass, Billy P.** 5.1804
Introduction to planetary geology / Billy P. Glass. — Cambridge [Cambridgeshire]; New York: Cambridge University Press, 1982. x, 469 p.,

[12] p. of plates: ill. (some col.); 25 cm. Includes index. 1. Planets — Geology I. T.
QB603.G46 G58 1982     559.9/2 19     *LC* 81-17057     *ISBN* 0521235790

**Guest, John.**     5.1805
Planetary geology / John Guest, with Paul Butterworth, John Murray, and William O'Donnell. — New York: Wiley, c1979. 208 p.: ill.; 25 cm. 'A Halsted Press book.' Includes index. 1. Planets — Geology — Pictorial works. 2. Lunar geology — Pictorial works. I. T.
QB603.G46 G83 1979     559.9/2 19     *LC* 80-106687     *ISBN* 0470268875

**Hubbard, William B.**     5.1806
Planetary interiors / William B. Hubbard. — New York, N.Y.: Van Nostrand Reinhold, c1984. ix, 334 p.: ill.; 24 cm. Includes index. 1. Planets — Internal structure I. T.
QB603.I53 H83 1984     559.9/2 19     *LC* 83-23296     *ISBN* 0442237049

**Ohring, George.**     • 5.1807
Weather on the planets: what we know about their atmospheres. — Garden City, N.Y.: Anchor Books, 1966. x, 144 p.: ill.; 18 cm. — (Science study series, S47. Selected topics in the atmospheric sciences) 1. Planetary meteorology I. T.
QB603.O36     523.4     *LC* 66-17455

**Elliot, James, 1943-.**     5.1808
Rings: discoveries from Galileo to Voyager / James Elliot and Richard Kerr. — Cambridge, Mass.: MIT Press, 1985 (c1984). xi, 209 p.: ill.; 24 cm. Includes index. 1. Planetary rings I. Kerr, Richard. II. T.
QB603.R55 E44     523.4 19     *LC* 84-9721     *ISBN* 0262050315

**Briggs, Geoffrey, 1941-.**     5.1809
The Cambridge photographic atlas of the planets / Geoffrey Briggs, Fredric Taylor. — Cambridge [Cambridgeshire]; New York: Cambridge University Press, 1982. 255 p.: ill. (some col.), maps; 31 cm. 1. Planets — Photographs I. Taylor, F. W. II. T.
QB605.B74 1982     523.4/9 19     *LC* 81-38529     *ISBN* 0521239761

**Chapman, Clark R.**     5.1810
The inner planets: new light on the rocky worlds of Mercury, Venus, Earth, the moon, Mars, and the asteroids / Clark R. Chapman. — New York: Scribner, c1977. xvi, 170 p.: ill.; 22 cm. Rev. ed. published as: Planets of rock and ice. 1982. Includes index. 1. Mercury (Planet) 2. Venus (Planet) 3. Earth 4. Mars (Planet) I. T.
QB611.C44     559.9     *LC* 76-58914     *ISBN* 0684148986

**Burgess, Eric.**     5.1811
Venus, an errant twin / Eric Burgess. — New York: Columbia University Press, 1985. 160 p.: ill.; 28 cm. Includes index. 1. Space flight to Venus 2. Venus (Planet) I. T.
QB621.B87 1985     523.4/2 19     *LC* 85-384     *ISBN* 023105856X

**Bodechtel, Johann.**     5.1812
[Weltraumbilder der Erde. English] The Earth from space / Johann Bodechtel and Hans–Gunter Gierloff–Emden; translated by Hildegard Mayhew and Lotte Evans. — New York: Arco Pub. Co., 1974. 176 p.: ill. (some col.); 31 cm. Translation of Weltraumbilder der Erde. 1. Earth — Photographs from space 2. Moon — Photographs from space I. Gierloff-Emden, Hans Günter. joint author. II. T.
QB637.B6313 1974b     910/.02/0222     *LC* 72-97584     *ISBN* 0668029609

**Mission to earth: Landsat views the world / Nicholas M. Short**     5.1813
**... [et al.].**
Washington: Scientific and Technical Office, National Aeronautics and Space Administration: for sale by the Supt. of Docs., U.S. Govt. Print. Off., 1976. ix, 459 p.: ill.; 36 cm. (NASA SP; 360) Includes index. 1. Astronautics in earth sciences 2. Earth — Photographs from space I. Short, Nicholas M.
QB637.M57     910/.02/0222     *LC* 76-608116

**Nicks, Oran W.**     5.1814
This island Earth, edited by Oran W. Nicks. Washington, Scientific and Technical Information Division, Office of Technology Utilization, National Aeronautics and Space Administration; [for sale by the Supt. of Docs., U.S. Govt. Print. Off.] 1970. viii, 182 p. illus. (part col.) 30 cm (NASA SP-250) 1. Earth — Photographs from space I. T.
QB637.N5     910/.02     *LC* 73-608969

**Baker, Victor R.**     5.1815
The channels of Mars / by Victor R. Baker. — 1st ed. — Austin: University of Texas Press, 1982. xiii, 198 p.: ill.; 29 cm. Includes index. 1. Geomorphology 2. Mars (Planet) — Surface I. T.
QB641.B23 1982     559.9/23 19     *LC* 81-7549     *ISBN* 0292710682

**Carr, M. H. (Michael H.)**     5.1816
The surface of Mars / Michael H. Carr. — New Haven: Yale University Press, c1981. xi, 232 p.: ill.; 29 cm. — (Yale planetary exploration series.) Includes index. 1. Mars (Planet) — Surface I. T. II. Series.
QB641.C363     559.9/23 19     *LC* 81-3425     *ISBN* 0300027508

**Moore, Patrick.**     5.1817
Mars [by] Patrick Moore and Charles A. Cross. — New York: Crown Publishers, [1973] 48 p.: illus.; 34 cm. 1. Mars (Planet) I. Cross, Charles A., 1920- joint author. II. T.
QB641.M58     919.9/23     *LC* 73-78847     *ISBN* 0517505274

**Morrison, David, 1940-.**     5.1818
Voyage to Jupiter / David Morrison and Jane Samz. — Washington, D.C.: Scientific and Technical Information Branch National Aeronautics and Space Administration: For sale by the Supt. of Docs., U.S. G.P.O., 1980. xi, 199 p.: ill. (some col.), charts; 26 cm. (NASA SP. 439) S/N 033-000-00797-3 Item 830-I 1. Project Voyager 2. Jupiter probes I. Samz, Jane. II. United States. National Aeronautics and Space Administration. Scientific and Technical Information Branch. III. T. IV. Series.
QB661.M67 1980     559.9/25 19     *LC* 80-600126

**Morrison, David, 1940-.**     5.1819
Voyages to Saturn / David Morrison. — Washington, D.C.: Scientific and Technical Information Branch, National Aeronautics and Space Administration: For sale by the Supt. of Docs., U.S. G.P.O., 1982. ix, 227 p.: ill., (some color); 26 cm. — (NASA SP. 451) Includes index. S/N 033-000-00842-2 Item 830-I 1. Saturn probes 2. Saturn (Planet) — Exploration. 3. Project Voyager 4. Pioneer (Space probes) I. United States. National Aeronautics and Space Administration. Scientific and Technical Information Branch. II. T. III. Series.
QB671.M67 1982     919.9/26 19     *LC* 81-600073

**Saturn / edited by Tom Gehrels, Mildred Shapley Matthews.**     5.1820
Tucson, Ariz.: University of Arizona Press, c1984. xi, 968 p.: ill.; 24 cm. — (Space science series.) Includes index. 1. Saturn (Planet) — Addresses, essays, lectures. I. Gehrels, Tom, 1925- II. Matthews, Mildred Shapley. III. Series.
QB671.S23 1984     523.4/6 19     *LC* 84-2517     *ISBN* 0816508291

**Tombaugh, Clyde William, 1906-.**     5.1821
Out of the darkness, the planet Pluto / Clyde W. Tombaugh, Patrick Moore. — Harrisburg, Pa.: Stackpole Books, c1980. 221 p.: ill.; 24 cm. Includes index. 1. Pluto (Planet) I. Moore, Patrick. joint author. II. T.
QB701.T65 1980     523.4/82     *LC* 80-36881     *ISBN* 0811711633

# QB721–790 Meteors. Interstellar Matter. Comets

**Comets / edited by Laurel L. Wilkening, with the assistance of**     5.1822
**Mildred Shapley Matthews; with 48 collaborating authors.**
Tucson, Ariz.: University of Arizona Press, c1982. x, 766 p.: ill.; 24 cm. — (Space science series.) 1. Comets I. Wilkening, Laurel L. II. Matthews, Mildred Shapley. III. Series.
QB721.C648 1982     523.6 19     *LC* 81-21814     *ISBN* 0816507694

**Whipple, Fred Lawrence, 1906-.**     5.1823
The mystery of comets / by Fred L. Whipple assisted by Daniel W.E. Green. — Washington, D.C.: Smithsonian Institution Press, 1985. xii, 276 p., [8] p. of plates: ill. (some col.); 24 cm. (Smithsonian library of the solar system.) Includes index. 1. Comets — Popular works. I. Green, Daniel W. E. II. T. III. Series.
QB721.4.W47 1985     523.6 19     *LC* 85-8343     *ISBN* 0874749689

**Wasson, John T.**     5.1824
Meteorites: their record of early solar–system history / John T. Wasson. — New York: W.H. Freeman, c1985. vii, 267 p.: ill.; 24 cm. 1. Meteorites 2. Solar system — History. I. T.
QB755.W374 1985     523.5/1 19     *LC* 85-1484     *ISBN* 071671700X

**Spitzer, Lyman, 1914-.**     5.1825
Searching between the stars / Lyman Spitzer, Jr. — New Haven, [Conn.]: Yale University Press, c1982. xv, 179 p.: ill.; 22 cm. — (Mrs. Hepsa Ely Silliman memorial lectures. 46) Includes index. 1. Interstellar matter 2. Astronautics in astronomy I. T. II. Series.
QB790.S68     523.1/12 19     *LC* 81-13138     *ISBN* 0300027095

# QB801–855 Stars. Clusters and Nebulae

**Gaposchkin, Cecilia Helena Payne, 1900-.**                              **5.1826**
Stars and clusters / Cecilia Payne–Gaposchkin. — Cambridge, Mass.: Harvard University Press, 1979. 262 p.: ill.; 25 cm. — (The Harvard books on astronomy) 1. Stars 2. Stars — Clusters I. T.
QB801.G24       523.8       *LC* 79-4472       *ISBN* 0674834402

**Kaplan, S. A. (Samuil Aronovich)**                                     **5.1827**
[Fizika zvezd. English] The physics of stars / by S.A. Kaplan; translated by Renata Feldman. — Chichester [Sussex]; New York: Wiley, [1983] c1982. viii, 158 p.: ill.; 24 cm. Translation of: Fizida zvezd. 3rd ed. Includes index. 1. Stars I. Feldman, Renata. II. T.
QB801.K2813 1983       523.8 19       *LC* 82-2651       *ISBN* 0471103276

**Narlikar, Jayant Vishnu, 1938-.**                                      **5.1828**
From black clouds to black holes / Jayant V. Narlikar. — Singapore; Philadelphia: World Scientific, c1985. viii, 147 p.: ill.; 22 cm. Includes index. 1. Stars 2. Black holes (Astronomy) 3. Astrophysics I. T.
QB801.N29 1985       523.8 19       *LC* 85-3334       *ISBN* 997197813X

**Page, Thornton.**                                                   • **5.1829**
Starlight: what it tells about the stars / edited by Thornton Page & Lou Williams Page. — New York: Macmillan, [1967] xiv, 337 p.: ill.; 23 cm. — (Sky and telescope library of astronomy, v. 5) 'Each of the articles ... is reproduced essentially as it originally appeared in sky and telescope or its predecessors, the sky and the telescope.' 1. Stars I. Page, Lou Williams. joint author. II. T.
QB801.P24       523.8       *LC* 67-12798

**Strand, K. Aage (Kaj Aage), 1907- ed.**                             • **5.1830**
Basic astronomical data. Chicago, University of Chicago Press [1963] 495 p. illus. 25 cm. (Stars and stellar systems, 3) 1. Stars. I. T.
QB801.S75       523.8       *LC* 63-11402

**Asimov, Isaac, 1920-.**                                             **5.1831**
The exploding suns: the secrets of the supernovas / Isaac Asimov; illustrated by D.F. Bach. — 1st ed. — New York: Dutton, c1985. x, 276 p.: ill.; 25 cm. 'Truman Talley books.' Includes index. 1. Stars — Popular works. 2. Supernovae — Popular works. 3. Cosmology — Popular works. I. T.
QB801.6.A85 1985       523.1 19       *LC* 84-21077       *ISBN* 0525243232

**Kippenhahn, Rudolf, 1926-.**                                        **5.1832**
[Hundert Milliarden Sonnen. English] 100 billion suns: the birth, life, and death of the stars / Rudolf Kippenhahn; translated by Jean Steinberg. — New York: Basic Books, c1983. viii, 264 p., [4] leaves of plates: ill. (some col.); 24 cm. Translation of: Hundert Milliarden Sonnen. Includes index. 1. Stars — Evolution I. T. II. Title: One hundred billion suns.
QB806.K5313 1983       521/.58 19       *LC* 82-72398       *ISBN* 0465052630

**Page, Thornton. comp.**                                             • **5.1833**
The evolution of stars: how they form, age, and die. Edited by Thornton Page & Lou Williams Page. New York: Macmillan [1967, c1968] xiv, 334 p.: ill., ports.; 23 cm. (Sky and telescope library of astronomy, v. 6) 'Each of the articles ... is reproduced essentially as it originally appeared in Sky and telescope or its predecessors, the Sky and the Telescope.' 1. Stars — Evolution I. Page, Lou Williams. joint comp. II. Sky & telescope. III. Sky. IV. Telescope. V. T.
QB806.P3       523.8       *LC* 67-28468

**Eichhorn, Heinrich K. (Heinrich Karl), 1927-.**                     **5.1834**
Astronomy of star positions: a critical investigation of star catalogues, the methods of their construction, and their purpose. — New York: Ungar, [1974] xvii, 357 p.; 26 cm. 1. Astrometry 2. Stars — Catalogs I. T.
QB807.E34       523.8/908       *LC* 73-81764       *ISBN* 0804441871

**Van de Kamp, Peter, 1901-.**                                        **5.1835**
Stellar paths: photographic astrometry with long–focus instruments / Peter Van de Kamp; with an introduction by Jean–Claude Pecker. — Dordrecht, Holland; Boston: D. Reidel Pub. Co.; Hingham, MA: Sold and distributed in the U.S.A. and Canada by Kluwer Boston, c1981. xxii, 155 p.: ill.; 25 cm. — (Astrophysics and space science library. v. 85) Includes index. 1. Astrometry I. T. II. Series.
QB807.V33       523.8/1 19       *LC* 81-8505       *ISBN* 9027712565

**Reddish, Vincent C.**                                               **5.1836**
The physics of stellar interiors: an introduction / V. C. Reddish. — Edinburgh: Edinburgh University Press, c1974. vii, 107 p.: ill.; 23 cm. 'The text of a course of fifteen lectures given to astronomy students at the Warner and Swasey Observatory, Case-Western Reserve University, Cleveland, Ohio, in the spring of 1969.' 1. Stars — Structure — Addresses, essays, lectures. I. T.
QB808.R42       523.8/6       *LC* 75-306524       *ISBN* 0852242700

**Greenstein, Jesse Leonard, 1909- ed.**                              • **5.1837**
Stellar atmospheres. [Chicago] University of Chicago Press [1961, c1960] xix, 724 p. illus., diagrs., tables. 25 cm. (Stars and stellar systems; compendium of astronomy and astrophysics, 6) 1. Stars — Atmospheres I. T.
QB809.G7       523.8       *LC* 61-9138

**Novotny, Eva.**                                                     **5.1838**
Introduction to stellar atmospheres and interiors. — New York: Oxford University Press, 1973. xii, 543 p.: illus.; 24 cm. 1. Stars — Atmospheres 2. Stars — Structure I. T.
QB809.N68       523.8       *LC* 72-86302

**Malin, David.**                                                     **5.1839**
Colours of the stars / by David Malin and Paul Murdin. — Cambridge; New York: Cambridge University Press, 1984. ix, 195 p.: ill. (some col.); 29 cm. Includes index. 1. Stars — Color I. Murdin, Paul. II. T.
QB816.M34 1984       523.8/2 19       *LC* 83-20928       *ISBN* 052125714X

**Blaauw, Adriaan. ed.**                                              • **5.1840**
Galactic structure, edited by Adriaan Blaauw and Maarten Schmidt. Contributors: Halton C. Arp [and others]. Chicago, University of Chicago Press [1965] xx, 606 p. illus. 24 cm. (Stars and stellar systems; compendium of astronomy and astrophysics, v. 5) 1. Milky Way I. Schmidt, Maarten. joint ed. II. T.
QB819.B55       523.113       *LC* 64-23428

**Page, Thornton. comp.**                                             • **5.1841**
Stars and clouds of the Milky Way: the structure and motion of our galaxy / edited by Thornton Page & Lou Williams Page. — New York: Macmillan, [1968] xvi, 361 p.: ill., charts, ports.; 23 cm. — (Sky and telescope library of astronomy, v. 7) Articles originally published in slightly different form in the Sky, in Sky and telescope, and in the Telescope. 1. Milky Way I. Page, Lou Williams. joint comp. II. The Sky. III. Sky & telescope. IV. The Telescope. V. T.
QB819.P27       523.1/13/08       *LC* 68-27037

**Hoffmeister, C. (Cuno), 1892-.**                                    **5.1842**
[Veränderliche Sterne. English] Variable stars / C. Hoffmeister, G. Richter, W. Wenzel; translated by S. Dunlop. — Berlin; New York: Springer-Verlag, c1985. xv, 328 p.: ill.; 23 cm. Translation of: Veränderliche Sterne. Includes indexes. 1. Stars, Variable I. Richter, Gerold. II. Wenzel, W. (Wolfgang), 1929- III. T.
QB835.H5913 1985       523.8/44 19       *LC* 85-7928       *ISBN* 0387134034

# QB843–855 SPECIAL TYPES OF STARS. CLUSTERS. NEBULAE

**Kaufmann, William J.**                                              **5.1843**
Black holes and warped spacetime / William J. Kaufmann, III. — San Francisco: W. H. Freeman, c1979. x, 221 p., [8] leaves of plates: ill.; 24 cm. Includes index. 1. Space and time I. T.
QB843.B55 K38       520       *LC* 79-18059       *ISBN* 0716711524

**Moore, Patrick.**                                                   **5.1844**
Black holes in space / Patrick Moore and Iain Nicolson. — New York: Norton, 1976. 126 p.: ill.; 22 cm. Includes index. 1. Black holes (Astronomy) I. Nicolson, Iain. II. T.
QB843.B55 M66 1976       523       *LC* 75-15604       *ISBN* 0393064050

**Shapiro, Stuart L. (Stuart Louis), 1947-.**                         **5.1845**
Black holes, white dwarfs, and neutron stars: the physics of compact objects / Stuart L. Shapiro, Saul A. Teukolsky. — New York: Wiley, c1983. xvii, 645 p.: ill.; 24 cm. 'A Wiley-Interscience publication.' Includes index. 1. Black holes (Astronomy) 2. White dwarfs 3. Neutron stars I. Teukolsky, Saul A. (Saul Arno), 1947- II. T.
QB843.B55 S5 1983       521/.5 19       *LC* 82-20112       *ISBN* 0471873179

**Shipman, Harry L.**                                                 **5.1846**
Black holes, quasars, and the universe / Harry L. Shipman. — 2d ed. — Boston: Houghton Mifflin, c1980. viii, 344 p.: ill.; 24 cm. Includes index. 1. Black holes (Astronomy) 2. Quasars 3. Cosmology I. T.
QB843.B55 S54 1980       523 19       *LC* 79-49834       *ISBN* 0395284996

**Hoffleit, Dorrit.**                                                 **5.1847**
The bright star catalogue: containing data compiled through 1979 / by Dorrit Hoffleit; with the collaboration of Carlos Jaschek. 4th rev. ed. New Haven, Conn.: Yale University Observatory, 1982. xv, 472 p.; 29 cm. Third rev. ed. published as: Catalogue of bright stars. 1. Stars, Brightest — Catalogs. I. Jaschek, Carlos. II. T. III. Title: Catalogue of bright stars.
QB843.B75 B74

**Manchester, Richard N.**     **5.1848**
Pulsars / Richard N. Manchester, Joseph H. Taylor. — San Francisco: W. H. Freeman, c1977. 281 p.: ill.; 25 cm. — (A Series of books in astronomy and astrophysics) Includes indexes. 1. Pulsars I. Taylor, Joseph H., joint author. II. T.
QB843.P8 M36     523     *LC* 77-4206     *ISBN* 0716703580

**Murdin, Paul.**     **5.1849**
Supernovae / Paul Murdin, Lesley Murdin. — Rev. ed. — Cambridge [Cambridgeshire]; New York: Cambridge University Press, 1985. 185 p.: ill.; 26 cm. Rev. ed. of: The new astronomy. c1978. Includes index. 1. Supernovae I. Murdin, Lesley. II. Murdin, Paul. New Astronomy. III. T.
QB843.S95 M87 1985     523 19     *LC* 84-23833     *ISBN* 052130038X

**Mallas, John H.**     **5.1850**
The Messier album: an observer's handbook / by John H. Mallas and Evered Kreimer. — Cambridge [Eng.]; New York: Cambridge University Press, 1979, c1978. viii, 216 p., [16] leaves of plates: ill.; 23 cm. 1. Messier, Charles. 2. Nebulae — Observations. 3. Stars — Clusters — Observations. I. Kreimer, Evered. joint author. II. T.
QB851.M34 1979     523.8/9     *LC* 79-16714     *ISBN* 0521230152

**Shapley, Harlow, 1885-1972.**     • **5.1851**
Galaxies. — [3rd ed.] Rev. by Paul W. Hodge. — Cambridge, Mass.: Harvard University Press, 1972. x, 232 p.: illus.; 25 cm. — (Harvard books on astronomy.) 1. Galaxies I. Hodge, Paul W. II. T. III. Series.
QB851.S47 1972     523.1/12     *LC* 77-169859     *ISBN* 0674340515

**Sulentic, Jack W.**     **5.1852**
The revised new general catalogue of nonstellar astronomical objects / [by] Jack W. Sulentic and William G. Tifft. — Tucson: University of Arizona Press [1973] xxiv, 384 p.; 31 cm. A revision of J. L. E. Dreyer's New general catalogue of nebulae and clusters of stars. 1. Stars — Clusters — Catalogs. 2. Nebulae — Catalogs. 3. Galaxies — Catalogs. I. Tifft, William G., joint author. II. Dreyer, J. L. E. (John Louis Emil), 1852-1926. New general catalogue of nebulae and clusters of stars. III. T.
QB851.S84     523.1/021/6     *LC* 73-83378

**Mitton, Simon, 1946-.**     **5.1853**
The Crab Nebula / Simon Mitton. — 1st U.S. ed. — New York: Scribner, 1979, c1978. 194 p.: ill.; 22 cm. Includes index. 1. Crab Nebula I. T.
QB855.M57 1979     523.1/12     *LC* 78-23381     *ISBN* 0684160773

# QB856–860 Galaxies. Quasars

**Kaufmann, William J.**     **5.1854**
Galaxies and quasars / William J. Kaufmann, III. — San Francisco: W. H. Freeman, c1979. x, 226 p.: ill.; 24 cm. 1. Galaxies 2. Quasars I. T.
QB857.K38     523.1/12     *LC* 79-10570     *ISBN* 0716711338

**Mitton, Simon, 1946-.**     **5.1855**
Exploring the galaxies / Simon Mitton. New York: Scribner, 1977 (c1976). 206 p., [8] leaves of plates: ill.; 23 cm. Includes indexes. 1. Galaxies I. T.
QB857.M57 1976b     523.1/12     *LC* 76-42913     *ISBN* 0684148625

**The Universe of galaxies / compiled by Paul W. Hodge.**     **5.1856**
New York: W.H. Freeman, c1984. 113 p.: ill. (some col.); 28 cm. 'Readings from Scientific American.' Includes index. 1. Galaxies I. Hodge, Paul W. II. Scientific American.
QB857.U55 1984     523.1/12 19     *LC* 84-4090     *ISBN* 0716716755

**Vaucouleurs, Gérard Henri de, 1918-.**     **5.1857**
Second reference catalogue of bright galaxies: containing information on 4364 galaxies with references to papers published between 1964 and 1975 / Gerard de Vaucouleurs, Antoinette de Vaucouleurs, Harold G. Corwin, Jr. — Austin: University of Texas Press, c1976. 396 p.; 29 cm. — (University of Texas monographs in astronomy. no. 2) First ed. published in 1964 under title: Reference catalogue of bright galaxies. 1. Galaxies — Catalogs. I. Vaucouleurs, Antoinette de. joint author. II. Corwin, Harold G. joint author. III. T. IV. Series.
QB857.V38 1976     523.1/12/0216     *LC* 75-44009     *ISBN* 0292755070

**Bok, Bart Jan, 1906-.**     **5.1858**
The Milky Way / Bart J. Bok and Priscilla F. Bok. — 5th ed. — Cambridge, Mass.: Harvard University Press, 1981. viii, 356 p.: ill.; 24 cm. — (The Harvard books on astronomy) Includes index. 1. Milky Way I. Bok, Priscilla Fairfield. joint author. II. T.
QB857.7.B64 1981     523.1/13 19     *LC* 80-22544     *ISBN* 0674575032

**Kühn, Ludwig.**     **5.1859**
[Milchstrassensystem. English] The Milky Way: the structure and development of our star system / Ludwig Kühn. — Chichester [West Sussex]; New York: Wiley, c1982. vii, 151 p.: ill.; 24 cm. Translation of: Das Milchstrassensystem. Includes index. 1. Milky Way I. T.
QB857.7.K8313 1982     523.1/13 19     *LC* 82-2820     *ISBN* 0471102776

**Burbidge, Geoffrey R.**     • **5.1860**
Quasi-stellar objects [by] Geoffrey Burbidge and Margaret Burbidge. — San Francisco: W.H. Freeman, [1967] viii, 235 p.: illus.; 21 cm. — (A Series of books in astronomy and astrophysics) 1. Quasars I. Burbidge, E. Margaret. joint author. II. T.
QB860.B87     523     *LC* 67-17457

**Kahn, F. D. (Franz Daniel)**     **5.1861**
Quasars: their importance in astronomy and physics / by F. D. Kahn and H. P. Palmer. [2nd ed.]. — Cambridge, Mass., Harvard University Press, 1968. 112 p. illus. 22 cm. 1. Quasars I. Palmer, H. P. (Henry Procter) joint author. II. T.
QB860.K3 1968     523

# QB980–991 Cosmogony. Cosmology

**The Very early universe: proceedings of the Nuffield workshop, Cambridge, 21 June to 9 July, 1982 / edited by G.W. Gibbons and S.W. Hawking and S.T.C. Siklos.**     **5.1862**
Cambridge [Cambridgeshire]; New York: Cambridge University Press, 1983. 480 p.: ill.; 24 cm. Proceedings of the Nuffield Workshop on 'The Very Early Universe.' 1. Cosmology — Congresses. I. Gibbons, G. W. II. Hawking, S. W. (Stephen W.) III. Siklos, S. T. C. IV. Title: Nuffield Workshop on 'The Very Early Universe' (1982: Cambridge, Cambridgeshire)
QB980.V46 1983     523.1 19     *LC* 83-7330     *ISBN* 0521253497

**Cosmology + 1: readings from Scientific American / with introd. by Owen Gingerich.**     **5.1863**
San Francisco: W. H. Freeman, c1977. 113 p.: ill.; 29 cm. 1. Cosmology — Addresses, essays, lectures. 2. Stars — Evolution — Addresses, essays, lectures. I. Gingerich, Owen. II. Scientific American.
QB981.C823     523.1/08     *LC* 77-1448     *ISBN* 0716700123

**Durham, Frank, 1935-.**     **5.1864**
Frame of the universe: a history of physical cosmology / Frank Durham, Robert D. Purrington. — New York: Columbia University Press, 1983. ix, 284 p.: ill.; 24 cm. Includes index. 1. Cosmology — History. I. Purrington, Robert D. II. T.
QB981.D89 1983     523.1/09 19     *LC* 82-12990     *ISBN* 0231053924

**Eddington, Arthur Stanley, Sir, 1882-1944.**     • **5.1865**
The expanding universe, by Sir Arthur Eddington ... New York, The Macmillan company; Cambridge, Eng., The University press, 1946. viii, [2], 127 p. 2 pl. (incl. front.) 19.5 cm. 'This book is an expanded version of a public letter delivered at the meeting of the International astronomical union at Cambridge (Massachusetts) in September 1932.'—Pref. 1. Nebulae 2. Cosmology I. T.
QB981.E3     523.1

**Fritzsch, Harald, 1943-.**     **5.1866**
[Vom Urknall zum Zerfall. English] The creation of matter: the universe from beginning to end / Harald Fritzsch; translated by Jean Steinberg. — New York: Basic Books, c1984. x, 307 p.: ill.; 22 cm. Translation of: Vom Urknall zum Zerfall. Includes index. 1. Cosmology 2. Big bang theory 3. Matter — Constitution I. T.
QB981.F7413 1984     523.1 19     *LC* 83-46089     *ISBN* 0465014461

**Gamow, George, 1904-1968.**     • **5.1867**
The creation of the universe. — Rev. ed. — New York: Viking Press, [1961] 147 p.: illus.; 22 cm. 1. Cosmogony I. T.
QB981.G3 1961     523.1     *LC* 61-7387

**Gribbin, John R.**     **5.1868**
White holes: cosmic gushers in the universe / John Gribbin. New York: Delacorte Press/E. Friede, c1977. viii, 296 p.: ill.; 21 cm. Includes index. 1. Cosmology 2. White holes (Astronomy) I. T.
QB981.G78 1977     523.1     *LC* 77-8508     *ISBN* 0440095298

**Hoyle, Fred.**     **5.1869**
From Stonehenge to modern cosmology. — San Francisco: W. H. Freeman, [1972] 96 p.: illus.; 22 cm. Based on lectures delivered in 1971 to the Faculty of Natural Sciences and Mathematics at the State University of New York at

Buffalo. 1. Cosmology — Addresses, essays, lectures. 2. Stonehenge — Addresses, essays, lectures. 3. Science and civilization — Addresses, essays, lectures. I. T.
QB981.H755    523.1/08    LC 72-10836    ISBN 0716703416

**Hoyle, Fred, Sir.**    **5.1870**
Ten faces of the universe / Fred Hoyle. — San Francisco: W. H. Freeman, c1977. ix, 207 p.: ill.; 24 cm. 1. Cosmology I. T.
QB981.H756    523.1    LC 76-44336    ISBN 0716703831 pbk

**Kant, Immanuel, 1724-1804.**    • **5.1871**
[Allgemeine Naturgeschichte und Theorie des Himmels. English] Kant's cosmogony: as in his essay on the retardation of the rotation of the earth and his Natural history and theory of the heavens / translated by W. Hastie; rev. and edited with an introd. and appendix by Willy Ley. — New York: Greenwood Pub. Corp. [1968] xx, 183 p.: port.; 21 cm. Translation of Allgemeine Naturgeschichte und Theorie des Himmels. 1. Nebular hypothesis 2. Earth — Rotation I. Hastie, W. (William), 1842-1903. tr. II. Ley, Willy, 1906-1969. ed. III. T.
QB981.K2 1968    523.1/2    LC 68-58918

**Kaufmann, William J.**    **5.1872**
Relativity and cosmology / William J. Kaufmann, III. — 2d ed. — New York: Harper & Row, c1977. vi, 154 p.: ill.; 24 cm. Includes index. 1. Cosmology 2. General relativity (Physics) I. T.
QB981.K3 1977    523    LC 76-41868    ISBN 0060435720

**Landsberg, Peter Theodore.**    **5.1873**
Mathematical cosmology: an introduction / Peter T. Landsberg and David A. Evans. — Oxford [Eng.]: Clarendon Press, 1978 (c1977). x, 309 p.: ill.; 24 cm. 1. Cosmology — Mathematics. I. Evans, D. A., joint author. II. T.
QB981.L287    523.1/0151    LC 78-305893    ISBN 0198511361

**Morris, Richard, 1939-.**    **5.1874**
The end of the world / Richard Morris. — 1st ed. — Garden City, N.Y.: Anchor Press, 1980. xi, 180 p., [8] leaves of plates: ill.; 21 cm. 1. Cosmology I. T.
QB981.M86    523.1    LC 79-8437    ISBN 0385155239

**Narlikar, Jayant Vishnu, 1938-.**    **5.1875**
Introduction to cosmology / Jayant V. Narlikar. — Boston: Jones and Bartlett, c1983. xv, 470 p., 2 p. of plates: ill. (some col.); 25 cm. Includes index. 1. Cosmology I. T.
QB981.N3 1983    523.1 19    LC 82-16940    ISBN 0867200154

**Peebles, P. J. E. (Phillip James Edwin)**    **5.1876**
Physical cosmology / by P. J. E. Peebles. — Princeton, N.J.: Princeton University Press, 1971. xvi, 282 p.; 24 cm. (Princeton series in physics) 1. Cosmology I. T.
QB981.P42    523.1    LC 74-181520    ISBN 0691081085

**Pellegrino, Charles R.**    **5.1877**
Darwin's universe: origins and crises in the history of life / Charles R. Pellegrino, Jesse A. Stoff. — New York: Van Nostrand Reinhold, c1983. xi, 208 p.: ill.; 24 cm. Includes index. 1. Darwin, Charles, 1809-1882. 2. Life — Origin 3. Cosmology I. Stoff, Jesse A. II. T.
QB981.P44 1983    577 19    LC 82-8352    ISBN 0442275269

**Ronan, Colin A.**    **5.1878**
Deep space / Colin A. Ronan. — 1st American ed. — New York: Macmillan, 1982. 208 p.: ill. (some col.); 30 cm. Includes index. 1. Cosmology 2. Outer space I. T.
QB981.R65 1982    523.1 19    LC 82-9966    ISBN 0026045109

**Rowan-Robinson, Michael.**    **5.1879**
Cosmology / Michael Rowan-Robinson. — 2nd ed. — Oxford: Clarendon Press, 1981. xii, 152 p.: ill.; 23 cm. — (Oxford physics series. 15) Includes indexes. 1. Cosmology I. T. II. Series.
QB981.R69 1981    523.1 19    LC 80-41980    ISBN 0198518579

**Wagoner, Robert V.**    **5.1880**
Cosmic horizons: understanding the universe / Robert V. Wagoner and Donald W. Goldsmith. — San Francisco: W.H. Freeman, c1983. ix, 195 p.: ill.; 24 cm. Reprint. Originally published: Stanford, Calif.: Stanford Alumni Association, 1982. (The Portable Stanford) Includes index. 1. Cosmology 2. Astronomy I. Goldsmith, Donald. II. T.
QB981.W233 1983    523.1 19    LC 82-20994    ISBN 0716714183

**Weinberg, Steven.**    **5.1881**
The first three minutes: a modern view of the origin of the universe / Steven Weinberg. New York: Basic Books, c1977. x, 188 p., [5] leaves of plates: ill.; 22 cm. Includes index. 1. Cosmology I. T.
QB981.W48    523.1/2    LC 76-7682    ISBN 0465024351

**Trefil, James S., 1938-.**    **5.1882**
The moment of creation: big bang physics from before the first millisecond to the present universe / James S. Trefil; illustrations by Gloria Walters. — New York: Scribner, c1983. vi, 234 p.: ill.; 24 cm. Includes index. 1. Big bang theory 2. Cosmology — History. 3. Nuclear astrophysics I. T.
QB991.B54 T7 1983    523.1/8 19    LC 83-9011    ISBN 0684179636

**Rowan-Robinson, Michael.**    **5.1883**
The cosmological distance ladder: distance and time in the universe / Michael Rowan-Robinson. — New York, NY: W.H. Freeman, 1985. ix, 355 p.: ill.; 24 cm. 1. Cosmological distances I. T.
QB991.C66 R68 1984    521 19    LC 84-4088    ISBN 0716715864

## QC1-75 COLLECTED WORKS. REFERENCE. GENERAL WORKS

**Bohr, Niels Henrik David, 1885-1962.**                    **5.1884**
Collected works. General editor: L. Rosenfeld. Amsterdam, North-Holland Pub. Co., 1972- <1985 >. <v. 1-6 > illus., ports. 27 cm. English and Danish. v. 6- : General editor, Erik Rüdinger. Vol. 1-5: Sole distributors for the U.S.A. and Canada: American Elsevier Pub. Co., New York, N.Y.; v. 6- : Sole distributors for the U.S.A. and Canada: Elsevier Science Pub. Co., New York, N.Y. 1. Physics — Collected works. I. Rosenfeld, L. (Leon), 1904-1974. II. T.
QC3.B584    *LC* 70-126498    *ISBN* 0720418003

✓**Fermi, Enrico, 1901-1954.**                    ● **5.1885**
Collected papers: (Note e memorie). [Chicago]: University of Chicago Press, [1962-. v.: ill., ports., facsims.; 27 cm. 1. Physics — Collected works. I. T.
QC3.F39    530.08    *LC* 60-12465

✓**Magie, William Francis, 1858-1943.**                    ● **5.1886**
A source book in physics. — Cambridge: Harvard University Press, 1963. xiv, 620 p.: illus.; 24 cm. — (Source books in the history of the sciences.) 1. Physics — Collected works. 2. Physics — History. I. T. II. Series.
QC3.M26 1963    530.82    *LC* 63-21307

**Szilard, Leo.**                    **5.1887**
The collected works of Leo Szilard / Bernard T. Feld and Gertrud Weiss Szilard, editors, with Kathleen R. Winsor; foreword by Jacques Monod; introductory essays: Carl Eckart [and others] London; Cambridge, Mass.: MIT Press, 1972. 737 p.: ill.; 26 cm. English or German. 1. Physics — Collected works. 2. Biology — Collected works. I. T.
QC3.S97    530/.08    *LC* 79-151153    *ISBN* 0262060396

**Encyclopaedic dictionary of physics: general, nuclear, solid**    **5.1888**
**state, molecular, chemical, metal and vacuum physics, astronomy, geophysics, biophysics, and related subjects / editor-in-chief: J. Thewlis; associate editors: R. C. Glass, D. J. Hughes, A. R. Meetham.**
Oxford: Pergamon Press, 1961-1964. 9 v.: ill. 1. Physics — Dictionaries. I. Thewlis, James.
QC5.E52    QC5.E56.    *LC* 60-7069

**Encyclopedia of physics / edited by Rita G. Lerner and George**    **5.1889**
**L. Trigg; foreword by Walter Sullivan.**
Reading, Mass.: Addison-Wesley Pub. Co., Advanced Book Program, c1981. xvi, 1157 p.: ill.; 29 cm. 1. Physics — Dictionaries. I. Lerner, Rita G. II. Trigg, George L.
QC5.E545    530/.03/21 19    *LC* 80-21175    *ISBN* 0201043130

✓**The Encyclopedia of physics / edited by Robert M. Besançon.**    **5.1890**
3rd ed. — New York: Van Nostrand Reinhold Co., c1985. xvii, 1378 p.: ill.; 27 cm. 1. Physics — Dictionaries. I. Besançon, Robert M. (Robert Martin)
QC5.E546 1985    530/.03/21 19    *LC* 84-13045    *ISBN* 0442257783

**McGraw-Hill dictionary of physics and mathematics / Daniel**    **5.1891**
**N. Lapedes, editor-in-chief.**
New York: McGraw-Hill, c1978. xvi, 1074, 46 p.: ill.; 24 cm. 1. Physics — Dictionaries. 2. Mathematics — Dictionaries 3. Science — Dictionaries I. Lapedes, Daniel N. II. Title: Dictionary of physics and mathematics.
QC5.M23    530/.03    *LC* 78-8983    *ISBN* 0070454809

**Rickards, Teresa.**                    **5.1892**
Barnes & Noble thesaurus of physics / Teresa Rickards; edited by R.C. Denney and Stephen Foster. — New York: Barnes & Noble, c1984. 256 p., [4] p. of plates: ill. (some col.); 20 cm. Includes index. 1. Physics — Dictionaries. I. Denney, Ronald C. II. Foster, Stephen. III. T. IV. Title: Thesaurus of physics.
QC5.R5 1984    530/.03/21 19    *LC* 83-47598    *ISBN* 0060152141

## QC6 Philosophy. Relativity

### QC6 A-C

**Abro, A. d'.**                    ● **5.1893**
The evolution of scientific thought from Newton to Einstein. — 2d ed., rev. and enl. — [New York]: Dover Publications, [1950] 481 p.: ports., diagrs.; 21 cm. 1. Relativity (Physics) 2. Science — Methodology I. T.
QC6.A3 1950    530.1    *LC* 50-9480

**American Association of Physics Teachers.**                    **5.1894**
Special relativity theory: selected reprints. — New York: Pub. for the American association of physics teachers by the American institute of physics [1963]. 108 p.: diagrs. — (American Association of Physics Teachers. Selected reprints) Cover-title. Includes Resource letter SRT-1 prepared by Gerald Holton for the Commission on college physics: p. 1-8. 'A project of the AAPT Committee on resource letters, 1963.' 1. Relativity (Physics) I. Holton, Gerald James. II. American Institute of Physics. III. T. IV. Series.
QC6.A44

✓**Anderson, James L.**                    ● **5.1895**
Principles of relativity physics [by] James L. Anderson. — New York: Academic Press, [1967] xvii, 484 p.: illus.; 24 cm. 1. Relativity (Physics) I. T.
QC6.A48 1967    530.11    *LC* 66-30140

✓**Bohm, David.**                    ● **5.1896**
Causality and chance in modern physics. Foreword by Louis de Broglie. Princeton, N.J., Van Nostrand [c1957] 170 p. illus. 23 cm. 1. Physics — Philosophy I. T.
QC6.B597 1957a    530.1    *LC* 58-1489

✓**Bohr, Niels Henrik David, 1885-1962.**                    ● **5.1897**
[Atomfysik og menneskelig erkendelse. English] Atomic physics and human knowledge. New York, Wiley [1958] viii, 101 p. diagrs. 24 cm. 'This collection of articles ... forms a sequel to earlier essays edited by the Cambridge University Press, 1934, in a volume titled Atomic theory and the description of nature.' 1. Physics — Philosophy 2. Nuclear physics — Addresses, essays, lectures. I. T.
QC6.B598    530.1    *LC* 58-9002

**Bohr, Niels Henrik David, 1885-1962.**                    ● **5.1898**
Essays, 1958-1962, on atomic physics and human knowledge. — [New York: Interscience Publishers, 1963] x, 100 p.: port.; 24 cm. 1. Physics — Philosophy — Addresses, essays, lectures. 2. Nuclear physics — Addresses, essays, lectures. I. T.
QC6.B599 1963    530.1    *LC* 63-21771

✓**Born, Max, 1882-1970.**                    **5.1899**
Einstein's theory of relativity. Rev. ed., prepared with the collaboration of Günther Leibfried and Walter Biem. New York: Dover Publications [c1965] vii, 376 p.: ill.; 21 cm. A revised and enlarged version of the work first published in 1924. 1. Einstein, Albert, 1879-1955. 2. Relativity (Physics) I. T.
QC6.B653 1965    530.11    *LC* 65-1214

**Bridgman, P. W. (Percy Williams), 1882-1961.**                    ● **5.1900**
The logic of modern physics / by P. W. Bridgmen. — New York: The Macmillan company, 1958 [c1927] xiv p., 1 l., 228 p.; 22 1/2 cm. 1. Physics — Philosophy I. T.
QC6.B68    *LC* 27-9657

✓**Bridgman, P. W. (Percy Williams), 1882-1961.**                    ● **5.1901**
The nature of physical theory / by P.W. Bridgman. — New York: Dover Publications, c1936. 138 p.; 21 cm. Published on the Louis Vanuxem Foundation. 1. Physics — Philosophy I. T. II. Title: Physical theory.
QC6.B683 1936a    *LC* 50-43518

✓**Bridgman, P. W. (Percy Williams), 1882-1961.**                    ● **5.1902**
A sophisticate's primer of relativity / prologue and epilogue by Adolf Grünbaum. — [1st ed.]. Middletown, Conn.: Wesleyan University Press, [1962] 191 p.: ill.; 22 cm. 1. Relativity (Physics) I. T.
QC6.B6836 1962    530.11    *LC* 62-18341

**Brillouin, Léon, 1889-.**      • **5.1903**
Relativity reexamined. — New York: Academic Press, 1970. xi, 111 p.: illus.; 21 cm. 1. Relativity (Physics) I. T.
QC6.B72    530.11    *LC* 74-107560    *ISBN* 0121349454

**Davies, P. C. W.**      **5.1904**
Superforce: the search for a grand unified theory of nature / Paul Davies. — New York: Simon and Schuster, c1984. 255 p.: ill.; 24 cm. Includes index. 1. Physics — Philosophy 2. Cosmology 3. Force and energy I. T.
QC6.D327 1984    530.1 19    *LC* 84-5473    *ISBN* 0671476858

## QC6 E–M

**Eddington, Arthur Stanley, Sir, 1882-1944.**      • **5.1905**
The philosophy of physical science. — [Ann Arbor]: University of Michigan Press, 1958. ix, 230 p.; 21 cm. — (Ann Arbor paperbacks, AA20.) "Substance of the course of lectures delivered as Tarner lecturer of Trinity College, Cambridge, in the Easter term 1938." 1. Science — Philosophy 2. Physics — Philosophy 3. Knowledge, Theory of I. T.
QC6.E3 1958    530.1    *LC* 58-14940

**Eddington, Arthur Stanley, Sir, 1882-1944.**      • **5.1906**
The mathematical theory of relativity / by A.S. Eddington ... 2d ed. Cambridge [Eng.]: The University Press, 1960. ix, 270 p.; 28 cm. 'A first draft of this book was published in 1921 as a mathematical supplement to the French edition of Space, time and gravitation.'—Pref. 1. Relativity (Physics) I. T.
QC6.E35 1960    530.1    *LC* 31-32716

**Eddington, Arthur Stanley, Sir, 1882-1944.**      • **5.1907**
Space, time, and gravitation; an outline of the general relativity theory. New York, Harper [1959] 213 p. illus. 21 cm. (Harper torchbooks, TB510. The science library) 1. Space and time 2. Gravitation 3. Relativity (Physics) I. T.
QC6.E4 1959    530.1    *LC* 59-13846

**Einstein, Albert, 1879-1955.**      • **5.1908**
[Über die spezielle und die allgemeine Relativitäts theorie. English] Relativity: the special and the general theory; a popular exposition. Authorized translation by Robert W. Lawson. [17th ed.] New York, Crown Publishers [1961] ix, 164 p. ports. 21 cm. (Bonanza paperback) 1. Relativity (Physics) I. T.
QC6    QC6.E5 1961.    530.1    *LC* 63-6904

**French, A. P. (Anthony Philip), 1920-.**      • **5.1909**
Special relativity [by] A. P. French. New York, Norton [1968] x, 286 p. illus. 24 cm. (The M.I.T. introductory physics series) 1. Special relativity (Physics) I. T.
QC6.F68    530.11    *LC* 68-12180

**Graves, John Cowperthwaite.**      • **5.1910**
The conceptual foundations of contemporary relativity theory / foreword by John Archibald Wheeler. — Cambridge, Mass.: M.I.T. Press, [1971] ix, 361 p.; 24 cm. 1. Relativity (Physics) 2. Science — Philosophy I. T.
QC6.G687    530.1/1    *LC* 77-122257    *ISBN* 0262070405

**Heisenberg, Werner, 1901-1976.**      • **5.1911**
Physics and philosophy; the revolution in modern science. — [1st ed.]. — New York: Harper, [1958] 206 p.; 20 cm. — (World perspectives, v. 19) 1. Physics — Philosophy 2. Quantum theory I. T.
QC6.H34    530.1    *LC* 58-6150

**Heisenberg, Werner, 1901-1976.**      **5.1912**
[Schritte über Grenzen. English] Across the frontiers. Translated from the German by Peter Heath. [1st ed.] New York, Harper & Row [1974] xxii, 229 p. 21 cm. (World perspectives, v. 48) Translation of Schritte über Grenzen. 1. Physics — Philosophy 2. Science — Philosophy I. T.
QC6.H34613 1974    530.1    *LC* 73-4087    *ISBN* 0060118245

**Lindsay, Robert Bruce, 1900-.**      **5.1913**
Foundations of physics [by] Robert Bruce Lindsay [and] Henry Margenau. New York, Dover Publications [1957] 542 p. illus. 22 cm. 'An unabridged republication of the first edition with corrections and a new reading list prepared by the authors.' 1. Physics — Philosophy I. Margenau, Henry, 1901- joint author. II. T.
QC6.L42 1957    530.1    *LC* 57-14416

**Lorentz, H. A. (Hendrik Antoon), 1853-1928.**      • **5.1914**
The principle of relativity: a collection of original memoirs on the special and general theory of relativity / by H. A. Lorentz, ... [et al.]; with notes by A. Sommerfeld; translated by W. Perrett and G. B. Jeffery.— London: Dover, 1952. viii, 216 p.: ill. 1. Relativity (Physics) I. Einstein, Albert, 1879-1955. II. Minkowski, H. (Hermann), 1864-1909. III. Weyl, Hermann, 1885-1955. IV. Sommerfeld, Arnold Johannes Wilhelm, 1868- V. Perrett, W. VI. Jeffery, George Barker, 1891- VII. T.
QC6.L86    *LC* a 52-9845

**Marder, Leslie.**      **5.1915**
Time and the space–traveller [by] L. Marder. — Philadelphia: University of Pennsylvania Press, 1972 (c1971) 208 p.: illus.; 23 cm. 1. Time dilatation I. T.
QC6.M35132    530.1/1    *LC* 77-182498    *ISBN* 0812276507

**Mermin, N. David.**      **5.1916**
Space and time in special relativity [by] N. David Mermin. New York, McGraw-Hill [1968] xii, 240 p. illus. 20 cm. (McGraw-Hill paperbacks in physics) 1. Special relativity (Physics) 2. Space and time I. T.
QC6.M367    530.11    *LC* 67-30052

**Muirhead, H. (Hugh)**      **5.1917**
The special theory of relativity / [by] H. Muirhead. — New York: Wiley [1973] xi, 163 p.: ill.; 24 cm. 'A Halsted Press book.' 1. Relativity (Physics) 2. Lorentz transformations 3. Symmetry (Physics) I. T.
QC6.M86    530.1/1    *LC* 72-6874

## QC6 N–Z

**Planck, Max, 1858-1947.**      • **5.1918**
The philosophy of physics, by Dr. Max Planck ... translated by H.W. Johnston. New York, W.W. Norton & Company, inc. [c1936] 128 p. 22 cm. 'First edition.' 1. Physics — Philosophy I. Johnston, Walter Henry, 1895- tr. II. T.
QC6.P625    530.1    *LC* 36-8178

**Powers, Jonathan.**      **5.1919**
Philosophy and the new physics / Jonathan Powers. — London; New York: Methuen, 1982. xvii, 203 p.; 20 cm. — (Ideas) (University paperbacks; 792) Includes indexes. 1. Physics — Philosophy I. T.
QC6.P694 1982    530/.01 19    *LC* 82-12486    *ISBN* 0416734707

**Reichenbach, Hans, 1891-1953.**      • **5.1920**
The direction of time / edited by Maria Reichenbach. — Berkeley: University of California Press, 1956. xi, 280 p.: diagrs., tables; 25 cm. 1. Space and time I. T.
QC6.R382    530.1    *LC* 55-9883

**Russell, Bertrand, 1872-1970.**      • **5.1921**
The ABC of relativity. Rev. ed. Edited by Felix Pirani. London: G. Allen & Unwin [1958] 139 p.: ill.; 23 cm. 1. Relativity (Physics) I. T.
QC6.R8 1958    530.1    *LC* 58-42601

**Schrödinger, Erwin, 1887-1961.**      • **5.1922**
Space–time structure. — Cambridge [Eng.]: University Press, 1950. viii, 119 p.: ill.; 23 cm. Erratum slip inserted. 1. Space and time 2. Relativity (Physics) I. T.
QC6.S428    *LC* 50-10960

**Shadowitz, Albert.**      • **5.1923**
Special relativity [by] A. Shadowitz. Philadelphia, Saunders Co., 1968. xiii, 203 p. illus. 24 cm. (Studies in physics and chemistry. no. 6) 1. Relativity (Physics) I. T. II. Series.
QC6.S473    530.11    *LC* 67-17454

**Taylor, Edwin F.**      • **5.1924**
Spacetime physics [by] Edwin F. Taylor [and] John Archibald Wheeler. — San Francisco: W. H. Freeman, [1966] 208 p.: ill., ports.; 27 cm. — (A Series of books in physics) 1. Relativity (Physics) 2. Space and time I. Wheeler, John Archibald, 1911- joint author. II. T.
QC6.T35    530.11    *LC* 65-13566

**Tolman, Richard Chace, 1881-1948.**      • **5.1925**
Relativity, thermodynamics and cosmology / by Richard C. Tolman. — Oxford: The Clarendon Press, 1934. xv, 501 p.: ill. — (The International series of monographs on physics) 1. Relativity (Physics) 2. Thermodynamics 3. Cosmology I. T.
QC6.T6

**Weinberg, Steven.**      • **5.1926**
Gravitation and cosmology: principles and applications of the general theory of relativity. — New York: Wiley, [1972] xxviii, 657 p.: illus.; 23 cm. 1. General relativity (Physics) 2. Gravitation 3. Cosmology I. T.
QC6.W47    530.1/1    *LC* 78-37175    *ISBN* 0471925675

## QC6.5 UNIFIED FIELD THEORIES

**Arzeliès, Henri, 1913-.**      **5.1927**
Relativistic point dynamics. Translated by P. W. Hawkes from a thoroughly rev. text, brought up to date. — Oxford; New York: Pergamon Press, [1972] xxxix, 376 p.: illus.; 25 cm. 'Translation based upon material drawn from ...

Dynamique relativiste, published ... in 1957 and 1958.' 1. Unified field theories 2. Electrodynamics I. T.
QC6.5.A7213 1971 530.1/42 *LC* 72-142173 *ISBN* 0080158420

# QC7–16 History. Biography. Directories

**Bellone, Enrico.** 5.1928
[Mondo di carta. English] A world on paper: studies on the second scientific revolution / Enrico Bellone; English translation by Mirella and Riccardo Giacconi. — Cambridge, Mass.: MIT Press, [1980] xiii, 220 p.; 24 cm. Translation of Il mondo di carta. 1. Physics — History. I. T.
QC7.B4313 530/.09 19 *LC* 80-10674 *ISBN* 0262021471

**Bernal, J. D. (John Desmond), 1901-.** 5.1929
The extension of man: a history of physics before the quantum. — Cambridge: M.I.T. Press, [1972] 317 p.: illus.; 23 cm. Originally given as lectures at Birkbeck College, University of London. 1. Physics — History. I. T.
QC7.B46 1972 530/.09 *LC* 72-178982 *ISBN* 0262020866

**Brush, Stephen G.** 5.1930
The temperature of history: phases of science and culture in the nineteenth century / by Stephen G. Brush. New York: B. Franklin, [1977] viii, 210 p.: ill., port.; 24 cm. — (Studies in the history of science; 4) 1. Physics — History. 2. Romanticism 3. Realism I. T. II. Series.
QC7.B78 530/.09/034 *LC* 77-11999 *ISBN* 089102073X

**Cohen, I. Bernard, 1914-.** 5.1931
The Newtonian revolution: with illustrations of the transformation of scientific ideas / I. Bernard Cohen. — Cambridge [Eng.]; New York: Cambridge University Press, 1981 (c1980). xv, 404 p.; 24 cm. Includes index. 1. Newton, Isaac, Sir, 1642-1727. Principia 2. Physics — History. 3. Science — History I. T.
QC7.C66 509 *LC* 79-18637 *ISBN* 0521229642

**Einstein, Albert, 1879-1955.** • 5.1932
The evolution of physics: the growth of ideas from early concepts to relativity and quanta, by Albert Einstein and Leopold Infeld. — New York: Simon and Schuster, 1938. x, 319, [1] p.: ill., III pl., diagrs.; 21 cm. 'About the author': p. [320] 1. Physics — History. 2. Relativity (Physics) 3. Quantum theory I. Infeld, Leopold, 1898-1968. joint author. II. T.
QC7.E5 530.9 *LC* 38-27272

**Harman, P. M. (Peter Michael), 1943-.** 5.1933
Energy, force, and matter: the conceptual development of nineteenth–century physics / P.M. Harman. — Cambridge; New York: Cambridge University Press, 1982. ix, 182 p.: ill.; 22 cm. — (Cambridge history of science.) Includes index. 1. Physics — History. 2. Force and energy — History. I. T. II. Series.
QC7.H257 530/.09/034 19 *LC* 81-17029 *ISBN* 0521246008

**McCormmach, Russell.** 5.1934
Night thoughts of a classical physicist / Russell McCormmach. — Cambridge, Mass.: Harvard University Press, 1982. 217 p., [2] leaves of plates: ill.; 25 cm. 1. Physics — History — Fiction. I. T.
QC7.M35 813/.54 19 *LC* 81-6674 *ISBN* 0674624602

**Physical thought from the Presocratics to the quantum** 5.1935
**physicists: an anthology / selected, introduced, and edited by Shmuel Sambursky.**
New York: Pica Press: distributed by Universe Books, 1975, c1974. xv, 584 p.: ill.; 24 cm. 1. Physics — History. 2. Physics — Philosophy 3. Science — History 4. Science — Philosophy I. Sambursky, Samuel, 1900-
QC7.P47 1975 530/.09 *LC* 74-12946 *ISBN* 0876637128

**Segrè, Emilio.** 5.1936
From falling bodies to radio waves: classical physicists and their discoveries / Emilio Segrè. — New York: W.H. Freeman, c1984. x, 298 p.: ill.; 24 cm. Includes indexes. 1. Physics — History. 2. Physicists — Biography I. T.
QC7.S435 1984 530/.09 19 *LC* 83-16584 *ISBN* 0716714825

**Segrè, Emilio.** 5.1937
[Personaggi e scoperte nella fisica contemporanea. English] From x–rays to quarks: modern physicists and their discoveries / Emilio Segrè. — San Francisco: W. H. Freeman, c1980. ix, 337 p.: ill.; 24 cm. Translation of Personaggi e scoperte nella fisica contemporanea. Includes indexes. 1. Physics — History. 2. Physicists — Biography I. T.
QC7.S4413 530/.09 *LC* 80-466 *ISBN* 071671146X

**Springs of scientific creativity: essays on founders of modern** 5.1938
**science / Rutherford Aris, H. Ted Davis, Roger H. Stuewer, editors.**
Minneapolis: University of Minnesota Press, c1983. viii, 342 p.: ill.; 24 cm. 1. Physics — History. 2. Physicists 3. Scientists 4. Creative ability in science I. Aris, Rutherford. II. Davis, H. Ted (Howard Ted) III. Stuewer, Roger H.
QC7.S77 1983 509/.2/2 19 *LC* 82-23715 *ISBN* 0816610878

**Rutherford and physics at the turn of the century / edited by** 5.1939
**Mario Bunge and William R. Shea.**
Kent, Eng.: Dawson; New York: Science History Publications, 1979. 184 p.: port.; 24 cm. 1. Rutherford, Ernest, 1871-1937. 2. Physics — History — Addresses, essays, lectures. 3. Physicists — Great Britain — Biography. I. Bunge, Mario Augusto. II. Shea, William R.
QC7.5.R87 1979 530/.09/041 *LC* 78-13986 *ISBN* 0882021842

**Pyenson, Lewis.** 5.1940
Cultural imperialism and exact sciences: German expansion overseas, 1900–1930 / Lewis Pyenson. — New York: P. Lang, c1985. xvi, 342 p.: ill.; 23 cm. (Studies in history and culture. vol. 1) 1. Physics — Argentina — Foreign influences — History. 2. Physics — Oceania — Foreign influences — History. 3. Physics — China — Foreign influences — History. 4. Astronomy — Argentina — Foreign influences — History. 5. Astronomy — Oceania — Foreign influences — History. 6. Astronomy — China — Foreign influences — History. 7. Germany — Foreign relations — History. I. T. II. Series.
QC9.G3 P94 1985 500/.2/0943 19 *LC* 84-47907 *ISBN* 0820401595

**Physics through the 1990's.** 5.1941
Washington, D.C.: National Academy Press, 1986. 8 v.
QC9.U5 P4x 1986

**The Biographical dictionary of scientists. Physicists / general** 5.1942
**editor, David Abbott.**
New York: P. Bedrick Books, 1984. 212 p.: ill.; 26 cm. Includes index. 1. Physicists — Biography I. Abbott, David, 1937- II. Title: Physicists.
QC15.B56 1984 530/.092/2 B 19 *LC* 84-9211 *ISBN* 0911745793

**MacDonald, David Keith Chalmers, 1920-.** 5.1943
Faraday, Maxwell, and Kelvin. — [1st ed.]. — Garden City, N.Y.: Doubleday, 1964. xvi, 143 p.: illus., ports., facsims.; 19 cm. — (Science study series. S33) 1. Faraday, Michael, 1791-1867. 2. Maxwell, James Clerk, 1831-1879. 3. Kelvin, William Thomson, Baron, 1824-1907. I. T. II. Series.
QC15.M27 925.3 *LC* 64-11313

**Weber, Robert L., 1913-.** 5.1944
Pioneers of science: nobel prize winners in physics / Robert L. Weber; edited by J.M.A. Lenihan. — Bristol: Institute of Physics, c1980. xviii, 272 p.: ill.; 24 cm. 1. Physicists — Biography 2. Nobel prizes I. Lenihan, J. M. A. II. T.
QC15.W4 530/.92/2 B 19 *LC* 81-108183 *ISBN* 0854980369

**Bernstein, Jeremy, 1929-.** 5.1945
Hans Bethe, prophet of energy / Jeremy Bernstein. — New York: Basic Books, c1980. xii, 212 p.; 22 cm. Based on articles written for the New Yorker. Includes index. 1. Bethe, Hans Albrecht, 1906- 2. Physicists — Biography 3. Nuclear energy — History. I. T.
QC16.B46 B47 539/.092/4 B *LC* 80-50555 *ISBN* 0465029035

**Einstein, Albert, 1879-1955.** 5.1946
Out of my later years / Albert Einstein. — New York: Philosophical Library, 1950. viii, 282 p.: port. — 1. Einstein, Albert, 1879-1955. I. T.
QC16E5 A3 QC16E5 A3. 081 *LC* 50-6859

**Pais, Abraham, 1918-.** 5.1947
'Subtle is the Lord—': the science and the life of Albert Einstein / Abraham Pais. — Oxford [Oxfordshire]; New York: Oxford University Press, 1982. xvi, 552 p., [9] p. of plates: ill.; 24 cm. 1. Einstein, Albert, 1879-1955. 2. Physicists — Biography 3. Physics — History. I. T.
QC16.E5 P26 1982 530/.092/4 B 19 *LC* 82-2273 *ISBN* 019853907X

**Some strangeness in the proportion: a centennial symposium to** 5.1948
**celebrate the achievements of Albert Einstein / edited by Harry Woolf.**
Reading, Mass.: Addison-Wesley Pub. Co., Advanced Book Program, 1980. xxxi, 539 p.: ill.; 25 cm. 1. Einstein, Albert, 1879-1955 — Congresses. 2. Relativity (Physics) — Congresses. 3. Quantum theory — Congresses. 4. Astrophysics — Congresses. I. Einstein, Albert, 1879-1955. II. Woolf, Harry.
QC16.E5 S63 530.1 19 *LC* 80-20111 *ISBN* 0201099241

**Elsasser, Walter M., 1904-.** 5.1949
Memoirs of a physicist in the atomic age / Walter M. Elsasser. — New York: Science History Publications, 1978. xii, 268 p.: ill.; 24 cm. 1. Elsasser, Walter M., 1904- 2. Physicists — United States — Biography. I. T.
QC16.E58 A35 530/.092/4 B *LC* 77-16583 *ISBN* 0882021788

**Feynman, Richard Phillips.**     **5.1950**
'Surely you're joking, Mr. Feynman!': adventures of a curious character / Richard P. Feynman as told to Ralph Leighton; edited by Edward Hutchings. — New York: W.W. Norton, c1985. 350 p.; 22 cm. Includes index. 1. Feynman, Richard Phillips. 2. Physicists — United States — Biography. 3. Science — Anecdotes I. Leighton, Ralph. II. Hutchings, Edward. III. T.
QC16.F49 A37 1985    530/.092/4 B 19    *LC* 84-14703    *ISBN* 0393019217

**Infeld, Leopold, 1898-1968.**     **5.1951**
Quest: an autobiography / Leopold Infeld. — 2d ed. — New York, N.Y.: Chelsea Pub. Co., 1980. 361 p.; 24 cm. 1. Infeld, Leopold, 1898-1968. 2. Physicists — Poland — Biography. I. T.
QC16.I6 A3 1980    530/.092/4 B 19    *LC* 79-55510    *ISBN* 0828403090

**Goldman, Martin.**     **5.1952**
The demon in the aether: the story of James Clerk Maxwell / Martin Goldman. — Edinburgh: P. Harris; Bristol: A. Hilger, 1983. 224 p., [12] p. of plates: ill., ports.; 24 cm. 1. Maxwell, James Clerk, 1831-1879. 2. Physicists — Great Britain — Biography. I. T.
QC16.M4 G65 1983    530/.092/4 B 19    *LC* 83-200363    *ISBN* 0862280265

**Kargon, Robert Hugh.**     **5.1953**
The rise of Robert Millikan: portrait of a life in American science / Robert H. Kargon. — Ithaca, N.Y.: Cornell University Press, 1982. 205 p.: ill.; 23 cm. Includes index. 1. Millikan, Robert Andrews, 1868-1953. 2. Physicists — United States — Biography. I. T.
QC16.M58 K37    530/.092/4 B 19    *LC* 81-15204    *ISBN* 0801414598

**Morse, Philip McCord, 1903-.**     **5.1954**
In at the beginnings: a physicist's life / Philip M. Morse. Cambridge, Mass.: MIT Press, c1977. vii, 375 p., [6] leaves of plates: ill.; 21 cm. Includes index. 1. Morse, Philip McCord, 1903- 2. Physicists — United States — Biography. I. T.
QC16.M66 A34    530/.092/4 B    *LC* 76-40010    *ISBN* 0262131242

**Andrade, E. N. da C. (Edward Neville da Costa), 1887-1971.**    • **5.1955**
Isaac Newton. New York: Chanticleer Press [1950] 111 p.: ill., ports.; 19 cm. (Personal portraits). 1. Newton, Isaac, Sir, 1642-1727. I. T. II. Series.
QC16.N7 A55    925.3    *LC* 50-7104

**Christianson, Gale E.**     **5.1956**
In the presence of the Creator: Isaac Newton and his times / Gale E. Christianson. — New York: Free Press; London: Collier Macmillan, c1984. xv, 623 p., [16] p. of plates: ill.; 25 cm. Includes index. 1. Newton, Isaac, Sir, 1642-1727. 2. Physicists — Great Britain — Biography. 3. Mathematicians — Great Britain — Biography. I. T.
QC16.N7 C49 1984    509/.24 B 19    *LC* 83-49211    *ISBN* 0029051908

**Guerlac, Henry.**     **5.1957**
Newton on the Continent / Henry Guerlac. — Ithaca, N.Y.: Cornell University Press, 1981. 169 p.: ill.; 25 cm. English and French. 1. Newton, Isaac, Sir, 1642-1727 — Addresses, essays, lectures. 2. Science — History — Addresses, essays, lectures. 3. Physicists — Great Britain — Biography — Addresses, essays, lectures. I. T.
QC16.N7 G82    509/.2/4 B 19    *LC* 81-3187    *ISBN* 0801414091

**Westfall, Richard S.**     **5.1958**
Never at rest: a biography of Isaac Newton / Richard S. Westfall. — Cambridge [Eng.]; New York: Cambridge University Press, 1981 (c1980). xviii, 908 p.: ill.; 24 cm. Includes indexes. 1. Newton, Isaac, Sir, 1642-1727. 2. Physicists — Great Britain — Biography. I. T.
QC16.N7 W35    509/.2/4 B    *LC* 79-26294    *ISBN* 0521231434

**Goodchild, Peter.**     **5.1959**
J. Robert Oppenheimer: shatterer of worlds / Peter Goodchild. — Boston: Houghton Mifflin, 1981. 301 p.: ill.; 25 cm. Published in conjunction with the BBC/WGBH television series Oppenheimer, produced by Peter Goodchild and written by Peter Prince. Includes index. 1. Oppenheimer, J. Robert, 1904-1967. 2. Physicists — United States — Biography. I. T.
QC16.O62 G66 1981    530/.092/4 B 19    *LC* 81-1331    *ISBN* 0395305306

**Major, John, 1936-.**     **5.1960**
The Oppenheimer hearing. New York, Stein and Day [1971] 336 p. illus. 23 cm. (Historic trials series) 1. Oppenheimer, J. Robert, 1904-1967. I. T.
QC16.O62 M3    353.0085/5397 19    *LC* 76-156939    *ISBN* 0812813952

**Nye, Mary Jo.**     **5.1961**
Molecular reality; a perspective on the scientific work of Jean Perrin. — London: Macdonald; New York: American Elsevier, [1972] xi, 201 p.: illus.; 24 cm. — (History of science library) 1. Perrin, Jean Baptiste, 1870-1942. 2. Atomic theory — History. 3. Molecules — History. I. T. II. Series.
QC16.P4 N9    539.7/092/4 B    *LC* 70-171234    *ISBN* 0444195963

**Heilbron, J. L.**     **5.1962**
The dilemmas of an upright man: Max Planck as spokesman for German science / J.L. Heilbron. — Berkeley: University of California Press, c1986. xiii, 238 p., [16] p. of plates: ill.; 22 cm. Includes index. 1. Planck, Max, 1858-1947. 2. Physics — Germany — History. 3. Physicists — Germany — Biography. I. T.
QC16.P6 H45 1986    530/.092/4 19    *LC* 85-24609    *ISBN* 0520057104

**Andrade, E. N. da C. (Edward Neville da Costa), 1887-1971.**     **5.1963**
Rutherford and the nature of the atom. [1st ed.] Garden City, N.Y.: Doubleday [1964] xix, 218 p.: ill., ports.; 19 cm. (Science study series. S35) 1. Rutherford, Ernest, 1871-1937. I. T. II. Series.
QC16.R8 A5    925.3    *LC* 64-11734

**Hilts, Philip J.**     **5.1964**
Scientific temperaments: three lives in contemporary science / Philip J. Hilts. — New York: Simon and Schuster, c1982. 302 p.; 23 cm. 1. Wilson, Robert R., 1914- 2. Ptashne, Mark. 3. McCarthy, John, 1927- 4. Fermi National Accelerator Laboratory — History. 5. Scientists — United States — Biography. 6. Biology — Research — History. 7. Artificial intelligence — History. I. T.
QC16.W56 H54 1982    509/.2/2 B 19    *LC* 82-10694    *ISBN* 0671225332

# QC20–28 Mathematical Physics

**Joos, Georg, 1894-1959.**     **5.1965**
Theoretical physics / With the collaboration of Ira M. Freeman. — 3d ed. — New York: Hafner Pub. Co., 1958? xxiii, 885 p. : ill. Translation of Lehrbuch der theoretischen Physik. 1. Mathematical physics I. T.
QC20.J62 1958    *LC* 58-4151

**Koonin, Steven E.**     **5.1966**
Computational physics / Steven E. Koonin. — Menlo Park, CA: Benjamin/Cummings Pub. Co., c1986. x, 409 p.: ill.; 25 cm. 1. Mathematical physics 2. Numerical analysis 3. Physics — Computer programs. 4. Differential equations — Numerical solutions I. T.
QC20.K665 1986    530.1/5/0285 19    *LC* 85-15052    *ISBN* 0805354301

**Longair, M. S., 1941-.**     **5.1967**
Theoretical concepts in physics: an alternative view of theoretical reasoning in physics for final–year undergraduates / M.S. Longair. — 1st ed. — Cambridge; New York: Cambridge University Press, 1984. xiii, 366 p.: ill.; 24 cm. Includes index. 1. Mathematical physics I. T.
QC20.L66 1984    530.1 19    *LC* 83-18928    *ISBN* 0521255503

**Morse, Philip McCord, 1903-.**    • **5.1968**
Methods of theoretical physics [by] Philip M. Morse [and] Herman Feshbach. — New York: McGraw-Hill, 1953. 2 v.: illus.; 24 cm. — (International series in pure and applied physics) 1. Mathematical physics I. Feshbach, Herman. joint author. II. T.
QC20.M6    530.151    *LC* 52-11515

**Roos, Bernard W.**    • **5.1969**
Analytic functions and distributions in physics and engineering [by] Bernard W. Roos. New York, Wiley [1969] xiv, 521 p. illus. 24 cm. 1. Mathematical physics 2. Magnetohydrodynamics 3. Neutron transport theory 4. Analytic functions 5. Distribution (Probability theory) I. T.
QC20.R67    530.15/7    *LC* 69-19241    *ISBN* 0471733342

**Sommerfeld, Arnold Johannes Wilhelm, 1868-1951.**    • **5.1970**
[Vorlesungen über theoretische Physik. English] Lectures on theoretical physics. New York, Academic Press, 1950-. v. illus. 24 cm. 1. Mathematical physics I. T.
QC20.S66    530.151    *LC* 50-8749

**Thirring, Walter E., 1927-.**     **5.1971**
[Lehrbuch der mathematischen Physik. English] A course in mathematical physics / Walter Thirring; translated by Evans M. Harrell. — New York: Springer-Verlag, c1978-c1979. 2 v.: ill.; 25 cm. Translation of: Lehrbuch der mathematischen Physik. 1. Mathematical physics I. T.
QC20.T4513    530.1/5 19    *LC* 78-16172    *ISBN* 0387814752

**Thompson, Colin J.**                                **5.1972**
Mathematical statistical mechanics / [by] Colin J. Thompson. — New York:
Macmillan, 1972. ix, 278 p.: ill.; 24 cm. — (A Series of books in applied
mathematics) 1. Mathematical physics 2. Statistical mechanics
3. Biomathematics I. T.
QC20.T47      530.1/32      LC 77-150071

**Trainor, Lynn E. H., 1921-.**                       **5.1973**
From physical concept to mathematical structure: an introduction to
theoretical physics / Lynn E. H. Trainor and Mark B. Wise. — Toronto;
Buffalo: University of Toronto Press, c1979. xviii, 399 p.: ill.; 24 cm. —
(Mathematical expositions. no. 22) 1. Mathematical physics I. Wise, Mark B.,
1953- joint author. II. T. III. Series.
QC20.T68      530.1/5      LC 78-11616      ISBN 0802054323

**Reed, Michael, 1942-.**                             **5.1974**
Methods of modern mathematical physics / Michael Reed, Barry Simon. —
Rev. and enl. ed. — New York: Academic Press, c1980-. v.: ill.; 24 cm.
1. Functional analysis 2. Mathematical physics I. Simon, Barry. joint author.
II. T.
QC20.7.F84 R43 1980      530.1/5 19      LC 80-39580      ISBN
0125850506

**Baker, George A. (George Allen), 1932-.**           **5.1975**
Essentials of Padé approximants [by] George A. Baker, Jr. New York,
Academic Press, 1975. xi, 306 p. illus. 24 cm. 1. Padé approximant I. T.
QC20.7.P3 B34      515/.235      LC 74-1632      ISBN 012074855X

**Berkeley physics course.**                          • **5.1976**
New York: McGraw-Hill, [1965-71, v. 5, 1967] 5 v.: illus.; 25 cm. The course is
being developed by an interuniversity group, of which Charles Kittel is
chairman. 1. Physics I. Kittel, Charles.
QC21.B4445      530      LC 64-66016      ISBN 0070048614

**Condon, Edward Uhler, 1902-1974.**                  • **5.1977**
Handbook of physics / edited by E. U. Condon [and] Hugh Odishaw. — 2d ed.
— New York: McGraw-Hill, [1967] 1 v. (various pagings): ill.; 26 cm.
1. Physics I. Odishaw, Hugh. joint author. II. T.
QC21.C7 1967      530      LC 66-20002

**Handbuch der Physik = [Encyclopedia of physics] /**   • **5.1978**
**Herausgegeben von S. Flügge.**
Berlin: Springer-Verlag, 1955-. v.: ill., diagrs. English, French of German.
Vols.1- have added t.p.: Encyclopedia of physics. Editor:1955- S. Flügge,
Siegfried 1. Physics I. Flügge, Siegfried II. Title: Encyclopedia of physics
QC21H43      LC 56-2942      ISBN 3540075127

**Landau, L. D. (Lev Davidovich), 1908-1968.**         • **5.1979**
[Kurs obshchei fiziki. English] General physics; mechanics and molecular
physics [by] L.D. Landau, A.I. Akhiezer [and] E.M. Lifshitz. Translated by
J.B. Sykes, A.D. Petford [and] C.L. Petford. [1st English ed.]. Oxford, New
York, Pergamon Press [1967] x, 372 p. illus. 23 cm. Translation of [Kurs
obshchei fiziki] 1. Physics I. Akhiezer, A. I. (Aleksandr Il'ich), 1911- joint
author. II. Lifshits, E. M. (Evgenii Mikhailovich) joint author. III. T.
QC21.L2713 1967      530      LC 67-30260

**Landau, L. D. (Lev Davidovich), 1908-1968.**         **5.1980**
Course of theoretical physics / by L. D. Landau and E. M. Lifshitz. — London:
Pergamon Press; Reading Mass.: Addison-Wesley Publishing Co., 1958-. v.: ill.;
24 cm. Translation of Teoreticheskaia fizika. I. T.
QC21.Lx

**Edgington, John Anthony.**                           **5.1981**
Physical science for biologists, [by] J. A. Edgington and H. J. Sherman. —
London: Hutchinson, 1971. xii, 225 p.,: illus.; 23 cm. 1. Physics I. Sherman,
Howard Jefferson, joint author. II. T.
QC21.2.E33      530      LC 71-868119      ISBN 0091078601

**Halliday, David, 1916-.**                           **5.1982**
Physics. Part Two / David Halliday, Robert Resnick. — 3rd ed., extended
version. — New York: Wiley, c1986. xiv, 565-1335, 42, 11 p.: ill.; 27 cm. 'We
have modified the last two chapters ... and have added five new ones'—Pref.
Includes index. 1. Physics I. Resnick, Robert, 1923- II. T.
QC21.2.H355 1986      530 19      LC 86-5606      ISBN 0471832022

**Kim, Sung Kyu, 1939-.**                             **5.1983**
Modern physics for scientists and engineers / S. K. Kim and E. N. Strait. —
New York: Macmillan, c1978. xiv, 466 p.: ill.; 26 cm. 1. Physics I. Strait, E.
N., joint author. II. T.
QC21.2.K49      530      LC 77-5365      ISBN 0023637803

**March, Robert H., 1937-.**                          **5.1984**
Physics for poets / Robert H. March. — 2d ed. — New York: McGraw-Hill,
c1978. x, 287 p.: ill. ; 24 cm. Includes index. 1. Physics I. T.
QC21.2.M36 1978      530      LC 77-2860      ISBN 0070402434

**Pais, Abraham, 1918-.**                             **5.1985**
Inward bound: of matter and forces in the physical world / Abraham Pais. —
Oxford [Oxfordshire]: Clarendon Press; New York: Oxford University Press,
1986. xiv, 666 p.; 25 cm. 1. Physics 2. Physics — History. I. T.
QC21.2.P35 1986      530 19      LC 85-21587      ISBN 0198519710

**Richardson, I. W., 1934-.**                         • **5.1986**
Physics for biology and medicine [by] I. W. Richardson [and] Ejler B.
Neergaard, with the assistance of Beverley B. Richardson. — London; New
York: Wiley-Interscience, [1972] x, 243 p.: illus.; 24 cm. 1. Physics 2. Medical
physics I. Neergaard, Ejler B., joint author. II. Richardson, Beverley B.
III. T.
QC21.2.R5      530      LC 76-180711      ISBN 0471719501

**Sears, Francis Weston, 1898-.**                     **5.1987**
University physics / Francis W. Sears, Mark W. Zemansky, Hugh D. Young.
— 7th ed. — Reading, Mass.: Addison-Wesley Pub. Co., 1986. p. cm. Includes
index. 1. Physics I. Zemansky, Mark Waldo, 1900- II. Young, Hugh D.
III. T.
QC21.2.S36 1986      530 19      LC 85-28801      ISBN 0201066815

**Shive, John N. (John Northrup), 1913-.**            **5.1988**
Similarities in physics / John N. Shive, Robert L. Weber. — New York: J.
Wiley, c1982. xiii, 277 p.: ill.; 25 cm. 'A Wiley-Interscience publication.'
Includes index. 1. Physics 2. Similarity (Physics) I. Weber, Robert L., 1913-
II. T.
QC21.2.S42 1982      530 19      LC 82-241448      0471897857

**Taylor, John Gerald, 1931-.**                       **5.1989**
The new physics [by] John G. Taylor. — New York: Basic Books, [1972] xi,
308 p.: illus.; 22 cm. 1. Physics I. T.
QC21.2.T38      539      LC 78-174817      ISBN 0465050662

**Bueche, F. (Frederick), 1923-.**                    **5.1990**
Principles of physics / F. Bueche. — 4th ed. — New York: McGraw-Hill,
c1982. xx, 839 p.: ill.; 24 cm. 1. Physics I. T.
QC23.B8496 1982      530 19      LC 81-12353      ISBN 0070088675

**Feynman, Richard Phillips.**                        • **5.1991**
The Feynman lectures on physics [by] Richard P. Feynman, Robert B.
Leighton [and] Matthew Sands. — Reading, Mass.: Addison-Wesley Pub. Co.,
[1963-65] 3 v.: illus.; 29 cm. Vol. 2 has subtitle: The electromagnetic field; 3 has
subtitle: Quantum mechanics. 1. Physics I. Leighton, Robert B., joint author.
II. Sands, Matthew Linzee, joint author. III. T. IV. Title: Lectures on
physics.
QC23.F47      530      LC 63-20717

**Ford, Kenneth William, 1926-.**                     **5.1992**
Classical and modern physics: a textbook for students of science and
engineering / [by] Kenneth W. Ford. — Lexington, Mass.: Xerox College Pub.,
1972. 543 p.: ill.; 26 cm. 1. Physics I. T.
QC23.F655      530      LC 76-161385      ISBN 0536007233

**Giancoli, Douglas C.**                              **5.1993**
Physics, principles with applications / Douglas C. Giancoli. — 2nd ed. —
Englewood Cliffs, N.J.: Prentice-Hall, c1985. xx, 811 p.: ill. (some col.); 26 cm.
Includes index. 1. Physics I. T.
QC23.G399 1985      530 19      LC 84-22250      ISBN 0136726275

**Holton, Gerald James.**                             **5.1994**
Introduction to concepts and theories in physical science / by Gerald Holton.
— 2nd ed., rev. and with new material / by Stephen G. Brush. — Princeton, NJ:
Princeton University Press, c1985. xix, 589 p.: ill.; 24 cm. Includes index.
1. Physics 2. Astronomy I. Brush, Stephen G. II. T.
QC23.H758 1985      500.2      LC 85-42663      ISBN 0691083843

**Rogers, Eric M.**                                   • **5.1995**
Physics for the inquiring mind; the methods, nature, and philosophy of physical
science. — Princeton, N.J.: Princeton University Press, 1960. 778 p.: illus.; 29
cm. 1. Physics I. T.
QC23.R68      530      LC 59-5603

**Ridley, B. K.**                                     **5.1996**
Time, space and things / B. K. Ridley. — Harmondsworth; New York [etc.]:
Penguin, 1977 (c1976). 169 p.: ill.; 20 cm. — (Peregrine books) Includes index.
1. Physics I. T.
QC24.5.R5      530      LC 77-361757      ISBN 0140551131

**Feynman, Richard Phillips.**                        • **5.1997**
The character of physical law [by] Richard Feynman. — Cambridge: M.I.T.
Press, [1965] 173 p.: illus.; 21 cm. — (The Messenger lectures, 1964) (The
M.I.T. Press paperback series, 66.) 1. Physics — Addresses, essays, lectures.
I. T.
QC28.F4 1965      LC 67-14527

# QC30–61 Study. Research. Problems. Measurements. Tables

**Graduate programs in physics, astronomy and related fields.** 5.1998
1977-78- . — New York: American Institute of Physics, 1977-. v.; 28 cm.
(AIP publication.) Annual. Title varies slightly. I. American Institute of
Physics. II. Series.
QC30.A51A2 *LC* sc 83-6264

**Epstein, Lewis C.** 5.1999
Thinking physics is gedanken physics / Lewis C. Epstein. — 2nd ed. — San
Francisco: Insight Press, 1983. 561 p.: ill.; 23 cm. 1. Physics — Problems,
exercises, etc. 2. Physics — Miscellanea. I. T.
QC32.E67 1983 530.02 *ISBN* 0953218041

**Problems and solutions for students, edited by L. Marton and** • 5.2000
**W. F. Hornyak.**
New York, Academic Press, 1969. xii, 281 p. illus. 24 cm. (Methods of
experimental physics. v. 8) 1. Physics — Problems, exercises, etc. I. Marton,
L. (Ladislaus), 1901- ed. II. Hornyak, William F. (William Frank), 1922- ed.
III. Series.
QC32.P7 530/.076 *LC* 69-13487 *ISBN* 0124759084

**Walker, Jearl, 1945-.** 5.2001
The flying circus of physics: with answers / Jearl Walker. — New York;
Toronto: Wiley, c1977. 295 p.: ill.; 24 cm. 1. Physics — Problems, exercises,
etc. I. T.
QC32.W2 530 *ISBN* 047102984X

**Low temperature physics: four lectures/ by F. E. Simon ... [et** • 5.2002
**al.]**
London: Pergamon Press, 1952. 132 p.: ill. 1. Low temperature research
2. Physics — Research I. Simon, Franz Eugen Simon, baron, 1893-
QC33.L6 *LC* 53-1620

**Bishop, Owen.** 5.2003
Yardsticks of the universe / Owen Bishop. — 1st American ed. — New York:
P. Bedrick Books: Distributed in the USA by Harper & Row, 1984 (c1982).
125 p.: ill.; 22 cm. Includes index. 1. Physical measurements I. T.
QC39.B57 1984 530.8 19 *LC* 83-15782 *ISBN* 0911745173

**Bridgman, P. W. (Percy Williams), 1882-1961.** • 5.2004
Dimensional analysis / by W. P. Bridgman. — New Haven: Yale university
press, 1931. 113 p. First pub., November 1922. Revised edition, March 1931.
1. Physical measurements I. T.
QC39.B7 1931 *LC* 32-18603

**Diagram Group.** 5.2005
Comparisons of distance, size, area, volume, mass, weight, density, energy,
temperature, time, speed and number throughout the universe / by the
Diagram Group. — New York: St. Martin's Press, c1980. 240 p.: ill.; 29 cm.
Includes indexes. 1. Physical measurements — Miscellanea. 2. Science —
Miscellanea. 3. Technology — Miscellanea. I. T.
QC39.D5 1980 530.8 *LC* 80-14251 *ISBN* 0312154844

**Rothman, Milton A.** 5.2006
Discovering the natural laws; the experimental basis of physics [by] Milton A.
Rothman. Illus. by the author. — [1st ed.]. — Garden City, N.Y.: Doubleday,
1972. xii, 227 p.: illus.; 22 cm. 1. Physical measurements 2. Physics —
Experiments I. T.
QC39.R68 530 *LC* 78-171318

**Royal Society (Great Britain). Discussion Meeting. (1983 May** 5.2007
**25-26: London, England)**
The constants of physics: proceedings of a Royal Society discussion meeting
held on 25 and 26 May 1983 / organized by W.H. McCrea, M.J. Rees and S.
Weinberg; and edited by W.H. McCrea and M.J. Rees. — London: The Society;
Great Neck, N.Y.: Distributed by Scholium International, 1983. 363 p.: ill.
Distributor from label on p. 2 of cover. First published in Philosophical
transactions of the Royal Society of London, series A, volume 310 (no. 1512),
pages 209-363'—T.p. verso. 1. Physical measurements — Congresses.
2. Astronomical constants — Congresses. 3. Units — Congresses. I. McCrea,
William Hunter. II. Rees, Martin J., 1942- III. Weinberg, Steven. IV. T.
QC39.R688 1983 530.8 19 *LC* 84-670182 *ISBN* 085403224X

**Zebrowski, Ernest.** 5.2008
Fundamentals of physical measurement / Ernest Zebrowski, Jr. — North
Scituate, Mass.: Duxbury Press, c1979. ix, 291 p.: ill.; 24 cm. Includes index.
1. Physical measurements I. T.
QC39.Z4 530/.8 *LC* 78-7315 *ISBN* 0878721738

**Cambridge physics in the thirties / edited and introduced by** 5.2009
**John Hendry.**
Bristol: A. Hilger, c1984. 209 p.: ill.; 24 cm. Includes index. 1. Cavendish
Laboratory (Cambridge, Cambridgeshire) — History. 2. Physics — England
— History. I. Hendry, John, 1952- II. Title: Cambridge physics in the 30's.
QC51.G72 C352 1984 507/.20426/59 19 *LC* 83-216483 *ISBN*
0852747616

**Crowther, J. G. (James Gerald), 1899-.** 5.2010
The Cavendish Laboratory, 1874–1974 [by] J. G. Crowther. New York, Science
History Publications [1974] xvi, 464 p. illus. 26 cm. 1. Cavendish Laboratory
(Cambridge, Cambridgeshire) I. T.
QC51.G72 C353 1974 530/.07/2042659 *LC* 74-13623 *ISBN*
0882020293

**American Institute of Physics.** 5.2011
American Institute of Physics handbook / section editors: Bruce H. Billings
[and others]; coordinating editor: Dwight E. Gray. — 3d ed. — New York:
McGraw-Hill, [1972] 1 v. (various pagings): ill.; 24 cm. 1. Physics —
Handbooks, manuals, etc. I. Gray, Dwight E., 1903- ed. II. T.
QC61.A5 1972 016.5301/5 *LC* 72-3248 *ISBN* 007001485X

**Fischbeck, Helmut J., 1928-.** 5.2012
Formulas, facts, and constants for students and professionals in engineering,
chemistry, and physics / Helmut J. Fischbeck, Kurt H. Fischbeck. — Berlin;
New York: Springer-Verlag, 1982. xii, 251 p.: ill.; 24 cm. Includes index.
1. Physics — Handbooks, manuals, etc. I. Fischbeck, Kurt, 1898- II. T.
QC61.F58 1982 530/.0212 19 *LC* 82-721 *ISBN* 0387113150

**Tuma, Jan J.** 5.2013
Handbook of physical calculations: definitions, formulas, technical
applications, physical tables, conversion tables, graphs, dictionary of physical
terms / Jan J. Tuma. — 2nd enl. and rev. ed. — New York: McGraw-Hill,
c1983. xiv, 478 p.: ill.; 24 cm. Includes index. 1. Physics — Handbooks,
manuals, etc. 2. Physical measurements — Handbooks, manuals, etc. I. T.
QC61.T85 1983 530/.02/02 19 *LC* 82-9002 *ISBN* 0070654395

# QC71–75 Addresses. Essays. Lectures

**Bondi, Hermann.** • 5.2014
Assumption and myth in physical theory, by H. Bondi. — London: Cambridge
U.P., 1967. vii, 88 p.: diagrs.; 21 cm. — (Tarner lectures. 1966]) 1. Physics —
Addresses, essays, lectures. I. T. II. Series.
QC71.B63 530.1 *LC* 67-21954 *ISBN* 0521042828

**Born, Max, 1882-1970.** • 5.2015
Physics in my generation. — [2d rev. ed.]. — New York: Springer-Verlag,
[1969] vii, 172 p.: illus.; 23 cm. — (Heidelberg science library.) 1. Physics —
Addresses, essays, lectures. I. T. II. Series.
QC71.B66 1969 530/.08 *LC* 68-59281

**Born, Max.** • 5.2016
Experiment and theory in physics. New York: Dover Publications, 1956. 43 p.;
21 cm. "Unabridged and unaltered republication of the original 1943 edition."
1. Physics — Addresses, essays, lectures. I. T.
QC71.B67 1956 530.4 *LC* 56-58690

**Compton, Arthur Holly, 1892-1962.** 5.2017
Scientific papers of Arthur Holly Compton; x–rays and other studies. Edited
and with an introd. by Robert S. Shankland. — Chicago: University of Chicago
Press, [1973] xxix, 777 p.: illus.; 27 cm. 1. Physics — Addresses, essays,
lectures. I. T.
QC71.C64 1973 539.7/222 *LC* 73-84189 *ISBN* 0226114309

**Dirac, P. A. M. (Paul Adrien Maurice), 1902-.** 5.2018
Directions in physics: lectures delivered during a visit to Australia and New
Zealand August/September 1975 / P. A. M. Dirac; edited by H. Hora and J. R.
Shepanski; with a foreword by Sir Mark Oliphant. — New York: Wiley, c1978.
ix, 95 p.: ill.; 24 cm. 'A Wiley-Interscience publication.' 1. Physics —
Addresses, essays, lectures. I. T.
QC71.D55 530 *LC* 77-24892 *ISBN* 0471029971

**On modern physics / [by] Werner Heisenberg [and others;** 5.2019
**English translation by M. Goodman and J.W. Binns].**
New York: C.N. Potter [c1961] 108 p.; 22 cm. 1. Physics — Addresses, essays,
lectures. 2. Science — Philosophy — Addresses, essays, lectures.
I. Heisenberg, Werner, 1901-1976.
QC71.O5 530 *LC* 60-14431

**Weisskopf, Victor Frederick, 1908-.**    **5.2020**
Physics in the twentieth century: selected essays [by] Victor F. Weisskopf. Foreword by Hans A. Bethe. — Cambridge, Mass.: MIT Press, [1972] xv, 368 p.: illus.; 22 cm. 1. Physics — Addresses, essays, lectures. I. T.
QC71.W44      530/.08     LC 76-39899     ISBN 0262230569

**Jammer, Max.**    • **5.2021**
Concepts of force; a study in the foundations of dynamics. Cambridge, Harvard University Press, 1957. 269 p. 22 cm. 1. Force and energy I. T.
QC73.J3      530     LC 57-7610

# QC81–114 WEIGHTS AND MEASURES

**Dresner, Stephen.**    **5.2022**
Units of measurement: an encyclopaedic dictionary of units, both scientific and popular, and the quantities they measure. — New York: Hastings House, [1972, c1971] xvi, 287 p.; 24 cm. 1. Units — Dictionaries. 2. Weights and measures — Dictionaries. I. T.
QC82.D74 1972      389/.03     LC 78-187316     ISBN 0803874960

**Jerrard, H. G.**    **5.2023**
A dictionary of scientific units: including dimensionless numbers and scales / H.G. Jerrard and D.B. McNeill. — 5th ed. — London; New York: Chapman and Hall, 1986. p. cm. (Science paperbacks. 210) Includes index. 1. Units — Dictionaries. I. McNeill, D. B. (Donald Burgess), 1911- II. T. III. Series.
QC82.J4 1986      530.8/03/21 19     LC 85-31431     ISBN 0412280906

**Klein, H. Arthur.**    **5.2024**
The world of measurements: masterpieces, mysteries and muddles of metrology / H. Arthur Klein. — New York: Simon and Schuster, [1974] 736 p.: ill.; 23 cm. Includes index. 1. Weights and measures 2. Weights and measures — History I. T.
QC88.K58      530/.8     LC 74-7656     ISBN 0671215655

**Petley, B. W. (Brian William)**    **5.2025**
The fundamental physical constants and the frontier of measurement / B.W. Petley. — Bristol; Boston: A. Hilger, c1985. x, 346 p.: ill.; 24 cm. Includes index. 1. Constants, Physical 2. Physical measurements I. T.
QC100.A2 P48 1985      530.8 19     LC 86-124318     ISBN 0852744277

# QC122–168 DESCRIPTIVE AND EXPERIMENTAL MECHANICS

**Cohen, I. Bernard, 1914-.**    **5.2026**
The birth of a new physics / by I. Bernard Cohen. — Rev. and updated. — New York: W.W. Norton, c1985. xiv, 258 p.: ill.; 22 cm. Includes index. 1. Mechanics 2. Mechanics, Celestial I. T.
QC122.C6 1985      530/.09 19     LC 84-25582     ISBN 0393019942

**Galilei, Galileo, 1564-1642.**    • **5.2027**
[De motu. English] On motion, and On mechanics; comprising De motu (ca. 1590) translated with introduction and notes by I.E. Drabkin, and Le meccaniche (ca. 1600) translated with introduction and notes by Stillman Drake. Madison, University of Wisconsin Press, 1960. viii, 193 p. illus. 24 cm. (Wisconsin. University. Publications in medieval science, 5) 1. Mechanics 2. Physics — Early works to 1800. I. Drabkin, I. E. (Israel Edward), 1905-1965. ed. and tr. II. Drake, Stillman. ed. and tr. III. Galilei, Galileo, 1564-1642. Delle meccaniche. English. 1960. IV. T.
QC123.G1153      531     LC 60-5658

**Galilei, Galileo, 1564-1642.**    **5.2028**
[Discorsi e dimostrazioni matematiche. English] Two new sciences, including centers of gravity & force of percussion. Translated with introd. and notes by Stillman Drake. [Madison] University of Wisconsin Press [1974] xxxix, 323 p. illus. 23 cm. Translation of Discorsi e dimostrazioni matematiche. 1. Mechanics — Early works to 1800. 2. Physics — Early works to 1800. I. Drake, Stillman. tr. II. T.
QC123.G13 1974      530     LC 73-2043     ISBN 029906400X ISBN 0299064042

**Casper, Barry M.**    **5.2029**
Revolutions in physics [by] Barry M. Casper and Richard J. Noer. — [1st ed.]. — New York: Norton, [1972] x, 479 p.: illus.; 25 cm. 1. Motion 2. Relativity (Physics) 3. Particles (Nuclear physics) I. Noer, Richard J., 1937- joint author. II. T.
QC125.2.C36      531/.11     LC 75-162931     ISBN 039309992X

**French, A. P. (Anthony Philip), 1920-.**    • **5.2030**
Newtonian mechanics [by] A. P. French. New York, W. W. Norton [1971] xiii, 743 p. illus. 25 cm. (The M.I.T. introductory physics series) 1. Mechanics I. T.
QC125.2.F74      531     LC 74-95528     ISBN 039309958X

**Kittel, Charles.**    **5.2031**
Mechanics [by] Charles Kittel, Walter D. Knight [and] Malvin A. Ruderman. Rev. by A. Carl Helmholz [and] Burton J. Moyer. — 2d ed. — New York: McGraw-Hill, [1973] xix, 426 p.: illus.; 24 cm. — (Berkeley physics course. v. 1) 1. Mechanics I. Knight, Walter D. joint author. II. Ruderman, Malvin A. joint author. III. Helmholz, A. Carl, ed. IV. Moyer, Burton J., ed. V. T. VI. Series.
QC125.2.K5x QC1.B375      530/.08 s 531     LC 72-7444     ISBN 0070048800

**Symon, Keith R.**    • **5.2032**
Mechanics [by] Keith R. Symon. — 3d ed. — Reading, Mass.: Addison-Wesley Pub. Co., [c1971] xii, 639 p.: illus.; 25 cm. — (Addison-Wesley series in physics) 1. Mechanics I. T.
QC125.2.S94 1971      531     LC 75-128910

**Main, Iain G., 1932-.**    **5.2033**
Vibrations and waves in physics / Iain G. Main. — 2nd ed. — Cambridge [Cambridgeshire]; New York: Cambridge University Press, 1984. xiii, 356 p.: ill.; 24 cm. Includes index. 1. Vibration 2. Waves I. T.
QC136.M34 1984      531/.32 19     LC 83-23999     ISBN 0521261244

**Pippard, A. B.**    **5.2034**
The physics of vibration / A. B. Pippard. — Cambridge; New York: Cambridge University Press, 1978. 431 p. 1. Vibration I. T.
QC136.P56      531/.32     LC 77-85685     ISBN 0521218993

**Pascal, Blaise, 1623-1662.**    • **5.2035**
The physical treatises of Pascal: the equilibrium of liquids and the weight of the mass of the air / translated by I.H.B. and A.G.H. Spiers; with introduction and notes by Frederick Barry. — New York: Columbia University Press, 1937. 181p. (Records of civilization; sources and studies, ed. under the auspices of the Dept. of history, Columbia university ... No. XXVIII) 1. Hydrostatics 2. Air 3. Atmospheric pressure I. Barry, Frederick, 1876-, ed. II. Stevin, Simon, 1548-1620 III. Galillei, Galileo, 1564-1642 IV. Torricelli, Evangelista, 1608-1647. V. T.
QC143 P33 1937      LC 38-410

**Barton, Allan F. M.**    **5.2036**
The dynamic liquid state / A. F. M. Barton. — London: Longman; New York: distributed by Longman Inc., 1975 (c1974). vii, 159 p.: ill.; 22 cm. 1. Liquids I. T.
QC145.2.B37      532     LC 73-90500     ISBN 0582442761

**Trefil, James S., 1938-.**    **5.2037**
Introduction to the physics of fluids and solids [by] J. S. Trefil. New York, Pergamon Press [1975] xiii, 304 p. illus. 24 cm. 1. Fluids 2. Solids I. T.
QC145.2.T73 1975      531     LC 74-2153     ISBN 008018104X

**Handbook of fluids in motion / edited by Nicholas P. Cheremisinoff, Ramesh Gupta.**    **5.2038**
Ann Arbor, Mich.: Butterworths, c1983. xiii, 1202 p.: ill.; 24 cm. 'An Ann Arbor Science book.' 1. Fluid mechanics — Handbooks, manuals, etc. I. Cheremisinoff, Nicholas P. II. Gupta, Ramesh, 1947-
QC145.3.H36 1983      532/.051 19     LC 82-70706     ISBN 0250404583

**Drake, Stillman.**    **5.2039**
Cause, experiment, and science: a Galilean dialogue, incorporating a new English translation of Galileo's Bodies that stay atop water, or move in it / Stillman Drake. — Chicago: University of Chicago Press, 1981. xxix, 237 p.; 21 cm. Includes index. 1. Hydrostatics I. Galilei, Galileo, 1564-1642. Discorso al serenissimo don Cosimo II, gran duca di Toscana, intorno alle cose, che stanno in su l'acque. English. 1981. II. T.
QC147.D7      532/.2 19     LC 81-2974     ISBN 0226162281

**Lighthill, M. J., Sir.**    **5.2040**
Waves in fluids / James Lighthill. — Cambridge [Eng.]; New York: Cambridge University Press, 1978. xv, 504 p.: ill.; 24 cm. Includes indexes. 1. Waves 2. Fluid dynamics 3. Wave-motion, Theory of I. T.
QC157.L53      532/.0593     LC 77-8174     ISBN 0521216893

**Keenan, Joseph Henry, 1900-.**    **5.2041**
Gas tables: thermodynamic properties of air products of combustion and component gases, compressible flow functions, including those of Ascher H.

Shapiro and Gilbert M. Edelman / by Joseph H. Keenan, Jing Chao, and Joseph Kaye. — 2d ed. — New York: Wiley, c1980. xiv, 217 p.: ill.; 26 cm. 'A Wiley-Interscience publication.' 1. Air — Tables. 2. Thermodynamics — Tables I. Chao, Jing. joint author. II. Kaye, Joseph, 1912- joint author. III. T. QC161.5.K43 1980    621.43/021/2 19    LC 79-15098    ISBN 0471022071

**Dushman, Saul, 1883-.**    • 5.2042
Scientific foundations of vacuum technique. — 2d ed. Revised by members of the research staff, General Electric Research Laboratory. J. M. Lafferty, editor. — New York: Wiley, [1962] 806 p.: illus.; 24 cm. 1. Vacuum 2. Gases, Kinetic theory of I. T.
QC166.D85 1962    533.5    LC 61-17361

# QC171–220 ATOMIC PHYSICS. CONSTITUTION AND PROPERTIES OF MATTER

**Abro, A. d'.**    • 5.2043
[Decline of mechanism] The rise of the new physics; its mathematical and physical theories. [2d ed. New York] Dover Publications [1952, c1951] 2 v. (ix, 982 p.) ports., diagrs. 21 cm. 'Formerly titled 'Decline of mechanism.'' 1. Quantum theory 2. Mathematical physics I. T.
QC171.A3 1952    530.1    LC 52-8895

**Born, Max, 1882-1970.**    • 5.2044
The restless universe / Figures by Otto Koenigsberger; authorized translation by Winifred M. Deans. — [2d ed., rev.]. — New York: Dover Publications, 1951. 315 p.: ill.; 25 cm. 1. Matter — Constitution 2. Physics I. T.
QC171.B63 1951    530.1    LC 51-13192

**Gamow, George, 1904-1968.**    • 5.2045
The atom and its nucleus. — [Englewood Cliffs, N.J.]: Prentice-Hall, [1961] 153 p.: ill.; 21 cm. — (A Spectrum book, S-St-1) 1. Matter 2. Atoms 3. Nuclear physics I. T.
QC171.G29    539    LC 61-6360

**Gottlieb, Milton.**    • 5.2046
Seven states of matter, by scientists of the Westinghouse Research Laboratories: Milton Gottlieb, Max Garbuny [and] Werner Emmerich. Sharon Banigan, executive editor. New York, Walker [1966] 247 p. illus., ports. 24 cm. (A Westinghouse search book) 1. Matter — Properties I. Garbuny, Max, 1912- joint author. II. Emmerich, Werner. joint author. III. Westinghouse Research Laboratories. IV. T.
QC171.G64    530.1    LC 66-13265

**Willmott, J. C. (John Charles)**    5.2047
Atomic physics / [by] J. C. Willmott. — London; New York: Wiley [1975] xiv, 357 p.: ill.; 24 cm. (The Manchester physics series) 1. Nuclear physics 2. Quantum theory I. T.
QC171.2.W54    539.7    LC 74-9580    ISBN 0471949302 ISBN 0471949310

# QC173 Nuclear Physics. Constitution of Matter and Antimatter

## QC173 A–F

**Arya, Atam Parkash.**    • 5.2048
Fundamentals of nuclear physics [by] Atam P. Arya. — Boston: Allyn and Bacon, 1966. xiv, 646 p.: illus.; 24 cm. 'Chart of the nuclides, Knolls Atomic Power Laboratory, operated by the General Electric Company under the direction of Naval Reactors, U.S. Atomic Energy Commission. Eighth edition—revised to March 1965' ([2] p. (on fold. l.)) in pocket. 1. Nuclear physics I. T.
QC173.A75    539.7    LC 66-25817

**Bethe, Hans Albrecht, 1906-.**    • 5.2049
Elementary nuclear theory / [by] Hans A. Bethe and Philip Morrison. 2d ed. New York: Wiley [1956] 274 p.: ill.; 24 cm. 1. Nuclear physics I. Morrison, Philip. joint author. II. T.
QC173.B48 1956    539.1 539.7*    LC 56-7152

**Beyer, Robert T. (Robert Thomas), 1920-.**    • 5.2050
Foundations of nuclear physics: facsimiles of thirteen fundamental studies as they were originally reported in the scientific journals / with a bibliography compiled by Robert T. Beyer. — New York: Dover Publications, c1949. 272 p.: ill.; 24 cm. — ('Foundations' series) 1. Nuclear physics I. T.
QC173.B485    539.1    LC 49-8636

**Bohr, Niels Hendrik David, 1885-.**    • 5.2051
Atomic theory and the description of nature / by Niels Bohr. — New York: The Macmillan company; Cambridge, Eng. . The University press, 1934-. v. Printed in Great Britain. 1. Atoms 2. Quantum theory I. T.
QC173.B535

**Broglie, Louis de, 1892-.**    • 5.2052
Matter and light; the new physics, tr. by W. H. Johnston. — New York, Dover, 1946. 300 p. diagrs. 20 cm. 'The undulatory aspects of the electron; [address delivered at Stockholm on receiving the Nobel prize, December 12, 1929]': p. [165]-179. 1. Matter — Constitution 2. Light 3. Wave mechanics 4. Physics — Philosophy I. Johnston, Walter Henry, 1895- tr. II. T.
QC173.B    QC173.B8532 1946.    530.1    LC A 48-8148 *

**Eisberg, Robert Martin.**    • 5.2053
Fundamentals of modern physics. — New York: Wiley, [1961] 729 p.: illus.; 24 cm. 1. Matter — Constitution 2. Quantum theory 3. Relativity (Physics) I. T.
QC173.E358    530.1    LC 61-6770

**Enge, Harald A.**    5.2054
Introduction to nuclear physics / Harald A. Enge. — Reading, Mass.: Addison-Wesley Pub. Co., c1966. x, 582 p.: ill.; 24 cm. (Addison-Wesley series in physics; 1870) 1. Nuclear physics I. T.
QC173.E53    LC 66-21268

**Fano, Ugo.**    • 5.2055
Basic physics of atoms and molecules [by] U. Fano and L. Fano. New York, Wiley [1959] 414 p. illus. 24 cm. 1. Matter — Constitution 2. Quantum theory 3. Nuclear physics — Problems, exercises, etc. I. Fano, L. joint author. II. T.
QC173.F3    539.1    LC 59-6765

**Flowers, Brian Hilton.**    • 5.2056
Properties of matter / [by] B. H. Flowers, E. Mendoza. — London; New York: J. Wiley and Sons, 1970. xiii, 319 p.: ill.; 24 cm. — (The Manchester physics series) 1. Matter — Properties I. Mendoza, Eric, joint author. II. T.
QC173.F59    539/.1    LC 70-118151    ISBN 0471264970

**French, A. P. (Anthony Philip), 1920-.**    • 5.2057
Principles of modern physics. New York, Wiley [1958] 355 p. illus. 24 cm. 1. Matter — Constitution 2. Relativity (Physics) 3. Quantum theory I. T.
QC173.F7217    530.1    LC 58-7898

**Frisch, Otto Robert, 1904-.**    5.2058
The nature of matter [by] Otto R. Frisch. London: Thames and Hudson; New York: Dutton, [1972] 216 p.: illus., (part col.) (The world of Science Library.) 1. Atoms 2. Atomic theory 3. Matter — Constitution I. T. II. Series.
QC173.F724    LC 70-180712    ISBN 0525164278

## QC173 G–K

**Gamow, George, 1904-1968.**    • 5.2059
Theory of atomic nucleus energy–sources / by G. Gamov and C. L. Critchfield; being the 3d ed. of Structure of atomic nucleus and nuclear transformations. — Oxford: Clarendon Press, 1949. vi, 344 p.: ill. — (International series of monographs on physics.) 1. Nuclear energy I. Critchfield, Charles Louis, 1910- II. T. III. Series.
QC173.G3 1949    LC 49-10627

**Gardner, Martin, 1914-.**    5.2060
The ambidextrous universe: mirror asymmetry and time–reversed worlds / Martin Gardner; illustrated by John Mackey. — 2d rev. updated ed. — New York: Scribner, c1979. 293 p.: ill; 21 cm. 1. Parity nonconservation 2. Symmetry (Physics) I. T.
QC173.G34 1979    501    LC 78-16984    ISBN 0684157896

**Gasiorowicz, Stephen.**    5.2061
The structure of matter: a survey of modern physics / Stephen Gasiorowicz. — Reading, Mass.: Addison-Wesley Pub. Co., c1979. xii, 525 p.: ill.; 24 cm. —

(Addison-Wesley series in physics.) Includes index. 1. Matter — Constitution 2. Physics I. T.
QC173.G348        530.1        LC 78-18645        ISBN 0201025116

**Heisenberg, Werner, 1901-1976.**                                    5.2062
Nuclear physics. New York, Philosophical Library [1953] 225 p. illus. 19 cm. Translation of Die Physik der Atomkerne. 1. Nuclear energy 2. Nuclear physics I. T.
QC173.H3854        541.2        LC 53-13280

**Heisenberg, Werner, 1901-1976.**                                  • 5.2063
[Teil und das Ganze. English] Physics and beyond; encounters and conversations. Translated from the German by Arnold J. Pomerans. [1st ed.] New York, Harper & Row [c1971] xviii, 247 p. 22 cm. (World perspectives. v. 42) Translation of Der Teil und das Ganze. 1. Nuclear physics 2. Physics — Philosophy I. T. II. Series.
QC173.H38613 1971        539.7        LC 78-95963

**Hirschfelder, Joseph Oakland, 1911-.**                            • 5.2064
Molecular theory of gases and liquids / [by] Joseph O. Hirschfelder, Charles F. Curtiss [and] R. Byron Bird; with the assistance of the staff of the former University of Wisconsin Naval Research Laboratory. — Corrected printing with notes added. [New York]: Wiley [1965, c1954] xxvi, 1249 p.: ill.; 24 cm. 1. Molecular theory 2. Gases 3. Liquids I. Curtiss, Charles F. (Charles Francis) joint author. II. Bird, R. Byron (Robert Byron), 1924- joint author. III. University of Wisconsin. Theoretical Chemistry Laboratory. IV. T.
QC173.H54 1965        532        LC 66-1476

**Hughes, Vernon W.**                                              • 5.2065
Atomic and electron physics. Edited by Vernon W. Hughes and Howard L. Schultz. — New York: Academic Press, 1967. 2 v.: illus.; 24 cm. — (Methods of experimental physics. v. 4) 1. Atoms 2. Nuclear physics I. Schultz, Howard Louis, joint author. II. T. III. Series.
QC173.H758 1967        539.7        LC 67-23170

**Irvine, John Maxwell.**                                          • 5.2066
Nuclear structure theory, by J. M. Irvine. — [1st ed.]. — Oxford; New York: Pergamon Press, [1972] xiii, 478 p.: illus.; 26 cm. — (International series of monographs in natural philosophy, v. 49) 1. Nuclear structure 2. Many-body problem I. T.
QC173.I73        539.7        LC 72-80303        ISBN 0080164013

**Jammer, Max.**                                                   • 5.2067
Concepts of mass, in classical and modern physics. Cambridge, Harvard University Press, 1961. 230 p. 22 cm. 1. Mass (Physics) I. T.
QC173.J28        531.54        LC 61-13737

**Kaplan, Irving, 1912-.**                                         • 5.2068
Nuclear physics. 2d ed. Reading, Mass.: Addison-Wesley Pub. Co. [1963] 770 p.: ill.; 24 cm. (Addison-Wesley series in nuclear science and engineering.) 1. Nuclear physics I. T. II. Series.
QC173.K27 1963        539.7        LC 62-9402

## QC173 L–Z

**Landau, L. D. (Lev Davidovich), 1908-1968.**                     5.2069
[Lektsii po teorii atomnogo iadra. English] Lectures on nuclear theory, by L.D. Landau and Ya. Smorodinsky. Translated from the Russian. Rev. ed. New York, Plenum Press, 1959. 108 p. illus. 24 cm. 1. Nuclear physics I. Smorodinskiĭ, IA. A. (IAkov Abramovich) joint author. II. T.
QC173.L2463 1959        539.7        LC 59-8865

**Livesey, Derek L. (Derek Leonard), 1923-.**                      • 5.2070
Atomic and nuclear physics [by] Derek L. Livesey. Waltham, Mass., Blaisdell Pub. Co. [1966] xi, 525 p. illus. 26 cm. (Blaisdell book in the pure and applied sciences.) 1. Nuclear physics I. T. II. Series.
QC173.L78        539        LC 65-17961

**Orear, Jay.**                                                    5.2071
Nuclear physics: a course given by Enrico Fermi at the University of Chicago / notes compiled by Jay Orear, A. H. Rosenfeld, and R. A. Schluter. — Rev. ed. — [Chicago]: University of Chicago Press, [1960, c1950] ix, 248 p.: ill.; 25 cm. 'Notes on lectures in Physics 262-3: Nuclear Physics, given by Enrico Fermi, Jan.-June 1949.' 1. Nuclear physics I. Fermi, Enrico, 1901-1954. II. Rosenfeld, Arthur H., 1926- joint author. III. Schluter, R. A., joint author. IV. T.
QC173.O56 1960        539.7        LC 75-277214

**Polkinghorne, J. C., 1930-.**                                    5.2072
The particle play: an account of the ultimate constituents of matter / J. C. Polkinghorne. — Oxford; San Francisco: W. H. Freeman, c1979. viii, 138 p.: ill.; 23 cm. Includes index. 1. Matter — Constitution 2. Quarks I. T.
QC173.P559        530        LC 79-17846        ISBN 071671177X

**Ramsey, Norman, 1915-.**                                         • 5.2073
Molecular beams. Oxford, Clarendon Press, 1956. 466 p. illus. 25 cm. (The International series of monographs on physics) 1. Molecular beams I. T.
QC173.R313        539        LC 56-3940

**Rutherford Centennial Symposium, University of Canterbury,**     5.2074
**1971.**
The structure of matter, edited by B. G. Wybourne. [Christchurch, N.Z.] University of Canterbury, 1972. 541 p. illus. 24 cm. Symposium held 7-9 July 1971 in honor of the centenary of the birth of Ernest Rutherford. English or French. 'Distributors for U.S.: International Scholarly Book Services, Portland, Oregon.' 1. Rutherford, Ernest, 1871-1937 — Congresses. 2. Matter — Constitution — Congresses. 3. Nuclear physics — Congresses. I. Wybourne, Brian G. ed. II. Rutherford, Ernest, 1871-1937. III. T.
QC173.R83 1971        539/.1        LC 79-185696        ISBN 0900322177

**Segrè, Emilio. ed.**                                             • 5.2075
Experimental nuclear physics. — New York: Wiley, [1953-59] 3 v.: illus.; 24 cm. 1. Nuclear physics I. T.
QC173.S313        539.1 539.7*        LC 52-5852

**Semat, Henry, 1900-.**                                           5.2076
Introduction to atomic and nuclear physics / [by] Henry Semat [and] John R. Albright. — 5th ed. — New York: Holt, Rinehart and Winston, [1972] xv, 712 p.: ill.; 25 cm. First ed. published in 1939 under title: Introduction to atomic physics. 1. Physics 2. Atoms 3. Nuclear physics I. Albright, John Rupp, 1937- joint author. II. T.
QC173.S315 1972        539.7        LC 70-155296        ISBN 0030854024

**Taylor, John Robert, 1939-.**                                    • 5.2077
Scattering theory: the quantum theory on nonrelativistic collisions [by] John R. Taylor. — New York: Wiley, [1972] xvi, 477 p.: illus.; 23 cm. 1. Scattering (Physics) I. T.
QC173.T33        539.7/54        LC 75-37938        ISBN 0471849006

**Woodgate, Gordon Kemble.**                                       5.2078
Elementary atomic structure / G. K. Woodgate. — 2d ed. — Oxford: Clarendon Press; New York: Oxford University Press, 1980. ix, 228 p.: graphs; 24 cm. 1. Atomic structure I. T.
QC173.W66 1980        539/.14        LC 79-41673        ISBN 0198511469

## QC173.3–173.39 PROPERTIES OF MATTER

**Brush, Stephen G.**                                              5.2079
Statistical physics and the atomic theory of matter: from Boyle and Newton to Landau and Onsager / by Stephen G. Brush. — Princeton, N.J.: Princeton University Press, c1983. ix, 356 p.: ill.; 25 cm. — (Princeton series in physics.) Includes index. 1. Matter — Properties 2. Quantum theory 3. Statistical physics 4. Atomic theory I. T. II. Series.
QC173.3.B78 1983        530.1 19        LC 82-61357        ISBN 0691083258

**Cotterill, Rodney, 1933-.**                                      5.2080
The Cambridge guide to the material world / Rodney Cotterill. — Cambridge [Cambridgeshire]; New York: Cambridge University Press, 1985. 352 p.: ill. (some col.); 30 cm. Includes index. 1. Matter — Properties I. T.
QC173.3.C66 1985        500 19        LC 84-7686        ISBN 0521246407

**Fraga, Serafin.**                                                5.2081
Handbook of atomic data / Serafin Fraga, Jacek Karwowski, K. M. S. Saxena. Amsterdam; New York: Elsevier Scientific Pub. Co., 1976. 551 p.; 25 cm. Includes index. 1. Atoms — Handbooks, manuals, etc. 2. Ions — Handbooks, manuals, etc. 3. Hartree-Fock approximation — Handbooks, manuals, etc. I. Karwowski, Jacek. joint author. II. Saxena, K. M. S. joint author. III. T.
QC173.397.F7        539.7/021/2        LC 76-16162        ISBN 0444414614

**Moses, Alfred James, 1921-.**                                    5.2082
The practicing scientist's handbook: a guide for physical and terrestrial scientists and engineers / Alfred J. Moses. — New York: Van Nostrand Reinhold Co., c1978. x, 1292 p.: ill.; 26 cm. Chiefly tables. 1. Matter — Properties — Handbooks, manuals, etc. 2. Materials — Handbooks, manuals, etc. I. T.
QC173.397.M67        530.4        LC 77-5866        ISBN 0442255845

## QC173.5–173.75 RELATIVITY PHYSICS

**Miller, Arthur I.**                                              5.2083
Albert Einstein's special theory of relativity: emergence (1905) and early interpretation, 1905–1911 / Arthur I. Miller. — Reading, Mass.: Addison-Wesley Pub. Co., Advanced Book Program, 1981. xxviii, 466 p.: ill.; 24 cm.

Includes index. 1. Einstein, Albert, 1879-1955. 2. Relativity (Physics) — History. 3. Physics — History. 4. Physicists — Biography I. T.
QC173.52.M54    530.1/1    *LC* 79-27495    *ISBN* 0201046806

**Bergmann, Peter Gabriel.**       **5.2084**
Introduction to the theory of relativity / by Peter Gabriel Bergmann; with a foreword by Albert Einstein. New York: Dover Publications, 1976. xii, 307 p.: ill.; 22 cm. 1. Relativity (Physics) I. T.
QC173.55.B47 1976    530.1/1    *ISBN* 0486632822

**Bergmann, Peter Gabriel.**       **5.2085**
The riddle of gravitation / Peter G. Bergmann. — Rev. and updated ed. — New York: Scribner, 1987, c1968. 1 v. Includes index. 1. Relativity (Physics) 2. Gravitation I. T.
QC173.55.B49 1987    530.1/1 19    *LC* 86-22090    *ISBN* 0684184605

**Calder, Nigel.**       **5.2086**
Einstein's universe / Nigel Calder. — New York: Viking Press, 1979. 154 p., [5] leaves of plates: ill.; 24 cm. Includes index. 1. Relativity (Physics) 2. Astrophysics 3. Cosmology I. T.
QC173.55.C34    521    *LC* 78-26087    *ISBN* 0670290769

**Einstein, Albert, 1879-1955.**       **5.2087**
The meaning of relativity / Albert Einstein. — 5th ed., including the Relativistic theory of the non-symmetric field. — Princeton: Princeton University Press, 1955 [c1956] 166 p.: diagrs.; 21 cm. Includes index. 'Translated by Edwin Plimpton Adams ... Ernst G. Straus ... [and] Sonja Bargmann.' The Stafford Little lectures, 1921. 1. Einstein, Albert, 1879-1955 — Biography. 2. Relativity (Physics) 3. Physicists — Biography I. T.
QC173.55.E384    530.1/1 19    *LC* 83-114212

**Frankel, Theodore, 1929-.**       **5.2088**
Gravitational curvature: an introduction to Einstein's theory / Theodore Frankel. — San Francisco: W. H. Freeman, c1979. xviii, 172 p.: ill.; 24 cm. Includes index. 1. Relativity (Physics) 2. Gravitation I. T.
QC173.55.F7    530.1/1    *LC* 78-12092    *ISBN* 0716710064

**Lilley, Sam.**       **5.2089**
Discovering relativity for yourself / with some help from Sam Lilley. — Cambridge [Eng.]; New York: Cambridge University Press, 1981. xi, 425 p.: ill.; 24 cm. Includes index. 1. Relativity (Physics) I. T.
QC173.55.L54    530.1/1    *LC* 80-40263    *ISBN* 0521230381

**Resnick, Robert, 1923-.**       **5.2090**
Basic concepts in relativity and early quantum theory. New York: Wiley [1972] xi, 244 p.: ill.; 26 cm. 1. Relativity (Physics) 2. Quantum theory I. T.
QC173.55.R46 1972    530.1/1    *LC* 78-39835    *ISBN* 0471717029 *ISBN* 0471717037

**Rindler, Wolfgang, 1924-.**       • **5.2091**
Essential relativity: special, general, and cosmological / Wolfgang Rindler. 2d ed. — New York: Springer-Verlag, c1977. xiv, 284 p.: ill.; 24 cm. (Texts and monographs in physics) 1. Relativity (Physics) I. T.
QC173.55.R56 1977    530.1/1    *LC* 76-28816    *ISBN* 038707970X

**Torretti, Roberto, 1930-.**       **5.2092**
Relativity and geometry / by Roberto Torretti. — 1st ed. — Oxford [Oxfordshire]; New York: Pergamon Press, 1983. x, 395 p.: ill.; 23 cm. — (Foundations and philosophy of science and technology series) Includes index. 1. Relativity (Physics) 2. Geometry, Differential 3. Geometry — Philosophy. I. T.
QC173.55.T67 1983    530.1/1 19    *LC* 82-9826    *ISBN* 0080267734

**Epstein, Lewis Carroll.**       **5.2093**
Relativity visualized / written and illustrated by Lewis Carroll Epstein. — San Francisco: Insight Press, c1983. xi, 199, [22] p.: ill. 1. Relativity (Physics) I. T.
QC173.57.E68    530.11    *LC* 82-84280    *ISBN* 0935218033

**Davies, P. C. W.**       **5.2094**
The physics of time asymmetry / P. C. W. Davies. — Berkeley: University of California Press, 1974. xviii, 214 p.: ill.; 24 cm. 1. Space and time I. T.
QC173.59.S65 D38 1974    530.1/1    *LC* 74-81536    *ISBN* 0520028252

**Davies, P. C. W.**       **5.2095**
Space and time in the modern universe / P. C. W. Davies. Cambridge; New York: Cambridge University Press, 1977. 232 p.: ill.; 23 cm. Includes index. 1. Space and time I. T.
QC173.59.S65 D39    530.1/1    *LC* 76-27902    *ISBN* 0521214459

**Salmon, Wesley C.**       **5.2096**
Space, time, and motion: a philosophical introduction / Wesley C. Salmon. — 2d ed., rev. — Minneapolis: University of Minnesota Press, c1980. 159 p.: ill.; 23 cm. Includes index. 1. Space and time 2. Motion 3. Physics — Philosophy I. T.
QC173.59.S65 S24 1980    530.1/1 19    *LC* 80-18423

**Sklar, Lawrence.**       **5.2097**
Space, time, and spacetime. — Berkeley: University of California, [1974] xii, 423 p.: ill.; 24 cm. 1. Space and time I. T.
QC173.59.S65 S55    114    *LC* 73-76096    *ISBN* 0520024338

**Adler, Ronald.**       **5.2098**
Introduction to general relativity [by] Ronald Adler, Maurice Bazin [and] Menahem Schiffer. — 2d ed. — New York: McGraw-Hill, [1975] xiv, 549 p.; 24 cm. — (International series in pure and applied physics) 1. General relativity (Physics) I. Bazin, Maurice, joint author. II. Schiffer, Menahem, joint author. III. T.
QC173.6.A34 1975    530.1/1    *LC* 74-18459    *ISBN* 0070004234

**Clarke, C.**       **5.2099**
Elementary general relativity / C. Clarke. — New York: Wiley, 1980, c1979. ix, 131 p.: ill.; 24 cm. 'A Halsted Press book.' Includes index. 1. General relativity (Physics) I. T.
QC173.6.C55 1980    530.1/1    *LC* 80-116224    *ISBN* 0470269308

**Foster, J.**       **5.2100**
A short course in general relativity / J. Foster and J. D. Nightingale. — London; New York: Longman, 1979. xv, 192 p.: ill.; 22 cm. — (Longman mathematical texts) Includes index. 1. General relativity (Physics) I. Nightingale, J. D. II. T.
QC173.6.F67    530.1/1    *LC* 78-40859    *ISBN* 0582441943

**Geroch, Robert.**       **5.2101**
General relativity from A to B / Robert Geroch. — Chicago: University of Chicago Press, 1978. xi, 225 p.: ill.; 21 cm. Includes index. 1. General relativity (Physics) I. T.
QC173.6.G47    530.1/1    *LC* 77-18908    *ISBN* 0226288633

**Kilmister, C. W. (Clive William)**       **5.2102**
General theory of relativity, by C. W. Kilmister. [1st ed.] Oxford, New York, Pergamon Press [1973] ix, 365 p. 21 cm. (The Commonwealth and international library. Selected readings in physics) 1. General relativity (Physics) I. T.
QC173.6.K54 1973    530.1/1    *LC* 73-7639    *ISBN* 0080176399 *ISBN* 0080176453

**Schutz, Bernard F.**       **5.2103**
A first course in general relativity / Bernard F. Schutz. — Cambridge [Cambridgeshire]; New York: Cambridge University Press, 1985. xiv, 376 p.: ill.; 24 cm. Includes index. 1. General relativity (Physics) 2. Astrophysics I. T.
QC173.6.S38 1985    530.1/1 19    *LC* 83-23205    *ISBN* 0521257700

**Wald, Robert M.**       **5.2104**
General relativity / Robert M. Wald. — Chicago: University of Chicago Press, 1984. xiii, 491 p.: ill.; 25 cm. Includes index. 1. General relativity (Physics) I. T.
QC173.6.W35 1984    530.1/1 19    *LC* 83-17969    *ISBN* 0226870324

**Rindler, Wolfgang, 1924-.**       **5.2105**
Introduction to special relativity / Wolfgang Rindler. — Oxford: Cambridge University, 1982. x, 185 p.: ill.; 22 cm. Includes index. 1. Special relativity (Physics) I. T.
QC173.65.R56 1982    530.1/1 19

# QC173.96–174.5 Quantum Theory. Quantum Mechanics

**Gribbin, John R.**       **5.2106**
In search of Schrödinger's cat: quantum physics and reality / John Gribbin. — Toronto; New York: Bantam Books, 1984. xvi, 302 p.: ill.; 21 cm. Includes index. 1. Schrödinger, Erwin, 1887-1961. 2. Quantum theory — History. 3. Reality I. T.
QC173.98.G75 1984    530.1/2/09 19    *LC* 84-2975    *ISBN* 0553341030

**Jammer, Max.**       **5.2107**
The philosophy of quantum mechanics: the interpretations of quantum mechanics in historical perspective. — New York: Wiley, [1974] xi, 536 p.; 24 cm. 'A Wiley-Interscience publication.' 1. Quantum theory — History. 2. Physics — Philosophy I. T.
QC173.98.J35    530.1/2    *LC* 74-13030    *ISBN* 0471439584

**Colston Research Society.**       **5.2108**
Observation and interpretation: a symposium of philosophers and physicists / edited by S. Körner in collaboration with M. H. L. Pryce. — New York: Academic Press, 1957. 218 p.: ill.; 26 cm. (Colston papers. v.9) Proceedings of the ninth symposium ... held in the University of Bristol, April 1-4, 1957.

1. Science — Philosophy 2. Science — Methodology 3. Observation (Psychology) I. Körner, Stephan, 1913- ed. II. T. III. Series.
QC174.C6x AS122.C62 vol. 9

**Bjorken, James D.**     • 5.2109
Relativistic quantum mechanics [by] James D. Bjorken [and] Sidney D. Drell. New York, McGraw-Hill [1964] x, 300 p. 23 cm. (International series in pure and applied physics.) 1. Quantum theory I. Drell, Sidney D. (Sidney David), 1926- joint author. II. T. III. Series.
QC174.1.B52     530.12     LC 63-21778

**Bohm, David, 1917-.**     • 5.2110
Quantum theory. — New York: Prentice-Hall, 1951. ix, 646 p.: ill. — (Prentice-Hall physics series) 1. Quantum theory I. T.
QC174.1.B6     LC 51-1683

**Cropper, William H.**     • 5.2111
The quantum physicists and an introduction to their physics / [by] William H. Cropper. — New York: Oxford University Press, 1970. ix, 257 p.: ill., port.; 23 cm. 1. Quantum theory I. T.
QC174.1.C7     530.12     LC 73-83037

**Heisenberg, Werner.**     • 5.2112
The physical principles of the quantum theory. New York: Dover Publications, [1950?, c1930]. 183p.,illus. 1. Quantum theory I. T.
QC174.1.H4 1950     530.1     LC 49-11952

**Jammer, Max.**     • 5.2113
The conceptual development of quantum mechanics. New York, McGraw-Hill [1966] xii, 399 p. illus. 24 cm. (International series in pure and applied physics.) 1. Quantum theory I. T. II. Series.
QC174.1.J26     530.123     LC 66-17914

**Jauch, Josef Maria, 1914-1974.**     5.2114
Are quanta real? A Galilean dialogue [by] J. M. Jauch. — Bloomington: Indiana University Press, [1973] xii, 106 p.: illus.; 25 cm. 1. Quantum theory I. T.
QC174.1.J27 1973     530.1/2     LC 72-79907     ISBN 0253308607

**Kittel, Charles.**     • 5.2115
Quantum theory of solids. New York, Wiley [1963] xi, 435 p. diagrs. 24 cm. 1. Quantum theory 2. Solid state physics I. T.
QC174.1.K54     530.12     LC 63-20633

**Mandl, F. (Franz), 1923-.**     • 5.2116
Quantum mechanics. 2d ed. New York, Academic Press, 1957. 267 p. 26 cm. 1. Quantum theory I. T.
QC174.1.M28 1957     530.1     LC 58-1453

**Merzbacher, Eugen.**     • 5.2117
Quantum mechanics [by] Eugen Merzbacher. — 2d ed. — New York: J. Wiley, [1970] x, 621 p.: illus.; 23 cm. 1. Quantum theory I. T.
QC174.1.M36 1970     530.12     LC 74-88316     ISBN 0471596701

**Mott, Nevill Francis, 1905- .**     • 5.2118
Wave mechanics and its applications / by N.F. Mott and I.N. Sneddon. — New York: Dover Publications, [1963] 393 p.: diagrs. (Dover books on advanced science) 'S1070'. 1. Quantum theory I. Sneddon, Ian Naismith. II. T. III. Series.
QC174.1.M65 1963

**Peierls, Rudolf Ernst, Sir, 1907-.**     • 5.2119
Quantum theory of solids / by R.E. Peierls. — 1st ed. — Oxford: Clarendon Press, 1955. viii, 229 p.: ill. — (International series of monographs on physics.) 1. Quantum theory 2. Solids I. T. II. Series.
QC174.1.P43

**Reichenbach, Hans, 1891-1953.**     • 5.2120
Philosophic foundations of quantum mechanics. Berkeley, University of California Press, 1946. x, 182 p. diagrs. 1. Quantum theory 2. Physics — Philosophy I. T.
QC174.1 R4 1946     LC 44-4471

**Schiff, Leonard I. (Leonard Isaac), 1915-.**     • 5.2121
Quantum mechanics / [by] Leonard I. Schiff. 3d ed. New York: McGraw-Hill [1968] xviii, 544 p.: ill.; 23 cm. (International series in pure and applied physics) 1. Quantum theory I. T.
QC174.1.S34 1968     530.12     LC 68-25665

**Slater, John Clarke, 1900-1976.**     • 5.2122
Quantum theory of matter [by] John C. Slater. — 2d ed. — New York: McGraw-Hill, [1968] 763 p.: illus.; 23 cm. — (International series in pure and applied physics) 1. Quantum theory I. T.
QC174.1.S55 1968     530.12     LC 68-11620

**Waerden, B. L. van der (Bartel Leendert), 1903- comp.**     • 5.2123
Sources of quantum mechanics, edited with a historical introd. by B. L. van der Waerden. New York, Dover Publications [1968, c1967] xi, 430 p. 22 cm. (Classics of science, v. 5) 1. Quantum theory — History — Sources. I. T.
QC174.1.W3 1968     530.12/3/08     LC 68-12916

**Wieder, Sol.**     5.2124
The foundations of quantum theory. — New York: Academic Press, [1973] xv, 399 p.: illus.; 25 cm. 1. Quantum theory I. T.
QC174.1.W475     530.1/2     LC 72-9422     ISBN 0127490507

**Ziman, J. M. (John M.), 1925-.**     • 5.2125
Elements of advanced quantum theory, by J. M. Ziman. — London: Cambridge U.P., 1969. xii, 269 p.: illus.; 24 cm. 1. Quantum theory I. T.
QC174.1.Z49     530.12     LC 69-16290     ISBN 0521074584

## QC174.12–174.35 GENERAL WORKS

**Bethe, Hans Albrecht, 1906-.**     5.2126
Intermediate quantum mechanics / Hans A. Bethe, Roman Jackiw. — 3rd ed. — Menlo Park, Calif.: Benjamin/Cummings Pub. Co., 1986. xviii, 396 p.; 24 cm. 1. Quantum theory I. Jackiw, Roman W. II. T.
QC174.12.B47 1986     530.1/2 19     LC 85-19010     ISBN 0805307575

**Bohm, David.**     5.2127
Wholeness and the implicate order / David Bohm. — London; Boston: Routledge & Kegan Paul, 1981, c1980. xv, 224 p.: ill.; 22 cm. 1. Quantum theory 2. Physics — Philosophy 3. Whole and parts (Philosophy) I. T.
QC174.12.B633 1981     530.1/2 19     LC 80-40026     ISBN 0710009712

**Cagnac, Bernard, 1931-.**     5.2128
Modern atomic physics: fundamental principles / B. Cagnac, J. C. Pebay-Peyroula; translated by J. S. Deech. — New York: Wiley, 1975. xxiv, 328 p.: ill.; 24 cm. Translation of v. 1 of Physique atomique. 'A Halsted Press book.' Includes index. 1. Nuclear physics 2. Atomic theory 3. Quantum theory I. Pebay-Peyroula, Jean Claude, 1930- joint author. II. T.
QC174.12.C3213 1975     539.7     LC 74-28161     ISBN 0470129204

**Davydov, A. S. (Aleksandr Sergeevich), 1912-.**     5.2129
[Kvantovaia mekhanika. English] Quantum mechanics / by A. S. Davydov; translated, edited, and with additions by D. ter Haar. — 2d ed. — Oxford; New York: Pergamon Press, 1976. xiii, 637 p.: ill.; 25 cm. — (International series in natural philosophy; v. 1) (Pergamon international library of science, technology, engineering, and social studies) Translation of Kvantovaia mekhanika. 1. Quantum theory I. T.
QC174.12.D3813 1976     530.1/2     LC 76-11628     ISBN 0080204384

**French, A. P. (Anthony Philip), 1920-.**     5.2130
An introduction to quantum physics / A. P. French, Edwin F. Taylor. — 1st ed. — New York: Norton, c1978. xviii, 670 p.: ill.; 24 cm. (The M.I.T. introductory physics series) Includes index. 1. Quantum theory I. Taylor, Edwin F. joint author. II. T.
QC174.12.F73     530.1/2     LC 78-4853     ISBN 0393090159

**Fromhold, A. T.**     5.2131
Quantum mechanics for applied physics and engineering / Albert Thomas Fromhold, Jr. — New York: Academic Press, 1981. xvi, 430 p.: ill.; 24 cm. Includes index. 1. Quantum theory 2. Engineering I. T.
QC174.12.F76     530.1/2 19     LC 80-19001     ISBN 0122691504

**Herbert, Nick.**     5.2132
Quantum reality: beyond the new physics / Nick Herbert. — Garden City, N.Y.: Anchor Press/Doubleday, 1985. xv, 268 p.: ill.; 22 cm. Includes index. 1. Quantum theory — Popular works. I. T.
QC174.12.H47 1985     530.1/2 19     LC 82-46033     ISBN 0385187041

**Jordan, Thomas F., 1936-.**     5.2133
Quantum mechanics in simple matrix form / Thomas F. Jordan. — New York: Wiley, c1986. xi, 259 p.: ill.; 23 cm. 'A Wiley-Interscience publication.' 1. Quantum theory 2. Matrices I. T.
QC174.12.J67 1986     530.1/2 19     LC 85-12121     ISBN 0471817511

**Landau, L. D. (Lev Davidovich), 1908-1968.**     5.2134
[Kvantovaia mekhanika. English] Quantum mechanics: non–relativistic theory / by L. D. Landau and E. M. Lifshitz; translated from the Russian by J. B. Sykes and J. S. Bell. — 3d ed., rev. and enl. — Oxford; New York: Pergamon Press, 1977. xiv, 673 p.: ill.; 25 cm. (Their Course of theoretical physics; v. 3) Translation of Kvantovaia mekhanika. 1. Quantum theory I. Lifshits, E. M. (Evgeniĭ Mikhaĭlovich) joint author. II. T.
QC174.12.L3513 1977     530.1/2     LC 76-18223     ISBN 0080209408. ISBN 008019012X pbk

**Morrison, Michael A., 1949-.**      **5.2135**
Quantum states of atoms, molecules, and solids / Michael A. Morrison, Thomas L. Estle, Neal F. Lane. — Englewood Cliffs, N.J.: Prentice-Hall, c1976. xv, 575 p.: ill.; 24 cm. (Prentice-Hall physics series) Includes index. 1. Quantum theory 2. Electrons 3. Atomic theory 4. Molecular theory 5. Energy-band theory of solids I. Estle, Thomas Leo, 1931- joint author. II. Lane, Neal F., 1938- joint author. III. T.
QC174.12.M68     530.1/2     *LC* 75-20246     *ISBN* 0137479808

**Pauling, Linus, 1901-.**      **5.2136**
Introduction to quantum mechanics: with applications to chemistry / by Linus Pauling and E. Bright Wilson, Jr. — New York, N.Y.: Dover Publications, 1985, c1963. xi, 468 p.: ill.; 22 cm. Reprint. Originally published: New York; London: McGraw-Hill, 1935. 1. Quantum theory 2. Wave mechanics 3. Chemistry, Physical and theoretical I. Wilson, E. Bright (Edgar Bright), 1908- II. T.
QC174.12.P39 1985     530.1/2 19     *LC* 84-25919     *ISBN* 0486648710

**Shankar, Ramamurti.**      **5.2137**
Principles of quantum mechanics / Ramamurti Shankar. — New York: Plenum Press, c1980. xviii, 612 p.: ill.; 24 cm. Includes index. 1. Quantum theory I. T.
QC174.12.S52     530.1/2     *LC* 79-24490     *ISBN* 0306403978

**Slater, John Clarke, 1900-1976.**      • **5.2138**
Quantum theory of molecules and solids [by] John C. Slater. — New York: McGraw-Hill, [1963-. v.: ill.; 24 cm. — (International series in pure and applied physics) 1. Quantum theory 2. Solids 3. Molecules I. T.
QC174.12.S55     530.1/2     *LC* 62-17647     *ISBN* 0070580383

**Pagels, Heinz R., 1939-.**      **5.2139**
The cosmic code: quantum physics as the language of nature / Heinz R. Pagels. — New York: Simon and Schuster, c1982. 370 p., [8] p. of plates: ill.; 25 cm. Includes index. 1. Quantum theory 2. Particles (Nuclear physics) 3. Science — Philosophy I. T.
QC174.13.P33 1982     530.1/2 19     *LC* 81-16525     *ISBN* 0671248022

**Joshi, A. W.**      **5.2140**
Elements of group theory for physicists / A.W. Joshi. — 3rd ed. — New York: J. Wiley, c1982. xiii, 334 p.: ill.; 23 cm. 'A Halsted Press book.' Spine title: Group theory for physicists. Includes index. 1. Groups, Theory of I. T. II. Title: Group theory for physicists.
QC174.17.G7 J67 1982     512/.2/02453 19     *LC* 82-200639

**Schulman, L. S. (Lawrence S.), 1941-.**      **5.2141**
Techniques and applications of path integration / L. S. Schulman. — New York: Wiley, c1981. xv, 359 p.: ill.; 24 cm. 'A Wiley-Interscience publication.' 1. Integrals, Path I. T.
QC174.17.P27 S38     530.1/2 19     *LC* 80-19129     *ISBN* 0471764507

**Ring, Peter, 1941-.**      **5.2142**
The nuclear many–body problem / Peter Ring, Peter Schuck; [editors, Wolf Beiglböck ... et al.]. — New York: Springer-Verlag, c1980. xvii, 716 p.; 25 cm. — (Texts and monographs in physics) Includes indexes. 1. Many-body problem 2. Nuclear physics I. Schuck, Peter. joint author. II. Beiglböck, W., 1939- III. T.
QC174.17.P7 R56     530.1/44     *LC* 79-25447     *ISBN* 0387098208

**Wess, Julius.**      **5.2143**
Supersymmetry and supergravity / by Julius Wess and Jonathan Bagger. — Princeton, N.J.: Princeton University Press, c1983. viii, 180 p.; 24 cm. — (Princeton series in physics.) 1. Supersymmetry 2. Supergravity I. Bagger, Jonathan, 1955- II. T. III. Series.
QC174.17.S9 W47 1983     530.1/43 19     *LC* 82-61394     *ISBN* 0691083274

## QC174.2–174.35 WAVE MECHANICS. MATRIX MECHANICS

**Broglie, Louis de, 1892-.**      • **5.2144**
New perspectives in physics / Louis De Broglie; translated by A. J. Pomerans. — New York: Basic Books, 1962. 291 p.: ill. Translation of Nouvelles perspectives en microphysique. 1. Wave mechanics — Addresses, essays, lectures. 2. Science — Addresses, essays, lectures. I. T.
QC174.2.B67453     530.124     *LC* 61-17662

**Heitler, Walter, 1904-.**      • **5.2145**
Elementary wave mechanics, with applications to quantum chemistry. 2d ed. Oxford, Clarendon Press, 1956. 193 p. illus. 19 cm. 1. Wave mechanics I. T.
QC174.2.H4 1956     530.1     *LC* 56-59037

**Przibram, Karl, 1878- comp.**      • **5.2146**
Letters on wave mechanics: Schrödinger, Planck, Einstein, Lorentz. Edited by K. Przibram for the Austrian Academy of Sciences; translated and with an introd. by Martin J. Klein. New York, Philosophical Library [1967] xv, 75 p. ports. 23 cm. 1. Wave mechanics I. Schrödinger, Erwin, 1887-1961. II. Planck, Max, 1858-1947. III. Einstein, Albert, 1879-1955. IV. Lorentz, H. A. (Hendrik Antoon), 1853-1928. V. T.
QC174.2.P73     530.12/4     *LC* 65-23493

**Schrödinger, Erwin, 1887-1961.**      **5.2147**
[Abhandlungen zur Wellenmechanik. English] Collected papers on wave mechanics / by E. Schrödinger. — 2d English ed. — New York: Chelsea Pub. Co., 1978. xiii, 146 p.: ill.; 24 cm. Translation of the 2d ed. of Abhandlungen zur Wellenmechanik. Reprint of the 1928 ed. published by Blackie, London. 1. Wave mechanics — Collected works. I. T.
QC174.2.S3213 1978     530.1/24     *LC* 78-11493     *ISBN* 0828403023

**Solitons** / edited by R. K. Bullough and P. J. Caudrey; with      **5.2148** contributions by R. K. Bullough ... [et al.].
Berlin; New York: Springer-Verlag, 1980. xviii, 389 p.: ill.; 25 cm. — (Topics in current physics. 17) 1. Solitons I. Bullough, R. K. (Robert Keith), 1929- II. Caudrey, P. J., 1943- III. Series.
QC174.26.W28 S63     530.1/24     *LC* 80-12790     *ISBN* 038709962X

**Chew, Geoffrey Foucar, 1924-.**      • **5.2149**
S–matrix theory of strong interactions: a lecture note and reprint volume / Geoffrey F. Chew. — New York: Benjamin, 1962. x, 182 p.: ill. — (Frontiers in physics) Lectures given in Les Houches and Edinburgh, 1960. 1. Matrix mechanics 2. S-matrix theory I. T.
QC174.3.C52 1962

**Dirac, P. A. M. (Paul Adrien Maurice), 1902-.**      • **5.2150**
The principles of quantum mechanics. 4th ed. Oxford, Clarendon Press, 1958. 312 p. 24 cm. (International series of monographs on physics) 1. Matrix mechanics 2. Quantum theory I. T.
QC174.3.D5 1958     530.1     *LC* 58-907

**Von Neumann, John, 1903-1957.**      • **5.2151**
Mathematical foundations of quantum mechanics / translated from the German ed. by Robert T. Beyer. — Princeton, N.J.: Princeton University Press, 1957. 1 v. (Investigations in physics; no. 2) 1. Matrix mechanics I. T. II. Series.
QC174.3.V613     *LC* 53-10143

## QC174.45–174.5 QUANTUM FIELD THEORY

**Bjorken, James D.**      • **5.2152**
Relativistic quantum fields [by] James D. Bjorken [and] Sidney D. Drell. New York, McGraw-Hill [1965] xiv, 396 p. illus. 23 cm. (International series in pure and applied physics.) 1. Quantum field theory I. Drell, Sidney D. (Sidney David), 1926- joint author. II. T. III. Series.
QC174.45.B55     530.12     *LC* 64-7726

**Bogoliubov, N. N. (Nikolaĭ Nikolaevich), 1909-.**      **5.2153**
[Kvantovye polia. English] Quantum fields / N.N. Bogoliubov, D.V. Shirkov. — 1st English ed. / authorized translation from the Russian edition by D.B. Pontecorvo. — Reading, Mass.: Benjamin/Cummings Pub. Co., Advanced Book Program/World Science Division, 1982, c1983. xv, 388 p.: ill.; 25 cm. Translation of: Kvantovye polia. Includes index. 1. Quantum field theory I. Shirkov, D. V. (Dmitriĭ Vasil'evich) II. T.
QC174.45.B5813 1983     530.1/43 19     *LC* 82-4366     *ISBN* 0805309837

**Harris, Edward G.**      • **5.2154**
A pedestrian approach to quantum field theory [by] Edward G. Harris. — New York: Wiley-Interscience, [1972] xii, 167 p.; 23 cm. 1. Quantum field theory I. T.
QC174.45.H28     530.1/43     *LC* 70-37646     *ISBN* 0471353205

**Itzykson, Claude.**      **5.2155**
Quantum field theory / Claude Itzykson and Jean–Bernard Zuber. — New York: McGraw-Hill International Book Co., 1980. xxii, 705 p.: ill.; 24 cm. — (International series in pure and applied physics) Includes index. 1. Quantum field theory I. Zuber, Jean Bernard. joint author. II. T.
QC174.45.I77     530.1/43     *LC* 78-40977     *ISBN* 0070320713

**Mandl, F. (Franz), 1923-.**      **5.2156**
Quantum field theory / F. Mandl and G. Shaw. — Chichester; New York: Wiley, c1984. xii, 354 p.: ill. 'A Wiley-Interscience publication.' 1. Quantum field theory I. Shaw, G. (Graham), 1942- II. T.
QC174.45.M32 1984     530.1/43 19     *LC* 84-5229     *ISBN* 0471105090

Nishijima, K. (Kazuhiko), 1926-.    • 5.2157
Fields and particles: field theory and dispersion relations / [by] K. Nishijima. — New York: W. A. Benjamin, 1969. ix, 465 p.; 24 cm. (Lecture notes and supplements in physics) 'Based on lectures delivered at the University of Illinois.' 1. Quantum field theory I. T.
QC174.45.N57    530.14/3    LC 69-12567

Ramond, Pierre, 1943-.    5.2158
Field theory: a modern primer / Pierre Ramond. — Reading, Mass.: Benjamin/Cummings Pub. Co., Advanced Book Program, 1981. xviii, 397 p.: ill.; 24 cm. — (Frontiers in physics. 51) Includes index. 1. Quantum field theory 2. Perturbation (Quantum dynamics) 3. Gauge fields (Physics) 4. Integrals, Path I. T. II. Series.
QC174.45.R35    530.1/43 19    LC 80-27067    ISBN 0805378928

Schweber, S. S. (Silvan S.)    • 5.2159
An introduction to relativistic quantum field theory. Foreword by Hans A. Bethe. Evanston, Ill., Row, Peterson [1961] 905 p. illus. 24 cm. 1. Quantum field theory I. T. II. Title: Relativistic quantum field theory.
QC174.45.S33    530.12    LC 61-3787

Streater, R. F.    • 5.2160
PCT, spin and statistics, and all that [by] R.F. Streater [and] A.S. Wightman. New York, W.A. Benjamin, 1964. viii, 181 p. diagrs. 24 cm. (Mathematical physics monograph series.) 1. Quantum field theory I. Wightman, A. S. joint author. II. T. III. Series.
QC174.45.S8    530.12    LC 63-22797

Barut, A. O. (Asim Orhan), 1926-.    • 5.2161
The theory of the scattering matrix for the interactions of fundamental particles [by] A.O. Barut. New York, Macmillan [1967] xiv, 350 p. illus. 24 cm. 1. S-matrix theory I. T.
QC174.5.B33    539.7/21    LC 67-15547

Hartree, Douglas R. (Douglas Rayner), 1897-1958.    • 5.2162
The calculation of atomic structures. New York, J. Wiley, 1957. 181 p. illus. 24 cm. (Structure of matter series.) 1. Wave mechanics 2. Numerical analysis I. T. II. Series.
QC174.5.H35    530.1    LC 57-5916

Mackey, George Whitelaw, 1916-.    • 5.2163
The mathematical foundations of quantum mechanics: a lecture–note volume. — New York: W.A. Benjamin, 1963. x, 137 p.; 24 cm. (Mathematical physics monograph series.) 1. Quantum theory 2. Mathematical physics I. T. II. Series.
QC174.5.M25    530.12    LC 63-21773

Thouless, D. J.    • 5.2164
The quantum mechanics of many–body systems [by] D. J. Thouless. — 2d ed. — New York: Academic Press, 1972. xi, 242 p.: illus.; 24 cm. — (Pure and applied physics. v. 11) 1. Many-body problem I. T. II. Series.
QC174.5.T5 1972    530.1/44    LC 76-182653    ISBN 0126915601

Tinkham, Michael.    • 5.2165
Group theory and quantum mechanics. New York: McGraw-Hill [c1964] xii, 340 p.: diagrs.; 23 cm. (International series in pure and applied physics.) 1. Quantum theory 2. Groups, Theory of I. T. II. Series.
QC174.5.T54    530.12    LC 63-19773

## QC174.7–174.8 STATISTICAL PHYSICS

Landau, L. D. (Lev Davidovich), 1908-1968.    5.2166
[Statisticheskaia fizika. English] Statistical physics / by L. D. Landau and E. M. Lifshitz; translated from the Russian by J. R. Sykes and M. J. Kearsley. — 3d ed. / by E.M. Lifshitz and L.P. Pitaevskiĭ. — Oxford; New York: Pergamon Press, c1980. x, 387 p.; 26 cm. — (Their Course of theoretical physics; v. 9, pt. 2) (Pergamon international library of science, technology, engineering, and social sciences) Translation of Statisticheskaia fizika. Includes index. 1. Statistical physics I. Lifshits, E. M. (Evgeniĭ Mikhaĭlovich) joint author. II. Pitaevskiĭ, L. P. (Lev Petrovich) III. T.
QC174.8.L3613 1980    530.1/33    LC 78-41328    ISBN 0080230733

Ma, Shang-keng, 1940-1983.    5.2167
[T'ung chi li hsüeh. English] Statistical mechanics / Shang–Keng Ma; translated by M.K. Fung. — Philadelphia: World Scientific, c1985. xxv, 548 p.: ill.; 23 cm. Translation of: T'ung chi li hsüeh. Includes index. 1. Statistical mechanics I. T.
QC174.8.M2513 1985    530.1/3 19    LC 85-2299    ISBN 9971966069

Mayer, Joseph Edward, 1904-.    5.2168
Statistical mechanics / Joseph Edward Mayer and Maria Goeppert Mayer. — 2d ed. — New York: Wiley, 1977. xv, 491p.: ill. 1. Statistical mechanics I. Mayer, Maria Goeppert, 1906-1972, joint author. II. T.
QC174.8.M37 1976    QC175 M3 1977.    530.1/32    LC 76-20668    ISBN 0471579858

Reichl, L. E.    5.2169
A modern course in statistical physics / by L. E. Reichl; foreword by Ilya Prigogine; [ill. by Pamela Vesterby]. — Austin: University of Texas Press, c1980. xii, 709 p.: ill.; 24 cm. 1. Statistical physics I. T.
QC174.8.R44    530.1/5/95    LC 79-15287    ISBN 029275051X

Universality in chaos: a reprint selection / compiled and    5.2170
introduced by Predrag Cvitanović.
Bristol: Adam Hilger, c1984. 511 p.: ill.; 25 cm. 1. Chaotic behavior in systems — Addresses, essays, lectures. I. Cvitanović, Predrag.
QC174.84.U55 1984    530.1/5 19    LC 84-121724    ISBN 0852747667

## QC175–175.45 Statistical Mechanics. Kinetic Theory of Gases and Liquids

Jeans, James Hopwood, Sir, 1877-1946.    • 5.2171
The dynamical theory of gases. — 4th ed. — [New York]: Dover Publications, [1954] 444 p.: diagrs.; 24 cm. 1. Gases, Kinetic theory of I. T.
QC175.A6 J4 1954    533.7    LC 55-14516    ISBN 0486601366

Baierlein, Ralph.    • 5.2172
Atoms and information theory; an introduction to statistical mechanics. — San Francisco: W. H. Freeman, [1971] xi, 486 p.; 25 cm. 1. Statistical mechanics I. T.
QC175.B33    530.1/3    LC 71-116369    ISBN 0716703327

Collie, C. H.    5.2173
Kinetic theory and entropy / C.H. Collie. — London; New York: Longman, 1982. x, 393 p.: ill.; 22 cm. 1. Gases, Kinetic theory of 2. Entropy I. T.
QC175.C58 1982    531/.113 19    LC 81-8332    ISBN 0582443687

Dennery, Philippe.    5.2174
[Introduction à la mécanique statistique. English] An introduction to statistical mechanics. New York, J. Wiley [1972] x, 118 p. illus. 23 cm. 'A Halsted Press book.' Translation of Introduction à la mécanique statistique. 1. Statistical mechanics I. T.
QC175.D3813    530.1/32    LC 72-4150    ISBN 0470209100

Dynamical aspects of critical phenomena. Edited by J. I.    5.2175
Budnick and M. P. Kawatra.
New York: Gordon and Breach, [1972] ix, 628 p.; 24 cm. 'Papers presented at a conference on dynamical aspects of critical phenomena held ... Fordham University ... June 9-11, 1970.' 1. Phase transformations (Statistical physics) — Congresses. I. Budnick, J. I., 1929- ed. II. Kawatra, M. P., 1935- ed.
QC175.D92    536/.401    LC 77-183846    ISBN 0677123507

Fowler, R.H. (Ralph Howard), 1889-.    • 5.2176
Statistical thermodynamics: a version of statistical mechanics for students of physics and chemistry / by R.H. Fowler ... and E.A. Guggenheim. — New York: Macmillan; Cambridge, Eng.: University Press, 1939. x, 693 p.: diagrs.; 27 cm. 'Printed in Great Britain'. 1. Statistical mechanics 2. Thermodynamics I. Guggenheim, E. A. (Edward Armand), 1901- II. T.
QC175.F64    LC 40-13528

Gibbs, J. Willard (Josiah Willard), 1839-1903.    • 5.2177
Elementary principles in statistical mechanics: developed with especial reference to the rational foundation of thermodynamics / by J. Willard Gibbs. — New York: Dover, 1960. xviii, 207 p.; 20 cm. "Unabridged and unaltered republication of the work first published in 1902." 1. Thermodynamics 2. Statistical mechanics I. T.
QC175.G5 1960    LC 61-387

Haar, D. ter.    • 5.2178
Elements of statistical mechanics. — New York: Rinehart, 1954. 468 p.: ill. 1. Statistical mechanics I. T. II. Title: Statistical mechanics.
QC175.H14    LC 54-5402

**Huang, Kerson, 1928-.**    • **5.2179**
Statistical mechanics. New York, Wiley [1963] 470 p. illus. 25 cm. 1. Statistical mechanics I. T.
QC175.H8     530.13     *LC* 63-11437

**Kennard, Earle Hesse, 1885- .**    • **5.2180**
Kinetic theory of gases, with an introduction to statistical mechanics / by Earle H. Kennard. — 1st ed. — New York; London: McGraw-Hill,1938. xiii, 483 p.: ill. (International series in physics) 1. Gases, Kinetic. 2. Statistical mechanics I. T.
QC175.K45     QC175.K5.     *LC* 38-6323

**Khinchin, Aleksandr IAkovlevich, 1894-1959.**    • **5.2181**
Mathematical foundations of statistical mechanics / tr. from the Russian by G. Gamow. — New York: Dover Publications, 1949. viii, 179 p. — (The Dover series in mathematics and physics) 'First American edition.' - Dust jacket. 1. Statistical mechanics I. T.
QC175.K52     *LC* 49-9707

**Loeb, Leonard B. (Leonard Benedict), 1891-.**    • **5.2182**
The kinetic theory of gases, being a text and reference book whose purpose is to combine the classical deductions with recent experimental advances in a convenient form for student and investigator. 3d ed. New York, Dover Publications [1961] 687 p. illus. 22 cm. 1. Gases, Kinetic theory of I. T.
QC175.L6 1961     533.7     *LC* 61-66220

**Reif, F. (Frederick), 1927-.**    • **5.2183**
Fundamentals of statistical and thermal physics [by] F. Reif. New York, McGraw-Hill [1965] x, 651 p. illus. 23 cm. (McGraw-Hill series in fundamentals of physics) 1. Statistical mechanics 2. Statistical thermodynamics I. T.
QC175.R43     530.13     *LC* 63-22730

**Brush, Stephen G.**    **5.2184**
The kind of motion we call heat: a history of the kinetic theory of gases in the 19th century / by Stephen G. Brush. — Amsterdam: North-Holland Pub. Co.; New York: American Elsevier, [1976] 2v. (769, xxxix, xxxix p.): ports.; 24 cm. — (Studies in statistical mechanics. v. 6) Includes indexes. 1. Gases, Kinetic theory of — History. 2. Statistical mechanics — History. 3. Physics — History. I. T. II. Series.
QC175.S77 vol.6     530.1/3/08 s 533/.7/09034     *LC* 75-31624     *ISBN* 0444110119

**Tabor, David.**    **5.2185**
Gases, liquids, and solids / D. Tabor. — 2d ed. — Cambridge [Eng.]; New York: Cambridge University Press, 1979. xiv, 333 p.: ill.; 24 cm. Includes index. 1. Gases, Kinetic theory of 2. Liquids 3. Solids I. T.
QC175.T3 1979     530.4     *LC* 78-26451     *ISBN* 0521223830

**Tolman, Richard Chace, 1881-1948.**    • **5.2186**
The principles of statistical mechanics / by Richard C. Tolman. — [London]: Oxford university press, [1948, c1938] xix, 660 p.: ill.; 25 cm. — (International series of monographs on physics.) 1. Statistical mechanics 2. Quantum statistics I. T. II. Series.
QC175.T62     *LC* 39-6793

**Williams, Dudley, 1912- ed.**    **5.2187**
Molecular physics / edited by Dudley Williams. — 2d ed. — New York: Academic Press, 1974-. v. : ill.; 24 cm. — (Methods of experimental physics. v. 3) 1. Molecules 2. Molecular theory I. T. II. Series.
QC175.16.M6 W553     539/.12     *LC* 73-8905     *ISBN* 0124760031

**Frenkel', IA. I. (IAkov Il'ich), 1894-1952.**    • **5.2188**
Kinetic theory of liquids. New York, Dover Publications [1955] 488 p. illus. 21 cm. 'An unabridged and unaltered republication of the first English translation published in 1946.' 1. Liquids, Kinetic theory of I. T.
QC175.3.F2 1955     532     *LC* 56-13521

# QC176–176.84 Solid State Physics

**The Beginnings of solid state physics: a symposium / organized**    **5.2189**
**by Sir Nevill Mott, held 30 April–2 May 1979.**
London: Royal Society; Great Neck, N.Y.: distributed by Scholium International, 1980. 177 p.: ill.; 25 cm. 'First published in Proceedings of the Royal Society of London, series A, volume 371 (no. 1744), pages 1-177.' Distributor from label on p. 2 of cover. 1. Solid state physics — Congresses. I. Mott, N. F. (Nevill Francis), Sir, 1905- II. Royal Society (Great Britain)
QC176.A1 B4     530.4/1 19     *LC* 80-670261     *ISBN* 085403143X

**Concise encyclopedia of solid state physics / edited by Rita G.**    **5.2190**
**Lerner, George L. Trigg; foreword by Conyers Herring.**
Reading, Mass.: Addison-Wesley Pub. Co., Advanced Book Program/World Science Division, c1983. xv, 311 p.: ill.; 29 cm. 'Articles chosen for this volume have been selected from the Encyclopedia of physics'—Pref. 1. Solid state physics — Dictionaries. I. Lerner, Rita G. II. Trigg, George L. III. Handbuch der Physik.
QC176.A3 C66 1983     530.4/1/0321 19     *LC* 82-18162     *ISBN* 020114204X

**Blakemore, J. S. (John Sydney), 1927-.**    **5.2191**
Solid state physics / J.S. Blakemore. — 2nd ed. — Cambridge [Cambridgeshire]; New York: Cambridge University Press, 1985. x, 506 p.: ill.; 26 cm. 1. Solid state physics I. T.
QC176.B63 1985     530.4/1 19     *LC* 85-47879     *ISBN* 0521309328

**Dalven, Richard.**    **5.2192**
Introduction to applied solid state physics: topics in the applications of semiconductors, superconductors, and the nonlinear optical properties of solids / Richard Dalven. — New York: Plenum Press, c1980. xiv, 330 p.: ill.; 24 cm. 1. Solid state physics 2. Semiconductors I. T.
QC176.D24     621.3/028 19     *LC* 79-21902     *ISBN* 0306403854

**Hall, Henry Edgar, 1928-.**    **5.2193**
Solid state physics / [by] H. E. Hall. — London; New York: Wiley, [1974] xvii, 351 p.: ill.; 24 cm. — (The Manchester physics series) 1. Solids I. T.
QC176.H24     530.4/1     *LC* 73-10743     *ISBN* 0471342807

**Hughes, A. E. (Antony Elwyn)**    **5.2194**
Real solids and radiation / A.E. Hughes and D. Pooley. — London: Wykeham Publications; New York: Springer-Verlag: Distributed in the United States by Crane, Russak, 1976. x, 196 p.: ill.; 22 cm. — (Wykeham science series. 35) Distributor from label on p. 3 of cover. Includes index. 1. Solids 2. Solids — Effect of radiation on 3. Crystals — Defects I. Pooley, D. (Derek) joint author. II. T. III. Series.
QC176.H83     530.4/1     *LC* 74-32348     *ISBN* 0387911235

**Kittel, Charles.**    **5.2195**
Introduction to solid state physics / Charles Kittel. — 6th ed. — New York: Wiley, c1986. x, 646 p.: ill.; 25 cm. 1. Solid state physics I. T.
QC176.K5 1986     530.4/1 19     *LC* 85-17812     *ISBN* 0471874744

**Patterson, James Deane, 1934-.**    • **5.2196**
Introduction to the theory of solid state physics [by] James D. Patterson. Reading, Mass.: Addison-Wesley Pub. Co., [1971] x, 388 p.: illus.; 25 cm. — (Addison-Wesley series in solid state sciences) 1. Solid state physics I. T.
QC176.P28     530.4/1     *LC* 79-109518

**Rosenberg, H. M. (Harold Max)**    **5.2197**
The solid state: an introduction to the physics of crystals for students of physics, materials science, and engineering / H. M. Rosenberg. — 2d ed. — Oxford: Clarendon Press, 1978. 274 p.: ill.; 23 cm. (Oxford physics series) Includes index. 1. Solid state physics 2. Crystals I. T.
QC176.R67 1978     530.4/1     *LC* 78-40482     *ISBN* 0198518447

**Seitz, Frederick, 1911-.**    • **5.2198**
The modern theory of solids / by Frederick Seitz. — 1st ed. — New York; London: McGraw-Hill book co., 1940. xv, 698 p.: ill. — (International series in physics; L. A. DuBridge, consulting editor) 1. Solids 2. Crystallography I. T.
QC176.S4x     *LC* 40-31693

**Taylor, Philip Lester.**    • **5.2199**
A quantum approach to the solid state [by] Philip L. Taylor. Englewood Cliffs, N.J.: Prentice-Hall, [1970] xii, 322 p.: ill.; 24 cm. 1. Solid state physics 2. Quantum theory I. T.
QC176.T36     530.4/1     *LC* 79-108738     *ISBN* 0137479646

**Wannier, Gregory H.**    • **5.2200**
Elements of solid state theory. Cambridge [Eng.] University Press, 1959. 270 p. illus. 22 cm. 1. Solid state physics I. T. II. Title: Solid state theory.
QC176.W3     531.7     *LC* 59-16341

**Wert, Charles Allen.**    • **5.2201**
Physics of solids [by] Charles A. Wert [and] Robb M. Thomson. 2d ed. New York, McGraw-Hill [1970] xi, 522 p. illus. 24 cm. (McGraw-Hill series in materials science and engineering) 1. Solid state physics I. Thomson, Robb M. (Robb Milton), 1925- joint author. II. T.
QC176.W45 1970     530.4/1     *LC* 77-98055

**Ziman, J. M. (John M.), 1925-.**    • **5.2202**
Electrons and phonons: the theory of transport phenomena in solids / by John Ziman. — Oxford: Clarendon Press, 1960. 554 p.: ill.; 25 cm. (The International series of monographs on physics) 1. Electrons 2. Phonons 3. Transport theory I. T.
QC176.Z5     531.7     *LC* 60-2430

Ziman, John M. (John M.), 1925-.    • 5.2203
Principles of the theory of solids, by J. M. Ziman. 2d ed. Cambridge [Eng.] University Press, 1972. xiii, 435 p. illus. 24 cm. 1. Solid state physics I. T.
QC176.Z53 1972    530.4/1    LC 72-80250    ISBN 0521083826

## QC176.8 SPECIAL TOPICS, A–Z

Hurd, C. M. (Colin Michael), 1937-.    5.2204
Electrons in metals: an introduction to modern topics / C. M. Hurd. — New York: Wiley, [1975] ix, 331 p.: ill.; 24 cm. 'A Wiley-Interscience publication.' 1. Free electron theory of metals 2. Metals I. T.
QC176.8.E4 H87    530.4/1    LC 75-20241    ISBN 0471422207

Jones, H. (Harry), 1905-.    5.2205
The theory of Brillouin zones and electronic states in crystals / by H. Jones. — 2d. rev. ed. — Amsterdam: North-Holland Pub. Co.; New York: American Elsevier, 1975. xii, 284 p.: ill.; 23 cm. Includes index. 1. Brillouin zones 2. Crystals — Electric properties I. T. II. Title: Brillouin zones and electronic states in crystals.
QC176.8.E4 J64 1975    548/.85    LC 74-75579    ISBN 0444106391

Mott, N. F. (Nevill Francis), Sir, 1905-.    5.2206
Electronic processes in non–crystalline materials / by N. F. Mott and E. A. Davis. — 2d ed. — Oxford: Clarendon Press; New York: Oxford University Press, 1979. xiv, 590 p.: ill.; 24 cm. (International series of monographs on physics) Includes index. 1. Energy-band theory of solids 2. Free electron theory of metals 3. Amorphous substances — Electric properties. I. Davis, Ewart Arthur, joint author. II. T.
QC176.8.E4 M67 1979    530.4/1    LC 78-40236    ISBN 0198512880

Pines, David, 1924-.    • 5.2207
Elementary excitations in solids: lectures on phonons, electrons, and plasmons / David Pines. — New York: W.A. Benjamin, 1964. xii, 299 p.: graphs; 24 cm. — (Lecture notes and supplements in physics.) 1. Solids 2. Quantum theory 3. Exciton theory I. T.
QC176.8.E9 P55    LC 63-19982

Cochran, William, F.R.S.    5.2208
The dynamics of atoms in crystals / [by] W. Cochran. New York: Crane, Russak, 1974 (c1973) 145 p.: ill.; 24 cm. (The Structures and properties of solids, 3) 1. Lattice dynamics I. T.
QC176.8.L3 C62 1973    548/.81    LC 73-78106    ISBN 0844802107 ISBN 0844802115

Handbook of optical constants of solids / edited by Edward D. Palik.    5.2209
Orlando: Academic Press, 1985. xviii, 804 p.: ill.; 25 cm. (Academic Press handbook series.) 1. Solids — Optical properties — Handbooks, manuals, etc. I. Palik, Edward D. II. Series.
QC176.8.O6 H36 1985    530.4/1 19    LC 84-15870    ISBN 0125444206

Prutton, M.    5.2210
Surface physics / M. Prutton. — 2nd ed. — Oxford: Clarendon Press; New York: Oxford University Press, 1983. x, 138 p.: ill.; 23 cm. — (Oxford physics series. 11) Includes index. 1. Solids — Surfaces 2. Surface chemistry I. T. II. Series.
QC176.8.S8 P78 1983    530.4/1 19    LC 84-105599    ISBN 0198518552

Berman, R. (Robert)    5.2211
Thermal conduction in solids / by R. Berman. — Oxford [Eng.]: Clarendon Press, 1976. xi, 193 p.: ill.; 24 cm. (Oxford studies in physics.) Includes index. 1. Solids — Thermal properties 2. Heat — Conduction I. T.
QC176.8.T4 B47    536/.23    LC 77-353358    ISBN 0198514298

## QC177–178 Theories of the Ether. Theories of Gravitation

Schaffner, Kenneth F.    5.2212
Nineteenth–century aether theories, by Kenneth F. Schaffner. — [1st ed.]. — Oxford; New York: Pergamon Press, [1972] ix, 278 p.; 20 cm. — (The Commonwealth and international library. Selected readings in physics) 1. Ether (of space) I. T.
QC177.S48 1972    530.1    LC 77-133397    ISBN 0080156746

Whittaker, E. T. (Edmund Taylor), 1873-1956.    • 5.2213
A history of the theories of aether and electricity / Edmund Whittaker. — New York: Philosophical Library, 1954-. v.: ill. 1. Electromagnetic theory 2. Electricity — History. 3. Ether (of space) 4. Vacuum I. T.
QC177.W63    530.1    LC 54-675

Bowler, M. G.    5.2214
Gravitation and relativity / by M. G. Bowler. — 1st ed. — Oxford; New York: Pergamon Press, 1976. x, 172 p.: ill.; 25 cm. (International series in natural philosophy; v. 86) 1. Gravitation 2. General relativity (Physics) I. T.
QC178.B64 1976    530.1/1    LC 75-42161    ISBN 0080205674. ISBN 0080204082 pbk

Misner, Charles W.    5.2215
Gravitation [by] Charles W. Misner, Kip S. Thorne [and] John Archibald Wheeler. — San Francisco: W. H. Freeman, [1973] xxvi, 1279 p.: illus.; 26 cm. 1. Gravitation 2. Astrophysics 3. General relativity (Physics) I. Thorne, Kip S. joint author. II. Wheeler, John Archibald, 1911- joint author. III. T.
QC178.M57    531/.14    LC 78-156043    ISBN 0716703343

Nicolson, Iain.    5.2216
Gravity, black holes and the universe / Iain Nicolson. — New York: J. Wiley, c1981. 264 p.: ill. Includes index. 1. Gravitation 2. Black holes (Astronomy) I. T.
QC178.N5    531/.5    ISBN 0470271116

Ohanian, Hans C.    5.2217
Gravitation and spacetime / Hans C. Ohanian. — 1st ed. — New York: Norton, c1976. xiv, 461 p.: ill.; 24 cm. Includes index. 1. Gravitation 2. Space and time I. T.
QC178.O35    530.1/1    LC 75-38991    ISBN 0393091988

Stephani, Hans.    5.2218
[Allgemeine Relativitätstheorie. English] General relativity: an introduction to the theory of the gravitational field / Hans Stephani; edited by John Stewart; translated by Martin Pollock and John Stewart. -- Cambridge [Cambridgeshire]; New York: Cambridge University Press, 1982. xvi, 298 p.: ill.; 24 cm. Rev. translation of: Allgemeine Relativitätstheorie. Includes index. 1. Gravitational fields 2. General relativity (Physics) I. Stewart, John M. II. T.
QC178.S8213 1982    530.1/1 19    LC 81-10115    ISBN 0521240085

## QC182–220 Special Properties of Matter and Antimatter

Einstein, Albert, 1879-1955.    • 5.2219
Investigations on the theory of the Brownian movement / by Albert Einstein; edited with notes by R. Fürth, translated by A.D. Cowper. — New York: Dover Publications Inc, 1956. 119, [18] p.; 21 cm. 1. Brownian movements I. Fürth, Reinhold, 1893- . II. T.
QC183 E53 [1956]    QC183 E543 1956.

Jost, Wilhelm, 1903-.    • 5.2220
Diffusion in solids, liquids, gases. 3d print., with addendum. New York: Academic Press, 1960. 558, 94 p.: ill.; 24 cm. (Physical chemistry; a series of monographs, v. 1) 1. Diffusion I. T.
QC185.J64 1960    541.341    LC 63-5834

Houwink, R. (Roelof), 1897-.    5.2221
Elasticity, plasticity and structure of matter / edited by R. Houwink and H. K. de Decker. 3d ed. Cambridge [Eng.]: University Press, 1971. xi, 470 p.: ill.; 24 cm. 1. Rheology I. DeDecker, H. K., 1915- II. T.
QC189.H68 1971    531/.113    LC 72-154515    ISBN 052107875X

Constantinescu, F. (Florin), 1938-.    5.2222
Problems in quantum mechanics / by F. Constantinescu and E. Magyari; translated by V. V. Grecu; edited by J. A. Spiers. Oxford; New York: Pergamon Press, 1976, c1971. vii, 419 p.; 25 cm. (International series in natural philosophy. v. 30) Translation of Mecanică cuantică. 'Reprinted with corrections.' Includes index. 1. Quantum theory — Problems, exercises, etc. I. Magyari, E., joint author. II. T. III. Series.
QC194.15.C5813 1976    530.1/2/076    ISBN 008006826X ISBN 0080190081 pbk

# QC221–246 Acoustics. Sound

**Rayleigh, John William Strutt, Baron, 1842-1919.**                    • 5.2223
The theory of sound / by John William Strutt, baron Rayleigh, with a historical introduction by Robert Bruce Lindsay. — 2d ed. rev. and enl. — New York: Dover publications, 1945. 2 v. in 1.: front. (port.), diagrs.; 22 cm. 'First American edition.' 1. Sound 2. Vibration 3. Waves I. Lindsay, Robert Bruce, 1900- II. T.
QC223.R262 1945          534.1          LC 45-8804

**Berg, Richard E.**                                                          5.2224
The physics of sound / Richard E. Berg, David G. Stork. — Englewood Cliffs, N.J.: Prentice-Hall, c1982. xiv, 370 p.: ill.; 24 cm. 1. Sound 2. Music — Acoustics and physics I. Stork, David G. II. T.
QC225.15.B47          781/.22 19          LC 81-13840          ISBN 0136742831

**Dowling, A. P. (Ann P.), 1952-.**                                          5.2225
Sound and sources of sound / A.P. Dowling and J.E. Ffowcs Williams. — Chichester: E. Horwood; New York: Halsted Press, 1983. 321 p.: ill.; 24 cm. (Ellis Horwood series in engineering science.) Includes index. 1. Sound 2. Sound-waves 3. Sound — Equipment and supplies I. Ffowcs Williams, John E. II. T. III. Series.
QC225.15.D68 1983          534 19          LC 82-15687          ISBN 0470273712

**Stevens, S. S. (Stanley Smith), 1906-1973.**                              5.2226
Sound and hearing / by S.S. Stevens, Fred Warshofsky, and the editors of Time–Life Books. — Revised edition. — Alexandria, Va.: Time-Life Books; Morristown, N.J.: School and library distribution by Silver Burdett Co., c1980. 200 p.: ill. (some col.); 29 cm. — (Life science library.) Includes index. 1. Sound — Popular works. 2. Hearing — Popular works. I. Warshofsky, Fred. II. Time-Life Books. III. T. IV. Series.
QC225.3.S73 1980          612/.85 19          LC 80-52113

**Lindsay, Robert Bruce, 1900- comp.**                                       5.2227
Physical acoustics. Edited by R. Bruce Lindsay. — Stroudsburg, Pa.: Dowden, Hutchinson & Ross, [1974] xiii, 480 p.: illus.; 26 cm. — (Benchmark papers in acoustics, v. 4) 1. Sound 2. Sound-waves I. T.
QC225.7.L56          534          LC 73-12619          ISBN 0879330406

**Fundamentals of acoustics / Lawrence E. Kinsler ... [et al.].**            5.2228
3rd ed. — New York: Wiley, c1982. xvi, 480 p.: ill.; 25 cm. Includes index. 1. Sound-waves 2. Sound — Equipment and supplies 3. Architectural acoustics 4. Underwater acoustics I. Kinsler, Lawrence E.
QC243.F86 1982          534 19          LC 81-7463          ISBN 0471097438

**Meyer, Erwin, 1899-.**                                                     5.2229
[Physikalische und technische Akustik. English] Physical and applied acoustics; an introduction [by] Erwin Meyer [and] Ernst–Georg Neumann. Translated by John M. Taylor, Jr. New York, Academic Press, 1972. xvii, 412 p. illus. 24 cm. Translation of Physikalische und technische Akustik. 1. Sound-waves 2. Acoustical engineering I. Neumann, Ernst-Georg, 1929- joint author. II. T.
QC243.M513 1972          534          LC 75-187239          ISBN 0124931502

**Temkin, Samuel, 1936-.**                                                   5.2230
Elements of acoustics / Samuel Temkin. — New York: Wiley, c1981. xii, 515 p.: ill.; 24 cm. Includes indexes. 1. Sound-waves I. T.
QC243.T46          534 19          LC 80-24416          ISBN 0471059900

# QC251–338 Heat

**Zemansky, Mark Waldo, 1900-.**                                             5.2231
Heat and thermodynamics: an intermediate textbook / Mark W. Zemansky, Richard H. Dittman. — 6th ed. — New York: McGraw-Hill, c1981. xv, 543 p.: ill.; 24 cm. Includes index. 1. Heat 2. Thermodynamics I. Dittman, Richard. joint author. II. T.
QC254.2.Z45 1981          536          LC 80-18253          ISBN 0070728089

**Benedict, Robert P.**                                                      5.2232
Fundamentals of temperature, pressure, and flow measurements / Robert P. Benedict. — 3rd ed. — New York: Wiley, c1984. xx, 532 p.: ill.; 25 cm. 'A Wiley-Interscience publication.' 1. Thermometers and thermometry 2. Pressure — Measurement 3. Fluid dynamic measurements I. T.
QC271.B47 1984          536/.5/028 19          LC 83-23558          ISBN 0471893838

**Quinn, T. J. (Terry J.)**                                                  5.2233
Temperature / T.J. Quinn. — London; New York: Academic Press, 1983. x, 416 p.: ill.; 24 cm. — (Monographs in physical measurement.) 1. Thermometers and thermometry I. T. II. Series.
QC271.Q85 1983          536/.5/0287 19          LC 82-72595          ISBN 0125696809

**McClintock, P. V. E.**                                                     5.2234
Matter at low temperatures / P.V.E. McClintock, D.J. Meredith, and J.K. Wigmore. — New York: Wiley, 1984. vi, 258 p.: ill.; 23 cm. 'A Wiley-Interscience publication.' 1. Low temperatures 2. Materials at low temperatures 3. Liquid helium I. Meredith, D. J. II. Wigmore, J. K. III. T.
QC278.M35 1984          536/.56 19          LC 84-7497          ISBN 047181315X

**Rose-Innes, Alistair Christopher.**                                        5.2235
Low temperature laboratory techniques: the use of liquid helium in the laboratory / A. C. Rose–Innes. — 2nd ed. — [London]: English Universities Press, 1973. 255 p.: ill.; 23 cm. (Applied physics guides) First ed. published in 1964 under title: Low temperature techniques. 1. Low temperatures 2. Liquid helium I. T.
QC278.R58 1973          536/.56          LC 75-315066          ISBN 034004778X

**White, Guy K. (Guy Kendall)**                                             5.2236
Experimental techniques in low–temperature physics / by Guy K. White. — 3d ed. — Oxford: Clarendon Press; New York: Oxford University Press, 1979. xii, 331 p., [2] leaves of plates: ill.; 23 cm. — (Monographs on the physics and chemistry of materials) 1. Low temperatures I. T.
QC278.W45 1979          536/.56/072          LC 79-321089          ISBN 0198513593

**Zemansky, Mark Waldo, 1900-.**                                            5.2237
Temperatures very low and very high / Mark W. Zemansky. — New York: Dover, 1981, c1964. viii, 127 p.: ill.; 22 cm. Unabridged and corrected republication of the work originally published by D. Van Nostrand Co. in 1964. Includes index. 1. Temperatures. I. T.
QC278.Z4          536.5          LC 80-69673          ISBN 048624072X

**Wilks, J. (John), 1922-.**                                                • 5.2238
An introduction to liquid helium / by J. Wilks. — Oxford: Clarendon P., 1970. ix, 165 p.: ill.; 22 cm. (Oxford library of the physical sciences) 1. Liquid helium I. T.
QC284.W65          536/.56          LC 78-526088          ISBN 0198514204

**Stanley, H. Eugene (Harry Eugene), 1941-.**                               5.2239
Introduction to phase transitions and critical phenomena, by H. Eugene Stanley. New York, Oxford University Press, 1971. xx, 308 p. illus. 24 cm. (The International series of monographs on physics) 1. Critical phenomena (Physics) 2. Phase rule and equilibrium I. T. II. Title: Phase transitions and critical phenomena.
QC307.S7 1971b          536/.401          LC 71-172087

# QC311–319 Thermodynamics

**Adkins, C. J. (Clement John)**                                            5.2240
Equilibrium thermodynamics / C. J. Adkins. — 2d ed. — London; New York: McGraw-Hill, [1975] xiii, 284 p.: ill.; 22 cm. — (European physics series) 1. Thermodynamic equilibrium I. T.
QC311.A3 1975          536/.7          LC 74-34392          ISBN 0070840571

**Bridgman, P. W. (Percy Williams), 1882-1961.**                            • 5.2241
The nature of thermodynamics / by P.W. Bridgman. — Cambridge, Mass.: Harvard University Press, 1943. xii, 229 p.: diagrs.; 22 cm. 1. Thermodynamics I. T.
QC311.B815          536.7          LC a 41-4663

**Callen, Herbert B.**                                                       • 5.2242
Thermodynamics: an introduction to the physical theories of equilibrium thermostatics and irreversible thermodynamics. — New York: Wiley, 1960. 376 p.: ill.; 24 cm. 1. Thermodynamics I. T.
QC311.C25          536.7          LC 60-5597

**Carnot, Sadi, 1796-1832.**                                                • 5.2243
[Réflexions sur la puissance motrice du feu. English] Reflections on the motive power of fire, by Sadi Carnot; and other papers on the second law of thermodynamics, by É. Clapeyron and R. Clausius. Edited with an introd. by E. Mendoza. New York, Dover Publications [1960] xxii, 152 p. illus., ports., facsim. 21 cm. 'Memoir on the motive power of heat, by É. Clapeyron': p. [71]-105. 'On the motive power of heat ... by R. Clausius': p. [107]-152. 1. Thermodynamics I. Clapeyron, E. (Emile), 1799-1864. Mémoire sur la puissance motrice de la chaleur. English. 1960. II. Clausius, R. (Rudolf), 1822-1888. Ueber die bewegende Kraft der Wärme. English. 1960. III. T.

IV. Title: Memoir on the motive power of heat. V. Title: On the motive power of heat.
QC311.C288    536.7    *LC* 60-50876

**Glansdorff, P.**      • **5.2244**
Thermodynamic theory of structure, stability and fluctuations [by] P. Glansdorff and I. Prigogine. London, New York, Wiley-Interscience [1971] xxiii, 306 p. illus. 24 cm. 1. Thermodynamics I. Prigogine, I. (Ilya) joint author. II. T. III. Title: Structure, stability and fluctuations.
QC311.G538    536/.7    *LC* 78-147070    *ISBN* 0471302805

**Guggenheim, E. A. (Edward Armand), 1901-.**    **5.2245**
Thermodynamics: an advanced treatment for chemists and physicists / by E. A. Guggenheim. — 6th ed. — Amsterdam; New York: North-Holland Pub. Co.; New York: distributed in the U.S.A. and Canada by Elsevier North-Holland, 1977, c1967. xxiv, 390 p.: graphs; 24 cm. Includes index. 1. Thermodynamics I. T.
QC311.G92 1977    536/.7    *LC* 77-371304

**Hatsopoulos, G. N. (George N.)**      • **5.2246**
Principles of general thermodynamics [by] George N. Hatsopoulos [and] Jospeh H. Keenan. New York, Wiley [1965] xiii, 788 p. illus. 24 cm. 1. Thermodynamics I. Keenan, Joseph Henry, 1900- joint author. II. T.
QC311.H328    536.7    *LC* 65-12709

**Jancovici, Bernard.**    **5.2247**
Statistical physics and thermodynamics / [by] B. Jancovici; problems by Yves Archambault; translated from the French by L. J. Carroll. — New York: Wiley, [1973] xi, 147 p.: ill.; 23 cm. 'A Halsted Press book.' Translation of Physique statistique et thermodynamique. 1. Thermodynamics 2. Statistical physics I. T.
QC311.J2813    536/.7    *LC* 72-12614    *ISBN* 0470439653

**Kestin, Joseph.**    **5.2248**
A course in thermodynamics / Joseph Kestin. — Washington: Hemisphere Pub. Corp., c1979. 2 v.: ill.; 25 cm. — (Series in thermal and fluids engineering) 1. Thermodynamics I. T.
QC311.K43 1978    536.7    *LC* 78-5491

**Lewis, Gilbert Newton, 1875-1946.**      • **5.2249**
[Thermodynamics and the free energy of chemical substances] Thermodynamics / [by] Gilbert Newton Lewis [and] Merle Randall; rev. by Kenneth S. Pitzer [and] Leo Brewer. — 2d ed. New York: McGraw-Hill, 1961. 723 p.: ill.; 24 cm. (McGraw-Hill series in advanced chemistry) First published in 1923 under title: Thermodynamics and the free energy of chemical substances. 1. Thermodynamics 2. Chemistry, Physical and theoretical I. Randall, Merle, 1888-1950, joint author.
QC311.L4 1961    541.369    *LC* 60-10604

**Owen, David R.**    **5.2250**
A first course in the mathematical foundations of thermodynamics / David R. Owen. — New York: Springer-Verlag, c1984. xvii, 134 p.: ill.; 25 cm. — (Undergraduate texts in mathematics.) Includes index. 1. Thermodynamics 2. Thermodynamics — Mathematics. I. T. II. Series.
QC311.O94 1984    536/.7 19    *LC* 83-14705    *ISBN* 0387908978

**Pippard, A. B.**      • **5.2251**
Elements of classical thermodynamics for advanced students of physics. Cambridge [Eng.]: University Press, 1957. 165 p.: ill.; 23 cm. 1. Thermodynamics I. T. II. Title: Classical thermodynamics for advanced students of physics.
QC311.P5    536.7    *LC* 57-14462

**Reiss, Howard.**      • **5.2252**
Methods of thermodynamics. New York, Blaisdell Pub. Co. [1965] xvii, 217 p. illus. 23 cm. (Blaisdell book in the pure and applied sciences.) 1. Thermodynamics I. T. II. Series.
QC311.R34    536.7    *LC* 65-17958

**Schrödinger, Erwin.**      • **5.2253**
Statistical thermodynamics: a course of seminar lectures delivered in January–March 1944, at the School of Theoretical Physics, Dublin Institute for Advanced Studies. — 2d ed. Cambridge [Eng.]: Cambridge U.P. 1952. 95 p.: ill.; 20 cm. 1. Thermodynamics 2. Statistical mechanics I. T.
QC311.S38 1952    536.7    *LC* 52-14738

**Sussman, Martin V.**    **5.2254**
Elementary general thermodynamics [by] Martin V. Sussman. — Reading, Mass.: Addison-Wesley Pub. Co., [1972] xx, 444 p.: illus.; 25 cm. — (Addison-Wesley series in chemical engineering) 1. Thermodynamics I. T.
QC311.S89    536/.7    *LC* 74-133896

**Wark, Kenneth, 1927-.**    **5.2255**
Thermodynamics / Kenneth Wark. — 4th ed. — New York: McGraw-Hill, c1983. xvi, 896 p.: ill.; 25 cm. 1. Thermodynamics I. T.
QC311.W3 1983    536/.7 19    *LC* 82-10031    *ISBN* 0070682844

**The Second law of thermodynamics / edited by Joseph Kestin.**    **5.2256**
Stroudsburg, Pa.: Dowden, Hutchinson & Ross; [New York]: exclusive distributor, Halsted Press, 1977 (c1976). xiii, 329 p.: ill.; 26 cm. — (Benchmark papers on energy; 5) 1. Thermodynamics — Addresses, essays, lectures. I. Kestin, Joseph.
QC311.19.S4    536/.71    *LC* 76-19059    *ISBN* 0879332425

**Kittel, Charles.**    **5.2257**
Thermal physics / Charles Kittel, Herbert Kroemer. — 2d ed. — San Francisco: W. H. Freeman, c1980. xvii, 473 p.: ill.; 24 cm. Includes index. 1. Statistical thermodynamics I. Kroemer, Herbert, 1928- joint author. II. T.
QC311.5.K52 1980    536/.7    *LC* 79-16677    *ISBN* 0716710889

**McClelland, B. J.**    **5.2258**
Statistical thermodynamics [by] B. J. McClelland. — London: Chapman and Hall [Distributed by Halsted Press, New York, 1973] xvi, 334 p.: illus.; 24 cm. — (Studies in chemical physics) 1. Statistical thermodynamics I. T.
QC311.5.M23 1973    536/.7    *LC* 73-13384    *ISBN* 0412103508

**Smith, Norman Obed, 1914-.**    **5.2259**
Elementary statistical thermodynamics: a problems approach / Norman O. Smith. — New York: Plenum Press, c1982. xiv, 216 p.: ill.; 21 cm. Includes index. 1. Statistical thermodynamics I. T.
QC311.5.S584 1982    536/.7/015195 19    *LC* 82-18131    *ISBN* 0306412055

**Haywood, R. W. (Richard Wilson)**    **5.2260**
Equilibrium thermodynamics for engineers and scientists / R. W. Haywood. — Chichester [Eng.]; New York: J. Wiley, c1980. xxv, 430 p.: ill.; 24 cm. 'A Wiley-Interscience publication.' 1. Thermodynamic equilibrium I. T.
QC318.T47 H39    536/.7    *LC* 79-40650    *ISBN* 0471276316

# QC319.8–338 Heat Transfer

**Heat transfer in flames. N. H. Afgan and J. M. Beer, editors.**    **5.2261**
Washington, Scripta Book Co., 1974. viii, 501 p. illus. 26 cm. (Advances in thermal engineering, 2) 'A Halsted Press book.' Selected papers from the 1973 international seminar organized by the International Centre for Heat and Mass Transfer. 1. Heat — Transmission — Congresses. 2. Mass transfer — Congresses. 3. Flame — Congresses. I. Afgan, Naim. ed. II. Beér, J. M. (János Miklós), 1923- ed. III. International Center for Heat and Mass Transfer.
QC319.8.H43    536/.2    *LC* 74-8747    *ISBN* 0470009314

**Chapman, Alan J. (Alan Jesse), 1925-.**    **5.2262**
Heat transfer / Alan J. Chapman. — 4th ed. — New York: Macmillan; London: Collier Macmillan, c1984. xv, 608 p.: ill.; 25 cm. 1. Heat — Transmission I. T.
QC320.C5 1984    536/.2 19    *LC* 83-144    *ISBN* 0023214708

**Eckert, E. R. G. (Ernst Rudolf Georg), 1904-.**    • **5.2263**
Analysis of heat and mass transfer [by] E. R. G. Eckert [and] Robert M. Drake, Jr. New York, McGraw-Hill [1971, c1972] xxi, 806 p. illus. 23 cm. (McGraw-Hill series in mechanical engineering) 1. Heat — Transmission 2. Mass transfer I. Drake, Robert M., 1920- joint author. II. T.
QC320.E27    536/.2    *LC* 73-159305    *ISBN* 0070189250

**Holman, J. P. (Jack Philip)**    **5.2264**
Heat transfer / J.P. Holman. — 6th ed. — New York: McGraw-Hill Book Co., c1986. xx, 676 p.: ill. (some col.); 24 cm. 1. Heat — Transmission I. T.
QC320.H64 1986    536/.2 19    *LC* 85-13783    *ISBN* 0070296200

**Incropera, Frank P.**    **5.2265**
Fundamentals of heat transfer / Frank P. Incropera, David P. DeWitt. — New York: Wiley, c1981. xxiii, 819 p.: ill.; 24 cm. 1. Heat — Transmission I. DeWitt, David P., 1934- joint author. II. T.
QC320.I45    536/.2    *LC* 80-17209    *ISBN* 047142711X

**Kreith, Frank.**    **5.2266**
Principles of heat transfer / Frank Kreith, Mark S. Bohn. — 4th ed. — New York: Harper & Row, c1986. xviii, 700 p.: ill.; 24 cm. 1. Heat — Transmission I. Bohn, Mark. II. T.
QC320.K7 1986    621.402/2 19    *LC* 86-331    *ISBN* 006043774X

**Rohsenow, Warren M.**    **5.2267**
Handbook of heat transfer / edited by Warren M. Rohsenow [and] J. P. Hartnett. — New York: McGraw-Hill, [c1973] 1 v. (various pagings): ill.; 23 cm. 1. Heat — Transmission — Handbooks, manuals, etc. I. Hartnett, J. P. (James P.) joint author. II. T.
QC320.R528    536/.2    *LC* 72-11529    *ISBN* 0070535760

**Thomas, Lindon C., 1941-.**    **5.2268**
Fundamentals of heat transfer / Lindon C. Thomas. — Englewood Cliff, N.J.: Prentice-Hall, c1980. xviii, 702 p.: ill.; 24 cm. Includes bibligraphical references and index. 1. Heat — Transmission I. T.
QC320.T49 1980    536/.2 19    *LC* 79-26073    *ISBN* 0133399036

**Whitaker, Stephen.**    **5.2269**
Fundamental principles of heat transfer / Stephen Whitaker. New York: Pergamon Press, c1977. xv, 556 p.: ill.; 29 cm. 1. Heat — Transmission I. T.
QC320.W46 1977    536/.2    *LC* 75-41701    *ISBN* 0080178669

**Siegel, Robert, 1927-.**    **5.2270**
Thermal radiation heat transfer / Robert Siegel, John R. Howell. — 2d ed. — Washington: Hemisphere Pub. Corp., c1981. xvi, 862 p.: ill.; 25 cm. — (Series in thermal and fluids engineering) 1. Heat — Radiation and absorption 2. Heat — Transmission 3. Materials — Thermal properties I. Howell, John R. joint author. II. T.
QC331.S55 1981    536/.33    *LC* 79-17242    *ISBN* 0070573166

# QC350–495 Optics. Light

## QC350–369 General Works

**Lasers and light: readings from Scientific American** / with introductions by Arthur L. Schawlow.    • **5.2271**
San Francisco: W. H. Freeman, [1969] vi, 376 p.: ill. (part col.); 29 cm. 1. Light — Collected works. 2. Lasers — Collected works. I. Schawlow, A. L., 1921- ed. II. Scientific American.
QC351.L35    535    *LC* 77-80079    *ISBN* 0716709856

**Swenson, Loyd S.**    • **5.2272**
The ethereal aether; a history of the Michelson–Morley–Miller aether-drift experiments, 1880–1930, by Loyd S. Swenson, Jr. With a foreword by Gerald Holton. — Austin: University of Texas Press, [1972] xxii, 361 p.: illus.; 24 cm. 1. Optics — History. 2. Ether (of space) — History. 3. Relativity (Physics) — History. I. T.
QC352.S93    535/.24/0724    *LC* 74-37253    *ISBN* 0292720009

**Newton, Isaac, Sir, 1642-1727.**    **5.2273**
[Selections. English & Latin. 1984] The optical papers of Isaac Newton / edited by Alan E. Shapiro. — Cambridge [Cambridgeshire]; New York: Cambridge University Press, 1984. 627 p.: ill.; 26 cm. English and Latin. Includes index. 1. Optics — Early works to 1800. 2. Optics — History — Sources. I. Shapiro, Alan E. (Alan Elihu), 1942- II. T.
QC353.N52 1984    535 19    *LC* 82-14751    *ISBN* 0521252482

**Newton, Isaac, Sir, 1642-1727.**    • **5.2274**
Opticks; or, A treatise of the reflections, refractions, inflections & colours of light. Based on the 4th ed., London, 1730; with a foreword by Albert Einstein, an introd. by Sir Edmund Whittaker, a pref. by I. Bernard Cohen, and an analytical table of contents prepared by Duane H. D. Roller. — New York: Dover Publications, [1952] cxv, 406 p.: illus., ports., facsims.; 19 cm. 1. Optics — Early works to 1800. I. T.
QC353.N57 1952    535    *LC* 52-12165

**Brown, Earle B.**    • **5.2275**
Modern optics [by] Earle B. Brown. New York, Reinhold [1965] vii, 645 p. illus. 24 cm. 1. Optics I. T.
QC355.B868    535    *LC* 65-27054

**Michelson, Albert Abraham, 1852-1931.**    • **5.2276**
Studies in optics. — Chicago, University of Chicago Press [1962, c1927] 176 p. illus. 21 cm. — (Phoenix science series) 1. Optics I. T.
QC355.M5 1962    535.2    *LC* 62-52412

**Born, Max, 1882-1970.**    **5.2277**
Principles of optics: electromagnetic theory of propagation, interference and diffraction of light / by Max Born and Emil Wolf, with contributions by A. B. Bhatia ... [et al.]. — 6th ed. — Oxford; New York: Pergamon Press, 1980. xxvii, 808 p.: ill.; 25 cm. 1. Optics 2. Electromagnetic theory I. Wolf, Emil. joint author. II. T.
QC355.2.B67 1980    535 19    *LC* 80-41470    *ISBN* 0080264816

**Ditchburn, R. W.**    **5.2278**
Light / R. W. Ditchburn. 3d ed. — London; New York: Academic Press, 1976. 2 v. (xviii, 775 p.): ill.; 23 cm. 1. Light I. T.
QC355.2.D57 1976    535    *LC* 75-19632    *ISBN* 0122181018

**Gerrard, Anthony.**    **5.2279**
Introduction to matrix methods in optics [by] A. Gerrard [and] J. M. Burch. — London; New York: Wiley, [1975] xiii, 355 p.: illus.; 24 cm. — (Wiley series in pure and applied optics) 'A Wiley-Interscience publication.' 1. Optics 2. Matrices I. Burch, James M., joint author. II. T.
QC355.2.G47    535    *LC* 72-21192    *ISBN* 0471296856

**Haken, H.**    **5.2280**
Light / H. Haken. — Amsterdam; New York: North-Holland Pub. Co.; New York: Sole distributors for the U.S.A. and Canada, Elsevier North-Holland, c1981-1985. 2 v.: ill.; 23 cm. Vol. 2, imprint: Amsterdam; New York: North-Holland Physics Pub. Includes indexes. 1. Light 2. Lasers 3. Nonlinear optics 4. Quantum optics I. T.
QC355.2.H33    535 19    *LC* 80-22397    *ISBN* 0444860207

**Jenkins, Francis Arthur, 1899-1960.**    **5.2281**
Fundamentals of optics / Francis A. Jenkins, Harvey E. White. — 4th ed. — New York: McGraw-Hill, c1976. xx, 746 p.: ill.; 25 cm. First ed. published in 1937 under title: Fundamentals of physical optics. Includes index. 1. Optics I. White, Harvey Elliott, 1902- joint author. II. T.
QC355.2.J46 1976    535    *LC* 75-26989    *ISBN* 0070323305

**Longhurst, R. S. (Richard Samuel)**    **5.2282**
Geometrical and physical optics / [by] R. S. Longhurst. — 3d ed. [London]: Longman, 1974 (c1973) xviii, 677 p.: ill.; 23 cm. (A Longman text) Label mounted on t.p.: Distributed in the U.S.A. by Longman Inc., New York. 1. Optics I. T.
QC355.2.L65 1973    535    *LC* 74-169158    *ISBN* 0582440998

**Meyer-Arendt, Jurgen R.**    **5.2283**
Introduction to classical and modern optics / Jurgen R. Meyer–Arendt. — 2nd ed. — Englewood Cliffs, N.J.: Prentice-Hall, c1984. xv, 559 p.: ill.; 25 cm. 1. Optics I. T.
QC355.2.M49 1984    535 19    *LC* 83-10902    *ISBN* 013479303X

**Nussbaum, Allen.**    **5.2284**
Contemporary optics for scientists and engineers / Allen Nussbaum and Richard A. Phillips. — Englewood Cliffs, N.J.: Prentice-Hall, c1976. xii, 511 p.: ill.; 24 cm. — (Solid state physical electronics series.) 1. Optics I. Phillips, Richard A., joint author. II. T. III. Series.
QC355.2.N87    535    *LC* 74-30210    *ISBN* 0131701835

**Welford, W. T.**    **5.2285**
Optics / W.T. Welford. — 2nd ed. — Oxford; New York: Oxford University Press, 1981. vii, 150 p.: ill.; 22 cm. — (Oxford physics series. 14) (Oxford science publications.) Includes index. 1. Optics I. T. II. Series. III. Series: Oxford science publications.
QC355.2.W44 1981    535 19    *LC* 80-41847    *ISBN* 0198518471

**Young, Matt, 1941-.**    **5.2286**
Optics and lasers: including fibers and optical waveguides / Matt Young. — 3rd rev. ed. — Berlin; New York: Springer-Verlag, c1986. xvi, 279 p.: ill.; 24 cm. (Springer series in optical sciences. v. 5) Includes index. 1. Optics 2. Lasers I. T. II. Series.
QC355.2.Y68 1986    621.36 19    *LC* 85-27795    *ISBN* 0387161279

**Stroke, George W.**    • **5.2287**
An introduction to coherent optics and holography [by] George W. Stroke. — 2d ed. — New York: Academic Press, 1969. xxi, 358 p.: illus.; 24 cm. Includes reprints of three papers by D. Gabor (p. [261]-[324]) 1. Coherence (Optics) 2. Holography I. Gabor, Dennis, 1900- II. T. III. Title: Coherent optics and holography.
QC357.S96 1969    535/.4    *LC* 78-4547

**Smith, F. Graham (Francis Graham), 1923-.**    **5.2288**
Optics [by] F. Graham Smith [and] J. H. Thomson. — London; New York: J. Wiley, [1971] xv, 350 p.: illus.; 24 cm. — (The Manchester physics series) 1. Optics I. Thomson. John Hunter, joint author. II. T.
QC357.2.S57    535    *LC* 71-146547    *ISBN* 047180360X

**Morris, Richard, 1939-.**    **5.2289**
Light / Richard Morris. — Indianapolis: Bobbs-Merrill, c1979. 200 p.: ill.; 22 cm. Includes index. 1. Light I. T.
QC358.5.M67    535    *LC* 78-11206    *ISBN* 0672525577

**American Association of Physics Teachers.**    **5.2290**
Quantum and statistical aspects of light: selected reprints. — New York: American Institute of Physics [1963] 92 p.: ill. Cover-title Includes Resource letter QSL-1 [by] P. Carruthers, p. 1-5 1. Photons I. American Institute of Physics. II. T.
QC361.A47x

**Optical shop testing / edited by Daniel Malacara.** 5.2291
New York: Wiley, c1978. xix, 523 p.: ill.; 24 cm. — (Wiley series in pure and applied optics) 1. Optical measurements 2. Interferometer I. Malacara, Daniel, 1937-
QC367.O59　　681/.4/028　　LC 77-13222　　ISBN 0471019739

# QC371–376 Optical Instruments and Apparatus

**Levi, Leo, 1926-.** 5.2292
Applied optics; a guide to optical system design. — New York: Wiley, 1980. 1128 p. (Wiley series in pure and applied optics) 1. Optics 2. Optical instruments I. T.
QC371.L48　　535/.33 19　　LC 67-29942　　ISBN 0471050547

# QC381 Geometrical Optics

**Kingslake, Rudolf.** 5.2293
Lens design fundamentals / Rudolf Kingslake. — New York: Academic Press, 1978. xii, 366 p.: ill.; 24 cm. 1. Lenses — Design and construction. I. T.
QC385.2.D47 K56　　681/.42　　LC 77-80788　　ISBN 0124086501

**Fowles, Grant R.** 5.2294
Introduction to modern optics / Grant R. Fowles. — 2d ed. — New York: Holt, Rinehart and Winston, [1975] viii, 328 p.: ill.; 25 cm. 1. Optics, Physical I. T.
QC395.2.F68 1975　　535/.2　　LC 74-23437　　ISBN 0030894042

# QC398–449 Physical Optics

**Tolansky, S. (Samuel), 1907-.** 5.2295
An introduction to interferometry [by] S. Tolansky. 2d ed. New York, Wiley [1973] x, 253 p. illus. 22 cm. 'A Halsted Press book.' 1. Interferometer I. T.
QC411.T58 1973　　535/.4　　LC 72-10729　　ISBN 0470876700

**American Association of Physics Teachers.** 5.2296
Polarized light: selected reprints. — New York: Published for the American Association of Physics Teachers by the American Institute of Physics [1963] 103 p.: ill., diagrs., tables; 27 cm. (Its Selected reprints) 1. Polarization (Light) I. American Institute of Physics. II. T.
QC441 A54

**Shurcliff, William A.** • 5.2297
Polarized light [by] William A. Shurcliff and Stanley S. Ballard. Princeton, N.J., Published for the Commission on College Physics [by] D. Van Nostrand [1964] 144 p. illus., plates. 21 cm. (Van Nostrand momentum book print 7) 1. Polarization (Light) I. Ballard, Stanley S. joint author. II. T.
QC441.S5 1964　　535.5　　LC 64-57904

**Goldin, Edwin, 1933-.** 5.2298
Waves and photons: an introduction to quantum optics / Edwin Goldin. — New York: Wiley, 1982. xi, 211 p.: ill.; 24 cm. — (Wiley series in pure and applied optics. 0277-2493) Includes index. 1. Quantum optics I. T. II. Series.
QC446.2.G64 1982　　535/.15 19　　LC 82-10991　　ISBN 0471085928

**Maitland, Arthur.** • 5.2299
Laser physics. By A. Maitland and M. H. Dunn. — Amsterdam: North-Holland Pub. Co., 1969 [1970] xii, 413 p.; 23 cm. Sole distributors for the Western Hemisphere; Wiley Interscience Division, J. Wiley & Sons, New York. 1. Lasers I. Dunn, Malcolm Harry, joint author. II. T.
QC446.2.M34　　535.5/8　　LC 76-97205　　ISBN 0720401534

**Zernike, Frits, 1930-.** 5.2300
Applied nonlinear optics [by] Frits Zernike and John E. Midwinter. — New York: Wiley, [1973] xi, 199 p.: illus.; 23 cm. — (Wiley series in pure and applied optics) 1. Nonlinear optics I. Midwinter, John E., joint author. II. T.
QC446.2.Z47　　535　　LC 72-8369　　ISBN 0471982121

# QC450–467 Spectroscopy

**Bingel, Werner A.** 5.2301
Theory of molecular spectra [by] Werner A. Bingel. — [Chichester, Eng.]: J. Wiley & Sons, 1971 (c1969) x, 180 p.: ill.; 21 cm. — (Chemical topics for students, 2) Translation of Theorie der Molekülspektren. 1. Molecular spectra I. T. II. Series.
QC451.B513　　535/.84　　LC 75-80980　　ISBN 0471073016

**Herzberg, Gerhard, 1904-.** • 5.2302
[Atomspektren und Atomstruktur. English] Atomic spectra and atomic structure / by Gerhard Herzberg; translated with the co-operation of the author by J. W. T. Spinks. — New York: Dover publications, 1944. xiii, [1], 257 p.: diagrs.; 22 cm. 'First edition, 1937. Second edition, 1944.' 1. Atomic spectroscopy 2. Atoms I. Spinks, J. W. T. (John William Tranter), 1908- tr. II. T.
QC451.H453 1944　　535.84　　LC 45-4509

**Herzberg, Gerhard, 1904-.** • 5.2303
[Molekülspektren und molekülstruktur. English] Molecular spectra and molecular structure, by Gerhard Herzberg, with the co-operation, in the 1st ed., of J.W.T. Spinks. 2d ed. New York, Van Nostrand [1950-. v. diagrs. 24 cm. 1. Molecular spectroscopy — Tables. 2. Molecular structure — Tables. I. T.
QC451.H464　　539.1　　LC 50-8347

**Howarth, Oliver.** 5.2304
Theory of spectroscopy; an elementary introduction. — New York: Wiley, [1973] x, 214 p.: illus.; 24 cm. 'A Halsted Press book.' 1. Spectrum analysis I. T. II. Title: Spectroscopy.
QC451.H83　　544/.6　　LC 73-35　　ISBN 047041667X

**Pauling, Linus, 1901-.** • 5.2305
The structure of line spectra / by Linus Pauling, and Samuel Goudsmit. — 1st ed. — New York: McGraw-Hill book company, inc., 1930. x, 263 p.: ill. — (International series in physics) 1. Spectrum analysis I. Goudsmit, Samuel Abraham, 1902- II. T. III. Title: Line spectra.
QC451.P3　　544.6　　LC 30-10392

**Sawyer, Ralph Alanson, 1895-.** • 5.2306
Experimental spectroscopy. 3d ed. New York, Dover Publications [1963] x, 358 p. illus., diagrs. 22 cm. 1. Spectrum analysis 2. Spectroscope I. T.
QC451.S28 1963　　LC 63-17915

**Spectrometric techniques / edited by George A. Vanasse; contributors, Doran Baker ... [et al.].** 5.2307
New York: Academic Press, 1977. 355 p.: ill.; 24 cm. 1. Spectrum analysis 2. Spectrum analysis — Instruments I. Vanasse, George A. II. Baker, Doran J.
QC451.S619　　535.8/4 19　　LC 76-13949　　ISBN 0127104011

**Spectroscopy, Part A / edited by Dudley Williams.** 5.2308
New York [etc.]; London: Academic Press, 1976. xvii, 366 p.: ill.; 24 cm. (Methods of experimental physics. vol.13) In 2 parts. 1. Spectrum analysis I. Williams, Dudley. II. Series.
QC451.S6x　　535/.84　　LC 76-6854　　ISBN 0124759130

**Spectroscopy / edited by B. P. Straughan and S. Walker.** 5.2309
London: Chapman and Hall; New York: Wiley; distributed in the U.S.A. by Halsted Press, 1976. 3v.　: ill.; 24 cm. Previous editions by S. Walker and H. Straw published in 1962 and 1967, entered under: Walker, Stanley. 1. Spectrum analysis I. Straughan, B. P. II. Walker, S. D. (Stanley D.) Spectroscopy.
QC451.W33 1976　　QC451 W33 1976.　　535/.84　　LC 75-45328
ISBN 0470150319

**White, Harvey Elliott, 1902-.** • 5.2310
Introduction to atomic spectra, by Harvey Elliott White. 1st ed. New York, London, McGraw-Hill book company, inc., 1934. xii, 457 p. illus., diagrs. 24 cm. (International series in physics) 1. Atomic spectroscopy I. T. II. Title: Atomic spectra.
QC451.W5　　535.84　　LC 34-38364

**Greenwood, Norman Neil.** 5.2311
Index of vibrational spectra of inorganic and organometallic compounds [by] N. N. Greenwood, E. J. F. Ross [and] B. P. Straughan. — Cleveland: CRC Press, [1972] 2 v.; 23 cm. — (International scientific series) 1. Vibrational spectra — Indexes. I. Ross, Euan James Ferguson, 1941- joint author. II. Straughan, B. P., joint author. III. T.
QC453.G74　　547/.308/5　　LC 72-133910

**Massachusetts Institute of Technology wavelength tables: with**     **5.2312**
**intensities in arc, spark, or discharge tube of more than 100,000**
**spectrum lines most strongly emitted by the atomic elements**
**under normal conditions of excitation between 10,000 A. and**
**2000 A., arranged in order of decreasing wavelengths /**
**measured and compiled under the direction of George R.**
**Harrison by staff members of the Spectroscopy Laboratory of**
**the Massachusetts Institute of Technology; assisted by the**
**Works Progress Administration.**
1969 ed. / with errata and certain revisions. — Cambridge, Mass.: M.I.T. Press, [1969]-c1982. 2 v.: front.; 26 cm. Vol. 2 has title: M.I.T. wavelength tables. 1. Spectrum analysis — Tables. I. Harrison, George Russell, 1898- II. Phelps, Frederick M. III. Massachusetts Institute of Technology. Spectroscopy Laboratory. IV. United States. Work Projects Administration. V. Title: Wavelength tables. VI. Title: M.I.T. wavelength tables. VII. Title: MIT wavelength tables.
QC453.M36 1969     535/.84/0212 19     *LC* 73-95288     *ISBN* 0262080028

**Condon, Edward Uhler, 1902-1974.**     • **5.2313**
The theory of atomic spectra / by E. U. Condon, and G. H. Shortley. — Cambridge, Eng.: The University press, 1935. xiv, 441 p.: ill. 1. Spectrum analysis 2. Quantum theory I. Shortley, George, 1910- II. T. III. Title: Atomic spectra.
QC454.C64     *LC* 35-22624

**Farrar, Thomas Clark, 1933-.**     • **5.2314**
Pulse and Fourier transform NMR; introduction to theory and methods [by] Thomas C. Farrar [and] Edwin D. Becker. — New York: Academic Press, 1971. xiv, 115 p.: illus.; 24 cm. 1. Nuclear magnetic resonance 2. Radiofrequency spectroscopy 3. Pulse techniques (Electronics) 4. Fourier transformations I. Becker, Edwin D. joint author. II. T.
QC454.F34 1971     538/.3     *LC* 78-159605     *ISBN* 0122496507

**Demtröder, W.**     **5.2315**
Laser spectroscopy: basic concepts and instrumentation / Wolfgang Demtröder. — 2nd corr. print. — Berlin; New York: Springer-Verlag, 1982. p. cm. — (Springer series in chemical physics. v. 5) Includes index. 1. Laser spectroscopy I. T. II. Series.
QC454.L3 D46 1982     535.5/8 19     *LC* 82-16890     *ISBN* 0387103430

**Townes, Charles H.**     **5.2316**
Microwave spectroscopy / C. H. Townes, A. L. Schawlow. — New York: Dover Publications, 1975. xviii, 698 p.: ill.; 21 cm. 'An unabridged and corrected republication of the work first published in 1955 by the McGraw-Hill Book Company.' Includes indexes. 1. Microwave spectroscopy 2. Gases — Spectra I. Schawlow, A. L., 1921- joint author. II. T.
QC454.M5 T68 1975     543/.085     *LC* 74-83620     *ISBN* 048661798X

**Macomber, James D., 1939-.**     **5.2317**
The dynamics of spectroscopic transitions: illustrated by magnetic resonance and laser effects / James D. Macomber. — New York: Wiley, c1976. xxiv, 332 p.: ill.; 24 cm. (Wiley-Interscience monographs in chemical physics) 'Wiley-Interscience publication.' 1. Nuclear spectroscopy 2. Magnetic resonance 3. Quantum optics I. T.
QC454.N8 M3     538/.3     *LC* 75-25852     *ISBN* 0471563005

**Shrader, Stephen R., 1942-.**     **5.2318**
Introductory mass spectrometry [by] Stephen R. Shrader. — Boston: Allyn and Bacon, [1971] x, 246 p.: illus.; 22 cm. — (Allyn and Bacon chemistry series) 1. Mass spectrometry I. T.
QC454.S515     539.6     *LC* 78-141227

**The Coblentz Society desk book of infrared spectra / Clara D.**     **5.2319**
**Craver, editor.**
2nd ed. — Kirkwood, MO (P.O. Box 9952, Kirkwood 63122): The Society, 1982, c1977. iii, 538 p.: ill.; 29 cm. Includes indexes. 1. Infrared spectroscopy — Handbooks, manuals, etc. I. Craver, Clara D. II. Coblentz Society. III. Title: Desk book of infared spectra.
QC457.C687 1982     544/.63 19     *LC* 82-71413

**Klöpffer, Walter, 1938-.**     **5.2320**
Introduction to polymer spectroscopy / Walter Klöpffer. — Berlin; New York: Springer-Verlag, 1984. xii, 190 p.: ill.; 25 cm. (Polymers, properties and applications. 7) 1. Polymers and polymerization — Spectra I. T. II. Series.
QC463.P5 K55 1984     547.7/028 19     *LC* 83-16700     *ISBN* 0387128506

# QC474–496 Radiation Physics

**Stimson, Allen.**     **5.2321**
Photometry and radiometry for engineers. — New York: Wiley, [1974] xiv, 446 p.: illus.; 24 cm. 'A Wiley-Interscience publication.' 1. Radiation — Measurement 2. Photometry I. T.
QC475.S74     535/.22     *LC* 74-11253     *ISBN* 047182531X

**Clark, George L. (George Lindenberg), 1892- ed.**     • **5.2322**
The encyclopedia of X–rays and gamma rays. New York, Reinhold Pub. Corp. [1963] xxvii, 1149 p. illus., diagrs., tables. 26 cm. 1. X-rays — Dictionaries. 2. Gamma rays — Dictionaries. 3. Radiology — Dictionaries. 4. Radiobiology — Dictionaries. I. T.
QC481.C475     537.535203     *LC* 63-13449

**James, Reginald William, 1891-.**     • **5.2323**
X–ray crystallography / with a general pref. by O. W. Richardson. — 5th ed. — London: Methuen; New York: Wiley, 1953. 101 p.: ill. — (Methuen's monographs on physical subjects) 1. X-rays 2. Cystallography. I. T.
QC481.J3 1953     QD/945.J28.     *LC* 53-10270

**Guinier, André.**     • **5.2324**
X–ray studies of materials [by] A. Guinier [and] D.L. Dexter. New York, Interscience Publishers, 1963. ix, 156 p. illus., diagrs. 21 cm. (Interscience tracts on physics and astronomy; 20) 1. X-ray spectroscopy I. Dexter, D. L. (David Lawrence), 1924- joint author. II. T.
QC482.G83     537.5352     *LC* 63-13594

**Agarwal, B. K. (Bipin Kumar), 1931-.**     **5.2325**
X–ray spectroscopy: an introduction / B. K. Agarwal. — Berlin; New York: Springer-Verlag, 1979. xiii, 418 p.: ill.; 24 cm. — (Springer series in optical sciences; v. 15) 1. X-ray spectroscopy I. T.
QC482.S6 A34     537.5/352     *LC* 79-415     *ISBN* 0387092684

**Hillas, A. M.**     **5.2326**
Cosmic rays, by A. M. Hillas. — [1st ed.]. — Oxford, New York, Pergamon Press [1972] x, 297 p. illus. 21 cm. — (The Commonwealth and international library. Selected readings in physics) 1. Cosmic rays I. T.
QC485.H53 1972     539.7/223/08     *LC* 70-181329     *ISBN* 0080167241

**Longair, M. S., 1941-.**     **5.2327**
High energy astrophysics: an informal introduction for students of physics and astronomy / M.S. Longair. — Cambridge [England]; New York: Cambridge University Press, 1981. viii, 412 p.: ill.; 24 cm. 1. Cosmic rays 2. Nuclear astrophysics I. T.
QC485.8.O7 L66     523.01/9 19     *LC* 81-7702     *ISBN* 0521235138

**American Institute of Physics.**     **5.2328**
Mössbauer effect: selected reprints. — New York: Published for the American Association of Physics Teachers by the American Institute of Physics [1962] 127 p.: ill.; 21 cm. Reprints of articles from various journals. 1. Mössbauer effect I. American Association of Physics Teachers. II. T.
QC490.Ax

**Wertheim, Gunther K.**     • **5.2329**
Mössbauer effect: principles and applications, by Gunther K. Wertheim. New York, Academic Press [1964] viii, 116 p. illus. 21 cm. (Academic paperbacks. Physics.) 1. Mössbauer effect I. T. II. Series.
QC490.W4 1964     535.35     *LC* 64-24667

**Frauenfelder, Hans, 1922-.**     • **5.2330**
The Mössbauer effect; a review, with a collection of reprints. New York, W.A. Benjamin, 1962. 336 p. illus. 23 cm. (Frontiers in physics: a lecture note and reprint series) 1. Mössbauer effect I. T.
QC491.F7     537.5/352     *LC* 61-18181

**Gibb, Terence Charles.**     **5.2331**
Principles of Mössbauer spectroscopy / T. C. Gibb. — London: Chapman and Hall; New York: Wiley, 1976. 254 p.: graphs; 24 cm. (Studies in chemical physics) 'A Halsted Press book.' Includes index. 1. Mössbauer spectroscopy I. T.
QC491.G52     537.5/352     *LC* 75-25878     *ISBN* 0470297433

## QC494–496 Color

**Evans, Ralph Merrill.**    • 5.2332
An introduction to color. — New York: J. Wiley, 1948. x, 340 p.: ill. 1. Color I. T.
QC495.E8    LC 48-7620

**Judd, Deane Brewster, 1900-1972.**    5.2333
Color in business, science, and industry / Deane B. Judd and Günter Wyszecki. — 3d ed. — New York: Wiley, [1975] xiii, 553 p.: ill.; 23 cm. (Wiley series in pure and applied optics) Includes indexes. 1. Color I. Wyszecki, Günter. joint author. II. T.
QC495.J79 1975    535.6    LC 75-6590    ISBN 0471452122

**Nassau, Kurt.**    5.2334
The physics and chemistry of color: the fifteen causes of color / Kurt Nassau. — New York: Wiley, c1983. xx, 454 p., [8] p. of plates: ill. (some col.); 24 cm. — (Wiley series in pure and applied optics. 0277-2493) 'A Wiley-Interscience publication.' Includes index. 1. Color 2. Chemistry, Physical and theoretical I. T. II. Series.
QC495.N35 1983    535.6 19    LC 83-10580    ISBN 0471867764

**Optical Society of America. Committee on Colorimetry.**    • 5.2335
The science of color. — New York: Crowell, 1953. xiii, 385 p., 25 p. of plates: ill. (part. col.); 26 cm. 1. Color I. T.
QC495.O6    535.6    LC 52-7039

## QC501–764 Electricity. Magnetism

## QC501–581 History. General Works

**Faraday, Michael, 1791-1867.**    • 5.2336
Experimental researches in electricity. — New York: Dover Publications, [1965] 3 v. in 2.: illus. (1 fold.); 22 cm. 'An unabridged and unaltered republication of the work originally published ... 1839-1855.' 1. Electricity — Collected works. 2. Electricity — Early works to 1850 I. T.
QC503.F21 1965    537    LC 63-19490

**Bordeau, Sanford P.**    5.2337
Volts to Hertz— the rise of electricity: from the compass to the radio through the works of sixteen great men of science whose names are used in measuring electricity and magnetism / Sanford P. Bordeau. — Minneapolis, Minn.: Burgess Pub. Co., c1982. ix, 308 p.: ill., facsims., plans, ports.; 26 cm. Includes index. 1. Electricity — History. 2. Magnetism — History. 3. Physicists — Biography I. T.
QC507.B73 1982    537/.09 19    LC 82-17702    ISBN 0808749080

**Franklin, Benjamin, 1706-1790.**    • 5.2338
Benjamin Franklin's experiments: a new edition of Franklin's experiments and observations on electricity / Edited, with a critical and historical introduction, by I. Bernard Cohen. — Cambridge, Mass: Harvard University Press, 1941. — xxviii, 453 p., [3] leaves of plates: ill., facsim.; 23 cm. Includes index. I. Cohen, I. Bernard, 1914- II. Cohen, I. Bernard, 1914- Experiments and observations on electricity. III. T.
QC516.F85 1941    LC 41-4483

**Cavendish, Henry, 1731-1810.**    • 5.2339
The electrical researches of the Honourable Henry Cavendish / ed. by J. Clerk Maxwell. — London: F. Cass, 1967. 454 p.: ill. (Cass library of science classics; 4) 1. Electricity — Early works to 1850 I. Maxwell, James Clerk, 1831-1879. ed. II. T. III. Series.
QC517.C35 1967

**Landau, L. D. (Lev Davidovich), 1908-1968.**    • 5.2340
[Ėlektrodinamika sploshnykh sred. English] Electrodynamics of continuous media / by L. D. Landau and E. M. Lifshitz; translated from the Russian by J. B. Sykes and J. S. Bell. — Oxford; New York: Pergamon Press, 1960. 417 p.: ill.; 26 cm. (Their Course of theoretical physics, v. 8) 1. Electricity 2. Electromagnetic theory I. Lifshits, Evgeniĭ Mikhaĭlovich, joint author. II. T.
QC518.L313    537.6    LC 60-14731

**Maxwell, James Clerk, 1831-1879.**    • 5.2341
A treatise on electricity and magnetism / by James Clerk Maxwell. — Unabridged 3d ed. — New York: Dover, 1954. 2v.: ill. 'Unabridged, slightly altered, republication of the third ed., pub. by the Clarendon Press in 1891.' 1. Electricity 2. Magnetism I. T.
QC518.M47 1954    ISBN 0486606368

**Panofsky, Wolfgang Kurt Hermann, 1919-.**    • 5.2342
Classical electricity and magnetism, by Wolfgang K.H. Panofsky and Melba Phillips. 2d ed. Reading, Mass., Addison-Wesley Pub. Co. [1962] 494 p. illus. 24 cm. (Addison-Wesley series in physics.) 1. Electricity 2. Electromagnetic theory 3. Relativity (Physics) I. Phillips, Melba, 1907- joint author. II. T. III. Series.
QC518.P337 1962    538.3    LC 61-10973

**Michels, Walter C. (Walter Christian), 1906-1975.**    • 5.2343
Electrical measurements and their applications. Princeton, N.J.: D. Van Nostrand [1957] 331 p.: ill.; 24 cm. 'Based on ... [the author's] Advanced electrical measurements.' 1. Electric measurements 2. Physical instruments I. T.
QC535.M52    537.7    LC 57-6969

**Smith, Arthur Whitmore, 1874-.**    • 5.2344
Electrical measurements [by] Arthur Whitmore Smith [and] M.L. Wiedenbeck. 5th ed. New York, McGraw-Hill, 1959. 307 p. illus. 24 cm. First ed. published in 1914 under title: Principles of electrical measurements. 1. Electric measurements I. Wiedenbeck, M. L. (Marcellus Lee) II. T.
QC535.S57 1959    621.37    LC 58-11193

**Crowley, Joseph M.**    5.2345
Fundamentals of applied electrostatics / Joseph M. Crowley. — New York: Wiley, c1986. xvi, 255 p.: ill.; 24 cm. 'A Wiley-Interscience publication.' 1. Electrostatics I. T.
QC571.C76 1986    537/.2 19    LC 85-17793    ISBN 0471803189

**Moore, Arthur Dearth, 1895-.**    5.2346
Electrostatics and its applications. A. D. Moore, editor. — New York: Wiley, [1973] xviii, 481 p.: illus.; 23 cm. 'A Wiley-Interscience publication.' 1. Electrostatics I. T.
QC571.M663    537.2    LC 72-13945    ISBN 0471614505

## QC601–612 Electric Current. Conductivity

**Dunlap, W. Crawford (William Crawford), 1918-.**    • 5.2347
An introduction to semiconductors. New York: Wiley [1957] 417 p.: ill.; 24 cm. 1. Semiconductors I. T.
QC611.D85    537.22    LC 56-8961

**Fraser, D. A.**    5.2348
The physics of semiconductor devices / D.A. Fraser. — 4th ed. — Oxford [Oxfordshire]: Clarendon Press; New York: Oxford University Press, c1986. x, 196 p.: ill. — (Oxford physics series. 16) Includes index. 1. Semiconductors I. T. II. Series.
QC611.F72 1986    537.5/22 19    LC 86-5325    ISBN 0198518676

**Seeger, Karlheinz.**    5.2349
Semiconductor physics: an introduction / Karlheinz Seeger. — 3rd ed. — Berlin; New York: Springer-Verlag, c1985. xiv, 476 p.: ill.; 24 cm. (Springer series in solid-state sciences. v. 40) Includes index. 1. Semiconductors I. T. II. Series.
QC611.S43 1985    621.3815/2/0153 19    LC 85-9944    ISBN 0387155783

**Shoenberg, D. (David).**    • 5.2350
Superconductivity. — 2d ed. — Cambridge: University Press, 1952. 256 p.: ill. — (Cambridge monographs on physics) 1. Electric conductivity 2. Low temperature research 3. Electromagnetic theory I. T.
QC611.S52 1952    LC 52-14732

**Smith, R. A. (Robert Allan), 1909-.**    5.2351
Semiconductors / R. A. Smith. — 2d ed. — Cambridge; New York: Cambridge University Press, 1978. xvii, 523 p.: ill.; 24 cm. Includes indexes. 1. Semiconductors I. T.
QC611.S59 1978    537.6/22    LC 77-28181    ISBN 0521218241. ISBN 0521293146 pbk

**Moll, John L.** • 5.2352
Physics of semiconductors / [by] John L. Moll. — New York: McGraw-Hill [1964] viii, 293 p.: ill.; 23 cm. (McGraw-Hill physical and quantum electronics series.) 1. Semiconductors I. T. II. Series.
QC612.S4 M57    621.3815    *LC* 63-23391

**Schrieffer, J. R. (John Robert), 1931-.** 5.2353
Theory of superconductivity / J.R. Schrieffer. — Rev. print. — Reading, Mass.: Benjamin/Cummings Pub. Co., [1983] xviii, 332 p.: ill.; 24 cm. — (Frontiers in physics; 20) 'With appendix: Nobel lectures, December 11, 1972, by J.R. Schrieffer, Leon N. Cooper, and John Bardeen'—T.p. verso. 1. Superconductivity I. T.
QC612.S8 S3 1983    537.6/23 19    *LC* 83-167315    *ISBN* 0805385029

**Tinkham, Michael.** 5.2354
Introduction to superconductivity / Michael Tinkham. — New York: McGraw-Hill, [1975] xiv, 296 p.: ill.; 25 cm. (International series in pure and applied physics) Includes indexes. 1. Superconductivity I. T.
QC612.S8 T49    537.6/23    *LC* 74-32166    *ISBN* 0070648778

**Williams, John Eric Charles.** • 5.2355
Superconductivity and its applications [by] J. E. C. Williams. — London: Pion, 1970. 213 p., 5 plates.: illus.; 24 cm. — (Acta polytechnica Scandinavica. Applied physics series. 4) 1. Superconductivity I. T. II. Series.
QC612.S8 W5    621.39    *LC* 75-854664    *ISBN* 0850860105

## QC630–667 Electrodynamics. Electric Waves. Electromagnetic Fields

**Grandy, Walter T., 1933-.** • 5.2356
Introduction to electrodynamics and radiation [by] Walter T. Grandy. — New York: Academic Press, 1970. xiii, 284 p.: illus.; 24 cm. — (Pure and applied physics. v. 34) 1. Electrodynamics 2. Quantum field theory 3. Radiation I. T. II. Series.
QC631.G73    537.6    *LC* 78-117077    *ISBN* 0122952502

**Jackson, John David, 1925-.** 5.2357
Classical electrodynamics / John David Jackson. — 2d ed. — New York: Wiley, c1975. xxii, 848 p.: ill.; 24 cm. Includes index. 1. Electrodynamics I. T.
QC631.J3 1975    537.6/01    *LC* 75-9962    *ISBN* 047143132X

**Hertz, Heinrich Rudolph, 1857-1894.** • 5.2358
Electric waves: being researches on the propagation of electric action with finite velocity through space / by Heinrich Hertz; authorised English translation by D. E. Jones with a preface by Lord Kelvin. — New York: Dover Publications, 1962. xv, 278 p.: ill.; 22 cm. Includes bibliographical references and index. Translation of Untersuchungen über die Ausbreitung der elektrischen Kraft. 1. Electric waves I. T.
QC661.H593 1962    *LC* 62-53081    *ISBN* 0486600572

**Landau, L. D. (Lev Davidovich), 1908-1968.** 5.2359
[Élektrodinamika sploshnykh sred. English] Electrodynamics of continuous media / by L.D. Landau and E.M. Lifshitz; translated from the Russian by J.B. Sykes, J.S. Bell, and M.J. Kearsley. — 2nd ed., rev. and enl. / by E.M. Lifshitz and L.P. Pitaevskii. — Oxford [Oxfordshire]; New York: Pergamon, 1984. xiii, 460 p.: ill.; 26 cm. (Pergamon international library of science, technology, engineering, and social studies.) (Course of theoretical physics; v. 8) Translation of: Élektrodinamika sploshnykh sred. 'Translated from the second edition ...: Izdatel'stvo 'Nauka', Moscow 1982.'—T.p. verso. Includes index. 1. Electromagnetic waves 2. Electrodynamics 3. Continuum mechanics I. Lifshits, E. M. (Evgeniĭ Mikhaĭlovich) II. Pitaevskiĭ, L. P. (Lev Petrovich) III. T. IV. Series.
QC661.L2413 1984    537 19    *LC* 83-24997    *ISBN* 0080302769

**Paris, Demetrius T., 1928-.** 5.2360
Basic electromagnetic theory [by] Demetrius T. Paris [and] F. Kenneth Hurd. — New York: McGraw-Hill, [1969] xiv, 591 p.: illus., ports.; 23 cm. — (McGraw-Hill physical and quantum electronics series) 1. Electromagnetic theory I. Hurd, Frank Kenneth, 1912- joint author. II. T.
QC661.P3    537.1/1    *LC* 68-8775

**Read, Frank Henry.** 5.2361
Electromagnetic radiation / F.H. Read. — Chichester [Eng.]; New York: J. Wiley, c1980. xiv, 331 p.: ill.; 34 cm. — (Manchester physics series) Based on a course of lectures given by the author at the University of Manchester. 1. Electromagnetic waves I. T.
QC661.R4    539.2 19    *LC* 79-41484    *ISBN* 0471277185

**Landau, L. D. (Lev Davidovich), 1908-1968.** 5.2362
[Teoriia polia. English] The classical theory of fields / L. D. Landau and E. M. Lifshitz; translated from the Russian by Morton Hamermesh. — 4th rev. English ed. — Oxford; New York: Pergamon Press, 1975. xi, 402 p.: ill.; 27 cm. (Course of theoretical physics; v. 2) Translated from the 6th rev. ed. of Teoriia polia. 1. Electromagnetic fields 2. Field theory (Physics) I. Lifshits, E. M. (Evgeniĭ Mikhaĭlovich) joint author. II. T.
QC665.E4 L3713 1975    530.1/4    *LC* 75-4737    *ISBN* 0080181767

**Maxwell, James Clerk, 1831-1879.** 5.2363
A dynamical theory of the electromagnetic field / James Clerk Maxwell; with an appreciation by Albert Einstein; edited and introduced by Thomas F. Torrance. — Edinburgh: Scottish Academic Press, c1982. xiii, 103 p.; 22 cm. 1. Electromagnetic fields I. Torrance, Thomas Forsyth, 1913- II. T.
QC665.E4 M38 1982    530.1/41 19    *LC* 83-140288    *ISBN* 0707303249

**Portis, Alan M., 1926-.** 5.2364
Electromagnetic fields: sources and media / Alan M. Portis. — New York: Wiley, c1978. xxiii, 775 p.; 24 cm. 1. Electromagnetic fields 2. Solids state physics. 3. Plasma (Ionized gases) I. T.
QC665.E4 P67    537    *LC* 78-7585    *ISBN* 0471019062

**Wangsness, Roald K.** 5.2365
Electromagnetic fields / Roald K. Wangsness. — New York: Wiley, c1979. 645 p. in various pagings: ill.; 26 cm. Includes index. 1. Electromagnetic fields I. T.
QC665.E4 W36    537    *LC* 78-15027    *ISBN* 0471041033

## QC669–675 Electromagnetic Theory

**Abraham, Max, 1875-1922.** • 5.2366
The classical theory of electricity and magnetism / by Max Abraham ... revised by Richard Becker ... authorized translation by John Dougall. — 2d ed. — London: Blackie, [1950] xiv, 289 p.: ill. — (Student's physics. v.5) Translation of Theorie der Elektrizität. v. 1, 14. Aufl., 1949. 1. Electromagnetic theory 2. Electricity 3. Magnetism I. Becker, Richard, 1887-1955. II. Dougall, John. III. T. IV. Series.
QC670.A15 1950    *LC* 53-2546

**Chirgwin, Brian H.** 5.2367
Elementary electromagnetic theory / [by] B. H. Chirgwin, C. Plumpton [and] C. W. Kilmister. — [1st ed.] Oxford; New York: Pergamon Press, [1971-73] 3 v. (viii, 602 p.): ill.; 23 cm. 1. Electromagnetic theory I. Plumpton, C. (Charles) joint author. II. Kilmister, C. W. (Clive William) joint author. III. T.
QC670.C4    530.1/41    *LC* 70-129631

**Clemmow, P. C.** 5.2368
An introduction to electromagnetic theory [by] P. C. Clemmow. — Cambridge [Eng.]: University Press, 1973. xi, 297 p.; 24 cm. 1. Electromagnetic theory I. T.
QC670.C44    530.1/41    *LC* 73-77174    *ISBN* 0521202396

**Heaviside, Oliver, 1850-1925.** • 5.2369
Electromagnetic theory. Including an account of Heaviside's unpublished notes for a fourth volume, and with a foreword by Edmund Whittaker. — 3d ed. — New York: Chelsea Pub. Co., [1971] 3 v.: illus.; 22 cm. 'The present work is an unabridged edition, in three volumes, of a work originally published at London in 1893, 1899, and 1912, respectively.' 1. Electromagnetic theory 2. Vector analysis 3. Electromagnetic waves I. T.
QC670.H42 1971    530.1/41    *LC* 74-118633    *ISBN* 082840237X

**Narayana Rao, Nannapaneni.** 5.2370
Elements of engineering electromagnetics / Nannapaneni Narayana Rao. — 2nd ed. — Englewood Cliffs, N.J.: Prentice-Hall, c1987. xiii, 593 p.: ill.; 25 cm. Includes index. 1. Electromagnetic theory I. T.
QC670.N3 1987    530.1/41 19    *LC* 86-5092    *ISBN* 0132641933

**Reitz, John R.** 5.2371
Foundations of electromagnetic theory / John R. Reitz, Frederick J. Milford, Robert W. Christy. — 3d ed. — Reading, Mass.: Addison-Wesley, c1979. x, 534 p.: ill.; 25 cm. — (Addison-Wesley series in physics.) 1. Electromagnetic theory I. Milford, Frederick J., joint author. II. Christy, Robert W. joint author. III. T. IV. Series.
QC670.R4 1979    530.1/41    *LC* 78-18649    *ISBN* 0201063328

**Wilson, J. (John), 1939-.** 5.2372
Optoelectronics, an introduction / J. Wilson, J.F.B. Hawkes. — Englewood Cliffs, N.J.: Prentice-Hall, c1983. xv, 445 p.: ill.; 24 cm. — (Prentice-Hall

international series in optoelectronics.) 1. Optoelectronics I. Hawkes, J. F. B., 1942- II. T. III. Series.
QC673.W54 1983     621.36 19     *LC* 82-16546     *ISBN* 0136383955

# QC680–689 Quantum Electrodynamics

**Akhiezer, A. I. (Aleksandr Il'ich), 1911-.**     **5.2373**
[Kvantovaia ėlektrodinamika. English] Quantum electrodynamics [by] A.I. Akhiezer [and] V.B. Berestetskiĭ. Authorized English ed., rev. and enl. by the authors. Translated from the 2d Russian ed., by G.M. Volkoff. New York, Interscience Publishers, 1965. xix, 868 p. illus. 24 cm. (Interscience monographs and texts in physics and astronomy. v. 11) 1. Quantum electrodynamics I. Berestetskiĭ, V. B. (Vladimir Borisovich) joint author. II. T. III. Series.
QC680.A313 1965     537.6     *LC* 63-17766

**Griffiths, David J. (David Jeffrey), 1942-.**     **5.2374**
Introduction to electrodynamics / David J. Griffiths. — Englewood Cliffs, N.J.: Prentice-Hall, 1981. x, 479 p.: ill.; 24 cm. Includes index. 1. Electrodynamics I. T.
QC680.G74     537.6     *LC* 80-11508     *ISBN* 013481374X

**Heitler, Walter, 1904-.**     • **5.2375**
The quantum theory of radiation / by W. Heitler. — 3rd ed. — New York: Dover Publications, 1984. xiii, 430 p.: ill.; 22 cm. Reprint. Originally published: 3rd ed. Oxford: Clarendon Press, 1954. (The International series of monographs on physics) 1. Quantum electrodynamics I. T.
QC680.H44 1984     537.6 19     *LC* 83-5201     *ISBN* 0486645584

**Jauch, Josef Maria, 1914-1974.**     **5.2376**
The theory of photons and electrons: the relativistic quantum field theory of charged particles with spin one–half / J. M. Jauch and F. Rohrlich. — 2d expanded ed. — New York: Springer-Verlag, 1976. xix, 553 p.: ill.; 24 cm. (Texts and monographs in physics) 1. Quantum electrodynamics I. Rohrlich, F. joint author. II. T.
QC680.J38 1976     530.1/43     *LC* 75-8890     *ISBN* 0387072950

**Schwinger, Julian Seymour, 1918- ed.**     • **5.2377**
Selected papers on quantum electrodynamics. New York: Dover Publications [1958] 424 p.: ill.; 24 cm. 1. Quantum electrodynamics I. T.
QC680.S35     537.6     *LC* 58-8524

**Corney, Alan.**     **5.2378**
Atomic and laser spectroscopy / Alan Corney. — [S.l.]: Oxford, 1977. xvii, 763 p.: ill.; 24 cm. 1. Quantum electronics 2. Atomic spectroscopy 3. Laser spectroscopy I. T.
QC688.C67     537/.5     *LC* 77-372597     *ISBN* 0198511388

**Svelto, Orazio.**     **5.2379**
[Principi dei laser. English] Principles of lasers / Orazio Svelto; translated from Italian and edited by David C. Hanna. — 2nd ed. — New York: Plenum Press, c1982. xv, 375 p.: ill.; 24 cm. Translation of: Principi dei laser. 1. Lasers I. Hanna, D. C. (David C.), 1941- II. T.
QC688.S913 1982     535.5/8 19     *LC* 82-484     *ISBN* 0306408627

# QC701–718 Electric Discharge. Plasma Physics. Ionized Gases

**American Association of Physics Teachers.**     **5.2380**
Plasma physics: selected reprints. — New York: Pub. by the American Institute of Physics for the American Association of Physics Teachers, 1963. 119 p.: ill., diagrs.; 27 cm. (American Association of Physics Teachers. Selected reprints) Cover title. Resource letter PP-1 prepared by Sanford C. Brown at the request of the Commission on college physics: p. 1-4. 'A project of the AAPT Committee on resource letters, 1963.' 1. Plasma (Ionized gases) I. Brown, Sanborn Conner, 1913- II. American Institute of Physics. III. T. IV. Series.
QC711.A44

**Loeb, Leonard B. (Leonard Benedict), 1891-.**     • **5.2381**
Basic processes of gaseous electronics. [2d ed., rev.] Berkeley, University of California Press, 1960 [c1955] 1028 p. illus. 25 cm. 1. Electric discharges through gases 2. Electronics I. T. II. Title: Gaseous electronics.
QC711.L67 1961     537.53     *LC* 60-50686

**Thomson, J. J. (Joseph John), Sir, 1856-1940.**     • **5.2382**
Conduction of electricity through gases, by J. J. Thomson and G. P. Thomson. — New York: Dover Publications, [1969] 2 v.: illus.; 22 cm. Reprint of the 3d ed., 1928-33. 1. Electric discharges through gases 2. Ionization of gases I. Thomson, G. P. (George Paget), Sir, 1892- joint author. II. T.
QC711.T5 1969     537.5/32     *LC* 68-8881

**Artsimovich, L. A. (Lev Andreevich), 1909-1973.**     • **5.2383**
[Elementarnaia fizika plazmy. English] Elementary plasma physics [by] Lev A. Arzimovich. [1st English ed.]. New York, Blaisdell Pub. Co. [1965] 188 p. illus. 21 cm. (A Blaisdell book in the pure and applied sciences, BP44) 1. Plasma (Ionized gases) I. T.
QC718.A713 1965     537.532     *LC* 65-14569

**Boley, Forrest I.**     • **5.2384**
Plasmas, laboratory and cosmic / [by] Forrest I. Boley. — Princeton, N.J.: Published for the Commission on College Physics [by] Van Nostrand [1966] 154 p.: ill.; 21 cm. (Van Nostrand momentum book no. 11) 1. Plasma (Ionized gases) I. Commission on College Physics. II. T.
QC718.B6     537.532     *LC* 65-28992

**Frank-Kamenetskiĭ, D. A. (David Al'bertovich)**     **5.2385**
[Plazma—chetvertoe sostoianie veshchestva. English] Plasma—the fourth state of matter [by] D. A. Frank–Kamenetskii. Translated from the Russian by Joseph Norwood, Jr. New York, Plenum Press, 1972. viii, 159 p. illus. 24 cm. Translation of Plazma—chetvertoe sostoianie veshchestva. 1. Plasma (Ionized gases) I. T.
QC718.F713     530.4/4     *LC* 71-165695     *ISBN* 0306305232

**Nicholson, Dwight R. (Dwight Roy)**     **5.2386**
Introduction to plasma theory / Dwight R. Nicholson. — New York: Wiley, c1983. xii, 292 p.: ill.; 25 cm. — (Wiley series in plasma physics. 0271-602X) 1. Plasma (Ionized gases) I. T. II. Series.
QC718.N53 1983     530.4/4 19     *LC* 82-13658     *ISBN* 047109045X

**Seshadri, S. R., 1925-.**     **5.2387**
Fundamentals of plasma physics [by] S. R. Seshadri. — New York: American Elsevier Pub. Co., [c1973] xiv, 545 p.: illus.; 26 cm. 1. Plasma (Ionized gases) I. T.
QC718.S44     530.4/4     *LC* 72-77559     *ISBN* 0444001255

**Birdsall, Charles K.**     **5.2388**
Plasma physics via computer simulation / Charles K. Birdsall, A. Bruce Langdon. — New York: McGraw-Hill, c1985. xxiii, 479 p.: ill.; 24 cm. Includes indexes. 1. Plasma (Ionized gases) — Simulation methods. 2. Computer simulation I. Langdon, A. Bruce. II. T.
QC718.4.B57 1985     530.4/4 19     *LC* 81-8296     *ISBN* 0070053715

# QC721 Physics of Particles

(see also: QC793-793.5)

**Anderson, David L.**     • **5.2389**
The discovery of the electron; the development of the atomic concept of electricity. — Princeton, N.J.: Published for the Commission on College Physics [by] Van Nostrand, [1964] vi, 138 p.: illus.; 21 cm. — (Van Nostrand momentum book, no. 3) 1. Electrons 2. Electricity 3. X-rays I. T.
QC721.A52     *LC* 64-372

**Elementary particles. Contributors: J. P. Blewett [and others] Edited by Luke C. L. Yuan.**     • **5.2390**
New York, Academic Press, 1971. xii, 314 p. illus. 24 cm. (Science, technology, and society) 1. Particles (Nuclear physics) I. Blewett, John P. (John Paul), 1910- II. Yuan, Luke C. L., ed. III. Series.
QC721.E436 1971     539.7/21     *LC* 77-84252     *ISBN* 0127748504

**Frisch, David H.**     • **5.2391**
Elementary particles [by] David H. Frisch and Alan M. Thorndike. — Princeton, N.J.: Published for the Commission on College Physics [by] D. Van Nostrand, [c1964] vi, 153 p.: illus., diagrs.; 21 cm. — (Van Nostrand momentum books, no. 1) 1. Particles (Nuclear physics) I. Thorndike, Alan M., joint author. II. T.
QC721.F87 1964     *LC* 64-282

**Gasiorowicz, Stephen.**     • **5.2392**
Elementary particle physics. — New York: Wiley, [1966] xx, 613 p.: ill.; 24 cm. 1. Particles (Nuclear physics) I. T.
QC721.G353     *LC* 66-17637

**Källén, Gunnar, 1926-1968.**      • **5.2393**
Elementary particle physics. Reading, Mass., Addison-Wesley Pub. Co. [1964] xiv, 546 p. illus. 24 cm. (A-W series in advanced physics.) 1. Particles (Nuclear physics) I. T. II. Series.
QC721.K18     539.72     LC 64-15565

**Longo, Michael J., 1935-.**      **5.2394**
Fundamentals of elementary particle physics / [by] Michael J. Longo. — New York: McGraw-Hill, [1973] xiii, 226 p.: ill.; 24 cm. — (McGraw-Hill series in fundamentals of physics.) 1. Particles (Nuclear physics) I. T. II. Series.
QC721.L8     539.7/21     LC 71-39635     ISBN 0070386897

**Lorentz, H. A. (Hendrik Antoon), 1853-1928.**      • **5.2395**
The Theory of electrons and its applications to the phenomena of light and radiant heat. — 2d ed. — New York: Dover, [1953,c1952]. 343 p. 'Student's edition.' 1. Electrons 2. Electromagnetic theory 3. Radiation I. T.
QC721.L89 1953     541.2     LC 53-3862

**Lurié, David.**      • **5.2396**
Particles and fields. — New York: Interscience Publishers, 1968. xii, 506 p.: illus.; 24 cm. 1. Particles (Nuclear physics) 2. Quantum field theory I. T.
QC721.L98     530.14/3     LC 68-22312     ISBN 0470556420

**Marshak, Robert Eugene, 1916-.**      • **5.2397**
Introduction to elementary particle physics [by] R.E. Marshak and E.C.G. Sudarshan. New York, Interscience Publishers, 1961. 231 p. 21 cm. (Interscience tracts on physics and astronomy, 11) 1. Particles (Nuclear physics) 2. Quantum theory I. Sudarshan, E. C. G. joint author. II. T. III. Title: Elementary particle physics.
QC721.M289     539.721     LC 61-11108

**Millikan, Robert Andrews, 1868-1953.**      • **5.2398**
Electrons (+ and –), protons, photons, neutrons, and cosmic rays / by Robert Andrews Millikan. — Chicago, Ill: University of Chicago Press [1935] x, 492 p.: ill., plates, diagrs.; 20 cm. (University of Chicago science series) The author has here revised his former work entitled The electron and added six new chapters. 1. Electrons 2. Atoms 3. Protons 4. Neutrons 5. Cosmic rays I. T.
QC721.M7     LC 35-1781

**Mott, N. F. (Nevill Francis), Sir, 1905-.**      **5.2399**
The theory of atomic collisions, by N.F. Mott and H.S.W. Massey. 3d ed. Oxford, Clarendon Press, 1965. xxii, 858 p. illus. 25 cm. (The International series of monographs on physics) 1. Atoms 2. Electrons 3. Ions 4. Quantum theory I. Massey, Harrie Stewart Wilson, Sir. joint author. II. T.
QC721.M88 1965     539.701     LC 66-1351

**Newton, Roger G.**      • **5.2400**
Scattering theory of waves and particles [by] Roger G. Newton. New York, McGraw-Hill [1966] xviii, 681 p. illus. 23 cm. (International series in pure and applied physics.) 1. Scattering (Physics) I. T. II. Series.
QC721.N4755     539.72     LC 65-26485

**Omnès, Roland.**      • **5.2401**
[Introduction à l'études des particules élémentaires. English] Introduction to particle physics. Translation: G. Barton. London, New York, Wiley-Interscience [c1971] xiii, 414 p. illus. 24 cm. Translation of Introduction à l'études des particules élémentaires. 1. Particles (Nuclear physics) I. T.
QC721.O52513     539.7/21     LC 75-172471     ISBN 0471653721

**Rutherford, Ernest, 1871-1937.**      • **5.2402**
Radiations from radioactive substances, by Sir Ernest Rutherford, James Chadwick, and C. D. Ellis. [Reprinted with corrections]. — Cambridge [Eng.] University Press, 1951. xi, 588 p. illus. 24 cm. 1. Radioactivity I. T.
QC721.R94 1951     539.7     LC 51-14724

**Segrè, Emilio.**      **5.2403**
Nuclei and particles: an introduction to nuclear and subnuclear physics. — New York: W.A. Benjamin, 1977. xx, 966 p.: ill.; 24 cm. 1. Nuclear physics 2. Particles (Nuclear physics) I. T.
QC721.S4475     539.7     LC 64-21231

**Yang, Chen Ning, 1922-.**      • **5.2404**
Elementary particles: a short history of some discoveries in atomic physics. — Princeton, N.J.: Princeton University Press, 1961 [c1962] 68 p.: ill.; 23 cm. (Vanuxem lectures. 1959) 1. Particles (Nuclear physics) I. T. II. Series.
QC721.Y273     539.721     LC 60-12285

## QC750–764 Magnetism. Nuclear Magnetism

**O'Dell, T. H. (Thomas Henry).**      **5.2405**
Ferromagnetodynamics: the dynamics of magnetic bubbles, domains, and domain walls / T. H. O'Dell. — New York: Wiley, c1981. vii, 230 p.: ill.; 25 cm. 'A Halsted Press book.' Includes indexes. 1. Magnetic bubbles 2. Domain structure 3. Ferromagnetism I. T.
QC754.2.M34 O32 1981     538/.44 19     LC 80-25331     ISBN 0470270845

**Booker, Henry G.**      **5.2406**
Energy in electromagnetism / Henry G. Booker. — London; New York: Peter Peregrinus on behalf of the Institution of Electrical Engineers, c1982. xiv, 360 p.: ill.; 23 cm. (IEE electromagnetic waves series. v. 13) 1. Electromagnetism 2. Force and energy 3. Power (Mechanics) I. T. II. Series.
QC760.B63 1982     537 19     LC 82-140530     ISBN 0906048591

**Lawden, Derek F.**      **5.2407**
Electromagnetism / D. F. Lawden. — London: George Allen and Unwin, 1975 [c1973] [vii], 96 p.: ill. — (Problem solvers; no.13) 1. Electromagnetism I. T.
QC760.L39     ISBN 0045380015

**Woodson, Herbert H.**      **5.2408**
Electromechanical dynamics [by] Herbert H. Woodson [and] James R. Melcher. — New York: Wiley, [1968] 1 v.: ill.; 23 cm. 1. Electromagnetism 2. Electromechanical devices — Dynamics I. Melcher, James R. joint author. II. T.
QC760.W87     537     LC 67-31215

**American Association of Physics Teachers.**      **5.2409**
NMR & EPR: selected reprints. — New York: American Institute of Physics [1965] 108 p.: ill., diagrs.; 27 cm. (AAPT committee on resource letters) 1. Nuclear magnetic resonance 2. Electron paramagnetic resonance I. T.
QC762.Ax

**Martin, Maryvonne L.**      **5.2410**
Practical NMR spectroscopy / Maryvonne L. Martin and Gerard J. Martin, Jean–Jacques Delpuech. — Philadelphia: Heyden, c1980. 460 p.: ill.; 24 cm. 1. Nuclear magnetic resonance spectroscopy I. Martin, Gérard J. joint author. II. Delpuech, Jean Jacques, joint author. III. T.
QC762 M27     ISBN 0855014628

**Paudler, William W., 1932-.**      **5.2411**
Nuclear magnetic resonance / William W. Paudler. — Boston: Allyn and Bacon, 1971. 241 p.: ill. — (Allyn and Bacon chemistry series) 1. Nuclear magnetic resonance I. T.
QC762.P38     538.3     LC 78-141228

**Paudler, William W., 1932-.**      **5.2412**
Nuclear magnetic resonance: general concepts and applications / William W. Paudler. — New York: Wiley, c1987. 241 p.: ill. 'A Wiley Interscience publication.' Includes index. 1. Nuclear magnetic resonance I. T.
QC762.P38 1987     538/.362 19     LC 86-26549     ISBN 0471839795

**Wertz, John E., 1916-.**      **5.2413**
Electron spin resonance; elementary theory and practical applications [by] John E. Wertz [and] James R. Bolton. New York, McGraw-Hill [1972] xiv, 497 p. illus. 23 cm. (McGraw-Hill series in advanced chemistry) 1. Electron paramagnetic resonance I. Bolton, James R., 1937- joint author. II. T.
QC762.W47     538/.3     LC 77-154239     ISBN 0070694540

## QC770–799 NUCLEAR AND PARTICLE PHYSICS. NUCLEAR ENERGY. RADIOACTIVITY

**Shalit, Amos de-, 1926-1969.**      **5.2414**
Theoretical nuclear physics [by] Amos deShalit [and] Herman Feshbach. — New York: Wiley, 1974. 979 p.: ill. 1. Nuclear physics — Collected works. 2. Nuclear reactions — Collected works. I. Feshbach, Herman. joint author. II. T.
QC771.S48     539.7     LC 73-17165     ISBN 0471203858

**Siegbahn, Kai, 1918- ed.** • **5.2415**
Alpha– beta– and gamma–ray spectroscopy. Amsterdam, North-Holland Pub. Co., 1965. 2 v. (lv, 1742 p.) illus. 25 cm. Stamped on t.p.: New York, Stechert-Hafner Service Agency, inc. Revised and expanded edition of the editor's Beta- and gamma-ray spectroscopy. 1. Nuclear physics — Addresses, essays, lectures. I. T.
QC771.S5 1965          539.7082          *LC* 65-2984

# QC773–774 History. Biography

**Compton, Arthur Holly, 1892-1962.** • **5.2416**
Atomic quest: a personal narrative. New York: Oxford University Press, 1956. 370 p.: ill.; 21 cm. 1. Nuclear energy — History. 2. Atomic bomb I. T.
QC773.A1 C65          623.451*          *LC* 56-11114

**Groves, Leslie R., 1896-1970.** • **5.2417**
Now it can be told; the story of the Manhattan project. [1st ed.]. New York, Harper [1962] xiv, 464 p. illus., ports. 22 cm. 1. United States. Army. Corps of Engineers. Manhattan District. 2. Atomic bomb — United States — History. I. T.
QC773.A1 G7          623.45119          *LC* 61-10208

**Jungk, Robert, 1913-.** • **5.2418**
[Heller als tausend Sonnen. English] Brighter than a thousand suns: a personal history of the atomic scientists / translated by James Cleugh. — [1st American ed.] New York: Harcourt Brace [1958] 369 p.; 21 cm. 1. Nuclear energy — History. 2. Atomic bomb — History. I. T.
QC773.J813          539.76*          *LC* 58-8581

**Romer, Alfred, 1906-.** • **5.2419**
The restless atom; [the awakening of nuclear physics. 1st ed.] Garden City, N.Y., Anchor Books; available through Wesleyan University Press, Columbus, Ohio, 1960. 198 p. illus. 19 cm. (Science study series, S12) 1. Nuclear physics 2. Atoms 3. Radiation I. T.
QC773.R6          539.7          *LC* 60-10681

**Smyth, Henry DeWolf, 1898-.** **5.2420**
[Atomic bombs] Atomic energy for military purposes: the official report on the development of the atomic bomb under the auspices of the United States Government, 1940–1945 / by Henry DeWolf Smyth. — 1st AMS ed. — New York: AMS Press, 1978. vii, 308 p., [4] leaves of plates: ill.; 23 cm. First published under title: Atomic bombs. Commonly known as the Smyth report. 'Written at the request of Maj. Gen. L. R. Groves, U.S.A.' Reprint of the 1948 ed. published by Princeton University Press, Princeton, N.J. Includes indexes. 1. Atomic bomb — United States — History. 2. Nuclear energy — United States — History. I. T. II. Title: Smyth report on military uses of atomic energy.
QC773.3.U5 S67 1978          623.4/5119          *LC* 75-41258          *ISBN* 0404147038

**Fermi, Laura.** • **5.2421**
Atoms in the family; my life with Enrico Fermi. — [Chicago]: University of Chicago Press, [1954] 267 p.: illus.; 24 cm. 1. Fermi, Enrico, 1901-1954. I. T.
QC774.F4 F4          925.3          *LC* 54-12114

# QC776–782 General Works

**Blatt, John Markus.** **5.2422**
Theoretical nuclear physics / John M. Blatt, Victor F. Weisskopf. — New York: Springer-Verlag, c1979. xiv, 864 p.: ill.; 24 cm. Includes index. 1. Nuclear physics I. Weisskopf, Victor Frederick, 1908- joint author. II. T.
QC776.B53 1979          539.7          *LC* 79-4268          *ISBN* 0387903828

**Bowler, M. G.** **5.2423**
Nuclear physics, by M. G. Bowler. — [1st ed.]. — Oxford; New York: Pergamon Press, [1973] xi, 420 p.: ill.; 26 cm. — (International series of monographs in natural philosophy, v. 53) 1. Nuclear physics I. T.
QC776.B68 1973          539.7          *LC* 72-13262          *ISBN* 008016983X

**Burge, Edward James.** **5.2424**
Atomic nuclei and their particles / E. J. Burge. — Oxford: Clarendon Press, 1977. [10], 194 p.: ill.; 23 cm. — (Oxford physics series; 13) Includes index. 1. Nuclear physics I. T.
QC776.B87          539.7          *LC* 78-312952          *ISBN* 019851834X

**Elton, L. R. B. (Lewis Richard Benjamin)** • **5.2425**
Introductory nuclear theory, by L.R.B. Elton. 2d ed. Philadelphia, Saunders, 1966 [c1965] xi, 332 p. illus. 23 cm. 1. Nuclear physics I. T.
QC776.E4 1966a          539.7          *LC* 66-18339

**Evans, Robley Dunglison, 1907-.** • **5.2426**
The atomic nucleus. — New York: McGraw-Hill, 1955. 972 p.: ill.; 24 cm. — (International series in pure and applied physics) 1. Nuclear physics I. T.
QC776.E8          539.1 539.7*          *LC* 55-7275

**Glasstone, Samuel, 1897-.** • **5.2427**
Sourcebook on atomic energy. 3d ed. Princeton, N.J.: Van Nostrand [1967] vii, 883 p.: ill., ports.; 24 cm. 'Published under the auspices of the Division of Technical Information, United States Atomic Energy Commission.' 1. Nuclear energy I. U.S. Atomic Energy Commission. II. T.
QC776.G6 1967          539.7          *LC* 67-29947

**Marmier, Pierre, 1922-.** • **5.2428**
Physics of nuclei and particles/ Pierre Marmier, Eric Sheldon. — New York: Academic Press, [1969-. v.: ill. 1. Nuclear physics I. Sheldon, Eric, 1930- II. T.
QC776.M3          539.7          *LC* 68-14644

**Burcham, W. E.** **5.2429**
Nuclear physics; an introduction [by] W. E. Burcham. 2d ed. [London] Longman [1973] xix, 686 p. illus. 24 cm. (A Longman text) 'Errata': leaf inserted. 1. Nuclear physics I. T.
QC777.B78 1973          539.7          *LC* 73-164480          *ISBN* 0582441102

**Lapp, Ralph Eugene, 1917-.** **5.2430**
Nuclear radiation physics / [by] Ralph E. Lapp [and] Howard L. Andrews. — 4th ed. — Englewood Cliffs, N.J.: Prentice-Hall, [1972] xiv, 447 p.: ill.; 24 cm. 1. Nuclear physics 2. Radiation I. Andrews, Howard Lucius, 1906- joint author. II. T.
QC777.L3 1972          539.7          *LC* 75-168620          *ISBN* 013625988X

**Spruch, Grace Marmor. comp.** **5.2431**
The ubiquitous atom. Edited and with an introd. by Grace Marmor Spruch and Larry Spruch. Illustrated with photos and with diagrams by Richard Liu. New York, Scribner [1974] xii, 458 p. illus. 24 cm. 'Based upon material from booklets in the series Understanding the atom, produced under the aegis of the United States Atomic Energy Commission.' 1. Atoms I. Spruch, Larry. joint comp. II. Understanding the atom. III. T.
QC777.S67          539.7          *LC* 74-507          *ISBN* 0684137739

**Trefil, James S., 1938-.** **5.2432**
From atoms to quarks: an introduction to the strange world of particle physics / James S. Trefil. — New York: Scribner, c1980. xi, 225 p.: ill.; 24 cm. 1. Nuclear physics 2. Particles (Nuclear physics) I. T.
QC777.T73          539.7          *LC* 80-11093          *ISBN* 0684164841

**Asimov, Isaac, 1920-.** **5.2433**
Worlds within worlds: the story of nuclear energy / Isaac Asimov; foreword by James Holahan. — Seattle, Wash.: University Press of the Pacific; Forest Grove, Or.: Distributed by International Scholarly Book Services, c1980. 156 p.: ill., ports.; 23 cm. Includes index. 1. Nuclear energy — Popular works. I. T.
QC778.A85 1980          539.7 19          *LC* 84-167298          *ISBN* 0898750016

**Calder, Nigel.** **5.2434**
The key to the universe: a report on the new physics / Nigel Calder. — New York: Viking Press, 1977. 199 p.: ill.; 26 cm. Includes index. 1. Nuclear physics — Popular works. 2. Astrophysics — Popular works. 3. Cosmology — Popular works. I. T.
QC778.C34 1977b          539          *LC* 76-51766          *ISBN* 0670412708

**Oppenheimer, J. Robert, 1904-1967.** • **5.2435**
The open mind: [lectures] — New York: Simon and Schuster, 1955. 146 p.; 21 cm. 1. Nuclear energy — Addresses, essays, lectures. 2. Science — Addresses, essays, lectures. I. T.
QC780.O6          504          *LC* 55-10043

# QC783–787 Handbooks. Tables. Instruments. Apparatus

**Moore, Charlotte Emma, 1898-.** • **5.2436**
Atomic energy levels as derived from the analyses of optical spectra. Washington: U.S. Dept. of Commerce, National Bureau of Standards, 1949-. v.;

30 cm. (Circular of the National Bureau of Standards, 467) 1. Atomic spectra — Tables. 2. Energy levels (Quantum mechanics) — Tables. I. T.
QC783.M6      535.84083      *LC* 53-60419

**Overman, Ralph T.**               • **5.2437**
Radioisotope techniques [by] Ralph T. Overman [and] Herbert M. Clark. — New York: McGraw-Hill, 1960. 476 p.: illus.; 24 cm. 1. Radioisotopes — Handbooks, manuals, etc. 2. Hot laboratories (Radioactive substances) I. Clark, Herbert M., joint author. II. T.
QC784.O9      541.38028      *LC* 59-10721

**England, J. B. A.**             **5.2438**
Techniques in nuclear structure physics [by] J. B. A. England. — New York: Wiley, 1974. 2 v.    : illus.; 24 cm. 'A Halsted Press book.' 1. Nuclear physics — Instruments I. T.
QC786.E54     QC786 E54.      539.7/028      *LC* 74-8171      *ISBN* 0470241616

**Livingston, M. Stanley (Milton Stanley)**      • **5.2439**
Particle accelerators [by] M. Stanley Livingston [and] John P. Blewett. New York, McGraw-Hill, 1962. 666 p. illus. 24 cm. (International series in pure and applied physics.) 1. Particle accelerators I. Blewett, John P. (John Paul), 1910- joint author. II. T. III. Series.
QC786.L52      539.73      *LC* 61-12960

**Persico, Enrico, 1900-.**          • **5.2440**
Principles of particle accelerators / Enrico Persico, Ezio Ferrari, Sergio E. Segre. — New York: W. A. Benjamin, 1968. x, 301 p.: ill.; 24 cm. 1. Particle accelerators I. Ferrari, Ezio. II. Segre, Sergio E III. T.
QC786.P38      *LC* 68-18558

**Profio, A. Edward, 1931-.**           **5.2441**
Experimental reactor physics / A. Edward Profio. — New York: Wiley, c1976. xi, 811 p.; ill.; 24 cm. 'A Wiley-Interscience publication.' 1. Nuclear reactors 2. Nuclear physics — Experiments. 3. Neutrons — Measurement 4. Radiation — Measurement I. T.
QC786.5.P76      621.48/31      *LC* 75-35735      *ISBN* 0471700959

**Knoll, Glenn F.**            **5.2442**
Radiation detection and measurement / Glenn F. Knoll. — New York: Wiley, c1979. xv, 816 p.; ill.; 24 cm. 1. Nuclear counters 2. Radiation — Measurement I. T.
QC787.C6 K56      539.7/7      *LC* 78-12387      *ISBN* 047149545X

**Price, William J. (William James), 1918-.**    • **5.2443**
Nuclear radiation detection [by] William J. Price. 2d ed. New York, McGraw-Hill [1964] ix, 430 p. illus. 23 cm. (McGraw-Hill series in nuclear engineering.) 1. Nuclear counters 2. Radioactivity I. T. II. Series.
QC787.C6 P7 1964      539.77      *LC* 63-23463

**Tait, W. H.**              **5.2444**
Radiation detection / W. H. Tait. — London; Boston: Butterworths, 1980. viii, 406 p.: ill.; 24 cm. 1. Nuclear counters 2. Ionizing radiation — Measurement I. T.
QC787.C6 T24      539.7/7 19      *LC* 80-501510      *ISBN* 040810645X

**Hetrick, David L., 1927-.**         • **5.2445**
Dynamics of nuclear reactors [by] David L. Hetrick. — Chicago: University of Chicago Press, [1971] x, 542 p.: illus.; 24 cm. 1. Nuclear reactors — Mathematical models. 2. Nuclear reactor kinetics I. T.
QC787.N8 H47      621.48/31/0184      *LC* 76-130309      *ISBN* 0226331660

**Goldsmith, Maurice.**            **5.2446**
Europe's giant accelerator: the story of the CERN 400 GeV Proton Synchrotron / [by] Maurice Goldsmith and Edwin Shaw. — London: Taylor and Francis, 1977. x, 261 p., xvi p. of plates: ill. (some col.), facsim., maps, ports.; 27 cm. Includes indexes. 1. European Organization for Nuclear Research. 2. Proton synchrotrons — Switzerland — Geneva region. I. Shaw, Edwin. joint author. II. T. III. Title: CERN proton synchrotron.
QC787.S9 G64      681/.753      *LC* 78-304420      *ISBN* 0850661218

**Symposium on the History of the ZGS (1979: Argonne National Laboratory)**          **5.2447**
History of the ZGS (Argonne, 1979) / editors, Joanne S. Day, Alan D. Krisch, Lazarus G. Ratner. — New York: American Institute of Physics, 1980. 453 p.: ill.; 25 cm. (AIP conference proceedings; no. 60) 'Sponsored by: Argonne Universities Association, Argonne National Laboratory, ZGS Users Group.' 1. Synchrotron, Zero gradient — History — Congresses. 2. Nuclear physics — Research — Illinois — Lemont — History — Congresses. I. Day, Joanne S. II. Krisch, A. D. III. Ratner, Lazarus G. IV. Argonne Universities Association. V. Argonne National Laboratory. VI. Argonne National Laboratory. ZGS Users Group. VII. T. VIII. Title: Zero gradient synchrotron.
QC787.S9 S92 1979      539.7/35 19      *LC* 80-67694      *ISBN* 0883181592

## QC790–792.7 Nuclear Fission. Nuclear Fusion. Atomic Energy

**Glasstone, Samuel, 1897-.**         • **5.2448**
Controlled thermonuclear reactions, an introduction to theory and experiment, by Samuel Glasstone and Ralph H. Lovberg. Princeton, N.J., Van Nostrand [1960] xvi, 523 p. illus. 24 cm. 'Prepared under the auspices of the Office of Technical Information, United States Atomic Energy Commission.' 1. Controlled fusion I. Lovberg, Ralph H. (Ralph Harvey) II. T.
QC791.G5      539.764      *LC* 60-50431

**Atomic and molecular physics of controlled thermonuclear**    **5.2449**
**fusion / edited by Charles J. Joachain and Douglass E. Post.**
New York: Plenum Press, c1983. x, 576 p.: ill.; 26 cm. — (NATO advanced science institutes series. Physics. v. 101) 'Published in cooperation with NATO Scientific Affairs Division.' 'Proceedings of a NATO advanced study institute, held July 19-30, 1982, at the Hotel Zagarella, Santa Flavia, Italy.'—Verso of t.p. 1. Controlled fusion — Congresses. I. Joachain, C. J. (Charles Jean) II. Post, D. E. (Douglass Edmund), 1945- III. North Atlantic Treaty Organization. Scientific Affairs Division. IV. Series.
QC791.7.A86 1983      539.7/64 19      *LC* 83-11128      *ISBN* 0306413981

**Bromberg, Joan Lisa.**           **5.2450**
Fusion: science, politics, and the invention of a new energy source / Joan Lisa Bromberg. — Cambridge, Mass.: MIT Press, c1982. xxvi, 344 p.: ill.; 24 cm. 1. Controlled fusion I. T.
QC791.73.B76 1982      333.79/24 19      *LC* 82-10039      *ISBN* 0262021803

**Hagler, M. O.**             **5.2451**
An introduction to controlled thermonuclear fusion / M. O. Hagler, M. Kristiansen. — Lexington, Mass.: Lexington Books, c1977. xviii, 188 p.: ill.; 24 cm. Includes index. 1. Controlled fusion 2. Fusion reactors I. Kristiansen, M. (Magne), 1932- joint author. II. T.
QC791.73.H33      621.48/4      *LC* 74-33596      *ISBN* 0669991198

**Clark, Ronald William.**           **5.2452**
The greatest power on earth: the international race for nuclear supremacy / Ronald W. Clark. — 1st U.S. ed. — New York: Harper & Row, [1981] c1980. ix, 342 p., [16] p. of plates; 24 cm. Includes index. 1. Nuclear energy — History. I. T.
QC791.96.C55 1981      355.8/25119/09 19      *LC* 80-7899      *ISBN* 0060148462

**Inglis, David Rittenhouse, 1905-.**        **5.2453**
Nuclear energy: its physics and its social challenge. Reading, Mass., Addison-Wesley Pub. Co. [1973] xiv, 395 p. illus. 21 cm. (Addison-Wesley series in physics) 1. Nuclear energy 2. Nuclear warfare — Social aspects I. T.
QC792.I55      539.7      *LC* 78-186840

**Pringle, Peter.**             **5.2454**
The nuclear barons / Peter Pringle and James Spigelman. — 1st ed. — New York: Holt, Rinehart and Winston, c1981. xii, 578 p.; 24 cm. Includes index. 1. Nuclear energy 2. Radiation — Safety measures 3. Nuclear energy — Social aspects. I. Spigelman, James Jacob, 1946- joint author. II. T.
QC792.7.P74      363.1/79 19      *LC* 80-26212      *ISBN* 0030419018

## QC793–793.5 Elementary Particle Physics

**Nobel Conference. 12th, Gustavus Adolphus College, 1976.**    **5.2455**
The nature of the physical universe: 1976 Nobel Conference / organized by Gustavus Adolphus College, St. Peter, Minnesota; edited by Douglas Huff, Omer Prewett. — New York: Wiley, c1979. xvii, 140 p.: ill.; 24 cm. 'A Wiley-Interscience publication.' 1. Particles (Nuclear physics) — Congresses. 2. Science — Philosophy — Congresses. 3. Cosmology — Congresses. I. Huff, Douglas, 1944- II. Prewett, Omer, 1939- III. Gustavus Adolphus College. IV. T.
QC793.N63 1976      500      *LC* 78-14788      *ISBN* 0471031909

**Pickering, Andrew.**            **5.2456**
Constructing quarks: a sociological history of particle physics / Andrew Pickering. — Chicago: University of Chicago Press, 1984. xi, 468 p.: ill.; 23 cm.

Includes index. 1. Particles (Nuclear physics) — History. 2. Quarks — History. I. T.
QC793.16.P53 1984     539.7/21/09 19     LC 84-235     ISBN 0226667987

**Bernstein, Jeremy, 1929-.**         • **5.2457**
Elementary particles and their currents. — San Francisco: W. H. Freeman, [1968] xi, 322 p.: illus.; 25 cm. — (A Series of books in physics) 1. Particles (Nuclear physics) I. T.
QC793.2.B47     539.7/21     LC 68-21404

**Dodd, J. E. (James Edmund), 1952-.**      **5.2458**
The ideas of particle physics: an introduction for scientists / J.E. Dodd. — Cambridge [Cambridgeshire]; New York: Cambridge University Press, 1984. ix, 202 p.: ill.; 26 cm. Includes indexes. 1. Particles (Nuclear physics) I. T.
QC793.2.D6 1984     539.7/21 19     LC 83-15227     ISBN 0521253381

**Frauenfelder, Hans, 1922-.**        **5.2459**
Nuclear and particle physics / Hans Frauenfelder, Ernest M. Henley. — Reading, Mass.: W. A. Benjamin, 1975. 573 p.: ill.; 25 cm. (Lecture notes and supplements in physics; no. 14) 1. Particles (Nuclear physics) 2. Nuclear physics I. Henley, Ernest M. joint author. II. T.
QC793.2.F7     539.7/21     LC 75-11876

**Gottfried, Kurt.**                   **5.2460**
Concepts of particle physics, v. 1 / Kurt Gottfried, Victor F. Weisskopf. — Oxford [Oxfordshire]: Clarendon Press; New York: Oxford University Press, 1984. 189 p. Includes index. 1. Particles (Nuclear physics) I. Weisskopf, Victor Frederick, 1908- II. T.
QC793.2.G68 1984     539.7/21 19     LC 83-17275     ISBN 0195033922

**Leon, Melvin, 1936-.**            **5.2461**
Particle physics: an introduction / [by] M. Leon. — New York: Academic Press, [1973] xii, 268 p.: ill.; 24 cm. 1. Particles (Nuclear physics) I. T.
QC793.2.L46     539.7/21     LC 72-77329     ISBN 0124438504

**Okun', L. B. (Lev Borisovich)**       **5.2462**
Particle physics: the quest for the substance of substance / L.B. Okun; translated from the Russian by V.I. Kisin. — Chur; New York: Harwood Academic Publishers, c1985. xiii, 223 p.: ill.; 24 cm. (Contemporary concepts in physics. 0272-2488; v. 2) Includes index. 1. Particles (Nuclear physics) I. T. II. Series.
QC793.2.O38 1985     539.7/2 19     LC 84-10735     ISBN 3718602288

**Perkins, Donald H.**              **5.2463**
Introduction to high energy physics / Donald H. Perkins. — 3rd ed. — Menlo Park, Calif.: Benjamin/Cummings Pub. Co., c1986. 1 v. 1. Particles (Nuclear physics) I. T.
QC793.2.P47 1986     539.7/21 19     LC 86-10916     ISBN 0805323163

**Sutton, Christine.**              **5.2464**
The particle connection: the most exciting scientific chase since DNA and the double helix / Christine Sutton. — New York: Simon and Schuster, c1984. 175 p.: ill.; 25 cm. 1. Particles (Nuclear physics) I. T.
QC793.2.S88 1984     539.7/2 19     LC 84-10595     ISBN 067149659X

**Weinberg, Steven.**              **5.2465**
The discovery of subatomic particles / Steven Weinberg. — New York: Scientific American Library, c1983. xiii, 206 p.: ill.; 24 cm. 1. Particles (Nuclear physics) I. T.
QC793.2.W44 1983     539.7/21 19     LC 82-23157     ISBN 0716714884

**Feinberg, Gerald, 1933-.**         **5.2466**
What is the world made of?: Atoms, leptons, quarks, and other tantalizing particles / Gerald Feinberg. 1st ed. — Garden City, N.Y.: Anchor Press/ Doubleday, 1977. xvi, 290 p., [4] leaves of plates: ill.; 22 cm. Includes index. 1. Particles (Nuclear physics) 2. Nuclear physics 3. Atomic theory I. T.
QC793.24.F44     539.7     LC 76-18342     ISBN 0385076932

**Particles and fields: readings from Scientific American / with an**    **5.2467**
introd. by William J. Kaufmann, III.
San Francisco: W. H. Freeman, c1980. vi, 139 p.: ill.; 30 cm. 1. Particles (Nuclear physics) — Addresses, essays, lectures. 2. Quarks — Addresses, essays, lectures. 3. Unified field theories — Addresses, essays, lectures. I. Kaufmann, William J. II. Scientific American.
QC793.28.P38     539.7/21     LC 80-10669     ISBN 0716712334

**Edmonds, A. R.**                 **5.2468**
Angular momentum in quantum mechanics / by A. R. Edmonds. — 3d print., with corrections. — Princeton, N.J.: Princeton University Press, 1974, c1960. viii, 146 p.; 25 cm. (Investigations in physics; 4) Includes index. 1. Angular momentum (Nuclear physics) I. T. II. Series.
QC793.3.A5 E35 1974     530.1/2     LC 77-39796     ISBN 0691079129

**American Association of Physics Teachers.**     **5.2469**
Molecular beams: selected reprints. — New York: Published for the AAPT by the American Institute of Physics, [1965]. 2 v.: ill. Cover title. 1. Molecular beams — Addresses, essays, lectures. 2. Atomic spectra — Addresses, essays, lectures. 3. Molecular spectra — Addresses, essays, lectures. I. American Institute of Physics. II. T.
QC793.3.B4 A46 QC173

**Davies, P. C. W.**                **5.2470**
The forces of nature / P. C. W. Davies. — Cambridge; New York: Cambridge University Press, 1979. viii, 246 p.: ill.; 24 cm. Includes index. 1. Nuclear forces (Physics) 2. Nuclear physics I. T.
QC793.3.B5 D38     539.7     LC 78-72084     ISBN 052122523X

**Moriyasu, K.**                 **5.2471**
An elementary primer for gauge theory / K. Moriyasu. — Singapore: World Scientific, c1983. xi, 177 p.: ill.; 22 cm. 1. Gauge fields (Physics) I. T.
QC793.3.F5 M67 1983     530.1/43 19     LC 84-147918     ISBN 9971950944

**Lichtenberg, D. B. (Don Bernett), 1928-.**     **5.2472**
Unitary symmetry and elementary particles / D. B. Lichtenberg. — 2d ed. — New York: Academic Press, 1978. xv, 275 p.: ill.; 24 cm. Includes index. 1. Eightfold way (Nuclear physics) I. T.
QC793.3.S6 L5 1978     539.7/21     LC 77-92306     ISBN 0124484603

**Jones, G. A. (Grenville Arthur)**       **5.2473**
The properties of nuclei / G.A. Jones. — 2nd ed. — Oxford [Oxfordshire]: Clarendon Press; New York: Oxford University Press, 1987, c1986. p. cm. (Oxford physics series. 12) Includes index. 1. Nuclear structure 2. Nuclear reactions I. T. II. Series.
QC793.3.S8 J66 1987     539.7/23 19     LC 86-17931     ISBN 0198518684

**Ryder, Lewis H., 1941-.**           **5.2474**
Elementary particles and symmetries / Lewis Ryder. — New York: Gordon and Breach Science Publishers, c1975. xxvii, 249 p.; 24 cm. (Documents on modern physics) 1. Symmetry (Physics) 2. Particles (Nuclear physics) I. T.
QC793.3.S9 R9     539.7/21/0151222     LC 73-92578     ISBN 0677051301

**Fritzsch, Harald, 1943-.**          **5.2475**
Quarks: the stuff of matter / Harald Fritzsch. — New York: Basic Books, c1983. xiii, 297 p.: ill.; 22 cm. Translation of: Quarks: Urstoff unserer Welt. Includes index. 1. Quarks I. T.
QC793.5.Q2522 F7413 1983     539.7/216 19     LC 82-72395     ISBN 0465067816

**Halzen, F. (Francis)**              **5.2476**
Quarks and leptons: an introductory course in modern particle physics / Francis Halzen, Alan D. Martin. — New York: Wiley, c1984. xvi, 396 p.: ill.; 24 cm. Includes index. 1. Quarks 2. Leptons (Nuclear physics) I. Martin, Alan D. (Alan Douglas) II. T.
QC793.5.Q2522 H34 1984     539.7/21 19     LC 83-14649     ISBN 0471887412

**Huang, Kerson, 1928-.**          **5.2477**
Quarks, leptons & gauge fields / Kerson Huang. — Singapore: World Scientific, c1982. x, 281 p.; 24 cm. 1. Quarks 2. Leptons (Nuclear physics) 3. Gauge fields (Physics) I. T. II. Title: Quarks, leptons and gauge fields.
QC793.5.Q2522 H83 1982     539.7/21 19     LC 82-941945     ISBN 9971950030

# QC793.9–794.8 Nuclear Interactions

**Gibson, W. M.**                 **5.2478**
The physics of nuclear reactions: a new edition of the author's Nuclear reactions, for use as a main text for an honours degree course in nuclear physics / by W.M. Gibson. — 1st ed. — Oxford; New York: Pergamon Press, 1980. ix, 338 p.: ill.; 22 cm. — (Pergamon international library of science, technology, engineering, and social studies.) Includes index. 1. Nuclear reactions I. T. II. Series.
QC794.G48 1980     539.7/5     LC 79-40063     ISBN 0080230784

**Goldberger, Marvin L.**        • **5.2479**
Collision theory [by] Marvin L. Goldberger [and] Kenneth M. Watson. New York, Wiley [1964] ix, 919 p. illus. 24 cm. (Structure of matter series.)

1. Collisions (Nuclear physics) 2. Scattering (Physics) I. Watson, Kenneth M. joint author. II. T. III. Series.
QC794.G62    539.72    *LC* 64-17819

**Jackson, Daphne F.**    • **5.2480**
Nuclear reactions / [by] Daphne F. Jackson. — London: Methuen, [1970] x, 260 p.: ill.; 24 cm. 'Distributed in the U.S.A. by Barnes & Noble.' 1. Nuclear reactions I. T.
QC794.J28    539.75    *LC* 75-504591    *ISBN* 0416117805

**Satchler, G. R. (George Raymond)**    **5.2481**
Introduction to nuclear reactions / G. R. Satchler. — New York: Wiley, 1980. xii, 316 p.: ill.; 24 cm. 'A Halsted Press book.' 1. Nuclear reactions I. T.
QC794.S26 1980    539.7/5    *LC* 79-26275    *ISBN* 0470264675

**Massey, Harrie Stewart Wilson, Sir.**    **5.2482**
Atomic and molecular collisions / Sir Harrie Massey. — London: Taylor & Francis; New York: Wiley, 1979. xviii, 309 p.: ill.; 24 cm. Includes index. 1. Collisions (Nuclear physics) 2. Atoms 3. Molecules I. T.
QC794.6.C6 M36    539.7/54    *LC* 79-11716    *ISBN* 0470267429

**Ross, Graham G.**    **5.2483**
Grand unified theories / Graham G. Ross. — Menlo Park, Calif.: Benjamin/ Cummings Pub. Co., 1984, c1985. xiv, 497 p.: ill.; 24 cm. (Frontiers in physics; no. 60) Includes index. 1. Grand unified theories (Nuclear physics) I. T.
QC794.6.G7 R67 1985    530.1/42 19    *LC* 84-20329    *ISBN* 0805369678

**Zee, A.**    **5.2484**
Unity of forces in the universe / A. Zee. — Singapore: World Scientific, c1982. 2 v. (xv, 1076 p.): ill.; 22 cm. 'Reprinted papers': v. 1, p. [43]-464; v. 2, p. [523]-1075. 1. Grand unified theories (Nuclear physics) 2. Cosmology 3. Nuclear astrophysics I. T.
QC794.6.G7 Z43 1982    539.7 19    *LC* 84-129195    *ISBN* 9971950391

**Dean, Nathan W.**    **5.2485**
Introduction to the strong interactions / Nathan W. Dean. New York: Gordon and Breach Science Publishers, c1976. xiv, 377 p.: ill.; 24 cm. 1. Nuclear reactions I. T.
QC794.8.S8 D4    539.7/54    *LC* 73-85292    *ISBN* 0677027508

**Commins, Eugene D.**    **5.2486**
Weak interactions of leptons and quarks / Eugene D. Commins, Philip H. Bucksbaum. — Cambridge [Cambridgeshire]; New York, NY: Cambridge University Press, 1983. x, 473 p.: ill.; 24 cm. Includes index. 1. Lepton interactions 2. Quarks 3. Weak interactions (Nuclear physics) I. Bucksbaum, Philip H. II. T.
QC794.8.W4 C65 1983    539.7/54 19    *LC* 82-4452    *ISBN* 0521230926

# QC794.95–796 Radioactivity. Radioactive Substances

**Tsoulfanidis, Nicholas, 1938-.**    **5.2487**
Measurement and detection of radiation / Nicholas Tsoulfanidis. — Washington: Hemisphere Pub. Corp.; New York: McGraw-Hill, c1983. xv,

571 p.: ill.; 24 cm. — (McGraw-Hill series in nuclear engineering.) 1. Radiation — Measurement 2. Nuclear counters I. T. II. Series.
QC795.42.T78 1983    539.7/7 19    *LC* 81-2940    *ISBN* 0070653976

**Kocher, David C.**    **5.2488**
Radioactive decay data tables: a handbook of decay data for application to radiation dosimetry and radiological assesments / David C. Kocher. — [Oak Ridge, Tenn.]: Technical Information Center, U.S. Dept. of Energy; Springfield, Va.: Available from National Technical Information Service, U.S. Dept. of Commerce, [1981] v, 221 p.: ill.; 28 cm. 'April 1981.' 'DOE/ TIC-11026.' 1. Radioactive decay — Tables. I. T.
QC795.8.D4 K62 1981    539.7/5 19    *LC* 81-607800    *ISBN* 0870791249

# QC801–809 Geophysics. Cosmic Physics

**International dictionary of geophysics: seismology,**    • **5.2489**
**geomagnetism, aeronomy, oceanography, geodesy, gravity, marine geophysics, meteorology, the earth as a planet and its evolution** / editors: S. K. Runcorn [and others]; with the editorial assistance of D. B. Stone.
Oxford; New York: Pergamon Press, [1967] 2 v.: ill., maps. and portfolio (2 fold. col. maps); 26 cm. 1. Geophysics — Dictionaries. I. Runcorn, S. K. ed. II. Title: Dictionary of geophysics.
QC801.9.I5 1967    551    *LC* 66-16369

**Stacey, F. D. (Frank D.)**    **5.2490**
Physics of the earth / Frank D. Stacey. — 2d ed. — New York: Wiley, c1977. ix, 414 p.: ill.; 24 cm. Includes indexes. 1. Geophysics I. T.
QC806.S65 1977    551    *LC* 76-41891    *ISBN* 0471819565

**Melchior, Paul J.**    **5.2491**
The tides of the planet earth / by Paul Melchior. — 2nd ed. — Oxford [Oxfordshire]; New York: Pergamon Press, 1983. xii, 641 p.: ill.; 24 cm. Includes indexes. 1. Earth tides I. T.
QC809.E2 M48 1983    551.1/4 19    *LC* 82-16567    *ISBN* 0080262481

**Budyko, M. I. (Mikhail Ivanovich)**    **5.2492**
[Klimat i zhizn'. English] Climate and life / by M. I. Budyko. — English ed. edited by David H. Miller. New York: Academic Press, 1974. xvii, 508 p.: ill.; 24 cm. (International geophysics series. 18) Translation of Klimat i zhizn'. 1. Heat budget (Geophysics) 2. Climatology 3. Bioclimatology I. T. II. Series.
QC809.E6 B813    551.6    *LC* 73-801    *ISBN* 0121394506

**Pedlosky, Joseph.**    **5.2493**
Geophysical fluid dynamics / Joseph Pedlosky. — 2nd ed. — New York: Springer-Verlag, c1987. xiv, 710 p.: ill.; 24 cm. Includes index. 1. Fluid dynamics 2. Geophysics I. T.
QC809.F5 P43 1987    551 19    *LC* 86-13941    *ISBN* 038796388X

**Greisen, Kenneth.**    **5.2494**
The physics of cosmic x–ray, γ–ray, and particle sources. — New York: Gordon and Breach, [1971] viii, 115 p.; 24 cm. — (Topics in astrophysics and space physics, 8) 'Originally appeared as a section of Astrophysics and general relativity, 1968 Brandeis University Summer Institute in Theoretical Physics, volume 2, published by Gordon and Breach in 1971.' 1. Nuclear astrophysics 2. Cosmic rays I. T.
QC809.N8 G74    523.01/9/7222    *LC* 78-135063    *ISBN* 067703380X

American Meteorological Society. Committee on the • 5.2495
Compendium of Meteorology.
Compendium of meteorology, prepared under the direction of the Committee on the Compendium of Meteorology; edited by Thomas F. Malone. Boston, American Meteorological Society, 1951. ix, 1334 p. illus., charts. 29 cm.
1. Meteorology — Collected works. I. Malone, Thomas F. ed. II. T.
QC852.A5 551.5082 LC 52-1692

The Encyclopedia of climatology / edited by John E. Oliver, 5.2496
Rhodes W. Fairbridge.
New York: Van Nostrand Reinhold, c1987. xvi, 986 p.: ill.; 27 cm. — (Encyclopedia of earth sciences. v. 11) 1. Meteorology — Dictionaries. 2. Climatology — Dictionaries. I. Oliver, John E. II. Fairbridge, Rhodes Whitmore, 1914- III. Series.
QC854.E525 1987 551.5/03/21 19 LC 86-11173 ISBN 0879330090

Glossary of meteorology / Edited by Ralph E. Huschke. • 5.2497
Boston: American Meteorological Society, 1959. viii, 638 p.; 24 cm. 'Sponsored by U.S. Department of Commerce, Weather Bureau [and others]'
1. Meteorology — Dictionaries. I. Huschke, R. E. (Ralph E.), 1925- ed. II. American Meteorological Society.
QC854.G55 551.503 LC 59-65380

Ludlum, David McWilliams, 1910-. • 5.2498
Early American tornadoes, 1586–1870 [by] David M. Ludlum. Boston, American Meteorological Society, 1970. 219 p. illus. 29 cm. (The History of American weather [4]) 1. Tornadoes — United States. I. T. II. Series.
QC857.U6 H56 no. 4 551.5/53/0973 LC 72-23901

Ludlum, David McWilliams, 1910-. 5.2499
Early American winters [by] David M. Ludlum. — Boston: American Meteorological Society, 1966-. v. : illus., maps.; 29 cm. — (The History of American weather, [2]) 1. Winter — United States. 2. Meteorology — United States. I. T.
QC857.U6 H56 no. 2 551.6 LC 67-7551

Berry, F. A. (Frederic Aroyce), 1906- ed. 5.2500
Handbook of meteorology, edited by F.A. Berry, jr. ... E. Bollay ... [and] Norman R. Beers ... 1st ed. New York, London, McGraw-Hill book company, inc., 1945. ix, 1068 p. incl. illus. (incl. charts) tables, diagrs. (part fold.) 23 cm.
1. Meteorology I. Bollay, Eugene, 1912- joint ed. II. Beers, Norman R., 1911- joint ed. III. T.
QC861.B43 551.5 LC 45-10426

Geiger, Rudolf, 1894-. • 5.2501
[Klima der bodennahen Luftschicht. English] The climate near the ground. Translated by Scripta Technica, inc. [from the 4th German ed.] Cambridge, Harvard University Press, 1965. xiv, 611 p. illus., charts. 24 cm.
1. Microclimatology 2. Meteorology, Agricultural I. T.
QC861.G453 1965 551.5 LC 64-23191

Humphreys, W. J. (William Jackson), 1862-1949. • 5.2502
Physics of the air / with a new pref. by Julius London. — New York: Dover Publications [1964] xvi, 676 p.: ill.; 22 cm. 'S1044' 1. Meteorology 2. Atmosphere 3. Climatology I. T.
QC861.H8 1964 551.5 LC 63-19493

Houghton, Henry G. 5.2503
Physical meteorology / Henry G. Houghton. — Cambridge, Mass.: MIT Press, c1985. viii, 442 p.: ill.; 24 cm. Includes index. 1. Atmospheric physics I. T.
QC861.2.H68 1985 551.5 19 LC 84-12225 ISBN 0262081466

Blumenstock, David I. (David Irving), 1913-1963. 5.2504
The ocean of air. New Brunswick, N.J., Rutgers University Press, 1959. 457 p. illus. 25 cm. 1. Meteorology 2. Weather I. T.
QC863.B55 551.5 LC 59-7509

Schaefer, Vincent J. 5.2505
A field guide to the atmosphere / text and photos. by Vincent J. Schaefer and John A. Day; drawings by Christy E. Day; sponsored by the National Audubon Society and National Wildlife Federation. — Boston: Houghton Mifflin, 1981. xx, 359 p., [8] leaves of plates: ill. (some col.); 20 cm. — (The Peterson field guide series; 26) Includes index. 1. Atmosphere 2. Meteorology 3. Weather I. Day, John A. joint author. II. T.
QC863.S346 551.5 19 LC 80-25473 ISBN 0395240808

Campbell, Ian M. (Ian McIntyre), 1941-. 5.2506
Energy and the atmosphere: a physical–chemical approach / by Ian M. Campbell. — London; New York: Wiley, c1977. ix, 398 p.: ill.; 23 cm. Includes index. 1. Atmosphere 2. Atmospheric chemistry 3. Fuel 4. Pollution 5. Energy. I. T.
QC866.C27 551.5/1 LC 76-57689 ISBN 0471994820. ISBN 0471994812 pbk

Corliss, William R. 5.2507
Tornados, dark days, anomalous precipitation, and related weather phenomena: a catalog of geophysical anomalies / compiled by William R. Corliss. — Glen Arm, MD: Sourcebook Project, c1983. vi, 196 p.: ill.; 27 cm.
1. Meteorology — Miscellanea. 2. Geophysics — Miscellanea. I. T. II. Title: Geophysical anomalies.
QC870.C67 1983 551.5 19 LC 82-63156 ISBN 0915554100

Remote sensing in meteorology, oceanography, and hydrology / 5.2508
editor, A.P. Cracknell.
Chichester, West Sussex: E. Horwood; New York: Halsted Press, 1981. 542 p.: ill.; 24 cm. Based on material presented at a postgraduate summer school sponsored by the European Association of Remote Sensing Laboratories held at the University of Dundee. 1. Meteorology — Remote sensing. 2. Oceanography — Remote sensing. 3. Hydrology — Remote sensing. I. Cracknell, Arthur P.
QC871.R44 1981 621.36/78 19 LC 81-4151 ISBN 0470271833

Middleton, W. E. Knowles (William Edgar Knowles), 1902-. 5.2509
Meteorological instruments, by W.E. Knowles Middleton and Athelstan F. Spilhaus. 3d ed., rev. [Toronto] University Press [1965, c1953] 286p.
1. Meteorological instruments I. Spilhaus Athelstan Frederick, jt. author II. T.
QC876 M5 1953

Goody, Richard M. 5.2510
The physics of the stratosphere. Cambridge [Eng.] University Press, 1954. 187 p. illus. 22 cm. (Cambridge monographs on physics.) 1. Atmosphere, Upper I. T. II. Series.
QC879.G68 LC 54-1205

## QC879.6–.8 ATMOSPHERIC CHEMISTRY

CRC handbook of high resolution infrared laboratory spectra of 5.2511
atmospheric interest / editors, David G. Murcray, Aaron Goldman.
Boca Raton, Fla.: CRC Press, c1981. 282 p.: chiefly ill., graphs; 26 cm.
1. Atmospheric chemistry — Handbooks, manuals, etc. 2. Infrared spectroscopy — Handbooks, manuals, etc. 3. Molecular spectroscopy — Handbooks, manuals, etc. 4. Absorption spectra — Handbooks, manuals, etc. I. Murcray, D. G. II. Goldman, Aaron. III. Title: Handbook of high resolution infrared laboratory spectra of atmospheric interest.
QC879.6.C17 551.5 19 LC 80-23134 ISBN 0849329507

Heicklen, Julian. 5.2512
Atmospheric chemistry / Julian Heicklen. New York: Academic Press, 1976. xiv, 406 p.: ill.; 24 cm. 1. Atmospheric chemistry I. T.
QC879.6.H44 551.5/11 LC 76-2944 ISBN 0123367409

Holland, Heinrich D. 5.2513
The chemical evolution of the atmosphere and oceans / Heinrich D. Holland. — Princeton, N.J.: Princeton University Press, c1984. xii, 582 p.: ill.; 25 cm. — (Princeton series in geochemistry.) 1. Atmospheric chemistry 2. Chemical oceanography 3. Chemical evolution I. T. II. Series.
QC879.6.H63 1984 551.5 19 LC 83-43077 ISBN 0691083487

The Photochemistry of atmospheres: Earth, the other planets, 5.2514
and comets / edited by Joel S. Levine.
Orlando, Fla.: Academic Press, 1985. xxiv, 518 p.: ill.; 24 cm. 1. Atmospheric chemistry 2. Photochemistry 3. Planets — Atmospheres 4. Atmosphere, Upper I. Levine, Joel S.
QC879.6.P48 1985 551.5/11 19 LC 84-12356 ISBN 0124449204

**Stratospheric ozone and man** / editors, Frank A. Bower, Richard B. Ward.     **5.2515**
Boca Raton, Fla.: CRC Press, 1982-. v.: ill.; 26 cm. 1. Atmospheric ozone 2. Stratosphere 3. Man — Influence of climate 4. Man — Influence on nature I. Bower, Frank A. II. Ward, Richard B.
QC879.7.S87 1982     363.7/392 19     *LC* 80-39562     *ISBN* 0849357535

**Kellogg, William W.**     **5.2516**
Climate change and society: consequences of increasing atmospheric carbon dioxide / William W. Kellogg and Robert Schware. — Boulder, Colo.: Westview Press, 1981. xiii, 178 p.: ill.; 24 cm. 1. Atmospheric carbon dioxide — Social aspects. 2. Climatic changes — Social aspects. I. Schware, Robert, 1952- II. T.
QC879.8.K44     363.7/392 19     *LC* 80-54157     *ISBN* 086531179X

# QC880–884 DYNAMIC METEOROLOGY

**Dutton, John A.**     **5.2517**
The ceaseless wind: an introduction to the theory of atmospheric motion / John A. Dutton. — New York: McGraw-Hill, c1976. xv, 579 p.: ill.; 25 cm. 1. Atmospheric circulation 2. Dynamic meteorology I. T.
QC880.D84     551.5/153     *LC* 75-22016     *ISBN* 0070184070

**Fleagle, Robert Guthrie, 1918-.**     **5.2518**
An introduction to atmospheric physics / Robert G. Fleagle, Joost A. Businger. — 2d ed. — New York: Academic Press, 1980. xiv, 432 p.: ill.; 24 cm. (International geophysics series. v. 25) Includes index. 1. Atmospheric physics I. Businger, Joost Alois. joint author. II. T. III. Series.
QC880.F53 1980     551.5 19     *LC* 80-766     *ISBN* 0122603559

**Holton, James R.**     **5.2519**
An introduction to dynamic meteorology / James R. Holton. — 2d ed. — New York: Academic Press, c1979. xii, 391 p.: ill.; 24 cm. — (International geophysics series; v. 23) Includes index. 1. Dynamic meteorology I. T.
QC880.H65 1979     551.5/153     *LC* 79-12918     *ISBN* 0122543606

**Atkinson, Bruce Wilson.**     **5.2520**
Meso–scale atmospheric circulations / B.W. Atkinson. — London; New York: Academic Press, 1981. xvii, 495 p.: ill.; 24 cm. 1. Atmospheric circulation 2. Mesometeorology I. T.
QC880.4.A8 A85 1981     551.5/17 19     *LC* 81-66386     *ISBN* 0120659603

**Pasquill, F.**     **5.2521**
Atmospheric diffusion / F. Pasquill and F.B. Smith. — 3rd ed. — Chichester, West Sussex: E. Horwood; New York: Halsted Press, 1983. 437 p.: ill.; 24 cm. — (Ellis Horwood series in environmental science.) Includes index. 1. Atmospheric diffusion 2. Air — Pollution I. Smith, F. B., 1932- II. T. III. Series.
QC880.4.D44 P37 1983     551.5/153 19     *LC* 83-219     *ISBN* 0853124264

**Brasseur, Guy.**     **5.2522**
Aeronomy of the middle atmosphere: chemistry and physics of the stratosphere and mesosphere / by Guy Brasseur and Susan Solomon. — 2nd rev. ed. — Dordrecht; Boston: D. Reidel Pub. Co.; Norwell, MA, U.S.A.: Sold and distributed in the U.S.A. and Canada by Kluwer Academic Publishers, c1986. xvi, 452 p.: ill.; 25 cm. — (Atmospheric sciences library.) 1. Stratosphere 2. Mesosphere 3. Middle atmosphere I. Solomon, Susan, 1956- II. T. III. Series.
QC881.2.S8 B73 1986     551.5/142 19     *LC* 86-20358     *ISBN* 9027723443

**Israël, H. (Hans), 1902-.**     **5.2523**
[Spurenstoffe in der Atmosphäre. English] Trace elements in the atmosphere / by H. Israël and G. W. Israël; translated by STS, inc. — [1st English language ed.] Ann Arbor, Mich.: Ann Arbor Science Publishers [1974] viii, 158 p.: ill.; 24 cm. Translation of Spurenstoffe in der Atmosphäre. 1. Atmosphere 2. Trace elements 3. Aerosols I. Israël, Gerhard W., joint author. II. T.
QC882.I8713     551.5/11     *LC* 73-86059     *ISBN* 0250400413

**Yoshino, Masatoshi, 1928-.**     **5.2524**
Climate in a small area: an introduction to local meteorology / Masatoshi M. Yoshino. — [Tokyo]: University of Tokyo Press, c1975. xvi, 549 p.: ill.; 27 cm. Completely revised and enlarged translation of Shōkikō. Includes indexes. 1. Micrometeorology I. T.
QC883.8.J3 Y6713     551.6/6     *LC* 75-330869     *ISBN* 0860081443

# QC884 Paleoclimatology

**Bradley, Raymond S., 1948-.**     **5.2525**
Quaternary paleoclimatology: methods of paleoclimatic reconstruction / R.S. Bradley. — Boston: Allen & Unwin, 1985. xvii, 472 p.: ill., maps; 24 cm. Includes index. 1. Paleoclimatology 2. Geology, Stratigraphic — Quaternary I. T.
QC884.B614 1985     551.6 19     *LC* 84-9281     *ISBN* 0045510679

**Brooks, C. E. P. (Charles Ernest Pelham)**     • **5.2526**
Climate through the ages; a study of the climatic factors and their variations [by] C. E. P. Brooks. 2d rev. ed. New York, Dover Publications [1970] 395 p. illus. 21 cm. 1. Climatology 2. Paleoclimatology I. T.
QC884.B65 1970     551.6     *LC* 74-100543     *ISBN* 0486222454

**Climate in earth history** / Geophysics Study Committee, Geophysics Research Board, Commission on Physical Sciences, Mathematics, and Resources, National Research Council.     **5.2527**
Washington, D.C.: National Academy Press, 1982. xiv, 198 p.: ill.; 28 cm. — (Studies in geophysics.) Papers presented at the American Geophysical Union meeting, held in Toronto, May 1980. 1. Paleoclimatology — Addresses, essays, lectures. 2. Historical geology — Addresses, essays, lectures. I. National Research Council (U.S.). Geophysics Study Committee. II. American Geophysical Union. Meeting. (1980: Toronto, Ont.) III. Series.
QC884.C574 1982     551.69 19     *LC* 82-18857     *ISBN* 0309033292

**NATO Advanced Research Workshop on Milankovitch and Climate (1982: Palisades, N.Y.)**     **5.2528**
Milankovitch and climate: understanding the response to astronomical forcing / edited by A. Berger ... [et al.]. — Dordrecht; Boston: D. Reidel Pub. Co.; Higham, MA, U.S.A.: Sold and distributed in the U.S.A. and Canada by Kluwer Academic Publishers, c1984. 2 v.: ill.; 25 cm. (NATO ASI series. Series C, Mathematical and physical sciences; v. 126, pt. 1-2) 'Published in cooperation with NATO Scientific Affairs Division.' 1. Milanković, Milutin. 2. Paleoclimatology — Congresses. 3. Astrophysics — Congresses. I. Berger, A. (André), 1942- II. T.
QC884.N185 1982     551.6 19     *LC* 84-6805     *ISBN* 902771777X

**Wernstedt, Frederick L.**     **5.2529**
World climatic data [by] Frederick L. Wernstedt. — [Lemont, Pa.]: Climatic Data Press, 1972. 522 p.; 31 cm. 1. Atmospheric temperature — Observations. 2. Precipitation (Meteorology) I. T.
QC901.A1 W472     551.5     *LC* 73-159472

# QC907–913 TEMPERATURE AND RADIATION

**Budyko, M. I. (Mikhail Ivanovich)**     • **5.2530**
[Teplovoĭ balans zemnoĭ poverkhnosti. English] The heat balance of the earth's surface / Translated by Nina A. Stepanova from Teplovoĭ balans zemnoĭ poverkhnosti. — Washington: U.S. Dept. of Commerce, Weather Bureau, 1958. 259 p.: ill.; 27 cm. 1. Heat budget (Geophysics) I. T.
QC907.B813     551.12     *LC* 58-61130

**National Research Council (U.S.). Committee on the Atmospheric Effects of Nuclear Explosions.**     **5.2531**
The effects on the atmosphere of a major nuclear exchange / Committee on the Atmospheric Effects of Nuclear Explosions, Commission on Physical Sciences, Mathematics, and Resources, National Research Council. — Washington, D.C.: National Academy Press, 1985. ix, 193 p.: ill.; 28 cm. 1. Nuclear energy and meteorology 2. Nuclear explosions — Environmental aspects. 3. Smoke — Environmental aspects. 4. Dust — Environmental aspects. 5. Fires — Environmental aspects. I. T. II. Title: Nuclear exchange.
QC913.N28 1985     551.5 19     *LC* 84-62739     *ISBN* 0309035287

**International Symposium on Humidity and Moisture. (1963: Washington, D.C.)**     **5.2532**
Humidity and moisture: measurement and control in science and industry. Arnold Wexler, editor-in-chief. New York, Reinhold Pub. Corp. [1965] 4 v. illus. 27 cm. 'Based on papers presented at the ... symposium ... Sponsored by National Bureau of Standards, U.S. Weather Bureau, American Society of Heating, Refrigerating and Air-conditioning Engineers, American Meteorological Society [and] Instrument Society of America.' 1. Humidity —

Addresses, essays, lectures. 2. Moisture — Addresses, essays, lectures. I. Wexler, Arnold. ed. II. United States. National Bureau of Standards. III. T.
QC915.I55 1963        551.57        *LC* 65-13613

# QC921–929 CLOUDS. RAIN. WEATHER CONTROL. SNOW

**Scorer, R. S. (Richard Segar), 1919-.**                              **5.2533**
Clouds of the world; a complete color encyclopedia, by Richard Scorer. — [Harrisburg, Pa.]: Stackpole Books, [1972] 176 p.: col. illus.; 34 cm. 1. Clouds — Pictorial books. I. T.
QC921.S357        551.5/76        *LC* 72-1115        *ISBN* 0811719618

**Ludlam, F. H.**                                                       **5.2534**
Clouds and storms: the behavior and effect of water in the atmosphere / F. H. Ludlam. — University Park: Pennsylvania State University Press, c1980. xv, 405 p., [30] leaves of plates: ill.; 29 cm. 1. Cloud physics I. T.
QC921.5.L83        551.5/76        *LC* 77-22281        *ISBN* 0271005157

**Mason, B. J. (Basil John)**                                          **5.2535**
Clouds, rain, and rainmaking / B. J. Mason. — 2d ed. — Cambridge [Eng.]; New York: Cambridge University Press, 1976 (c1975). 189 p.: ill.; 22 cm. Includes index. 1. Cloud physics 2. Weather control I. T.
QC921.5.M28 1975        551.5/7        *LC* 74-16991        *ISBN* 0521206502

**Mason, B. J. (Basil John)**                                        • **5.2536**
The physics of clouds, by B. J. Mason. 2nd ed. Oxford, Clarendon Press, 1971. xvi, 671, [1] p., 41 plates. illus. 25 cm. (Oxford monographs on meteorology) 1. Cloud physics I. T.
QC921.5.M3 1971        551.5/76        *LC* 70-27326        *ISBN* 0198516037

**World Meteorological Organization.**                                 **5.2537**
International cloud atlas / World Meteorological Organization. Rev. ed. — Geneva: Secretariat of the World Meteorological Organization, 1975-. v.: ill.; 29 cm. (WMO [publications]; no. 407) Includes index. 1. Clouds 2. Clouds — Atlases. I. T.
QC922.W6x        551.5/08 s 551.5/76        *LC* 77-356574        *ISBN* 9263104077

**Dennis, Arnett S.**                                                  **5.2538**
Weather modification by cloud seeding / by Arnett S. Dennis. — New York: Academic Press, 1980. xv, 267 p.: ill.; 24 cm. — (International geophysics series. v. 24) Includes index. 1. Weather control 2. Rain-making I. T. II. Series.
QC928.D46        551.68/76        *LC* 79-8539        *ISBN* 0122106504

**Hess, Wilmot N.**                                                    **5.2539**
Weather and climate modification, edited by W. N. Hess. — New York: Wiley, [1974] xiii, 842 p.: illus.; 26 cm. 'A Wiley-Interscience publication.' 1. Weather control I. T.
QC928.H47        551.6/8        *LC* 73-21829        *ISBN* 0471374539

**Huschke, R. E. (Ralph E.), 1925-.**                                  **5.2540**
Glossary of terms frequently used in weather modification / [compiled by Ralph E. Huschke]. — Boston, Mass.: American Meteorological Society, [1968] 1972 printing. iii, 59 p. Cover title. Prepared for the Seminar for Science Writers on Weather Modification, New York, N.Y., 25 April 1968. 1. Weather control — Dictionaries I. Seminar for Science Writers on Weather Modification, 2d, New York, 1968 II. T.
QC928 H87 1972

**Bell, Corydon, 1894-.**                                            • **5.2541**
The wonder of snow. [1st ed.] New York: Hill and Wang [1957] 269 p.; 22 cm. 1. Snow I. T.
QC929.S7 B36        *LC* 57-5837

**Handbook of snow: principles, processes, management & use /**        **5.2542**
edited by D.M. Gray, D.H. Male.
Willowdale, Ont.: Pergamon Press Canada, c1981. xx, 776 p.: ill., maps; 24 cm. 1. Snow 2. Snow mechanics I. Gray, D. M. (Donald Maurice), 1929- II. Male, D. H. (David Harold), 1939-
QC929.S7 H35        551.57/84 19        *ISBN* 008025375X

# QC935–968 WINDS. STORMS. ATMOSPHERIC ELECTRICITY

**Reiter, Elmar R.**                                                 • **5.2543**
Jet–stream meteorology. — Chicago: University of Chicago Press, 1963. xiv, 515 p.: ill. 1. Jet stream I. T.
QC935.R413        *LC* 63-13074

**Eagleman, Joe R.**                                                   **5.2544**
Severe and unusual weather / Joe R. Eagleman. — New York: Van Nostrand Reinhold Co., c1983. xi, 372 p.: ill., maps; 24 cm. Includes index. 1. Storms 2. Weather 3. Weather control I. T.
QC941.E17 1983        551.5/5 19        *LC* 81-14672        *ISBN* 0442261950

**Kutzbach, Gisela.**                                                  **5.2545**
The thermal theory of cyclones: a history of meteorological thought in the nineteenth century / Gisela Kutzbach. — Boston: American Meteorological Society, c1979. xiv, 255 p.: ill.; 27 cm. — (Historical monograph series) Based on the author's thesis. Includes index. 1. Cyclones 2. Atmospheric thermodynamics 3. Meteorology — History. I. T.
QC941.K87        551.5/53        *LC* 79-51009        *ISBN* 0933876483

**Storm data for the United States, 1970–1974: a quinquennial**        **5.2546**
**compilation of the U.S. Environmental Data Service's official**
**monthly reports of storm activity logged by the National**
**Weather Service with damage extent estimates and counts of**
**injuries and deaths.**
Detroit, Mich.: Gale Research Co., c1982. 884 p.; 29 cm. — (Gale weather series.) Compiled from the Service's Storm data monthly pamphlets. 1. Storms — United States. I. United States. Environmental Data Service. II. Storm data. III. Series.
QC943.5.U6 S83 1982        551.5/5/0973 19        *LC* 81-13436        *ISBN* 0810311402

**Storm data for the United States, 1975–1979: a quinquennial**        **5.2547**
**compilation of the U.S. Environmental Data Service's official**
**monthly reports of storm activity logged by the National**
**Weather Service with damage extent estimates and counts of**
**injuries and deaths.**
Detroit, Mich.: Gale Research Co., c1982. 946 p.; 29 cm. — (Gale weather series.) Compiled from the service's Storm data monthly pamphlets. 1. Storms — United States — Handbooks, manuals, etc. I. United States. Environmental Data Service. II. United States. Environmental Data and Information Service. III. Storm data. IV. Series.
QC943.5.U6 S84 1982        551.5/5/0973 19        *LC* 81-13474        *ISBN* 0810311399

**Ludlum, David McWilliams, 1910-.**                                 • **5.2548**
Early American hurricanes, 1492–1870 / David M. Ludlum. — Boston: American Meteorological Society [c1963] xii, 198 p.: maps, charts; 29 cm. (The History of American weather; no. 1) 1. Storms — United States. 2. Hurricanes I. T. II. Series.
QC945.L82 1963        551.5520973        *LC* 64-188

**CRC handbook of atmospherics / editor, Hans Volland.**               **5.2549**
Boca Raton, Fla.: CRC Press, c1982. 2 v.: ill.; 26 cm. 1. Atmospherics I. Volland, Hans.
QC961.C73 1982        551.5/6 19        *LC* 81-674        *ISBN* 0849332265

**Salanave, Leon E., 1917-.**                                          **5.2550**
Lightning and its spectrum: an atlas of photographs / Leon E. Salanave. — Tucson, Ariz.: University of Arizona Press, c1980. xvii, 136 p.: ill.; 24 x 31 cm. Includes index. 1. Lightning — Atlases. I. T.
QC966.S37        551.5/63/0222        *LC* 80-18882        *ISBN* 0816503745

**Singer, Stanley, 1925-.**                                          • **5.2551**
The nature of ball lightning. New York: Plenum Press 1971. ix, 169 p.: ill. (part col.); 24 cm. 1. Ball lightning I. T.
QC966 S55        *LC* 70-128512        *ISBN* 0306304945

**Thunderstorms—a social, scientific, & technological**                **5.2552**
**documentary / Edwin Kessler, editor.**
[Boulder, Colo.?]: U.S. Dept. of Commerce, National Oceanic and Atmospheric Administration, Environmental Research Laboratories: For sale by the Supt. of Docs., U.S. G.P.O., 1981-1982. 3 v.: ill. (some col.), maps; 28 cm. 'September 1981.' Description based on vol. 1. S/N 003-017-00497-0 Item 207-C-1 1. Thunderstorms — United States. 2. Thunderstorms — Social aspects — United States. I. Kessler, Edwin. II. Environmental Research Laboratories (U.S.) III. Title: Thunderstorm in human affairs.
QC968.T48 1981        363.3/492 19        *LC* 82-601021

## QC973.5–976 Radar Meteorology. Meteorological Optics

**Battan, Louis J.**     **5.2553**
Radar observation of the atmosphere / Louis J. Battan. Rev. ed. — Chicago: University of Chicago Press, 1973. x, 324 p.: ill.; 24 cm. First ed. published in 1959 under title: Radar meteorology. Includes index. 1. Radar meteorology I. T.
QC973.5.B3 1973     551.6/353     LC 72-84405     ISBN 0226039196

**Minnaert, M. G. J. (Marcel Gilles Jozef), 1893-.**     • **5.2554**
[Natuurkunde van 't vrije veld. English] The nature of light & colour in the open air. Translation [by] H. M. Kremer–Priest, revision [by] K. E. Brian Jay. [New York] Dover Publications [1954] 362 p. illus. 21 cm. Translation of Licht en Kleur in het landschap, pt. 1 of De natuurkunde van 't vrije veld. 1. Meteorological optics 2. Light 3. Color I. T.
QC975.M552 1954     535     LC 54-10021

**Greenler, Robert, 1929-.**     **5.2555**
Rainbows, halos, and glories / Robert Greenler. — Cambridge; New York: Cambridge University Press, 1980. x, 195 p., [16] leaves of plates: ill.; 27 cm. 1. Meteorological optics 2. Rainbow 3. Halos (Meteorology) I. T. II. Title: Glories.
QC975.2.G73     551.5/6     LC 80-14722     ISBN 0521236053

**Corliss, William R.**     **5.2556**
Lightning, auroras, nocturnal lights, and related luminous phenomena: a catalog of geophysical anomalies / compiled by William R. Corliss. — Glen Arm, MD: Sourcebook Project, c1982. v, 242 p.: ill.; 27 cm. 1. Meteorological optics — Handbooks, manuals, etc. I. T.
QC975.8.C67 1982     551.5/6 19     LC 82-99902     ISBN 0915554097

**Corliss, William R.**     **5.2557**
Rare halos, mirages, anomalous rainbows, and related electromagnetic phenomena: a catalog of geophysical anomalies / compiled by William R. Corliss. — Glen Arm, MD: Sourcebook Project, c1984. vi, 238 p.: ill.; 27 cm. 1. Meteorological optics — Handbooks, manuals, etc. 2. Halos (Meteorology) — Handbooks, manuals, etc. 3. Mirages — Handbooks, manuals, etc. 4. Rainbow — Handbooks, manuals, etc. 5. Magnetic anomalies — Handbooks, manuals, etc. I. T.
QC975.8.C68 1984     551.5/6 19     LC 84-50491     ISBN 0915554127

## QC980–994 Climatology

## QC980–981 General Works

**World survey of climatology / editor in chief, H.E. Landsberg.**     **5.2558**
Amsterdam; New York: Elsevier Scientific Pub. Co., 1984. 16 v.: ill.; 30 cm. 1. Climatology — Collected works. I. Landsberg, Helmut Erich, 1906-
QC980.15.W67     551.69 19     LC 78-477739

**Battan, Louis J.**     **5.2559**
Weather / Louis J. Battan. — 2nd ed. — Englewood Cliffs, N.J.: Prentice-Hall, c1985. 135 p.: ill.; 24 cm. (Prentice-Hall foundations of earth science series.) Includes index. 1. Weather I. T. II. Series.
QC981.B33 1985     551.5 19     LC 84-17844     ISBN 0139476989

**Holford, Ingrid.**     **5.2560**
The Guinness book of weather facts & feats / Ingrid Holford. — 2nd ed. — Enfield, Middlesex: Guinness Superlatives, c1982. 253 p.: ill. (some col.); 25 cm. Includes index. 1. Weather 2. Weather — Handbooks, manuals, etc. I. T. II. Title: Weather facts and feats.
QC981.H593 1982     551.5 19     LC 82-242995     ISBN 0851122434

**Kendrew, W. G. (Wilfrid George)**     **5.2561**
The climates of the continents. 5th ed. Oxford, Clarendon Press, 1961. 608 p. illus., maps, tables. 23 cm. 1. Climatology I. T.
QC981.K4 1961     551.59     LC 61-19753

**Lamb, H. H.**     • **5.2562**
Climate: present, past and future / [by] H. H. Lamb. — London: Methuen, 1972-. v.: ill., charts, maps.; 26 cm. 'Distributed in the U.S.A. by Barnes and Noble Inc.'; v. 2 has imprint: London, Methuen; New York, Barnes & Noble Books. 1. Climatology 2. Paleoclimatology 3. Weather forecasting I. T.
QC981.L28     551.5     LC 72-183843     ISBN 0416115306

**Mather, John Russell, 1923-.**     **5.2563**
Climatology: fundamentals and applications [by] John R. Mather. — New York: McGraw-Hill, [1974] xiii, 412 p.: illus.; 24 cm. — (McGraw-Hill series in geography) 1. Climatology I. T.
QC981.M43     551.5     LC 73-23082     ISBN 0070408912

**Oliver, John E.**     **5.2564**
Climatology, an introduction / John E. Oliver, John J. Hidore. — Columbus [Ohio]: Merrill, c1984. xiv, 381 p.: ill.; 27 cm. Includes index. 1. Climatology I. Hidore, John J. II. T.
QC981.O395 1984     551.6 19     LC 83-63079     ISBN 0675201446

**Sellers, William D.**     • **5.2565**
Physical climatology [by] William D. Sellers. Chicago, University of Chicago Press [1965] viii, 272 p. illus., maps. 25 cm. 1. Climatology I. T.
QC981.S4     551.6     LC 65-24983

**Study of Man's Impact on Climate, Stockholm, 1970.**     **5.2566**
Inadvertent climate modification; report. Cambridge, Mass., MIT Press [1971] xxi, 308 p. illus. 22 cm. Sponsored by the Massachusetts Institute of Technology and hosted by the Royal Swedish Academy of Sciences and the Royal Swedish Academy of Engineering Sciences. 1. Climatic changes 2. Weather control 3. Man — Influence on nature I. Massachusetts Institute of Technology. II. Kungl. Svenska vetenskapsakademien. III. Ingenjörsvetenskapsakademien (Sweden) IV. T.
QC981.S77 1970     551.6/8     LC 79-170861     ISBN 0262191016     ISBN 0262690330

**Trewartha, Glenn Thomas, 1896-.**     **5.2567**
The Earth's problem climates / Glenn T. Trewartha. — 2d ed. — Madison, Wis.: University of Wisconsin Press, 1981. xi, 371 p.: ill.; 26 cm. Includes index. 1. Climatology I. T.
QC981.T648 1981     551.6     LC 80-5120     ISBN 029908230X

**Trewartha, Glenn Thomas, 1896-.**     **5.2568**
An introduction to climate / Glenn T. Trewartha, Lyle H. Horn; cartography by Randall D. Sale. — 5th ed. — New York: McGraw-Hill, c1980. xii, 416 p.: ill.; 24 cm. — (McGraw-Hill series in geography) 1. Climatology 2. Weather I. Horn, Lyle H., joint author. II. T.
QC981.T65 1980     551.5     LC 79-14203     ISBN 0070651523

**Theory of climate: proceedings of a symposium commemorating the two–hundredth anniversary of the Academy of Sciences of Lisbon, October 12–14, 1981, Lisbon, Portugal / edited by Barry Saltzman.**     **5.2569**
New York; London: Academic Press, 1983. xii, 505 p.: ill. Advances in geophysics, vol. 25. Includes index. 1. Climatology — Addresses, essays, lectures. I. Saltzman, Barry.
QC981.4.T44 1983     ISBN 012088252

**Oke, T. R.**     **5.2570**
Boundary layer climates / T. R. Oke. — London: Methuen; New York: Wiley, 1978. xxi, 372 p.: ill.; 24 cm. 'A Halsted Press book.' Includes indexes. 1. Microclimatology 2. Planetary boundary layer I. T.
QC981.7.M5 O34 1978     551.6/6     LC 77-25266     ISBN 0470993642

**Landsberg, Helmut Erich, 1906-.**     **5.2571**
The urban climate / Helmut E. Landsberg. — New York: Academic Press, 1981. x, 275 p.: ill.; 24 cm. — (International geophysics series. v. 28) 1. Urban climatology I. T. II. Series.
QC981.7.U7 L36     551.5/09173/2 19     LC 80-2766     ISBN 0124359604

**Budyko, M. I. (Mikhail Ivanovich)**     **5.2572**
[Klimat v proshlom i budushchem. English] The Earth's climate, past and future / M.I. Budyko; translated by the author. — New York: Academic Press, 1982. x, 307 p.: ill.; 24 cm. — (International geophysics series. v. 29) Translation of Klimat v proshlom i budushchem. Includes index. 1. Climatic changes 2. Man — Influence on nature I. T. II. Series.
QC981.8.C5 B8313 1982     551.6 19     LC 81-17673     ISBN 0121394603

**Calder, Nigel.**     **5.2573**
The weather machine / Nigel Calder. New York: Viking Press, 1975, c1974. 143 p.: ill.; 26 cm. Includes index. 1. Climatic changes I. T.
QC981.8.C5 C34 1975     551.6     LC 75-1087     ISBN 0670754250

# QC982–994 By Region or Country

**Conway, H. McKinley (Hobart McKinley), 1920- ed.**          **5.2574**
The weather handbook: a summary of weather statistics for selected cities
throughout the United States and around the world / edited by H. McKinley
Conway and Linda L. Liston. — Rev. ed. — Atlanta: Conway Research, 1974.
255 p.: maps.; 24 cm. Chiefly tables. Includes index. 1. Climatology — Tables.
I. Liston, Linda L. joint author. II. T.
QC982.5.C6 1974          551.6/9/1732          *LC* 74-187773

**Climates of the states: National Oceanic and Atmospheric**          **5.2575**
**Administration narrative summaries, tables, and maps for each**
**state, with overview of state climatologist programs / new**
**material by James A. Ruffner.**
3rd ed. — Detroit, Mich.: Gale Research Co., c1985. v. <1 >: maps; 29 cm.
Published also as no. 60, Parts 1-52 (part 50 vacant) 1976-1978, in the series
Climates of the States, Climatology [i.e. Climatography] of the United States.
1. United States — Climate — Charts, diagrams, etc. I. Ruffner, James A.
II. United States. National Oceanic and Atmospheric Administration.
QC983.C56 1985          551.6973 19          *LC* 85-25271          *ISBN* 0810310422

**The Weather almanac.**          **5.2576**
5th ed. (1987)-     . — Detroit: Gale Research Co., c1987-. v.: ill.; 24 cm.
1. Air quality — United States — Handbooks, manuals, etc. 2. United States
— Climate — Handbooks, manuals, etc.
QC983.W38          551.6973 19          *LC* 81-644322          *ISBN* 0810314975 1987

**Weather of U.S. cities / James A. Ruffner and Frank E. Bair,**          **5.2577**
**editors.**
3rd ed. — Detroit, Mich.: Gale Research Co., c1987. v. <1-2 >; 29 cm.
Subtitle: A compilation of weather records for 281 key cities and weather
observation points in the United States and its island territories to provide
insight into their diverse climates and normal weather tendencies, supplies
narrative statements about the various cities' climates, and complements the
descriptions with statistical cumulations to quantify 'normals, means, and
extremes' for each. 1. Urban climatology — United States — Handbooks,
manuals, etc. 2. United States — Climate — Handbooks, manuals, etc.
I. Ruffner, James A. II. Bair, Frank E. III. Gale Research Company.
IV. Title: Weather of US cities.
QC983.W393 1987          551.6973 19          *LC* 87-11869          *ISBN* 0810321025

**Anderson, Bette Roda, 1945-.**          **5.2578**
Weather in the West: from the midcontinent to the Pacific / by Bette Roda
Anderson. — 1st ed. — Palo Alto, Calif.: American West Pub. Co., [1975]
223 p.: ill. (some col.); 28 cm. (Great West series) Includes index. 1. Weather
2. West (U.S.) — Climate. I. T.
QC984.W38 A5          551.6/9/78          *LC* 73-90799          *ISBN* 0910118485

**Hare, F. Kenneth (Frederick Kenneth)**          **5.2579**
Climate Canada / F. Kenneth Hare, Morley K. Thomas. — 2nd ed. —
Toronto; New York: J. Wiley & Sons Canada, c1979. 230 p.: ill. (some col.), col.
maps; 25 cm. 1. Canada — Climate. I. Thomas, Morley K. II. T.
QC985.H37 1979          551.6971 19          *LC* 81-151093          *ISBN* 047199796X

**Riehl, Herbert, 1915-.**          **5.2580**
Climate and weather in the tropics / Herbert Riehl. — London; New York:
Academic Press, 1979. xii, 611 p.: ill.; 23 cm. 1. Tropics — Climate I. T.
QC993.5.R54 1979          551.6913 19          *LC* 78-73890          *ISBN* 0125881800

**Barry, Roger Graham.**          **5.2581**
Mountain weather and climate / Roger G. Barry. — London; New York:
Methuen, 1981. xii, 313 p.: ill.; 24 cm. 1. Mountain climate I. T.
QC993.6.B37 1981          551.6914/3 19          *LC* 80-42348          *ISBN*
0416737307

# QC995–998 WEATHER FORECASTING

**Haltiner, George J.**          **5.2582**
Numerical prediction and dynamic meteorology / George J. Haltiner, Roger
Terry Williams. — 2d ed. — New York: Wiley, c1980. xvii, 477 p.: ill.; 24 cm.
First ed. (1971) published under title: Numerical weather prediction. Includes
indexes. 1. Numerical weather forecasting 2. Dynamic meteorology
I. Williams, Roger Terry, 1936- joint author. II. T.
QC996.H35 1980          551.6/34          *LC* 79-25544          *ISBN* 0471059714

**Richardson, Lewis Fry, 1881-1953.**          **• 5.2583**
Weather prediction by numerical process. With a new introd. by Sydney
Chapman. New York, Dover Publications [1965] xvi, 236 p. illus., maps. 24 cm.
First published in 1922. Includes bibliographies. 1. Numerical weather
forecasting I. T.
QC996.R65 1965          551.634          *LC* 65-27019

**Inwards, Richard, 1840-1937.**          **• 5.2584**
Weather lore: the unique bedside book; Taken from the world's literature and
the age–old wisdom of farmers, mariners, bird watchers, concerning flowers,
plants, trees, butterflies, birds, animals, fish, tides, clouds, rainbows, stars, mock
suns, mock moons, haloes; Ed. rev. and amplified for the Royal Meteorological
Society / by E.L. Hawke. — 4th ed. — London: Rider, 1950. 251 p.: ill.
1. Weather — Folklore I. T.
QC998.I64 1950

# QD    Chemistry

## QD1–66 Reference. General Works

**Chemical abstracts.**    5.2585
v. 1- Jan. 1, 1907-. [Columbus, Ohio, etc.] American Chemical Society. Weekly. Individual issues, 1934- have subtitle: Key to the world's chemical literature. 'A publication of the Chemical Abstracts Service.' 1. Chemistry — Abstracts — Periodicals. 2. Chemistry — Bibliography — Periodicals. I. American Chemical Society. Chemical Abstracts Service.
QD1.A51    540/.05    LC 09-4698

**Annual review of physical chemistry.**    • 5.2586
v. 1- 1950-. Palo Alto, Calif. [etc.] Annual Reviews, inc. v. ill. 23 cm. Annual. Available on microfilm from University Microfilms. 1. Chemistry, Physical and theoretical — Periodicals. 2. Chemistry, Physical and theoretical — Bibliography — Periodicals. I. Rollefson, Gerhard Krohn, 1900- ed.
QD1.A732    541.058    LC a 51-1658

**Leicester, Henry Marshall, 1906-.**    • 5.2587
A source book in chemistry, 1400–1900 / [by] Henry M. Leicester and Herbert S. Klickstein. — Cambridge, Mass.: Harvard University Press, 1963 [c1952] xvi, 554 p.: ill.; 24 cm. — (Source books in the history of the sciences.) 1. Chemistry — Collected works. I. Klickstein, Herbert S. joint author. II. T. III. Series.
QD3.L47 1963    540.82    LC 63-16776

**Leicester, Henry Marshall, 1906-.**    • 5.2588
Source book in chemistry, 1900–1950. Edited by Henry M. Leicester. — Cambridge, Mass.: Harvard University Press, 1968. xvii, 408 p.: illus.; 24 cm. — (Source books in the history of the sciences.) 1. Chemistry — Collected works. I. T. II. Series.
QD3.L472    540/.8    LC 68-14263

## QD5 Dictionaries

**Callaham, Ludmilla Ignatiev.**    5.2589
[Russian-English technical and chemical dictionary] Russian–English chemical and polytechnical dictionary / Ludmilla Ignatiev Callaham. — 3d ed. — New York: Wiley, [1975] xxviii, 852 p.; 24 cm. First ed. published in 1947 under title: Russian-English technical and chemical dictionary. 'A Wiley-Interscience publication.' 1. Chemistry — Dictionaries — Russian. 2. Technology — Dictionaries — Russian. 3. Russian language — Dictionaries — English. I. T.
QD5.C33 1975    540/.3    LC 75-5982    ISBN 0471129984

**Condensed chemical dictionary.**    5.2590
Hawley's condensed chemical dictionary. — 11th ed. / rev. by N. Irving Sax and Richard J. Lewis. — New York: Van Nostrand Reinhold, c1987. xv, 1288 p.: ill.; 24 cm. Rev. ed. of: The Condensed chemical dictionary. 10th ed. / rev. by Gessner G. Hawley. 1981. Includes index. 1. Chemistry — Dictionaries. I. Hawley, Gessner Goodrich, 1905- II. Sax, N. Irving (Newton Irving) III. Lewis, Richard J., Sr. IV. T.
QD5.C5 1987    540/.3/21 19    LC 86-23333    ISBN 0442280971

**Hackh, Ingo W. D. (Ingo Waldemar Dagobert), 1890-1938.**    5.2591
[Chemical dictionary] Grant & Hackh's chemical dictionary: American, international, European, and British usage: containing the words generally used in chemistry, and many of the terms used in the related sciences of physics, medicine, engineering, biology, pharmacy, astrophysics, agriculture, mineralogy, etc., based on recent scientific literature. — 5th ed. / completely rev. and edited by Roger Grant and Claire Grant. — New York: McGraw-Hill, c1987. p. cm. Rev. ed. of: Chemical dictionary. 4th ed. 1969. 1. Chemistry — Dictionaries. I. Grant, Roger L. II. Grant, Claire. III. T. IV. Title: Grant and Hackh's chemical dictionary. V. Title: Chemical dictionary.
QD5.H3 1987    540/.3 19    LC 86-7496    ISBN 0070240671

**Hampel, Clifford A.**    5.2592
Glossary of chemical terms / Clifford A. Hampel and Gessner G. Hawley. — 2nd ed. — New York: Van Nostrand Reinhold, c1982. ix, 306 p.; 23 cm. 1. Chemistry — Dictionaries. I. Hawley, Gessner Goodrich, 1905- II. T.
QD5.H34 1982    540/.3/21 19    LC 81-11482    ISBN 0442238711

**Kingzett, Charles Thomas, 1852-1935.**    • 5.2593
[Popular chemical dictionary] Kingzett's chemical encyclopaedia: a digest of chemistry & its industrial applications / general editor: D. H. Hey; assistant editors: I. R. Beattie [and others]; foreword by Sir Eric Rideal. — 9th ed. Princeton, N.J.: Van Nostrand [1967] xi, 1092 p.: ill.; 25 cm. First published in 1919 under title: Popular chemical dictionary. 1. Chemistry — Dictionaries. I. Hey, Donald Holroyde. ed. II. T. III. Title: Chemical encyclopaedia.
QD5.K4 1967    540/.3    LC 67-2238

**Patterson, Austin M. (Austin McDowell), 1876-1956.**    • 5.2594
A French–English dictionary for chemists. 2d ed. New York: Wiley [1954] xiv, 476 p.; 19 cm. 1. Chemistry — Dictionaries — French. 2. French language — Dictionaries — English. I. T.
QD5.P25 1954    540.3    LC 54-6661

**Patterson, Austin M. (Austin McDowell), 1876-1956.**    • 5.2595
A German–English dictionary for chemists. 3d ed. New York, Wiley [1950] xviii, 541 p. 18 cm. 1. Chemistry — Dictionaries — German. 2. German language — Dictionaries — English. I. T.
QD5.P3 1950    540.3    LC 50-4541

**Van Nostrand Reinhold encyclopedia of chemistry / Douglas M.**    5.2596
**Considine, editor–in–chief; Glenn D. Considine, managing editor.**
4th ed. — New York: Van Nostrand Reinhold, c1984. vii, 1082 p.: ill.; 29 cm. Rev. ed. of: The Encyclopedia of chemistry. 3rd ed. 1973. 1. Chemistry — Dictionaries. I. Considine, Douglas Maxwell. II. Considine, Glenn D. III. Encyclopedia of chemistry.
QD5.V37 1984    540/.3/21 19    LC 83-23336    ISBN 0442225725

## QD7–8.5 Nomenclature. Terminology. Chemical Information

**Cahn, R. S. (Robert Sidney), 1899-.**    5.2597
Introduction to chemical nomenclature / R. S. Cahn, O. C. Dermer. — 5th ed. — London; Boston: Butterworths, 1979. 200 p.: ill.; 23 cm. 1. Chemistry — Nomenclature I. Dermer, Otis C. (Otis Clifford), 1909- joint author. II. T.
QD7.C2 1979    540/.1/4    LC 79-40303    ISBN 0408106085

**Fieser, Louis Frederick, 1899-.**    • 5.2598
Style guide for chemists / [by] Louis F. Fieser [and] Mary Fieser. — New York: Reinhold [1960] 116 p.: ill.; 24 cm. 1. Technical writing 2. Chemistry — Terminology. I. Fieser, Mary, 1909- joint author. II. T.
QD7.F5    540.149    LC 60-11201

**The ACS style guide: a manual for authors and editors / Janet**    • 5.2599
**S. Dodd, editor; Marianne C. Brogan, advisory editor.**
Washington, DC: American Chemical Society, 1986. xvii 264 p. — Includes index. 1. Chemical literature — Authorship — Handbooks, manuals, etc. 2. English language — Style — Handbooks, manuals, etc. I. Dodd, Janet S., 1944- II. Brogan, Marianne C. III. American Chemical Society.
QD8.5.A25 1986    808/.06654 19    LC 85-21472    ISBN 0841209170

**Bottle, R. T. ed.**    5.2600
Use of chemical literature / editor, R. T. Bottle. — 3d ed. — London; Boston: Butterworths, 1979. xiv, 306 p.; 23 cm. — (Information sources for research and development) 1. Chemical literature I. T.
QD8.5.B6 1979    QD8.5 B6 1979.    540/.7    LC 79-41061    ISBN 0408384522

**Maizell, Robert E. (Robert Edward), 1924-.**    5.2601
How to find chemical information: a guide for practicing chemists, educators, and students / Robert E. Maizell. — 2nd ed. — New York: J. Wiley, c1986. p. cm. 'A Wiley-Interscience publication.' 1. Chemical literature I. T.
QD8.5.M34 1986    540/.7 19    LC 86-15687    ISBN 0471867675

**Mellon, M. G. (Melvin Guy), 1893-.**    5.2602
Chemical publications, their nature and use / M.G. Mellon. — 5th ed. — New York: McGraw-Hill, c1982. xii, 419 p.: ill.; 25 cm. 1. Chemical literature 2. Chemistry — Study and teaching 3. Bibliography — Best books — Chemistry. I. T.
QD8.5.M44 1982    540/.72 19    *LC* 81-20947    *ISBN* 0070415145

**Wolman, Yecheskel, 1935-.**    5.2603
Chemical information: a practical guide to utilization / Yecheskel Wolman. — Chichester [West Sussex]; New York: Wiley, c1983. xiv, 191 p.: ill.; 24 cm. 'A Wiley-Interscience publication.' Includes index. 1. Chemical literature 2. Chemistry — Information services I. T.
QD8.5.W64 1983    540/.72 19    *LC* 82-2763    *ISBN* 0471103195

# QD11–23 History. Biography. Directories

## QD11–15 History. General Works. Alchemy

**Asimov, Isaac, 1920-.**    • 5.2604
A short history of chemistry. — [1st ed.]. — Garden City, N.Y.: Anchor Books, 1965. 263 p.: ill.; 19 cm. — (Science study series, S41) 1. Chemistry — History I. T.
QD11.A8    540.9    *LC* 65-10641

**Farber, Eduard, 1892-.**    • 5.2605
The evolution of chemistry; a history of its ideas, methods, and materials. — 2d ed. — New York: Ronald Press Co., [1969] vii, 437 p.: illus.; 24 cm. 1. Chemistry — History I. T.
QD11.F34 1969    540/.9    *LC* 69-14669

**Hannaway, Owen.**    5.2606
The chemists and the word: the didactic origins of chemistry / Owen Hannaway. — Baltimore: Johns Hopkins University Press, [1975] xiii, 165 p.; 23 cm. 1. Chemistry — History — Sources. I. T.
QD11.H27    540/.9    *LC* 74-24380    *ISBN* 0801816661

**Ihde, Aaron John, 1909-.**    5.2607
The development of modern chemistry / Aaron J. Ihde. — New York: Dover, c1984. xii, 851 p.: ill.; 22 cm. Reprint. Originally published: New York: Harper & Row, 1970 printing. With updated appendix. Includes indexes. 1. Chemistry — History I. T.
QD11.I44 1984    540/.9 19    *LC* 82-18245    *ISBN* 0486642356

**Leicester, Henry Marshall, 1906-.**    5.2608
The historical background of chemistry. — New York: Wiley, 1956. 260 p.: ill. 1. Chemistry — History I. T.
QD11.L4    *LC* 56-8001

**Partington, J. R. (James Riddick), 1886-1965.**    • 5.2609
A history of chemistry / by J.R. Partington. — London: Macmillan, 1961-. v.: ill., ports.; 26 cm. Vol. 1, pt. 1 has title: Theoretical background. Vol. 1, pt. 1, pt. 2, pt. 3, pt. 4. Errata (leaf) inserted. 1. Chemistry — History 2. Chemists — Biography I. T.
QD11.P28    *LC* 62-1666

**Partington, James Riddick.**    • 5.2610
A short history of chemistry / [by] James Partington. — 3d ed., rev. and enl. London: Macmillan; New York: St. Martin's Press, 1960. 415 p.: ill.; 21 cm. 1. Chemistry — History I. T.
QD11.P3    540.9P273    *LC* 61-3050

**Stillman, John Maxson, 1852-1923.**    5.2611
[Story of early chemistry] The story of alchemy and early chemistry (The story of early chemistry) New York, Dover Publications [1960] 566 p. 21 cm. 'An unabridged and unaltered republication of the first edition of the work which first appeared in 1924 under the title The story of early chemistry.' 1. Chemistry — History I. T. II. Title: Alchemy and early chemistry.
QD11.S84 1960    540.1    *LC* 60-3183

**Holmyard, Eric John, 1891-1959.**    5.2612
Alchemy. — Baltimore: Penguin Books, [1968] 288 p.: ill.; 19 cm. — (Pelican books, A348) Reprint of the 1957 ed. 1. Alchemy I. T.
QD13.H64 1968    540.1    *LC* 68-6870

**Multhauf, Robert P.**    • 5.2613
The origins of chemistry [by] Robert P. Multhauf. — New York: F. Watts, [1967] 412 p.; 25 cm. — (The Watts history of science library) 1. Chemistry — History I. T.
QD14.M97 1967a    540/.9    *LC* 67-24564

**Farber, Eduard, 1892- comp.**    • 5.2614
Milestones of modern chemistry; original reports of the discoveries. — New York: Basic Books, [1966] ix, 237 p.: illus.; 22 cm. — (Science & discovery books) 1. Chemistry — History I. T.
QD15.F3    540.9    *LC* 66-23492

## QD21–22 Biography

**Farber, Eduard, 1892- ed.**    • 5.2615
Great chemists. New York: Interscience Publishers, 1961. 1642 p.: ill.; 25 cm. 1. Chemists 2. Chemistry — History I. T.
QD21.F35    925.4    *LC* 60-16809

**Farber, Eduard, 1892-.**    • 5.2616
Nobel prize winners in chemistry, 1901–1961. Rev. ed. London; New York: Abelard-Schuman [1963] 341 p.: ill.; 23 cm. (The Life of science library, no. 41) 1. Chemists 2. Nobel prizes I. T.
QD21.F37 1963    925.4    *LC* 62-17263

**Jaffe, Bernard, 1896-.**    5.2617
Crucibles: the story of chemistry from ancient alchemy to nuclear fission / Bernard Jaffe. — New rev. and updated 4th ed. — New York: Dover Publications, 1976. viii, 368 p.: ill.; 22 cm. 1. Chemists — Biography 2. Chemistry — History I. T.
QD21.J3 1976    540/.9    *LC* 75-38070    *ISBN* 0486233421

**Nachmansohn, David, 1899-.**    5.2618
German–Jewish pioneers in science, 1900–1933: highlights in atomic physics, chemistry, and biochemistry / David Nachmansohn. — Berlin; New York: Springer-Verlag, c1979. xx, 388 p.: ports.; 24 cm. 1. Chemists — Germany — Biography. 2. Biochemists — Germany — Biography. 3. Physicists — Germany — Biography. 4. Jews — Germany — Biography. I. T.
QD21.N33    509/.2/2 B    *LC* 79-10550    *ISBN* 0387904026

**Thackray, Arnold, 1939-.**    5.2619
John Dalton: critical assessments of his life and science. — Cambridge: Harvard University Press, 1972. xiv, 190 p.: ill.; 24 cm. — (Harvard monographs in the history of Science) 1. Dalton, John, 1766-1844. I. T. II. Series.
QD22.D2 T47    540/.92/4 B    *LC* 72-75403    *ISBN* 0674475259

## QD23 Directories

**Directory of graduate research.**    5.2620
[Washington]: American Chemical Society. v.; 30 cm. Biennial. 1. Chemistry — Bio-bibliography — Directories. 2. Chemical engineering — Bio-bibliography — Directories. 3. Dissertations, Academic — Bio-bibliography — Directories. 4. Biochemical engineering — Bio-bibliography — Directories. I. American Chemical Society. Committee on Professional Training. II. Title: ACS directory of graduate research.
QD23.A5    *LC* 79-3432

# QD27–31 General Works to 1969

**Boyle, Robert, Hon. 1627-1691.**    • 5.2621
The sceptical chymist / by the Hon. Robert Boyle. — London: J. M. Dent.; New York: E. P. Dutton, 1911. xxii, 230 p. — (Everyman's library; Science; no.559) Introduction by M. M. Pattison Muir. 1. Chemistry — Early works to 1800. I. T.
QD27.B65    *LC* a 12-670

**Gould, Edwin S.**    • 5.2622
Inorganic reactions and structure. — Rev. ed. — New York: Holt, Rinehart and Winston, [1962] 513 p.: ill.; 24 cm. 1. Chemistry, Inorganic I. T.
QD31.G68 1962    546    *LC* 62-9519

**Mellor, Joseph William, 1873-1938.**    • 5.2623
A comprehensive treatise on inorganic and theoretical chemistry.: with supplemental volumes. — London; New York: Longmans, Green [1946-52; v. 16, 1947] v.; ill. 1. Chemistry, Inorganic 2. Chemistry, Physical and theoretical I. T.
QD31 M52

# QD31.2 General Works, 1970–

**Bowen, Humphrey John Moule.**     **5.2624**
Environmental chemistry of the elements / H. J. M. Bowen. — London; New York: Academic Press, 1979. xv, 333 p.: ill.; 24 cm. Revision of Trace elements in biochemistry. Includes index. 1. Environmental chemistry I. T.
QD31.2.B68     574.5/2     *LC* 79-50305     *ISBN* 0121204502

**Brady, James E., 1938-.**     **5.2625**
General chemistry, principles and structure / James E. Brady, Gerard E. Humiston. — 3rd ed. — New York: Wiley, c1982. xvii, 831 p., [12] p. of plates: ill.; 27 cm. Includes index. 1. Chemistry I. Humiston, Gerard E., 1939- II. T.
QD31.2.B7 1982     540 19     *LC* 81-16162     *ISBN* 0471078069

**Chemical principles / Richard E. Dickerson ... [et al.].**     **5.2626**
4th ed. — Menlo Park, Calif.: Benjamin/Cummings Pub. Co., c1984. xv, 930, 63, 14 p.: ill. (some col.); 25 cm. Rev. ed. of: Chemical principles / Richard E. Dickerson, 3rd ed. 1979. 1. Chemistry I. Dickerson, Richard Earl. II. Dickerson, Richard Earl. Chemical principles.
QD31.2.C375 1984     540 19     *LC* 84-360     *ISBN* 0805324224

**Chemistry of the environment / R. A. Bailey ... [et al.].**     **5.2627**
New York: Academic Press, 1978. x, 575 p.: ill.; 24 cm. 1. Environmental chemistry I. Bailey, Ronald Albert, 1933-
QD31.2.C4313     540     *LC* 78-11293     *ISBN* 0120730502

**Horne, Ralph Albert, 1929-.**     **5.2628**
The chemistry of our environment / R. A. Horne. — New York: Wiley, c1978. ix, 869 p.: ill.; 26 cm. 'A Wiley-Interscience publication.' 1. Environmental chemistry I. T.
QD31.2.H64     301.31     *LC* 77-1156     *ISBN* 0471409448

**Masterton, William L., 1927-.**     **5.2629**
Chemical principles / William L. Masterton, Emil J. Slowinski, Conrad L. Stanitski. — 6th ed. — Philadelphia: Saunders College Pub., c1985. xvii, 861, 54, 21, 10, [16] p. of plates: ill. (some col.); 26 cm. (Saunders golden sunburst series) Includes index. 1. Chemistry I. Slowinski, Emil J. II. Stanitski, Conrad L. III. T.
QD31.2.M38 1985     540 19     *LC* 84-22217     *ISBN* 0030707447

**Moore, John W.**     **5.2630**
Environmental chemistry / John W. Moore, Elizabeth A. Moore. — New York: Academic Press, 1976. xv, 500 p.: ill.; 24 cm. Includes index. 1. Environmental chemistry I. Moore, Elizabeth A., joint author. II. T.
QD31.2.M63     540     *LC* 75-26348     *ISBN* 012505050X

**Pauling, Linus, 1901-.**     **5.2631**
Chemistry / Linus Pauling, Peter Pauling. — San Francisco: W. H. Freeman, [1975] xi, 767 p.: ill.; 24 cm. (A Series of books in chemistry) 1. Chemistry I. Pauling, Peter, joint author. II. T.
QD31.2.P38 1975     540     *LC* 74-34071     *ISBN* 0716701766

**Thibodeaux, Louis J.**     **5.2632**
Chemodynamics, environmental movement of chemicals in air, water, and soil / Louis J. Thibodeaux. — New York: Wiley, c1979. xxiii, 501 p.: ill.; 24 cm. 'A Wiley-Interscience publication.' 1. Environmental chemistry I. T.
QD31.2.T47     574.5/2     *LC* 78-31637     *ISBN* 0471047201

# QD40–66 Laboratories. Handbooks

## QD40–45 Study and Teaching

**Chemical research faculties: an international directory, 1984 / Gisella Linder Pollock, project editor.**     **5.2633**
Washington, D.C.: American Chemical Society, c1984. xxxv, 407, [117] p.; 29 cm. Includes indexes. 1. Chemistry — Research — Directories. 2. Chemistry — Study and teaching (Higher) — Directories. 3. Chemists — Directories. I. Pollock, Gisella Linder. II. American Chemical Society.
QD40.C4317 1984     540/.72 19     *LC* 83-22323     *ISBN* 0841208174

**Benson, Sidney William, 1918-.**     • **5.2634**
Chemical calculations: an introduction to the use of mathematics in chemistry / [by] Sidney W. Benson. — 3d ed. — New York: Wiley, [1971] xix, 279 p.: ill.; 23 cm. 1. Chemistry — Mathematics. I. T.
QD42.B453 1971     540/.1/51     *LC* 76-146670     *ISBN* 0471067695

**Adams, David Michael.**     • **5.2635**
Advanced practical inorganic chemistry / by D. M. Adams and J. B. Raynor. — London; New York: Wiley, 1965. xiv, 182 p.: ill. 1. Chemistry, Inorganic — Laboratory manuals I. Raynor, John Barrie. II. T.
QD45.A27     543     *LC* 65-23104

**Research in chemistry at undergraduate institutions: a directory of work in progress by the faculty of 151 chemistry departments, along with background data on each department / Brian Andreen, editor.**     **5.2636**
3rd ed. — Tucson, Ariz. (6840 E. Broadway Blvd., Tucson 85710): Council on Undergraduate Research, 1985. vii, 414 p.; 28 cm. Rev. ed. of: Research in chemistry at private undergraduate colleges. 2nd ed. 1981. 'April 1985.' 1. Chemistry — Research — United States — Directories. 2. Universities and colleges — United States — Directories. I. Andreen, Brian. II. Council on Undergraduate Research (U.S.) III. Research in chemistry at private undergraduate colleges.
QD47.R475 1985     540/.72/073 19     *LC* 85-170803

## QD51–66 Laboratories. Techniques. Handbooks

**Assembly of Mathematical and Physical Sciences (U.S.). Committee on Hazardous Substances in the Laboratory.**     **5.2637**
Prudent practices for handling hazardous chemicals in laboratories / Committee on Hazardous Substances in the Laboratory, Assembly of Mathematical and Physical Sciences, National Research Council. — Washington, D.C.: National Academy Press, 1981. xiv, 291 p.: ill. (in pocket); 24 cm. 1. Chemical laboratories — Safety measures. I. T.
QD51.A88 1981     542/.028/9 19     *LC* 80-26877     *ISBN* 0309031281

**Green, Michael E.**     **5.2638**
Safety in working with chemicals / Michael E. Green, Amos Turk. — New York: Macmillan, c1978. ix, 166 p.: ill.; 24 cm. Includes index. 1. Chemical laboratories — Safety measures. I. Turk, Amos. joint author. II. T.
QD51.G73     542     *LC* 78-5122     *ISBN* 0023464208

**Steere, Norman V., comp.**     • **5.2639**
CRC handbook of laboratory safety / edited by Norman V. Steere. — 2d ed. — Cleveland: Chemical Rubber Co., [1971] xv, 854 p.: ill. (part col.); 28 cm. 1. Chemical laboratories — Safety measures. I. Chemical Rubber Company. II. T. III. Title: Handbook of laboratory safety.
QD51.S88 1971     542/.1     *LC* 79-22327

**Shugar, Gershon J., 1918-.**     **5.2640**
Chemical technicians' ready reference handbook / [by] Gershon J. Shugar, Ronald A. Shugar [and] Lawrence Bauman. — New York: McGraw-Hill, [1973] xi, 463 p.: ill.; 26 cm. 1. Chemistry — Manipulation — Handbooks, manuals, etc. I. Shugar, Ronald A., joint author. II. Bauman, Lawrence, joint author. III. T.
QD61.S58     542     *LC* 73-2585     *ISBN* 0070571759

**Techniques of chemistry. [Arnold Weissberger, editor].**     • **5.2641**
New York: Wiley-Interscience [1970-72; v. 1. pt. 1, 1971] 3 v. in 12: ill.; 24 cm. Based on Technique of organic chemistry.
QD61.T4     *LC* sn 83-7084

**Laser–induced chemical processes / edited by Jeffrey I. Steinfeld.**     **5.2642**
New York: Plenum Press, c1981. xii, 276 p.: ill.; 24 cm. 1. Lasers in chemistry I. Steinfeld, Jeffrey I.
QD63.L3 L37     541.3 19     *LC* 80-20478     *ISBN* 0306405873

**Miller, James Monroe.**     **5.2643**
Separation methods in chemical analysis / [by] James M. Miller. New York; London [etc.]: Wiley-Interscience, 1975. x, 309 p.: ill.; 24 cm. Text on lining papers. Index. 1. Separation (Technology) 2. Chemistry, Analytic I. T.
QD63.S4     544     *LC* 74-13781     *ISBN* 0471604909

**Karger, Barry L., 1939-.**     **5.2644**
An introduction to separation science [edited by Barry L. Karger, Lloyd R. Snyder [and] Csaba Horvath. New York, Wiley [1973] xix, 586 p. illus. 23 cm. 'A Wiley-Interscience publication.' 1. Separation (Technology) I. Snyder, Lloyd R. joint author. II. Horváth, Csaba, 1930- joint author. III. T.
QD63.S4 K37     544     *LC* 73-4016     *ISBN* 0471458600

**Morris, C. J. O. R. (Colin John Owen Rhonabwy)**    5.2645
Separation methods in biochemistry / C.J.O.R. Morris and P. Morris. — 2d ed. — New York: Wiley, 1976. 1045 p.: ill.; 24 cm. 'A Halsted Press book.' 1. Separation (Technology) 2. Biochemistry — Technique I. Morris, P., joint author. II. T.
QD63.S4 M6 1976    547/.34/92    *LC* 73-9380    *ISBN* 0470615796

**Aylward, G. H.**    5.2646
SI chemical data / G. H. Aylward, T. J. V. Findlay. — 2d ed. — Sydney; New York: J. Wiley, 1974, c1971. xiii, 136 p.; 25 cm. Published in 1966 under title: Chemical data book. 1. Chemistry — Tables. I. Findlay, T. J. V. (Triston John Victor) joint author. II. T.
QD65.A9 1974    540/.21/2    *LC* 74-189512    *ISBN* 0471038512

**Bauer, Edward L.**    5.2647
A statistical manual for chemists [by] Edward L. Bauer. — 2d ed. — New York: Academic Press, 1971. xiv, 193 p.: illus.; 22 cm. 1. Chemistry — Tables. 2. Mathematical statistics I. T.
QD65.B29 1971    540/.01/5195    *LC* 73-154404    *ISBN* 0120827565

**Gordon, Arnold J.**    5.2648
The chemist's companion: a handbook of practical data, techniques, and references [by] Arnold J. Gordon and Richard A. Ford. — New York: Wiley, [1972] xii, 537 p.: illus.; 28 cm. 'A Wiley-Interscience publication.' 1. Chemistry — Handbooks, manuals, etc. I. Ford, Richard A., joint author. II. T.
QD65.G64    542    *LC* 72-6660    *ISBN* 0471315907

**Handbook of chemistry and physics: a ready–reference book of**    5.2649
**chemical and physical data / editor–in–chief, Robert C. Weast; associate editors, Melvin J. Astle, William H. Beyer.**
66th ed. — Boca Raton, Fla.: CRC Press, c1985-6. 1 v. (various pagings); 26 cm. (CRC handbook series) 1. Chemistry — Tables. 2. Physics — Tables. I. Weast, Robert C. II. Astle, Melvin J. III. Beyer, William H. IV. Chemical Rubber Company. V. Title: Handbook of chemistry and physics.
QD65.H3    *LC* 13-11056    *ISBN* 0849304660

**Lange, Norbert Adolph, 1892-1970.**    5.2650
Lange's Handbook of chemistry / editor, John A. Dean; formerly compiled and edited by Norbert Adolph Lange. — 13th ed. — New York: McGraw-Hill, c1985. 1 v. (various pagings): ill. 1. Chemistry — Handbooks, manuals, etc. I. Dean, John Aurie, 1921- II. T. III. Title: Handbook of chemistry.
QD65.L3x 1985    TP151 L3 1979.    540/.2/02    *ISBN* 0070161925

**Linke, William F., 1924-.**    • 5.2651
Solubilities: inorganic and metal–organic compounds; a compilation of solubility data from the periodical literature. 4th ed. by William F. Linke. Washington, American Chemical Society, 1958-. v. 24 cm. 'A revision and continuation of the compilation originated by Atherton Seidell.' 1. Solubility — Tables. I. Seidell, Atherton, 1878- Solubilities of inorganic and organic substances II. T.
QD66.L5    *LC* 65-6490

---

# QD71–142 ANALYTICAL
# CHEMISTRY

## QD71–77 General Works

**Feigl, Fritz, 1891-.**    • 5.2652
Chemistry of specific, selective, and sensitive reactions / translated by Ralph E. Oesper. — New York: Academic Press, 1949. xiv, 740 p. 1. Chemistry, Analytic 2. Chemical reactions I. T.
QD73.F4    *LC* 49-10034

**Surrey, Alexander Robert, 1914-.**    • 5.2653
Name reactions in organic chemistry. 2d ed., rev. and enl. New York: Academic Press, 1961. 278 p.: ill.; 24 cm. Includes bibliography. 1. Chemical reactions 2. Chemistry, Organic I. T.
QD73.S8 1961    547.2    *LC* 61-65187

**Wilson, Cecil Leeburn.**    • 5.2654
Comprehensive analytical chemistry / edited by Cecil L. Wilson and David W. Wilson. — Amsterdam; New York: Elsevier Pub. Co., 1959-. v.: ill., diagrs., tables.; 24 cm. Vols. 9- < 10, 12A, 12C, 14 > edited by G. Svehla, have title: Wilson and Wilson's Comprehensive analytical chemistry. 1. Chemistry,

Analytic I. Wilson, David Woodburn, 1917- II. Svehla, G. III. T. IV. Title: Wilson and Wilson's Comprehensive analytical chemistry.
QD75.W75    543 19    *LC* 58-10158

**Budevsky, O.**    5.2655
Foundations of chemical analysis / O. Budevsky; translation editors: R. A. Chalmers & M. R. Masson. — Chichester: Ellis Horwood Ltd., 1979. 372 p.: ill.; 24 cm. — (Ellis Horwood series in analytical chemistry) 1. Chemistry, Analytic I. Chalmers, Robert Alexander. II. Masson, M. R. (Mary R.) III. T. IV. Title: Chemical analysis.
QD75.2 B83    *LC* 79-40240    *ISBN* 0853121133

**Kolthoff, I. M. (Izaak Maurits), 1894-.**    5.2656
Treatise on analytical chemistry / edited by I.M. Kolthoff and Philip J. Elving. — 2d ed. — New York: Wiley, c1978-. v.: ill.; 25 cm. Pt. 1, v. 8- : edited by Philip J. Elving; associated editor, Edward J. Meehan. 'An Interscience publication.' 1. Chemistry, Analytic I. Elving, Philip Juliber, 1913- II. Meehan, Edward J. III. T.
QD75.2.K64 1978    543    *LC* 78-1707    *ISBN* 047103438X

**Methodicum chimicum: a critical survey of proven methods and**    5.2657
**their application in chemistry, natural science, and medicine / editor–in–chief, Friedhelm Korte; volume editors, H. Aebi ... [et al.].**
New York: Academic Press, 1974-. v. in    : ill.; 28 cm. 1. Chemistry, Analytic I. Korte, Friedhelm. II. Aebi, Hugo.
QD75.2.M47    543

**Physical methods in modern chemical analysis / edited by**    5.2658
**Theodore Kuwana.**
New York: Academic Press, 1978. v. : ill.; 24 cm. 1. Chemistry, Analytic I. Kuwana, Theodore.
QD75.2.P49    543    *LC* 77-92242    *ISBN* 0124308015

**The Analytical approach / edited by Jeanette G. Grasselli.**    5.2659
Washington, D.C.: American Chemical Society, 1983. x, 239 p.: ill.; 29 cm. 1. Chemistry, Analytic — Addresses, essays, lectures. I. Grasselli, Jeanette G.
QD75.25.A5 1983    543 19    *LC* 82-22618    *ISBN* 0841207534

**Miller, J. C. (Jane Charlotte)**    5.2660
Statistics for analytical chemistry / J.C. Miller and J.N. Miller. — Chichester: E. Horwood; New York: Halsted Press, 1984. 202 p.: ill.; 24 cm. (Ellis Horwood series in analytical chemistry.) 1. Chemistry, Analytic — Statistical methods. I. Miller, J. N. (James N.), 1943- II. T. III. Series.
QD75.4.S8 M55 1984    543/.0028 19    *LC* 84-19271    *ISBN* 0853126623

**American Chemical Society.**    5.2661
Reagent chemicals: American Chemical Society specifications, official from January 1, 1987. — 7th ed. — Washington, DC: ACS, 1986. xiii, 713 p.; 24 cm. Includes index. 1. Chemical tests and reagents I. T.
QD77.A54 1986    543/.01 19    *LC* 86-20569    *ISBN* 084120991X

**Welcher, Frank Johnson, 1907-.**    • 5.2662
Organic analytical reagents / by Frank J. Welcher. — New York: D. Van Nostrand company, inc., 1947-. v.; 24 cm. Includes bibliographies. 1. Chemical tests and reagents 2. Chemistry, Analytic 3. Chemistry, Organic I. T.
QD77.W415    544.11    *LC* 47-2480

---

# QD79 Chromatography.
# Instrumental Analysis. Thermal
# Analysis

**Chromatography: fundamentals and applications of**    5.2663
**chromatographic and electrophoretic methods / edited by E. Heftmann.**
Amsterdam; New York: Elsevier Scientific Pub. Co.; New York, NY: Distributors for the United States and Canada, Elsevier Science Pub. Co., 1983. 2 v.: ill.; 25 cm. — (Journal of chromatography library. v. 22A-B) 1. Chromatographic analysis I. Heftmann, Erich. II. Series.
QD79.C4 C485 1983    543/.089 19    *LC* 84-129336    *ISBN* 0444420452

**Stock, Ralph.**    5.2664
Chromatographic methods / R. Stock, C. B. F. Rice. — 3d ed. — London: Chapman and Hall; New York: distributed by Halsted Press, 1975 (c1974). viii, 383 p.: ill.; 23 cm. Includes index. 1. Chromatographic analysis I. Rice, Cedric Bertram Fitzsimons, joint author. II. T.
QD79.C4 S76    544/.92    *LC* 75-315040    *ISBN* 0412105608

**Jennings, Walter, 1922-.**    5.2665
Gas chromatography with glass capillary columns / Walter Jennings. — 2d ed. — New York: Academic Press, 1980. xiii, 320 p.: ill.; 24 cm. 1. Gas chromatography 2. Capillarity I. T.
QD79.C45 J46 1980    543/.0896 19    *LC* 79-8851    *ISBN* 012384360X

**High–performance liquid chromatography / John H. Knox ... [et**    5.2666
**al.].**
Edinburgh: Edinburgh University Press, [1979] viii, 205 p.: ill.; 24 cm. 1. High performance liquid chromatography I. Knox, John H.
QD79.C454 H53    544/.924    *LC* 79-338437    *ISBN* 0852243413

**Snyder, Lloyd R.**    5.2667
Introduction to modern liquid chromatography / L. R. Snyder, J. J. Kirkland. — 2d ed. — New York: Wiley, c1979. xix, 863 p.: ill.; 24 cm. 'A Wiley-Interscience publication.' 1. Liquid chromatography I. Kirkland, J. J. (Joseph Jack), 1925- joint author. II. T.
QD79.C454 S58 1979    544/.924    *LC* 79-4537    *ISBN* 0471038229

**Ewing, Galen Wood, 1914-.**    5.2668
Instrumental methods of chemical analysis / Galen W. Ewing. — 5th ed. — New York: McGraw-Hill, c1985. xvi, 538 p.: ill.; 25 cm. 1. Instrumental analysis I. T.
QD79.I5 E95 1985    543/.08 19    *LC* 84-12209    *ISBN* 0070198578

**Willard, Hobart Hurd, 1881-.**    5.2669
Instrumental methods of analysis / Hobart H. Willard ... [et al.]. — 6th ed. — New York: Van Nostrand, c1981. xxiv, 1030 p.: ill.; 25 cm. Previous ed.: Hobart H. Willard, Lynne L. Merritt, Jr., John A. Dean. 5th ed. 1974. 1. Instrumental analysis I. T.
QD79.I5 I52 1981    543/.08 19    *LC* 80-51096    *ISBN* 0442245025

**Wendlandt, Wesley William.**    5.2670
Thermal analysis / Wesley Wm. Wendlandt. — 3rd ed. — New York: Wiley, c1986. xviii, 814 p.: ill.; 24 cm. (Chemical analysis. 0069-2883; v. 19) 'A Wiley-Interscience publication.' Includes bibliographies and index. 1. Thermal analysis I. T. II. Series.
QD79.T38 W45 1986    543/.086 19    *LC* 85-12419    *ISBN* 0471884774

---

# QD81–98 Qualitative Analysis

**Feigl, Fritz, 1891-.**    • 5.2671
[Qualitative Analyse mit Hilfe von Tüpfelreaktionen. English] Spot tests in inorganic analysis, by Fritz Feigl, and Vinzenz Anger. Translated by Ralph E. Oesper. 6th English ed., rev. & enl. Amsterdam, New York, Elsevier Pub. Co., 1972. xxix, 669 p. illus. 23 cm. Translation of the first part of a work originally published under title: Qualitative Analyse mit Hilfe von Tüpfelreaktionen. 1. Chemistry, Analytic — Qualitative 2. Spot tests (Chemistry) I. Anger, Vinzenz, joint author. II. T.
QD81.F453 1972    544/.834    *LC* 76-135494    *ISBN* 0444409297

**Vogel, Arthur Israel.**    5.2672
[Qualitative inorganic analysis] Vogel's qualitative inorganic analysis. — 6th ed. / rev. by G. Svehla. — Harlow, Essex, England: Longman Scientific & Technical; New York: Wiley, 1987. ix, 310 p.: ill.; 24 cm. Previous ed. as: Vogel's textbook of macro and semimicro qualitative inorganic analysis. 1979. 1. Chemistry, Analytic — Qualitative 2. Chemistry, Inorganic I. Svehla, G. II. Vogel, Arthur Israel. Textbook of macro and semimicro qualitative inorganic analysis. III. T. IV. Title: Qualitative inorganic analysis.
QD81.V6 1987    544 19    *LC* 86-10453    *ISBN* 0470207108

**Moeller, Therald.**    5.2673
Ions in aqueous systems; an introduction to chemical equilibrium and solution chemistry [by] Therald Moeller [and] Rod O'Connor. — New York: McGraw-Hill, [1971, c1972] x, 367 p.: illus.; 23 cm. 1. Chemistry, Analytic — Qualitative 2. Ionic solutions 3. Chemical equilibrium I. O'Connor, Rod, 1934- joint author. II. T.
QD83.M8    544    *LC* 70-147163    *ISBN* 0070426473

## QD95–96 Spectrum Analysis

**Crooks, J. E.**    5.2674
The spectrum in chemistry / J.E. Crooks. — London: Academic Press, 1978. x, 313 p.: ill.; 23 cm. 1. Spectrum analysis I. T.
QD95.C72    QD95 C72.    *LC* 77-81375    *ISBN* 0121955508

**Jaffé, Hans H.**    • 5.2675
Theory and applications of ultraviolet spectroscopy [by] H. H. Jaffé and Milton Orchin. — New York: Wiley, [1962] 624 p.: illus.; 24 cm. 1. Ultraviolet spectroscopy I. Orchin, Milton, 1914- joint author. II. T. III. Title: Ultraviolet spectroscopy.
QD95.J24    544.6    *LC* 62-15181

**Kirkbright, G. F.**    5.2676
Atomic absorption and fluorescence spectroscopy / G. F. Kirkbright, M. Sargent. — London; New York: Academic Press, 1975 (c1974). ix, 798 p.: ill.; 24 cm. 1. Atomic absorption spectroscopy 2. Fluorescence spectroscopy I. Sargent, M., joint author. II. T.
QD96.A8 K57    QD96A8 K57.    543/.085    *LC* 75-305689    *ISBN* 0124097502

**Symons, M. C. R.**    5.2677
Chemical and biochemical aspects of electron–spin resonance spectroscopy / Martyn Symons. — New York: J. Wiley, c1978. xiii, 190 p.: ill.; 24 cm. 'A Halsted Press book.' 1. Electron paramagnetic resonance spectroscopy I. T.
QD96.E4 S95    543/.085    *LC* 78-2837    *ISBN* 0740263598

**Nakamoto, Kazuo, 1922-.**    5.2678
Infrared and Raman spectra of inorganic and coordination compounds / Kazuo Nakamoto. — 4th ed. — New York: Wiley, c1986. xi, 484 p.: ill.; 24 cm. 'A Wiley-Interscience publication.' 1. Infrared spectroscopy 2. Raman spectroscopy I. T.
QD96.I5 N33 1986    543/.08583 19    *LC* 86-1345    *ISBN* 0471010669

**Pouchert, Charles J.**    5.2679
The Aldrich library of infrared spectra / Charles J. Pouchert. — Ed. 3. — Milwaukee, Wis. (940 W. St. Paul Ave., Milwaukee 53233): Aldrich Chemical Co., c1981. xxiii, 1873 p.: chiefly ill.; 32 cm. Includes indexes. 1. Infrared spectroscopy — Tables. I. Aldrich Chemical Company. II. T.
QD96.I5 P67 1981    547.3/08583 19    *LC* 81-67533

**Rose, M. E.**    5.2680
Mass spectrometry for chemists and biochemists / M.E. Rose, R.A.W. Johnstone. — Cambridge [Cambridgeshire]; New York: Cambridge University Press, 1982. xiii, 307 p.: ill.; 24 cm. — (Cambridge texts in chemistry and biochemistry.) Includes index. 1. Mass spectrometry I. Johnstone, R. A. W. (Robert Alexander Walker) II. T. III. Series.
QD96.M3 R67 1982    543/.0873 19    *LC* 81-10122    *ISBN* 0521237297

**Becker, Edwin D.**    5.2681
High resolution NMR: theory and chemical applications / Edwin D. Becker. — 2d ed. — New York: Academic Press, 1980. xiv, 354 p.: ill.; 24 cm. 1. Nuclear magnetic resonance spectroscopy I. T.
QD96.N8 B43 1980    538/.3    *LC* 79-26540    *ISBN* 0120846608

**Breitmaier, E.**    5.2682
[$^{13}$C-NMR-Spektroskopie. English] $^{13}$C NMR spectroscopy: a working manual with exercises / Eberhard Breitmaier and Gerhard Bauer; translated from the German by Bruce K. Cassels. — Chur [Switzerland]; New York: Harwood Academic Publishers, c1984. x, 356 p.: ill.; 24 cm. (MMI Press polymer monograph series. 0275-7265; v. 3) Translation of: $^{13}$C-NMR-Spektroskopie. Includes index. 1. Nuclear magnetic resonance spectroscopy — Handbooks, manuals, etc. 2. Carbon — Isotopes — Spectra — Handbooks, manuals, etc. I. Bauer, Gerhard. II. T. III. Series.
QD96.N8 B7313 1984    543/.0877 19    *LC* 84-8942    *ISBN* 3718600226

**Pouchert, Charles J.**    5.2683
The Aldrich library of NMR spectra / Charles J. Pouchert. — Ed. 2. — Milwaukee, Wis. (P.O. Box 355, Milwaukee 53201): Aldrich Chemical Co., c1983. 2 v.: chiefly ill.; 32 cm. Includes indexes. 1. Nuclear magnetic resonance spectroscopy — Tables. I. Aldrich Chemical Company. II. T. III. Title: Aldrich library of N.M.R. spectra.
QD96.N8 P68 1983    538/.362 19    *LC* 83-70633

**Ghosh, Pradip K.**    5.2684
Introduction to photoelectron spectroscopy / Pradip K. Ghosh. — New York: Wiley, [1983] x, 377 p.: ill.; 24 cm. — (Chemical analysis. 0069-2883: v. 67) Rev. ed. of: A whiff of photoelectron spectroscopy. 1970. 'A Wiley-Interscience publication.' 1. Photoelectron spectroscopy I. T. II. Series.
QD96.P5 G48 1983    543/.0858 19    *LC* 82-17374    *ISBN* 0471064270

**Grasselli, Jeanette G.**    5.2685
Chemical applications of Raman spectroscopy / Jeanette G. Grasselli and Marcia K. Snavely, Bernard J. Bulkin. — New York: Wiley, c1981. x, 198 p.: ill.; 24 cm. 'A Wiley-Interscience publication.' 1. Raman spectroscopy I. Snavely, Marcia K. II. Bulkin, Bernard J. III. T.
QD96.R34 G7    543/.08584 19    *LC* 81-1326    *ISBN* 0471085413

## QD98 Other Special Methods

**Cheronis, Nicholas Dimitrius, 1896-1962.**                • **5.2686**
Semimicro qualitative organic analysis: the systematic identification of organic compounds / [by] Nicholas D. Cheronis, John B. Entrikin [and] Ernest M. Hodnett. — 3d ed. New York: Interscience Publishers, [1965] xi, 1060 p.: ill.; 25 cm. 1. Chemistry, Analytic — Qualitative 2. Chemistry, Organic — Tables. 3. Microchemistry I. Entrikin, John Bennett, 1899- joint author. II. Hodnett, Ernest Matelle, 1914- joint author. III. T.
QD98.C45 1965        547.348        LC 64-25892

## QD101–142 Quantitative Analysis

**Fritz, James S. (James Sherwood), 1924-.**                **5.2687**
Quantitative analytical chemistry / James S. Fritz, George H. Schenk. — 4th ed. — Boston: Allyn and Bacon, c1979. x, 661 p.: ill.; 24 cm. Includes index. 1. Chemistry, Analytic — Quantitative I. Schenk, George H. joint author. II. T.
QD101.2.F74 1979        545        LC 78-21616        ISBN 0205065279

**Laitinen, Herbert August, 1915-.**                **5.2688**
Chemical analysis; an advanced text and reference [by] Herbert A. Laitinen [and] Walter E. Harris. — 2d ed. — New York: McGraw-Hill, [1975] xix, 611 p.: illus.; 24 cm. — (McGraw-Hill series in advanced chemistry) 1. Chemistry, Analytic — Quantitative I. Harris, Walter Edgar, 1915- joint author. II. T.
QD101.2.L34 1975        545        LC 74-11497        ISBN 0070360863

**Skoog, Douglas A.**                **5.2689**
Analytical chemistry, an introduction [by] Douglas A. Skoog [and] Donald M. West. 2d ed. New York, Holt, Rinehart and Winston [1974] ix, 598 p. illus. 24 cm. 1. Chemistry, Analytic — Quantitative I. West, Donald M. joint author. II. T.
QD101.2.S55 1974        545        LC 73-16072        ISBN 0030019761

**Marczenko, Zygmunt.**                **5.2690**
Separation and spectrophotometric determination of elements / Zygmunt Marczenko; translation editor Mary Masson. — Chichester: E. Horwood; New York: Halsted Press, 1986. 678 p.: ill.; 25 cm. — Zygmunt Marczenko; translation editor Mary Masson. — (Ellis Horwood series in analytical chemistry.) Rev. ed. of: Spectrophotometric determination of elements. 1. Colorimetry 2. Chemical elements I. T. II. Series.
QD113.M38 1986        543/.0852 19        LC 86-2911        ISBN 047020334X

**Laboratory techniques in electroanalytical chemistry / editors,**        **5.2691**
**Peter T. Kissinger, William R. Heineman.**
New York: Dekker, c1984. xv, 751 p.: ill.; 24 cm. — (Monographs in electroanalytical chemistry and electrochemistry.) 1. Electrochemical analysis — Laboratory manuals. I. Kissinger, Peter T., 1944- II. Heineman, William R. III. Series.
QD115.L23 1984        543/.0871 19        LC 84-4274        ISBN 082471864X

**Engelhardt, Heinz, 1936-.**                **5.2692**
[Hochdruck-Flüssigkeits-Chromatographie. English] High performance liquid chromatography / Heinz Engelhardt; translated from the German by George Gutnikov. — Berlin; New York: Springer-Verlag, c1979. xii, 248 p.: ill.; 25 cm. (Chemical laboratory practice) 'Enlarged and revised translation of the 2nd edition [1977] of Hochdruck-Flüssigkeits-Chromatographie.' 1. Liquid chromatography I. Gutnikov, George, 1938- II. T.
QD117.C5 E5313        544/.924        LC 78-22002        ISBN 0387090053

**Standard methods of chemical analysis.**                • **5.2693**
6th ed. — Princeton, N.J.: Van Nostrand, [1962-66] 3 v. in 5.: illus. (part col.); 24 cm. Previous editions edited by W. W. Scott. 1. Chemistry, Analytic 2. Chemistry, Technical I. Furman, N. Howell (Nathaniel Howell), 1892-1965. ed. II. Welcher, Frank Johnson, 1907- ed. III. Scott, Wilfred Welday, 1876-1932, ed. Standard methods of chemical analysis.
QD131.S68        545        LC 62-2869

**Paul, A. (Amal)**                **5.2694**
Chemistry of glasses / A. Paul. — London; New York: Chapman and Hall, 1982. ix, 293 p.: ill.; 25 cm. 1. Glass I. T.
QD139.G5 P38 1982        620.1/44 19        LC 81-16793        ISBN 0412230208

## QD147–199 INORGANIC CHEMISTRY

## QD147–154 Reference Works. General Works

**Advances in inorganic chemistry and radiochemistry.**                • **5.2695**
v. 1- 1959-. New York, Academic Press. v. ill. 24 cm. Irregular. 1. Chemistry, Inorganic — Collected works. 2. Radiochemistry — Collected works. I. Eméleus, H. J. (Harry Julius) ed. II. Sharpe, A. G. ed.
QD151.A45        546.082        LC 59-7692

**Phillips, C. S. G. (Courtenay Stanley Goss)**                • **5.2696**
Inorganic chemistry / [by] C. S. G. Phillips and R. J. P. Williams. New York: Oxford University Press, 1965-1966. 2 v.: ill.; 24 cm. 1. Chemistry, Inorganic I. Williams, R. J. P. (Robert Joseph Paton) joint author. II. T.
QD151.P47        546        LC 65-27666

**Comprehensive inorganic chemistry. Editorial board: J. C.**        **5.2697**
**Bailar, Jr., H. J. Eméleus, Sir Ronald Nyholm [and] A. F.**
**Trotman–Dickenson (executive editor).**
[1st ed.]. — [Oxford]: Pergamon Press; distributed by Compendium Publishers [Elmsford, N.Y., 1973] 5 v.: illus.; 26 cm. 1. Chemistry, Inorganic I. Bailar, John Christian, 1904- ed. II. Trotman-Dickenson, A. F., ed.
QD151.2.C64        546        LC 77-189736        ISBN 008017275X

**Cotton, F. Albert (Frank Albert), 1930-.**                **5.2698**
Advanced inorganic chemistry: a comprehensive text / F. Albert Cotton and Geoffrey Wilkinson. — 4th ed., completely rev. from the original literature. — New York: Wiley, c1980. xvi, 1396 p.: ill.; 24 cm. 'A Wiley-Interscience publication.' 1. Chemistry, Inorganic I. Wilkinson, Geoffrey, Sir, 1921- joint author. II. T.
QD151.2.C68 1980        546        LC 79-22506        ISBN 0471027758

**Huheey, James E.**                **5.2699**
Inorganic chemistry: principles of structure and reactivity / James E. Huheey. — 3rd ed. — New York: Harper & Row, c1983. xvi, 936, [118] p.: ill.; 25 cm. Includes index. 1. Chemistry, Inorganic I. T.
QD151.2.H84 1983        546 19        LC 83-253        ISBN 0060429879

**Inorganic chemistry, series one / Consultant editor: H. J.**        **5.2700**
**Eméleus.**
London: Butterworths; Baltimore: University Park Press, 1972. 11 v.: ill.; 25 cm. — (MTP international review of science.) 1. Chemistry, Inorganic — Collected works. I. Eméleus, H. J. (Harry Julius) ed. II. Series.
QD151.2.I5        546        LC 76-37370

**Moeller, Therald.**                **5.2701**
Inorganic chemistry, a modern introduction / Therald Moeller. — New York: Wiley, c1982. viii, 846 p.: ill.; 24 cm. 'A Wiley-Interscience publication.' 1. Chemistry, Inorganic I. T.
QD151.2.M63 1982        546 19        LC 81-16455        ISBN 0471612308

**Purcell, Keith F., 1932-.**                **5.2702**
Inorganic chemistry / Keith F. Purcell, John C. Kotz. Philadelphia: Saunders, 1977. xix, 1116 p.: ill.; 27 cm. (Saunders golden sunburst series) 1. Chemistry, Inorganic I. Kotz, John C. joint author. II. T.
QD151.2.P87        546        LC 76-8585        ISBN 0721674070

**Douglas, Bodie Eugene, 1924-.**                **5.2703**
Problems for inorganic chemistry / Bodie E. Douglas, Darl H. McDaniel, John J. Alexander. — New York: Toronto: J. Wiley, 1983. 298 p.: ill.; 24 cm. 1. Chemistry, Inorganic — Examinations, questions, etc. I. McDaniel, Darl H. II. Alexander, John J. III. T.
QD154.D73 1983        ISBN 0471895059

**Angelici, Robert J.**                **5.2704**
Synthesis and technique in inorganic chemistry / Robert J. Angelici. 2d ed. — Philadelphia: Saunders, 1977. xiv, 237 p.: ill.; 24 cm. (Saunders golden sunburst series) 1. Chemistry, Inorganic — Laboratory manuals I. T.
QD155.A53 1977        546/.028        LC 76-4244        ISBN 0721612814

# QD156 Inorganic Synthesis

**Inorganic syntheses.** • **5.2705**
v. 1-. New York [etc.] McGraw-Hill [etc.] 1939-. v. ill. 24 cm. 'Initiated at the Chicago meeting of the American Chemical Society, Sept. 1933.' 1. Chemistry, Inorganic — Synthesis — Periodicals. I. Booth, Harold Simmons, 1891- II. American Chemical Society.
QD156.I56    541/.39    *LC* 39-23015

**Jolly, William L.** • **5.2706**
The synthesis and characterization of inorganic compounds [by] William L. Jolly. — Englewood Cliffs, N.J.: Prentice-Hall, [1970] xi, 590 p.: illus.; 24 cm. — (Prentice-Hall international series in chemistry) 1. Chemistry, Inorganic — Synthesis I. T.
QD156.J65    541/.39    *LC* 78-100587    *ISBN* 0138799326

**Preparative inorganic reactions / Editor: William L. Jolly.** • **5.2707**
New York: Interscience Publishers, 1964-. 6 v.: ill.; 24 cm. Vols. 6- have imprint: New York, Wiley-Interscience. 1. Chemistry, Inorganic — Synthesis I. Jolly, William L. ed.
QD156.P74    541/.39    *LC* 64-17052    *ISBN* 0471446882

# QD162–181 Gases. Metals. Special Elements

**Basolo, Fred, 1920-.** • **5.2708**
Mechanisms of inorganic reactions; a study of metal complexes in solution [by] Fred Basolo and Ralph G. Pearson. — 2d ed. — New York: Wiley, [1967] xi, 701 p.: illus.; 24 cm. 1. Chemistry, Inorganic 2. Chemical reactions 3. Metals I. Pearson, Ralph G. joint author. II. T.
QD171.B32 1967    546.3    *LC* 66-28755

**Parish, Richard Vernon, 1934-.** **5.2709**
The metallic elements / R. V. Parish. — London; New York: Longman, 1977. xii, 254 p.: ill.; 25 cm. 1. Metals I. T.
QD171.P33    546/.3    *LC* 76-54330    *ISBN* 0582442788

**Brown, Herbert Charles, 1912-.** **5.2710**
Boranes in organic chemistry, by Herbert C. Brown. — Ithaca [N.Y.]: Cornell University Press, [1972] xiv, 462 p.: illus.; 24 cm. — (George Fisher Baker non-resident lectureship in chemistry at Cornell University.) 1. Borane 2. Chemistry, Organic — Synthesis I. T. II. Series.
QD181.B1 B73    547/.05/671    *LC* 79-165516    *ISBN* 0801406811

**Emsley, J. (John)** **5.2711**
The chemistry of phosphorus: environmental, organic, inorganic, biochemical, and spectroscopic aspects / John Emsley & Dennis Hall. New York: Wiley, c1976. xi, 563 p.: ill.; 26 cm. 'A Halsted Press book.' 1. Phosphorus I. Hall, Dennis. joint author. II. T.
QD181.P1 E45 1976    546/.712    *LC* 75-17432    *ISBN* 0470238690

**Goldwhite, Harold.** **5.2712**
Introduction to phosphorus chemistry / Harold Goldwhite. — Cambridge [Eng.]; New York: Cambridge University Press, 1981. xiv, 113 p.: ill.; 24 cm. — (Cambridge texts in chemistry and biochemistry.) Includes index. 1. Phosphorus I. T. II. Series.
QD181.P1 G67    546/.712    *LC* 79-27141    *ISBN* 0521229782

**Liebau, Friedrich, 1926-.** **5.2713**
Structural chemistry of silicates: structure, bonding, and classification / Friedrich Liebau. — Berlin; New York: Springer-Verlag, c1985. xii, 347 p.: 136 ill.; 25 cm. Includes indexes. 1. Silicates I. T.
QD181.S6 L614 1985    546/.68324 19    *LC* 84-23532    *ISBN* 0387137475

# QD241–449 ORGANIC CHEMISTRY

# QD241–257 General Works

**Comprehensive organic chemistry: the synthesis and reactions of organic compounds / chairman and deputy chairman of the editorial board, Sir Derek Barton and W. David Ollis.** **5.2714**
1st ed. — Oxford; New York: Pergamon Press, 1979. 6 v.: ill.; 28 cm. 1. Chemistry, Organic — Collected works. I. Barton, Derek, Sir, 1918- II. Ollis, W. David.
QD245.C65 1979    547    *LC* 78-40502    *ISBN* 0080213197

**Dictionary of organic compounds.** **5.2715**
5th ed. — New York: Chapman and Hall, 1982. 5 v.: ill.; 29 cm. Includes two unnumbered index volumes. 1. Chemistry, Organic — Dictionaries.
QD246.D5 1982    547/.003/21 19    *LC* 82-2280    *ISBN* 0412170000

**Gould, Edwin S.** • **5.2716**
Mechanism and structure in organic chemistry. New York: Holt [1959] 790 p.: ill.; 25 cm. 1. Chemistry, Organic I. T.
QD251.G6    547.139    *LC* 59-8696

**Organic reactions.** • **5.2717**
v. 1-. New York, John Wiley & Sons, 1942-. v. ill., tables. 24 cm. 'Editorial board [v. 1- ] Roger Adams, editor-in-chief, Werner E. Buchmann, Louis F. Fieser [and others].' 1. Chemistry, Organic — Collected works. I. Adams, Roger, 1889-1971. ed.
QD251.O7    547    *LC* 42-20265

**Rodd, E. H. ed.** • **5.2718**
[Chemistry of carbon compounds] Rodd's Chemistry of carbon compounds; a modern comprehensive treatise. 2d ed., edited by S. Coffey. Amsterdam, New York, Elsevier Pub. Co., 1964- <86 >. < v. 1, pts. A-G; v. 2, pts. A-E; v. 3, pts. A-H; v. 4, pts. A-H, K-L; in 30 > illus. 24 cm. Vol. IV, pt. C- edited by Martin F. Ansell. 1. Chemistry, Organic 2. Carbon compounds I. Coffey, S. (Samuel) II. Ansell, Martin F. (Martin Frederick) III. T. IV. Title: Chemistry of carbon compounds.
QD251.R6 1964    547    *LC* 64-4605    *ISBN* 0444406646

**Carey, Francis A., 1937-.** **5.2719**
Advanced organic chemistry. / Francis A. Carey and Richard J. Sundberg. — 2nd ed. — New York: Plenum Press, c1984 [pt. B. 1983]. 2 v.: ill.; 26 cm. 1. Chemistry, Organic I. Sundberg, Richard J., 1938- II. T.
QD251.2.C36 1984    547/.2 19    *LC* 83-6278    *ISBN* 0306410885

**Gordon, John E., 1931-.** **5.2720**
How to succeed in organic chemistry / John E. Gordon. — New York: Wiley, c1979. xiv, 594 p.: ill.; 26 cm. — (Wiley self-teaching guides) Includes index. 1. Chemistry, Organic — Programmed instruction. I. T.
QD251.2.G67    547/.007/7    *LC* 78-21496    *ISBN* 0471030104

**March, Jerry, 1929-.** **5.2721**
Advanced organic chemistry: reactions, mechanisms, and structure / Jerry March. — 3rd ed. — New York: Wiley, c1985. xiii, 1346 p.: ill.; 25 cm. 'A Wiley-Interscience publication.' 1. Chemistry, Organic I. T.
QD251.2.M37 1985    547 19    *LC* 84-15311    *ISBN* 0471888419

**Morrison, Robert Thornton, 1918-.** **5.2722**
Organic chemistry / Robert Thornton Morrison, Robert Neilson Boyd. — 5th ed. — Boston: Allyn and Bacon, c1987. xxvii, 1434 p.: ill. (some col.); 27 cm. Includes index. 1. Chemistry, Organic I. Boyd, Robert Neilson. II. T.
QD251.2.M67 1987    547 19    *LC* 87-1003    *ISBN* 0205084532

**Roberts, John D., 1918-.** **5.2723**
Basic principles of organic chemistry / John D. Roberts, Marjorie C. Caserio. — 2d ed. — Menlo Park, Calif.: W. A. Benjamin, c1977. xix, 1596 p.: ill.; 25 cm. 1. Chemistry, Organic I. Caserio, Marjorie C., joint author. II. T.
QD251.2.R6 1977    547    *LC* 77-76749    *ISBN* 0805383298

**Streitwieser, Andrew, 1927-.** • **5.2724**
Molecular orbital theory for organic chemists. New York, Wiley [1961] 489 p. illus. 24 cm. 1. Chemistry, Organic 2. Molecular orbitals I. T.
QD255.S88    547.122    *LC* 61-17363

**Grasselli, Jeanette G.** **5.2725**
Atlas of spectral data and physical constants for organic compounds / editors, Jeanette G. Grasselli, William M. Ritchey. — 2d ed. — Cleveland: CRC Press, [1975] 6 v.: ill.; 32 cm. At head of title: CRC. First ed. (1973), edited by J. G.

Grasselli, has title: CRC atlas of spectral data and physical constants for organic compounds. 1. Chemistry, Organic — Tables. 2. Spectrum analysis — Tables. I. Ritchey, William M., joint author. II. Chemical Rubber Company. III. CRC atlas of spectral data and physical constants for organic compounds. IV. T.
QD257.7.G7 1975    547/.0021/2    LC 75-2452    ISBN 0878193170

# QD258–281 Operations in Organic Chemistry

**Huyser, Earl S., 1927-.**      • **5.2726**
Free–radical chain reactions [by] Earl S. Huyser. New York, Wiley-Interscience [1970] vii, 387 p. 23 cm. 1. Free radical reactions I. T.
QD258.H95    547/.1/39    LC 77-106013    ISBN 0471425966

**Adams, Roger, 1889-1971.**      **5.2727**
[Elementary laboratory experiments in organic chemistry] Laboratory experiments in organic chemistry / Roger Adams, John R. Johnson, Charles F. Wilcox. — 7th ed. — New York: Macmillan, c1979. xviii, 538 p.: ill.; 24 cm. First published in 1928 under title: Elementary laboratory experiments in organic chemistry. Includes index. 1. Chemistry, Organic — Laboratory manuals I. Johnson, John Raven, 1900- joint author. II. Wilcox, Charles F., 1930- joint author. III. T.
QD261.A2 1979    547/.0028    LC 78-4482    ISBN 0023005904

**Fieser, Louis Frederick, 1899-.**      **5.2728**
Organic experiments / Louis F. Fieser, Kenneth L. Williamson. — 6th ed. — Lexington, Mass.: D.C. Heath, c1987. xiii, 495, xv p.: ill.; 24 cm. 1. Chemistry, Organic — Laboratory manuals I. Williamson, Kenneth L. II. T.
QD261.F5 1987    547/.0078 19    LC 86-81267    ISBN 0669121843

**Newman, Melvin Spencer.**      **5.2729**
An advanced organic laboratory course / [by] Melvin S. Newman. — New York: Macmillan, [1971, c1972] xvi, 229 p.: ill.; 24 cm. — (A Series of books in chemistry) 1. Chemistry, Organic — Laboratory manuals I. T.
QD261.N46    547/.0028    LC 70-155927

**Vogel, Arthur Israel.**      **5.2730**
Vogel's Textbook of practical organic chemistry, including qualitative organic analysis. — 4th ed. / rev. by the following members of the School of Chemistry, Thames (formerly Woolwich) Polytechnic, B. S. Furniss ...[et al.]. — London; New York: Longman, 1978. xxxv, 1368 p.: ill.; 24 cm. Third ed. published in 1956 under title: A text-book of practical organic chemistry, including qualitative organic analysis. 1. Chemistry, Organic — Laboratory manuals 2. Chemistry, Analytic — Qualitative I. Furniss, Brian Stanley. II. T. III. Title: Practical organic chemistry, including qualitative organic analysis.
QD261.V63 1978    547 19    LC 77-23559    ISBN 0582442508

## QD262 Organic Synthesis

**Buehler, Calvin Adam, 1896-.**      • **5.2731**
Survey of organic syntheses [by] Calvin A. Buehler [and] Donald E. Pearson. — New York: Wiley-Interscience, [1970]-c1976. 2 v.: illus.; 24 cm. 1. Chemistry, Organic — Synthesis I. Pearson, Donald Emanual, 1914- joint author. II. T.
QD262.B78    547/.2    LC 73-112590    ISBN 047111670X

**Fieser, Louis Frederick, 1899-.**      • **5.2732**
Reagents for organic synthesis [by] Louis F. Fieser [and] Mary Fieser. New York: Wiley [1967-<c1986 >. v. <1-12 >: ill.; 24 cm. Authors' names in reverse order in v. 2-7. Vols. 8, <10-12 > by Mary Fieser. Vol. 9 by Mary Fieser, Rick L. Danheiser, William Roush. Vols. 8-<12 > have title: Fieser and Fieser's Reagents for organic synthesis. Vols. 2-3 have imprint: New York, Wiley-Interscience. Vols. 4-<12 > A Wiley-Interscience publication. 1. Chemistry, Organic — Synthesis 2. Chemical tests and reagents I. Fieser, Mary, 1909- joint author. II. T. III. Title: Fieser and Fieser's Reagents for organic synthesis.
QD262.F5    547/.2 19    LC 66-27894    ISBN 0471258768

**Fleming, Ian, 1935-.**      **5.2733**
Selected organic syntheses; a guidebook for organic chemists. — London; New York: Wiley, [1973] viii, 227 p.; 24 cm. 1. Chemistry, Organic — Synthesis I. T.
QD262.F58    547/.2    LC 72-615    ISBN 0471263907

**Greene, Theodora W., 1931-.**      **5.2734**
Protective groups in organic synthesis / Theodora W. Greene. — New York: Wiley, c1981. xiii, 349 p.; 24 cm. 'A Wiley-Interscience publication.' 1. Chemistry, Organic — Synthesis 2. Protective groups (Chemistry) I. T.
QD262.G665    547/.2 19    LC 80-25348    ISBN 0471057649

**Harrison, Ian T.**      **5.2735**
Compendium of organic synthetic methods [by] Ian T. Harrison and Shuyen Harrison. — New York: Wiley-Interscience, [1971]-. v.; 24 cm. 1. Chemistry, Organic — Synthesis I. Harrison, Shuyen, joint author. II. T.
QD262.H32    547/.2    LC 71-162800    ISBN 047135550X

**House, Herbert O.**      • **5.2736**
Modern synthetic reactions [by] Herbert O. House. — 2d ed. — Menlo Park, Calif.: W. A. Benjamin, 1972. 856 p.; 24 cm. — (Organic chemistry monograph series.) 1. Chemistry, Organic — Synthesis 2. Chemical reactions I. T. II. Series.
QD262.H67 1972    547/.2    LC 78-173958

**Norman, R. O. C. (Richard Oswald Chandler)**      **5.2737**
Principles of organic synthesis / R. O. C. Norman. — 2d ed. — London: Chapman and Hall; New York: Wiley, 1978. xiii, 800 p.: ill.; 24 cm. 'A Halsted Press book.' 1. Chemistry, Organic — Synthesis I. T.
QD262.N6 1978    547/.2    LC 78-784    ISBN 0470263172

**Organic syntheses.**      • **5.2738**
v. 1- 1921-. New York [etc.] J. Wiley & Sons, inc. [etc.] v. ill., diagrs. 24 cm. Annual. 'An annual publication of satisfactory methods for the preparation of organic chemicals.' 1. Chemistry, Organic — Synthesis I. Adams, Roger, 1889-1971. ed. II. Clarke, Hans Thacher, 1887-1972. joint ed. III. Conant, James Bryant, 1893-1978 joint ed. IV. Kamm, Oliver, b. 1888. joint ed.
QD262.O7    547.058    LC 21-17747

**Organic syntheses. Collective volume.**      • **5.2739**
v. 1-. New York [etc.] J. Wiley and Sons, Inc. [etc.] 1932-. v. ill. 24 cm. Irregular. Bibliographical footnotes. Each vol. is a revision of 10 of the annual volumes. 1. Chemistry, Organic — Synthesis — Collected works.
QD262.O722    LC 42-5730

**Pizey, J. S.**      **5.2740**
Synthetic reagents [by] S. [i.e. J.] S. Pizey. Chichester, E. Horwood; New York, Halsted Press [1974]- <1985 >. v. <1, 3-6 > 24 cm. 1. Chemistry, Organic — Synthesis 2. Chemical tests and reagents I. T.
QD262.P58    547/.2    LC 73-14417    ISBN 0470691042

**Swan, John Melvin.**      **5.2741**
Organometallics in organic synthesis [by] J. M. Swan [and] D. St. C. Black. — London: Chapman and Hall [Distributed in the U.S.A. by Halsted Press, New York, 1974] 158 p.: illus.; 21 cm. — (Chapman and Hall chemistry textbook series) 1. Chemistry, Organic — Synthesis 2. Organometallic compounds I. Black, David St. Clair, joint author. II. T.
QD262.S89 1974    547/.05    LC 74-165116    ISBN 0412108704

**Warren, Stuart G.**      **5.2742**
Organic synthesis, the disconnection approach / Stuart Warren. — Chichester; New York: Wiley, c1982. xii, 391 p.: ill.; 24 cm. Includes index. 1. Chemistry, Organic — Synthesis I. T.
QD262.W284 1982    547/.2 19    LC 81-19694    ISBN 0471101605

## QD271–272 Organic Analysis

**Hamming, Mynard C.**      **5.2743**
Interpretation of mass spectra of organic compounds [by] Mynard C. Hamming [and] Norman G. Foster. — New York: Academic Press, 1972. xiv, 694 p.: illus.; 24 cm. 1. Mass spectrometry 2. Organic compounds — Spectra. I. Foster, Norman G., joint author. II. T.
QD271.H318 1972    547/.308/5    LC 72-87228    ISBN 0123221501

**Lyman, Warren J.**      **5.2744**
Handbook of chemical property estimation methods: environmental behavior of organic compounds / Warren J. Lyman, William F. Reehl, David H. Rosenblatt. — New York: McGraw-Hill, c1982. 977 p. in various pagings: ill.; 24 cm. 1. Organic compounds — Analysis. I. Reehl, William F. II. Rosenblatt, David Hirsch. III. T.
QD271.L95 1982    547.3 19    LC 81-23662    ISBN 0070391750

**Siggia, Sidney.**      **5.2745**
Instrumental methods of organic functional group analysis. Edited by Sidney Siggia. — New York: Wiley-Interscience, [1972] ix, 428 p.: illus.; 23 cm. 1. Chemistry, Organic 2. Instrumental analysis I. T.
QD271.S597    547/.308    LC 77-168642    ISBN 0471791105

**Cooper, James William, 1943-.**      **5.2746**
Spectroscopic techniques for organic chemists / James W. Cooper. — New York: Wiley, c1980. xv, 376 p.: ill.; 24 cm. 'A Wiley-Interscience publication.' 1. Spectrum analysis 2. Chemistry, Organic I. T.
QD272.S6 C66    547/.308/5 19    LC 79-23952    ISBN 0471051667

**Silverstein, Robert M. (Robert Milton), 1916-.**    **5.2747**
Spectrometric identification of organic compounds / Robert M. Silverstein, G. Clayton Bassler, Terence C. Morrill. — 4th ed. — New York: Wiley, c1981. 442 p.: ill.; 29 cm. 1. Spectrum analysis 2. Chemistry, Organic I. Bassler, G. Clayton. joint author. II. Morrill, Terence C. joint author. III. T. QD272.S6 S55 1981    54.3/0858 19    *LC* 80-20548    *ISBN* 0471029904

## QD281 Other Special Methods

**Olah, George A. (George Andrew), 1927-.**    **5.2748**
Friedel–Crafts chemistry, by George A. Olah. New York, Wiley [1973] 581 p. illus. 23 cm. (Interscience monographs on organic chemistry) 'A Wiley-Interscience publication.' Based on Friedel-Crafts and related reactions, edited by the author. 1. Friedel-Crafts reaction I. T. QD281.A5 O43    547/.21    *LC* 73-754    *ISBN* 0471653152

**Freifelder, Morris, 1907-.**    **5.2749**
Catalytic hydrogenation in organic synthesis: procedures and commentary / Morris Freifelder. — New York: Wiley, c1978. xiv, 191 p.: ill.; 24 cm. 'A Wiley-Interscience publication.' 1. Hydrogenation 2. Catalysis 3. Chemistry, Organic — Synthesis I. T. QD281.H8 F73    547/.23    *LC* 78-9458    *ISBN* 0471029459

**Oxidation in organic chemistry / edited by Kenneth B. Wiberg.**    **5.2750**
New York: Academic Press, 1965- < 1982 >. v. < 1-4 >: ill.; 24 cm. — (Organic chemistry; v. 5) Pts. B-<D > edited by Walter S. Trahanovsky. 1. Oxidation 2. Chemistry, Organic I. Wiberg, Kenneth B. II. Trahanovsky, Walter S., 1938- QD281.O9 W5    547/.23 19    *LC* 65-26047    *ISBN* 0126972508

**Flory, Paul J.**    **5.2751**
Principles of polymer chemistry. — Ithaca, N.Y.: Cornell University Press, 1953. 672p.,illus. (George Fisher Baker non-resident lectureship in chemistry at Cornell University.) 1. Polymers and polymerization I. T. II. Title: Polymer chemistry III. Series. QD281.P6 F58    541.7    *LC* 53-13473

**Sandler, Stanley R., 1935-.**    **5.2752**
Polymer syntheses [by] Stanley R. Sandler [and] Wolf Karo. New York, Academic Press, 1974-1980. 3 v. illus. 24 cm. (Organic chemistry; a series of monographs, v. 29) 1. Polymers and polymerization I. Karo, Wolf, 1924- joint author. II. T. QD281.P6 S27    547/.84    *LC* 73-2073    *ISBN* 0126185013

**Hudlicky, Milos, 1919-.**    **5.2753**
Reductions in organic chemistry / Milŏs Hudlický. — Chichester [West Sussex]: E. Horwood; New York: Halstead Press, 1984. xvi, 309 p.: ill.; 24 cm. — (Ellis Horwood books in organic chemistry.) Includes indexes. 1. Reduction, Chemical 2. Chemistry, Organic I. T. II. Series. QD281.R4 H83 1984    547/.23 19    *LC* 84-3768    *ISBN* 0853123454

## QD291 Indexes. Tables

**Rappoport, Zvi.**    • **5.2754**
Handbook of tables for organic compound identification. Compiled by Zvi Rappoport. 3d ed. Cleveland, Chemical Rubber Co. [1967] ix, 564 p. 28 cm. Previous editions, compiled by M. Frankel, published under Title: Tables for indentification of organic compounds. 1. Chemistry, Organic — Tables. I. Frankel, Max. Tables for indentification of organic compounds. II. T. QD291.R28 1967    547/.0021/2    *LC* 67-7118

## QD301–412 Compounds. Polymers

**The Chemistry of diazonium and diazo groups / edited by Saul Patai.**    **5.2755**
Chichester; Toronto: Wiley, 1978. 2 v. (xiv, 1069 p.); 24 cm. — (The Chemistry of functional groups; [v. 20]) 1. Diazo compounds I. Patai, Saul, 1918- II. Series. QD 245.C53    QD305.A9 C47.    547/.043    *LC* 75-6913    *ISBN* 0471994154

**Organic peroxides. Daniel Swern, editor.**    **5.2756**
New York: Wiley-Interscience, [1970-72] 3 v.: illus.; 23 cm. 1. Peroxides I. Swern, Daniel, 1916- ed. QD305.E7 O7    547 19    *LC* 72-84965    *ISBN* 0471839604

**Pines, Herman, 1902-.**    **5.2757**
Base–catalyzed reactions of hydrocarbons and related compounds / Herman Pines, Wayne M. Stalick. — New York: Academic Press, 1977. xi, 587 p.: ill.; 24 cm. 1. Hydrocarbons 2. Catalysis I. Stalick, Wayne M., joint author. II. T. QD305.H5 P55    547/.41    *LC* 76-27450    *ISBN* 012557150X

**Patai, Saul.**    • **5.2758**
The chemistry of alkenes / edited by Saul Patai. — London; New York: Interscience Publishers, 1964-1970. 2 v.: ill.; 24 cm. (Chemistry of functional groups.) Vol. 2 edited by Jacob Zabicky. 1. Olefins I. Zabicky, Jacob. II. T. III. Series. QD305.H7 P3    547.412    *LC* 64-25218

**The Chemistry of the carbon–carbon triple bond / edited by Saul Patai.**    **5.2759**
Chichester [Eng.]; New York: J. Wiley, 1978. 2 v. (xiv, 1065 p.): ill.; 24 cm. — (Chemistry of functional groups.) 1. Acetylene compounds I. Patai, Saul. II. Series. QD305.H8 C43    QD305H8 C43.    547/.413

**Patai, Saul.**    • **5.2760**
The chemistry of the carbon–nitrogen double bond; edited by Saul Patai. — London; New York: Interscience Publishers, 1970. xiii, 794 p.: illus.; 24 cm. — (Chemistry of functional groups.) 1. Organonitrogen compounds 2. Methylenimine. 3. Schiff bases I. T. II. Series. QD305.I6 P3    547/.044    *LC* 70-104166    *ISBN* 0471669423

**Patai, Saul.**    **5.2761**
The chemistry of the thiol group / Edited by Saul Patai. — London; New York: Wiley, 1975 (c1974). 2 v. (xiii, 956 p.): ill.; 24 cm. — (Chemistry of functional groups.) 'An Interscience publication.' 1. Thiols I. T. II. Series. QD305.T45 P37    547/.46/3    *LC* 74-3876    *ISBN* 0471669490

**The Carbohydrates: chemistry and biochemistry / edited by Ward Pigman, Derek Horton; assistant editor, Anthony Herp.**    **5.2762**
2nd ed. — New York: Academic Press, 1970-1980. 2 v. in 4: ill.; 24 cm. Vol. 1B edited by W. Pigman, D. Horton, and J. Wander. 1. Carbohydrates I. Pigman, William Ward, 1910- II. Horton, Derek, 1932- III. Herp, Anthony. QD321.P6243    547/.7/8 19    *LC* 68-26647    *ISBN* 0125563027

**Watson, James D., 1928-.**    • **5.2763**
The double helix; a personal account of the discovery of the structure of DNA, by James D. Watson. — [1st ed.]. — New York: Atheneum, 1968. xvi, 226 p.: illus., facsims., ports.; 22 cm. Autobiographical. 1. Watson, James D., 1928- 2. DNA I. T. QD341.A2 W315    547/.596    *LC* 68-16217

## QD380–388 Polymers

**Billmeyer, Fred W.**    **5.2764**
Textbook of polymer science / Fred W. Billmeyer, Jr. — 3rd ed. — New York: Wiley, c1984. xviii, 578 p.: ill.; 24 cm. 'A Wiley-Interscience publication.' 1. Polymers and polymerization I. T. QD381.B52 1984    668.9 19    *LC* 83-19870    *ISBN* 0471031968

**Mandelkern, Leo.**    **5.2765**
An introduction to macromolecules. — London: English Universities Press; New York: Springer-Verlag, 1973 (c1972). x, 161 p.: illus.; 23 cm. — (Heidelberg science library. v. 17) 1. Macromolecules I. T. II. Series. QD381.M37    547/.7    *LC* 72-83670    *ISBN* 0387900454

**Morawetz, Herbert.**    **5.2766**
Polymers: the origins and growth of a science / Herbert Morawetz. — New York: Wiley, c1985. xvi, 306 p.: ill.; 25 cm. 'A Wiley-Interscience publication.' Includes indexes. 1. Polymers and polymerization — History. I. T. QD381.M663 1985    547.7/09 19    *LC* 84-26996    *ISBN* 0471896381

**Price, Charles C. (Charles Coale), 1913-.**    **5.2767**
Geometry of molecules [by] Charles C. Price. New York, McGraw-Hill [1971] x, 118 p. illus. (part col.) 21 cm. (Chemistry-biology interface series) 1. Polymers and polymerization 2. Stereochemistry 3. Chemical bonds I. T. QD381.P68    547/.84    *LC* 77-159314

**Richards, E. G. (Edward Graham).**    **5.2768**
An introduction to the physical properties of large molecules in solution / E. G. Richards, with an additional chapter, The scattering of radiation by macromolecules [by] S. D. Dover. — Cambridge [Eng.]; New York: Cambridge University Press, 1980. xvii, 266 p.: ill.; 24 cm. (IUPAB biophysics series; 3)

Includes index. 1. Polymers and polymerization 2. Solution (Chemistry) I. Dover, S. D. (Stanley David) joint author. II. T.
QD381.R52     547.8/4     LC 79-41583     ISBN 0521231108

**Tobolsky, Arthur Victor.**     5.2769
Polymer science and materials. Edited by Arthur V. Tobolsky [and] Herman F. Mark. New York, Wiley-Interscience [1971-. v. illus. 23 cm. 1. Polymers and polymerization I. Mark, H. F. (Herman Francis), 1895- joint author. II. T.
QD381.T6     547/.84     LC 70-155908     ISBN 0471875813

**Williams, David John, 1937-.**     5.2770
Polymer science and engineering [by] David J. Williams. — Englewood Cliffs, N.J.: Prentice-Hall, [1971] xiii, 401 p.: illus.; 24 cm. — (Prentice-Hall international series in the physical and chemical engineering sciences) 1. Polymers and polymerization I. T.
QD381.W55     547/.84     LC 75-160255     ISBN 0136856365

**Cullis, C. F.**     5.2771
The combustion of organic polymers / by C.F. Cullis and M.M. Hirschler. — Oxford: Clarendon Press; New York: Oxford University Press, 1981. x, 419 p.: ill.; 24 cm. — (International series of monographs on chemistry.) Includes indexes. 1. Polymers and polymerization — Combustion. I. Hirschler, M. M. II. T. III. Series.
QD381.8.C84     547.7/04561 19     LC 80-41799     ISBN 0198513518

**Schnabel, W.**     5.2772
Polymer degradation: principles and practical applications / W. Schnabel. — New York: Macmillan, c1981. 227 p.: ill.; 24 cm. 1. Polymers and polymerization — Deterioration I. T.
QD381.8.S32 1981     LC 81-85158     ISBN 0029496403

**Brandrup, J., ed.**     5.2773
Polymer handbook. J. Brandrup, E. H. Immergut, editors. With the collaboration of W. McDowell. 2d ed. New York, Wiley [1975] 1 v. (various pagings) 29 cm. 'A Wiley Interscience publication.' 1. Polymers and polymerization — Tables. I. Immergut, E. H. joint ed. II. McDowell, W., joint ed. III. T.
QD388.B7 1975     547/.84/0202     LC 74-11381     ISBN 0471098043

## QD390–412 Other Organic Compounds

**Ring systems handbook.**     5.2774
1984 ed.-     . — Columbus, Ohio: American Chemical Society, c1984-. v.; 29 cm. 'A publication of Chemical Abstracts Service.' Vol. for 1984- issued in 4 parts: Ring formula file I; Ring systems file II; Ring formula index, Ring name index; and Ring WLN index. Updated by semiannual cumulative supplements. 1. Ring formation (Chemistry) — Collected works. 2. Cyclic compounds — Collected works. I. American Chemical Society. Chemical Abstracts Service.
QD390.R56     547/.5 19     LC 84-647353

**Comprehensive heterocyclic chemistry: the structure, reactions, synthesis, and uses of heterocyclic compounds / chairman of the editorial board, Alan R. Katritzky; co-chairman of the editorial board, Charles W. Rees.**     5.2775
1st ed. — Oxford [Oxfordshire]; New York: Pergamon Press, 1984. 8 v.: ill.; 28 cm. Includes indexes. 1. Heterocyclic compounds I. Katritzky, Alan R. II. Rees, Charles W. (Charles Wayne)
QD400.C65 1984     547/.59 19     LC 83-4264     ISBN 0080262007

**Paquette, Leo A.**     • 5.2776
Principles of modern heterocyclic chemistry [by] Leo A. Paquette. — New York: Benjamin, 1968. xiv, 401 p.; 22 cm. — (Organic chemistry monograph series.) 1. Heterocyclic compounds I. T. II. Series.
QD400.P34     547/.59     LC 68-11542

**The Porphyrins / edited by David Dolphin.**     5.2777
New York: Academic Press, 1978-c1979. 7 v.: ill.; 24 cm. 1. Porphyrin and porphyrin compounds I. Dolphin, David.
QD401.P825     547/.593     LC 77-14197     ISBN 0122201019

**Fieser, Louis Frederick, 1899-.**     • 5.2778
Steroids / Louis F. Fieser and Mary Fieser. — New York: Reinhold Pub. Corp., 1959. 945 p.: ill. Replaces the authors' Natural products related to phenanthrene (3d ed., 1949) 1. Steroids I. Fieser, Mary, 1909- II. T.
QD405.F44     LC 59-12534

**Collman, James P. (James Paddock) 1932-.**     5.2779
Principles and applications of organotransition metal chemistry / James P. Collman, Louis S. Hegedus; [editor, Aidan Kelly]. — Mill Valley, Calif.: University Science Books, c1980. 715 p.: ill.; 24 cm. 1. Organometallic compounds 2. Transition metal compounds I. Hegedus, Louis S. joint author. II. T.
QD411.C64     QD411 C64.     547/.056 19     LC 79-57228     ISBN 0935702032

**Comprehensive organometallic chemistry: the synthesis, reactions, and structures of organometallic compounds / editor, Sir Geoffrey Wilkinson, deputy editor, F. Gordon A. Stone, executive editor, Edward W. Abel.**     5.2780
1st ed. — Oxford [Oxfordshire]; New York: Pergamon Press, 1982. 9 v.: ill.; 28 cm. 1. Organometallic chemistry I. Wilkinson, Geoffrey, Sir, 1921- II. Stone, F. Gordon A. (Francis Gordon Albert), 1925- III. Abel, Edward W.
QD411.C65 1982     547/.05 19     LC 82-7595     ISBN 0080252699

**Dictionary of organometallic compounds.**     5.2781
London; New York: Chapman and Hall, 1984. 3 v.: ill. Includes index. 1. Organometallic compounds — Dictionaries. I. Chapman and Hall.
QD411.D53 1984     547/.05/0321 19     LC 84-19952     ISBN 0412247100

**Lukehart, Charles M., 1946-.**     5.2782
Fundamental transition metal organometallic chemistry / Charles M. Lukehart. — Monterey, Calif.: Brooks/Cole, c1985. xiv, 447 p.: ill.; 24 cm. 1. Organometallic chemistry 2. Transition metal compounds I. T.
QD411.L857 1985     547/.05 19     LC 84-12135     ISBN 0534038018

**Brown, Herbert Charles, 1912-.**     5.2783
Organic syntheses via boranes / Herbert C. Brown; with techniques by Gary W. Kramer, Alan B. Levy, M. Mark Midland. — New York, [1975] xix, 283 p.: ill.; 23 cm. 'A Wiley-Interscience publication.' 1. Organoboron compounds 2. Chemistry, Organic — Synthesis I. T.
QD412.B1 B77 1975     547/.05/671     LC 74-20520     ISBN 0471112801

**The Organic chemistry of iron / edited by Ernst A. Koerner von Gustorf, Friedrich–Wilhelm Grevels, Ingrid Fischler.**     5.2784
New York: Academic Press, 1978. 673 p.: ill.; 24 cm. — (Organometallic chemistry) 1. Organoiron compounds I. Koerner von Gustorf, Ernst A., 1932-1975. II. Grevels, Friedrich-Wilhelm. III. Fischler, Ingrid.
QD412.F4 O73     547/.05/621     LC 77-16071     ISBN 012417101X

**Wakefield, Basil John, 1934-.**     5.2785
The chemistry of organolithium compounds [by] B. J. Wakefield. — [1st ed.]. — Oxford; New York: Pergamon Press, [1974] x, 335 p.: illus.; 25 cm. 1. Organolithium compounds I. T.
QD412.L5 W34 1974     547/.05/381     LC 73-10091     ISBN 0080176402

**Sidgwick, Nevil Vincent, 1873-1952.**     • 5.2786
The organic chemistry of nitrogen, by the late N. V. Sidgwick. — 3rd ed. newly revised and rewritten by Ian T. Millar and H. D. Springall. — Oxford: Clarendon P., 1966 [i.e. 1967] xii, 909 p.: front. (port.), tables, diagrs.; 25 cm. 1. Organonitrogen compounds I. Millar, Ian T. II. Springall, H. D. III. T.
QD412.N1 S5 1966     547/.04     LC 67-77211

**Kosolapoff, G. M. (Gennady M.)**     5.2787
Organic phosphorus compounds [edited by] G. M. Kosolapoff and L. Maier. — New York: Wiley-Interscience, 1972. 4 v.: ill.; 23 cm. 1950 ed. published under title: Organophosphorus compounds. 1. Organophosphorus compounds I. Maier, L., joint author. II. T.
QD412.P1 K55 1972     547/.07     LC 72-1359     ISBN 0471504408

**Organic chemistry of sulfur / edited by S. Oae.**     5.2788
New York: Plenum Press, c1977. ix, 713 p.: ill.; 24 cm. 1. Organosulphur compounds — Addresses, essays, lectures. I. Ōae, Shigeru.
QD412.S1 O67     547/.06     LC 75-20028     ISBN 0306307405

**Organometallic chemistry reviews: organosilicon reviews / edited by D. Seyferth ... [et al.].**     5.2789
Amsterdam; New York: Elsevier Scientific Pub. Co.; New York: distributors for the United States and Canada, Elsevier North-Holland, 1976. 404 p.: ill.; 25 cm. (Journal of organometallic chemistry library. 2) 1. Organosilicon compounds — Addresses, essays, lectures. I. Seyferth, Dietmar, 1929- II. Series.
QD412.S6 O73     547/.05/683     LC 76-27869     ISBN 0444414886

## QD415–436 Biological Chemistry

**The Chemistry of natural products / edited by R.H. Thomson.**     5.2790
Glasgow: Blackie; New York: Distributed in the USA by Chapman and Hall, 1985. xii, 467 p.: ill.; 24 cm. 1. Natural products I. Thomson, R. H. (Ronald Hunter)
QD415.C483 1985     547.7 19     LC 84-9412     ISBN 0412007819

**Comprehensive biochemistry / edited by Marcel Florkin and** • **5.2791**
**Elmer H. Stotz.**
Amsterdam; New York: Elsevier Pub. Co., 1962- < 1986 > . < 1-16, 18-19B, pt.
1, 20-22, 24-29, 32-33, 35 > v. in < 36 > : ill.; 23 cm. Each vol. has also special
title. General and vol. editors vary. Vol. 13, 2nd ed. Vols. < 19A, 19B, pt. 1 >
published by Elsevier Scientific Pub. Co. 1. Biochemistry I. Florkin, Marcel.
II. Stotz, Elmer Henry, 1911-
QD415.F54    574.19/2 19    LC 62-10359    ISBN 0444801510

**Natural products chemistry / edited by Koji Nakanishi ... [et** **5.2792**
**al.].**
Tokyo: Kodansha; New York: Academic Press, c1974-. v.    : ill.; 26 cm.
(Kodansha scientific books) 1. Biochemistry I. Nakanishi, Kōji, 1925-
QD415.N35    547/.7    LC 74-6431    ISBN 0125139012

**Plummer, David T.** **5.2793**
An introduction to practical biochemistry / David T. Plummer. — 2d ed. —
London; New York: McGraw-Hill, c1978. xxiii, 362 p.: ill.; 23 cm.
1. Biochemistry — Laboratory manuals. I. T.
QD415.5.P57 1978    547    LC 77-30195    ISBN 0070840741

**Neurath, Hans, 1909- ed.** **5.2794**
The proteins, edited by Hans Neurath [and] Robert L. Hill. Assisted by Carol-
Leigh Boeder. — 3d ed. — New York: Academic Press, 1975-. v.    : illus.; 24
cm. 1. Proteins I. Hill, Robert L. 1928- joint ed. II. T.
QD431.N453    547/.75    LC 74-10195    ISBN 0125163010

**Bloomfield, Victor A.** **5.2795**
Physical chemistry of nucleic acids [by] Victor A. Bloomfield, Donald M.
Crothers [and] Ignacio Tinoco, Jr. — New York: Harper & Row, [1974] x,
517 p.: ill.; 24 cm. 1. Nucleic acids I. Crothers, Donald M. joint author.
II. Tinoco, Ignacio. joint author. III. T.
QD433.B44    547/.596    LC 73-8373    ISBN 0060407794

**Ts'o, Paul O. P. (Paul On Pong), 1929-.** **5.2796**
Basic principles in nucleic acid chemistry. — New York: Academic Press, 1974.
2 v.: ill. I. T.
QD433.T77    LC 72-13612    ISBN 0127019014

# QD450–655 PHYSICAL AND THEORETICAL CHEMISTRY

**Physical chemistry, an advanced treatise. Edited by Henry** • **5.2797**
**Eyring.**
New York, Academic Press, 1967-. v. illus. 24 cm. 1. Chemistry, Physical and
theoretical — Collected works. I. Eyring, Henry, 1901- ed.
QD453.P55    LC 67-4203

**Atkins, P. W. (Peter William), 1940-.** **5.2798**
Physical chemistry / P.W. Atkins; with introductory problems by J.C. Morrow.
— 3rd ed. — New York: W.H. Freeman, c1986. xxiv, 857 p.: ill.; 26 cm.
1. Chemistry, Physical and theoretical I. T.
QD453.2.A88 1986    541.3 19    LC 85-7048    ISBN 0716717492

**Barrow, Gordon M.** **5.2799**
Physical chemistry for the life sciences [by] Gordon M. Barrow. — New York:
McGraw-Hill, [1974] x, 405 p.: illus.; 24 cm. 1. Chemistry, Physical and
theoretical I. T.
QD453.2.B373    541/.3/024574    LC 73-18289    ISBN 0070038554

**Berry, R. Stephen, 1931-.** **5.2800**
Physical chemistry / R. Stephen Berry, Stuart A. Rice, John Ross, with the
assistance of George P. Flynn, Joseph N. Kushick. — New York: Wiley, c1980.
xvi, 1264, [40] p.: ill.; 26 cm. Includes bibliographies and index. 1. Chemistry,
Physical and theoretical I. Rice, Stuart Alan, 1932- joint author. II. Ross,
John, 1926- joint author. III. T.
QD453.2.B48 1980b    541.3 19    LC 79-790    ISBN 0471048291

**Brand, J. C. D. (John Charles Drury)** **5.2801**
Molecular structure: the physical approach / by J. C. D. Brand and J. C.
Speakman. — 2d ed. / rev. by J. C. Speakman and J. K. Tyler. — New York:
Wiley, 1975. 367 p.: ill.; 23 cm. 'A Halsted Press book.' 1. Chemistry, Physical
and theoretical 2. Molecules I. Speakman, J. Clare (James Clare), 1907- joint
author. II. Tyler, John K. III. T.
QD453.2.B69 1975    541/.22    LC 75-8507    ISBN 0470097957

**Bromberg, J. Philip, 1936-.** **5.2802**
Physical chemistry / J. Philip Bromberg. — Boston: Allyn and Bacon, c1980.
xiv, 882 p.: ill.; 24 cm. — (Allyn and Bacon chemistry series.) Includes index.
1. Chemistry, Physical and theoretical I. T. II. Series.
QD453.2.B76    541/.3    LC 79-10480    ISBN 0205065724

**Alberty, Robert A.** **5.2803**
Physical chemistry / Robert A. Alberty. — 7th ed. — New York: Wiley, c1987.
x, 934 p.: ill.; 24 cm. 1. Chemistry, Physical and theoretical I. T.
QD453.2.D36 1987    541.3 19    LC 86-15681    ISBN 0471825778

**Levine, Ira N., 1937-.** **5.2804**
Physical chemistry / Ira N. Levine. — 2nd ed. — New York: McGraw-Hill,
c1983. xix, 890 p.: ill.; 25 cm. Includes index. 1. Chemistry, Physical and
theoretical I. T.
QD453.2.L48 1983    541.3 19    LC 82-14939    ISBN 007037421X

**Moore, Walter John, 1918-.** • **5.2805**
Physical chemistry [by] Walter J. Moore. — 4th ed. — Englewood Cliffs, N.J.:
Prentice-Hall, [1972] xiii, 977 p.: illus.; 25 cm. 1. Chemistry, Physical and
theoretical I. T.
QD453.2.M65    541/.3    LC 70-156983    ISBN 0136659683

**Everdell, M. H.** **5.2806**
Statistical mechanics and its chemical applications / M. H. Everdell. —
London; New York: Academic Press, 1975. xxii, 305 p.: ill.; 24 cm. Includes
index. 1. Chemistry, Physical and theoretical — Mathematics. 2. Statistical
thermodynamics I. T.
QD455.3.M3 E93    541/.369    LC 75-19634    ISBN 0122444507

**Mortimer, Robert G.** **5.2807**
Mathematics for physical chemistry / Robert G. Mortimer. — New York:
Macmillan, c1981. x, 405 p.: ill.; 24 cm. 1. Chemistry, Physical and theoretical
— Mathematics. I. T.
QD455.3.M3 M67    510/.24541    LC 80-16615    ISBN 0023840005

**Daniels, Farrington, 1889-1972.** **5.2808**
Experimental physical chemistry [by] Farrington Daniels [and others]. — 7th
ed. — New York: McGraw-Hill, [1970] xiii, 669 p.: illus.; 24 cm. 1. Chemistry,
Physical and theoretical — Laboratory manuals. I. T.
QD457.D25 1970    541/.3/028    LC 75-77952

**Experiments in physical chemistry / David P. Shoemaker ... [et** **5.2809**
**al.].**
4th ed. — New York: McGraw-Hill, c1981. xii, 787 p.: ill.; 25 cm. First-2d ed.
by D. P. Shoemaker and C. W. Garland; 3d ed. by D. P. Shoemaker, C. W.
Garland, and J. I. Steinfeld. 1. Chemistry, Physical and theoretical —
Laboratory manuals. I. Shoemaker, David P. II. Shoemaker, David P.
Experiments in physical chemistry.
QD457.S56 1981    541.3/078 19    LC 80-20081    ISBN 0070570051

**Dreisbach, Robert Rickert.** • **5.2810**
Physical properties of chemical compounds. Washington: American Chemical
Society, 1955-59. 2 v.: tables; 24 cm. (Advances in chemistry series, no. 15, 22)
1. Chemistry, Organic — Tables. I. T.
QD458.D7    547.083    LC 55-2887

# QD461 Atomic and Molecular Theory

**Bacon, G. E. (George Edward), 1917-.** **5.2811**
Neutron scattering in chemistry / G. E. Bacon. — London; Boston:
Butterworths, 1977. 186 p.: ill.; 24 cm. Includes index. 1. Atomic theory
2. Neutrons — Scattering I. T.
QD461.B22    541/.28    LC 76-49474    ISBN 0408708004

**Companion, Audrey L.** **5.2812**
Chemical bonding/ Audrey L. Companion. — 2d ed. — New York: McGraw-
Hill, 1979. x, 179 p.: ill.; 21 cm. 1. Chemical bonds I. T.
QD461.C63 1979    QD461 C63 1979.    541/.224    LC 78-17081
    ISBN 0070123837

**Cotton, F. Albert (Frank Albert), 1930-.** • **5.2813**
Chemical applications of group theory [by] F. Albert Cotton. 2d ed. New York,
Wiley-Interscience [1971] xiv, 386 p. illus. 23 cm. 1. Molecular theory
2. Groups, Theory of I. T.
QD461.C65 1971    541/.22/0151222    LC 76-129657    ISBN
0471175706

**Flygare, W. H., 1936-.**    **5.2814**
Molecular structure and dynamics / W. H. Flygare. — Englewood Cliffs, N.J.: Prentice-Hall, c1978. xviii, 696 p.: ill.; 25 cm. 1. Molecular theory 2. Quantum chemistry I. T.
QD461.F58    541/.28    *LC* 77-16786    *ISBN* 0135997534

**Hall, Lowell H., 1937-.**    • **5.2815**
Group theory and symmetry in chemistry / [by] Lowell H. Hall. — New York: McGraw-Hill, [1969] xiii, 370 p.: ill.; 23 cm. 1. Groups, Theory of 2. Symmetry (Physics) I. T.
QD461.H17    541/.2    *LC* 69-13607

**Jorgensen, William L.**    **5.2816**
The organic chemist's book of orbitals [by] William L. Jorgensen [and] Lionel Salem. — New York: Academic Press, 1973. xi, 305 p.: ill.; 24 cm. A revised German ed. published in 1974 under title: Orbitale organischer Moleküle. 1. Molecular orbitals — Charts, diagrams, etc. 2. Chemistry, Organic — Charts, diagrams, etc. I. Salem, Lionel. joint author. II. T.
QD461.J68    547/.1/28    *LC* 72-9990    *ISBN* 0123902509

**Kihara, Tarō.**    **5.2817**
[Bunshikanryoku. English] Intermolecular forces / T. Kihara; translated by S. Ichimaru. — Chichester; New York: Wiley, c1978. vii, 182 p.: ill.; 24 cm. Translation of Bunshikanryoku. Includes indexes. 1. Molecular theory I. T.
QD461.K42513    541/.226    *LC* 77-12353    *ISBN* 0471995835

**Lehmann, Walter J., 1926-.**    **5.2818**
Atomic and molecular structure: the development of our concepts [by] Walter J. Lehmann. — New York: Wiley, [1972] xix, 449 p.: illus.; 23 cm. 1. Atomic structure 2. Molecular structure I. T.
QD461.L5    541/.22    *LC* 70-37434    *ISBN* 0471524409

**Woodward, R. B. (Robert Burns), 1917-1979.**    • **5.2819**
The conservation of orbital symmetry / [by] R. B. Woodward and R. Hoffmann. — [Weinheim/Bergstr.]: Verlag Chemie, 1970. 177 p.: ill. (part col.); 21 cm. 1. Conservation of orbital symmetry I. Hoffmann, Roald, joint author. II. T.
QD461.W75    541/.224    *LC* 79-103636

**Murrell, J. N. (John Norman)**    **5.2820**
The chemical bond / John N. Murrell, Sydney F. A. Kettle, John M. Tedder. — Chichester; New York: Wiley, c1978. xi, 310 p.: ill.; 24 cm. 1. Chemical bonds I. Kettle, S. F. A. (Sidney Francis Alan) joint author. II. Tedder, John M. (John Michael) joint author. III. T.
QD461.M84    541/.224    *LC* 77-21728    *ISBN* 0471995770. *ISBN* 0471995789 pbk

**Murrell, J. N. (John Norman)**    **5.2821**
Semi–empirical self–consistent–field molecular orbital theory of molecules / [by] J. N. Murrell and A. J. Harget. — London; New York: Wiley-Interscience, 1972. 180 p.: ill.; 24 cm. 1. Molecular orbitals 2. Self-consistent field theory I. Harget, Alan John, joint author. II. T.
QD461.M85    541/.28    *LC* 71-172470    *ISBN* 0471626805

**Sanderson, R. T. (Robert Thomas), 1912-.**    **5.2822**
Chemical bonds and bond energy / R. T. Sanderson. — 2d ed. — New York: Academic Press, 1976. xii, 218 p.: ill.; 24 cm. (Physical chemistry, a series of monographs; v. 21) 1. Chemical bonds I. T.
QD461.S33 1976    541/.224    *LC* 75-26353    *ISBN* 0126180601

**Streitwieser, Andrew, 1927-.**    **5.2823**
Orbital and electron density diagrams; an application of computer graphics [by] Andrew Streitwieser, Jr. [and] Peter H. Owens. — New York: Macmillan, [1973] xiv, 159 p.: illus.; 28 cm. 1. Molecular orbitals — Charts, diagrams, etc. 2. Chemical bonds — Charts, diagrams, etc. 3. Computer graphics 4. Electron distribution — Charts, diagrams, etc. I. Owens, Peter H., joint author. II. T.
QD461.S89    539/.6    *LC* 72-86795

**Van Wazer, John R.**    **5.2824**
Electron densities in molecules and molecular orbitals / John R. Van Wazer, Ilyas Absar. — New York: Academic Press, 1975. x, 101 p.: ill.; 29 cm. (Physical chemistry, a series of monographs; v. 35) 1. Molecular structure 2. Molecular orbitals I. Absar, Ilyas, joint author. II. T.
QD461.V32    539/.6    *LC* 74-30809    *ISBN* 0127145508

## QD462 Quantum Chemistry

**Atkins, P. W. (Peter William), 1940-.**    **5.2825**
Molecular quantum mechanics / P.W. Atkins. — 2nd ed. — Oxford [Oxfordshire]; New York: Oxford University Press, 1983. xiii, 471 p.: ill.; 26 cm. 1. Quantum chemistry I. T.
QD462.A84 1983    541.2/8 19    *LC* 82-18998    *ISBN* 0198551711

**Flurry, Robert L.**    **5.2826**
Quantum chemistry: an introduction / R.L. Flurry, Jr. — Englewood Cliffs, N.J.: Prentice-Hall, c1983. xv, 399 p.: ill.; 25 cm. 1. Quantum chemistry I. T.
QD462.F583 1983    541.2/8 19    *LC* 82-7715    *ISBN* 0137478321

**Levine, Ira N., 1937-.**    **5.2827**
Quantum chemistry / Ira N. Levine. — 3rd ed. — Boston: Allyn and Bacon, c1983. x, 566 p.: ill.; 25 cm. — (Allyn and Bacon chemistry series.) Includes index. 1. Quantum chemistry I. T. II. Series.
QD462.L48 1983    541.2/8 19    *LC* 82-24291    *ISBN* 0205077935

**Lowe, John P.**    **5.2828**
Quantum chemistry / John P. Lowe. — New York: Academic Press, c1978. xvi, 599 p.: ill.; 24 cm. 1. Quantum chemistry I. T.
QD462.L69    541/.28    *LC* 77-6602    *ISBN* 0124575501

## QD466–470 Chemical Elements

**Donohue, Jerry, 1920-.**    **5.2829**
The structures of the elements. — New York: Wiley, [1974] xi, 436 p.: ill.; 23 cm. 'A Wiley-Interscience publication.' 1. Chemical structure I. T.
QD466.D6    546    *LC* 73-13788    *ISBN* 0471217883

**Greenwood, N. N. (Norman Neill)**    **5.2830**
Chemistry of the elements / N.N. Greenwood and A. Earnshaw. — 1st ed. — Oxford [Oxfordshire]; New York: Pergamon Press, 1984. xxi, 1542 p.: ill.; 26 cm. 1. Chemical elements I. Earnshaw, A. (Alan) II. T.
QD466.G74 1984    546 19    *LC* 83-13346    *ISBN* 0080220568

**Hampel, Clifford A.**    • **5.2831**
The encyclopedia of the chemical elements / edited by Clifford A. Hampel. — New York: Reinhold Book Corp., [1968] viii, 849 p.: ill.; 27 cm. 1. Chemical elements — Dictionaries. I. T.
QD466.H295    546/.11/03    *LC* 68-29938

**Table of isotopes.**    **5.2832**
7th ed. / editors, C. Michael Lederer, Virginia S. Shirley; principal authors, Edgardo Browne, Janis M. Dairiki, Raymond E. Doebler, authors, Adnan A. Shihab-Eldin ... [et al.]. — New York: Wiley, c1978. 1628 p. in various pagings: ill.; 28 cm. 'A Wiley-interscience publication.' Sixth ed. by C. M. Lederer, J. M. Hollander, and I. Perlman. 'Prepared under U.S. Department of Energy contract no. 7405-ENG-48.' 1. Isotopes — Tables, etc. I. Lederer, Charles Michael. Table of isotopes. II. Shirley, Virginia S. III. Browne, Edgardo.
QD466.L37 1978    QD466 L37 1978.    541/.388    *LC* 78-14938    *ISBN* 0471041793

**Weeks, Mary Elvira, 1892-.**    • **5.2833**
Discovery of the elements / completely rev. and new material added by Henry M. Leicester; illus. collected by F. B. Dains. — 7th ed. — [Easton, Pa.]: Journal of chemical education, [1968] x, 896 p.: ill., ports.; 24 cm. 1. Chemical elements 2. Chemists I. Leicester, Henry Marshall, 1906- ed. II. T.
QD466.W4 1968    546/.11    *LC* 68-15217

**Mazurs, Edward G.**    **5.2834**
Graphic representations of the periodic system during one hundred years / Edward G. Mazurs. — Rev. 2d ed. — University, Ala.: University of Alabama Press, 1974. xii, 251 p.: ill.; 27 cm. 1. Periodic law 2. Chemical elements I. T.
QD467.M35 1974    541/.901    *LC* 73-8051    *ISBN* 0817332006

**Cartmell, Edward.**    **5.2835**
Valency and molecular structure / E. Cartmell and G. W. A. Fowles. — 4th ed. — London; Boston: Butterworths, 1977. 341 p.: ill.; 24 cm. 1. Valence (Theoretical chemistry) 2. Molecular structure I. Fowles, Gerald Wilfred Albert, joint author. II. T. III. Title: Molecular structure.
QD469.C3 1977    541/.224    *LC* 77-30013    *ISBN* 0408708093

**Coulson, C. A. (Charles Alfred), 1910-1974.**    **5.2836**
[Valence] Coulson's Valence / Roy McWeeny. — 3d ed. — Oxford; New York: Oxford University Press, 1979. x, 434 p.: ill.; 25 cm. 1. Valence (Theoretical chemistry) I. McWeeny, R. II. T.
QD469.C74 1979    541/.224    *LC* 78-40323    *ISBN* 0198551444

**Pauling, Linus, 1901-.**    **5.2837**
The nature of the chemical bond and the structure of molecules and crystals: an introduction to modern structural chemistry. — 3d ed. — Ithaca, N.Y.: Cornell University Press, 1960. 644 p.: ill.; 25 cm. — (George Fisher Baker non-resident lectureship in chemistry at Cornell University. [v. 18]) 1. Chemical bonds 2. Quantum chemistry 3. Molecules 4. Crystallography I. T. II. Title: Chemical bond. III. Series.
QD469.P38 1960    541.396    *LC* 60-16025

**Stranges, Anthony N. (Anthony Nicholas), 1936-.**    **5.2838**
Electrons and valence: development of the theory, 1900–1925 / by Anthony N. Stranges. — 1st ed. — College Station: Texas A&M University Press, c1982. xii,

291 p. [2] leaves of plates: ill.; 24 cm. Includes index. 1. Valence (Theoretical chemistry) I. T.
QD469.S73 1982     541.2/24 19     LC 81-48378     ISBN 0890961247

## QD471–475 Chemical Compounds. Properties and Structures

**Bailar, John Christian, 1904-.**        • **5.2839**
The chemistry of the coordination compounds / Daryle H. Busch, editorial assistant. New York: Reinhold Pub. Corp., 1956. x, 834 p. (Monograph series (American Chemical Society) no. 131) 1. Coordination compounds I. T. II. Series.
QD471.B23     LC 56-6686

**Basolo, Fred, 1920-.**        • **5.2840**
Coordination chemistry: the chemistry of metal complexes / [by] Fred Basolo [and] Ronald C. Johnson. — New York: W. A. Benjamin, 1964. xii, 180 p.: ill. (part col.); 22 cm. — (The General chemistry monograph series) 1. Coordination compounds I. Johnson, Ronald C. joint author. II. T.
QD471.B316     541.396     LC 64-22273

**Figgis, B. N.**        **5.2841**
Introduction to ligand fields [by] B.N. Figgis. New York, Interscience Publishers [1966] ix, 351 p. illus. 24 cm. 'Based on a course of lectures delivered to the Inorganic Chemistry Graduate School at the University of Texas in 1961.' 1. Ligand field theory 2. Complex ions I. T. II. Title: Ligand fields.
QD471.F57     541.22     LC 65-24309

**Kettle, S. F. A. (Sidney Francis Alan)**        **5.2842**
Symmetry and structure / S.F.A. Kettle. — Chichester [West Sussex]; New York: Wiley, c1985. x, 330 p.: ill.; 24 cm. Includes index. 1. Chemical structure 2. Symmetry (Physics) 3. Groups, Theory of 4. Chemical bonds 5. Molecules I. T.
QD471.K47516 1985     541.2/2 19     LC 84-17365     ISBN 0471905011

**Tanford, Charles, 1921-.**        • **5.2843**
Physical chemistry of macromolecules. — New York: Wiley, [1961] 710 p.: illus.; 24 cm. 1. Macromolecules 2. Chemistry, Physical and theoretical I. T.
QD471.T24     541.345     LC 61-11511

**Coordination chemistry. Edited by Arthur E. Martell.**        **5.2844**
New York, Van Nostrand Reinhold [1971]-78. 2 v. illus. 24 cm. (ACS monograph 168, 174 0065-7719) Vol. 2 published by American Chemical Society, Washington. 1. Coordination compounds I. Martell, Arthur Earl, 1916- ed.
QD474.C66     541/.2242     LC 74-151255     ISBN 0841202923

**Day, Marion Clyde, 1927-.**        • **5.2845**
Theoretical inorganic chemistry [by] M. Clyde Day, Jr. [and] Joel Selbin. — 2d ed. — New York: Reinhold Book Corp., [1969] xviii, 590 p.: illus.; 24 cm. — (Reinhold chemistry textbook series) 1. Chemistry, Inorganic 2. Chemistry, Physical and theoretical I. Selbin, Joel, 1931- joint author. II. T.
QD475.D3 1969     541/.2     LC 68-55805

**Douglas, Bodie Eugene, 1924-.**        **5.2846**
Concepts and models of inorganic chemistry / Bodie E. Douglas, Darl H. McDaniel, John J. Alexander. — 2nd ed. — New York: Wiley, c1983. xii, 800 p.: ill.; 25 cm. 1. Chemistry, Inorganic I. McDaniel, Darl Hamilton, 1928- II. Alexander, John J. III. T.
QD475.D65 1983     546 19     LC 82-2606     ISBN 0471219843

### QD476 PHYSICAL ORGANIC CHEMISTRY

**Advances in physical organic chemistry.**        • **5.2847**
v. 1- 1963-. London, New York, Academic Press. v. ill., diagrs. 24 cm. Annual. 1. Chemistry, Physical organic — Collected works. I. Gold, Victor. ed.
QD476.A4     547.1082     LC 62-22125

**Benfey, O. Theodor (Otto Theodor), 1925-.**        • **5.2848**
From vital force to structural formulas / [by] O. Theodor Benfey. — Boston: Houghton Mifflin Co. [1964] xi, 115 p.: ill.; 23 cm. (Classic researches in organic chemistry, 0-1) 1. Chemistry, Organic 2. Chemistry, Physical and theoretical I. T. II. Series.
QD476.B4 1964     547.12     LC 64-4822

**The Chemistry of double–bonded functional groups / edited by Saul Patai.**        **5.2849**
London; New York: Wiley, 1977. 2 v. (xv, 1343 p.): ill.; 24 cm. (The Chemistry of functional groups: Supplement A; pts. 1-2) 1. Chemistry, Physical organic I. Patai, Saul. II. Series.
QD476.C53     547     LC 77-364680     ISBN 0471669407

**Ferguson, Lloyd N.**        • **5.2850**
The modern structural theory of organic chemistry. — Englewoods Cliffs, N.J.: Prentice-Hall, [1963] 600 p.: illus.; 24 cm. — (Prentice-Hall chemistry series) 1. Chemistry, Organic 2. Chemistry, Physical organic I. T.
QD476.F42     547.12     LC 63-10542

**Gilchrist, T. L. (Thomas Lonsdale)**        **5.2851**
Organic reactions and orbital symmetry / T. L. Gilchrist and R. C. Storr. — 2d ed. — Cambridge [Eng.]: New York: Cambridge University Press, 1979. vii, 311 p.: ill.; 24 cm. (Cambridge texts in chemistry and biochemistry.) 1. Chemistry, Physical organic 2. Chemical reaction, Conditions and laws of 3. Molecular orbitals 4. Symmetry (Physics) I. Storr, R. C., joint author. II. T. III. Series.
QD476.G54 1979     547/.1/39     LC 78-54578     ISBN 0521220149

**Hammett, Louis Plack, 1894-.**        • **5.2852**
Physical organic chemistry: reaction rates, equilibria, and mechanisms / [by] Louis P. Hammett. — 2d ed. — New York: McGraw-Hill, [1970] 420 p.: illus.; 23 cm. — (McGraw-Hill series in advanced chemistry) 1. Chemistry, Physical organic I. T.
QD476.H33 1970     547/.1/3     LC 73-91680

**Hine, Jack Sylvester, 1923-.**        • **5.2853**
Physical organic chemistry. — 2d ed. — New York: McGraw-Hill, 1962. 552 p.: illus.; 24 cm. — (McGraw-Hill series in advanced chemistry) 1. Chemistry, Physical organic I. T.
QD476.H5 1962     547.1     LC 61-18627

**Ingold, Christopher, Sir, 1893-.**        • **5.2854**
Structure and mechanism in organic chemistry / by C. K. Ingold. — 2d ed. — Ithaca: Cornell University Press [1969] ix, 1266 p.: ill.; 25 cm. 1. Chemistry, Physical organic I. T.
QD476.I55 1969     547/.1/3     LC 69-12426     ISBN 0801404991

**Isaacs, Neil S., 1934-.**        **5.2855**
Reactive intermediates in organic chemistry [by] N. S. Isaacs. — London; New York: Wiley, [1974] xiii, 550 p.: illus.; 23 cm. 1. Chemistry, Physical organic I. T.
QD476.I85     547/.2     LC 73-8194     ISBN 0471428612

**Lowry, Thomas H.**        **5.2856**
Mechanism and theory in organic chemistry / Thomas H. Lowry and Kathleen Schueller Richardson. — 3rd ed. — New York: Harper & Row, c1987. 748 p. 1. Chemistry, Physical organic I. Richardson, Kathleen Schueller. II. T.
QD476.L68 1987     547.1/3 19     LC 86-22851     ISBN 0060440848

**Pasto, Daniel J., 1936-.**        • **5.2857**
Organic structure determination [by] Daniel J. Pasto [and] Carl R. Johnson. — Englewood Cliffs, N.J.: Prentice-Hall, [1969] xiii, 513 p.: illus.; 25 cm. — (Prentice-Hall international series in chemistry) 1. Chemistry, Physical organic I. Johnson, Carl R., 1937- joint author. II. T.
QD476.P35     547/.1/2     LC 69-15046     ISBN 0136408540

**Progress in physical organic chemistry.**        • **5.2858**
v. 1-. New York, Wiley [etc.], 1963-. v. diagrs., tables. 24 cm. 'An Interscience publication.' Suspended 1977-80. 1. Chemistry, Physical organic — Collected works. I. Cohen, Saul G., ed. II. Streitwieser, Andrew, 1927- ed. III. Taft, Robert W. ed.
QD476.P74     547.1     LC 63-19364

**Sykes, Peter.**        **5.2859**
The search for organic reaction pathways. — New York: Wiley, [1972] xii, 247 p.; 22 cm. 'A Halsted Press book'. 1. Chemistry, Physical organic 2. Chemical reaction, Conditions and laws of I. T.
QD476.S9 1972b     547/.1/39     LC 72-4192     ISBN 0470841303

## QD477 Acids and Bases

**Finston, H. L.**        **5.2860**
A new view of current acid–base theories / Harmon L. Finston and Allen C. Rychtman. — New York: Wiley, c1982. viii, 216 p.: ill.; 24 cm. 'A Wiley-Interscience publication.' 1. Acid-base equilibrium I. Rychtman, Allen C. II. T.
QD477.F56 1982     541.3/94 19     LC 81-16030     ISBN 0471084727

**Ho, Tse-Lok.**        **5.2861**
Hard and soft acids and bases principle in organic chemistry / Tse Lok Ho. — New York: Academic Press, 1977. xii, 209 p.: ill.; 24 cm. 1. Acids 2. Bases (Chemistry) 3. Chemistry, Organic 4. Chemical reactions I. T.
QD477.H6     547/.1/39     LC 76-13939     ISBN 0123500508

**Jensen, William B.**                                              **5.2862**
The Lewis acid–base concepts: an overview / William B. Jensen. — New York: Wiley, c1980. xi, 364 p.: ill.; 24 cm. 'A Wiley-Interscience publication.' Includes indexes. 1. Acid-base equilibrium I. T.
QD477.J46      546/.24      *LC* 79-15561      *ISBN* 0471039020

**Pearson, Ralph G. comp.**                                        **5.2863**
Hard and soft acids and bases. Edited by Ralph G. Pearson. — Stroudsburg, Pa.: Dowden, Hutchinson & Ross, [1973] xiii, 480 p.: illus.; 27 cm. — (Benchmark papers in inorganic chemistry) 1. Acids — Addresses, essays, lectures. 2. Bases (Chemistry) — Addresses, essays, lectures. I. T.
QD477.P39      546/.24      *LC* 72-93262      *ISBN* 087933021X

# QD478 Solid State Chemistry. Chemical Models

**Adams, David Michael.**                                          **5.2864**
Inorganic solids; an introduction to concepts in solid–state structural chemistry [by] D. M. Adams. — London; New York: Wiley, [1974] xvi, 336 p.: illus.; 23 cm. 1. Solid state chemistry I. T.
QD478.A3      541/.042/1      *LC* 73-16863      *ISBN* 0471004707

**Hannay, N. B. (Norman Bruce), 1921-.**                           **5.2865**
Treatise on solid state chemistry / edited by N. B. Hannay. — New York: Plenum Press, [1973-76]. 6 v. in 7: ill.; 26 cm. — 1. Solid state chemistry I. T.
QD478.H35 QD505.5      541/.042/1 s 541/.042/1      *LC* 73-13799
    *ISBN* 0306350505

**West, Anthony R.**                                               **5.2866**
Solid state chemistry and its applications / Anthony R. West. — Chichester [West Sussex]; New York: Wiley, c1984. vii, 734 p.: ill.; 24 cm. 1. Solid state chemistry I. T.
QD478.W47 1984      540/.421 19      *LC* 83-21607      *ISBN* 0471903779

**Suckling, Colin J., 1947-.**                                     **5.2867**
Chemistry through models: concepts and applications of modelling in chemical science, technology, and industry / Colin J. Suckling, Keith E. Suckling, and Charles W. Suckling. — Cambridge; New York: Cambridge University Press, 1978. xii, 321 p.: ill.; 24 cm. 1. Chemical models I. Suckling, Keith E., 1947- joint author. II. Suckling, C. W., joint author. III. T.
QD480.S82      540/.22/8      *LC* 77-41429      *ISBN* 0521216613

# QD481 Stereochemistry

**Eliel, Ernest Ludwig, 1921-.**                                 • **5.2868**
Conformational analysis [by] Ernest L. Eliel [and others]. New York, Interscience Publishers [1965] xiii, 524 p. illus. 24 cm. 1. Conformational analysis I. T.
QD481.E517      547.16      *LC* 65-14028

**Eliel, Ernest Ludwig, 1921-.**                                 • **5.2869**
Stereochemistry of carbon compounds. — New York: McGraw-Hill, 1962. 486 p.: illus.; 24 cm. — (McGraw-Hill series in advanced chemistry) 1. Stereochemistry 2. Chemistry, Organic I. T.
QD481.E52      547.16      *LC* 61-14354

**Gillespie, Ronald J. (Ronald James)**                            **5.2870**
Molecular geometry [by] R. J. Gillespie. London, New York, Van Nostrand Reinhold, 1972. ix, 228 p. fold. leaf. illus. 24 cm. 1. Stereochemistry 2. Chemistry, Inorganic I. T.
QD481.G52      541/.223      *LC* 77-160198      *ISBN* 0442026935 *ISBN* 0442026978

**Klyne, William.**                                                **5.2871**
Atlas of stereochemistry: absolute configurations of organic molecules / W. Klyne and J. Buckingham. — 2d ed. — New York: Oxford University Press, 1978. 2 v. Includes indexes. 1. Stereochemistry — Atlases. I. Buckingham, J. joint author. II. T.
QD481.K64 1978b      547/.1/223

**Lister, David G.**                                               **5.2872**
Internal rotation and inversion: an introduction to large amplitude motions in molecules / David G. Lister, John N. Macdonald, and Noel L. Owen. — London; New York: Academic Press, 1978. xii, 246 p.: ill.; 24 cm. 1. Molecular rotation I. Macdonald, John N. joint author. II. Owen, Noel L. joint author. III. T.
QD481.L59      541/.22      *LC* 77-15322      *ISBN* 0124522505

**Mislow, Kurt.**                                                • **5.2873**
Introduction to stereochemistry / Kurt Mislow. — New York: W. A. Benjamin, 1965. xii, 193 p.: ill. — (Organic chemistry monograph series.) 1. Stereochemistry I. T. II. Series.
QD481.M53      547.1223      *LC* 65-10940

**Ramsay, O. Bertrand (Ogden Bertrand), 1932-.**                   **5.2874**
Stereochemistry / O. Bertrand Ramsay. — London; Philadelphia: Heyden, c1981. xv, 256 p.: ill.; 21 cm. — (Nobel prize topics in chemistry.) Includes indexes. 1. Stereochemistry I. T. II. Series.
QD481.R24 1981      541.2/23 19      *LC* 82-106278      *ISBN* 0855016825

**Topics in stereochemistry.**                                     **5.2875**
v. 1-. New York, John Wiley & Sons [etc.] 1967-. v. 24 cm. 1. Stereochemistry — Collected works. I. Allinger, Norman L. ed. II. Eliel, Ernest Ludwig, 1921- ed.
QD481.T6      547/.1223      *LC* 67-13943

**Wells, A. F. (Alexander Frank), 1912-.**                         **5.2876**
Structural inorganic chemistry / A.F. Wells. — 5th ed. — Oxford [Oxfordshire]: Clarendon Press; New York: Oxford University Press, 1984, c1975. xxxi, 1382 p., [7] p. of plates: ill.; 24 cm. 1. Chemical structure 2. Stereochemistry 3. Crystallography I. T.
QD481.W44 1984      546/.252 19      *LC* 82-18866      *ISBN* 0198553706

# QD501–505 Conditions and Laws of Chemical Change

**Atwood, Jim D., 1940-.**                                         **5.2877**
Inorganic and organometallic reaction mechanisms / Jim D. Atwood. — Monterey, Calif.: Brooks/Cole Pub. Co., c1985. xi, 322 p.: ill.; 24 cm. 1. Chemical reactions, Conditions and laws of. 2. Organometallic compounds I. T.
QD501.A89 1985      541.3/9 19      *LC* 84-19904      *ISBN* 0534037771

**Bell, R. P. (Ronald Percy)**                                   • **5.2878**
The proton in chemistry. Ithaca, N.Y.: Cornell University Press, 1959. vii, 223 p.: ill.; 25 cm. (George Fisher Baker non-resident lectureship in chemistry at Cornell University. 1958) 1. Chemical reaction, Conditions and laws of 2. Protons I. T. II. Series.
QD501.B386      541.3      *LC* 60-49

**Bender, Myron L., 1924-.**                                     • **5.2879**
Mechanisms of homogeneous catalysis from protons to proteins [by] Myron L. Bender. New York, Wiley-Interscience [1971] x, 686 p. illus. 23 cm. 1. Catalysis 2. Enzymes I. T.
QD501.B3872      547/.1/395      *LC* 73-153080      *ISBN* 0471065005

**Cannon, R. D. (Roderick David), 1938-.**                         **5.2880**
Electron transfer reactions / R.D. Cannon. — London: Butterworths, 1980. 351 p.: ill.; 24 cm. 1. Chemical reaction, Conditions and laws of 2. Electrons I. T.
QD 501 C22 1980      QD501 C36 1980.      *LC* 79-41278      *ISBN* 0408106468

**Eyring, Henry, 1901-.**                                        • **5.2881**
Modern chemical kinetics [by] Henry Eyring and Edward M. Eyring. — New York: Reinhold Pub. Corp., [1963] 114 p.: illus.; 19 cm. 1. Chemical reaction, Rate of I. Eyring, Edward M., joint author. II. T.
QD501.E9      541.39      *LC* 63-9650

**Jencks, William P., 1927-.**                                     **5.2882**
Catalysis in chemistry and enzymology [by] William P. Jencks. — New York: McGraw-Hill, [1969] xvi, 644 p.: ill.; 23 cm. — (McGraw-Hill series in advanced chemistry) 1. Catalysis 2. Enzymes I. T.
QD501.J43      547/.1/395      *LC* 68-31661

**Jordan, Peter C.**                                               **5.2883**
Chemical kinetics and transport / Peter C. Jordan. — New York: Plenum Press, c1979. xvi, 368 p.: ill.; 24 cm. 1. Chemical reaction, Rate of 2. Transport theory I. T.
QD501.J7573      541/.39      *LC* 78-20999      *ISBN* 0306401223

**Klotz, Irving M. (Irving Myron), 1916-.**                      • **5.2884**
Energy changes in biochemical reactions [by] Irving M. Klotz. New York, Academic Press, 1967. x, 108 p. illus. 21 cm. 1. Bioenergetics I. T.
QD501.K7557      574.1/92      *LC* 66-30088

**Laidler, Keith James, 1916-.**     **5.2885**
Theories of chemical reaction rates [by] Keith J. Laidler. — New York: McGraw-Hill, [1969] vii, 234 p.: illus.; 23 cm. — (McGraw-Hill series in advanced chemistry) 1. Chemical reaction, Rate of I. T.
QD501.L19     541/.394     *LC* 78-85165

**Miller, G. Tyler (George Tyler), 1931-.**     **5.2886**
Energetics, kinetics, and life; an ecological approach [by] G. Tyler Miller. Belmont, Calif., Wadsworth Pub. Co. [1971] 360 p. illus. 26 cm. 1. Thermodynamics 2. Chemical reaction, Rate of 3. Bioenergetics I. T.
QD501.M748     541/.369     *LC* 70-163983     *ISBN* 053400136X

## QD502–505 Reaction Rates and Mechanisms. Chemical Equilibrium and Thermodynamics. Catalysis

**Hill, Charles G., 1937-.**     **5.2887**
An introduction to chemical engineering kinetics & reactor design / Charles G. Hill, Jr. — New York: Wiley, c1977. xi, 594 p.: ill.; 25 cm. 1. Chemical reaction, Rate of 2. Chemical reactors — Design and construction. I. T.
QD502.H54     660.2/83     *LC* 77-8280     *ISBN* 0471396095

**Johnson, Colin D.**     **5.2888**
The Hammett equation [by] C. D. Johnson. — Cambridge [Eng.]: University Press, 1973. vii, 196 p.: illus.; 22 cm. — (Cambridge chemistry texts) 1. Hammett equation I. T.
QD502.J63     547/.1/394     *LC* 72-93140     *ISBN* 0521201381

**Menger, Fredric M., 1937-.**     **5.2889**
Electronic interpretation of organic chemistry: a problems–oriented text / Fredric M. Menger and Leon Mandell. — New York: Plenum Press, c1980. vii, 216 p.: ill.; 24 cm. 1. Chemical reactions 2. Chemistry, Organic I. Mandell, Leon. joint author. II. T.
QD502.M46     547/.1/39     *LC* 79-21718     *ISBN* 030640379X

**Moore, John W.**     **5.2890**
Kinetics and mechanism. — 3rd ed. / John W. Moore, Ralph G. Pearson. — New York: Wiley, c1981. xv, 455 p.: ill.; 24 cm. Revision of: 2nd ed. / Arthur A. Frost, Ralph G. Pearson. 1961. A Wiley-Interscience publication.' 1. Chemical reaction, Rate of I. Pearson, Ralph G. II. Frost, Arthur Atwater, 1909- Kinetics and mechanism. III. T.
QD502.M66 1981     541.3/94 19     *LC* 81-981     *ISBN* 0471035580

**Skinner, Gordon.**     **5.2891**
Introduction to chemical kinetics [by] Gordon B. Skinner. — New York: Academic Press, 1974. x, 214 p.: illus.; 24 cm. 1. Chemical reaction, Rate of I. T.
QD502.S55     541/.39     *LC* 73-18979     *ISBN* 0126478503

**Smith, Ian W. M.**     **5.2892**
Kinetics and dynamics of elementary gas reactions / Ian W. M. Smith. — London; Boston: Butterworths, 1980. xii, 387 p.: ill.; 24 cm. — (Butterworths monographs in chemistry and chemical engineering.) 1. Chemical reaction, Rate of 2. Gases, Kinetic theory of I. T. II. Series.
QD502.S57     541/.39     *LC* 79-40533     *ISBN* 0408707909

**Hartley, F. R.**     **5.2893**
Solution equilibria / F. R. Hartley, C. Burgess, and R. M. Alcock. — Chichester: E. Horwood; New York: Halsted Press, 1980. 361 p.: ill.; 24 cm. 1. Chemical equilibrium 2. Solution (Chemistry) I. Burgess, C. (Christopher) joint author. II. Alcock, R. M. joint author. III. T.
QD503.H37 1980     541.3/9     *LC* 79-42956     *ISBN* 0853121486

**Klotz, Irving M. (Irving Myron), 1916-.**     **5.2894**
Chemical thermodynamics: basic theory and methods / Irving M. Klotz, Robert M. Rosenberg. — 4th ed. — Menlo Park, Calif.: Benjamin/Cummings Pub. Co., c1986. xiv, 512 p.: ill.; 25 cm. 1. Thermodynamics I. Rosenberg, Robert M., 1926- II. T.
QD504.K55 1986     541.3/69 19     *LC* 86-3303     *ISBN* 0805355014

**Tamaru, Kenji, 1923-.**     **5.2895**
Dynamic heterogeneous catalysis / K. Tamaru. — London: Academic Press, 1978. xiii, 140 p.: ill.; 23 cm. 1. Heterogeneous catalysis I. T.
QD505.T342     QD505 T342.     *LC* 77-71841     *ISBN* 0126841500

## QD506 Surface Chemistry

**Adamson, Arthur W.**     **5.2896**
Physical chemistry of surfaces / Arthur W. Adamson. — 4th ed. — New York: J. Wiley, c1982. xviii, 664 p.: ill.; 24 cm. 'A Wiley-Interscience publication.' 1. Surface chemistry 2. Chemistry, Physical and theoretical I. T.
QD506.A3 1982     541.3/453 19     *LC* 82-2711     *ISBN* 0471078778

**Jaycock, M. J.**     **5.2897**
Chemistry of interfaces / M. J. Jaycock and G. D. Parfitt. — Chichester, Eng.: E. Horwood; New York: Halsted Press, 1981. 279 p.: ill.; 23 cm. — (Ellis Horwood series in physical chemistry) 1. Surface chemistry I. Parfitt, G. D. II. T.
QD506.J39     541.3/453     *LC* 80-40387     *ISBN* 0470270969

**Mikhail, Raouf Shaker.**     **5.2898**
Microstructure and thermal analysis of solid surfaces / Raouf Sh. Mikhail and Erich Robens. — Chichester [West Sussex]; New York: Wiley, c1983. x, 496 p.: ill.; 24 cm. 'A Wiley-Heyden publication.' Includes indexes. 1. Surface chemistry 2. Thermal analysis I. Robens, Erich. II. T.
QD506.M54 1983     541.3/453 19     *LC* 82-17507     *ISBN* 0471262307

**Roberts, M. W. (Meirion Wynn)**     **5.2899**
Chemistry of the metal–gas interface / by M. W. Roberts and C. S. McKee. — Oxford: Clarendon Press; New York: Oxford University Press, 1979 (c1978). xiv, 594 p.: ill.; 23 cm. (Monographs on the physics and chemistry of materials) 1. Surface chemistry 2. Metals — Surfaces 3. Gases in metals I. McKee, C. S. joint author. II. T.
QD506.R63     541.3/453 19     *LC* 77-30413     *ISBN* 0198513399

**Somorjai, Gabor A.**     **5.2900**
Chemistry in two dimensions: surfaces / by Gabor A. Somorjai. — Ithaca: Cornell University Press, 1981. 575 p.: ill.; 23 cm. — (The George Fisher Baker non-resident lectureship in chemistry at Cornell University) 1. Surface chemistry I. T.
QD506.S588     541.3/453 19     *LC* 80-21443     *ISBN* 0801411793

**Somorjai, Gabor A.**     **5.2901**
Principles of surface chemistry [by] G. A. Somorjai. — Englewood Cliffs, N.J.: Prentice-Hall, [1972] xviii, 283 p.: illus.; 24 cm. — (Fundamental topics in physical chemistry) 1. Surface chemistry I. T.
QD506.S59     541/.3453     *LC* 79-172890     *ISBN* 0137106084

## QD510–536 Thermochemistry

**Glassman, Irvin.**     **5.2902**
Combustion / Irvin Glassman. — 2nd ed. — Orlando [Fla.]: Academic Press, 1987. xix, 501 p.: ill.; 25 cm. Includes indexes. 1. Combustion I. T.
QD516.G55 1987     541.3/61 19     *LC* 86-13975     *ISBN* 0122858514

**Kanury, A. Murty.**     **5.2903**
Introduction to combustion phenomena: (for fire, incineration, pollution, and energy applications) / A. Murty Kanury. — New York: Gordon and Breach, c1975. xvii, 411 p.; 24 cm. — (Combustion science and technology book series. v. 2) 1. Combustion I. T. II. Series.
QD516.K29     541/.361     *LC* 73-81393     *ISBN* 0677026900

**Kuo, Kenneth K.**     **5.2904**
Principles of combustion / Kenneth Kuan-yun Kuo. — New York: Wiley, c1986. xxiii, 810 p.: ill.; 25 cm. 'A Wiley-Interscience publication.' 1. Combustion I. T.
QD516.K86 1986     541.3/61 19     *LC* 85-22627     *ISBN* 0471098523

**Utermark, Walther, 1898-.**     • **5.2905**
[Schmelzpunkt-Tabellen organischer Verbindungen] Melting point tables of organic compounds / [by] Walther Utermark [and] Walter Schicke. — 2d, rev. and supplemented ed. New York: Interscience Publishers, 1963. xxxii, 715 p.; 25 cm. Added t.p. in German, French and Russian. Tables in German, with prefatory matter and index of special terms in German, English, French and Russian. 'Titres des colonnes du tableau': 2 slips inserted in pocket. 1. Melting points I. Schicke, Walter, joint author. II. T.
QD518.U7 1963     547.1362     *LC* 63-5577

## QD541–544 Theory of Solution

**Hildebrand, Joel Henry, 1881-.**                                    • 5.2906
Regular solutions / [by] Joel H. Hildebrand [and] Robert L. Scott. —
Englewood Cliffs, N. J.: Prentice-Hall, 1962. 180 p.: ill.; 24 cm. (Prentice-Hall
international series in chemistry) Includes bibliography. 1. Solution
(Chemistry) I. Scott, Robert Lane, 1922- joint author. II. T.
QD541.H5 1970      541.34      LC 62-11984

**Marcus, Y.**                                    5.2907
Introduction to liquid state chemistry / Y. Marcus. — London; New York:
Wiley, c1977. xviii, 357 p.: ill.; 24 cm. 'A Wiley-Interscience publication.'
1. Liquids I. T.
QD541.M338      541/.042/2      LC 76-40230      ISBN 0471994480

**Murrell, J. N. (John Norman)**                                    5.2908
Properties of liquids and solutions / J.N. Murrell and E.A. Boucher. —
Chichester [West Sussex]; New York: Wiley, c1982. x, 288 p.: ill.; 24 cm.
Includes index. 1. Liquids 2. Solution (Chemistry) I. Boucher, E. A. II. T.
QD541.M9 1982      541/.0422 19      LC 81-21921      ISBN 0471102016

**Hildebrand, Joel Henry, 1881-.**                                    • 5.2909
Solubility of nonelectrolytes / by Joel H. Hildebrand and Robert L. Scott. — 3d
ed. — New York: Dover, 1964. 488 p.: ill., diagr.; 21 cm. — (Dover books on
chemistry and physical chemistry) Originally published, New York, Reinhold,
1950 in series: American Chemical Society. Monograph series, 17. 1. Solubility
2. Solution (Chemistry) I. Scott, Robert Lane. II. T.
QD543.H5 1964      541.34      LC 64-15503

**Acree, William E. (William Eugene)**                                    5.2910
Thermodynamic properties of nonelectrolyte solutions / William E. Acree, Jr.
— Orlando: Academic Press, 1984. x, 308 p.: graphs; 24 cm. Includes index.
1. Nonaqueous solvents — Thermal properties. 2. Solution (Chemistry) —
Thermal properties. I. T.
QD544.5.A26 1984      541.3/416 19      LC 83-9998      ISBN 0120430207

## QD551–591 Electrochemistry

**Bard, Allen J.**                                    5.2911
Electrochemical methods: fundamentals and applications / Allen J. Bard,
Larry R. Faulkner. — New York: Wiley, c1980. xviii, 718 p.: ill.; 24 cm.
1. Electrochemistry I. Faulkner, Larry R., 1944- II. T.
QD553.B37      541/.37      LC 79-24712      ISBN 0471055425

**Bockris, J. O'M. (John O'M.), 1923-.**                                    5.2912
Electro–chemical science [by] J. O'M. Bockris and D. M. Dražić. London,
Taylor and Francis, 1972. viii, 300 p. illus. 25 cm. Distributed in the U.S.A. by
Barnes & Noble Books, New York. 1. Electrochemistry I. Dražić, Dragutin
M., joint author. II. T.
QD553.B62      541/.37      LC 73-156189      ISBN 0850660513

**Crow, David Richard.**                                    5.2913
Principles and applications of electrochemistry / D. R. Crow. — 2d ed. —
London: Chapman and Hall; New York: Wiley, 1979. 232 p.: ill.; 21 cm. —
(Chapman and Hall chemistry textbook series) 'A Halsted Press book.'
1. Electrochemistry I. T.
QD553.C92 1979      541/.37      LC 79-75      ISBN 0470266740

**Sawyer, Donald T.**                                    5.2914
Experimental electrochemistry for chemists [by] Donald T. Sawyer [and] Julian
L. Roberts, Jr. — New York: Wiley, [1974] x, 435 p.: illus.; 23 cm. 'A Wiley-
Interscience publication.' 1. Electrochemistry I. Roberts, Julian L., joint
author. II. T.
QD553.S32      541/.37      LC 74-3235      ISBN 0471755605

**Albert, Adrien.**                                    5.2915
The determination of ionization constants: a laboratory manual [by] Adrien
Albert [and] E. P. Serjeant. — 2nd ed. — London: Chapman and Hall, 1971. x,
115 p.: illus.; 25 cm. First ed. published in 1962 under title: Ionization constants
of acids and bases. Distributed in the USA by Barnes & Noble, Inc.
1. Ionization constants — Measurement — Laboratory manuals. 2. Acids
3. Bases (Chemistry) I. Serjeant, E. P. joint author. II. T.
QD561.A366 1971      541/.3722/028      LC 72-304765      ISBN
0412103001

## QD601–731 Radiation Chemistry. Photochemistry

**Choppin, Gregory R.**                                    5.2916
Nuclear chemistry: theory and applications / by Gregory R. Choppin and Jan
Rydberg. — 1st ed. — Oxford [Eng.]; New York: Pergamon Press, 1980. viii,
667 p.: ill.; 26 cm. 1. Nuclear chemistry 2. Radiochemistry 3. Radiation
chemistry I. Rydberg, Jan, joint author. II. T.
QD601.2.C47 1980      541/.38      LC 79-40371      ISBN 0080238262

**Turro, Nicholas J., 1938-.**                                    5.2917
Modern molecular photochemistry / Nicholas J. Turro. — Menlo Park, Calif.:
Benjamin/Cummings Pub. Co., c1978. 628 p.: ill.; 25 cm. 1. Photochemistry
2. Chemical reactions 3. Chemistry, Organic I. T.
QD601.2.T87      541/.35      LC 78-57151      ISBN 0805393536

**Faires, R. A. (Ronald Arthur), 1910-.**                                    5.2918
Radioisotope laboratory techniques [by] R. A. Faires and B. H. Parks. With a
chapter by R. D. Stubbs. [3d ed.] New York, Halsted Press Division, Wiley
[1973] 312 p. illus. 23 cm. 1. Radiochemical laboratories 2. Radioisotopes —
Laboratory manuals. I. Parks, Bertram Hasloch, 1913- joint author. II. T.
QD604.8.F35 1973      621.48/37      LC 72-2292      ISBN 0470251506

**Photochemistry: an introduction / by D. R. Arnold [and others].**    5.2919
New York: Academic Press, 1974. vii, 283 p.: ill.; 24 cm. 1. Photochemistry
I. Arnold, Donald Robert, 1935-
QD708.2.P46      541/.35      LC 74-4442      ISBN 0120633507

**Barltrop, J. A.**                                    5.2920
Excited states in organic chemistry / J. A. Barltrop and J. D. Coyle. — London;
New York: Wiley, [1975] xii, 376 p.: ill.; 24 cm. 1. Photochemistry
2. Chemistry, Physical organic I. Coyle, J. D. (John D.) joint author. II. T.
QD715.B37      547/.1/3      LC 74-22400      ISBN 0471049956

## QD901–999 Crystallography

## QD905–908 Reference Works

**Phillips, Frank Coles, 1902-.**                                    5.2921
An introduction to crystallography [by] F. C. Phillips. — 4th ed. — New York:
Wiley, [1972, c1971] 351 p.: ill.; 24 cm. 1. Crystallography I. T.
QD905.2.P55 1972      548      LC 77-127036      ISBN 0582443210

**Smith, Joseph V.**                                    5.2922
Geometrical and structural crystallography / Joseph V. Smith. — New York:
Wiley, c1982. xii, 450 p.: ill.; 25 cm. — (Smith and Wyllie intermediate geology
series.) Includes indexes. 1. Crystallography I. T. II. Series.
QD905.2.S64 1982      549 19      LC 82-2058      ISBN 0471861685

**Edington, Jeffrey William.**                                    5.2923
Practical electron microscopy in materials science / J. W. Edington. New York:
Van Nostrand Reinhold Co., 1977. xii, 344 p.: ill.; 31 cm. Originally published
as separate monographs, 1974 to 1976, by the Macmillan Press Ltd., London
and Basingstoke, under titles: The operation and calibration of the electron
microscope; Electron diffraction in the electron microscope; Interpretation of
transmission electron micrographs; and Typical electron microscope
investigations. 1. Crystallography 2. Electron microscopy I. T.
QD906.7.E37 E34 1977      502/.8      LC 76-7010      ISBN 0442222300

## QD921 Crystal Structure and Growth

**Brown, Penelope Jane.**                                    5.2924
The crystal structure of solids [by] P. J. Brown, J. B. Forsyth. — London:
Edward Arnold; New York: Crane, Russak, 1973. [12], 172 p.: illus.; 24 cm. —

(The Structures and properties of solids [2]) Includes index. 1. Crystallography 2. Solids I. Forsyth, John Bruce, joint author. II. T.
QD921.B787 1973      548/.81      *LC* 73-76883      *ISBN* 0844802042

**Holden, Alan.**                                                      **5.2925**
Crystals and crystal growing / Alan Holden and Phylis Morrison; introduction by Philip Morrison. — 1st MIT Press ed. — Cambridge, Mass.: MIT Press, 1982. 318 p., [32] p. of plates: ill.; 21 cm. Includes index. 1. Crystals 2. Crystals — Growth I. Morrison, Phylis, 1927- II. T.
QD921.H58 1982      548 19      *LC* 81-23639      *ISBN* 0262580500

**Hull, Derek.**                                                       **5.2926**
Introduction to dislocations / by D. Hull and D.J. Bacon. — 3rd ed. — Oxford [Oxfordshire]; New York: Pergamon Press, 1984. xiii, 257 p.: ill.; 24 cm. — (International series on materials science and technology. v. 37) (Pergamon international library of science, technology, engineering, and social studies.) 1. Dislocations in crystals I. Bacon, D. J. II. T. III. Series. IV. Series: Pergamon international library of science, technology, engineering, and social studies.
QD921.H84 1984      548/.842 19      *LC* 83-13321      *ISBN* 0080287212

**Kennon, Noel F.**                                                    **5.2927**
Patterns in crystals / Noel F. Kennon. — Chichester [Eng.]; New York: Wiley, c1978. 197 p.: ill.; 24 cm. Includes index. 1. Crystals I. T.
QD921.K52      548/.81      *LC* 78-4531      *ISBN* 047199748X

**Parsonage, N. G. (Neville George)**                                  **5.2928**
Disorder in crystals / by N. G. Parsonage and L. A. K. Staveley. — Oxford: Clarendon Press; New York: Oxford University Press, 1979 (c1978). xxviii, 926 p.: ill.; 25 cm. (International series of monographs on chemistry.) 1. Crystals — Defects I. Staveley, L. A. K., 1914- joint author. II. T. III. Series.
QD921.P34      548/.842      *LC* 77-30456      *ISBN* 0198556047

# QD941–999 Optical Properties of Crystals. X–Ray Crystallography

**Wahlstrom, Ernest Eugene, 1909-.**                                   **5.2929**
Optical crystallography / Ernest E. Wahlstrom. — 5th ed. — New York: Wiley, c1979. 488 p.: ill.; 24 cm. 1. Crystal optics I. T.
QD941.W28 1979      548/.9      *LC* 78-13695      *ISBN* 0471047910

**Blundell, T. L.**                                                    **5.2930**
Protein crystallography / T. L. Blundell and L. N. Johnson. New York: Academic Press, 1976. xiv, 565 p.: ill.; 24 cm. (Molecular biology, an international series of monographs and textbooks) Includes index. 1. X-ray crystallography 2. Proteins I. Johnson, L. N., joint author. II. T. III. Series.
QD945.B57      547/.75/028      *LC* 76-1068      *ISBN* 0121083500

**Dunitz, Jack D.**                                                    **5.2931**
X-ray analysis and the structure of organic molecules / by Jack D. Dunitz. — Ithaca: Cornell University Press, c1979. 514 p.: ill.; 24 cm. — (George Fisher Baker non-resident lectureship in chemistry at Cornell University.) 1. X-ray crystallography 2. Molecular structure I. T. II. Series.
QD945.D84 1979      547/.1/22      *LC* 78-15588      *ISBN* 0801411157

**Glusker, Jenny Pickworth.**                                          **5.2932**
Crystal structure analysis: a primer / Jenny Pickworth Glusker, Kenneth N. Trueblood. — 2nd ed. — New York: Oxford University Press, 1985. xvii, 269 p.: ill.; 25 cm. Includes index. 1. X-ray crystallography I. Trueblood, Kenneth N. II. T.
QD945.G58 1985      547/.83 19      *LC* 84-14823      *ISBN* 0195035313

**Ladd, M. F. C. (Marcus Frederick Charles)**                          **5.2933**
Structure determination by X-ray crystallography / M.F.C. Ladd and R.A. Palmer. — 2nd ed. — New York: Plenum Press, c1985. xxii, 502 p.: ill.; 24 cm. 1. X-ray crystallography I. Palmer, R. A. (Rex Alfred), 1936- II. T.
QD945.L32 1985      548/.83 19      *LC* 84-24811      *ISBN* 0306418789

**Lipson, Henry Solomon, 1920-.**                                      **5.2934**
Crystals and X-rays / by H. S. Lipson. — London: Wykeham, 1970. xiv, 197 p.: illus.; 22 cm. — (The Wykeham science series, 13) Distributed in the United States of America by Springer-Verlag New York Inc., New York. 1. X-ray crystallography I. T.
QD945.L48      548/.83      *LC* 72-853799      *ISBN* 0851091504

**Sherwood, Dennis.**                                                  **5.2935**
Crystals, X–rays, and proteins / Dennis Sherwood. New York: Wiley, 1976. xxii, 702 p.: ill.; 24 cm. 'A Halsted Press book.' Includes index. 1. X-ray crystallography 2. Proteins I. T.
QD945.S46 1976      548/.83      *LC* 73-7098      *ISBN* 047078590X

**Stout, George H., 1932-.**                                         • **5.2936**
X–ray structure determination: a practical guide / [by] George H. Stout [and] Lyle H. Jensen. — New York: Macmillan, [1968] xi, 467 p.: ill.; 24 cm. 1. X-ray crystallography I. Jensen, Lyle H., joint author. II. T.
QD945.S8      548/.83      *LC* 68-10385

**Wyckoff, Ralph W. G. (Ralph Walter Graystone), 1897-.**              **5.2937**
Crystal structures. — 2d ed. — New York: Interscience Publishers, [c1963-1971] 6 v. in 7: illus.; 24 cm. 1. Crystallography I. T.
QD951.W82      548.8      *LC* 63-22897

# QE    Geology

## QE1–7 REFERENCE WORKS

**Mather, Kirtley F. (Kirtley Fletcher), 1888- comp.** • **5.2938**
Source book in geology, 1900–1950. Edited by Kirtley F. Mather. Cambridge, Harvard University Press, 1967. xv, 435 p. illus. 24 cm. (Source books in the history of the sciences.) Sequel to a source book in geology published in 1939, reprinted in 1964. 1. Geology — History 2. Geology — Collected works. I. T. II. Series.
QE3.M38 1967    550    LC 67-12100

**Bates, Robert Latimer, 1912-.** **5.2939**
Glossary of geology / Robert L. Bates and Julia A. Jackson, editors. — 3rd ed. — Alexandria, Va.: American Geological Institute, 1987. x, 788 p. 1. Geology — Dictionaries. I. Jackson, Julia A., 1939- II. T.
QE5.B38 1987    550/.3/21 19    LC 87-3579    ISBN 0913312894

**Challinor, John.** **5.2940**
[Dictionary of geology] Challinor's dictionary of geology / edited by Antony Wyatt. — 6th ed. — Cardiff: University of Wales Press; New York: Oxford University Press, 1986. xviii, 374 p.; 22 cm. Rev. ed. of: A dictionary of geology. 5th ed. 1978. Includes index. 1. Geology — Dictionaries. I. Wyatt, Antony. II. Challinor, John. Dictionary of geology III. T. IV. Title: Dictionary of geology.
QE5.C45 1986    550/.3/21 19    LC 85-21828    ISBN 0195205065

**The Encyclopedia of applied geology / edited by Charles W.** **5.2941**
**Finkl, Jnr.**
New York: Van Nostrand Reinhold, c1984. xxviii, 644 p.: ill.; 26 cm. — (Encyclopedia of earth sciences. v. 13) 1. Geology — Dictionaries. I. Finkl, Charles W., 1941- II. Series.
QE5.E5 1984    624.1/51/0321 19    LC 83-12765    ISBN 0442225377

**Fairbridge, Rhodes Whitmore, 1914-.** **5.2942**
The encyclopedia of world regional geology / edited by Rhodes W. Fairbridge. — Stroudsburg, Pa.: Dowden, Hutchinson & Ross; [New York]: distributed by Halsted Press, [1975]. xv, 704 p.: ill., maps; 26 cm. — (Encyclopedia of earth sciences. v. 8) 1. Geology — Dictionaries. I. T. II. Series.
QE5.F33    550/.9    LC 75-1406    ISBN 047025145X

**McGraw–Hill encyclopedia of the geological sciences / Daniel** **5.2943**
**N. Lapedes, editor in chief.**
New York: McGraw-Hill, c1978. 915 p.: ill.; 29 cm. Includes index. 1. Geology — Dictionaries. I. Lapedes, Daniel N.
QE5.M29    550/.3    LC 78-18425    ISBN 0070452652

**McGraw–Hill dictionary of earth sciences / Sybil P. Parker,** **5.2944**
**editor in chief.**
New York: McGraw-Hill, c1984. 837 p.; 24 cm. 1. Earth sciences — Dictionaries. I. Parker, Sybil P. II. McGraw-Hill Book Company. III. Title: Dictionary of earth sciences.
QE5.M365 1984    550/.3/21 19    LC 83-20362    ISBN 0070452520

**Wilmarth, Mary Grace, 1866-1949.** • **5.2945**
Lexicon of geologic names of the United States (including Alaska) Washington, U.S. Govt. Print. Off., 1938. Grosse Pointe, Mich., Scholarly Press, 1968. 2 v. (2396 p.) 24 cm. (United States. Geological Survey. Bulletin 896) 'Also includes the names and ages, but not the definitions of the named geologic units of Canada, Mexico, the West Indies, Central America, and Hawaii.' 1. Geology — United States — Nomenclature. I. T.
QE5.W5 1968    551.7/003    LC 71-3260

**North American stratigraphic code / The North American** **5.2946**
**Commission on Stratigraphic Nomenclature.**
[Tulsa, Okla.: American Association of Petroleum Geologists, 1983] p. 841-875: ill. Cover title. 'Reprinted in July, 1983 from the American Association of Petroleum Geologists bulletin, volume 67, number 5 (May, 1983).' 1. Geology, Stratigraphic — Nomenclature 2. Geology — North America — Nomenclature. I. North American Commission on Stratigraphic Nomenclature. II. AAPG bulletin; v. 67, no. 5
QE7.N677

## QE11–23 HISTORY. BIOGRAPHY. DIRECTORIES

**Adams, Frank D. (Frank Dawson), 1859-1942.** • **5.2947**
The birth and development of the geological sciences. — Baltimore: William & Wilkins, 1938. v, 506 p.: illus., ports., facsims.; 21 cm. 1. Geology — History 2. Geology — History — Sources. I. T. II. Title: Geological sciences.
QE11.A3    550.9    LC 39-2208

**Albritton, Claude C., 1913- comp.** **5.2948**
Philosophy of geohistory, 1785–1970. Edited by Claude C. Albritton, Jr. — Stroudsburg, Pa.: Dowden, Hutchinson & Ross, [1975] xiii, 386 p.: illus.; 26 cm. — (Benchmark papers in geology, v. 13) 1. Earth sciences — History — Addresses, essays, lectures. I. T.
QE11.A42    550/.9    LC 74-10559    ISBN 0471020524

**Faul, Henry.** **5.2949**
It began with a stone: a history of geology from the Stone Age to the age of plate tectonics / Henry Faul, Carol Faul. — New York: J. Wiley, c1983. xvii, 270 p.: ill.; 26 cm. 'A Wiley-Interscience publication.' Includes index. 1. Geology — History I. Faul, Carol. II. T.
QE11.F38 1983    550/.9 19    LC 83-3683    ISBN 0471896055

**Geikie, Archibald, Sir, 1835-1924.** • **5.2950**
The founders of geology. — 2d ed. — New York: Dover Publications, [1962] 486 p.; 22 cm. 'An unabridged and unaltered republication of the second (1905) edition of the work first published ... in 1897.' 1. Geology — History I. T.
QE11.G3 1962    550.9    LC 63-2681

**Greene, Mott T., 1945-.** **5.2951**
Geology in the nineteenth century: changing views of a changing world / by Mott T. Greene. — Ithaca, N.Y.: Cornell University Press, 1982. 324 p.: ill., maps; 24 cm. — (Cornell history of science series) Includes index. 1. Geology — History I. T. II. Series.
QE11.G73 1982    550/.9/034 19    LC 82-7456    ISBN 0801414679

**Hallam, A. (Anthony), 1933-.** **5.2952**
Great geological controversies / A. Hallam. — Oxford; New York: Oxford University Press, 1983. vii, 182 p.; 24 cm. — (Oxford science publications.) 1. Geology — History I. T. II. Series.
QE11.H35 1983    551/.09 19    LC 83-2357    ISBN 0198544316

**Zittel, Karl Alfred, ritter von, 1839-1904.** • **5.2953**
History of geology and palæontology to the end of the nineteenth century / by Karl Alfred von Zittel ... Tr. by Maria M. Ogilvie–Gordon ... With thirteen portraits. — London: W. Scott; New York: C. Scribner's sons, 1901. xiii, 1 l., 562 p.: front., ports., ill.; 19 cm. (The contemporary science series ... [42]) 1. Geology — History 2. Paleontology — History I. Gordon, Maria Matilda (Ogilvie) Dame, d. 1939, tr. II. T.
QE11.Z8    LC 02-12497

**Porter, Roy, 1946-.** **5.2954**
The making of geology: earth science in Britain, 1660–1815 / Roy Porter. Cambridge [Eng.]; New York: Cambridge University Press, 1977. x, 288 p.; 23 cm. Includes index. 1. Geology — Great Britain — History. I. T.
QE13.G7 P67    550/.941    LC 76-56220    ISBN 0521215218

**Merrill, George P. (George Perkins), 1854-1929.** • **5.2955**
The first one hundred years of American geology, by George P. Merrill. New York, Hafner Pub. Co., 1964 [c1924] xxi, 773 p. illus., maps, ports. 24 cm. 'Facsimile of the edition of 1924.' 1. Geology — History 2. Geology — United States 3. Geologists — United States. I. T.
QE13.U6 M6 1964    550    LC 64-20222

**New Hampshire Bicentennial Conference on the History of** **5.2956**
**Geology, University of New Hampshire, 1976.**
Two hundred years of geology in America: proceedings of the New Hampshire Bicentennial Conference on the History of Geology / Cecil J. Schneer, editor. — Hanover, N.H.: Published for the University of New Hampshire by the University Press of New England, 1979. 385 p.: ill.; 24 cm. 1. Geology — United States — History. I. Schneer, Cecil J., 1923- II. University of New Hampshire. III. T.
QE13.U6 N48 1976    550/.973    LC 78-63149    ISBN 0874511607

**Tinsley, Elizabeth J.** 5.2957
Worldwide directory of national earth–science agencies and related international organizations: a listing of governmental earth–science agencies and selected major international organizations whose functions are similar to those of the U.S. Geological Survey / compiled by E.J. Tinsley and Joyce P. Hollander. — Washington: U.S. G.P.O.; Alexandria, VA: Distribution Branch, Text Products Section, U.S. Geological Survey [distributor], 1984. iv, 102 p.: maps; 26 cm. (U.S. Geological Survey circular. 934) 1. Earth sciences — Directories. 2. Geological surveys — Directories. I. Hollander, Joyce P. II. T. III. Series.
QE23.T56 1984     351.85/55 19     LC 84-600161

# QE26–61 General Works

**Grabau, Amadeus William, 1870-1946.** • 5.2958
Principles of stratigraphy / With a prefatory note by Marshall Kay. — [New ed.]. — New York: Dover Publications, [1960] 2 v.: ill.; 21 cm. — (Dover books on science, S686-S687) 'Unabridged and unaltered republication of the last revised edition published in 1924.' 1. Geology, Stratigraphic I. T.
QE26.G8 1960     551.7     LC 60-51875

**Shelton, John S.** • 5.2959
Geology illustrated [by] John S. Shelton. Drawings by Hal Shelton. — San Francisco: W. H. Freeman, [1966] xii, 434 p.: illus., maps.; 28 cm. 1. Geology I. T.
QE26.S5     550     LC 66-16380

**The Cambridge encyclopedia of earth sciences / editor in chief,** 5.2960
**David G. Smith.**
New York, N.Y.: Crown Publisher/Cambridge University Press, 1982 (c1981). 496 p.: ill. (some col.); 27 cm. Includes index. 1. Earth sciences I. Smith, David G. (David Graham)
QE26.2.C35 1981     550 19     LC 81-3313     ISBN 0517543702

**Van Andel, Tjeerd H. (Tjeerd Hendrik), 1923-.** 5.2961
New views on an old planet: continental drift and the history of earth / Tjeerd H. van Andel. — Cambridge [Cambridgeshire]; New York: Cambridge University Press, 1985. xii, 324 p.: ill.; 26 cm. 1. Geology 2. Continental drift I. T.
QE26.2.V36 1985     551.1/36 19     LC 84-14251     ISBN 0521300843

**Wyllie, Peter J., 1930-.** 5.2962
The dynamic earth: textbook in geosciences [by] Peter J. Wyllie. — New York: Wiley, [1971] xiv, 416 p.: illus.; 26 cm. 1. Earth sciences I. T.
QE26.2.W9     551     LC 73-155909     ISBN 0471968897

**Jacobs, J. A. (John Arthur), 1916-.** 5.2963
A textbook on geonomy [by] J. A. Jacobs. — New York: Wiley, [1975, c1974] ix, 328 p.: illus.; 26 cm. 'A Halsted Press book.' 1. Earth sciences 2. Astronomy I. T.
QE28.J32 1975     550     LC 74-9662     ISBN 0470434457

**Lahee, Frederic Henry, 1884-.** • 5.2964
Field geology. — 6th ed. — New York: McGraw-Hill Book Co., 1961. 926 p.: ill.; 20 cm. 1. Geology — Field work. I. T.
QE28.L2 1961     550     LC 60-15291

**Hamblin, W. Kenneth (William Kenneth), 1928-.** 5.2965
The Earth's dynamic systems: a textbook in physical geology / by W. Kenneth Hamblin. — 4th ed. — Minneapolis, Minn.: Burgess Pub., c1985. xii, 528 p.: ill. (some col.); 29 cm. 1. Physical geology I. T.
QE28.2.H35 1985     551 19     LC 85-6636     ISBN 0808747428

**Holmes, Arthur, 1890-1965.** 5.2966
[Principles of physical geology] Holmes Principles of physical geology / Arthur Holmes. — 3d ed. / rev. by Doris L. Holmes. — New York: Wiley, c1978. 730 p.: ill.; 24 cm. Previous ed. published in 1965 under title: Principles of physical geology. 'A Halsted Press book.' 1. Physical geology I. Holmes, Doris L., 1899- II. T. III. Title: Principles of physical geology.
QE28.2.H64 1978     551     LC 78-2508     ISBN 0471072516

**Press, Frank.** 5.2967
Earth / Frank Press, Raymond Siever. — 4th ed. — New York: W.H. Freeman, c1986. xviii, 656 p., [16] p. of plates: ill. (some col.); 29 cm. Map on lining papers. I. Siever, Raymond. II. T.
QE28.2.P7 1986     550 19     LC 85-20581     ISBN 0716717433

**Spencer, Edgar Winston.** 5.2968
Physical geology / Edgar W. Spencer. — Reading, MA: Addison-Wesley Pub. Co., c1983. ix, 611 p.: ill.; 29 cm. 1. Physical geology I. T.
QE28.2.S646 1983     551 19     LC 82-18415     ISBN 0201064235

**Dott, Robert H., 1929-.** 5.2969
Evolution of the earth / Robert H. Dott, Jr., Roger L. Batten; maps and diagrs. by Randall D. Sale. — 3d ed. — New York: McGraw-Hill, c1981. vii, 573, I13 p.: ill.; 26 cm. 1. Historical geology I. Batten, Roger Lyman. joint author. II. T.
QE28.3.D68 1981     551.7     LC 80-18876     ISBN 0070176256

**Ozima, Minoru.** 5.2970
[Chikyu-shi. English] The earth: its birth and growth / Minoru Ozima; translated by Judy Wakabayashi. — Cambridge: Cambridge University Press, 1981. x, 117 p.: ill.; 22 cm. Translation of: Chikyu-shi by Iwanami Shoten, Tokyo, 1979. 1. Historical geology I. T.
QE28.3.O95     QE28.3 O95.     LC 80-41807     ISBN 0521235006

**Stanley, Steven M.** 5.2971
Earth and life through time / Steven M. Stanley. — New York: W.H. Freeman, c1986. xi, 690 p.: ill. (some col.); 29 cm. Map on lining paper. 1. Historical geology I. T.
QE28.3.S73 1986     551.7 19     LC 84-21098     ISBN 0716716771

# QE33–36 Special Topics, A–Z. Maps

**Flawn, Peter Tyrell.** • 5.2972
Environmental geology: conservation, land–use planning, and resource management [by] Peter T. Flawn. — New York: Harper & Row, [1970] xix, 313 p.: illus., maps.; 24 cm. — (Harper's geoscience series) 1. Geology 2. Conservation of natural resources I. T.
QE33.F5     550     LC 75-103915

**Moore, Carl Allphin, 1911-.** • 5.2973
Handbook of subsurface geology. New York: Harper & Row [c1963] xiii, 235 p.: ill., maps, profiles; 25 cm. (Harper's geoscience series.) 1. Geology, Structural 2. Prospecting 3. Petroleum — Geology I. T. II. Title: Subsurface geology. III. Series.
QE33.M57     622.18282     LC 64-10009

**ERTS–I: a new window on our planet / Richard S. Williams,** 5.2974
**Jr., and William D. Carter, editors; cooperating organizations,**
**U.S. Department of the Interior ... [et al.].**
Washington: U.S. Govt. Print. Off., 1976. xix, 362 p.: ill. (some col.); 29 cm. (Geological Survey professional paper; 929) 1. Astronautics in earth sciences I. Williams, Richard S. II. Carter, William Douglas, 1926-
QE33.2.A7 E17     550     LC 75-37451

**Cheeney, R. F.** 5.2975
Statistical methods in geology for field and lab decisions / R.F. Cheeney. — London; Boston: Allen & Unwin, 1983. xvi, 169 p.: ill.; 23 cm. Includes index. 1. Geology — Statistical methods I. T.
QE33.2.M3 C48 1983     550/.72 19     LC 83-7647     ISBN 0045500290

**Remote sensing in geology / edited by Barry S. Siegal, Alan R.** 5.2976
**Gillespie.**
New York: Wiley, c1980. xviii, 702 p., [16] leaves of plates: ill.; 29 cm. 1. Geology — Remote sensing. I. Siegal, Barry S., 1947- II. Gillespie, Alan R.
QE33.2.R4 R44     550/.28     LC 79-17967     ISBN 0471790524

**Albritton, Claude C., 1913- ed.** • 5.2977
The fabric of geology. Prepared under the direction of a committee of the Geological Society of America, in commemoration of the society's 75th anniversary. — Reading, Mass.: Addison-Wesley Pub. Co., [1963] x, 372 p.: illus.; 25 cm. 1. Geology — Addresses, essays, lectures. I. Geological Society of America. II. T.
QE35.A45     550.82     LC 63-17126

**Levorsen, Arville Irving, 1894-1965.** 5.2978
Paleogeologic maps. San Francisco, W.H. Freeman [1960] 174 p. illus. 25 cm. (Series of geology texts.) 1. Geology — Maps I. T. II. Series.
QE36.L4     551.7084     LC 60-11325

**Moseley, F.** 5.2979
Advanced geological map interpretation / Frank Moseley. — New York: Wiley, 1979. 79, [1] p.: ill.; 27 cm. 'A Halsted Press book.' 1. Geology — Maps I. T.
QE36.M67 1979     550/.2/22     LC 79-11243     ISBN 0470267089

**Roberts, John L. (John Leonard), 1936-.**                        **5.2980**
Introduction to geological maps and structures / John L. Roberts. — 1st ed. — Oxford; New York: Pergamon Press, 1982. vii, 332 p.: ill.; 24 cm. — (Pergamon international library of science, technology, engineering, and social studies.) Includes index. 1. Geology — Maps 2. Geology, Structural I. T. II. Series.
QE36.R63 1982      550/.222 19      LC 81-21018      ISBN 008023982X

# QE39 Special Fields. Submarine Geology. Urban Geology

**Burk, Creighton A.**                                             **5.2981**
The geology of continental margins, edited by Creighton A. Burk and Charles L. Drake. — New York: Springer-Verlag, [1974] xiii, 1009 p.: illus.; 29 cm. 1. Continental margins 2. Submarine geology I. Drake, Charles L., 1924- joint author. II. T.
QE39.B85      551.4/608      LC 74-16250      ISBN 038706866X

**Kennett, James P.**                                             **5.2982**
Marine geology / James P. Kennett. — Englewood Cliffs, N.J.: Prentice-Hall, c1982. xv, 813 p.: ill.; 25 cm. Includes indexes. 1. Submarine geology I. T.
QE39.K46      551.46/08 19      LC 81-10726      ISBN 0135569362

**Nairn, A. E. M.**                                               **5.2983**
The ocean basins and margins, edited by Alan E. M. Nairn and Francis G. Stehli. New York: Plenum Press, 1974. 598 p.: ill. 1. Submarine geology 2. Continental margins I. Stehli, Francis Greenough. joint author. II. T.
QE39.N27      551.4/608      LC 72-83046      ISBN 0306377713

**Seibold, Eugen.**                                               **5.2984**
The sea floor: an introduction to marine geology / E. Seibold, W.H. Berger. — Berlin; New York: Springer-Verlag, 1982. vii, 288 p.: ill.; 25 cm. Includes indexes. 1. Submarine geology I. Berger, Wolfgang H. II. T.
QE39.S38      551.46/08 19      LC 81-18434      ISBN 0387112561

**Shepard, Francis Parker, 1897-.**                              **5.2985**
Geological oceanography: evolution of coasts, continental margins & the deep-sea floor / Francis P. Shepard. — New York: Crane, Russak, c1977. ii, 214 p., [2] leaves of plates: ill.; 26 cm. 1. Submarine geology 2. Coast changes I. T.
QE39.S539      551.4/6      LC 76-54533      ISBN 0844810649

**Leveson, David, 1934-.**                                       **5.2986**
Geology and the urban environment / David Leveson: original ill. drafted by Margaret Leveson. — New York: Oxford University Press, 1980. viii, 386 p.: ill.; 25 cm. Includes index. 1. Urban geology 2. Land use — Planning I. T.
QE39.5.U7 L48 1980      550/.9173/2      LC 78-31256      ISBN 0195025784

# QE40–61 Study and Teaching

**Earth and astronomical sciences research centres: a world**      **5.2987**
**directory of organizations and programmes / consultant editor,**
**Jennifer M. Fitch.**
1st ed. — Harlow, Essex, UK: Longman; Detroit, MI, USA: Distributed exclusively in USA, its possessions, and Canada by Gale Research Co., 1984. 742 p.; 25 cm. (Reference on research.) Includes indexes. 1. Earth sciences — Research — Directories. 2. Astronomy — Research — Directories. I. Fitch, Jennifer M. II. Series.
QE40.E25 1984      550/.72 19      LC 84-209608      ISBN 0582900204

**American Geological Institute. Conference (1959: Duluth,**      **• 5.2988**
**Minn.)**
Geology and earth sciences sourcebook for elementary and secondary schools / Robert L. Heller, editor; prepared under the guidance of the American Geological Institute, National Academy of Sciences–National Research Council. — New York: Holt, Rinehart and Winston [1962] 496 p.: ill.; 23 cm. Held on the Duluth campus of the University of Minnesota. 1. Geology — Study and teaching. I. Heller, Robert L. (Robert Leo), 1919- ed. II. National Academy of Sciences (U.S.) III. University of Minnesota, Duluth. IV. T.
QE41.A55      550.7      LC 62-10549

**Compton, Robert R.**                                           **5.2989**
Geology in the field / Robert R. Compton. — New York: Wiley, c1985. xi, 398 p.: ill.; 22 cm. 1. Geology — Field work. I. T.
QE45.C63 1985      551/.0723 19      LC 85-2325      ISBN 0471829021

**Low, Julian William, 1904-.**                                  **• 5.2990**
Geologic field methods. New York, Harper [1957] 489 p. illus. 20 cm. (Harper's geoscience series.) 1. Geology — Field work. I. T. II. Series.
QE45.L6      550.72      LC 57-8063

**Davis, John C.**                                               **5.2991**
Statistics and data analysis in geology / John C. Davis. — 2nd ed. — New York: Wiley, c1986. x, 646 p.: ill.; 25 cm. + 1 computer program on 1 computer disk (5 1/4 in.) System requirements for floppy disk: PC with PC-DOS or MS-DOS (version 2.10); 128K; color or monochrome monitor; DOS-compatible line printer. 1. Geology — Data processing 2. Geology — Statistical methods I. T.
QE48.8.D38 1986      550/.72 19      LC 85-12331      ISBN 0471080799

**Loudon, T. V.**                                                **5.2992**
Computer methods in geology / T. V. Loudon. — London; New York: Academic Press, 1979. x, 269 p.: ill.; 24 cm. 1. Geology — Data processing I. T.
QE48.8.L68      550/.028/54      LC 78-18025      ISBN 0124569501

# QE65–350 GEOLOGY OF SPECIAL REGIONS

# QE71–288 The Americas. Europe

**Eardley, A. J. (Armand John), 1901-.**                         **• 5.2993**
Structural geology of North America. 2d ed. New York: Harper & Row [c1962] xv, 743 p.: ill., maps (part col.); 22 x 30 cm. (Harper's geoscience series.) 1. Geology — North America. 2. Geology, Structural I. T. II. Series.
QE71.E17 1962      551.8      LC 62-17482

**King, Philip Burke, 1903-.**                                   **5.2994**
The evolution of North America / by Philip B. King. — Rev. ed. — Princeton, N.J.: Princeton University Press, 1977. xv, 197 p.: ill. (1 fold.); 29 cm. 1. Geology — North America. I. T.
QE71.K54 1977      557      LC 77-71987      ISBN 0691081956

**North American geology: early writings / edited by Robert M.**   **5.2995**
**Hazen.**
Stroudsburg, Pa.: Dowden, Hutchinson & Ross; [New York]: distributed world wide by Academic Press, c1979. xvii, 356 p.; 26 cm. — (Benchmark papers in geology; 51) 1. Geology — North America — Addresses, essays, lectures. I. Hazen, Robert M., 1948-
QE71.N67      557 19      LC 79-708      ISBN 0879333456

**Geological Survey (U.S.). Office of the Data Administrator.**   **5.2996**
Scientific and technical, spatial, and bibliographic data bases and systems of the U.S. Geological Survey, 1983: including other federal agencies / compiled by the Office of the Data Administrator; prepared with the cooperation of the Bureau of Land Management and the Minerals Management Service. — Rev. ed. — Alexandria, VA (604 S. Pickett St., Alexandria 22304): Distribution Branch, Text Products Section, U.S. Geological Survey, [1984] 438 p. in various pagings; 26 cm. (Geological Survey circular. 817) Spine title: Data bases and systems of the U.S. Geological Survey, 1983. Rev. ed. of: Scientific and technical, spatial, and bibliographic data bases of the U.S. Geological Survey, 1979 / compiled by the Office of the Data Base Administrator. 1980. Includes indexes. 1. Information storage and retrieval systems — Earth sciences. I. United States. Bureau of Land Management. II. United States. Minerals Management Service. III. Geological Survey (U.S.). Office of the Data Base Administrator. Scientific and technical, spatial, and bibliographic data bases of the U.S. Geological Survey, 1979. IV. T. V. Title: Data bases and systems of the U.S. Geological Survey, 1983. VI. Series.
QE75.C5 no. 817 1984 QE48.8      557.3 s 025/.0655 19      LC 84-601610

**Dodd, Kurt.**                                                  **5.2997**
Guide to obtaining USGS information / compiled by Kurt Dodd, H. Kit Fuller, and Paul F. Clarke. — [Washington]: U.S. Geological Survey, 1985. 35 p.; 28 cm. (U.S. Geological Survey circular; 900) Supersedes Circular 777. Rev. ed. of: A guide to obtaining information from the USGS, 1978 / compiled by Paul F. Clarke, Helen F. Hodgson, and Gary W. North. 1978. 1. Geology — United States — Information. 2. Hydrology — United States — Information services. I. Fuller, H. Kit. II. Clarke, Paul F. III. Clarke, Paul F. Guide to obtaining information from the USGS, 1978. IV. Geological Survey (U.S.) V. T.
QE75.C5 no. 900 QE47.A1      557.3 s 557.3/072 19      LC 85-600161

Thornbury, William D. (William David), 1900-.    • 5.2998
Regional geomorphology of the United States [by] William D. Thornbury. New York, Wiley [1965] viii, 609 p. illus., maps. 26 cm. 1. Geology — United States 2. Physical geography — United States. I. T.
QE77.T5     551.40973     LC 65-12698

McPhee, John A.                    5.2999
In suspect terrain / John McPhee. — New York: Farrar, Straus, Giroux, 1982. 209 p.; 22 cm. 1. Geology — Northeastern States. I. T.
QE78.3.M36 1983     550 19     LC 82-21031     ISBN 0374176507

McPhee, John A.                    5.3000
Basin and range / John McPhee. — New York: Farrar, Straus, Giroux, [1980]. 215 p.; 22 cm. 1. Geology — The West. I. T.
QE79.M28 1981     557.9 19     LC 80-28679     ISBN 0374109141

McPhee, John A.                    5.3001
Rising from the plains / John McPhee. — New York: Farrar, Straus, Giroux, c1986. 213 p., [1] p. of plates: ill.; 22 cm. Illustrations on lining papers. 1. Geology — Rocky Mountains. 2. Geology — History I. T.
QE79.M29 1986     557.8 19     LC 86-14891     ISBN 0374250820

Jenks, William Furness, 1909-.          • 5.3002
Handbook of South American geology: an explanation of the geologic map of South America / William F. Jenks; containing papers by A. I. de Oliveira ... [et al.]. — New York: Geological Society of America, 1956. xix, 378 p., 11 l. of plates: ill., maps; 26 cm. — (Memoir / Geological Society of America; 65) 1. Geology — South America I. Oliveira, Avelino Ignacio de, 1891- II. Geological Society of America. III. T.
QE230.J4     LC 56-58161

Ager, D. V. (Derek Victor)           5.3003
The geology of Europe: a regional approach / Derek V. Ager. — New York: Halsted Press, 1981 (c1980). xix, 535 p.: ill.; 25 cm. 1. Geology — Europe. I. T.
QE260.A37 1980     554     LC 80-40318     ISBN 0470269901

Brinkmann, Roland, 1898-.          • 5.3004
[Abriss der Geologie. English] Geologic evolution of Europe. Translated from the German by John E. Sanders. Stuttgart, F. Enke; New York, Hafner Pub. Co., 1960. vi, 161 p. illus., ports., maps. 25 cm. 'Condensed version of the second volume of the 8th edition of the Abriss der Geologie.' 1. Geology — Europe. 2. Geology, Stratigraphic I. T.
QE260.B723     554     LC 60-4061

Nalivkin, D. V. (Dmitriĭ Vasil'evich), 1889-.       5.3005
[Geologiia SSSR. English] Geology of the U.S.S.R. / D.V. Nalivkin; translated from the Russian by N. Rast; edited by N. Rast and T.S. Westoll. — Toronto; Buffalo: University of Toronto Press, 1974 (c1973). xxviii, 855 p., [12] fold. leaves of plates: ill. (part fold.), maps (part fold.), ports.; 27 cm. Translation of Geologiia SSSR. Includes indexes. 1. Geology — Russia. 2. Mines and mineral resources — Russia. I. T.
QE276.N2813     554.7     LC 75-317194     ISBN 0802019846

## QE289–350 Asia. Africa. Australia. Oceans

Furon, Raymond, 1898-.          • 5.3006
[Géologie de l'Afrique. English] Geology of Africa / translated by A. Hallam and L.A. Stevens. — New York: Hafner Pub. Co. [1963] 377 p.: ill.; 23 cm. 1. Geology — Africa. 2. Geology, Stratigraphic I. T.
QE320.F813     556     LC 63-2498

Tectonics of Africa / co-ordinated by G. Choubert and A.    5.3007
Faure-Muret.
Paris: Unesco, 1972. 602 p.: ill., maps (1 fold. col. in pocket); 28 cm. (Sciences de la terre. Earth sciences; 6) 'SC.70/XVII.6/AF.' English or French, with summaries in French or English. Label mounted on t.p.: Unipub, New York, distributor. 1. Geology — Africa. I. Title: Tectonics of Africa.
QE320.T2x     551.8/096     LC 72-75842

Brown, David Alexander.          • 5.3008
The geological evolution of Australia & New Zealand, by D. A. Brown, K. S. W. Campbell [and] K. A. W. Crook. [1st ed.] Oxford, New York, Pergamon Press [1968] x, 409 p. illus., maps. 23 cm. (The Commonwealth and international library. Geology division) 1. Geology — Australia 2. Geology — New Zealand. 3. Geology, Stratigraphic I. Campbell, K. S. W. (Kenton Stewart Wall) II. Crook, K. A. W. III. T.
QE340.B7 1968     551.7/00994     LC 66-29583

## QE351–399 MINERALOGY

## QE351–366 Reference. General Works

The Encyclopedia of mineralogy / edited by Keith Frye.    5.3009
Stroudsburg, Pa.: Hutchinson Ross Pub. Co., c1981. xx, 794 p.: ill.; 26 cm. — (Encyclopedia of earth sciences. v. 4B) 1. Mineralogy — Dictionaries. I. Frye, Keith, 1935- II. Series.
QE355.E49     549/.03/21 19     LC 81-982     ISBN 0879331844

A Manual of new mineral names, 1892–1978 / edited by Peter    5.3010
G. Embrey and John P. Fuller.
London: British Museum (Natural History); New York: Oxford University Press, 1980. ix, 467 p.; 24 cm. Includes index. 1. Mineralogy — Nomenclature. I. Embrey, Peter G. II. Fuller, John P.
QE357.M36 1980     549/.03     LC 80-40204     ISBN 0198585012

Mitchell, Richard Scott, 1929-.          5.3011
Mineral names: what do they mean? / By Richard Scott Mitchell, assisted by John Reese Henley. — New York: Van Nostrand Reinhold Co., c1979. xv, 229 p.; 24 cm. Includes index. 1. Mineralogy — Names. I. Henley, John Reese. joint author. II. T.
QE357.M57     549/.01/4     LC 78-26141     ISBN 0442245939

Dana, James Dwight, 1813-1895.          • 5.3012
The system of mineralogy of James Dwight Dana and Edward Salisbury Dana, Yale University, 1837–1892. — 7th ed., / entirely rewritten and greatly enlarged by Charles Palache, Harry Berman, and Clifford Frondel. — New York: Wiley; London: Chapman and Hall, [1944-. v.: ill. 1. Mineralogy I. Dana, Edward Salisbury, 1849-1935. II. Palache, Charles, 1869- III. Berman, Harry M , 1902-1944. IV. Frondel, Clifford, 1907- V. T.
QE362.D23 1944     LC 44-8346

Berry, L. G. (Leonard Gascoigne), 1914-.          5.3013
Mineralogy, concepts, descriptions, determinations / L.G. Berry, Brian Mason. — 2nd ed. / revised by R.V. Dietrich. — San Francisco: Freeman, c1983. xi, 561 p.: ill.; 25 cm. 1. Mineralogy I. Mason, Brian Harold, 1917- II. Dietrich, Richard Vincent, 1924- III. T.
QE363.2.B4 1983     549 19     LC 82-16008     ISBN 0716714248

Zoltai, Tibor.          5.3014
Mineralogy: concepts and principles / Tibor Zoltai and James H. Stout. — Minneapolis, Minn.: Burgess Pub. Co., c1984. x, 505 p.: ill.; 29 cm. 1. Mineralogy I. Stout, James H. II. T.
QE363.2.Z65 1984     549 19     LC 83-20992     ISBN 0808726064

Deer, W. A. (William Alexander)          • 5.3015
An introduction to the rock-forming minerals / [by] W. A. Deer, R. A. Howie [and] J. Zussman. — New York: Wiley [1966] x, 528 p.: ill.; 23 cm. Includes bibliographies. 1. Mineralogy 2. Rocks I. Howie, R. A. (Robert Andrew) joint author. II. Zussman, J. joint author. III. T.
QE364.D37 1966a     549.6     LC 66-7468

Simon and Schuster's Guide to rocks and minerals / edited by    5.3016
Martin Prinz, George Harlow, and Joseph Peters.
New York: Simon and Schuster, [1978] 607 p.: ill.; 19 cm. — (A Fireside book) Translation of Minerali e rocce, by A. Mottana, R. Crespi, and G. Liborio. Includes index. 1. Rocks — Collectors and collecting 2. Mineralogy — Collectors and collecting I. Prinz, Martin. II. Harlow, George. III. Peters, Joseph, 1951- IV. Mottana, Annibale. Minerali e rocce.
QE366.2.M6713     552/.075     LC 78-8610     ISBN 0671243969

## QE367–399 Determinative and Descriptive Mineralogy

Zussman, J. ed.          5.3017
Physical methods in determinative mineralogy / edited by J. Zussman. — 2d ed. — London; New York: Academic Press, 1977. xiv, 720 p.: ill.; 24 cm. 1. Mineralogy, Determinative — Methodology. I. T.
QE367.Z8 1977     549/.12     LC 77-76850     ISBN 0127829601

**Pough, Frederick H.**     **5.3018**
A field guide to rocks and minerals / by Frederick H. Pough. 4th ed. — Boston: Houghton Mifflin, 1976. xix, 317 p., [49] leaves of plates: ill.; 19 cm. (The Peterson field guide series; 7) Includes index. 1. Mineralogy, Determinative 2. Rocks I. T.
QE367.2.P68 1976     549/.1     *LC* 75-22364     *ISBN* 0395081068

**Phillips, William Revell, 1929-.**     **5.3019**
Optical mineralogy: the nonopaque minerals / Wm. Revell Phillips, Dana T. Griffen. — San Francisco: W. H. Freeman, c1981. xi, 677 p.: ill.; 25 cm. — (A Series of books in geology) 1. Optical mineralogy I. Griffen, Dana T., 1943- joint author. II. T.
QE369.O6 P44     549/.125     *LC* 80-12435     *ISBN* 071671129X

**Dana, Edward Salisbury, 1849-1935.**     • **5.3020**
A textbook of mineralogy: with an extended treatise on crystallography and physical mineralogy / by Edward Salisbury Dana. — 4th ed., rev. and enl., by William E. Ford. — New York: J. Wiley, 1948, c1932. xi, 851 p.: ill. Includes indexes. 1. Mineralogy 2. Crystallography I. Ford, W. E. (William Ebenezer), 1878- II. T.
QE372.D18     549

**Dana, James Dwight, 1813-1895.**     **5.3021**
Manual of mineralogy (after James D. Dana) / Cornelis Klein, Cornelius S. Hurlbut, Jr. — 20th ed. — New York: Wiley, c1985. xi, 596 p., [4] p. of plates: ill. (some col.); 29 cm. 1. Mineralogy I. Klein, Cornelis, 1937- II. Hurlbut, Cornelius Searle, 1906- III. T.
QE372.D2 1985     549 19     *LC* 84-19556     *ISBN* 0471805807

**Craig, James R., 1940-.**     **5.3022**
Ore microscopy and ore petrography / James R. Craig, David J. Vaughan. — New York: Wiley, c1981. xii, 406 p.: ill.; 24 cm. 'A Wiley-Interscience publication.' 1. Ores 2. Thin sections (Geology) I. Vaughan, David J., 1946- joint author. II. T.
QE390.C7     549/.12 19     *LC* 80-39786     *ISBN* 0471085960

**Guilbert, John M.**     **5.3023**
The geology of ore deposits / John M. Guilbert, Charles F. Park, Jr. — New York: W.H. Freeman, c1986. xiv, 985 p.: ill.; 25 cm. Based on Ore deposits / Charles F. Park, Jr., Roy A. MacDiarmid. 3rd ed. 1975. 1. Ore deposits 2. Geology I. Park, Charles Frederick, 1903- II. Park, Charles Frederick, 1903- Ore deposits. III. T. IV. Title: Ore deposits.
QE390.G85 1986     553.4 19     *LC* 85-10099     *ISBN* 0716714566

**Marine manganese deposits / edited by G. P. Glasby.**     **5.3024**
Amsterdam; New York: Elsevier Scientific Pub. Co.; New York: distributors for the U.S. and Canada, Elsevier/North-Holland, c1977. 523 p.: ill.; 25 cm. — (Elsevier oceanography series; 15) Includes index. 1. Manganese nodules I. Glasby, G. P.
QE390.2.M35 M37     553/.462     *LC* 76-48895     *ISBN* 0444415246

**Webster, Robert.**     **5.3025**
Gems, their sources, descriptions, and identification / Robert Webster. — 4th ed. / revised by B.W. Anderson. — London; Boston: Butterworths, 1983. xxii, 1006 p., [17] p. of plates: ill. (some col.); 25 cm. Includes indexes. 1. Precious stones. 2. Jewelry. I. Anderson, B. W. (Basil William), 1901- II. T.
QE392.W37 1983     553.8 19     *LC* 83-182288     *ISBN* 0408011483

**Deer, W. A. (William Alexander)**     **5.3026**
Rock–forming minerals [by] W.A. Deer, R.A. Howie and J. Zussman. New York, Wiley [1962–<63 >. v. <1 > illus. 26 cm. 1. Rock-forming minerals 2. Silicate minerals 3. Rocks I. T.
QE397.D44 1962     549     *LC* 62-5735

**Deer, W. A. (William Alexander)**     **5.3027**
Rock–forming minerals / W. A. Deer, R. A. Howie, J. Zussman. — 2nd ed. — London: Longman; New York: Halsted Press, 1978- v.: ill.; 24 cm. V. 1A published in 1982. 1. Silicate minerals 2. Rocks 3. Rock-forming minerals I. Howie, R. A. (Robert Andrew) II. Zussman, J. III. T.
QE397.D44 1978     549     *LC* 79-310837     *ISBN* 0582465265

**MacKenzie, W. S.**     **5.3028**
Atlas of rock–forming minerals in thin section / W. S. MacKenzie and C. Guilford. — New York: Halsted Press, 1980. v, 98 p.: ill. (some col.); 28 cm. Includes index. 1. Rock-forming minerals — Pictorial work. 2. Thin sections (Geology) — Pictorial works. I. Guilford, C. joint author. II. T.
QE397.M33 1980b     549/.114 19     *LC* 79-27822     *ISBN* 0470269219

**Barnes, Virgil E. (Virgil Everett), 1903- comp.**     **5.3029**
Tektites / edited by Virgil E. and Mildred A. Barnes. — Stroudsburg, Pa.: Dowden, Hutchinson & Ross [1973] xv, 445 p.: ill.; 26 cm. (Benchmark papers in geology) 1. Tektite — Addresses, essays, lectures. I. Barnes, Mildred, joint comp. II. T.
QE399.B34     523.5/1     *LC* 72-95942     *ISBN* 0879330279

# QE420–499 PETROLOGY. ROCKS

**Mitchell, Richard Scott, 1929-.**     **5.3030**
Dictionary of rocks / Richard Scott Mitchell. — New York: Van Nostrand Reinhold, c1985. xi, 228 p., [4] p. of plates: ill. (some col.); 27 cm. 1. Petrology — Dictionaries. I. T.
QE423.M58 1985     552/.003/21 19     *LC* 84-22062     *ISBN* 0442263287

**Barth, Tom. F. W. (Tom. Fredrik Weiby), 1899-1971.**     • **5.3031**
Theoretical petrology. 2d ed. New York: Wiley [1962] 416 p.: ill.;c24 cm. 1. Petrology I. T.
QE431.B38 1962     552     *LC* 62-18349

**Moorhouse, W. W. (Walter Wilson), 1913-1969.**     • **5.3032**
The study of rocks in thin section. New York: Harper [1959] 514 p.: ill.; 25 cm. (Harper's geoscience series.) 1. Petrology 2. Thin sections (Geology) I. T. II. Series.
QE431.M68     552.8     *LC* 59-7027

**Spock, Leslie Erskine, 1900-.**     • **5.3033**
Guide to the study of rocks. 2d ed. New York: Harper [1962] 298 p.: ill.; 25 cm. (Harper's geoscience series.) 1. Petrology I. T. II. Series.
QE431.S75 1962     552     *LC* 62-11472

**Dietrich, Richard Vincent, 1924-.**     **5.3034**
Rocks and rock minerals / Richard V. Dietrich, Brian J. Skinner. — New York: Wiley, c1979. xi, 319 p.: ill.; 24 cm. 1. Petrology 2. Mineralogy I. Skinner, Brian J., 1928- joint author. II. T.
QE431.2.D53     552     *LC* 79-1211     *ISBN* 0471029343

**Ehlers, Ernest G.**     **5.3035**
Petrology: igneous, sedimentary, and metamorphic / Ernest G. Ehlers, Harvey Blatt. — San Francisco: Freeman, c1982. xvi, 732 p.: ill.; 24 cm. 1. Petrology I. Blatt, Harvey. II. T.
QE431.2.E38     552 19     *LC* 81-12517     *ISBN* 0716712792

**Ernst, W. G. (Wallace Gary), 1931-.**     **5.3036**
Petrologic phase equilibria / W. G. Ernst. — San Francisco: W. H. Freeman, c1976. viii, 333 p.: ill.; 24 cm. — (A series of books in geology) Includes indexes. 1. Phase rule and equilibrium 2. Petrology I. T.
QE431.5.E76     552     *LC* 76-3699     *ISBN* 0716702797

**Shrock, Robert Rakes, 1904-.**     • **5.3037**
Sequence in layered rocks: a study of features and structures useful for determining top and bottom or order of succession in bedded and tabular rock bodies / Robert R. Shrock. — 1st ed. — New York: McGraw-Hill, 1948. xiii, 507 p.: ill., diagrs.; 24 cm. 1. Rocks 2. Geology, Structural 3. Geology — Field work. I. T.
QE431.5.S45     QE431.5 S45.     552     *LC* 48-7904

**Physical properties of rocks and minerals / edited by Y. S.**     **5.3038**
**Touloukian, W. R. Judd, R. F. Roy.**
New York: McGraw-Hill, c1981. xx, 548 p.: ill.; 29 cm. (McGraw-Hill/ CINDAS data series on material properties; v. II-2) 1. Rocks 2. Mineralogy I. Touloukian, Y. S. (Yeram Sarkis), 1918- II. Judd, William R. III. Roy, Robert F. IV. Series.
QE431.6.P5 P48     552/.06     *LC* 80-17963     *ISBN* 0070650322

**Hutchison, Charles S. (Charles Strachan), 1933-.**     **5.3039**
Laboratory handbook of petrographic techniques / [by] Charles S. Hutchison. — New York: Wiley [1974] xxvii, 527 p.: ill.; 26 cm. 'A Wiley-Interscience publication.' 1. Petrology — Laboratory manuals. I. T.
QE433.H87     552/.0028     *LC* 73-17336     *ISBN* 0471425508

**Heinrich, E. William (Eberhardt William), 1918-.**     • **5.3040**
Microscopic petrography. New York: McGraw-Hill, 1956. 296 p.: ill.; 24 cm. (McGraw-Hill series in the geological sciences.) 1. Rocks — Analysis I. T. II. Series.
QE434.H4     552.8     *LC* 55-11171

**Williams, Howel, 1898-.**     **5.3041**
Petrography: an introduction to the study of rocks in thin sections / Howel Williams, Francis J. Turner, Charles M. Gilbert. — 2nd ed. — San Francisco: W.H. Freeman, c1982. xiv, 626 p.: ill.; 25 cm. 1. Petrology 2. Thin sections (Geology) I. Turner, Francis J. II. Gilbert, Charles M., 1910- III. T.
QE434.W73 1982     552 19     *LC* 82-5072     *ISBN* 0716713764

**Jeffery, P. G. (Paul Geoffrey)**     **5.3042**
Chemical methods of rock analysis / by P.G. Jeffery and D. Hutchison. — 3rd ed., repr. with corrections. — Oxford; New York: Pergamon Press, 1983,

c1981. xvi, 379 p.: ill.; 24 cm. — (Pergamon series in analytical chemistry. v. 4)
1. Rocks — Analysis I. Hutchison, D. II. T. III. Series.
QE438.J44 1981      552/.06 19      *LC* 81-81234      *ISBN* 0080238068

# QE461–462 Igneous Rocks

**Best, Myron G.**          **5.3043**
Igneous and metamorphic petrology / Myron G. Best. — San Francisco:
Freeman, c1982. xviii, 630 p.: ill.; 25 cm. 1. Rocks, Igneous 2. Rocks,
Metamorphic I. T.
QE461.B53 1982      552/.1 19      *LC* 81-17530      *ISBN* 0716713357

**Bowen, Norman Levi, 1887-1956.**          • **5.3044**
The evolution of the igneous rocks / with a new introd. by J. F. Schairer. —
New York: Dover Publications, 1956. [18] 332 p.: ill., map; 22 cm. 1. Rocks,
Igneous I. T.
QE461.B6 1956      QE461.B78 1956.      *LC* 56-14011

**Fisher, Richard V. (Richard Virgil), 1928-.**          **5.3045**
Pyroclastic rocks / R.V. Fisher, H.–U. Schmincke. — Berlin; New York:
Springer-Verlag, 1984. xiv, 472 p.: ill.; 25 cm. Includes indexes. 1. Volcanic
ash, tuff, etc. I. Schmincke, Hans-Ulrich. II. T.
QE461.F55 1984      552/.23 19      *LC* 83-20042      *ISBN* 0387127569

**Hatch, F. H. (Frederick Henry), 1864-1932.**          **5.3046**
Petrology of the igneous rocks / F.H. Hatch, A.K. Wells, and M.K. Wells. —
Rewritten 13th ed. — London: G. Allen & Unwin, [1983], c1972. 551 p.: ill.; 22
cm. — (Textbook of petrology; v. 1) Includes index. 1. Rocks, Igneous
I. Wells, A. K. (Alfred Kingsley) II. Wells, M. K. (Maurice Kingsley), 1921-
III. T.
QE461.H3 1983      552/.1 19      *LC* 83-3890      *ISBN* 0045520097

**Hyndman, Donald W.**          **5.3047**
Petrology of igneous and metamorphic rocks / Donald W. Hyndman. — 2nd
ed. — New York: McGraw-Hill, c1985. x, 786 p.: ill.; 24 cm. — (International
series in the earth and planetary sciences.) Includes index. 1. Rocks, Igneous
2. Rocks, Metamorphic I. T. II. Series.
QE461.H98 1985      552/.1 19      *LC* 84-15760      *ISBN* 0070316589

**Shand, S. James (Samuel James), b. 1882.**          • **5.3048**
Eruptive rocks: their genesis, composition, classification, and their relation to
ore–deposits, with a chapter on meteorites / by S. James Shand. — New York:
Hafner Pub. Co., 1969. xvi, 488 p.: ill., maps.; 24 cm. Reprint of the 1947 ed.
1. Rocks, Igneous 2. Ore deposits 3. Meteorites I. T.
QE461.S48 1969      552/.1      *LC* 76-76363

**Turner, Francis John, 1904-.**          • **5.3049**
Igneous and metamorphic petrology / Francis J. Turner, John Verhoogen. —
2d ed. — New York: McGraw-Hill, 1960. 694 p.: ill. — (International series in
the earth sciences) 1. Rocks, Igneous 2. Rocks, Crystalline and metamorphic.
I. Verhoogen, John, 1912- II. T.
QE461.T9 1960      *LC* 59-10726

# QE471–472 Sedimentary Rocks

**Adams, A. E.**          **5.3050**
Atlas of sedimentary rocks under the microscope / A.E. Adams, W.S.
MacKenzie, and C. Guilford. — New York: Wiley, 1984. 104 p.: ill. (some col.);
28 cm. 'A Halsted Press book.' 1. Rocks, Sedimentary — Atlases.
I. MacKenzie, W. S. II. Guilford, C. III. T.
QE471.A28 1984      552/.5/0222 19      *LC* 83-12379      *ISBN*
047027476X

**Blatt, Harvey.**          **5.3051**
Origin of sedimentary rocks / Harvey Blatt, Gerard Middleton, Raymond
Murray. — 2d ed. — Englewood Cliffs, N.J.: Prentice-Hall, c1980. xvii, 782 p.:
ill.; 24 cm. 1. Rocks, Sedimentary I. Middleton, Gerard V. joint author.
II. Murray, Raymond C. joint author. III. T.
QE471.B65 1980      552/.5      *LC* 79-15661      *ISBN* 0136427103

**Blatt, Harvey.**          **5.3052**
Sedimentary petrology / Harvey Blatt. — San Francisco: W.H. Freeman,
c1982. xii, 564 p.: ill.; 24 cm. 1. Rocks, Sedimentary I. T.
QE471.B653 1982      552/.5 19      *LC* 81-22147      *ISBN* 0716713543

**Carver, Robert E., 1931-.**          **5.3053**
Procedures in sedimentary petrology / edited by Robert E. Carver. — New
York: Wiley-Interscience, [1971] xiii, 653 p.: ill.; 23 cm. 1. Rocks, Sedimentary
— Analysis. I. T.
QE471.C37      552/.5      *LC* 75-138907      *ISBN* 047113855X

**The Encyclopedia of sedimentology / edited by Rhodes W.**          **5.3054**
**Fairbridge, Joanne Bourgeois.**
Stroudsburg, Pa.: Dowden, Hutchinson & Ross; [New York]: distributed world
wide by Academic Press, c1978. xvi, 901 p.: ill.; 26 cm. (Encyclopedia of
earth sciences. v. 6) 1. Sedimentology — Dictionaries. I. Fairbridge, Rhodes
Whitmore, 1914- II. Bourgeois, Joanne. III. Series.
QE471.E49      551.3/03      *LC* 78-18259      *ISBN* 0879331526

**Friedman, Gerald M.**          **5.3055**
Principles of sedimentology / Gerald M. Friedman, John E. Sanders. — New
York: Wiley, c1978. xiii, 792 p.: ill.; 29 cm. Includes index. 1. Sedimentology
I. Sanders, John Essington, 1926- joint author. II. T.
QE471.F72      552/.5      *LC* 78-5355      *ISBN* 0471752452

**Miall, Andrew D.**          **5.3056**
Principles of sedimentary basin analysis / Andrew D. Miall. — New York:
Springer-Verlag, c1984. xii, 490 p.: ill.; 28 cm. 1. Sedimentology
2. Stratigraphic correlation 3. Paleogeography I. T.
QE471.M44 1984      551.3 19      *LC* 84-1249      *ISBN* 0387909419

**Pettijohn, F. J. (Francis John), 1904-.**          **5.3057**
Atlas and glossary of primary sedimentary structures / by F. J. Pettijohn and
Paul Edwin Potter; translations into Spanish, French, and German by Juan
Carlos Riggi, Marie–Hélène Sachet, and Hans–Ulrich Schmincke. — Berlin;
New York: Springer-Verlag, 1964. xv, 370 p.: ill.; 28 cm. 1. Sedimentary
structures I. Potter, Paul Edwin. joint author. II. T.
QE471.P44      552.5084      *LC* 63-21507

**Pettijohn, F. J. (Francis John), 1904-.**          **5.3058**
Sedimentary rocks [by] F. J. Pettijohn. 3d ed. New York, Harper & Row [1975]
xii, 628 p. illus. 26 cm. 1. Rocks, Sedimentary 2. Sedimentation and deposition
I. T.
QE471.P46 1975      552/.5      *LC* 74-12043      *ISBN* 0060451912

**Reineck, Hans-Erich.**          **5.3059**
Depositional sedimentary environments, with reference to terrigenous clastics /
H.–E. Reineck, I. B. Singh. — 2d, rev. and updated ed. — Berlin; New York:
Springer-Verlag, 1980. xix, 549 p.: ill.; 27 cm. 'Springer study edition.' Includes
index. 1. Rocks, Sedimentary 2. Sedimentary structures 3. Sediments
(Geology) I. Singh, I. B. (Indra Bir) joint author. II. T.
QE471.R425 1980      551.3/03 19      *LC* 80-20429      *ISBN* 0387101896

**Sedimentary environments and facies / edited by H.G. Reading.**          **5.3060**
2nd ed. — Oxford: Blackwell Scientific, 1986. xi, 615 p.: ill., maps; 24 cm.
1. Sedimentation and deposition 2. Rocks, Sedimentary 3. Facies (Geology)
I. Reading, H. G.
QE471 S4 1986      551.3/04 19      *ISBN* 0632015721

**Selley, Richard C., 1939-.**          **5.3061**
Ancient sedimentary environments and their sub–surface diagnosis / Richard
C. Selley. — 3rd ed. — Ithaca, N.Y.: Cornell University Press, 1985. xii, 317 p.:
ill.; 24 cm. 1. Rocks, Sedimentary 2. Geology, Stratigraphic I. T.
QE471.S42 1985      551.3/03 19      *LC* 85-17424      *ISBN* 0801418712

**Bathurst, Robin G. C.**          **5.3062**
Carbonate sediments and their diagenesis / by Robin G. C. Bathurst. — 2d enl.
ed. — Amsterdam; New York: Elsevier Scientific Pub. Co., 1975. xix, 658 p.:
ill.; 25 cm. (Developments in sedimentology. 12) Includes index. 1. Rocks,
Carbonate 2. Diagenesis I. T. II. Series.
QE471.15.C3 B37 1975      552/.5      *LC* 76-350244      *ISBN* 0444413510

**Pettijohn, F. J. (Francis John), 1904-.**          **5.3063**
Sand and sandstone / F.J. Pettijohn, P.E. Potter, R. Siever. — 2nd ed. — New
York: Springer-Verlag, c1987. xviii, 553 p.: ill.; 28 cm. 1. Sand 2. Sandstone
I. Potter, Paul Edwin. II. Siever, Raymond. III. T.
QE471.2.P47 1987      552/.5 19      *LC* 86-17925      *ISBN* 0387963553

**Collinson, J. D. (John David)**          **5.3064**
Sedimentary structures / J.D. Collinson, D.B. Thompson. — London; Boston:
Allen & Unwin, 1982. xiv, 194 p.: ill.; 25 cm. 1. Sedimentary structures
I. Thompson, D. B. (David B.) II. T.
QE472.C64 1982      552/.5 19      *LC* 81-19110      *ISBN* 0045520178

**Potter, Paul Edwin.**          **5.3065**
Paleocurrents and basin analysis / P. E. Potter, F. J. Pettijohn. — 2d corr. and
updated ed. — Berlin; New York: Springer-Verlag, 1977. xiii, 425 p., [17] leaves
of plates: ill.; 24 cm. 1. Paleocurrents 2. Sedimentary structures
3. Sedimentation and deposition I. Pettijohn, F. J. (Francis John), 1904- joint
author. II. T.
QE472.P67 1977      551.4/701      *LC* 76-30293      *ISBN* 0387079521

# QE475–499 Metamorphic Rocks

**The Evolution of the crystalline rocks** / edited by D. K. Bailey **5.3066**
and R. MacDonald.
London; New York: Academic Press, 1976. ix, 484 p.: ill.; 24 cm. 1. Rocks, Crystalline I. Bailey, D. K. (David Kenneth), 1931- II. Macdonald, R. (Robert)
QE475.A2 E95　　　552　　　LC 75-46326　　　ISBN 0120734508

**Mason, Roger, 1941-.** **5.3067**
Petrology of the metamorphic rocks / Roger Mason. — London; Boston: G. Allen & Unwin, 1978. xiii, 254 p.: ill.; 24 cm. — (Textbook of petrology; v. 3) Includes index. 1. Rocks, Metamorphic I. T.
QE475.A2 M394　　　552/.4　　　LC 78-326606　　　ISBN 0045520135

**Miyashiro, Akiho.** **5.3068**
[Henseigan to henseitai. English] Metamorphism and metamorphic belts / by Akiho Miyashiro. — London; Boston: G. Allen & Unwin, c1973, 1979 printing. 492 p.: ill.; 23 cm. Revised translation of: Henseigan to henseitai / Miyashiro Akiho. Tokyo: Iwanami Shoten. 1965. Includes index. 1. Metamorphism (Geology) I. T.
QE475.A2 M5813 1979　　　552/.4 19　　　LC 85-241728　　　ISBN 0045500177

**Suk, Miloš.** **5.3069**
[Petrologie metamorfovaných hornin. English] Petrology of metamorphic rocks / by M. Suk. — Amsterdam; New York: Elsevier Scientific Pub. Co., 1983. 322 p.: ill.; 25 cm. — (Developments in petrology. 9) Translation of: Petrologie metamorfovaných hornin. Errata slip inserted. Includes index. 1. Rocks, Metamorphic I. T. II. Series.
QE475.A2 S8913 1983　　　552/.4 19　　　LC 82-20962　　　ISBN 0444996648

**Vernon, R. H. (Ronald Holden)** **5.3070**
Metamorphic processes: reactions and microstructure development / R. H. Vernon. — New York: Wiley, 1975. 247 p.: ill.; 25 cm. 'A Halsted Press book.' 1. Metamorphism (Geology) I. T.
QE475.A2 V47 1975　　　552/.4　　　LC 75-9139　　　ISBN 0470906553

**Winkler, Helmut G. F., 1915-.** **5.3071**
[Genese der metamorphen Gesteine. English] Petrogenesis of metamorphic rocks / Helmut G. F. Winkler. — 5th ed. — New York: Springer-Verlag, c1979. x, 348 p.: ill.; 24 cm. Translation of Die Genese der metamorphen Gesteine. 'Springer study edition.' 1. Rocks, Metamorphic I. T.
QE475.A2 W5613 1979　　　552/.4　　　LC 79-14704　　　ISBN 0387904131

**Pitcher, Wallace S. ed.** **5.3072**
Controls of metamorphism: a symposium / edited by Wallace S. Pitcher and Glenys W. Flinn. — New York: Wiley [1965] 368 p.: ill.; 27 cm. (Geological journal. Special issue no. 1) 'Held in the Department of Geology, University of Liverpool, in January 1964, under the auspices of the Liverpool Geological Society.' 1. Metamorphism (Geology) I. Flinn, Glenys W. joint ed. II. University of Liverpool. Dept. of Geology. III. Liverpool Geological Society. IV. T.
QE475.P5 1965a　　　LC 67-3973

**Turner, Francis J.** **5.3073**
Metamorphic petrology: mineralogical, field, and tectonic aspects / Francis J. Turner. — 2d ed. — Washington: Hemisphere Pub. Corp.; New York: McGraw-Hill, c1981. xv, 524 p.: ill.; 25 cm. — (McGraw-Hill international series in the earth and planetary sciences) 1. Rocks, Metamorphic I. T.
QE475.T89 1981　　　552/.4　　　LC 79-27497

# QE500–625 DYNAMIC AND STRUCTURAL GEOLOGY

# QE501–505 General Works

**Jacobs, J. A. (John Arthur), 1916-.** **5.3074**
Physics and geology / [by] J. A. Jacobs, R. D. Russell [and] J. Tuzo Wilson. 2d ed. New York: McGraw-Hill, [1974] xvi, 622 p.: ill.; 24 cm. (International series in the earth and planetary sciences.) 1. Geophysics I. Russell, R. D. (Richard

Doncaster), 1929- joint author II. Wilson, J. Tuzo (John Tuzo), 1908- III. T. IV. Series.
QE 501 J17 1974　　　LC 73-6621　　　ISBN 0070321485

**Jeffreys, Harold, Sir, 1891-.** **5.3075**
The earth: its origin, history, and physical constitution / Harold Jeffreys. — 6th ed. — Cambridge [Eng.]; New York: Cambridge University Press, 1976. xii, 574 p., 2 fold. leaves, x leaves of plates: ill.; 24 cm. Includes index. 1. Earth I. T.
QE501.J4 1976　　　551　　　LC 74-19527　　　ISBN 0521206480

**Sitter, L. U. de (Lamoraal Ulbo), 1902-.** **• 5.3076**
Structural geology [by] L.U. de Sitter. 2d ed. New York, McGraw-Hill [1964] xii, 551 p. illus., maps. 23 cm. (International series in the earth sciences) 1. Geology, Structural I. T.
QE501.S54 1964　　　551.8　　　LC 63-23533

**Takeuchi, Hitoshi, 1921-.** **• 5.3077**
Debate about the earth: approach to geophysics through analysis of continental drift / [by] H. Takeuchi, S. Uyeda [and] H. Kanamori; translated by Keido Kanamori; illustrated by James K. Levorsen. — San Francisco: Freeman, Cooper [1967] 253 p.: ill., maps, ports.; 24 cm. Translation and expansion of [Chikyū no kagaku] 1. Continental drift I. Uyeda, Seiya, 1929- joint author. II. Kanamori, H. (Hiroo), 1936- joint author. III. T.
QE501.T313　　　551.1　　　LC 67-21261

**Verhoogen, John, 1912-.** **• 5.3078**
The earth; an introduction to physical geology [by] John Verhoogen [and others]. — New York: Holt, Rinehart and Winston, [1970] vii, 748 p.: illus., maps.; 25 cm. Part of illustrative matter is colored. 1. Geology I. T.
QE501.V39　　　551　　　LC 77-96846　　　ISBN 0030796555

**Elder, John, 1933-.** **5.3079**
The bowels of the earth / John Elder. London; New York: Oxford University Press, 1976. vii, 222 p.: ill.; 24 cm. Includes index. 1. Geodynamics I. T.
QE501.2.E4　　　551.1　　　LC 76-375937　　　ISBN 019854412X

**Sharma, P. Vallabh.** **5.3080**
Geophysical methods in geology / P.V. Sharma. — 2nd ed. — New York: Elsevier, c1986. xviii, 442 p.: ill.; 24 cm. 1. Geophysics 2. Prospecting — Geophysical methods 3. Geology — Methodology. I. T.
QE501.3.S48 1986　　　551/.028 19　　　LC 85-25360　　　ISBN 0444008365

**Faure, Gunter.** **5.3081**
Principles of isotope geology / Gunter Faure. — 2nd ed. — New York: Wiley, c1986. xv, 589 p.: ill.; 24 cm. 1. Isotope geology I. T.
QE501.4.N9 F38 1986　　　550/.28 19　　　LC 86-9147　　　ISBN 0471864129

# QE508–509 Geological Time

**Albritton, Claude C., 1913-.** **5.3082**
The abyss of time, changing conceptions of the earth's antiquity after the sixteenth century / Claude C. Albritton, Jr. — San Francisco, CA: Freeman, Cooper, c1980. 251 p.: ill.; 24 cm. Includes indexes. 1. Geological time 2. Geology — History I. T.
QE508.A47　　　551.7 19　　　LC 79-57131　　　ISBN 0877353417

**Berry, William B. N.** **5.3083**
Growth of a prehistoric time scale: based on arganic evolution / William B.N. Berry. — Rev. ed. — Palo Alto, CA: Blackwell Scientific Publications, 1986. 158 p. Includes index. 1. Geological time I. T.
QE508.B53 1986　　　551.7/01 19　　　LC 86-24453　　　ISBN 0865423261

**Burchfield, Joe D.** **5.3084**
Lord Kelvin and the age of the earth [by] Joe D. Burchfield. — New York: Science History Publications, 1975. xii, 260 p.: port.; 24 cm. 1. Kelvin, William Thomson, Baron, 1824-1907. 2. Earth — Age I. T.
QE508.B83 1975　　　551.7　　　LC 74-5754　　　ISBN 0882020137

**A Geologic time scale** / W.B. Harland ... [et al.]; assisted by **5.3085**
K.E. Fancett.
Cambridge [England]; New York: Cambridge University Press, 1982. xi, 131 p.: ill.; 31 cm. — (Cambridge earth science series.) Includes index. 1. Geological time I. Harland, W. B. (Walter Brian), 1917- II. Series.
QE508.G3956 1982　　　551.7/01 19　　　LC 82-4333　　　ISBN 0521247284

**Gould, Stephen Jay.** **5.3086**
Time's arrow, time's cycle: myth and metaphor in the discovery of geological time / Stephen Jay Gould. — Cambridge, Mass.: Harvard University Press, 1987. xiii, 222 p.: ill.; 24 cm. — (Jerusalem-Harvard lectures.) Includes index.

1. Burnet, Thomas, 1635?-1715. Telluris theoria sacra 2. Hutton, James, 1726-1797. Theory of the earth. 3. Lyell, Charles, Sir, 1797-1875. 4. Geological time — Study and teaching — History. I. T. II. Series.
QE508.G68 1987     551.7/01/09 19     *LC* 86-29485     *ISBN* 0674891988

# QE509–511 Earth Structure

**Bolt, Bruce A., 1930-.**         **5.3087**
Inside the earth: evidence from earthquakes / Bruce A. Bolt; [artist, Eric Hieber]. — San Francisco: W.H. Freeman, c1982. xi, 191 p.: ill.; 24 cm. Includes index. 1. Seismology 2. Earth — Internal structure I. T.
QE509.B69 1982     551.1/1 19     *LC* 81-17431     *ISBN* 0716713594

**Bott, Martin Harold Phillips, 1926-.**         **5.3088**
The interior of the earth: its structure, constitution and evolution / Martin H.P. Bott. — 2nd ed. — New York: Elsevier, 1982. ix, 403 p.: ill.; 26 cm. 1. Geophysics 2. Earth — Crust 3. Earth — Mantle 4. Earth — Internal structure I. T.
QE 509 B75 1982     QE511.B56 1982.

**Brown, G. C. (Geoff C.)**         **5.3089**
The inaccessible earth / G.C. Brown, A.E. Mussett. — London; Boston: Allen & Unwin, 1981. xii, 235 p.: ill., maps; 25 cm. Includes index. 1. Earth — Internal structure I. Mussett, A. E. (Alan E.) II. T.
QE509.B89     551.1/1 19     *LC* 81-169473     *ISBN* 0045500274

**Bucher, Walter H. (Walter Herman), 1888-.**       **• 5.3090**
The deformation of the earth's crust; an inductive approach to the problems of diastrophism. With a new pref. — New York: Hafner Pub. Co., 1957, [c1933] xiii, 518 p. illus., maps (1 fold.) tables. 24 cm. Bibliographical footnotes. 1. Geophysics 2. Geology, Structural 3. Earth — Surface I. T.
QE511.B8 1957     551.13     *LC* 57-11469

# QE511.4–511.7 Plate Tectonics

**Cox, Allan, 1926-1987. comp.**         **5.3091**
Plate tectonics and geomagnetic reversals; readings, selected, edited, and with introductions by Allan Cox. — San Francisco: W. H. Freeman, [1973] vii, 702 p.: illus.; 26 cm. — (A Series of books in geology) 1. Plate tectonics — Addresses, essays, lectures. 2. Paleomagnetism — Addresses, essays, lectures. 3. Heat budget (Geophysics) — Addresses, essays, lectures. I. T.
QE511.4.C68     551.1/3     *LC* 73-4323     *ISBN* 0716702592

**Hallam, A. (Anthony), 1933-.**         **5.3092**
A revolution in the earth sciences: from continental drift to plate tectonics / [by] A. Hallam. — New York: Oxford, 1975, [c1973] ix, 127 p.: ill., maps; 25 cm. 1. Continental drift — History. 2. Plate tectonics — History. I. T.
QE511.4.H34     551.1/3     *LC* 73-165995     *ISBN* 0198581440

**Continents adrift and continents aground: readings from**     **5.3093**
**Scientific American / with introductions by J. Tuzo Wilson.**
San Francisco: W. H. Freeman, c1976. vii, 230 p.: ill.; 29 cm. 1. Continental drift — Addresses, essays, lectures. 2. Plate tectonics — Addresses, essays, lectures. I. Wilson, J. Tuzo (John Tuzo), 1908- II. Scientific American.
QE511.5.C65 1976     551.1/3     *LC* 76-46564     *ISBN* 0716702819. *ISBN* 0716702800 pbk

**King, Lester Charles.**         **5.3094**
Wandering continents and spreading sea floors on an expanding earth / Lester C. King. — Chichester [West Sussex]; New York: Wiley, c1983. xi, 232 p.: ill.; 24 cm. 'A Wiley-Intersicence publication.' Includes index. 1. Continental drift 2. Sea-floor spreading 3. Expanding earth I. T.
QE511.5.K53 1983     551.1/36 19     *LC* 83-1345     *ISBN* 0471901563

**Marvin, Ursula B.**         **5.3095**
Continental drift: the evolution of a concept / [by] Ursula B. Marvin. — Washington: Smithsonian Institution Press; [distributed by G. Braziller], 1973. 239 p.: ill.; 29 cm. 1. Continental drift 2. Geophysics I. T.
QE511.5.M37     551.4/1     *LC* 72-9575     *ISBN* 0874741297

**Sullivan, Walter.**         **5.3096**
Continents in motion: the new earth debate. — New York: McGraw-Hill, [1974] xiv, 399 p.: ill.; 29 cm. 1. Continental drift I. T.
QE511.5.S93     551.1/3     *LC* 73-17315     *ISBN* 0070624127

**Tarling, D. H. (Donald Harvey)**         **5.3097**
Continental drift: a study of the earth's moving surface / Don and Maureen Tarling. — Rev. ed. — Garden City, N.Y.: Anchor Press, 1975. xiv, 142 p.: ill.; 18 cm. (Science study series. S65) Includes index. 1. Continental drift I. Tarling, Maureen P. joint author. II. T. III. Series.
QE511.5.T35 1975     551.1/3     *LC* 74-12858     *ISBN* 0385063849

**Uyeda, Seiya, 1929-.**         **5.3098**
[Atarashii chikyūkan. English] The new view of the Earth: moving continents and moving oceans / Seiya Uyeda; translated by Masako Ohnuki. — San Francisco: W. H. Freeman, c1978. v, 217 p.: ill.; 24 cm. Translation of Atarashii chikyūkan. Includes index. 1. Continental drift I. T.
QE511.5.U9313     551.1/3     *LC* 77-9900     *ISBN* 0716702835. *ISBN* 0716702827 pbk

**Windley, B. F. (Brian F.)**         **5.3099**
The evolving continents / Brian F. Windley. — 2nd ed. — Chichester [West Sussex]; New York: Wiley, c1984. xx, 399 p.: ill.; 26 cm. Includes index. 1. Continental drift 2. Geodynamics I. T.
QE511.5.W56 1984     551.1/36 19     *LC* 83-21597     *ISBN* 0471903760

**Rona, Peter A.**         **5.3100**
Hydrothermal processes at seafloor spreading centers / edited by Peter A. Rona ... [et al.]. — New York: Published in cooperation with NATO Scientific Affairs Division [by] Plenum Press, c1983. xiv, 796 p., [10] p. of plates: ill. (some col.); 26 cm. — (NATO conference series. Marine sciences. v. 12) 'Proceedings of a NATO Advanced Research Institute, held April 5-8, 1982, at the Department of Earth Sciences of Cambridge, University, England'—T.p. verso. 1. Sea-floor spreading — Congresses. 2. Hydrothermal deposits — Congresses. 3. Heat budget (Geophysics) — Congresses. 4. Chemical oceanography — Congresses. 5. Hydrothermal vent ecology — Congresses. I. T. II. Series.
QE511.7.H93 1983     551.46/08 19     *LC* 83-17747     *ISBN* 0306414821

# QE515 Geochemistry

**Fairbridge, Rhodes Whitmore, 1914-.**       **• 5.3101**
The encyclopedia of geochemistry and environmental sciences / edited by Rhodes W. Fairbridge. — New York: Van Nostrand Reinhold Co., [1972] xxi, 1321 p.: ill.; 26 cm. — (Encyclopedia of earth sciences. v. 4A) 1. Geochemistry — Dictionaries. 2. Pollution — Dictionaries. I. T. II. Series.
QE515.F24     551.8/03     *LC* 75-152326     *ISBN* 0879331801

**Garrels, Robert Minard, 1916-.**         **5.3102**
Solutions, minerals, and equilibria [by] Robert M. Garrels [and] Charles L. Christ. New York, Harper & Row [1965] xiii, 450 p. illus. 25 cm. (Harper's geoscience series.) Based on Mineral equilibria at low temperatures and pressure, by R.M. Garrels, published in 1960. 1. Geochemistry I. Christ, Charles L. (Charles Louis) joint author. II. T. III. Series.
QE515.G32     551.9     *LC* 65-12674

**Goldschmidt, Victor Moritz, 1888-1947.**       **• 5.3103**
Geochemistry / edited by Alex Muir. — Oxford: Clarendon Press, 1954. xi, 730 p.: ill. — (International series of monographs on physics.) Errata slip inserted. 1. Geochemistry I. T. II. Series.
QE515.G69     QE515.G62.     *LC* 54-3115

**Krauskopf, Konrad Bates, 1910-.**         **5.3104**
Introduction to geochemistry / Konrad B. Krauskopf. — 2d ed. — New York: McGraw-Hill, c1979. xiii, 617 p.: ill.; 24 cm. — (McGraw-Hill international series in the earth and planetary sciences) 1. Geochemistry I. T.
QE515.K7 1979     551.9     *LC* 78-10432     *ISBN* 0070354472

**Origin and distribution of the elements: proceedings of the**     **5.3105**
**second symposium, Paris, May 1977 / editor, L.H. Ahrens.;**
**editorial assistant, G. Protas.**
1st ed. — Oxford; New York: Pergamon Press, 1979. xi, 909 p.: ill.; 26 cm. — (Physics and chemistry of the earth. v. 11) (International series in earth sciences. v. 34) 1. Geochemistry — Congresses. 2. Cosmochemistry — Congresses. I. Ahrens, L. H. (Louis Herman), 1918- II. Series. III. Series: International series in earth sciences. v. 34
QE515.S9x 1979 QE514     551.9     *LC* 78-40583     *ISBN* 0080229476

**Wedepohl, Karl Hans.**         **5.3106**
Handbook of geochemistry. Executive editor: K. H. Wedepohl. Editorial board: C. W. Correns [and others]. — Berlin; Heidelberg; New York: Springer, 1969-1978. 2 v. in 6 with illus.; 26 cm. Vol. 2 loose-leaf. 1. Geochemistry I. T.
QE515.W42     551.9     *LC* 78-85402     unpriced

## QE521–545 Volcanoes. Earthquakes. Seismology

**Blong, R. J. (Russell J.)**                                    **5.3107**
Volcanic hazards: a sourcebook on the effects of eruptions / R.J. Blong. — Sydney; Orlando, Fla.: Academic Press, c1984. xvi, 424 p.: ill., maps; 24 cm. Includes index. 1. Volcanoes 2. Natural disasters I. T.
QE522.B6 1984      363.3/495 19      LC 83-73405      ISBN 0121071804

**Bullard, Fred M. (Fred Mason), 1901-.**                                    **5.3108**
Volcanoes of the Earth / by Fred M. Bullard. — 2nd rev. ed. — Austin: University of Texas Press, 1984. 629 p., [16] p. of plates: ill. (some col.); 26 cm. — (Dan Danciger publication series.) Includes index. 1. Volcanoes I. T. II. Series.
QE522.B87 1984      551.2/1 19      LC 83-21738      ISBN 0292787065

**Cotton, Charles Andrew, 1885-.**                                    **5.3109**
Volcanoes as landscape forms, by C. A. Cotton. — New York: Hafner Pub. Co., 1969. 415 p.: illus.; 23 cm. Reprint of the 2d ed., 1952. 1. Volcanoes 2. Landforms I. T.
QE522.C6 1969      551.2/1      LC 75-76360

**Explosive volcanism: inception, evolution, and hazards /**                                    **5.3110**
**Geophysics Study Committee, Geophysics Research Forum, Commission on Physical Sciences, Mathematics, and Resources, National Research Council.**
Washington, D.C.: National Academy Press, 1984. xii, 176 p.: ill.; 29 cm. — (Studies in geophysics.) Col. maps in pocket ([3] folded leaves of plates) 1. Volcanism — Addresses, essays, lectures. I. Geophysics Research Forum (U.S.). Geophysics Study Committee. II. Series.
QE522.E97 1984      551.2/1 19      LC 83-23610      ISBN 0309033934

**Macdonald, Gordon Andrew, 1911-.**                                    **5.3111**
Volcanoes [by] Gordon A. Macdonald. — Englewood Cliffs, N.J.: Prentice-Hall, [1972] xii, 510 p.: illus.; 25 cm. 1. Volcanoes I. T.
QE522.M18      551.2/1      LC 78-37404      ISBN 0139422196

**Krakatau, 1883—the volcanic eruption and its effects / [edited**                                    **5.3112**
**by] Tom Simkin and Richard S. Fiske; with the collaboration of Sarah Melcher and Elizabeth Nielsen.**
Washington, D.C.: Smithsonian Institution Press, 1983. 464 p.: ill. (some col.), ports., maps; 29 cm. Includes index. 1. Krakatoa (Indonesia) — Eruption, 1883. I. Simkin, Tom. II. Fiske, Richard S.
QE523.K73 K7 1983      551.2/1/09598 19      LC 83-14818      ISBN 0874748429

**Rosenfeld, Charles.**                                    **5.3113**
Earthfire: the eruption of Mount St. Helens / Charles Rosenfeld and Robert Cooke. — Cambridge, Mass.: MIT Press, c1982. 155 p.: ill.; 23 x 28 cm. Includes index. 1. Saint Helens, Mount (Wash.) — Eruption, 1980 I. Cooke, Robert, 1935- II. T.
QE523.S23 R67 1982      551.2/1/0979784 19      LC 82-9969      ISBN 0262181061

**Båth, Markus.**                                    **5.3114**
Introduction to seismology / Markus Båth. — 2d rev. ed. — Boston: Birkhauser, 1979. 428 p.: ill.; 23 cm. ([Science and civilization; v. 27]) Includes indexes. 1. Seismology I. T.
QE534.2.B313 1979      551.2/2      LC 79-18231      ISBN 3764309563

**Bolt, Bruce A., 1930-.**                                    **5.3115**
Earthquakes / Bruce A. Bolt. — Rev. and updated. — New York: W.H. Freeman, c1988. xvii, 282 p.: ill.; 23 cm. Includes index. 1. Earthquakes I. T.
QE534.2.B64 1988      551.2/2 19      LC 86-31982      ISBN 0716719096

**Eiby, G. A.**                                    **5.3116**
Earthquakes / G. A. Eiby. — New York: Van Nostrand Reinhold Co., c1980. 209 p.: ill.; 29 cm. Includes index. 1. Earthquakes I. T.
QE534.2.E36      551.2/2      LC 80-10786      ISBN 0442251912

## QE565 Coral Reefs and Islands

**Darwin, Charles.**                                    **5.3117**
The structure and distribution of coral reefs / [by] Charles Darwin; foreword by H.W. Menard. Berkeley [etc.]; London: University of California Press, 1976. xii, 214, [4] p., [21] p. of plates: ill., maps (some col.); 21 cm. (California library

reprint series.) Originally published: as 'The geology of the voyage of the 'Beagle''. Part 1. London: Smith, Elder, 1842. 1. Coral reefs and islands I. T. II. Title: Geological observations on coral reefs, volcanic islands, and on South America. Part 1. III. Series.
QE565.D3x      551.4/2      ISBN 0520032829

## QE570–599 Weathering. Erosion. Deposition

**Berner, Robert A., 1935-.**                                    **5.3118**
Early diagenesis: a theoretical approach / Robert A. Berner. — Princeton, N.J.: Princeton University Press, c1980. xii, 241 p.: ill.; 25 cm. — (Princeton series in geochemistry.) Includes index. 1. Diagenesis I. T. II. Series.
QE571.B47      552/.5      LC 80-7510      ISBN 0691082588

**Embleton, Clifford. comp.**                                    **5.3119**
Glaciers and glacial erosion. — [London]: Macmillan, 1973 (c1972) 287 p.: ill.; 23 cm. — (Geographical readings series) 1. Glacial erosion — Addresses, essays, lectures. 2. Glaciers — Addresses, essays, lectures. I. T.
QE576.E46 1972      551.3/12      LC 73-154614      ISBN 0333126556

**Davis, Richard A. (Richard Albert), 1937-.**                                    **5.3120**
Depositional systems: a genetic approach to sedimentary geology / Richard A. Davis, Jr. — Englewood Cliffs, N.J.: Prentice-Hall, c1983. xvii, 669 p.: ill.; 24 cm. Includes index. 1. Sedimentation and deposition I. T.
QE581.D38 1983      551.3 19      LC 82-24125      ISBN 013198960X

**Bagnold, Ralph A. (Ralph Alger), 1896-.**                                    **• 5.3121**
The physics of blown sand and desert dunes / by R. A. Bagnold. — London: Methuen, 1941. xxiv, 265, [1] p.: ill.; 22 cm. 1. Sand-dunes 2. Winds 3. Ripple-marks I. T.
QE597.B3 1941      551.37      LC 41-15623

**Sharpe, Charles Farquharson Stewart, 1907-.**                                    **• 5.3122**
Landslides and related phenomena: a study of mass–movements of soil and rock. — Paterson, N.J.: Pageant Books, 1960 (c1938). 137 p.: ill.; 24 cm. (Columbia geomorphic studies, no. 2.) 1. Earth movements 2. Landslides I. T. II. Series.
QE599.A2 S5 1960      LC 60-10229

## QE601–606 Structural Geology

**Billings, Marland Pratt, 1902-.**                                    **• 5.3123**
Structural geology [by] Marland P. Billings. — 3d ed. — Englewood Cliffs, N.J.: Prentice-Hall, [1972] xv, 606 p.: illus.; 24 cm. 1. Geology, Structural I. T.
QE601.B5 1972      551.8      LC 73-167628      ISBN 0138538468

**The Encyclopedia of structural geology and plate tectonics /**                                    **5.3124**
**edited by Carl K. Seyfert.**
New York: Van Nostrand Reinhold, c1987. p. cm. — (Encyclopedia of earth sciences. v. 10) Includes index. 1. Geology, Structural — Dictionaries. 2. Plate tectonics — Dictionaries. I. Seyfert, Carl K., 1938- II. Series.
QE601.E53 1987      551.8/03/21 19      LC 87-18879      ISBN 0442281250

**Hills, E. Sherbon (Edwin Sherbon)**                                    **• 5.3125**
Outlines of structural geology. — 3d ed. rev. — London: Methuen; New York: Wiley, 1953. 182 p.: ill. 1. Geology, Structural I. T.
QE601.H5 1953      QE601.H65 1953.      LC 53-9541

**Hobbs, Bruce E.**                                    **5.3126**
An outline of structural geology / Bruce E. Hobbs, Winthrop D. Means, Paul F. Williams. — New York: Wiley, c1976. xviii, 571 p.: ill.; 24 cm. Includes index. 1. Geology, Structural I. Means, Winthrop Dickinson, joint author. II. Williams, Paul Frederick, 1938- joint author. III. T.
QE601.H6      551.8      LC 75-20393      ISBN 0471401560

**Turner, Francis J.**                                    **5.3127**
Structural analysis of metamorphic tectonites / [by] Francis J. Turner and Lionel E. Weiss. — New York: McGraw-Hill [1963] 545 p.: ill.; 24 cm. (International series in the earth sciences.) 1. Geology, Structural 2. Rocks, crystalline and metamorphic. I. Weiss, Lionel E. (Lionel Edward), 1927- joint author. II. T. III. Series.
QE601.T87      551.8      LC 62-18522

**Fabric of ductile strain / edited by M.R. Stauffer.** **5.3128**
Stroudsburg, Pa.: Hutchinson Ross Pub. Co.; New York, N.Y.: Distributed
worldwide by Van Nostrand Reinhold, c1983. xi, 400 p.: ill.; 27 cm. —
(Benchmark papers in geology. 75) 1. Rock deformation — Addresses, essays,
lectures. I. Stauffer, M. R. II. Series.
QE604.F3 1983    551.8 19    LC 82-23199    ISBN 0879334428

# QE640–700 STRATIGRAPHY

# QE640–653 General Works

√ **Ager, D. V. (Derek Victor)** **5.3129**
The nature of the stratigraphical record / Derek V. Ager. — 2d ed. — New
York: Wiley, 1981. xiv, 122 p., [10] leaves of plates: ill.; 22 cm. 'A Halsted Press
book.' Includes index. 1. Geology, Stratigraphic I. T.
QE651.A37 1981    551.7 19    LC 80-22559    ISBN 0470270527

**Concepts and methods of biostratigraphy / edited by Erle G.** **5.3130**
**Kauffman and Joseph E. Hazel, with the assistance of Barbara**
**Duffy Heffernan.**
Stroudsburg, Pa.: Dowden, Hutchinson & Ross; [New York]: distributed by
Halsted Press, c1977. xiii, 658 p.: ill.; 24 cm. Includes index. 1. Geology,
Stratigraphic 2. Paleontology, Stratigraphic I. Kauffman, Erle Galen, 1933-
II. Hazel, Joseph E., 1933- III. Heffernan, Barbara Duffy. IV. Title:
Biostratigraphy.
QE651.C67    551.7/01    LC 76-42248    ISBN 0879332468

**Dunbar, Carl Owen, 1891-.** **5.3131**
Principles of stratigraphy [by] Carl O. Dunbar [and] John Rodgers. — New
York: Wiley, [1957] 356 p.: illus.; 27 cm. 1. Geology, Stratigraphic I. Rodgers,
John, 1914- joint author. II. T.
QE651.D8    551.7    LC 57-8883

**Facies models / edited by Roger G. Walker.** **5.3132**
2nd ed. — Toronto: Geological Association of Canada, 1984. — 317 p.: ill.; 28
cm. — (Geoscience Canada reprint series. 1) 'A fully rewritten version of the
first edition, with several new contributions. Most of the papers in the first
edition appeared originally in Geoscience Canada, 1976-1979, published by the
Geological Association of Canada.' 1. Facies (Geology) 2. Geology,
Stratigraphic I. Walker, Roger G. II. Geological Association of Canada.
III. Series.
QE651.F33 1984    ISBN 0919216250

**Hallam, A. (Anthony), 1933-.** **5.3133**
Facies interpretation and the stratigraphic record / A. Hallam. — Oxford; San
Francisco: W. H. Freeman, c1981. xii, 291 p.: ill.; 25 cm. Includes indexes.
1. Facies (Geology) 2. Geology, Stratigraphic I. T.
QE651.H18    551.7 19    LC 80-24276    ISBN 0716712911

**International Union of Geological Sciences. International** **5.3134**
**Subcommission on Stratigraphic Classification.**
International stratigraphic guide: a guide to stratigraphic classification,
terminology, and procedure / by International Subcommission on Stratigraphic
Classification of IUGS Commission on Stratigraphy; Hollis D. Hedberg, editor.
— New York: Wiley, [1976] xii, 200 p.: ill. 'A Wiley-Interscience publication.'
Includes index. 1. Geology, Stratigraphic I. Hedberg, Hollis Dow, 1903-
II. T.
QE651.I57 1976    QE651 I57 1976.    551.7    LC 75-33086    ISBN
0471367435

√ **Krumbein, William Christian, 1902-.** **5.3135**
Stratigraphy and sedimentation / by W. C. Krumbein and L. L. Sloss. — 2d ed.
San Francisco: W. H. Freeman [1963] xvi, 660 p.: ill., charts (part col.); 25 cm.
(A Geology series) 1. Geology, Stratigraphic 2. Sedimentation and deposition
I. Sloss, L. L. (Laurence Louis), 1913- joint author. II. T.
QE651.K7 1963    551.7    LC 61-11422

# QE654–700 Geological Eras

√ **Holland, C. H. (Charles Hepworth)** • **5.3136**
Cambrian of the new world / edited by C. H. Holland. — London; New York:
Wiley-Interscience [1971] 456 p.: ill., maps; 28 cm. (Lower Palaeozoic rocks of

the world. v. 1) 1. Geology, Stratigraphic — Cambrian 2. Geology —
America. I. T. II. Series.
QE656.H6    551.7/2/097    LC 70-122342    ISBN 0471406244

**Secord, James A.** **5.3137**
Controversy in Victorian geology: the Cambrian–Silurian dispute / James A.
Secord. — Princeton, N.J.: Princeton University Press, c1986. xvii, 363 p.: ill.;
25 cm. Includes index. 1. Geology, Stratigraphic — Cambrian — History.
2. Geology, Stratigraphic — Silurian — History. 3. Geology — Wales —
History. I. T.
QE656.S4 1986    551.7/23 19    LC 85-43310    ISBN 0691084173

**Rudwick, M. J. S.** **5.3138**
The great Devonian controversy: the shaping of scientific knowledge among
gentlemanly specialists / Martin J.S. Rudwick. — Chicago: University of
Chicago Press, c1985. xxxiii, 494 p.: ill., ports.; 26 cm. (Science and its
conceptual foundations) Includes index. 1. Geology, Stratigraphic —
Devonian 2. Science — History 3. Geology — History 4. Geology — England
— Devon. I. T. II. Series.
QE665.R83 1985    551.7/4 19    LC 84-16199    ISBN 0226731014

√ **Arkell, William Joscelyn, 1904-1958.** • **5.3139**
Jurassic geology of the world. New York, Hafner Pub. Co. [1956] xv, 806 p.
illus., 46 plates, maps. 26 cm. 1. Geology, Stratigraphic — Jurassic
2. Geology, Stratigraphic — Bibliography. I. T.
QE681.A6 1956    551.76    LC 56-3105

**Hallam, A. (Anthony), 1933-.** **5.3140**
Jurassic environments / A. Hallam. — Cambridge [Eng.]; New York:
Cambridge University Press, 1975. ix, 269 p.: ill.; 24 cm. — (Cambridge earth
science series) Includes index. 1. Geology, Stratigraphic — Jurassic
2. Paleontology — Jurassic I. T.
QE681.H34    551.7/6    LC 74-80359    ISBN 0521205557

**Geological background to fossil man: recent research in the** **5.3141**
**Gregory Rift Valley, East Africa / edited by Walter W. Bishop.**
Edinburgh: Published for the Geological Society of London by Scottish
Academic Press , 1978. ix, 585 p., [7] leaves of plates (5 fold.): ill., 26 cm.
1. Geology, stratigraphic — Cenozoic — Congresses. 2. Geology — Africa,
East — Congresses. 3. Gregory Rift Valley — Congresses. I. Bishop, Walter
W. II. Geological Society of London.
QE690.G44    551.8/7    LC 78-323378    ISBN 0707301432

**Charlesworth, J. K. (John Kaye), 1889-.** • **5.3142**
The Quaternary era: with special reference to its glaciation. — London: E.
Arnold [1957] 2 v. (xlvii, 1700 p.): ill., maps (1 fold.) charts, profiles; 25 cm.
1. Geology, Stratigraphic — Quaternary 2. Glacial epoch I. T.
QE696.C53 1957    551.79 551.78*    LC 57-2105

√ **Flint, Richard Foster, 1902-.** • **5.3143**
Glacial and Pleistocene geology. New York, Wiley [1957] xiii, 553 p. illus.,
maps (5 fold.) 24 cm. Based on the author's Glacial geology and the Pleistocene
epoch. 1. Geology, Stratigraphic — Pleistocene 2. Glaciology I. T.
QE696.F54    551.79    LC 57-8884

**Flint, Richard Foster, 1902-.** • **5.3144**
Glacial and Quaternary geology. — New York: Wiley, [1971] xii, 892 p.: ill.; 24
cm. 1. Glacial epoch 2. Geology, Stratigraphic — Quaternary I. T.
QE696.F553    551.7/9    LC 74-141198    ISBN 0471264350

**Late–Quaternary environments of the United States / H.E.** **5.3145**
**Wright, Jr., editor.**
Minneapolis: University of Minnesota Press, c1983. 2 v.: ill., maps; 29 cm.
1. Geology, Stratigraphic — Quaternary — Congresses. 2. Geology — United
States — Congresses. I. Wright, H. E. (Herbert Edgar), 1917- II. Porter,
Stephen C.
QE696.L29 1983    551.7/9/0973 19    LC 83-5804    ISBN
0816612528

**Wright, H. E. (Herbert Edgar), 1917-.** **5.3146**
The Quaternary of the United States; a review volume for the VII Congress of
the International Association for Quaternary Research [by] H. E. Wright, Jr.
and David G. Frey, editors. Princeton, N.J., Princeton University Press, 1965.
x, 922 p. illus., maps. 29 cm. 1. Geology, Stratigraphic — Quaternary
2. Geology — United States I. Frey, David G. (David Grover), 1915-
II. International Association for Quaternary Research. III. T.
QE696.W93    LC 65-14304

# QE701–760 PALEONTOLOGY

## QE701–716 Reference. General Works

The Encyclopedia of paleontology / edited by Rhodes W. **5.3147**
Fairbridge, David Jablonski.
Stroudsburg, Pa.: Dowden, Hutchinson & Ross; [New York]: distributed by Academic Press, c1979. xiii, 886 p.: ill.; 28 cm. — (Encyclopedia of earth sciences. v. 7) 1. Paleontology I. Fairbridge, Rhodes Whitmore, 1914- II. Jablonski, David, 1953- III. Series.
QE703.E52     560/.3     LC 79-11468     *ISBN* 0879331852

Rudwick, M. J. S.                                      **5.3148**
The meaning of fossils: episodes in the history of palaeontology / Martin J. S. Rudwick. — 2d rev. ed. — New York: Science History Publications, 1976. 287 p.: ill.; 24 cm. — (History of science library) Includes index. 1. Paleontology — History. I. T.
QE705.A1 R8 1976     560/.903     LC 76-40050     *ISBN* 088202163X

Shaw, Alan B.                                          **5.3149**
Time in stratigraphy / [by] Alan B. Shaw. — New York: McGraw-Hill [1964] xiv, 365 p.: ill.; 23 cm. (International series in the earth sciences.) 1. Paleontology, Stratigraphic 2. Geology, Stratigraphic I. T. II. Series.
QE711.S46     560.17     LC 63-22158

Grzimek's Encyclopedia of evolution / editor–in–chief, Bernhard   **5.3150**
Grzimek.
New York: Van Nostrand Reinhold Co., c1976. 560 p.: ill. (some col.); 25 cm. 1. Paleontology 2. Evolution 3. Historical geology I. Grzimek, Bernhard. II. Title: Encyclopedia of evolution.
QE711.2.G79     QE711.2 G79.     575/.003     LC 76-9296

Raup, David M.                                         **5.3151**
Principles of paleontology / David M. Raup, Steven M. Stanley. — 2d ed. — San Francisco: W. H. Freeman, c1978. x, 481 p.: ill.; 24 cm. Includes indexes. 1. Paleontology I. Stanley, Steven M. joint author. II. T.
QE711.2.R37 1978     560     LC 77-17443     *ISBN* 0716700220

Simpson, George Gaylord, 1902-.                        **5.3152**
Fossils and the history of life / George Gaylord Simpson. — New York: Scientific American Library, c1983. 239 p.: ill. (some col.); 24 cm. Includes index. 1. Paleontology I. T.
QE711.2.S55 1983     560 19     LC 83-4423     *ISBN* 0716715643

## QE719–760 Micropaleontology. Paleoecology

Brasier, M. D.                                         **5.3153**
Microfossils / M. D. Brasier. — London: G. Allen & Unwin, 1980. xii, 193 p.: ill.; 26 cm. Includes indexes. 1. Micropaleontology I. T.
QE719.B72     560 19     LC 79-40772     *ISBN* 0045620016

Introduction to marine micropaleontology / edited by Bilal U.     **5.3154**
Haq, Anne Boersma; contributors, W. A. Berggren ... [et al.].
New York: Elsevier, c1978. 376 p.: ill.; 28 cm. Errata slip inserted. 1. Micropaleontology 2. Marine sediments I. Haq, Bilal U. II. Boersma, Anne. III. Berggren, William A.
QE719.I57     560/.92     LC 78-4516     *ISBN* 0444002677

Dodd, J. Robert (James Robert), 1934-.                 **5.3155**
Paleoecology, concepts and applications / J. Robert Dodd, Robert J. Stanton, Jr. — New York: Wiley, c1981. xiv, 559 p.: ill.; 24 cm. 'A Wiley-Interscience publication.' Includes index. 1. Paleoecology I. Stanton, Robert J. joint author. II. T.
QE720.D62     560/.45 19     LC 80-19623     *ISBN* 0471041718

The Ecology of fossils: an illustrated guide / edited by W. S.    **5.3156**
McKerrow; [community reconstructions drawn by Elizabeth Winson, cartographic reconstructions drawn by Peter Deussen].
Cambridge, Mass.: MIT Press, 1978. 384 p.: ill.; 26 cm. — (Alphabook) Includes index. 1. Paleoecology 2. Paleontology, Stratigraphic 3. Animal communities I. McKerrow, W. S.
QE720.E26 1978b     560     LC 78-52250     *ISBN* 0262131447

Laporte, Léo F.                                        **5.3157**
Ancient environments / Léo F. Laporte. — 2d ed. — Englewood Cliffs, N.J.: Prentice-Hall, c1979. 163 p.: ill.; 24 cm. — (The Prentice-Hall foundations of earth science series) Bibliography: p. 151-152. Includes index. 1. Paleoecology — Addresses, essays, lectures. I. T.
QE720.L36 1979     560     LC 79-737     *ISBN* 0130363928

Frey, Robert W.                                        **5.3158**
The study of trace fossils: a synthesis of principles, problems, and procedures in ichnology / edited by Robert W. Frey. — New York: Springer-Verlag, 1975. xiv, 562 p.: ill.; 27 cm. 1. Trace fossils I. T.
QE720.5.F73     560     LC 74-30164     *ISBN* 0387068708

Patterns of evolution as illustrated by the fossil record / edited   **5.3159**
by A. Hallam.
Amsterdam; New York: Elsevier Scientific Pub. Co.: distributors for the U.S. and Canada, Elsevier North-Holland, 1977. xiii, 591 p.: ill.; 25 cm. — (Developments in palaeontology and stratigraphy. 5) 1. Paleontology 2. Evolution I. Hallam, A. (Anthony), 1933- II. Series.
QE721.P34     575     LC 77-2819     *ISBN* 0444414959

Schopf, Thomas J. M.                                   **5.3160**
Models in paleobiology, edited by Thomas J. M. Schopf. — San Francisco: Freeman, Cooper, [1972] vi, 250 p.: illus.; 24 cm. 1. Paleontology — Simulation methods — Congresses. I. T.
QE721.S36     560/.1/84     LC 72-78387     *ISBN* 0877353255

Stanley, Steven M.                                     **5.3161**
Extinction / Steven M. Stanley. — New York: Scientific American Library: Distributed by W.H. Freeman, c1987. 242 p.: ill. (some col.); 25 cm. Includes index. 1. Extinction (Biology) I. T.
QE721.2.E97 S73 1987     575/.7 19     LC 86-22027     *ISBN* 0716750147

Earth's earliest biosphere: its origin and evolution / edited by J.   **5.3162**
William Schopf.
Princeton, N.J.: Princeton University Press, c1983. xxv, 543 p., [36] p. of plates: ill. (some col.); 29 cm. Includes index. 1. Paleontology — Pre-Cambrian I. Schopf, J. William, 1941-
QE724.E27 1983     560/.1/71 19     LC 82-61383     *ISBN* 0691083231

Quaternary extinctions: a prehistoric revolution / Paul S.        **5.3163**
Martin, Richard G. Klein, editors.
Tucson, Ariz.: University of Arizona Press, c1984. x, 892 p.: ill.; 27 cm. 1. Paleontology — Quaternary 2. Extinction (Biology) I. Martin, Paul S. (Paul Schultz), 1928- II. Klein, Richard G.
QE741.Q29 1984     560/.1/78 19     LC 83-18053     *ISBN* 0816508127

Shimer, Hervey Woodburn, 1872-.                    • **5.3164**
Index fossils of North America: a new work based on the complete revision and reillustration of Grabau and Shimer's 'North American index fossils,' by Hervey W. Shimer and Robert R. Shrock. A publication of the Technology press, Massachusetts institute of technology. — New York: J. Wiley & Sons, inc.; London: Chapman & Hall, limited, [1948, c1944] ix, 837 p.: illus.; 28 cm. 1. Paleontology — North America. 2. Invertebrates, Fossil I. Shrock, Robert Rakes, 1904- joint author. II. Grabau, Amadeus William, 1870- North American index fossils. III. Massachusetts Institute of Technology. IV. T.
QE745.S48     562     LC 44-5139

# QE761–882 PALEOZOOLOGY

## QE770–840 Invertebrates

Clarkson, E. N. K. (Euan Neilson Kerr), 1937-.         **5.3165**
Invertebrate palaeontology and evolution / E.N.K. Clarkson. — 2nd ed. — London; Boston: Allen & Unwin, 1985. xiii, 382 p.: ill. Includes index. 1. Invertebrates, Fossil I. T.
QE770.C56 1985     562 19     LC 85-20037     *ISBN* 0045600090

**Glaessner, Martin F. (Martin Fritz), 1906-.**                          **5.3166**
The dawn of animal life: a biohistorical study / Martin F. Glaessner. —
Cambridge; New York: Cambridge University Press, 1984. xi, 244 p.: ill.; 24
cm. — (Cambridge earth science series.) Includes indexes. 1. Invertebrates,
Fossil 2. Marine invertebrates — Evolution. 3. Paleontology — Pre-Cambrian
I. T. II. Series.
QE770.G54 1984        562 19        LC 83-5188        ISBN 0521235073

**Moore, Raymond Cecil, 1892-.**                                    **• 5.3167**
Invertebrate fossils / Raymond C. Moore, Cecil G. Lalicker, Alfred G. Fischer.
— New York: McGraw-Hill Book Co., 1952. xiii, 766 p.: ill. 1. Invertebrates,
Fossil I. Lalicker, Cecil G. II. Fischer, Alfred G. III. T.
QE770.M6        LC 51-12632

# QE841–899 Vertebrates

**Colbert, Edwin Harris, 1905-.**                                    **5.3168**
Evolution of the vertebrates: a history of the backboned animals through time /
Edwin H. Colbert. — 3d ed. — New York: J. Wiley, c1980. xvi, 510 p.: ill.; 24
cm. 'A Wiley-Interscience publication.' Includes index. 1. Vertebrates, Fossil
2. Vertebrates — Evolution 3. Phylogeny I. T.
QE841.C68 1980        566        LC 79-27621        ISBN 0471049662

**Romer, Alfred Sherwood, 1894-.**                                    **• 5.3169**
Vertebrate paleontology. — 3d ed. — Chicago: University of Chicago Press,
[1966] viii, 468 p.: illus.; 29 cm. 1. Vertebrates, Fossil 2. Vertebrates —
Anatomy I. T. II. Title: Notes and comments on Vertebrate paleontology.
QE841.R6 1966        566        LC 66-13886

**Colbert, Edwin Harris, 1905-.**                                    **• 5.3170**
The age of reptiles [by] Edwin H. Colbert. — New York: Norton, [1965] 228 p.:
illus., maps.; 25 cm. — (The World naturalist) 1. Reptiles, Fossil I. T.
QE861.C72        568.1        LC 65-13325

**Desmond, Adrian J., 1947-.**                                    **5.3171**
The hot–blooded dinosaurs: a revolution in palaeontology / Adrian J.
Desmond. — New York: Dial Press, 1976, c1975. 238 p.: ill.; 26 cm. Includes
index. 1. Dinosaurs 2. Paleontology — History. 3. Body temperature I. T.
QE862.D5 D45 1976        567.9/1 19        LC 76-190        ISBN 0803737556

**Kurtén, Björn.**                                    **5.3172**
Pleistocene mammals of North America / Björn Kurtén and Elaine Anderson.
— New York: Columbia University Press, 1980. xvii, 442 p.: ill.; 26 cm.

Includes indexes. 1. Mammals, Fossil 2. Paleontology — Pleistocene
3. Paleontology — North America. I. Anderson, Elaine. joint author. II. T.
QE881.K82        569/.097        LC 79-26679        ISBN 0231037333

# QE901–996 PALEOBOTANY

**Andrews, Henry Nathaniel, 1910-.**                                    **5.3173**
The fossil hunters: in search of ancient plants / Henry N. Andrews. — Ithaca,
N.Y.: Cornell University Press, c1980. 421 p.: ill.; 24 cm. Includes index.
1. Paleobotany — History. 2. Paleobotanists — Biography. I. T.
QE904.A1 A5        561/.09        LC 79-24101        ISBN 080141248X

**Andrews, Henry Nathaniel, 1910-.**                                    **• 5.3174**
Studies in paleobotany. With a chapter on palynology by Charles J. Felix. —
New York: Wiley, [1961] 487 p.: illus.; 24 cm. 1. Paleobotany I. T.
QE905.A72        561        LC 61-6768

**Banks, Harlan Parker, 1913-.**                                    **5.3175**
Evolutions and plants of the past [by] Harlan P. Banks. — Belmont, Calif.:
Wadsworth Pub. Co., [1970] x, 170 p.: ill.; 24 cm. — (Fundamentals of botany
series) 1. Paleobotany I. T.
QE905.B3        561        LC 77-131873

**Seward, A. C. (Albert Charles), 1863-1941.**                          **• 5.3176**
Plant life through the ages: a geological and botanical retrospect; including 9
reconstructions of ancient landscapes drawn for the author by Edward
Vulliamy. — New York: Hafner, 1959. 603 p.: ill.; 24 cm. 1. Paleobotany
2. Geology I. T.
QE905.S53 1959        QE905.S51 1959.        LC 59-10943

**Stewart, Wilson N. (Wilson Nichols), 1917-.**                          **5.3177**
Paleobotany and the evolution of plants / Wilson N. Stewart. — Cambridge
[Cambridgeshire]; New York: Cambridge University Press, 1983. x, 405 p.: ill.;
27 cm. 1. Paleobotany 2. Plants — Evolution I. T.
QE905.S73 1983        561 19        LC 82-21986        ISBN 0521233151

**Tschudy, Robert H.**                                    **5.3178**
Aspects of palynology. Robert H. Tschudy [and] Richard A. Scott, editors.
New York, Wiley-Interscience [1969] vii, 510 p. illus. 26 cm. 1. Palynology
I. Scott, Richard A. (Richard Albert), 1921- joint author. II. T.
QE993.T74        561/.13        LC 73-84968        ISBN 0471892203

The Beagle record: selections from the original pictorial records    **5.3179**
and written accounts of the voyage of H.M.S. Beagle / edited
by Richard Darwin Keynes.
Cambridge; New York: Cambridge University Press, 1979. xiv, 409 p.: ill.; 29
cm. Includes index. 1. Darwin, Charles, 1809-1882. 2. Beagle Expedition
(1831-1836) 3. Naturalists — England — Biography. 4. Naturalists —
England — Correspondence. I. Keynes, R. D.
QH11.B43    500.9/8    LC 77-82500    *ISBN* 0521218225

**Darwin, Charles, 1809-1882.**    • **5.3180**
Journal of researches into the geology and natural history of the various
countries visited by H.M.S. Beagle / by Charles Darwin, 1839. — New York:
Hafner, 1952. xiv, 615 p., [16] leaves of plates: ill.; 24 cm. — (Pallas; v. 2)
Facsim. of original t.p. Includes index. 1. Beagle Expedition (1831-1836)
2. Natural history 3. Voyages around the world 4. Geology 5. South America
— Description and travel I. T.
QH11.D2 1839a    LC 53-2985

## QH13 REFERENCE WORKS

**Abercrombie, M. (Michael), 1912-1979.**    **5.3181**
The Penguin dictionary of biology / [by] M. Abercrombie, C. J. Hickman, and
M. L. Johnson. — [New ed.]. — London: Allen Lane; New York: Viking Press,
1977. 3-311 p.: ill.; 23 cm. First-6th ed. published under title: A dictionary of
biology. 1. Biology — Dictionaries. I. Hickman, C. J. joint author.
II. Johnson, M. L. joint author. III. T.
QH13.A25 1977    574/.03    LC 77-77778    *ISBN* 0670272221

**Gray, Peter, 1908-.**    • **5.3182**
The dictionary of the biological sciences. — New York: Reinhold Pub. Corp.,
[1967] xx, 602 p.: illus.; 26 cm. 1. Biology — Dictionaries. I. T.
QH13.G68    574/.03    LC 67-24690

**Gray, Peter, 1908- ed.**    • **5.3183**
The encyclopedia of the biological sciences. — 2d ed. — New York: Van
Nostrand Reinhold Co., [1970] xxv 1027 p.: illus.; 26 cm. 1. Biology —
Dictionaries. I. T.
QH13.G7 1970    574/.03    LC 77-81348

**Jaeger, Edmund Carroll, 1887-.**    • **5.3184**
The biologist's handbook of pronunciations / illus. by Morris Van Dame and
the author. — Springfield, Ill.: Thomas [1960] 317 p.: ill.; 20 cm. 1. Biology —
Dictionaries. I. T.
QH13.J3 1960    574.03    LC 59-14924

**The Oxford dictionary of natural history / edited by Michael**    **5.3185**
**Allaby; foreword by David Attenborough.**
Oxford; New York: Oxford University Press, 1985. xiv, 688 p.; 25 cm.
1. Natural history — Dictionaries. I. Allaby, Michael.
QH13.O9 1985    508/.03/21 19    LC 85-13758    *ISBN* 0192177206

**Steen, Edwin Benzel, 1901-.**    **5.3186**
Dictionary of biology [by] Edwin B. Steen. — New York: Barnes & Noble,
[1971] vii, 630 p.; 21 cm. — (Everyday handbooks, no. 321) 1. Biology —
Dictionaries. I. T.
QH13.S74    574/.03    LC 70-156104    *ISBN* 0389003336

## QH15–44 HISTORY. BIOGRAPHY

**Elman, Robert.**    **5.3187**
First in the field: America's pioneering naturalists / by Robert Elman; foreword
by Dean Amadon. New York: Mason/Charter, 1977. xx, 231 p., [8] leaves of
plates: ill.; 24 cm. Includes index. 1. Naturalists — United States — Biography.
I. T.
QH26.E44    500.9/2/2 B    LC 77-3437    *ISBN* 0884054993

**Kastner, Joseph.**    **5.3188**
A species of eternity / Joseph Kastner. — 1st ed. — New York: Knopf, 1977.
xiv, 350 p., [8] leaves of plates: ill.; 25 cm. Includes index. 1. Naturalists —
United States — Biograph. I. T.
QH26.K38 1977    500.92/2 3    LC 77-74983    *ISBN* 0394490339

## QH31 Individual Biography, A–Z

### QH31 A–B

**Bartram, John, 1699-1777.**    • **5.3189**
John and William Bartram's America; selections from the writings of the
Philadelphia naturalists. Edited with an introd. by Helen Gere Cruickshank.
Foreword by B. Bartram Cadbury. Illustrated by Francis Lee Jacques. New
York, Devin-Adair Co., 1957. xxii, 418 p. illus., maps, plates, ports. (American
naturalists series) 1. Naturalists — Correspondence, reminiscences, etc.
2. Natural history — United States 3. United States — Description and travel
— To 1783 I. Bartram, William, 1739-1823. (jt. author) II. Cruickshank,
Helen Gere. III. T.
QH31.B23    LC 57-8862

### QH31.D2 DARWIN
### (see also: QH365)

**Darwin, Charles, 1809-1882.**    • **5.3190**
Autobiography: with original omissions restored / edited with appendix and
notes by his grand–daughter, Nora Barlow. — [1st American ed.] New York:
Harcourt, Brace [1959, c1958] 253 p.: ports., facsim., geneal. table; 22 cm.
I. Barlow, Nora. ed. II. T.
QH31.D2 A16 1958    925.9    LC 59-6418

**Darwin, Charles, 1809-1882.**    • **5.3191**
The life and letters of Charles Darwin, including an autobiographical chapter.
Edited by his son, Francis Darwin. London, J. Murray, 1888. New York,
Johnson Reprint Corp. [1969] 3 v. ports. 23 cm. (The Sources of science, no.
102) I. Darwin, Francis, Sir, 1848-1925. ed. II. T.
QH31.D2A2 1969    575/.00924 B    LC 77-12465

**Darwin, Charles, 1809-1882.**    **5.3192**
[Correspondence] The correspondence of Charles Darwin / [editors, Frederick
Burkhardt, Sydney Smith]. — Cambridge [Cambridgeshire]; New York:
Cambridge University Press, 1985. 702 p.: ill.; 24 cm. 1. Darwin, Charles,
1809-1882. 2. Naturalists — England — Correspondence. I. Burkhardt,
Frederick, 1912- II. Smith, Sydney, 1911- III. T.
QH31.D2 A33 1985    575/.0092/4 B 19    LC 84-45347    *ISBN*
0521255872

**Darwin, Charles, 1809-1882.**    **5.3193**
The red notebook of Charles Darwin / edited and with an introd. and notes by
Sandra Herbert. — [London]: British Museum (Natural History); Ithaca:
Cornell University Press, 1980. 164 p.: ill.; 26 cm. (Bulletin of the British
Museum (Natural History). Historical series; v. 7) Includes indexes. 1. Darwin,
Charles, 1809-1882. 2. Natural history 3. Naturalists — England —
Biography. I. Herbert, Sandra. II. T.
QH31.D2 A37    575/.0092/4    LC 78-74215    *ISBN* 0801412269

**Allan, Mea.**    **5.3194**
Darwin and his flowers: the key to natural selection / Mea Allan. — New York:
Taplinger Pub. Co., 1977. 318 p.: ill.; 24 cm. Includes index. 1. Darwin,
Charles, 1809-1882. 2. Natural selection 3. Plant genetics 4. Naturalists —
England — Biography. 5. Botanists — England — Biography. I. T.
QH31.D2 A78 1977    575/.009/24 B    LC 77-155104    *ISBN*
0800821130

**Autobiographies / Charles Darwin, Thomas Henry Huxley;**    **5.3195**
**edited with an introd. by Gavin de Beer.**
London; New York: Oxford University Press, 1974. xxvi, 123 p., [6] leaves of
plates: ill.; 25 cm. — (Oxford English memoirs and travels) Includes index.
1. Darwin, Charles, 1809-1882. 2. Huxley, Thomas Henry, 1825-1895.
3. Naturalists — Biography. I. Darwin, Charles, 1809-1882. II. Huxley,
Thomas Henry, 1825-1895. III. De Beer, Gavin, Sir, 1899-1972. IV. Series.
QH31.D2 A93    575/.0092/4 B    LC 75-321823    *ISBN* 0192554107

**Clark, Ronald William.**    **5.3196**
The survival of Charles Darwin: a biography of a man and an idea / Ronald W. Clark. — 1st ed. — New York: Random House, 1985 (c1984). x, 449 p., [16] p. of plates: ill.; 24 cm. Includes index. 1. Darwin, Charles, 1809-1882. 2. Evolution — History. 3. Naturalists — England — Biography. I. T. QH31.D2 C57 1984    575/.0092/4 19    *LC* 84-42507    *ISBN* 039452134X

**Darwin on man: A psychological study of Scientific creativity,**    **5.3197**
**by Howard E. Gruber, together with Darwin's early and unpublished notebooks, transcribed and annotated by Paul H. Barrett. Foreword by Jean Piaget.**
[1st ed.] New York, E. P. Dutton, 1974. xxv, 495 p. illus. 25 cm. 1. Darwin, Charles, 1809-1882. 2. Evolution 3. Psychology, Comparative 4. Creative ability in science 5. Naturalists — England — Biography. I. Gruber, Howard E. A psychological study of scientific creativity. 1974. II. Darwin, Charles, 1809-1882. Selected works. 1974. III. Barrett, Paul H. QH31.D2 D37 1974    575/.0092/4    *LC* 76-122778    *ISBN* 0525088776

**Gillespie, Neal C., 1933-.**    **5.3198**
Charles Darwin and the problem of creation / Neal C. Gillespie. — Chicago: University of Chicago Press, c1979. xiii, 201 p.; 24 cm. Includes index. 1. Darwin, Charles, 1809-1882. 2. Life — Origin 3. Naturalists — England — Biography. I. T. QH31.D2 G55    575/.0092/4 19    *LC* 79-11231    *ISBN* 0226293742

**Himmelfarb, Gertrude.**    **5.3199**
Darwin and the Darwinian revolution. [1st ed.]. Garden City, N.Y., Doubleday, 1959. 480 p. 22 cm. 1. Darwin, Charles, 1809-1882. 2. Evolution I. T. QH31.D2 H57    925.9    *LC* 59-7908

**Irvine, William, 1906-1964.**    • **5.3200**
Apes, angels, and Victorians: Darwin, Huxley, and evolution / William Irvine. — New York: Meridian Books, 1959, c1955. 399 p.; 19 cm. — (Meridian books; M78) 1. Darwin, Charles, 1809-1882. 2. Huxley, Thomas Henry, 1825-1895. 3. Evolution I. T. QH31.D2 I7 1959    *LC* 59-12909

**Miller, Jonathan, 1934-.**    **5.3201**
Darwin for beginners / Jonathan Miller & Borin Van Loon. — 1st American ed. — New York: Pantheon Books, c1982. 176 p.: ill.; 21 cm. 1. Darwin, Charles, 1809-1882. 2. Naturalists — England — Biography. I. Van Loon, Borin. II. T. QH31.D2 M54 1982    575/.0092/4 B 19    *LC* 82-47888    *ISBN* 0394748476

**Ospovat, Dov.**    **5.3202**
The development of Darwin's theory: natural history, natural theology, and natural selection, 1838–1859 / Dov Ospovat. — Cambridge; New York: Cambridge University Press, 1981. xii, 301 p.: ill.; 24 cm. 1. Darwin, Charles, 1809-1882. 2. Natural selection — History. 3. Natural history — History. 4. Biology — History. 5. Naturalists — England — Biography. I. T. QH31.D2 O74    575.01/62 19    *LC* 81-4077    *ISBN* 0521238188

## QH31 H–Z

**Clark, Ronald William.**    **5.3203**
JBS: the life and work of J. B. S. Haldane [by] Ronald W. Clark. — [1st American ed.]. — New York: Coward-McCann, [1969, c1968] 326 p.: ports.; 23 cm. 1. Haldane, J. B. S. (John Burdon Sanderson), 1892-1964. I. T. QH31.H27 C55 1969    575.00924 B    *LC* 68-11875

**Huxley, Julian, 1887-1975.**    **5.3204**
Memories II / [by] Julian Huxley. — [1st U.S. ed.]. — New York: Harper & Row, 1974 (c1973). 269 p.: ill.; 24 cm. — (A Cass Canfield book) Autobiographical. Vol. 2 does not have edition statement and series statement. 1. Huxley, Julian, 1887-1975. 2. Huxley, Julian, 1887-1975. I. T. QH31.H88 A3 1973    574/.092/4 B

**Huxley, Thomas Henry, 1825-1895.**    • **5.3205**
Life and letters of Thomas Henry Huxley / By his son Leonard Huxley. — New York: D. Appleton, 1900. 2 v.: fronts., 1 ill. plates, ports, facsims.; 22 cm. I. Huxley, Leonard, 1860-1933. II. T. QH31.H9 A2 1900

**Bibby, Cyril.**    **5.3206**
Scientist extraordinary: the life and scientific work of Thomas Henry Huxley, 1825–1895 / by Cyril Bibby. — New York: St. Martin's Press [1972] xi, 208 p.: ill.; 22 cm. 1. Huxley, Thomas Henry, 1825-1895. I. T. QH31.H9 B48 1972b    574/.092/4 B    *LC* 72-77611

**Burkhardt, Richard Wellington, 1944-.**    **5.3207**
The spirit of system: Lamarck and evolutionary biology / Richard W. Burkhardt, Jr. Cambridge, Mass.: Harvard University Press, 1977. 285 p.; 25 cm. Includes index. 1. Lamarck, Jean Baptiste Pierre Antoine de Monet de, 1744-1829. 2. Evolution — History. 3. Biologists — France — Biography. I. T. QH31.L2 B87    575.01/66/0924    *LC* 76-53804    *ISBN* 0674833171

**Antony van Leeuwenhoek and his 'Little animals': being some**    • **5.3208**
**account of the father of protozoology and bacteriology and his multifarious discoveries in these disciplines / collected, translated, and edited from his printed works, unpublished manuscripts, and contemporary records by Clifford Dobell.**
New York: Dover, 1960. 435 p., [28] leaves of plates: ill., ports. 1. Leeuwenhoek, Antoni van, 1632-1723. 2. Protozoa 3. Bacteria I. Leeuwenhoek, Antoni van, 1632-1723. II. Dobell, Clifford, 1886-1949 QH31L55 D6 1960    *LC* 60-2548    *ISBN* 0486605949

**Orel, Vítězslav.**    **5.3209**
[Mendel. English] Mendel / Vítězslav Orel; translated by Stephen Finn. — Oxford [Oxfordshire]; New York: Oxford University Press, 1984. vii, 111 p.; 23 cm. (Past masters.) Includes index. 1. Mendel, Gregor, 1822-1884. 2. Geneticists — Austria — Biography. I. T. II. Series. QH31.M45 O6813 1984    575.1/1/0924 B 19    *LC* 84-10089    *ISBN* 0192876252

**Graustein, Jeannette E.**    • **5.3210**
Thomas Nuttall, naturalist; explorations in America, 1808–1841 [by] Jeannette E. Graustein. Cambridge, Harvard University Press, 1967. xiii, 481 p. illus., port. 25 cm. 'Biographical sketches of Thomas Nuttall': p. 401. Bibliographical references included in 'Notes' (p. 403-458) 1. Nuttall, Thomas, 1786-1859. I. T. QH31.N8 G7    574/.0924 B    *LC* 67-13253

**Raven, Charles E. (Charles Earle), 1885-1964.**    • **5.3211**
John Ray, naturalist, his life and works. [2d ed.] Cambridge [Eng.] University Press, 1950. xix, 506 p. port. 24 cm. 'Sources': p. [xiii]—xv. Bibliographical footnotes. 1. Ray, John, 1627-1705. I. T. QH31.R2R3    *LC* A 53-9835

**Brooks, John Langdon, 1920-.**    **5.3212**
Just before the origin: Alfred Russel Wallace's theory of evolution / John Langdon Brooks. — New York: Columbia University Press, 1984. xiii, 284 p., [1] folded leaf: ill., maps; 24 cm. Maps on lining papers. Includes index. 1. Wallace, Alfred Russel, 1823-1913. 2. Evolution — History. 3. Naturalists — England — Biography. I. T. QH31.W2 B76 1984    575.01/62/0924 B 19    *LC* 83-7710    *ISBN* 0231056761

**White, Gilbert, 1720-1793.**    **5.3213**
The portrait of a tortoise / extracted from the jounals & letters of Gilbert White; with an introduction & notes by Sylvia Townsend Warner. — London: Chatto & Windus, 1946. 63 p.: ports. 1. Turtles I. Warner, Sylvia Townsend, 1893-II. T. QH31W58 A5    QH31W58 A5.    598.13    *LC* 47-20173

## QH44 LINNÉ

**Goerke, Heinz.**    **5.3214**
[Carl von Linné. English] Linnaeus / translated from the German by Denver Lindley. — New York: Scribner [1973] xi, 178 p.: ill.; 25 cm. 1. Linné, Carl von, 1707-1778. I. T. QH44.G5413    581/.092/4 B    *LC* 70-37209    *ISBN* 0684127776

**Linnaeus, the man and his work / edited by Tore Frängsmyr;**    **5.3215**
**with contributions by Sten Lindroth, Gunnar Eriksson, Gunnar Broberg.**
Berkeley: University of California Press, c1983. xii, 202 p., [12] p. of plates: ill.; 24 cm. 1. Linné, Carl von, 1707-1778. 2. Naturalists — Sweden — Biography. I. Frängsmyr, Tore, 1938- II. Lindroth, Sten. III. Eriksson, Gunnar, 1931- IV. Broberg, Gunnar, 1942- QH44.L56 1983    580/.92/4 B 19    *LC* 82-2044    *ISBN* 0520045688

# QH45–83 NATURAL HISTORY. NATURE CONSERVATION

**Morholt, Evelyn.**    **5.3216**
A sourcebook for the biological sciences [by Evelyn Morholt, Paul F. Brandwein [and] Alexander Joseph. 2d ed. New York, Harcourt, Brace &

World [1966] xxi, 795 p. illus. 24 cm. (Teaching science series) First published in 1958 under title: Teaching high school science. 1. Biology — Study and teaching 2. Biology — Outlines, syllabi, etc. I. Brandwein, Paul Franz, 1912- joint author. II. Joseph, Alexander. joint author. III. T.
QH53.M67 1966     574 19     *LC* 66-13536

**Conservation biology: an evolutionary–ecological perspective /**     **5.3217**
**edited by Michael E. Soulé and Bruce A. Wilcox.**
Sunderland, Mass.: Sinauer Associates, c1980. xv, 395 p.: ill.; 23 cm. Includes index. 1. Nature conservation — Congresses. I. Soulé, Michael E. II. Wilcox, Bruce A., 1948-
QH75.C66     333.9/5     *LC* 79-26463     *ISBN* 0878938001

**Conservation biology: the science of scarcity and diversity /**     **5.3218**
**edited by Michael E. Soulé.**
Sunderland, Mass.: Sinauer Associates, c1986. xiii, 584 p.: ill.; 24 cm. Includes index. 1. Nature conservation 2. Population biology 3. Ecology I. Soulé, Michael E.
QH75.C664 1986     574.5 19     *LC* 86-1902     *ISBN* 0878937943

**Frankel, O. H. (Otto Herzberg), 1900-.**     **5.3219**
Conservation and evolution / O.H. Frankel and Michael E. Soulé. — Cambridge [England]; New York: Cambridge University Press, 1981. viii, 327 p.: ill.; 24 cm. Includes index. 1. Nature conservation 2. Ecological genetics I. Soulé, Michael E. II. T.
QH75.F73     639.9 19     *LC* 80-40528     *ISBN* 0521232759

**Genetics and conservation: a reference for managing wild animal**     **5.3220**
**and plant populations / edited by Christine M. Schonewald–Cox**
**... [et al.].**
Menlo Park, Calif.: Benjamin/Cummings, 1983. xxii, 722 p.: ill.; 24 cm. — (Biological conservation series. 1) Includes indexes. 1. Germplasm resources 2. Population genetics I. Schonewald-Cox, Christine M. II. Series.
QH75.G45 1983     639.9 19     *LC* 83-3922     *ISBN* 0805377646

**Harris, Larry D.**     **5.3221**
The fragmented forest: island biogeography theory and the preservation of biotic diversity / Larry D. Harris; with a foreword by Kenton R. Miller. — Chicago: University of Chicago Press, 1984. xviii, 211 p.: ill.; 22 cm. — (A Chicago original paperback) Includes indexes. 1. Nature conservation 2. Biogeography 3. Island ecology I. T.
QH75.H37 1984     639.9 19     *LC* 84-144     *ISBN* 0226317641

**Myers, Norman.**     **5.3222**
A wealth of wild species: storehouse for human welfare / Norman Myers. — Boulder, Colo: Westview Press, 1983. xiii, 274 p.: ill.; 24 cm. Includes index. 1. Nature conservation — Economic aspects. 2. Biology, Economic I. T.
QH75.M93 1983     333.7/2 19     *LC* 82-20121     *ISBN* 0865311323

**Naveh, Zeev.**     **5.3223**
Landscape ecology: theory and application / Zev Naveh, Arthur S. Lieberman; with a foreword by Arthur M. Schultz; with an epilogue by Frank E. Egler. — New York: Springer-Verlag, c1984. xviii, 356 p.: ill.; 24 cm. — (Springer series on environmental management.) 1. Landscape protection 2. Ecology I. Lieberman, Arthur S. II. T. III. Series.
QH75.N3594 1984     333.7/2 19     *LC* 83-4284     *ISBN* 0387908498

**Odell, Rice.**     **5.3224**
Environmental awakening: the new revolution to protect the earth / Rice Odell; foreword by Edmond S. Muskie. — [Washington, D.C.]: Conservation Foundation; Cambridge, Mass.: Ballinger Pub. Co., c1980. xiv, 330 p.: ill.; 24 cm. 'Material in this book was drawn from several dozen issues of the Conservation Foundation letter.' Includes index. 1. Nature conservation 2. Environmental protection I. T.
QH75.O33     333.7     *LC* 80-10990     *ISBN* 0884106306

**Allin, Craig W. (Craig Willard)**     **5.3225**
The politics of wilderness preservation / Craig W. Allin. — Westport, Conn.: Greenwood Press, 1982. 304 p.; 25 cm. — (Contributions in political science. 0147-1066; no. 64) Includes index. 1. Nature conservation — Political aspects — United States. 2. Wilderness areas — Political aspects — United States. I. T. II. Series.
QH76.A44 1982     333.78/216/0973 19     *LC* 81-6234     *ISBN* 0313214581

**Fox, Stephen R.**     **5.3226**
John Muir and his legacy: the American conservation movement / Stephen Fox. — 1st ed. — Boston: Little, Brown, c1981. xii, 436 p.: ill.; 24 cm. 1. Muir, John, 1838-1914. 2. Nature conservation — United States — History. 3. Conservationists — United States — Biography. 4. Naturalists — United States — Biography. I. T.
QH76.F69     333.95/0973 19     *LC* 81-1852     *ISBN* 0316291102

**Mitchell, Lee Clark, 1957-.**     **5.3227**
Witnesses to a vanishing America: the nineteenth–century response / Lee Clark Mitchell. — Princeton, N.J.: Princeton University Press, c1981. xvii, 320 p.: ill.;

24 cm. Includes index. 1. Nature conservation — United States — History. 2. Conservation of natural resources — United States — History. 3. Frontier and pioneer life — United States. 4. Indians of North America — Public opinion 5. Ethnology — United States — History. I. T.
QH76.M54     333.95/0973 19     *LC* 80-8567     *ISBN* 069106461X

**Huth, Hans, 1892-.**     **5.3228**
Nature and the American: three centuries of changing attitudes. — Berkeley: University of California Press, 1957. xvii, 250 p.: ill. (part mounted col.) 64 plates (incl. ports.); 27 cm. 1. Nature conservation — United States — History. 2. Conservation of natural resources — United States — History. I. T.
QH77.U6 H8     574.973     *LC* 57-12393

**Gould, Stephen Jay.**     **5.3229**
The flamingo's smile: reflections in natural history / Stephen Jay Gould. — 1st ed. — New York: Norton, c1985. 476 p.: ill.; 21 cm. Includes index. 1. Natural history — Addresses, essays, lectures. I. T.
QH81.G673 1985     508 19     *LC* 85-4916     *ISBN* 0393022285

**Leopold, Aldo, 1886-1948.**     ● **5.3230**
A Sand County almanac, and Sketches here and there; illus. by Charles W. Schwartz. — New York: Oxford Univ. Press, 1949. xiii, 226 p.: illus.; 22 cm. 1. Natural history — Outdoor books 2. Natural history — United States. 3. Wildlife conservation I. T. II. Title: Sketches here and there.
QH81.L56     574     *LC* 49-11164

**Prishvin, Mikhail Mikhaĭlovich, 1873-1954.**     **5.3231**
[Zhen'-shen', koren' zhizni. English] The root of life / Mikhail Prishvin; translated from the Russian by Alice Stone Nakhimovsky and Alexander Nakhimovsky; ill. by Stefen Bernath. — New York: Macmillan; London: Collier Macmillan, c1980. 115 p.: ill.; 22 cm. 1. Nature 2. Deer — Anecdotes. I. T.
QH81.P8613     891.78/4207     *LC* 80-10428

# QH83 BIOLOGY. CLASSIFICATION.
## TERMINOLOGY

**Humphries, Christopher John.**     **5.3232**
Cladistic biogeography / Christopher J. Humphries and Lynne R. Parenti. — Oxford: Clarendon Press; New York: Oxford University Press, 1986. xii, 98 p.: ill.; 25 cm. — (Oxford monographs on biogeography.) (Oxford science publications.) Includes indexes. 1. Cladistic analysis 2. Biogeography I. Parenti, Lynne R. II. T. III. Series. IV. Series: Oxford science publications.
QH83.H86 1986     575 19     *LC* 85-9711     *ISBN* 0198545762

**Jeffrey, Charles.**     **5.3233**
Biological nomenclature / [by] Charles Jeffrey for the Systematics Association; foreword by V. H. Heywood. — 2nd ed. — New York: Crane,Russak, [1977] viii, 72 p.; 24 cm. Includes index. 1. Biology — Nomenclature I. Systematics Association. II. T.
QH83.J43 1977     574/.01/4     *LC* 78-301399     *ISBN* 0713126140

**Margulis, Lynn, 1938-.**     **5.3234**
Five kingdoms: an illustrated guide to the phyla of life on earth / Lynn Margulis, Karlene V. Schwartz. — San Francisco: W.H. Freeman, c1982. xiv, 338 p.: ill.; 25 cm. 1. Biology — Classification I. Schwartz, Karlene V., 1936- II. T.
QH83.M36     574/.012 19     *LC* 81-7845     *ISBN* 0716712121

**Nelson, Gareth J.**     **5.3235**
Systematics and biogeography: cladistics and vicariance / Gareth Nelson and Norman Platnick. — New York: Columbia University Press, 1981. xi, 567 p.: ill.; 24 cm. Includes indexes. 1. Biology — Classification 2. Biogeography 3. Cladistic analysis I. Platnick, Norman I. joint author. II. T. III. Title: Cladistics and vicariance.
QH83.N4     574/.012 19     *LC* 80-20828     *ISBN* 0231045743

**Synopsis and classification of living organisms / Sybil P.**     **5.3236**
**Parker, editor in chief.**
New York: McGraw-Hill, c1982. 2 v.: ill. (some col.); 29 cm. 1. Biology — Classification I. Parker, Sybil P.
QH83.S89     574.012 19     *LC* 81-13653     *ISBN* 0070790310

## QH84–199 GEOGRAPHICAL DISTRIBUTION. BIOGEOGRAPHY

**Brown, James H.**       5.3237
Biogeography / James H. Brown, Arthur C. Gibson. — St. Louis: Mosby, 1983. xi, 643 p.: ill.; 25 cm. Includes index. 1. Biogeography I. Gibson, Arthur C. II. T.
QH84.B76 1983     574.9 19     LC 82-14121     ISBN 0801608244

**Cox, C. Barry (Christopher Barry), 1931-.**       5.3238
Biogeography: an ecological and evolutionary approach / C. Barry Cox, Peter D. Moore. — 3d ed. — New York: Wiley, 1980. xi, 234 p.: ill.; 24 cm. 'A Halsted Press book.' 1. Biogeography I. Moore, Peter D. joint author. II. T.
QH84.C65 1980     574.5/2     LC 79-22636     ISBN 047026893X

**Furley, Peter A. (Peter Anthony), 1935-.**       5.3239
Geography of the biosphere: an introduction to the nature, distribution and evolution of the world's life zones / Peter A. Furley, Walter W. Newey with a contribution from R.P. Kirby, J.McG. Hotson. — London: Butterworths, 1983. xi, 413 p.: ill., maps; 31 cm. Includes index. 1. Biogeography I. Newey, Walter W. II. T.
QH84.F8x 1983    QH84.F87 1983.     574.9 19     ISBN 0408708018

**MacArthur, Robert H.**       5.3240
Geographical ecology: patterns in the distribution of species / Robert H. MacArthur. — Princeton, N.J.: Princeton University Press, [1984], c1972. p. cm. Reprint. Originally published: New York: Harper & Row, 1972. Includes index. 1. Biogeography 2. Ecology I. T.
QH84.M23 1984     574.5/24 19     LC 83-24477     ISBN 0691083533

**Simmons, I. G. (Ian Gordon), 1937-.**       5.3241
Biogeography: natural and cultural / I. G. Simmons. — London: E. Arnold, 1979. xiii, 400 p.: ill.; 24 cm. Includes index. 1. Biogeography 2. Man — Influence on nature I. T.
QH84.S55 1979     574.9 19     LC 80-492727     ISBN 0713162457

**Aubert de La Rüe, E. (Edgar), 1901-.**       • 5.3242
[Tropiques. English] The tropics / by Edgar Aubert de La Rüe, François Bourlière and Jean–Paul Harroy. — New York: Knopf, 1957. 208 p.: ill., col. plates; 29 cm. 1. Natural history — Tropics — Pictorial works. I. T.
QH84.5.A813     574.084     LC 57-13821

**MacArthur, Robert H.**       • 5.3243
The theory of island biogeography [by] Robert H. MacArthur and Edward O. Wilson. — Princeton, N.J.: Princeton University Press, 1967. xi, 203 p.: ill.; 23 cm. — (Monographs in population biology. [1]) 1. Biogeography I. Wilson, Edward Osborne, 1929- joint author. II. T. III. Title: Island biogeography. IV. Series.
QH85.M3     574.91     LC 67-24102

**Jaeger, Edmund Carroll, 1887-.**       • 5.3244
The North American deserts. With a chapter by Peveril Meigs and illus. by John D. Briggs [and others]. — Stanford, Calif.: Stanford University Press, 1957. vii, 308 p.: illus.; 24 cm. 1. Desert ecology 2. Deserts I. T.
QH88.J3     575.32653 574.5*     LC 57-9307

## QH90–100 Marine Biology. Fresh Water Biology

**Carson, Rachel, 1907-1964.**       • 5.3245
The edge of the sea. With illus. by Bob Hines. Boston, Houghton Mifflin, 1955. 276 p. illus. 22 cm. 1. Seashore biology I. T.
QH91.C3     591.921     LC 54-10759

**Idyll, C. P. (Clarence P.)**       5.3246
Abyss: the deep sea and the creatures that live in it / by C. P. Idyll. — 3d rev. ed. — New York: Crowell, [1976] p. cm. Includes index. 1. Marine biology 2. Ocean 3. Abyssal zone 4. Fishes, Deep-sea I. T.
QH91.I3 1976     574.92     LC 76-4081     ISBN 069001175X

**Marshall, Norman Bertram.**       5.3247
Deep–sea biology: developments and perspectives / N. B. Marshall. — 1st U.S. ed. — New York: Garland STPM Press, 1980. 566 p., [2] leaves of plates: ill. (some col.); 23 cm. Includes indexes. 1. Marine biology 2. Benthos I. T.
QH91.M29 1980     574.92     LC 79-25526     ISBN 0824072286

**McConnaughey, Bayard Harlow, 1916-.**       5.3248
Introduction to marine biology / Bayard H. McConnaughey, Robert Zottoli. — 4th ed. — St. Louis: Mosby, c1983. xi, 638 p.: ill. (some col.); 29 cm. Includes index. 1. Marine biology I. Zottoli, Robert. II. T.
QH91.M38 1983     574.92 19     LC 82-12511     ISBN 0801632595

**Nybakken, James Willard.**       5.3249
Marine biology: an ecological approach / James W. Nybakken. — New York: Harper & Row, c1982. xvii, 446 p., [8] p. of plates: ill. (some col.); 25 cm. 1. Marine biology 2. Marine ecology I. T.
QH91.N9 1982     574.5/2636 19     LC 81-7236     ISBN 0060448490

**Thurman, Harold V.**       5.3250
Marine biology / Harold V. Thurman, Herbert H. Webber. — Columbus, Ohio: C.E. Merrill, c1984. xiv, 446 p., [8] p. of plates: ill. (some col.); 29 cm. 1. Marine biology I. Webber, Herbert H. II. T.
QH91.T5 1984     574.92 19     LC 83-62582     ISBN 067520139X

**Cousteau, Jacques Yves.**       5.3251
The ocean world / Jacques Cousteau. — New York: H. N. Abrams, 1979. 446 p.: ill.; 34 cm. A condensation of the author's 20-vol. series with the same title, first published 1972-1974 by World Pub., New York. Includes index. 1. Marine biology 2. Ocean I. T.
QH91.15.C652     574.92 19     LC 77-20197     ISBN 0810907771

**Primary productivity in the sea / edited by Paul G. Falkowski.**       5.3252
New York: Plenum Press, c1980. ix, 531 p.: ill.; 26 cm. — (Brookhaven symposia in biology. no. 31) (Environmental science research; v. 19) 1. Primary productivity (Biology) — Congresses. 2. Marine productivity — Congresses. I. Falkowski, Paul G. II. Series.
QH91.8.P7 P74     581.5/2636 19     LC 80-24664     ISBN 0306406233

**Perkins, Eric John.**       5.3253
The biology of estuaries and coastal waters / E. J. Perkins. — London; New York: Academic Press, 1974. ix, 678 p.: ill.; 24 cm. 1. Estuarine biology 2. Seashore biology 3. Coastal zone management I. T.
QH95.9.P47     574.92     LC 73-9473     ISBN 012550750X

**Coker, Robert Ervin, 1876-.**       • 5.3254
Streams, lakes, ponds. — Chapel Hill: University of North Carolina Press, [1954] 327 p.: illus.; 24 cm. 1. Freshwater biology 2. Water 3. Rivers 4. Limnology I. T.
QH96.C6     574.929     LC 54-13071

**Edmondson, Walles Thomas, 1916- ed.**       • 5.3255
Fresh–water biology. — 2d ed. — New York: Wiley, [1959] xx, 1248 p.: ill.; 24 cm. At head of title: The late Henry Baldwin Ward [and the late George Chandler Whipple. First ed., by H. B. Ward and G. C. Whipple, with the collaboration of a staff of specialists, published in 1918. 1. Freshwater biology I. Ward, Henry Baldwin, 1865-1945. Fresh-water biology. II. T.
QH96.E33     574.929     LC 59-6781

**Frey, David G. (David Grover), 1915- ed.**       • 5.3256
Limnology in North America. Madison, University of Wisconsin Press, 1963. xvii, 734 p. illus., ports., maps. 27 cm. 1. Limnology — North America — Collected works. I. T.
QH96.F7     551.48097     LC 63-7540

**Welch, Paul Smith, 1882-.**       • 5.3257
Limnological methods. — Philadelphia: Blakiston Co., [1948] xviii, 381 p.: ill.; 24 cm. 1. Freshwater biology — Research. 2. Limnology I. T.
QH96.W39     574.929     LC 48-9828

**Wetzel, Robert G.**       5.3258
Limnology/ Robert G. Wetzel. — 2nd ed. — Philadelphia: Saunders, c1983. xii, 767, 81, 10 p.; 23 cm. Includes index. 1. Limnology I. T.
QH96.W47 1983     551.48/2 19     LC 81-53073     ISBN 0030579139

**Bardach, John E.**       • 5.3259
Downstream: a natural history of the river. — [1st ed.]. — New York: Harper & Row, [1964] ix, 278 p.: illus., maps. diagrs.; 22 cm. 1. Freshwater biology 2. Rivers 3. Natural history I. T.
QH97.B37     574.929     LC 62-14596

**Hutchinson, G. Evelyn (George Evelyn), 1903-.**       • 5.3260
A treatise on limnology. New York, Wiley [1957-. v. illus., maps, diagrs., tables. 24 cm. Vol. 3- : A Wiley-Interscience publication. 1. Limnology I. T.
QH98.H82     574.929     LC 57-8888

# QH101–199 Regions. Countries

## QH101–132 The Americas

**Dice, Lee Raymond, 1887-.**                                                • 5.3261
The biotic provinces of North America / by Lee R. Dice. — Ann Arbor: University of Michigan Press, 1943. viii, 78 p.: fold. map; 26 cm. 1. Natural history — North America 2. Botany — Ecology 3. Animal ecology I. T. QH102.D5       *LC* 43-52995

**Shelford, Victor Ernest, 1877-.**                                          • 5.3262
The ecology of North America. — Urbana: University of Illinois Press, 1963. xxii, 610 p.: illus., maps.; 27 cm. 1. Ecology — North America. I. T. QH102.S5       574.5097       *LC* 63-7255

**U.S. Fish and Wildlife Service.**                                          5.3263
Classification of wetlands and deepwater habitats of the United States / by Lewis M. Cowardin ... [et al.]. — Washington: Fish and Wildlife Service, U.S. Dept. of the Interior: for sale by the Supt. of Docs., U.S. Govt. Print Off., 1979. v, 103 p.: ill.; 26 cm. 'Biological services program FWS/OBS-79/31.' 1. Wetlands — United States — Classification. 2. Wetland ecology — United States. 3. Aquatic ecology — United States. I. Cowardin, Lewis M. II. Biological Services Program (U.S.) III. T. QH104.U5 1979       574.5/0973 s 574.5/2632       *LC* 79-607795

**Wright, Henry A.**                                                         5.3264
Fire ecology, United States and southern Canada / Henry A. Wright and Arthur W. Bailey. — New York: Wiley, c1982. xxi, 501 p.: ill.; 25 cm. 'A Wiley-Interscience publication.' 1. Fire ecology — United States. 2. Fire ecology — Canada. 3. Botany — United States — Ecology. 4. Botany — Canada — Ecology. 5. Prescribed burning — United States. 6. Prescribed burning — Canada. I. Bailey, Arthur W. II. T. QH104.W74       581.5/222 19       *LC* 81-14770       *ISBN* 0471090336

**Mitchell, John Hanson.**                                                   5.3265
A field guide to your own back yard / John Hanson Mitchell; illustrations by Laurel Molk. — 1st ed. — New York: Norton, c1985. 288 p.: ill.; 21 cm. Includes index. 1. Urban ecology (Biology) — Northeastern States. 2. Natural history — Northeastern States. I. T. QH104.5.N58 M58 1985       574.974 19       *LC* 84-14760       *ISBN* 0393019233

**Convergent evolution in warm deserts: an examination of**                  5.3266
**strategies and patterns in deserts of Argentina and the United States / edited by Gordon H. Orians, Otto T. Solbrig.**
Stroudsburg, Pa.: Dowden, Hutchinson & Ross; [New York]: exclusive distributor Halsted Press, c1977. xiv, 333 p.: ill.; 25 cm. — (US/IBP synthesis series; 3) Includes indexes. 1. Desert ecology — Southwest, New. 2. Desert ecology — Argentine Republic. 3. Evolution 4. Convergence (Biology) I. Orians, Gordon H. II. Solbrig, Otto T. III. Series. QH104.5.S6 C66       574.5/265       *LC* 76-56261       *ISBN* 087933276X

**Krutch, Joseph Wood, 1893-1970.**                                          • 5.3267
The desert year / Joseph Wood Krutch; decorations by Rudolf Freund. — New York: Sloane, 1952. 270 p.: ill.; 22 cm. 1. Natural history — Southwest, New. 2. Desert fauna 3. Desert flora I. T. QH104.5.S6.K7       574.978       *LC* 52-8150

**An Arctic ecosystem: the coastal tundra at Barrow, Alaska /**              5.3268
**edited by Jerry Brown ... [et al.].**
Stroudsburg, Pa.: Dowden, Hutchinson & Ross: distributed world-wide by Academic Press, c1980. xxv, 571 p.: ill.; 25 cm. — (US/IBP synthesis series; 12) Includes index. 1. Tundra ecology — Alaska — Barrow. 2. Coastal ecology — Alaska — Barrow. 3. Ecology — Arctic regions. I. Brown, Jerry, 1936- II. Series. QH105.A4 A77       574.5/26       *LC* 79-22901       *ISBN* 0879333707

**Conkling, Philip W.**                                                      5.3269
Islands in time: a natural and human history of the islands of Maine / by Philip W. Conkling; drawings by Katherine Hall Fitzgerald; photographs by George Putz, Jim Kosinski, and Rick Perry. — Camden, Me.: Down East Books, c1981. xvii, 222 p.: ill.; 26 cm. 1. Island ecology — Maine. 2. Islands — Maine — History. 3. Maine — History I. T. QH105.M2 C66       917.41/0942 19       *LC* 80-70610       *ISBN* 0892721111

**Bormann, F. Herbert, 1922-.**                                             5.3270
Pattern and process in a forested ecosystem: disturbance, development, and the steady state based on the Hubbard Brook ecosystem study / F. Herbert Bormann, Gene E. Likens. — New York: Springer-Verlag, c1979. xi, 253 p.: ill.;

24 cm. Includes index. 1. Forest ecology — New Hampshire — Hubbard Brook Valley. I. Likens, Gene E., 1935- joint author. II. T. QH105.N4 B67       574.5/264       *LC* 78-6015       *ISBN* 0387903216

**An Ecosystem approach to aquatic ecology: Mirror Lake and its**            5.3271
**environment / edited by Gene E. Likens.**
New York: Springer-Verlag, c1985. xiv, 516 p.: ill.; 28 cm. Includes indexes. 1. Lake ecology — New Hampshire — Mirror Lake (Grafton County) 2. Limnology — New Hampshire — Mirror Lake (Grafton County) 3. Freshwater ecology — New Hampshire — Mirror Lake Watershed (Grafton County) 4. Mirror Lake (Grafton County, N.H.) I. Likens, Gene E., 1935- QH105.N4 E3 1985       574.5/26322/097423 19       *LC* 84-26686       *ISBN* 0387961062

**Wilkinson, Douglas, 1919-.**                                               • 5.3272
The Arctic coast. — [Toronto: N.S.L. Natural Science of Canada Ltd., 1970] 160 p.: illus. (part col.), col. maps.; 25 x 27 cm. — (The Illustrated natural history of Canada) 1. Natural history — Canada, Northern. 2. Natural history — Arctic regions. I. T. QH106.W54       500.9712       *LC* 76-109047

**Island biogeography in the Sea of Cortéz / edited by Ted J.**              5.3273
**Case, Martin L. Cody.**
Berkeley: University of California Press, c1983. x, 508 p., [8] p. of plates: ill.; 26 cm. Based on a symposium held in 1977 at the University of California, Los Angeles. 1. Island ecology — Mexico — California, Gulf of — Congresses. 2. Biogeography — Mexico — California, Gulf of — Congresses. 3. California, Gulf of (Mexico) — Congresses. I. Case, Ted J. II. Cody, Martin L., 1941- QH107.I84 1983       574.5/267/091641 19       *LC* 82-16036       *ISBN* 0520047990

**Sarmiento, Guillermo.**                                                    5.3274
[Estructura y funcionamiento de sabanas neotropicales. English] The ecology of neotropical savannas / Guillermo Sarmiento; translated by Otto Solbrig. — Cambridge, Mass.: Harvard University Press, 1984. xii, 235 p.: ill.; 24 cm. Translation of: Estructura y funcionamiento de sabanas neotropicales. Includes index. 1. Savanna ecology — Venezuela. 2. Savanna ecology I. T. QH130.S2713 1984       574.5/2643/098 19       *LC* 83-12904       *ISBN* 0674224604

## QH135–199 Europe. Asia. Africa. Other Regions

**Ecology of European rivers / edited by B.A. Whitton.**                     5.3275
Oxford; Boston: Blackwell Scientific, 1984. 644 p.: ill.; 25 cm. 1. Stream ecology — Europe. I. Whitton, B. A. QH135.E26 1984       574.5/26323/094 19       *LC* 84-208600       *ISBN* 0632008164

**Production ecology of British moors and montane grasslands /**             5.3276
**edited by O. W. Heal and D. F. Perkins, assisted by Wendy M. Brown.**
Berlin; New York: Springer-Verlag, 1978. xii, 426 p.: ill.; 25 cm. — (Ecological studies. v. 27) Includes index. 1. Biological productivity — Great Britain. 2. Grassland ecology — Great Britain. 3. Moor ecology — Great Britain. 4. Mountain ecology — Great Britain. I. Heal, O. W. II. Perkins, Donald Francis, 1935- III. Brown, Wendy M. IV. Series. QH137.P75       574.5/264       *LC* 77-17853       *ISBN* 0387084576

**White, Gilbert, 1720-1793.**                                               • 5.3277
[Journals of Gilbert White] Journals / Edited by Walter Johnson. New York: Taplinger Pub. Co. [1970] xlviii, 463 p.: ill., facsim., maps; 23 cm. Extracts from the author's unpublished Naturalist's journal. Reprint of the 1931 ed., published under title: Journals of Gilbert White. 1. Natural history — England — Selborne. I. Johnson, Walter, 1867- ed. II. T. QH138.S4 W27 1970       500.9       *LC* 73-105555       *ISBN* 0800832639

**White, Gilbert, 1720-1793.**                                               • 5.3278
The natural history of Selborne / Gilbert White. — London: Dent; New York: Dutton, 1949. xxiii, 289 p. — (Everyman's library; 48) 1. Natural history — England — Selborne. 2. Selborne (England) I. T. QH138.S4 W5 1949       500.9/422/76

**Whitmore, T. C. (Timothy Charles)**                                        5.3279
Tropical rain forests of the Far East / T.C. Whitmore; with a chapter on soils by C.P. Burnham. — 2nd ed. — Oxford [Oxfordshire]: Clarendon Press, 1984. xvi, 352 p.: ill., maps; 26 cm. (Oxford science publications.) Maps on lining papers. Includes indexes. 1. Rain forest ecology — Asia, Southeastern. 2. Rain forests — Asia, Southeastern. 3. Forests and forestry — Asia, Southeastern. I. T. II. Series. QH193.S6 W47 1984       574.5/2642/0959 19       *LC* 83-13441       *ISBN* 0198541368

**Beadle, L. C. (Leonard C.)**          **5.3280**
The inland waters of tropical Africa: an introduction to tropical limnology / L.C. Beadle. — 2nd ed. — London; New York: Longman, 1981. x, 475 p.: ill.; 24 cm. Includes index. 1. Limnology — Africa. 2. Limnology — Tropics. I. T.
QH194.B4 1981     574.5/2632/0967 19     *LC* 80-41376     *ISBN* 0582463416

**Endean, R.**          **5.3281**
Australia's Great Barrier Reef / Robert Endean. — St. Lucia [Brisbane, Qld.]; New York: University of Queensland Press, c1982. xx, 348 p.: ill. (some col.); 27 cm. Includes index. 1. Coral reef biology — Australia — Great Barrier Reef (Qld.) 2. Great Barrier Reef (Qld.) I. T.
QH197.E53 1982     508.943 19     *LC* 82-2063     *ISBN* 070221678X

**Guthrie-Smith, Herbert, 1861-1940.**      **5.3282**
Tutira: the story of a New Zealand sheep station / by H. Guthrie–Smith. — 3rd ed. — Edinburgh: W. Blackwood & Sons, 1953. xxxi, 444 p., [22] leaves of plates: ill. port., maps (some folded); 25 cm. 1. Natural history — New Zealand — Hawke's Bay (Province) 2. Acclimatization 3. Plant succession — New Zealand — Hawke's Bay (Province) 4. Weeds — New Zealand — Hawkes Bay (Province) I. T.
QH197.G8 1953     574.9/931/25     *LC* 54-33276

**Williams, W. D. (William David)**      **5.3283**
Life in inland waters / W.D. Williams. — Melbourne; Boston: Blackwell Scientific Publications; St Louis, Mo.: Blackwell Mosby Book Distributors, 1983. ix, 252 p.: ill.; 22 cm. Includes index. 1. Freshwater biology — Australia. I. T.
QH197.W63 1983     574.92/9/94 19     *LC* 83-164319     *ISBN* 0867930888

**Halle, Louis Joseph, 1910-.**      **5.3284**
The sea and the ice: a naturalist in Antarctica, by Louis J. Halle. With an introd. by Les Line. — Boston: Published in cooperation with the National Audubon Society by Houghton Mifflin, 1973. xv, 286 p.: illus.; 23 cm. — (The Audubon library) 1. Natural history — Antarctic regions. 2. Birds — Antarctic regions. I. National Audubon Society. II. T. III. Series.
QH199.5.H34     500.9/98/9     *LC* 72-6813     *ISBN* 0395154707

# QH201–278 Microscopy

**Gray, Peter, 1908-.**      **5.3285**
The encyclopedia of microscopy and microtechnique / edited by Peter Gray. — New York: Van Nostrand Reinhold, [1973] xi, 638 p.: ill.; 26 cm. 1. Microscope and microscopy — Technique — Dictionaries. I. T.
QH203.G8     502/.8     *LC* 73-164     *ISBN* 0442228120

**Ford, Brian J.**      **5.3286**
Single lens: the story of the simple microscope / Brian J. Ford. — 1st American ed. — New York: Harper & Row, 1985. x, 182 p.: 31 ill., ports.; 25 cm. Includes indexes. 1. Leeuwenhoek, Antoni van, 1632-1723. 2. Microscope and microscopy — History. 3. Biologists — Netherlands — Biography. I. T.
QH204.F65 1985     502/.8/22 19     *LC* 84-48161     *ISBN* 0060153660

**Curry, Alan.**      **5.3287**
Under the microscope / Alan Curry, Robin F. Grayson, Geoffrey R. Hosey. — New York: Van Nostrand Reinhold Co., c1982. 160 p. [4] p. of plates: ill. (some col); 23 cm. Includes index. 1. Microscope and microscopy I. Grayson, Robin F. II. Hosey, Geoffrey R. III. T.
QH205.2.C87 1982     502/.8/2 19     *LC* 82-19973     *ISBN* 0442215983

**Spence, John C. H.**      **5.3288**
Experimental high–resolution electron microscopy / John C. H. Spence. — Oxford: Clarendon Press; New York: Oxford University Press, 1981 (c1980). xii, 370 p.: ill.; 23 cm. — (Monographs on the physics and chemistry of materials) 1. Electron microscope, Transmission 2. Electron microscopy I. T.
QH212.T7 S68     535/.3325     *LC* 79-41669     *ISBN* 0198513658

# QH301–705 General Biology

# QH301–304 Reference Works

**Biological abstracts.**      **5.3289**
v. 1- Dec. 1926-. [Philadelphia] BioSciences Information Service of Biological Abstracts [etc.] v. 27 cm. Semimonthly. Vols. for 1939-62 published also in sections: Section A: General biology; Section B: Basic medical sciences; Section C: Microbiology, immunology, public health, and parasitology; Section D: Plant sciences; Section E: Animal sciences. 1. Biology — Abstracts — Periodicals. I. Schramm, Jacob Richard, 1885- ed. II. BioSciences Information Service of Biological Abstracts. III. Union of American Biological Societies.
QH301.B37     570.5     *LC* 31-13663

**Dictionary of life sciences / edited by E.A. Martin.**      **5.3290**
2nd ed., rev. — New York: Pica Press: Distributed by Universe Books, 1984, c1983. 396 p.: ill.; 23 cm. 1. Biology — Dictionaries. I. Martin, E. A. (Elizabeth A.)
QH302.5.D52 1984     574/.03/21 19     *LC* 83-13258     *ISBN* 0876637403

**Holmes, Sandra, 1945-.**      **5.3291**
Henderson's dictionary of biological terms / Sandra Holmes. — 9th ed. — New York: Van Nostrand Reinhold Co., [1986], c1979. xi, 510 p.; 20 cm. 1. Biology — Dictionaries. I. T.
QH302.5.H65 1986     574/.03/21 19     *LC* 86-4118     *ISBN* 0442231601

**Roe, Keith E.**      **5.3292**
Dictionary of theoretical concepts in biology / Keith E. Roe & Richard G. Frederick. — Metuchen, N.J.: Scarecrow Press, 1981. xli, 267 p.; 23 cm. 1. Biology — Dictionaries. 2. Biology — Philosophy — History — Sources. 3. Biology — Bibliography 4. Biology — Indexes. I. Frederick, Richard G. joint author. II. T.
QH302.5.R63     574/.03/21 19     *LC* 80-19889     *ISBN* 081081353X

**Bottle, R. T.**      **5.3293**
The use of biological literature / editors: R. T. Bottle [and] H. V. Wyatt. — [2d ed. Hamden, Conn.]: Archon Books, 1972 (c1971) xii, 379 p.; 23 cm. (Information sources for research and development) 1. Biological literature I. Wyatt, H. V. (Harold Vivian) joint author. II. T.
QH303.B6 1971     016.574     *LC* 72-200914     *ISBN* 0208012214

**Smith, Roger Cletus, 1888-.**      **5.3294**
[Guide to the literature of the life sciences] Smith's Guide to the literature of the life sciences / Roger C. Smith, W. Malcolm Reid, Arlene E. Luchsinger. — 9th ed. — Minneapolis, Minn.: Burgess Pub. Co., c1980. xi, 223 p.: ill.; 24 cm. 1. Biological literature I. Reid, W. Malcolm, 1910- joint author. II. Luchsinger, Arlene E. joint author. III. T. IV. Title: Guide to the literature of the life sciences.
QH303.S6 1980     574/.07 19     *LC* 79-55580     *ISBN* 0808735764

**CBE Style Manual Committee.**      **5.3295**
CBE style manual: a guide for authors, editors, and publishers in the biological sciences / prepared by CBE Style Manual Committee. — 5th ed., rev. and expanded. — Bethesda, Md.: Council of Biology Editors, c1983. xx, 324 p.: ill.; 24 cm. Rev. and expanded ed. of: Council of Biology Editors style manual. 4th ed. c1978. Includes index. 1. Biology — Authorship. 2. Printing, Practical — Style manuals I. T. II. Title: C.B.E. style manual.
QH304.C33 1983     808/.02 19     *LC* 83-7172     *ISBN* 0914340042

# QH305 History

**Allen, Garland E.**      **5.3296**
Life science in the twentieth century / Garland E. Allen. — New York: Wiley, [1975] xxv, 258 p.: ill.; 22 cm. (History of science) Includes index. 1. Biology — History. I. T.
QH305.A44     574/.09/04     *LC* 74-31295     *ISBN* 0471023361

**Coleman, William, 1934-.**                                    5.3297
Biology in the nineteenth century: problems of form, function, and transformation [by] William Coleman. — New York: Wiley, [1971] vii, 187 p.: illus., facsims.; 22 cm. — (History of science) 1. Biology — History. I. T. QH305.C54     574/.09/034 19     *LC* 73-151725     *ISBN* 0471164968

**Mayr, Ernst, 1904-.**                                          5.3298
The growth of biological thought: diversity, evolution, and inheritance / Ernst Mayr. — Cambridge, Mass.: Belknap Press, 1982. ix, 974 p.; 25 cm. Includes index. 1. Biology — History. 2. Biology — Philosophy — History. I. T. QH305.M26 1982     574/.09 19     *LC* 81-13204     *ISBN* 0674364457

# QH307–313 General Works

**Lotka, Alfred J. (Alfred James), 1880-1949.**                 • 5.3299
[Elements of physical biology] Elements of mathematical biology. New York: Dover Publications [c1956] 465 p.: ill.; 21 cm. 'An unabridged republication of the first edition of the work first published under the title Elements of physical biology.' 1. Biology 2. Biomathematics I. T. II. Title: Mathematical biology. QH307.L75 1956     574.0151     *LC* 57-2438

**Luria, S. E. (Salvador Edward), 1912-.**                      5.3300
36 lectures in biology / [by] S. E. Luria. — Cambridge, Mass.: MIT Press [1975] xvii, [2], 439 p.: ill.; 26 cm. 1. Biology 2. Genetics I. T. QH308.2.L87     574     *LC* 74-19136     *ISBN* 0262120682 *ISBN* 0262620294

**Purves, William K. (William Kirkwood), 1934-.**              5.3301
Life, the science of biology / William K. Purves, Gordon H. Orians. — 2nd ed. — Sunderland, Mass.: Sinauer Associates, c1987. xxi, 1271 p.: ill. (some col.); 29 cm. 1. Biology I. Orians, Gordon H. II. T. QH308.2.P87 1987     574 19     *LC* 86-31340     *ISBN* 0878937331

**Bates, Marston, 1906-1974.**                                  • 5.3302
The nature of natural history. Rev. ed. New York, Scribner [1962, c1961] 309 p. 21 cm. (The Scribner library, SL48) Includes bibliography. 1. Biology I. T. QH309.B34 1962     574     *LC* 62-1061

**Altman, Philip L. ed.**                                       • 5.3303
Environmental biology / compiled and edited by Philip L. Altman and Dorothy S. Dittmer; prepared under the auspices of the Committee on Biological Handbooks. — Bethesda, Md.: Federation of American Societies for Experimental Biology, [1966] xxi, 694 p.: ill.; 29 cm. — (Biological handbooks) 1. Biology — Handbooks, manuals, etc. I. Katz, Dorothy Dittmer. joint ed. II. T. QH310.A395     574     *LC* 66-27592

**Medawar, P. B. (Peter Brian), 1915-.**                        • 5.3304
The uniqueness of the individual. New York: Basic Books [1957] 191 p.: ill.; 21 cm. 1. Biology — Addresses, essays, lectures. 2. Evolution — Addresses, essays, lectures. I. T. QH311.M42 1957a     574.04     *LC* 57-10538

# QH315–318.5 Study and Teaching. Field Work

**Biological Sciences Curriculum Study.**                       5.3305
Biology teachers' handbook / Biological Sciences Curriculum Study; William V. Mayer, editor. — 3d ed. — New York: Wiley, c1978. viii, 585 p.: ill.; 24 cm. 1. Biology — Study and teaching (Secondary) I. Mayer, William V. II. T. QH315.B586 1978     574/.07/12     *LC* 77-27548     *ISBN* 0471019453

**Cox, Donald D.**                                              5.3306
The context of biological education: the case for change [by] Donald D. Cox and Lary V. Davis. [Washington] Commission on Undergraduate Education in Biological Sciences; [available from American Institute of Biological Sciences, Education Division] 1972. ix, 147 p. 23 cm. (The Commission on Undergraduate Education in the Biological Sciences. Publication no. 34.) 1. Biology — Study and teaching (Higher) I. Davis, Lary V., joint author. II. T. III. Title: The case for change. QH315.C6x QH301.C66 no. 34     574/.07/11 s 574/.07/11     *LC* 72-84011

**Hurd, Paul DeHart, 1905-.**                                   • 5.3307
Biological education in American secondary schools, 1890–1960. Washington, American Institute of Biological Sciences [1961] ix, 263 p. front. 24 cm. (American Institute of Biological Sciences. Biological Sciences Curriculum Study. Bulletin no. 1) 1. Biology — Study and teaching (Secondary) — United States. I. T. QH315.H87     574.071273     *LC* 61-11432

**Voss, Burton E. (Burton Elmer), 1927-.**                      • 5.3308
Biology as inquiry; a book of teaching methods [by] Burton E. Voss [and] Stanley B. Brown. Saint Louis, Mosby, 1968. xvi, 239 p. illus. 26 cm. 1. Biology — Study and teaching I. Brown, Stanley Barber, 1919- joint author. II. T. QH315.V6     574/.07     *LC* 68-19897

## QH323.5–324 Biomathematics. Research Techniques

**Batschelet, Edward.**                                         5.3309
Introduction to mathematics for life scientists. — Berlin; New York: Springer-Verlag, 1972 (c1971). xiv, 495 p.: illus.; 24 cm. — (Biomathematics, v. 2) 1. Biomathematics I. T. QH323.5.B37     510/.24/574     *LC* 70-167852     *ISBN* 3540055223

**Dudley, Brian A. C.**                                         5.3310
Mathematical and biological interrelations / Brian A. C. Dudley. — Chichester; New York: Wiley, c1977. x, 319 p.: ill.; 23 cm. 1. Biomathematics I. T. QH323.5.D8     574/.01/51     *LC* 77-7284     *ISBN* 0471994847

**Jones, D. S. (Douglas Samuel)**                              5.3311
Differential equations and mathematical biology / D.S. Jones and B.D. Sleeman. — London; Boston: Allen & Unwin, 1983. xii, 339 p.: ill.; 25 cm. Includes index. 1. Biomathematics 2. Differential equations I. Sleeman, B. D. II. T. QH323.5.J65 1983     574/.0151535 19     *LC* 82-6701     *ISBN* 004515001X

**Sokal, Robert R.**                                            5.3312
Biometry: the principles and practice of statistics in biological research / Robert R. Sokal and F. James Rohlf. — 2d ed. — San Francisco: W. H. Freeman, c1981. xviii, 859 p.: ill.; 24 cm. Includes index. 1. Biometry I. Rohlf, F. James, 1936- joint author. II. T. QH323.5.S63 1981     574/.072 19     *LC* 81-4     *ISBN* 0716712547

**Sokal, Robert R.**                                            5.3313
Introduction to biostatistics / Robert R. Sokal and F. James Rohlf. — 2nd ed. — New York: Freeman, c1987. xii, 363 p.: ill.; 24 cm. Includes index. 1. Biometry I. Rohlf, F. James, 1936- II. T. QH323.5.S633 1987     574/.072 19     *LC* 86-31838     *ISBN* 0716718057

**Thom, René, 1923-.**                                          5.3314
[Stabilité structurelle et morphogénèse. English] Structural stability and morphogenesis; an outline of a general theory of models. Translated from the French ed., as updated by the author, by D. H. Fowler. With a foreword by C. H. Waddington. [1st English ed.] Reading, Mass., W. A. Benjamin, 1975. 348 p. illus. 25 cm. 1. Biology — Mathematical models 2. Morphogenesis — Mathematical models. 3. Topology I. T. QH323.5.T4813     574.4/01/514     *LC* 74-8829     *ISBN* 0805392769 *ISBN* 0805392777

**Fisher, Ronald Aylmer, Sir, 1890-1962.**                      • 5.3315
Statistical tables for biological, agricultural, and medical research, by Ronald A. Fisher and Frank Yates. 6th ed., rev. and enl. New York, Hafner Pub. Co. [1963] x, 146 p. 29 cm. 1. Statistics — Charts, diagrams, etc. 2. Mathematical statistics 3. Biomathematics I. Yates, Frank. joint author. II. T. QH324.F52 1963     311.2     *LC* 63-22899

**Methods of enzymatic analysis / editor–in–chief, Hans Ulrich**   5.3316
**Bergmeyer, editors, Jürgen Bergmeyer and Marianne Grassl.**
3rd ed. — Weinheim; Deerfield Beach, Fla.: Verlag Chemie, c1983-. v. : ill.; 25 cm. Errata slip inserted, v. 2. 1. Enzymatic analysis — Collected works. I. Bergmeyer, Hans Ulrich. II. Bergmeyer, Jürgen. III. Grassl, Marianne. QH324.9.E5 M48 1983     543 19     *LC* 84-105641     *ISBN* 0895732319

**Campbell, Iain D.**                                           5.3317
Biological spectroscopy / Iain D. Campbell and Raymond A. Dwek. — Menlo Park, Calif.: Benjamin/Cummings Pub. Co., c1984. xviii, 404 p.: ill.; 25 cm. — (Biophysical techniques series) Includes index. 1. Spectrum analysis 2. Biology — Technique I. Dwek, Raymond A. II. T. III. Series. QH324.9.S6 C35 1984     574/.028 19     *LC* 84-6232     *ISBN* 080531847X

## QH325–332 Life: Origin

**Calvin, Melvin, 1911-.** • 5.3318
Chemical evolution: molecular evolution towards the origin of living systems on the earth and elsewhere. — Oxford: Clarendon P., 1969. ix, 278 p.: 8 plates, ill. (incl. 8 col.), chart, facsims., map.; 25 cm. 1. Life — Origin 2. Geochemistry 3. Molecular biology I. T.
QH325.C26      577      *LC* 70-415289      *ISBN* 0198553420

**Fox, Sidney W.** 5.3319
Molecular evolution and the origin of life / Sidney W. Fox, Klaus Dose; with a foreword by A. Oparin. — Rev. ed. — New York: M. Dekker, c1977. xv, 370 p., [1] leaf of plates: ill.; 24 cm. — (Biology; v. 2) 1. Life — Origin 2. Chemical evolution I. Dose, Klaus. joint author. II. T. III. Series.
QH325.F66 1977      577      *LC* 77-21434      *ISBN* 0824766199

**Margulis, Lynn, 1938-.** 5.3320
Early life / Lynn Margulis. — Boston, Mass.: Science Books International, c1982. xiv, 160 p.: ill.; 23 cm. — (A Series of books in biology) 1. Life — Origin 2. Life (Biology) I. T. II. Series.
QH325.M29 1982      577 19      *LC* 81-18337      *ISBN* 0867200057

**Molecular evolution and protobiology / edited by Koichiro** 5.3321
**Matsuno ... [et al.].**
New York: Plenum Press, c1984. ix, 470 p.: ill.; 26 cm. 1. Chemical evolution 2. Life — Origin I. Matsuno, Kōichirō.
QH325.M64 1984      577 19      *LC* 83-24465      *ISBN* 0306415097

**Oparin, Aleksandr Ivanovich, 1894-1980.** • 5.3322
Life, its nature, origin and development / Translated from the Russian by Ann Synge. — New York: Academic Press, 1961. 207 p.: ill.; 23 cm. 1. Life (Biology) I. T.
QH325.O633 1961      574      *LC* 62-13112

**Orgel, Leslie E.** 5.3323
The origins of life: molecules and natural selection [by] L. E. Orgel. — New York: Wiley, [1973] vi, 237 p.: illus.; 21 cm. 1. Life — Origin 2. Chemical evolution I. T.
QH325.O68      577      *LC* 72-10534      *ISBN* 0471656925

**Blum, Harold Francis, 1899-.** • 5.3324
Time's arrow and evolution, by Harold F. Blum. — [3d ed.]. — Princeton, N.J.: Princeton University Press, 1968. xiii, 232 p.: illus.; 21 cm. 1. Evolution 2. Thermodynamics 3. Cosmogony I. T.
QH331.B55 1968      575      *LC* 68-31676

**Burnet, Frank Macfarlane, Sir, 1899-.** 5.3325
Dominant mammal; the biology of human destiny [by] Sir Macfarlane Burnet. — New York: St. Martin's Press, [1972, c1971] 205 p.; 22 cm. 1. Biology — Philosophy 2. Human ecology 3. Man I. T.
QH331.B887 1972      301.31      *LC* 70-183879

**Hull, David L.** 5.3326
Philosophy of biological science [by] David L. Hull. — Englewood Cliffs, N.J.: Prentice-Hall, [1974] xi, 148 p.: illus.; 23 cm. — (Prentice-Hall foundations of philosophy series) 1. Biology — Philosophy I. T.
QH331.H84      574/.01      *LC* 73-12981      *ISBN* 0136636158

**Towards a liberatory biology / the Dialectics of Biology Group;** 5.3327
**general editor, Steven Rose.**
London; New York: Allison & Busby; New York, N.Y.: Distributed in the USA by Schocken Books, 1982. 161 p.; 20 cm. Papers presented at a conference held in Bressanone, Italy, Mar. 26-30, 1980. 1. Biology — Philosophy — Congresses. I. Rose, Steven Peter Russell, 1938- II. Dialectics of Biology Group.
QH331.T66 1982      574/.01 19      *LC* 82-198992      *ISBN* 0850314267

## QH332 Bioethics

**Encyclopedia of bioethics / Warren T. Reich, editor in chief.** 5.3328
New York: Free Press, c1978. 4 v. (xxxix, 1933 p.); 29 cm. 1. Bioethics — Dictionaries. 2. Medical ethics — Dictionaries. I. Reich, Warren T.
QH332.E52      174/.2      *LC* 78-8821      *ISBN* 0029260604

**Kieffer, George H., 1930-.** 5.3329
Bioethics: a textbook of issues / George H. Kieffer. — Reading, Mass.: Addison-Wesley Pub. Co., c1979. x, 454 p.: ill.; 25 cm. 1. Bioethics 2. Medical ethics I. T.
QH332.K53      174/.9574      *LC* 78-55822      *ISBN* 0201038919

## QH345 Biological Chemistry

**Florkin, Marcel. ed.** • 5.3330
Comparative biochemistry: a comprehensive treatise. Edited by Marcel Florkin [and] Howard S. Mason. New York: Academic Press, 1960-64. 7 v.: ill., tables; 24 cm. 1. Biochemistry 2. Physiology, Comparative I. Mason, Howard S. joint ed. II. T.
QH345.F495      574.192      *LC* 59-13830

**Freifelder, David, 1935-.** 5.3331
Physical biochemistry: applications to biochemistry and molecular biology / David Freifelder. — 2nd ed. — San Francisco: W.H. Freeman, c1982. xii, 761 p.: ill.; 24 cm. 1. Biochemistry — Technique 2. Molecular biology — Technique 3. Biophysics — Technique. I. T.
QH345.F72 1982      574.19/283 19      *LC* 81-19521      *ISBN* 0716714442

**Handbook of biochemistry and molecular biology / editor,** 5.3332
**Gerald D. Fasman.**
3d ed. — Cleveland: CRC Press, c1975-1977. 9 v.: ill.; 26 cm. Previous editions published under title: Handbook of biochemistry. At head of title: CRC. 1. Biochemistry — Handbooks, manuals, etc. 2. Molecular biology — Handbooks, manuals, etc. I. Fasman, Gerald D. II. Chemical Rubber Company.
QH345.H347 1975      574.1/92/0212      *LC* 75-29514      *ISBN* 0878195033

**Lehninger, Albert L.** 5.3333
Biochemistry: the molecular basis of cell structure and function / Albert L. Lehninger. — 2d ed. — New York: Worth Publishers, 1975. xxiii, 1104 p.: ill.; 29 cm. 1. Biochemistry I. T.
QH345.L38 1975      574.1/92      *LC* 75-11082      *ISBN* 0879010479

**Marshall, Alan G., 1944-.** 5.3334
Biophysical chemistry: principles, techniques, and applications / Alan G. Marshall. — New York: Wiley, c1978. xv, 812 p.: ill.; 24 cm. Erratum slip tipped in. 1. Biochemistry 2. Chemistry, Physical and theoretical I. T.
QH345.M325      541/.3/024574      *LC* 77-19136      *ISBN* 0471027189

**Metzler, David E.** 5.3335
Biochemistry: the chemical reactions of living cells / David E. Metzler. — New York: Academic Press, c1977. xxxii, 1129 p.: ill.; 24 cm. 1. Biochemistry 2. Cytochemistry I. T.
QH345.M39      574.8/76      *LC* 75-3231      *ISBN* 0124925502

**Tinoco, Ignacio.** 5.3336
Physical chemistry: prinicples and applications in biological sciences / Ignacio Tinoco, Jr., Kenneth Sauer, James C. Wang. — Englewood Cliffs, N.J.: Prentice-Hall, c1978. xv, 624 p.: ill.; 24 cm. 1. Biochemistry 2. Chemistry, Physical and theoretical I. Sauer, Kenneth, 1931- joint author. II. Wang, James C. joint author. III. T.
QH345.T56      541/.02/4574      *LC* 77-25417      *ISBN* 0136659012

## QH352 Population Biology

**Begon, Michael.** 5.3337
Population ecology: a unified study of animals and plants / Michael Begon, Martin Mortimer. — Sunderland, Mass.: Sinauer Associates, 1981. vii, 200 p.: ill.; 25 cm. Includes indexes. 1. Population biology 2. Ecology I. Mortimer, Martin. II. T.
QH352.B43 1981      574.5/248 19      *LC* 81-5641      *ISBN* 0878930663

**Caughley, Graeme.** 5.3338
Analysis of vertebrate populations / Graeme Caughley. London; New York: Wiley, c1977. ix, 234 p.: ill.; 24 cm. 'A Wiley-Interscience publication.' Includes indexes. 1. Animal populations I. T.
QH352.C38      596/.05/24      *LC* 76-913      *ISBN* 0471017051

**Kingsland, Sharon E.** 5.3339
Modeling nature: episodes in the history of population ecology / Sharon E. Kingsland. — Chicago: University of Chicago Press, c1985. ix, 267 p.: ports.; 24 cm. (Science and its conceptual foundations.) Includes index. 1. Population biology — History. 2. Population biology — Mathematical models — History. I. T. II. Series.
QH352.K56 1985      574.5/248 19      *LC* 85-1414      *ISBN* 0226437264

# QH359–420 EVOLUTION

## QH359–366 General Works

**Evolution from molecules to men / edited by D.S. Bendall on behalf of Darwin College.**　　5.3340
Cambridge [Cambridgeshire]; New York: Cambridge University Press, 1983. xiii, 594 p.: ill.; 24 cm. Revised papers first presented at a conference entitled 'Evolution of molecules and men', Darwin College, Cambridge, 27 June-2 July 1982. 1. Evolution — Congresses. I. Bendall, D. S. II. Darwin College.
QH359.E92 1983　　575 19　　LC 82-22020　　ISBN 0521247535

**Bowler, Peter J.**　　5.3341
The eclipse of Darwinism: anti–Darwinian evolution theories in the decades around 1900 / Peter J. Bowler. — Baltimore: Johns Hopkins University Press, c1983. xi, 291 p.; 24 cm. Includes index. 1. Evolution — History. I. T.
QH361.B68 1983　　575.01/6 19　　LC 82-21170　　ISBN 0801829321

**Bowler, Peter J.**　　5.3342
Evolution, the history of an idea / Peter J. Bowler. — Berkeley: University of California Press, c1984. xiv, 412 p.; 24 cm. Includes index. 1. Evolution — History. I. T.
QH361.B69 1984　　575/.009 19　　LC 83-5909　　ISBN 0520048806

**Conference on the Comparative Reception of Darwinism, Austin, Tex., 1972.**　　5.3343
The comparative reception of Darwinism. Edited by Thomas F. Glick. Austin, University of Texas Press [1974] ix, 505 p. 23 cm. (The Dan Danciger publication series) 'Held ... under the joint sponsorship of the American Council of Learned Societies and the University of Texas at Austin.' 1. Evolution — History — Congresses. I. Glick, Thomas F. ed. II. American Council of Learned Societies. III. University of Texas at Austin. IV. T.
QH361.C67 1972　　301.15/43/5750162　　LC 74-10797　　ISBN 0292710151

**Eiseley, Loren C., 1907-1977.**　　• 5.3344
Darwin's century: evolution and the men who discovered it. — [1st ed.]. — Garden City, N.Y.: Doubleday, 1958. 378 p.: ill.; 22 cm. — (Doubleday anchor books) 1. Evolution — History. I. T.
QH361.E35　　575.09　　LC 58-6638

**Gould, Stephen Jay.**　　5.3345
Ever since Darwin: reflections in natural history / Stephen Jay Gould. — 1st ed. — New York: Norton, c1977. 285 p.: ill.; 22 cm. Includes index. 1. Evolution — History. 2. Natural selection — Histor. I. T.
QH361.G65 1977　　575.01/62　　LC 77-22504　　ISBN 0393064255

**Gould, Stephen Jay.**　　5.3346
The panda's thumb: more reflections in natural history / Stephen Jay Gould. — 1st ed. — New York: Norton, c1980. 343 p.: ill.; 22 cm. Includes index. 1. Evolution — History. 2. Natural selection — History. I. T.
QH361.G66 1980　　575.01/62　　LC 80-15952　　ISBN 0393013804

**Greene, John C.**　　• 5.3347
The death of Adam; evolution and its impact on Western thought. Ames, Iowa State University Press [1959] 388 p. illus. 27 cm. 1. Evolution — History. 2. Religion and science — 1946- I. T.
QH361.G7　　575.09　　LC 59-11784

**Provine, William B.**　　5.3348
Sewall Wright and evolutionary biology / by William B. Provine. — Chicago: University of Chicago Press, c1987. 1 v. (unpaged): ill.. (Science and its conceptual foundations.) Includes index. 1. Wright, Sewall, 1889- 2. Evolution — History. 3. Genetics — History. 4. Geneticists — United States — Biography. 5. Biologists — United States — Biography. I. T. II. Series.
QH361.P87 1987　　575/.092/4 B 19　　LC 85-24651　　ISBN 0226684741

**Ruse, Michael.**　　5.3349
The Darwinian revolution: science red in tooth and claw / Michael Ruse. — Chicago: University of Chicago Press, 1979. xv, 320 p.: ill.; 24 cm. Includes index. 1. Darwin, Charles, 1809-1882. 2. Darwin, Charles, 1809-1882. On the origin of species 3. Evolution — History. I. T.
QH361.R87　　575/.009　　LC 78-25826　　ISBN 0226731642

**Evolution versus Creationism: the public education controversy / edited by J. Peter Zetterberg.**　　5.3350
Phoenix, AZ: Oryx Press, 1983. xi, 516 p.; 24 cm. Includes index / compiled by Frederick Ramey. 1. Evolution — Study and teaching — Addresses, essays, lectures. 2. Creationism — Study and teaching — Addresses, essays, lectures. I. Zetterberg, J. Peter.
QH362.E86 1983　　575/.007 19　　LC 82-18795　　ISBN 0897740610

## QH365 Darwin
(see also: QH31.D2)

**Darwin, Charles, 1809-1882.**　　• 5.3351
Evolution by natural selection / [by] Charles Darwin and Alfred Russel Wallace; with a foreword by Sir Gavin de Beer. Cambridge, Published for the XV International Congress of Zoology and the Linnean Society of London at the University Press, 1958. — New York: Johnson Reprint Corp., 1971. viii, 287 p.; 23 cm. 1. Evolution 2. Natural selection I. Wallace, Alfred Russel, 1823-1913. II. T.
QH365.A1 1971　　575.01/62　　LC 74-155108

**Darwin, Charles, 1809-1882.**　　5.3352
[Selected works. 1977] The collected papers of Charles Darwin / edited by Paul H. Barrett; with a foreword by Theodosius Dobzhansky. — Chicago: University of Chicago Press, 1977. 2 v.: ill.; 24 cm. 1. Darwin, Charles, 1809-1882. 2. Natural history — Collected works. 3. Naturalists — England — Correspondence. I. T.
QH365.A1 1977　　575/.008　　LC 76-606　　ISBN 0226136574

**Darwin, Charles, 1809-1882.**　　5.3353
[On the origin of species] Charles Darwin's natural selection: being the second part of his big species book written from 1856 to 1858 / edited from manuscript by R. C. Stauffer. — London; New York: Cambridge University Press, 1975. xii, 692 p.: ill.; 24 cm. Includes index. 1. Natural selection 2. Evolution I. Stauffer, Robert C., 1913- II. T. III. Title: Natural selection.
QH365.O15 1975　　QH365 O15 1975.　　575.01/62　　LC 75-306275　　ISBN 0521201632

**Darwin, Charles, 1809-1882.**　　• 5.3354
On the origin of species. A facsim. of the 1st ed., with an introd. by Ernst Mayr. Cambridge, Harvard University Press, 1964. xxvii, ix, 502 p. 1 illus., port. 22 cm. 1. Evolution 2. Natural selection I. T.
QH365.O2 1859a　　575.0162　　LC 63-17196

**Hull, David L. comp.**　　5.3355
Darwin and his critics; the reception of Darwin's theory of evolution by the scientific community [by] David L. Hull. Cambridge, Mass., Harvard University Press, 1973. xii, 473 p. 24 cm. 1. Darwin, Charles, 1809-1882. On the origin of species 2. Darwin, Charles, 1809-1882. The descent of man. 3. Evolution I. T.
QH365.O8 H84　　575.01/62 19　　LC 72-81274　　ISBN 0674192753

## QH366 General Works, 1861–1969

**Dobzhansky, Theodosius Grigorievich, 1900-1975.**　　• 5.3356
Genetics and the origin of species. 3d ed., rev. New York, Columbia University Press, 1959. x, 364 p. illus., maps. 24 cm. (Columbia biological series. 11) 1. Evolution I. T. II. Series.
QH366.D6 1959　　575　　LC 51-14816

**Fisher, Ronald Aylmer, Sir, 1890-1962.**　　• 5.3357
The genetical theory of natural selection. — [2d rev. ed.]. — New York: Dover Publications, [1958] 291 p.: ill.; 21 cm. — (Dover books on science, S466) 1. Natural selection I. T.
QH366.F5 1958　　575.423 574.5*　　LC 58-13362

**Goldschmidt, Richard Benedict, 1878-1958.**　　5.3358
The material basis of evolution. — New Jersey: Pageant Books, 1960, c1940. 436 p.: ill. 1. Evolution 2. Genetics I. T.
QH366.G53 1960

**Haldane, J. B. S. (John Burdon Sanderson), 1892-1964.**　　• 5.3359
The causes of evolution / by J.B.S. Haldane. — New York: Harper & Brothers, [1932] 234 p.: ill., plates; 20 cm. 1. Evolution I. T.
QH366.H45

**Rensch, Bernhard, 1900-.**　　• 5.3360
[Neuere Probleme der Abstammungslehre. English] Evolution above the species level. [Translated by Dr. Altevogt] New York, Columbia University Press, 1960[c1959] xvii, 419 p. illus., maps, tables. 25 cm. (Columbia biological series. no. 19) Translation of Neuere Probleme der Abstammungslehre. 1. Evolution 2. Phylogeny I. T. II. Series.
QH366.R473 1960　　591.38　　LC 58-13505

**Simpson, George Gaylord, 1902-.** • **5.3361**
The major features of evolution. — New York: Columbia University Press, 1953. xx, 434 p.: ill.; 24 cm. — (Columbia biological series. no. 17) Based on the author's Tempo and mode of evolution. 1. Evolution I. T. II. Series.
QH366.S57      575.01      LC 53-10263

**Simpson, George Gaylord, 1902-.** • **5.3362**
Tempo and mode in evolution. New York, Hafner Pub. Co., 1965 [c1944] xviii, 237 p. illus., map. 24 cm. (Columbia biological series, no. 15) 'Facsimile of 1944 edition.' Bibliography: p. [219]-226. 1. Evolution I. T.
QH366.S59 1965      575.01      LC 65-28698

**Tax, Sol, 1907- ed.** • **5.3363**
Evolution after Darwin: the University of Chicago centennial. — [Chicago]: University of Chicago Press, [1960] 3 v.: ill., ports., maps, diagrs., facsims., tables; 25 cm. Papers presented at the University of Chicago Darwin centennial celebration in November 1959. Vol. 3 includes index for the set and a record of the celebration. 1. Evolution 2. Social evolution I. T.
QH366.T3      LC 60-10575

## QH366.2 1970–

**Attenborough, David, 1926-.** **5.3364**
Life on Earth: a natural history / David Attenborough. — 1st American ed. — Boston: Little, Brown, 1981 (c1979). 319 p.: ill. (some col.); 26 cm. Includes index. 1. Evolution 2. Zoology — Miscellanea. I. T.
QH366.2.A87      575 19      LC 79-90108      ISBN 0316057452

**Ayala, Francisco José, 1934-.** **5.3365**
Evolving: the theory and processes of organic evolution / Francisco J. Ayala, James W. Valentine. — Menlo Park, Calif.: Benjamin/Cummings Pub. Co., c1979. xii, 452 p.: ill.; 24 cm. Includes index. 1. Evolution I. Valentine, James W. joint author. II. T.
QH366.2.A97      575      LC 79-788      ISBN 0805303103

**Beyond neo–Darwinism: an introduction to the new evolutionary** **5.3366**
**paradigm / edited by Mae–Wan Ho, Peter T. Saunders.**
London; Orlando: Academic Press, 1984. xiv, 376 p.: ill.; 24 cm. 1. Evolution I. Ho, Mae-Wan. II. Saunders, P. T. (Peter Timothy), 1939-.
QH366.2.B486 1984      575 19      LC 83-72403      ISBN 012350080X

**The Evolutionary synthesis: perspectives on the unification of** **5.3367**
**biology / edited by Ernst Mayr and William B. Provine.**
Cambridge, Mass.: Harvard University Press, 1980. xi, 487 p.; 24 cm. 1. Evolution 2. Evolution — History. I. Mayr, Ernst, 1904- II. Provine, William B.
QH366.2.E87      575      LC 80-13973      ISBN 0674272250

**Futuyma, Douglas J., 1942-.** **5.3368**
Evolutionary biology / Douglas J. Futuyma. — 2nd ed. — Sunderland, Mass.: Sinauer Associates, 1986. p. cm. Includes index. 1. Evolution I. T.
QH366.2.F87 1986      575 19      LC 86-15531      ISBN 0878931880

**Gould, Stephen Jay.** **5.3369**
Hen's teeth and horse's toes / Stephen Jay Gould. — 1st ed. — New York: Norton, c1983. 413 p.: ill.; 22 cm. Includes index. 1. Evolution I. T.
QH366.2.G66 1983      575 19      LC 82-22259      ISBN 0393017168

**Grant, Verne.** **5.3370**
The evolutionary process: a critical review of evolutionary theory / Verne Grant. — New York: Columbia University Press, 1985. xii, 499 p.: ill.; 24 cm. Includes indexes. 1. Evolution I. T.
QH366.2.G67 1985      575 19      LC 85-7733      ISBN 0231057520

**Margulis, Lynn, 1938-.** **5.3371**
Symbiosis in cell evolution: life and its environment on the early Earth / Lynn Margulis. — San Francisco: W. H. Freeman, c1981. xxii, 419 p.: ill.; 24 cm. Includes index. 1. Cells — Evolution. 2. Life — Origin 3. Symbiosis I. T.
QH366.2.M36      577 19      LC 80-26695      ISBN 0716712555

**Maynard Smith, John, 1920-.** **5.3372**
On evolution. — Edinburgh: Edinburgh University Press, 1972. viii, 125 p.: illus.; 20 cm. 1. Evolution I. T.
QH366.2.M3919      575      LC 72-77391      ISBN 0852242298

**Mayr, Ernst, 1904-.** **5.3373**
Evolution and the diversity of life: selected essays / Ernst Mayr. Cambridge, Mass.: Belknap Press of Harvard University press, 1976. ix, 721 p.: ill.; 24 cm. 1. Evolution — Addresses, essays, lectures. 2. Species — Addresses, essays, lectures. I. T.
QH366.2.M393      575/.008      LC 75-42131      ISBN 0674271041

**Salthe, Stanley N.** **5.3374**
Evolutionary biology / [by] Stanley N. Salthe. — New York: Holt, Rinehart and Winston, [1972] viii, 437 p.: illus.; 24 cm. 1. Evolution I. T.
QH366.2.S25      575      LC 76-183650      ISBN 0030821916

**Stanley, Steven M.** **5.3375**
Macroevolution, pattern and process / Steven M. Stanley; [artists, John and Judy Waller]. — San Francisco: W. H. Freeman, c1979. xi, 332 p.: ill.; 24 cm. Includes index. 1. Evolution 2. Paleontology I. T.
QH366.2.S68      575      LC 79-15464      ISBN 0716710927

## QH368 Human Evolution

**Ardrey, Robert.** • **5.3376**
African genesis; a personal investigation into the animal origins and nature of man. Drawings by Berdine Ardrey. — [1st American ed.]. — New York: Atheneum, 1961. 380 p.: illus.; 25 cm. 1. Man — Origin 2. Human evolution 3. Psychology, Comparative I. T.
QH368.A68      573.2      LC 61-15889

**Bates, Marston, 1906-1974.** • **5.3377**
Man in nature. — 2d ed. — Englewood Cliffs, N.J.: Prentice-Hall, [1964] x, 116 p.: ill., maps, ports.; 24 cm. — (Foundations of modern biology series) 1. Man — Origin 2. Biology, Economic I. T.
QH368.B334 1964      573.2      LC 64-17070

**Cohen, Yehudi A. comp.** **5.3378**
Man in adaptation / edited by Yehudi A. Cohen. — Chicago: Aldine Pub. Co., [1968] 2 v.: ill. 1. Anthropology — Addresses, essays, lectures. 2. Human evolution I. T.
QH368.C537      390      LC 68-18325

**Dobzhansky, Theodosius Grigorievich, 1900-1975.** • **5.3379**
Mankind evolving; the evolution of the human species. New Haven, Yale University Press, 1962. 381 p. illus. 25 cm. (Yale University. Mrs. Hepsa Ely Silliman memorial lectures) 1. Human evolution 2. Man — Origin 3. Human genetics I. T.
QH368.D6      575      LC 62-8243

**Huxley, Thomas Henry, 1825-1895.** • **5.3380**
[Evidence as to man's place in nature] Man's place in nature. Introd. by Ashley Montagu. [Ann Arbor] University of Michigan Press [1959] 184 p. illus. 21 cm. (Ann Arbor paperbacks, AA24) First published in 1863 under title: Evidence as to man's place in nature. 1. Man — Origin I. T.
QH368.H96      573      LC 59-16099

**Moore, Ruth E.** • **5.3381**
Man, time, and fossils: the story of evolution / by Ruth Moore; drawings by Sue Richert. — 2d ed., significantly rev. and enl. — New York: Knopf, 1961. 436 p.: ill.; 22 cm. 1. Human evolution 2. Fossil man I. T.
QH368.M8 1961      573.2      LC 61-15043

## QH368.5–373 Evolution: Special Aspects

**Grant, Verne.** **5.3382**
Plant speciation / Verne Grant. — 2nd ed. — New York: Columbia University Press, 1981. xii, 563 p.: ill.; 24 cm. Includes indexes. 1. Plants — Evolution 2. Species I. T.
QH368.5.G7 1981      581.3/8 19      LC 81-6159      ISBN 0231051123

**Smith, Homer William, 1895-1962.** • **5.3383**
From fish to philosopher. — [1st ed.]. — Boston: Little, Brown, [1953] 264 p.: ill.; 21 cm. 1. Evolution 2. Kidneys 3. Consciousness I. T.
QH369.S58      575.6      LC 53-7332

**Brooks, D. R. (Daniel R.), 1951-.** **5.3384**
Evolution as entropy: toward a unified theory of biology / Daniel R. Brooks and E.O. Wiley. — Chicago: University of Chicago Press, 1986. xiv, 335 p.; 24 cm. — (Science and its conceptual foundations.) Includes index. 1. Evolution 2. Entropy I. Wiley, E. O. II. T. III. Series.
QH371.B69 1986      575.01/6 19      LC 85-8544      ISBN 0226075818

**Coevolution** / edited by Douglas J. Futuyma and Montgomery    **5.3385**
Slatkin; with the assistance of Bruce R. Levin and Jonathan
Roughgarden.
Sunderland, Mass.: Sinauer Associates, c1983. x, 555 p.: ill. (some col.); 24 cm.
Includes index. 1. Coevolution I. Futuyma, Douglas J., 1942- II. Slatkin,
Montgomery.
QH371.C73 1983     575 19     *LC* 82-19496     *ISBN* 0878932283

**Did the Devil make Darwin do it?: modern perspectives on the**    **5.3386**
**creation–evolution controversy** / edited by David B. Wilson with
the assistance of Warren D. Dolphin.
1st ed. — Ames: Iowa State University Press, 1983. xxii, 241 p.: ill.; 24 cm.
1. Evolution 2. Creationism I. Wilson, David B. II. Dolphin, Warren D.
QH371.D52 1983     231.7/65 19     *LC* 82-23205     *ISBN* 0813804337

**Eigen, M. (Manfred), 1927-.**    **5.3387**
The hypercycle, a principle of natural self–organization / M. Eigen, P.
Schuster. — Berlin; New York: Springer-Verlag, 1979. viii, 92 p.: ill.; 27 cm.
Includes index. 1. Chemical evolution 2. Genetic translation I. Schuster, P.
(Peter), 1941- joint author. II. T.
QH371.E33     575     *LC* 79-1315     *ISBN* 0387092935

**Eldredge, Niles.**    **5.3388**
Time frames: the rethinking of Darwinian evolution and the theory of
punctuated equilibria / Niles Eldredge. — New York: Simon and Schuster,
c1985. 240 p.: ill.; 24 cm. Includes index. 1. Evolution I. T. II. Title:
Punctuated equilibria.
QH371.E44 1985     575.01/62 19     *LC* 84-23632     *ISBN* 0671495550

**Gould, Stephen Jay.**    **5.3389**
Ontogeny and phylogeny / Stephen Jay Gould. Cambridge, Mass.: Belknap
Press of Harvard University Press, 1977. ix, 501 p.: ill.; 25 cm. Includes index.
1. Phylogeny 2. Ontogeny I. T.
QH371.G68     575.01     *LC* 76-45765     *ISBN* 0674639405

**Jacob, François, 1920-.**    **5.3390**
The possible and the actual / François Jacob. — Seattle: University of
Washington Press, c1982. viii, 71 p.; 25 cm. — (Jessie and John Danz lectures.)
1. Evolution — Addresses, essays, lectures. I. T. II. Series.
QH371.J2     575 19     *LC* 81-16452     *ISBN* 029595888X

**Kimura, Motoo, 1924-.**    **5.3391**
The neutral theory of molecular evolution / Motoo Kimura. — Cambridge
[Cambridgeshire]; New York: Cambridge University Press, 1983. xv, 367 p.:
ill.; 24 cm. Includes indexes. 1. Chemical evolution I. T.
QH371.K53 1983     575.01/6 19     *LC* 82-22225     *ISBN* 0521231094

**Kitcher, Philip, 1947-.**    **5.3392**
Abusing science: the case against creationism / Philip Kitcher. — Cambridge,
Mass.: MIT Press, c1982. x, 213 p.; 24 cm. Includes index. 1. Evolution
2. Evolution — Religious aspects 3. Creation I. T.
QH371.K57 1982     575.01 19     *LC* 82-9912     *ISBN* 0262110857

**Krebs, J. R. (John R.)**    **5.3393**
An introduction to behavioural ecology / by J.R. Krebs and N.B. Davies;
drawings by Jan Parr. — 2nd ed. — Sunderland, Mass.: Sinauer Associates Inc.,
1986. x, 292 p.: ill.; 24 cm. Includes indexes. 1. Behavior evolution 2. Animal
behavior 3. Human behavior 4. Animal ecology 5. Human ecology I. Davies,
N. B. (Nicholas B.), 1952- joint author. II. T.
QH371.K73     591.51 19

**Margulis, Lynn, 1938-.**    **5.3394**
Microcosmos: four billion years of evolution from our microbial ancestors /
Lynn Margulis and Dorion Sagan; foreword by Lewis Thomas. — New York:
Summit Books, c1986. 301 p.: ill.; 23 cm. Includes index. 1. Evolution
2. Microorganisms — Evolution I. Sagan, Dorion, 1959- II. T.
QH371.M28 1986     575 19     *LC* 86-4432     *ISBN* 0671441698

**Mayr, Ernst, 1904-.**    • **5.3395**
Animal species and evolution. — Cambridge: Belknap Press of Harvard
University Press, 1963. xiv, 797 p.: maps, diagrs., tables.; 24 cm. 1970 ed.
published under title: Populations, species, and evolution. 1. Species
2. Zoology — Variation 3. Evolution I. T.
QH371.M33     575     *LC* 63-9552

**Mayr, Ernst, 1904-.**    • **5.3396**
Populations, species, and evolution: an abridgment of Animal species and
evolution. — Cambridge, Mass.: Belknap Press of Harvard University Press,
1970. xv, 453 p.: ill., maps.; 25 cm. 1963 ed. published under title: Animal
species and evolution. 1. Species 2. Zoology — Variation 3. Evolution I. T.
QH371.M33 1970     591.3/8     *LC* 79-111486     *ISBN* 0674690109

**McGowan, Christopher.**    **5.3397**
In the beginning—: a scientist shows why the creationists are wrong / Chris
McGowan. — Buffalo, N.Y.: Prometheus Books, 1984. xiii, 208 p.: ill.; 23 cm.
Includes index. 1. Evolution 2. Creationism I. T.
QH371.M34 1984     575 19     *LC* 83-62997     *ISBN* 0879752408

**Molecular evolution: an annotated reader** / [edited by] E.A.    **5.3398**
Terzaghi, A.S. Wilkins, D. Penny.
Boston: Jones and Bartlett, c1984. xiii, 409 p.: ill.; 29 cm. (A Series of books in
biology) 1. Chemical evolution I. Terzaghi, E. A. (Eric A.), 1936- II. Wilkins,
A. S. (Adam S.), 1945- III. Penny, D. (David), 1938-
QH371.M75 1984     577 19     *LC* 83-17541     *ISBN* 0867200219

**Ruse, Michael.**    **5.3399**
Taking Darwin seriously: a naturalistic approach to philosophy / Michael
Ruse. — New York, NY: Blackwell, 1986. xv, 303 p.: ill.; 24 cm. Includes
index. 1. Evolution — Philosophy. I. T.
QH371.R77 1986     575.01/62 19     *LC* 85-15094     *ISBN* 0631135421

**Williams, George Christopher, 1926-.**    **5.3400**
Sex and evolution [by] George C. Williams. — Princeton, N.J.: Princeton
University Press, 1975. x, 200 p.: illus.; 23 cm. — (Monographs in population
biology. 8) 1. Evolution 2. Sex (Biology) I. T. II. Series.
QH371.W54     575     *LC* 74-2985     *ISBN* 0691081476

**Convergent evolution in Chile and California: Mediterranean**    **5.3401**
**climate ecosystems** / edited by Harold A. Mooney.
Stroudsburg, Pa.: Dowden, Hutchinson & Ross; [New York]: exclusive
distributor Halsted Press, c1977. xii, 224 p.: ill.; 25 cm. (US/IBP synthesis
series; 5) Includes indexes. 1. Convergence (Biology) 2. Ecology — California.
3. Ecology — Chile. 4. Mediterranean climate I. Mooney, Harold A.
II. Series.
QH373.C66     575     *LC* 77-1884     *ISBN* 0879332794

# QH375–408 Natural Selection. Variation

**Dawkins, Richard, 1941-.**    **5.3402**
The extended phenotype: the gene as the unit of selection / Richard Dawkins.
— Oxford [Oxfordshire]; San Francisco: Freeman, c1982. viii, 307 p.; 25 cm.
Includes indexes. 1. Natural selection 2. Gene expression 3. Genetics
4. Evolution I. T.
QH375.D38 1982     575 19     *LC* 81-9889     *ISBN* 0716713586

**Genes, organisms, populations: controversies over the units of**    **5.3403**
**selection** / edited by Robert N. Brandon and Richard M.
**Burian.**
Cambridge, Mass.: MIT Press, c1984. xiv, 329 p.: ill.; 24 cm. 'Bradford
books'–P. [ii] 1. Natural selection — Addresses, essays, lectures. I. Brandon,
Robert N. II. Burian, Richard M.
QH375.G46 1984     575.01/62 19     *LC* 83-24838     *ISBN* 0262022052

**Murray, Joseph James, 1930-.**    **5.3404**
Genetic diversity and natural selection / [by] James Murray. — Edinburgh:
Oliver and Boyd, 1972. viii, 128 p.: ill.; 23 cm. (University reviews in biology,
15) 1. Natural selection 2. Variation (Biology) I. T.
QH401.M87     575.2     *LC* 72-304689     *ISBN* 0050024574 *ISBN*
005002457X

**Hanson, Earl D.**    **5.3405**
Animal diversity [by] Earl D. Hanson. — 3d ed. — Englewood Cliffs, N.J.:
Prentice-Hall, [1972] x, 164 p.: ill.; 23 cm. — (Foundations of modern biology
series) 1. Zoology — Variation 2. Evolution 3. Phylogeny I. T.
QH408.H27 1972     591.3/8     *LC* 72-15     *ISBN* 0130371688

# QH421–499 Genetics

**Stern, Curt, 1902- ed.**    • **5.3406**
The origin of genetics; a Mendel source book, edited by Curt Stern and Eva R.
Sherwood. — San Francisco: W. H. Freeman, [c1966] xi, 179 p.: illus., port.; 22
cm. 1. Mendel, Gregor, 1822-1884. 2. Genetics — History. I. Sherwood, Eva
R., joint ed. II. T.
QH421.S7     575.1/09     *LC* 66-27948

**Mendel, Gregor, 1822-1884.**    • **5.3407**
[Versuche über Pflanzenhybriden. English] Experiments in plant hybridisation / [Translation made by the Royal Horticultural Society of London]; with a foreword by Paul C. Mangelsdorf. — Cambridge: Harvard University Press, 1965. vii, 41 p.: port.; 23 cm. 'The original paper was published in the Verh. naturf. Ver. in Brunn, Abhandlungen, IV 1865, which appeared in 1866.' 1. Plant genetics 2. Hybridization, Vegetable I. T.
QH423.M5313 1965a     LC 67-9611

# QH426–430 Reference. General Works

**King, Robert C.**    **5.3408**
A dictionary of genetics / Robert C. King, William D. Stansfield. — 3rd ed. — New York: Oxford University Press, 1985. vi, 480 p.: ill.; 25 cm. 1. Genetics — Dictionaries. I. Stansfield, William D., 1930- II. T.
QH427.K55 1985     575.1/0321 19     LC 84-29575     *ISBN* 0195034945

**Rieger, Rigomar.**    **5.3409**
Glossary of genetics and cytogenetics: classical and molecular / R. Rieger, A. Michaelis, M. M. Green. 4th completely rev. ed. — Berlin; New York: Springer-Verlag, 1976. 647 p.: ill.; 20 cm. 'The first and second editions of this book were published in German ... under the title: Genetisches und cytogenetisches Wörterbuch.' 'Springer study edition.' 1. Genetics — Dictionaries. 2. Cytogenetics — Dictionaries. I. Michaelis, Arnd. joint author. II. Green, Melvin M. joint author. III. T.
QH427.R54 1976     575.1/03     LC 76-16183     *ISBN* 0387076689

**Hoagland, Mahlon B.**    **5.3410**
Discovery, the search for DNA's secrets / Mahlon Hoagland. — Boston: Houghton Mifflin, 1981. xiv, 198 p.: ill.; 22 cm. Includes index. 1. Genetics — History. 2. Molecular genetics — History. 3. DNA I. T.
QH428.H63     574.87/3282 19     LC 81-6560     *ISBN* 0395305101

**Jacob, François, 1920-.**    **5.3411**
[Logique du vivant. English] The logic of life: a history of heredity / translated by Betty E. Spillmann. — [1st American ed.] New York: Pantheon Books [1974, c1973] viii, 348 p.; 22 cm. Translation of La logique du vivant. 1. Genetics — History. 2. Biology — History. 3. Life (Biology) I. T.
QH428.J313 1974     575.1     LC 73-18010     *ISBN* 0394472462

**Keller, Evelyn Fox, 1936-.**    **5.3412**
A feeling for the organism: the life and work of Barbara McClintock / Evelyn Fox Keller. — San Francisco: W.H. Freeman, c1984. xix, 235 p.: ill., ports; 22 cm. 1. McClintock, Barbara, 1902- 2. Geneticists — United States — Biography. I. T.
QH429.2.M38 K44     575.1/092/4 B 19     LC 82-21066     *ISBN* 0716714337

**Carlson, Elof Axel.**    **5.3413**
Genes, radiation, and society: the life and work of H.J. Muller / Elof Axel Carlson. — Ithaca: Cornell University Press, 1981. xiv, 457 p.: ill.; 24 cm. 1. Muller, H. J. (Hermann Joseph), 1890-1967. 2. Genetics — Social aspects — History. 3. Geneticists — United States — Biography. I. T.
QH429.2.M84 C37     575.1/092/4 B 19     LC 81-5486     *ISBN* 0801413044

**Crow, James F.**    **5.3414**
Genetics notes: an introduction to genetics / by James F. Crow. — 8th ed. — Minneapolis, Minn.: Burgess, c1983. vii, 306 p.: ill.; 23 cm. Includes index. 1. Genetics I. T.
QH430.C76 1983     575.1 19     LC 82-70471     *ISBN* 080874805X

**An Introduction to genetic analysis / David T. Suzuki ... [et al.].**    **5.3415**
3rd ed. — New York: W.H. Freeman, c1986. x, 612 p.: ill. (some col.); 29 cm. Rev. ed. of: An introduction to genetic analysis / David T. Suzuki. 2nd ed. c1981. Includes index. 1. Genetics 2. Genetics — Methodology. I. Suzuki, David T., 1936- II. Suzuki, David T., 1936- Introduction to genetic analysis.
QH430.I62 1986     575.1 19     LC 85-12978     *ISBN* 0716717050

**Lewin, Benjamin.**    **5.3416**
Genes / Benjamin Lewin. — 3rd ed. — New York: Wiley, 1987. 1 v. (unpaged): ill. 1. Genetics I. T.
QH430.L487 1987     575.1 19     LC 86-18959     *ISBN* 0471832782

**Nei, Masatoshi.**    **5.3417**
Molecular evolutionary genetics / Masatoshi Nei. — New York: Columbia University Press, 1987. x, 512 p.: ill.; 24 cm. 1. Molecular genetics 2. Evolution I. T.
QH430.N45     574.87/328 19     LC 86-17599     *ISBN* 0231063202

**Snyder, Leon A.**    **5.3418**
General genetics / Leon A. Snyder, David Freifelder, Daniel L. Hartl. — Boston: Jones and Bartlett Publishers, c1985. xiv, 666 p.: ill. (some col.); 25 cm. Includes index. 1. Genetics I. Freifelder, David, 1935- II. Hartl, Daniel L. III. T.
QH430.S69 1985     575.1 19     LC 84-21292     *ISBN* 0867200502

**Stent, Gunther Siegmund, 1924-.**    **5.3419**
Molecular genetics: an introductory narrative / Gunther S. Stent, Richard Calendar. — 2d ed. — San Francisco: W. H. Freeman, c1978. xiii, 773 p.: ill.; 24 cm. 1. Molecular genetics I. Calendar, Richard. joint author. II. T.
QH430.S73 1978     574.8/732     LC 78-688     *ISBN* 0716700484

**Strickberger, Monroe W.**    **5.3420**
Genetics / Monroe W. Strickberger. — 3rd ed. — New York: Macmillan; London: Collier Macmillan, c1985. xxi, 842 p.: ill. (some col.); 26 cm. 1. Genetics I. T.
QH430.S87 1985     575.1 19     LC 84-26162     *ISBN* 002418120X

**Swanson, Carl P.**    **5.3421**
Cytogenetics: the chromosome in division, inheritance, and evolution / Carl P. Swanson, Timothy Merz, William J. Young. — 2d ed. — Englewood Cliffs, NJ: Prentice-Hall, c1981. xiv, 577 p.: ill.; 24 cm. 1. Cytogenetics 2. Chromosomes I. Merz, Timothy. joint author. II. Young, William J. joint author. III. T.
QH430.S98 1981     574.87/3223     LC 79-27393     *ISBN* 0131966189

# QH431 Human Genetics

## QH431 A–J

**Bresler, Jack Barry, 1923- comp.**    **5.3422**
Genetics and society. Edited by Jack B. Bresler. — Reading, Mass.: Addison-Wesley Pub. Co., [1973] xv, 280 p.: illus.; 21 cm. — (Addison-Wesley series in life science) 1. Human genetics — Social aspects — Addresses, essays, lectures. I. T.
QH431.B672     573.2/1/08     LC 72-2650

**Carlson, Elof Axel.**    • **5.3423**
The gene: a critical history. — Philadelphia: Saunders, 1966. xi, 301 p.: ill.; 25 cm. 1. Genetics — History. I. T.
QH431.C246     575.109     LC 66-18495

**Cavalli-Sforza, Luigi Luca, 1922-.**    **5.3424**
The genetics of human populations [by] L. L. Cavalli–Sforza [and] W. F. Bodmer. San Francisco, W. H. Freeman [1971] xvi, 965 p. illus. 26 cm. (A Series of books in biology) 1. Human population genetics I. Bodmer, W. F. (Walter Fred), 1936- joint author. II. T.
QH431.C394     573.2/1     LC 72-120303     *ISBN* 0716706814

**Crow, James F.**    **5.3425**
An introduction to population genetics theory / [by] James F. Crow [and] Motoo Kimura. — New York: Harper & Row, [1970]. xiv, 591 p.: ill.; 24 cm. 1. Population genetics I. Kimura, Motoo, 1924- joint author. II. T.
QH431.C886     575.1/01/82     LC 78-103913

**Ephrussi, Boris, 1901-.**    **5.3426**
Hybridization of somatic cells. — Princeton, N.J.: Princeton University Press, [1972] x, 175 p.: ill.; 25 cm. 1. Somatic hybrids 2. Cell hybridization I. T.
QH431.E64     575.2/8     LC 79-39783     *ISBN* 069108114X

**Fincham, J. R. S.**    **5.3427**
Genetic complementation / [by] J.R.S. Fincham. — New York: W.A. Benjamin, 1966. xii, 143 p.: ill.; 24 cm. (Microbial and molecular biology series.) 1. Complementation (Genetics) I. T. II. Series.
QH431.F55     575.1     LC 66-10908

**Harris, Harry.**    **5.3428**
The principles of human biochemical genetics / Harry Harris. — 3d rev. ed. — Amsterdam; New York: Elsevier/North-Holland Biomedical Press; New York: sole distributors for the U.S.A. and Canada, Elsevier/North-Holland, 1980. xv, 554 p.: ill.; 24 cm. Includes index. 1. Human genetics 2. Biochemical genetics I. T.
QH431.H292 1980     611/.01816 19     LC 80-20730     *ISBN* 0444802568

**Harris, Henry, 1925-.**      5.3429
Cell fusion. Oxford, Clarendon P., 1970. [10], 108 p. illus. 22 cm. (Dunham lectures. 1969) 1. Cell hybridization I. T. II. Series.
QH431.H2923     574.8/7     *LC* 72-194000

**Hsu, T. C. (Tao-Chiuh), 1917-.**      5.3430
Human and mammalian cytogenetics: an historical perspective / T. C. Hsu. — New York: Springer-Verlag, c1979. xi, 186 p.: ill.; 24 cm. (Heidelberg science library.) Includes index. 1. Human cytogenetics — History. 2. Mammals — Genetics — History. 3. Cytogenetics — History. I. T. II. Series.
QH431.H755     575.2/1     *LC* 79-14681     *ISBN* 038790364X

**Huxley, Julian, 1887-1975.**      • 5.3431
Heredity, East and West: Lysenko and world science. — New York: H. Schuman [1949] x, 246 p.: port.; 22 cm. 'Literature cited': p. 235-238. 1. Lysenko, Trofim Denisovich, 1898-1976. 2. Genetics I. T.
QH431.H89     575.1     *LC* 49-50254 *

## QH431 K–R

**Kuspira, John, 1928-.**      5.3432
Genetics: questions and problems [by] John Kuspira [and] G. W. Walker. — New York: McGraw-Hill, [1973] viii, 776 p.: illus.; 23 cm. 1. Genetics — Problems, exercises, etc. I. Walker, George William, 1913- joint author. II. T.
QH431.K89     575.1/076     *LC* 72-6855     *ISBN* 0070356726

**Lindegren, Carl C. (Carl Clarence), 1896-.**      5.3433
The cold war in biology [by] Carl C. Lindegren. Ann Arbor, Mich., Planarian Press [c1966] vii, 113 p. illus. 29 cm. 1. Genetics 2. Evolution I. T.
QH431.L424     575.1     *LC* 66-29217

**Medvedev, Zhores A., 1925-.**      • 5.3434
The rise and fall of T. D. Lysenko [by] Zhores A. Medvedev. Translated by I. Michael Lerner, with the editorial assistance of Lucy G. Lawrence. New York, Columbia University Press, 1969. xvii, 284 p. illus., ports. 23 cm. 1. Lysenko, Trofim Denisovich, 1898-1976. 2. Genetics I. T.
QH431.M3613     575.1/0947     *LC* 79-77519

**Peters, James Arthur, 1922- ed.**      • 5.3435
Classic papers in genetics. — Englewood Cliffs, N.J.: Prentice-Hall, 1959. 282 p.: illus.; 23 cm. — (Prentice-Hall biological science series) 1. Genetics — Addresses, essays, lectures. I. T.
QH431.P43     575.1082     *LC* 59-14106

**Pontecorvo, G.**      5.3436
Trends in genetic analysis. New York, Columbia University Press, 1958. 145 p. illus. 24 cm. (Columbia biological series. no. 18) 1. Genetics I. T. II. Series.
QH431.P754     575.1     *LC* 58-8805

**Provine, William B. comp.**      5.3437
The origins of theoretical population genetics / [compiled by] William B. Provine. — Chicago: University of Chicago Press, [1971] xi, 201 p.; 23 cm. — (Chicago history of science and medicine.) 1. Population genetics — History. I. T. II. Series.
QH431.P797     575.1     *LC* 73-153711     *ISBN* 0226684652

**Robinson, Gloria.**      5.3438
A prelude to genetics: theories of a material substance of heredity: Darwin to Weismann / by Gloria Robinson. — Lawrence, Kan.: Coronado Press, 1979. xvi, 260 p.: ill.; ports. 1. Human genetics 2. Heredity, Human I. T.
QH431.R695     QH431 R636.     *ISBN* 0872911276

## QH431 S–Z

**Sager, Ruth.**      • 5.3439
Cell heredity / [by] Ruth Sager [and] Francis J. Ryan. — New York: Wiley [1961] 411 p.: ill.; 24 cm. 1. Cytogenetics I. Ryan, Francis J. (Francis Joseph), 1916- joint author. II. T.
QH431.S262     574.87     *LC* 61-11498

**Sager, Ruth.**      5.3440
Cytoplasmic genes and organelles. — New York: Academic Press, [1972] xiv, 405 p.: illus.; 24 cm. 1. Cytoplasmic inheritance 2. Mitochondria 3. Chloroplasts I. T.
QH431.S263 1972     575.1/2     *LC* 71-182609     *ISBN* 0126146500

**Srb, Adrian M.**      • 5.3441
General genetics [by] Adrian M. Srb, Ray D. Owen [and] Robert E. Edgar. — 2d ed. — San Francisco: W. H. Freeman, [1965] x, 557 p.: illus. (part col.); 25 cm. — (A Series of books in biology) 1. Genetics I. Owen, Ray David, 1915- joint author. II. Edgar, Robert S., joint author. III. T.
QH431.S69 1965     575.1     *LC* 65-19558

**Vogel, Friedrich, 1925-.**      5.3442
Human genetics: problems and approaches / F. Vogel, A.G. Motulsky. — 2nd ed., completely rev. — Berlin; New York: Springer-Verlag, c1986. xxxiv, 807 p.: ill.; 28 cm. Includes indexes. 1. Human genetics I. Motulsky, Arno G., 1923- II. T.
QH431.V59 1986     573.2/1 19     *LC* 86-3957     *ISBN* 0387164111

**Wagner, Robert P.**      • 5.3443
Genetics and metabolism [by] Robert P. Wagner [and] Herschel K. Mitchell. 2d ed. New York, J. Wiley [1964] ix, 673 p. illus., diagrs., tables. 24 cm. 1. Genetics 2. Metabolism I. Mitchell, Herschel K. joint author. II. T.
QH431.W28 1964     *LC* 63-18630

**Wallace, Bruce, 1920-.**      • 5.3444
Genetic load, its biological and conceptual aspects. — Englewood Cliffs, N.J.: Prentice-Hall, [c1970] xi, 116 p.: ill.; 24 cm. — (Concepts of modern biology series) 1. Genetic load I. T.
QH431.W288     575.1/2     *LC* 78-82908     *ISBN* 0133511979

**Whitehouse, H. L. K. (Harold L. K.)**      • 5.3445
Towards an understanding of the mechanism of heredity [by] H. L. K. Whitehouse. Foreword by G. Pontecorvo. New York, St. Martin's Press, 1965 [i. e. 1966] xii, 372 p. illus. 24 cm. Bibliography: p. 333-362. 1. Genetics I. T.
QH431.W459     575.1     *LC* 65-28391

**Wilson, Edward Osborne, 1929-.**      5.3446
A primer of population biology / [by] Edward O. Wilson and William H. Bossert. — [1st ed.]. — Stamford, Conn.: Sinauer Associates, [1971] 192 p.: ill.; 22 cm. 1. Population biology 2. Ecology I. Bossert, William H., 1937- joint author. II. T.
QH431.W493     575.1     *LC* 73-155365     *ISBN* 0978939261

**Woese, Carl R.**      • 5.3447
The genetic code: the molecular basis for genetic expression / [by] Carl R. Woese. — New York: Harper & Row [1967] viii, 200 p.: ill.; 24 cm. (Modern perspectives in biology.) 1. Genetic code I. T. II. Series.
QH431.W58     575.2/1     *LC* 67-15793

# QH433–438 Plant and Microbial Genetics. Heredity

**Birge, Edward A. (Edward Asahel)**      5.3448
Bacterial and bacteriophage genetics: an introduction / Edward A. Birge. — New York: Springer-Verlag, c1983. xvi, 359 p.: ill.; 24 cm. — (Springer series in microbiology.) 1. Bacterial genetics 2. Bacteriophage — Genetics I. T. II. Series.
QH434.B57     589.9/015 19     *LC* 81-151     *ISBN* 0387905049

**Davis, Ronald W. (Ronald Wayne), 1941-.**      5.3449
Advanced bacterial genetics / Ronald W. Davis, David Botstein, John R. Roth. — Cold Spring Harbor, N.Y.: Cold Spring Harbor Laboratory, 1980 (1981 printing) x, 254 p.: ill.; 28 cm. — (Manual for genetic engineering.) 1. Bacterial genetics — Laboratory manuals. 2. Bacterial genetics — Experiments. 3. Genetic engineering — Laboratory manuals. 4. Genetic engineering — Experiments. I. Botstein, David. II. Roth, John R., 1939- III. Cold Spring Harbor Laboratory. IV. T. V. Series.
QH434.D38 1980     589.9/087322 19     *LC* 80-25695     *ISBN* 0879691301

**Lin, E. C. C.**      5.3450
Bacteria, plasmids, and phages: an introduction to molecular biology / E.C.C. Lin, Richard Goldstein, Michael Syvanen. — Cambridge, Mass.: Harvard University Press, 1984. ix, 316 p.: ill.; 24 cm. 1. Microbial genetics 2. Molecular genetics I. Goldstein, Richard (Richard N.) II. Syvanen, Michael. III. T.
QH434.L56 1984     576/.139 19     *LC* 83-22784     *ISBN* 0674581652

**Dawkins, Richard, 1941-.**      5.3451
The selfish gene / Richard Dawkins. New York: Oxford University Press, 1976. xi, 224 p.; 23 cm. Includes index. 1. Genetics 2. Evolution 3. Behavior genetics I. T.
QH437.D38     591.5     *LC* 76-29168     *ISBN* 019857519X

**Edwards, A. W. F. (Anthony William Fairbank), 1935-.**      5.3452
The foundations of mathematical genetics / A. W. F. Edwards. — Cambridge; New York: Cambridge University Press, 1977. viii, 119 p.: ill.; 23 cm. Includes index. 1. Population genetics — Mathematical models I. T.
QH438.4.M3 E37     575.1     *LC* 76-9168     *ISBN* 0521213258

**Mather, Kenneth.**　5.3453
Biometrical genetics: the study of continuous variation / Sir Kenneth Mather, John L. Jinks. — 3rd ed. — London; New York: Chapman and Hall, 1982. xiv, 396 p.: ill.; 24 cm. Includes index. 1. Genetics — Statistical methods. 2. Variation (Biology) — Statistical methods. 3. Biometry I. Jinks, John L. II. T.
QH438.4.S73 M37 1982　　575.2/072 19　*LC* 82-217100　*ISBN* 0412228904

**Baer, Adela S., 1931- comp.**　5.3454
Heredity and society: readings in social genetics / edited by Adela S. Baer. — New York: Macmillan, [1973] ix, 382 p.: ill.; 25 cm. 1. Human genetics — Social aspects — Addresses, essays, lectures. I. T.
QH438.7.B3　　301.24/3　*LC* 70-189726

**Stansfield, William D., 1930-.**　5.3455
Schaum's outline of theory and problems of genetics / by William D. Stansfield. — 2nd ed. — New York: McGraw-Hill, c1983. 392 p.: ill.; 28 cm. — (Schaum's outline series) Includes index. 1. Genetics — Problems, exercises, etc. I. T.
QH440.3.S7 1983　　575.1/076 19　*LC* 82-15275　*ISBN* 0070608458

**Miller, Jeffrey H.**　5.3456
Experiments in molecular genetics [by] Jeffrey H. Miller. — [Cold Spring Harbor, N.Y.]: Cold Spring Harbor Laboratory, 1972. xvi, 466 p.: illus.; 27 cm. 1. Molecular genetics — Experiments. I. T.
QH440.4.M54　　575.2/1　*LC* 72-78914　*ISBN* 0879691069

## QH442 Genetic Engineering

**Etzioni, Amitai.**　5.3457
Genetic fix. — New York: Macmillan, [1973] 276 p.; 22 cm. 1. Genetic engineering — Social aspects. 2. Human genetics — Social aspects. I. T.
QH442.E88　　301.24/3　*LC* 73-7350

**Lappé, Marc.**　5.3458
Broken code: the exploitation of DNA / Marc Lappé. — San Francisco: Sierra Club Books, c1984. xiii, 354 p.: ill.; 22 cm. 1. Genetic engineering — Social aspects. 2. Recombinant DNA — Social aspects. 3. Genetic engineering 4. Recombinant DNA I. T.
QH442.L38 1984　　303.4/83 19　*LC* 84-22190　*ISBN* 0871568357

**Old, R. W.**　5.3459
Principles of gene manipulation: an introduction to genetic engineering / R. W. Old, S. B. Primrose. — Berkeley: University of California Press, 1980. ix, 138 p.: ill.; 24 cm. — (Studies in microbiology; v. 2) Includes index. 1. Genetic engineering I. Primrose, S. B. joint author. II. T.
QH442.O42　　575.1　*LC* 79-25736　*ISBN* 0520041437

**Rodriguez, Raymond L.**　5.3460
Recombinant DNA techniques: an introduction / Raymond L. Rodriguez and Robert C. Tait; foreword by Wacław Szybalski. — Menlo Park, Ca.: Benjamin/Cummings, 1983. xviii, 236 p.: ill.; 28 cm. 1. Recombinant DNA 2. Genetic engineering — Technique. I. Tait, Robert C. II. T. III. Title: Recombinant D.N.A. techniques.
QH442.R6 1983　　660/.62 19　*LC* 83-11864　*ISBN* 0201108704

**Watson, James D., 1928-.**　5.3461
The DNA story: a documentary history of gene cloning / James D. Watson, John Tooze. — San Francisco: W.H. Freeman and Co., c1981. xii, 605 p.: ill.; 29 cm. Includes index. 1. Recombinant DNA — Research — History — Addresses, essays, lectures. 2. Cloning — Research — History — Addresses, essays, lectures. I. Tooze, John. II. T.
QH442.W37　　574.87/3282 19　*LC* 81-3299　*ISBN* 071671292X

**Maniatis, Tom.**　5.3462
Molecular cloning: a laboratory manual / T. Maniatis, E.F. Fritsch, J. Sambrook. — Cold Spring Harbor, N.Y.: Cold Spring Harbor Laboratory, 1982. x, 545 p.: ill.; 28 cm. Includes index. 1. Molecular cloning 2. Eukaryotic cells I. Fritsch, E. F. II. Sambrook, Joseph. III. T.
QH442.2.M26 1982　　574.87/3224 19　*LC* 81-68891　*ISBN* 0879691360

**McKinnell, Robert Gilmore.**　5.3463
Cloning of frogs, mice, and other animals / Robert Gilmore McKinnell. — Rev. ed. — Minneapolis: University of Minnesota Press, c1985. ix, 127 p.: ill.; 24 cm. Rev. ed. of: Cloning. c1979. Includes index. 1. Cloning 2. Cell nuclei — Transplantation 3. Embryology, Experimental I. McKinnell, Robert Gilmore. Cloning. II. T.
QH442.2.M32 1985　　596/.016 19　*LC* 85-2541　*ISBN* 0816613605

**Genetic maps.**　5.3464
Vol. 1 (Mar. 1980)-　. — Bethesda, Md.: Laboratory of Viral Carcinogenesis, National Cancer Institute, National Institutes of Health, 1980-. v.: ill.; 28 cm. 'Previous volumes ... become obsolete with each subsequent issue.' Published: Cold Spring Harbor, N.Y.: Cold Spring Harbor Laboratory, 1982- I. Cold Spring Harbor Laboratory. II. Laboratory of Viral Carcinogenesis (National Cancer Institute)
QH445.2 G46　*LC* sn 83-10922

## QH448–452 Genetic Recombination. Genetic Regulation

**Stahl, Franklin W.**　5.3465
Genetic recombination: thinking about it in phage and fungi / Franklin W. Stahl. — San Francisco: W. H. Freeman, c1979. xi, 333 p.: ill.; 24 cm. — (A Series of books in biology) 1. Genetic recombination 2. Bacteriophage — Genetics 3. Fungi — Genetics I. T.
QH448.S7　　575.1　*LC* 79-13378　*ISBN* 0716710374

**Lewin, Benjamin.**　5.3466
Gene expression [by] Benjamin Lewin. London, New York, Wiley [1974-. v. illus. 24 cm. 'A Wiley-Interscience publication.' 1. Gene expression 2. Molecular genetics I. T.
QH450.L48　　575.2/1　*LC* 73-14382　*ISBN* 0471531677

**The Operon / edited by Jeffrey H. Miller, William S. Reznikoff.**　5.3467
2d ed. — Cold Spring Harbor, N.Y.: Cold Spring Harbor Laboratory, 1980. vi, 469 p. [2] p. of plates: ill.; 23 cm. (Cold Spring Harbor monograph series.) 1. Operons I. Miller, Jeffrey H. II. Reznikoff, William S. III. Series.
QH450.2.O63 1980　　574.87/322　*LC* 80-15490　*ISBN* 0879691336

**Stent, Gunther Siegmund, 1924-.**　5.3468
The double helix: a personal account of the discovery of the structure of DNA / James D. Watson; edited by Gunther S. Stent. — 1st ed. — New York: Norton, c1980. xxv, 298 p.: ill.; 21 cm. (A Norton critical edition) 1. Watson, James D., 1928- The Double Helix — Reviews. 2. DNA 3. Genetic code 4. Molecular biology — History. I. Watson, James D., 1928- II. T.
QH450.2.W37　　574.87/3282　*LC* 80-10770　*ISBN* 039301245X

**Somatic cell hybridization. Edited by Richard L. Davidson and Felix F. de la Cruz.**　5.3469
New York, Raven Press [1974] xvii, 295 p. illus. 25 cm. (A monograph of the National Institute of Child Health and Human Development) Proceedings of a conference sponsored by the National Institute of Child Health and Human Development; held Mar. 11-14, 1973, Winter Park, Fla. 1. Somatic hybrids — Congresses. I. Davidson, Richard L. ed. II. De La Cruz, Felix F. ed. III. National Institute of Child Health and Human Development (U.S.)
QH451.S65　　599/.01/51　*LC* 74-75725　*ISBN* 0911216758

## QH452.7–470 Quantitative Genetics. Population Genetics

**Falconer, D. S. (Douglas Scott)**　5.3470
Introduction to quantitative genetics / D.S. Falconer. — 2nd ed., repr. with amendments. — Burnt Mill, Harlow, Essex, England: Longman; New York, N.Y.: Wiley, 1986, c1981. p. cm. Includes index. 1. Quantitative genetics I. T.
QH452.7.F34 1986　　575.1 19　*LC* 86-15251　*ISBN* 0470204745

**Crow, James F.**　5.3471
Basic concepts in population, quantitative, and evolutionary genetics / James F. Crow. — New York: W.H. Freeman, c1986. xii, 273 p.: ill.; 24 cm. Includes index. 1. Population genetics 2. Quantitative genetics 3. Evolution I. T.
QH455.C76 1986　　575 19　*LC* 85-15893　*ISBN* 071671759X

**Hartl, Daniel L.**　5.3472
Principles of population genetics / Daniel L. Hartl. — Sunderland, Mass.: Sinauer Associates, c1980. xvi, 488 p.: ill.; 24 cm. Includes indexes. 1. Population genetics 2. Quantitative genetics I. T.
QH455.H37　　575.1　*LC* 79-28384　*ISBN* 0878932720

Lewontin, Richard C., 1929-.                          5.3473
The genetic basis of evolutionary change [by] R. C. Lewontin. — New York:
Columbia University Press, 1974. xiii, 346 p.: illus.; 23 cm. — (Columbia
biological series. no. 25) 1. Population genetics 2. Evolution 3. Variation
(Biology) I. T. II. Series.
QH455.L48        575.1        LC 73-19786        ISBN 0231033923

Roughgarden, Jonathan.                               5.3474
Theory of population genetics and evolutionary ecology: an introduction /
Jonathan Roughgarden. — New York: Macmillan, c1979. x, 634 p.: ill.; 26 cm.
Includes index. 1. Population genetics 2. Population biology 3. Evolution
I. T.
QH455.R68        575.1        LC 78-7245        ISBN 0024031801

Spiess, Eliot B.                                     5.3475
Genes in populations / Eliot B. Spiess. New York: Wiley, c1977. xi, 780 p.: ill.;
26 cm. Includes indexes. 1. Population genetics I. T.
QH455.S6779      575.1        LC 77-3990        ISBN 0471816124

Wallace, Bruce, 1920-.                               5.3476
Basic population genetics / Bruce Wallace. — New York: Columbia University
Press, 1981. xii, 688 p.: ill.; 24 cm. Includes index. 1. Population genetics I. T.
QH455.W34        575.1/5 19    LC 80-39504       ISBN 0231050429

Wright, Sewall, 1889-.                               5.3477
Evolution and the genetics of populations: a treatise. — Chicago: University of
Chicago Press, [1968-78] 4 v.: ill.; 24 cm. 1. Population genetics 2. Evolution
I. T.
QH455.W76        575.1        LC 67-25533

Merrell, David J.                                    5.3478
Ecological genetics / David J. Merrell. — Minneapolis: University of
Minnesota Press, c1981. xii, 500 p.: ill.; 24 cm. Includes index. 1. Ecological
genetics I. T.
QH456.M47        575.1/5 19    LC 81-14789       ISBN 0816610193

The Genetics and biology of Drosophila / edited by M.          5.3479
Ashburner and E. Novitski.
London; New York: Academic Press, 1976- <c1986 >. v. < 1a-c, 2a-d, 3a-3e
> : ill.; 24 cm. Vol. 3a- <3e > edited by M. Ashburner, H.L. Carson, and J.N.
Thompson, Jr. 1. Drosophila melanogaster — Collected works. 2. Drosophila
melanogaster — Genetics — Collected works. 3. Drosophila 4. Drosophila —
Genetics — Collected works. 5. Insects — Genetics I. Ashburner, M.
II. Novitski, Edward.
QH470.D7 G46     595.7/74      LC 75-19614       ISBN 0120649012

# QH471–499 Reproduction.
# Development. Regeneration

Farley, John, 1936-.                                 5.3480
Gametes & spores: ideas about sexual reproduction, 1750–1914 / John Farley.
— Baltimore: Johns Hopkins University Press, c1982. x, 299 p.: ill., ports.; 24
cm. 1. Reproduction — Research — History. 2. Reproduction I. T. II. Title:
Gametes and spores.
QH471.F37 1982       574.1/6 19     LC 82-87        ISBN 0801827388

Forsyth, Adrian.                                     5.3481
A natural history of sex: the ecology and evolution of sexual behavior / Adrian
Forsyth. — New York: Scribner's, c1986. xiv, 190 p.; 22 cm. Includes index.
1. Sex (Biology) 2. Sex (Psychology) 3. Behavior evolution I. T.
QH471.F69 1986       591.5/6 19     LC 86-1826      ISBN 0684183382

Margulis, Lynn, 1938-.                               5.3482
Origins of sex: three billion years of genetic recombination / Lynn Margulis,
Dorion Sagan. — New Haven: Yale University Press, c1986. xiii, 258 p.: ill.; 25
cm. — (Bio-origins series.) Includes index. 1. Sex (Biology) 2. Genetic
recombination I. Sagan, Dorion, 1959- II. T. III. Series.
QH481.M27 1986       575.1 19       LC 85-8385      ISBN 0300033400

Maynard Smith, John, 1920-.                          5.3483
The evolution of sex / John Maynard Smith. — Cambridge [Eng.]; New York:
Cambridge University Press, 1978. x, 222 p.: ill.; 23 cm. Includes indexes.
1. Sex (Biology) 2. Evolution 3. Population genetics I. T.
QH481.M28        574.1/66      LC 77-85689       ISBN 052121887X

Biology of fertilization / edited by Charles B. Metz, Alberto          5.3484
Monroy.
Orlando: Academic Press, 1985. 3 v.: ill.; 24 cm. 1. Fertilization (Biology)
I. Metz, Charles B. II. Monroy, Alberto.
QH485.B53 1985       574.1/66 19    LC 84-10982      ISBN 0124926010

Bonner, John Tyler.                                  • 5.3485
Morphogenesis: an essay on development. — Princeton: Princeton University
Press, 1952. vi, 296 p.: ill. 1. Morphogenesis I. T.
QH491.B6         QH491.B71.    LC 52-5847

Bonner, John Tyler.                                  5.3486
On development; the biology of form. — Cambridge, Mass.: Harvard
University Press, 1974. 282 p.: illus.; 24 cm. 'A Commonwealth Fund book.'
1. Developmental biology I. T.
QH491.B62        574.3        LC 73-88053       ISBN 0674634101

Explorations in developmental biology / [compiled by] Chandler          5.3487
Fulton and Attila O. Klein.
Cambridge, Mass.: Harvard University Press, 1976. xv, 704 p.: ill.; 29 cm.
1. Developmental biology — Addresses, essays, lectures. 2. Biology
3. Embryology I. Fulton, Chandler, 1934- II. Klein, Attila O., 1930-
QH491.E97        574.3        LC 75-25775       ISBN 0674278526

Schubert, David, 1943-.                              5.3488
Developmental biology of cultured nerve, muscle, and glia / David Schubert. —
New York: Wiley, c1984. xiv, 315 p.: ill.; 24 cm. 'A Wiley-Interscience
publication.' Includes index. 1. Developmental cytology 2. Cell culture I. T.
QH491.S38 1984       591.1/88 19     LC 83-26115      ISBN 0471865923

Ord, Margery G.                                      5.3489
Cell and tissue regeneration: a biochemical approach / Margery G. Ord, Lloyd
A. Stocken. — New York: Wiley, c1984. xvii, 221 p.: ill.; 24 cm. — (Cell
biology; v. 2) 'A Wiley-Interscience publication.' Includes index.
1. Regeneration (Biology) 2. Cytochemistry 3. Histochemistry I. Stocken,
Lloyd A. II. T.
QH499.O73 1984       591.8 19       LC 84-3536      ISBN 0471862487

# QH501–531 LIFE: BIOLOGY

Hanawalt, Philip C., 1931- comp.                     5.3490
The chemical basis of life: an introduction to molecular and cell biology;
readings from Scientific American / with introductions by Philip C. Hanawalt
and Robert H. Haynes. — San Francisco: W. H. Freeman, [1973] viii, 405 p.:
ill.; 30 cm. 1. Molecular biology — Addresses, essays, lectures. 2. Cytology —
Addresses, essays, lectures. I. Haynes, Robert H., 1931- joint comp.
II. Scientific American. III. T.
QH501.H35        574.8/8       LC 73-8899       ISBN 0716708825

Nobel Conference. 13th, Gustavus Adolphus College, 1977.          5.3491
The nature of life / XIIIth Nobel Conference; edited by William H. Heidcamp;
with contributions by René Dubos ... [et al.]. — Baltimore: University Park
Press, c1978. x, 180 p.: ill.; 23 cm. 'Proceedings of the XIIIth Nobel Conference
... held at Gustavus Adolphus College, St. Peter, Minnesota, October 4-5, 1977.'
1. Life (Biology) — Congresses. I. Heidcamp, William H., 1944- II. Dubos,
René J. (René Jules), 1901- III. Gustavus Adolphus College. IV. T.
QH501.N63 1977       577        LC 78-9316       ISBN 0839112807

# QH505–506 Biophysics. Molecular
# Biology

Ackerman, Eugene, 1920-.                             5.3492
Biophysical science / Eugene Ackerman, Lynda B. Ellis, Lawrence E.
Williams. — 2d ed. — Englewood Cliffs, N.J.: Prentice-Hall, 1979. xviii, 634 p.:
ill.; 24 cm. 1. Biophysics I. Ellis, Lynda B. M. joint author. II. Williams,
Lawrence E. joint author. III. T.
QH505.A25 1979       574.1/91      LC 78-18682      ISBN 0130769010

Davidovits, Paul.                                    5.3493
Physics in biology and medicine / Paul Davidovits. — Englewood Cliffs, N.J.:
Prentice-Hall, [1975] xviii, 298 p.: ill.; 24 cm. — (Prentice-Hall physics series)
Includes index. 1. Biophysics 2. Medical physics I. T.
QH505.D36        574.1/91      LC 74-31231       ISBN 0136723527

Metcalf, Harold J.                                   5.3494
Topics in classical biophysics / Harold J. Metcalf. — Englewood Cliffs, N.J.:
Prentice-Hall, c1980. xiv, 286 p.: ill.; 23 cm. 1. Biology — Research I. T.
QH505.M47 1980       574.1/91      LC 79-10383      ISBN 013925255X

**Rashevsky, Nicolas, 1899-.**    • 5.3495
Mathematical biophysics; physico–mathematical foundations of biology. 3d rev. ed. New York, Dover Publications [1960] 2 v. illus. 21 cm. Includes bibliography. 1. Biomathematics 2. Biophysics 3. Cells I. T.
QH505.R3 1960     574.191     *LC* 60-2545

**Setlow, Richard B. (Richard Burton)**    • 5.3496
Molecular biophysics, by Richard B. Setlow and Ernest C. Pollard. Reading, Mass., Addison-Wesley Pub. Co. [1962] 545 p. illus. 24 cm. (Addison-Wesley series in the life sciences.) 1. Molecular biology 2. Molecules I. Pollard, Ernest C. (Ernest Charles), 1906- joint author. II. T. III. Series.
QH505.S45     574.191     *LC* 61-5025

**Sybesma, C.**    5.3497
An introduction to biophysics / C. Sybesma. — New York: Academic Press, 1977. x, 278 p.: ill.; 24 cm. Includes index. 1. Biophysics I. T.
QH505.S86     574.1/91     *LC* 76-13953     *ISBN* 0126797501

**Van Holde, K. E. (Kensal Edward), 1928-.**    5.3498
Physical biochemistry / K.E. van Holde. — 2nd ed. — Englewood Cliffs, NJ: Prentice-Hall, c1985. xii, 287 p.: ill.; 24 cm. 1. Biophysics 2. Biochemistry 3. Chemistry, Physical organic I. T.
QH505.V27 1985     574.19/283 19     *LC* 84-8266     *ISBN* 0136662722

**Vincent, Julian F. V.**    5.3499
Structural biomaterials / Julian F.V. Vincent. — New York: Halsted Press, c1982. vii, 206 p.: ill.; 24 cm. Includes index. 1. Biomechanics 2. Molecular biology I. T. II. Title: Biomaterials.
QH505.V48 1982     574.19 19     *LC* 81-6797     *ISBN* 0470271744

**Introduction to molecular biology / [by] G. H. Haggis;**    5.3500
**including material contributed to the 1st ed. by D. Mitchie [and others]; a new appendix on X–ray diffraction, by B. M. Blow, and a section on tumor viruses, by Rose Sheinin.**
2d ed. — New York: Wiley, [1974, c1964] x, 428 p.: ill.; 24 cm. 'A Halsted Press book.' 1. Molecular biology I. Haggis, G. H.
QH506.I55 1974     574.8/8     *LC* 73-6393     *ISBN* 0470338741

**Molecular biology of the gene / James D. Watson ... [et al.].**    5.3501
4th ed. — Menlo Park, Calif.: Benjamin/Cummings, c1987-. v. < 1 > : ill. (some col.); 29 cm. 1. Molecular biology 2. Molecular genetics I. Watson, James D., 1928-
QH506.M6627 1987     574.87/328 19     *LC* 86-24500     *ISBN* 0805396128

**Nobel lectures in molecular biology, 1933–1975 / with a**    5.3502
**foreword, David Baltimore.**
New York: Elsevier North-Holland, c1977. ix, 534 p.: ill.; 23 cm. 1. Molecular biology — Addresses, essays, lectures. 2. Molecular genetics — Addresses, essays, lectures. I. Baltimore, David.
QH506.N58     574.8/8/08     *LC* 77-22255     *ISBN* 0444002367

**Olby, Robert C. (Robert Cecil)**    5.3503
The path to the double helix. Foreword by Francis Crick. Seattle, University of Washington Press [1974] xxiii, 510 p. illus. 24 cm. 1. Molecular biology — History. 2. DNA I. T.
QH506.O45     574.8/732     *LC* 74-10676     *ISBN* 0295953594

**Segel, Lee A.**    5.3504
Modeling dynamic phenomena in molecular and cellular biology / Lee A. Segel. — Cambridge; New York: Cambridge University Press, 1984. xx, 300 p.: ill.; 24 cm. Includes index. 1. Molecular biology — Mathematical models. 2. Cytology — Mathematical models. 3. Molecular biology — Data processing. 4. Cytology — Data processing I. T.
QH506.S44 1984     574.87/0724 19     *LC* 83-15172     *ISBN* 0521254655

**Vol'kenshteĭn, M. V. (Mikhail Vladimirovich), 1912-.**    5.3505
[Molekuliarnaia biofizika. English] Molecular biophysics / M. V. Volkenstein. — New York: Academic Press, 1977. ix, 621 p.: ill.; 24 cm. Translation of Molekuliarnaia biofizika. 1. Molecular biology 2. Biophysics I. T.
QH506.V5813     574.8/8     *LC* 73-18990     *ISBN* 0127231501

# QH511–530 Growth. Aging. Death

**Lehninger, Albert L.**    • 5.3506
Bioenergetics: the molecular basis of biological energy transformations. — 2d ed. — Menlo Park, Calif.: W. A. Benjamin, c1971. x, 245 p.: ill. 1. Bioenergetics I. T.
QH511.L4 1971     *LC* 71-140831     *ISBN* 0805361030

**Hochachka, Peter W.**    5.3507
Metabolic arrest and the control of biological time / Peter W. Hochachka and Michael Guppy. — Cambridge, Mass.: Harvard University Press, 1987. xiii, 227 p.: ill.; 25 cm. Includes index. 1. Dormancy (Biology) 2. Metabolism I. Guppy, Michael. II. T.
QH523.H63 1987     591.1/33 19     *LC* 86-14860     *ISBN* 0674569768

**The Genetics of aging / edited by Edward L. Schneider.**    5.3508
New York: Plenum Press, c1978. xvi, 424 p.: ill.; 24 cm. 1. Aging — Genetic aspects I. Schneider, Edward L.
QH529.G46     612.6/7/0157321     *LC* 78-28     *ISBN* 0306311003

**Swift, M. J. (Michael John), 1939-.**    5.3509
Decomposition in terrestrial ecosystems / M. J. Swift, O. W. Heal & J. M. Anderson. — Oxford: Blackwell, 1979. xii, 372 p.: ill.; 25 cm. (Studies in ecology; v. 5) Includes index. 1. Biodegradation I. Heal, O. W. joint author. II. Anderson, J. M. joint author. III. T.
QH530.5.S94     574.5/264     *LC* 80-481543     *ISBN* 0632003782

# QH540–549 ECOLOGY
(see also: Botany: Ecology, QK901-977)

# QH540 Dictionaries

**Lincoln, Roger J.**    5.3510
A dictionary of ecology, evolution, and systematics / R.J. Lincoln, G.A. Boxshall, and P.F. Clark. — Cambridge; New York: Cambridge University Press, 1982. 298 p.: ill.; 24 cm. 1. Ecology — Dictionaries. 2. Evolution — Dictionaries. 3. Biology — Classification — Dictionaries. I. Boxshall, Geoffrey Allan. II. Clark, P. F. III. T.
QH540.4.L56 1982     574.5/03/21 19     *LC* 81-18013     *ISBN* 0521239575

**McGraw–Hill encyclopedia of environmental science / Sybil P.**    5.3511
**Parker, editor in chief.**
2d ed. — New York: McGraw-Hill Book Co., c1980. 858 p.: ill.; 29 cm. 'Some of the material in this volume has been published previously in the McGraw-Hill encyclopedia of science and technology, fourth edition.' 1. Ecology — Dictionaries. 2. Man — Influence on nature — Dictionaries. 3. Environmental protection — Dictionaries. I. Parker, Sybil P. II. McGraw-Hill Book Company. III. McGraw-Hill encyclopedia of science and technology. IV. Title: Encyclopedia of environmental science.
QH540.4.M3 1980     304.2/03     *LC* 79-28098     *ISBN* 0070452644

# QH541 General Works

### QH541 A–O

**Andrewartha, H. G. (Herbert George), 1907-.**    5.3512
The ecological web: more on the distribution and abundance of animals / H.G. Andrewartha and L.C. Birch. — Chicago: University of Chicago Press, 1985 (c1984). xiv, 506 p.: ill.; 25 cm. Includes indexes. 1. Animal ecology 2. Zoogeography I. Birch, L. Charles, 1918- II. T.
QH541.A524 1984     591.5 19     *LC* 84-70     *ISBN* 0226020339

**Bates, Marston, 1906-1974.**                                              • 5.3513
The forest and the sea: a look at the economy of nature and the ecology of man.
— New York: Random House, [1960] 277 p.; 21 cm. 1. Ecology I. T.
QH541.B3      574.5      *LC* 60-5564

**Begon, Michael.**                                                        5.3514
Ecology: individuals, populations, and communities / Michael Begon, John L.
Harper, Colin R. Townsend. — Sunderland, Mass.: Sinauer Associates, c1986.
xii, 876 p.: ill. (some col.); 26 cm. Includes indexes. 1. Ecology I. Harper, John
L. II. Townsend, Colin R. III. T.
QH541.B415 1986      574.5 19      *LC* 85-22168      *ISBN* 0878930515

**Community ecology / edited by Jared Diamond, Ted J. Case.**              5.3515
New York: Harper & Row, c1986. xxii, 665 p.: ill.; 25 cm. Includes index.
1. Biotic communities 2. Ecology I. Diamond, Jared M. II. Case, Ted J.
QH541.C644 1986      574.5/24 19      *LC* 85-8477      *ISBN* 006041202X

**Elton, Charles S. (Charles Sutherland), 1900-.**                         • 5.3516
The ecology of invasions by animals and plants. London, Methuen; [1958]
181 p. illus., maps. 22 cm. 1. Ecology 2. Biogeography I. T.
QH541.E4 1958a      *LC* 58-4723

**Forman, Richard T. T.**                                                  5.3517
Landscape ecology / Richard T.T. Forman, Michel Godron. — New York:
Wiley, c1986. xix, 619 p.: ill.; 25 cm. Includes index. 1. Ecology 2. Landscape
protection 3. Human ecology I. Godron, Michel. II. T.
QH541.F67 1986      712 19      *LC* 85-12306      *ISBN* 0471870374

**Grzimek's Encyclopedia of ecology / editor–in–chief, Bernhard**          5.3518
**Grzimek.**
New York: Van Nostrand Reinhold Co., c1976. 705 p.: ill. (some col.); 25 cm.
Includes index. 1. Ecology I. Grzimek, Bernhard. II. Title: Encyclopedia of
ecology.
QH541.G79      574.5/03      *LC* 76-9297      *ISBN* 0442229488

**Handbook of contemporary developments in world ecology /**              5.3519
**edited by Edward J. Kormondy and J. Frank McCormick.**
Westport, Conn.: Greenwood Press, 1981. xxviii, 776 p.: ill.; 24 cm. Includes
index. 1. Ecology I. Kormondy, Edward John, 1926- II. McCormick, J.
Frank, 1935-
QH541.H243      574.5 19      *LC* 80-1797      *ISBN* 031321381X

**Hutchinson, G. Evelyn (George Evelyn), 1903-.**                          5.3520
An introduction to population ecology / G. Evelyn Hutchinson. — New
Haven: Yale University Press, 1978. xi, 260 p.: ill.; 28 cm. 1. Ecology 2. Biotic
communities I. T.
QH541.H87      574.5/24      *LC* 77-11005      *ISBN* 0300021550

**McIntosh, Robert P. (Robert Patrick)**                                   5.3521
The background of ecology: concept and theory / Robert P. McIntosh. —
Cambridge [Cambridgeshire]; New York: Cambridge University Press, 1985.
xiii, 383 p.; 24 cm. (Cambridge studies in ecology.) Includes indexes.
1. Ecology I. T. II. Series.
QH541.M386 1985      574.5 19      *LC* 84-27490      *ISBN* 052124935X

**Odum, Eugene Pleasants, 1913-.**                                         5.3522
Basic ecology / Eugene P. Odum. — Philadelphia: Saunders College Pub.,
c1983. x, 613 p.: ill.; 25 cm. Updated ed. of pt. 1 of: Fundamentals of ecology.
3rd ed. 1971. Includes index. 1. Ecology I. T.
QH541.O312 1983      574.5 19      *LC* 82-60633      *ISBN* 0030584140

## QH541 P–Z

**Association of American Geographers. Commission on College**             5.3523
**Geography. Panel on Environmental Education.**
Perspectives on environment; essays requested by the Panel on Environmental
Education, Commission on College Geography. Edited by Ian R. Manners and
Marvin W. Mikesell. — Washington: [Association of American Geographers,
1974] v, 395 p.: illus.; 26 cm. — (Association of American Geographers.
Commission on College Geography. Publication, no. 13) 1. Ecology 2. Man —
Influence on nature I. Manners, Ian R. ed. II. Mikesell, Marvin W. ed.
III. Panel on Environmental Education. IV. T. V. Series.
QH541.P43      301.31      *LC* 73-88849

**Pianka, Eric R.**                                                        5.3524
Evolutionary ecology / Eric R. Pianka. — 3rd ed. — New York: Harper &
Row, c1983. xii, 416 p.: ill.; 24 cm. 1. Ecology 2. Evolution
I. T.
QH541.P5 1983      574.5/2 19      *LC* 82-6118      *ISBN* 0060452323

**Ricklefs, Robert E.**                                                    5.3525
Ecology / Robert E. Ricklefs. — 2d ed. — New York: Chiron Press, c1979. xii,
966 p.: ill., maps; 24 cm. — 1. Ecology I. T.
QH541.R53 1979      574.5      *LC* 78-60315      *ISBN* 0913462071

**Smith, Robert Leo.**                                                     5.3526
Ecology and field biology / Robert Leo Smith. — 3d ed. — New York: Harper
& Row, c1980. xii, 835 p.: ill.; 27 cm. Includes index. 1. Ecology 2. Biology —
Field work I. T.
QH541.S6 1980      574.5 19      *LC* 79-28390      *ISBN* 0060463295

**Theoretical ecology: principles and applications / edited by**           5.3527
**Robert M. May.**
2d ed. — Sunderland, MA: Sinauer Associates, c1981. ix, 489 p.: ill.; 24 cm.
Includes index. 1. Ecology 2. Ecology — Mathematical models. I. May,
Robert M.
QH541.T49 1981      574.5 19      *LC* 80-19344      *ISBN* 0878935142

**Westman, Walter E., 1945-.**                                             5.3528
Ecology, impact assessment, and environmental planning / Walter E.
Westman. — New York: Wiley, c1985. xi, 532 p.: ill., maps; 24 cm.
(Environmental science and technology. 0194-0287) 'A Wiley-Interscience
publication.' 1. Ecology 2. Environmental impact analysis 3. Land use —
Planning I. T. II. Series.
QH541.W43 1985      333.7 19      *LC* 84-11867      *ISBN* 0471896217

**Whittaker, Robert Harding, 1920-.**                                      5.3529
Communities and ecosystems / Robert H. Whittaker. — 2d ed. — New York:
Macmillan, [1975] xviii, 385 p.: ill.; 24 cm. 1. Ecology I. T.
QH541.W44 1975      574.5/24      *LC* 74-6636      *ISBN* 0024273902

**Worster, Donald, 1941-.**                                                5.3530
Nature's economy: a history of ecological ideas / Donald Worster. — [New
ed.]. — Cambridge [Cambridgeshire]; New York: Cambridge University Press,
1985, c1977. xviii, 404 p.; 25 cm. (Studies in environment and history.) Includes
index. 1. Ecology — History. I. T. II. Series.
QH541.W638 1985      574.5/09 19      *LC* 84-15551      *ISBN* 0521267927

**Worster, Donald, 1941-.**                                                5.3531
Nature's economy: the roots of ecology / Donald Worster. — San Francisco:
Sierra Club Books, c1977. xii, 404 p.; 24 cm. Includes index. 1. Ecology —
History. I. T.
QH541.W64      574.5/09      *LC* 77-7579      *ISBN* 0871561972

# QH541.145–.15 Addresses, Essays, Lectures. Special Aspects

**Global ecology / edited by Charles H. Southwick.**                       5.3532
Sunderland, Mass.: Sinauer Associates, 1985. xi, 323 p.: ill.; 24 cm. 1. Ecology
— Addresses, essays, lectures. 2. Pollution — Environmental aspects —
Addresses, essays, lectures. 3. Man — Influence on nature — Addresses,
essays, lectures. I. Southwick, Charles H.
QH541.145.G584 1985      304.2/8 19      *LC* 85-1800      *ISBN*
0878938109

**Whittaker, Robert Harding, 1920- comp.**                                 5.3533
Niche: theory and application / edited by Robert H. Whittaker and Simon A.
Levin. — Stroudsburg, Pa.: Dowden, Hutchinson & Ross; [New York]:
distributed by Halsted Press, 1976 (c1975) xv, 448 p.: ill.; 26 cm. (Benchmark
papers in ecology; 3) 1. Ecology — Addresses, essays, lectures. 2. Species —
Addresses, essays, lectures. 3. Biotic communities — Addresses, essays,
lectures. I. Levin, Simon A. joint comp. II. T.
QH541.145.W47      574.5/22      *LC* 74-23328      *ISBN* 0470941170

**Ecosystem modeling in theory and practice: an introduction with**       5.3534
**case histories / edited by Charles A. S. Hall, John W. Day, Jr.**
New York: Wiley, c1977. xxiii, 684 p.: ill.; 24 cm. 'A Wiley-Interscience
publication.' 1. Ecology — Data processing. 2. Ecology — Mathematical
models. 3. Biological models I. Hall, Charles A. S. II. Day, John W.
QH541.15.E45 E26      574.5/01/84      *LC* 76-57204      *ISBN* 0471341657

**Kitching, R. L. (Roger Laurence), 1945-.**                               5.3535
Systems ecology: an introduction to ecological modelling / R.L. Kitching. —
St. Lucia [Qld.]; New York: University of Queensland Press, 1984. xx, 280 p.:
ill.; 24 cm. Includes index. 1. Ecology — Data processing. 2. Ecology —
Mathematical models. I. T.
QH541.15.E45 K57 1983      574.5/0724 19

**Smith, John Maynard, 1920-.**                                            5.3536
Models in ecology / [by] J. Maynard Smith. — Cambridge [Eng.]: University
Press, [1975, c1974]. xii, 145 p.; 22 cm. 1. Ecology — Mathematical models.
I. T.
QH541.15.M3 S6      574.5/01/84      *LC* 74-155344      *ISBN* 0521202620

# QH541.28 Study and Teaching. Research

**Brower, James E.**      5.3537
Field & laboratory methods for general ecology / James E. Brower, Jerrold H. Zar. — 2nd ed. — Dubuque, Iowa: W.C. Brown Publishers, c1984. xi, 226 p.: ill.; 28 cm. Rev. ed. of: Field and laboratory methods for general ecology. c1977. 1. Ecology — Field work. 2. Ecology — Laboratory manuals. I. Zar, Jerrold H., 1941- II. Brower, James E. Field and laboratory methods for general ecology. III. T. IV. Title: Field and laboratory methods for general ecology.
QH541.28.B76 1984    574.5/07/8 19    LC 84-70027    ISBN 0069746575

**Krebs, Charles J.**      5.3538
Ecology: the experimental analysis of distribution and abundance / Charles J. Krebs. — 3rd ed. — New York: Harper & Row, c1985. xi, 800 p.: ill.; 25 cm. Includes index. 1. Ecology — Methodology. 2. Population biology — Methodology. 3. Biogeography — Methodology. I. T.
QH541.28.K74 1985    574.5 19    LC 84-10845    ISBN 0060437782

# QH541.5 By Type of Environment, A–Z

## QH541.5 A–J

**Ecological processes in coastal and marine systems / edited by**      5.3539
**Robert J. Livingston.**
New York: Plenum Press, c1979. xi, 548 p.: ill.; 26 cm. — (Marine science; v. 10) 'Proceedings of a conference ... conducted by the Florida State University Graduate Research Council, the Department of Biological Science (Florida State University) and the Center for Professional Development and Public Service, and held at the Florida State University, Tallahassee, April 13-15, 1978.' 1. Coastal ecology — Congresses. 2. Marine ecology — Congresses. I. Livingston, Robert J. II. Florida State University. Graduate Research Council. III. Florida State University. Dept. of Biological Science. IV. Florida State University. Center for Professional Development and Public Service.
QH541.5.C65 E26    574.5/26    LC 79-21388    ISBN 0306403188

**Mann, K. H. (Kenneth Henry), 1923-.**      5.3540
Ecology of coastal waters: a systems approach / by K.H. Mann. — Berkeley: University of California Press, 1982. x, 322 p.: ill.; 24 cm. — (Studies in ecology; v. 8) Includes index. 1. Coastal ecology I. T.
QH541.5.C65 M36 1982    574.5/2638 19    LC 81-40321    ISBN 0520045262

**Arid–land ecosystems: structure, functioning and management,**      5.3541
**Vol.1 / edited by D.W. Goodall, R.A. Perry with the assistance of K.M.W. Howes.**
Cambridge [etc.]: Cambridge University Press, 1979. xxvii, 881 p.: ill., charts, maps; 24 cm. In 2 vols. 'International Biological Programme [16]'. English text, French, Russian and Spanish contents lists. Index. 1. Arid regions I. Goodall, David William. II. Perry, R. A. III. International Biological Programme.
QH541.5.D4    574.5/265    LC 77-84810    ISBN 052121842X

**Estuaries and enclosed seas / edited by Bostwick H. Ketchum.**      5.3542
Amsterdam; New York: Elsevier Scientific Pub. Co.; New York: Distributors for the U.S. and Canada, Elsevier Science Pub. Co., 1983. xii, 500 p.: ill., maps; 27 cm. — (Ecosystems of the world. 26) Col. map on lining papers. 1. Estuarine ecology 2. Marine ecology I. Ketchum, Bostwick H., 1912- II. Title: Enclosed seas. III. Series.
QH541.5.E8 E84 1983    574.5/26365 19    LC 81-9853    ISBN 0444419217

**McLusky, Donald Samuel.**      5.3543
The estuarine ecosystem / Donald S. McLusky. — New York: Wiley, 1981. viii, 150 p.: ill.; 21 cm. — (Tertiary level biology) 'A Halsted Press book.' Includes index. 1. Estuarine ecology I. T.
QH541.5.E8 M32    574.5/26365 19    LC 80-28199    ISBN 0470271272

**Forest island dynamics in man–dominated landscapes / edited**      5.3544
**by Robert L. Burgess and David M. Sharpe; contributors, M.C. Bruner ... [et al.].**
New York: Springer-Verlag, c1981. xvii, 310 p.: ill.; 25 cm. (Ecological studies. 41) Includes index. 1. Forest ecology 2. Forest ecology — United States. I. Burgess, Robert Lewis, 1931- II. Sharpe, David M. III. Bruner, M. C. (Marc C.) IV. Series.
QH541.5.F6 F67    581.5/2642 19    LC 81-2248    ISBN 0387905847

**The Functioning of freshwater ecosystems / edited by E. D. Le**      5.3545
**Cren and R. H. Lowe–McConnell.**
Cambridge [Eng.]; New York: Cambridge University Press, 1979. xxix, 588 p.: ill.; 24 cm. — (International Biological Programme; 22) Text in English with Contents pages in English, French, Russian, and Spanish. Includes index. 1. Freshwater productivity 2. Freshwater ecology I. Le Cren, E. D. II. Lowe-McConnell, R. H. III. Series.
QH541.5.F7 F86    574.5/2632    LC 79-50504    ISBN 0521225078

**Leadley Brown, Alison.**      5.3546
Ecology of fresh water. — Cambridge, Mass.: Harvard University Press, 1971. xi, 129 p.: illus.; 21 cm. 1. Freshwater ecology I. T.
QH541.5.F7 L4 1971b    574.5/2632    LC 75-156140    ISBN 0674224477

**Macan, T. T. (Thomas Townley)**      5.3547
Freshwater ecology [by] T. T. Macan. 2d ed. New York, Wiley [1974] viii, 343 p. illus. 22 cm. 'A Halsted Press book.' 1. Freshwater ecology I. T.
QH541.5.F7 M3 1974    574.5/2632    LC 73-14419    ISBN 0470561491

**Williamson, M. H. (Mark Herbert)**      5.3548
Island populations / Mark Williamson. — Oxford; New York: Oxford University Press, 1981. xi, 286 p.; 24 cm. — (Oxford science publications.) Includes indexes. 1. Island ecology 2. Population biology I. T. II. Series.
QH541.5.I8 W54    574.5/267 19    LC 80-41507    ISBN 0198541341

## QH541.5 M–R

**Freshwater wetlands: ecological processes and management**      5.3549
**potential / edited by Ralph E. Good, Dennis F. Whigham, Robert L. Simpson; technical editor, Crawford G. Jackson, Jr.**
New York: Academic Press, 1978. xvii, 378 p.: ill.; 24 cm. Proceedings of a conference held at Rutgers University, New Brunswick, N.J., Feb. 13-16, 1977. 1. Wetland ecology — Congresses. 2. Wetland conservation — Congresses. I. Good, Ralph E. II. Whigham, Dennis F. III. Simpson, Robert L. (Robert Lee), 1942-
QH541.5.M3 F74    574.5/2632    LC 78-2836    ISBN 0122901509

**Mires — swamp, bog, fen, and moor / edited by A.J.P. Gore.**      5.3550
Amsterdam; New York: Elsevier Scientific Pub. Co., 1983. 2 v.: ill. — (Ecosystems of the world. 4A-B) 1. Wetland ecology I. Gore, A. J. P. (Anthony John Poynter) II. Series.
QH541.5.M3 M57    QH541.5M3 M57.    574.5/26325 19    LC 81-15162    ISBN 0444420053

**Heathlands and related shrublands / edited by R. L. Specht.**      5.3551
Amsterdam; New York: Elsevier Scientific Pub. Co.; New York: Distributors for the U.S. and Canada, Elsevier North-Holland, Inc., 1979-1981. 2 v.: ill.; 27 cm. (Ecosystems of the world. 9A, 9B) 1. Moor ecology 2. Shrubland ecology I. Specht, R. L. (Raymond Louis), 1924- II. Series.
QH541.5.M6 H42    574.5/264 19    LC 79-13938    ISBN 044441701X

**Zwinger, Ann.**      5.3552
Land above the trees: a guide to American alpine tundra / by Ann H. Zwinger and Beatrice E. Willard; with line drawings by Ann H. Zwinger and photos. by Herman Zwinger and Beatrice Willard. — [1st ed.]. — New York: Harper & Row, [1972] xviii, 489 p.: ill. (part col.); 26 cm. 1. Mountain ecology — United States. 2. Alpine flora — United States. I. Willard, Beatrice E. joint author. II. T.
QH541.5.M65 Z85    574.5/264    LC 72-79702    ISBN 0060148233

**Macan, T. T. (Thomas Townley)**      5.3553
Ponds and lakes / [by] T. T. Macan. — New York: Crane, Russak, [1974, c1973] 148 p.: ill.; 23 cm. 1. Pond ecology 2. Limnology I. T.
QH541.5.P63 M28 1974    574.5/2632    LC 73-91602

**Grassland ecosystems of the world: analysis of grasslands and**      5.3554
**their uses / edited by R. T. Coupland.**
Cambridge [Eng.]; New York: Cambridge University Press, 1979. xxviii, 401 p.: ill.; 24 cm. — (International Biological Programme; 18) Includes index. 1. Grassland ecology I. Coupland, R. T. II. Series.
QH541.5.P7 G712    574.5/264    LC 77-83990    ISBN 0521218675

**Grasslands, systems analysis, and man / edited by A. I.**   **5.3555**
**Breymeyer and G. M. Van Dyne.**
Cambridge [Eng.]; New York: Cambridge University Press, 1980. xxiv, 950 p.: ill.; 24 cm. — (International Biological Programme; 19) 1. International Biological Programme. 2. Grassland ecology 3. Grassland ecology — Mathematical models. I. Breymeyer, A. I. (Alicja I.), 1932- II. Van Dyne, George M., 1932- III. Series.
QH541.5.P7 G74     574.5/264     *LC* 77-28249     *ISBN* 0521218721

**Tropical savannas / edited by François Bourlière.**   **5.3556**
Amsterdam; New York: Elsevier Scientific Pub. Co.; New York: Distributors for the U.S. and Canada, Elsevier Science Pub. Co., 1983. xii, 730 p.: ill., maps; 27 cm. — (Ecosystems of the world. 13) Col. map on lining papers. 1. Savanna ecology — Tropics. I. Bourlière, François, 1913- II. Series.
QH541.5.P7 T76 1983     574.5/2643/0913 19     *LC* 81-19415     *ISBN*
0444420355

**Tropical rain forest ecosystems: structure and function / edited**   **5.3557**
**by F.B. Golley.**
Amsterdam; New York: Elsevier Scientific Pub. Co., 1982. xi, 381 p.: ill.; 27 cm. — (Ecosystems of the world. 14A) 1. Rain forest ecology I. Golley, Frank B. II. Series.
QH541.5.R27 T76 1982     574.5/2642 19     *LC* 81-7861     *ISBN*
0444419861

## QH541.5 S–Z

**The Ecology of a salt marsh / edited by L.R. Pomeroy and**   **5.3558**
**R.G. Wiegert.**
New York: Springer-Verlag, c1981. xiv, 271 p.: ill.; 25 cm. (Ecological studies. v. 38) Includes index. 1. Tidemarsh ecology I. Pomeroy, Lawrence R., 1925- II. Wiegert, Richard G. III. Series.
QH541.5.S24 E26     574.5/2636 19     *LC* 80-29676     *ISBN*
0387905553

**Teal, John.**   • **5.3559**
Life and death of the salt marsh, by John and Mildred Teal. Illustrated by Richard G. Fish. — [1st ed.]. — Boston: Little, Brown, [1969] x, 278 p.: illus., map.; 24 cm. 'An Atlantic monthly press book.' 1. Marshes, Tide 2. Marsh ecology I. Teal, Mildred. joint author. II. Fish, Richard G. illus. III. T.
QH541.5.S24 T4     500.9     *LC* 70-86614

**Wet coastal ecosystems / edited by V. J. Chapman.**   **5.3560**
Amsterdam: Elsevier Scientific Pub. Co.; New York: distributors for the United States and Canada, Elsevier/North Holland, 1977. xi, 428 p.: ill.; 27 cm. (Ecosystems of the world. 1) 1. Tidemarsh ecology 2. Coastal ecology I. Chapman, V. J. (Valentine Jackson), 1910- II. Series.
QH541.5.S24 W47     574.5/26     *LC* 77-342     *ISBN* 0444415602

**The Ecology of the seas / edited by D. H. Cushing and J. J.**   **5.3561**
**Walsh.**
Philadelphia: W. B. Saunders Co., c1976. x, 467 p.: ill.; 25 cm. Includes indexes. 1. Marine ecology I. Cushing, D. H. II. Walsh, John Joseph, 1942-
QH541.5.S3 E25     574.5/2636     *LC* 76-9641     *ISBN* 0721628125

**Kinne, Otto.**   **5.3562**
Marine ecology: a comprehensive, integrated treatise on life in oceans and coastal waters / editor Otto Kinne. — London; New York: Wiley-Interscience, 1970-1984. 5 v. in 13: ill., charts, maps; 26 cm. Vol. 5 published: Chichester [West Sussex]; New York: Wiley. 'A Wiley-Interscience publication'—V. 5. 1. Marine ecology — Collected works. I. T.
QH541.5.S3 K5     574.5/2636     *LC* 79-121779     *ISBN* 0471480010

**Upwelling ecosystems / edited by R. Boje and M. Tomczak;**   **5.3563**
**contributors, R. T. Barber ... [et al.].**
Berlin; New York: Springer-Verlag, 1978. x, 303 p.: ill.; 24 cm. 1. Marine ecology 2. Upwelling (Oceanography) I. Boje, R., 1934- II. Tomczak, M., 1941-
QH541.5.S3 U57     574.5/2636     *LC* 78-15685     *ISBN* 0387088229

**Eltringham, S. K. (Stewart Keith)**   **5.3564**
Life in mud and sand [by] S. K. Eltringham. New York, Crane, Russak [c1971] vi, 218 p. illus. 22 cm. 1. Seashore ecology I. T.
QH541.5.S35 E45 1971b     574.909/4/6     *LC* 72-79457     *ISBN*
0844800074

**Mediterranean–type shrublands / edited by Francesco di Castri,**   **5.3565**
**David W. Goodall, and Raymond Specht.**
Amsterdam; New York: Elsevier Scientific Pub. Co.: distributors for the United States and Canada, Elsevier North-Holland, 1981. xii, 643 p.: ill.; 27 cm. (Ecosystems of the world. 11) 1. Shrubland ecology 2. Mediterranean climate I. Di Castri, Francesco. II. Goodall, David W., 1914- III. Specht, R. L. (Raymond Louis), 1924- IV. Series.
QH541.5.S55 M42     574.5/264     *LC* 80-15879     *ISBN* 044441858X

**Hynes, Hugh Bernard Noel, 1917-.**   **5.3566**
The ecology of running waters / [by] H. B. N. Hynes. — [Toronto]: University of Toronto Press, 1970. xxiv, 555 p.: ill.; 25 cm. 1. Stream ecology 2. Limnology 3. Freshwater biology I. T.
QH541.5.S7 H9     574.5/2632     *LC* 79-156298     *ISBN* 0802016898

**International Symposium on Regulated Streams. 1st, Erie, Pa.,**   **5.3567**
**1979.**
The ecology of regulated streams: [proceedings of the first International Symposium on Regulated Streams held in Erie, Pa., April 18–20, 1979] / edited by James V. Ward and Jack A. Stanford. — New York: Plenum Press, c1979. xi, 398 p.: ill.; 26 cm. Errata slip inserted. 1. Stream ecology — Congresses. 2. Rivers — Regulation — Environmental aspects — Congresses. I. Ward, James V. II. Stanford, Jack Arthur, 1947- III. T.
QH541.5.S7 I57 1979     574.5/2632     *LC* 79-21632     *ISBN*
030640317X

**Perspectives in running water ecology / edited by Maurice A.**   **5.3568**
**Lock and D. Dudley Williams.**
New York: Plenum Press, c1981. x, 430 p.: ill.; 26 cm. 1. Stream ecology I. Lock, M. A. II. Williams, D. Dudley.
QH541.5.S7 P47     574.5/26323 19     *LC* 81-17838     *ISBN*
0306408988

**Whitton, B. A.**   **5.3569**
River ecology / edited by B.A. Whitton. — Berkeley: University of California Press, 1975. x, 725 p.: ill. — (Studies in ecology (University of California Press) 2) 1. Stream ecology I. T. II. Series.
QH541.5S7 W45     *LC* 75-10884     *ISBN* 0520030168

**Tundra ecosystems: a comparative analysis / edited by L. C.**   **5.3570**
**Bliss, O. W. Heal, J. J. Moore.**
Cambridge [Eng.]; New York: Cambridge University Press, 1981. xxxvi, 813 p.: ill.; 24 cm. (International Biological Programme; 25) 1. Tundra ecology I. Bliss, L. C. (Lawrence C.) II. Heal, O. W. III. Moore, J. J. (John J.) IV. International Biological Programme. V. Series.
QH541.5.T8 T86     574.5/2644     *LC* 79-41580     *ISBN* 0521227763

# QH543–549 Bioclimatology. Environmental Influence. Adaptation

**Lowry, William P., 1927-.**   • **5.3571**
Weather and life; an introduction to biometeorology [by] William P. Lowry. — New York: Academic Press, [1969] xiii, 305 p.: illus.; 21 cm. 1. Bioclimatology I. T.
QH543.L69     574.1/91     *LC* 69-18334

**Mediterranean type ecosystems: origin and structure / edited by**   **5.3572**
**Francesco di Castri and Harold A. Mooney.**
Berlin; New York: Springer-Verlag, 1973. xii, 405 p.: ill.; 25 cm. — (Ecological studies. v. 7) 1. Bioclimatology 2. Mediterranean climate I. Di Castri, Francesco. ed. II. Mooney, Harold A. ed. III. Series.
QH543.M46     574.5/42     *LC* 72-95688     *ISBN* 0387061061

**Hazard assessment of chemicals: current developments / edited**   **5.3573**
**by Jitendra Saxena, Farley Fisher.**
Vol. 1-  . — New York: Academic Press, 1981-. v.: ill.; 24 cm. Annual. 1. Pollution — Environmental aspects — Periodicals. 2. Environmental impact analysis — Periodicals.
QH545.A1 H38     363.7/384     *LC* 82-640828

**Tinsley, Ian J., 1929-.**   **5.3574**
Chemical concepts in pollutant behavior / Ian J. Tinsley. — New York: Wiley, c1979. xiv, 265 p.: ill.; 24 cm. (Environmental science and technology) 'A Wiley-Interscience publication.' 1. Agricultural chemicals — Environmental aspects. 2. Pollution — Environmental aspects I. T.
QH545.A25 T56     551.9     *LC* 78-24301     *ISBN* 0471038253

**Environmental effects of off–road vehicles: impacts and**   **5.3575**
**management in arid regions / edited by Robert H. Webb,**
**Howard G. Wilshire.**
New York: Springer-Verlag, c1983. xxi, 534 p.: ill.; 24 cm. (Springer series on environmental management.) 1. All terrain vehicles — Environmental aspects. 2. Arid regions ecology I. Webb, Robert H. II. Wilshire, Howard Gordon, 1926- III. Series.
QH545.A43 E58 1983     574.5/222 19     *LC* 82-10479     *ISBN*
0387907378

**Gates, David Murray, 1921-.**							**5.3576**
Energy and ecology / David M. Gates. — Sunderland, Mass.: Sinauer Associates, 1985. xii, 377 p.: ill.; 25 cm. Includes index. 1. Energy industries — Environmental aspects. 2. Power resources I. T.
QH545.E53 G38 1985			333.79 19			LC 84-27471			ISBN 0878932305

**The Ecology of natural disturbance and patch dynamics / edited**			**5.3577**
**by S.T.A. Pickett, P.S. White.**
Orlando, Fla.: Academic Press, 1985. xiv, 472 p.: ill.; 24 cm. Includes index. 1. Natural disasters — Environmental aspects. 2. Biotic communities I. Pickett, S. T. A. II. White, P. S. III. Title: Patch dynamics.
QH545.N3 E28 1985			574.5/22 19			LC 84-18599			ISBN 0125545207

**Conference on the Long-Term Worldwide Biological**			**5.3578**
**Consequences of Nuclear War (1983: Washington, D.C.)**
The cold and the dark: the world after nuclear war: the Conference on the Long–Term Worldwide Biological Consequences of Nuclear War / Paul R. Ehrlich ... [et al.]; foreword by Lewis Thomas. — 1st ed. — New York: Norton, c1984. xxxv, 229 p., [4] p. of plates: ill. (some col.); 22 cm. Conference held Oct. 31-Nov. 1, 1983 at the Sheraton Washington Hotel in Washington, D.C. 1. Nuclear warfare — Environmental aspects — Congresses. I. Ehrlich, Paul R. II. T.
QH545.N83 C66 1983			574.5 19			LC 84-6070			ISBN 0393018709

**Dunlap, Thomas R., 1943-.**							**5.3579**
DDT: scientists, citizens, and public policy / Thomas R. Dunlap. — Princeton, N.J.: Princeton University Press, c1981. 318 p.; 22 cm. Includes index. 1. DDT (Insecticide) — Environmental aspects — United States — History. 2. Pesticides policy — United States — History. I. T.
QH545.P4 D86			363.7/384 19			LC 80-8546			ISBN 0691046808

**Herbicides in war: the long–term ecological and human**			**5.3580**
**consequences / edited by Arthur H. Westing; [prepared by]**
**Stockholm International Peace Research Institute.**
London; Philadelphia: Taylor & Francis, 1984. xiv, 210 p.: ill.; 24 cm. Work contains selected papers that were presented at the International Symposium on Herbicides and Defoliants in War that was held in Ho Chi Minh City, Jan. 13-20, 1983. Includes index. 1. Herbicides — Environmental aspects — Addresses, essays, lectures. 2. Herbicides — Environmental aspects — Vietnam — Addresses, essays, lectures. 3. Herbicides — Toxicology — Addresses, essays, lectures. 4. Herbicides — Toxicology — Vietnam — Addresses, essays, lectures. 5. Herbicides — War use — Addresses, essays, lectures. 6. Herbicides — Vietnam — War use — Addresses, essays, lectures. I. Westing, Arthur H. II. Stockholm International Peace Research Institute. III. International Symposium on Herbicides and Defoliants in War (1983: Ho Chi Minh City, Vietnam)
QH545.P4 H47 1984			574.5/2642/09597 19			LC 84-2468			ISBN 0850662656

**Portmann, Adolf, 1897-.**							• **5.3581**
[Tarnung im Tierreich. English] Animal camouflage. [Translated by A. J. Pomerans] Ann Arbor, University of Michigan Press [1959] 111 p. illus. 22 cm. (Ann Arbor science library) 1. Camouflage (Biology) I. T.
QH546.P653			591.57			LC 59-5066

**Wickler, Wolfgang.**							• **5.3582**
Mimicry in plants and animals / Translated from the German by R. D. Martin. — New York: McGraw-Hill, [1968] 253 p.: ill. (part col.); 20 cm. — (World university library) 1. Mimicry (Biology) I. T.
QH546.W513 1968b			574.5/7			LC 67-26359

**Pontin, A. J.**							**5.3583**
Competition and coexistence of species / A.J. Pontin. — Boston: Pitman Advanced Pub. Program, c1982. vii, 102 p.: ill.; 24 cm. 1. Competition (Biology) I. T. II. Title: Coexistence of species.
QH546.3.P66 1982			574.5 19			LC 81-1654			ISBN 0273084895

**The Biology of mutualism: ecology and evolution / edited by**			**5.3584**
**Douglas H. Boucher.**
New York: Oxford University Press, 1985. x, 388 p.: ill.; 23 cm. 1. Mutualism (Biology) 2. Evolution I. Boucher, Douglas H.
QH548.3.B56 1985			574.5/2482 19			LC 85-7264			ISBN 0195204832

# QH573–671 THE CELL. CYTOLOGY

## QH573–581 General Works, Through 1969

**Allen, John M. (John Morgan), 1924- ed.**			• **5.3585**
The nature of biological diversity. New York, McGraw-Hill [1963] vii, 304 p. illus. 24 cm. (University of Michigan. Institute of Science and Technology. Series [of lectures] 1961) 1. Cytology — Addresses, essays, lectures. 2. Histochemistry — Addresses, essays, lectures. 3. Morphology (Animals) I. T.
QH573.A42			574.87082			LC 62-20182

**Bonner, David M. ed.**			• **5.3586**
Control mechanisms in cellular processes [by] Sigmund R. Suskind [and others]. New York, Ronald Press [1961] v, 248 p. illus., diagrs. 24 cm. 'The Society of General Physiologists: seventh annual symposium, the Marine Biological Laboratory, Woods Hole, Massachusetts, September, 1960.' 1. Cytology — Collected works. 2. Biochemistry — Collected works. I. Suskind, Sigmund R. II. Society of General Physiologists. III. T.
QH573.B59			574.87082			LC 61-18434

**Bourne, Geoffrey H. (Geoffrey Howard), 1909- ed.**			• **5.3587**
Cytology and cell physiology, edited by Geoffrey H. Bourne. Contributors: R. Barer [and others] 3d ed. New York, Academic Press, 1964. xvii, 780 p. illus. 24 cm. 1. Cytology 2. Cell physiology I. T.
QH573.B6 1964			574.87			LC 64-15267

**Mazia, Daniel, 1912- ed.**			**5.3588**
General physiology of cell specialization [by] Daniel Mazia [and] Albert Tyler. New York, McGraw-Hill [c1963] xiv, 434 p. illus. (part col.) 24 cm. (McGraw-Hill publications in the biological sciences. Series in organism biology.) Papers from a symposium held at Oregon State University, Corvallis, Aug. 26-29, 1962 and sponsored by the Society of General Physiologists and others. 1. Cell physiology — Addresses, essays, lectures. I. Tyler, Albert, 1906- joint ed. II. Society of General Physiologists. III. Oregon State University. IV. T. V. Series.
QH573.M3			574.87082			LC 63-15026

**Brachet, J. (Jean), 1909- ed.**			• **5.3589**
The cell: biochemistry, physiology, morphology. Edited by Jean Brachet [and] Alfred E. Mirsky. New York, Academic Press, 1959-64. 6 v. illus. 24 cm. 1. Cytology I. Mirsky, Alfred E. joint ed. II. T.
QH581.B72			574.87082			LC 59-7677

**Fawcett, Don Wayne, 1917-.**			• **5.3590**
An atlas of fine structure: the cell, its organelles, and inclusions [by] Don W. Fawcett. Philadelphia, W. B. Saunders Co., 1966. vii, 448 p. illus. 27 cm. Second ed. published in 1981 under title: The cell. 1. Cytology — Atlases. I. T. II. Title: The cell, its organelles and inclusions.
QH581.F3			591.8			LC 66-10500

**Jensen, William A.**			• **5.3591**
Cell ultrastructure [by] William A. Jensen [and] Roderic B. Park. — Belmont, Calif.: Wadsworth Pub. Co., [1967] iv, 60 p.: illus.; 31 cm. 1. Cells I. Park, Roderic B., joint author. II. T.
QH581.J4			574.8/72			LC 67-21430

**Swanson, Carl P.**			• **5.3592**
Cytology and cytogenetics. Englewood Cliffs, N.J., Prentice-Hall, 1957. 596 p. illus. 24 cm. 1. Cytology 2. Cytogenetics I. T.
QH581.S9			576.3 574.8*			LC 57-9976

**Willmer, E. N. (Edward Nevill)**			• **5.3593**
Cytology and evolution [by] E. N. Willmer. 2d ed. New York, Academic Press, 1970. x, 649 p. illus. (part col.) 24 cm. 1. Cytology 2. Evolution I. T.
QH581.W74 1970			591.8			LC 68-26637

**Wilson, Edmund B. (Edmund Beecher), 1856-1939.**			**5.3594**
The cell in development and inheritance. — 3rd ed., rev. and enl. — New York, Macmillan, 1925. 1232 p.: ill. 1. Cells I. T.
QH581.W75 1925

## QH581.2 1970–

**Altman, Philip L.**                                                                 **5.3595**
Cell biology / compiled and edited by Philip L. Altman and Dorothy Dittmer
Katz. — Bethesda, Md.: Federation of American Societies for Experimental
Biology, c1976. xix, 454 p.; 27 cm. — (Biological handbooks. 1) Chiefly tables.
1. Cytology — Handbooks, manuals, etc. 2. Cytology — Tables. I. Katz,
Dorothy Dittmer. II. Federation of American Societies for Experimental
Biology. III. T. IV. Series.
QH581.2.C42       574.8/7       *LC* 77-361036       *ISBN* 0913822108

**The Cell in medical science / edited by F. Beck and J. B.**              **5.3596**
**Lloyd.**
London; New York: Academic Press, 1975 (c1974) 2 v.: ill.; 24 cm. 1. Cytology
2. Pathology, Cellular I. Beck, F. (Felix) II. Lloyd, John Benjamin.
QH581.2.C44       611/.0181/08       *LC* 78-172366       *ISBN* 0120842017

**Darnell, James E.**                                                              **5.3597**
Molecular cell biology / James Darnell, Harvey Lodish, David Baltimore. —
New York: Scientific American Books: Distributed by W.H. Freeman, c1986.
xxxv, 1187 p.: ill. (some col.); 29 cm. 1. Cytology 2. Molecular biology
I. Lodish, Harvey F. II. Baltimore, David. III. T.
QH581.2.D37 1986       574.87/6042 19       *LC* 86-1881       *ISBN*
0716714485

**De Duve, Christian.**                                                            **5.3598**
A guided tour of the living cell / Christian de Duve; illustrated by Neil O.
Hardy. — New York: Scientific American Library: Distributed by W.H.
Freeman Co., c1984. 2 v. (xii, 423 p.): ill. (some col.); 24 cm. Spine title: The
living cell. 'This book is published in collaboration with the Rockefeller
University Press.' Errata slip inserted, v. 2. Includes indexes. 1. Cells I. Hardy,
Neil O. II. T. III. Title: Living cell.
QH581.2.D43 1984       574.87 19       *LC* 84-5534       *ISBN* 0716750023

**Dyson, Robert D.**                                                               **5.3599**
Cell biology: a molecular approach / Robert D. Dyson. — 2d ed. — Boston:
Allyn and Bacon, c1978. xviii, 616 p.: ill.; 24 cm. 1. Cytology I. T.
QH581.2.D95 1978       574.8/7       *LC* 77-17813       *ISBN* 0205059422

**Novikoff, Alex Benjamin, 1913-1987.**                                   **5.3600**
Cells and organelles / Eric Holtzman, Alex B. Novikoff. — 3rd ed. —
Philadelphia: Saunders College Pub., c1984. ix, 660, xlix p.: ill.; 24 cm. Rev. ed.
of: Cells and organelles / Alex B. Novikoff, Eric Holtzman. 2nd ed. c1976.
Cover title: Cells & organelles. 1. Cytology 2. Cell organelles I. Holtzman,
Eric, 1939- II. T. III. Title: Cells & organelles.
QH581.2.H64 1984       574.8/7 19       *LC* 83-7583       *ISBN* 0030494613

**Molecular biology of the cell / Bruce Alberts ... [et al.].**              **5.3601**
New York: Garland Pub., c1983. xxxix, 1146, 35 p.: ill. (some col.); 29 cm.
1. Cytology 2. Molecular biology I. Alberts, Bruce.
QH581.2.M64 1983       574.87 19       *LC* 82-15692       *ISBN* 0824072820

**De Robertis, Eduardo D. P., 1913-.**                                        **5.3602**
Cell and molecular biology / E.D.P. De Robertis, E.M.F. De Robertis, Jr. —
8th ed. — Philadelphia: Lea & Febiger, 1987. xxix, 734 p.: ill. (some col.); 27
cm. 1. Cytology 2. Molecular biology I. De Robertis, E. M. F. II. T.
QH581.2.R613 1987       574.87 19       *LC* 86-123       *ISBN* 0812110129

**Swanson, Carl P.**                                                               **5.3603**
The cell / Carl P. Swanson, Peter L. Webster. — 5th ed. — Englewood Cliffs,
N.J.: Prentice-Hall, c1985. x, 374 p.: ill.; 25 cm. Includes index. 1. Cytology
I. Webster, Peter L., 1940- II. T.
QH581.2.S89 1985       574.87 19       *LC* 84-17812       *ISBN* 013121781X

**White, M. J. D. (Michael James Denham), 1910-.**                      **5.3604**
Animal cytology and evolution [by] M. J. D. White. 3d ed. Cambridge, [Eng.]
University Press, 1973. viii, 961 p. illus. 24 cm. 1. Cytology 2. Evolution I. T.
QH581.2.W45 1973       591.8/7       *LC* 79-190418       *ISBN* 0521070716

**Wolfe, Stephen L.**                                                              **5.3605**
Biology of the cell / Stephen L. Wolfe. — 2d ed. — Belmont, Calif.: Wadsworth
Pub. Co., c1981. ix, 544 p.: ill.; 26 cm. Includes index. 1. Cytology I. T.
QH581.2.W64 1981       574.87 19       *LC* 80-26301       *ISBN* 053400900X

**Wolfe, Stephen L.**                                                              **5.3606**
Introduction to cell biology / Stephen L. Wolfe. — Belmont, Calif.: Wadsworth
Pub. Co., c1983. vii, 408 p.: ill.; 27 cm. 1. Cytology I. T.
QH581.2.W645 1983       574.87 19       *LC* 82-13594       *ISBN* 0534012701

## QH600–608 Chromosomes. Cell Membranes. Cell Division. Cell Differentiation

**DuPraw, Ernest J., 1931-.**                                                   **5.3607**
DNA and chromosomes / [by] E. J. DuPraw. — New York: Holt, Rinehart and
Winston, [1970] xi, 340 p.: ill.; 23 cm. — (Holt, Rinehart and Winston
molecular and cellular biology series) 1. Chromosomes 2. DNA I. T.
QH600.D8       574.8/732       *LC* 78-132096       *ISBN* 030841313(pbk)

**White, M. J. D. (Michael James Denham), 1910-.**                      **5.3608**
The chromosomes [by] M. J. D. White. 6th ed. London, Chapman and Hall,
distributed by Halsted Press, New York [1973] 214 p. illus. 23 cm.
1. Chromosomes I. T.
QH600.W46 1973       574.8/732       *LC* 73-7337       *ISBN* 0412119307

**Finean, J. B.**                                                                  **5.3609**
Membranes and their cellular functions / J.B. Finean, R. Coleman, and R.H.
Michell; illustrations by T.A. Bramley. — 3rd ed. — Oxford [Oxfordshire];
Boston: Blackwell Scientific Publications, 1984. vii, 227 p.: ill.; 24 cm. 1. Cell
membranes I. Coleman, R. (Roger), 1938- II. Michell, R. H. III. T.
QH601.F56 1984       574.87/5 19       *LC* 85-204172       *ISBN* 0632012048

**Quinn, Peter J.**                                                                **5.3610**
The molecular biology of cell membranes / Peter J. Quinn. — Baltimore:
University Park Press, 1976. x, 229 p.: ill.; 24 cm. 1. Cell membranes
2. Molecular biology I. T.
QH601.Q56 1976       574.8/75       *LC* 76-5817       *ISBN* 0839609296

**Robertson, R. N.**                                                               **5.3611**
The lively membranes / R.N. Robertson. — Cambridge; New York: Cambridge
University Press, 1983. ix, 206 p.: ill.; 24 cm. 1. Membranes (Biology) I. T.
QH601.R58 1983       574.87/5 19       *LC* 82-22011       *ISBN* 0521237475

**Lehninger, Albert L.**                                                        • **5.3612**
The mitochondrion; molecular basis of structure and function [by] Albert L.
Lehninger. — New York: W. A. Benjamin, 1964. xx, 263 p.: illus.; 24 cm.
1. Mitochondria I. T.
QH603.M5 L4       574.8764       *LC* 64-13923

**Tzagoloff, Alexander, 1937-.**                                              **5.3613**
Mitochondria / Alexander Tzagoloff. — New York: Plenum Press, c1982. xiv,
342 p.: ill.; 26 cm. — (Cellular organelles.) 1. Mitochondria I. T. II. Series.
QH603.M5 T94 1982       574.87/342 19       *LC* 81-23373       *ISBN*
030640799X

**Baserga, Renato.**                                                              **5.3614**
The biology of cell reproduction / Renato Baserga. — Cambridge, Mass.:
Harvard University Press, 1985. xi, 251 p.: ill.; 24 cm. Includes index. 1. Cell
proliferation 2. Cell cycle I. T.
QH605.B327 1985       574.87/62 19       *LC* 84-12902       *ISBN* 0674074068

**Makino, Sajirō, 1906-.**                                                     • **5.3615**
An atlas of the chromosome numbers in animals. — 2d ed. (1st American ed.)
rev. and enl. from the original Tokyo ed. — Ames: Iowa State College Press,
[1951] xxviii, 290 p.; 24 cm. 1. Chromosome numbers 2. Zoology I. T.
QH605.M334 1951       576.3323       *LC* 51-1602

**Prescott, David M., 1926-.**                                               **5.3616**
Reproduction of eukaryotic cells / David M. Prescott. — New York: Academic
Press, 1976. ix, 177 p.: ill.; 24 cm. Includes index. 1. Cell cycle 2. Cell
proliferation I. T.
QH605.P7       574.8/762       *LC* 75-36654       *ISBN* 0125641508

**Maclean, Norman, 1932-.**                                                  **5.3617**
The differentiation of cells / Norman Maclean. — Baltimore: University Park
Press, 1977. viii, 216 p.: ill.; 22 cm. — (Genetics, principles and perspectives; 1)
Includes index. 1. Cell differentiation I. T. II. Series.
QH607.M3 1977       574.8/761       *LC* 77-16202       *ISBN* 0839111940

**Truman, D. E. S. (Donald Ernest Samuel), 1936-.**                    **5.3618**
The biochemistry of cytodifferentiation / by D. E. S. Truman. — New York:
Wiley, [1974] vi, 122 p.: ill.; 24 cm. 'A Halsted Press book.' 1. Cell
differentiation 2. Biochemistry I. T.
QH607.T78       574.8/761       *LC* 73-21785       *ISBN* 0470891904

## QH611–647 Physical, Chemical, and Physiological Properties

**Glick, David, 1908-.**     • **5.3619**
Quantitative chemical techniques of histo– and cytochemistry. With a foreword by Heinz Holter. New York, Interscience Publishers [1962-63] 2 v. illus. 24 cm. 1. Cytochemistry — Technique 2. Histochemistry — Technique. I. T.
QH611.G55     574.192     *LC* 61-17319

**Jellinck, P. H.**     • **5.3620**
The cellular role of macromolecules [by] P.H. Jellinck. [Glenview, Ill.] Scott, Foresman [1967] 117 p. illus. 23 cm. (Scott, Foresman series in undergraduate biology. v. 2) 1. Macromolecules 2. Molecular biology I. T. II. Series.
QH611.J4     574.8/76     *LC* 67-15478

**Troyer, Henry.**     **5.3621**
Principles and techniques of histochemistry / Henry Troyer. — 1st ed. — Boston: Little, Brown, c1980. xv, 431 p.: ill.; 25 cm. 1. Histochemistry I. T.
QH613.T76     599.08/212 19     *LC* 80-80592     *ISBN* 0316853100

**Giese, Arthur Charles, 1904-.**     **5.3622**
Cell physiology / Arthur C. Giese. — 5th ed. — Philadelphia: Saunders, 1979. xviii, 609, xxxv p.: ill.; 27 cm. 1. Cell physiology I. T.
QH631.G5 1979     574.8/76     *LC* 79-4728     *ISBN* 0721641202

**Ling, Gilbert N., 1919-.**     **5.3623**
In search of the physical basis of life / Gilbert N. Ling. — New York: Plenum Press, c1984. xxx, 791 p.: ill.; 26 cm. Includes index. 1. Cell physiology 2. Life (Biology) I. T.
QH631.L56 1984     574.87 19     *LC* 83-26919     *ISBN* 0306414090

**Molecular organization and cell function / editor, Robert F. Goldberger.**     **5.3624**
New York: Plenum Press, c1980. xvi, 620 p.; 26 cm. — (Biological regulation and development. v. 2) 1. Cell physiology 2. Molecular biology 3. Biological control systems I. Goldberger, Robert F. II. Series.
QH631.M57     574.87/6 19     *LC* 80-19935     *ISBN* 0306404869

**Lackie, J. M.**     **5.3625**
Cell movement and cell behaviour / J.M. Lackie. — London; Boston: Allen & Unwin, 1986. xv, 316 p.: ill.; 24 cm. Includes index. 1. Cells — Motility I. T.
QH647.L33 1986     575.87/64 19     *LC* 85-20041     *ISBN* 0045740356

## QH650–671 Environmental Effects on Cells

**Symposium on Light and Life (1960: Johns Hopkins University)**     • **5.3626**
A Symposium on Light and Life. Edited by William D. McElroy and Bentley Glass. Baltimore, Johns Hopkins Press, 1961. xii, 924 p. illus., diagrs., tables. 24 cm. (Contribution of the McCollum-Pratt Institute. no. 302) 1. Photobiology — Congresses. I. McElroy, William David, 1917- ed. II. Glass, Bentley, 1906- ed. III. T. IV. Title: Light and life. V. Series.
QH651.S9 1960     574.52     *LC* 60-16544

**Coggle, J. E.**     **5.3627**
Biological effects of radiation / J.E. Coggle. — 2nd ed. — New York: International Publications Service, Taylor & Francis, 1983. xii, 247 p.: ill.; 24 cm. Includes index. 1. Radiobiology 2. Radiation — Physiological effect I. T.
QH652.C56 1983     599/.024 19     *LC* 83-80179     *ISBN* 0800230752

**Wallace, Bruce, 1920-.**     **5.3628**
Radiation, genes, and man, by Bruce Wallace and Th. Dobzhansky. — New York: Holt, [1959] 205 p.: illus.; 22 cm. 1. Radiogenetics 2. Genetics — Popular works. I. Dobzhansky, Theodosius Grigorievich, 1900-1975. joint author. II. T.
QH652.W3     575.131     *LC* 59-14275

# QK    Botany

Steele, Arthur Robert.    5.3629
Flowers for the king; the expedition of Ruiz and Pavon and the Flora of Peru. Durham, N.C., Duke University Press, 1964. xv, 378 p. illus., ports., maps, facsims. 24 cm. (Duke historical publications.) 1. Ruiz, Hipólito, 1754-1816. 2. Pavón, José, 1754-1840. 3. Botany — Peru. 4. Botany — Chile. I. T. II. Series.
QK5.S74    580.75    LC 64-11428

## QK9–13 REFERENCE WORKS

Jackson, Benjamin Daydon, 1846-1927.    • 5.3630
A glossary of botanic terms: with their derivation and accent. — 4th ed., rev. and enl. — London: Duckworth [1949] x, 481 p.; 20 cm. 1. Botany — Dictionaries I. T.
QK9.J3 1949    LC 50-558

Little, R. John.    5.3631
A dictionary of botany / R. John Little, C. Eugene Jones; ill. by Raymond B. Smith. — New York: Van Nostrand Reinhold Co., c1980. 400 p.: ill.; 24 cm. 1. Botany — Dictionaries I. Jones, C. Eugene. joint author. II. T.
QK9.L735    581/.03    LC 79-14968    ISBN 0442241690

Stearn, William Thomas, 1911-.    5.3632
Botanical Latin: history, grammar, syntax, terminology, and vocabulary / William T. Stearn. — 3rd ed., rev. — Newton Abbot, Devon; North Pomfret, Vt.: David & Charles, 1983. xiv, 566 p.: ill.; 23 cm. English and Latin. Includes index. 1. Botany — Terminology 2. Latin language I. T.
QK10.S7 1983    581/.014 19    LC 84-129534    ISBN 0715385488

Index kewensis plantarum phanerogamarum nomina et    • 5.3633
synonyma omnium generum et specierum a Linnaeo usque ad annum MDCCCLXXXV complectens nomine recepto auctore patria unicuique plantae subjectis / sumptibus beati Caroli Roberti Darwin ductu et consilio Josephi D. Hooker confecit B. Daydon Jackson.
Oxonii: e prelo Clarendoniano, 1895. 2 v. Added t.p. in English. Vol. 1 issued in 4 parts; v.2 in 2 parts. 1. Botany — Nomenclature. 2. Phanerogams I. Hookers, Joseph Datton, Sir, 1817-1916. II. Jackson, Benjamin Daydon, 1846-1927. III. Royal Botanic Gardens, Kew.
QK11.I4    LC 09-16876

Willis, J. C. (John Christopher), 1868-1958.    5.3634
[Manual and dictionary of the flowering plants and ferns] A dictionary of the flowering plants and ferns. 8th ed. revised by H. K. Airy Shaw. Cambridge [Eng.]: University Press, 1973. xxii, 1245, lxvi p.; 23 cm. First published under title: A manual and dictionary of the flowering plants and ferns. 1. Botany — Nomenclature I. Shaw, Herbert Kenneth Airy. II. T.
QK11.W53 1973    581/.03    LC 72-83581    ISBN 052108699X ISBN 0521097908

## QK15–35 HISTORY. BIOGRAPHY

Arber, Agnes Robertson, 1879-1960.    • 5.3635
Herbals, their origin and evolution; a chapter in the history of botany, 1470–1670. 2d ed. rewritten and enl. Darien, Hafner, 1970. xxiv, 325 p. 157 illus., facsims., ports. 22 cm. Facsimile of the 1938 ed. 1. Herbals — Europe — History. 2. Botany — Europe — History. I. T.
QK15.A8 1938a    582.1/2    LC 70-125789

Ewan, Joseph Andorfer, 1909-.    • 5.3636
A short history of botany in the United States / edited by Joseph Ewan; with contributions by Chester A. Arnold [and others]. — New York: Hafner Pub. Co., 1969. ix, 174 p.; 24 cm. 1. Botany — U.S. — History. I. Arnold, Chester Arthur, 1901- II. T. III. Title: Botany in the United States.
QK21.U5 E9    581/.0973    LC 74-75143

Berkeley, Edmund.    5.3637
The life and travels of John Bartram from Lake Ontario to the River St. John / Edmund Berkeley and Dorothy Smith Berkeley. — Tallahassee: University Presses of Florida, c1982. xv, 376 p.: ill.; 24 cm. 'A Florida State University book.' Includes index. 1. Bartram, John, 1699-1777. 2. Botanists — Pennsylvania — Biography. 3. Botany — United States — History. I. Berkeley, Dorothy Smith. II. T.
QK31.B3 B47    581/.092/4 B 19    LC 81-4083    ISBN 0813007003

Dupree, A. Hunter.    • 5.3638
Asa Gray, 1810–1888. — Cambridge: Belknap Press of Harvard University Press, 1959. x, 505 p.: illus., ports.; 24 cm. 1. Gray, Asa, 1810-1888. I. T.
QK31.G8 D8    925.8    LC 59-12967

Hooker, Joseph Dalton, Sir, 1817-1911.    • 5.3639
Life and letters of Sir Joseph Dalton Hooker, O.M., G.C.S.J.: based on materials collected and arranged by Lady Hooker / by Leonard Huxley. — London: J. Murray, 1918. 2 v.: ill.; 23 cm. Includes index. 1. Botanists — Great Britain — Biography. I. Huxley, Leonard, 1860-1933. II. Hooker, Hyacinth Symonds, Lady. III. T. IV. Title: Life and letters of Sir Joseph Dalton Hooker.
QK31.H66 A4 1918    LC 18-19306

Rodgers, Denny, 1900-.    5.3640
John Torrey, a story of North American botany. Princeton, Princeton Univ. Press, 1942. 352 p. Illustrated title-page. 1. Torrey, John, 1796-1873. 2. Botany — History I. T.
QK31.T7R6

## QK41–100 GENERAL WORKS

Bold, Harold Charles, 1909-.    5.3641
The plant kingdom / Harold C. Bold, John W. La Claire II. — 5th ed. — Englewood Cliffs, N.J.: Prentice-Hall, c1987. x, 309 p.: ill.; 23 cm. Includes index. 1. Botany I. La Claire, John W., 1951- II. T.
QK47.B73 1987    581 19    LC 86-17009    ISBN 0136803989

Raven, Peter H.    5.3642
Biology of plants / Peter H. Raven, Ray F. Evert, Susan E. Eichhorn. — 4th ed. — New York, N.Y.: Worth Publishers, c1986. xvi, 775 p.: ill. (some col.); 29 cm. 1. Botany I. Evert, Ray Franklin. II. Eichhorn, Susan E. III. T.
QK47.R25 1986    580 19    LC 85-51292    ISBN 087901315X

De Laubenfels, David J., 1925-.    5.3643
Mapping the world's vegetation: regionalization of formations and flora / David J. de Laubenfels. — 1st ed. — Syracuse, N.Y.: Syracuse University Press, 1975. xvii, 246 p.: ill.; 25 cm. (Syracuse geographical series; no. 4) Includes index. 1. Vegetation mapping 2. Phytogeography I. T. II. Series.
QK63.D44    581.9    LC 75-25934    ISBN 0815621728

## QK71–89 Botanical Gardens. Herbaria

Prest, John M.    5.3644
The Garden of Eden: the botanic garden and the re–creation of paradise / John Prest. — New Haven: Yale University Press, c1981. 121 p.: ill. (some col.); 27 cm. Includes index. 1. Botanical gardens — Europe — History. I. T.
QK73.E85 P73 1981    712/.5 19    LC 81-11365    ISBN 0300027265

The Biological aspects of rare plant conservation / edited by    5.3645
Hugh Synge.
Chichester [West Sussex]; New York: Wiley, c1981. xxviii, 558 p.: ill.; 24 cm. Proceedings of an international conference held at King's College, Cambridge, July 14-19, 1980, and sponsored by the Linnean Society of London and the Botanical Society of the British Isles. 'A Wiley-Interscience publication.' 1. Rare plants — Congresses. 2. Plant conservation — Congresses. I. Synge, Hugh. II. Linnean Society of London. III. Botanical Society of the British Isles.
QK86.A1 B56    639.9/9 19    LC 80-42067    ISBN 0471280046

**Koopowitz, Harold.**           5.3646
Plant extinction: a global crisis / Harold Koopowitz and Hilary Kaye. — Washington, D.C.: Stone Wall Press; Harrisburg, PA: Distributed by Stackpole Books, c1983. 239 p.: ill.; 24 cm. Includes index. 1. Plants — Extinction 2. Plant conservation 3. Botany, Economic I. Kaye, Hilary. II. T.
QK86.A1 K66 1983     581 19     LC 82-62894     ISBN 0913276448

**Ayensu, Edward S.**           5.3647
Endangered and threatened plants of the United States / Edward S. Ayensu and Robert A. DeFilipps, with the assistance of Sam E. Fowler ... [et al.]. — Washington: Smithsonian Institution, 1978. xv, 403 p.; 29 cm. Ed. of 1975, by the Smithsonian Institution, published under title: Report on endangered and threatened plant species of the United States. 1. Rare plants — United States. 2. Plant conservation — United States. I. DeFilipps, Robert A. joint author. II. Smithsonian Institution. III. Smithsonian Institution. Report on endangered and threatened plant species of the United States. IV. T.
QK86.U6 A93 1978     333.9/5     LC 77-25138     ISBN 0874742226

**Mohlenbrock, Robert H., 1931-.**           5.3648
Where have all the wildflowers gone?: a region–by–region guide to threatened or endangered U.S. wildflowers / Robert H. Mohlenbrock; illustrations by Mark Mohlenbrock. — New York: Macmillan; London: Collier Macmillan, c1983. xiv, 239 p., [8] p. of plates: ill.; 22 cm. Includes index. 1. Rare plants — United States. 2. Wild flowers — United States. 3. Endangered species — United States. I. T.
QK86.U6 M63 1983     581 19     LC 82-23411     ISBN 002585450X

# QK91–100 Classification

**Benson, Lyman David, 1909-.**          • 5.3649
Plant taxonomy: methods and principles. — New York: Ronald Press Co., [1962] 494 p.: illus.; 24 cm. — (A Chronica botanica publication) 1. Botany — Classification I. T.
QK95.B44     580.12     LC 62-11646

**Harborne, J. B. (Jeffrey B.)**           5.3650
Plant chemosystematics / J.B. Harborne and B.L. Turner. — London: Academic Press, 1984. x, 562 p.: ill.; 24 cm. Includes indexes. 1. Botany — Classification 2. Biochemistry I. Turner, B. L. (Billie Lee), 1925- II. T.
QK95.H3x     581/.012 19     ISBN 0123246407

**Jeffrey, Charles.**           5.3651
An introduction to plant taxonomy / C. Jeffrey. — 2nd ed. — Cambridge [Cambridgeshire]; New York: Cambridge University Press, 1982. vii, 154 p.: ill.; 23 cm. Includes index. 1. Botany — Classification I. T.
QK95.J43 1982     581/.012 19     LC 81-17090     ISBN 0521245427

**Jones, Samuel B., 1933-.**           5.3652
Plant systematics / Samuel B. Jones, Jr., Arlene E. Luchsinger. — 2nd ed. — New York: McGraw-Hill, c1986. xiii, 512 p.: ill.; 25 cm. Includes indexes. 1. Botany — Classification I. Luchsinger, Arlene E. II. T.
QK95.J63 1986     581/.01/2 19     LC 85-23048     ISBN 0070327963

**Plant biosystematics / edited by William F. Grant.**      5.3653
Toronto; New York: Academic Press, 1984. xv, 674 p.: ill.; 24 cm. Proceedings of a symposium sponsored by the International Organization of Plant Biosystematists and held at McGill University in July 1983. 1. Botany — Classification — Congresses. I. Grant, William F. II. International Organization of Plant Biosystematists.
QK95.P545 1984     580/.12 19     LC 84-6490     ISBN 012295680X

**International Botanical Congress. (13th: 1981: Sydney, N.S.W.)**     5.3654
International code of botanical nomenclature = Code international de la nomenclature botanique = Internationaler Code der botanischen Nomenklatur / adopted by the Thirteenth International Botanical Congress, Sydney, August 1981; prepared and edited by E.G. Voss ... [et al.]. — Utrecht: Bohn, Scheltema & Holkema; Boston: W. Junk, 1983. xv, 472 p.; 25 cm. — (Regnum vegetabile. v. 111) Includes indexes. 1. Botany — Nomenclature — Congresses. I. Voss, Edward G. (Edward Groesbeck), 1929- II. T. III. Title: Code international de la nomenclature botanique. IV. Title: Internationaler Code der botanischen Nomenklatur. V. Series.
QK96.R4 vol. 111     581/.012 s 581/.012 19     LC 83-12277     ISBN 9031305723

**Benson, Lyman David, 1909-.**           5.3655
Plant classification / Lyman Benson; principal plant dissections and ill. by Jerome D. Laudermilk. — 2d ed. — Lexington, Mass.: Heath, c1979. xxiii, 901 p.: ill.; 24 cm. 1. Botany — Classification I. T.
QK97.B45 1979     581/.01/2     LC 78-61856     ISBN 0669014893

**Hutchinson, J. (John), 1884-1972.**           5.3656
The families of flowering plants: arranged according to a new system based on their probable phylogeny / by J. Hutchinson. — 3d ed. — Oxford: Clarendon Press, 1973. –. xviii, 968 p.: ill.; 24 cm. — 1. Botany — Classification 2. Angiosperms I. T.
QK97.H82 1973     582/.13/012     LC 74-155307     ISBN 0198543778

**Sturtevant, E. Lewis (Edward Lewis), 1842-1898.**      5.3657
Sturtevant's edible plants of the world / edited by U. P. Hedrick. — New York: Dover Publications [1972] vii, 686 p.: port.; 24 cm. Reprint of the 1919 ed. published by J. B. Lyon Co., Albany, for the State of New York, as the Dept. of Agriculture's 27th Annual report, v. 2, pt. 2 (Report of the New York Agricultural Experiment Station for 1919), under title: Sturtevant's notes on edible plants. 1. Sturtevant, E. Lewis (Edward Lewis), 1842-1898. 2. Plants, Edible I. T.
QK98.5.A1 S78 1972     581.6/32     LC 76-184690     ISBN 0486204596

**Nicholson, Barbara.**          • 5.3658
The Oxford book of food plants; illustrations by B. E. Nicholson, text by S. G. Harrison, G. B. Masefield [and] Michael Wallis. London, Oxford U.P., 1969. viii, 206 p. illus. (chiefly col). 25 cm. 1. Plants, Edible 2. Vegetables 3. Fruit 4. Plants, Cultivated I. Harrison, Sydney Gerald. II. Masefield, G. B. (Geoffrey Bussell) III. Wallis, Michael. IV. T.
QK98.5.N5     581.6/32     LC 71-458825     ISBN 0199100063

**Peterson, Lee.**           5.3659
A field guide to edible wild plants of Eastern and Central North America / by Lee Peterson; line drawings by Lee Peterson and Roger Tory Peterson; photos. by Lee Peterson. — Boston: Houghton Mifflin, 1978, c1977. xiii, 330 p., 15 leaves of plates: ill. (some col.); 19 cm. (The Peterson field guide series; no. 23) Includes index. 1. Wild plants, Edible — United States — Identification. 2. Wild plants, Edible — Canada — Identification. I. Peterson, Roger Tory, 1908- II. T.
QK98.5.U6 P47     581.6/32/0973     LC 77-27323     ISBN 0395204453

**Le Strange, Richard.**           5.3660
A history of herbal plants / Richard le Strange; illustrated by Derek Cork; foreword by Anthony Huxley. — New York: Arco Pub. Co., c1977. xxi, 304 p.: ill.; 24 cm. Includes indexes. 1. Botany, Medical — History. 2. Herbs — Therapeutic use — History. I. T.
QK99.A1 L4 1977     615/.321     LC 77-3360     ISBN 0668042478

**Elliott, Douglas B.**           5.3661
Roots: an underground botany and forager's guide / written and illustrated by Douglas B. Elliott. — Old Greenwich, Conn.: Chatham Press, c1976. 128 p.: ill.; 21 x 23 cm. Includes index. 1. Medicinal plants — North America. 2. Wild plants, Edible — North America — Identification. 3. Roots (Botany) — Identification. 4. Plants — Folklore I. T.
QK99.N67 E44     581.6/3     LC 75-46234     ISBN 0856991325

**Tampion, John.**           5.3662
Dangerous plants / John Tampion. New York: Universe Books, 1977. 176 p.: ill.; 24 cm. Includes indexes. 1. Poisonous plants — Identification. 2. Poisonous plants — Toxicology 3. Allergens I. T.
QK100.A1 T35 1977b     581.6/9     LC 76-55116     ISBN 0876632800

# QK101–474 Geographical Distribution. Plant Geography

**Daubenmire, Rexford F., 1904-.**           5.3663
Plant geography: with special reference to North America / Rexford Daubenmire. — New York: Academic Press, 1978. vi, 338 p.: ill.; 24 cm. — (Physiological ecology) Includes index. 1. Phytogeography 2. Botany — North America. I. T.
QK101.D26     QK101 D26.     581.9     LC 77-75570     ISBN 012204150X

**Eyre, S. R.**          • 5.3664
Vegetation and soils: a world picture / by S. R. Eyre. — 2d ed. — Chicago: Aldine Pub. Co., [1968] xvi, 328 p.: ill., maps; 24 cm. 1. Botany — Ecology 2. Plant-soil relationships 3. Phytogeography I. T.
QK101.E87 1968b     581.5     LC 68-19885

**Good, Ronald, 1896-.**           5.3665
The geography of the flowering plants / by Ronald Good. [4th ed. London]: Longman [1974] xvi, 557 p.: ill.; 24 cm. Label mounted on t.p.: Distributed in the U.S.A. by Longman Inc., New York, N.Y. 1. Phytogeography 2. Botany — Ecology I. T.
QK101.G6 1974     582/.13/09     LC 73-85684     ISBN 0582466113

**Kellman, Martin C.**                                                  **5.3666**
Plant geography / Martin C. Kellman. — 2d ed. — New York: St. Martin's
Press, 1980. xii, 181 p., [4] leaves of plates: ill.; 24 cm. Includes index.
1. Phytogeography 2. Botany — Ecology I. T.
QK101.K44 1980      581.5 19      LC 80-5079      ISBN 0312614616

**Stott, Philip Anthony.**                                              **5.3667**
Historical plant geography: an introduction / Philip Stott. — London; Boston:
Allen & Unwin, 1981. xii, 151 p.: ill.; 24 cm. Includes index.
1. Phytogeography 2. Phytogeography — Methodology. I. T.
QK101.S76      581.9 19      LC 80-41627      ISBN 0045800103

**Fassett, Norman Carter, 1900-.**                                    • **5.3668**
A manual of aquatic plants / With Revision appendix by Eugene C. Ogden. —
[Rev. ed.]. — Madison: University of Wisconsin Press, 1957. 405 p.: ill.; 24 cm.
1. Freshwater flora — United States. I. T. II. Title: Aquatic plants.
QK105.F3 1957      581.92973      LC 57-6593

# QK108–280 The Americas

**Bailey, L. H. (Liberty Hyde), 1858-1954.**                          • **5.3669**
Manual of cultivated plants most commonly grown in the continental United
States and Canada, by L. H. Bailey and the staff of the Bailey Hortorium at
Cornell University. Rev. ed., completely restudied. New York, Macmillan Co.,
1949. 1116 p. illus. 22 cm. 1. Botany — United States. 2. Botany — Canada.
3. Plants, Cultivated I. T.
QK110.B3 1949      581.97      LC 49-9666

**Physiological ecology of North American plant communities /**       **5.3670**
edited by Brian F. Chabot and Harold A. Mooney.
New York: Chapman and Hall, 1985. xiv, 351 p.: ill.; 26 cm. 1. Botany —
North America — Ecology. 2. Plant communities — North America. 3. Plant
physiology I. Chabot, Brian F. II. Mooney, Harold A.
QK110.P49 1985      581.5/097 19      LC 84-9586      ISBN 0412232405

**Rickett, Harold William, 1896-.**                                  • **5.3671**
Wild flowers of the United States / general editor, William C. Steele;
collaborators: Rogers McVaugh [and others. — 1st ed.] New York: McGraw-
Hill [1966-1973] 6 v. in 14 pts.: ill., col. map (on lining papers) col. plates.; 33
cm. 'Publication of the New York Botanical Garden.' 1. Wild flowers —
United States — Pictorial works. I. Steere, William Campbell, 1907- ed.
II. McVaugh, Rogers, 1909- III. New York Botanical Garden. IV. T.
QK115.R5      582.130973      LC 66-17920

**Gleason, Henry A. (Henry Allan), 1882-.**                          • **5.3672**
Manual of vascular plants of Northeastern United States and adjacent Canada
[by] Henry A. Gleason and Arthur Cronquist. Princeton, N.J., Van Nostrand
[1963] li, 810 p. 23 cm. 1. Botany — United States. 2. Botany — Canada.
I. Cronquist, Arthur. II. T. III. Title: Vascular plants of Northeastern United
States and adjacent Canada.
QK117.G49      581.937      LC 63-640

**Gleason, Henry A. (Henry Allan), 1882-.**                          • **5.3673**
The new Britton and Brown illustrated flora of the Northeastern United States
and adjacent Canada / by Henry A. Gleason with the assistance of specialists in
certain groups. — 3d print., slightly rev. — New York: Published for the New
York Botanical Garden by Hafner Pub. Co., 1963, c1952. 3 v. ill. 1. Botany —
Northeastern States. 2. Botany — Canada. I. Britton, Nathaniel Lord,
1859-1934. Illustrated flora of the Northern United States, Canada, and the
British possessions. II. New York Botanical Garden. III. T. IV. Title:
Illustrated flora of the Northeastern United States and adjacent Canada.
QK117.G5 1963      LC 63-16478

**Gray, Asa, 1810-1888.**                                            • **5.3674**
Gray's Manual of botany: a handbook of the flowering plants and ferns of the
central and northeastern United States and adjacent Canada / largely rewritten
and expanded by Merritt Lyndon Fernald; wtih assistance of specialists in some
groups. — 8th (centennial) edition, illustrated. — New York: American Book
Company, 1950. lxiv, 1632 p.: ill.; 24 cm. First edition published in 1848 under
title: A manual of the botany of the northern United States. 1. Botany —
United States I. Fernald, Merritt Lyndon, 1873- II. T. III. Title: Manual of
botany
QK117.G75 1950      LC 50-9007

**Newcomb, Lawrence.**                                               **5.3675**
[Wildflower guide] Newcomb's Wildflower guide: an ingenious new key system
for quick, positive field identification of the wildflowers, flowering shrubs and
vines of Northeastern and North Central North America / Lawrence
Newcomb; illustrated by Gordon Morrison; foreword by Roland C. Clement.
— 1st ed. — Boston: Little, Brown, c1977. xxii, 490 p.: ill.; 21 cm. Includes
index. 1. Wild flowers — Northeastern States — Identification. 2. Shrubs —

Northeastern States — Identification. 3. Climbing plants — Northeastern
States — Identification. I. T. II. Title: Wildflower guide.
QK118.N42      582/.13/0974      LC 77-47      ISBN 0316604410

**Peterson, Roger Tory, 1908-.**                                      **5.3676**
A field guide to wildflowers of Northeastern and North-Central North
America; a visual approach arranged by color, form, and detail, by Roger Tory
Peterson and Margaret McKenny. Illus. by Roger Tory Peterson. Boston,
Houghton Mifflin, 1968. xxviii, 420 p. illus. (part col.) 20 cm. (The Peterson
field guide series, 17) 1. Wild flowers — United States — Pictorial works.
I. McKenny, Margaret. joint author. II. T.
QK118.P5      582.13/097      LC 67-13042

**Analysis of coniferous forest ecosystems in the Western United**    **5.3677**
**States / edited by Robert L. Edmonds.**
Stroudsburg, Pa.: Hutchinson Ross Pub. Co.; [New York]: distributed
worldwide by Academic Press, c1982. xvii, 419 p.: ill.; 24 cm. — (US/IBP
synthesis series; v. 14) Includes index. 1. Forest ecology — West (U.S.)
2. Conifers — West (U.S.) — Ecology. 3. Stream ecology — West (U.S.)
4. Lake ecology — West (U.S.) I. Edmonds, Robert L. II. Series.
QK133.A5 1982      581.5/2642/0978 19      LC 80-26699      ISBN
0879333820

**Cronquist, Arthur.**                                               **5.3678**
Intermountain flora: vascular plants of the intermountain west, U.S.A, vol. 1 /
by Arthur Cronquist and others. — New York: Hafner, for New York
Botanical Garden, 1972. 270 p. illus., maps. I. Holmgren, Arthur H
II. Holmgren, Noel H. III. Reveal, James L. IV. T.
QK141.I58      LC 73-134298

**Abrams, Le Roy, 1874-1956.**                                       • **5.3679**
An illustrated flora of the Pacific States: Washington, Oregon, and California.
Stanford University, Stanford University Press, 1923-[60] 4 v. illus. 28 cm. Vol.
4 by Roxana Stinchfield Ferris. 1. Botany — Pacific States. I. Ferris, Roxana
S. (Roxana Stinchfield), 1895- II. T.
QK143.A3      LC 23-9934

**Mount St. Helens, 1980: botanical consequences of the explosive**   **5.3680**
**eruptions / edited by David E. Bilderback.**
Berkeley: University of California Press, c1987. vii, 360 p.: ill.; 25 cm. Papers
presented at a symposium held in June, 1981 during the 62nd Annual Meeting
of the Pacific Division of the American Association for the Advancement of
Science and sponsored by the Pacific Section of the Botanical Society of
America and the Western Section of the Ecological Society of America.
Includes index. 1. Botany — Washington (State) — Saint Helens, Mount,
Region — Ecology — Congresses. 2. Plant communities — Washington (State)
— Saint Helens, Mount, Region — Congresses. 3. Vegetation dynamics —
Washington (State) — Saint Helens, Mount, Region — Congresses. 4. Saint
Helens, Mount — Eruption, 1980 — Congresses. I. Bilderback, David E.
II. Botanical Society of America. Pacific Section. III. Ecological Society of
America. Western Section. IV. Title: Mount Saint Helens, 1980.
QK192.M68 1987      581.5/222 19      LC 85-24650      ISBN 0520056086

# QK475–495 Spermatophyta

# QK475–493 Trees. Shrubs

**Leathart, Scott.**                                                  **5.3681**
Trees of the world / Scott Leathart. — New York: A & W Pub., 1977. 224 p.:
ill. (chiefly col.), map; 33 cm. Col. ill. on lining papers. Includes index. 1. Trees
I. T.
QK475.L365      582/.16      LC 76-52282      ISBN 0894790005

**The Oxford encyclopedia of trees of the world / consultant**        **5.3682**
**editor, Bayard Hora.**
Oxford; New York: Oxford University Press, 1981. 288 p.: col. ill.; 29 cm.
Includes indexes. 1. Trees I. Hora, Bayard.
QK475.O93      582.16 19      LC 81-129929      ISBN 0192177125

**Zimmermann, Martin Huldrych, 1926-.**                               **5.3683**
Trees: structure and function / [by] Martin H. Zimmermann [and] Claud L.
Brown; with a chapter on irreversible thermodynamics of transport phenomena
by Melvin T. Tyree. — New York: Springer-Verlag, 1971. xii, 336 p.: illus.; 26
cm. 1. Trees — Physiology I. Brown, Claud L., 1925- II. Tyree, Melvin T.
III. T.
QK475.Z54      582.16/01      LC 70-163210      ISBN 0387053670

**Dirr, Michael A.**     **5.3684**
Manual of woody landscape plants: their identification, ornamental characteristics, culture, propagation and uses / Michael A. Dirr. — Rev. [ed]. — Champaign, Ill.: Stipes Pub. Co., 1977, c1975. 536 p.: ill. 1. Woody plants — Identification. 2. Ornamental woody plants — Handbooks, manuals, etc. I. T.
QK477.2.I4 D52 1977     QK477.2I4 D52 1977.     *ISBN* 0875631371

**Elias, Thomas S.**     **5.3685**
The complete trees of North America: field guide and natural history / by Thomas S. Elias; drawings by Ruth T. Brunstetter, Charles Edward Faxon, Mary W. Gill; cartography by Delos D. Rowe Associates. — New York: Outdoor Life/Nature Books: Van Nostrand Reinhold, c1980. xii, 948 p.: ill.; 22 cm. Includes index. 1. Trees — North America — Identification. I. T. II. Title: Trees of North America.
QK481.E38     582.16097 19     *LC* 77-12451     *ISBN* 0442238622

**Little, Elbert Luther.**     **5.3686**
The Audubon Society field guide to North American trees / Elbert L. Little; photos. by Sonja Bullaty and Angelo Lomeo, and others; visual key by Susan Rayfield and Olivia Buehl. — Chanticleer Press ed. — New York: Knopf: distributed by Random House, c1980. 2 v.: ill. (some col.); 20 cm. Includes indexes. 1. Trees — United States — Identification. 2. Trees — Canada — Identification. I. Bullaty, Sonja. II. Lomeo, Angelo. III. National Audubon Society. IV. T.
QK481.L49 1980     582.16097 19     *LC* 79-3474

**Rehder, Alfred, 1863-1949.**     ● **5.3687**
Manual of cultivated trees and shrubs hardy in North America exclusive of the subtropical and warmer temperate regions. — 2d ed. rev. and enl. — New York: Macmillan, 1940. xxix, 996 p.: map (frontis.) 1. Woody plants — North America. I. T.
QK481.R4 1940     *LC* 40-12709

**Sargent, Charles Sprague, 1841-1927.**     ● **5.3688**
Manual of the trees of North America (exclusive of Mexico) With 783 illus. by Charles Edward Faxon and Mary W. Gill. — 2d corr. ed. — New York: Dover Publications, [1961, c1949] 2 v. (xxvi, 910 p.): illus., maps.; 21 cm. 1. Trees — North America. I. Faxon, Charles Edward, 1846-1918. illus. II. Gill, Mary (Wright) illus. III. T.
QK481.S21 1961     582.16097     *LC* 61-65275

**Petrides, George A.**     **5.3689**
A field guide to trees and shrubs: field marks of all trees, shrubs, and woody vines that grow wild in the northeastern and north–central United States and in southeastern and south–central Canada / by George A. Petrides; illus. by George A. Petrides [and] Roger Tory Peterson. — 2d ed. — Boston: Houghton Mifflin, 1972. xxxii, 428 p.: ill. (part col.); 19 cm. — (The Peterson field guide series, 11) 1. Trees — North America — Identification. 2. Shrubs — North America — Identification. 3. Climbing plants — North America — Identification. I. T.
QK482.P43 1972     582/.1609/7     *LC* 76-157132     *ISBN* 0395136512

# QK495 Angiosperms

**Cronquist, Arthur.**     **5.3690**
An integrated system of classification of flowering plants / Arthur Cronquist. — New York: Columbia University Press, 1981. xviii, 1262 p.: ill.; 24 cm. 1. Angiosperms — Classification. I. T.
QK495.A1 C76     582.13/012 19     *LC* 80-39556     *ISBN* 0231038801

**Metcalfe, C. R. (Charles Russell)**     ● **5.3691**
Anatomy of the dicotyledons: leaves, stem, and wood in relation to taxonomy with notes on economic uses / by C. R. Metcalfe and L. Chalk; with the assistance of M. M. Chattaway ... [et al.]. — Oxford: Clarendon Press, 1950. 2 v. (lxiv, 1500 p.): ill.; 25 cm. 1. Dicotyledons 2. Botany — Anatomy I. Chalk, Laurence II. T.
QK495.A12 M48     *LC* a 51-8940

**Cronquist, Arthur.**     ● **5.3692**
The evolution and classification of flowering plants. Boston, Houghton Mifflin [1968] x, 396 p. illus., ports. 24 cm. (Riverside studies in biology) 1. Angiosperms — Evolution. 2. Angiosperms — Classification. 3. Plants — Evolution 4. Botany — Classification I. T.
QK495.A56 C7     582.13     *LC* 68-4883

**Takhtadzhian, A. L. (Armen Leonovich)**     ● **5.3693**
[Proiskhozhdenie pokrytosemennykh rasteniĭ. English] Flowering plants: origin and dispersal / [by] Armen Takhtajan; authorised translation from the Russian by C. Jeffrey. — City of Washington: Smithsonian Institution Press [c1969] x, 310 p.: ill., maps (1 fold.), plates.; 23 cm. Translation of

Proiskhozhdenie pokrytosemennykh rasteniĭ (romanized form) 1. Angiosperms 2. Plants — Evolution I. T.
QK495.A56 T323 1969b     582.13     *LC* 74-7292

**Benson, Lyman David, 1909-.**     **5.3694**
The cacti of the United States and Canada / Lyman Benson; with line drawings by Lucretia Breazeale Hamilton. — Stanford, Calif.: Stanford University Press, 1982. ix, 1044, [48] pages of plates: ill. (some col.); 29 cm. Includes index. 1. Cactus — United States. 2. Cactus — Canada. 3. Botany — United States. 4. Botany — Canada. I. T.
QK495.C11 B354 1982     583/.47/0973 19     *LC* 73-80617     *ISBN* 0804708630

**Dallimore, William.**     ● **5.3695**
A handbook of Coniferae and Ginkgoaceae / by W. Dallimore, A. Bruce Jackson; rev. by S. G. Harrison; with drawings by Miss G. Lister, H. R. W. Herbert. — 4th ed. — New York: St Martin's Press, 1967. xix, 729 p.: ill. 1. Conifers 2. Ginkgo I. Jackson, Albert Bruce, 1876- II. Harrison, Sydney Gerald. III. T.
QK495.C75 D3 1967     *LC* 67-11838

**Hitchcock, A. S. (Albert Spear), 1865-1935.**     **5.3696**
Manual of the grasses of the United States. 2d ed., rev. by Agnes Chase. New York, Dover Publications [1971] 2 v. illus., maps. 24 cm. Reprint of the 1950 ed. 1. Grasses — United States — Identification. I. Chase, Agnes, 1869-1963. II. T.
QK495.G74 H525 1971     584/.9/0973     *LC* 70-142876     *ISBN* 0486227170

**Chamberlain, Charles Joseph, 1863-.**     ● **5.3697**
Gymnosperms: structure and evolution. — New York: Dover Publications, [1966] xi, 484 p.: illus.; 22 cm. 1. Gymnosperms I. T.
QK495.G9 C5 1966     585     *LC* 66-20503

# QK504–635 Cryptogams

**Nonvascular plants: an evolutionary survey / R.F. Scagel ... [et al.].**     **5.3698**
Belmont, Calif.: Wadsworth Pub. Co., c1982. vi, 570 p.: ill.; 25 cm. 'A comprehensive revision and expansion of the nonvascular plant section (including bryophytes) of An evolutionary survey of the plant kingdom'—Pref. 1. Cryptogams 2. Cryptogams — Evolution 3. Plants — Phylogeny I. Scagel, Robert Francis, 1921-
QK505.N66 1982     586 19     *LC* 81-24066     *ISBN* 0534010296

## QK520–532 Ferns

**Sporne, K. R.**     ● **5.3699**
The morphology of pteridophytes: the structure of ferns and allied plants. — 2nd ed. — London: Hutchinson, 1966. 192 p. . ill. (Hutchinson university library. Biological sciences.) 1. Pteridophyta 2. Botany — Morphology I. T. II. Series.
QK521.S68 1966     *LC* 66-71401

**Tryon, Rolla Milton, 1916-.**     **5.3700**
Ferns and allied plants: with special reference to tropical America / Rolla M. Tryon, Alice F. Tryon; habitat photography principally by Walter H. Hodge. — New York: Springer-Verlag, c1982. xii, 857 p.: ill., maps; 28 cm. 1. Ferns — America — Classification. 2. Pteridophyta — America — Classification. 3. Ferns — Tropics — Classification. 4. Pteridophyta — Tropics — Classification. I. Tryon, Alice F. II. Hodge, W. H. (Walter Henricks), 1912- III. T.
QK524.4.T78 1982     587/.097 19     *LC* 82-3248     *ISBN* 038790672X

**Lellinger, David B.**     **5.3701**
A field manual of the ferns & fern–allies of the United States & Canada / David B. Lellinger; with photographs by A. Murray Evans. — Washington, D.C.: Smithsonian Institution Press, c1985. ix, 389 p., [45] p. of plates: ill. (some col.); 27 cm. Includes index. 1. Ferns — United States — Identification. 2. Ferns — Canada — Identification. 3. Pteridophyta — United States — Identification. 4. Pteridophyta — Canada — Identification. I. T. II. Title: Ferns & fern-allies of the United States & Canada. III. Title: Ferns and fern-allies of the United States and Canada.
QK524.5.L45 1985     587 19     *LC* 84-22216     *ISBN* 0874746027

**Cobb, Boughton.**     **5.3702**
A field guide to the ferns and their related families of northeastern and central North America with a section on species also found in the British Isles and western Europe. Illustrated by Laura Louise Foster. — Boston: Houghton

Mifflin, 1956. xviii, 281 p.: illus.; 20 cm. — (The Peterson field guide series, 10) 1. Ferns — North America — Identification. I. T.
QK525.C75　　587.3　　*LC* 55-10024

## QK533–563 Bryophyta. Mosses. Liverworts

**Conard, Henry Shoemaker, 1874-.**　　　　　　　**5.3703**
How to know the mosses and liverworts / Henry S. Conard. — 2d ed., rev. / by Paul L. Redfearn, Jr. — Dubuque, Iowa: W. C. Brown Co., c1979. xi, 302 p.: ill.; 24 cm. — (Pictured key nature series) Includes index. 1. Bryophytes — North America — Identification. 2. Mosses — North America — Identification. 3. Liverworts — North America — Identification. I. Redfearn, Paul L. II. T. III. Title: Mosses and liverworts.
QK533.84.N67 C66 1979　　588/.097　　*LC* 78-52712　　*ISBN* 0697047687

**Richardson, D. H. S. (David H. S.)**　　　　　　**5.3704**
The biology of mosses / by D.H.S. Richardson. — New York: Wiley, 1981. xii, 220 p.: ill.; 24 cm. 'A Halsted Press book.' 1. Mosses I. T.
QK537.R53 1981　　588/.2 19　　*LC* 81-3029　　*ISBN* 0470271906

**Crum, Howard Alvin, 1922-.**　　　　　　　　**5.3705**
Mosses of Eastern North America / Howard A. Crum and Lewis E. Anderson. — New York: Columbia University Press, 1981. 2 v. (1328 p.): ill.; 27 cm. 1. Mosses — United States. 2. Mosses — Canada. I. Anderson, Lewis Edward, 1912- joint author. II. T.
QK541.C78 1981　　588/.2/097　　*LC* 79-24789　　*ISBN* 0231045166

## QK565–580 Algae

**Pringsheim, Ernst Georg, 1881-.**　　　　　　• **5.3706**
Pure cultures of algae, their preparation & maintenance. — New York: Hafner, 1964. xii, 119 p.: illus., port.; 21 cm. 1. Algae — Cultures and culture media I. T.
QK565.P77 1964　　589.3　　*LC* 63-12514

**Fogg, G. E. (Gordon Elliott), 1919-.**　　　　　　**5.3707**
Algal cultures and phytoplankton ecology / G. E. Fogg. — 2d ed. — Madison: University of Wisconsin Press, 1975. xv, 175 p.: ill.; 22 cm. Includes index. 1. Algae — Cultures and culture media 2. Phytoplankton — Ecology. I. T.
QK565.2.F63 1975　　589/.3　　*LC* 74-27308　　*ISBN* 0299067602

**Handbook of phycological methods: physiological and**　　**5.3708**
**biochemical methods / edited by Johan A. Hellebust and J. S.**
**Craigie; sponsored by the Phycological Society of America, Inc.**
Cambridge: Cambridge University Press, 1978. 512 p.: ill.; 24 cm. 1. Algology — Technique. I. Hellebust, Johan A. II. Craigie, J. S. III. Phycological Society of America. IV. Title: Physiological and biochemical methods.
QK 565.2 H23 1978　　*LC* 73-79496　　*ISBN* 0521200490

**Bold, Harold Charles, 1909-.**　　　　　　　　**5.3709**
Introduction to the algae: structure and reproduction / Harold C. Bold, Michael J. Wynne. — 2nd ed. — Englewood Cliffs, N.J.: Prentice-Hall, c1985. xvi, 720 p.: ill.; 25 cm. Includes index. 1. Algology 2. Algae — Anatomy 3. Algae — Reproduction. I. Wynne, Michael James. II. T.
QK566.B64 1985　　589.3 19　　*LC* 84-4696　　*ISBN* 0134777468

**Lee, Robert Edward, 1942-.**　　　　　　　　**5.3710**
Phycology / Robert Edward Lee. — Cambridge; New York: Cambridge University Press, 1980. x, 478 p.: ill.; 24 cm. 1. Algology I. T.
QK566.L44　　589.3　　*LC* 79-25402　　*ISBN* 0521225302

**Chapman, V. J. (Valentine Jackson), 1910-.**　　　　**5.3711**
The algae. [By] V. J. Chapman and D. J. Chapman. [2d ed.] [London] Macmillan, [1973] 497 p. illus., maps. 24 cm. 1. Algology I. Chapman, David J. II. T.
QK 567 C46 1973　　*LC* 73-161503　　*ISBN* 0333142705

**Humm, Harold Judson.**　　　　　　　　　　**5.3712**
Introduction and guide to the marine bluegreen algae / Harold J. Humm, Susanne R. Wicks. — New York: Wiley, c1980. x, 194 p.; ill.; 24 cm. 'A Wiley-Interscience publication.' Includes indexes. 1. Cyanobacteria 2. Marine algae 3. Cyanobacteria — Identification. 4. Marine algae — Identification. I. Wicks, Susanne R. joint author. II. T.
QK569.C96 H85　　589/.46　　*LC* 79-24488　　*ISBN* 0471052175

**Dawson, Elmer Yale, 1918-1966.**　　　　　　　**5.3713**
How to know the seaweeds / Isabella A. Abbott, E. Yale Dawson. — 2d ed. — Dubuque, Iowa: W. C. Brown Co., c1978. viii, 141 p.: ill.; 24 cm. — (The Pictured key nature series) Includes index. 1. Marine algae — United States — Identification. I. Abbott, Isabella Aiona. joint author. II. T. III. Title: Seaweeds.
QK571.D35 1978　　589/.39/214　　*LC* 76-24691　　*ISBN* 0697048950

## QK581–625 Lichens. Fungi

**Hale, Mason E.**　　　　　　　　　　　　　**5.3714**
The biology of lichens / Mason E. Hale, Jr. — 3rd ed. — London; Baltimore, Md., U.S.A.: E. Arnold, 1983. 190 p.: ill.; 23 cm. (Series of student texts in contemporary biology.) Includes index. 1. Lichens I. T. II. Series.
QK583.H35 1983　　589.1 19　　*LC* 85-128739　　*ISBN* 0713128674

**Hawksworth, D. L.**　　　　　　　　　　　　**5.3715**
The lichen–forming fungi / David L. Hawksworth, David J. Hill. — Glasgow: Blackie; New York: Distributed in the USA by Chapman and Hall in association with Methuen, 1984. vii, 158 p.: ill.; 21 cm. (Tertiary level biology.) Includes index. 1. Lichens 2. Fungi I. Hill, David J., D. Phil. II. T. III. Series.
QK583.H39 1984　　589.1 19　　*LC* 84-1020　　*ISBN* 0412006316

**Lawrey, James D., 1949-.**　　　　　　　　　**5.3716**
Biology of lichenized fungi / James D. Lawrey. — New York: Praeger, 1984. x, 408 p.: ill. Includes indexes. 1. Lichens 2. Fungi I. T. II. Title: Lichenized fungi.
QK583.L38 1984　　589.1 19　　*LC* 84-9908　　*ISBN* 0030600472

**Hale, Mason E.**　　　　　　　　　　　　　**5.3717**
How to know the lichens / Mason E. Hale. — 2d ed. — Dubuque, Iowa: W. C. Brown Co., c1979. viii, 246 p., [1] leaf of plates: ill.; 24 cm. — (The Pictured key nature series) Includes index. 1. Lichens — United States — Identification. 2. Lichens — North America — Identification. I. T.
QK587.H25 1979　　QK587 H25 1979.　　589/.1/097　　*LC* 78-55751
　　*ISBN* 0697047628

**Garraway, Michael O. (Michael Oliver)**　　　　　**5.3718**
Fungal nutrition and physiology / Michael O. Garraway, Robert C. Evans. — New York: Wiley, c1984. vii, 401 p.: ill.; 24 cm. 'A Wiley-Interscience publication.' 1. Fungi — Physiology 2. Fungi — Nutrition. I. Evans, Robert C. (Robert Church) II. T.
QK601.G27 1984　　589.2/0413 19　　*LC* 83-23450　　*ISBN* 0471058440

**Fincham, J. R. S.**　　　　　　　　　　　　**5.3719**
Fungal genetics / J. R. S. Fincham, P. R. Day, A. Radford. — 4th ed. — Berkeley: University of California Press, 1979. xvi, 636 p.: ill.; 24 cm. — (Botanical monographs. v. 4) Includes index. 1. Fungi — Genetics I. Day, Peter R., 1928- joint author. II. Radford, Albert E. joint author. III. T. IV. Series.
QK602.F5 1979b　　589.2/0415　　*LC* 79-112291　　*ISBN* 0520038185

**Alexopoulos, Constantine John, 1907-.**　　　　　**5.3720**
Introductory mycology / Constantine J. Alexopoulos, Charles W. Mims; artwork by Sung–Huang Sun and Raymond W. Scheetz. — 3d ed. — New York: Wiley, c1979. xvii, 632 p.: ill.; 25 cm. 1. Mycology I. Mims, Charles W. joint author. II. T.
QK603.A55 1979　　589/.2　　*LC* 79-12514　　*ISBN* 0471022144

**Moore-Landecker, Elizabeth.**　　　　　　　　**5.3721**
Fundamentals of the fungi. — Englewood Cliffs, N.J.: Prentice-Hall, [1972] xi, 482 p.: illus.; 24 cm. — (Prentice-Hall biological science series) 1. Mycology 2. Fungi I. T.
QK603.M62　　589/.2　　*LC* 75-160527　　*ISBN* 0133392678

**Ross, Ian K.**　　　　　　　　　　　　　　**5.3722**
Biology of the fungi, their development, regulation, and associations / Ian K. Ross. — New York: McGraw-Hill, c1979. xii, 499 p.: ill.; 25 cm. — (McGraw-Hill series in organismic biology) Includes index. 1. Fungi 2. Mycology I. T.
QK603.R67　　589/.2　　*LC* 78-23201　　*ISBN* 007053870X

**Webster, John, 1925-.**　　　　　　　　　　**5.3723**
Introduction to fungi / John Webster. — 2d ed. — Cambridge [Eng.]; New York: Cambridge University Press, 1980. x, 669 p.: ill.; 24 cm. Includes index. 1. Fungi 2. Fungi — Classification. I. T.
QK603.W4 1980　　589/.2　　*LC* 79-52856　　*ISBN* 0521228883

**Cooke, William Bridge.**　　　　　　　　　　**5.3724**
The ecology of fungi / William Bridge Cooke. — Boca Raton, Fla.: CRC Press, c1979. 274 p.: ill.; 26 cm. Includes index. 1. Fungi — Ecology I. T.
QK604.C637　　589/.2/045　　*LC* 78-27812　　*ISBN* 0849353432

**Henrici, Arthur Trautwein, 1889-1943.**　　　　　• **5.3725**
Henrici's Molds, yeasts, and actinomycetes: a handbook for students of bacteriology / by Charles E. Skinner, Chester W. Emmons [and] Henry M. Tsuchiya. — 2d ed. — New York: J. Wiley & sons, inc.; London: Chapman & Hall, 1947. xiv, 409 p.: ill. 1. Molds (Botany) 2. Yeast. 3. Actinomyces. I. Skinner, Charles Edward, 1897- II. Emmons, Chester Wilson, 1900- III. Tsuchiya, Henry Mitsumara. IV. T.
QK604.H55 1947　　*LC* 47-2478

**Miller, Orson K.**      **5.3726**
Mushrooms of North America [by] Orson K. Miller, Jr. — New York: Dutton,
[1972] 360 p.: illus.; 27 cm. 'A Chanticleer Press edition.' 1. Mushrooms —
North America — Identification. I. T.
QK617.M55    589/.222/097    *LC* 72-82162    *ISBN* 0525161651

**Smith, Alexander Hanchett, 1904-.**      **5.3727**
The mushroom hunter's field guide / Alexander H. Smith and Nancy Smith
Weber. — All col. and enl. — Ann Arbor: University of Michigan Press, c1980.
316 p.: ill.; 28 cm. Includes index. 1. Mushrooms — United States —
Identification. 2. Mushrooms — Canada — Identification. I. Weber, Nancy S.
joint author. II. T.
QK617.S56 1980    589.2/097    *LC* 80-10514    *ISBN* 0472856103

## QK635 Myxomycetes

**Martin, G. W. (George Willard), 1886-1971.**      **5.3728**
The genera of Myxomycetes / G.W. Martin, C.J. Alexopoulos, M.L. Farr;
illustrations by Ruth McVaugh Allen. — Iowa City: University of Iowa Press,
c1983. xi, 102 p., p. 479-560: col. ill.; 27 cm. 'Page numbers for the plates follow
the original pagination of 1969 edition'—P. vii. Includes index.
1. Myxomycetes 2. Myxomycetes — Classification. 3. Fungi — Classification.
I. Alexopoulos, Constantine John, 1907- II. Farr, Marie Leonore, 1927-
III. T.
QK635.A1 M37 1983    589.2/9 19    *LC* 83-5092    *ISBN* 0877451249

**Bonner, John Tyler.**      • **5.3729**
The cellular slime molds. — 2d ed., rev. and augm. — Princeton, N.J.:
Princeton University Press, 1967. x, 205 p.: illus.; 23 cm. 1. Acrasiales I. T.
QK635.B6 1967    589.29    *LC* 66-22732

## QK641–707 Morphology.
## Anatomy. Embryology

**Bold, Harold Charles, 1909-.**      **5.3730**
Morphology of plants and fungi / Harold C. Bold, Constantine J. Alexopoulos,
Theodore Delevoryas. — 5th ed. — New York: Harper & Row, c1987. x,
912 p.: ill.; 25 cm. Includes index. 1. Botany — Morphology 2. Plants —
Reproduction I. Alexopoulos, Constantine John, 1907- II. Delevoryas,
Theodore, 1929- III. T.
QK641.B596 1987    581.4 19    *LC* 86-14294    *ISBN* 0060408391

**Eames, Arthur Johnson, 1881-.**      • **5.3731**
Morphology of vascular plants: lower groups, Psilophytales to Filicales / by
Arthur J. Eames. — New York: McGraw-Hill, 1936. xviii, 433 p.: ill.; 24 cm. —
(McGraw-Hill publications in the botanical sciences) 1. Cryptogams
2. Botany — Morphology 3. Paleobotany I. T. II. Title: Vascular plants.
QK641.E33

**Foster, Adriance Sherwood, 1901-1973.**      **5.3732**
Comparative morphology of vascular plants [by] Adriance S. Foster [and]
Ernest M. Gifford, Jr. — 2d ed. — San Francisco: W. H. Freeman, [1974] viii,
751 p.: illus.; 26 cm. 1. Botany — Morphology I. Gifford, Ernest M. joint
author. II. T.
QK641.F6 1974    581.4    *LC* 73-22459    *ISBN* 0716707128

**Eames, Arthur Johnson, 1881-.**      • **5.3733**
Morphology of the angiosperms. — New York: McGraw-Hill, 1961. 518 p.:
illus.; 24 cm. — (McGraw-Hill publications in the botanical sciences)
1. Angiosperms 2. Botany — Morphology I. T.
QK643.A5 E2    582.13    *LC* 60-15757

**Sporne, K. R.**      • **5.3734**
The morphology of gymnosperms; the structure and evolution of primitive
seed–plants [by] K.R. Sporne. London, Hutchinson University Library [1965]
216 p. illus. 20 cm. Imprint covered by label, New York, Hillary House.
1. Gymnosperms 2. Botany — Morphology I. T.
QK643.G99 S65    585    *LC* 66-1105

**Metcalfe, C. R. (Charles Russell)**      • **5.3735**
Anatomy of the monocotyledons / edited by C.R. Metcalfe. — Oxford:
Clarendon Press, 1960. v.: ill.; 24 cm. 1. Monocotyledons 2. Botany —
Anatomy I. T.
QK643.M7 M4    *LC* 60-52155

**Bewley, J. Derek, 1943-.**      **5.3736**
Seeds: physiology of development and germination / J. Derek Bewley and
Michael Black. — New York: Plenum Press, c1985. xiii, 367 p.: ill.; 24 cm.
1. Seeds — Physiology 2. Germination I. Black, Michael. II. T.
QK661.B49 1985    582/.0467 19    *LC* 84-13444    *ISBN* 0306416875

**Kozlowski, T. T. (Theodore Thomas), 1917-.**      **5.3737**
Seed biology. Edited by T. T. Kozlowski. New York, Academic Press, 1972. 3 v.
illus. 24 cm. (Physiological ecology) 1. Seeds I. T.
QK661.K69    582/.03/34    *LC* 71-182641    *ISBN* 0124243010

**Esau, Katherine, 1898-.**      • **5.3738**
Plant anatomy. — 2d ed. — New York: Wiley, [1965] xx, 767 p.: ill.; 24 cm.
1. Botany — Anatomy 2. Botany — Morphology I. T.
QK671.E8 1965    581.4    *LC* 65-12713

**Davis, Gwenda L.**      • **5.3739**
Systematic embryology of the angiosperms [by] Gwenda L. Davis. — New
York: Wiley, [1966] viii, 528 p.; 24 cm. 1. Angiosperms 2. Botany —
Embryology I. T.
QK693.A5 D3    582.13    *LC* 66-26739

## QK710–899 Plant Physiology

## QK710–745 General Works

**Bidwell, R. G. S. (Roger Grafton Shelford), 1927-.**      **5.3740**
Plant physiology / R. G. S. Bidwell. — 2d ed. — New York: Macmillan, c1979.
xx, 726 p.: ill.; 26 cm. — (The Macmillan biology series) 1. Plant physiology
I. T.
QK711.2.B54 1979    581.1    *LC* 78-6504    *ISBN* 0023094303

**Galston, Arthur William, 1920-.**      **5.3741**
The life of the green plant / Arthur W. Galston, Peter J. Davies, Ruth L. Satter.
— 3d ed. — Englewood Cliffs, N.J.: Prentice-Hall, c1980. xv, 464 p.: ill.; 24 cm.
1. Plant physiology I. Davies, Peter J., 1940- joint author. II. Satter, Ruth L.
joint author. III. T.
QK711.2.G34 1980    581.1    *LC* 79-16227    *ISBN* 0135363268

**Noggle, Glen Ray, 1914-.**      **5.3742**
Introductory plant physiology / G. Ray Noggle, George J. Fritz. — Englewood
Cliffs, N.J.: Prentice-Hall, c1976. xiv, 688 p.: ill.; 25 cm. — (Prentice-Hall
biological sciences series) 1. Plant physiology I. Fritz, George J. (George
John), 1919- joint author. II. T.
QK711.2.N63    582/.01 19    *LC* 75-44357    *ISBN* 0135021871

**Salisbury, Frank B.**      **5.3743**
Plant physiology / Frank B. Salisbury, Cleon W. Ross. — 3rd ed. — Belmont,
Calif.: Wadsworth Pub. Co., c1985. xv, 540 p.: ill.; 29 cm. Includes indexes.
1. Plant physiology I. Ross, Cleon W., 1934- II. T.
QK711.2.S23 1985    581.1 19    *LC* 84-20953    *ISBN* 0534044824

**The Molecular biology of plant cells / edited by H. Smith.**      **5.3744**
Berkeley: University of California Press, 1978 (c1977). x, 496 p.: ill.; 25 cm.
(Botanical monographs. v. 14) Includes index. 1. Plant cells and tissues
2. Molecular biology I. Smith, H. (Harry), 1935- II. Series.
QK725.M75    581.8/7    *LC* 77-73503    *ISBN* 0520034651

**Leopold, A. Carl (Aldo Carl), 1919-.**      **5.3745**
Plant growth and development / A. Carl Leopold, Paul E. Kriedemann. — 2d.
ed. — New York: McGraw-Hill, [1975] xiv, 545 p.: ill.; 25 cm. (McGraw-Hill
series in organismic biology) Includes index. 1. Growth (Plants) 2. Plants —
Development 3. Plant physiology I. Kriedemann, Paul E., joint author. II. T.
QK731.L44 1975    582/.03    *LC* 74-20970    *ISBN* 0070372004

**Moore, Thomas C.**      **5.3746**
Biochemistry and physiology of plant hormones / Thomas C. Moore. — New
York: Springer-Verlag, c1979. xii, 274 p.: ill.; 24 cm. 1. Plant hormones I. T.
QK731.M66    581.1/4    *LC* 79-11492    *ISBN* 0387904018

**Thimann, Kenneth Vivian, 1904-.**      **5.3747**
Hormone action in the whole life of plants / Kenneth V. Thimann. — Amherst:
University of Massachusetts Press, 1977. x, 448 p.: ill.; 24 cm. Includes indexes.
1. Plant hormones 2. Growth (Plants) I. T.
QK731.T48    581.1/927    *LC* 76-26641    *ISBN* 087023224X

# QK746–769 Chemical and Physical Effects

**Air pollution and plant life** / edited by **Michael Treshow.**    **5.3748**
Chichester [West Sussex]; New York: Wiley, c1984. xii, 486 p.: ill.; 24 cm. — (Environmental monographs and symposia.) 'A Wiley-Interscience publication.' 1. Plants, Effect of air pollution on 2. Air — Pollution — Environmental aspects. I. Treshow, Michael. II. Series.
QK751.A36 1984     581.5/222 19     *LC* 83-5905     *ISBN* 0471901032

**Levitt, J. (Jacob), 1911-.**    **5.3749**
Responses of plants to environmental stresses / J. Levitt. — 2d ed. — New York: Academic Press, 1980. 2 v.: ill.; 24 cm. (Physiological ecology.) 1. Plants, Effect of stress on 2. Plants — Hardiness 3. Botany — Ecology I. T. II. Series.
QK754.L42 1980     581.2/4     *LC* 79-51680     *ISBN* 0124455018

# QK861–899 Phytochemistry

**The Biochemistry of plants: a comprehensive treatise** / edited by    **5.3750**
**P. K. Stumpf and E. E. Conn.**
New York: Academic Press, 1980. 8 v.: ill.; 25 cm. 1. Botanical chemistry I. Stumpf, Paul K. (Paul Karl), 1919- II. Conn, Eric E.
QK861.B48     581.19/2 19     *LC* 80-13168     *ISBN* 0126754020

**Bonner, James Frederick, 1910-.**    **5.3751**
Plant biochemistry / edited by James Bonner and Joseph E. Varner. — 3d ed. — New York: Academic Press, 1976. xvi, 925 p.: ill. 1. Botanical chemistry I. Varner, J. E. II. T.
QK861.B6 1976     QK861 B6 1976.     581.1/92     *LC* 76-21693
    *ISBN* 0121148602

**Jensen, William A.**    • **5.3752**
Botanical histochemistry: principles and practice / drawings by Evanell M. Towne. — San Francisco: W. H. Freeman [1962] 408 p.: ill.; 25 cm. (A Series of biology books) 1. Plant histochemistry I. T.
QK861.J4     581.1     *LC* 62-12268

**Epstein, Emanuel.**    **5.3753**
Mineral nutrition of plants: principles and perspectives. — New York: Wiley, 1972. ix, 412 p.: illus., port; 24 cm. 1. Plants — Nutrition 2. Plants, Effect of minerals on 3. Plants — Assimilation I. T.
QK867.E66     QK867 E66 1972.     581.1/335     *LC* 75-165018
    *ISBN* 047124340X

**Hewitt, Eric John.**    **5.3754**
Plant mineral nutrition [by] E. J. Hewitt [and] T. A. Smith. — New York: Wiley, [1975, c1974] 298 p.: illus.; 24 cm. 'A Halsted Press book.' 1. Plants — Nutrition 2. Plants, Effect of minerals on I. Smith, Terence A. (Terence Arthur) joint author. II. T.
QK867.H48 1975     581.1/335     *LC* 73-16544     *ISBN* 0470383852

**Flooding and plant growth** / edited by **T.T. Kozlowski.**    **5.3755**
Orlando, Fla.: Academic Press, 1984. xiv, 356 p.: ill.; 24 cm. — (Physiological ecology.) 1. Plants, Effect of floods on 2. Floodplain flora 3. Floods I. Kozlowski, T. T. (Theodore Thomas), 1917- II. Series.
QK870.F58 1984     581.5/263 19     *LC* 83-15811     *ISBN* 0124241204

**Kozlowski, Theodore Thomas.**    **5.3756**
Water deficits and plant growth / edited by T.T. Kozlowski. — v.1- 1968-. New York [etc.]; London: Academic Press, 1968. ill.; 24 cm. 1. Plants — Water requirements 2. Growth (Plants) I. T.
QK870.W38     581.3/1     *LC* 68-14658     *ISBN* 0124241557

## QK882 Photosynthesis

**Danks, Susan M.**    **5.3757**
Photosynthetic systems: structure, function, and assembly / Susan M. Danks, E. Hilary Evans, and Peter A. Whittaker. — Chichester [Sussex]; New York: Wiley, c1983. xi, 162 p.: ill.; 24 cm. 1. Photosynthesis 2. Chloroplasts I. Evans, E. Hilary. II. Whittaker, Peter A., 1939- III. T.
QK882.D36 1983     581.1/3342 19     *LC* 83-5831     *ISBN* 0471102504

**Edwards, Gerry.**    **5.3758**
C3, C4: mechanisms, and cellular and environmental regulation of photosynthesis / Gerry Edwards, David Walker. — Berkeley: University of California Press, c1983. x, 542 p.: ill.; 24 cm. 'A Packard Publishing Limited book.' 1. Photosynthesis — Regulation 2. Carbon — Metabolism. 3. Plants — Assimilation I. Walker, David, 1928- II. T.
QK882.E295 1983     581.1/3342 19     *LC* 82-49298

**Foyer, Christine H.**    **5.3759**
Photosynthesis / Christine H. Foyer. — New York: Wiley, c1984. xvii, 219 p.: ill.; 24 cm. — (Cell biology; v. 1) 'A Wiley-Interscience publication.' 1. Photosynthesis I. T.
QK882.F64 1984     581.1/3342 19     *LC* 83-21764     *ISBN* 0471864730

**Gregory, Richard Paul Fitzgerald, 1938-.**    **5.3760**
Biochemistry of photosynthesis [by] R. P. F. Gregory. — London; New York: Wiley-Interscience, [1971] xii, 202 p.: illus.; 24 cm. 1. Photosynthesis I. T.
QK882.G83     581.1/3342     *LC* 77-165955     *ISBN* 0471326755

**Harry Steenbock Symposium. 5th, Madison, Wis., 1975.**    **5.3761**
$CO_2$ metabolism and plant productivity: [proceedings of the fifth annual Harry Steenbock Symposium, held in Madison, Wisconsin, on June 9–11, 1975] / edited by R. H. Burris and C. C. Black. — Baltimore: University Park Press, c1976. xi, 431 p.; ill.; 24 cm. 1. Carbon dioxide — Metabolism — Congresses. 2. Plants — Metabolism — Congresses. 3. Primary productivity (Biology) — Congresses. I. Burris, Robert H. (Robert Harza), 1914- II. Black, Clanton C. III. T.
QK882.H25 1975     581.1/33     *LC* 76-14996     *ISBN* 0839108944

**Photosynthesis** / edited by **Govindjee.**    **5.3762**
New York: Academic Press, 1982. 799 p.: ill. (Cell biology.) 1. Photosynthesis I. Govindjee, 1933- II. Series.
QK882.P546 1982     581.1/3342 19     *LC* 82-8702     *ISBN* 0122943015

# QK891–898 Respiration. Special Plant Constituents

**The Physiology and biochemistry of plant respiration** / edited    **5.3763**
**by J.M. Palmer.**
Cambridge [Cambridgeshire]; New York: Cambridge University Press, 1985. ix, 195 p.: ill.; 24 cm. (Seminar series / Society for Experimental Biology; 20) 1. Plants — Respiration I. Palmer, J. M. (John Michael), 1936-
QK891.P483 1985     581.1/2 19

**Harwood, John L.**    **5.3764**
Lipids in plants and microbes / John L. Harwood, Nicholas J. Russell. — London; Boston: G. Allen & Unwin, 1984. 162 p.: ill.; 24 cm. Includes index. 1. Plant lipids 2. Microbial lipids I. Russell, Nicholas J. II. T.
QK898.L56 H37 1984     581.19/247 19     *LC* 84-9156     *ISBN* 0045740216

# QK901–977 PLANT ECOLOGY

# QK901–909 General Works

**Braun-Blanquet, J. (Josias), 1884-.**    • **5.3765**
[Pflanzensoziologie. English] Plant sociology; the study of plant communities. Authorized English translation of Pflanzensoziologie by J. Braun-Blanquet. Translated, rev. and ed. by George D. Fuller and Henry S. Conard. New York, Hafner Pub. Co., 1965. xviii, 439 p. illus., maps. 24 cm. A reprint of the 1932 ed. 1. Plant communities I. Fuller, George D. (George Damon), 1869- ed. and tr. II. Conard, Henry Shoemaker, 1874- ed. and tr. III. T.
QK901.B652 1965     581.55     *LC* 65-27077

**Green planet: the story of plant life on earth** / edited by **David**    **5.3766**
**M. Moore.**
Cambridge [Cambridgeshire]; New York: Cambridge University Press, 1982. 288 p.: ill.; 29 cm. Includes indexes. 1. Botany — Ecology 2. Phytogeography I. Moore, D. M. (David Moresby)
QK901.G82 1982     581.5 19     *LC* 82-4287     *ISBN* 0521246105

**Larcher, W. (Walter), 1929-.**    **5.3767**
[Ökologie der Pflanzen. English] Physiological plant ecology / W. Larcher; translated by M. A. Biederman–Thorson. — 2d totally rev. ed. — Berlin; New

York: Springer-Verlag, 1980. xvii, 303 p.: ill.; 23 cm. Translation of Ökologie der Pflanzen. Includes index. 1. Botany — Ecology 2. Plant physiology I. T.
QK901.L3513 1980    581.5    *LC* 79-26396    *ISBN* 0387097953

**Tivy, Joy.**                         **5.3768**
Biogeography: a study of plants in the ecosphere / Joy Tivy. — 2nd ed. — London; New York: Longman, 1982. xvii, 459 p.: ill.; 22 cm. 1. Botany — Ecology 2. Phytogeography 3. Biogeography I. T.
QK901.T58 1982    581.5 19    *LC* 80-41366    *ISBN* 0582300096

# QK910–929 Vegetation Dynamics (Plant Populations)

**Perspectives on plant population ecology / edited by Rodolfo**    **5.3769**
**Dirzo and José Sarukhán.**
Sunderland, Mass.: Sinauer Associates, 1984. xviii, 478 p.: ill.; 24 cm. Includes index. 1. Plant populations 2. Botany — Ecology I. Dirzo, Rodolfo. II. Sarukhán, José.
QK910.P47 1984    581.5/248 19    *LC* 83-20182    *ISBN* 0878931422

**Silvertown, Jonathan W.**            **5.3770**
Introduction to plant population ecology / Jonathan W. Silvertown. — London; New York: Longman, 1982. 209 p.: ill.; 24 cm. Includes index. 1. Plant populations 2. Vegetation dynamics 3. Botany — Ecology I. T.
QK910.S54 1982    581.5/248 19    *LC* 81-15595    *ISBN* 0582442656

**The Role of terrestrial and aquatic organisms in decomposition**    **5.3771**
**processes: the 17th symposium of the British Ecological Society,**
**15–18 April 1975 / edited by J. M. Anderson and A.**
**Macfadyen.**
Oxford: Blackwell Scientific, 1976. xii, 3-474 p.: ill.; 25 cm. (Symposium of the British Ecological Society; 17th) Distributed in the U.S.A. by Halsted Press, New York. 1. Biodegradation — Congresses. 2. Biogeochemical cycles — Congresses. 3. Decomposition (Chemistry) — Congresses. I. Anderson, J. M. II. Macfadyen, A. (Amyan) III. British Ecological Society.
QK911.B7 A35 no. 17 1976 QP517.B5    574.5/08 s 574.5/3    *LC* 77-358784    *ISBN* 063200018X

**European Ecological Symposium. 1st, Norwich, Eng., 1977.**    **5.3772**
Ecological processes in coastal environments: the first European Ecological Symposium and the 19th symposium of the British Ecological Society, Norwich, 12–16 September, 1977 / edited by R. L. Jefferies and A. J. Davy; sponsoring societies, the British Ecological Society ... [et al.]. — Oxford [Eng.]: Blackwell Scientific Publications; New York: distributed by Halsted Press, 1979. xvii, 684 p., [1] fold. leaf of plates: ill.; 24 cm. — (British Ecological Society symposia; 19) Summaries also in French. 1. Coastal ecology — Congresses. I. Jefferies, R. L. II. Davy, A. J. III. British Ecological Society. IV. T.
QK911.B7 A35 no. 19 QH541.5.C65    574.5/08 s 574.5/26    *LC* 79-319345    *ISBN* 063200472X

**Harper, John L.**                     **5.3773**
Population biology of plants / John L. Harper. — London; New York: Academic Press, 1977. xxiv, 892 p.: ill.: 24 cm. Includes indexes. 1. Plant populations 2. Population biology I. T.
QK911.H35    581.5/24    *LC* 76-16973    *ISBN* 0123258502

**Schnell, Donald E., 1936-.**           **5.3774**
Carnivorous plants of the United States and Canada / by Donald E. Schnell. Winston-Salem, N.C.: J. F. Blair, c1976. ix, 125 p.: ill.; 24 cm. Includes index. 1. Insectivorous plants — United States. 2. Insectivorous plants — Canada. I. T.
QK917.S36    583/.121/0973    *LC* 76-26883    *ISBN* 0910244901

**Meeuse, Bastiaan.**                **5.3775**
The sex life of flowers / Bastiaan Meeuse and Sean Morris; photographs by Oxford Scientific Films; drawings by Michael Woods. — New York: Facts on File, 1984. 152 p.: ill. (some col.); 29 cm. Ill. on lining papers. Includes index. 1. Pollination 2. Plants, Sex in 3. Flowers I. Morris, Sean. II. T.
QK926.M418 1984    582.13/04166 19    *LC* 84-4044    *ISBN* 0871969076

# QK930–940 Physiographic Regions

**Dawes, Clinton J.**                 **5.3776**
Marine botany / Clinton J. Dawes. — New York: Wiley, c1981. x, 628 p.: ill.; 24 cm. 'A Wiley-Interscience publication.' 1. Marine flora 2. Botany — Ecology I. T.
QK931.D38    581.92 19    *LC* 81-7527    *ISBN* 0471078441

**Riemer, Donald N.**                 **5.3777**
Introduction to freshwater vegetation / Donald N. Riemer. — Westport, Conn.: AVI Pub. Co., c1984. xi, 207 p.: ill.; 24 cm. 1. Freshwater flora 2. Aquatic weeds — Control 3. Freshwater ecology I. T. II. Title: Freshwater vegetation.
QK932.R54 1984    581.5/2632 19    *LC* 83-22477    *ISBN* 0870554484 0870554884

**Phytoplankton manual / edited by A. Sournia.**    **5.3778**
Paris: Unesco, 1978. xvi, 337 p.: ill.; 25 cm. (Monographs on oceanographic methodology; 6) Includes index. 1. Phytoplankton — Research. 2. Phytoplankton — Handbooks, manuals, etc. 3. Marine phytoplankton — Research. 4. Marine phytoplankton — Handbooks, manuals, etc. I. Sournia, Alain. II. Series.
QK933.P49    589/.4    *LC* 79-309840    *ISBN* 9231015729

**Reynolds, C. S.**                 **5.3779**
The ecology of freshwater phytoplankton / C. S. Reynolds. — Cambridge; New York: Cambridge University Press, 1984. x, 384 p.: ill.; 24 cm. — (Cambridge studies in ecology.) Includes indexes. 1. Freshwater phytoplankton — Ecology. I. T. II. Series.
QK935.R45 1984    589.4/0916/9 19    *LC* 83-7211    *ISBN* 0521237823

**Ecology of coastal vegetation: proceedings of a symposium,**    **5.3780**
**Haamstede, March 21–25, 1983 / edited by W.G. Beeftink, J.**
**Rozema & A.H.L. Huiskes.**
Dordrecht [Netherlands]; Boston: W. Junk, 1985. xx, 598 p.: ill.; 27 cm. — (Advances in vegetation science. 6) 'Reprinted from Vegetatio, volumes 61/62.' Includes indexes. 1. Coastal flora — Ecology — Congresses. 2. Coastal flora — Europe — Ecology — Congresses. 3. Plant communities — Congresses. 4. Plant communities — Europe — Congresses. 5. Botany — Ecology — Congresses. 6. Botany — Europe — Ecology — Congresses. I. Beeftink, W. G. II. Rozema, J. III. Huiskes, A. H. L. IV. Series.
QK938.C6 E25 1985    581.5/2638 19    *LC* 85-9931    *ISBN* 9061935318

**Braun, E. Lucy (Emma Lucy), 1889-.**      ● **5.3781**
Deciduous forests of eastern North America, by E.Lucy Braun. — New York: Hafner Pub. Co., 1964 [c1950] xiv, 596 p.: illus., maps (1 fold.); 24 cm. 1. Forests and forestry — North America. 2. Forest ecology 3. Botany — North America. I. T.
QK938.F6 B7 1964    581.5264    *LC* 64-20220

**Forest succession: concepts and application / edited by Darrell**    **5.3782**
**C. West, Herman H. Shugart, Daniel B. Botkin.**
New York: Springer-Verlag, c1981. xv, 517 p.: ill.; 25 cm. — (Springer advanced texts in life sciences.) Papers presented at a conference held at Mountain Lake, Va., in June 1980. Includes index. 1. Forest ecology — Congresses. 2. Plant succession — Congresses. I. West, D. C. II. Botkin, Daniel B. III. Shugart, H. H. IV. Series.
QK938.F6 F674    581.5/2642 19    *LC* 81-16707    *ISBN* 0387905979

**Neal, Ernest G.**                 ● **5.3783**
Woodland ecology. — 2d ed. — Cambridge: Harvard University Press, 1960 [c1958] 117 p.: illus.; 19 cm. 1. Forest ecology I. T.
QK938.F6 N4 1960    581.5264    *LC* a 62-8632

**Richards, Paul Westmacott.**        ● **5.3784**
The tropical rain forest: an ecological study / by P. W. Richards. — Cambridge, [Eng.]: University Press, 1952. xviii, 450 p.: ill., fold, map; 25 cm. 1. Forest ecology 2. Forests and forestry — Tropics. I. T.
QK938.F6 R5    574.5264    *LC* 52-14310    *ISBN* 0521060796

**Spurr, Stephen Hopkins.**           **5.3785**
Forest ecology / Stephen H. Spurr, Burton V. Barnes. — 3d ed. — New York: Wiley, c1980. x, 687 p.: ill.; 24 cm. Includes index. 1. Forest ecology I. Barnes, Burton Verne, 1930- joint author. II. T.
QK938.F6 S68 1980    574.5/264    *LC* 79-10007    *ISBN* 0471047325

**Weaver, John E. (John Ernest), 1884-1966.**                • **5.3786**
Grasslands of the Great Plains: their nature and use, by J.E. Weaver and F.W. Albertson, with special chapters by B.W. Allred and Arnold Heerwagen. Lincoln, Neb., Johnsen Pub. Co. [1956] ix, 395 p. illus., maps. 24 cm. 1. Grasslands — Great Plains. 2. Botany — Great Plains. 3. Botany — Ecology I. Albertson, F. W. (Frederick William) joint author. II. T.
QK938.P7 W37      581.52645      *LC* 56-9095

**Weaver, John E. (John Ernest), 1884-1966.**                • **5.3787**
North American prairie / by J.E. Weaver. — Lincoln, Neb.: Johnsen Pub. Co., 1954. xi, 348 p.: ill. 1. Prairies 2. Botany — North America. I. T.
QK938.P7 W4      *LC* 54-4501

**Chapman, V. J. (Valentine Jackson), 1910-.**                **5.3788**
Salt marshes and salt deserts of the world / by V. J. Chapman. — 2d, supplemented reprint ed. — Lehre [Ger.]: J. Cramer, 1974. 102, xvi, 392 p.: ill.; 23 cm. Label mounted on verso of t.p.: Distributed by ISBS, Inc., Forest Grove, Or. Includes original t.p. 1. Tidemarsh flora 2. Marshes, Tide 3. Halophytes 4. Alkali lands 5. Reclamation of land I. T.
QK938.S27 C45 1974      581.5/2636      *LC* 77-351046      *ISBN* 3768209274

# QK980–989 PLANT EVOLUTION

**Darlington, C. D. (Cyril Dean), 1903-.**                **5.3789**
Chromosome botany and the origins of cultivated plants [by] C. D. Darlington. — 3d rev. ed. — New York: Hafner Press, 1973. xvii, 237 p.: illus.; 21 cm. 1. Plants — Evolution 2. Plants, Cultivated 3. Chromosomes I. T.
QK980.D37 1973      581.8/732      *LC* 73-80913      *ISBN* 0028436709

**Briggs, D. (David), 1936-.**                **5.3790**
Plant variation and evolution / D. Briggs, S.M. Walters. — 2nd ed. — Cambridge [Cambridgeshire]; New York: Cambridge University, 1984. xv, 412 p.: ill.; 24 cm. Includes index. 1. Botany — Variation 2. Plants — Evolution I. Walters, S. M. (Stuart Max) II. T.
QK983.B73 1984      581.1/5 19      *LC* 83-14310      *ISBN* 0521257069

# QL    Zoology

**Grzimek, Bernhard.**                                    5.3791
[Tierleben. English] Grzimek's Animal life encyclopedia. Bernhard Grzimek, editor–in–chief. New York, Van Nostrand Reinhold Co. [1972-75; v. 13, 1972] 13 v. illus. 25 cm. Translation of Tierleben. 1. Zoology — Collected works. I. T. II. Title: Animal life encyclopedia.
QL3.G7813      591      *LC* 79-183178

**Macmillan illustrated animal encyclopedia / edited by Philip**     5.3792
**Whitfield; American consultant, Edward S. Ayensu; foreword by**
**Gerald Durrell.**
New York: Macmillan, c1984. 600 p.: col. ill.; 30 cm. Includes index. 1. Zoology I. Whitfield, Philip. II. Ayensu, Edward S.
QL7.M33 1984      591/.03/21 19      *LC* 84-3956      *ISBN* 0026276801

**Leftwich, A. W.**                                        • 5.3793
A dictionary of zoology [by] A. W. Leftwich. — [3d ed.]. — London: Constable, [1973] ix, 478 p.; 23 cm. 1. Zoology — Dictionaries. I. T.
QL9.L4 1973      591/.03      *LC* 73-161027      *ISBN* 0094549729

**Pennak, Robert W. (Robert William)**                     • 5.3794
Collegiate dictionary of zoology. New York: Ronald Press Co. [1964] vi, 583 p.; 26 cm. 1. Zoology — Dictionaries. I. T.
QL9.P4      590.3      *LC* 64-13331

**Chancellor, John, 1927 July 1-.**                         5.3795
Audubon: a biography / by John Chancellor. — New York: Viking Press, 1978. 224 p.: ill.; 26 cm. — (A Studio book) Includes index. 1. Audubon, John James, 1785-1851. 2. Ornithologists — United States — Biography. I. T.
QL31.A9 C43      598.2/092/4 B      *LC* 78-8465      *ISBN* 0670140538

**Rothschild, Miriam.**                                     5.3796
Dear Lord Rothschild: birds, butterflies, and history / Miriam Rothschild. — Philadelphia: Balaban; London: Hutchinson; Philadelphia: Distributed by ISI, c1983. xx, 398 p., [106] p. of plates: ill. (some col.); 25 cm. Includes index. 1. Rothschild, Lionel Walter Rothschild, Baron, 1868-1937. 2. Zoologists — England — Biography. I. T.
QL31.R67 R63 1983      590/.92/4 B 19      *LC* 83-8760      *ISBN* 086689019X

**Aristotle.**                                             5.3797
[De animalium motu. English] Aristotle's De motu animalium: text with translation, commentary, and interpretive essays / by Martha Craven Nussbaum. — Princeton, N.J.: Princeton University Press, 1978. xxiii, 430 p.; 23 cm. Includes indexes. 1. Zoology — Pre-Linnean works 2. Animal locomotion — Early works to 1800. I. Nussbaum, Martha Craven, 1947- II. T. III. Title: De motu animalium.
QL41.A719 1978      591 19      *LC* 77-72132      *ISBN* 0691072248

**Boolootian, Richard A.**                                  5.3798
College zoology / Richard A. Boolootian, Karl A. Stiles. — 10th ed. — New York: Macmillan, c1981. x, 803 p.: ill.; 25 cm. 1. Zoology I. Stiles, Karl Amos, 1897-1968. joint author. II. T.
QL45.2.H4 1981      591 19      *LC* 80-22446      *ISBN* 002311990X

**Kershaw, Diana R.**                                       5.3799
Animal diversity / Diana R. Kershaw; with illustrations by Brian Price Thomas. — Slough: University Tutorial Press, 1983. 428 p.: ill.; 28 cm. Includes index. 1. Zoology 2. Anatomy I. T.
QL45.2.K47 1983      591 19      *LC* 83-186966      *ISBN* 0723108471

**General zoology / Tracy I. Storer ... [et al.].**          5.3800
6th ed. — New York: McGraw-Hill, c1979. ix, 902 p.: ill.; 25 cm. 1. Zoology I. Storer, Tracy Irwin, 1889-
QL47.2.G46 1979      591      *LC* 78-12558      *ISBN* 0070617805

**Hickman, Cleveland Pendleton, 1895-.**                    5.3801
Biology of animals [by] Cleveland P. Hickman [and] Cleveland P. Hickman, Jr. — Saint Louis: C. V. Mosby Co., 1972. x, 522 p.: illus.; 27 cm. 1. Zoology I. Hickman, Cleveland P. joint author. II. T.
QL47.2.H53      591      *LC* 76-175188      *ISBN* 0801621658

**Villee, Claude Alvin, 1917-.**                            5.3802
General zoology [by] Claude A. Villee, Warren F. Walker, Jr. [and] Robert D. Barnes. — 4th ed. — Philadelphia: Saunders, 1973. xviii, 912 p.: ill.; 27 cm. 1. Zoology I. Walker, Warren Franklin. joint author. II. Barnes, Robert D. joint author. III. T.
QL47.2.V5 1973      591      *LC* 72-82815      *ISBN* 0721690386

**Weisz, Paul B., 1921-.**                                  5.3803
The science of zoology [by] Paul B. Weisz. — 2d ed. — New York: McGraw-Hill, [1972] xvi, 727 p.: illus. (part col.); 25 cm. 1. Zoology I. T.
QL47.2.W45 1973      591      *LC* 72-4172      *ISBN* 0070691355

**The New Larousse encyclopedia of animal life / [based on La**     5.3804
**vie des animaux by Léon Bertin with contributions by Maurice**
**and Robert Burton ... et al.; foreword to revised edition by**
**Maurice Burton, to first edition by Robert Cushman Murphy;**
**all photographs supplied by Bruce Coleman Ltd.].**
New York: Larousse, 1980. 640 p.: col. ill.; 30 cm. Includes index. 1. Zoology I. Bertin, Léon, 1896-1956. Vie des animaux. II. Burton, Maurice, 1898-
QL50.N48 1980      591 19      *LC* 79-91865      *ISBN* 0883321327

**Culture methods for invertebrate animals: a compendium /**     • 5.3805
**prepared cooperatively by American zoologists under the**
**direction of a committee from Section F of the American**
**association for the advancement of science: Paul S. Galtsoff,**
**Frank E. Lutz, Paul S. Welch, James G. Needham, chairmen;**
**assisted by many specialists.**
Ithaca, N. Y.: Comstock, 1937. xxxii, 590 p.: ill. 1. Invertebrates 2. Zoological specimens — Collection and preservation I. Galtsoff, Paul Simon, 1887- II. Lutz, Frank Eugene, 1879-1943. III. Welch, Paul Smith, 1882- IV. Needham, James George, 1868- V. American Association for the Advancement of Science.
QL62.C8      *LC* 37-2789

**International zoo yearbook.**                              5.3806
v. 1- 1959-. London, Zoological Society of London. v. ill. 25 cm. Annual. 1. Zoos — Yearbooks. I. Jarvis, Caroline, ed. II. Morris, Desmond. ed. III. Zoological Society of London.
QL76.I55      591      *LC* 63-28248

**Wildlife conservation evaluation / edited by Michael B. Usher.**     5.3807
London; New York: Chapman and Hall, 1986. xii, 394 p.: ill.; 24 cm. Includes indexes. 1. Wildlife conservation — Evaluation. 2. Nature conservation — Evaluation. I. Usher, Michael B., 1941-
QL82.W53 1986      333.95 19      *LC* 85-26964      *ISBN* 0412267500

**Leeds, Anthony, 1925- ed.**                               5.3808
Man, culture, and animals; the role of animals in human ecological adjustments. Edited by Anthony Leeds [and] Andrew P. Vayda. Washington [American Association for the Advancement of Science] 1965. vii, 304 p. illus., maps. 24 cm. (American Association for the Advancement of Science. Publication no. 78) Includes most of the papers presented at the Denver meeting of the American Association for the Advancement of Science, Dec. 30, 1961, and papers by additional contributors. 1. Human-animal relationships — Addresses, essays, lectures. I. Vayda, Andrew Peter. joint ed. II. American Association for the Advancement of Science. III. T.
QL85.L35      301.24      *LC* 65-23451

**Toynbee, J. M. C. (Jocelyn M. C.), d. 1985.**             5.3809
Animals in Roman life and art / [by] J. M. C. Toynbee. — Ithaca, N.Y.: Cornell University Press, [1973] 431 p.: ill.; 23 cm. — (Aspects of Greek and Roman

life) 1. Animals and civilization 2. Animals in art 3. Animals in literature 4. Zoology — Italy — Rome. 5. Rome — Antiquities I. T. II. Series.
QL87.T68          704.94/32          *LC* 73-1762          *ISBN* 0801407850

**Caras, Roger A.**                                                                5.3810
Venomous animals of the world [by] Roger Caras. — Englewood Cliffs, N.J.: Prentice-Hall, [1974] xix, 362 p.: illus.; 29 cm. 1. Poisonous animals I. T.
QL100.C37          591.6/9          *LC* 74-8633          *ISBN* 0139415262

**Halstead, Bruce W.**                                                            5.3811
Poisonous and venomous marine animals of the world / by Bruce W. Halstead; with the editorial assistance of Linda G. Halstead. — Rev. ed. — Princeton, N.J.: Darwin Press, c1978. xlvi, 1043, 283 p.: ill.; 29 cm. Erratum slip tipped in. 1. Dangerous marine animals 2. Poisonous animals I. Halstead, Linda G. II. T.
QL100.H33 1978          591.6/9/09162          *LC* 72-177977          *ISBN* 087850012X

# QL101–345 GEOGRAPHICAL DISTRIBUTION. ZOOGEORAPHY

**Beaufort, L. F. de (Lieven Ferdinand de), 1879-.**              • 5.3812
Zoogeography of the land and inland waters. — London: Sidgwick and Jackson, 1951. 208 p.: maps; 23 cm. (Text-books of animal biology) 1. Zoogeography I. T.
QL101.B39          *LC* 51-6520

**Darlington, Philip Jackson, 1904-.**                            • 5.3813
Zoogeography: the geographical distribution of animals. — [New York: Wiley, 1957] 675 p.: illus.; 24 cm. 1. Zoogeography I. T.
QL101.D3          591.9          *LC* 57-8882

**Hesse, Richard, 1868-1944.**                                    • 5.3814
[Tiergeographie auf ökologischer Grundlage. English] Ecological animal geography. An authorized ed., rewritten and rev.; based on Tiergeographie auf oekologischer Grundlage, by Richard Hesse. 2d ed. [by] W. C. Allee and Karl P. Schmidt. New York: Wiley [1951] xiii, 715 p.: ill.; 24 cm. 1. Zoogeography 2. Animal ecology I. Allee, Warder Clyde, 1885- ed. and tr. II. T.
QL101.H48 1951          591.9          *LC* 51-12300

**Simpson, George Gaylord, 1902-.**                               • 5.3815
The geography of evolution; collected essays. — [1st ed.]. — Philadelphia: Chilton Books, [1965] x, 249 p.: illus., maps.; 21 cm. 1. Zoogeography 2. Evolution I. T.
QL101.S55          575.7          *LC* 65-22541

**Wallace, Alfred Russel, 1823-1913.**                            • 5.3816
The geographical distribution of animals: with a study of the relations of living and extinct faunas as elucidating the past changes of the earth's surface / by Alfred Russel Wallace. — New York: Hafner Pub. Co., 1962. 2 v.: ill., col. maps (1 fold.), tables. 1. Zoogeography 2. Paleontology I. T.
QL101.W18 1962          *LC* 62-15789

**Wallwork, John Anthony, 1932-.**                                5.3817
The distribution and diversity of soil fauna / John A Wallwork. — London; New York: Academic Press, 1976. xii, 355 p.: ill.; 24 cm. Errata slip inserted. 1. Soil fauna I. T.
QL110.W33          591.5/2/6          *LC* 75-19684          *ISBN* 0127333509

**Daiber, Franklin C.**                                           5.3818
Animals of the tidal marsh / Franklin C. Daiber. — New York: Van Nostrand Reinhold, c1982. x, 422 p.: ill.; 24 cm. Includes index. 1. Tidemarsh fauna I. T.
QL114.D34          591.52/636 19          *LC* 80-26403          *ISBN* 0442248547

**Adaptation to environment: essays on the physiology of marine**   5.3819
**animals / edited by R. C. Newell.**
London; Boston: Butterworths, 1976. 539 p.: ill.; 24 cm. 1. Marine fauna — Physiology 2. Adaptation (Physiology) I. Newell, R. C. (Richard Charles)
QL121.A24          591.5/2636          *LC* 75-33894          *ISBN* 040870778X

**George, J. David (John David)**                                 5.3820
Marine life: an illustrated encyclopedia of invertebrates in the sea / by J. David George and Jennifer J. George; with a foreword by Sir Eric Smith. — New York: Wiley, c1979. 288 p.: ill. (some col.); 31 cm. 'A Wiley-Interscience publication.' Includes index. 1. Marine invertebrates I. George, Jennifer J. joint author. II. T.
QL121.G4          592/.09/2          *LC* 79-10976          *ISBN* 0471056758

**MacGinitie, George Eber, 1889-.**                               • 5.3821
Natural history of marine animals [by] G. E. MacGinitie [and] Nettie MacGinitie. — 2d ed. — New York: McGraw-Hill, [1968] xii, 523 p.: illus.; 23 cm. 1. Marine fauna I. MacGinitie, Nettie, joint author. II. T.
QL121.M2 1968          591.9/2          *LC* 67-24441

**Spoel, S. van der.**                                            5.3822
A comparative atlas of zooplankton: biological patterns in the oceans / S. van der Spoel, R.P. Heyman. — Berlin; New York: Springer-Verlag, 1983. 186 p.: ill., maps. Includes index. Map in pocket. 1. Marine zooplankton — Geographical distribution I. Heyman, R. P. (Robert Pieter), 1952- II. T.
QL123.S75 1983          QL123 S75 1983.          592 19          *LC* 83-10440
   *ISBN* 0387125736

**Ricketts, Edward Flanders, 1896-1948.**                         5.3823
Between Pacific tides / Edward F. Ricketts, Jack Calvin, and Joel W. Hedgpeth. — 5th ed. / revised by David W. Phillips. — Stanford, Calif.: Stanford University Press, 1985. xxvi, 652 p.: ill.; 24 cm. Includes index. 1. Marine invertebrates — Pacific Coast (U.S.) 2. Intertidal ecology — Pacific Coast (U.S.) 3. Seashore biology — Pacific Coast (U.S.) 4. Animals — Habitations I. Calvin, Jack. II. Hedgpeth, Joel Walker, 1911- III. Phillips, David W. IV. T.
QL138.R5 1985          591.926 19          *LC* 83-40620          *ISBN* 0804712298

**Green, J. (James), 1928-.**                                     • 5.3824
The biology of estuarine animals / [by] J. Green. — Seattle: University of Washington [1968] x, 401 p.: ill.; 22 cm. (Biology series) 1. Marine fauna 2. Estuarine biology I. T.
QL139.G73 1968          591.9/2          *LC* 68-21828

**Pennak, Robert W. (Robert William)**                            5.3825
Fresh–water invertebrates of the United States / by Robert W. Pennak. — 2d ed. — New York: Wiley, c1978. xv, 803 p.: ill.; 26 cm. 'A Wiley-Interscience publication.' 1. Freshwater invertebrates — United States. I. T.
QL141.P45 1978          592/.09/2973          *LC* 78-8130          *ISBN* 0471042498

**Collins, Henry Hill, 1905-1961.**                               5.3826
The complete field guide to North American wildlife, Eastern edition / assembled by Henry Hill Collins, Jr.; ill. by Paul Donahue ... [et al.]. — 1st ed. — New York: Harper & Row, c1981. 714 p., 110 pages of plates: ill. Includes index. 1. Zoology — North America. 2. Zoology — Atlantic States. 3. Animals — Identification I. T.
QL151.C62 1981          591.974 19          *LC* 80-8198          *ISBN* 0061811637

**Ransom, Jay Ellis, 1914-.**                                     5.3827
Harper & Row's Complete field guide to North American wildlife, Western edition / assembled by Jay Ellis Ransom; ill. by Biruta Akerbergs ... [et al.]. — 1st ed. — New York: Harper & Row, c1981. xi, 809 p., [64] leaves of plates: ill.; 23 cm. Includes index. 1. Zoology — North America. 2. Zoology — West (U.S.) 3. Animals — Identification I. T. II. Title: Complete field guide to North American wildlife, Western edition.
QL151.R36 1981          591.978 19          *LC* 79-2635          *ISBN* 0061817155

**Serengeti, dynamics of an ecosystem / edited by A. R. E.**       5.3828
**Sinclair and M. Norton–Griffiths.**
Chicago: University of Chicago Press, 1979. xii, 389 p., [16] leaves of plates: ill.; 25 cm. Includes index. 1. Animal ecology — Tanzania — Serengeti Plain. 2. Serengeti National Park (Tanzania) I. Sinclair, A. R. E. (Anthony Ronald Entrican) II. Norton-Griffiths, M.
QL337.T3 S43          574.5/264          *LC* 79-10146          *ISBN* 0226760286

# QL351 CLASSIFICATION

**Mayr, Ernst, 1904-.**                                           • 5.3829
Principles of systematic zoology. — New York: McGraw-Hill, [1969] xi, 428 p.: illus., maps, ports.; 23 cm. 1. Zoology — Classification I. T.
QL351.M29          591/.01/2          *LC* 68-54937

**Neave, Sheffield Airey, 1879-1961. ed.**                        5.3830
Nomenclator zoologicus: a list of the names of genera and subgenera in zoology from the tenth edition of Linnaeus, 1758, to the end of 1935 / edited by Sheffield Airey Neave. — London: Pub. for the proprietors by the Zoological society of London, 1939-1950. 5 v.; 24 cm. 1. Zoology — Nomenclature I. Zoological Society of London. II. T.
QL354.N4          590.1432          *LC* 39-24906

## QL362–601 INVERTEBRATES

**Barnes, Robert D.**      **5.3831**
Invertebrate zoology / Robert D. Barnes. — 5th ed. — Philadelphia: Saunders College Pub., 1986. p. cm. 1. Invertebrates I. T.
QL362.B27 1986     592 19     *LC* 86-10023     *ISBN* 003008914X

**Buchsbaum, Ralph Morris, 1907-.**      **5.3832**
Animals without backbones. — 3rd ed. / Ralph Buchsbaum ... [et al.]. — Chicago: University of Chicago Press, 1987. x, 572 p.: ill.; 24 cm. Includes index. 1. Invertebrates I. T.
QL362.B93 1987     592 19     *LC* 86-7046     *ISBN* 0226078736

**Engemann, Joseph G.**      **5.3833**
Invertebrate zoology / Joseph G. Engemann, Robert W. Hegner. — 3d ed. — New York: Macmillan; London: Collier Macmillan Publishers, c1981. xxi, 746 p.: ill.; 26 cm. In the 2d ed. Hegner's name appeared first on t.p. 1. Invertebrates I. Hegner, Robert William, 1880-1942. joint author. II. T.
QL362.H4 1981     592     *LC* 80-12063     *ISBN* 002333780X

**Lutz, Paul E.**      **5.3834**
Invertebrate zoology / Paul E. Lutz. — Reading, Mass.: Addison-Wesley Pub. Co., c1986. xvii, 734 p.: ill.; 25 cm. 1. Invertebrates I. T.
QL362.L85 1986     592 19     *LC* 85-4040     *ISBN* 0201168308

**Gosner, Kenneth L., 1925-.**      **5.3835**
Guide to identification of marine and estuarine invertebrates; Cape Hatteras to the Bay of Fundy [by] Kenneth L. Gosner. — New York: Wiley-Interscience, [1971] xix, 693 p.: illus.; 23 cm. 1. Marine invertebrates — Identification. I. T.
QL362.5.G68     592/.09/214     *LC* 70-149771     *ISBN* 0471318973

**Winsor, Mary P.**      **5.3836**
Starfish, jellyfish, and the order of life: issues in nineteenth–century science / Mary P. Winsor. — New Haven: Yale University Press, c1976. 228 p.: ill.; 25 cm. (Yale studies in the history of science and medicine. 10) Includes index. 1. Invertebrates — Classification — History. I. T. II. Series.
QL362.5.W56     593/.01/2     *LC* 74-29739     *ISBN* 0300016352

## QL366–369 Protozoa

**Hall, Richard P. (Richard Pinkham), 1900-.**      • **5.3837**
Protozoology. New York, Prentice-Hall, 1953. 682 p. illus. 24 cm. (Prentice-Hall animal science series) 1. Protozoology I. T.
QL366.H3     593.1     *LC* 52-14030

**Biochemistry and physiology of protozoa / edited by Michael**      **5.3838**
**Levandowsky, S. H. Hutner; consulting editor, Luigi Provasoli.**
2d ed. — New York: Academic Press, 1979. 462 p.: ill.; 24 cm. First ed. published in 1951-64, entered under A. Lwoff. 1. Protozoa — Physiology I. Levandowsky, Michael. II. Hutner, S. H. (Seymour Herbert), 1911- III. Lwoff, André, 1902- ed. Biochemistry and physiology of protozoa.
QL369.2.L87 1979     593.1/041 19     *LC* 78-20045     *ISBN* 0124446019

## QL371–379 Coelenterata

**Bergquist, Patricia R.**      **5.3839**
Sponges / Patricia R. Bergquist. — Berkeley: University of California Press, c1978. 268 p., [6] leaves of plates: ill.; 25 cm. Includes index. 1. Sponges I. T.
QL371.B47 1978     593/.4     *LC* 77-93466     *ISBN* 0520036581

## QL386–394 Vermes

**Edwards, C. A. (Clive Arthur), 1925-.**      **5.3840**
Biology of earthworms [by] C. A. Edwards [and] J. R. Lofty. London: Chapman and Hall, 1973 (c1972) xv, 283 p.: ill.; 23 cm. Distributed in the

U.S.A. by Harper & Row Publishers, Barnes & Noble Import Division. 1. Opisthophora. I. Lofty, J. R., joint author. II. T.
QL391.A6 E33     595/.146     *LC* 73-152755     *ISBN* 0412110601

**Physiology of annelids / edited by P. J. Mill.**      **5.3841**
London; New York: Academic Press, 1978. xvi, 683 p.: ill.; 24 cm. 1. Annelida — Physiology. I. Mill, P. J. (Peter John)
QL391.A6 P52     595/.14/041     *LC* 77-81376

**Nicholas, Warwick L.**      **5.3842**
The biology of free–living nematodes / by Warwick L. Nicholas. — 2nd ed. — Oxford: Clarendon Press; Oxford; New York: Oxford University Press, 1984. ix, 251 p.: ill.; 24 cm. — (Oxford science publications.) Includes indexes. 1. Nematoda I. T. II. Series.
QL391.N4 N5 1984     595.1/82 19     *LC* 83-11437     *ISBN* 0198575874

**Wright, Christopher Amyas, 1928-.**      **5.3843**
Flukes and snails [by] C. A. Wright. [1st American ed.] New York: Hafner Press [1973, c1971] 168 p.: ill.; 22 cm. (Science of biology series, no. 4) 1. Digenea 2. Mollusks — Parasites I. T.
QL391.P7 W74 1973     595/.122     *LC* 73-82829     *ISBN* 002855020X

**Erasmus, David A.**      **5.3844**
The biology of trematodes [by] David A. Erasmus. — New York: Crane, Russak, [1972] viii, 312 p.: illus.; 26 cm. 1. Trematoda I. T.
QL391.T7 E58 1972b     595/.122     *LC* 72-82877     *ISBN* 0844800619

## QL401–432 Mollusca. Shells

**Abbott, R. Tucker (Robert Tucker), 1919-.**      **5.3845**
Kingdom of the seashell / by R. Tucker Abbott. — New York: Crown Publishers [1972] 256 p.: ill. (part col.); 29 cm. 'A Rutledge book.' 1. Shells 2. Mollusks I. T.
QL403.A22 1972     594/.04/7     *LC* 74-160575

**Abbott, R. Tucker (Robert Tucker), 1919-.**      **5.3846**
American seashells: the marine molluska of the Atlantic and Pacific coasts of North America / [by] R. Tucker Abbott. — 2d ed. New York: Van Nostrand Reinhold [1974] 663 p.: ill. (part col.); 29 cm. 1. Mollusks — North America. I. T.
QL411.A19 1974     594/.04/7     *LC* 74-7267     *ISBN* 0442202288

**Morris, Percy A., 1899-.**      **5.3847**
[Field guide to the shells of our Atlantic Coast] A field guide to shells, of the Atlantic and gulf coasts and the West Indies / by Percy A. Morris; illustrated with photos; edited by William J. Clench. — 3d ed. [completely rewritten and enlarged] Boston: Houghton Mifflin, 1973. xxviii, 330 p.: ill. (part col.); 19 cm. (The Peterson field guide series, 3) Sponsored by the National Audubon Society and National Wildlife Federation. First published in 1947 under title: A field guide to the shells of our Atlantic Coast. 1. Shells — Atlantic Coast (U.S.) — Identification. 2. Shells — Mexico, Gulf of — Identification. 3. Shells — West Indies — Identification. I. T.
QL416.M6 1973     594/.04/7     *LC* 72-75612     *ISBN* 0395168090

**Morris, Percy A., 1899-.**      **5.3848**
A field guide to shells of the Pacific Coast and Hawaii, including shells of the Gulf of California, by Percy A. Morris. Illustrated with photos. — 2d ed., rev. and enl. — Boston: Houghton Mifflin, 1966. xxxiii, 297 p.: illus. (part col.); 20 cm. — (The Peterson field guide series, no. 6) 1. Shells — Identification. 2. Shells — Pacific coast. 3. Shells — Hawaii. I. T.
QL417.M72 1966     594     *LC* 66-10192

## QL434–601 Arthropoda

**Snodgrass, R. E. (Robert E.), 1875-1962.**      • **5.3849**
A textbook of arthropod anatomy / by R. E. Snodgrass. — New York: Hafner, 1965. viii, 363 p.: ill.; 24 cm. 1. Arthropoda I. T. II. Title: Arthropod anatomy.
QL434.S43     QL434.S67.     *LC* 65-25216

**Boudreaux, H. Bruce, 1914-.**      **5.3850**
Arthropod phylogeny with special reference to insects / H. Bruce Boudreaux. — New York: Wiley, c1979. viii, 320 p.: ill.; 24 cm. 'A Wiley-Interscience

publication.' Includes index. 1. Arthropoda — Evolution. 2. Insects — Evolution 3. Phylogeny I. T.
QL434.35.B68      595/.2/0438      *LC* 78-16638      *ISBN* 0471042900

## QL435–445 Crustacea

**The Biology and management of lobsters** / edited by J. Stanley      **5.3851**
**Cobb, Bruce F. Phillips.**
New York: Academic Press, 1980. 2 v.: ill.; 23 cm. 1. Lobsters 2. Lobster fisheries I. Cobb, J. Stanley. II. Phillips, Bruce F.
QL444.M33 B56      595.3/841 19      *LC* 79-6803      *ISBN* 0121774015

**Crane, Jocelyn.**      **5.3852**
Fiddler crabs of the world (Ocypodidae: genus Uca). — Princeton, N.J.: Princeton University Press, [1975] xxiii, 736 p.: illus.; 29 cm. 1. Fiddler-crabs I. T.
QL444.M33 C7      595/.3842      *LC* 73-16781      *ISBN* 0691081026

## QL449–.92 Myriapoda

**Lewis, J. G. E. (John Gordon Elkan)**      **5.3853**
The biology of centipedes / J.G.E. Lewis. — Cambridge [Eng.]; New York: Cambridge University Press, 1981. [vii], 476 p.: ill.; 23 cm. Includes index. 1. Centipedes I. T.
QL449.5.L48      595.6/2 19      *LC* 80-49958      *ISBN* 0521234131

## QL451–459 Arachnida

**Comstock, John Henry, 1849-1931.**      • **5.3854**
The spider book: a manual for the study of the spiders and their near relatives, the scorpions, psuedoscorpions, whip–scorpions, harvestmen, and other members of the class Arachnida, found in America north of Mexico, with analytical keys for their classification and popular accounts of their habits. — Rev. and ed. by W. J. Gertsch. — Ithaca, N.Y.: Comstock Pub. Co., 1948, 1975 printing. xi, 729 p.: ill.; 24 cm. — (Handbooks of American natural history) 1. Arachnida — North America. I. T.
QL457.1.C7      595.4      *LC* 49-4798

**Gertsch, Willis John, 1906-.**      **5.3855**
American spiders / by Willis J. Gertsch. — 2d ed. — New York: Van Nostrand Reinhold, [1978] xiii, 274 p., [64] p. of plates: ill. (some col.) Includes index. 1. Spiders — North America. 2. Arachnida — North America. I. T.
QL458.4.G47 1978      595/.44/097      *LC* 78-6646      *ISBN* 0442226497

## QL461–601 Insects. Entomology

**Borror, Donald Joyce, 1907-.**      • **5.3856**
An introduction to the study of insects [by] Donald J. Borror [and] Dwight M. De Long. — Rev. ed. — New York: Holt, Rinehart and Winston, [1964] xi, 819 p.: illus.; 26 cm. 1. Entomology 2. Insects — United States. I. De Long, Dwight Moore, 1892- joint author. II. T.
QL463.B69 1964      595.7      *LC* 64-11978

**Imms, A. D. (Augustus Daniel), 1880-1949.**      **5.3857**
[General textbook of entomology] Imms' General textbook of entomology. — 10th ed. / O. W. Richards and R. G. Davies. — London: Chapman and Hall; New York: Wiley: distributed in the U.S.A. by Halsted Press, 1977. 2 v.: ill.; 24 cm. 1. Entomology I. Richards, Owain Westmacott, 1901- II. Davies, Richard Gareth. III. T. IV. Title: General textbook of entomology.
QL463.I57 1977      595.7      *LC* 76-47011      *ISBN* 0470991224

**Price, Peter W.**      **5.3858**
Insect ecology / Peter W. Price. — New York: Wiley, [1975] xii, 514 p.: ill.; 24 cm. 'A Wiley-Interscience publication.' Includes indexes. 1. Insects — Ecology. I. T.
QL463.P73      595.7/05      *LC* 75-12720      *ISBN* 0471697214

**Ross, Herbert Holdsworth, 1908-.**      **5.3859**
A textbook of entomology / Herbert H. Ross, Charles A. Ross, June R.P. Ross. — 4th ed. — New York: Wiley, c1982. viii, 666, [30] p.: ill.; 25 cm. 1. Entomology I. Ross, Charles Alexander. II. Ross, June R. P. III. T.
QL463.R68 1982      595.7 19      *LC* 81-16097      *ISBN* 0471736945

**Borror, Donald Joyce, 1907-.**      **5.3860**
A field guide to the insects of America north of Mexico / by Donald J. Borror and Richard E. White; color and shaded drawings by Richard E. White; line drawings by the authors. — Boston: Houghton Mifflin, 1970. xi, 404 p.: ill. (part col.); 19 cm. — (The Peterson field guide series, 19) 1. Insects — U.S. — Identification. I. White, Richard E. joint author. II. T.
QL464.B65      595.7/09/73      *LC* 70-80420

**Thornhill, Randy.**      **5.3861**
The evolution of insect mating systems / Randy Thornhill and John Alcock. — Cambridge, Mass.: Harvard University Press, 1983. ix, 547 p.: ill.; 25 cm. Includes indexes. 1. Insects — Evolution 2. Insects — Reproduction I. Alcock, John, 1942- II. T.
QL468.7.T46 1983      595.7/056 19      *LC* 82-21351      *ISBN* 0674271807

**Milne, Lorus Johnson, 1912-.**      **5.3862**
The Audubon Society field guide to North American insects and spiders / Lorus and Margery Milne; visual key by Susan Rayfield. — New York: Knopf: distributed by Random House, c1980. 989 p.: ill. (some col.); 20 cm. — (The Audubon Society field guide series) 'A Chanticleer Press edition.' Includes index. 1. Insects — North America — Identification. 2. Spiders — North America — Identification. 3. Arachnida — North America — Identification. I. Milne, Margery Joan Greene, 1914- joint author. II. T. III. Title: Field guide to North American insects and spiders.
QL473.M54 1980      595.7097 19      *LC* 80-7620      *ISBN* 0394507630

**Arnett, Ross H.**      **5.3863**
American insects: a handbook of the insects of America north of Mexico / Ross H. Arnett, Jr. — New York: Van Nostrand Reinhold, c1985. xiii, 850 p.: ill.; 29 cm. 1. Insects — United States. 2. Insects — Canada. I. T.
QL474.A76 1985      595.7097 19      *LC* 84-15320      *ISBN* 0442208669

**Snodgrass, R. E. (Robert E.), 1875-1962.**      • **5.3864**
Principles of insect morphology / by R. E. Snodgrass. — 1st ed. — New York; London: McGraw-Hill, 1935. ix, 667 p.: ill. — (McGraw-Hill publications in the zoölogical sciences, A. F. Shull, consulting editor) 1. Insects — Anatomy I. T. II. Title: Insect morphology.
QL494.S65      *LC* 35-13531

**Chemical ecology of insects** / edited by William J. Bell and      **5.3865**
**Ring T. Cardé.**
Sunderland, Mass.: Sinauer Associates, Inc., 1984. xvi, 524 p.: ill.; 25 cm. 1. Insects — Physiology 2. Insects — Ecology. 3. Chemical senses I. Bell, William J. II. Cardé, Ring T.
QL495.C47 1984      595.7/05 19      *LC* 83-20212      *ISBN* 0878930698

**Dethier, V. G. (Vincent Gaston), 1915-.**      • **5.3866**
The physiology of insect senses. London, Methuen; New York, Wiley [1963] ix, 266 p. illus. 23 cm. (Methuen's monographs on biological subjects) 1. Insects — Physiology 2. Senses and sensation I. T.
QL495.D4      595.701      *LC* 64-9657

**Roeder, Kenneth D. (Kenneth David), 1908-.**      • **5.3867**
Insect physiology Raimon L. Beard...[et al.] — New York: Wiley, 1953. xiv, 1100 p.: ill. 1. Insects — Physiology I. T.
QL495.R6      *LC* 52-11489

**Wigglesworth, Vincent B. (Vincent Brian), Sir, 1899-.**      **5.3868**
Insect physiology / V.B. Wigglesworth. — 8th ed. — London; New York: Chapman and Hall, 1984. x, 191 p.: ill.; 23 cm. 1. Insects — Physiology I. T.
QL495.W5 1984      595.7/01 19      *LC* 84-7782      *ISBN* 0412264609

**Wigglesworth, Vincent B. (Vincent Brian), Sir, 1899-.**      **5.3869**
The principles of insect physiology, by V. B. Wigglesworth. 7th ed. London, Chapman and Hall [1972] vii, 827 p. illus. 26 cm. 1. Insects — Physiology I. T.
QL495.W53 1972      595.7/01      *LC* 73-152566      *ISBN* 0412114909

**Defensive mechanisms in social insects** / edited by Henry R.      **5.3870**
**Hermann.**
New York: Praeger, 1984. xii, 259 p.: ill.; 25 cm. 1. Insect societies 2. Animal defenses I. Hermann, Henry R.
QL496.D44 1984      595.7/057 19      *LC* 83-24798      *ISBN* 0030570026

**Matthews, Robert W., 1942-.**      **5.3871**
Insect behavior / Robert W. Matthews, Janice R. Matthews. — New York: Wiley, c1978. xiii, 507 p.: ill.; 24 cm. 'A Wiley-Interscience publication.' 1. Insects — Behavior I. Matthews, Janice R., 1943- joint author. II. T.
QL496.M39      595.7/05      *LC* 78-7869      *ISBN* 0471576859

**Variable plants and herbivores in natural and managed systems**      **5.3872**
/ edited by Robert F. Denno, Mark S. McClure.
New York: Academic Press, 1983. xvi, 717 p.: ill; 24 cm. 1. Insects — Host plants 2. Insect-plant relationships 3. Insect pests — Control 4. Botany — Variation 5. Insects — Variation. I. Denno, Robert F. II. McClure, Mark S.
QL496.V37 1983      581.5/264 19      *LC* 82-22666      *ISBN* 0122091604

**Wigglesworth, Vincent B. (Vincent Brian), Sir, 1899-.**      • **5.3873**
The physiology of insect metamorphosis. — Cambridge, Eng.: University Press, 1954. vii, 151 p.: ill. — (Cambridge monographs in experimental biology. no. 1) 1. Insects — Development 2. Insects — Physiology I. T. II. Series.
QL496.W62      *LC* 55-1618

**Nachtigall, Werner.** 5.3874
[Gläserne Schwingen. English] Insects in flight; a glimpse behind the scenes in biophysical research. Translators: Harold Oldroyd, Roger H. Abbott [and] Marguerite Biederman–Thorson. New York, McGraw-Hill [1974] 150 p. illus. 29 cm. Translation of Gläserne Schwingen. 1. Flight 2. Wings 3. Insects — Anatomy 4. Animal mechanics I. T.
QL496.7.N313    595.7/01/852    *LC* 70-172030    *ISBN* 0070457360

**The American cockroach / edited by William J. Bell and K. G.** 5.3875
**Adiyodi.**
London: Chapman and Hall, c1981. xvi, 529 p.: ill. 1. Cockroaches — Addresses, essays, lectures I. Bell, William J. II. Adiyodi, K. G.
QL505.6A1 A47    *ISBN* 0412161400

**Otte, Daniel.** 5.3876
The North American grasshoppers / Daniel Otte. — Cambridge, Mass.: Harvard University Press, 1981. 275 p.: ill., maps. 1. Locusts — North America — Identification — Collected works. 2. Insects — Identification — Collected works. 3. Insects — North America — Identification — Collected works. I. T.
QL508.A2 O88    595.7/26 19    *LC* 81-6806    *ISBN* 0674626605

**Dixon, A. F. G. (Anthony Frederick George)** 5.3877
Biology of aphids / [by] A. F. G. Dixon. — London: Edward Arnold, 1974 (c1973). [5], 58 p., 4 p. of plates: ill.; 23 cm. (Studies in biology; no. 44) 1. Aphididae I. T.
QL527.A64 D58 1973    595.7/52    *LC* 74-186695    *ISBN* 0713124210

**Caste differentiation in social insects / guest editors, J.A.L.** 5.3878
**Watson; B.M. Okot–Kotber, and Ch. Noirot.**
1st ed. — Oxford [Oxfordshire]; New York: Pergamon Press, 1985. xiv, 405 p.: ill.; 24 cm. (Current themes in tropical science. v. 3) 'Based on the International Study Workshop on Termite Caste Differentiation, held at the International Centre of Insect Physiology and Ecology (ICIPE), in Nairobi, Kenya, on 7-12 November 1982'–Pref. 1. Termites — Behavior — Congresses. 2. Insect societies — Congresses. 3. Insects — Behavior — Congresses. I. Watson, J. A. L. II. Okot-Kotber, B. M. III. Noirot, Ch. IV. International Study Workshop on Termite Caste Differentiation (1982: International Centre of Insect Physiology and Ecology) V. Series.
QL529.C37 1985    595.7/0524 19    *LC* 84-11055    *ISBN* 0080307833

### QL541–562 Lepidoptera. Butterflies. Moths

**The Biology of butterflies / edited by R.I. Vane–Wright and** 5.3879
**P.R. Ackery.**
London; Orlando: Published for The Royal Entomological Society by Academic Press, 1984. xxiv, 429 p., [4] p. of plates: ill. (some col.), port.; 31 cm. (Symposium of the Royal Entomological Society of London, 0080-4363; no. 11) 'Dedicated to E.B. Ford.' Includes indexes. 1. Butterflies — Congresses. I. Vane-Wright, Richard Irwin. II. Ackery, Phillip Ronald. III. Ford, E. B. (Edmund Briscoe), 1901- IV. Royal Entomological Society of London.
QL541.B56 1984    595.78/9 19    *LC* 83-71684    *ISBN* 0127137505

**Howe, William H.** 5.3880
The Butterflies of North America / William H. Howe, coordinating editor and illustrator & twenty contributors—contributors, David L. Bauer ... [et al.]. — Garden City, N.Y.: Doubleday, 1975. xiii, 633 p., 97 leaves of plates: ill. (some col.); 27 cm. Includes indexes. 1. Butterflies — North America. 2. Insects — North America. I. Bauer, David L. II. T.
QL548.B8    595.7/89/097    *LC* 73-15276    *ISBN* 0385049269

**Klots, Alexander Barrett, 1903-.** 5.3881
A field guide to the butterflies of North America, east of the Great Plains. Illustrated with color paintings of 247 species by Marjorie Statham, and 232 photos. by Florence Longworth. — Boston: Houghton Mifflin, 1951. xvi, 349 p.: illus. (part col.); 19 cm. — (The Peterson field guide series) 1. Butterflies — North America. I. T.
QL548.K55    595.789    *LC* 51-10190

**Pyle, Robert Michael.** 5.3882
The Audubon Society field guide to North American butterflies / Robert Michael Pyle; visual key by Carol Nehring and Jane Opper. — New York: Knopf, c1981. 916 p.: ill. (some col.),map. — (Audubon Society field guide series.) 'A Chanticleer Press edition'. 1. Butterflies — North America. I. T. II. Title: Field guide to North American butterflies. III. Series.
QL548.P9    595.78    *LC* 80-84240    *ISBN* 0394519140 pa

**Covell, Charles V.** 5.3883
A field guide to the moths of eastern North America / Charles V. Covell, Jr.; photographic plates by Tatiana Dominick and Harold H. Norvell; drawings by Elaine R. Snyder Hodges and Charles V. Covell, Jr. — Boston: Houghton Mifflin, 1984. xv, 496 p.: ill. (some col.); 19 cm. — (Peterson field guide series.) Includes index. 1. Moths — Atlantic States — Identification. 2. Moths — United States — Identification. 3. Insects — Identification. 4. Insects —

Atlantic States — Identification. 5. Insects — United States — Identification. I. T. II. Series.
QL551.A75 C68 1984    595.78/1097 19    *LC* 83-26523    *ISBN* 0395260566

### QL563–569 Hymenoptera. Bees. Ants

**Frisch, Karl von, 1886-.** • 5.3884
Bees: their vision, chemical senses, and language. — Rev. ed. — Ithaca: Cornell University Press, [1971] xviii, 157 p.: illus.; 21 cm. 1. Bees I. T.
QL568.A6 F62 1971    595.79/9    *LC* 71-148718    *ISBN* 0801406285

**Michener, Charles Duncan, 1918-.** 5.3885
The social behavior of the bees; a comparative study, by Charles D. Michener. — Cambridge, Mass.: Belknap Press of Harvard University Press, 1974. xii, 404 p.: illus.; 26 cm. 1. Bees — Behavior. 2. Social behavior in animals I. T.
QL568.A6 M557    595.7/99/045    *LC* 73-87379    *ISBN* 0674811755

**Snodgrass, R. E. (Robert E.), 1875-1962.** • 5.3886
Anatomy of the honey bee. Ithaca, N.Y.: Comstock Pub. Associates, 1956. xiv, 334 p.: ill.; 25 cm. 1. Bees — Anatomy I. T.
QL568.A6 S68    595.799    *LC* 56-14047

**Maeterlinck, Maurice, 1862-1949.** 5.3887
The life of the ant, translated by Bernard Miall. New York, The John Day Company [c1930] 282 p. 20 cm. 1. Ants I. Miall, Bernard, 1876- tr. II. T.
QL568.F7 M3    *LC* 31-26089

**Schneirla, T. C. (Theodore Christian), 1902-1968.** 5.3888
Army ants: a study in social organization / edited by Howard R. Topoff. — San Francisco: W. H. Freeman, [1971] xx, 349 p.: ill. (part col.); 25 cm. 1. Army ants 2. Ants — Behavior I. Topoff, Howard R. ed. II. T.
QL568.F7 S3    595.79/6    *LC* 70-149408    *ISBN* 0716709333

### QL571–597 Coleoptera. Beetles

**White, Richard E.** 5.3889
A field guide to the beetles of North America: text and illustrations / by Richard E. White. — Boston: Houghton Mifflin, 1983. xii, 368 p.: ill.; 19 cm. — (Peterson field guide series. 29) Includes index. 1. Beetles — North America — Identification. 2. Insects — Identification. 3. Insects — North America — Identification. I. T. II. Series.
QL581.W47 1983    595.76/097 19    *LC* 83-60    *ISBN* 0395318084

# QL605–739 Vertebrates

**Alexander, R. McNeill.** 5.3890
The chordates / R. McNeill Alexander. — 2d ed. — Cambridge [Eng.]; New York: Cambridge University Press, 1981. 510 p.: ill.; 24 cm. 1. Chordata I. T.
QL605.A384 1980    596 19    *LC* 80-41275    *ISBN* 0521281415

**Blair, W. Frank, 1912-.** • 5.3891
Vertebrates of the United States [by] W. Frank Blair [and others]. — 2d ed. — New York: McGraw-Hill, [1968] ix, 616 p.: illus.; 24 cm. 1. Vertebrates — United States — Identification. I. T.
QL605.B58 1968    596/.09/73    *LC* 67-18322

**Goodrich, Edwin S. (Edwin Stephen), 1868-1946.** • 5.3892
[Studies on the structure & development of vertebrates] Studies on the structure and development of vertebrates. New York: Dover Publications [1958] 2 v.: ill.; 21 cm. 'An unabridged and unaltered republication of the first edition.' 1. Vertebrates — Anatomy I. T.
QL605.G6 1958    596    *LC* 58-3213

**Young, J. Z. (John Zachary), 1907-.** 5.3893
The life of vertebrates / J.Z. Young. — 3rd ed. — Oxford: Clarendon Press, 1981. xv, 645 p.: ill.; 25 cm. Includes indexes. 1. Vertebrates 2. Vertebrates, Fossil I. T.
QL605.Y68 1981    596 19    *LC* 81-206006    *ISBN* 0198571720

**Stahl, Barbara J.** 5.3894
Vertebrate history: problems in evolution [by] Barbara J. Stahl. — New York: McGraw-Hill, [1973, c1974] ix, 594 p.: illus.; 24 cm. — (McGraw-Hill series in population biology) 1. Vertebrates — Evolution 2. Vertebrates, Fossil I. T.
QL607.5.S7    596/.03/8    *LC* 73-13997    *ISBN* 0070606986

# QL614–639.6 Icthyology. Fishes

**Bond, Carl E.**                                              **5.3895**
Biology of fishes / Carl E. Bond. — Philadelphia: W. B. Saunders Co., 1979. vii, 514 p.: ill.; 26 cm. 1. Ichthyology 2. Fishes I. T.
QL615.B67      597      *LC* 77-84665      *ISBN* 0721618391

**Ichthyology / Karl F. Lagler ... [et al.]; illustrated by William**      **5.3896**
**L. Brudon.**
2d ed. — New York: Wiley, c1977. xv, 506 p.: ill.; 24 cm. First ed. by K. F. Lagler, J. E. Bardach, and R. R. Miller. 1. Fishes I. Lagler, Karl Frank, 1912- Ichthyology.
QL615.L3 1977      597      *LC* 76-50114      *ISBN* 0471511668

**Marshall, Norman Bertram.**                                • **5.3897**
The life of fishes / [by] N. B. Marshall. — Cleveland: World Pub. Co., [1966] 402 p.: ill., maps, plates (part col.); 25 cm. 1. Fishes I. T.
QL615.M34 1966      597      *LC* 66-11276

**Migdalski, Edward C.**                                        **5.3898**
The fresh & salt water fishes of the world / by Edward C. Migdalski and George S. Fichter; ill. by Norman Weaver. 1st ed. — New York: Knopf: distributed by Random House, 1976. 316 p.: ill. (some col.); 32 cm. Includes index. 1. Fishes I. Fichter, George S. joint author. II. Weaver, Norman. III. T.
QL615.M49      597      *LC* 76-13704      *ISBN* 0394492390

**Moyle, Peter B.**                                            **5.3899**
Fishes: an introduction to ichthyology / Peter B. Moyle, Joseph J. Cech, Jr. — Englewood Cliffs, N.J.: Prentice-Hall, c1982. xiv, 593 p.: ill.; 24 cm. Includes index. 1. Fishes 2. Ichthyology I. Cech, Joseph J. II. T.
QL615.M64      597 19      *LC* 81-12185      *ISBN* 0133197239

**Norman, J. R. (John Roxborough), 1898-1944.**                **5.3900**
A history of fishes / J. R. Norman; ill. by W. P. C. Tenison. — 3d ed. / by P. H. Greenwood. — New York: Wiley, [1975] xxiv, 467 p.: ill.; 24 cm. 'A Halsted Press book.' Includes index. 1. Fishes I. Greenwood, Peter Humphry. II. T.
QL615.N6 1975      597      *LC* 74-26626      *ISBN* 0470326417

**Curtis, Brian.**                                             **5.3901**
The life story of the fish / by Brian Curtis; introduction by William Beebe. — New York: D. Appleton-Century [c1938] xiv, 260 p.: ill., plates, diagrs.; 22 cm. 1. Fishes I. T.
QL617.C85      597      *LC* 38-27296

**Nelson, Joseph S.**                                          **5.3902**
Fishes of the world / Joseph S. Nelson. — 2nd ed. — New York: Wiley, c1984. xv, 523 p.: ill.; 24 cm. 'A Wiley-Interscience publication.' Includes index. 1. Fishes — Classification I. T.
QL618.N4 1984      597/.001/2 19      *LC* 83-19684      *ISBN* 0471864757

**Marshall, Norman Bertram.**                                  **5.3903**
Explorations in the life of fishes [by] N. B. Marshall. — Cambridge: Harvard University Press, 1971. 204 p.: ill.; 25 cm. — (Harvard books in biology. no. 7) 1. Fishes 2. Fishes, Deep-sea 3. Convergence (Biology) I. T. II. Series.
QL618.2.M37      597.5      *LC* 75-129122      *ISBN* 0674279514

**Cushing, D. H.**                                             **5.3904**
Fisheries biology: a study in population dynamics / D. H. Cushing. — 2d ed. — Madison: University of Wisconsin Press, 1981. xvi, 295 p.: ill.; 24 cm. Includes index. 1. Fish populations I. T.
QL618.3.C86 1981      597/.05/248 19      *LC* 79-5405      *ISBN* 0299081109

**Ecology of freshwater fish production / edited by Shelby D.**   **5.3905**
**Gerking.**
New York: Wiley, 1978. xiv, 520 p.: ill.; 25 cm. 'A Halsted Press book.' 1. Fish populations 2. Fishes — Growth 3. Fishes — Behavior 4. Fish-culture I. Gerking, Shelby Delos, 1918-
QL618.3.E27 1978      639/.31      *LC* 77-92407      *ISBN* 0470993626

**Robins, C. Richard.**                                        **5.3906**
A field guide to Atlantic Coast fishes of North America / C. Richard Robins, G. Carleton Ray; illustrations by John Douglass and Rudolf Freund; sponsored by the National Audubon Society and the National Wildlife Federation. — Boston: Houghton Mifflin, 1986. xi, 354 p., [127] p. of plates: ill. (some col.); 19 cm. (Peterson field guide series. 32) Includes index. 1. Fishes — Atlantic Coast (North America) — Identification. I. Ray, G. Carleton. II. Douglass, John. III. Freund, Rudolf. IV. National Audubon Society. V. National Wildlife Federation. VI. T. VII. Series.
QL621.5.R63 1986      597.092/14 19      *LC* 85-18144      *ISBN* 0395318521

**Eschmeyer, William N.**                                      **5.3907**
A field guide to Pacific Coast fishes of North America: from the Gulf of Alaska to Baja, California / William N. Eschmeyer, Earl S. Herald; illustrations by Howard Hammann, Katherine P. Smith, associate illustrator. — Boston: Houghton Mifflin, 1983. xii, 336 p., 48 leaves of plates: ill. (some col.); 19 cm. — (Peterson field guide series.) Includes index. 1. Fishes — Pacific Coast (North America) — Identification. I. Herald, Earl Stannard. II. T. III. Series.
QL623.4.E83 1983      597.0979 19      *LC* 82-11989      *ISBN* 0395331889

**The Audubon Society field guide to North American fishes,**    **5.3908**
**whales, and dolphins / Herbert T. Boschung, Jr. ... [et al.].**
New York: Knopf: Distributed by Random House, [1983] 848 p.: col. ill.; 20 cm. — (Audubon Society field guide series.) 'A Chanticleer Press edition.' Includes index. 1. Fishes — North America — Identification. 2. Cetacea — North America — Identification. 3. Mammals — North America — Identification. I. Boschung, Herbert T. II. Series.
QL625.A93 1983      597.097 19      *LC* 83-47962      *ISBN* 0394534050

**Water quality criteria for freshwater fish / [edited by] J.S.**  **5.3909**
**Alabaster, assisted by R. Lloyd.**
2d ed. — London; Boston: Published by arrangement with the Food and Agriculture Organization of the United Nations by Butterworths, 1982 (1984 printing) xix, 361 p.: ill.; 25 cm. 1. Fishes, Fresh-water — Europe — Effect of water quality on. 2. Water quality — Europe. I. Alabaster, John S. II. Lloyd, R. (Richard), 1930- III. Food and Agriculture Organization of the United Nations.
QL633.A1 W38 1984      597/.052632 19      *LC* 84-238177      *ISBN* 0408108495

**Lowe-McConnell, R. H.**                                      **5.3910**
Fish communities in tropical freshwaters: their distribution, ecology, and evolution / R. H. Lowe-McConnell. London; New York: Longman, 1975. xvii, 337 p.: ill.; 23 cm. Includes indexes. 1. Fishes, Fresh-water — Tropics. 2. Fishes — Ecology I. T.
QL637.5.L68      597/.05/26320913      *LC* 74-75103      *ISBN* 0582443482

**Netboy, Anthony.**                                           **5.3911**
The salmon: their fight for survival / by Anthony Netboy; illustrated with photos; maps by Samuel H. Bryant. — Boston: Houghton Mifflin, 1974 [c1973] xxii, 613 p.: ill.; 24 cm. 1. Salmon 2. Salmon-fisheries 3. Salmon-fishing I. T.
QL638.S2 N49      333.9/5      *LC* 72-9022      *ISBN* 0395140137

**Castro, José I. (José Ignacio), 1948-.**                     **5.3912**
The sharks of North American waters / by José I. Castro; drawings by D. Bryan Stone III. — 1st ed. — College Station: Texas A&M University Press, c1983. 180 p.: ill.; 24 cm. — (W.L. Moody, Jr., natural history series. no. 5) Includes index. 1. Sharks — North America — Identification. 2. Sharks — Identification. 3. Fishes — Identification 4. Fishes — North America — Identification. I. T. II. Series.
QL638.9.C35 1983      597/.31/097 19      *LC* 82-16720      *ISBN* 0890961409

**Brown, M. E. (Margaret Elizabeth) ed.**                     • **5.3913**
The physiology of fishes. — New York: Academic Press, 1957. 2 v.: illus., diagrs., tables.; 24 cm. 1. Fishes — Physiology I. T.
QL639.B77      597      *LC* 56-6602

**Alexander, R. McNeill.**                                     **5.3914**
Functional design in fishes [by] R. McN. Alexander. — 3d. ed. — London: Hutchinson, c1974. 160 p.: illus., diagrs.; 22 cm. — (Hutchinson university library: Biological sciences) 1. Fishes — Physiology I. T.
QL639.1.A56 1974      597/.01      *ISBN* 009104751X

**Hoar, William Stewart, 1913-.**                              **5.3915**
Fish physiology / edited by W. S. Hoar and D. J. Randall. Contributors: Frank P. Conte [and others] New York: Academic Press, 1969-1984. 10 v.: ill.; 24 cm. Vols. 8- < 10 > edited by W.S. Hoar [et al.] 1. Fishes — Physiology — Collected works. I. Randall, D. J. II. Conte, Frank P., 1929- III. T.
QL639.1.H6      597/.01      *LC* 76-84233      *ISBN* 0123504058

# QL640–669.2 Reptilia. Amphibia

**Morphology and biology of reptiles / edited by A. d'A. Bellairs**   **5.3916**
**and C. Barry Cox.**
London: Published for the Linnean Society of London by Academic Press, c1976. xi, 290 p., [5] leaves of plates: ill.; 27 cm. (Linnean Society symposium series; no. 3) Papers presented at a symposium held in the rooms of the Linnean Society in London, Sept. 9-10, 1975. 1. Reptiles — Congresses. I. Bellairs, Angus d'A. II. Cox, C. Barry (Christopher Barry), 1931- III. Linnean Society of London.
QL640.M67      598.1      *LC* 76-11703      *ISBN* 0120858509

**Bellairs, Angus d'A.**      • **5.3917**
The life of reptiles [by] Angus Bellairs. — New York: Universe Books, [1970] 2 v. (xi, 590 p.): illus.; 25 cm. — (The Universe natural history series) 1. Reptiles I. T.
QL641.B38 1970     598.1     *LC* 70-99976     *ISBN* 0876631138

**Gans, Carl, 1923-.**      • **5.3918**
Biology of the reptilia / edited by Carl Gans. — London; New York: Academic Press, 1969-. v. 1-15    : ill.; 24 cm. Vol. 14, 15 published by: New York: Wiley. 1. Reptiles — Collected works. I. T.
QL641.G3     598.1     *LC* 68-9113

**Porter, Kenneth R.**      **5.3919**
Herpetology [by] Kenneth R. Porter. — Philadelphia: Saunders, 1972. xi, 524 p.: illus.; 27 cm. 1. Herpetology I. T.
QL641.P63     598.1     *LC* 75-188390     *ISBN* 0721672957

**Conant, Roger, 1909-.**      **5.3920**
A field guide to reptiles and amphibians of Eastern and Central North America / illustrated by Isabelle Hunt Conant. — [2d ed.]. — Boston: Houghton Mifflin, 1975. xviii, 429 p.: ill., 48 plates (part col.); 19 cm. — (The Peterson field guide series, 12) First published in 1958 under title: A field guide to reptiles and amphibians of the United States and Canada east of the 100th meridian. 1. Reptiles — North America. 2. Amphibians — North America. 3. Reptiles — Identification. 4. Amphibians — Identification I. T.
QL651.C65 1975     598.1/097     *LC* 74-13425     *ISBN* 0395199794

**King, Wayne.**      **5.3921**
The Audubon Society field guide to North American reptiles and amphibians / F. Wayne King, John Behler. — New York: Knopf: distributed by Random House, 1979. 719 p.: ill. (chiefly col.), maps; 19 cm. Includes index. 1. Reptiles — North America — Identification. 2. Amphibians — North America — Identification. I. Behler, John, joint author. II. National Audubon Society. III. T.
QL651.K56 1979     598.1/097     *LC* 79-2217     *ISBN* 0394508246

**Leviton, Alan E.**      • **5.3922**
Reptiles and amphibians of North America / [by] Alan E. Leviton. — New York: Doubleday, [1971] 250 p.: ill. (part col.); 23 cm. — (Animal life of North America series) 'A Chanticleer Press edition.' 1. Reptiles — North America. 2. Amphibians — North America. I. T.
QL651.L42     598.1/097     *LC* 71-147351

**Stebbins, Robert C. (Robert Cyril), 1915-.**      **5.3923**
A field guide to western reptiles and amphibians: field marks of all species in western North America, including Baja California / text and illustrations by Robert C. Stebbins; sponsored by the National Audubon Society and National Wildlife Federation. — 2nd ed. rev. — Boston: Houghton Mifflin, 1985. xiv, 336 p.: ill.; 19 cm. (Peterson field guide series. 16) Ill. on lining papers. Includes index. 1. Reptiles — North America — Identification. 2. Reptiles — West (U.S.) — Identification. 3. Amphibians — North America — Identification. 4. Amphibians — West (U.S.) — Identification. I. National Audubon Society. II. National Wildlife Federation. III. T. IV. Title: Western reptiles and amphibians. V. Series.
QL651.S783 1985     597.6/0978 19     *LC* 84-25125     *ISBN* 0395382548

**Carr, Archie Fairly.**      • **5.3924**
Handbook of turtles; the turtles of the United States, Canada, and Baja California. Ithaca, N.Y.: Comstock Pub. Associates, 1952. 542p.,illus.,maps. (Handbooks of American natural history) 1. Turtles 2. Reptiles — North America. I. T. II. Series.
QL666.C5 C34     598.13     *LC* 52-9126     *ISBN* 0801400643

**Ernst, Carl H.**      **5.3925**
Turtles of the United States [by] Carl H. Ernst & Roger W. Barbour. — [Lexington]: The University Press of Kentucky, [c1972] x, 347 p.: illus.; 28 cm. 1. Turtles — United States. I. Barbour, Roger William, 1919- joint author. II. T.
QL666.C5 E76     598.1/3/0973     *LC* 72-81315     *ISBN* 0813112729

**Klauber, Laurence Monroe, 1883-1968.**      **5.3926**
Rattlesnakes: their habits, life histories, and influence on mankind. — 2d ed. — Berkeley: Published for the Zoological Society of San Diego by the University of California Press, 1972. 2 v. (xxx, 1533 p.): illus.; 27 cm. 1. Rattlesnakes 2. Poisonous snakes — Venom I. T.
QL666.O6 K56 1972     598.1/2     *LC* 78-188573     *ISBN* 0520017757

**Minton, Sherman A.**      **5.3927**
Venomous reptiles / Sherman A. Minton, Jr., Madge Rutherford Minton. — Rev. ed. — New York: Scribner, c1980. xii, 308 p., [8] leaves of plates: ill.; 22 cm. Includes index. 1. Poisonous snakes 2. Poisonous snakes — Venom I. Minton, Madge Rutherford. joint author. II. T.
QL666.O6 M66 1980     597.96/0469     *LC* 80-17015     *ISBN* 0684166267

**Parker, Hampton Wildman, 1897-1968.**      **5.3928**
Snakes: a natural history / H. W. Parker. — 2d ed., rev. and enl. / by A. G. C. Grandison; illustrator, B. C. Groombridge. — London: British Museum (Natural History); Ithaca [N.Y.]: Cornell University Press, 1977. 108 p., [8] leaves of plates: ill. (some col.); 22 cm. Includes index. 1. Snakes I. Grandison, Alice Georgie Cruickshank. II. T.
QL666.O6 P293 1977     598.1/2     *LC* 76-54625     *ISBN* 0801410959

**Wright, Albert Hazen, 1879-.**      • **5.3929**
Handbook of snakes of the United States and Canada / by Albert Hazen Wright and Anna Allen Wright. — Ithaca, N.Y.: Comstock Pub. Associates, 1957-. v.: ill. map. — (Handbooks of American natural history) 1. Snakes — North America. I. Wright, Anna (Allen), 1882- II. T. III. Series.
QL666O6 W77     598.12     *LC* 57-1635     *ISBN* 0801404630

**Duellman, William Edward, 1930-.**      **5.3930**
Biology of amphibians / William E. Duellman, Linda Trueb; illustrated by Linda Trueb. — New York: McGraw Hill, c1986. xvii, 670 p.: ill.; 27 cm. Includes index. 1. Amphibians I. Trueb, Linda. II. T.
QL667.D84 1986     597.6 19     *LC* 85-14916     *ISBN* 0070179778

**Wright, Anna (Allen) 1882-.**      • **5.3931**
Handbook of frogs and toads of the United States and Canada, by Albert Hazen Wright and Anna Allen Wright. — 3d ed. — Ithaca, N.Y.: Comstock Pub. Co., 1949. xii, 640 p.: illus., maps.; 24 cm. — (Handbooks of American natural history [v. 1]) Authors' names in reverse order in previous editions. 1. Frogs 2. Toads — North America. 3. Amphibians — North America. I. Wright, Albert Hazen, 1879- joint author. II. T. III. Series.
QL668.E2 W8 1949     597.8     *LC* 49-1510

**Ryan, Michael J. (Michael Joseph), 1953-.**      **5.3932**
The túngara frog: a study in sexual selection and communication / Michael J. Ryan; with a foreword by Peter Marler. — Chicago: University of Chicago Press, c1985. xv, 230 p.: ill.; 24 cm. Includes index. 1. Physalaemus pustulosus — Behavior. 2. Physalaemus pustulosus — Reproduction. 3. Amphibians — Behavior 4. Amphibians — Reproduction. 5. Amphibians — Latin America. I. T.
QL668.E257 R93 1985     597.8/7 19     *LC* 84-24110     *ISBN* 0226732282

**Noble, Gladwyn Kingsley, 1894-1940.**      • **5.3933**
The biology of the amphibia. — [New York]: Dover Publications, [c1954] 577 p.: illus.; 21 cm. 'An unabridged republication of the first edition with a new biographical note on the author.' 1. Amphibians I. T.
QL669.N6 1954     597.6     *LC* 55-14430

**Romer, Alfred Sherwood, 1894-.**      **5.3934**
Osteology of the reptiles. Chicago, University of Chicago Press [1956] xxi, 772 p. illus. 25 cm. 1. Reptiles — Anatomy 2. Skeleton I. T.
QL669.R58     598.1     *LC* 55-5143

# QL671–699 Birds. Ornithology

## QL671–674 GENERAL WORKS

**A Dictionary of birds / edited by Bruce Campbell and Elizabeth Lack.**      **5.3935**
Vermillion, S.D.: Published for the British Ornithologists' Union [by] Buteo Books, 1985. xxx, 670 p.: ill.; 29 cm. 1. Ornithology — Dictionaries. I. Campbell, Bruce, 1912- II. Lack, Elizabeth. III. British Ornithologists' Union.
QL672.2.D53 1985     598/.03/21 19     *LC* 84-72101     *ISBN* 0931130123

**Alexander, Wilfrid Backhouse, 1885-.**      • **5.3936**
Birds of the ocean: containing descriptions of all the seabirds of the world, with notes on their habits and guides to their identification. — New and rev. [i.e. 2d] ed. — New York: Putnam, [1963, c1954] 306 p.: ill.; 18 cm. — (A Putnam nature field book) 1. Sea birds I. T.
QL673.A37 1963     598.4     *LC* 63-4339

**Austin, Oliver Luther, 1903-.**      • **5.3937**
Birds of the world: a survey of the twenty–seven orders and one hundred and fifty–five families / illustrated by Arthur Singer; edited by Herbert S. Zim. — New York: Golden Press [1961] 316 p.: col. ill., col. maps; 35 cm. 1. Birds I. T.
QL673.A88     598.2     *LC* 61-13290

**Avian biology** / edited by Donald S. Farner [and] James R.        **5.3938**
King; Taxonomic editor: Kenneth C. Parkes; Contributors: N.
Philip Ashmole [and others]
New York: Academic Press, 1971-1985. 8 v.: ill.; 24 cm. Vols. 8- published in
Orlando. 1. Ornithology — Collected works. I. Farner, Donald Sankey, 1915-
ed. II. King, James Roger, 1927- ed.
QL673.A9      598.2      *LC* 79-178216      *ISBN* 0122494016

**Dorst, Jean, 1924-.**                                        **5.3939**
The life of birds / translated by I. C. J. Galbraith. — New York: Columbia
University Press, 1974. 2 v. (717 p.): ill.; 25 cm. French translation has title: La
vie des oiseaux. 1. Birds 2. Birds — Behavior I. T.
QL673.D58 1974      598.2/5      *LC* 74-8212      *ISBN* 0231039093

**Encyclopedia of birds** / edited by Christopher M. Perrins and        **5.3940**
Alex. L.A. Middleton.
New York, N.Y.: Facts on File, 1985. xxxi, 445 p.: ill. (some col.); 29 cm. 'A
Equinox book'—T.p. verso. Includes index. 1. Birds I. Perrins, Christopher
M. II. Middleton, Alex L. A.
QL673.E53 1985      598 19      *LC* 84-26024      *ISBN* 0816011508

**Harrison, Peter, 1946 Oct. 16-.**                                        **5.3941**
Seabirds, an identification guide / by Peter Harrison; illustrated by the author.
— Boston: Houghton Mifflin, 1983. 448 p.: ill. (some col.); 24 cm. Includes
indexes. 1. Sea birds — Identification. 2. Birds — Identification. I. T.
QL673.H29 1983      598.29/24 19      *LC* 82-15564      *ISBN* 0395332532

**Perrins, Christopher M.**                                        **5.3942**
Avian ecology / C.M. Perrins, T.R. Birkhead. — Glasgow: Blackie; New York:
Distributed in the USA by Chapman and Hall, 1983. x, 221 p.: ill.; 21 cm. —
(Tertiary level biology.) Includes index. 1. Birds — Ecology. I. Birkhead, T.
R. II. T. III. Series.
QL673.P46 1983      598.25 19      *LC* 83-7875      *ISBN* 0412004119

**Stresemann, Erwin, 1889-1972.**                                        **5.3943**
[Entwicklung der Ornithologie von Aristoteles bis zur Gegenwart. English]
Ornithology from Aristotle to the present / Erwin Stresemann; translated by
Hans J. and Cathleen Epstein; edited by G. William Cottrell; with a foreword
and an epilogue on American ornithology by Ernst Mayr. — Cambridge, Mass.:
Harvard University Press, 1975. xii, 432 p.: ill.; 24 cm. Translation of Die
Entwicklung der Ornithologie von Aristoteles bis zur Gegenwart.
1. Ornithology — History. I. T.
QL673.S8513 1975      598.2/09      *LC* 74-25035      *ISBN* 0674644859

**Audubon, John James, 1785-1851.**                               • **5.3944**
The original water–color paintings / by John James Audubon for The birds of
America; reproduced in color for the first time from the collection at the New
York Historical Society; introd. by Marshall B. Davidson. — [Original ed.]
New York: American Heritage Pub. Co.; distributed to booksellers by
Houghton Mifflin Co., Boston, 1966. 2 v.: ill. (part col.) facsim., 431 col. plates
(part fold.) ports. (1 col.); 35 cm. M. B. Davidson edited the descriptive
captions, which include many quotations from Audubon's Ornithological
biography. 1. Birds — North America. 2. Birds — Pictorial works.
I. Davidson, Marshall B. ed. II. Audubon, John James, 1785-1851. Birds of
America III. T.
QL674.A9 1966      598.2973 19      *LC* 66-17926

## QL677 CLASSIFICATION. EVOLUTION

**Gruson, Edward S.**                                        **5.3945**
Checklist of the world's birds: a complete list of the species, with names,
authorities, and areas of distribution / Edward S. Gruson, with the assistance of
Richard A. Forster. — New York: Quadrangle/New York Times Book Co.,
1976. xii, 212 p.: map (on lining papers); 25 cm. Includes index. 1. Birds —
Classification. 2. Birds — Nomenclature (Popular) I. Forster, Richard A.,
joint author. II. T. III. Title: World's birds.
QL677.G76      598.2/021/6      *LC* 72-85239      *ISBN* 0812902963

**Howard, Richard.**                                        **5.3946**
A complete checklist of the birds of the world / Richard Howard, Alick Moore;
with a foreword by Leslie Brown. — Oxford; New York: Oxford University
Press, 1980. 701 p.; 23 cm. 1. Birds — Classification. I. Moore, Alick. joint
author. II. T.
QL677.H75      598/.012 19      *LC* 79-41431      *ISBN* 0192176811

**Feduccia, J. Alan.**                                        **5.3947**
The age of birds / Alan Feduccia. — Cambridge, Mass.: Harvard University
Press, 1980. 196 p.: ill.; 29 cm. Includes index. 1. Birds — Evolution 2. Birds
— Classification. 3. Birds, Fossil I. T.
QL677.3.F42      598      *LC* 80-11926      *ISBN* 0674009754

**Kress, Stephen W.**                                        **5.3948**
The Audubon Society handbook for birders / Stephen W. Kress; drawings by
Anne Senechal Faust; foreword by Olin Sewall Pettingill, Jr. — New York:
Scribner, c1981. xiii, 322 p.: ill.; 24 cm. 1. Bird watching I. National Audubon
Society. II. T.
QL677.5.K73      598/.07/234 19      *LC* 81-205      *ISBN* 0684168383

**Lack, David Lambert.**                                        • **5.3949**
Population studies of birds / by David Lack. — Oxford: Clarendon P., 1966. v,
341 p.: front., illus., tables, diagrs.; 24 cm. 1. Bird populations — Europe.
2. Birds — Europe. I. T.
QL677.5.L3      598.255      *LC* 66-73610

## QL678–695 GEOGRAPHICAL
## DISTRIBUTION

**Audubon, John James.**                                        **5.3950**
Audubon's Birds of America / [edited] by Roger Tory Peterson & Virginia
Marie Peterson. — New York: Abbeville Press, c1981. [44] p., 435 p. of col.
plates (some folded): chiefly col. ill. At head of title: The Audubon Society baby
elephant folio. 1. Birds — North America — Pictorial works. 2. Artists —
North America — Biography. I. Peterson, Roger Tory. II. Peterson, Virginia
Marie, 1925- III. National Audubon Society. IV. T. V. Title: Birds of
America.
QL681.A97 1981      598.2973 19      *LC* 81-12884      *ISBN* 0896592316

**The Audubon Society master guide to birding** / John Farrand,        **5.3951**
Jr., editor.
Chanticleer Press ed. — New York: Knopf: Distributed by Random House,
c1983. 3 v.: ill. (some col.); 22 cm. Includes indexes. 1. Birds — North America
— Identification. I. Farrand, John. II. National Audubon Society. III. Title:
Master guide to birding.
QL681.A986 1983      598.297 19      *LC* 83-47945      *ISBN* 0394533828

**Field guide to the birds of North America** / Thomas B. Allen ...        **5.3952**
[et al.], writers; Teresa S. Purvis, index; contributions by
Caroline Hottenstein ... [et al.].
1st ed. — Washington, D.C.: National Geographic Society, c1983. 464 p.: col.
ill.; 21 cm. Includes index. 1. Birds — North America — Identification.
I. Allen, Thomas B. II. Hottenstein, Caroline. III. National Geographic
Society (U.S.) IV. Title: Birds of North America.
QL681.F53 1983      598.297 19      *LC* 83-13262      *ISBN* 0870444727

**Palmer, Ralph S. (Ralph Simon), 1914- ed.**                        • **5.3953**
Handbook of North American birds. New Haven: Yale University Press, 1962-.
3 v.: ill., plates (part col.) maps; 26 cm. 'Sponsored by the American
Ornithologists' Union and New York State Museum and Science Service.'
1. Birds — North America. I. T.
QL681.P35      598.297      *LC* 62-8259      *ISBN* 0300019025

**Peterson, Roger Tory, 1908-.**                                        • **5.3954**
A field guide to the birds: giving field marks of all species found east of the
Rockies / text and illustrations by Roger Tory Peterson. — 2d rev. and enl. ed.
Sponsored by National Audubon Society. — Boston: Houghton Mifflin Co.,
1947. xxiv, 290 p.: illus., plates. (part col.) map.; 19 cm. 1. Birds — North
America. I. T.
QL681.P45 1947      598.297      *LC* 47-5163

**Pough, Richard Hooper, 1904-.**                                        • **5.3955**
Audubon water bird guide: water, game and large land birds, eastern and
central North America, from southern Texas to central Greenland / color illus.
by Don Eckelberry; line drawings by Earl L. Poole. — [1st ed.]. — Garden City,
N.Y.: Doubleday, 1951. xxviii, 352 p.: ill. (part col.) maps.; 19 cm. 'Sponsored
by National Audubon Society.' 1. Water-birds I. T.
QL681.P69      598.2973      *LC* 51-10952

**Robbins, Chandler S.**                                        **5.3956**
Birds of North America: a guide to field identification / by Chandler S.
Robbins, Bertel Bruun, and Herbert S. Zim; illustrated by Arthur Singer. —
Expanded, rev. ed. — New York: Golden Press, c1983. 360 p.: ill. (some col.);
20 cm. — (Golden field guide series.) Includes index. 1. Birds — North
America — Identification. I. Bruun, Bertel. II. Zim, Herbert Spencer, 1909-
III. T. IV. Series.
QL681.R59 1983      598.297 19      *LC* 83-60422      *ISBN* 030737002X

**Terres, John K.**                                        **5.3957**
The Audubon Society encyclopedia of North American birds / by John K.
Terres; with a foreword by Dean Amadon. — 1st ed. — New York: Knopf:
distributed by Random House, 1980. 1109 p.: ill.; 29 cm. 1. Birds — North
America — Dictionaries. 2. Ornithology — Dictionaries. I. National
Audubon Society. II. T. III. Title: Encyclopedia of North American birds.
QL681.T43 1980      598.297/03/21      *LC* 80-7617      *ISBN* 0394466519

**Udvardy, Miklos D. F., 1919-.**         **5.3958**
The Audubon Society field guide to North American birds—western region /
M. D. F. Udvardy; visual key developed by Susan Rayfield. — New York:
Knopf: distributed by Random House, c1977. 855 p.: ill.; 20 cm. 'A Chanticleer
Press edition.' Includes index. 1. Birds — North America — Identification.
2. Birds — West (U.S.) — Identification. I. T.
QL681.U33 1977     598.2/97     LC 76-47938     *ISBN* 0394414101

**Pough, Richard Hooper, 1904-.**         • **5.3959**
Audubon western bird guide: land, water, and game birds, western North
America, including Alaska, from Mexico to Bering Strait and the Arctic Ocean
/ by Richard H. Pough; col. illus. by Don Eckelberry; line drawings by Terry
M. Shortt; sponsored by National Audubon Society. — [1st ed.] Garden City,
N.Y.,: Doubleday, 1957. xxxvi, 316 p.: ill., diagrs., map, col. plates. 1. Birds —
The West 2. Birds — Northwest, Canadian I. Eckelberry, Don Richard, 1921-
II. National Audubon Society. III. T.
QL683.W4     LC 56-7948

**Peterson, Roger Tory, 1908-.**         • **5.3960**
A field guide to western birds: field marks of all species found in North America
west of the 100th meridian, with a section on the birds of the Hawaiian Islands /
text and illus. by Roger Tory Peterson. — 2d ed., rev. and enl. Boston:
Houghton Mifflin, 1961. 366 p.: ill.; 20 cm. (The Peterson field guide series, 2)
1. Birds — West (U.S.) I. T.
QL683.W4 P4 1961     598.2978     *LC* 60-12250

**Lack, David Lambert.**         **5.3961**
Island biology, illustrated by the land birds of Jamaica / David Lack. —
Berkeley: University of California Press, 1976. xvi, 445 p.: ill.; 25 cm. (Studies in
ecology; v. 3) Includes index. 1. Birds — Jamaica. 2. Island fauna — Jamaica.
I. T.
QL688.J2 L3     598.2/97292     *LC* 75-7194     *ISBN* 0520030079

## QL696 Systematic Groups, A–Z

**Delacour, Jean, 1890-.**         • **5.3962**
The waterfowl of the world / with plates in colour by Peter Scott. — London:
Country Life, 1954-1964. 4 v.: diagrs., maps, col. plates; 26 cm. 1. Anatidae
I. T.
QL696.A5     *LC* 55-600//rev.

**Bent, Arthur Cleveland, 1866-1954.**         • **5.3963**
Life histories of North American wild fowl. — New York: Dover Publications,
[1962] 2 v.: illus.; 22 cm. 'Unabridged and unaltered republication of the work
first published ... in 1923 ... [and] in 1925.' 1. Anatidae 2. Birds — North
America. 3. Birds — Behavior I. T.
QL696.A5 B4 1962     598.2     *LC* 68-51885

**Tinbergen, Niko, 1907-.**         • **5.3964**
The herring gull's world; a study of the social behavior of birds. Illustrated with
51 photos. taken by the author, 58 drawings and diagrs. [Rev. ed.] New York,
Basic Books [1961, c1960] 255 p. illus. 21 cm. (The New naturalist [monograph.
M9]) 1. Herring-gull 2. Birds — Behavior 3. Social behavior in animals I. T.
QL696.L3 T5 1961     598.33     *LC* 61-5466

**Lack, David Lambert.**         • **5.3965**
Darwin's finches; an essay on the general biological theory of evolution. — New
York: Harper, 1961, c1947. 204 p.: ill.; 21 cm. (Harper torchbooks. The science
library) 1. Fringillidae 2. Evolution I. T. II. Series.
QL696.P2 L2

## QL697–698 Anatomy. Physiology. Behavior

**Form and function in birds / edited by A. S. King, J.**     **5.3966**
**McLelland.**
London; New York: Academic Press, 1979-1985. 3 v.: ill.; 27 cm. 1. Birds —
Anatomy — Collected works. 2. Birds — Physiology — Collected works.
I. King, Anthony Stuart. II. McLelland, J. (John)
QL697.F58     598.2/4 19     *LC* 79-50523     *ISBN* 0124075010

**Acoustic communication in birds / edited by Donald E.**     **5.3967**
**Kroodsma, Edward H. Miller; taxonomic editor, Henri Ouellet.**
New York: Academic Press, 1983 (c1982) 2 v.: ill.; 24 cm. — (Communication
and behavior.) 1. Bird-song 2. Animal communication I. Kroodsma, Donald
E. II. Miller, Edward H. III. Ouellet, Henri. IV. Series.
QL698.5.A26 1982     598.2/59 19     *LC* 82-6736     *ISBN* 0124268013

**Bird vocalisations: their relations to current problems in biology**   • **5.3968**
**and psychology; essays presented to W. H. Thorpe / edited by**
**R. A. Hinde.**
London: Cambridge U.P., 1969. xv, 394 p.: 34 plates, ill.; 24 cm. 1. Bird-song
— Addresses, essays, lectures. 2. Birds — Behavior — Addresses, essays,
lectures. I. Thorpe, W. H. (William Homan), 1902- II. Hinde, Robert A. ed.
QL698.5.B56     598.2/59     *LC* 69-19376     *ISBN* 0521074096

**Thielcke, Gerhard.**         **5.3969**
[Vogelstimmen. English] Bird sounds / by Gerhard A. Thielcke. — Ann Arbor:
University of Michigan Press, c1976. viii, 190 p.: ill.; 22 cm. — (Ann Arbor
science library) Translation of Vogelstimmen. Includes index. 1. Bird-song
I. T.
QL698.5.T4813     598.2/5/9     *LC* 73-80579     *ISBN* 0472001213.
*ISBN* 0472050214 pbk

**Baker, Robin, 1944-.**         **5.3970**
Bird navigation: the solution of a mystery? / R. Robin Baker. — New York:
Holmes and Meier, 1984. x, 256 p.: ill.; 24 cm. Includes indexes. 1. Bird
navigation I. T.
QL698.8.B35 1984     598.2/18 19     *LC* 83-22498     *ISBN* 0841909466

**Griffin, Donald Redfield, 1915-.**         **5.3971**
Bird migration / by Donald R. Griffin; ill. by Helen C. Lyman. — New York:
Dover Publications, [1974] x, 180 p.: ill.; 22 cm. Includes index. 1. Birds —
Migration I. T.
QL698.9.G7 1974     598.2/5/2     *LC* 74-76321     *ISBN* 0486205290

# QL700–739 Mammals

## QL700–708 General Works

**The Encyclopedia of mammals / edited by David Macdonald.**     **5.3972**
New York, NY: Facts on File, 1984. xv, 895, [xvi]-xlviii p.: col. ill.; 29 cm.
Includes index. 1. Mammals I. Macdonald, David W. (David Whyte)
QL703.E53 1984     599 19     *LC* 84-1631     *ISBN* 0871968711

**Morris, Desmond.**         • **5.3973**
The mammals; a guide to the living species. — [1st ed.]. — New York: Harper
& Row, [1965] 448 p.: illus., maps.; 26 cm. I. T.
QL703.M68 1965     599     *LC* 65-20508

**Orders and families of recent mammals of the world / edited by**     **5.3974**
**Sydney Anderson, J. Knox Jones, Jr.; sponsored by the**
**American Society of Mammalogists.**
New York: Wiley, 1984. xii, 686 p.: ill.; 25 cm. 'A Wiley-Interscience
publication.' Includes index. 1. Mammals I. Anderson, Sydney, 1927-
II. Jones, J. Knox. III. American Society of Mammalogists.
QL703.O73 1984     599 19     *LC* 83-21806     *ISBN* 047108493X

**Vaughan, Terry A.**         **5.3975**
Mammalogy / Terry A. Vaughan. — 3rd ed. — Philadelphia: Saunders College
Pub., c1986. vii, 576 p.: ill.; 25 cm. Includes index. 1. Mammals I. T.
QL703.V38 1986     599 19     *LC* 85-10754     *ISBN* 0030584744

**Walker, Ernest P. (Ernest Pillsbury), 1891-.**         **5.3976**
[Mammals of the world] Walker's Mammals of the world. — 4th ed. / by
Ronald M. Nowak and John L. Paradiso. — Baltimore: Johns Hopkins
University Press, 1983. 2 v. (xliv, 1362, xxv p.): ill. Rev. ed. of: Mammals of the
world. 3rd ed. 1975. Includes index. 1. Mammals 2. Mammals —
Bibliography. I. Nowak, Ronald M. II. Paradiso, John L. III. T. IV. Title:
Mammals of the world.
QL703.W222 1983     QL703 W22 1983.     599 19     *LC* 82-49056
   *ISBN* 0801825253

**Young, J. Z. (John Zachary), 1907-.**         • **5.3977**
The life of mammals. — New York: Oxford University Press, 1957. 820 p.: ill.
1. Mammals I. T.
QL703.Y6     *LC* 57-12715

**Corbet, G. B. (Gordon Barclay)**         **5.3978**
A world list of mammalian species / G. B. Corbet and J. E. Hill. — London:
British Museum (Natural History); Ithaca, N.Y.: Comstock Pub. Associates,
1980. viii, 226 p.; 24 cm. 1. Mammals — Nomenclature. 2. Mammals —
Classification. I. Hill, John Edwards. joint author. II. T.
QL708.C67 1980     599/.001/2     *LC* 79-53396     *ISBN* 0801412609

## QL711–736 GEOGRAPHICAL DISTRIBUTION

**Handbook of marine mammals / edited by Sam H. Ridgway and**                    **5.3979**
**Richard J. Harrison.**
London; New York: Academic Press, 1985. 3 v.: ill.; 23 cm. 1. Marine
mammals — Collected works. I. Ridgway, Sam H. II. Harrison, Richard
John, 1920-
QL713.2.H34        599 19        *LC* 80-42010        *ISBN* 0125885016

**Marine mammals and fisheries / edited by J.R. Beddington,**                    **5.3980**
**R.J.H. Beverton, and D.M. Lavigne.**
London; Boston: G. Allen & Unwin, 1985. xxi, 354 p.: ill.; 25 cm. 1. Marine
mammals 2. Fisheries — Environmental aspects. 3. Fishery management
I. Beddington, J. R. II. Beverton, R. J. H. III. Lavigne, D. M.
QL713.2.M35 1985        333.95/9 19        *LC* 85-6008        *ISBN* 0046390030

**Scheffer, Victor B.**                    **5.3981**
A natural history of marine mammals / Victor B. Scheffer; ill. by Peter Parnall.
New York: Scribner, c1976. xi, 157 p.: ill.; 24 cm. Includes index. 1. Marine
mammals I. Parnall, Peter. II. T.
QL713.2.S33        599/.09/2        *LC* 76-14820        *ISBN* 0684145766

## QL715–724 North America

**Big game of North America: ecology and management /**                    **5.3982**
**compiled and edited by John L. Schmidt and Douglas L.**
**Gilbert; illustrated by Charles W. Schwartz; technical editors,**
**Richard E. McCabe and Laurence R. Jahn.**
Harrisburg, Pa.: Stackpole Books, c1978. xv, 494 p., [4] leaves of plates: ill.; 26
cm. 'A Wildlife Management Institute book.' Includes index. 1. Big game
animals — North America. 2. Wildlife management — North America.
3. Mammals — North America. I. Schmidt, John L., 1943- II. Gilbert,
Douglas L.
QL715.B53        639/.979        *LC* 78-14005        *ISBN* 0811702448

**Burt, William Henry, 1903-.**                    **5.3983**
A field guide to the mammals: field marks of all North American species found
north of Mexico / text and maps by William Henry Burt; ill. by Richard Philip
Grossenheider; sponsored by the National Audubon Society and National
Wildlife Federation. — 3d ed. — Boston: Houghton Mifflin, 1976. xxv, 289 p.,
[28] leaves of plates: ill.; 19 cm. — (The Peterson field guide series; 5) Includes
index. 1. Mammals — North America — Identification. I. Grossenheider,
Richard Philip. II. T.
QL715.B8 1976        599/.09/73        *LC* 75-26885        *ISBN* 0395240824

**Cahalane, Victor Harrison, 1901-.**                    • **5.3984**
Mammals of North America / by Victor H. Cahalane, with drawings by
Francis L. Jaques. — New York: The Macmillan company, 1961 (c1947). x,
682 p.: ill.; 25 cm. 1. Mammals — North America. I. Jaques, Francis Lee,
1887-1969. illus. II. T.
QL715.C3        599        *LC* 47-4195

**Hall, E. Raymond (Eugene Raymond), 1902-.**                    **5.3985**
The mammals of North America / E. Raymond Hall. — 2d ed. — New York:
Wiley, 1981. 2 v.: ill.; 29 cm. 'A Wiley-Interscience publication.' Includes
indexes. 1. Mammals — North America. 2. Mammals — West Indies. I. T.
QL715.H15 1981        599/.097        *LC* 79-4109        *ISBN* 0471054437

**Whitaker, John O.**                    **5.3986**
The Audubon Society field guide to North American mammals / John O.
Whitaker, Jr.; Robert Elman, text consultant; visual key by Carol Nehring. —
New York: Knopf: distributed by Random House, c1980. 745 p.: ill. (some
col.); 20 cm. — (The Audubon Society field guide series) 'A Chanticleer Press
edition.' Includes index. 1. Mammals — North America — Identification.
I. Elman, Robert. II. National Audubon Society. III. T. IV. Title: Field
guide to North American mammals.
QL715.W48        599.097 19        *LC* 79-3525        *ISBN* 0394507622

**Wild mammals of North America: biology, management, and**                    **5.3987**
**economics / edited by Joseph A. Chapman and George A.**
**Feldhamer.**
Baltimore: Johns Hopkins University Press, c1982. xiii, 1147 p.: ill.; 26 cm.
1. Mammals — North America. 2. Wildlife management — North America.
I. Chapman, Joseph A. II. Feldhamer, George A.
QL715.W56 1982        639.9/79097 19        *LC* 81-8209        *ISBN*
0801823536

**Banfield, Alexander William Francis, 1918-.**                    **5.3988**
The mammals of Canada / A. W. F. Banfield; ill. by Allan Brooks ... [et al.];
cartography by Geoffrey Matthews and Jennifer Wilcox. — Toronto; Buffalo:
Published for the National Museum of Natural Sciences, National Museums of
Canada by University of Toronto Press, [1974] xxv, 438 p., [13] leaves of plates:

ill. (some col.); 28 cm. 1. Mammals — Canada. I. National Museum of
Natural Sciences (Canada) II. T.
QL721.B32        599/.09/71        *LC* 73-92298        *ISBN* 0802021379

**Simpson, George Gaylord, 1902-.**                    **5.3989**
Splendid isolation: the curious history of South American mammals / George
Gaylord Simpson. — New Haven: Yale University Press, 1980. ix, 266 p.: ill.;
24 cm. 1. Mammals — South America — Evolution. 2. Mammals, Fossil I. T.
QL725.A1 S58        599/.03/8098        *LC* 79-17630        *ISBN* 0300024347

## QL737 SYSTEMATIC GROUPS, A–Z

## QL737.C2 CARNIVORA

**Denis, Armand.**                    • **5.3990**
Cats of the world. — Boston: Houghton Mifflin, 1964. xv, 144 p.: illus. (part
col.); 26 cm. — (World wildlife series, 1) 1. Felidae I. T. II. Series.
QL737.C2 D4        599.7442        *LC* 64-23231

**Ewer, R. F.**                    **5.3991**
The carnivores / [by] R. F. Ewer. — Ithaca, N.Y.: Cornell University Press,
[1973] xv, 494 p.: ill.; 25 cm. 1. Carnivora I. T.
QL737.C2 E93        599/.744        *LC* 72-6263        *ISBN* 0801407451

**Fox, Michael W., 1937-.**                    • **5.3992**
Behaviour of wolves, dogs, and related canids, by Michael W. Fox. [1st U.S. ed.]
New York, Harper & Row [1972, c1971] 220 p. illus. 24 cm. 1. Canidae —
Behavior. 2. Mammals — Behavior I. T.
QL737.C22 F69 1972        599/.74442/045        *LC* 74-160662        *ISBN*
0060113219

**Fox, Michael W., 1937-.**                    **5.3993**
The wild canids: their systematics, behavioral ecology, and evolution / edited
by M. W. Fox; foreword by Konrad Lorenz. — New York: Van Nostrand
Reinhold, [1974, c1975] xvi, 508 p.: ill.; 24 cm. (Behavioral science series)
Includes indexes. 1. Canidae I. T.
QL737.C22 F694        599/.74442        *LC* 74-23194        *ISBN* 0442224303

**Mech, L. David.**                    • **5.3994**
The wolf: the ecology and behavior of an endangered species / by L. David
Mech. — [1st ed.] Garden City, N.Y.: Published for the American Museum of
Natural History by the Natural History Press [1970] xx, 384 p.: ill., maps; 24
cm. 1. Wolves I. American Museum of Natural History. II. T.
QL737.C22 M4        599.7/4442        *LC* 73-100043

**Wolves of the world: perspectives of behavior, ecology, and**                    **5.3995**
**conservation / edited by Fred H. Harrington and Paul C.**
**Paquet.**
Park Ridge, N.J.: Noyes Publications, c1982. xx, 474 p.: ill.; 25 cm. — (Noyes
series in animal behavior, ecology, conservation, and management.) Most of the
papers included were originally presented at the 1979 Portland International
Wolf Symposium. Includes index. 1. Wolves — Congresses. I. Harrington,
Fred H. II. Paquet, Paul C. III. Portland International Wolf Symposium
(1979) IV. Series.
QL737.C22 W65 1982        599.74/442 19        *LC* 82-3397        *ISBN*
0815509057

**Zimen, Erik, 1941-.**                    **5.3996**
[Wolf, Mythos und Verhalten. English] The wolf, a species in danger / Erik
Zimen; translated from the German by Eric Mosbacher. — New York:
Delacorte Press, c1981. vi, 373 p., [8] leaves of plates: ill. (some col.); 24 cm.
Translation of Der Wolf, Mythos und Verhalten. Includes index. 1. Wolves
I. T.
QL737.C22 Z5513        599.74/442 19        *LC* 80-20962        *ISBN*
0440096197

**Crouch, James Ensign, 1908-.**                    **5.3997**
Text–atlas of cat anatomy / [by] James E. Crouch; illustrated by Martha B.
Lackey. — Philadelphia: Lea & Febiger, 1969. xvi, 399 p.: ill. (part col.); 32 cm.
1. Cats — Anatomy I. T. II. Title: Cat anatomy.
QL737.C23 C7        599.7/4428        *LC* 68-25206

**Field, Hazel Elizabeth, 1891-.**                    **5.3998**
An atlas of cat anatomy / [by] Hazel E. Field and Mary E. Taylor. — 2d ed. rev.
and enl. by Bernard B. Butterworth. — Chicago: University of Chicago Press,
[1969] 77 p.: ill.; 33 cm. 1. Cats — Anatomy I. Taylor, Mary E., joint author.
II. Butterworth, Bernard B., 1923- III. T.
QL737.C23 F5 1969        599.7/4428        *LC* 69-16998        *ISBN* 0226248178

**Gilbert, Stephen G.**                                                    **5.3999**
Pictorial anatomy of the cat / illustrations & text by Stephen G. Gilbert. —
Rev. ed. — Seattle: University of Washington Press, 1975. vii, 120 p.: ill. (some
col.); 28 cm. Includes index. 1. Cats — Anatomy 2. Dissection I. T.
QL737.C23 G5         599.7/4428       *LC* 67-21200       *ISBN* 029595454X

**Guggisberg, C. A. W. (Charles Albert Walter), 1913-.**                   **5.4000**
Wild cats of the world / c. A. W. Guggisberg. — 1st ed. — New York:
Taplinger Pub. Co., 1975. 328 p., [10] leaves of plates: ill.; 24 cm. Includes
index. 1. Felidae I. T.
QL737.C23 G83 1975     599/.74428     *LC* 74-21020       *ISBN*
0800883241

**Schaller, George B.**                                                    **5.4001**
The Serengeti lion: a study of predator–prey relations / [by] George B. Schaller;
drawings by Richard Keane. — Chicago: University of Chicago Press [1972]
xiii, 480 p.: ill.; 25 cm. (Wildlife behavior and ecology) 'Publication no. 86 of the
Serengeti Research Institute.' 1. Lions — Behavior. 2. Predation (Biology)
3. Mammals — Tanzania — Serengeti Plain. 4. Serengeti National Park
(Tanzania) I. T.
QL737.C23 S298       599/.74428       *LC* 78-180043     *ISBN* 0226736393

**Kruuk, H. (Hans)**                                                       **5.4002**
The spotted hyena: a study of predation and social behavior. — Chicago:
University of Chicago Press [1972] xvi, 335 p.: ill.; 25 cm. (Wildlife behavior
and ecology) 1. Spotted hyena — Behavior. 2. Predation (Biology) 3. Social
behavior in animals I. T.
QL737.C24 K78        599/.74427       *LC* 70-175304     *ISBN* 0226455076

**Chanin, Paul.**                                                          **5.4003**
The natural history of otters / Paul Chanin. — New York, N.Y.: Facts on File,
c1985. xi, 179 p., [8] p. of plates: ill. (some col.); 24 cm. Includes index.
1. Otters I. T.
QL737.C25 C43 1985   599.74/447 19    *LC* 85-6858        *ISBN*
0816012881

## QL737.C4 CETACEA

**Ellis, Richard, 1938-.**                                                 **5.4004**
The book of whales / written and illustrated by Richard Ellis. — New York:
Knopf, 1985. xvii, 202 p., [24] p. of plates: ill. (some col.); 31 cm. 1. Whales
2. Whaling I. T.
QL737.C4 E25 1985    599.5 19         *LC* 86-172220     *ISBN* 0394733711

**Gaskin, D. E. (David Edward), 1939-.**                                   **5.4005**
The ecology of whales and dolphins / D.E. Gaskin. — London; Exeter, N.H.:
Heinemann, 1982. xii, 459 p.: ill.; 25 cm. 1. Cetacea — Ecology. I. T.
QL737.C4 G24 1982    599.5/045 19     *LC* 82-11703      *ISBN*
0435622862

**International Symposium on Cetacean Research. (1st: 1963:**              **5.4006**
**Washington, D.C.)**
Whales, dolphins, and porpoises: [proceedings] / edited by Kenneth S. Norris.
— Berkeley: University of California Press, 1966. xv, 789 p.: ill., maps; 26 cm.
Symposium held in Washington, D.C., in August, 1963; conducted by the
American Institute of Biological Sciences. 1. Cetacea — Addresses, essays,
lectures. I. Norris, Kenneth S. (Kenneth Stafford) ed. II. American Institute
of Biological Sciences. III. T.
QL737.C4 I5 1963     599.5          *LC* 65-21983

**Lockley, R. M. (Ronald Mathias), 1903-.**                               **5.4007**
Whales, dolphins and porpoises / Ronald M. Lockley; with ill. by Elizabeth
Sutton. — 1st American ed. — New York: W.W. Norton, 1979. 200 p.: ill.
(some col.); 26 cm. Includes index. 1. Whales 2. Dolphins 3. Porpoises I. T.
QL737.C4 L6          599.5        *LC* 79-88317       *ISBN* 0393012832

**Minasian, Stanley M., 1948-.**                                           **5.4008**
The world's whales: the complete illustrated guide / Stanley M. Minasian,
Kenneth C. Balcomb III, Larry Foster. — 1st ed. — Washington, D.C.:
Smithsonian Books; New York: Distributed by W.W. Norton, c1984. 224 p.: ill.
(some col.); 27 cm. Includes index. 1. Cetacea I. Balcomb, Kenneth C., 1940-
II. Foster, Larry, 1934- III. T.
QL737.C4 M66 1984    599.5 19        *LC* 84-14142     *ISBN* 0895990148

**Scheffer, Victor B.**                                                  • **5.4009**
The year of the whale / by Victor B. Scheffer; decorations by Leonard Everett
Fisher. — New York: Scribner, [1969] viii, 213 p.: ill.; 23 cm. 1. Sperm whale
I. T.
QL737.C435 S3        599.5/3         *LC* 68-57084

## QL737.C5 CHIROPTERA

**Ecology of bats / edited by Thomas H. Kunz.**                            **5.4010**
New York: Plenum Press, c1982. xviii, 425 p.: ill.; 24 cm. 1. Bats — Ecology.
2. Mammals — Ecology. I. Kunz, Thomas H.
QL737.C5 E33 1982    599.4/045 19    *LC* 82-10157     *ISBN*
030640950X

**Hill, John Edwards.**                                                    **5.4011**
Bats: a natural history / John E. Hill and James D. Smith. — 1st ed. — Austin:
University of Texas Press, 1984. 243 p.: ill.; 25 cm. 'Published in co-operation
with the British Museum (Natural History).' Includes indexes. 1. Bats
I. Smith, James Dale. II. T.
QL737.C5 H55 1984    599.4 19        *LC* 83-51654     *ISBN* 0292707525

## QL737.I5 INSECTIVORA

**Mellanby, Kenneth.**                                                     **5.4012**
The mole. — New York: Taplinger Pub. Co., [1973] 159 p.: illus.; 21 cm. —
([The New naturalist]) 1. Moles (Animals) I. T.
QL737.I57 M45 1973   599/.33         *LC* 72-2186      *ISBN* 0800853164

## QL737.M3 MARSUPIALA

**Lee, Anthony K. (Anthony Kingston), 1933-.**                             **5.4013**
Evolutionary ecology of marsupials / Anthony K. Lee, Andrew Cockburn. —
Cambridge [Cambridgeshire]; New York: Cambridge University Press, 1985.
viii, 274 p.: ill.; 24 cm. (Monographs on marsupial biology.) Includes indexes.
1. Marsupialia — Ecology. 2. Marsupialia — Evolution. 3. Mammals —
Ecology. 4. Mammals — Evolution I. Cockburn, Andrew, 1954- II. T.
III. Series.
QL737.M3 L44 1985    599.2/0438 19   *LC* 84-9440      *ISBN*
052125292X

## QL737.P9–.P955 PRIMATES. GENERAL WORKS

**Behavioral regulators of behavior in primates. Edited by C. R.**         **5.4014**
**Carpenter.**
Lewisburg [Pa.] Bucknell University Press [1973] 303 p. illus. 27 cm. (The
Primates) Selected papers, rewritten and extensively edited, originally
presented at the 8th International Congress of Anthropological and
Ethnological Sciences, held in Tokyo, and at the 2d International Congress of
Primatology, held in Atlanta, Ga. 1. Primates — Behavior I. Carpenter, C.
Ray (Clarence Ray), 1905- ed. II. International Congress of Anthropological
and Ethnological Sciences. 8th, Tokyo and Kyoto, 1968. III. International
Congress of Primatology. (2nd: 1968: Atlanta, Ga.)
QL737.P9 B39         599/.8/045      *LC* 72-3602      *ISBN* 0838710999

**Bramblett, Claud A.**                                                    **5.4015**
Patterns of primate behavior / Claud A. Bramblett. — 1st ed. — Palo Alto,
Calif.: Mayfield Pub. Co., 1976. xii, 320 p.: ill.; 21 cm. Includes index.
1. Primates — Behavior 2. Mammals — Behavior I. T.
QL737.P9 B747        599/.8/045      *LC* 75-44695     *ISBN* 087484326X

**Comparative reproduction of nonhuman primates. Edited by E.**           **5.4016**
**S. E. Hafez.**
Springfield, Ill.: Thomas, [1971] xiv, 557 p.: illus.; 24 cm. 1. Primates
2. Reproduction 3. Sexual behavior in animals I. Hafez, E. S. E. (Elsayed
Saad Eldin), 1922- ed.
QL737.P9 C58         599.8/04/1662   *LC* 74-161162

**DeVore, Irven. ed.**                                                   • **5.4017**
Primate behavior: field studies of monkeys and apes / contributors: Jarvis R.
Bastian [and others] — New York: Holt, Rinehart and Winston [1965] xiv,
654 p.: ill., maps; 24 cm. 'One result of nine-month 'Primate project' held at the
Center for Advanced Study in the Behavioral Sciences, Stanford, California,
during 1962-1963. Organized by Sherwood L. Washburn and David A.
Hamburg, and supported by a grant (no. M-5502) from the National Institutes
of Health.' 1. Primates — Behavior I. Center for Advanced Study in the
Behavioral Sciences (Stanford, Calif.) II. T. III. Title: Field studies of
monkeys and apes.
QL737.P9 D48         599.8          *LC* 65-12817

**Kavanagh, Michael.**                                                     **5.4018**
A complete guide to monkeys, apes and other primates / Michael Kavanagh;
introduced by Desmond Morris. — New York: Viking Press, 1984,c1983.

224 p.: ill. (some col.), maps; 25 cm. Includes index. 1. Primates I. T. II. Title: Monkeys, apes and other primates.
QL737.P9 K39   *ISBN* 0670435430

**Malayan forest primates: ten years' study in tropical rain forest**   **5.4019**
/ edited by David J. Chivers.
New York: Plenum Press, c1980. xxiv, 364 p.: ill.; 26 cm. Includes index. 1. Primates — Malaysia — Kerau Game Preserve, Pahang. 2. Primates — Behavior 3. Mammals — Behavior 4. Mammals — Malaysia — Kerau Game Preserve, Pahang. 5. Kerau Game Preserve, Pahang. I. Chivers, David John.
QL737.P9 M275   599.8/09595 19   *LC* 80-25181   *ISBN* 0306406268

**Poirier, Frank E., 1940-.**   **5.4020**
Primate socialization / edited by Frank E. Poirier. — [1st ed.]. — New York: Random House, [1972] x, 260 p.: ill.; 24 cm. 1. Primates — Behavior 2. Social behavior in animals I. T.
QL737.P9 P64   599.8/045/24   *LC* 78-173907   *ISBN* 0394311124

**Primate behavior.**   • **5.4021**
v. 1-4. New York, Academic Press, 1970-1975. 4 v. ill. 24 cm. 'Developments in field and laboratory research.' 1. Primates — Behavior — Collected works. I. Rosenblum, Leonard A. ed.
QL737.P9 P67   599.8/045   *LC* 79-127677

**Primate bio–social development: biological, social, and ecological**   **5.4022**
determinants / edited by Suzanne Chevalier–Skolnikoff, Frank E. Poirier.
New York: Garland Pub., 1977. xix, 636 p.: ill.; 26 cm. 1. Primates — Behavior 2. Social behavior in animals I. Chevalier-Skolnikoff, Suzanne. II. Poirier, Frank E., 1940-
QL737.P9 P6714   599/.05   *LC* 76-25748   *ISBN* 0824099001

**Primate evolution and human origins / [selected by] Russell L.**   **5.4023**
Ciochon, John G. Fleagle.
Menlo Park, Calif.: Benjamin/Cummings Pub. Co., c1985. viii, 396 p.: ill.; 29 cm. 1. Primates — Evolution 2. Human evolution I. Ciochon, Russell L. II. Fleagle, John G.
QL737.P9 P67249 1985   599.8/0438 19   *LC* 84-21644   *ISBN* 080532240X

**Reynolds, Vernon.**   • **5.4024**
The apes: the gorilla, chimpanzee, orangutan, and gibbon; their history and their world. — [1st ed.]. — New York: Dutton, 1967. 296 p.: illus., facsims., maps.; 25 cm. 1. Apes I. T.
QL737.P9 R48   599.8/8   *LC* 66-21302

**Richard, Alison F.**   **5.4025**
Primates in nature / Alison F. Richard. — New York: W.H. Freeman, c1985. x, 558 p.: ill.; 24 cm. Includes index. 1. Primates I. T.
QL737.P9 R54 1985   599.8 19   *LC* 84-18802   *ISBN* 071671647X

**Rosen, Stephen I., 1943-.**   **5.4026**
Introduction to the primates: living and fossil [by] S. I. Rosen. — Englewood Cliffs, N.J.: Prentice-Hall, [1974] x, 245 p.: illus.; 23 cm. 1. Primates 2. Primates, Fossil 3. Human evolution I. T.
QL737.P9 R67   599/.8   *LC* 73-14802   *ISBN* 0134934601

**Rowell, Thelma.**   **5.4027**
The social behaviour of monkeys. — Harmondsworth: Penguin, 1972. 203 p.: illus., map.; 18 cm. — (Penguin education) (Penguin science of behaviour. Social psychology) 1. Primates — Behavior 2. Social behavior in animals I. T.
QL737.P9 R68   599/.8/045   *LC* 73-154918   *ISBN* 0140807063

**Wolfheim, Jaclyn H.**   **5.4028**
Primates of the world: distribution, abundance, and conservation / Jaclyn H. Wolfheim. — Seattle: University of Washington Press, c1983. xxiii, 831 p.: ill., maps; 25 cm. 1. Primates I. T.
QL737.P9 W64 1983   599.8 19   *LC* 82-13464   *ISBN* 0295958995

**Zuckerman, Solly Zuckerman, Baron, 1904-.**   **5.4029**
The social life of monkeys and apes / S. Zuckerman. — 2nd ed. — London; Boston: Routledge & K. Paul, 1981. xx, 511 p.: ill.; 23 cm. 'Re-issue of 1932 edition together with a postscript.' Includes index. 1. Monkeys — Behavior 2. Apes — Behavior. 3. Social behavior in animals 4. Mammals — Behavior I. T.
QL737.P9 Z8 1981   599.8/0451 19   *LC* 80-40991   *ISBN* 0710006918

**Moynihan, M.**   **5.4030**
The New World primates: adaptive radiation and the evolution of social behavior, languages, and intelligence / Martin Moynihan. — Princeton, N.J.: Princeton University Press, 1976. x, 262 p.: ill.; 23 cm. Includes index. 1. Cebidae — Behavior. 2. Callitrichidae — Behavior. 3. Mammals — Latin America. I. T.
QL737.P92 M68   599/.82   *LC* 75-3467   *ISBN* 0691081689

**Terborgh, John, 1936-.**   **5.4031**
Five New World primates: a study in comparative ecology / John Terborgh. — Princeton, N.J.: Princeton University Press, c1983. xiv, 260 p.: ill.; 25 cm. — (Monographs in behavior and ecology.) Includes indexes. 1. Cebidae — Ecology. 2. Mammals — Ecology. 3. Mammals — Peru — Ecology. I. T. II. Title: 5 New World primates. III. Series.
QL737.P925 T46 1983   599.8/2 19   *LC* 83-42596   *ISBN* 0691083371

**Dunbar, R. I. M. (Robin Ian MacDonald), 1947-.**   **5.4032**
Reproductive decisions: an economic analysis of gelada baboon social strategies / R.I.M. Dunbar. — Princeton, N.J.: Princeton University Press, 1985 (c1984). x, 265 p.: ill.; 25 cm. (Monographs in behavior and ecology.) Includes indexes. 1. Gelada baboon — Reproduction. 2. Gelada baboon — Behavior. 3. Social behavior in animals 4. Mammals — Reproduction 5. Mammals — Behavior I. T. II. Series.
QL737.P93 D76 1984   599.8/2 19   *LC* 84-42584   *ISBN* 0691083606

# QL737.P96 Apes

**Fossey, Dian.**   **5.4033**
Gorillas in the mist / Dian Fossey. — Boston, Mass.: Houghton Mifflin, 1983. xviii, 326 p., [80] p. of plates: ill.; 24 cm. Includes index. 1. Gorillas — Behavior 2. Mammals — Behavior I. T.
QL737.P96 F67 1983   599.88/460451 19   *LC* 82-23332   *ISBN* 0395282179

**Goodall, Jane, 1934-.**   **5.4034**
The chimpanzees of Gombe: patterns of behavior / Jane Goodall. — Cambridge, Mass.: Belknap Press of Harvard University Press, 1986. 673 p., [8] p. of plates: ill. (some col.); 29 cm. Includes indexes. 1. Gombe Stream National Park (Tanzania) 2. Chimpanzees — Behavior. 3. Mammals — Behavior 4. Mammals — Tanzania — Gombe Stream National Park — Behavior. I. T.
QL737.P96 G585 1986   599.88/440451 19   *LC* 85-20030   *ISBN* 0674116496

**The Great apes / edited by David A. Hamburg and Elizabeth R.**   **5.4035**
McCown.
Menlo Park, Calif.: Benjamin/Cummings Pub. Co., c1979. xiii, 554 p.: ill.; 24 cm. — (Perspectives on human evolution; v. 5) (Benjamin/Cummings series in anthropology) 'A publication of the Society for the Study of Human Evolution.' Includes indexes. 1. Apes — Behavior. 2. Mammals — Behavior I. Hamburg, David A., 1925- II. McCown, Elizabeth R. III. Society for the Study of Human Evolution. IV. Series. V. Series: Benjamin/Cummings series in anthropology
QL737.P96G7x   573.2/008 s 599/.88/045   *LC* 79-11361   *ISBN* 0805336699

**Maple, Terry.**   **5.4036**
Orang-utan behavior / Terry L. Maple. — New York: Van Nostrand Reinhold Co., c1980. xii, 268 p., [2] leaves of plates: ill. (some col.); 24 cm. — (Van Nostrand Reinhold primate behavior and development series.) Includes indexes. 1. Orangutan — Behavior. 2. Mammals — Behavior I. T. II. Series.
QL737.P96 M36 1980   599/.884   *LC* 79-22233   *ISBN* 0442251548

**Terrace, Herbert S., 1936-.**   **5.4037**
Nim / Herbert S. Terrace. — 1st ed. — New York: Knopf: distributed by Random House, 1979. x, 303 p.: ill.; 24 cm. Includes index. 1. Chimpanzees — Psychology. 2. Human-animal communication 3. Sign language 4. Nim Chimpsky (Chimpanzee) 5. Mammals — Psychology. I. T.
QL737.P96 T47 1979   156/.3   *LC* 79-2157   *ISBN* 0394402502

**Yerkes, Robert Mearns, 1876-1956.**   • **5.4038**
The great apes: a study of anthropoid life / by Robert M. Yerkes and Ada W. Yerkes. New Haven, Yale University Press, 1929. — New York: Johnson Reprint Corp., 1970. xix, 652 p.: ill.; 24 cm. — (Landmarks in anthropology) 1. Apes — Behavior. 2. Psychology, Comparative I. Yerkes, Ada (Watterson) joint author. II. T.
QL737.P96 Y4 1970   599.8/8/045   *LC* 75-139379

# QL737.P98–.Z Other Mammals

**Douglas-Hamilton, Iain.**   **5.4039**
Among the elephants / Iain and Oria Douglas–Hamilton; foreword by Niko Tinbergen. New York: Viking Press, 1975. 285 p., [36] leaves of plates: ill.; 25 cm. Includes index. 1. African elephant — Behavior. I. Douglas-Hamilton, Oria. joint author. II. T.
QL737.P98 D68 1975   599/.61   *LC* 74-7502   *ISBN* 0670122084

**Laws, Richard M.**      **5.4040**
Elephants and their habitats: the ecology of elephants in North Bunyoro, Uganda / R. M. Laws, I. S. C. Parker, R. C. B. Johnstone. — Oxford [Eng.]: Clarendon Press, 1975. xii, 376 p.: ill.; 24 cm. Includes indexes. 1. African elephant 2. Mammals — Uganda — Bunyoro — Ecology. I. Parker, I. S. C. (Ian S. C.), 1936- joint author. II. Johnstone, Ronald C. B., joint author. III. T.
QL737.P98 L34     599/.61     LC 75-325917     ISBN 0198543875

**Barnett, S. A. (Samuel Anthony), 1915-.**      **5.4041**
The rat: a study in behavior / S. A. Barnett. — Rev. ed. — Chicago: University of Chicago Press, 1975. xiv, 318 p.: ill.; 25 cm. Includes index. 1. Rats — Psychology. I. T.
QL737.R666 B37 1975     599/.3233     LC 74-33509     ISBN 0226037401

**Walther, Fritz R.**      **5.4042**
Communication and expression in hoofed mammals / Fritz R. Walther. — Bloomington: Indiana University Press, c1984. xx, 423 p.: ill. — (Animal communication.) Includes index. 1. Ungulata — Behavior. 2. Animal communication 3. Mammals — Behavior I. T. II. Series.
QL737.U4 W25 1983    QL737U4 W25 1984.    599.3/0451 19     LC 82-49011    ISBN 0253313805

**Geist, Valerius.**      **5.4043**
Mountain sheep; a study in behavior and evolution. — Chicago: University of Chicago Press, [1971] xv, 383 p.: illus.; 25 cm. — (Wildlife behavior and ecology) 1. Mountain sheep — Behavior. I. T.
QL737.U53 G44     599/.7358     LC 77-149596     ISBN 0226285723

**Schaller, George B.**      **5.4044**
Mountain monarchs: wild sheep and goats of the Himalaya / Geroge B. Schaller. — Chicago: University of Chicago Press, 1977. xviii 425 p., [16] leaves of plates: ill.; 25 cm. — (Wildlife behavior and ecology) Includes index. 1. Bovidae 2. Alpine fauna — Himalaya Mountains. 3. Mammals — Himalaya Mountains. I. T.
QL737.U53 S3     599/.7358     LC 77-1336     ISBN 0226736415

**Calef, George W. (George Waller), 1944-.**      **5.4045**
Caribou and the barren–lands / George Calef. — Ottawa: Canadian Arctic Resources Committee, c1981. 176 p.: col. ill., maps. 1. Caribou — Canada, Northern. 2. Caribou — Alaska. 3. Mammals — Canada, Northern. 4. Mammals — Alaska. I. Canadian Arctic Resources Committee. II. T.
QL737U55 C23     599.73/57 19     ISBN 0919996205

**Dagg, Anne Innis.**      **5.4046**
The giraffe: its biology, behavior, and ecology / Anne Innis Dagg, J. Bristol Foster. — New York: Van Nostrand Reinhold Co., c1976. xiii, 210 p.: ill.; 24 cm. Includes index. 1. Giraffes I. Foster, J. Bristol. joint author. II. T.
QL737.U56 D3     599/.7357     LC 75-33181     ISBN 0442224311

## QL739–.3 MAMMALIAN ANATOMY. PHYSIOLOGY. BEHAVIOR

**Mammalian cell membranes / edited by G. A. Jamieson and D. M. Robinson.**      **5.4047**
London; Boston: Butterworths, 1976-1977. 5 v.: ill.; 24 cm. 1. Mammals — Cytology 2. Cell membranes I. Jamieson, G. A. (Graham A.), 1929- II. Robinson, David Mason, 1932-
QL739.15.M35     599/.08/75     LC 75-33317     ISBN 0408707224

**Pheromones and reproduction in mammals / edited by John G. Vandenbergh.**      **5.4048**
New York: Academic Press, 1983. xiv, 298 p.: ill.; 24 cm. Includes bibliographies and index. 1. Mammals — Reproduction 2. Pheromones I. Vandenbergh, John G.
QL739.2.P48 1983     599/.016 19     LC 82-22776     ISBN 0127107800

**Reproduction in mammals / edited by C.R. Austin, R.V. Short; drawings by John R. Fuller.**      **5.4049**
2nd ed. — Cambridge [Cambridgeshire]; New York: Cambridge University Press, 1982. 4 v.: ill.; 26 cm. 1. Mammals — Reproduction — Collected works. I. Austin, C. R. (Colin Russell), 1914- II. Short, Roger Valentine, 1930-
QL739.2.R46 1982     599.01/6 19     LC 81-18060     ISBN 0521246288

**Young, J. Z. (John Zachary), 1907-.**      **5.4050**
The life of mammals: their anatomy and physiology. — 2nd ed. / [by] J. Z. Young, with the assistance of M. J. Hobbs. — Oxford: Clarendon Press, 1975. xv, 528 p.: ill., map; 26 cm. Includes indexes. 1. Mammals — Physiology 2. Mammals — Anatomy I. Hobbs, Michael John. II. T.
QL739.2.Y68 1975     599/.01     LC 76-357378     ISBN 0198571569

**Parental care in mammals / edited by David J. Gubernick and Peter H. Klopfer.**      **5.4051**
New York: Plenum Press, c1981. xix, 459 p.; 24 cm. 1. Mammals — Behavior 2. Parental behavior in animals I. Gubernick, David J. II. Klopfer, Peter H.
QL739.3.P37     599.05/6     LC 80-36692     ISBN 0306405334

## QL750–799 ANIMAL BEHAVIOR

**Alcock, John, 1942-.**      **5.4052**
Animal behavior: an evolutionary approach / John Alcock. — 3rd ed. — Sunderland, Mass.: Sinauer Associates, c1984. 596 p.: ill.; 27 cm. Col. ill. on lining papers. 1. Animal behavior 2. Evolution I. T.
QL751.A58 1984     591.51 19     LC 83-14420     ISBN 0878930213

**Andrewartha, H. G. (Herbert George), 1907-.**      **• 5.4053**
The distribution and abundance of animals / by H. G. Andrewartha and L. C. Birch. — Chicago: University of Chicago Press, 1954. xv, 782 p.: ill., maps. 25 cm. 1. Physiology, Comparative 2. Animal ecology 3. Zoogeography I. Birch, L. Charles, 1918- II. T.
QL751.A642     LC 54-13016

**Behavioural ecology: an evolutionary approach / edited by J.R. Krebs and N.B. Davies.**      **5.4054**
2nd ed. — Sunderland, Mass.: Sinauer Associates, 1984, c1978. xi, 493 p.: ill.; 26 cm. Includes indexes. 1. Animal behavior 2. Animal ecology 3. Behavior evolution I. Krebs, J. R. (John R.) II. Davies, N. B. (Nicholas B.), 1952- III. Title: Behavioral ecology.
QL751.B345 1984     591.51 19     LC 83-20267     ISBN 0878931325

**Eisner, Thomas, 1929- comp.**      **5.4055**
Animal behavior: readings from Scientific American / selected and introduced by Thomas Eisner, Edward O. Wilson. — San Francisco: W. H. Freeman, [1975] iv, 339 p.: ill.; 29 cm. Includes index. 1. Animal behavior — Addresses, essays, lectures. I. Wilson, Edward Osborne, 1929- joint comp. II. Scientific American. III. T.
QL751.6.E37     591.5     LC 75-2383     ISBN 0716705117. ISBN 0716705109 pbk

**Elton, Charles S. (Charles Sutherland), 1900-.**      **5.4056**
Animal ecology [by] Charles Elton. New York, October House [1966] xvi, 207 p. illus. 23 cm. (Biology series) First published in 1927. 1. Animal ecology I. T.
QL751.E5 1966     591.5     LC 66-21099

**Grzimek's Encyclopedia of ethology / editor–in–chief, Bernhard Grzimek.**      **5.4057**
New York: Van Nostrand Reinhold Co., c1977. xx, 705 p.: ill. (some col.); 25 cm. Includes index. 1. Animal behavior I. Grzimek, Bernhard. II. Title: Encyclopedia of ethology.
QL751.G8945     591.5     LC 76-9298     ISBN 0442229461

**Hinde, Robert A.**      **5.4058**
Animal behaviour; a synthesis of ethology and comparative psychology [by] Robert A. Hinde. 2d ed. New York, McGraw-Hill [1970] xvi, 876 p. illus. 23 cm. 1. Animal behavior 2. Psychology, Comparative I. T.
QL751.H49 1970     156     LC 77-95806

**Kikkawa, Jiro.**      **5.4059**
The behaviour of animals [by] Jiro Kikkawa [and] Malcolm J. Thorne. New York, Taplinger Pub. Co. [1972, c1971] viii, 223 p. illus. 24 cm. 1. Animal behavior I. Thorne, Malcolm J., joint author. II. T.
QL751.K47 1972     591.5     LC 70-172983     ISBN 0800807154

**Klopfer, Peter H.**      **5.4060**
An introduction to animal behavior: ethology's first century / [by] Peter H. Klopfer. — 2d ed. Englewood Cliffs, N.J.: Prentice-Hall [1974] xiv, 332 p.: ill.; 24 cm. (Prentice-Hall biological science series) 1. Animal behavior 2. Animal behavior — History. I. T.
QL751.K593 1974     591.5     LC 73-22467     ISBN 0134779355

**Krutch, Joseph Wood, 1893-1970.**      **• 5.4061**
The great chain of life. With illus. by Paul Landacre. Boston, Houghton Mifflin, 1957 [c1956] 227 p. illus. 22 cm. 1. Animal behavior 2. Evolution I. T.
QL751.K87     574     LC 56-13184

**Lorenz, Konrad, 1903-.**      **• 5.4062**
King Solomon's ring: new light on animal ways / illustrated by the author and with a foreword by Julian Huxley; [translation from the German by Marjorie

Kerr Wilson]. — New York: Crowell [1952] 202 p.: ill.; 22 cm. 1. Animal
behavior I. T.
QL751.L695     591.5     LC 52-7373

**Maier, Richard A., 1933-.**             **5.4063**
Comparative animal behavior [by] Richard A. Maier [and] Barbara M. Maier.
Belmont, Calif., Brooks/Cole Pub. Co. [1970] viii, 459 p. illus. 25 cm. (Core
books in psychology) 1. Animal behavior I. Maier, Barbara M., joint author.
II. T.
QL751.M217     591.5     LC 78-95056

**Morse, Douglass H., 1938-.**             **5.4064**
Behavioral mechanisms in ecology / Douglass H. Morse. — Cambridge, Mass.:
Harvard University Press, 1980. viii, 383 p.: ill.; 25 cm. Includes index.
1. Animal behavior 2. Animal ecology I. T.
QL751.M876     591.51     LC 80-12130     ISBN 0674064607

**Mortenson, F. Joseph.**             **5.4065**
Animal behavior, theory and research / F. Joseph Mortenson. — Monterey,
Calif.: Brooks/Cole Pub. Co., [1975] x, 193 p.: ill.; 23 cm. — (Basic concepts in
psychology series) Includes index. 1. Animal behavior I. T.
QL751.M88     596/.05     LC 75-24161     ISBN 0818501472

**Sparks, John.**             **5.4066**
The discovery of animal behaviour / John Sparks. — 1st American ed. —
Boston: Little, Brown, c1982. 288 p.: ill. (some col.); 26 cm. Based on the BBC
television series, The Discovery of animal behaviour. Includes index. 1. Animal
behavior I. Discovery of animal behaviour (Television program) II. T.
III. Title: Animal behaviour.
QL751.S674 1982     591.5/1 19     LC 82-82622     ISBN 0316804924

**Tinbergen, Niko, 1907-.**             **5.4067**
The animal in its world: explorations of an ethologist, 1932–1972 / [by] Niko
Tinbergen; foreword by Sir Peter Medawar. — Cambridge, Mass.: Harvard
University Press, 1972-73. 2 v.: ill.; 23 cm. Includes papers translated from the
German. 1. Animal behavior I. T.
QL751.T543 1972b     591.5     LC 72-94876     ISBN 0674037251

**Tinbergen, Niko, 1907-.**             • **5.4068**
Curious naturalists. New York, Basic Books [c1958] 280 p. illus. 23 cm.
1. Birds — Behavior 2. Insects — Behavior I. T.
QL751.T55 1958a     591.51     LC 59-13750

**Quantitative ethology / edited by Patrick W. Colgan.**          **5.4069**
New York: Wiley, c1978. xiv, 364 p.: ill.; 24 cm. 'A Wiley-Interscience
publication.' Includes indexes. 1. Animal behavior — Mathematical models.
I. Colgan, Patrick W.
QL751.65.M3 Q36     591.5     LC 78-999     ISBN 0471022365

---

# QL752–785 Special Topics

## QL752 Animal Populations

**Andrewartha, H. G. (Herbert George), 1907-.**      • **5.4070**
Introduction to the study of animal populations [by] H. G. Andrewartha. 2nd
ed. London, Methuen, 1970. xiv, 283 p. illus., map. 22 cm. 1. Animal
populations I. T.
QL752.A63 1970     591.5/24     LC 77-557051     ISBN 0416129706

**Elton, Charles S. (Charles Sutherland), 1900-.**      • **5.4071**
Voles, mice and lemmings / by Charles Elton / (Authorized) reprint ([der
Ausg.] Oxford 1942.). — Weinheim: Cramer; Codicote/Herts., Wheldon and
Wesley; New York: Stechert-Hafner, 1965. 496 p.: ill., maps. (Histoire naturalis
classica; t. 32) 1. Animal populations 2. Microtus 3. Mice 4. Lemmings I. T.
II. Series.
QL752.E45 1965

**Lack, David Lambert.**             • **5.4072**
The natural regulation of animal numbers, by David Lack. Oxford, Clarendon
P., 1967. viii, 343 p. col. front., illus., maps, tables, diagrs. 25 cm.
Bibliography: p. [281]-32o. 1. Animal populations 2. Bird populations I. T.
QL752.L3 1967     591.5/5     LC 67-111082

**MacArthur, Robert H.**             • **5.4073**
The biology of populations [by] Robert H. MacArthur [and] Joseph H. Connell.
— New York: Wiley, [1966] xv, 200 p.: ill.; 24 cm. 1. Animal populations
I. Connell, Joseph H., joint author. II. T.
QL752.M2     591.5     LC 66-21070

**Macfadyen, A. (Amyan)**             • **5.4074**
Animal ecology: aims and methods. [2d ed.]. New York: Pitman Pub. Corp.
[1963] 344 p.: ill.; 23 cm. (Zoology series.) 1. Animal ecology 2. Animal
populations I. T. II. Series.
QL752.M22 1963     591.5     LC 62-21996

## QL753–763 Habits. Behavior

**Morgan, Ann Haven, 1882-.**             • **5.4075**
Field book of animals in winter / by Ann Haven Morgan. — New York:
Putnam's Sons, c1939. xv, 527 p.: ill., (some col.) 1. Animal behavior
2. Animal behavior 3. Hibernation I. T. II. Title: Animals in winter
QL753.M67     LC 39-27745

**Animal migration, orientation, and navigation / edited by**      **5.4076**
**Sidney A. Gauthreaux, Jr.**
New York: Academic Press, 1980. xii, 387 p.: ill.; 24 cm. — (Physiological
ecology.) 1. Animal migration 2. Animal orientation 3. Animal navigation
I. Gauthreaux, Sidney A. II. Series.
QL754.A56     591.52/5 19     LC 80-1680     ISBN 0122777506

**Street, Philip, 1915-.**             **5.4077**
Animal migration and navigation / Philip Street. — New York: Scribner,
c1976. 144 p.: ill.; 23 cm. Includes index. 1. Animal migration 2. Animal
navigation I. T.
QL754.S77 1976     591.5/2     LC 75-30276     ISBN 0684145162

**External construction by animals / edited by Nicholas E.**      **5.4078**
**Collias and Elsie C. Collias.**
Stroudsburg, Pa.: Dowden, Hutchinson & Ross; New York: distributed by
Halsted Press, c1976. xv, 413 p.: ill.; 26 cm. (Benchmark papers in animal
behavior; v. 4) 1. Animals — Habitations I. Collias, Nicholas E. (Nicholas
Elias), 1914- II. Collias, Elsie C.
QL756.E9     591.5/6     LC 75-34185     ISBN 047016543X

**Chappell, Leslie H.**             **5.4079**
Physiology of parasites / Leslie H. Chappell. — New York: Wiley, 1980, c1979.
x, 230 p.: ill.; 21 cm. — (Tertiary level biology) 'A Halsted Press book.' Includes
index. 1. Parasites — Physiology I. T.
QL757.C46 1980     591.5/24     LC 79-20237     ISBN 0470268581

**Cheng, Thomas C. (Thomas Clement)**          **5.4080**
General parasitology / Thomas C. Cheng. — 2nd ed. — Orlando, Fla.:
Academic Press, 1986. xix, 827 p., [4] p. of plates: ill. (some col.)
1. Parasitology 2. Parasites I. T.
QL757 C49 1986     LC 86-70105     ISBN 0121707555

**Noble, Elmer Ray, 1909-.**             **5.4081**
Parasitology: the biology of animal parasites / Elmer R. Noble, Glenn A.
Noble. — 5th ed. — Philadelphia: Lea & Febiger, 1982. viii, 522 p., [4] leaves of
plates: ill. (some col.); 26 cm. 1. Parasitology I. Noble, Glenn Arthur, 1909-
II. T.
QL757.N6 1982     574.5/249 19     LC 81-20686     ISBN 0812108191

**Olsen, O. Wilford (Oliver Wilford), 1901-.**          **5.4082**
Animal parasites: their life cycles and ecology [by] O. Wilford Olsen. Illus. by
the author. 3d ed. Baltimore, University Park Press [1974] xii, 562 p. illus. 29
cm. 1. Parasitology I. T.
QL757.O4 1974     591.5/24     LC 73-17411     ISBN 0839106432

**Read, Clark P., 1921-.**             **5.4083**
Animal parasitism [by] Clark P. Read. — Englewood Cliffs, N.J.: Prentice-
Hall, [1972] ix, 182 p.: ill.; 24 cm. — (Concepts of modern biology series)
(Prentice-Hall biological science series) 1. Parasitism 2. Host-parasite
relationships I. T.
QL757.R34     591.5/24     LC 72-39331     ISBN 013037671X

**Taylor, Robert J., 1945-.**             **5.4084**
Predation / Robert J. Taylor. — New York: Chapman and Hall, 1984. viii,
166 p.: ill. — (Population and community biology.) Includes index.
1. Predation (Biology) I. T. II. Series.
QL758.T38 1984     574.5/3 19     LC 84-4974     ISBN 0412250608

**Conference on Sex and Behavior, Berkeley, Calif.**       • **5.4085**
Sex and behavior. Frank A. Beach, editor. New York, Wiley [1965] xvi, 592 p.
illus. 24 cm. 'Represents the end product of two conferences held in 1961 and
1962 at the University of California in Berkeley. The meetings were organized
and sponsored by the Committee for Research in Problems of Sex, National
Academy of Sciences-National Research Council.' 1. Sex — Congresses.
2. Sexual behavior in animals — Congresses. I. Beach, Frank Ambrose, 1911-
ed. II. National Research Council. Committee for Research in Problems of
Sex. III. University of California, Berkeley. IV. T.
QL761.C65     LC 65-24286

**Rheingold, Harriet L. (Harriet Lange) ed.** • **5.4086**
Maternal behavior in mammals. New York: Wiley [1963] viii, 349 p.: ill., map, diagrs.; 24 cm. 1. Parental behavior in animals 2. Mammals — Behavior 3. Animals — Infancy I. T.
QL763.R5      591.51      *LC* 63-20638

## QL765–767 Sound Production

**Griffin, Donald Redfield, 1915-.** • **5.4087**
Listening in the dark: the acoustic orientation of bats and men. — New Haven: Yale University Press, 1958. 413 p.: ill.; 25 cm. 1. Bats 2. Echolocation (Physiology) 3. Bioacoustics 4. Animal orientation I. T.
QL765.G7      599.32      *LC* 58-5458

**Symposium on Animal Sounds and Communication (1958:** • **5.4088**
**Indiana University)**
Animal sounds and communication; [proceedings] Edited by W.E. Lanyon and W.N. Tavolga. Washington, American Institute of Biological Sciences [c1960] xiii, 443 p. illus. 24 cm. and phonodisc (2 s. 12 in. 33 1/3 rpm. microgroove) in container. (American Institute of Biological Sciences. Publication no. 7) 1. Sound production in animals 2. Animal communication I. Lanyon, Wesley E. ed. II. Tavolga, William N., 1922- ed. III. T.
QL765.S9 1958      591.59      *LC* 60-13370

## QL768 Animal Tracks

**Murie, Olaus Johan, 1889-1963.**      **5.4089**
A field guide to animal tracks / text and illus. by Olaus J. Murie. — 2d ed. Boston: Houghton Mifflin, 1974. 1 v. (The Peterson field guide series, 9) 1. Animal tracks 2. Zoology — North America. 3. Zoology — Central America. I. T.
QL768.M87 1974      591.5      *LC* 74-6294      *ISBN* 0395080371

## QL775 Social Relations

**Bonner, John Tyler.**      **5.4090**
The evolution of culture in animals / John Tyler Bonner; original drawings by Margaret La Farge. — Princeton, N.J.: Princeton University Press, c1980. 216 p.: ill.; 16 x 24 cm. Includes index. 1. Social behavior in animals 2. Sociobiology 3. Culture I. T.
QL775.B58      591.5/2/4      *LC* 79-3190      *ISBN* 0691082502

**Chance, Michael Robin Alexander, 1915-.** • **5.4091**
Social groups of monkeys, apes, and men [by] Michael R. A. Chance [and] Clifford J. Jolly. — New York: Dutton, 1970. 224 p.: illus.; 24 cm. 1. Social behavior in animals 2. Primates — Behavior 3. Social groups I. Jolly, Clifford J., 1939- II. T.
QL775.C45 1970b      599.8/04/524      *LC* 72-119714      *ISBN* 0525206582

**Chauvin, Rémy.** • **5.4092**
[Sociétés animales de l'abeille au gorille. English] Animal societies from the bee to the gorilla / by Rémy Chauvin; translated by George Ordish. — [1st American ed.] New York: Hill and Wang [1968] 281 p.: ill.; 21 cm. Translation of Les sociétés animales de l'abeille au gorille. 1. Animal societies I. T.
QL775.C513 1968b      591.5/5      *LC* 68-14791

**Tinbergen, Niko, 1907-.** • **5.4093**
Social behaviour in animals with special reference to vertebrates [by] N. Tinbergen. [London] Methuen [1966] xi, 150 p. illus. 19 cm. (Science paperbacks, 1) 1. Social behavior in animals 2. Vertebrates — Behavior. I. T.
QL775.T5 1966      591.5      *LC* 67-6130

**Wilson, Edward Osborne, 1929-.**      **5.4094**
Sociobiology: the new synthesis / Edward O. Wilson. Cambridge, Mass.: Belknap Press of Harvard University Press, 1975. ix, 697 p.: ill.; 26 cm. Includes index. 1. Sociobiology 2. Social behavior in animals I. T.
QL775.W54      591.5      *LC* 74-83910      *ISBN* 0674816218

## QL776 Communications

**Davis, Flora.**      **5.4095**
Eloquent animals: a study in animal communication: how chimps lie, whales sing, and slime molds pass the message along / Flora Davis. — New York: Coward, McCann & Geoghegan, c1978. 223 p.; 22 cm. Includes index. 1. Animal communication I. T.
QL776.D38 1978      591.5/9      *LC* 77-18021      *ISBN* 0698108922

**Lewis, D. Brian.**      **5.4096**
Biology of communication / D. Brian Lewis and D. Michael Gower. — New York: Wiley, 1980. viii, 239 p.: ill.; 21 cm. — (Tertiary level biology) 'A Halsted Press book.' Includes index. 1. Animal communication 2. Neurophysiology I. Gower, D. Michael, joint author. II. T.
QL776.L49 1980      591.5/9      *LC* 79-20920      *ISBN* 047026859X

**Sales, Gillian.**      **5.4097**
Ultrasonic communication by animals / [by] Gillian Sales [and] David Pye. — London: Chapman and Hall; New York: Wiley, [1974] x, 281 p.: ill.; 24 cm. 'A Halsted Press Book.' 1. Animal communication 2. Animal sounds 3. Ultrasonics in biology I. Pye, David, 1932- joint author. II. T.
QL776.S24 1974      591.5/9      *LC* 73-15213      *ISBN* 0470749857

**Shorey, Harry H.**      **5.4098**
Animal communication by pheromones / H. H. Shorey. New York: Academic Press, 1976. viii, 167 p.: ill.; 24 cm. Includes indexes. 1. Animal communication 2. Pheromones I. T.
QL776.S54      591.5/9      *LC* 75-44765      *ISBN* 012640450X

## QL781–785 Instinct. Psychology. Animal Intelligence

**Tinbergen, Niko, 1907-.** • **5.4099**
The study of instinct / by N. Tinbergen. — 1st ed. 2nd impression; with a new introduction. Oxford: Clarendon P., 1969. xx, 228 p.: 2 plates, ill.; 25 cm. 1. Instinct 2. Animal behavior I. T.
QL781.T58 1969      591.5/1      *LC* 74-452984      *ISBN* 019857343X

**Anderson, E. W. (Edward William), 1908-.**      **5.4100**
Animals as navigators / E.W. Anderson. — New York, N.Y.: Van Nostrand Reinhold, c1983. 206 p., [8] p. of plates: ill.; 23 cm. 1. Animal navigation I. T.
QL782.A53 1983      591.1 19      *LC* 82-21898      *ISBN* 0442208820

**Griffin, Donald Redfield, 1915-.**      **5.4101**
The question of animal awareness: evolutionary continuity of mental experience / Donald R. Griffin. — Rev. and enl. ed. — New York: Rockefeller University Press, 1981. xi, 209 p.; 24 cm. Includes indexes. 1. Animal intelligence 2. Animal communication 3. Animal behavior I. T.
QL785.G72 1981      156/.3 19      *LC* 81-51221      *ISBN* 0874700353

**Mackintosh, N. J. (Nicholas John), 1935-.**      **5.4102**
The psychology of animal learning / N. J. Mackintosh. — London; New York: Academic Press, 1974. xiv, 730 p.: ill.; 24 cm. Includes indexes. 1. Animal intelligence 2. Learning, Psychology of I. T.
QL785.M17 1974      156/.3/15      *LC* 73-19009      *ISBN* 0124646506

**Nato Advanced Study Institute on Animal Learning,**      **5.4103**
**Reisensburg, Ger., 1976.**
Animal learning: survey and analysis / M. E. Bitterman ... [et al.]; with a foreword by Gabriel Horn. — New York: Plenum Press, c1979. xi, 510 p.: ill.; 26 cm. — (NATO advanced study institutes series. Life sciences. v. 19) 1. Animal intelligence 2. Learning, Psychology of I. Bitterman, M. E. II. North Atlantic Treaty Organization. III. T. IV. Series.
QL785.N37 1976      156/.3/1      *LC* 78-9894      *ISBN* 0306400618

**Staddon, J. E. R.**      **5.4104**
Adaptive behavior and learning / J.E.R. Staddon. — Cambridge [Cambridgeshire]; New York: Cambridge University Press, 1983. xiii, 555 p.: ill.; 25 cm. Includes indexes. 1. Learning in animals 2. Adaptation (Biology) I. T.
QL785.S8 1983      591.51 19      *LC* 83-5206      *ISBN* 0521256992

**Cognitive processes of nonhuman primates. Edited by Leonard** • **5.4105**
**E. Jarrard. Contributors: Norman Geschwind [and others]**
New York, Academic Press, 1971. xii, 188 p. illus. 24 cm. 'Based on the sixth annual Symposium on Cognition ... held at Carnegie-Mellon University, March 26 and 27, 1970.' 1. Primates — Behavior — Congresses. 2. Cognition in animals — Congresses. I. Jarrard, Leonard E., 1930- ed. II. Geschwind, Norman. III. Symposium on Cognition. 6th, Carnegie-Mellon University, 1970.
QL785.5.P7 C6      156/.3/4      *LC* 77-154377      *ISBN* 0123808502

**The Ontogeny of vertebrate behavior. Edited by Howard Moltz.**      **5.4106**
**[Contributors: P. P. G. Bateson and others]**
New York, Academic Press, 1971. xi, 500 p. illus. 24 cm. 1. Vertebrates — Behavior. 2. Ontogeny I. Bateson, P. P. G. (Paul Patrick Gordon), 1938- II. Moltz, Howard. ed.
QL785.5.V4 O58 1971      596/.05/22      *LC* 79-159616      *ISBN* 0125043503

# QL799–950 Morphology. Anatomy

**Olson, Everett Claire, 1910-.**    • **5.4107**
Morphological integration / by Everett C. Olson and Robert L. Miller. — [Chicago]: University of Chicago Press [1958] 317 p.: ill.; 25 cm. 1. Morphology (Animals) 2. Evolution I. Miller, Robert Lee, 1920- II. T.
QL799.O45    591.4    *LC* 58-5116

**Schmidt-Nielsen, Knut, 1915-.**    **5.4108**
Scaling, why is animal size so important? / Knut Schmidt–Nielsen. — Cambridge; New York: Cambridge University Press, 1984. xi, 241 p.: ill.; 24 cm. Includes index. 1. Body size 2. Morphology (Animals) I. T.
QL799.S34 1984    596 19    *LC* 84-5841    *ISBN* 0521266572

**Hildebrand, Milton, 1918-.**    **5.4109**
Analysis of vertebrate structure / Milton Hildebrand; illustrated by Viola and Milton Hildebrand. — 2nd ed. — New York: Wiley, c1982. xiv, 654 p.: ill.; 25 cm. Includes index. 1. Vertebrates — Anatomy 2. Morphology (Animals) I. T.
QL805.H64 1982    596/.04 19    *LC* 81-13049    *ISBN* 0471090581

**Romer, Alfred Sherwood, 1894-.**    **5.4110**
The vertebrate body / Alfred Sherwood Romer, Thomas S. Parsons. — 6th ed. — Philadelphia: Saunders College Pub., c1986. vii, 679 p.: ill. (some col.); 25 cm. (Saunders series in organismic biology.) Includes index. 1. Vertebrates — Anatomy I. Parsons, Thomas Sturges, 1930- II. T. III. Series.
QL805.R65 1986    596/.01 19    *LC* 85-8196    *ISBN* 0030584469

**Weichert, Charles K. (Charles Kipp), 1902-.**    **5.4111**
Elements of chordate anatomy [by] Charles K. Weichert [and] William Presch. 4th ed. New York: McGraw-Hill [1975] viii, 526 p.: ill.; 24 cm. (McGraw-Hill series in organismic biology) A condensed version of C. K. Weichert's Anatomy of the chordates. 1. Chordata — Anatomy. 2. Anatomy, Comparative I. Presch, William, joint author. II. T.
QL805.W4 1975    596/.04    *LC* 74-17151    *ISBN* 0070690081

**Stubbs, George, 1724-1806.**    **5.4112**
The anatomical works of George Stubbs / [text by] Terence Doherty. — Boston: D.R. Godine, 1975, c1974. ix, 345 p.: chiefly ill., facsims., ports. (1 col.); 37 cm. 1. Anatomy — Early works to 1800 — Atlases. I. Doherty, Terence. II. T.
QL806.S8 1974    599/.04    *LC* 74-15259    *ISBN* 0879231173

**Kessel, Richard G., 1931-.**    **5.4113**
Tissues and organs: a text–atlas of scanning electron microscopy / Richard G. Kessel, Randy H. Kardon. — San Francisco: W. H. Freeman, c1979. ix, 317 p.: ill.; 25 x 29 cm. Includes index. 1. Histology — Atlases. 2. Ultrastructure (Biology) — Atlases. I. Kardon, Randy H., 1954- II. T.
QL807.K47    611/.018    *LC* 78-23886    *ISBN* 0716700913

**Allen, B. L.**    **5.4114**
Basic anatomy: a laboratory manual: the human skeleton, the cat / B.L. Allen. — 2nd ed. — New York: W.H. Freeman, c1980. xv, 171 p.: ill. 1. Anatomy, Comparative — Laboratory manuals 2. Anatomy, Human — Laboratory manuals 3. Cats — Anatomy — Laboratory manuals. I. T.
QL812.A42 1980    *ISBN* 0716710919

**Walker, Warren Franklin.**    **5.4115**
Vertebrate dissection / Warren F. Walker. — 7th ed. — Philadelphia: Saunders College Pub., c1986. xii, 391 p.: ill.; 28 cm. Includes index. 1. Anatomy, Comparative — Laboratory manuals 2. Vertebrates — Anatomy — Laboratory manuals. 3. Dissection I. T.
QL812.5.W35 1986    596/.04/028 19    *LC* 85-8201    *ISBN* 003004782X

**Bullock, Theodore Holmes.**    • **5.4116**
Structure and function in the nervous systems of invertebrates [by] Theodore Holmes Bullock and G. Adrian Horridge. With chapters by Howard A. Bern, Irvine R. Hagadorn [and] J. E. Smith. — San Francisco: W. H. Freeman, [1965] 2 v. (xx, 1719 p.): illus. (part col.); 28 cm. — (A Series of books in biology) 1. Nervous system — Invertebrates. I. Horridge, G. Adrian. joint author. II. T.
QL925.B85    592.018    *LC* 65-7965

**Spearman, R. I. C. (Richard Ian Campbell)**    **5.4117**
The integument: a textbook of skin biology / [by] R. I. C. Spearman. — London: Cambridge University Press, 1973. vii, 208, [8] p.: ill.; 24 cm. (Biological structure and function. 3) Includes index. 1. Skin I. T. II. Series.
QL941.S67    591.1/858    *LC* 72-88612    *ISBN* 0521200482

**Ramón y Cajal, Santiago, 1852-1934.**    **5.4118**
The structure of the retina. Compiled and translated by Sylvia A. Thorpe and Mitchell Glickstein. — Springfield, Ill.: C. C. Thomas, [1972] xxxix, 196 p.: illus.; 24 cm. 'First published in 1892 in the ... journal La Cellule.' 1. Retina I. T.
QL949.R2513    596/.01/823    *LC* 70-175083    *ISBN* 0398023859

# QL951–991 Embryology

## QL953–957 History. General Works. Laboratory Manuals

**Needham, Joseph, 1900-.**    • **5.4119**
A history of embryology. 2d ed., rev. with the assistance of Arthur Hughes. New York, Abelard-Schuman [1959] 303 p. illus., ports., diagrs., facsim. 24 cm. 1. Embryology — History. 2. Embryology — Bibliography. I. T.
QL953.N4 1959    591.3309    *LC* 59-6081

**Oppenheimer, Jane M. (Jane Marion), 1911-.**    • **5.4120**
Essays in the history of embryology and biology [by] Jane M. Oppenheimer. Cambridge, Mass., M.I.T. Press [1967] xi, 374 p. 24 cm. 1. Embryology — History. I. T.
QL953.O6    574.3    *LC* 67-14098

**Arey, Leslie Brainerd, 1891-.**    • **5.4121**
Developmental anatomy: a textbook and laboratory manual of embryology. — 7th ed. — Philadelphia: Saunders, 1965. xi, 695 p.: illus. (part col.); 27 cm. 1. Embryology I. T.
QL955.A7 1965    611.013    *LC* 65-12317

**Balinsky, B. I. (Boris Ivan), 1905-.**    **5.4122**
An introduction to embryology / B.I. Balinsky; assisted by B.C. Fabian. — 5th ed. — Philadelphia: Saunders College Pub., c1981. xiv, 768 p.: ill.; 25 cm. Includes index. 1. Embryology I. Fabian, B. C. II. T.
QL955.B184 1981    591.3/3 19    *LC* 80-53915    *ISBN* 0030577128

**Berrill, N. J. (Norman John), 1903-.**    **5.4123**
Development / N. J. Berrill, Gerald Karp. — New York: McGraw-Hill, c1976. viii, 566 p.: ill.; 25 cm. 1. Developmental biology 2. Embryology I. Karp, Gerald. joint author. II. T.
QL955.B37    591.3    *LC* 75-26740    *ISBN* 007005021X

**Saunders, John Warren, 1919-.**    • **5.4124**
Patterns and principles of animal development [by] John W. Saunders, Jr. — [New York]: Macmillan, [1970] xiii, 282 p.: illus.; 26 cm. — (The Macmillan biology series) 1. Embryology 2. Developmental genetics I. T.
QL955.S38    591.3    *LC* 75-79031

**Waddington, Conrad Hal, 1905-.**    • **5.4125**
Principles of development and differentiation [by] C. H. Waddington. — New York: Macmillan, [1966] x, 115 p.: illus.; 24 cm. — (Current concepts in biology series) 1. Embryology 2. Developmental genetics 3. Cytology I. T.
QL955.W33    574.3    *LC* 66-15030

**Hamburger, Viktor, 1900-.**    • **5.4126**
A manual of experimental embryology. — Rev. ed. — [Chicago]: University of Chicago Press, [1960] 220 p.: illus.; 25 cm. 1. Embryology — Laboratory manuals. I. T.
QL957.H25 1960    591.33072    *LC* 60-14069

## QL958–959 Invertebrates. Vertebrates

**Hörstadius, Sven Otto, 1898-.**    **5.4127**
Experimental embryology of echinoderms [by] Sven Hörstadius. — Oxford [Eng.]: Clarendon Press, 1973. 192 p.: ill.; 25 cm. 1. Sea urchin embryo 2. Embryology, Experimental I. T.
QL958.H67    593/.95    *LC* 73-181011    *ISBN* 0198573731

**Lillie, Frank Rattray, 1870-1947.**                                    • **5.4128**
Development of the chick, an introduction to embryology. Rev. by Howard L. Hamilton; advisory editor, B. H. Willier. — 3d ed. — New York: Holt, [1952] xv, 624 p.: illus. (part col.) port.; 22 cm. 1. Embryology 2. Chick embryo I. T.
QL959.L7 1952      591.33      *LC* 52-7484

**Nelsen, Olin Everett, 1898-.**                                         • **5.4129**
Comparative embryology of the vertebrates; with 2057 drawings and photos. grouped as 380 illus. — New York: Blakiston, [1953] 982 p.: illus.; 24 cm. 1. Embryology — Vertebrates. I. T.
QL959.N4      591.33      *LC* 52-11811

**Patten, Bradley Merrill, 1889-1971.**                                  • **5.4130**
Early embryology of the chick [by] Bradley M. Patten. 5th ed. New York, McGraw-Hill [1971] xvi, 284 p. illus. 24 cm. 1. Embryology 2. Chick embryo I. T.
QL959.P23 1971      598.6/1      *LC* 76-133808      *ISBN* 0070487960

**Patten, Bradley Merrill, 1889-1971.**                                  • **5.4131**
Embryology of the pig. — 3d ed. / with col. front. and 186 ill. in the text, containing 412 figures, of which 6 are in color. — Philadelphia: Blakiston Co., [1948] xiii, 352 p.: ill. (some col.) 1. Embryology — Mammals. 2. Swine I. T.
QL959.P25 1948      *LC* 48-10874

**Romanoff, Alexis Lawrence, 1892-.**                                    • **5.4132**
The avian embryo; structural and functional development. New York, Macmillan [1960] xvi, 1305 p. illus., diagrs., tables. 25 cm. 'A complementary and companion volume to The avian egg, published in 1949.' 1. Embryology — Birds I. T.
QL959.R819      598.233      *LC* 59-7975

# QL961–971 Special Topics

**Willier, Benjamin Harrison, 1890- ed.**                                **5.4133**
Foundations of experimental embryology. Edited by Benjamin H. Willier and Jane M. Oppenheimer. 2d ed., enl. and with a new introd. by Jane M.

Oppenheimer. New York, Hafner Press [1974] xxiv, 277 p. illus. 24 cm. 1. Embryology, Experimental — Addresses, essays, lectures. I. Oppenheimer, Jane M. (Jane Marion), 1911- joint ed. II. T.
QL961.W5 1974      591.3/3/072      *LC* 74-11271      *ISBN* 0028498607

**Brachet, J. (Jean), 1909-.**                                          • **5.4134**
The biochemistry of development. — London; New York: Pergamon Press, 1960. 320 p.: ill. — (International series of monographs on pure and applied biology. Division: Modern trends in physiological sciences; v. 2) 1. Chemical embryology I. T.
QL963.B7      *LC* 59-14176

**International Lecture Course, 4th, Wageningen, 1965.**                 • **5.4135**
Cell differentiation and morphogenesis; international lecture course, Wageningen, The Netherlands, April 26–29, 1965 [by] W. Beermann [and others]. — Amsterdam: North-Holland Pub. Co., 1966. viii, 212 p.: illus.; 23 cm. 'Organized by the Agricultural University of Wageningen.' 1. Cell differentiation — Congresses. 2. Morphogenesis — Congresses. I. Beermann, W. II. Wageningen. Landbouwhoogeschool. III. T.
QL963.5.I5 1965a      574.3      *LC* 68-102013

**Needham, Joseph, 1900-.**                                             • **5.4136**
Chemical embryology. — New York: Hafner, 1963. 3 v. (xxi, 2021 p.): ill., port. 1. Chemical embryology 2. Chemical embryology — Bibliography. I. T.
QL963.N4 1963      *LC* 63-14242

**Saunders, John Warren, 1919-.**                                       • **5.4137**
Animal morphogenesis [by] John W. Saunders, Jr. — New York: Macmillan, [1968] ix, 118 p.: illus.; 24 cm. — (Current concepts in biology) 1. Morphogenesis I. T.
QL963.S37      591.3/3      *LC* 68-10297

**Saxén, Lauri.**                                                       • **5.4138**
Primary embryonic induction [by] Lauri Saxén [and] Sulo Toivonen. London, Logos Press; Englewood Cliffs, N.J., Prentice-Hall [c1962] 271 p. illus. 23 cm. (Scientific monographs on experimental biology.) 1. Embryology I. Toivonen, Sulo. joint author. II. T. III. Series.
QL971.S25      591.33      *LC* 63-4898

## QM21–101 GENERAL WORKS. ATLASES

**Harvey, William, 1578-1657.**                                     • 5.4139
[Prelectiones anatomiae universalis. English] Lectures on the whole of anatomy: an annotated translation of Prelectiones anatomiae universalis / by C.D. O'Malley, F.N.L. Poynter [and] K.F. Russell. — Berkeley: University of California Press, 1961. 239 p.: ill., col. port., facsims.; 24 cm. 1. Anatomy, Human — Early works to 1800. I. O'Malley, Charles Donald. tr. II. T.
QM21.H313      611      LC 61-16879

**Fowler, Ira.**                                                    5.4140
Human anatomy / Ira Fowler. — Belmont, Calif.: Wadsworth Pub. Co., c1984. xv, 615 p.: ill. (some col.); 26 cm. 1. Anatomy, Human I. T.
QM23.2.F68 1984      611 19      LC 83-16991      ISBN 0534027466

**Gray, Henry, 1825-1861.**                                         5.4141
Anatomy of the human body / by Henry Gray. — 30th American ed. / edited by Carmine D. Clemente. — Philadelphia: Lea & Febiger, 1985. xvii, 1676 p.: ill. (some col.); 27 cm. Cover title: Gray's Anatomy. 1. Anatomy, Human I. Clemente, Carmine D. II. T. III. Title: Gray's Anatomy.
QM23.2.G73 1985      611 19      LC 84-5741      ISBN 081210644X

**Spence, Alexander P., 1929-.**                                    5.4142
Basic human anatomy / Alexander P. Spence; illustrations by Fran Milner. — 2nd ed. — Menlo Park, Calif.: Benjamin/Cummings Pub. Co., c1986. xvii, 688 p.: ill. (some col.); 29 cm. (Benjamin/Cummings series in the life sciences.) Includes index. 1. Anatomy, Human I. T. II. Series.
QM23.2.S68 1986      611 19      LC 85-18489      ISBN 0805369864

**Anson, Barry Joseph, 1894-.**                                     • 5.4143
An atlas of human anatomy. 2d ed. Philadelphia, Saunders [1963] xvii, 632 p. illus., part col. 28 cm. 1. Anatomy, Human — Atlases I. T.
QM25.A49 1963      611.084      LC 63-7036

**Baillière's atlas of male anatomy.**                              • 5.4144
5th ed. revised by Katherine F. Armstrong; coloured plates by Douglas J. Kidd; foreword by Sir Cecil Wakeley. — London: Baillière, Tindall & Cassell, 1967. 34 p.: 7 plates, 80 illus. (incl. 30 col.); 44 cm. Text tipped in on lining paper, plates on right. 1. Anatomy, Human — Atlases I. Armstrong, Katherine Fairlie, 1892- II. Title: Atlas of male anatomy.
QM25.B3x      611      LC 68-69730

**Crelin, Edmund S., 1923-.**                                       5.4145
Anatomy of the newborn: an atlas / [by] Edmund S. Crelin. — Philadelphia: Lea & Febiger, 1969. xiii, 256 p.: (chiefly ill. (part col.)); 32 cm. 1. Infants (Newborn) — Anatomy — Atlases. 2. Anatomy, Human — Atlases I. T.
QM25.C7 1969      611      LC 68-55357

**McMinn, R. M. H. (Robert Matthew Hay)**                           5.4146
Color atlas of human anatomy / R. M. H. McMinn, R. T. Hutchings. — Chicago: Year Book Medical Publishers, c1977. 352 p.: ill (col.); 32 cm. Includes index. 1. Anatomy, Human — Atlases I. Hutchings, R. T. joint author. II. T.
QM25.M23      611/.0022/2      LC 76-23581      ISBN 0815158238

**Yokochi, Chihiro.**                                               5.4147
Photographic anatomy of the human body / Chihiro Yokochi, Johannes W. Rohen. — 2d ed. — Baltimore: University Park Press, c1978. 102 p.: ill.; 31 cm. 1. Anatomy, Human — Atlases I. Rohen, Johannes W. (Johannes Wilhelm) II. T.
QM25.Y613 1978      611/.0022/2      LC 77-4976      ISBN 0839111045

**Baillière's atlas of female anatomy / by Katharine F.**           • 5.4148
**Armstrong; coloured plates by Douglas J. Kidd.**
7th ed. — London: Baillière, Tindall and Cassell, [1969] 32 p.: ill., col. plates.; 44 cm. 1. Women — Health and hygiene I. Armstrong, Katharine Fairlie, 1892- II. Title: Atlas of female anatomy.
QM26.B3x      611      LC 72-497372      ISBN 0702002976

## QM101 Skeleton

**Goldberg, Kathy E. (Kathy Ellen), 1953-.**                        5.4149
The skeleton: fantastic framework / by Kathy E. Goldberg and the editors of U.S. News Books. — Washington, D.C.: U.S. News Books, c1982. 165 p.: ill. (some col.); 29 cm. — (The Human body) Includes index. 1. Skeleton I. U.S. News Books. II. T. III. Series.
QM101.G63 1982      611/.71 19      LC 81-23098      ISBN 089193605X

## QM451–455 NERVOUS SYSTEM. BRAIN

**Crosby, Elizabeth Caroline, 1888-.**                              • 5.4150
Correlative anatomy of the nervous system [by] Elizabeth C. Crosby, Tryphena Humphrey [and] Edward W. Lauer, with contributions by J. Ariëns Kappers [and others]. New York, Macmillan [1962] 731 p. illus. 29 cm. 1. Neuroanatomy I. T.
QM451.C7      611.8      LC 62-7511

**Bonin, Gerhardt von, 1890-.**                                     • 5.4151
The evolution of the human brain. [Chicago] University of Chicago Press [1963] 92 p. illus. 23 cm. (The Scientist's library: Biology and medicine) 1. Brain — Evolution 2. Human evolution I. T.
QM455. B58      611.81      LC 63-13062

**Nieuwenhuys, R., 1927-.**                                         5.4152
The human central nervous system: a synopsis and atlas / R. Nieuwenhuys, J. Voogd, Chr. van Huijzen. — Berlin; New York: Springer-Verlag, 1978. vi, 253 p.: ill.; 27 cm. Includes index. 1. Central nervous system — Atlases. 2. Histology — Atlases. 3. Neuroanatomy — Atlases. I. Voogd, J. joint author. II. Huijzen, Chr. van. joint author. III. T.
QM455.N48      612/.82/0222      LC 78-15493      ISBN 0387089039

## QM550–575 NORMAL HISTOLOGY

**Andrew, Warren.**                                                 5.4153
Histology of the vertebrates: a comparative text / [by] Warren Andrew [and] Cleveland P. Hickman. — Saint Louis: Mosby, 1974. vii, 439 p.: ill.; 27 cm. 1. Histology 2. Anatomy, Comparative I. Hickman, Cleveland Pendleton, 1895- joint author. II. T.
QM551.A52      596/.08/24      LC 73-17378      ISBN 0801602475

**Andrew, Warren, 1910-.**                                          • 5.4154
Textbook of comparative histology. New York: Oxford University Press, 1959. 652 p.: ill.; 24 cm. 1. Histology I. T. II. Title: Comparative histology.
QM551.A54      574.82      LC 58-9461

**Arey, Leslie Brainerd, 1891-.**                                   • 5.4155
Human histology; a textbook in outline form. — 3d ed. — Philadelphia: Saunders, 1968. ix, 328 p.: illus. (part col.); 27 cm. 1. Histology I. T.
QM551.A7 1968      611/.018      LC 68-11625

**Cowdry, E. V. (Edmund Vincent), 1888-1975.**                      • 5.4156
A textbook of histology: functional significance of cells and intercellular substances / by John C. Finerty and E.V. Cowdry. — 5th ed. Philadelphia: Lea & Febiger, 1960. 573 p.: ill.; 26 cm. Previous editions by E.V. Cowdry. 1. Histology I. Finerty, John C. II. T.
QM551.C65 1960      611.018      LC 60-11112

**Fawcett, Don Wayne, 1917-.**                                      5.4157
A textbook of histology / Don W. Fawcett. — 11th ed. — Philadelphia: Saunders, 1986. xi, 1017 p.: ill. (some col.); 27 cm. At head of title: Bloom and

Fawcett. Rev. ed. of: Textbook of histology / William Bloom, Don W. Fawcett. 10th ed. 1975. 1. Histology I. Bloom, William, 1899- Textbook of histology. 10th ed. II. T. III. Title: Histology.
QM551.F34 1986      611/.018 19      *LC* 85-8218      *ISBN* 0721617298

**Histology / [edited by] Leon Weiss, Roy O. Greep.**                    **5.4158**
4th ed. — New York: McGraw-Hill, c1977. xv, 1209 p., [12] leaves of plates: ill.; 25 cm. First-2d ed. edited by R. O. Greep; 3d ed. edited by R. O. Greep and L. Weiss. 1. Histology I. Weiss, Leon. II. Greep, Roy Orval, 1905- III. Greep, Roy Orval, 1905- ed. Histology.
QM551.G73 1977      599/.08/2      *LC* 76-42251      *ISBN* 007069091X

**Davenport, Harold Alvin, 1895-.**                    • **5.4159**
Histological and histochemical technics. Philadelphia, Saunders, 1960. 401 p. illus. 25 cm. 1. Histology — Laboratory manuals. 2. Histochemistry — Technique. I. T.
QM555.D27      578.9      *LC* 60-5059

**Baker, John Randal, 1900-.**                    • **5.4160**
Cytological technique: the principles underlying routine methods [by] John R. Baker. — 5th ed. — London: Methuen; New York: Wiley, 1966. xi, 149 p.: tables, diagrs.; 20 cm. — (Methuen's monographs on biological subjects) 1. Histology — Technique I. T.
QM556.B27 1966      578.6      *LC* 67-72760

**Humason, Gretchen L.**                    **5.4161**
Animal tissue techniques / Gretchen L. Humason. — 4th ed. — San Francisco: W. H. Freeman, c1979. xiii, 661 p.; 25 cm. Includes index. 1. Histology — Technique 2. Stains and staining (Microscopy) 3. Histochemistry — Technique. I. T.
QM556.H85 1979      578/.9      *LC* 78-17459      *ISBN* 0716702991

**Matthews, J. Les (James Les), 1926-.**                    **5.4162**
Atlas of human histology and ultrastructure [by] J. L. Matthews and J. H. Martin. Philadelphia, Lea & Febiger, 1971. xiii, 382 p. illus. 29 cm. 1. Histology — Atlases. I. Martin, James Harold, 1938- joint author. II. T.
QM557.M37      611/.018/0222      *LC* 72-157470      *ISBN* 0812103475

# QM601–699 HUMAN EMBRYOLOGY

**Allan, Frank D.**                    • **5.4163**
Essentials of human embryology [by] Frank D. Allan. — 2d ed. — New York: Oxford University Press, 1969. xii, 344 p.: illus.; 24 cm. 1. Embryology, Human I. T.
QM601.A4 1969      612.64      *LC* 69-10492

**Blechschmidt, Erich, 1904-.**                    • **5.4164**
[Vorgeburtlichen Entwicklungsstadien des Menschen. English & German] The stages of human development before birth: an introduction to human embryology. — Philadelphia: Saunders, 1961. 684 p.: ill.; 28 cm. German and English. 1. Embryology, Human I. T.
QM601.B553      612.64      *LC* 61-10163

**Hamilton, William James, 1903-.**                    • **5.4165**
[Human embryology; prenatal development of form and function] Hamilton, Boyd and Mossman's human embryology; prenatal development of form and function. 4th ed.; by W. J. Hamilton and H. W. Mossman. Cambridge, Heffer, 1972. xii, 646 p. illus. (some col.). 25 cm. 1. Embryology, Human I. Boyd, James Dixon, 1907-1968. II. Mossman, Harland W. (Harland Winfield), 1898- joint author. III. T. IV. Title: Human embryology; prenatal development of form and function.
QM601.H3 1972      612.6/4      *LC* 72-171158      *ISBN* 0852700830

**Patten, Bradley Merrill, 1889-1971.**                    **5.4166**
[Human embryology] Patten's Human embryology: elements of clinical development / Clark Edward Corliss. — New York: McGraw-Hill, c1976. viii, 469 p.: ill.; 24 cm. 'A Blakiston publication.' 1. Embryology, Human I. Corliss, Clark Edward. II. T. III. Title: Human embryology.
QM601.P2 1976      611/.013      *LC* 75-45235      *ISBN* 0070131503

**Tuchmann-Duplessis, Herbert.**                    **5.4167**
Illustrated human embryology. — New York: Springer-Verlag, 1972-. 3 v.: ill. (some col.); 27 cm. Translation of Embryologie: travaux pratiques et enseignement dirigé. 1. Embryology, Human — Atlases. I. T.
QM602.E4313      611/.013      *LC* 76-355442      *ISBN* 0387900209

**Paré, Ambroise, 1510?-1590.**                    **5.4168**
[Des monstres et prodiges. English] On monsters and marvels / Ambroise Paré; translated with an introduction and notes by Janis L. Pallister. — Chicago: University of Chicago Press, 1982. xxxii, 224 p., [1] p. of plates: ill., port.; 24 cm. Translation of: Des monstres et prodiges. Includes index. 1. Abnormalities, Human — Early works to 1800. 2. Animals — Abnormalities — Early works to 1800. I. Pallister, Janis L. II. T.
QM691.P3713 1982      599.02/2 19      *LC* 81-16297      *ISBN* 0226645622

**Smith, David W., 1926-1981.**                    • **5.4169**
Recognizable patterns of human malformation: genetic, embryologic, and clinical aspects / by David W. Smith. — Philadelphia: Saunders, 1970. xv, 368 p.: ill.; 27 cm. (Major problems in clinical pediatrics, v. 7) 1. Abnormalities, Human — Etiology 2. Human mechanics 3. Morphogenesis 4. Birth injuries 5. Growth disorders I. T.
QM691.S57      611/.012      *LC* 76-92146

# QP    Physiology

## QP6–31 General Works

### QP6–29 Reference Works. History. Biography

**Handbook of physiology (1959 ed.): a critical, comprehensive presentation of physiological knowledge and concepts** / Editor-in-chief: John Field.    • 5.4170
Washington: American Physiological Society; [distributed by Williams & Wilkins, Baltimore] 1959-. v. in    : ill., col. plate, ports.; 29 cm. Section 10-published in Bethesda, Md. 1. Physiology — Collected works. I. Field, John, 1902- ed. II. American Physiological Society (1887- )
QP6.H25    612.082    *LC* 60-4587

**Frank, Robert Gregg, 1943-.**    5.4171
Harvey and the Oxford physiologists: scientific ideas and social interaction / by Robert G. Frank, Jr. — Berkeley: University of California Press, 1981 (c1980). xviii, 368 p., [6] leaves of plates: ill.; 26 cm. 1. Harvey, William, 1578-1657. 2. University of Oxford. 3. Physiology — England — History. 4. Physiologists — England — Biography. I. T.
QP21.F76    599.01/0942    *LC* 79-63553    *ISBN* 0520039068

**Hall, Thomas Steele, 1909-.**    • 5.4172
Ideas of life and matter; studies in the history of general physiology, 600 B.C.–1900 A.D. [by] Thomas S. Hall. Chicago: University of Chicago Press, [1969] 2 v.; 24 cm. Published in 1975 under title: History of general physiology, 600 B.C. to A.D. 1900. 1. Physiology — History. I. T.
QP21.H34    577/.2/09    *LC* 69-16999

**Sayre, Anne.**    5.4173
Rosalind Franklin and DNA / Anne Sayre. 1st ed. — New York: Norton, [1975] 221 p.: port.; 21 cm. 1. Franklin, Rosalind, 1920-1958. 2. DNA I. T.
QP26.F68 S29 1975    574.8/732/0924 B    *LC* 75-11737    *ISBN* 0393074935

**William Harvey and his age: the professional and social context of the discovery of the circulation** / edited by Jerome J. Bylebyl.    5.4174
Baltimore: Johns Hopkins University Press, c1979. xii, 154 p.: ill.; 24 cm. — (Henry E. Sigerist supplements to the Bulletin of the history of medicine. new ser., no. 2) Papers from a conference held in Kansas City, May 13, 1978, at the annual meeting of the American Association for the History of Medicine. 1. Harvey, William, 1578-1657. 2. Blood — Circulation — History — Congresses. 3. Physiologists — England — Biography. 4. Physicians — England — Biography. I. Bylebyl, Jerome J. II. American Association for the History of Medicine. III. Series.
QP26.H3 W544    612/.1/0924 B    *LC* 78-20526    *ISBN* 0801822130

**Babkin, Boris Petrovich, 1877-.**    • 5.4175
Pavlov, a biography. — [Chicago]: University of Chicago Press, [1949] xiii, 364 p.: illus., ports.; 22 cm. 1. Pavlov, Ivan Petrovich, 1849-1936. I. T.
QP26.P35 B3    926.12    *LC* 49-11887

**Darwin, Erasmus, 1731-1802.**    5.4176
Zoonomia. With a new pref. by Thom Verhave and Paul R. Bindler. — New York: AMS Press, 1974. 2 v.: illus.; 24 cm. — (Language, man, and society) Reprint of the 1794-96 ed. printed for J. Johnson, London. 1. Physiology — Early works to 1800. 2. Pathology — Early works to 1800. I. T.
QP29.D22 1974    612    *LC* 79-147964    *ISBN* 0404082157

**Descartes, René, 1596-1650.**    5.4177
[Homme. English and French] Treatise of man. French text with translation and commentary by Thomas Steele Hall. Cambridge, Harvard University Press, 1972. xlviii, 232 p. illus. 24 cm. (Harvard monographs in the history of science) Includes 'facsimile of the first French edition': p. [119]-[225] also paged 1-107. 1. Physiology — Early works to 1800. I. Hall, Thomas Steele, 1909-II. T. III. Series.
QP29.D44 1972    612    *LC* 76-173412    *ISBN* 0674907108

## QP31 General Works, to 1969

**Ramsay, James Arthur.**    • 5.4178
Physiological approach to the lower animals [by] J. A. Ramsay. — 2nd ed. — London: Cambridge U.P., 1968. x, 150 p.: 49 illus.; 23 cm. 1. Physiology, Comparative 2. Invertebrates — Physiology I. T.
QP31.R3 1968    591.1    *LC* 68-21398    *ISBN* 0521071852

**Scheer, Bradley T. (Bradley Titus), 1914- comp.**    • 5.4179
Comparative physiology [compiled by] Bradley T. Scheer. Dubuque, Iowa, W. C. Brown Co. [1968] vii, 236 p. illus. 23 cm. (Brown biology readings series) 1. Physiology, Comparative I. T.
QP31.S27 1968    591.1    *LC* 68-22964

## QP31.2 1970–

**Eckert, Roger.**    5.4180
Animal physiology: mechanisms and adaptations / Roger Eckert, with chapters 13 and 14 by David Randall. — 2nd ed. — San Francisco: W.H. Freeman, c1983. xviii, 830 p.: ill.; 25 cm. 1. Physiology I. Randall, David J., 1938- II. T.
QP31.2.E24 1983    591.1 19    *LC* 82-18372    *ISBN* 071671423X

**Prosser, C. Ladd (Clifford Ladd), 1907-.**    5.4181
Comparative animal physiology / edited by C. Ladd Prosser. — 3d ed. Philadelphia: Saunders, 1973. xxii, 966, xlv p.: ill.; 27 cm. 1. Physiology, Comparative I. T.
QP31.2.P78 1973    591.1    *LC* 72-80793    *ISBN* 0721673813

**Schmidt-Nielsen, Knut, 1915-.**    • 5.4182
Animal physiology [by] Knut Schmidt-Nielsen. — 3d ed. — Englewood Cliffs, N.J.: Prentice-Hall, [1970] x, 145 p.: illus. (part col.); 24 cm. — (Prentice-Hall foundations of modern biology series) 1. Physiology I. T.
QP31.2.S36 1970    591.1    *LC* 71-110093    *ISBN* 0130373907

**Schmidt-Nielsen, Knut, 1915-.**    5.4183
Animal physiology: adaptation and environment / Knut Schmidt-Nielsen. — 3rd ed. — Cambridge [Cambridgeshire]; New York: Cambridge University Press, 1983. xii, 619 p.: ill.; 24 cm. 1. Physiology I. T.
QP31.2.S363 1983    591.1 19    *LC* 83-7766    *ISBN* 0521259738

**Schmidt-Nielsen, Knut, 1915-.**    5.4184
How animals work / by Knut Schmidt-Nielsen. — Cambridge [Eng.]: University Press, 1972. vi, 114 p.: ill.; 22 cm. 1. Physiology I. T.
QP31.2.S37    591.1    *LC* 77-174262    *ISBN* 0521084172

## QP33 Comparative Physiology

**Gordon, Malcolm S.**    5.4185
Animal physiology: principles and adaptations / Malcolm S. Gordon, in collaboration with George A. Bartholomew ... [et al.]. — 4th ed. — New York: Macmillan; London: Collier Macmillan, c1982. xvii, 635 p.: ill.; 25 cm. 1. Physiology, Comparative 2. Adaptation (Physiology) 3. Animal ecology I. T.
QP33.G65 1982    591.1 19    *LC* 81-8227    *ISBN* 0023453206

**Hoar, William Stewart, 1913-.**    5.4186
General and comparative physiology / William S. Hoar. — 3rd ed. — Englewood Cliffs, N.J.: Prentice-Hall, c1983. xii, 851 p.: ill.; 25 cm. Includes index. 1. Physiology, Comparative I. T.
QP33.H6 1983    591.1 19    *LC* 82-24076    *ISBN* 0133493083

**Cannon, Walter B. (Walter Bradford), 1871-1945.**    • 5.4187
The wisdom of the body [by] Walter B. Cannon ... New York, W. W. Norton & company, inc. [c1939] xviii, 19-333 p. illus., pl., diagrs. 22.5 cm. 'Revised and

enlarged edition.' 'References' at end of each chapter; 'A list of publications from the physiological laboratory in Harvard university, on which the present account is based': p. 325-327. 1. Physiology I. T.
QP33.5.C3 1939    612    *LC* 39-27360

**Griffin, Donald Redfield, 1915- comp.**      **5.4188**
Animal engineering; readings from Scientific American, with introductions by Donald R. Griffin. — San Francisco: W. H. Freeman, [1974] 120 p.: illus.; 30 cm. 1. Biophysics — Addresses, essays, lectures. 2. Bioengineering — Addresses, essays, lectures. 3. Animal mechanics — Addresses, essays, lectures. I. Scientific American. II. T.
QP33.5.G74 1974    591.1/9/108    *LC* 74-12112    *ISBN* 0716705095

# QP34–38 HUMAN PHYSIOLOGY

**Gordon, Malcolm S.**      • **5.4189**
Animal function; principles and adaptations [by] Malcolm S. Gordon in collaboration with George A. Bartholomew [and others]. — New York: Macmillan, [1968] xvi, 560 p.: illus.; 26 cm. — (The Macmillan core series in biology) Second-(3d) ed. published under title: Animal physiology. 1. Physiology, Comparative 2. Animal ecology I. T.
QP34.G57    591.1    *LC* 68-10218

**Starling, Ernest Henry, 1866-1927.**      • **5.4190**
Principles of human physiology [by] Starling and Lovatt Evans. — 14th ed. Edited by Hugh Davson and M. Grace Eggleton. With a foreword and historical notes by Sir Charles Lovatt Evans. — Philadelphia: Lea & Febiger, 1968. xv, 1668 p.: illus.; 25 cm. 1. Physiology I. Evans, Charles Arthur Lovatt, Sir, 1884- II. T.
QP34.S75 1968    612    *LC* 79-157

**Best, Charles Herbert, 1899-.**      **5.4191**
[Physiological basis of medical practice] Best and Taylor's Physiological basis of medical practice. — 11th ed. / edited by John B. West. — Baltimore: Williams & Wilkins, c1985. xxvi, 1340 p.: ill.; 29 cm. Erratum ([1] leaf) inserted. 1. Human physiology I. Taylor, Norman Burke, 1885- II. West, John B. (John Burnard) III. T. IV. Title: Physiological basis of medical practice.
QP34.5.B47 1985    612 19    *LC* 83-6613    *ISBN* 0683089447

**Bleier, Ruth, 1923-.**      **5.4192**
Science and gender: a critique of biology and its theories on women / Ruth Bleier. — New York: Pergamon Press, c1984. xii, 220 p.: ill.; 24 cm. — (Athene series.) 1. Women — Physiology — Philosophy. 2. Human biology — Philosophy. 3. Sex discrimination against women 4. Feminism 5. Sexism I. T. II. Series.
QP34.5.B55 1984    305.4/2 19    *LC* 83-22054    *ISBN* 0080309720

**Grollman, Sigmund.**      **5.4193**
The human body: its structure and physiology / Sigmund Grollman. — 4th ed. — New York: Macmillan, c1978. ix, 662 p.: ill.; 24 cm. 1. Human physiology 2. Anatomy, Human I. T.
QP34.5.G76 1978    612    *LC* 76-30626    *ISBN* 0023480807

**Guyton, Arthur C.**      **5.4194**
Textbook of medical physiology / Arthur C. Guyton. — 7th ed. — Philadelphia: Saunders, 1986. xxviii, 1057 p.: ill. (some col.); 29 cm. 1. Human physiology 2. Physiology, Pathological I. T. II. Title: Medical physiology.
QP34.5.G9 1986    612 19    *LC* 85-18294    *ISBN* 0721612601

**Singer, Sam, 1944-.**      **5.4195**
The biology of people / Sam Singer, Henry R. Hilgard. — San Francisco: W. H. Freeman, c1978. xii, 546 p.: ill.; 28 cm. — (A Series of books in biology) Includes index. 1. Human physiology 2. Human biology 3. Human genetics I. Hilgard, Henry R. joint author. II. T.
QP34.5.S56    612    *LC* 77-17893    *ISBN* 0716700263

**Strand, Fleur L.**      **5.4196**
Physiology: a regulatory systems approach / Fleur L. Strand. — New York: Macmillan, c1978. xiv, 602 p.: ill.; 29 cm. 1. Human physiology 2. Biological control systems I. T.
QP34.5.S8    612    *LC* 77-933    *ISBN* 0024176702

**Tortora, Gerard J.**      **5.4197**
Principles of human anatomy / Gerard J. Tortora. — 4th ed. — New York: Harper & Row, c1986. xxi, 713, 38, 25 p.: ill. (some col.); 29 cm. Includes index. 1. Human physiology 2. Anatomy, Human I. T.
QP34.5.T68 1986    612 19    *LC* 85-8545    *ISBN* 0060466235

**Vander, Arthur J., 1933-.**      **5.4198**
Human physiology: the mechanisms of body function / Arthur J. Vander, James H. Sherman, Dorothy S. Luciano. — 4th ed. — New York: McGraw-Hill, c1985. 715, [85] p.: ill.; 24 cm. Includes index. 1. Human physiology I. Sherman, James H., 1936- II. Luciano, Dorothy S. III. T.
QP34.5.V36 1985    612 19    *LC* 84-21828    *ISBN* 007066966X

**Women look at biology looking at women: a collection of**      **5.4199**
**feminist critiques / edited by Ruth Hubbard, Mary Sue Henifin, and Barbara Fried, with the collaboration of Vicki Druss and Susan Leigh Star.**
Boston: G. K. Hall, c1979. xxii, 268 p.: ill.; 25 cm. 1. Women — Physiology — Philosophy. 2. Feminism 3. Sexism I. Hubbard, Ruth, 1924- II. Henifin, Mary Sue, 1953- III. Fried, Barbara, 1951-
QP34.5.W65 1979    301.41/2    *LC* 79-1445    *ISBN* 0816190033

# QP71 ESSAYS

**Krebs, Hans Adolf, Sir.**      • **5.4200**
Energy transformations in living matter; a survey, by H.A. Krebs and H.L. Kornberg. With an appendix by K. Burton. Berlin, Springer, 1957. 213-298 p. illus. 25 cm. 'Sonderabdruck aus Ergebnisse der Physiologie, biologischen Chemie und experimentellen Pharmakologie, neunundvierzigster Band.' 1. Physiology — Addresses, essays, lectures. 2. Biochemistry I. Kornberg, H. L. joint author. II. T.
QP71.K7    *LC* 62-2363

# QP81–87 SPECIAL ASPECTS OF LIFE IN GENERAL

# QP81.5 Gender

**Fausto-Sterling, Anne, 1944-.**      **5.4201**
Myths of gender: biological theories about women and men / Anne Fausto-Sterling. — New York: Basic Books, c1985. xi, 258 p.: ill.; 25 cm. Includes index. 1. Sex differences 2. Feminism 3. Sexism 4. Human biology — Philosophy. 5. Prejudices I. T.
QP81.5.F38 1985    155.33 19    *LC* 85-47561    *ISBN* 0465047904

# QP82–82.2 Influence of the Environment

**Edholm, O. G. (Otto Gustaf)**      • **5.4202**
The physiology of human survival / edited by O.G. Edholm and A.L. Bacharach. — London; New York: Academic Press, 1965. xxii, 581 p.: ill.; 24 cm. Consists mainly of papers presented at a symposium held in London in 1963 at the offices of the Zoological Society and organized by the Physiological Society, the Society for the Study of Human Biology and the Zoological Society of London. 1. Man — Influence of environment 2. Stress (Physiology) 3. Adaptation (Biology) I. Bacharach, A. L. (Alfred Louis), 1891-1966. joint ed. II. Physiological Society (Great Britain) III. Society for the Study of Human Biology. IV. Zoological Society of London. V. T.
QP82.E3    612    *LC* 65-27088

**Environmental physiology of animals / editors, J. Bligh, J. L.**      **5.4203**
**Cloudsley–Thompson, A. G. MacDonald.**
New York: Wiley: distributed in the United States of America by Halsted Press, 1976. viii, 456 p.: ill.; 24 cm. 1. Adaptation (Physiology) 2. Bioclimatology 3. Evolution I. Bligh, J. II. Cloudsley-Thompson, J. L. III. Macdonald, A. G. (Alister Gordon)
QP82.E59 1976    591.1    *LC* 76-25459    *ISBN* 0470989238

**Folk, G. Edgar (George Edgar), 1914-.**      • **5.4204**
Introduction to environmental physiology; environmental extremes and mammalian survival [by] G. Edgar Folk, Jr. Philadelphia, Lea & Febiger, 1966. 308 p. illus. 26 cm. Second ed. published in 1973 under title: Environmental

physiology. 1. Bioclimatology 2. Stress (Physiology) 3. Mammals — Physiology I. T.
QP82.F62       599.054      LC 66-16619

**Hochachka, Peter W.**                           5.4205
Biochemical adaptation / Peter W. Hochachka, George N. Somero. — Princeton, N.J.: Princeton University Press, c1984. xx, 537 p.: ill.; 24 cm. Includes index. 1. Adaptation (Physiology) 2. Biochemistry I. Somero, George N. II. T.
QP82.H63 1984     574.5 19     LC 83-43076     ISBN 0691083436

**Variations in human physiology** / edited by R.M. Case;     5.4206
**contributions by D.E. Evans ... [et al.].**
Manchester, UK; Dover, N.H., USA: Manchester University Press, c1985. vii, 241 p.: ill.; 25 cm. 1. Adaptation (Physiology) 2. Human physiology 3. Variation (Biology) I. Case, R. Maynard (Richard Maynard) II. Evans, D. E.
QP82.V37 1985     612 19     LC 85-11301     ISBN 0719010861

**Becker, Robert O.**                          5.4207
Electromagnetism and life / Robert O. Becker, Andrew A. Marino. — Albany: State University of New York Press, c1982. xiii, 211 p.: ill.; 24 cm. 1. Electromagnetism — Physiological effect 2. Electrophysiology I. Marino, Andrew A. II. T.
QP82.2.E43 B42     574.19/17 19     LC 81-9286     ISBN 0873955609

**Psychobiology of stress: a study of coping men** / edited by     5.4208
**Holger Ursin, Eivind Baade, Seymour Levine.**
New York: Academic Press, 1978. xv, 236 p.: ill.; 24 cm. — (Behavioral biology) 1. Norway. Hæren — Parachute troops. 2. Stress (Physiology) 3. Parachuting — Physiological aspects. 4. Psychobiology I. Ursin, Holger. II. Baade, Eivind. III. Levine, Seymour.
QP82.2.S8 P79     612/.042     LC 78-8119     ISBN 0127092501

**Stress and human health: analysis and implications of research:**     5.4209
**a study** / by the Institute of Medicine, National Academy of
**Sciences; Glen R. Elliott, Carl Eisdorfer, editors.**
New York: Springer Pub. Co., c1982. xxv, 372 p.: ill.; 24 cm. — (Springer series on psychiatry. 1) 1. Stress (Physiology) 2. Health 3. Stress (Psychology) 4. Medicine, Psychosomatic I. Elliott, Glen R. II. Eisdorfer, Carl. III. Institute of Medicine (U.S.) IV. Series.
QP82.2.S8 S86 1982     616.07 19     LC 82-50101     ISBN 0826141102

# QP84 Growth. Biological Rhythms

**Cheek, Donald B.**                        • 5.4210
Human growth; body composition, cell growth, energy, and intelligence [by] Donald B. Cheek. Philadelphia, Lea & Febiger, 1968. xxx, 781 p. illus. 24 cm. 1. Human growth 2. Children — Growth 3. Developmental psychology I. T.
QP84.C43     612.6     LC 67-25087

**Cloudsley-Thompson, J. L.**                  • 5.4211
Rhythmic activity in animal physiology and behaviour. New York: Academic Press, 1961. 236 p.: ill.; 24 cm. (Theoretical and experimental biology. v. 1) 1. Biological rhythms 2. Animal behavior I. T. II. Series.
QP84.C53     591.5     LC 61-10699

**Thompson, D'Arcy Wentworth, 1860-1948.**         • 5.4212
On growth and form. 2d ed., reprinted. Cambridge [Eng.] University Press, 1952. 2 v. (1116 p.) illus. 23 cm. 1. Growth I. T.
QP84.T4     LC 52-12032

**Reinberg, Alain.**                          5.4213
Biological rhythms and medicine: cellular, metabolic, physiopathologic, and pharmacologic aspects / Alain Reinberg, Michael H. Smolensky; with contributions by H. von Mayersbach ... [et. al.]. — New York: Springer-Verlag, c1983. x, 305 p.: ill.; 27 cm. — (Topics in environmental physiology and medicine) 1. Biological rhythms 2. Metabolism I. Smolensky, Michael H. II. T. III. Series.
QP84.6.R44 1983     599/.01882 19     LC 82-19675     ISBN 0387907912

# QP85–86 Longevity. Aging

**Benet, Sula, 1903-.**                        5.4214
How to live to be 100: the life–style of the people of the Caucasus / Sula Benet. — New York: Dial Press, 1976. xii, 201 p., [8] leaves of plates: ill.; 23 cm. Includes index. 1. Longevity 2. Caucasus — Social life and customs. I. T. II. Title: The life-style of the people of the Caucasus.
QP85.B45     612.6/8     LC 75-40471     ISBN 080373834X

**The Biology of aging** / edited by John A. Behnke, Caleb E.     5.4215
**Finch, and Gairdner B. Moment.**
New York: Plenum Press, c1978. xi, 388 p.: ill.; 24 cm. 'A Publication of the American Institute of Biological Sciences.' 1. Aging I. Behnke, John A. II. Finch, Caleb Ellicott. III. Moment, Gairdner Bostwick, 1905-
QP86.B518     574.3/72     LC 78-19012     ISBN 0306311399

**Handbook of the biology of aging** / editors, Caleb E. Finch,     5.4216
**Edward L. Schneider, with the assistance of associate editors,**
**Richard C. Adelman, George M. Martin, Edward J. Masoro.**
2nd ed. — New York: Van Nostrand Reinhold, c1985. xvi, 1025 p.: ill.; 27 cm. (Handbooks of aging.) 1. Aging — Handbooks, manuals, etc. I. Finch, Caleb Ellicott. II. Schneider, Edward L. III. Series.
QP86.H35 1985     574.3/72 19     LC 84-27052     ISBN 0442225296

**Kohn, Robert Rothenberg, 1925-.**                5.4217
Principles of mammalian aging / Robert R. Kohn. — 2d ed. — Englewood Cliffs, N.J.: Prentice-Hall, c1978. xii, 240 p.: ill.; 24 cm. — (Prentice-Hall foundations of developmental biology series) 1. Aging 2. Mammals — Physiology I. T.
QP86.K58 1978     599/.03/72     LC 77-20289     ISBN 0137093527

**Palmore, Erdman Ballagh, 1930- comp.**          5.4218
Normal aging: reports from the Duke longitudinal study / edited by Erdman Palmore. — Durham, N.C.: Duke University Press, 1970-1985. 3 v.: ill.; 25 cm. Research project of the Duke University Center for the Study of Aging and Human Development. 1. Aging I. Duke University. Center for the Study of Aging and Human Development. II. T.
QP86.P3     612.6/7     LC 74-132028     ISBN 0822302381

# QP88–90 TISSUES. BONE

**Umbreit, Wayne William, 1913-.**               • 5.4219
[Manometric techniques and related methods for the study of tissue metabolism] Manometric & biochemical techniques; a manual describing methods applicable to the study of tissue metabolism [by] W. W. Umbreit, R. H. Burris [and] J. F. Stauffer. Chapters on specialized techniques by M. J. Johnson [and others] Contributions by H. F. DeLuca, H. A. Lardy and G. A. LePage. 5th ed. Minneapolis, Burgess Pub. Co., 1972. v, 387 p. illus. 27 cm. First ed. published in 1945 under title: Manometric techniques and related methods for the study of tissue metabolism. 1. Tissue metabolism 2. Manometer 3. Physiology — Technique. I. Burris, Robert H. (Robert Harza), 1914- II. Stauffer, John Frederick. III. T.
QP88.U5 1972     574.8/21     LC 73-174880     ISBN 080872102X

**Bourne, Geoffrey H. (Geoffrey Howard), 1909- ed.**     • 5.4220
The biochemistry and physiology of bone. Edited by Geoffrey H. Bourne. 2d ed. New York: Academic Press, 1971-. v. ill.; 24 cm. 1. Bone I. T.
QP88.2.B62     596/.01/852     LC 70-154375

**Shipman, Pat, 1949-.**                      5.4221
The human skeleton / Pat Shipman, Alan Walker, David Bichell. — Cambridge, Mass.: Harvard University Press, 1986 (c1985). x, 343 p.: ill.; 24 cm. Includes index. 1. Bones 2. Human skeleton 3. Anthropometry I. Walker, Alan, 1938- II. Bichell, David. III. T.
QP88.2.S45     612/.75 19     LC 85-5497     ISBN 0674416104

**Moore, Francis D. (Francis Daniels), 1913-.**        • 5.4222
Transplant: the give and take of tissue transplantation [by] Francis D. Moore. [Rev. ed.] New York, Simon and Schuster [1972] 364 p. illus. 25 cm. First ed. published in 1964 under title: Give and take, the development of tissue transplantation. 1. Transplantation immunology I. T.
QP89.M64 1972     617/.95     LC 78-139649     ISBN 0671208713

## QP91–135 Blood. Cardiovascular System. Circulation

## QP91–110 Blood. Circulation

**Davenport, Horace Willard, 1912-.**      **5.4223**
The ABC of acid–base chemistry: the elements of physiological blood–gas chemistry for medical students and physicians / Horace W. Davenport. — 6th ed., rev. — Chicago: University of Chicago Press, 1974. 124 p.: ill.; 24 cm. 1. Acid-base equilibrium 2. Blood — Analysis I. T. II. Title: Acid-base chemistry.
QP93.D38 1974     612/.015     *LC* 73-90943     *ISBN* 0226137058 *ISBN* 0226137031 pbk

**Ingram, Vernon M.**      • **5.4224**
The hemoglobins in genetics and evolution. New York, Columbia University Press, 1963. 165 p. illus. 24 cm. (Columbia biological series. no. 22) 1. Hemoglobin 2. Hemoglobinopathy — Genetic aspects I. T. II. Series.
QP96.5.I6     612.111     *LC* 63-10416

**Race, Robert Russell.**      **5.4225**
Blood groups in man / R. R. Race and Ruth Sanger; with a foreword by Sir Ronald Fisher. — 6th ed. — Oxford: Blackwell Scientific Publications; Philadelphia: distributed by J. B. Lippincott, 1975. xix, 659 p.: ill.; 24 cm. 1. Blood groups I. Sanger, Ruth, joint author. II. T.
QP98.R3 1975     612/.11825     *LC* 75-330416     *ISBN* 0632004312

**Harvey, William, 1578-1657.**      • **5.4226**
The circulation of the blood and other writings / William Harvey; translated by Kenneth J. Franklin. — London: Dent; New York: Dutton, 1963. xvii, 236 p. — (Everyman's Library; 262) Translation of De circulatione sanguinis. 1. Blood — Circulation I. T.
QP101.H36 1963     *LC* 63-5486

**Respiration and circulation / compiled and edited by the**      **5.4227**
**auspices of the Committee on Biological Handbooks.**
Bethesda, Md.: Federation of American Societies for Experimental Biology, [c1971] xxv, 930 p.: ill.; 29 cm. (Biological handbooks) A revision and combination of the Handbook of respiration (1958) and the Handbook of circulation (1959) compiled by P. L. Altman and others. 1. Blood — Circulation — Handbooks, manuals, etc. 2. Cardiovascular system — Handbooks, manuals, etc. 3. Respiration — Handbooks, manuals, etc. 4. Plants — Respiration — Handbooks, manuals, etc. I. Altman, Philip L. ed. II. Katz, Dorothy Dittmer. ed.
QP101.R47     574.1/1     *LC* 70-137563

**Microcirculation / edited by Gabor Kaley and Burton M.**      **5.4228**
**Altura.**
Baltimore; London [etc.]: University Park Press, 1977. xiv, 528 p.: ill., port.; 24 cm. In 3 vols. '... a volume on microcirculation ... to honor Benjamin W. Zweifach' - Preface. Index. 1. Microcirculation I. Kaley, Gabor. II. Altura, Burton M. III. Zweifach, Benjamin William.
QP106.6.M5     596/.01/1     *LC* 76-53805     *ISBN* 0839109660

## QP121 Respiration

**Dejours, Pierre.**      **5.4229**
Principles of comparative respiratory physiology / Pierre Dejours. — 2nd rev ed. — Amsterdam; New York: Elsevier/North-Holland Biomedical Press; New York: sole distributors for the U.S.A. and Canada, Elsevier North-Holland, 1981. xvi, 265 p.: ill.; 25 cm. Includes index. 1. Respiration 2. Physiology, Comparative I. T.
QP121.D36 1981     596/.012 19     *LC* 81-4913     *ISBN* 0444802797

**Krogh, August, 1874-1949.**      • **5.4230**
The comparative physiology of respiratory mechanisms. — New York: Dover Publications, [1968, c1941] vii, 172 p.: illus.; 22 cm. 'Contains the substance of the series of lectures delivered at Swarthmore [College] in the spring of 1939.' 1. Respiration I. T.
QP121.K8 1968     591.1/2     *LC* 68-55068

**Weibel, Ewald R.**      **5.4231**
The pathway for oxygen: structure and function in the mammalian respiratory system / Ewald R. Weibel. — Cambridge, Mass.: Harvard University Press, 1984. xv, 425 p.: ill.; 24 cm. Includes index. 1. Respiration 2. Oxygen in the body I. T.
QP121.W395 1984     612/.2 19     *LC* 83-18622     *ISBN* 0674657918

**Robertshaw, D.**      **5.4232**
Environmental physiology. Edited by D. Robertshaw. — London: Butterworths; Baltimore: University Park Press, [1974] 326 p.: illus.; 25 cm. — (Physiology, v. 7) (MTP international review of science.) 1. Body temperature — Regulation 2. Temperature — Physiological effect 3. Altitude, Influence of I. T. II. Series. III. Series: MTP international review of science.
QP1.P62 vol. 7 QP135.R6x     599/.01/08 s 599/.01/91     *LC* 73-16055     *ISBN* 0839110561

## QP141–185 Nutrition

**Human nutrition.**      **5.4233**
New York: Plenum Press. v.: ill.; 26 cm. Began with v. 1 in 1979. Description based on: Vol. 2. 1. Nutrition — Collected works. 2. Nutrition disorders — Collected works. I. Alfin-Slater, Roslyn, 1916- II. Kritchevsky, David, 1920-
QP141.A1 H84     613.2 19     612 11     *LC* 86-644454

**Chaney, Margaret Stella, 1892-.**      **5.4234**
Nutrition / Margaret S. Chaney, Margaret L. Ross, Jelia C. Witschi. — 9th ed. — Boston: Houghton Mifflin, c1979. xi, 559 p.: ill.; 25 cm. 1. Nutrition I. Ross, Margaret Louise. joint author. II. Witschi, Jelia C. joint author. III. T.
QP141.C5 1979     613/.2     *LC* 78-69546     *ISBN* 0395254485

**Garrison, Robert H.**      **5.4235**
The nutrition desk reference: NDR / Robert H. Garrison, Jr., and Elizabeth Somer. — New Canaan, Conn.: Keats Pub., 1985. xiv, 245 p.: ill.; 26 cm. 1. Nutrition — Handbooks, manuals, etc. 2. Drug-nutrient interactions — Handbooks, manuals, etc. 3. Cardiovascular system — Diseases — Nutritional aspects — Handbooks, manuals, etc. 4. Cancer — Nutritional aspects — Handbooks, manuals, etc. I. Somer, Elizabeth. II. T.
QP141.G33 1985     613.2 19     *LC* 84-26098     *ISBN* 0879833289

**Hamilton, Eva May Nunnelley.**      **5.4236**
Nutrition, concepts and controversies / Eva May Nunnelley Hamilton, Eleanor Noss Whitney, Frances Sienkiewicz Sizer. — 3rd ed. / prepared by Eleanor Noss Whitney and Frances Sienkiewicz Sizer. — St. Paul: West Pub., c1985. xv, 475, 133 p.: ill. (some col.); 25 cm. 1. Nutrition 2. Food I. Sizer, Frances Sienkiewicz. II. Whitney, Eleanor Noss. III. T.
QP141.H34 1985     613.2 19     *LC* 84-17297     *ISBN* 0314852433

**Handbook of dietary fiber in human nutrition / editor, Gene A.**      **5.4237**
**Spiller.**
Boca Raton, Fla.: CRC Press, 1986. 1 v. 1. Fiber in human nutrition — Handbooks, manuals, etc. I. Spiller, Gene A.
QP141.H346 1986     613.2/8 19     *LC* 86-14780     *ISBN* 0849335302

**Kleiber, Max, 1893-.**      • **5.4238**
The fire of life; an introduction to animal energetics. — New York: Wiley, [1961] 454 p.: illus.; 24 cm. 1. Bioenergetics 2. Starvation I. T.
QP141.K56     591.191     *LC* 61-15416

**Modern nutrition in health and disease / [edited by] Maurice E.**      **5.4239**
**Shils, Vernon R. Young.**
7th ed. — Philadelphia: Lea & Febiger, 1987. p. cm. 1. Nutrition 2. Diet therapy I. Shils, Maurice E. (Maurice Edward), 1914- II. Young, Vernon R. (Vernon Robert), 1937-
QP141.M64 1987     613.2 19     *LC* 86-15314     *ISBN* 0812109848

**Nutrition, an integrated approach / [edited by] Ruth L. Pike,**      **5.4240**
**Myrtle L. Brown.**
3rd ed. — New York: Wiley, c1984. xiv, 1068 p.: ill.; 25 cm. Includes index. 1. Nutrition I. Pike, Ruth L. II. Brown, Myrtle L. (Myrtle Laurestine), 1926-
QP141.N776 1984     613.2 19     *LC* 83-16766     *ISBN* 0471090042

**Nutrition in the 20th century / edited by Myron Winick.**      **5.4241**
New York: J. Wiley, c1984. viii, 197 p.: ill.; 24 cm. (Current concepts in nutrition. 0090-0443; v. 13) 'A Wiley-Interscience publication.' 1. Nutrition I. Winick, Myron. II. Series.
QP141.N794 1984     613.2 19     *LC* 84-13044     *ISBN* 0471811653

**Whitney, Eleanor Noss.**     5.4242
Understanding nutrition / Eleanor Noss Whitney and Eva May Nunnelley Hamilton. — 4th ed. / revised by Eleanor Noss Whitney with Marie A. Boyle. — St. Paul: West Pub. Co., c1987. 1 v. Includes index. 1. Nutrition 2. Metabolism I. Hamilton, Eva May Nunnelley. II. Boyle, Marie A. (Marie Ann) III. T.
QP141.W46 1987     613.2 19     *LC* 86-28236     *ISBN* 0314242473

**Wilson, Eva D.**     5.4243
Principles of nutrition / Eva D. Wilson, Katherine H. Fisher, Pilar A. Garcia. — 4th ed. — New York: Wiley, c1979. ix, 607 p.: ill.; 24 cm. 1. Nutrition I. Fisher, Katherine H., joint author. II. Garcia, Pilar A. joint author. III. T.
QP141.W52 1979     641.1     *LC* 78-11710     *ISBN* 0471026956

# QP187 ENDOCRINOLOGY

**Barrington, Ernest James William.**     5.4244
An introduction to general and comparative endocrinology / E. J. W. Barrington. — 2d ed. — Oxford: Clarendon Press, 1975. x, 281 p.: ill.; 26 cm. Includes index. 1. Endocrinology, Comparative I. T. II. Title: General and comparative endocrinology.
QP187.B354 1975     591.1/42     *LC* 75-333196     *ISBN* 0198541201

**Comparative endocrinology / Aubrey Gorbman ... [et al.].**     5.4245
New York: Wiley, c1983. xvi, 572 p.: ill.; 25 cm. 'A Wiley-Interscience publication.' Errata slip inserted. 1. Endocrinology, Comparative I. Gorbman, Aubrey, 1914-
QP187.C5966 1983     596/.0142 19     *LC* 82-13455     *ISBN* 0471062669

**Gerontological Society.**     • 5.4246
Endocrines and aging; a symposium presented before the Gerontological Society seventeenth annual meeting, Minneapolis, Minnesota. Compiled and edited by Leo Gitman. Springfield, Ill., Thomas [1968, c1967] xvi, 305 p. illus. 24 cm. (American lecture series. publication no. 662) 1. Endocrinology 2. Aging I. Gitman, Leo. ed. II. T. III. Series.
QP187.G386     612/.4     *LC* 66-18931

**Hadley, Mac E.**     5.4247
Endocrinology / Mac E. Hadley. — Englewood Cliffs, N.J.: Prentice-Hall, c1984. xxvi, 547 p.: ill.; 25 cm. Includes index. 1. Endocrinology I. T.
QP187.H17 1984     599/.0142 19     *LC* 83-8701     *ISBN* 0132771373

**Turner, Clarence Donnell, 1903-.**     5.4248
[Introduction to general endocrinology] General endocrinology / C. Donnell Turner, Joseph T. Bagnara. — 6th ed. — Philadelphia: Saunders, 1976. x, 596 p.: ill.; 26 cm. First published in 1941 under title: An introduction to general endocrinology. 1. Endocrinology I. Bagnara, Joseph T. (Joseph Thomas), 1929- II. T.
QP187.T8 1976     596/.01/42     *LC* 75-38156     *ISBN* 0721689337

**Riegel, Jay Arthur.**     5.4249
Comparative physiology of renal excretion [by] J. A. Riegel. New York, Hafner Pub. Co., 1972. xi, 204 p. illus. 22 cm. (University reviews in biology, 14) 1. Kidneys 2. Urination 3. Physiology, Comparative I. T.
QP211.R56 1972b     591.1/49     *LC* 73-152578     *ISBN* 0050024558 *ISBN* 005002454X

**Smith, Homer William, 1895-1962.**     • 5.4250
The kidney: structure and function in health and disease. New York: Oxford University Press, 1951. xxii, 1049 p.: ill.; 24 cm. (Oxford medical publications.) 1. Kidneys I. T. II. Series.
QP211.S618     *LC* 51-3902

**Smith, Homer William, 1895-1962.**     • 5.4251
Principles of renal physiology. New York, Oxford University Press, 1956. 237 p. illus. 23 cm. 1. Kidneys I. T. II. Title: Renal physiology.
QP211.S632     612.46     *LC* 56-6992

# QP251–285 REPRODUCTION. PHYSIOLOGY OF SEX

**Asdell, S. A. (Sydney Arthur), 1897-.**     • 5.4252
Patterns of mammalian reproduction / by S.A. Asdell. 2d ed. Ithaca, N.Y.: Comstock Publishing Associates [1964] viii, 670 p.; 25 cm. 1. Reproduction 2. Mammals — Physiology I. T.
QP251.A7 1964     599.016     *LC* 64-25162

**Cole, H. H. (Harold Harrison), 1897- ed.**     • 5.4253
Reproduction in domestic animals, edited by H. H. Cole and P. T. Cupps. 2d ed. New York, Academic Press, 1969. xvii, 657 p. illus. 24 cm. 1. Reproduction 2. Veterinary physiology I. Cupps, P. T. joint ed. II. T.
QP251.C67 1969     596/.01/6     *LC* 68-26645

**Corea, Gena.**     5.4254
The mother machine: reproductive technologies from artificial insemination to artificial wombs / Gena Corea. — 1st ed. — New York: Harper & Row, c1985. x, 374 p.; 25 cm. Includes index. 1. Human reproduction — Political aspects. 2. Artificial insemination, Human — Social aspects. 3. Women's rights I. T.
QP251.C78 1985     306.8/5 19     *LC* 84-48150     *ISBN* 0060153903

**Human reproduction: physiology, population, and family**     5.4255
**planning / Howard C. Taylor, editor; Fédération Internationale de Gynécologie et d'Obstrétrique, Geneva, The Population Council, New York.**
Cambridge, Mass.: MIT Press, 1977 (c1976). 3 v. (588 p.): ill.; 28 cm. 1. Human reproduction 2. Population 3. Birth control I. Taylor, Howard Canning, 1900- II. International Federation of Gynecology and Obstetrics. III. Population Council.
QP251.H843     612.6     *LC* 76-7378     *ISBN* 026270014X

**Jones, Richard E. (Richard Evan), 1940-.**     5.4256
Human reproduction and sexual behavior / Richard E. Jones. — Englewood Cliffs, N.J.: Prentice-Hall, c1984. xiii, 545 p.: ill.; 24 cm. 1. Human reproduction 2. Sex I. T.
QP251.J635 1984     612/.6 19     *LC* 83-567     *ISBN* 0134475240

**Masters, William H.**     • 5.4257
Human sexual response [by] William H. Masters, research director [and] Virginia E. Johnson, research associate, the Reproductive Biology Research Foundation, St. Louis, Missouri. [1st ed.] Boston, Little, Brown [1966] xiii, 366 p. illus. 25 cm. Bibliography: p. 317-335. 1. Sex (Biology) 2. Sex (Psychology) I. Johnson, Virginia E. joint author. II. Reproductive Biology Research Foundation. III. T.
QP251.M35     612.6     *LC* 66-18370

**Young, William Caldwell, 1899- ed.**     • 5.4258
Sex and internal secretions / contributors: A. Albert [and others]; foreword by George W. Corner. — 3d ed. — Baltimore: Williams & Wilkins, 1961. 2 v. (xxiv, 1609 p.): ill. (part col.); 26 cm. Previous editions edited by Edgar Allen. 1. Sex (Biology) 2. Endocrinology I. Allen, Edgar, 1892-1943, ed. Sex and internal secretions. II. T.
QP251.Y6 1961     591.14     *LC* 60-12279

**Sherfey, Mary Jane, 1933-.**     5.4259
The nature and evolution of female sexuality. — [1st ed.]. — New York: Random House, [1972-. 188 p.: illus. 1. Sex (Biology) 2. Sex (Psychology) 3. Generative organs, Female I. T.
QP259.S53     612.62     *LC* 69-16458     *ISBN* 0394465393

**Asso, Doreen.**     5.4260
The real menstrual cycle / Doreen Asso. — Chichester [West Sussex]; New York: Wiley, c1983. xv, 214 p.: ill.; 24 cm. Includes indexes. 1. Menstruation 2. Menopause I. T.
QP263.A77 1983     612/.662 19     *LC* 83-5890     *ISBN* 0471900435

# QP301–348 Movements. Speech. Muscle. Nerves

## QP301 General Works

**Alexander, R. McNeill.**                                                  **5.4261**
Locomotion of animals / R. McNeill Alexander. — New York: Wiley, 1982. p. cm. — (Tertiary level biology.) 'A Halsted Press book.' Includes index. 1. Animal locomotion I. T. II. Series.
QP301.A297      591.1/852 19      LC 81-21844      ISBN 0470273135

**The Body at work: biological ergonomics / edited by W.T.      5.4262
Singleton.**
Cambridge [Cambridgeshire]; New York: Cambridge University Press, 1982. x, 430 p.: ill.; 23 cm. 1. Work — Physiological aspects 2. Kinesiology I. Singleton, W. T. (William Thomas)
QP301.B48 1982      612/.044 19      LC 81-18096      ISBN 0521240875

**Broer, Marion Ruth.**                                                   **5.4263**
Efficiency of human movement / Marion R. Broer, Ronald F. Zernicke. — 4th ed. — Philadelphia: Saunders, 1979. xi, 427 p.: ill.; 26 cm. 1. Human mechanics 2. Man — Attitude and movement 3. Kinesiology 4. Sports — Physiological aspects I. Zernicke, Ronald F. joint author. II. T.
QP301.B88 1979      612/.76      LC 79-125      ISBN 0721620884

**Grandjean, E. (Etienne)**                                               **5.4264**
[Physiologische Arbeitsgestaltung. English] Fitting the task to the man: an ergonomic approach / E. Grandjean; [translated by Harold Oldroyd]. — [3d ed.]. — London: Taylor & Francis, 1980. vii, 379 p.: ill.; 24 cm. Translation of Physiologische Arbeitsgestaltung. Includes index. 1. Work — Physiological aspects 2. Human mechanics 3. Human engineering 4. Industrial hygiene I. T.
QP301.G6513 1980      620.8 19      LC 80-485627      ISBN 0850661919

**Granit, Ragnar, 1900-.**                                              • **5.4265**
The basis of motor control; integrating the activity of muscles, alpha and gamma motoneurons and their leading control systems. London, New York, Academic Press, 1970. vii, 346 p. illus. 24 cm. 1. Human mechanics 2. Muscles — Motility 3. Neuromuscular transmission 4. Motor neurons I. T.
QP301.G66      612/.74      LC 71-117122      ISBN 0122953509

**International Symposium on Biochemistry of Exercise. (5th:      5.4266
1982: Boston, Mass.)**
Biochemistry of exercise / scientific editors, Howard G. Knuttgen, James A. Vogel, Jacques Poortmans. — Champaign, IL: Human Kinetics Publishers, c1983. xxxii, 926 p.: ill.; 24 cm. — (International series on sport sciences. v. 13) 'Proceedings of the Fifth International Symposium on the Biochemistry of Exercise, June 1-5, 1982, Boston, Massachusetts'—Half t.p. 1. Exercise — Physiological aspects — Congresses. 2. Biochemistry — Congresses. I. Knuttgen, Howard G. II. Vogel, James A. III. Poortmans, J. R. IV. T. V. Series.
QP301.I57 1982      612/.044 19      LC 82-84696      ISBN 0931250412

**Mechanics and energetics of animal locomotion / edited by R.      5.4267
McN. Alexander and G. Goldspink.**
London: Chapman and Hall; New York: distributed by Halsted Press, 1977. xii, 346 p.: ill.; 24 cm. 1. Animal locomotion 2. Animal mechanics 3. Bioenergetics I. Alexander, R. McNeill. II. Goldspink, G.
QP301.M38      591.1/852      LC 77-6737      ISBN 0470991852

**Morehouse, Laurence Englemohr, 1913-.**                                **5.4268**
Physiology of exercise / Laurence E. Morehouse, Augustus T. Miller, Jr. — 7th ed. — Saint Louis: Mosby, 1976. xi, 364 p.: ill.; 26 cm. 1. Exercise — Physiological effect. I. Miller, Augustus Taylor, 1910- joint author. II. T.
QP301.M65 1976      612/.76      LC 75-22186      ISBN 0801634857

**Shephard, Roy J.**                                                      **5.4269**
Endurance fitness / Roy J. Shephard. 2d ed. — Toronto: University of Toronto Press, c1977. xiv, 380 p.: ill.; 24 cm. Includes index. 1. Physical fitness 2. Exercise — Physiological effect. I. T.
QP301.S48 1977      613.7      LC 76-23257      ISBN 0802022502

**Shephard, Roy J.**                                                      **5.4270**
Human physiological work capacity / R. J. Shephard. — Cambridge, [Eng.]; New York: Cambridge University Press, 1978. xiii, 303 p.: ill.; 24 cm. —

(International biological programme; 15) Includes index. 1. Work — Physiological aspects 2. Human biology I. T. II. Series.
QP301.S49      612/.042      LC 77-80847      ISBN 0521217814

**Shephard, Roy J.**                                                      **5.4271**
Physiology and biochemistry of exercise / Roy J. Shephard. — New York, N.Y.: Praeger, 1982. viii, 672 p.: ill.; 27 cm. Includes index. 1. Exercise — Physiological aspects 2. Biochemistry I. T.
QP301.S494 1982      612/.04 19      LC 81-1833      ISBN 0030592895

**Todd, Mabel Elsworth.**                                              • **5.4272**
The thinking body: a study of the balancing forces of dynamic man / foreword by E. G. Brackett. — Brooklyn: Dance Horizons [pref. 1968, c1959] xxviii, 314 p.: ill.; 21 cm. (Series of republications by Dance Horizons, 14) First published in 1937. 1. Posture 2. Animal mechanics I. T.
QP301.T6 1968      612/.75      LC 68-28048

## QP303 Mechanics. Kinesiology

**Frankel, Victor H.**                                                  • **5.4273**
Orthopaedic biomechanics; the application of engineering to the musculoskeletal system [by] Victor H. Frankel [and] Albert H. Burstein. — Philadelphia: Lea & Febiger, 1970. vii, 188 p.: illus.; 25 cm. 1. Human mechanics I. Burstein, Albert H., joint author. II. T.
QP303.F67      612/.76      LC 77-78537      ISBN 0812100905

**Gans, Carl, 1923-.**                                                    **5.4274**
Biomechanics: an approach to vertebrate biology / Carl Gans. — Ann Arbor: University of Michigan Press, [1980] c1974. x, 261 p.: ill.; 22 cm. 1. Animal mechanics 2. Morphology (Animals) 3. Vertebrates — Anatomy I. T.
QP303.G33 1980      596/.01852      LC 80-18705      ISBN 0472080164

**Gray, James, Sir, 1891-1975.**                                          **5.4275**
Animal locomotion. — New York: Norton, [c1968] xi, 479 p.: illus.; 25 cm. — (The World naturalist) 1. Animal locomotion I. T.
QP303.G7 1968b      591.1/8      LC 68-31974

**Hay, James G., 1936-.**                                                 **5.4276**
The anatomical and mechanical bases of human motion / James G. Hay, J. Gavin Reid. — Englewood Cliffs, N.J.: Prentice-Hall, c1982. xv, 443 p.: ill.; 24 cm. 1. Human mechanics 2. Kinesiology I. Reid, J. Gavin. II. T.
QP303.H389      612/.76 19      LC 81-8601      ISBN 0130351393

**Luttgens, Kathryn, 1926-.**                                            **5.4277**
Kinesiology: scientific basis of human motion / Kathryn Luttgens, Katharine F. Wells. — 7th ed. — Philadelphia: Saunders College Pub., c1982. xv, 656 p.: ill.; 24 cm. Rev. ed. of: Kinesiology / Katharine F. Wells, Kathryn Luttgens. 6th ed. 1976. 1. Kinesiology I. Wells, Katharine F. II. Wells, Katharine F. Kinesiology. III. T.
QP303.L87 1982      612/.76 19      LC 81-53074      ISBN 0030583586

## QP306 Voice and Speech

**Fletcher, Harvey, 1884-.**                                           • **5.4278**
Speech and hearing in communication. — 2d ed. — Princeton, N. J.: Van Nostrand, 1958. x, 461 p.: ill. — (The Bell Telephone Laboratory series) 1. Speech 2. Hearing 3. Phonetics 4. Sound 5. Music — Acoustics and physics I. T.
QP306.F6 1958

**Fry, Dennis Butler.**                                                   **5.4279**
The physics of speech / D. B. Fry. — Cambridge [Eng.]; New York: Cambridge University Press, 1979. 148 p.: ill.; 24 cm. — (Cambridge textbooks in linguistics) Includes index. 1. Speech 2. Sound-waves I. T.
QP306.F8 1979      612/.78      LC 78-56752      ISBN 0521221730

**Minifie, Fred D.**                                                   • **5.4280**
Normal aspects of speech, hearing, and language. Edited by Fred D. Minifie, Thomas J. Hixon [and] Frederick Williams. Contributing authors: David J. Broad [and others]. — Englewood Cliffs, N.J.: Prentice-Hall, [1973] xii, 509 p.: illus.; 25 cm. 1. Speech — Physiological aspects 2. Hearing 3. Language and languages I. Hixon, Thomas J., 1940- joint author. II. Williams, Frederick, 1933- joint author. III. Broad, David J. IV. T.
QP306.M617      612/.78      LC 73-2567      ISBN 0136237029

**Paget, Richard Arthur Surtees, Sir, bart., 1869-.** • **5.4281**
Human speech; some observations, experiments, and conclusions as to the nature, origin, purpose and possible improvement of human speech, by Sir Richard Paget, bart. ... — London, K. Paul, Trench, Trubner & co., ltd.; New York, Harcourt, Brace & company, 1930. xiv, 360 p. ill., plates. (International library of psychology, philosophy and scientific method) 'Polynesian language, by Dr. J. Rae': p. 318-353. I. T.
QP306.P3        *LC* 30-12680

**Laws, Kenneth.**                                                        **5.4282**
The physics of dance / Kenneth Laws; photographs by Martha Swope. — New York: Schirmer Books, c1984. xv, 160 p.: ill.; 25 cm. 1. Dancing — Physiological aspects. 2. Ballet dancing — Physiological aspects. 3. Human mechanics 4. Biophysics I. T.
QP310.D35 L39 1984        792.8/01 19        *LC* 83-20462        *ISBN* 002872030X

## QP310.F5 Flight

**Ward-Smith, A. J. (Alfred John)**                                     **5.4283**
Biophysical aerodynamics and the natural environment / A.J. Ward-Smith. — Chichester [West Sussex]; New York: Wiley, c1984. x, 172 p.: ill.; 24 cm. 'A Wiley-Interscience publication.' Includes index. 1. Animal flight 2. Biophysics 3. Aerodynamics I. T.
QP310.F5 W37 1984        591.1/852 19        *LC* 84-11870        *ISBN* 0471904368

## QP321 Muscle

**Needham, Dorothy (Moyle) 1896-.**                                     **5.4284**
Machina carnis; the biochemistry of muscular contraction in its historical development, by Dorothy M. Needham. — Cambridge [Eng.]: University Press, 1971. xv, 782 p.: illus.; 24 cm. 1. Muscle contraction — History. I. T.
QP321.N42        612/.744/09        *LC* 75-142959        *ISBN* 0521079748

**Szent-Györgyi, Albert, 1893-.**                                        • **5.4285**
Nature of life: a study on muscle / by A. Szent-Györgyi. — New York: Academic Press, 1948. 91 p., 7 p. de planches: ill., graphiques. Cours donnés au University of Birmingham et au Massachusetts Institute of Technology. I. University of Birmingham II. Massachusetts Institute of Technology III. T.
QP321.S96        G12.74        *LC* 48-1989

## QP331–341 Electrophysiology

**Eccles, John C. (John Carew), Sir, 1903-.**                            • **5.4286**
The physiology of nerve cells. Baltimore: Johns Hopkins Press [1968] ix, 270 p.: ill.; 21 cm. (Johns Hopkins paperback JH-47) Reprint of the 1957 ed., with a new introd. by the author. 1. Neurons I. T.
QP331.E3 1968        612/.81        *LC* 68-9181

**Horridge, G. Adrian.**                                                 • **5.4287**
Interneurons: their origin, action, specificity, growth, and plasticity [by] G. Adrian Horridge. — London; San Francisco: W. H. Freeman, 1968. xxii, 436 p.: illus.; 25 cm. — (A series of books in biology) 1. Neurons I. T.
QP331.H66        612/.811        *LC* 68-13053

**Plonsey, Robert.**                                                     **5.4288**
Bioelectric phenomena. With the introd. and first chapter by David G. Fleming. — New York: McGraw-Hill, [1969] xiv, 380 p.: illus.; 23 cm. — (McGraw-Hill series in bioengineering) 1. Electrophysiology I. Fleming, David G., 1926- II. T.
QP341.P73        591.1/91/7        *LC* 69-17189

**Stein, R. B., 1940-.**                                                 **5.4289**
Nerve and muscle: membranes, cells and systems / R.B. Stein. — New York: Plenum Press, c1980. ix, 265 p.: ill.; 24 cm. Includes index. 1. Electrophysiology 2. Nerves 3. Muscles I. T.
QP341.S78        599/.01/852        *LC* 80-15028        *ISBN* 0306405121

# QP351–499 NEUROPHYSIOLOGY. NEUROPSYCHOLOGY

## QP352–356 History. General Works

**American Association for the Advancement of Science. Section** • **5.4290**
**on Medical Sciences.**
Evolution of nervous control from primitive organisms to man: a symposium organized by the Section on Medical Sciences of the American Association for the Advancement of Science and presented at the New York meeting on December 29-30, 1956 / arr. by Bernard B. Brodie and Allan D. Bass; edited by Allan D. Bass. — Washington, 1959. vii, 231 p.: ill., ports., diagrs.; 24 cm. (Publication of the American Association for the Advancement of Science, no. 52) 1. Neurology — Collected works. I. Bass, Allan D. ed. II. T.
QP352.A5 1956        591.1802        *LC* 59-10142

**Isaacson, Robert Lee, 1928-.**                                         • **5.4291**
Basic readings in neuropsychology. — New York: Harper & Row, [c1964]. xi, 429 p.: ill., diagrs.; 21 cm. Pagination differs. 1. Psychophysiology — Addresses, essays, lectures. I. T.
QP355.I7        131.082        *LC* 64-10949

**Sherrington, Charles Scott, Sir, 1857-1952.**                          • **5.4292**
The integrative action of the nervous system. [2d ed.] New Haven: Yale University Press [1947] xxiv, 433 p.: ill., port.; 22 cm. (Yale University. Hepsa Ely Silliman Memorial lectures) 'Has as its basis a course of lectures given at Yale University under the Hepsa Ely Silliman Memorial Endowment.' Includes facsimilie t.-p. of 1906 ed. 1. Nervous system 2. Psychophysiology I. T.
QP355.S55x        *LC* a 48-5984

**Skinner, B. F. (Burrhus Frederic), 1904-.**                            • **5.4293**
The behavior of organisms: and experimental analysis / by B.F. Skinner. — New York: Appleton-Century-Crofts [c196-? c1938] xv, 457 p.: ill.; 21 cm. (The Century psychology series) 1. Psychophysiology 2. Rats I. T.
QP355.S7        152        *LC* 66-28616

**Troland, Leonard Thompson, 1889-.**                                    • **5.4294**
The principles of psychophysiology: a survey of modern scientific psychology / by Leonard T. Troland. — New York: Greenwood Press, [1969, c1929-32] 3 v.: ill.; 23 cm. 1. Psychophysiology I. T.
QP355.T75        152        *LC* 68-57643

**Milner, Peter M.**                                                     • **5.4295**
Physiological psychology [by] Peter M. Milner. — New York: Holt, Rinehart and Winston, [1970] x, 531 p.: illus.; 26 cm. 1. Psychophysiology I. T.
QP355.2.M56        152        *LC* 78-107876        *ISBN* 0030809746

**Shepherd, Gordon M., 1933-.**                                          **5.4296**
Neurobiology / Gordon M. Shepherd. — New York: Oxford University Press, 1983. xvii, 611 p.: ill.; 26 cm. 1. Neurobiology I. T.
QP355.2.S52 1983        599.01/88 19        *LC* 82-7938        *ISBN* 0195030540

**Uttal, William R.**                                                    **5.4297**
Cellular neurophysiology and integration: an interpretive introduction / William R. Uttal. — Hillsdale, N.J.: L. Erlbaum Associates; New York: distributed by Halsted Press, 1975. xviii, 310 p.: ill.; 24 cm. Includes indexes. 1. Neurophysiology 2. Neurons I. T.
QP355.2.U88        612/.8        *LC* 75-4673        *ISBN* 0470896558

**Beach, Frank Ambrose, 1911-.**                                         • **5.4298**
Hormones and behavior: a survey of interrelationships between endocrine secretions and patterns of overt response / with a foreword by Earl T. Engle. — [2d. ed.] New York: Cooper Square Publishers, 1961 [c1948] 368 p.; 24 cm. 1. Hormones 2. Psychophysiology I. T.
QP356.B35 1961        *LC* 61-8158

**Selye, Hans, 1907-.**                                                  **5.4299**
The stress of life / by Hans Selye. — Rev. ed. — New York: McGraw-Hill, c1976. xxvii, 515 p.: ill.; 21 cm. Includes index. 1. Stress (Physiology) 2. Adaptation (Physiology) I. T.
QP356.S44 1976        616.07        *LC* 75-12746        *ISBN* 0070562083

**Bradford, H. F. (Harry F.)**        5.4300
Chemical neurobiology: an introduction to neurochemistry / H.F. Bradford. — New York: W.H. Freeman, c1986. xvi, 507 p.: ill.; 25 cm. 1. Neurochemistry 2. Brain chemistry I. T.
QP356.3.B73 1986     612/.8042 19     *LC* 85-7037     *ISBN* 0716716941

**Cooper, Jack R., 1924-.**        5.4301
The biochemical basis of neuropharmacology / Jack R. Cooper, Floyd E. Bloom, Robert H. Roth. — 5th ed. — New York: Oxford University Press, 1986. xi, 400 p.: ill. 1. Neurochemistry 2. Neuropharmacology I. Bloom, Floyd E. II. Roth, Robert H., 1939- III. T.
QP356.3.C66 1986     615/.78 19     *LC* 85-29803     *ISBN* 019504035X

**Endocrinology and human behaviour: proceedings of a**     • 5.4302
**conference held at the Institute of Psychiatry, London, 9 to 11 May 1967 / edited by Richard P. Michael; with a foreword by Sir Aubrey Lewis.**
London; New York [etc.]: Oxford U.P., 1968. xvi, 349 p.: ill.; 25 cm. (Oxford medical publications) 1. Neuroendocrinology — Addresses, essays, lectures. 2. Psychophysiology — Addresses, essays, lectures. I. Michael, Richard Phillip, ed. II. University of London. Institute of Psychiatry.
QP356.3.E9x     155.2/34     *LC* 79-360066     *ISBN* 0192633104

**Katz, Bernard, 1911-.**        • 5.4303
Nerve, muscle, and synapse / [by] Bernard Katz. — New York: McGraw-Hill [1966] ix, 193 p.: ill. (part col.); 21 cm. (McGraw-Hill series in the new biology) 1. Neurochemistry 2. Electrophysiology 3. Muscles 4. Synapses I. T.
QP356.3.K3     591.1/8     *LC* 66-14815

# QP360 Neuropsychology

**Boddy, John.**        5.4304
Brain systems and psychological concepts / John Boddy. — Chichester; New York: Wiley, c1978. xvi, 461 p.: ill.; 25 cm. Includes index. 1. Neuropsychology 2. Brain I. T.
QP360.B624     152     *LC* 77-21203     *ISBN* 0471996017

**Camhi, Jeffrey M., 1941-.**        5.4305
Neuroethology: nerve cells and the natural behavior of animals / Jeffrey M. Camhi. — Sunderland, Mass.: Sinauer Associates, c1984. xv, 416 p.: ill.; 27 cm. Includes index. 1. Neuropsychology 2. Animal behavior I. T.
QP360.C34 1984     591.5/1 19     *LC* 83-14957     *ISBN* 0878930752

**Gazzaniga, Michael S.**        5.4306
Handbook of psychobiology / edited by Michael S. Gazzaniga, Colin Blakemore. — New York: Academic Press, 1975. xvi, 639 p.: ill.; 24 cm. 1. Psychobiology I. Blakemore, Colin. joint author. II. T.
QP360.G38     596/.01/88     *LC* 74-10193     *ISBN* 0122786564

**Greenfield, Norman S.**        5.4307
Handbook of psychophysiology / editors: Norman S. Greenfield [and] Richard A. Sternbach. — New York: Holt, Rinehart and Winston, [1972] xii, 1011 p.: ill.; 27 cm. 1. Psychophysiology I. Sternbach, Richard A. joint author. II. T.
QP360.G74     612/.8     *LC* 72-158478     *ISBN* 0030866561

**Guthrie, D. M. (David Maltby)**        5.4308
Neuroethology: an introduction / D.M. Guthrie. — New York: Wiley, 1981 (c1980). viii, 221 p.: ill.; 24 cm. 'A Halsted Press book.' 1. Neuropsychology I. T.
QP360.G87     591.5 19     *LC* 81-121517     *ISBN* 0470269936

**Hebb, D. O. (Donald Olding)**        5.4309
The conceptual nervous system / edited by Henry A. Buchtel. — 1st ed. — Oxford [Oxfordshire]; New York: Pergamon Press, 1982. xii, 196 p.: ill.; 26 cm. — (Foundations & philosophy of science & technology series) Includes index. 1. Neuropsychology I. Buchtel, Henry A. II. T.
QP360.H388 1982     153 19     *LC* 82-16509     *ISBN* 0080274188

**Kandel, Eric R.**        5.4310
Cellular basis of behavior: an introduction to behavioral neurobiology / Eric R. Kandel. San Francisco: W. H. Freeman, c1976. xx, 727 p.: ill.; 24 cm. (A Series of books in psychology) Includes indexes. 1. Neurobiology 2. Psychophysiology I. T.
QP360.K37     591.1/88     *LC* 76-8277     *ISBN* 0716705230

**Luriia, A. R. (Aleksandr Romanovich), 1902-.**        5.4311
The working brain: an introduction to neuropsychology / [by] A. R. Luria; translated by Basil Haigh. — New York: Basic Books, 1974 (c1973) 398 p.: ill.; 21 cm. 1. Neuropsychology I. T.
QP360.L8713 1973     612/.82     *LC* 72-95540     *ISBN* 0465092071

**Psychophysiology / edited by Stephen W. Porges and Michael**     5.4312
**G. H. Coles.**
Stroudsburg, Pa.: Dowden, Hutchinson & Ross; New York: exclusive distributor, Halsted Press, c1976. xv, 365 p.: ill.; 26 cm. — (Benchmark papers in animal behavior; 6) 1. Psychophysiology — Addresses, essays, lectures. 2. Animal behavior — Addresses, essays, lectures. 3. Psychology, Comparative — Addresses, essays, lectures. I. Porges, Stephen W. II. Coles, Michael G. H.
QP360.P77     152/.08     *LC* 76-17287     *ISBN* 0879332018

**Sperry, Roger Wolcott, 1913-.**        5.4313
Science and moral priority: merging mind, brain, and human values / Roger Sperry. — New York: Columbia University Press, 1983. xiv, 150 p.; 24 cm. — (Convergence) 1. Neuropsychology — Philosophy. 2. Ethics 3. Intellect 4. Science — Philosophy I. T.
QP360.S63 1983     174/.95 19     *LC* 81-24206     *ISBN* 0231054068

**Taylor, Gordon Rattray.**        5.4314
The natural history of the mind / Gordon Rattray Taylor. — 1st American ed. — New York: Dutton, 1979. xii, 370 p.: ill.; 25 cm. Includes index. 1. Neuropsychology 2. Brain 3. Mind and body I. T.
QP360.T39 1979     152     *LC* 79-88891     *ISBN* 0525164243

**Van Toller, C.**        5.4315
The nervous body: an introduction to the autonomic nervous system and behaviour / C. Van Toller. — Chichester; New York: Wiley, c1979. xii, 176 p.: ill.; 24 cm. 1. Neuropsychology 2. Nervous system, Autonomic I. T.
QP360.V38     599/.01/88     *LC* 78-16758     *ISBN* 047199703X

# QP361–426 Nervous System. Brain

## QP361–363 Nervous System. General Works

**Bullock, Theodore Holmes.**        5.4316
Introduction to nervous systems / Theodore Holmes Bullock, with the collaboration of Richard Orkand, Alan Grinnell. — San Francisco: W. H. Freeman, c1977. xiv, 559 p.: ill.; 24 cm. — (A Series of books in biology) Includes index. 1. Neurobiology I. Orkand, Richard, joint author. II. Grinnell, Alan, 1936- joint author. III. T.
QP361.B92     612/.8     *LC* 76-3735     *ISBN* 071670577X

**Clarke, Edwin.**        • 5.4317
The human brain and spinal cord; a historical study illustrated by writings from antiquity to the twentieth century [by] Edwin Clarke and C. D. O'Malley. — Berkeley: University of California Press, 1968. xiii, 926 p.: illus., ports.; 26 cm. 1. Central nervous system I. O'Malley, Charles Donald. joint author. II. T.
QP361.C57     612/.82/08     *LC* 68-11275

**Gardner, Ernest Dean, 1915-.**        5.4318
Fundamentals of neurology: a psychophysiological approach / Ernest Gardner. — 6th ed. — Philadelphia: Saunders, 1975. xiii, 460 p.: ill.; 26 cm. 1. Nervous system 2. Neurology I. T. II. Title: Neurology.
QP361.G36 1975     612/.8     *LC* 74-6681     *ISBN* 0721640028

**Griffith, J. S. (John Stanley)**        • 5.4319
Mathematical neurobiology: an introduction to the mathematics of the nervous system [by] J.S. Griffith. — London; New York: Academic Press, 1971. ix, 161 p.: ill.; 24 cm. 1. Nervous system — Mathematical models. 2. Human information processing I. T.
QP361.G68 1971     612.8/01/51     *LC* 71-141725     *ISBN* 0123030501

**Nathan, Peter Wilfred.**        5.4320
The nervous system / Peter Nathan. — 2nd ed., With corrections. — Oxford; New York: Oxford University Press, 1982. xv, 298 p., [8] p. of plates: ill.; 20 cm. — (Oxford medical publications.) (Oxford paperbacks) Includes index. 1. Nervous system I. T. II. Series.
QP361.N37 1983     612/.8 19     *LC* 83-4223     *ISBN* 0192860275

**The Neurosciences: a study program, planned and edited by**     • 5.4321
**Gardner C. Quarton, Theodore Melnechuk, Francis O. Schmitt, and the associates and staff of the Neurosciences Research Program.**
New York: Rockefeller University Press, 1967. xiii, 962 p.: illus.; 29 cm. An outgrowth of the NRP's first intensive study program in the neurosciences held in the summer of 1966 at the University of Colorado. 1. Neurobiology

2. Nervous system 3. Learning, Psychology of 4. Memory I. Quarton, Gardner C., ed. II. Melnechuk, Theodore. ed. III. Schmitt, Francis Otto, 1903- ed. IV. Neurosciences Research Program.
QP361.N48      574.18      *LC* 67-30343

**Ottoson, David, 1918-.**      5.4322
Physiology of the nervous system / by David Ottoson. — New York: Oxford University Press, 1983. xiv, 527 p.: ill.; 26 cm. Includes index. 1. Neurophysiology I. T.
QP361.O874 1983      612/.8 19      *LC* 82-14171      *ISBN* 0195204093

**Schadé, J. P.**      5.4323
Basic neurology; an introduction to the structure and function of the nervous system [by] J. P. Schadé and Donald H. Ford. — 2d rev. ed. — Amsterdam; New York: Elsevier Scientific Pub., 1973. 269 p.: illus.; 28 cm. 1. Neurology I. Ford, Donald Herbert, 1921- joint author. II. T.
QP361.S25 1973      596/.01/88      *LC* 77-168914      *ISBN* 0444409408

**Hodgkin, Alan Lloyd.**      • 5.4324
The conduction of the nervous impulse. Springfield, Ill., C. C. Thomas [1964] 108 p. illus. 22 cm. 1. Nervous system I. T.
QP363.H62      *LC* 64-7355

**Hopkins, W. G.**      5.4325
Development of nerve cells and their connections / W.G. Hopkins, M.C. Brown. — Cambridge [Cambridgeshire]; New York: Cambridge University Press, 1984. 137 p.: ill.; 24 cm. 1. Developmental neurology 2. Nerves 3. Neurons 4. Nerve endings I. Brown, M. C. (Michael Charles) II. T.
QP363.5.H66 1984      591.1/88 19      *LC* 83-10097      *ISBN* 0521253446

## QP372 CENTRAL NERVOUS SYSTEM. REFLEXES. CONDITIONAL RESPONSE

**Konorski, Jerzy.**      • 5.4326
Conditioned reflexes and neuron organization / translated from the Polish MS. under the author's supervision by Stephen Garry. — Facsim. reprint of the 1948 ed., with a new foreword and supplementary chapter. — New York: Hafner Pub. Co., 1968. xx, 277 p.; 22 cm. — (Cambridge biological studies) 1. Conditioned response I. T.
QP372.K6195 1968      612/.81      *LC* 68-54065

**Sokolov, E. N. (Evgeniĭ Nikolaevich), 1920-.**      • 5.4327
[Vospriiatie i uslovnyĭ refleks. English] Perception and the conditioned reflex. Translated by Stefan W. Waydenfeld. Scientific editors: Robin Worters [and] A. D. B. Clarke. Oxford, New York, Pergamon Press, 1963. x, 309 p. illus., diagrs. 24 cm. 1. Perception 2. Conditioned response I. T.
QP372.S633 1963      152      *LC* 62-22210

## QP376–430 BRAIN

**Bachelard, H. S.**      5.4328
Brain biochemistry [by] H. S Bachelard. — London: Chapman and Hall; New York: Wiley, [1974] 71 p.: illus.; 21 cm. — (Outline studies in biology) 'A Halsted Press book.' 1. Brain chemistry I. T.
QP376.B2 1974      612/.822      *LC* 74-4105      *ISBN* 0470039817

**The Brain.**      5.4329
San Francisco: W. H. Freeman, c1979. 149 p.: ill.; 30 cm. 'A Scientific American book.' 'The chapters ... originally appeared as articles in the September 1979 issue of Scientific American.' Includes index. 1. Brain — Addresses, essays, lectures. I. Scientific American.
QP376.B695      612/.82      *LC* 79-21012      *ISBN* 0716711508

**Eccles, John C. (John Carew), Sir, 1903-.**      5.4330
The human mystery / John C. Eccles. — Berlin; New York: Springer-Verlag, 1979. xvi, 255 p.: ill.; 24 cm. (Gifford lectures. 1977-1978.) Includes index. 1. Brain 2. Life — Origin 3. Human evolution 4. Anthroposophy 5. Natural theology I. T. II. Series.
QP376.E265      573      *LC* 78-12095      *ISBN* 0387090169

**Eccles, John C. (John Carew), Sir, 1903-.**      5.4331
The understanding of the brain / John C. Eccles. — 2d ed. — New York: McGraw-Hill, c1977. xii, 244 p.: ill.; 23 cm. 'A Blakiston publication.' 'Based on the thirty-third series of lectures on the Patten Foundation delivered at the Bloomington Campus, Indiana University.' Includes index. 1. Brain I. T.
QP376.E27 1977      612/.82      *LC* 76-14941      *ISBN* 0070188653

**Furst, Charles.**      5.4332
Origins of the mind: mind-brain connections / Charles Furst. — Englewood Cliffs, N.J.: Prentice-Hall, c1979. x, 262 p.: ill.; 21 cm. — (A Spectrum book) 1. Brain 2. Mind and body 3. Consciousness I. T.
QP376.F85 1979      153      *LC* 78-23185      *ISBN* 0136427774

**Granit, Ragnar, 1900-.**      5.4333
The purposive brain / Ragnar Granit. — Cambridge, Mass.: MIT Press, c1977. x, 244 p.: ill., graph. 1. Brain 2. Neurophysiology 3. Neurophysiology — Philosophy. I. T.
QP376.G69      QP376 G62.      152.3      *LC* 77-2347      *ISBN* 0262070693

**Jastrow, Robert, 1925-.**      5.4334
The enchanted loom: mind in the universe / Robert Jastrow. — New York: Simon and Schuster, c1981. 183 p.: ill.; 24 cm. Includes index. 1. Intellect — Evolution. 2. Brain — Evolution 3. Human evolution 4. Artificial intelligence 5. Cosmology I. T.
QP376.J36      153 19      *LC* 81-13532      *ISBN* 0671433083

**Konorski, Jerzy.**      • 5.4335
Integrative activity of the brain: an interdisciplinary approach. — Chicago: University of Chicago Press [1967] xii, 531 p.: ill. (part col.) 24 cm. 1. Brain 2. Conditioned response I. T.
QP376.K65      612/.82      *LC* 67-16776

**Luriia, A. R. (Aleksandr Romanovich), 1902-.**      • 5.4336
[Mozg cheloveka i psikhicheskie protsessy. English] Human brain and psychological processes / by A.R. Luria; translated by Basil Haigh. — New York: Harper & Row [1966] xix, 587 p.: ill.; 22 cm. 1. Brain 2. Psychology I. T.
QP376.L813      616.8      *LC* 66-13158

**Magoun, Horace Winchell, 1907-.**      • 5.4337
The waking brain. — 2d ed. — Springfield, Ill.: Thomas, [1963] 188 p.: illus.; 24 cm. 1. Brain I. T.
QP376.M28 1963      612.821      *LC* 62-21324

**Meltzer, Herbert L., 1921-.**      5.4338
The chemistry of human behavior / Herbert L. Meltzer; ill. by Francesca de Majo. — Chicago: Nelson-Hall, c1979. viii, 261 p.: ill.; 23 cm. Includes index. 1. Brain chemistry 2. Human behavior I. T.
QP376.M525      612/.82      *LC* 77-19195      *ISBN* 0882291777

**Ornstein, Robert Evans.**      5.4339
The amazing brain / Robert Ornstein and Richard F. Thompson; illustrated by David Macaulay. — Boston: Houghton Mifflin, 1984. 182 p.: ill.; 26 cm. 1. Brain I. Thompson, Richard F. II. T.
QP376.O76 1984      612/.82 19      *LC* 84-12907      *ISBN* 0395354862

**Penfield, Wilder, 1891-.**      5.4340
The mystery of the mind: a critical study of consciousness and the human brain / by Wilder Penfield, with discussions by William Feindel, Charles Hendel, and Charles Symonds. — Princeton, N.J.: Princeton University Press, [1975] xxix, 123 p.: ill.; 23 cm. Includes index. 1. Brain 2. Consciousness I. T.
QP376.P39      612/.82      *LC* 74-25626      *ISBN* 069108159X

**Russell, William Ritchie.**      5.4341
Explaining the brain / W. Ritchie Russell, with A. J. Dewar. — London; New York: Oxford University Press, 1975. x, 157 p.: ill.; 21 cm. 'Chapters 9 and 10 were written in conjunction with Dr. A. J. Dewar.' Includes index. 1. Brain I. Dewar, A. J., joint author. II. T.
QP376.R88      612/.82      *LC* 76-356988      *ISBN* 0192176501

**Wooldridge, Dean E.**      • 5.4342
The machinery of the brain. — New York: McGraw-Hill, [1963] 252 p.: ill.; 21 cm. 1. Brain I. T.
QP376.W8      591.18      *LC* 63-13940

## QP381–385 Cerebrum. Localization of Functions

**Pavlov, Ivan Petrovich, 1849-1936.**      • 5.4343
[Dvadtsatiletnii opyt ob7ektivnogo izucheniia vyssheĭ nervnoĭ deiatel'nosti zhivotnykh. English] Conditioned reflexes; an investigation of the physiological activity of the cerebral cortex. Translated and edited by G.V. Anrep. New York, Dover Publications [1960] xv, 430 p. illus. 21 cm. Translation of Dvadtsatiletnii opyt ob7ektivnogo izucheniia vyssheĭnervnoĭ deiatel'nosti zhivotnykh. 1. Classical conditioning 2. Cerebral cortex 3. Brain — Localization of functions I. T.
QP381.P3 1960      158.423      *LC* 60-2546

**Luriia, A. R. (Aleksandr Romanovich), 1902-.**   5.4344
[Vysshie korkovye funktsii cheloveka i ikh narusheniia pri lokal'nykh porazheniiakh mozga. English.] Higher cortical functions in man / Aleksandr Romanovich Luria; prefaces to the English edition by Hans–Lukas Teuber and Karl H. Pribram; authorized translation from the Russian by Basil Haigh. — 2d ed., rev. and expanded. — New York: Basic Books: Consultants Bureau, c1980. xxii, 634 p.: ill.; 24 cm. Translation of Vysshie korkovye funktsii cheloveka i ikh narusheniia pri lokal'nykh porazheniiakh mozga. Includes indexes. 1. Cerebral cortex 2. Higher nervous activity 3. Neuropsychology I. T.
QP383.L87 1980    612/.825 19    *LC* 77-20421    *ISBN* 0465029604

**Penfield, Wilder, 1891-.**   • 5.4345
Speech and brain–mechanisms / by Wilder Penfield and Lamar Roberts. — Princeton, N.J., Princeton University Press, 1959. 286 p.: ill. 25 cm. 'The general conclusions embodied in this monograph were presented by Wilder Penfield in the Vanuxem lectures at Princeton University in February, 1956.' 1. Brain — Localization of functions 2. Speech 3. Speech, Disorders of I. Roberts, Lamar. II. T.
QP385.P38    612.8252    *LC* 59-5602

**Symposium on the Frontal Granular Cortex and Behavior (1962:**   • 5.4346
**Pennsylvania State University)**
The frontal granular cortex and behavior. A symposium edited by J.M. Warren [and] K. Akert. Consulting editors: J. Konorski [and others]. New York, McGraw-Hill [1964] x, 492 p. illus., diagrs. 24 cm. 1. Cerebral cortex 2. Neuropsychology — Congresses. I. Warren, J. M. (John M.) ed. II. Akert, Konrad. ed. III. Pennsylvania State University. IV. T.
QP385.S9 1962    591.18    *LC* 63-20816

## QP401–425 Emotions. Memory. Consciousness. Sleep

**Cannon, Walter B. (Walter Bradford), 1871-1945.**   • 5.4347
Bodily changes in pain, hunger, fear and rage; an account of recent researches into the function of emotional excitement. 2d ed. College Park, Md., McGrath Pub. Co., 1970 [c1929] xvi, 404 p. illus. 23 cm. 1. Emotions 2. Mind and body I. T.
QP401.C25 1970    612    *LC* 75-119223    *ISBN* 0843400781

**Darwin, Charles, 1809-1882.**   • 5.4348
The expression of the emotions in man and animals / with a pref. by Konrad Lorenz. — Chicago: University of Chicago Press [1965] xiii, 372 p.: ill., port.; 21 cm. 'Reprinted from the Authorized edition of D. Appleton and Company, New York and London.' 1. Emotions 2. Psychology, Comparative 3. Instinct I. T.
QP401.D3 1965    157.2    *LC* 65-17286

**Hardy, James Daniel, 1904-.**   • 5.4349
Pain sensations and reactions / James D. Hardy, Harold G. Wolff, Helen Goodell; with a foreword by Edwin G. Boring. — New York: Hafner, 1967. xv, 435 p.: ill. 1. Pain I. Wolff, Harold G. (Harold George), 1898- joint author. II. Goodell, Helen, joint author. III. T.
QP401.H3x    612/.88    *LC* 67-22374

**Baddeley, Alan D., 1934-.**   5.4350
Your memory, a user's guide / Alan Baddeley. — 1st American ed. — New York: Macmillan, 1982. 222 p.: ill. (some col.); 26 cm. 1. Memory I. T.
QP406.B33 1982    153.1 19    *LC* 82-7226    *ISBN* 0025046608

**Neural mechanisms of learning and memory / Mark R.**   5.4351
**Rosenzweig and Edward L. Bennett, editors; prepared with the**
**support of the National Institute of Education.**
Cambridge, Mass.: MIT Press, c1976. xiii, 637 p.: ill.; 29 cm. Papers presented at a conference held at Asilomar, Calif., June 24-28, 1974. 1. Memory — Congresses. 2. Learning — Physiological aspects 3. Information theory in biology — Congresses. 4. Neuropsychology — Congresses. I. Rosenzweig, Mark R. II. Bennett, Edward L. III. National Institute of Education (U.S.)
QP406.N48    612/.82    *LC* 75-35780    *ISBN* 0262180766

**Harth, Erich.**   5.4352
Windows on the mind: reflections on the physical basis of consciousness / Erich Harth. — 1st ed. — New York: Morrow, 1982. 285 p.: ill.; 25 cm. 1. Consciousness 2. Intellect 3. Brain I. T.
QP411.H37    153 19    *LC* 81-11158    *ISBN* 0688007511

**Dement, William Charles, 1928-.**   5.4353
Some must watch while some must sleep / by William C. Dement. — San Francisco: W. H. Freeman; trade distributor: Scribner, New York, [1974] xiii, 148 p.: ill.; 24 cm. Reprint of the 1972 ed. published by Stanford Alumni Association, Stanford, Calif., in series: The Portable Stanford. 1. Sleep 2. Dreams I. T.
QP425.D44 1974    612/.821    *LC* 74-7334    *ISBN* 0716707691

**Freemon, Frank R.**   5.4354
Sleep research; a critical review, by Frank R. Freemon. — Springfield, Ill.: Thomas, [1972] ix, 205 p.: illus.; 24 cm. 1. Sleep — Physiological aspects I. T.
QP425.F74    612/.821    *LC* 72-75915    *ISBN* 0398025401

**Kleitman, Nathaniel, 1895-.**   • 5.4355
Sleep and wakefulness. Rev. and enl. ed. Chicago, University of Chicago Press [1963] x, 552 p. diagrs., tables. 25 cm. 1. Sleep 2. Physiology I. T.
QP425.K53 1963    612.8217    *LC* 63-17845

## QP431–495 The Senses

## QP431–445 GENERAL WORKS

**Brown, Evan L.**   5.4356
Perception and the senses / Evan L. Brown, Kenneth Deffenbacher. — New York: Oxford University Press, 1979. xii, 520 p., [1] leaf of plates: ill.; 26 cm. Includes indexes. 1. Senses and sensation 2. Perception I. Deffenbacher, Kenneth. joint author. II. T.
QP431.B72    152.1    *LC* 78-26552    *ISBN* 0195025040

**Carr, Donald Eaton, 1903-.**   5.4357
The forgotten senses / [by] Donald E. Carr. — [1st ed.]. — Garden City, N.Y.: Doubleday, 1972. xi, 347 p.; 22 cm. 1. Senses and sensation 2. Psychology, Comparative 3. Extrasensory perception I. T.
QP431.C28    591.1/82    *LC* 70-157578

**Moncrieff, R. W.**   • 5.4358
The chemical senses. [2d ed.] London, L. Hill, 1951. vii, 538 p. illus. 22 cm. 1. Senses and sensation 2. Biochemistry I. T.
QP431.M6 1951    *LC* 52-3572

**Uttal, William R.**   5.4359
The psychobiology of sensory coding [by] William R. Uttal. — New York: Harper & Row, [1973] xvi, 679 p.: illus.; 25 cm. — (Physiological psychology series) 1. Senses and sensation 2. Neural transmission 3. Psychobiology I. T.
QP431.U87    612/.8    *LC* 73-15972    *ISBN* 0060467371

**Von Békésy, Georg, 1899-1972.**   • 5.4360
Sensory inhibition. — Princeton, N.J.: Princeton University Press, 1967. x, 265 p.: illus.; 23 cm. — (The Herbert Sidney Langfeld memorial lectures, 1965) 1. Senses and sensation 2. Inhibition I. T. II. Series.
QP431.V58    152.1    *LC* 66-17713

**Mach, Ernst, 1838-1916.**   • 5.4361
The analysis of sensations and the relation of the physical to the psychical / by Ernst Mach; translated from the 1st German ed. by C.M. Williams. — Rev. and supplemented from the 5th German ed. / by Sydney Waterlow; with a new introd. by Thomas S. Szasz. — New York: Dover Publications; 1959. xlii, 380 p.; ill., music; 21 cm. 1. Senses and sensations. I. T.
QP435.M133 1959    *LC* 59-4170

**Somjen, George G.**   5.4362
Sensory coding in the mammalian nervous system. [New York] Appleton-Century-Crofts [1972] xix, 386 p. illus. 25 cm. (Neuroscience series, no. 4) 1. Senses and sensation 2. Neurophysiology 3. Central nervous system I. T.
QP435.S62    599/.01/82    *LC* 72-78258

**Symposium on Principles of Sensory Communication, Endicott**   • 5.4363
**House, 1959.**
Sensory communication, contributions. Walter A. Rosenblith, editor. — [Cambridge]: M.I.T. Press, Massachusetts Institute of Technology, 1961. xiv, 844 p.: illus., diagrs.; 24 cm. 1. Communication 2. Senses and sensation I. Rosenblith, Walter A., ed. II. T.
QP435.S9 1959    152.082    *LC* 61-8798

**International Symposium on Skin Senses. 1st, Florida State**   • 5.4364
**University, 1966.**
The skin senses; proceedings. Compiled and edited by Dan R. Kenshalo. Springfield, Ill., Thomas [1968] xvii, 636 p. illus., port. 26 cm. Held at the Florida State University in Tallahassee, March, 1966. 1. Senses and sensation — Congresses. 2. Skin — Innervation — Congresses. I. Kenshalo, Dan R. ed. II. Florida State University. III. T.
QP450.I57 1966    599.01/827 19    *LC* 67-21770

**Melzack, Ronald.**   5.4365
The challenge of pain / Ronald Melzack and Patrick D. Wall. — Completely rev. ed. — New York: Basic Books, 1983, c1982. 447 p.: ill.; 22 cm. Rev. ed. of:

The puzzle of pain. 1973. Includes index. 1. Pain — Physiological aspects 2. Pain — Prevention. I. Wall, Patrick D. II. T.
QP451.4.M44 1983    616/.0472 19    *LC* 82-70851    *ISBN* 0465009069

## QP461–471 Hearing

**Bioacoustics, a comparative approach / edited by Brian Lewis.**    **5.4366**
London; New York: Academic Press, 1983. x, 493 p.: ill.; 24 cm. Includes indexes. 1. Hearing — Physiological aspects. 2. Sound production by animals 3. Bioacoustics 4. Physiology, Comparative I. Lewis, D. Brian.
QP461.B57 1983    591.1/825 19    *LC* 82-72339    *ISBN* 0124465501

**Dallos, Peter.**    **5.4367**
The auditory periphery; biophysics and physiology. — New York: Academic Press, 1973. xii, 548 p.: illus.; 24 cm. 1. Hearing 2. Biophysics I. T.
QP461.D3    612/.854    *LC* 72-9324

**Deutsch, Lawrence J.**    **5.4368**
Elementary hearing science / by Lawrence J. Deutsch and Alan M. Richards. — Baltimore: University Park Press, c1979. viii, 191 p.: ill.; 23 cm. 1. Hearing I. Richards, Alan M. joint author. II. T.
QP461.D46    612/.85    *LC* 79-419    *ISBN* 0839112556

**Durrant, John D.**    **5.4369**
Bases of hearing science / John D. Durrant, Jean H. Lovrinic. — 2nd ed. — Baltimore: Williams & Wilkins, c1984. xxiv, 276 p.; 26 cm. 1. Hearing 2. Psychoacoustics I. Lovrinic, Jean H. II. T.
QP461.D87 1984    612/.85 19    *LC* 83-21869    *ISBN* 0683027360

**Gelfand, Stanley A., 1948-.**    **5.4370**
Hearing: an introduction to psychological and physiological acoustics / Stanley A. Gelfand. — New York: M. Dekker, c1981. xi, 379 p.; 24 cm. 1. Hearing 2. Psychoacoustics I. T.
QP461.G28    612/.85 19    *LC* 80-27882    *ISBN* 0824711890

**Jerger, James. ed.**    **5.4371**
Modern developments in audiology. — 2d ed. — New York: Academic Press, [1973] xvi, 521 p.: illus.; 24 cm. 1. Audiology I. T.
QP461.J4 1973    612/.85    *LC* 72-82660

**Stebbins, William C., 1929-.**    **5.4372**
The acoustic sense of animals / William C. Stebbins. — Cambridge, Mass.; London, England: Harvard University Press, 1983. 168 p.: ill.; 25 cm. Includes index. 1. Hearing — Physiological aspects. I. T.
QP461.S68 1983    591.1/825 19    *LC* 82-21350    *ISBN* 0674003268

**Stevens, S. S. (Stanley Smith), 1906-1973.**    • **5.4373**
Sound and hearing / by S. S. Stevens, Fred Warshofsky, and the editors of Life. New York: Time, Inc. [1965] 200 p.: ill. (part col.) ports.; 28 cm. (Life science library) 1. Hearing 2. Sound I. Warshofsky, Fred. joint author. II. Life (Chicago) III. T.
QP461.S72    612.85    *LC* 65-28353

**Von Békésy, Georg, 1899-1972.**    • **5.4374**
Experiments in hearing. Translated and edited by E.G. Wever. New York, McGraw-Hill, 1960. 745 p. illus. 24 cm. (McGraw-Hill series in psychology.) 1. Hearing — Experiments. 2. Audiometry I. T. II. Series.
QP461.V64    612.85072    *LC* 59-9411

## QP474–495 Vision

**Ali, M. A. (Mohamed Ather), 1932-.**    **5.4375**
Vision in vertebrates / M.A. Ali and M.A. Klyne. — New York: Plenum Press, c1985. x, 272 p.: ill.; 24 cm. Includes indexes. 1. Vision 2. Eye 3. Vertebrates — Physiology I. Klyne, M. A. II. T.
QP475.A45 1985    596/.01/823 19    *LC* 85-12141    *ISBN* 0306420651

**Brewster, David, Sir, 1781-1868.**    **5.4376**
Brewster and Wheatstone on vision / edited by Nicholas J. Wade. — London; New York: Published for Experimental Psychology Society by Academic Press, 1983. xii, 358 p., [1] leaf of plates: ill.; 24 cm. Includes indexes. 1. Vision — Addresses, essays, lectures. 2. Photography, Stereoscopic — Addresses, essays, lectures. I. Wheatstone, Charles, Sir, 1802-1875. II. Wade, Nicholas. III. Experimental Psychology Society. IV. T.
QP475.B74 1983    612/.84 19    *LC* 83-70172    *ISBN* 012729550X

**The Eye / edited by Hugh Davson.**    **5.4377**
3rd ed. — Orlando, Fla.: Academic Press, 1984-. < v. 1; in 2 >: ill.; 24 cm. 1. Eye — Collected works. I. Davson, Hugh, 1909-
QP475.E92 1984    612/.84 19    *LC* 83-73325    *ISBN* 0122069013

**Graham, Clarence Henry, 1906- ed.**    • **5.4378**
Vision and visual perception. Clarence H. Graham, editor. [Contributors:] Neil R. Bartlett [and others]. — New York: Wiley, [1965] vii, 637 p.: illus.; 26 cm. 1. Visual perception 2. Color vision I. T.
QP475.G65    152.14    *LC* 65-12711

**Helmholtz, Hermann Ludwig Ferdinand von, 1821-1894.**    • **5.4379**
[Handbuch der physiologischen Optik. English] Helmholtz's treatise on physiological optics / translated from the 3d German ed.; edited by James P. C. Southall. — New York: Dover Publications [1962] 3 v. in 2: ill. (part col.) port., diagrs., facsims.; 21 cm. Translation of Handbuch der physiologischen Optik, with additions made in 1924 by Southall. 'An unabridged and corrected republication of the English translation first published ... in 1924[-25]' 1. Optics, Physiological I. Southall, James Powell Cocke, 1871- II. T. III. Title: Treatise on physiological optics.
QP475.H48613 1962    612/.84    *LC* 63-1421

**Le Grand, Yves, 1908-.**    • **5.4380**
[Optique physiologique. t. 2. Lumière et couleurs. English] Light, colour and vision / approved translation [from the French] by R. W. G. Hunt, J. W. T. Walsh and F. R. W. Hunt. — English 2nd ed. London: Chapman & Hall, 1968. xiii, 564 p.: ill.; 23 cm. 'Distribution in the U.S.A. by Barnes and Noble.' Translation of Lumière et couleurs, published as v. 2 of the author's Optique physiologique. 1. Optics, Physiological I. T.
QP475.L473 1968    612/.84    *LC* 68-68889

**Mueller, Conrad George, 1920-.**    • **5.4381**
Light and vision / by Conrad G. Mueller, Mae Rudolph, and the editors of Life. — New York: Time, inc., [1966] 200 p.: illus. (part col.) ports.; 28 cm. — (Life science library.) 1. Vision 2. Light I. Rudolph, Mae, joint author. II. Life (Chicago) III. T. IV. Series.
QP475.5.M8    152.1/4    *LC* 66-27561

**Cornsweet, Tom N.**    • **5.4382**
Visual perception [by] Tom N. Cornsweet. — New York: Academic Press, [1970] xiii, 475 p.: ill. (part col.); 26 cm. 1. Visual perception I. T.
QP481.C67    612/.84    *LC* 71-107570    *ISBN* 0121897508

**Hering, Ewald, 1834-1918.**    • **5.4383**
[Grundzüge der Lehre vom Lichtsinn. English] Outlines of a theory of the light sense / translated by Leo M. Hurvich and Dorothea Jameson. — Cambridge, Mass.: Harvard University Press, 1964. xxvii, 317 p.: ill. (part col.); 25 cm. 1. Optics, Physiological I. T.
QP481.H4813    612.84    *LC* 64-11130

**Hurvich, Leo Maurice, 1910-.**    • **5.4384**
The perception of brightness and darkness [by] Leo M. Hurvich and Dorothea Jameson. — Boston: Allyn and Bacon, 1966. ix, 141 p.: ill.; 22 cm. (Contemporary topics in experimental psychology.) 1. Vision I. Jameson, Dorothea, 1920- joint author. II. T. III. Series.
QP481.H85    152.143    *LC* 66-15487

**NATO Advanced Study Institute on Photoreceptors (1981:**    **5.4385**
**Erice, Sicily)**
Photoreceptors / edited by A. Borsellino and L. Cervetto. — New York: Plenum Press, c1984. ix, 373 p.: ill.; 26 cm. (NATO ASI series. Life sciences. v. 75) 'Proceedings of a NATO Advanced Study Institute on Photoreceptors, held July 1-12, 1981, in Erice, Sicily, Italy'—T.p. verso. 'Published in cooperation with NATO Scientific Affairs Division.' 1. Photoreceptors — Congresses. I. Borsellino, Antonio. II. Cervetto, L. III. North Atlantic Treaty Organization. Scientific Affairs Division. IV. T. V. Series.
QP481.N345 1981    591.1/823 19    *LC* 84-2131    *ISBN* 0306416298

**Ittelson, William H.**    • **5.4386**
Visual space perception. New York, Springer Pub. Co. [1960] 212 p. illus. 24 cm. 1. Space perception I. T.
QP491.I85    152.1    *LC* 60-15818

**Coren, Stanley.**    **5.4387**
Seeing is deceiving: the psychology of visual illusions / Stanley Coren, Joan Stern Girgus. — Hillsdale, N.J.: Lawrence Erlbaum Associates; New York: distributed by Halsted Press, 1978. xiii, 255 p.: ill.; 24 cm. Includes indexes. 1. Optical illusions 2. Optical illusions — Psychological aspects. I. Girgus, Joan S., 1942- joint author. II. T.
QP495.C67    152.1/48    *LC* 78-13509    *ISBN* 0470265221

**Luckiesh, Matthew, 1883-.**    • **5.4388**
Visual illusions: their causes, characteristics, and applications / by M. Luckiesh; with a new introd. by William H. Ittelson. — New York: Dover Publications, [1965] xxi, 252 p.: ill.; 22 cm. 'An unabridged and unaltered republication of the work originally published ... in 1922.' 1. Optical illusions I. T.
QP495.L8 1965    612.843    *LC* 65-27432

# QP501–801 BIOLOGICAL CHEMISTRY

## QP501–521 Reference. General Works

**Annual review of biochemistry.**         • 5.4389
v. 1- 1932-. Palo Alto, Calif., Annual Reviews, inc. [etc.] v. diagr. 23 cm. Annual. 1. Biochemistry — Yearbooks. I. Luck, James Murray, ed.
QP501.A7      LC 32-25093

**Paul, John, 1922-.**             5.4390
Biochemistry of cell differentiation / edited by J. Paul. — London: Butterworths; Baltimore: University Park Press, [1974] 380 p.: ill.; 24 cm. — (Biochemistry, series one, v. 9) (MTP international review of science.) 1. Cell differentiation 2. Cytochemistry I. T. II. Series. III. Series: MTP international review of science.
QP501.B527 vol. 9 QH607     574.1/92/08 s 574.8/761     LC 74-6296
    ISBN 0839110480

**Fruton, Joseph Stewart, 1912-.**         5.4391
Molecules and life; historical essays on the interplay of chemistry and biology [by] Joseph S. Fruton. — New York: Wiley-Interscience, [1972] x, 579 p.; 23 cm. 1. Biochemistry — History. I. T.
QP511.F78     574.1/92     LC 72-3095     ISBN 0471284483

**Leicester, Henry Marshall, 1906-.**        5.4392
Development of biochemical concepts from ancient to modern times [by] Henry M. Leicester. — Cambridge, Mass.: Harvard University Press, 1974. 286 p.; 24 cm. — (Harvard monographs in the history of science) 1. Biochemistry — History. I. T. II. Series.
QP511.L44     574.1/92/09     LC 73-83965     ISBN 0674200187

**Chargaff, Erwin.**            5.4393
Heraclitean fire: sketches from a life before nature / Erwin Chargaff. — New York: Rockefeller University Press, 1978. 252 p.; 23 cm. Includes index. 1. Chargaff, Erwin. 2. Biochemists — United States — Biography. I. T.
QP511.8.C45 A33     574.1/92/0924 B     LC 77-95216     ISBN 0874700299

**Stenesh, J., 1927-.**           5.4394
Dictionary of biochemistry / J. Stenesh. — New York: Wiley, [1975] viii, 344 p.; 26 cm. 'A Wiley-Interscience publication.' 1. Biochemistry — Dictionaries. I. T.
QP512.S73     574.1/92/03     LC 75-23037     ISBN 0471821055

**Conn, Eric E.**            5.4395
Outlines of biochemistry / Eric E. Conn ... [et al.]. — 5th ed. — New York: Wiley, c1987. p. cm. Includes index. 1. Biochemistry I. T.
QP514.2.C65 1987     574.19/2 19     LC 86-24688     ISBN 0471052884

**Gabler, Raymond.**          5.4396
Electrical interactions in molecular biophysics: an introduction / Raymond Gabler. — New York: Academic Press, 1978. xi, 352 p.: ill.; 24 cm. 1. Biochemistry 2. Biophysics 3. Molecular biology 4. Electrostatics I. T.
QP514.2.G3     574.1/92     LC 77-6595     ISBN 0122713508

**Lehninger, Albert L.**         5.4397
Short course in biochemistry [by] Albert L. Lehninger. — [New York]: Worth Publishers, [1973] 420, xliv p.: ill.; 25 cm. An elementary version of the author's Biochemistry. 1. Biochemistry I. T.
QP514.2.L43     574.1/92     LC 72-93199     ISBN 087901024X

**Stryer, Lubert.**           5.4398
Biochemistry / Lubert Stryer. — 2d ed. — San Francisco: W. H. Freeman, c1981. xxvii, 949 p.: ill.; 27 cm. 1. Biochemistry I. T.
QP514.2.S66 1981     574.19/2 19     LC 80-24699     ISBN 0716712261

**White, Abraham, 1908-.**        5.4399
Principles of biochemistry [by] Abraham White, Philip Handler [and] Emil L. Smith. — 5th ed. — New York: McGraw-Hill, [1973] xv, 1295 p.: illus.; 25 cm. 'A Blakiston publication.' 1. Biochemistry I. Handler, Philip, 1917- joint author. II. Smith, Emil L., 1911- joint author. III. T.
QP514.2.W49 1973     612/.015     LC 73-6745     ISBN 0070697582

**Handbook of biochemistry; Selected data for molecular biology.**     • 5.4400
Editor: Herbert A. Sober; Advisory Board chairman: Robert A. Harte; compiler: Eva K. Sober, in collaboration with a large number of scientists ...
2d ed. Cleveland, Chemical Rubber Co. [1970] 1 v. (various pagings) illus. (1 fold. col. in pocket) 28 cm. Third ed. published in 1975 under title: Handbook of biochemistry and molecular biology. 1. Biochemistry — Tables. I. Sober, Herbert Alexander, 1918- ed. II. Chemical Rubber Company.
QP516.H3 1970     574.1/92/0212     LC 70-20735

**Parker, Frank S., 1921-.**         5.4401
Applications of infrared, raman, and resonance raman spectroscopy in biochemistry / Frank S. Parker. — New York: Plenum Press, c1983. xiv, 550 p.: ill.; 26 cm. 1. Spectrum analysis 2. Biochemistry — Technique I. T. II. Title: Biochemistry.
QP519.9.S6 P37 1983     574.19/285 19     LC 83-11012     ISBN 0306412063

## QP525–801 Special Substances

### QP535 INORGANIC SUBSTANCES

**Bezkorovainy, Anatoly.**         5.4402
Biochemistry of nonheme iron / Anatoly Bezkorovainy; with a chapter contributed by Dorice Narins. — New York: Plenum Press, c1980. xviii, 435 p.: ill.; 24 cm. (Biochemistry of the elements. v. 1) 1. Iron — Metabolism 2. Iron proteins 3. Biochemistry I. Narins, Dorice. II. T. III. Series.
QP535.F4 B46     599.01/9214     LC 80-16477     ISBN 0306405016

**Denton, Derek A.**          5.4403
The hunger for salt: an anthropological, physiological, and medical analysis / Derek Denton. — Berlin; New York: Springer-Verlag, 1982. xix, 650 p.: ill.; 28 cm. 1. Salt in the body 2. Appetite I. T.
QP535.N2 D46 1982     612/.01524 19     LC 82-3336     ISBN 0387112863

### QP551–572 PROTEINS. INSULIN

**Haschemeyer, Rudy Harm, 1930-.**       5.4404
Proteins: a guide to study by physical and chemical methods [by] Rudy H. Haschemeyer [and] Audrey E. V. Haschemeyer. — New York: Wiley, [1973] ix, 445 p.: illus.; 23 cm. 'A Wiley-Interscience publication.' 1. Proteins 2. Biochemistry — Technique I. Haschemeyer, Audrey E. V., 1936- joint author. II. T.
QP551.H37     574.1/9245     LC 72-13134     ISBN 0471358509

**Kornberg, Arthur, 1918-.**        • 5.4405
Enzymatic synthesis of DNA. New York, Wiley, 1961 [c1962] 103 p. illus. 19 cm. (Ciba lectures in microbial biochemistry, 1961) Edition of 1974 published under title: DNA synthesis. 1. DNA 2. Enzymes I. T.
QP551.K795     574.193     LC 62-20165

**Schulz, Georg E., 1939-.**        5.4406
Principles of protein structure / G. E. Schulz, R. H. Schirmer. — New York: Springer-Verlag, c1979. x, 314 p.: ill.; 24 cm. — (Springer advanced texts in chemistry.) 1. Proteins I. Schirmer, R. Heiner, 1942- joint author. II. T. III. Series.
QP551.S4255     547/.75     LC 78-11500     ISBN 0387903860

**Bliss, Michael.**           5.4407
The discovery of insulin / Michael Bliss. — Chicago: University of Chicago Press, 1982. 304 p., [16] p. of plates: ill.; 24 cm. Includes index. 1. Insulin — History. 2. Diabetes — Research — History. 3. Medicine — Research — History. I. T.
QP572.I5 B58 1982     615/.365 19     LC 82-50911     ISBN 0226058972

### QP601 ENZYMES

**Advances in enzymology and related subjects.**      • 5.4408
v. 1-  ; 1941-. New York: Interscience, 1941-. v. ill.; 24 cm. Annual. 1. Enzymes — Collected works I. Nord, Friedrich Franz, 1889- II. Werkman, Chester Hamlin, 1893-
QP601.A1 A3

**Bruice, Thomas C.**     5.4409
Bioorganic mechanisms / [by] Thomas C. Bruice [and] Stephen J. Benkovic. — New York: W. A. Benjamin, 1966-. v. : ill.; 24 cm. (Frontiers in chemistry) 1. Biorganic chemistry. 2. Enzymes 3. Chemistry, Physical organic I. Benkovic, Stephen J., joint author. II. T.
QP601.B845     574.1925     LC 66-13993

**Methods in enzymology, edited by Sidney P. Colowick and**   • 5.4410
**Nathan O. Kaplan.**
New York: Academic Press, 1955-. v. in     : illus.; 24 cm. 1. Enzymes — Collected works. 2. Biochemistry — Technique — Collected works. I. Colowick, Sidney P. ed. II. Kaplan, Nathan Oram, 1917- ed.
QP601.C733     612/.0151     LC 54-9110     ISBN 0121818799

**The Enzymes. Edited by Paul D. Boyer.**   • 5.4411
3d ed. New York, Academic Press, 1970-< 1983 >. v. < 1-16 > illus. 24 cm. 1. Enzymes — Collected works. I. Boyer, Paul D. ed.
QP601.E523     574.1/925     LC 75-117107     ISBN 0121227022

**Fersht, Alan, 1943-.**     5.4412
Enzyme structure and mechanism / Alan Fersht. — Reading [Eng.]; San Francisco: W. H. Freeman, c1977. xvii, 371 p.: ill.; 24 cm. 1. Enzymes I. T.
QP601.F42     574.19/25 19     LC 77-6441     ISBN 0716701898. ISBN 071670188X pbk

**Friedrich, Peter.**     5.4413
Supramolecular enzyme organization: quaternary structure and beyond / Peter Friedrich. — New York: Oxford University Press, 1984. xvi, 300 p.: ill.; 25 cm. Includes index. 1. Enzymes I. T. II. Title: Quaternary structure and beyond.
QP601.F75 1984     574.19/25 19     LC 84-11080     ISBN 0080263763

**International Union of Biochemistry. Nomenclature Committee.**     5.4414
Enzyme nomenclature, 1978: recommendations of the Nomenclature Committee of the International Union of Biochemistry on the nomenclature and classification of enzymes. — New York: Academic Press, 1979. v, 606 p.; 24 cm. 'Published for the International Union of Biochemistry.' Revision of Enzyme nomenclature; recommendations (1972) of the Commission on Biochemical Nomenclature published in 1973. Includes index. 1. Enzymes — Nomenclature. 2. Enzymes — Classification. I. International Union of Biochemistry. II. Commission on Biochemical Nomenclature. Enzyme nomenclature. III. T.
QP601.I54 1979     574.1/925/014     LC 79-1466     ISBN 0122271602

**Segel, Irwin H., 1935-.**     5.4415
Enzyme kinetics: behavior and analysis of rapid equilibrium and steady state enzyme systems / Irwin H. Segel. — New York: Wiley, [1975] xxii, 957 p.: ill.; 23 cm. 'A Wiley-Interscience publication.' 1. Enzymes I. T.
QP601.S45     574.1/925     LC 74-26546     ISBN 0471774251

**Wong, Jeffrey Tze-Fei, 1937-.**     5.4416
Kinetics of enzyme mechanisms / J. Tze–Fei Wong. — London; New York: Academic Press, 1975. xiii, 294 p.: ill.; 26 cm. Includes index. 1. Enzymes — Mathematical models. I. T.
QP601.W736 1975     574.1/925     LC 74-18511     ISBN 0127622500

## QP620–625 Nucleic Acids

**Adams, R. L. P. (Roger Lionel Poulter)**     5.4417
The biochemistry of the nucleic acids / Roger L.P. Adams, John T. Knowler, David P. Leader. — 10th ed. — London; New York: Chapman and Hall, 1986. xviii, 526 p.: ill.; 26 cm. 1. Nucleic acids I. Knowler, John T., 1942- II. Leader, David P., 1943- III. T.
QP620.B56 1986     574.87/328 19     LC 86-9749     ISBN 0412272709

**Judson, Horace Freeland.**     5.4418
The eighth day of creation: makers of the revolution in biology / by Horace Freeland Judson. — New York: Simon and Schuster, c1979. 686 p., [16] plates: ill.; 25 cm. Includes bibliographical references and index. 1. DNA — History. 2. Molecular biology — History. I. T.
QP624.J82     574.8/732     LC 78-12139     ISBN 0671225405

**Kornberg, Arthur, 1918-.**     5.4419
DNA replication / Arthur Kornberg. — San Francisco: W. H. Freeman, c1980. x, 724 p.: ill.; 25 cm. Edition of 1974 published under title: DNA synthesis. 1. DNA — Synthesis I. T.
QP624.K66     574.8/732     LC 79-19543     ISBN 0716711028

**Portugal, Franklin H.**     5.4420
A century of DNA: a history of the discovery of the structure and function of the genetic substance / Franklin H. Portugal and Jack S. Cohen. — Cambridge, Mass.: MIT Press, c1977. xiii, 384 p.; ill.; 24 cm. 1. DNA — History. 2. Molecular genetics — History. 3. Molecular biologists — Biography. I. Cohen, Jack S. joint author. II. T.
QP624.P67     574.8/732     LC 77-7340     ISBN 0262160676

**Nucleotide sequences 1984: a compilation from the GenBank**     5.4421
**and EMBL data libraries.**
Oxford: IRL, 1984. 2 v. (1200) p.; 28 cm. 'A special supplement to 'Nucleic Acids Research" 1. Nucleotide sequence I. Nucleic acids research.
QP625.N89     547/.596 19     ISBN 0904147657

## QP701–801 Carbohydrates. Lipids. Amino Acids

**Roehrig, Karla L.**     5.4422
Carbohydrate biochemistry and metabolism / Karla L. Roehrig. — Westport, Conn.: AVI Pub. Co., c1984. xiii, 205 p.: ill.; 24 cm. 1. Carbohydrates — Metabolism 2. Carbohydrates — Metabolism — Disorders I. T.
QP701.R58 1984     599/.01/33 19     LC 83-22476     ISBN 0870554476

**Gurr, M. I. (Michael Ian)**     5.4423
Lipid biochemistry: an introduction / M.I. Gurr, A.T. James. — 3rd ed. — London; New York: Chapman and Hall, 1980. vii, 247 p.: ill.; 21 cm. 1. Lipids I. James, A. T. II. T.
QP751.G87 1980     574.19/247 19     LC 80-40425     ISBN 0412226200

**Meister, Alton.**   • 5.4424
Biochemistry of the amino acids. 2d ed. New York: Academic Press, 1965. 2 v.: ill.; 24 cm. 1. Amino acids I. T.
QP801.A5 M372     574.19296     LC 65-12768

**Thimann, Kenneth Vivian, 1904- ed.**   • 5.4425
The action of hormones in plants and invertebrates. New York, Academic Press, 1952. viii, 228 p. illus. 24 cm. 'Reprinted, with additions and supplementary bibliographies, from 'The hormones' [edited by G. Pincus and K.V. Thimann] vol. 1.' 1. Plant hormones 2. Hormones 3. Insects — Physiology 4. Crustacea I. T.
QP801.H7 T4     574.194     LC 51-14024

**Michelson, A. M.**     5.4426
The chemistry of nucleosides and nucleotides. London, New York, Academic Press, 1963. 622 p. illus. 24 cm. 1. Nucleosides 2. Nucleotides 3. Nucleic acids I. T.
QP801.N8 M5     547.596     LC 62-21476

## QP903–981 Experimental Pharmacology

**Current research in marijuana; proceedings of a symposium held**     5.4427
**at the Aeronautic Center, Oklahoma City, Okla., June 13–15,**
**1972. Edited by Mark F. Lewis.**
New York: Academic Press, 1972. ix, 219 p.: illus.; 24 cm. 1. Marihuana — Physiological effect. I. Lewis, Mark F. ed.
QP917.C25 C87     615/.782     LC 72-88343     ISBN 0124470505

**Marijuana and health hazards: methodological issues in current**     5.4428
**research / edited by Jared R. Tinklenberg.**
New York: Academic Press, 1975. ix, 178 p.; 24 cm. Proceedings of a conference sponsored by the Drug Abuse Council and held in Washington, D. C., on Jan. 6, 1975. 1. Marihuana — Physiological effect — Congresses. I. Tinklenberg, Jared R. II. Drug Abuse Council (Washington, D.C.)
QP981.C14 M37     615.9/52/3962     LC 75-13085     ISBN 0126913501

## QR1–58 Reference. General Works. History

**Cowan, Samuel Tertius.**                                    **5.4429**
A Dictionary of microbial taxonomy / S. T. Cowan; edited by L. R. Hill. — Cambridge [Eng.]; New York: Cambridge University Press, 1978. xii, 285 p.; 24 cm. 1. Microbiology — Classification — Dictionaries. I. Hill, Leslie Rowland, 1935- II. T.
QR9.C66    576/.01/2    *LC* 77-85705    *ISBN* 052121890X

**Singleton, Paul.**                                          **5.4430**
Dictionary of microbiology / Paul Singleton, Diana Sainsbury. — Chichester [Eng.]; New York: Wiley, c1978. 481 p.: ill.; 24 cm. 'A Wiley Interscience publication.' 1. Microbiology — Dictionaries. I. Sainsbury, Diana. joint author. II. T.
QR9.S56    576/.03    *LC* 78-4532    *ISBN* 0471996580

**De Kruif, Paul, 1890-1971.**                               • **5.4431**
Microbe hunters. Text ed. Edited by Harry G. Grover. New York, Chicago, Harcourt, Brace and company, 1932. xiii, 368 p. illus. 20 cm. At head of title: Paul De Kruif. 1. Scientists 2. Bacteriology — History. 3. Microorganisms I. Grover, Harry Greenwood, 1881- ed. II. T.
QR31.A1 D4 1932d    925    *LC* 32-10382

**Dubos, René J. (René Jules), 1901-.**                      **5.4432**
The professor, the institute, and DNA / by René J. Dubos. — New York: Rockefeller University Press, 1976. 238 p., [7] leaves of plates: ill.; 25 cm. Includes index. 1. Avery, Oswald Theodore, 1877-1955. 2. Rockefeller University — History. 3. Microbiologists — New York (City) — Biography. 4. Medical scientists — New York (City) — Biography. I. T.
QR31.A9 D8    576/.092/4 B    *LC* 76-26812    *ISBN* 0874700221

**Luria, S. E. (Salvador Edward), 1912-.**                   **5.4433**
A slot machine, a broken test tube: an autobiography / S.E. Luria. — 1st ed. — New York: Harper & Row, c1984. x, 228 p.: ill.; 24 cm. — (Alfred P. Sloan Foundation series). Includes index. 1. Luria, S. E. (Salvador Edward), 1912- 2. Virologists — United States — Biography. 3. Virologists — Italy — Biography. I. T. II. Series.
QR31.L84 A37 1984    576/.64/0924 B 19    *LC* 83-48366    *ISBN* 0060152605

**The Bacteria; a treatise on structure and function, edited by I.C.**    • **5.4434**
**Gunsalus [and others].**
New York, Academic Press, 1960- < 1986 > . v. < 1-3, 5-10 > illus., diagrs. 24 cm. Vols. < 8-10 > have as editors: consulting editor, I.C. Gunsalus; editors-in-chief, J.R. Sokatch, L. Nicholas Ornston. 1. Bacteriology — Collected works. I. Gunsalus, I. C. (Irwin Clyde), 1912- II. Sokatch, J. R. (John Robert), 1928- III. Ornston, L. Nicholas.
QR41.B23 1960    589.9    *LC* 59-13831    *ISBN* 0123072085

**Brock, Thomas D.**                                         **5.4435**
Biology of microorganisms / Thomas D. Brock, David W. Smith, Michael T. Madigan. — 4th ed. — Englewood Cliffs, N.J.: Prentice-Hall, c1984. xvi, 847 p., 8 p. of plates: ill. (some col.); 24 cm. 1. Microbiology I. Smith, David W., 1948- II. Madigan, Michael T., 1949- III. T.
QR41.2.B77 1984    576 19    *LC* 83-24506    *ISBN* 0130781134

**CRC Handbook of Microbiology / editors, Allen I. Laskin,**    **5.4436**
**Hubert A. Lechevalier.**
2d ed. — Cleveland: CRC Press, 1977. v.: ill. — (CRC handbook of microbiology; v. 1-6) 1. Bacteria I. Lechevalier, Hubert A. joint author. II. Laskin, Allen I., 1928- joint author
QR6.C2 1977 vol. 1 QR412    QR41.2 C2 1977.    576/.08 589.9    *LC* 77-12459    *ISBN* 0849372011

**The Microbial world / Roger Y. Stanier .... [et al.].**    **5.4437**
5th ed. — Englewood Cliffs, N.J.: Prentice-Hall, c1986. xiv, 689 p.: ill. (some col.); 26 cm. Rev. ed. of: The microbial world / Roger Y. Stanier, Edward A. Adelberg, John L. Ingraham. 4th ed. c1976. 1. Microbiology I. Stanier, Roger Y. II. Stanier, Roger Y. Microbial world.
QR41.2.M464 1986    576 19    *LC* 85-28189    *ISBN* 0135810426

**Pelczar, Michael J. (Michael Joseph), 1916-.**             **5.4438**
Microbiology / Michael J. Pelczar, Jr., E.C.S. Chan, Noel R. Krieg, with the assistance of Merna Foss Pelczar. — 5th ed. — New York: McGraw-Hill, c1986. ix, 918 p., [8] p. of plates: ill. (some col.); 24 cm. Col. ill. on lining papers. 1. Microbiology I. Chan, E. C. S. (Eddie Chin Sun). II. Krieg, Noel R. III. T.
QR41.2.P4 1986    576 19    *LC* 84-28932    *ISBN* 0070492344

**Burrows, William, 1908-.**                                 **5.4439**
[Textbook of microbiology] Burrows Textbook of microbiology / Bob A. Freeman. — 22nd ed. — Philadelphia: W.B. Saunders Co., 1985. xii, 1038 p.: ill. (some col.); 27 cm. 1. Medical microbiology I. Freeman, Bob A. II. T. III. Title: Textbook of microbiology.
QR46.B84 1985    616/.01 19    *LC* 83-18902    *ISBN* 0721638686

**Microbiology, including immunology and molecular genetics /**    **5.4440**
**Bernard D. Davis ... [et al.].**
3d ed. — Hagerstown, Md.: Harper & Row, c1980. p. cm. 1. Medical microbiology 2. Immunology 3. Molecular genetics I. Davis, Bernard David, 1916-
QR46.M5393 1980    616/.01    *LC* 80-13433

**Reid, Robert William.**                                    **5.4441**
Microbes and men / Robert Reid. — [New York]: Saturday Review Press, 1975 [c1974]. 170 p.: ill.; 24 cm. 1. Medical microbiology — History. 2. Microbiologists — Biography. I. T.
QR46.R43 1975    616.01/09    *LC* 74-24326    *ISBN* 0841503486

**Crueger, Wulf.**                                           **5.4442**
[Lehrbuch der angewandten Mikrobiologie. English] Biotechnology: a textbook of industrial microbiology / Wulf Crueger, Anneliese Crueger; editor of the English edition, Thomas D. Brock. — Sunderland, MA: Sinauer Associates; Madison, WI: Science Tech, 1984. x, 308 p.: ill.; 24 cm. Translation of: Lehrbuch der angewandten Mikrobiologie. 1. Industrial microbiology I. Crueger, Anneliese. II. Brock, Thomas D. III. T.
QR53.C7813 1984    660/.62 19    *LC* 84-1340    *ISBN* 0878931260

**Dixon, Bernard.**                                          **5.4443**
Magnificent microbes / Bernard Dixon. 1st American ed. — New York: Atheneum, 1976. 251 p.; 22 cm. Includes index. 1. Microorganisms I. T.
QR56.D59 1976    576    *LC* 75-14678    *ISBN* 0689106777

**Brock, Thomas D. ed. and tr.**                            • **5.4444**
Milestones in microbiology. — Englewood Cliffs, N.J.: Prentice-Hall, 1961. 275 p.: illus.; 23 cm. 1. Microbiology — Addresses, essays, lectures. 2. Microbiology — History — Addresses, essays, lectures. I. T.
QR58.B7    576.082    *LC* 61-7270

## QR65–82 Technique. Classification

**Laboratory procedures in clinical microbiology / edited by John**    **5.4445**
**A. Washington; with contributions by members of the Section of**
**Clinical Microbiology, Department of Laboratory Medicine,**
**Mayo Clinic, Rochester, Minnesota.**
2nd ed. — New York: Springer-Verlag, c1985. xiv, 885 p., [8] p. of plates: ill. (some col.); 25 cm. 1. Diagnostic microbiology — Laboratory manuals. I. Washington, John A., 1936- II. Mayo Clinic. Section of Clinical Microbiology.
QR67.L33 1985    616/.01/028 19    *LC* 84-23659

**Difco manual: dehydrated culture media and reagents for**    **5.4446**
**microbiology.**
10th ed. — Detroit: Difco Laboratories, c1984. vii, 1155 p.: ill. — 'Completely revised and rewritten.' 1. Bacteriology — Cultures and culture media I. Difco Laboratories. II. Title: Dehydrated culture media and reagents for microbiology.
QR71.D57 1953    *ISBN* 0961316993

**Clowes, Royston C., 1921-.**                               **5.4447**
Experiments in microbial genetics / edited by R. C. Clowes and W. Hayes. — Oxford; Edinburgh: Blackwell Scientific Publications, [c1968] xii, 244 p.: ill.; 23

cm. 1. Microbial genetics — Experiments. I. Hayes, William. joint author. II. T.
QR73.C55        576.1/1/50724        *LC* 77-357974        *ISBN* 0632010800

**Hayes, William.**                                                    • **5.4448**
The genetics of bacteria and their viruses: studies in basic genetics and molecular biology. — 2d ed. — New York: Wiley, [1968] xvi, 925 p.: ill. (part col.); 23 cm. 1. Microbial genetics 2. Molecular genetics I. T.
QR73.H3 1968b        589.9/01/5        *LC* 69-16699

**Wollman, Élie L.**                                                   • **5.4449**
[Sexualité des bactéries. English] Sexuality and the genetics of bacteria / [by] François Jacob and Élie L. Wollman. — New York: Academic Press, 1961. 374 p.: ill.; 24 cm. Translation and revision of La sexualité des bactéries, in which the authors' names appear in reverse order. 1. Bacterial genetics 2. Sex (Biology) I. Jacob, François, 1920- joint author. II. T.
QR73.W613        589.9/01/5        *LC* 61-16625

**Broda, Paul, 1939-.**                                                **5.4450**
Plasmids / Paul Broda. — Oxford [Eng.]; San Francisco: W. H. Freeman, c1979. viii, 197 p.: ill.; 24 cm. Includes indexes. 1. Plasmids I. T.
QR76.6.B76        589.9        *LC* 79-10665        *ISBN* 0716711117

**Rogers, H. J.**                                                      **5.4451**
Microbial cell walls and membranes / H.J. Rogers, H.R. Perkin, J.B. Ward. — London: Chapman and Hall, 1980. 564 p.: ill.; 24 cm. 1. Bacterial cell walls 2. Cell membranes I. Perkin, H. R. (Harold Robert), 1924- II. Ward, J. B. (J. Barrie) III. T.
QR 77.3 R72 1980        QR77.3 R72 1980.        *LC* 80-40517        *ISBN* 0-412-12030-5

**Bergey's manual of systematic bacteriology / Noel R. Krieg,**        **5.4452**
**editor, volume 1; John G. Holt, editor–in–chief.**
Baltimore: Williams & Wilkins, c1984- < c1986 >. v. < 1-2 >: ill.; 29 cm. Based on: Bergey's manual of determinative bacteriology. Vol. 2: Peter H.A. Sneath, editor; Nicholas S. Mair, M. Elisabeth Sharpe, associate editors. Includes indexes. 1. Bacteriology — Classification — Collected works. I. Bergey, D. H. (David Hendricks), 1860-1937. II. Krieg, Noel R. III. Holt, John G. IV. Bergey's manual of determinative bacteriology.
QR81.B46 1984        589.9/0012 19        *LC* 82-21760        *ISBN* 0683041088

## QR84–151 BACTERIA. MICROBIAL ECOLOGY

**Rose, Anthony H.**                                                   **5.4453**
Chemical microbiology: an introduction to microbial physiology / Anthony H. Rose. — 3d ed. — New York: Plenum Press, 1976. ix, 469 p.: ill.; 23 cm. 1. Microorganisms — Physiology 2. Microbiological chemistry I. T.
QR84.R66 1976        576/.11/92        *LC* 75-29515        *ISBN* 0306308886

**Spore Conference.**                                                  • **5.4454**
Spores. [1]-2. Minneapolis, Minn. [etc.] Burgess Pub. Co. [etc.] 1957-[1961] 2 v. ill. 24 cm. ([1]: Publication - American Institute of Biological Sciences, no. 5) 1. Spores (Bacteria) — Congresses. I. University of Illinois (Urbana-Champaign campus) II. United States. Office of Naval Research. III. T.
QR84.S63        589.9/01/65        *LC* 57-14449

**Ingraham, John L.**                                                  **5.4455**
Growth of the bacterial cell / John L. Ingraham, Ole Maaløe, Frederick C. Neidhardt. — Sunderland, Mass.: Sinauer Associates, c1983. xi, 435 p.: ill.; 26 cm. 1. Bacterial growth 2. Escherichia coli — Growth. I. Maaløe, Ole. II. Neidhardt, Frederick C. III. T.
QR86.I53 1983        589.9/.031 19        *LC* 83-496        *ISBN* 0878933522

**Sprent, Janet I.**                                                   **5.4456**
The biology of nitrogen–fixing organisms / Janet I. Sprent. — London; New York: McGraw-Hill, c1979. 196 p.: ill.; 24 cm. — (European plant biology series) 1. Nitrogen-fixing microorganisms 2. Nitrogen — Fixation I. T.
QR89.7.S67        589        *LC* 78-40897        *ISBN* 0070840873

**A treatise on dinitrogen fixation, Section 3: Biology / general**    **5.4457**
**editor R.W.F. Hardy; section III editor W.S. Silver.**
New York; London [etc.]: Wiley, 1977. xiii, 675 p.: ill.; 24 cm. 'A Wiley-Interscience publication'. 1. Nitrogen — Fixation I. Hardy, Ralph Wilbur Frederick. II. Silver, W. S.
QR89.7.T73        581.1/33        *LC* 76-15278        *ISBN* 0471351385

**Atlas, Ronald M., 1946-.**                                           **5.4458**
Microbial ecology: fundamentals and applications / Ronald M. Atlas, Richard Bartha. — Reading, Mass.: Addison-Wesley Pub. Co., c1981. xi, 560 p.: ill.; 24 cm. — (Addison-Wesley series in the life sciences) 1. Microbial ecology I. Bartha, Richard. joint author. II. T.
QR100.A87        576/.15        *LC* 80-13684        *ISBN* 0201000512

## QR101–129 By Environment. Air. Food

**Gregory, Philip Herries.**                                           **5.4459**
The microbiology of the atmosphere [by] P. H. Gregory. — 2d ed. — New York: Wiley, [1973] xxi, 377 p.: illus. (part col.); 24 cm. — (A Plant science monograph) 'A Halsted Press book.' 1. Air — Microbiology 2. Palynology I. T.
QR101.G7 1973        576        *LC* 72-7718        *ISBN* 0471326712

**Banwart, George J.**                                                 **5.4460**
Basic food microbiology / George J. Banwart. — Abridged textbook edition. Westport, Conn.: AVI Pub. Co., c1981. ix, 519 p. 1. Food — Microbiology I. T.
QR115.B34        664/.001/576        *LC* 79-10571        *ISBN* 0870553224

## QR180–189 IMMUNOLOGY

**Medawar, P. B. (Peter Brian), 1915-.**                               **5.4461**
Memoir of a thinking radish: an autobiography / Peter Medawar. — Oxford; New York: Oxford University Press, 1986. 209 p., [8] p. of plates: ill.; 23 cm. Includes index. 1. Medawar, P. B. (Peter Brian), 1915- 2. Immunologists — Great Britain — Biography. I. T.
QR180.72.M43 A3 1986        616.07/9/0924 B 19        *LC* 85-26009
    *ISBN* 0192177370

**Clark, William R., 1938-.**                                          **5.4462**
The experimental foundations of modern immunology / William R. Clark. — New York: Wiley, c1980. 372 p.: ill.; 24 cm. 1. Immunology 2. Immunology, Experimental I. T.
QR181.C62        616.07/9        *LC* 80-13565        *ISBN* 0471040886

**Golub, Edward S., 1934-.**                                           **5.4463**
Immunology, a synthesis / Edward S. Golub. — Sunderland, Mass.: Sinauer Associates, c1987. xxi, 551 p.: ill.; 25 cm. 1. Immunology 2. Immunologic diseases I. T.
QR181.G66 1987        616.079 19        *LC* 86-26079        *ISBN* 0878932682

**Hyde, Richard M.**                                                   **5.4464**
Immunology / Richard M. Hyde, Robert A. Patnode. — Reston, Va.: Reston Pub. Co., c1978. viii, 280 p.: ill.; 25 cm. 1. Immunology I. Patnode, Robert A. joint author. II. T.
QR181.H83        616.07/9        *LC* 77-26152        *ISBN* 0879093854

**An Introduction to immunology / edited by E. M. Lance, P. B.**       **5.4465**
**Medawar, E. Simpson.**
New York: McGraw-Hill, 1977. xii, 158 p.; 20 cm. 'A Blakiston publication.' Includes index. 1. Immunology I. Lance, Eugene Mitchell. II. Medawar, P. B. (Peter Brian), 1915- III. Simpson, Edmond.
QR181.I515        616.07/9        *LC* 77-2160        *ISBN* 0070361088

**Manning, Margaret J.**                                               **5.4466**
Comparative immunobiology / Margaret J. Manning and Rodney J. Turner. — New York: Wiley, 1976. viii, 184 p.: ill.; 21 cm. (Tertiary level biology) 'A Halsted Press book.' Includes index. 1. Immunology, Comparative I. Turner, Rodney J., joint author. II. T.
QR181.M34 1976        596/.02/9        *LC* 75-42363        *ISBN* 0470149957

**Immunology: readings from Scientific American / with**               **5.4467**
**introductions and additional material by F. M. Burnet.**
San Francisco: W. H. Freeman, c1976. viii, 275 p.: ill. (some col.); 30 cm. Includes index. 1. Immunology — Addresses, essays, lectures. I. Burnet, Frank Macfarlane, Sir, 1899- II. Scientific American.
QR181.5.I46        616.07/9/08        *LC* 75-19356        *ISBN* 0716705257

**Goodfield, June, 1927-.**                                        **5.4468**
An imagined world: a story of scientific discovery / by June Goodfield. — 1st
U.S. ed. — New York: Harper & Row, c1981. x, 240 p.; 25 cm. 1. Immunology
— Research 2. Medicine — Research I. T.
QR182.5.G66 1981      616.07/9/072 19      *LC* 79-1664      *ISBN*
0060116412

**Immunogenetics / Marek B. Zaleski ... [et al.].**                **5.4469**
Boston: Pitman, c1983. xvi, 514 p.: ill.; 25 cm. Errata slip inserted.
1. Immunogenetics I. Zaleski, Marek B.
QR184.I443 1983      616.07/9 19      *LC* 82-22486      *ISBN* 0273019252

**Snustad, D. Peter.**                                            **5.4470**
Genetics experiments with bacterial viruses / [by] D. Peter Snustad [and]
Donald S. Dean. — San Francisco: W. H. Freeman, [1971] viii, 65 p.: ill.; 28 cm.
1. Bacteriophage — Experiments. 2. Viral genetics — Experiments. I. Dean,
Donald Stewart, 1916- joint author. II. T.
QR185.B4 S64      576/.6482      *LC* 72-183230      *ISBN* 0716701618

**Panem, Sandra, 1946-.**                                         **5.4471**
The interferon crusade / Sandra Panem. — Washington, D.C.: Brookings
Institution, c1984. x, 109 p.: ill.; 24 cm. 1. Interferon — Research — History.
I. T.
QR187.5.P36 1984      616.99/4061 19      *LC* 84-17629      *ISBN*
0815769008

**Smith, Kenneth Manley, 1892-.**                                 **5.4472**
Plant viruses [by] Kenneth M. Smith. — 5th ed. — London: Chapman and
Hall; [distributed in the U.S.A. by Halsted Press, New York, 1974] vii, 211 p.:
illus.; 22 cm. — (Science paperbacks, no. 99) 1. Plant viruses 2. Virus diseases
of plants I. T.
QR351.S63 1974      576/.6483      *LC* 74-165269      *ISBN* 0412121301

# QR355–484 VIROLOGY

**Hughes, Sally Smith.**                                          **5.4473**
The virus: a history of the concept / Sally Smith Hughes. — London:
Heinemann Educational Books; New York: Science History Publications, 1977.
xix, 140 p.: ill.; 24 cm. Includes index. 1. Virology — History. I. T.
QR359.H84 1977      616.01/94/09      *LC* 77-512      *ISBN* 0882021680

**Andrewes, Christopher Howard, Sir, 1896-.**                     **5.4474**
Viruses of vertebrates / Sir Christopher Andrewes, H. G. Pereira [and] P.
Wildy. — 4th ed. — London: Baillière Tindall, 1978. 421 p.; 24 cm. 1. Viruses
2. Virus diseases 3. Vertebrates — Diseases. I. Pereira, H. G. II. Wildy, Peter
III. T.
QR360 A6 1978      *ISBN* 0702006785

**Burnet, Frank Macfarlane, Sir, 1899-.**                        • **5.4475**
The viruses: biochemical, biological, and biophysical properties / edited by F.
M. Burnet [and] W. M. Stanley. — New York: Academic Press,c1959. 3 v.: ill.
1. Viruses I. Stanley, Wendell Meredith, 1904- II. T.
QR360.B83      *LC* 59-7923

**Martin, S. J. (Samuel John), 1936-.**                           **5.4476**
The biochemistry of viruses / S. J. Martin. — Cambridge; New York:
Cambridge University Press, 1978. x, 145 p.: ill.; 22 cm. — (Cambridge texts in
chemistry and biochemistry.) 1. Viruses 2. Microbiological chemistry I. T.
II. Series.
QR467.M37      576/.64      *LC* 77-8231      *ISBN* 0521216788

# R Medicine

## R Medicine: General

### R15–120 Societies. General Works

**Campion, Frank D., 1921-.**                                   **5.4477**
The AMA and U.S. health policy since 1940 / Frank D. Campion. — 1st ed. — Chicago: Chicago Review Press, c1984. ix, 603 p.: ill.; 25 cm. Includes index. 1. American Medical Association — History — 20th century. 2. Medical policy — United States — History — 20th century. 3. Medical care — United States — History — 20th century. I. T. II. Title: A.M.A. and US health policy since 1940.
R15.A55 C36 1984     610/.6/073 19     LC 84-7817     ISBN 0914091573

**Osler, William, Sir, 1849-1919.**                            • **5.4478**
Aequanimitas: with other addresses to medical students, nurses and practitioners of medicine, by Sir William Osler, bt. ... 3d impression, 2d ed., with three additional addresses. — Philadelphia: P. Blakiston's Son & Co., 1914. x, 475 p.; 21 cm. 1. Medicine — Addresses, essays, lectures. I. T.
R117.O8 1914     610.4     LC 36-25408

**Perspectives in biology and medicine.**                      • **5.4479**
Life and disease: new perspectives in biology and medicine / edited by Dwight J. Ingle. — New York: Basic Books [1963] 441 p.: ill.; 24 cm. Includes bibliography. 1. Medicine — Addresses, essays, lectures. 2. Biology — Addresses, essays, lectures. I. Ingle, Dwight Joyce, 1907- ed. II. T.
R117.P426     616.082     LC 63-12527

**Virchow, Rudolf Ludwig Karl, 1821-1902.**                    • **5.4480**
Disease, life, and man, selected essays. Translated and with an introd. by Lelland J. Rather. — Stanford, Calif.: Stanford University Press, 1958. viii, 273 p.; 23 cm. — (Stanford studies in the medical sciences, 9) 1. Medicine — Addresses, essays, lectures. 2. Pathology — Addresses, essays, lectures. 3. Life (Biology) — Addresses, essays, lectures. I. T. II. Series.
R117.V5     610.4     LC 58-13534

**Kreps, Gary L.**                                             **5.4481**
Health communication: theory and practice / Gary L. Kreps, Barbara C. Thornton. — New York: Longman, c1984. xi, 287 p.: ill.; 23 cm. — (Communication and careers.) Includes index. 1. Communication in medicine — Case studies. I. Thornton, Barbara C., 1936- II. T. III. Series.
R118.K73 1984     610/.141 19     LC 83-958     ISBN 0582284112

**Medical and health information directory: a guide to**       **5.4482**
associations, agencies, companies, institutions, research centers, hospitals, clinics, treatment centers, educational programs, publications, audiovisuals, data banks, libraries, and information services in clinical medicine, basic bio–medical sciences, and the technological and socio–economic aspects of health care.
3rd. ed. / Anthony T. Kruzas, Kay Gill, and Karen Backus, editors. — Detroit, Mich.: Gale Research Co., c1985. v. Includes index. Vol. 3 revises and replaces the Health services directory. 1. Information services — United States — Directories. 2. Medicine — United States — Directories. 3. Medical care — United States — Directories. I. Kruzas, Anthony Thomas. II. Gill, Kay. III. Backus, Karen.
R118.4.U6 M38 1985     LC 85-148281     ISBN 0810302683

**Fishbein, Morris, 1889-.**                                   • **5.4483**
Medical writing; the technic and the art. — 4th ed. — Springfield, Ill.: Thomas, [1972] xi, 203 p.: illus.; 24 cm. 1. Medical writing I. T.
R119.F55 1972     808/.066/61021     LC 73-165883     ISBN 0398022798

## R121–125 Dictionaries. Terminology

**Blakiston's Gould medical dictionary: a modern comprehensive**  **5.4484**
dictionary of the terms used in all branches of medicine and allied sciences, with illustrations and tables / [editorial board, Alfonso R. Gennaro ... et al.].
4th ed. — New York: McGraw-Hill, c1979. xxvi, 1632 p., [13] leaves of plates: ill.; 26 cm. Based on Gould's medical dictionary. 1. Medicine — Dictionaries. I. Gennaro, Alfonso R. II. Gould, George M. (George Milbry), 1848-1922. Gould's medical dictionary III. Title: Gould medical dictionary.
R121.B62 1979     610/.3     LC 78-21929     ISBN 0070057001. ISBN 0070057036

**Dorland's Illustrated medical dictionary.**                  **5.4485**
26th ed. — Philadelphia; Toronto: W. B. Saunders, c1985. xxix, 1485 p.: ill. Earlier editions published under title: The American illustrated medical dictionary. 1. Medicine — Dictionaries. I. Dorland, William Alexander Newman, 1864-1956. II. Title: Medical dictionary.
R121.D73 1981     610.3     LC 78-50050     ISBN 0721616453

**International dictionary of medicine and biology / editorial**  **5.4486**
board, E. Lovell Becker ... [et al.]; consulting editor, Alexandre Manuila; editor–in–chief, Sidney I. Landau.
New York: Wiley, c1986. 3 v. (li, 3200 p.); 26 cm. (Wiley medical publication.) Includes index. 1. Medicine — Dictionaries. 2. Biology — Dictionaries. I. Becker, E. Lovell (Ernest Lovell), 1923- II. Landau, Sidney I. III. Manuila, Alexandre. IV. Series.
R121.I58 1986     610/.3/21 19     LC 85-16867     ISBN 047101849X

**Jablonski, Stanley.**                                        **5.4487**
Illustrated dictionary of eponymic syndromes, and diseases, and their synonyms. — Philadelphia: Saunders, [1969] viii, 335 p.: illus.; 26 cm. 1. Medicine — Dictionaries. 2. Diseases — Nomenclature. 3. Eponyms — Dictionaries. I. T. II. Title: Eponymic syndromes, and diseases, and their synonyms.
R121.J24     610/.3     LC 69-12884

**The Oxford companion to medicine / edited by John Walton,**    **5.4488**
Paul B. Beeson, Ronald Bodley Scott; associate editors and principal contributors, S.G. Owen, Philip Rhodes.
Oxford [Oxfordshire]; New York: Oxford University Press, 1986. 2 v.: ill.; 24 cm. 1. Medicine — Dictionaries. 2. Medicine — Biography — Dictionaries. I. Walton, John Nicholas. II. Beeson, Paul B. (Paul Bruce), 1908- III. Scott, Ronald Bodley. IV. Owen, S. G. (Samuel Griffith) V. Rhodes, Philip.
R121.O88 1986     610/.3/21 19     LC 85-29846     ISBN 0192611917

**Stedman, Thomas Lathrop, 1853-1938.**                        **5.4489**
[Medical dictionary] Stedman's Medical dictionary. — 24th ed. — Baltimore: Williams & Wilkins, c1982. xlvii, 1678 p.: ill.; 26 cm. 1. Medicine — Dictionaries. I. T. II. Title: Medical dictionary.
R121.S8 1982     610/.3/21     LC 81-3021     ISBN 0683079158

**Taber, Clarence Wilbur, 1870-.**                             **5.4490**
[Cyclopedic medical dictionary] Taber's Cyclopedic medical dictionary. — Ed. 15 / edited by Clayton L. Thomas. — Philadelphia: F.A. Davis, c1985. xxix, 2170 p.: ill. Includes index. 1. Thomas, Clayton L., 1921- 2. Medicine — Dictionaries. I. T. II. Title: Cyclopedic medical dictionary.
R121.T144 1985     610/.3/21 19     LC 84-3137     ISBN 080368309X

**Thomson, William A.R. (William Archibald Robson), 1906-.**     **5.4491**
Black's medical dictionary / William A. R. Thomson. — 34th ed. — Totowa, N.J.: Barnes & Noble, 1984. 982 p.: ill.; 23 cm. 1. Medicine — Dictionaries. I. T. II. Title: Medical dictionary.
R121.T47 1976     LC 79-167     ISBN 038920496X

**Skinner, Henry Alan.**                                       • **5.4492**
The origin of medical terms. — 2d ed. Reprinted with corrections. — New York: Hafner Pub. Co., 1970 [c1961] x, 438 p.: ill.; 26 cm. 1. Medicine — Terminology 2. English language — Etymology — Dictionaries I. T.
R123.S54 1970     610/.1/4     LC 73-105705

Wain, Harry, 1907-.                                                    • 5.4493
The story behind the word; some interesting origins of medical terms.
Springfield, Ill., Thomas [1958] viii, 342 p. 27 cm. 1. Medicine — Dictionaries
2. Medicine — Terminology I. T.
R123.W2 1958      LC 57-12557

# R126–684 History. Biography

Hippocrates.                                                              5.4494
[Selected works. English. 1978] Hippocratic writings / edited with an
introduction by G. E. R. Lloyd; translated [from the Greek] by J. Chadwick and
W. N. Mann ... [et al.]. — [New] ed.; with additional material. —
Harmondsworth; New York: Penguin, 1978. 380 p.; 18 cm. (Pelican classics)
First ed. published in 1950 under title: Medical works. Includes indexes.
1. Medicine, Greek and Roman — Collected works. I. Lloyd, G. E. R.
(Geoffrey Ernest Richard), 1933- II. Chadwick, John, 1920- III. Mann,
William Neville. IV. Hippocrates. Spurious and doubtful works. V. T.
R126.H54 1978     610/.938    LC 78-377839     ISBN 0140400311

Levine, Edwin Burton, 1920-.                                             5.4495
Hippocrates. — New York: Twayne Publishers, [1971] 172 p.; 22 cm. —
(Twayne's world author's series, TWAS 165. Greece) 1. Hippocrates.
2. Medicine, Greek and Roman I. T.
R126.H8 L4      610/.938     LC 70-120489

Scientific American medicine / Edward Rubenstein, editor in              5.4496
chief, Daniel D. Federman, editor.
New York: Scientific American, c1978. 2 v.: ill. (some col.); 31 cm. Loose-leaf
for updating. 1. Medicine I. Rubenstein, Edward, 1924- II. Federman, Daniel
D. III. Scientific American, inc.
R129.S35      616     LC 77-92625     ISBN 0894540009

Ackerknecht, Erwin Heinz, 1906-.                                       • 5.4497
History and geography of the most important diseases / by Erwin H.
Ackerknecht; pref. by George Rosen. — [1st ed.]. — New York: Hufner Pub.
Co., 1965. xii, 210 p.; 22 cm. 1. Medicine — History 2. Medical geography
I. T.
R131.A173     610.9      LC 65-20093

Ackerknecht, Erwin Heinz, 1906-.                                        5.4498
A short history of medicine / Erwin H. Ackerknecht. — Rev. ed. — Baltimore:
Johns Hopkins University Press, 1982. xx, 277 p.: ill.; 23 cm. Includes index.
1. Medicine — History I. T.
R131.A34 1982     610/.9 19     LC 81-48194     ISBN 0801827264

Clendening, Logan, 1884-1945. ed.                                      • 5.4499
Source book of medical history. — New York: Dover Publications, [1960,
c1942] 685 p.; 24 cm. 1. Medicine — History I. T.
R131.C613 1960     610.9     LC 60-2873

Dolan, John Patrick.                                                     5.4500
Health and society: a documentary history of medicine / John P. Dolan and
William N. Adams–Smith. — New York: Seabury Press, 1978. xi, 244 p.; 24
cm. — (A Continuum book) Includes index. 1. Medicine — History
2. Medicine — History — Sources. I. Adams-Smith, William N., 1929- joint
author. II. T.
R131.D64      610/.9     LC 77-13478     ISBN 0816493243

Garrison, Fielding H. (Fielding Hudson), 1870-1935.                    • 5.4501
An introduction to the history of medicine: with medical chronology,
suggestions for study and bibliographic data / by Fielding H. Garrison. — 4th
ed., rev. and enl. Philadelphia: W.B. Saunders, 1929. 996 p.: illus.(incl.ports.)
1. Medicine — History I. T. II. Title: History of medicine.
R131.G3 1929      LC 29-3665     ISBN 0721640303

Hudson, Robert P.                                                        5.4502
Disease and its control: the shaping of modern thought / Robert P. Hudson. —
Westport, Conn.: Greenwood Press, 1983. xvii, 259 p.; 22 cm. —
(Contributions in medical history. 0147-1058; no. 12) 1. Medicine — History
2. Medicine — Philosophy I. T. II. Series.
R131.H825 1983     616/.009 19     LC 82-21135     ISBN 0313238065

King, Lester Snow, 1908-.                                               5.4503
Medical thinking: a historical preface / Lester S. King. — Princeton, N.J.:
Princeton University Press, c1982. vii, 336 p.; 24 cm. 1. Medicine — History
2. Medicine — Philosophy 3. Medical logic 4. Tuberculosis — History. I. T.
R131.K48 1982     610/.9 19     LC 81-11965     ISBN 0691082979

Lehrer, Steven.                                                         5.4504
Explorers of the body / Steven Lehrer. — 1st ed. — Garden City, N.Y.:
Doubleday, 1979. ix, 463 p., [4] leaves of plates: ill.; 22 cm. Includes index.
1. Medicine — History I. T.
R131.L42      610/.9     LC 78-14685     ISBN 0385134975

Lyons, Albert S.                                                         5.4505
Medicine: an illustrated history / by Albert S. Lyons and R. Joseph Petrucelli
II, with special sections by Juan Bosch ... [et al.], and contributions by Alan H.
Barnert ... [et al.]. — New York: H. N. Abrams, [1978] 616 p.: ill.; 34 cm.
Includes index. 1. Medicine — History I. Petrucelli, R. Joseph. joint author.
II. T.
R131.L95      610/.9     LC 77-12912     ISBN 0810910543

Temkin, Owsei, 1902-.                                                   5.4506
The double face of Janus and other essays in the history of medicine / Owsei
Temkin. Baltimore: Johns Hopkins University Press, c1977. x, 543 p.; 24 cm.
1. Medicine — History — Collected works. I. T.
R131.T4      610/.9     LC 76-47380     ISBN 0801818591

Clarke, Edwin.                                                         • 5.4507
Modern methods in the history of medicine; edited by Edwin Clarke. —
London: Athlone Press, 1971. xiv, 389 p., 4 plates.: illus.; 23 cm. 1. Medicine —
Historiography I. T.
R133.C53      610/.9     LC 70-501553     ISBN 0485111217

Foucault, Michel.                                                       5.4508
[Naissance de la clinique. English] The birth of the clinic; an archaeology of
medical perception. Translated from the French by A. M. Sheridan Smith. [1st
American ed.] New York, Pantheon Books [1973] xix, 215 p. 25 cm. (World of
man) Translation of Naissance de la clinique. 1. Medicine — History
2. Medicine — Philosophy I. T.
R133.F6913     362.1/1     LC 73-3493     ISBN 0394483219

International medical who's who: a biographical guide in the            5.4510
biomedical sciences.
2nd ed. — London: Longman, 1985. 2 v. — (Longman reference on research
series.) 1. Medical scientists — Biography.
R134.I5x 1985     610/.92/2 19     ISBN 058290112X

Majno, Guido.                                                           5.4511
The healing hand: man and wound in the ancient world / Guido Majno. —
Cambridge, Mass.: Harvard University Press, 1975. xxiii, 571 p., [6] leaves of
plates: ill. (some col.); 29 cm. 'A Commonwealth Fund book.' Includes index.
1. Medicine, Ancient 2. Wounds and injuries — Treatment — History.
3. Surgery — History. I. T.
R135.M34     617/.14/093     LC 74-80730     ISBN 0674383303

Rosner, Fred.                                                           5.4512
Medicine in the Bible and the Talmud: selections from classical Jewish sources /
by Fred Rosner. — New York: Ktav Pub. House, 1977. xiii, 247 p., [2] leaves of
plates: ill.; 24 cm. — (The Library of Jewish law and ethics; 5) 1. Medicine in
the Bible 2. Medicine in the Talmud 3. Medical ethics I. T.
R135.5.R67     296.1     LC 76-58505     ISBN 0870683268

Kealey, Edward J.                                                       5.4513
Medieval medicus: a social history of Anglo–Norman medicine / by Edward J.
Kealey. — Baltimore: Johns Hopkins University Press, c1981. x, 211 p.: ill.; 24
cm. Includes index. 1. Medicine, Medieval — England. 2. Physicians —
England — Biography. 3. Hospitals, Medieval — England. 4. England —
Social conditions — Medieval period, 1066-1485 I. T.
R141.K4     362.1/0942 19     LC 80-21870     ISBN 0801825334

Ullmann, Manfred.                                                       5.4514
Islamic medicine / Manfred Ullmann; [translated by Jean Watt]. — Edinburgh:
Edinburgh University Press, c1978. xiv, 138 p., [4] leaves of plates: ill.; 21 cm.
— (Islamic surveys; 11) Includes indexes. 1. Medicine, Arabic I. T. II. Series.
R143.U5x      909/.09/7671 s 610/.917/671     LC 78-310925     ISBN
0852243251

Reiser, Stanley Joel.                                                   5.4515
Medicine and the reign of technology / Stanley Joel Reiser. — Cambridge; New
York: Cambridge University Press, 1978. xi, 317 p.: ill.; 24 cm. Includes index.
1. Medicine — History 2. Medical technology — History. 3. Diagnosis —
History. 4. Medical innovations — Social aspects I. T.
R145.R44      610/.9/03     LC 77-87389     ISBN 0521219078

King, Lester Snow, 1908-.                                               5.4516
The philosophy of medicine: the early eighteenth century / Lester S. King. —
Cambridge, Mass.: Harvard University Press, 1978. viii, 291 p.; 25 cm.
1. Medicine — 15th-18th centuries 2. Medicine — Philosophy — History.
I. T.
R148.K515     610/.1     LC 77-24645     ISBN 0674665856

**King, Lester Snow, 1908-.**                                    • 5.4517
The road to medical enlightenment, 1650–1695, by Lester S. King. — London: Macdonald & Co.; New York: American Elsevier, 1970. iii-x, 209 p.; 25 cm. — (History of science library) 1. Medicine — History I. T. II. Series.
R148.K52        610/.9/032        LC 79-111293        ISBN 444196854

**Shryock, Richard Harrison, 1893-1972.**                        • 5.4518
Medicine and society in America, 1660–1860. [New York]: New York University Press, 1960. 182 p.; 22 cm. (Anson G. Phelps lectureship on early American history.) 1. Medicine — History 2. Medicine — United States I. T. II. Series.
R148.S45        610.973        LC 60-6417

**Sourkes, Theodore L.**                                        • 5.4519
Nobel Prize winners in medicine and physiology, 1901–1965, by Theodore L. Sourkes. — [New and rev. ed.]. — London; New York: Abelard-Schuman, [1967, c1966] ix, 464 p.: ports.; 23 cm. — (The Life of science library, no. 45) Revision of Lloyd G. Stevenson's Nobel Prize winners in medicine and physiology, 1901-1950. 1. Physicians 2. Physiologists 3. Nobel prizes I. Stevenson, Lloyd G. Nobel Prize winners in medicine and physiology, 1901-1950. II. T.
R149.S6 1967        610/.922        LC 65-24774

## R150–684 BY COUNTRY OR REGION

## R151–363 United States

**Bordley, James, 1900-.**                                      5.4520
Two centuries of American medicine, 1776–1976 / James Bordley III, A. McGehee Harvey. — Philadelphia: Saunders, 1976. xv, 844 p.: ill.; 27 cm. Includes index. 1. Medicine — United States — History. I. Harvey, A. McGehee (Abner McGehee), 1911- joint author. II. T.
R151.B58        610/.973        LC 75-19841        ISBN 0721618731

**Brieger, Gert H., comp.**                                     • 5.4521
Medical America in the nineteenth century: readings from the literature / edited by Gert H. Brieger. — Baltimore: Johns Hopkins Press, [1972] x, 338 p.; 24 cm. 1. Medicine — United States — Addresses, essays, lectures. I. T.
R151.B75        610/.973        LC 76-165053        ISBN 0801812372

**Kett, Joseph F.**                                             • 5.4522
The formation of the American medical profession; the role of institutions, 1780–1860, by Joseph F. Kett. — New Haven: Yale University Press, 1968. xi, 217 p.; 24 cm. 1. Medicine — United States — History — 18th century. 2. Medicine — United States — History — 19th century. I. T.
R151.K47        610/.973        LC 68-13914

**Rothstein, William G.**                                       5.4523
American physicians in the nineteenth century: from sects to science [by] William G. Rothstein. — Baltimore: Johns Hopkins University Press, [1972] xv, 362 p.; 24 cm. 1. Medicine — United States I. T.
R151.R68        610.69/52/0973        LC 77-186517        ISBN 0801812429

**Stevens, Rosemary.**                                          5.4524
American medicine and the public interest. — New Haven: Yale University Press, 1971. xiii, 572 p.; 25 cm. 1. Medicine — United States 2. Medicine — Specialties and specialists — United States. 3. Medical care — United States I. T.
R151.S8        362.1        LC 77-151592        ISBN 0300014198

**Brown, E. Richard.**                                          5.4525
Rockefeller medicine men: medicine and capitalism in America / E. Richard Brown. — Berkeley: University of California Press, c1979. xii, 283 p., [3] leaves of plates: ill.; 24 cm. 1. Rockefeller Foundation — History. 2. Carnegie Foundation for the Advancement of Teaching — History. 3. Medicine — United States — History — 20th century. 4. Medical policy — United States — Business community participation — History — 20th century. 5. Charities, Medical — United States — History — 20th century. 6. Medical economics — United States — History — 20th century. 7. Medical education — United States — History — 20th century. 8. United States — Economic conditions — 1865-1918 I. T.
R152.B73        362.1/0973        LC 78-65461        ISBN 0520038177

**Burrow, James Gordon, 1922-.**                                5.4526
Organized medicine in the progressive era: the move toward monopoly / James G. Burrow. — Baltimore: Johns Hopkins University Press, c1977. ix, 218 p.; 24 cm. Includes index. 1. Medicine — United States — History — 20th century. 2. Medical societies — United States — Political activity — History — 20th century. 3. Medical economics — United States — History — 20th century. 4. Progressivism (United States politics) I. T.
R152.B8        362.1/0973        LC 77-894        ISBN 0801819180

**Haller, John S.**                                             5.4527
American medicine in transition 1840–1910 / by John S. Haller, Jr. — Urbana: University of Illinois Press, c1981. xii, 457 p., [5] leaves of plates: ill.; 24 cm. Includes index. 1. Medicine — United States — History — 19th century. 2. Medicine — History — 19th century. I. T.
R152.H354        610/.9/034 19        LC 80-14546        ISBN 0252008065

**Rosen, George, 1910-.**                                       5.4528
The structure of American medical practice, 1875–1941 / George Rosen; Charles E. Rosenberg, editor. — Philadelphia: University of Pennsylvania Press, 1983. viii, 152 p., [4] p. of plates: ill.; 23 cm. Based on the author's 1976 Richard H. Shryock lectures sponsored by the University of Pennsylvania Dept. of History. Includes index. 1. Medicine — United States — History. I. Rosenberg, Charles E. II. T.
R152.R67 1983        610/.973 19        LC 83-10461        ISBN 0812211537

**Dictionary of American medical biography / Martin Kaufman,        5.4529
Stuart Galishoff, Todd L. Savitt, editors; Joseph Carvalho III, editorial associate.**
Westport, Conn.: Greenwood Press, 1984. 2 v. (xvi, 1027 p.); 25 cm. Includes index. 1. Medicine — United States — Biography. 2. Public health personnel — United States — Biography. 3. Healers — United States — Biography. I. Kaufman, Martin, 1940- II. Galishoff, Stuart. III. Savitt, Todd L., 1942-
R153.D53 1984        610/.92/2 B 19        LC 82-21110        ISBN 031321378X

**Hamilton, Alice, 1869-1970.**                                 5.4530
Exploring the dangerous trades: the autobiography of Alice Hamilton, M.D. / with a foreword by Barbara Sicherman; with illustrations by Norah Hamilton. — Boston, Mass.: Northeastern University Press, 1985. xx, 433 p., [9] leaves of plates: ill.; 22 cm. Reprint. Originally published: Boston: Little, Brown, 1943. Includes index. 1. Hamilton, Alice, 1869-1970. 2. Women physicians — United States — Biography. 3. Toxicologists — United States — Biography. 4. Medicine, Industrial — United States — History. I. T.
R154.H238 A34 1985        616.9/803/0924 B 19        LC 85-18876        ISBN 0930350812

**Sicherman, Barbara.**                                         5.4531
Alice Hamilton, a life in letters / Barbara Sicherman. — Cambridge, Mass.: Harvard University Press, 1984. xiv, 460 p.: ill., ports.; 25 cm. 'A Commonwealth Fund book.' Includes index. 1. Hamilton, Alice, 1869-1970. 2. Physicians — United States — Biography. 3. Toxicologists — United States — Biography. I. Hamilton, Alice, 1869-1970. II. T.
R154.H238 S53 1984        616.9/803/0924 B 19        LC 83-26521        ISBN 0674015533

**Thomas, Lewis, 1913-.**                                       5.4532
The youngest science: notes of a medicine–watcher / Lewis Thomas. — New York: Viking Press, 1983. xvi, 270 p.; 22 cm. — (Alfred P. Sloan Foundation series.) 1. Thomas, Lewis, 1913- 2. Physicians — United States — Biography. I. T. II. Series.
R154.T48 A36 1983        610/.92/4 B 19        LC 82-50736        ISBN 067079533X

## R461–684 Other Countries

**Health, medicine, and mortality in the sixteenth century /        5.4533
edited by Charles Webster.**
Cambridge [Eng.]; New York: Cambridge University Press, 1979. 394 p.: ill.; 24 cm. — (Cambridge monographs on the history of medicine.) 1. Medicine — England — History — 16th century. 2. Public health — England — History — 16th century. 3. Mortality — England — History — 16th century. I. Webster, Charles, 1936- II. Series.
R487.H42        610/.942        LC 78-73234        ISBN 0521226430

**Baxby, Derrick.**                                             5.4534
Jenner's smallpox vaccine: the riddle of vaccinia virus and its origin / Derrick Baxby. — London: Heinemann Educational Books, c1981. xiv, 214 p.: ill., port.; 23 cm. 1. Jenner, Edward, 1749-1823. 2. Smallpox — Preventive inoculation — History 3. Physicians — Great Britain — Biography I. T.
R489.J5 B3        R489J5 B39.        ISBN 043554072

**Fisher, Richard B.**                                          5.4535
Joseph Lister, 1827–1912 / Richard B. Fisher. — New York: Stein and Day, 1977. 351 p., [8] leaves of plates: ill.; 25 cm. Includes index. 1. Lister, Joseph, Baron, 1827-1912. 2. Surgeons — Great Britain — Biography. 3. Surgery, Aseptic and antiseptic — History. I. T.
R489.L75 F5 1977        617/.092/4 B        LC 76-50614        ISBN 0812821564

**Osler, William, Sir, 1849-1919.**                                      **5.4536**
Selected writings, 12 July 1849 to 20 December 1919; with an introd. by G.L.
Keynes. London, New York, Oxford University Press, 1951. xx, 278 p. illus.,
ports. 22 cm. 1. Physicians — Correspondence. I. T.
R489.O7 A16 1951        610.4        *LC* 51-3479

**Unschuld, Paul U. (Paul Ulrich), 1943-.**                              **5.4537**
Medicine in China: a history of ideas / Paul U. Unschuld. — Berkeley:
University of California Press, c1985. xi, 423 p.; 24 cm. (Comparative studies of
health systems and medical care.) Includes index. 1. Medicine, Chinese —
Philosophy. I. T. II. Series.
R602.U56 1985        362.1/0951 19        *LC* 84-2415        *ISBN* 0520050231

**Unschuld, Paul U. (Paul Ulrich), 1943-.**                              **5.4538**
[Medizin und Ethik. English] Medical ethics in Imperial China: a study in
historical anthropology / Paul U. Unschuld. — Berkeley: University of
California Press, c1979. viii, 141 p.; 23 cm. — (Comparative studies of health
systems and medical care.) Rev. and expanded translation of Medizin und
Ethik. Includes index. 1. Medicine, Chinese — Practice — History. 2. Medical
ethics — China — History. 3. Physicians — China — History. 4. Philosophy,
Confucian — History. I. T. II. Series.
R602.U5713        174/.2/0951        *LC* 77-80479        05200354307

# R690–728 Medicine as a Profession. Directories

**Drachman, Virginia G., 1948-.**                                       **5.4539**
Hospital with a heart: women doctors and the paradox of separatism at the New
England Hospital, 1862–1969 / Virginia G. Drachman. — Ithaca: Cornell
University Press, 1984. 258 p.: ill.; 24 cm. Includes index. 1. New England
Hospital for Women and Children — History. 2. Women physicians — United
States — History — 20th century. 3. Women physicians — United States —
History — 19th century. 4. Sex discrimination in medical education — United
States — History. 5. Sex discrimination against women — United States —
History. I. T.
R692.D73 1984        305.4/3616/0974461 19        *LC* 83-45930        *ISBN*
0801416248

**In her own words: oral histories of women physicians / edited**       **5.4540**
**by Regina Markell Morantz, Cynthia Stodola Pomerleau, and**
**Carol Hansen Fenichel.**
Westport, Conn.: Greenwood Press, 1982. xiv, 284 p.: ill.; 24 cm.
(Contributions in medical history. 0147-1058; no. 8) Interviews with women
physicians. Includes index. 1. Women physicians — United States —
Interviews. 2. Physicians — United States — Interviews. I. Morantz-Sanchez,
Regina Markell. II. Pomerleau, Cynthia S. III. Fenichel, Carol. IV. Series.
R692.I5 1982        610/.92/2 B 19        *LC* 81-13349        *ISBN* 0313226865

**Lopate, Carol.**                                                     • **5.4541**
Women in medicine. Baltimore, Published for the Josiah Macy, Jr., Foundation
by the Johns Hopkins Press [1968] xvii, 204 p. 24 cm. 1. Women physicians
I. Josiah Macy, Jr. Foundation. II. T.
R692.L65        610/.23        *LC* 68-19526

**Morantz-Sanchez, Regina Markell.**                                    **5.4542**
Sympathy and science: women physicians in American medicine / Regina
Markell Morantz-Sanchez. — New York: Oxford University Press, 1985. xii,
464 p.; 25 cm. Includes index. 1. Women physicians — United States —
History. 2. Medicine — United States — History. 3. Social medicine — United
States — History. I. T.
R692.M64 1985        610.6952/088042 19        *LC* 85-10464        *ISBN*
0195036271

**Curtis, James L., 1922-.**                                          • **5.4543**
Blacks, medical schools, and society [by] James L. Curtis. Ann Arbor,
University of Michigan Press [1971] xv, 169 p. 23 cm. 1. Afro-Americans in
medicine 2. Medical education — United States. I. T.
R695.C86 1971        610/.71/173        *LC* 76-148249        *ISBN* 0472269003

**Cartwright, Frederick Fox.**                                          **5.4544**
Disease and history, by Frederick F. Cartwright in collaboration with Michael
D. Biddiss. — New York: Crowell, [1972] viii, 247 p.; 22 cm. 1. Medicine —
History 2. Epidemics — History. 3. World history I. T.
R702.C37        614.4/9        *LC* 73-184972        *ISBN* 069024116X

**McKeown, Thomas.**                                                    **5.4545**
The modern rise of population / Thomas McKeown. — New York: Academic
Press, 1976. 168 p.: graphs; 24 cm. 1. Communicable diseases — Mortality —
History. 2. Population — History 3. Medicine — History 4. Public health —
History. 5. Diet — History. I. T.
R702.M3 1976        301.32/9        *LC* 76-13391        *ISBN* 0124855504

**Ransford, Oliver, 1914-.**                                           **5.4546**
'Bid the sickness cease': disease in the history of black Africa / Oliver Ransford.
— London: J. Murray, 1984 (c1983). x, 235 p., [8] p. of plates: ill.; 23 cm.
Includes index. 1. Diseases and history — Africa. 2. Epidemics — Africa, Sub-
Saharan — History. 3. Tropical medicine — Africa, Sub-Saharan — History.
4. Medical geography — Africa, Sub-Saharan — History. I. T.
R702.R36        614.4/267 19        *LC* 83-241100        *ISBN* 0719539862

**Strauss, Maurice Benjamin, 1904- comp.**                            • **5.4547**
Familiar medical quotations / edited by Maurice B. Strauss. — [1st ed.]. —
Boston: Little, Brown, [1968] xix, 968 p.; 25 cm. 1. Medicine — Quotations,
maxims, etc. I. T.
R707.S75        610/.2        *LC* 68-21620

**American medical directory.**                                         **5.4548**
1st- ed. Chicago, American Medical Association [etc.] 1906-. v. 28-30 cm.
'Directory of physicians in the United States, Canal Zone, Puerto Rico, Virgin
Islands, certain Pacific islands and U.S. physicians temporarily located in
foreign countries.' Vols. for 1973-<79> issued in four parts: pt. 1,
Alphabetical index of physicians, pts. 2-4, Geographical register of physicians.
Special supplement accompanies issue for 1931. 1. Physicians — United States
— Directories. I. American Medical Association. II. American medical
directory update.
R712.A1 A6        610/.257        *LC* 07-10295

**Directory of medical specialists.**                                   **5.4549**
1st(1940-41)-. Chicago: Marquis Who's Who [etc.]. v. Earlier editions have
expanded title: Directory of medical specialists holding certification by
American Boards. Issued in 2 vols. 1. Medicine — Specialties and specialists —
Directories. 2. Physicians — United States — Directories. 3. Physicians —
Canada — Directories. I. American Board of Medical Specialties.
R712.A1 D5        *LC* 40-9671

# R723–726 Philosophy. Ethics. Psychology

**Brody, Howard.**                                                      **5.4550**
Placebos and the philosophy of medicine: clinical, conceptual, and ethical issues
/ Howard Brody. — Chicago: University of Chicago Press, 1980. vii, 164 p.; 21
cm. Revision of the author's thesis, Michigan State University, 1977. Includes
index. 1. Medicine — Philosophy 2. Placebo (Medicine) 3. Mind and body
I. T.
R723.B68 1980        610/.1        *LC* 79-18481        *ISBN* 0226075311

**Dubos, René J. (René Jules), 1901-.**                               • **5.4551**
Man adapting / by René Dubos. — New Haven: Yale University Press, 1965.
xxii, 527 p.: ill.; 24 cm. (Yale University. Mrs. Hepsa Ely Silliman memorial
lectures) 1. Medicine — Philosophy 2. Man — Influence of environment
3. Adaptation (Biology) 4. Environmental health I. T.
R723.D77        610 19        *LC* 65-22317

**The Encyclopaedia of medical ignorance: exploring the frontiers**     **5.4552**
**of medical knowledge / edited by Ronald Duncan and Miranda**
**Weston-Smith.**
1st ed. — Oxford; New York: Pergamon Press, 1984. vii, 253 p.: ill.; 26 cm.
1. Medicine — Philosophy — Addresses, essays, lectures. I. Duncan, Ronald
Frederick Henry, 1914- II. Weston-Smith, Miranda.
R723.E53 1984        616 19        *LC* 83-4785        *ISBN* 0080245153

**Maxmen, Jerrold S.**                                                  **5.4553**
The post-physician era: medicine in the twenty-first century / Jerrold S.
Maxmen. — New York: Wiley, c1976. x, 300 p.; 22 cm. (Health, medicine, and
society: A Wiley-Interscience series) 'A Wiley-Interscience publication.'
1. Medicine — Philosophy 2. Medical innovations 3. Medical personnel
4. Twenty-first century — Forecasts I. T.
R723.M34        610.69/6        *LC* 76-2442        *ISBN* 0471578800

**Medical choices, medical chances: how patients, families, and**       **5.4554**
**physicians can cope with uncertainty / Harold Bursztajn ... [et**
**al.].**
New York: Delacorte Press/Seymour Lawrence, c1981. xxii, 456 p.: ill.; 24 cm.
'A Merloyd Lawrence book.' Includes index. 1. Medicine — Philosophy
2. Medical logic 3. Medicine — Decision making. 4. Probabilities
5. Uncertainty 6. Physician and patient I. Bursztajn, Harold.
R723.M36        610/.1/9 19        *LC* 80-22631        *ISBN* 0440057507

**Moore, Michael C., 1947-.**                                          **5.4555**
The complete handbook of holistic health / Michael C. Moore, Lynda J.
Moore. — Englewood Cliffs, N.J.: Prentice-Hall, 1983. xiii, 253 p.; 23 cm. 'A

Spectrum book.' 1. Holistic medicine 2. Health 3. Consumer education
I. Moore, Lynda J., 1948- II. T.
R723.M617 1983        615.5 19        LC 82-13284        ISBN 0131610260

**Pellegrino, Edmund D., 1920-.**                                    **5.4556**
Humanism and the physician / Edmund D. Pellegrino. — 1st ed. — Knoxville:
University of Tennessee Press, c1979. xiii, 248 p.; 24 cm. 1. Medicine —
Philosophy 2. Medicine and the humanities 3. Humanism 4. Medical ethics
5. Medical education — Philosophy. I. T.
R723.P38        610/.1        LC 78-23174        ISBN 0870492187

**Pellegrino, Edmund D., 1920-.**                                    **5.4557**
A philosophical basis of medical practice: toward a philosophy and ethic of the
healing professions / Edmund D. Pellegrino, David C. Thomasma. — New
York: Oxford University Press, 1981. xvii, 341 p.; 22 cm. 1. Medicine —
Philosophy I. Thomasma, David C., 1939- joint author. II. T.
R723.P3813        610/.1        LC 80-36735        ISBN 0195027906

## R724–725.5 MEDICAL ETHICS

**Barry, Vincent E.**                                                **5.4558**
Moral aspects of health care / Vincent Barry. — Belmont, Calif.: Wadsworth
Pub. Co., c1982. x, 510 p.; 24 cm. 1. Medical ethics I. T.
R724.B33        174/.2 19        LC 81-21854        ISBN 0534010903

**Chapman, Carleton B.**                                             **5.4559**
Physicians, law, and ethics / Carleton B. Chapman. — New York: New York
University Press, 1984. xviii, 192 p.: ill.; 24 cm. Includes index. 1. Medical
ethics — History. 2. Medical laws and legislation — History. I. T.
R724.C45 1984        174/.2 19        LC 84-2130        ISBN 0814713920

**Ethics in medicine: historical perspectives and contemporary**     **5.4560**
**concerns / edited by Stanley Joel Reiser, Arthur J. Dyck, and**
**William J. Curran.**
Cambridge, Mass.: MIT Press, c1977. xiii, 679 p.; 28 cm. 1. Medical ethics —
Addresses, essays, lectures. 2. Medical ethics — History — Sources. I. Reiser,
Stanley Joel. II. Dyck, Arthur J., 1932- III. Curran, William J.
R724.E823        174/.2        LC 77-1876        ISBN 0262180812

**Fletcher, Joseph Francis, 1905-.**                                 **5.4561**
Humanhood: essays in biomedical ethics / Joseph Fletcher. — Buffalo:
Prometheus Books, 1979. xii, 204 p.; 24 cm. 1. Medical ethics — Addresses,
essays, lectures. 2. Bioethics — Addresses, essays, lectures. 3. Philosophical
anthropology — Addresses, essays, lectures. I. T.
R724.F54        174/.2        LC 79-1756        ISBN 0879751126

**Intervention and reflection: basic issues in medical ethics:**     **5.4562**
**[readings / selected by] Ronald Munson.**
3rd ed. — Belmont, Calif.: Wadsworth Pub. Co., 1987. ix, 602 p.; 25 cm.
Includes index. 1. Medical ethics I. Munson, Ronald, 1939-
R724.I57 1987        174/.2 19        LC 86-28259        ISBN 053408088X

**Kass, Leon.**                                                      **5.4563**
Toward a more natural science: biology and human affairs / Leon R. Kass. —
New York: Free Press, c1985. xiv, 370 p.: ill.; 25 cm. Includes index.
1. Medical ethics 2. Bioethics 3. Science and ethics I. T.
R724.K318 1985        174/.2 19        LC 85-1570        ISBN 0029183405

**McLean, Sheila.**                                                  **5.4564**
Medicine, morals, and the law / Sheila McLean and Gerry Maher. —
Aldershot, Hampshire, England: Gower, c1983. ix, 214 p.; 23 cm. 1. Medical
ethics 2. Medical laws and legislation — Great Britain. I. Maher, Gerry. II. T.
R724.M2923 1983        174/.2 19        LC 83-174750        ISBN 0566005336

**Medical ethics: a clinical textbook and reference for the health**  **5.4565**
**care professions / edited by Natalie Abrams, Michael D.**
**Buckner.**
Cambridge, Mass.: MIT Press, c1983. xvii, 694 p.; 26 cm. 'A Bradford book.'
1. Medical ethics I. Abrams, Natalie. II. Buckner, Michael D.
R724.M2928 1983        174/.2 19        LC 82-42556        ISBN 0262010682

**Medical ethics and the law: implications for public policy /**     **5.4566**
**[compiled by] Marc D. Hiller.**
Cambridge, Mass.: Ballinger Pub. Co., [1981] xxiii, 471 p.; 24 cm. 1. Medical
ethics 2. Medical policy — United States. 3. Medical laws and legislation —
United States. I. Hiller, Marc D.
R724.M293        174/.2 19        LC 81-3890        ISBN 0884107078

**Phillips, Melanie, 1951-.**                                        **5.4567**
Doctors' dilemmas: medical ethics and contemporary science / Melanie
Phillips, John Dawson. — New York: Methuen, 1985. ix, 230 p.; 23 cm.

Includes index. 1. Medical ethics 2. Social medicine 3. Medicine — Political
aspects. I. Dawson, John, 1946- II. T.
R724.P47 1985        174/.2 19        LC 85-3039        ISBN 041601111X

**Ramsey, Paul.**                                                    **5.4568**
Ethics at the edges of life: medical and legal intersections / Paul Ramsey. —
New Haven: Yale University Press, 1978. xvii, 353 p.; 24 cm. — (The Bampton
lectures in America) Includes index. 1. Medical ethics 2. Life and death,
Power over 3. Medical laws and legislation — United States. 4. Christian
ethics 5. Medical policy — United States. I. T.
R724.R3        174/.2        LC 77-76308        ISBN 0300021372

**Ramsey, Paul.**                                                  • **5.4569**
The patient as person; explorations in medical ethics. — New Haven: Yale
University Press, 1970. xxii, 283 p.; 25 cm. — (The Lyman Beecher lectures at
Yale university) 1. Medical ethics I. T.
R724.R33        174/.2        LC 77-118737        ISBN 0300013574

**Szasz, Thomas Stephen, 1920-.**                                    **5.4570**
The theology of medicine: the political–philosophical foundations of medical
ethics / Thomas Szasz. 1st ed. — New York: Harper & Row, 1977. xxii, 170 p.;
21 cm. (Harper colophon books; CN 545) 1. Medical ethics — Addresses,
essays, lectures. 2. Psychiatric ethics — Addresses, essays, lectures. I. T.
R724.S97 1977        174/.2        LC 76-13332        ISBN 006090545X

**United States. President's Commission for the Study of Ethical**   **5.4571**
**Problems in Medicine and Biomedical and Behavioral Research.**
Making health care decisions: a report on the ethical and legal implications of
informed consent in the patient–practitioner relationship. — Washington,
D.C.: President's Commission for the Study of Ethical Problems in Medicine
and Biomedical and Behavioral Research: For sale by the Supt. of Docs., U.S.
G.P.O., 1982. 3 v.: ill.; 23 cm. 'October 1982.' S/N 040-000-00459-9 Item 851-J
1. Medical ethics — United States. 2. Informed consent (Medical law) —
United States. 3. Physician and patient — United States. I. T.
R724.U55 1982        362.1/042 19        LC 82-600637

**Value conflicts in health care delivery / edited by Bart**         **5.4572**
**Gruzalski and Carl Nelson.**
Cambridge, Mass.: Ballinger, c1982. xvi, 230 p.; 24 cm. 1. Medical ethics —
Addresses, essays, lectures. I. Gruzalski, Bart. II. Nelson, Carl William, 1943-
R724.V33 1982        174/.22 19        LC 82-3896        ISBN 0884107353

**Childress, James F.**                                              **5.4573**
Who should decide?: Paternalism in health care / James F. Childress. — New
York: Oxford University Press, 1982. xiv, 250 p.; 24 cm. 1. Medical ethics
2. Paternalism I. T.
R725.5.C48 1982        174/.2 19        LC 82-7945        ISBN 019503127X

## R726 PROLONGING OR TERMINATING CARE. EUTHANASIA

**The Dilemmas of euthanasia / edited by John A. Behnke and**         **5.4574**
**Sissela Bok.**
1st ed. — Garden City, N.Y.: Anchor Press, 1975. viii, 187 p.; 18 cm.
1. Euthanasia — Addresses, essays, lectures. 2. Euthanasia — United States
— Addresses, essays, lectures. 3. Terminal care — Addresses, essays, lectures.
I. Behnke, John A. II. Bok, Sissela.
R726.D54        174/.24        LC 75-5267        ISBN 0385097301

**Ethical issues in death and dying / Robert F. Weir, editor.**      **5.4575**
2nd ed. — New York: Columbia University Press, 1986. x, 388 p.; 24 cm.
1. Medical ethics 2. Terminal care — Moral and ethical aspects 3. Death —
Proof and certification 4. Euthanasia — Moral and ethical aspects. 5. Suicide
— Moral and ethical aspects. I. Weir, Robert F., 1943-
R726.E77 1986        174/.2 19        LC 86-4191        ISBN 0231062222

**Kluge, Eike-Henner W.**                                            **5.4576**
The ethics of deliberate death / Eike-Henner W. Kluge. — Port Washington,
N.Y.: Kennikat Press, 1981. 154 p.; 22 cm. — (Multi-disciplinary studies in the
law.) (National university publications) Includes index. 1. Euthanasia I. T.
II. Series.
R726.K58        174/.24        LC 80-36834        ISBN 0804692602

**Maguire, Daniel C.**                                               **5.4577**
Death by choice [by] Daniel C. Maguire. — [1st ed.]. — Garden City, N.Y.:
Doubleday, 1974. 224 p.; 22 cm. 1. Death 2. Euthanasia I. T.
R726.M28        174/.24        LC 73-81441        ISBN 0385076428

**Russell, Olive Ruth.**                                             **5.4578**
Freedom to die: moral and legal aspects of euthanasia / by O. Ruth Russell. —
Rev. ed. — New York: Human Sciences Press, 1977, c1975. 413 p.; 22 cm.

'Supplement to the first edition: development from early 1974 to late 1976': p. 337-396. Includes index. 1. Euthanasia I. T.
R726.R8 1977     174/.24     *LC* 77-3383     *ISBN* 0877053111

**United States. President's Commission for the Study of Ethical**     5.4579
**Problems in Medicine and Biomedical and Behavioral Research.**
Deciding to forego life–sustaining treatment: a report on the ethical, medical, and legal issues in treatment decisions. — Washington, DC: President's Commission for the Study of Ethical Problems in Medicine and Biomedical and Behavioral Research: For sale by the Supt. of Docs., U.S. G.P.O., 1983. 554 p.: ill., maps, forms; 23 cm. 'March 1983.' S/N 040-000-00470-0 Item 851-J
1. Euthanasia — Moral and ethical aspects. 2. Right to die — Moral and ethical aspects. 3. Terminal care — Moral and ethical aspects 4. Infants (Newborn) — Diseases — Treatment — Moral and ethical aspects. 5. Medical ethics 6. Medical laws and legislation — United States. I. T.
R726.U55 1983     362.1 19     *LC* 83-600503

**Veatch, Robert M.**     5.4580
Death, dying, and the biological revolution: our last quest for responsibility / Robert M. Veatch. — New Haven: Yale University Press, 1976. ix, 323 p.; 25 cm. Includes index. 1. Terminal care — Religious aspects 2. Terminal care — Moral and ethical aspects 3. Medical policy — United States. 4. Death I. T.
R726.V4     174/.24     *LC* 75-43337     *ISBN* 0300019491

**Walton, Douglas N.**     5.4581
Ethics of withdrawal of life–support systems: case studies on decision–making in intensive care / Douglas N. Walton. — Westport, Conn.: Greenwood Press, 1983. xv, 257 p.; 22 cm. (Contributions in philosophy. 0084-926X; no. 23) Includes index. 1. Euthanasia — Moral and ethical aspects — Case studies. 2. Terminal care — Moral and ethical aspects — Case studies. 3. Life support systems (Critical care) — Moral and ethical aspects — Case studies. 4. Critical care medicine — Moral and ethical aspects — Case studies. 5. Critical care medicine — Decision-making — Case studies. I. T. II. Series.
R726.W34 1983     174/.24 19     *LC* 82-15662     *ISBN* 0313237522

## R726.5–726.8 MEDICINE AND PSYCHOLOGY. TERMINAL CARE

**Behavioral medicine: the biopsychosocial approach / edited by**     5.4582
**Neil Schneiderman, Jack T. Tapp.**
Hillsdale, N.J.: L. Erlbaum Associates, 1985. xxi, 663 p.: ill.; 24 cm. (Environment and health.) 1. Medicine and psychology 2. Medicine, Psychosomatic I. Schneiderman, Neil. II. Tapp, Jack T., 1934- III. Series.
R726.5.B4258 1985     616.08 19     *LC* 83-14105     *ISBN* 0898592925

**Compliance in health care / edited by R. Brian Haynes, D.**     5.4583
**Wayne Taylor, and David L. Sackett.**
Baltimore: Johns Hopkins University Press, c1979. xvi, 516 p.; 24 cm. Completely rev. and expanded ed. of Compliance with therapeutic regimens. Includes index.. 1. Patient compliance — Congresses. I. Haynes, R. Brian. II. Taylor, D. Wayne. III. Sackett, David L. IV. Compliance with therapeutic regimens.
R726.5.C65 1979     613     *LC* 78-20527     *ISBN* 0801821622

**Gatchel, Robert J., 1947-.**     5.4584
An introduction to health psychology / Robert J. Gatchel, Andrew Baum; foreword by Jerome E. Singer. — Reading, Mass.: Addison-Wesley, c1983. xvii, 381 p.: ill.; 24 cm. Includes index. 1. Medicine and psychology 2. Medicine, Psychosomatic I. Baum, Andrew. II. T.
R726.5.G38 1983     616.08 19     *LC* 82-73548     *ISBN* 0201113600

**Health and behavior: frontiers of research in the biobehavioral**     5.4585
**sciences / edited by David A. Hamburg, Glen R. Elliott, and**
**Delores L. Parron.**
Washington, D.C.: National Academy Press, 1982. xiii, 359 p.: ill.; 23 cm. — (IOM publication. 82-010) 1. Medicine and psychology 2. Social medicine I. Hamburg, David A., 1925- II. Elliott, Glen R. III. Parron, Delores L. IV. Series.
R726.5.H43 1982     616.07/1 19     *LC* 82-81830     *ISBN* 0309032792

**Viney, Linda L.**     5.4586
Images of illness / Linda L. Viney. — Original ed. — Malabar, Fla.: Krieger, 1983. 150 p.; 24 cm. Includes index. 1. Sick — Psychology 2. Imagery (Psychology) I. T.
R726.5.V55 1983     155.9/16 19     *LC* 83-19     *ISBN* 0898746124

**A Hospice handbook: a new way to care for the dying / edited**     5.4587
**by Michael P. Hamilton and Helen F. Reid.**
Grand Rapids: Eerdmans, c1980. xii, 196 p.: ill.; 21 cm. 1. Hospice care 2. Hospices (Terminal care) I. Hamilton, Michael Pollock, 1927- II. Reid, Helen F.
R726.8.H67     362.1     *LC* 79-19518     *ISBN* 0802818021

**The Life–threatened elderly / edited by Margot Tallmer ... [et**     5.4588
**al.]; with the editorial assistance of Lillian G. Kutscher.**
New York: Columbia University Press, 1984. xi, 359 p.: ill.; 24 cm. (Columbia University Press/Foundation of Thanatology series.) 1. Terminal care 2. Aged — Psychology 3. Death — Psychological aspects I. Tallmer, Margot. II. Series.
R726.8.L54 1984     362.1/75 19     *LC* 83-14263     *ISBN* 0231049668

**Munley, Anne.**     5.4589
The hospice alternative: a new context for death and dying / Anne Munley. — New York: Basic Books, c1983. xviii, 349 p.; 22 cm. Includes index. 1. Hospice care I. T.
R726.8.M85 1983     362.1/75 19     *LC* 82-72402     *ISBN* 0465030602

**Pattison, E. Mansell, 1933-.**     5.4590
The experience of dying / E. Mansell Pattison. — Englewood Cliffs, N.J.: Prentice-Hall, c1977. xiii, 335 p.: ill.; 21 cm. — (A Spectrum book) Includes index. 1. Terminal care 2. Death — Psychological aspects I. T.
R726.8.P37     362.1     *LC* 76-44542     *ISBN* 0132946297

## R727–733 Medical Personnel and the Public. Medical Practice

**Arney, William Ray.**     5.4591
Medicine and the management of living: taming the last great beast / William Ray Arney & Bernard J. Bergen. — Chicago: University of Chicago Press, c1984. 202 p.; 21 cm. Includes index. 1. Physician and patient 2. Power (Social sciences) 3. Social medicine I. Bergen, Bernard J. II. T.
R727.3.A76 1984     362.1/042 19     *LC* 83-24380     *ISBN* 0226027929

**Katz, Jay, 1922-.**     5.4592
The silent world of doctor and patient / Jay Katz. — New York: Free Press; London: Collier Macmillan, c1984. xxi, 263 p.; 25 cm. 1. Physician and patient 2. Medicine — Decision making. 3. Trust (Psychology) 4. Paternalism I. T.
R727.3.K34 1984     610.69/6 19     *LC* 83-48830     *ISBN* 0029170109

**National Symposia on Patient Education.**     5.4593
Patient education: an inquiry into the state of the art / Wendy D. Squyres, editor. — New York: Springer Pub. Co., c1980. xx, 359 p.: ill.; 23 cm. — (Springer series on health care and society. 4) 1. Patient education I. Squyres, Wendy D. II. T. III. Series.
R727.4.N37 1980     610/.7     *LC* 79-27556     *ISBN* 0826131204

**Lander, Louise.**     5.4594
Defective medicine: risk, anger, and the malpractice crisis / Louise Lander. — 1st ed. — New York: Farrar, Straus, and Giroux, 1978. xiii, 242 p.; 22 cm. 1. Medicine — Practice — United States. 2. Physicians — Malpractice — United States. 3. Physician and patient 4. Medical care — United States I. T.
R729.L36 1978     346/.73/033     *LC* 78-5577     *ISBN* 0374136270

**Wechsler, Henry, 1932-.**     5.4595
Handbook of medical specialties / Henry Wechsler. — New York: Human Sciences Press, c1976. 315 p.: ill.; 21 cm. — (Health services series) 1. Medicine — Specialties and specialists — United States. I. T.
R729.5.S6 W4     331.1/26     *LC* 74-19051     *ISBN* 0877052328

**Weil, Andrew.**     5.4596
Health and healing: understanding conventional and alternative medicine / Andrew Weil. — Boston: Houghton Mifflin, 1984 (c1983). 296 p.; 22 cm. 1. Alternative medicine 2. Medicine 3. Health I. T.
R733.W44     615.5/3 19     *LC* 83-10845     *ISBN* 0395344301

## R735–864 Medical Education. Medical Research. Medical Records

**Handbook of health professions education / Christine H.**     5.4597
**McGuire ... [et al.].**
1st ed. — San Francisco: Jossey-Bass, 1983. xxvi, 543 p.: ill.; 26 cm. — (Jossey-Bass higher education series.) (Jossey-Bass health series.) 'Responding to new realities in medicine, dentistry, pharmacy, nursing, allied health, and public health'—P. [iii]. 1. Medical education 2. Paramedical education I. McGuire, Christine H. II. Series. III. Series: Jossey-Bass health series.
R735.H28 1983     610/.7/11 19     *LC* 83-48160     *ISBN* 0875895794

**Broadhead, Robert S., 1947-.** 5.4598
The private lives and professional identity of medical students / Robert S. Broadhead. — New Brunswick, U.S.A.: Transaction Books, c1983. x, 128 p.; 24 cm. (New observations) Includes index. 1. Medical students — Psychology. 2. Medical education — Social aspects 3. Professional socialization 4. Medical students — United States — Family relationships. 5. Medical students — United States — Psychology. I. T.
R737.B69 1983      305/.961 19      LC 82-19502      ISBN 0878554785

**Puschmann, Th. (Theodor), 1844-1899.** • 5.4599
A history of medical education / introd. by Erwin H. Ackerknecht. — New York: Hafner Pub. Co., 1966. 650 p.; 24 cm. (History of medicine series. no. 28.) First published 1891. 1. Medical education — History. 2. Education, Medical — History. I. T. II. Series.
R737.P8      LC 65-21774

**The Visual arts and medical education / edited by Geri Berg;** 5.4600
**with Eric Avery ... [et al.].**
Carbondale: Southern Illinois University Press, c1983. xxii, 147 p.: ill.; 23 cm. — (Medical humanities series.) (Report #16 of the Institute on Human Values in Medicine) 1. Medical education 2. Medicine and art I. Berg, Geri, 1946- II. Avery, Eric. III. Series.
R737.V53 1983      610/.7 19      LC 82-19217      ISBN 0809310384

**Zabarenko, Ralph N.** 5.4601
The doctor tree: developmental stages in the growth of physicians / Ralph N. Zabarenko, Lucy M. Zabarenko. — Pittsburgh: University of Pittsburgh Press, c1978. xiv, 173 p.: ill.; 21 cm. — (Contemporary community health series.) 1. Medical education — Psychological aspects. 2. Medical students — Psychology. 3. Physicians — Psychology I. Zabarenko, Lucy, joint author. II. T. III. Series.
R737.Z3      610/.7/3      LC 77-18340      ISBN 0822933705

**McGovern, John P.** • 5.4602
Wm. Osler: the continuing education [edited] by John P. McGovern and Charles G. Roland. Springfield, Ill., Thomas [c1969] xvii, 365 p. illus., ports. 24 cm. A selection of 14 addresses by W. Osler, each with a commentary prepared by an essayist selected by the editors. 1. Medical education — Addresses, essays, lectures. I. Osler, William, Sir, 1849-1919. II. Roland, Charles G. joint author. III. T.
R740.M24      610/.71      LC 70-100428

**Flexner, Abraham, 1866-1959.** • 5.4603
Medical education in the United States and Canada; a report to the Carnegie Foundation for the Advancement of Teaching. — New York: Arno Press, 1972 [c1910] xvii, 346 p.: illus.; 24 cm. — (Medicine & society in America) Original ed. issued as Bulletin no. 4 of the Carnegie Foundation for the Advancement of Teaching. 1. Medical education — United States. 2. Medical education — Canada. I. Carnegie Foundation for the Advancement of Teaching. II. T. III. Series.
R745.F57 1972      610/.7/117      LC 78-180575      ISBN 0405039522

**Ludmerer, Kenneth M.** 5.4604
Learning to heal: the development of American medical education / Kenneth M. Ludmerer. — New York: Basic Books, c1985. xv, 346 p.; 24 cm. Includes index. 1. Medical education — United States — History. I. T.
R745.L84 1985      610/.7/1173 19      LC 85-47554      ISBN 0465038808

**Millis, John S., 1903-.** • 5.4605
A rational public policy for medical education and its financing: a report to the Board of Directors, the National Fund for Medical Education / by John S. Millis. — [Cleveland: National Fund for Medical Education], 1971. ix, 158 p.; 22 cm. 1. Medical education — U.S. I. National Fund for Medical Education. Board of Directors. II. T.
R745.M614      610/.71/173      LC 71-171690

**Jones, James H. (James Howard), 1943-.** 5.4606
Bad blood: the Tuskegee syphilis experiment / James H. Jones. — New York: Free Press; London: Collier Macmillan Publishers, c1981. xii, 272 p., [8] leaves of plates: ill.; 24 cm. Includes indexes. 1. Tuskegee Syphilis Study 2. Human experimentation in medicine — Alabama — Macon County — History. 3. Syphilis — Research — Alabama — Macon County — History. 4. Syphilis — Alabama — Macon County — History. 5. Afro-American men — Diseases — Alabama — Macon County — History. I. Tuskegee Institute. II. T.
R853.H8 J66 1981      364.1/42 19      LC 80-69281      ISBN 0029166705

**Ramsey, Paul.** 5.4607
The ethics of fetal research / Paul Ramsey. — New Haven: Yale University Press, 1975. xxi, 104 p.; 21 cm. — (A Yale fastback; 15) 1. Human experimentation in medicine — Moral and religious aspects. 2. Fetus — Research — Moral and religious aspects. 3. Medicine — Research — Moral and religious aspects. I. T.
R853.H8 R35 1975      174/.2      LC 74-27633      ISBN 0300018797

**Research on human subjects; problems of social control in** 5.4608
**medical experimentation [by] Bernard Barber [and others].**
New York: Russell Sage Foundation, [1973] viii, 263 p.; 24 cm. 1. Human experimentation in medicine — Moral and religious aspects. 2. Human experimentation in medicine — Social aspects. 3. Social control I. Barber, Bernard.
R853.H8 R47      174/.2      LC 72-83831      ISBN 0871540908

**Banta, H. David (Henry David), 1938-.** 5.4609
Toward rational technology in medicine: considerations for health policy / H. David Banta, Clyde J. Behney, Jane Sisk Willems; foreword by Edward M. Kennedy. — New York: Springer, c1981. xiv, 242 p.: ill.; 24 cm. — (Springer series on health care and society. v. 5) Includes index. 1. Medical innovations — United States. 2. Medical policy — United States. 3. Medical care — United States I. Behney, Clyde J. joint author. II. Willems, Jane Sisk. joint author. III. T. IV. Series.
R854.U5 B36      362.1/068/2 19      LC 80-27512      ISBN 0826132006

**Davis, Audrey B.** 5.4610
Medicine and its technology: an introduction to the history of medical instrumentation / Audrey B. Davis. — Westport, Conn.: Greenwood Press, 1981. xiv, 285 p.: ill.; 29 cm. — (Contributions in medical history. no. 7 0147-1058) 1. Medical instruments and apparatus — History. 2. Medical innovations — History. I. T. II. Series.
R856.A5 D38      610/.28 19      LC 80-25202      ISBN 0313228078

**Medical instrumentation: application and design / John G.** 5.4611
**Webster, editor; contributing authors, John W. Clark ... [et al.].**
Boston: Houghton Mifflin, c1978. xvi, 729 p.: ill.; 25 cm. 1. Medical instruments and apparatus I. Webster, John G., 1932- II. Clark, John William, 1936-
R856.M376      610/.28      LC 77-76419      ISBN 0395254116

**Lang, Gerald S.** 5.4612
The practice–oriented medical record / Gerald S. Lang and Kenneth J. Dickie. — Germantown, Md.: Aspen Systems Corp., 1978. xx, 287 p.: ill.; 24 cm. 1. Medical records I. Dickie, Kenneth J. joint author. II. T.
R864.L36      651.5      LC 78-1931      ISBN 0894430327

**Westin, Alan F.** 5.4613
Computers, health records, and citizen rights / Alan F. Westin. — New York: Petrocelli, [1977] 318 p.: ill. Study sponsored by the Institute for Computer Sciences and Technology of the National Bureau of Standards. 1. Medical records — United States — Data processing 2. Medical records — United States — Access control. 3. Privacy, Right of — United States. I. Institute for Computer Sciences and Technology. II. T.
R864.W4x QC100.U556 no. 157      602/.1 s 651.5      LC 76-608322

# R895 Medical Physics

**Cameron, John R.** 5.4614
Medical physics / John R. Cameron and James G. Skofronick. — New York: Wiley, c1978. xviii, 615 p.: ill.; 24 cm. 'A Wiley-Interscience publication.' 1. Medical physics I. Skofronick, James G. joint author. II. T.
R895.C28      612/.014      LC 77-26909      ISBN 0471131318

**Damask, A. C.** 5.4615
Medical physics / A. C. Damask. — New York: Academic Press, 1978-1984. 3 v.: ill.; 24 cm. 1. Medical physics 2. Biophysics I. Swenberg, Charles E. II. T.
R895.D35      612/.014      LC 78-205      ISBN 0122012011

# RA Public Aspects of Medicine

**Miles, Rufus E.** 5.4616
The Department of Health, Education, and Welfare [by] Rufus E. Miles, Jr. — New York: Praeger, [1974] viii, 326 p.: illus.; 22 cm. — (The Praeger library of U.S. Government departments and agencies, no. 39) 1. United States. Dept. of Health, Education, and Welfare. I. T.
RA5.M54      353.84      LC 72-88986

# RA390–409 Medicine and State. Regulation. Licensure. Statistics

**Rutstein, David D.**      5.4617
Blueprint for medical care [by] David D. Rutstein. — Cambridge, Mass.: MIT Press, [1974] xxiv, 284 p.: illus.; 21 cm. 1. Health planning I. T.
RA393.R87    362.1/0973    *LC* 73-21474    *ISBN* 0262180650

**Santé rationnée? English.**      5.4618
The end of an illusion: the future of health policy in Western industrialized nations / edited by Jean de Kervasdoué, John R. Kimberly, and Victor G. Rodwin. — Berkeley: University of California Press, c1984. xxii, 292 p.; 24 cm. (Comparative studies of health systems and medical care.) Translation of: La Santé rationnée? 1. Medical policy 2. Health planning I. Kervasdoué, Jean de. II. Kimberly, John. III. Rodwin, Victor. IV. T. V. Series.
RA393.S2813 1984    362.1 19    *LC* 83-18030    *ISBN* 0520047265

**Spiegel, Allen D.**      5.4619
Basic health planning methods / Allen D. Spiegel, Herbert Harvey Hyman. — Germantown, Md.: Aspen Systems Corp., 1978. viii, 500 p.; 24 cm. Includes index. 1. Health planning I. Hyman, Herbert Harvey. joint author. II. T.
RA393.S67    362.1    *LC* 78-10780    *ISBN* 0894430777

**Health care in big cities** / edited by Leslie H. W. Paine.      5.4620
New York: St. Martin's Press, 1978. 368 p.; 23 cm. 1. Health services administration 2. Medical care 3. Metropolitan areas I. Paine, Leslie.
RA394.H4    362.1/09173/2    *LC* 78-7783    *ISBN* 0312365233

**Ambulatory care: problems of cost and access** / edited by Stuart      5.4621
**H. Altman, Joanna Lion, Judith LaVor Williams.**
Lexington, Mass.: LexingtonBooks, c1983. xi, 227 p.; 24 cm. — (University Health Policy Consortium series.) 1. Ambulatory medical care — United States. 2. Ambulatory medical care — United States — Costs. I. Altman, Stuart H. II. Lion, Joanna. III. Williams, Judith LaVor. IV. Series.
RA395.A3 A495 1983    338.4/33621/2 19    *LC* 82-49054    *ISBN* 0669064017

**Handbook of health, health care, and the health professions** /      5.4622
**edited by David Mechanic.**
New York: Free Press, c1983. xxiii, 806 p.: ill.; 26 cm. 1. Medical care — United States 2. Social medicine — United States. 3. Medical policy — United States. 4. Medical care — Research I. Mechanic, David, 1936-
RA395.A3 H36 1983    362.1/0973 19    *LC* 82-71149    *ISBN* 0029206901

**Introduction to health services** / edited by Stephen J. Williams,      5.4623
**Paul R. Torrens.**
2nd ed. — New York: Wiley, c1984. xxii, 498 p.: ill.; 24 cm. (Wiley series in health services. 0195-3907) (Wiley medical publication.) 1. Medical care — United States 2. Health services administration — United States. I. Williams, Stephen Joseph, 1948- II. Torrens, Paul R. (Paul Roger), 1934- III. Series. IV. Series: Wiley medical publication.
RA395.A3 I57 1984    362.1/0973 19    *LC* 83-14831    *ISBN* 0471869007

**Mechanic, David, 1936-.**      5.4624
Future issues in health care: social policy and the rationing of medical services / David Mechanic. — New York: Free Press, c1979. xiii, 194 p.; 24 cm. Includes index. 1. Medical care — United States 2. Medical policy — United States. 3. Social medicine — United States. 4. Medical care — Research I. T.
RA395.A3 M416    362.1/0973    *LC* 78-63413    *ISBN* 002920710X

**Reforming medicine: lessons of the last quarter century** / edited      5.4625
**by Victor W. Sidel and Ruth Sidel.**
1st ed. — New York: Pantheon Books, c1984. 311 p.; 22 cm. 1. Medical care — United States I. Sidel, Victor W. II. Sidel, Ruth.
RA395.A3 R38 1984    362.1/043 19    *LC* 83-42814    *ISBN* 0394502132

**Sidel, Victor W.**      5.4626
A healthy state: an international perspective on the crisis in United States medical care / by Victor W. Sidel and Ruth Sidel. — 1st ed. — New York: Pantheon Books, c1977. xxxv, 347 p.: ill.; 22 cm. Includes index. 1. Medical care — United States I. Sidel, Ruth. joint author. II. T.
RA395.A3 S52    362.1/0973    *LC* 77-5196    *ISBN* 0394407601

**Starr, Paul, 1949-.**      5.4627
The social transformation of American medicine / Paul Starr. — New York: Basic Books, 1983 (c1982). xiv, 514 p.; 24 cm. 1. Medical care — United States

— History. 2. Social medicine — United States — History. 3. Physicians — United States — History. I. T.
RA395.A3 S77    305/.961/0973 19    *LC* 81-68412    *ISBN* 0465079342

**Gross, Stanley J.**      5.4628
Of foxes and hen houses: licensing and the health professions / Stanley J. Gross. — Westport, Conn.: Quorum Books, 1984. xvi, 204 p.; 25 cm. Includes index. 1. Medical personnel — Licenses — United States. I. T.
RA396.A3 G73 1984    610/.7 19    *LC* 83-11218    *ISBN* 0899300596

**Medical risks: patterns of mortality and survival: a reference**      5.4629
**volume / sponsored by the Association of Life Insurance**
**Medical Directors of America and the Society of Actuaries;**
**editors, Richard B. Singer, Louis Levinson, editorial committee,**
**John O. Alden ... [et al.].**
D. C.: Heath, 1976. 662 p. in various pagings; 29 cm. Includes indexes. 1. Mortality 2. Death — Causes — Tables. 3. Life expectancy — Tables. 4. Medical statistics I. Singer, Richard B. II. Levinson, Louis. III. Association of Life Insurance Medical Directors of America. IV. Society of Actuaries.
RA407.M4    312/.2    *LC* 74-31609    *ISBN* 0669982285

**Erhardt, Carl L.**      5.4630
Mortality and morbidity in the United States / Carl L. Erhardt and Joyce E. Berlin, editors. — Cambridge, Mass.: Harvard University Press, 1974. xxv, 289 p.; 25 cm. — (Vital and health statistics monographs) 1. Diseases — United States — Statistics. 2. Mortality — United States 3. United States — Statistics, Medical 4. United States — Statistics, Vital I. Berlin, Joyce E., joint author. II. T. III. Series.
RA407.3.E73    312/.2/0973    *LC* 74-83140    *ISBN* 0674587405

# RA410–415 Medical Economics

**Abel-Smith, Brian.**      5.4631
Value for money in health services: a comparative study / Brian Abel-Smith. — New York: St. Martin's Press, 1976. 230 p.; 23 cm. 1. Medical economics 2. Medical care 3. Health planning I. T.
RA410.A23 1976    362.1    *LC* 75-37423

**Fuchs, Victor R.**      5.4632
The health economy / Victor R. Fuchs. — Cambridge, Mass.: Harvard University Press, 1986. viii, 401 p.: ill.; 25 cm. Includes index. 1. Medical economics — Addresses, essays, lectures. 2. Medical policy — Addresses, essays, lectures. I. T.
RA410.F83 1986    338.4/73621/0973 19    *LC* 85-16442    *ISBN* 0674383400

**Critical issues in medical technology** / edited by Barbara J.      5.4633
**McNeil, Ernest G. Cravalho.**
Boston, Mass.: Auburn House Pub. Co., c1982. xvi, 432 p.: ill.; 24 cm. 1. Medical innovations — Economic aspects — United States. 2. Medical innovations — Government policy — United States. 3. Medical innovations — Social aspects — United States. 4. Medical innovations — Evaluation. 5. Technology assessment — United States. I. Cravalho, Ernest G. II. McNeil, Barbara J., 1941-
RA410.53.C75    306/.4 19    *LC* 81-7900    *ISBN* 0865690707

**Enthoven, Alain C., 1930-.**      5.4634
Health plan: the only practical solution to the soaring cost of medical care / Alain C. Enthoven. — Reading, Mass.: Addison-Wesley Pub. Co., c1980. xxv, 196 p.: ill.; 25 cm. 1. Medical economics — United States. 2. Insurance, Health — United States 3. Medical policy — United States. I. T.
RA410.53.E57    338.4/7/36210973    *LC* 79-25583    *ISBN* 0201031434

**Fuchs, Victor R.**      5.4635
Who shall live? Health, economics, and social choice [by] Victor R. Fuchs. New York, Basic Books [1975, c1974] vi, 168 p. 22 cm. 1. Medical economics — United States. 2. Medical care — United States I. T.
RA410.53.F82 1975    338.4/7/36210973    *LC* 74-79283    *ISBN* 0465091857

**Menzel, Paul T., 1942-.**      5.4636
Medical costs, moral choices: a philosophy of health care economics in America / Paul T. Menzel. — New Haven: Yale University Press, c1983. xi, 260 p.; 24 cm. Includes index. 1. Medical care, Cost of — United States — Moral and ethical aspects. 2. Medical care — United States — Cost control. I. T.
RA410.53.M46 1983    338.4/33621/0973 19    *LC* 83-3450    *ISBN* 0300029608

**Miller, Irwin.**   5.4637
The health care survival curve: competition and cooperation in the marketplace / Irwin Miller. — Homewood, Ill.: Dow Jones-Irwin, c1984. xv, 144 p.; 24 cm. Includes index. 1. Medical economics — United States. 2. Health maintenance organizations — United States. 3. Medical policy — United States. 4. Voluntarism — United States. 5. Competition — United States. I. T.
RA410.53.M55 1984   338.4/73621/0973 19   *LC* 83-73714   *ISBN* 0870944819

**A New approach to the economics of health care / edited by**   5.4638
**Mancur Olson.**
Washington, D.C.: American Enterprise Institute for Public Policy Research, c1981. xvi, 502 p.: ill.; 23 cm. (AEI symposia. 81E) Proceedings of a conference sponsored by the Center for Health Policy Research of the American Enterprise Institute, held Sept. 25-26, 1980 in Washington, D.C. 1. Medical economics — United States — Congresses. 2. Medical care, Cost of — United States — Congresses. 3. Medical policy — United States — Congresses. 4. Medical economics — Congresses. I. Olson, Mancur. II. American Enterprise Institute for Public Policy Research. Center for Health Policy Research. III. Series.
RA410.53.N47   338.4/73621/0973 19   *LC* 81-14980   *ISBN* 084472212X

**Pauly, Mark V., 1941-.**   5.4639
Doctors and their workshops: economic models of physician behavior / Mark V. Pauly. — Chicago: University of Chicago Press, 1980. ix, 132 p.; 24 cm. (National Bureau of Economic Research monograph.) 1. Medical economics — United States. 2. Physicians — United States 3. Medical care — United States — Utilization. 4. Physician and patient — United States. I. T. II. Series.
RA410.53.P36   338.4/561/36210973   *LC* 80-16112   *ISBN* 0226650448

**Toward a national health policy: public policy and the control of**   5.4640
**health–care costs / edited by Kenneth M. Friedman, Stuart H. Rakoff.**
Lexington, Mass.: Lexington Books, c1977. xiii, 257 p.; 24 cm. 1. Medical care — United States — Cost control. 2. Medical care, Cost of — United States. 3. Medical policy — United States. I. Friedman, Kenneth Michael. II. Rakoff, Stuart H.
RA410.53.T68   362.1/0973   *LC* 75-42931   *ISBN* 0669005630

**Wohl, Stanley.**   5.4641
The medical industrial complex / Stanley Wohl. — 1st ed. — New York: Harmony Books, c1984. 218 p.; 24 cm. Includes index. 1. Medical care, Cost of — United States. 2. Health facilities, Proprietary — United States. 3. Medical corporations — United States. I. T.
RA410.53.W64 1984   338.4/73621/0973 19   *LC* 83-26509   *ISBN* 0517553511

**Mizrahi, Andrée.**   5.4642
[Socio-économie de la santé. English] Medical care, morbidity, and costs: graphic presentations of health statistics / Andrée Mizrahi, Arié Mizrahi, Simone Sandier; foreword by Kerr L. White; preface by Pierre Laroque. — 1st ed. — Oxford, England; Elmsford, N.Y., U.S.A.: Pergamon, 1983. 190 p.: col. ill.; 27 cm. Translation of: Socio-économie de la santé. 1. Medical care, Cost of — France — Charts, diagrams, etc. 2. Medical economics — France — Charts, diagrams, etc. 3. France — Statistics, Medical — Charts, diagrams, etc. 4. Medical economics — Charts, diagrams, etc. I. Mizrahi, Arié. II. Sandier, S. III. T.
RA410.55.F8 M5913 1983   362.1/0212 19   *LC* 83-6321   *ISBN* 0080312950

**Brown, Lawrence D. (Lawrence David), 1947-.**   5.4643
Politics and health care organization: HMOs as federal policy / Lawrence D. Brown. — Washington, D.C.: Brookings Institution, c1983. xv, 540 p.; 24 cm. 1. Health maintenance organizations — United States. 2. Medical policy — United States. I. T.
RA413.5.U5 B76 1983   362.1/0425 19   *LC* 81-70466   *ISBN* 0815711581

# RA418–418.5 Medicine and Society. Medical Sociology

**Duff, Raymond S., 1923-.**   • 5.4644
Sickness and society [by] Raymond S. Duff and August B. Hollingshead. — [1st ed.]. — New York: Harper & Row, [1968] xiii, 390 p.; 25 cm. 1. Social medicine 2. Hospitals — Sociological aspects I. Hollingshead, August de Belmont. joint author. II. T.
RA418.D8   301.2/46   *LC* 68-15988

**Illich, Ivan, 1926-.**   5.4645
Medical nemesis: the expropriation of health / Ivan Illich. — 1st American ed. — New York: Pantheon Books, c1976. viii, 294 p.; 22 cm. 1. Social medicine 2. Medicine — Philosophy 3. Medical care 4. Iatrogenic diseases I. T.
RA418.I44 1976   362.1   *LC* 75-38118   *ISBN* 0394402251

**Horrobin, David F.**   5.4646
Medical hubris: a reply to Ivan Illich / David F. Horrobin. — Montreal: Eden Press, c1977. 146 p.; 22 cm. Includes index. 1. Illich, Ivan, 1926- Medical nemesis. 2. Medicine — Philosophy 3. Medical care 4. Iatrogenic diseases I. T.
RA418.I44 H67   362.1   *LC* 80-66836   *ISBN* 0888310013

**Rosen, George, 1910- comp.**   5.4647
From medical police to social medicine: essays on the history of health care. — [1st ed.]. — New York: Science History Publications, 1974. 327 p.: illus.; 23 cm. 1. Social medicine — Addresses, essays, lectures. 2. Medical care — History — Addresses, essays, lectures. I. T.
RA418.R67   362.1/09   *LC* 74-10819   *ISBN* 0882020153

**The Use and abuse of medicine / edited by Marten W. de Vries,**   5.4648
**Robert L. Berg, Mack Lipkin, Jr.**
New York, N.Y.: Praeger, 1982. xx, 296 p.; 24 cm. 1. Social medicine — Addresses, essays, lectures. 2. Medical anthropology — Addresses, essays, lectures. 3. Medical care — Addresses, essays, lectures. I. De Vries, Marten W. II. Berg, Robert L. III. Lipkin, Mack.
RA418.U75 1982   362.1 19   *LC* 82-7563   *ISBN* 0030617022

**Whorton, James, 1942-.**   5.4649
Crusaders for fitness: the history of American health reformers / James C. Whorton. — Princeton, N.J.: Princeton University Press, c1982. 359 p., [4] leaves of plates: ill.; 23 cm. 1. Health reformers — United States — History. 2. Health attitudes — United States — History. I. T.
RA418.3.U6 W5 1982   613/.0973 19   *LC* 82-47621   *ISBN* 0691046948

**Ellison, David L.**   5.4650
The bio–medical fix: human dimensions of bio–medical technologies / David L. Ellison. — Westport, Conn.: Greenwood Press, 1978. xiii, 171 p.; 22 cm. Includes index. 1. Medical innovations — Social aspects 2. Diagnosis — Data processing — Social aspects. 3. Genetic engineering — Social aspects. 4. Hemodialysis — Social aspects I. T.
RA418.5.M4 E44   362.1/042   *LC* 77-91104   *ISBN* 0313200386

**Davis, Karen, 1942-.**   5.4651
Health and the war on poverty: a ten–year appraisal / Karen Davis and Cathy Schoen. — Washington: Brookings Institution, c1978. xiv, 230 p.; 24 cm. — (Studies in social economics.) 1. Poor — Medical care — United States 2. Poor — Health and hygiene — United States. 3. Medical policy — United States. I. Schoen, Cathy. joint author. II. T. III. Series.
RA418.5.P6 D38   362.1/9/0973   *LC* 77-91832   *ISBN* 081571758X

# RA421–772 Public Health. Preventive Medicine. Environmental Health

**Cipolla, Carlo M.**   5.4652
Public health and the medical profession in the Renaissance / Carlo M. Cipolla. — Cambridge [Eng.]; New York: Cambridge University Press, 1976. viii, 136 p.: ill.; 23 cm. Includes index. 1. Public health — Italy — History. 2. Medicine — 15th-18th centuries 3. Medicine — Tuscany — History. 4. Physicians — Tuscany. I. T.
RA424.C57   362.1/0945   *LC* 75-22984   *ISBN* 0521209595

**Hobson, William.**   5.4653
The theory and practice of public health / edited by W. Hobson. — 5th ed. — Oxford; New York: Oxford University Press, 1979. xiii, 785 p.: ill.; 29 cm. — (Oxford medical publications) 1. Public health I. T.
RA425.H57 1979   614   *LC* 79-40184   *ISBN* 0192642278

**Kark, Sidney L.**   5.4654
The practice of community–oriented primary health care / Sidney L. Kark. — New York: Appleton-Century-Crofts, c1981. x, 253 p.: graphs; 23 cm. 1. Community health services I. T.
RA425.K357   362.1/0425   *LC* 80-17639   *ISBN* 0838577733

**Imperato, Pascal James.**                                    5.4655
Acceptable risks / Pascal James Imperato, Greg Mitchell. — New York, N.Y.:
Viking, 1985. xix, 286 p.; 22 cm. Includes index. 1. Medicine, Preventive
2. Safety education 3. Health I. Mitchell, Greg. II. T.
RA431.I46 1985      613 19      *LC* 83-40634      *ISBN* 0670102059

# RA440–564.9 By Region, Ethnic Group, Age, etc

**Willgoose, Carl E.**                                    5.4656
Health teaching in secondary schools / Carl E. Willgoose. — 3rd ed. —
Philadelphia: Saunders College Pub., c1982. v, 426 p.: ill.; 25 cm. 1. Health
education (Secondary) 2. Health education I. T.
RA440.W48 1982      613/.07/12 19      *LC* 81-53101      *ISBN*
0030584930

**The Demand for primary health services in the Third World /**      5.4657
**John S. Akin ... [et al.].**
Totowa, NJ: Rowman & Allanheld, 1985. xiv, 252 p.: ill. Includes index.
1. Community health services — Developing countries 2. Community health
services — Economic aspects — Developing countries. 3. Community health
services — Supply and demand — Developing countries. I. Akin, John S.
RA441.5.D46 1984      362.1/09172/4 19      *LC* 84-18153      *ISBN*
0847673553

**Rosen, George, 1910-.**                                    5.4658
Preventive medicine in the United States, 1900–1975: trends and interpretations
/ George Rosen. — 1st ed. — New York: Science History Publications, 1975.
94 p., [8] leaves of plates: ill.; 23 cm. 1. Medicine, Preventive — United States
— History. 2. Public health — United States — History. I. T.
RA445.R76      362.1/04/2      *LC* 75-35978      *ISBN* 0882021036

**The Scientific basis of health and safety regulation / Robert W.**      5.4659
**Crandall and Lester B. Lave, editors.**
Washington, D.C.: Brookings Institution, c1981. xiv, 309 p.: ill.; 24 cm. —
(Studies in the regulation of economic activity.) 1. Public health — United
States — Decision making — Case studies. 2. Environmental health —
Government policy — United States — Decision making — Case studies.
3. Traffic safety — Government policy — United States — Decision making —
Case studies. 4. Policy sciences — Case studies. I. Crandall, Robert W.
II. Lave, Lester B. III. Series.
RA445.S43      363.1/0973 19      *LC* 81-10224      *ISBN* 0815716001

**Leavitt, Judith Walzer.**                                    5.4660
The healthiest city: Milwaukee and the politics of health reform / Judith
Walzer Leavitt. — Princeton, N.J.: Princeton University Press, c1982. xvii,
294 p.: ill.; 23 cm. Includes index. 1. Public health — Wisconsin — Milwaukee
— History. 2. Public health administration — Wisconsin — Milwaukee —
History. 3. Urban health — Wisconsin — Milwaukee — History.
4. Milwaukee (Wis.) — Politics and government. I. T.
RA448.M5 L4 1982      614.4/4/0977595 19      *LC* 81-47932      *ISBN*
0691082987

**Ethnicity and medical care / Alan Harwood, editor.**      5.4661
Cambridge, Mass.: Harvard University Press, c1981. xii, 523 p.; 24 cm. 'A
Commonwealth Fund book.' 1. Minorities — Medical care — United States.
2. Medical anthropology — United States. 3. Ethnology — United States
4. Ethnicity — United States. I. Harwood, Alan.
RA448.4.E83      362.1 19      *LC* 80-19339      *ISBN* 0674268652

**Transcultural health care / editors, George Henderson, Martha**      5.4662
**Primeaux.**
Menlo Park, Calif.: Addison-Wesley Pub. Co., Medical/Nursing Division,
c1981. xxv, 323 p.; 24 cm. 1. Minorities — Medical care — United States.
2. Medical anthropology 3. Medical anthropology — United States. 4. Folk
medicine — United States I. Henderson, George, 1932- II. Primeaux, Martha,
1930-
RA448.4.T7      362.1/0973 19      *LC* 80-39991      *ISBN* 0201032376

**Kunitz, Stephen J.**                                    5.4663
Disease change and the role of medicine: the Navajo experience / Stephen J.
Kunitz. — Berkeley: University of California Press, c1983. x, 227 p.; 24 cm. —
(Comparative studies of health systems and medical care.) Includes index.
1. Navajo Indians — Diseases. 2. Navajo Indians — Mortality. 3. Navajo
Indians — Medical care. 4. Navajo Indians — Medicine. 5. Indians of North
America — Southwest, New — Diseases. 6. Indians of North America —
Southwest, New — Mortality. 7. Indians of North America — Southwest, New
— Medical care. 8. Indians of North America — Southwest, New — Medicine.
I. T. II. Series.
RA448.5.I5 K85 1983      362.1/08997 19      *LC* 83-47663      *ISBN*
0520049268

**Sidel, Ruth.**                                    5.4664
The health of China / Ruth Sidel and Victor W. Sidel; with a chapter on
education by Mark Sidel. — Boston, Mass.: Beacon Press, c1982. xix, 251 p.; 21
cm. Includes index. 1. Public health — China. 2. Public welfare — China.
3. Medical policy — China. 4. China — Social policy. I. Sidel, Victor W.
II. Sidel, Mark. III. T.
RA527.S495 1982      362.4/0951 19      *LC* 81-68353      *ISBN*
0807021601

**Aging and public health / Harry T. Phillips, Susan A. Gaylord,**      5.4665
**editors; foreword by Michael A. Ibrahim.**
New York: Springer Pub. Co., c1985. xxiv, 325 p.: ill.; 24 cm. 1. Aged — Care
and hygiene — United States. 2. Aged — United States — Social conditions.
3. Aged — Services for — United States. 4. Aging — Psychological aspects
I. Phillips, Harry T., 1915- II. Gaylord, Susan A.
RA564.8.A397 1985      362.1/9897/00973 19      *LC* 85-2815      *ISBN*
0826143806

**Brody, Elaine M.**                                    5.4666
Mental and physical health practices of older people: a guide for health
professionals / Elaine M. Brody with the assistance of Morton H. Kleban and
William E. Oriol; foreword by Barry D. Lebowitz. — New York: Springer Pub.
Co., c1985. xv, 272 p.: ill.; 24 cm. Includes index. 1. Aged — Care and hygiene.
2. Aged — Mental health 3. Aged — Diseases I. Kleban, Morton H.
II. Oriol, William E. III. T.
RA564.8.B76 1985      613/.0438 19      *LC* 84-22154      *ISBN*
0826148700

**Double exposure: women's health hazards on the job and at**      5.4667
**home / edited by Wendy Chavkin; preface by Eula Bingham.**
New York: Monthly Review Press, c1984. xi, 276 p.: ill.; 21 cm. — (New
feminist library.) 1. Women — Health and hygiene — Addresses, essays,
lectures. 2. Industrial hygiene — Addresses, essays, lectures. 3. Housing and
health — Addresses, essays, lectures. I. Chavkin, Wendy. II. Series.
RA564.85.D68 1984      613.6/2 19      *LC* 83-42525      *ISBN*
085345633X

# RA565–618 Environmental Health

**Salvato, Joseph A.**                                    5.4668
Environmental engineering and sanitation / Joseph A. Salvato. — 3rd ed. —
New York: Wiley, c1982. xxiv, 1163 p.: ill.; 25 cm. — (Environmental science
and technology. 0194-0287) 'A Wiley-Interscience publication.'
1. Environmental health 2. Environmental engineering 3. Sanitary
engineering 4. Sanitation I. T. II. Series.
RA565.S3 1982      628 19      *LC* 81-11509      *ISBN* 0471049425

**Calabrese, Edward J., 1946-.**                                    5.4669
Nutrition and environmental health: the influence of nutritional status on
pollutant toxicity and carcinogenicity / Edward J. Calabrese. — New York:
Wiley, c1980-c1981. 2 v.: ill.; 23 cm. (Environmental science and technology)
'A Wiley-Interscience publication.' 1. Pollutants — Toxicology.
2. Environmentally induced diseases — Nutritional aspects. 3. Vitamins in
human nutrition I. T.
RA566.C28      614.7 19      *LC* 79-21089      *ISBN* 047104833X

**Turiel, Isaac.**                                    5.4670
Indoor air quality and human health / Isaac Turiel. — Stanford, Calif.:
Stanford University Press, 1985. xiv, 173 p.: ill.; 24 cm. Includes index.
1. Ventilation — Hygienic aspects. 2. Air — Pollution, Indoor — Toxicology.
3. Air quality I. T.
RA575.5.T87 1985      613/.5 19      *LC* 84-50638      *ISBN* 0804712557

**Dick, George, 1914-.**                                    5.4671
Immunisation / George Dick. — London; Fort Lee, N.J.: Update Books, 1978.
152 p.: ill.; 24 cm. Includes index. 1. Immunization I. T.
RA638.D5      614.4/7      *LC* 79-306893      *ISBN* 0906141109

# RA639–653 Transmission of Disease. Epidemics

**American Public Health Association.**                                    5.4672
Control of communicable diseases in man / Abram S. Benenson, editor. — 14th
ed. — Washington: The Association, 1985. 485 p. Published in 1918 under title:
The control of communicable diseases. 'An official report of the American
Public Health Association.' 1. Communicable diseases — Prevention
I. Benenson, Abram S., 1914- II. T.
RA643.A5 1985      RA643 A5 1981.      614.4

**Chase, Allan, 1913–.**     **5.4673**
Magic shots: a human and scientific account of the long and continuing struggle to eradicate infectious diseases by vaccination / Allan Chase. — 1st ed. — New York: Morrow, 1982. 576 p.; 25 cm. 1. Communicable diseases — Prevention — History. 2. Vaccination — History. I. T.
RA643.C44 1982     614.4/7/09 19     *LC* 82-12505     *ISBN* 0688007872

**Ettling, John, 1944–.**     **5.4674**
The germ of laziness: Rockefeller philanthropy and public health in the New South / John Ettling. — Cambridge, Mass.: Harvard University Press, 1981. x, 236 p.; 24 cm. 1. Rockefeller Sanitary Commission for the Eradication of Hookworm Disease — History. 2. Hookworm disease — Southern States — Prevention — History — 20th century. 3. Public health — Southern States — History — 20th century. I. T.
RA644.H65 E88     362.1/969654 19     *LC* 81-4174     *ISBN* 0674349903

**Silverstein, Arthur M.**     **5.4675**
Pure politics and impure science: the swine flu affair / Arthur M. Silverstein. — Baltimore: Johns Hopkins University Press, c1981. xv, 176 p.: ill.; 24 cm. Includes index. 1. Swine influenza — Preventive inoculation — Political aspects — United States. 2. Swine influenza — United States — Preventive inoculation. 3. Medical policy — United States. I. T.
RA644.I6 S54     614.5/18 19     *LC* 81-47590     *ISBN* 0801826322

**Harrison, Gordon A.**     **5.4676**
Mosquitoes, malaria, and man: a history of the hostilities since 1880 / Gordon Harrison; [line drawings by Wynne Brown]. — 1st ed. — New York: Dutton, c1978. viii, 314 p.: ill.; 25 cm. Includes index. 1. Malaria — Prevention — History. 2. Mosquitoes — Control — History. 3. Malaria — Transmission. 4. Mosquitoes as carriers of disease I. T.
RA644.M2 H37 1978     614.5/3/2009     *LC* 77-21725     *ISBN* 0525160256

**Slack, Paul.**     **5.4677**
The impact of plague in Tudor and Stuart England / Paul Slack. — London; Boston: Routledge & K. Paul, 1985. xvi, 443 p.: maps; 23 cm. Includes index. 1. Plague — England — History. 2. Plague — England — Case studies. 3. Plague — Social aspects — England. 4. Great Britain — History — Tudors, 1485-1603 5. Great Britain — History — Stuarts, 1603-1649. I. T.
RA644.P7 S65 1985     942.05 19     *LC* 84-27574     *ISBN* 0710204698

**Reforming the long–term–care system: financial and**     **5.4678**
**organizational options / edited by James J. Callahan, Jr., Stanley S. Wallack (University Health Policy Consortium).**
Lexington, Mass.: Lexington Books, c1981. ix, 261 p.; 24 cm. — (University Health Policy Consortium series.) 1. Long-term care of the sick — United States — Administration. 2. Long-term care of the sick — United States — Finance. 3. Medical policy — United States. I. Callahan, James J. II. Wallack, Stanley. III. University Health Policy Consortium (Mass.) IV. Series.
RA644.6.R45     362.1/8/068 19     *LC* 80-8366     *ISBN* 0669040401

**Adams, Paul.**     **5.4679**
Health of the state / Paul Adams; foreword by S.M. Miller. — New York: Praeger, 1982. x, 198 p.; 24 cm. — (Praeger special studies in social welfare.) Includes index. 1. War — Medical aspects 2. War and society 3. Medical policy — United States. 4. Medical policy — Great Britain. 5. United States — Social policy 6. Great Britain — Social policy. I. T. II. Series.
RA646.A3 1982     362.1/042 19     *LC* 81-22647     *ISBN* 0030586283

**The Medical implications of nuclear war / Institute of**     **5.4680**
**Medicine/National Academy of Sciences; Fredric Solomon and Robert Q. Marston, editors; with a foreword by Lewis Thomas.**
Washington, D.C.: National Academy Press, 1986. p. cm. Based on papers presented at a symposium held at the National Academy of Sciences, Washington, D.C., Sept. 20-22, 1985 and organized under the auspices of the Institute of Medicine. Includes index. 1. Nuclear warfare — Hygienic aspects — Congresses. 2. Emergency medical services — Congresses. 3. Nuclear warfare — Environmental aspects — Congresses. 4. Nuclear warfare — Psychological aspects — Congresses. 5. Nuclear warfare — Social aspects — Congresses. I. Solomon, Fredric. II. Marston, Robert Q., 1923- III. Institute of Medicine (U.S.)
RA648.3.M445 1986     363.3/498 19     *LC* 86-18134     *ISBN* 0309036925

**McNeill, William Hardy, 1917-.**     **5.4681**
Plagues and peoples / William H. McNeill. — 1st ed. — Garden City, N.Y.: Anchor Press, 1976. viii, 369 p.: map; 22 cm. 1. Epidemics — History. 2. Civilization — History I. T.
RA649.M3     614.4/9     *LC* 76-2798     *ISBN* 0385112564

**Disease in African history: an introductory survey and case**     **5.4682**
**studies / Mario Joaquim Azevedo ... [et al.]; edited by Gerald W. Hartwig and K. David Patterson.**
Durham, N.C.: Duke University Press, 1978. xiv, 258 p.: ill.; 24 cm. ([Publication] - Duke University Center for Commonwealth and Comparative Studies; no. 44) Includes index. 1. Epidemics — Africa, Sub-Saharan — History. 2. Diseases and history — Africa, Sub-Saharan. 3. Medical geography — Africa, Sub-Saharan — History. I. Azevedo, Mario Joaquim. II. Hartwig, Gerald W. III. Patterson, K. David (Karl David), 1941-
RA650.8.S82 D57     614.4/26     *LC* 78-52421     *ISBN* 0822304104

**Biocultural aspects of disease / edited by Henry Rothschild;**     **5.4683**
**coordinating editor Charles F. Chapman.**
New York: Academic Press, 1981. xix, 653 p.: ill.; 24 cm. 1. Epidemiology 2. Health and race 3. Medical anthropology 4. Medical geography I. Rothschild, Henry, 1932-
RA651.B53     616.07/1 19     *LC* 81-12714     *ISBN* 012598720X

**Mausner, Judith S.**     **5.4684**
Epidemiology: an introductory text / Judith S. Mausner, Shira Kramer; with contributions by Peter Gann, G. Stephen Bowen; with the collaboration of Richard Morton. — 2nd ed. — Philadelphia: Saunders, 1985. xii, 361 p.: ill.; 23 cm. At head of title: Mausner & Bahn. 1. Epidemiology I. Kramer, Shira. II. Bahn, Anita K. III. T.
RA651.M33 1985     614.4 19     *LC* 83-20292     *ISBN* 0721661815

**Vogt, Thomas M.**     **5.4685**
Making health decisions: an epidemiologic perspective on staying well / Thomas M. Vogt. — Chicago: Nelson-Hall, c1983. xi, 210 p.: ill.; 23 cm. Includes index. 1. Epidemiology 2. Health 3. Health behavior 4. Medicine, Preventive I. T.
RA651.V6 1983     614.4 19     *LC* 83-6260     *ISBN* 0830410015

## RA770–772 OTHER PUBLIC HEALTH TOPICS

**Health care of homeless people / Philip W. Brickner ... [et al.],**     **5.4686**
**editors.**
New York: Springer Pub. Co., c1985. xiii, 349 p.: ill.; 24 cm. 1. Homelessness — Hygienic aspects — United States — Addresses, essays, lectures. 2. Poor — Medical care — United States — Addresses, essays, lectures. 3. Mentally ill — Care and treatment — United States — Addresses, essays, lectures. I. Brickner, Philip W., 1928-
RA770.H43 1985     362.1/0425 19     *LC* 84-23625     *ISBN* 0826149901

**Hassinger, Edward Wesley.**     **5.4687**
Rural health organization: social networks and regionalization / Edward W. Hassinger. — 1st ed. — Ames: Iowa State University Press, 1982. ix, 194 p.; 23 cm. Includes index. 1. Rural health services — Administration. 2. Regional medical programs I. T.
RA771.H35 1982     362.1/0425 19     *LC* 82-15323     *ISBN* 0813815894

**Kryter, Karl D.**     **5.4688**
The effects of noise on man / by Karl D. Kryter. — 2nd ed. — New York: Academic Press, 1985. xi, 688 p.: ill.; 24 cm. Originally published: Washington, D.C.: National Aeronautics and Space Administration, Scientific and Technical Information Branch, 1984. (NASA reference publication; 1115). 'January 10, 1983.' 1. Noise — Hygienic aspects. 2. Noise — Physiological aspects. 3. Noise — Social aspects. 4. Noise pollution 5. Deafness, Noise induced I. T.
RA772.N7 K78 1985     616.9/896 19     *LC* 83-3892     *ISBN* 0124274609

## RA773–788 Personal Health and Hygiene. Exercise. Nutrition

**The New our bodies, ourselves: a book by and for women / the**     **5.4689**
**Boston Women's Health Book Collective.**
New York: Simon & Schuster, c1984. xx, 647 p.: ill.; 28 cm. (A Touchstone book) Rev. ed. of: Our bodies, ourselves. 2nd ed., completely rev. and expanded. c1976. 1. Women — Health and hygiene 2. Women — Diseases 3. Women — Psychology I. Boston Women's Health Book Collective. II. Our bodies, ourselves.
RA778.N67 1984     613/.04244 19     *LC* 84-5545     *ISBN* 0671460889

**Woman's health and medical guide / edited by Patricia J.**   **5.4690**
**Cooper; illustrations by Sandra McMahon and Lianne M.**
**Krueger; black and white photography by Fred Lyon; [exercise**
**illustrations by Joe Isom; color photographs by Mike Dieter].**
1st ed. — Des Moines, Iowa: Meredith Corp., c1981. 696 p.: ill. (some col.); 28
cm. — (Better homes and gardens books.) At head of title: Better homes and
gardens. Includes index. 1. Women — Health and hygiene 2. Women —
Diseases 3. Women — Physiology I. Cooper, Patricia J. II. Better homes and
gardens. III. Series.
RA778.W73      613/.0424 19      *LC* 79-55161      *ISBN* 0696002752

**Women and health in America: historical readings / edited by**   **5.4691**
**Judith Walzer Leavitt.**
Madison, Wis.: University of Wisconsin Press, 1984. ix, 526 p.: ill.; 24 cm.
Includes index. 1. Women — Health and hygiene — United States — History
— Addresses, essays, lectures. 2. Women — United States — Sexual behavior
— History — Addresses, essays, lectures. 3. Women — Diseases — United
States — History — Addresses, essays, lectures. 4. Women in medicine —
United States — History — Addresses, essays, lectures. I. Leavitt, Judith
Walzer.
RA778.W744 1984      362.1/088042 19      *LC* 83-40267      *ISBN*
0299096408

**The Complete book of exercises / Diagram Group.**   **5.4692**
New York: Van Nostrand Reinhold, 1984. p. cm. Rev. ed. of: The Complete
encyclopedia of exercises / the Diagram Group. 1981, c1979. Includes index.
1. Exercise 2. Physical fitness I. Diagram Group. II. Complete encyclopedia
of exercises.
RA781.C57 1984      613.7/1 19      *LC* 83-1358      *ISBN* 0442219709

**Cooper, Kenneth H.**   **5.4693**
The aerobics program for total well–being: exercise, diet, emotional balance /
Kenneth H. Cooper. — New York: M. Evans, c1982. 320 p.: ill.; 24 cm.
1. Aerobic exercises 2. Physical fitness I. T.
RA781.15.C657 1982      613.7/1 19      *LC* 82-16361      *ISBN*
0871313804

# RA790 Mental Health

**Chamberlin, Judi.**   **5.4694**
On our own: patient–controlled alternatives to the mental health system / by
Judi Chamberlin. — New York: Hawthorn Books, c1978. xvii, 236 p.; 24 cm.
Includes index. 1. Mental health services I. T.
RA790.C56      362.2/04/25      *LC* 76-56520      *ISBN* 080155523X

**Coan, Richard W.**   **5.4695**
Hero, artist, sage, or saint?: A survey of views on what is variously called mental
health, normality, maturity, self–actualization, and human fulfillment /
Richard W. Coan. New York: Columbia University Press, 1977. xiii, 322 p.; 24
cm. 1. Mental health I. T.
RA790.C663      150/.19      *LC* 76-57751      *ISBN* 0231038062

**DeYoung, Carol D.**   **• 5.4696**
The nurse's role in community mental health centers; out of uniform and into
trouble [by] Carol D. DeYoung [and] Margene Tower. Contributing authors:
Jody Glittenberg [and others] Saint Louis, Mosby, 1971. xvi, 117 p. 25 cm.
1. Psychiatric nursing 2. Community mental health services I. Tower,
Margene. joint author. II. T. III. Title: Out of uniform and into trouble.
RA790.5.D48      610.73/68/023      *LC* 70-140950      *ISBN* 0801612772

**Armour, Philip K.**   **5.4697**
The cycles of social reform: mental health policy making in the United States,
England, and Sweden / Philip K. Armour. — Washington, D.C.: University
Press of America, c1981. v, 364 p.; 22 cm. Based on the author's thesis
(University of California, Berkeley) Includes index. 1. Mental health policy —
United States. 2. Mental health policy — England. 3. Mental health policy —
Sweden. 4. Mental health policy — History. I. T.
RA790.6.A77 1981      362.2/094 19      *LC* 81-16216      *ISBN*
0819120332

**Brown, Phil.**   **5.4698**
The transfer of care: psychiatric deinstitutionalization and its aftermath / Phil
Brown. — Boston: Routledge & Kegan Paul, 1985. xiii, 275 p.; 23 cm. Includes
indexes. 1. Mentally ill — Care — United States. 2. Mental health services —
United States. 3. Mental health policy — United States. I. T.
RA790.6.B78 1985      362.2/0973 19      *LC* 84-9797      *ISBN*
0710099002

**Delworth, Ursula.**   **5.4699**
Crisis center/hotline; a guidebook to beginning and operating. Edited by Ursula
Delworth, Edward H. Rudow [and] Janet Taub. With a foreword by Weston

Morrill. — Springfield, Ill.: Thomas, [1972] xii, 144 p.; 24 cm. 1. Community
mental health services — United States. I. Rudow, Edward H., joint author.
II. Taub, Janet, joint author. III. T.
RA790.6.D44      362.2/2      *LC* 72-79187      *ISBN* 0398025614

**Levine, Murray, 1928-.**   **5.4700**
The history and politics of community mental health / Murray Levine. — New
York: Oxford University Press, 1981. 232 p.; 21 cm. Includes indexes.
1. Community mental health services — United States — History. 2. Mental
health services — United States — History. 3. Mental health policy — United
States — History. 4. Mental health services — Law and legislation — United
States. I. T.
RA790.6.L49      362.2/0973 19      *LC* 81-1113      *ISBN* 0195029550

**Naparstek, Arthur.**   **5.4701**
Neighborhood networks for humane mental health care / Arthur J. Naparstek,
David E. Biegel, and Herzl R. Spiro with Joseph Coffey and John Andreozzi. —
New York: Plenum Press, c1982. xiv, 223 p.; 24 cm. Includes index.
1. Community mental health services — United States. 2. Community
psychology I. Biegel, David E. II. Spiro, Herzl R., 1935- III. T.
RA790.6.N44 1982      362.2/0425 19      *LC* 82-18149      *ISBN*
0306410516

**Racism and mental health; essays. Charles V. Willie, Bernard**   **5.4702**
**M. Kramer [and] Bertram S. Brown, editors.**
[Pittsburgh] University of Pittsburgh Press [1973] xviii, 604 p. 21 cm.
(Contemporary community health series.) Based on a series of conferences at
Syracuse University, 1970-71, and conducted by the university's Dept. of
Sociology. 1. Mental health — United States — Congresses. 2. Racism —
Congresses. 3. Afro-Americans — Psychology — Congresses. 4. United States
— Race relations — Congresses. I. Willie, Charles Vert, 1927- ed. II. Kramer,
Bernard M., ed. III. Brown, Bertram S. ed. IV. Syracuse University. Dept. of
Sociology. V. Series.
RA790.6.R3      362.8/4      *LC* 72-78933      *ISBN* 0822932520 *ISBN*
0822952335

**Reaching the underserved: mental health needs of neglected**   **5.4703**
**populations / edited by Lonnie R. Snowden.**
Beverly Hills, Calif.: Sage Publications, c1982. 303 p.; 23 cm. — (Sage annual
reviews of community mental health. v. 3) 1. Mental health services — United
States. 2. Minorities — Mental health services — United States. 3. Poor —
Mental health services — United States. I. Snowden, Lonnie R., 1947-
II. Series.
RA790.6.R418 1982      362.2/042/0973 19      *LC* 82-10722      *ISBN*
0803918569

**Pyle, Gerald F.**   **5.4704**
Applied medical geography / Gerald F. Pyle. — Washington: V. H. Winston;
New York: distributed solely by Halsted Press, 1979. xiv, 282 p.: ill.; 24 cm.
(Scripta series in geography.) 1. Medical geography I. T. II. Series.
RA792.P94 1979      614.4/2      *LC* 78-27856      *ISBN* 0470266430

# RA960–999 Hospitals. Nursing Homes

**Ley, P.**   **• 5.4705**
Communicating with the patient / P. Ley and M. S. Spelman. — St. Louis:
Green, [c1967] 128 p.: ill. 1. Communication 2. Physician-Patient Relations.
I. Spelman, M S II. T.
RA965.L4 1967b      *LC* 67-27243

**Thompson, John D.**   **5.4706**
The hospital: a social and architectural history / John D. Thompson and Grace
Goldin. New Haven: Yale University Press, 1975. xxvii, 349 p.: ill.; 29 cm.
Includes index. 1. Yale-New Haven Hospital. 2. Hospitals — Design and
construction — History. 3. Hospital wards 4. Hospitals — Sociological
aspects 5. Hospital care I. Goldin, Grace. joint author. II. T.
RA967.T5      725/.51/09      *LC* 74-19574      *ISBN* 0300018290

**The Theory and practice of infection control / edited by Inge**   **5.4707**
**Gurevich, Patricia Tafuro, Burke A. Cunha.**
New York: Praeger, 1984. xx, 419 p.: ill.; 25 cm. 1. Nosocomial infections —
Prevention. 2. Hospitals — Sanitation 3. Hospitals — Disinfection
4. Communicable diseases — Prevention I. Gurevich, Inge. II. Tafuro,
Patricia. III. Cunha, Burke A.
RA969.T47 1984      614.4/4 19      *LC* 84-6850      *ISBN* 0030636264

**Aaron, Henry J.**   **5.4708**
The painful prescription: rationing hospital care / Henry J. Aaron and William
B. Schwartz. — Washington, D.C.: Brookings Institution, c1984. xii, 161 p.; 24
cm. — (Studies in social economics.) 'A study sponsored jointly by the Tufts

University School of Medicine and the Brookings Institution.' 1. Hospital care — United States. 2. Hospital care — Great Britain. 3. Hospital utilization — United States 4. Hospital utilization — Great Britain. 5. Medical policy — United States. 6. Medical policy — Great Britain. I. Schwartz, William B. II. Tufts University. School of Medicine. III. Brookings Institution. IV. T. V. Series.
RA981.A2 A5 1984    362.1/1/0973 19    LC 83-45962    ISBN 0815700342

**Joskow, Paul L.**                                                    **5.4709**
Controlling hospital costs: the role of government regulation / Paul L. Joskow. — Cambridge, Mass.: MIT Press, c1981. 211 p.; 24 cm. — (MIT Press series in health and public policy. 2) Includes index. 1. Hospitals — United States — Cost control. 2. Hospitals — Economic aspects — United States. 3. Hospitals — Cost control — Law and legislation — United States. I. T. II. Series.
RA981.A2 J65    362.1/1/0681 19    LC 81-14289    ISBN 026210024X

**Vogel, Morris J.**                                                   **5.4710**
The invention of the modern hospital, Boston, 1870–1930 / Morris J. Vogel. — Chicago: University of Chicago Press, c1980. ix, 171 p.; 24 cm. 1. Hospitals — United States — History — 19th century. 2. Hospitals — United States — History — 20th century. 3. Boston (Mass.) — Hospitals — History — 19th century. 4. Boston (Mass.) — Hospitals — History — 20th century. I. T.
RA982.B7 V63    362.1/1/0974461 19    LC 79-26052    ISBN 0226862402

**Rosner, David, 1947-.**                                             **5.4711**
A once charitable enterprise: hospitals and health care in Brooklyn and New York, 1885–1915 / David Rosner. — Cambridge [Cambridgeshire]; New York: Cambridge University Press, 1982. ix, 234 p.: ill.; 24 cm. — (Interdisciplinary perspectives on modern history.) Includes index. 1. Hospital care — New York (N.Y.) — History. 2. Hospital and community — New York (N.Y.) — History. 3. Hospitals, Voluntary — New York (N.Y.) — History. 4. New York (N.Y.) — Hospitals — History. 5. Brooklyn (N.Y.) — Hospitals — History. I. T. II. Series.
RA982.N49 R676 1982    362.1/1/097471 19    LC 81-21725    ISBN 0521242177

**Henderson, Gail, 1949-.**                                           **5.4712**
The Chinese hospital: a socialist work unit / Gail E. Henderson and Myron S. Cohen. — New Haven: Yale University Press, c1984. xvi, 183 p., 12 p. of plates: ill.; 25 cm. Includes index. 1. Hu-pei sheng i hsüeh yüan. Fu shu ti 2 i yüan. 2. Hospitals — China — Sociological aspects. I. Cohen, Myron S. II. T. III. Title: Danwei.
RA990.C5 H46 1984    362.1/1/095121 19    LC 83-16943    ISBN 0300030630

**Gubrium, Jaber F.**                                                 **5.4713**
Living and dying at Murray Manor / Jaber F. Gubrium. — New York: St. Martin's Press, c1975. 221 p.; 22 cm. 1. Nursing home care 2. Nursing homes — United States. I. T.
RA997.G77    362.6/15/0973    LC 74-23279

# RA1001–1171 Forensic Medicine. Medical Jurisprudence

**Medicine, law, & public policy / edited by Nicholas N. Kittrie,**    **5.4714**
**Harold L. Hirsh, Glen Wegner; with a foreword by Walter F. Mondale.**
New York: AMS Press, c1975. 605 p.: ill.; 24 cm. 1. Medical jurisprudence — United States — Congresses. 2. Medical laws and legislation — United States — Congresses. 3. Medical policy — United States — Congresses. I. Kittrie, Nicholas N., 1928- II. Hirsh, Harold L. III. Wegner, Glen.
RA1016.M42    344/.73/04    LC 75-793    ISBN 0404104266

**Glaister, John, 1892-.**                                            **5.4715**
[Medical jurisprudence and toxicology] Glaister's medical jurisprudence and toxicology. 13th ed.; edited by the late Edgar Rentoul and Hamilton Smith; foreword by Gilbert Forbes. Edinburgh: Churchill Livingstone, 1973. xiv, 780 p.: ill.; 23 cm. 1. Medical jurisprudence 2. Toxicology I. Rentoul, Edgar, joint author. II. Smith, Hamilton, joint author. III. T. IV. Title: Medical jurisprudence and toxicology.
RA1051.G5 1973    614/.19    LC 73-595966    ISBN 0443008949

**Waltz, Jon R.**                                                   • **5.4716**
Medical jurisprudence [by] Jon R. Waltz [and] Fred E. Inbau. — New York: Macmillan, [1971] xiv, 398 p.: illus.; 24 cm. 1. Medical jurisprudence I. Inbau, Fred Edward. joint author. II. T.
RA1051.W35    614/.19    LC 77-133563

**Lewis, Howard R.**                                                • **5.4717**
The medical offenders [by] Howard R. and Martha E. Lewis. With a pref. by James L. Goddard. New York: Simon and Schuster, [1970] 377 p.; 24 cm. 1. Physicians — United States — Malpractice. I. Lewis, Martha E. joint author. II. T.
RA1056.5.L47    616    LC 68-28916    ISBN 0671201301

**Walton, Douglas N.**                                                **5.4718**
Brain death: ethical considerations / by Douglas N. Walton. — West Lafayette, Ind.: Purdue University, 1980. ix, 95 p.; 22 cm. (Science and society ; v. 5) Includes index. 1. Brain death 2. Brain death — Moral and religious aspects. I. T.
RA1063.3.W36    174/.24 19    LC 80-80845    ISBN 0931682126

# RA1195–1270 Toxicology

**National Research Council (U.S.). Steering Committee on**            **5.4719**
**Identification of Toxic and Potentially Toxic Chemicals for**
**Consideration by the National Toxicology Program.**
Toxicity testing: strategies to determine needs and priorities / Steering Committee on Identification of Toxic and Potentially Toxic Chemicals for Consideration by the National Toxicology Program, Board on Toxicology and Environmental Health Hazards, Commission on Life Sciences, National Research Council. — Washington, D.C.: National Academy Press, 1984. xiii, 382 p.: ill.; 28 cm. 1. National Toxicology Program (U.S.) 2. Toxicity testing — United States. 3. Toxicity testing I. T.
RA1199.N375 1984    615.9/07 19    LC 84-60095    ISBN 0309034337

**Casarett, Louis J.**                                                **5.4720**
Toxicology: the basic science of poisons / edited by Louis J. Casarett, John Doull. — New York: Macmillan, [1975] xiii, 768 p.: ill.; 26 cm. 1. Toxicology 2. Poisoning 3. Poisons I. Doull, John, 1923- joint author. II. T.
RA1211.C296    615.9    LC 74-7704    ISBN 0023199601

**Deichmann, William B.**                                           • **5.4721**
Toxicology of drugs and chemicals / by William B. Deichmann and Horace W. Gerarde. — [4th ed.] New York: Academic Press, 1969. xvi, 805 p.: ill.; 24 cm. First-2d ed. published under title: Signs, symptoms, and treatment of certain acute intoxications. Third ed. published in 1964 under title: Symptomatology and therapy of toxicological emergencies. 1. Toxicological emergencies — Handbooks, manuals, etc. I. Gerarde, Horace W. joint author. II. T.
RA1211.D42 1969    615.9/002/02    LC 69-12282    ISBN 0122088565

**Gray, C. H. (Charles Horace) ed.**                               • **5.4722**
Laboratory handbook of toxic agents / C. H. Gray, editor in chief. — 2nd ed. London: Royal Institute of Chemistry, 1966. ix, 190 p.: ill., tables; 28 cm. 1. Industrial toxicology I. Royal Institute of Chemistry. II. T. III. Title: R. I. C. laboratory handbook of toxic agents.
RA1211.G7 1966    LC 66-78933

**Kaye, Sidney.**                                                     **5.4723**
Handbook of emergency toxicology: a guide for the identification, diagnosis, and treatment of poisoning / by Sidney Kaye. — 4th ed. — Springfield, Ill.: Thomas, c1980. xxviii, 565 p.: ill.; 24 cm. — (American lecture series; publication no. 1034) Includes index. 1. Poisoning I. T.
RA1211.K3 1980    615.9/08    LC 79-17565    ISBN 0398039607

**Dreisbach, Robert H. (Robert Hastings), 1916-.**                    **5.4724**
Handbook of poisoning: prevention, diagnosis, treatment / Robert H. Dreisbach. — 10th ed. — Los Altos, Calif.: Lange Medical Publications, 1980. 578 p.: ill.; 18 cm. (A Concise medical library for practitioner and student) On spine: Poisoning. 1. Poisoning — Handbooks, manuals, etc. I. T. II. Title: Poisoning.
RA1215.D73 1980    615.9 19    LC 79-92918    ISBN 0870410733

**Registry of toxic effects of chemical substances.**                 **5.4725**
Cincinnati, Ohio: U.S. Dept. of Health and Human Services, Public Health Service, Center for Disease Control, National Institute for Occupational Safety and Health; Washington, D.C.: For sale by the Supt. of Docs., U.S. G.P.O. v.; 28 cm. (-1978: DHEW publication; no. (NIOSH) (DHHS (NIOSH) publication) Annual. Began with 1975. Description based on: 1979 ed. Vols. for < 1980- > issued in parts. 1. Poisons — Tables — Periodicals. 2. Industrial toxicology — Periodicals. I. National Institute for Occupational Safety and Health. II. Tracor Jitco, Inc.
RA1215.N37a    615.9/02/0212    LC 75-649213

**Documentation of the threshold limit values.**                      **5.4726**
4th ed. — Cincinnati, Ohio: American Conference of Governmental Industrial Hygienists, 1980. vii, 486 p.: ill.; 30 cm. Previously published as:

Documentation of the threshold limit values for substances in workroom air / American Conference of Governmental Industrial Hygienists. 3rd. ed. Cincinnati, Ohio: American Conference of Governmental Industrial Hygienists, 1971. On spine: Documentation of TLVs. 1. Threshold limit values (Industrial toxicology) 2. Industrial toxicology 3. Industrial hygiene I. American Conference of Governmental Industrial Hygienists. II. Title: Documentation of TLVs. III. Title: Threshold limit values.
RA1229.D6 1980      615.9/02 19      *LC* 81-112373

**Hamilton, Alice, 1869-1970.**                                          **5.4727**
Hamilton and Hardy's industrial toxicology. — 4th ed. / rev. by Asher J. Finkel. — Boston: J. Wright, 1983. xii, 428 p.; 26 cm. Rev. ed. of: Industrial toxicology. 2nd ed., rev. and enl. [1949] 1. Industrial toxicology I. Hardy, Harriet Louise, 1906- II. Finkel, Asher J. III. T. IV. Title: Industrial toxicology.
RA1229.H35 1983      615.9/02 19      *LC* 82-8613      *ISBN* 0723670277

**Mutagenicity, carcinogenicity, and teratogenicity of industrial**      **5.4728**
**pollutants / edited by Micheline Kirsch–Volders.**
New York: Plenum Press, c1984. xiv, 336 p.: ill.; 24 cm. 'Published in conjunction with the Belgian Environmental Mutagen Society.' 1. Industrial toxicology 2. Pollutants — Toxicology. 3. Chemical mutagenesis 4. Carcinogens 5. Teratogenic agents I. Kirsch-Volders, Micheline. II. Belgian Environmental Mutagen Society.
RA1229.M87 1984      615.9/02 19      *LC* 83-11126      *ISBN* 0306411482

**Gofman, John W.**                                          **5.4729**
Radiation and human health / by John W. Gofman; [ill. by Jon Goodchild]. — San Francisco: Sierra Club Books, c1981. xiv, 908 p.: ill.; 24 cm. Includes index. 1. Ionizing radiation — Toxicology. 2. Tumors, Radiation-induced 3. Radiation — Dosage I. T.
RA1231.R2 G56      616.9/897 19      *LC* 80-26484      *ISBN* 0871562758

**Apfel, Roberta J., 1938-.**                                          **5.4730**
To do no harm: DES and the dilemmas of modern medicine / Roberta J. Apfel, Susan M. Fisher. — New Haven: Yale University Press, c1984. x, 199 p.; 22 cm. Includes index. 1. Diethylstilbestrol — Toxicology. 2. Vagina — Cancer — Psychological aspects. 3. Physician and patient 4. Trust (Psychology) 5. Iatrogenic diseases — Psychological aspects. I. Fisher, Susan M., 1937- II. T.
RA1242.D48 A64 1984      363.1/94 19      *LC* 84-5089      *ISBN* 0300031920

**Formaldehyde toxicity / edited by James E. Gibson.**                                          **5.4731**
Washington: Hemisphere Pub. Corp., c1983. xxii, 312 p.: ill.; 23 cm. — (Chemical Industry Institute of Toxicology series.) 'Third CIIT Conference on Toxicology' — Pref. 1. Formaldehyde — Toxicology. I. Gibson, James E., 1941- II. Chemical Industry Institute of Toxicology. Conference. III. Series.
RA1242.F6 F67 1983      615.9/5136 19      *LC* 82-6189      *ISBN* 0891162755

**Lampe, Kenneth F.**                                          **5.4732**
AMA handbook of poisonous and injurious plants / Kenneth F. Lampe, Mary Ann McCann. — Chicago, Ill.: American Medical Association: Distributed by Chicago Review Press, c1985. xi, 432 p.: col. ill.; 21 cm. 1. Poisonous plants — Toxicology — Handbooks, manuals, etc. 2. Skin — Inflammation — Handbooks, manuals, etc. 3. Poisonous plants — United States — Identification. 4. Poisonous plants — Canada — Identification. 5. Poisonous plants — Caribbean Area — Identification. I. McCann, Mary Ann. II. American Medical Association. III. T.
RA1250.L27 1985      615.9/52 19      *LC* 84-28532      *ISBN* 0899701833

**Hayes, Wayland J., 1917-.**                                          **5.4733**
Pesticides studied in man / Wayland J. Hayes, Jr. — Baltimore: Williams & Wilkins, c1982. xiii, 672 p.; 29 cm. 1. Pesticides — Toxicology I. T.
RA1270.P4 H37      615.9/02 19      *LC* 81-7410      *ISBN* 0683038966

**Whorton, James, 1942-.**                                          **5.4734**
Before Silent spring; pesticides and public health in pre–DDT America [by] James Whorton. — Princeton, N.J.: Princeton University Press, [1975, c1974] xv, 288 p.; 23 cm. 1. Pesticides — Toxicology. 2. Pesticide residues in food — United States. 3. Food contamination 4. Food adulteration and inspection — United States — History. I. T.
RA1270.P4 W45 1975      632/.95/042      *LC* 74-11071      *ISBN* 0691081395

# RB Pathology

**Major, Ralph Hermon, 1884-.**                                          **5.4735**
Classic descriptions of disease, with biographical sketches of the authors, by Ralph H. Major. [3d. ed.] Springfield, Ill., C. C. Thomas [1945] xxxii, 679 p.,

illus., port. 26 cm. 1. Pathology — Collected works. 2. Pathology — Early works to 1800. 3. Pathology — History I. T.
RB6.M3 1945      *LC* 45-302

**Virchow, Rudolf Ludwig Karl, 1821-1902.**                                          **5.4736**
[Cellularpathologie. English] Cellular pathology as based upon physiological and pathological histology / translated from the 2d German ed. by Frank Chance; with a new introductory essay by L. J. Rather. — New York: Dover Publications [1971] xxvii, 554 p.: ill.; 22 cm. Translation of Die Cellularpathologie in ihrer Begründung auf physiologische und pathologische Gewebelehre. Reprint of the 1863 ed. 1. Pathology, Cellular 2. Histology, Pathological I. T.
RB25.V82 1971      611/.0181      *LC* 76-143679      *ISBN* 0486226980

**Netter, Frank Henry, 1906-.**                                          • **5.4737**
The Ciba collection of medical illustrations. Summit, N.J.: Ciba Pharmaceutical Products, [1953-. 1 v.: illus. (part col.); 32 cm. 1. Pathology — Atlases. 2. Medicine — Pictorial works. 3. Anatomy, Human — Atlases I. Ciba Pharmaceutical Products, inc. II. T.
RB33.N42      612/.022/2      *LC* 53-2151

**Laboratory tests: implications for nursing care / C. Judith**      **5.4738**
**Byrne ... [et al.].**
2nd ed. — Menlo Park, Calif.: Addison-Wesley Pub. Co., Health Sciences Division, c1986. xxi, 756 p.; 24 cm. 1. Diagnosis, Laboratory 2. Nursing I. Byrne, C. Judith (Claire Judith), 1944-
RB37.L276 1986      616.07/5 19      *LC* 85-13555      *ISBN* 0201126702

**Grouchy, Jean de.**                                          **5.4739**
[Atlas des maladies chromosomiques. English] Clinical atlas of human chromosomes / Jean de Grouchy, Catherine Turleau; foreword by Victor McKusick. — 2nd ed. — New York: Wiley, c1984. xx, 487 p.: ill.; 25 cm. (A Wiley medical publication) Translation of: Atlas des maladies chromosomiques. Deuxième éd. 1. Human chromosome abnormalities — Atlases. 2. Human cytogenetics — Atlases. 3. Medical genetics — Atlases. 4. Abnormalities, Human — Atlases. I. Turleau, Catherine. II. T.
RB44.G7613 1984      616/.042 19      *LC* 83-16839      *ISBN* 047189205X

**Robbins, Stanley L. (Stanley Leonard), 1915-.**                                          **5.4740**
Basic pathology / Stanley L. Robbins. — 4th ed. — Philadelphia: Saunders, 1987. p. cm. 1. Pathology I. Kumar, Vinay. II. T.
RB111.R6 1987      616.07 19      *LC* 86-21984      *ISBN* 0721618146

**Beveridge, W. I. B. (William Ian Beardmore), 1908-.**                                          • **5.4741**
Frontiers in comparative medicine / [by] W. I. B. Beveridge; foreword by Robert A. Good. — Minneapolis: University of Minnesota Press, [1972] 104 p.; 23 cm. (The Wesley W. Spink lectures on comparative medicine, v. 1) 1. Pathology, Comparative 2. Medicine, Comparative I. T. II. Series.
RB114.B48 1972      619      *LC* 72-79500      *ISBN* 0816606439

**Leader, Robert W., 1919-.**                                          • **5.4742**
Dictionary of comparative pathology and experimental biology [by] Robert W. Leader [and] Isabel Leader. — Philadelphia: Saunders, 1971. vi, 238 p.: illus.; 26 cm. 1. Pathology, Comparative — Dictionaries. I. Leader, Isabel, joint author. II. T. III. Title: Comparative pathology and experimental biology.
RB114.L4      596/.02/03      *LC* 72-118591      *ISBN* 0721656595

**Busch, Harris. ed.**                                          • **5.4743**
Biochemical frontiers in medicine. [1st ed.] Boston, Little, Brown [1963] 364 p. illus. 24 cm. 1. Biochemistry — Addresses, essays, lectures. 2. Physiology, Pathological — Addresses, essays, lectures. I. T.
RB121.B86      *LC* 63-16148

**Meinhart, Noreen T.**                                          **5.4744**
Pain, a nursing approach to assessment and analysis / Noreen T. Meinhart, Margo McCaffery. — Norwalk, Conn.: Appleton-Century-Crofts, c1983. ix, 390 p.: ill.; 24 cm. 1. Pain 2. Pain — Nursing. I. McCaffery, Margo. II. T.
RB127.M44 1983      616/.0472 19      *LC* 82-22779      *ISBN* 0838577032

**Steinberg, Franz U., 1913-.**                                          **5.4745**
The immobilized patient: functional pathology and management / Franz U. Steinberg. — New York: Plenum Medical Book Co., c1980. ix, 156 p.: ill.; 24 cm. — (Topics in bone and mineral disorders) 1. Hypokinesia 2. Hypokinesia — Physiological aspects. I. T. II. Series.
RB135.S73      616.7      *LC* 79-25903      *ISBN* 0306403722

**Bordicks, Katherine J.**                                          **5.4746**
Patterns of shock: implications for nursing care / Katherine J. Bordicks. — 2d ed. — New York: Macmillan, c1980. xx, 279 p.: ill.; 24 cm. 1. Shock 2. Shock — Nursing. I. T.
RB150.S5 B6 1980      617/.21      *LC* 79-9824      *ISBN* 0023124504

Shock, a nursing guide / [edited by] Jacqueline M. Carolan.    **5.4747**
Oradell, N.J.: Medical Economics Books, c1984. xi, 209 p.: ill.; 23 cm. 1. Shock
2. Shock — Nursing. I. Carolan, Jacqueline M.
RB150.S5 S475 1984      616/.047 19      LC 83-13238      *ISBN*
0874893461

## RB151–155 Theories of Disease. Medical Genetics

King, Lester Snow, 1908-.                                   • **5.4748**
The growth of medical thought. — [Chicago]: University of Chicago Press,
1963. xi, 254 p. — (Midway reprints) 1. Diseases — Causes and theories of
causation 2. Medicine — History I. T.
RB151.K5      LC 63-9729

Mims, Cedric A.                                             **5.4749**
The pathogenesis of infectious disease / Cedric A. Mims. London: Academic
Press; New York: Grune & Stratton, 1976. x, 246 p.: ill.; 24 cm. 1. Infection
2. Pathology I. T.
RB153.M55      616.01      LC 76-1092      *ISBN* 0124982506

Genetic counseling / editors, Herbert A. Lubs, Felix de la Cruz.    **5.4750**
New York: Raven Press, 1977. xvii, 598 p.: ill.; 25 cm. — (A monograph of the
National Institute of Child Health and Human Development.) 1. Genetic
counseling — Congresses. I. Lubs, Herbert Augustus, 1929- II. De La Cruz,
Felix F.
RB155.G36      613.9      LC 76-52601      *ISBN* 0890041504

Genetic counseling: psychological dimensions / edited by    **5.4751**
Seymour Kessler; with a foreword by Charles J. Epstein.
New York: Academic Press, 1979. xix, 248 p.; 24 cm. 1. Genetic counseling —
Psychological aspects. I. Kessler, Seymour.
RB155.G373      362.1/9/6042      LC 78-87879      *ISBN* 0124056504

Muir, Bernice L.                                            **5.4752**
Essentials of genetics for nurses / Bernice L. Muir. — New York: Wiley, c1983.
xii, 400 p.: ill.; 24 cm. — (Wiley medical publication.) 'This work includes some
material previously published by the same author in a book entitled
Pathophysiology'—P. 1. Medical genetics 2. Nursing I. T. II. Series.
RB155.M84 1983      616/.042/024613 19      LC 82-10841      *ISBN*
0471082384

## RC INTERNAL MEDICINE. PRACTICE OF MEDICINE

The Principles and practice of medicine.                    **5.4753**
21st ed. / edited by A. McGehee Harvey ... [et al.]. — Norwalk, Conn.:
Appleton-Century-Crofts, c1984. xxiii, 1596 p.: ill.; 29 cm. Based on: The
principles and practice of medicine / William Osler. 1. Internal medicine
I. Harvey, A. McGehee (Abner McGehee), 1911- II. Osler, William, Sir,
1849-1919. Principles and practice of medicine.
RC46.P89 1984      616 19      LC 84-3087      *ISBN* 0838579280

Textbook of medicine / [edited by] Cecil.                   **5.4754**
17th ed. / edited by James B. Wyngaarden, Lloyd H. Smith, Jr.; editor for
neurologic and behavioral diseases, Fred Plum; consulting editors, Thomas E.
Andreoli ... [et al.]. — Philadelphia: Saunders, 1985. xxxi, 2341, xcv p., 8 p. of
plates: ill. (some col.); 29 cm. Simultaneously published in 2 v. 1. Internal
medicine I. Cecil, Russell L. (Russell La Fayette), 1881-1965.
II. Wyngaarden, James B., 1924- III. Smith, Lloyd H. (Lloyd Holly), 1924-
IV. Title: Cecil Textbook of medicine.
RC46.T35 1985b      616 19      LC 84-20226      *ISBN* 0721696260

The Merck manual of diagnosis and therapy / Robert Berkow,    • **5.4755**
editor.
13th ed. — Rahway , N.J.: Published by Merck Sharp & Dohme Research
Laboratories, Division of Merck & Co., inc., 1977. 2165 p.: ill.; 20 cm.
1. Diagnosis 2. Therapeutics 3. Medicine — Handbooks, manuals, etc.
I. Merck & Co.
RC55.M4      *ISBN* 0911910026

The American Medical Association family medical guide /    **5.4756**
editor–in–chief, Jeffrey R.M. Kunz.
1st ed. — New York: Random House, c1982. 831 p.: ill.; 24 cm. (American
Medical Association home health library.) Includes indexes. 1. Medicine,
Popular I. Kunz, Jeffrey R. M. II. Series.
RC81.A543 1982      616 19      LC 82-3873      *ISBN* 0394510151

## RC86–88 Medical Emergencies. First Aid

American Medical Association.                               **5.4757**
The American Medical Association's handbook of first aid and emergency care
/ developed by the American Medical Association; medical advisors, Gail V.
Anderson, Christine E. Haycock, Stanley M. Zydlo; text by Martha Ross
Franks; ill. by Richard Lowe. — 1st ed. — New York: Random House, c1980.
xii, 234 p.: ill.; 21 cm. 1. First aid in illness and injury 2. Medical emergencies
I. Franks, Martha Ross. II. T.
RC86.7.A47 1980      616.02/52      LC 80-5310      *ISBN* 0394736680

## RC91–320 Diseases

T-W-Fiennes, Richard N. (Richard Nathaniel), 1909-.    **5.4758**
Zoonoses and the origins and ecology of human disease / by Richard N. T–W–
Fiennes. — London; New York: Academic Press, 1979 (c1978). xv, 196 p.: ill.;
23 cm. 1. Ecology 2. Zoonoses I. T.
RC112 F48      LC 77-93212      *ISBN* 0122560507

Beaver, Paul Chester, 1905-.                               **5.4759**
Clinical parasitology / Paul Chester Beaver, Rodney Clifton Jung, Eddie
Wayne Cupp. — 9th ed. — Philadelphia: Lea & Febiger, 1984. viii, 825 p.: ill.;
27 cm. Rev. ed. of: Craig and Faust's Clinical parasitology / Charles Franklin
Craig. 8th ed. 1970. 1. Medical parasitology I. Jung, Rodney Clifton, 1920-
II. Cupp, Eddie Wayne. III. Craig, Charles Franklin, 1872-1950. Craig and
Faust's Clinical parasitology. IV. T.
RC119.B35 1984      616.9/6 19      LC 83-11338      *ISBN* 0812108760

Markell, Edward K.                                         **5.4760**
Medical parasitology / Edward K. Markell, Marietta Voge, David J. John. —
6th ed. — Philadelphia: Saunders, 1986. iv, 383 p.: ill.; 27 cm. 1. Medical
parasitology I. Voge, Marietta, 1918- II. John, David T. III. T.
RC119.M3 1986      616.9/6 19      LC 85-18272      *ISBN* 072161857X

Animal agents and vectors of human disease / [edited by] Paul    **5.4761**
Chester Beaver, Rodney Clifton Jung.
5th ed. — Philadelphia: Lea & Febiger, 1985. viii, 281 p., [6] leaves of plates: ill.
(some col.); 27 cm. Rev. ed. of: Animal agents and vectors of human disease /
Ernest Carroll Faust, Paul Chester Beaver, Rodney Clifton Jung. 4th ed. 1975.
1. Medical parasitology 2. Animals as carriers of disease I. Beaver, Paul
Chester, 1905- II. Jung, Rodney Clifton, 1920- III. Faust, Ernest Carroll,
1890- Animal agents and vectors of human disease.
RC119.A54 1985      616.9/6 19      LC 85-183      *ISBN* 0812109872

Morris, R. J. (Robert John)                                **5.4762**
Cholera, 1832: the social response to an epidemic / R. J. Morris. New York:
Holmes & Meier Publishers, c1976. 228 p.: ill.; 23 cm. Includes index.
1. Cholera, Asiatic — Great Britain, 1832. I. T.
RC133.G6 M67 1976      614.5/14/0941      LC 76-25452      *ISBN*
0841902887

Collier, Richard, 1924-.                                   **5.4763**
The plague of the Spanish lady: the influenza pandemic of 1918–1919 / Richard
Collier. — 1st American ed. — New York: Atheneum, 1974. 376 p., [4] leaves
of plates: ill.; 23 cm. 1. Influenza — History. I. T.
RC150.4.C64 1974      614.5/18/09041      LC 73-91632      *ISBN*
0689105924

Brody, Saul Nathaniel.                                     **5.4764**
The disease of the soul: leprosy in medieval literature. — Ithaca [N.Y.]: Cornell
University Press, [1974] 223 p.: ill.; 23 cm. 1. Leprosy — History. 2. Leprosy
— Miscellanea. I. T.
RC154.1.B76      616.9/98/00902      LC 73-8407      *ISBN* 0801408040

Ziegler, Philip.                                           **5.4765**
The Black Death. New York, John Day Co. [1969] 319 p. map. 22 cm. 1. Black
death 2. Civilization, Medieval I. T.
RC171.Z55      940.1/7      LC 78-78627

**Cipolla, Carlo M.** 5.4766
[Chi ruppe i rastelli a Monte Lupo? English] Faith, reason, and the plague in seventeenth–century Tuscany / Carlo M. Cipolla; translated by Muriel Kittel. — Ithaca, N.Y.: Cornell University Press, 1980 (c1979). 113 p., [4] leaves of plates: ill.; 23 cm. Translation of Chi ruppe i rastelli a Monte Lupo? 1. Plague — Italy — Montelupo Fiorentino. 2. Public health — Italy — Montelupo Fiorentino — History. 3. Montelupo Fiorentino (Italy) — History — 17th century. I. T.
RC178.I9 M66213 1979     614.5/73/2/094551     LC 79-2479     ISBN 0801412307

**Hopkins, Donald R.** 5.4767
Princes and peasants: smallpox in history / Donald R. Hopkins; with a foreword by George I. Lythcott. — Chicago: University of Chicago Press, 1983. xx, 380 p., [15] pages of plates: maps, ports.; 24 cm. Includes index. 1. Smallpox — History. I. T.
RC183.1.H66 1983     614.5/21/09 19     LC 83-6472     ISBN 0226351769

### RC200–203 Venereal Diseases

**Kassler, Jeanne.** 5.4768
Gay men's health: a guide to the AID syndrome and other sexually transmitted diseases / Jeanne Kassler. — 1st ed. — New York: Harper & Row, c1983. x, 166 p.: ill.; 21 cm. Includes index. 1. Sexually transmitted diseases 2. Gay men — Diseases. 3. AIDS (Disease) I. T.
RC200.2.K37 1983     616.95/1 19     LC 82-48669     ISBN 0060910577

**Brandt, Allan M.** 5.4769
No magic bullet: a social history of venereal disease in the United States since 1880 / Allan M. Brandt. — New York: Oxford University Press, 1985. viii, 245 p., [14] p. of plates: ill.; 24 cm. 1. Sexually transmitted diseases — United States — History. I. T.
RC201.47.B73 1985     362.1/9695/100973 19     LC 84-18991     ISBN 0195034694

### RC254–282 Neoplasms. Cancer

**Cairns, John.** 5.4770
Cancer: science and society / John Cairns. — San Francisco: W. H. Freeman, c1978. xi, 199 p.: ill.; 25 cm. — (A Series of books in biology) 1. Cancer I. T.
RC261.C252     616.9/94     LC 78-16960     ISBN 0716700980

**Maugh, Thomas H.** 5.4771
Seeds of destruction: the Science report on cancer research / Thomas H. Maugh II and Jean L. Marx. — New York: Plenum Press, [1975] xiii, 251 p.: ill.; 24 cm. 'Part of the material ... originally appeared as a series in the Research News section of Science, the Journal of the American Association for the Advancement of Science.' Includes index. 1. Cancer 2. Carcinogenesis I. Marx. Jean L., joint author. II. Science. III. T.
RC261.M434     616.9/94     LC 75-15860     ISBN 0306308363

**Diet, nutrition, and cancer / Committee on Diet, Nutrition, and Cancer, Assembly of Life Sciences, National Research Council.** 5.4772
Washington, D.C.: National Academy Press, 1982. 1 v. (various pagings): ill.; 28 cm. 1. Cancer — Nutritional aspects 2. Food habits I. Assembly of Life Sciences (U.S.). Committee on Diet, Nutrition, and Cancer.
RC262.D5 1982     616.99/4071 19     LC 82-81777     ISBN 0309032806

**Concepts of oncology nursing / Donna L. Vredevoe ... [et al.] with contribution by Carol A. Brainerd.** 5.4773
Englewood Cliffs, N.J.: Prentice-Hall, c1981. xii, 401 p.; 24 cm. 1. Cancer — Nursing I. Vredevoe, Donna L.
RC266.C66     610.73/698 19     LC 80-27886     ISBN 0131665871

**Donovan, Marilee Ivers.** 5.4774
Cancer care nursing / Marilee Ivers Donovan, Sandra Erdene Girton; co-author, chapter 9—Cancer rehabilitation, Susan Dean–Baar. — 2nd ed. — Norwalk, Conn.: Appleton-Century-Crofts, c1984. x, 582 p.: ill.; 24 cm. 1. Cancer — Nursing I. Girton, Sandra Erdene. II. Dean-Baar, Susan. III. T.
RC266.D66 1984     610.73/698 19     LC 83-11771     ISBN 0838510329

**Cancer, the outlaw cell / Richard E. LaFond, editor.** 5.4775
Washington: American Chemical Society Publication, 1978. xv, 192 p.: ill.; 26 cm. 'Based on articles published in Chemistry (1977) vol. 50, no. 1-6-' 1. Cancer — Research 2. Cancer cells I. LaFond, Richard E. II. Chemistry.
RC267.C37     616.9/94     LC 78-2100     ISBN 0841204055 ISBN 0841204314 pbk

**Diet, nutrition, and cancer: a critical evaluation / editors, Bandaru S. Reddy, Leonard A. Cohen.** 5.4776
Boca Raton, Fla.: CRC Press, c1986. 2 v.: ill.; 27 cm. 1. Cancer — Nutritional aspects I. Reddy, Bandaru S. II. Cohen, Leonard A.
RC268.45.D54 1986     616.99/4 19     LC 85-15172     ISBN 0849363322

**Koocher, Gerald P.** 5.4777
The Damocles syndrome: psychosocial consequences of surviving childhood cancer / Gerald P. Koocher and John E. O'Malley. — New York: McGraw-Hill, c1981. xx, 219 p.; 24 cm. Includes indexes. 1. Tumors in children — Psychological aspects. 2. Tumors in children — Social aspects. I. O'Malley, John E. joint author. II. T.
RC281.C4 K64     362.1/9892/994 19     LC 80-22462     ISBN 0070353409

### RC311.1 Scrofula

**Bloch, Marc Léopold Benjamin, 1886-1944.** 5.4778
[Rois thaumaturges. English] The royal touch; sacred monarchy and scrofula in England and France. Translated by J. E. Anderson. [S.l.]: McGill-Queen's, 1973. xi, 441 p. illus. 25 cm. Translation of Les rois thaumaturges. 1. Royal touch I. T.
RC311.1.B5513     616.9/95/46     LC 72-91245     ISBN 0710073550

# RC321–571 Neurology and Psychiatry. Neuropsychiatry

**International encyclopedia of psychiatry, psychology, psychoanalysis & neurology / Benjamin B. Wolman, editor.** 5.4779
New York: Produced for Aesculapius Publishers by Van Nostrand Reinhold Co., c1977. 12 v.: ill.; 29 cm. 1. Psychiatry — Dictionaries. 2. Psychology — Dictionaries. 3. Psychoanalysis — Dictionaries. 4. Neurology — Dictionaries. I. Wolman, Benjamin B.
RC334.I57     616.8/9/003     LC 76-54527     ISBN 0918228018

**Rubins, Jack L.** 5.4780
Karen Horney: gentle rebel of psychoanalysis / Jack L. Rubins. — New York: Dial Press, c1978. xviii, 362 p., [8] leaves of plates: ill.; 24 cm. Includes index. 1. Horney, Karen, 1885-1952. 2. Psychoanalysts — Biography. I. T.
RC339.52.H67 R8     616.8/917/0924     LC 78-9339     ISBN 0803744250

**Evans, Richard Isadore, 1922-.** 5.4781
R. D. Laing, the man and his ideas / Richard I. Evans. — 1st ed. — New York: Dutton, 1976. lxxv, 170 p.; 21 cm. (Dialogues with notable contributors to personality theory; v. 10) Includes index. 1. Laing, R. D. (Ronald David), 1927- 2. Psychiatrists — England — Biography. 3. Psychiatry. 4. Psychology. I. Laing, R. D. (Ronald David), 1927- II. T.
RC339.52.L34 E9 1976     616.8/9/00924     LC 75-14294     ISBN 0525187650

**Biological foundations of psychiatry / edited by Robert G. Grenell, Sabit Gabay.** 5.4782
New York: Raven Press, c1976. 2 v. (xxiv, 1044 p.): ill.; 25 cm. 1. Neuropsychiatry 2. Higher nervous activity 3. Neurophysiology 4. Psychopharmacology I. Grenell, Robert G. (Robert Gordon), 1916- II. Gabay, Sabit.
RC343.B48     616.8/9/07     LC 74-15664     ISBN 0911216960

**Freud, Sigmund, 1856-1939.** • 5.4783
[Zur Geschichte der psychoanalytischen Bewegung. English] The history of the psychoanalytic movement, by Prof. Dr. Sigmund Freud ... authorized English translation by A. A. Brill ... New York, The Nervous and Mental Disease Publishing Company, 1917. 2 p.l., 58 p. 25 cm. (Nervous and mental disease monograph series, no. 25) 1. Psychoanalysis — History. I. Brill, A. A. (Abraham Arden), 1874-1948. tr. II. T. III. Series.
RC343.F75     LC 17-7058

**Horney, Karen, 1885-1952.** • 5.4784
The neurotic personality of our time, by Dr. Karen Horney. — New York: W. W. Norton & company, inc., [1937] xii, 13-299 p.; 23 cm. 'First edition.' 1. Neuroses 2. Psychoanalysis 3. Personality I. T.
RC343.H65     616.8     LC 37-3732     ISBN 0393010120

**Classics of neurology (from Emerson C. Kelly's 'Medical classics').** • 5.4785
Huntington, N.Y.: R. E. Krieger Pub. Co., 1971. v, 377 p.: illus., facsims., ports.; 24 cm. 1. Neurology 2. Neurologists I. Medical classics.
RC344.C55     616.8/08     LC 78-158127

**Davis, Joan E., 1945-.**        **5.4786**
Neurologic critical care / Joan E. Davis, Celestine B. Mason. — New York: Van Nostrand Reinhold, c1979. ix, 291 p.: ill.; 24 cm. 1. Neurological nursing 2. Critical care medicine I. Mason, Celestine B. joint author. II. T.
RC350.5.D38     610.73/6     *LC* 79-4379     *ISBN* 0442220049

**Neurologic disorders.**        **5.4787**
Springhouse, Pa.: Springhouse Corp., c1984. 192 p.: ill. (some col.); 29 cm. (Nurse's clinical library.) 'Nursing84 books.' Includes index. 1. Neurological nursing I. Series.
RC350.5.N48 1984     610.73/68 19     *LC* 84-5504     *ISBN* 0916730727

**Temkin, Owsei, 1902-.**        **5.4788**
The falling sickness; a history of epilepsy from the Greeks to the beginnings of modern neurology. 2d ed., rev. Baltimore, Johns Hopkins Press [1971] xv, 467 p. illus. 24 cm. 1. Epilepsy — History. I. T.
RC372.T45 1971     616.85/3/009     *LC* 70-139522     *ISBN* 0801812119

**McFie, John, M.D.**        **5.4789**
Assessment of organic intellectual impairment / John McFie. — London; New York: Academic Press, 1975. xii, 164 p.: ill.; 24 cm. Includes index. 1. Brain damage — Diagnosis 2. Intelligence tests 3. Brain damage — Case studies. I. T.
RC386.5.M22     616.8/5884     *LC* 75-19663     *ISBN* 0124819508

## RC423–427 SPEECH AND LANGUAGE DISORDERS

**Human communication disorders: an introduction / edited by**    **5.4790**
**George H. Shames and Elisabeth H. Wiig.**
2nd ed. — Columbus; Toronto: C.E. Merrill Pub. Co., c1986. xi, 649 p.: ill., maps. 1. Communicative disorders I. Shames, George H., 1926- II. Wiig, Elisabeth H.
RC423.H847     616.85/5     *LC* 85-43192     *ISBN* 0675205204

**Travis, Lee Edward, 1896- ed.**        ● **5.4791**
Handbook of speech pathology and audiology. — New York: Appleton-Century-Crofts, [1971] ix, 1312 p.: illus.; 26 cm. First published in 1957 under title: Handbook of speech pathology. 1. Speech, Disorders of I. T. II. Title: Speech pathology and audiology.
RC423.T67 1971     616.85/5     *LC* 74-146360     *ISBN* 0390885398

**Van Riper, Charles, 1905-.**        **5.4792**
Speech correction: an introduction to speech pathology and audiology / Charles Van Riper, Lon Emerick. — 7th ed. — Englewood Cliffs, N.J.: Prentice-Hall, c1984. xi, 468 p.: ill.; 25 cm. 1. Speech, Disorders of 2. Speech therapy 3. Audiology I. Emerick, Lon L. II. T.
RC423.V35 1984     616.8/554 19     *LC* 83-13905     *ISBN* 013829531X

**Jonas, Gerald, 1935-.**        **5.4793**
Stuttering, the disorder of many theories / Gerald Jonas. — New York: Farrar, Straus & Giroux, c1977. 67 p.; 21 cm. 'Most of the material ... first appeared in The New Yorker.' 1. Stuttering I. T.
RC424.J768 1977     616.8/554     *LC* 77-9040     *ISBN* 0374271186

**Sommers, Ronald K.**        **5.4794**
Articulation disorders / Ronald K. Sommers. — Englewood Cliffs, N.J.: Prentice-Hall, c1983. xv, 220 p.: ill.; 24 cm. — (Remediation of communication disorders.) Includes index. 1. Articulation disorders 2. Articulation disorders in children I. T. II. Series.
RC424.7.S65 1983     616.85/5 19     *LC* 82-12381     *ISBN* 0130490806

**Albert, Martin L., 1939-.**        **5.4795**
The bilingual brain: neuropsychological and neurolinguistic aspects of bilingualism / Martin L. Albert, Loraine K. Obler. — New York: Academic Press, 1978. xi, 302 p.; 24 cm. (Perspectives in neurolinguistics and psycholinguistics) Includes indexes. 1. Aphasia 2. Bilingualism — Physiological aspects. 3. Bilingualism — Psychological aspects. 4. Neurolinguistics I. Obler, Loraine K. joint author. II. T.
RC425.A43     616.8/552     *LC* 78-51243     *ISBN* 0120487500

## RC435–576 PSYCHIATRY. PSYCHOTHERAPY. PSYCHOANALYSIS. PSYCHOPATHOLOGY. MENTAL RETARDATION

### RC435–473 Psychiatry

**American handbook of psychiatry / Silvano Arieti, editor-in-**    **5.4796**
**chief.**
2nd ed. — New York: Basic Books, 1975. 6 v.: ill.; 27 cm. 1. Psychiatry — Collected works. I. Arieti, Silvano.
RC435.A562     616.8/9/008     *LC* 73-78893     *ISBN* 0465001475

**American Psychiatric Association. Joint Commission on Public**    **5.4797**
**Affairs.**
A psychiatric glossary / American Psychiatric Association; edited by a subcommittee of the Joint Commission on Public Affairs, Arnold Werner, chairman. — 5th ed. — Boston: Little, Brown, c1980. ix, 142 p.; 19 cm. Previous editions edited by the subcommittee of the Committee on Public Information. 1. Psychiatry — Dictionaries. I. Werner, Arnold, 1938- II. American Psychiatric Association. Committee on Public Information. Psychiatric glossary. III. T.
RC437.A5 1980     616.89/003/21 19     *LC* 79-55869

**Campbell, Robert Jean.**        **5.4798**
Psychiatric dictionary / Robert Jean Campbell. — 5th ed. — New York: Oxford University Press, 1981. 693 p.; 24 cm. Fourth ed. by L. E. Hinsie and R. J. Campbell. 1. Psychiatry — Dictionaries. I. Hinsie, Leland Earl, 1895- Psychiatric dictionary. II. T.
RC437.H5 1981     616.89/003/21     *LC* 80-18738     *ISBN* 0195028171

**Gross, Martin L. (Martin Louis), 1925-.**        **5.4799**
The psychological society: a critical analysis of psychiatry, psychotherapy, psychoanalysis and the psychological revolution / Martin L. Gross. — 1st ed. — New York: Random House, c1978. 369 p.; 24 cm. 1. Psychiatry — Philosophy 2. Psychology — Philosophy 3. Civilization, Modern — 20th century I. T.
RC437.5.G75     616.8/9/001     *LC* 77-90288     *ISBN* 0394462335

**Siegler, Miriam.**        **5.4800**
Models of madness, models of medicine [by] Miriam Siegler [and] Humphry Osmond. — New York: Macmillan, [1974] xxi, 287 p.; 24 cm. 1. Psychiatry — Methodology I. Osmond, Humphry. joint author. II. T.
RC437.5.S53     616.8/9/07     *LC* 74-8429     *ISBN* 0025940007

**Szasz, Thomas Stephen, 1920-.**        **5.4801**
The therapeutic state: psychiatry in the mirror of current events / Thomas Szasz. — Buffalo, N.Y.: Prometheus Books, 1984. 360 p.; 24 cm. Chiefly reprints of articles originally published 1965-1983. 1. Psychiatry — United States — Methodology — Addresses, essays, lectures. 2. Mental illness — Social aspects — Addresses, essays, lectures. I. T.
RC437.5.S927 1984     616.89 19     *LC* 83-63057     *ISBN* 0879752394

**Alexander, Franz, 1891-.**        ● **5.4802**
The history of psychiatry; an evaluation of psychiatric thought and practice from prehistoric times to the present, by Franz G. Alexander and Sheldon T. Selesnick. [1st ed.] New York, Harper & Row [1966] xvi, 471 p. illus., ports. 25 cm. 1. Psychiatry — History. I. Selesnick, Sheldon T., joint author. II. T.
RC438.A39     616.89009     *LC* 64-18048

**Hunter, Richard Alfred. ed.**        ● **5.4803**
Three hundred years of psychiatry, 1535–1860; a history presented in selected English texts [by] Richard Hunter [and] Ida Macalpine. London, New York, Oxford University Press, 1963. xxvi, 1107 p. illus., ports., facsims. 25 cm. 1. Psychiatry — Great Britain — History — Addresses, essays, lectures. 2. Psychiatry — History — Addresses, essays, lectures. 3. Psychiatry — Addresses, essays, lectures. 4. Psychology, Pathological — Addresses, essays, lectures. I. Macalpine, Ida. joint ed. II. T.
RC438.H84     616.89/00941 19     *LC* 63-2062

**MacDonald, Michael, 1945-.**        **5.4804**
Mystical Bedlam: madness, anxiety, and healing in seventeenth-century England / Michael MacDonald. — Cambridge; New York: Cambridge University Press, 1981. xvi, 323 p.: ill.; 24 cm. — (Cambridge monographs on the history of medicine.) Includes indexes. 1. Psychiatry — History — 17th century. 2. Mental illness — Great Britain — Public opinion — History — 17th century. 3. Mental illness — Great Britain — History — 17th century. 4. Family — Great Britain — History — 17th century. 5. Public opinion — Great Britain — History — 17th century. I. T. II. Series.
RC438.M27     362.2/0942 19     *LC* 80-25787     *ISBN* 0521231701

**Simon, Bennett, 1933-.**       **5.4805**
Mind and madness in ancient Greece: the classical roots of modern psychiatry / Bennett Simon. — Ithaca, N.Y.: Cornell University Press, 1978. 336 p.: ill.; 24 cm. 1. Psychology, Pathological — History. 2. Psychiatry — Greece — History. 3. Greece — Intellectual life — History. I. T.
RC438.S55     616.8/9/0938     *LC* 77-90911     *ISBN* 0801408598

**Zilboorg, Gregory, 1890-1959.**       • **5.4806**
A history of medical psychology [by] Gregory Zilboorg, M.D., in collaboration with George W. Henry, M.D. — New York: W. W. Norton & company, inc., [c1941] 606 p.: illus., ports., facsims.; 24 cm. 'First edition.' 1. Psychiatry — History. I. Henry, George William, 1889- II. T. III. Title: Medical psychology.
RC438.Z5     616.809     *LC* 41-24603

## RC439–451 Hospitals. Treatment

**Stanton, Alfred H.**       • **5.4807**
The mental hospital; a study of institutional participation in psychiatric illness and treatment [by] Alfred H. Stanton and Morris S. Schwartz. [1st ed.] New York, Basic Books [1954] xx, 492 p. diagrs., plan, tables. 24 cm. 1. Psychiatric hospital care I. Schwartz, Morris S., joint author. II. T.
RC439.S77     362.2     *LC* 54-12017

**State mental hospitals, what happens when they close / edited**       **5.4808**
**by Paul I. Ahmed and Stanley C. Plog.**
New York: Plenum Medical Book Co., c1976. xiv, 219 p.; 24 cm. — (Current topics in mental health) 1. Psychiatric hospitals 2. Community mental health services I. Ahmed, Paul I. II. Plog, Stanley C.
RC439.S78     362.1/1/0973     *LC* 76-21706     *ISBN* 0306308975

**Budson, Richard D.**       **5.4809**
The psychiatric halfway house: a handbook of theory and practice / Richard D. Budson. — Pittsburgh: University of Pittsburgh Press, c1978. xix, 278 p.: ill.; 21 cm. — (Contemporary community health series.) Includes index. 1. Mentally ill — Rehabilitation 2. Halfway houses I. T. II. Series.
RC439.5.B8     362.2/2     *LC* 77-74548     *ISBN* 0822933500

**Estroff, Sue E.**       **5.4810**
Making it crazy: an ethnography of psychiatric clients in an American community / Sue E. Estroff; foreword by H. Richard Lamb. — Berkeley: University of California Press, c1981. xxi, 328 p.: map; 24 cm. Includes index. 1. Mentally ill — Rehabilitation — United States. 2. Community mental health services — United States. 3. Sheltered workshops — United States. 4. Supplemental security income program — United States. 5. Psychiatry — Research — Field work. I. T.
RC439.5.E84     362.2/2/0973 19     *LC* 79-64660     *ISBN* 0520039637

**Grob, Gerald N., 1931-.**       **5.4811**
Mental illness and American society, 1875–1940 / Gerald N. Grob. — Princeton, N.J.: Princeton University Press, c1983. xiii, 428 p.; 25 cm. Includes index. 1. Mental illness — Treatment — United States — History. 2. Psychiatry — United States — History. 3. Mental health policy — United States — History. 4. Psychiatric hospital care — United States — History. I. T.
RC443.G75 1983     362.2/0973 19     *LC* 83-3047     *ISBN* 0691083320

**Grob, Gerald N., 1931-.**       **5.4812**
Mental institutions in America; social policy to 1875 [by] Gerald N. Grob. — New York: Free Press, [1973] xiii, 458 p.: illus.; 21 cm. 1. Mentally ill — Care and treatment — United States — History. 2. Psychiatric hospitals — United States — History. I. T.
RC443.G76     362.2/1/0973     *LC* 72-92868

### RC451.4–451.5 BY AGE, SEX, OR ETHNIC GROUP

**Mental health interventions for the aging / Arthur MacNeill**       **5.4813**
**Horton, Jr. and contributors.**
Brooklyn, N.Y.: Praeger, 1982. viii, 198 p.: ill.; 24 cm. 'A J.F. Bergin Publishers book.' 1. Geriatric psychiatry I. Horton, Arthur MacNeill, 1947-
RC451.4.A5 M455 1982     618.97/689 19     *LC* 81-10176     *ISBN* 0030616077

**Psychopathology of aging / edited by Oscar J. Kaplan.**       **5.4814**
New York: Academic Press, 1979. xiv, 316 p.; 24 cm. 1. Geriatric psychiatry I. Kaplan, Oscar J.
RC451.4.A5 P778     618.97/689 19     *LC* 79-21829     *ISBN* 0123969506

**Counseling men / edited by Thomas M. Skovholt, Paul G.**       **5.4815**
**Schauble, Richard Davis.**
Monterey, Calif.: Brooks/Cole Pub. Co., c1980. x, 207 p.; 23 cm. — (Brooks/Cole series in counseling psychology) 1. Men — Counseling of 2. Sex role

3. Men — Mental health I. Skovholt, Thomas M. II. Schauble, Paul G. III. Davis, Richard, 1945-
RC451.4.M45 C68     362.8     *LC* 79-29722     *ISBN* 0818503726

**Chesler, Phyllis.**       **5.4816**
Women and madness. — [1st ed.]. — Garden City, N.Y.: Doubleday, [1972] xxiii, 359 p.: illus.; 22 cm. 1. Women — Health and hygiene — Sociological aspects 2. Mental illness 3. Women — Psychology 4. Sex role I. T.
RC451.4.W6 C47     616.8/9     *LC* 72-76136     *ISBN* 0385026714

**Scarf, Maggie, 1932-.**       **5.4817**
Unfinished business: pressure points in the lives of women / Maggie Scarf. — 1st ed. — Garden City, N.Y.: Doubleday, 1980. xvi, 581 p.; 24 cm. Includes index. 1. Women — Mental health 2. Depression, Mental I. T.
RC451.4.W6 S34     155.6/33     *LC* 78-22352     *ISBN* 0385122489

**Women and psychotherapy: an assessment of research and**       **5.4818**
**practice / edited by Annette M. Brodsky and Rachel T. Hare–**
**Mustin.**
New York: Guilford Press, c1980. xvii, 428 p.; 24 cm. 'Based on the work of the participants in a conference held March 20-22, 1979, in Washington D.C. ... The conference was part of a contract by the National Institute of Mental Health to the American Psychological Association.' 1. Women — Mental health — Congresses. 2. Psychotherapy — Philosophy — Congresses. 3. Psychotherapy — Research — Congresses. I. Brodsky, Annette M. II. Hare-Mustin, Rachel T., 1928- III. National Institute of Mental Health (U.S.) IV. American Psychological Association.
RC451.4.W6 W65     616.89/1/088042     *LC* 80-14842     *ISBN* 0898626056

**Ethnicity and family therapy / edited by Monica McGoldrick,**       **5.4819**
**John K. Pearce and Joseph Giordano.**
New York: Guilford Press, c1982. xxiii, 600 p.; 24 cm. — (Guilford family therapy series.) 1. Family psychotherapy — United States 2. Minorities — Mental health services — United States. I. McGoldrick, Monica. II. Pearce, John K., 1935- III. Giordano, Joseph. IV. Series.
RC451.5.A2 E83 1982     616.89/156 19     *LC* 81-20198     *ISBN* 0898620406

**Mental health and people of color: curriculum development and**       **5.4820**
**change / edited by Jay C. Chunn II, Patricia J. Dunston,**
**Fariyal Ross–Sheriff.**
Washington, D.C.: Howard University Press, 1983. xxi, 472 p.: ill.; 24 cm. Cover title: Mental health & people of color. 1. Minorities — Mental health — United States — Study and teaching. 2. Mental health education — United States. I. Chunn, Jay C., 1938- II. Dunston, Patricia J., 1947- III. Ross-Sheriff, Fariyal, 1940- IV. Title: Mental health & people of color.
RC451.5.A2 M46 1983     362.2/089 19     *LC* 83-295     *ISBN* 0882580973

**Sue, Stanley.**       **5.4821**
The mental health of Asian Americans / Stanley Sue, James K. Morishima. — 1st ed. — San Francisco: Jossey-Bass, 1982. xvi, 222 p.: ill.; 24 cm. — (Jossey-Bass social and behavioral science series.) Includes index. 1. Asian Americans — Mental health 2. Asian Americans — Mental health services 3. Mental health services — United States. I. Morishima, James K. II. T. III. Series.
RC451.5.A75 S93 1982     362.2/08995073 19     *LC* 82-48060     *ISBN* 0875895352

**Behavior modification in Black populations: psychosocial issues**       **5.4822**
**and empirical findings / edited by Samuel M. Turner and**
**Russell T. Jones.**
New York: Plenum Press, c1982. xviii, 330 p.: ill.; 24 cm. 1. Afro-Americans — Mental health 2. Psychotherapy 3. Behavior modification I. Turner, Samuel M., 1944- II. Jones, Russell T., 1950-
RC451.5.N4 B43 1982     362.2/08996073 19     *LC* 82-3746     *ISBN* 0306408678

## RC454–464 General Works. Clinical Cases. Clinical Psychology

**The Harvard guide to modern psychiatry / edited by Armand**       **5.4823**
**M. Nicholi, Jr.**
Cambridge, Mass.: Belknap Press of Harvard University Press, 1978. 691 p.; 26 cm. 1. Psychiatry I. Nicholi, Armand M., 1928-
RC454.H36     616.8/9     *LC* 77-11036     *ISBN* 0674375661

**Lewis, Helen Block.**       **5.4824**
Freud and modern psychology / Helen Block Lewis. — New York: Plenum Press, c1981-c1983. 2 v.; 24 cm. — (Emotions, personality, and psychotherapy.)

1. Freud, Sigmund, 1856-1939. 2. Emotions 3. Interpersonal relations 4. Psychology, Pathological 5. Psychoanalysis I. T. II. Series.
RC454.L48 1981    616.89/001/9 19    *LC* 80-20937    *ISBN* 0306405253

**Menninger, Karl, 1893-.**      • **5.4825**
The vital balance: the life process in mental health and illness / [by] Karl Menninger with Martin Mayman and Paul Pruyser. — New York: Viking Press, [1963] 531 p.; 25 cm. 1. Psychiatry I. T.
RC454.M38    616.8/9    *LC* 63-17075

**Werlinder, Henry, 1937-.**      **5.4826**
Psychopathy: a history of the concepts: analysis of the origin and development of a family of concepts in psychopathology / Henry Werlinder. — Uppsala: Univ.; Stockholm: Almqvist & Wiksell international (distr.), 1978. 218 p.; 23 cm. — (Uppsala studies in education; 6 0347-1314) 1. Psychology, Pathological — History. I. T.
RC454.W45    616.8/582    *LC* 79-309504    *ISBN* 915540782X

**White, Robert Winthrop.**      **5.4827**
The abnormal personality / Robert W. White, Norman F. Watt. — 5th ed. — New York: Wiley, c1981. xiii, 793 p.: ill.; 24 cm. Includes indexes. 1. Psychology, Pathological 2. Psychotherapy I. Watt, Norman F. joint author. II. T.
RC454.W488 1981    157 19    *LC* 80-22055    *ISBN* 0471045993

**Eysenck, H. J. (Hans Jurgen), 1916- ed.**      **5.4828**
Handbook of abnormal psychology. Edited by H. J. Eysenck. [2d ed.] San Diego, Calif., R. R. Knapp [1973] xvi, 906 p. illus. 25 cm. 1. Psychology, Pathological 2. Psychology, Experimental I. T.
RC454.4.E95 1973    157    *LC* 72-97452    *ISBN* 0912736135

**Goldstein, Arnold P.**      **5.4829**
Structured learning therapy: toward a psychotherapy for the poor [by] Arnold P. Goldstein. New York, Academic Press, 1973. xviii, 421 p. 24 cm. 1. Psychotherapy 2. Poverty — Psychological aspects 3. Poor — Mental health services. 4. Schizophrenia I. T.
RC454.4.G64    616.8/914    *LC* 72-12197    *ISBN* 0122887506

**Park, Clara Claiborne.**      **5.4830**
You are not alone: understanding and dealing with mental illness: a guide for patients, families, doctors, and other professionals / by Clara Claiborne Park, with Leon N. Shapiro. — 1st ed. — Boston: Little, Brown, c1976. xiii, 496 p.; 24 cm. 'An Atlantic Monthly Press book.' Includes indexes. 1. Psychiatry 2. Mental health services 3. Mental health laws 4. Insurance, Mental health 5. Consumer education I. Shapiro, Leon N., joint author. II. T.
RC454.4.P37    362.2    *LC* 76-3423    *ISBN* 0316690732

**Hollingshead, August de Belmont.**      • **5.4831**
Social class and mental illness; a community study [by] August B. Hollingshead [and] Frederick C. Redlich. — New York: Wiley, [1958] ix, 442 p.: diagrs., tables.; 24 cm. 1. Mental illness 2. Social classes I. Redlich, Frederick Carl, 1910- joint author. II. T.
RC455.H6    616.8    *LC* 58-6076

**Joint Commission on Mental Illness and Health.**      • **5.4832**
Action for mental health; final report, 1961. New York, Basic Books [1961] xxxviii, 338 p. illus. 24 cm. 1. Social psychiatry — United States. 2. Psychology, Pathological — United States. I. T.
RC455.J6    131.3    *LC* 61-7488

**Myers, Jerome K. (Jerome Keeley), 1921-.**      • **5.4833**
A decade later: a follow–up of Social class and mental illness / [by] Jerome K. Meyers and Lee L. Bean; in collaboration with Max P. Pepper. — New York, Wiley [1968] xii, 250 p. 24 cm. This study is a follow-up to Social class and mental illness, by A. Hollingshead and F. Redlich, published in 1958. 1. Mental illness 2. Social classes I. Bean, Lee L. joint author. II. Pepper, Max P., joint author. III. Hollingshead, August de Belmont. Social class and mental illness. IV. T.
RC455.M87    301.47/689    *LC* 67-28949

**The Practice of mental health consultation / edited by Fortune**      **5.4834**
**V. Mannino, Beryce W. MacLennan, Milton F. Shore; foreword by Bertram S. Brown; introd. by James G. Kelley.**
New York: Gardner Press: distributed by Halsted Press, [1975] x, 255 p.; 24 cm. 1. Mental health consultation — Practice. I. Mannino, Fortune V. (Fortune Vincent), 1928- II. MacLennan, Beryce W. III. Shore, Milton F. IV. Title: Mental health consultation.
RC455.P694 1975    362.2/2    *LC* 75-25848    *ISBN* 0470567740

**Psychiatric disorder and the urban environment; report of the**      **5.4835**
**Cornell Social Science Center [i.e. Seminar] Berton H. Kaplan, editor, in collaboration with Alexander H. Leighton, Jane M. Murphy, and Nicholas Freydberg.**
New York: Behavioral Publications, [1971] x, 310 p.; 22 cm. — (Social problems series) 1. Social psychiatry 2. City and town life I. Kaplan, Berton H., 1930- ed.
RC455.P758    616.89    *LC* 77-140050    *ISBN* 0877050201

**Scheper-Hughes, Nancy.**      **5.4836**
Saints, scholars, and schizophrenics: mental illness in rural Ireland / by Nancy Scheper–Hughes. — Berkeley: University of California Press, c1979. xiv, 245 p.; 21 x 24 cm. Includes index. 1. Social psychiatry — Ireland. 2. Mental illness — Ireland — Statistics. 3. National characteristics, Irish I. T.
RC455.S27    301.29/419/6    *LC* 77-71067    *ISBN* 0520034449

**The Social setting of mental health / edited by Alfred Dean,**      **5.4837**
**Alan M. Kraft, Bert Pepper.**
New York: Basic Books, c1976. ix, 405 p.; 24 cm. 1. Social psychiatry 2. Therapeutic community 3. Mental illness — Diagnosis 4. Mental health services I. Dean, Alfred, 1933- II. Kraft, Alan M., 1925- joint author. III. Pepper, Bert, 1932- joint author.
RC455.S623    362.2/04/2    *LC* 76-3487    *ISBN* 0465079180

**Ethical issues in sex therapy and research / Reproductive**      **5.4838**
**Biology Research Foundation conference; edited by William H. Masters, Virginia E. Johnson, Robert C. Kolodny.**
1st ed. — Boston: Little, Brown, c1977. xix, 227 p.; 25 cm. Proceedings of a conference held Jan. 22-23, 1976. 1. Psychiatric ethics — Congresses. 2. Sex therapy — Congresses. 3. Psychiatry — Research — Congresses. I. Masters, William H. II. Johnson, Virginia E. III. Kolodny, Robert C. IV. Reproductive Biology Research Foundation (U.S.)
RC455.2.E8 E83    RC455.2E8 E83.    174/.2    *LC* 77-70467    *ISBN* 0316549835

**Arieti, Silvano.**      **5.4839**
On schizophrenia, phobias depression, psychotherapy, and the farther shores of psychiatry: selected papers of Silvano Arieti. — New York: Brunner/Mazel, c1978. xiv, 505 p.; 24 cm. Includes index. 1. Psychiatry — Addresses, essays, lectures. I. T.
RC458.A73    616.8/9    *LC* 77-25333    *ISBN* 0876301618

**Mental illness: changes and trends / edited by Philip Bean.**      **5.4840**
Chichester [Sussex]; New York: Wiley, c1983. xvi, 482 p.: ill.; 24 cm. 1. Mental illness — Addresses, essays, lectures. 2. Psychotherapy — Addresses, essays, lectures. 3. Mental health services — Addresses, essays, lectures. I. Bean, Philip.
RC458.M46 1983    362.2 19    *LC* 82-8603    *ISBN* 0471102407

**Sullivan, Harry Stack, 1892-1949.**      • **5.4841**
Conceptions of modern psychiatry. With a foreword by the author and a critical appraisal of the theory by Patrick Mullahy. — [2d ed.]. — New York, W. W. Norton [1961? c1953] 298 p. 22 cm. — (William Alanson White memorial lectures, 1st) 1. Psychiatry — Addresses, essays, lectures. I. Mullahy, Patrick. II. T.
RC458.S77x    616.89081    *LC* A 62-8621

**Sullivan, Harry Stack.**      • **5.4842**
Fusion of psychiatry and social science / with introd. and commentaries by Helen Swick Perry. — New York: Norton, 1964. xxxv, 346 p.: ill.; 22 cm. 1. Psychiatry — Addresses, essays, lectures. 2. Sociology — Addresses, essays, lectures. I. T.
RC458.S85 1964    301.15    *LC* 64-11151

# RC465–469 Diagnosis

**Wallerstein, Robert S.**      **5.4843**
Forty–two lives in treatment: a study of psychoanalysis and psychotherapy / by Robert S. Wallerstein. — New York: Guilford Press, c1986. xv, 784 p.; 27 cm. (Guilford psychoanalysis series.) 'The report of the Psychotherapy Research Project of the Menninger Foundation, 1954-1982.' Includes indexes. 1. Psychotherapy — Case studies. 2. Psychoanalysis — Case studies. I. Menninger Foundation. Psychotherapy Research Project. II. T. III. Series.
RC465.W35 1986    616.89/14/0926 19    *LC* 84-22409    *ISBN* 0898623251

**Allison, Joel.**      **5.4844**
The interpretation of psychological tests [by] Joel Allison, Sidney J. Blatt [and] Carl N. Zimet. New York, Harper & Row [1968] x, 342 p. illus. 22 cm. 1. Clinical psychology I. Blatt, Sidney J. (Sidney Jules). joint author. II. Zimet, Carl N., joint author. III. T.
RC467.A4 1968    155.28    *LC* 68-10801

Clinical psychology and behavioral medicine: overlapping **5.4845**
disciplines / Robert J. Gatchel, Andrew Baum, and Jerome E.
Singer (editors).
Hillsdale, N.J.: L. Erlbaum Associates, 1982. xiii, 533 p.; 24 cm. — (Handbook
of psychology and health. v. 1) 1. Clinical psychology 2. Medicine and
psychology I. Gatchel, Robert J., 1947- II. Baum, Andrew. III. Singer,
Jerome E. IV. Series.
RC467.C5x RC454.H353 vol. 1    610/.1/9 s 616.89 19    *LC* 82-1415
*ISBN* 089859183X

Reisman, John M. **5.4846**
A history of clinical psychology / by John M. Reisman. — Enl. ed. of The
development of clinical psychology. — New York: Irvington Publishers:
distributed by Halsted Press, c1976. ix, 420 p.; 24 cm. — (The Century
psychology series) 1. Clinical psychology — History. I. T.
RC467.R4 1976    616.89/009 19    *LC* 75-40102    *ISBN* 047015229X

The Broad scope of ego function assessment / edited by Leopold **5.4847**
Bellak, Lisa A. Goldsmith.
New York: Wiley, c1984. xx, 577 p.: ill.; 24 cm. — (Wiley series in general and
clinical psychiatry.) 'A Wiley-Interscience publication.' 1. Mental illness —
Diagnosis 2. Personality assessment 3. Ego (Psychology) I. Bellak, Leopold,
1916- II. Goldsmith, Lisa A. III. Series.
RC469.B76 1984    616.89/075 19    *LC* 84-3726    *ISBN* 0471891983

Rapaport, David. **5.4848**
Diagnostic psychological testing / by David Rapaport, Merton M. Gill, and
Roy Schafer; edited by Robert R. Holt. — Rev. ed. — New York: International
Universities Press, [1968] x, 562 p.; 24 cm. Revised and abridged from the
complete ed. published 1945-46. 1. Psychodiagnostics I. Schafer, Roy. joint
author. II. Gill, Merton Max, 1914- joint author. III. Holt, Robert R. ed.
IV. T.
RC469.R37    155.28    *LC* 68-16993

# RC475-489 Psychotherapy

Wolpe, Joseph. ed. • **5.4849**
The conditioning therapies: the challenge in psychotherapy / edited by Joseph
Wolpe, Andrew Salter [and] L. J. Reyna. — New York: Holt, Rinehart and
Winston [1964] viii, 192 p.: ill.; 24 cm. Papers of the University of Virginia
conference held April, 1962. 1. Behavior therapy — Congresses.
2. Psychotherapy — Congresses. I. University of Virginia. II. T.
RC475.W65    151.3    *LC* 64-18610

Driscoll, Richard. **5.4850**
Pragmatic psychotherapy / Richard Driscoll. — New York: Van Nostrand
Reinhold, c1984. xii, 266 p.; 24 cm. Includes index. 1. Psychotherapy I. T.
RC480.D74 1984    616.89/14 19    *LC* 83-10422    *ISBN* 0442219830

Frank, Jerome David, 1909-. **5.4851**
Persuasion and healing; a comparative study of psychotherapy [by] Jerome D.
Frank. Rev. ed. Baltimore, Johns Hopkins University Press [1973] xx, 378 p. 24
cm. 1. Psychotherapy I. T.
RC480.F67 1973    616.89/14 19    *LC* 72-4015    *ISBN* 080181443X

Fromm-Reichmann, Frieda. • **5.4852**
Principles of intensive psychotherapy. Chicago: U.of Chicago P., 1950. 245p.
1. Psychotherapy 2. Psychiatrists I. T.
RC480.F7x    616.8    *LC* 50-9782    *ISBN* 0226265986

Haley, Jay. **5.4853**
Ordeal therapy / Jay Haley. — 1st ed. — San Francisco: Jossey-Bass, 1984. xiv,
213 p.; 24 cm. — (Jossey-Bass social and behavioral science series.) Includes
index. 1. Psychotherapy 2. Family psychotherapy 3. Psychotherapy, Brief
I. T. II. Series.
RC480.H26 1984    616.89/14 19    *LC* 83-49262    *ISBN* 0875895956

Handbook of psychotherapy and behavior change / editors, Sol **5.4854**
L. Garfield, Allen E. Bergin.
3rd ed. — New York: Wiley, c1986. xvi, 886 p.: ill.; 26 cm. 1. Psychotherapy
2. Psychotherapy — Research I. Garfield, Sol L. (Sol Louis), 1918- II. Bergin,
Allen E., 1934-
RC480.H286 1986    616.89/14 19    *LC* 86-7817    *ISBN* 0471799955

Mahrer, Alvin R. • **5.4855**
The goals of psychotherapy, edited by Alvin R. Mahrer. — New York:
Appleton-Century-Crofts, [1967] viii, 301 p.; 24 cm. — (The Century
psychology series) 1. Psychotherapy I. T.
RC480.M33    616.89    *LC* 66-29064

Meltzoff, Julian. • **5.4856**
Research in psychotherapy [by] Julian Meltzoff and Melvin Kornreich. — [1st
ed.]. — New York: Atherton Press, 1970. ix, 561 p.; 24 cm. 1. Psychotherapy
— Research I. Kornreich, Melvin, joint author. II. T.
RC480.M45    616.89/1    *LC* 74-105610

Sifneos, Peter E. (Peter Emanuel), 1920-. • **5.4857**
Short-term psychotherapy and emotional crisis [by] Peter E. Sifneos.
Cambridge, Mass., Harvard University Press, 1972. xvii, 299 p. 22 cm.
1. Psychotherapy, Brief 2. Anxiety I. T.
RC480.S46    616.8/914    *LC* 78-172323    *ISBN* 0674807200

Tennov, Dorothy. **5.4858**
Psychotherapy: the hazardous cure / by Dorothy Tennov. — New York:
Abelard-Schuman, [1975] xviii, 314 p.; 24 cm. Includes index.
1. Psychotherapy I. T.
RC480.T44 1975    616.8/914    *LC* 75-9856    *ISBN* 0200040286

Truax, Charles B. • **5.4859**
Toward effective counseling and psychotherapy: training and practice, by
Charles B. Truax and Robert R. Carkhuff. — Chicago: Aldine Pub. Co., [1967]
xiv, 416 p.: illus.; 24 cm. — (Modern applications in psychology)
1. Psychotherapy 2. Counseling I. Carkhuff, Robert R. joint author. II. T.
RC480.T7    616.89    *LC* 66-15211

Bockoven, J. Sanbourne. • **5.4860**
Moral treatment in community mental health, by J. Sanbourne Bockoven. —
New York: Springer Pub. Co., [1972] xi, 305 p.; 22 cm. An enl. ed. of the
author's Moral treatment in American psychiatry, published in 1963.
1. Psychotherapy — History. 2. Community mental health services —
History. 3. Psychotherapy ethics — History. I. T.
RC480.5.B6 1972    362.2/0425    *LC* 70-189446    *ISBN* 0826112803

Gottman, John Mordechai. **5.4861**
How to do psychotherapy and how to evaluate it: a manual for beginners [by]
John Mordechai Gottman [and] Sandra Risa Leiblum. With pref. by Leonard
Ullmann. New York: Holt, Rinehart and Winston, [1974] viii, 184 p.: illus.; 23
cm. — (The Person in psychology series) 1. Psychotherapy — Evaluation.
I. Leiblum, Sandra Risa. joint author. II. T.
RC480.5.G64    616.8/914    *LC* 73-15978    *ISBN* 003007651X

Hart, Joseph Truman, 1937-. **5.4862**
Modern eclectic therapy: a functional orientation to counseling and
psychotherapy: including a twelve-month manual for therapists / Joseph Hart;
with the assistance of John Hart. — New York: Plenum Press, c1983. xiv,
394 p.: ill.; 24 cm. Includes index. 1. Psychology, Pathological — Eclectic
treatment. 2. Functionalism (Psychology) 3. Counseling 4. Psychotherapy
I. T.
RC480.5.H343 1983    616.89/14 19    *LC* 83-11088    *ISBN*
0306412136

The History of psychotherapy: from healing magic to encounter **5.4863**
/ edited by Jan Ehrenwald.
New York: J. Aronson, c1976. 589 p.; 24 cm. Includes index. 1. Psychotherapy
— History. 2. Psychotherapy I. Ehrenwald, Jan, 1900-
RC480.5.H54    616.8/914/09    *LC* 76-26565    *ISBN* 0876682808

Kadushin, Charles. • **5.4864**
Why people go to psychiatrists. — [1st ed.]. — New York: Atherton Press,
1969. x, 373 p.: illus.; 25 cm. 1. Mental illness 2. Psychotherapy I. T.
RC480.5.K32    616.89/1    *LC* 68-16405

Paul, Gordon L. **5.4865**
Insight vs. desensitization in psychotherapy: an experiment in anxiety reduction
/ Gordon L. Paul. —. Stanford, Calif.: Stanford U.P., 1966. 148 p.: ill.; 23 cm.
"Based on the author's doctoral dissertation in psychology for the University of
Illinios." 1. Psychotherapy 2. Anxiety I. T.
RC480.5.P33    616.891    *LC* 65-26824

Perls, Frederick S. • **5.4866**
Gestalt therapy verbatim [by] Frederick S. Perls. Compiled and edited by John
O. Stevens. — [Lafayette, Calif.: Real People Press, 1969] 279 p.; 24 cm.
1. Gestalt therapy I. T.
RC480.P45    150.19/82    *LC* 79-80835    *ISBN* 0911226028

Reynolds, David K. **5.4867**
The quiet therapies: Japanese pathways to personal growth / David K.
Reynolds; afterword by George DeVos. — Honolulu: University Press of
Hawaii, c1980. viii, 135 p.: ill.; 22 cm. 1. Psychotherapy 2. Psychotherapy —
Japan I. T.
RC480.5.R39    616.89/14/0952    *LC* 80-17611    *ISBN* 0824806905

**Rogers, Carl R. (Carl Ransom), 1902-.**                    • 5.4868
On becoming a person: a therapist's view of psychotherapy. — Boston:
Houghton Mifflin [1961] 420 p.: ill.; 23 cm. 1. Client-centered psychotherapy
I. T.
RC480.5.R62        131.322      *LC* 61-4718

**Zilbergeld, Bernie.**                                       5.4869
The shrinking of America: myths of psychological change / Bernie Zilbergeld.
— 1st ed. — Boston: Little, Brown, c1983. 307 p.; 24 cm. Includes index.
1. Psychotherapy — United States. 2. Personality change 3. Psychotherapy
— Evaluation. 4. United States — Social conditions I. T.
RC480.5.Z54 1983        616.89/14 19        *LC* 82-21712        *ISBN*
0316987948

**Golan, Naomi.**                                             5.4870
Passing through transitions: a guide for practitioners / Naomi Golan. — New
York: Free Press; London: Collier Macmillan Publishers, c1981. xxii, 330 p.; 24
cm. Includes index. 1. Crisis intervention (Psychiatry) 2. Adulthood —
Psychological aspects. I. T.
RC480.6.G63        158/.3 19        *LC* 80-70837        *ISBN* 0029120705

**Golan, Naomi.**                                             5.4871
Treatment in crisis situations / Naomi Golan. — New York: Free Press, c1978.
xv, 266 p.; 22 cm. — (Treatment approaches in the human services.) Includes
index. 1. Crisis intervention (Psychiatry) I. T. II. Series.
RC480.6.G64        362.2      *LC* 77-85350        *ISBN* 0029120608

**Handbook of interpersonal psychotherapy / edited by Jack C.**    5.4872
**Anchin, Donald J. Kiesler.**
New York: Pergamon Press, c1982. xxi, 346 p.: ill.; 26 cm. — (Pergamon
general psychology series. 101) 1. Psychotherapist and patient
2. Psychotherapy I. Anchin, Jack C. (Jack Charles), 1951- II. Kiesler, Donald
J. III. Series.
RC480.8.H36 1982        616.89/14 19        *LC* 81-8499        *ISBN* 0080259596

## RC481–499 SPECIAL THERAPIES

**Rogers, Carl R. (Carl Ransom), 1902-.**                    • 5.4873
Client–centered therapy, its current practice, implications, and theory, by Carl
R. Rogers, with chapters contributed by Elaine Dorfman, Thomas Gordon
[and] Nicholas Hobbs. Boston, Houghton Mifflin [1951] xii, 560 p. 23 cm. (The
Houghton Mifflin psychological series) 1. Client-centered psychotherapy I. T.
RC481.R55x        616.8      *LC* 51-9139

**Rogers, Carl R. (Carl Ransom), 1902-.**                    • 5.4874
Counseling and psychotherapy; newer concepts in practice, by Carl R. Rogers.
Boston, New York [etc.] Houghton Mifflin company [1942] xiv, 450 p. 23 cm.
'Under the editorship of Leonard Carmichael.' 1. Client-centered
psychotherapy I. Carmichael, Leonard, 1898- ed. II. T.
RC481.R59        616.89/17 19        *LC* 42-24693

**Rogers, Carl R. (Carl Ransom), 1902-.**                    • 5.4875
Person to person: the problem of being human; a new trend in psychology [by]
Carl R. Rogers and Barry Stevens. With contributions from: Eugene T.
Gendlin, John M. Shlien [and] Wilson Van Dusen. [Walnut Creek, Calif., Real
People Press, 1967] 276 p. 23 cm. 1. Client-centered psychotherapy —
Addresses, essays, lectures. 2. Psychology — Addresses, essays, lectures.
I. Stevens, Barry, 1902- joint author. II. T.
RC481.R6        616.89/1        *LC* 67-26674

**Legal and ethical issues in human research and treatment:**    5.4876
**psychopharmacologic considerations / edited by Donald M.**
**Gallant and Robert Force.**
Jamaica, N.Y.: Spectrum Publications; New York: distributed by Halsted
Press, c1978. 186 p.; 24 cm. Papers of a symposium sponsored by the American
College of Neuropsychopharmacology and held in Dec. 17, 1976.
1. Psychopharmacology — Congresses. 2. Psychiatric ethics — Congresses.
3. Psychiatry — Research — Law and legislation — United States —
Congresses. 4. Informed consent (Medical law) — United States —
Congresses. I. Gallant, Donald M., 1929- II. Force, Robert, 1934-
III. American College of Neuropsychopharmacology.
RC483.L38        615/.78/072      *LC* 77-12628        *ISBN* 0893350397. *ISBN*
0470263547

**Janosik, Ellen Hastings.**                                  5.4877
Life cycle group work in nursing / Ellen Hastings Janosik, Lenore Bolling
Phipps. — Monterey, Calif.: Wadsworth Health Sciences Division, c1982. xviii,
394 p.: ill.; 24 cm. 1. Group psychotherapy 2. Psychiatric nursing I. Phipps,
Lenore Bolling. II. T.
RC488.J36 1982        616.89/152 19        *LC* 80-71075        *ISBN* 0534010970

**Kaplan, Harold I., 1927-.**                                 • 5.4878
Comprehensive group psychotherapy, edited by Harold I. Kaplan [and]
Benjamin J. Sadock. Baltimore, Williams & Wilkins, 1971. xvi, 911 p. illus. 26
cm. 1. Group psychotherapy I. Sadock, Benjamin J., 1933- joint author. II. T.
RC488.K36        616.89/15        *LC* 70-155935

**Rose, Sheldon D.**                                          5.4879
Group therapy: a behavioral approach / Sheldon D. Rose. Englewood Cliffs,
N.J.: Prentice-Hall, c1977. xi, 308 p.: ill.; 24 cm. Includes indexes. 1. Group
psychotherapy 2. Behavior therapy I. T.
RC488.R65        616.8/915        *LC* 76-27689        *ISBN* 0133652394

**Families of the slums; an exploration of their structure and**    • 5.4880
**treatment [by] Salvador Minuchin [and others]**
New York, Basic Books [1967] xiv, 460 p. illus. 25 cm. 'Grew out of a research
project in family therapy conducted at the Wiltwyck School for Boys.'
1. Family psychotherapy 2. Problem families I. Minuchin, Salvador.
II. Wiltwyck School for Boys, Esopus, N.Y.
RC488.5.F3        362.8/2      *LC* 67-28507

**Family therapy: theory and practice / edited by Philip J.**    5.4881
**Guerin, Jr., for American Orthopsychiatric Association.**
New York: Gardner Press: distributed by Halsted Press, c1976. xi, 553 p.: ill.;
24 cm. 1. Family psychotherapy I. Guerin, Philip J. II. American
Orthopsychiatric Association.
RC488.5.F35        616.8/915        *LC* 76-8409        *ISBN* 0470150890

**Marriage and marital therapy: psychoanalytic, behavioral, and**    5.4882
**systems theory perspectives / edited by Thomas J. Paolino, Jr.,**
**and Barbara S. McCrady.**
New York: Brunner/Mazel, c1978. xxiii, 586 p.: ill.; 24 cm. 1. Marital
psychotherapy — Addresses, essays, lectures. 2. Psychoanalysis — Addresses,
essays, lectures. 3. Behaviorism (Psychology) — Addresses, essays, lectures.
4. Social systems — Addresses, essays, lectures. 5. Marriage — Addresses,
essays, lectures. I. Paolino, Thomas J., 1940- II. McCrady, Barbara S.
RC488.5.M365        362.8/286 19        *LC* 78-17398        *ISBN* 0876301715

**Minuchin, Salvador.**                                       5.4883
Family therapy techniques / Salvador Minuchin, H. Charles Fishman. —
Cambridge, Mass.: Harvard University Press, 1981. 303 p.; 24 cm. 1. Family
psychotherapy I. Fishman, H. Charles (Herman Charles), 1946- joint author.
II. T.
RC488.5.M56        616.89/156 19        *LC* 80-25392        *ISBN* 0674294106

**Nichols, Michael P.**                                       5.4884
Family therapy, concepts and methods / Michael P. Nichols; with a foreword
by Philip J. Guerin, Jr. and David R. Chabot. — New York: Gardner Press,
c1984. xvii, 609 p.: ill.; 24 cm. 1. Family psychotherapy I. T.
RC488.5.N53 1984        616.89/156 19        *LC* 83-16492        *ISBN*
0898760933

**Papp, Peggy.**                                              5.4885
The process of change / Peggy Papp; foreword by Donald A. Bloch. — New
York: Guilford Press, c1983. xv, 248 p.; 24 cm. — (Guilford family therapy
series.) Includes index. 1. Family psychotherapy 2. Change (Psychology) I. T.
II. Series.
RC488.5.P36 1983        616.89/156 19        *LC* 83-12814        *ISBN*
089862052X

## RC489 Special Therapies, A–Z

**Feder, Elaine.**                                            5.4886
The expressive arts therapies / Elaine & Bernard Feder. — Englewood Cliffs,
N.J.: Prentice-Hall, c1981. vi, 249 p.: ill.; 24 cm. — (A Spectrum book) 1. Art
therapy 2. Music therapy 3. Dance therapy I. Feder, Bernard. joint author.
II. T.
RC489.A7 F43        616.89/165 19        *LC* 80-23887        *ISBN* 0132980428

**Ayllon, Teodoro, 1929-.**                                   • 5.4887
The token economy: a motivational system for therapy and rehabilitation / [by]
Teodoro Ayllon [and] Nathan Azrin.— New York: Appleton-Century-Crofts,
[1968] viii, 288 p.; 21 cm. — (The Century psychology series) 1. Token
economy (Psychology) I. Azrin, Nathan H., 1930- joint author. II. T.
RC489.B4 A9        616.89/1        *LC* 69-12160

**Bandura, Albert, 1925-.**                                   • 5.4888
Principles of behavior modification. — New York: Holt, Rinehart and Winston,
[1969] ix, 677 p.: illus.; 24 cm. 1. Behavior therapy 2. Personality change I. T.
RC489.B4 B3        616.89/1        *LC* 74-81173        *ISBN* 0030811511

**Erwin, Edward, 1937-.**                                     5.4889
Behavior therapy: scientific, philosophical, and moral foundations / Edward
Erwin. — Cambridge; New York: Cambridge University Press, 1978. 250 p.

1. Behavior therapy 2. Behavior therapy — Philosophy. 3. Psychiatric ethics I. T.
RC489.B4 E77    616.8/914    *LC* 78-17623    *ISBN* 0521222931

**Ballou, Mary B., 1949-.**                  **5.4890**
A feminist position on mental health / by Mary Ballou and Nancy W. Gabalac, with David Kelley. — Springfield, Ill.: Thomas, c1985. ix, 180 p.; 24 cm. Includes index. 1. Feminist therapy 2. Women — Mental health 3. Women — Psychology I. Gabalac, Nancy W. II. Kelley, David. III. T.
RC489.F45 B35 1985    616.89/14/088042 19    *LC* 84-8495    *ISBN* 0398050406

**Eichenbaum, Luise.**                     **5.4891**
Understanding women: a feminist psychoanalytic approach / Luise Eichenbaum, Susie Orbach. — New York: Basic Books, c1983. xi, 212 p.; 22 cm. Expanded version of: Outside in, inside out. 1982. Includes index. 1. Feminist therapy 2. Psychoanalysis — Social aspects. 3. Women and psychoanalysis I. Orbach, Susie, 1946- II. T.
RC489.F45 E38 1983    616.89/14/088042 19    *LC* 82-72545    *ISBN* 0465088643

**Perls, Frederick S.**                     **5.4892**
[Gestalt approach] The gestalt approach & Eye witness to therapy, by Fritz Perls. [Ben Lomond, Calif.,] Science & Behavior Books [1973] xv, 206 p. 25 cm. Two books on which the author was working at the time of his death, published as one. 1. Gestalt therapy I. Perls, Frederick S. Eye witness to therapy. 1973. II. T. III. Title: Eye witness to therapy.
RC489.G4 P47 1973    616.8/914    *LC* 73-76971    *ISBN* 083140034X

**Meditation, classic and contemporary perspectives / Deane H.**    **5.4893**
**Shapiro, Jr., Roger N. Walsh, editors.**
New York: Aldine Pub. Co., c1984. xxii, 722 p.: ill.; 27 cm. Includes index. 1. Meditation — Therapeutic use. I. Shapiro, Deane H. II. Walsh, Roger N.
RC489.M43 M43 1984    615.8/51 19    *LC* 84-300    *ISBN* 0202251365

**Greenberg, Ira A., 1924- comp.**             **5.4894**
Psychodrama: theory and therapy, edited by Ira A. Greenberg. — New York: Behavioral Publications, 1974. xvi, 496 p.; 22 cm. 1. Psychodrama I. T.
RC489.P7 G72    616.8/915    *LC* 73-20227    *ISBN* 0877051100

**Handbook of rational–emotive therapy / Albert Ellis and**    **5.4895**
**Russell Grieger, with contributors.**
New York: Springer Pub. Co., c1977-<c1986 >. v. <1-2 >; 23 cm. 1. Rational-emotive psychotherapy I. Ellis, Albert. II. Grieger, Russell.
RC489.R3 H36    616.8/914    *LC* 77-21410    *ISBN* 0826122000

**Berne, Eric.**                         **5.4896**
What do you say after you say hello? The psychology of human destiny. — New York: Grove Press, [1972] xvii, 457 p.: illus.; 24 cm. 1. Transactional analysis I. T.
RC489.T7 B47    301.11/2    *LC* 77-187888    *ISBN* 0394479955

**Transactional analysis after Eric Berne: teachings and practices**    **5.4897**
**of three TA schools / Graham Barnes, editor; contributors,**
**Michael Brown ... [et al.].**
New York: Harper's College Press, c1977. xv, 543 p.: ill.; 25 cm. Includes index. 1. Transactional analysis I. Barnes, Graham. II. Brown, Michael, 1947-
RC489.T7 T69    158    *LC* 77-4754    *ISBN* 0061684120

## RC490–495 Hypnosis

**Ericksonian approaches to hypnosis and psychotherapy / edited**    **5.4898**
**by Jeffrey K. Zeig.**
New York: Brunner/Mazel, c1982. xxvi, 518 p.: ill.; 24 cm. Proceedings of the International Congress on Ericksonian Approaches to Hypnosis and Psychotherapy, held Dec. 3-8, 1980, in Phoenix, Ariz. 1. Erickson, Milton H — Congresses. 2. Hypnotism — Therapeutic use — Congresses. 3. Psychotherapy — Congresses. I. Zeig, Jeffrey K., 1947- II. International Congress on Ericksonian Approaches to Hypnosis and Psychotherapy (1980: Phoenix, Ariz.)
RC490.5.E75 E75    616.89/14 19    *LC* 81-18115    *ISBN* 0876302762

**Ambrose, Gordon.**                    • **5.4899**
A handbook of medical hypnosis; an introduction for practitioners and students [by] Gordon Ambrose [and] George Newbold. — 3d ed. — Baltimore: Williams and Wilkins Co., [1968] xiv, 312 p.; 22 cm. 1. Hypnotism — Therapeutic use I. Newbold, George, joint author. II. T. III. Title: Medical hypnosis.
RC495.A5x    615/.8512    *LC* 68-5920    *ISBN* 0702002311

**Barber, Theodore Xenophon, 1927-.**          **5.4900**
Hypnosis, imagination, and human potentialities [by] Theodore X. Barber, Nicholas P. Spanos, and John F. Chaves. New York, Pergamon Press [1974] ix, 189 p. 23 cm. (Pergamon general psychology series, 46) 1. Hypnotism —

Therapeutic use I. Spanos, Nicholas P., joint author. II. Chaves, John F., joint author. III. T.
RC495.B34 1974    615/.8512    *LC* 73-19539    *ISBN* 0080179320
*ISBN* 0080179312

## RC500–509 Psychoanalysis

**Rapaport, David. ed. and tr.**               • **5.4901**
Organization and pathology of thought: selected sources. — New York: Columbia University Press, 1951. xviii, 786 p.; 24 cm. (Austen Riggs Foundation. Monograph no. 1) Bibliography: p. [731]-770. 1. Psychoanalysis — Collected works. 2. Thought and thinking I. T.
RC501.R3    153.082    *LC* 51-10861 rev

**Brenner, Charles, 1913-.**                • **5.4902**
An elementary textbook of psychoanalysis. — Rev. ed. — New York: International Universities Press, [1973] ix, 280 p.; 23 cm. 1. Psychoanalysis I. T.
RC504.B74 1973    616.8/917    *LC* 72-86658    *ISBN* 0823616207

**Fancher, Raymond E.**                 • **5.4903**
Psychoanalytic psychology; the development of Freud's thought [by] Raymond E. Fancher. — [1st ed.] — New York: Norton, [1973] xi, 241 p.: illus.; 21 cm. 1. Freud, Sigmund, 1856-1939. 2. Psychoanalysis I. T.
RC504.F32 1973    616.8/917/0924    *LC* 73-1273    *ISBN* 0393011011

**Kernberg, Otto F., 1928-.**                **5.4904**
Object–relations theory and clinical psychoanalysis / Otto F. Kernberg. — New York: J. Aronson, c1976. 299 p.; 24 cm. (Classical psychoanalysis and its applications) Includes index. 1. Psychoanalysis 2. Object relations (Psychoanalysis) I. T.
RC504.K47    150/.19/5    *LC* 75-42548    *ISBN* 0876682476

**Luborsky, Lester, 1920-.**                **5.4905**
Principles of psychoanalytic psychotherapy: a manual for supportive-expressive treatment / Lester Luborsky. — New York: Basic Books, c1984. xxiv, 270 p.: ill.; 22 cm. Includes index. 1. Psychoanalysis 2. Supportive psychotherapy I. T.
RC504.L83 1984    616.89/17 19    *LC* 83-45377    *ISBN* 0465063284

**Menninger, Karl, 1893-.**                • **5.4906**
Theory of psychoanalytic technique. — New York: Basic Books, [1958] 206 p.: illus.; 25 cm. — (Menninger Clinic monograph series, no. 12) 1. Psychoanalysis I. T. II. Series.
RC504.M4 1958    131.342    *LC* 58-9932

**Reich, Wilhelm, 1897-1957.**              **5.4907**
[Charakteranalyse. English] Character analysis. Newly translated by Vincent R. Carfagno. 3d, enl. ed. New York, Farrar, Straus and Giroux [1972] xxvii, 545 p. illus. 21 cm. Translation of Charakteranalyse, and of Psychischer Kontakt und vegetative Strömung. To these have been added two articles: The expressive language of the living, and The schizophrenic split. 1. Psychoanalysis 2. Sex (Psychology) I. T.
RC504.R4513 1972    150/.19/5    *LC* 70-163663    *ISBN* 0374120749

**Weiss, Joseph, 1924-.**                 **5.4908**
The psychoanalytic process: theory, clinical observation, and empirical research / Joseph Weiss, Harold Sampson, and the Mount Zion Psychotherapy Research Group; foreword by Morris N. Eagle. — New York: Guilford Press, c1986. xxiii, 423 p.; 24 cm. Includes index. 1. Psychoanalysis 2. Psychoanalysis — Research. I. Sampson, Harold. II. Mount Zion Psychotherapy Research Group. III. T.
RC504.W45 1986    150.19/5 19    *LC* 85-30548    *ISBN* 0898626706

**Wolman, Benjamin B.**                • **5.4909**
Psychoanalytic techniques: a handbook for the practicing psychoanalyst / edited by Benjamin B. Wolman. — New York: Basic Books, [1967] x, 596 p.; 25 cm. 1. Psychoanalysis I. T.
RC504.W55    616.89/17    *LC* 67-19469

**Empirical studies of psychoanalytical theories / edited by**    **5.4910**
**Joseph Masling.**
Hillsdale, N.J.: Analytic Press: Distributed by L. Erlbaum, 1983-. v. <1 >: ill.; 24 cm. 1. Psychoanalysis — Research. I. Masling, Joseph M.
RC506.E46 1983    150.19/5 19    *LC* 82-11536    *ISBN* 0881630004

**Freud, Sigmund, 1856-1939.**             • **5.4911**
[Correspondence. English] The Freud/Jung letters; the correspondence between Sigmund Freud and C. G. Jung. Edited by William McGuire. Translated by Ralph Manheim and R. F. C. Hull. [Princeton, N.J.] Princeton University Press [1974] xlii, 650 p. illus. 25 cm. (Bollingen series. 94) 'Translated from the unpublished letters in German.' 1. Freud, Sigmund, 1856-1939. 2. Jung, C. G. (Carl Gustav), 1875-1961. 3. Psychoanalysts —

Europe — Correspondence. I. Jung, C. G. (Carl Gustav), 1875-1961.
II. McGuire, William, 1917- ed. III. T. IV. Series.
RC506.F69713     150.19/52 B 19     *LC* 76-166373     *ISBN* 0691098905

**Kohut, Heinz.**            **5.4912**
The analysis of the self; a systematic approach to the psychoanalytic treatment of narcissistic personality disorders. — New York: International Universities Press, [1971] xvi, 368 p.; 23 cm. — (The Psychoanalytic study of the child. Monograph no. 4) 1. Transference (Psychology) 2. Narcissism 3. Personality, Disorders of I. T. II. Series.
RC506.K64     616.85/83     *LC* 70-143392

**Schlessinger, Nathan.**         **5.4913**
A developmental view of the psychoanalytic process: follow–up studies and their consequences / by Nathan Schlessinger, Fred P. Robbins. — New York, N.Y.: International Universities Press, c1983. viii, 228 p.; 23 cm. Includes index. 1. Psychoanalysis — Longitudinal studies. I. Robbins, Fred P. II. T.
RC506.S297 1983     616.89/17 19     *LC* 83-225     *ISBN* 0823612570

**Spence, Donald P.**           **5.4914**
Narrative truth and historical truth: meaning and interpretation in psychoanalysis / Donald P. Spence. — 1st ed. — New York: W.W. Norton, c1982. 320 p.; 22 cm. Includes index. 1. Psychoanalytic interpretation 2. Meaning (Psychology) 3. Truth — Psychological aspects. 4. Psychotherapist and patient 5. Psychotherapy — Research I. T.
RC506.S66 1982     150.19/5 19     *LC* 81-22311     *ISBN* 0393015882

**Abraham, Karl, 1877-1925.**       **5.4915**
[Selections. English.] Clinical papers and essays on psycho–analysis / by Karl Abraham; with a pref. by Ernest Jones; edited by Hilda C. Abraham; translated by Hilda C. Abraham and D. R. Ellison with the assistance of Hilda Maas and Anna Hackel. — New York: Brunner/Mazel, [1979] c1955. 336 p., [1] leaf of plates: ill.; 23 cm. — (Brunner/Mazel classics in psychoanalysis; no. 4) Reprint of the ed. published by Hogarth Press, London, which was issued as no. 49 in The International psycho-analytical library. 1. Psychoanalysis — Addresses, essays, lectures. I. Abraham, Hilda C. II. T. III. Series.
RC509.A3213 1979     616.89/17 19     *LC* 79-11099     *ISBN* 087630207X

**Classics in psychoanalytic technique / Robert Langs, ed.**      **5.4916**
New York: J. Aronson, c1981. xii, 523 p. — (Classical psychoanalysis and its applications.) 1. Psychoanalysis 2. Transference (Psychology) 3. Psychotherapy 4. Psychotherapist and patient I. Langs, Robert, 1928- II. Series.
RC509.C5x     *LC* 80-66919     *ISBN* 0876684177

**Freud, Anna, 1895-.**          • **5.4917**
The psycho–analytical treatment of children: technical lectures and essays / Pt. 1 and 2 translated from the German by Nancy Procter–Gregg. — New York: International Universities Press, [1959, c1946] 98 p. 1. Psychoanalysis — Addresses, essays, lectures. 2. Child psychiatry I. T.
RC509.F7 1959     *LC* 60-43246

**Schafer, Roy.**            **5.4918**
The analytic attitude / Roy Schafer. — New York: Basic Books, c1983. xiv, 316 p.; 24 cm. Includes index. 1. Psychoanalysis — Addresses, essays, lectures. I. T.
RC509.S347 1983     616.89/17 19     *LC* 82-16245     *ISBN* 0465002676

**Schafer, Roy.**            **5.4919**
Language and insight / Roy Schafer. — New Haven: Yale University Press, 1978. xiv, 208 p.; 21 cm. — (The Sigmund Freud memorial lectures; 1975-1976) Includes index. 1. Psychoanalysis — Addresses, essays, lectures. 2. Psycholinguistics — Addresses, essays, lectures. 3. Insight in psychotherapy — Addresses, essays, lectures. I. T. II. Series.
RC509.S35     616.8/917     *LC* 77-20940     *ISBN* 0300021739

**From group dynamics to group psychoanalysis: therapeutic**     **5.4920**
**applications of group dynamic understanding / edited by Morton Kissen.**
Washington: Hemisphere Pub. Corp.; New York: distributed solely by Halsted Press, c1976. xv, 362 p.; 24 cm. (The Series in clinical and community psychology) Includes indexes. 1. Group psychoanalysis 2. Small groups I. Kissen, Morton.
RC510.F76     616.8/915     *LC* 76-14844     *ISBN* 0470151323

## RC512–553 Psychopathology. Psychoses. Neuroses

**Bowers, Malcolm B.**           **5.4921**
Retreat from sanity; the structure of emerging psychosis [by] Malcolm B. Bowers, Jr. — New York: Human Sciences Press, [1974] 245 p.; 22 cm. 1. Psychoses I. T.
RC512.B67     616.8/9     *LC* 73-20296     *ISBN* 0877051348

**Frosch, John.**            **5.4922**
The psychotic process / John Frosch. — New York: International Universities Press, c1983. xiii, 521 p.; 24 cm. Includes index. 1. Psychoses 2. Psychoanalysis I. T.
RC512.F76 1983     616.89 19     *LC* 82-21392     *ISBN* 082365690X

**Arieti, Silvano.**           **5.4923**
Interpretation of schizophrenia / Silvano Arieti. — 2nd ed., completely rev. and expanded. — New York: Basic Books, c1974. xvii, 756 p.: ill.; 25 cm. 1. Schizophrenia I. T.
RC514.A7 1974     616.8/982     *LC* 73-91078     *ISBN* 0465034292

**Bernheim, Kayla F.**          **5.4924**
Schizophrenia: symptoms, causes, treatments / Kayla F. Bernheim, Richard R. J. Lewine. — 1st ed. — New York: Norton, c1979. xii, 256 p.; 21 cm. Includes index. 1. Schizophrenia I. Lewine, Richard R. J. joint author. II. T.
RC514.B47     616.8/982     *LC* 78-13040     *ISBN* 0393011747

**Kernberg, Otto F., 1928-.**        **5.4925**
Borderline conditions and pathological narcissism / Otto F. Kernberg. — New York: J. Aronson, c1975. xvi, 361 p.; 24 cm. — (Classical psychoanalysis and its applications) 1. Borderline personality disorder 2. Narcissism I. T.
RC514.K4     616.8/982     *LC* 75-5616     *ISBN* 0876682050

**Scheflen, Albert E.**          **5.4926**
Levels of schizophrenia / by Albert E. Scheflen. — New York, N.Y.: Brunner/Mazel, c1981. xvii, 171 p.; 24 cm. Includes index. 1. Schizophrenia I. T.
RC514.S319     616.89/82 19     *LC* 80-21030     *ISBN* 0876302525

**Eysenck, H. J. (Hans Jurgen), 1916-.**     • **5.4927**
The causes and cures of neurosis: an introduction to modern behaviour therapy based on learning theory and the principles of conditioning / by H. J. Eysenck and S. Rachman. — [1st ed.] San Diego, Calif.: R. R. Knapp [1965] xii, 318 p.: ill.; 22 cm. 1. Neuroses 2. Behavior therapy I. Rachman, Stanley. joint author. II. T.
RC530.E9     616.85     *LC* 64-21700

**Gray, Melvin.**            **5.4928**
Neuroses: a comprehensive and critical view / Melvin Gray. — New York: Van Nostrand Reinhold, 1980, c1978. xvi, 341 p.: diagrs.; 24 cm. 1. Neuroses I. T.
RC530.G685     616.8/5     *LC* 77-25002     *ISBN* 0442228147

**Shapiro, David, 1926-.**         • **5.4929**
Neurotic styles. Foreword by Robert P. Knight. — New York: Basic Books, [1965] xii, 207 p.; 22 cm. — (The Austen Riggs Center. Monograph series, no. 5) 1. Neuroses I. T.
RC530.S5     616.89075     *LC* 65-23044

**Hysterical personality / edited by Mardi J. Horowitz.**     **5.4930**
New York: J. Aronson, c1977. xii, 441 p.: ill.; 24 cm. — (Classical psychoanalysis and its applications) Includes index. 1. Hysteria I. Horowitz, Mardi Jon, 1934-
RC532.H9     616.8/52     *LC* 77-73010     *ISBN* 0876682646

**Depression in the elderly: an interdisciplinary approach / edited**     **5.4931**
**by G. Maureen Chaisson–Stewart.**
New York: Wiley, c1985. xviii, 377 p.: ill.; 24 cm. — (Wiley medical publication.) 1. Depression, Mental 2. Geriatric psychiatry I. Chaisson-Stewart, G. Maureen (Grace Maureen) II. Series.
RC537.D4434 1985     618.97/68527 19     *LC* 84-26952     *ISBN* 0471870595

**Essential papers on depression / James C. Coyne, editor.**     **5.4932**
New York: New York University Press, 1986. xi, 507 p.: ill.; 24 cm. (Essential papers in psychoanalysis.) 1. Depression, Mental — Addresses, essays, lectures. 2. Depression, Mental — Etiology — Addresses, essays, lectures. I. Coyne, James C., 1947- II. Series.
RC537.E78 1986     616.85/27 19     *LC* 85-21498     *ISBN* 081471398X

**Handbook of affective disorders / edited by E.S. Paykel.**     **5.4933**
New York: Guilford Press, 1982. 457 p.: ill.; 26 cm. 1. Affective disorders I. Paykel, Eugene S.
RC537.H337 1982     616.85/27 19     *LC* 82-1049     *ISBN* 0898626226

**Handbook of studies on depression / edited by Graham D.**    5.4934 ✓
**Burrows.**
Amsterdam; New York: Excerpta Medica; New York: sole distributors for the
U.S.A., Elsevier/North-Holland, 1977. xiii, 433 p.: ill.; 25 cm. 1. Depression,
Mental 2. Psychopharmacology I. Burrows, Graham D.
RC537.H34      616.8/52      *LC* 77-8103      *ISBN* 9021921081

**Wolff, Harold G. (Harold George), 1898-.**              • 5.4935
Stress and disease. 2d ed. Rev. and edited by Stewart Wolf and Helen Goodell.
Springfield, Ill., Thomas [1968] xv, 277 p. illus. 24 cm. 1. Diseases — Causes
and theories of causation 2. Stress (Physiology) 3. Stress (Psychology)
I. Wolf, Stewart, 1914- ed. II. Goodell, Helen, ed. III. T.
RC539.W6 1968      616.07      *LC* 66-21439

**Grinker, Roy R. (Roy Richard), 1900-.**                • 5.4936
Men under stress. New York, McGraw-Hill [1963] 484 p. 21 cm.
1. Aeronautics, Military — Psychology 2. War neuroses I. Spiegel, John Paul,
1911- joint author. II. T.
RC550.G7 1963      *LC* 63-12127

## RC552–553 SPECIFIC NEUROSES. PATHOLOGICAL STATES

**Abraham, Suzanne.**                                5.4937
Eating disorders: the facts / Suzanne Abraham and Derek Llewellyn–Jones. —
Oxford, [Oxfordshire]; New York: Oxford University Press, 1985 (c1984).
162 p.: ill.; 23 cm. Spine title: Eating disorders, the facts. Includes index.
1. Anorexia nervosa 2. Bulimia 3. Obesity I. Llewellyn-Jones, Derek. II. T.
III. Title: Eating disorders, the facts.
RC552.A5 A37 1984      616.85/2 19      *LC* 84-782      *ISBN* 0192614592

**Anorexia nervosa & bulimia: diagnosis and treatment / James**    5.4938
**E. Mitchell, editor.**
Minneapolis: University of Minnesota Press, c1985. viii, 214 p.: ill.; 24 cm.
(University of Minnesota continuing medical education. v. 3) (Publications in
the health sciences.) 1. Anorexia nervosa 2. Bulimia I. Mitchell, James E.
(James Edward), 1947- II. Title: Anorexia nervosa and bulimia. III. Series.
IV. Series: Publications in the health sciences.
RC552.A5 S754 1985      616.85/2 19      *LC* 84-26933      *ISBN*
0816613885

**Bruch, Hilde, 1904-.**                             5.4939
The golden cage: the enigma of anorexia nervosa / Hilde Bruch. — Cambridge,
Mass.: Harvard University Press, 1978. xii, 150 p.; 24 cm. 1. Anorexia nervosa
I. T.
RC552.A5 B78      616.8/5      *LC* 77-10674      *ISBN* 0674356500

**Garfinkel, Paul E., 1946-.**                       5.4940
Anorexia nervosa: a multidimensional perspective / Paul E. Garfinkel and
David M. Garner. — New York: Brunner/Mazel; Montreal: Book Center,
c1982. xii, 379 p.; 24 cm. 1. Anorexia nervosa I. Garner, David M., 1947-
II. T.
RC552.A5 G37 1982      616.85/2 19      *LC* 82-1337      *ISBN*
0876302975

**Minuchin, Salvador.**                              5.4941
Psychosomatic families: anorexia nervosa in context / Salvador Minuchin,
Bernice L. Rosman, Lester Baker, with a contribution by Ronald Liebman. —
Cambridge, Mass.: Harvard University Press, 1978. viii, 351 p.: ill.; 24 cm.
1. Anorexia nervosa 2. Medicine, Psychosomatic 3. Family psychotherapy
I. Rosman, Bernice L. joint author. II. Baker, Lester. joint author. III. T.
RC552.A5 M56      616.8/5      *LC* 78-1742      *ISBN* 0674722205

**Krueger, David W.**                                5.4942
Success and the fear of success in women / David W. Krueger. — New York:
Free Press, c1984. xv, 180 p.; 25 cm. Includes index. 1. Fear of success
2. Women — Mental health I. T.
RC552.F43 K78 1984      158.1/088042 19      *LC* 83-48706      *ISBN*
0029180406

**Millman, Marcia.**                                 5.4943
Such a pretty face: being fat in America / Marcia Millman; with photos. by
Naomi Bushman. — 1st ed. — New York: Norton, c1980. xv, 252 p.: ill.; 22 cm.
1. Obesity — Psychological aspects 2. Obesity — Social aspects — United
States. 3. Femininity (Psychology) I. T.
RC552.O25 M54 1980      616.3/98/0019      *LC* 79-21064      *ISBN*
0393013170

**Psychological aspects of obesity: a handbook / Benjamin B.**    5.4944
**Wolman, editor; Stephen DeBerry, editorial associate.**
New York: Van Nostrand Reinhold, c1982. ix, 318 p.: ill.; 24 cm. 1. Obesity —
Psychological aspects I. Wolman, Benjamin B. II. DeBerry, Stephen.
RC552.O25 P75 1982      616.3/98/0019 19      *LC* 81-1917      *ISBN*
0442226098

**Trauma and its wake: the study and treatment of post–traumatic**    5.4945 ✓
**stress disorder / edited by Charles R. Figley.**
New York: Brunner/Mazel, c1985. xxvi, 457 p.: ill.; 24 cm. (Brunner/Mazel
psychosocial stress series. no. 4) 1. Post-traumatic stress disorder I. Figley,
Charles R., 1944- II. Series.
RC552.P67 T73 1985      616.85/21 19      *LC* 84-29344      *ISBN*
0876303858

**The Trauma of war: stress and recovery in Viet Nam veterans /**    5.4946
**edited by Stephen M. Sonnenberg, Arthur S. Blank, Jr., John**
**A. Talbott.**
Washington, D.C.: American Psychiatric Press, c1985. xxi, 453 p.; 24 cm.
1. Post-traumatic stress disorder 2. Veterans — Mental health services —
United States. 3. Vietnamese Conflict, 1961-1975 — Psychological aspects.
I. Sonnenberg, Stephen M., 1940- II. Blank, Arthur S., 1936-
RC552.P67 T75 1985      616.85/212 19      *LC* 85-6094      *ISBN*
0880480483

**Essential papers on narcissism / Andrew P. Morrison, editor.**    5.4947
New York: New York University Press, 1986. viii, 491 p.; 24 cm. (Essential
papers in psychoanalysis.) Includes indexes. 1. Narcissism — Addresses,
essays, lectures. I. Morrison, Andrew P., 1937- II. Series.
RC553.N36 E77 1986      616.85/82 19      *LC* 85-25845      *ISBN*
0814753949

## RC555 SEXUAL PROBLEMS

**Handbook of sex therapy / edited by Joseph LoPiccolo and**    5.4948 ✓
**Leslie LoPiccolo.**
New York: Plenum Press, c1978. xx, 531 p.: ill.; 26 cm. — (Perspectives in
sexuality) 1. Sex therapy — Addresses, essays, lectures. I. LoPiccolo, Joseph.
II. LoPiccolo, Leslie.
RC555.H36      616.6/06      *LC* 77-18818      *ISBN* 0306310740

**Schreiber, Flora Rheta.**                          5.4949 ✓
Sybil. — Chicago: Regnery, [1973] 359 p.; 24 cm. 1. Multiple personality —
Personal narratives. I. T.
RC555.S37      616.8/582/09      *LC* 72-11188      *ISBN* 0809200015

**Kaplan, Helen Singer, 1929-.**                     5.4950 ✓
The new sex therapy; active treatment of sexual dysfunctions. — New York:
Brunner/Mazel, [1974] xvi, 544 p.: illus.; 24 cm. 1. Sex therapy I. T.
RC556.K33      616.6      *LC* 73-87724      *ISBN* 0876300832

**Kaplan, Helen Singer, 1929-.**                     5.4951 ✓
Disorders of sexual desire and other new concepts and techniques in sex therapy
/ Helen Singer Kaplan. — New York: Brunner/Mazel, c1979. xx, 237 p.; 24
cm. — (Her The new sex therapy; v. 2) 1. Sexual disorders 2. Sexual disorders
— Case studies. 3. Sex therapy 4. Sex therapy — Case studies. I. T.
RC556.K33 vol. 2      616.6 s 616.6      *LC* 79-18908      *ISBN* 0876302126

**Masters, William H.**                              • 5.4952 ✓
Human sexual inadequacy [by] William H. Masters [and] Virginia E. Johnson.
— [1st ed.] — Boston: Little, Brown, [1970] x, 467 p.: illus.; 25 cm. 1. Sexual
disorders I. Johnson, Virginia E. joint author. II. T.
RC556.M37      616.6      *LC* 71-117043      *ISBN* 070000193X

**Tollison, C. David, 1949-.**                       5.4953 ✓
Sexual disorders: treatment, theory, and research / C. David Tollison and
Henry E. Adams. — New York: Gardner Press, c1979. xxi, 439 p.: ill.; 24 cm.
Includes indexes. 1. Sexual disorders I. Adams, Henry E., 1931- joint author.
II. T.
RC556.T64      616.8/583      *LC* 79-20853      *ISBN* 0898760291

**Finkelhor, David.**                                5.4954
Child sexual abuse: new theory and research / David Finkelhor. — New York:
Free Press, c1984. xii, 260 p.; 25 cm. Includes index. 1. Child molesting
2. Sexually abused children I. T.
RC560.C46 F55 1984      *LC* 84-47889      *ISBN* 0029100208

## RC563–568 DRUG ABUSE. SUBSTANCE ABUSE. ALCOHOLISM

**The Addictions: multidisciplinary perspectives and treatments /**    5.4955
**edited by Harvey B. Milkman, Howard J. Shaffer.**
Lexington, Mass.: Lexington Books, c1985. xviii, 204 p.: ill.; 24 cm. Based on
the proceedings of a national conference entitled: The addictions: an
interdisciplinary synthesis of concepts and treatments, held in Denver, Colo.,
Oct. 28-29, 1983. 1. Substance abuse — Congresses. I. Milkman, Harvey.
II. Shaffer, Howard, 1948-
RC564.A293 1985      616.86 19      *LC* 84-47871      *ISBN* 0669087394

**Austin, Gregory A.**                                                5.4956
Drug use and abuse: a guide to research findings / Gregory A. Austin, Michael L. Prendergast; foreword by Dan J. Lettieri. — Santa Barbara, Calif.: ABC-Clio Information Services, c1984. 2 v.; 29 cm. Includes indexes. 1. Drug abuse — Abstracts. 2. Psychotropic drugs — Abstracts. 3. Drug abuse — Periodicals — Indexes. 4. Psychotropic drugs — Periodicals — Indexes. I. Prendergast, Michael L., 1946- II. T.
RC564.A95 1984      616.86/3 19      *LC* 84-3015      *ISBN* 0874364140

**Peele, Stanton.**                                                  5.4957
The meaning of addiction: compulsive experience and its interpretation / Stanton Peele. — Lexington, Mass.: Lexington Books, c1985. xiv, 203 p.: ill.; 24 cm. Includes indexes. 1. Substance abuse 2. Alcoholism 3. Compulsive behavior 4. Substance abuse — Treatment — United States. 5. Substance abuse — Government policy — United States. I. T.
RC564.P45 1985      616.86 19      *LC* 84-54208      *ISBN* 0669029521

**Beauchamp, Dan E.**                                                5.4958
Beyond alcoholism: alcohol and public health policy / Dan E. Beauchamp. — Philadelphia: Temple University Press, 1980. xi, 222 p.: ill.; 22 cm. Includes index. 1. Alcoholism — Social aspects. 2. Alcoholism — United States 3. Mental health policy — United States. I. T.
RC565.B38      362.2/92      *LC* 80-15122      *ISBN* 0877221898

✓ **Kissin, Benjamin, 1917-.**                                       5.4959
The biology of alcoholism. Edited by Benjamin Kissin and Henri Begleiter. New York, Plenum Press, 1971-[77] 5 v. illus. 24 cm. 1. Alcoholism I. Begleiter, Henri. joint author. II. T.
RC565.K52      616.86/1 19      *LC* 74-131883      *ISBN* 0306371111

**Medical and social aspects of alcohol abuse / edited by Boris**    5.4960
**Tabakoff, Patricia B. Sutker, and Carrie L. Randall.**
New York: Plenum Press, c1983. xvi, 403 p.; 24 cm. 1. Alcoholism 2. Alcohol — Physiological aspects. I. Tabakoff, Boris, 1942- II. Sutker, Patricia B. III. Randall, Carrie L., 1947-
RC565.M346 1983      616.86/1 19      *LC* 83-4786      *ISBN* 0306412217

**The Misuse of alcohol: crucial issues in dependence, treatment,**  5.4961
**& prevention / edited by Nick Heather, Ian Robertson, & Phil**
**Davies on behalf of New Directions in the Study of Alcohol**
**Group.**
New York: New York University Press, 1985. 284 p.: ill.; 23 cm. 1. Alcoholism — Treatment 2. Alcoholism — Prevention I. Heather, Nick. II. Robertson, Ian, 1951- III. Davies, Phil, 1950- IV. New Directions in the Study of Alcohol Group (Great Britain)
RC565.M544 1985      616.86/106 19      *LC* 85-3113      *ISBN* 0814734324

**Sobell, Mark B.**                                                  5.4962
Behavioral treatment of alcohol problems: individualized therapy and controlled drinking / Mark B. Sobell and Linda C. Sobell. — New York: Plenum Press, c1978. xv, 225 p.: ill.; 24 cm. — (The Plenum behavior therapy series) Includes index. 1. Alcoholism 2. Behavior therapy I. Sobell, Linda C. joint author. II. T.
RC565.S6      616.8/61/06      *LC* 77-12381      *ISBN* 0306310570

**Vaillant, George E., 1934-.**                                      5.4963
The natural history of alcoholism / George E. Vaillant. — Cambridge, Mass.: Harvard University Press, 1983. xi, 359 p.: ill.; 24 cm. Includes index. 1. Alcoholism — Psychological aspects 2. Men — Mental health I. T.
RC565.V33 1983      616.86/1 19      *LC* 82-11696      *ISBN* 0674603753

**Rosenbaum, Marsha, 1948-.**                                        5.4964
Women on heroin / Marsha Rosenbaum. — New Brunswick, N.J.: Rutgers University Press, c1981. x, 196 p.; 24 cm. — (Crime, law, and deviance series.) Includes index. 1. Heroin habit 2. Women — Mental health I. T. II. Series.
RC568.H4 R67      362.2/93/088042 19      *LC* 80-29566      *ISBN* 0813509211

✓ **Essential papers on borderline disorders: one hundred years at**  5.4965
**the border / Michael H. Stone, editor.**
New York: New York University Press, 1986. x, 580 p.; 24 cm. (Essential papers in psychoanalysis.) Includes indexes. 1. Borderline personality disorder — Addresses, essays, lectures. I. Stone, Michael H., 1933- II. Series.
RC569.5.B67 E87 1986      616.89 19      *LC* 85-15384      *ISBN* 0814778496

**Parke, Ross D.**                                                   5.4966
Child abuse: an interdisciplinary analysis [by] Ross D. Parke and Candace Whitmer Collmer. — University of Chicago Press, [1975] 79 p. 1. Child abuse I. Collmer, Candace Whitmer. II. T. III. Title: Review of child development research.
RC569.5.C55P3x      362.71      *LC* 75-26043

**Campbell, Jacquelyn.**                                             5.4967
Nursing care of victims of family violence / Jacquelyn Campbell, Janice Humphreys. — Reston, Va.: Reston Pub. Co., c1984. xx, 444 p.; 24 cm. Includes index. 1. Family violence 2. Nursing I. Humphreys, Janice. II. T.
RC569.5.F3 C35 1984      362.8/283 19      *LC* 83-13979      *ISBN* 0835950425

**Crabtree, Adam.**                                                  5.4968
Multiple man: explorations in possession and multiple personality / by Adam Crabtree. — New York: Praeger, 1985. 278 p. Includes index. 1. Multiple personality — History. 2. Demoniac possession 3. Demoniac possession — Case studies. I. T.
RC569.5.M8 C73 1985      616.85/236 19      *LC* 85-3512      *ISBN* 0030051797

**In response to aggression: methods of control and prosocial**       5.4969
**alternatives / by Arnold P. Goldstein ... [et al.].**
New York: Pergamon Press, 1981. p. cm. — (Pergamon general psychology series. v. 98) 1. Aggressiveness (Psychology) 2. Violence 3. Control (Psychology) 4. Social control I. Goldstein, Arnold P. II. Series.
RC569.5.V55 I5 1981      303.6 19      *LC* 81-2385      *ISBN* 0080255809

## RC569.7–573 Mental Retardation

**Learning and cognition in the mentally retarded / edited by**       5.4970
**Penelope H. Brooks, Richard Sperber, Charley McCauley.**
Hillsdale, N.J.: L. Erlbaum Associates, 1984. xvii, 541 p.: ill.; 24 cm. (NICHD-Mental retardation research centers series.) 'Proceedings of the conference ... held at George Peabody College of Vanderbilt University; sponsored by the National Institute of Child Health and Human Development of the United States Public Health Service.' 1. Mental retardation — Congresses. I. Brooks, Penelope H. II. Sperber, Richard. III. McCauley, Charley. IV. National Institute of Child Health and Human Development (U.S.) V. Series.
RC569.9.L43 1984      616.85/88 19      *LC* 84-10289      *ISBN* 0898593743

**Baroff, George S.**                                                5.4971
Mental retardation: nature, cause, and management / George S. Baroff. — 2nd ed. — Washington [D.C.]: Hemisphere Pub. Corp., c1986. vi, 541 p.: ill.; 24 cm. Includes index. 1. Mental retardation 2. Mentally handicapped — Care I. T.
RC570.B27 1986      616.85/88 19      *LC* 85-8525      *ISBN* 0891162631

**Carter, Charles H.**                                               5.4972
Handbook of mental retardation syndromes, by Charles H. Carter. 3d ed. Springfield, Ill., Thomas [1975] xii, 416 p. illus. 24 cm. 1. Mental retardation I. T.
RC570.C28 1975      616.8/5884      *LC* 73-20240      *ISBN* 0398030901

**Classification in mental retardation / editor, Herbert J.**         5.4973
**Grossman; contributors, Michael J. Begab ... [et al.].**
Washington, DC: American Association on Mental Deficiency, c1983. v, 228 p.: graphs; 24 cm. Includes index. 1. Mental retardation — Classification. I. Grossman, Herbert J., 1923- II. Begab, Michael J. III. American Association on Mental Deficiency.
RC570.C515 1983      616.85/88/0012 19      *LC* 83-8779      *ISBN* 0940898128

**Ellis, Norman R. ed.**                                             5.4974
Handbook of mental deficiency: psychological theory and research / edited by Norman R. Ellis. — 2d ed. — Hillsdale, N.J.: L. Erlbaum Associates; New York: distributed by the Halsted Press Division of Wiley, 1979. xxix, 785 p.: ill.; 26 cm. 1. Mental retardation I. T.
RC570.E43 1979      616.8/588      *LC* 79-18991      *ISBN* 0898590027

**Jordan, Thomas Edward.**                                           5.4975
The mentally retarded / Thomas E. Jordan. — 4th ed. — Columbus, Ohio: Merrill, c1976. vii, 734 p.; 24 cm. 1. Mental retardation 2. Mentally handicapped — Care I. T.
RC570.J6 1976      616.8/588      *LC* 75-41716      *ISBN* 0675086167

**Clarke, Ann M. (Ann Margaret).**                                   5.4976
Mental deficiency: the changing outlook / edited by Ann M. Clarke, Alan D.B. Clarke, and Joseph M. Berg. — 4th ed., 1st American ed. — New York: Free Press, 1985. xxiv, 834 p.; 24 cm. 1. Mental retardation I. Clarke, A. D. B. (Alan Douglas Benson) II. Berg, Joseph M. III. T.
RC570. M373 1985      616.85/88 19      *LC* 85-20736      *ISBN* 0029059704

**Mental retardation, the developmental–difference controversy /**    5.4977
**edited by Edward Zigler, David Balla.**
Hillsdale, N.J.: L. Erlbaum Associates, 1982. viii, 333 p.: ill.; 24 cm. 1. Mental retardation I. Zigler, Edward, 1930- II. Balla, David A.
RC570.M424 1982      616.85/88 19      *LC* 82-8798      *ISBN* 0898591708

**Scheerenberger, R. C.**        **5.4978**
A history of mental retardation / R.C. Scheerenberger. — Baltimore: P.H. Brookes Pub. Co., c1983. xvii, 311 p.: ill., ports.; 27 cm. Includes index. 1. Mental retardation — History. 2. Mentally handicapped — Services for — History. I. T.
RC570.S25 1983    362.3/09 19    *LC* 82-9489    *ISBN* 0933716273

**Zigler, Edward, 1930-.**        **5.4979**
Understanding mental retardation / Edward Zigler and Robert M. Hodapp. — Cambridge; New York: Cambridge University Press, 1986. xii, 292 p.: ill.; 24 cm. Includes indexes. 1. Mental retardation I. Hodapp, Robert M. II. T.
RC570.Z54 1986    616.85/88 19    *LC* 85-31444    *ISBN* 0521318785

**Gibson, David, 1926-.**        **5.4980**
Down's syndrome: the psychology of mongolism / David Gibson. — [1st ed.]. — Cambridge; New York: Cambridge University Press, 1979 (c1978). xiii, 366 p.: ill.; 24 cm. Includes index. 1. Down's syndrome I. T.
RC571.G5    616.8/58842    *LC* 77-87381    *ISBN* 0521219140

## RC576 AFTER–CARE REHABILITATION

**Glasscote, Raymond M.**        • **5.4981**
Halfway houses for the mentally ill; a study of programs and problems [by] Raymond M. Glasscote, Jon E. Gudeman [and] J. Richard Elpers, in collaboration with Donald Miles [and others] Foreword by Bertram S. Brown. — Washington: Joint Information Service of the American Psychiatric Association and the National Association for Mental Health, 1971. xiii, 224 p.: illus., forms.; 24 cm. 1. Mentally ill — Rehabilitation 2. Community mental health services I. Gudeman, Jon E., 1936- joint author. II. Elpers, J. Richard, 1938- joint author. III. Joint Information Service of the American Psychiatric Association and the National Association for Mental Health. IV. T.
RC576.G55    362.2/2    *LC* 70-153492

## RC581–607 Immunologic Diseases. Allergy

**Adverse reactions to foods: American Academy of Allergy and**        **5.4982**
**Immunology Committee on Adverse Reactions to Foods, National Institute of Allergy and Infectious Disease.**
[Bethesda, Md.?]: U.S. Dept. of Health and Human Services, Public Health Service, National Institutes of Health, 1984. xv, 101 p.: ill.; 28 cm. (NIH publication; no. 84-2442) 'July 1984.' Includes indexes. Item 505-A-1 1. Food allergy I. National Institute of Allergy and Infectious Diseases (U.S.)
RC596.A45 1984    616.97/5 19    *LC* 84-603142

**AIDS: a self–care manual / Aids Project Los Angeles; editors,**        **5.4983**
**Betty Clare Moffatt ... [et al.]**
Santa Monica, CA: IBS Press, 1987. — xiv, 306 p. Includes index. 1. AIDS (Disease) I. Moffatt, Betty Clare II. AIDS Project Los Angeles
RC607.A26.M6x    616.9792 19    *ISBN* 0961660511

**What to do about AIDS: physicians and mental health**        **5.4984**
**professionals discuss the issues / edited by Leon McKusick.**
Berkeley: University of California Press, c1986. xvii, 202 p.; 24 cm. Papers from a conference convened in San Francisco, Sept. 13-14, 1985, by the AIDS Clinical Research Center at the University of California, San Francisco. 1. AIDS (Disease) — Psychological aspects — Congresses. I. McKusick, Leon. II. University of California, San Francisco. AIDS Clinical Research Center.
RC607.A26 W49 1986    616.97/92/0019 19    *LC* 86-16189    *ISBN* 0520059352

## RC620–627 Nutritional Diseases

**Adverse effects of foods / edited by E. F. Patrice Jelliffe and**        **5.4985**
**Derrick B. Jelliffe.**
New York: Plenum, c1982. xv, 614 p.: ill.; 26 cm. 1. Nutrition disorders 2. Food poisoning 3. Food contamination I. Jelliffe, E. F. Patrice. II. Jelliffe, Derrick Brian.
RC620.5.A38 1982    615.9/54 19    *LC* 82-566    *ISBN* 0306408708

**Nutritional toxicology / edited by John N. Hathcock.**        **5.4986**
New York: Academic Press, 1982. 515 p.: ill. — (Nutrition, basic and applied science.) 1. Nutritionally induced diseases — Collected works. 2. Nutrition —

Collected works. 3. Food additives — Toxicology — Collected works. I. Hathcock, John N. II. Series.
RC622.N894 1982    616.3/99 19    *LC* 82-4036    *ISBN* 012332601X

**Roe, Daphne A., 1923-.**        **5.4987**
A plague of corn; the social history of pellagra [by] Daphne A. Roe. Ithaca [N.Y.] Cornell University Press [1973] xiii, 217 p. illus. 22 cm. 1. Pellagra — History. 2. Social history I. T.
RC625.R64    616.3/93/009    *LC* 72-12408    *ISBN* 0801407737

## RC633–665 Blood Diseases. Endocrinology

**Edelstein, Stuart J.**        **5.4988**
The sickled cell: from myths to molecules / Stuart J. Edelstein. — Cambridge, Mass.: Harvard University Press, 1986. x, 197 p.: ill.; 24 cm. Includes index. 1. Sickle cell anemia 2. Sickle cell anemia — Africa. I. T.
RC641.7.S5 E34 1986    614.5/91527 19    *LC* 86-2003    *ISBN* 0674807375

**Textbook of endocrinology (Philadelphia, Pa.)**        **5.4989**
Textbook of endocrinology / edited by Robert H. Williams; with contributions by forty–nine authorities. — 6th ed. — Philadelphia: Saunders, 1981. xxiii, 1270 p.: ill.; 29 cm. 1. Endocrine glands — Diseases 2. Endocrinology I. Williams, Robert Hardin. II. T.
RC648.T46 1981    616.4    *LC* 79-67306    *ISBN* 0721693989

**Endocrine disorders.**        **5.4990**
Springhouse, Pa.: Springhouse Corp., 1984. 192 p.: ill.; 29 cm. — (Nurse's clinical library.) 'Nursing84 books.' Includes index. 1. Endocrine glands — Diseases 2. Endocrine glands — Diseases — Nursing. I. Series.
RC649.E5137 1984    616.4 19    *LC* 84-5509    *ISBN* 0916730719

## RC666–935 Diseases, by Body System

## RC666–681 Cardiovascular System. Heart

**American Heart Association.**        **5.4991**
Heartbook: a guide to prevention and treatment of cardiovascular diseases / American Heart Association; illus. by Ilil Arbel. — 1st ed. — New York: Dutton, c1980. xiv, 370 p.: ill.; 29 cm. Includes index. 1. Cardiovascular system — Diseases 2. Heart — Diseases I. T.
RC672.A44 1980    616.1    *LC* 79-17334    *ISBN* 0525930566

**DeBakey, Michael E. (Michael Ellis), 1908-.**        **5.4992**
The living heart / Michael DeBakey and Antonio Gotto; illustrated by Herbert R. Smith. — New York: D. McKay Co., c1977. xiv, 256 p.: ill.; 26 cm. Includes index. 1. Cardiovascular system — Diseases 2. Cardiovascular system I. Gotto, Antonio M. joint author. II. T.
RC672.D4    616.1    *LC* 76-47013    *ISBN* 067950575X

**Cardiovascular disorders.**        **5.4993**
Springhouse, Pa.: Springhouse Corp., c1984. 192 p.: ill. (some col.); 29 cm. (Nurse's clinical library.) 'Nursing84 books.' Includes index. 1. Cardiovascular disease nursing I. Series.
RC674.C363 1984    616.1 19    *LC* 83-17004    *ISBN* 0916730565

**Classics of cardiology: a collection of classic works on the heart**        • **5.4994**
**and circulation with comprehensive biographic accounts of the authors: fifty–two contributions by fifty–one authors / [edited] by Fredrick A. Williams and Thomas E. Keys.**
New York: Henry Schuman: Dover, 1961-. v.: ill., ports; 21 cm. 1. Cardiology 2. Cardiovascular system 3. Heart — Diseases I. Williams, Fredrick A. II. Keys, Thomas E. (Thomas Edward), 1908-
RC681.C53 1961

**Hypertension.**      5.4995
Springhouse, Pa.: Springhouse Corp., c1984. 136 p.: ill. (some col.); 26 cm. — (Nursing now series.) 'Nursing 84 books.' Includes index. 1. Hypertension — Nursing. I. Springhouse Corporation. II. Series.
RC685.H8 H7675 1984    610.73/691 19    *LC* 84-1315    *ISBN* 0916730778

## RC705–779 Respiratory System

**Rarey, Kanute P.**      5.4996
Respiratory patient care / Kanute P. Rarey, John W. Youtsey. — Englewood Cliffs, N.J.: Prentice-Hall, c1981. xvi, 400 p.: ill.; 24 cm. 1. Respiratory therapy I. Youtsey, John W. joint author. II. T.
RC735.I5 R37    615.8/36 19    *LC* 80-39946    *ISBN* 0137746040

**Respiratory emergencies.**      5.4997
Springhouse, Pa.: Springhouse Corp., 1985 (c1984). 128 p.: ill. (some col.); 27 cm. (Nursing now series.) 'Nursing84 books.' Includes index. 1. Respiratory disease nursing 2. Emergency nursing I. Series.
RC735.5.R467 1984    610.73/692 19    *LC* 84-20306    *ISBN* 0916730808

## RC799–869 Gastrointestinal System

**Gastrointestinal disorders.**      5.4998
Springhouse, Pa.: Springhouse Corp., c1985. 192 p.: col. ill.; 29 cm. (Nurse's clinical library.) 'Nursing85 books.' Includes index. 1. Gastrointestinal system — Diseases 2. Gastrointestinal system — Diseases — Nursing. I. Series.
RC802.G375 1985    616.3/3 19    *LC* 84-20242    *ISBN* 0916730751

**Renal and urologic disorders.**      5.4999
Springhouse, Pa.: Springhouse Corp., c1984. 192 p.: ill. (some col.); 29 cm. (Nurse's clinical library.) 'Nursing84 books.' Includes index. 1. Urological nursing I. Springhouse Corporation. II. Series.
RC874.7.R46 1984    616.6 19    *LC* 84-14104    *ISBN* 0916730743

**Wedeen, Richard P., 1934-.**      5.5000
Poison in the pot: the legacy of lead / Richard P. Wedeen. — Carbondale: Southern Illinois University Press, c1984. xi, 274 p.: ill.; 24 cm. Includes index. 1. Nephritis, Interstitial — Etiology. 2. Lead — Toxicology 3. Occupational diseases I. T.
RC918.N37 W43 1984    616.6/12 19    *LC* 84-2296    *ISBN* 0809311569

## RC925–935 Musculoskeletal System

**Rheumatic diseases: rehabilitation and management / edited by**      5.5001
**Gail Kershner Riggs and Eric P. Gall.**
Boston: Butterworth Publishers, c1984. xxv, 485 p.: ill.; 24 cm. 1. Arthritis — Rehabilitation. 2. Arthritis — Treatment. 3. Rheumatism — Treatment. I. Riggs, Gail Kershner. II. Gall, Eric P. (Eric Papineau), 1940-
RC933.R37 1984    616.7/2206 19    *LC* 83-15195    *ISBN* 0409950513

## RC952–954 Geriatrics

**Geriatric medicine / edited by Christine K. Cassel, John R.**      5.5002
**Walsh.**
New York: Springer-Verlag, c1984. 2 v.: ill. 1. Geriatrics I. Cassel, Christine K. II. Walsh, John R. (John Richard), 1926-
RC952.G393 1984    618.97 19    *LC* 84-1332    0387909443

**Cognition, stress, and aging / James E. Birren and Judy**      5.5003
**Livingston, editors; Donna E. Deutchman, Editorial Coordinator.**
Englewood Cliffs, N.J.: Prentice-Hall, c1985. xii, 212 p.: ill.; 24 cm. Based on research by Fellows of the Andrew Norman Institute at the Andrus Gerontology Center, University of Southern California. 'The ANI series on aging'—Jacket. 1. Aged — Diseases — Psychosomatic aspects. 2. Cognition — Age factors 3. Stress (Psychology) 4. Aging — Psychological aspects I. Birren, James E. II. Livingston, Judy. III. Ethel Percy Andrus Gerontology Center. IV. Title: ANI series on aging.
RC952.5.C59 1985    618.97/08 19    *LC* 84-13296    *ISBN* 0131398253

**Nutrition in the middle and later years / edited by Elaine B.**      5.5004
**Feldman.**
Boston: J. Wright-PSG, 1983. x, 342 p.: ill.; 24 cm. 1. Geriatrics 2. Middle age — Nutrition 3. Aged — Nutrition 4. Nutrition disorders I. Feldman, Elaine B., 1926-
RC952.5.N88 1983    613.2/0880565 19    *LC* 82-13618    *ISBN* 0723670463

**Handbook of gerontological nursing / edited by Bernita M.**      5.5005
**Steffl.**
New York, N.Y.: Van Nostrand Reinhold, c1984. xiv, 567 p.: ill.; 27 cm. 1. Geriatric nursing I. Steffl, Bernita M.
RC954.H35 1984    618.97/0024/613 19    *LC* 83-10478    *ISBN* 0442278454

**Nursing and the aged / edited by Irene Mortenson Burnside.**      5.5006
2d ed. — New York: McGraw-Hill, c1981. xxi, 710 p.: ill.; 25 cm. Includes indexes. 1. Geriatric nursing I. Burnside, Irene Mortenson, 1923-
RC954.N87 1981    610.73/65    *LC* 80-11056    *ISBN* 0070092117

**Primary health care of the older adult / May Futrell ... [et al.].**      5.5007
N. Scituate, Mass.: Duxbury Press, c1980. xiv, 494 p.: ill.; 24 cm. 1. Geriatric nursing 2. Aged — Care and hygiene. I. Futrell, May DiPietro.
RC954.P75    610.73/65    *LC* 79-15816    *ISBN* 087872236X

**Old, sick, and helpless: where therapy begins / Robert J.**      5.5008
**Kastenbaum ... [et al.].**
Cambridge, Mass.: Ballinger Pub. Co., 1981. vii, 222 p.; 24 cm. — (Cushing Hospital series on aging and terminal care.) 1. Aged — Hospital care 2. Aged — Rehabilitation. 3. Holistic medicine 4. Gerontology I. Kastenbaum, Robert. II. Series.
RC954.3.O43    362.1/9897 19    *LC* 81-3557    *ISBN* 0884107175

## RC963–969 Industrial Medicine. Industrial Hygiene

**Environmental and occupational medicine / editor, William N.**      5.5009
**Rom; assistant editors, Attilio D. Renzetti, Jr., Jeffrey S. Lee, Victor E. Archer.**
1st ed. — Boston: Little, Brown, c1983. xxv, 1015 p.: ill.; 27 cm. 1. Medicine, Industrial 2. Environmentally induced diseases I. Rom, William N.
RC963.E58 1983    616.9/8 19    *LC* 82-81957    *ISBN* 0316755605

**Occupational health: recognizing and preventing work–related**      5.5010
**disease / edited by Barry S. Levy, David H. Wegman; foreword by Anthony Robbins.**
1st ed. — Boston: Little, Brown, c1983. xxii, 526 p.: ill.; 24 cm. 1. Medicine, Industrial I. Levy, Barry S. II. Wegman, David H.
RC963.O22 1983    616.9/803 19    *LC* 82-80773    *ISBN* 0316522341

**Occupational medicine: principles and practical applications /**      5.5011
**[edited by] Carl Zenz.**
2nd ed. — Chicago: Year Book Medical Publishers, c1987. 944 p. 1. Medicine, Industrial I. Zenz, Carl, 1923-
RC963.O23 1987    616.9/803 19    *LC* 86-24598    *ISBN* 0815198655

**Encyclopaedia of occupational health and safety / technical**      5.5012
**editor, Luigi Parmeggiani.**
3rd rev. ed. — Geneva: International Labour Office, 1983. 2 v.: ill.; 31 cm. Prepared under the auspices of the International Labour Organisation. Errata slip inserted in v. 2. 1. Medicine, Industrial — Dictionaries. 2. Industrial hygiene — Dictionaries. I. Parmeggiani, Luigi. II. International Labour Organisation.
RC963.3.E53 1983    613.6/2/0321 19    *LC* 83-219118    *ISBN* 9221032892

**McCann, Michael, 1943-.**      5.5013
Artist beware / by Michael McCann. — New York: Watson-Guptill Publications, 1979. xvi, 378 p.: ill.; 24 cm. Includes index. 1. Artists — Diseases and hygiene. 2. Artisans — Diseases and hygiene. 3. Artists' materials — Toxicology. I. T.
RC963.6.A78 M32 1979    702/.8    *LC* 79-18982    *ISBN* 0823002950

**Hunter, Donald, 1898-.**      5.5014
The diseases of occupations / Donald Hunter. — 6th ed. — London: Hodder and Stoughton, 1978. xxii, 1257 p.: ill.; 23 cm. 1. Occupational diseases I. T.
RC964.H8 1978    616.9/803    *LC* 79-315897    *ISBN* 0340220848

**Stellman, Jeanne Mager, 1947-.**      **5.5015**
Work is dangerous to your health; a handbook of health hazards in the
workplace and what you can do about them [by] Jeanne M. Stellman [and]
Susan M. Daum. With contributions by James L. Weeks, Steven D. Stellman
[and] Michael E. Green. With illus. by Lyda Pola. [1st ed.] New York,
Pantheon Books [1973] xxiii, 448 p. illus. 22 cm. 1. Occupational diseases
2. Industrial hygiene I. Daum, Susan M., 1941- joint author. II. T.
RC964.S7 1972b    613.6/2    *LC* 72-12386    *ISBN* 0394485254

**Stellman, Jeanne Mager, 1947-.**      **5.5016**
Office work can be dangerous to your health: a handbook of office health and
safety hazards and what you can do about them / Jeanne Stellman and Mary
Sue Henifin; illustrations by Lyda Pola. — 1st ed. — New York: Pantheon
Books, c1983. xiv, 239 p.: ill.; 22 cm. Includes index. 1. Offices — Hygienic
aspects. 2. White collar workers — Diseases and hygiene. I. Henifin, Mary
Sue, 1953- II. T.
RC965.O3 S83 1983    613.6/2 19    *LC* 83-42956    *ISBN* 0394511603

**Brown, Mary Louise, 1916-.**      **5.5017**
Occupational health nursing: principles and practices / Mary Louise Brown. —
New York: Springer Pub. Co., c1981. xii, 340 p.; 24 cm. 1. Industrial nursing
I. T.
RC966.B73    610.73/46 19    *LC* 80-21024    *ISBN* 0826122507

**Burgess, William A., 1924-.**      **5.5018**
Recognition of health hazards in industry: a review of materials and processes /
William A. Burgess. — New York: Wiley, c1981. xiii, 275 p.: ill.; 24 cm. 'A
Wiley-Interscience publication.' 1. Industrial hygiene 2. Manufacturing
processes — Hygienic aspects. I. T.
RC967.B83    620.8/5 19    *LC* 81-2132    *ISBN* 0471063398

**Gill, F. S. (Frank S.)**      **5.5019**
Monitoring for health hazards at work / by Frank S. Gill and Indira Ashton;
foreword by Ricards Warburton. — London: Grant McIntyre, Medical and
Scientific; Scarborough, Ont.: Distributed by Blackwell Mosby, 1982. xiv,
155 p.: ill. RoSPA, The Royal Society for the Prevention of Accidents
1. Industrial safety 2. Industrial hygiene I. Ashton, Indira. II. Royal Society
for the Prevention of Accidents. III. T.
T55 G45    RC967.G5x.    *ISBN* 0862860296

**Industrial hygiene aspects of plant operations / Lester V.**      **5.5020**
**Cralley, Lewis J. Cralley, editors.**
New York: Macmillan, c1982-1985. 3 v.: ill.; 24 cm. Associate editors: v. 2,
John E. Mutchler; v. 3, Knowlton J. Caplan. 1. Industrial hygiene
2. Manufacturing processes — Hygienic aspects. I. Cralley, Lester V.
II. Cralley, Lewis J., 1911-
RC967.I48 1982    620.8/5 19    *LC* 82-80255    *ISBN* 0029493501

**Page, Joseph A.**      **5.5021**
Bitter wages: Ralph Nader's study group report on disease and injury on the
job, by Joseph A. Page and Mary–Win O'Brien. — New York: Grossman
Publishers, 1973. xvii, 314 p.; 22 cm. On spine: The Nader report: bitter wages.
1. Industrial hygiene 2. Occupational diseases I. O'Brien, Mary-Win, joint
author. II. Nader, Ralph. III. T. IV. Title: The Nader report: bitter wages.
RC967.P33    616.9/803    *LC* 72-112512    *ISBN* 0670170488

**Patty, F. A. (Frank Arthur), 1897-.**      **5.5022**
[Industrial hygiene and toxicology] Patty's Industrial hygiene and toxicology /
George D. Clayton, Florence E. Clayton, editors; contributors, M. C. Battigelli
... [et al.]. — 3d rev. ed. — New York: Wiley, c1978-1985. 3 v. in 5: ill.; 24 cm.
Vol. 3 edited by L.V. Cralley, L.J. Cralley. 'A Wiley-Interscience publication.'
1. Industrial hygiene 2. Industrial toxicology I. Clayton, George D.
II. Clayton, Florence E. III. Battigelli, Mario C. IV. T. V. Title: Industrial
hygiene and toxicology.
RC967.P37 1978    613.6/2    *LC* 77-17515    *ISBN* 0471160466

# RC1000–1015 Submarine
# Medicine

**Hempleman, H. V.**      **5.5023**
The physiology of diving in man and other animals / H. V. Hempleman, A. P.
M. Lockwood. — London: E. Arnold, 1978. 56, [2] p.: ill.; 23 cm. (The Institute
of Biology's studies in biology; no. 99) 1. Underwater physiology 2. Diving,
Submarine — Physiological aspects 3. Marine mammals — Physiology.
4. Water-birds — Physiology. I. Lockwood, A. P. M. (Antony Peter Murray),
1931- joint author. II. T.
RC1015.H45    599/.01/9135    *LC* 79-307465    *ISBN* 0713126914

# RC1200–1238 Sports Medicine.
# Physiology of Sports

**Falls, Harold B.**      **5.5024**
Essentials of fitness / Harold B. Falls, Ann M. Baylor, Rod K. Dishman. —
Philadelphia: Saunders College, 1980. xiv, 317 p.: ill.; 26 cm. 1. Sports
medicine 2. Physical fitness 3. Exercise therapy I. Baylor, Ann M. joint
author. II. Dishman, Rod K. joint author. III. T.
RC1210.F26    613.7 19    *LC* 79-66714    *ISBN* 0030567777

**Athletic training and sports medicine / [editorial board: Arthur**      **5.5025**
**E. Ellison ... et al.].**
1st ed. — Chicago, Ill.: American Academy of Orthopaedic Surgeons, 1984. vii,
602 p.: ill. (some col.). 1. Sports medicine — Addresses, essays, lectures
2. Physical education and training — Safety measure — Addresses, essays,
lectures I. Ellison, Arthur E. II. American Academy of Orthopaedic
Surgeons.
RC1215 A87 1984    *ISBN* 089203002X

**Kostrubala, Thaddeus, 1930-.**      **5.5026**
The joy of running / Thaddeus Kostrubala. — 1st ed. — Philadelphia:
Lippincott, c1976. 158 p.; 24 cm. 1. Running — Physiological aspects.
2. Coronary heart disease I. T.
RC1220.R8 K67    613.7/1    *LC* 76-9835    *ISBN* 0397011105

**Newsholme, E. A.**      **5.5027**
The runner: energy and endurance / by Eric Newsholme & Tony Leech; preface
by Sir Roger Bannister. — Roosevelt, N.J.: Fitness Books, [1983] vii, 152 p.: ill.;
22 cm. Includes index. 1. Running — Psychological aspects. I. Leech, A. R.
II. T.
RC1220.R8 N49 1983    613.7/1 19    *LC* 84-220265    *ISBN*
0913115002

**Sharkey, Brian J.**      **5.5028**
Physiology of fitness: prescribing exercise for fitness, weight control, and health
/ Brian J. Sharkey. — 2nd ed. — Champaign, Ill.: Human Kinetics Publishers,
c1984. xv, 365 p.: ill.; 23 cm. Includes index. 1. Sports — Physiological aspects
2. Physical fitness 3. Exercise — Physiological aspects I. T.
RC1235.S52 1984    613.7 19    *LC* 84-3850    *ISBN* 0931250668

**Wells, Christine L., 1938-.**      **5.5029**
Women, sport & performance: a physiological perspective / Christine L. Wells.
— Champaign, Ill.: Human Kinetics Publishers, c1985. xi, 333 p.: ill.; 24 cm.
Includes index. 1. Sports — Physiological aspects 2. Women — Physiology
3. Exercise for women I. T.
RC1235.W45 1985    612/.044 19    *LC* 84-25255    *ISBN* 0931250870

# RD Surgery. Orthopedia

**Wangensteen, Owen Harding, 1898-.**      **5.5030**
The rise of surgery: from empiric craft to scientific discipline / by Owen H.
Wangensteen and Sarah D. Wangensteen. — Minneapolis: University of
Minnesota Press, c1978. xviii, 785 p.: ill.; 25 cm. Includes indexes. 1. Surgery
— History. I. Wangensteen, Sarah D. joint author. II. T.
RD19.W36    *LC* 77-87933

**Billings, John Shaw, 1838-1913.**      • **5.5031**
The history and literature of surgery. — [New York]: Argosy-Antiquarian,
1970. 132 p.; 25 cm. Reprint of the 1895 ed. 1. Surgery — History. 2. Surgery
— Bibliography. I. T.
RD21.B55 1970    617/.09    *LC* 78-115407    *ISBN* 0872660389

**Bosk, Charles L.**      **5.5032**
Forgive and remember: managing medical failure / Charles L. Bosk. —
Chicago: University of Chicago Press, 1979. x, 236 p.; 23 cm. Includes index.
1. Surgery — Study and teaching (Graduate) — Social aspects. 2. Surgical
errors 3. Surgery — Quality control. 4. Surgeons 5. Social control I. T.
RD28.A1 B67    617    *LC* 78-16596    *ISBN* 0226066797

**Woodruff, Michael F. A., Sir.**      **5.5033**
On science and surgery / Michael Woodruff. Edinburgh: Edinburgh University
Press, c1977. viii, 154 p.; 21 cm. 1. Surgery — Addresses, essays, lectures.
2. Medicine — Addresses, essays, lectures. I. T.
RD39.W66    610    *LC* 77-675824    *ISBN* 0852243030

**Pernick, Martin S.**      5.5034
A calculus of suffering: pain, professionalism, and anesthesia in nineteenth–century America / Martin S. Pernick. — New York: Columbia University Press, 1985. xiii, 421 p.; ill.; 24 cm. Includes index. 1. Anesthesia — United States — History — 19th century. 2. Medicine — United States — History — 19th century. 3. Surgery — United States — History — 19th century. 4. Pain — Social aspects — United States — History — 19th century. I. T.
RD80.3.P47 1985     617/.96/0973 19     *LC* 84-12664     *ISBN* 0231051867

**Mannon, James M., 1942-.**      5.5035
Caring for the burned: life and death in a hospital burn center / by James M. Mannon. — Springfield, Ill., U.S.A.: Thomas, c1985. vii, 262 p.; 24 cm. Includes index. 1. Burn care units — Social aspects. 2. Burn care units — Psychological aspects. I. T.
RD96.4.M35 1985     362.1/9711 19     *LC* 84-16294     *ISBN* 0398050899

**Electronic devices for rehabilitation / edited by John G.**      5.5036
**Webster ... [et al.].**
New York: Wiley, c1985. xii, 446 p.; ill.; 24 cm. — (Medical instrumentation and clinical engineering series.) (Wiley medical publication.) 1. Self-help devices for the disabled 2. Medical electronics I. Webster, John G., 1932- II. Series. III. Series: Wiley medical publication.
RD755.E54 1985     617 19     *LC* 84-15171     *ISBN* 0471808989

**The use of technology in the care of the elderly and the**      5.5037
**disabled: tools for living / edited by Jean Bray and Sheila**
**Wright; foreword by H. S. Wolff.**
English language ed. — Westport, Conn.: Greenwood Press, c1980. xii, 267 p.; ill.; 24 cm. Based on papers read at two symposia held in London and Berlin in 1979 under the sponsorship of the Commission of the European Communities. 1. Orthopedic apparatus — Congresses. 2. Self-help devices for the disabled — Congresses. 3. Physically handicapped — Rehabilitation — Congresses. 4. Aged — Rehabilitation — Congresses. I. Bray, Jean, 1932- II. Wright, Sheila, 1919- III. Commission of the European Communities.
RD755.U83     617/.9     *LC* 80-17847     *ISBN* 0313226164

**DeLoach, Charlene.**      5.5038
Adjustment to severe physical disability: a metamorphosis / Charlene DeLoach, Bobby G. Greer. — New York: McGraw-Hill, c1981. xv, 310 p.; 25 cm. — (McGraw-Hill series in special education) Includes indexes. 1. Physically handicapped — Psychology 2. Adjustment (Psychology) 3. Social adjustment 4. Physically handicapped — Rehabilitation I. Greer, Bobby G. joint author. II. T.
RD798.D4     362.4/01/9     *LC* 80-17612     *ISBN* 0070162816

# RF AUDIOLOGY

**Martin, Frederick N.**      5.5039
Introduction to audiology / Frederick N. Martin. — 3rd ed. — Englewood Cliffs, N.J.: Prentice-Hall, c1986. xii, 452 p.; ill.; 25 cm. 1. Hearing disorders 2. Audiometry 3. Audiology I. T.
RF290.M34 1986     617.8 19     *LC* 85-12107     *ISBN* 0134781732

**Newby, Hayes A.**      5.5040
Audiology / Hayes A. Newby, Gerald R. Popelka. — 5th ed. — Englewood Cliffs, N.J.: Prentice-Hall, c1985. vi, 472 p.; ill.; 24 cm. 1. Audiology 2. Hearing disorders I. Popelka, Gerald R. II. T.
RF290.N47 1985     617.8/9 19     *LC* 84-17958     *ISBN* 0130508659

**Northern, Jerry L.**      5.5041
Hearing in children / Jerry L. Northern, Marion P. Downs. — 3rd ed. — Baltimore: Williams & Wilkins, c1984. xi, 391 p.; ill.; 26 cm. Includes index. 1. Hearing disorders in children I. Downs, Marion P. II. T.
RF291.5.C45 N67 1984     618.92/0978 19     *LC* 83-10378     *ISBN* 0683065734

# RG GYNECOLOGY. OBSTETRICS

**Ruzek, Sheryl Burt.**      5.5042
The women's health movement: feminist alternatives to medical control / Sheryl Burt Ruzek. — New York: Praeger, 1978. xviii, 351 p.; 25 cm. Includes indexes. 1. Women's health services — United States. 2. Women's health services — Political aspects — United States. 3. Feminism — United States. I. T.
RG14.U6 R88 1978     362.1     *LC* 78-15483     *ISBN* 0030414369

**Shorter, Edward.**      5.5043
A history of women's bodies / Edward Shorter. — New York: Basic Books, c1982. xiv, 398 p.; 25 cm. 1. Childbirth — History. 2. Obstetrics — History. 3. Women — Physiology — History. 4. Sex customs — History. I. T.
RG51.S48 1982     362.1/088042 19     *LC* 82-70856     *ISBN* 0465030297

**English Trotula. English & English (Middle English)**      5.5044
Medieval woman's guide to health: the first English gynecological handbook: Middle English text / with introd. and modern English translation by Beryl Rowland. — Kent, Ohio: Kent State University Press, 1981. xvii, 192 p.; ill.; 24 cm. A Middle English treatise associated with Trotula; edited from British Library ms. Sloane 2463. Includes index. 1. Gynecology — Early works to 1800. 2. Obstetrics — Early works to 1800. 3. Medicine, Medieval 4. English language — Middle English, 1100-1500 — Texts. I. Rowland, Beryl. II. British Museum. MSS (Sloane 2463) III. Trotula. IV. T.
RG85.E53 1980     618 19     *LC* 80-82201     *ISBN* 0873382439

**Sexual and reproductive aspects of women's health care / edited**      5.5045
**by Malkah T. Notman and Carol C. Nadelson.**
New York: Plenum Press, c1978. xii, 363 p.; 24 cm. — (The woman patient, medical and psychological interfaces; v. 1) (Women in context.) 1. Gynecology — Psychological aspects 2. Pregnancy — Psychological aspects 3. Gynecology 4. Sexual disorders 5. Women's health services I. Notman, Malkah T. II. Nadelson, Carol C. III. Series. IV. Series: Women in context.
RG103.5.S49     618     *LC* 78-17972     *ISBN* 0306311518

**Shephard, Bruce D., 1944-.**      5.5046
The complete guide to women's health / Bruce D. Shephard, Carroll A. Shephard. — Tampa, Fla.: Mariner Pub. Co., c1982. xxii, 419 p.; ill.; 26 cm. Includes index. 1. Gynecology — Popular works. 2. Obstetrics — Popular works. 3. Women — Diseases I. Shephard, Carroll A., 1944- II. T.
RG121.S533 1982     618 19     *LC* 82-14802     *ISBN* 093616607X

**Sloane, Ethel.**      5.5047
Biology of women / Ethel Sloane. — 2nd ed. — New York: Wiley, c1985. xiii, 656 p.; ill.; 24 cm. (Wiley medical publication.) 1. Women — Health and hygiene 2. Women — Physiology 3. Gynecology — Popular works. I. T. II. Series.
RG121.S637 1985     613/.04244 19     *LC* 84-25726     *ISBN* 0471879398

**O'Donovan, Oliver.**      5.5048
Begotten or made? / Oliver O'Donovan. — Oxford [Oxfordshire]: Clarendon Press; New York: Oxford University Press, 1984. ix, 88 p.; 20 cm. 1. Artificial insemination, Human — Moral and ethical aspects. 2. Fertilization in vitro, Human — Moral and ethical aspects. 3. Sex change — Moral and ethical aspects. 4. Christian ethics 5. Ethics, Jewish I. T.
RG134.O36 1984     174/.2 19     *LC* 84-9638     *ISBN* 0198266782

**Grobstein, Clifford, 1916-.**      5.5049
From chance to purpose: an appraisal of external human fertilization / Clifford Grobstein. — Reading, Mass.: Addison-Wesley Pub. Co., 1981. 207 p. Includes index. 1. Fertilization in vitro, Human 2. Fertilization in vitro, Human — Moral and religious aspects. 3. Fertilization in vitro, Human — Government policy. 4. Human biology I. T.
RG135.G76     618.1/78 19     *LC* 81-1918     *ISBN* 0201045850

**Singer, Peter.**      5.5050
Making babies: the new science and ethics of conception / Peter Singer and Deane Wells. — New York: C. Scribner's Sons, 1985. ix, 245 p.; 22 cm. Rev. ed. of: The reproduction revolution. 1st ed. 1984. Includes index. 1. Fertilization in vitro, Human 2. Surrogate mothers 3. Sex preselection 4. Cloning 5. Genetic engineering 6. Fertilization in vitro, Human — Moral and ethical aspects. 7. Surrogate mothers — Moral and ethical aspects. 8. Sex preselection — Moral and ethical aspects. 9. Cloning — Moral and ethical aspects. 10. Genetic engineering — Moral and ethical aspects. I. Wells, Deane. II. Singer, Peter. Reproduction revolution. III. T.
RG135.S557 1985     613.9/4 19     *LC* 84-29823     *ISBN* 0684183714

**Birth control and controlling birth: women–centered perspectives**      5.5051
**/ edited by Helen B. Holmes, Betty B. Hoskins, and Michael**
**Gross.**
Clifton, N.J.: Humana Press, c1980. xiv, 338 p.; ill.; 24 cm. — (Contemporary issues in biomedicine, ethics, and society.) 1. Contraceptives — Research — Congresses. 2. Contraception — Congresses. 3. Obstetrics — Technological innovations — Congresses. 4. Obstetrics — Social aspects — Congresses. 5. Childbirth — Congresses. 6. Women's health services — United States — Congresses. I. Holmes, Helen B. II. Hoskins, Betty B. III. Gross, Michael, 1948- IV. Series.
RG136.A2 B54     613.9/4 19     *LC* 80-82173     *ISBN* 0896030237

**Djerassi, Carl.**      **5.5052**
The politics of contraception / Carl Djerassi. — New York: Norton, c1979. 274 p.: ill. Reprint of the 1979 ed. published by the Stanford Alumni Association, Stanford, Calif., in series: The Portable Stanford. Includes index. 1. Contraception 2. Contraception — Research. 3. Oral contraceptives I. T.
RG136.D57 1979     RG136 D57 1979.     613.9/4     LC 79-21845
    ISBN 0393012646

**Shapiro, Howard I.**      **5.5053**
The birth control book / by Howard I. Shapiro. — New York: St. Martin's Press, c1977. 318 p.: ill.; 25 cm. Includes index. 1. Contraception I. T.
RG136.S48     613.9/4     LC 76-62792     ISBN 0312081723

**Harper, Michael J. K.**      **5.5054**
Birth control technologies: prospects by the year 2000 / by Michael J.K. Harper. — 1st ed. — Austin: University of Texas Press, 1983. vi, 271 p.; 24 cm. Includes index. 1. Contraceptives — Research. I. T.
RG137.H37 1983     613.9/4 19     LC 82-15940     ISBN 0292707398

**Merkin, Donald H.**      **5.5055**
Pregnancy as a disease: the pill in society / Donald H. Merkin. — Port Washington, N.Y.: Kennikat Press, 1976. xv, 134 p.; 23 cm. — (National university publications) Includes index. 1. Oral contraceptives — Social aspects 2. Oral contraceptives — Side effects 3. Diethylstilbestrol 4. Drugs — Law and legislation — United States. I. T.
RG137.5.M45     613.9/432     LC 76-12971     ISBN 080469138X

**Gannon, Linda.**      **5.5056**
Menstrual disorders and menopause: biological, psychological, and cultural research / Linda R. Gannon. — New York: Praeger, 1985. xii, 285 p.: ill. Includes indexes. 1. Menstruation disorders 2. Menopause I. T.
RG161.G35 1985     618.1/72 19     LC 85-3629     ISBN 0030632439

**The Menopause / edited by Herbert J. Buchsbaum.**      **5.5057**
New York: Springer-Verlag, c1983. xiv, 225 p.: ill.; 28 cm. (Clinical perspectives in obstetrics and gynecology.) 1. Menopause I. Buchsbaum, Herbert J., 1934- II. Series.
RG186.M434 1983     618.1/72 19     LC 83-405     ISBN 0387908250

**Rothenberg, Robert E.**      **5.5058**
The complete book of breast care / by Robert E. Rothenberg. — New York: Crown Publishers, [1975] xi, 244 p.: ill.; 24 cm. 'A Medbook publication.' 1. Breast — Care and hygiene 2. Breast — Diseases I. T.
RG493.R67 1975     618.1/9     LC 74-30108     ISBN 0517519097

**Oakley, Ann.**      **5.5059**

# RG500–991 Obstetrics

The captured womb: a history of the medical care of pregnant women / Ann Oakley. — Oxford [Oxfordshire]; New York, N.Y.: B. Blackwell, 1984. 352 p.: ill.; 24 cm. Includes index. 1. Prenatal care — Great Britain — History — 20th century. I. T.
RG516.O2 1984     362.1/982/00941 19     LC 84-8856     ISBN 0631141529

**Donegan, Jane B. (Jan Bauer), 1933-.**      **5.5060**
Women & men midwives: medicine, morality, and misogyny in early America / Jane B. Donegan. — Westport, Conn.: Greenwood Press, 1978. viii, 316 p.: ill.; 22 cm. — (Contributions in medical history; no. 2 0147-1058) Includes index. 1. Obstetrics — United States — History. 2. Midwives — United States — History. 3. Women in medicine — United States — History. 4. Sex discrimination in medicine — United States — History. 5. Sex discrimination against women — United States — History. 6. Women — United States — Social conditions. 7. Misogyny — United States — History. I. T.
RG518.U5 D66     618.2     LC 77-87968     ISBN 0837198682

**Leavitt, Judith Walzer.**      **5.5061**
Brought to bed: childbearing in America, 1750 to 1950 / Judith Walzer Leavitt. — New York: Oxford University Press, 1986. ix, 284 p.: ill.; 25 cm. Includes index. 1. Obstetrics — United States — History — 18th century. 2. Obstetrics — United States — History — 19th century. 3. Obstetrics — United States — History — 20th century. 4. Childbirth — United States — History — 18th century. 5. Childbirth — United States — History — 19th century. 6. Childbirth — United States — History — 20th century. I. T.
RG518.U5 L4 1986     618.2/00973 19     LC 85-30967     ISBN 0195038436

**Arms, Suzanne.**      **5.5062**
Immaculate deception: a new look at women and childbirth in America / Suzanne Arms. — Boston: Houghton Mifflin, 1975. xiii, 318 p.: ill.; 16 x 23 cm.

'A San Francisco Book Company/Houghton Mifflin book.' Includes index. 1. Childbirth 2. Obstetrics — United States. I. T.
RG525.A79     618.2/00973     LC 74-28129     ISBN 0395198933

**Parfitt, Rebecca Rowe, 1942-.**      **5.5063**
The birth primer: a source book of traditional and alternative methods in labor and delivery / Rebecca Rowe Parfitt. — Philadelphia: Running Press, c1977. xiv, 259 p.: ill.; 26 cm. Includes index. 1. Childbirth 2. Obstetrics — Popular works. I. T.
RG525.P248     618.4 19     LC 77-12403     ISBN 0894710028 pbk

**Simkin, Penny, 1938-.**      **5.5064**
Pregnancy, childbirth, and the newborn: a complete guide for expectant parents / by Penny Simkin, Janet Whalley, and Ann Keppler. — Deephaven, MN: Meadowbrook Books, 1984. iv, 282 p.: ill.; 24 cm. Includes index. 1. Pregnancy 2. Childbirth 3. Infants (Newborn) — Care and hygiene. I. Whalley, Janet, 1945- II. Keppler, Ann, 1946- III. T.
RG525.S585 1984     618.2 19     LC 83-21941     ISBN 0881660043

**Arney, William Ray.**      **5.5065**
Power and the profession of obstetrics / William Ray Arney. — Chicago: University of Chicago Press, 1983. xi, 290 p.: ill. 1. Obstetrics — Social aspects 2. Obstetrics — Practice 3. Midwives 4. Physician and patient 5. Power (Social sciences) I. T.
RG526.A76 1982     RG526 A76 1982.     362.1/982 19     LC 82-8410
    ISBN 0226027287

**Test–tube women: what future for motherhood? / edited by Rita**      **5.5066**
**Arditti, Renate Duelli Klein, and Shelley Minden.**
London; Boston: Pandora Press, 1984. x, 482 p.; 20 cm. Includes index. 1. Pregnancy — Social aspects — Addresses, essays, lectures. 2. Human reproduction — Social aspects — Addresses, essays, lectures. 3. Medical innovations — Social aspects — Addresses, essays, lectures. 4. Pro-choice movement — Addresses, essays, lectures. I. Arditti, Rita, 1934- II. Duelli-Klein, Renate. III. Minden, Shelley.
RG556.T47 1984     304.6/32 19     LC 84-4282     ISBN 0863580300

**Hees-Stauthamer, Jellemieke C. (Jellemieke Christine), 1950-.**      **5.5067**
The first pregnancy: an integrating principle in female psychology / by Jellemieke C. Hees–Stauthamer. — Ann Arbor, Mich.: UMI Research Press, c1985. xvi, 174 p.: ill.; 24 cm. (Research in clinical psychology. no. 13) Includes index. 1. Pregnancy — Psychological aspects 2. Children, First-born 3. Pregnant women — Attitudes. I. T. II. Series.
RG560.H44 1985     618.2/001/9 19     LC 85-5791     ISBN 0835716570

**Oakley, Ann.**      **5.5068**
Women confined: towards a sociology of childbirth / Ann Oakley. — New York: Schocken Books, 1980. ix, 334 p.; 21 cm. Includes index. 1. Pregnancy — Psychological aspects 2. Childbirth — Psychological aspects 3. Childbirth — Social aspects. 4. Mothers 5. Obstetrics — Social aspects I. T.
RG560.O25     618.4/01/9     LC 79-26267     ISBN 0805237437

**Volpe, E. Peter (Erminio Peter)**      **5.5069**
Patient in the womb / by E. Peter Volpe. — Macon, GA.: Mercer, c1984. x, 157 p.: ill.; 24 cm. — (Mercer's sesquicentennial series.) 1. Fetus — Diseases — Genetic aspects. 2. Fetus — Abnormalities 3. Prenatal diagnosis I. T. II. Series.
RG626.V6 1984     618.3 19     LC 84-10746     ISBN 0865541221

**Smith, David W., 1926-1981.**      **5.5070**
Recognizable patterns of human malformation: genetic, embryologic, and clinical aspects / by David W. Smith with the assistance of Kenneth Lyons Jones. — 3rd ed. — Philadelphia: Saunders, 1982. xvii, 653 p.: ill.; 27 cm. — (Major problems in clinical pediatrics. v. 7) 1. Abnormalities, Human — Etiology 2. Human mechanics 3. Morphogenesis 4. Birth injuries 5. Growth disorders I. Jones, Kenneth Lyons. II. T. III. Series.
RG627.5.S58 1982     616/.043 19     LC 81-50624     ISBN 0721683819

**Young, Diony, 1938-.**      **5.5071**
Changing childbirth: family birth in the hospital / Diony Young. — Rochester, N.Y.: Childbirth Graphics, 1982. xvii, 516 p.: ill.; 22 cm. 1. Childbirth 2. Labor (Obstetrics) 3. Family 4. Hospitals, Gynecologic and obstetric — Psychological aspects. I. T.
RG651.Y68 1982     618.4 19     LC 82-9492     ISBN 0943114004

**Sandelowski, Margarete.**      **5.5072**
Pain, pleasure, and American childbirth: from the twilight sleep to the read method, 1914–1960 / Margarete Sandelowski. — Westport, Conn.: Greenwood Press, 1984. xix, 152 p.; 22 cm. — (Contributions in medical history. 0147-1058; no. 13) Includes index. 1. Childbirth — United States — History — 20th century. 2. Natural childbirth — United States — History — 20th century. 3. Pain 4. Childbirth — Psychological aspects I. T. II. Series.
RG652.S243 1984     618.4/5 19     LC 83-18510     ISBN 0313240760

**Dick-Read, Grantly, 1890-1959.** • 5.5073
The natural childbirth primer. — New York: Harper, [1956, c1955] 52 p.: ill.; 22 cm. First published in London in 1955 under title: Antenatal illustrated. 1. Childbirth — Psychology. I. T.
RG661.D5 1956    618.4    *LC* 56-6913

**Rothman, Barbara Katz.** 5.5074
In labor: women and power in the birthplace / Barbara Katz Rothman. — 1st ed. — New York: Norton, c1982. 320 p.; 22 cm. 1. Maternal health services — United States. 2. Childbirth — United States. 3. Midwives — United States. 4. Obstetrics — Social aspects — United States. I. T.
RG960.R67 1982    362.1/982 19    *LC* 81-19027    *ISBN* 039301584X

# RJ PEDIATRICS

**Developmental–behavioral pediatrics / Melvin D. Levine ... [et** 5.5075
**al.].**
Philadelphia: Saunders, 1983. xxviii, 1253 p.: ill.; 27 cm. Some ill. on lining papers. 1. Pediatrics 2. Pediatrics — Psychological aspects. I. Levine, Melvin D.
RJ47.D48 1983    618.92/8 19    *LC* 82-40187    *ISBN* 0721657443

**Goodman, Richard M. (Richard Merle), 1932-.** 5.5076
The malformed infant and child: an illustrated guide / Richard M. Goodman, Robert J. Gorlin; medical illustrator, Deborah Meyer. — New York: Oxford University Press, 1983. ix, 460 p.: ill.; 27 cm. Includes index. 1. Children — Diseases — Diagnosis 2. Infants — Diseases — Diagnosis 3. Abnormalities, Human — Diagnosis. I. Gorlin, Robert J., 1923- II. T.
RJ50.G65 1983    618.92/0043 19    *LC* 82-14085    *ISBN* 0195032543

**Spock, Benjamin, 1903-.** 5.5077
Baby and child care / Benjamin Spock and Michael B. Rothenberg; consultants, Lawrence R. Berger, Kathryn A. Mikesell; illustrations by Dorothea Fox. — Rev. and updated ed. — New York: E.P. Dutton, c1985. xxi, 647 p.: ill.; 22 cm. First published in 1946 under title: Common sense book of baby and child care. Includes index. 1. Infants — Care and hygiene. 2. Children — Care and hygiene. I. Rothenberg, Michael B. II. Spock, Benjamin, 1903- Common sense book of baby and child care. III. T.
RJ61.S76 1985    649/.1 19    *LC* 85-60149    *ISBN* 0525243127

**Medical problems in the classroom: the teacher's role in** 5.5078
**diagnosis and management / edited by Robert H.A. Haslam and**
**Peter J. Valletutti.**
2nd ed. — Austin, Tex.: PRO-ED, c1985. xi, 481 p.: ill.; 23 cm. 1. Children — Diseases — Addresses, essays, lectures. 2. School children — Health and hygiene — Addresses, essays, lectures. 3. Exceptional children — Education — Addresses, essays, lectures. I. Haslam, Robert H. A., 1936- II. Valletutti, Peter J.
RJ71.M42 1985    618.92/00024372 19    *LC* 85-3521    *ISBN* 0936104740

**Advocacy for child mental health / edited by Irving N. Berlin.** 5.5079
New York: Brunner/Mazel, [1975] 338 p.; 22 cm. 1. Child mental health 2. Child mental health services I. Berlin, Irving Norman, 1917-
RJ111.A33    362.7/8/20425    *LC* 74-78716    *ISBN* 0876300964

**Leach, Penelope.** 5.5080
Babyhood: stage by stage, from birth to age two: how your baby develops physically, emotionally, mentally / Penelope Leach. — 1st American ed. — New York: Knopf distributed by Random House, 1976. xix, 344, xiii p.; 25 cm. Includes index. 1. Infants — Development I. T.
RJ131.L37 1976    612.6/5    *LC* 76-13676    *ISBN* 0394498429

**Tanner, J. M. (James Mourilyan)** 5.5081
Foetus into man: physical growth from conception to maturity / J. M. Tanner. — Cambridge, Mass.: Harvard University Press, 1978. 250 p.: ill.; 22 cm. Includes indexes. 1. Children — Growth I. T.
RJ131.T29    612.6    *LC* 77-13728    *ISBN* 0674307038

**Batshaw, Mark L., 1945-.** 5.5082
Children with handicaps: a medical primer / by Mark L. Batshaw and Yvonne M. Perret; drawings by Elaine Kasmer. — Baltimore: Brookes Pub. Co., c1981. xiii, 447 p.: ill.; 24 cm. 1. Handicapped children — Care 2. Developmentally disabled children — Care and treatment. 3. Child development deviations I. Perret, Yvonne M., 1946- II. T.
RJ138.B37    618.92 19    *LC* 81-9961    *ISBN* 0933716168

**Physically handicapped children: a medical atlas for teachers /** 5.5083
**edited by Eugene E. Bleck, Donald A. Nagel.**
2nd ed. — New York: Grune & Stratton, c1982. xxii, 530 p.: ill.; 29 cm. 1. Physically handicapped children 2. Children — Diseases 3. Physically handicapped children — Education I. Bleck, E. E. (Eugene Edmund), 1923- II. Nagel, Donald A.
RJ138.P45 1982    618.92/7 19    *LC* 81-6804    *ISBN* 0808913913

**Sussman, George D., 1943-.** 5.5084
Selling mothers' milk: the wet–nursing business in France, 1715–1914 / George D. Sussman. — Urbana: University of Illinois Press, c1982. xi, 210 p., [4] leaves of plates: ill.; 24 cm. Includes index. 1. Wet-nurses — France — History — 18th century. 2. Wet-nurses — France — History — 19th century. 3. France — Social conditions — 18th century 4. France — Social conditions — 19th century I. T.
RJ216.S9 1982    338.4/76493 19    *LC* 81-16277    *ISBN* 0252009193

**Mahan, L. Kathleen.** 5.5085
Nutrition in adolescence / L. Kathleen Mahan, Jane Mitchell Rees. — St. Louis: Times Mirror/Mosby College Pub., 1984. xv, 331 p.: ill.; 24 cm. 1. Youth — Nutrition I. Rees, Jane Mitchell. II. T.
RJ235.M33 1984    613.2/088055 19    *LC* 83-9124    *ISBN* 0801630703

**Beuf, Ann H., 1938-.** 5.5086
Biting off the bracelet: a study of children in hospitals / Ann Hill Beuf. — [Philadelphia]: University of Pennsylvania Press, 1979. ix, 164 p.; 21 cm. Includes index. 1. Children — Hospital care 2. Children — Hospitals — Sociological aspects. 3. Hospitals — Sociological aspects I. T.
RJ242.B47    362.7/8/11    *LC* 79-13411    *ISBN* 081227766X

**Whaley, Lucille F., 1923-.** 5.5087
Nursing care of infants and children / Lucille F. Whalry, Donna L. Wong. — 3rd ed. — St. Louis: Mosby, 1986. p. cm. 1. Pediatric nursing I. Wong, Donna L., 1948- II. T.
RJ245.W47 1986    618.92/00024613 19    *LC* 86-23850    *ISBN* 0801654076

**Crelin, Edmund S., 1923-.** 5.5088
Functional anatomy of the newborn [by] Edmund S. Crelin. — New Haven: Yale University Press, 1973. xii, 87 p.: illus.; 27 cm. 1. Infants (Newborn) I. T.
RJ252.C74    611    *LC* 72-91292    *ISBN* 0300016328

**Lyon, Jeff.** 5.5089
Playing God in the nursery / Jeff Lyon. — 1st ed. — New York: W.W. Norton, c1985. 366 p.; 24 cm. An outgrowth of a series of articles written for the Chicago tribune in 1983. Includes index. 1. Neonatal intensive care — Moral and ethical aspects 2. Infanticide — Moral and ethical aspects. 3. Medical ethics I. T.
RJ253.5.L96 1985    174/.24 19    *LC* 84-25457    *ISBN* 0393018989

**Weir, Robert F., 1943-.** 5.5090
Selective nontreatment of handicapped newborns: moral dilemmas in neonatal medicine / Robert F. Weir. — New York: Oxford University Press, 1984. xii, 292 p.; 25 cm. 1. Neonatal intensive care — Moral and ethical aspects 2. Infants (Newborn) — Legal status, laws, etc. 3. Infanticide 4. Medical ethics I. T. Title: Handicapped newborns.
RJ253.5.W44 1984    174/.24 19    *LC* 83-19376    *ISBN* 0195033965

**Zimmerman, David R.** 5.5091
Rh: the intimate history of a disease and its conquest [by] David R. Zimmerman. — New York: Macmillan, [1973] xviii, 371 p.: illus.; 24 cm. 1. Erythroblastosis fetalis 2. Rh factor I. T.
RJ270.Z55    618.3/2    *LC* 72-90280

**Physical disabilities and health impairments: an introduction /** 5.5092
**John Umbreit, editor.**
Columbus: C.E. Merrill Pub. Co., c1983. xvi, 301 p.: ill.; 29 cm. Includes bibliographies and index. 1. Musculoskeletal system — Abnormalities. 2. Neuromuscular diseases in children 3. Children — Diseases I. Umbreit, John.
RJ480.P48 1983    618.92 19    *LC* 82-62477    *ISBN* 0675200458

**National Institute of Mental Health Conference on Dyslexia,** 5.5093
**Rockville, Md., 1977.**
Dyslexia: an appraisal of current knowledge / edited by Arthur L. Benton, David Pearl. — New York: Oxford University Press, 1978. xvii, 544 p.: ill.; 24 cm. Papers from National Institute of Mental Health Conference on Dyslexia, March 7 and 8, 1977.' Includes index. 1. Dyslexia — Congresses. I. Benton, Arthur Lester, 1909- II. Pearl, David, 1921- III. National Institute of Mental Health (U.S.) IV. T.
RJ496.A5 N37 1977    616.8/553    *LC* 78-3483    *ISBN* 0195023846

**Eisenson, Jon, 1907-.** 5.5094
Aphasia in children. — New York: Harper & Row, [1972] viii, 216 p.: illus.; 22 cm. 1. Aphasic children I. T.
RJ496.A6 E57 618.9/28/552 *LC* 78-174529 *ISBN* 0060418818

**Handbook of minimal brain dysfunctions: a critical view /** 5.5095
**edited by Herbert E. Rie, Ellen D. Rie.**
New York: J. Wiley, c1980. xxii, 744 p.: ill.; 26 cm. — (Wiley series on personality processes) 'A Wiley-Interscience publicaton.' 1. Minimal brain dysfunction in children I. Rie, Herbert E., 1931- II. Rie, Ellen D.
RJ496.B7 H36 618.9/28/58 19 *LC* 78-25656 *ISBN* 0471029599

# RJ499–506 Mental Disorders of Children

**Basic handbook of child psychiatry / Joseph D. Noshpitz,** 5.5096
**editor-in-chief.**
New York: Basic Books, c1979. 4 v.; 27 cm. 1. Child psychiatry I. Noshpitz, Joseph D.
RJ499.B33 618.92/89 19 *LC* 78-7082

**Bettelheim, Bruno.** • 5.5097
Truants from life; the rehabilitation of emotionally disturbed children. — Glencoe, Ill.: Free Press, [1955] 511 p.: illus.; 22 cm. 1. Sonia Shankman Orthogenic School. 2. Mentally ill children I. T.
RJ499.B48 136.708 *LC* 55-7331

**Burlingham, Dorothy.** • 5.5098
Psychoanalytic studies of the sighted and the blind. — New York: International Universities Press, [1972] vi, 396 p.; 23 cm. 1. Mother and child. 2. Child psychiatry 3. Blind — Psychology. 4. Child analysis I. T.
RJ499.B73 618.9/28/91708 *LC* 76-184213 *ISBN* 082364510X

**Elkind, David, 1931-.** 5.5099
The hurried child: growing up too fast too soon / David Elkind. — Reading, Mass.: Addison-Wesley Pub. Co., 1982 (c1981). xiii, 210 p.; 25 cm. 1. Child mental health 2. Stress (Psychology) I. T.
RJ499.E415 305.2/3 19 *LC* 81-14842 *ISBN* 0201039664

**Freud, Anna, 1895-.** 5.5100
Normality and pathology in childhood; assessments of development. — New York: International Universities Press, [1965] xii, 273 p.; 23 cm. 1. Child psychiatry 2. Child study. 3. Child analysis I. T.
RJ499.F78 618.9289 *LC* 65-17007

**Joint Commission on Mental Health of Children.** 5.5101
Child mental health in international perspective; report. Edited by Henry P. David. — [1st ed.]. — New York: Harper & Row, [1972] xiii, 522 p.; 25 cm. 1. Child mental health — Addresses, essays, lectures. 2. Mentally ill children — Care and treatment — United States — Addresses, essays, lectures. 3. Mentally ill children — Care and treatment — Europe — Addresses, essays, lectures. I. David, Henry Philip, 1923- ed. II. T.
RJ499.J57 362.7/8/2 *LC* 70-181614 *ISBN* 0060122277

**Mahler, Margaret S.** 5.5102
The selected papers of Margaret S. Mahler, M.D. — New York: J. Aronson, c1979. 2 v.; 24 cm. Includes indexes. 1. Child psychiatry 2. Child psychology 3. Separation-individuation I. T.
RJ499.M234 618.92/89 19 *LC* 79-51915 *ISBN* 0876683715

**Ross, Alan O.** 5.5103
Psychological disorders of children; a behavioral approach to theory, research, and therapy [by] Alan O. Ross. — New York: McGraw-Hill, [1974] xviii, 360 p.: illus.; 23 cm. — (McGraw-Hill series in psychology) 1. Child psychiatry I. T.
RJ499.R66 618.9/28/9 *LC* 73-6617 *ISBN* 0070538670

**Winnicott, D. W. (Donald Woods), 1896-1971.** 5.5104
Therapeutic consultations in child psychiatry / [by] D. W. Winnicott. — New York: Basic Books [1971] 410 p.: ill.; 24 cm. 1. Child psychiatry 2. Child analysis I. T.
RJ499.W49 1971 618.92/8/917 *LC* 70-158448 *ISBN* 0465085113

**Spitz, René A. (René Arpad), 1887-1974.** 5.5105
René A. Spitz, dialogues from infancy: selected papers / edited by Robert N. Emde. — New York: International Universities Press, c1983. x, 484 p.; 24 cm. Includes index. 1. Infant psychiatry — Addresses, essays, lectures. I. Emde, Robert N. II. T. III. Title: Dialogues from infancy.
RJ502.5.S65 1983 618.92/89 19 *LC* 83-26461 *ISBN* 0823657876

**Greenspan, Stanley I.** 5.5106
The clinical interview of the child / Stanley I. Greenspan with the collaboration of Nancy Thorndike Greenspan. — New York: McGraw-Hill, c1981. 203 p.; 24 cm. Includes index. 1. Child psychopathology — Diagnosis. 2. Interviewing in psychiatry 3. Child psychology I. Greenspan, Nancy Thorndike. joint author. II. T.
RJ503.5.G73 618.92/89075 19 *LC* 80-39736 *ISBN* 0070243409

**Klein, Melanie.** 5.5107
[Psychoanalyse des Kindes. English] The psycho-analysis of children / by Melanie Klein; authorized translation by Alix Strachey; revised in collaboration with Alix Strachney by H.A. Thorner. — Free Press ed. — New York: Free Press, 1984, c1975. xvi, 326 p.; 25 cm. — (The Writings of Melanie Klein; v. 2) Translation of: Die Psychoanalyse des Kindes. Includes index. 1. Child analysis 2. Personality in children 3. Psychoanalysis I. T. II. Title: Psychoanalysis of children.
RJ504.2.K4413 1984 618.92/8917 19 *LC* 84-13774 *ISBN* 0029184304

**Graziano, Anthony M., 1932-.** 5.5108
Children and behavior therapy / Anthony M. Graziano, Kevin C. Mooney. — New York: Aldine, c1984. xii, 486 p.; 24 cm. Spine title: Children & behavior therapy. Includes index. 1. Behavior therapy for children 2. Child psychotherapy I. Mooney, Kevin C., 1955- II. T. III. Title: Children & behavior therapy.
RJ505.B4 G723 1984 618.92/89142 19 *LC* 83-25724 *ISBN* 0202260879

## RJ506 SPECIFIC DISORDERS, A–Z

**Autism, a reappraisal of concepts and treatment / edited by** 5.5109
**Michael Rutter and Eric Schopler.**
New York: Plenum Press, c1978. xii, 540 p.; 24 cm. 'Based on papers presented at the International Symposium on Autism held in St. Gallen, Switzerland, July 12-15, 1976.' 1. Autism — Congresses. I. Rutter, Michael. II. Schopler, Eric. III. International Symposium on Autism. (1976: Saint Gall, Switzerland)
RJ506.A9 A89 618.9/28/982 *LC* 77-26910 *ISBN* 0306310961

**Bettelheim, Bruno.** • 5.5110
The empty fortress: infantile autism and the birth of the self. — New York: Free Press, [1967] xiv, 484 p.: ill.; 24 cm. 1. Autism I. T.
RJ506.A9 B4 618.9289 *LC* 67-10886

**Lovaas, O. Ivar (Ole Ivar), 1927-.** 5.5111
The autistic child: language development through behavior modification / by O. Ivar Lovaas. — New York: Irvington Publishers: distributed by Halsted Press, c1977. viii, 246 p.: ill.; 25 cm. Includes indexes. 1. Autism 2. Mentally ill children — Education — Language arts. 3. Behavior modification I. T.
RJ506.A9 L68 371.9/2 *LC* 76-5890 *ISBN* 0470150653

**McKnew, Donald H.** 5.5112
Why isn't Johnny crying: coping with depression in children / Donald H. McKnew, Leon Cytryn, Herbert C. Yahraes; with a foreword by Reginald Lourie. — 1st ed. — New York: W.W. Norton, c1983. 187 p.: ill. Includes index. 1. Depression in children I. Cytryn, Leon. II. Yahraes, Herbert C. III. T.
RJ506.D4 M34 1983 618.92/8527 19 *LC* 82-22556 *ISBN* 0393017249

**Hyperactive children: the social ecology of identification and** 5.5113
**treatment / edited by Carol K. Whalen, Barbara Henker.**
New York: Academic Press, 1980. xxiv, 407 p.: ill.; 24 cm. Includes index. 1. Hyperactive children I. Whalen, Carol K. II. Henker, Barbara A.
RJ506.H9 H963 618.92/8589 *LC* 80-324 *ISBN* 0127459502

**Winnicott, D. W. (Donald Woods), 1896-1971.** 5.5114
Deprivation and delinquency / D.W. Winnicott; edited by Clare Winnicott, Ray Shepherd, and Madeleine Davis. — London; New York: Tavistock Publications; New York: Tavistock Publications in association with Methuen, 1984. vi, 294 p.; 23 cm. Includes indexes. 1. Juvenile delinquency 2. Antisocial personality disorders 3. Deprivation (Psychology) 4. Parental deprivation 5. Child psychotherapy — Residential treatment 6. World War, 1939-1945 — Children — Great Britain. 7. World War, 1939-1945 — Evacuation of civilians — Great Britain. I. Winnicott, Clare. II. Shepherd, Ray. III. Davis, Madeleine. IV. T.
RJ506.J88 W56 1984 616.85/82071/088055 19 *LC* 84-8837 *ISBN* 0422791709

**Advances in learning and behavioral disabilities.** 5.5115
Vol. 1 (1982)- . — Greenwich, Conn.: JAI Press, c1982-. v.; 24 cm. Annual. 'A research annual.' 1. Learning disabilities — Periodicals. 2. Problem children — Periodicals. I. Gadow, Kenneth D. II. Bialer, Irv, 1919-
RJ506.L4 A33 618.92/89 19 *LC* 82-645749

**Mulliken, Ruth K.**                                                    **5.5116**
Assessment of multihandicapped and developmentally disabled children / Ruth K. Mulliken, John J. Buckley. — Rockville, Md.: Aspen Systems Corp., 1983. x, 343 p.; 24 cm. 'An Aspen publication.' 1. Mentally handicapped children — Psychological testing 2. Developmentally disabled children — Testing. I. Buckley, John J. (John Jay), 1947- II. T.
RJ506.M4 M84 1983    618.92/8588075 19    *LC* 83-3739    *ISBN* 089443876X

**Robinson, Nancy M.**                                                    **5.5117**
The mentally retarded child: a psychological approach / Nancy M. Robinson, Halbert B. Robinson; with contributions by Gilbert S. Omenn, Joseph C. Campione. — 2d ed. — New York: McGraw-Hill, c1976. xvi, 592 p.: ill.; 25 cm. (McGraw-Hill series in psychology) Order of authors' names reversed in 1965 ed. Includes indexes. 1. Mentally handicapped children 2. Mental retardation I. Robinson, Halbert B. joint author. II. T.
RJ506.M4 R62 1976    618.9/28/588    *LC* 75-30903    *ISBN* 0070532028

**Massie, Henry N.**                                                      **5.5118**
Childhood psychosis in the first four years of life / Henry N. Massie, Judith Rosenthal. — New York: McGraw-Hill, c1984. x, 315 p.: ill.; 24 cm. Includes index. 1. Psychoses in children 2. Infant psychiatry I. Rosenthal, Judith. II. T.
RJ506.P69 M37 1984    618.92/89 19    *LC* 83-26799    *ISBN* 0070407657

**Cantor, Sheila, 1939-.**                                               **5.5119**
The schizophrenic child: a primer for parents and professionals / Sheila Cantor; with a preface by Peter Tanguay. — 1st ed. — Montréal: Eden Press, c1982. vii, 129 p.; 22 cm. 1. Schizophrenia in children I. T.
RJ506.S3 C35    618.92/8982 19    *ISBN* 0920792138

# RK Dentistry

**Wiles, Cheryl B.**                                                      **5.5120**
Communication for dental auxiliaries / Cheryl B. Wiles, William J. Ryan. — Reston, Va.: Reston Pub. Co., c1982. xx, 231 p.: ill.; 23 cm. 1. Communication in dentistry 2. Dental personnel and patient 3. Dental teams 4. Dental auxiliary personnel I. Ryan, William J. II. T.
RK28.3.W54 1982    617.6/01/07 19    *LC* 81-19254    *ISBN* 0835908976

**Ring, Malvin E.**                                                       **5.5121**
Dentistry: an illustrated history / Malvin E. Ring. — New York: Abrams; Toronto: C. V. Mosby Co., 1985. 319 p.: ill. (some col.) Includes index. 1. Dentistry — History I. T.
RK29.R54 1985    617.6/009 19    *LC* 85-3883    *ISBN* 0810911000

**Maury, F.**                                                            **5.5122**
Treatise on the dental art founded on actual experience / by F. Maury; translated from the French with notes and additions by J.B. Savier. — Boston: Milford House, 1972. 324 p.: ill. 1. Dentistry I. T.
RK50.M3    *LC* 72-92721    *ISBN* 0878210253

**Garfield, Sydney, 1915-.**                                        • **5.5123**
Teeth, teeth, teeth: a treatise on teeth ... — New York: Simon and Schuster, [1971, c1969] 448 p.: ill., ports.; 25 cm. 1. Dentistry 2. Teeth I. T.
RK51.5.G36 1971    617/.6    *LC* 74-162711    *ISBN* 0671210971

**International dental care delivery systems: issues in dental** **5.5124**
**health policies: proceedings of a colloquium / edited by John I.**
**Ingle, Patricia Blair.**
Cambridge, Mass.: Published for the W. K. Kellogg Foundation, Battle Creek, Mich. [by] Ballinger Pub. Co., c1978. xxi, 263 p.: ill.; 24 cm. At head of title: The Institute of Medicine and the Pan American Health Organization. 1. Dental care — Congresses. 2. Dental policy — Congresses. I. Ingle, John Ide, 1919- II. Blair, Patricia Wohlgemuth. III. Institute of Medicine (U.S.) IV. Pan American Health Organization.
RK52.I57    362.1/9/76    *LC* 78-13352    *ISBN* 0884105296

**Dunning, James Morse, 1904-.**                                         **5.5125**
Dental care for everyone: problems and proposals / James M. Dunning. — Cambridge: Harvard University Press, 1976. xii, 234 p.; 24 cm. 1. Dental care — United States. 2. Dental economics — United States. I. T.
RK52.2.D86    362.1/9/7600973    *LC* 75-40216    *ISBN* 0674197909

**Davis, Peter B.**                                                      **5.5126**
The social context of dentistry / Peter Davis. — London: Croom Helm, c1980. 189 p.; 23 cm. Includes index. 1. Dentistry — Social aspects I. T.
RK52.5.D38    306/.4 19    *LC* 80-511085    0709905126

**Fluorides and dental caries: contemporary concepts for** **5.5127**
**practitioners and students / edited by Ernest Newbrun; with a**
**foreword by Yngve Ericsson.**
3rd ed. — Springfield, Ill., U.S.A.: Thomas, c1986. xx, 289 p.: ill.; 27 cm. 1. Dental caries — Prevention 2. Fluorides — Physiological effect 3. Water — Fluoridation I. Newbrun, Ernest.
RK331.F56 1986    617.6/7061 19    *LC* 85-24520    *ISBN* 0398051968

# RM Therapeutics. Pharmacology

**The Pharmacological basis of therapeutics / editors, Louis S.** **5.5128**
**Goodman, Alfred Gilman, associate editors, Alfred G. Gilman,**
**George B. Koelle.**
5th ed. — New York: Macmillan, [1975] xvi, 1704 p.: ill.; 27 cm. 1. Pharmacology 2. Chemotherapy I. Goodman, Louis Sanford, 1906- II. Gilman, Alfred, 1908-
RM101.P53 1975    615/.7    *LC* 75-15903    *ISBN* 0023447818

**Bodinski, Lois H.**                                                    **5.5129**
The nurse's guide to diet therapy / Lois H. Bodinski. — 2nd ed. — New York: Wiley, c1987. xix, 492 p.; 24 cm. — (Wiley medical publication.) 'First edition prepared in consultation with Roba Ritt.' 1. Diet therapy 2. Nursing I. T. II. Series.
RM216.B658 1987    615.8/54 19    *LC* 86-24629    *ISBN* 0471011967

**Krause, Marie V.**                                                     **5.5130**
Food, nutrition, and diet therapy: a textbook of nutritional care / Marie V. Krause, L. Kathleen Mahan. — 7th ed. — Philadelphia: Saunders, 1984. xiii, 1010 p.: ill.; 28 cm. Cover title: Food, nutrition & diet therapy. 1. Diet therapy 2. Nutrition 3. Food I. Mahan, L. Kathleen. II. T. III. Title: Food, nutrition & diet therapy.
RM216.K74 1984    615.8/54 19    *LC* 83-20384    *ISBN* 0721655149

**Bennett, William, 1941-.**                                             **5.5131**
The dieter's dilemma: eating less and weighing more / William Bennett & Joel Gurin. — New York: Basic Books, c1982. xiv, 315 p.; 22 cm. 1. Reducing diets 2. Obesity 3. Body image 4. Body, Human — Social aspects I. Gurin, Joel, 1953- II. T.
RM222.2.B443 1982    613.2/5/019 19    *LC* 81-68403    *ISBN* 0465016529

**Chernin, Kim.**                                                        **5.5132**
The obsession: reflections on the tyranny of slenderness / Kim Chernin. — 1st ed. — New York: Harper & Row, c1981. xi, 206 p. 1. Reducing — Social aspects. 2. Reducing — Psychological aspects. I. T.
RM222.2.C47 1981    RM222.2 C25 1981.    391/.62/0973 19    *LC* 81-47224    *ISBN* 0060148845

**Brody, Jane E.**                                                       **5.5133**
[Good food book] Jane Brody's Good food book: living the high–carbohydrate way / by Jane E. Brody; illustrations by Ray Skibinski. — New York: Norton, c1985. xxviii, 700 p.: ill.; 25 cm. Includes index. 1. High-carbohydrate diet — Recipes I. T. II. Title: Good food book.
RM237.59.B76 1985    613.2/8 19    *LC* 85-2966    *ISBN* 0393022102

**Lappé, Marc.**                                                         **5.5134**
Germs that won't die: medical consequences of the misuse of antibiotics / Marc Lappé. — 1st ed. — Garden City: Anchor Press/Doubleday, 1982. xvi, 246 p.: ill.; 22 cm. Includes index. 1. Antibiotics 2. Drug resistance in microorganisms 3. Medication abuse — Complications and sequelae I. T.
RM267.L36    615/.329 19    *LC* 81-43146    *ISBN* 0385150938

**American Medical Association. Division of Drugs.**                     **5.5135**
AMA drug evaluations / prepared by the AMA Division of Drugs, in cooperation with the American Society for Clinical Pharmacology and Therapeutics. — 5th ed. — [Chicago, Ill.: distributed by American Medical Association; Philadelphia: distributed worldwide by W.B. Saunders Co., 1983. 1884 p.: ill.; 26 cm. 1. Drugs I. American Society for Clinical Pharmacology and Therapeutics. II. T. III. Title: Drug evaluations.
RM300.A553    *LC* sn 84-12107    *ISBN* 0721611079

**Clinical pharmacology: basic principles in therapeutics / edited**    **5.5136**
**by Kenneth L. Melmon and Howard F. Morrelli.**
2d ed. — New York: Macmillan, c1978. xiv, 1146 p.: ill.; 26 cm.
1. Pharmacology I. Melmon, Kenneth L., 1934- II. Morrelli, Howard F.,
1935-
RM300.C55 1978    615/.58    *LC* 77-5690    *ISBN* 0023802308

**Folb, Peter I., 1938-.**    **5.5137**
The safety of medicines, evaluation and prediction / Peter I. Folb; foreword by
J. R. Trounce. — Berlin; New York: Springer-Verlag, 1980. xi, 103 p.; 21 cm.
1. Drugs — Side effects 2. Drugs — Safety measures. 3. Drugs — Testing
4. Drug utilization — Evaluation I. T.
RM302.5.F64    615/.7/0287    *LC* 80-17994    *ISBN* 0387101438

**Bush, Patricia J.**    **5.5138**
Drugs, alcohol, & sex / Patricia J. Bush. — New York, N.Y.: R. Marek, c1980.
287 p.; 24 cm. 'How you can help or harm your sex life with alcohol, prescribed
and over-the-counter medicines, and recreational drugs, includes aphrodisiacs,
the pill, marijuana, uppers, downers, psychedelics, hormones,
antihypertensives, steroids, volatile inhalants, and feminine hygiene products.'
1. Generative organs — Effect of drugs on. 2. Drugs — Physiological effect
3. Alcohol — Physiological effect I. T.
RM380.B87    613.9/5    *LC* 80-15481    *ISBN* 0399900802

**Van der Zee, Barbara.**    **5.5139**
Green pharmacy: a history of herbal medicine / Barbara Griggs. — New York:
Viking Press, 1982, c1981. xii, 379 p.; 24 cm. Includes index. 1. Herbs —
Therapeutic use — History. 2. Materia medica, Vegetable — History. I. T.
RM666.H33 V36 1982    615/.321/09 19    *LC* 81-51885    *ISBN*
0670354341

**Huxley, Aldous, 1894-1963.**    **5.5140**
The doors of perception. [1st ed. New York] Harper [1954] 79 p. 20 cm.
1. Peyote 2. Mescaline I. T.
RM666.P48 H9    615.323471    *LC* 54-5833

**Physicians' desk reference for nonprescription drugs.**    **5.5141**
7th ed. 1st- ed.; 1980-. Oradell, N.J.: Medical Economics Co., 1986. 1 v.: ill.; 26
cm. 1. Drugs, Nonprescription — Periodicals.
RM671.A1 P48    615/.1/05    *LC* 80-644575

**Occupational therapy strategies and adaptations for independent**    **5.5142**
**daily living / Florence S. Cromwell, editor.**
New York: Haworth Press, c1984. 186 p.: ill.; 23 cm. 'Has also been published
as Occupational therapy in health care, volume 1, number 4, winter 1984'—T.p.
verso. 1. Occupational therapy — Addresses, essays, lectures. 2. Life skills —
Addresses, essays, lectures. I. Cromwell, Florence S.
RM735.36.O29 1984    615.8/515 19    *LC* 84-19157    *ISBN*
0866563504

**Kraus, Richard G.**    **5.5143**
Therapeutic recreation service: principles and practices / Richard Kraus. —
3rd ed. — Philadelphia: Saunders College Pub., c1983. x, 454 p.: ill.; 24 cm.
Includes index. 1. Recreational therapy 2. Handicapped — Recreation
3. Aged — Recreation 4. Recreation and juvenile delinquency I. T.
RM736.7.K7 1983    362.1/78 19    *LC* 82-24059    *ISBN* 0030628520

**Cusack, Odean.**    **5.5144**
Pets and the elderly: the therapeutic bond / Odean Cusack, Elaine Smith. —
New York: Haworth Press, c1984. 257 p., [1] leaf of plates: ill.; 23 cm. 'Has also
been published as Activities, adaptation & aging, volume 4, numbers 2/3,
January 1984'—T.p. verso. Includes index. 1. Pets — Therapeutic use.
2. Aged — Rehabilitation. I. Smith, Elaine. II. T.
RM931.A65 C88 1984    615.8/515 19    *LC* 83-26409    *ISBN*
0866562591

# RS Pharmacy. Materia Medica

**The Merck index: an encyclopedia of chemicals, drugs, and**    **5.5145**
**biologicals / Martha Windholz, editor; Susan Budavari, co-**
**editor; Rosemary F. Blumetti, associate editor; Elizabeth S.**
**Otterbein, assistant editor.**
10th ed. — Rahway, N.J., U.S.A.: Merck, 1983. 2179 p. in various pagings: ill.;
26 cm. 1. Drugs — Dictionaries. 2. Chemicals — Dictionaries. I. Windholz,
Martha. II. Merck & Co.
RS51.M4 1983    615/.1/0321 19    *LC* 83-61075    *ISBN* 0911910271

**Krochmal, Arnold, 1919-.**    **5.5146**
A guide to the medicinal plants of the United States [by] Arnold & Connie
Krochmal. — [New York]: Quadrangle, [1973] 259 p.: illus.; 24 cm. 1. Materia

medica, Vegetable — United States. 2. Botany, Medical — United States.
I. Krochmal, Connie. joint author. II. T.
RS81.K76 1973    581.6/34/0973    *LC* 72-83289    *ISBN* 0812902610

**Remington's practice of pharmacy.**    • **5.5147**
[1st]- ed. Easton, Pa.: Mack Pub. Co., 1885-. 1. Pharmacy — Handbooks,
manuals, etc. I. Remington, Joseph Price, 1847-1918.
RS91.R4    *LC* 60-53334

**Wardell, William M.**    **5.5148**
Regulation and drug development / William M. Wardell and Louis Lasagna. —
Washington: American Enterprise Institute for Public Policy Research, 1975.
181 p.; 23 cm. (Evaluative studies; 21) 1. Drugs — Research — United States.
2. Drugs — Law and legislation — United States. 3. Pharmaceutical industry
— United States. 4. Pharmaceutical policy — United States. I. Lasagna,
Louis, 1923- joint author. II. T.
RS122.W37    615/.1/072073    *LC* 75-18947    *ISBN* 0844731676

**National formulary.**    • **5.5149**
1st- ed.;1888-. Washington, DC.: American Pharmaceutical Association.
v.: ill.; 24 cm. Separately paged supplements accompany some vols.
1. Medicine — Formulae, receipts, prescriptions — Periodicals. I. American
Pharmaceutical Association. II. American Pharmaceutical Association.
Committee on National Formulary. III. American Pharmaceutical
Association. National Formulary Board.
RS141.2.N3    615/.13/73 19    *LC* 55-4116

**The Pharmacopoeia of the United States of America.**    • **5.5150**
1820-1979. Easton, Pa. [etc.] 1820- [19— Vols. for 1830-19 called [1st]-
revision. Supplements accompany some volumes. 1. Pharmacopoeias —
United States. I. United States Pharmacopoeial Convention.
RS141.2.P5    *LC* 35-37146

**Lewis, Walter Hepworth.**    **5.5151**
Medical botany: plants affecting man's health / Walter H. Lewis, Memory P. F.
Elvin–Lewis. — New York: Wiley, c1977. xv, 515 p.: ill.; 26 cm. 'A Wiley-
Interscience publication.' Includes index. 1. Botany, Medical 2. Materia
medica, Vegetable I. Elvin-Lewis, Memory P. F., 1933- joint author. II. T.
RS164.L475    615/.32    *LC* 76-44376    *ISBN* 0471533203

**Clarke, Frank H.**    **5.5152**
Calculator programming for chemistry and the life sciences / Frank H. Clarke.
— New York: Academic Press, 1981. vii, 226 p.: ill.; 24 cm. 1. Chemistry,
Pharmaceutical — Computer programs. 2. Biology — Research — Computer
programs. 3. Programmable calculators I. T.
RS418.C55    542/.8 19    *LC* 81-15046    *ISBN* 0121753204

# RT Nursing

**Bridges, Daisy Caroline.**    • **5.5153**
A history of the International Council of Nurses, 1899–1964: the first sixty–five
years. — Philadelphia: Lippincott, [1967] xxvi, 254 p.: ill., ports.; 23 cm.
1. International Council of Nurses. I. T.
RT1.I6782    610.73/062/1    *LC* 67-7938

**Kalisch, Beatrice J., 1943-.**    **5.5154**
Politics of nursing / Beatrice J. Kalisch, Philip A. Kalisch; foreword by Daniel
K. Inouye. — Philadelphia: Lippincott, c1982. xv, 512 p.: ill.; 24 cm. Includes
index. 1. Nursing — Political aspects — United States. 2. Nursing —
Government policy — United States. 3. Medical policy — United States.
4. Nurses — United States — Political activity. I. Kalisch, Philip Arthur.
II. T.
RT4.K33    362.1/7 19    *LC* 81-8471    *ISBN* 0397542453

**Kalisch, Philip Arthur.**    **5.5155**
The advance of American nursing / Philip A. Kalisch, Beatrice J. Kalisch. —
2nd ed. — Boston: Little, Brown, c1986. x, 851 p.: ill.; 24 cm. Includes index.
1. Nursing — United States — History. I. Kalisch, Beatrice J., 1943- II. T.
RT4.K34 1986    362.1/73/0973 19    *LC* 85-19719    *ISBN*
0316482293

**Power and influence: a source book for nurses / edited by**    **5.5156**
**Kathleen R. Stevens.**
New York: Wiley, c1983. xxii, 304 p.; 22 cm. — (Wiley medical publication.)
1. Nursing — United States. 2. Nursing — Political aspects — United States.
3. Job satisfaction I. Stevens, Kathleen R. II. Series.
RT4.P68 1983    362.1/73 19    *LC* 82-13397    *ISBN* 0471088706

**Reverby, Susan.**                                                                 5.5157
Ordered to care: the dilemma of American nursing, 1850–1945 / Susan Reverby. — Cambridge; New York: Cambridge University Press, 1987. 1 v. (Cambridge history of medicine.) Includes index. 1. Nursing — United States — History — 19th century. 2. Nursing — United States — History — 20th century. I. T. II. Title: Dilemma of American nursing, 1850-1945. III. Series.
RT4.R45 1987      610.73/069 19      *LC* 86-26815      *ISBN* 0521256046

**Roberts, Mary M.**                                                           • 5.5158
American nursing; history and interpretation. New York, Macmillan, 1954. 688 p. illus. 22 cm. 1. Nurses and nursing — United States. I. T.
RT4.R6      *LC* 54-12563

---

# RT31–37 History. Biography

**Bullough, Vern L.**                                                                 5.5159
The care of the sick: the emergence of modern nursing / Vern and Bonnie Bullough. — New York: Prodist, 1978. 311 p.; 24 cm. Includes index. 1. Nursing — History. I. Bullough, Bonnie. joint author. II. T.
RT31.B813 1978      610.73/09      *LC* 78-14238      *ISBN* 0882021834

**Dolan, Josephine A.**                                                                 5.5160
Nursing in society: a historical perspective / Josephine A. Dolan, M. Louise Fitzpatrick, Eleanor Krohn Herrmann. — 15th ed. — Philadelphia: Saunders, 1983. viii, 417 p.: ill.; 26 cm. 1. Nursing — History. 2. Nursing — Social aspects — History. I. Fitzpatrick, M. Louise. II. Herrmann, Eleanor Krohn. III. T.
RT31.D64 1983      362.1/73 19      *LC* 82-48503      *ISBN* 0721631355

**Nutting, M. Adelaide (Mary Adelaide), 1858-1948.**                      • 5.5161
A history of nursing; the evolution of nursing systems from the earliest times to the foundation of the first English and American training schools for nurses. New York, London, G. P. Putnam's sons, 1907-12. 4 v. fronts., illus., plates, ports. 21 cm. 1. Nurses and nursing — History. I. Dock, Lavinia L., 1858-1956. joint author. II. T.
RT31.N95      *LC* 07-41533

**Stewart, Isabel Maitland.**                                                    • 5.5162
A history of nursing, from ancient to modern times; a world view. 5th ed. by Isabel M. Stewart and Anne L. Austin. New York, Putnam [1962] 516 p. illus. 22 cm. First ed., by L. L. Dock and I. M. Stewart, published in 1920 under title: A short history of nursing. 1. Nursing — History. I. Austin, Anne L., 1891- joint author. II. T.
RT31.S7      610.7309      *LC* 62-12843

**Cohn, Victor.**                                                                 5.5163
Sister Kenny: the woman who challenged the doctors / by Victor Cohn. — Minneapolis: University of Minnesota Press, 1976 (c1975). 302 p., [8] leaves of plates: ill., map; 24 cm. Includes index. 1. Kenny, Elizabeth. 2. Poliomyelitis — History. I. T.
RT37.K39 C63 1975      616.8/35/0620924 B      *LC* 75-15401      *ISBN* 0816607559

**Huxley, Elspeth Joscelin Grant, 1907-.**                                         5.5164
Florence Nightingale. New York, G. P. Putnam's Sons [1975] 254 p. ill. 26 cm. 1. Nightingale, Florence, 1820-1910. I. T.
RT 37 N68 H98 1975a      *LC* 74-19237      *ISBN* 0399114807

**Nightingale, Florence, 1820-1910.**                                          • 5.5165
Notes on nursing: what it is, and what it is not. — Philadelphia: University of Pennsylvania Printing Office, 1965. 79 p.; 23 cm. Facsim. of 1st ed., London, Harrison & Sons, 1860. 'Reproduction...upon the occasion of the two hundredth anniversary of the School of Medicine of the University of Pennsylvania ...1765-1965.' 1. Nursing I. T.
RT40.N5 1965      610.73      *LC* 64-23264

---

# RT41–69 General Works, 1901–

**Carnevali, Doris L.**                                                                 5.5166
Nursing care planning: diagnosis and management / Doris L. Carnevali. — 3rd ed. — Philadelphia: Lippincott, c1983. xviii, 333 p.: ill.; 24 cm. Rev. ed. of: Nursing care planning / Dolores E. Little. 2nd ed. c1976. 1. Nursing 2. Nursing care plans I. Little, Dolores E. Nursing care planning. II. T.
RT41.C288 1983      610.73 19      *LC* 82-13108      *ISBN* 0397544219

**Henderson, Virginia.**                                                                 5.5167
Principles and practice of nursing / Virginia Henderson, Gladys Nite. — 6th ed. — New York: Macmillan, c1978. xiii, 2119 p.: ill.; 26 cm. Editions for 1922-1955 by B. Harmer published under title: Textbook of the principles and practice of nursing; 4th ed. (1939) by B. Harmer and V. Henderson and 5th ed. (1955) rev. by V. Henderson. 1. Nursing I. Nite, Gladys, joint author. II. Harmer, Bertha. Textbook of the principles and practice of nursing. III. T.
RT41.H24 1978      610.73      *LC* 76-17020      *ISBN* 0023535806

**Introduction to nursing: an adaptation model / [edited by]**           5.5168
**Callista Roy.**
2nd ed. — Englewood Cliffs, N.J.: Prentice-Hall, c1984. xxi, 580 p.: ill.; 24 cm. 1. Nursing 2. Nursing — Psychological aspects I. Roy, Callista. II. Title: An adaptation model.
RT41.I57 1984      610.73 19      *LC* 83-24496      *ISBN* 0134912748

**Leddy, Susan.**                                                                 5.5169
Conceptual bases of professional nursing / Susan Leddy, J. Mae Pepper, contributors, Marie G. Finamore, Susan E. Gordon, Eleanor Rudick. — Philadelphia: Lippincott, c1985. xi, 330 p.; 24 cm. 1. Nursing I. Pepper, J. Mae. II. T.
RT41.L53 1985      610.73 19      *LC* 84-7903      *ISBN* 0397543964

**Little, Dolores E.**                                                           • 5.5170
Nursing care planning [by] Dolores E. Little [and] Doris L. Carnevali. Philadelphia, Lippincott [1969] x, 245 p. forms. 23 cm. 1. Nursing 2. Nursing care plans I. Carnevali, Doris L. joint author. II. T.
RT41.L75      *LC* 73-77965

**The Nurse's almanac / editor, Howard S. Rowland; director of**           5.5171
**research, Beatrice L. Rowland.**
2nd ed. — Rockville, Md.: Aspen Systems Corp., 1984. xiv, 849 p.: ill.; 24 cm. 'An Aspen publication.' 1. Nursing 2. Nursing — United States. I. Rowland, Howard S. II. Rowland, Beatrice L.
RT41.N85 1984      610.73 19      *LC* 84-12296      *ISBN* 089443599X

**Henderson, Virginia.**                                                           • 5.5172
The nature of nursing; a definition and its implications for practice, research, and education. — New York: Macmillan, [1966] vii, 84 p.: illus.; 24 cm. 'Contents grew out of a Clare Dennison memorial lecture at the University of Rochester School of Nursing ... 1964. A condensed version was published in The American journal of nursing in August, 1964.' 1. Nursing — Philosophy. I. T.
RT42.H4      610.73      *LC* 66-11434

**Rogers, Martha E.**                                                           • 5.5173
An introduction to the theoretical basis of nursing [by] Martha E. Rogers. Philadelphia, F. A. Davis Co. [1970] xii, 144 p. illus. 24 cm. (Nursing science, 1) 1. Nursing — Philosophy. I. T. II. Title: Theoretical basis of nursing.
RT42.R64      610.73/01      *LC* 71-103539

**Assessing vital functions accurately.**                                         5.5174
2nd ed. — Springhouse, Pa.: Springhouse Corp., 1983. 192 p.: ill. (some col.); 24 cm. — (New nursing skillbook.) 'Nursing 83 books.' Includes index. 1. Physical diagnosis 2. Vital signs — Measurement. 3. Nursing I. Series.
RT48.A85 1983      616.07/54 19      *LC* 83-20023      *ISBN* 0916730654

**Burns, Kenneth R.**                                                                 5.5175
Health assessment in clinical practice / Kenneth R. Burns, Patricia J. Johnson. — Englewood Cliffs, N.J.: Prentice-Hall, c1980. x, 452 p.: ill.; 28 cm. 1. Physical diagnosis 2. Nursing I. Johnson, Patricia J. joint author. II. T.
RT48.B87      616.07/5/024613      *LC* 79-15907      *ISBN* 0133850544

**Treseler, Kathleen Morrison.**                                                    5.5176
Clinical laboratory tests: significance and implications for nursing / Kathleen Morrison Treseler. — Englewood Cliffs, N.J.: Prentice-Hall, c1982. xxvi, 548 p.: ill.; 23 cm. Includes index. 1. Nursing 2. Diagnosis, Laboratory I. T.
RT48.T73 1982      616.07/56 19      *LC* 81-21091      *ISBN* 0131377604

**The Handbook of nursing / editors, Jeanne Howe ... [et al.];**           5.5177
**consulting editor, Margaret E. Armstrong.**
New York: Wiley, c1984. xv, 1756 p.: ill.; 26 cm. (Wiley medical publication.) 1. Nursing — Handbooks, manuals, etc. I. Howe, Jeanne. II. Armstrong, Margaret E. III. Series.
RT51.H36 1984      610.73 19      *LC* 83-25942      *ISBN* 0471895245

**Murphy, Lois Barclay, 1902-.**                                                    5.5178
The home hospital: how a family can cope with catastrophic illness / Lois Barclay Murphy. — New York: Basic Books, c1982. xx, 348 p.; 22 cm. Includes index. 1. Home nursing 2. Home nursing — Psychological aspects. 3. Sick — Psychology 4. Sick — Family relationships. I. T.
RT61.M88 1982      649.8 19      *LC* 82-70852      *ISBN* 0465030416

**Current issues in nursing** / edited by Joanne Comi McCloskey,    **5.5179**
Helen Kennedy Grace.
2nd ed. — Boston: Blackwell Scientific Publications; St. Louis, MO:
Distributors USA, Blackwell Mosby Book Distributors, 1985. xxvi, 1138 p.: ill.;
24 cm. 1. Nursing — Addresses, essays, lectures. 2. Nursing — United States
— Addresses, essays, lectures. I. McCloskey, Joanne Comi. II. Grace, Helen
K.
RT63.C87 1985      610.73 19      *LC* 84-28340      *ISBN* 086542019X

**Nightingale, Florence, 1820-1910.**        • **5.5180**
[Selections. 1954] Selected writings of Florence Nightingale / compiled by Lucy
Ridgely Seymer. — New York: Macmillan, c1954. xvi, 396 p. 1. Nursing —
Addresses, essays, lectures. 2. Nurses — Addresses, essays, lectures.
I. Seymer, Lucy Ridgely (Buckler). II. T.
RT63.N5      *LC* 54-4820

**The Management of common human miseries: a text for primary**    **5.5181**
**health care practitioners** / Bonnie Bullough, editor; with
contributors.
New York: Springer Pub. Co., c1979. ix, 484 p.; 24 cm. 1. Medicine
2. Ambulatory medical care 3. Nurse practitioners I. Bullough, Bonnie.
RT65.M35      616      *LC* 78-24072      *ISBN* 082612190X

# RT71–81.5 Study. Teaching. Research

**Brown, Esther Lucile, 1898-.**        • **5.5182**
Nursing for the future, a report prepared for the National Nursing Council.
New York, Russell Sage Foundation, 1948. 198 p. 24 cm. 1. Nursing
2. Nursing — Study and teaching I. National Nursing Council. II. T.
RT71.B752      610.73069      *LC* 48-8562

**Van Ort, Suzanne R.**        **5.5183**
Teaching in collegiate schools of nursing / Suzanne R. Van Ort, Arlene M.
Putt. — Boston: Little, Brown, c1985. xv, 254 p.: ill.; 24 cm. 1. Nursing —
Study and teaching 2. Nursing — Study and teaching (Graduate) I. Putt,
Arlene M. II. T.
RT71.V36 1985      610.73/07/11 19      *LC* 84-21804      *ISBN*
0316897159

**Institute of Medicine (U.S.). Division of Health Care Services.**    **5.5184**
Nursing and nursing education: public policies and private actions / Division of
Health Care Services, Institute of Medicine. — Washington, D.C.: National
Academy Press, 1983. xxi, 311 p.: ill.; 27 cm. 1. Nursing — Study and teaching
— Government policy — United States. 2. Federal aid to nursing education —
United States. I. T.
RT79.I57 1983      610.73/07/1173 19      *LC* 83-60053      *ISBN*
0309033462

**Abdellah, Faye G.**        **5.5185**
Better patient care through nursing research / Faye G. Abdellah, Eugene
Levine. — 3rd ed. — New York, N.Y.: Macmillan, c1986. p. cm. Includes
index. 1. Nursing — Research — Methodology. I. Levine, Eugene. II. T.
RT81.5.A25 1986      610.73/072 19      *LC* 85-23051      *ISBN*
0023000805

**Brink, Pamela J.**        **5.5186**
Basic steps in planning nursing research: from question to proposal / Pamela J.
Brink, Marilynn J. Wood. — 2nd ed. — Monterey, Calif.: Wadsworth Health
Sciences Division, c1983. xii, 305 p.; 23 cm. 1. Nursing — Research I. Wood,
Marilynn J. II. T.
RT81.5.B74 1983      610.73/072 19      *LC* 82-17426      *ISBN* 0534012418

**Dempsey, Patricia Ann.**        **5.5187**
The research process in nursing / Patricia Ann Dempsey, Arthur D. Dempsey.
— 2nd ed. — Boston: Jones and Bartlett, c1986. xii, 276 p.: ill.; 24 cm.
1. Nursing — Research — Methodology. I. Dempsey, Arthur D. II. T.
RT81.5.D46 1986      610.73/072 19      *LC* 85-22535      *ISBN*
0867203501

**Polit, Denise F.**        **5.5188**
Nursing research: principles and methods / Denise F. Polit, Bernadette P.
Hungler. — 3rd ed. — Philadelphia: Lippincott, c1987. p. cm. 1. Nursing —
Research — Methodology. I. Hungler, Bernadette P. II. T.
RT81.5.P64 1987      610.73/072 19      *LC* 86-10251      *ISBN* 0397546319

**Readings for nursing research** / edited by Sydney D. Krampitz,    **5.5189**
Natalie Pavlovich.
St. Louis: C. V. Mosby Co., 1981. xii, 285 p.: ill.; 28 cm. 1. Nursing —
Research — Addresses, essays, lectures. I. Krampitz, Sydney Diane.
II. Pavlovich, Natalie, 1940-
RT81.5.R4      610.73/072      *LC* 80-18125      *ISBN* 0801627478

# RT82–86 Philosophy. Ethics. Psychological Aspects

**The Nursing profession: a time to speak** / edited by Norma L.    **5.5190**
Chaska.
New York: McGraw-Hill, c1983. xxx, 914 p.; 24 cm. 1. Nursing 2. Nursing —
United States. I. Chaska, Norma L. II. Title: Time to speak.
RT82.N868 1983      610.73 19      *LC* 82-6620      *ISBN* 0070106967

**Crisis theory: a framework for nursing practice** / Mary Sue    **5.5191**
Infante, editor.
Reston, Va.: Reston Pub. Co., 1982. ix, 675 p.; 25 cm. 1. Nursing —
Philosophy. I. Infante, Mary Sue, 1939-
RT84.5.C74 1982      610.73/01 19      *LC* 82-3800      *ISBN* 0835911799

**Nursing theories: the base for professional nursing practice** /    **5.5192**
**Julia B. George, editor; the Nursing Theories Conference**
**Group.**
2nd ed. — Englewood Cliffs, N.J.: Prentice-Hall, c1985. xiii, 354 p.; 23 cm.
1. Nursing — Philosophy — Congresses. I. George, Julia B. II. Nursing
Theories Conference Group.
RT84.5.N89 1985      610.73/01 19      *LC* 84-17919      *ISBN* 0136274072

**Orem, Dorothea E. (Dorothea Elizabeth), 1914-.**        **5.5193**
Nursing: concepts of practice / Dorothea E. Orem. — 3rd ed. — New York:
McGraw-Hill, c1985. ix, 303 p.: ill.; 23 cm. Includes index. 1. Nursing —
Philosophy. I. T.
RT84.5.O73 1985      610.73 19      *LC* 84-20086      *ISBN* 0070475253

**Riehl-Sisca, Joan.**        **5.5194**
Conceptual models for nursing practice / [edited by] Joan P. Riehl, Callista
Roy. — 2d ed. — New York: Appleton-Century-Crofts, c1980. xvi, 416 p.: ill.;
23 cm. 1. Nursing — Philosophy. I. Roy, Callista. II. T.
RT84.5.R53 1980      610.73/01      *LC* 79-28305      *ISBN* 0838512003

**Davis, Anne J., 1931-.**        **5.5195**
Ethical dilemmas and nursing practice / Anne J. Davis, Mila A. Aroskar. —
New York: Appleton-Century-Crofts, c1978. ix, 238 p.: 23 cm. 1. Nursing
ethics 2. Medical ethics I. Aroskar, Mila A. joint author. II. T.
RT85.D33      174/.2      *LC* 78-51072      *ISBN* 0838522734

**Davitz, Joel Robert.**        **5.5196**
Inferences of patients' pain and psychological distress: studies of nursing
behaviors / Joel R. Davitz, Lois Leiderman Davitz. — New York: Springer
Pub. Co., c1981. xi, 209 p.; 24 cm. Includes index. 1. Nursing — Psychological
aspects 2. Pain — Psychological aspects. 3. Pain — Nursing. 4. Nurse and
patient 5. Suffering 6. Inference I. Davitz, Lois Jean. joint author. II. T.
RT86.D37      610.73/01/9 19      *LC* 80-23830      *ISBN* 0826133606

**Hall, John.**        **5.5197**
Psychology for nurses and health visitors / John Hall. — London: Macmillan,
1982. x, 373 p.; 26 cm. — (Psychology for professional groups) 1. Nursing —
Psychological aspects I. T. II. Series.
RT86.H35      *ISBN* 0333318633

**Peplau, Hildegard E.**        • **5.5198**
Interpersonal relations in nursing, a conceptual frame of reference for
psychodynamic nursing. Foreword by R. Louise McManus. — New York:
Putnam, [1952] 330 p.: illus.; 21 cm. — (Modern nursing series) 1. Nurse and
patient 2. Interpersonal relations I. T.
RT86.P4      610.73      *LC* 52-7077

**Archer, Sarah Ellen.**        **5.5199**
Nurses, a political force / by Sarah Ellen Archer, Patricia A. Goehner. —
Monterey, Calif.: Wadsworth Health Sciences Division, c1982. xi, 451 p.: ill.; 24
cm. Includes index. 1. Nursing — Political aspects — United States. 2. Nurses
— United States — Political activity. 3. United States — Politics and
government I. Goehner, Patricia A. II. T.
RT86.5.A73      322/.2 19      *LC* 81-16206      *ISBN* 0818505133

# RT87–90 Special Topics

**Pain.**                                                                            **5.5200**
Springhouse, Pa.: Springhouse Corp., 1985. 128 p.: ill. (some col.); 27 cm.
(Nursing now) 'Nursing85 books.' Includes index. 1. Pain — Nursing.
RT87.P35 P32 1985      616/.0472 19      *LC* 84-26727      *ISBN*
0916730816

**Human sexuality in nursing process / edited by Elizabeth M.**      **5.5201**
**Lion.**
New York: Wiley, c1982. xiv, 496 p.: ill.; 24 cm. — (Wiley medical publication.)
1. Sex 2. Nursing 3. Sexual disorders — Nursing. 4. Sick — Sexual behavior
I. Lion, Elizabeth M. II. Series.
RT87.S49 H85      613.9/5/024613 19      *LC* 81-16201      *ISBN*
0471038695

**Nursing and thanatology / edited by Elsa Poslusny ... [et al.].**      **5.5202**
New York, N.Y.: Arno Press, 1981. 244 p.: ill.; 24 cm. — (Foundation of
Thanatology-Arno Press continuing series on thanatology.) 1. Nursing
2. Terminal care 3. Nursing — Psychological aspects 4. Death —
Psychological aspects I. Poslusny, Elsa. II. Series.
RT87.T45 N87 1981      610.73/61 19      *LC* 80-671      *ISBN* 0405130953

**Downie, Patricia A.**                                                              **5.5203**
Lifting, handling and helping patients / by Patricia A. Downie and Pat
Kennedy; with a foreword by Theodora Turner. — London: Faber, 1981.
143 p.: ill.; 21 cm. 1. Transport of sick and wounded I. Kennedy, Pat. II. T.
RT87.T72      610.73 18      610.73 19      *ISBN* 0571116302

**Narrow, Barbara W.**                                                               **5.5204**
Patient teaching in nursing practice: a patient and family–centered approach /
Barbara W. Narrow. — New York: Wiley, c1979. xii, 219 p.; 23 cm. — (A
Wiley medical publication) Includes index. 1. Patient education 2. Nurse and
patient I. T.
RT90.N37 1979      610.73      *LC* 78-10241      *ISBN* 0471040355

# RT98 Community Health Nursing

**Benson, Evelyn Rose.**                                                             **5.5205**
Community health and nursing practice / Evelyn Rose Benson, Joan Quinn
McDevitt. — 2d ed. — Englewood Cliffs, N.J.: Prentice-Hall, c1980. xiii,
370 p.: ill.; 25 cm. 1. Community health nursing I. McDevitt, Joan Quinn.
joint author. II. T.
RT98.B46 1980      362.1/04/25      *LC* 79-20546      *ISBN* 0131531719

**Clark, Mary Jo Dummer.**                                                          **5.5206**
Community nursing: health care for today and tomorrow / Mary Jo Dummer
Clark. — Reston, Va.: Reston Pub. Co., c1984. xix, 552 p.: ill.; 25 cm.
1. Community health nursing I. T.
RT98.C545 1984      610.73/43 19      *LC* 83-17782      *ISBN* 0835908429

**Freeman, Ruth B.**                                                                 **5.5207**
Community health nursing practice / Ruth B. Freeman, Janet Heinrich. — 2d
ed. — Philadelphia: Saunders, 1981. vii, 592 p.: ill.; 24 cm. 1. Community
health nursing I. Heinrich, Janet. joint author. II. T.
RT98.F73 1981      610.73/43/0973 19      *LC* 80-52769      *ISBN*
0721638775

**Petrowski, Dorothy D.**                                                            **5.5208**
Handbook of community health nursing: essentials for clinical practice /
Dorothy D. Petrowski, with contributors; foreword by Ruth B. Freeman. —
New York: Springer Pub. Co., c1984. xv, 391 p.: ill.; 24 cm. 1. Community
health nursing — Handbooks, manuals, etc. I. T.
RT98.P47 1984      610.73/43 19      *LC* 83-16767      *ISBN* 0826142109

# RT120 Emergency Nursing

**Emergencies.**                                                                     **5.5209**
Springhouse, Pa.: Springhouse Corp., c1985. xxvii, 832 p.: ill. (some col.); 23
cm. (Nurse's reference library.) 'Nursing85 books.' 1. Emergency nursing —
Hanbooks, manuals, etc. I. Springhouse Corporation. II. Series.
RT120.E4 E42 1985      616/.025 19      *LC* 84-14122      *ISBN*
0916730859

**Fought, Sharon Gavin.**                                                            **5.5210**
Psychosocial nursing care of the emergency patient / Sharon Gavin Fought,
Anita Narciso Throwe. — New York: Wiley, c1984. xiv, 247 p.: ill.; 23 cm. 'A
Wiley medical publication.' 1. Emergency nursing 2. Psychiatric nursing
I. Throwe, Anita Narciso. II. T.
RT120.E4 F68 1984      610.73/61 19      *LC* 84-12024      *ISBN*
0471875627

**Nursing critically ill patients confidently.**                                     **5.5211**
2nd ed. — Springhouse, Pa.: Springhouse, 1984. 192 p.: ill.; 24 cm. (New
nursing skillbook series) 'Nursing84 books'. Includes index. 1. Intensive care
nursing
RT120.I5 N88 1984      610.73/61 19      *LC* 84-5635      *ISBN*
0916730670

# RZ OTHER SYSTEMS OF MEDICINE

**Gevitz, Norman.**                                                                  **5.5212**
The D.O.'s: osteopathic medicine in America / Norman Gevitz. — Baltimore:
Johns Hopkins University Press, c1982. x, 183 p.: ill.; 24 cm. 1. Osteopathy —
United States — History. I. T. II. Title: DO's.
RZ325.U6 G48 1982      615.5/33/0973 19      *LC* 82-47978      *ISBN*
0801827779

**Krippner, Stanley, 1932-.**                                                        **5.5213**
The realms of healing / Stanley Krippner, Alberto Villoldo; introd. by Evan
Harris Walker. Millbrae, Calif.: Celestial Arts, 1976. ix, 336 p.: ill.; 22 cm.
Includes index. 1. Spiritual healing 2. Medicine — Religious aspects
I. Villoldo, Alberto, 1949-. II. T.
RZ400.K74      615/.851      *LC* 76-377123      *ISBN* 0890871124

**Roth, Julius A.**                                                                  **5.5214**
Health purifiers and their enemies: a study of the natural health movement in
the United States with a comparison to its counterpart in Germany / Julius A.
Roth, with the collaboration of Richard R. Hanson. New York: Prodist, 1977.
130 p.; 23 cm. 1. Naturopathy — United States — History. 2. Naturopathy —
Germany — History. I. Hanson, Richard R. II. T.
RZ440.R67      615/.535/0973      *LC* 77-2210      *ISBN* 0882021176

# S1–760 AGRICULTURE: GENERAL

## S1–523 Reference Works. General Works

**United States. Dept. of Agriculture.**    • 5.5215
Yearbook of agriculture. 1894-. Washington: U.S. Govt. Print. Off. v.: ill., ports., maps; 24 cm. Annual. Since 1936 each volume has also a special title. Beginning with 1930 the Yearbook is designated by the year in which it is published. Consequently there is no issue bearing date 1929. Vols. for 1943-1947, 1950-1951 issued combined. 1. Agriculture — United States 2. Agriculture — Yearbooks. I. United States. Dept. of Agriculture. II. T.
S21.A35    LC 04-18127

**U. S. Dept. of Agriculture. Agricultural History Branch.**    • 5.5216
Century of service: the first 100 years of the United States Department of Agriculture. [by Gladys L. Baker, and others. Washington] Centennial Committee, U. S. Dept. of Agriculture: [for sale by the Superintendent of Documents, U. S. Govt. Print. Off., 1963] xv, 560 p. illus., 24 cm. 'Literature cited': p. 419-439. 1. Agriculture and state — United States 2. United States. Dept. of Agriculture. 3. United States — Dept. of Agriculture — History. I. Baker, Gladys, 1910- II. United States. Dept. of Agriculture. Centennial Committee. III. T.
S21.C8 1963    630.6173    LC agr63-175

**Harding, T. Swann (Thomas Swann), 1890.**    • 5.5217
Two blades of grass, a history of scientific development in the U. S. Department of Agriculture, by T. Swann Harding. Norman, University of Oklahoma Press, 1947. 352 p. ill. 'First edition.' 1. United States. Dept. of Agriculture. 2. Agriculture — Research 3. Scientists, American. I. T. II. Title: Scientific development in the U. S. Department of agriculture.
S21.C9 H3    630.72    LC agr47-159

**Moore, Ernest G.**    • 5.5218
The Agricultural Research Service [by] Ernest G. Moore. — New York: Praeger, [1967] xii, 244 p.: illus.; 22 cm. — (Praeger library of U.S. Government departments and agencies) 1. United States. Agricultural Research Service. I. T.
S21.C9 M6    630/.72/073    LC 67-22294

**Rasmussen, Wayne David, 1915-.**    • 5.5219
The Department of Agriculture [by] Wayne D. Rasmussen and Gladys L. Baker. New York, Praeger [1972] xii, 257 p. illus. 22 cm. (Praeger library of U.S. Government departments and agencies, no. 32) 1. United States. Dept. of Agriculture. I. Baker, Gladys L., 1910- joint author. II. T.
S21.C9 R37    353.81    LC 77-117476

**The State of food and agriculture.**    • 5.5220
1947- . — Rome: Food and Agriculture Organization of the United Nations. — v. Annual. 1. Food supply — Periodicals. 2. Agriculture — Periodicals. I. Food and Agriculture Organization of the United Nations. II. Title: World outlook and state of food and agriculture.
S401.U6 A317    LC 48-2563

**Dalal-Clayton, D. B. (D. Barry)**    5.5221
Black's agricultural dictionary / D.B. Dalal–Clayton. — London: A. & C. Black, 1981. xii, 499 p.: ill.; 23 cm. 1. Agriculture — Dictionaries. I. T. II. Title: Agricultural dictionary.
S411.D245 1981    630/.3/21 19    LC 82-121547    ISBN 0713621303

**A Dictionary of agricultural and allied terminology / John N.**    • 5.5222
**Winburne, editor–in–chief.**
[East Lansing]: Michigan State University Press, 1962. 905 p.; 25 cm. 1. Agriculture — Dictionaries. I. Winburne, John N. (John Newton), 1911-
S411.D57    630.3    LC 62-9169

# S415–417 Biography

**Holt, Rackham.**    • 5.5223
George Washington Carver, an American biography. — Rev. ed. — Garden City, N.Y.: Doubleday, [1963] 360 p.: illus.; 22 cm. 1. Carver, George Washington, 1864?-1943. I. T.
S417.C3 H6 1963    925    LC 62-11430

**McMurry, Linda O.**    5.5224
George Washington Carver, scientist and symbol / Linda O. McMurry. — New York: Oxford University Press, 1981. x, 367 p.: ill.; 22 cm. 1. Carver, George Washington, 1864?-1943. 2. Agriculturists — United States — Biography. I. T.
S417.C3 M3    630/.92/4 B 19    LC 81-4896    ISBN 0195029712

**Winters, Donald L.**    • 5.5225
Henry Cantwell Wallace, as Secretary of Agriculture, 1921–1924. University of Illinois Press [1970] 313 p. 1. Wallace, Henry Cantwell, 1866-1924. I. United States. Dept. of Agriculture. II. T.
S417.W34 W55    LC 76-630796

**Young, Arthur, 1741-1820.**    5.5226
Arthur Young and his times / edited by G. E. Mingay. — Toronto: Macmillan of Canada/Maclean-Hunter Press, 1975. 264 p.: maps; 23 cm. 'The works of Arthur Young': p. [251]-255. Includes index. 1. Young, Arthur, 1741-1820. 2. Agriculturists — Correspondence, reminiscences, etc. 3. Agriculture — Great Britain. 4. Agriculture — Europe. 5. Europe — Description and travel — 17th-18th centuries I. Mingay, G. E. II. T.
S417.Y6 A28 1975    S417Y6 A28 1975.    338.1/0941    ISBN 0770513549

# S419–481 History

## S419–439 GENERAL WORKS

**Gras, Norman Scott Brien, 1884-1956.**    • 5.5227
A history of agriculture in Europe and America, by Norman Scott Brien Gras ... 2d ed. New York, F. S. Crofts & co., 1940. xxvii, 496 p. illus. (plans) diagrs. 22 cm. 'Second printing, March, 1940.' 'This edition contains a new chapter covering the period 1920-40. Minor changes have been made in several chapters.'—p. viii. 'Suggestions for further study' at end of each chapter. 1. Agriculture — Europe — History. 2. Agriculture — United States — History. I. T.
S419.G8 1940    630.9    LC 40-27443

**Sauer, Carl Ortwin, 1889-.**    • 5.5228
Agricultural origins and dispersals. New York, American Geographical Society, 1952. v, 110 p. fold. col. maps. 23 cm. (Bowman memorial lectures, ser. 2) 1. Plants, Cultivated — History 2. Domestic animals — History. I. T. II. Series.
S421.S3    LC agr52-86

**White, K. D.**    • 5.5229
Roman farming [by] K. D. White. — Ithaca, N.Y.: Cornell University Press, [1970] 536 p.: illus., maps, plans.; 23 cm. — (Aspects of Greek and Roman life) 1. Agriculture — Rome. I. T. II. Series.
S431.W46    630/.937    LC 77-119592    ISBN 0801405750

**Grigg, David B.**    5.5230
The agricultural systems of the world: an evolutionary approach / D. B. Grigg. — London; New York: Cambridge University Press, 1974. ix, 358 p.: maps; 24 cm. (Cambridge geographical studies. 5) Includes index. 1. Agricultural geography 2. Agriculture — History I. T. II. Series.
S439.G788    630/.9    LC 73-82451    ISBN 0521202698

## S441 United States: General

**American husbandry. Edited by Harry J. Carman.**                • 5.5231
[New ed.] Port Washington, N. Y., Kennikat Press [1964, c1939] lxi, 582 p.
With reproductions of the original title pages, London, 1775. Authorship not
definitely established; evidence indicates that the author may have been either
John Mitchell or Arthur Young. Cf. introd. 1. Agriculture — North America.
2. Agriculture — West Indies, British. I. Carman, Harry James, 1884-1964.
II. Mitchell, John, 1711-1768. III. Young, Arthur, 1741-1820.
S441.A5 1964      LC 64-15535

**Bidwell, Percy Wells, 1888-.**                • 5.5232
History of agriculture in the northern United States, 1620–1860, by Percy Wells
Bidwell...and John I. Falconer... Washington, The Carnegie institution of
Washington, 1925. xii, 512 p.: ill., 2 pl., maps, diagrs.; 26 cm. — (Carnegie
institution of Washington. Publication no.358) Half-title: Contributions to
American economic history, [v.5]. 1. Agriculture — United States I. Falconer,
John Ironside, 1888- II. T.
S441.B5      630.973      LC 25-13458

**Danhof, Clarence H., 1911-.**                • 5.5233
Change in agriculture; the northern United States, 1820–1870 [by] Clarence H.
Danhof. — Cambridge: Harvard University Press, 1969. x, 322 p.: illus.; 25 cm.
1. Agricultural innovations — U.S. — History. 2. Agriculture — U.S. —
History. I. T.
S441.D3      530/.973      LC 70-75430      ISBN 0674107705

**Ebeling, Walter, 1907-.**                5.5234
The fruited plain: the story of American agriculture / Walter Ebeling. —
Berkeley: University of California Press, c1979. xiii, 433 p.: ill.; 27 cm. Includes
index. 1. Agriculture — United States I. T.
S441.E23      338.1/0973      LC 78-62837      ISBN 0520037510

**Hargreaves, Mary Wilma M.**                • 5.5235
Dry farming in the northern Great Plains, 1900–1925. Cambridge, Harvard
University Press, 1957. xi, 587 p. maps, charts, diagrs., tables. 22 cm. (Harvard
ecomonic studies, v. 101) 1. Agriculture — Great Plains — History.
2. Agriculture — Economic aspects — Great Plains. 3. Dry farming I. T.
II. Series.
S441.H29      LC 56-11281

**Hayter, Earl W.**                • 5.5236
The troubled farmer, 1850–1900; rural adjustment to industrialism [by] Earl W.
Hayter. — Dekalb: Northern Illinois University Press, [1968] vii, 349 p.:
facsims., ports.; 24 cm. 1. Agriculture — United States — History. 2. United
States — Rural conditions I. T.
S441.H36      630.11/73      LC 67-26267

**Hurt, R. Douglas.**                5.5237
The Dust Bowl: an agricultural and social history / R. Douglas Hurt. —
Chicago: Nelson-Hall, 1982 (c1981). x, 214 p.; 23 cm. Includes index.
1. Agriculture — Great Plains — History — 20th century. 2. Droughts —
Great Plains — History — 20th century. 3. Dust storms — Great Plains —
History — 20th century. 4. Depressions — 1929 — United States 5. Great
Plains — History. 6. Great Plains — Social conditions. I. T.
S441.H92      338.1/0978 19      LC 81-4031      ISBN 0882295411

**Rasmussen, Wayne David, 1915- ed.**                • 5.5238
Readings in the history of American agriculture. Urbana, University of Illinois
Press [c1960] 340 p. illus. 1. Agriculture — United States — History. I. T.
S441.R34      LC 60-8342

**Rossiter, Margaret W.**                5.5239
The emergence of agricultural science: Justus Liebig and the Americans,
1840–1880 / Margaret W. Rossiter. — New Haven: Yale University Press,
1975. xiv, 275 p., [2] leaves of plates: ill.; 25 cm. — (Yale studies in the history of
science and medicine. 9) Includes index. 1. Liebig, Justus, Freiherr von,
1803-1873. 2. Agricultural chemistry — History. 3. Agriculture — United
States — History. 4. Agriculture — Research — United States — History.
I. T. II. Series.
S441.R63 1975      630/.24/0973      LC 74-29737      ISBN 0300017219

**Sachs, Carolyn E., 1950-.**                5.5240
The invisible farmers: women in agricultural production / Carolyn E. Sachs. —
Totowa, N.J.: Rowman & Allanheld, 1983. xiv, 153 p.: ill.; 22 cm. Includes
index. 1. Women farmers — United States — History. 2. Women farmers —
United States. I. T.
S441.S25 1983      305.4/33/0973 19      LC 82-22824      ISBN
0865980942

**Schapsmeier, Edward L.**                5.5241
Encyclopedia of American agricultural history / Edward L. Schapsmeier,
Frederick H. Schapsmeier. — Westport, Conn.: Greenwood Press, 1976
(c1975). xii, 467 p.; 25 cm. Includes indexes. 1. Agriculture — United States —

History — Dictionaries. 2. Agriculture — Dictionaries. I. Schapsmeier,
Frederick H. joint author. II. T.
S441.S36      630/.973      LC 74-34563      ISBN 0837179580

### S443–451 SECTIONS. STATES

**Gray, Lewis Cecil, 1881-.**                • 5.5242
History of agriculture in the southern United States to 1860, by Lewis Cecil
Gray, assisted by Esther Katherine Thompson, with an introductory note by
Henry Charles Taylor ... Washington, The Carnegie institution of Washington,
1933. 2 v. illus. (Carnegie institution of Washington. Publication no. 430) Half-
title: Contributions to American economic history, [v.6]. Paged continously.
1. Agriculture — United States 2. Agriculture — United States —
Bibliography I. Thompson, Esther Katherine. II. T.
S445.G8      630.975      LC 33-6309

**Range, Willard, 1910-.**                • 5.5243
A century of Georgia agriculture, 1850–1950 / by Willard Range; foreword by
George H. King. — Athens: University of Georgia Press, c1954. xii, 333 p.:
maps, diagrs.; 24 cm. 1. Agriculture — Georgia — History. 2. Agriculture —
Economic aspects — Georgia. I. T.
S451.G3 R3      LC 53-13266

**Malin, James Claude, 1893-.**                • 5.5244
Winter wheat in the golden belt of Kansas; a study in adaption to subhumid
geographical environment, by James C. Malin. — New York: Octagon Books,
1973 [c1944] 290 p.: illus.; 24 cm. Reprint of the ed. published by the University
of Kansas Press, Lawrence. 1. Agriculture — Kansas — History. 2. Wheat —
Kansas. 3. Kansas — Climate. I. T.
S451.K2 M3 1973      338.1/7/31109781      LC 73-4648      ISBN
0374952612

**Moore, John Hebron.**                • 5.5245
Agriculture in ante–bellum Mississippi. — New York: Octagon Books, 1971
[c1958] 268 p.; 24 cm. 1. Agriculture — Mississippi — History. 2. Mississippi
— Economic conditions — History. I. T.
S451.M7 M6 1971      630/.9762      LC 70-154666      ISBN 0374958300

**Craven, Avery Odelle, 1886-.**                • 5.5246
Soil exhaustion as a factor in the agricultural history of Virginia and Maryland,
1606–1860, Avery Odelle Craven ... Urbana, The University of Illinois [c1926]
179 p. 24 cm. (University of Illinois studies in the social sciences, vol. XIII, no.
1) 1. Agriculture — Virginia. 2. Agriculture — Maryland. 3. Soil exhaustion
I. T.
S451.V8 C7      LC 27-7898

## S452–469 Europe

**Chambers, Jonathan David, 1898-1970.**                • 5.5247
The agricultural revolution, 1750–1880 [by] J. D. Chambers [and] G. E.
Mingay. New York, Schocken Books [1966] vii, 222 p. illus., maps (1 fold.) 23
cm. Includes bibliographies. 1. Agriculture — Great Britain — History.
I. Mingay, G. E. joint author. II. T.
S455.C43 1966a      630.942      LC 66-11369

**Ernle, Rowland Edmund Prothero, Baron, 1851-1937.**                • 5.5248
English farming, past and present / with introductions by G. E. Fussell and O.
R. McGregor. — New 6th ed. — Chicago: Quadrangle Books, [1961] cxlv,
559 p.; 23 cm. 'The edition ... here reprinted is the fifth published in 1936, edited
and revised by Sir Daniel Hall ... [with] critical and bibliographical
introductions in the form of commentaries [supplied]. 1. Agriculture —
England — History. 2. Agriculture — Economic aspects — England. I. Hall,
Daniel, Sir, 1864-1942. II. Fussell, G. E. (George Edwin), 1889-
III. McGregor, O. R. (Oliver Ross), 1921- IV. T.
S455.E7 1961b      630/.942      LC 61-13075

**Kerridge, Eric.**                5.5249
The farmers of old England. — Totowa, N.J.: Rowman and Littlefield, [1973]
180 p.: illus.; 23 cm. 1. Agriculture — England — History. 2. Farmers —
England — History. I. T.
S455.K47 1973      630/.942      LC 72-13820      ISBN 087471169X

**Thirsk, Joan.**                • 5.5250
English peasant farming: the agrarian history of Lincolnshire from Tudor to
recent times. — London: Routledge & K. Paul, 1957. xv, 350 p.: ill., maps
(part fold.) tables; 23 cm. 1. Agriculture — England — Lincolnshire —
History. 2. Peasantry — England — Lincolnshire. I. T.
S457.L5 T48 1957

**Volin, Lazar, 1896-1966.**                • 5.5251
A century of Russian agriculture; from Alexander II to Khrushchev.
Cambridge, Mass., Harvard University Press, 1970. viii, 644 p. 24 cm. (Russian

Research Center studies, no. 63) 1. Agriculture — Soviet Union — History. I. T.
S469.R9 V57     630/.947     LC 72-119075     ISBN 0674106210

## S470–481 Other Countries, Regions, A–Z

**Scobie, James R     1929-.**        • 5.5252
Revolution on the Pampas: a social history of Argentine wheat, 1860–1910 / by James R. Scobie. — Austin: Published for the Institute of Latin American Studies by the University of Texas Press, 1964. x, 206 p., [7] leaves of plates: ill., maps. — (Latin American monographs; no.1) 1. Agriculture — Argentine Republic — History. 2. Wheat — Argentine Republic. I. T.
S471.A7 S35     LC 64-22387

**Jasbir Singh, 1932-.**           5.5253
An agricultural atlas of India: a geographical analysis. — Kurukshetra: Vishal Publications, 1974. xxvi, 356 p.: maps.; 25 cm. Sponsored by the Indian Council of Social Science Research. 1. Agricultural geography — India. I. Jasbir Singh, 1932- The green revolution in India: how green it is. 1974. II. Indian Council of Social Science Research. III. T.
S471.I3 J38     630/.954     LC 74-901096

**Agricultural change in tropical Africa / Kenneth R. M. Anthony**     5.5254
**... [et al.].**
Ithaca: Cornell University Press, 1979. 326 p.: ill.; 24 cm. Includes indexes. 1. Agriculture — Africa, Sub-Saharan. 2. Agricultural innovations — Africa, Sub-Saharan. 3. Agriculture — Economic aspects — Africa, Sub-Saharan. 4. Agricultural productivity — Africa, Sub-Saharan. 5. Agriculture — Research — Africa, Sub-Saharan. I. Anthony, Kenneth R. M.
S472.A1 A34     338.1/0967     LC 78-58039     ISBN 0801411599

## S493–520 General Works

**Bailey, L. H. (Liberty Hyde), 1858-1954. ed.**        • 5.5255
Cyclopedia of American agriculture: a popular survey of agricultural conditions, practices and ideals in the United States and Canada / ed. by L.H. Bailey; with one hundred full page plates and more than two thousand illustrations in the text ... New York: The Macmillan company; London: Macmillan & co., ltd., 1907-1909. 4 v.: fronts., ill. (incl. maps) plates; 27 cm. 'Biographies': v. 4, p. 547-628. 1. Agriculture — North America. 2. Agriculture — North America — Biography. I. T.
S493.B2     LC 07-8529

**Technical change and social conflict in agriculture: Latin**     5.5256
**American perspectives / edited by Martín Piñeiro and Eduardo Trigo.**
Boulder, Colo.: Westview Press, 1984 (c1983). xvi, 248 p.: ill.; 28 cm. — (A Westview replica edition) 'Presents the intellectual production of the first phase of the Cooperative Research Project on Agricultural Technology in Latin America (PROTAAL) and the most relevant papers presented by invitees at a meeting held in San Jose, Costa Rica in September 1981'—P. xv. 1. Agricultural innovations — Latin America. 2. Agricultural innovations — Social aspects — Latin America. 3. Agricultural innovations — Economic aspects — Latin America. 4. Agriculture — Research — Latin America. 5. Agriculture and state — Latin America. 6. Agriculture — Latin America. 7. Agriculture — Economic aspects — Latin America. I. Piñeiro, Martín. II. Trigo, Eduardo. III. Cooperative Research Project on Agricultural Technology in Latin America.
S494.5.I5 T43 1983     338.1/098 19     LC 83-50881     ISBN 0865318026

**Grigg, David B.**          5.5257
An introduction to agricultural geography / David Grigg. — London; Dover, N.H., USA: Hutchinson, 1984. 204 p.: ill.; 25 cm. (Hutchinson university library.) Series statement from jacket. 1. Agricultural geography I. T. II. Series.
S495.G79 1984     338.1 19     LC 84-12824     ISBN 0091567106

## S521 Essays. Country Life

**Buel, Jesse, 1778-1839.**        • 5.5258
Jesse Buel, agricultural reformer; selections from his writings, edited, with introd. by Harry J. Carman. New York Columbia University Press 1947. xxxvi,

609 p.: front. (port.) ill.; 22 cm. (Columbia University Studies in the history of American agriculture, no. 12) 1. Buel, Jesse, 1778-1839 — Bibliography 2. Agriculture — Addresses, essays, lectures I. Carman, Harry James, 1884-1969, ed. II. T. III. Series.
S521 B88

**Fussell, G. E. (George Edwin), 1889-.**        • 5.5259
The English countryman, his life and work, A.D. 1500–1900. London A. Melrose [1955] 172p. 1. Farm life — England 2. Country life — England I. Fussell, K. R. jt. author II. T.
S521 F85

## S530–539 Agricultural Education

**Baker, Gladys, 1910-.**        • 5.5260
The county agent ... by Gladys Lucille Baker. Chicago, Ill., The University of Chicago press, 1939. xxi, 226 p. incl. tables. (Studies in public administration, vol. 11) Published also without thesis note on t.-p. 1. County agricultural agents I. T.
S533.Bx

## S590–599 Soils. Soil Science

### S591–592 General Works.
### Encyclopedias

**Brady, Nyle C.**          5.5261
The nature and properties of soils / Nyle C. Brady. — 9th ed. — New York: Macmillan; London: Collier Macmillan, c1984. xvii, 750 p.: ill., some col.; 25 cm. 1. Soil science I. T.
S591.B79 1984     631.4 19     LC 83-19545     ISBN 0023133406

**Buol, S. W.**          5.5262
Soil genesis and classification / S. W. Buol, F. D. Hole, R. J. McCracken. — 2d ed. — Ames: Iowa State University Press, 1980. x, 404 p.: ill.; 24 cm. 1. Soil science 2. Soil formation 3. Soils — Classification I. Hole, Francis Doan, 1913- joint author. II. McCracken, R. J. joint author. III. T.
S591.B887 1979     631.4     LC 79-15992     ISBN 081381460X

**Foth, H. D.**          5.5263
Soil geography and land use / Henry D. Foth, John W. Schafer. — New York: J. Wiley, c1980. 484 p.: ill.; 24 cm. 1. Soil geography 2. Land use I. Schafer, John W. joint author. II. T.
S591.F68 1980     631.4/7     LC 79-27731     ISBN 0471017108

**Hole, Francis Doan, 1913-.**          5.5264
Soil landscape analysis / Francis D. Hole, James B. Campbell. — Totowa, N.J.: Rowman & Allanheld, 1985. xvi, 196 p.: ill.; 25 cm. Includes index. 1. Soil geography 2. Soils 3. Landscape I. Campbell, James B., 1944- II. T.
S591.H69 1985     641.4/9 19     LC 83-24418     ISBN 086598140X

**Pedogenesis and soil taxonomy / edited by L.P. Wilding, N.E.**     5.5265
**Smeck, and G.F. Hall.**
Amsterdam; New York: Elsevier; New York: Distributors for the U.S. and Canada, Elsevier Science Pub. Co., 1983. 2 v.: ill.; 25 cm. — (Developments in soil science. 11A-11B) 1. Soil science — Collected works 2. Soils — Classification — Collected works. 3. Soil formation — Collected works. I. Wilding, L. P. II. Smeck, N. E. III. Hall, G. F. IV. Series.
S591.P39 1983     631.4/4 19     LC 82-24198     ISBN 0444421009

**Russell, Edward J. (Edward John), Sir, 1872-1965.**     5.5266
[Soil conditions and plant growth] Russell's soil conditions and plant growth. — 11th ed. / edited by Alan Wild. — Burnt Mill, Harlow, Essex, England: Longman Scientific & Technical; New York: Wiley, 1987. 1 v. Rev. ed. of: Soil conditions and plant growth. 10th ed. 1973. Includes indexes. 1. Soil science 2. Crops and soils I. Wild, Alan. II. Russell, Edward J. (Edward John), Sir, 1872-1965. Soil conditions and plant growth III. T. IV. Title: Soil conditions and plant growth.
S591.R84 1987     631.4 19     LC 86-27391     ISBN 0470207965

**The Encyclopedia of soil science / edited by Rhodes W.**    5.5267
**Fairbridge, Charles W. Finkl, Jnr.**
Stroudsburg, Pa.: Dowden, Hutchinson & Ross: distributed world wide by
Academic Press, c1979-. v.: ill.; 26 cm. (Encyclopedia of earth sciences; v. 12)
1. Soil science — Dictionaries. I. Fairbridge, Rhodes Whitmore, 1914-
II. Finkl, Charles W., 1941-
S592.E52     631.4/03     LC 78-31233     ISBN 0879331763

## S592.14–592.2 SOIL SURVEYS. SOIL
## CLASSIFICATION AND FORMATION

**Olson, Gerald W.**    5.5268
Field guide to soils and the environment: applications of soil surveys / Gerald
W. Olson. — New York: Chapman and Hall, 1984. xvii, 219 p.: ill.; 29 cm.
(Environmental resource management series.) 'A Dowden and Culver book.'
1. Soil surveys 2. Soil science I. T. II. Series.
S592.14.O36 1984     631.4 19     LC 84-5050     ISBN 0412259605

**International Society of Soil Science. International Conference.**    5.5269
**(1981: Jerusalem)**
Aridic soils and geomorphic processes: proceedings of the International
Conference of the International Society of Soil Science, Jerusalem, Israel,
March 29–April 4, 1981 / Dan H. Yaalon (ed.). — Cremlingen, W. Germany:
Catena, c1982. 219 p.: ill.; 24 cm. (Catena supplement. 0722-0723; 1) 1. Desert
soils — Congresses. 2. Arid regions — Congresses. 3. Soil formation —
Congresses. I. Yaalon, Dan H. II. T. III. Series.
S592.17.D47 I58 1981     551.6/0915/4 19     LC 83-210606     ISBN
392338100X

**Birkeland, Peter W.**    5.5270
Soils and geomorphology / Peter W. Birkeland. — New York: Oxford
University Press, 1984. xiv, 372 p.: ill.; 25 cm. Rev. ed. of: Pedology,
weathering, and geomorphological research. 1974. 1. Soil formation
2. Weathering 3. Soil science 4. Geology, Stratigraphic — Quaternary
I. Birkeland, Peter W. Pedology, weathering, and geomorphological research.
II. T.
S592.2.B57 1984     551.3/05 19     LC 83-13345     ISBN 0195033981

**Jenny, Hans, 1899-.**    5.5271
The soil resource: origin and behavior / Hans Jenny. — New York: Springer-
Verlag, c1980. xx, 377 p.: ill.; 25 cm. — (Ecological studies. v. 37) 1. Soil
formation 2. Soil ecology I. T. II. Series.
S592.2.J46     631.4     LC 80-11785     038790453X

## S592.3–596.5 SOIL PHYSICS AND
## CHEMISTRY

**Hillel, Daniel.**    5.5272
Applications of soil physics / Daniel Hillel. — New York: Academic Press,
1980. xiv, 385 p.: ill.; 24 cm. Includes index. 1. Soil physics 2. Soil moisture
3. Soil management I. T.
S592.3.H53     631.4/3     LC 80-535     ISBN 0123485800

**Hillel, Daniel.**    5.5273
Fundamentals of soil physics / Daniel Hillel. — New York: Academic Press,
1980. xvii, 413 p.: ill.; 24 cm. Includes index. 1. Soil physics I. T.
S592.3.H54     631.4/3     LC 80-16688     ISBN 0123485606

**Hillel, Daniel.**    5.5274
Introduction to soil physics / Daniel Hillel. — New York: Academic Press,
1982. xiii, 364 p. Based on the author's Applications of soil physics and
Fundamentals of soil physics. Includes index. 1. Soil physics I. T.
S592.3.H55     631.4/3 19     LC 81-10848     ISBN 0123485207

**Bohn, Hinrich L., 1934-.**    5.5275
Soil chemistry / Hinrich L. Bohn, Brian L. McNeal, George A. O'Connor. —
2nd ed. — New York: Wiley, c1985. xiii, 341 p.: ill.; 24 cm. 'A Wiley-
Interscience publication.' 1. Soil chemistry I. McNeal, Brian Lester, 1938-
II. O'Connor, George A., 1944- III. T.
S592.5.B63 1985     631.4/1 19     LC 85-3221     ISBN 0471822175

**Gieseking, John Eldon, 1905-.**    5.5276
Soil components, edited by John E. Gieseking. — New York: Springer-Verlag,
1975. 2 v.: ill.; 27 cm. 1. Soils — Composition I. T.
S592.5.G53     631.4/1     LC 73-14742     ISBN 0387068619

**Stevenson, F. J.**    5.5277
Cycles of soil: carbon, nitrogen, phosphorus, sulfur, micronutrients / F.J.
Stevenson. — New York: Wiley, c1986. xviii, 380 p.: ill.; 24 cm. 'A Wiley-

Interscience publication.' 1. Soil biochemistry 2. Biogeochemical cycles
3. Soil ecology I. T.
S592.7.S73 1986     631.4/1 19     LC 85-12042     ISBN 0471822183

## S596.7–621 SOILS AND CROPS.
### DRAINAGE

**Barber, Stanley A.**    5.5278
Soil nutrient bioavailability: a mechanistic approach / Stanley A. Barber. —
New York: Wiley, c1984. xiii, 398 p.: ill.; 24 cm. 'A Wiley-Interscience
publication.' 1. Crops and soils — Mathematical models. 2. Crops —
Nutrition — Mathematical models. 3. Soil fertility — Mathematical models.
I. T.
S596.7.B37 1984     631.4 19     LC 83-23331     ISBN 0471090328

**Nye, Peter Hague.**    5.5279
Solute movement in the soil–root system / P. H. Nye, P. B. Tinker. — Berkeley:
University of California Press, 1977. xiv, 342 p.: ill.; 25 cm. (Studies in ecology;
v. 4) Includes indexes. 1. Crops and soils — Mathematical models. 2. Plant-
soil relationships — Mathematical models. 3. Crops — Nutrition —
Mathematical models. 4. Plants — Nutrition — Mathematical models.
5. Roots (Botany) — Physiology — Mathematical models. I. Tinker, Philip
Bernard Hague. joint author. II. T.
S596.7.N93     582/.01/32     LC 77-71490     ISBN 0520034511

**Allison, Franklin Elmer, 1892-1972.**    5.5280
Soil organic matter and its role in crop production. — Amsterdam; New York:
Elsevier Scientific Pub. Co., 1973. vi, 639 p.; 25 cm. — (Developments in soil
science. 3) 1. Humus 2. Soil science 3. Organic farming I. T. II. Series.
S598.A5997     631.4/17     LC 72-83193     ISBN 0444410171

**Soil organic matter / edited by M. Schnitzer and S. U. Khan.**    5.5281
Amsterdam; New York: Elsevier Scientific Pub. Co.; New York: distributors
for the U.S. and Canada, Elsevier/North-Holland, 1978. xiii, 319 p.: ill.; 25 cm.
— (Developments in soil science. 8) 1. Humus I. Schnitzer, M. II. Khan,
Shahamat U. III. Series.
S598.S6     631.4/17     LC 78-1906     ISBN 0444416102

**Sánchez, Pedro A., 1940-.**    5.5282
Properties and management of soils in the tropics / Pedro A. Sanchez. — New
York: Wiley, c1976. x, 618 p.: ill.; 24 cm. 'A Wiley-Interscience publication.'
1. Soils — Tropics. 2. Plant-soil relationships — Tropics. 3. Soil science
4. Agriculture — Tropics I. T.
S599.9.T76 S26     631.4/913     LC 76-22761     ISBN 0471752002

**Soil physical properties and crop production in the tropics /**    5.5283
**edited by R. Lal and D. J. Greenland.**
Chichester [Eng.]; New York: J. Wiley, c1979. xiv, 551 p., [4] leaves of plates:
ill.; 24 cm. 'A Wiley-Interscience publication.' 1. Soils — Tropics. 2. Soil
physics 3. Crops and soils — Tropics. I. Lal, R. II. Greenland, D. J.
S599.9.T76 S65     631.4/3 19     LC 79-40583     ISBN 0471997579

**United States. Soil Conservation Service.**    5.5284
Drainage of agricultural land; a practical handbook for the planning, design,
construction, and maintenance of agricultural drainage systems. — Port
Washington, N.Y.: Water Information Center, [1973] 430 p.: illus.; 26 cm.
'Reproduced ... from section 16—drainage of agricultural land of the national
engineering handbook ... issued in 1971 by the Soil Conservation Service, U.S.
Department of Agriculture.' 1. Drainage I. T.
S621.U64     631.6/2     LC 72-92351     ISBN 0912394064

# S622–627 Soil Conservation

**Simms, D. Harper (Denton Harper), 1912-.**    • 5.5285
The Soil Conservation Service [by] D. Harper Simms. New York, Praeger
[1970] ix, 238 p. illus. 22 cm. (Praeger library of U.S. Government departments
and agencies, no. 23) 1. United States. Soil Conservation Service. I. T.
S622.S44     631.4/9/73     LC 73-101485

**International Conference on Soil Conservation (1980: National**    5.5286
**College of Agricultural Engineering)**
Soil conservation: problems and prospects / edited by R.P.C. Morgan. —
Chichester; New York: J. Wiley, c1981. xvi, 576 p.: ill.; 24 cm. 'A Wiley-
Interscience publication.' 'This volume is the Proceedings of Conservation 80,
the International Conference on Soil Conservation, held at the National College
of Agricultural Engineering, Silsoe, Bedford, UK, 21st-25th July, 1980'—p. ii.

1. Soil conservation — Congresses. I. Morgan, R. P. C. (Royston Philip Charles), 1942- II. National College of Agricultural Engineering. III. T.
S622.2.I57 1981    631.4/5 19     LC 80-42351     ISBN 0471278823

**National Conference on Soil Erosion, Purdue University, 1976.**    **5.5287**
Soil erosion: prediction and control: the proceedings of a National Conference on Soil Erosion, May 24–26, 1976, Purdue University, West Lafayette, Indiana. Ankeny, Iowa: Soil Conservation Society of America, c1977. xiii, 393 p.: ill.; 26 cm. (Special publication - Soil Conservation Society of America; no. 21) 1. Soil erosion — Congresses. 2. Soil conservation — Congresses. I. T.
S622.2.N38 1976    631.4/5    LC 77-74183

**Soil erosion and conservation / edited by S.A. El–Swaify, W.C.**    **5.5288**
**Moldenhauer, and Andrew Lo.**
Ankeny, Iowa: Soil Conservation Society of America, c1985. xxviii, 793 p.: ill.; 24 cm. 'This volume is based on 'Mālama 'Āina '83,' the International Conference on Soil Erosion and Conservation, held January 16-22, 1983, in Honolulu, Hawaii'—P. ii. 1. Soil erosion — Congresses. 2. Soil conservation — Congresses. 3. Sediment control — Congresses. I. El-Swaify, S. A. (Samir Aly) II. Moldenhauer, W. C. III. Lo, Andrew. IV. Soil Conservation Society of America. V. International Conference on Soil Erosion and Conservation (1983: Honolulu, Hawaii)
S622.2.S65 1985    631.4 19    LC 85-2507    ISBN 0935734112

**Morgan, R. P. C. (Royston Philip Charles), 1942-.**    **5.5289**
Soil erosion / R. P. C. Morgan. — London; New York: Longman, 1979. 113 p.: ill.; 23 cm. (Topics in applied geography.) Includes index. 1. Soil erosion 2. Soil conservation 3. Soil erosion — Malaysia — Malaya. 4. Soil conservation — Malaysia — Malaya. I. T. II. Series.
S623.M68    631.4/5 19    LC 77-25911    ISBN 0582486920

**Hardin, Charles Meyer.**    • **5.5290**
The politics of agriculture: soil conservation and the struggle for power in rural America. — Glencoe, Ill.: Free Press, [1952] 282 p. 1. Soil conservation — United States 2. Agriculture and state — United States I. T.
S624.A1 H3    LC 52-8160

**National Symposium on Erosion and Soil Productivity (1984:**    **5.5291**
**New Orleans, La.)**
Erosion and soil productivity: proceedings of the National Symposium on Erosion and Soil Productivity, December 10–11, 1984, Hyatt Regency New Orleans, New Orleans, Louisiana. — St. Joseph, Mich.: American Society of Agricultural Engineers, c1985. vii, 289 p.: ill.; 23 cm. (ASAE publication; 8-85) 1. Soil erosion — United States — Congresses. 2. Soil productivity — United States — Congresses. 3. Soil erosion — Congresses. 4. Soil productivity — Congresses. I. American Society of Agricultural Engineers. II. T.
S624.A1 N46 1984    631.4/5 19    LC 85-70630    ISBN 0916150690

# S631–667 Fertilizers

**Follett, Roy H.**    **5.5292**
Fertilizers and soil amendments / Roy H. Follett, Larry S. Murphy, Roy L. Donahue. — Englewood Cliffs, N.J.: Prentice-Hall, c1981. xv, 557 p.: ill.; 25 cm. 1. Fertilizers 2. Soil amendments 3. Crops — Nutrition I. Murphy, Larry S. joint author. II. Donahue, Roy Luther, 1908- joint author. III. T.
S633.F62    631.8 19    LC 80-25799    ISBN 0133143368

**Jones, Ulysses S.**    **5.5293**
Fertilizers and soil fertility / Ulysses S. Jones. — Reston, Va.: Reston Pub. Co., c1979. xii, 368 p.; ill.; 25 cm. 1. Fertilizers and manures. 2. Soil fertility I. T.
S633.J76    631.8/1 19    LC 79-870    ISBN 0835919609

**Tisdale, Samuel L.**    **5.5294**
Soil fertility and fertilizers / Samuel L. Tisdale, Werner L. Nelson, James D. Beaton. — 4th ed. — New York: Macmillan; London: Collier Macmillan, c1985. xiv, 754 p.: ill.; 27 cm. 1. Fertilizers 2. Soil fertility 3. Crops — Nutrition I. Nelson, Werner L. II. Beaton, James D., 1930- III. T.
S633.T66 1985    631.4/2 19    LC 83-9902    ISBN 0024208302

# S671–790 Farm Machinery. Farm Buildings

**Blandford, Percy W.**    **5.5295**
Old farm tools and machinery: an illustrated history / by Percy W. Blandford. — Fort Lauderdale, Fla.: Gale Research Co., c1976. 188 p.: ill.; 23 cm. Includes index. 1. Agricultural machinery — History. 2. Agricultural implements —

History. 3. Agricultural machinery — Pictorial works. 4. Agricultural implements — Pictorial works. I. T.
S674.5.B55 1976    631.3/09    LC 75-44376    ISBN 0810320193

**White, K. D.**    • **5.5296**
Agricultural implements of the Roman world [by] K. D. White. — London: Cambridge U.P., 1967. xvi, 232 p.: 16 plates, illus.; 25 cm. 1. Agricultural implements — Rome — History. 2. Agriculture — Rome. 3. Rome — Antiquities I. T.
S676.W5    631.3/0937    LC 67-10350    ISBN 0521069122

**International Conference on Robotics and Intelligent Machines**    **5.5297**
**in Agriculture. (1st: 1983: Tampa, Fla.)**
Robotics and intelligent machines in agriculture: proceedings of the first International Conference on Robotics and Intelligent Machines in Agriculture, October 2–4, 1983, Curtis Hixon Convention Center, Tampa, Florida. — St. Joseph, Mich.: American Society of Agricultural Engineers, c1984. v, 155 p.: ill.; 23 cm. (ASAE publication. 4-84) 1. Robotics — Congresses. 2. Agricultural machinery — Congresses. 3. Artificial intelligence — Congresses. I. T. II. Series.
S678.65.I58 1983    631.3/7 19    LC 83-73657    ISBN 0916150607

**Rogin, Leo 1893-.**    • **5.5298**
The introduction of farm machinery in its relation to the productivity of labor in the agriculture of the United States during the nineteenth century. Berkeley, Ca., University of California Press, 1931. 260 p. illus. 27 cm. (University of California publications in economics, v.9) 'Index of authors cited': p. 244-251. 1. Farm mechanization 2. Wheat — United States I. T.
S751.R6 1931a    LC a 31-750

**Harvey, Nigel, 1916-.**    **5.5299**
A history of farm buildings: in England and Wales / Nigel Harvey. — New ed. — Newton Abbot: David & Charles, 1984. 279 p.: ill., plans; 24 cm. 1. Farm buildings — England — History. I. T.
S787.G7    631.2/0942 19    ISBN 0715383833

# S900–972 CONSERVATION OF NATURAL RESOURCES

**Nash, Roderick. comp.**    **5.5300**
The American environment: readings in the history of conservation / edited by Roderick Nash. — 2d ed. — Reading, Mass.: Addison-Wesley Pub. Co., c1976. xx, 364 p.: ill.; 22 cm. (Themes and social forces in American history series) 1. Conservation of natural resources — United States — History — Sources. I. T.
S930.N36 1976    333.7/2/0973    LC 75-10913    ISBN 0201052393

**Roosevelt, Franklin D. (Franklin Delano), 1882-1945.**    • **5.5301**
Franklin D. Roosevelt & conservation, 1911–1945. Compiled and edited by Edgar B. Nixon. Hyde Park, N.Y.: General Services Administration, National Archives and Records Service, Franklin D. Roosevelt Library, 1957. 2 v. group port. 24 cm. (Use and abuse of America's natural resources) 1. Roosevelt, Franklin D. (Franklin Delano), 1882-1945. 2. Conservation of natural resources — United States I. Nixon, Edgar Burkhardt, 1902- ed. II. T. III. Series.
S930.R66    333.7/2/0973    LC 72-2861    ISBN 0405045255

**Swain, Donald C.**    • **5.5302**
Federal conservation policy, 1921–1933. Berkeley, University of California Press, 1963. 221 p. ports. 24 cm. (University of California publications in history, v.76) 1. Natural resources — United States I. T.
S930.S9 E173.C15 vol. 76    LC 63-63900

**Udall, Stewart L.**    • **5.5303**
The quiet crisis. Introd. by John F. Kennedy. — [1st ed.] — New York: Holt, Rinehart and Winston, [1963] xiii, 209 p.: illus. (part col.) ports. (part col.); 24 cm. 1. Conservation of natural resources — United States — History. I. T.
S930.U3    333.720973    LC 63-21463

**Pryde, Philip R.**    **5.5304**
Conservation in the Soviet Union [by] Philip R. Pryde. Cambridge [Eng.] University Press, 1972. xv, 301 p. illus. 24 cm. 1. Conservation of natural resources — Soviet Union. 2. Natural areas — Soviet Union. I. T.
S934.R9 P76    333.7/2/0947    LC 72-182025    ISBN 0521084326

**Jackson, W. A. Douglas (William Arthur Douglas), 1923-.**    **5.5305**
Soviet resource management and the environment / edited by W.A. Douglas Jackson. — Columbus, Ohio: Anchor Press, c1978. xiv, 239 p.: ill., maps.

1. Conservation of natural resources — Russia 2. Environmental policy — Russia I. T.
S934.R9 S66

**Dasmann, Raymond Fredric, 1919-.**       5.5306
Environmental conservation / Raymond F. Dasmann; [illustrations by John Balbalis with the assistance of the Wiley Illustration Department]. — 5th ed. — New York: Wiley, c1984. x, 486 p.: ill.; 24 cm. 1. Conservation of natural resources 2. Ecology 3. Human ecology 4. Conservation of natural resources — United States 5. Ecology — United States. 6. Human ecology — United States. I. T.
S938.D37 1984     333.7/2 19     LC 83-21767     ISBN 047189141X

**Pinchot, Gifford, 1865-1946.**       • 5.5307
The fight for conservation. Introd. by Gerald D. Nash. — Seattle: University of Washington Press, [1967, c1910] xxvii, 152 p.; 23 cm. — (Americana library, 5) 1. Conservation of natural resources — United States 2. United States — Economic conditions — 1865-1918 I. T.
S942.P5     333.7/2/0973     LC 68-1821

## S960–964 Wildlife Conservation

**Murphy, Robert William, 1902-.**       • 5.5308
Wild sanctuaries; our national wildlife refuges; a heritage restored, by Robert Murphy. Foreword by Stewart L. Udall. — New York: Dutton, 1968. 288 p.: illus. (part col.), maps.; 29 cm. 1. Wildlife refuges — U.S. I. T.
S962.M8     333.7/8     LC 67-20543

# SB PLANT CULTURE. HORTICULTURE

## SB1–106 Reference. General Works

**Stephenson, Joseph W.**       • 5.5309
The gardener's directory. [1st ed.] Garden City, N.Y.: Hanover House, 1960. 454 p.; 22 cm. 1. Horticulture — Directories. 2. Horticulture — Bibliography 3. Horticulture — Societies, etc. 4. Botanical gardens I. T.
SB44.S8     635.9058     LC 60-10683

**Bailey, L. H. (Liberty Hyde), 1858-1954. ed.**       • 5.5310
The standard cyclopedia of horticulture; a discussion, for the amateur, and the professional and commerical grower, of the kinds, characteristics and methods of cultivation of the species of plants grown in the regions of the United States and Canada for ornament, for fancy, for fruit and for vegetables; with keys to the natural families and genera, descriptions of the horticultural capabilities of the states and provinces and dependent islands, and sketches of eminent horticulturists, by L.H. Bailey. Illustrated with colored plates, four thousand engravings in the text, and ninety-six full-page cuts ... New York, The Macmillan company, 1937. 3 v. col. fronts., illus. (incl. ports., maps) plates (part col.) 27 cm. Paged continuously. 'Popular edition, published October, 1935; November, 1935; October, 1937.' First published under title: Cyclopedia of American horticulture. 1. Gardening — Dictionaries. I. T.
SB45.B17 1937     630.3     LC 39-2472

**Bailey, L. H. (Liberty Hyde), 1858-1954.**       5.5311
Hortus third: a concise dictionary of plants cultivated in the United States and Canada / initially compiled by Liberty Hyde Bailey and Ethel Zoe Bailey; revised and expanded by the staff of the Liberty Hyde Bailey Hortorium. — New York: Macmillan, c1976. xiv, 1290 p.: ill.; 29 cm. Includes index. 1. Plants, Cultivated — North America — Dictionaries. 2. Gardening — North America — Dictionaries. I. Bailey, Ethel Zoe. joint author. II. Liberty Hyde Bailey Hortorium. III. T.
SB45.B22 1976     582/.06/1     LC 77-352066

## SB107–112 Economic Botany

**Baker, Herbert G.**       • 5.5312
Plants and civilization [by] Herbert G. Baker. — 2d ed. — Belmont, Calif.: Wadsworth Pub. Co., [1970] xi, 194 p.: illus.; 24 cm. — (Fundamentals of botany series) 1. Botany, Economic I. T.
SB107.B3 1970     581.6     LC 76-93490

**Berrie, A. M. M.**       5.5313
An introduction to the botany of the major crop plants / Alex M. M. Berrie. — London; Bellmawr, N.J.: Heyden, c1977. x, 220 p.: ill.; 25 cm. — (Botanical sciences series) Includes index. 1. Botany, Economic 2. Plants, Cultivated I. T. II. Series.
SB107.B47     581.6/1     LC 78-301727     ISBN 085501220X

**Candolle, Alphonse de, 1806-1893.**       • 5.5314
Origin of cultivated plants / by Alphonse de Candolle. — New York: Hafner Pub. Co., 1959. — 468 p.; 23 cm. — (International scientific series (London, Eng.). v. 49) 1. Plants, Cultivated 2. Botany, Economic I. T. II. Series.
SB107.C213 1959     LC 59-7042

**Gill, Norman Thorpe.**       5.5315
Agricultural botany / N.T. Gill and K.C. Vear. — 3d ed. rev. / by K.C. Vear and D.J. Barnard. — London: Duckworth, 1980-. 6 v.: ill.; 24 cm. 1. Botany, Economic 2. Agriculture I. Vear, Kenneth Charles. joint author. II. Barnard, D. J. III. T.
SB107.G47 1980     630/.2/81 19     LC 81-459897     ISBN 0715612506

**Brengle, K. G.**       5.5316
Principles and practices of dryland farming / K.G. Brengle. — Boulder, Colo.: Colorado Associated University Press, c1982. xii, 178 p.: ill.; 24 cm. Includes index. 1. Dry farming I. T.
SB110.B685 1982     631.5/86 19     LC 80-70691     ISBN 0870810952

**Cobley, Leslie S.**       5.5317
An introduction to the botany of tropical crops / Leslie S. Cobley. 3rd edition. — London; New York: Longman, 1977. xvi, 371 p.: ill.; 22 cm. 1. Tropical crops 2. Botany — Tropics. I. T.
SB111.C62 1977     581.6/1/0913

## SB119–171 Plant Propagation. Genetic Engineering

**Hartmann, Hudson Thomas, 1914-.**       5.5318
Plant propagation: principles and practices / Hudson T. Hartmann, Dale E. Kester. — 4th ed. — Englewood Cliffs, N.J.: Prentice-Hall, c1983. viii, 727 p.: ill.; 25 cm. 1. Plant propagation I. Kester, Dale E. II. T.
SB119.H3 1983     631.5/3 19     LC 82-16551     ISBN 0136810071

**Genetic engineering of plants: agricultural research opportunities and policy concerns / Board on Agriculture, National Research Council.**       5.5319
Washington, D.C.: National Academy Press, 1984. x, 83 p.: ill.; 26 cm. Includes index. 1. Plant genetic engineering 2. Plant-breeding 3. Agriculture — Research 4. Plant genetic engineering — United States. 5. Plant-breeding — United States. 6. Agriculture — Research — United States. I. National Research Council (U.S.). Board on Agriculture.
SB123.G375 1984     631.5/2 19     LC 83-63138     ISBN 0309034345

**Welsh, James R., 1933-.**       5.5320
Fundamentals of plant genetics and breeding / James R. Welsh. — New York, N.Y.: Wiley, c1981. xiv, 290 p.: ill.; 24 cm. 1. Plant-breeding 2. Plant genetics I. T.
SB123.W4     631.5/3     LC 80-14638     ISBN 0471028622

**Gene banks and the world's food / Donald L. Plucknett ... [et al.].**       5.5321
Princeton, N.J.: Princeton University Press, c1987. xv, 247 p.: ill.; 25 cm. Includes index. 1. Gene banks, Plant 2. Food crops — Germplasm resources. I. Plucknett, Donald L., 1931-
SB123.3.G46 1987     631.5/2 19     LC 86-42841     ISBN 0691084386

**Nickell, Louis G., 1921-.**       5.5322
Plant growth regulators: agricultural uses / Louis G. Nickell. — Berlin; New York: Springer-Verlag, 1982. xii, 173 p.: ill.; 25 cm. 1. Plant regulators I. T.
SB128.N52     631.8 19     LC 81-9320     ISBN 0387109730

# SB188–305 Food Crops

**Briggs, D. E. (Dennis Edward)**     5.5323
Barley / D. E. Briggs. — New York: Wiley, 1978. xviii, 612 p.: ill.; 24 cm. 'A Halsted Press book.' 1. Barley I. T.
SB191.B2 B75     633/.16     LC 78-7314     ISBN 0470263938

**Jugenheimer, Robert W.**     5.5324
Corn: improvement, seed production, and uses / Robert W. Jugenheimer. — New York: Wiley, c1976. xvii, 670 p.: ill.; 24 cm. 'Completely rewritten and expanded revision of the book entitled Hybrid maize breeding and seed production, published in 1958 by the Food and Agriculture Organization of the United Nations, Rome.' 'A Wiley-Interscience publication.' Includes index. 1. Corn — Breeding 2. Corn — Seeds 3. Hybrid corn 4. Corn — Utilization I. T.
SB191.M2 J86     633.1/52 19     LC 75-32414     ISBN 0471453153

**Maize breeding and genetics / edited by David B. Walden.**     5.5325
New York: Wiley, c1978. xv, 794 p.: ill.; 24 cm. 'A Wiley-Interscience publication.' Includes index. 1. Corn 2. Corn — Breeding 3. Corn — Genetics I. Walden, David B., 1932-
SB191.M2 M325     633/.15/3     LC 78-6779     ISBN 0471918059

**Rice—production and utilization / [edited by] Bor S. Luh.**     5.5326
Westport, Conn.: AVI Pub. co., c1980. xii, 925 p.: ill.; 24 cm. 1. Rice 2. Rice — Processing I. Luh, Bor Shiun, 1916-
SB191.R5 R497     633/.18     LC 79-13864     ISBN 0870553321

**Walton, Peter D.**     5.5327
Production and management of cultivated forages / Peter D. Walton. — Reston, Va.: Reston Pub. Co., c1983. xvi, 336 p.: ill.; 24 cm. 1. Forage plants I. T.
SB193.W26 1983     633.2 19     LC 82-12306     ISBN 0835956229

**Stubbendieck, James L.**     5.5328
North American range plants / J. Stubbendieck, Stephan L. Hatch, and Kathie J. Kjar. — 2nd ed. — Lincoln: University of Nebraska Press, c1982. xi, 464 p.: ill.; 26 cm. Includes index. 1. Range plants — North America — Identification. 2. Forage plants — North America — Identification. 3. Range plants — North America. 4. Forage plants — North America. I. Hatch, Stephan L., 1945- II. Hirsch, Kathie J., 1954- III. T.
SB193.3.N67 S88 1982     582/.06 19     LC 82-8560     ISBN 0803291329

**Soybean physiology, agronomy, and utilization / edited by A. Geoffrey Norman.**     5.5329
New York: Academic Press, 1978. xii, 249 p.: ill.; 24 cm. 1. Soybean I. Norman, Arthur Geoffrey, 1905-
SB205.S7 S535     635/.655     LC 78-18399     ISBN 0125211600

**Barnes, Arthur Chapman, 1891-.**     5.5330
The sugar cane. [2d ed.] New York, Wiley [1974] 572 p. illus. 24 cm. 1. Sugarcane I. T.
SB 231 B26 1973     LC 72-7590     ISBN 0470053305

**Spices / J. W. Purseglove ... [et al.].**     5.5331
London; New York: Longman, 1981. 2 v. (xi, 813 p.): ill.; 22 cm. (Tropical agriculture series) 1. Spices 2. Spice trade I. Purseglove, J. W. (John William), 1921-
SB305.S67     633.8/3     LC 80-40349     ISBN 0582468116

# SB317–319 Horticulture

**Handbook of legumes of world economic importance / [edited by] James A. Duke.**     5.5332
New York: Plenum Press, 1981 [c1980] xi, 345 p.: ill.; 28 cm. 1. Legumes I. Duke, James A., 1929-
SB317.L43 H36     633.3     LC 80-16421     ISBN 0306404060

**North American horticulture, a reference guide / compiled by the American Horticultural Society; project director Jane S. Keough; publications director Judy Powell; editor Barbara W. Ellis.**     5.5333
New York: Scribner, c1982. xvi, 367 p.; 29 cm. Includes index. 1. Horticulture — United States — Societies, etc. — Directories. 2. Gardening — United States — Societies, etc. — Directories. 3. Conservation of natural resources — United States — Societies, etc. — Directories. 4. Horticulture — Canada —

Societies, etc. — Directories. 5. Gardening — Canada — Societies, etc. — Directories. 6. Conservation of natural resources — Canada — Societies, etc. — Directories. I. Keough, Jane S. II. Powell, Judy. III. Ellis, Barbara W. IV. American Horticultural Society.
SB317.56.U6 N67 1982     635/.02573 19     LC 82-5762     ISBN 0684176041

**Everett, Thomas H.**     5.5334
The New York Botanical Garden illustrated encyclopedia of horticulture / Thomas H. Everett. — New York: Garland Pub., 1981. 10 v.: ill. (some col.); 32 cm. 1. Horticulture — Dictionaries. 2. Gardening — Dictionaries. 3. Plants, Ornamental — Dictionaries. 4. Plants, Cultivated — Dictionaries. I. New York Botanical Garden. II. T. III. Title: Encyclopedia of horticulture.
SB317.58.E94     SB317.58 E94.     635.9/03/21     LC 80-65941     ISBN 0824072316

**Soule, James.**     5.5335
Glossary for horticultural crops / James Soule; sponsored by the American Society for Horticultural Science. — New York: Wiley, c1985. xxvi, 898 p.: ill.; 27 cm. Includes indexes. 1. Horticulture — Terminology. I. American Society for Horticultural Science. II. T.
SB317.58.S68 1985     635/.014 19     LC 84-20927     ISBN 0471884995

**Janick, Jules, 1931-.**     5.5336
Horticultural science / Jules Janick. — 4th ed. — New York: W.H. Freeman, c1986. xi, 746 p.: ill.; 25 cm. 1. Horticulture I. T.
SB318.J35 1986     635 19     LC 85-20521     ISBN 0716717425

**Poincelot, Raymond P., 1944-.**     5.5337
Horticulture: principles and practical applications / Raymond P. Poincelot. — Englewood Cliffs, N.J.: Prentice-Hall, c1980. xv, 652 p.: ill.; 24 cm. 1. Horticulture I. T.
SB318.P64     635     LC 79-28307     ISBN 0133948099

# SB320–402 Vegetables. Fruit

**Yamaguchi, Mas.**     5.5338
World vegetables: principles, production, and nutritive values / Mas Yamaguchi. — Westport, Conn.: AVI Pub. Co., c1983. xv, 415 p.: ill.; 24 cm. — (Plant science textbook series.) 1. Vegetables I. T. II. Series.
SB320.9.Y25 1983     635 19     LC 83-6422     ISBN 0870554336

**Splittstoesser, Walter E.**     5.5339
Vegetable growing handbook / Walter E. Splittstoesser. — 2nd ed. — Westport, Conn.: AVI Pub. Co., c1984. x, 325 p.: ill.; 24 cm. 1. Vegetable gardening I. T.
SB321.S645 1984     635 19     LC 83-22515     ISBN 087055445X

**Bultitude, John.**     5.5340
Apples: a guide to the identification of international varieties / John Bultitude. — Seattle: University of Washington Press, 1983. 323, [2] p.: ill. (some col.); 26 cm. 1. Apple — Varieties 2. Apple — Identification. I. T.
SB363.3.A1 B85 1983     634/.117 19     LC 83-232669     ISBN 0295960418

**Food and Agriculture Organization of the United Nations.**     5.5341
Modern olive production / Food and Agriculture Organization of the United Nations, Instituto Nacional de Investigaciones Agrarias (INIA) Ministry of Agriculture, Spain. — Rome: United Nations Development Programme, Food and Agriculture Organization of the United Nations, 1977. xi, 251 p.: ill.; 28 cm. 'Prepared for the Centre for the Improvement and Demonstration of Olive Production Techniques.' 1. Olive I. Instituto Nacional de Investigaciones Agrarias. II. Centro de Mejora y Demostracion de las Tecnicas Oleicolas. III. T.
SB367.F663     634.63     ISBN 9251002495 pbk

**Citrus science and technology / edited by Steven Nagy, Philip E. Shaw, Matthew K. Veldhuis.**     5.5342
Westport, Conn.: Avi Pub. Co., c1977. 2 v.: ill.; 24 cm. 1. Citrus fruits 2. Citrus fruits — By-products I. Nagy, Steven. II. Shaw, Philip E. III. Veldhuis, Matthew K.
SB369.C53     641.3/4/3     LC 77-4438     ISBN 087055221X

# SB403–450.87 Ornamental Plants. Floriculture

**McDaniel, Gary L.**     **5.5343**
Ornamental horticulture / Gary L. McDaniel. — 2nd ed. — Reston, Va.: Reston Pub. Co., c1982. xiv, 526 p.: ill.; 24 cm. 1. Ornamental horticulture — Vocational guidance. 2. Ornamental horticulture I. T.
SB403.45.M35 1982   635.9 19   *LC* 81-23397   *ISBN* 0835953483

**Coats, Alice M.**     • **5.5344**
[Quest for plants] The plant hunters; being a history of the horticultural pioneers, their quests, and their discoveries from the Renaissance to the twentieth century [by] Alice M. Coats. New York, McGraw-Hill [1970, c1969] 400 p. illus., maps, ports. 26 cm. First published in 1969 under title: The quest for plants. 1. Plants, Ornamental — Collection and preservation — History. 2. Plant introduction — History. 3. Horticulturists 4. Botanists I. T.
SB404.5.C63 1970   581/.0922 B   *LC* 77-101380

**The Ball red book: greenhouse growing / Vic Ball, editor.**     **5.5345**
14th ed. — Reston, Va.: Reston Pub. Co., c1985. xiv, 720 p.: ill.; 24 cm. 1. Floriculture 2. Plants, Ornamental 3. Ornamental plant industry I. Ball, Vic.
SB405.B254 1985   635.9 19   *LC* 84-11559   *ISBN* 0835903826

**Introduction to floriculture / edited by Roy A. Larson.**     **5.5346**
New York: Academic Press, c1980. xviii, 607 p.: ill.; 24 cm. 1. Floriculture I. Larson, Roy A.
SB405.I55   635.9   *LC* 80-10769   *ISBN* 0124376509

**Graf, Alfred Byrd.**     • **5.5347**
[Exotica] Exotica 4: pictorial cyclopedia of exotic plants and trees. Century ed. Rutherford, N.J.: Roehrs Co., 1985. 1 v. First published in 1957 under title: Exotica. 1. Tropical plants — Pictorial works. 2. Plants, Ornamental — Pictorial works. 3. House plants — Pictorial works. I. T.
SB407.G7   635.96/5   *LC* 74-92881

**Graf, Alfred Byrd.**     **5.5348**
Tropica: color cyclopedia of exotic plants and trees for warm–region horticulture—in cool climate the summer garden or sheltered indoors / Alfred Byrd Graf. — 2nd ed., rev. and enl. — East Rutherford, N.J.: Roehrs Co., 1981. 1136 p.: col. ill., map; 27 cm. Map on lining papers. Includes indexes. 1. Plants, Ornamental — Pictorial works. 2. Tropical plants — Pictorial works. 3. House plants — Pictorial works. I. T.
SB407.G73 1981   635.9/52 19   *LC* 81-112593   *ISBN* 091126616X

**Bechtel, Helmut.**     **5.5349**
[Orchideenatlas. English] The manual of cultivated orchid species / Helmut Bechtel, Phillip Cribb, Edmund Launert. — 1st MIT Press ed. — Cambridge, Mass.: MIT Press, 1981. 444 p.: ill. (some col.); 28 cm. Translation of Orchideenatlas. Includes index. 1. Orchids 2. Orchids — Classification. 3. Orchids — Pictorial works. 4. Orchid culture I. Cribb, Phillip. II. Launert, Edmund. III. T.
SB409.B4213 1981   635.9/3415 19   *LC* 80-29634   *ISBN* 0262021625

**Padilla, Victoria.**     **5.5350**
Bromeliads; a descriptive listing of the various genera and the species most often found in cultivation. — New York: Crown Publishers, [c1973] 134 p.: illus. (part col.); 29 cm. 1. Bromeliaceae I. T.
SB413.B7 P3 1973   584/.22   *LC* 72-84287   *ISBN* 0517500450

**Elwes, Henry John, 1846-1922.**     **5.5351**
Lilies. — A revision of Elwes' Monograph of the genus Lilium and its supplements / compiled by Patrick M. Synge, with the aid of members of the Lily Committee of the Royal Horticultural Society and other experts in association with the Royal Horticultural Society; introd. by Jan de Graaff. — New York: Universe Books, 1980. 276 p., [27] leaves of plates: ill.; 26 cm. Also contains articles by O. E. P. Wyatt and others. Includes index. 1. Lilies 2. Liliaceae I. Synge, Patrick Millington. II. Royal Horticultural Society (Great Britain). Lily Committee. III. Royal Horticultural Society (Great Britain) IV. T.
SB413.L7 E48 1980   635.9/34324 19   *LC* 79-9682   *ISBN* 0876633408

**Treseder, Neil G.**     **5.5352**
Magnolias / Neil G. Treseder. — London; Boston: Faber & Faber published in collaboration with the Royal Horticultural Society, 1978. xviii, 243 p., [4] leaves of plates: ill. (some col.); 26 cm. Includes indexes. 1. Magnolia 2. Magnolia — Varieties. I. T.
SB413.M34 T73   635.9/773/114   *LC* 79-305910   *ISBN* 0571096190

**Hybrids and hybridizers, rhododendrons and azaleas for Eastern North America / edited by Philip A. Livingston and Franklin H. West; introd. by David Goheen Leach.**     **5.5353**
Newtown Square, Pa.: Harrowood Books, c1978. xvi, 256 p., [12] leaves of plates: ill.; 29 cm. Includes indexes. 1. Rhododendron — Breeding. 2. Azalea — Breeding. 3. Plant breeders — United States — Biography. 4. Rhododendron — Varieties 5. Azalea — Varieties 6. Hybridization, Vegetable I. Livingston, Philip A., 1901- II. West, Franklin H., 1921-
SB413.R47 H9   635.9/33/62   *LC* 77-16822   *ISBN* 0915180049

## SB419 Indoor Gardening

**Poincelot, Raymond P., 1944-.**     **5.5354**
Gardening indoors with house plants [by] Raymond P. Poincelot. — Emmaus, Pa.: Rodale Press, Book Division, [1974] xi, 266 p.: illus.; 23 cm. 1. House plants I. T.
SB419.P62   635.9/65   *LC* 74-16238   *ISBN* 0878570853

**Rodale's encyclopedia of indoor gardening / edited by Anne M. Halpin.**     **5.5355**
Emmaus, PA: Rodale Press, c1980. vii, 902 p.: ill.; 24 cm. Includes indexes. 1. Indoor gardening 2. House plants 3. Organic gardening I. Halpin, Anne Moyer. II. Title: Encyclopedia of indoor gardening.
SB419.R74   635.9/65   *LC* 80-17019   *ISBN* 0878573194

## SB421–439 Classes of Plants

**McMillan Browse, P. D. A.**     **5.5356**
The commercial production of climbing plants / P.D.A. McMillan Browse. — London: Grower, 1981. x, 97 p.: ill.; 30 cm. 1. Climbing plants 2. Plant propagation I. T.
SB427.B7x   635.9/74 18   635.9/74 19   *ISBN* 0901361496

**Ouden, P. den (Pieter den), 1874-1964.**     • **5.5357**
Manual of cultivated conifers; hardy in the cold–and warm–temperate zone, by P. den Ouden, in collaboration with B.K. Boom. The Hague, M. Nijhoff, 1965. x, 526 p. illus. 27 cm. 1. Ornamental conifers 2. Conifers 3. Ornamental conifers — Varieties. 4. Conifers — Varieties. I. Boom, B. K. (Boudewijn Karel), 1891- joint author. II. T.
SB428.O8   635.9/752 19   *LC* 67-2348

**Foliage plant production / Jasper N. Joiner, editor.**     **5.5358**
Englewood Cliffs, N.J.: Prentice-Hall, c1981. xix, 614 p.: ill.; 24 cm. 1. Foliage plants I. Joiner, Jasper N.
SB431.F64   635.9/75 19   *LC* 80-21797   *ISBN* 0133228673

**Koreshoff, Deborah R.**     **5.5359**
Bonsai: its art, science, history and philosophy / written and illustrated by Deborah R. Koreshoff; photography by Penny Wright. Brisbane, Australia: Boolarong; Portland, Or.: Timber Press, c1984. xvii, 255 p., [31] p. of plates: ill. (some col.) map; 31 cm. 1. Bonsai I. T.
SB433.5.K67   *ISBN* 0917304683

## SB435–439 Shrubs and Ornamental Trees. Wild Flowers

**Krüssmann, Gerd.**     **5.5360**
[Handbuch der Laubgehölze. English] Manual of cultivated broad–leaved trees & shrubs / written by Gerd Krüssmann; translated by Michael E. Epp; technical editor, Gilbert S. Daniels. — Beaverton, Or.: Timber Press, in cooperation with the American Horticultural Society, 1984-. 3 v.: ill., maps; 29 cm. Translation of: Handbuch der Laubgehölze. 'Alphabetical reference to the botanical terminology.' v. 1, p. [33]-39. 1. Trees — Handbooks, manuals etc. 2. Shrubs — Handbooks, manuals etc. 3. Plants, Cultivated 4. Woody plants I. American Horticultural Society. II. T. III. Title: Cultivated broad-leaved trees & shrubs. IV. Title: Manual of cultivated broad-leaved trees and shrubs. V. Title: Cultivated broad-leaved trees and shrubs.
SB435.K94   *ISBN* 0917304780

**Flint, Harrison L. (Harrison Leigh), 1929-.**     **5.5361**
Landscape plants for eastern North America: exclusive of Florida and the immediate Gulf Coast / Harrison L. Flint; drawings by Jenny M. Lyverse. — New York: Wiley, 1983. ix, 677 p.: ill.; 27 cm. 'A Wiley-Interscience publication.' Includes index. 1. Ornamental woody plants — United States. 2. Ground cover plants — United States. 3. Landscape gardening — United States. 4. Ornamental woody plants — Canada. 5. Ground cover plants — Canada. 6. Landscape gardening — Canada. I. Lyverse, Jenny M. II. T. III. Title: Eastern North America.
SB435.5.F55 1983   635.9/7 19   *LC* 82-16068   *ISBN* 0471869058

**Plants that merit attention** / the Garden Club of America; Janet   **5.5362**
Meakin Poor, editor ... [et al.].
Portland, Or.: Timber Press, 1984. 1 v.: ill. (some col.); 29 cm. Includes index.
1. Trees — United States. 2. Shrubs — United States. I. Poor, Janet Meakin.
II. Garden Club of America.
SB435.5.P69 1984     635.9     *ISBN* 0917304756

**Grey, Gene W., 1931-.**      **5.5363**
Urban forestry / Gene W. Grey, Frederick J. Deneke. — 2nd ed. — New York:
Wiley, c1986. xv, 299 p.: ill.; 24 cm. 1. Urban forestry I. Deneke, Frederick J.,
1942- II. T.
SB436.G73 1986     635.9/77 19     *LC* 85-12333     *ISBN* 0471088137

**Phillips, Harry R.**      **5.5364**
Growing and propagating wild flowers / by Harry R. Phillips; with
contributions by Rob Gardner and Charlotte A. Jones-Roe in collaboration
with the staff of the North Carolina Botanical Garden; edited by C. Ritchie Bell
and Ken Moore; illustrations by Dorothy S. Wilbur. — Chapel Hill: University
of North Carolina Press, c1985. x, 331 p., [8] p. of plates: ill. (some col.); 24 cm.
Includes index. 1. Wild flower gardening 2. Wild flowers — Propagation.
I. Gardner, Rob. II. Jones-Roe, Charlotte A. III. Bell, C. Ritchie.
IV. Moore, Ken. V. North Carolina Botanical Garden. VI. T.
SB439.P48 1985     635.9/676 19     *LC* 84-25734     *ISBN* 0807816485

# SB450.9–467 Gardens and Gardening

**Wyman, Donald, 1903-.**      **5.5365**
[Gardening encyclopedia] Wyman's Gardening encyclopedia / by Donald
Wyman. — New expanded 2nd ed. — New York: Macmillan; London: Collier
Macmillan Publishers, c1986. 1 v. 1. Gardening — Dictionaries. 2. Plants,
Cultivated — Dictionaries. I. T. II. Title: Gardening encyclopedia.
SB450.95.W96 1986     635/.03/21 19     *LC* 86-12509     *ISBN*
0026320703

**Bush-Brown, James.**      **5.5366**
America's garden book / by James and Louise Bush-Brown; rev. ed. by the
New York Botanical Garden. — New York: Scribner, [1980] c1965. 819 p.: ill.;
24 cm. Previous ed. entered under L. Carter Bush-Brown. Includes index.
1. Gardening 2. Gardening — United States. I. Bush-Brown, Louise Carter,
1897- joint author. II. New York Botanical Garden. III. T.
SB453.B9 1979     635.9/0973     *LC* 79-17303     *ISBN* 0684162709

**Crockett, James Underwood.**      **5.5367**
Crockett's victory garden / by James Underwood Crockett; photography by
Lee Lockwood/Black Star. — 1st ed. — Boston: Little, Brown, c1977. 326 p.:
ill.; 27 cm. Based on the television show Crockett's victory garden. Includes
index. 1. Gardening 2. Vegetable gardening I. T. II. Title: Victory garden.
SB453.C778     635/.0973     *LC* 77-2336     *ISBN* 0316161209

**Ortho's complete guide to successful gardening** / project editor,   **5.5368**
Barbara Ferguson; project writer, Deni W. Stein; art director,
James Stockton.
San Francisco, CA: Ortho Books, c1983. 504 p.: col. ill.; 29 cm. Includes index.
1. Gardening I. Ferguson, Barbara J. II. Stein, Deni W. III. Ortho Books.
IV. Title: Successful gardening.
SB453.O65 1983     635.9 19     *LC* 83-61313     *ISBN* 0897210182

**Keswick, Maggie.**      **5.5369**
The Chinese garden: history, art & architecture / Maggie Keswick;
contributions and conclusion by Charles Jencks. — New York: Rizzoli, 1978.
216 p.: ill. (some col.); 32 cm. Includes index. 1. Gardens, Chinese 2. Gardens
— China I. Jencks, Charles. joint author. II. T.
SB457.55.K47 1978     712     *LC* 78-57898     *ISBN* 0847801934

**Morris, Edwin T.**      **5.5370**
The gardens of China: history, art, and meanings = [Chung-hua yüan lin] /
Edwin T. Morris. — New York: Scribner, c1983. xii, 273 p., [8] p. of plates: ill.
(some col.); 28 cm. Parallel title in Chinese characters. Includes index.
1. Gardens, Chinese 2. Gardens — China I. T. II. Title: Chung-hua yüan lin.
SB457.55.M66 1983     712/.0951 19     *LC* 83-14181     *ISBN*
0684179598

**Watkin, David, 1941-.**      **5.5371**
The English vision: the picturesque in architecture, landscape, and garden
design / David Watkin. — 1st U.S. Ed. — New York: Harper & Row, c1982. xi,
227 p., [1] p. of plates: ill.; 29 cm. (Icon editions.) Includes index. 1. Gardens,
English — History. 2. Architecture, English — History. 3. Picturesque, The
I. T. II. Title: Picturesque in architecture, landscape, and garden design.
III. Series.
SB457.6.W37 1982     720/.942 19     *LC* 82-47548     *ISBN* 0064388751

**Bring, Mitchell.**      **5.5372**
Japanese gardens: design and meaning / Mitchell Bring, Josse Wayembergh. —
New York: McGraw-Hill, c1981. ix, 214 p., [4] leaves of plates: ill.; 24 cm. —
(McGraw-Hill series in landscape and landscape architecture.) Includes index.
1. Gardens, Japanese 2. Gardens — Japan — Kyoto. I. Wayembergh, Josse.
joint author. II. T. III. Series.
SB458.B74     712/.0952     *LC* 79-27286     *ISBN* 0070078254

**Itō, Teiji, 1922-.**      **5.5373**
The gardens of Japan / text by Teiji Itoh. — 1st ed. — Tokyo; New York:
Kodansha International; [New York, N.Y.: Distributed by Kodansha
International/USA through Harper & Row, 1984] 228 p.: ill. (some col.); 37
cm. Includes index. 1. Gardens, Japanese 2. Gardens — Japan I. T.
SB458.I833 1984     712/.0952 19     *LC* 83-48882     *ISBN* 0870116487

**Foster, H. Lincoln.**      **5.5374**
Rock gardening: a guide to growing alpines and other wildflowers in the
American garden / by H. Lincoln Foster; with drawings by Laura Louise
Foster. — Boston: Houghton Mifflin, 1968. xxviii, 466 p.: ill. 23 cm. 1. Rock
gardens 2. Rock gardens — United States. 3. Rock plants I. T.
SB459.F6     635.96/72     *LC* 66-18804

**Thacker, Christopher.**      **5.5375**
The history of gardens / Christopher Thacker. — Berkeley: Universityof
California Press, c1979. 288 p.: ill.; 27 cm. Includes index. 1. Gardens —
History 2. Gardens — Design — History. I. T.
SB465.T47 1979     712/.09     *LC* 78-59446     *ISBN* 0520037367

**Wiebenson, Dora.**      **5.5376**
The picturesque garden in France / Dora Wiebenson. — Princeton, N.J.:
Princeton University Press, c1978. xviii, 137 p., [44] leaves of plates: ill.; 29 cm.
Includes index. 1. Gardens, English — France. 2. Gardens, English
3. Gardens — France 4. Picturesque, The I. T.
SB466.F8 W53     712/.0944     *LC* 77-22704     *ISBN* 0691039305

**Strong, Roy C.**      **5.5377**
The Renaissance garden in England / Roy Strong. — London: Thames and
Hudson, c1979. 240 p.: ill.; 27 cm. 1. Gardens, Renaissance — England —
History. 2. Gardens — England — History. I. T.
SB466.G75 E57     712/.0942     *LC* 78-55191     *ISBN* 0500012091

# SB469–477 Landscape Gardening. Landscape Architecture

**Stroud, Dorothy.**      **5.5378**
Capability Brown / Dorothy Stroud; with an introduction by Christopher
Hussey. — London; Boston: Faber and Faber, 1984. 262 p., [69] p. of plates: ill.,
plans, ports.; 24 cm. Includes index. 1. Brown, Lancelot, 1716-1783.
2. Landscape architects — England — Biography. I. Brown, Lancelot,
1716-1783. II. T.
SB470.B7 S7 1984     712/.092/4 B 19     *LC* 84-13541     *ISBN*
057113405X

**Roper, Laura Wood.**      **5.5379**
FLO: A biography of Frederick Law Olmsted. — Baltimore: Johns Hopkins
University Press, [1973] xvii, 555 p.: illus.; 25 cm. 1. Olmsted, Frederick Law,
1822-1903. 2. Landscape architecture — United States. I. T.
SB470.O5 R66     712/.092/4 B     *LC* 73-8125     *ISBN* 0801815088

**Newton, Norman T., 1898-.**      **5.5380**
Design on the land; the development of landscape architecture [by] Norman T.
Newton. — Cambridge, Mass.: Belknap Press of Harvard University Press,
1971. xxiv, 714 p.: illus., maps, plans.; 26 cm. 1. Landscape architecture —
History. I. T.
SB470.5.N47     712/.09     *LC* 70-134955     *ISBN* 0674198700

**Carpenter, Philip L. (Philip Lee), 1933-.**      **5.5381**
Plants in the landscape / Philip L. Carpenter, Theodore D. Walker, Frederick
O. Lanphear. — San Francisco: W. H. Freeman, [1976] vii, 481 p.: ill.; 22 x 29
cm. 1. Landscape gardening 2. Plants, Ornamental I. Walker, Theodore D.
joint author. II. Lanphear, Frederick O., joint author. III. T.
SB472.C27     712

**Hussey, Christopher, 1899-.**      **5.5382**
English gardens and landscapes, 1700-1750. — London: Country Life, 1967.
174 p.: front., illus., 96 plates, maps; 28 1/2 cm. 1. Gardens — England —
History. 2. Landscape architecture — England — History. 3. Gardens,
English — History. I. T.
SB477.E5 H8     712/.6/0942     *LC* 68-70833

**Kirby, Rosina Greene.**      5.5383
Mexican landscape architecture from the street and from within. — Tucson: University of Arizona Press, [1972] 167 p.: illus.; 24 x 32 cm. 1. Landscape architecture — Mexico. I. T.
SB477.M6 K57      712/.0972      LC 72-83818      ISBN 0816503273

# SB481–485 Parks

**World Congress on National Parks (1982: Bali, Indonesia)**      5.5384
National parks, conservation, and development: the role of protected areas in sustaining society: proceedings of the World Congress on National Parks, Bali, Indonesia, 11–22 October 1982 / edited by Jeffrey A. McNeely and Kenton R. Miller; International Union for Conservation of Nature and Natural Resources in cooperation with the United Nations Environment Programme ... [et al.]. — Washington, D.C.: Smithsonian Institution Press, c1984. xiii, 825 p.: ill.; 28 cm. 1. National parks and reserves — Congresses. 2. Natural areas — Congresses. 3. Nature conservation — Congresses. 4. Conservation of natural resources — Congresses. I. McNeely, Jeffrey A. II. Miller, Kenton. III. International Union for Conservation of Nature and Natural Resources. IV. T.
SB481.A2 W67 1982      333.78/3 19      LC 84-600007      ISBN 0874746639

**Lykes, Ira B.**      5.5385
Fundamentals of park technology / by Ira B. Lykes. — Gaithersburg, Md.: Associated Faculty Press, Inc., 1981. v,253 p.: ill., maps; 23 cm. 1. Parks — Management I. T.
SB481.L94 1981      639.95      LC 80-70104      ISBN 0867330090

**Rutledge, Albert J.**      5.5386
Anatomy of a park: the essentials of recreation area planning and design / Donald J. Molnar with Albert J. Rutledge; illustrations by Donald J. Molnar. — 2nd ed. — New York: McGraw-Hill, c1986. xii, 190 p.: ill.; 29 cm. Authors' names reversed on previous ed. Includes index. 1. Parks — Design and construction. 2. Parks — Planning. 3. Landscape architecture 4. Recreation areas — Design and construction. 5. Recreation areas — Planning. I. Molnar, Donald J. II. T.
SB481.R86 1986      712/.5 19      LC 85-19817      ISBN 0070543496

**United States. National Park Service.**      • 5.5387
Parks for America; a survey of park and related resources in the fifty States and a preliminary plan. [Washington, For sale by the Superintendent of Documents, U.S. Govt. Print. Off.] 1964. xiv, 485 p. illus., maps. (part col.) 29 cm. 1. Parks — United States. 2. Recreation areas — United States I. T.
SB482.A3 1964b      LC 64-62654

**Everhart, William C.**      5.5388
The National Park Service / William C. Everhart; foreword by Russell E. Dickenson. — Boulder, Colo.: Westview Press, 1983. x, 197 p.: ill.; 24 cm. — (Westview library of federal departments, agencies, and systems.) Includes index. 1. United States. National Park Service. 2. National parks and reserves — United States I. T. II. Series.
SB482.A4 E95 1983      353.0086/3 19      LC 82-10884      ISBN 0865311307

**Ise, John, 1885-.**      5.5389
Our national park policy / John Ise. — New York: Arno Press, 1979, c1961. xiii, 701 p., [9] leaves of plates: ill.; 24 cm. — (The Development of public land law in the United States) Reprint of the 1967 ed. published for Resources for the Future by the Johns Hopkins Press, Baltimore. 1. National parks and reserves — United States — History. I. T.
SB482.A4 I83 1979      333.7/8/0973      LC 78-53548      ISBN 0405113773

# SB599–999 Pests. Diseases

## SB599–618 General Works. Weeds. Poisonous Plants

**Pirone, Pascal Pompey, 1907-.**      5.5390
Diseases and pests of ornamental plants / Pascal P. Pirone. — 5th ed. — New York: Wiley, c1978. x, 566 p.: ill.; 25 cm. 'A Wiley-Interscience publication.' Includes index. 1. Plants, Ornamental — Diseases and pests. I. T.
SB603.5.P57 1978      635.9/2      LC 77-26893      ISBN 0471072494

**Crafts, Alden Springer, 1897-.**      5.5391
Modern weed control / by Alden S. Crafts. — Berkeley: University of California Press, c1975. 440 p.: ill.; 24 cm. Previous editions by W. W. Robbins, published under title: Weed control. 1. Weeds — Control I. Robbins, Wilfred William, 1884-1952. Weed control. II. T.
SB611.R6 1975      632/.58      LC 74-76383      ISBN 0520027337

**Crockett, Lawrence J.**      5.5392
Wildly successful plants: a handbook of North American weeds / by Lawrence J. Crockett; ill. by Joanne Bradley. New York: Macmillan, c1977. xii, 268 p.: ill.; 24 cm. 1. Weeds — United States — Identification. 2. Weeds — Canada — Identification. I. T.
SB612.A2 C72      581.6/5      LC 76-54687      ISBN 0025288504

**Muenscher, Walter Conrad Leopold, 1891-1963.**      5.5393
Weeds / Walter Conrad Muenscher; [new] foreword and appendixes by Peter A. Hyypio. — Ithaca: Comstock Pub. Associates, 1980, c1955. xviii, 586 p.: ill.; 22 cm. Reprint of the 2d ed., published by Macmillan, New York. 1. Weeds — United States — Identification. 2. Weeds — Canada — Identification. 3. Weeds — Control I. T.
SB612.A2 M8 1980      632/.58/097      LC 79-48017      ISBN 0801412668

**Kingsbury, John Merriam, 1928-.**      • 5.5394
Poisonous plants of the United States and Canada. — Englewood Cliffs, N.J.: Prentice-Hall, [1964] xiii, 626 p.: illus. (part col.); 24 cm. — (Prentice-Hall biological science series) 1. Poisonous plants 2. Botany — North America. I. T.
SB617.K5      581.69      LC 64-14394

## SB731–738 Plant Pathology. General Works

**Ainsworth, G. C. (Geoffrey Clough), 1905-.**      5.5395
Introduction to the history of plant pathology / G. C. Ainsworth. — Cambridge [Eng.]; New York: Cambridge University Press, 1981. xii, 315 p., [1] leaf of plates: ill.; 24 cm. Includes index. 1. Plant diseases — History. I. T.
SB731.A37      632/.3/09 19      LC 80-40476      ISBN 0521230322

**Dickinson, C. H.**      5.5396
Plant pathology and plant pathogens / C.H. Dickinson, J.A. Lucas. — 2nd ed. — Oxford; Boston: Blackwell Scientific Publications; St. Louis, Mo.: Blackwell Mosby Book Distributors, 1982. viii, 229 p.: ill.; 24 cm. — (Basic microbiology. v. 6) 1. Plant diseases 2. Phytopathogenic microorganisms — Host plants 3. Phytopathogenic microorganisms 4. Host-parasite relationships I. Lucas, John Alexander. II. T. III. Series.
SB731.D5 1982      581.2/3 19      LC 84-113734      ISBN 0632009187

**Lucas, G. B.**      5.5397
Introduction to plant diseases: identification and management / G.B. Lucas, C.L. Campbell, L.T. Lucas. — Westport, Conn.: AVI pub. Co., c1985. xvii, 313 p.: ill.; 20 cm. Includes index. 1. Plant diseases 2. Phytopathogenic microorganisms — Control. I. Campbell, C. L. (C. Lee) II. Lucas, L. T. III. T.
SB731.L83 1985      632/.3 19      LC 85-1325      ISBN 0870554735

**Nyvall, Robert F.**      5.5398
Field crop diseases handbook / Robert F. Nyvall. — Westport, Conn.: AVI Pub. Co., c1979. xxxi, 436 p.: ill.; 27 cm. — (AVI sourcebook and handbook series.) 1. Field crops — Diseases and pests 2. Plant diseases 3. Phytopathogenic microorganisms — Control. I. T. II. Series.
SB731.N94      633/.08/9      LC 79-17944      ISBN 0870553364

**Roberts, Daniel A. (Daniel Altman), 1922-.**      5.5399
Fundamentals of plant pathology / Daniel A. Roberts, Carl W. Boothroyd. — 2nd ed. — New York: W.H. Freeman and Co., c1984. xvi, 432 p.: ill.; 25 cm. Includes bibliographies and index. 1. Plant diseases I. Boothroyd, Carl W. (Carl William), 1915- II. T.
SB731.R56 1984      632 19      LC 83-20694      ISBN 0716715058

**Westcott, Cynthia, 1898-.**      5.5400
[Plant disease handbook] Westcott's Plant disease handbook. — 4th ed. / rev. by R. Kenneth Horst. — New York: Van Nostrand Reinhold, c1979. xx, 803 p., [4] leaves of plates: ill.; 24 cm. Includes index. 1. Plant diseases 2. Plant diseases — United States. I. Horst, R. Kenneth (Ralph Kenneth), 1935- II. T. III. Title: Plant disease handbook.
SB731.W47 1979      632      LC 78-15312      ISBN 0442235437

**Zoosporic plant pathogens: a modern perspective / edited by S.T. Buczacki.**      5.5401
London; New York: Academic Press, 1983. x, 352 p.: ill.; 24 cm. Includes index. 1. Fungi, Phytopathogenic — Addresses, essays, lectures. 2. Fungi — Zoospores — Addresses, essays, lectures. 3. Fungal diseases of plants —

Addresses, essays, lectures. 4. Fungi, Phytopathogenic — Control —
Addresses, essays, lectures. I. Buczacki, S. T.
SB733.Z66 1983      632/.4 19      *LC* 82-72596      *ISBN* 0121391809

## SB741–750 SPECIFIC DISEASES

**The Downy mildews / edited by D.M. Spencer.**                           **5.5402**
London; New York: Academic Press, 1981. xxi, 636 p.: ill.; 24 cm. 1. Downy
mildew diseases 2. Peronosporaceae — Control. I. Spencer, D. M. (Douglas
Malcolm), 1927-
SB741.D68 D68      632/.452 19      *LC* 81-66686      *ISBN* 012656860X

**Littlefield, Larry J.**                                                **5.5403**
Biology of the plant rusts: an introduction / Larry J. Littlefield. — 1st ed. —
Ames: Iowa State University Press, 1981. ix, 103 p., [3] leaves of plates: ill.
(some col.); 24 cm. 1. Rust fungi 2. Fungal diseases of plants I. T.
SB741.R8 L39      632/.425 19      *LC* 81-3734      *ISBN* 081381670X

**The Dynamics of host defence / edited by John A. Bailey, B.J**          **5.5404**
**Deverall.**
Sydney; New York: Academic Press, 1983. ix, 233 p.: ill.; 24 cm. 1. Plants —
Disease and pest resistance 2. Phytopathogenic microorganisms — Host plants
I. Bailey, John A. II. Deverall, Brian J.
SB750.D96 1983      581.2/9 19      *LC* 83-70713      *ISBN* 0120734605

## SB761 DISEASES AND PESTS OF TREES AND SHRUBS

**Coulson, Robert N. (Robert Norris), 1943-.**                           **5.5405**
Forest entomology: ecology and management / Robert N. Coulson, John A.
Witter. — New York: Wiley, c1984. x, 669 p.: ill.; 24 cm. 'A Wiley-Interscience
publication.' 1. Forest insects 2. Forest insects — Control I. Witter, John A.
II. T.
SB761.C68 1984      634.9/67 19      *LC* 83-23492      *ISBN* 0471025739

## SB931–950 ECONOMIC ENTOMOLOGY

**Introduction to insect pest management / edited by Robert L.**          **5.5406**
**Metcalf, William H. Luckmann.**
2nd ed. — New York: Wiley, c1982. xiv, 577 p.: ill.; 24 cm. — (Environmental
science and technology. 0194-0287) 'A Wiley-Interscience publication.'
1. Insect pests — Control I. Metcalf, Robert Lee, 1916- II. Luckmann,
William Henry, 1926- III. Series.
SB931.I58 1982      632/.7 19      *LC* 82-4794      *ISBN* 0471085472

**Pfadt, Robert E. ed.**                                                 **5.5407**
Fundamentals of applied entomology. With chapters by Christian C. Burkhardt
[and others] Edited by Robert E. Pfadt. 2d ed. New York, Macmillan [1971] x,
693 p. illus. 24 cm. 1. Beneficial insects 2. Insect pests — Control
I. Burkhardt, Christian C., 1924- II. T.
SB931.P45 1971      632/.7      *LC* 73-133562

**Urban entomology, interdisciplinary perspectives / edited by**         **5.5408**
**G.W. Frankie and C.S. Koehler.**
New York, NY: Praeger, 1983. xii, 493 p.: ill.; 25 cm. 1. Beneficial insects
2. Insect pests 3. Insects 4. Urban fauna I. Frankie, G. W. II. Koehler,
Carlton S.
SB931.U73 1983      628.9/657 19      *LC* 83-2407      *ISBN* 0030575729

**New technology of pest control / edited by Carl B. Huffaker;**         **5.5409**
**sponsored by the International Center for Integrated and**
**Biological Control, the University of California.**
New York: Wiley, c1980. xvi, 500 p., [1] leaf of plates: ill.; 24 cm.
(Environmental science and technology) 'A Wiley-Interscience publication.'
1. Pests — Integrated control 2. Insect pests — Control I. Huffaker, C. B.,
1914- II. International Center for Integrated and Biological Control.
SB950.N48      632/.7      *LC* 79-4369

**Sill, Webster H., 1916-.**                                            **5.5410**
Plant protection: an integrated interdisciplinary approach / Webster H. Sill, Jr.
— 1st ed. — Ames, Iowa: Iowa State University Press, 1982. xiii, 297 p.: ill.; 24
cm. Includes index. 1. Plants, Protection of 2. Pests — Integrated control
I. T.
SB950.S54      632 19      *LC* 81-12323      *ISBN* 0813816653

**Sill, Webster H., 1916-.**                                            **5.5411**
The plant protection discipline: problems and possible developmental strategies
/ by Webster H. Sill, Jr. — Montclair, N.J.: Allanheld, Osmun & Co.; New
York: distribution Halsted Press, c1978. x, 190 p.; 24 cm. Includes index.
1. Plants, Protection of I. T.
SB950.S55      632      *LC* 78-59171      *ISBN* 0470264438

## SB951–989 PESTICIDES. PLANT PROTECTION

**Cremlyn, Richard James William Campbell-Davys.**                       **5.5412**
Pesticides: preparation and mode of action / R. Cremlyn. — Chichester; New
York: Wiley, c1978. ix, 240 p., [12] leaves of plates: ill.; 24 cm. 1. Pesticides
I. T.
SB951.C68      632/.95      *LC* 77-28590      *ISBN* 0471996319

**McEwen, Freeman Lester, 1926-.**                                       **5.5413**
The use and significance of pesticides in the environment / F. L. McEwen, G. R.
Stephenson. — New York: Wiley, c1979. xiv, 538 p.: ill.; 24 cm. 'A Wiley-
Interscience publication.' Includes index. 1. Pesticides 2. Pesticides —
Environmental aspects I. Stephenson, Gerald Robert, 1942- joint author.
II. T.
SB951.M38      363      *LC* 78-23368      *ISBN* 0471039039

**Mel'nikov, Nikolaĭ Nikolaevich.**                                      **5.5414**
Chemistry of pesticides / by N.N. Melnikov; edited by Frances A. Gunther and
Jane Davies Gunther; translated from the Russian by Ruth L. Busbey. — New
York: Springer-Verlag, 1971. ix, 480 p. — (Residue reviews. v.36) Translation
of Khimiia pestutsidov. 1. Pesticides I. Gunther, Frances A. II. Gunther,
Jane Davies. III. T. IV. Series.
SB951.M4413 1971      *LC* 62-18595      *ISBN* 0387900314

**Marsh, R. W.**                                                        **5.5415**
Systemic fungicides. Edited by R. W. Marsh, with the assistance of R. J. W.
Byrde and D. Woodcock. — New York: Wiley, [1972] xii, 321 p.: illus.; 22 cm.
'A Halsted Press book.' 1. Systemic fungicides I. Byrde, Robert Jocelyn
Walter. II. Woodcock, David. III. T.
SB951.3.M36 1972b      632/.952      *LC* 72-4058      *ISBN* 0470572507

**Carson, Rachel, 1907-1964.**                                     ● **5.5416**
Silent spring. Drawings by Lois and Louis Darling. Boston, Houghton Mifflin,
1962. 368 p. illus. 22 cm. 1. Pesticides — Toxicology 2. Pesticides and wildlife
3. Insect pests — Biological control I. T.
SB959.C3      301.3      *LC* 60-5148

**The Encyclopedia of natural insect & disease control: the most**       **5.5417**
**comprehensive guide to protecting plants—vegetables, fruit,**
**flowers, trees, and lawns—without toxic chemicals / edited by**
**Roger B. Yepsen, Jr.**
Emmaus, Pa.: Rodale Press, c1984. 490 p.: ill. (some col.); 24 cm. Rev. ed of:
Organic plant protection. c1976. Includes index. 1. Plants, Protection of
2. Organic gardening 3. Garden pests — Control. I. Yepsen, Roger B.
II. Organic plant protection. III. Title: The Encyclopedia of natural insect and
disease control. IV. Title: Natural insect & disease control.
SB974.E53 1984      635/.0494 19      *LC* 83-24643      *ISBN* 0878574883

**Swan, Lester A.**                                                 ● **5.5418**
Beneficial insects; nature's alternatives to chemical insecticides: animal
predation, parasitism, disease organisms. [1st ed.] New York, Harper & Row
[1964] xvii, 429 p. illus. 22 cm. 1. Insect pests — Biological control I. T.
SB975.S92      632.9      *LC* 64-12705

## SD FORESTRY

**Clepper, Henry Edward, 1901-1987.**                                    **5.5419**
Professional forestry in the United States [by] Henry Clepper. — Baltimore:
Published for Resources for the Future by the Johns Hopkins Press, [1971] ix,
337 p.; 24 cm. 1. Forests and forestry — U.S. — History. I. Resources for the
Future. II. T.
SD143.C56      634.9/0973      *LC* 70-171107      *ISBN* 080181331X

**Clark, Thomas Dionysius, 1903-.**                                      **5.5420**
The greening of the South: the recovery of land and forest / Thomas D. Clark.
— Lexington, Ky.: University Press of Kentucky, c1984. xvi, 168 p., [24] p. of
plates: ill.; 24 cm. (New perspectives on the South.) Includes index. 1. Forests
and forestry — Southern States — History. 2. Lumbering — Southern States
— History. 3. Forest management — Southern States — History.

4. Deforestation — Southern States — History. 5. Reforestation — Southern States — History. 6. Forest conservation — Southern States — History. I. T. II. Series.
SD144.A15 C53 1984        333.75/0975 19        *LC* 84-17301        *ISBN* 0813103053

**Forestry handbook** / edited for the Society of American        **5.5421**
**Foresters by Karl F. Wenger.**
2nd ed. — New York: Wiley, c1984. xix, 1335 p.: ill.; 25 cm. — (SAF publication. 84-01) 'A Wiley-Interscience publication.' 1. Forests and forestry — Handbooks, manuals, etc. I. Wenger, Karl F., 1918- II. Society of American Foresters. III. Series.
SD373.F58 1984        634.9 19        *LC* 83-17110        *ISBN* 0471062278

**Leuschner, William A.**        **5.5422**
Introduction to forest resource management / William A. Leuschner. — New York: Wiley, c1984. vi, 298 p.: ill.; 25 cm. Includes index. 1. Forest management I. T.
SD373.L45 1984        634.9/28 19        *LC* 83-21602        *ISBN* 0471086681

**Sharpe, Grant William.**        **5.5423**
Introduction to forestry / Grant W. Sharpe, Clare W. Hendee, Wenonah F. Sharpe. — 5th ed. — New York: McGraw-Hill, c1986. ix, 629 p.: ill.; 24 cm. (McGraw-Hill series in forest resources.) 1. Forests and forestry 2. Forests and forestry — United States. I. Hendee, Clare W. (Clare Worden), 1908- II. Sharpe, Wenonah. III. T. IV. Series.
SD373.S56 1986        634.9/0973 19        *LC* 85-13318        *ISBN* 0070564825

**Stoddard, Charles Hatch, 1912-.**        **5.5424**
Essentials of forestry practice / Charles H. Stoddard, Glenn M. Stoddard. — 4th ed. — New York: Wiley, c1987. 387 p. Includes index. 1. Forests and forestry 2. Forests and forestry — United States. I. Stoddard, Glenn M. II. T.
SD373.S79 1987        634.9/0973 19        *LC* 86-22408        *ISBN* 0471842370

**Armson, Kenneth Avery, 1927-.**        **5.5425**
Forest soils: properties and processes / K. A. Armson. — Toronto: University of Toronto Press, 1977. xii, 390 p.: ill., diagrs., tables (part. col.) Includes index. 1. Forest soils I. T.
SD390 A698        631.4        *ISBN* 0802022650

**Pritchett, William L.**        **5.5426**
Properties and management of forest soils / William L. Pritchett, Richard F. Fisher. — 2nd ed. — New York: Wiley, c1986. p. cm. Includes index. 1. Forest soils 2. Soil management 3. Forest management I. Fisher, Richard F. II. T.
SD390.P74 1986        634.9 19        *LC* 86-22421        *ISBN* 0471895725

**Wilson, Brayton F. (Brayton Fuller), 1934-.**        **5.5427**
The growing tree / Brayton F. Wilson. — Rev. ed. — Amherst: University of Massachusetts Press, 1984. 138 p.: ill.; 24 cm. 1. Trees — Growth I. T.
SD396.W55 1984        582.16/031 19        *LC* 84-3577        *ISBN* 0870234234

# SD411–425 Conservation and Utilization

**Pyne, Stephen J., 1949-.**        **5.5428**
Introduction to wildland fire: fire management in the United States / Stephen J. Pyne. — New York: Wiley, c1984. xxii, 455 p.: ill.; 25 cm. 'A Wiley-Interscience publication.' 1. Wildfires 2. Wildfires — Prevention and control 3. Wildfires — United States. 4. Wildfires — United States — Prevention and control. I. T.
SD421.P94 1984        363.3/7 19        *LC* 83-17100        *ISBN* 047109658X

**Pyne, Stephen J., 1949-.**        **5.5429**
Fire in America: a cultural history of wildland and rural fire / Stephen J. Pyne. — Princeton, N.J.: Princeton University Press, c1982. xvi, 654 p.: ill.; 25 cm. Includes index. 1. Wildfires — United States — History. 2. Fires — United States — History. I. T.
SD421.3.P96 1982        304/.2 19        *LC* 81-47945        *ISBN* 0691083002

**Core, H. A.**        **5.5430**
Wood structure and identification / H. A. Core, W. A. Côté, and A. C. Day. 1st ed. — Syracuse, N.Y.: Syracuse University Press, 1976. xii, 168 p.: ill.; 26 cm. (Syracuse wood science series; 6) Errata slip inserted. Includes index. 1. Wood — Identification 2. Wood — Anatomy — Atlases. 3. Timber — United States — Identification. I. Côté, Wilfred A. joint author. II. Day, A. C. joint author. III. T. IV. Series.
SD536.C67        674/.12        *LC* 76-26938        *ISBN* 0815650418

**Husch, Bertram, 1923-.**        **5.5431**
Forest mensuration / Bertram Husch, Charles I. Miller, Thomas W. Beers. — 3rd ed. — New York: J. Wiley, c1982. vii, 402 p.: ill.; 25 cm. Includes index. 1. Forests and forestry — Mensuration 2. Forest surveys I. Miller, Charles I. II. Beers, Thomas W. III. T.
SD555.H8 1982        634.9/285 19        *LC* 82-4811        *ISBN* 0471044237

**Clawson, Marion, 1905-.**        **5.5432**
Forests for whom and for what? / Marion Clawson. — Baltimore: Published for Resources for the Future by Johns Hopkins University Press, [1975] xi, 175 p.; 23 cm. Includes index. 1. Forest policy — United States. 2. Forests and forestry — United States. I. Resources for the Future. II. T.
SD565.C58        333.7/5/0973        *LC* 74-24399        *ISBN* 080181698X

**Dana, Samuel Trask, 1883-.**        **5.5433**
Forest and range policy, its development in the United States / Samuel Trask Dana, Sally K. Fairfax, assistance from Mark Rey and Barbara T. Andrews on chapters 9 and 10. — 2d ed. — New York: McGraw-Hill, c1980. xviii, 458 p.: ill.; 24 cm. (McGraw-Hill series in forest resources) 1. Forest policy — United States. 2. Range policy — United States — History. I. Fairfax, Sally K. II. T.
SD565.D3 1980        333.7/4/0973        *LC* 79-13652        *ISBN* 0070152888

**Enarson, Elaine Pitt, 1949-.**        **5.5434**
Woods–working women: sexual integration in the U.S. Forest Service / Elaine Pitt Enarson. — [Tuscaloosa, Ala.]: University of Alabama Press, c1984. x, 174 p.; 25 cm. Includes index. 1. United States. Forest Service — Officials and employees. 2. Women — Employment — United States. 3. Affirmative action programs — United States. 4. Forest reserves — Oregon I. T.
SD565.E5 1984        331.4/133 19        *LC* 83-6725        *ISBN* 0817301887

**Frome, Michael.**        • **5.5435**
The Forest Service. New York, Praeger [1971] xiii, 241 p. illus. 22 cm. (Praeger library of U.S. Government departments and agencies, no. 30) 1. United States. Forest Service. 2. Forest conservation — United States. I. T.
SD565.F7        634.9/0973        *LC* 68-30834

**Kaufman, Herbert, 1922-.**        • **5.5436**
The forest ranger: a study in administrative behavior / by Herbert Kaufman. — Baltimore: Published for Resources for the Future by Johns Hopkins Press, 1960. xviii, 259 p.: ill., fold. map. 1. Foresters — United States. 2. Industrial management — Case studies. I. T.
SD 565.K3        *LC* 60-6650

**Robinson, Glen O.**        **5.5437**
The Forest Service: a study in public land management / Glen O. Robinson. — Baltimore: Published for Resources for the Future, inc. by the Johns Hopkins University Press, [1975] xv, 337 p.: ill.; 23 cm. 1. United States. Forest Service. 2. United States — Public lands I. Resources for the Future. II. T.
SD565.R6        353.008/233        *LC* 75-11352        *ISBN* 0801817234

**Steen, Harold K.**        **5.5438**
The U.S. Forest Service: a history / Harold K. Steen. Seattle: University of Washington Press, c1976. xvi, 356 p., [8] leaves of plates: ill.; 25 cm. Includes index. 1. United States. Forest Service — History. I. T.
SD565.S75        353.008/233        *LC* 76-15932        *ISBN* 0295955236

# SF1–593 ANIMAL CULTURE

**Battaglia, Richard A.**        **5.5439**
Handbook of livestock management techniques / Richard A. Battaglia, Vernon B. Mayrose. — Minneapolis, MN: Burgess Pub. Co., CEPCO Division, c1981. xi, 595 p.: ill.; 29 cm. Includes index. 1. Livestock — Handbooks, manuals, etc. I. Mayrose, Vernon B. II. T.
SF65.2.B38 1981        636 19        *LC* 80-70003        *ISBN* 0808729578

**McNitt, J. I. (James I.)**        **5.5440**
Livestock husbandry techniques / J.I. McNitt. — London: Granada, 1983. viii, 280 p.: ill.; 24 cm. Includes index. 1. Livestock I. T.
SF71.2 M3x        636.08/3 19        *ISBN* 0246118717

**Rice, Victor Arthur, 1890-1964.**        • **5.5441**
Breeding and improvement of farm animals / Victor Arthur Rice ... [et al.] — 6th ed. — New York: McGraw-Hill, [1967] xiv, 477 p.: ill. — (McGraw-Hill publications in the agricultural sciences) 1. Stock and stock-breeding. I. T.
SF105.R5 1967        636.08/2        *LC* 67-14677

**Winogrand, Garry, 1928-.**        **5.5442**
Stock photographs: the Fort Worth Fat Stock Show and Rodeo / by Garry Winogrand; with an essay on the Southwestern Exposition and Fat Stock Show by Ron Tyler. — Austin: University of Texas Press, c1980. 117 p.: chiefly ill.; 23

x 29 cm. 1. Winogrand, Garry, 1928- 2. Southwestern Exposition and Fat Stock Show, Fort Worth, Tex. — Pictorial works. I. T.
SF117.65.T42 F678      779/.9636 19      *LC* 80-53004      *ISBN* 0292724330

**Swatland, H. J., 1944-.**            5.5443
Structure and development of meat animals / H.J. Swatland. — Englewood Cliffs, N.J.: Prentice-Hall, c1984. xi, 436 p.: ill.; 25 cm. 1. Livestock — Carcasses 2. Veterinary anatomy 3. Meat 4. Muscles 5. Muscles I. T.
SF140.C37 S9 1984      636.089/2 19      *LC* 83-13938      *ISBN* 0138543984

# SF191–275 Cattle

**Perry, Tilden Wayne.**            5.5444
Beef cattle feeding and nutrition / Tilden Wayne Perry. — New York: Academic Press, 1980. xv, 383 p.: ill.; 24 cm. — (Animal feeding and nutrition) 1. Beef cattle — Feeding and feeds I. T.
SF203.P46      636.2/13      *LC* 79-8537      *ISBN* 0125520506

# SF277–359 Horses

**Ensminger, M. Eugene.**            5.5445
The complete encyclopedia of horses / M. E. Ensminger. — South Brunswick: A. S. Barnes, c1977. 487 p.: ill.; 29 cm. 'Breed magazines': p. 475-476. 1. Horses — Dictionaries. I. T.
SF278.E57      636.1/003      *LC* 74-9282      *ISBN* 0498015084

**Summerhays, R. S. (Reginald Sherriff), 1881-.**      • 5.5446
[Encyclopaedia for horsemen] Summerhays' encyclopaedia for horsemen / compiled by R. S. Summerhays; assisted by Stella A. Walker. — [5th rev. ed.] London; New York: F. Warne [1970] xvi, 385 p.: ill.; 21 cm. Previous editions published under title: Encyclopaedia for horsemen. 1. Horses — Dictionaries. 2. Horsemanship — Dictionaries. I. T. II. Title: Encyclopaedia for horsemen.
SF278.S8 1970      636.1/003      *LC* 79-114792      *ISBN* 0723212619

# SF375, 395 Sheep. Swine

**Ensminger, M. Eugene.**            • 5.5447
[Sheep husbandry] Sheep and wool science, by M. E. Ensminger. 4th ed. Danville, Ill., Interstate Printers & Publishers [1970] 948 p. illus., maps, ports. 24 cm. (His Animal agriculture series) First published in 1952 under title: Sheep husbandry. 1. Sheep 2. Goats I. T.
SF375.E57 1970      636.3      *LC* 73-79612

**Fraser, Allan.**            • 5.5448
Sheep husbandry and diseases / by Allan Fraser and John T. Stamp. — 5th ed. — London: Lockwood, 1969. xii, 438 p.: 56 plates, ill., map (on lining paper); 23 cm. 1. Sheep 2. Sheep — Gt. Brit. I. Stamp, John Trevor, joint author. II. T.
SF375.F8x      636.3      *LC* 72-360966      *ISBN* 0258966963

**Sheep breeding / edited by G.J. Tomes, D.E. Robertson, and**      5.5449
**R.J. Lightfoot; rev. by William Haresign.**
2d ed. — London; Boston: Butterworths, c1979. 580 p.: ill.; 25 cm. (Studies in the agricultural and food sciences) Earlier ed. (1976) issued as the proceedings of the International Sheep Breeding Congress with title: Sheep breeding. 1. Sheep breeding — Congresses. I. Tomes, G. J. II. Robertson, D. E. III. Lightfoot, R. J. IV. Haresign, William. V. International Sheep Breeding Congress, Muresk and Perth, Australia, 1976. Sheep breeding.
SF376.2.S53 1979      636.3/08/2      *LC* 78-41188      *ISBN* 0408106336

**Krider, J. L. (Jake Luther), 1913-.**      • 5.5450
Swine production [by] J. L. Krider [and] W. E. Carroll. 4th ed. New York, McGraw-Hill Book Co. [c1971] x, 528 p. illus. 23 cm. (McGraw-Hill publications in the agricultural sciences) Third ed. by W. E. Carroll, J. L. Krider, and F. N. Andrews. 1. Swine I. Carroll, W. E. (William Ernest), 1882- joint author. II. T.
SF395.K7 1971      636.4      *LC* 78-126748

**Whittemore, Colin Trengove.**            5.5451
Pig production: the scientific and practical principles / Colin T. Whittemore. — London; New York: Longman, 1980. 145 p.: ill.; 14 x 22 cm. — (Longman handbooks in agriculture.) Includes index. 1. Swine I. T. II. Series.
SF395.W47      636.083      *LC* 79-42758      *ISBN* 0582455901

# SF406 Laboratory Animals

**Arrington, Lewis R., 1919-.**      • 5.5452
Introductory laboratory animal science: the breeding, care, and management of experimental animals / [by] L. R. Arrington. — Danville, Ill.: Interstate Printers & Publishers, [1972] xi, 203 p.: ill.; 24 cm. 1. Laboratory animals I. T.
SF406.A77      636.08/85      *LC* 73-169003

# SF411–459 Dogs. Cats. Aquarium Fishes

**Dangerfield, Stanley, 1911-.**            5.5453
The international encyclopedia of dogs / edited by Stanley Dangerfield and Elsworth Howell; with special contributions by Maxwell Riddle. — New York: Howell Book House, 1974. 479, [1] p.: ill. (some col.); 29 cm. 1. Dogs — Dictionaries. I. Howell, Elsworth S. joint author. II. T.
SF422.D28 1974      636.7/003      *LC* 74-19842

**The Complete dog book: the photograph, history, and official**      5.5454
**standard of every breed admitted to AKC registration, and the**
**selection, training, breeding, care, and feeding of pure–bred**
**dogs.**
17th ed. — New York, N.Y.: Howell Book House, 1985. 768 p.: ill. (some col.); 25 cm. 'Official publication of the American Kennel Club.' Includes index. 1. Dogs 2. Dog breeds 3. Dogs — Standards — United States. I. American Kennel Club.
SF426.C66 1985      636.7 19      *LC* 85-4296      *ISBN* 0876054637

**The Book of the cat / edited by Michael Wright and Sally**      5.5455
**Walters; designed by Celia Welcomme; original paintings by**
**Peter Warner; consulting editors, Barbara S. Stein, Sidney R.**
**Thompson.**
1st American ed. — New York: Summit Books, c1980. 256 p.: ill. (some col.); 29 cm. Includes indexes. 1. Cats I. Wright, Michael, 1941- II. Walters, Sally.
SF442.B66 1980      636.8 19      *LC* 80-23570      *ISBN* 067144753X

**The Aquarium encyclopedia / [edited by] Günther Sterba;**      5.5456
**English editor, Dick Mills; translated by Susan Simpson.**
1st MIT Press ed. — Cambridge, Mass.: MIT Press, 1983. 605, [2] p.: ill. (some col.); 28 cm. Translation of: Lexicon der Aquaristik und Ichthyologie. 1. Aquariums — Dictionaries. 2. Aquarium fishes — Dictionaries. 3. Fishes — Dictionaries. 4. Aquarium plants — Dictionaries. 5. Aquatic animals — Dictionaries. 6. Aquatic plants — Dictionaries. I. Sterba, Günther. II. Mills, Dick.
SF456.5.L4913 1983      639.3/4/0321 19      *LC* 82-247      *ISBN* 0262192071

# SF487 Poultry

**Banks, Stuart.**            5.5457
The complete handbook of poultry–keeping / Stuart Banks. — New York: Van Nostrand Reinhold Co., 1979. 216 p.: ill.; 25 cm. Includes index. 1. Poultry 2. Chickens I. T. II. Title: Poultry-keeping.
SF487.B182 1979      636.5/08      *LC* 79-14305      *ISBN* 0442233825

# SF521–539 Bee Culture

**Jaycox, Elbert R.**            5.5458
Beekeeping in the Midwest / Elbert R. Jaycox. — Rev. ed. — Urbana: University of Illinois Press, c1976. 168 p.: ill.; 24 cm. (Circular - Illinois

Cooperative Extension Service; 1125) Includes index. 1. Bee culture — Middle West. I. T.
SF523.J39 1976      638/.1/0977      LC 76-40887      ISBN 0252006380

**Crane, Eva.**                                                                    **5.5459**
The archaeology of beekeeping / Eva Crane. — Ithaca, N.Y.: Cornell University Press, 1984 (c1983). 360 p.: ill.; 24 cm. Includes index. 1. Bee culture — History. I. T.
SF524.C73      638/.1/09 19      LC 82-74021      ISBN 0801416094

# SF600–998 Veterinary Medicine

**Black's veterinary dictionary / edited by Geoffrey P. West.**      **5.5460**
15th ed. — Totowa, N.J.: Barnes & Noble, 1985. 896 p.: ill.; 23 cm. 1. Veterinary medicine — Dictionaries. I. West, Geoffrey P. (Geoffrey Philip) II. Title: Veterinary dictionary.
SF609.B53 1985      636.089/03/21 19      LC 85-172278      ISBN 0389205559

**Schwabe, Calvin W.**                                                           **5.5461**
Veterinary medicine and human health / Calvin W. Schwabe. — 3rd ed. — Baltimore: Williams & Wilkins, c1984. xix, 680 p.: ill.; 29 cm. 1. Veterinary medicine 2. Public health 3. Veterinary public health I. T.
SF740.S38 1984      636.089 19      LC 83-6628      ISBN 0683075942

**The Merck veterinary manual: a handbook of diagnosis, therapy,**      **5.5462**
**and disease prevention and control for the veterinarian /**
**Clarence M. Fraser, editor; Asa Mays, associate editor; Harold**
**E. Amstutz ... [et al.].**
6th ed. — Rahway, N.J., U.S.A.: Merck, 1986. xxvii, 1677 p.: ill.; 22 cm. Includes index. 1. Veterinary medicine — Handbooks, manuals, etc. I. Fraser, Clarence M.
SF748.M47 1986      636.089 19      LC 85-62725      ISBN 0911910530

**Hafez, E. S. E. (Elsayed Saad Eldin), 1922- ed.**      **5.5463**
The behavior of domestic animals / edited by E. S. E. Hafez. — 3d ed. — Baltimore: Williams and Wilkins, 1975. xii, 532 p., [15] leaves of plates: ill.; 24 cm. 1. Domestic animals — Behavior I. T.
SF756.7.H33 1975      636      LC 76-368301

**Carlson, Delbert G.**                                                           **5.5464**
Cat owner's home veterinary handbook / by Delbert G. Carlson and James M. Giffin. — 1st ed. — New York: Howell Book House, c1983. 391 p.: ill.; 24 cm. Includes index. 1. Cats — Diseases — Handbooks, manuals, etc. I. Giffin, James M. II. T.
SF985.C29 1983      636.8/0896 19      LC 82-23383      ISBN 0876058144

**Carlson, Delbert G.**                                                           **5.5465**
Dog owner's home veterinary handbook / by Delbert G. Carlson and James M. Giffin. — 1st ed. — New York: Howell Book House, c1980. xviii, 364 p.: ill.; 24 cm. Includes index. 1. Dogs — Diseases — Handbooks, manuals, etc. I. Giffin, James M. joint author. II. T.
SF991.C25      636.7/089      LC 80-13912      ISBN 0876057644

# SH Aquaculture. Fisheries

**Bardach, John E.**                                                             **5.5466**
Aquaculture; the farming and husbandry of freshwater and marine organisms [by] John E. Bardach, John H. Ryther and William O. McLarney. — New York: Wiley-Interscience, [1972] xii, 868 p.: illus.; 23 cm. 1. Aquaculture I. Ryther, John H. joint author. II. McLarney, William O. joint author. III. T.
SH135.B37      639/.3      LC 72-2516      ISBN 0471048259

**Brown, E. Evan.**                                                              **5.5467**
World fish farming: cultivation and economics / E. Evan Brown. — 2nd ed. — Westport, Conn.: AVI Pub. Co., c1983. xviii, 516 p.: ill.; 24 cm. 1. Aquaculture industry I. T.
SH135.B76 1983      338.3/713 19      LC 83-338      ISBN 0870554271

**Stickney, Robert R.**                                                          **5.5468**
Principles of warmwater aquaculture / Robert R. Stickney. — New York: Wiley, c1979. xii, 375 p.: ill.; 24 cm. 'A Wiley-Interscience publication.' 1. Aquaculture 2. Channel catfish I. T.
SH135.S75      639/.34      LC 78-25642      ISBN 047103388X

**Iversen, Edwin S.**                                                            **5.5469**
Farming the edge of the sea / E. S. Iversen. — 2d ed. — Farnham, Eng.: Fishing News Books, c1976. 436 p.: ill.; 22 cm. Includes index. 1. Mariculture I. T.
SH138.I93 1976      630/.9162      LC 77-369142      ISBN 0852380798

**Hickling, Charles Frederick.**                                      ● **5.5470**
The farming of fish, by C. F. Hickling. — [1st ed.]. — Oxford; New York: Pergamon Press, [1968] vii, 88 p.: illus.; 20 cm. — (Commonwealth and international library. Biology in action series) 1. Fish-culture I. T.
SH151.H56 1968      639/.3      LC 67-31503

**Bennett, George W. (George William), 1908-.**      **5.5471**
Management of lakes and ponds / George W. Bennett. — 2nd ed. — [S.l.]: AVI Publishing Co., Inc., 1983. xx, 375 p.: ill.; 24 cm. 1. Fish-culture 2. Fishery management 3. Fish ponds I. T.
SH159.B38 1983      639.3/11 19      LC 83-6091      ISBN 0898746264

**Disease diagnosis and control in North American marine**      **5.5472**
**aquaculture / edited by Carl J. Sindermann.**
Amsterdam; New York: Elsevier Scientific Pub. Co., c1977. xi, 329 p.: ill.; 24 cm. — (Developments in aquaculture and fisheries science. 6) 1. Shellfish — Diseases. 2. Fishes — Diseases 3. Sea turtles — Diseases. 4. Mariculture I. Sindermann, Carl J. II. Series.
SH179.S5 D57      639/.34      LC 77-22524      ISBN 0444002375

# SH201–400 Fisheries

**Firth, Frank E.**                                                          ● **5.5473**
The encyclopedia of marine resources / Edited by Frank E. Firth. — New York: Van Nostrand Reinhold Co., [1969] xi, 740 p.: ill., maps.; 27 cm. 1. Fisheries — Dictionaries. 2. Marine resources — Dictionaries. I. T.
SH201.F56 1969      551.4/6/003      LC 70-78014

**World fisheries policy: multidisciplinary views / edited by Brian**      **5.5474**
**J. Rothschild.**
Seattle: University of Washington Press, 1973 (c1972) xix, 272 p.: ill.; 25 cm. (Public policy issues in resource management. v. 4) Based on papers presented at a series of seminars sponsored by the Graduate School of Public Affairs, University of Washington. 1. Fishery policy I. Rothschild, Brian J., 1934- ed. II. University of Washington. Graduate School of Public Affairs. III. Series.
SH323.W67      338.3/72/7      LC 72-8927      ISBN 0295952326

**Fish population dynamics / edited by J. A. Gulland.**      **5.5475**
London; New York: Wiley, c1977. xi, 372 p.: ill.; 24 cm. 'A Wiley-Interscience publication.' 1. Fishery resources 2. Fish populations I. Gulland, J. A.
SH327.5.F57      597/.05/24      LC 75-45094      ISBN 047101575X

**Cushing, D. H.**                                                               **5.5476**
Fisheries resources of the sea and their management / David Cushing. — London: Oxford University Press, 1975. 87 p.: ill.; 22 cm. — (Science and engineering policy series) Includes index. 1. Fishery management, International I. T.
SH328.C87      333.9/5      LC 76-351443      ISBN 0198583206

**Fisheries management / edited by Robert T. Lackey and Larry**      **5.5477**
**A. Nielsen.**
New York: Wiley, 1980. x, 422 p.: ill.; 24 cm. 'A Halsted Press book.' 1. Fishery management I. Lackey, Robert T. II. Nielsen, Larry A.
SH328.F56      333.95/6 19      LC 80-20028      ISBN 047027056X

**Gulland, J. A.**                                                               **5.5478**
The management of marine fisheries, by J. A. Gulland. — Seattle: University of Washington Press, 1974. viii, 198 p.: illus.; 23 cm. 1. Fishery management I. T.
SH328.G84 1974      338.3/72/7      LC 74-2473      ISBN 0295953357

**McHugh, J. L.**                                                                **5.5479**
Fishery management / J.L. McHugh. — Berlin; New York: Springer-Verlag, 1984. iv, 207 p.: ill.; 25 cm. — (Lecture notes on coastal and estuarine studies. #10) 1. Fishery management I. T. II. Series.
SH328.M4 1984      338.3/72/068 19      LC 84-14031      ISBN 0387960627

**Everhart, W. Harry (Watson Harry), 1918-.**      **5.5480**
Principles of fishery science / W. Harry Everhart, William D. Youngs. — 2d ed. — Ithaca: Comstock Pub. Associates, 1981. 349 p.: ill.; 22 cm. 1. Fishery

management 2. Fish populations 3. Fish-culture I. Youngs, William D. joint author. II. T.
SH328.R69 1981      639.3      *LC* 80-15603      *ISBN* 0801413346

**Royce, William F.**                                             **5.5481**
Introduction to the practice of fishery science / William F. Royce. — Orlando: Academic Press, 1984. xi, 428 p.: ill.; 24 cm. Includes index. 1. Fisheries I. T.
SH331.R68 1984      639/.2 19      *LC* 84-9224      *ISBN* 0126009600

**Anderson, Lee G.**                                              **5.5482**
The economics of fisheries management / Lee G. Anderson. — Rev. and enl. ed. — Baltimore: Johns Hopkins University Press, c1986. xx, 296 p.: ill.; 24 cm. Includes index. 1. Fisheries — Economic aspects 2. Fishery management — Economic aspects. I. T.
SH334.A53 1986      338.3/727 19      *LC* 85-24061      *ISBN* 0801832535

**Modern fishing gear of the world / edited by Hilmar**          **5.5483**
**Kristjonsson.**
Surrey, England: Published by arrangement with the Food and Agriculture Organization of the United Nations by Fishing News Books, c1959. 1 v. Includes abstracts in English, French and Spanish. 1. Fisheries — Equipment and supplies — Congresses I. Kristjonsson, Hilmar II. Food and Agriculture Organization of the United Nations. III. FAO World Fishing Gear Congress (2nd: 1963: London, England)
SH344 M6      *LC* 61-23702      *ISBN* 085238016X

**Crutchfield, James Arthur.**                                   • **5.5484**
The Pacific salmon fisheries; a study of irrational conservation [by] James A. Crutchfield and Giulio Pontecorvo. [Baltimore] Published for Resources for the Future by Johns Hopkins Press [1969] xii, 220 p. illus., maps. 24 cm. 1. Pacific salmon fisheries — Alaska. 2. Pacific salmon fisheries — Washington (State) — Puget Sound. 3. Fishery management — Northwest, Pacific. I. Pontecorvo, Giulio, 1923- joint author. II. Resources for the Future. III. T.
SH348.C77      333.9      *LC* 72-75180      *ISBN* 0801810256

**Stackpole, Edouard A., 1905-.**                                **5.5485**
Whales & destiny: the rivalry between America, France, and Britain for control of the southern whale fishery, 1785–1825 / [by] Edouard A. Stackpole. — [Amherst]: University of Massachusetts Press, [1972] xii, 427 p.: ill.; 25 cm. 1. Whaling — History. I. T.
SH383.S7      338.3/72/95      *LC* 72-77567

**Tønnessen, J. N. (Johan Nicolay), 1901-.**                     **5.5486**
[Moderne hvalfangst historie. English] The history of modern whaling / J.N. Tønnessen, A.O. Johnsen; translated from the Norwegian by R.I. Christophersen. — Berkeley: University of California Press, c1982. xx, 798 p.: ill.; 25 cm. Translation and shortened version of: Den moderne hvalfangst historie. Includes index. 1. Whaling — History. I. Johnsen, Arne Odd, 1909- II. T.
SH383.T6413 1982      338.3/7295/09 19      *LC* 79-64657      *ISBN* 0520039734

**Allen, Everett S.**                                            **5.5487**
Children of the light: the rise and fall of New Bedford whaling and the death of the arctic fleet / [by] Everett S. Allen. — [1st ed.] — Boston: Little, Brown, [1973] viii, 302 p.: ill.; 24 cm. 1. Whaling — Massachusetts — New Bedford — History. I. T.
SH383.2.A44      338.3/72/950974485      *LC* 73-9694      *ISBN* 0316034223

# SH401–691 Angling

**McClane, A. J. (Albert Jules), 1922- ed.**                     **5.5488**
McClane's new standard fishing encyclopedia and international angling guide / edited by A. J. McClane; illustrated by Richard E. Younger and Frances Watkins. — Enl. and rev. [2d] ed. New York: Holt, Rinehart and Winston [1974] 1156 p.: ill. (part col.); 29 cm. First ed. published in 1965 under title: McClane's standard fishing encyclopedia and international angling guide. 1. Fishing — Dictionaries. I. T. II. Title: New standard fishing encyclopedia and international angling guide.
SH411.M18 1974      799.1/03      *LC* 74-6108      *ISBN* 0030603250

**Walton, Izaak, 1593-1683.**                                    • **5.5489**
The compleat angler / by Izaak Walton and Charles Cotton; with an introduction by John Buchan. — London: Oxford University Press: H. Milford [1935] xxiv, 322 p., 1 l.,: incl. ill., 2 facsims.; 16 cm. (The world's classics. CCCCXXX) 'The first part of the 'Compleat angler' was published in 1653. Cotton's second part appeared for the first time with the fifth edition of the former in 1678.' Includes facsimile reproductions of the title-pages of pt. I, 5th ed., London, 1676 and pt. II, London, 1676. 1. Fishing I. Cotton, Charles, 1630-1687. II. T.
SH433.A1935      799.12      *LC* 35-27372

# SK1–579 HUNTING. WILDLIFE CONSERVATION

**Brander, Michael.**                                            • **5.5490**
Hunting & shooting, from earliest times to the present day. — New York: Putnam, [1971] 255 p.: illus., col. plates.; 26 cm. 1. Hunting — History. I. T.
SK21.B68      799.29      *LC* 71-153992

**Bauer, Erwin A.**                                              • **5.5491**
Treasury of big game animals. Text and photos. by Erwin A. Bauer. — New York: Outdoor Life, [1972] ix, 398 p.: illus. (part col.); 27 cm. — (An Outdoor life book) 1. Big game hunting 2. Big game animals 3. Photography of animals I. T.
SK33.B36      799.2/77      *LC* 72-90933      *ISBN* 0060102438

**The Complete book of hunting / Robert Elman, supervising**     **5.5492**
**editor; with contributions by Erwin Bauer ... [et al.].**
New York: Abbeville Press, c1980. 320 p.: ill. (some col.) Includes index. 1. Hunting I. Elman, Robert.
SK33.C585      799.2 19      *LC* 80-21486      *ISBN* 0896591743

**The New hunter's encyclopedia.**                               **5.5493**
Updated new print. of 3d. ed. — New York: Galahad Books, [1974?] xx, 1054 p.: ill.; 29 cm. Published in 1948 under title: The Hunter's encyclopedia. Originally published by Stackpole Books, Harrisburg, Pa. Includes index. 1. Hunting — North America. 2. Hunting — Dictionaries. 3. Game and game-birds — North America.
SK33.H945 1974      799.2/97      *LC* 73-92819      *ISBN* 0883651939

**Trippensee, Reuben Edwin, 1894-.**                             • **5.5494**
Wildlife management / by Reuben Edwin Trippensee. — New York: McGraw-Hill Book Co., 1948-53. 2 v.: ill., maps. (American forestry series.) 1. Game and gamebirds — North America. 2. Wildlife conservation — North America. 3. Wildlife management — North America. I. T. II. Series.
SK353.T75      *LC* 48-285      *ISBN* 0070651957

**Shaw, James H.**                                               **5.5495**
Introduction to wildlife management / James H. Shaw. — New York: McGraw-Hill, c1985. xvii, 316 p.: ill.; 24 cm. (McGraw-Hill series in forest resources.) Includes index. 1. Wildlife management I. T. II. Series.
SK355.S46 1985      639.9 19      *LC* 84-9713      *ISBN* 0070564817

**Allen, Durward Leon, 1910-.**                                  • **5.5496**
Our wildlife legacy. — Rev. ed. — New York: Funk & Wagnalls, [1962] 422 p.: illus.; 22 cm. 1. Wildlife conservation — United States. 2. Wildlife management I. T.
SK361.A66 1962      799      *LC* 62-7980

**Anderson, Stanley H.**                                         **5.5497**
Managing our wildlife resources / Stanley H. Anderson. — Columbus: C.E. Merrill Pub. Co., c1985. xiii, 514 p.: ill.; 25 cm. 1. Wildlife management — United States. I. T.
SK361.A74 1985      639.9 19      *LC* 84-61743      *ISBN* 0675203376

# SK601 CAMPING. OUTDOOR LIFE

**Brower, David R.**                                             **5.5498**
The Sierra Club wilderness handbook / edited by David Brower. — 1st ed. — New York: Ballantine Books, 1967. xvi, 272 p. 1. Camping I. T. II. Title: Wilderness handbook.
SK 601.B845

# T    Technology. Engineering

## T TECHNOLOGY: GENERAL

### T10.5–11 Technical Information. Technical Writing

**A Guide for better technical presentations** / edited by Robert    **5.5499**
M. Woelfle.
New York: IEEE Press, c1975. vi, 229 p.: ill.; 28 cm. (IEEE Press selected reprint series) 1. Communication of technical information I. Woelfle, Robert M.
T10.5.G8    808    *LC* 74-19559    *ISBN* 0879420553

**Information sources in engineering** / editor, L.J. Anthony.    **5.5500**
2nd ed. — London; Boston: Butterworths, 1985. vii, 579 p.: ill.; 23 cm. (Butterworths guides to information sources.) Rev. ed. of: Use of engineering literature. 1976. 1. Technical literature I. Anthony, L. J. II. Use of engineering literature. III. Series.
T10.7.I54 1985    620/.007 19    *LC* 85-11002    *ISBN* 0408114754

**Mount, Ellis.**    **5.5501**
Guide to basic information sources in engineering / by Ellis Mount. New York: Wiley; distributed by Halsted Press, c1976. viii, 196 p.; 22 cm. (Information resources series) Includes index. 1. Technical literature 2. Engineering — Bibliography. 3. Technology — Information services I. T.
T10.7.M68 1976    607    *LC* 75-43261    *ISBN* 0470150130

**Schenk, Margaret T., 1919-.**    **5.5502**
What every engineer should know about engineering information resources / Margaret T. Schenk, James K. Webster. — New York: M. Dekker, c1984. viii, 216 p.: ill.; 24 cm. — (What every engineer should know. v. 13) 1. Technology — Information services 2. Technical literature I. Webster, James K. II. T. III. Series.
T10.7.S34 1984    620/.0072 19    *LC* 84-11350    *ISBN* 082477244X

**Subramanyam, K.**    **5.5503**
Scientific and technical information resources / Krishna Subramanyam. — New York: M. Dekker, c1981. ix, 416 p.: ill.; 24 cm. — (Books in library and information science. v. 33) Includes indexes. 1. Technical literature 2. Scientific literature 3. Reference books — Technology — Bibliography. 4. Reference books — Science — Bibliography. I. T. II. Series.
T10.7.S93    507    *LC* 80-28531    *ISBN* 0824713567

**Brusaw, Charles T.**    **5.5504**
Handbook of technical writing / Charles T. Brusaw, Gerald J. Alred, Walter E. Oliu. — 2nd ed. — New York: St. Martin's Press, c1982. xxxviii, 696 p.: ill.; 21 cm. Includes index. 1. Technical writing — Handbooks, manuals, etc. I. Alred, Gerald J. II. Oliu, Walter E. III. T.
T11.B78 1982    808/.0666 19    *LC* 81-51836    *ISBN* 0312358083

**Day, Robert A., 1924-.**    **5.5505**
How to write and publish a scientific paper / Robert A. Day. — 2d ed. — Philadelphia: ISI Press, c1983. xv, 181 p.: ill.; 24 cm. — (Professional writing series.) Includes index. 1. Technical writing I. T. II. Series.
T11.D33 1983    808/.0665021 19    *LC* 83-8460    *ISBN* 0894950215

**A Guide for writing better technical papers** / edited by Craig    **5.5506**
Harkins, Daniel L. Plung.
New York: IEEE Press: Sole worldwide distributor (exclusive of IEEE): Wiley, c1982. vi, 219 p.: ill.; 28 cm. — (IEEE Press selected reprint series) 1. Technical writing I. Harkins, Craig. II. Plung, Daniel L.
T11.G84    808/.0666 19    *LC* 81-20042    *ISBN* 0879421584

**Schoff, Gretchen H., 1931-.**    **5.5507**
Writing & designing operator manuals: including service manuals and manuals for international markets / Gretchen H. Schoff, Patricia A. Robinson. — Belmont, Calif.: Lifetime Learning Publications, c1984. xiii, 162 p.: ill.; 25 cm. 1. Technical writing I. Robinson, Patricia A., 1948- II. T. III. Title: Writing and designing operator manuals.
T11.S376 1984    808/.0666 19    *LC* 84-3865    *ISBN* 0534033628

**Ulman, Joseph N.**    ● **5.5508**
Technical reporting / [by] Joseph N. Ulman, Jr. [and] Jay R. Gould. — 3d ed. — New York: Holt, Rinehart and Winston, [1971, c1972] xix, 419 p.: ill.; 25 cm. 1. Technical writing 2. Report writing I. Gould, Jay Reid. joint author. II. T.
T11.U4 1972    808/.066/6021    *LC* 70-158149    *ISBN* 0030810035

**Weiss, Edmond H.**    **5.5509**
The writing system for engineers and scientists / Edmond H. Weiss. — Englewood Cliffs, NJ: Prentice-Hall, c1982. xiv, 274 p.: ill.; 24 cm. Includes index. 1. Technical writing I. T.
T11.W44    808/.06662021 19    *LC* 81-775    *ISBN* 0139716068

## T12 Industrial Directories

**Thomas register of American manufacturers.**    ● **5.5510**
New York: Thomas Pub. Co., 1969-. v.; 37 cm. Title varies slightly. 1. Industrialists — United States — Directories.
T 12 T46    *LC* 06-43937

## T14 Philosophy. Social Aspects

**Barbour, Ian G.**    ● **5.5511**
Science & secularity: the ethics of technology / [by] Ian G. Barbour. — [1st ed.]. — New York: Harper & Row, [1970] 151 p.; 22 cm. 1. Technology — Philosophy 2. Ethics I. T.
T14.B36 1970    174/.9/6    *LC* 77-109886

**Ellul, Jacques.**    ● **5.5512**
[Technique. English] The technological society / translated from the French by John Wilkinson; with an introd. by Robert K. Merton. — [1st American ed.] New York: Knopf, 1964. xxxvi, 449 p.; 25 cm. Translation of La technique; ou, L'enjeu du siècle. 1. Technology — Philosophy 2. Technology and civilization I. T.
T14.E553 1964    301.24    *LC* 62-15562

**Florman, Samuel C.**    **5.5513**
The existential pleasures of engineering / Samuel C. Florman. — New York: St. Martin's Press, c1976. xi, 160 p.; 22 cm. 1. Technology — Philosophy 2. Engineering I. T.
T14.F56    601    *LC* 75-9480

**Appropriate technology and social values** / edited by Franklin    **5.5514**
A. Long, Alexandra Oleson.
Cambridge: Ballinger Pub. Co., pub. in association with the American Academy of Arts and sciences, 1980. viii, 215 p. 1. Technology — Social aspects — Addresses, essays, lectures. 2. Underdeveloped areas — Technology — Addresses, essays, lectures. I. Long, Franklin A., 1910- II. Oleson, Alexandra, 1939-
T14.5.A67    T14.5 A67.    301.24/3    *LC* 79-18528    *ISBN* 0884103730

**Boyle, Charles.**    **5.5515**
People, science, and technology: a guide to advanced industrial society / Charles Boyle, Peter Wheale, Brian Surgess [sic]. — Totowa, N.J.: Barnes & Noble Books, 1984. x, 265 p.; 23 cm. 1. Technology — Social aspects 2. Science — Social aspects I. Sturgess, Brian T. II. Wheale, Peter. III. T.
T14.5.B69 1984    303.4/83 19    *LC* 83-24368    *ISBN* 0389204552

**Braun, Ernest, 1925-.**    **5.5516**
Wayward technology / Ernst Braun. — Westport, Conn.: Greenwood Press, 1984. x, 224 p.: ill.; 24 cm. (Contributions in sociology. 0084-9278; no. 48) 1. Technology — Social aspects I. T. II. Series.
T14.5.B73 1984    600 19    *LC* 83-22586    *ISBN* 0313243980

**Collingridge, David.**     5.5517
The social control of technology / David Collingridge. — New York: St. Martin's Press, 1981 (c1980). 200 p.: ill.; 23 cm. 1. Technology — Social aspects 2. Technology assessment I. T.
T14.5.C64 1980    303.4/83 19    *LC* 80-21944    *ISBN* 031273168X

**Controversy: politics of technical decisions / edited by Dorothy**    5.5518
**Nelkin.**
2nd ed. — Beverly Hills: Sage Publications, c1984. 283 p.; 23 cm. (Sage focus editions; v. 8) 1. Technology — Social aspects 2. Science — Social aspects I. Nelkin, Dorothy.
T14.5.C665 1984    361.6/13 19    *LC* 83-24737    *ISBN* 0803922507

**Dickson, David, 1947-.**     5.5519
[Alternative technology and the politics of technical change] The politics of alternative technology / David Dickson. — New York: Universe Books, 1975, c1974. 224 p.; 22 cm. First published under title: Alternative technology and the politics of technical change. 1. Technology — Social aspects I. T.
T14.5.D52 1975    301.24/3    *LC* 75-7919    *ISBN* 087663224X

**Kasson, John F., 1944-.**     5.5520
Civilizing the machine: technology and republican values in America, 1776–1900 / John F. Kasson. — New York: Grossman Publishers, 1976. xiv, 274 p.: ill. 1. Technology — Social aspects — United States — History. 2. United States — Civilization — 19th century I. T.
T14.5.K37   T14.5 K37.   301.24/3/0973   *LC* 76-3730   *ISBN* 0670224847

**Machina ex dea: feminist perspectives on technology / [edited**    5.5521
**by] Joan Rothschild.**
New York: Pergamon Press, c1983. xxx, 233 p.; 24 cm. — (Athene series.) 1. Technology — Social aspects 2. Feminism I. Rothschild, Joan. II. Series.
T14.5.M3 1983    303.4/83 19    *LC* 83-8353    *ISBN* 0080294049

**Noble, David F.**     5.5522
America by design: science, technology, and the rise of corporate capitalism / by David F. Noble. — 1st ed. — New York: Knopf, 1977. xxvi, 384 p.; 22 cm. 1. Technology — Social aspects — United States. 2. Production (Economic theory) 3. Capitalism — United States. 4. Science and industry — United States. 5. United States — History I. T.
T14.5.N6 1977    301.24/3    *LC* 76-47928    *ISBN* 0394499832

**Rochlin, Gene I. comp.**     5.5523
Scientific technology and social change; readings from Scientific American, with introductions by Gene I. Rochlin. — San Francisco: W. H. Freeman, [1974] 403 p.: illus.; 30 cm. 1. Technology — Social aspects — Addresses, essays, lectures. I. Scientific American. II. T.
T14.5.R62    301.24/3    *LC* 74-3282    *ISBN* 071670501X

**Stanley, Manfred.**     5.5524
The technological conscience: survival and dignity in an age of expertise / Manfred Stanley. — New York: Free Press, c1978. xix, 281 p.; 24 cm. Includes index. 1. Technology — Social aspects I. T.
T14.5.S7    301.24/3    *LC* 78-428    *ISBN* 0029306108

**Teich, Albert H. comp.**     • 5.5525
Technology and man's future / Albert H. Teich, editor. — New York: St. Martin's Press, [1972] xiv, 274 p.: ill.; 22 cm. 1. Technology — Social aspects — Addresses, essays, lectures. 2. Technology assessment — Addresses, essays, lectures. I. T.
T14.5.T45    301.24/3/08    *LC* 73-190777

**Winner, Langdon.**     5.5526
Autonomous technology: technics–out–of–control as a theme in political thought / by Langdon Winner. Cambridge, Mass.: MIT Press, c1977. x, 386 p.; 21 cm. 1. Technology — Social aspects 2. Technology — Philosophy 3. Technocracy I. T.
T14.5.W56    301.24/3    *LC* 76-40100    *ISBN* 026223078X

## T15–40 History. Industrial Archaeology

**Burke, James, 1936-.**     5.5527
Connections / James Burke. — 1st American ed. — Boston: Little, Brown, 1979 (c1978). 304 p.: ill.; 26 cm. Includes index. 1. Technology — History. I. T.
T15.B76 1978    609    *LC* 78-21662    *ISBN* 0316116815

**Clark, Ronald William.**     5.5528
Works of man / Ronald W. Clark. — 1st American ed. — New York, N.Y., U.S.A.: Viking, 1985. 352 p.: ill. (some col.); 26 cm. Includes index. 1. Technology — History. 2. Inventions — History. I. T.
T15.C56 1985    609 19    *LC* 85-40027    *ISBN* 0670804835

**Daumas, Maurice. ed.**     5.5529
[Histoire générale des techniques. English] A history of technology & invention: progress through the ages / edited by Maurice Daumas; translated by Eileen B. Hennessy. — New York: Crown Publishers, 1980 (c1979) 758 p.: ill., facsims., maps; 26 cm. Translation of Histoire générale des techniques. 1. Technology — History. I. T.
T15.D2613    609    *LC* 71-93403

**Derry, T. K. (Thomas Kingston), 1905-.**     • 5.5530
A short history of technology from the earliest times to A.D. 1900 / by T.K. Derry and Trevor I. Williams. — New York: Oxford University Press, 1961 [c1960] 782 p.: ill.; 22 cm. 1. Technology — History. I. Williams, Trevor Illtyd. joint author. II. T.
T15.D4 1961    609    *LC* 61-1920

**Kranzberg, Melvin. comp.**     • 5.5531
Technology and culture; an anthology. Edited by Melvin Kranzberg and William H. Davenport. — New York: Schocken Books, [1972] 364 p.; 21 cm. 1. Technology — History — Addresses, essays, lectures. 2. Technology and civilization — Addresses, essays, lectures. I. Davenport, William Henry, 1908- joint comp. II. T.
T15.K7    301.24/3/08    *LC* 73-185318    *ISBN* 0805234454

**The twentieth century, c. 1900 to c. 1950 / edited by Trevor I.**    5.5532
**Williams.**
Oxford: Clarendon Press, 1979 (c1978). 2 v.: ill. (part col.) port., maps.; 26 cm. (A history of technology) 1. Technology — History. 2. Civilization — History I. Williams, Trevor Illtyd. II. Series.
T15.S53    609    *LC* a 55-8645    *ISBN* 0198581513

**Singer, Charles, 1876-.**     • 5.5533
A History of technology / edited by Charles Singer, E. J. Holmyard, A. R. Hall ... [et al.]. — Oxford: Clarendon Press, 1954-1958. 5 v.: ill. (certaines en coul.); 26 cm. 1. Technology — History. 2. Civilization — History I. T.
T15.S56    *LC* 55-8645

**Technology in Western civilization / edited by Melvin**    • 5.5534
**Kranzberg [and] Carroll W. Pursell, Jr.; executive editors: Paul**
**J. Grogan [and] Donald F. Kaiser.**
New York: Oxford University Press, 1967. 2 v.: ill., maps, ports.; 24 cm. 1. Technology — History. 2. Technology and civilization I. Kranzberg, Melvin. ed. II. Pursell, Carroll W. ed.
T15.T43    609    *LC* 67-15129

**White, K. D.**     5.5535
Greek and Roman technology / K.D. White. — Ithaca, N.Y.: Cornell University Press, 1984. 272 p.: ill.; 28 cm. — (Aspects of Greek and Roman life) Includes index. 1. Technology — History. I. T.
T16.W45 1984    609/.38 19    *LC* 82-74518    *ISBN* 0801414393

**White, Lynn Townsend, 1907-.**     5.5536
Medieval religion and technology: collected essays / Lynn White, Jr. — Berkeley: University of California Press, c1978. xxiv, 360 p., [23] leaves of plates: ill.; 24 cm. — (Publications of the Center for Medieval and Renaissance Studies, UCLA; 13) 1. Technology — Religious aspects — History. 2. Religion and science — History I. T.
T17.W47    609/.4    *LC* 77-83113    *ISBN* 0520035666

**Williams, Trevor Illtyd.**     5.5537
A short history of twentieth–century technology c. 1900–c. 1950 / Trevor I. Williams. — Oxford [Oxfordshire]: Clarendon Press; New York: Oxford University Press, 1982. xix, 411 p.: ill.; 25 cm. Sequel to: A short history of technology from the earliest times to A.D. 1900 / by T.K. Derry and Trevor I. Williams. 1. Technology — History — 20th century. I. Derry, T. K. (Thomas Kingston), 1905- Short history of technology from the earliest times to A.D. 1900. II. T.
T20.W55 1982    609/.04 19    *LC* 82-4362    *ISBN* 0198581599

**Morison, Elting Elmore.**     5.5538
From know–how to nowhere: the development of American technology / [by] Elting E. Morison. — New York: Basic Books, [1975, c1974] xiii, 199 p.: ill.; 22 cm. 1. Technology — History — United States. I. T.
T21.M7 1975    609/.73    *LC* 74-79279    *ISBN* 0465025803

**Science, technology, and national policy / edited by Thomas J.**    5.5539
**Kuehn, Alan L. Porter.**
Ithaca, N.Y.: Cornell University Press, c1981. 530 p.: ill.; 24 cm. Includes index. 1. Technology and state — United States — Addresses, essays, lectures.

2. Science and state — United States — Addresses, essays, lectures. I. Kuehn, Thomas J., 1948- II. Porter, Alan L.
T21.S35      338.4/76/0973 19      *LC* 80-66900      *ISBN* 0801413435

**Technological frontiers and foreign relations** / National      **5.5540**
Academy of Sciences, National Academy of Engineering,
Council on Foreign Relations; Anne G. Keatley, editor.
Washington, D.C.: National Academy Press, 1985. vi, 306 p.: ill.; 23 cm.
1. Technology — United States. 2. United States — Foreign relations — 1977-
I. Keatley, Anne G. II. National Academy of Sciences (U.S.) III. National
Academy of Engineering. IV. Council of Foreign Relations.
T21.T4 1985      *LC* 85-61129      *ISBN* 0309035414

**Bracegirdle, Brian.**      **5.5541**
The archaeology of the Industrial Revolution [by] Brian Bracegirdle with Brian
Bowers [and others. — 1st American ed.]. — Rutherford [N.J.]: Fairleigh
Dickinson University Press, [1973] 207 p.: illus. (some col.); 29 cm.
1. Industrial archaeology — Great Britain. I. T.
T26.G7 B76 1973b      609/.42      *LC* 73-8287      *ISBN* 0838614248

**Hudson, Kenneth.**      **5.5542**
Industrial archaeology: a new introduction / [by] Kenneth Hudson. 3rd revised
and reset ed. — London: J. Baker, 1976. 240 p.: ill., facsims., maps, plans; 26
cm. Includes index. 1. Industrial archaeology — Great Britain. I. T.
T26.G7 H8 1976      609/.41      *LC* 76-376064      *ISBN* 0212970143

**The Technological level of Soviet industry** / edited by Ronald      **5.5543**
Amann, Julian Cooper and R. W. Davies, with the assistance of
Hugh Jenkins.
New Haven: Yale University Press, 1977. xxxii, 575 p.: ill.; 26 cm.
1. Technology — Russia. I. Amann, Ronald, 1943- II. Cooper, Julian, 1945-
III. Davies, R. W. (Robert William), 1925-
T26.R9 T44      338.4/7      *LC* 77-76298      *ISBN* 0300020767

**Nayar, Baldev Raj.**      **5.5544**
India's quest for technological independence / Baldev Raj Nayar. — New
Delhi, India: Lancers Publishers, 1983. 2 v.: ill., map; 23 cm. 1. Technology
and state — India. I. T.
T27.I4 N39 1983      338.954 19      *LC* 83-904666

**Hudson, Kenneth.**      **5.5545**
World industrial archaeology / Kenneth Hudson. — Cambridge [Eng.]; New
York: Cambridge University Press, 1979. 247 p.: ill.; 25 cm. — (New studies in
archaeology.) Includes index. 1. Industrial archaeology I. T. II. Series.
T37.H84      609      *LC* 77-94225      *ISBN* 0521219914. *ISBN* 0521293308
pbk

**Who's who in technology today.**      **5.5546**
Highland Park, Ill., [etc.]: J. Dick [etc.] v.; 26 cm. Issues for 1980-84 published
in 5 or more vols. 1. Technologists — United States — Biography —
Periodicals.
T39.W5      609/.2/2      *LC* 80-644137

**Heydenreich, Ludwig Heinrich, 1903-.**      **5.5547**
Leonardo the inventor / Ludwig H. Heydenreich, Bern Dibner, Ladislao Reti.
— New York: McGraw-Hill, 1980. 192 p.: ill.; 21 cm. Essays originally
published in The unknown Leonardo, edited by Ladislao Reti, with additional
illustrations. 1. Leonardo, da Vinci, 1452-1519. 2. Leonardo, da Vinci,
1452-1519 — Knowledge — Engineering. 3. Leonardo, da Vinci, 1452-1519 —
Knowledge — Military engineering. 4. Leonardo, da Vinci, 1452-1519 —
Knowledge — Mechanics. I. Dibner, Bern. joint author. II. Reti, Ladislao.
joint author. III. Reti, Ladislao. Unknown Leonardo IV. T.
T40.L46 H49      620/.0092/4      *LC* 80-10668      *ISBN* 0070286108

# T49 Formulas

**Hiscox, Gardner Dexter, 1822?-1908. ed.**      **5.5548**
Henley's twentieth century book of formulas, processes and trade secrets: a
valuable reference book for the home, factory, office, laboratory and the
workshop ... — New rev. and enl. ed. by T. O'Conor Sloane. Rev. 1956 by
Harry E. Eisenson. — Cornwells Heights, PA: Publishers Agency, 1981. 867,
[67] p.: ill.; 22 cm. Previously published under titles: Henley's twentieth century
book of recipes, formulas and processes; Henley's twentieth century formulas,
recipes and processes; Fortunes in formulas. 1. Industrial arts 2. Recipes
I. Sloane, T. O'Conor (Thomas O'Conor), 1851-1940 II. Eisenson, Harry E.
III. T.
T49.H6 1981      602/.02      *LC* 76-18904

# T49.5 Special Topics

**Pacey, Arnold.**      **5.5549**
The culture of technology / Arnold Pacey. — 1st MIT Press ed. — Cambridge,
Mass.: MIT Press, 1983. viii, 210 p.: ill.; 24 cm. Includes index. 1. Technology
I. T.
T49.5.P3 1983      306/.46 19      *LC* 83-11393      *ISBN* 0262160935

**Technology and international affairs** / edited by Joseph S.      **5.5550**
Szyliowicz.
New York: Praeger, 1981. xii, 287 p.: ill.; 24 cm. 1. Technology and
international affairs I. Szyliowicz, Joseph S.
T49.5.T43 1981      303.4/83 19      *LC* 81-13985      *ISBN* 003053321X

# T54–55.3 Industrial Safety

**Perrow, Charles.**      **5.5551**
Normal accidents: living with high–risk technologies / Charles Perrow. — New
York: Basic Books, c1984. x, 386 p.: ill.; 24 cm. Includes index. 1. Industrial
accidents 2. Accidents 3. Risk I. T.
T54.P47 1984      363.1 19      *LC* 83-45256      *ISBN* 046505143X

**Gloss, David S.**      **5.5552**
Introduction to safety engineering / David S. Gloss, Miriam Gayle Wardle. —
New York: Wiley, c1984. xv, 612 p.: ill.; 24 cm. 'A Wiley-Interscience
publication.' 1. Industrial safety 2. System safety I. Wardle, Miriam Gayle.
II. T.
T55.G584 1984      363.1/1/0973 19      *LC* 83-16751      *ISBN*
0471876674

**Hammer, Willie.**      **5.5553**
Occupational safety management and engineering / Willie Hammer. — 3rd ed.
— Englewoods Cliffs, N.J.: Prentice-Hall, c1985. xvi, 511 p.: ill.; 24 cm.
(Prentice-Hall international series in industrial and systems engineering.)
1. Industrial safety 2. Accidents — Prevention I. T. II. Series.
T55.H273 1985      363.1/1 19      *LC* 84-18358      *ISBN* 0136294375

**National Safety Council.**      **5.5554**
Accident prevention manual for industrial operations: engineering and
technology / Frank E. McElroy, editor in chief. — 8th ed. — Chicago, Ill.:
National Safety Council, c1980. vii, 760 p.: ill.; 25 cm. — (Its Occupational
safety and health series) Companion volume to Accident prevention manual for
industrial operations: administration and programs. Previous editions of these 2
works were published as one volume under title: Accident prevention manual
for industrial operations. 1. Industrial safety 2. Accidents — Prevention
I. McElroy, Frank E. II. T. III. Series.
T55.N3 1980      363.1/1 19      *LC* 80-81376      *ISBN* 0879120266

**Petersen, Dan.**      **5.5555**
Techniques of safety management / Dan Petersen. — 2d ed. — New York:
McGraw-Hill, c1978. xv, 314 p.: ill.; 24 cm. 1. Industrial safety I. T.
T55.P37 1978      614.8/52      *LC* 77-9384      *ISBN* 0070495963

**Bretherick, L.**      **5.5556**
Handbook of reactive chemical hazards / L. Bretherick. — 3rd ed. — London;
Boston: Butterworths, 1985. xxvi, 22, 1852 p.: ill.; 25 cm. Includes index.
1. Hazardous substances — Handbooks, manuals, etc. 2. Chemicals — Safety
measures — Handbooks, manuals, etc. I. T.
T55.3.H3 B73 1985      660.2/804 19      *LC* 85-7922      *ISBN* 0408013885

**Sax, N. Irving (Newton Irving)**      **5.5557**
Dangerous properties of industrial materials / N. Irving Sax; assisted by
Benjamin Feiner ... [et al.]. — 6th ed. — New York: Van Nostrand Reinhold,
c1984. xxiii, 3124 p.: ill.; 29 cm. 1. Hazardous substances I. Feiner, Benjamin.
II. T.
T55.3.H3 S3 1984      604.7 19      *LC* 83-21766      *ISBN* 0442283040

**Toxic substances sourcebook.**      **5.5558**
[New York: Environment Information Center, Toxic Substances Reference
Dept.] 1978. 554 p.; 29 cm. (EIC sourcebook series: 1) 1. Hazardous substances
— Periodicals. 2. Poisons — Periodicals. 3. Pollutants — Periodicals.
I. Environment Information Center. Toxic Substances Reference Dept.
T55.3.H3 T69      615.9      *LC* 79-640076

# T55.4–60.8 Industrial Engineering

**Metcalf, Henry Clayton, 1867-.**      **5.5559**
Dynamic administration: the collected papers of Mary Parker Follett / edited by Henry C. Metcalf and L. Urwick. — [S.l.]: Harper, 1941. 320 p. 1. Industrial organization 2. Personnel management 3. Business I. Urwick, L. (Lyndall), 1891- II. T.
T56.F62 1965     *LC* 42-25133

**Handbook of industrial engineering / edited by Gavriel**      **5.5560**
**Salvendy.**
New York: Wiley, c1982. 1 v. (various pagings): ill.; 24 cm. 'A Wiley-Interscience publication.' 1. Industrial engineering — Handbooks, manuals, etc. I. Salvendy, Gavriel, 1938-
T56.23.H36 1982    658.5 19     *LC* 81-23059     *ISBN* 0471058416

**Burman, Peter J.**      **5.5561**
Precedence networks for project planning and control, [by] P. J. Burman. — London; New York: McGraw-Hill, 1972. xii, 374, [3] p. (3 fold.).: illus., forms, map, plans.; 26 cm. 1. Industrial project management 2. Network analysis (Planning) I. T.
T56.8.B87    658.4/032     *LC* 73-157176     *ISBN* 0070844011

**Moder, Joseph J.**      **5.5562**
Project management with CPM and PERT / [by] Joseph J. Moder [and] Cecil R. Phillips. — 2d ed. New York: Van Nostrand Reinhold Co. [1970] xviii, 360 p.: ill.; 24 cm. Rev. ed. published as: Project management with CPM, PERT, and precedence diagramming. 3rd ed. c1983. 1. Network analysis (Planning) 2. Industrial project management I. Phillips, Cecil R. joint author. II. T.
T56.8.M63 1970    658.4/04 19     *LC* 70-108654

## T57.6–57.62 Operations Research. System Analysis. Simulation

**Andrew, A. M.**      **5.5563**
Computational techniques in operations research / A.M. Andrew. — Tunbridge Well, Kent; Cambridge, Mass.: Abacus Press, 1985. 201 p.: ill.; 24 cm. — (Computer language and programming series.) Includes indexes. 1. Operations research — Data processing I. T. II. Series.
T57.6.A55 1985    001.4/24/0285 19     *LC* 85-9110     *ISBN* 0856264253

**Conolly, Brian.**      **5.5564**
Techniques in operational research / Brian Conolly. — Chichester: Horwood; New York: Halsted Press, 1981. 2 v.: ill.; 24 cm. — (Ellis Horwood series in mathematics and its applications.) 1. Operations research I. T. II. Series.
T57.6.C655    001.4/24 19     *LC* 80-41741     *ISBN* 0470271302

**DeMarco, Tom.**      **5.5565**
Structured analysis and system specification / by Tom DeMarco; foreword by P. J. Plauger. — Englewood Cliffs, N.J.: Prentice-Hall, c1979. xiv, 352 p.: ill.; 24 cm. — (Prentice-Hall software series.) 'A Yourdon book.' Includes index. 1. System analysis 2. Flow charts I. T. II. Series.
T57.6.D45 1979    658.4/032     *LC* 79-14655     *ISBN* 0138543801

**Developments in operational research / edited by R.W. Eglese**      **5.5566**
**and G.K. Rand.**
1st ed. — Oxford [Oxfordshire]; New York: Pergamon Press, 1984. vii, 110 p.: ill.; 28 cm. (Frontiers of operational research and applied systems analysis.) 1. Operations research — Addresses, essays, lectures. I. Eglese, R. W. II. Rand, G. K. (Graham K.) III. Series.
T57.6.D49 1984    658.4/03/4 19     *LC* 84-16641     *ISBN* 0080318290

**Ghosal, A.**      **5.5567**
Examples & exercises in operations research / by A. Ghosal, S. G. Loo and N. Singh. — London; New York: Gordon and Breach Science Publishers, [1975]. vii, 262 p.; 24 cm. (Studies in operations research; 4) 1. Operations research I. Loo, Sonny G., joint author. II. Singh, Nau Nihal, 1923- joint author. III. T. IV. Series.
T57.6.G5412    001.4/24     *LC* 74-76113     *ISBN* 0677039107

**Handbook of operations research / edited by Joseph J. Moder**      **5.5568**
**and Salah E. Elmaghraby.**
New York: Van Nostrand Reinhold, c1978. 2 v.: ill.; 24 cm. 1. Operations research I. Moder, Joseph J. II. Elmaghraby, Salah Eldin, 1927-
T57.6.H35    001.4/24     *LC* 77-21580     *ISBN* 0442245955

**Hillier, Frederick S.**      **5.5569**
Introduction to operations research / Frederick S. Hillier, Gerald J. Lieberman. — 4th ed. — Oakland, Calif.: Holden-Day, c1986. xviii, 888 p.: ill.; 25 cm. Includes index. 1. Operations research I. Lieberman, Gerald J. II. T.
T57.6.H54 1986    001.4/24 19     *LC* 86-80560     *ISBN* 0816238715

**Lientz, Bennet P.**      **5.5570**
Computer applications in operations analysis [by] Bennet P. Lientz. Englewood Cliffs, N.J.: Prentice-Hall, [1974, c1975] xiv, 289 p.: ill.; 24 cm. 1. Operations research — Data processing I. T.
T57.6.L53    658.4/034/02854     *LC* 74-8959     *ISBN* 0131641034

**Martin, James, 1933-.**      **5.5571**
Diagramming techniques for analysts and programmers / James Martin, Carma McClure. — Englewood Cliffs, N.J.: Prentice-Hall, c1985. xvi, 396 p.: ill.; 25 cm. 1. System analysis 2. Electronic digital computers — Programming 3. Flow charts I. McClure, Carma L. II. T.
T57.6.M3484 1985    001.64/23 19     *LC* 84-17262     *ISBN* 0132087944

**Operations research support methodology / edited by Albert G.**      **5.5572**
**Holzman.**
New York: M. Dekker, c1979. ix, 647 p.: ill.; 26 cm. — (Industrial engineering. v. 2) 'These articles originally appeared in the Encyclopedia of computer science and technology, volumes 1-10.' 1. Operations research I. Holzman, Albert George. II. Encyclopedia of computer science and technology. III. Series.
T57.6.O646    658.4/034     *LC* 79-101     *ISBN* 0824767713

**Rivett, Patrick.**      **5.5573**
Principles of model building: the construction of models for decision analysis. — London; New York: Wiley, 1972. [10], 141 p.: ill.; 24 cm. 1. Operations research 2. Decision-making 3. Mathematical models I. T.
T57.6.R58    658.4/033     *LC* 72-2642     *ISBN* 0471724653

**Taha, Hamdy A.**      **5.5574**
Operations research: an introduction / Hamdy A. Taha. — 3rd ed. — New York: Macmillan, c1982. xiv, 848 p.: ill.; 26 cm. Includes index. 1. Operations research 2. Programming (Mathematics) I. T.
T57.6.T3 1982    001.4/24 19     *LC* 81-5984     *ISBN* 0024188603

**Thesen, Arne.**      **5.5575**
Computer methods in operations research / Arne Thesen. — New York: Academic Press, 1978. xiii, 268 p.: ill.; 24 cm. — (Operations research and industrial engineering series) 1. Operations research — Data processing I. T.
T57.6.T47    001.4/24/02854     *LC* 77-74063     *ISBN* 0126861501

**Weinberg, Gerald M.**      **5.5576**
Rethinking systems analysis and design / Gerald M. Weinberg. — Boston: Little, Brown, c1982. xiv, 193 p.: ill.; 24 cm. — (Little, Brown computer systems series.) Includes index. 1. System analysis 2. System design I. T. II. Series.
T57.6.W425 1982    003 19     *LC* 82-228     *ISBN* 0316928445

**Whitaker, David.**      **5.5577**
OR on the micro / David Whitaker. — Chichester [West Sussex]; New York: Wiley, c1984. viii, 197 p.: ill.; 24 cm. 1. Operations research — Data processing 2. Microcomputers — Programming I. T. II. Title: O.R. on the microcomputer.
T57.6.W587 1984    658.4/034/028542 19     *LC* 82-17463     *ISBN* 0471900834

**Shannon, Robert E., 1932-.**      **5.5578**
Systems simulation: the art and science / Robert E. Shannon. — Englewood Cliffs, N.J.: Prentice-Hall, [1975] xii, 387 p.: ill.; 24 cm. 1. Simulation methods I. T.
T57.62.S47    601/.84     *LC* 75-1174     *ISBN* 0138818398

## T57.7–57.95 Programming. Networks. Decision Theory

**Hayhurst, George.**      **5.5579**
Mathematical programming for management and business / [by] G. Hayhurst. London: Edward Arnold, 1976. [6], 161 p.: ill.; 22 cm. 1. Programming (Mathematics) I. T.
T57.7.H39    519.7/002/465     *LC* 76-362251     *ISBN* 0713133554

**Kaufmann, A. (Arnold), 1911-.**      **5.5580**
[Méthodes et modèles de la recherche opérationnelle. Vol. 3. English] Integer and mixed programming: theory and applications / Arnold Kaufmann, Arnaud Henry–Labordère; translated by Henry C. Sneyd. — New York: Academic Press, 1977. ix, 379 p.: ill.; 24 cm. (Mathematics in science and engineering. v.

137) Translation of v. 3 of Méthodes et modèles de la recherche opérationnelle. Includes index. 1. Integer programming I. Henry-Labordère, A. II. T. III. Series.
T57.7.K3913      519.7/7      *LC* 75-32029      *ISBN* 0124023657

**Luenberger, David G., 1937-.**                                                      **5.5581**
Linear and nonlinear programming / David G. Luenberger. — 2nd ed. — Reading, Mass.: Addison-Wesley, c1984. xv, 491 p.: ill.; 25 cm. Rev. ed. of: Introduction to linear and nonlinear programming. Includes index. 1. Linear programming 2. Nonlinear programming I. Luenberger, David G., 1937- Introduction to linear and nonlinear programming. II. T.
T57.7.L8 1984      519.7/2 19      *LC* 83-11830      *ISBN* 0201157942

**McMillan, Claude.**                                                                 **5.5582**
Mathematical programming / Claude McMillan, Jr. — 2d ed. — New York: Wiley, [1975] xi, 650 p.: ill.; 23 cm. (The Wiley series in management and administration) 1. Programming (Mathematics) I. T.
T57.7.M35 1975      519.7      *LC* 74-23273      *ISBN* 0471585726

**Nicholson, T. A. J.**                                                               **5.5583**
Optimization in industry / [by] T. A. J. Nicholson. — London: Longman, 1971. 2 v.: ill.; 24 cm. — (London Business School series) 1. Programming (Mathematics) 2. Mathematical optimization I. T.
T57.7.N53 1971b      658.4/033      *LC* 72-193245      *ISBN* 0582445981

**Taha, Hamdy A.**                                                                    **5.5584**
Integer programming: theory, applications, and computations / Hamdy A. Taha. — New York: Academic Press, 1975. xii, 380 p.: ill.; 24 cm. (Operations research and industrial engineering) Includes index. 1. Integer programming I. T.
T57.7.T33      519.7/7      *LC* 74-10205      *ISBN* 012682150X

**Williams, H. P.**                                                                   **5.5585**
Model building in mathematical programming / H. P. Williams. — Chichester; New York: Wiley, c1978. xiv, 330 p.: ill.; 24 cm. 'A Wiley-Interscience publication.' Includes indexes. 1. Programming (Mathematics) 2. Mathematical models I. T.
T57.7.W55      519.7      *LC* 77-7380      *ISBN* 0471995266

**Bazaraa, M. S., 1943-.**                                                            **5.5586**
Linear programming and network flows / Mokhtar S. Bazaraa, John J. Jarvis. New York: Wiley, c1977. x, 565 p.: ill.; 24 cm. Includes index. 1. Linear programming 2. Network analysis (Planning) I. Jarvis, John J., joint author. II. T.
T57.74.B39      519.7/2      *LC* 76-42241      *ISBN* 0471060151

**Chvátal, Vašek, 1946-.**                                                            **5.5587**
Linear programming / Vašek Chvátal. — New York: W.H. Freeman, c1983. xiii, 478 p.: ill.; 24 cm. — (Series of books in the mathematical sciences.) Includes index. 1. Linear programming I. T. II. Series.
T57.74.C54 1983      519.7/2 19      *LC* 82-21132      *ISBN* 0716711958

**Gass, Saul I.**                                                                     **5.5588**
Linear programming: methods and applications / Saul I. Gass. — 5th ed. — New York: McGraw-Hill, c1985. xi, 532 p.: ill.; 24 cm. Includes index. 1. Linear programming I. T.
T57.74.G3 1985      519.7/2 19      *LC* 84-14354      *ISBN* 0070229821

**Greenberg, Michael R.**                                                             **5.5589**
Applied linear programming for the socioeconomic and environmental sciences / Michael R. Greenberg. — New York: Academic Press, 1978. xv, 327 p.: ill.; 24 cm. — (Operations research and industrial engineering) 1. Linear programming 2. Social sciences — Linear programming. 3. Environmental engineering — Linear programming. I. T.
T57.74.G73      001.4/24      *LC* 78-6295      *ISBN* 012299650X

**Murtagh, Bruce A.**                                                                 **5.5590**
Advanced linear programming: computation and practice / Bruce A. Murtagh. — New York; London: McGraw-Hill International Book Co., c1981. xii, 202 p.: ill.; 24 cm. Includes index. 1. Linear programming I. T.
T57.74.M86      519.7/2      *LC* 79-42644      *ISBN* 0070440956

**Salkin, Harvey M.**                                                                 **5.5591**
Integer programming / Harvey M. Salkin. — Reading, Mass.: Addison-Wesley Pub. Co., [1975] xx, 537 p.: ill.; 24 cm. 1. Linear programming 2. Integer programming I. T.
T57.74.S26      519.7/7      *LC* 74-5999      *ISBN* 0201068419

**Thompson, Gerald E.**                                                               **5.5592**
Linear programming; an elementary introduction [by] Gerald E. Thompson. — New York: Macmillan, [1971] vii, 384 p.: illus.; 24 cm. 1. Linear programming I. T.
T57.74.T45      519/.72      *LC* 75-123886

**Avriel, M.**                                                                        **5.5593**
Nonlinear programming: analysis and methods / Mordecai Avriel. — Englewood Cliffs, N.J.: Prentice-Hall, c1976. xv, 512 p.: ill.; 24 cm. — (Prentice-Hall series in automatic computation) 1. Nonlinear programming I. T.
T57.8.A9      519.7/6 19      *LC* 75-45324      *ISBN* 0136236030

**Bazaraa, M. S., 1943-.**                                                            **5.5594**
Nonlinear programming: theory and algorithms / Mokhtar S. Bazaraa, C. M. Shetty. — New York: Wiley, c1979. xiv, 560 p.: ill.; 24 cm. Includes index. 1. Nonlinear programming I. Shetty, C. M., 1929- joint author. II. T.
T57.8.B39 1979      519.7/6      *LC* 78-986      *ISBN* 0471786101

**Himmelblau, David Mautner, 1923-.**                                                 **5.5595**
Applied nonlinear programming [by] David M. Himmelblau. — New York: McGraw-Hill, [1972] xi, 498 p.: illus.; 23 cm. 1. Nonlinear programming I. T.
T57.8.H55      519.7/6      *LC* 76-148127      *ISBN* 0070289212

**Elmaghraby, Salah Eldin, 1927-.**                                                   **5.5596**
Activity networks: project planning and control by network models / Salah E. Elmaghraby. — New York: Wiley, c1977. xvii, 443 p.: ill.; 24 cm. 'A Wiley-Interscience publication.' Includes indexes. 1. Network analysis (Planning) I. T.
T57.85.E42      658.4/032      *LC* 77-9501      *ISBN* 0471238619

**Jensen, Paul A., 1936-.**                                                           **5.5597**
Network flow programming / Paul A. Jensen, J. Wesley Barnes. — New York: Wiley, c1980. xiv, 408 p.: ill.; 24 cm. Includes index. 1. Network analysis (Planning) 2. Programming (Mathematics) I. Barnes, J. Wesley. joint author. II. T.
T57.85.J39      658.4/032      *LC* 79-26939      *ISBN* 0471044717

**Smith, David K.**                                                                   **5.5598**
Network optimisation practice: a computational guide / David K. Smith. — Chichester: Ellis Horwood; Toronto: J. Wiley, 1982. 237 p.; 24 cm. (Ellis Horwood series in mathematics and its applications) I. T. II. Series.
T57.85.S57 1982      658.4/03/2 19      *LC* 82-3028      *ISBN* 0853124035

**Gross, Donald.**                                                                    **5.5599**
Fundamentals of queueing theory / Donald Gross, Carl M. Harris. — 2nd ed. — New York: Wiley, 1985. xii, 587 p.: ill.; 24 cm. (Wiley series in probability and mathematical statistics.) Includes indexes. 1. Queuing theory I. Harris, Carl M., 1940- II. T. III. Series.
T57.9.G76 1985      519.8/2 19      *LC* 84-21011      *ISBN* 0471890677

**Keeney, Ralph L., 1944-.**                                                          **5.5600**
Decisions with multiple objectives: preferences and value tradeoffs / Ralph L. Keeney and Howard Raiffa, with a contribution by Richard F. Meyer. — New York: Wiley, c1976. xxviii, 569 p. — (Wiley series in probability and mathematical statistics) Includes index. 1. Decision-making I. Raiffa, Howard, 1924- joint author. II. T.
T57.95.K43      T57.95 K43.      658.4/03      *LC* 76-7895      *ISBN* 0471465100

## T58–60 Management. Information. Work Environment

**Gilbreth, Frank Bunker, 1868-1924.**                                                **5.5601**
Motion study, a method for increasing the efficiency of the workman. New York, D. Van Nostrand company, 1911. xxiii, 116 p. illus. 20 cm. 1. Efficiency, Industrial I. Kent, Robert Thurston. II. T.
T58.G38      *LC* 11-1772

**Gilbreth, Lillian Moller, 1878-1972.**                                          ● **5.5602**
The psychology of management: the function of the mind in determining, teaching and installing methods of least waste. — New York: Sturgis & Walton co., 1914. 344 p. 1. Psychology, Industrial 2. Efficiency, Industrial 3. Personnel management I. T.
T58G65      658.5

**Roethlisberger, Fritz Jules, 1898-1974.**                                       ● **5.5603**
Management and the worker: an account of a research program conducted by the Western electric company, Hawthorne works, Chicago / by F. J. Roethlisberger and William J. Dickson; with the assistance and collaboration of Harold A. Wright. — Cambridge, Mass.: Harvard university press, 1939. xxiv, 615 p., incl. tables, diagrs.: 5 pl. on 4 l.; 24 cm. 'About twelve years ago the Western electric company, at its Hawthorne plant, began the series of inquiries into the human effect of work and working conditions described in this book ... [which] offers for the first time a continuous history of the entire series ... It also relates together many different inquiries.'—Pref. 1. Personnel management 2. Psychology, Industrial 3. Research, Industrial I. Dickson, William John,

1904- joint author. II. Wright, Harold A. III. Western Electric Company.
IV. T.
T58.R62     658.3     *LC* 39-25984

**Taylor, Frederick Winslow, 1856-1915.**        5.5604
The principles of scientific management / by Frederick Winslow Taylor. —
New York; London: Harper & brothers, 1911. 77 p.; 23 cm. 'This special edition
printed in February 1911, for confidential circulation among the members of
the American society of mechanical engineers, with the compliments of the
author.' 1. Efficiency, Industrial I. T.
T58.T4 A3 1911     *LC* 11-10339

**Burch, John G.**        5.5605
Information systems: theory and practice / John Burch, Gary Grudnitski. —
4th ed. — New York: Wiley, c1986. xiii, 674 p.: ill.; 25 cm. 1. Management
information systems I. Grudnitski, Gary. II. T.
T58.6.B87 1986     658.4/038 19     *LC* 85-26492     *ISBN* 047183758X

**Connor, Denis, 1934-.**        5.5606
Information system specification and design road map / Denis Connor. —
Englewood Cliffs, N.J.: Prentice-Hall, c1985. xix, 236 p.: ill.; 25 cm. —
1. Management information systems — Design and construction. I. T.
T58.6.C668 1985     658.4/038 19     *LC* 84-24979     *ISBN* 0134648684

**Dickson, Gary W.**        5.5607
The management of information systems / Gary W. Dickson, James C.
Wetherbe. — New York: McGraw-Hill, c1985. xviii, 493 p.: ill.; 24 cm.
(McGraw-Hill series in management information systems.) 1. Management
information systems — Management. I. Wetherbe, James C. II. T. III. Series.
T58.6.D45 1985     658.4/0388 19     *LC* 84-767     *ISBN* 0070168253

**Hicks, James O.**        5.5608
Management information systems: a user perspective / James O. Hicks, Jr. —
2nd ed. — St. Paul: West Pub. Co., c1987. xxvii, 623 p.: ill. (some col.); 27 cm.
Includes index. 1. Management information systems I. T.
T58.6.H49 1987     658.4/038 19     *LC* 86-22432     *ISBN* 031428494X

**Kroeber, Donald W.**        5.5609
Computer–based information systems: a management approach / Donald W.
Kroeber, Hugh J. Watson. — 2nd ed. — New York: Macmillan; London:
Collier Macmillan, c1987. xv, 600 p.: ill.; 24 cm. 1. Management information
systems I. Watson, Hugh J. II. T.
T58.6.K757 1987     658.4/038 19     *LC* 85-23711     *ISBN* 0023668709

**Lucas, Henry C.**        5.5610
The analysis, design, and implementation of information systems / Henry C.
Lucas, Jr. — 3rd ed. — New York: McGraw-Hill, c1985. xii, 495 p.: ill.; 24 cm.
(McGraw-Hill series in management information systems.) Includes index.
1. Management information systems 2. System analysis I. T. II. Series.
T58.6.L79 1985     658.4/038 19     *LC* 84-11238     *ISBN* 0070389292

**McFarlan, F. Warren (Franklin Warren)**        5.5611
Corporate information systems management: the issues facing senior executives
/ F. Warren McFarlan, James L. McKenney. — Homewood, Ill.: R.D. Irwin,
1983. ix, 211 p.: ill.; 24 cm. 'Also published as the text portion of Corporate
information systems management: text and cases by Cash, McFarlan &
McKenney'—T.p. verso. Includes index. 1. Management information systems
I. McKenney, James L. II. T.
T58.6.M397 1983     658.4/038 19     *LC* 82-82122

**McLeod, Raymond.**        5.5612
Management information systems / Raymond McLeod, Jr. — 3rd ed. —
Chicago: Science Research Associates, c1986. xiii, 842 p.: ill.; 24 cm.
1. Management information systems I. T.
T58.6.M424 1986     658.4/038 19     *LC* 85-19585     *ISBN* 0574219951

**Scott, George M.**        5.5613
Principles of management information systems / George M. Scott. — New
York: McGraw-Hill, c1986. xviii, 618 p.: ill.; 25 cm. (McGraw-Hill series in
management information systems.) 1. Management information systems I. T.
II. Series.
T58.6.S38 1986     658.4/0388 19     *LC* 84-21849     *ISBN* 0070561036

**Thierauf, Robert J.**        5.5614
Effective management information systems: accent on current practices /
Robert J. Thierauf. — Columbus, Ohio: C.E. Merrill, c1984. v, 558 p.: ill.; 24
cm. 1. Management information systems I. T.
T58.6.T46 1984     658.4/038 19     *LC* 83-62901     *ISBN* 0675201071

**Zmud, Robert W., 1946-.**        5.5615
Information systems in organizations / Robert W. Zmud. — Glenview, Ill.:
Scott, Foresman & Co., c1983. xiii, 445 p.: ill.; 24 cm. 1. Management
information systems I. T.
T58.6.Z578 1983     658.4/0388 19     *LC* 82-20534     *ISBN* 0673154386

**Ergonomic design for people at work: a source book for human**        5.5616
**factors practitioners in industry including safety, design, and**
**industrial engineers, medical, industrial hygiene, and industrial**
**relations personnel, and management / by the Human Factors**
**Section, Health, Safety, and Human Factors Laboratory,**
**Eastman Kodak Company.**
Belmont, Calif.: Lifetime Learning Publications, c1983. 406 p.: ill.; 24 cm.
1. Human engineering — Handbooks, manuals, etc. I. Eastman Kodak
Company. Human Factors Section. II. Eastman Kodak Company.
Ergonomics Group.
T59.7.E714 1983     620.8/2 19     *LC* 83-719     *ISBN* 0534979629

**National Institute for Occupational Safety and Health.**        5.5617
The industrial environment—its evaluation & control. — [3d ed.]. —
Washington;: for sale by the Supt. of Docs., U.S. Govt. Print. Off., 1973. x,
719 p.: illus.; 29 cm. Second ed. published in 1965 by the U.S. Public Health
Service, Division of Occupational Health. 1. Work environment 2. Industrial
hygiene I. United States. Public Health Service. Division of Occupational
Health. The industrial environment: its evaluation and control. II. T.
T59.77.N37 1973     613.6/2     *LC* 74-601580

**The Physical environment at work / edited by D.J. Oborne and**        5.5618
**M.M. Gruneberg.**
Chichester [Sussex]; New York: J. Wiley, c1983. xv, 236 p.: ill.; 24 cm. (Wiley
series in psychology and productivity at work.) 1. Work environment
2. Human engineering I. Oborne, David J. II. Gruneberg, Michael M.
III. Series.
T59.77.P5 1983     620.8/2 19     *LC* 82-23743     *ISBN* 0471901237

**Aft, Lawrence S.**        5.5619
Productivity measurement and improvement / Lawrence S. Aft. — Reston,
Va.: Reston Pub. Co., c1983. xiii, 429 p.: ill.; 24 cm. 1. Time study 2. Motion
study 3. Industrial productivity I. T.
T60.4.A34 1983     658.5/15 19     *LC* 82-16587     *ISBN* 0835956202

**Barnes, Ralph Mosser, 1900-.**        5.5620
Motion and time study: design and measurement of work / Ralph M. Barnes.
— 7th ed. — New York: Wiley, c1980. xi, 689 p.: ill.; 24 cm. Includes index.
1. Motion study 2. Time study I. T.
T60.4.B39 1980     658.5/42     *LC* 80-173     *ISBN* 0471059056

**Niebel, Benjamin W.**        5.5621
Motion and time study / Benjamin W. Niebel. — 7th ed. — Homewood, Ill.:
R.D. Irwin, 1982. xi, 756 p.: ill.; 24 cm. — (Irwin series in management and the
behavioral sciences.) 1. Motion study 2. Time study 3. Wages I. T. II. Series.
T60.7.N54 1982     658.5/42 19     *LC* 81-84839     *ISBN* 0256025274

**Automation and work design: a study / prepared by the**        5.5622
**International Labour Office; edited by Federico Butera and**
**Joseph E. Thurman.**
Amsterdam; New York: North-Holland; New York, N.Y., U.S.A.: Sole
distributors for the U.S.A. and Canada, Elsevier Science Pub. Co., 1984. xvii,
758 p.: ill.; 25 cm. 1. Work design 2. Automation I. Butera, Federico, 1940-
II. Thurman, Joseph E. III. International Labour Office.
T60.8.A8 1984     658.5/14 19     *LC* 84-8169     *ISBN* 0444875387

## T61–171 TECHNICAL EDUCATION

**Safford, Frank, 1935-.**        5.5623
The ideal of the practical: Colombia's struggle to form a technical elite / Frank
Safford. — Austin: University of Texas Press, c1976. xv, 373 p.: ill.; 24 cm.
(Latin American monographs; no. 39) Includes index. 1. Technical education
— Colombia — History. 2. Colombia — Economic conditions I. T.
T95.S2     607/.861     *LC* 75-16072     *ISBN* 029273803X

**Venables, Peter Percy Frederick Ronald, Sir, 1904-.**        5.5624
Higher education developments: the technological universities, 1956–1976 /
Peter Venables. — London; Boston: Faber and Faber, 1978. 406 p.: ill.; 23 cm.
— (Society today and tomorrow) 1. Technical education — Great Britain.
I. T.
T107.V398     378.41 19     *LC* 79-313403     *ISBN* 0571102832

## T173–185 Technological Change

**York, Neil Longley.**        5.5625
Mechanical metamorphosis: technological change in revolutionary America /
Neil Longley York; foreword by Brooke Hindle. — Westport, Conn.:
Greenwood Press, 1985. xviii, 240 p.: ill.; 25 cm. (Contributions in America

studies, 0084-9227; no. 78) 1. Technological innovations — United States — History. 2. United States — History — Revolution, 1775-1783 I. T. II. Series.
T173.4.Y67 1985     609.73 19     *LC* 84-11845     *ISBN* 0313244758

**Gabor, Dennis, 1900-.**     • **5.5626**
Innovations: scientific, technological, and social. — New York: Oxford University Press, 1970. vi, 113 p.; 21 cm. 1. Technological innovations I. T.
T173.8.G3 1970     301.2/43     *LC* 72-176613     *ISBN* 0195194128

**Sahal, Devendra.**     **5.5627**
Patterns of technological innovation / Devendra Sahal; foreword by Richard R. Nelson. — Reading, Mass.: Addison-Wesley Pub. Co., Advanced Book Program/World Science Division, 1981. xvi, 381 p.: ill.; 25 cm. 1. Technological innovations I. T.
T173.8.S24     608 19     *LC* 81-7967     *ISBN* 0201066300

**Gee, Sherman.**     **5.5628**
Technology transfer, innovation, and international competitiveness / Sherman Gee. — New York: Wiley, c1981. x, 228 p.: ill.; 24 cm. 'A Wiley-Interscience publication.' Includes index. 1. Technology transfer 2. Technological innovations — United States. I. T.
T174.3.G42     338.4/76 19     *LC* 80-22786     *ISBN* 0471084689

**Technology crossing borders: the choice, transfer, and**     **5.5629**
**management of international technology flows / contributors,**
**Michel Amsalem ... [et al.]; edited by Robert Stobaugh and**
**Louis T. Wells, Jr.; foreword by Michael Y. Yoshino.**
Boston, Mass.: Harvard Business School Press, c1984. xii, 329 p.: ill.; 25 cm. 1. Technology transfer — Addresses, essays, lectures. I. Amsalem, Michel A. II. Stobaugh, Robert B. III. Wells, Louis T.
T174.3.T375 1984     338.9/26 19     *LC* 83-26591     *ISBN* 0875841589

**Collingridge, David.**     **5.5630**
Technology in the policy process: controlling nuclear power / David Collingridge. — New York: St. Martin's Press, 1983. xvii, 254 p.: ill.; 23 cm. 1. Technology assessment 2. Breeder reactors I. T.
T174.5.C64 1983     333.79/24/068 19     *LC* 83-9801     *ISBN* 0312790171

**Hazards: technology and fairness / National Academy of**     **5.5631**
**Engineering.**
Washington, D.C.: National Academy Press, 1986. viii, 225 p.: ill.; 23 cm. (Series on technology and social priorities.) Consists of papers based on the Symposium on Hazards: Technology and Fairness, held June 3-4, 1985. 1. Technology assessment — Congresses. 2. Health risk assessment — Congresses. 3. Risk — Congresses. I. National Academy of Engineering. II. Symposium on Hazards: Technology and Fairness (1985: Washington, D.C.) III. Series.
T174.5.H39 1986     363.1 19     *LC* 86-2412     *ISBN* 0309036445

**International Conference on Technology Assessment, Monaco,**     **5.5632**
**1975.**
Technology assessment and the oceans: proceedings of the International Conference on Technology Assessment, Monaco, 26–30 October 1975 / edited by Philip D. Wilmot, Aart Slingerland. — Guildford, Eng.: IPC Science and Technology Press; Boulder, Colo.: Westview Press, 1977. x, 259 p.: ill.; 29 cm. — (ISTA Documentation series; no. 1) Sponsored by Eurocéan and the International Society for Technology Assessment. 1. Technology assessment — Congresses. 2. Marine resources — Congresses. 3. Ocean — Congresses. I. Wilmot, Philip D. II. Slingerland, Aart. III. Association européenne océanique. IV. International Society for Technology Assessment. V. T. VI. Series.
T174.5.I57 1975     303.4/83 19     *LC* 77-73026     *ISBN* 089158725X

**International Congress on Technology Assessment. 2d,**     **5.5633**
**University of Michigan, 1976.**
Technology assessment: creative futures: perspectives from and beyond the second international congress / prepared by Mark A. Boroush, Kan Chen and Alexander N. Christakis; [sponsored by the International Society for Technology Assessment]. — New York: North Holland, c1980. xviii, 405 p.: ill.; 24 cm. — (North Holland series in system science and engineering; v. 5) 1. Technology assessment — Congresses. I. Boroush, Mark A. II. Chen, Kan, 1928- III. Christakis, Alexander N. IV. International Society for Technology Assessment. V. T.
T174.5.I57 1976     301.24/3/018     *LC* 79-17366     *ISBN* 0444003282

**Lawless, Edward W.**     **5.5634**
Technology and social shock / Edward W. Lawless. — New Brunswick, N.J.: Rutgers University Press, c1977. xii, 616 p.: graphs; 23 cm. 1. Technology assessment — Case studies. 2. Technology — Public opinion — Case studies. 3. Technology — Social aspects — Case studies. 4. Social history — 194- I. T.
T174.5.L38     301.15/43/6     *LC* 75-44184     *ISBN* 0813507804

**Risk evaluation and management / edited by Vincent T. Covello**     **5.5635**
**and Joshua Menkes and Jeryl Mumpower.**
New York: Plenum Press, c1986. xi, 544 p.: ill.; 26 cm. — (Contemporary issues in risk analysis. v. 1) 1. Technology assessment 2. Risk I. Covello, Vincent T. II. Menkes, Joshua. III. Mumpower, Jeryl, 1949- IV. Series.
T174.5.R56 1986     363.1 19     *LC* 86-4895     *ISBN* 0306419785

**Design since 1945 / editors, Kathryn B. Hiesinger and George**     **5.5636**
**H. Marcus; contributing authors, Max Bill ... [et. al.].**
[Philadelphia]: Philadelphia Museum of Art; New York: Rizzoli, 1983. xxiv, 251 p.: ill. (some col.). Catalog of the exhibition held at the Philadelphia Museum of Art, Oct. 16, 1983-Jan. 8, 1984. Includes index. 1. Design, Industrial — Exhibitions. I. Hiesinger, Kathryn B., 1943- II. Marcus, George H. III. Philadelphia Museum of Art.
T180.P47 P473 1983     745.2/074/014811 19     *LC* 83-17414     *ISBN* 0847805190

**The Trouble with technology: explorations in the process of**     **5.5637**
**technological change / edited by Stuart Macdonald, D.McL.**
**Lamberton, Thomas Mandeville.**
New York: St. Martin's Press, 1983. x, 224 p.; 24 cm. 1. Technology — Addresses, essays, lectures. I. Macdonald, Stuart. II. Lamberton, D. M. (Donald McLean), 1927- III. Mandeville, T. D.
T185.T76 1983     338.4/76 19     *LC* 83-10961     *ISBN* 0312819854

# T201–324 Inventions. Patents

**Grubb, Philip W.**     **5.5638**
Patents for chemists / by Philip W. Grubb. — Oxford: Clarendon Press; New York: Oxford University Press, c1982. x, 273 p.: ill.; 24 cm. — (Oxford science publications.) Includes index. 1. Patents 2. Chemistry — Patents. I. T. II. Series.
T211.G78 1982     346.04/86/02466 342.648602466 19     *LC* 82-195143     *ISBN* 0198551533

**Fenner, Terrence W.**     • **5.5639**
Inventor's handbook [by] Terrence W. Fenner and James L. Everett. — New York: Chemical Pub. Co., 1969. xi, 309 p.: illus.; 23 cm. 1. Inventions 2. Patents 3. Industrial management I. Everett, James L., joint author. II. Associated Ideas, inc. III. T.
T212.F44     608.7     *LC* 73-5567

**Jewkes, John, 1902-.**     • **5.5640**
The sources of invention / by John Jewkes, David Sawers [and] Richard Stillerman. — 2d ed. [rev. and enl.]. — New York: W. W. Norton, [c1969] 372 p.: ports.; 20 cm. — (The Norton library N502) 1. Inventions I. Sawers, David. joint author. II. Stillerman, Richard, joint author. III. T.
T212.J4 1969b     608.7     *LC* 79-90986     *ISBN* 039300502X

**Trade names dictionary: a guide to approximately 220,000**     **5.5641**
**consumer–oriented trade names, brand names, product names,**
**coined names, model names, and design names, and names and**
**addresses of their manufacturers, importers, marketers, or**
**distributors / Donna Wood, editor.**
5th ed., 1986-87. — Detroit: Gale Research Co., c1986. 2 v. (1828 p.); 29 cm. 1. Trademarks — United States. 2. Business names — United States. I. Wood, Donna, 1949-
T223.V4 A25     658.827     *ISBN* 0810306867

**Trade names dictionary: company index / Donna Wood, editor.**     **5.5642**
5th ed., 1986-87. — Detroit: Gale Research Co., 1986. 2 v. (1838 p.); 29 cm. 'A companion volume to Trade names dictionary, with each company-and-address entry followed by an alphabetical listing of its brands.' 1. Trademarks — United States. 2. Business names — United States. I. Wood, Donna, 1949-
T223.V4 A253     658.827     *LC* 82-642841     *ISBN* 0810306875

# T352–385 Engineering Graphics

**Stitt, Fred A.**     **5.5643**
Systems graphics: breakthroughs in drawing production and project management for architects, designers, and engineers / Fred A. Stitt. — New York: McGraw-Hill, c1984. viii, 261 p.: ill.; 29 cm. — (McGraw-Hill designing with systems series.) Includes index. 1. Drawing-room practice 2. Copying processes 3. Engineering graphics I. T. II. Series.
T352.S74 1984     604.2 19     *LC* 83-866     *ISBN* 0070615519

**Stitt, Fred A.** 5.5644
Systems drafting: creative reprographics for architects and engineers / Fred A. Stitt. — New York: McGraw-Hill, c1980. ix, 245 p.: ill.; 28 cm. Includes index. 1. Structural drawing 2. Architectural drawing 3. Mechanical drawing 4. Copying processes 5. Overlay drafting systems I. T.
T355.S75    604/.2    *LC* 79-20128    *ISBN* 0070615500

**Demel, John T.** 5.5645
Introduction to computer graphics / John T. Demel and Michael J. Miller. — Monterey, Calif.: Brooks/Cole Engineering Division, c1984. xi, 427 p., [8] p. of plates: ill. (some col.); 24 cm. Includes index. 1. Computer graphics I. Miller, Michael J. II. T. III. Title: Computer graphics.
T385.D46 1984    001.64/43 19    *LC* 83-25202    *ISBN* 053403053X

**Enderle, G. (Günter), 1944-.** 5.5646
Computer graphics programming: GKS, the graphics standard / G. Enderle, K. Kansy, G. Pfaff. — Berlin; New York: Springer-Verlag, 1984. xvi, 542 p.: ill. (some col.); 25 cm. — (Symbolic computation. Computer graphics.) Includes index. 1. Computer graphics — Standards. I. Kansy, K. (Klaus), 1945- II. Pfaff, G. (Günther), 1951- III. T. IV. Series.
T385.E53 1984    001.64/43 19    *LC* 83-12438    *ISBN* 0387115250

**Foley, James D., 1942-.** 5.5647
Fundamentals of interactive computer graphics / James D. Foley, Andries van Dam. — Reading, Mass.: Addison-Wesley Pub. Co., c1982. xx, 664 p.: ill.; 24 cm. — (The Systems programming series) Includes index. 1. Computer graphics 2. Interactive computer systems I. Van Dam, Andries, 1938- joint author. II. T.
T385.F63    001.64/43 19    *LC* 80-24311    *ISBN* 0201144689

**Giloi, Wolfgang.** 5.5648
Interactive computer graphics: data structures, algorithms, languages / Wolfgang K. Giloi. — Englewood Cliffs, N.J.: Prentice-Hall, c1978. xiii, 354 p.: ill.; 24 cm. Includes index. 1. Computer graphics 2. Interactive computer systems 3. Algorithms 4. Programming languages (Electronic computers) 5. Data structures (Computer science) I. T.
T385.G54    001.6/443    *LC* 78-5425    *ISBN* 013469189X

**Hubbard, Stuart W.** 5.5649
The computer graphics glossary / by Stuart W. Hubbard. — Phoenix, AZ: Oryx Press, 1984 (c1983). vi, 94 p.: ill.; 24 cm. 1. Computer graphics — Dictionaries. I. T.
T385.H78 1983    001.64/43 19    *LC* 82-42918    *ISBN* 0897740726

**Mufti, Aftab A.** 5.5650
Elementary computer graphics / Aftab A. Mufti. — Reston, Va.: Reston Pub. Co., c1983. xiv, 210 p.: ill.; 24 cm. 1. Computer graphics I. T.
T385.M83 1983    001.64/43 19    *LC* 82-20468    *ISBN* 0835916545

**Newman, William M., 1939-.** 5.5651
Principles of interactive computer graphics / William M. Newman, Robert F. Sproull. — 2d ed. — New York: McGraw-Hill, c1979. xvi, 541 p., [1] leaf of plates: ill.; 24 cm. (McGraw-Hill computer science series) Includes index. 1. Computer graphics 2. Interactive computer systems I. Sproull, Robert F. joint author. II. T.
T385.N48 1979    001.55    *LC* 78-23825    *ISBN* 0070463387

**Pavlidis, Theodosios.** 5.5652
Algorithms for graphics and image processing / Theo Pavlidis. — Rockville, MD: Computer Science Press, c1982. xv, 416 p., 29 p. of plates: ill.; 24 cm. 1. Computer graphics 2. Image processing 3. Pattern recognition systems 4. Algorithms I. T.
T385.P38 1982    001.55 19    *LC* 81-9832    *ISBN* 091489465X

**Tutorial, computer graphics / [compiled by] John C. Beatty,** 5.5653
**Kellogg S. Booth.**
2d ed. — Silver Spring, MD: IEEE Computer Society Press; Los Angeles, CA: Order from IEEE Computer Society, c1982. vi, 570 p.: ill. (some col.); 28 cm. 'IEEE catalog number EH0194-1.' 1. Computer graphics — Addresses, essays, lectures. I. Beatty, John C. II. Booth, Kellogg S. III. IEEE Computer Society. IV. Title: Computer graphics.
T385.T876 1982    001.64/43 19    *LC* 82-80837

# T395 Exhibitions

**Altick, Richard Daniel, 1915-.** 5.5654
The shows of London / Richard D. Altick. — Cambridge, Mass.: Belknap Press, 1978. 553 p.: ill.; 26 cm. 1. London (England) — Exhibitions — History. I. T.
T395.5.G7 A45    942.1    *LC* 77-2755    *ISBN* 0674807316

**Rydell, Robert W.** 5.5655
All the world's a fair: visions of empire at American international expositions, 1876–1916 / Robert W. Rydell. — Chicago: University of Chicago Press, 1984. x, 328 p.: ill.; 24 cm. Includes index. 1. Exhibitions — History. I. T.
T395.5.U6 R93 1984    909.81/074/013 19    *LC* 84-2674    *ISBN* 0226732398

**Alles, Alfred.** 5.5656
Exhibitions: universal marketing tools. — New York: Wiley, [1973] 260 p.; 25 cm. — (Cassell/Associated Business Programmes marketing library) 'A Halsted Press book.' 1. Exhibitions 2. Marketing I. T.
T396.A38    658.8/2    *LC* 73-1796    *ISBN* 0470023325

**Burg, David F.** 5.5657
Chicago's White City of 1893 / David F. Burg. — Lexington: University Press of Kentucky, 1976. xv, 381 p.: ill. 1. World's Columbian Exposition (1893: Chicago, Ill.) 2. Chicago (Ill.) — Exhibitions. I. T. II. Title: White City of 1893.
T500.B1 B8    T500.B1 B8.    *LC* 75-3542    *ISBN* 0813113318

# TA–TH General Engineering. Civil Engineering Group

# TA Engineering: General. Civil Engineering: General

**Scott, John S., 1915-.** 5.5658
Dictionary of civil engineering / John S. Scott; illustrated by Clifford Bayliss. — 3d ed. — New York: Halsted Press, 1980. 308 p.: ill.; 23 cm. 1. Civil engineering — Dictionaries. I. T.
TA9.S35 1980    624/.03/21 19    *LC* 80-24419    *ISBN* 047027087X

**Hill, Donald Routledge.** 5.5659
A history of engineering in classical and medieval times / Donald Hill. — La Salle, Ill.: Open Court Pub. Co., c1984. 263 p.: ill.; 23 cm. Includes index. 1. Engineering — Europe — History. 2. Engineering — Asia — History. I. T.
TA16.H55 1984    620/.009/01 19    *LC* 84-7339    *ISBN* 0875484220

**Stephens, John H. (John Hall), 1925-.** 5.5660
Towers, bridges, and other structures / John H. Stephens. — New York: Sterling Pub. Co., 1976. 288 p.: ill. (some col.); 25 cm. 'One of the Guinness family of books.' Includes index. 1. Civil engineering — History. I. T.
TA19.S84 1976    624/.09    *LC* 76-19809    *ISBN* 0806900962. *ISBN* 0806900970 lib. bdg.

**Schodek, Daniel L., 1941-.** 5.5661
Landmarks in American civil engineering / Daniel L. Schodek. — Cambridge, Mass.: MIT Press, c1987. xviii, 383 p.: ill.; 31 cm. Includes index. 1. Civil engineering — United States. 2. United States — Public works I. T.
TA23.S36 1987    624/.0973 19    *LC* 86-20162    *ISBN* 026219256X

**Carvill, James.** 5.5662
Famous names in engineering / James Carvill. — London; Boston: Butterworths, 1981. 93 p.: ill.; 26 cm. 1. Engineers — Biography. I. T.
TA139.C37 1981    509/.2/2 B 19    *LC* 80-41705    *ISBN* 0408005394

**Who's who in engineering.** 5.5663
3d- ed. New York: American Association of Engineering Societies [etc.], 1977-. v.: ill.; 29 cm. Biennial. 1. Engineers — United States — Biography. 2. Engineers — United States — Directories. I. American Association of Engineering Societies. II. Engineers Joint Council.
TA139.E37    620/.0092/2 B    *LC* 78-640547

**Great engineers and pioneers in technology / editors, Roland** 5.5664
**Turner and Steven L. Goulden, assistant editor, Barbara**
**Sheridan.**
New York: St. Martin's Press, c1981-. v. < 1- >: ill.; 26 cm. Includes index. 1. Engineers — Biography. 2. Engineering — History. I. Turner, Roland. II. Goulden, Steven L.
TA139.G7 1981    620/.0092/2 19    *LC* 80-28986    *ISBN* 0312345747

**Robinson, Eric, 1924- comp.** 5.5665
Partners in science: letters of James Watt and Joseph Black / edited with introductions and notes by Eric Robinson and Douglas McKie. — London: Constable [1970] xvi, 502 p.: facsims.; 23 cm. Includes James Watt's notebook of his experiments with heat: p. 431-479. 1. Engineers — Correspondence

2. Chemists — Correspondence I. McKie, Douglas. joint comp. II. Watt, James, 1736-1819. III. Black, Joseph, 1728-1799. IV. T.
TA140.W3 R58      621.1/0924      *LC* 78-474560      *ISBN* 0094516405

## TA144–160 REFERENCE. STUDY

**CRC handbook of tables for applied engineering science.**                **5.5666**
**Editors: Ray E. Bolz [and] George L. Tuve.**
2d ed. Cleveland, Ohio, CRC Press [1973] 1166 p. illus. 27 cm. 1. Engineering — Tables. I. Bolz, Ray E., 1918- ed. II. Tuve, George Lewis. ed. III. Chemical Rubber Company. IV. Title: Handbook of tables for applied engineering science.
TA151.C2 1973      620/.0021/2      *LC* 73-166251      *ISBN* 0878192522

**Civil engineer's reference book / edited by L. S. Blake; with**                **5.5667**
**specialist contributors.**
3d ed., completely rev. and reset. — London: Newnes-Butterworths, 1975. 1725 p. in various pagings: ill.; 23 cm. First-2d ed. published in 1951 and 1961 respectively under title: Civil engineering reference book, edited by E. H. Probst and J. Comrie. 1. Civil engineering — Handbooks, manuals, etc. 2. Civil engineering — Tables. I. Blake, Leslie Spencer, 1925- II. Probst, Emil Heinrich, 1877-1950. ed. Civil engineering reference book.
TA151.C58 1975      624      *LC* 75-309179      *ISBN* 0408704756

**Eshbach, Ovid Wallace, 1893-1958, ed.**                **5.5668**
Handbook of engineering fundamentals / prepared by a staff of specialists under the editorship of Mott Souders and Ovid W. Eshbach. — 3d ed. — New York: Wiley, [c1975] x, 1562 p.: ill.; 22 cm. — (Wiley engineering handbook series) Includes index. 1. Engineering — Handbooks, manuals, etc. I. Souders, Mott, 1904- II. T.
TA151.E8 1974      620/.002/02      *LC* 74-7467      *ISBN* 0471245534

**Handbook of heavy construction. Edited by John A. Havers and     • 5.5669
Frank W. Stubbs, Jr.**
2d ed. — New York: McGraw-Hill, [1971] 1 v. (various pagings): illus.; 24 cm. First ed. edited by F. W. Stubbs, Jr. 1. Engineering — Handbooks, manuals, etc. I. Havers, John Alan, 1925- ed. II. Stubbs, Frank Whitworth, 1898-1967. Handbook of heavy construction.
TA151.H29 1971      624/.02/02      *LC* 77-107297      *ISBN* 0070272786

**Heisler, Sanford I.**                **5.5670**
The Wiley engineer's desk reference: a concise guide for the professional engineer / Sanford I. Heisler. — New York: J. Wiley, 1984. xvi, 567 p.: ill.; 25 cm. 'A Wiley-Interscience publication.' 1. Engineering — Handbooks, manuals, etc. I. John Wiley & Sons. II. T. III. Title: Engineer's desk reference.
TA151.H424 1984      620 19      *LC* 83-21690      *ISBN* 0471866326

**Souders, Mott, 1904-.**                • **5.5671**
The engineer's companion: a concise handbook of engineering fundamentals. — New York: Wiley [1966] viii, 426 p.: ill.; 22 cm. 1. Engineering — Handbooks, manuals, etc. I. T.
TA151.S57      621.00202      *LC* 65-26851      *ISBN* 0471813958

**Standard handbook for civil engineers / Frederick S. Merritt,**                **5.5672**
**editor.**
3rd ed. — New York: McGraw-Hill, c1983. 1 v. (various pagings): ill.; 25 cm. 1. Civil engineering — Handbooks, manuals, etc. I. Merritt, Frederick S.
TA151.S8 1983      624 19      *LC* 82-14902      *ISBN* 0070415153

**Bowker, Albert Hosmer, 1919-.**                • **5.5673**
Engineering statistics [by] Albert H. Bowker [and] Gerald J. Lieberman. — 2d ed. — Englewood Cliffs, N.J.: Prentice-Hall, [1972] xviii, 641 p.; 24 cm. 1. Engineering — Statistical methods I. Lieberman, Gerald J. joint author. II. T.
TA153.B67 1972      620/.001/5195      *LC* 72-39106      *ISBN* 0132794551

**Davidson, Frank Paul, 1918-.**                **5.5674**
Macro: a clear vision of how science and technology will shape our future / Frank P. Davidson with John Stuart Cox; photo research by Vincent Virga. — 1st ed. — New York: W. Morrow, 1983. 450 p.: ill.; 25 cm. Includes index. 1. Engineering 2. Technological forecasting I. Cox, John Stuart. II. T.
TA153.D38 1983      620 19      *LC* 83-62049      *ISBN* 0688021824

**Thring, M. W. (Meredith Wooldridge), 1915-.**                **5.5675**
The engineer's conscience / [by] M.W. Thring. — [Bury-St-Edmunds]: Northgate Pub. Co. Ltd., 1980. xii, 240 p., [12] p. of plates: ill., map; 23 cm. 1. Engineering — Social aspects. I. T.
TA153.T48      303.4/83 19      *LC* 81-105578      *ISBN* 0852984332

**Billmeyer, Fred W.**                **5.5676**
Entering industry: a guide for young professionals / Fred W. Billmeyer, Jr., and Richard N. Kelley. — New York: Wiley, [1975] xi, 281 p.: ill.; 23 cm. 'A Wiley-

Interscience publication.' 1. Engineering — Vocational guidance 2. Chemical engineering — Vocational guidance I. Kelley, Richard N., 1940- joint author. II. T.
TA157.B5      620/.0023      *LC* 75-22283      *ISBN* 0471072850

**Eckard, Joseph D., 1942-.**                **5.5677**
Professional engineer's license guide: what you need to know and do to obtain PE (and EIT) registration / Joseph D. Eckard, Jr.; introd. by James T. Cobb, Jr. — 3d ed. — Boston: Herman Publishing, c1978. xix, 108 p.: ill.; 24 cm. — (Herman's career management guides) Includes index. 1. Engineers — Licenses — United States. I. T.
TA157.E26 1978      620/.0023      *LC* 78-17249      *ISBN* 0890470200

**Layton, Edwin T., 1928-.**                • **5.5678**
The revolt of the engineers: social responsibility and the American engineering profession / [by Edwin T. Layton, Jr. — Cleveland: Press of Case Western Reserve University, 1971] xiv, 286 p.; 24 cm. 1. Engineering — Vocational guidance I. T.
TA157.L38      620/.0062/73      *LC* 71-116385      *ISBN* 0829502009

**Mechanical technician's handbook / Maurice J. Webb, editor–**                **5.5679**
**in–chief.**
New York: McGraw-Hill, c1983. viii, [467 p.]: ill.; 24 cm. 'A James Peter book.' Includes index. 1. Technicians in industry — Handbooks, manuals, etc. I. Webb, Maurice J.
TA158.M4 1983      620 19      *LC* 81-23652      *ISBN* 0070688028

**Baldwin, Allen J.**                **5.5680**
A programmed review of engineering fundamentals / Allen J. Baldwin, Karen M. Hess. — New York: Van Nostrand Reinhold Co., c1978. xiii, 287 p.: ill.; 29 cm. Includes index. 1. Engineering — Programmed instruction. 2. Engineering — Examinations, questions, etc. I. Hess, Kären M., 1939- joint author. II. T.
TA159.B34      620/.007/7      *LC* 78-1823      *ISBN* 0442202393

**La Londe, William S.**                **5.5681**
Professional engineers' examination questions and answers / William S. La Londe, Jr., William J. Stack-Staikidis. — 4th ed. — New York: McGraw-Hill, c1984. xiii, 539 p.: ill.; 21 cm. 1. Engineering — Examinations, questions, etc. 2. Engineers — Licenses — United States. I. Stack-Staikidis, William J., 1929- II. T.
TA159.L3 1984      620/.0076 19      *LC* 82-23393      *ISBN* 0070360995

## TA165 ENGINEERING INSTRUMENTS

**Beckwith, T. G. (Thomas G.)**                **5.5682**
Mechanical measurements / Thomas G. Beckwith, N. Lewis Buck, Roy D. Marangoni. — 3d ed. — Reading, Mass.: Addison-Wesley Pub. Co., c1982. xvi, 730 p.: ill.; 24 cm. 1. Engineering instruments 2. Measuring instruments I. Buck, N. Lewis (Nelson Lewis) joint author. II. Marangoni, Roy D. joint author. III. T.
TA165.B38 1982      620/.0044 19      *LC* 80-26718      *ISBN* 0201000369

**Morrison, Ralph.**                **5.5683**
Instrumentation fundamentals and applications / Ralph Morrison. — New York: Wiley, c1984. xiii, 144 p.: ill.; 24 cm. 'A Wiley-Interscience publication.' Includes index. 1. Engineering instruments I. T.
TA165.M64 1984      681/.2 19      *LC* 83-21696      *ISBN* 0471881813

**Norton, Harry N.**                **5.5684**
Sensor and analyzer handbook / Harry N. Norton. — Englewood Cliffs, NJ: Prentice-Hall, c1982. xiii, 562 p.: ill.; 25 cm. 1. Measuring instruments 2. Transducers I. T.
TA165.N6      621.3815/48 19      *LC* 81-15844      *ISBN* 0138067600

**Soisson, Harold E.**                **5.5685**
Instrumentation in industry / Harold E. Soisson. — New York: Wiley, [1975] xii, 563 p.: ill.; 23 cm. 'A Wiley-Interscience publication.' 1. Engineering instruments I. T.
TA165.S725      681      *LC* 74-23222      *ISBN* 0471810495

## TA166–174 HUMAN ENGINEERING.
## SYSTEMS ENGINEERING. DESIGN

**Handbook of human factors / [edited by] Gavriel Salvendy.**                **5.5686**
New York: Wiley, c1987. xxiv, 1874 p.: ill.; 24 cm. 'A Wiley-Interscience publication.' 1. Human engineering — Handbooks, manuals, etc. I. Salvendy, Gavriel, 1938-
TA166.H275 1987      620.8/2 19      *LC* 86-9083      *ISBN* 0471880159

**McCormick, Ernest J. (Ernest James)**      **5.5687**
Human factors in engineering and design / Mark S. Sanders, Ernest J. McCormick. — 6th ed. — New York: McGraw-Hill, c1987. 491 p.: ill. Includes indexes. 1. Human engineering I. Sanders, Mark S. II. T.
TA166.M39 1987     620.8/2 19     LC 86-10679     ISBN 0070449031

**Roebuck, John Arthur, 1929-.**      **5.5688**
Engineering anthropometry methods / J. A. Roebuck, Jr., K. H. E. Kroemer, W. G. Thomson. — New York: Wiley-Interscience, [1975] xv, 459 p.: ill.; 23 cm. (Wiley series in human factors) Includes index. 1. Human engineering 2. Anthropometry I. Kroemer, K. H. E., 1933- joint author. II. Thomson, Walter Gary, 1939- joint author. III. T.
TA166.R63     620.8/2     LC 74-34272     ISBN 0471729752

**Brown, Robert Goodell.**      **5.5689**
Smoothing, forecasting and prediction of discrete time series. Englewood Cliffs, N.J., Prentice-Hall [1963] 468 p. illus. 24 cm. (Prentice-Hall international series in management) (Prentice-Hall quantitative methods series.) 1. Time-series analysis 2. Electronic digital computers — Programming 3. Systems engineering I. T.
TA168.B68 1963     519.9     LC 63-13271

**Doebelin, Ernest O.**      **5.5690**
System modeling and response: theoretical and experimental approaches / Ernest O. Doebelin. — New York: Wiley, [1980] xiii, 587 p.: ill.; 24 cm. 1. Systems engineering — Mathematical models. 2. Systems engineering — Data processing. I. T.
TA168.D593     620.7/2     LC 79-27609     ISBN 0471032115

**Motil, John M.**      **5.5691**
Digital systems fundamentals [by] John M. Motil. — New York: McGraw-Hill, [1972] xx, 390 p.: illus.; 23 cm. — (McGraw-Hill series in electronic systems) 1. Systems engineering 2. Switching theory 3. Digital electronics I. T.
TA168.M68     620/.7     LC 75-172029     ISBN 0070435154

**Truxal, John G.**      **5.5692**
Introductory system engineering / [by] John G. Truxal. — New York: McGraw-Hill, [1972] xi, 596 p.: ill.; 23 cm. — (McGraw-Hill series in electronic systems) 1. Systems engineering I. T.
TA168.T78     620/.72     LC 76-172265     ISBN 0070653178

**Wymore, A. Wayne.**      **5.5693**
Systems engineering methodology for interdisciplinary teams / A. Wayne Wymore. — New York: Wiley, c1976. ix, 431 p.: ill.; 24 cm. 'A Wiley-Interscience publication.' Includes indexes. 1. Systems engineering I. T.
TA168.W92     620/.7     LC 75-31929     ISBN 047196901X

**Beakley, George C.**      **5.5694**
Introduction to engineering design and graphics [by] George C. Beakley [and] Ernest G. Chilton. With contributions by Michael J. Nielsen. — New York: Macmillan, [1973] xii, 818 p.: illus.; 24 cm. 1. Engineering design 2. Engineering graphics I. Chilton, Ernest G., joint author. II. T.
TA174.B4     620/.0042     LC 77-186438

**Besant, C. B.**      **5.5695**
Computer–aided design and manufacture / C.B. Besant, C.W.K. Lui. — 3rd ed. — Chichester [West Sussex]: E. Horwood; New York: Halsted Press, 1986. 410 p.: ill.; 24 cm. (Ellis Horwood series in mechanical engineering.) 1. Engineering design — Data processing 2. Manufacturing processes — Data processing 3. Computer-aided design I. Lui, C. W. K., 1955- II. T. III. Series.
TA174.B46 1986     670/.285 19     LC 85-27185

**CAD, principles and applications / Paul C. Barr ... [et al.].**      **5.5696**
Englewood Cliffs, NJ: Prentice Hall, c1985. ix, 206 p.: ill.; 25 cm. Includes index. 1. Engineering design — Data processing 2. Computer-aided design I. Barr, Paul C. II. Title: C.A.D., principles and applications.
TA174.C26 1985     620/.00425/02854 19     LC 84-15937     ISBN 0131101986

**Fuchs, H. O. (Henry Otten), 1907- comp.**      **5.5697**
10 cases in engineering design / edited by H. O. Fuchs and R. F. Steidel, Jr. [London]: Longman, [1973] x, 399 p.: ill.; 28 cm. 1. Engineering design — Case studies. I. Steidel, Robert F., 1926- joint comp. II. T.
TA174.F83     620/.004/2     LC 73-178311     ISBN 0582441447 ISBN 0582441455

**Ostrofsky, Benjamin, 1925-.**      **5.5698**
Design, planning, and development methodology / Benjamin Ostrofsky. Englewood Cliffs, N.J.: Prentice-Hall, c1977. xiii, 401 p.: ill.; 24 cm. 1. Engineering design 2. System analysis 3. Decision-making I. T.
TA174.O87     620/.004/2     LC 76-162     ISBN 0132002469

## TA177–194 Engineering Economy. Management

**David, F. W.**      **5.5699**
Experimental modelling in engineering / F.W. David and H. Nolle. — London; Boston: Butterworths, 1982. 185 p.: ill.; 25 cm. 1. Engineering models I. Nolle, H. II. T.
TA177.D38 1982     620/.00724 19     LC 82-144057     ISBN 0408011394

**Grant, Eugene Lodewick, 1897-.**      **5.5700**
Principles of engineering economy / Eugene L. Grant, W. Grant Ireson, Richard S. Leavenworth. — 7th ed. — New York: Wiley, 1982. x, 687 p.: ill.; 24 cm. Includes index. 1. Engineering economy I. Ireson, William Grant, 1914- II. Leavenworth, Richard S. III. T.
TA177.4.G7 1982     658.1/5 19     LC 81-10399     ISBN 047106436X

**Kurtz, Max, 1920-.**      **5.5701**
Handbook of engineering economics: guide for engineers, technicians, scientists, and managers / Max Kurtz; with a section on linear programming coauthored by Ruth I. Kurtz. — New York: McGraw-Hill, c1984. 257, 570, 155, [116] p.: ill.; 24 cm. 1. Engineering economy — Handbooks, manuals, etc. I. Kurtz, Ruth I. II. T.
TA177.4.K873 1984     658.1/5 19     LC 83-13551     ISBN 0070356599

**Thuesen, G. J., 1938-.**      **5.5702**
Engineering economy. — 6th ed. / G.J. Thuesen, W.J. Fabrycky. — Englewood Cliffs, N.J.: Prentice-Hall, c1984. xvi, 633 p.: ill.; 24 cm. — (Prentice-Hall international series in industrial and systems engineering.) Rev. ed. of: Engineering economy. 5th ed. /H.G. Thuesen, W.J. Fabrycky, G.J. Thuesen. c1977. Includes index. 1. Engineering economy I. Fabrycky, W. J. (Wolter J.), 1932- II. Thuesen, H. G. (Holger George), 1898- Engineering economy. III. T. IV. Series.
TA177.4.T47 1984     658.1/5 19     LC 83-15979     ISBN 0132777231

**Handbook of engineering management / John E. Ullmann, editor, Donald A. Christman, Bert Holtje, associate editors.**      **5.5703**
New York: Wiley, c1986. xvi, 848 p.: ill.; 23 cm. 'A James Peter book.' 'A Wiley-Interscience publication.' 1. Engineering — Management I. Ullmann, John E. II. Christman, Donald A. III. Holtje, Bert.
TA190.H36 1986     620/.0068 19     LC 85-22805     ISBN 0471878286

**Parker, David. Henry W.**      **• 5.5704**
Methods improvement for construction managers [by] Henry W. Parker [and] Clarkson H. Oglesby. — New York: McGraw-Hill, [1972] xi, 300 p.: illus.; 23 cm. — (McGraw-Hill series in construction engineering and management) 1. Engineering — Management I. Oglesby, Clarkson Hill, 1908- joint author. II. T.
TA190.P28     658/.92     LC 73-172031     ISBN 0070485038

**Antill, James M.**      **5.5705**
Critical path methods in construction practice [by] James M. Antill [and] Ronald W. Woodhead. — 2d ed. — New York: Wiley-Interscience, [1970] xii, 414 p.: illus.; 23 cm. 1. Critical path analysis 2. Engineering — Management I. Woodhead, Ronald W. joint author. II. T.
TA194.A57 1970     658.92     LC 79-121902     ISBN 0471032468

**Handbook of applied meteorology / edited by David D. Houghton.**      **5.5706**
New York: Wiley, c1985. xv, 1461 p.: ill.; 25 cm. 'A Wiley Interscience publication.' 1. Engineering meteorology — Handbooks, manuals, etc. 2. Meteorology — Handbooks, manuals, etc. I. Houghton, David D.
TA197.H36 1985     551.5 19     LC 84-11915     ISBN 0471084042

## TA329–348 Engineering Mathematics

### TA330–332 General Works. Tables

**Engineering mathematics / [by] A.J.M. Spencer ... [et al.].**      **5.5707**
New York; London [etc.]: Van Nostrand Reinhold, 1977. v.: ill.; 25 cm. Includes bibliographies and index. ISBN 0-442-30147-2 Pbk: £5.50. 1. Engineering mathematics I. Spencer, Antony James Merrill.
TA330.E53     510/.2/462     LC 76-45663     ISBN 0442301464

**Kaplan, Wilfred, 1915-.**      **5.5708**
Advanced mathematics for engineers / Wilfred Kaplan. — Reading, Mass.: Addison-Wesley Pub. Co., c1981. xix, 929 p.: ill.; 25 cm. Includes index. 1. Engineering mathematics I. T.
TA330.K32     515 19     LC 80-19492     ISBN 0201037734

**Mathematical methods in engineering / edited by Glyn A.O.**    **5.5709**
**Davies.**
Chichester [West Sussex]; New York: Wiley, c1984. xiv, 458 p.: ill.; 23 cm.
(Handbook of applicable mathematics. Guidebook. 5) 'A Wiley-Interscience
publication.' Includes index. 1. Engineering mathematics I. Davies, Glyn A.
O. II. Series.
TA330.M32 1984    620/.001/51 19    *LC* 83-23250    *ISBN*
0471103314

**Noble, Ben.**    • **5.5710**
Applications of undergraduate mathematics in engineering, written and edited
by Ben Noble. [Buffalo?] Mathematical Association of America [1967] xvii,
364 p. illus. 24 cm. 1. Engineering mathematics I. T.
TA330.N6 1967    620.00151    *LC* 66-27577

**Smith, Alan A.**    **5.5711**
Civil engineering systems analysis and design / Alan A. Smith, Ernest Hinton,
and Roland W. Lewis. — Chichester [West Sussex]; New York: Wiley, c1983.
xii, 473 p.: ill.; 23 cm. 'A Wiley-Interscience publication.' Includes index.
1. Civil engineering 2. System analysis 3. System design I. Hinton, E.
(Ernest) II. Lewis, R. W. (Roland Wynne) III. T.
TA330.S63 1983    624 19    *LC* 82-13640    *ISBN* 0471900605

**ASM handbook of engineering mathematics / by faculty**    **5.5712**
**members of the Department of Mechanical Engineering, the**
**University of Akron, Mamerto L. Chu ... [et al.] and by Samuel**
**J. Brown; editorial coordinator, William G. Belding.**
Metals Park, Ohio: American Society for Metals, c1983. xiv, 697 p.: ill.; 24 cm.
1. Engineering mathematics — Handbooks, manuals, etc. I. Chu, Mamerto L.
II. Brown, S. J. (Samuel J.) III. Belding, William G. IV. University of Akron.
Dept. of Mechanical Engineering. V. American Society for Metals. VI. Title:
A.S.M. handbook of engineering mathematics.
TA332.A79 1983    510/.2462 19    *LC* 82-22664    *ISBN* 087170157X

**Standard handbook of engineering calculations / Tyler G.**    **5.5713**
**Hicks, editor; S. David Hicks, coordinating editor.**
2nd ed. — New York: McGraw-Hill, c1985. 1 v. (various pagings): ill.; 24 cm.
Includes index. 1. Engineering mathematics — Handbooks, manuals, etc.
I. Hicks, Tyler Gregory, 1921-
TA332.S73 1985    620/.00212 19    *LC* 84-28929    *ISBN* 007028735X

### TA335–343 NUMERICAL AND STATISTICAL METHODS. MODELS

**Ferziger, Joel H.**    **5.5714**
Numerical methods for engineering application / Joel H. Ferziger. — New
York: Wiley, c1981. xii, 270 p.: ill.; 25 cm. 'A Wiley-Interscience publication.'
Includes index. 1. Engineering mathematics 2. Numerical analysis I. T.
TA335.F47    515/.02462 19    *LC* 81-1260    *ISBN* 0471063363

**Guttman, Irwin.**    **5.5715**
Introductory engineering statistics [by] Irwin Guttman, S. S. Wilks [and] J.
Stuart Hunter. 2d ed. New York, Wiley [1971] xix, 549 p. illus. 24 cm. (Wiley
series in probability and mathematical statistics) 1. Engineering — Statistical
methods I. Wilks, S. S. (Samuel Stanley), 1906-1964. joint author. II. Hunter,
J. Stuart, 1923- joint author. III. T.
TA340.G8 1971    620/.001/82    *LC* 72-160214    *ISBN* 0471337706

**Larson, Harold J., 1934-.**    **5.5716**
Probabilistic models in engineering sciences / Harold J. Larson, Bruno O.
Shubert. — New York: Wiley, c1979. 544 p. 1. Engineering — Statistical
methods 2. Probabilities 3. Stochastic processes I. Shubert, Bruno O. joint
author. II. T.
TA340.L37    620/.001/5192    *LC* 79-755    *ISBN* 0471017515

**McCuen, Richard H., 1941-.**    **5.5717**
Statistical methods for engineers / Richard H. McCuen. — Englewood Cliffs,
N.J.: Prentice-Hall, c1985. xviii, 439 p.: ill.; 24 cm. Includes bibliographies and
index. 1. Engineering — Statistical methods I. T.
TA340.M28 1985    519.5/02462 19    *LC* 84-13356    *ISBN*
0138449031

**Osyczka, Andrzej.**    **5.5718**
Multicriterion optimization in engineering with FORTRAN programs /
Andrzej Osyczka; translation editor B.J. Davies. — Chichester, W. Sussex: E.
Horwood; New York: Halsted Press, 1984. viii, 178 p.: ill.; 24 cm. — (Ellis
Horwood series in mechanical engineering.) (Ellis Horwood series in
engineering science.) Translated from the Polish. Includes indexes.
1. Engineering — Mathematical models. 2. Engineering — Data processing
3. FORTRAN (Computer program language) I. T. II. Series. III. Series:
Ellis Horwood series in engineering science.
TA342.O89 1984    620/.0042 19    *LC* 83-25478    *ISBN* 0853124817

**Speckhart, Frank H., 1940-.**    **5.5719**
A guide to using CSMP—the Continuous system modeling program: a program
for simulating physical systems / Frank H. Speckhart, Walter L. Green. —
Englewood Cliffs, N.J.: Prentice-Hall, c1976. x, 325 p.: ill.; 24 cm. 1. CSMP
(Computer program) 2. Digital computer simulation 3. Engineering — Data
processing I. Green, Walter L., 1934- joint author. II. T.
TA343.S64    001.6/424    *LC* 75-19498    *ISBN* 0133713776

### TA345 ELECTRONIC DATA PROCESSING

**Borse, G. J. (Garold J.)**    **5.5720**
FORTRAN 77 and numerical methods for engineers / G.J. Borse. — Boston:
PWS Engineering, c1985. xiv, 656 p.: ill.; 25 cm. Includes index. 1. Engineering
— Data processing 2. FORTRAN (Computer program language) I. T.
II. Title: FORTRAN 77.
TA345.B67 1985    620/.0028/5424 19    *LC* 85-531    *ISBN*
053404638X

**McCracken, Daniel D.**    **5.5721**
Computing for engineers and scientists with Fortran 77 / Daniel D.
McCracken. — New York: Wiley, c1984. xi, 361 p.: ill.; 26 cm. Includes index.
1. Engineering — Data processing 2. Science — Data processing
3. FORTRAN (Computer program language) I. T.
TA345.M395 1984    620/.0028/4 19    *LC* 83-23473    *ISBN*
0471097012

**Shoup, Terry E., 1944-.**    **5.5722**
A practical guide to computer methods for engineers / Terry E. Shoup. —
Englewood Cliffs, N.J.: Prentice-Hall, c1979. xii, 255 p.: ill.; 24 cm.
1. Engineering — Data processing 2. Engineering — Mathematical models.
I. T.
TA345.S56 1979    620/.00285/4    *LC* 78-10467    *ISBN* 0136906516

### TA347 OTHER SPECIFIC ANALYTICAL AIDS

**Ames, William F.**    **5.5723**
Nonlinear partial differential equations in engineering, by W. F. Ames. New
York, Academic Press, 1965-72. 2 v. illus. 24 cm. (Mathematics in science and
engineering. 18) 1. Differential equations, Partial 2. Differential equations,
Nonlinear I. T. II. Series.
TA347.D45 A43    515/.353    *LC* 65-22767

**Taylor, Edward S., 1943-.**    **5.5724**
Dimensional analysis for engineers / Edward S. Taylor. — Oxford [Eng.]:
Clarendon Press, 1974. xi, 162 p.; 24 cm. Includes index. 1. Dimensional
analysis I. T.
TA347.D5 T33    621/.0153/08    *LC* 74-188131    *ISBN* 0198561229

**Bathe, Klaus-Jürgen.**    **5.5725**
Numerical methods in finite element analysis / Klaus–Jürgen Bathe, Edward L.
Wilson. — Englewood Cliffs, N.J.: Prentice-Hall, c1976. xv, 528 p.: ill.; 24 cm.
(Prentice-Hall civil engineering and engineering mechanics series) 1. Finite
element method 2. Numerical analysis I. Wilson, Edward L., 1931- joint
author. II. T.
TA347.F5 B37    624/.171/01515    *LC* 75-46522    *ISBN* 0136271901

**Davies, Alan J.**    **5.5726**
The finite element method: a first approach / Alan J. Davies. — Oxford:
Clarendon Press; New York: Oxford University Press, 1980. xii, 287 p.: ill.; 23
cm. — (Oxford applied mathematics and computing science series.) Includes
index. 1. Finite element method I. T. II. Series.
TA347.F5 D38    515.3/53 19    *LC* 79-40673    *ISBN* 0198596308

**Huebner, Kenneth H., 1942-.**    **5.5727**
The finite element method for engineers / Kenneth H. Huebner, Earl A.
Thornton. — 2nd ed. — New York: Wiley, c1982. xxii, 623 p.: ill.; 24 cm. 'A
Wiley-Interscience publication.' 1. Finite element method I. Thornton, Earl
A. (Earl Arthur), 1936- II. T.
TA347.F5 H83 1982    620/.0042 19    *LC* 82-8379    *ISBN*
0471091596

**Livesley, R. K.**    **5.5728**
Finite elements: an introduction for engineers / R.K. Livesley. — Cambridge;
New York: Cambridge University Press, 1983. x, 199 p.: ill.; 24 cm. 1. Finite
element method I. T.
TA347.F5 L58 1983    620/.001/515353 19    *LC* 82-22155    *ISBN*
0521243149

**Reddy, J. N. (Junuthula Narasimha), 1945-.**    **5.5729**
An introduction to the finite element method / J.N. Reddy. — New York:
McGraw-Hill, c1984. xiii, 495 p.: ill.; 25 cm. 1. Finite element method I. T.
II. Title: Finite element method.
TA347.F5 R4 1984    620/.001/515353 19    *LC* 83-7923    *ISBN*
0070513465

State–of–the–art surveys on finite element technology /          5.5730
sponsored by the Applied Mechanics Division; edited by Ahmed
K. Noor, Walter D. Pilkey.
New York, N.Y. (345 E. 47th St., New York 10017): American Society of
Mechanical Engineers, c1983. xvi, 530 p.: ill.; 26 cm. 1. Finite element method
I. Noor, Ahmed Khairy, 1938- II. Pilkey, Walter D. III. American Society of
Mechanical Engineers. Applied Mechanics Division.
TA347.F5 S73 1983      515.3/53 19      LC 83-82420

Muth, Eginhard J., 1928-.                                       5.5731
Transform methods: with applications to engineering and operations research /
Eginhard J. Muth. Englewood Cliffs, N.J.: Prentice-Hall, c1977. xi, 372 p.: ill.;
24 cm. Includes index. 1. Laplace transformation 2. Z transformation
3. Engineering 4. Operations research I. T.
TA347.T7 M87      515/.723      LC 76-25914      ISBN 0139288619

# TA350–358 Mechanics of Engineering

## TA350 Applied Mechanics

Beer, Ferdinand Pierre, 1915-.                                  5.5732
Vector mechanics for engineers: statics and dynamics / Ferdinand P. Beer, E.
Russell Johnston, Jr. — New York: McGraw-Hill, c1984. xxi, 926 p.:
ill. (some col.); 24 cm. Also issued in two separate volumes: Vector mechanics
for engineers, statics, 4th ed., and Vector mechanics for engineers, dynamics,
4th ed. Ill. on back lining paper. Includes index. 1. Mechanics, Applied
2. Vector analysis 3. Statics 4. Dynamics I. Johnston, E. Russell (Elwood
Russell), 1925- II. T.
TA350.B3552 1984b      620.1/05 19      LC 84-3886      ISBN 0070044384

Malvern, Lawrence E., 1916-.                                    5.5733
Engineering mechanics / Lawrence E. Malvern. — Englewood Cliffs, N.J.:
Prentice-Hall, c1976. 2 v. (x, 665, lxx p.): ill.; 24 cm. Includes indexes.
1. Mechanics, Applied I. T.
TA350.M343      620.1      LC 75-31958      ISBN 013278663X

Massachusetts Institute of Technology. Dept. of Mechanical     • 5.5734
Engineering.
An introduction to the mechanics of solids [by] Robert R. Archer [and others].
— 2d ed. edited by Thomas J. Lardner. — New York: McGraw-Hill, [1972] xii,
628 p.: illus.; 23 cm. 1. Mechanics, Applied 2. Solids I. Archer, Robert R.
II. Lardner, Thomas J., ed. III. T.
TA350.M37 1972      620.1/05      LC 78-175183      ISBN 0070134367

Richards, T. H.                                                 5.5735
Energy methods in stress analysis: with an introduction to finite element
techniques / T. H. Richards. — Chichester: Horwood; New York: Halsted
Press, 1978 [c1976]. xxi, 410 p.: ill.; 24 cm. — (Ellis Horwood series in
engineering science.) 1. Mechanics, Applied 2. Finite element method I. T.
II. Series.
TA350.R55      620.1/04      LC 76-29647      ISBN 0470989602

## TA351–355 Applied Statics and Dynamics. Vibration

Hibbeler, R. C.                                                 5.5736
Engineering mechanics—statics / R.C. Hibbeler. — 3rd ed. — New York:
Macmillan; London: Collier Macmillan, c1983. xii, 449 p.: ill.; 24 cm.
Companion volume to Engineering mechanics—dynamics. These two works
are also published together as Engineering mechanics—statics and dynamics.
Includes index. 1. Statics I. T.
TA351.H5 1983      531/.2/02462 19      LC 82-6536      ISBN 0023543108

Kraut, George P.                                                5.5737
Statics and strength of materials / George P. Kraut. — Reston, Va.: Reston
Pub. Co., c1984. x, 678 p.: ill.; 25 cm. Includes index. 1. Statics 2. Strength of
materials I. T.
TA351.K7 1984      620.1/03 19      LC 83-17739      ISBN 0835971120

Meriam, J. L. (James L.)                                        5.5738
Statics [by] J. L. Meriam. — 2d ed., SI-version. — New York: Wiley, [1975] xiv,
381 p.: illus.; 26 cm. 1. Statics 2. Mechanics, Applied I. T.
TA351.M4 1975      620.1/03      LC 74-11459      ISBN 0471596043

Stevens, Karl K., 1939-.                                        5.5739
Statics and strength of materials / Karl K. Stevens. — 2nd ed. — Englewood
Cliffs, N.J.: Prentice-Hall, c1987. p. cm. Includes index. 1. Statics 2. Strength
of materials I. T.
TA351.S73 1987      620.1/12 19      LC 86-22498      ISBN 0138446717

Hibbeler, R. C.                                                 5.5740
Engineering mechanics—dynamics / R.C. Hibbeler. — 3rd ed. — New York:
Macmillan; London: Collier Macmillan, c1983. xii, 512 p.: ill.; 24 cm.
Companion volume to Engineering mechanics—statics. These two works are
also published together as Engineering mechanics—statics and dynamics.
Includes index. 1. Dynamics I. T.
TA352.H5 1983      531/.3/02462 19      LC 82-6541      ISBN 0023542500

Kane, Thomas R.                                                 5.5741
Dynamics, theory and applications / Thomas R. Kane, David A. Levinson. —
New York: McGraw-Hill, c1985. xv, 379 p.: ill.; 25 cm. (McGraw-Hill series in
mechanical engineering.) Includes index. 1. Dynamics I. Levinson, David A.
II. T. III. Series.
TA352.K36 1985      531/.11 19      LC 84-21802      ISBN 0070378460

Meriam, J. L. (James L.)                                        5.5742
Dynamics [by] J. L. Meriam. — 2d ed. — New York: Wiley, [1971] xiii, 480 p.:
ill.; 26 cm. 1. Dynamics I. T.
TA352.M45 1971      620.1/04      LC 71-142138      ISBN 0471596019

Blevins, Robert D.                                              5.5743
Flow–induced vibration / Robert D. Blevins. New York: Van Nostrand
Reinhold Co., c1977. xiii, 363 p.: ill.; 24 cm. 1. Vibration 2. Fluid dynamics
I. T.
TA355.B52      620.3      LC 76-56249      ISBN 0442208286

Den Hartog, J. P. (Jacob Pieter), 1901-.                        5.5744
Mechanical vibrations / J.P. Den Hartog. — New York: Dover Publications,
1985. xi, 436 p.; 22 cm. (Dover books on engineering.) Reprint. Originally
published: 4th ed. New York: McGraw-Hill, 1956. With a new preface.
Includes index. 1. Vibration 2. Mechanics, Applied I. T. II. Series.
TA355.D4 1985      620.3 19      LC 84-18806      ISBN 0486647854

Harris, Cyril M., 1917- ed.                                     5.5745
Shock and vibration handbook / edited by Cyril M. Harris and Charles E.
Crede. — 2d ed. — New York: McGraw-Hill, c1976. 1218 in various pagings:
ill.; 24 cm. — (McGraw-Hill handbooks) 1. Vibration — Handbooks, manuals,
etc. 2. Shock (Mechanics) — Handbooks, manuals, etc. I. Crede, Charles E.,
joint ed. II. T.
TA355.H35 1976      620.3      LC 76-55      ISBN 0070267995

Steidel, Robert F., 1926-.                                      5.5746
An introduction to mechanical vibrations / Robert F. Steidel, Jr. — 2d ed. —
New York: Wiley, c1979. xiv, 395 p.: ill.; 24 cm. Includes index. 1. Vibration
I. T.
TA355.S74 1979      620.3      LC 78-9589      ISBN 0471820830

Timoshenko, Stephen, 1878-1972.                                5.5747
Vibration problems in engineering / [by] S. Timoshenko, in collaboration with
D. H. Young. — 3d ed. — New York: Van Nostrand, 1955. — ix, 468 p.: ill.; 24
cm. 1. Vibration I. Young, Donovan Harold, 1904- II. T.
TA355.T55 1955      LC 54-10381

## TA357–358 Applied Fluid Mechanics

Blevins, Robert D.                                              5.5748
Applied fluid dynamics handbook / Robert D. Blevins. — New York, N.Y.:
Van Nostrand Reinhold Co., c1984. x, 558 p.: ill.; 29 cm. 1. Fluid dynamics —
Handbooks, manuals, etc. I. T.
TA357.B57 1984      620.1/064 19      LC 83-14517      ISBN 0442212968

Dynamics of polymeric liquids.                                 5.5749
New York: Wiley, c1977. 470 p.: ill. 1. Polymers and polymerization —
Mechanical properties 2. Polymers and polymerization I. Bird, R. Byron
(Robert Byron), 1924-
TA357.D95      620.1/06      LC 76-15408      ISBN 047107375X

Merzkirch, Wolfgang.                                           5.5750
Flow visualization / Wolfgang Merzkirch. — 2nd ed. — Orlando: Academic
Press, 1987. p. cm. Includes index. 1. Flow visualization I. T.
TA357.M47 1987      620.1/064 19      LC 86-22279      ISBN 0124913512

Reynolds, A. J.                                                5.5751
Turbulent flows in engineering [by] A. J. Reynolds. — London; New York:
John Wiley, [1974] xvii, 462 p.: illus.; 24 cm. 'A Wiley-Interscience
publication.' 1. Fluid mechanics 2. Turbulence I. T.
TA357.R49      620.1/064      LC 73-8464      ISBN 0471717827

United Kingdom Atomic Energy Authority. Research Group.        5.5752
Two–phase flow and heat transfer / edited by D. Butterworth and G. F. Hewitt.
— Oxford; New York: Oxford University Press, 1977. xxv, 514 p.: ill.; 25 cm. —
(Harwell series) 1. Fluid mechanics 2. Two-phase flow 3. Heat —
Transmission I. Butterworth, D. (David) II. Hewitt, G. F. (Geoffrey
Frederick) III. T.
TA357.U57 1977      621.4/022      LC 78-303117      ISBN 0198517157

**Welty, James R.**     5.5753
Fundamentals of momentum, heat, and mass transfer / James R. Welty, Charles E. Wicks, Robert E. Wilson. — 3rd ed. — New York: Wiley, c1984. xxii, 803 p.: ill.; 25 cm. Includes indexes. 1. Fluid mechanics 2. Heat — Transmission 3. Mass transfer I. Wicks, Charles E. II. Wilson, Robert E. (Robert Elliott) III. T.
TA357.W45 1984     532 19     *LC* 83-17065     *ISBN* 0471874973

**Glass, I. I., 1918-.**     5.5754
Shock waves & man, by I. I. Glass. — Toronto: University of Toronto Institute for Aerospace Studies, 1974. xii, 169 p.: illus.; 24 cm. 1. Shock waves I. T.
TA358.G55     620.1/04     *LC* 74-77074     *ISBN* 0969048807

## TA368 STANDARDS

**Glie, Rowen, comp.**     5.5755
Speaking of standards. — Boston: Cahners Books, [1972] xxv, 302 p.; 24 cm. 'Sponsored by the Metropolitan New York Section of the Standards Engineers Society.' 1. Standards, Engineering I. Standards Engineers Society. Metropolitan New York Section. II. T.
TA368.G56     620     *LC* 70-185561     *ISBN* 0843603070

## TA401–495 MATERIALS OF ENGINEERING AND CONSTRUCTION

### TA401–403.6 GENERAL WORKS

**American Society for Testing and Materials.**     5.5756
Annual book of ASTM standards. — Philadelphia, Pa.: ASTM. v.: ill.; 24 cm. Annual. Began with vol. for 1970. Description based on: 1982, pt. 7. Each vol. issued in parts. 1. Materials — Standards — United States — Periodicals. 2. Materials — Testing — Standards — United States — Periodicals. I. T.
TA401.A653     620.1/1/0218 19     *LC* 83-641658

**Ashby, M. F.**     5.5757
Engineering materials: an introduction to their properties and applications / by Michael F. Ashby and David R.H. Jones. — 1st ed. — Oxford; New York: Pergamon Press, 1980. x, 278 p.: ill.; 26 cm. — (International series on materials science and technology; v. 34) (Pergamon international library of science, technology, engineering, and social studies) Includes bibliographies and index. 1. Materials I. Jones, David Rayner Hunkin, 1945- joint author. II. T.
TA403.A69 1980     620.1/1     *LC* 80-40623     *ISBN* 0080261396

**Askeland, Donald R.**     5.5758
The science and engineering of materials / by Donald R. Askeland. — Monterey, CA: Brooks/Cole Engineering Division, c1984. xv, 748, 14 p.: ill.; 24 cm. Includes index. 1. Materials I. T.
TA403.A74 1984     *LC* 83-24060     *ISBN* 0534029574

**Brady, George Stuart, 1887-.**     • 5.5759
Materials handbook: an encyclopedia for managers, technical professionals, purchasing and production managers, technicians, supervisors, and foremen / George S. Brady, Henry R. Clauser. — 12th ed. — New York; Montreal: McGraw-Hill, 1986. ix, 1038 p. 1. Materials — Dictionaries. I. Clauser, Henry R. II. T.
TA403     TA403.B75.     620.1/1/03     *ISBN* 0070070717

**Budinski, Kenneth G.**     5.5760
Engineering materials: properties and selection / Kenneth G. Budinski. — 2nd ed. — Reston, Va.: Reston Pub. Co., c1983. viii, 486 p.: ill.; 25 cm. 1. Materials I. T.
TA403.B787 1983     620.1/12 19     *LC* 82-10148     *ISBN* 0835916928

**Guy, Albert G.**     5.5761
Essentials of materials science / A. G. Guy. — New York: McGraw-Hill, c1976. x, 468 p.: ill.; 24 cm. 1. Materials I. T.
TA403.G87     620.1/12     *LC* 75-17767     *ISBN* 007025351X

**Harris, Bryan, 1936-.**     5.5762
Structure and properties of engineering materials / B. Harris and A. R. Bunsell. — London; New York: Longman Group Ltd., 1977. xv, 347 p.: ill.; 23 cm. — (Introductory engineering series) 1. Materials I. Bunsell, A. R. joint author. II. T.
TA403.H373     620.1/12     *LC* 76-41771     *ISBN* 0582440009

**Hornbostel, Caleb.**     5.5763
Construction materials: types, uses, and applications / Caleb Hornbostel. — New York: Wiley, c1978. ix, 878 p.: ill.; 29 cm. 'A Wiley-Interscience publication.' Includes index. 1. Building materials I. T.
TA403.H59     624/.18     *LC* 78-6278     *ISBN* 0471409405

**Jastrzebski, Zbigniew D.**     5.5764
The nature and properties of engineering materials / Zbigniew D. Jastrzebski. — 3rd ed. — New York: Wiley, c1987. p. cm. 1. Materials I. T.
TA403.J35 1987     620.1/1 19     *LC* 86-24673     *ISBN* 0471818410

**Pollack, Herman W.**     5.5765
Materials science and metallurgy / Herman W. Pollack. — 3d ed. — Reston, Va.: Reston Pub. Co., c1981. xiii, 527 p.: ill.; 24 cm. 1. Materials 2. Metals I. T.
TA403.P569 1981     620.1/1     *LC* 80-36710     *ISBN* 0835942805

**Rosenthal, Daniel M.**     5.5766
Introduction to properties of materials [by] Daniel Rosenthal [and] Robert M. Asimow. 2d ed. New York, Van Nostrand Reinhold [1971] xxvi, 534 p. illus. 24 cm. (University series in basic engineering) 1. Materials I. Asimow, Robert M. II. T.
TA403.R573 1971     620.1/1     *LC* 79-152327

**Treatise on materials science and technology / edited by**     5.5767
**Herbert Herman.**
New York: Academic Press, 1972-. 26 v.: ill.; 24 cm. Vols. 3, 6-7, 9- < 26 > have also special titles. 1. Materials I. Herman, Herbert. ed.
TA403.T74     620.1/1 19     *LC* 77-182672     *ISBN* 0123418011

**Van Vlack, Lawrence H.**     5.5768
Elements of materials science and engineering / Lawrence H. Van Vlack. — 5th ed. — Reading, Mass.: Addison-Wesley Pub. Co., c1984. xix, 633 p.: ill.; 24 cm. (Addison-Wesley series in metallurgy and materials engineering.) Includes index. 1. Materials 2. Solids I. T. II. Series.
TA403.V35 1984     620.1/1 19     *LC* 83-25648     *ISBN* 0201080869

**Van Vlack, Lawrence H.**     • 5.5769
Materials science for engineers [by] Lawrence H. Van Vlack. — Reading, Mass.: Addison-Wesley Pub. Co., [1970] xii, 545 p.: illus.; 25 cm. — (Addison-Wesley series in metallurgy and materials) 1. Materials I. T.
TA403.V36 1970     620.1/1     *LC* 74-91151

**CRC handbook of materials science / editor, Charles T. Lynch.**     5.5770
Cleveland: CRC Press, [1974]- < 1980 >. v. < 1-4 >: ill.; 26 cm. Part of illustrative matter in pocket. 1. Materials — Handbooks, manuals, etc. I. Lynch, Charles T. II. Summitt, Robert, 1935- III. Sliker, Alan, 1936- IV. Chemical Rubber Company. V. Title: Handbook of materials science.
TA403.4.L94     620.1/12     *LC* 73-90240     0878192344

**An Introduction to computer simulation in applied science.**     5.5771
**Edited by Farid F. Abraham and William A. Tiller.**
New York: Plenum Press, 1972. xiv, 219 p.: illus.; 24 cm. 'This set of lectures is the outgrowth of a ... course in the Department of Materials Science at Stanford University.' 1. Materials — Mathematical models. 2. Materials — Data processing 3. Quantum chemistry — Data processing 4. Numerical weather forecasting I. Abraham, Farid F., ed. II. Tiller, William A., ed.
TA403.6.I57     501/.84     *LC* 72-83047     *ISBN* 0306305798

### TA405–409 STRENGTH OF MATERIALS

**Beer, Ferdinand Pierre, 1915-.**     5.5772
Mechanics of materials / Ferdinand P. Beer, E. Russell Johnston, Jr. — New York: McGraw-Hill, c1981. xv, 616 p.: ill.; 25 cm. Includes index. 1. Strength of materials I. Johnston, E. Russell (Elwood Russell), 1925- joint author. II. T.
TA405.B39     620.1/12 19     *LC* 80-23582     *ISBN* 0070042845

**Den Hartog, J. P. (Jacob Pieter), 1901-.**     • 5.5773
Mechanics. New York, Dover Publications [1961, c1948] 462 p. illus. 21 cm. 'An unabridged and corrected republication of the first edition published ... in 1948.' 1. Mechanics I. T.
TA405.D39 1961     531     *LC* 61-1958

**Dieter, George Ellwood.**     5.5774
Mechanical metallurgy / George E. Dieter. — 3rd ed. — New York: McGraw-Hill, c1986. xxiii, 751 p.: ill.; 24 cm. — (McGraw-Hill series in materials science and engineering) 1. Strength of materials 2. Physical metallurgy I. T. II. Series.
TA405.D53 1986     620.1/63 19     *LC* 85-18229     *ISBN* 0070168938

**Felbeck, David K.**     5.5775
Strength and fracture of engineering solids / David K. Felbeck, Anthony G. Atkins. — Englewood Cliffs, NJ: Prentice-Hall, c1984. xiv, 542 p.: ill.; 24 cm.

1. Strength of materials 2. Fracture mechanics I. Atkins, Anthony G., 1939-
II. T.
TA405.F418 1984     620.1/12 19     *LC* 83-9488     *ISBN* 0138517096

**Gere, James M.**            **5.5776**
Mechanics of materials / James M. Gere, Stephen P. Timoshenko. — 2nd ed. —
Monterey, Calif.: Brooks/Cole Engineering Division, c1984. xvi, 762 p.: col.
ill.; 25 cm. Authors' names in reverse order on 1st ed. Includes indexes.
1. Strength of materials I. Timoshenko, Stephen, 1878-1972. II. T.
TA405.G44 1984     620.1/1 19     *LC* 83-24308     *ISBN* 0534030998

**Mechanics of materials / Archie Higdon ... [et al.].**     **5.5777**
4th ed. — New York: Wiley, c1985. xvii, 744 p.: ill.; 25 cm. Includes index.
1. Strength of materials I. Higdon, Archie, 1905-
TA405.M515 1985     620.1/12 19     *LC* 84-7583     *ISBN* 0471890448

**Popov, E. P. (Egor Paul), 1913-.**        **• 5.5778**
Introduction to mechanics of solids [by] Egor P. Popov. Englewood Cliffs, N.J.,
Prentice-Hall [1968] xix, 571 p. illus. 24 cm. (Civil engineering and engineering
mechanics series) Based on the author's Mechanics of materials. 1. Strength of
materials I. T. II. Title: Mechanics of solids.
TA405.P678     620.1/12     *LC* 68-10135

**Sandor, Bela Imre.**            **5.5779**
Strength of materials / Bela I. Sandor. — Englewood Cliffs, N.J.: Prentice Hall,
c1978. xiv, 432 p.: ill.; 24 cm. Includes index. 1. Strength of materials I. T.
TA405.S28     620.1/12     *LC* 77-15506     *ISBN* 0138524181

**Timoshenko, Stephen.**          **5.5780**
Elements of strength of materials / [by] S. Timoshenko [and] D.H. Young. —
5th ed. New York: Van Nostrand [1968] x, 377 p.: ill.; 24 cm. 1. Strength of
materials I. Young, Donovan Harold, 1904- , joint author. II. Young,
Donovan Harold, joint author. III. T.
TA405. T52 1968     620.112     *LC* 68-1158

**Ugural, A. C.**             **5.5781**
Advanced strength and applied elasticity / A. C. Ugural, S. K. Fenster. — New
York: American Elsevier Pub. Co., [1975] xii, 433 p.: ill.; 24 cm. 1. Strength of
materials 2. Elasticity I. Fenster, Saul K., 1933- joint author. II. T.
TA405.U42     620.1/12     *LC* 74-27388     *ISBN* 0444001603

**Dally, James William.**           **5.5782**
Experimental stress analysis / [by] James W. Dally, William F. Riley. — 2nd
ed. — New York; London [etc.]: McGraw-Hill, 1978. xix, 571 p.: ill.; 25 cm.
1. Strains and stresses I. Riley, William Franklin. II. T.
TA407.D32 1978     620.1/123     *LC* 76-393     *ISBN* 0070152047

**Reid, C. N.**               **5.5783**
Deformation geometry for materials scientists, by C. N. Reid. [1st ed.] Oxford,
New York, Pergamon Press [1973] viii, 211 p. illus. 21 cm. (International series
on materials science and technology, v. 11) 1. Materials 2. Deformations
(Mechanics) I. T.
TA407.R413 1973     620.1/123     *LC* 73-4716     *ISBN* 0080172377
*ISBN* 008017745X

**Sandor, Bela Imre.**            **5.5784**
Fundamentals of cyclic stress and strain [by] Bela I. Sandor. — [Madison]:
University of Wisconsin Press, [1972] xvi, 167 p.: illus.; 24 cm. 1. Materials —
Fatigue 2. Strains and stresses I. T. II. Title: Cyclic stress and strain.
TA407.S23     620.1/123     *LC* 70-176415     *ISBN* 0299061000

**Barsom, John M., 1938-.**        **5.5785**
Fracture and fatigue control in structures: applications of fracture mechanics /
John M. Barsom, Stanley T. Rolfe. — 2nd ed. — Englewood Cliffs, N.J.:
Prentice-Hall, c1987. p. cm. (Prentice-Hall international series in civil
engineering and engineering mechanics.) Rev. ed. of: Fracture and fatigue
control in structures / Stanley T. Rolfe, John M. Barsom. 1977. 1. Fracture
mechanics 2. Metals — Fatigue I. Rolfe, S. T. (Stanley Theodore), 1934-
II. Rolfe, S. T. (Stanley Theodore), 1934- Fracture and fatigue control in
structures. III. T. IV. Series.
TA409.B37 1987     620.1/126 19     *LC* 86-16870     *ISBN* 0133298639

**Broek, David.**             **5.5786**
Elementary engineering fracture mechanics / David Broek. — 3rd rev. ed. —
The Hague; Boston: Martinus Nijhoff; Hingham, Mass.: Distributed by Kluwer
Boston, 1984. xiv, 469 p.: ill.; 23 cm. 1. Fracture mechanics I. T.
TA409.B76 1982     620.1/126 19     *LC* 82-45135     *ISBN* 9024725801

**Knott, J. F. (John Frederick)**      **5.5787**
Fundamentals of fracture mechanics [by] J. F. Knott. New York, Wiley [1973]
273 p. illus. 24 cm. 'A Halsted Press book.' 1. Fracture mechanics 2. Metals —
Fracture I. T.
TA409.K66     620.1/126     *LC* 73-15844     *ISBN* 0470495650

## TA417–418.9 Properties of Materials

**Silk, M. G. (Maurice G.)**          **5.5788**
Ultrasonic transducers for nondestructive testing / M.G. Silk. — Bristol: A.
Hilger, c1984. xiv, 162 p.: ill.; 24 cm. Includes indexes. 1. Ultrasonic testing
I. T.
TA417.4.S55 1984     620.1/1274 19     *LC* 84-235088     *ISBN*
0852744366

**Hertzberg, Richard W., 1937-.**      **5.5789**
Deformation and fracture mechanics of engineering materials / Richard W.
Hertzberg. — 2nd ed. — New York: Wiley, c1983. xviii, 697 p.: ill.; 25 cm.
1. Deformations (Mechanics) 2. Fracture mechanics I. T.
TA417.6.H46 1983     620.1/123 19     *LC* 83-5881     *ISBN* 0471086096

**Johnson, W. (William), 1922-.**      **5.5790**
Engineering plasticity / W. Johnson and P.B. Mellor. — Chichester, West
Sussex, England: E. Horwood; New York: Halsted Press, 1983. xviii, 646 p., [2]
folded leaves of plates: ill.; 23 cm. — (Ellis Horwood series in engineering
science.) 1. Plasticity 2. Metal-work I. Mellor, P. B. (Peter Bassindale), 1929-
II. T. III. Series.
TA418.14.J633 1983     620.1/633 19     *LC* 83-18446     *ISBN*
047020012X

**Wigley, D. A.**             **5.5791**
Mechanical properties of materials at low temperatures [by] D. A. Wigley. —
New York: Plenum Press, 1971. xiv, 325 p.: illus.; 24 cm. — (International
cryogenics monograph series.) 1. Materials at low temperatures — Congresses.
I. T. II. Series.
TA418.24.W54     620.1/1216     *LC* 70-157929     *ISBN* 0306305143

**Corrosion and corrosion protection handbook / edited by Philip**     **5.5792**
**A. Schweitzer.**
New York: M. Dekker, c1983. xi, 521 p.: ill.; 24 cm. — (Mechanical
engineering (Marcel Dekker, Inc.) 19) 1. Corrosion and anti-corrosives —
Handbooks, manuals, etc. I. Schweitzer, Philip A. II. Series.
TA418.74.C5928 1983     620.1/1223 19     *LC* 83-1885     *ISBN*
0824717058

**Handbook of composites / edited by George Lubin.**     **5.5793**
New York: Van Nostrand Reinhold, c1982. x, 786 p.: ill.; 27 cm. Rev. ed. of:
Handbook of fiberglass and advanced plastics composites. 1969. 1. Composite
materials — Handbooks, manuals, etc. 2. Fibrous composites — Handbooks,
manuals, etc. I. Lubin, George. II. Handbook of fiberglass and advanced
plastics composites.
TA418.9.C6 H33 1982     620.1/18 19     *LC* 81-10341     *ISBN*
0442248970

**Hull, Derek.**             **5.5794**
An introduction to composite materials / Derek Hull. — Cambridge; New
York: Cambridge University Press, 1981. x, 246 p.: ill.; 23 cm. — (Cambridge
solid state science series.) 1. Composite materials I. T. II. Series.
TA418.9.C6 H85 1981     620.1/18 19     *LC* 80-42039     *ISBN*
0521239915

**Jones, Robert M., 1939-.**         **5.5795**
Mechanics of composite materials [by] Robert M. Jones. — New York:
McGraw-Hill, [1975] xiv, 355 p.: ill.; 24 cm. 1. Composite materials
2. Laminated materials I. T.
TA418.9.C6 J59     620.1/1     *LC* 74-14576     *ISBN* 0070327904

## TA419–495 Special Materials

### TA419–455 Wood. Ceramics. Concrete. Glass. Plastics

**Spencer, Albert G.**           **5.5796**
Wood and wood products / Albert G. Spencer, Jack A. Luy. — Columbus,
Ohio: Merrill, [1975] x, 246 p.: ill.; 29 cm. (The Merrill series in career
programs) 1. Wood 2. Forest products I. Luy, Jack A., joint author. II. T.
TA419.S73     674     *LC* 74-75406     *ISBN* 0675087988

**Van Vlack, Lawrence H.**        **• 5.5797**
Physical ceramics for engineers / Lawrence H. Van Vlack. — Reading, Mass.:
Addison-Wesley Pub. Co., [1964]. 342 p.: ill. — (Addison-Wesley series in
metallurgy and materials) Addison-Wesley series in ceramics. 1. Ceramic
materials I. T.
TA430.V3 1964     *LC* 64-11886

**Handbook of structural concrete** / edited by F.K. Kong ... [et    **5.5798**
al.].
New York: McGraw-Hill, 1983. 1 v. (various pagings); 24 cm. 1. Concrete —
Handbooks, manuals, etc. I. Kong, F. K.
TA439.H275 1983     620.1/36 19     *LC* 83-802     *ISBN* 0070115737

**Mindess, Sidney.**                       **5.5799**
Concrete / Sidney Mindess, J. Francis Young. — Englewood Cliffs, N.J.:
Prentice-Hall, c1981. xvi, 671 p.: ill.; 24 cm. — (Civil engineering and
engineering mechanics series) 1. Concrete I. Young, J. Francis. joint author.
II. T.
TA439.M49     624.1/834 19     *LC* 80-17389     *ISBN* 0131671065

**Neville, Adam M.**                     **5.5800**
Properties of concrete / A. M. Neville. — 3d ed. — London; Marshfield, Mass.:
Pitman Pub., 1981. xii, 779 p.: ill.; 25 cm. 1. Concrete I. T.
TA439.N48 1981     620.1/36 19     *LC* 80-25198     *ISBN* 0273016415

**Popovics, Sandor, 1921-.**              **5.5801**
Fundamentals of Portland cement concrete—a quantitative approach / Sandor
Popovics. — New York: Wiley, c1982-. v. < 1 > : ill.; 24 cm. 'A Wiley-
Interscience publication.' 1. Concrete 2. Portland cement I. T.
TA439.P77 1982     620.1/36 19     *LC* 82-2796     *ISBN* 0471862177

**Holloway, Dennis Glyn.**              **5.5802**
The physical properties of glass [by] D. G. Holloway. New York, Springer-
Verlag, 1973. xii, 220 p. illus. 22 cm. Includes index. 1. Glass I. T.
TA450.H65     620.1/44     *LC* 74-165652     *ISBN* 0851093205

**MacDermott, Charles P., 1920-.**        **5.5803**
Selecting thermoplastics for engineering applications / Charles P.
MacDermott. — New York: M. Dekker, c1984. x, 171 p.: ill.; 24 cm. —
(Plastics engineering; 5) Includes index. 1. Thermoplastics I. T.
TA455.P5 M23 1984     620.1/923 19     *LC* 84-7048     *ISBN*
0824770994

**Physical properties of polymers** / James E. Mark ... [et al.].    **5.5804**
Washington, D.C.: American Chemical Society, 1984. ix, 246 p.: ill.; 26 cm.
1. Polymers and polymerization 2. Chemistry, Physical and theoretical
I. Mark, James E., 1934- II. American Chemical Society.
TA455.P58 P474 1984     620.1/92 19     *LC* 84-10958     *ISBN*
0841208514

**Williams, J. G. (James Gordon), 1938-.**     **5.5805**
Fracture mechanics of polymers / J.G. Williams. — Chichester: E. Horwood;
New York: Halsted Press, 1984. 302 p.: ill.; 24 cm. (Ellis Horwood series in
engineering science.) 1. Polymers and polymerization — Fracture 2. Fracture
mechanics I. T. II. Series.
TA455.P58 W538 1984     620.1/920426 19     *LC* 83-26593     *ISBN*
0853126852

**Williams, J. G. (James Gordon), 1938-.**     **5.5806**
Stress analysis of polymers / J. G. Williams. — 2d ed. — Chichester: E.
Horwood; New York: Halsted Press, 1980. 360 p.: ill.; 24 cm. — (Ellis
Horwood series in engineering science.) 1. Polymers and polymerization —
Mechanical properties 2. Strains and stresses I. T. II. Series.
TA455.P58 W54 1980     620.1/920423 19     *LC* 80-40144

## TA459–480 METALS. ALLOYS

**Metals handbook** / edited by Howard E. Boyer, Timothy L.    **5.5807**
**Gall.**
9th ed. — Metals Park, Ohio: American Society for Metals, [1984] c1985. 1 v.
(various pagings): ill.; 29 cm. 1. Metals — Handbooks, manuals, etc. I. Boyer,
Howard E. II. Gall, Timothy L. III. American Society for Metals.
TA459.M43 1985     669 19     *LC* 84-71465     *ISBN* 087170188X

**Seitz, Frederick, 1911-.**            • **5.5808**
The physics of metals / by Frederick Seitz ... 1st ed. New York; London:
McGraw-Hill Book Company, inc., 1943. xiii, 330 p.: diagrs.; 21 cm.
(Metallurgy and metallurgical engineering series) 'Periodic chart of the
elements' on end lining-papers. 1. Metals I. T.
TA459.S47     *LC* 43-12641

**Colangelo, Vito J.**                 **5.5809**
Analysis of metallurgical failures / V.J. Colangelo, F.A. Heiser. — 2nd ed. —
New York: Wiley, c1987. 361 p.: ill. 'A Wiley-Interscience publication.'
Includes index. 1. Metals — Fatigue 2. Metals — Fracture 3. Metals —
Testing I. Heiser, F. A. (Francis A.) II. T.
TA460.C62 1987     620.1/63 19     *LC* 86-22406     *ISBN* 0471891681

**Fuchs, H. O. (Henry Otten), 1907-.**       **5.5810**
Metal fatigue in engineering / H. O. Fuchs, R. I. Stephens. — New York:
Wiley, c1980. xii, 318 p.: ill.; 25 cm. 'A Wiley-Interscience publication.'
1. Metals — Fatigue I. Stephens, R. I. (Ralph Ivan) joint author. II. T.
TA460.F78     620.1/63     *LC* 80-294     *ISBN* 0471052647

**Honeycombe, R. W. K. (Robert William Kerr)**    **5.5811**
The plastic deformation of metals / R.W.K. Honeycombe. — 2nd ed. —
London; Baltimore, Md., U.S.A.: E. Arnold, 1984. xiii, 483 p.: ill.; 23 cm.
Includes bibliographical references and indexes. 1. Metals — Plastic properties
I. T.
TA460.H57 1984     620.1/633 19     *LC* 85-124042     *ISBN* 0713134682

**Kocańda, Stanisław.**               **5.5812**
[Zmeczeniowe niszczenie metali. English] Fatigue failure of metals / S.
Kocańda. — Alphen aan den Rijn: Sijthoff & Noordhoff International
Publishers, c1978. xii, 367 p.: ill.; 25 cm. — (Series on fatigue and fracture. v. 1)
Rev. English version of Zmeczeniowe niszczenie metali. Includes index.
1. Metals — Fatigue 2. Metals — Fracture I. T. II. Series.
TA460.K5313     620.1/6/3     *LC* 78-378428     *ISBN* 9028600256

**Meyers, Marc A.**                 **5.5813**
Mechanical metallurgy: principles and applications / Marc André Meyers,
Krishan Kumar Chawla. — Englewood Cliffs, N.J.: Prentice-Hall, c1984. xxi,
761 p.: ill.; 24 cm. 1. Metals — Mechanical properties 2. Physical metallurgy
I. Chawla, Krishan Kumar, 1942- II. T.
TA460.M466 1984     620.1/6 19     *LC* 83-552     *ISBN* 0135698634

**Unified numbering system for metals and alloys: and cross index**    **5.5814**
**of chemically–similar specifications** / a joint activity of the
**Society of Automotive Engineers, inc., American Society for**
**Testing and Materials.**
2d ed. — Warrendale, Pa.: SAE, 1977. x, 275 p.; 28 cm. 'SAE HS108a, ASTM
DS-56A.' 1. Metals — Notation 2. Alloys — Notation. I. Society of
Automotive Engineers. II. American Society for Testing and Materials.
TA461.U58 1977     669/.0012 19     *LC* 77-89064

**Evans, Ulick Richardson.**            **5.5815**
An introduction to metallic corrosion / Ulick R. Evans. — 3d ed. — London:
E. Arnold; Metals Park, Ohio: American Society for Metals, 1982, c1981.
302 p.: ill.; 24 cm. 1. Corrosion and anti-corrosives I. T.
TA462.E83 1982     620.1/623 19     *LC* 81-17651     *ISBN* 0871701324

**Scully, J. C.**                    **5.5816**
The fundamentals of corrosion / J. C. Scully. — 2d ed. — Oxford; New York:
Pergamon Press, 1975. xi, 234 p.: ill.; 21 cm. (International series of
monographs on materials science and technology; v. 17) Includes index.
1. Corrosion and anti-corrosives I. T.
TA462.S39 1975     620.1/1223     *LC* 74-28581     *ISBN* 0080180817

**Angus, H. T. (Harold T.)**           **5.5817**
Cast iron: physical and engineering properties / H. T. Angus. — 2d ed. —
London; Boston: Butterworths, 1976. 542 p.: ill.; 24 cm. Published in 1960
under title: Physical and engineering properties of cast iron. 1. Cast-iron I. T.
TA474.A6 1976     620.1/7     *LC* 75-31960     *ISBN* 0408706880

**Copper in iron and steel** / [edited by] Iain Le May, L.    **5.5818**
**McDonald Schetky.**
New York: Wiley, c1982. xix, 423 p.: ill.; 24 cm. 'A Wiley-Interscience
publication.' 1. Copper steel 2. Iron-copper alloys I. Le May, Iain.
II. Schetky, L. McDonald.
TA479.C7 C594 1982     669/.961 19     *LC* 82-17615     *ISBN*
0471059137

**Superalloys** / compiled by consulting editor, Matthew J.    **5.5819**
**Donachie, Jr.**
Metals Park, Ohio: American Society for Metals, c1984. 412 p.: ill.; 29 cm. —
(Source book / American Society for Metals) Includes index. 1. Chromium-
cobalt-nickel-molybdenum alloys — Addresses, essays, lectures. I. Donachie,
Matthew J. II. American Society for Metals.
TA480.C5 S87 1984     620.1/88 19     *LC* 83-71812     *ISBN*
0871701707

## TA501–625 SURVEYING

**Brinker, Russell C. (Russell Charles), 1908-.**     **5.5820**
Elementary surveying / Russell C. Brinker, Paul R. Wolf. — 7th ed. — New
York: Harper & Row, c1984. xvi, 608 p.: ill. (some col.); 24 cm. 1. Surveying
I. Wolf, Paul R. II. T.
TA545.B86 1984     526.9 19     *LC* 83-18462     *ISBN* 0060409827

**Herubin, Charles A., 1931-.**    5.5821
Principles of surveying / Charles A. Herubin. — 3rd ed. — Reston, Va.: Reston Pub. Co., c1982. x, 342 p.: ill.; 24 cm. Includes index. 1. Surveying I. T.
TA545.H47 1982    526.9 19    *LC* 82-283    *ISBN* 0835956164

**Kavanagh, Barry F.**    5.5822
Surveying: principles and applications / Barry F. Kavanagh, S.J. Glenn Bird. — Reston, Va.: Reston Pub. Co., c1984. xi, 900 p.: ill.; 25 cm. Includes index. 1. Surveying I. Bird, S. J. Glenn. II. T.
TA545.K37 1984    526.9 19    *LC* 84-2115    *ISBN* 0835974057

**McCormac, Jack C.**    5.5823
Surveying / Jack C. McCormac. — Englewood Cliffs, N.J.: Prentice-Hall, c1983. xix, 522 p.: ill., maps; 24 cm. 1. Surveying I. T.
TA545.M33 1983    526.9 19    *LC* 82-3765    *ISBN* 013878843X

**Schmidt, Milton O. (Milton Otto), 1910-.**    5.5824
Fundamentals of surveying / Milton O. Schmidt, Kam W. Wong. — 3rd ed. — Boston: PWS Engineering, 1985. xiii, 683 p.: ill.; 25 cm. 1. Surveying I. Wong, Kam W., 1940- II. T.
TA545.S257 1985    526.9 19    *LC* 84-23687    *ISBN* 0534041612

**Schofield, W. (Wilfred)**    5.5825
Engineering surveying: theory and examination problems for students / W. Schofield. — 2d ed. — London; Boston: Newnes-Butterworths, 1978-1984. 2 v.: ill.; 22 cm. Includes index. 1. Surveying I. T.
TA545.S263 1978    526.9/02/462    *LC* 78-318335

**Whyte, W. S. (Walter S.)**    5.5826
Basic metric surveying / W.S. Whyte and R.E. Paul. — 3rd ed. — London; Boston: Butterworths, 1985. ix, 355 p.: ill.; 24 cm. Includes index. 1. Surveying 2. Metric system I. Paul, R. E. II. T.
TA545.W69 1985    526.9/024624 19    *LC* 85-3819    *ISBN* 0408013540

**Mikhail, Edward M.**    5.5827
Analysis and adjustment of survey measurements / Edward M. Mikhail, Gordon Gracie. — New York: Van Nostrand Reinhold Co., c1981. xii, 340 p.; 24 cm. Includes index. 1. Surveying 2. Mensuration I. Gracie, Gordon, 1930- joint author. II. T.
TA549.M537    526.9    *LC* 79-26047    *ISBN* 0442253699

**Milne, P. H.**    5.5828
BASIC programs for land surveying / P.H. Milne. — London; New York: E. & F.N. Spon, 1984. xiii, 442 p.: ill.; 23 cm. Includes index. 1. Surveying — Computer programs. 2. BASIC (Computer program language) 3. Apple II (Computer) — Programming 4. Apple II (Computer) — Programming I. T. II. Title: B.A.S.I.C. programs for land surveying.
TA549.M5374 1984    526.9/028/5425 19    *LC* 84-1296    *ISBN* 0419130004

**American Society of Photogrammetry.**    5.5829
Manual of photogrammetry / editor–in–chief, Chester C. Slama, associate editors, Charles Theurer, Soren W. Henriksen. — 4th ed. — Falls Church, Va.: American Society of Photogrammetry, c1980. xv, 1056 p.: ill.; 26 cm. 1. Photographic surveying — Handbooks, manuals, etc. 2. Photogrammetry — Handbooks, manuals, etc. I. Slama, Chester C. II. Theurer, Charles. III. Henriksen, Soren W. IV. T.
TA593.25.A48 1980    526.9/82 19    *LC* 80-21514    *ISBN* 0937294012

**Laurila, Simo H. (Simo Heikki), 1920-.**    5.5830
Electronic surveying and navigation / Simo H. Laurila. — New York: Wiley, c1976. xiv, 545 p.: ill.; 24 cm. 'A Wiley-Interscience publication.' 1. Electronics in surveying 2. Electronics in navigation 3. Geodesy I. T.
TA595.L38    526/.028    *LC* 75-41461    *ISBN* 0471518654

## TA630–901 Structural Engineering: General

## TA633–636 General Works

**White, Richard N.**    5.5831
Structural engineering [by] Richard N. White, Peter Gergely [and] Robert G. Sexsmith. — New York: Wiley, [1972-. v.    : illus.; 24 cm. 1. Structural engineering I. Gergely, Peter. joint author. II. Sexsmith, Robert G. joint author. III. T.
TA633.W47    624/.17    *LC* 75-174772    *ISBN* 0471940682

**Gaylord, Edwin Henry.**    5.5832
Structural engineering handbook / edited by Edwin H. Gaylord, Jr., Charles N. Gaylord. — 2d ed. — New York: McGraw-Hill, c1979. ca. 600 p. in various pagings: ill.; 24 cm. 1. Structural engineering — Handbooks, manuals, etc. I. Gaylord, Charles N. II. T.
TA635.G3 1979    624/.1    *LC* 78-25705

**Augusti, Giuliano.**    5.5833
Probabilistic methods in structural engineering / Giuliano Augusti, Alesandro Baratta, Fabio Casciati. — London; New York: Chapman and Hall, 1984. xxvi, 556 p.: ill.; 24 cm. Includes index. 1. Structural engineering — Statistical methods. 2. Engineering mathematics 3. Probabilities I. Baratta, Alessandro. II. Casciati, Fabio. III. T.
TA636.A93 1984    624.1/7/015192 19    *LC* 83-7589    *ISBN* 0412222302

**Billington, David P.**    5.5834
The tower and the bridge: the new art of structural engineering / David P. Billington. — New York: Basic Books, c1983. xx, 306 p.: ill.; 25 cm. 1. Structural engineering 2. Towers — Design and construction. 3. Bridges — Design I. T.
TA636.B54 1983    624/.2 19    *LC* 83-70758    *ISBN* 0465086772

## TA640–646 Computational and Matrix Methods. Structural Analysis

**Ural, Oktay.**    5.5835
Finite element method: basic concepts and applications. — New York: Intext Educational Publishers, [1973] xiii, 272 p.: illus.; 25 cm. — (The Intext series in civil engineering) 1. Structures, Theory of 2. Finite element method 3. Matrices I. T.
TA640.2.U7    624/.17    *LC* 73-6838    *ISBN* 0700224289

**Zienkiewicz, O. C.**    5.5836
The finite element method / O. C. Zienkiewicz. — 3d expanded and rev. ed. — London; New York: McGraw-Hill, c1977. xv, 787 p.: ill.; 24 cm. First ed. (1967) published under title: The finite element method in structural and continuum mechanics; 2d ed. (1971) published under title: The finite element method in engineering science. 1. Structures, Theory of 2. Continuum mechanics 3. Finite element method I. T.
TA640.2.Z5 1977    620/.001/515353    *LC* 77-30152    *ISBN* 0070840725

**McGuire, William, 1920-.**    5.5837
Matrix structural analysis / William McGuire and Richard H. Gallagher. — New York: Wiley, c1979. xix, 460 p.: ill.; 25 cm. 1. Structures, Theory of — Matrix methods I. Gallagher, Richard H. joint author. II. T.
TA642.M25    624/.171/01512943    *LC* 78-8471    *ISBN* 0471030597

**Gerstle, Kurt H.**    5.5838
Basic structural analysis [by] Kurt H. Gerstle. — Englewood Cliffs, N.J.: Prentice-Hall, [1974] xiii, 498 p.: illus.; 23 cm. — (Civil engineering and engineering mechanics series) 1. Structures, Theory of I. T.
TA645.G44    624/.171    *LC* 73-8912    *ISBN* 0130693936

**Gordon, J. E. (James Edward), 1913-.**    5.5839
Structures: or, Why things don't fall down / J. E. Gordon. — New York: Plenum Press, c1978. 395 p., [12] leaves of plates: ill.; 23 cm. Includes index. 1. Structures, Theory of 2. Structural engineering I. T.
TA645.G65 1978b    624/.17    *LC* 78-19068    *ISBN* 0306400251

**Hibbeler, R. C.**    5.5840
Structural analysis / Russell C. Hibbeler. — New York: Macmillan; London: Collier Macmillan, c1985. xi, 527 p.: ill.; 24 cm. 1. Structures, Theory of I. T.
TA645.H47 1985    624.1/71 19    *LC* 84-12247    *ISBN* 0023544600

**Norris, Charles Head, 1910-.**    5.5841
Elementary structural analysis / Charles Head Norris, John Benson Wilbur, Senol Utku. — 3d ed. — New York: McGraw-Hill, c1976. xxiii, 673 p.: ill.; 24 cm. Previous editions are entered under J. B. Wilbur. 1. Structures, Theory of I. Wilbur, John Benson, 1905- joint author. II. Utku, Senol, joint author. III. T. IV. Title: Structural analysis.
TA645.N58 1976    624/.171    *LC* 76-2407    *ISBN* 0070472564

**Oden, J. Tinsley (John Tinsley), 1936-.**    5.5842
Mechanics of elastic structures / J. T. Oden and E. A. Ripperger. — 2d ed. — Washington: Hemisphere Pub. Corp.; New York: McGraw-Hill, c1981. xv, 460 p.: ill.; 24 cm. Includes index. 1. Structures, Theory of I. Ripperger, E. A. joint author. II. T.
TA645.O3 1981    624/.17    *LC* 79-25261    *ISBN* 0070475075

**Tauchert, Theodore R., 1935-.**    5.5843
Energy principles in structural mechanics / [by] Theodore R. Tauchert. New York: McGraw-Hill [1974] xii, 380 p.: ill.; 23 cm. 1. Structures, Theory of I. T.
TA645.T37    624.17    LC 73-17205    ISBN 0070629250

**Timoshenko, Stephen, 1878-1972.**    5.5844
Theory of structures / S. P. Timoshenko, D. H. Young. — 2d ed. — New York; Toronto: McGraw-Hill, c1965. x, 629 p.: ill. 1. Structures, Theory of I. Young, Donovan Harold, 1904- II. T.
TA645.T52 1965    LC 64-7941

**Venkatraman, B.**    5.5845
Structural mechanics with introductions to elasticity and plasticity [by] B. Venkatraman [and] Sharad A. Patel. New York, McGraw-Hill [1970] xiii, 648 p. illus. 23 cm. 1. Structures, Theory of 2. Elasticity 3. Plasticity I. Patel, Sharad A. joint author. II. T.
TA645.V4    624/.17    LC 71-81613

**Weaver, William, 1929-.**    5.5846
Matrix analysis of framed structures / William Weaver, Jr., James M. Gere. — 2nd ed. — New York: D. Van Nostrand Co., c1980. xii, 492 p.: ill.; 24 cm. Rev. ed. of: Analysis of framed structures / James M. Gere and William Weaver, Jr. 1965. Includes index. 1. Structures, Theory of 2. Matrices I. Gere, James M. II. Gere, James M. Analysis of framed structures. III. T.
TA645.W36 1980    624.1/773 19    LC 79-65701    ISBN 0442257732

**West, Harry H., 1936-.**    5.5847
Analysis of structures: an integration of classical and modern methods / Harry H. West. — New York: Wiley, 1980. xix, 689 p.: ill.; 24 cm. 1. Structures, Theory of I. T.
TA645.W43    624/.17    LC 78-27290    ISBN 0471020362

**Yang, T. Y.**    5.5848
Finite element structural analysis / T.Y. Yang. — Englewood Cliffs, N.J.: Prentice-Hall, c1986. xiv, 543 p.: ill.; 24 cm. (Prentice-Hall international series in civil engineering and engineering mechanics.) 1. Structures, Theory of 2. Finite element method I. T. II. Series.
TA645.Y36 1986    624.1/7 19    LC 85-12278    ISBN 0133171167

**Cheung, Y. K.**    5.5849
Finite strip method in structural analysis / by Y. K. Cheung. — 1st ed. — Oxford; New York: Pergamon Press, 1976. x, 232 p.: ill.; 22 cm. — (Structures and solid body mechanics series) (Pergamon international library of science, technology, engineering and social studies.) 1. Structures, Theory of I. T.
TA646.C48 1976    624/.171    LC 75-19483    ISBN 0080183085

**Cook, Robert Davis.**    5.5850
Concepts and applications of finite element analysis / Robert D. Cook. — 2d ed. — New York: Wiley, c1981. xix, 537 p.: ill.; 24 cm. 1. Structures, Theory of 2. Finite element method I. T.
TA646.C66 1981    624.1/71 19    LC 80-26255    ISBN 0471030503

**The Finite element method; a basic introduction [by] K. C.**    5.5851
**Rockey [and others]**
New York, Wiley [1975] 239 p.: ill.; 24 cm. 'A Halsted Press book.' 1. Structures, Theory of 2. Finite element method I. Rockey, K. C. (Kenneth Charles)
TA646.F5    624/.171    LC 74-6671    ISBN 0470729279

**Gallagher, Richard H.**    5.5852
Finite element analysis: fundamentals [by] Richard H. Gallagher. — Englewood Cliffs, N.J.: Prentice-Hall, [1974, c1975] xix, 420 p.: illus.; 24 cm. — (Prentice-Hall civil engineering and engineering mechanics series) 1. Finite element method 2. Structures, Theory of I. T.
TA646.G33    624/.171    LC 74-4339    ISBN 0133172481

## TA648–654.6 Static and Dynamic Loading

**Salvadori, Mario George, 1907-.**    5.5853
Statics and strength of structures [by] Mario Salvadori. In collaboration with Jeremiah Eck and Giuseppe de Campoli. — Englewood Cliffs, N.J.: Prentice-Hall, [1971] xi, 323 p.: illus.; 24 cm. — (Prentice-Hall international series in architecture) 1. Structures, Theory of 2. Statics I. T.
TA648.S24    624/.171    LC 70-138821

**Blevins, Robert D.**    5.5854
Formulas for natural frequency and mode shape / Robert D. Blevins. — New York: Van Nostrand Reinhold Co., c1979. xi, 492 p.: ill.; 26 cm. 1. Structural dynamics — Handbooks, manuals, etc. 2. Vibration — Handbooks, manuals, etc. 3. Hydraulics — Handbooks, manuals, etc. I. T.
TA654.B54    620.3    LC 79-556    ISBN 0442207107

**Clough, Ray W., 1920-.**    5.5855
Dynamics of structures / Ray W. Clough, Joseph Penzien. New York: McGraw-Hill, [1975] xxii, 634 p.: ill.; 24 cm. Includes index. 1. Structural dynamics I. Penzien, Joseph. joint author. II. T.
TA654.C6    624/.171    LC 74-26963    ISBN 0070113920

**Levy, Samuel, 1912-.**    5.5856
The component element method in dynamics: with application to earthquake and vehicle engineering / Samuel Levy and John P. D. Wilkinson. New York: McGraw-Hill International Book Co., c1976. xiv, 363 p.: ill.; 25 cm. 1. Structural dynamics — Data processing. 2. Finite element method I. Wilkinson, John P. D., joint author. II. T.
TA654.L47    624/.171    LC 76-16551    ISBN 0070373981

**Paz, Mario.**    5.5857
Structural dynamics: theory and computation / Mario Paz. — 2nd ed. — New York, N.Y.: Van Nostrand Reinhold, c1985. xx, 561 p.: ill.; 24 cm. 1. Structural dynamics I. T.
TA654.P39 1985    624.1/71 19    LC 84-7360    ISBN 0442275358

**Simiu, Emil.**    5.5858
Wind effects on structures: an introduction to wind engineering / Emil Simiu, Robert H. Scanlan. — 2nd ed. — New York: Wiley, c1986. xi, 589 p.: ill.; 24 cm. 'A Wiley-Interscience publication.' 1. Wind-pressure 2. Buildings — Aerodynamics 3. Structural dynamics I. Scanlan, Robert H. II. T.
TA654.5.S55 1986    624.1/76 19    LC 85-10598    ISBN 047186613X

**Newmark, N. M. (Nathan Mortimore), 1910-1981.**    5.5859
Fundamentals of earthquake engineering [by] Nathan M. Newmark [and] Emilio Rosenblueth. Englewood Cliffs, N.J.: Prentice-Hall [1971] xvi, 640 p.: ill.; 25 cm. (Civil engineering and engineering mechanics series) 1. Earthquake engineering 2. Structural dynamics 3. Structural design I. Rosenblueth, Emilio, 1926- joint author. II. T.
TA654.6.N49    624/.176    LC 70-150108    ISBN 013336206X

## TA656–664 Structural Stability and Design

**Blockley, D. I.**    5.5860
The nature of structural design and safety / D.I. Blockley. — Chichester, Eng.: E. Horwood; New York: Halsted Press, 1980. 365 p.: ill.; 24 cm. — (Ellis Horwood series in engineering science.) 1. Structural stability 2. Structural design 3. Safety factor in engineering I. T. II. Series.
TA656.B56 1980    624.1/771    LC 80-40028    ISBN 0470270470

**Thompson, J. M. T.**    5.5861
Elastic instability phenomena / J.M.T. Thompson and G.W. Hunt. — Chichester; New York: Wiley, c1984. xii, 209 p.: ill.; 24 cm. 'A Wiley-Interscience publication.' Includes index. 1. Structural stability 2. Buckling (Mechanics) 3. Elasticity I. Hunt, G. W. II. T.
TA656.T48 1984    624.1/71 19    LC 83-14514    ISBN 0471902799

**Brush, Don Orr.**    5.5862
Buckling of bars, plates, and shells [by] Don O. Brush [and] Bo O. Almroth. New York, McGraw-Hill [1975] xvii, 379 p. illus. 24 cm. 1. Buckling (Mechanics) 2. Structures, Theory of I. Almroth, Bo O. joint author. II. T.
TA656.2.B78    624/.171    LC 74-9932    ISBN 0070085935

**Optimum structural design; theory and applications. Edited by**    5.5863
**R. H. Gallagher and O. C. Zienkiewicz.**
London; New York: Wiley, [1973] xiv, 358 p.: illus.; 24 cm. 'The separate chapters of this book were presented at an international symposium on optimization of structural design held at the University of Wales, Swansea, in January 1972.' 1. Structural design 2. Programming (Mathematics) I. Gallagher, Richard H. ed. II. Zienkiewicz, O. C. ed.
TA658.2.O67    624/.1771    LC 72-8600    ISBN 0471290505

**Kenner, Hugh.**    5.5864
Geodesic math and how to use it / by Hugh Kenner. — Berkeley: University of California Press, c1976. xi, 172 p.: ill.; 22 cm. 1. Geodesic domes — Mathematical models. 2. Polyhedra — Tables. I. T.
TA660.D6 K46    516/.23    LC 74-27292    ISBN 0520029240

**Pugh, Anthony.**    5.5865
An introduction to tensegrity / by Anthony Pugh. — Berkeley: University of California Press, c1976. x, 121, [1] p.: ill.; 23 cm. — (The Dome series) 1. Geodesic domes 2. Polyhedra I. T. II. Series.
TA660.D6 P83 1976    624/.1775    LC 75-5951    ISBN 0520029968

**Baker, E. H., 1937-.**    5.5866
Structural analysis of shells [by] E. H. Baker, L. Kovalevsky [and] F. L. Rish. — New York: McGraw-Hill, [1972] xiii, 351 p.: illus.; 24 cm. 1. Shells

(Engineering) I. Kovalevsky, L., 1916- joint author. II. Rish, F. L., 1929- joint author. III. T.
TA660.S5 B34     624/.1776     *LC* 78-130678     *ISBN* 0070033544

**Billington, David P.**                       **5.5867**
Thin shell concrete structures / David P. Billington. — 2nd ed. — New York: McGraw-Hill, 1982. xviii, 373 p.: ill.; 24 cm. '1st edition, 1965.' 1. Shells, Concrete 2. Reinforced concrete construction I. T.
TA660.S5 B52 1982     624.1/83462 19     *LC* 81-5073     *ISBN* 0070052794

**Bushnell, D. (David), 1938-.**                 **5.5868**
Computerized buckling analysis of shells / by D. Bushnell. — Dordrecht; Boston: M. Nijhoff Hingham, MA: Distributors for the U.S. and Canada, Kluwer Academic, 1985. xvii, 423 p.: ill.; 25 cm. (Mechanics of elastic stability. 9) Includes indexes. 1. Shells (Engineering) — Data processing. 2. Buckling (Mechanics) — Data processing. I. T. II. Series.
TA660.S5 B87 1985     624.1/7762 19     *LC* 84-27376     *ISBN* 9024730996

**Flügge, Wilhelm, 1904-.**                     **5.5869**
Stresses in shells. — 2d ed. — Berlin; New York: Springer-Verlag, 1973. xi, 525 p.: illus.; 24 cm. 1. Shells (Engineering) I. T.
TA660.S5 F58 1973     624/.1776     *LC* 74-183604     *ISBN* 0387053220

**Łukasiewicz, Stanisław, doc. dr. hab. inż.**       **5.5870**
[Obciążenia skupione w płytach, tarczach i powłokach. nglish] Local loads in plates and shells / Stanisław Łukasiewicz. — Alphen aan den Rijn: Sijthoff & Noordhoff, c1979. xvii, 569 p.: ill.; 24 cm. — (Mechanics of surface structures; 4) (Monographs and textbooks on mechanics of solids and fluids) Translation of Obciążenia skupione w płytach, tarczach i powłokach. 1. Thin-walled structures 2. Strains and stresses 3. Shells (Engineering) 4. Plates (Engineering) I. T.
TA660.T5 L8413     624.1/776     *LC* 79-322868     *ISBN* 9028600477

# TA663–695 Construction, by Material

**Handbook of composite construction engineering / edited by**    **5.5871**
**Gajanan M. Sabnis.**
New York: Van Nostrand Reinhold Co., c1979. xviii, 380 p.: ill.; 26 cm. 1. Composite construction I. Sabnis, Gajanan M.
TA664.H36     624/.18     *LC* 78-18354     *ISBN* 0442277350

**Koerner, Robert M., 1933-.**                 **5.5872**
Construction and geotechnical engineering using synthetic fabrics / Robert M. Koerner, Joseph P. Welsh. — New York: Wiley, c1980. xvii, 267 p.: ill.; 24 cm. — (Wiley series of practical construction guides) 'A Wiley-Interscience publication.' 1. Synthetic fabrics in building 2. Textile fibers, Synthetic I. Welsh, Joseph P., 1933- joint author. II. T.
TA668.K63     624/.189/7     *LC* 79-21733     *ISBN* 0471047767

## TA680–683.9 Concrete Construction

**Handbook of concrete engineering / edited by Mark Fintel.**    **5.5873**
2nd ed. — New York: Van Nostrand Reinhold, c1985. xiv, 892 p.: ill.; 29 cm. 1. Concrete construction — Handbooks, manuals, etc. I. Fintel, Mark.
TA682.H36 1985     624.1/834 19     *LC* 84-7359     *ISBN* 0442226233

**Cross, Hardy, 1885-.**                       **5.5874**
Continuous frames of reinforced concrete / by Hardy Cross and Newlin Dolbey Morgan. — New York: Wiley, 1932. x, 343 p.: ill. 1. Reinforced concrete construction 2. Framing (Building) I. Morgan, Newlin Dolbey, 1888- II. T.
TA683.C87 1954

**Bresler, Boris.**                           **5.5875**
Reinforced concrete engineering / edited by Boris Bresler. — New York: Wiley, 1974. 529 p.: ill.; 23 cm. 'A Wiley-Interscience publication.' 1. Reinforced concrete construction I. T.
TA683.2.B69     624/.1834     *LC* 73-19862     *ISBN* 0471102792

**Ferguson, Phil Moss, 1899-.**                 **5.5876**
Reinforced concrete fundamentals / Phil M. Ferguson. — 4th ed. — New York: Wiley, c1979. viii, 724 p.: ill.; 24 cm. 1. Reinforced concrete construction I. T.
TA683.2.F4 1979     624/.1834     *LC* 78-21555     *ISBN* 0471014591

**Park, R. (Robert), 1933-.**                  **5.5877**
Reinforced concrete structures / R. Park and T. Paulay. — New York: Wiley, [1975] xvii, 769 p.: ill.; 24 cm. 'A Wiley-interscience publication.' '[Based on] two editions of seminar notes entitled Ultimate strength design of reinforced concrete structures, vol. 1, printed by the University of Canterbury for extension study seminars conducted for practicing structural engineers in New

Zealand.' 1. Reinforced concrete construction I. Paulay, T., 1923- joint author. II. T.
TA683.2.P28     624/.1834     *LC* 74-28156     *ISBN* 0471659177

**Parker, Harry, 1887-.**                       **5.5878**
Simplified design of reinforced concrete / Harry Parker. — 5th ed. / prepared by James Ambrose. — New York: Wiley, c1984. xiv, 250 p.: ill.; 22 cm. 'A Wiley-Interscience publication.' Includes index. 1. Reinforced concrete construction I. Ambrose, James E. II. T.
TA683.2.P3 1984     693/.54 19     *LC* 84-10462     *ISBN* 0471803499

**Wang, Chu-Kia, 1917-.**                     **5.5879**
Reinforced concrete design / Chu–kia Wang, Charles G. Salmon. — 4th ed. — New York: Harper & Row, c1985. x, 947 p.: ill.; 25 cm. 1. Reinforced concrete construction I. Salmon, Charles G. II. T.
TA683.2.W3 1985     624.1/8341 19     *LC* 84-12973     *ISBN* 0060468963

**Winter, George, 1907-.**                     **5.5880**
Design of concrete structures / Arthur H. Nilson, George Winter. — 10th ed. — New York: McGraw-Hill, c1986. xii, 730 p.: ill.; 25 cm. Rev. ed. of: Design of concrete structures / George Winter, Arthur H. Nilson. 9th ed. c1979. 1. Reinforced concrete construction 2. Prestressed concrete construction I. Nilson, Arthur H. II. T.
TA683.2.W48 1986     624.1/8341 19     *LC* 85-16618     *ISBN* 0070465614

**Structural design guide to the ACI building code / Paul F. Rice**    **5.5881**
**... [et al.].**
3rd ed. — New York: Van Nostrand Reinhold Co., c1985. ix, 477 p.: ill.; 24 cm. 1. Reinforced concrete construction — Contracts and specifications — United States. I. Rice, Paul F., 1921-
TA683.24.S77 1985     624.1/8341/0218 19     *LC* 85-3129     *ISBN* 0442276338

**Lin, T. Y. (Tung Yen), 1911-.**               **5.5882**
Design of prestressed concrete structures / T. Y. Lin, Ned H. Burns. — 3d ed. — New York: Wiley, c1981. vii, 646 p.: ill.; 24 cm. 1. Prestressed concrete construction I. Burns, N. H. (Ned Hamilton), 1932- joint author. II. T.
TA683.9.L5 1981     693/.542 19     *LC* 80-20619     *ISBN* 0471018988

**Nilson, Arthur H.**                         **5.5883**
Design of prestressed concrete / Arthur H. Nilson. — New York: Wiley, c1978. xiii, 526 p.: ill.; 24 cm. 1. Prestressed concrete construction I. T.
TA683.9.N54     624/.1834     *LC* 78-4929     *ISBN* 0471020346

## TA684–690 Metal Construction

**Disque, Robert O.**                         **5.5884**
Applied plastic design in steel [by] Robert O. Disque. — New York: Van Nostrand Reinhold Co., [1971] xi, 243 p.: illus.; 24 cm. 1. Building, Iron and steel 2. Plastic analysis (Theory of structures) I. T.
TA684.D58     624/.1821     *LC* 79-153190

**Johnston, Bruce Gilbert, 1905-.**             **5.5885**
Basic steel design / Bruce G. Johnston, Fung–Jen Lin, T. V. Galambos. — 2d ed. — Englewood Cliffs, N.J.: Prentice-Hall, c1980. xiii, 352 p.: ill.; 24 cm. — (Civil engineering and engineering mechanics series) 1. Building, Iron and steel 2. Structural design I. Lin, Fung-Jen. joint author. II. Galambos, T. V. (Theodore V.) joint author. III. T.
TA684.J6 1980     624/.1821     *LC* 79-13902     *ISBN* 0130693448

**Parker, Harry, 1887-.**                       **5.5886**
Simplified design of structural steel / Harry Parker. — 5th ed. / prepared by James Ambrose. — New York: Wiley, c1983. xiv, 401 p.: ill.; 22 cm. 'A Wiley-Interscience publication.' Includes index. Bibliography: p. 318. 1. Building, Iron and steel 2. Steel, Structural I. Ambrose, James E. II. T.
TA684.P33 1983     624.1/821 19     *LC* 83-1180     *ISBN* 0471897663

**Salmon, Charles G.**                        **5.5887**
Steel structures: design and behavior / [by] Charles G. Salmon [and] John E. Johnson. — Scranton: Intext Educational Publishers, [1971] xiv, 946 p.: ill.; 24 cm. — (The Intext series in civil engineering) 1. Building, Iron and steel 2. Steel, Structural I. Johnson, John Edwin, 1931- joint author. II. T.
TA684.S24     624/.1821     *LC* 72-160683     *ISBN* 070022341X

**Mazzolani, Federico M.**                    **5.5888**
Aluminum alloy structures / Federico M. Mazzolani. — Boston: Pitman, 1985. xviii, 430 p.: ill. (Surveys in structural engineering and structural mechanics. 3) Includes index. 1. Aluminum construction 2. Aluminum alloys I. T. II. Series.
TA690.M38 1985     620.1/86 19     *LC* 84-26599     *ISBN* 0273086537

# TA705–775 ENGINEERING GEOLOGY. SOIL MECHANICS. EARTHWORK FOUNDATIONS

**Bell, F. G. (Frederic Gladstone)**                    **5.5889**
Fundamentals of engineering geology / F.G. Bell. — London; Boston: Butterworth, 1983. 648 p.: ill.; 25 cm. 1. Engineering geology 2. Geology I. T.
TA705.B334 1983      624.1/51 19      LC 83-157776      ISBN 0408011696

**Environmental geology / edited by Frederick Betz, Jr.**     **5.5890**
Stroudsburg, Pa.: Dowden, Hutchinson & Ross; New York: distributed by Halsted Press, c1975. xv, 390 p.: ill.; 26 cm. (Benchmark papers in geology; 25) 1. Engineering geology — Addresses, essays, lectures. 2. Environmental protection — Addresses, essays, lectures. 3. Man — Influence of environment — Addresses, essays, lectures. 4. Man — Influence on nature — Addresses, essays, lectures. I. Betz, Frederick, 1915-
TA705.E64      301.31      LC 75-29646      ISBN 0470071702

**Hunt, Roy E.**                                    **5.5891**
Geotechnical engineering investigation manual / Roy E. Hunt. — New York: McGraw-Hill, c1984. xiii, 983 p.: ill., maps; 25 cm. — (McGraw-Hill series in geotechnical engineering.) 1. Engineering geology — Handbooks, manuals, etc. I. T. II. Series.
TA705.H86 1984      624.1/51 19      LC 82-22886      ISBN 0070313091

**Legget, Robert Ferguson.**                        **5.5892**
Handbook of geology in civil engineering / Robert F. Legget, Paul F. Karrow. — 3rd ed. — New York: McGraw-Hill, c1983. xiv, [1308] p.: ill., maps, port.; 25 cm. Enl. ed. of: Geology and engineering. 2nd ed. 1962. Maps on lining papers. 1. Engineering geology I. Karrow, Paul Frederick, 1930- II. T.
TA705.L4 1983      624.1/51 19      LC 81-17218      ISBN 0070370613

**International Society of Soil Mechanics and Foundation**     **5.5893**
**Engineering.**
Technical terms, symbols, and definitions in English, French, German, Italian, Portuguese, Russian, Spanish and Swedish used in soil mechanics and foundation engineering. — 5th ed. — [Zurich]: The Society, 1981. v, 245 p.; 27 cm. Spine and cover title: Lexicon in 8 languages. 1. Soil mechanics — Dictionaries — Polyglot. 2. Civil engineering — Dictionaries — Polyglot. 3. Dictionaries, Polyglot I. T. II. Title: Lexicon in 8 languages.
TA710.A1 I5968 1981      624/.03      LC 76-492543

**American Society of Civil Engineers. Committee on Sampling**     • **5.5894**
**and Testing.**
Subsurface exploration and sampling of soils for civil engineering purposes: report on a research project, sponsored by the Engineering Foundation, the Graduate School of Engineering, Harvard University [and] the Waterways Experiment Station, Corps of Engineers, U.S. Army. Report prepared by M. Juul Hvorslev [member of the committee] Edited and printed by Waterways Experiment Station, Vicksburg, Miss. [Vicksburg?] 1949. 521p. 1. Soil mechanics 2. Soil — Analysis I. Hvorslev, Mikael Juul, 1895- II. T.
TA710 A49      LC 51-3820

**Das, Braja M., 1941-.**                            **5.5895**
Principles of geotechnical engineering / Braja M. Das. — Boston: PWS Engineering, 1985. xv, 571 p.: ill.; 25 cm. 1. Soil mechanics I. T.
TA710.D264 1985      624.1/5136 19      LC 84-14237      ISBN 0534037658

**Dunn, I. S. (Irving S.), 1923-.**                  **5.5896**
Fundamentals of geotechnical analysis / Irving S. Dunn, Loren R. Anderson, Fred W. Kiefer. — New York: Wiley, c1980. xv, 414 p.: ill.; 24 cm. Includes indexes. 1. Soil mechanics I. Anderson, L. R. (Loren Runar), 1941- joint author. II. Kiefer, F. W. (Fred William), 1925- joint author. III. T.
TA710.D87      624/.1513      LC 79-13583      ISBN 0471036986

**Gray, Donald H.**                                  **5.5897**
Biotechnical slope protection and erosion control / Donald H. Gray, Andrew T. Leiser. — New York: Van Nostrand Reinhold Co., c1982. xiv, 271 p.: ill.; 29 cm. Includes index. 1. Slopes (Soil mechanics) 2. Soil stabilization 3. Soil erosion 4. Soil-binding plants I. Leiser, Andrew T. II. T.
TA710.G6287 1982      624.1/51363 19      LC 81-16149      ISBN 0442212224

**Holtz, R. D. (Robert D.)**                         **5.5898**
An introduction to geotechnical engineering / Robert D. Holtz, William D. Kovacs. — Englewood Cliffs, N.J.: Prentice-Hall, c1981. xiv, 733 p.: ill.; 24 cm. Includes index. 1. Soil mechanics 2. Rock mechanics I. Kovacs, William D. joint author. II. T.
TA710.H564      624.1/513 19      LC 80-23292      ISBN 0133539121

**Lambe, T. William.**                               **5.5899**
Soil mechanics, SI version / T. William Lambe, Robert V. Whitman; with the assistance of H. G. Poulos. — New York: Wiley, c1979. xiii, 553 p., [1] fold leaf

of plates: ill.; 29 cm. — (Series in soil engineering) Includes index. 1. Soil mechanics I. Whitman, Robert V., 1928- joint author. II. T.
TA710.L246      624/.1513      LC 77-14210      ISBN 0471024910

**Lee, I. K. (Ian Kenneth)**                         **5.5900**
Geotechnical engineering / Ian K. Lee, Weeks White, Owen G. Ingles. — Boston: Pitman, c1983. xxviii, 508 p.: ill.; 29 cm. Includes indexes. 1. Soil mechanics I. White, Weeks. II. Ingles, O. G. III. T.
TA710.L34 1983      624.1/5136 19      LC 81-13787      ISBN 027301756X

**Mitchell, James Kenneth, 1930-.**                  **5.5901**
Fundamentals of soil behavior / James K. Mitchell. — New York: Wiley, 1976. xvi, 422 p.: ill.; 29 cm. (Series in soil engineering) Includes indexes. 1. Soil mechanics I. T.
TA710.M577      624/.1513      LC 75-28096      ISBN 0471611689

**Schofield, A. N. (Andrew Noel), 1930-.**           **5.5902**
Critical state soil mechanics [by] Andrew Schofield and Peter Wroth. New York, McGraw-Hill [1968] xix, 310 p. illus. 23 cm. (European civil engineering series) 1. Soil mechanics I. Wroth, Peter. joint author. II. T.
TA710.S28      624/.151      LC 68-2178

**Schroeder, W. L. (Warren Lee), 1939-.**            **5.5903**
Soils in construction / W.L. Schroeder. — 3rd ed. — New York: Wiley, c1984. xii, 330 p.: ill.; 25 cm. 1. Soil mechanics 2. Foundations 3. Building I. T.
TA710.S286 1984      624.1/5136 19      LC 83-14569      ISBN 0471865818

**Scott, Ronald F.**                                 • **5.5904**
Principles of soil mechanics / by Ronald F. Scott. — Reading, Mass.: Addison-Wesley, 1963. x, 550 p.: ill.; 24 cm. 1. Soil mechanics I. T.
TA710.S36      LC 62-9404

**Singh, Alam, 1927-.**                              **5.5905**
Soil engineering in theory and practice / Alam Singh. — 1st ed. — New York, N.Y.: Apt Books, 1982 (c1981) 742 p.: ill.; 25 cm. Includes index. 1. Soil mechanics 2. Soils 3. Civil engineering I. T.
TA710.S52 1982      624.1/51 19      LC 82-215261      ISBN 0865900248

**Sowers, George F.**                                **5.5906**
Introductory soil mechanics and foundations: geotechnical engineering / George F. Sowers. — 4th ed. — New York: Macmillan, c1979. xvii, 621 p.: ill.; 24 cm. Third ed., published in 1970, by G. B. Sowers and G. F. Sowers. 1. Soil mechanics 2. Foundations I. Sowers, George B. Introductory soil mechanics and foundations. II. T.
TA710.S67 1979      624/.15      LC 78-19069      ISBN 0024138703

**Spangler, Merlin Grant, 1894-.**                   **5.5907**
Soil engineering / Merlin G. Spangler, Richard L. Handy. — 4th ed. — New York: Harper & Row, c1982. xxvi, 819 p.: ill.; 25 cm. — (Harper & Row series in civil engineering.) 1. Soil mechanics I. Handy, Richard Lincoln, 1929- II. T. III. Series.
TA710.S7 1982      624.1/5136 19      LC 82-1115      ISBN 0700225331

**Terzaghi, Karl, 1883-1963.**                       • **5.5908**
Soil mechanics in engineering practice [by] Karl Terzaghi [and] Ralph B. Peck. — 2d ed. — New York: Wiley, [1967] xx, 729 p.: illus.; 24 cm. 1. Soil mechanics I. Peck, Ralph Brazleton, joint author. II. T.
TA710.T39 1967      624/.151      LC 67-17356

**Terzaghi, Karl, 1883-1963.**                       • **5.5909**
Theoretical soil mechanics / by Karl Terzaghi. — New York: Wiley, 1943. xvii, 510 p.: ill. 1. Soil mechanics I. T.
TA710.T4      620.19      LC 43-7652      ISBN 0471853054

**Head, K. H.**                                      **5.5910**
Manual of soil laboratory testing / K. H. Head. — New York: Wiley, 1980. 339 p.: ill.; 26 cm. 'A Halsted Press book.' 1. Soils — Testing — Laboratory manuals. I. T.
TA710.5.H4      620.1/91/0287      LC 80-12258      ISBN 0470269731

**Parker, Albert D.**                                • **5.5911**
Planning and estimating underground construction [by] Albert D. Parker. — New York: McGraw-Hill, [1970] xvi, 300 p.: illus.; 23 cm. 1. Underground construction — Estimates and costs. I. T.
TA712.P32      624/.19      LC 71-90018

**TSytovich, N. A. (Nikolaĭ Aleksandrovich)**        **5.5912**
[Mekhanika merzlykh gruntov. English] The mechanics of frozen ground / N.A. Tsytovich; edited by George K. Swinzow, Gregory P. Tschebotarioff, advisory editor. — Washington: Scripta Book Co., [1975] xvii, 426 p.: ill.; 24 cm. — (McGraw-Hill series in modern structures) Translation of Mekhanika merzlykh gruntov. Includes index. 1. Frozen ground 2. Soil mechanics I. T.
TA713.T72813      624/.1513      LC 74-32196      ISBN 0070654107

**Mitchell, R. J. (Robert J.)**                                                5.5913
Earth structures engineering / R.J. Mitchell. — Boston: Allen & Unwin, 1983.
xiii, 265 p.: ill.; 24 cm. Includes index. 1. Earthwork 2. Soil mechanics I. T.
TA715.M53 1983        624.1/891 19        *LC* 83-2621        *ISBN* 0046240039

**Church, Horace K.**                                                            5.5914
Excavation handbook / Horace K. Church. — New York: McGraw-Hill,
c1981. ca. 1000 p. in various pagings: ill.; 24 cm. 1. Excavation 2. Engineering
geology I. T.
TA730.C48        624.1/52 19        *LC* 80-19630        *ISBN* 0070108404

**Barkan, D. D.**                                                             • 5.5915
Dynamics of bases and foundations / D. D. Barkan; translated from the
Russian by L. Drashevska; translation edited by G. P. Tschebotarioff. — New
York: McGraw-Hill, c1962. xxxii, 434 p.: ill. Translation of Dinamika
osnovaniĭ i fundamentov. 1. Foundations I. T.
TA775.B333        *LC* 62-15743

**Bowles, Joseph E.**                                                            5.5916
Foundation analysis and design / Joseph E. Bowles. — 3rd ed. — New York:
McGraw-Hill, c1982. xiv, 816 p.: ill.; 25 cm. Includes indexes. 1. Foundations
2. Soil mechanics I. T.
TA775.B63 1982        624.1/5 19        *LC* 81-13649        *ISBN* 0070067708

**Das, Braja M., 1941-.**                                                        5.5917
Principles of foundation engineering / Braja M. Das. — Boston: PWS
Engineering, c1984. xvii, 595 p.: ill.; 24 cm. 1. Foundations I. T.
TA775.D227 1984b        624.1/5 19

**Leonards, G. A.**                                                           • 5.5918
Foundation engineering / edited by G. A. Leonards. — New York: McGraw-
Hill, 1962. ix, 1136 p.: ill. — (McGraw-Hill civil engineering series)
1. Foundations I. T.
TA775.L44        *LC* 61-9112

**Peck, Ralph B. (Ralph Brazelton)**                                             5.5919
Foundation engineering [by] Ralph B. Peck, Walter E. Hanson [and] Thomas
H. Thornburn. 2d ed. New York, Wiley [1974] xxiii, 514 p. illus. 26 cm.
1. Foundations I. Hanson, Walter Edmund, 1916- joint author.
II. Thornburn, Thomas Hampton, joint author. III. T.
TA775.P4 1974        624/.15        *LC* 73-9877        *ISBN* 0471675857

**Tschebotarioff, Gregory Porphyriewitch, 1899-.**                           • 5.5920
Foundations: retaining and earth structures: the art of design and construction
and its scientific basis in soil mechanics / [by] Gregory P. Tschebotarioff. — 2d
ed. — New York: McGraw-Hill, [1973] xxix, 642 p.: ill.; 23 cm. First ed.
published in 1951 under title: Soil mechanics, foundations, and earth structures.
1. Foundations 2. Soil mechanics 3. Earthwork I. T.
TA775.T78 1973        624.1/5 19        *LC* 72-11824        *ISBN* 0070653771

**Winterkorn, Hans Friedrich, 1905-.**                                          5.5921
Foundation engineering handbook, edited by Hans F. Winterkorn [and] Hsai–
Yang Fang. — New York: Van Nostrand Reinhold, [1975] xvi, 751 p.: illus.; 29
cm. 1. Foundations — Handbooks, manuals, etc. 2. Soil mechanics —
Handbooks, manuals, etc. I. Fang, Hsai-Yang. joint author. II. T.
TA775.W54        624/.15        *LC* 74-1066        *ISBN* 0442295642

**Xanthakos, Petros P.**                                                         5.5922
Slurry walls / Petros P. Xanthakos. — New York: McGraw-Hill, c1979. xvi,
622 p.: ill.; 25 cm. — (McGraw-Hill series in modern structures) 1. Slurry
trench construction 2. Concrete walls 3. Foundations I. T.
TA775.X36        624/.1834        *LC* 79-10095        *ISBN* 0070722150

# TA1000–1280 TRANSPORTATION
# ENGINEERING

**Hay, William Walter, 1908-.**                                                  5.5923
An introduction to transportation engineering / William W. Hay. — 2d ed. —
New York: Wiley, c1977. xvi, 652 p., [2] fold. leaves of plates: ill.; 24 cm.
1. Transportation I. T.
TA1145.H35 1977        380.5        *LC* 77-9293        *ISBN* 0471364339

**Heggie, Ian Graeme.**                                                          5.5924
Transport engineering economics / [by] Ian G. Heggie. — London; New York:
McGraw-Hill, 1972. ix, 265 p.: ill., maps; 26 cm. 1. Transportation
2. Engineering economy I. T.
TA1145.H37        380.5        *LC* 73-157982        *ISBN* 0070844054

**Money, Lloyd J., 1920-.**                                                      5.5925
Transportation energy and the future / Lloyd J. Money. — Englewood Cliffs,
N.J.: Prentice-Hall, c1984. xii, 142 p.: ill.; 24 cm. — (Prentice-Hall series in

energy.) Includes index. 1. Transportation 2. Power resources 3. Petroleum
I. T. II. Series.
TA1145.M56 1984        629.04 19        *LC* 83-19212        *ISBN* 0139302301

**Morlok, Edward K.**                                                            5.5926
Introduction to transportation engineering and planning / Edward K. Morlok.
— New York: McGraw-Hill, c1978. xvi, 767 p.: ill.; 25 cm. 1. Transportation
I. T.
TA1145.M58        380.5        *LC* 77-16450        *ISBN* 0070431329

**Paquette, Radnor Joseph.**                                                     5.5927
Transportation engineering: planning and design / Radnor J. Paquette,
Norman J. Ashford, Paul H. Wright. — 2nd ed. — New York: Wiley, c1982.
vii, 679 p.: ill.; 24 cm. 1. Transportation 2. Civil engineering I. Ashford,
Norman. II. Wright, Paul H. III. T.
TA1145.P34 1982        629.04 19        *LC* 81-11700        *ISBN* 047104878X

**Yu, Jason C.**                                                                 5.5928
Transportation engineering: introduction to planning, design, and operations /
Jason C. Yu. — New York: Elsevier, c1982. xiv, 462 p.: ill.; 24 cm. Includes
index. 1. Transportation engineering 2. Transportation — Planning I. T.
TA1145.Y8 1982        380.5/068 19        *LC* 81-12507        *ISBN* 0444005641

**Advanced urban transport** / [by] Ian Black ... [et al.; for the              5.5929
**Urban Transport Research Group, University of Warwick].**
Farnborough, Hants.: Saxon House; Lexington, Mass.: Lexington Books, 1975.
xi, 212 p.: ill., maps; 24 cm. 1. Local transit I. Black, Ian. II. University of
Warwick. Urban Transport Research Group.
TA1205.A36        388.4        *LC* 75-3834        *ISBN* 0347010814

**Anderson, John Edward.**                                                       5.5930
Transit systems theory / J. Edward Anderson. — Lexington, Mass.: Lexington
Books, c1978. xxii, 340 p.: ill.; 24 cm. 1. Urban transportation 2. Local transit
I. T.
TA1205.A5        388.4        *LC* 77-11856        *ISBN* 066901902X

**Creighton, Roger.**                                                         • 5.5931
Urban transportation planning / by Roger L. Creighton. — Urbana: University
of Illinois Press [1970] xxviii, 375 p.: ill., maps; 24 cm. 1. Urban transportation
I. T.
TA1205.C7        711/.7        *LC* 71-90452        *ISBN* 0252000692

**McGean, Thomas.**                                                              5.5932
Urban transportation technology / Thomas McGean. — Lexington, Mass.:
Lexington Books, c1976. xx, 295 p.: ill.; 24 cm. Includes bibliographical
references and index. 1. Urban transportation I. T.
TA1205.M25        629.04        *LC* 75-10228        *ISBN* 0669999113

**Tomazinis, Anthony R.**                                                        5.5933
Productivity, efficiency, and quality in urban transportation systems / Anthony
R. Tomazinis. — Lexington, Mass.: Lexington Books, [1975] xiv, 237 p.: ill.; 24
cm. Includes index. 1. Urban transportation I. T.
TA1205.T6        388.4        *LC* 75-19550        *ISBN* 0669001422

**Weigelt, Horst, 1928-.**                                                       5.5934
[Stadtverkehr der Zukunft. English] City traffic: a systems digest / Horst R.
Weigelt, Rainer E. Götz, Helmut H. Weiss; translated by Gunther F. Wengatz.
— New York: Van Nostrand Reinhold, 1977. xi, 244 p.: ill.; 24 cm. Translation
of Stadtverkehr der Zukunft. 1. Urban transportation I. Weiss, Helmut H.,
1937- joint author. II. Götz, Rainer E., 1943- joint author. III. T.
TA1205.W4413        388.4        *LC* 77-23360        *ISBN* 0442292597

**Automated people movers: engineering and management in major**               5.5935
**activity centers: proceedings of a conference / sponsored by the**
**Urban Transportation Division of the American Society of Civil**
**Engineers in cooperation with the Advanced Transit Association**
**... [et al.], Miami, Florida, March 25–28, 1985; edited by**
**Edward S. Neumann and Murthy V.A. Bondada.**
New York, N.Y.: ASCE, c1985. 846 p.: ill.; 22 cm. Includes indexes.
1. Personal rapid transit — Congresses. I. Neumann, Edward S. II. Bondada,
Murthy V. A. III. American Society of Civil Engineers. Urban Transportation
Division. IV. Advanced Transit Association (Washington, D.C.)
TA1207.A98 1985        625/.4 19        *LC* 85-72342        *ISBN* 0872624889

**Irving, Jack H., 1920-.**                                                      5.5936
Fundamentals of personal rapid transit: based on a program of research,
1968–1976 at the Aerospace Corporation, El Segundo, California / editor and
principal author, Jack H. Irving, associate authors, Harry Bernstein, C. L.
Olson, Jon Buyan. — Lexington, Mass.: Lexington Books, c1978. xviii, 322 p.:
ill.; 24 cm. 1. Personal rapid transit I. Aerospace Corporation. II. T.
TA1207.I79        625.4/4        *LC* 78-13604        *ISBN* 0669025208

## TA1501–1820 APPLIED OPTICS

**Cathey, W. Thomas, 1937-.**     5.5937
Optical information processing and holography / [by] W. Thomas Cathey. — New York: Wiley, [1974] xiv, 398 p.: ill.; 23 cm. (Wiley series in pure and applied optics) 1. Optical data processing 2. Optical pattern recognition 3. Holography I. T.
TA1630.C37     621.36     LC 73-14604     ISBN 0471140783

**Adams, M. J.**     5.5938
An introduction to optical waveguides / M.J. Adams. — Chichester; New York: Wiley, c1981. xv, 401 p.: ill.; 26 cm. 'A Wiley-Interscience publication.' 1. Optical wave guides I. T.
TA1632.A26 1981     535.8/9 19     LC 80-42059     ISBN 0471279692

**Ballard, Dana Harry.**     5.5939
Computer vision / Dana H. Ballard, Christopher M. Brown. — Englewood Cliffs, N.J.: Prentice-Hall, c1982. xx, 523 p., [2] leaves of plates: ill. (some col.); 25 cm. 1. Computer vision I. Brown, Christopher M. II. T.
TA1632.B34 1982     621.38/0414 19     LC 81-20974     ISBN 0131653164

**Hord, R. Michael, 1940-.**     5.5940
Digital image processing of remotely sensed data / R. Michael Hord. — New York: Academic Press, 1982. xiii, 256 p.: ill.; 24 cm. — (Notes and reports in computer science and applied mathematics. 5) Includes index. 1. Image processing — Digital techniques 2. Remote sensing I. T. II. Series.
TA1632.H67 1982     621.36/78 19     LC 82-16267     ISBN 0123556201

**Levine, Martin D., 1938-.**     5.5941
Vision in man and machine / Martin D. Levine. — New York: McGraw-Hill, c1985. xvi, 574 p.: ill. (some col.); 24 cm. (McGraw-Hill series in electrical engineering. Computer engineering.) 1. Image processing — Digital techniques I. T. II. Series.
TA1632.L48 1985     001.53/4 19     LC 84-21827     ISBN 0070374465

**Moik, Johannes G.**     5.5942
Digital processing of remotely sensed images / Johannes G. Moik. — Washington: Scientific and Technical Information Branch, National Aeronautics and Space Administration: for sale by the Supt. of Docs., U.S. Govt. Print. Off., 1980. vii, 330 p.: ill.; 24 cm. (NASA SP; 431) 1. Image processing 2. Remote sensing I. T.
TA1632.M64     621.36/7     LC 79-16727

**Schowengerdt, Robert A.**     5.5943
Techniques for image processing and classification in remote sensing / Robert A. Schowengerdt. — New York: Academic Press, 1983. xv, 249 p., [3] p. of plates: ill. (some col.); 24 cm. 1. Image processing 2. Remote sensing I. T.
TA1632.S3 1983     621.36/78 19     LC 83-11769     ISBN 0126289808

## TA1660–1705 INTEGRATED OPTICS, LASERS, AND LASER APPLICATIONS

**Laser applications / edited by Monte Ross; contributors:**     5.5944
**Frederick Aronowitz [and others].**
New York: Academic Press, 1971. 308 p.: ill.; 24 cm. 1. Lasers I. Ross, Monte. ed. II. Aronowitz, Frederick.
TA1660.L37     621.366     LC 79-154380     ISBN 0124319017

**Beesley, M. J.**     5.5945
Lasers and their applications / M. J. Beesley. 2d ed. — London: Taylor and Francis; New York: Halsted Press, 1976. xii, 253 p.: ill.; 24 cm. 1. Lasers I. T.
TA1675.B43 1976     621.36/6     LC 76-25393     ISBN 0470151668

**Hallmark, Clayton L.**     5.5946
Lasers, the light fantastic / by Clayton L. Hallmark. — 1st ed. — Blue Ridge Summit, Pa.: Tab Books, c1979. 294 p.: ill.; 22 cm. Includes index. 1. Lasers I. T.
TA1675.H34     621.36/6     LC 78-11176     ISBN 0830698574

**Harry, John E., 1940-.**     5.5947
Industrial lasers and their applications [by] John E. Harry. London; New York: McGraw Hill, [1974] xii, 189 p.: illus.; 26 cm. 1. Lasers — Industrial applications. I. T.
TA1675.H37     621.36/6     LC 74-8197     ISBN 0070844437

**Hecht, Jeff.**     5.5948
Laser, supertool of the 1980s / Jeff Hecht and Dick Teresi. — New York: Ticknor & Fields, c1982. 264 p.: ill.; 23 cm. 1. Lasers — Popular works. I. Teresi, Dick. II. T.
TA1675.H43 1982b     621.36/6 19     LC 83-24261     ISBN 0899192866

**Verdeyen, Joseph Thomas.**     5.5949
Laser electronics / Joseph T. Verdeyen. — Englewood Cliffs, N.J.: Prentice-Hall, c1981. xvi, 444 p.: ill.; 24 cm. — (Solid state physical electronics series) 1. Lasers I. T.
TA1675.V47     621.36/6 19     LC 80-24531     ISBN 0135237386

**Yariv, Amnon.**     5.5950
Introduction to optical electronics / Amnon Yariv. — 2d ed. — New York: Holt, Rinehart and Winston, c1976. ix, 438 p.: ill.; 25 cm. 1. Lasers 2. Electro-optics. 3. Quantum electronics I. T.
TA1675.Y37 1976     621.36 19     LC 76-11773     ISBN 0030898927

**Mallow, Alex.**     5.5951
Laser safety handbook / Alex Mallow, Leon Chabot. — New York: Van Nostrand Reinhold Co., c1978. xiii, 353 p.: ill.; 24 cm.. 1. Lasers — Safety measures. I. Chabot, Leon. joint author. II. T.
TA1677.M34     621.36/6/028     LC 78-1484     ISBN 0442250924

**Ready, John F., 1932-.**     5.5952
Industrial applications of lasers / John F. Ready. — New York: Academic Press, 1978. xv, 588 p.: ill.; 24 cm. 1. Lasers — Industrial applications. I. T.
TA1677.R4     621.389/6     LC 77-6611     ISBN 012583960X

**Sliney, David.**     5.5953
Safety with lasers and other optical sources: a comprehensive handbook / David Sliney and Myron Wolbarsht. — New York: Plenum Press, c1980. xxviii, 1035 p.: ill.; 26 cm. 1. Lasers — Safety measures. 2. Lasers — Physiological effect. 3. Light — Physiological effect 4. Electric lamps — Safety measures. 5. Welding — Safety measures I. Wolbarsht, Myron. joint author. II. T.
TA1677.S44     621.36/6     LC 80-16591     ISBN 0306404346

**Light and its uses: making and using lasers, holograms,**     5.5954
**interferometers, and instruments of dispersion: readings from**
**Scientific American / with introductions by Jearl Walker.**
San Francisco: W. H. Freeman, 1980. viii, 147 p.: ill.; 29 cm. At head of title: The amateur scientist. Includes index. 1. Lasers — Addresses, essays, lectures. 2. Holography — Addresses, essays, lectures. 3. Interferometer — Addresses, essays, lectures. 4. Spectrum analysis — Instruments — Addresses, essays, lectures. I. Walker, Jearl, 1945- II. Scientific American.
TA1688.L53     621.36     LC 79-27551     ISBN 0716711842

**Thompson, G. H. B. (George Horace Brooke)**     5.5955
Physics of semiconductor laser devices / G. H. B. Thompson. — Chichester [Eng.]; New York: J. Wiley, c1980. xxv, 549 p.: ill.; 24 cm. 'A Wiley-Interscience publication.' 1. Semiconductor lasers I. T.
TA1700.T45     535.5/8     LC 79-41217     ISBN 0471276855

**Koechner, Walter, 1937-.**     5.5956
Solid state laser engineering / Walter Koechner. New York: Springer-Verlag, 1976. xi, 620 p.: ill.; 24 cm. (Springer series in optical sciences; v. 1) 1. Solid-state lasers I. T.
TA1705.K63     621.36/61     LC 75-40054     ISBN 0387901671

## TA1750–1820 OTHER TOPICS

**Fynn, G. W.**     5.5957
The cutting and polishing of electro-optic materials / G. W. Fynn and W. J. A. Powell. — New York: Wiley, c1979. xv, 215 p.: ill.; 29 cm. 'A Halsted Press book.' 1. Electrooptics — Materials. 2. Optical materials 3. Cutting 4. Grinding and polishing I. Powell, W. J. A. joint author. II. T.
TA1750.F96 1979     621.38/0414     LC 78-21139     ISBN 0470266074

**Seippel, Robert G.**     5.5958
Optoelectronics / Robert G. Seippel. — Reston, Va.: Reston Pub. Co., c1981. xiv, 354 p.: ill.; 25 cm. Includes index. 1. Optoelectronics I. T.
TA1750.S44     621.36 19     LC 80-22288     ISBN 083595255X

**International Conference on Optical Fibre Sensors. (1st: 1983:**     5.5959
**London, England)**
First International Conference on Optical Fibre Sensors, 26–28 April 1983 / organised by the Electronics Division of the Institution of Electrical Engineers in association with the Associazione Elettrotecnica ed Elettronica Italiana, Italy ... [et al.], with the support of the Convention of National Societies of Electrical Engineers of Western Europe (EUREL), venue, the Institution of Electrical Engineers. — London; New York: The Institution, c1983. viii, 216 p.: ill.; 30 cm. — (Conference publication, 0537-9989; no. 221) Cover title: Optical fibre sensors. 1. Fiber optics — Congresses. 2. Optical detectors — Congresses. I. Institution of Electrical Engineers. Electronics Division. II. Associazione elettrotecnica ed elettronica italiana. III. Convention of National Societies of Electrical Engineers of Western Europe. IV. T. V. Title: Optical fibre sensors.
TA1800.I58 1983     621.36/92 19     LC 83-172818     ISBN 0852962746

**Snyder, Allan W., 1940-.** 5.5960
Optical waveguide theory / Allan W. Snyder, John D. Love. — London; New York: Chapman and Hall, 1983. viii, 734 p.: ill.; 24 cm. (Science paperbacks. 190) 1. Optical wave guides I. Love, J. D. (John D.) II. T. III. Series.
TA1800.S69 1983    621.36/9 19    *LC* 83-7463    *ISBN* 0412099500

**Unger, Hans-Georg, 1926-.** 5.5961
Planar optical waveguides and fibres / by H.–G. Unger. — Oxford [Eng.]; New York: Clarendon Press, 1977. xvii, 751 p.: ill.; 24 cm. — (Oxford engineering science series) 1. Fiber optics 2. Optical wave guides I. T.
TA1800.U53    621.36/9    *LC* 78-313615    *ISBN* 0198561334

# TC Hydraulic Engineering. Ocean Engineering

**Linsley, Ray K.** 5.5962
Water–resources engineering / Ray K. Linsley, Joseph B. Franzini. — 3d ed. — New York: McGraw-Hill, c1979. xii, 716 p.: ill.; 24 cm. — (McGraw-Hill series in water resources and environmental engineering) 1. Hydraulic engineering 2. Water resources development I. Franzini, Joseph B. joint author. II. T.
TC145.L55 1979    627    *LC* 78-4498    *ISBN* 0070379653

## TC147–180 HYDRAULICS. HYDRODYNAMICS

**Charlier, Roger Henri.** 5.5963
Tidal energy / Roger Henri Charlier. — New York: Van Nostrand Reinhold, c1982. xi, 351 p.: ill.; 24 cm. Includes index. 1. Tidal power I. T.
TC147.C58 1982    621.31/2134 19    *LC* 81-13111    *ISBN* 0442244258

**International Conference on the Utilization of Tidal Power, Nova Scotia Technical College, 1970.** 5.5964
Tidal power; proceedings. Edited by T. J. Gray and O. K. Gashus. — New York: Plenum Press, 1972. x, 630 p.: illus.; 26 cm. Conference held May 24-29, 1970. 1. Tidal power — Congresses. I. Gray, Thomas James, 1917- ed. II. Gashus, O. K., ed. III. T.
TC147.I58 1970    621.312/134    *LC* 70-179031    *ISBN* 0306305593

**Brater, Ernest Fredrick, 1912-.** 5.5965
Handbook of hydraulics for the solution of hydraulic engineering problems. — 6th ed. / Ernest F. Brater, Horace Williams King. — New York: McGraw-Hill, c1976. [591] p. in various pagings: ill.; 20 cm. First-4th ed. (1918-54) by H. W. King (4th ed. rev. by E. F. Brater), published under title: Handbook of hydraulics for the solution of hydraulic problems; 5th ed. (1963) by H. W. King and E. F. Brater, published under title: Handbook of hydraulics for the solution of hydrostatic and fluid-flow problems. 1. Hydraulics I. King, Horace Williams, 1874-1951. joint author. II. T.
TC160.K5 1976    620.1/06    *LC* 76-6486    *ISBN* 0070072434

**Morris, Henry Madison, 1918-.** 5.5966
Applied hydraulics in engineering / [by] Henry M. Morris [and] James M. Wiggert. — 2d ed. — New York: Ronald Press Co., [1972] v, 629 p.: ill.; 24 cm. 1. Hydraulics I. Wiggert, James M., joint author. II. T.
TC160.M76 1972    627    *LC* 77-163950

**Mahoney, Gene, 1923-.** 5.5967
Fire department hydraulics / Eugene F. Mahoney. — Boston: Allyn and Bacon, c1980. xiv, 550 p.: ill.; 24 cm. Includes index. 1. Hydraulics 2. Fire extinction — Water-supply 3. Fire-departments — Equipment and supplies I. T.
TC163.M25    628.9/252    *LC* 78-31235    *ISBN* 0205065635

**Graf, Walter Hans, 1936-.** 5.5968
Hydraulics of sediment transport. — New York: McGraw-Hill, 1972 (c1971) xi, 513 p.: illus.; 23 cm. — (McGraw-Hill series in water resources and environmental engineering) 1. Sediment transport I. T.
TC175.2.G7    627/.042    *LC* 79-128788    *ISBN* 0070239002

**Domenico, P. A. (Patrick A.)** 5.5969
Concepts and models in groundwater hydrology [by] Patrick A. Domenico. New York, McGraw-Hill [1972] ix, 405 p. illus. 23 cm. (McGraw-Hill international series in the earth and planetary sciences) 1. Groundwater flow — Mathematical models. 2. Water, Underground — Mathematical models. I. T.
TC176.D64    551.4/9/0184    *LC* 79-168751    *ISBN* 0070175357

**Wang, Herbert.** 5.5970
Introduction to groundwater modeling: finite difference and finite element methods / Herbert F. Wang, Mary P. Anderson. — San Francisco: W.H. Freeman, c1982. x, 237 p.: ill.; 24 cm. Includes index. 1. Groundwater flow — Mathematical models. 2. Difference equations 3. Finite element method I. Anderson, Mary P. II. T.
TC176.W36    551.49/0724 19    *LC* 81-2665    *ISBN* 0716713039

**International Symposium on Risk and Reliability in Water Resources (1978: University of Waterloo)** 5.5971
Inputs for risk analysis in water systems / edited by Edward A. McBean, Keith W. Hipel and T. E. Unny. — Fort Collins, Colo.: Water Resources Publications, 1979. viii, 480 p.: ill.; 24 cm. Selected papers of the International Symposium on Risk and Reliability in Water Resources held at the University of Waterloo, Waterloo, Ontario, from June 26-28, 1978. 1. Hydraulic structures — Design and construction — Statistical methods — Congresses. 2. Risk — Statistical methods — Congresses. 3. Reliability (Engineering) — Statistical methods — Congresses. I. McBean, Edward A. II. Hipel, Keith W. III. Unny, T. E. IV. T.
TC180.I54 1978    627    *LC* 79-64192

## TC203–381 HARBORS AND COAST PROTECTIVE WORKS

**Agerschou, Hans.** 5.5972
Planning and design of ports and marine terminals / Hans Agerschou, Helge Lundgren, and Torben Sørensen, in collaboration with Torben Ernst ... [et al.]. — Chichester [West Sussex]; New York: Wiley, c1983. x, 320 p.: ill.; 25 cm. 'Wiley Interscience publication.' Errata slip inserted. 1. Harbors — Design and construction 2. Marine terminals — Design and construction. I. Lundgren, Helge, 1914- II. Sørensen, Torben. III. T.
TC205.A33 1983    627/.2 19    *LC* 83-7032    *ISBN* 0471901911

**Bruun, Per.** 5.5973
Port engineering. — Houston, Tex.: Gulf Pub. Co., [1973] ix, 436 p.: illus.; 27 cm. An expanded report on eight seminars held by the Dept. of Ocean Engineering at the University of Hawaii in 1969. 1. Harbors I. Hawaii. University, Honolulu. Dept. of Ocean Engineering. II. T.
TC205.B78    627/.2    *LC* 76-184682    *ISBN* 0872017389

## TC405–1645 WATER RESOURCES DEVELOPMENT. OCEAN ENGINEERING

**Goodman, Alvin S.** 5.5974
Principles of water resources planning / Alvin S. Goodman; with the assistance of David C. Major ... [et al.]. — Englewood Cliffs, N.J.: Prentice-Hall, c1984. xii, 563 p.: ill.; 25 cm. 1. Water resources development I. Major, David C. II. T.
TC405.G633 1984    333.91/15 19    *LC* 83-4575    *ISBN* 0137106165

**Mather, John Russell, 1923-.** 5.5975
Water resources: distribution, use, and management / John R. Mather. — New York: Wiley; Silver Spring, Md.: V.H. Winston, c1984. xv, 439 p.: ill.; 25 cm. — (Environmental science and technology. 0194-0287) Includes indexes. 1. Water resources development I. T. II. Series.
TC405.M38 1984    333.91 19    *LC* 83-21795    *ISBN* 047189401X

**Hall, M. J.** 5.5976
Urban hydrology / M.J. Hall. — London: Elsevier Applied Science, c1984. xi, 299 p.: ill., 1 chart; 23 cm. 1. Urban hydrology I. T.
TC409.H3x    551.48/09173/2 19    *ISBN* 0853342687

**Goldman, Charles Remington, 1930-.** 5.5977
Environmental quality and water development, edited by Charles R. Goldman, James McEvoy III [and] Peter J. Richerson. — San Francisco: W. H. Freeman, [1973] vii, 510 p.: illus.; 26 cm. 1. Water resources development — United States. 2. Human ecology — United States. I. McEvoy, James, 1940- joint author. II. Richerson, Peter J. joint author. III. T.
TC423.G64    333.9/1/00973    *LC* 72-83739    *ISBN* 0716702568

**Grigg, Neil S.** 5.5978
Water resources planning / Neil S. Grigg. — New York: McGraw-Hill, c1985. xii, 328 p.: ill.; 24 cm. 1. Water resources development — United States. I. T.
TC423.G75 1985    333.91 19    *LC* 84-28868    *ISBN* 0070247714

**Viessman, Warren.** 5.5979
Water management: technology and institutions / Warren Viessman, Jr., Claire Welty. — New York: Harper & Row, c1985. xix, 618 p.: ill.; 24 cm. 1. Water

resources development — United States. 2. Water-supply — United States — Management. I. Welty, Claire, 1954- II. T.
TC423.V54 1985     333.91/00973 19     *LC* 84-10864     *ISBN* 0060468181

**Handbook of dam engineering / edited by Alfred R. Golze.**     5.5980
New York: Van Nostrand Reinhold Co., c1977. xii, 793 p.: ill.; 26 cm. 1. Dams — Design and construction — Handbooks, manuals, etc. I. Golzé, Alfred R., 1905-
TC540.H28     627/.8     *LC* 77-8687     *ISBN* 0442227523

**Anguizola, G. A., 1927-.**     5.5981
Philippe Bunau–Varilla, the man behind the Panama Canal / Gustave Anguizola. — Chicago: Nelson-Hall, 1980. x, 472 p., [8] leaves of plates: ill., map (on lining papers); 23 cm. Includes index. 1. Bunau-Varilla, Philippe, 1859-1940. 2. Civil engineers — France — Biography. 3. Panama Canal (Panama) — History. I. T.
TC774.A67     386/.444/09     *LC* 79-13673     *ISBN* 0882293974

**Gaythwaite, John.**     5.5982
The marine environment and structural design / John Gathtwaithe. — New York: Van Nostrand Reinhold Co., c1981. xvi, 313 p.: ill.; 24 cm. 1. Ocean engineering 2. Structural design I. T.
TC1645.G39     627 19     *LC* 80-29583     *ISBN* 0442248342

# TD Environmental Technology. Sanitary Engineering

## TD9–145 REFERENCE. GENERAL WORKS

**Encyclopedia of environmental science and engineering / [edited**     5.5983
**by] J.R. Pfafflin, E.N. Ziegler.**
2nd rev. and updated ed. — New York: Gordon and Breach Science Publishers, c1983. 3 v. (xxiii, 1254 p.): ill.; 28 cm. 1. Environmental engineering — Dictionaries. I. Pfafflin, J. R. (James R.) II. Ziegler, E. N. (Edward N.)
TD9.E5 1983     628.5 19     *LC* 83-16452     *ISBN* 0677064306

**Glossary: water and wastewater control engineering / prepared**     5.5984
**by joint editorial board representing American Public Health**
**Association [and others] William T. Ingram: chairman.**
[New York]: American Public Health Association, 1969. xi, 387 p.; 24 cm. 1. Sanitary engineering — Dictionaries. I. American Public Health Association. II. Title: Water and wastewater control engineering.
TD9.G55     628.1/03/21 19     *LC* 71-9055

**Scott, John S., 1915-.**     5.5985
Dictionary of waste and water treatment / John S. Scott, Paul G. Smith. — London; Boston: Butterworths, 1981, c1980. 359 p.: ill.; 22 cm. 1. Sanitary engineering — Dictionaries. I. Smith, Paul G., M.Sc. II. T.
TD9.S37 1981     628/.03/21 19     *LC* 82-101572     *ISBN* 0408004959

**Environmental engineers' handbook. Béla G. Lipták, editor.**     5.5986
[1st ed.]. — Radnor, Pa.: Chilton Book Co., [1973-74] 3 v.: illus.; 25 cm. 1. Environmental engineering — Handbooks, manuals, etc. 2. Pollution — Handbooks, manuals, etc. I. Lipták, Béla G. ed.
TD145.E57 1973     628     *LC* 72-14241     *ISBN* 0801956927

**Peavy, Howard S.**     5.5987
Environmental engineering / Howard S. Peavy, Donald R. Rowe, George Tchobanoglous. — New York: McGraw-Hill, c1985. xiv, 699, 20 p.: ill.; 24 cm. — (McGraw-Hill series in water resources and environmental engineering.) 1. Environmental engineering I. Rowe, Donald R. II. Tchobanoglous, George. III. T. IV. Series.
TD145.P43 1985     628 19     *LC* 84-3854     *ISBN* 0070491348

## TD159–167 MUNICIPAL ENGINEERING

**Handbook of municipal administration and engineering /**     5.5988
**William S. Foster, editor.**
New York: McGraw-Hill, c1978. ca. 350 p. in various pagings: ill.; 26 cm. 1. Municipal engineering — Handbooks, manuals, etc. 2. Municipal government — Handbooks, manuals, etc. I. Foster, William S.
TD159.H36     628     *LC* 77-14128     *ISBN* 0070216304

**Dunne, Thomas, 1943-.**     5.5989
Water in environmental planning / Thomas Dunne, Luna B. Leopold. — San Francisco: W. H. Freeman, c1978. xxvii, 818 p.: ill.; 24 cm. 1. Environmental engineering 2. Regional planning 3. Hydrology I. Leopold, Luna Bergere, 1915- joint author. II. T.
TD160.D85     333.9/1     *LC* 78-8013     *ISBN* 0716700794

## TD170–196 ENVIRONMENTAL POLLUTION

**Chanlett, Emil T.**     5.5990
Environmental protection / Emil T. Chanlett. — 2d ed. — New York: McGraw-Hill, c1979. xx, 585 p.: ill.; 25 cm. — (McGraw-Hill series in water resources and environmental engineering) 1. Environmental protection 2. Environmental health I. T.
TD170.C47 1979     363.6     *LC* 78-16357     *ISBN* 0070105316

**Environmental trends.**     5.5991
Washington, D.C.: Council on Environmental Quality, Executive Office of the President: For sale by the Supt. of Docs., U.S. G.P.O., 1981. v, 346 p.: col. ill., maps; 21 x 28 cm. 'Geological Survey, U.S. Department of the Interior.' 'July 1981.' S/N 041-011-00058-1 Item 856-E 1. Environmental protection — United States 2. Environmental monitoring — United States. I. Geological Survey (U.S.) II. Council on Environmental Quality (U.S.)
TD171.E574 1981     333.7/0973 19     *LC* 81-604053

**State of the environment: an assessment at mid–decade: a report**     5.5992
**from the Conservation Foundation.**
Washington, D.C.: The Foundation, c1984. xxxiv, 586 p.: ill.; 23 cm. Includes index. 1. Environmental protection — United States 2. Environmental policy — United States. I. Conservation Foundation.
TD171.S74 1984     363.7 19     *LC* 84-12651     *ISBN* 0891640843

**Komarov, Boris.**     5.5993
[Unichtozhenie prirody. English] The destruction of nature in the Soviet Union / Boris Komarov; foreword by Marshall I. Goldman. — White Plains, N.Y.: M. E. Sharpe, c1980. x, 150 p.; 24 cm. Translation of Unichtozhenie prirody. 1. Pollution — Russia. 2. Ecology — Russia. I. T.
TD186.5.R9 K6513     363.7/32/0947     *LC* 80-5452     *ISBN* 087332157X

**Black, Peter E.**     5.5994
Environmental impact analysis / Peter E. Black. — New York, N.Y.: Praeger, 1981. xii, 146 p.: ill.; 24 cm. Includes index. 1. Environmental impact analysis — United States. I. T.
TD194.6.B53     333.7/1/0973 19     *LC* 81-7339     *ISBN* 0030596181

**Canter, Larry W.**     5.5995
Environmental impact assessment / Larry W. Canter. New York: McGraw-Hill, c1977. xiv, 331 p.: ill.; 25 cm. (McGraw-Hill series in water resources and environmental engineering) 1. Environmental impact analysis 2. Environmental impact statements I. T.
TD194.6.C36     333.7     *LC* 76-42480     *ISBN* 007009764X

**Stratford, Alan H.**     5.5996
Airports and the environment: a study of air transport development and its impact upon the social and economic well–being of the community / Alan H. Stratford. — New York: St. Martin's Press, 1974. xiii, 158 p., [2] leaves of plates: ill.; 23 cm. 1. Airports — Environmental aspects I. T.
TD195.A36 S77     363.6     *LC* 74-82530

**Glasstone, Samuel, 1897-.**     5.5997
Nuclear power and its environmental effects / Samuel Glasstone, Walter H. Jordan. — La Grange Park, Ill.: American Nuclear Society, c1980. xii, 395 p.: ill.; 24 cm. 1. Nuclear power plants — Environmental aspects I. Jordan, Walter H. joint author. II. American Nuclear Society. III. T.
TD195.E4 G55     363.7 19     *LC* 80-67303     *ISBN* 0894480227

**Sagan, Leonard A.**     5.5998
Human and ecologic effects of nuclear power plants. Edited by Leonard A. Sagan, with an introd. by Rolf Eliassen. Springfield, Ill., Thomas [1974] xix, 536 p. illus. 26 cm. 1. Nuclear power plants — Environmental aspects I. T.
TD195.E4 S2     621.48/1     *LC* 73-8614     *ISBN* 0398029296

**The Social costs of power production: prepared for the Electric**     5.5999
**Power Task Force of the Scientists' Institute for Public**
**Information and the Power Study Group of the American**
**Association for the Advancement of Science Committee on**
**Environmental Alterations / edited by Barry Commoner,**
**Howard Boksenbaum, Michael Corr.**
New York: Macmillan Information, [1975] xx, 217 p.: ill.; 24 cm. (Energy and human welfare; v. 1) 1. Electric power-plants — Environmental aspects — Addresses, essays, lectures. I. Commoner, Barry, 1917- II. Boksenbaum,

Howard. III. Corr, Michael. IV. Scientists' Institute for Public Information. Electric Power Task Force. V. American Association for the Advancement of Science. Committee on Environmental Alterations. Power Study Group. VI. Series.
TD195.E4 S6    363.6    *LC* 75-8986    *ISBN* 0024684201

**Inhaber, Herbert, 1941-.**    **5.6000**
Energy risk assessment / Herbert Inhaber. — New York: Gordon and Breach, c1982. xxvi, 395 p.: ill.; 24 cm. 1. Energy development — Environmental aspects. 2. Environmental impact analysis 3. Health risk assessment 4. Risk I. T.
TD195.E49 I53 1982    333.79/1 19    *LC* 82-3060    *ISBN* 0677059809

**Watkins, L. H.**    **5.6001**
Environmental impact of roads and traffic / L.H. Watkins. — London; Englewood, New Jersey: Applied Science, c1981. viii, 268 p.: ill.; 23 cm. 1. Roads — Environmental aspects — Great Britain. 2. Traffic noise — Great Britain. 3. Automobiles — Environmental aspects — Great Britain. I. T.
TD195.R63 W37 1981    363.7/01 19    *LC* 81-167609    *ISBN* 0853349630

**Cohn, Louis F. (Louis Franklin), 1948-.**    **5.6002**
Environmental analysis of transportation systems / Louis F. Cohn, Gary R. McVoy. — New York: Wiley, c1982. xii, 374 p.: ill.; 29 cm. 'A Wiley-Interscience publication.' 1. Transportation — Environmental aspects. I. McVoy, Gary R. (Gary Richard), 1951- II. T.
TD195.T7 C63 1982    380.5 19    *LC* 81-14637    *ISBN* 0471080985

**Acid deposition, atmospheric processes in eastern North**    **5.6003**
**America: a review of current scientific understanding /**
**Committee on Atmospheric Transport and Chemical**
**Transformation in Acid Precipitation ... [et al.].**
Washington, D.C.: National Academy Press, 1983. xiv, 375 p.: ill. 1. Acid rain — Canada, Eastern 2. Acid rain — Northeastern States I. National Research Council (U.S.). Committee on Atmospheric Transport and Chemical Transformation in Acid Precipitation.
TD196A25 A24 1983    *LC* 83-61851    *ISBN* 0309033896

**Acid rain and transported air pollutants: implications for public**    **5.6004**
**policy / Office of Technology Assessment, Congress of the**
**United States.**
New York: UNIPUB, 1985. vii, 323 p., [1] leaf of plates: ill.; 27 cm. Originally published: Washington, D.C.: Congress of the U.S., Office of Technology Assessment, [1984] 'Published in cooperation with the Office of Technology Assessment, Congress of the United States'—T.p. verso. 1. Acid rain — United States. 2. Air — Pollution — United States. 3. Environmental policy — United States. I. United States. Congress. Office of Technology Assessment.
TD196.A25 A2823 1985    363.7/386/0973 19    *LC* 84-52370    *ISBN* 0890590443

**Acid rain information book / edited by David V. Bubenick.**    **5.6005**
2nd ed. — Park Ridge, N.J., USA: Noyes Publications, 1984. xiii, 397 p.: ill.; 24 cm. Rev. ed. of: Acid rain information book / Frank A. Record. 1982. 1. Acid rain I. Bubenick, David V. II. Record, Frank. Acid rain information book.
TD196.A25 A29 1984    363.7/394 19    *LC* 83-21986    *ISBN* 0815509677

**Verschueren, Karel.**    **5.6006**
Handbook of environmental data on organic chemicals / Karel Verschueren. — 2nd ed. — New York: Van Nostrand Reinhold Co., c1983. vi, 1310 p.: ill.; 24 cm. Includes index. 1. Organic compounds — Environmental aspects — Handbooks, manuals, etc. I. T.
TD196.O73 V47 1983    363.7/384 19    *LC* 82-10994    *ISBN* 0442288026

**Barlett, Donald L.**    **5.6007**
Forevermore, nuclear waste in America / Donald L. Barlett and James B. Steele. — 1st ed. — New York: W.W. Norton, c1985. 352 p.: ill.; 22 cm. Includes index. 1. Radioactive pollution — United States. 2. Radioactive waste disposal — Environmental aspects — United States. I. Steele, James B. II. T.
TD196.R3 B37 1985    363.7/28 19    *LC* 84-22761    *ISBN* 0393019209

## TD201–500 WATER SUPPLY. WATER QUALITY. POLLUTION

**Groundwater contamination / Geophysics Study Committee,**    **5.6008**
**Geophysics Research Forum, Commission on Physical Sciences,**
**Mathematics, and Resources, National Research Council.**
Washington, D.C.: National Academy Press, 1984. xii, 179 p.: ill.; 28 cm. — (Studies in geophysics.) 1. Water, Underground — Pollution — United States.

I. Geophysics Research Forum (U.S.). Geophysics Study Committee. II. Series.
TD223.G75 1984    628.2/68 19    *LC* 83-27249    *ISBN* 0309034418

**Groundwater contamination from hazardous wastes / Princeton**    **5.6009**
**University Water Resources Program; Eric F. Wood, Director**
**... [et al.].**
Englewood Cliffs, N.J.: Prentice-Hall, 1985. xii, 159 p.: ill.; 25 cm. 1. Water, Underground — Pollution — United States. 2. Hazardous wastes — Environmental aspects — United States. 3. Hazardous waste sites — Environmental aspects — United States. I. Wood, Eric F. II. Princeton University. Water Resources Program.
TD223.G76 1985    628.4/4564 19    *ISBN* 0133662861

**Handbook of public water systems / Culp/Wesner/Culp; edited**    **5.6010**
**by Robert B. Williams, Gordon L. Culp.**
New York: Van Nostrand Reinhold, c1986. xiv, 1113 p.: ill.; 24 cm. — (Van Nostrand Reinhold environmental engineering series.) 1. Municipal water supply — United States. 2. Water quality — United States 3. Water — Purification I. Williams, Robert B. II. Culp, Gordon L. III. Culp/Wesner/Culp. IV. Series.
TD223.H27 1986    628.1 19    *LC* 85-26458    *ISBN* 0442215975

**Handbook of water quality management planning / edited by**    **5.6011**
**Joseph L. Pavoni.**
New York: Van Nostrand Reinhold, c1977. xviii, 419 p.: ill.; 24 cm. — (Van Nostrand Reinhold environmental engineering series) 1. Water quality management — United States. I. Pavoni, Joseph L.
TD223.H29 1977    333.9/1/50973    *LC* 77-21601    *ISBN* 0442232829

**Lake, Elizabeth E.**    **5.6012**
Who pays for clean water?: The distribution of water pollution control costs / by Elizabeth E. Lake, William M. Hanneman, and Sharon M. Oster. — Boulder, Colo.: Westview Press, 1979. xxiii, 244 p.: ill.; 24 cm. (An Urban systems research report) (A Westview replica edition) 1. Water quality management — United States — Finance. 2. Water quality management — United States — Costs. 3. Sewage disposal — United States — Finance. 4. Sewage disposal — United States — Costs. 5. Municipal finance — United States. I. Hanneman, William M. joint author. II. Oster, Sharon. joint author. III. T. IV. Series.
TD223.L28    614.7/72    *LC* 79-5152    *ISBN* 0891585869

**Al-Layla, Muhammad Anis H.**    **5.6013**
Water supply engineering design / M. Anis Al–Layla, Shamim Ahmad, and E. Joe Middlebrooks. Ann Arbor, Mich.: Ann Arbor Science Publishers, c1977. vii, 284 p.: ill.; 24 cm. 1. Water-supply engineering I. Shamīm, Ahmad. joint author. II. Middlebrooks, E. Joe. joint author. III. T.
TD345.A44    628.1    *LC* 76-46026    *ISBN* 0250401479

**Clark, John William.**    **5.6014**
Water supply and pollution control / John W. Clark, Warren Viessman, Jr., Mark J. Hammer. — 3d ed. — New York: IEP—Dun-Donnelley, Harper & Row, c1977. xvii, 857 p.: ill.; 24 cm. 1. Water-supply 2. Sewage I. Viessman, Warren. joint author. II. Hammer, Mark J., 1931- joint author. III. T.
TD345.C58 1977    628.1 19    *LC* 76-57126    *ISBN* 0700224955

**Todd, David Keith, 1923-.**    • **5.6015**
The water encyclopedia: a compendium of useful information on water resources / edited by David Keith Todd. — Port Washington, N.Y.: Water Information Center [1970] x, 559 p.: ill., maps; 26 cm. 1. Water-supply — Tables. 2. Hydrology — Tables. I. T.
TD351.T63    551.4/8/0212    *LC* 76-140311

**Krenkel, Peter A.**    **5.6016**
Water quality management / Peter A. Krenkel, Vladimir Novotny. — New York: Academic Press, 1980. xii, 671 p.: ill.; 24 cm. 1. Water quality management I. Novotny, Vladimir, 1938- joint author. II. T.
TD365.K73    628.1/68 19    *LC* 80-516    *ISBN* 0124261507

**Mathematical modeling of water quality: streams, lakes, and**    **5.6017**
**reservoirs / edited by Gerald T. Orlob.**
Chichester [West Sussex]; New York: Wiley, c1983. xx, 518 p.: ill.; 24 cm. — (International series on applied systems analysis. 12) 'A Wiley-Interscience publication. International Institute for Applied Systems Analysis.' 1. Water quality — Mathematical models. I. Orlob, Gerald T. II. International Institute for Applied Systems Analysis. III. Series.
TD365.M27 1983    363.7/394/0724 19    *LC* 82-17457    *ISBN* 0471100315

**Tchobanoglous, George.**    **5.6018**
Water quality: characteristics, modeling, modification / George Tchobanoglous, Edward D. Schroeder. — Reading, Mass.: Addison-Wesley, c1985. xxix, 768 p.: ill.; 25 cm. (Water quality management. v. 1) 1. Water quality I. Schroeder, Edward D. II. T. III. Series.
TD365.T38 1985    363.7/394 19    *LC* 84-11120    *ISBN* 0201054337

**An introduction to water quality modelling / edited by A.**                **5.6019**
**James.**
Chichester [West Sussex]; New York: Wiley, c1984. ix, 234 p.: ill.; 24 cm. 'A Wiley-Interscience publication.' Includes index. 1. Water quality — Measurement — Mathematical models. I. James, A.
TD367.I58 1984        628.1/0724 19        *LC* 83-16921        *ISBN* 0471903566

**American Public Health Association.**                **5.6020**
Standard methods for the examination of water and wastewater / Prepared and published jointly by the American Public Health Association, American Water Works Association, Water Pollution Control Federation. — 16th ed. — Washington, D. C.: American Public Health Association, 1985. xlix, 1268 p.: ill.; 24 cm. — 1. Water — Analysis 2. Sewage — Analysis I. American Water Works Association. II. Water Pollution Control Federation. III. T.
TD 380 A51 1985        *ISBN* 0875531318

**A Guide to marine pollution. Compiled by Edward D. Goldberg.**        **5.6021**
New York: Gordon and Breach Science Publishers, [c1972] x, 168 p.: illus.; 24 cm. 'This volume is an expansion of the final report of the Seminar on Methods of Detection, Measurement and Monitoring of Pollutants in the Marine Environment ... organized by FAO ... held in conjunction with the FAO Technical Conference on Marine Pollution and its Effects on Living Resources and Fishing, Rome, 9-18 December, 1970.' 1. Water — Pollution — Measurement — Addresses, essays, lectures. 2. Marine pollution — Measurement — Addresses, essays, lectures. I. Goldberg, Edward D. ed. II. Food and Agriculture Organization of the United Nations. III. Seminar on Methods of Detection, Measurement and Monitoring of Pollutants in the Marine Environment, Rome, 1970.
TD380.G84        628.1/686/162        *LC* 75-187038        *ISBN* 0677125003

**Kneese, Allen V.**                                        • **5.6022**
The economics of regional water quality management / by Allen V. Kneese. — Baltimore: Published for Resources for the Future by the Johns Hopkins Press, 1964. xii, 215 p.: ill., map. 1. Water — Pollution — Economic aspects. I. Resources for the Future. II. T.
TD423.K5        *LC* 64-18737

**Canter, Larry W.**                                        **5.6023**
Ground water pollution control / by Larry W. Canter and Robert C. Knox. — Chelsea, Mich.: Lewis Publishers, c1986. xxv, 526 p.: ill.; 24 cm. Includes index. 1. Water, Underground — Pollution I. Knox, Robert C. II. T.
TD426.C36 1986        363.7/394 19        *LC* 84-28927        *ISBN* 0873710142

**Ground water quality / edited by C.H. Ward, W. Giger. P.L.**        **5.6024**
**McCarty.**
New York: Wiley, c1985. xviii, 547 p.: ill.; 24 cm. (Environmental science and technology.) 'A Wiley-Interscience publication.' Papers presented at the First International Conference on Ground Water Quality Research, Oct. 7-10, 1981 at Rice University in Houston, Tex., sponsored by the National Center for Ground Water Research. 1. Water, Underground — Pollution — Congresses. 2. Water quality — Congresses. I. Ward, C. H. (Calvin Herbert), 1933- II. Giger, W. (Walter) III. McCarty, Perry L. IV. National Center for Ground Water Research (U.S.) V. Series.
TD426.G72 1985        363.7/394 19        *LC* 84-25661        *ISBN* 0471815977

**Nyer, Evan K.**                                        **5.6025**
Groundwater treatment technology / Evan K. Nyer. — New York: Van Nostrand Reinhold, c1985. x, 188 p.: ill.; 24 cm. 1. Water, Underground — Purification I. T.
TD426.N94 1985        628.1/62 19        *LC* 84-29099        *ISBN* 0442267061

**Weber, Walter J., 1934-.**                                **5.6026**
Physicochemical processes for water quality control / [by] Walter J. Weber, Jr.; with contributions by Jack A. Borchardt [and others]. — New York: Wiley-Interscience, [1972] xxvi, 640 p.: ill.; 23 cm. — (Environmental science and technology) 1. Water — Purification I. T.
TD430.W42        628.1/6        *LC* 77-37026        *ISBN* 0471924350

**Synthetic membrane processes: fundamentals and water**        **5.6027**
**applications / edited by Georges Belfort.**
Orlando, Fla.: Academic Press, 1984. xiii, 552 p.: ill.; 24 cm. — (Water pollution.) 1. Saline water conversion — Reverse osmosis process 2. Saline water conversion — Electrodialysis process 3. Membranes (Technology) I. Belfort, Georges. II. Series.
TD480.4.S94 1984        628.1/64 19        *LC* 83-2654        *ISBN* 0120854805

## TD511–812 Sewage. Refuse. Solid
## Wastes

**Metcalf & Eddy.**                                        **5.6028**
Wastewater engineering: collection, treatment, disposal / [by] Metcalf & Eddy, inc. — New York: McGraw-Hill [1972] xiii, 782 p.: ill.; 23 cm. (McGraw-Hill series in water resources and environmental engineering) Accompanied by

'Solutions manual, prepared by George Tchobanoglous' (102 p. illus. 23 cm.) published: New York, McGraw-Hill [1972]. 1. Sewerage 2. Sewage disposal I. Tchobanoglous, George. II. T.
TD645.M57        628/.2        *LC* 75-172262        *ISBN* 0070416753

**Nemerow, Nelson Leonard.**                                **5.6029**
Industrial water pollution: origins, characteristics, and treatment / Nelson L. Nemerow. — Reading, Mass.: Addison-Wesley Pub. Co., c1978. xiii, 738 p.: ill.; 25 cm. Published in 1971 under title: Liquid waste of industry. 1. Sewage 2. Water — Pollution I. T.
TD730.N45 1978        628.1/683        *LC* 76-46612        *ISBN* 0201052466

**Patterson, James William, 1940-.**                        **5.6030**
Wastewater treatment technology / James W. Patterson. — Ann Arbor, Mich.: Ann Arbor Science, c1975. v, 265 p.: ill.; 24 cm. 1. Sewage — Purification 2. Water — Purification I. T.
TD745.P32 1975        628/.3        *LC* 74-28653        *ISBN* 0250400863

**Benefield, Larry D.**                                        **5.6031**
Biological process design for wastewater treatment / Larry D. Benefield, Clifford W. Randall. — Englewood Cliffs, NJ: Prentice-Hall, c1980. xiv, 526 p.: ill.; 24 cm. — (Prentice-Hall series in environmental sciences) 1. Sewage — Purification — Biological treatment 2. Sewage disposal plants — Design and construction I. Randall, Clifford W. joint author. II. T.
TD755.B36 1980        628/.3        *LC* 79-13745        *ISBN* 013076406X

**Mudrack, K. (Klaus), 1924-.**                                **5.6032**
[Biologie der Abwasserreinigung. English] Biology of sewage treatment and water pollution control / K. Mudrack, and S. Kunst; translator, B.D. Hemmings; translation editor, E.B. Pike. — New York: Wiley, 1986. viii, 193 p.: ill.; 25 cm. Translation of: Biologie der Abwasserreinigung. Includes index. 1. Sewage — Purification — Biological treatment 2. Sewage sludge I. Kunst, Sabine. II. T.
TD755.M7313 1986        628.3/51 19        *LC* 85-27285        *ISBN* 0853129126

**Velz, Clarence J.**                                        **5.6033**
Applied stream sanitation / Clarence J. Velz. — 2nd ed. — New York: Wiley, c1984. viii, 800 p.: ill.; 24 cm. 'A Wiley-Interscience publication.' 1. Stream self-purification I. T.
TD764.V4 1984        628.1/68 19        *LC* 83-23555        *ISBN* 0471864161

**Vesilind, P. Aarne.**                                        **5.6034**
Treatment and disposal of wastewater sludges / P. Aarne Vesilind. — Rev. ed. — Ann Arbor: Ann Arbor Science Publishers, c1979. xi, 323 p.: ill.; 24 cm. 1. Sewage sludge I. T.
TD767.V47 1979        628/.36        *LC* 78-71431        *ISBN* 0250402904

**Pavoni, Joseph L.**                                        **5.6035**
Handbook of solid waste disposal: materials and energy recovery / Joseph L. Pavoni, John E. Heer, Jr., D. Joseph Hagerty. — New York: Van Nostrand Reinhold Co., [1975] xv, 549 p.: ill.; 23 cm. — (Van Nostrand Reinhold environmental engineering series) 1. Refuse and refuse disposal 2. Recycling (Waste, etc.) 3. Refuse as fuel I. Heer, John E. joint author. II. Hagerty, D. Joseph. joint author. III. T.
TD791.P3        628/.44        *LC* 74-26777        *ISBN* 0442230273

**Wilson, David C.**                                        **5.6036**
Waste management: planning, evaluation, technologies / David C. Wilson. — Oxford: Clarendon Press; New York: Oxford University Press, 1981. xxi, 530 p.: ill.; 24 cm. Includes index. 1. Refuse and refuse disposal I. T.
TD791.W54 1981        363.7/28 19        *LC* 80-41812

**Hecht, N. L. (Norman L.)**                                **5.6037**
Design principles in resource recovery engineering / by Norman L. Hecht. — Boston: Butterworths, c1983. xiv, 159 p.: ill.; 24 cm. 'An Ann Arbor science book.' 1. Recycling (Waste, etc.) I. T.
TD794.5.H43 1983        628.4/458 19        *LC* 82-46060        *ISBN* 0250403153

**Vesilind, P. Aarne.**                                        **5.6038**
Unit operations in resource recovery engineering / P. Aarne Vesilind, Alan E. Rimer. — Englewood Cliffs, N.J.: Prentice-Hall, c1981. x, 452 p.: ill.; 24 cm. 1. Recycling (Waste, etc.) 2. Refuse and refuse disposal 3. Separation (Technology) 4. Refuse as fuel I. Rimer, Alan E. joint author. II. T.
TD794.5.V47 1981        628/.445        *LC* 79-25757        *ISBN* 0139379533

**Epstein, Samuel S.**                                        **5.6039**
Hazardous waste in America / Samuel S. Epstein, Lester O. Brown, Carl Pope. — San Francisco: Sierra Club Books, c1982. xii, 593 p.; 24 cm. 1. Hazardous wastes — United States. 2. Hazardous wastes — Law and legislation — United States. I. Brown, Lester O. II. Pope, Carl. III. T.
TD811.5.E67 1982        363.7/28 19        *LC* 82-3304        *ISBN* 0871562944

**Kiang, Yen-Hsiung, 1947-.**      5.6040
Hazardous waste processing technology / by Yen–hsiung Kiang, Amir A. Metry. — Ann Arbor, Mich.: Ann Arbor Science Publishers, c1982. xviii, 549 p.: ill.; 24 cm. 1. Hazardous wastes I. Metry, Amir. II. T.
TD811.5.K5 1982    628.4/45 19    LC 81-69070    ISBN 0250404117

## TD878–893 OTHER TYPES OF POLLUTION

### TD881–890 Air Pollution

**Fundamentals of air pollution [by] Arthur C. Stern [and others]**   5.6041
New York, Academic Press [1973] xiv, 492 p. illus. 27 cm. 1. Air — Pollution I. Stern, Arthur C.
TD883.F86    628.5/3    LC 72-82650    ISBN 0126665605

**Industrial air pollution handbook / editor, Albert Parker.**    5.6042
1st ed. — London; New York: McGraw-Hill, c1978. xix, 657 p.: ill.; 26 cm. 1. Air — Pollution 2. Air — Pollution — Great Britain. 3. Flue gases — Purification I. Parker, Albert.
TD883.I394    628.5/3/0941    LC 77-30126    ISBN 0070844860

**Seinfeld, John H.**      5.6043
Air pollution: physical and chemical fundamentals [by] John H. Seinfeld. — New York: McGraw-Hill, [1974, c1975] xv, 523 p.: illus.; 24 cm. 1. Air — Pollution I. T.
TD883.S4    628.5/3    LC 74-4296    ISBN 0070560420

**Air pollution / edited by Arthur C. Stern.**      5.6044
3d. ed. — New York: Academic Press, 1976. 6 v.: ill.; 24 cm. — (Environmental sciences) 1. Air — Pollution — Collected works. I. Stern, Arthur C. II. Series.
TD883.S83 1976    363.6    LC 76-8256    ISBN 0126666016

**Wark, Kenneth, 1927-.**      5.6045
Air pollution, its origin and control / Kenneth Wark, Cecil F. Warner. — New York: IEP, c1976. xvi, 519 p.: ill.; 24 cm. — (The IEP series in mechanical engineering) 1. Air — Pollution I. Warner, Cecil Francis, 1915- joint author. II. T.
TD883.W28    363.7/392 19    LC 75-38668    ISBN 0700224882

**Meyer, Beat.**      5.6046
Indoor air quality / Beat Meyer. — Reading, Mass.: Addison-Wesley Pub. Co., 1983. xiii, 434 p.: ill.; 24 cm. Includes indexes. 1. Indoor air pollution 2. Air quality management I. T.
TD883.1.M49 1983    363.7/392 19    LC 82-8911    ISBN 0201050943

**Wadden, R. A.**      5.6047
Indoor air pollution: characterization, prediction, and control / Richard A. Wadden and Peter A. Scheff. — New York: Wiley, c1983. xi, 213 p.: ill.; 24 cm. — (Environmental science and technology. 0194-0287) 'A Wiley-Interscience publication.' 1. Indoor air pollution I. Scheff, Peter A. II. T. III. Series.
TD883.1.W33 1983    363.7/392 19    LC 82-11153    ISBN 0471876739

**Springer, George S.**      5.6048
Engine emissions; pollutant formation and measurement. Edited by George S. Springer and Donald J. Patterson. — New York: Plenum Press, 1973. xii, 371 p.: illus.; 24 cm. 1. Automobiles — Motors — Exhaust gas 2. Diesel motor exhaust gas 3. Aircraft exhaust emissions I. Patterson, Donald J. joint author. II. T.
TD886.5.S68    629.04    LC 71-188716    ISBN 0306305852

**Brenchley, David L.**      5.6049
Industrial source sampling [by] David L. Brenchley, C. David Turley [and] Raymond F. Yarmac. — Ann Arbor, Mich.: Ann Arbor Science, [1973] xxii, 484 p.: illus.; 25 cm. 1. Air — Pollution — Measurement 2. Gases — Analysis I. Turley, C. David, joint author. II. Yarmac, Raymond F., joint author. III. T.
TD890.B7    628.5/3    LC 72-96908    ISBN 025040012X

**Handbook of air pollution analysis / edited by Roy M. Harrison and Roger Perry.**      5.6050
2nd ed. — London; New York: Chapman and Hall, 1986. xxii, 634 p.: ill.; 24 cm. 1. Air — Pollution — Measurement — Handbooks, manuals, etc. 2. Environmental chemistry — Handbooks, manuals, etc. I. Harrison, Roy M., 1948- II. Perry, Roger, 1940-
TD890.H36 1986    628.5/3 19    LC 85-26011    ISBN 0412244101

### TD892 Noise

**Harris, Cyril M., 1917-.**      5.6051
Handbook of noise control / edited by Cyril M. Harris. — 2d ed. — New York: McGraw-Hill, c1979. ca. 600 p. in various pagings: ill.; 24 cm. 1. Noise control I. T.
TD892.H37 1979    620.2/3    LC 78-6764    ISBN 0070268142

**Noise control: handbook of principles and practices / edited by David M. Lipscomb, Arthur C. Taylor.**      5.6052
New York: Van Nostrand Reinhold Co., c1978. xvii, 375 p.: ill.; 24 cm. — (Van Nostrand Reinhold environmental engineering series) 1. Noise control — Handbooks, manuals, etc. I. Lipscomb, David M. II. Taylor, Arthur C.
TD892.N6514    620.2/3    LC 77-20200    ISBN 0442248113

## TD895–899 INDUSTRIAL AND FACTORY SANITATION. RADIOACTIVE WASTE

**Koziorowski, B.**      5.6053
[Ścieki przemysłowe. English] Industrial waste disposal, by B. Koziorowski and J. Kucharski. Translated from the Polish by J. Bandrowski. Translation edited by G. R. Nellist. [1st English ed.] Oxford, New York, Pergamon Press [1972] vii, 369 p. illus. 27 cm. Translation of Ścieki przemysłowe. 1. Factory and trade waste I. Kucharski, Józef, joint author. II. T.
TD897.K6813 1972    628.5/4    LC 77-138807    ISBN 0080158684

**Equity issues in radioactive waste management / edited by Roger E. Kasperson; with the assistance of Mimi Berberian; with contributions from Shaul Ben–David ... [et al.].**      5.6054
Cambridge, Mass.: Oelgeschlager, Gunn & Hain, 1984. 416 p. 1. Radioactive waste disposal — Social aspects — Addresses, essays, lectures. I. Kasperson, Roger E. II. Berberian, Mimi.
TD898.E68 1983    363.7/28 19

**Heckman, Richard A.**      5.6055
Nuclear waste management abstracts / Richard A. Heckman and Camille Minichino. — New York: IFI/Plenum, c1982. vii, 104 p.: ill.; 29 cm. — (IFI data base library.) Includes indexes. 1. Radioactive waste disposal — Abstracts. I. Minichino, Camille. II. T. III. Series.
TD898.H43 1982    363.7/28 19    LC 81-19868    ISBN 0306652021

**Lipschutz, Ronnie D.**      5.6056
Radioactive waste: politics, technology, and risk / Ronnie D. Lipschutz. — Cambridge, Mass.: Ballinger Pub. Co., c1980. xvii, 247 p.: ill.; 24 cm. 'A report of the Union of Concerned Scientists.' Includes index. 1. Radioactive waste disposal I. Union of Concerned Scientists. II. T.
TD898.L56    614.7/6    LC 79-19649    ISBN 0884106217

**Resnikoff, Marvin.**      5.6057
The next nuclear gamble: transportation and storage of nuclear waste / by Marvin Resnikoff; with Lindsay Audin; assisted by Nancy Bernstein, Leslie Birnbaum. — New York, N.Y.: Council on Economic Priorities, c1983. 378 p.: ill.; 23 cm. 1. Radioactive waste disposal — United States. 2. Radioactive wastes — Transportation 3. Radioactive wastes — Storage. I. Council on Economic Priorities. II. T.
TD898.R475 1983    621.48/38 19    LC 83-157630    ISBN 0878710205

**Shapiro, Fred C.**      5.6058
Radwaste / by Fred C. Shapiro. — 1st ed. — New York: Random House, c1981. 288 p.; 22 cm. Includes index. 1. Radioactive waste disposal — United States. I. T.
TD898.S48    363.7/28 19    LC 81-40238    ISBN 039451159X

# TE Highway Engineering. Roads

**Oglesby, Clarkson Hill, 1908-.**      5.6059
Highway engineering / Clarkson H. Oglesby, R. Gary Hicks. — 4th ed. — New York: Wiley, c1982. xiii, 844 p., [1] folded leaf: ill.; 25 cm. 1. Highway engineering I. Hicks, Russell G. II. T.
TE145.O675 1982    625.7 19    LC 81-12949    ISBN 047102936X

**Winfrey, Robley, 1899-.**      • 5.6060
Economic analysis for highways. — Scranton, Pa.: International Textbook Co., [1969] xii, 923 p.: illus.; 24 cm. — (International textbooks in civil engineering) 1. Highway engineering 2. Engineering economy 3. Transportation,

Automotive — U.S. — Finance. 4. Express highways — Economic aspects — U.S. I. T.
TE145.W57     338.4/7/3881     *LC* 69-16620     *ISBN* 0700222448

**Woods, Kenneth Brady, 1905- ed.**     • **5.6061**
Highway engineering handbook. Kenneth B. Woods, editor–in–chief; Donald S. Berry, associate editor; William H. Goetz, associate editor. 1st ed. New York, McGraw-Hill, 1960. 1 v. (various pagings) illus., maps, diagrs. 24 cm. (McGraw-Hill handbooks) 1. Highway engineering — Handbooks, manuals, etc. I. T.
TE145.W65     625.7     *LC* 58-59682

**Wright, Paul H.**     **5.6062**
Highway engineering / Paul H. Wright, Radnor J. Paquette. — 5th ed. — New York: Wiley, c1987. 838 p. Includes indexes. 1. Highway engineering I. Paquette, Radnor Joseph. II. T.
TE145.W74 1987     625.7 19     *LC* 86-15720     *ISBN* 0471826243

**Lapinski, Michael.**     **5.6063**
Road and bridge construction handbook / Michael Lapinski. — New York: Van Nostrand Reinhold Co., c1978. ix, 156 p.: ill.; 24 cm. Includes index. 1. Road construction 2. Bridge construction I. T.
TE153.L32     625.7     *LC* 78-1475     *ISBN* 0442246811

**Krebs, Robert D., 1931-.**     **5.6064**
Highway materials [by] Robert D. Krebs [and] Richard D. Walker. — New York: McGraw-Hill, [c1971] xvi, 428 p.: illus., map.; 23 cm. 1. Road materials 2. Roads — Subgrades I. Walker, Richard D., 1931- joint author. II. T.
TE200.K72     625.7/35     *LC* 78-119824

**Meyer, Carl F.**     **5.6065**
Route surveying and design / Carl F. Meyer, David W. Gibson. — 5th ed. — New York: Harper & Row, c1980. viii, 548 p.: ill.; 21 cm. — (Series in civil engineering) Includes index. 1. Roads — Surveying 2. Railroads — Surveying 3. Route surveying I. Gibson, David W., 1944- joint author. II. T.
TE209.M48 1980     625     *LC* 79-15267     *ISBN* 0700225242

**Kell, James H.**     **5.6066**
Manual of traffic signal design / James H. Kell, Iris J. Fullerton. — Englewood Cliffs, N.J.: Prentice-Hall, c1982. x, 259 p.: ill.; 29 cm. At head of title: Institute of Transportation Engineers. Includes index. 1. Traffic signs and signals I. Fullerton, Iris J. II. Institute of Transportation Engineers. III. T.
TE228.K44 1982     625.7/94 19     *LC* 82-60988     *ISBN* 0135543606

**Sargious, Michel.**     **5.6067**
Pavements and surfacings for highways and airports / Michel Sargious. — New York: Wiley, [1975] xviii, 619 p.: ill.; 23 cm. 'A Halsted Press book.' 1. Pavements I. T.
TE250.S25     625.8     *LC* 75-11891     *ISBN* 0470754184

**Haas, R. C. G. (Ralph C. G.)**     **5.6068**
Pavement management systems / Ralph Haas, W. Ronald Hudson. — New York: McGraw-Hill, c1978. xvi, 457 p.: ill.; 25 cm. 1. Pavements — Design and construction. 2. Pavements — Evaluation. I. Hudson, W. Ronald. joint author. II. T.
TE251.H26     625.8     *LC* 77-8672     *ISBN* 0070253919

**Yoder, Eldon J. (Eldon Joseph)**     **5.6069**
Principles of pavement design / E. J. Yoder, M. W. Witczak. — 2d ed. — New York: Wiley, [1975] xiii, 711 p.: ill.; 26 cm. 'A Wiley-Interscience publication.' 1. Pavements — Design and construction. I. Witczak, Matthew W., joint author. II. T.
TE251.Y6 1975     625.8     *LC* 75-12555     *ISBN* 0471977802

# TF Railroad Engineering

**Allen, G. Freeman (Geoffrey Freeman)**     **5.6070**
Railways: past, present & future / G. Freeman Allen; foreword by Sir Peter Parker. — 1st ed. — New York: Morrow, 1982. 303 p.: ill. (some col.); 30 cm. Includes index. 1. Railroads — History I. T.
TF15.A424 1982     385/.09 19     *LC* 82-60816     *ISBN* 0688006361

**Hastings, Paul, 1933-.**     **5.6071**
Railroads; an international history. — New York: Praeger, [1972] 144 p.: illus.; 23 cm. 1. Railroads — History I. T.
TF15.H38     385/.09/034     *LC* 77-179924

**Hay, William Walter, 1908-.**     **5.6072**
Railroad engineering / William W. Hay. — 2nd ed. — New York: Wiley, c1982. xvi, 758 p., [2] folded leaves of plates: ill.; 24 cm. 'A Wiley-Interscience publication.' 1. Railroad engineering I. T.
TF200.H38 1982     625.1 19     *LC* 81-23117     *ISBN* 0471364002

**Railroad track: theory and practice: material properties, cross–     5.6073
sections, welding, and treatment / edited by Fritz Fastenrath; translated by Walter Grant.**
New York: F. Ungar Pub. Co., c1981. xx, 457 p.: ill.; 24 cm. Translation of Die Eisenbahnschiene. 1. Railroads — Rails I. Fastenrath, Fritz.
TF258.E3713     625.1/5 19     *LC* 80-5340     *ISBN* 0804442312

**Behrend, George.**     **5.6074**
Luxury trains from the Orient Express to the TGV / George Behrend. — New York: Vendome Press: Distributed in the U.S. of America by the Viking Press, 1982, c1977. 232 p.: ill. (some col.); 26 cm. 1. Railroads — Express-trains I. T.
TF573.B43 1982     385/.37 19     *LC* 81-10366     *ISBN* 0865650160

**Cudahy, Brian J.**     **5.6075**
Under the sidewalks of New York: the story of the greatest subway system in the world / by Brian J. Cudahy. — Brattleboro, Vt.: S. Greene Press, c1979. 176 p.: ill.; 25 cm. Includes index. 1. Subways — New York (N.Y.) 2. Local transit — New York (N.Y.) I. T.
TF725.N5 C8     388.4/2/097471     *LC* 79-15221     *ISBN* 0828903522

**Nene, Vilas D.**     **5.6076**
Advanced propulsion systems for urban rail vehicles / Vilas D. Nene. — Englewood Cliffs, N.J.: Prentice-Hall, c1985. xii, 228 p.: ill.; 24 cm. Includes index. 1. Electric railway motors 2. Electric railroads — Power supply I. T.
TF935.N46 1985     625/.4 19     *LC* 84-4769     *ISBN* 0130129313

# TG Bridge Engineering

**Steinman, D. B. (David Barnard), 1886-1960.**     **5.6077**
Bridges and their builders / David B. Steinman & Sara Ruth Watson. — [Rev. and expanded ed.] — New York: Dover Publications, 1957. 401 p.: ill. 1. Bridges — History. 2. Engineers I. Watson, Sara Ruth. II. T.
TG15.S8 1957     *LC* 57-13151

**McCullough, David G.**     **5.6078**
The Great Bridge [by] David McCullough. New York, Simon and Schuster [1972] 636 p. illus. 25 cm. 1. Brooklyn Bridge (New York, N.Y.) I. T.
TG25.N53 M32     624.5/5/097471     *LC* 72-81823     *ISBN* 0671212133

**Heins, Conrad P.**     **5.6079**
Design of modern concrete highway bridges / Conrad P. Heins, Richard A. Lawrie. — New York: J. Wiley, c1984. xvii, 635 p.: ill.; 24 cm. 'A Wiley-Interscience publication.' 1. Bridges, Concrete — Design and construction. I. Lawrie, Richard A. II. T.
TG335.H46 1984     624/.2 19     *LC* 83-6748     *ISBN* 0471875449

**Heins, Conrad P.**     **5.6080**
Design of modern steel highway bridges / C. P. Heins, D. A. Firmage. — New York: Wiley, c1979. ix, 463 p.: ill.; 24 cm. 'A Wiley-Interscience publication.' 1. Bridges, Iron and steel — Design and construction. I. Firmage, D. Allan (David Allan), 1918- joint author. II. T.
TG350.H43     624.2     *LC* 78-9084     *ISBN* 0471042633

**Vlasov, V. Z. (Vasiliĭ Zakharovich)**     **5.6081**
[Tonkostennye uprugie sterzhni. English] Thin–walled elastic beams. 2d ed. rev. and augm. Translated from Russian [by] Y. Schectman]. Jerusalem: Published for the National Science Foundation, Washington, D.C., by the Israel Program for Scientific Translations, 1961; [available from the Office of Technical Services, U.S. Dept of Commerce, Washington], 1961. 493 p. illus., port., diagrs., tables. 25 cm. 1. Girders 2. Elasticity I. T.
TG350.V573 1961     *LC* 62-61955

**Podolny, Walter.**     **5.6082**
Construction and design of prestressed concrete segmental bridges / Walter Podolny, Jr., Jean M. Muller. — New York: Wiley, c1982. xi, 561 p., [1] folded leaf of plates: ill.; 29 cm. — (Wiley series of practical construction guides. 0271-6011) 'A Wiley-Interscience publication.' 1. Bridges, Concrete — Design and construction. 2. Prestressed concrete construction I. Muller, Jean M. II. T. III. Series.
TG355.P63 1982     624.2 19     *LC* 81-13025     *ISBN* 0471056588

**Fisher, John W., 1931-.**     **5.6083**
Fatigue and fracture in steel bridges: case studies / John W. Fisher. — New York: Wiley, c1984. xix, 315 p.: ill.; 24 cm. 'A Wiley-Interscience publication.'

1. Bridges, Iron and steel 2. Steel, Structural — Fatigue 3. Steel, Structural — Fracture. I. T.
TG380.F57 1984    624/.252 19    *LC* 83-23495    *ISBN* 047180469X

**Podolny, Walter.**        **5.6084**
Construction and design of cable–stayed bridges / Walter Podolny, Jr. and John B. Scalzi. — 2nd ed. — New York: Wiley, c1986. xv, 336 p.: ill.; 29 cm. — (Wiley series of practical construction guides.) 'A Wiley-Interscience publication.' Includes indexes. 1. Bridges, Cable–stayed — Design and construction. I. Scalzi, John B. II. T. III. Series.
TG405.P6 1986    624/.55 19    *LC* 85-26622    *ISBN* 0471826553

# TH Building Construction

## TH1–915 BUILDING CONSTRUCTION. GENERAL WORKS

**Mainstone, R. J. (Rowland J.), 1923-.**        **5.6085**
Developments in structural form / Rowland Mainstone. — 1st American ed. — Cambridge, Mass.: M.I.T. Press, 1975. 350 p.: ill.; 31 cm. Includes index. 1. Building 2. Structural engineering 3. Architecture I. T.
TH145.M2796 1975b    721    *LC* 74-3472    *ISBN* 0262131110

**Clayton, C. R. I.**        **5.6086**
Site investigation / C.R.I. Clayton, N.E. Simons, and M.C. Matthews. — New York: Halsted Press, 1982. 424 p.: ill.; 26 cm. 'A Halsted Press Book.' Includes index. 1. Building sites — Handbooks, manuals, etc. 2. Soil mechanics — Handbooks, manuals, etc. I. Simons, N. E. II. Matthews, M. C. III. T.
TH375.C58 1982    624.1/51 19    *LC* 81-21973    *ISBN* 0470273283

**Adrian, James J.**        **5.6087**
Construction estimating: an accounting and productivity approach / James J. Adrian. — Reston, Va.: Reston Pub. Co., c1982. xiii, 528 p.: ill.; 24 cm. Includes index. 1. Building — Estimates I. T.
TH435.A3 1982    624 19    *LC* 82-321    *ISBN* 0835909255

**Advances in tall buildings / Council on Tall Buildings and**    **5.6088**
**Urban Habitat; Lynn S. Beedle, editor–in–chief.**
New York: Van Nostrand Reinhold Co., c1986. xx, 693 p.: ill.; 24 cm. Includes indexes. 1. Tall buildings — Addresses, essays, lectures. 2. Structural engineering — Addresses, essays, lectures. I. Beedle, Lynn S. II. Council on Tall Buildings and Urban Habitat.
TH845.A45 1986    721/.042 19    *LC* 85-17826    *ISBN* 0442215991

**Council on Tall Buildings and Urban Habitat.**        **5.6089**
Structural design of tall concrete and masonry buildings / group coordinators, Raymond C. Reese ... [et al.]; group editors, James G. MacGregor, Inge Lyse. — [New York: American Society of Civil Engineers, c1978] xxii, 938 p.: ill.; 24 cm. — (Monograph on planning and design of tall buildings; v. CB) Includes indexes. 1. Tall buildings — Design and construction — Collected works. 2. Reinforced concrete construction — Collected works. 3. Masonry — Design and construction — Collected works. 4. Structural design — Collected works. I. Reese, Raymond C. II. MacGregor, James Grierson, 1934- III. Lyse, Inge, 1898- IV. T. V. Series.
TH845.C68 1978 vol. CB    721/.042 s 690    *LC* 78-60643

**Salvadori, Mario George, 1907-.**        **5.6090**
Structural design in architecture / Mario Salvadori, Matthys Levy; with example and problem solutions by Howard H. M. Hwang. — 2d ed. — Englewood Cliffs, N.J.: Prentice-Hall, c1981. xxii, 458 p.: ill.; 24 cm. Includes index. 1. Structural design I. Levy, Matthys. joint author. II. T.
TH845.S32 1981    729/.3    *LC* 80-11550    *ISBN* 013853473X

**Salvadori, Mario George, 1907-.**        **5.6091**
Why buildings stand up: the strength of architecture / Mario Salvadori; ill. by Saralinda Hooker and Christopher Ragus. — 1st ed. — New York: Norton, c1980. 311 p.: ill.; 25 cm. Includes index. 1. Structural engineering I. Hooker, Saralinda. II. Ragus, Christopher. III. T.
TH845.S33 1980    624.1/7    *LC* 80-16285    *ISBN* 0393014010

**Schueller, Wolfgang, 1934-.**        **5.6092**
High–rise building structures / Wolfgang Schueller. — 2nd ed. — Malabar, Fla.: R.E. Krieger Pub. Co., 1986. xiii, 274 p.: ill.; 25 cm. Includes index. 1. Tall buildings 2. Structural engineering I. T.
TH845.S37 1986    721/.042 19    *LC* 84-27809    *ISBN* 0898748356

## TH1061–4970 BUILDING CONSTRUCTION SYSTEMS. DESIGN. USES

**Ground movements and their effects on structures / edited by**    **5.6093**
**P.B. Attewell and R.K. Taylor.**
London: Surrey University Press; New York: Distributed in the USA by Chapman and Hall, 1984. xviii, 441 p.: ill.; 24 cm. 1. Earth movements and building 2. Mine subsidences 3. Earthquake engineering I. Attewell, P. B. II. Taylor, R. K.
TH1095.G76 1984    624.1/5 19    *LC* 84-9428

**Herbert, Gilbert.**        **5.6094**
Pioneers of prefabrication: the British contribution in the nineteenth century / Gilbert Herbert. — Baltimore: Johns Hopkins University Press, c1978. xii, 228 p.: ill.; 25 cm. — (The Johns Hopkins studies in nineteenth-century architecture) Includes index. 1. Buildings, Prefabricated — Great Britain — History. I. T. II. Series.
TH1098.H47    693.9/7/0941    *LC* 76-47372    *ISBN* 0801818524

**Hansen, Hans Jürgen, 1921-.**        **5.6095**
[Holzbaukunst. English] Architecture in wood; a history of wood building and its techniques in Europe and North America. Edited by Hans Jürgen Hansen. Translated by Janet Seligman. With contributions by Arne Berg [and others] New York, Viking Press [1971] 288 p. illus. (part col.) 31 cm. (A Studio book) Translation of Holzbaukunst; eine Geschichte der abendländischen Holzarchitektur und ihrer Konstruktionselemente. 1. Building, Wooden 2. Woodwork I. Berg, Arne, 1917- II. T.
TH1101.H2913    721/.0448/09    *LC* 71-101786    *ISBN* 0670131482

**Croome, Derek J.**        **5.6096**
Noise, buildings, and people / by Derek J. Croome. — 1st ed. — Oxford; New York: Pergamon Press, 1977. xx, 613 p.: ill.; 25 cm. — (International series in heating, ventilation, and refrigeration; v. 11) Includes indexes. 1. Soundproofing 2. Noise control 3. Buildings — Environmental engineering. I. T.
TH1725.C76 1977    693.8/34    *LC* 75-40156    *ISBN* 008019690X.
*ISBN* 0080198163 flexicover

**Ramaswamy, G. S., 1923-.**        **5.6097**
Design and construction of concrete shell roofs [by] G. S. Ramaswamy. — New York: McGraw-Hill, [1968] x, 641 p.: illus.; 23 cm. 1. Roofs, Shell 2. Reinforced concrete construction I. T.
TH2416.R29    624/.95    *LC* 66-18478

**Small and mini hydropower systems: resource assessment and**    **5.6098**
**project feasibility / Jack J. Fritz [editor].**
New York: McGraw-Hill, c1984. 1 v. (various pagings): ill.; 24 cm. 1. Hydroelectric power plants — Design and construction. I. Fritz, Jack J.
TH4581.S53 1984    621.31/2134 19    *LC* 83-13595    *ISBN* 0070224706

## TH6014–7975 ENVIRONMENTAL ENGINEERING. HEATING. VENTILATING

**ASHRAE handbook.**        **5.6099**
1981-. Atlanta, Ga.: American Society of Heating, Refrigerating and Air-Conditioning Engineers, Inc., 1981-. v.: ill.; 29 cm. Annual. Issued in 4 vols.: Fundamentals, Applications, Equipment, Systems. 'Will be revised on a four year cycle.' 1. Refrigeration and refrigerating machinery 2. Air conditioning 3. Ventilation 4. Heat engineering I. American Society of Heating, Refrigerating and Air-Conditioning Engineers.
TH7011.A21

**American Conference of Governmental Industrial Hygienists.**    **5.6100**
**Committee on Industrial Ventilation.**
Industrial ventilation: a manual of recommended practice. — 1st- ed. Lansing, Mich.: [s.n.], [1951- v.: ill., diagrs.; 29 cm. annual (irregular) 1. Factories — Heating and ventilation I. T.
TH7392 M6 A5    *LC* 62-12929

## TH7413–7414 Solar Heating
(See also: TJ810)

**Anderson, Bruce, 1947-.**        **5.6101**
The solar home book: heating, cooling, and designing with the sun / by Bruce Anderson with Michael Riordan; art direction by Linda Goodman, ill. by Edward A. Wong, pencil drawings by Rachel Dutton. — Harrisville, N.H.: Cheshire Books; Rockville, MD: distributed by RPM Distributors, c1976.

297 p.: ill.; 22 x 28 cm. Includes index. 1. Solar houses 2. Solar energy I. Riordan, Michael. joint author. II. T.
TH7413.A53    697/.78 19    *LC* 76-29494    *ISBN* 0917352017

**Beckman, William A.**       **5.6102**
Solar heating design, by the f–chart method / William A. Beckman, Sanford A. Klein, John A. Duffie. — New York: Wiley, c1977. xv, 200 p.: ill.; 24 cm. 'A Wiley-Interscience publication.' Includes index. 1. Solar heating 2. FCHART (Computer program) I. Klein, Sanford A., 1950- joint author. II. Duffie, John A. joint author. III. T.
TH7413.B4    697/.78    *LC* 77-22168    *ISBN* 0471034061

**Jones, Robert W. (Robert William), 1940-.**       **5.6103**
The sunspace primer: a guide for passive solar heating / Robert W. Jones, Robert D. McFarland. — New York: Van Nostrand Reinhold, c1984. xiv, 285 p.: ill.; 24 cm. 1. Solar heating — Passive systems I. McFarland, Robert D. II. T.
TH7413.J66 1984    697/.78 19    *LC* 83-16776    *ISBN* 0442245750

**Kreider, Jan F., 1942-.**       **5.6104**
Solar heating and cooling: engineering, practical design, and economics / Jan F. Kreider, Frank Kreith. — Washington: Scripta Book Co., [1975] ix, 342 p.: ill.; 25 cm. Includes index. 1. Solar heating 2. Solar air conditioning I. Kreith, Frank. joint author. II. T.
TH7413.K73 1975    697/.78    *LC* 75-6646    *ISBN* 0070354731

**Lebens, Ralph M.**       **5.6105**
Passive solar heating design / Ralph M. Lebens. — London: Applied Science Publishers; New York: Halsted Press, 1980. xv, 234 p.: ill.; 23 cm. 1. Solar heating — Passive systems I. T.
TH7413.L43    697/.78    *LC* 80-40255

**Passive solar design handbook.**       **5.6106**
New York: Van Nostrand Reinhold Co., c1984. 750 p.: ill.; 29 cm. Includes index. 1. Solar houses — Design and construction. 2. Solar energy — Passive systems I. Anderson, Bruce, 1947- II. Total Environmental Action, inc. III. Los Alamos Scientific Laboratory. IV. Los Alamos National Laboratory.
TH7414.P26 1984    690/.869 19    *LC* 83-21805    *ISBN* 0442208103

## TH9025–9745 PROTECTION OF BUILDINGS. FIRE PREVENTION

**Marshall, J. Lawrence, 1913-.**       **5.6107**
Lightning protection [by] J. L. Marshall. — New York: Wiley, [1973] xiii, 190 p.: ill.; 23 cm. 'A Wiley-Interscience publication.' 1. Lightning protection I. T.
TH9057.M37    643    *LC* 73-4415    *ISBN* 0471573051

**The National electrical code handbook: based on the 1987**       **5.6108**
**edition of the National electrical code / Joseph A. Ross, editor;**
**Wilford I. Summers, technical consultant.**
4th ed. — Boston, Mass.: National Fire Protection Association, c1986. Includes index. 1. Electric engineering — Law and legislation — United States. I. Ross, Joseph A. II. Summers, Wilford I. III. National Fire Protection Association. National Electrical Code, 1981
TH9115.N28 no. SPP-6C KF5704    363.3/77 s 343.73/0786213 363.3/77 s 347.303786213 19    *LC* 85-63883    *ISBN* 0877653267

**Fire protection handbook.**       **5.6109**
16th ed. — Boston, Mass.: National Fire Protection Association, 1986. 1 v. (various pagings): ill.; 29 cm. 1. Fire prevention — Handbooks, manuals, etc. 2. Fire extinction — handbooks, manuals, etc. I. National Fire Protection Association.
TH9150.F47    614.84    *LC* 62-12655

**Meyer, Eugene, 1938-.**       **5.6110**
Chemistry of hazardous materials / Eugene Meyer. Englewood Cliffs, N.J.: Prentice-Hall, c1976. xiv, 370 p.: ill.; 25 cm. 1. Hazardous substances — Fires and fire prevention. 2. Hazardous substances I. T.
TH9446.H38 M48    604/.7/0154    *LC* 76-18686    *ISBN* 0131292390

## TJ MECHANICAL ENGINEERING. AUTOMATION

## TJ1–211 General Works

**Hottel, Hoyt C. (Hoyt Clarke), 1903-.**       **5.6111**
New energy technology—some facts and assessments [by] H. C. Hottel and J. B. Howard. Cambridge, Mass.: MIT Press, 1972 (c1971) xi, 364 p. illus. 24 cm. 1. Power resources — United States. I. Howard, J. B. (Jack Benny), 1937- joint author. II. T.
TJ23.H67    621.4    *LC* 70-37654    *ISBN* 0262080524 *ISBN* 0262580195

**Mechanical engineers' handbook.**       • **5.6112**
1st- ed.; 1916-. New York: McGraw-Hill. v.: ill.; 18-24 cm. 'Based on the Hütte.' 1. Mechanical engineering — Handbooks, manuals, etc. I. Marks, Lionel S. (Lionel Simeon), 1871- II. Baumeister, Theodore, 1897- III. Akademischer Verein Hütte, Berlin. 'Hütte,' des Ingenieurs Taschenbuch.
TJ151.M37    *LC* 16-12915

**Hupping, Carol.**       **5.6113**
Producing your own power; how to make nature's energy sources work for you. Edited by Carol Hupping Stoner. Technical consultants: Eugene and Sandra Fulton Eccli. Illus.: Erick Ingraham. Emmaus, PA, Rodale Press, Book Division [1974] 322 p. illus. 23 cm. (An Organic gardening and farming book) 1. Power resources I. T.
TJ153.H85    621.4    *LC* 74-10765    *ISBN* 0878570888

**McMullan, J. T. (John T.)**       **5.6114**
Energy resources and supply / J. T. McMullan, R. Morgan, R. B. Murray. — London; New York: Wiley, c1976. xii, 508 p.: ill.; 24 cm. 'A Wiley-Interscience publication.' 1. Power resources 2. Power (Mechanics) I. Morgan, R. joint author. II. Murray, R. B. joint author. III. T.
TJ153.M183    333.7    *LC* 75-6973    *ISBN* 0471589756

**Renewable energy resources and rural applications in the**       **5.6115**
**developing world / edited by Norman L. Brown.**
Boulder, Colo.: Westview Press for the American Association for the Advancement of Science, 1978. xviii, 168 p.: ill.; 24 cm. (AAAS selected symposia series; 6) 1. Renewable energy sources — Developing countries I. Brown, Norman L.
TJ163.R46    333.7    *LC* 77-18549    *ISBN* 0891584331

## TJ163.15–163.5 POWER RESOURCES. ENERGY CONSERVATION

### TJ163.15–163.16 Symposia. Reference Works

**Alternative energy sources: international symposium of the**       **5.6116**
**Kuwait Foundation / edited by Jamal T. Manassah.**
New York: Academic Press, 1981. 2 v. (xi, 922): ill.; 24 cm. Proceedings of a symposium sponsored by the Kuwait Foundation for the Advancement of Sciences, and held in Kuwait Feb. 9-13, 1980. 1. Renewable energy sources — Congresses. 2. Power resources — Congresses. I. Manassah, Jamal T. II. Mu'assasat al-Kuwayt lil-Taqaddum al-'Ilmī.
TJ163.15.A475 1981    662/.6 19    *LC* 80-27710    *ISBN* 0124671012

**International Energy Symposium. (1st: 1980: Knoxville, Tenn.)**       **5.6117**
World energy production and productivity: proceedings of the International Energy Symposium I, October 14, 1980 / symposium chairman, John C. Sawhill; edited by Robert A. Bohm, Lillian A. Clinard, Mary R. English. — Cambridge, Mass.: Ballinger Pub. Co., c1981. xxxiv, 410 p.: ill.; 24 cm. — (International energy symposia series) 1. Power resources — Congresses. 2. Energy policy — Congresses. I. Sawhill, John C., 1936- II. Bohm, Robert A. III. Clinard, Lillian A. IV. English, Mary R. V. T. VI. Series.
TJ163.15.I5635 1980    333.79 19    *LC* 81-12863    *ISBN* 0884106497

**International Energy Symposium. (2nd: 1981: Knoxville, Tenn.)**       **5.6118**
Improving world energy production and productivity: proceedings of the International Energy Symposium II, November 3–6, 1981 / edited by Lillian A. Clinard, Mary R. English, Robert A. Bohm. — Cambridge, Mass.: Ballinger, c1982. xxxviii, 663 p.: ill.; 24 cm. — (International energy symposia series. v. 2)

1. Power resources — Congresses. 2. Energy policy — Congresses. I. Clinard, Lillian A. II. English, Mary R. III. Bohm, Robert A. IV. T. V. Series.
TJ163.15.I5635 1981      333.79 19      *LC* 82-6869      *ISBN* 0884108775

**United Nations. Statistical Office.**         • **5.6119**
World energy supplies. no. 1- 1929-50— New York, United Nations, Department of International Economic and Social Affairs, Statistical Office. v. maps, diagrs., tables. 28 cm. (Its Statistical Papers, ser. J) Annual. Issued with the United Nations publications sales numbers. 1. Serial publications 2. Power resources — Statistics. I. T. II. Series.
TJ163.15.U5x      338.272      *LC* 58-680

**Dictionary of energy** / general editor, Malcolm Slesser; subject    **5.6120**
editors, D.J. Bennet ... [et al.]; special assistants, P. Howell, C. Lewis.
1st American ed. — New York: Schocken Books, 1983, c1982. 299 p.: ill.; 25 cm. 1. Power resources — Dictionaries. 2. Power (Mechanics) — Dictionaries. I. Slesser, Malcolm.
TJ163.16.D5 1983      621.042/03/21 19      *LC* 82-10252      *ISBN* 0805238166

## TJ163.2 General Works

**Carr, Donald Eaton, 1903-.**         **5.6121**
Energy and the earth machine / Donald E. Carr. — 1st ed. — New York: Norton, c1976. x, 275 p.; 24 cm. Includes index. 1. Power resources 2. Human ecology 3. Energy policy 4. Energy conservation I. T.
TJ163.2.C37 1976      333.7      *LC* 75-44431      *ISBN* 0393064077

**Dorf, Richard C.**         **5.6122**
Energy, resources & policy / Richard C. Dorf. — Reading, Mass.: Addison-Wesley Pub. Co., c1978. xvii, 486 p.: ill.; 25 cm. 1. Power resources 2. Energy policy I. T.
TJ163.2.D67      333.7      *LC* 76-45151      *ISBN* 0201016737

**Energy and man: technical and social aspects of energy** / edited    **5.6123**
by M. Granger Morgan.
New York: IEEE Press, c1975. xi, 521 p.: ill.; 28 cm. (IEEE Press selected reprint series) 1. Power resources 2. Energy consumption 3. Power (Mechanics) 4. Energy policy — Social aspects I. Morgan, Millett Granger, 1941-
TJ163.2.E46      333.9      *LC* 74-27680      *ISBN* 087942043X

**Energy and people: social implications of different energy**    **5.6124**
futures / edited by Mark Diesendorf; assistant editors Roger Bartell ... [et al.].
Canberra: Society for Social Responsibility in Science (A.C.T.), 1979. 176 p.; 30 cm. 1. Power resources — Social aspects. 2. Energy policy — Social aspects I. Diesendorf, Mark. II. Society for Social Responsibility in Science (A.C.T.).
TJ163.2.E462      333.79/0994      *LC* 80-670075      0909509125

**Energy management handbook** / edited by Wayne C. Turner.    **5.6125**
New York: Wiley, c1982. xxiii, 714 p.: ill.; 24 cm. 'A Wiley-Interscience publication.' 1. Power resources — Handbooks, manuals, etc. 2. Energy conservation — Handbooks, manuals, etc. I. Turner, Wayne C., 1942-
TJ163.2.E4827      621.042/0685 19      *LC* 81-10351      *ISBN* 047108252X

**Energy: readings from Scientific American** / with introductions    **5.6126**
by S. Fred Singer.
San Francisco: W. H. Freeman, c1979. vi, 221 p.: ill.; 29 cm. Includes index. 1. Power resources 2. Power (Mechanics) I. Singer, S. Fred (Siegfried Fred), 1924- II. Scientific American.
TJ163.2.E4842      333.7      *LC* 78-31979      *ISBN* 071671082X

**Energybook** / edited by John Prenis.         **5.6127**
Philadelphia: Running Press, 1975. 112 p.: ill.; 34 cm. 1. Power resources 2. Power (Mechanics) I. Prenis, John.
TJ163.2.E5      621.4      *LC* 74-84854      *ISBN* 0914294210

**Handbook of energy technology and economics** / edited by    **5.6128**
Robert A. Meyers.
New York: Wiley, c1983. xiv, 1089 p.: ill.; 25 cm. 'A Wiley-Interscience publication.' 1. Energy development — Handbooks, manuals, etc. I. Meyers, Robert A. (Robert Allen), 1936-
TJ163.2.H355 1983      333.79 19      *LC* 82-8477      *ISBN* 0471082090

**International Conference on Energy Options. (4th: 1984:**    **5.6129**
London)
Fourth International Conference on Energy Options: the role of alternatives in the world energy scene, 3–6 April 1984 / organised by the Science, Education & Technology Divisions of the Institution of Electrical Engineers, in association with the British Wind Energy Society ... [et al.]. — London: The Institution of Electrical Engineers, 1984. 421 p.: ill. (Conference publication / Institution of Electrical Engineers; no. 233) 1. Renewable energy sources 2. Energy policy

I. T. II. Title: Energy options. III. Title: Role of alternatives in the world energy scene.
TJ163.2.I54 1984      *ISBN* 0852962908

**International Institute for Applied Systems Analysis. Energy**    **5.6130**
**Systems Program Group.**
Energy in a finite world: report / by the Energy Systems Program Group of the International Institute for Applied Systems Analysis; Wolf Häfele, program leader; written by Jeanne Anderer with Alan McDonald and Nebojsa Nakicenovic. — Cambridge, Mass.: Ballinger Pub. Co., c1981. 2 v.: ill.; 26 cm. 1. Power resources 2. Energy policy I. Häfele, Wolf. II. Anderer, Jeanne. III. McDonald, Alan T. IV. Nakicenovic, Nebojsa. V. T.
TJ163.2.I55 1981      333.79 19      *LC* 80-20057      *ISBN* 0884106411

**McGraw–Hill encyclopedia of energy** / Sybil P. Parker, editor    **5.6131**
in chief.
2d ed. — New York: McGraw-Hill Book Co., c1981. viii, 838 p.: ill.; 29 cm. 1. Power resources — Dictionaries. 2. Power (Mechanics) — Dictionaries. I. Parker, Sybil P. II. Title: Encyclopedia of energy.
TJ163.2.M3 1981      333.79/03/21      *LC* 80-18078      *ISBN* 0070452687

**McMullan, J. T. (John T.)**         **5.6132**
Energy resources / J. T. McMullan, R. Morgan, and R. B. Murray. — New York: Wiley, 1978 (c1977). viii, 177 p.: ill.; 22 cm. (Resource and environmental sciences series) 'A Halsted Press book.' Includes index. 1. Power resources I. Morgan, R. joint author. II. Murray, R. B. joint author. III. T. IV. Series.
TJ163.2.M34      333.7      *LC* 77-26748      *ISBN* 0470993774

**Perspectives on energy: issues, ideas, and environmental**    **5.6133**
dilemmas / edited by Lon C. Ruedisili, Morris W. Firebaugh.
New York: Oxford University Press, 1975. xii, 527 p.: ill.; 24 cm. 1. Power resources 2. Power (Mechanics) 3. Energy policy I. Ruedisili, Lon C. II. Firebaugh, Morris W.
TJ163.2.P47      333.7      *LC* 74-22886      *ISBN* 0195018796 pbk

**Ramage, Janet, 1932-.**         **5.6134**
Energy, a guidebook / Janet Ramage. — Oxford [Oxfordshire]; New York: Oxford University Press, 1983. xx, 345 p.: ill.; 23 cm. — (OPUS) Includes index. 1. Power resources 2. Power (Mechanics) I. T. II. Series.
TJ163.2.R345 1983      333.79 19      *LC* 82-14207      *ISBN* 0192191691

**Rider, Don K., 1918-.**         **5.6135**
Energy, hydrocarbon fuels and chemical resources / Don K. Rider. — New York: Wiley, c1981. x, 493 p.: ill.; 24 cm. 'A Wiley-Interscience publication'. 1. Power resources 2. Energy policy 3. Feedstock I. T.
TJ163.2.R52      333.8/2 19      *LC* 81-196      *ISBN* 0471059153

**Starr, Chauncey.**         **5.6136**
Current issues in energy: a selection of papers / by Chauncey Starr. — 1st ed. — Oxford; New York: Pergamon Press, 1979. xvi, 202 p., [1] leaf of plates: ill.; 26 cm. — (Pergamon international library of science, technology, engineering, and social studies) 1. Power resources 2. Energy policy I. T.
TJ163.2.S734 1979      333.7 19      *LC* 78-40695      *ISBN* 0080232434

**Teller, Edward, 1908-.**         **5.6137**
Energy from heaven and earth: in which a story is told about energy from its origins 15,000,000,000 years ago to its present adolescence—turbulent, hopeful, beset by problems, and in need of help / Edward Teller. — San Francisco: W. H. Freeman, c1979. xiv, 322 p.: ill.; 25 cm. Based on lectures given by the author during 1975 for the Harvey Prize Lectures at Technion, Haifa, Israel; the Distinguished Visiting Lectures of the Faculty of Natural Sciences and Mathematics, State University of New York at Buffalo; and a lecture delivered at Acadia University, Wolfville, Nova Scotia. 1. Power resources I. T.
TJ163.2.T4      333.7      *LC* 79-4049      *ISBN* 0716710633

**Voegeli, Henry E. (Henry Edward)**         **5.6138**
Survival 2001: scenario from the future / Henry E. Voegeli, John J. Tarrant. — New York: Van Nostrand Reinhold, [1975] 115 p.: ill.; 28 cm. 1. Power resources 2. Power (Mechanics) 3. Energy conservation I. Tarrant, John J. joint author. II. T.
TJ163.2.V63      621      *LC* 74-29310      *ISBN* 0442284063

## TJ163.235 Handbooks. Tables

**Glasstone, Samuel, 1897-.**         **5.6139**
Energy deskbook / by Samuel Glasstone. — New York: Van Nostrand Reinhold Co., c1983. xii, 453 p.; 26 cm. 1. Power resources — Handbooks, manuals, etc. 2. Power (Mechanics) — Handbooks, manuals, etc. I. T.
TJ163.235.G53 1983      621.042/0321 19      *LC* 82-24864      *ISBN* 0442229283

**Loftness, Robert L.**         **5.6140**
Energy handbook / Robert L. Loftness. — 2nd ed. — New York: Van Nostrand Reinhold, c1984. ix, 763 p.: ill.; 23 x 31 cm. 1. Power resources —

Handbooks, manuals, etc. 2. Power (Mechanics) — Handbooks, manuals, etc.
I. T.
TJ163.235.L64 1984     333.79 19     *LC* 83-21834     *ISBN* 0442259921

## TJ163.25 Special Regions

**Campbell, Robert Wellington.**          **5.6141**
Soviet energy technologies: planning, policy, research, and development /
Robert W. Campbell. — Bloomington: Indiana University Press, c1980. x,
268 p.: graphs; 25 cm. Includes index. 1. Energy development — Russia.
2. Energy policy — Russia. 3. Power resources — Research — Russia. I. T.
TJ163.25.R9 C36     333.79/0947     *LC* 80-7562     *ISBN* 0253159652

**Dienes, Leslie.**          **5.6142**
The Soviet energy system: resource use and policies / Leslie Dienes and
Theodore Shabad. — Washington: V. H. Winston; New York: distributed
solely by Halsted Press, a division of Wiley, c1979. vii, 298 p.: ill.; 24 cm. —
(Scripta series in geography.) 1. Power resources — Russia. 2. Energy policy
— Russia. I. Shabad, Theodore. joint author. II. T. III. Series.
TJ163.25.R9 D53     333.7     *LC* 78-20814     *ISBN* 0470266295

**Cuff, David J.**          **5.6143**
The United States energy atlas / David J. Cuff, William J. Young. — 2nd ed. —
New York: Macmillan Pub. Co.; London: Collier Macmillan, c1986. p. cm.
Includes index. 1. Power resources — United States. I. Young, William J.
(William Jack), 1935- II. T.
TJ163.25.U6 C83 1986     333.99/0973 19     *LC* 85-4867     *ISBN* 0026912406

**Energy research programs.**          **5.6144**
1st ed. (1980)-     . — New York: R.R. Bowker, c1980-. v.; 29 cm. Annual.
Includes sections on the United States, Canada, Mexico. 1. Power resources —
Research — United States — Directories. I. Jaques Cattell Press.
TJ163.25.U6 E52     621.042/072073 19     *LC* 80-648739

**Energy resources in an uncertain future: coal, gas, oil, and**          **5.6145**
**uranium supply forecasting** / M.A. Adelman ... [et al.].
Cambridge, Mass.: Ballinger Pub. Co., c1983. xxix, 434 p.: ill.; 24 cm. Includes
index. 1. Power resources — United States. 2. Coal — United States. 3. Gas,
Natural — United States 4. Petroleum — United States 5. Uranium — United
States. I. Adelman, Morris Albert.
TJ163.25.U6 E528 1983     553.2/0973 19     *LC* 81-10969     *ISBN* 0884106446

**Energy resource recovery in arid lands** / edited by Klaus D.      **5.6146**
**Timmerhaus.**
1st ed. — Albuquerque: University of New Mexico Press, c1981. x, 118 p.: ill.;
24 cm. (Contributions of the Committee on Desert and Arid Zones Research of
the Southwestern and Rocky Mountain Division of the American Association
for the Advancement of Science. [18]) 1. Power resources — West (U.S.) —
Addresses, essays, lectures. 2. Energy development — West (U.S.) —
Addresses, essays, lectures. 3. Arid regions — West (U.S.) — Addresses,
essays, lectures. I. Timmerhaus, Klaus D. II. Series.
TJ163.25.U6 E54     333.79/0978 19     *LC* 80-54573     *ISBN* 0826305644

**Gibbons, John H., 1929-.**          **5.6147**
Energy, the conservation revolution / John H. Gibbons and William U.
Chandler. — New York: Plenum Press, c1981. xv, 258 p.: ill.; 24 cm. —
(Modern perspectives in energy.) 1. Power resources — United States.
2. Energy conservation — United States. I. Chandler, William U., 1950- joint
author. II. T. III. Series.
TJ163.25.U6 G52     333.79/16/0973 19     *LC* 80-28431     *ISBN* 0306406705

**National Research Council (U.S.). Committee on Nuclear and**      **5.6148**
**Alternative Energy Systems.**
Energy in transition, 1985–2010: final report of the Committee on Nuclear and
Alternative Energy Systems, National Research Council, National Academy of
Sciences. — San Francisco: W. H. Freeman, c1980. xxxvii, 677 p.: ill.; 24 cm.
1. Power resources — United States. 2. Energy policy — United States. I. T.
TJ163.25.U6 N382 1980     333.79 19     *LC* 79-27389     *ISBN* 071671227X

**University of Oklahoma. Science and Public Policy Program.**      **5.6149**
Energy from the West: a technology assessment of Western energy resource
development / by Science and Public Policy Program, University of Oklahoma,
Michael D. Devine ... [et al.]. — Norman: University of Oklahoma Press,
c1981. xvii, 362 p.: ill.; 27 cm. Based largely on the results of a study conducted
from 1975 through 1979 for the Office of Energy, Minerals, and Industry of the
Environmental Protection Agency. 1. Energy development — West (U.S.)
2. Energy policy — West (U.S.) 3. Environmental protection — West (U.S.)

I. Devine, Michael D. II. United States. Environmental Protection Agency.
Office of Energy, Minerals, and Industry. III. T.
TJ163.25.U6 O35 1981     333.79/0978 19     *LC* 80-5936     *ISBN*
0806117508

**Sant, Roger W.**          **5.6150**
Creating abundance: America's least–cost energy strategy / Roger W. Sant,
Dennis W. Bakke, Roger F. Naill; James Bishop, Jr., editor. — New York:
McGraw-Hill, c1984. xiii, 176 p.: ill.; 23 cm. 1. Power resources — United
States. 2. Energy policy — United States. I. Bakke, Dennis. II. Naill, Roger
F. III. Bishop, James. IV. T.
TJ163.25.U6 S26 1984     333.79/.0973 19     *LC* 83-24853     *ISBN*
0070415188

## TJ163.3–163.5 Energy Conservation

**Efficient electricity use: a practical handbook for an energy**      **5.6151**
**constrained world** / Craig B. Smith, editor.
New York: Pergamon Press, c1976. xxvi, 960 p.: ill.; 28 cm. 'Applied
Nucleonics Company, Inc., Santa Monica, California, was selected by the
Electric Power Research Institute to conduct a research program to compile
efficient methods of using energy, particularly electricity.' 1. Energy
conservation — Handbooks, manuals, etc. 2. Electric power — Handbooks,
manuals, etc. 3. Energy consumption — Handbooks, manuals, etc. I. Smith,
Craig B. II. Applied Nucleonics Company. III. Electric Power Research
Institute.
TJ163.3.E3 1976     333.7     *LC* 75-44373     *ISBN* 008020869X

**Smith, Craig B.**          **5.6152**
Energy management principles: applications, benefits, savings / Craig B. Smith.
— New York: Pergamon Press, c1981. xx, 495 p.: ill.; 24 cm. 1. Energy
conservation 2. Power resources I. T.
TJ163.3.S545 1981     333.79/16 19     *LC* 81-5167     *ISBN* 0080280366

**Zackrison, Harry B.**          **5.6153**
Energy conservation techniques for engineers / Harry B. Zackrison, Jr. — New
York: Van Nostrand Reinhold, c1984. xiv, 332 p.: ill.; 24 cm. Includes index.
1. Energy conservation 2. Buildings — Energy conservation 3. Power
resources I. T.
TJ163.3.Z3 1984     696 19     *LC* 82-23691     *ISBN* 0442293925

**An Efficient energy future: prospects for Europe and North**      **5.6154**
**America.**
London; Boston: United Nations Economic Commission for Europe:
Buterworths, 1983. viii, 258 p.: ill.; 31 cm. 1. Energy conservation — Europe.
2. Energy conservation — North America. I. United Nations. Economic
Commission for Europe.
TJ163.4.E8 E35 1983     333.79/12 19     *LC* 83-127232     *ISBN*
0408013281

**Energy conservation in heating, cooling, and ventilating**      **5.6155**
**buildings: heat and mass transfer techniques and alternatives** /
edited by C. J. Hoogendoorn and N. H. Afgan.
Washington: Hemisphere Pub. Corp., c1978. 2 v. (xii, 901 p.): ill.; 24 cm. —
(Series in thermal and fluids engineering) Lectures and papers presented at a
seminar sponsored by the International Centre for Heat and Mass Transfer,
held at Dubrovnik, Yugoslavia, Aug. 29-Sept. 2, 1977. 1. Buildings — Energy
conservation — Congresses. 2. Heat — Transmission — Congresses. 3. Mass
transfer — Congresses. I. Hoogendoorn, C. J. II. Afgan, Naim.
III. International Center for Heat and Mass Transfer.
TJ163.5.B84 E528     697     *LC* 78-1108     *ISBN* 0891160949

**Retrofitting of commercial, institutional, and industrial buildings**    **5.6156**
**for energy conservation** / edited by Milton Meckler.
New York: Van Nostrand Reinhold, c1984. xii, 414 p.: ill.; 26 cm. 1. Buildings
— Energy conservation I. Meckler, Milton.
TJ163.5.B84 R47 1984     696 19     *LC* 83-1148     *ISBN* 0442262264

**Saving energy in the home: Princeton's experiments at Twin**      **5.6157**
**Rivers** / edited by Robert H. Socolow.
Cambridge, Mass.: Ballinger Pub. Co., c1978. xxvii, 330 p.: ill.; 24 cm. Reports
of research conducted by the Center for Environmental Studies, Princeton
University. 'Also being published by Elsevier Sequoia S.A. as a special issue of
Energy and buildings, vol. 1, no. 3.' 1. Dwellings — New Jersey — Twin Rivers
— Energy conservation. I. Socolow, Robert H. II. Princeton University.
Center for Environmental Studies.
TJ163.5.D86 S28     696     *LC* 78-2598     *ISBN* 0884100804

## TJ163.6–164 Power (Mechanics). Power Plants

**Harder, Edwin L. (Edwin Leland), 1905-.** 5.6158
Fundamentals of energy production / Edwin L. Harder. — New York: Wiley, c1982. xvi, 368 p.: ill.; 29 cm. — (Alternate energy.) 'A Wiley-Interscience publication.' 1. Power (Mechanics) 2. Power resources I. T. II. Series.
TJ163.9.H37 1982    333.79 19    LC 81-16257    *ISBN* 0471083569

**Purcell, John Francis, 1916-.** 5.6159
From hand ax to laser: man's growing mastery of energy / by John Purcell; illustrated by Judy Skorpil. — New York: Vanguard Press, c1982. xi, 308 p.: ill.; 24 cm. Includes indexes. 1. Power (Mechanics) — History. 2. Science — History I. T.
TJ163.9.P87 1982    621.042 19    LC 81-16389    *ISBN* 0814908608

**Thumann, Albert.** 5.6160
Fundamentals of energy engineering / Albert Thumann. — Atlanta, Ga.: Fairmont Press; Englewood Cliffs, N.J.: Prentice-Hall, 1984. v, 446 p.: ill.; 24 cm. 1. Power (Mechanics) 2. Power resources I. T.
TJ163.9.T54 1984    621.042 19    LC 83-20518    *ISBN* 013338327X

## TJ173–211 Mechanical Dynamics. Kinematics. Robots

**Lindsay, James F.** 5.6161
Dynamics of physical circuits and systems / James F. Lindsay, Silas Katz; [ill. by Scientific Illustrators]. — Champaign, Ill.: Matrix Publishers; Forest Grove, OR: exclusive distributor, ISBS, Inc., c1978. xi, 459 p.: ill.; 24 cm. — (Matrix series in circuits and systems) 1. Dynamics I. Katz, Silas, joint author. II. T.
TJ173.L56    620.1/04    LC 78-53838    *ISBN* 0916460215

**Hirschhorn, Jeremy.** • 5.6162
Dynamics of machinery / by Jeremy Hirschhorn. — New York: Barnes & Noble, [1968, c1967] xvi, 447 p.: ill.; 24 cm. 1. Machinery, Kinematics of 2. Mechanical movements 3. Machinery — Vibration 4. Machinery, Dynamics of I. T.
TJ175.H684 1968    621.8/11    LC 68-2245

**Dudley, Darle W.** 5.6163
Handbook of practical gear design / Darle W. Dudley. — New York: McGraw-Hill, c1984. 675 p. in various pagings: ill.; 24 cm. Rev. ed. of: Practical gear design. 1st ed. 1954. Includes index. 1. Gearing — Handbooks, manuals, etc. I. Dudley, Darle W. Practical gear design II. T.
TJ184.D784 1984    621.8/33 19    LC 84-3860    *ISBN* 0070179514

**The World yearbook of robotics research and development.** 5.6164
1st ed. — London, England: Kogan Page; Detroit, Mich.: Gale Research Co., 1985-. v.; 24 cm. 'The concept of the book is based on a section of The International Robotics Yearbook (Kogan Page, London; Ballinger, Boston -1983).' 1. Robotics — Research — Periodicals. 2. Robots — Periodicals. 3. Robotics — Directories. 4. Robots, Industrial — Periodicals. I. Gale Research Company.
TJ210.2.W67    629.8/92 19    LC 86-641028

**Robotics research: the second international symposium / edited** 5.6165
**by Hideo Hanafusa and Hirochika Inoue.**
Cambridge, Mass.: MIT Press, c1985. xx, 530 p.: ill.; 29 cm. (MIT Press series in artificial intelligence.) Papers presented at the Second International Symposium on Robotics Research, held Aug. 20-23, 1984, in Kyoto, Japan. 1. Robotics — Research — Congresses. I. Hanafusa, Hideo, 1923- II. Inoue, Hirochika, 1942- III. International Symposium on Robotics Research. (2nd: 1984: Kyoto, Japan) IV. Series.
TJ210.3.R64 1985    629.8/92 19    LC 85-6    *ISBN* 0262081512

**Robotics research: the third international symposium / edited by** 5.6166
**O.D. Faugeras and Georges Giralt.**
Cambridge, Mass.: MIT Press, c1986. vii, 404 p.: ill.; 29 cm. — (MIT Press series in artificial intelligence.) Proceedings of the Third International Symposium on Robotics Research held at the Château Monvillargenes in Gouvieux, France, 10/7-11/85. '3'—Cover. 1. Robotics — Research — Congresses. I. Faugeras, O. D. II. Giralt, Georges. III. International Symposium on Robotics Research. (3rd: 1985: Gouvieux, France) IV. Series.
TJ210.3.R643 1986    629.8/92 19    LC 86-20901    *ISBN* 0262061015

**Waldman, Harry.** 5.6167
Dictionary of robotics / Harry Waldman. — New York: Macmillan; London: Collier Macmillan, c1985. viii, 303 p.: ill.; 25 cm. 1. Robotics — Dictionaries. 2. Robots — Dictionaries. I. T.
TJ210.4.W35 1985    629.8/92/0321 19    LC 84-23070    *ISBN* 0029485304

**Koren, Yoram.** 5.6168
Robotics for engineers / by Yoram Koren. — New York: McGraw-Hill, c1985. xvii, 347 p.: ill.; 24 cm. 1. Robotics 2. Robots, Industrial I. T.
TJ211.K66 1985    629.8/92 19    LC 84-21316    *ISBN* 0070353999

**Raibert, Marc H.** 5.6169
Legged robots that balance / Marc H. Raibert. — Cambridge, Mass.: MIT Press, 1986. xiii, 233 p.: ill.; 24 cm. — (MIT Press series in artificial intelligence.) Includes index. 1. Robotics 2. Artificial intelligence I. T. II. Series.
TJ211.R35 1986    629.8/92 19    LC 85-23888    *ISBN* 0262181177

**Robot motion: planning and control / [edited by] Michael Brady** 5.6170
**... [et al.].**
Cambridge, Mass.: MIT Press, c1982. xv, 585 p.: ill.; 24 cm. — (MIT Press series in artificial intelligence.) 1. Robots — Motion 2. Manipulators (Mechanism) I. Brady, Michael, 1945- II. Series.
TJ211.R54 1982    629.8/92 19    LC 82-23929    *ISBN* 026202182X

**Robotics research: the first international symposium / edited by** 5.6171
**Michael Brady and Richard Paul.**
Cambridge, Mass.: MIT Press, c1984. xiv, 1001 p.: ill.; 27 cm. — (MIT Press series in artificial intelligence.) Papers presented at the First International Symposium on Robotics Research held at Bretton Woods, N.H., Aug. 25-Sept. 2, 1983. 1. Robotics — Research — Congresses. 2. Artificial intelligence — Congresses. I. Brady, Michael, 1945- II. Paul, Richard P. III. International Symposium on Robotics Research. (1st: 1983: Bretton Woods, N.H.) IV. Series.
TJ211.R568 1984    629.8/92 19    LC 83-25592    *ISBN* 0262022079

**Todd, D. J.** 5.6172
Walking machines: an introduction to legged robots / D.J. Todd. — New York: Chapman and Hall, 1985. 190 p.: ill.; 24 cm. Includes index. 1. Robots I. T.
TJ211.T63 1985    629.8/92 19    *ISBN* 041201131X

**Tutorial on robotics / [edited by] C.S.G. Lee, R.C. Gonzalez,** 5.6173
**K.S. Fu.**
2nd ed. — Washington, D.C.: IEEE Computer Society Press, c1986. xii, 731 p.: ill.; 28 cm. 'IEEE Computer Society order number 658.' 'IEEE catalog number EH0241-0.' 1. Robotics 2. Robots, Industrial I. Lee, C. S. G. (C. S. George) II. Gonzalez, Rafael C. III. Fu, K. S. (King Sun), 1930-
TJ211.T88 1986    629.8/92 19    LC 85-82545    *ISBN* 0818606584

**Young, John Frederick.** 5.6174
Robotics [by] John F. Young. New York: Wiley, 1974 (c1973) 303 p. illus. 23 cm. 'A Halsted Press book.' 1. Robotics I. T.
TJ211.Y68    629.8/92    LC 72-6308    *ISBN* 0470979909

**Horn, Berthold.** 5.6175
Robot vision / Berthold Klaus Paul Horn. — MIT Press ed. — Cambridge, Mass.: MIT Press; New York: McGraw-Hill, c1986. x, 509 p.: ill.; 24 cm. (MIT electrical engineering and computer science series.) Includes index. 1. Robot vision I. T. II. Series.
TJ211.3.H67 1986    629.8/92 19    LC 85-18137    *ISBN* 0262081598

## TJ212–225 Control Engineering. Automatic Control Systems

**Athans, Michael.** 5.6176
Optimal control: an introduction to the theory and its applications / [by] Michael Athans [and] Peter L. Falb. — New York: McGraw-Hill, [1966] xiv, 879 p.: ill. — (Lincoln Laboratory publications) 1. Automatic control I. Falb, Peter L. II. T.
TJ213.A865    LC 65-21570

**Cassell, Douglas A.** 5.6177
Microcomputers and modern control engineering / by Douglas A. Cassell. — Reston, Va.: Reston Pub. Co., c1983. xvii, 590 p.: ill.; 24 cm. Includes index. 1. Automatic control 2. Microcomputers I. T.
TJ213.C294 1983    629.8/95 19    LC 82-25040    *ISBN* 0835943658

**Kuo, Benjamin C., 1930-.** 5.6178
Automatic control systems / Benjamin C. Kuo. — 5th ed. — Englewood Cliffs, NJ: Prentice-Hall, 1987. p. cm. 1. Automatic control 2. Control theory I. T.
TJ213.K8354 1987    629.8/3 19    LC 86-17047    *ISBN* 0130548421

**Lentz, Kendrick W.** 5.6179
Design of automatic machinery / Kendrick W. Lentz, Jr. — New York: Van Nostrand Reinhold, c1985. xv, 336 p.: ill.; 24 cm. Includes index.

1. Machinery, Automatic — Design and construction. 2. Automatic control I. T.
TJ213.L366 1985 621.8 19 *LC* 84-3513 *ISBN* 0442260326

**Mayr, Otto.** • **5.6180**
[Zur Frühgeschichte der technischen Regelungen. English] The origins of feedback control. Cambridge, M.I.T. Press [1970] vii, 151 p. illus. 24 cm. Translation of Zur Frühgeschichte der technischen Regelungen. 1. Automatic control — History. I. T.
TJ213.M3413 628.8 *LC* 72-123250 *ISBN* 026213067X

**Dorf, Richard C.** **5.6181**
Modern control systems / Richard C. Dorf. — 4th ed. — Reading, Mass.: Addison-Wesley, c1986. xvi, 539 p.: ill.; 25 cm. (Addison-Wesley series in electrical engineering.) 1. Feedback control systems I. T. II. Series.
TJ216.D67 1986 629.8/3 19 *LC* 85-7532 *ISBN* 0201053268

**Franklin, Gene F.** **5.6182**
Digital control of dynamic systems / Gene F. Franklin, J. David Powell. — Reading, Mass.: Addison-Wesley Pub. Co., c1980. xvi, 335 p.: ill.; 24 cm. Includes index. 1. Digital control systems 2. Dynamics I. Powell, J. David, 1938- joint author. II. T.
TJ216.F72 1980 629.8/95 *LC* 79-16377 *ISBN* 0201028913

**Hostetter, G. H., 1939-.** **5.6183**
Design of feedback control systems / Gene H. Hostetter, Clement J. Savant, Jr., Raymond Stefani. — [New York]: Holt, Rinehart & Winston, [1982] xvi, 541 p.: ill.; 24 cm. — (HRW series in electrical and computer engineering.) 1. Feedback control systems I. Savant, C. J. II. Stefani, Raymond T. III. T. IV. Series.
TJ216.H63 1982 629.8/312 19 *LC* 81-6371 *ISBN* 0030575931

**Jacquot, Raymond G., 1938-.** **5.6184**
Modern digital control systems / Raymond G. Jacquot. — New York: M. Dekker, c1981. xii, 355 p.: ill.; 24 cm. — (Electrical engineering and electronics. 11) 1. Digital control systems I. T. II. Series.
TJ216.J29 629.8/95 19 *LC* 81-7834 *ISBN* 0824713222

**Kuo, Benjamin C., 1930-.** **5.6185**
Digital control systems / Benjamin C. Kuo. — [2d ed.]. — New York: Holt, Rinehart and Winston, 1980. xiv, 730 p.: ill.; 25 cm. (HRW series in electrical and computer engineering.) 1. Digital control systems I. T. II. Series.
TJ216.K812 1980 629.8/043 *LC* 80-16455 *ISBN* 0030575680

**Schwarzenbach, J.** **5.6186**
System modelling and control / J. Schwarzenbach, K.F. Gill. — 2nd ed. — London; Baltimore, Md.: E. Arnold, 1984. xi, 322 p.: ill.; 23 cm. 1. Feedback control systems — Mathematical models. 2. System analysis I. Gill, K. F. II. T.
TJ216.S38 1984 629.8/314 19 *LC* 84-71791 *ISBN* 0713135182

**Vande Vegte, J. (John)** **5.6187**
Feedback control systems / John van de Vegte. — Englewood Cliffs, NJ: Prentice-Hall, c1986. xiv, 433 p.: ill.; 25 cm. Includes index. 1. Feedback control systems I. T.
TJ216.V26 1986 629.8/3 19 *LC* 85-6567 *ISBN* 0133129500

**Applied digital control / edited by Spyros G. Tzafestas.** **5.6188**
Amsterdam; New York: North-Holland; New York, N.Y., U.S.A.: Sole distributors for the U.S.A. and Canada, Elsevier Science Pub. Co., 1985. xx, 305 p.: ill.; 24 cm. (North-Holland systems and control series. v. 7) 1. Digital control systems I. Tzafestas, S. G., 1939- II. Series.
TJ223.M53 A67 1985 629.8/95 19 *LC* 85-25243 *ISBN* 0444878823

**Houpis, Constantine H.** **5.6189**
Digital control systems—theory, hardware, software / Constantine H. Houpis, Gary B. Lamont. — New York: McGraw-Hill, c1985. xix, 667 p.: ill.; 25 cm. (McGraw-Hill series in electrical engineering. Control theory.) Includes index. 1. Digital control systems I. Lamont, Gary B. II. T. III. Series.
TJ223.M53 H68 1985 629.8/95 19 *LC* 84-9644 *ISBN* 0070304807

**Phillips, Charles L.** **5.6190**
Digital control system analysis and design / Charles L. Phillips, H. Troy Nagle, Jr. — Englewood Cliffs, N.J.: Prentice-Hall, c1984. xv, 556 p.: ill.; 24 cm. 1. Digital control systems 2. Electric filters, Digital 3. INTEL 8086 (Computer) I. Nagle, H. Troy, 1942- II. T.
TJ223.M53 P47 1984 629.8/95 19 *LC* 83-9531 *ISBN* 0132120437

# TJ227–254 Machine Design

**Mechanical design and systems handbook / Harold A. Rothbart,** **5.6191**
**editor in chief.**
2nd ed. — New York: McGraw-Hill, c1985. 1 v. (various pagings): ill.; 24 cm. 1. Machinery — Design — Handbooks, manuals, etc. I. Rothbart, Harold A.
TJ230.M43 1985 621.8/15 19 *LC* 84-20128 *ISBN* 0070540209

**Shigley, Joseph Edward.** **5.6192**
Mechanical engineering design / Joseph Edward Shigley, Larry D. Mitchell. — 4th ed. — New York: McGraw-Hill, c1983. xix, 869 p.: ill.; 25 cm. — (McGraw-Hill series in mechanical engineering) 1. Machinery — Design I. Mitchell, Larry D. II. T.
TJ230.S5 1983 621.8/15 19 *LC* 82-10044 *ISBN* 007056888X

**Shigley, Joseph Edward.** **5.6193**
Mechanical engineering design: metric edition / Joseph Edward Shigley. — 1st metric ed. — New York: McGraw-Hill, [1985], c1986. xvii, 699 p.: ill.; 24 cm. 1. Machinery — Design I. T.
TJ230.S5 1986 621.8/15 19 *LC* 85-44 *ISBN* 0070568987

**Spotts, Merhyle Franklin, 1895-.** **5.6194**
Design of machine elements: incorporates both U.S. customary and SI units / M.F. Spotts. — 6th ed. — Englewood Cliffs, N.J.: Prentice-Hall, c1985. xviii, 730 p.: ill.; 24 cm. 1. Machinery — Design I. T.
TJ230.S82 1985 621.8/15 19 *LC* 84-13377 *ISBN* 013200593X

# TJ255–567 Heat Engines. Steam Engineering

## TJ260–265 HEAT TRANSFER.
### THERMODYNAMICS

**Arpaci, Vedat S., 1928-.** **5.6195**
Conduction heat transfer, by Vedat S. Arpaci. — Reading, Mass., Addison-Wesley Pub. Co. [1966] ix, 550 p. illus. 25 cm. — (Addison-Wesley series in mechanics and thermodynamics) 1. Heat — Conduction 2. Heat engineering I. T.
TJ260.A7 621.4022 *LC* 66-25602 *ISBN* 0201003597

**Handbook of heat and mass transfer / Nicholas P.** **5.6196**
**Cheremisinoff, editor.**
Houston: Gulf Pub. Co., c1986. 2 v.: ill.; 24 cm. 1. Heat — Transmission — Handbooks, manuals, etc. 2. Mass transfer — Handbooks, manuals, etc. I. Cheremisinoff, Nicholas P.
TJ260.H36 1986 621.402/2 19 *LC* 84-25338 *ISBN* 0872014118

**Welty, James R.** **5.6197**
Engineering heat transfer / James R. Welty. — SI version. — New York: Wiley, c1978. xiii, 510 p.: ill.; 24 cm. 1. Heat — Transmission 2. Heat — Transmission — Data processing I. T.
TJ260.W38 1978 621.4/022 *LC* 78-5179 *ISBN* 0471028606

**White, Frank M.** **5.6198**
Heat transfer / Frank M. White. — Reading, Mass.: Addison-Wesley, c1984. xvii, 588 p.: ill.; 25 cm. 1. Heat — Transmission I. T.
TJ260.W48 1984 621.402/2 19 *LC* 82-16404 *ISBN* 0201083248

**Wong, H. Y.** **5.6199**
Handbook of essential formulae and data on heat transfer for engineers / H. Y. Wong. — London; New York: Longman, 1977. xi, 236 p.: ill.; 22 cm. 1. Heat — Transmission — Handbooks, manuals, etc. I. T.
TJ260.W66 621.4/022/0202 *LC* 77-5681 *ISBN* 0582460506

**Fraas, Arthur P.** **5.6200**
Heat exchanger design [by] Arthur P. Fraas [and] M. Necati Ozisik. New York, Wiley [1965] vii, 386 p. illus. 29 cm. 1. Heat exchangers — Design and construction. I. Özişik, M. Necati. joint author. II. T.
TJ263.F7 621.4022 *LC* 65-21441

**Kubo, Ryōgo, 1920-.** • 5.6201
Thermodynamics: an advanced course with problems and solutions / Ryogo Kubo; in cooperation with Hiroshi Ichimura, Tsunemaru Usui, Natsuki Hashitsume. — Amsterdam: North-Holland, 1968. xii, 300 p. Translation of part of the book Netsugaku, tōkei-rikigaku. 1. Thermodynamics I. T.
TJ265.K7613    660/.29/69    LC 67-26462

**Reynolds, William Craig, 1933-.** 5.6202
Engineering thermodynamics / William C. Reynolds, Henry C. Perkins. — 2d ed. — New York: McGraw-Hill, c1977. xii, 690 p.: ill.; 24 cm. 1. Thermodynamics I. Perkins, Henry C. (Henry Crawford) II. T.
TJ265.R38 1977    621.4/021    LC 76-43284    ISBN 0070520461

**Sonntag, Richard Edwin.** 5.6203
Introduction to thermodynamics: classical and statistical [by] Richard E. Sonntag [and] Gordon J. Van Wylen. — New York: Wiley, [1971] xvii, 813 p.: illus.; 24 cm. — (Series in thermal and transport sciences) 1. Thermodynamics 2. Statistical thermodynamics I. Van Wylen, Gordon John. joint author. II. T.
TJ265.S66    536/.7    LC 72-129053    ISBN 0471813656

**Van Wylen, Gordon John.** 5.6204
Fundamentals of classical thermodynamics / Gordon J. Van Wylen and Richard E. Sonntag. — 3rd ed., English/SI version. — New York: Wiley, c1986. xiv, 749 p.: ill.; 24 cm. Includes index. 1. Thermodynamics I. Sonntag, Richard Edwin. II. T.
TJ265.V23 1986    536/.7 19    LC 85-26338    ISBN 0471861731

## TJ266-485 TURBINES. STEAM ENGINES. GEOTHERMAL ENERGY

**Wilson, David Gordon.** 5.6205
The design of high-efficiency turbomachinery and gas turbines / David Gordon Wilson. — Cambridge, Mass.: MIT Press, c1984. xvi, 496 p.: ill. 1. Turbomachines — Design and cosntruction 2. Gas-turbines — Design and construction I. T.
TJ266 W54 1984    LC 84-18741    ISBN 026223114X

**Haar, Lester.** 5.6206
NBS/NRC steam tables: thermodynamic and transport properties and computer programs for vapor and liquid states of water in SI units / Lester Haar, John S. Gallagher, George S. Kell. — Washington, [D.C.]: Hemisphere Pub. Corp., c1984. xii, 320 p.: ill.; 27 cm. 'Tables ... approved by the Office of Standard Reference Data of the National Bureau of Standards and incorporated into the National Standard Reference Data System'—Foreword. 1. Steam — Tables 2. Steam — Thermal properties — Computer programs. I. Gallagher, John S. (John Scott), 1933- II. Kell, George S., d. 1983. III. National Standard Reference Data System (U.S.) IV. T. V. Title: N.B.S./N.R.C. steam tables.
TJ270.H3 1984    621.1/8/0212 19    LC 84-663    ISBN 0891163549

**Briggs, Asa, 1921-.** 5.6207
The power of steam: an illustrated history of the world's steam age / Asa Briggs. — Chicago: University of Chicago Press, 1982. 208 p.: ill. (some col.); 27 cm. 1. Steam engineering — History. I. T.
TJ275.B825 1982    621.1/09 19    LC 82-40321    ISBN 0226074951

**Armstead, H. Christopher H.** 5.6208
Geothermal energy: its past, present, and future contributions to the energy needs of man / H. Christopher H. Armstead. — 2nd ed. — London; New York: E. & F.N. Spon, c1983. xxxviii, 404 p.: ill.; 24 cm. Includes index. 1. Geothermal engineering 2. Geothermal resources I. T.
TJ280.7.A74 1983    333.79/2 19    LC 83-337    ISBN 0419122206

**Grant, Malcolm A.** 5.6209
Geothermal reservoir engineering / Malcolm A. Grant, Ian G. Donaldson, Paul F. Bixley. — New York: Academic Press, 1982. xiii, 369 p.: ill.; 24 cm. — (Energy science and engineering) Includes indexes. 1. Geothermal engineering I. Donaldson, Ian G. II. Bixley, Paul F. III. T. IV. Series.
TJ280.7.G7 1982    621.44 19    LC 82-4105    ISBN 0122956206

**Handbook of geothermal energy** / editors, L.M. Edwards ... [et 5.6210 al.].
Houston: Gulf Pub. Co., c1982. ix, 613 p.: ill.; 24 cm. 1. Geothermal engineering — Handbooks, manuals, etc. 2. Geothermal resources — Handbooks, manuals, etc. I. Edwards, L. M.
TJ280.7.H36 1982    621.44 19    LC 81-20246    ISBN 0872013227

**Wahl, Edward F.** 5.6211
Geothermal energy utilization / Edward F. Wahl. New York: Wiley, c1977. xiv, 302 p., [1] leaf of plates: ill.; 24 cm. 'A Wiley-Interscience publication.' 1. Geothermal engineering I. T.
TJ280.7.W33    621.4    LC 77-546    ISBN 0471023043

**Gilchrist, James Duncan.** 5.6212
Fuels, furnaces, and refractories / J. D. Gilchrist. 1st ed. — New York: Pergamon Press, 1977. xiii, 353 p.: ill.; 21 cm. (International series on materials science and technology; v. 21) (Pergamon international library of science, technology, engineering and social studies) A combined revision of the author's Fuels and refractories and Furnaces. Includes index. 1. Furnaces 2. Refractory materials 3. Fuel I. Gilchrist, James Duncan. Fuels and refractories. II. Gilchrist, James Duncan. Furnaces. III. T.
TJ320.G49 1977    621.4/025    LC 76-5865    ISBN 0080204309

**Boulton, Matthew, 1728-1809.** 5.6213
The selected papers of Boulton & Watt / edited by Jennifer Tann. — Cambridge, Mass.: MIT Press, 1981-. v. <1 >; 24 cm. Includes index. 1. Steam-engines — History — Sources. I. Watt, James, 1736-1819. II. Tann, Jennifer, 1939- III. T.
TJ461.B68 1981    621.1 19    LC 81-3695    ISBN 0262021676

**Von Tunzelmann, G. N.** 5.6214
Steam power and British industrialization to 1860 / G. N. von Tunzelmann. — [S.l.]: Oxford, 1978. x, 344 p.: ill.; 23 cm. Includes index. 1. Steam-engines — History. 2. Great Britain — Industry — History. I. T.
TJ461.V66    338.4/7/621160941    LC 77-30200    ISBN 0198282737

**Rolt, L. T. C., 1910-1974.** 5.6215
The steam engine of Thomas Newcomen / L. T. C. Rolt & J. S. Allen. — Hartington, Eng.: Moorland Pub. Co.; New York: Science History Publications, 1977. 160 p.: ill.; 24 cm. Includes index. 1. Newcomen, Thomas, 1663-1729. 2. Steam-engines — History. I. Allen, John Scott, 1925- joint author. II. T.
TJ485.N48 R64 1977    621.1/64    LC 77-22930    ISBN 0882021710

## TJ603-830 Other Motors and Engines

**Hosny, A. N.** 5.6216
Propulsion systems / [by] A. N. Hosney. — Rev. ed., expanded. — Columbia: University of South Carolina Press, [1974] xiv, 551 p.: ill.; 23 cm. 1. Jet propulsion I. T.
TJ759.H58 1974    629.1    LC 73-18277    ISBN 0872493105

**Walker, G. (Graham), 1930-.** 5.6217
Stirling-cycle machines, [by] G. Walker. Oxford, Clarendon Press, 1973. ix, 156 p. illus. 24 cm. Includes index. 1. Stirling engines I. T.
TJ765.W34    621.4    LC 73-174571    ISBN 0198561121

**Bathie, William W.** 5.6218
Fundamentals of gas turbines / William W. Bathie. — New York: Wiley, c1984. x, 358 p.: ill.; 25 cm. 1. Gas-turbines I. T.
TJ778.B34 1984    621.43/3 19    LC 83-21609    ISBN 0471862851

**Cohen, Henry, 1921 Sept. 29-.** 5.6219
Gas turbine theory / H. Cohen, G.F.C. Rogers, H.I.H. Saravanamuttoo. — 3rd ed. — Burnt Mill, Harlow, Essex, England: Longman Scientific & Technical; New York: Wiley, 1987. p. cm. Includes index. 1. Gas-turbines I. Rogers, G. F. C. (Gordon Frederick Crichton) II. Saravanamuttoo, H. I. H. III. T.
TJ778.C6 1987    621.43/3 19    LC 86-21478    ISBN 0470207051

**Benson, Rowland.** 5.6220
Internal combustion engines: a detailed introduction to the thermodynamics of spark and compression ignition engines, their design and development / Rowland S. Benson and N.D. Whitehouse. — First ed. — Oxford: Pergamon Press, 1979. 430 p.: ill.; 25 cm. — (Thermodynamics and fluid mechanics series) 1. Internal combustion engines I. Whitehouse, N. D. (Norman Dan) II. T.
TJ785 B4    LC 79-40360    ISBN 0080227171

**Taylor, Charles Fayette, 1894-.** 5.6221
The internal-combustion engine in theory and practice / by Charles Fayette Taylor. — 2nd ed., rev. — Cambridge, Mass.: M.I.T. Press, 1985. 2 v.: ill.; 24 cm. Four folded leaves of ill. in pocket of v. 1. 1. Internal combustion engines I. T.
TJ785.T382 1985    621.43 19    LC 84-28885    ISBN 0262200511

**Fuel economy of the gasoline engine: fuel, lubricant, and other** 5.6222
**effects** / edited by D. R. Blackmore and A. Thomas; contributors, W. S. Affleck ... [et al.].
New York: Wiley, 1977. xi, 268 p.: ill.; 25 cm. 'A Halsted Press book.' 1. Internal combustion engines, Spark ignition — Fuel consumption I. Blackmore, David Richard, 1938- II. Thomas, Alan, 1925- III. Affleck, W. S.
TJ789.F78 1977    621.43/4    LC 77-3916    ISBN 0470991321

**Design and applications in diesel engineering** / editor–in–chief,    **5.6223**
S.D. Haddad; associate editor, N. Watson.
Chichester, West Sussex: E. Horwood; New York: [Distributed by] Halsted Press, 1984. 339 p.: ill.; 24 cm. — (Ellis Horwood series in mechanical engineering.) 1. Diesel motor — Design 2. Automobiles — Motors (Diesel) I. Haddad, S. D. (Sam David), 1939- II. Watson, N. (Neil), 1939- III. Series.
TJ795.D41355 1984    621.43/6 19    LC 84-4576    ISBN 047020074X

**The modern diesel: development and design.**    **5.6224**
14th ed.: edited by D. S. D. Williams, R. J. B. Keig [and] John M. Dickson-Simpson. — London: Newnes-Butterworths, 1972. [7], 248 p.: illus.; 25 cm. Previous ed. edited by Donald Harry Smith. London, Iliffe, 1959. 1. Diesel motor I. Williams, Denys Stephen Dodsley, 1897- ed. II. Keig, Robert Joseph Brook, ed. III. Dickson-Simpson, John Marmaduke, ed.
TJ795.M55 1972    629.04    LC 73-155317    ISBN 0408000759

## TJ810–825 Solar Energy. Windmills
(see also: TH7413-7414)

**Crowther, Richard L.**    **5.6225**
Sun/Earth: how to use solar and climatic energies / by Richard L. Crowther, concepts, text, Paul Karius, graphics, text, Lawrence Atkinson, text, cover design, Donald J. Frey, text, editing. — New York: Scribner, c1977. vii, 232 p.: ill.; 17 x 28 cm. — (Lyceum editions) (Scribner library; SL 753) Includes index. 1. Solar energy 2. Power resources 3. Buildings — Energy conservation I. T.
TJ810.C76 1977    621.47    LC 77-20006    ISBN 0684155451

**Katzman, Martin T.**    **5.6226**
Solar and wind energy: an economic evaluation of current and future technologies / Martin T. Katzman. — Totowa, N.J.: Rowman & Allanheld, 1984. xx, 187 p.: ill.; 25 cm. Includes index. 1. Solar energy — Economic aspects. 2. Wind power — Economic aspects. I. T.
TJ810.K28 1984    333.79/23 19    LC 83-23044    ISBN 0865981523

**Kreith, Frank.**    **5.6227**
Principles of solar engineering / Frank Kreith, Jan F. Kreider. — Washington: Hemisphere Pub. Corp., c1978. xii, 778 p.: ill.; 24 cm. (Series in thermal and fluids engineering) Includes indexes. 1. Solar energy I. Kreider, Jan F., 1942- joint author. II. T.
TJ810.K73    621.47    LC 77-27861    ISBN 0070354766

**McVeigh, J. C.**    **5.6228**
Sun power: an introduction to the applications of solar energy / by J.C. McVeigh. — 2nd ed. — Oxford; New York: Pergamon Press, c1983. xii, 259 p.: ill.; 24 cm. — (Pergamon international library of science, technology, engineering, and social studies.) 1. Solar energy I. T. II. Series.
TJ810.M34 1983    621.47 19    LC 82-9852    ISBN 0080261485

**Norton, Thomas W.**    **5.6229**
Solar energy experiments for high school and college students / Thomas W. Norton, author; Donald C. Hunter, consultant; Roger J. Cheng, project coordinator. — Emmaus, Pa.: Rodale Press, c1977. xiv, 129 p.: ill.; 28 cm. Includes index. 1. Solar energy — Experiments — Juvenile literature. I. T.
TJ810.N67 1977    621.47    LC 77-4918    ISBN 0878571795

**Schiffman, Yale M.**    **5.6230**
Limits to solar and biomass energy growth / Yale M. Schiffman, Gregory J. D'Alessio. — Lexington, Mass.: Lexington Books, c1983. xxx, 286 p.: ill.; 24 cm. 1. Solar energy 2. Solar energy — Environmental aspects. I. D'Alessio, Gregory J. II. T.
TJ810.S34 1983    333.79/23 19    LC 81-48071    ISBN 0669052531

**Solar energy: chemical conversion and storage** / edited by    **5.6231**
Richard R. Hautala, R. Bruce King, and Charles Kutal.
Clifton, N.J.: Humana Press, c1979. x, 419 p.: ill.; 24 cm. — (Contemporary issues in science and society.) Based on an American Chemical Society symposium held in Savannah, Georgia, in November, 1978. 1. Solar energy — Addresses, essays, lectures. 2. Chemical processes — Addresses, essays, lectures. 3. Energy storage — Addresses, essays, lectures. I. Hautala, Richard R. II. King, R. Bruce. III. Kutal, Charles. IV. American Chemical Society. V. Series.
TJ810.S4885    621.47    LC 79-87568    ISBN 0896030067

**The Solar energy directory** / Sandra Oddo, senior editor;    **5.6232**
Martin McPhillips, associate editor; Richard Gottlieb, general editor.
New York, N.Y.: Grey House Pub., c1983. viii, 312 p.; 29 cm. Includes index. 1. Solar energy — United States — Directories. I. Oddo, Sandra. II. McPhillips, Martin. III. Gottlieb, Richard.
TJ810.S622 1983    621.47/025/73 19    LC 83-5498    ISBN 0939300060

**Solar energy handbook** / Jan F. Kreider, editor–in–chief, and    **5.6233**
Frank Kreith.
New York: McGraw-Hill, c1981. ca. 1100 p. in various pagings: ill.; 23 cm. — (McGraw-Hill series in modern structures) 1. Solar energy — Handbooks, manuals, etc. I. Kreider, Jan F., 1942- II. Kreith, Frank.
TJ810.S6244    621.47    LC 79-22570    ISBN 007035474X

**Welford, W. T.**    **5.6234**
The optics of nonimaging concentrators: light and solar energy / W. T. Welford, R. Winston. — New York: Academic Press, 1978. xi, 200 p.: ill.; 24 cm. Includes index. 1. Solar collectors I. Winston, Roland. joint author. II. T.
TJ810.W44    621.47/028    LC 77-25634    ISBN 0127453504

**Baker, T. Lindsay.**    **5.6235**
A field guide to American windmills / by T. Lindsay Baker; foreword by Donald E. Green. — 1st ed. — Norman: University of Oklahoma Press, c1985. xii, 516 p.: ill.; 23 x 29 cm. Includes index. 1. Windmills — United States. I. T.
TJ825.B25 1985    621.4/5 19    LC 84-40272    ISBN 0806119012

**Wortman, Andrze J.**    **5.6236**
Introduction to wind turbine engineering / by Andrze J. Wortman. — Boston: Butterworth Publishers, c1983. xii, 130 p.: ill.; 24 cm. 'An Ann Arbor Science book.' 1. Air-turbines 2. Wind power I. T.
TJ825.W87 1983    621.4/5 19    LC 83-71593    ISBN 0250405628

## TJ840–935 Hydraulic Machinery. Fluids

**McCloy, D.**    **5.6237**
The control of fluid power [by] D. McCloy [and] H. R. Martin. — New York: Wiley, [1973] 367 p.: illus.; 25 cm. 'A Halsted Press book.' 1. Fluid power technology 2. Hydraulic control I. Martin, Hugh Robert. joint author. II. T.
TJ843.M22    620.1/06    LC 72-5349    ISBN 0471581956

**Kirshner, Joseph M.**    **5.6238**
Design theory of fluidic components [by] Joseph M. Kirshner and Silas Katz. — New York: Academic Press, 1975. xi, 479 p.: ill.; 24 cm. 1. Fluidic devices I. Katz, Silas, joint author. II. T.
TJ853.K57    629.8/04/2    LC 73-18940    ISBN 0124102506

## TJ935 Flow of Fluids. Air Flow

**Benedict, Robert P.**    **5.6239**
Fundamentals of pipe flow / Robert P. Benedict. — New York: Wiley, c1980. xix, 531 p.: ill.; 24 cm. 'A Wiley-Interscience publication.' 1. Pipe — Fluid dynamics I. T.
TJ935.B46    621.8/67 19    LC 79-23924    ISBN 0471033758

**Durst, F.**    **5.6240**
Principles and practice of laser–Doppler anemometry / F. Durst, A. Melling, and J.H. Whitelaw. — 2nd ed. — London; New York: Academic Press, 1981. ix, 437 p.: ill.; 28 cm. Includes index. 1. Laser Doppler velocimeter I. Melling, A. II. Whitelaw, James H. III. T.
TJ935.D83 1981    681/.2 19    LC 81-201710    ISBN 0122252608

## TJ1040–1570 Machinery

**Society of Automotive Engineers.**    **5.6241**
Universal joint and driveshaft design manual / [illustrators, Gilbert B. Arnold, Vincent Platek]. — Warrendale, PA: Society of Automotive Engineers, c1979. 440 p.: ill.; 29 cm. (Advances in engineering series. no. 7) Includes index. 1. Universal joints (Mechanics) — Design and construction. 2. Shafting — Design and construction. 3. Power transmission I. T. II. Series.
TJ1059.S62 1979    621.8/25    LC 79-63005

**Dowson, D.**    **5.6242**
Elasto–hydrodynamic lubrication / by D. Dowson and G. R. Higginson, chapters 9 and 10 by J. F. Archard and A. W. Crook. — SI ed. — Oxford [Eng.]; New York: Pergamon Press, 1977. xiv, 235 p.: ill.; 22 cm. — (International series on materials science and technology; v. 23) (Pergamon international library of science, technology, engineering and social studies.)

Includes indexes. 1. Roller bearings — Lubrication 2. Gearing — Lubrication I. Higginson, G. R. joint author. II. T.
TJ1071.D64 1977      621.8/9      *LC* 76-58388      *ISBN* 0080213030

**Billett, Michael.**                                                          **5.6243**
Industrial lubrication: a practical handbook for lubrication and production engineers / by Michael Billett. — Oxford; New York: Pergamon Press, 1979. viii, 136 p.: ill.; 26 cm. Includes index. 1. Lubrication and lubricants I. T.
TJ1075.B48 1979      621.8/9      *LC* 79-40526      *ISBN* 0080242324

**Cameron, A. (Alastair), 1917-.**                                            **5.6244**
Basic lubrication theory / A. Cameron; with additional material by C. M. Mc.Ettles. — 3rd ed. — Chichester: E. Horwood; New York: Halsted Press, 1981. 256 p.: ill.; 24 cm. — (Ellis Horwood series in engineering science) Includes indexes. 1. Lubrication and lubricants I. Ettles, C. M. Mc. II. T.
TJ1075.C26 [1981]      621.8/9      *LC* 79-41817      *ISBN* 085312177X

**CRC handbook of lubrication: (theory and practice of tribology)**           **5.6245**
/ editor, E. Richard Booser.
Boca Raton, Fla.: CRC Press, c1983-c1984. 2 v.: ill.; 26 cm. Sponsored by the American Society of Lubrication Engineers. 1. Lubrication and lubricants — Handbooks, manuals, etc. I. Booser, E. Richard. II. American Society of Lubrication Engineers. III. Title: C.R.C. handbook of lubrication.
TJ1075.C7 1984      621.8/9 19      *LC* 82-4552      *ISBN* 0849339014

**Fuller, Dudley D.**                                                         **5.6246**
Theory and practice of lubrication for engineers / Dudley D. Fuller. — 2nd ed. — New York: Wiley, c1984. xviii, 682 p.: ill.; 24 cm. 'A Wiley-Interscience publication.' 1. Lubrication and lubricants I. T.
TJ1075.F8 1984      621.8/9 19      *LC* 83-27394      *ISBN* 0471047031

**Bézier, Pierre.**                                                           **5.6247**
[Emploi des machines à commande numérique. English] Numerical control: mathematics and applications / [by] P. Bézier; appendixes by A. R. Forrest; translated by A. R. Forrest and Anne F. Pankhurst. — London; New York: J. Wiley, [1972] xvi, 240 p.: ill.; 24 cm. (Wiley series in computing) Translation of Emploi des machines à commande numérique. 1. Machine-tools — Numerical control I. T.
TJ1189.B4713      621.9/02      *LC* 70-39230      *ISBN* 0471071951

**Krutz, Gary.**                                                             **5.6248**
Design of agricultural machinery / Gary Krutz, Lester Thompson, Paul Claar. — New York: Wiley, c1984. vii, 472 p.: ill.; 24 cm. 1. Agricultural machinery — Design and construction. I. Thompson, Lester. II. Claar, Paul. III. T.
TJ1480.K73 1984      681/.763 19      *LC* 83-23251      *ISBN* 047108672X

# TK ELECTRICAL ENGINEERING. ELECTRONICS. NUCLEAR ENGINEERING

## TK1–441 Reference. History. General Works

**IEEE standard dictionary of electrical and electronics terms /**            **5.6249**
Frank Jay, editor in chief.
3rd ed. — New York, NY: Institute of Electrical and Electronics Engineers: Distributed in cooperation with Wiley-Interscience, c1984. 1173 p.: ill.; 27 cm. 'ANSI/IEEE std 100-1984.' 1. Electric engineering — Dictionaries. 2. Electronics — Dictionaries. I. Jay, Frank. II. American National Standards Institute. III. Institute of Electrical and Electronics Engineers. IV. Title: I.E.E.E. standard dictionary of electrical and electronics terms.
TK9.I35 1984      621.3/03/21 19      *LC* 84-81283      *ISBN* 0471807877

**McMahon, A. Michal (Adrian Michal), 1937-.**                               **5.6250**
The making of a profession: a century of electrical engineering in America / A. Michal McMahon. — New York: Institute of Electrical and Electronics Engineers, 1985 (c1984). xv, 304 p.: ill.; 24 cm. 1. Institute of Electrical and Electronics Engineers — History. 2. Electric engineering — United States — History. I. T.
TK23.M39 1984      621.3/0973 19      *LC* 84-22425      *ISBN* 0879421738

**Ryder, John Douglas, 1907-.**                                             **5.6251**
Engineers & electrons: a century of electrical progress / John D. Ryder, Donald G. Fink. — New York: IEEE Press, c1984. xix, 251 p.: ill., ports.; 25 cm.

1. Electric engineering — United States — History. I. Fink, Donald G. II. T. III. Title: Engineers and electrons.
TK23.R9 1984      621.3/0973 19      *LC* 83-22681      *ISBN* 087942172X

**Turning points in American electrical history / edited by James**          **5.6252**
**E. Brittain.**
New York: IEEE Press: distributor Wiley, c1977. xi, 399 p.: ill.; 28 cm. — (IEEE Press selected reprint series) 1. Electric engineering — United States — History — Addresses, essays, lectures. 2. Telecommunication — United States — History — Addresses, essays, lectures. I. Brittain, James E., 1931-
TK23.T83      621.3/0973      *LC* 76-18433      *ISBN* 0879420812

**Wachhorst, Wyn.**                                                          **5.6253**
Thomas Alva Edison, an American myth / Wyn Wachhorst. — Cambridge, Mass.: MIT Press, c1981. ix, 328 p.: ill.; 24 cm. Includes index. 1. Edison, Thomas A. (Thomas Alva), 1847-1931. 2. Inventors — United States — Biography. I. T.
TK140.E3 W3      621.3/092/4 B 19      *LC* 81-751      *ISBN* 0262231085

## TK145–441 HANDBOOKS. STANDARDS AND MEASUREMENTS. MANAGEMENT

**Laughton, M. A.**                                                          **5.6254**
Electrical engineer's reference book / edited by M. A. Laughton and M. G. Say with specialist contributors. — 14th ed. — London; Toronto: Butterworths, 1985. ~1100 p. in various pagings.: ill.; 25 cm. 1. Electric engineering — Handbooks, manuals, etc. I. Say, M. G. (Maurice George), 1902- II. T.
TK145      TK145.E43 1985.      621.3 19      *ISBN* 0408004320

**Johnk, Carl Theodore Adolf, 1919-.**                                       **5.6255**
Engineering electromagnetic fields and waves [by] Carl T. A. Johnk. — New York: Wiley, [1975] xv, 655 p.: illus.; 23 cm. 1. Electric engineering 2. Electromagnetic fields 3. Electromagnetic waves I. T.
TK145.J56      621.3      *LC* 74-13567      *ISBN* 0471442895

**Jordan, Edward C. (Edward Conrad)**                                        **5.6256**
Electromagnetic waves and radiating systems [by] Edward C. Jordan [and] Keith G. Balmain. — 2d ed. — Englewood Cliffs, N.J.: Prentice-Hall, [1968] xiii, 753 p.: illus.; 24 cm. — (Prentice-Hall electrical engineering series) 1. Electric engineering I. Balmain, Keith George, joint author. II. T.
TK145.J6 1968      621.3      *LC* 68-16319

**Shultz, Richard D.**                                                       **5.6257**
Introduction to electric power engineering / Richard D. Shultz, Richard A. Smith. — New York: Harper & Row, c1985. viii, 264 p.: ill.; 24 cm. Includes index. 1. Electric engineering I. Smith, Richard A. (Richard Allan), 1951- II. T.
TK145.S555 1985      621.31 19      *LC* 84-4554      *ISBN* 0060461314

**Starr, William.**                                                         **5.6258**
Electrical wiring and design: a practical approach / William Starr. — New York: Wiley, c1983. xi, 412 p.: ill.; 24 cm. Includes index. 1. Electric engineering 2. Buildings — Electric equipment I. T.
TK145.S76 1983      621.31/924 19      *LC* 82-21936      *ISBN* 0471051314

**Standard handbook for electrical engineers.**                             **5.6259**
12th ed. / Donald G. Fink, editor, H. Wayne Beaty, editor. — New York; London: McGraw-Hill, c1987. 2248 p.in various pagings: ill., 2 charts, maps; 24 cm. 1. Electric engineering I. Fink, Donald G. II. Beaty, H. Wayne.
TK145.S7x      621.3 19      *LC* 56-6964      *ISBN* 0070209758

**Fundamentals handbook of electrical and computer engineering**            **5.6260**
/ [edited by] Sheldon S.L. Chang.
New York: Wiley, c1982. 707 p.: ill. 'A Wiley-Interscience publication.' 1. Electric engineering — Handbooks, manuals, etc. 2. Computer engineering — Handbooks, manuals, etc. I. Chang, Sheldon S. L.
TK151.F86 1982      621.3 19      *LC* 82-4872      *ISBN* 0471862150

**Korn, Granino Arthur, 1922-.**                                          • **5.6261**
Basic tables in electrical engineering / Granino A. Korn. — New York: McGraw-Hill, 1965. x, 370 p.: ill. 1. Electric engineering — Tables I. T.
TK151.K6      621.302      *LC* 64-66023

**Pender, Harold, 1879- ed.**                                             • **5.6262**
[American handbook for electrical engineers] Electrical engineers' handbook, prepared by a staff of specialists; Harold Pender and William A. Del Mar, editors. 4th ed. New York, Wiley [1949-50] 2 v. illus. 22 cm. (Wiley engineering handbook series) Vol. 2 edited by H. Pender and K. McIlwain. First ed. published in 1914 under title: American handbook for electrical engineers. 1. Electric engineering — Handbooks, manuals, etc. I. Del Mar, William Arthur, 1880- joint ed. II. T.
TK151.P42      621.302      *LC* 49-11664

**Siemens Aktiengesellschaft.**    5.6263
Electrical engineering handbook. [London] Heyden & Son [1976] xii, 749 p. illus., tables. Translated from German by Able Translations Ltd. Title of German original: Handbuch der Elektrotechnik. First published in 1969. 1. Electrical engineering — Handbooks, manuals, etc. 2. Electric engineering — Tables I. T.
TK151.S5 1976    ISBN 0855012315

**Shen, Liang Chi.**    5.6264
Applied electromagnetism / Liang Chi Shen, Jin Au Kong. — Monterey, CA: Brooks/Cole Engineering Division, c1983. xv, 507 p.: ill.; 24 cm. Includes index. 1. Electric engineering 2. Electromagnetic theory I. Kong, Jin Au, 1942- II. T.
TK153.S475 1983    621.34 19    LC 82-17884    ISBN 0534013589

**Silvester, P. (Peet)**    5.6265
Finite elements for electrical engineers / P.P. Silvester, R.L. Ferrari. — Cambridge [Cambridgeshire]; New York: Cambridge University Press, 1983. ix, 209 p.: ill.; 24 cm. 1. Electric engineering — Mathematics 2. Finite element method I. Ferrari, R. L. (Ronald L.) II. T.
TK153.S53 1983    621.3/01/515353 19    LC 82-23550    ISBN 0521273102

**Kidwell, Walter.**    5.6266
Electrical instruments and measurements. — New York: McGraw-Hill, [1969] x, 449 p.: illus.; 23 cm. 1. Electric measurements 2. Electric meters I. T.
TK275.K47    621.37    LC 69-11938

**Meland, Sam.**    5.6267
Electrical project management / Sam Meland. — New York: McGraw-Hill, c1984. ix, 287 p.: ill.; 24 cm. Includes index. 1. Electric engineering — Management. 2. Industrial project management I. T.
TK441.M4 1984    621.3/068 19    LC 83-957    ISBN 007041338X

## TK454 ELECTRICAL CIRCUITS. NETWORKS

**Adby, P. R.**    5.6268
Applied circuit theory: matrix and computer methods / P. R. Adby. — Chichester [Eng.]: E. Horwood; New York: Halsted Press, 1980. 490 p.: ill.; 24 cm. — (Ellis Horwood series in electrical and electronic engineering.) 1. Electric circuits 2. Matrices 3. Electric engineering — Mathematics 4. Electric engineering — Data processing I. T. II. Series.
TK454.A32    621.319/2/015129434    LC 79-41458    ISBN 0470269081

**Boylestad, Robert L.**    5.6269
Introductory circuit analysis / Robert L. Boylestad. — 4th ed. — Columbus, Ohio: C.E. Merrill Pub. Co., c1982. xii, 788 p.: ill.; 26 cm. — (Merrill's international series in electrical and electronics technology.) Includes index. 1. Electric circuits I. T. II. Series.
TK454.B68 1982    621.3815/3 19    LC 81-82530    ISBN 0675099382

**Hayt, William Hart, 1920-.**    5.6270
Engineering circuit analysis / William H. Hayt, Jr., Jack E. Kemmerly. — 4th ed. — New York: McGraw-Hill, c1986. xvi, 653 p.: ill. (some col.); 25 cm. (McGraw-Hill series in electrical engineering.) Includes index. 1. Electric circuit analysis 2. Electric network analysis I. Kemmerly, Jack E., 1924- II. T. III. Series.
TK454.H4 1986    621.319/2 19    LC 85-9635    ISBN 0070273979

**Ivison, J. M.**    5.6271
Electric circuit theory / J. M. Ivison. — New York: Van Nostrand Reinhold Co., 1977. 118 p.: ill.; 30 cm. Includes index. 1. Electric circuits I. T.
TK454.I88    621.319/2    LC 76-45659    ISBN 0442302010

**Jackson, Herbert W.**    5.6272
Introduction to electric circuits / Herbert W. Jackson. — 6th ed. — Englewood Cliffs, N.J.: Prentice-Hall, c1986. xiv, 786 p.: col. ill.; 24 cm. Includes index. 1. Electric circuits I. T.
TK454.J28 1986    621.319/2 19    LC 85-24422    ISBN 0134814258

**Lago, Gladwyn Vaile, 1917-.**    5.6273
Circuit and system theory / Gladwyn Lago, Lloyd M. Benningfield. — New York: Wiley, c1979. xi, 575 p.: ill.; 24 cm. 1. Electric circuits 2. System analysis 3. Electric engineering — Mathematics 4. Engineering mathematics I. Benningfield, Lloyd M. joint author. II. T.
TK454.L33    621.319/2    LC 79-10878    ISBN 0471049271

**Siebert, William McC.**    5.6274
Circuits, signals, and systems / William McC. Siebert. — Cambridge, Mass.: MIT Press; New York: McGraw-Hill, c1986. xvi, 651 p.: ill.; 23 cm. (MIT

electrical engineering and computer science series.) Includes index. 1. Electric circuits 2. Discrete-time systems 3. Linear time invariant systems I. T. II. Series.
TK454.S57 1986    621.319/2 19    LC 85-4302    ISBN 0262192292

**Chen, Wai-Kai, 1936-.**    5.6275
Linear networks and systems / Wai–Kai Chen. — Monterey, Calif.: Brooks/ Cole Engineering Division, c1983. xiv, 686, A12 p.: ill.; 25 cm. 1. Electric networks I. T.
TK454.2.C425 1983    621.319/2 19    LC 82-20647    ISBN 0534013430

**Director, Stephen W., 1943-.**    5.6276
Circuit theory: a computational approach / Stephen W. Director. — New York: Wiley, [1975] xvi, 679 p.: ill.; 23 cm. Includes index. 1. Electric networks 2. Electric circuits 3. Electric engineering — Data processing 4. Electric engineering — Mathematics I. T.
TK454.2.D57    621.319/2    LC 75-2016    ISBN 0471215805

**Gabel, Robert A.**    5.6277
Signals and linear systems / Robert A. Gabel, Richard A. Roberts. — 3rd ed. — New York: Wiley, c1987. xvii, 470 p.; 25 cm. Includes index. 1. Electric network analysis 2. Linear systems I. Roberts, Richard A., 1935- II. T.
TK454.2.G22 1987    620.7/2 19    LC 86-7748    ISBN 0471825131

**Gupta, Someshwar Chander.**    5.6278
Circuit analysis with computer applications to problem solving / [by] Someshwar C. Gupta, Jon W. Bayless [and] Behrouz Peikari. — Scranton: Intext Educational Publishers [1972] xiii, 546 p.: ill; 24 cm. (The Intext series in circuits, systems, communications, and computers) 1. Electric network analysis — Data processing I. Bayless, Jon W., joint author. II. Peikari, Behrouz. joint author. III. T.
TK454.2.G79    621.319/2    LC 70-177301    ISBN 070022405X

**Hostetter, G. H., 1939-.**    5.6279
Engineering network analysis / Gene H. Hostetter. — New York: Harper & Row, c1984. xxii, 888 p.: ill. (some col.); 24 cm. Includes index. 1. Electric network analysis I. T.
TK454.2.H668 1984    621.319/2 19    LC 83-22765    ISBN 0060429070

**Skilling, Hugh Hildreth, 1905-.**    5.6280
Electric networks. — New York: Wiley, [1974] xviii, 483 p.: illus.; 23 cm. 1. Electric networks I. T.
TK454.2.S58 1974    621.319/2    LC 73-14870    ISBN 0471794201

**Van Valkenburg, M. E. (Mac Elwyn), 1921-.**    5.6281
Network analysis / [by] M. E. Van Valkenburg. 3d ed. Englewood Cliffs, N.J.: Prentice-Hall [1974] xv, 571 p.: ill.; 25 cm. 1. Electric network analysis I. T.
TK454.2.V36 1974    621.319/2    LC 73-12705    ISBN 0136110959

# TK1001–1841 Production of Electrical Energy or Power

## TK1001–1005 GENERAL WORKS

**Bergen, Arthur R.**    5.6282
Power systems analysis / Arthur R. Bergen. — Englewood Cliffs, N.J.: Prentice-Hall, c1986. xiv, 529 p.: ill.; 25 cm. (Prentice-Hall series in electrical and computer engineering.) Includes index. 1. Electric power systems I. T. II. Series.
TK1001.B44 1986    621.31 19    LC 85-9300    ISBN 0136878644

**Eaton, J. Robert (James Robert), 1902-.**    5.6283
Electric power transmission systems / J. Robert Eaton, Edwin Cohen. — 2nd ed. — Englewood Cliffs, N.J.: Prentice-Hall, c1983. xiv, 415 p.: ill.; 24 cm. Includes index. 1. Electric power systems I. Cohen, Edwin, 1934- II. T.
TK1001.E27 1983    621.31/9 19    LC 82-21514    ISBN 0132473046

**Healy, Timothy J.**    5.6284
Energy, electric power, and man [by] Timothy J. Healy. — San Francisco, Calif.: Boyd & Fraser Pub. Co., [1974] xiii, 355 p.: illus.; 25 cm. 1. Electric power production 2. Power resources I. T.
TK1001.H4    621.31    LC 73-86050    ISBN 0878350411

**Hill, Philip Graham, 1910-.**     **5.6285**
Power generation: resources, hazards, technology, and costs / Philip G. Hill. — Cambridge: MIT Press, c1977. xiv, 402 p.: ill.; 24 cm. 1. Electric power production 2. Electric power-plants — Environmental aspects 3. Power resources 4. Fuel I. T.
TK1001.H63    621.312    *LC* 76-54739    *ISBN* 0262080915

**Anderson, Paul M., 1926-.**     **5.6286**
Power system control and stability / P. M. Anderson, A. A. Fouad. — 1st ed. — Ames: Iowa State University Press, 1977-. v.: ill.; 26 cm. 1. Electric power systems 2. System analysis I. Fouad, Abdel-Aziz A., joint author. II. T.
TK1005.A7    621.3    *LC* 76-26022    *ISBN* 0813812453

**Gross, Charles A.**     **5.6287**
Power system analysis / Charles A. Gross. — 2nd ed. — New York: Wiley, c1986. xiv, 593 p.: ill.; 25 cm. 1. Electric power systems I. T.
TK1005.G76 1986    621.31 19    *LC* 85-17995    *ISBN* 0471862061

**Hughes, Thomas Parke.**     **5.6288**
Networks of power: electrification in Western society, 1880–1930 / Thomas P. Hughes. — Baltimore: Johns Hopkins University Press, c1983. xi, 474 p.: ill.; 26 cm. 1. Electric power systems — United States — History. 2. Electric power systems — Great Britain — History. 3. Electric power systems — Germany — History. I. T.
TK1005.H83 1983    363.6/2 19    *LC* 82-14858    *ISBN* 0801828732

**Kusic, George L., 1935-.**     **5.6289**
Computer–aided power systems analysis / George L. Kusic. — Englewood Cliffs, N.J.: Prentice-Hall, c1986. ix, 403 p.: ill.; 24 cm. 1. Electric power systems — Data processing I. T.
TK1005.K87 1986    621.31 19    *LC* 85-19173    *ISBN* 0131645269

**Rechowicz, M.**     **5.6290**
Electric power at low temperatures / M. Rechowicz. — Oxford [Eng.]: Clarendon Press, 1975. xiv, 138 p.: ill.; 24 cm. (Monographs in electrical and electronic engineering) Includes index. 1. Electric power production 2. Electric power transmission 3. Low temperature engineering I. T.
TK1005.R32    621.31    *LC* 76-350187    *ISBN* 0198593120

## TK1041–1841 POWER PRODUCTION. POWER SOURCES. POWER PLANTS

**Armstead, H. Christopher H.**     **5.6291**
Geothermal energy: review of research and development; edited by H. Christopher H. Armstead. — Paris: Unesco, 1973. 186 p.: illus.; 27 cm. — (Earth sciences. 12) Label mounted on t.p.: Unipub, Inc., New York. 1. Geothermal engineering — Congresses. 2. Steam power-plants — Congresses. 3. Geothermal resources — Congresses. I. T. II. Series.
TK1041.A7    621.4    *LC* 72-97138

**Aschner, Fritz.**     **5.6292**
Planning fundamentals of thermal power plants / F. S. Aschner. — New York: Wiley, 1978 (c1977). xii, 738 p.: diag.; 24 cm. 'A Halsted Press book.' 1. Electric power-plants I. T.
TK1041.A8 1977    621.312/13    *LC* 77-16591    *ISBN* 0470993561

**Cogeneration sourcebook / compiled and edited by F. William Payne.**     **5.6293**
Atlanta, Ga.: Fairmont Press, c1985. 290 p.: ill.; 24 cm. 1. Cogeneration of electric power and heat I. Payne, F. William, 1924-
TK1041.C634 1985    333.79/3 19    *LC* 84-48530    *ISBN* 0881730025

**Geothermal energy; resources, production, stimulation. Edited by Paul Kruger and Carel Otte.**     **5.6294**
Stanford, Calif.: Stanford University Press, 1973. x, 360 p.: illus.; 24 cm. Based on papers presented at the Special Session on Geothermal Energy held at the American Nuclear Society annual meeting, June 19-20, 1972, in Las Vegas, Nev. 1. Geothermal engineering — Congresses. 2. Electric power-plants — Congresses. 3. Geothermal resources — Congresses. I. Kruger, Paul, 1925- ed. II. Otte, Carel, 1922- ed. III. American Nuclear Society.
TK1041.G4    333.7    *LC* 72-85700    *ISBN* 0804708223

**Hu, S. David.**     **5.6295**
Cogeneration / S. David Hu. — Reston, Va.: Reston Pub. Co., c1985. xviii, 428 p.: ill.; 24 cm. Bibliography: p. 396-415. Includes index. 1. Cogeneration of electric power and heat I. T.
TK1041.H8 1985    621.1/9 19    *LC* 84-15053    *ISBN* 0835907716

**Duderstadt, James J., 1942-.**     **5.6296**
Nuclear power: technology on trial / James J. Duderstadt and Chihiro Kikuchi. — Ann Arbor: University of Michigan Press, c1979. x, 228 p.: ill.; 23 cm.

Includes index. 1. Nuclear power plants 2. Nuclear energy I. Kikuchi, Chihiro, 1914- joint author. II. T.
TK1078.D83    621.48/3    *LC* 79-16455    *ISBN* 0472093118

**Green, A. E. (Arthur Eric)**     **5.6297**
Safety systems reliability / A.E. Green. — Chichester, [Sussex]; New York: Wiley, 1984 (c1983). xi, 293 p.: ill.; 24 cm. 'A Wiley-Interscience publication.' 1. Nuclear power plants — Reliability. 2. Nuclear power plants — Safety measures. 3. System safety I. T.
TK1078.G74 1983    621.48/35 19    *LC* 82-24863    *ISBN* 047190144X

**International Atomic Energy Agency.**     **5.6298**
Operating experience with nuclear power stations in member states in 1975. — Vienna: International Atomic Energy Agency, 1976. 289 p.; 30 cm. Began with vol. for 1970. 1. Nuclear power plants — Yearbooks. I. T.
TK1078.I57a    333.7    *LC* 76-641148

**Planning for rare events: nuclear accident preparedness and management: proceedings of an international workshop, January 28–31, 1980 / John W. Lathrop, editor.**     **5.6299**
1st ed. — Oxford; New York: Pergamon Press, 1981. xi, 268 p.: ill.; 26 cm. (IIASA proceedings series. v. 14) Sponsored by the International Institute for Applied Systems Analysis. 1. Nuclear power plants — Accidents — Congresses. I. Lathrop, John W. II. International Institute for Applied Systems Analysis. III. Series.
TK1078.P5 1981    363.1/79 19    *LC* 81-17768    *ISBN* 0080287034

**McCormick, Michael E., 1936-.**     **5.6300**
Ocean wave energy conversion / Michael E. McCormick. — New York: Wiley, c1981. xxiv, 233 p.: ill.; 24 cm. — (Alternate energy). 'A Wiley-Interscience publication.' 1. Ocean wave power I. T. II. Series.
TK1081.M39    621.31/2134 19    *LC* 81-494    *ISBN* 047108543X

**Martin, Daniel, 1948-.**     **5.6301**
Three Mile Island: prologue or epilogue? / By Daniel Martin. — Cambridge, Mass.: Ballinger Pub. Co., c1980. ix, 253 p.: ill.; 24 cm. 1. Three Mile Island Nuclear Power Plant (Pa.) 2. Nuclear power plants — Pennsylvania — Harrisburg Region — Accidents. I. T.
TK1345.H37 M37    363.1/79 19    *LC* 80-11067

**The Three Mile Island accident: diagnosis and prognosis / L.M. Toth ... [et al.], editors.**     **5.6302**
Washington, D.C.: American Chemical Society, 1986. ix, 301 p.: ill.; 24 cm. — (ACS symposium series. 0097-6156; 293) 'Developed from a symposium sponsored by the Division of Nuclear Chemistry and Technology at the 189th Meeting of the American Chemical Society, Miami Beach, Florida, April 28-May 3, 1985.' 1. Three Mile Island Nuclear Power Plant (Pa.) — Congresses. 2. Nuclear power plants — Pennsylvania — Accidents — Congresses. I. Toth, L. M. (Louis McKenna), 1941- II. American Chemical Society. Division of Nuclear Chemistry and Technology. III. American Chemical Society. Meeting. (189th: 1985: Miami Beach, Fla.) IV. Series.
TK1345.H37 T45 1986    363.1/79 19    *LC* 85-26852    *ISBN* 0841209480

**Lilienthal, David Eli, 1899-1981.**     • **5.6303**
TVA: democracy on the march / by David E. Lilienthal. — 20th anniversary ed. — New York: Harper, 1953. xxiv, 294 p. . ill., map. , 22 cm. 1. Tennessee Valley Authority. I. T.
TK1425.M8 L53 1953    627.1    *LC* 53-7202

**Hackleman, Michael A.**     **5.6304**
Wind and windspinners: a nuts and bolts approach to wind–electric systems / by Michael A. Hackleman. — Culver City, Calif.: Peace Press, c1974. 115 p.: ill.; 28 cm. An Earthmind/Peace Press publication. 1. Wind power 2. Electric power-plants I. T.
TK1541.H22    621.312/136    *LC* 74-196087    *ISBN* 0915238020 pa

**Hunt, V. Daniel.**     **5.6305**
Windpower: a handbook on wind energy conversion systems / V. Daniel Hunt. — New York: Van Nostrand Reinhold Co., c1981. xvii, 610 p.: ill.; 26 cm. 1. Wind power I. T.
TK1541.H86    621.4/5    *LC* 80-12581    *ISBN* 0442273894

**Johnson, Gary L.**     **5.6306**
Wind energy systems / Gary L. Johnson. — Englewood Cliffs, N.J.: Prentice-Hall, c1985. viii, 360 p.: ill.; 24 cm. 1. Wind power I. T.
TK1541.J64 1985    621.4/5 19    *LC* 83-24779    *ISBN* 0139577548

# TK2000–2970 Dynamoelectric Machinery and Auxiliaries

**Smith, R. T. (Richard Thomas), 1925-.**                         **5.6307**
Analysis of electrical machines / Richard T. Smith. — New York: Pergamon Press, c1982. ix, 229 p.: ill.; 24 cm. 1. Electric machinery I. T.
TK2000.S6 1982      621.31/042 19      LC 81-4541      ISBN 008027174X

**Fitzgerald, A. E. (Arthur Eugene), 1909-.**                         **5.6308**
Electric machinery / A.E. Fitzgerald, Charles Kingsley, Jr., Stephen D. Umans. — 4th ed. — New York: McGraw-Hill, c1983. xii, 571 p.: ill.; 25 cm. — (McGraw-Hill series in electrical engineering. Power and energy.) Includes index. 1. Electric machinery I. Kingsley, Charles, 1904- II. Umans, Stephen D. III. T. IV. Series.
TK2181.F5 1983      621.31/042 19      LC 82-7763      ISBN 0070211450

**Kosow, Irving L.**                         **5.6309**
Electric machinery and transformers [by] Irving L. Kosow. — Englewood Cliffs, N.J.: Prentice-Hall, [1972] xx, 635 p.: illus.; 24 cm. — (Prentice-Hall series in electronic technology) 1. Electric machinery 2. Electric transformers I. T.
TK2181.K663      621.31/042      LC 79-164665      ISBN 0132472058

**Krause, Paul C.**                         **5.6310**
Analysis of electric machinery / Paul C. Krause. — New York: McGraw-Hill, c1986. xvi, 564 p.: ill.; 24 cm. (McGraw-Hill series in electrical engineering. Power and energy.) 1. Electric machinery I. T. II. Series.
TK2181.K72 1986      621.31/042 19      LC 85-11015      ISBN 0070354367

## TK2511–2805 Motors. Alternating Current Machinery

**Electric motor handbook / editor, E. H. Werninck.**                         **5.6311**
London; New York: McGraw-Hill, c1978. xvi, 629 p.: ill.; 26 cm. 1. Electric motors — Handbooks, manuals, etc. I. Werninck, E. H.
TK2511.E42      621.4/62      LC 77-30474      ISBN 0070844887

**Lloyd, Thomas Cox.**                         **5.6312**
Electric motors and their applications [by] Tom C. Lloyd. — New York: Wiley-Interscience, [1969] ix, 332 p.: illus.; 23 cm. 1. Electric motors I. T.
TK2511.L55      621.313      LC 70-77834      ISBN 0471542350

**Veinott, Cyril G. (Cyril George)**                         **5.6313**
Fractional and subfractional horsepower electric motors: available types, basic operating principles, selection, and maintenance / Cyril G. Veinott, Joseph E. Martin. — 4th ed. — New York: McGraw-Hill, c1986. xxvi, 477 p.: ill.; 24 cm. 1. Electric motors, Fractional horsepower I. Martin, Joseph E. II. T.
TK2537.V38 1986      621.46/2 19      LC 85-12487      ISBN 0070673934

**Kenjō, Takashi.**                         **5.6314**
[Mekatoronikusu no tame no DC sābo mōta. English] Permanent–magnet and brushless DC motors / T. Kenjo and S. Nagamori. — Oxford: Clarendon Press; New York: Oxford University Press, 1985. viii, 194 p.: ill.; 24 cm. — (Monographs in electrical and electronic engineering. 18) (Oxford science publications.) Translation of: Mekatoronikusu no tame no DC sābo mōta. Includes index. 1. Electric motors, Direct current 2. Servomechanisms I. Nagamori, Shigenobu, 1944- II. T. III. Series. IV. Series: Oxford science publications.
TK2681.K4613 1985      621.46/2 19      LC 85-8862      ISBN 0198562144

**Say, M. G. (Maurice George), 1902-.**                         **5.6315**
Alternating current machines / M.G. Say. — 5th ed. — New York: Wiley, c1983. xii, 632 p.: ill.; 23 cm. 'A Halsted Press book.' 1. Electric machinery — Alternating current 2. Electric transformers I. T.
TK2711.S3 1983      621.31/33 19      LC 83-10719      ISBN 0470274514

**Adkins, Bernard.**                         **5.6316**
The general theory of alternating current machines: S.I. application to practical problems / Bernard Adkins and Ronald G. Harley. — 2d ed. — London: Chapman and Hall; New York: Halsted Press, [1975] xvi, 279 p.: ill.; 24 cm. First ed. published in 1957 under title: The general theory of electrical machines. Includes index. 1. Electric machinery — Alternating current 2. Electric machinery I. Flanagan, Harley. Ronald G., joint author. II. T. III. Title: The general theory of electrical machines.
TK2712.A34 1975      621.313/3      LC 75-2107      ISBN 0470008709

**Yamamura, Sakae, 1918-.**                         **5.6317**
Theory of linear induction motors. — New York: Wiley, [1972] xi, 161 p.: illus.; 24 cm. 'A Halsted Press book.' 1. Electric motors, Induction 2. Electric motors, Linear I. T.
TK2785.Y35      621.46/2      LC 72-5208      ISBN 0470970901

## TK2811–2970 Auxiliary Apparatus. Batteries

**Switchgear and control handbook / Robert W. Smeaton, editor.**                         **5.6318**
New York: McGraw-Hill, c1977. 957 p. in various pagings: ill.; 24 cm. 1. Electric switchgear — Handbooks, manuals, etc. 2. Electric controllers — Handbooks, manuals, etc. 3. Automatic control — Handbooks, manuals, etc. I. Smeaton, Robert W.
TK2821.S88      621.31/7      LC 76-17925      ISBN 0070584397

**Kosow, Irving L.**                         **5.6319**
Control of electric machines [by] Irving L. Kosow. — Englewood Cliffs, N.J.: Prentice-Hall, [1973] xvii, 376 p.: illus.; 25 cm. — (Prentice-Hall series in electronic technology) 1. Electric controllers 2. Electric driving 3. Automatic control I. T.
TK2851.K66      621.31/7      LC 72-3359      ISBN 0131717855

**Kusko, Alexander, 1921-.**                         **5.6320**
Solid–state DC motor drives. — Cambridge, Mass.: M.I.T. Press, [1969] ix, 126 p.: ill.; 24 cm. — (Monographs in modern electrical technology, 1) 1. Electric controllers 2. Electric motors, Direct current 3. Thyristors I. T.
TK2851.K87      621.313/2      LC 70-86271      ISBN 0262110318

**Ravindranath, B.**                         **5.6321**
Power system protection and switchgear / B. Ravindranath, M. Chander; with a foreword by C. S. Jha. — New York: Wiley, c1977. xvi, 444 p., [4] leaves of plates: ill.; 24 cm. 'A Halsted Press book.' Includes index. 1. Protective relays 2. Electric circuit-breakers 3. Electric power systems — Protection I. Chander, M. joint author. II. T.
TK2861.R28      621.31/7      LC 77-12056      ISBN 0470993111

**Angrist, Stanley W.**                         **5.6322**
Direct energy conversion / Stanley W. Angrist. — 4th ed. — Boston: Allyn and Bacon, c1982. vii, 468 p.: ill.; 25 cm. — (Allyn and Bacon series in mechanical engineering and applied mechanics.) 1. Direct energy conversion I. T. II. Series.
TK2896.A6 1982      621.31/24 19      LC 81-20591      ISBN 0205077587

**Handbook of batteries and fuel cells / David Linden, editor in chief.**                         **5.6323**
New York: McGraw-Hill, c1984. 1 v. (various pagings): ill.; 24 cm. 1. Electric batteries — Handbooks, manuals, etc. 2. Fuel cells — Handbooks, manuals, etc. I. Linden, David.
TK2901.H36 1984      621.31/242 19      LC 82-23999      ISBN 0070378746

**The primary battery / edited by George W. Heise and N. Corey Cahoon.**                         **5.6324**
New York; London [etc.]: Wiley-Interscience, 1976. 2 v.: ill., port.; 24 cm. (Electrochemical Society series.) 1. Electric batteries I. Heise, George William. II. Cahoon, Nelson Corey. III. Series.
TK2921.P75      621.35/3      LC 73-121906      ISBN 0471129232

**Schallenberg, Richard H., 1943-1980.**                         **5.6325**
Bottled energy: electrical engineering and the evolution of chemical energy storage / Richard H. Schallenberg. — Philadelphia: American Philosophical Society, c1982. xvi, 420 p.: ill.; 23 cm. — (Memoirs of the American Philosophical Society. 0065-9738; v. 148) Includes indexes. 1. Storage batteries — History. I. T. II. Series.
TK2941.S3x Q11.P612 vol. 148      081 s 621.31/2424/09 19      LC 80-68493      ISBN 0871691485

## TK2960 Solar Batteries

**Buresch, Matthew.**                         **5.6326**
Photovoltaic energy systems: design and installation / Matthew Buresch. — New York: McGraw-Hill, c1983. xiii, 335 p.: ill.; 24 cm. Includes index. 1. Photovoltaic power generation I. T.
TK2960.B87 1983      621.31/244 19      LC 82-17150      ISBN 0070089523

**Chopra, Kasturi L., 1933-.**    5.6327
Thin film solar cells / Kasturi Lal Chopra and Suhit Ranjan Das. — New York: Plenum Press, c1983. xvi, 607 p.: ill.; 24 cm. 1. Solar cells 2. Thin films I. Das, Suhit Ranjan, 1931- II. T.
TK2960.C48 1983    621.31/244 19    *ISBN* 0306411415

**Green, Martin A.**    5.6328
Solar cells: operating principles, technology, and system applications / Martin A. Green. — Englewood Cliffs, NJ: Prentice-Hall, c1982. xiv, 274 p.: ill.; 24 cm. — (Prentice-Hall series in solid state physical electronics.) Includes index. 1. Solar cells 2. Photovoltaic power generation I. T. II. Series.
TK2960.G73    621.31/244 19    *LC* 81-4355    *ISBN* 0138222703

**Zweibel, Kenneth.**    5.6329
Basic photovoltaic principles and methods / Solar Energy Research Institute. — New York: Van Nostrand Reinhold, c1984. xv, 249 p.: ill.; 24 cm. 'The principal authors of this document are Kenneth Zweibel (Photovoltaics Program Office) and Paul Hersch (Technical Information Branch)'—P. ix. Includes index. 1. Solar cells I. Hersch, Paul. II. Solar Energy Research Institute. III. T.
TK2960.Z94 1984    621.31/244 19    *LC* 83-21853    *ISBN* 0442281269

## TK3000–3511 Electric Power Distribution

**Beeman, Donald, ed.**    5.6330
Industrial power systems handbook. — 1st ed. — New York: McGraw-Hill, 1955. 971 p.: illus.; 24 cm. — (McGraw-Hill handbooks) 1. Electric power distribution I. T.
TK3001.B4    621.319    *LC* 54-10629

**Gönen, Turan.**    5.6331
Electric power distribution system engineering / Turan Gönen. — New York: McGraw-Hill, c1986. x, 739 p.: ill.; 25 cm. (McGraw-Hill series in electrical engineering. Power and energy.) 1. Electric power distribution I. T. II. Series.
TK3001.G58 1986    621.319 19    *LC* 85-79    *ISBN* 0070237077

**Pansini, Anthony J.**    5.6332
Electrical distribution engineering / Anthony J. Pansini. — New York: McGraw-Hill, c1983. xxi, 435 p.: ill.; 24 cm. Includes index. 1. Electric power distribution I. T.
TK3001.P28 1983    621.319/2 19    *LC* 82-20814    *ISBN* 0070484546

## TK3221–3351 Electric Lines. Networks. Wiring

**Kurtz, Edwin Bernard, 1894-.**    5.6333
The lineman's and cableman's handbook / Edwin B. Kurtz, Thomas M. Shoemaker. — 7th ed. — New York: McGraw-Hill Book, c1986. 1 v. (various pagings): ill.; 24 cm. Includes index. 1. Electric lines — Handbooks, manuals, etc. 2. Electric cables — Handbooks, manuals, etc. I. Shoemaker, Thomas M., 1921- II. T.
TK3221.K83 1986    621.319/22 19    *LC* 85-17120    *ISBN* 0070356866

**Balabanian, Norman, 1922-.**    5.6334
Linear network theory: analysis, properties, design and synthesis / Norman Balabanian and Theodore A. Bickart. — Beaverton, Or.: Matrix Publishers, 1981. x, 638 p.: ill. — (Matrix series in circuits and systems.) 1. Electric networks 2. Electric circuits 3. Matrices I. Bickart, Theodore A., 1935- II. T. III. Series.
TK3226 B25    *LC* 80-85066    *ISBN* 091646010X

**Brown, Homer E., 1909-.**    5.6335
Solution of large networks by matrix methods / Homer E. Brown. — 2nd ed. — New York: Wiley, c1985. xv, 320 p.: ill.; 24 cm. 'A Wiley-Interscience publication.' 1. Electric network analysis — Data processing 2. Electric power systems — Data processing 3. Short circuits 4. Matrices I. T.
TK3226.B763 1985    621.319/2/01512943 19    *LC* 85-5380    *ISBN* 0471800740

**McPartland, Joseph F.**    5.6336
Handbook of practical electrical design / J.F. McPartland; assistant editors, Brian J. McPartland ... [et al.]. — New York: McGraw-Hill, c1984. 1 v. (various pagings): ill.; 25 cm. 'Conforms to prevailing National electrical code requirements.' Includes index. 1. Electric wiring — Handbooks, manuals, etc. I. McPartland, Brian J. II. T.
TK3271.M35 1984    621.31 19    *LC* 82-20798    *ISBN* 007045695X

## TK4001–4661 Applications: Lighting, Heating

**Illuminating Engineering Society of North America.**    5.6337
IES lighting handbook / John E. Kaufman (editor). — New York, N.Y.: Illuminating Engineering Society of North America, 1981. 2 v.: ill.; 27 cm. Fifth ed. published in 1972 by Illuminating Engineering Society. 1. Electric lighting I. Kaufman, John E. II. Illuminating Engineering Society. IES lighting handbook. III. T. IV. Title: Lighting handbook.
TK4161.I46 1981    621.32/2 19    *LC* 80-84964    *ISBN* 0879950072

**Helms, Ronald N.**    5.6338
Illumination engineering for energy efficient luminous environments / Ronald N. Helms. — Englewood Cliffs, N.J.: Prentice-Hall, c1980. xiii, 322 p.: ill.; 25 cm. 1. Electric lighting 2. Lighting 3. Electric power — Conservation I. T.
TK4175.H45    621.32/2    *LC* 79-14866    *ISBN* 0134508092

**Murdoch, Joseph B., 1927-.**    5.6339
Illumination engineering—from Edison's lamp to the laser / Joseph B. Murdoch. — New York: Macmillan Pub. Co.; London: Collier Macmillan Publishers, c1985. xiv, 541 p.: ill.; 25 cm. 1. Electric lighting 2. Lighting I. T.
TK4175.M87 1985    621.32/1 19    *LC* 84-20134    *ISBN* 0029485800

**Sorcar, Prafulla C.**    5.6340
Energy saving lighting systems / Prafulla C. Sorcar. — New York: Van Nostrand Reinhold, c1982. xiii, 346 p.: ill.; 24 cm. 1. Electric lighting 2. Electric lighting — Energy conservation. I. T.
TK4188.S59 1982    621.32/2 19    *LC* 81-19773    *ISBN* 0442264305

**Frier, John P.**    5.6341
Industrial lighting systems / John P. Frier and Mary E. Gazley Frier. — New York: McGraw-Hill, c1980. xii, 322 p.: ill.; 24 cm. 1. Industrial buildings — Lighting. 2. Electric discharge lighting I. Frier, Mary E. Gazley. joint author. II. T.
TK4399.F2 F74    621.32/25/4    *LC* 79-23138    *ISBN* 0070224579

**Barber, H.**    5.6342
Electroheat / H. Barber. — London; New York: Granada; White Plains, NY: Distributed in the USA by Sheridan House, 1983. v, 302 p.: ill.; 24 cm. 1. Electric heating I. T.
TK4601.B37 1983    621.402 19    *LC* 83-135345    *ISBN* 0246117397

## TK5101–5865 Telecommunications. Telegraph

### TK5101 General Works

**Bennett, William R. (William Ralph), 1904-.**    • 5.6343
Introduction to signal transmission [by] William R. Bennett. New York, McGraw-Hill [1970] xvi, 266 p. illus. 23 cm. (McGraw-Hill electrical and electronic engineering series) 1. Telecommunication I. T.
TK5101.B39    621.38    *LC* 78-98484

**Beranek, Leo Leroy, 1914-.**    • 5.6344
Acoustics. — New York: McGraw-Hill, 1954. 481 p.: ill.; 24 cm. — (McGraw-Hill electrical and electronic engineering series) 1. Sound 2. Telecommunication I. T.
TK5101.B4    *LC* 53-12426

**Carne, E. Bryan, 1928-.**    5.6345
Modern telecommunication / E. Bryan Carne. — New York: Plenum Press, c1984. xii, 293 p.: ill.; 24 cm. (Applications of communications theory.) Includes index. 1. Telecommunication I. T. II. Series.
TK5101.C2986 1984    621.38 19    *LC* 84-16103    *ISBN* 030641841X

**Chorafas, Dimitris N.**    5.6346
Telephony: today and tomorrow / Dimitris N. Chorafas. — Englewood Cliffs, N.J.: Prentice-Hall, c1984. xii, 292 p.: ill.; 23 cm. — (Prentice-Hall series in

data processing management.) Includes index. 1. Telecommunication — Technological innovations. 2. Telephone — Technological innovations. I. T. II. Series.
TK5101.C496 1984     621.385 19     LC 83-3271     ISBN 0139027009

**Freeman, Roger L.**            5.6347
Telecommunication transmission handbook / Roger L. Freeman. — 2nd ed. — New York: Wiley, c1981. xxvii, 706 p.: ill.; 24 cm. 'A Wiley-Interscience publication.' 1. Telecommunication I. T.
TK5101.F66 1981     621.38 19     LC 81-7499     ISBN 0471080292

**Haykin, Simon S., 1931-.**            5.6348
Communication systems / Simon Haykin. — 2nd ed. — New York: Wiley, c1983. xvi, 653 p.: ill.; 24 cm. 1. Telecommunication 2. Signal theory (Telecommunication) I. T.
TK5101.H37 1983     621.38/0413 19     LC 82-17593     ISBN 0471096911

**Lathi, B. P. (Bhagwandas Pannalal)**            5.6349
Modern digital and analog communication systems / B.P. Lathi. — New York: Holt, Rinehart, and Winston, c1983. xii, 708 p.: ill.; 24 cm. — (HRW series in electrical and computer engineering.) Includes index. 1. Telecommunication systems 2. Digital communications 3. Statistical communication theory I. T. II. Series.
TK5101.L333 1983     621.38/0413 19     LC 82-23224     ISBN 003058969X

**Martin, James, 1933-.**            5.6350
Future developments in telecommunications / James Martin. — 2d ed. — Englewood Cliffs, N.J.: Prentice-Hall, c1977. xviii, 668 p.: ill.; 25 cm. — (Prentice-Hall series in automatic computation) 1. Telecommunication I. T.
TK5101.M325 1977     621.38     LC 76-40103     ISBN 0133458504

**Pierce, John Robinson, 1910-.**            5.6351
Introduction to communication science and systems / John R. Pierce and Edward C. Posner. — New York: Plenum Press, c1980. xvi, 390 p.: ill.; 24 cm. — (Applications of communications theory.) 1. Telecommunication I. Posner, Edward C., 1933- joint author. II. T. III. Series.
TK5101.P53     621.38     LC 80-14877     ISBN 0306404923

**Schwartz, Mischa.**            5.6352
Information transmission, modulation, and noise: a unified approach to communication systems / Mischa Schwartz. — 3d ed. — New York: McGraw-Hill, c1980. xv, 646 p.: ill.; 24 cm. — (McGraw-Hill series in electrical engineering.) (Communications and information theory) 1. Telecommunication 2. Digital communications 3. Modulation (Electronics) 4. Electronic noise I. T. II. Series. III. Series: Communications and information theory
TK5101.S3 1980     621.38     LC 80-11555     ISBN 0070557829

**Shanmugam, K. Sam.**            5.6353
Digital and analog communication systems / K. Sam Shanmugam. — New York: Wiley, c1979. xviii, 600 p.: ill.; 24 cm. 1. Telecommunication 2. Digital communications 3. Information theory 4. Signal theory (Telecommunication) I. T.
TK5101.S445     621.38     LC 78-26191     ISBN 0471030902

**Shannon, Claude E., 1916-.**          • 5.6354
The mathematical theory of communication. — Urbana: University of Illinois Press, 1949. v (i.e. vii), 117 p.: diagrs.; 24 cm. 'The first paper is reprinted from the Bell System technical journal, July and October, 1948 ... The second ... appeared [in condensed form] in Scientific American July, 1949.' 1. Telecommunication 2. Mathematical physics I. Weaver, Warren, 1894- II. T.
TK5101.S45     621.381     LC 49-11922

**Singleton, Loy A.**            5.6355
Telecommunications in the information age: a nontechnical primer on the new technologies / Loy A. Singleton. — Cambridge, Mass.: Ballinger Pub. Co., c1983. viii, 239 p.: ill.; 24 cm. Includes index. 1. Telecommunication I. T.
TK5101.S535 1983     384 19     LC 83-11742     ISBN 0884104281

**Stanley, William D.**            5.6356
Electronic communications systems / William D. Stanley. — Reston, Va.: Reston Pub. Co., c1982. ix, 566 p.: ill.; 24 cm. Includes index. 1. Telecommunication 2. Information theory I. T.
TK5101.S66 1982     621.38 19     LC 81-15837     ISBN 0835916669

**Stark, Henry, 1938-.**            5.6357
Modern electrical communications: theory and systems / Henry Stark, Franz B. Tuteur. — Englewood Cliffs, N.J.: Prentice-Hall, c1979. xvi, 601 p.: ill.; 24 cm. 1. Telecommunication I. Tuteur, Franz B., joint author. II. T.
TK5101.S67 1979     621.38     LC 78-8635     ISBN 0135932025

**Stremler, Ferrel G.**            5.6358
Introduction to communication systems / Ferrel G. Stremler. — 2nd ed. — Reading, Mass.: Addison-Wesley Pub. Co., c1982. xiv, 702 p.: ill.; 24 cm. — (Addison-Wesley series in electrical engineering.) 1. Telecommunication 2. Signal theory (Telecommunication) I. T. II. Series.
TK5101.S75 1982     621.38 19     LC 81-7917     ISBN 0201072513

**Taub, Herbert, 1918-.**            5.6359
Principles of communication systems / Herbert Taub, Donald L. Schilling. — 2nd ed. — New York: McGraw-Hill, c1986. xix, 759 p.: ill.; 25 cm. (McGraw-Hill series in electrical engineering. Communications and signal processing.) 1. Telecommunication systems I. Schilling, Donald L. II. T. III. Series.
TK5101.T28 1986     621.38 19     LC 85-11638     ISBN 0070629552

**Ziemer, Rodger E.**            5.6360
Principles of communications: systems, modulation, and noise / R. E. Ziemer and W. H. Tranter. — Boston: Houghton Mifflin, c1976. xii, 513 p.: ill.; 25 cm. Includes indexes. 1. Telecommunication 2. Signal theory (Telecommunication) I. Tranter, William H. joint author. II. T.
TK5101.Z57     621.38     LC 75-25015     ISBN 0395206030

## TK5102 DICTIONARIES. ENCYCLOPEDIAS

**Graham, John, 1936-.**            5.6361
The Facts on File dictionary of telecommunications / by John Graham. — New York, N.Y.: Facts on File Inc., 1983. 199 p.: ill.; 22 cm. 1. Telecommunication — Dictionaries. I. T. II. Title: Dictionary of telecommunications.
TK5102.G73 1983     384/.03/21 19     LC 82-15675     ISBN 0871961202

**Weik, Martin H.**            5.6362
Fiber optics and lightwave communications standard dictionary / Martin H. Weik. — New York: Van Nostrand Reinhold Co., c1981. x, 284 p.: ill.; 24 cm. 1. Optical communications — Dictionaries. 2. Fiber optics — Dictionaries. I. T.
TK5102.W44 1981     621.36/92/0321     LC 80-12765     ISBN 0442256582

## TK5102.5 SPECIAL WORKS, A–F

**Applications of digital signal processing / Alan V. Oppenheim, editor.**            5.6363
Englewood Cliffs, N.J.: Prentice-Hall, c1978. xii, 499 p.: ill.; 24 cm. — (Prentice-Hall signal processing series) 1. Signal processing I. Oppenheim, Alan V., 1937-
TK5102.5.A68     621.38/043     LC 77-8547     ISBN 0130391158

**Array signal processing / Simon Haykin, editor; James H. Justice ... [et al.].**            5.6364
Englewood Cliffs, N.J.: Prentice-Hall, c1985. ix, 433 p.: ill.; 25 cm. — (Prentice-Hall signal processing series.) 1. Signal processing I. Haykin, Simon S., 1931- II. Justice, James H., 1941- III. Series.
TK5102.5.A73 1985     621.38/043 19     LC 84-6974     ISBN 0130464821

**Blahut, Richard E.**            5.6365
Fast algorithms for digital signal processing / Richard E. Blahut. — Reading, Mass.: Addison-Wesley Pub. Co., c1985. xiv, 441 p.; 24 cm. 1. Signal processing — Digital techniques 2. Algorithms I. T.
TK5102.5.B535 1985     621.38/043 19     LC 83-25702     ISBN 0201101556

**Cadzow, James A.**            5.6366
Signals, systems, and transforms / James A. Cadzow, Hugh F. Van Landingham. — Englewood Cliff, N.J.: Prentice-Hall, c1985. xi, 348 p.: ill.; 25 cm. Includes index. 1. Signal theory (Telecommunication) 2. System analysis 3. Fourier transformations I. Van Landingham, Hugh F., 1935- II. T.
TK5102.5.C24 1985     003 19     LC 84-22841     ISBN 0138095426

**Carlson, A. Bruce, 1937-.**            5.6367
Communication systems: an introduction to signals and noise in electrical communication / A. Bruce Carlson. — 3rd ed. — New York: McGraw-Hill, c1986. xvii, 686 p.: ill.; 25 cm. (McGraw-Hill series in electrical engineering. Communications and signal processing.) Includes index. 1. Signal theory (Telecommunication) 2. Modulation (Electronics) 3. Digital communications I. T. II. Series.
TK5102.5.C3 1986     621.38/043 19     LC 85-4314     ISBN 007009960X

**Cooper, George R.**      **5.6368**
Modern communications and spread spectrum / George R. Cooper, Clare D. McGillem. — New York: McGraw-Hill, c1986. xvi, 436 p.: ill.; 25 cm. (McGraw-Hill series in electrical engineering. Communications and signal processing.) 1. Telecommunication 2. Signal processing 3. Spread spectrum communications I. McGillem, Clare D. II. T. III. Series.
TK5102.5.C66 1986      621.38 19      *LC* 84-20092      *ISBN* 0070129517

**Data compression / edited by Lee D. Davisson and Robert M.**      **5.6369**
**Gray.**
Stroudsburg, Pa.: Dowden, Hutchinson & Ross; [New York]: distributed by Halsted Press, c1976. xv, 407 p.: ill.; 26 cm. (Benchmark papers in electrical engineering and computer science; 14) 1. Data compression (Telecommunication) 2. Coding theory I. Davisson, Lee D. II. Gray, Robert M., 1943-
TK5102.5.D335 1976      621.38      *LC* 76-3629      *ISBN* 0879330899

**Davidson, Colin William.**      **5.6370**
Transmission lines for communications / C. W. Davidson. — New York: Wiley, c1978. vi, 218 p.: ill.; 24 cm. 'A Halsted Press book.' 1. Telecommunication lines I. T.
TK5102.5.D363 1978      621.38/028      *LC* 78-4546      *ISBN* 0470991607

**Dixon, Robert C. (Robert Clyde), 1932-.**      **5.6371**
Spread spectrum systems / Robert C. Dixon. — 2nd ed. — New York: J. Wiley, c1984. xv, 422 p.: ill.; 24 cm. 'A Wiley-Interscience publication.' Includes index. 1. Spread spectrum communications I. T.
TK5102.5.D55 1984      621.38/043 19      *LC* 83-26080      *ISBN* 0471883093

**Dudgeon, Dan E.**      **5.6372**
Multidimensional digital signal processing / Dan E. Dudgeon, Russell M. Mersereau. — Englewood Cliffs, NJ: Prentice-Hall, 1983. xv, 400 p.: ill.; 25 cm. — (Prentice-Hall signal processing series.) 1. Signal processing — Digital techniques I. Mersereau, Russell M. II. T. III. Series.
TK5102.5.D83 1983      621.38/043 19      *LC* 83-3135      *ISBN* 0136049591

**Goodyear, Colin Crosland.**      **5.6373**
Signals and information [by] C. C. Goodyear. — New York: Wiley-Interscience, [1972, c1971] 310 p.: illus.; 23 cm. 1. Signal theory (Telecommunication) I. T.
TK5102.5.G65 1972      621.38/043      *LC* 74-38234      *ISBN* 0471315206

**Jayant, Nuggehally S., 1946-.**      **5.6374**
Digital coding of waveforms: principles and applications to speech and video / N.S. Jayant, Peter Noll. — Englewood Cliffs, N.J.: Prentice-Hall, c1984. xvi, 688 p.: ill.; 25 cm. — (Prentice-Hall signal processing series.) 1. Signal processing — Digital techniques 2. Coding theory I. Noll, Peter, 1936- II. T. III. Series.
TK5102.5.J39 1984      621.38/043 19      *LC* 83-22170      *ISBN* 0132119137

**Lynn, Paul A.**      **5.6375**
An introduction to the analysis and processing of signals [by] Paul A. Lynn. — New York: Wiley, [1973] x, 222 p.: illus.; 24 cm. 'A Halsted Press book.' 1. Signal theory (Telecommunication) 2. Digital filters (Mathematics) I. T.
TK5102.5.L94 1973      621.38/043      *LC* 73-7050      *ISBN* 0470557362

**McClellan, James H., 1947-.**      **5.6376**
Number theory in digital signal processing / James H. McClellan, Charles M. Rader. — Englewood Cliffs, N.J.: Prentice-Hall, c1979. xii, 276 p.: ill.; 29 cm. — (Prentice-Hall signal processing series) Includes index. 1. Signal processing — Digital techniques 2. Numbers, Theory of 3. Convolutions (Mathematics) 4. Fourier transformations I. Rader, Charles M. joint author. II. T.
TK5102.5.M216 1979      621.38/043      *LC* 78-12313      *ISBN* 0136273491

**Morris, David Joseph.**      **5.6377**
Introduction to communication command and control systems / by David J. Morris. — 1st ed. — Oxford; New York: Pergamon Press, 1977. ix, 308 p.: ill.; 26 cm. 1. Command and control systems 2. Telecommunication I. T. II. Title: Communication command and control systems.
TK5102.5.M67 1977      621.38      *LC* 76-21681      *ISBN* 0080203787

**Oppenheim, Alan V., 1937-.**      **5.6378**
Digital signal processing [by] Alan V. Oppenheim [and] Ronald W. Schafer. — Englewood Cliffs, N.J.: Prentice-Hall, [1975] xiv, 585 p.: illus.; 24 cm. 1. Signal theory (Telecommunication) 2. Digital electronics I. Schafer, Ronald W., 1938- joint author. II. T.
TK5102.5.O245      621.3819/58/2      *LC* 74-17280      *ISBN* 0132146355

**Papoulis, Athanasios, 1921-.**      **5.6379**
Signal analysis / Athanasios Papoulis. New York: McGraw-Hill, c1977. ix, 431 p.: ill.; 25 cm. 1. Signal processing I. T.
TK5102.5.P35      621.38/043      *LC* 76-54353      *ISBN* 0070484600

**Signal processor chips / David Quarmby, editor.**      **5.6380**
Englewood Cliffs, N.J.: Prentice-Hall, c1985. viii, 179 p.: ill.; 25 cm. 'A Spectrum book.' 1. Signal processing — Digital techniques 2. Integrated circuits I. Quarmby, David.
TK5102.5.S543 1985      621.38/043 19      *LC* 84-18287      *ISBN* 0138094500

**Stearns, Samuel D.**      **5.6381**
Digital signal analysis / Samuel D. Stearns. — Rochelle Park, N.J.: Hayden Book Co., [1975] 280 p.: ill.; 24 cm. 1. Signal processing — Digital techniques I. T.
TK5102.5.S698      621.38/043      *LC* 75-19319      *ISBN* 0810458284

**Widrow, Bernard, 1929-.**      **5.6382**
Adaptive signal processing / Bernard Widrow, Samuel D. Stearns. — Englewood Cliffs, N.J.: Prentice-Hall, c1985. xviii, 474 p.: ill.; 25 cm. (Prentice-Hall signal processing series.) 1. Adaptive signal processing I. Stearns, Samuel D. II. T. III. Series.
TK5102.5.W537 1985      621.38/043 19      *LC* 84-18057      *ISBN* 0130040290

**Young, Thomas, 1934-.**      **5.6383**
Linear systems and digital signal processing / Thomas Young. — Englewood Cliffs, NJ: Prentice-Hall, c1985. x, 357 p.: ill.; 24 cm. 1. Signal processing — Digital techniques 2. Analog-to-digital converters 3. Linear systems I. T.
TK5102.5.Y68 1985      621.38/043 19      *LC* 84-18375      *ISBN* 0135373662

## TK5103 Apparatus and Supplies

**Freeman, Roger L.**      **5.6384**
Telecommunication system engineering: analog and digital network design / Roger L. Freeman. — New York: Wiley, c1980. xxii, 480 p.: ill.; 24 cm. 'A Wiley-Interscience publication.' 1. Telecommunication systems — Design and construction. 2. Telephone systems — Design and construction. I. T.
TK5103.F68      621.38      *LC* 79-26661      *ISBN* 0471029556

**Hardy, James K.**      **5.6385**
High frequency circuit design / by James K. Hardy; with ill. by Patricia Hardy. — Reston, Va.: Reston Pub. Co., c1979. xi, 353 p.: ill.; 24 cm. 1. Telecommunication — Apparatus and supplies — Design and construction. 2. Electronic circuit design 3. Amplifiers (Electronics) 4. Oscillators, Electric 5. Electric filters I. T.
TK5103.H38      621.3815/3      *LC* 78-27778      *ISBN* 0835928241

**Hills, Michael Turner.**      **5.6386**
Telecommunications switching principles / M. T. Hills. — Cambridge, Mass.: MIT Press, 1979. xiii, 327 p.: ill.; 25 cm. 1. Telecommunication — Switching systems I. T.
TK5103.H55 1979      621.38      *LC* 78-61815      *ISBN* 0262080923

**Optical communications: a telecommunications review.**      **5.6387**
Berlin: Siemens Aktiengesellschaft; Chichester: Wiley, 1983. — 220 p.: ill. (some col.); 30 cm. Special issue of Telecom report, v. 6, 1983. 1. Telecommunication — Apparatus and supplies I. Siemens Aktiengesellschaft. II. Telecom report.
TK5103.O6 1983      621.38 19      *ISBN* 3800938359

## TK5103.59–5103.7 Optical and Digital Communication

**Gowar, John, 1945-.**      **5.6388**
Optical communication systems / John Gowar. — Englewood Cliffs, NJ: Prentice/Hall International, c1984. xiv, 577 p.: ill.; 24 cm. — (Prentice-Hall international series in optoelectronics.) 1. Optical communications I. T. II. Series.
TK5103.59.G68 1984      621.38/0414 19      *LC* 83-8694      *ISBN* 0136380565

**Personick, Stewart D.**      **5.6389**
Optical fiber transmission systems / Stewart D. Personick. — New York: Plenum Press, c1981. xi, 179 p.: ill.; 24 cm. — (Applications of communications theory.) 1. Optical communications 2. Fiber optics I. T. II. Series.
TK5103.59.P47      621.36/92 19      *LC* 80-20684      *ISBN* 0306405806

**Digital communications by satellite: modulation, multiple access,**   **5.6390**
**and coding / Vijay K. Bhargava ... [et al.].**
New York: Wiley, c1981. xxi, 569 p.: ill.; 24 cm. 'A Wiley-Interscience
publication.' 1. Digital communications 2. Artificial satellites in
telecommunication I. Bhargava, Vijay K., 1948-
TK5103.7.D53      621.38/0422 19      LC 81-10276      ISBN 047108316X

**Feher, Kamilo.**                                           **5.6391**
Digital communications: microwave applications / Kamilo Feher. —
Englewood Cliffs, N.J.: Prentice-Hall, c1981. xviii, 269 p.: ill.; 24 cm. 1. Digital
communications 2. Microwave communication systems I. T.
TK5103.7.F43 1981      621.38/0413      LC 80-13904      ISBN
0132140802

**Kobayashi, Kōji, 1907-.**                               **5.6392**
[C&C modern communications. English] Computers and communications: a
vision of C&C / Kōji Kobayashi. — Cambridge, Mass.: MIT Press, c1986. xvi,
190 p.: ill.; 22 cm. Translation of: C&C modern communications. 1. Digital
communications 2. Computer networks I. T.
TK5103.7.K6313 1986      384.3 19      LC 85-24144      ISBN
026211111X

**Ziemer, Rodger E.**                                       **5.6393**
Digital communications and spread spectrum systems / Rodger E. Ziemer,
Roger L. Peterson. — New York: Macmillan; London: Collier Macmillan,
c1985. xviii, 750 p.: ill.; 27 cm. 1. Digital communications 2. Spread spectrum
communications I. Peterson, Roger L. II. T.
TK5103.7.Z54 1985      621.38/0413 19      LC 84-17141      ISBN
0024316709

## TK5104 ARTIFICIAL TELECOMMUNICATION SATELLITES

**Baylin, Frank.**                                             **5.6394**
Satellites today / by Frank Baylin, with Amy Toner. — [Boulder, Colo.]:
ConSol Network Inc., 1985, c1984. 163 p.: ill.; 21 cm. 1. Artificial satellites in
telecommunication 2. Television 3. Telecommunication I. Toner, Amy.
II. T.
TK5104.B39      LC 84-70697      ISBN 0917893018

**Gagliardi, Robert M., 1934-.**                            **5.6395**
Satellite communications / Robert M. Gagliardi. — Belmont, Calif.: Lifetime
Learning Publications, c1984. xviii, 474 p.: ill.; 24 cm. 1. Artificial satellites in
telecommunication — Congresses. I. T.
TK5104.G33 1984      621.38/0422 19      LC 83-19905      ISBN
0534029760

**The INTELSAT global satellite system / edited by Joel Alper,**   **5.6396**
**Joseph N. Pelton.**
New York, N.Y.: American Institute of Aeronautics and Astronautics, c1984.
ix, 425 p.: ill.; 24 cm. (Progress in astronautics and aeronautics. v. 93)
1. Artificial satellites in telecommunication I. Alper, Joel. II. Pelton, Joseph
N. III. Title: I.N.T.E.L.S.A.T. global satellite system. IV. Series.
TK5104.I5x      629.1 s 384 19      LC 84-18524      ISBN 0915928906

**Martin, James, 1933-.**                                     **5.6397**
Communications satellite systems / James Martin. — Englewood Cliffs, N.J.:
Prentice-Hall, c1978. xv, 398 p.: ill.; 24 cm. — (Prentice-Hall series in
automatic computation) 1. Artificial satellites in telecommunication I. T.
TK5104.M37      621.38/0422      LC 78-5247      ISBN 0131531638

## TK5105 DATA TRANSMISSION SYSTEMS

**Bylanski, P.**                                              **5.6398**
Digital transmission systems / P. Bylanski and D.G.W. Ingram. — Rev. ed. —
Stevenage, Herts.: P. Pergrinus on behalf of the Institution of Electrical
Engineers, c1980. xiii, 431 p.: ill. (IEE telecommunications series. 4) 1. Data
transmission systems 2. Digital electronics I. Ingram, Derek George
Woodward. II. Institution of Electrical Engineers. III. T. IV. Series.
TK5105.B9x 1980      ISBN 0906048427

**McNamara, John E.**                                     **5.6399**
Technical aspects of data communication / John E. McNamara. — 2nd ed. —
Bedford, Mass.: Digital Press, c1982. xi, 330 p.: ill.; 24 cm. Includes index.
1. Data transmission systems I. T.
TK5105.M4 1982      621.38 19      LC 81-17433      ISBN 0932376185

**Mosco, Vincent.**                                         **5.6400**
Pushbutton fantasies: critical perspectives on videotex and information
technology / Vincent Mosco. — Norwood, N.J.: Ablex Pub. Corp., c1982. xi,

195 p.: ill.; 24 cm. (Communication and information science.) 1. Videotex
systems — Social aspects. I. T. II. Series.
TK5105.M68 1982      303.4/833 19      LC 82-11601      ISBN
0893911259

**Owen, Frank F. E.**                                      **5.6401**
PCM and digital transmission systems / Frank F.E. Owen. — New York:
McGraw-Hill, c1982. xi, 295 p.: ill.; 26 cm. — (Texas Instruments electronics
series.) Includes index. 1. Data transmission systems 2. Pulse-code modulation
3. Digital electronics I. T. II. Title: P.C.M. and digital transmission systems.
III. Series.
TK5105.O94      621.38/0413 19      LC 81-5988      ISBN 0070479542

**Roden, Martin S.**                                       **5.6402**
Analog and digital communication systems / Martin S. Roden. — 2nd ed. —
Englewood Cliffs, N.J.: Prentice-Hall, c1985. xiv, 456 p.: ill.; 25 cm. Includes
index. 1. Telecommunication 2. Digital communications I. T.
TK5105.R64 1985      621.38/0413 19      LC 84-18114      ISBN
0130328227

**Rosner, Roy D., 1943-.**                                 **5.6403**
Distributed telecommunications networks via satellites and packet switching /
Roy D. Rosner. — Belmont, Calif.: Lifetime Learning Publications, c1982. xiii,
235 p.: ill.; 24 cm. 1. Telecommunication systems 2. Packet switching (Data
transmission) 3. Artificial satellites in telecommunication I. T.
TK5105.R66 1982      621.38/0413 19      LC 82-4675      ISBN
0534979335

**Sippl, Charles J.**                                       **5.6404**
Dictionary of data communications / Charles J. Sippl. — 2nd ed. — New York:
Wiley, c1985. 532 p.; 24 cm. Rev. ed. of: Data communications dictionary /
Charles J. Sippl. c1976. 'A Halsted Press book.' 1. Data transmission systems
— Dictionaries. 2. Electronic data processing — Dictionaries. I. Sippl,
Charles J. Data communications dictionary. II. T.
TK5105.S36 1985      001.64/4 19      LC 85-5392      ISBN 0470201827

**Schwartz, Mischa.**                                      **5.6405**
Computer–communication network design and analysis / Mischa Schwartz. —
Englewood Cliffs, N.J.: Prentice-Hall, c1977. xi, 372 p.: ill.; 24 cm. Includes
index. 1. Data transmission systems 2. Computer networks I. T.
TK5105.S38      621.38      LC 76-54691      ISBN 013165134X

**Stallings, William.**                                      **5.6406**
Data and computer communications / William Stallings. — New York:
Macmillan Pub. Co.; London: Collier Macmillan, c1985. xiv, 594 p.: ill.; 27 cm.
Includes index. 1. Data transmission systems 2. Computer networks I. T.
TK5105.S73 1985      384 19      LC 84-7914      ISBN 0024154407

**Uzunoglu, Vasil.**                                       **5.6407**
Analysis and design of digital systems / Vasil Uzunoglu, with James C.
Morakis. — New York: Gordon and Breach, [1975] ix, 506 p.: ill.; 24 cm.
1. Data transmission systems 2. Digital electronics I. Morakis, James C., joint
author. II. T.
TK5105.U95      621.38/0413      LC 78-186587      ISBN 0677041004

## TK5105.5 COMPUTER NETWORKS

**Ahuja, Vijay.**                                          **5.6408**
Design and analysis of computer communication networks / Vijay Ahuja. —
New York: McGraw-Hill, c1982. xiv, 306 p.: ill.; 25 cm. — (McGraw-Hill
computer science series.) 1. Computer networks I. T. II. Series.
TK5105.5.A39      001.64/404 19      LC 81-11826      ISBN 0070006970

**Chorafas, Dimitris N.**                                  **5.6409**
Designing and implementing local area networks / Dimitris N. Chorafas. —
New York: McGraw-Hill, c1984. xii, 354 p.: ill.; 24 cm. Includes index.
1. Local networks (Computer networks) I. T.
TK5105.5.C486 1984      001.64/404 19      LC 83-11965      ISBN
0070108196

**Computer communications / editor, Wushow Chou; contributors,**   **5.6410**
**Wushow Chou ... [et al.].**
Englewood Cliffs, NJ: Prentice-Hall, c1983-c1985. 2 v.: ill.; 24 cm.
1. Computer networks 2. Data transmission systems I. Chou, Wushow.
TK5105.5.C637 1983      004.6 19      LC 82-3833      ISBN 0131650432

**Computer network architectures and protocols / edited by Paul**   **5.6411**
**E. Green, Jr.**
New York: Plenum Press, c1982. xvii, 718 p.: ill.; 23 cm. — (Applications of
communications theory.) 1. Computer networks I. Green, Paul Eliot, 1924-
II. Series.
TK5105.5.C638 1982      001.64/404 19      LC 82-5227      ISBN
0306407884

**IAkubaĭtis, Éduard Aleksandrovich.**    **5.6412**
[Arkhitektura vychislitel′nykh seteĭ. English] Network architectures for distributed computing = Arkhitektura vychislitelnykh setei / Eduard A. Yakubaitis; translated by Martin Morell. — New York: Allerton Press, c1983. x, 415 p.: ill.; 24 cm. Translation of: Arkhitektura vychislitel′nykh seteĭ. 'The present translation is based on the author's updated and revised manuscript which reflects his view of the state of the art at end of 1982'—T.p. verso. 1. Computer networks 2. Electronic data processing — Distributed processing I. T. II. Title: Arkhitektura vychislitelnykh setei.
TK5105.5.I1813 1983     001.64/404 19     *LC* 83-70666     *ISBN* 0898640059

**Laver, F. J. M.**    **5.6413**
Computers, communications and society / Murray Laver. London; New York: Oxford University Press, 1975. 99 p.: ill.; 22 cm. (Science and engineering policy series) Includes index. 1. Computer networks 2. Data transmission systems 3. Telecommunication I. T.
TK5105.5.L38     301.24/3     *LC* 75-313246     *ISBN* 0198583230

**Pužman, Josef.**    **5.6414**
Communication control in computer networks / Josef Puzman, Radoslav Porizek. — Chichester [Eng.]; New York: J. Wiley, c1980. 296 p.; 24 cm. — (Wiley series in computing.) 'A Wiley-Interscience publication.' Includes index. 1. Computer networks I. Porizek, Radoslav. joint author. II. T. III. Series.
TK5105.5.P89     001.64/404 19     *LC* 80-41259     *ISBN* 0471278947

**Tanenbaum, Andrew S., 1944-.**    **5.6415**
Computer networks / Andrew S. Tanenbaum. — Englewood Cliffs, N.J.: Prentice-Hall, c1981. xv, 517 p.: ill.; 24 cm. Includes index. 1. Computer networks I. T.
TK5105.5.T36     001.64/404 19     *LC* 80-23283     *ISBN* 0131651838

**Techo, Robert.**    **5.6416**
Data communications: an introduction to concepts and design / Robert Techo. — New York: Plenum Press, c1980. x, 293 p.: ill.; 24 cm. — (Applications of modern technology in business.) 1. Computer networks 2. Data transmission systems I. T. II. Series.
TK5105.5.T42     001.6/44/04     *LC* 79-24613     *ISBN* 0306403986

# TK6001–6720 Telephone. Radio. Radar. Television

## TK6001–6525 Telephone

**AT & T Bell Laboratories. Technical Publication Dept.**    **5.6417**
Engineering and operations in the Bell System / prepared by members of the technical staff and the Technical Publication Department, AT&T Bell Laboratories; R.F. Rey, technical editor. — 2nd ed. reorganized and rewritten telecommunications in the Bell System in 1982-1983. — Murray Hill, N.J.: AT&T Bell Laboratories, 1983. xvi, 884 p.: ill.; 25 cm. Includes index. 1. Telephone — United States I. Rey, R. F. II. T.
TK6023.A8 1983     621.385/0973 19     *LC* 83-72956     *ISBN* 0932764045

**A History of engineering and science in the Bell System / prepared by members of the technical staff, Bell Telephone Laboratories; M.D. Fagen, editor.**    **5.6418**
[New York]: The Laboratories, 1975- <c1985 >. v. <1-7 >: ill.; 25 cm. Vol. 3 prepared by A.E. Joel, Jr. and other members of the technical staff, Bell Telephone Laboratories; G.E. Schindler, Jr., editor. 1. American Telephone and Telegraph Company — History. 2. Telephone — United States — History. 3. Telecommunication — United States — History. 4. Electronics — United States — History. I. Fagen, M. D. II. Joel, Amos E. III. Schindler, G. E. IV. Bell Telephone Laboratories, inc.
TK6023.H57 1975     621.385/0973 19     *LC* 75-31499     *ISBN* 0932764002

**Kuecken, John A.**    **5.6419**
Talking computers and telecommunications / John A. Kuecken. — New York: Van Nostrand Reinhold Co., c1983. x, 237 p.: ill.; 24 cm. Includes index. 1. Telephone I. T.
TK6161.K83 1983     621.385 19     *LC* 82-2715     *ISBN* 0442247214

**Briley, Bruce E. (Bruce Edwin), 1936-.**    **5.6420**
Introduction to telephone switching / Bruce E. Briley. — Reading, Mass.: Addison-Wesley, Advanced Book Program, 1983. xx, 253 p.: ill.; 25 cm. 1. Telephone systems 2. Telephone, Automatic I. T.
TK6397.B67 1983     621.385/7 19     *LC* 83-8835     *ISBN* 0201112469

**World radio TV handbook.**    **5.6421**
London; New York: Billboard Publications. v.: ports., maps, music; 22 cm. Annual. Description based on: 1982; title from cover. 'A complete directory of international radio and television.' 1. Radio broadcasting — Directories. 2. Radio stations — Directories. 3. Television stations — Directories.
TK6450 W67     *LC* sn 82-4544

# TK6540–6571 Radio

**Aitken, Hugh G. J.**    **5.6422**
Syntony and spark: the origins of radio / Hugh G. J. Aitken. — New York: Wiley, c1976. xvi, 347 p.: ill.; 24 cm. (Science, culture, and society) 'A Wiley-Interscience publication.' 1. Radio — History I. T.
TK6547.A46     621.3841/09     *LC* 75-34247     *ISBN* 0471018163

**Aitken, Hugh G. J.**    **5.6423**
The continuous wave: technology and American radio, 1900–1932 / Hugh G.J. Aitken. — Princeton, N.J.: Princeton University Press, c1985. xvii, 588 p.: ill.; 24 cm. 1. Radio — United States — History. I. T.
TK6548.U6 A65 1985     384.6/0973 19     *LC* 84-22265     *ISBN* 0691083762

**De Forest, Lee, 1873-1961.**    • **5.6424**
Father of radio: the autobiography of Lee de Forest. Chicago: Wilcox & Follett, 1950. 502 p.: ill.; 21 cm. Includes index. I. T.
TK6548.U6D4x

**Terman, Frederick Emmons, 1900-.**    • **5.6425**
[Radio engineering] Electronic and radio engineering / [by] Frederick Emmons Terman; assisted by Robert Arthur Helliwell [and others] — 4th ed. New York: McGraw-Hill, 1955. 1078 p.: ill.; 24 cm. (McGraw-Hill electrical and electronic engineering series) Previous editions published under title: Radio engineering. 1. Radio 2. Electronics I. T.
TK6550.T4 1955     621.3841     *LC* 55-6174

**Clarke, R. H. (Richard Henry)**    **5.6426**
Diffraction theory and antennas / R.H. Clarke and John Brown. — Chichester, Eng.: E. Horwood; New York, N.Y.: Halsted Press, 1980. 292 p.: ill.; 24 cm. — (Ellis Horwood series in electrical and electronic engineering.) Includes index. 1. Radio waves — Diffraction 2. Radio — Antennas I. Brown, John, 1923- II. T. III. Series.
TK6553.C53 1980     621.3841/1     *LC* 80-40388     *ISBN* 0853121826

**Picquenard, Armel.**    **5.6427**
Radio wave propagation. New York: Wiley [1974] vi, 343 p.: ill.; 25 cm. (Philips technical library.) 'A Halsted Press book.' 1. Radio waves I. T. II. Series.
TK6553.P5313 1974     621.3841/1     *LC* 72-2046     *ISBN* 0470689218

**Ross, John F.**    **5.6428**
Handbook for radio engineering managers / J.F. Ross. — London: Butterworths, 1980. 947 p.: ill.; 24 cm. 1. Radio 2. Engineering — Management I. T.
TK6553.R6x     658/.92/13841 18     621.3841/068 19     *ISBN* 040800424X

**Smith, Jack, 1935-.**    **5.6429**
Modern communication circuits / Jack Smith. — New York: McGraw-Hill, c1986. xix, 557 p.: ill.; 25 cm. (McGraw-Hill series in electrical engineering. Communications and signal processing.) 1. Radio circuits I. T. II. Series.
TK6553.S5595 1986     621.3841/2 19     *LC* 84-26166     *ISBN* 0070587302

**Antenna engineering handbook.**    **5.6430**
2nd ed / editors Richard C. Johnson, Henry Jasik. — New York; London: McGraw-Hill, c1984. 1 v. (various pagings): ill.; 24 cm. 1. Radio — Antennas I. Johnson, Richard C. II. Jasik, Henry.
TK6565.A6     621.3841/35 19     *LC* 59-14455     *ISBN* 0070322910

**Cantril, Hadley, 1906-1969.**    • **5.6431**
The psychology of radio, by Hadley Cantril ... and Gordon W. Allport ... New York, London, Harper & Brothers, 1935. x, 276 p. diagrs. 24 cm. 'An analysis of the general psychological and cultural factors that shape radio programs and determine the reponses of the listeners to these broadcasts.'—Pref. 'First edition.' 1. Radio broadcasting 2. Radio — United States. 3. Social psychology I. Allport, Gordon W. (Gordon Willard), 1897-1967. joint author. II. T. III. Title: Radio, The psychology of.
TK6570.B7 C34     *LC* 35-19535

**Jakes, William C.**    **5.6432**
Microwave mobile communications / Edited by William C. Jakes, Jr. — New York: Wiley, [1974] ix, 642 p.: ill.; 23 cm. 'A Wiley-Interscience publication.'

1. Mobile communication systems 2. Microwave communication systems I. T.
TK6570.M6 J34      621.3841/65      *LC* 74-13401      *ISBN* 0471437204

**Prentiss, Stan.**                                                          **5.6433**
Introducing cellular communications: the new mobile telephone system / by Stan Prentiss. — 1st ed. — Blue Ridge Summit, Pa.: Tab Books, c1984. vii, 216 p.: ill.; 22 cm. 'No. 1682.' Includes index. 1. Cellular radio I. T.
TK6570.M6 P74 1984      384.5/3 19      *LC* 83-24186      *ISBN* 0830606823

## TK6573–6595 RADAR

**Radar technology / [edited by] Eli Brookner.**                            **5.6434**
Dedham, Mass.: Artech House, c1977. 432 p.: ill.; 29 cm. An outgrowth of 4 lectures delivered 1972-76. 1. Radar I. Brookner, Eli, 1931-
TK6575.B75      621.3848      *LC* 77-13055      *ISBN* 0890060215

**Hovanessian, Shahen A., 1931-.**                                          **5.6435**
Radar detection and tracking systems / by S. A. Hovanessian. — Dedham, Mass.: Artech House, [c1973] 1 v. (various pagings): illus.; 24 cm. — 1. Radar I. T.
TK6575.H68      621.3848      *LC* 73-81238      *ISBN* 0890060185

**Massachusetts Institute of Technology. Radar School.**            • **5.6436**
Principles of radar / by members of the staff /by J. Francis Reintjes [and] Godfrey T. Coate. — 3d ed. — New York: McGraw-Hill, 1952. xv, 985 p.: ill. 1. Radar 2. Racon I. Reintjes, J. Francis. II. Coate, Godfrey T. III. T.
TK6575.M3 1952      *LC* 52-5996

**Tzannes, N. S. (Nicolaos S.), 1937-.**                                    **5.6437**
Communication and radar systems / Nicolaos S. Tzannes. — Englewood Cliffs, N.J.: Prentice-Hall, c1985. xv, 413 p.: ill.; 24 cm. Includes index. 1. Radar 2. Telecommunication I. T.
TK6575.T95 1985      621.3848 19      *LC* 84-2005      *ISBN* 0131535455

## TK6630–6720 TELEVISION
(See also: HE8700, PN1992)

**International television & video almanac.**                               **5.6438**
32nd ed. (1987)-      . — New York: Quigley Pub. Co., 1987-. v.: ill.; 24 cm. Annual. 1. Television broadcasting — United States — Periodicals. 2. Video recordings — United States — Periodicals. 3. Television broadcasting — United States — Biography — Periodicals. 4. Video recordings — United States — Biography — Periodicals.
TK6630.A1 I6x.      *LC* 87-644123

**Television engineering handbook / K. Blair Benson, editor–in–**           **5.6439**
**chief.**
New York: McGraw-Hill, c1986. 1 v. (various pagings): ill.; 24 cm. Includes index. 1. Television — Handbooks, manuals, etc. I. Benson, K. Blair.
TK6642.T437 1986      621.388 19      *LC* 85-4293      *ISBN* 0070047790

**The Small television studio, equipment and facilities / Alan**           **5.6440**
**Bermingham ... [et al.].**
New York: Hastings House, c1975. 163 p.: ill.; 22 cm. (Communication arts books) (Media manuals) 'A Focal Press book.' 1. Television stations I. Bermingham, Alan.
TK6646.S6 1975      791.45      *LC* 75-6058      *ISBN* 0803867255

**Color television picture tubes / A. M. Morrell ... [et al.].**           **5.6441**
New York: Academic Press, 1974. x, 226 p.: ill.; 24 cm. (Advances in image pickup and display: Supplement; 1) 1. Television picture tubes 2. Color television I. Morrell, Albert M. II. Series.
TK6655.P5 C64      621.388/36/1      *LC* 73-18958      *ISBN* 0120221519

**Millerson, Gerald.**                                                      **5.6442**
Video production handbook / Gerald Millerson. — London; Boston: Focal Press, 1987. xii, 216 p.: ill.; 25 cm. Includes index. 1. Video tape recorders and recording 2. Video recordings — Production and direction I. T.
TK6655.V5 M55 1987      621.388/332 19      *LC* 86-20757      *ISBN* 024051260X

**Murray, Michael, 1932-.**                                                 **5.6443**
The videotape book: a basic guide to portable TV production / Michael Murray. — New York: Taplinger Pub. Co., c1975. 248 p.: ill.; 21 cm. Includes index. 1. Video tape recorders and recording I. T.
TK6655.V5 M87 1975      778.59      *LC* 75-8413      *ISBN* 080088020X

**White, Gordon.**                                                          **5.6444**
Video recording; record and replay systems. — New York: Crane, Russak, [c1972] 208 p.: ill.; 23 cm. 1. Video tape recorders and recording I. T.
TK6655.V5 W49 1972b      778.59      *LC* 72-81492      *ISBN* 0844800589

**Grant, William, 1925-.**                                                  **5.6445**
Cable television / William Grant. — Reston, Va.: Reston Pub. Co., c1983. xx, 362 p.: ill.; 24 cm. Includes index. 1. Cable television I. T.
TK6675.G73 1983      621.388/5 19      *LC* 83-8649      *ISBN* 0835906167

# TK7800–8360 Electronics

## TK7800–7866 REFERENCE. GENERAL WORKS

**Carter, Harley.**                                                         **5.6446**
Dictionary of electronics. — [2d ed.]. — Blue Ridge Summit, Pa.: Tab Books, [1972, c1963] vi, 410 p.: illus.; 23 cm. 'No. 300.' 1. Electronics — Dictionaries. I. T.
TK7804.C34 1972      621.381/03      *LC* 72-90780      *ISBN* 083062300X

**Graf, Rudolf F.**                                                         **5.6447**
Modern dictionary of electronics / Rudolf F. Graf. — 6th ed. — Indianapolis, Ind., USA: H.W. Sams, c1984. 1152 p.: ill.; 23 cm. '22041'—Cover. 1. Electronics — Dictionaries. I. T.
TK7804.G67 1984      621.381/03/21 19      *LC* 83-51223      *ISBN* 0672220415

**Traister, John E.**                                                       **5.6448**
Encyclopedic dictionary of electronic terms / John E. Traister, Robert J. Traister. — Englewood Cliffs, N.J.: Prentice-Hall, c1984. iii, 604 p.: 477 ill.; 24 cm. 1. Electronics — Dictionaries. I. Traister, Robert J. II. T.
TK7804.T7 1984      621.381/03/21 19      *LC* 84-2107      *ISBN* 0132769980

**Horowitz, Paul, 1942-.**                                                  **5.6449**
The art of electronics / Paul Horowitz, Winfield Hill. — Cambridge, [Eng.]; New York: Cambridge University Press, 1980. xviii, 716 p.: ill.; 26 cm. Includes index. 1. Electronics 2. Electronic circuit design I. Hill, Winfield. joint author. II. T.
TK7815.H67 1980      621.381      *LC* 79-27170      *ISBN* 0521231515

**Malvino, Albert Paul.**                                                   **5.6450**
Electronic principles / Albert Paul Malvino. — 3rd ed. — New York: McGraw-Hill, c1984. xiv, 754 p.: ill.; 25 cm. Includes index. 1. Electronics I. T.
TK7816.M25 1984      621.381 19      *LC* 83-19987      *ISBN* 0070399123

**Electronics engineers' handbook / Donald G. Fink, editor–in–**           **5.6451**
**chief, Donald Christiansen, associate editor.**
2nd ed. — New York: McGraw-Hill, c1982. 1 v. (various pagings): ill.; 25 cm. 'Companion volume to the Standard handbook for electrical engineers ... 11th edition'—Pref. 1. Electronics — Handbooks, manuals, etc. I. Fink, Donald G. II. Christiansen, Donald.
TK7825.E34 1982      621.381/0202 19      *LC* 81-3756      *ISBN* 0070209812

**Handbook of modern electronics and electrical engineering /**            **5.6452**
**editor–in–chief, Charles Belove; associate editors, Phillip**
**Hopkins ... [et al.].**
New York: Wiley, c1986. xxviii, 2401 p.: ill.; 25 cm. 'A Wiley-Interscience publication.' 1. Electronics — Handbooks, manuals, etc. 2. Electric engineering — Handbooks, manuals, etc. I. Belove, Charles. II. Hopkins, Phillip.
TK7825.H38 1986      621.3 19      *LC* 85-29450      *ISBN* 0471097543

**Colclaser, Roy A.**                                                       **5.6453**
Materials and devices for electrical engineers and physicists / Roy A. Colclaser and Sherra Diehl–Nagle. — New York: McGraw-Hill, c1985. xiv, 284 p.: ill.; 25 cm. — (McGraw-Hill series in electrical engineering. Electronics and electronic circuits.) 1. Electronics — Materials 2. Semiconductors I. Diehl-Nagle, Sherra. II. T. III. Series.
TK7835.C564 1985      621.381/028 19      *LC* 84-927      *ISBN* 0070116938

**Gatland, Howard Bruce.**                                                  **5.6454**
Electronic engineering applications of two–port networks / by H. B. Gatland. — 1st ed. — Oxford; New York: Pergamon Press, 1976. xv, 324 p.: ill.; 21 cm.

(Applied electricity and electronics division) Includes index. 1. Electronics 2. Electric networks, Two-port I. T.
TK7835.G37 1976    621.381    *LC* 75-6562    *ISBN* 0080180698

**Lacy, Edward A., 1935-.**      **5.6455**
Handbook of electronic safety procedures / Edward A. Lacy. Englewood Cliffs, N.J.: Prentice-Hall, c1977. xiv, 269 p.: ill.; 24 cm. 1. Electronics — Safety measures. 2. Electronic industries — Safety measures. I. T.
TK7835.L33    621.381/028    *LC* 75-44230    *ISBN* 0133773418

**Wang, Shyh, 1925-.**      • **5.6456**
Solid–state electronics. New York: McGraw-Hill [1966] xxi, 778 p.: ill.; 24 cm. (International series in pure and applied physics) 'Based on lecture notes of courses taught by the author at the University of California, Berkeley.' 1. Solid state electronics I. T.
TK7835.W3    621.381    *LC* 65-28136

**Kaplinsky, Raphael.**      **5.6457**
Computer–aided design: electronics, comparative advantage and development / Raphael Kaplinsky. — New York: Macmillan, c1982. 144 p.: ill.; 24 cm. Includes index. 1. Electronic industries — Developing countries. 2. Engineering design — Data processing 3. Computer-aided design I. T.
TK7836.K35 1982    338.4/762000425/091724 19    *LC* 82-14816
     *ISBN* 0029495202

# TK7867 ELECTRONIC CIRCUITS

**Boylestad, Robert L.**      **5.6458**
Electronic devices and circuit theory / Robert Boylestad, Louis Nashelsky. — 4th ed. — Englewood Cliffs, NJ: Prentice-Hall, 1987, c1986. p. cm. Includes index. 1. Electronic circuits 2. Electronic apparatus and appliances I. Nashelsky, Louis. II. T.
TK7867.B66 1987    621.38 19    *LC* 86-22661    *ISBN* 0132505568

**Chua, Leon O., 1936-.**      **5.6459**
Computer–aided analysis of electronic circuits: algorithms and computational techniques / Leon O. Chua, Pen–Min Lin. — Englewood Cliffs, N.J.: Prentice-Hall, [1975] xxvi, 737 p.: ill.; 24 cm. — (Prentice-Hall series in electrical and computer engineering) 1. Electronic circuit design — Data processing 2. Electronic circuits — Mathematical models. I. Lin, Pen-Min, 1928- joint author. II. T.
TK7867.C49    621.3815/3/02854    *LC* 75-1388    *ISBN* 0131654152

**Fidler, J. K. (John Kelvin)**      **5.6460**
Computer aided circuit design / J. K. Fidler, C. Nightingale. — New York: Wiley, c1978. viii, 254 p.: ill.; 24 cm. 'A Halsted Press book.' 1. Electronic circuit design — Data processing I. Nightingale, C. joint author. II. T.
TK7867.F5 1978    621.3815/3    *LC* 77-19300    *ISBN* 0470262915

**Handbook of circuit analysis languages and techniques / editors,**      **5.6461**
**Randall W. Jensen, Lawrence P. McNamee.**
Englewood Cliffs, N.J.: Prentice-Hall, c1976. xxii, 809 p.: ill.; 25 cm. 1. Electronic circuit design — Data processing 2. Programming languages (Electronic computers) I. Jensen, Randall W. II. McNamee, Lawrence P., 1934-
TK7867.H35    621.3815/3    *LC* 75-23235    *ISBN* 0133726495

**Jones, Martin Hartley, 1942-.**      **5.6462**
A practical introduction to electronic circuits / Martin Hartley Jones. — 2nd ed. — Cambridge [Cambridgeshire]; New York: Cambridge University Press, 1985. xvi, 278 p.: ill.; 25 cm. Includes index. 1. Electronic circuits I. T.
TK7867.J62 1985    621.3815/3 19    *LC* 85-7718    *ISBN* 0521307856

**Robinson, Vester.**      **5.6463**
Manual of solid state circuit design and troubleshooting / Vester Robinson. Reston, Va.: Reston Pub. Co., [1976] c1977. xii, 413 p.: ill.; 24 cm. Includes index. 1. Electronic circuit design 2. Semiconductors 3. Electronic circuits — Testing 4. Semiconductors — Testing I. T.
TK7867.R6    621.3815/3/042    *LC* 76-26555    *ISBN* 0879094648

**Schilling, Donald L.**      **5.6464**
Electronic circuits, discrete and integrated / Donald L. Schilling, Charles Belove. — 2d ed. — New York: McGraw-Hill, c1979. xix, 811 p.: ill.; 24 cm. (Electronics and electronic circuits) (McGraw-Hill series in electrical engineering) 1. Electronic circuits I. Belove, Charles. joint author. II. T.
TK7867.S33 1979    621.381/53    *LC* 78-12142    *ISBN* 0070552940

**Sedra, Adel S.**      **5.6465**
Microelectronic circuits / Adel S. Sedra, Kenneth C. Smith. — 2nd ed. — New York: Holt, Rinehart, and Winston, c1987. 1 v. 1. Electronic circuits 2. Integrated circuits I. Smith, Kenneth Carless. II. T.
TK7867.S39 1987    621.3815/3 19    *LC* 86-25645    *ISBN* 0030073286

**Vlach, Jiří.**      **5.6466**
Computer methods for circuit analysis and design / Jiří Vlach, Kishore Singhal. — New York: Van Nostrand Reinhold, c1983. xxix, 594 p.: ill.; 24 cm. — (Van Nostrand Reinhold electrical/computer science and engineering series.) Includes index. 1. Electronic circuits 2. Electronic circuit design — Data processing I. Singhal, Kishore. II. T. III. Series.
TK7867.V58 1983    621.3815/3 19    *LC* 82-16018    *ISBN* 0442281080

**Wong, Yu Jen, 1945-.**      **5.6467**
Function circuits: design and applications / Yu Jen Wong, William E. Ott. — New York: McGraw-Hill, c1976. xii, 291 p.: ill.; 24 cm. — (The BB electronics series) 1. Electronic circuits I. Ott, William E., 1945- joint author. II. T. III. Series.
TK7867.W66    621.3815/3    *LC* 76-43060    *ISBN* 007071570X

# TK7868 SPECIAL CIRCUITS, A–Z

**Breuer, Melvin A.**      **5.6468**
Diagnosis and reliable design of digital systems / Melvin A. Breuer, Arthur D. Friedman. Woodland Hills, Calif.: Computer Science Press, c1976. ix, 308 p.: ill.; 24 cm. (Digital system design series). 1. Digital electronics 2. Electronic apparatus and appliances — Testing 3. Electronic circuit design I. Friedman, Arthur D. joint author. II. T. III. Series.
TK7868.D5 B73    621.3815    *LC* 76-19081    *ISBN* 0914894579

**Cowan, Sam, 1943-.**      **5.6469**
Handbook of digital logic ... with practical applications / Sam Cowan. — Englewood Cliffs, N.J.: Prentice-Hall, c1985. x, 309 p.: ill.; 24 cm. Includes index. 1. Digital electronics 2. Logic circuits I. T.
TK7868.D5 C68 1985    621.3815 19    *LC* 84-16049    *ISBN* 0133771938

**Hodges, David A., 1937-.**      **5.6470**
Analysis and design of digital integrated circuits / David A. Hodges, Horace G. Jackson. — New York: McGraw-Hill, c1983. xiii, 434 p.: ill.; 25 cm. — (McGraw-Hill series in electrical engineering. Electronics and electronic circuits.) 1. Digital electronics 2. Integrated circuits I. Jackson, Horace G. II. T. III. Series.
TK7868.D5 H63 1983    621.381/73 19    *LC* 82-14907    *ISBN* 0070291535

**Middleton, Robert Gordon, 1908-.**      **5.6471**
New digital troubleshooting techniques: a complete, illustrated guide / Robert G. Middleton. — Englewood Cliffs, N.J.: Prentice-Hall, Business and Professional Division, c1984. 279 p.: ill.; 25 cm. Includes index. 1. Digital electronics 2. Electronic apparatus and appliances — Maintenance and repair I. T.
TK7868.D5 M524 1984    621.381/028/8 19    *LC* 83-16157    *ISBN* 0136122752

**Porat, Dan I.**      **5.6472**
Introduction to digital techniques / Dan I. Porat, Arpad Barna. — New York: Wiley, c1979. x, 527 p.: ill.; 24 cm. — (Electronic technology series) Includes index. 1. Digital electronics I. Barna, Arpad. joint author. II. T.
TK7868.D5 P67    621.38/0413    *LC* 78-17696    *ISBN* 0471029246

**Taub, Herbert, 1918-.**      **5.6473**
Digital circuits and microprocessors / Herbert Taub. — New York: McGraw-Hill Book Co., c1982. xvii, 541 p.: ill.; 25 cm. — (McGraw-Hill series in electrical engineering. Computer engineering and switching theory.) Includes index. 1. Digital electronics 2. Microprocessors I. T. II. Series.
TK7868.D5 T36    621.3815/3 19    *LC* 81-3729    *ISBN* 0070629455

**Taub, Herbert, 1918-.**      **5.6474**
Digital integrated electronics / Herbert Taub, Donald Schilling. New York: McGraw-Hill, c1977. xx, 650 p.: ill.; 24 cm. (McGraw-Hill electrical and electronic engineering series) 1. Digital electronics 2. Integrated circuits I. Schilling, Donald L. joint author. II. T.
TK7868.D5 T37    621.381    *LC* 76-4585    *ISBN* 0070629218

**Bennetts, R. G.**      **5.6475**
Design of testable logic circuits / R.G. Bennetts. — London; Reading, Mass.: Addison-Wesley Pub. Co., c1984. xii, 164 p.: ill.; 25 cm. (Microelectronics systems design series.) 1. Logic circuits 2. Logic circuits — Testing. I. T. II. Series.
TK7868.L6 B45 1984    621.3819/535 19    *LC* 83-11768    *ISBN* 0201144034

**Towers, T. D., 1914-.**      **5.6476**
Practical solid–state DC power supplies / by T. D. Towers. 1st ed. — Blue Ridge Summit, Pa.: G/L Tab Books, c1976. 192 p.: ill.; 22 cm. Includes index.

1. Electronic apparatus and appliances — Power supply — Direct current I. T.
TK7868.P6 T68     621.38/028     *LC* 76-45068     *ISBN* 0830668918

**Allen, P. E. (Phillip E.)** 5.6477
Switched capacitor circuits / Phillip E. Allen, Edgar Sánchez–Sinencio. — New York: Van Nostrand Reinhold, c1984. xv, 759 p.: ill.; 24 cm. — (Van Nostrand Reinhold electrical/computer science and engineering series.) Includes index. 1. Switched capacitor circuits I. Sánchez-Sinencio, Edgar. II. T. III. Series.
TK7868.S88 A38 1984     621.3815/3 19     *LC* 83-10507     *ISBN* 0442208731

**Hill, Fredrick J.** 5.6478
Introduction to switching theory and logical design / Frederick [sic] J. Hill, Gerald R. Peterson. — 3d ed. — New York: Wiley, c1981. xv, 617 p.: ill.; 24 cm. 1. Switching circuits 2. Digital electronics 3. Logic design I. Peterson, Gerald R. joint author. II. T.
TK7868.S9 H5 1981     621.3815/37 19     *LC* 80-20333     *ISBN* 0471042730

## TK7870–7871 APPARATUS AND MATERIALS

**Bell Telephone Laboratories, inc.** • 5.6479
Physical design of electronic systems. Prepared by members of the technical staff, Bell Telephone Laboratories, Inc., under the general direction of: D. Baker [and others]. — Englewood Cliffs, N.J.: Prentice-Hall, [1970-72] 4 v.: illus.; 25 cm. — (Prentice-Hall electrical engineering series) 1. Electronic systems — Design and construction. I. Baker, Donn, 1928- II. T.
TK7870.B43 1970     621.381     *LC* 74-76873     *ISBN* 0136663540

**Jones, Thomas H., 1926-.** 5.6480
Electronic components handbook / Thomas H. Jones. — Reston, Va.: Reston Pub. Co., c1978. xviii, 391 p.: ill.; 24 cm. 1. Electronic apparatus and appliances — Handbooks, manuals, etc. I. T.
TK7870.J65     621.3815     *LC* 77-22341     *ISBN* 087909222X

**Millman, Jacob, 1911-.** • 5.6481
Pulse, digital, and switching waveforms: devices and circuits for their generation and processing / [by] Jacob Millman [and] Herbert Taub. — New York: McGraw-Hill, [1965] xiv, 958 p.: illus.; 24 cm. 1. Electronic circuits 2. Delay lines 3. Switching circuits 4. Pulse circuits I. Taub, Herbert, 1918- joint author. II. T.
TK7870.M53     621.3815     *LC* 64-66293

**Villanucci, Robert S., 1944-.** 5.6482
Electronic techniques; shop practices and construction [by] Robert S. Villanucci, Alexander W. Avtgis [and] William F. Megow. — Englewood Cliffs, N.J.: Prentice-Hall, [1974] xvi, 569 p.: illus.; 25 cm. — (Prentice-Hall series in electronic technology) 1. Electronic apparatus and appliances — Design and construction I. Avtgis, Alexander W., 1931- joint author. II. Megow, William F., 1936- joint author. III. T.
TK7870.V497     621.381     *LC* 73-9814     *ISBN* 0132524945

**Middleton, Robert Gordon, 1908-.** 5.6483
Troubleshooting electronic equipment without service data / Robert G. Middleton. — Englewood Cliffs, N.J.: Prentice-Hall, Business and Professional Division, c1984. 303 p.: ill.; 24 cm. Includes index. 1. Electronic apparatus and appliances — Maintenance and repair I. T.
TK7870.2.M535 1984     621.381/028/8 19     *LC* 83-13772     *ISBN* 0139310975

**Ellison, Gordon N.** 5.6484
Thermal computations for electronic equipment / Gordon N. Ellison. — New York: Van Nostrand Reinhold Co., c1984. xv, 397 p.: ill.; 26 cm. 1. Electronic apparatus and appliances — Cooling 2. Heat — Transmission I. T.
TK7870.25.E4 1984     621.402/2/028542 19     *LC* 82-21863     *ISBN* 0442219237

## TK7871.2–7871.58 AMPLIFIERS. LASERS. MASERS

**Carson, Ralph S.** 5.6485
High-frequency amplifiers / Ralph S. Carson. — 2nd ed. — New York: Wiley, c1982. xii, 291 p.: ill.; 24 cm. 'A Wiley-Interscience publication.' Includes index. 1. Transistor amplifiers 2. Smith charts I. T.
TK7871.2.C35 1982     621.3815/35 19     *LC* 82-4723     *ISBN* 0471868329

**Faber, Rodney B.** 5.6486
Linear circuits: discrete and integrated [by] Rodney B. Faber. — Columbus, Ohio: Merrill, [1974] xiv, 509 p.: illus.; 26 cm. — (Merrill's international series in electrical and electronics technology) 1. Amplifiers (Electronics) 2. Integrated circuits 3. Electronic circuits I. T.
TK7871.2.F33     621.3815/35     *LC* 73-87839     *ISBN* 0675088615

**Lengyel, Bela A. (Bela Adalbert), 1910-.** • 5.6487
Lasers [by] Bela A. Lengyel. 2d ed. New York, Wiley-Interscience [1971] xii, 386 p. illus. 24 cm. (Wiley series in pure and applied optics) 1. Lasers I. T.
TK7871.3.L45 1971     621.36/6     *LC* 77-139279     *ISBN* 0471526207

**Siegman, A. E.** • 5.6488
An introduction to lasers and masers [by] A. E. Siegman. — New York: McGraw-Hill, [c1971] xiii, 520 p.: illus.; 24 cm. — (McGraw-Hill series in the fundamentals of electronic science) 1. Lasers 2. Masers I. T.
TK7871.3.S55     621.36/6     *LC* 79-123189

**Yariv, Amnon.** 5.6489
Introduction to optical electronics. New York: Holt, Rinehart and Winston, [1971] x, 342 p.: illus.; 25 cm. — (HRW series in electrical engineering, electronics, and systems) 1. Lasers 2. Optoelectronic devices 3. Quantum electronics I. T.
TK7871.3.Y35     537.5/6     *LC* 74-139995     *ISBN* 0030846943

**Bertolotti, Mario.** 5.6490
Masers and lasers: an historical approach / M. Bertolotti. — Bristol: A. Hilger, c1983. xii, 268 p.: ill.; 24 cm. 1. Masers — History. 2. Lasers — History. I. T.
TK7871.4.B47 1983     621.36/6 19     *LC* 83-105489     *ISBN* 0852745362

## TK7871.6 ANTENNAS

**Balanis, Constantine A., 1938-.** 5.6491
Antenna theory: analysis and design / Constantine A. Balanis. — New York: Harper & Row, c1982. xvii, 790 p.: ill.; 25 cm. — (Harper & Row series in electrical engineering.) 1. Antennas (Electronics) I. T. II. Series.
TK7871.6.B353 1982     621.38/028/3 19     *LC* 81-20248     *ISBN* 0060404582

**Collin, Robert E.** 5.6492
Antennas and radiowave propagation / Robert E. Collin. — New York: McGraw-Hill, c1985. xii, 508 p.: ill.; 24 cm. (McGraw-Hill series in electrical engineering. Radio, television, radar, and antennas.) Includes indexes. 1. Antennas (Electronics) 2. Radio wave propagation I. T. II. Series.
TK7871.6.C62 1985     621.3841/1 19     *LC* 84-17108     *ISBN* 0070118086

**The Handbook of antenna design: v. 2. / editors, A.W. Rudge ... [et al.].** 5.6493
London: P. Peregrinus on behalf of the Institution of Electrical Engineers, c1983. 945 p.: ill. (IEE electromagnetic waves series. 16.) 1. Antennas (Electronics) — Design and construction. I. Rudge, A. W. (Alan W.) II. Series.
TK7871.6.H34     621.38/028/3 19     *LC* 83-114959     *ISBN* 0906048826

**The Handbook of antenna design: v. 1 / editors, A.W. Rudge ... [et al.].** 5.6494
London: P. Peregrinus on behalf of the Institution of Electrical Engineers, c1982. 708 p.: ill. (IEE electromagnetic waves series. 15.) 1. Antennas (Electronics) — Design and construction. I. Rudge, A. W. (Alan W.) II. Series.
TK7871.6.H34 1982     621.38/028/3 19     *LC* 83-114959     *ISBN* 0906048826

**Milligan, Thomas A.** 5.6495
Modern antenna design / Thomas A. Milligan. — New York: McGraw-Hill, c1985. xv, 408 p.: ill.; 24 cm. 1. Antennas (Electronics) — Design and construction. I. T.
TK7871.6.M54 1985     621.38/028/3 19     *LC* 84-17131     *ISBN* 0070423180

**Stutzman, Warren L.** 5.6496
Antenna theory and design / Warren L. Stutzman, Gary A. Thiele. — New York: Wiley, c1981. x, 598 p.: ill.; 24 cm. 1. Antennas (Electronics) I. Thiele, Gary A. joint author. II. T.
TK7871.6.S77     621.38/028/3 19     *LC* 80-23498     *ISBN* 047104458X

## TK7871.85–7871.99 Semiconductors. Transistors. Thermistors

**Gray, Paul E.**      • 5.6497
Electronic principles: Physics, models, and circuits / [by] Paul E. Gray and Campbell L. Searle. — New York: Wiley, [1969] xxiii, 1016 p.: ill. (part col.); 24 cm. 1. Semiconductors 2. Transistor circuits I. Searle, Campbell L., joint author. II. T.
TK7871.85.G67     621.381/5     LC 78-107884     ISBN 0471323985

**Navon, David H.**      5.6498
Electronic materials and devices / David H. Navon. — Boston: Houghton Mifflin, [1975] xi, 404 p.: ill.; 25 cm. 1. Semiconductors 2. Solids 3. Electronic apparatus and appliances I. T.
TK7871.85.N39     621.3815/2     LC 74-11948     ISBN 0395189179

**Streetman, Ben G.**      5.6499
Solid state electronic devices / Ben G. Streetman. — 2d ed. — Englewood Cliffs, N.J.: Prentice-Hall, 1980. xvii, 461 p.: ill.; 24 cm. 1. Semiconductors I. T.
TK7871.85.S77 1980     621.3815/2 19     LC 79-16994     ISBN 0138221715

**Sze, S. M., 1936-.**      5.6500
Physics of semiconductor devices / S.M. Sze. — 2nd ed. — New York: Wiley, c1981. xii, 868 p.: ill.; 24 cm. 'A Wiley-Interscience publication.' 1. Semiconductors I. T.
TK7871.85.S988 1981     537.6/22 19     LC 81-213     ISBN 0471056618

**Sze, S. M., 1936-.**      5.6501
Semiconductor devices, physics and technology / S.M. Sze. — New York: Wiley, c1985. xi, 523 p.: ill.; 25 cm. 1. Semiconductors I. T.
TK7871.85.S9883 1985     621.381/52 19     LC 85-3217     ISBN 0471874248

**Yang, Edward S.**      5.6502
Fundamentals of semiconductor devices / Edward S. Yang. — New York: McGraw-Hill, c1978. xi, 355 p.: ill.; 25 cm. 1. Semiconductors I. T.
TK7871.85.Y36     621.3815/2     LC 77-11021     ISBN 0070722366

**Feldman, James M.**      5.6503
The physics and circuit properties of transistors [by] James M. Feldman. — New York: Wiley, [1972] x, 604 p.: illus.; 23 cm. 1. Transistors I. T.
TK7871.9.F45     621.3815/28     LC 71-39722     ISBN 0471257060

**Gottlieb, Irving M.**      5.6504
Solid–state high–frequency power / Irving M. Gottlieb. — Reston, Va.: Reston Pub. Co., c1982. x, 246 p.: ill.; 24 cm. Includes index. 1. Power transistors 2. Amplifiers, Radio frequency 3. Transistor amplifiers I. T.
TK7871.9.G65 1982     621.3815/28 19     LC 81-12128     ISBN 0835970485

**Ritchie, G. J. (Gordon James)**      5.6505
Transistor circuit techniques: discrete and integrated / G.J. Ritchie. — Wokingham, Berkshire, England: Van Nostrand Reinhold (UK), c1983. x, 168 p.: ill.; 26 cm. (Tutorial guides in electronic engineering. 1) 1. Transistor circuits I. T. II. Series.
TK7871.9.R58 1983     621.3815/30422 19     LC 82-11090     ISBN 0442305311

**Getreu, Ian E.**      5.6506
Modeling the bipolar transistor / Ian E. Getreu. — Amsterdam; New York: Elsevier Scientific Pub. Co., 1978 (c1976). x, 261 p.: ill.; 25 cm. — (Computer-aided design of electronic circuits; 1) 1. Bipolar transistors — Data processing. 2. Bipolar transistors — Mathematical models. 3. Transistor circuits — Design and construction — Data processing. I. T. II. Series.
TK7871.96.B55 G47     621.381/5/28     LC 78-17599     ISBN 0444417222

**Nicollian, E. H.**      5.6507
MOS (metal oxide semiconductor) physics and technology / E.H. Nicollian, J.R. Brews. — New York: Wiley, c1982. xv, 906 p.: ill.; 25 cm. 'A Wiley-Interscience publication.' 1. Metal oxide semiconductors I. Brews, J. R. II. T.
TK7871.99.M44 N52 1982     621.3815/2 19     LC 81-7607     ISBN 0471085006

**Ong, DeWitt G.**      5.6508
Modern MOS technology: processes, devices, and design / DeWitt G. Ong. — New York: McGraw-Hill, c1984. xii, 366 p.: ill.; 24 cm. 1. Metal oxide semicondutors. 2. Integrated circuits I. T. II. Title: Modern M.O.S. technology.
TK7871.99.M44 O53 1984     621.381/73042 19     LC 83-11339     ISBN 0070477094

## TK7872 Other Semiconductors, A–Z

**Dewan, S. B.**      5.6509
Power semiconductor circuits / S. B. Dewan, A. Straughen. — New York: Wiley, [1975] xv, 523 p.: ill.; 23 cm. 'A Wiley-Interscience publication.' 1. Electric current converters 2. Thyristors 3. Diodes, Semiconductor 4. Electric switchgear I. Straughen, A. joint author. II. T.
TK7872.C8 D48     621.3815/32     LC 75-8911     ISBN 047121180X

**Adaptive filters / edited by C.F.N. Cowan and P.M. Grant; with**      5.6510
**contributions from P.F. Adams ... [et al.].**
Englewood Cliffs, N.J.: Prentice-Hall, c1985. xx, 308 p.: ill.; 24 cm. (Prentice-Hall signal processing series.) Includes index. 1. Adaptive filters I. Cowan, C. F. N. (Colin F. N.) II. Grant, Peter M. III. Adams, P. F. (Peter F.) IV. Series.
TK7872.F5 A33 1985     621.3815/324 19     LC 84-18039     ISBN 0130040371

**Daniels, Richard W., 1942-.**      5.6511
Approximation methods for electronic filter design; with applications to passive, active, and digital networks [by] Richard W. Daniels. — New York: McGraw-Hill, [1974] xvii, 388 p.: illus.; 24 cm. 1. Electric filters — Design and construction — Approximation methods 2. Approximation theory I. T.
TK7872.F5 D36     621.3815/32     LC 74-8091     ISBN 0070153086

**Haykin, Simon S., 1931-.**      5.6512
Introduction to adaptive filters / Simon Haykin. — New York: Macmillan; London: Collier Macmillan, c1984. xii, 217 p.: ill.; 25 cm. 1. Adaptive filters I. T.
TK7872.F5 H37 1984     621.3815/324 19     LC 84-11234     ISBN 0029494605

**Humpherys, DeVerl S.**      • 5.6513
The analysis, design, and synthesis of electrical filters [by] DeVerl S. Humpherys. — Englewood Cliffs, N.J.: Prentice-Hall, [1970] xi, 675 p.: illus.; 24 cm. — (Prentice-Hall networks series) 1. Electric filters I. T.
TK7872.F5 H84     621.381/532     LC 79-108809     ISBN 0130329043

**Jackson, Leland B.**      5.6514
Digital filters and signal processing / by Leland B. Jackson. — Boston: Kluwer Academic Publishers, c1986. xi, 259 p.: ill.; 25 cm. Includes index. 1. Electric filters, Digital 2. Signal processing — Digital techniques I. T.
TK7872.F5 J33 1986     621.38/043 19     LC 85-9812     ISBN 0898381746

**Van Valkenburg, M. E. (Mac Elwyn), 1921-.**      5.6515
Analog filter design / M.E. Van Valkenburg. — New York: Holt, Rinehart, and Winston, c1982. xi, 608 p.: ill.; 25 cm. — (HRW series in electrical and computer engineering.) Includes index. 1. Electric filters, Active 2. Operational amplifiers I. T. II. Series.
TK7872.F5 V38     621.3815/324 19     LC 81-23774     ISBN 0030592461

**Egan, William F.**      5.6516
Frequency synthesis by phase lock / William F. Egan. — New York: Wiley, c1981. xix, 279 p.: ill.; 24 cm. 'A Wiley-Interscience publication.' Includes index. 1. Frequency synthesizers 2. Phase-locked loops I. T.
TK7872.F73 E32     621.3815/36     LC 80-16917     ISBN 0471082023

**Shaw, Melvin P.**      5.6517
The Gunn–Hilsum effect / Melvin P. Shaw, Harold L. Grubin, and Peter R. Solomon. — New York: Academic Press, 1979. xviii, 250 p.: ill.; 24 cm. 1. Gunn effect 2. Semiconductors 3. Solid state physics I. Grubin, Harold L. joint author. II. Solomon, Peter R., 1939- joint author. III. T.
TK7872.G8 S5     621.3815/2     LC 76-45995     ISBN 0126383502

**Frerking, Marvin E.**      5.6518
Crystal oscillator design and temperature compensation / Marvin E. Frerking. — New York: Van Nostrand, c1978. xiii, 240 p.: ill.; 24 cm. 1. Oscillators, Crystal 2. Oscillators, Transistor 3. Frequency stability 4. Temperature control I. T.
TK7872.O7 F73     621.3815/33     LC 77-17876     ISBN 0442224591

**Gibbons, Gerard.**      5.6519
Avalanche–diode microwave oscillators [by] G. Gibbons. Oxford, Clarendon Press, 1973. xi, 138 p. 24 cm. (Monographs in electrical and electronic engineering) 1. Oscillators, Microwave 2. Diodes, Avalanche I. T.
TK7872.O7 G53     621.381/32/3     LC 73-173643     ISBN 0198593147

**Blanchard, Alain, 1938-.**      5.6520
Phase–locked loops: application to coherent receiver design / Alain Blanchard. New York: Wiley, c1976. xiv, 389 p.: ill.; 24 cm. 'A Wiley-Interscience publication.' 1. Phase-locked loops I. T.
TK7872.P38 B56     621.38/043     LC 75-30941     ISBN 0471079413

**Todd, Carl David.**       **5.6521**
The potentiometer handbook: users' guide to cost–effective applications / written for Bourns, Inc. by Carl David Todd; associate editors, W. T. Hardison, W. E. Galvan. — New York: McGraw-Hill, [1975] xv, 300 p.: ill.; 27 cm. Includes index. 1. Potentiometer — Handbooks, manuals, etc. 2. Electric resistors — Handbooks, manuals, etc. I. Bourns, Inc. II. T.
TK7872.P6 T63    621.37/43    *LC* 75-20010    *ISBN* 0070066906

# TK7874 MICROELECTRONICS.
## INTEGRATED CIRCUITS

**Augarten, Stan.**       **5.6522**
State of the art: a photographic history of the integrated circuit / Stan Augarten; foreword by Ray Bradbury. — New Haven: Ticknor & Fields, 1983. xv, 79 p.: col. ill.; 21 x 24 cm. 1. Integrated circuits — Popular works. I. T.
TK7874.A84 1983    621.381/73 19    *LC* 83-669    *ISBN* 0899192068

**Chirlian, Paul M.**       **5.6523**
Analysis and design of integrated electronic circuits / Paul M. Chirlian. — New York: Harper & Row, c1981. xvi, 1072 p.: ill.; 25 cm. 1. Integrated circuits I. T.
TK7874.C544    621.381/73    *LC* 80-18067    *ISBN* 0060412666

**Connelly, Joseph Alvin, 1942-.**       **5.6524**
Analog integrated circuits: devices, circuits, systems, and applications / J. A. Connelly, contributing editor; prepared from contributions by the engineering staff of Harris Semiconductor. — New York: Wiley, [1975] xxi, 401 p.: ill.; 24 cm. 'A Wiley-Interscience publication.' Includes index. 1. Linear integrated circuits I. Harris Semiconductor (Firm) II. T.
TK7874.C66    621.381/73    *LC* 74-20947    *ISBN* 0471168548

**Designer's handbook of integrated circuits / Arthur B.**       **5.6525**
**Williams, editor in chief.**
New York: McGraw-Hill, c1984. 1 v. (various pagings): ill.; 24 cm. 1. Integrated circuits — Handbooks, manuals, etc. I. Williams, Arthur Bernard, 1940-
TK7874.D476 1984    621.381/73 19    *LC* 82-14955    *ISBN* 007070435X

**Digital integrated circuits and operational–amplifier and**       **5.6526**
**optoelectronic circuit design / edited by Bryan Norris.**
New York: McGraw-Hill, c1976. 206 p.: ill.; 26 cm. (Texas Instruments electronics series) 1. Digital integrated circuits 2. Operational amplifiers 3. Optoelectronic devices I. Norris, Bryan.
TK7874.D53    621.381/73/042    *LC* 76-43099    *ISBN* 0070637539

**Elmasry, Mohamed I., 1943-.**       **5.6527**
Digital bipolar integrated circuits / Mohamed I. Elmasry. — New York: Wiley, c1983. xiv, 322 p.: ill.; 24 cm. 'A Wiley-Interscience publication.' 1. Digital integrated circuits 2. Bipolar transistors I. T.
TK7874.E5 1983    621.381/73 19    *LC* 82-21868    *ISBN* 0471055719

**Glaser, Arthur B.**       **5.6528**
Integrated circuit engineering: design, fabrication, and applications / Arthur B. Glaser, Gerald E. Subak–Sharpe. — Reading, Mass.: Addison-Wesley Pub. Co., c1977. xvii, 811 p.: ill.; 25 cm. 1. Integrated circuits 2. Microelectronics I. Subak-Sharpe, Gerald E. joint author. II. T.
TK7874.G57    621.381/73    *LC* 77-73945    *ISBN* 0201074273

**Gray, Paul R., 1942-.**       **5.6529**
Analysis and design of analog integrated circuits / Paul R. Gray, Robert G. Meyer. — 2nd ed. — New York: Wiley, c1984. xvii, 771 p.: ill.; 25 cm. 1. Linear integrated circuits 2. Metal oxide semiconductors 3. Bipolar transistors I. Meyer, Robert G., 1942- II. T.
TK7874.G688 1984    621.381/73 19    *LC* 83-17098    *ISBN* 0471874930

**Grebene, Alan B., 1939-.**       **5.6530**
Analog integrated circuit design / [by] Alan B. Grebene. — New York: Van Nostrand Reinhold Co., [1972] xi, 401 p.: ill.; 23 cm. — (Microelectronics series) 1. Linear integrated circuits 2. Electronic analog computers — Circuits 3. Electronic circuit design I. T.
TK7874.G69    621.3819/57/35    *LC* 72-3869    *ISBN* 0442228279

**Hardware and software concepts in VLSI / edited by Guy**       **5.6531**
**Rabbat.**
New York: Van Nostrand Reinhold, c1983. xiv, 559 p.: ill.; 24 cm. (Van Nostrand Reinhold electrical/computer science and engineering series.) 1. Integrated circuits — Very large scale integration I. Rabbat, Guy. II. Series.
TK7874.H384 1983    621.381/73 19    *LC* 82-17604    *ISBN* 0442225385

**Herpy, Miklós.**       **5.6532**
Analog integrated circuits: operational amplifiers and analog multipliers / Miklós Herpy; [translated by I. L. Moller]. — Chichester; New York: Wiley, c1980. 479 p.: ill.; 25 cm. 'A Wiley-Interscience publication.' 'Revised version of the Hungarian 'Analóg integráltáramkörök' Muszaki Könyvkiadó, Budapest.' Includes index. 1. Linear integrated circuits I. T.
TK7874.H44    621.381/73 19    *LC* 77-21008    *ISBN* 0471996041

**International Symposium on Methods and Materials in**       **5.6533**
**Microelectronic Technology (1982: Bad Neuenahr-Ahrweiler,**
**Germany)**
Methods and materials in microelectronic technology / edited by Joachim Bargon. — New York: Plenum Press, c1984. viii, 367 p.: ill.; 26 cm. (IBM research symposia series.) 'Proceedings of the International Symposium on Methods and Materials in Microelectronic Technology, held September 29-October 1, 1982, in Bad Neuenahr, Federal Republic of Germany'—T.p. verso. 1. Integrated circuits — Very large scale integration — Design and construction — Congresses. 2. Photolithography — Congresses. 3. Ion beam lithography — Congresses. 4. X-ray lithography — Congresses. I. Bargon, Joachim. II. T. III. Title: Microelectronic technology. IV. Series.
TK7874.I5924 1982    621.381/7 19    *LC* 84-13352    *ISBN* 0306418037

**Lenk, John D.**       **5.6534**
Handbook of integrated circuits: for engineers and technicians / John D. Lenk. — Reston, Va.: Reston Pub. Co., c1978. xiii, 480 p.: ill.; 24 cm. Includes index. 1. Integrated circuits I. T.
TK7874.L37    621.381/73    *LC* 78-7260    *ISBN* 083592744X

**Marcus, R. B. (Robert B.)**       **5.6535**
Transmission electron microscopy of silicon VLSI circuits and structures / R.B. Marcus and T.T. Sheng. — New York: Wiley, c1983. x, 217 p.: ill.; 29 cm. 'A Wiley-Interscience publication.' 1. Integrated circuits 2. Electron microscopy 3. Electron microscope, Transmission I. Sheng, T. T. (Tai Tsu) II. T.
TK7874.M26 1983    621.381/73 19    *LC* 83-3469    *ISBN* 0471092517

**Mead, Carver.**       **5.6536**
Introduction to VLSI systems / Carver Mead, Lynn Conway. — Reading, Mass.: Addison-Wesley, c1980. xvi, 396 p., [8] leaves of plates: ill.; 24 cm. 1. Integrated circuits — Large scale integration 2. Microcomputers 3. Digital electronics 4. Computer architecture I. Conway, Lynn. joint author. II. T.
TK7874.M37    621.381/73 19    *LC* 78-74688    *ISBN* 0201043580

**Microcircuit engineering / edited by H. Ahmed and W. C.**       **5.6537**
**Nixon.**
Cambridge [Eng.]; New York: Cambridge University Press, 1980. x, 585 p.: ill.; 24 cm. 1. Integrated circuits 2. Microelectronics I. Ahmed, H. II. Nixon, W. C.
TK7874.M45    621.381/73    *LC* 79-41451    *ISBN* 0521231183

**Millman, Jacob, 1911-.**       **5.6538**
Integrated electronics: analog and digital circuits and systems [by] Jacob Millman [and] Christos C. Halkias. — New York: McGraw-Hill, [1972] xix, 911 p.: illus.; 24 cm. — (McGraw-Hill electrical and electronic engineering series) 1. Integrated circuits 2. Digital electronics 3. Electronic analog computers — Circuits I. Halkias, Christos C., joint author. II. T.
TK7874.M525    621.381/73    *LC* 79-172657    *ISBN* 0070423156

**Morgan, D. V.**       **5.6539**
An introduction to microelectronic technology / D.V. Morgan, K. Board; adapted by Richard H. Cockrum. — New York: Wiley & Sons, c1985. xvi, 207 p.: ill.; 25 cm. Includes index. 1. Microelectronics I. Board, K. II. Cockrum, Richard H. III. T.
TK7874.M53357 1985    621.381/7 19    *LC* 84-26951    *ISBN* 0471810738

**Muroga, Saburo.**       **5.6540**
VLSI system design: when and how to design very–large–scale integrated circuits / Saburo Muroga. — New York: Wiley, c1982. xiii, 496 p.: ill.; 24 cm. Includes index. 1. Integrated circuits — Very large scale integration I. T. II. Title: V.L.S.I. system design.
TK7874.M87 1982    621.381/73 19    *LC* 82-8598    *ISBN* 0471860905

**Till, William C.**       **5.6541**
Integrated circuits: materials, devices, and fabrication / William C. Till, James T. Luxon. — Englewood Cliffs, N.J.: Prentice-Hall, c1982. xiii, 462 p.: ill.; 24 cm. 1. Microelectronics 2. Integrated circuits I. Luxon, James T. II. T.
TK7874.T55    621.381/7 19    *LC* 81-5929    *ISBN* 0134690311

**Tutorial—VLSI testing & validation techniques / [compiled by]**       **5.6542**
**Hassan K. Reghbati.**
Washington, D.C.: IEEE Computer Society Press; Los Angeles, CA: Order from IEEE Computer Society, 1985. ix, 603 p.: ill.; 28 cm. 1. Integrated circuits

— Very large scale integration — Testing. I. Reghbati, Hassan K., 1949- II. Title: VLSI testing & validation techniques. III. Title: Tutorial—VLSI texting and validation techniques.
TK7874.T8855 1985      621.395/028/7 19      LC 85-80876      ISBN 0818606681

**Tutorial: VLSI, the coming revolution in applications and design**     **5.6543**
/ [edited by] Rex Rice.
New York, N.Y.: Institute of Electrical and Electronics Engineers; Long Beach, CA: available from IEEE Computer Society, c1980. vi, 315 p.: ill.; 28 cm. 'Initially presented at February 25-28 spring 80 Compcon, twentieth IEEE Computer Society international conference, Jack Tar Hotel, San Francisco.' 1. Integrated circuits — Large scale integration — Addresses, essays, lectures. 2. Microelectronics — Addresses, essays, lectures. I. Rice, Rex. II. IEEE Computer Society. III. Compcon. 20th, San Francisco, 1980.
TK7874.T887      621.381/73 19      LC 79-93146

**United Technical Publications.**      **5.6544**
Modern applications of linear IC's [by the] editorial staff, United Technical Publications. — [1st ed.]. — Blue Ridge Summit, Pa.: G/L Tab Books, [1974] 276 p.: illus.; 23 cm. 1. Integrated circuits 2. Electronic circuit design I. T.
TK7874.U54 1974      621.381/73      LC 73-90737      ISBN 0830647082

**Veronis, Andrew.**      **5.6545**
Integrated circuit fabrication technology / Andrew Veronis. — Reston, Va.: Reston Pub. Co., c1979. x, 193 p.: ill.; 24 cm. Includes index. 1. Integrated circuits I. T.
TK7874.V47      621.381/73      LC 78-31381      ISBN 0835930920

**VLSI handbook / Norman G. Einspruch.**      **5.6546**
Orlando, Fla.: Academic Press, 1985. xxvi, 902 p.: ill.; 25 cm. (Handbooks in science and technology.) 1. Integrated circuits — Very large scale integration — Handbooks, manuals, etc. I. Einspruch, Norman G. II. Series.
TK7874.V563 1985      621.3819/5835 19      LC 84-20373      ISBN 0122341007

## TK7876–7882 Microwaves. Electronic Measurements. Applications of Electronics

**Davis, W. Alan.**      **5.6547**
Microwave semiconductor circuit design / W. Alan Davis. — New York: Van Nostrand Reinhold Co., c1984. xii, 415 p.: ill. 1. Microwave circuits 2. Microwave devices 3. Semiconductors I. T.
TK7876.D38 1983      621.381/32 19      LC 83-6669      ISBN 0442272111

**Gandhi, Om P., 1935-.**      **5.6548**
Microwave engineering and applications / Om P. Gandhi. — New York: Pergamon Press, c1981. xvi, 543 p.: ill.; 25 cm. 1. Microwave devices I. T.
TK7876.G36 1981      621.381/33 19      LC 80-29202      ISBN 0080255892

**White, Joseph F., 1938-.**      **5.6549**
Microwave semiconductor engineering / Joseph F. White. — New York: Van Nostrand Reinhold, c1982. xvii, 558 p.: ill.; 24 cm. — (Van Nostrand Reinhold electrical/computer science and engineering series.) Originally published as: Semiconductor control. c1977. 1. Microwave devices — Design and construction. 2. Semiconductors I. T. II. Series.
TK7876.W49      621.381/33 19      LC 81-10498      ISBN 0442291442

**Bell, David A., 1930-.**      **5.6550**
Electronic instrumentation and measurements / David A. Bell. — Reston, Va.: Reston Pub. Co., c1983. x, 531 p.: ill.; 25 cm. Includes index. 1. Electronic measurements 2. Electronic instruments I. T.
TK7878.B45 1983      621.3815/48 19      LC 82-25176      ISBN 0835916693

**Wedlock, Bruce D., 1934-.**      • **5.6551**
Electronic components and measurements / [by] Bruce D. Wedlock [and] James K. Roberge. — Englewood Cliffs, N.J.: Prentice-Hall, [1969] xiii, 338 p.: ill.; 24 cm. — (Prentice-Hall electrical engineering series) 1. Electronic instruments 2. Electronic measurements I. Roberge, James K., 1938- joint author. II. T.
TK7878.4.W42      621.381      LC 79-13618      ISBN 0132504642

**Wilmshurst, T. H.**      **5.6552**
Signal recovery from noise in electronic instrumentation / T.H. Wilmshurst. — Bristol; Boston: A. Hilger, c1985. x, 193 p.: ill.; 25 cm. Includes index. 1. Electronic instruments — Noise. I. T.
TK7878.4.W55 1985      621.38/0436 19      LC 85-179058      ISBN 0852747837

**Wobschall, Darold.**      **5.6553**
Circuit design for electronic instrumentation: for signal processing, data transmission, displays, and instrumentation / by Darold Wobschall. — 2nd ed. — New York: McGraw-Hill, 1987. p. cm. Includes index. 1. Electronic instruments — Design and construction. I. T.
TK7878.4.W62 1987      621.3815/3 19      LC 86-20866      ISBN 007071231X

**Lenk, John D.**      **5.6554**
Handbook of oscilloscopes: theory and application / John D. Lenk. — Rev. and enl. — Englewood Cliffs, N.J.: Prentice-Hall, c1982. xii, 340 p.: ill.; 24 cm. Includes index. 1. Cathode ray oscilloscope I. T.
TK7878.7.L38 1982      621.37/47 19      LC 81-10680      ISBN 013380576X

**Bose, Bimal K.**      **5.6555**
Power electronics and ac drives / B.K. Bose. — Englewood Cliffs, N.J.: Prentice-Hall, c1986. xiv, 402 p.: ill.; 25 cm. 1. Power electronics 2. Electric machinery — Alternating current I. T.
TK7881.15.B67 1987      621.31/7 19      LC 85-28184      ISBN 0136868827

**Larson, Boyd, 1934-.**      **5.6556**
Power control electronics / Boyd Larson. — Englewood Cliffs, N.J.: Prentice-Hall, c1983. xi, 164 p.: ill.; 25 cm. Includes index. 1. Power electronics I. T.
TK7881.15.L37 1983      621.31/7 19      LC 82-15028      ISBN 0136871860

**Pearman, Richard A.**      **5.6557**
Power electronics: solid state motor control / Richard A. Pearman. — Reston, Va.: Reston Pub. Co., c1980. x, 287 p.: ill.; 24 cm. Includes index. 1. Power electronics 2. Electric motors — Electronic control I. T.
TK7881.15.P4      621.313      LC 79-25283      ISBN 0835955850

## TK7881.4 Sound Recording

**Handbook for sound engineers: the new audio cyclopedia / Glen**     **5.6558**
**Ballou, editor.**
1st ed.— Indianapolis: H.W. Sams & Co., 1987. xv, 1247 p.: ill.; 26 cm. — (Audio library) Includes bibliographical references and index. 1. Electroacoustics 2. Electronics 3. Sound — Recording and reproducing I. Ballou, Glen.
TK7881.4 H37      621.3893 19      LC 85-50023      ISBN 0672219832

**Nisbett, Alec.**      **5.6559**
The technique of the sound studio: for radio, recording studio, television, and film / by Alec Nisbett. — 4th ed. — London: Focal Press; New York: Focal/Hastings House, 1979. 560 p.: ill.; 23 cm. (Library of communication techniques) Includes index. 1. Sound — Recording and reproducing 2. Sound studios 3. Radio broadcasting — Sound effects 4. Television broadcasting — Sound studios. I. T.
TK7881.4.N5 1979      621.389/3      LC 79-315393      ISBN 0803872038

**Olson, Harry Ferdinand, 1901-.**      **5.6560**
Modern sound reproduction [by] Harry F. Olson. — New York: Van Nostrand Reinhold, [1972] xiii, 335 p.: illus.; 23 cm. 1. Sound — Recording and reproducing 2. Electro-acoustics I. T.
TK7881.4.O45      621.389/33      LC 71-185982      ISBN 0442262809

**Sound recording practice: a handbook / compiled by the**     **5.6561**
**Association of Professional Recording Studios; edited by John Borwick.**
London; New York: Oxford University Press, 1976. xix, 440 p.: ill.; 24 cm. Includes index. 1. Sound — Recording and reproducing 2. Sound recording industry 3. Magnetic recorders and recording I. Borwick, John. II. Association of Professional Recording Studios.
TK7881.4.S68      621.389/3      LC 76-371050      ISBN 0193119153

**Lowman, Charles E., 1918-.**      **5.6562**
Magnetic recording [by] Charles E. Lowman. — New York: McGraw-Hill, [1972] xiv, 285 p.: illus.; 23 cm. 1. Magnetic recorders and recording I. T.
TK7881.6.L69      621.389/32      LC 72-4057      ISBN 0070388458

**Burris-Meyer, Harold, 1902-.**      **5.6563**
Sound in the theatre / Harold Burris–Meyer, Vincent Mallory, and Lewis S. Goodfriend. — Rev., expanded ed. — New York: Theatre Arts Books, c1979. 94 p.: ill.; 28 cm. Includes index. 1. Theaters — Electronic sound control 2. Auditoriums — Electronic sound control I. Mallory, Vincent. joint author. II. Goodfriend, Lewis S. joint author. III. T.
TK7881.9.B87 1979      621.389/2      LC 78-66064      ISBN 0878301577

## TK882 Other Applications, A–Z

**Bylander, E. G.**                                                                   **5.6564**
Electronic displays / E. G. Bylander. — New York: McGraw-Hill, c1979. ix, 175 p.: ill.; 26 cm. — (Texas Instruments electronic series) 1. Information display systems I. T.
TK7882.I6 B94      621.3815/42      *LC* 78-31849      *ISBN* 0070095108

**Sherr, Sol.**                                                                       **5.6565**
Electronic displays / Sol Sherr. — New York: Wiley, c1979. viii, 636 p.: ill.; 23 cm. 'A Wiley-Interscience publication.' 1. Information display systems I. T.
TK7882.I6 S49 1979      621.3819/534      *LC* 78-10390      *ISBN* 0471029416

**Teletext and videotex in the United States: market potential,**     **5.6566**
**technology, public policy issues / John Tydeman ... [et al.]**
**(Institute for the Future, Menlo Park, California).**
New York, N.Y.: Data Communications, McGraw-Hill, c1982. xii, 314 p.: ill.; 25 cm. (McGraw-Hill data communications book series.) Includes index. 1. Teletext systems — United States. 2. Videotex systems — United States. I. Tydeman, John. II. Institute for the Future. III. Series.
TK7882.I6 T43 1982      384 19      *LC* 82-9970      *ISBN* 0070004277

**Handbook of pattern recognition and image processing / edited**     **5.6567**
**by Tzay Y. Young and King–Sun Fu.**
Orlando: Academic Press, 1986. xx, 705 p.: ill.; 25 cm. — edited by Tzay Y. Young and King-Sun Fu. — (Handbooks in science and technology.) 1. Pattern recognition systems 2. Image processing I. Young, Tzay Y., 1933- II. Fu, K. S. (King Sun), 1930- III. Series.
TK7882.P3 H36 1986      621.3819/598 19      *LC* 85-13381      *ISBN* 0127745602

**Bristow, Geoff.**                                                                   **5.6568**
Electronic speech synthesis: techniques, technology, and applications / Geoff Bristow. — New York: McGraw-Hill, c1984. xxi, 346 p.: ill. — 1. Speech synthesis I. T.
TK7882.S65 B75 1984      621.3819/5832 19      *LC* 84-3943      *ISBN* 0070079129

**Rabiner, Lawrence R., 1943-.**                                                     **5.6569**
Digital processing of speech signals / Lawrence R. Rabiner, Ronald W. Schafer. — Englewood Cliffs, N.J.: Prentice-Hall, c1978. xvi, 512 p.: ill.; 25 cm. — (Prentice-Hall signal processing series) 1. Speech processing systems 2. Digital electronics I. Schafer, Ronald W., 1938- joint author. II. T.
TK7882.S65 R3      621.38/0412      *LC* 78-8555      *ISBN* 0132136031

## TK7885–7895 COMPUTER ENGINEERING

**Hordeski, Michael F.**                                                             **5.6570**
The illustrated dictionary of microcomputers / by Michael Hordeski. — 2nd ed. — Blue Ridge Summit, PA: TAB Professional and Reference Books, c1986. viii, 352 p.: ill.; 25 cm. Rev. ed. of: Illustrated dictionary of microcomputer terminology. 1st ed. c1978. 1. Microcomputers — Dictionaries. I. Hordeski, Michael F. Illustrated dictionary of microcomputer terminology. II. T.
TK7885.A2 H67 1986      004.16/03/21 19      *LC* 85-27672      *ISBN* 083060488X

**Goldstine, Herman Heine, 1913-.**                                                  **5.6571**
The computer from Pascal to von Neumann [by] Herman H. Goldstine. — [Princeton, N.J.]: Princeton University Press, [1972] x, 378 p.: illus.; 25 cm. 1. Computers — History. I. T.
TK7885.A5 G64      621.3819/5/09      *LC* 70-173755      *ISBN* 0691081042

**Bartee, Thomas C.**                                                                **5.6572**
Digital computer fundamentals / Thomas C. Bartee. — 6th ed. — New York: McGraw-Hill, c1985. xii, 610 p.: ill.; 25 cm. Includes index. 1. Electronic digital computers I. T.
TK7885.B317 1985      621.3819/58 19      *LC* 84-10054      *ISBN* 0070038996

**Booth, Taylor L.**                                                                 **5.6573**
Introduction to computer engineering: hardware and software design / Taylor L. Booth. — 3rd ed. — New York: Wiley, c1984. xxiv, 656 p.: ill.; 24 cm. Rev. ed. of: Digital networks and computer systems. 2nd ed. c1978. 1. Computer engineering I. Booth, Taylor L. Digital networks and computer systems. II. T. III. Title: Introduction to computer engineering hardware and software design.
TK7885.B583 1984      001.64 19      *LC* 84-2252      *ISBN* 0471873217

**Kidder, Tracy.**                                                                   **5.6574**
The soul of a new machine / Tracy Kidder. — 1st ed. — Boston: Little, Brown, c1981. 293 p.; 22 cm. 'An Atlantic Monthly Press book.' 1. Data General Corporation. 2. Computer engineering — Popular works. I. T.
TK7885.4.K53      621.3819/582 19      *LC* 81-6044      *ISBN* 0316491705

**Eadie, Donald.**                                                                   **5.6575**
A user's guide to computer peripherals / Donald Eadie. — Eaglewood Cliffs, NJ: Prentice-Hall, 1982. x, 244 p.: ill.; 24 cm. Includes index. 1. Computer input-output equipment I. T.
TK7887.5.E22 1982      001.64/4 19      *LC* 81-8482      *ISBN* 0139396608

**Seyer, Martin D.**                                                                 **5.6576**
RS–232 made easy: connecting computers, printers, terminals, and modems / Martin D. Seyer. — Englewood Cliffs, N.J.: Prentice Hall, c1984. xiii, 214 p.: ill.; 24 cm. Includes index. 1. Computer interfaces — Standards — United States. I. T.
TK7887.5.S48 1984      001.64/404 19      *LC* 83-13939      *ISBN* 0137834802

**Analog–digital conversion handbook / by the engineering staff**     **5.6577**
**of Analog Devices, Inc.; edited by Daniel H. Sheingold.**
3rd ed. — Englewood Cliffs, NJ: Prentice-Hall, c1986. xxi, 672, xxiii-xliii p.: ill.; 25 cm. (Analog Devices technical handbooks.) Includes index. 1. Analog-to-digital converters I. Sheingold, Daniel H. II. Analog Devices, inc. III. Series.
TK7887.6.A525 1986      621.398/14 19      *LC* 85-62726      *ISBN* 0130328480

**Clayton, G. B. (George Burbridge)**                                               **5.6578**
Data converters / G.B. Clayton. — New York: Wiley; London: Macmillan, 1982. ix, 242 p.: ill.; 24 cm. 'A Halsted Press book.' 1. Analog-to-digital converters 2. Digital-to-analog converters I. T.
TK7887.6.C55 1982      621.3819/596 19      *LC* 81-20109      *ISBN* 0470273216

**Hnatek, Eugene R.**                                                                **5.6579**
A user's handbook of D/A and A/D converters / Eugene R. Hnatek. — New York: Wiley, c1976. xiv, 472 p.: ill.; 26 cm. 'A Wiley-Interscience publication.' 1. Digital-to-analog converters 2. Analog-to-digital converters I. T.
TK7887.6.H58      621.398/14 19      *LC* 75-14341      *ISBN* 0471401099

## TK7888.3–7895 Digital Computers. Special Computers

**Hwang, Kai.**                                                                      **5.6580**
Computer arithmetic: principles, architecture, and design / Kai Hwang. — New York: Wiley, c1979. xiii, 423 p.: ill.; 24 cm. 1. Electronic digital computers 2. Computer arithmetic and logic units 3. Computer arithmetic I. T.
TK7888.3.H9      621.3819/58/2      *LC* 78-18922      *ISBN* 0471034967

**Kraft, George D., 1937-.**                                                         **5.6581**
Mini/microcomputer hardware design / George D. Kraft, Wing N. Toy. — Englewood Cliffs, N.J.: Prentice-Hall, c1979. xiv, 514 p.: ill.; 25 cm. 1. Minicomputers — Design and construction. 2. Microcomputers — Design and construction. I. Toy, Wing N., 1926- joint author. II. T.
TK7888.3.K7 1979      621.3819/58      *LC* 78-13605      *ISBN* 013583807X

**Lala, Parag K., 1948-.**                                                           **5.6582**
Fault tolerant and fault testable hardware design / Parag K. Lala. — Englewood Cliffs, N.J.: Prentice-Hall International, c1985. xiv, 263 p.: ill.; 24 cm. Includes index. 1. Electronic digital computers — Reliability 2. Fault-tolerant computing I. T.
TK7888.3.L27 1985      621.3819/583 19      *LC* 84-8316      *ISBN* 0133082482

**McGlynn, Daniel R.**                                                               **5.6583**
Microprocessors: technology, architecture, and applications / Daniel R. McGlynn. — New York: Wiley, c1976. xi, 207 p.: ill.; 24 cm. 'A Wiley-Interscience publication.' Includes index. 1. Microprocessors 2. Minicomputers I. T.
TK7888.3.M26      001.6/4      *LC* 76-137      *ISBN* 0471584142

**Mano, M. Morris, 1927-.**                                                          **5.6584**
Digital design / M. Morris Mano. — Englewood Cliffs, N.J.: Prentice-Hall, c1984. xi, 492 p.: ill.; 24 cm. Chapters 1-7 and 10 originally published as part of the author's Digital logic and computer design, c1979. 1. Electronic digital computers — Circuits 2. Logic circuits 3. Logic design 4. Digital integrated circuits I. Mano, M. Morris, 1927- Digital logic and computer design. II. T.
TK7888.3.M343 1984      621.3815/37 19      *LC* 83-24734      *ISBN* 0132123339

**Myers, Glenford J., 1946-.**       **5.6585**
Digital system design with LSI bit–slice logic / Glenford J. Myers. — New York: Wiley, c1980. xi, 338 p.: ill.; 25 cm. 'A Wiley-Interscience publication.' 1. Electronic digital computers — Design and construction. 2. Digital electronics 3. Logic circuits 4. Logic design 5. Integrated circuits — Large scale integration 6. Microprogramming I. T.
TK7888.3.M93    621.3819/58/3 19    *LC* 79-26258    *ISBN* 0471053767

**O'Connor, Patrick J. (Patrick Joseph), 1947-.**    **5.6586**
Understanding digital electronics: how microcomputers and microprocessors work / Patrick J. O'Connor. — Englewood Cliffs, NJ: Prentice-Hall, c1984. vi, 266 p.: ill.; 24 cm. Includes index. 1. Microcomputers 2. Microprocessors I. T.
TK7888.3.O28 1984    621.3819/58 19    *LC* 83-21206    *ISBN* 0139369643

**Prosser, Franklin P.**       **5.6587**
The art of digital design: an introduction to top–down design / Franklin P. Prosser, David E. Winkel. — 2nd ed. — Englewood Cliffs, N.J.: Prentice-Hall, 1986. xvii, 525 p.: ill.; 25 cm. Order of author's names reversed on previous ed. 1. Electronic digital computers — Design and construction. 2. Minicomputers — Design and construction. I. Winkel, David E. II. Winkel, David E. Art of digital design. III. T.
TK7888.3.P77 1986    004.2/1 19    *LC* 86-5042    *ISBN* 0130467804

**Knowles, Roy.**       **5.6588**
Automatic testing: systems and applications / Roy Knowles. — London; New York: McGraw-Hill, c1976. ix, 246 p.: ill.; 24 cm. 1. Automatic checkout equipment I. T.
TK7895.A8 K56    681.2    *LC* 75-34197    *ISBN* 0070844615

**Johnson, James B.**       **5.6589**
The multibus design guidebook: structures, architectures, and applications / James B. Johnson, Steve Kassel. — New York: McGraw-Hill, c1984. xvii, 424 p.: ill.; 24 cm. 1. Microcomputers — Buses 2. Computer architecture I. Kassel, Steve. II. T.
TK7895.B87 J63 1984    621.3819/535 19    *LC* 83-16258    *ISBN* 0070325995

**Isailović, Jordan, 1945-.**       **5.6590**
Videodisc and optical memory systems / Jordan Isailović. — Englewood Cliffs, N.J.: Prentice-Hall, c1985. xiv, 350 p.: ill.; 25 cm. 1. Optical storage devices 2. Video discs I. T.
TK7895.M4 I83 1985    621.3819/5833 19    *LC* 84-17957    *ISBN* 0139420533

**McKay, Charles W., 1943-.**       **5.6591**
Experimenting with MSI, LSI, IO, and modular memory systems / Charles W. McKay. — Englewood Cliffs, N.J.: Prentice-Hall, c1981. xiii, 272 p.: ill.; 24 cm. Includes index. 1. Computer storage devices 2. Computer input-output equipment 3. Integrated circuits 4. Microcomputers I. T.
TK7895.M4 M33 1981    621.3819/583    *LC* 80-16738    *ISBN* 013295477X

**Byers, T. J.**       **5.6592**
Microprocessor support chips: theory, design, and applications / T.J. Byers. — New York, N.Y.: Micro Text: McGraw-Hill, c1983. 224 p.: ill.; 29 cm. Includes index. 1. Microprocessors — Catalogs. I. T.
TK7895.M5 B93 1983    621.3819/58 19    *LC* 82-60432    *ISBN* 0070095183

**Hordeski, Michael F.**       **5.6593**
The design of microprocessor, sensor, and control systems / Michael F. Hordeski. — Reston, Va.: Reston Pub. Co., c1985. xv, 376 p.: ill.; 25 cm. Includes index. 1. Microprocessors 2. Process control 3. Transducers I. T.
TK7895.M5 H66 1985    629.8/95 19    *LC* 84-6897    *ISBN* 0835912698

**Microprocessor applications handbook / David F. Stout, editor–in–chief.**    **5.6594**
New York: McGraw-Hill, c1982. 477 p. in various pagings: ill.; 24 cm. 1. Microprocessors I. Stout, David F.
TK7895.M5 M463    621.3819/58 19    *LC* 81-11787    *ISBN* 0070617988

**Wist, Abund Ottokar.**       **5.6595**
Electronic design of microprocessor–based instruments and control systems / Abund Ottokar Wist and Z.H. Meiksin. — Englewood Cliffs, N.J.: Prentice-Hall, Business and Professional Division, c1986. xii, 287 p.: ill.; 24 cm. Includes index. 1. Microprocessors 2. Electronic instruments — Design and construction. 3. Electronic controllers — Design and construction. I. Meiksin, Z. H. II. T.
TK7895.M5 W57 1986    621.381 19    *LC* 85-3586    *ISBN* 0132505312

## TK8304 ELECTRONIC VISION

**Rose, Albert, 1910-.**       **5.6596**
Vision: human and electronic. — New York: Plenum Press [c1973] xv, 197 p.: ill. — (Optical physics and engineering.) 1. Visual perception 2. Vision 3. Optics I. T. II. Series.
TK8304.R67    *LC* 73-97422    *ISBN* 0306307324

# TK9001–9401 Nuclear Engineering

**Fermi, Laura.**       ● **5.6597**
Atoms for the world: United States participation in the Conference on the Peaceful Uses of Atomic Energy. — [Chicago]: University of Chicago Press [1957] xii, 227 p.: ill.; 24 cm. 1. International Conference on the Peaceful Uses of Atomic Energy. Geneva, 1955. I. T.
TK9006.I5 1955j    539.76    *LC* 57-6977/L

**Cohen, Bernard Leonard, 1924-.**       **5.6598**
Before it's too late: a scientist's case for nuclear energy / Bernard L. Cohen. — New York: Plenum Press, c1983. xvi, 290 p.; 22 cm. 1. Nuclear energy I. T.
TK9145.C576 1983    333.79/24 19    *LC* 83-11083    *ISBN* 0306414252

**Evans, Nigel, 1954-.**       **5.6599**
Nuclear power: futures, costs and benefits / Nigel Evans and Chris Hope. — Cambridge [Cambridgeshire]; New York: Cambridge University Press, 1984. xviii, 171 p.: ill.; 24 cm. Includes index. 1. Nuclear energy I. Hope, Chris. II. T.
TK9145.E9 1984    333.79/24 19    *LC* 84-1806    *ISBN* 0521261910

**Foster, Arthur R.**       **5.6600**
Basic nuclear engineering / Arthur R. Foster, Robert L. Wright, Jr. — 4th ed. — Boston: Allyn and Bacon, c1983. xii, 611 p.: ill.; 25 cm. — (Allyn and Bacon series in engineering.) 1. Nuclear engineering I. Wright, Robert L. II. T. III. Series.
TK9145.F6 1983    621.48 19    *LC* 82-11577    *ISBN* 0205078869

**A Guide to nuclear power technology: a resource for decision making / Frank J. Rahn ... [et al.].**    **5.6601**
New York: Wiley, c1984. xi, 985 p.: ill.; 25 cm. 'A Wiley-Interscience publication.' 1. Nuclear engineering I. Rahn, Frank J.
TK9145.G82 1984    621.48/3 19    *LC* 84-7362    *ISBN* 0471889148

**Hunt, Stanley Ernest.**       **5.6602**
Fission, fusion and the energy crisis [by] S. E. Hunt. [1st ed.] Oxford, New York, Pergamon Press 1975 (c1974) ix, 164 p. illus. 22 cm. (Pergamon energy series, v. 1) 1. Nuclear energy I. T.
TK9145.H86    621.48    *LC* 74-9926    *ISBN* 0080181023 *ISBN* 0080180795

**Knief, Ronald Allen, 1944-.**       **5.6603**
Nuclear energy technology: theory and practice of commercial nuclear power / Ronald Allen Knief. — Washington: Hemisphere Pub. Corp.; New York: McGraw-Hill, c1981. xv, 605 p.: ill.; 24 cm. (McGraw-Hill series in nuclear engineering) Includes indexes. 1. Nuclear engineering 2. Nuclear energy I. T.
TK9145.K58 1981    621.48 19    *LC* 80-25862

**Seaborg, Glenn Theodore, 1912-.**       ● **5.6604**
Man and atom: building a new world through nuclear technology / by Glenn T. Seaborg and William R. Corliss. — [1st ed.] New York: E. P. Dutton, 1971. 411 p.: ill.; maps; 24 cm. 1. Nuclear engineering 2. Nuclear energy I. Corliss, William R. joint author. II. T.
TK9145.S4 1971    621.48    *LC* 70-122795    *ISBN* 0525150994

**Murray, Raymond LeRoy, 1920-.**       **5.6605**
Nuclear energy: an introduction to the concepts, systems, and applications of nuclear processes / Raymond L. Murray. — 2d ed. (in SI/metric units). — Oxford; New York: Pergamon Press, 1980. xix, 317 p.: ill.; 24 cm. (Pergamon unified engineering series; v. 22) (Pergamon international library of science, technology, engineering, and social studies) 1. Nuclear engineering 2. Nuclear energy I. T.
TK9146.M87 1980    621.48    *LC* 79-41701    *ISBN* 0080247512

**Nuclear power safety / edited by James H. Rust and Lynn E. Weaver.**    **5.6606**
New York: Pergamon Press, 1977 (c1976). viii, 410 p.: ill.; 28 cm. — (Georgia Institute of Technology series in nuclear engineering.) (Progress in nuclear energy new series; series 4) 1. Nuclear engineering — Safety measures —

Addresses, essays, lectures. 2. Nuclear power plants — Safety measures — Addresses, essays, lectures. I. Rust, James H. II. Weaver, Lynn E.
TK9152.N79 1976     TK9152 N79 1976.     621.48/35     LC 76-44475
    ISBN 0080214177

**DeLeon, Peter.**                                                                    5.6607
Development and diffusion of the nuclear reactor: a comparative analysis / Peter deLeon. — Cambridge, Mass.: Ballinger Pub. Co., c1979. xviii, 325 p.; 24 cm. 'A Rand Graduate Institute book.' Originally presented as the author's thesis, Rand Graduate Institute for Policy Studies, 1978. Includes index. 1. Nuclear engineering — Research. 2. Nuclear reactors 3. Technology and state I. T.
TK9153.D44 1979     338.4/7/62148     LC 79-12988     ISBN 0884106829

**Hoyle, Fred, Sir.**                                                                5.6608
Energy or extinction?: The case for nuclear energy / Fred Hoyle. — London: Heinemann, 1977. vii, 81 p.: ill.; 22 cm. 1. Nuclear energy 2. Power resources I. T.
TK9153.H69     621.48     LC 77-376795     ISBN 0435544306

**Nader, Ralph.**                                                                    5.6609
The menace of atomic energy / Ralph Nader, John Abbotts. — 1st ed. — New York: Norton, c1977. 414 p.: ill.; 22 cm. 1. Nuclear energy I. Abbotts, John. joint author. II. T.
TK9153.N28 1977     614.8/39     LC 77-2197     ISBN 0393087735

**Nuclear power: assessing and managing hazardous technology /**                     5.6610
**edited by Martin J. Pasqualetti and K. David Pijawka with the**
**assistance of Sara J. Frischknecht.**
Boulder, Colo.: Westview Press, 1984. xvii, 423 p.: ill.; 23 cm. (A Westview replica edition) 1. Nuclear energy — Addresses, essays, lectures. 2. Technology assessment — Addresses, essays, lectures. I. Pasqualetti, Martin J., 1945- II. Pijawka, K. D. (K. David)
TK9155.N77 1984     333.79/24 19     LC 83-21797     ISBN 0865318115

## TK9202–9401 Nuclear Reactors

**Cameron, I. R.**                                                                   5.6611
Nuclear fission reactors / I.R. Cameron. — New York: Plenum Press, c1982. ix, 389 p.: ill.; 24 cm. Bibliography: p. 375-381. Includes index. 1. Nuclear reactors 2. Nuclear energy I. T.
TK9202.C17 1982     621.48/3 19     LC 82-18128     ISBN 0306410737

**El-Wakil, M. M. (Mohamed Mohamed), 1921-.**                                        5.6612
Nuclear energy conversion [by] M. M. El–Wakil. Scranton, Intext Educational Publishers [1971] xiv, 666 p. illus. 24 cm. 1. Nuclear reactors 2. Nuclear power plants 3. Direct energy conversion I. T.
TK9202.E46     621.48/1     LC 77-144356     ISBN 070022310X

**Nero, Anthony V.**                                                                 5.6613
A guidebook to nuclear reactors / Anthony V. Nero, Jr. — Berkeley: University of California Press, c1979. xiii, 289 p.: ill.; 29 cm. 1. Nuclear reactors I. T.
TK9202.N45     621.48/3     LC 77-76183     ISBN 0520034821. ISBN 0520036611 pbk

**Duderstadt, James J., 1942-.**                                                     5.6614
Inertial confinement fusion / James J. Duderstadt, Gregory A. Moses. — New York: Wiley, c1982. x, 347 p.: ill.; 25 cm. 'A Wiley-Interscience publication.' 1. Pellet fusion I. Moses, Gregory A. II. T.
TK9204.D82     621.48/4 19     LC 81-11472     ISBN 0471090506

**Heppenheimer, T. A., 1947-.**                                                      5.6615
The man–made sun: the quest for fusion power / T.A. Heppenheimer. — 1st ed. — Boston: Little, Brown, c1984. xvi, 347 p., [16] p. of plates: ill.; 24 cm. 'An Omni Press book.' Includes index. 1. Fusion reactors I. T.
TK9204.H47 1984     621.48/4 19     LC 83-22240     ISBN 0316357936

**Harvey, John F.**                                                                  5.6616
Theory and design of modern pressure vessels [by] John F. Harvey. — 2d ed. — New York: Van Nostrand Reinhold, [1974] xii, 436 p.: illus.; 23 cm. Edition of 1963 published under title: Pressure vessel design; ed. of 1980 published under title: Pressure component construction. 1. Pressure vessels — Design and construction. I. T.
TK9211.5.H37 1974     681/.766     LC 74-4320     ISBN 0442231849

**Benedict, Manson.**                                                               5.6617
Nuclear chemical engineering / Manson Benedict, Thomas H. Pigford, Hans Wolfgang Levi. — 2d ed. — New York: McGraw-Hill, c1981. xv, 1008 p.: ill.; 24 cm. — (McGraw-Hill series in nuclear engineering) 1. Nuclear engineering 2. Nuclear chemistry I. Pigford, Thomas H. joint author. II. Levi, Hans Wolfgang. joint author. III. T.
TK9350.B4 1981     621.48 19     LC 80-21538     ISBN 0070045313

**Graves, Harvey W.**                                                               5.6618
Nuclear fuel management / Harvey W. Graves, Jr. — New York: Wiley, c1979. xvi, 327 p.: ill.; 24 cm. 1. Nuclear fuels I. T.
TK9360.G73     621.48/335     LC 78-19119     ISBN 0471031364

**Nuclear safeguards analysis: nondestructive and analytical**                       5.6619
**chemical techniques: based on a symposium / sponsored by the**
**Division of Nuclear Chemistry and Technology at the 175th**
**meeting of the American Chemical Society, Anaheim, CA,**
**March 13–17, 1978; E. Arnold Hakkila, editor.**
Washington: The Society, 1978. x, 213 p.: ill.; 24 cm. (ACS symposium series; 79) 1. Nuclear fuels — Testing — Congresses. 2. Nuclear fuels — Analysis — Congresses. 3. Nuclear industry — Security measures — Congresses. I. Hakkila, E. Arnold, 1931- II. American Chemical Society. Division of Nuclear Chemistry and Technology.
TK9360.N854     621.48/35     LC 78-12706     ISBN 0841204497

**Patterson, Walter C., 1936-.**                                                    5.6620
The plutonium business and the spread of the bomb / Walter C. Patterson for the Nuclear Control Institute. — San Francisco: Sierra Club Books, c1984. xvi, 272 p.; 22 cm. Includes index. 1. Plutonium 2. Breeder reactors 3. Nuclear nonproliferation I. Nuclear Control Institute (Washington, D.C.) II. T.
TK9360.P38 1984     333.79/24 19     LC 84-22181     ISBN 0871568373

# TL Motor Vehicles. Bicycles. Aeronautics. Astronautics

## TL1–480 Motor Vehicles

## TL1–175 General Works

**Georgano, G. N.**                                                                 5.6621
Encyclopedia of American automobiles / edited by G. N. Georgano; contributors: Glenn Baechler [and others]. — New York: Dutton, [1971] 222 p.: ill. (part col.); 26 cm. 'Material ... extracted from [the editor's] The complete encyclopedia of motorcars.' 1. Automobiles — United States — History. I. Baechler, Glenn. II. Georgano, G. N. The complete encyclopedia of motorcars. III. T. IV. Title: American automobiles.
TL23.G46     629.22/22/0973     LC 79-147885     ISBN 0525097929

**S.A.E. handbook.**                                                                5.6622
Warrendale, Pa. [etc.]: Society of Automotive Engineers, Inc. ill., plates, diagrs.; 18-22 cm. Annual. 1924, v. 1, loose-leaf edition. Earlier data sheets were published by the society in loose-leaf form under cover-title: Standards and data sheets. [New York, 1917] 2 v. Two supplements to the 1931 edition, issued 1931 and January 1932, and loose-leaf sheets including additions adopted in June 1932, take the place of the regular 1932 issue. A supplement to the 1933 edition, issued August 1934, takes the place of the regular 1934 issue. 1. Automobiles — Handbooks, manuals, etc. I. Society of Automotive Engineers.
TL151.S62     LC 25-16527

**The Passenger car power plant of the future: conference**                         5.6623
**sponsored by the Combustion Engines Group and the**
**Automobile Division of the Institution of Mechanical Engineers,**
**London 2–4 October 1979.**
London: published by Mechanical Engineering Publications for the Institution of Mechanical Engineers, 1979. xiii, 182 p.: ill. — (I Mech E conference publications; 1979/13) 1. Automobiles — Fuel consumption — Congresses. 2. Automobiles — Technological innovations — Congresses. I. Institution of Mechanical Engineers (Great Britain). Combustion Engines Group. II. Institution of Mechanical Engineers (Great Britain). Automobile Division.
TL151.6.P37 1979     TL151.6 P37 1979.

**Crouse, William Harry, 1907-.**                                                   5.6624
Automotive technician's handbook / William H. Crouse and Donald L. Anglin. — New York: McGraw-Hill, c1979. vii, 664 p.: ill.; 29 cm. Includes index. 1. Motor vehicles — Maintenance and repair I. Anglin, Donald L. joint author. II. T.
TL152.C692     629.28/7     LC 79-14274     ISBN 0070147515

**Johnson, W. (William), 1922-.**                                                   5.6625
Crashworthiness of vehicles: an introduction to aspects of collision of motor cars, ships, aircraft and railway coaches / [by] W. Johnson and A. G. Mamalis.

— London: Mechanical Engineering Publications, 1978. 129 p.: ill., plans; 21 cm. 1. Vehicles — Crashworthiness. I. Mamalis, A. G. joint author. II. T.
TL154.J57     629.04     *LC* 79-302018     *ISBN* 0852983867

## TL210–229 CONSTRUCTION DETAILS. MOTORS. ENGINES

**Ayres, Robert U.**             **5.6626**
Alternatives to the internal combustion engine; impacts on environmental quality, by Robert U. Ayres and Richard P. McKenna. Baltimore: Published for Resources for the Future by the Johns Hopkins University Press, [1972] xvi, 324 p.: illus.; 24 cm. 1. Motor vehicles — Motors 2. Internal combustion engines 3. Automobiles, Electric 4. Environmental policy I. McKenna, Richard P., joint author. II. Resources for the Future. III. T.
TL210.A96     629.2/5     *LC* 74-181555     *ISBN* 0801813697

**Dark, Harris, 1922-.**            **5.6627**
Auto engines of tomorrow: power alternatives for cars to come / Harris Edward Dark. — Bloomington: Indiana University Press, [1975] ix, 180 p.: ill.; 24 cm. Includes index. 1. Automobiles — Motors I. T.
TL210.D33 1975     629.2/5     *LC* 74-6518     *ISBN* 0253104904

**Nunney, Malcolm James.**        **5.6628**
The automotive engine / [by] M. J. Nunney. — London: Newnes-Butterworths, 1975. [7], 280 p.: ill.; 25 cm. Label mounted on t.p.: Sole distributor for the U.S.A., Transatlantic Arts, Levittown, N.Y. Includes index. 1. Automobiles — Motors I. T.
TL210.N86     621.2/504     *LC* 76-367616     *ISBN* 040800178X

**Vehicle engines: fuel consumption and air pollution / edited by**     **5.6629**
**M. S. Janota.**
Stevenage, Eng.: P. Peregrinus, 1975 (c1974) v, 154 p.: ill.; 24 cm. (Mankind and the engineer; v. 3) Papers from a conference held at Queen Mary College, London in April 1973. 1. Motor vehicles — Motors — Congresses. I. Janota, M. S.
TL210.V36     629.2/5     *LC* 74-83030     *ISBN* 0901223611

**Wakefield, Ernest Henry, 1915-.**        **5.6630**
The consumer's electric car / Ernest H. Wakefield. — Ann Arbor, Mich.: Ann Arbor Science Publishers, c1977. xiv, 136 p.: ill.; 24 cm. 1. Automobiles, Electric I. T.
TL220.W34     629.22/93     *LC* 76-50984     *ISBN* 025040155X

**Norbye, Jan P.**             **5.6631**
The gas turbine engine: design, development, applications / Jan P. Norbye. — 1st ed. — Radnor, Pa.: Chilton Book Co., [1975] xvi, 570 p.: ill.; 24 cm. Includes index. 1. Automotive gas turbines 2. Automobiles, Gas-turbine I. T.
TL227.N67 1975     629.2/503     *LC* 75-6733     *ISBN* 0801957532

## TL230–257 SPECIAL TYPES. DESIGN. SAFETY STANDARDS

**Setright, L. J. K.**             **5.6632**
The Grand Prix, 1906 to 1972 [by] L. J. K. Setright. — [1st American ed.]. — New York: Norton, [1973] 320 p.: illus.; 26 cm. 1. Automobiles, Racing 2. Grand Prix racing — History. I. T.
TL236.S46 1973b     796.7/2/0904     *LC* 74-163640     *ISBN* 0393086801

**Seiffert, Ulrich.**             **5.6633**
The future for automotive technology / Ulrich Seiffert, Peter Walzer. — London; Dover, N.H.: F. Pinter (Publishers), 1984. xvi, 197 p.: ill.; 24 cm. (Future for science and technology series.) Includes index. 1. Automobiles — Design and construction 2. Automobiles — Technological innovations I. Walzer, Peter. II. T. III. Series.
TL240.S357 1984     629.2 19     *LC* 84-42620     *ISBN* 0861874609

**Wong, Jo Yung.**             **5.6634**
Theory of ground vehicles / J. Y. Wong. — New York: Wiley, c1978. xxi, 330 p.: ill.; 24 cm. 'A Wiley-Interscience publication.' 1. Motor vehicles — Design and construction 2. Ground-effect machines — Design and construction. I. T.
TL240.W66     629.22     *LC* 78-16714     *ISBN* 0471034703

**Nader, Ralph.**            • **5.6635**
Unsafe at any speed: the designed–in dangers of the American automobile. — [Expanded ed.]. — New York: Grossman, 1972. xciii, 417 p.: ill.; 22 cm. At head of title: Updated. 1. Automobiles — Design and construction

2. Automobiles — Safety measures I. T. II. Title: Updated Unsafe at any speed.
TL242.N3 1972     629.2/3     *LC* 79-179071     *ISBN* 0670741590

**Automotive aerodynamics: selected SAE papers through 1977 /**     **5.6636**
**prepared under the auspices of the Vehicle Configuration Committee of the Automobile Body Activity, SAE Engineering Activity Board.**
Warrendale, Pa.: Society of Automotive Engineers, c1978. v, 281 p.: ill.; 29 cm. — (Progress in technology series; v. 16) 1. Automobiles — Aerodynamics — Addresses, essays, lectures. I. Society of Automotive Engineers.
TL245.A87     629.2/31     *LC* 78-57059

**Ellinger, Herbert E.**            **5.6637**
Automotive suspension, steering, and brakes / Herbert E. Ellinger and Richard B. Hathaway. — Englewood Cliffs, N.J.: Prentice-Hall, 1980. xi, 305 p.: ill.; 28 cm. Includes index. 1. Automobiles — Springs and suspension — Maintenance and repair. 2. Automobiles — Steering-gear — Maintenance and repair. 3. Automobiles — Brakes — Maintenance and repair. I. Hathaway, Richard B., 1947- joint author. II. T.
TL257.E44 1980     629.2/4     *LC* 78-32045     *ISBN* 0130542881

## TL400–437 BICYCLES
(see also: GV1040-1059)

**DeLong, Fred.**            **5.6638**
[Guide to bicycles & bicycling] DeLong's guide to bicycles & bicycling: the art & science. [1st ed.] Radnor, Pa., Chilton Book Co. [1974] x, 278 p. illus. 29 cm. 1. Bicycles 2. Cycling I. Guide to bicycles & bicycling. II. T.
TL410.D44 1974     796.6     *LC* 74-4133     *ISBN* 0801958461

**Sharp, Archibald, 1862-1934.**        **5.6639**
Bicycles and tricycles: an elementary treatise on their design and construction / by Archibald Sharp. — Cambridge, Mass.: MIT Press, c1977. xviii, 536 p.: ill.; 19 cm. Reprint of the 1896 ed. published by Longmans, Green, London, New York. Includes index. 1. Bicycles 2. Tricycles I. T.
TL410.S5 1977     629.22/72     *LC* 77-4928     *ISBN* 0262191563

# TL500–777 Aeronautics. Aeronautical Engineering

## TL501–514 REFERENCE

**Jane's all the world's aircraft.**        • **5.6640**
[1st] issue (1909)- . — London: S. Low, Marston; 1909-. v.: ill., ports., maps, diagrs. Annual. Imprint varies. Founded in 1909 by Fred T. Jane. 1. Aeronautics — Yearbooks. 2. Airplanes — Yearbooks. I. Jane, Fred T., 1865-1916 II. Title: All the world's airships. III. Title: All the world's aircraft. IV. Title: Jane's aircraft.
TL501.J3     *LC* 10-8268

**Encyclopedia of aviation.**            **5.6641**
New York: Scribner, 1977. 218 p.: ill.; 29 cm. Includes index. 1. Aeronautics — Dictionaries. I. Charles Scribner's Sons.
TL509.E55 1977     387.7/03     *LC* 77-72699     *ISBN* 0684148404

**Ocran, Emanuel Benjamin.**        **5.6642**
Dictionary of air transport and traffic control / E.B. Ocran. — London; New York: Granada, 1984. ix, 243 p.; 23 cm. Includes indexes. 1. Aeronautics, Commercial — Dictionaries. 2. Air traffic control — Dictionaries. I. T.
TL509.O53 1984     387.7/03/21 19     *LC* 84-164542     *ISBN* 0246123605

## TL515–540 HISTORY. BIOGRAPHY

**American heritage.**           • **5.6643**
The American heritage history of flight, by the editors of American heritage. Editor in charge: Alvin M. Josephy, Jr. Narrative by Arthur Gordon. With 2 chapters by Marvin W. McFarland. Introd. by Carl Spaatz [and] Ira C. Eaker. — [New York]: American Heritage Pub. Co.; book trade distribution by Simon

& Schuster, [1962] 416 p.: illus. (part col.) ports. (part col.); 29 cm. 1. Aeronautics — History I. Gordon, Arthur. II. T.
TL515.A624    629.1309    *LC* 62-17517

**Friedlander, Mark P.**    5.6644
Higher, faster, and farther, by Mark P. Friedlander, Jr. and Gene Gurney. — New York: Morrow, 1973. 349 p.: illus.; 22 cm. 1. Aeronautics — Flights 2. Aeronautics — Competitions I. Gurney, Gene. joint author. II. T.
TL515.F755    629.13/09    *LC* 73-9377    *ISBN* 0688002048

**Gibbs-Smith, Charles Harvard, 1909-.**    • 5.6645
Aviation: an historical survey from its origins to the end of World War II. London, H.M.S.O., 1970. xvi, 316 p., 28 plates (5 fold.) illus. 26 cm. At head of title: Science Museum. First ed. published in 1960 under title: The Aeroplane. 1. Aeronautics — History 2. Airplanes — History. I. Science Museum (Great Britain) II. T.
TL515.G48 1970    629.13/09/04    *LC* 76-548741    *ISBN* 0112900135

**Gibbs-Smith, Charles Harvard, 1909-.**    5.6646
Flight through the ages: a complete, illustrated chronology from the dreams of early history to the age of space exploration / by C. H. Gibbs-Smith. — New York: Crowell, 1974. 240 p.: ill. (some col.); 31 cm. Includes index. 1. Aeronautics — History I. T.
TL515.G495 1974    629.1/09    *LC* 74-8389    *ISBN* 0690006071

**Crouch, Tom D.**    5.6647
A dream of wings: Americans and the airplane, 1875–1905 / Tom D. Crouch. — 1st ed. — New York: Norton, c1981. 349 p.: ill.; 24 cm. Includes index. 1. Aeronautics — United States — History. I. T.
TL521.C65 1981    629.13/00973    *LC* 80-18077    *ISBN* 0393013855

**Kryter, Karl D.**    5.6648
Physiological, psychological, and social effects of noise / Karl D. Kryter. — Washington, D.C.: National Aeronautics and Space Administration, Scientific and Technical Information Branch; Springfield, Va.: For sale by the National Technical Information Service, 1984. — v, 654 p.: ill.; 28 cm. (NASA reference publication; 1115) 'July 1984'—Cover. 1. Noise — Physiological effect 2. Noise — Social aspects. 3. Noise pollution 4. Noise — Psychological aspects. I. U.S. National Aeronautics and Space Administration. Scientific and Technical Information Branch. II. T.
TL521.3.N32 no. 1115    *LC* gp 85-19747

**Jackson, A. J. (Aubrey Joseph)**    5.6649
British civil aircraft since 1919, by A. J. Jackson. 2nd ed. London, Putnam, 1973-74. 3 v. illus. 23 cm. First ed., published 1959-60 under title: British civil aircraft, 1919-1959. 1. Aeronautics — Great Britain — History. 2. Airplanes — History. 3. Airplanes, Private I. T.
TL526.G7 J32    387.7/33/40942    *LC* 73-157828    *ISBN* 0370100069

**Grierson, John, 1909-1977.**    • 5.6650
Challenge to the poles: highlights of Arctic and Antarctic aviation / John Grierson; with foreword by Charles A. Lindbergh. — Hamden, Conn.: Archon Books, 1964. 695 p., [26] leaves of plates: ill., maps, ports.; 22.1 x 13.6 cm. 1. Aeronautics — Polar regions. I. T.
TL532.G7    629.130998    *LC* 64-9858

## TL539–540 Biography

**Wolko, Howard S.**    5.6651
In the cause of flight: technologists of aeronautics and astronautics / Howard S. Wolko. — Washington: Smithsonian Institution Press, 1981. iii, 121 p.; 28 cm. — (Smithsonian studies in air and space. no. 4) Includes index. 1. Aeronautics — Biography 2. Rocketry — Biography I. T. II. Series.
TL539.W67 1981    629.13/0092/2 B 19    *LC* 80-19749

**Lindbergh, Anne Morrow, 1906-.**    5.6652
Hour of gold, hour of lead: diaries and letters of Anne Morrow Lindbergh, 1929–1932. — [1st ed.]. — New York: Harcourt Brace Jovanovich, [1973] xi, 340 p.: ill.; 22 cm. 'A Helen and Kurt Wolff book.' Continuation of the author's Bring me a Unicorn. Continued by the author's Locked rooms and open doors. 1. Lindbergh, Anne Morrow, 1906- — Diaries. 2. Lindbergh, Anne Morrow, 1906- — Correspondence. 3. Lindbergh, Anne Morrow, 1906- 4. Air pilots — Correspondence, reminiscences, etc. I. T.
TL540.L49 A4 1973    818/.5/209 B    *LC* 72-88792    *ISBN* 0151421765

**Shute, Nevil, 1899-1960.**    • 5.6653
Slide rule: the autobiography of an engineer / Nevil Shute. — New York: Morrow, 1954. 240 p.: ill. 1. Shute, Nevil, 1899-1960. 2. Engineers — Biography. I. T.
TL540.N6A3    350

**Cate, Curtis, 1924-.**    • 5.6654
Antoine de Saint–Exupéry. — New York: Putnam, [1970] xvi, 608 p.: illus., facsims., ports.; 25 cm. 1. Saint-Exupéry, Antoine de, 1900-1944. I. T.
TL540.S18 C37 1970    629.13/0924 B    *LC* 70-81650

**Daley, Robert.**    5.6655
An American saga: Juan Trippe and his Pan Am empire / Robert Daley. — 1st ed. — New York: Random House, c1980. x, 529 p., [8] leaves of plates: ill.; 24 cm. Includes index. 1. Trippe, J. T. (Juan Terry), 1899- 2. Pan American World Airways, inc. 3. Aeronautics — United States — Biography. I. T.
TL540.T7 D34 1980    387.7/092/4 B    *LC* 79-4792    *ISBN* 039450223X

**Von Kármán, Theodore, 1881-1963.**    • 5.6656
The wind and beyond; Theodore von Kármán, pioneer in aviation and pathfinder in space, by Theodore von Kármán with Lee Edson. — [1st ed.]. — Boston: Little, Brown, [1967] 376 p.: illus., ports.; 24 cm. I. Edson, Lee. II. T.
TL540.V67 A3    629.1/0924    *LC* 67-11227

## TL554–568 General Works. Meteorology. Research

**Van Sickle, Neil D. ed.**    • 5.6657
Modern airmanship, edited by Neil D. Van Sickle. 4th ed. New York, Van Nostrand-Reinhold Co. [1971] xiii, 909 p. illus. 24 cm. 1. Aeronautics 2. Airplanes — Piloting I. T.
TL545.V3 1971    629.132/524    *LC* 71-143545

**Hallion, Richard.**    5.6658
Supersonic flight; the story of the Bell X–1 and Douglas D–558. Introd. by Michael Collins and Melvin B. Zisfein. — New York: Macmillan, [1972] xxii, 248 p.: illus.; 24 cm. 1. High-speed aeronautics — History. 2. Supersonic planes — History. 3. Bell X-1 (Supersonic planes) 4. Skystreak (Supersonic planes) I. T.
TL551.5.H3    629.13/09/04    *LC* 72-88809

**United States. Weather Bureau.**    • 5.6659
Aviation weather, for pilots and flight operations personnel. — Washington: For sale by the Supt. of Docs., U. S. Govt. Print Off., 1965. viii, 299 p.: ill. (some col.) Supersedes and replaces Technical manual no. 104 [Pilot's weather handbook, by J. T. Lee and Carl M. Reber] and is a joint publication of the Federal Aviation Agency's Flight Standards Service and the Department of Commerce, Weather Bureau ... [It] was prepared in the Weather Bureau by William P. Nash, meteorologist-pilot, with the assistance of other members of the Weather Bureau. 1. Meteorology in aeronautics I. Nash, William P II. Lee, J. T. (Jean Theodore), 1922- Pilot's weather handbook. III. United States. Flight Standards Service. IV. T.
TL556. U67    *LC* 65-61704

**Koppes, Clayton R., 1945-.**    5.6660
JPL and the American space program: a history of the Jet Propulsion Laboratory / Clayton R. Koppes. — New Haven: Yale University Press, c1982. xiii, 299 p., [6] p. of plates: ill. (some col.); 25 cm. — (Yale planetary exploration series.) 1. Jet Propulsion Laboratory (U.S.) — History. 2. Astronautics — United States — History. I. T. II. Title: J.P.L. and the American space program. III. Series.
TL568.J47 K66 1982    629.4/072079493 19    *LC* 82-40162    *ISBN* 0300024088

## TL570–589 Mechanics of Flight: Aerodynamics

**Bertin, John J., 1938-.**    5.6661
Aerodynamics for engineers / John J. Bertin and Michael L. Smith. — Englewood Cliffs, N.J.: Prentice-Hall, c1979. xvi, 410 p.: ill.; 25 cm. 1. Aerodynamics I. Smith, Michael L., 1943- joint author. II. T.
TL570.B42 1979    629.132/3    *LC* 78-24219    *ISBN* 0130182346

**Etkin, Bernard.**    5.6662
Dynamics of atmospheric flight. New York, Wiley [1972] xii, 579 p. illus. 24 cm. 1. Aerodynamics 2. Stability of airplanes 3. Flight I. T.
TL570.E74    629.132/3    *LC* 73-165946    *ISBN* 0471246204

**Küchemann, Dietrich, 1911-1976.**    5.6663
The aerodynamic design of aircraft: a detailed introduction to the current aerodynamic knowledge and practical guide to the solution of aircraft design problems / D. Küchemann. — Oxford; New York: Pergamon Press, 1978. x, 564 p.: ill.; 26 cm. — (Pergamon international library of science, technology,

engineering, and social studies) 'In SI/Metric Units.' Includes index. 1. Aerodynamics 2. Airplanes — Design and construction I. T.
TL570.K75 1978    629.132/3 19    *LC* 78-40505    *ISBN* 0080205151

**Shevell, Richard Shepherd.**          **5.6664**
Fundamentals of flight / Richard S. Shevell. — Englewood Cliffs, N.J.: Prentice-Hall, c1983. xxiv, 405 p.: ill.; 25 cm. 1. Aerodynamics I. T.
TL570.S462 1983    629.132/3 19    *LC* 82-13193    *ISBN* 0133390934

**Von Mises, Richard, 1883-1953.**        ● **5.6665**
Theory of flight / by Richard von Mises; with the collaboration of W. Prager, and Gustav Kuerti; with a new introd. by Kurt H. Hohenemser. — New Yorl+k: Dover Publications, c1959. xvi, 629 p.: ill. — (Dvoer books on engineering and engineering physics) (Dover books on engineering and engineering physics) 1. Aerodynamics 2. Flight 3. Airplanes I. Prager, Willy, 1903- II. Kuerti, Gustav III. T.
TL570 V64 1959    *LC* 59-4203      *ISBN* 0486605418

# TL600–777 AIRCRAFT. AIRPORTS

**Aviation space dictionary / editor, Ernest J. Gentle; co–editor,**    **5.6666**
**Lawrence W. Reithmaier.**
6th ed. — Fallbrook, Cal.: Aero Publishers, Inc., 1980. 272 p.: ill.; 28 cm. 1. Aeronautics — Dictionaries. 2. Astronautics — Dictionaries I. Gentle, Ernest J. II. Reithmaier, Lawrence W.
TL600.A85 1980    TL600 A85 1980.    629.1303    *LC* 80-67567
   *ISBN* 0816830029

**Taylor, Michael John Haddrick.**        **5.6667**
Encyclopedia of aircraft / edited by Michael J. H. Taylor & John W. R. Taylor. — New York: Putnam, c1978. 253 p.: ill. (some col.); 31 cm. Includes index. 1. Airplanes — History. 2. Airplanes — Dictionaries. I. Taylor, John William Ransom. II. T.
TL670.3.E52    629.133/34/03    *LC* 78-53408

**Crawford, Donald R.**        **5.6668**
A practical guide to airplane performance and design / by Donald R. Crawford. — Rev. print. — Torrance, Ca.: Crawford Aviation, 1981. xiii, 206 p.: ill.; 28 cm. 'Published to help the beginning designer through some of the preliminary phases of aircraft design.' Template and graph paper inserted. Includes index. 1. Airplanes — Design and construction I. T.
TL671.2.C7 1981    629.134/1 19    *LC* 81-67801    *ISBN* 0960393404

**Stinton, Darrol, 1927-.**        **5.6669**
The design of the aeroplane: which describes common–sense mechanics of design as they affect the flying qualities of aeroplanes needing only one pilot / Darrol Stinton. — New York: Van Nostrand Reinhold, 1983. xxix, 642 p.: ill.; 26 cm. Errata slip inserted. 1. Airplanes — Design and construction I. T.
TL671.2.S773 1983    629.134/1 19    *LC* 82-13635    *ISBN* 0442282494

**Cutler, John.**        **5.6670**
Understanding aircraft structures / John Cutler. — London; Toronto: Granada, c1981. v, 170 p.: ill.; 25 cm. 1. Airframes — Terminology. 2. Airframes I. T.
TL 671.6 C98 1981      *ISBN* 0246113103

**Megson, T. H. G. (Thomas Henry Gordon)**        **5.6671**
Aircraft structures for engineering students [by] T. H. G. Megson. London, Edward Arnold, 1972. ix, 485 p. illus. 24 cm. 1. Airframes 2. Aeroelasticity 3. Airplanes — Airworthiness I. T.
TL671.6.M36    629.134/31    *LC* 73-151581    *ISBN* 0713132760

**Green, William.**        **5.6672**
Observer's directory of military aircraft / William Green, Gordon Swanborough. — New York (N.Y.): Arco, c1982. 256 p.: ill. 1. Airplanes, Military I. Swanborough, Gordon. II. T. III. Title: Directory of military aircraft.
TL685.3 G798 1982    623.746    *LC* 82-71835    *ISBN* 0668056495

# TL701–716 Motors. Aircraft Operation

**McMahon, Patrick Joseph.**        **5.6673**
Aircraft propulsion / [by] P. J. McMahon; with a foreword by S. G. Hooker. — London: Pitman, 1972 (c1971) xi, 379 p.: ill.; 23 cm. (Pitman aeronautical engineering series) 1. Airplanes — Motors 2. Aircraft gas-turbines I. T.
TL701.M17    629.134/35    *LC* 73-578893    *ISBN* 027342324X

**Hill, Philip G.**        ● **5.6674**
Mechanics and thermodynamics of propulsion [by] Philip G. Hill [and] Carl R. Peterson. Reading, Mass., Addison-Wesley Pub. Co. [1965] x, 563 p. illus. 25

cm. (Addison-Wesley series in aerospace science) Includes bibliographical references. 1. Airplanes — Jet propulsion 2. Rocket engines 3. Space vehicles — Propulsion systems I. Peterson, Carl R., joint author. II. T.
TL709.H5    629.42    *LC* 65-10408

**The Jet age: forty years of jet aviation / edited by Walter J.**    **5.6675**
**Boyne and Donald S. Lopez; with contributions by Anselm**
**Franz ... [et al.].**
Washington: National Air and Space Museum, Smithsonian Institution: distributed by Smithsonian Institution Press, 1979. vii, 190 p.: ill.; 26 cm. Lectures presented at a symposium held Oct. 26, 1979 and sponsored by the National Air and Space Museum. 1. Airplanes — Jet propulsion — History — Congresses. I. Boyne, Walter J., 1929- II. Lopez, Donald S., 1923- III. Franz, Anselm. IV. National Air and Space Museum.
TL709.J46    629.133/349    *LC* 79-20216    *ISBN* 087474248X

**Kerrebrock, Jack L.**        **5.6676**
Aircraft engines and gas turbines / Jack L. Kerrebrock. — Cambridge, Mass.: MIT Press, c1977. x, 285 p.: ill.; 24 cm. 1. Aircraft gas-turbines I. T.
TL709.K46    629.134/353    *LC* 77-4428    *ISBN* 0262110644

**Constant, Edward W.**        **5.6677**
The origins of the turbojet revolution / Edward W. Constant II. — Baltimore: Johns Hopkins University Press, 1981 (c1980). xiv, 311 p.: ill.; 24 cm. — (Johns Hopkins studies in the history of technology. new ser., no. 5) 1. Airplanes — Turbojet engines — History. I. T. II. Series.
TL709.3.T83 C64    621.43/52    *LC* 80-11802    *ISBN* 080182222X

## TL716 Helicopters

**Fay, John.**        **5.6678**
The helicopter: history, piloting, and how it flies / by John Fay; illustrated by Lucy Raymond, David Gibbings, Dulcie Legg. 3d rev. ed. — Newton Abbot; North Pomfret, Vt.: David & Charles, 1977 (c1976). xiii, 194 p., [4] leaves of plates: ill.; 23 cm. Previous ed. published under title: The helicopter and how it flies. Includes index. 1. Helicopters I. T.
TL716.F35 1976    629.133/35    *LC* 77-360773    *ISBN* 0715372491

**Gregory, Hollingsworth Franklin, 1906-.**        **5.6679**
The helicopter / H. F. Gregory. — South Brunswick: A. S. Barnes, c1976. 223 p.: ill.; 32 cm. Published in 1944 under title: Anything a horse can do: the story of the helicopter. Includes index. 1. Helicopters I. T.
TL716.G68 1976    629.133/35    *LC* 74-30720    *ISBN* 0498016706

**Johnson, Wayne, 1946-.**        **5.6680**
Helicopter theory / Wayne Johnson. — Princeton, N.J.: Princeton University Press, c1980. xxii, 1089 p.: ill.; 24 cm. Includes index. 1. Helicopters I. T.
TL716.J63    629.133/352 19    *LC* 79-83995

## TL725–733 Airports

**Ashford, Norman.**        **5.6681**
Airport operations / Norman Ashford, H.P. Martin Stanton, Clifton A. Moore. — New York: Wiley, c1984. ix, 476 p.: ill.; 24 cm. 'A Wiley-Interscience publication.' 1. Airports — Management I. Stanton, H. P. Martin. II. Moore, Clifton A. III. T.
TL725.3.M2 A83 1984    387.7/36 19    *LC* 83-10371    *ISBN* 0471896136

**Singer, Jerry A.**        **5.6682**
Small airport management handbook / Jerry A. Singer. — Athens, GA: Carl Vinson Institute of Government, University of Georgia, 1985. 166 p.: ill.; 28 cm. 1. Airports — Management — Handbooks, manuals, etc. I. T.
TL725.3.M2 S56 1985    387.7/36/068 19    *LC* 84-22173    *ISBN* 0898540992

**Ashford, Norman.**        **5.6683**
Airport engineering / Norman Ashford, Paul H. Wright. — 2nd ed. — New York: Wiley, c1984. ix, 433 p.: ill.; 24 cm. 'A Wiley-Interscience publication.' 1. Airports — Planning I. Wright, Paul H. II. T.
TL725.3.P5 A83 1984    629.136 19    *LC* 83-23494    *ISBN* 0471865680

**De Neufville, Richard, 1939-.**        **5.6684**
Airport systems planning: a critical look at the methods and experience / Richard De Neufville; with prefaces by Norman J. Payne and John R. Wiley. 1st American ed. — Cambridge, Mass.: MIT Press, 1976. xvi, 201 p.; 23 cm. Includes index. 1. Airports — Planning I. T.
TL725.3.P5 D46 1976    387.7/36    *LC* 76-5994    *ISBN* 0262040514

**Horonjeff, Robert.**        **5.6685**
Planning and design of airports / Robert Horonjeff and Francis X. McKelvey. — 3rd ed. — New York: McGraw-Hill, c1983. xii, 616 p.: ill.; 24 cm. —

(McGraw-Hill series in transportation.) 1. Airports — Planning 2. Airports — Design and construction. I. McKelvey, Francis X. II. T. III. Series.
TL725.3.P5 H6 1983      629.136 19      *LC* 82-14859      *ISBN* 0070303673

## TL760–769 Gliders. Ultralight Aircraft

**Ellison, Norman.**                                                    5.6686
British gliders and sailplanes, 1922–1970. — New York: Barnes & Noble, [1971] 296 p.: illus.; 25 cm. 1. Gliders (Aeronautics) — History. 2. Gliding and soaring — History — Gt. Brit. I. T.
TL760.E57      629.133/33      *LC* 79-29407      *ISBN* 0389041629

**Piggott, Derek.**                                                    5.6687
Understanding gliding: the principles of soaring flight / Derek Piggott; with illustrations by the author. — 2nd ed. — London: Black, 1987. [257] p.: ill., charts, maps; 25 cm. 1. Gliding and soaring I. T.
TL760.P5x      629.132/31 19      *ISBN* 0713655682

**Grosser, Morton.**                                                    5.6688
Gossamer odyssey: the triumph of human–powered flight / Morton Grosser. — Boston: Houghton Mifflin, 1981. xxi, 298 p., [16] leaves of plates: ill.; 24 cm. Includes index. 1. Human powered aircraft I. T.
TL769.G76      629.133/34 19      *LC* 80-39634      *ISBN* 0395305314

# TL780–4050 Rockets. Astronautics. Space Flights

## TL780–785 ROCKETS

**Von Braun, Wernher, 1912-1977.**                               • 5.6689
History of rocketry & space travel / [by] Wernher Von Braun [and] Frederick I. Ordway, III; original illus. by Harry H. K. Lange; introd. by Frederick C. Durant, III. — Rev. ed. — New York: Crowell, [1969] xi, 276 p.: ill. (part col.), facsims., ports.; 29 cm. 1. Rocketry — History. 2. Astronautics — History. I. Ordway, Frederick Ira, 1927- joint author. II. T.
TL781.V6 1969      629.4/09      *LC* 76-94786

**Sutton, George Paul.**                                               5.6690
Rocket propulsion elements: an introduction to the engineering of rockets / George P. Sutton. — 5th ed. — New York: Wiley, c1986. vii, 361 p.: ill.; 24 cm. 'A Wiley-Interscience publication.' 1. Rocket engines I. T.
TL782.S8 1986      629.134/354 19      *LC* 85-20398      *ISBN* 0471800279

## TL787–795 ASTRONAUTICS: GENERAL

**Space and society: challenges and choices: proceedings of a**      5.6691
**conference held April 14–16, 1982 at the University of Texas at**
**Austin / edited by Paul Anaejionu, Nathan C. Goldman, Philip**
**J. Meeks.**
San Diego, Calif.: Published for the American Astronautical Society by Univelt, c1984. xii, 429 p.: ill.; 25 cm. (Science and technology series, 0278-4017; v. 59) 'Symposium sponsored by College of Liberal Arts, University of Texas at Austin ... [et al.]'—P. vii. 1. Astronautics — Social aspects — Congresses. I. Anajionu, Paul. II. Goldman, Nathan C. III. Meeks, Phillip J. IV. University of Texas at Austin. College of Liberal Arts. V. American Astronautical Society.
TL787.S628 1984      338.4/76294 19      *LC* 84-233635      *ISBN* 0877032041

**The Illustrated encyclopedia of space technology: a**               5.6692
**comprehensive history of space exploration / Kenneth Gatland,**
**consultant and chief author; with a foreword by Arthur C.**
**Clarke.**
1st U.S. ed. — New York: Harmony Books, c1981. 289 p.: ill. (some col.); 31 cm. — (A Salamander book) Spine title: Space technology. 1. Astronautics — Dictionaries I. Gatland, Kenneth William, 1924- II. Title: Space technology.
TL788.I44 1981      629.4/03/21 19      *LC* 80-28533      *ISBN* 0517542587

## TL789–789.3 UFO's

**UFO's—a scientific debate. Edited by Carl Sagan and Thornton**      5.6693
**Page.**
Ithaca [N.Y.]: Cornell University Press, [1972] xxxi, 310 p.: illus.; 23 cm. Papers presented at a symposium sponsored by the American Association for the Advancement of Science, held in Boston on Dec. 26-27, 1969. 1. Unidentified flying objects — Congresses. I. Sagan, Carl, 1934- ed. II. Page, Thornton. ed. III. American Association for the Advancement of Science.
TL789.A1 U23      001.9/4      *LC* 72-4572      *ISBN* 0801407400

**Condon, Edward Uhler, 1902-1974.**                              • 5.6694
Final report of the scientific study of uniedentified flying objects / [by] Edward U. Condon; Daniel S. Gillmor, editor; with an introd. by Walter Sullivan. — New York: Dutton, 1969. xxiv, 967 p.: ill.; 22 cm. Commonly known as the Condon report. Conducted by the University of Colorado under contract F44620-67-C-0035 to the Air Force Office of Scientific Research, Office of Aerospace Research, USAF. 1. Unidentified flying objects I. Colorado. University II. T. III. Title: Scientific study of unidentified flying objects. IV. Title: Condon report on unidentified flying objects.
TL789.C658 1969      001/.94      *LC* 73-77914

**Hynek, J. Allen (Joseph Allen), 1910-.**                          5.6695
The UFO experience; a scientific inquiry [by] J. Allen Hynek. — Chicago: H. Regnery Co., [1972] xii, 276 p.: illus.; 24 cm. 1. Unidentified flying objects I. T.
TL789.H9      001.9/4      *LC* 76-183827

**Jacobs, David Michael, 1942-.**                                   5.6696
The UFO controversy in America / David Michael Jacobs. — Bloomington: Indiana University Press, [1975] xvi, 362 p., [3] leaves of plates: ill.; 24 cm. Includes index. 1. Unidentified flying objects I. T.
TL789.J26 1975      001.9/42      *LC* 74-11886      *ISBN* 0253190061

**Klass, Philip J.**                                                 5.6697
UFOs: the public deceived / Philip J. Klass. — Buffalo, N.Y.: Prometheus Books, 1983. viii, 310 p., [12] p. of plates: ill.; 24 cm. 1. Unidentified flying objects I. T. II. Title: U.F.O.s.
TL789.K575 1983      001.9/42 19      *LC* 83-60202      0879752014

**Menzel, Donald Howard, 1901-.**                                  5.6698
The UFO enigma: the definitive explanation of the UFO phenomenon / Donald H. Menzel & Ernest H. Taves; introd. by Fred L. Whipple. — 1st ed. — Garden City, N.Y.: Doubleday, 1977. xiv, 297 p., [8] leaves of plates: ill.; 22 cm. 1. Unidentified flying objects I. Taves, Ernest H. (Ernest Henry), 1916- joint author. II. T.
TL789.M458      001.9/42      *LC* 76-16255      *ISBN* 0385035969

**Randles, Jenny.**                                                 5.6699
Science and the UFOs / Jenny Randles and Peter Warrington. — Oxford, UK; New York, NY, USA: B. Blackwell, 1985. viii, 215 p., [8] p. of plates: ill.; 24 cm. Includes index. 1. Unidentified flying objects I. Warrington, Peter. II. T. III. Title: Science and the U.F.O.s.
TL789.R325 1985      001.9/42 19      *LC* 84-20319      *ISBN* 0631135634

**Salisbury, Frank B.**                                             5.6700
The Utah UFO display: a biologist's report / by Frank B. Salisbury; with data from the files of Joseph Junior Hicks; foreword by J. Allen Hynek. — Old Greenwich, Conn.: Devin-Adair Co., [1974] xxiv, 286 p., [8] leaves of plates: ill.; 22 cm. Includes index. 1. Unidentified flying objects — Sightings and encounters — Utah. I. Hicks, Joseph Junior. II. T.
TL789.S18      001.9/42      *LC* 74-75389      *ISBN* 0815970005

## TL879.8 Astronautics, by Country

**Oberg, James E., 1944-.**                                         5.6701
Red star in orbit / James E. Oberg. — 1st ed. — New York: Random House, c1981. xiii, 272 p., [8] leaves of plates: ill.; 22 cm. Includes index. 1. Astronautics — Soviet Union I. T.
TL789.8.R9 O24      387.8 19      *LC* 80-6033      *ISBN* 0394514297

**McDougall, Walter A., 1946-.**                                   5.6702
The heavens and the earth: a political history of the space age / Walter A. McDougall. — New York: Basic Books, c1985. xviii, 555 p.: ill.; 25 cm. Includes index. 1. Astronautics and state — United States. 2. Astronautics and state — Soviet Union. 3. Astronautics — United States — History. 4. Astronautics — Soviet Union — History. I. T.
TL789.8.U5 M34 1985      338.4/76294/0973 19      *LC* 84-45314      *ISBN* 046502887X

**Oberg, James E., 1944-.**                                         5.6703
The new race for space: the U.S. and Russia leap to the challenge for unlimited rewards / James E. Oberg; foreword by Ben Bova. — Harrisburg, PA:

Stackpole Books, c1984. xiv, 210 p.: ill.; 23 cm. Includes index. 1. Astronautics — United States 2. Astronautics — Soviet Union I. T.
TL789.8.U5 O24 1984    629.4/0947 19    *LC* 84-2576    *ISBN* 0811721779

**Taylor, L. B.**            **5.6704**
For all mankind: America's space programs of the 1970s and beyond / L. B. Taylor, Jr.; foreword by Wernher von Braun. — 1st ed. — New York: Dutton, 1974. xii, 307 p.: ill.; 22 cm. 'A Sunrise book.' Includes index. 1. Astronautics — United States 2. Outer space — Exploration — United States. I. T.
TL789.8.U5 T36 1974    508.9/9    *LC* 74-9109    *ISBN* 0876901151

**Murray, Bruce C.**            **5.6705**
Flight to Mercury / Bruce Murray and Eric Burgess. New York: Columbia University Press, 1977. xi, 162 p.: ill.; 28 cm. 1. Project Mariner 2. Mercury probes 3. Venus probes I. Burgess, Eric. joint author. II. T.
TL789.8.U6 M3496    629.43/54/1    *LC* 76-25017    *ISBN* 0231039964

**Collins, Michael, 1930-.**            **5.6706**
Carrying the fire; an astronaut's journeys. With a foreword by Charles A. Lindbergh. New York: Farrar, Straus and Giroux, [1974] xvii, 478 p.: illus.; 24 cm. 1. Collins, Michael, 1930- 2. Apollo 11 (Spacecraft) 3. Project Apollo I. T.
TL789.85.C64 A33 1974    629.45/0092/4 B    *LC* 74-7211    *ISBN* 0374119171

## TL790–953 SPACE FLIGHT. ARTIFICIAL SATELLITES

**Grey, Jerry.**            **5.6707**
Beachheads in space: a blueprint for the future / Jerry Grey. — New York: Macmillan, c1983. xi, 274 p.; 22 cm. 1. Astronautics 2. Astronautics, Military 3. Space stations I. T.
TL790.G76 1983    629.4/09048 19    *LC* 83-815    *ISBN* 0025455907

**Lovell, Bernard, Sir, 1913-.**            **5.6708**
The origins and international economics of space exploration [by] Sir Bernard Lovell. New York, Wiley [1973] viii, 104 p. illus. 22 cm. 'A Halsted Press book.' Expansion of a lecture delivered at the University of Edinburgh on 6 Mar. 1973. 1. Astronautics 2. Outer space — Exploration I. T.
TL790.L68    629.4    *LC* 73-18325    *ISBN* 0470548517

**Jane's spaceflight directory / [edited by] Reginald Turnill.**            **5.6709**
2nd ed. — London: Jane's Publishing Company, c1986. 453 p.: ill.; 33 cm. Includes index. 1. Space flight — History — Directories. 2. Manned space flight — History. I. Title: Spaceflight directory.
TL790.T87 1984    629.47    *ISBN* 0710603673

**Allen, Joseph P.**            **5.6710**
Entering space: an astronaut's odyssey / by Joseph P. Allen, with Russell Martin; design by Hans Teensma. — New York: Stewart, Tabori & Chang: Distributed by Workman Pub., c1984. 223 p.: col. ill.; 26 cm. Includes index. 1. Astronautics I. Martin, Russell. II. T.
TL793.A454 1984    629.45 19    *LC* 84-2561    *ISBN* 0941434532

**United States. Earth Resources Observation Systems Data Center.**            **5.6711**
Landsat data users handbook / prepared by the U.S. Geological Survey, EROS Data Center, and NASA Goddard Space Flight Center. — 3rd rev. ed. [Sioux Falls, S. D.]: U.S. Geological Survey, 1979. 1 v.: ill., maps; 30 cm. Loose-leaf for updating. 1. Remote sensing systems. 2. Astronautics in earth sciences 3. Scientific satellites — Handbooks, manuals, etc. 4. Remote sensing — Handbooks, manuals, etc. I. Goddard Space Flight Center. II. T.
G70.4.U558    TL796.L3 1979x.

**Wilding-White, T. M.**            **5.6712**
Jane's pocket book of space exploration / T. M. Wilding–White. New York: Collier Books, 1977. 238 p.: ill.; 11 x 18 cm. Includes index. 1. Artificial satellites 2. Space probes 3. Launch vehicles (Astronautics) I. T.
TL796.W48 1977    629.47/021/2    *LC* 76-23520

**Barrett, E. C. (Eric Charles)**            **5.6713**
Climatology from satellites / [by] E.C. Barrett. — London: Methuen, 1979. xii, 418 p., leaf of plate, [16] p. of plates: ill., charts, maps; 24 cm. Index. 1. Meteorological satellites I. T.
TL798.M4    551.6/354    *ISBN* 0416721508 pa

**The Case for Mars: proceedings of a conference held April 29–May 2, 1981 at University of Colorado, Boulder, Colorado / edited by Penelope J. Boston.**            **5.6714**
San Diego, Calif.: Published for the American Astronautical Society by Univelt, c1984. xxv, 322 p.: ill.; 25 cm. (Science and technology series, 0278-4017; v. 57) 1. Space flight to Mars — Congresses. 2. Mars (Planet) — Exploration — Congresses. I. Boston, Penelope J. II. University of Colorado, Boulder.
TL799.M3 C37 1984    629.45/53 19    *LC* 84-251281    *ISBN* 0877031975

**Oberg, James E., 1944-.**            **5.6715**
Mission to Mars: plans and concepts for the first manned landing / James E. Oberg. — Harrisburg, PA: Stackpole, c1982. 221 p.: ill.; 24 cm. Includes index. 1. Space flight to Mars I. T.
TL799.M3 O23 1982    629.45/53 19    *LC* 82-5689    *ISBN* 0811704327

**Baker, David, 1944-.**            **5.6716**
The history of manned space flight / David Baker. — 1st ed. — New York: Crown Publishers, 1982. 544 p.: ill. (some col.); 34 cm. Includes index. 1. Manned space flight — History. I. T.
TL873.B33 1982    387.8/09 19    *LC* 81-3101    *ISBN* 051754377X

## TL1050–3280 ASTRODYNAMICS. SPACE NAVIGATION

**Herrick, Samuel, 1911-.**            **5.6717**
Astrodynamics. — London; New York: Van Nostrand Reinhold Co., [1971-. v. ; 24 cm. 1. Astrodynamics I. T.
TL1050.H47    629.4/1    *LC* 78-125199    *ISBN* 0442033702

**Mallan, Lloyd.**            • **5.6718**
Suiting up for space: the evolution of the space suit. — New York: John Day Co., [1971] ix, 262 p.: illus., ports.; 26 cm. 1. Space suits I. T.
TL1550.M35    629.47/72    *LC* 75-89308

**Deep space telecommunications systems engineering / edited by Joseph H. Yuen.**            **5.6719**
New York: Plenum Press, 1983. xx, 603 p.: ill.; 24 cm. — (Applications of communications theory.) 'Prepared by the Jet Propulsion Laboratory, California Institute of Technology, under contract with the National Aeronautics and Space Administration'—T.p. verso. Originally published: Pasadena, Calif.: Jet Propulsion Laboratory, California Institute of Technology, 1982. 1. Astronautics — Communications systems. I. Yuen, Joseph H. II. Jet Propulsion Laboratory (U.S.) III. Series.
TL3025.D44 1983    629.46/43 19    *LC* 83-17830    *ISBN* 0306414899

## TN MINING ENGINEERING. METALLURGY

## TN1–259 Reference. General Works

**Thrush, Paul W.**            • **5.6720**
A dictionary of mining, mineral, and related terms / compiled and edited by Paul W. Thrush and the staff of the Bureau of Mines. — [Washington: U.S. Bureau of Mines; for sale by the Supt. of Docs., U.S. Govt. Print. Off.], 1968. vii, 1269 p.; 30 cm. 1. Mining engineering — Dictionaries. 2. Mineral industries — Dictionaries I. U.S. Bureau of Mines. II. T.
TN9.T5    622/.03    *LC* 68-67091

**Gregory, Cedric Errol.**            **5.6721**
A concise history of mining / Cedric E. Gregory. — New York: Pergamon Press, c1980. xviii, 259 p.: ill.; 24 cm. Includes index. 1. Mining engineering — History. I. T.
TN15.G73 1980    622/.09    *LC* 80-13925    *ISBN* 0080238823

**Cameron, Eugene N. (Eugene Nathan), 1910-.**                    **5.6722**
At the crossroads: the mineral problems of the United States / Eugene N. Cameron. — New York: Wiley, c1986. xxi, 320 p.: ill.; 26 cm. 1. Mines and mineral resources — United States. I. T.
TN23.C36 1986        333.8/5/0973 19        *LC* 85-29587        *ISBN* 0471839833

**United States. Bureau of Mines.**                    • **5.6723**
Mineral facts and problems / by staff, Bureau of mines. — [1st ed.] (1956)- .
— Washington, D.C.: U.S. Govt. Print. Off., 1956-. v.: Ill.; 26 cm. (Bulletin / Bureau of Mines; 556, 585, 630, 667,) 1. Mines and mineral resources — United States. 2. Mineral industries — United States. I. États-Unis. Bureau of Mines. II. T.
TN23.U4        *LC* 56-60859

**Minerals yearbook.**                    • **5.6724**
1932/33-. Washington, Dept. of the Interior, Bureau of Mines; for sale by the Supt. of Docs., U.S. Govt. Print. Off. v. ill., maps. 24 cm. Annual. 1976, v. 2. Chapters that will later be included in the bound vols. are issued as preprints in advance of publication as they are completed. CONTENTS: V. 2. Area reports: Domestic. Issued in three vols., 1952-62; four vols., 1963-69; three vols., 1970- 1. Mineral industries — United States — Statistics — Yearbooks. 2. Mines and mineral resources — United States — Statistics — Yearbooks. I. United States. Bureau of Mines.
TN23.U612        338.2/0973        *LC* gp 80-18868

**SME mining engineering handbook / Arthur B. Cummins,**                    **5.6725**
**chairman, editorial board; Ivan A. Given, editor.**
New York: Society of Mining Engineers, American Institute of Mining, Metallurgical, and Petroleum Engineers, 1973. 2 v.: ill.; 24 cm. — (Mudd series) 1. Mining engineering — Handbooks, manuals, etc. I. Cummins, Arthur B. II. Given, Ivan A., ed. III. Society of Mining Engineers of AIME.
TN151.S18        622/.02/02        *LC* 72-86922

**Blunden, John.**                    **5.6726**
Mineral resources and their management / John Blunden. — London; New York: Longman, 1985. 302 p.: ill. — (Themes in resource management.) Includes index. 1. Mines and mineral resources 2. Conservation of natural resources I. T. II. Series.
TN153.B58 1985        333.8/5 19        *LC* 84-10061        *ISBN* 0582300584

**International minerals: a national perspective / edited by Allen**                    **5.6727**
**F. Agnew.**
Boulder, Colo.: Published by Westview Press for the American Association for the Advancement of Science, 1983. xv, 164 p.: ill.; 24 cm. — (AAAS selected symposia series; 90) 'Based on a symposium which was held ... in Washington, D.C., January 3-8 [1982] ... sponsored by the American Geological Institute and by AAAS Section E (Geology and Geography)'—T.p. verso. 1. Mines and mineral resources 2. Mines and mineral resources — United States. 3. Strategic materials — United States. I. Agnew, Allen Francis, 1918- II. American Geological Institute. III. American Association for the Advancement of Science. Section E—Geology and Geography.
TN153.I49 1983        333.8/5 19        *LC* 83-60538        *ISBN* 0865316228

# TN260–271 Economic Geology. Prospecting

**Jensen, Mead LeRoy, 1925-.**                    **5.6728**
Economic mineral deposits / Mead L. Jensen, Alan M. Bateman. — 3d ed. rev. print. — New York: Wiley, c1981. — viii, 593 p.: ill.; 29 cm. 1. Geology, Economic 2. Mines and mineral resources I. Bateman, Alan Mara II. T.
TN260.B3        *ISBN* 0471090433

**Jensen, Mead LeRoy, 1925-.**                    **5.6729**
Economic mineral deposits / Mead L. Jensen, Alan M. Bateman. — 3d ed. — New York: Wiley, c1979. viii, 593 p.: ill.; 29 cm. Second ed. by A. M. Bateman. Includes index. 1. Geology, Economic 2. Mines and mineral resources I. Bateman, Alan Mara, joint author. II. Bateman, Alan Mara. Economic mineral deposits. III. T.
TN260.B3 1979        553        *LC* 78-9852        *ISBN* 0471017698

**Economic geology and geotectonics / edited by D. H. Tarling.**                    **5.6730**
New York: Wiley, 1981. x, 213 p.: ill.; 25 cm. 'A Halsted Press book.' 1. Geology, Economic 2. Geology, Structural I. Tarling, D. H. (Donald Harvey)
TN260.E28        553 19        *LC* 81-673        *ISBN* 0470271450

**Mining geology / edited by Willard C. Lacy.**                    **5.6731**
Stroudsburg, Pa.: Hutchinson Ross Pub. Co.; New York: Distributed worldwide by Van Nostrand Reinhold Publishing Co., c1983. xiii, 466 p.: ill.; 26

cm. — (Benchmark papers in geology. 69) 1. Mining geology — Addresses, essays, lectures I. Lacy, W. C. (Willard C.) II. Series.
TN260.M57 1983        553 19        *LC* 82-968        *ISBN* 0879334266

**Peters, William C.**                    **5.6732**
Exploration mining and geology / William C. Peters. — New York: Wiley, c1978. xxiii, 696 p.: ill.; 24 cm. Cover title: Exploration and mining geology. Includes index. 1. Mining geology 2. Prospecting I. T. II. Title: Exploration and mining geology.
TN260.P47        622/.1        *LC* 77-14006        *ISBN* 0471682616

**Hutchison, Charles S. (Charles Strachan), 1933-.**                    **5.6733**
Economic deposits and their tectonic setting / Charles S. Hutchison. — New York: J. Wiley, c1983. x, 365 p.: ill.; 26 cm. Includes index. 1. Ore deposits 2. Geology, Economic 3. Geology, Structural I. T.
TN263.H87 1983        553 19        *LC* 83-136755        *ISBN* 0471872814

**Sawkins, Frederick J.**                    **5.6734**
Metal deposits in relation to plate tectonics / F.J. Sawkins. — Berlin; New York: Springer-Verlag, 1984. xiv, 325 p.: ill., maps; 24 cm. — (Minerals and rocks. 17) Includes index. 1. Ore deposits 2. Plate tectonics I. T. II. Series.
TN263.S27 1984        553.4 19        *LC* 83-16890        *ISBN* 0387127526

**Cronan, D. S. (David Spencer)**                    **5.6735**
Underwater minerals / by D.S. Cronan. — London; New York: Academic Press, 1980. xv, 362 p.: ill.; 24 cm. — (Ocean science, resources, and technology, an international series) Includes index. 1. Marine mineral resources 2. Mineral resources in submerged lands I. T. II. Series.
TN264.C76        553/.09162 19        *LC* 80-49966        *ISBN* 0121974804

**Edwards, Richard, 1940-.**                    **5.6736**
Ore deposit geology and its influence on mineral exploration / Richard Edwards and Keith Atkinson. — London; New York: Chapman and Hall, 1986. xvi, 466 p.: ill.; 26 cm. 1. Ore deposits 2. Geology 3. Prospecting I. Atkinson, Keith, 1942- II. T.
TN265.E33 1986        553/.1 19        *LC* 85-11713        *ISBN* 0412246902

**Applied geophysics / W. M. Telford ... [et al.].**                    **5.6737**
London; New York: Cambridge University Press, 1976. xvii, 860 p.: ill.; 24 cm. 1. Prospecting — Geophysical methods I. Telford, W. M. (William Murray), 1917-
TN269.A663        622/.15        *LC* 74-16992        *ISBN* 0521206707

**Dobrin, Milton Burnett.**                    **5.6738**
Introduction to geophysical prospecting / Milton B. Dobrin. — 3d ed. — New York: McGraw-Hill, c1976. ix, 630 p.: ill.; 24 cm. 1. Prospecting — Geophysical methods I. T.
TN269.D6 1976        622/.15        *LC* 75-37603        *ISBN* 0070171955

**Robinson, Enders A.**                    **5.6739**
Geophysical signal processing / Enders A. Robinson, Tariq S. Durrani, with a chapter by Lloyd G. Peardon. — Englewood Cliffs, N.J.: Prentice-Hall, c1986. xi, 481 p.: ill.; 24 cm. Includes index. 1. Seismic prospecting 2. Seismology 3. Digital filters (Mathematics) 4. Signal processing I. Durrani, Tariq S. II. Peardon, Lloyd G. III. T.
TN269.R553 1986        551/.028 19        *LC* 85-12085        *ISBN* 0133526674

**Seismic stratigraphy: applications to hydrocarbon exploration /**                    **5.6740**
**edited by Charles E. Payton.**
Tulsa, Okla.: American Association of Petroleum Geologists, 1977. vii, 516 p.: ill.; 25 cm. — (Memoir - American Association of Petroleum Geologists; 26) 1. Seismic reflection method 2. Petroleum 3. Geology, Stratigraphic I. Payton, Charles E.
TN269.S37        622/.18/28        *LC* 77-91023        *ISBN* 0891813020

**Waters, Kennth Harold, 1913-.**                    **5.6741**
Reflection seismology: a tool for energy resource exploration / Kenneth H. Waters. — 3rd ed. — New York: Wiley, [1986] 377 p.: ill. 'A Wiley-Interscience publication.' 1. Seismic reflection method I. T.
TN269.W37 1986        622/.159 19        *LC* 86-15809        *ISBN* 0471011444

**Mineral exploration / edited by Willard C. Lacy.**                    **5.6742**
Stroudsburg, Pa.: Hutchinson Ross Pub. Co.; [New York]: Distributed world wide by Van Nostrand Reinhold Co., c1983. xiii, 433 p.: ill.; 26 cm. — (Benchmark papers in geology. 70) 1. Prospecting — Addresses, essays, lectures. I. Lacy, Willard C. II. Series.
TN270.M655 1983        622/.1 19        *LC* 82-969        *ISBN* 0879334258

**Claerbout, Jon F.**                    **5.6743**
Fundamentals of geophysical data processing: with applications to petroleum prospecting / Jon F. Claerbout. — Palo Alto, CA: Blackwell Scientific Publications, c1985. xiii, 274 p.: ill.; 25 cm. Includes index. 1. Prospecting — Geophysical methods — Data processing 2. Petroleum — Geology — Data processing I. T.
TN271.P4 C6 1985        622/.15/02854 19        *LC* 84-28343        *ISBN* 0865423059

**Unconventional methods in exploration for petroleum and**    **5.6744**
**natural gas II: a symposium under the auspices of the Institute**
**for the Study of Earth and Man, Southern Methodist University**
**/ edited by Benjamin M. Gottlieb.**
Dallas: SMU Press, c1981. ix, 257 p.: ill.; 29 cm. + 1 atlas ([22] leaves of plates:
all col. ill. (some folded); 29 cm.) Proceedings of the Second Symposium on
Unconventional Methods in Exploration for Petroleum and Natural Gas held
in Dallas, Tex. Sept. 13-14, 1979. Atlas in case. 1. Prospecting — Congresses.
2. Petroleum — Congresses. 3. Gas, Natural — Congresses. I. Gottlieb,
Benjamin M., 1912- II. Southern Methodist University. Institute for the Study
of Earth and Man. III. Symposium on Unconventional Methods in
Exploration for Petroleum and Natural Gas. (2nd: 1979: Dallas, Tex.)
TN271.P4 U53      622/.1828 19      LC 81-8805      ISBN 0870741799

# TN272–580 Mining. Ore Deposits. Ore Dressing

**Economic evaluation of mineral property / edited by Sam L.**    **5.6745**
**VanLandingham.**
Stroudsburg, Pa.: Hutchinson Ross Pub. Co., c1983. xi, 385 p.: ill.; 27 cm. —
(Benchmark papers in geology. 67) Includes indexes. 1. Mine valuation —
Addresses, essays, lectures. I. VanLandingham, Sam L. II. Series.
TN272.E32 1983      333.33/9 19      LC 82-1025      ISBN 0879334231

**Elements of practical coal mining / Douglas F. Crickmer, David**    **5.6746**
**A. Zegeer, editors.**
2nd ed. New York: Society of Mining Engineers of the American Institute of
Mining, Metallurgical, and Petroleum Engineers, 1981. v, 847 p.: ill.; 24 cm.
'Coal Division of SME-AIME [and] Howard N. Eavenson Award Fund of
AIME, co-sponsors.' 1. Coal mines and mining I. Crickmer, Douglas F.
II. Zegeer, David A. III. Society of Mining Engineers of AIME. Coal
Division.
TN275.E44 1981      622/.33      LC 79-57346      ISBN 0895202700

**Thomas, L. J.**    **5.6747**
An Introduction to mining: exploration, feasibility, extraction, rock mechanics
/ L. J. Thomas. — [2d ed.]. — New York: Halsted Press, 1978. ix, 471 p.: ill.,
diagrs., maps on end papers; 24 cm. 1. Mining engineering 2. Prospecting
3. Rock mechanics I. T.
TN275.T48 1978      TN275 T48 1978.      622      ISBN 0454000871

**Langefors, U.**    **5.6748**
The modern technique of rock blasting / by U. Langefors and B. Kihlström. —
3d ed. — New York: Wiley, c1978. 438 p.: ill.; 24 cm. 'A Halsted Press book.'
1. Blasting I. Kihlström, Björn. joint author. II. T.
TN279.L314 1978      624/.152      LC 77-23895      ISBN 0470992824

**Peng, Syd S., 1939-.**    **5.6749**
Coal mine ground control / Syd S. Peng. — New York: Wiley, c1978. xiii,
450 p.: ill.; 24 cm. 'A Wiley-Interscience publication.' 1. Ground control
(Mining) 2. Coal mines and mining — Safety measures I. T.
TN288.P46      622/.8      LC 78-8965      ISBN 0471041211

**Borgese, Elisabeth Mann.**    **5.6750**
The mines of Neptune: minerals and metals from the sea / by Elisabeth Mann
Borgese; foreword by Jan Tinbergen. — New York: H.N. Abrams, 1985. 158 p.:
ill. (some col.), maps; 29 cm. 1. Ocean mining 2. Mineral resources in
submerged lands I. T.
TN291.5.B67 1985      553/.09162 19      LC 84-14451      ISBN
0810913224

**Morrell, William Parker, 1899-.**    • **5.6751**
The gold rushes, by W. P. Morrell. — 2nd ed. — London: Black, 1968. xi,
427 p.: plates, 8 maps.; 23 cm. — (The Pioneer histories) 1. Gold mines and
mining — History. I. T.
TN420.M7 1968      904/.7      LC 68-141030      ISBN 0713601868

**Fisher, John Robert.**    **5.6752**
Silver mines and silver miners in colonial Peru, 1776–1824 / by J. R. Fisher. —
[Liverpool]: Centre for Latin-American Studies, University of Liverpool, [1977]
150 p.: ill.; 30 cm. (Monograph series - Centre for Latin-American Studies,
University of Liverpool; no. 7) Includes index. 1. Silver mines and mining —
Peru — History. I. T.
TN434.P5 F57      338.2/7/4210985      LC 78-308232      ISBN
0902806068

**Kelly, Errol G.**    **5.6753**
Introduction to mineral processing / Errol G. Kelly, David J. Spottiswood. —
New York: Wiley, c1982. xxiv, 491 p.: ill.; 29 cm. 'A Wiley-Interscience
publication.' 1. Ore-dressing I. Spottiswood, David J. II. T.
TN500.K44 1982      622/.7 19      LC 82-2807      ISBN 0471033790

# TN600–799 Metallurgy

**Sorby Centennial Symposium on the History of Metallurgy**    • **5.6754**
**(1963: Cleveland, Ohio)**
The Sorby Centennial Symposium on the History of Metallurgy, Cleveland,
Ohio, October 22–23, 1963: proceedings / edited by Cyril Stanley Smith. —
New York: Gordon and Breach, 1965. xxii, 558 p.: ill., facsims., ports.; 24 cm.
— (Metallurgical Society conferences; v. 27) Sponsored by the Society for the
History of Technology, American Society for Metals, and the Metallurgical
Society, American Institute of Mining, Metallurgical and Petroleum Engineers.
1. Metallurgy — History — Congresses. I. Smith, Cyril Stanley, 1903-
II. Sorby, Henry Clifton, 1826-1908. III. Society for the History of
Technology. IV. American Society for Metals. V. Metallurgical Society of
A.I.M.E. VI. T. VII. Series.
TN605.S62 1963      LC 65-17635

**Merriman, Arthur Douglas.**    • **5.6755**
A dictionary of metallurgy / by A. D. Merriman. — London: MacDonald &
Evans, 1958. xv, 401 p.: ill.; 29 cm. 1. Metallurgy — Dictionaries. I. T.
TN609.M475      LC 59-480

**Aitchison, Leslie.**    • **5.6756**
A history of metals / by Leslie Aitchison. — New York : Interscience
Publishers, 1960. 2v. (xxi, 647 p.): ill., facsims, maps; 29cm. 1. Metallurgy —
History. 2. Metal-work — History. 3. Art metal-work — History. I. T.
TN615.A5      669.09

**Dennis, William Herbert, 1904-.**    • **5.6757**
A hundred years of metallurgy. Chicago: Aldine Pub. Co., 1964,c1963. ix,
342 p.: ill.; 23 cm. 1. Metallurgy — History. I. T.
TN615.D4 1964      LC 64-12248

**Parr, J. Gordon (James Gordon), 1927-.**    • **5.6758**
Man, metals, and modern magic. — Cleveland: American Society for Metals,
1958. 238 p.: ill. 1. Metallurgy — History. 2. Metals I. T.
TN615.P3      LC 58-8631

**Tylecote, R. F.**    **5.6759**
A history of metallurgy / R. F. Tylecote. London: Metals Society, c1976. ix,
182 p.: ill.; 30 cm. 1. Metallurgy — History. I. T.
TN615.T94      669/.009      LC 77-361332      ISBN 0904357066

**Agricola, Georg, 1494-1555.**    • **5.6760**
De re metallica / Translated from the first Latin ed. of 1556, with biographical
introd., annotations, and appendices... by Herbert Clark Hoover and Lou
Henry Hoover. [New ed.] New York: Dover, 1950. xxxi, 638 p.: ill., facsim,; 28
cm. 1. Metallurgy — Early works to 1800. 2. Mineral industries — Early
works to 1800. I. Hoover, Herbert, 1874-1964. II. T.
TN617.A4 1950      LC 51-8994      ISBN 0486600068

**Gilchrist, James Duncan.**    **5.6761**
Extraction metallurgy / J. D. Gilchrist. — 2d ed. — Oxford; New York:
Pergamon Press, 1980. x, 456 p.: ill.; 22 cm. — (International series on
materials science and technology; v. 30) (Pergamon international library of
science, technology, engineering, and social studies) Includes index.
1. Metallurgy I. T.
TN665.G48 1980      669      LC 78-40820      ISBN 0080217117

**Nutt, Merle Caro.**    **5.6762**
Metallurgy & plastics for engineers / Merle C. Nutt. — Phoenix: Associated
Lithographers, c1976. xv, 550 p.: ill. 1. Metallurgy 2. Metals 3. Powder
metallurgy 4. Plastics I. T.
TN665 N79

**Pehlke, Robert D.**    **5.6763**
Unit processes of extractive metallurgy [by] Robert D. Pehlke. — New York:
American Elsevier Pub. Co., [c1973] xiv, 396 p.: illus.; 26 cm. 1. Metallurgy
I. T.
TN665.P422      669      LC 72-87210      ISBN 0444001301

**Tottle, C. R.**    **5.6764**
An encyclopaedia of metallurgy and materials / C.R. Tottle. — London: Metals
Society; Plymouth: Macdonald & Evans, 1984. ci, 380 p.: ill.; 29 cm.
1. Metallurgy — Dictionaries. I. T.
TN665.T6x      669/.003/21 19      ISBN 0712105719

**Smithells, Colin J. (Colin James)**    **5.6765**
Smithells metals reference book. — 6th ed. / editor Eric A. Brandes. —
London: Butterworths, 1983. 1 v. (various pagings): ill.; 26 cm. 1. Metals —
Handbooks, manuals, etc. I. Brandes, Eric A. (Eric Adolph) II. T. III. Title:
Metals reference book.
TN671.S6x      669/.00212 19      ISBN 0408710535

**Hyslop, Marjorie R.**                                5.6766
A brief guide to sources of metals information, by Marjorie R. Hyslop. — Washington: Information Resources Press, 1973. xi, 180 p.; 24 cm. 1. Metallurgy — Information services. I. T. II. Title: Metals information.
TN675.4.H95    669/.007    LC 72-87893    ISBN 0878150080

**Shewmon, Paul G.**                                  5.6767
Transformation in metal [by] Paul G. Shewmon. — New York: McGraw-Hill, [1969] xii, 394 p.: illus.; 23 cm. — (McGraw-Hill series in materials science and engineering) 1. Physical metallurgy I. T.
TN688.S46    669.9/4    LC 69-18723

## TN689.2–700 METALLOGRAPHY.
## PHYSICAL METALLURGY

**NATO Advanced Study Institute on Surface Modification and**    5.6768
**Alloying (1981: Trevi, Italy)**
Surface modification and alloying by laser, ion, and electron beams / edited by J.M. Poate, G. Foti, and D.C. Jacobson. — New York: Published in cooperation with NATO Scientific Affairs Division [by] Plenum Press, c1983. x, 414 p.: ill.; 26 cm. — (NATO conference series. Materials science. v. 8) Proceedings of a NATO Advanced Study Institute on Surface Modification and Alloying, held Aug. 24-28, 1981, in Trevi, Italy. 1. Metals — Surfaces — Congresses. 2. Metals — Effect of radiation on — Congresses. 3. Alloys — Congresses. 4. Laser beams — Congresses. 5. Ion bombardment — Congresses. 6. Electron beams — Congresses. I. Poate, J. M. II. Foti, G. III. Jacobson, D. C. IV. North Atlantic Treaty Organization. Scientific Affairs Division. V. T. VI. Series.
TN689.2.N35 1981    671.7 19    LC 83-9465    ISBN 0306413736

**Symposium on Metallography in Failure Analysis, Houston,**    5.6769
**Tex., 1977.**
Metallography in failure analysis: [proceedings of a Symposium on Metallography in Failure Analysis / sponsored by the American Society for Metals and the International Metallographic Society, held in Houston, Texas, July 17–18, 1977]; edited by James L. McCall and P. M. French. — New York: Plenum Press, c1978. vii, 301 p.: ill.; 26 cm. Includes indexes. 1. Metallography — Congresses. 2. Fracture mechanics — Congresses. I. McCall, James L. II. French, P. M. (Peter Michael), 1935- III. American Society for Metals. IV. International Metallographic Society. V. T.
TN689.2.S88 1977    620.1/6/3    LC 78-7224    ISBN 030640012X

**Andrews, Kenneth William.**                         5.6770
Physical metallurgy: techniques and applications / by K. W. Andrews. — New York: Wiley, 1973. 2 v.: ill.; 24 cm. 'A Halsted Press book.' 1. Physical metallurgy I. T.
TN690.A64    669/.9    LC 72-11308    ISBN 0470031506

**Devereux, Owen F. (Owen Francis), 1937-.**          5.6771
Topics in metallurgical thermodynamics / Owen F. Devereux. — New York: Wiley, c1983. xiii, 494 p.: ill.; 24 cm. 'A Wiley-Interscience publication.' 1. Physical metallurgy 2. Thermodynamics I. T.
TN690.D47 1983    669/.9 19    LC 83-1115    ISBN 0471869635

**Elliott, Roy, Ph. D.**                              5.6772
Eutectic solidification processing: crystalline and glassy alloys / Roy Elliott. — London; Boston: Butterworths, 1983. 370 p.: ill.; 24 cm. — (Butterworths monographs in metals) 1. Eutectic alloys 2. Solidification I. T.
TN690.E536 1983    669/.94 19    LC 83-7464    ISBN 0408107146

**Flemings, Merton C., 1929-.**                       5.6773
Solidification processing [by] Merton C. Flemings. — New York: McGraw-Hill, [1974] x, 364 p.: illus.; 24 cm. — (McGraw-Hill series in materials science and engineering) 1. Solidification 2. Alloys I. T.
TN690.F59    669/.9    LC 73-4261    ISBN 007021283X

**Guy, Albert G.**                                    5.6774
Elements of physical metallurgy [by] Albert G. Guy and John J. Hren. — 3d ed. — Reading, Mass.: Addison-Wesley, [1974] xv, 618 p.: illus.; 25 cm. — (Addison-Wesley series in metallurgy and materials) 1. Physical metallurgy I. Hren, John J. joint author. II. T.
TN690.G895 1974    669/.9    LC 72-9315    ISBN 0201026333

**Martin, J. W. (John Wilson), 1926-.**               5.6775
Stability of microstructure in metallic systems / J. W. Martin, R. D. Doherty. — Cambridge [Eng.]; New York: Cambridge University Press, 1976. x, 298 p.: ill.; 22 cm. (Cambridge solid state science series) Includes index. 1. Physical metallurgy I. Doherty, R. D., joint author. II. T.
TN690.M2664    669/.94    LC 75-38189

**Murr, Lawrence Eugene.**                            5.6776
Interfacial phenomena in metals and alloys / Lawrence E. Murr; with a foreword by Morris Cohen. — Reading, Mass.: Addison-Wesley Pub. Co.,

Advanced Book Program, 1975. xiv, 376 p.: ill.; 24 cm. 1. Physical metallurgy 2. Surfaces (Technology) 3. Metals 4. Alloys I. T.
TN690.M87    669/.95    LC 74-30394    ISBN 0201048841

**Physical metallurgy / edited by R.W. Cahn, P. Haasen.**    5.6777
3rd rev. and enl. ed. — Amsterdam; New York: North-Holland Physics Pub.; New York, N.Y., U.S.A.: Sole distributors for the USA and Canada, Elsevier Science Pub. Co., 1983. 2 v. (xxxiv, 1957, 16 p.): ill.; 25 cm. 1. Physical metallurgy I. Cahn, R. W. (Robert W.), 1924- II. Haasen, P. (Peter)
TN690.P44 1983    669/.94 19    LC 83-17292    ISBN 0444866280

**Reed-Hill, Robert E.**                              5.6778
Physical metallurgy principles [by] Robert E. Reed-Hill. — 2d ed. — New York: Van Nostrand, [1972, c1973] xiii, 920 p.: illus.; 24 cm. — (University series in basic engineering) 1. Physical metallurgy I. T.
TN690.R43 1973    669/.9    LC 79-181094    ISBN 0442068646

**Smallman, R. E.**                                   5.6779
Modern physical metallurgy / R.E. Smallman. — 4th ed. — London; Boston: Butterworths, 1985. 530 p.: ill.; 24 cm. 1. Physical metallurgy I. T.
TN690.S56 1985    669/.9 19    LC 84-23884    ISBN 0408710500

**Verhoeven, John D., 1934-.**                        5.6780
Fundamentals of physical metallurgy / John D. Verhoeven. — New York: Wiley, [1975] xiii, 567 p.: ill.; 23 cm. 1. Physical metallurgy I. T.
TN690.V46    669/.9    LC 75-4600    ISBN 0471906166

**Westbrook, J. H. (Jack Hall), 1924- ed.**           5.6781
Intermetallic compounds / edited by J. H. Westbrook. — Huntington, N.Y.: R. E. Krieger Pub. Co., 1977, c1967. xvii, 663 p.: ill.; 24 cm. Reprint of the ed. published by Wiley, New York, in series: Wiley series on the science and technology of materials. 1. Intermetallic compounds I. T.
TN690.W47 1977    669/.94    LC 76-30325    ISBN 0882754947

**Mondolfo, L. F. (Lucio F.)**                        5.6782
Aluminum alloys: structure and properties / L. F. Mondolfo. — London; Boston: Butterworths, 1976. ix, 971 p.: ill.; 24 cm. Errata slip inserted. 1. Aluminum alloys I. T.
TN693.A5 M58    669/.722    LC 76-373472    ISBN 0408706805

**Leslie, William C., 1920-.**                        5.6783
The physical metallurgy of steels / William C. Leslie. — Washington: Hemisphere Pub. Corp.; New York: McGraw-Hill, c1981. xii, 396 p.: ill.; 24 cm. — (McGraw-Hill series in materials science and engineering) 1. Steel — Metallurgy I. T.
TN693.I7 L45    669/.96142 19    LC 80-28332    ISBN 0070377804

**Collings, E. W.**                                   5.6784
Applied superconductivity, metallurgy, and physics of titanium alloys / E.W. Collings. — New York: Plenum Press, c1986. 2 v.: ill.; 24 cm. (International cryogenics monograph series.) 1. Titanium alloys — Electric properties. 2. Titanium alloys — Metallurgy. 3. Superconductivity I. T. II. Series.
TN693.T5 C625 1986    673/.7322 19    LC 85-12063    ISBN 0306416905

## TN703–757 IRON AND STEEL
## METALLURGY

**Dennis, William Herbert, 1904-.**                 • 5.6785
Metallurgy of the ferrous metals / by W. H. Dennis. — London: Pitman, 1963. xi, 393 p.: ill.; 23 cm. 1. Iron — Metallurgy 2. Steel — Metallurgy I. T.
TN705.D47    LC 65-1208

**Peacey, J. G.**                                     5.6786
The iron blast furnace: theory and practice / by G. Peacey, W. G. Davenport. — Oxford; New York: Pergamon Press, 1979. xiii, 251 p.: ill.; 22 cm. — (International series on materials science and technology; v. 31) (Pergamon international library of science, technology, engineering, and social studies) 1. Blast-furnaces I. Davenport, W. G. (William George) joint author. II. T.
TN713.P42 1979    669/.1413    LC 78-40823    ISBN 0080232183

**The Making, shaping, and treating of steel / edited by William**    5.6787
**T. Lankford, Jr. ... [et al.]; United States Steel.**
10th ed. — [Pittsburgh, Pa.]: Association of Iron and Steel Engineers, c1985. xvii, 1572 p.: ill.; 28 cm. 1. Steel — Metallurgy I. Lankford, William T. II. United States Steel Corporation. III. Association of Iron and Steel Engineers.
TN730.M35 1985    669.1/42 19    LC 84-81539    ISBN 0930767004

## TN758–799 METALLURGY OF NON-FERROUS METALS

**Dennis, William Herbert, 1904-.**     • **5.6788**
Metallurgy of the non-ferrous metals. — London: Pitman, 1954. 647 p.: ill.
1. Nonferrous metals — Metallurgy I. T.
TN758.D44    TN758.D41.    *LC* 55-558

**Topics in non-ferrous extractive metallurgy / edited by A. R.**    **5.6789**
**Burkin.**
New York: Wiley, 1980. x, 134 p.: ill.; 24 cm. — (Critical reports on applied
chemistry. v. 1) 'A Halsted Press book.' 1. Nonferrous metals — Metallurgy
I. Burkin, A. R. (Alfred Richard) II. Series.
TN758.T65 1980    669    *LC* 80-17435    *ISBN* 0470270160

**Barry, B. T. K.**    **5.6790**
Tin and its alloys and compounds / B.T.K. Barry and C.J. Thwaites. —
Chichester: Ellis Horwood; New York: Halsted Press, 1983. 268 p.: ill.; 24 cm.
— (Ellis Horwood series in industrial metals.) 1. Tin 2. Tin alloys 3. Tin
compounds I. Thwaites, C. J. (Colin John), 1927- II. T. III. Series.
TN793.B37 1983    669/.6 19    *LC* 83-12760    *ISBN* 0470274808

**Betteridge, W. (Walter), 1911-.**    **5.6791**
Nickel and its alloys / W. Betteridge. — Chichester, West Sussex, England:
Ellis Horwood; New York: Halsted Press, 1984. 211 p.: ill.; 24 cm. — (Ellis
Horwood series in industrial metals.) 'Expanded version of an earlier text'—
Pref. 1. Nickel 2. Nickel alloys I. T. II. Series.
TN799.N6 B45 1984    669/.7332 19    *LC* 84-12796    *ISBN*
0853127298

## TN799.5–948 Nonmetallic Minerals

**Harben, P. W.**    **5.6792**
Geology of the nonmetallics / Peter W. Harben, Robert L. Bates. — 1st ed. —
New York, N.Y.: Metal Bulletin Inc., 1984. — vi, 392 p.: ill., maps; 24 cm.
1. Nonmetallic minerals — Handbooks, manuals, etc. I. Bates, Robert
Latimer, 1912- II. T.
TN799.5.H37 1984    *ISBN* 0913333026

## TN800–879 COAL. PETROLEUM

**Coal and modern coal processing: an introduction / edited by G.**    **5.6793**
**J. Pitt and G. R. Millward.**
London: Academic Press, 1979. xiii, 210 p.: ill.; 24 cm. 1. Coal I. Pitt, G. J.
II. Millward, G. R.
TN800.C6    *LC* 78-75271    *ISBN* 0125578504

**Simeons, Charles.**    **5.6794**
Coal, its role in tomorrow's technology: a sourcebook on global coal resources /
by Charles Simeons. — Oxford; New York: Pergamon Press, 1978. xv, 313 p.:
ill.; 26 cm. Includes index. 1. Coal I. T.
TN800.S49 1978    553.2    *LC* 78-40827    *ISBN* 0080227120

**Coal age operating handbook of underground mining / edited by**    **5.6795**
**Nicholas P. Chironis.**
New York: Coal Age Mining Informational Services, c1977. vi, 410 p.: ill.; 29
cm. — (Coal age library of operating handbooks. v. 1) Includes index. 1. Coal
mines and mining — Handbooks, manuals, etc. I. Chironis, Nicholas P.
II. Series.
TN802.C64    622/.33    *LC* 77-85375    *ISBN* 0070114579

**Britton, Scott G., 1954-.**    **5.6796**
Practical coal mine management / Scott G. Britton. — New York: Wiley,
c1981. xi, 233 p.: ill.; 24 cm. 'A Wiley-Interscience Publication.' Includes index.
1. Coal mines and mining — Management. I. T.
TN803.B75    622/.334/0685 19    *LC* 81-11426    *ISBN* 0471090352

**Schmidt, Richard A.**    **5.6797**
Coal in America: an encyclopedia of reserves, production, and use / by Richard
A. Schmidt. — New York: Coal Week, McGraw-Hill Publications Co., c1979.
xv, 458 p.: ill.; 25 cm. 1. Coal — United States. I. T.
TN805.A5 S35    333.8/2    *LC* 78-11372

**Tver, David F.**    **5.6798**
The petroleum dictionary / David F. Tver, Richard W. Berry. — New York:
Van Nostrand Reinhold Co., c1980. vi, 374 p.: ill.; 24 cm. 1. Petroleum —
Dictionaries. I. Berry, Richard W., 1933- joint author. II. T.
TN865.T83    553/.282/03    *LC* 79-19346    *ISBN* 0442240465

**Whitehead, Harry.**    **5.6799**
An A–Z of offshore oil & gas: an illustrated international glossary and reference
guide to the offshore oil & gas industries and their technology / Harry
Whitehead. — 2nd ed. — Houston, Tex.: Gulf Pub. Co., Book Division, 1983.
438 p.: ill.; 29 cm. 1. Petroleum in submerged lands — Dictionaries. 2. Gas,
Natural, in submerged lands — Dictionaries. 3. Offshore oil industry —
Directories. 4. Offshore gas industry — Directories. I. T. II. Title: A to Z of
offshore oil and gas.
TN865.W48 1983    622/.338/09162 19    *LC* 82-84656    *ISBN*
087201052X

**Amyx, James W.**    **5.6800**
Petroleum reservoir engineering / James W. Amyx, Daniel M. Bass, Jr., Robert
L. Whiting. — New York: McGraw-Hill, 1960-. v.: ill.; 24 cm. 1. Oil fields
2. Petroleum engineering I. T.
TN870.A66    *LC* 59-13191

**Archer, J. S. (John S)**    **5.6801**
Petroleum engineering: principles and practice / J.S. Archer and C.G. Wall. —
London: Graham & Trotman, 1986. 362 p.: ill. 1. Petroleum engineering
I. Wall, C. G. (Colin G) II. T.
TN870    TN870 A74 1986.    622/.3382 19    *ISBN* 0860106659

**Institute of Petroleum (Great Britain)**    **5.6802**
Modern petroleum technology. Edited by G. D. Hobson, in collaboration with
W. Pohl. 4th ed. New York, Wiley [1973] xiii, 996 p. illus. 26 cm. 'A Halsted
Press book.' 1. Petroleum engineering I. Hobson, George Douglas. ed. II. T.
TN870.I48 1973    665/.5    *LC* 73-1020    *ISBN* 0470401559

**Landes, Kenneth Knight, 1899-.**    • **5.6803**
Petroleum geology. — 2d ed. — New York: Wiley, 1959. 443 p.: ill., maps.
1. Petroleum — Geology I. T.
TN870.L25 1959    *LC* 59-14987

**Pratt, Wallace Everett, 1885-.**    • **5.6804**
World geography of petroleum / edited by Wallace E. Pratt and Dorothy Good.
— [Princeton]: Published for the American Geographical Society by Princeton
University Press, 1950. xvii, 464 p.: ill., maps (1 fold. col.). — (American
Geographical Society. Special publication; no. 31) 1. Petroleum I. Good,
Dorothy. II. T.
TN870.P73    TN870.P91.    *LC* 50-11069

**Riva, Joseph P.**    **5.6805**
World petroleum resources and reserves / Joseph P. Riva, Jr. — Boulder, Colo.:
Westview Press, 1983. xxiii, 355 p.: ill.; 24 cm. — (A Westview special study)
1. Petroleum 2. Petroleum — Reserves I. T.
TN870.R53 1983    333.8/23 19    *LC* 82-13625    *ISBN* 0865314462

**Peaceman, Donald W.**    **5.6806**
Fundamentals of numerical reservoir simulation / Donald W. Peaceman. —
Amsterdam; New York: Elsevier Scientific Pub. Co.: distributors for the U.S.
and Canada, Elsevier North-Holland, 1977. xiii, 176 p.: ill.; 25 cm. —
(Developments in petroleum science. 6) Includes index. 1. Oil reservoir
engineering — Mathematical models. 2. Oil reservoir engineering — Data
processing. I. T. II. Series.
TN871.P37    622/.18/282    *LC* 77-4771    *ISBN* 0444415785

**Subsurface geology: petroleum, mining, construction.**    **5.6807**
5th ed. / edited by L.W. LeRoy ... [et al.]. — Golden, Colo.: Colorado School of
Mines, 1987. 1156 p. Includes index. 1. Petroleum — Geology 2. Engineering
geology 3. Mining geology I. LeRoy, L. W. (Leslie Walter), 1909-
TN871.15.S9 1987    622/.01/55 19    *LC* 86-18806    *ISBN*
0918062683

# TP CHEMICAL TECHNOLOGY

## TP1–151 General Works

**Chemical and process technology encyclopedia / editor–in–chief,**    5.6808
**Douglas M. Considine.**
New York: McGraw-Hill, [1974] xxix, 1261 p.: ill.; 24 cm. 1. Chemistry,
Technical — Dictionaries. I. Considine, Douglas Maxwell. ed.
TP9.C49    660/.03    *LC* 73-12913    *ISBN* 007012423X

**Encyclopedia of chemical technology / editorial board, Herman**    5.6809
**F. Mark ... [et al.]; executive editor, Martin Grayson, associate**
**editor, David Eckroth.**
3d ed. — New York: Wiley, c1978-c1984. 31 v.: ill.; 26 cm. At head of title:
Kirk-Othmer. 'A Wiley-Interscience publication.' Errata slips inserted.
Includes supplement volume issued in 1984 and separately published index
volumes for v. 1-4, 5-8, 9-12, 13-16, 17-20; and a cumulative index to v. 1-24 and
the supplement volume. 1. Chemistry, Technical — Dictionaries. I. Kirk,
Raymond E. (Raymond Eller), 1890-1957. II. Othmer, Donald F. (Donald
Frederick), 1904- III. Grayson, Martin. IV. Eckroth, David. V. Title: Kirk-
Othmer encyclopedia of chemical technology.
TP9.E685 1978    660/.03/21 19    *LC* 77-15820    *ISBN* 0471020370

**Gardner, William, d. 1943.**    5.6810
Chemical synonyms and trade names: a dictionary and commercial handbook
containing over 35,500 definitions / by William Gardner. — 8th ed., rev. and
enl. / by Edward I. Cooke and Richard W.I. Cooke. — Oxford: Technical
Press, c1978. 769 p.; 25 cm. Includes index. 1. Chemicals — Dictionaries.
2. Chemicals — Trademarks. I. Cooke, Edward Ingram. II. Cooke, Richard
W. I. III. T.
TP9.G28 1978    660/.03    *LC* 77-85232    *ISBN* 029139678X

**Haynes, Williams, 1886-1960.**    • 5.6811
American chemical industry. New York, Van Nostrand, 1945-[54; v. 1, 1954] 6
v. illus., ports. 25 cm. 1. Chemicals — Manufacture and industry — United
States. I. T.
TP23.H37    660.973    *LC* 46-359

**Clausen, Chris A., 1940-.**    5.6812
Principles of industrial chemistry / Chris A. Clausen III, Guy Mattson. — New
York: Wiley, c1978. xiv, 412 p.: ill.; 24 cm. 'A Wiley-Interscience publication.'
1. Chemistry, Technical I. Mattson, Guy. joint author. II. T.
TP145.C67    660.2    *LC* 78-9450    *ISBN* 047102774X

**Holland, Charles Donald.**    5.6813
Fundamentals of chemical reaction engineering / Charles D. Holland, Rayford
G. Anthony. — Englewood Cliffs, N.J.: Prentice-Hall, c1979. xiv, 541 p.: ill.; 24
cm. — (Prentice-Hall international series in the physical and chemical
engineering sciences) 1. Chemical engineering 2. Chemical reactions
I. Anthony, Rayford Gaines, 1935- joint author. II. T.
TP145.H64    660.2/9/9    *LC* 78-18372    *ISBN* 0133355969

**Reuben, B. G.**    5.6814
The chemical economy: a guide to the technology and economics of the
chemical industry / [by] B. G. Reuben and M. L. Burstall. — [London]:
Longmans [1974] xix, 530 p.: ill.; 26 cm. 1. Chemistry, Technical 2. Chemical
industry I. Burstall, M. L. joint author. II. T.
TP145.R47    338.4/7/66    *LC* 73-85210    *ISBN* 0582463076

**Riegel, Emil Raymond, 1882-1963.**    5.6815
[Handbook of industrial chemistry] Riegel's Handbook of industrial chemistry.
— 8th ed. / edited by James A. Kent. — New York: Van Nostrand Reinhold
Co., c1983. ix, 979 p.: ill.; 26 cm. 1. Chemistry, Technical I. Kent, James
Albert, 1922- II. T. III. Title: Handbook of industrial chemistry.
TP145.R54 1983    660 19    *LC* 82-4806    *ISBN* 0442201648

**Austin, D. G.**    5.6816
Chemical engineering drawing symbols / D. G. Austin. — London: G.
Godwin; New York: J. Wiley, 1979. xv, 96 p.: ill.; 31 cm. Includes index.
1. Chemical engineering — Notation. 2. Engineering drawings I. T.
TP149.A97 1979    604/.2/6602148    *LC* 79-317439    *ISBN*
0470266015

**Caglioti, Luciano.**    5.6817
[Due volti della chimica. English] The two faces of chemistry / Luciano
Caglioti; translated by Mirella Giacconi. — Cambridge, Mass.: MIT Press,

c1983. xvi, 218 p.: ill.; 24 cm. Translation of: I due volti della chimica. Includes
index. 1. Chemical engineering — Social aspects. I. T.
TP149.C2513 1983    363.1/72 19    *LC* 82-12706    *ISBN* 0262030888

**Handbook of chemical engineering calculations / Nicholas P.**    5.6818
**Chopey, editor, Tyler G. Hicks, series editor.**
New York: McGraw-Hill, c1984. 1 v. (various pagings): ill.; 24 cm.
1. Chemical engineering — Mathematics. I. Chopey, Nicholas P.
TP149.H285 1984    660.2/0212 19    *LC* 83-9435    *ISBN* 0070108056

**Hinchen, John D.**    • 5.6819
Practical statistics for chemical research, by John D. Hinchen. — London:
Methuen, and Science Paperbacks, 1969. vii, 116 p.: illus.; 23 cm. Distributed in
U.S.A. by Barnes & Noble. 1. Chemical engineering — Statistical methods.
I. T.
TP149.H55    519/.024/54    *LC* 71-409992    *ISBN* 0416466702

**Reklaitis, G. V., 1942-.**    5.6820
Introduction to material and energy balances / G.V. Reklaitis; with
contributions by Daniel R. Schneider. — New York: Wiley, c1983. xiv, 683 p.:
ill.; 25 cm. 1. Chemical engineering — Mathematics. 2. Mathematical
optimization 3. Nonlinear programming I. Schneider, Daniel R. II. T.
TP149.R44 1983    620/.0042 19    *LC* 82-23800    *ISBN* 0471041319

**Smith, J. M. (Joseph Mauck), 1916-.**    5.6821
Introduction to chemical engineering thermodynamics / J.M. Smith, H.C. Van
Ness. — 4th ed. — New York: McGraw-Hill, c1987. xii, 698 p.: ill.; 25 cm. —
(McGraw-Hill chemical engineering series.) 1. Thermodynamics 2. Chemical
engineering I. Van Hess, H.C. (Hendrick C.) II. T. III. Series.
TP149.S582 1987    660.2/969 19    *LC* 86-7184    *ISBN* 0070587035

## TP151 HANDBOOKS. TABLES

**The Chemical formulary: a condensed collection of valuable,**    5.6822
**timely, practical formulae for making thousands of products in**
**all fields of industry / editor–in–chief, H. Bennett.**
New York: Chemical Pub. Co., 1933-. 20 v.; 23 cm. Includes indexes.
1. Chemistry, Technical — Formulae, receipts, prescriptions I. Bennett,
Harry.
TP151.B35

**Chemical Technician Curriculum Project. Writing Team.**    5.6823
Chemical technology handbook: guidebook for industrial chemical
technologists and technicians / by the Writing Team for the Chemical
Technician Curriculum Project; edited by Robert L. Pecsok, Kenneth
Chapman and Wade H. Ponder. — Washington: American Chemical Society,
1975. 215 p.: ill.; 25 cm. 'The Chemical technology handbook is the revised
version, with additional chapters, of the guidebook from the series, 'Modern
chemical technology,' which was developed by the Chemical Technician
Curriculum Project (ChemTeC).' 1. Chemistry, Technical — Handbooks,
manuals, etc. I. Pecsok, Robert L. II. Chapman, Kenneth. III. Ponder, Wade
H. IV. T.
TP151.C575 1975    660    *LC* 75-22497    *ISBN* 0841202427

**Himmelblau, David Mautner, 1923-.**    5.6824
Basic principles and calculations in chemical engineering / David M.
Himmelblau. — 4th ed. — Englewood Cliffs, N.J.: Prentice-Hall, c1982. xii,
628 p.: ill. (1 fold. in pocket); 24 cm. (Prentice-Hall international series in the
physical and chemical engineering sciences). 1. Chemical engineering —
Tables. I. T. II. Series.
TP151.H5 1982    660.2 19    *LC* 81-19175    *ISBN* 0130664987

**Hopp, Vollrath.**    5.6825
[Chemie Kompendium für das Selbstudium. English] Handbook of applied
chemistry: facts for engineers, scientists, technicians, and technical managers /
Vollrath Hopp, Ingo Hennig. — Washington: Hemisphere Pub. Corp.; New
York: McGraw-Hill, c1983. 1 v. (various pagings): ill.; 24 cm. Translation of:
Chemie Kompendium für das Selbstudium. 1. Chemistry, Technical —
Handbooks, manuals, etc. I. Hennig, Ingo. II. T.
TP151.H5813 1983    660.2 19    *LC* 83-310    *ISBN* 0070303207

**Mel'nik, B. D. (Boris Davydovich)**    5.6826
[Kratkiĭ inzhenernyĭ spravochnik po tekhnologii neorganicheskikh veshchestv.
English] Technology of inorganic compounds [by] B.D. Mel'nik and E.B.
Mel'nikov. Translated from Russian by R. Kondor. Translation edited by D.
Slutzkin. Jerusalem, Israel Program for Scientific Translations, 1970. iv, 248 p.
illus. 25 cm. Translation of Kratkiĭ inzhenernyĭ spravochnik po tekhnologii
neorganicheskikh veshchestv. 1. Chemical engineering — Graphic methods.
2. Chemicals — Manufacture and industry. I. Mel'nikov, E. B. (Evgeniĭ
Borisovich) joint author. II. T.
TP151.M413    661/.0021/2    *LC* 72-175914

**Perry's Chemical engineers' handbook.**      **5.6827**
6th ed. / prepared by a staff of specialists under the editorial direction of late editor Robert H. Perry; editor, Don W. Green; assistant editor, James O. Maloney. — New York: McGraw-Hill, c1984. 1 v. (various pagings): 1846 ill.; 27 cm. Rev. ed. of: Chemical engineers' handbook. 5th ed. 1973. 1. Chemical engineering — Handbooks, manuals, etc. I. Perry, Robert H., 1924- II. Green, Don W. III. Maloney, James O. IV. Chemical engineers' handbook.
TP151.P45 1984     660.2/8 19     *LC* 84-837     *ISBN* 0070494797

**Strauss, Howard J.**      **5.6828**
Handbook for chemical technicians / Howard J. Strauss; edited by Milton Kaufman. New York: McGraw-Hill, c1976. 455 p. in various pagings: ill.; 24 cm. Includes index. 1. Chemistry, Technical — Handbooks, manuals, etc. I. T.
TP151.S89     542     *LC* 76-10459     *ISBN* 0070621640

# TP155–197 Chemical Engineering

**Coulson, J. M. (John Metcalfe)**      **5.6829**
Chemical engineering / by J.M. Coulson and J.F. Richardson. — 2nd ed. (SI units). — Oxford; New York: Pergamon Press, < 1979- > . 6 v.: ill.; 26 cm. — (Pergamon international library of science, technology, engineering, and social studies.) 1. Chemical engineering I. Richardson, J. F. (John Francis) II. T. III. Series.
TP155.C69 1979     660.2 19     *LC* 79-40177     *ISBN* 0080238181

**Franks, Roger G. E.**      **5.6830**
Modeling and simulation in chemical engineering [by] Roger G. E. Franks. — New York: Wiley-Interscience, 1972. xiii, 411 p.: illus.; 24 cm. 1. Chemical engineering — Mathematical models. 2. Digital computer simulation I. T.
TP155.F724     660/.2/0184     *LC* 72-39717     *ISBN* 0471275352

**Myers, Alan L., 1932-.**      **5.6831**
Introduction to chemical engineering and computer calculations / Alan L. Myers and Warren D. Seider. — Englewood Cliffs, N.J.: Prentice-Hall, c1976. xx, 524 p.: ill.; 24 cm. (Prentice-Hall international series in the physical and chemical engineering sciences) 1. Chemical engineering 2. Chemical engineering — Mathematics. 3. Chemical engineering — Data processing I. Seider, Warren D. joint author. II. T.
TP155.M9     660.2     *LC* 75-15984     *ISBN* 0134792386

**Sherwood, Thomas Kilgore, 1903-1976.**      **5.6832**
A course in process design. Cambridge, Mass.: M.I.T. Press, 1963. 254 p. illus. 24 cm. 1. Chemical engineering I. T.
TP155.S45     660.28     *LC* 63-18727

**Luyben, William L.**      **5.6833**
Process modeling, simulation, and control for chemical engineers [by] W. L. Luyben. New York, McGraw-Hill [1973] xvii, 558 p. illus. 24 cm. (McGraw-Hill chemical engineering series) 1. Chemical processes — Mathematical models. 2. Chemical processes — Data processing 3. Chemical process control I. T.
TP155.7.L88     660.2/81     *LC* 74-173713     *ISBN* 0070391572

**Perlmutter, Daniel D.**      **5.6833a**
Introduction to chemical process control / Daniel D. Perlmutter. — New York: Wiley, 1965. xii, 204 p.: ill.; 24 cm. 1. Chemical process control 2. Process control I. T.
TP155.7.P38     660.2/84     *LC* 65-24925

**Resnick, William, 1922-.**      **5.6834**
Process analysis and design for chemical engineers / William Resnick. — New York: McGraw-Hill, c1981. xix, 363 p.: ill.; 25 cm. — (McGraw-Hill chemical engineering series) Includes index. 1. Chemical processes I. T.
TP155.7.R47     660.2     *LC* 80-10678     *ISBN* 0070518874

**Rudd, Dale F.**      **5.6835**
Process synthesis [by] Dale F. Rudd, Gary J. Powers [and] Jeffrey J. Siirola. — Englewood Cliffs, N.J.: Prentice-Hall, [1973] xi, 320 p.: illus.; 25 cm. — (Prentice-Hall international series in the physical and chemical engineering sciences) 1. Chemical processes 2. Chemical engineering I. Powers, Gary J., 1945- joint author. II. Siirola, Jeffrey J., 1945- joint author. III. T.
TP155.7.R83     660.2/8     *LC* 73-3331     *ISBN* 0137233531

**Ulrich, Gael D.**      **5.6836**
A guide to chemical engineering process design and economics / Gael D. Ulrich. — New York: Wiley, 1983. viii, 472 p.: ill.; 27 cm. 1. Chemical processes I. T.
TP155.7.U46 1983     660.2/81 19     *LC* 83-6919     *ISBN* 0471082767

**Stephanopoulos, George.**      **5.6837**
Chemical process control: an introduction to theory and practice / George Stephanopoulos. — Englewood Cliffs, N.J.: Prentice-Hall, c1984. xxi, 696 p.: ill.; 24 cm. — (Prentice-Hall international series in the physical and chemical engineering sciences.) 1. Chemical process control I. T. II. Series.
TP155.75.S73 1984     660.281 19     *LC* 83-11206     *ISBN* 0131286293

**Ruthven, Douglas M. (Douglas Morris), 1938-.**      **5.6838**
Principles of adsorption and adsorption processes / Douglas M. Ruthven. — New York: Wiley, c1984. xxiv, 433 p.: ill.; 24 cm. 'A Wiley-Interscience publication.' Includes indexes. 1. Adsorption 2. Separation (Technology) I. T.
TP156.A35 R8 1984     660.2/8423 19     *LC* 83-16904     *ISBN* 0471866067

**Satterfield, Charles N.**      **5.6839**
Heterogeneous catalysis in practice / Charles N. Satterfield. — New York: McGraw-Hill, c1980. xvi, 416 p.: ill.; 25 cm. — (McGraw-Hill chemical engineering series) Includes index. 1. Heterogeneous catalysis I. T.
TP156.C35 S27     660.2/995     *LC* 80-10513     *ISBN* 0070548757

**Cussler, E. L.**      **5.6840**
Diffusion, mass transfer in fluid systems / E.L. Cussler. — Cambridge [Cambridgeshire]; New York: Cambridge University Press, 1984. xii, 525 p.: ill.; 24 cm. 1. Diffusion 2. Mass transfer 3. Fluids I. T.
TP156.D47 C878 1984     660.2/8423 19     *LC* 83-1905     *ISBN* 052123171X

**Rademaker, O.**      **5.6841**
Dynamics and control of continuous distillation units / O. Rademaker, J. E. Rijnsdorp, and A. Maarleveld. — Amsterdam; New York: Elsevier Scientific Pub. Co., 1975. 726 p.: ill.; 25 cm. Includes index. 1. Distillation 2. Automatic control I. Rijnsdorp, John E. joint author. II. Maarleveld, A., joint author. III. T.
TP156.D5 R3     660.2/8425     *LC* 74-83315     *ISBN* 0444412344

**Azbel, David.**      **5.6842**
Two–phase flows in chemical engineering / David Azbel; with editorial assistance by Philip Kemp–Pritchard. — Cambridge; New York: Cambridge University Press, 1981. xx, 311 p.: ill.; 24 cm. 1. Two-phase flow 2. Chemical engineering I. Kemp-Pritchard, Philip. II. T.
TP156.F6 A98     660.2 19     *LC* 80-20936     *ISBN* 0521237726

**Fluidization / edited by J.F. Davidson, R. Clift, D. Harrison.**      **5.6843**
2nd ed. — London; Orlando: Academic Press, 1985. xiv, 733 p.: ill.; 24 cm. 1. Fluidization I. Davidson, J. F. (John Frank) II. Clift, R. (Roland) III. Harrison, D. (David).
TP156.F65 F564 1985     660.2/84292 19     *LC* 84-10962     *ISBN* 0122055527

**Yates, J. G.**      **5.6844**
Fundamentals of fluidized–bed chemical processes / J. G. Yates. — London: Rutterworth, 1983. xiii, 222 p.: ill. (Butterworths monographs in chemical engineering) 1. Fluidization I. T. II. Series.
TP156.F65 Y2x 1983     660.2/842 19     *ISBN* 040870909X

**Treybal, Robert Ewald, 1915-.**      **5.6845**
Mass–transfer operations / Robert E. Treybal. — 3d ed. — New York: McGraw-Hill, c1980. xiv, 784 p.: ill.; 25 cm. — (McGraw-Hill chemical engineering series) 1. Chemical engineering 2. Mass transfer I. T.
TP156.M3 T7 1980     660.2/8422     *LC* 78-27876     *ISBN* 0070651760

**Oldshue, James Y.**      **5.6846**
Fluid mixing technology / James Y. Oldshue. — New York, N.Y.: Chemical Engineering, McGraw-Hill Publications Co., c1983. xvi, 574 p.: ill.; 24 cm. 1. Mixing 2. Fluids I. T.
TP156.M5 O4 1983     660.2/84292 19     *LC* 82-22160     *ISBN* 0076067149

**Handbook of powder science and technology / edited by M.E.**      **5.6847**
**Fayed, L. Otten.**
New York: Van Nostrand Reinhold Co., c1984. xiv, 850 p.: ill.; 26 cm. 1. Particles 2. Powders I. Fayed, M. E. (Muhammad E.) II. Otten, L. (Lambert)
TP156.P3 H35 1984     620/.43 19     *LC* 83-6828     *ISBN* 0442226101

**Perrin, D. D. (Douglas Dalzell), 1922-.**      **5.6848**
Purification of laboratory chemicals / D. D. Perrin and W. L. F. Armarego and D. R. Perrin. — 2d ed. — Oxford; New York: Pergamon Press, 1980. x, 568 p.; 26 cm. Includes index. 1. Chemicals — Purification. I. Armarego, W. L. F. joint author. II. Perrin, Dawn R. joint author. III. T.
TP156.P83 P47 1980     542     *LC* 79-41708     *ISBN* 0080229611

**Brian, P. L. Thibaut, 1930-.**      **5.6849**
Staged cascades in chemical processing [by] P. L. Thibaut Brian. — Englewood Cliffs, N.J.: Prentice-Hall, [1972] xi, 275 p.: illus.; 24 cm. — (Prentice Hall

international series in the physical and chemical engineering sciences) 1. Separation (Technology) 2. Chemical processes I. T.
TP156.S45 B75    660.2/8424    *LC* 79-181496    *ISBN* 0138402809

**Handbook of separation techniques for chemical engineers /**    **5.6850**
**Philip A. Schweitzer, editor–in–chief.**
New York: McGraw-Hill, 1979. ca. 1200 p. in various pagings: ill.; 24 cm. 'A James Peter book.' 1. Separation (Technology) — Handbooks, manuals, etc. I. Schweitzer, Philip A.
TP156.S45 H35    660.2/842    *LC* 79-4096    *ISBN* 007055790X

**Solid–liquid separation / editor, J. Gregory.**    **5.6851**
Chichester [West Sussex]: Published for the Society of Chemical Industry, London, by E. Horwood; New York, N.Y.: Distributors, North and South America, Halsted Press, 1984. 363 p.: ill.; 24 cm. Papers of a symposium organized by the Society of Chemical Industry and held at University College London Sept. 19-21, 1983. 1. Separation (Technology) I. Gregory, J. (John), 1938- II. Society of Chemical Industry (Great Britain)
TP156.S45 S64 1984    660.2/842 19    *LC* 83-22731    *ISBN* 0853126844

**Geankoplis, Christie J.**    **5.6852**
Transport processes and unit operations / Christie J. Geankoplis. — Boston: Allyn and Bacon, c1978. x, 650 p.: ill.; 25 cm. 1. Transport theory I. T.
TP156.T7 G4    660.2/842    *LC* 77-16642    *ISBN* 0205059392

**Chemical reaction and reactor engineering / edited by James J.**    **5.6853**
**Carberry, Arvind Varma.**
New York: M. Dekker, c1986. p. cm. Includes index. 1. Chemical reactors I. Carberry, James J. II. Varma, Arvind.
TP157.C416 1986    660.2/83 19    *LC* 86-19673    *ISBN* 0824775430

**Levenspiel, Octave.**    **5.6854**
Chemical reaction engineering. — 2d ed. — New York: Wiley, [1972] xxi, 578 p.: illus.; 23 cm. 1. Chemical reactors I. T.
TP157.L4 1972    660.2/83    *LC* 72-178146    *ISBN* 0471530166

**Westerterp, K. R.**    **5.6855**
Chemical reactor design and operation / K.R. Westerterp, W.P.M. van Swaaij, A.A.C.M. Beenackers. — [2nd ed.]. — Chichester [Sussex]; New York: Wiley, c1984. xxxii, 767 p.: ill.; 24 cm. Rev. ed. of: Elements of chemical reactor design and operation / H. Kramers and K.R. Westerterp. 1963. 1. Chemical reactors I. Swaaij, W. P. M. van II. Beenackers, A. A. C. M. III. Kramers, H. Elements of chemical reactor design and operation. IV. T.
TP157.W43 1984    660.2/81 19    *LC* 83-5769    *ISBN* 0471901830

**Pinkava, Jan.**    • **5.6856**
Handbook of laboratory unit operations for chemists and chemical engineers. English translation [edited by] J. Bryant. — New York: Gordon and Breach, [c1970] 470 p.: illus.; 25 cm. Revised translation of Laboratorní technika kontinuálních chemických procesů. 1. Chemical engineering — Laboratory manuals. 2. Chemical processes I. T.
TP161.P5613 1970b    660/.2842    *LC* 74-122851

# TP200–248 Chemicals. Chemical Manufacture

**Chemical technology: an encyclopedic treatment; the economic**    • **5.6857**
**application of modern technological developments.**
New York, Barnes & Noble [1969- v. 1, c1968] v. illus. 25 cm. 1968 ed. published under title: Materials and technology. Based on Warenkennis en technologie, by J. F. van Oss. 1. Chemical industry 2. Commercial products I. Oss, Jacob Frederik van, 1875- Warenkennis en technologie.
TP200.M3642    661    *LC* 68-31037    *ISBN* 0064911063

**Yaws, Carl L.**    **5.6858**
Physical properties: a guide to the physical, thermodynamic, and transport property data of industrially important chemical compounds / Carl L. Yaws. — New York: Chemical engineering, c1977. 239 p.: ill.; 29 cm. 1. Chemicals I. T.
TP200.Y38    541/.3    *LC* 77-14825

**Conference on the Marine Transportation, Handling, and**    **5.6859**
**Storage of Bulk Chemicals. (6th: 1985: London, England)**
MariChem 85: Conference on the Marine Transportation, Handling, and Storage of Bulk Chemicals, London, June 25-27, 1985. — Rickmansworth, Herts., England: Gastech, c1985. — vi, 292 p., [4] leaves of plates: ill.; 30 cm. Spine title: Marichem 85 proceedings. 1. Chemicals — Transportation — Congresses. 2. Chemicals — Storage — Congresses. I. T. II. Title: Marichem 85 proceedings.
TP201.C66 1985    387.5/44 19    *LC* 84-239252    *ISBN* 0904930319

**Reid, Robert C.**    **5.6860**
The properties of gases and liquids / Robert C. Reid, John M. Prausnitz, Thomas K. Sherwood. 3d ed. — New York: McGraw-Hill, c1977. xv, 688 p.: graphs; 24 cm. (McGraw-Hill chemical engineering series) 1. Gases 2. Liquids I. Prausnitz, J. M. joint author. II. Sherwood, Thomas Kilgore, 1903-1976. joint author. III. T.
TP242.R4 1977    660/.04/2    *LC* 76-42204    *ISBN* 0070517908

**Audrieth, L. F. (Ludwig Frederick), 1901-.**    • **5.6861**
Non–aqueous solvents: applications as media for chemical reactions / Ludwig F. Audrieth, Jacob Kleinberg. — New York: Wiley, 1953. 284 p.: ill. 1. Solvents I. Kleinberg, Jacob, 1914- II. T.
TP247.5.A85    *LC* 52-12057

**Durrans, Thomas H. (Thomas Harold)**    • **5.6862**
Solvents, [by] Thomas H. Durrans. 8th ed.; revised by Eric H. Davies. London, Chapman and Hall, 1971. iii-ix, 267 p. illus. 23 cm. 'Distributed in the U.S.A. by Barnes and Noble, inc.' 1. Solvents I. Davies, Eric H. II. T.
TP247.5.D8 1971    667/.75    *LC* 77-883875    *ISBN* 0412096803

**Lagowski, J. J. ed.**    **5.6863**
The chemistry of non–aqueous solvents, edited by J. J. Lagowski. — New York: Academic Press, 1966-1978. 5 v. in 6.: illus.; 24 cm. 1. Nonaqueous solvents I. T.
TP247.5.L3    660.2/9/482    *LC* 66-16441    *ISBN* 0124338046

**Marsden, Cyril.**    • **5.6864**
Solvents guide / compiled and edited by C. Marsden; with the collaboration of Seymour Mann. — 2d ed., rev. and extended. — New York: Interscience Publishers, [1963]. 633 p. 1. Solvents I. T.
TP247.5.M3 1963

# TP248.1–248.9 Biotechnology

**Prentis, Steve.**    **5.6865**
Biotechnology: a new industrial revolution / Steve Prentis; foreword by Magnus Pyke. — New York: G. Braziller, 1984. 192 p., [8] p. of plates: ill.; 24 cm. Includes index. 1. Biotechnology I. T.
TP248.2.P74 1984    660/.62 19    *LC* 83-26571    *ISBN* 0807610941

**Yoxen, Edward.**    **5.6866**
The gene business: who should control biotechnology? / Edward Yoxen. — 1st U.S. ed. — New York: Harper & Row, 1984, c1983. ix, 230 p.; 24 cm. Includes index. 1. Biotechnology 2. Genetic engineering 3. Biotechnology — Social aspects. 4. Genetic engineering — Social aspects. I. T.
TP248.2.Y68 1984    174/.957487/3282 19    *LC* 83-48809    *ISBN* 0060153032

**Aiba, Shuichi, 1923-.**    **5.6867**
Biochemical engineering, by Shuichi Aiba, Arthur E. Humphrey [and] Nancy F. Millis. — [2d ed.]. — New York: Academic Press, 1973. xvii, 434 p.: illus.; 27 cm. 1. Biochemical engineering 2. Fermentation I. Humphrey, Arthur Earl, joint author. II. Millis, Nancy F., joint author. III. T.
TP248.3.A42 1973    660/.63    *LC* 73-12447    *ISBN* 0120450526

**Sylvester, Edward J.**    **5.6868**
The gene age: genetic engineering and the next industrial revolution / Edward J. Sylvester and Lynn C. Klotz. — New York: Scribner, c1983. xii, 208 p.: ill.; 22 cm. 1. Genetic engineering I. Klotz, Lynn C. II. T.
TP248.6.S94 1983    575.1 19    *LC* 83-11486    *ISBN* 0684179504

# TP250–267 Industrial Electrochemistry

**Kuhn, A. T.**    • **5.6869**
Industrial electrochemical processes, edited by A. T. Kuhn. — Amsterdam; New York: Elsevier Pub. Co., 1971. xxiii, 632 p. with illus.; 25 cm. 1. Electrochemistry, Industrial I. T.
TP255.K84    660/.29/7    *LC* 70-118254    *ISBN* 0444408851

**Pletcher, Derek.**    **5.6870**
Industrial electrochemistry / Derek Pletcher. — London; New York: Chapman and Hall, 1982. xii, 325 p.: ill.; 25 cm. 1. Electrochemistry, Industrial I. T.
TP255.P57 1982    660.2/97 19    *LC* 82-6280    *ISBN* 0412165007

# TP315–365 Fuel

**Alternative technologies for power production: prepared for the Electric Power Task Force of the Scientists' Institute for Public Information and the Power Study Group of the American Association for the Advancement of Science Committee on Environmental Alterations / edited by Barry Commoner, Howard Boksenbaum, Michael Corr.** 5.6871
New York: Macmillan Information, [1975] xviii, 213 p.: ill.; 24 cm. (Energy and human welfare; v. 2) 1. Fuel — Addresses, essays, lectures. 2. Electric power production — Addresses, essays, lectures. 3. Power resources — Addresses, essays, lectures. I. Commoner, Barry, 1917- II. Boksenbaum, Howard. III. Corr, Michael. IV. Scientists' Institute for Public Information. Electric Power Task Force. V. American Association for the Advancement of Science. Committee on Environmental Alterations. Power Study Group. VI. Series.
TP319.A56    662/.6    LC 75-8987    ISBN 0024684309

**Tillman, David A.** 5.6872
Wood as an energy resource / David A. Tillman. — New York: Academic Press, 1978. xiv, 252 p.: ill.; 24 cm. 1. Fuelwood I. T.
TP324.T54    333.7/5    LC 78-8252    ISBN 0126912602

**Berkowitz, N. (Norbert), 1923-.** 5.6873
An introduction to coal technology / N. Berkowitz. — New York: Academic Press, 1979. xiv, 345 p.: ill.; 24 cm. — (Energy science and engineering.) 1. Coal I. T. II. Series.
TP325.B46    662/.62    LC 78-19663    ISBN 0120919508

**Coal / edited by Mones E. Hawley.** 5.6874
Stroudsburg, Pa.: Dowden, Hutchinson & Ross; [New York]: distributed by Halsted Press, [1976] 2 v.: ill. — (Benchmark papers on energy; 3-4) 1. Coal — Addresses, essays, lectures. I. Hawley, Mones E.
TP325.C514    TP325 C514.    553/.2/08    LC 76-10855    ISBN 0879332190

**Grainger, Leslie.** 5.6875
Coal utilisation: technology, economics and policy / L. Grainger and J. Gibson. — New York: Halsted Press, 1982 (c1981). xxii, 503 p.: ill.; 25 cm. Includes index. 1. Coal I. Gibson, J. (Joseph) II. T.
TP325.G732 1981    553.2/4 19    LC 81-7249    ISBN 0470272724

**Smoot, L. Douglas (Leon Douglas)** 5.6876
Coal combustion and gasification / L. Douglas Smoot and Philip J. Smith. — New York: Plenum Press, c1985. xvi, 443 p.: ill.; 24 cm. (Plenum chemical engineering series.) Includes index. 1. Coal — Combustion 2. Coal gasification I. Smith, Philip J. II. T. III. Series.
TP325.S57 1985    662.6/2 19    LC 84-17937    ISBN 0306417502

**Symposium on Future Automotive Fuels—Prospects, Performance, and Perspective, General Motors Research Laboratories, 1975.** 5.6877
Future automotive fuels: prospects, performance, perspective: [proceedings of the Symposium on Future Automotive Fuels—Prospects, Performance, and Perspective, held at the General Motors Research Laboratories, Warren, Michigan, October 6–7, 1975] / edited by Joseph M. Colucci and Nicholas E. Gallopoulos. — New York: Plenum Press, 1977. ix, 380 p.: ill.; 26 cm. 1. Motor fuels — Congresses. I. Colucci, Joseph M. II. Gallopoulos, Nicholas E. III. General Motors Corporation. Research Laboratories. IV. T.
TP343.S88 1975    662/.6 19    LC 76-30757    ISBN 0306310171

**Rothman, Harry.** 5.6878
Energy from alcohol: the Brazilian experience / Harry Rothman, Rod Greenshields, and Francisco Rosillo Callé. — Lexington, Ky.: University Press of Kentucky, c1983. 188 p.: ill., map; 23 cm. Includes indexes. 1. Alcohol as fuel 2. Fuel — Brazil. I. Greenshields, Rod, 1933- II. Rosillo Callé, Francisco, 1945- III. T.
TP358.R667 1983    333.79/3 19    LC 82-21956    ISBN 0813114799

**Hoffmann, Peter, 1935-.** 5.6879
The forever fuel: the story of hydrogen / Peter Hoffmann. — Boulder, Colo.: Westview Press, [1981] xiv, 271 p.: ill. Includes index. 1. Hydrogen as fuel I. T.
TP359.H8 H63    TP359H8 H63.    665.8/1 19    LC 80-20965    ISBN 0891585818

**Williams, L. O.** 5.6880
Hydrogen power: an introduction to hydrogen energy and its applications / L. O. Williams. — 1st ed. — Oxford; New York: Pergamon Press, 1980. ix, 158 p.: ill.; 26 cm. — (Pergamon international library of science, technology, engineering, and social studies) 1. Hydrogen as fuel I. T.
TP359.H8 W54 1980    665.8/1    LC 80-40434    ISBN 0080247830

**Bungay, Henry R. (Henry Robert), 1928-.** 5.6881
Energy, the biomass options / Henry R. Bungay. — New York: Wiley, c1981. viii, 347 p.: ill.; 24 cm. (Alternate energy.) 'A Wiley-Interscience publication.' Includes index. 1. Biomass energy I. T. II. Series.
TP360.B86    662/.8 19    LC 80-19645    ISBN 0471043869

**Handbook of synfuels technology / Robert A. Meyers, editor in chief.** 5.6882
New York: McGraw-Hill, c1984. 906 p. in various pagings: ill.; 24 cm. 1. Synthetic fuels — Handbooks, manuals, etc. I. Meyers, Robert A. (Robert Allen), 1936-
TP360.H36 1984    662/.66 19    LC 83-17505    ISBN 0070417628

**International Conference on Biomass. (2nd: 1982: Berlin, Germany: West)** 5.6883
Energy from biomass: 2nd E.C. Conference: proceedings of the International Conference on Biomass, held in Berlin, Federal Republic of Germany, 20–23 September 1982 / edited by A. Strub, P. Chartier, and G. Schleser. — London; New York: Applied Science Publishers; New York, N.Y.: Sole distributor in USA and Canada, Elsevier Science Pub. Co., c1983. xxxii, 1148 p.: ill.; 23 cm. English, French, and German. Organized by the Commission of the European Communities. 1. Biomass energy — Congresses. I. Strub, A. S. (Albert S.) II. Chartier, P. (Pierre) III. Schleser, G. IV. Commission of the European Communities. V. T.
TP360.I56 1982    662/.8 19    LC 83-101717    ISBN 0853341966

# TP363 Heating, Drying, Cooling, Evaporating Processes

**Masters, K. (Keith)** 5.6884
Spray drying handbook / K. Masters. — 4th ed. — New York: Halsted Press, 1985. xiv, 696 p.: ill.; 23 cm. 1. Spray drying I. T.
TP363.M35 1985    660.2/8426 19    LC 84-28999    ISBN 0470201517

# TP368–659 Food Processing and Technology

**Potter, Norman N.** 5.6885
Food science / Norman N. Potter. — 4th ed. — Westport, Conn.: AVI Pub. Co., c1986. xvi, 735 p.: ill.; 24 cm. 1. Food industry and trade I. T.
TP370.P58 1986    664 19    LC 85-30654    ISBN 0870554964

**Pyke, Magnus.** 5.6886
Synthetic food. — New York: St. Martin's Press, [1971] viii, 145 p.: illus.; 23 cm. 1. Food, Artificial I. T.
TP370.P93 1971    664    LC 77-162369

**Green, Maurice B. (Maurice Berkeley)** 5.6887
Eating oil: energy use in food production / Maurice B. Green. Boulder, Colo.: Westview Press, [1977] 205 p. Includes index. 1. Food industry and trade — Energy consumption 2. Agriculture — Energy consumption I. T.
TP370.5.G73    338.1/6    LC 77-21577    ISBN 0891582444

**Microbiology of fermented foods / edited by Brian J.B. Wood.** 5.6888
London; New York: Elsevier Applied Science Publishers; New York, NY, USA: Sole distributor in the USA and Canada, Elsevier Science Pub. Co., c1985. 2 v.: ill.; 23 cm. 1. Food, Fermented — Microbiology. I. Wood, Brian J. B.
TP371.44.M53 1985    664/.024 19    LC 85-237508    ISBN 0853343349

**Jul, Mogens.** 5.6889
The quality of frozen foods / Mogens Jul. — London; Orlando: Academic Press, 1984. xiii, 292 p.: ill.; 24 cm. Includes index. 1. Food, Frozen I. T.
TP372.3.J84 1984    664/.02853 19    LC 83-73403    ISBN 0123919800

**Control of food quality and food analysis / edited by G.G. Birch and K.J. Parker.** 5.6890
London: Elsevier Applied Science Publishers, 1984. — xi, 332 p.: ill.; 24 cm. Conference papers. 1. Food industry and trade — Quality control — Congresses. I. Birch, G. G. (Gordon Gerard), 1934- II. Parker, K. J. (Kenneth John), 1926-
TP372.5.C6x    664/.07 19    ISBN 0853342393

## TP490–498 Refrigeration

**International Institute of Refrigeration.**                    **5.6891**
New international dictionary of refrigeration. Paris: International Institute of Refrigeration, [1976?] xxxvii, 560 p.; 29 cm. Text in English, Danish, French, German, Italian, Russian, and Spanish. First ed. published 1961 under title: International dictionary of refrigeration; 1962 ed. published under title: International dictionary of refrigeration in six languages. Includes indexes. 3000.00F 1. Refrigeration and refrigerating machinery — Dictionaries — Polyglot. 2. Dictionaries, Polyglot I. T.
TP490.4.I57 1976        621.5/6/03        LC 76-373634

## TP500–659 Fermentation Industries. Wines

**Lichine, Alexis, 1913-.**                    **5.6892**
[Encyclopedia of wines & spirits] Lichine's encyclopedia of wines & spirits / [by Alexis Lichine] in collaboration with William Fifield and with the assistance of ... [others]. — Enlarges and completely revised ed. — London: Cassell, 1979. xv, 716, [1] p.: maps; 29 cm. 1974 ed. published under title: Alex Lichine's New encyclopedia of wines & spirits. Includes index. 1. Wine and wine making — Dictionaries. I. Fifield, William, 1916- II. T. III. Title: Encyclopedia of wines & spirits.
TP546.L5 1979        641.2/22/0321        LC 79-322909        0340302783

**Johnson, Hugh.**                    **5.6893**
[Modern encyclopedia of wine] Hugh Johnson's Modern encyclopedia of wine / [illustrations, Paul Hogarth; grape illustrations, John Davis; colour maps, Eugene Fleury]. — New York: Simon and Schuster, c1983. 544 p.: ill. (some col.); 27 cm. Includes index. 1. Wine and wine making I. T. II. Title: Modern encyclopedia of wine.
TP548.J632 1983        641.2/2/0321 19        LC 82-3203        ISBN 0671451340

## TP670–699 Oils, Fats, and Waxes. Petroleum

**Bailey, Alton Edward, 1907-1953.**                    **5.6894**
[Industrial oil and fat products] Bailey's Industrial oil and fat products / edited by Daniel Swern; authors, Marvin W. Formo ... [et al.]. — 4th ed. — New York: Wiley, c1979. 1 v.: ill.; 24 cm. 'A Wiley-Interscience publication.' Vol. 3 edited by Thomas H. Applewhite. 1. Oils and fats I. Swern, Daniel, 1916- II. Formo, Marvin W. III. Applewhite, Thomas H. IV. T. V. Title: Industrial oil and fat products.
TP670.B28 1979        665/.3 19        LC 78-31275        ISBN 0471839574

## TP690–699 Petroleum Refining and Products

**Sittig, Marshall.**                    **• 5.6895**
Organic chemical process encyclopedia, 1969. — 2d ed. — Park Ridge, N.J.: Noyes Development Corp., [1969] 712 p.: illus.; 29 cm. 1. Chemical processes — Handbooks, manuals, etc. 2. Petroleum products — Handbooks, manuals, etc. I. T.
TP690.S56 1969        661/.804        LC 71-89540        ISBN 0815502850

**Waddams, Austen Lawrence.**                    **5.6896**
Chemicals from petroleum: an introductory survey / A. Lawrence Waddams. — 4th ed. — Houston: Gulf Pub. Co., Book Division, 1980, c1978. vii, 376 p.: ill.; 21 cm. Includes index. 1. Petroleum chemicals I. T.
TP692.3.W3 1980        661/.804 19        LC 79-56811        ISBN 0872011046

## TP785–889 Clay Industries. Ceramics. Glass

**Dodd, A. E. (Arthur Edward)**                    **5.6897**
Dictionary of ceramics: pottery, glass, vitreous enamels, refractories, cement buildng materials, cement and concrete, electroceramics, special ceramics, by A.E. Dodd. 2nd ed., rev. and enl. London, Newnes, 1967. vi, 362 p. ill., tables, diagrs. 1. Ceramics — Dictionaries I. T.
TP788 D6 1967        LC 67-114884

**O'Bannon, Loran S., 1910-.**                    **5.6898**
Dictionary of ceramic science and engineering / Loran S. O'Bannon. — New York: Plenum Press, c1984. xvi, 302 p.; 26 cm. Includes index. 1. Ceramics — Dictionaries. I. T.
TP788.O2 1984        666/.03/21 19        LC 83-13936        ISBN 0306413248

**Sanders, Herbert H.**                    **5.6899**
The world of Japanese ceramics / by Herbert H. Sanders, with the collaboration of Kenkichi Tomimoto. — Tokyo: Kodansha International, 1982, c1968. — 267 p.: ill., map; 26 cm. 1. Pottery, Japanese I. Tomimoto, Kenkichi, 1886-1963. II. T.
TP804.J3 S3 1982        738.0952        ISBN 087011557X

**Kingery, W. D.**                    **5.6900**
Introduction to ceramics / W. D. Kingery, H. K. Bowen, D. R. Uhlmann. — 2d ed. — New York: Wiley, c1976. xii, 1032 p.: ill.; 24 cm. (Wiley series on the science and technology of materials) 'A Wiley-Interscience publication.' 1. Ceramics I. Bowen, Harvey Kent, joint author. II. Uhlmann, D. R. (Donald Robert) joint author. III. T.
TP807.K52 1975        666        LC 75-22248        ISBN 0471478601

**Rado, Paul.**                    **5.6901**
An introduction to the technology of pottery. — [1st ed.]. — Oxford; New York: Pergamon Press, [1969] xx, 258 p.: illus. (part col.); 20 cm. — (The Commonwealth and international library. Materials science and technology (Ceramics division) 1. Pottery I. T.
TP807.R27 1969        666/.3        LC 79-90454        ISBN 0080064582

**Grimshaw, Rex W.**                    **• 5.6902**
The chemistry and physics of clays and allied ceramic materials, by Rex W. Grimshaw. — 4th ed. rev. — New York: Wiley-Interscience, [1971] 1024 p.: illus.; 24 cm. Previous editions, written by A. B. Searle and R. W. Grimshaw, have title: The chemistry and physics of clays and other ceramic materials. 1. Clay 2. Ceramic materials I. Searle, Alfred Broadhead, 1877-1967. The chemistry and physics of clays and other ceramic materials. II. T.
TP810.5.G75 1971        666/.4/2        LC 76-178139        ISBN 0471327808

**Doremus, R. H.**                    **5.6903**
Glass science [by] Robert H. Doremus. — New York: Wiley, [1973] viii, 349 p.: illus.; 23 cm. — (Wiley series on the science and technology of materials) 'A Wiley-Interscience publication.' 1. Glass 2. Glass manufacture I. T.
TP857.D67        666/.1        LC 73-2730        ISBN 0471219002

## TP890–1185 Textiles. Plastics

**Pettit, Florence Harvey.**                    **5.6904**
America's indigo blues; resist–printed and dyed textiles of the eighteenth century, by Florence H. Pettit. With 106 photos., 8 color plates, and 44 woodcuts, engravings, and drawings. New York, Hastings House [1974] 251 p. illus. (part col.) 26 cm. 1. Textile printing — History. 2. Dyes and dyeing — Textile fibers — History. 3. Indigo — History. 4. Textile fabrics, American — History. 5. Resist-dyed textiles — United States — History — 18th century. I. T.
TP930.P468 1974        667/.26        LC 74-10778        ISBN 0803803761

**Encyclopedia of polymer science and engineering / editorial**                    **5.6905**
board, Herman F. Mark ... [et al.]; editor–in–chief, Jacqueline I. Kroschwitz.
2nd ed. — New York: Wiley, c1985- <c1986 > . v. < 1-5 > : ill.; 26 cm. Rev. ed. of: Encyclopedia of polymer science and technology. 1964- 'A Wiley-Interscience publication.' 1. Polymers and polymerization — Dictionaries. I. Mark, H. F. (Herman Francis), 1895- II. Kroschwitz, Jacqueline I. III. Encyclopedia of polymer science and technology.
TP1087.E46 1985        668.9 19        LC 84-19713        ISBN 0471895407

**Holmes-Walker, W. A., 1926-.**                                      **5.6906**
Polymer conversion / W. A. Holmes–Walker. — New York: Wiley, [1975] viii, 286 p.: ill.; 23 cm. 'A Halsted Press book.' 1. Polymers and polymerization 2. Plastics I. T.
TP1087.H64        668.4/2        LC 74-11510        ISBN 0470407670

**Tadmor, Zehev, 1937-.**                                            **5.6907**
Principles of polymer processing / Zehev Tadmor, Costas G. Gogos. — New York: Wiley, c1979. xv, 736 p.: ill.; 26 cm. (SPE monographs) 'A Wiley-Interscience publication.' 1. Polymers and polymerization I. Gogos, Costas G. joint author. II. T.
TP1087.T32        668        LC 78-17859        ISBN 0471843202

**DuBois, J. Harry (John Harry), 1903-.**                             **5.6908**
Plastics / J. Harry DuBois, Frederick W. John. — 6th ed. — New York: Van Nostrand Reinhold, c1981. xiii, 461 p.: ill.; 24 cm. Includes index. 1. Plastics I. John, Frederick W. joint author. II. T.
TP1120.D8 1981        668.4 19        LC 80-21775        ISBN 0442262639

**Roff, W. J. (William John)**                                       **5.6909**
[Fibres, films, plastics, and rubbers] Handbook of common polymers: fibres, films, plastics, and rubbers. Compiled by W. J. Roff and J. R. Scott, with the assistance of J. Pacitti. Cleveland, CRC Press [1971] 688 p. illus. 25 cm. (International scientific series) 1956 ed. published under title: Fibres, plastics, and rubbers. This rev. and updated version first published in 1971 in London under title: Fibres, films, plastics, and rubbers. 1. Plastics 2. Rubber 3. Textile fibers, Synthetic I. Scott, John Richard, joint author. II. T.
TP1120.R64 1971b        620.1/92        LC 74-173090        ISBN 0878199330

**Handbook of plastics and elastomers / Charles A. Harper,**          **5.6910**
**editor–in–chief.**
New York: McGraw-Hill, [1975] 1008 p. in various pagings: ill.; 24 cm. 1. Plastics — Handbooks, manuals, etc. 2. Elastomers — Handbooks, manuals, etc. I. Harper, Charles A.
TP1130.H36        668.4/02/02        LC 75-9790        ISBN 0070266816

**Society of the Plastics Industry.**                                **5.6911**
Plastics engineering handbook of the Society of the Plastics Industry, inc. / edited by Joel Frados. 4th ed. — New York: Van Nostrand Reinhold, c1975. xvi, 909 p.: ill.; 27 cm. First ed. published in 1947 under title: SPI handbook; 2d-3d editions published under title: SPI plastics engineering handbook. Includes index. 1. Plastics — Handbooks, manuals, etc. I. Frados, Joel. II. T.
TP1130.S58        668.4/1        LC 75-26508        ISBN 0442224699

# TR PHOTOGRAPHY

## TR1–195 General Works

**Witkin, Lee D.**                                                   **5.6913**
The photograph collector's guide / Lee D. Witkin, Barbara London; foreward by Alan Shestack. — 1st ed. — Boston: New York Graphic Society, c1979. x, 438 p., [4] leaves of plates: ill.; 29 cm. Includes index. 1. Photographs — Collectors and collecting. I. London, Barbara, 1936- II. T.
TR6.5.W57        770/.75        LC 79-17019        ISBN 0821206818

## TR9 REFERENCE WORKS

**The Focal encyclopedia of photography.**                          • **5.6914**
Revised desk ed. — London; New York: Focal P., 1969. xi, 1699 p.: illus.; 22 cm. 1. Photography — Dictionaries.
TR9.F6 1969        770/.3        LC 77-381067        ISBN 0240506804

**The ICP encyclopedia of photography / International Center of**     **5.6915**
**Photography.**
1st ed. — New York: Crown, c1984. 607 p.: ill. (some col.) 'A Pound Press book.' 1. Photography — Dictionaries. I. International Center of Photography.
TR9.I24 1984        770/.3/21 19        LC 84-1856        ISBN 051755271X

**Stroebel, Leslie D.**                                             **5.6916**
Dictionary of contemporary photography / by Leslie Stroebel & Hollis N. Todd. — Dobbs Ferry, N.Y.: Morgan & Morgan, [1974] 217 p.: ill.; 27 cm. 1. Photography — Dictionaries. I. Todd, Hollis N. joint author. II. T.
TR9.S88        770/.3        LC 73-93536        ISBN 0871000652

## TR15 HISTORY

**Gassan, Arnold.**                                                 • **5.6917**
A chronology of photography: a critical survey of the history of photography as a medium of art. — Athens, Ohio: Handbook Co., [distributed by Light Impressions, Rochester, N.Y., 1972] 373 p.: ill.; 23 cm. 1. Photography — History. I. T.
TR15.G33        770/.9        LC 72-83426        ISBN 0912808012

**Gernsheim, Helmut, 1913-.**                                       • **5.6918**
The history of photography from the camera obscura to the beginning of the modern era [by] Helmut Gernsheim, in collaboration with Alison Gernsheim. [2d ed.] New York, McGraw-Hill [1969] 599 p. illus., facsims., ports. 31 cm. First ed. published in 1955 under title: The history of photography from the earliest use of the camera obscura in the eleventh century up to 1914. Rev. ed. published as: The origins of photography. 1982. 1. Photography — History. I. Gernsheim, Alison. joint author. II. T.
TR15.G37 1969        770/.9        LC 69-18726

**Newhall, Beaumont, 1908-.**                                         **5.6919**
The history of photography: from 1839 to the present / Beaumont Newhall. — Completely rev. and enl. ed. — New York: Museum of Modern Art; Boston: Distributed by New York Graphic Society Books, c1982. 319 p.: ill. (some col.); 29 cm. Includes index. 1. Photography — History. I. T.
TR15.N47 1982        770/.9 19        LC 82-81430        ISBN 0870703803

**Pollack, Peter.**                                                   **5.6920**
The picture history of photography, from the earliest beginnings to the present day. — Rev. and enl. ed. — New York: H. N. Abrams, [1969] 708 p.: illus. (part col.), ports.; 29 cm. 1. Photography — History. I. T.
TR15.P55 1969        779        LC 76-76556

**Rosenblum, Naomi.**                                                 **5.6921**
A world history of photography / by Naomi Rosenblum. — 1st ed. — New York: Abbeville Press, c1984. 671 p.: ill. (some col.); 30 cm. Includes index. 1. Photography — History. I. T.
TR15.R67 1984        770/.9 19        LC 83-73417        ISBN 0896594386

**Schwarz, Heinrich, 1894-1974.**                                     **5.6922**
Art and photography: forerunners and influences: selected essays / by Heinrich Schwarz; edited by William E. Parker. — Layton, UT: Peregrine Smith Books in association with Visual Studies Workshop Press, 1985. 158 p.: ill., ports.; 23 cm. 1. Photography — History — Addresses, essays, lectures. I. Parker, William E. (William Edward), 1932- II. T.
TR15.S395 1985        770/.9 19        LC 84-5112        ISBN 0879051884

**Green, Jonathan.**                                                  **5.6923**
American photography: a critical history 1945 to the present / by Jonathan Green; pictures selected and sequenced by Jonathan Green and James Friedman. — New York: H.N. Abrams, 1984. 247 p.: ill. (some col.); 31 cm. Includes index. 1. Photography — United States — History. I. T.
TR23.G73 1984        770/.973 19        LC 83-15532        ISBN 0810918145

**The Golden age of British photography, 1839–1900: photographs**      **5.6924**
**from the Victoria and Albert Museum, London, with selections**
**from the Philadelphia Museum of Art, Royal Archives, Windsor**
**Castle, The Royal Photographic Society, Bath, Science**
**Museum, London, Scottish National Portrait Gallery, Edinburgh**
**/ edited and introduced by Mark Haworth–Booth.**
Millerton, N.Y.: Aperture in association with the Philadelphia Museum of Art; New York: distributed in the U.S. by Viking Penguin, c1984. 189 p.: ill.; 30 cm. Includes index. 1. Photography — Great Britain — History. I. Haworth-Booth, Mark. II. Victoria and Albert Museum. III. Aperture, Inc. IV. Philadelphia Museum of Art.
TR57.G65 1984        770/.941 19        LC 84-70357        ISBN 0893811440

## TR139–145 BIOGRAPHY

**Browne, Turner.**                                                   **5.6925**
Macmillan biographical encyclopedia of photographic artists & innovators / Turner Browne, Elaine Partnow. — New York: Macmillan; London: Collier Macmillan, c1983. xiii, 722 p., [104] p. of plates: ill.; 24 cm. 1. Photographers — Biography. I. Partnow, Elaine. II. T.
TR139.B767 1983        770/.92/2 B 19        LC 82-4664        ISBN 0025175009

**Contemporary photographers / editors, George Walsh, Colin**          **5.6926**
**Naylor, Michael Held.**
New York: St. Martin's Press, [1982] 837 p.: ill.; 31 cm. (Contemporary arts series) 1. Photographers — Biography. 2. Photography, Artistic I. Walsh, George. II. Held, Michael. III. Naylor, Colin.
TR139.C66 1982        770/.92/2 B 19        LC 82-3337        ISBN 0312167911

**Willis-Thomas, Deborah, 1948-.**                                    **5.6927**
Black photographers, 1840–1940: an illustrated bio–bibliography / Deborah Willis–Thomas. — New York: Garland, 1985. xviii, 141 p.: ill.; 29 cm. (Garland reference library of the humanities. v. 401) Includes indexes. 1. Photography — Bio-bibliography. 2. Afro-American photographers I. T. II. Series.
TR139.W55 1985        770/.92/2 19        *LC* 82-49145        *ISBN* 0824091477

**Gernsheim, Helmut, 1913-.**                                    • **5.6928**
L. J. M. Daguerre: the history of the diorama and the daguerreotype / by Helmut and Alison Gernsheim. — New York: Dover Publications, [1968] xxii, 226 p.: ill., facsims., ports.; 24 cm. 'An unabridged and revised republication of the work originally published ... in 1956 [under title: L. J. M. Daguerre (1787-1851), the world's first photographer] A new preface has been written by the authors for this edition.' 1. Daguerre, Louis Jacques Mandé, 1787-1851. I. Gernsheim, Alison. joint author. II. T.
TR140.D3 G47 1968        770/.924 B        *LC* 68-8044        *ISBN* 048622290X

**Phillips, Sandra S., 1945-.**                                    **5.6929**
André Kertész: of Paris and New York / Sandra S. Phillips, David Travis, and Weston J. Naef. — Chicago, Ill.: Art Institute of Chicago, 1985. 288 p.: ill.; 28 cm. Catalog of an exhibition held May 10-July 14, 1985, Art Institute of Chicago and Dec. 19, 1985-Feb. 23, 1986, Metropolitan Museum of Art, New York, N.Y. Includes index. 1. Kertész, André. 2. Photographers — United States — Biography. I. Travis, David, 1948- II. Naef, Weston J., 1942- III. Art Institute of Chicago. IV. Metropolitan Museum of Art (New York, N.Y.) V. T.
TR140.K4 P47 1985        770/.92/4 B 19        *LC* 84-72764        *ISBN* 050054106X

**Siskind, Aaron.**                                    • **5.6930**
Aaron Siskind, photographer / edited with an introduction by Nathan Lyons; essays by Henry Holmes Smith and Thomas B. Hess; statement by Aaron Siskind. — New York: Eastman House; New York: [distributed by Horizon Press], 1965. 74 p.: ill.; 26 x 27 cm. — (George Eastman House monograph; no. 5) 1. Photography, Artistic I. Lyons, Nathan. II. Smith, Henry Holmes. III. Hess, Thomas B. IV. T. V. Series.
TR140.S54 A3        *LC* 65-20164

**Buckland, Gail.**                                    **5.6931**
Fox Talbot and the invention of photography / Gail Buckland. — Boston: D. R. Godine, 1980. 216 p.: ill. (some col.); 28 cm. Includes index. 1. Talbot, William Henry Fox, 1800-1877. 2. Photography — History. 3. Photographers — England — Biography. I. T.
TR140.T3 B83        770/.92/4 B        *LC* 79-90358        *ISBN* 0879233079

**Edward Weston omnibus: a critical anthology / edited and with**                **5.6932**
**introductions by Beaumont Newhall and Amy Conger.**
Salt Lake City: G.M. Smith: Peregrine Smith Books, 1984. xiii, 209 p., [32] p. of plates: ill., ports. 1. Weston, Edward, 1886-1958. I. Weston, Edward, 1886-1958. II. Newhall, Beaumont, 1908- III. Conger, Amy, 1942-
TR140.W45 E38 1984        770/.92/4 19        *LC* 84-3214        *ISBN* 0879051310

## TR145 General Works, 1850–

**Adams, Ansel, 1902-.**                                    **5.6933**
The New Ansel Adams photography series. — Boston: New York Graphic Society, c1980-<c1983 >. v. <1-3 >: ill.; 25 cm. Includes index. 1. Photography — Collected works. I. T.
TR145.A38        770 19        *LC* 80-11401        *ISBN* 0821210920

**Neblette, Carroll Bernard.**                                    **5.6934**
[Photography, its principles and practice] Neblette's Handbook of photography and reprography: materials, processes, and systems. — 7th ed. / edited by John M. Sturge. — New York: Van Nostrand Reinhold, c1977. ix, 641 p.: ill.; 29 cm. First published in 1927 under title: Photography, its principles and practice. 1. Photography 2. Copying processes I. Sturge, John M. II. T. III. Title: Handbook of photography and reprography.
TR145.N4 1977        770        *LC* 76-43356        *ISBN* 0442259484

**Photographic materials and processes / Leslie Stroebel ... [et**                **5.6935**
**al.].**
Boston: Focal Press, c1986. xx, 585 p.: ill. (some col.); 29 cm. Includes index. 1. Photography I. Stroebel, Leslie D.
TR145.P47 1986        770 19        *LC* 85-1543        *ISBN* 0240517520

**Thinking photography / edited by Victor Burgin.**                **5.6936**
London: Macmillan Press, 1982. 239 p.: ill., ports. — (Communications and culture) 1. Photography I. Burgin, Victor. II. Series.
TR145.T5        *ISBN* 0333271947

**Time-Life Books.**                                    **5.6937**
Life library of photography / by the editors of Time–Life Books. Morristown, N.J.: School and library distribution by Silver Burdett, 1981-. v.: ill.; 21 cm. 1. Photography I. T.
TR145.T5x        770/.1/6

**White, Minor.**                                    **5.6938**
Zone system manual: previsualization, exposure, development, printing: the Ansel Adams zone system as a basis of intuitive photography. — [New rev. ed.]. — Hasting-on-Hudson, N.Y.: Morgan & Morgan, [c1968] 112 p.: ill.; 19 cm. 1. Photography — Handbooks, manuals, etc. I. T.
TR146.W42 1968        770.28        *LC* 77-1830

**Darkroom / Wynn Bullock .. [et al.]; edited by Eleanor Lewis.**                **5.6939**
[New York]: Lustrum Press; Rochester, N.Y.: distributed by Light Impressions Corp., c1977. 183 p.: ill.; 27 cm. 1. Photography — Special effects 2. Photography — Processing I. Bullock, Wynn. II. Lewis, Eleanor, 1938-
TR148.D28        770/.28        *LC* 76-57201        *ISBN* 0912810203

**Langford, Michael John, 1933-.**                                    **5.6940**
The master guide to photography / Michael Langford. — New York: Knopf: Distributed by Random House, 1982. 432 p.: ill. (some col.); 27 cm. Includes index. 1. Photography — Handbooks, manuals, etc. I. T.
TR150.L364 1982        770 19        *LC* 82-80133        *ISBN* 0394508734

**Lester, Henry M.**                                    • **5.6941**
Photo-lab index. 1st- ed; 1939-. New York: Morgan & Lester. v.: ill. (incl. plans), tables, diagrs.; 19-21 cm. Loose-leaf. The cumulative formulary of standard recommended photographic procedures. 1. Photography — Formulae I. T.
TR151.L4        *LC* 40-847

**Sontag, Susan, 1933-.**                                    **5.6942**
On photography / Susan Sontag. — New York: Farrar, Straus and Giroux, c1977. 207 p.; 22 cm. 1. Photography, Artistic I. T.
TR183.S65 1977        770/.1        *LC* 77-11916        *ISBN* 0374226261

**Photography, essays & images: illustrated readings in the**                **5.6943**
**history of photography / edited by Beaumont Newhall.**
New York: Museum of Modern Art; Boston: Distributed by New York Graphic Society, c1980. 327 p.: ill.; 28 cm. 1. Photography — Addresses, essays, lectures. I. Newhall, Beaumont, 1908- II. Title: Photography, essays and images.
TR185.P487        770 19        *LC* 80-83434        *ISBN* 0870703854

## TR250–285 Cameras

**Adams, Ansel, 1902-.**                                    **5.6944**
Polaroid Land photography / Ansel Adams, with the collaboration of Robert Baker. — 1st rev. ed. — Boston: New York Graphic Society, c1978. xi, 307 p.: ill.; 25 cm. First published in 1963 under title: Polaroid Land photography manual. Includes index. 1. Polaroid Land camera 2. Instant photography 3. Photography — Handbooks, manuals, etc. I. Baker, Robert. II. T.
TR263.P6 A3 1978        771.3/1        *LC* 78-7069        *ISBN* 0821207296

**Horne, Douglas F. (Douglas Favel), 1915-.**                **5.6945**
Lens mechanism technology / D. F. Horne. — New York: Crane, Russak, 1975. xiv, 266 p.: ill.; 29 cm. Includes indexes. 1. Lens mounts — Design and construction. 2. Camera shutters — Design and construction. I. T.
TR270.H67 1975        681/.418        *LC* 76-355807        *ISBN* 0844807702

## TR287–500 Photographic Processing

**Shaw, Susan, 1946-.**                                    **5.6946**
Overexposure: health hazards in photography / Susan Shaw; edited by David Featherstone. — Carmel, Calif.: Friends of Photography, c1983. 329 p.: ill.; 24 cm. Includes indexes. 1. Photography — Processing — Hygienic aspects. 2. Photography — Developing and developers — Hygienic aspects. I. Featherstone, David. II. T.
TR287.S48 1983        770/.28/3 19        *LC* 83-81548        *ISBN* 093328635X

**Crawford, William, 1948-.**                                    **5.6947**
The keepers of light: a history & working guide to early photographic processes / William Crawford. — Dobbs Ferry, N.Y.: Morgan & Morgan, c1979. 318 p.,

[12] leaves of plates: ill. (some col.); 24 cm. Includes index. 1. Photography —
Printing processes 2. Photography — Printing processes — History. I. T.
TR330.C68     770/.28     *LC* 79-88815     *ISBN* 0871001586

**Darkroom dynamics: a guide to creative darkroom techniques /**     **5.6948**
**Jim Stone, editor.**
Marblehead, Mass.: Curtin & London; Toronto: Van Nostrand Reinhold, 1979.
ix, 199 p.: ill. (some col.): 29 cm. Includes index. 1. Photography — Printing
processes I. Stone, Jim.
TR330.D37     770/.28     *LC* 78-23902     *ISBN* 0930764072

**Newhall, Beaumont, 1908-.**     **5.6949**
The daguerreotype in America / by Beaumont Newhall. 3d rev. ed. — New
York: Dover Publications, 1976. 175 p., [48] leaves of plates: ill.; 29 cm.
Includes index. 1. Daguerreotype — History. 2. Photography — United States
— History. I. T.
TR365.N4 1976     772/.12     *LC* 76-691     *ISBN* 0486233227

**Brettell, Richard R.**     **5.6950**
Paper and light: the calotype in France and Great Britain, 1839–1870 / Richard
R. Brettell, with Roy Flukinger, Nancy Keeler, and Sydney Mallett Kilgore. —
Boston: D.R. Godine, 1984. 216 p.: ill.; 30 cm. 'In association with the Museum
of Fine Arts, Houston, and the Art Institute of Chicago.' 1. Calotype —
History. 2. Photographers — France — Biography. 3. Photographers —
Great Britain — Biography. I. Museum of Fine Arts, Houston. II. Art
Institute of Chicago. III. T.
TR395.B74 1984     772/.16/0941 19     *LC* 83-47983     *ISBN*
0879234857

**Weinstein, Robert A.**     **5.6951**
Collection, use, and care of historical photographs / Robert A. Weinstein and
Larry Booth. Nashville: American Association for State and Local History,
c1977. 222 p.: ill.; 25 cm. Includes index. 1. Photographs — Conservation and
restoration 2. Photographs — Collectors and collecting. I. Booth, Larry, joint
author. II. T.
TR465.W44     770/.28     *LC* 76-27755     *ISBN* 091005021X

# TR590–620 Lighting

**Edgerton, Harold Eugene, 1903-.**     **5.6952**
Moments of vision: the stroboscopic revolution in photography / Harold E.
Edgerton and James R. Killian, Jr. — Cambridge, Mass.: MIT Press, c1979.
177 p.: ill. (some col.); 24 x 30 cm. 1. Edgerton, Harold Eugene, 1903-
2. Photography, Electronic flash 3. Stroboscope I. Killian, James Rhyne,
1904- II. T.
TR593.E33     778.3/7     *LC* 79-11647     *ISBN* 0262050226

# TR640–685 Artistic Photography

**Barthes, Roland.**     **5.6953**
[Chambre claire. English] Camera lucida: reflections on photography / Roland
Barthes; translated by Richard Howard. — 1st American ed. — New York: Hill
and Wang, 1981. 119 p., [1] leaf of plates: ill.; 22 cm. Translation of: La
chambre claire. 1. Photography, Artistic 2. Photography — Philosophy. I. T.
II. Title: Reflections on photography.
TR642.B3713 1981     770/.1 19     *LC* 81-4649     *ISBN* 0809033402

**The Camera viewed: writings on twentieth–century photography**     **5.6954**
**/ edited by Peninah R. Petruck.**
1st ed. — New York: E. P. Dutton, c1979. 2 v.: ill.; 21 cm. 1. Photography,
Artistic — Addresses, essays, lectures.
TR642.C35 1979     700/.9/04     *LC* 78-55776     *ISBN* 0525475354

**Homer, William Innes.**     **5.6955**
Alfred Stieglitz and the photo–secession / William Innes Homer. 1st ed. New
York: New York Graphic Society Books; Boston; Little, Brown, c1983. 180 p.:
ill.; 28 cm. Includes index. 1. Stieglitz, Alfred, 1864-1946. 2. Photography,
Artistic — History. I. T.
TR642.H65 1983     770/.973 19     *LC* 82-25975     *ISBN* 0821215256

**A Photographic vision: pictorial photography, 1889–1923 /**     **5.6956**
**edited by Peter C.Bunnell.**
Santa Barbara: P. Smith, 1980. — viii, 212 p.: ill. 1. Photography, Artistic —
Addresses, essays, lectures. I. Bunnell, Peter C.
TR642.P45     770 19     *LC* 80-20481     *ISBN* 0879050594

**New York (City). Metropotitan Museum of Art.**     **5.6957**
The collection of Alfred Stieglitz: fifty pioneers of modern photography /
Weston J. Naef. — New York: Metropolitan Museum of Art, 1978. xi, 529 p.:
ill. — (A Studio book) 1. Stieglitz, Alfred, 1864-1946 — Photograph
collections. 2. Photographers I. Naef, Weston J., 1942- II. T.
TR646.U6 N484     TR646U6 N484.     770/.92/2     *LC* 78-6850
*ISBN* 0670670510

# TR647 Works of Individual
# Photographers, A–Z

**Arbus, Diane, 1923-1971.**     **5.6958**
Diane Arbus. — Millerton, N.Y.: [Aperture, 1972] 15 p., 80 plates.; 29 cm.
'Published in conjunction with a major exhibition of the photographs of Diane
Arbus at the Museum of Modern Art. Edited and designed by Doon Arbus ...
and Marvin Israel.' 1. Photography, Artistic — Exhibitions. I. T.
TR647.A7 A69     779/.2/0924     *LC* 72-93191     *ISBN* 0912334401

**Evans, Walker, 1903-1975.**     • **5.6959**
Walker Evans. With an introd. by John Szarkowski. New York, Museum of
Modern Art; distributed by New York Graphic Society, Greenwich, Conn.
[1971] 189 p. (chiefly illus.) 27 cm. Book of photographs to accompany an
exhibition. 1. Photography, Artistic — Exhibitions. I. Museum of Modern Art
(New York, N.Y.) II. T.
TR647.E9 A57     779/.0924     *LC* 71-146835     *ISBN* 0870703129

**Ray, Man, 1890-1976.**     **5.6960**
[Man Ray. English] Man Ray: photographs / introduction by Jean–Hubert
Martin; with three texts by Man Ray; [translated from the French, Man Ray,
photographe, by Carolyn Breakspear]. — New York, N.Y.: Thames and
Hudson, 1982. 255 p.: ill.; 31 cm. 'Based on an exhibition of Man Ray
photographs, held at the Centre national d'art et de culture Georges Pompidou,
Paris, from December 1981 to April 1982'—T.p. verso. Includes index. 1. Ray,
Man, 1890-1976. 2. Photography, Artistic — Exhibitions. I. Centre Georges
Pompidou. II. T.
TR647.R3813 1982     779/.092/4 19     *LC* 81-53058     *ISBN*
0500540799

**Stieglitz, Alfred, 1864-1946.**     **5.6961**
Alfred Stieglitz, photographs & writings / Sarah Greenough, Juan Hamilton.
— 1st ed. — Washington: National Gallery of Art, [1983] 246 p.: ill., ports.; 36
cm. 'Calloway editions.' 'Published as a complement to the exhibition to be
mounted by the National Gallery of Art, 30 January-1 May 1983'—
1. Stieglitz, Alfred, 1864-1946. 2. Photography, Artistic — Exhibitions.
I. Greenough, Sarah, 1951- II. Hamilton, Juan. III. National Gallery of Art
(U.S.) IV. T.
TR647.S84 1983     770/.92/4 19     *LC* 82-7925     *ISBN* 0894680277

**White, Minor.**     • **5.6962**
Mirrors, messages, manifestations. — [New York]: Aperture, [1969] 242 p.
(chiefly illus.); 32 cm. 'An Aperture monograph.' 'Comments by Beaumont
Newhall, Meyer Schapiro, Peter Bunnell, Jonathan Williams, Barbara Morgan,
Ansel Adams': [11] p. in pocket. 1. Photography, Artistic I. T.
TR647.W46 A2 1969     779.0924     *LC* 77-99253

# TR650–654 Collections

## TR650–652 1800-1900

**Brandt, Bill.**     • **5.6963**
Shadow of light: a collection of photographs from 1931 to the present / With an
introd. by Cyril Connolly and notes by Marjorie Beckett. — New York: Viking
Press, (1966) 128 p.: (chiefly illus.) (Studio book.) 1. Photography, Artistic
I. T. II. Series.
TR650.B68

**Brassaï, 1899-.**     • **5.6964**
Brassaï. With an introductory essay by Lawrence Durell. New York, Museum
of Modern Art; distributed by New York Graphic Society, Greenwich, Conn.
[1968] 79, [1] p. (chiefly illus., ports.) 23 cm. 1. Photography, Artistic 2. Paris
(France) — Description — Views. I. Durrell, Lawrence. II. Museum of
Modern Art (New York, N.Y.) III. T.
TR650.B683     770/.924     *LC* 68-54161

**Doty, Robert M.**     **5.6965**
Photo–secession: Stieglitz and the fine-art movement in photography / Robert
Doty; with a foreword by Beaumont Newhall. — New York: Dover
Publications, 1978. 139 p.: ill.; 28 cm. Reprint of the 1960 ed. published by
George Eastman House, New York, which was issued as George Eastman

House monograph no. 1. 1. Stieglitz, Alfred, 1864-1946. 2. Photography, Artistic I. T.
TR650.G36 1978     770/.1     *LC* 77-20467     *ISBN* 0486235882

**Moholy-Nagy, László, 1895-1946.**          • **5.6966**
[Malerei, Fotografie, Film. English] Painting, photography, film / with a note by Hans M. Wingler and a postscript by Otto Stelzer; translated by Janet Seligman. — Cambridge, Mass.: M.I.T. Press [1969] 150 p.: ill.; 26 cm. ([A Bauhaus book]) Translation of Malerei, Fotografie, Film. 1. Photography, Artistic 2. Art and photography 3. Form (Aesthetics) I. T.
TR650.M6183 1969b     779     *LC* 69-20302

**Photodiscovery: masterworks of photography, 1840–1940 /**     **5.6967**
[collected] by Bruce Bernard; with notes on the photographic processes by Valerie Lloyd; [project director, Robert Morton; editor, Margaret Donovan].
New York: H. N. Abrams, 1980. 262 p.: ill. (some col.); 32 cm. 1. Photography, Artistic 2. Photography — History. I. Bernard, Bruce. II. Donovan, Margaret.
TR650.P46     779     *LC* 80-12590     *ISBN* 0810914530

**Strand, Paul, 1890-1976.**          **5.6968**
Paul Strand: a retrospective monograph. — [Millerton, N.Y.]: Aperture, 1971. 2 v.: (chiefly illus.); 32 cm. 1. Photography, Artistic I. T.
TR650.S74     779/.0924     *LC* 78-178221

**Szarkowski, John.**          • **5.6969**
The photographer's eye. — New York: Museum of Modern Art; distributed by Doubleday, Garden City, N.Y., [1966] 155 p.; 24 cm. 1. Photography, Artistic I. T.
TR650.S92     779     *LC* 65-25724

**White, Minor.**          **5.6970**
Minor White: rites & passages: his photographs accompanied by excerpts from his diaries and letters / biographical essay by James Baker Hall. — Millerton, N.Y.: Aperture, 1978. 141 p., [1] leaf of plates: ill.; 30 cm. 1. White, Minor. 2. Photography, Artistic 3. Photographers — United States — Biography. I. T.
TR650.W48     770/.92/4 B     *LC* 77-80023     *ISBN* 0893810223

## TR653 1901-1950

**Kertész, André.**          **5.6971**
André Kertész: sixty years of photography, 1912–1972. Edited by Nicolas Ducrot. — New York: Grossman, 1972. 224 p. (chiefly illus.); 25 x 28 cm. 1. Photography, Artistic I. T.
TR653.K47 1972     779/.092/4     *LC* 72-77700     *ISBN* 0670123854

**Lange, Dorothea.**          **5.6972**
Photographs of a lifetime / Dorothea Lange; with an essay by Robert Coles; afterword by Therese Heyman. — Millerton, N.Y.: Aperture; [S.l.]: Distributed by Viking Penguin, c1982. 182 p.: chiefly ill.; 31 cm. 1. Lange, Dorothea. 2. Photography, Documentary 3. Photographers — United States — Biography. I. Coles, Robert. II. T.
TR653.L35 1982     779/.092/4 B 19     *LC* 82-70769     *ISBN* 0893811009

**Szarkowski, John.**          **5.6973**
The work of Atget / John Szarkowski, Maria Morris Hambourg. — New York: Museum of Modern Art; Boston: Distributed by New York Graphic Society, c1985. 182 p.: ill.; 31 cm. (Springs Mills series on the art of photography.) (v. 2-4: Springs Industries series on the art of photography) 1. Atget, Eugène, 1856-1927. 2. Photography, Artistic I. Hambourg, Maria Morris. II. Atget, Eugène, 1856-1927. III. Museum of Modern Art (New York, N.Y.) IV. T. V. Series.
TR653.S93     770/.92/4 19     *LC* 81-80130     *ISBN* 087070205X

**Weston, Edward, 1886-1958.**          **5.6974**
Edward Weston, his life and photographs: the definitive volume of his photographic work / illustrated biography by Ben Maddow; afterword by Cole Weston. — Rev. ed. — Millerton, N.Y.: Aperture, c1979. 299 p.: ill.; 32 x 35 cm. Edition for 1973 published under title: Edward Weston, fifty years. 1. Weston, Edward, 1886-1958. 2. Photography, Artistic 3. Photographers — United States — Biography. I. Maddow, Ben, 1909- II. T.
TR653.W457 1979     770/.92/4 B     *LC* 79-7058     *ISBN* 0893810436

## TR654 1951-

**Adams, Ansel, 1902-.**          **5.6975**
The portfolios of Ansel Adams / introd. by John Szarkowski; [edited by Tim Hill]. — Boston: New York Graphic Society, c1977. xii, 124 p.: chiefly ill.; 28 cm. 1. Adams, Ansel, 1902- 2. Photography, Artistic I. T.
TR654.A34     779/.092/4     *LC* 77-71628     *ISBN* 0821207237

**Cartier-Bresson, Henri, 1908-.**          **5.6976**
[Henri Cartier Bresson, photographie. English] Henri Cartier Bresson, photographer. — 1st U.S. ed. — Boston: New York Graphic Society, c1979. 155 p.: ill.; 30 x 31 cm. Translation of: Henri Cartier Bresson, photographe. Includes index. 1. Cartier-Bresson, Henri, 1908- 2. Photography, Artistic I. T.
TR654.C36713 1979     779/.092/4 19     *LC* 79-88493     *ISBN* 0821207563

**Ray, Man, 1890-1976.**          **5.6977**
[Man Ray, l'immagine fotografica. English] Man Ray, the photographic image / edited by Janus; translator, Murtha Baca. — 1st U.S. ed. — Woodbury, N.Y.: Barron's, 1980, c1977. 227 p.: ill.; 25 cm. Translation of Man Ray, l'immagine fotografica. 1. Ray, Man, 1890-1976. 2. Photography, Composite 3. Photography, Artistic I. Janus, fl. 1972- II. T. III. Title: Photographic image.
TR654.R3713 1980     779     *LC* 80-12415     *ISBN* 0812053745

**Weston, Brett.**          **5.6978**
Brett Weston, photographs from five decades / profile by R.H. Cravens. — Millerton, N.Y.: Aperture, Inc.; [New York]: Distributed in U.S. by Harper & Row, c1980. 131 p.: ill.; 35 cm. 1. Weston, Brett. 2. Photography, Artistic I. Cravens, Richard H. II. T.
TR654.W43     770/.092/4 19     *LC* 80-68712     *ISBN* 0893810657

## TR660 LANDSCAPE PHOTOGRAPHY

**Jussim, Estelle.**          **5.6979**
Landscape as photograph / Estelle Jussim, Elizabeth Lindquist–Cock. — New Haven: Yale University Press, c1985. xv, 168 p., [8] p. of plates: ill. (some col.); 24 x 27 cm. Includes index. 1. Photography — Landscapes I. Lindquist-Cock, Elizabeth. II. T.
TR660.J87 1985     778.9/36 19     *LC* 84-40671     *ISBN* 0300032218

**Thoreau, Henry David, 1817-1862.**          **5.6980**
[Selections. 1962] In wildness is the preservation of the world, from Henry David Thoreau / selections & photos by Eliot Porter; introd. by Joseph Wood Krutch. — San Francisco: Sierra Club [1962] 167 p.: col. ill.; 35 cm. ([Sierra Club exhibit format series, 4]) I. Porter, Eliot, 1901- II. Sierra Club. III. T.
TR660.T5     779.93     *LC* 62-20527

**Adams, Ansel, 1902-.**          **5.6981**
Yosemite and the range of light / Ansel Adams; introd. by Paul Brooks. — Boston: New York Graphic Society, 1979. 28 p., [55] leaves of plates: 116 ill.; 32 x 39 cm. 1. Adams, Ansel, 1902- 2. Yosemite National Park (Calif.) — Description and travel — Views. 3. Photography — Landscapes I. T.
TR660.5.A33     779/.36/0979447     *LC* 78-72074     *ISBN* 0821207504

**Garnett, William.**          **5.6982**
The extraordinary landscape: aerial photographs of America / by William Garnett; introduction by Ansel Adams. — Boston: Little, Brown, c1982. xvii, 183 p.: ill. (some col.); 30 cm. 'A New York Graphic Society book.' 1. Garnett, William. 2. Photography — Landscapes I. T.
TR660.5.G37 1982     779/.36/0924 19     *LC* 82-60887

**Second view: the Rephotographic Survey Project / Mark Klett,**     **5.6983**
**chief photographer; Ellen Manchester, project director; JoAnn Verburg, project coordinator; Gordon Bushaw and Rick Dingus, project photographers; with an essay by Paul Berger.**
1st ed. — Albuquerque: University of New Mexico Press, c1984. ix, 211 p.: chiefly ill.; 24 x 32 cm. 1. Photography — Landscapes 2. Photography in geography 3. West (U.S.) — Description and travel — Views. I. Klett, Mark, 1952- II. Manchester, Ellen. III. Verburg, JoAnn.
TR660.5.S43 1984     778.9/36/0973 19     *LC* 84-3600     *ISBN* 0826307515

## TR674–681 HUMAN FIGURES.
### PORTRAITS

**Brandt, Bill.**          **5.6984**
Nudes, 1945–1980: photographs / by Bill Brandt; introd. by Michael Hiley. — 1st U.S. ed. — Boston: New York Graphic Society, 1980. 12, 100 p.: chiefly ill.; 30 cm. 1. Brandt, Bill. 2. Photography of the nude I. T.
TR675.B65 1980     779/.24/0924 19     *LC* 80-82724     *ISBN* 0821210971

**Darrah, William Culp, 1909-.**     **5.6985**
Cartes de visite in nineteenth century photography / William C. Darrah. — Gettysburg Pa.: W.C. Darrah, c1981. 221 p.: ill.; 29 cm. Includes indexes. 1. Carte de visite photographs. I. T.
TR680.D28    770/.9/034 19    *LC* 81-69489    *ISBN* 091311605X

**Eisenstaedt, Alfred.**     **5.6986**
People. — New York: Viking Press, [1973] 259 p.: ill.; 34 cm. — (A Studio book) 1. Eisenstaedt, Alfred. 2. Photography — Portraits I. T.
TR680.E33 1973    779/.2/0924    *LC* 73-5332    *ISBN* 0670547018

**Newman, Arnold, 1918-.**     **5.6987**
Artists, portraits from four decades / by Arnold Newman; foreword by Henry Geldzahler; introd. by Arnold Newman. — 1st ed. — Boston: New York Graphic Society, c1980. 140 p.: ill. Includes index. 1. Artists — United States — Portraits. 2. Artists — Europe — Portraits. I. T.
TR681.A7 N48    779/.2/0924 19    *LC* 80-23961    *ISBN* 0821210998

# TR692–835 Scientific and Technical Applications

**Darius, Jon.**     **5.6988**
Beyond vision / Jon Darius. — Oxford [Oxfordshire]; New York: Oxford University Press, 1984. 224 p.: ill. (some col.); 28 cm. Includes indexes. 1. Photography — Scientific applications I. T.
TR692.D37 1984    778.3 19    *LC* 84-4405    *ISBN* 0198532458

**Blaker, Alfred A., 1928-.**     **5.6989**
Handbook for scientific photography / Alfred A. Blaker. — San Francisco: W. H. Freeman, c1977. xxii, 319 p., [4] leaves of plates: ill. (some col.); 24 cm. 'A greatly expanded revision of [the author's] Photography for scientific publication ... published in 1965.' Includes index. 1. Photography — Scientific applications 2. Scientific illustration I. T.
TR692.5.B55 1977    778.3    *LC* 77-24661    *ISBN* 0716702851

**Wolf, Paul R.**     **5.6990**
Elements of photogrammetry, with air photo interpretation and remote sensing / Paul R. Wolf. — 2nd ed. — New York: McGraw-Hill, c1983. xi, 628 p.: ill.; 24 cm. 1. Photogrammetry 2. Aerial photography 3. Photographic interpretation 4. Remote sensing I. T.
TR693.W64 1983    526.9/82 19    *LC* 82-4700    *ISBN* 0070713456

## TR721–729 Nature Photography

**Blaker, Alfred A., 1928-.**     **5.6991**
Field photography: beginning and advanced techniques / Alfred A. Blaker. — San Francisco: W. H. Freeman, c1976. xxi, 451 p., [6] leaves of plates: ill. (some col.); 24 cm. & field manual. Includes index. 1. Outdoor photography I. T.
TR721.B55    778    *LC* 75-33382    *ISBN* 0716705184

## TR780 Stereophotography

**Darrah, William Culp, 1909-.**     **5.6992**
The world of stereographs / William C. Darrah. — Gettysburg, Pa: Darrah, 1977. 246 p.: ill. (some col.); 29 cm. Includes index. 1. Photography, Stereoscopic I. T.
TR780.D35    778.4/09    *LC* 77-92123    *ISBN* 0913116041

## TR810 Aerial Photography

**Avery, Thomas Eugene.**     **5.6993**
Interpretation of aerial photographs / Thomas Eugene Avery, Graydon Lennis Berlin. — 4th ed. — Minneapolis, Minn.: Burgess Pub. Co., c1985. ix, 554 p., 12 p. of plates: ill. (some col.); 24 cm. 1. Photographic interpretation 2. Photography, Aerial I. Berlin, Graydon Lennis, 1943- II. T.
TR810.A9 1985    778.3/5 19    *LC* 84-23249    *ISBN* 0808700960

# TR820 Photojournalism

**Benson, Harry.**     **5.6994**
Harry Benson on photojournalism / photographs by Harry Benson; text by Gigi and Harry Benson. — 1st ed. — New York: Harmony Books, c1982. 176 p.: ill.; 29 cm. 1. Photography, Journalistic I. Benson, Gigi. II. T.
TR820.B425 1982    778.9/907 19    *LC* 82-1005    *ISBN* 0517544490

**Weegee, 1899-1968.**     **5.6995**
Weegee / edited and with an introd. by Louis Stettner. — 1st ed. — New York: Knopf, 1977. 183 p.: chiefly ill.; 29 cm. A selection of photographs taken between 1930-1965. 1. Weegee, 1899-1968. 2. Photography, Journalistic I. Stettner, Louis, 1922- II. T.
TR820.F45 1977    779/.092/4    *LC* 77-75356    *ISBN* 0394407709

**Hurley, F. Jack (Forrest Jack)**     **5.6996**
Portrait of a decade; Roy Stryker and the development of documentary photography in the thirties [by] F. Jack Hurley. Photographic editing by Robert J. Doherty. Baton Rouge, Louisiana State University Press [1972] ix, 196 p. illus. 29 cm. 1. Stryker, Roy Emerson, 1893-1975. 2. United States. Farm Security Administration. 3. Photography, Documentary — United States. I. T.
TR820.5.H87    779/.9/917303916    *LC* 72-79331    *ISBN* 0807102350

**Smith, W. Eugene, 1918-.**     **5.6997**
W. Eugene Smith, master of the photographic essay / edited with commentary by William S. Johnson; foreword by James L. Enyeart. — Millerton, N.Y.: Aperture; [New York, N.Y.]: Distributed by Harper & Row, c1981. 223 p.: chiefly ill.; 31 cm. 1. Smith, W. Eugene, 1918- 2. Photography, Documentary I. Johnson, William, 1940- II. T.
TR820.5.S543 1981    770/.92/4 19    *LC* 80-68723    *ISBN* 0893810703

# TR845–899 Cinematography. Motion Pictures

## TR845–852 General Works

**Beaver, Frank Eugene.**     **5.6998**
Dictionary of film terms / Frank E. Beaver. — New York: McGraw-Hill, c1983. viii, 392 p.: ill.; 18 cm. Includes indexes. 1. Cinematography — Dictionaries. I. T.
TR847.B43 1983    791.43/03/21 19    *LC* 82-14046    *ISBN* 0070042160

**Fielding, Raymond. comp.**     **5.6999**
A technological history of motion pictures and television; an anthology from the pages of the Journal of the Society of Motion Picture and Television Engineers. Berkeley University of California Press 1967. 255p. 1. Cinematography — History — Addresses, essays, lectures 2. Television — History — Addresses, essays, lectures I. Society of Motion Picture and Television Engineers. Journal II. T.
TR848 F5

**Holm, Bill, 1925-.**     **5.7000**
Edward S. Curtis in the land of the war canoes: a pioneer cinematographer in the Pacific Northwest / Bill Holm and George Irving Quimby. — Seattle: University of Washington Press, c1980. 132 p.: ill.; 23 x 29 cm. — (Thomas Burke Memorial Washington State Museum monograph. 2) Includes index. 1. Curtis, Edward S., 1868-1952. 2. Cinematographers — United States — Biography. I. Quimby, George Irving, 1913- joint author. II. T. III. Series.
TR849.C87 H64 1980    778.5/3/0924    *LC* 80-12172    *ISBN* 0295957085

**Hendricks, Gordon.**     **5.7001**
Eadweard Muybridge: the father of the motion picture / Gordon Hendricks. — New York: Grossman Publishers, 1975. xvi, 271 p.: ill.; 28 cm. Includes index. 1. Muybridge, Eadweard, 1830-1904. 2. Chronophotography — History. I. T.
TR849.M87 H46    770/.92/4 B    *LC* 73-16572    *ISBN* 0670286796

**American cinematographer manual / Edited by Fred H. Detmers.**     **5.7002**
6th ed. — Hollywood, Calif.:The ASC Press, 1986. (32), 393, (9) p.: ill. (some col.), charts, forms; 19cm.— Includes index. 1. Cinematography — Handbooks, manuals etc. I. Detmers, Fred H. II. American Society of Cinematographers.
TR850 A57 1986    *LC* 79-93439    *ISBN* 0935578072

**Lipton, Lenny, 1940-.**       **5.7003**
Independent filmmaking / Lenny Lipton; introduction by Stan Brakhage. — Rev. ed. — New York: Simon and Schuster, 1983. 445 p.: ill.; 24 cm. 'A Fireside book.' Includes index. 1. Cinematography I. T.
TR850.L62 1983    778.5/3 19     *LC* 83-475     *ISBN* 067146258X

**Roberts, Kenneth H.**       **5.7004**
A primer for film–making; a complete guide to 16 mm and 35 mm film production [by] Kenneth H. Roberts and Win Sharples, Jr. — New York: Pegasus, [1971] xiii, 546 p.: illus.; 28 cm. 1. Cinematography 2. Motion pictures — Production and direction I. Sharples, Winston, joint author. II. T.
TR850.R6    778.5/3     *LC* 70-91620

**Lipton, Lenny, 1940-.**       **5.7005**
The super 8 book / by Lenny Lipton; edited by Chet Roaman; designed and illustrated by Christopher Swan. — San Francisco: Straight Arrow Books; [New York]: distributed by Simon and Schuster, c1975. 308 p.: ill.; 23 cm. Includes index. 1. Cinematography 2. Motion picture cameras I. T.
TR851.L56    778.5/3     *LC* 75-9430     *ISBN* 0879320915

**Mathias, Harry.**       **5.7006**
Electronic cinematography: achieving photographic control over the video image / Harry Mathias & Richard Patterson. — Belmont, Calif.: Wadsworth Pub. Co., c1985. xv, 251 p.: ill.; 24 cm. Includes index. 1. Electronic cameras 2. Cinematography I. Patterson, Richard. II. T.
TR882.M38 1985    778.59 19     *LC* 84-17309     *ISBN* 0534042813

## TR892–899 APPLIED CINEMATOGRAPHY. SOUND MOTION PICTURES

**Laybourne, Kit.**       **5.7007**
The animation book: a complete guide to animated filmmaking, from filp–books to sound cartoons / Kit Laybourne; pref. by George Griffin; introd. by Derek Lamb. — New York: Crown Publishers, 1979. xiv, 272 p., [8] p. of plates: ill.; 29 cm. Includes index. 1. Animation (Cinematography) I. T.
TR897.5.L39 1979    778.5/347     *LC* 79-12774     *ISBN* 0517529467

**Perisic, Zoran.**       **5.7008**
The focalguide to shooting animation / Zoran Perisic. — London; New York: Focal Press, c1978. 224 p.: ill. (some col.); 19 cm. Includes index. 1. Animation (Cinematography) I. T.
TR897.5.P48    778.5/347     *LC* 78-307441     *ISBN* 0240509730

**Millerson, Gerald.**       **5.7009**
The technique of lighting for television and motion pictures / by Gerald Millerson. — 2nd ed. — London: Focal Press, 1982. 391 p.: ill.; 23 cm. — (Library of communication techniques.) Includes index. 1. Television — Lighting 2. Cinematography — Lighting I. T. II. Series.
TR899.M48 1982    778.59 778.5/3 18     778.59 778.5/343 19     *LC* 80-42086     *ISBN* 024051128X

**Rosenblum, Ralph.**       **5.7010**
When the shooting stops ... the cutting begins: a film editor's story / Ralph Rosenblum and Robert Karen. — New York: Viking Press, 1979. viii, 310 p.: ill.; 24 cm. Includes index. 1. Motion pictures — Editing I. Karen, Robert. joint author. II. T.
TR899.R67 1979    778.5/35     *LC* 79-11991     *ISBN* 0670759910

## TR925–1045 Photomechanical Processes. Xerography

**Goldschmidt, Lucien.**       **5.7011**
The truthful lens: a survey of the photographically illustrated book, 1844–1914 / Lucien Goldschmidt and Weston J. Naef. — 1st ed. — New York: Grolier Club, 1980. xii, 241 p.: ill.; 29 cm. Based on an exhibition held at the Grolier Club, Dec. 1974. Includes index. 1. Photomechanical processes — Exhibitions. 2. Illustration of books — Exhibitions I. Naef, Weston J., 1942- II. Grolier Club. III. T.
TR925.G73    779 19     *LC* 80-66237

**Williams, Edgar M.**       **5.7012**
The physics and technology of xerographic processes / Edgar M. Williams. — New York: Wiley, c1984. xiv, 288 p.: ill.; 25 cm. 'A Wiley-Interscience publication.' Includes indexes. 1. Xerography I. T.
TR1045.W55 1984    686.4/4 19     *LC* 83-26077     *ISBN* 0471880809

## TS MANUFACTURES

## TS1–149 General Works. Industrial Design History

**Pulos, Arthur J.**       **5.7013**
American design ethic: a history of industrial design to 1940 / Arthur J. Pulos. — Cambridge, Mass.: MIT Press, c1983. 441 p.: ill.; 29 cm. Includes index. 1. Design, Industrial — United States — History. I. T.
TS23.P84 1983    745.2/0973 19     *LC* 82-4625     *ISBN* 0262160854

**Goodison, Nicholas.**       **5.7014**
Ormolu: the work of Matthew Boulton. [London] Phaidon, [distributed by Praeger Publishers, New York, 1974] xii, 398 p. illus. 29 cm. 1. Boulton, Matthew, 1728-1809. 2. Art metal-work — Birmingham, Eng. 3. Gilding 4. Birmingham (West Midlands, England) — Industries. I. T.
TS140.B68 G66    739.2     *LC* 78-165860     *ISBN* 0714815896

**Loewy, Raymond, 1893-1986.**       **5.7015**
Industrial design / Raymond Loewy. — Woodstock, N.Y.: Overlook Press, 1979. 250 p.: ill. (some col.): 28 cm. Includes index. 1. Loewy, Raymond, 1893-1986. 2. Industrial designers — Biography. I. T.
TS140.L63 A34    745.2/092/4 B     *LC* 79-15104     *ISBN* 0879510986

**Dreyfuss, Henry, 1904-.**       • **5.7016**
Designing for people. — [New ed.]. — New York: Paragraphic Books, 1967] 230 p.: ill.; 28 cm. 1. Design, Industrial 2. Human engineering I. T.
TS149.D678 1967    620.8     *LC* 67-12937

**Hounshell, David A.**       **5.7017**
From the American system to mass production, 1800–1932: the development of manufacturing technology in the United States / David A. Hounshell. — Baltimore: Johns Hopkins University Press, c1984. xxi, 411 p.: ill.; 26 cm. — (Studies in industry and society. 4) Includes index. 1. Mass production — United States — History. I. T. II. Series.
TS149.H68 1984    338.6/5/0973 19     *LC* 83-16269     *ISBN* 0801829755

## TS155–199 Production Management. Operations Management

**Apple, James MacGregor, 1915-.**       **5.7018**
Plant layout and material handling / James M. Apple. — 3d ed. New York: John Wiley & Sons, 1977. 488 p.: ill., graph. 1. Factories — Design and construction 2. Materials handling 3. Factories — Design and construction 4. Materials handling I. T.
TS155.A58 1977    *ISBN* 0471071714

**Computers in manufacturing: how to understand metalworking's**       **5.7019**
**newest tools— and their use to improve output / by the editors of American machinist.**
New York: American Machinist, McGraw-Hill, c1983. vi, 299 p.: ill.; 28 cm. Selected articles, mostly from the past 3 years, from the American machinist. Includes index. 1. Production management — Data processing 2. Production engineering — Data processing I. American machinist.
TS155.C59 1983    670/.285/4 19     *LC* 83-8798     *ISBN* 007001549X

**Johnson, Lynwood A.**       **5.7020**
Operations research in production planning, scheduling, and inventory control [by] Lynwood A. Johnson [and] Douglas C. Montgomery. — New York: Wiley, [1974] xiv, 525 p.: illus.; 23 cm. 1. Production management — Mathematical models. 2. Inventory control — Mathematical models. 3. Operations research I. Montgomery, Douglas C. joint author. II. T.
TS155.J56    658.5/03     *LC* 73-17331     *ISBN* 0471446181

**Production and inventory control handbook / James H. Greene,**       **5.7021**
**editor in chief.**
2nd ed. — New York: McGraw-Hill, c1987. 1 v. (various paagings): ill.; 24 cm. 'Prepared under the supervision of the Handbook Editorial Board of the American Production and Inventory Control Society (APICS)' 1. Production

management — Handbooks, manuals, etc. 2. Inventory control — Handbooks, manuals, etc. I. Greene, James H. (James Harnsberger), 1915- II. American Production and Inventory Control Society. Handbook Editorial Board.
TS155.P74 1987      658.5 19      *LC* 86-7195      *ISBN* 0070243212

**Reed, Ruddell.**      **5.7022**
Plant location, layout, and maintenance. — Homewood, Ill.: R. D. Irwin, 1967. viii, 193 p.: ill. (The Irwin series in operations management) 1. Factories — Location 2. Plant layout 3. Plant maintenance I. T.
TS155.R363      658.2      *LC* 67-17049

**Skinner, Wickham.**      **5.7023**
Manufacturing, the formidable competitive weapon / Wickham Skinner. — New York: Wiley, [1985] xviii, 330 p.: ill.; 24 cm. Includes index. 1. Production management I. T.
TS155.S553 1985      658.5 19      *LC* 85-3290      *ISBN* 0471817392

# TS155.6–170 Quality Control.
## Process Control. Scheduling

**CAD/CAM handbook / Eric Teicholz, editor–in–chief.**      **5.7024**
New York: McGraw-Hill, c1985. 1 v. (various pagings): ill.; 29 cm. (McGraw-Hill designing with systems series.) 1. CAD/CAM systems — Handbooks, manuals, etc. I. Teicholz, Eric. II. Title: C.A.D./C.A.M. handbook. III. Series.
TS155.6.C36 1985      620/.00425/02854 19      *LC* 84-4365      *ISBN* 0070634033

**Groover, Mikell P., 1939-.**      **5.7025**
CAD/CAM: computer–aided design and manufacturing / Mikell P. Groover, Emory W. Zimmers, Jr. — Englewood Cliffs, N.J.: Prentice-Hall, c1984. xix, 489 p.: ill. (some col.); 24 cm. 1. CAD/CAM systems I. Zimmers, Emory W. II. T. III. Title: C.A.D./C.A.M.
TS155.6.G76 1984      670/.28/54 19      *LC* 83-11132      *ISBN* 0131101307

**Buffa, Elwood Spencer, 1923-.**      **5.7026**
Production–inventory systems: planning and control / Elwood S. Buffa, Jeffrey G. Miller. — 3d ed. — Homewood, Ill.: Richard D. Irwin, 1979. xii, 744 p.: ill.; 24 cm. 1. Production control 2. Inventory control I. Miller, Jeffrey G. joint author. II. T.
TS155.8.B84 1979      658.7/87      *LC* 78-61186      *ISBN* 0256020418

**Hax, Arnoldo C.**      **5.7027**
Production and inventory management / Arnoldo C. Hax, Dan Candea. — Englewood Cliffs, N.J.: Prentice-Hall, 1960. x, 513 p.: ill.; 24 cm. 1. Production control 2. Inventory control I. Candea, Dan. II. T.
TS155.8.H38 1984      658.5 19      *ISBN* 0137248806

**Orlicky, Joseph.**      **5.7028**
Material requirements planning; the new way of life in production and inventory management. — New York: McGraw-Hill, [1975] xx, 292 p.: illus.; 24 cm. 1. Production control — Data processing 2. Inventory control — Data processing I. T.
TS155.8.O74      658.7      *LC* 74-10904      *ISBN* 0070477086

**Duncan, Acheson J. (Acheson Johnston), 1904-.**      **5.7029**
Quality control and industrial statistics / Acheson J. Duncan. — 5th ed. — Homewood, Ill.: Irwin, 1986. xxii, 1123 p.: ill.; 24 cm. Includes index. 1. Quality control — Statistical methods. 2. Sampling (Statistics) I. T.
TS156.D83 1986      658.5/62 19      *LC* 85-81998      *ISBN* 0256035350

**Halpern, Siegmund, 1918-.**      **5.7030**
The assurance sciences: an introduction to quality control and reliability / Siegmund Halpern. — Englewood Cliffs, N.J.: Prentice-Hall, c1978. xii, 431 p.: ill.; 25 cm. Includes index. 1. Quality control 2. Reliability (Engineering) 3. Maintainability (Engineering) I. T.
TS156.H3      620/.0045      *LC* 77-2967      *ISBN* 0130496014

**Johnson, Curtis D., 1939-.**      **5.7031**
Microprocessor–based process control / Curtis D. Johnson. — Englewood Cliffs, N.J.: Prentice-Hall, c1984. x, 259 p.: ill. Includes index. 1. Process control 2. Microprocessors I. T.
TS156.8.J628 1984      629.8/95 19      *LC* 83-17832      *ISBN* 0135806542

**Patrick, Dale R.**      **5.7032**
Industrial process control systems / by Dale R. Patrick and Stephen W. Fardo. — Englewood Cliffs, N.J.: Prentice-Hall, 1985, c1979. 200 p.: ill.; 28 cm. 1. Process control I. Fardo, Stephen W. II. T.
TS156.8.P25      670.42/7 19      *LC* 79-65744      *ISBN* 0134629876

**Process instruments and controls handbook / Douglas M.**      **5.7033**
**Considine, editor–in–chief; Glenn D. Considine, managing editor.**
3rd ed. — New York: McGraw-Hill, c1985. 1766 p. in various pagings: ill.; 24 cm. 1. Process control — Handbooks, manuals, etc. 2. Automatic control — Handbooks, manuals, etc. 3. Engineering instruments — Handbooks, manuals, etc. I. Considine, Douglas Maxwell. II. Considine, Glenn D.
TS156.8.P764 1985      629.8 19      *LC* 84-10044      *ISBN* 0070124361

**Bedworth, David D.**      **5.7034**
Integrated production control systems: management, analysis, design / David D. Bedworth, James E. Bailey. — 2[nd] e[d.]. — New York: Wiley, c1987. xiv, 477 p.: ill.; 24 cm. 1. Production control — Data processing I. Bailey, James Edward, 1942- II. T.
TS157.B43 1987      658.5/0028/5 19      *LC* 86-23379      *ISBN* 0471821799

**Baker, Kenneth R., 1943-.**      **5.7035**
Introduction to sequencing and scheduling [by] Kenneth R. Baker. — New York: Wiley, [1974] ix, 305 p.: illus.; 23 cm. 1. Scheduling (Management) I. T.
TS157.5.B34      TS157.5 B34.      658.5/1      *LC* 74-8010      *ISBN* 0471045551

**Lang, Douglas Wallace.**      **5.7036**
Critical path analysis / [by] Douglas W. Lang. — 2nd ed. — [Sevenoaks]: Teach Yourself Books, 1977. xi, 217 p.: ill.; 18 cm. — (Teach yourself books) Includes index. 1. Critical path analysis I. T.
TS158.L36 1977      309.2/62      *LC* 77-371563      *ISBN* 0340212780

**Brown, Robert Goodell.**      **5.7037**
Materials management systems: a modular library / Robert Goodell Brown. — New York: Wiley, c1977. xii, 436 p.: ill.; 24 cm. 'A Wiley-Interscience publication.' Includes index. 1. Materials management 2. Materials management — Data processing I. T.
TS161.B76      658.7/028/54      *LC* 77-8281      *ISBN* 0471111821

**Tersine, Richard J.**      **5.7038**
Modern materials management / Richard J. Tersine, John H. Campbell. — New York: North-Holland, c1977. xii, 281 p.: ill.; 24 cm. Includes index. 1. Materials management I. Campbell, John Hardin, 1946- joint author. II. T.
TS161.T48      658.7      *LC* 77-2291      *ISBN* 0444002286

# TS171–175 Product Design.
## Industrial Design. Product Safety

**Niebel, Benjamin W.**      **5.7039**
Product design and process engineering [by] Benjamin W. Niebel [and] Alan B. Draper. — New York: McGraw-Hill, [1974] xii, 833 p.: illus.; 24 cm. 1. Design, Industrial 2. Production engineering 3. Manufacturing processes I. Draper, Alan B., joint author. II. T.
TS171.N53      620/.004/2      *LC* 74-4294      *ISBN* 0070465355

**Lucie-Smith, Edward.**      **5.7040**
A history of industrial design / Edward Lucie–Smith. — New York: Van Nostrand Reinhold, c1983. 240 p.: ill. (some col.); 29 cm. Includes index. 1. Design, Industrial — History. I. T.
TS171.4.L83 1983      745.2/09 19      *LC* 83-5861      *ISBN* 0442258046

**Pye, David W., 1914-.**      **5.7041**
The nature and art of workmanship [by] David Pye. — London: Studio Vista; New York: Van Nostrand Reinhold, 1971. 96 p.: illus., facsim.; 20 cm. Originally published, London: Cambridge University Press, 1968. 1. Design, Industrial I. T.
TS171.4.P9 1971      745.2      *LC* 78-141444      *ISBN* 0289701422

**Dhillon, B. S.**      **5.7042**
Engineering reliability: new techniques and applications / B. S. Dhillon, Chanan Singh. — New York: Wiley, c1981. xix, 339 p.: ill.; 24 cm. — (Wiley series on systems engineering and analysis) 'A Wiley-interscience publication.' 1. Reliability (Engineering) I. Singh, Chanan. joint author. II. T.
TS173.D48      620/.00452      *LC* 80-18734      *ISBN* 0471050148

**Henley, Ernest J.**      **5.7043**
Reliability engineering and risk assessment / Ernest J. Henley, Hiromitsu Kumamoto. — Englewood Cliffs, N.J.: Prentice-Hall, c1981. xxiv, 568 p.: ill.; 24 cm. 1. Reliability (Engineering) 2. Health risk assessment I. Kumamoto, Hiromitsu. joint author. II. T.
TS173.H47 1981      620/.00452      *LC* 80-381      *ISBN* 0137722516

**Hammer, Willie.**      **5.7044**
Product safety management and engineering / Willie Hammer. — Englewood Cliffs, N.J.: Prentice-Hall, c1980. xii, 324 p.: ill.; 29 cm. — (Prentice-Hall

international series in industrial and systems engineering.) Includes index.
1. Product safety I. T. II. Series.
TS175.H35 1980     658.5/6     *LC* 79-11058     *ISBN* 0137241046

## TS176–195 Manufacturing Engineering. Process Engineering. Packaging

**Bolz, Roger William.**       **5.7045**
Production processes: the productivity handbook / Roger W. Bolz. — 5th ed. — Winston-Salem, N.C.: Conquest Publications, c1977. 1,092 p. in various pagings: ill.; 27 cm. Cover title: The productivity handbook. 1. Production engineering 2. Manufacturing processes I. T. II. Title: Productivity handbook.
TS176.B64 1977     658.5 19     *LC* 76-24032

**Halevi, Gideon, 1928-.**       **5.7046**
The role of computers in manufacturing processes / Gideon Halevi. — New York: Wiley, c1980. xiv, 502 p.: ill.; 24 cm. 'A Wiley-Interscience publication.' 1. Production engineering — Data processing I. T.
TS176.H33     658.5/0028/54     *LC* 80-11378     *ISBN* 0471043834

**Owen, A. E.**       **5.7047**
Flexible assembly systems: assembly by robots and computerized integrated systems / A.E. (Tony) Owen. — New York: Plenum Press, c1984. xi, 231 p.: ill.; 24 cm. Includes index. 1. Assembly-line methods 2. Robots, Industrial 3. Automation I. T.
TS178.4.O94 1984     670.42/7 19     *LC* 84-4852     *ISBN* 0306415275

**Groover, Mikell P., 1939-.**       **5.7048**
Automation, production systems, and computer–aided manufacturing / Mikell P. Groover. — Englewood Cliffs, N.J.: Prentice-Hall, c1980. xix, 601 p.: ill.; 25 cm. 1. Manufacturing processes — Automation. 2. Production control 3. CAD/CAM systems 4. Robots, Industrial 5. Group technology I. T.
TS183.G76 1980     629.8 19     *LC* 79-23492     *ISBN* 0130546682

**Handbook of industrial robotics / Shimon Y. Nof, editor; with a**    **5.7049**
**foreword by Isaac Asimov.**
New York: J. Wiley, c1985. xvii, 1358 p.: ill.; 25 cm. 1. Robots, Industrial — Handbooks, manuals, etc. I. Nof, Shimon Y., 1946-
TS191.8.H36 1985     629.8/92 19     *LC* 84-20969     *ISBN* 0471896845

**Kafrissen, Edward.**       **5.7050**
Industrial robots and robotics / Edward Kafrissen, Mark Stephans. — Reston, Va.: Reston Pub. Co., c1984. xiv, 396 p.: ill.; 25 cm. Includes index. 1. Robots, Industrial 2. Robotics I. Stephans, Mark. II. T.
TS191.8.K34 1984     629.8/92 19     *LC* 83-17723     *ISBN* 0835930718

**Mann, Lawrence.**       **5.7051**
Maintenance management / Lawrence Mann, Jr. — Rev. ed. — Lexington, Mass.: LexingtonBooks, c1983. xxv, 480 p.: ill.; 24 cm. Includes index. 1. Plant maintenance I. T.
TS192.M38 1983     658.2/02 19     *LC* 81-47628     *ISBN* 0669047155

**Hanlon, Joseph F.**       **5.7052**
Handbook of package engineering / Joseph F. Hanlon. — 2nd ed. — New York: McGraw-Hill, c1984. viii, 538 p. in various pagings: ill.; 24 cm. Includes index. 1. Packaging — Handbooks, manuals, etc. I. T. II. Title: Package engineering.
TS195.H35 1984     688.8 19     *LC* 83-13589     *ISBN* 0070259941

## TS200–770 Metal Manufactures. Metalworking. Welding

**Backofen, Walter A.**       **5.7053**
Deformation processing [by] Walter A. Backofen. — Reading, Mass.: Addison-Wesley Pub. Co., [c1972] 326 p.: illus.; 25 cm. — (Addison-Wesley series in metallurgy and materials) 1. Metal-work 2. Deformations (Mechanics) I. T.
TS213.B23     671.3     *LC* 71-132054

**Harris, John Noel.**       **5.7054**
Mechanical working of metals: theory and practice / by John Noel Harris. — 1st ed. — Oxford; New York: Pergamon Press, 1983. viii, 243 p.: ill.; 23 cm. (International series on materials science and technology. v. 36) (Pergamon international library of science, technology, engineering, and social studies.)

1. Metal-work I. T. II. Series. III. Series: Pergamon international library of science, technology, engineering, and social studies.
TS213.H29 1983     671.3 19     *LC* 81-19957     *ISBN* 0080254640

**Metal forming and impact mechanics: William Johnson**    **5.7055**
**commemorative volume / edited by S.R. Reid.**
1st ed. — Oxford [Oxfordshire]; New York: Pergamon Press, 1985. xliv, 348 p., [1] leaf of plates: ill., port.; 24 cm. 1. Metal-work 2. Deformations (Mechanics) 3. Impact I. Johnson, W. (William), 1922- II. Reid, S. R.
TS213.M385 1985     671.3 19     *LC* 85-12292     *ISBN* 0080316794

**Forging handbook / Thomas G. Byrer, editor; S.L. Semiatin,**    **5.7056**
**associate editor; Donald C. Vollmer, associate editor.**
Cleveland, Ohio: Forging Industry Association; Metals Park, Ohio: American Society for Metals, c1985. ix, 296 p.: ill.; 29 cm. 1. Forging — Handbooks, manuals, etc. I. Byrer, Thomas G. II. Semiatin, S. L. III. Vollmer, Donald C.
TS225.F549 1985     671.3/32 19     *LC* 85-71789     *ISBN* 0871701944

**Davies, A. C. (Arthur Cyril).**       **5.7057**
The science and practice of welding / A.C. Davies. — 8th ed. — Cambridge [Cambridgeshire]; New York: Cambridge University Press, 1984. 2 v.: ill.; 24 cm. Includes index. 1. Welding I. T.
TS227.D22 1984     671.5/2 19     *LC* 83-23225     *ISBN* 0521261139

**Dawson, R. J. C.**       **5.7058**
Fusion welding and brazing of copper and copper alloys [by] R. J. C. Dawson. — New York: Wiley, [1973] 139 p.: illus.; 23 cm. 'A Halsted Press book.' 1. Copper — Welding 2. Copper alloys — Welding 3. Copper — Brazing 4. Copper alloys — Brazing I. T.
TS227.D34     673/.3/52     *LC* 73-7969     *ISBN* 0470199814

**Houldcroft, Peter Thomas.**       **5.7059**
Welding process technology / P. T. Houldcroft. — Cambridge, Eng.: Cambridge University Press, 1977. ix, 313 p.: ill.; 24 cm. Successor to the author's Welding processes. 1. Welding I. T.
TS227.H678     671.5/2     *LC* 76-47408     *ISBN* 0521215307

**Lindberg, Roy A.**       **5.7060**
Welding and other joining processes / Roy A. Lindberg, Norman R. Braton. — Boston: Allyn and Bacon, c1976. vii, 541 p.: ill.; 24 cm. 1. Welding 2. Metal bonding 3. Fasteners I. Braton, Norman R. joint author. II. T.
TS227.L58     671.5     *LC* 75-30745     *ISBN* 020505000X

**Welding processes / Ivan H. Griffin ... [et al.].**       **5.7061**
3rd ed. — Albany, N.Y.: Delmar Publishers, c1984. ix, 309 p.: ill. (some col.); 27 cm. Rev. ed. of: Welding processes / Ivan H. Griffin, Edward M. Roden, Charles W. Briggs. 2nd ed. 1978. Includes index. 1. Welding I. Griffin, Ivan H. II. Griffin, Ivan H. Welding processes. 2nd ed.
TS227.W413 1984     671.5/2 19     *LC* 84-4302     *ISBN* 0827321333

**The Physics of welding / International Institute of Welding =**    **5.7062**
**Institut international de la soudure; edited by J.F. Lancaster.**
2nd ed. — Oxford; New York: Pergamon, 1986. xix, 340 p.: ill.; 24 cm. 1. Welding 2. Physics I. Lancaster, J. F. (John Frederick) II. International Institute of Welding.
TS227.2.P49 1986     671.5/2 19     *LC* 86-9441     *ISBN* 0080340768

**Schwartz, Mel M.**       **5.7063**
Metals joining manual / M. M. Schwartz. — New York: McGraw-Hill, c1979. 556 p. in various pagings: ill.; 24 cm. 1. Welding — Handbooks, manuals, etc. 2. Brazing — Handbooks, manuals, etc. 3. Solder and soldering — Handbooks, manuals, etc. I. T.
TS227.2.S38     671.5/02/02     *LC* 78-27886     *ISBN* 0070557209

**Wilson, Robert, chief metallurgist.**       **5.7064**
Metallurgy and heat treatment of tool steels / Robert Wilson. — London; New York: McGraw-Hill, [1975] xi, 378 p.: ill.; 26 cm. 1. Tool-steel I. T.
TS320.W63     669/.142     *LC* 74-32061     *ISBN* 0070844534

## TS500–549 Instruments. Clocks

**Horne, Douglas F. (Douglas Favel), 1915-.**       **5.7065**
Optical production technology [by] D. F. Horne. New York, Crane, Russak [1972, c1962] 567 p. illus. 29 cm. 1. Optical instruments — Design and construction I. T.
TS513.H67     681/.42     *LC* 72-79282     *ISBN* 0844800082

**Landes, David S.**       **5.7066**
Revolution in time: clocks and the making of the modern world / David S. Landes. — Cambridge, Mass.: Belknap Press of Harvard University Press, 1983. xviii, 482 p., [40] p. of plates: ill. (some col.); 25 cm. 1. Clocks and watches — History. 2. Horology — History. I. T.
TS542.L24 1983     681.1/13/09 19     *LC* 83-8489     *ISBN* 0674768000

## TS653–770 Metal Finishing. Precious Metals. Jewelry

**Lowenheim, Frederick Adolph, 1909-.** 5.7067
Electroplating / Frederick A. Lowenheim; sponsored by the American Electroplaters' Society. — New York: McGraw-Hill, c1978. xii, 594 p.: ill.; 24 cm. Includes index. 1. Electroplating I. American Electroplaters' Society. II. T.
TS670.L67 671.7/32 LC 77-11993 ISBN 0070388369

**Morton, Philip.** 5.7068
Contemporary jewelry: a studio handbook / Philip Morton. — Rev. and expanded. — New York: Holt, Rinehart and Winston, c1976. xii, 348 p.: ill.; 27 cm. Includes index. 1. Jewelry — History — 20th century 2. Jewelry making I. T.
TS740.M67 1976 739.27 LC 75-25851 ISBN 0030899249

**Sinkankas, John.** 5.7069
Gemstone & mineral data book: a compilation of data, recipes, formulas, and instructions for the mineralogist, gemologist, lapidary, jeweler, craftsman, and collector / John Sinkankas. — New York: Van Nostrand Reinhold Co., 1981, c1972. 352 p.; 23 cm. Includes index. Originally published: New York: Winchester Press, 1972. 1. Gem cutting — Handbooks, manuals, etc. 2. Mineralogy — Handbooks, manuals, etc. I. T. II. Title: Gemstone and mineral data book.
TS752.5.S56 1981 736/.2/028 19 LC 80-52974 ISBN 0442247095

## TS800–915 Wood Products. Furniture

**Wilk, Christopher.** 5.7070
Thonet: 150 years of furniture / Christopher Wilk. — Woodbury, N.Y.: Barron's, c1980. 143 p.: ill.; 22 x 24 cm. 1. Thonet, Michael, 1796-1871. 2. Gebrüder Thonet. 3. Furniture industry and trade — Austria — Vienna — Biography. 4. Vienna (Austria) — Industries. I. T.
TS810.A9 W53 684.1/3 19 LC 80-27891 ISBN 0812053842

**Hayward, Helena.** 5.7071
William and John Linnell, eighteenth century London furniture makers / Helena Hayward, Pat Kirkham. — New York: Rizzoli in association with Christie's, c1980. 2 v.: ill. (some col.); 29 cm. Includes index. 1. Linnell, William, ca. 1703-1763. 2. Linnell, John, 1729-1796. 3. Furniture industry and trade — England — London — History. 4. Furniture industry and trade — England — London — Biography. 5. London (England) — Industries. I. Kirkham, Pat. II. T.
TS810.G7 H39 684.1/0092/2 B 19 LC 80-51404 ISBN 0847803252

**Billcliffe, Roger.** 5.7072
Charles Rennie Mackintosh: the complete furniture, furniture drawings & interior designs / Roger Billcliffe. — New York: Taplinger Pub. Co., 1979. 252 p., [7] leaves of plates: ill. (some col.); 34 cm. Includes index. 1. Mackintosh, Charles Rennie, 1868-1928. 2. Furniture design I. T.
TS885.B54 1979 749.2/9411 LC 78-72303 ISBN 0800817737

**Greenberg, Cara.** 5.7073
Mid–century modern: furniture of the 1950's / by Cara Greenberg; new photography by Tim Street–Porter. — 1st ed. — New York: Harmony Books, c1984. 175 p.: ill. (some col.); 26 cm. Includes index. 1. Furniture — History — 20th century. I. T. II. Title: Furniture of the 1950s.
TS885.G68 1984 683.1/09/045 19 LC 84-3777 ISBN 0517554119

## TS1080–1268 Paper Manufacturing and Trade

**Hunter, Dard, 1883-1966.** 5.7074
Papermaking: the history and technique of an ancient craft / by Dard Hunter. — New York: Dover Publications, 1978, c1947. xxiv, 611, xxxvii p.: ill.; 22 cm. 'Unabridged republication of the second edition of this work as published by Alfred A. Knopf, New York.' Includes index. 1. Papermaking — History. 2. Water-marks — History. I. T.
TS1090.H816 1978 676/.2/09 LC 77-92477 ISBN 0486236196

**Saltman, David.** 5.7075
Paper basics: forestry, manufacture, selection, purchasing, mathematics and metrics, recycling / David Saltman. — New York: Van Nostrand Reinhold Co., c1978. xiv, 223 p.: ill.; 24 cm. Includes index. 1. Paper I. T.
TS1105.S23 676 LC 78-1476 ISBN 0442252211

## TS1300–1865 Textile Industries

**Warming, Wanda, 1947-.** 5.7076
The world of Indonesian textiles / text and photos. by Wanda Warming and Michael Gaworski; line drawings by Richard Flavin. — 1st ed. — Tokyo; New York: Kodansha International, 1981. 200 p.: ill. (some col.); 31 cm. Includes index. 1. Textile fabrics — Indonesia. I. Gaworski, Michael, 1950- joint author. II. T.
TS1413.I55 W37 677/.09598 19 LC 80-82526 ISBN 0870114328

**Encyclopedia of textiles / by the editors of American fabrics and fashions magazine.** 5.7077
3d ed. — Englewood Cliffs, N.J.: Prentice-Hall, c1980. xvi, 636 p.: ill.; 31 cm. 'Plus a comprehensive dictionary of textile terms.' Second ed. published under title: AF encyclopedia of textiles. Includes index. 1. Textile industry 2. Textile fabrics 3. Textile industry — Dictionaries. 4. Textile fabrics — Dictionaries. I. American fabrics and fashions. II. Title: AF encyclopedia of textiles.
TS1445.A18 1980 677 LC 79-26497 ISBN 0132765764

**American Home Economics Association. Textiles and Clothing Section.** 5.7078
Textile handbook. — 5th ed. — Washington: American Home Economics Association, [1974] v, 121 p.: ill.; 25 cm. Includes index. 1. Textile fabrics I. T.
TS1445.A46 1974 677/.002/02 LC 74-31289 ISBN 0846116111

**Emery, Irene.** 5.7079
The primary structures of fabrics: an illustrated classifications / by Irene Emery. — Washington, D.C.: Textile Museum, 1980. xxvi, 341 p.: ill.; 32 cm. Includes index. 1. Textile fabrics — Classification. I. Textile Museum (Washington, D.C.) II. T.
TS1449.E42 1980 677.6 19 LC 80-52671

**Albers, Anni.** • 5.7080
On weaving. — [1st ed.]. — Middletown, Conn.: Wesleyan University Press, [1965] 204 p.: illus. (part col.); 29 cm. 1. Textile design 2. Weaving I. T.
TS1475.A42 677.022 LC 65-19855

**Montgomery, Florence M.** 5.7081
Textiles in America, 1650-1870: a dictionary based on original documents: prints and paintings, commercial records, American merchants' papers, shopkeepers' advertisements, and pattern books with original swatches of cloth / Florence M. Montgomery. — 1st ed. — New York: Norton, [1984]. xviii, 412 p.: ill. (some col.); 26 cm. — 'A Winterthur/Barra Book.' 1. Textile fabrics — United States — History. 2. Textile fabrics — United States — Dictionaries. I. T.
TS1767.M66 1984 677/.02864/0973 19 LC 83-25339 ISBN 0393017036

## TS1870–2301 Rubber Industry. Other Industries

**Blackley, D. C.** 5.7082
Synthetic rubbers: their chemistry and technology / D.C. Blackley. — London; New York: Applied Science Publishers; New York, N.Y.: Sole distributor in the USA and Canada, Elsevier Science, c1983. ix, 372 p.: ill.; 23 cm. Includes index. 1. Rubber, Artificial I. T.
TS1925.B55 1983 678/.72 19 LC 82-222429 ISBN 0853341524

**Meat and poultry inspection: the scientific basis of the Nation's Program / prepared by the Committee on the Scientific Basis of the Nation's Meat and Poultry Inspection Program, Food and Nutrition Board, Commission on Life Sciences, National Research Council.** 5.7083
Washington, D.C.: National Academy Press, 1985. xii, 209 p. 1. Meat inspection — United States 2. Poultry — Inspection — United States I. National Research Council (U.S.). Committee on the Scientific Basis of the Nation's Meat and Poultry Inspection Program.
TS1975 M53 1985 LC 85-71993 ISBN 0309035821

**Read, Oliver.**                                                                    **5.7084**
From tin foil to stereo: evolution of the phonograph / by Oliver Read and Walter L. Welch. — 2d ed. — Indianapolis: H. W. Sams, 1976. xxii, 550 p., [8] leaves of plates: ill.; 22 cm. Includes index. 1. Phonograph — History. 2. Sound — Recording and reproducing — History. I. Welch, Walter Leslie, 1901- joint author. II. T.
TS2301.P3 R4 1976     621.389/33     *LC* 75-5412     *ISBN* 0672212064

# TT HANDICRAFTS. ARTS AND CRAFTS

**Harvey, John Hooper.**                                                              **5.7085**
Mediaeval craftsmen / John Harvey. — London: Batsford, 1975. vii, 231 p., [24] leaves of plates: ill.; 23 cm. Includes indexes. 1. Handicraft — Europe — History. 2. Artisans — Europe. 3. Middle Ages I. T.
TT55.H37 1974b     338.6/42/094     *LC* 75-317236     *ISBN* 0713429348

**Lever, Jill.**                                                                      **5.7086**
Architects' designs for furniture / Jill Lever. — New York: Rizzoli, 1982. 142 p.: ill. (some col.); 25 cm. Published in association with RIBA's British Architectural Library Drawings Collection. Includes index. 1. Furniture design 2. Architectural drawing 3. Architect-designed furniture I. British Architectural Library. II. T.
TT196.L46 1982     749.22 19     *LC* 82-236951     *ISBN* 0847804429

**Manko, Howard H.**                                                                  **5.7087**
Solders and soldering: materials, design, production, and analysis for reliable bonding / Howard H. Manko. — 2d ed. — New York: McGraw-Hill, c1979. xv, 350 p.: ill.; 24 cm. 1. Solder and soldering I. T.
TT267.M26 1979     671.5/6     *LC* 79-9714     *ISBN* 0070398976

**Gioello, Debbie Ann.**                                                              **5.7088**
Fashion production terms / Debbie Ann Gioello, Beverly Berke. — New York: Fairchild Publications, c1979. xi, 340 p.: ill.; 29 cm. (Language of fashion series.) Includes index. 1. Clothing trade — Terminology. 2. Fashion — Terminology. I. Berke, Beverly. joint author. II. T. III. Series.
TT494.G56     687/.01/4     *LC* 78-62284     *ISBN* 0870052004

**Kidwell, Claudia B.**                                                               **5.7089**
Suiting everyone: the democratization of clothing in America [by] Claudia B. Kidwell [and] Margaret C. Christman. — Washington: Published for the National Museum of History and Technology by the Smithsonian Institution Press; [for sale by the Supt. of Docs., U.S. Govt. Print. Off.], 1974. 208 p.: illus.; 23 x 28 cm. — (Smithsonian Institution Press publication no. 5176) 1. Clothing trade — United States — History. 2. Costume — United States — History. I. Christman, Margaret C. S. joint author. II. National Museum of History and Technology. III. T.
TT497.K44     391/.00973     *LC* 74-16239

**De Marly, Diana.**                                                                  **5.7090**
The history of haute couture, 1850–1950 / Diana de Marly. — New York: Holmes and Meier, c1980. 216 p., [4] leaves of plates: ill.; 26 cm. Includes index. 1. Fashion — History — 19th century. 2. Fashion — History — 20th century. I. T.
TT504.D45     391/.07/2     *LC* 79-22987     *ISBN* 084190586X

**Waugh, Norah.**                                                                • **5.7091**
The cut of men's clothes, 1600–1900. — New York, Theatre Arts Books [1964] 160 p.: illus. (part col.) 26 cm. Bibliography: p. 157. 1. Tailoring — Hist. I. T.
TT504.W38     391.109     *LC* 64-21658

**Waugh, Norah.**                                                                     **5.7092**
The cut of women's clothes, 1600–1930. With line diagrs. by Margaret Woodward. — New York: Theatre Arts Books, [1968] 336 p.: illus., ports. (1 col.); 29 cm. 1. Dressmaking — History. 2. Tailoring (Women's) — History. I. Woodward, Margaret. II. T.
TT504.W385 1968     391/.2/09     *LC* 68-13408

**LaVine, W. Robert.**                                                                **5.7093**
In a glamorous fashion: the fabulous years of Hollywood costume design / W. Robert LaVine, special assistant and photo consultant, Allen Florio. — New York: Scribner, c1980. xi, 259 p.: ill.; 28 cm. Includes index. 1. Costume design — California — Hollywood — History. 2. Costume designers — California — Hollywood. I. Florio, Allen. II. T.
TT507.L36     791.43/026/0979494     *LC* 80-16512     *ISBN* 0684166100

**The Psychology of fashion** / edited by Michael R. Solomon.                         **5.7094**
Lexington, Mass.: Lexington Books, c1985. xii, 428 p.: ill.; 24 cm. (Advances in retailing series.) 1. Fashion — Psychological aspects. I. Solomon, Michael R. II. Series.
TT507.P84 1985     391/.2/019 19     *LC* 84-48079     *ISBN* 0066901286

**Swan, Susan Burrows.**                                                              **5.7095**
Plain & fancy: American women and their needlework, 1700–1850 / Susan Burrows Swan. — 1st ed. — New York: Holt, Rinehart and Winston, c1977. 240 p.: ill.; 24 cm. 'A Rutledge book.' Includes index. 1. Needlework — United States — History. I. T.
TT715.S9     301.41/2     *LC* 77-1627     *ISBN* 003015121X

**Black, Mary E.**                                                                    **5.7096**
The key to weaving: a textbook of hand weaving for the beginning weaver / Mary E. Black. — 2d rev. ed. — New York: Macmillan, c1980. xvii, 698 p.: ill.; 25 cm. Edition for 1957 published under title: New key to weaving. Includes index. 1. Hand weaving I. T.
TT848.B5 1980     746.1/4     *LC* 79-26177     *ISBN* 0025111701

**Burnham, Harold B.**                                                                **5.7097**
Keep me warm one night: early handweaving in eastern Canada [by] Harold B. Burnham and Dorothy K. Burnham. [Toronto] University of Toronto Press in cooperation with the Royal Ontario Museum [c1972] xv, 387 p. illus. (part col.) 32 cm. 1. Hand weaving — Canada, Eastern. 2. Hand weaving — Patterns I. Burnham, Dorothy K. joint author. II. Royal Ontario Museum. III. T.
TT848.B85     746.1/4/0971     *LC* 72-83388     *ISBN* 0802018963 *ISBN* 0802002390

**Regensteiner, Else, 1906-.**                                                        **5.7098**
Weaver's study course, ideas and techniques / Else Regensteiner. — New York: Van Nostrand Reinhold Co., [1975] 144 p.: ill.; 29 cm. Rev. ed. published as: Weaving sourcebook. 2nd ed. 1983. Includes index. 1. Weaving I. T.
TT848.R44     746.1/4     *LC* 74-19755     *ISBN* 0442268718

**Olsen, Frederick L.**                                                               **5.7099**
The kiln book: materials, specifications, and construction / Frederick L. Olsen. — 2nd ed. — Radnor, Pa.: Chilton Book Co., c1983. xix, 291 p.: ill.; 24 cm. Includes index. 1. Kilns I. T.
TT924.O44 1983     738.1/3 19     *LC* 81-71090     *ISBN* 0801970717

# TX HOME ECONOMICS

## TX1–339 General Works. The House

**Cowan, Ruth Schwartz, 1941-.**                                                      **5.7100**
More work for mother: the ironies of household technology from the open hearth to the microwave / Ruth Schwartz Cowan. — New York: Basic Books, c1983. xiv, 257 p.: ill.; 25 cm. Includes index. 1. Home economics — United States — History. 2. Household appliances — United States — History. 3. Housewives — United States — History. I. T. II. Title: Household technology from the open hearth to the microwave.
TX23.C64 1983     640/.973 19     *LC* 83-70759     *ISBN* 0465047319

**Strasser, Susan, 1948-.**                                                           **5.7101**
Never done: a history of American housework / Susan Strasser. — 1st ed. — New York: Pantheon Books, c1982. xvi, 365 p.: ill.; 24 cm. Includes index. 1. Home economics — United States — History. 2. Housewives — United States — History. I. T.
TX23.S77 1982     640/.973 19     *LC* 81-48234     *ISBN* 0394510240

**Cohen, Daniel.**                                                                    **5.7102**
The last hundred years, household technology / by Daniel Cohen. — New York: M. Evans, 1983 (c1982). 184 p.: ill.; 22 cm. Includes index. 1. Household appliances — United States — History — Juvenile literature. 2. Technology — United States — History — Juvenile literature. I. T. II. Title: Last 100 years, household technology.
TX298.C58 1982     683/.8 19     *LC* 82-15442     *ISBN* 0871313863

# TX341–641 Nutrition. Foods and Food Supply

## TX349–350 DICTIONARIES. ENCYCLOPEDIAS

**Bender, Arnold E.**                                    5.7103
Dictionary of nutrition and food technology / Arnold E. Bender. — 5th ed. — London; Boston: Butterworths, 1982. 309 p.: ill.; 23 cm. 1. Nutrition — Dictionaries. 2. Food — Dictionaries. I. T.
TX349.B4 1982    641/.03/21 19    *LC* 83-201568    *ISBN* 040810855X

**Foods and food production encyclopedia / Douglas M.**    5.7104
**Considine, editor-in-chief; Glenn D. Considine, managing editor.**
New York: Van Nostrand Reinhold, c1982. xvi, 2305 p., [5] p. of plates: ill.; 29 cm. 1. Food — Dictionaries. 2. Agriculture — Dictionaries. 3. Food industry and trade — Dictionaries. I. Considine, Douglas Maxwell.
TX349.F58 1982    664/.03/21 19    *LC* 81-19728    *ISBN* 0442216122

**Larousse gastronomique / sous la direction de Robert J.**    5.7105
**Courtine.**
Paris: Larousse, c1984. 1142 p.: ill. (some col.); 27 cm. 1. Cookery — Dictionaries — French. 2. Food — Dictionaries — French. 3. Cookery, French I. Courtine, Robert J.
TX349.L36 1984    641.5/03/41 19    *LC* 84-172455    *ISBN* 2035063019

**Martin, Ruth Marion Somers, 1914-.**    5.7106
International dictionary of food and cooking [by] Ruth Martin. — New York: Hastings House, [1974, c1973] 311 p.; 21 cm. 1. Food — Dictionaries — Polyglot. 2. Cookery — Dictionaries — Polyglot. 3. Dictionaries, Polyglot I. T.
TX349.M33 1974    641.5/03    *LC* 73-21522    *ISBN* 0803833881

**Simon, André Louis, 1877-1970.**    • 5.7107
A dictionary of gastronomy [by] André L. Simon and Robin Howe. — New York: McGraw-Hill, [1970] 400 p.: illus. (part col.); 28 cm. 1. Food — Dictionaries. 2. Cookery — Dictionaries. I. Howe, Robin. joint author. II. T.
TX349.S53 1970    641/.03    *LC* 72-89318

## TX353 GENERAL WORKS, 1800-

**Deatherage, Fred E., 1913-.**    5.7108
Food for life / F. E. Deatherage. — New York: Plenum Press, [1975] xii, 422 p.: ill.; 24 cm. 1. Food 2. Food supply I. T.
TX353.D38 1975    641.3    *LC* 75-15502    *ISBN* 0306308169

**Frank, Robyn C.**    5.7109
Directory of food and nutrition information services and resources / edited by Robyn C. Frank. — [Phoenix, AZ]: Oryx Press, 1984. vi, 287 p.; 28 cm. Includes indexes. 1. Food — Information services — United States — Directories. 2. Nutrition — Information services — United States — Directories. I. T.
TX353.F75 1984    641/.072073 19    *LC* 83-42505    *ISBN* 0897740785

**Nutrition reviews' present knowledge in nutrition.**    5.7110
5th ed. — Washington, D.C.: Nutrition Foundation, 1984. xxii, 900 p., [2] p. of plates: ill. (some col.); 22 cm. 1. Nutrition I. Nutrition reviews. II. Title: Present knowledge in nutrition.
TX353.N88 1984    613.2 19    *LC* 84-60427    *ISBN* 093536840X

**Borgstrom, Georg, 1912-.**    • 5.7111
Principles of food science. — New York, Macmillan [1968] 2 v. illus. 26 cm. 1. Food 2. Food industry and trade I. T.
TX354.B64    664    *LC* 68-14715

**Charley, Helen.**    5.7112
Food science / Helen Charley. — 2nd ed. — New York: Wiley, c1982. 564 p.: ill.; 24 cm. 1. Food 2. Nutrition 3. Cookery I. T.
TX354.C47 1982    641.3 19    *LC* 81-11366    *ISBN* 0471062065

**Guthrie, Helen Andrews.**    5.7113
Introductory nutrition / Helen A. Guthrie. — 5th ed. — St. Louis: Mosby, 1983. vii, 675 p.: ill.; 29 cm. 1. Nutrition I. T.
TX354.G8 1983    613.2 19    *LC* 82-8084    *ISBN* 0801619971

**Lee, Frank A.**    5.7114
Basic food chemistry / Frank A. Lee. — 2nd ed. — Westport, Conn.: AVI Pub. Co., c1983. xi, 564 p.: ill.; 24 cm. — (Food science and technology textbook series.) 1. Food 2. Food — Composition I. T. II. Series.
TX354.L43 1983    641.3/001/54 19    *LC* 83-9186    *ISBN* 0870554166

**The Nutrition debate: sorting out some answers / [compiled by]**    5.7115
**Joan Dye Gussow and Paul R. Thomas.**
Palo Alto, Calif.: Bull Pub. Co.; New York, NY: Distributed in the U.S. by Kampmann, c1986. x, 411 p.: ill.; 23 cm. Consists, primarily, of articles reprinted from various sources, but includes some previously unpublished materials. 1. Nutrition 2. Diet 3. Food I. Gussow, Joan Dye. II. Thomas, Paul R., 1953-
TX355.5.N86 1986    613.2 19    *LC* 86-21616    *ISBN* 0915950669

**Sanjur, Diva.**    5.7116
Social and cultural perspectives in nutrition / Diva Sanjur. — Englewood Cliffs, N.J.: Prentice-Hall, c1982. xiv, 336 p.: ill.; 25 cm. 1. Nutrition — Social aspects. 2. Diet — Social aspects. 3. Food habits — Social aspects. I. T.
TX357.S27    641.1 19    *LC* 81-8693    *ISBN* 0138156476

**Reutlinger, Shlomo.**    5.7117
Malnutrition and poverty: magnitude and policy options / Shlomo Reutlinger, Marcelo Selowsky. — Baltimore: Published for the World Bank [by] Johns Hopkins University Press, c1976. xii, 82 p.: ill.; 23 cm. (World Bank staff occasional papers; no. 23) 1. Nutrition policy — Developing countries 2. Nutrition — Developing countries. I. Selowsky, Marcelo. joint author. II. T. III. Series.
TX359.R48    362.5    *LC* 76-17240    *ISBN* 0801818680

## TX360–361 DIET AND FOOD SUPPLY

**European diet from pre-industrial to modern times / edited by**    5.7118
**Elborg and Robert Forster.**
New York: Harper and Row, 1975. xiv, 112 p.; 21 cm. (Basic conditions of life) (Harper torchbooks; TB 1863) 1. Diet — Europe — History — Addresses, essays, lectures. I. Forster, Elborg, 1931- II. Forster, Robert, 1926-
TX360.E8 E87 1975    641.3/094    *LC* 74-18114    *ISBN* 0061318639

**DeWalt, Kathleen Musante.**    5.7119
Nutritional strategies and agricultural change in a Mexican community / by Kathleen Musante DeWalt. — Ann Arbor, MI: UMI Research Press, c1983. xx, 211 p.: ill.; 24 cm. — (Studies in cultural anthropology. no. 6) Revision of thesis (Ph. D.)—University of Connecticut, 1979. Includes index. 1. Diet — Mexico — Temascalcingo de José María Velasco. 2. Nutrition surveys — Mexico — Temascalcingo de José María Velasco. 3. Food habits — Mexico — Temascalcingo de José María Velasco. 4. Mazahua Indians — Food. 5. Indians of Mexico — Temascalcingo de José María Velasco — Food. 6. Temascalcingo de José María Velasco (Mexico) — Social life and customs. I. T. II. Series.
TX360.M4 D48 1983    306 19    *LC* 83-18303    *ISBN* 0835715167

**Lawrie, R. A. (Ralston Andrew)**    5.7120
Meat science, by R. A. Lawrie. 2d ed. Oxford, New York, Pergamon Press [1974] xviii, 419 p. illus. 21 cm. (The Commonwealth and international library. Food science and technology) 1. Meat I. T.
TX373.L3 1974    641.3/6    *LC* 73-4328    *ISBN* 0080171338 *ISBN* 0080178111

**Lappé, Frances Moore.**    5.7121
Diet for a small planet / Frances Moore Lappé; illustrations by Marika Hahn. — 10th anniversary ed., completely rev. & updated. — New York: Ballantine Books, 1982. xiv, 496 p.: ill.; 21 cm. Includes index. 1. Vegetarianism 2. Proteins in human nutrition 3. Vegetarian cookery I. T.
TX392.L27 1982    641.5/63 19    *LC* 82-1655    *ISBN* 0345306910

## TX531–597 FOOD ANALYSIS

**Analysis of foods and beverages: modern techniques / edited by**    5.7122
**George Charalambous.**
Orlando: Academic Press, 1984. xviii, 652 p.: ill.; 24 cm. — (Food science and technology.) 1. Food — Analysis 2. Beverages — Analysis. I. Charalambous, George, 1922- II. Series.
TX541.A76 1984    664/.07 19    *LC* 83-11783    *ISBN* 0121691608

**Bowes, Anna De Planter.**                                  5.7123
[Food values of portions commonly used] Bowes and Church's Food values of portions commonly used. — 14th ed. / revised by Jean A.T. Pennington and Helen Nichols Church. — New York: Harper & Row, c1985. 257 p. (A Harper colophon book) Spine title: Food values of portions commonly used. Chiefly tables. Includes index. 1. Food — Composition — Tables. 2. Nutrition — Tables. I. Church, Charles Frederick, 1902- II. Pennington, Jean A. Thompson. III. Church, Helen Nichols. IV. T. V. Title: Food values of portions commonly used.
TX551.B64 1985      641.1 19      LC 83-48373      ISBN 0060910933 pbk

**Handbook of nutritive value of processed food / Miloslav**      5.7124
**Rechcigl, Jr., editor.**
Boca Raton, Fla.: CRC Press, c1982. 2 v.: ill.; 26 cm. — (CRC series in nutrition and food.) 1. Food — Composition — Collected works. 2. Feeds — Composition — Collected works. 3. Food industry and trade — Collected works. 4. Feed processing — Collected works. 5. Nutrition — Collected works. 6. Animal nutrition — Collected works. I. Rechcígl, Miloslav. II. Series.
TX551.H264 1982      641.1 19      LC 80-21652      ISBN 0849339510

**National Research Council. Committee on Dietary Allowances.**      5.7125
Recommended dietary allowances / Committee on Dietary Allowances. — 9th rev. ed. — Washington: National Academy of Sciences, 1980. ix, 185 p.: ill. Study supported by the National Institutes of Health, contract no. NO1-AM-4-2209. 1. Diet I. National Research Council. Food and Nutrition Board. II. T.
TX551 N36 1980      LC 63-65472      ISBN 0309029411

**Watt, Bernice K. (Bernice Kunerth), 1910-.**      5.7126
[Composition of foods] Handbook of the nutritional contents of foods / prepared by Bernice K. Watt and Annabel L. Merrill, with the assistance of Rebecca K. Pecot ... [et al.] for the United States Department of Agriculture. — New York: Dover Publications, 1975. 190 p.; 31 cm. Reprint of the 1964 ed. published by Consumer and Food Economics Research Division, Agricultural Research Service, U.S. Dept of Agriculture, Washington, which was issued as Agriculture handbook no. 8 under title: Composition of foods: raw, processed, prepared. Chiefly tables. 1. Food — Composition — Tables. I. Merrill, Annabel Laura, 1905- joint author. II. T.
TX551.W37 1975      641.1      LC 75-2616      ISBN 0486213420

**Schwimmer, Sigmund.**      5.7127
Source book of food enzymology / Sigmund Schwimmer. — Westport, Conn.: AVI Pub. Co., c1981. xv, 967 p.: ill.; 26 cm. — (AVI sourcebook and handbook series) Includes indexes. 1. Enzymes 2. Food — Composition I. T.
TX553.E6 S38      664/.001/547758 19      LC 80-25116      ISBN 0870553690

**Gurr, M. I. (Michael Ian)**      5.7128
Role of fats in food and nutrition / M. I. Gurr. — London: Elsevier Applied Science, 1984. ix, 170 p. 1. Nutrition 2. Fat I. T.
TX553.F3      613.2/8 19      ISBN 0853342989

**Wolf, Walter James, 1927-.**      5.7129
Soybeans as a food source / authors, W. J. Wolf, J. C. Cowan. — Rev. ed. — Cleveland: CRC Press, [1975] 101 p.: ill.; 26 cm. 1. Soybean as food I. Cowan, John Charles, 1911- joint author. II. T.
TX558.S7 W65 1975      664/.8      LC 75-9535      ISBN 0878191127

## TX631–840 GASTRONOMY. COOKERY

**Beard, James, 1903-.**      5.7130
[Theory and practice of good cooking] James Beard's theory & practice of good cooking / [James Beard]; in collaboration with José Wilson; ill. by Karl Stuecklen. — 1st ed. — New York: Knopf, 1977. ix, 465 p.: ill.; 24 cm. Includes index. 1. Cookery I. T. II. Title: Theory and practice of good cooking.
TX651.B37 1977      641.5      LC 76-47701

**Franey, Pierre.**      5.7131
The New York times 60–minute gourmet / Pierre Franey; with an introd. by Craig Claiborne. — New York: Times Books, c1979. xi, 339 p.: ill.; 24 cm. Includes index. 1. Cookery I. T. II. Title: 60-minute gourmet.
TX652.F67 1979      641.5/55      LC 75-51427      ISBN 0812908341

**Anderson, Jean, 1929-.**      5.7132
The grass roots cookbook / Jean Anderson. — New York: Times Books, c1977. xvi, 334 p.; 24 cm. Includes index. 1. Cookery, American I. T.
TX715.A56643 1977      641.5/973      LC 77-4472      ISBN 0812906934

**Farmer, Fannie Merritt, 1857-1915.**      5.7133
The Fannie Farmer cookbook. — 12th ed. rev. / by Marion Cunningham with Jeri Laber; illustrated by Lauren Jarrett. — New York: Knopf: distributed by Random House, 1979. xiv, 811 p.: ill.; 24 cm. Includes index. 1. Cookery, American I. Cunningham, Marion. II. Laber, Jeri. III. T.
TX715.F234 1979      641.5      LC 79-2097      ISBN 0394406508

**Rombauer, Irma von Starkloff, 1877-1962.**      5.7134
Joy of cooking / Irma S. Rombauer, Marion Rombauer Becker; illustrated by Ginnie Hofmann and Ikki Matsumoto. — Indianapolis: Bobbs-Merrill, [1975] xii, 915 p.: ill.; 24 cm. Includes index. 1. Cookery, American I. Becker, Marion Rombauer. joint author. II. T.
TX715.R75 1975      641.5      LC 75-10772      ISBN 0672518317

**Child, Julia.**      5.7135
Mastering the art of French cooking / by Julia Child, Louisette Bertholle, Simone Beck. — Updated ed. — New York: Knopf, 1983. 2 v.: ill.; 26 cm. Vol. 2 by Julia Child and Simone Beck. Rev. ed. of: Mastering the art of French cooking / by Simone Beck, Louisette Bertholle, Julia Child. [1st ed]. 1961-1970. Includes index. 1. Cookery, French I. Bertholle, Louisette. II. Beck, Simone. III. Beck, Simone. Mastering the art of French cooking. IV. T.
TX719.C454 1983      641.5944 19      LC 83-48113      ISBN 0394721144

**Toklas, Alice B.**                                      • 5.7136
The Alice B. Toklas cook book / Illustrations by Sir Francis Rose. — New York: Harper, c1954. 288 p.: ill. 1. Cookery, French I. T.
TX719.T6      LC 54-8997

**Hazan, Marcella.**      5.7137
[Italian kitchen] Marcella's Italian kitchen/ by Marcella Hazan. — 1st ed. — New York: Knopf: Distributed by Random House, 1986. xii, 349 p., [12] p. of plates: col. ill.; 24 cm. Includes index. 1. Cookery, Italian I. T. II. Title: Italian kitchen.
TX723.H3424 1986      641.5945 19      LC 86-45268      ISBN 0394508920

**Claiborne, Craig.**      5.7138
The Chinese cookbook / Craig Claiborne & Virginia Lee; drawings by Barbara and Roderick Wells. — Philadelphia: Lippincott, [1976] c1972. xxi, 451 p.: ill.; 23 cm. Includes index. 1. Cookery, Chinese I. Lee, Virginia, fl. 1972- joint author. II. T.
TX724.5.C5 C6 1976      641.5/951      LC 76-10418      ISBN 0397007876

**Foods of the world.**      5.7139
[New York]: Time-Life Books, [1968-. v.: ill.; 29 cm. 1. Cookery, International 2. Menus I. Time-Life Books.
TX725.A1 F62      LC 70-16607

**The Gourmet cookbook.**      5.7140
Rev., 1st Knopf ed. — New York: Knopf: Distributed by Random House, 1984-. v. < 1 >: col. ill.; 26 cm. Prepared by the editors of the magazine, Gourmet. Reprint. Originally published: Rev. New York: Gourmet Books, 1965. Includes indexes. 1. Cookery, International I. Gourmet. II. Title: Gourmet cook book.
TX725.A1 G58 1984      641.59 19      LC 84-47897      ISBN 0394540301

**Claiborne, Craig.**      5.7141
The New York times international cook book / by Craig Claiborne; drawings by James J. Spanfeller. — [1st ed.]. — New York: Harper & Row, 1971. xxvii, 599 p.: ill. (part col.); 24 cm. 1. Cookery, International I. Spanfeller, James J. II. T. III. Title: International cookbook.
TX725.A1 N48 1971      641.5      LC 70-156514      ISBN 006010788X

**New York Times.**                                      • 5.7142
The New York Times cook book / edited by Craig Claiborne. — New York: Harper & Row, 1961. x, 717 p.: ill. Includes index. 1. Cookery, International 2. Cookery, American I. Claiborne, Craig. II. T.
TX725.N46 1961      641.59      LC 61-10840

## TX901–946 Hotels. Youth Hostels

**Hotel & travel index.**      5.7143
[New York, etc.: Ziff-Davis Pub. Co., Public Transportation and Travel Division, etc.] v.: ill.; 31 cm. Quarterly. Began in 1938. Cf. Union list of serials. 1. Hotels, taverns, etc — Directories. 2. Motels — Directories.
TX907.H59      647/.025      LC 68-3672

# U Military Science

## U MILITARY SCIENCE: GENERAL

**Kreidberg, Marvin, A.**                                          • 5.7144
History of military mobilization in the United States Army: 1775–1945 / by
Marvin A. Kreidberg and Merton G. Henry. — Washington, D.C.:
Department of the Army, 1955. xvii, 721 p.: ill., maps, ports.; 24 cm. —
(Department of the Army pamphlet; no. 20-212) 1. United States. Army —
Demobilization 2. United States. Army — Recruiting, enlistment, etc.
3. United States. Army — Mobilization. I. Henry, Merton G. II. United
States. Dept. of the Army. III. T.
U15.U64 no. 20-212    *LC* 56-60717

**Howard, Michael Eliot, 1922- ed.**                              • 5.7145
The theory and practice of war; essays presented to B. H. Liddell Hart on his
seventieth birthday. — New York, F. A. Praeger [1966, c1965] x, 376, [1] p. 22
cm. Includes bibliographical references. 1. Military art and science —
Addresses, essays, lectures. I. Liddell Hart, Basil Henry, Sir, 1895-1970. II. T.
U19.H75    355.0008    *LC* 66-13987

## U21–22 War: Sociology. Psychology

**Gray, J. Glenn (Jesse Glenn), 1913-1977.**                      • 5.7146
The warriors; reflections on men in battle. [1st ed.] New York, Harcourt, Brace
[1959] 242 p. 21 cm. 1. War 2. World War, 1939-1945 — Personal narratives,
American. I. T.
U21.G75    940.548    *LC* 59-7536

**Toynbee, Arnold Joseph, 1889-1975.**                            • 5.7147
War and civilization / Arnold J. Toynbee; selected by Albert Vann Fowler from
A Study of history. — New York: Oxford University Press, 1950. xii, 165 p.; 22
cm. 'Issued under the auspices of the Royal Institute of International Affairs.'
1. Militarism I. Fowler, Albert Vann, 1904- II. Toynbee, Arnold Joseph,
1889-1975. Study of history. III. T.
U21.T69    355.01    *LC* 50-9539

**Wright, Quincy, 1890-1970.**                                    5.7148
A study of war. — 2d ed., with a commentary on war since 1942. — Chicago,
University of Chicago Press [1965] xiii, 1637 p. illus., maps. 24 cm.
Bibliography: p. 1564-1577. 1. War 2. Military art and science I. T.
U21.W7 1965    355.02    *LC* 65-5396

**Aron, Raymond, 1905-.**                                         5.7149
[Penser la guerre, Clausewitz. English] Clausewitz, philosopher of war /
Raymond Aron; translated by Christine Booker and Norman Stone. —
Englewood Cliffs, N.J.: Prentice-Hall, c1985. xi, 418 p.; 24 cm. Translation of:
Penser la guerre, Clausewitz. Includes index. 1. Clausewitz, Carl von,
1780-1831. 2. War 3. Military art and science I. T.
U21.2.C54 A7613 1985    355/.02 19    *LC* 84-26569    *ISBN*
0131363425

**Johnson, James Turner.**                                        5.7150
Can modern war be just? / James Turner Johnson. — New Haven: Yale
University Press, c1984. xi, 215 p.; 22 cm. Includes index. 1. War — Moral and
ethical aspects 2. Just war doctrine I. T.
U21.2.J627 1984    172/.42 19    *LC* 84-3523    *ISBN* 0300031653

**Mansfield, Sue.**                                               5.7151
The gestalts of war: an inquiry into its origins and meanings as a social
institution / Sue Mansfield. — New York: Dial Press, c1982. xi, 274 p.; 23 cm.
Includes index. 1. War — Psychological aspects I. T.
U21.2.M34    355/.0275 19    *LC* 81-12592    *ISBN* 0385272197

**Otterbein, Keith F.**                                           5.7152
The evolution of war; a cross–cultural study [by] Keith F. Otterbein. With a
foreword by Robert L. Carneiro. — [n.p.]: H[uman] R[elations] A[rea] F[iles]
Press, 1970. 165 p.; 23 cm. 1. War I. T.
U21.2.O88    355.02/2    *LC* 79-87852

**Phillips, Robert L. (Robert Lester), 1938-.**                   5.7153
War and justice / by Robert L. Phillips. — 1st ed. — Norman: University of
Oklahoma Press, 1984. xv, 159 p.; 22 cm. Includes index. 1. Just war doctrine
2. Guerrilla warfare — Moral and ethical aspects. 3. Deterrence (Strategy) —
Moral and ethical aspects. 4. War (International law) I. T.
U21.2.P47 1984    341.6/2 19    *LC* 84-40278    *ISBN* 0806118938

**Pre-congress Conference on War, Its Causes and Correlates,**    5.7154
**University of Notre Dame, 1973.**
War, its causes and correlates / editor, Martin A. Nettleship, R. Dale Givens,
Anderson Nettleship. — The Hague: Mouton; Chicago: distributed by Aldine,
c1975. xviii, 813 p., [2] leaves of plates: ill.; 24 cm. — (World anthropology.)
'Organized under the aegis of the IXth International Congress of
Anthropological and Ethnological Sciences.' 1. War — Congresses.
I. Nettleship, Martin A., 1936- II. Givens, R. Dale, 1928- III. Nettleship,
Anderson. IV. International Congress of Anthropological and Ethnological
Sciences. 9th, Chicago, 1973. V. T. VI. Series.
U21.2.P62 1973    355.02    *LC* 75-331030    *ISBN* 9027976597

**Pre-congress Conference on War, Its Causes and Correlates,**    5.7155
**University of Notre Dame, 1973.**
Discussions on war and human aggression / ed. R. Dale Givens, Martin A.
Nettleship. The Hague: Mouton; Chicago: distributed in the USA and Canada
by Aldine, [1976] xvi, 231 p.; 24 cm. (World anthropology.) A companion to
War, its causes and correlates. Includes indexes. 1. War — Congresses.
I. Givens, R. Dale, 1928- II. Nettleship, Martin A., 1936- III. Pre-congress
Conference on War, Its Causes and Correlates, University of Notre Dame,
1973. War, its causes and correlates. IV. T. V. Series.
U21.2.P62 1973a    355.02    *LC* 76-381173    *ISBN* 0202900320

**War, strategy, and maritime power / edited by B. Mitchell**    5.7156
**Simpson III.**
New Brunswick, N.J.: Rutgers University Press, c1977. x, 356 p.; 24 cm.
1. War — Addresses, essays, lectures. 2. Strategy — Addresses, essays,
lectures. 3. Sea-power — Addresses, essays, lectures. 4. United States —
Armed Forces — Addresses, essays, lectures. I. Simpson, B. Mitchell
(Benjamin Mitchell), 1932-
U21.2.W38    359/.009    *LC* 77-3247    *ISBN* 0813508428

**Doorn, Jacobus Adrianus Antonius van, 1925-.**                  5.7157
The soldier and social change: comparative studies in the history and sociology
of the military / Jacques van Doorn. — Beverly Hills, Calif.: Sage Publications,
c1975. xii, 189 p.; 24 cm. (Sage series on armed forces and society; v. 7)
1. Sociology, Military 2. Armed Forces I. T.
U21.5.D63    301.5/93    *LC* 74-31573    *ISBN* 0803999488

**Janowitz, Morris.**                                             • 5.7158
The military in the political development of new nations; an essay in
comparative analysis. Chicago: University of Chicago Press, [1964] vii, 134 p.;
23 cm. Expanded ed. published in 1977 under title: Military institutions and
coercion in the developing nations. 1. Armed Forces — Political activity
2. States, New — Politics and government I. T.
U21.5.J3    355    *LC* 64-13952

**Johnson, John J., 1912- ed.**                                   • 5.7159
The role of the military in underdeveloped countries. Princeton, N.J., Princeton
University Press, 1962. viii, 427 p. 23 cm. Papers of a conference sponsored by
the Rand Corporation at Santa Monica, Calif., in August 1959. 1. Sociology,
Military — Congresses. 2. Developing countries — Armed Forces — Political
activity — Congresses. I. Rand Corporation. II. T.
U21.5.J6    322/.5/091724 19    *LC* 62-7406

**Perlmutter, Amos.**                                             5.7160
The military and politics in modern times: on professionals, praetorians, and
revolutionary soldiers / Amos Perlmutter. New Haven: Yale University Press,
1977. xix, 335 p.: ill.; 24 cm. 'Written under the auspices of the Center for
International Affairs, Harvard University.' 1. Sociology, Military 2. Armed
Forces — Political activity I. Harvard University. Center for International
Affairs. II. T.
U21.5.P36    301.5/93    *LC* 76-45769    *ISBN* 0300020457

**Radine, Lawrence B.**                                           5.7161
The taming of the troops: social control in the United States Army / Lawrence
B. Radine. — Westport, Conn.: Greenwood Press, 1977. xii, 276 p.; 22 cm. —
(Contributions in sociology; no. 22) 1. United States. Army — Personnel
management 2. Sociology, Military 3. Social control I. T.
U21.5.R32    301.5/93    *LC* 76-5262    *ISBN* 083718911X

**Enloe, Cynthia H., 1938-.**      **5.7162**
Does khaki become you?: the militarisation of women's lives / Cynthia Enloe. — 1st ed. — Boston, Mass.: South End Press, c1983. vii, 262 p.; 20 cm. Includes index. 1. Women and the military I. T.
U21.75.E55 1983b    355/.0088042 19    *LC* 84-164990    *ISBN* 0896081834

**Dollard, John, 1900-.**      • **5.7163**
Fear in battle / by John Dollard; with the assistance of Donald Horton. — Washington: Infantry journal, 1944. vii, 64 p.: diagrs.; 19 cm. — (Fighting forces series) First revised edition. 1. Fear I. Horton, Donald, 1910- II. Infantry journal. III. T.
U22.D6 1944    355

**Hartigan, Richard Shelly.**      **5.7164**
The forgotten victim: a history of the civilian / Richard Shelly Hartigan. — Chicago, Ill.: Precedent Pub., 1982. xi, 173 p.; 24 cm. Includes index. 1. War — Moral and ethical aspects 2. War — Casualties (Statistics, etc.) 3. Just war doctrine I. T.
U22.H37 1982    172/.42 19    *LC* 77-91278    *ISBN* 0913750190

**Paskins, Barrie.**      **5.7165**
The ethics of war / Barrie Paskins & Michael Dockrill. — Minneapolis: University of Minnesota Press, 1979. xii, 332 p.; 24 cm. Includes index. 1. Military ethics 2. War — Moral and ethical aspects I. Dockrill, M. L. (Michael L.) joint author. II. T.
U22.P37    172/.4    *LC* 79-10798    *ISBN* 0816608857

**Richardson, Frank M.**      **5.7166**
Fighting spirit: a study of psychological factors in war / [by] F. M. Richardson; with a foreword by Sir Peter Hunt. — New York: Crane, Russak, 1978. xv, 189 p.; 24 cm. Includes index. 1. Morale 2. Psychology, Military I. T.
U22.R57 1978b    355.02/019    *LC* 77-83809    *ISBN* 0844812617

**Stouffer, Samuel Andrew, 1900-.**      **5.7167**
The American soldier / by Samuel A. Stouffer ... [et al.]. — Princeton: Princeton University Press, 1949. 2 v.: ill.; 25 cm. — (Studies in social psychology in World War II; v.1-2) 1. Soldiers — United States. 2. Psychology, Military. I. T. II. Series.
U22.A5 1977    U22.S8 v.1,etc.    *LC* 52-174    *ISBN* 089126034X *ISBN* 0891260358

**Studies in social psychology in World War II ... prepared and**    • **5.7168**
**edited under the auspices of a special committee of the Social Science Research Council.**
[Princeton, Princeton University Press, 1949-50] 4 v. illus. 25 cm. 'Data ... collected by the Research Branch, Information and Education Division, War Department.' 1. Soldiers — United States 2. Social psychology I. Social Science Research Council (U.S.) II. United States. Army Service Forces. Information and Education Division.
U22.S8    355.1    *LC* 49-2480

**Merton, Robert King, 1910-.**      • **5.7169**
Continuities in social research; studies in the scope and method of 'The American soldier.' Edited by Robert K. Merton and Paul F. Lazarsfeld. Glencoe, Ill., Free Press, 1950. 255 p. 22 cm. 1. Stouffer, Samuel Andrew, 1900- The American soldier. I. Lazarsfeld, Paul Felix. II. T.
U22.S83 M4    355.1    *LC* 51-9172

**Watson, Peter.**      **5.7170**
War on the mind: the military uses and abuses of psychology / Peter Watson. — New York: Basic Books, c1978. 534 p.: ill.; 25 cm. 1. Psychology, Military 2. Psychological warfare I. T.
U22.3.W37    355/.001/9    *LC* 77-75237    *ISBN* 0465090656

# U24 Dictionaries

**Hayward, Philip Henry Cecil.**      **5.7171**
Jane's dictionary of military terms / compiled by P. H. C. Hayward. London: Macdonald and Jane's, 1976 (c1975). [4], 201 p.; 23 cm. 1. Military art and science — Dictionaries 2. Naval art and science — Dictionaries I. T.
U24.H38    355/.003    *LC* 76-361572    *ISBN* 035608261X

**United States. Joint Chiefs of Staff.**      **5.7172**
Department of Defense dictionary of military and associated terms: incorporating the NATO and IADB dictionaries. — Washington, D.C.: Joint Chiefs of Staff: [for sale by the Supt. of Docs., U.S. Govt. Print. Off.], 1986. vii, 399 p.; 26 cm. — (JCS publication; 1) Cover title. 1. Military art and science — Dictionaries I. T. II. Title: Dictionary of military and associated terms. III. Series.
U24U57    355/.003/21

# U27–55 History. Biography

**Brodie, Bernard, 1910-.**      **5.7173**
From crossbow to H–bomb [by] Bernard and Fawn M. Brodie. — New York,: Dell Pub. Co., 1962. 288 p.: illus.; 20 cm. — 1. Military art and science — History I. Brodie, Fawn McKay, 1915- joint author. II. T.
U27.B76 1973    355/.009

**Delbrück, Hans, 1848-1929.**      • **5.7174**
[Geschichte der Kriegskunst im Rahmen der politischen Geschichte. English] History of the art of war within the framework of political history / by Hans Delbrück; translated from the German by Walter J. Renfroe, Jr. — Westport, Conn.: Greenwood Press, 1975, c1985. 4 v.: maps; 24 cm. (Contributions in military history; no. 9, 20, 26, 39 0084-9251) Translation of: Geschichte der Kriegskunst im Rahmen der politischen Geschichte. 1. Military art and science — History 2. Naval art and science — History 3. War — History. I. T.
U27.D34213 1975    355/.009 s 355/.009    *LC* 72-792    *ISBN* 083716365X

**Montross, Lynn, 1895-1961.**      • **5.7175**
War through the ages. — Rev. and enl. 3d ed. Decorations by L. K. Hartzell. — New York: Harper, [1960] 1063 p.: illus.; 22 cm. 1. Military art and science — History 2. Military history I. T.
U27.M6 1960    355    *LC* 60-7533

**Wintringham, Thomas Henry, 1898-1949.**      **5.7176**
Weapons and tactics / Tom Wintringham and J. N. Blashford–Snell. — Harmondsworth, Eng.; Baltimore: Penguin Books, 1973. 285 p.; 18 cm. Pt. 1 by T. H. Wintringham first published in 1943; pt. 2 by J. N. Blashford-Snell first published in 1973. 1. Military art and science — History 2. Arms and armor — History. 3. Tactics — History. I. Blashford-Snell, John. II. T.
U27.W52 1973    355.4/09    *LC* 74-186316    *ISBN* 0140215220 pbk

**Yadin, Yigael, 1917-1984.**      • **5.7177**
[Torat ha-milhamah be-artsot ha-Mikra. English] The art of warfare in Biblical lands in the light of archaeological study. New York, McGraw-Hill [1963] 2 v. (484 p.): illus. (part col.) maps (part col.) plans; 28 cm. 1. Military art and science — History 2. Middle East — History, Military. I. T.
U29.Y3 1963    *LC* 63-8720

**Connolly, Peter.**      **5.7178**
Greece and Rome at war / Peter Connolly. — 1st American ed. — Englewood Cliffs, NJ: Prentice-Hall, 1981. 320 p.: col. ill., maps; 29 cm. Includes index. 1. Military art and science — Greece — History. 2. Military art and science — Rome — History. 3. Arms and armor, Ancient — Greece — History. 4. Arms and armor, Ancient — Rome — History. 5. Military history, Ancient — Greece. 6. Military history, Ancient — Rome. I. T.
U33.C647 1981    355/.00938 19    *LC* 81-178595    *ISBN* 0133649768

**Garlan, Yvon.**      **5.7179**
[Guerre dans l'Antiquité. English] War in the ancient world: a social history / Yvon Garlan; translated from the French by Janet Lloyd. — New York: Norton, c1975. 200 p.: maps; 21 cm. (Ancient culture and society) Translation of La Guerre dans l'Antiquité. Includes index. 1. Military art and science — History 2. Greece — Military antiquities. 3. Rome — Military antiquities I. T.
U33.G3513    355/.00938    *LC* 75-20463    *ISBN* 0393055663

**Greenhalgh, P. A. L.**      **5.7180**
Early Greek warfare; horsemen and chariots in the Homeric and Archaic Ages [by] P. A. L. Greenhalgh. — Cambridge [Eng.]: University Press, 1973. xvi, 212 p.: illus.; 24 cm. 1. Military art and science — History 2. Greece — History, Military. I. T.
U33.G7    355/.00938    *LC* 72-87437    *ISBN* 0521200563

**Pritchett, W. Kendrick (William Kendrick), 1909-.**      **5.7181**
The Greek state at war. Berkeley: University of California Press, [1971-1985] v. 25 cm. Vol. 1 first published in 1971 under title: Ancient Greek military practices. 1. Military art and science — History 2. Greece — History, Military. I. T. II. Title: Ancient Greek military practices.
U 33 P95 1971    *LC* 75-312653    *ISBN* 0520025652

**Tarn, William Woodthorpe, Sir, 1869-1957.**      • **5.7182**
Hellenistic military & naval developments. New York, Biblo and Tannen, 1966. vii, 170 p. 21 cm. 1. Military art and science — History 2. Naval art and science — History I. T.
U33.T3 1966    *LC* 66-15217

**Luttwak, Edward.**      **5.7183**
The grand strategy of the Roman Empire from the first century A.D. to the third / Edward N. Luttwak. Baltimore: Johns Hopkins University Press, c1976.

xii, 255 p.: ill.; 24 cm. Includes index. 1. Strategy 2. Military history, Ancient 3. Rome. Army. I. T.
U35.L8      355.03/303/7      *LC* 76-17232      *ISBN* 080181863X

**Watson, George Ronald.**            • **5.7184**
The Roman soldier [by] G. R. Watson. — Ithaca, N.Y.: Cornell University Press, [1969] 256 p.: illus.; 23 cm. — (Aspects of Greek and Roman life) 1. Soldiers — Rome. I. T. II. Series.
U35.W35 1969b      355.1/00937      *LC* 69-11153      *ISBN* 080140519X

**Webster, Graham.**            **5.7185**
The Roman Imperial Army of the first and second centuries A.D. / Graham Webster. — 3rd ed. — Totowa, N.J.: Barnes & Noble Books, 1985. xv, 343 p., [32] p. of plates: ill., maps; 26 cm. Spine title: The Roman Imperial Army. Includes indexes. 1. Rome. Army. 2. Rome — History, Military — 30 B.C.-476 A.D. 3. Rome — Military antiquities 4. Rome — Antiquities I. T. II. Title: Roman Imperial Army.
U35.W48 1985      355/.00937 19      *LC* 85-15696      *ISBN* 0389205907

**Beeler, John.**            • **5.7186**
Warfare in feudal Europe, 730–1200. — Ithaca: Cornell University Press, [1971] xvi, 272 p.: maps; 22 cm. 1. Military art and science — Europe — History. 2. Military history, Medieval I. T.
U37.B44      355/.0094      *LC* 74-148018      *ISBN* 0801406382

**Contamine, Philippe.**            **5.7187**
[Guerre au Moyen Age. English] War in the Middle Ages / Philippe Contamine; translated by Michael Jones. — New York, NY, USA: B. Blackwell, 1984. xvi, 387 p., [16] p. of plates: ill.; 24 cm. Translation of: La guerre au Moyen Age. Includes index. 1. Military art and science — Europe — History. 2. Middle Ages — History 3. Europe — History, Military I. T.
U37.C6513 1984      355/.0094 19      *LC* 84-14647      *ISBN* 0631131426

**Oman, Charles William Chadwick, Sir, 1860-1946.**      • **5.7188**
The art of war in the Middle Ages, A.D. 378–1515; revised and edited by John H. Beeler. Ithaca, Cornell University Press [1953] xviii, 176 p. ill. 1. Military art and science — History 2. Military history, Medieval I. T.
U37.O5 1953      *LC* 53-11909

**Chandler, David G.**            **5.7189**
The art of warfare in the age of Marlborough / David Chandler. — New York: Hippocrene Books, c1976. 317 p., [8] leaves of plates: ill.; 24 cm. Includes index. 1. Military art and science — History 2. Europe — History, Military I. T.
U39.C48      355/.0094      *LC* 75-26934      *ISBN* 0882543660

**Falls, Cyril Bentham, 1888-.**            • **5.7190**
The art of war: from the age of Napoleon to the present day. New York, Oxford University Press, 1961. 240 p. illus. 21 cm. (A Hesperides book, HS3) Includes bibliography. 1. Military art and science — History I. T.
U39.F3      355.09      *LC* 61-19637

**Fuller, J. F. C. (John Frederick Charles), 1878-1966.**      • **5.7191**
The conduct of war, 1789–1961; a study of the impact of the French, industrial, and Russian revolutions on war and its conduct. New Brunswick, N.J., Rutgers University Press, 1961. 352 p. illus. 23 cm. 1. Military art and science — History 2. Military history, Modern I. T.
U39.F8      355/.009 19      *LC* 61-10261

**Ropp, Theodore, 1911-.**            • **5.7192**
War in the modern world. — Durham, N. C., Duke University Press, 1959. 400 p. 24 cm. Includes bibliography. 1. Military art and science — Hist. 2. Military history, Modern I. T.
U39.R6      355.0903      *LC* 60-5274

**Rothenberg, Gunther Erich, 1923-.**            **5.7193**
The art of warfare in the age of Napoleon / Gunther E. Rothenberg. — Bloomington: Indiana University Press, c1978. 272 p., [4] leaves of plates: ill.; 24 cm. Includes index. 1. Military art and science — History 2. Military history, Modern — 18th century 3. Military history, Modern — 19th century 4. Europe — History, Military — 18th century 5. Europe — History, Military — 19th century I. T.
U39.R65      355/.0094      *LC* 77-86495      *ISBN* 0253310768

**Hale, J. R. (John Rigby), 1923-.**            **5.7194**
War and society in Renaissance Europe, 1450–1620 / J.R. Hale. — New York: St. Martin's Press, 1985. 282 p.; 22 cm. Includes index. 1. Military art and science — Europe — History. 2. Sociology, Military — Europe. 3. Renaissance 4. Europe — History, Military I. T.
U43.E95 H35 1985      306/.27/094 19      *LC* 85-40404      *ISBN* 0312856032

**Howard, Michael Eliot, 1922-.**            **5.7195**
War in European history / Michael Howard. — London; New York: Oxford University Press, 1976. x, 165 p.; 21 cm. Includes index. 1. Military art and science — History 2. War 3. Europe — History, Military I. T.
U43.E95 H68      355/.0094      *LC* 76-372794      *ISBN* 0192115642

**Strachan, Hew.**            **5.7196**
European armies and the conduct of war / Hew Strachan. — London; Boston: Allen & Unwin, 1983. 224 p.: ill., maps; 24 cm. Includes index. 1. Military art and science — Europe — History. 2. War 3. Military history, Modern I. T.
U43.E95 S76 1983      355/.0094 19      *LC* 83-8787      *ISBN* 004940069X

**Garthoff, Raymond L.**            • **5.7197**
Soviet military doctrine / by Raymond L. Garthoff; with a pref. by H.A. De Weerd. — Glencoe, Ill.: Free Press, 1953. xviii, 587 p.: ill., maps. 'A contribution to the research program conducted for the United States Air Force by the Rand Corporation.' British ed. has title: How Russia makes war. 1. Military art and science 2. Soviet Union — Politics and government I. Rand Corporation. II. T.
U43.R9 G3      *LC* 53-7394

**The War lords: military commanders of the twentieth century /**      **5.7198**
**edited by Sir Michael Carver.**
1st American ed. — Boston: Little, Brown, c1976. xvi, 624 p., [8] leaves of plates: ill.; 24 cm. Includes index. 1. Military biography 2. Military history, Modern — 20th century I. Carver, Michael, 1915-
U51.W32 1976      355.3/31/0922 B      *LC* 76-14402      *ISBN* 0316130605

**Dictionary of American military biography / Roger J. Spiller,**      **5.7199**
**editor, Joseph G. Dawson III, associate editor, T. Harry**
**Williams, consulting editor.**
Westport, Conn.: Greenwood Press, 1984. 3 v. (xv, 1368 p.); 25 cm. Includes index. 1. United States — Armed Forces — Biography 2. United States — Biography I. Spiller, Roger J. II. Dawson, Joseph G., 1945-
U52.D53 1984      355/.0092/2 B 19      *LC* 83-12674      *ISBN* 0313214336

**Fuller, J. F. C. (John Frederick Charles), 1878-1966.**      • **5.7200**
The generalship of Alexander the Great. New Brunswick, N.J., Rutgers University Press [1960] 336 p. illus. 25 cm. 1. Alexander, the Great, 356-323 B.C. 2. Military art and science — History 3. Macedonia — Army. I. T.
U55.A45 F8 1960      355.48      *LC* 59-15620

**Bankwitz, Philip Charles Farwell.**            • **5.7201**
Maxime Weygand and civil–military relations in modern France. — Cambridge: Harvard University Press, 1967. xiii, 445 p.; 22 cm. — (Harvard historical studies. v. 81) 1. Weygand, Maxime, 1867-1965. 2. France. Armée — Political activity. I. T. II. Series.
U55.W45 B3      944.081/0924 B      *LC* 67-22860

---

# U101–108 General Works

**Machiavelli, Niccolò, 1469-1527.**            **5.7202**
[Arte della guerra. English] The art of war. A rev. ed. of the Ellis Farneworth translation; with an introd. by Neal Wood. Indianapolis, Bobbs-Merrill [1965] lxxxvii, 247 p. illus. 21 cm. (The Library of liberal arts, 196) 1. Military art and science — Early works to 1800. 2. War 3. Torpedoes I. Wood, Neal. ed. II. T.
U101.M16 1965      355      *LC* 64-66078

**Sun-tzu, 6th cent. B.C.**            • **5.7203**
The art of war. Translated and with an introd. by Samuel B. Griffith. With a foreword by B. H. Liddell Hart. New York, Oxford University Press [c1963] xvi, 197 p. illus., maps. (UNESCO collection of representative works. Chinese series.) 1. Military art and science — Early works to 1800. I. Griffith, Samuel B., tr. II. T. III. Series.
U101.S95 1963b      *LC* 65-8619

**Vegetius Renatus, Flavius.**            • **5.7204**
The military institutions of the Romans / [by] Flavius Vegetius Renatus, translated from the Latin by Lieutenant John Clark, edited by Brig. Gen. Thomas R. Phillips, U.S.A. — Harrisburg, Pa.: The Military service pub. co., 1944. 114 p.: ill.; 20 cm. (Military classics.) 'This edition includes the first three books of Vegetius, omitting only repititions.' p. 10. 1. Military art and science — Early works to 1800. I. Clarke, John, lieutenant of marines. II. Phillips, Thomas Raphael, 1892- III. T. IV. Series.
U101.V4      *LC* 44-51414

**Bush, Vannevar, 1890-1974.**            • **5.7205**
Modern arms and free men: a discussion of the role of science in preserving democracy. New York, Simon and Schuster, 1949. 273 p. 23 cm. 1. Military art and science 2. World politics — 1945- 3. Munitions 4. War I. T.
U102.B985      355      *LC* 49-48841

**Clausewitz, Karl von, 1780-1831.**            **5.7206**
[Vom Kriege. English] On war / Carl von Clausewitz; edited and translated by Michael Howard and Peter Paret; introductory essays by Peter Paret, Michael

Howard, and Bernard Brodie; with a commentary by Bernard Brodie; index by Rosalie West. — Rev. ed. — Princeton, N.J.: Princeton University Press, 1984, c1976. 732 p. Translation of: Vom Kriege. 1. Military art and science 2. War I. Howard, Michael Eliot, 1922- II. Paret, Peter. III. T.
U102.C65 1984     355 19     *LC* 84-3401     *ISBN* 0691056579

**Frederick II, King of Prussia, 1712-1786.**     • **5.7207**
Frederick the Great on the art of war. Edited and translated by Jay Luvaas. — New York, Free Press [1966] xvi, 391 p. illus., maps. 21 cm. Excerpts from the author's military and political writings. Bibliography: p. 375-378. 1. Military art and science I. Luvaas, Jay. ed. and tr. II. T.
U102.F838     355     *LC* 66-12893

**Inter-university Seminar on Armed Forces and Society.**     **5.7208**
Handbook of military institutions. Roger W. Little, editor. — Beverly Hills, Calif.: Sage Publications, [1971] 607 p.; 25 cm. — (Sage series on armed forces and society) 1. Military art and science 2. Sociology, Military I. Little, Roger William, 1922- ed. II. T.
U102.I65     301.5/98     *LC* 78-127989     *ISBN* 0803900783

**Jomini, Henri, baron, 1779-1869.**     • **5.7209**
[Précis de l'art de la guerre. English] The art of war. Translated from the French by G. H. Mendell and W. P. Craighill. A new ed., with appendices and maps. Westport, Conn., Greenwood Press [1971] 410 p. illus., maps (3 fold.) 23 cm. (The West Point military library) Translation of Précis de l'art de la guerre. 'Originally published in 1862.' 1. Military art and science I. T.
U102.J78 1971     355     *LC* 68-54793     *ISBN* 0837150140

**Jane's weapon systems. 1st- (1969–70)- .**     • **5.7210**
New York: McGraw-Hill, 1970-. v.: ill. Imprint varies. 1. Weapons systems — Yearbooks.
U104.J35     *LC* 79-12909

# U161–167.5 Strategy. Tactics

**Phillips, Thomas Raphael, 1892- ed.**     • **5.7211**
Roots of strategy; a collection of military classics... Harrisburg, Pa., The Military service publishing company [c1940] 448 p. illus. (plans) 20 cm. 1. Strategy 2. Military art and science — Early works to 1800. I. Sun-tzu, 6th cent. B.C. II. Vegetius Renatus, Flavius. De re militari III. Saxe, Maurice, comte de, 1696-1750. Mes rêveries. IV. Frederick II, King of Prussia, 1712-1786. Die general-principia vom kriege. V. Napoleon I, Emperor of the French, 1769-1821. Maximes de guerre. VI. Giles, Lionel, 1875-1958. tr. VII. Clarke, John, lieutenant of marines, tr. VIII. T.
U161.P5 1940     *LC* 40-9718

**Chandler, David G.**     **5.7212**
Atlas of military strategy / David G. Chandler. — New York: Free Press, c1980. 208 p.: ill., maps, ports. 1. Strategy 2. Tactics 3. Military history, Modern I. T.
U162.C45 1980     355.4/3     *ISBN* 0029057507

**Luttwak, Edward.**     **5.7213**
Strategy and politics / Edward N. Luttwak. — New Brunswick, N.J.: Transaction Books, c1980. viii, 328 p.; 24 cm. — (Collected essays / Edward N. Luttwak; v. 1) 1. Strategy — Addresses, essays, lectures. 2. Military policy — Addresses, essays, lectures. 3. World politics — Addresses, essays, lectures. I. T.
U162.L87     355.03/3/08     *LC* 79-65224     *ISBN* 0878553460

**Makers of modern strategy: from Machiavelli to the nuclear age**     **5.7214**
**/ edited by Peter Paret with Gordon A. Craig and Felix Gilbert.**
Princeton, N.J.: Princeton University Press, c1986. vii, 941 p.; 24 cm. — (Princeton paperbacks) Includes index. 1. Strategy 2. Military art and science 3. Military history, Modern I. Paret, Peter. II. Craig, Gordon Alexander, 1913- III. Gilbert, Felix, 1905-
U162.M25 1986     355/.02 19     *LC* 85-17029     *ISBN* 0691092354

**Sokolovskiĭ, Vasiliĭ Danilovich, 1897-.**     **5.7215**
[Voennaia strategiia. English] Soviet military strategy / V. D. Sokolovskiy; edited, with an analysis and commentary, by Harriet Fast Scott. — 3d ed. — New York: Crane, Russak, [1975] vlvii, 494 p.; 24 cm. Translation of Voennaia strategiia. Includes index. 1. Strategy 2. War 3. Soviet Union — Military policy. 4. Soviet Union — Armed Forces I. T.
U162.S613 1975     355.4/3/0947     *LC* 73-94042     *ISBN* 0844803111

**Strategic survey / The Institute for Strategic Studies.**     **5.7216**
London: The Institute. v.; 25 cm. Annual. Began in 1966. Description based on: 1967. 1. Strategy — Yearbooks. 2. World politics — Yearbooks. I. Institute

for Strategic Studies (London, England) II. International Institute for Strategic Studies.
U162.S77     355.4/3     *LC* 70-363446

**Strategic thought in the nuclear age / editor, Laurence Martin;**     **5.7217**
**general editor, Hossein Amirsadeghi; contributors, Coral Bell.**
Baltimore: Johns Hopkins University Press, c1979. ix, 233 p.; 24 cm. 1. Strategy — Addresses, essays, lectures. 2. World politics — 1945- — Addresses, essays, lectures. I. Martin, Laurence W. II. Bell, Coral.
U162.S774     355.4/307     *LC* 79-2979     *ISBN* 0801823307

**Naroll, Raoul.**     **5.7218**
Military deterrence in history; a pilot cross–historical survey [by] Raoul Naroll, Vern L. Bullough [and] Frada Naroll. — [Albany]: State University of New York Press, [1974] lxii, 416 p.: illus.; 24 cm. 1. Deterrence (Strategy) 2. Military history I. Bullough, Vern L. joint author. II. Naroll, Frada, joint author. III. T.
U162.6.N37 1974     355.03/35/09     *LC* 69-14647     *ISBN* 087395047X

**The Security gamble: deterrence dilemmas in the nuclear age /**     **5.7219**
**edited by Douglas MacLean.**
Totowa, N.J.: Rowman & Allanheld, 1984. xix, 170 p.; 25 cm. (Maryland studies in public philosophy.) 1. Deterrence (Strategy) — Addresses, essays, lectures. 2. Nuclear weapons — Addresses, essays, lectures. 3- Military policy — Addresses, essays, lectures. I. MacLean, Douglas, 1947- II. Series.
U162.6.S33 1984     355/.0217 19     *LC* 84-15080     *ISBN* 0847673294

**Betts, Richard K., 1947-.**     **5.7220**
Surprise attack: lessons for defense planning / Richard K. Betts. — Washington, D.C.: Brookings Institution, c1982. xii, 318 p.; 24 cm. 1. Strategy 2. Surprise 3. Military history, Modern — 20th century I. T.
U163.B38 1982     355.4/3 19     *LC* 82-70887     *ISBN* 0815709307

**Strategic military deception / edited by Donald C. Daniel,**     **5.7221**
**Katherine L. Herbig.**
New York: Pergamon Press, c1982. xiii, 378 p.: ill.; 24 cm. — (Pergamon policy studies on security affairs.) 1. Strategy — Addresses, essays, lectures. 2. Deception — Addresses, essays, lectures. I. Daniel, Donald C. (Donald Charles), 1944- II. Herbig, Katherine L. (Katherine Lydigsen) III. Series.
U163.S76 1982     355.4/3 19     *LC* 81-14364     *ISBN* 0080272193

**Griffith, Paddy.**     **5.7222**
Forward into battle: fighting tactics from Waterloo to Vietnam / Paddy Griffith; with an introduction by John Keegan. — Chichester [West Sussex]: A. Bird, 1982 (c1981). 156 p., [8] p. of plates: ill.; 24 cm. Includes index. 1. Tactics — History — 19th century. 2. Tactics — History — 20th century. 3. Military history, Modern — 19th century 4. Military history, Modern — 20th century I. T.
U165.G69     355.4/2/09034 19     *LC* 81-215537     *ISBN* 0907319017

**Heilbrunn, Otto.**     • **5.7223**
Warfare in the enemy's rear. New York: Praeger, 1964, c1963. 231 p.; 23 cm. 1. Guerrilla warfare 2. Unified operations (Military science) 3. Psychological warfare 4. Parachute troops I. T.
U167.5.R4 H4     355.425     *LC* 63-20394

**Huston, James A. (James Alvin), 1918-.**     • **5.7224**
The sinews of war: Army logistics, 1775–1953, by James A. Huston. Washington, Office of the Chief of Military History, United States Army; [for sale by the Superintendent of Documents, U.S. Govt. Print. Off.] 1966. xxlii, 789 p. illus., maps (1 fold. col.) ports. 26 cm. (Army historical series) Bibliography: p. [703]-735. 1. Logistics I. T. II. Title: Army logistics.
U168.H8     355.41     *LC* 66-60015

**Van Creveld, Martin L.**     **5.7225**
Supplying war: logistics from Wallenstein to Patton / Martin Van Creveld. — Cambridge; New York: Cambridge University Press, 1977. viii, 284 p.: maps; 22 cm. Includes index. 1. Logistics — History. 2. Military art and science — History 3. Military history, Modern I. T.
U168.V36     355.4/1/094     *LC* 77-5550     *ISBN* 052121730X

# U240–241 Guerrilla Warfare. Counterinsurgency

**Asprey, Robert B.**     **5.7226**
War in the shadows; the guerrilla in history, by Robert B. Asprey. — [1st ed.]. — Garden City, N.Y.: Doubleday, [1975] 2 v. (lvii, 1622 p.): maps (1 on lining papers); 25 cm. 1. Guerrilla warfare — History. 2. Vietnamese Conflict, 1961-1975 I. T.
U240.A86     355.02/184/09     *LC* 72-92400     *ISBN* 0385034709

**Guevara, Ernesto, 1928-1967.**                                    ● 5.7227
[Guerra de guerrillas. English] Guerrilla warfare [by] Che Guevara. New York,
M[onthly] R[eview] Press, 1961. 127 p. illus. 23 cm. 1. Revolutions
2. Guerrilla warfare 3. Cuba — History — 1933-1959 I. T.
U240.G833      355.425      LC 61-14052

**Kitson, Frank.**                                                  ● 5.7228
Low intensity operations; subversion, insurgency, peace–keeping. — [1st ed. —
Harrisburg, Pa.]: Stackpole Books, [1971] xi, 208 p.; 23 cm. 1. Guerrilla
warfare 2. Subversive activities 3. Insurgency I. T.
U240.K53 1971      355.02/184      LC 72-162452      ISBN 0811709574

**Laqueur, Walter, 1921-.**                                         5.7229
Guerrilla: a historical and critical study / Walter Laqueur. — 1st ed. — Boston:
Little, Brown, c1976. xii, 462 p.; 24 cm. Includes index. 1. Guerrilla warfare —
History. I. T.
U240.L36      355.02/184/09      LC 76-22552      ISBN 0316514691

**Mao, Tse-tung, 1893-1976.**                                      ● 5.7230
Basic tactics. Translated and with an introd. by Stuart R. Schram. Foreword by
Samuel B. Griffith, II. — New York: Praeger, [1966] viii, 149 p.; 21 cm.
1. Guerrilla warfare I. Schram, Stuart R. ed. and tr. II. T.
U240.M28 1966      355.425      LC 66-18912

**Thompson, Robert Grainger Ker, Sir, 1916-.**                     ● 5.7231
Defeating Communist insurgency; the lessons of Malaya and Vietnam [by] Sir
Robert Thompson. New York, F. A. Praeger [1966] 171 p. maps. 22 cm.
(Studies in international security, 10) The 1st vol. of the author's trilogy, the 2d
of which is No exit from Vietnam; the 3d, Revolutionary war in world strategy,
1945-1969. 1. Counterinsurgency — Vietnam. 2. Revolutions 3. Insurgency
4. Vietnamese Conflict, 1961-1975 5. Malaya — History — Malayan
Emergency, 1948-1960 I. T. II. Series.
U240.T56 1966a      355.425      LC 66-14507

**Shackley, Theodore.**                                            5.7232
The third option: an American view of counterinsurgency operations /
Theodore Shackley. — New York: Reader's Digest Press: McGraw-Hill, c1981.
xiii, 185 p.; 22 cm. Includes index. 1. Counterinsurgency — Case studies.
2. World politics — 1975-1985 3. World politics — 1965-1975 4. United
States — Military policy I. T.
U241.S43      355/.02184/0926 19      LC 80-26947      ISBN 0070563829

# U260 Joint Operations

**Creswell, John.**                                                ● 5.7233
Generals and admirals; the story of amphibious command. London Longmans,
Green [1952] 192p. 1. Amphibious warfare 2. Military history, Modern I. T.
U260 C74

# U263–264 Nuclear Warfare.
# Nuclear Weapons

**The Environmental effects of nuclear war / edited by Julius**     5.7234
**London and Gilbert F. White.**
Boulder, Colo.: Westview Press, 1984. xii, 203 p.: ill.; 23 cm. (AAAS selected
symposium. 98) 1. Nuclear warfare — Environmental aspects. I. London,
Julius, 1917- II. White, Gilbert Fowler, 1911- III. Series.
U263.E58 1984      363.3/498 19      LC 84-19699      ISBN 0813370140

**Harwell, Mark A.**                                               5.7235
Nuclear winter: the human and environmental consequences of nuclear war /
Mark A. Harwell, with contributions by Joseph Berry ... [et al.]; with a
foreword by Russell W. Peterson. — New York: Springer-Verlag, c1984. xix,
179 p.: ill.; 25 cm. Includes index. 1. Nuclear warfare — Environmental
aspects 2. Nuclear winter I. T.
U263.H37 1984      355/.0217 19      LC 84-22126      ISBN 0387960937

**Hawks, doves, and owls: an agenda for avoiding nuclear war /**    5.7236
**Graham T. Allison, Albert Carnesale, Joseph S. Nye, Jr.,**
**editors.**
1st ed. — New York: Norton, c1985. xii, 282 p.; 22 cm. Includes index.
1. Nuclear warfare 2. Nuclear disarmament I. Allison, Graham T.
II. Carnesale, Albert. III. Nye, Joseph S.
U263.H39 1985      327.1/74 19      LC 84-29485      ISBN 0393019950

**Kahn, Herman, 1922-.**                                           5.7237
Thinking about the unthinkable in the 1980s / Herman Kahn. — New York:
Simon and Schuster, c1984. 250 p.; 25 cm. 1. Nuclear warfare 2. Deterrence
(Strategy) I. T.
U263.K33 1984      355/.0217 19      LC 84-1432      ISBN 0671475444

**Dyson, Freeman J.**                                              5.7238
Weapons and hope / by Freeman Dyson. — 1st ed. — New York: Harper &
Row, c1984. viii, 340 p.; 24 cm. 'A Cornelia & Michael Bessie book.' 1. Dyson,
Freeman J. 2. Nuclear warfare 3. Munitions 4. Arms race 5. Nuclear
disarmament 6. World politics — 1975-1985 7. Nuclear weapons I. T.
U264.D97 1984      327.1/74 19      LC 83-48343      ISBN 006039031X

**Boatner, Mark Mayo, 1921-.**                                     ● 5.7239
Military customs and traditions. Illustrated by Lachlan M. Field. New York,
D. McKay Co. [1956] 176 p. illus. 21 cm. 1. Military ceremonies, honors, and
salutes — United States. I. T.
U353.B6      355.1      LC 56-14010

# U400–773 Military Education.
# Military Life

**Lovell, John P., 1932-.**                                        5.7240
Neither Athens nor Sparta?: The American service academies in transition /
John P. Lovell. — Bloomington: Indiana University Press, c1979. xviii, 362 p.;
24 cm. 1. United States. Military Academy, West Point — History. 2. United
States Naval Academy — History. 3. United States Air Force Academy —
History. 4. United States Coast Guard Academy — History.. 5. Military
education — United States — History. I. T.
U408.L67      355/.007/1173      LC 78-9509      ISBN 0253129559

**Ambrose, Stephen E.**                                            ● 5.7241
Duty, honor, country: a history of West Point. — Baltimore, Johns Hopkins
Press [c1966] xv, 357 p. ill., ports.; 24 cm. Bibliography: p. 335-342. I. T.
U410.L1 A7      LC 66-14372

**Rommel, Erwin, 1891-1944.**                                      5.7242
[Infanterie greift an. English] Attacks / Erwin Rommel. — 1st ed. — Vienna,
Va.: Athena Press, c1979. viii, 325 p., [1] leaf of plates: ill.; 24 cm. Translation of
Infanterie greift an. 1. Rommel, Erwin, 1891-1944. 2. Infantry drill and tactics
3. World War, 1914-1918 — Personal narratives, German. 4. World War,
1914-1918 — Campaigns I. T.
U738.R6513      940.4/143/0924 B      LC 79-52022      ISBN 0960273603

**Ingraham, Larry H.**                                             5.7243
The boys in the barracks: observations on American military life / Larry H.
Ingraham; with critical commentary by Frederick J. Manning. — Philadelphia:
Institute for the Study of Human Issues, c1984. xxi, 242 p.: ill.; 24 cm.
1. United States. Army — Military life 2. Sociology, Military — United States.
3. Soldiers — United States I. Manning, Frederick J. II. T.
U766.I73 1983      355.1/0973 19      LC 83-250      ISBN 0897270487

# U800–897 History of Arms and
# Armor

**Oakeshott, R. Ewart.**                                           ● 5.7244
The archaeology of weapons. New York, Praeger [1960] 358 p.: illus.; 23 cm.
1. Arms and armor — History. 2. Military history I. T.
U800.O3      LC 60-11279

**Weller, Jac.**                                                   ● 5.7245
Weapons and tactics; Hastings to Berlin. New York, St. Martin's Press [1966]
238 p. maps, plates, ports. 23 cm. 1. Armed Forces 2. Arms and armor
3. Tactics I. T.
U800.W4 1966a      LC 66-14030

**Enciclopedia ragionata delle armi. English.**                   5.7246
The complete encyclopedia of arms & weapons / edited by Leonid Tarassuk and
Claude Blair; [translated from the Italian by Sylvia Mulcahy, Simon Pleasance,
and Hugh Young]. — New York: Simon and Schuster, [c1982] 544 p.: ill. (some
col.); 27 cm. Translation of: Enciclopedia ragionata delle armi. 1. Arms and
armor — Dictionaries. I. Tarassuk, Leonid. II. Blair, Claude. III. T.
IV. Title: Complete encyclopedia of arms and weapons. V. Title: Arms &
weapons. VI. Title: Arms and weapons.
U815.E5313 1982      355.8/24/03 19      LC 80-5922      067142557X

# UA ARMIES. MILITARY POLICY

**Kaufmann, William W.**           **5.7247**
The McNamara strategy / William W. Kaufmann. — 1st ed. — New York: Harper & Row, 1969. x, 339 p.; 22 cm. 1. McNamara, Robert S., 1916- 2. United States. Dept. of Defense. 3. United States — Military policy I. T.
UA2A23.K37     *LC* 64-12672

## UA10–19 General Works

**Berghahn, Volker Rolf.**          **5.7248**
Militarism: the history of an international debate, 1861–1979 / Volker R. Berghahn. — New York: St. Martin's Press, 1982. 132 p.; 22 cm. Includes index. 1. Militarism 2. Civil-military relations 3. Sociology, Military I. T.
UA10.B47 1982    355/.0213 19    *LC* 81-48630    *ISBN* 0312532326

**Howard, Michael Eliot, 1922- ed.**       **• 5.7249**
Soldiers and governments; nine studies in civil–military relations. Pref. by George Fielding Eliot. — Bloomington, Indiana University Press, 1959. 192 p. 23 cm. 1. Militarism 2. World politics I. T.
UA10.H6 1959    355.082    *LC* 59-11094

**World armaments and disarmament: SIPRI yearbook.**    **5.7250**
1972-      . — Stockholm: Almquist & Wiksell; New York: Humanities Press, c1972-. v.: ill.; 24 cm. Annual. 1. Armaments — Periodicals. 2. Disarmament — Periodicals. I. Stockholm International Peace Research Institute.
UA10.S69a    355/.033/0047 19    *LC* 83-643843

**National security policy: the decision–making process / edited**    **5.7251**
**by Robert L. Pfaltzgraff, Jr., Uri Ra'anan.**
Hamden, Conn.: Archon Books, 1984. xiii, 311 p.; 24 cm. Proceedings of a conference sponsored by the International Security Studies Program of the Fletcher School of Law and Diplomacy, held April 27-29, 1983. 1. National security — Decision making — Addresses, essays, lectures. 2. Military policy — Decision making — Addresses, essays, lectures. I. Pfaltzgraff, Robert L. II. Ra'anan, Uri, 1926- III. Fletcher School of Law and Diplomacy. International Security Studies Program.
UA10.5.N295 1984    355/.0335 19    *LC* 84-2932    *ISBN* 0208020039

**Brodie, Bernard, 1910-.**          **• 5.7252**
Strategy in the missile age. Princeton, N. J., Princeton University Press, 1959. vii, 423 p. 23 cm. 'This study was undertaken by the Rand Corporation as a part of its research program for the United States Air Force.' Bibliographical footnotes. 1. Strategy 2. Military policy 3. Nuclear warfare 4. United States — Military policy I. Rand Corporation. II. T.
UA11.B7    355.43    *LC* 58-6102

**Foot, M. R. D. (Michael Richard Daniel), 1919-.**    **• 5.7253**
Men in uniform: military manpower in modern industrial societies / by M.R.D. Foot; with a foreword by Alastair Buchan. — New York: Praeger for the Institute for Strategic Studies, 1961. x, 161 p.: ill.; 22 cm. — (Studies in international security; 3) 1. Military policy 2. Armed Forces I. T. II. Series.
UA11.F6 1961a

**Halperin, Morton H.**          **• 5.7254**
Limited war in the nuclear age. — New York, Wiley [1963] ix, 191 p. 24 cm. 'Written under the auspices of the Center for International Affairs, Harvard University.' 1. Military policy 2. Strategy 3. Nuclear warfare I. T.
UA11.H34    355    *LC* 63-18625

**Huntington, Samuel P.**          **• 5.7255**
Changing patterns of military politics / edited by Samuel P. Huntington. — [New York]: Free Press of Glencoe, c1962. 272 p.; 24 cm. — (Internatonal yearbook of political behaviour research; v.3) 1. Military policy 2. World politics I. T. II. Series.
UA11.H8    *LC* 61-18255

**Kahn, Herman, 1922-.**          **• 5.7256**
On escalation: metaphors and scenarios. New York, Praeger [1965] xvii, 308 p. 22 cm. (Hudson Institute. Series on national security and international order, no. 1) 1. Military policy 2. Escalation (Military science) I. T. II. Series.
UA11.K32    355/.0335 19    *LC* 65-18080

**Snyder, Glenn Herald.**          **• 5.7257**
Deterrence and defense: toward a theory of national security / by Glenn H. Snyder. — Princeton, N. J.: Princeton University Press, 1961. ix, 294 p. 1. Military policy 2. Deterrence (Strategy) 3. Nuclear warfare I. T.
UA11.S56    355.4/307    *LC* 61-12102

**Dupuy, Trevor Nevitt, 1916-.**          **5.7258**
The almanac of world military power / Trevor N. Dupuy, Grace P. Hayes, John A. C. Andrews; Gay Hammerman, coordinating editor. — 4th ed. — San Rafael, Calif.: Presidio Press, c1980. 432 p. 1. Armed Forces 2. Armaments I. Hayes, Grace P. joint author. II. Andrews, John A. C., joint author. III. Hammerman, Gay M. IV. T.
UA15.D9 1980    355/.033/0047    *LC* 80-11844    *ISBN* 0891410708

**The Reference handbook of the armed forces of the world.**    **5.7259**
**1971-.**
Washington, Praeger. v. 24 cm. Editor: 1971-    R. C. Sellers. 1. Armed Forces I. Sellers (Robert C.) & Associates, Washington. II. Title: Armed forces of the world.
UA15.R43x

**Williams, Walter L.**          **5.7260**
Intergovernmental military forces and world public order [by] Walter L. Williams. — Leiden: A. W. Sijthoff; Dobbs Ferry, N.Y.: Oceana Publications, 1971. xiii, 703 p.; 25 cm. 1. Armed Forces 2. International relations I. T.
UA15.W55    341/.72    *LC* 75-167280

## UA21–876 Military Situation, by Country

### UA22–42 UNITED STATES

**Betts, Richard K., 1947-.**          **5.7261**
Soldiers, statesmen, and cold war crises / Richard K. Betts. — Cambridge: Harvard University Press, c1977. xi, 292 p.; 25 cm. Includes index. 1. United States — Military policy 2. United States — Armed Forces 3. United States — Foreign relations — 1945- I. T.
UA23.B46    355.03/35/73    *LC* 77-8068    *ISBN* 0674817419

**Brown, Harold, 1927-.**          **5.7262**
Thinking about national security: defense and foreign policy in a dangerous world / Harold Brown. — Boulder, Colo.: Westview Press; New York: Distributed by Hearst Books, 1983. xvi, 288 p.; 24 cm. Includes index. 1. United States — National security I. T.
UA23.B7845 1983    355/.033073 19    *LC* 82-23859    *ISBN* 0865315485

**Clarfield, Gerard H.**          **5.7263**
Nuclear America: military and civilian nuclear power in the United States, 1940–1980 / Gerard H. Clarfield and William M. Wiecek. — 1st ed. — New York: Harper & Row, c1984. ix, 518 p.; 22 cm. Includes index. 1. Nuclear weapons 2. Nuclear energy — United States. 3. United States — Military policy I. Wiecek, William M., 1938- II. T.
UA23.C558 1984    355/.0335/73 19    *LC* 84-47565    *ISBN* 0060153369

**Congressional Quarterly, inc.**          **5.7264**
U.S. defense policy: weapons, strategy, and commitments; [editor, John L. Moore]. — 2d ed. — Washington, D.C.: Congressional Quarterly, c1980. 130, 89 p.: ill.; 28 cm. — (A Contemporary affairs report) Includes index. 1. Munitions 2. Military assistance, American 3. United States — Military policy 4. United States — Foreign relations — 1977- I. Moore, John Leo, 1927- II. T.
UA23.C654 1980    355/.033073 19    *LC* 80-607772    0871871582

**Enthoven, Alain C., 1930-.**          **• 5.7265**
How much is enough? Shaping the defense program, 1961–1969 [by] Alain C. Enthoven and K. Wayne Smith. — [1st ed.]. — New York: Harper & Row, [1971] xv, 364 p.; 23 cm. 1. U.S. — Military policy. I. Smith, K. Wayne. joint author. II. T.
UA23.E63    355.03/35/73    *LC* 78-127840

**Etzold, Thomas H.**          **5.7266**
Defense or delusion?: America's military in the 1980s / by Thomas H. Etzold. — 1st ed. — New York: Harper & Row, c1982. x, 259 p.; 24 cm. 1. United States — Military policy 2. United States — Armed Forces I. T.
UA23.E89 1982    355/.033073 19    *LC* 81-47655    *ISBN* 006038011X

**Fallows, James M.**     **5.7267**
National defense / James Fallows. — 1st ed. — New York: Random House, c1981. xvii, 204 p.; 24 cm. 1. United States — Military policy 2. United States — Defenses I. T.
UA23.F343     355/.033073 19     *LC* 80-6006     *ISBN* 0394518241

**Feld, Werner J.**     **5.7268**
Congress and national defense: the politics of the unthinkable / Werner J. Feld, John K. Wildgen. — New York: Praeger, 1985. xiii, 126 p.; ill.; 24 cm. 1. United States. Congress. 2. Nuclear arms control 4. United States — Military policy I. Wildgen, John K. II. T.
UA23.F39 1985     355/.0335/73 19     *LC* 84-16007     *ISBN* 0030697514

**Fulbright, J. William (James William), 1905-.**     • **5.7269**
The Pentagon propaganda machine [by] J. W. Fulbright. — New York: Liveright, [1970] vii, 166 p.; 22 cm. 1. United States. Dept. of Defense — Public relations. I. T.
UA23.F84     355.03/35/73     *LC* 79-131268     *ISBN* 0871405229

**Gregor, A. James (Anthony James), 1929-.**     **5.7270**
The iron triangle: a U.S. security policy for northeast Asia / A. James Gregor, Maria Hsia Chang. — Stanford, Calif.: Hoover Institution Press, Stanford University, c1984. x, 160 p.; 24 cm. (Hoover international studies.) Includes index. 1. United States — Military relations — Japan. 2. United States — Military relations — Taiwan. 3. United States — Military relations — Korea (South) 4. Japan — Military relations — United States. 5. Taiwan — Military relations — United States. 6. Korea (South) — Military relations — United States. I. Chang, Maria Hsia. II. T. III. Series.
UA23.G79 1984     355/.03305 19     *LC* 84-630     *ISBN* 0817979212

**Herken, Gregg, 1947-.**     **5.7271**
Counsels of war / Gregg Herken. — 1st ed. — New York: Knopf, 1985. xvi, 409 p.; 25 cm. Includes index. 1. Nuclear weapons 2. Military research — United States — History — 20th century. 3. United States — Military policy I. T.
UA23.H45 1985     355/.0335/73 19     *LC* 84-47876     *ISBN* 0394527356

**Huntington, Samuel P.**     • **5.7272**
The soldier and the state; the theory and politics of civil–military relations. — Cambridge: Belknap Press of Harvard University Press, 1957. xiii, 534 p.; 25 cm. 1. Militarism — United States. 2. Civil supremacy over the military — United States. I. T.
UA23.H95     342.73     *LC* 57-6349

**Janowitz, Morris.**     • **5.7273**
Sociology and the military establishment / by Morris Janowitz. — New York: Russell Sage Foundation, 1959. — 112 p. 1. United States. Dept. of Defence. 2. Sociology 3. United States — Defenses 4. United States — Armed Forces I. American Sociological Society. II. T.
UA23.J3     355.3     *LC* 59-10151

**Krepon, Michael, 1946-.**     **5.7274**
Strategic stalemate: nuclear weapons and arms control in American politics / Michael Krepon. — New York, NY: St. Martin's Press, 1984. xvi, 191 p.; 23 cm. 'A Council of Foreign Relations book.' Includes index. 1. Nuclear weapons 2. Strategic Arms Limitation Talks. 3. World politics — 1975-1985 4. United States — Military policy 5. United States — Politics and government — 1981- I. T.
UA23.K777 1984     355/.0335/73 19     *LC* 84-13323     *ISBN* 0312764340

**Lyons, Gene Martin.**     • **5.7275**
Schools for strategy; education and research in national security affairs by Gene M. Lyons and Louis Morton. New York: Praeger, 1965. 356p. 1. Universities and colleges — United States 2. Research — United States 3. United States — Military policy I. Morton, Louis. II. T.
UA23 L95     *LC* 65-14056

**McNaugher, Thomas L.**     **5.7276**
Arms and oil: U.S. military strategy and the Persian Gulf / Thomas L. McNaugher. — Washington, D.C.: Brookings Institution, c1985. xiii, 226 p.; 24 cm. 1. United States — Military policy 2. Persian Gulf Region — Strategic aspects I. T.
UA23.M43 1985     355/.0335/73 19     *LC* 84-45850     *ISBN* 0815756240

**Millis, Walter, 1899-1968. ed.**     • **5.7277**
American military thought. — Indianapolis: Bobbs-Merrill, [1966] liii, 554 p.; 22 cm. — (The American heritage series) 1. United States — Military policy 2. United States — History, Military I. T.
UA23.M565     355.033573     *LC* 66-14831

**Sherry, Michael S., 1945-.**     **5.7278**
Preparing for the next war: American plans for postwar defense, 1941–45 / Michael S. Sherry. New Haven: Yale University Press, 1977. x, 260 p.; 25 cm. (Yale historical publications. Miscellany. 114) Originally presented as the author's thesis, Yale, 1975. Includes index. 1. United States — Military policy 2. United States — Armed Forces I. T. II. Series.
UA23.S47 1977     355.03/307/3     *LC* 76-27853     *ISBN* 0300020317

**Smoke, Richard.**     **5.7279**
National security and the nuclear dilemma: an introduction to the American experience / Richard Smoke. — Reading, Mass.: Addison-Wesley Pub. Co., c1984. xiv, 271 p.; 21 cm. 1. Nuclear weapons 2. Nuclear disarmament 3. United States — Foreign relations — 1945- 4. United States — National security 5. United States — Military policy I. T.
UA23.S524 1984     355/.033073 19     *LC* 83-17916     *ISBN* 0201164205

**Stein, Jonathan B.**     **5.7280**
From H–bomb to star wars: the politics of strategic decision making / Jonathan B. Stein. — Lexington, Mass.: Lexington Books, c1984. xiii, 118 p.; 23 cm. Includes index. 1. Arms race — History — 20th century. 2. Hydrogen bomb 3. Space weapons 4. Ballistic missile defenses — United States 5. United States — Military policy — Decision making. I. T.
UA23.S685 1984     355/.0335/73 19     *LC* 84-47938     *ISBN* 0669089680

**Taylor, Maxwell D. (Maxwell Davenport), 1901-1987.**     • **5.7281**
The uncertain trumpet. [1st ed.] New York, Harper [c1960] 203 p. 22 cm. 1. United States — Military policy 2. United States — Defenses I. T.
UA 23 T242     *LC* 59-13290L

**Geelhoed, E. Bruce, 1948-.**     **5.7282**
Charles E. Wilson and controversy at the Pentagon, 1953 to 1957 / E. Bruce Geelhoed. — Detroit: Wayne State University Press, 1979. 216 p.; ill.; 24 cm. Includes index. 1. Wilson, Charles Erwin, 1890-1961. 2. United States. Dept. of Defense — History. 3. United States — Politics and government — 1953-1961 I. T.
UA23.6.G43     353.6/092/4 B     *LC* 79-9756     *ISBN* 0814316352

**Gabriel, Richard A.**     **5.7283**
Crisis in command: mismanagement in the Army / Richard A. Gabriel and Paul L. Savage. — 1st ed. — New York: Hill and Wang, 1978. xii, 242 p.; 22 cm. 1. United States. Army. 2. United States. Army — Officers 3. Military ethics — United States. I. Savage, Paul L. joint author. II. T.
UA25.G26     355.3/3/0973     *LC* 77-18689     *ISBN* 0809037114

**Stanton, Shelby L., 1948-.**     **5.7284**
Order of battle, U.S. Army, World War II / Shelby L. Stanton. — Novato, CA: Presidio, c1984. xiv, 620 p., [8] p. of plates: ill. (some col.); 32 cm. Spine title: Order of battle WW II. 1. United States. Army — Organization 2. United States. Army — History — World War, 1939-1945 I. T. II. Title: Order of battle, US Army, World War II. III. Title: Order of battle WW II. IV. Title: Order of battle WW 2. V. Title: Order of battle WW Two.
UA25.S767 1984     355.3/0973 19     *LC* 84-8299     *ISBN* 089141195X

**Utley, Robert Marshall, 1929-.**     • **5.7285**
Frontiersmen in blue; the United States Army and the Indian, 1848–1865, by Robert M. Utley. New York, Macmillan [1967] xv, 384 p. illus. 24 cm. 1. United States. Army — History 2. Indians of North America — Wars — 1815-1875 3. West (U.S.) — History I. T.
UA25.U8     355.3/51/0973     *LC* 67-19682

**Weigley, Russell Frank.**     **5.7286**
History of the United States Army / Russell F. Weigley. — Enl. ed. — Bloomington: Indiana University Press, c1984. vi, 730 p.; 24 cm. 'A Midland book'—Cover. 1. United States. Army — History 2. United States — History, Military I. T.
UA25.W35 1984     355.3/0973 19     *LC* 83-49010     *ISBN* 0253203236

**Weigley, Russell Frank.**     • **5.7287**
Towards an American army; military thought from Washington to Marshall. New York, Columbia University Press, 1962. xi, 297 p. 24 cm. 1. United States. Army — History 2. United States — Military policy I. T.
UA25.W4     *LC* 62-15388

**Wright, Robert K., 1946-.**     **5.7288**
The Continental Army / by Robert K. Wright, Jr. — Washington, D.C.: Center of Military History, U.S. Army: For sale by the Supt. of Docs., U.S. G.P.O., 1983. xvii, 451 p.::ill. (some col.); 26 cm. — (Army lineage series) Includes index. 1. United States. Continental Army — History 2. United States — History — Revolution, 1775-1783 — Campaigns and battles. I. T. II. Series.
UA25.W84 1983     355.3/0973 19     *LC* 82-16472

**Thompson, Neil B., 1921-.**     **5.7289**
Crazy Horse called them walk–a–heaps: the story of the foot soldier in the prairie Indian Wars / Neil Baird Thompson. — Saint Cloud, Minn.: North Star

Press, c1979. vi, 150 p., [2] leaves of plates: ill.; 24 cm. Includes index. 1. United States. Army — History — 19th century. 2. Indians of North America — Great Plains — Wars — 1866-1895. 3. Great Plains — History, Military. I. T.
UA26.G675 T46        301.6/334/0973        *LC* 79-120364        *ISBN* 0878390111

## UA42 National Guard

**Hill, Jim Dan, 1897-.**                                                        ● **5.7290**
The minute man in peace and war: a history of the National Guard / foreword by George Fielding Eliot. — [1st ed.] Harrisburg, Pa.: Stackpole Co. [1964] xx, 585 p.: ill.; 24 cm. -Copy 2. 1. United States — Militia 2. United States — National Guard I. T.
UA42.H5        *LC* 63-22141

**Mahon, John K.**                                                               **5.7291**
History of the militia and the National Guard / John K. Mahon. — New York: Macmillan; London: Collier Macmillan, c1983. 374 p., [16] p. of plates: ill.; 25 cm. (Macmillan wars of the United States.) Includes index. 1. United States — Militia — History. 2. United States — National Guard — History. I. T. II. Series.
UA42.M33 1983        355.3/7/0973 19        *LC* 82-24902        *ISBN* 0029197503

## UA600–876 OTHER COUNTRIES

## UA602.3–645 Latin America

**Nunn, Frederick M., 1937-.**                                                   **5.7292**
Yesterday's soldiers: European military professionalism in South America, 1890–1940 / Frederick M. Nunn. — Lincoln: University of Nebraska Press, c1983. xiii, 365 p.; 22 cm. 1. Sociology, Military — South America. 2. Military art and science — South America — History. 3. Europe — Military relations — South America. 4. South America — Military relations — Europe. I. T.
UA612.N86 1983        306/.27/098 19        *LC* 82-6961        *ISBN* 0803233051

**Potash, Robert A., 1921-.**                                                    **5.7293**
The army & politics in Argentina [by] Robert A. Potash. Stanford, Calif.: Stanford University Press, 1969-1980. 2 v.: ill., facsim., plan, ports.; 24 cm. Includes index. 1. Irigoyen, Hipólito, 1852-1933. 2. Perón, Juan Domingo, 1895-1974. 3. Argentina. Ejército — Political activity. 4. Argentina — Politics and government — 1910-1943 I. T.
UA613.P67        320.9/82        *LC* 69-13182        *ISBN* 0804710562

## UA646–829 Europe. NATO

**Corvisier, André.**                                                            **5.7294**
[Armées et sociétés en Europe de 1494 à 1789. English] Armies and societies in Europe, 1494–1789 / André Corvisier; translated by Abigail T. Siddall. — Bloomington: Indiana University Press, c1979. ix, 209 p.; 22 cm. Translation of Armées et sociétés en Europe de 1494 à 1789. Includes index. 1. Armies — History. 2. Sociology, Military 3. Europe — History, Military I. T.
UA646.C6813        301.5/93/094        *LC* 78-62419        *ISBN* 0253129850

**Gooch, John.**                                                                 **5.7295**
Armies in Europe / John Gooch. — London; Boston: Routledge & Kegan Paul, 1980. x, 286 p.; 23 cm. Includes index. 1. Armies — Europe — History. I. T.
UA646.G59        355/.0094        *LC* 79-41297        *ISBN* 0710004621

**Mendl, Wolf.**                                                                 **5.7296**
Western Europe & Japan between the superpowers / Wolf Mendl. — New York: St. Martin's Press; London: Croom Helm, 1984. 181 p.; 23 cm. 1. World politics — 1945- 2. Japan — National security. 3. Europe — National security. I. T. II. Title: Western Europe and Japan between the superpowers.
UA646.M43 1984        355/.033/0047 19        *LC* 84-40047        *ISBN* 0312864019

**Osgood, Robert Endicott.**                                                     ● **5.7297**
NATO, the entangling alliance / by Robert Endicott Osgood. — Chicago: University of Chicago Press, 1962. 416 p. 24 cm. 1. North Atlantic Treaty Organization. 2. World politics — 1945- I. T.
UA646.3.O8        355        *LC* 62-8348

**Buchan, Alastair.**                                                            ● **5.7298**
NATO in the 1960's; the implications of interdependence. With a foreword by John Slessor. New York, Praeger for the Institute for Strategic Studies, London

[1960] xii, 131 p. 22 cm. (Studies in international security, 1) 1. North Atlantic Treaty Orgaization. I. T. II. Series.
UA646.3.B7        355        *LC* 60-10484

**Schwartz, David N., 1956-.**                                                   **5.7299**
NATO's nuclear dilemmas / David N. Schwartz. — Washington, D.C.: Brookings Institution, c1983. x, 270 p.; 24 cm. Includes index. 1. North Atlantic Treaty Organization. 2. Nuclear weapons 3. Deterrence (Strategy) — History — 20th century. 4. Cruise missiles 5. Intermediate-range ballistic missiles I. T.
UA646.3.S38 1983        355/.031/097821 19        *LC* 83-11911        *ISBN* 0815777728

## UA647–668 Britain

**British defence policy in a changing world / edited by John**                  **5.7300**
**Baylis.**
London: Croom Helm, c1977. 295 p.; 23 cm. Includes index. 1. Great Britain — Defenses — Addresses, essays, lectures. 2. Great Britain — Military policy — Addresses, essays, lectures. 3. Great Britain — Foreign relations — 1945- — Addresses, essays, lectures. I. Baylis, John.
UA647.B85        355.03/3041        *LC* 78-301391        *ISBN* 0856643742

**Jaffe, Lorna S.**                                                              **5.7301**
The decision to disarm Germany: British policy towards postwar German disarmament, 1914–1919 / Lorna S. Jaffe. — Boston: Allen & Unwin, 1985. xiii, 286 p.; 23 cm. Includes index. 1. World War, 1914-1918 — Great Britain 2. World War, 1914-1918 — Germany. 3. Great Britain — Military policy. 4. Great Britain — Military relations — Germany. 5. Germany — Military relations — Great Britain. I. T.
UA647.J34 1985        355/.0335/41 19        *LC* 84-12351        *ISBN* 0049430343

**Preston, Richard Arthur.**                                                     ● **5.7302**
Canada and imperial defense; a study of the origins of the British Commonwealth's defense organization, 1867–1919 [by] Richard A. Preston. Durham, N.C., Published for the Duke University Commonwealth-Studies Center [by] Duke University Press, 1967. xxi, 576 p. 24 cm. (Duke University Commonwealth-Studies Center Publication no. 29) 1. Great Britain — Defenses. 2. Canada — Defenses. I. T.
UA647.P68        355.03/09171/242        *LC* 66-29550

**Shay, Robert Paul, 1947-.**                                                    **5.7303**
British rearmament in the thirties: politics and profits / Robert Paul Shay, Jr. Princeton, N.J.: Princeton University Press, c1977. xiii, 315 p.: ill.; 23 cm. Includes index. 1. Great Britain — Defenses. 2. Great Britain — Politics and government — 20th century 3. Great Britain — Foreign relations — 20th century I. T.
UA647.S37        355.03/3041        *LC* 76-45911        *ISBN* 0691052484

**Cruickshank, Charles Greig.**                                                  ● **5.7304**
Elizabeth's army, by C. G. Cruickshank. — 2nd ed. — London: Oxford U.P., 1968. xii, 316 p.; 20 cm. — (Oxford paperbacks, 148) 1. Great Britain. Army. 2. Military administration I. T.
UA649.C75 1968        355/.00942        *LC* 70-356991        *ISBN* 0198811489

**Firth, C. H. (Charles Harding), 1857-1936.**                                   ● **5.7305**
Cromwell's army; a history of the English soldier during the civil wars, the Commonwealth and the Protectorate; with a new introd. by P. H. Hardacre. London, Methuen; New York, Barnes & Noble [1962] 432 p. 22 cm. (Ford lectures delivered in the University of Oxford, 1900-1) Reprint from 3d ed. 1. Great Britain. Army. 2. Great Britain — History, Military I. T.
UA649.F52 1962        942.062        *LC* 62-5713

**Spiers, Edward M.**                                                            **5.7306**
The army and society, 1815–1914 / Edward M. Spiers. — London; New York: Longman, 1980. 318 p.; 23 cm. — (Themes in British social history) Includes index. 1. Great Britain. Army — History. 2. Sociology, Military — Great Britain. I. T.
UA649.S73        301.5/93/0941        *LC* 79-40042        *ISBN* 0582485657

**A Nation in arms: a social study of the British Army in the**                  **5.7307**
**First World War / edited by Ian F.W. Beckett and Keith**
**Simpson.**
Manchester; Dover, N.H.: Manchester University Press, c1985. x, 276 p.: ill.; 23 cm. Includes index. 1. Great Britain. Army — history — European War, 1914-1918. 2. Sociology, Military — Great Britain — History — 20th century. I. Beckett, I. F. W. (Ian Frederick William) II. Simpson, Keith, 1949-
UA649.3.N38 1985        306/.27/0941 19        *LC* 84-25048        *ISBN* 0719017378

**Liddell Hart, Basil Henry, 1895-.**                                            ● **5.7308**
The tanks; the history of the Royal tank regiment and its predecessors, Heavy branch Machine-gun corps, Tank corps and Royal tank corps, 1914–1945, by Captain B.H. Liddell Hart, with a foreword by Field–Marshal Viscount

Montgomery of Alamein. New York, Praeger [1959] 2 v. ill. 1. Great Britain. Army. Royal Tank Regiment. I. T.
UA656.R72 L5    358.3

## UA700–709 France

**Challener, Richard D.**                                    **5.7309**
The French theory of the nation in arms, 1866–1939. New York, Columbia University Press, 1955 [c1952] 305 p. 23 cm. 1. Draft — France. 2. France — Military policy. 3. France — History, Military I. T.
H31.C7 no. 579 UA700.C5    LC 54-11914

**Gaulle, Charles de, 1890-1970.**                          • **5.7310**
The army of the future, by General Charles de Gaulle, foreword by Walter Millis. Philadelphia, J. B. Lippincott company [c1941] 179 p. ill. 1. France. Army 2. France — Defenses. I. T.
UA700.G32 1941    355.0944    LC 41-51695

**Kennett, Lee B.**                                          • **5.7311**
The French armies in the Seven Years' War: a study in military organization and administration / Lee Kennett. — Durham, N. C.: Duke University Press, 1967. xvi, 165 p.; 23 cm. 1. France. Armée — History. 2. Seven Years' War, 1756-1763 I. T.
UA700.K4    355.3/1/0944    LC 67-18529

**Paret, Peter.**                                            • **5.7312**
French revolutionary warfare from Indochina to Algeria, the analysis of a political and military doctrine. New York Published for the Center of International Studies, Princeton University, by F.A. Praeger [1964] 163p. (Princeton studies in world politics. 6) 1. France — Military policy 2. Revolutions 3. Indochina, French — History — 1945- 4. Algeria — History — 1945- I. T. II. Series.
UA700 P36

**Horne, Alistair.**                                         **5.7313**
The French Army and politics, 1870–1970 / Alistair Horne. — 1st American ed. — New York: Peter Bedrick Books: Distributed in the USA by Harper & Row, c1984. xvii, 109 p.; 23 cm. Includes index. 1. France. Armée — Political activity. 2. France. Armée — History — 19th century. 3. France. Armée — History — 20th century. 4. France — Politics and government — 19th century 5. France — Politics and government — 20th century I. T.
UA702.H67 1984    322/.5/0944 19    LC 83-13453    ISBN 0911745157

**Lynn, John A. (John Albert), 1943-.**                      **5.7314**
The bayonets of the Republic: motivation and tactics in the army of Revolutionary France, 1791–94 / John A. Lynn. — Urbana: University of Illinois Press, c1984. xii, 356 p.: ill., maps; 24 cm. Includes index. 1. France. Armée — History — 18th century. 2. Tactics — History — 18th century. 3. Military art and science — France — History — 18th century. I. T.
UA702.L95 1984    355/.00944 19    LC 83-9093    ISBN 0252010914

**Mitchell, Allan.**                                         **5.7315**
Victors and vanquished: the German influence on army and church in France after 1870 / by Allan Mitchell. — Chapel Hill: University of North Carolina Press, c1984. xvii, 354 p.; 24 cm. Sequel to: The German influence in France after 1870. Includes index. 1. France. Armée — History — 19th century. 2. Catholic Church — France — History — 19th century. 3. Church and state — France — History — 19th century. 4. France — Church history — 19th century 5. Germany — Relations — France 6. France — Relations — Germany 7. France — Politics and government — 1870-1940 8. France — History, Military — 19th century I. T.
UA702.M5 1984    944.081 19    LC 83-25917    ISBN 0807816035

**Quimby, Robert S.**                                        • **5.7316**
The background of Napoleonic warfare; the theory of military tactics in eighteenth–century France. New York, Columbia University Press, 1957. 385 p. (Columbia studies in the social sciences, no.596) 1. France. Armée — History. 2. Military art and science — History 3. Tactics — History. 4. France — History, Military — 18th century I. T. II. Series.
UA702.Q5    LC 57-11105

## UA710–719 Germany

**Addington, Larry H.**                                      **5.7317**
The blitzkrieg era and the German General Staff, 1865–1941 [by] Larry H. Addington. — New Brunswick, N.J.: Rutgers University Press, [1971] xvii, 285 p.: maps.; 24 cm. 1. Halder, Franz, 1884- 2. Germany. Heer. Generalstab. 3. Lightning war 4. Germany — History, Military I. T.
UA712.A594    355/.00943    LC 75-163955    ISBN 0813507049

**O'Neill, Robert John.**                                    • **5.7318**
The German Army and the Nazi Party, 1933–1939 [by] Robert J. O'Neill. Foreword by Captain Sir Basil Liddell Hart. New York, J. H. Heineman [1967,

c1966] 286 p. illus., facsims., maps, ports. 26 cm. 1. Germany. Heer — History. 2. Nationalsozialistische Deutsche Arbeiter-Partei. I. T.
UA712.O5 1966    355.3/51/0943    LC 67-11678

**Van Creveld, Martin L.**                                   **5.7319**
Fighting power: German and US Army performance, 1939–1945 / Martin van Creveld. — Westport, Conn.: Greenwood Press, 1982. xi, 198 p.; 25 cm. (Contributions in military history. 0084-9251; no. 32) Includes index. 1. Germany. Heer — Evaluation. 2. United States. Army — Evaluation. 3. Germany. Heer — History — World War, 1939-1945. 4. United States. Army — History — World War, 1939-1945 5. Germany. Heer — Statistics. 6. United States. Army — Statistics I. T. II. Series.
UA712.V256 1982    355/.02 19    LC 81-23732    ISBN 0313233330

**Duffy, Christopher, 1936-.**                               **5.7320**
Army of Frederick the Great. — New York: Hippocrene Books, 1974. 272 p.: ill. (Historic armies and navies.) 1. Frederick II, King of Prussia, 1712-1786. 2. Prussia. Armiee — History. I. T. II. Series.
UA718P9 D83 1974    355.3'0943    LC 74-80439    ISBN 088254277X

**Shanahan, William Oswald, 1913-.**                         • **5.7321**
Prussian military reforms, 1786–1813, by William O. Shanahan. New York Columbia University Press 1945. 270p. (Studies in history, economics and public law, no. 520) 1. Prussia (Kingdom). Armee — History 2. Prussia — History, Military 3. Draft — Germany I. T.
UA718 P9 S5

## UA770–779 Soviet Union

**Berman, Robert P., 1950-.**                                **5.7322**
Soviet strategic forces: requirements and responses / Robert P. Berman and John C. Baker. — Washington, D.C.: Brookings Institution, c1982. xi, 171 p.: ill.; 24 cm. — (Studies in defense policy.) 1. Strategic forces — Soviet Union. 2. Soviet Union — Military policy. 3. United States — Military policy I. Baker, John C., 1949- II. T. III. Series.
UA770.B45 1982    358/.17/0947 19    LC 82-70889    ISBN 0815709269

**Dinerstein, Herbert Samuel, 1919-.**                       • **5.7323**
War and the Soviet Union; nuclear weapons and the revolution in Soviet military and political thinking. New York, Praeger [1959] 268 p. 24 cm. (Praeger publications in Russian history and world communism, no. 79) (Books that matter) 1. Nuclear warfare 2. Soviet Union — Military policy. I. T.
UA770.D5    LC 59-7696

**Holloway, David, 1943-.**                                  **5.7324**
The Soviet Union and the arms race / David Holloway. — New Haven: Yale University Press, 1983. x, 211 p.; 23 cm. 1. World politics — 1945- 2. Arms race — History — 20th century. 3. Soviet Union — Military policy. 4. Soviet Union — Defenses. 5. Soviet Union — Armed Forces I. T.
UA770.H63 1983    355/.033047 19    LC 82-20050    ISBN 0300029632

**Kaplan, Stephen S.**                                       **5.7325**
Diplomacy of power: Soviet Armed Forces as a political instrument / Stephen S. Kaplan, with Michel Tatu ... [et al.]. — Washington, D.C.: Brookings Institution, c1981. xvi, 733 p.; 24 cm. Includes index. 1. World politics — 1945- 2. Russia — Armed Forces — History — 20th century. 3. Russia — Foreign relations — 1945- 4. Russia — Military policy. I. T.
UA770.K28    327.1/17/0947 19    LC 80-25006    ISBN 0815748248

**Kolkowicz, Roman.**                                        • **5.7326**
The Soviet military and the Communist Party. Princeton, N.J., Princeton University Press, 1967. xvi, 429 p. 25 cm. 1. Kommunisticheskaia partiia Sovetskogo Soiuza. 2. Civil supremacy over the military — Soviet Union. 3. Soviet Union — Armed Forces — Political activity. I. T.
UA770.K6    355.03/32/47    LC 67-14410

**Porter, Bruce D.**                                         **5.7327**
The USSR in Third World conflicts: Soviet arms and diplomacy in local wars, 1945–1980 / Bruce D. Porter. — Cambridge [Cambridgeshire]; New York: Cambridge University Press, 1984. viii, 248 p.; 24 cm. Revision of author's thesis (Ph. D.)—Harvard University, 1979. 1. Developing countries — Military relations — Soviet Union. 2. Military history, Modern — 20th century 3. World politics — 1945- 4. Soviet Union — Military policy. 5. Soviet Union — Military relations — Developing countries. I. T. II. Title: U.S.S.R. in Third World conflicts.
UA770.P666 1984    355/.0335/47 19    LC 83-26265    ISBN 0521263085

**Rosefielde, Steven.**                                      **5.7328**
False science: underestimating the Soviet arms buildup: an appraisal of the CIA's direct costing effort, 1960–80 / Steven Rosefielde; foreword by Patrick Parker. — New Brunswick, NJ: Transaction Books, c1982. xii, 321 p.; 23 cm.

Includes index. 1. United States. Central Intelligence Agency. 2. Soviet Union — Armed Forces — Appropriations and expenditures. I. T.
UA770.R6 1982    355.6/22/0947 19    *LC* 81-1050    *ISBN* 0878554270

**Warner, Edward L.**                    **5.7329**
The military in contemporary Soviet politics: an institutional analysis / Edward L. Warner III. — New York: Praeger, 1977. viii, 314 p.; 25 cm. — (Praeger special studies in international politics and government) Includes index. 1. Russia — Military policy. 2. Russia — Armed Forces. 3. Russia — Politics and government — 1953- I. T.
UA770.W27 1977    355.03/35/47    *LC* 77-83476    *ISBN* 0030403464

**Erickson, John.**                    • **5.7330**
The Soviet high command; a military–political history, 1918–1941. [New York] St Martin's Press, 1962. xv, 889 p. port., maps., diagrs. 23 cm. Bibliography: p. 809-834. 1. Soviet Union. Armiia — History. 2. Soviet Union — Military policy. 3. Soviet Union — History, Military — 1917- I. T.
UA772.E7    355    *LC* 62-6671

**Liddell Hart, Basil Henry, 1895- ed.**                    • **5.7331**
The Red Army: the Red Army, 1918 to 1945; the Soviet Army, 1946 to the present, edited by B. H. Liddell Hart. Gloucester, Mass., P. Smith, 1968 [c1956] xiv, 480 p. illus., maps. 21 cm. 1. Soviet Union. Raboche-Krest'ianskaia Krasnaia Armiia — History. 2. Russia — History, Military. I. T.
UA772.L5 1968    355/.00947    *LC* 74-2182

**Suvorov, Viktor.**                    **5.7332**
Inside the Soviet army / Viktor Suvorov; foreword by Sir John Hackett. — California: Berkley Books; 1984. 446 p., [16] p. of plates: ill.; 18 cm. I. T.
UA772.SX    355/.00947 19    *ISBN* 0586059784

## UA780–789 Spain

**Payne, Stanley G.**                    • **5.7333**
Politics and the military in modern Spain [by] Stanley G. Payne. — Stanford, Calif.: Stanford University Press, 1967. xiii, 574 p.: 6 maps.; 25 cm. 1. Spain. Ejército. 2. Spain — Politics and government I. T.
UA782.P3    946.08    *LC* 66-17564

## UA830–853 Asia. Middle East

**Lebra-Chapman, Joyce, 1925-.**                    **5.7334**
Japanese–trained armies in Southeast Asia: independence and volunteer forces in World War II / Joyce C. Lebra. — New York: Columbia University Press, 1977. iv, 226 p., [2] leaves of plates: ill.; 23 cm. Includes index. 1. Military education — Asia, Southeastern — History. 2. Asia, Southeastern — Armed Forces — History. 3. Asia, Southeastern — History — Japanese occupation. I. T.
UA830.L4 1977    355.3/0959    *LC* 75-16116    *ISBN* 0231039956

**Chinese defence policy / edited by Gerald Segal and William T.**                    **5.7335**
**Tow.**
Urbana: University of Illinois Press, c1984. xxii, 286 p.; 23 cm. 1. China — Military policy — Addresses, essays, lectures. 2. China — Defenses — Addresses, essays, lectures. 3. China — Armed Forces — Addresses, essays, lectures. I. Segal, Gerald, 1953- II. Tow, William T.
UA835.C448 1984    355/.033051 19    *LC* 83-24229    *ISBN* 025201135X

**Smith, Richard J. (Richard Joseph), 1944-.**                    **5.7336**
Mercenaries and Mandarins: the Ever–Victorious Army in nineteenth century China / Richard J. Smith; foreword by John K. Fairbank. — Millwood, N.Y.: KTO Press, c1978. xxiii, 271 p.: ill.; 24 cm. (KTO studies in American history) Based on the author's thesis, University of California at Davis. Includes index. 1. China. Lu chün. Ch'ang sheng chün. 2. Taiping Rebellion, 1850-1864. I. T. II. Series.
UA838.C4 S54    951/.03    *LC* 78-6394    *ISBN* 0527839507

**George, Alexander L.**                    • **5.7337**
The Chinese Communist Army in action; the Korean War and its aftermath, by Alexander L. George. New York, Columbia University Press, 1967. xii, 255 p. illus. 24 cm. 1. China. Chung-kuo jen min chieh fang chün. 2. Korean War, 1950-1953 I. T.
UA839.3.G4    355/.00951    *LC* 67-12659

**Griffith, Samuel B.**                    • **5.7338**
The Chinese People's Liberation Army [by] Samuel B. Griffith, II. [1st ed.] New York, Published for the Council on Foreign Relations by McGraw-Hill [1967] xiv, 398 p. 3 fold. illus. (in pocket), maps. 22 cm. (The United States and China in world affairs) 1. China. Chung-kuo jen min chieh fang chün. I. Council on Foreign Relations. II. T. III. Series.
UA839.3.G7    355.3/1/0951    *LC* 67-16302

**Cohen, Stephen P., 1936-.**                    • **5.7339**
The Indian army; its contribution to the development of a nation [by] Stephen P. Cohen. — Berkeley: University of California Press, 1971. x, 216 p.; 24 cm. 1. India (Republic). Army — History. I. T.
UA842.C6    355.3/0954    *LC* 77-111421    *ISBN* 0520016971

**Mason, Philip.**                    **5.7340**
A matter of honour. — New York: Holt, Rinehart and Winston, [1974] 580 p.: illus.; 24 cm. 1. India. Army — History. I. T.
UA842.M33    355/.00954    *LC* 74-244    *ISBN* 0030129117

**The Modern Japanese military system / edited by James H.**                    **5.7341**
**Buck.**
Beverly Hills, [Calif.]: Sage Publications, c1975. 253 p.; 24 cm. (Sage research progress series on war, revolution, and peacekeeping; v. 5) 1. Japan — Armed Forces — Addresses, essays, lectures. 2. Japan — Defenses — Addresses, essays, lectures. 3. Japan — Military policy — Addresses, essays, lectures. I. Buck, James Harold.
UA845.M6    355/.00952    *LC* 75-14628    *ISBN* 0803905130

**Tsurutani, Taketsugu.**                    **5.7342**
Japanese policy and east Asian security / Taketsugu Tsurutani. — New York, N.Y.: Praeger, 1981. xi, 208 p.; 24 cm. Includes index. 1. Japan — National security. 2. East Asia — Defenses. I. T.
UA845.T85 1981    355/.033052 19    *LC* 81-11884    *ISBN* 0030598060

**Israeli security planning in the 1980s: its politics and economics**                    **5.7343**
**/ edited by Zvi Lanir.**
New York: Praeger, 1984. x, 271 p.: ill.; 25 cm. 'A JCSS book.' 1. Israel — Defenses. 2. Arab countries — Defenses. 3. Israel — Economic policy. I. Lanir, Zvi. II. Merkaz le-mehkarim estrategiyim 'al shem Yafeh.
UA853.I8 I87 1984    355/.03305694 19    *LC* 83-23124    *ISBN* 003063802X

**Luttwak, Edward.**                    **5.7344**
The Israeli Army: 1948–1973 / Edward N. Luttwak and Daniel Horowitz. — Cambridge, Mass.: Abt Books, c1983. x, 398 p.: ill., maps; 24 cm. 1. Israel — Armed Forces. I. Horowitz, Dan. II. T.
UA853.I8 L87 1983    355/.0095694 19    *LC* 83-2609    *ISBN* 0890115850

**Rothenberg, Gunther Erich, 1923-.**                    **5.7345**
The anatomy of the Israeli army / Gunther E. Rothenberg. — London: B. T. Batsford, 1979. 256 p., [8] leaves of plates: ill.; 24 cm. Includes index. 1. Israel — Armed Forces — History. I. T.
UA853.I8 R67    355/.0095694    *LC* 79-321715    *ISBN* 0713419660

**Farwell, Byron.**                    **5.7346**
The Gurkhas / Byron Farwell. — 1st ed. — New York: Norton, c1984. 317 p.: ill.; 22 cm. Includes index. 1. Gurkha soldiers I. T.
UA853.N35 F37 1984b    356/.1 19    *LC* 83-11271    *ISBN* 0393017737

**Cordesman, Anthony H.**                    **5.7347**
The Gulf and the search for strategic stability: Saudi Arabia, the military balance in the Gulf, and trends in the Arab–Israeli military balance / Anthony H. Cordesman. — Boulder, Colo.: Westview Press; London, England: Mansell, 1984. xxiii, 1041 p.: ill.; 24 cm. — (Westview's special studies on the Middle East) Includes index. 1. Persian Gulf Region — Strategic aspects 2. Arabian Peninsula — Strategic aspects. 3. Saudi Arabia — Military relations — United States. 4. United States — Military relations — Saudi Arabia. I. T.
UA853.P47 C66 1984    355/.0330536 19    *LC* 83-10341    *ISBN* 0865316198

## UA855–868 Africa

**Arlinghaus, Bruce E.**                    **5.7348**
Military development in Africa: the political and economic risks of arms transfers / Bruce E. Arlinghaus. — Boulder, Colo.: Westview Press, 1984. xiv, 152 p.; 24 cm. — (Westview special studies on Africa.) Includes index. 1. Munitions — Africa. 2. Africa — Military policy. 3. Africa — Politics and government — 1960- I. T. II. Series.
UA855.A74 1984    355/.03306 19    *LC* 83-23275    *ISBN* 0865314349

**Frankel, Philip H.**                    **5.7349**
Pretoria's praetorians: civil–military relations in South Africa / Philip H. Frankel. — Cambridge [Cambridgeshire]; New York: Cambridge University Press, 1985. xxii, 215 p.: ill.; 24 cm. Includes index. 1. Sociology, Military — South Africa. 2. Civil-military relations — South Africa. 3. South Africa — Armed Forces — History — 20th century. 4. South Africa —

Politics and government — 1978- 5. South Africa — Politics and government — 1961-1978 I. T.
UA856.F73 1984       322/.5/0968 19       *LC* 84-5040       *ISBN* 0521264405

## UA917–927 DEMOBILIZATION. CIVIL DEFENSE

**Ballard, Jack S.**                                                                5.7350
The shock of peace: military and economic demobilization after World War II / Jack Stokes Ballard. — Washington, D.C.: University Press of America, c1983. x, 259 p.: ill.; 23 cm. Includes index. 1. United States — Armed Forces — Demobilization — History — 20th century. 2. United States — Economic conditions — 1945- I. T.
UA917.U5 B34 1983       355.2/9/0973 19       *LC* 82-24860       *ISBN* 081913029X

## UB MILITARY ADMINISTRATION

**Hammond, Paul Y.**                                                              • 5.7351
Organizing for defense; the American military establishment in the twentieth century. Princeton, N. J., Princeton University Press, 1961. xi, 403 p. 25 cm. Bibliographical footnotes. 1. United States. Dept. of Defense. 2. United States — Armed Forces — Organization I. T.
UB23.H3       355.0973       *LC* 61-7398

**Straight, Michael Whitney.**                                                     5.7352
Trial by television: illustrated by Robert Osborn. — Boston: Beacon Press, c1954. 282 p.: ill. 1. McCarthy-Army controversy, 1954 2. United States — Politics and government — 1945- I. T.
UB23 S79       *LC* 54-11624

**Sweetman, John.**                                                                5.7353
War and administration: the significance of the Crimean War for the British Army / John Sweetman. — Edinburgh: Scottish Academic Press, 1984. 174 p., [2] p. of plates: maps, charts; 26 cm. Charts on lining papers. 1. Great Britain. Army — Management — History — 19th century. 2. Crimean War, 1854-1856. I. T.
UB58 1854-1856.S94 1984       355/.00941 19       *LC* 83-220916       *ISBN* 070730332X

**Thompson, I. A. A.**                                                             5.7354
War and government in Habsburg Spain, 1560–1620 / by I. A. A. Thompson. London: Athlone Press; [Atlantic Highlands] N. J.: distributed by Humanities Press, 1976. 374 p.; 23 cm. Includes index. 1. Military administration — History. 2. Spain — Armed Forces — History. 3. Spain — History — House of Austria, 1516-1700 I. T.
UB87.T48       355.6/0946       *LC* 77-355582       *ISBN* 0485111667

**Janowitz, Morris.**                                                             • 5.7355
The professional soldier, a social and political portrait. — Glencoe, Ill.: Free Press, [1960] 464 p.; 22 cm. 1. Soldiers — United States 2. Leadership 3. United States — Armed Forces — Officers 4. United States — Armed Forces — Military life I. T.
UB147.J3       355.069       *LC* 60-7090

**Blair, Bruce G., 1947-.**                                                        5.7356
Strategic command and control: redefining the nuclear threat / Bruce G. Blair. — Washington, D.C.: Brookings Institution, c1985. xiv, 341 p.: ill.; 24 cm. 1. Command and control systems — United States. 2. Strategic forces — United States. 3. Military policy — United States. I. T.
UB212.B5 1985       355.3/3041/0973 19       *LC* 84-73164       *ISBN* 081570982X

**Hittle, James Donald, 1915-.**                                                  • 5.7357
The military staff, its history and development / J. D. Hittle. — 3rd ed. — Harrisburgh, Pa.: Military Service Division, Stackpole Co., 1961. 326 p.; 22 cm. Includes index. 1. Armies — Staffs I. T.
UB220.H5 1961       355.3/31       *LC* 61-9092

**Korb, Lawrence J., 1939-.**                                                      5.7358
The Joint Chiefs of Staff: the first twenty–five years / Lawrence J. Korb. — Bloomington: Indiana University Press, c1976. xiii, 210 p.; 22 cm. 1. United States. Joint Chiefs of Staff — History. I. T.
UB223.K67 1976       353.6       *LC* 75-16839       *ISBN* 0253331692

## UB250–277 Intelligence. Psychological Warfare

**Buranelli, Vincent.**                                                            5.7359
Spy/counterspy: an encyclopedia of espionage / Vincent and Nan Buranelli. — New York: McGraw-Hill, c1982. xvi, 361 p.; 24 cm. 1. Espionage — Dictionaries. I. Buranelli, Nan, 1917- II. T.
UB250.B87 1982       327.1/2/0321 19       *LC* 81-23666       *ISBN* 0070089159

**Knowing one's enemies: intelligence assessment before the two**                  5.7360
**world wars / edited by Ernest R. May.**
Princeton, N.J.: Princeton University Press, 1985 (c1984). xiii, 561 p.; 25 cm. 1. Intelligence service — History — 20th century — Addresses, essays, lectures. 2. Military intelligence — History — 20th century — Addresses, essays, lectures. I. May, Ernest R.
UB250.K58       327.1/2/09 19       *LC* 84-42573       *ISBN* 0691047170

**Bamford, James.**                                                                5.7361
The puzzle palace: a report on America's most secret agency / James Bamford. — Boston: Houghton Mifflin, 1982. 465 p.; 24 cm. 1. United States. National Security Agency. I. T.
UB251.U5 B35 1982       327.1/2/06073 19       *LC* 82-3056       *ISBN* 0395312868

**Freedman, Lawrence.**                                                            5.7362
U.S. intelligence and the Soviet strategic threat / Lawrence Freedman. — Boulder, Colo.: Westview Press, 1977. xv, 235 p.: ill.; 22 cm. Includes index. 1. Military intelligence — United States. 2. Strategic forces — Soviet Union. I. T.
UB251.U5 F73       327/.174       *LC* 77-7525       *ISBN* 0891587489

**Intelligence requirements for the 1980's.**                                      5.7363
Washington, D.C.: National Strategy Information Center, 1979-. v.; 23 cm. At head of title: Consortium for the Study of Intelligence. Vols. 2-5 distributed by Transaction Books, New Brunswick. Vols. 6-7 published by Lexington Books. Each volume distictively titled. 1. Intelligence service — United States — Collected works. I. National Strategy Information Center. II. Consortium for the Study of Intelligence.
UB251.U5 I56       UB251U5 I56.       327.1/2/0973 19       *LC* 79-91051

**Dulles, Allen Welsh, 1893-1969.**                                               • 5.7364
The craft of intelligence. — [1st ed.]. — New York: Harper & Row, [1963] viii, 277 p.: illus., ports.; 22 cm. 1. Espionage 2. Spies I. T.
UB270.D8       327.1       *LC* 63-16507

## UB320–405 Military Service. Veterans

**U.S. President's Commission on an All-Volunteer Armed Force.**                   • 5.7365
The report of the President's Commission on an All–Volunteer Armed Force. — [New York]: Collier Books, [1970] 218 p.; 22 cm. Commonly known as the Gates report. 1. U.S. — Armed Forces — Recruiting, enlistment, etc. I. T. II. Title: Gates report on an all-volunteer armed force.
UB323.A5 1970       355.2/23/0973       *LC* 79-12775

**Conscripts and volunteers: military requirements, social justice,**             5.7366
**and the all–volunteer force / edited by Robert K. Fullinwider.**
Totowa, N.J.: Rowman & Allanheld, c1983. vi, 250 p.; 24 cm. — (Maryland studies in public philosophy.) 1. Military service, Voluntary — United States — Addresses, essays, lectures. 2. United States — Armed Forces — Recruiting, enlistment, etc. — Addresses, essays, lectures. I. Fullinwider, Robert K., 1942- II. Series.
UB323.C59 1983       355.2/2362/0973 19       *LC* 83-3095       *ISBN* 0847672247

**The Military draft: selected readings on conscription / edited by**             5.7367
**Martin Anderson, with Barbara Honegger.**
Stanford, Calif.: Hoover Institution Press, c1982. xvi, 668 p.; 24 cm. (Hoover Press publication; 258) 1. Draft — Addresses, essays, lectures. 2. Draft — United States — Addresses, essays, lectures. I. Anderson, Martin. II. Honegger, Barbara.
UB340.M55 1982       355.2/2363 19       *LC* 81-84641       *ISBN* 0817975810

**Murdock, Eugene Converse.** • 5.7368
Patriotism limited, 1862–1865; the Civil War draft and the bounty system. — [1st ed. — Kent, Ohio]: Kent State University Press, [1967] viii, 270 p.: illus., ports.; 24 cm. 1. Draft — United States — History. 2. Bounties, Military — United States — History. I. T.
UB343.M8      355.2/2      LC 67-64665

**Pearlman, Michael, 1944-.** 5.7369
To make democracy safe for America: patricians and preparedness in the Progressive Era / Michael Pearlman. — Urbana: University of Illinois Press, c1984. 297 p., [12] p. of plates: ill.; 24 cm. Includes index. 1. Draft — United States — History — 20th century. 2. Military education — United States — History — 20th century. 3. United States — Politics and government — 20th century 4. United States — Armed Forces — Operational readiness I. T.
UB353.P42 1984      355.2/2363/0973 19      LC 83-1107      ISBN 0252010191

**Brende, Joel Osler.** 5.7370
Vietnam veterans: the road to recovery / Joel Osler Brende and Erwin Randolph Parson. — New York: Plenum Press, c1985. xx, 270 p.; 22 cm. Includes indexes. 1. Veterans — United States — Psychology — Addresses, essays, lectures. 2. Vietnamese Conflict, 1961-1975 — United States — Addresses, essays, lectures. 3. Post-traumatic stress disorder — Addresses, essays, lectures. I. Parson, Erwin Randolph. II. T.
UB357.B74 1985      355.1/156/0973 19      LC 84-26396      ISBN 0306419661

**Woloch, Isser, 1937-.** 5.7371
The French veteran from the Revolution to the Restoration / by Isser Woloch. — Chapel Hill: University of North Carolina Press, c1979. xix, 392 p.: ill.; 24 cm. Includes index. 1. Hôtel des invalides (France) — History. 2. Veterans — France — History — 18th century. 3. Veterans — France — History — 19th century. 4. France — Social policy. I. T.
UB359.F8 W64      355.1/15/0944      LC 78-26444      ISBN 0807813567

**Demeter, Karl, 1889-.** • 5.7372
The German officer–corps in society and state, 1650–1945. Translated from the German by Angus Malcolm. Introd. by Michael Howard. — New York, Praeger [1965] xiv, 414 p. 23 cm. Translation of Das deutsche Offizierkorps in Gesellschaft und Staat, 1650-1945, originally published under title: Das deutsche Offizierkorps in seinen historisch-soziologischen Grundiagen. Bibliographical references included in 'Notes' (p. 371-404) 1. Germany. Heer — Organization. 2. Germany. Heer — Officers. I. T.
UB415.G4D413 1965      355.3320943      LC 65-14178

# UB416–418 Minorities, Women in Armed Forces

**Enloe, Cynthia H., 1938-.** 5.7373
Ethnic soldiers: state security in divided societies / Cynthia H. Enloe. — Athens: University of Georgia Press, c1980. xii, 276 p.; 23 cm. 1. Armed Forces 2. Ethnic groups 3. National security 4. Sociology, Military I. T.
UB416.E54      306/.2      LC 79-5418      ISBN 0820305073

**Female soldiers—combatants or noncombatants?: historical and** 5.7374
**contemporary perspectives / edited by Nancy Loring Goldman.**
Westport, Conn.: Greenwood Press, c1982. xix, 307 p.; 24 cm. (Contributions in women's studies. 0147-104X; no. 33) Includes index. 1. Women soldiers — Addresses, essays, lectures. 2. Combat — Addresses, essays, lectures. I. Goldman, Nancy L. II. Series.
UB416.F45 1982      355.1/088042 19      LC 81-13318      ISBN 0313231176

**Blacks in the military: essential documents / edited by Bernard** 5.7375
**C. Nalty and Morris J. MacGregor.**
Wilmington, Del.: Scholarly Resources, c1981. xi, 367 p.; 26 cm. 1. Afro-American soldiers — History — Sources. I. Nalty, Bernard C. II. MacGregor, Morris J., 1931-
UB418.A47 B55 1981      355.1/08996073 19      LC 80-54664      ISBN 0842021833

**MacGregor, Morris J., 1931-.** 5.7376
Integration of the Armed Forces, 1940–1965 / by Morris J. MacGregor, Jr. — Washington, D.C.: Center of Military History, U.S. Army: for sale by the Supt. of Docs., U.S. Govt. Print. Off., 1981. xx, 647 p.: ill.; 26 cm. — (Defense studies series) Includes index. 1. Afro-American soldiers 2. United States — Race relations I. T. II. Series.
UB418.A47 M33      355.3/3 19      LC 80-607077

**Holm, Jeanne, 1921-.** 5.7377
Women in the military: an unfinished revolution / Jeanne Holm. — Novato, CA: Presidio Press, c1982. xvii, 435 p.: ill.; 24 cm. Includes index. 1. United States — Armed Forces — Women I. T.
UB418.W65 H64 1982      355/.0088/042 19      LC 82-12324      ISBN 0891410783

**Rogan, Helen.** 5.7378
Mixed company: women in the modern army / Helen Rogan. — New York: Putnam, c1981. 333 p.; 24 cm. 1. United States — Armed Forces — Women I. T.
UB418.W65 R63 1981      355.1/088042 19      LC 81-10662      ISBN 0399126546

**Grundy, Kenneth W.** 5.7379
Soldiers without politics: Blacks in the South African armed forces / Kenneth W. Grundy. — Berkeley: University of California Press, c1983. xiv, 297 p.; 22 cm. — (Perspectives on Southern Africa. 33) 1. Soldiers, Black — South Africa. 2. Soldiers, Black — Namibia. I. T. II. Series.
UB419.S6 G78 1983      322/.5/089968 19      LC 82-2584      ISBN 0520047109

# UD–UE Infantry. Cavalry

**Ross, Steven T.** 5.7380
From flintlock to rifle: infantry tactics, 1740–1866 / Steven Ross. — Rutherford, N.J.: Fairleigh Dickinson University Press, 1979. 218 p.: ill.; 22 cm. Includes index. 1. Infantry drill and tactics — History — 18th century. 2. Infantry drill and tactics — History — 19th century. 3. Armies — Europe — History — 18th century. 4. Armies — Europe — History — 19th century. I. T.
UD15.R6      356/.1      LC 77-74397      ISBN 0838620515

**Denison, George T. (George Taylor), 1839-1925.** • 5.7381
A history of cavalry from the earliest times, with lessons for the future. 2d ed. London, Macmillan and co., limited, 1913. xxxi, 468 p. maps (part fold.) plans (part fold.) 23 cm. 1. Cavalry I. T.
UE15.D4 1913      LC 13-18690

# UF Artillery. Nuclear Weapons

**Batchelor, John, 1942-.** 5.7382
Artillery / [by] John Batchelor [and] Ian Hogg. — New York: Scribner, 1972. 158 p.: ill. (some col.); 28 cm. 1. Artillery — History I. Hogg, Ian V. II. T.
UF15.H54      623.4/1/09      LC 72-6654      ISBN 0684130920

**Carman, W. Y.** • 5.7383
A history of firearms, from earliest times to 1914. New York, St. Martin's Press [c1955] 207 p. illus. 23 cm. 1. Ordnance I. T.
UF520.C3x      LC 56-10694

**Brodie, Bernard, 1910- ed.** 5.7384
The absolute weapon: atomic power and world order, by Frederick S. Dunn [and others] ... Edited by Bernard Brodie. New York, Harcourt, Brace and company [1946] 3 p.l., 214 p. 21 cm. 'First edition.' Half-title: Institute of international studies, Yale university. 1. Nuclear energy 2. Atomic bomb 3. International organization I. Dunn, Frederick Sherwood, 1893-1962. II. Wolfers, Arnold, 1892- III. Corbett, Percy Ellwood, 1892- IV. Fox, William T. R. (William Thornton Rickert), 1912- V. Yale University. Institute of International Studies. VI. T.
UF767.B7 1946a      623.45      LC 46-4538

**Kahn, Herman, 1922-.** • 5.7385
On thermonuclear war. — Princeton, N.J.: Princeton University Press, 1960. 651 p.: illus.; 25 cm. 1. Nuclear warfare I. T.
UF767.K25 1960      358.39      LC 60-5751

**Teller, Edward, 1908-.** • 5.7386
The legacy of Hiroshima, by Edward Teller with Allen Brown. [1st ed.] Garden City, N. Y., Doubleday, 1962. 325 p. 22 cm. 1. Nuclear warfare 2. Nuclear disarmament 3. United States — Defenses I. T.
UF767.T4      341.672      LC 62-7686

# UG1–620 MILITARY ENGINEERING. FORTIFICATION

**Hill, Forest Garrett, 1919-.**      • **5.7387**
Roads, rails & waterways; the army engineers and early transportation. [1st ed.] Norman, University of Oklahoma Press [1957] 248 p. illus. 22 cm. 1. United States. Army. Corps of Engineers. 2. Transportation — United States — History. 3. United States — Public works I. T.
UG 23 H64      *LC* 57-11195L

**Hogg, Ian V., 1926-.**      **5.7388**
Fortress: a history of military defence / Ian V. Hogg. — New York: St. Martin's Press, 1977, c1975. 160 p.: ill.; 28 cm. Includes index. 1. Fortification — History. 2. Military architecture — History. I. T.
UG401.H66 1977      623/.109      *LC* 76-62774

**Fuller, J. F. C. (John Frederick Charles), 1878-1966.**      • **5.7389**
Armored warfare: an annotated edition of Lectures on F.S.R. III (operations between mechanized forces) / by J.F.C. Fuller; foreword by S.L.A. Marshall. — Westport, Conn.: The Military service publishing company, 1943. xix, 189 p.: ill.; 22 cm. Harrisburg, Pa.: Military Service Pub. Co., 1943. 1. Tank warfare 2. Mechanization, Military 3. Strategy I. Fuller, J. F. C. (John Frederick Charles), 1878-1966. Lectures on F.S.R. III (operations between mechanized forces) II. T.
UG446.5.F78      358/.18 19      *LC* 43-14026      *ISBN* 0313240671

**Ogorkiewicz, Richard M.**      • **5.7390**
Armor; a history of mechanized forces. New York, Praeger [1960] 475 p. illus. 25 cm. 1. Tank warfare 2. Motorization, Military 3. Arms and armor I. T.
UG446.5.O5 1960      *LC* 60-11276

**Hughes, James Quentin.**      **5.7391**
Military architecture / Quentin Hughes. — New York: St. Martin's Press, 1975, c1974. 256 p., [4] leaves of plates: ill.; 25 cm. — (Excursions into architecture) Includes index. 1. Military architecture — History. 2. Fortification — History. I. T.
UG460.H84 1975      725/.18      *LC* 74-25217

**Hecht, Jeff.**      **5.7392**
Beam weapons: the next arms race / Jeff Hecht. — New York: Plenum Press, c1984. xi, 363 p.: ill.; 22 cm. 1. Directed-energy weapons I. T.
UG486.5.H43 1984      355.8/2595 19      *LC* 83-24713      *ISBN* 0306415461

# UG622–1245 AIR FORCES. AIR WARFARE

**Douhet, Giulio, 1869-1930.**      **5.7393**
The command of the air, by Giulio Douhet; translated by Dino Ferrari. New York, Coward-McCann, inc., [c1942]. 394 p. Translated from the 2d ed., 1927. 1. Aeronautics, Military I. T.
UG630.D62      358.9      *LC* 42-50172

**Emme, Eugene Morlock. ed.**      **5.7394**
The impact of air power: national security and world politics. — Princeon, N.J.: Van Nostrand, [1969] 914 p.: maps (1 fold.) 1. Air power 2. Air warfare 3. Military policy 4. World politics 5. United States — Military policy I. T.
UG630.E5

**Higham, Robin D. S.**      **5.7395**
Air power; a concise history [by] Robin Higham. — New York: St. Martin's Press, [1972] xii, 282 p.: illus.; 24 cm. 1. Air power I. T.
UG630.H58 1972      358.4      *LC* 72-79066

**Janis, Irving Lester, 1918-.**      • **5.7396**
Air war and emotional stress; psychological studies of bombing and civilian defense. The Rand Corporation. 1st ed. New York, McGraw-Hill, 1951. ix, 280 p. 24 cm. (Rand note.) 1. Civil defense 2. Air warfare — Psychological aspects. I. T. II. Series.
UG630.J26      *LC* 51-13330

**Burgess, Eric.**      • **5.7397**
Long–range ballistic missiles. [1st American ed.] New York, Macmillan [1962, c1961] 255 p. illus. 22 cm. 1. Ballistic missiles I. T.
UG633.B84 1962      *LC* 61-17856

**De Seversky, Alexander Procofieff, 1894-.**      • **5.7398**
Air Power: Key to survival. New York, Simon and Schuster, 1950. 376 p.: illus., ports., col. map.; 22 cm. 1. Air warfare 2. United States — Air defenses I. T.
UG633.D44      *LC* 50-14963

**Futrell, Robert Frank.**      **5.7399**
Ideas, concepts, doctrine: a history of basic thinking in the United States Air Force, 1907–1964 / by Robert Frank Futrell. — Maxwell Air Force Base, Ala.: Air University, 1971. viii, 520 p.; 27 cm. 1. United States. Air Force — History 2. United States — Military policy — History. I. T.
UG633.F84      358.4/00973      *LC* 75-603315

**Goldberg, Alfred, 1918- ed.**      • **5.7400**
A history of the United States Air Force, 1907–1957. — [New York]: Arno Press, [1972, c1957] ix, 277 p.: illus.; 31 cm. — (Literature and history of aviation) 1. United States. Air Force — History I. T. II. Series.
UG633.G6 1972      358.4/13/0973      *LC* 71-169418      *ISBN* 0405037635

**Holley, I. B. (Irving Brinton), 1919-.**      • **5.7401**
Ideas and weapons: exploitation of the aerial weapon by the United States during World War I; a study in the relationship of technological advance, military doctrine, and the development of weapons, by I. B. Holley, Jr. Hamden, Conn., Archon Books, 1971 [c1953] xii, 222 p. 23 cm. 1. Aeronautics, Military — United States 2. World War, 1914-1918 — Aerial operations, American. I. T.
UG633.H6 1971      358.4/00973      *LC* 79-122410      *ISBN* 0208010904

**Kelsey, Benjamin S., d. 1981.**      **5.7402**
The dragon's teeth?: the creation of United States air power for World War II / Benjamin S. Kelsey. — Washington, D.C.: Smithsonian Institution Press, 1983 (c1982). 148 p.: ill.; 24 cm. Includes index. 1. United States. Army. Air Corps — History. I. T.
UG633.K43      358.4/00973 19      *LC* 82-600279      *ISBN* 0874745748

**Hurley, Alfred F.**      • **5.7403**
Billy Mitchell: crusader for air power / by Alfred F. Hurley. — New York: F. Watts, 1964. x, 180 p.: ill., ports. — (Watts aerospace library) 1. Mitchell, William, 1879-1936. 2. United States. Army — Biography 3. Air pilots I. T. II. Series.
UG633. M45H8      923.573      *LC* 64-11917

**Wise, S. F. (Sydney F.), 1924-.**      **5.7404**
The official history of the Royal Canadian Air Force / by Sydney F. Wise. — [Toronto]: University of Toronto Press in co-operation with the Dept. of National Defence and the Canadian Govt. Pub. Centre, Supply and Services Canada, c1980. v., plates: ill., maps (some col.); 25 cm. — 1. Canada. Royal Canadian Air Force — History — World War, 1914-1918. 2. World War, 1914-1918 — Aerial operations, Canadian. I. T.
UG635.C2 W57 D607.C2      358.4/00971 s 940.4/4971 19      *LC* 81-122577      *ISBN* 0802023797

**Slessor, John Cotesworth, 1897-.**      • **5.7405**
Air power and armies / by Wing Commander J. C. Slessor. — London: Oxford University Press, 1936. xx, 231 p.: 3 fold. maps (1 in pocket); 22 cm. 'This book is based on a series of lectures delivered at the Staff college at Chamberley between 1931 and 1934.' 1. Aeronautics, Military 2. World War, 1914-1918 — Aerial operations 3. Aeronautics, Military — Great Britain. I. T.
UG 635 G7 S63 1936      *LC* 37-5510

**Lee, Asher.**      • **5.7406**
The Soviet Air Force / foreword by Alexander P. Seversky. — New York: J.Day Co., 1962. 288 p.: ill. 1. Aeronautics, Military — Russia. 2. World War, 1939-1945 — Aerial operations, Russian. I. T.
UG635.R9 L43 1962

**Soviet aviation and air power: a historical view / edited by Robin Higham and Jacob W. Kipp.**      **5.7407**
London: Brassey's; Boulder, Colo.: Westview Press, 1978. xii, 328 p.: ill.; 26 cm. Includes index. 1. Aeronautics, Military — Russia — History — Addresses, essays, lectures. 2. Aeronautics — Russia — History — Addresses, essays, lectures. 3. Air power — Addresses, essays, lectures. I. Higham, Robin D. S. II. Kipp, Jacob W.
UG635.R9 S596 1978      358.4/00947      *LC* 76-30815      *ISBN* 0891581162

**Kennett, Lee B.**      **5.7408**
A history of strategic bombing / Lee Kennett. — New York: Scribner, c1982. x, 222 p., [24] p. of plates: ill.; 22 cm. 1. Bombing, Aerial — History. 2. World War, 1939-1945 — Aerial operations I. T.
UG700.K46 1982      358.4/14/09 19      *LC* 82-10673      *ISBN* 0684177811

**Ballistic missile defense / Ashton B. Carter and David N.**      **5.7409**
**Schwartz, editors.**
Washington, D.C.: Brookings Institution, c1984. xiii, 455 p.: ill.; 24 cm. 'A study jointly sponsored by the Brookings Institution and the Massachusetts Institute of Technology.' 1. Ballistic missile defenses — Addresses, essays, lectures. 2. Ballistic missile defenses — United States — Addresses, essays, lectures. 3. Ballistic missile defenses — Soviet Union — Addresses, essays, lectures. I. Carter, Ashton B. II. Schwartz, David N., 1956- III. Brookings Institution. IV. Massachusetts Institute of Technology.
UG740.B35 1984      358/.17 19      *LC* 83-24064      *ISBN* 0815713126

**Hallion, Richard.**      **5.7410**
Rise of the fighter aircraft, 1914–18 / Richard P. Hallion; foreword by Jay W. Hubbard. — Annapolis, MD: Nautical & Aviation Pub. Co. of America, [1984] vi, 200 p.: ill.; 24 cm. Includes index. 1. Airplanes, Military — History. 2. Fighter planes — History. 3. World War, 1914-1918 — Aerial operations I. T.
UG1240.H35 1984      358.4/3/09 19      *LC* 83-26947      *ISBN* 0933852428

**Knaack, Marcelle Size, 1921-.**      **5.7411**
Encyclopedia of US Air Force aircraft and missile systems / by Marcelle Size Knaack. — Washington: Office of Air Force History: for sale by the Supt. of Docs., U.S. Govt. Print. Off., 1978 (c1977) 358 p.: ill. Includes index. 1. United States. Air Force — Collected works. 2. Airplanes, Military — United States — Collected works. 3. Guided missiles — Collected works. I. United States.

Air Force. Office of Air Force History. II. T. III. Title: Encyclopedia of U.S. Air Force aircraft and missile systems.
UG1243.K53      358.4/3      *LC* 77-22377

**Stares, Paul B.**      **5.7412**
The militarization of space: U.S. policy, 1945–1984 / Paul B. Stares. — Ithaca, N.Y.: Cornell University Press, 1985. 334 p.; 25 cm. (Cornell studies in security affairs.) Includes index. 1. Astronautics, Military — United States — History. 2. United States — Military policy I. T. II. Series.
UG1523.S83 1985      358.4/03/0973 19      *LC* 85-47501      *ISBN* 0801418100

# UH OTHER SERVICES

**Woodham Smith, Cecil Blanche Fitz Gerald, 1896-.**      • **5.7413**
Florence Nightingale, 1820–1910 / Cecil Woodham–Smith. — London: Constable, 1950. vii, 615 p.: ill. 1. Nightingale, Florence, 1820-1910. I. T.
UH347.N6 W6 1950      *LC* 50-39338

**Ginzberg, Eli, 1911-.**      • **5.7414**
Psychiatry and military manpower policy, a reappraisal of the experience in World War II, by Eli Ginzberg, John L. Herma, and Sol W. Ginsburg. New York King's Crown Press 1953. 66p. (Columbia University. Graduate School of Business. Human resources studies) 1. Psychiatry, Military 2. United States — Armed Forces — Recruiting, enlistment, etc. I. Herma, John Leonard, 1911-, jt. author II. Ginsburg, Soloman Wiener, 1899-1960, jt. author III. T. IV. Series.
UH629.3 G5

# V Naval Science

## V23–24 Reference

**Blackburn, Graham, 1940-.**      **5.7415**
The Overlook illustrated dictionary of nautical terms / written & illustrated by Graham Blackburn. — Woodstock, N.Y.: Overlook Press, 1982 (c1981). 349 p. 1. Naval art and science — Dictionaries I. T.
V23.B58    623.8/03/21 19    *LC* 80-39640    *ISBN* 0879511249

**Jane's dictionary of naval terms / compiled by Joseph Palmer.**    **5.7416**
London: Macdonald and Jane's, 1976 (c1975). [4], 342 p.; 23 cm. 1. Naval art and science — Dictionaries 2. Naval art and science — Dictionaries I. Palmer, Joseph, Commander. II. Title: Dictionary of naval terms.
V23.J36    358.4/03    *LC* 76-370529    *ISBN* 035608258X

**Noel, John Vavasour, 1912-.**      **5.7417**
The VNR dictionary of ships & the seas / John V. Noel. — New York: Van Nostrand Reinhold, 1980. vi, 393 p. 1. Naval art and science — Dictionaries I. T.
V23.N63    359/.003/21    *LC* 80-15276    *ISBN* 0442256310

**The Oxford companion to ships & the sea / edited by Peter**    **5.7418**
**Kemp; [line drawings by Peter Milne and the OUP drawing office].**
London: Oxford University Press, 1976. viii, 972 p.: ill. (some col.), chart, maps, plans, ports.; 24 cm. 1. Naval art and science — Dictionaries 2. Naval history — Dictionaries. I. Kemp, Peter Kemp.
V23.O96    387/.03    *LC* 77-352082    *ISBN* 0192115537

**The Visual encyclopedia of nautical terms under sail / principal**    **5.7419**
**advisers, George P. B. Naish...[et al.].**
New York: Crown Publishers, 1978. ca. 300 p. in various pagings: ill. (some col.), plans; 27 cm. 1. Naval art and science — Dictionaries 2. Naval art and science — Terminology I. Naish, George Prideaux Brabant. II. Bathe, Basil W. III. Title: The country life book of nautical terms under sail.
V23.V58    623.8203    *LC* 77-28560    *ISBN* 0517533170

## V27–64 History

**Willmott, H. P.**      **5.7420**
Sea warfare: weapons, tactics and strategy / H.P. Willmott; with an epilogue by Admiral of the fleet the Lord Hill–Norton, GCB. — New York: Hippocrene Books, 1982, c1981. 165 p. [8] pages of plates: ill. 1. Naval art and science — History 2. Naval tactics I. T.
V53.W54 1982    359.009    *ISBN* 0882546961

**Command under sail: makers of the American naval tradition,**    **5.7421**
**1775–1850 / edited by James C. Bradford.**
Annapolis, Md.: Naval Institute Press, c1985. xvi, 333 p.: ill.; 24 cm. Includes index. 1. United States. Navy — Officers — Biography — Addresses, essays, lectures. 2. United States — History, Naval — To 1900 — Addresses, essays, lectures. I. Bradford, James C.
V62.C662 1985    359/.0092/2 B 19    *LC* 84-29584    *ISBN* 0870211374

**Maloney, Linda M.**      **5.7422**
The captain from Connecticut: the life and naval times of Isaac Hull / Linda M. Maloney. — Boston: Northeastern University Press, c1986. xviii, 549 p.: ill.; 25 cm. Includes index. 1. Hull, Isaac, 1773-1843. 2. United States. Navy — Biography 3. Admirals — United States — Biography. I. T.
V63.H85 M35 1986    359/.0092/4 B 19    *LC* 85-10552    *ISBN* 0930350790

**Buell, Thomas B.**      **5.7423**
The quiet warrior: a biography of Admiral Raymond A. Spruance, by Thomas B. Buell. — [1st ed.]. — Boston: Little, Brown, [1974] xviii, 486 p.: illus.; 24 cm. 1. Spruance, Raymond Ames, 1886-1969. I. T.
V63.S68 B8    940.54/5/0924 B    *LC* 74-1181    *ISBN* 0316114707

**The Bluejackets' manual. [1st]– ed.; 1902–.**    • **5.7424**
Annapolis: United States Naval Institute, 1902-. v.: ill. Originally compiled by R. McLean for the United States Naval Institute. Some issues in rev. editions. 1. United States. Navy — Seamen's handbooks I. McLean, Ridley, 1872-1933, comp. II. United States Naval Institute. III. United States. Navy.
V113.B55    *LC* 03-1595

**Fioravanzo, Giuseppe, 1891-.**      **5.7425**
[Storia del pensiero tattico navale. English] A history of naval tactical thought / Giuseppe Fioravanzo; translated by Arthur W. Holst. — [Annapolis]: Naval Institute Press, c1979. x, 251 p.: ill.; 22 cm. Translation of Storia del pensiero tattico navale. On spine: Naval tactical thought. Includes index. 1. Naval tactics — History. I. T. II. Title: Naval tactical thought.
V167.F5613    359.4/2/09    *LC* 78-70966    *ISBN* 0870212710

**Robison, Samuel Shelburne, 1867-.**    • **5.7426**
A history of naval tactics from 1530 to 1930; the evolution of tactical maxims, by Rear Admiral S. S. Robison ... and Mary L. Robison. — Annapolis, Md., The U. S. Naval institute [c1942] 956 p. ill. 1. Naval tactics 2. Naval history 3. Naval battles I. Robison, Mary Louis (Clark) II. United States Naval Institute. III. T.
V167.R6    359    *LC* 42-16602

**Creswell, John.**      **5.7427**
British admirals of the eighteenth century: tactics in battle. — London: Allen and Unwin, 1972. 3-263 p.: ill., maps, plans; 23 cm. 1. Naval tactics 2. Naval battles — Great Britain. I. T.
V169.C7    359.4/2/0942    *LC* 72-197343    *ISBN* 0049010190

**Winton, John.**      **5.7428**
Convoy: the defence of sea trade, 1890–1990 / John Winton. — London: M. Joseph, 1983. 378 p., [16] p. of plates: ill.; 24 cm. Includes index. 1. Naval convoys — History — 19th century. 2. Naval convoys — History — 20th century. I. T.
V182.W56 1983    359.3/26 19    *LC* 83-199609    *ISBN* 0718121635

**Stafford, Edward Peary.**    • **5.7429**
The far and the deep. / With a foreword by Charles A. Lockwood. — New York: Putnam, [1967] 384 p.: ill., ports.; 22 cm. 1. Submarine boats I. T.
V210.S692    359.32/57    *LC* 67-23135

## V750–995 War Vessels: Construction, etc

**Conway's All the world's fighting ships, 1922–1946 / [editor**    **5.7430**
**Roger Chesneau].**
London: Conway Maritime Press, 1980. [8], 456 p.: ill.; 32 cm. Continued by: Conway's All the world's fighting ships, 1947-1982. Includes index. 1. Warships 2. Navies I. Chesneau, Roger. II. Title: All the world's fighting ships, 1922-1946.
V765.C66    359.3/25/0904 19    *LC* 81-103282    *ISBN* 0851771467

**Conway's All the world's fighting ships, 1947–1982 / [editor,**    **5.7431**
**Robert Gardiner; contributors, Norman Friedman ... et al.].**
Annapolis, Md.: Naval Institute Press, c1983-. v. <1-2 >: ill.; 32 cm. Continues: Conway's All the world's fighting ships, 1922-1946. 1. Warships 2. Navies I. Gardiner, Robert, 1949- II. Friedman, Norman, 1946- III. Title: All the world's fighting ships, 1947-1982.
V765.C663 1983    359.3/25/0904 19    *LC* 82-42936    *ISBN* 0870219235

**Lavery, Brian.**      **5.7432**
The ship of the line / Brian Lavery. — Annapolis, Md.: Naval Institute Press, 1984 (c1983) 2 v.: ill.; 31 cm. 1. Ships of the line — Great Britain. 2. Ships of the line I. T.
V767.L35 1983    623.8/2/00941 19    *LC* 83-43279    *ISBN* 0870216317

**Baxter, James Phinney, 1893-.**    • **5.7433**
The introduction of the ironclad warship. — [Hamden, Conn.]: Archon Books, 1968 [c1933] x, 398 p.: illus.; 24 cm. 1. United States. Navy — History — Civil

War, 1861-1865 2. Armored vessels 3. Battleships I. T. II. Title: The ironclad warship.
V799.B3 1968     359.32/52/0973    *LC* 68-16330

**Conway's all the world's fighting ships, 1860–1905** / [editors,   **5.7434**
Roger Chesneau, Eugene M. Kolesnik; contributors, N.J.M.
Campbell ...[et al.]; line drawings by John Roberts].
1st American ed. — New York: Mayflower Books, c1979. 440 p.: ill.; 32 cm.
1. Warships — History. 2. Armored vessels — History. 3. Navies — History.
I. Chesneau, Roger. II. Kolesnik, Eugène M. III. Campbell, N. J. M.
IV. Title: All the world's fighting ships, 1860-1905.
V799.C66 1979b    359.3/2/509    *LC* 79-11466    *ISBN* 0831703024

**Conway's All the world's fighting ships, 1906–1921** / [editorial   **5.7435**
director, Robert Gardiner; editor, Randal Gray; contributors,
Przemysław Budzbon ... et al.].
London: Conway Maritime Press, 1985. 439 p.: ill.; 32 cm. Includes index.
1. Warships I. Gardiner, Robert, 1949- II. Gray, Randal. III. Budzbon,
Przemysław IV. Title: All the world's fighting ships, 1906-1921.
V800.C66 1985    359.3/25/09 19    *LC* 85-204543    *ISBN*
0851772455

**Raven, Alan.**    **5.7436**
British battleships of World War Two: the development and technical history of
the Royal Navy's battleships and battlecruisers from 1911 to 1946 / by Alan
Raven and John Roberts. — Annapolis: Naval Institute Press, 1977 (c1976).
436 p.: ill.; 26 cm. Includes index. 1. Great Britain. Royal Navy — History —
World War, 1939-1945. 2. Battle cruisers — Great Britain. 3. Battleships —
Great Britain. 4. World War, 1939-1945 — Naval operations, British.
I. Roberts, John Arthur, 1945- II. T.
V800.R38    359.8/3    *LC* 76-22915    *ISBN* 0870218174

**Reilly, John C.**    **5.7437**
American battleships, 1886–1923: predreadnought design and construction /
by John C. Reilly, Jr., and Robert L. Scheina. — Annapolis, Md.: Naval
Institute Press, c1980. 259 p. [4] fold. leaves of plates: ill.; 29 cm. Includes
index. 1. United States. Navy — History 2. Battleships — United States —
History. I. Scheina, Robert L. joint author. II. T.
V815.3.R44    359.3/252/0973    *LC* 79-91326    *ISBN* 0870215248

**Preston, Antony, 1938-.**    **5.7438**
Cruisers / Antony Preston. — 1st US ed. — Englewood Cliffs, N.J.: Prentice
Hall, c1980. 191 p.: ill. (some col.); 31 cm. 'A Bison book.' Includes index.
1. Cruisers (Warships) — History. I. T.
V820.P73 1980    359.8/3 19    *LC* 79-89592    *ISBN* 0131949020

**Preston, Antony, 1938-.**    **5.7439**
Destroyers / Antony Preston. — 1st U.S. ed. — Englewood Cliffs, N.J.:
Prentice-Hall, 1977. 224 p.: ill.; 31 cm. 'A Bison book.' Includes index.
1. Destroyers (Warships) — History. 2. Naval history, Modern I. T.
V825.P73 1977    359.3/2/540904    *LC* 77-82132    *ISBN* 0132021277

**Compton-Hall, Richard.**    **5.7440**
Submarine boats: the beginnings of underwater warfare / Richard Compton-
Hall. — New York: Arco Pub., 1984. 192 p.: ill.; 25 cm. Includes index.
1. Submarine boats — History. I. T.
V857.C65 1984    359.3/257/09 19    *LC* 83-7128    *ISBN* 0668059249

**Showell, Jak P. Mallmann.**    **5.7441**
U-boats under the Swastika: an introduction to German submarines 1935–1945
/ J. P. Mallmann Showell. — New York: Arco Pub. Co., 1974, c1973. 167 p.:
ill.; 25 cm. 1. Germany. Kriegsmarine — Submarine forces. 2. Submarine
boats 3. World War, 1939-1945 — Naval operations — Submarine 4. World
War, 1939-1945 — Naval operations, German I. T.
V859.G3 S5 1974    940.54/51    *LC* 73-93152    *ISBN* 0668034572

**Polmar, Norman.**    • **5.7442**
Aircraft carriers: a graphic history of carrier aviation and its influence on world
events / by Norman Polmar; in collaboration with Minoru Genda, Eric M.
Brown [and] Robert M. Langdon. — [1st ed.]. — Garden City, N.Y.:
Doubleday, 1969. viii, 788 p.: ill.; maps, plans, ports.; 29 cm. 1. Aircraft
carriers I. T.
V874.P6    359.32/55    *LC* 69-12186

**Friedman, Norman, 1946-.**    **5.7443**
U.S. aircraft carriers: an illustrated design history / by Norman Friedman; ship
plans by A.D. Baker III. — Annapolis, Md.: Naval Institute Press, c1983. viii,
427 p.: ill.; 29 cm. 1. Aircraft carriers — United States. I. T.
V874.3.F74 1983    623.8/255/0973 19    *LC* 82-14357    *ISBN*
0870217399

**Melhorn, Charles M.**    **5.7444**
Two-block fox: the rise of the aircraft carrier, 1911–1929 / [by] Charles M.
Melhorn. — Annapolis, Md.: Naval Institute Press, [1974] 181 p.; 24 cm.

1. United States. Navy — History 2. Aircraft carriers — History. 3. United
States — History, Naval I. T.
V874.3.M44    359.3/2/550973    *LC* 73-91169    *ISBN* 0870217089

**Sapolsky, Harvey M.**    **5.7445**
The Polaris system development: bureaucratic and programmatic success in
government / [by] Harvey M. Sapolsky. — Cambridge, Mass.: Harvard
University Press, 1972. xviii, 261 p.; 24 cm. 1. Polaris (Missile) I. T.
V993.S26    359.6/21    *LC* 72-79311    *ISBN* 0674682254

# VA NAVIES. NAVAL SITUATION

**Jane's fighting ships.**    **5.7446**
1898-. New York [etc.] McGraw-Hill Book Co. [etc.] illus. 19-33 cm. 1. Navies
— Yearbooks. 2. Warships — Yearbooks. I. Jane, Fred T. (Frederick
Thomas), 1865-1916. ed.
VA40.J34    623.82/5    *LC* 72-9090

# VA49–395 United States

**Mahan, A. T. (Alfred Thayer), 1840-1914.**    **5.7447**
The interest of America in sea power, present and future. — Boston: Little,
Brown, 1897. 314 p.: 2 fold. maps. 1. Sea-power 2. United States. Navy. I. T.
VA50.M3

**Miller, Nathan, 1927-.**    **5.7448**
The U.S. Navy: an illustrated history / by Nathan Miller. — New York:
American Heritage Pub. Co.: book trade distribution by Simon and Schuster,
[1977] 408 p.: ill.; 29 cm. Includes index. 1. United States. Navy — History
I. T.
VA55.M55    359/.00973 19    *LC* 77-24139    *ISBN* 0671229842

**Chapelle, Howard Irving.**    **5.7449**
The history of the American sailing Navy: the ships and their development. —
[1st ed.] New York: Norton [1949] xxiii, 558 p.: ill., port., plans (part fold.); 26
cm. 1. United States. Navy — History 2. Warships I. T. II. Title: The
American sailing Navy.
VA56.C5    *LC* 49-48709

**Coletta, Paolo Enrico, 1916-.**    **5.7450**
The United States Navy and defense unification, 1947–1953 / Paolo E. Coletta.
— Newark: University of Delaware Press, c1981. 367 p.: ill.; 24 cm. Includes
index. 1. United States. Navy — History — 20th century. 2. United States —
Military policy 3. United States — Politics and government — 1945-1953 I. T.
VA58.C75    359.6/0973    *LC* 79-3111    *ISBN* 087413126X

**Alden, John Doughty, 1921-.**    **5.7451**
The American steel navy: a photographic history of the U.S. Navy from the
introduction of the steel hull in 1883 to the cruise of the Great White Fleet,
1907–1909 / by John D. Alden; photographic research and editorial supervision
by Ed Holm; fifty warship profiles by Arthur D. Baker. — Annapolis, Md.:
Naval Institute Press, [1972] 396 p.: illus.; 31 cm. 1. United States. Navy —
Illustrations. I. T.
VA59.A65    359.3/2/50973    *LC* 76-163111    *ISBN* 0870216813

**Martin, Tyrone G.**    **5.7452**
A most fortunate ship: a narrative history of 'Old Ironsides' / by Tyrone G.
Martin. — Chester, Conn.: Globe Pequot Press, c1980. viii, [9] leaves of
plates: ill.; 27 cm. Includes index. 1. Constitution (Frigate) I. T.
VA65.C7 M33    359.3/225 19    *LC* 79-52490    *ISBN* 0871060337

**Wells, Tom Henderson.**    **5.7453**
The Confederate Navy: a study in organization. — University: University of
Alabama Press, [1971] ix, 182 p.; 24 cm. 1. Confederate States of America.
Navy — Organization. I. T.
VA393.W45    359.3/0975    *LC* 72-169496    *ISBN* 0817351051

**The RCN in retrospect, 1910–1968** / edited by James A.    **5.7454**
**Boutilier.**
Vancouver: University of British Columbia Press, c1982. xxx, 373 p., [48] p. of
plates: ill.; 24 cm. 1. Canada. Royal Canadian Navy — History — Addresses,
essays, lectures. 2. Canada — History, Naval — Addresses, essays, lectures.
I. Boutilier, James A. II. Title: R.C.N. in retrospect, 1910-1968.
VA400.R38 1982    359/.00971 19    *LC* 82-181801    *ISBN*
0774801522

**Kemp, Peter Kemp.**      • **5.7455**
History of the Royal Navy / edited by P. K. Kemp. — [1st American ed.] New
York: Putnam [1969] 304 p.: ill. (part col.), maps, ports.; 29 cm. 1. Great
Britain. Royal Navy — History. I. T.
VA454.K42 1969    359/.00942    *LC* 76-84572

**Marcus, Geoffrey Jules, 1906-.**      **5.7456**
Heart of oak: a survey of British sea power in the Georgian era / G. J. Marcus.
— London; New York: Oxford University Press, 1975. xi, 308 p.: ill.; 24 cm.
Includes index. 1. Great Britain. Royal Navy — History. 2. Seamen — Great
Britain. 3. Navigation — Great Britain — History. 4. Great Britain —
History, Naval I. T.
VA454.M319    359/.00941    *LC* 76-354759    *ISBN* 0192158120

**Marcus, Geoffrey Jules, 1906-.**      **5.7457**
A naval history of England. — Boston: Little, Brown, 1961-. 3 v.: maps; 23 cm.
Bibliography: v. 1, p. 465-480. 1. Great Britain. Royal Navy — Hist. 2. Gt.
Brit. — History, Naval. I. T.
VA454.M32    942    *LC* 62-9357

**Marder, Arthur Jacob.**      • **5.7458**
The anatomy of British sea power; a history of British naval policy in the pre-
dreadnought era, 1880–1905, by Arthur J. Marder. New York: Octagon Books,
1973. xix, 580, xv p. 24 cm. Reprint of the 1940 ed. published by Knopf, New
York. 1. Great Britain. Royal Navy — History. 2. Sea-power 3. Great Britain
— History, Naval — 19th century I. T.
VA454.M34    359/.00942    *LC* 73-2954    *ISBN* 0374952841

**Marder, Arthur Jacob.**      **5.7459**
From the Dardanelles to Oran: studies of the Royal Navy in war and peace,
1915–1940 / Arthur J. Marder. — London; New York: Oxford University
Press, 1974. xvi, 301 p., [5] leaves of plates: ill., fold. maps; 22 cm. 1. Great
Britain. Royal Navy — History. 2. Great Britain — History, Naval I. T.
VA454.M345    359/.00941    *LC* 75-302105    *ISBN* 0192158023

**Marder, Arthur Jacob.**      • **5.7460**
From the dreadnought to Scapa Flow: the Royal Navy in the Fisher era,
1904–1919 / by Arthur J. Marder. — London: Oxford University Press,
1961-1970. 5 v.: ill., maps.; 23 cm. 1. Fisher, John Arbuthnot Fisher, Baron,
1841-1920. 2. Great Britain. Royal Navy — History 3. World War, 1914-1918
— Naval operations 4. Great Britain — History, Naval. I. T.
VA454.M35    *LC* 61-19563    *ISBN* 0192151878

**Padfield, Peter.**      **5.7461**
Rule Britannia: the Victorian and Edwardian Navy / Peter Padfield. —
London; Boston: Routledge & Kegan Paul, 1981. 246 p.: ill.; 25 cm. Includes
index. 1. Great Britain. Royal Navy — History — 19th century. 2. Great
Britain. Royal Navy — History — 20th century. I. T.
VA454.P24    359/.00941 19    *LC* 81-198788    *ISBN* 0710007744

**Parkes, Oscar.**      **5.7462**
British battleships: 'Warrior' 1860 to 'Vanguard' 1950: a history of design,
construction and armament / Oscar Parkes; with a foreword by Admiral of the
Fleet, the Earl Mountbatten of Burma. — New & rev. ed. — Hamden, Conn.:
Archon books, 1972, c1971. xv, 701 p.: ill. 1. Great Britain. Royal Navy.
2. Warships I. T.
VA454.P28 1966    623.8252    *LC* 67-72751    *ISBN* 0208012532

**Pepys, Samuel, 1633-1703.**      • **5.7463**
[Memoires of the Royal Navy, 1679-1688] Pepys' Memoires of the Royal Navy,
1679–1688. Edited by J. R. Tanner. New York, Haskell House, 1971. xviii,
131 p. 23 cm. (Tudor & Stuart library) Reprint of the 1906 facsimile
reproduction. 1. Great Britain. Royal Navy — History. I. Tanner, J. R.
(Joseph Robson), 1860-1931. ed. II. T. III. Series.
VA454.P46 1971    359.3/0942    *LC* 68-25260    *ISBN* 0838302289

**Hamill, Ian.**      **5.7464**
The strategic illusion: the Singapore strategy and the defence of Australia and
New Zealand, 1919–1942 / Ian Hamill. — [Singapore]: Singapore University
Press, c1981. ix, 387 p.: maps; 23 cm. Includes index. 1. Singapore Naval Base
(Singapore) — History. 2. Great Britain — Colonies — Asia — Defenses.
3. Great Britain — Defenses. 4. Australia — Defenses. 5. New Zealand —
Defenses. I. T.
VA459.S5 H36 1981    359.7/09595/7 19    *LC* 81-941281    *ISBN*
997169008X

**Coad, J. G.**      **5.7465**
Historic architecture of the Royal Navy: an introduction / J.G. Coad. —
London: V. Gollancz, 1983. 160 p.: ill.; 26 cm. Includes index. 1. Navy-yards
and naval stations — Great Britain. 2. Military architecture — Great Britain
— History. I. T.
VA460.A1 C6 1983    623/.64/0941 19    *LC* 83-185428    *ISBN*
0575032774

**Showell, Jak P. Mallmann.**      **5.7466**
The German Navy in World War Two: a reference guide to the Kriegsmarine,
1935–1945 / Jak P. Mallmann Showell. — [Annapolis, Maryland]: Naval
Institute Press, [1979] 224 p.: ill.; 26 cm. Includes index. 1. Germany.
Kriegsmarine — History. 2. Warships — Germany — History. 3. World War,
1939-1945 — Naval operations, German I. T.
VA513.S52 [1979]    359/.00943    *LC* 79-84933    *ISBN* 0870219332

**Steinberg, Jonathan.**      • **5.7467**
Yesterday's deterrent: Tirpitz and the birth of the German battle fleet / by
Jonathan Steinberg; foreword by Commander Saunders. — New York:
Macmillan, 1966, c1965. 240 p.: ill., ports.; 21 cm. 1. Tirpitz, Alfred von,
1849-1930. 2. Germany. Kriegsmarine — History I. T.
VA513.S74 1966    359.00943    *LC* 66-27011

**Fairhall, David.**      • **5.7468**
Russian sea power. Boston, Gambit, 1971. 286 p. illus. 24 cm. 1. Soviet Union.
Voenno-Morskoĭ Flot. 2. Merchant marine — Russia. 3. Sea-power I. T.
VA573.F34 1971    387/.0947    *LC* 71-118209    *ISBN* 0876450400

**Gorshkov, Sergeĭ Georgievich, 1910-.**      **5.7469**
Red star rising at sea / Sergei G. Gorshkov; translated by Theodore A. Neely,
Jr. from a series of articles originally published in Morskoi sbornik; edited for
publication by Herbert Preston. — [Annapolis, Md.]: Naval Institute Press,
c1974. 150 p.: ill.; 29 cm. 1. Russia. Voennyĭ flot — History. 2. Naval history
3. Sea-power I. Morskoĭ sbornik. II. T.
VA573.G6613    359/.00947    *LC* 75-304584    *ISBN* 0870212449

**Guide to Far Eastern navies / edited by Barry M. Blechman**      **5.7470**
**and Robert P. Berman.**
Annapolis: Naval Institute Press, c1978. xiv, 586 p.: ill.; 16 x 24 cm. 1. Navies
— East Asia. I. Blechman, Barry M. II. Berman, Robert P., 1950-
VA620.G84    359/.0095    *LC* 77-87942    *ISBN* 0870217976

**Howarth, Stephen.**      **5.7471**
The fighting ships of the Rising Sun: the drama of the Imperial Japanese Navy,
1895–1945 / Stephen Howarth. — 1st American ed. — New York: Atheneum,
1983. xii, 398 p., [20] p. of plates: ill.; 25 cm. 'Published in Great Britain under
the title: Morning glory'—T.p. verso. Includes index. 1. Japan. Kaigun —
History. 2. Japan — History, Naval I. T.
VA653.H64 1983    359/.00952 19    *LC* 83-45076    *ISBN* 0689114028

**Jentschura, Hansgeorg.**      **5.7472**
Warships of the Imperial Japanese Navy, 1869–1945 / Hansgeorg Jentschura,
Dieter Jung, and Peter Mickel; translated by Antony Preston and J. D. Brown.
Annapolis, Md.: Naval Institute Press, c1977. 284 p.: ill.; 26 cm. A translation
with revisions of Die japanischen Kriegsschiffe, 1869-1945. Includes index.
1. Japan. Kaigun. 2. Warships I. Jung, Dieter. joint author. II. Mickel, Peter,
joint author. III. T.
VA653.J4513 1977b    623.82/5/0952    *LC* 77-366267    *ISBN*
087021893X

# VB Naval Administration

**American Secretaries of the Navy / edited by Paolo E. Coletta.**      **5.7473**
Annapolis, Md.: Naval Institute Press, c1980. 2 v. (xxx, 1028 p.): ports.; 26 cm.
1. United States. Navy — Management — History. 2. United States. Navy
Dept — History. 3. United States. Navy Dept — Biography. I. Coletta, Paolo
Enrico, 1916-
VB23.A57    353.7/092/2 B    *LC* 78-70967    *ISBN* 0870210734

**Horsfield, John.**      **5.7474**
The art of leadership in war: the Royal Navy from the age of Nelson to the end
of World War II / John Horsfield. — Westport, Conn.: Greenwood Press, 1980.
xiv, 240 p.: ill.; 22 cm. — (Contributions in military history. no. 21 0084-9251)
Includes index. 1. Great Britain. Royal Navy — History. 2. Admirals —
Great Britain. 3. Leadership I. T. II. Series.
VB205.G7 H67    359    *LC* 79-54059    *ISBN* 0313209197

**Calvert, James.**      • **5.7475**
The naval profession. — Rev. ed. — New York: McGraw-Hill, [1971] xiv,
250 p.: illus.; 22 cm. 1. U.S. Navy — Vocational guidance. I. T.
VB259.C28 1971    359/.0023    *LC* 71-152002    *ISBN* 0070096570

**Herwig, Holger H.**      **5.7476**
The German naval officer corps: a social and political history, 1890–1918 / [by]
Holger H. Herwig. — Oxford: Clarendon Press, 1973. xiv, 298 p.; 22 cm.
Revised German ed. (1977) published under title: Das Elitekorps des Kaisers.
1. Germany. Kriegsmarine — Officers. 2. Germany. Kriegsmarine — History.

3. Germany — Politics and government — 1881-1918. 4. Germany — Social conditions I. T.
VB315.G4 H47      359.3/3/20943      *LC* 74-158685      *ISBN* 0198225172

# VE–VG Marines. Naval Aviation

**Simmons, Edwin H., 1921-.**                                    **5.7477**
The United States Marines, 1775–1975 / by Edwin H. Simmons; foreword by R. E. Cushman, Jr.; maps by Charles Waterhouse, from sketches by the author. — New York: Viking Press, 1976. x, 342 p.: ill.; 20 cm. Includes index. 1. United States. Marine Corps — History I. T.
VE21.S55 1976      359.9/6/0973      *LC* 75-35719      *ISBN* 0670741019

**Heinl, Robert Debs, 1916-.**                                    • **5.7478**
Soldiers of the sea; the United States Marine Corps, 1775–1962. Annapolis, United States Naval Institute [1962] 692 p. illus. 25 cm. 1. United States. Marine Corps — History I. T.
VE23.H4      *LC* 61-18078

**Millett, Allan Reed.**                                    **5.7479**
Semper fidelis: the history of the United States Marine Corps / Allan R. Millett. — New York: Macmillan Pub. Co., c1980. xviii, 782 p., [8] leaves of plates: ill.; 25 cm. — (The Macmillan Wars of the United States) Includes index. 1. United States. Marine Corps — History I. T.
VE23.M54      359.9/6/0973 19      *LC* 80-1059      *ISBN* 0029215903

**History of the Naval Weapons Center, China Lake, California.**   **5.7480**
Washington: Naval History Division; [for sale by the Supt. of Docs., U.S. Govt. Print. Off.], 1971. 303 p.: ill., ports.; 26 cm. 1. Naval Weapons Center — History — Collected works. I. Christman, Albert B.
VF373.H58      623.4      *LC* 75-173042

**Layman, R. D., 1928-.**                                    **5.7481**
To ascend from a floating base: shipboard aeronautics and aviation, 1783–1914 / R. D. Layman. — Rutherford: Fairleigh Dickinson University Press, c1979. 271 p.: ill.; 22 cm. Includes index. 1. Naval aviation — History. I. T.
VG90.L38      358.4/009      *LC* 77-89782      *ISBN* 0838620787

**Robinson, Douglas Hill, 1918-.**                                    **5.7482**
Up ship!: a history of the U.S. Navy's rigid airships 1919–1935 / by Douglas H. Robinson and Charles L. Keller. — Annapolis, Md.: Naval Institute Press, c1982. xiii, 236 p.: ill.; 29 cm. Includes index. 1. United States. Navy — Aviation — History. 2. Airships — History. I. Keller, Charles L. II. T.
VG93.R6 1982      358.4/00973 19      *LC* 82-6374      *ISBN* 0870217380

**Van Vleet, Clarke.**                                    **5.7483**
United States naval aviation, 1910–1980 / prepared at the direction of the Deputy Chief of Naval Operations (Air Warfare) and the Commander, Naval Air Systems Command. — [3rd ed.]. — [Washington, D.C.]: Dept. of the Navy, United States of America: For sale by the Supt. of Docs., U.S. G.P.O., 1981. xv, 547 p.: ill.; 29 cm. Authors: Clarke Van Vleet, Wm. J. Armstrong. 'NAVAIR 00-80P-1.' 'Supersedes NAVWEPS 00-80P-1 dated 1970.' Includes indexes. 1. United States. Navy — Aviation — Chronology. I. Armstrong, William J. II. United States. Office of the Chief of Naval Operations. III. United States. Naval Air Systems Command. IV. T.
VG93.V33 1981      358.4/00973 19      *LC* 82-603674

**Cree, Edward H. (Edward Hodges), 1814-1901.**                  **5.7484**
[Cree journals] Naval surgeon: the voyages of Dr. Edward H. Cree, Royal Navy, as related in his private journals, 1837–1856 / illustrated by the author; edited and with an introduction by Michael Levien; [maps by Jennifer Johnson]. — 1st ed. — New York: E.P. Dutton, 1982, c1981. 275 p.: ill. (some col.); 25 cm. British ed. published as: The Cree journals. 1. Cree, Edward H. (Edward Hodges), 1814-1901. 2. Great Britain. Royal Navy — Biography. 3. Surgery, Naval — Great Britain — History — 19th century. I. Levien, Michael, 1927- II. T.
VG228.G7 C733 1982      359.3/45/0924 B 19      *LC* 81-69225      *ISBN* 0525241213

# VK Navigation. Merchant Marine

**Parry, J. H. (John Horace), 1914-.**                                    **5.7485**
Romance of the sea / [by J.H. Parry]; [prepared by National Geographic Book Service]. — 1st ed. — Washington, D.C.: National Geographic Society, c1981. 312 p.: ill.; 28 x 36 cm. Includes index. 1. Navigation — History 2. Ships — History. 3. Naval art and science — History 4. Seafaring life — History. I. National Geographic Book Service. II. T.
VK15.P4      *LC* 80-29569      *ISBN* 0870443461

**Rougé, Jean.**                                    **5.7486**
[Marine dans l'Antiquité. English] Ships and fleets of the ancient Mediterranean / by Jean Rougé; translated from the French by Susan Frazer. — 1st ed. — Middletown, Conn.: Wesleyan University Press, c1981. 228 p.: ill.; 22 cm. Translation of: La marine dans l'Antiquité. Includes index. 1. Navigation — Mediterranean region — History. 2. Naval history, Ancient I. T.
VK16.R6413      387/.0093 19      *LC* 81-4927      *ISBN* 0819550558

**Villiers, Alan John, 1903-.**                                    • **5.7487**
The way of a ship: being some account of the ultimate development of the ocean-going square-rigged sailing vessel, and the manner of her handling, her voyage-making, her personnel, her economics, her performance, and her end / by Alan Villiers; illustrated with the author's photos., and diagrs. and drawings by Harold A. Underhill. — New York: Scribner, 1970. xvii, 429 p.: ill., charts (1 fold.), ports.; 25 cm. 1. Sailing ships 2. Shipping — History. I. T.
VK18.V5 1970      387.2/2      *LC* 70-106543

**Cutler, Carl C., 1878-1966.**                                    • **5.7488**
Greyhounds of the sea; the story of the American clipper ship. With a foreword by Charles Francis Adams. Annapolis, United States Naval Institute [1961, c1930] 592 p. illus. 27 cm. 1. Clipper-ships 2. Merchant marine — United States I. T.
VK23.C8 1961      387.22      *LC* 60-16873

**Lloyd, Christopher, 1906-.**                                    • **5.7489**
The British seaman 1200–1860: a social survey. — London: Collins, 1968. 319 p.: 20 plates, illus., facsims.; 23 cm. 1. Seamen — Great Britain — History. I. T.
VK57.L55      359/.00942      *LC* 68-132004

**Knight, Austin Melvin, 1854-1927.**                                    **5.7490**
[Modern seamanship] Knight's Modern seamanship. — 17th ed. / revised by John V. Noel. — New York: Van Nostrand Reinhold, c1984. xi, 740 p.: ill.; 24 cm. Includes bibliographical references and index. 1. Seamanship I. Noel, John Vavasour, 1912- II. T. III. Title: Modern seamanship.
VK541.K73 1984      623.88 19      *LC* 82-23714      *ISBN* 0442268637

**Cotter, Charles H.**                                    • **5.7491**
A history of nautical astronomy [by] Charles H. Cotter. London, Sydney [etc.] Hollis & Carter, 1968. xii, 387 p. 8 plates, illus., facsims., map, port. 22 cm. 1. Nautical astronomy — History. I. T. II. Title: Nautical astronomy.
VK549.C63      527/.09      *LC* 68-12049      *ISBN* 0370004604 63/-

**Taylor, E. G. R. (Eva Germaine Rimington), 1879-.**                  • **5.7492**
The haven-finding art; a history of navigation from Odysseus to Captain Cook [by] E. G. R. Taylor. With a foreword by K. St. B. Collins. Appendix by Joseph Needham. New York, American Elsevier Pub. Co., 1971. xii, 310 p. illus. 23 cm. 1. Navigation — History I. T.
VK549.T39 1971b      623.89/09      *LC* 76-151853      *ISBN* 0444196080

**American practical navigator.**                                    • **5.7493**
Washington: Govt. Print. Off. v.: ill.,maps,diagrs.,charts. (Defense Mapping Agency. Hydrographic Centre. Publication; no.9) (H.O. pub. no.9.) Vols. for 1900-1971 issued as U.S. Hydrographic Office Publication no. 9. Vols. for 1972- issued as Defense Mapping Agency Hydrographic Centre Publication no. 9. Title varies. Imprint varies. 1. Navigation 2. Nautical astronomy I. Series. II. Series: H.O. pub. no.9.
VK555.A48      527      *LC* 50-46844

**Dutton, Benjamin, 1883-1937.**                                    **5.7494**
[Navigation & piloting] Dutton's Navigation & piloting. — 14th ed. / by Elbert S. Maloney. — Annapolis, Md.: Naval Institute Press, c1985. viii, 588, 52 p.: ill. (some col.); 28 cm. Includes index. 1. Navigation 2. Nautical astronomy I. Maloney, Elbert S. II. T. III. Title: Navigation and piloting. IV. Title: Dutton's Navigation and piloting.
VK555.D96 1985      623.89 19      *LC* 85-3004      *ISBN* 0870211579

Holland, F. Ross (Francis Ross), 1927-.                    • 5.7495
America's lighthouses; their illustrated history since 1716. Brattleboro, Vt., S.
Greene Press [1972] x, 226 p. illus. 29 cm. 1. Lighthouses — United States.
I. T.
VK1023.H65      387     *LC* 74-170080      *ISBN* 0828901481

# VM Naval Architecture. Ship Building

Albion, Robert Greenhalgh, 1896-.                          5.7496
Five centuries of famous ships: from the Santa Maria to the Glomar Explorer /
Robert G. Albion; with a foreword by Benjamin Labaree. — New York:
McGraw-Hill, c1978. viii, 435 p.: ill.; 24 cm. Includes index. 1. Ships —
History. I. T.
VM15.A5      387.2/09/03      *LC* 77-4904      *ISBN* 0070009538

Anderson, Romola.                                          • 5.7497
The sailing–ship; six thousand years of history, by Romola & R. C. Anderson.
New York, B. Blom, 1971. 211 p. illus. 22 cm. Reprint of the 1926 ed. 1. Sailing
ships 2. Clipper-ships I. Anderson, R. C. (Roger Charles), b. 1883. joint
author. II. T.
VM15.A6 1971      387.2/1      *LC* 79-177507

Casson, Lionel, 1914-.                                     • 5.7498
Ships and seamanship in the ancient world. — Princeton, N.J.: Princeton
University Press, 1971. xxviii, 441 p.: illus., plans.; 24 cm. 1. Ships — History.
2. Seamanship — History. I. T.
VM15.C35      623.82/1      *LC* 78-112996      *ISBN* 0691035369

Greenhill, Basil.                                          5.7499
Archaeology of the boat: a new introductory study / [by] Basil Greenhill; with
chapters by J. S. Morrison and Sean McGrail; ... drawings by Eric McKee;
introduced by W. F. Grimes. Middletown, Conn.: Wesleyan University Press,
c1976. 320 p.: ill., maps, plans, port.; 25 cm. Includes index. 1. Boats and
boating — History. 2. Boatbuilding — History. 3. Archaeology I. T.
VM15.G72      623.82/1      *LC* 76-22928      *ISBN* 0819550027

Haws, Duncan.                                              5.7500
Ships and the sea: a chronological review / by Duncan Haws. [New York]:
Crowell, [1975] 240 p.: ill.; 31 cm. Includes indexes. 1. Ships — History.
2. Navigation — History 3. Shipping — History. I. T.
VM15.H33 1975      387.2/09      *LC* 75-13686      *ISBN* 0690009682

Brøgger, A. W. (Anton Wilhelm), 1884-.                     5.7501
[Vikingeskipene. English] The Viking ships; their ancestry and evolution [by]
A. W. Brøgger [and] Haakon Shetelig. [English translation by Katherine John]
New York, Twayne Publishers 1972, c1971. 192 p. illus. 28 cm. Translation of
Vikingeskipene. 1. Viking ships I. Shetelig, Haakon, 1877-1955. II. T.
VM17.B715      623.82/1      *LC* 72-181704

Millar, John Fitzhugh.                                     5.7502
American ships of the Colonial and Revolutionary periods / John F. Millar. —
1st ed. — New York: Norton, c1978. viii, 356 p.: ill.; 22 x 28 cm. Includes
indexes. 1. Ships — History — 17th century. 2. Ships — History — 18th
century. 3. North America — History — Colonial period, ca. 1600-1775
4. United States — History — Revolution, 1775-1783 I. T.
VM22.M54      623.82/2/0973      *LC* 78-18742      *ISBN* 0393032221

Chapelle, Howard Irving.                                   • 5.7503
The history of American sailing ships, by Howard I. Chapelle; with drawings by
the author, and George C. Wales and Henry Rusk. New York, W. W. Norton &
company, 1935. xvii p., 1 l., 400 p. illus., plates, plans (part double) 27 cm.
Colored title vignette. 'First trade edition after printing a limited edition of 121
copies.' 1. Sailing ships 2. Shipbuilding — United States — History.
3. Shipping — United States — History. I. T. II. Title: American sailing
ships.
VM23.C53 1935a      623.8220973      *LC* 35-27469

Hutchins, John Greenwood Brown, 1909-.                     5.7504
The American maritime industries and public policy, 1789–1914: an economic
history / by John G. B. Hutchins. — New York: Russell & Russell [1969,
c1941] xxi, 627 p.; 23 cm. (Harvard economic studies. v. 71) 1. Shipbuilding —
United States — History. 2. Merchant marine — United States I. T. II. Series.
VM23.H85 1969      387.5/0973      *LC* 68-27065

Bamford, Paul Walden, 1921-.                               5.7505
Fighting ships and prisons; the Mediterranean galleys of France in the age of
Louis XIV [by] Paul W. Bamford. With drawings by John W. Ekstrom. —
Minneapolis: University of Minnesota Press, [1973] x, 380 p.: illus.; 24 cm.
1. Louis XIV, King of France, 1638-1715. 2. Galleys I. T.
VM71.B35      387.2/1      *LC* 72-92334      *ISBN* 0816606552

Hutcheon, Wallace, 1933-.                                  5.7506
Robert Fulton, pioneer of undersea warfare / by Wallace Hutcheon. —
Annapolis, Md.: Naval Institute Press, c1981. xii, 191 p.: ill.; 24 cm. Includes
index. 1. Fulton, Robert, 1765-1815. 2. Naval art and science 3. Naval
architects — United States — Biography. I. T.
VM140.F9 H87      623.8/25/0924 B 19      *LC* 80-81094      *ISBN*
0870215477

Chapelle, Howard Irving.                                   5.7507
The search for speed under sail, 1700–1855, by Howard I. Chapelle. — New
York: Norton, [1983] xviii, 453 p.: illus.; 26 cm. 1. Sailing ships 2. Naval
architecture I. T.
VM144.C28 1983      623.82/03      *LC* 67-11090

Bhattacharyya, Rameswar.                                   5.7508
Dynamics of marine vehicles / Rameswar Bhattacharyya. — New York: Wiley,
c1978. x, 498 p.: ill.; 29 cm. — (Ocean engineering, a Wiley series) 'A Wiley-
Interscience publication.' 1. Ships — Seakeeping I. T.
VM156.B49      623.8/1      *LC* 78-950      *ISBN* 0471072060

Bloomster, Edgar L.                                        • 5.7509
Sailing and small craft down the ages / drawings and text by Edgar L.
Bloomster. — [2d ed.]. — Annapolis, Md.: United States Naval Institute,
[1969] 116 p.: ill.; 30 cm. 1. Ships 2. Ships — Pictorial works I. T.
VM307.B6 1969      623.82/2      *LC* 70-11099

Marchaj, Czesław A.                                        5.7510
Aero–hydrodynamics of sailing / C. A. Marchaj. — New York: Dodd, Mead,
1980, c1979. xv, 701 p.: ill.; 28 cm. 1. Sailboats — Hydrodynamics 2. Sailboats
— Aerodynamics 3. Sails — Aerodynamics I. T.
VM331.M36 1980      623.8/12043      *LC* 79-27724      *ISBN* 0396077390

Chapman, Charles Frederic, 1881-.                          5.7511
Piloting, seamanship and small boat handling. 1922-. [New York]: Motor
boating & sailing [etc.] v.: ill.; 29-31 cm. (1922- < 48 > : Motor boating's Ideal
series, v. 5 (VM341.M9) 1. Motorboats — Collected works. 2. Seamanship —
Collected works. 3. Navigation — Collected works. I. T.
VM341.C63      VM341.M9.      623.88/2.3105      *LC* 42-49646

Zadig, Ernest A., 1899-.                                   5.7512
The complete book of boating: an owner's guide to design, construction,
piloting, operation, and maintenance / Ernest A. Zadig. — 3rd ed. —
Englewood Cliffs, N.J.: Prentice-Hall, c1985. 640 p.: ill.; 29 cm. 'A Spectrum
book'—T.p. verso. Includes index. 1. Boats and boating I. T.
VM341.Z33 1985      623.8/231 19      *LC* 84-26407      *ISBN* 0131574965

Friedman, Norman, 1946-.                                   5.7513
Submarine design and development / Norman Friedman. — Annapolis, Md.:
Naval Institute Press, c1984. 192 p.: ill.; 29 cm. 1. Submarine boats I. T.
VM365.F76 1984      623.8/257 19      *LC* 83-43278      *ISBN* 0870219545

Cousteau, Jacques Yves.                                    5.7514
[Calypso] Jacques Cousteau's Calypso / by Jacques Cousteau and Alexis
Sivirine. — New York: H.N. Abrams, 1983. 192 p.: col. ill.; 30 cm. Includes
index. 1. Calypso (Ship) 2. Oceanography — Research 3. Underwater
exploration I. Sivirine, Alexis. II. T. III. Title: Calypso.
VM453.C67 1983      551.4/6/00723 19      *LC* 83-3751      *ISBN*
0810907887

Toss, Brion.                                               5.7515
The rigger's apprentice / Brion Toss. — Camden, Me.: International Marine
Pub. Co., c1984. xi, 195 p.: ill.; 29 cm. 1. Knots and splices 2. Masts and
rigging I. T.
VM533.T58 1984      623.88/82 19      *LC* 84-47755      *ISBN* 087742165X

Rowland, K. T.                                             • 5.7516
Steam at sea: a history of steam navigation / [by] K. T. Rowland. — New York:
Praeger, [1970] 240 p.: ill., ports.; 23 cm. 1. Steam-navigation — History. I. T.
VM615.R85 1970b      623.82/04      *LC* 77-130458

Woodward, John B.                                          5.7517
Marine gas turbines / John B. Woodward. — New York: Wiley, [1975] xxii,
390 p.: ill.; 24 cm. (Ocean engineering, a Wiley series) 'A Wiley-Interscience
publication.' 1. Marine gas-turbines I. T.
VM740.W6      623.87/23/3      *LC* 74-31383      *ISBN* 0471959626

## Z4–8 HISTORY OF BOOKS AND BOOKMAKING

**Febvre, Lucien Paul Victor, 1878-1956.**                        **5.7518**
The coming of the book; the impact of printing 1450–1800 [by] Lucien Lebvre [and] Henri–Jean Martin. Translated by David Gerard. Edited by Geoffrey Nowell–Smith and David Wooton. London, NLB; Atlantic Highlands, N.J., Humanities Press [1976] 378 p. 22 cm. (Foundations of history library) Original title: L'apparition du livre. Includes bibliographic references. 1. Books — History I. Martin, Henri Jean, 1924- joint author. II. T.
Z4.F413    *ISBN* 0902308173

## Z40–115 WRITING. CALLIGRAPHY. CRYPTOGRAPHY. PALEOGRAPHY

**Anderson, Donald M.**                        **5.7519**
The art of written forms; the theory and practice of calligraphy [by] Donald M. Anderson. New York, Holt, Rinehart and Winston [1969] ix, 358 p. illus., facsims., maps. 28 cm. 1. Calligraphy I. T.
Z40.A5    741    *LC* 68-21782    *ISBN* 030686253 10.95

**Fairbank, Alfred J.**                        • **5.7520**
The story of handwriting; origins and development [by] Alfred Fairbank. — New York: Watson-Guptill, [1970] 108 p.: illus. (part col.); 22 cm. 1. Writing — History 2. Penmanship I. T.
Z40.F33    745.6/1    *LC* 77-84820

**Reynolds, Leighton Durham.**                        **5.7521**
Scribes and scholars: a guide to the transmission of Greek and Latin literature / by L. D. Reynolds and N. G. Wilson. — 2nd ed., revised and enlarged. — Oxford: Clarendon Press, 1974. x, 275 p., xvi p. of plates: facsims.; 21 cm. 1. Transmission of texts 2. Learning and scholarship — History I. Wilson, Nigel Guy. joint author. II. T.
Z40.R4 1974    Z40 R4 1974.    001.2    *LC* 75-308361    *ISBN* 0198143710

**Autographs and manuscripts, a collector's manual / Edmund**                        **5.7522**
**Berkeley, Jr., editor, Herbert E. Klingelhofer and Kenneth W.**
**Rendell, coeditors; sponsored by the Manuscript Society.**
New York: Scribner, c1978. xviii, 565 p.: ill.; 24 cm. Includes index. 1. Autographs — Collectors and collecting. I. Berkeley, Edmund, 1937- II. Klingelhofer, Herbert E. III. Rendell, Kenneth W. IV. Manuscript Society (U.S.)
Z41.A92    929.8    *LC* 78-8177    *ISBN* 0684156229

**Bickham, George, d. 1769.**                        **5.7523**
The universal penman / engraved by George Bickham; with an introductory essay by Philip Hofer. — New York: Dover Publications; Toronto: General Pub. Co., c1968. [5] 212 p.: ill. 'This Dover edition, first published in 1954, is an unabridged and unaltered republication of the 212 plates comprising The universal penman as published by George Bickham, London, circa 1740-1741.' 1. Penmanship 2. Business 3. Calligraphy I. T.
Z43.B58 1968    652.1    *LC* 54-13017    *ISBN* 0486206165

**Day, Lewis Foreman, 1845-1910.**                        **5.7524**
Penmanship of the XVI, XVII & XVIIIth centuries: a series of typical examples from English and foreign writing books / selected by Lewis F. Day. — New York: Taplinger Pub. Co., 1979, c1978. ca. 150 p.: ill.; 25 cm. 'A Pentalic book.' 1. Penmanship 2. Calligraphy I. T.
Z43.D27 1979    745.6/197    *LC* 78-58919    *ISBN* 0800862775

**International calligraphy today / foreword by Hermann Zapf;**                        **5.7525**
**introduction by Philip Grushkin and Jeanyee Wong.**
New York: Watson-Guptill Publications, 1982. 192 p.: ill. (some col.); 29 cm. Based on a show organized by International Typeface Corporation. Includes index. 1. Calligraphy 2. Calligraphy — Exhibitions I. International Typeface Corporation.
Z43.I7 1982    745.6/1977 19    *LC* 82-8513    *ISBN* 082302556X

**Johnston, Edward, 1872-1944.**                        **5.7526**
Formal penmanship and other papers. Edited by Heather Child. — [1st ed.]. — New York: Hastings House, [1971] 156 p.: illus.; 29 cm. — (Visual communication books) 1. Calligraphy I. T.
Z43.J776    745.6/1    *LC* 75-159047    *ISBN* 0803822820

**Mahoney, Dorothy.**                        **5.7527**
The craft of calligraphy / Dorothy Mahoney. — 1st pbk. ed. — New York: Taplinger Pub. Co., 1982, c1981. 128 p.: ill.; 24 cm. 'A Pentalic book.' Includes index. 1. Calligraphy I. T.
Z43.M25 1982    745.6/197 19    *LC* 81-23238    *ISBN* 0800819705

**Peabody Institute, Baltimore. Library.**                        **5.7528**
Calligraphy & handwriting in America, 1710–1962. [Exhibition] assembled and shown by the Peabody Institute Library, Baltimore, Maryland, November, 1961–January, 1962. [Compiled by P. W. Filby, assistant director] Caledonia, N.Y., Italimuse, 1963. 1 v. (unpaged) illus., facsims. 28 cm. 1. Calligraphy — Exhibitions I. Filby, P. William, 1911- II. T.
Z43.P37    652.1    *LC* 63-16341

**Konheim, Alan G., 1934-.**                        **5.7529**
Cryptography, a primer / Alan G. Konheim. — New York: Wiley, c1981. xiv, 432 p.: ill.; 24 cm. 'A Wiley-interscience publication.' Includes index. 1. Cryptography 2. Computers — Access control 3. Telecommunication — Security measures I. T.
Z103.K66    001.54/36 19    *LC* 80-24978    *ISBN* 0471081329

**Meyer, Carl H.**                        **5.7530**
Cryptography: a new dimension in computer data security: a guide for the design and implementation of secure systems / Carl H. Meyer, Stephen M. Matyas. — New York: Wiley, 1982. xxi, 755 p.: ill.; 26 cm. 1. Cryptography — Handbooks, manuals, etc. I. Matyas, Stephen M. II. T.
Z103.M55 1982    001.54/36 19    *LC* 82-2831    *ISBN* 0471048925

**Weber, Ralph Edward.**                        **5.7531**
United States diplomatic codes and ciphers, 1775–1938 / Ralph E. Weber. — Chicago: Precedent Pub., 1979. xviii, 633 p., [4] leaves of plates: facsims.; 23 cm. Includes index. 1. Cryptography — United States — History. 2. United States — Diplomatic and consular service — History. I. T.
Z103.W4    652/.8    *LC* 78-65854    *ISBN* 0913750204

**Ullman, B. L. (Berthold Louis), 1882-1965.**                        • **5.7532**
Ancient writing and its influence. Cambridge, Mass., M.I.T. Press [1969] xviii, 240 p. facsims. 19 cm. Reprint of the 1932 ed., with a new introd. by Julian Brown. 1. Paleography 2. Alphabet 3. Writing — History I. T.
Z105.U4 1969    411/.09    *LC* 78-6001

**Jackson, Donald, 1938-.**                        **5.7533**
The story of writing / Donald Jackson. — New York, N.Y.: Taplinger Pub. Co.; [Janesville, Wis.]: Parker Pen Co., 1981. 176 p.: ill. (some col.); 26 cm. Includes index. 1. Paleography 2. Writing — History I. T.
Z107.J3 1981b    417/.7 19    *LC* 80-53236    *ISBN* 0800801725

**Thompson, Edward Maunde, Sir, 1840-1929.**                        • **5.7534**
An introduction to Greek and Latin palaeography. — New York: B. Franklin, [1965] xvi, 600 p.: facsims.; 26 cm. — (Burt Franklin bibliography and reference series, #71) Reprint of the 1912 ed. 1. Paleography, Latin 2. Paleography, Greek I. T.
Z114.T472 1965    481/.7    *LC* 74-6461

## Z116 The Modern Printed Book: Treatises

**Gaskell, Philip.**                        **5.7535**
A new introduction to bibliography / Philip Gaskell. — [1st ed.] reprinted with corrections. — Oxford: Clarendon Press, 1974. xxv, 438 p.: ill., facsims.; 24 cm. Includes index. 1. Printing — History 2. Book industries and trade — History. 3. Bibliography — Methodology 4. Books — Bibliography. I. T.
Z116.A2 G27 1974    686.2/09    *LC* 75-330050    *ISBN* 0198181507

**Lee, Marshall, 1921-.**     5.7536
Bookmaking: the illustrated guide to design/production/editing / Marshall Lee. — 2d ed.. — New York: Bowker, 1980. 485 p.: ill.; 26 cm. — (A Balance House book) Includes index. 1. Books 2. Book industries and trade I. T.
Z116.A2 L44 1979    686     LC 79-65014     ISBN 0835210979

**Williamson, Hugh Albert Fordyce, 1918-.**     5.7537
Methods of book design: the practice of an industrial craft / Hugh Williamson. — 3rd ed. — New Haven: Yale University Press, 1983. xiv, 391 p.: ill.; 25 cm. Includes index. 1. Book design 2. Book industries and trade I. T.
Z116.A3 W5 1983    686 19     LC 83-3610     ISBN 0300026633

# Z117–265 Printing

## Z117–127 General Works

**ABHB: annual bibliography of the history of the printed book and libraries.**     5.7538
v.1- 1970-. The Hague, Nijhoff, 1973-. 1. Libraries — History — Bibliography. 2. Books — History — Bibliography. 3. Printing — Bibliography.
Z117.A12

**The Bookman's glossary / edited by Jean Peters.**     5.7539
6th ed., rev. and enl. — New York: Bowker, 1983. ix, 223 p.; 24 cm. 1. Book industries and trade — Dictionaries. 2. Printing — Dictionaries 3. Bibliography — Dictionaries 4. Library science — Dictionaries I. Peters, Jean, 1935- II. R.R. Bowker Company.
Z118.B75 1983    070.5/03 19     LC 83-2775     ISBN 0835216861

**Glaister, Geoffrey Ashall.**     5.7540
[Glossary of the book] Glaister's Glossary of the book: terms used in papermaking, printing, bookbinding and publishing with notes on illuminated manuscripts and private presses / Geoffrey Ashall Glaister. — 2d ed., completely rev. — Berkeley: University of California Press, 1980 (c1979). 551 p.: ill.; 26 cm. The 1960 ed. published under title: Glossary of the book. 1. Books — Dictionaries. 2. Printing — Dictionaries 3. Publishers and publishing — Dictionaries. I. T. II. Title: Glossary of the book.
Z118.G55    686.2/03 19     LC 76-47975     ISBN 0520033647

**Printing and the mind of man: assembled at the British Museum and at Earls Court, London, 16–27 July 1963.**     • 5.7541
[London]: F.W. Bridges; obtainable from the British Museum, [1963]. 125, 61 p., [24] leaves of plates: ill., facsims.; 24 cm. 'Catalogue of a display of printing mechanisms and printed materials, arranged to illustrate the history of Western civilization and the means of the multiplication of literary texts since the XV century. Organized in connexion with the Eleventh International Printing Machinery and Allied Trades Exhibition.' 'Printing and the mind of man, an exhibition of fine printing in the King's Library of the British Museum, July-September 1963, published by the Trustees of the British Museum' (61 p. at end) available separately. 1. Book industries and trade — Exhibitions 2. Printing — Specimens — Fine books — Bibliography. 3. Bibliographical exhibitions I. British Museum. Dept. of Printed Books. King's Library. II. International Printing Machinery and Allied Trades Exhibition (1963: London, England)
Z121.L73 1963    LC 64-4374

**Eisenstein, Elizabeth L.**     5.7542
The printing press as an agent of change: communications and cultural transformations in early modern Europe / Elizabeth L. Eisenstein. — Cambridge [Eng.]; New York: Cambridge University Press, 1979. 2 v. (xxi, 794 p.); 24 cm. Includes index. 1. Printing — Influence. 2. Reformation 3. Renaissance 4. Technology and civilization I. T.
Z124.E37    686.2     LC 77-91083     ISBN 0521220440

**Eisenstein, Elizabeth L.**     5.7543
The printing revolution in early modern Europe / Elizabeth L. Eisenstein. — Cambridge [Cambridgeshire]; New York: Cambridge University Press, 1984 (c1983). xiv, 297 p.: ill.; 28 cm. Includes index. 1. Printing — History 2. Technology and civilization 3. Europe — Intellectual life — History. I. T.
Z124.E374    686.2/09 19     LC 83-10145     ISBN 0521258588

**Lewis, John Noel Claude, 1912-.**     • 5.7544
Anatomy of printing: the influences of art and history on its design [by] John Lewis. — New York: Watson-Guptill Publications, [1970] 228 p.: illus. (part col.), facsims. (part col.), plates (part col.); 29 cm. 1. Printing — History 2. Art — History I. T.
Z124.L66 1970b    686/.2/094     LC 78-114197     ISBN 0823050254

**Steinberg, S. H. (Sigfrid Henry), 1899-1969.**     5.7545
Five hundred years of printing / by S. H. Steinberg; with a foreword by Beatrice Warde. — 3d ed. — Harmondsworth, Eng.; Baltimore: Penguin Books, 1974. 400 p.: facsims.; 19 cm. — (Pelican books; A343) Includes index. 1. Printing — History I. T.
Z124.S8 1974    686.2/09     LC 74-187755     ISBN 0140203435

## Z131–225 By Country

**Bennett, H. S. (Henry Stanley), 1889-.**     • 5.7546
English books & readers, 1475 to 1557: being a study in the history of the book trade from Caxton to the incorporation of the Stationers' Company, by H. S. Bennett. — 2nd ed. — London: Cambridge U.P., 1969. xiv, 337 p.; 22 cm. Appendices (p. 239-319):—I. Handlist of publications by Wynkyn de Worde, 1492-1535.—II. Trial list of translations into English printed between 1475-1560. 1. Worde, Wynkyn de, d. 1534? 2. Book industries and trade — Gt. Brit. — History. 3. Printing — History — Gt. Brit. 4. English literature — Translations from foreign literature — Bibliography. I. T.
Z151.B4 1969    658.8/096555/73     LC 70-85712     ISBN 0521076099

**McLean, Ruari.**     • 5.7547
Modern book design, from William Morris to the present day. Fair Lawn, N.J.: Essential Books, 1959 [c1958] 115p. 1. Printing — History — Great Britain 2. Private presses I. T.
Z151 M3 1959    LC 59-1267

**Ransom, Will, 1878-1955.**     • 5.7548
Private presses and their books, by Will Ransom. — New York: R.R. Bowker company, 1929. 493, [1] p.: illus. (incl. facsims.); 24 cm. 'Printed in a limited edition of twelve hundred copies for America and England.' A history of the private press movement in England and America with detailed check-lists of the publications, arranged chronologically under the name of the press, with index to presses, books, and individuals recorded. 1. Private presses — History. 2. Privately printed books — Bibliography. I. T.
Z151.R21    LC 29-24889

**Plant, Marjorie.**     • 5.7549
The English book trade: an economic history of the making and sale of books / by Marjorie Plant. 3rd ed. — London: Allen & Unwin, 1974. 3-520 p. [16] leaves of plates: ill., facsim., ports.; 23 cm. 1. Book industries and trade — England — History. 2. Printing — England — History. I. T.
Z152.E5 P55 1974    338.4/7/0705730942     LC 75-307309     ISBN 0046550127

**Carter, Thomas Francis, 1882-1925.**     • 5.7550
The invention of printing in China and its spread westward. Rev. by L. Carrington Goodrich. — 2d ed. — New York, Ronald Press Co. [1955] xxiv, 293 p. illus., port., facsims. 24 cm. Bibliography: p. 255-278. 1. Printing — Hist. — Origin and antecedents. 2. Printing — Hist. — China. I. T.
Z186.C5C3 1955    655.151     LC 55-5418

**Thomas, Isaiah, 1749-1831.**     • 5.7551
The history of printing in America with a biography of printers & an account of newspapers / by Isaiah Thomas; edited by Marcus A. McCorison from the 2d ed. — Imprint ed. — Barre, Mass.: Imprint Society, 1970. xxi, 650 p., [1] leaf of plates: port.; 26 cm. Includes an original leaf from the 1st ed. (Worcester, 1810) 1. Printing — History — United States. 2. Printing — History — Canada. I. T.
Z205.T56 1970    686.2/0973     LC 75-100491     ISBN 0876360096

**Silver, Rollo Gabriel, 1909-.**     • 5.7552
The American printer, 1787–1825 [by] Rollo G. Silver. — Charlottesville: Published for the Bibliographical Society of the University of Virginia [by] the University Press of Virginia, [1967] xii, 189 p.: illus.; 27 cm. 1. Printing — History — United States. I. T.
Z208.S5    655.1/73     LC 67-22310

**Wroth, Lawrence C. (Lawrence Counselman), 1884-1970.**     5.7553
The colonial printer, by Lawrence C. Wroth. Portland, Me., The Southworth-Anthoensen press, 1938. xxiv, 368 p., 2 l. plates, facsims., diagr. 25 cm. In case. 'Second edition, revised and enlarged.' 'This edition of fifteen hundred copies ... was completed in May, 1938.' 'Works referred to in notes': p. [331]-347. 1. Printing — History — United States. 2. Book industries and trade — United States 3. Printing as a trade — United States. I. T.
Z208.W95 1938    655.173     LC 38-14676

**Cave, Roderick.**     5.7554
The private press / Roderick Cave. — 2nd ed., rev. and enl. — New York: R.R. Bowker, 1983. xvi, 389 p.: ill.; 29 cm. Includes index. 1. Private presses — History. I. T.
Z231.5.P7 C37 1983    686.2/09 19     LC 83-7163     ISBN 0835216950

**Painter, George Duncan, 1914-.**                            **5.7555**
William Caxton: a biography / by George D. Painter. 1st American ed. — New York: Putnam, 1977, c1976. xi, 227 p., [4] leaves of plates: ill.; 25 cm. Includes index. 1. Caxton, William, ca. 1422-1491. 2. Printers — England — Biography. 3. Printing — History — England. I. T.
Z232.C38 P33 1976      686.2/092/4 B      *LC* 76-41134      *ISBN* 0399118888

**Wheat, Carl I. (Carl Irving), 1892-1966.**                  **5.7556**
Mapping the Transmississippi West, 1540–1861. — San Francisco: Institute of Historical Cartography, 1957-1963. 5 v.: maps (part fold., part col.); 37 cm. Bibliocartography: v. 1, p. [185]-254. Vol. 1. printed by Edwin and Robert Grabhorn. 1. Cartography — The West. I. T.
Z 239 G7 A13 v.45      *LC* 57-59400

## Z240–242 Incunabula

**Goff, Frederick Richmond, 1916- ed.**                       • **5.7557**
Incunabula in American libraries; a third census of fifteenth–century books recorded in North American collections. Reproduced from the annotated copy maintained by Frederick R. Goff, compiler and editor. — Millwood, N.Y.: Kraus Reprint Co., 1973 [c1964] lxiii, 798 p.; 29 cm. Reprint of the ed. published by the Bibliographical Society of America, New York; annotated and corrected, with new introd. and list of dealers. 1. Incunabula — Bibliography — Union lists. 2. Catalogs, Union — United States. 3. Catalogs, Union — Canada. 4. Books — Prices 5. Antiquarian booksellers — Directories. I. T.
Z240.G58 1973      016.093      *LC* 72-10463

## Z243–265 Practical Printing. Style Manuals

**Kelber, Harry.**                                           **5.7558**
Union printers and controlled automation [by] Harry Kelber and Carl Schlesinger. — London: Collier-Macmillan; New York: Free Press, [c1967] xix, 299 p.: illus.; 24 cm. 1. International Typographical Union of North America. Union no. 6, New York. 2. Printing industry — New York (City) I. Schlesinger, Carl, joint author. II. T.
Z243.U6 N52      331.881/55      *LC* 67-19236

**Meggs, Philip B.**                                         **5.7559**
A history of graphic design / Philip B. Meggs. — New York: Van Nostrand Reinhold, c1983. 511 p.: ill.; 29 cm. Includes index. 1. Printing, Practical — History. 2. Graphic arts — History. I. T.
Z244.5.M42 1983      686.2/09 19      *LC* 82-2826      *ISBN* 0442262213

**Moran, James.**                                           **5.7560**
Printing presses; history and development from the fifteenth century to modern times. — Berkeley: University of California Press, [1973] 263 p.: illus.; 29 cm. 1. Printing-press — History. I. T.
Z249.M748 1973      *LC* 72-75519      *ISBN* 0520022459

**Updike, Daniel Berkeley, 1860-1941.**                      • **5.7561**
Printing types, their history, forms, and use: a study in survivals. — 3d ed. — Cambridge, Mass.: Belknap Press, 1962. 2 v.: ill., facsims.; 25 cm. 1. Type and type-founding 2. Printing — History 3. Printing — Specimens I. T.
Z250.A2 U6 1962      *LC* 62-5866

**Morison, Stanley, 1889-1967.**                             • **5.7562**
Four centuries of fine printing: one hundred and ninety–two facsimiles of pages from books printed at presses established between 1465 and 1924, / with an historical introduction by Stanley Morison.— New ed. [4th rev. (reset) ed.]— New York: Barnes & Noble, 1960. 254 p. (pp. 59-250 facsimilés); 23 cm. I. T.
Z250.M86 1960      655.24      *LC* 60-3397

**University of Chicago. Press.**                            • **5.7563**
The Chicago manual of style: for authors, editors, and copywriters. — 13th ed., rev. and expanded. — Chicago: University of Chicago Press, 1982. ix, 737 p.: ill.; 24 cm. Rev. ed. of: A manual of style. 12th ed., rev. c1969. Includes index. 1. Printing, Practical — Style manuals 2. Authorship — Handbooks, manuals, etc. I. T.
Z253.U69 1982      808/.02 19      *LC* 82-2832      *ISBN* 0226103900

**Von Ostermann, George F. (George Frederick), 1873-1952.**  • **5.7564**
Manual of foreign languages for the use of librarians, bibliographers, research workers, editors, translators, and printers, by Georg[e] F. von Ostermann. 4th ed., rev. and enl. New York, Central Book Co., 1952. 414 p. illus. 24 cm. First

published in 1934 as supplement to Style manual of the United States Government Printing Office under title: Foreign languages for the use of printers and translators. 1. Printing, Practical — Style manuals I. United States. Government Printing Office. Foreign languages for the use of printers and translators. II. T.
Z253.V94 1952      402/.02      *LC* 52-2409

## Z266–276 Bookbinding

**Comparato, Frank E.**                                      **5.7565**
Books for the millions: a history of the men whose methods and machines packaged the printed word [by] Frank E. Comparato. — Harrisburg, Pa.: Stackpole Co., [1971] ix, 374 p.: illus.; 25 cm. 1. Bookbinding machinery — History. 2. Bookbinders I. T.
Z269.C65      686.3/03/09      *LC* 71-162441      *ISBN* 0811702634

**Walters Art Gallery.**                                     • **5.7566**
The history of bookbinding, 525–1950 A.D.; an exhibition held at the Baltimore Museum of Art, November 12, 1957, to January 12, 1958, organized by the Walters Art Gallery and presented in cooperation with the Baltimore Museum of Art. Baltimore, The Trustees of the Walters Art Gallery, 1957. xi, 275 p. 106 plates. 28 cm. 'Catalogue': p. 1-267. 1. Bookbinding — Exhibitions. I. T.
Z269.W24      686.074 655.45074*      *LC* 58-1915

**Bookbinding in America: three essays / by Hellmut Lehmann–Haupt, editor.**   • **5.7567**
New York: R. R. Bowker, 1967. xix, 293 p., 30 leaves of plates: ill. Includes index. 1. Bookbinding — United States. 2. Books — Conservation and restoration I. Lehmann-Haupt, Hellmut, 1903- II. French, Hannah Dustin, 1907- III. Rogers, Joseph William, 1906-
Z270.U5 L4 1967      *LC* 67-13796

## Z278–550 Bookselling. Publishing

### Z278–285 GENERAL WORKS

**The Business of book publishing: papers by practitioners /**   **5.7568**
**edited by Elizabeth A. Geiser, Arnold Dolin with Gladys S.**
**Topkis.**
Boulder, Colo.: Westview Press, 1985. x, 446 p.: ill.; 24 cm. 1. Publishers and publishing 2. Book industries and trade I. Geiser, Elizabeth A. II. Dolin, Arnold. III. Topkis, Gladys S. IV. Title: Book publishing.
Z278.B96 1985      070.5 19      *LC* 84-13230      *ISBN* 0891589988

**Dessauer, John P.**                                        **5.7569**
Book publishing: what it is, what it does / John P. Dessauer. — 2nd ed. — New York: R.R. Bowker, 1981. xiii, 230 p.: ill.; 24 cm. Includes index. 1. Publishers and publishing I. T.
Z278.D47 1981      070.5 19      *LC* 81-10065      *ISBN* 0835213250

**The Future of the printed word: the impact and the implications**   **5.7570**
**of the new communications technology / edited by Philip Hills.**
Westport, Conn.: Greenwood Press, 1980. 172 p.: ill.; 22 cm. 1. Publishers and publishing — Technological innovations — Addresses, essays, lectures. 2. Printing — Addresses, essays, lectures. 3. Information networks — Addresses, essays, lectures. 4. Information storage and retrieval systems — Addresses, essays, lectures. 5. Micropublishing — Addresses, essays, lectures. 6. Communication — Addresses, essays, lectures. 7. Electronic publishing I. Hills, Philip James.
Z278.F87      070.5/028/54 19      *LC* 80-1716      *ISBN* 0313226938

**Taubert, Sigfred.**                                        **5.7571**
The book trade of the world; edited by Sigfred Taubert. — Hamburg: Verlag für Buchmarkt-Forschung; New York: R. R. Bowker, [1972-. v. : maps.; 23 cm. Vol. 3 published by K. G. Saur, Munchen. 1. Book industries and trade I. T.
Z278.T34      338.4/7/070573      *LC* 72-142165      *ISBN* 357806596X

**Directory of poetry publishers: 1985–86 / ed. by Len Fulton and**   **5.7572**
**Ellen Ferber.**
1st. ed. (1985-86)- . — [Paradise, Calif.]: Dustbooks, 1985. 218 p. Annual. 'More than 1,000 markets for poets.' 1. Poetry — Authorship — Handbooks, manuals, etc. 2. Publishers and publishing — Directories. 3. Poetry —

Publishing — Directories. 4. Poetry — Marketing — Directories. I. Fulton, Len. II. Ferber, Ellen, 1939-
Z282.D57    *LC* sn 86-38082

**Publishers international directory. Internationales**    **5.7573**
**Verlagsadressbuch.**
1-, 1964-. New York, R. R. Bowker Co., 1964-. v. 22-30 cm. Fourth-8th ed. issued in two parts. *Other editions available:* Internationales Verlagsaddressbuch 0074-9877 gw (DLC) 64047570 (OCoLC)1781897 1. Publishers and publishing — Directories. I. Saur, Klaus Gerhard, comp. II. International ISBN publishers' index.
Z282.P78    070.5/025    *LC* 79-649088

**Brownstone, David M.**    **5.7574**
The dictionary of publishing / David M. Brownstone, Irene M. Franck. — New York: Van Nostrand Reinhold, c1982. vii, 302 p.; 24 cm. 'A Hudson Group book.' 1. Publishers and publishing — Dictionaries. I. Franck, Irene M. II. Van Nostrand Reinhold Company. III. T. IV. Title: The V.N.R. dictionary of publishing.
Z282.5.B76 1982    070.5/03 19    *LC* 81-11676    *ISBN* 0442258747

**Bodian, Nat G., 1921-.**    **5.7575**
Book marketing handbook / Nat G. Bodian. — 1st ed. — New York: R.R. Bowker, 1980-< 1983 >. v. < 1-2 >: ill.; 27 cm. Vol. 2 lacks ed. statement. Includes indexes. 1. Book industries and trade — Handbooks, manuals, etc. 2. Advertising — Books — Handbooks, manuals, etc. I. T.
Z283.B58    070.5/2 19    *LC* 80-17504    *ISBN* 0835212866

**Henderson, Bill, 1941- comp.**    **5.7576**
The publish–it–yourself handbook; literary tradition & how–to without commercial or vanity publishers. — [1st ed.]. — Yonkers, N.Y.: Pushcart Book Press, [1973] 362 p.: illus.; 23 cm. 1. Self-publishing 2. Privately printed books I. T.
Z285.5.H45    658.8/09/07    *LC* 73-76940

## Z286 SPECIAL TOPICS, A–Z

**Computer publishers & publications.**    **5.7577**
1984 ed.-    . — New Rochelle, N.Y.: Communications Trends, Inc., c1984-. v.; 28 cm. Annual. *Other editions available:* Computer publishers & publications North American library edition 1. Computer science literature — Publishing — Directories. 2. Computers — Periodicals — Publishing — Directories. I. Communications Trends, Inc.
Z286.C65 C66    *LC* 84-645503

**Electronic publishing plus: media for a technological future /**    **5.7578**
**edited by Martin Greenberger.**
[Washington, D.C.]: Washington Program—Annenberg School of Communications; White Plains, N.Y.: Knowledge Industry Publications, c1985. xv, 365 p.: ill.; 24 cm. (Communications library.) 'The contributions were drawn largely from a closed forum sponsored by the Washington Program of the Annenberg Schools of Communication in May 1984'–P. xiv. 1. Electronic publishing — Addresses, essays, lectures. I. Greenberger, Martin, 1931- II. Series.
Z286.E43 E438 1985    070.5/028/54 19    *LC* 85-12613    *ISBN* 086729146X

**Allin, Janet.**    **5.7579**
Map sources directory / compiled by Janet Allin. — Toronto: Office of Library Coordination, Council of Ontario Universities, 1978. 175 p. in various pagings; 28 cm. Includes index. 1. Map industry and trade — Directories. I. T.
Z286.M3 A44    338.4/7686283/025 19    *LC* 81-470492    *ISBN* 0887990983

**Meckler, Alan M., 1945-.**    **5.7580**
Micropublishing: a history of scholarly micropublishing in America, 1938–1980 / Alan Marshall Meckler. — Westport, Conn.: Greenwood Press, 1982. xiv, 179 p.; 22 cm. — (Contributions in librarianship and information science. 0084-9243; no. 40) Includes index. 1. Micropublishing — United States — History. I. T. II. Series.
Z286.M5 M4 1982    070.5/795/0973 19    *LC* 81-6955    *ISBN* 031323096X

**Machlup, Fritz, 1902-.**    **5.7581**
Information through the printed word: the dissemination of scholarly, scientific, and intellectual knowledge / Fritz Machlup, Kenneth Leeson, and associates. — New York: Praeger Publishers, 1978. 3 v.; 25 cm. 1. Scholarly publishing — Collected works. 2. Book industries and trade — Collected works. 3. Scholarly periodicals — Collected works. 4. Libraries — Collected works. I. Leeson, Kenneth. joint author. II. T.
Z286.S37 M3    070.5 19    *LC* 78-19460    *ISBN* 0030474019

## Z287–550 SPECIAL WORKS, BY REGION OR COUNTRY

**Publishing in the Third World: knowledge and development /**    **5.7582**
**edited by Philip G. Altbach, Amadio A. Arboleda, S. Gopinathan.**
Portsmouth, N.H.; London: Mansell, Heineman, 1985. xii, 226 p.; 24 cm. Includes index. 1. Publishers and publishing — Developing countries 2. Book industries and trade — Developing countries I. Altbach, Philip G. II. Arboleda, Amadio Antonio. III. Gopinathan, Saravanan.
Z289.P82 1985    070.5/091724 19    *LC* 84-27920    *ISBN* 0435080067

### Z291–444 Europe

**Official publications of Western Europe / edited by Eve**    **5.7583**
**Johansson.**
London: Mansell; Bronx, N.Y.: Distributed in the United States and Canada by H.W. Wilson, 1984. xvi, 313 p.; 24 cm. 1. Libraries — Special collections — Government publications. 2. Acquisition of European publications 3. Europe — Government publications. 4. Europe — Government publications — Bibliography — Methodology. 5. Europe — Government publications — Library resources. I. Johansson, Eve.
Z291.O38 1984    011/.53 19    *LC* 83-22246    *ISBN* 0720116236

### Z471–479 United States

**Coser, Lewis A., 1913-.**    **5.7584**
Books: the culture and commerce of publishing / Lewis A. Coser, Charles Kadushin, Walter W. Powell. — New York: Basic Books, c1982. xiii, 411 p.; 25 cm. 1. Publishers and publishing — United States. 2. Book industries and trade — United States I. Kadushin, Charles. II. Powell, Walter W. III. T.
Z471.C69    070.5/0973 19    *LC* 81-66100    *ISBN* 0465007457

**Joyce, Donald F.**    **5.7585**
Gatekeepers of black culture: black–owned book publishing in the United States, 1817–1981 / Donald Franklin Joyce. — Westport, Conn.: Greenwood Press, 1983. xiv, 249 p.; 22 cm. — (Contributions in Afro-American and African studies. 0069-9624; no. 70) Includes indexes. 1. Publishers and publishing — United States. 2. Book industries and trade — United States 3. Afro-American business enterprises — United States. I. T. II. Series.
Z471.J69 1983    070.5/08996073 19    *LC* 82-9227    *ISBN* 0313233322

**Elson, Robert T.**    **5.7586**
Time Inc.; the intimate history of a publishing enterprise/ by Robert T. Elson. Edited by Duncan Norton–Taylor. New York, Atheneum, 1968-1986. 3 v. illus. 24 cm. V.3 by Curtis Prendergast with Geoffrey Colvin; edited by Robert Lubar. V.2-3 have title: The world of Time Inc. I. Norton-Taylor, Duncan. II. Prendergast, Curtis III. Colvin, Geoffrey IV. T. V. Title: The intimate history of a publishing enterprise. VI. Title: The world of Time Inc.
Z473.E48    070    *LC* 68-16868    *ISBN* 068910555X

**Lehmann-Haupt, Hellmut, 1903-.**    • **5.7587**
The book in America; a history of the making and selling of books in the United States, by Hellmut Lehmann–Haupt in collaboration with Lawrence C. Wroth and Rollo G. Silver. — 2d [rev. and enl. American] ed. — New York, Bowker, 1951. xiv, 493 p. 24 cm. First published in Leipzig in 1937 under title: Das amerikanische Buchwesen. 1. Printing — Hist. — U.S. 2. Booksellers and bookselling — U.S. 3. Publishers and publishing — U.S. 4. Libraries — U.S. 5. Book collectors — U.S. I. T.
Z473.L522 1951    655.473    *LC* 51-11308

**Madison, Charles Allan.**    **5.7588**
Jewish publishing in America: the impact of Jewish writing on American culture / Charles A. Madison. — New York: Hebrew Publishing Co., 1976. x, 294 p.: ill.; 24 cm. Includes index. 1. Jews — United States — Publishing — History. 2. Yiddish literature — United States — History and criticism. 3. Jewish periodicals — United States — History. 4. United States — Intellectual life I. T.
Z473.M214    071/.3    *LC* 76-21272    *ISBN* 0884829022

**Stern, Madeleine B., 1912-.**    **5.7589**
Books and book people in 19th–century America / by Madeleine B. Stern. — New York: Bowker, 1978. xii, 341 p.: ill.; 24 cm. 1. Publishers and publishing — United States — History — 19th century — Addresses, essays, lectures. 2. Book industries and trade — United States — History — 19th century — Addresses, essays, lectures. I. T.
Z473.S856    070.5/0973    *LC* 78-12197    *ISBN* 0835211096

**Tebbel, John William, 1912-.**                                    • 5.7590
A history of book publishing in the United States, by John Tebbel. New York, R. R. Bowker Co. [1972]-1981. 4 v. 26 cm. 1. Publishers and publishing — United States — History. I. T.
Z473.T42        070.5/0973        *LC* 71-163903        *ISBN* 0835204898

**American book trade directory.**                                  • 5.7591
1st ed. (1915) -        . — New York: R.R. Bowker, 1915-        . — Irregular. 1. Book industries — Directories. and trade — United States — Directories. 2. Book collectors — United States 3. Publishers and publishing — United States — Directories.
Z475.A5

**Publishers directory.**                                            5.7592
5th ed. (1984-85)-. Detroit, Mich.: Gale Research Co., c1984-. Issued in parts. Vols. for 1984-85— accompanied by supplement. 1. Publishers and publishing — United States — Directories 2. Publishers and publishing — Canada — Directories 3. Booksellers and bookselling — United States — Directories 4. Booksellers and bookselling — Canada — Directories I. Gale Research Company.
Z475 B672

**Publishers, distributors, & wholesalers of the United States.**    5.7593
3rd ed.-        . — New York: R.R. Bowker, c1981-. v.; 28 cm. Annual. 1. Publishers and publishing — United States — Directories. 2. Book industries and trade — United States — Directories. I. R.R. Bowker Company. Dept. of Bibliography. II. R.R. Bowker Company. Publications Systems Dept.
Z475.P86        070.5/025/73 19        *LC* 82-644990

**The Book publishing annual / by the Book Division, R.R.**          5.7594
**Bowker Company, in collaboration with the staff of Publishers weekly.**
1984 ed.-        . — New York: R.R. Bowker, 1984-. v.: ill.; 29 cm. Annual. 'Highlights, analyses & trends.' 1. Book industries and trade — United States — Yearbooks. 2. Publishers and publishing — United States — Yearbooks. I. R. R. Bowker Company. Book Division. II. Publishers weekly.
Z477.P96        *LC* 85-645245

**Davis, Kenneth C.**                                                5.7595
Two–bit culture: the paperbacking of America / Kenneth C. Davis. — Boston: Houghton Mifflin, 1984. xvi, 430 p.: ill.; 23 cm. Includes index. 1. Paperbacks — Publishing — United States. 2. Book industries and trade — United States 3. Books and reading — United States 4. Popular literature — United States. 5. Publishers and publishing — United States — History — 20th century. 6. United States — Popular culture I. T.
Z479.D38 1984        070.5/73/0973 19        *LC* 83-22767        *ISBN* 0395343984

**Nemeyer, Carol A., 1929-.**                                        • 5.7596
Scholarly reprint publishing in the United States / [by] Carol A. Nemeyer. — New York: R. R. Bowker Co., 1972. ix, 262 p.; 24 cm. 1. Scholarly publishing — United States. 2. Reprints (Publications) I. T.
Z479.N44        070.5/73        *LC* 74-163901        *ISBN* 0835204855

# Z657–659 Freedom of the Press. Censorship

(see also: KF4774-4775)

**Censorship and obscenity / edited by Rajeev Dhavan and**           5.7597
**Christie Davies.**
Totowa, N.J.: Rowman and Littlefield, 1978. x, 187 p.: ill.; 23 cm. On spine: Law in society. 1. Censorship 2. Obscenity (Law) I. Dhavan, Rajeev. II. Davies, Christie. III. Title: Law in society.
Z657.C43        363.3/1        *LC* 78-106033        *ISBN* 0847660540

**The first freedom today: critical issues relating to censorship**  5.7598
**and intellectual freedom / edited by Robert B. Downs and**
**Ralph E. McCoy.**
Chicago: American Library Association, 1984. xv, 341 p.; 26 cm. Rev. ed. of: The First freedom. 1960. Includes index. 1. Censorship — United States — Addresses, essays, lectures. 2. Freedom of information — United States — Addresses, essays, lectures. 3. Freedom of speech — United States — Addresses, essays, lectures. 4. Freedom of the press — United States — Addresses, essays, lectures. I. Downs, Robert Bingham, 1903- II. McCoy, Ralph E. (Ralph Edward), 1915- III. First freedom.
Z658.U5 F57 1984        323.44/5 19        *LC* 84-461        *ISBN* 0838904122

**Woods, L. B., 1938-.**                                             5.7599
A decade of censorship in America: the threat to classrooms and libraries, 1966–1975 / L. B. Woods. — Metuchen, N.J.: Scarecrow Press, 1979. xii, 183 p.: ill.; 23 cm. Includes index. 1. Censorship — United States. I. T.
Z658.U5 W66        098/.12/0973        *LC* 79-20960        *ISBN* 0810812606

**Busha, Charles H.**                                                5.7600
An intellectual freedom primer / Charles H. Busha, editor. — Littleton, Colo.: Libraries Unlimited, 1977. 221 p.; 24 cm. 1. Censorship — Addresses, essays, lectures. 2. Liberty — Addresses, essays, lectures. 3. Computers — Access control — Addresses, essays, lectures. I. T.
Z659.I57        323.44        *LC* 77-7887        *ISBN* 087287172X

# Z662–1000 LIBRARIES. LIBRARY SCIENCE

# Z665–674 General Works

**Butler, Pierce, 1886-1953.**                                       • 5.7601
An introduction to library science. With an introd. by Lester E. Asheim. — [Chicago] University of Chicago Press [1961, c1933] 118 p. 21 cm. — (Phoenix books, P59) 1. Library science I. T.
Z665.B98 1961        020        *LC* 63-6623

**Line, Maurice Bernard.**                                           5.7602
Library surveys: an introduction to the use, planning procedure, and presentation of surveys / Maurice B. Line. — 2nd ed. / revised by Sue Stone. — London: C. Bingley, 1982. 162 p.: ill.; 23 cm. Includes index. 1. Library surveys I. Stone, Sue. II. T.
Z665.L75 1982        027/.00723 19        *LC* 82-126316        *ISBN* 0851573460

**Purcell, Gary R.**                                                 5.7603
Reference sources in library and information services: a guide to the literature / Gary R. Purcell with Gail Ann Schlachter; foreword by Charles A. Bunge. — Santa Barbara, Calif.: ABC-Clio Information Services, c1984. xxvi, 359 p.; 24 cm. Includes indexes. 1. Reference books — Library science. 2. Reference books — Information science. 3. Library science — Bibliography 4. Information science — Bibliography I. Schlachter, Gail A. II. T.
Z666.P96 1984        011/.02 19        *LC* 83-19700        *ISBN* 0874363551

**Busha, Charles H.**                                                5.7604
Research methods in librarianship: techniques and interpretation / Charles H. Busha, Stephen P. Harter. — New York: Academic Press, 1980. xii, 417 p.: ill.; 24 cm. — (Library and information science) 1. Library science — Research — Handbooks, manuals, etc. I. Harter, Stephen P. joint author. II. T.
Z669.7.B87        020/.7/2        *LC* 79-8864        *ISBN* 0121475506

**Fang, Josephine R.**                                               5.7605
International guide to library, archival, and information science associations / Josephine Riss Fang and Alice H. Songe. — 2d ed. — New York: R. R. Bowker, 1980. xxv, 448 p.; 25 cm. Includes indexes. 1. Library science — Societies, etc — Directories. 2. Information science — Societies, etc. — Directories. 3. Archives — Societies, etc. — Directories. I. Songe, Alice H. joint author. II. T.
Z673.A1 F33 1980        020/.621 19        *LC* 80-21721        *ISBN* 0835212858

**American Library Association.**                                    5.7606
The A.L.A. yearbook: a review of library events, 1975. — 1976 centennial ed. 1976-. Chicago: American Library Association, 1976. 494 p.: ill. Annual. 'A review of library events.' 1. American Library Association. I. American Library Association. Yearbook. II. T.
Z673.A5 A14        020/.622/73        *LC* 76-647548

**Encyclopedia of information systems and services.**               5.7607
1st ed.-        . — Ann Arbor, Mich.: Edwards Bros., c1971-. 5 v.; 29 cm. Sixth ed. published in 2 v.: International volume; and: United States volume; 7th ed.- published in 3 v.: v. 1, United States listings, v. 2, International listings, v. 3, Indexes. Kept up to date by periodic supplements with title: New information systems and services. 1. Information services — Directories. 2. Information storage and retrieval systems — Directories. 3. Electronic publishing — Directories. 4. Data libraries — Directories. I. Gale Research Company. II. New information systems and services.
Z674.3.E53        025/.04/025 19        *LC* 84-648860

**Information America: sources of print and nonprint materials**   **5.7608**
available from organizations, industry, government agencies, and
specialized publishers—master volume / compiled by Tracy
Davis and Patricia A. Young.
New York: Neal-Schuman Publishers, c1985. vi, 815 p.; 29 cm. Includes
indexes. 1. Information services — United States — Directories. I. Davis,
Tracy. II. Young, Patricia A.
Z674.5.U5 I52 1985     020/.25/73 19     *LC* 85-2953     *ISBN*
0918212790

## Z675 Classes of Libraries

**Subject directory of special libraries and information centers.**   **5.7609**
1st ed.-     . — Detroit, Mich.: Gale Research Co., c1975-. v.; 29 cm.
Contents: v. 1. Business and law libraries — v. 2. Education and information
science libraries — v. 3. Health sciences libraries — v. 4. Social sciences and
humanities libraries — v. 5. Science and technology libraries. 1. Libraries,
Special — United States — Directories. 2. Libraries, Special — Canada —
Directories. 3. Information services — United States — Directories.
4. Information services — Canada — Directories. I. Directory of special
libraries and information centers.
Z675.A2 S83     026/.00025/73 19     *LC* 85-645199

**Mount, Ellis.**   **5.7610**
University science and engineering libraries / Ellis Mount. — 2nd ed. —
Westport, Conn.: Greenwood Press, 1985. x, 303 p.: ill.; 22 cm. (Contributions
in librarianship and information science. 0084-9243; no. 49) Includes index.
1. Libraries, University and college 2. Scientific libraries 3. Engineering
libraries I. T. II. Series.
Z675.U5 M68 1985     026/.5 19     *LC* 84-6530     *ISBN* 0313239495

## Z678–686 Library Administration

**Lancaster, F. Wilfrid (Frederick Wilfrid), 1933-.**   **5.7611**
The measurement and evaluation of library services / by F. W. Lancaster, with
the assistance of M. J. Joncich. — Washington: Information Resources Press,
c1977. xii, 395 p.: ill.; 24 cm. 1. Libraries — Evaluation I. T.
Z678.85.L36     025.1     *LC* 77-72081     *ISBN* 087815017X

**Matthews, Joseph R.**   **5.7612**
Directory of automated library systems / Joseph R. Matthews. — New York:
Neal-Schuman Publishers, c1985. viii, 217 p.; 28 cm. (Library automation
planning guide series; no. 2) Includes indexes. 1. Libraries — Automation —
Directories. 2. Library science — Computer programs — Directories.
3. Microcomputers — Library applications — Directories. 4. Information
storage and retrieval systems — Directories. I. T. II. Series.
Z678.9.A3 M38 1985     025/.04 19     *LC* 84-25490     *ISBN*
0918212820

**Saffady, William, 1944-.**   **5.7613**
Introduction to automation for librarians / William Saffady. — Chicago:
American Library Association, 1983. viii, 304 p.: ill.; 27 cm. 1. Libraries —
Automation 2. Library science — Data processing 3. Information storage and
retrieval systems I. T.
Z678.9.S25 1983     025/.0028/5 19     *LC* 83-7164     *ISBN* 083890386X

**Mason, Ellsworth.**   **5.7614**
Mason on library buildings / Ellsworth Mason. — Metuchen, N.J.: Scarecrow
Press, 1980. ix, 333 p.: ill.; 29 cm. 1. Library buildings 2. Library architecture
I. T. II. Title: On library buildings.
Z679.M22     022/.3     *LC* 80-12029     *ISBN* 0810812916

**Metcalf, Keyes DeWitt, 1889-.**   **5.7615**
Planning academic and research library buildings / Keyes D. Metcalf. — 2nd
ed. / Philip D. Leighton, David C. Weber, eds. — Chicago: American Library
Association, 1986. p. cm. v. Includes index. 1. Library planning 2. Library
buildings 3. Libraries, University and college 4. Research libraries
5. Libraries — Space utilization I. Leighton, Philip D. II. Weber, David C.,
1924- III. T.
Z679. M49 1986     022/.317 19     *LC* 85-11207     *ISBN* 0838933203

**Cohen, Aaron, 1935-.**   **5.7616**
Designing and space planning for libraries: a behavioral guide / Aaron Cohen,
Elaine Cohen. — New York: R. R. Bowker Co., 1979. 250 p.: ill.; 26 cm.
Includes index. 1. Library planning 2. Library architecture 3. Libraries —
Space utilization I. Cohen, Elaine, 1938- joint author. II. T.
Z679.5.C64     022/.3     *LC* 79-12478     *ISBN* 0835211509

**Friends of libraries sourcebook / edited by Sandy Dolnick.**   **5.7617**
Chicago: American Library Association, 1980. x, 165 p.: ill.; 23 cm. Includes
index. 1. Friends of the library — Handbooks, manuals, etc. I. Dolnick,
Sandy.
Z681.5.F78     021.7 19     *LC* 80-24643     *ISBN* 0838932452

**Financial planning for libraries / Murray S. Martin, editor.**   **5.7618**
New York: Haworth Press, c1983. 131 p.; 23 cm. Previously published in
Journal of library administration, v. 3, no. 3-4. 1. Library finance 2. Library
administration I. Martin, Murray S.
Z683.F49 1983     025.1/1 19     *LC* 82-23346     *ISBN* 0866561188

## Z687–715 The Collections

**American Library Association. Collection Development**   **5.7619**
**Committee.**
Guidelines for collection development / Collection Development Committee,
Resources and Technical Services Division, American Library Association;
David L. Perkins, editor. — Chicago: American Library Association, 1979. vi,
78 p.; 23 cm. 1. Collection development (Libraries) I. Perkins, David, 1939-
II. T.
Z687.A518 1979     025.2     *LC* 79-16971     *ISBN* 0838932312

**Collection development in libraries: a treatise / edited by**   **5.7620**
**Robert D. Stueart, George B. Miller, Jr.**
Greenwich, Conn.: Jai Press, c1980. 2 v. (xxiv, 602 p.); 24 cm. — (Foundations
in library and information science. v. 10) 1. Collection development (Libraries)
I. Stueart, Robert D. II. Miller, George Bertram, 1926- III. Series.
Z687.C64     025.2     *LC* 79-93165     *ISBN* 0892321067

**Broadus, Robert N.**   **5.7621**
Selecting materials for libraries / Robert N. Broadus. — 2nd ed. — New York:
H.W. Wilson Co., 1981. x, 469 p.; 24 cm. 1. Book selection I. T.
Z689.B86 1981     025.20 19     *LC* 81-650     *ISBN* 0824206592

**Katz, William A., 1924-.**   **5.7622**
Collection development: the selection of materials for libraries / William A.
Katz. — New York: Holt, Rinehart and Winston, c1980. xvi, 352 p.; 24 cm.
1. Collection development (Libraries) 2. Book selection 3. Selection of non-
book materials. I. T.
Z689.K32     025.2     *LC* 79-19861     *ISBN* 0030502667

**Selection of library materials in the humanities, social sciences**   **5.7623**
**and sciences / Patricia A. McClung, editor; section editors,**
**William Hepfer ... [et al.].**
Chicago: American Library Association, 1985. xiv, 405 p.; 24 cm. 1. Book
selection 2. Collection development (Libraries) 3. Acquistions (Libraries)
I. McClung, Patricia A.
Z689.S354 1985     025.2/1 19     *LC* 85-20084     *ISBN* 083893305X

**Saffady, William, 1944-.**   **5.7624**
Micrographics / William Saffady. — 2nd ed. — Littleton, Colo.: Libraries
Unlimited, 1985. xii, 254 p.: ill.; 25 cm. (Library science text series.)
1. Libraries — Special collections — Microforms 2. Micrographics — Library
applications 3. Library science — Technological innovations. I. T. II. Series.
Z692.M5 S24 1985     686.4/3 19     *LC* 84-28863     *ISBN* 0872874532

**Osborn, Andrew Delbridge, 1902-.**   **5.7625**
Serial publications, their place and treatment in libraries / Andrew D. Osborn.
— 3d ed. — Chicago: American Library Association, 1980. xxii, 486 p.: ill.; 25
cm. Includes index. 1. Periodicals 2. Serials control systems I. T.
Z692.S5 O8 1980     025.17/3     *LC* 80-11686     *ISBN* 0838902995

## Z693–698 Cataloging. Indexing.
### Classification

**Foundations of cataloging: a sourcebook / edited by Michael**   **5.7626**
**Carpenter and Elaine Svenonius.**
Littleton, Colo.: Libraries Unlimited, 1985. xii, 276 p.: ill.; 25 cm. 1. Cataloging
— Addresses, essays, lectures. I. Carpenter, Michael, 1940- II. Svenonius,
Elaine.
Z693.F68 1985     025.3/2 19     *LC* 85-10333     *ISBN* 0872875113

**Wynar, Bohdan S.**   **5.7627**
Introduction to cataloging and classification / Bohdan S. Wynar. — 7th ed. / by
Arlene G. Taylor. — Littleton, Colo.: Libraries Unlimited, 1985. xvi, 641 p.; 25

cm. — (Library science text series) 1. Anglo-American cataloguing rules. 2. Cataloging 3. Classification — Books I. Taylor, Arlene G., 1941- II. T.
Z693.W94 1985      025.3 19      *LC* 85-23147      *ISBN* 0872875121

**Anglo–American cataloguing rules / prepared by the American**      **5.7628**
**Library Association ... [et al.]; edited by Michael Gorman and**
**Paul W. Winkler.**
2d ed. — Chicago: ALA, 1978. xvii, 620 p.; 26 cm. Originally published (1967) in two versions under the following titles: Anglo-American cataloging rules. North American text; Anglo-American cataloguing rules. British text. 1. Descriptive cataloging — Rules I. Gorman, Michael, 1941- II. Winkler, Paul W. (Paul Walter) III. American Library Association.
Z694.A5 1978      025.3/2      *LC* 78-13789      *ISBN* 083893210X

**Foskett, A. C. (Antony Charles)**      **5.7629**
The subject approach to information / A.C. Foskett. — 4th ed. — London: C. Bingley; Hamden, Conn.: Linnet Books, 1982. xvii, 574 p.: ill.; 23 cm. 1. Subject cataloging 2. Indexing I. T.
Z695.F66 1982      025.4/7 19      *LC* 82-228016      *ISBN* 0208019340

**Library of Congress. Subject Cataloging Division.**      **5.7630**
Library of Congress subject headings / Subject Cataloging Division, Processing Services. — 10th ed. — Washington: Library of Congress, 1986. 2 v. (xxxi, 3543); 31 cm. Incorporates material through December 1984. 1. Subject headings I. T.
Z695.L695 1986      025.4/9 19      *LC* 85-600211      *ISBN* 0844405108

**Sears, Minnie Earl, 1873-1933.**      **5.7631**
Sears list of subject headings. — 13th ed. / edited by Carmen Rovira and Caroline Reyes. — New York: Wilson, 1986. p. cm. 1. Subject headings I. Rovira, Carmen. II. Reyes, Caroline. III. T. IV. Title: List of subject headings.
Z695.S43 1986      025.4/9 19      *LC* 86-7734      *ISBN* 0824207300

**Educational Research Information Center (U.S.)**      **5.7632**
Thesaurus of ERIC descriptors / James E. Houston, editor/lexicographer; introduction by Lynn Barnett. — 11th ed. — Phoenix, Ariz.: Oryx Press, 1987 [i.e. 1986] xxvi, 588 p.; 29 cm. 1. Subject headings — Education. I. Houston, James E. II. T.
Z695.1.E3 E34 1986      025.4/937 19      *LC* 86-42555      *ISBN* 0897741595

**Thesaurus of psychological index terms.**      **5.7633**
4th ed. — Washington, D.C.: American Psychological Association, c1985. v, 263 p.; 29 cm. 1. Subject headings — Psychology. I. American Psychological Association.
Z695.1.P7 T48 1985      025.4/915 19      *LC* 85-169784

**American Library Association. Filing Committee.**      **5.7634**
ALA filing rules / Filing Committee, Resources and Technical Services Division, American Library Association. — Chicago: American Library Association, 1980. ix, 50 p.; 23 cm. 'Successor to A.L.A. rules for filing catalog cards (1942) and ALA rules for filing catalog cards, second edition (1968).' Includes index. 1. Library filing rules I. T.
Z695.95.A52 1980      025.3/17 19      *LC* 80-22186      *ISBN* 083893255X

**Dewey, Melvil, 1851-1931.**      **5.7635**
[Decimal classification and relativ index] Dewey decimal classification and relative index / devised by Melvil Dewey. — Ed. 19 / edited under the direction of Benjamin A. Custer. — Albany: Forest Press, 1979. 3 v.; 25 cm. First published anonymously in 1876 under title: A classification and subject index. 2d ed. published under title: Decimal classification and relativ index. 1. Classification, Dewey decimal I. Custer, Benjamin Allen, 1912- II. T.
Z696.D519 1979      025.4/31 19      *LC* 77-27967      0910608199

**Sayers, W. C. Berwick (William Charles Berwick), 1881-1960.**      **5.7636**
[Manual of classification for librarians and bibliographers] Sayers' Manual of classification for librarians. — 5th ed. / [revised by] Arthur Maltby. — London: Deutsch, 1975. 336 p., plate: port.; 23 cm. (A Grafton book) Originally published in 1926 under title: A manual of classification for librarians and bibliographers. 1. Classification — Books I. Maltby, Arthur. II. T. III. Title: Manual of classification for librarians.
Z696.S2925 1975      025.4      *LC* 75-317605      *ISBN* 023396603X

**United States. Library of Congress. Subject Cataloging Division.**      **5.7637**
[Schedules] Washington, D.C.: Cataloguing Distribution Service, 19-. v.; cm. 1. Classification, Library of Congress. I. T.
Z696.U5x

## Z699 MACHINE METHODS OF INFORMATION STORAGE AND RETRIEVAL

**Annual review of information science and technology.**      **5.7638**
v. 1- 1966-. [Washington, etc.] American Society for Information Science [etc.] v. 24 cm. Annual. 1. Information science — Collections. 2. Information storage and retrieval systems — Collections. 3. Libraries — Automation — Collections. I. Cuadra, Carlos A., ed. II. American Society for Information Science. III. American Documentation Institute.
Z699.A1 A65      029.708      *LC* 66-25096

**Fenichel, Carol H.**      **5.7639**
Online searching: a primer / by Carol H. Fenichel, Thomas H. Hogan. — 2nd. ed. — Marlton, N.J.: Learned Information, 1984. 188 p.: ill.; 22 cm. Includes index. 1. On-line bibliographic searching 2. Information retrieval I. Hogan, Thomas H. II. T.
Z699.F38 1984      025.5/24 19

**Key papers in information science / edited by Belver C. Griffith.**      **5.7640**
White Plains, N.Y.: Published for the American Society for Information Science by Knowledge Industry Publications, c1980. viii, 439 p.: ill.; 24 cm. 1. Information science — Addresses, essays, lectures. I. Griffith, Belver C. II. American Society for Information Science.
Z699.K422      029      *LC* 79-24288      *ISBN* 0914236504

**Computer–readable databases: a directory and data sourcebook /**      **5.7641**
**Martha E. Williams, editor–in–chief; Laurence Lannom,**
**managing editor; Carolyn G. Robins, data acquisitions editor.**
Chicago: American Library Association, 1985. 2 v.; 28 cm. 1. Information storage and retrieval systems — Directories. 2. Machine-readable bibliographic data — Directories. I. Williams, Martha E. II. Lannom, Laurence. III. Robins, Carolyn G. IV. Title: Computer-readable data bases.
Z699.22.C66 1985      025.3/028/54 19      *LC* 84-18577      *ISBN* 0838904157

**Directory of online databases.**      **5.7642**
Vol. 1, no. 1 (fall 1979)-      . — Santa Monica, Calif.: Cuadra Associates, c1979-. v.; 22-28 cm. Quarterly. Published jointly by: Cuadra Associates and Elsevier Science Publishing, 1986- Two issues yearly are directory issues and two are updates; each directory issue supersedes previous directory issue and update. 1. Information storage and retrieval systems — Directories.
Z699.22.D56      025/.04/025 19      *LC* 85-648743

**Directory of periodicals online: indexed, abstracted & full–text**      **5.7643**
**/ edited by Catherine Chung.**
Washington: Federal Document Retrieval, 1985. 524 p. 1. On-line bibliographic searching — Directories. 2. Information storage and retrieval systems — Periodicals — Directories. 3. Periodicals, On-line — Directories. 4. Newspapers, On-line — Directories. I. Chung, Catherine II. Federal Document Retrieval, Inc. III. Title: Periodicals online
Z699.5P43 D56 1985

**Powell, Ronald R.**      **5.7644**
Basic research methods for librarians / Ronald R. Powell. — Norwood, N.J.: Ablex Pub. Corp., c1985. x, 188 p.: ill.; 24 cm. (Libraries and information science series.) 1. Library science — Research — Methodology. I. T. II. Series.
Z669.7.P68 1985      020/.72 19      *LC* 84-28401      *ISBN* 0893911542

## Z700–703 CONSERVATION. STORAGE

**Cunha, George Daniel Martin.**      • **5.7645**
Conservation of library materials; a manual and bibliography on the care, repair, and restoration of library materials, by George Martin Cunha and Dorothy Grant Cunha. 2d ed. Metuchen, N.J., Scarecrow Press, 1971-72. 2 v. illus. 22 cm. 1. Library materials — Conservation and restoration. 2. Library materials — Conservation and restoration — Bibliography. I. Cunha, Dorothy Grant. joint author. II. T.
Z701.C782      025.7 19      *LC* 77-163871      *ISBN* 0810804271

**Cunha, George Daniel Martin.**      **5.7646**
Library and archives conservation: 1980s and beyond / George Martin Cunha and Dorothy Grant Cunha; assisted by Suzanne Elizabeth Henderson. — Metuchen, N.J.: Scarecrow Press, 1983. 2 v.: ill.; 23 cm. Vol. 2 has title: Bibliography. 'A supplement to ... the bibliography in Conservation of library materials'—Vol. 2, introd. Includes indexes. 1. Library materials — Conservation and restoration. 2. Archival materials — Conservation and restoration. I. Cunha, Dorothy Grant. II. Henderson, Suzanne Elizabeth. III. T.
Z701.C784 1983      025.7 19      *LC* 82-10806      *ISBN* 0810815877

**The Library preservation program: models, priorities,**    **5.7647**
**possibilities: proceedings of a conference, April 29, 1983,**
**Washington, D.C. / [sponsored by] Resources and Technical**
**Services Division, American Library Association with the**
**cooperation of the Library of Congress, National Preservation**
**Program; edited by Jan Merrill–Oldham and Merrily Smith.**
Chicago: ALA, 1985. vii, 117 p.: ill.; 23 cm. 1. Library materials —
Conservation and restoration — Congresses. 2. Books — Conservation and
restoration — Congresses. 3. Library administration — Congresses.
4. Libraries, University and college — United States — Administration —
Congresses. I. Merrill-Oldham, Jan, 1947- II. Smith, Merrily A.
III. American Library Association. Resources and Technical Services
Division. IV. Library of Congress. National Preservation Program Office.
Z701.L55 1985      025.7 19      *LC* 84-28270      *ISBN* 0838933157

## Z710–716.3 REFERENCE. CIRCULATION. PUBLIC RELATIONS

**Beaubien, Anne K.**      **5.7648**
Learning the library: concepts and methods for effective bibliographic
instruction / Anne K. Beaubien, Sharon A. Hogan, Mary W. George. — New
York: Bowker, 1982. x, 269 p.; 24 cm. Includes index. 1. Library orientation —
Handbooks, manuals, etc. 2. Searching, Bibliographical — Handbooks,
manuals, etc. I. Hogan, Sharon A. II. George, Mary W., 1948- III. T.
Z710.B37 1982      025.5/6 19      *LC* 82-4262      *ISBN* 0835215059

**Katz, William A., 1924-.**      **5.7649**
Introduction to reference work / William A. Katz. — 4th ed. — New York:
McGraw-Hill, c1982-. v. < 1 >; 24 cm. — (McGraw-Hill series in library
education.) 1. Reference services (Libraries) 2. Reference books I. T.
II. Series.
Z711.K32 1982      025.5/2 19      *LC* 81-12432      *ISBN* 0070333335

**Katz, William A., 1924-.**      **5.7650**
Reference and online services handbook: guidelines, policies, and procedures
for libraries / edited by Bill Katz and Anne Clifford. — New York: Neal-
Schuman, c1982-1986. 2 v.; 24 cm. Includes index. Vol. 2 edited by Bill Katz.
1. Reference services (Libraries) — United States — Handbooks, manuals, etc.
2. On-line bibliographic searching — Handbooks, manuals, etc. I. Clifford,
Anne (Anne Marie) II. T.
Z711.K33 1982      025.5/2 19      *LC* 81-11290      *ISBN* 0918212499

**American Library Association. Commission on Freedom and**    **5.7651**
**Equality of Access to Information.**
Freedom and equality of access to information: a report to the American
Library Association / Commission on Freedom and Equality of Access to
Information; Dan M. Lacy, chair. — Chicago: ALA, 1986. xx, 124 p.; 23 cm.
Includes index. 1. Libraries and readers 2. Freedom of information
3. Information services and state — United States. 4. Government information
— United States. I. Lacy, Dan Mabry, 1914- II. T.
Z711.4.A57 1986      025.5/23 19      *LC* 86-3655      *ISBN* 0838933327

**Geller, Evelyn.**      **5.7652**
Forbidden books in American public libraries, 1876–1939: a study in cultural
change / Evelyn Geller. — Westport, Conn.: Greenwood Press, 1984. xxi,
234 p.; 24 cm. — (Contributions in librarianship and information science.
0084-9243; no. 46) Includes index. 1. Public libraries — United States —
Censorship — History. 2. Censorship — United States — History. 3. Library
science — United States — History. 4. Books and reading — United States —
History. 5. Freedom of information — United States — History. I. T.
II. Series.
Z711.4.G44 1984      025.2/1874/0973 19      *LC* 83-12566      *ISBN*
0313238081

**Intellectual freedom manual / compiled by the Office for**    **5.7653**
**Intellectual Freedom of the American Library Association.**
2nd ed. — Chicago: The Association, 1983. xxx, 210 p.; 23 cm. 1. Libraries —
Censorship — Handbooks, manuals, etc. 2. Censorship — Handbooks, manuals,
manuals, etc. 3. Freedom of information — Handbooks, manuals, etc.
I. American Library Association. Office for Intellectual Freedom.
II. American Library Association.
Z711.4.I57 1983      025.2/13 19      *LC* 83-9958      *ISBN* 0838932835

**Morris, Leslie R.**      **5.7654**
Interlibrary loan policies directory / Leslie R. Morris and Patsy Fowler
Brautigam. — 2nd ed. — Chicago: American Library Association, 1984. iv,
448 p.; 21 x 26 cm. Rev. ed. of: Interlibrary loan policies directory / Sarah
Katharine Thomson. 1975. Includes index. 1. Inter-library loans — United
States 2. Libraries — United States — Directories. I. Brautigam, Patsy
Fowler. II. Thomson, Sarah Katharine, 1928- Interlibrary loan policies
directory. III. American Library Association. IV. T.
Z713.5.U6 M67 1984      025.6/2 19      *LC* 83-11897      *ISBN*
0838903932

**Edsall, Marian S.**      **5.7655**
Library promotion handbook / by Marian S. Edsall. — Phoenix, AZ: Oryx
Press, 1980. 244 p.: ill.; 28 cm. — (A Neal-Schuman professional book)
Includes index. 1. Public relations — Libraries — Handbooks, manuals, etc.
I. T.
Z716.3.E3      021.7      *LC* 79-26984      *ISBN* 0912700157

## Z719–880 Directories. History. Statistics

**Jackson, Sidney L. (Sidney Louis), 1914-1979.**      **5.7656**
Libraries and librarianship in the West: a brief history [by] Sidney L. Jackson.
— New York: McGraw-Hill, [1974] xiv, 489 p.: illus.; 23 cm. — (McGraw-Hill
series in library education) 1. Libraries — History 2. Library science —
History. I. T.
Z721.J245      021/.009      *LC* 73-13619      *ISBN* 0070321183

**Steele, Colin.**      **5.7657**
Major libraries of the world: a selective guide / Colin Steele. — London; New
York: Bowker, c1976. xix, 479 p.: ill.; 24 cm. 1. Libraries — Directories. I. T.
Z721.S82 1976      021/.0025      *LC* 77-369002      *ISBN* 0859350126

**World guide to libraries = Internationales Bibliotheks–**    **5.7658**
**Handbuch.**
7th ed. — München: K.G. Saur, 1986. xxxiii, 1203 p. — (Handbook of
international documentation and information = Handbuch der internationalen
Dokumentation und Information; v. 8) Includes index. English and German.
1. Libraries — Directories. I. Title: Internationales Bibliotheks-Handbuch.
Z721.W7 1986      *ISBN* 3598205317

**The Bowker annual of library and book trade information.**    • **5.7659**
1955/56-. New York, R. R. Bowker. v. Annual. 1. Book industries and trade
— United States — Yearbooks 2. Libraries — United States — Yearbooks
I. R. R. Bowker Company, New York II. Council of National Library
Associations. III. Library journal. IV. Title: American library annual.
V. Title: American library & book trade annual.
Z731.A47      *LC* 55-12434 rev

**American library directory; a classified list of libraries in the**    • **5.7660**
**United States and Canada, with personnel and statistical data.**
1923-. New York, R.R. Bowker. v. 27-29 cm. Annual. Subtitle varies slightly.
Vols. for 1951- called 19th- ed. Directory for 1927 accompanied by
supplementary volume 'comprising subject index to special collections in
American libraries and greater libraries overseas, subject index to library
literature recorded in 1927.' 1. Libraries — Directories. 2. Libraries — United
States — Directories. 3. Libraries — Canada — Directories. I. R.R. Bowker
Company. II. Jaques Cattell Press.
Z731.A53      021/.0025/73      *LC* 23-3581

**Ash, Lee.**      **5.7661**
Subject collections: a guide to special book collections and subject emphases as
reported by university, college, public, and special libraries and museums in the
United States and Canada / compiled by Lee Ash and William G. Miller, with
the collaboration of Barbara J. McQuitty. — 6th ed., rev. and enl. — New York:
R.R. Bowker Co., 1985. 2 v. (x, 2196 p.); 30 cm. 1. Library resources — United
States — Directories. 2. Library resources — Canada — Directories. I. Miller,
William G. (William Gerald) II. McQuitty, Barbara J. III. T.
Z731.A78 1985      026/.00025/7 19      *LC* 85-126315      *ISBN*
0835219178

**Directory of special libraries and information centers.**      **5.7662**
1st ed.- . — Detroit, Mich.: Gale Research Co., c1963-. v.; 29 cm. Each
volume separately titled: v. 1, Directory of special libraries and information
centers in the United States and Canada, 2nd-7th; Descriptive listings, 8th ed-
; v. 2, Geographic and personnel indexes, 2nd- < 8th ed. > Second
ed.- < 8th ed. > issued in 3 vols. Volume 1 of each ed. kept up to date by periodic
supplement: designated as v. 3, with title: New special libraries. 1. Libraries,
Special — United States — Directories. 2. Libraries, Special — Canada —
Directories. 3. Information services — United States — Directories.
4. Information services — Canada — Directories. I. New special libraries.
Z731.D56      026/.00025/73 19      *LC* 84-640165

**Garrison, Dee.**      **5.7663**
Apostles of culture: the public librarian and American society, 1876–1920 / by
Dee Garrison. — New York: Free Press, c1979. xvi, 319 p.; 25 cm. 1. Public
libraries — United States — History. 2. Libraries and society — United States.
I. T.
Z 731 G24 1979      *LC* 78-66979      *ISBN* 0026938502

**Williams, Sam P.**        **5.7664**
Guide to the research collections of the New York Public Library / compiled by Sam P. Williams under the direction of William Vernon Jackson and James W. Henderson, with the editorial assistance of Harvey Simmonds, Rowe Portis, and William L. Coakley. — Chicago: American Library Association, 1975. xxxi, 336 p.; 27 cm. Replaces A guide to the reference collections of the New York Public Library, compiled by Karl Brown. Includes index. 1. New York Public Library. 2. Library resources — New York (N.Y.) I. New York Public Library. A guide to the reference collections of the New York Public Library. II. T.
Z733.N6 W54    027.4/747/1    *LC* 75-15878    *ISBN* 0838901255

**Downs, Robert Bingham, 1903-.**        **5.7665**
British and Irish library resources: a bibliographical guide / Robert B. Downs, assisted by Elizabeth C. Downs. — London: Mansell; Bronx, N.Y.: Distributed in the U.S. and Canada by H.W. Wilson, 1981. xiv, 427 p.; 29 cm. Rev. and updated ed. of: British library resources. 1973. Includes indexes. 1. Library resources — British Isles — Catalogs — Bibliography. 2. Manuscripts — British Isles — Catalogs — Bibliography. 3. Bibliography — Bibliography I. Downs, Elizabeth C. (Elizabeth Crooks) II. Downs, Robert Bingham, 1903- British library resources. III. T.
Z791.A1 D68 1981    016.0252/07 19    *LC* 82-210249    *ISBN* 072011604X

# Z881–981 Library Catalogs

**National union catalog / compiled by the Library of Congress**     • **5.7666**
**with the cooperation of the Committee on Resources of American Libraries of the American Library Association.**
1956-    . — New York: Roman and Littlefield, 1963-. v.; 28 cm. (Library of Congress catalogs.) Monthly. First quinquennial cumulation covers 1958-62; the entries for 1956-57 were combined with the 1953-55 annual vols. of the Library of Congress catalog ... —Books: authors in a cumulation published in 1958 by J. W. Edwards, Ann Arbor, Mich. 1. Catalogs, Union — United States — Periodicals. I. Library of Congress. Catalog Publication Division. II. Library of Congress. Catalog Publication Division. III. Series.
Z881.A1 U372    *LC* 56-60041

**The National union catalog, pre–1956 imprints; a cumulative**    • **5.7667**
**author list representing Library of Congress printed cards and titles reported by other American libraries. Compiled and edited with the cooperation of the Library of Congress and the National Union Catalog Subcommittee of the Resources Committee of the Resources and Technical Services Division, American Library Association.**
London, Mansell, 1968-1981. 754 v. 36 cm. Vols. 686-754 comprise a supplement. 1. Catalogs, Union — United States. I. Library of Congress. II. American Library Association. Committee on Resources of American Libraries. National Union Catalog Subcommittee.
Z881.A1 U518    021.6/4    *LC* 67-30001

**Library of Congress.**        **5.7668**
Library of Congress catalog. Books: subjects; a cumulative list of works represented by Library of Congress printed cards. 1950-1974. Washington, Library of Congress. 100 v. 29 cm. Quarterly. 1. Catalogs, Subject I. T.
Z881.U49 A22    *LC* 50-60682

**Library of Congress.**        **5.7669**
Monographic series / [compiled and edited by the Catalog Publication Division, Library of Congress]. — -1982. Washington: The Library, -1983. v.; 27 cm. (Library of Congress catalogs.) Quarterly. Began with Jan./Mar. 1974. Description based on: Vol. 1, A-Czech (1975). 1. Children's literature in series — Catalogs. 2. Monographic series — Bibliography — Catalogs. I. Library of Congress. Catalog Publication Division. II. T. III. Series.
Z881.U49 U54a    *LC* 74-652501

**British Library.**        **5.7670**
The British Library general catalogue of printed books to 1975. — London: C. Bingley; London; New York: K.G. Saur, 1979-1987. 360 v.; 31 cm. On spine: BLC to 1975. Vols. 76-360 have imprint: London; New York: K.G. Saur. Includes England, subheadings index and England, titles index. 1. British Library. Dept. of Printed Books — Catalogs. I. T. II. Title: General catalogue of printed books to 1975. III. Title: BLC to 1975.
Z921.L553 B74 1979    018/.1 19    *LC* 79-40543    *ISBN* 085157520X

# Z987–997 Book Collecting

**Aungerville, Richard, known as Richard de Bury, Bp. of**    • **5.7671**
**Durham, 1287-1345.**
Philobiblon / the text and translation of E.C. Thomas / edited with a foreword by Michael Maclaglan. — Oxford: Published for the Shakespeare Head Press by B. Blackwell, [1960] lxxxiii, 191 p. English and Latin. Limited edition. 1. Book collecting I. Thomas, Ernest Chester, 1850-1892. II. T.
Z992.A91 1960    *LC* 61-66174

**Jackson, Holbrook, 1874-1948.**    • **5.7672**
The anatomy of bibliomania. — New York: Farrar, Straus, [1950] 668 p. 1. Bibliomania 2. Books. 3. Books and reading I. T.
Z992.J162    *LC* 50-7626

# Z998–1000 Booksellers' Catalogs. Book Prices

**American book–prices current: a record of literary properties**    • **5.7673**
**sold at auction in the United States.**
v.1-    ; 1894/95-. New York: R. R. Bowker Co. v. Annual. Subtitle varies. Imprint varies. Editors vary. 1. Books — Prices 2. Manuscripts — Prices 3. Autographs — Prices 4. Bibliography — Rare books.
Z1000.A51

**Bookman's price index.**        **5.7674**
Vol. 1 (1964)- . — Detroit, Mi.: Gale Research Co., c1964-. v.; 29 cm. Annual. 'An annual guide to the values of rare and other out-of-print books and sets of periodicals.' (varies) 1. Books — Prices — Periodicals. 2. Periodicals — Prices — Periodicals. 3. Catalogs, Booksellers' — Indexes. I. Gale Research Company.
Z1000.B74    018    *LC* 64-8723

**Guide to reprints.**        **5.7675**
1967-. [Washington] Microcard Editions. 28 cm. Annual. 1. Bibliography — Editions 2. Out-of-print books I. Diaz, Albert James. ed.
Z1000.5.G8    011    *LC* 66-29279

# Z1001–1121 General Bibliography

**Bowers, Fredson Thayer.**    • **5.7676**
Principles of bibliographical description. New York: Russell, 1962, c1949. 505 p.: ill. 1. Bibliography — Methodology I. T.
Z1001.B78 1962    010.1    *LC* 62-13826    *ISBN* 0846201305

**Esdaile, Arundell James Kennedy, 1880-1956.**    **5.7677**
[Manual of bibliography] Esdaile's Manual of bibliography / Roy Stokes. — 5th rev. ed. — London: Allen & Unwin, 1967 [i.e. 1968] 336 p.: plates, ill., facsims.; 23 cm. 1. Bibliography 2. Library science I. Stokes, Roy Bishop, 1915- II. T. III. Title: Manual of bibliography.
Z1001.E75    010/.7 19    *LC* 81-9088    *ISBN* 0810814625

**Krummel, Donald William, 1929-.**    **5.7678**
Bibliographies, their aims and methods / D.W. Krummel. — London; New York: Mansell; Bronx, New York, U.S.A.: Distributed in the U.S. and Canada by H.W. Wilson Co., 1984. x, 192 p.; 23 cm. 1. Bibliography 2. Bibliography — Methodology 3. Bibliography — Bibliography I. T.
Z1001.K86 1984    011/.44 19    *LC* 83-22177    *ISBN* 0720116872

**Library of Congress. General Reference and Bibliography**    • **5.7679**
**Division.**
Current national bibliographies, compiled by Helen F. Conover. Washington, 1955. v, 132 p. 27 cm. 1. Bibliography, National — Bibliography. 2. Bibliography — Bibliography I. Conover, Helen Field. II. T.
Z1002.A2 U52    016.01    *LC* 55-60025

**Besterman, Theodore.**                                        • 5.7680
A world bibliography of bibliographies and of bibliographical catalogues,
calendars, abstracts, digests, indexes, and the like. — 4th ed. rev. and greatly
enl. throughout. — Lausanne: Societas bibliographica, [1965-66] 5 v. (8425
columns); 28 cm. Vol. 5: Index. 1. Bibliography — Bibliography I. T.
Z1002.B5635     016.01     LC 71-7401

**Bibliographic index: a cumulative bibliography of bibliographies.**     • 5.7681
v. 1 (1937/42)- . — New York: H.W. Wilson, [1942?]-. v. 27 cm. Cumulated
from quarterly numbers and annual cumulations, the annual being the last
quarterly issue. 1. Bibliography — Bibliography — Periodicals I. H.W.
Wilson Company.
Z1002.B595     016.016     LC 46-41034 rev*

**Downs, Robert Bingham, 1903-.**                               • 5.7682
American library resources: a bibliographical guide / Robert B. Downs. —
Chicago: American Library Association, 1951. 428 p. 'Sponsored by the
American Library Association Board on Resources of American Libraries'.
Classified and annotated. Includes index. 1. Library resources — United States
— Bibliography. 2. Bibliography — Bibliography I. American Library
Association. Board on Resources of American Libraries. II. T.
Z1002.D6     LC 51-11156

**Downs, Robert Bingham, 1903-.**                               • 5.7683
Bibliography; current state and future trends, edited by Robert B. Downs and
Frances B. Jenkins. Urbana, University of Illinois Press, 1967. vii, 611 p. 24 cm.
(Illinois contributions to librarianship, no. 8) 'Appeared originally in the
Janaury and April 1967 issues of Library trends.' 1. Bibliography —
Bibliography I. Jenkins, Frances B. (Frances Briggs), 1905- joint author. II. T.
III. Series.
Z1002.D62     016.016     LC 67-21851

**Gray, Richard A.**                                            • 5.7684
Serial bibliographies in the humanities and social sciences. Compiled by
Richard A. Gray. With the assistance of Dorothy Villmow. — Ann Arbor,
Mich.: Pierian Press, 1969. xxiv, 345 p.; 27 cm. 1. Bibliography —
Bibliography — Periodicals. I. T.
Z1002.G814     016.01605     LC 68-58895

**Hackman, Martha L., 1912-.**                                  5.7685
The practical bibliographer [by] Martha L. Hackman. Englewood Cliffs, N.J.,
Prentice-Hall [1970] x, 118 p. illus. 24 cm. 1. Bibliography — Bibliography
2. Bibliography — Methodology I. T.
Z1002.H2     010     LC 73-102281     ISBN 0136874592


# Z1003 Books and Reading

**Altick, Richard Daniel, 1915-.**                              5.7686
English common reader: a social history of the mass reading public, 1800-1900.
— Chicago: U. of Chicago P., 1957. 430 p. Apprendices (p.379-396) 1. Books
and reading. 2. Publishers and publishing — Great Britain. 3. English
literature — History and criticism. I. T.
Z1003.A57     028.9     LC 57-6975

**Hart, James David, 1911-.**                                   • 5.7687
The popular book; a history of America's literary taste. — New York: Oxford
University Press, 1950. 351 p.; 24 cm. 1. Books and reading — United States
2. United States — Intellectual life I. T.
Z1003.H328     028     LC 50-9417

**Karetzky, Stephen, 1946-.**                                   5.7688
Reading research and librarianship: a history and analysis / Stephen Karetzky.
— Westport, Conn.: Greenwood Press, 1982. xxi, 385 p.; 24 cm. —
(Contributions in librarianship and information science. no. 36 0084-9243)
Includes index. 1. Books and reading — Research — United States — History.
2. Readership surveys — United States — History. 3. Library science —
Research — United States — History. I. T. II. Series.
Z1003.2.K37 1982     028/.9 19     LC 80-1715     ISBN 0313222266

**Norvell, George Whitefield, 1885-1970.**                      5.7689
The reading interests of young people. — [Rev. ed. — East Lansing]: Michigan
State University Press, 1974 c1973. viii, 516 p.; 25 cm. 1. Youth — United
States — Books and reading. 2. Reading interests — United States. 3. Reading
(Secondary education) I. T.
Z1003.2.N67 1973     028.5     LC 73-75997     ISBN 087013177X

**Davis, Richard Beale.**                                       5.7690
A colonial Southern bookshelf: reading in the eighteenth century / Richard
Beale Davis. — Athens: University of Georgia Press, c1979. x, 140 p.; 23 cm.
(Mercer University Lamar memorial lectures; no. 21) Includes index. 1. Books

and reading — Southern States — History — 18th century. 2. Southern States
— Intellectual life — Colonial period, ca. 1600-1775 I. T.
Z1003.3.S85 D38     028/.9     LC 78-3832     ISBN 0820304506

**Mehnert, Klaus, 1906-.**                                      5.7691
The Russians & their favorite books / Klaus Mehnert. — Stanford, Calif.:
Hoover Institution Press, Stanford University, c1983. xv, 280 p.; 25 cm.
1. Books and reading — Soviet Union. 2. Popular literature — Soviet Union.
3. Russian fiction — 20th century — Stories, plots, etc. 4. Authors, Russian —
20th century — Biography. I. T. II. Title: Russians and their favorite books.
Z1003.5.S62 M43 1983     028/.9/0947 19     LC 83-6108     ISBN
0817978216


# Z1006–1010 Dictionaries. Bibliographies

**ALA world encyclopedia of library and information services /**     5.7692
**[Robert Wedgeworth, editor].**
2nd ed. — Chicago: American Library Association, 1986. p. cm. 1. Library
science — Dictionaries 2. Information science — Dictionaries.
I. Wedgeworth, Robert. II. American Library Association.
Z1006.A18 1986     020/.3 19     LC 86-10894     ISBN 0838904270

**The ALA glossary of library and information science / Heartsill**     5.7693
**Young, editor, with the assistance of Terry Belanger ... [et al.].**
Chicago: American Library Association, 1983. xvi, 245 p.; 27 cm. 1. Library
science — Dictionaries 2. Information science — Dictionaries. I. Young,
Heartsill, 1917- II. Belanger, Terry. III. Title: A.L.A. glossary of library and
information science.
Z1006.A48 1983     020/.3 19     LC 82-18512     ISBN 0838903711

**Carter, John, 1905-1975.**                                    • 5.7694
ABC for book–collectors. — [3d ed., rev.] — London: R. Hart-Davis, [1961]
208 p. 1. Bibliography — Dictionaries 2. Book collecting — Dictionaries.
I. T.
Z1006.C37 1961     LC 62-6733

**Encyclopedia of library and information science. Editors: Allen**     5.7695
**Kent and Harold Lancour. Assistant editor: William Z. Nasri.**
New York, M. Dekker [1968]- <c1986 >. v. <1-40 > : ill., facsims.; 27 cm.
Vols. 10-32 have executive editors: A. Kent, H. Lancour, J.E. Daily; assistant
editor: W.Z. Nasri. Vol. 33 has executive editors: A. Kent, J.E. Dailey; assistant
editor: W.Z. Nasri. Vols. 36-< 40 > also numbered supplement 1-< 5 >
1. Library science — Dictionaries 2. Information science — Dictionaries.
I. Kent, Allen. II. Lancour, Harold, 1908- ed. III. Nasri, William Z. ed.
IV. Daily, Jay Elwood. ed.
Z1006.E57     020/.3     LC 68-31232     ISBN 0824720040

**Harrod, Leonard Montague, 1905-.**                            5.7696
[Librarians' glossary of terms used in librarianship, documentation and the
book crafts, and reference book] Harrod's Librarians' glossary of terms used in
librarianship, documentation and the book crafts, and reference book. — 5th
ed. /rev. and updated by Ray Prytherch. — Aldershot, Hants.; Brookfield, Vt.,
U.S.A.: Gower, 1984. xi, 861 p.; 23 cm. 'Advisory editor Leonard Montague
Harrod.' 'A Grafton book.' Rev. ed. of: The librarians' glossary of terms used in
librarianship, documentation and the book crafts, and reference book. 4th rev.
ed. 1977. Includes index. 1. Library science — Dictionaries 2. Information
science — Dictionaries. 3. Bibliography — Dictionaries 4. Book industries
and trade — Dictionaries. I. Prytherch, Raymond John. II. T. III. Title:
Librarians' glossary of terms used in librarianship, documentation and the book
crafts, and reference book.
Z1006.H32 1984     020/.3 19     LC 83-17174     ISBN 0566034603

**Longley, Dennis.**                                            5.7697
Dictionary of information technology / Dennis Longley and Michael Shain. —
New York: Wiley, 1983. 379 p.: ill.; 24 cm. 'A Wiley-Interscience publication.'
1. Information science — Dictionaries. I. Shain, Michael. II. T. III. Title:
Information technology.
Z1006.L66 1982     020/.3 19     LC 82-51103     ISBN 0471895741

**Tayyeb, R.**                                                  5.7698
A dictionary of acronyms and abbreviations in library and information science
/ compiled by R. Tayyeb and K. Chandna. — 2nd ed. — Ottawa: Canadian
Library Association, c1985. iii, 279 p.; 23 cm. 1. Library science —
Abbreviations. 2. Library science — Acronyms. 3. Information science —
Abbreviations. 4. Information science — Acronyms. I. Chandna, K. II. T.
Z1006.T37 1985     020/.148 19     LC 87-107788     ISBN 088802195X

# Z1019–1033 Special Classes of Books

**Perrin, Noel.**                                              • 5.7699
Dr. Bowdler's legacy; a history of expurgated books in England and America. — [1st ed.]. — New York: Atheneum, 1969. xvi, 296 p.; 22 cm. 1. Bowdler, Thomas, 1782-1856. 2. Expurgated books I. T.
Z1019.P4    098    LC 70-86546

**Rare books, 1983–84: trends, collections, sources / edited by**    5.7700
**Alice D. Schreyer.**
New York: R.R. Bowker, 1984. x, 581 p.; 24 cm. 1. Rare books — Bibliography — Addresses, essays, lectures. 2. Rare books — Collectors and collecting — Addresses, essays, lectures. 3. Libraries — Special collections — Rare books — Addresses, essays, lectures. 4. Rare books — Library resources — United States — Directories. 5. Antiquarian booksellers — United States — Directories. 6. Antiquarian booksellers — Canada — Directories. 7. Manuscripts — Collectors and collecting — Addresses, essays, lectures. I. Schreyer, Alice D.
Z1029.R36 1984    011/.31 19    LC 84-174331    ISBN 0835217566

**Mott, Frank Luther, 1886-1964.**                              5.7701
Golden multitudes; the story of best sellers in the United States. — New York, Macmillan Co., 1947. xii, 357 p. 25 cm. Includes bibliographies. 1. Bibliography — Best sellers. 2. Books and reading I. T.
Z1033.B3M6    016    LC 47-11742 *

**Small press record of books in print.**                        5.7702
5th- ed.; 1975-. [Paradise, CA., Dustbooks] v. 21 cm. Annual. 1. Little press books — Catalogs. I. Fulton, Len.
Z1033.L73 S52    070.5/93    LC 77-644297

**Guide to microforms in print.**                                5.7703
1961-77. Englewood, Colo. [etc.] Microcard Editions. 17 v. 26 cm. Annual. 1. Microforms — Catalogs 2. Microcards — Catalogs I. Diaz, Albert James. ed.
Z1033.M5 G8    011.36 19    LC 61-7082

**Subject guide to microforms in print.**                        • 5.7704
1962/63-. Washington, Microcard Editions. v. 28 cm. Annual. 1. Microforms — Catalogs I. Diaz, Albert James.
Z1033.M5 S8    016.099    LC 62-21624

**Paperbound books in print: an index to 4500 inexpensive**      • 5.7705
**reprints and originals with selective subject guide.**
v.1-    summer 1955-. New York, R.R. Bowker. v.: ill.; 18 cm. Semiannual. 1. Bibliography — Paperback editions — Periodicals. I. R.R. Bowker Company.
Z1033.P3 P32

# Z1035 Best Books. Book Reviews. Reference Books

**Book review index.**                                           • 5.7706
v. 1- Jan. 1965-. Detroit, Gale Research Co. v. 27 cm. 1. Books — Reviews — Indexes — Periodicals. I. Gale Research Company.
Z1035.A1 B6    LC 65-9908

**The Reader's adviser.**                                        • 5.7707
[1st]- ed.; 1921-. New York, R. R. Bowker Co. v. 22-27 cm. 1. Bibliography — Best books I. Graham, Bessie, 1883- comp. II. Hoffman, Hester Rosalyn Jacoby, 1895- comp.
Z1035.B7    011    LC 57-13277

**Good reading: a guide for serious readers / Arthur Waldhorn,**    5.7708
**Olga S. Weber, Arthur Zeiger, editors.**
22nd ed. — New York: R.R. Bowker, 1985. xix, 419 p.; 24 cm. Includes index. 1. Bibliography — Best books 2. Books and reading I. Waldhorn, Arthur, 1918- II. Weber, Olga S. III. Zeiger, Arthur, 1916-
Z1035.G63 1985    011/.7 19    LC 85-17459    ISBN 0835221008

**Encyclopedia buying guide.**                                   5.7709
[1st]-3rd ed.; 1975/76-1982. New York, Bowker. 3 v. 24 cm. Triennial. 'A consumer guide to general encyclopedias in print.' 1. Encyclopedias and dictionaries — Bibliography.
Z1035.W267    016.03    LC 76-645701

**American reference books annual.**                             • 5.7710
1970-. Littleton, Colo., Libraries Unlimited. v. 24 cm. Annual. 1970- < 79 > issued in 2 vols.: v. 1, General reference, social sciences, history, economics, business; v. 2, Fine arts, humanities, science and engineering. 1. Reference books — Bibliography — Periodicals.
Z1035.1.A55    011/.02    LC 75-120328

**Best reference books, 1981–1985: titles of lasting value selected**    5.7711
**from American reference books annual / edited by Bohdan S.**
**Wynar.**
Littleton, Colo.: Libraries Unlimited, 1986. xxi, 504 p.; 26 cm. Includes indexes. 1. Reference books — Reviews. 2. Reference books — Bibliography 3. Bibliography — Best books — Reference books. I. Wynar, Bohdan S. II. American reference books annual.
Z1035.1.B5342 1986    028.1/2 19    LC 86-15316    ISBN 0872875547

**Cheney, Frances Neel, 1906-.**                                 • 5.7712
Fundamental reference sources. — Chicago: American Library Association, 1971. x, 318 p.; 25 cm. 1. Reference books — Bibliography I. T.
Z1035.1.C5    011/.02    LC 73-151051    ISBN 083890081X

**Sheehy, Eugene P. (Eugene Paul), 1922-.**                      5.7713
Guide to reference books / Eugene P. Sheehy. — 10th ed. — Chicago: American Library Association, 1986. p. cm. Includes index. 1. Reference books — Bibliography I. T.
Z1035.1.S43 1986    011/.02 19    LC 85-11208    ISBN 0838903908

**Reference and subscription books reviews / prepared by the**    5.7714
**American Library Association, Reference and Subscription**
**Books Review Committee.**
-1982-1983. — Chicago: American Library Association, 1956-. v.; 25 cm. Annual. Began with: 1968-1970. Reprinted from The Booklist, v. 65-66- (called in v. 65, The Booklist and subscription books bulletin). Description based on: 1981-1982. 1. Reference books — Reviews — Periodicals. I. American Library Association. Reference and Subscription Books Review Committee. II. Booklist (Chicago, Ill.: 1969) III. Booklist and subscription books bulletin.
Z1035.1.S922    028.1/2 19    LC 73-159565

**Walford's guide to reference material / edited by A. J. Walford,**    5.7715
**with the assistance of Joan M. Harvey and L. J. Taylor.**
4th ed. — London: Library Association, 1980-86. 3 v. Includes indexes. 1. Reference books — Bibliography I. Harvey, Joan M. II. Taylor, L. J. III. Walford, Albert John. IV. Title: Guide to reference material.
Z1035.1.W33 1980    011/.02 19    LC 80-489414    ISBN 0853655642

# Z1037–1039 Books for Special Classes of Readers

**Bingham, Jane.**                                               5.7716
Fifteen centuries of children's literature: an annotated chronology of British and American works in historical context / Jane Bingham and Grayce Scholt. — Westport, Conn.: Greenwood Press, c1980. L, 540 p.: ill.; 25 cm. Includes index. 1. Children's literature, English — Bibliography. 2. Children's literature, American — Bibliography. 3. Children's literature, English — History and criticism. 4. Children's literature, American — History and criticism. 5. Children — Books and reading — History. I. Schott, Grayce. II. T.
Z1037.A1 B582 PN1009.A1    028.52    LC 79-8584    ISBN 0313221642

**Haviland, Virginia, 1911-.**                                   • 5.7717
Children's literature; a guide to reference sources. Washington, Library of Congress; [for sale by the Superintendent of Documents, U.S. Govt. Print. Off.] 1966. x, 341 p. illus. 24 cm. Compiled by Virginia Haviland, Elisabeth Wenning Davidson, and Barbara Quinnam of the Children's Book Section. 1. Children's literature — History and criticism — Bibliography. 2. Reference books — Children's literature — Bibliography. I. Wenning, Elisabeth. II. Quinnam, Barbara. III. Coughlan, Margaret N., 1925- IV. Library of Congress. Children's Book Section. V. T.
Z1037.A1 H35    016.8098/928/2    LC 66-62734    ISBN 084440022X

**Crago, Maureen, 1939-.**                                       5.7718
Prelude to literacy: a preschool child's encounter with picture and story / Maureen and Hugh Crago. — Carbondale: Southern Illinois University Press,

1983. xxxiii, 294 p.: ill.; 26 cm. 1. Children — Books and reading 2. Picture-books for children 3. Storytelling 4. Language arts (Preschool) I. Crago, Hugh, 1946- II. T.
Z1037.C918 1983 PN1009.A1     155.4/13 19     *LC* 82-19235     *ISBN* 0809310775

**Hunt, Mary Alice.**         **5.7719**
A Multimedia approach to children's literature: a selective list of films (and videocassettes), filmstrips, and recordings based on children's books / edited by Mary Alice Hunt; with a foreword by Ellin Greene. — 3rd ed. — Chicago: American Library Association, 1983. xxix, 182 p.; 23 cm. Rev. ed. of: A multimedia approach to children's literature / compiled and edited by Ellin Greene. 2nd ed. 1977. 'Materials selected by a committee of the Association for Library Service to Children.' Includes indexes. I. Greene, Ellin, 1927- A multimedia approach to children's literature. II. Association for Library Service to Children. III. T.
Z1037.M94 1983 PN1009.A1     011/.37 19     *LC* 83-15517     *ISBN* 0838932894

**Norton, Donna E.**         **5.7720**
Through the eyes of a child: an introduction to children's literature / Donna E. Norton. — Columbus, Ohio: C.E. Merrill Pub. Co., c1983. xxi, 664 p., [16] p. of plates: ill. (some col.); 24 cm. 1. Children — Books and reading 2. Children's literature — History and criticism. I. T.
Z1037.N78 1983     809/.89282 19     *LC* 82-62479     0675098327

**Peterson, Linda Kauffman.**         **5.7721**
Newbery and Caldecott Medal and Honor books: an annotated bibliography / Linda Kauffman Peterson, Marilyn Leathers Solt. — Boston, Mass.: G.K. Hall, 1982. xxxi, 427 p., [10] p. of plates: ill.; 25 cm. Includes indexes. 1. Children — Books and reading — Bibliography. 2. Children's literature — Bibliography 3. Literary prizes I. Solt, Marilyn Leathers. II. T.
Z1037.P45 1982 PN1009.A1     011/.62/079 19     *LC* 82-2880     *ISBN* 0816184488

**University of Victoria Symposium on Children's Response to a**         **5.7722**
**Literate Environment: Literacy before Schooling (1982)**
Awakening to literacy: the University of Victoria Symposium on Children's Response to a Literate Environment: Literacy before Schooling / edited by Hillel Goelman, Antoinette A. Oberg, and Frank Smith. — Exeter, N.H.: Heinemann Educational Books, 1984. xv, 240 p.: ill.; 23 cm. Includes indexes. 1. Children — Books and reading — Congresses. 2. Reading (Preschool) — Congresses. 3. Literacy — Congresses. I. Goelman, Hillel, 1951- II. Oberg, Antoinette A. III. Smith, Frank, 1928- IV. University of Victoria (B.C.). V. T.
Z1037.U74 1982     028.5/30543 19     *LC* 84-727     *ISBN* 0435082078

**Wilkin, Binnie Tate, 1933-.**         **5.7723**
Survival themes in fiction for children and young people / by Binnie Tate Wilkin; with a foreword by Jerome Cushman. — Metuchen, N.J.: Scarecrow Press, 1978. vi, 256 p.; 23 cm. Includes index. 1. Children's literature — Bibliography 2. Children's literature — History and criticism. I. T.
Z1037.W67     028.52     *LC* 77-14295     *ISBN* 0810810484

**Friedberg, Joan Brest, 1927-.**         **5.7724**
Accept me as I am: best books of juvenile nonfiction on impairments and disabilities / Joan Brest Friedberg, June B. Mullins, Adelaide Weir Sukiennik. — New York: Bowker, 1985. xiii, 363 p.: ill.; 24 cm. (Serving special needs series.) Includes indexes. 1. Children's literature — Bibliography 2. Bibliography — Best books — Children's literature. 3. Physically handicapped — Juvenile literature — Bibliography. 4. Mentally handicapped — Juvenile literature — Bibliography. 5. Mentally ill — Juvenile literature — Bibliography. I. Mullins, June B., 1927- II. Sukiennik, Adelaide Weir, 1938- III. T. IV. Series.
Z1037.9.F73 1985 PN1009.A1     011/.62/0880826 19     *LC* 85-3778
    *ISBN* 0835219747

**Radway, Janice A., 1949-.**         **5.7725**
Reading the romance: women, patriarchy, and popular literature / Janice A. Radway. — Chapel Hill: University of North Carolina Press, c1984. x, 274 p. Includes index. 1. Women — Books and reading 2. Women — Psychology 3. Women in literature 4. Sex role in literature 5. Love stories — Appreciation. 6. Love stories — Publishing. 7. Popular literature 8. Patriarchy I. T.
Z1039.W65 R32 1984     028/.9/024042 19     *LC* 83-23596     *ISBN* 0807841250

# Z1041–1107 Anonyms.
Pseudonyms

**Bates, Susannah, 1941-.**         **5.7726**
The PENDEX: an index of pen names and house names in fantastic, thriller, and series literature / Susannah Bates. — New York: Garland Pub., 1981. 233 p.; 23 cm. (Garland reference library of the humanities. v. 227) Includes index. 1. Anonyms and pseudonyms — Indexes. I. T. II. Series.
Z1041.B37 1981     014/.1 19     *LC* 80-8486     *ISBN* 0824095014

**Room, Adrian.**         **5.7727**
Naming names: stories of pseudonyms and name changes with a who's who / by Adrian Room. — Jefferson, N.C.: McFarland, 1981. ix, 349 p.; 24 cm. 1. Anonyms and pseudonyms I. T.
Z1041.R66     929.4 19     *LC* 80-27801     *ISBN* 0899500250

**Halkett, Samuel, 1814-1871.**         **5.7728**
A dictionary of anonymous and pseudonymous publications in the English language / Halkett and Laing. — 3rd rev. and enl. ed. / John Horden, editor. — Harlow: Longman, 1980-. v. < 1 >; 31 cm. Previous ed. published in 7 vols. as: Dictionary of anonymous and pseudonymous English literature. 1. Anonyms and pseudonyms, English I. Laing, John, 1809-1880. II. Horden, John. III. T.
Z1065.H18 1980     014/.2 19     *LC* 81-127850     *ISBN* 0582555213

# Z1201–5000 NATIONAL
BIBLIOGRAPHY

# Z1201–1361 America. United States

**American book publishing record.**         • **5.7729**
1965-. New York: Bowker. v. Annual. Replaced by five year cumulations issued under title: American book publishing record, BPR cumulative. 1. United States — Imprints
Z1201.A52     015.73     *LC* 66-19741

**Sabin, Joseph, 1821-1881.**         **5.7730**
Bibliotheca Americana; a dictionary of books relating to America, from its discovery to the present time. Begun by Joseph Sabin, continued by Wilberforce Eames and completed by R.W.G. Vail for the Bibliographical Society of America. Amsterdam, N. Israel, 1961-62. 29 v. in 15. illus. Imprint varies. Title varies: v. 1-19, and v. 20, pt. 1/2, A dictionary of books relating to America from its discovery to the present time. (Half-title: Bibliotheca Americana); v. 20-29, Bibliotheca Americana. A dictionary of books relating to America. 'Library location symbols': v. 29, p. [299]-305. 1. American literature — Bibliography 2. America — Bibliography I. Eames, Wilberforce, 1855-1937. II. Vail, R. W. G. (Robert William Glenroie), 1890-1966. III. Bibliographical Society of America. IV. T. V. Title: A dictionary of books relating to America
Z1201.S2     *LC* 01-26958

**Molnar, John Edgar.**         **5.7731**
Author–title index to Joseph Sabin's Dictionary of books relating to America. — Metuchen, N.J.: Scarecrow Press, 1974. 3 v. (vi, 3196 p.); 22 cm. 1. Sabin, Joseph, 1821-1881. A dictionary of books relating to America — Indexes. I. Sabin, Joseph, 1821-1881. A dictionary of books relating to America. II. T.
Z1201.S222     016.9173     *LC* 74-6291     *ISBN* 0810806525

**Thompson, Lawrence Sidney, 1916-.**         **5.7732**
The new Sabin; books described by Joseph Sabin and his successors, now described again on the basis of examination of originals, and fully indexed by title, subject, joint authors, and institutions and agencies, by Lawrence S. Thompson. Troy, N.Y., Whitston Pub. Co., 1974-1983. 10 v.; 24 cm. Accompanied by yearly indexes which are replaced every 5 years by a cumulative index volume. 1. America — Bibliography I. Sabin, Joseph, 1821-1888. Dictionary of books relating to America. II. T.
Z1201.T45 E18     016.973     *LC* 73-85960     *ISBN* 0878750495

**Brumble, H. David.**         **5.7733**
An annotated bibliography of American Indian and Eskimo autobiographies / H. David Brumble III. — Lincoln: University of Nebraska Press, c1981. 177 p.;

24 cm. Includes indexes. 1. Indians of North America — Biography — Bibliography. 2. Eskimos — Biography — Bibliography. I. T.
Z1209.B78 E89     016.970004/97 19     *LC* 80-23449     *ISBN*
0803211759

**Clements, William M., 1945-.**     5.7734
Native American folklore, 1879–1979: an annotated bibliography / compiled by William M. Clements, Frances M. Malpezzi. — Athens, Ohio: Swallow Press, c1984. xxiii, 247 p.; 29 cm. Includes indexes. 1. Indians of North America — Folklore — Bibliography. 2. Folklore — North America — Bibliography. I. Malpezzi, Frances M., 1946- II. T.
Z1209.C57 1984 E98.F6     016.398/08997073 19     *LC* 83-6672
*ISBN* 0804008310

**Haas, Marilyn L.**     5.7735
Indians of North America: methods and sources for library research / Marilyn L. Haas. — Hamden, CT: Library Professional Publications, 1983. xi, 163 p.: ill.; 23 cm. Includes index. 1. Indians of North America — Bibliography 2. Indians of North America — Library resources — United States. 3. Reference books — Indians of North America. 4. Indians of North America — Research — Methodology. I. T.
Z1209.H22 1983 E77     016.970004/97 19     *LC* 83-14007     *ISBN*
0208019804

**United States. National Archives and Records Service.**     5.7736
American Indians: a select catalog of National Archives microfilm publications. — Washington, D.C.: National Archives Trust Fund Board, General Services Administration, 1984. xii, 91 p.; 29 cm. Rev. ed. of: The American Indian. 1972. Includes index. 1. United States. National Archives and Records Service — Microform catalogs. 2. Indians of North America — Government relations — Sources — Bibliography — Microform catalogs. 3. Indians of North America — Government relations — Manuscripts — Microform catalogs. 4. Documents on microfilm — Catalogs. I. United States. National Archives and Records Service. American Indian. II. T.
Z1209.U53 1984 E93     016.3058/97/073 19     *LC* 83-13412     *ISBN*
0911333096

**Corley, Nora T.**     5.7737
Resources for native peoples studies / by Nora T. Corley. — Ottawa: National Library of Canada, Resources Survey Division, 1984. 342, 341 p.: map; 28 cm. (Research collections in Canadian libraries. Special studies; 9) Text in English and French with French text on inverted pages. Title on added t.p.: Ressources sur les études autochtones. Includes index. Folded maps in pockets. Errata sheet inserted between p. 102-103. 1. Indians of North America — Library resources — Canada — Directories. 2. Indians of North America — Periodicals — Bibliography — Union lists. 3. Catalogs, Union — Canada. 4. Reference books — Indians of North America — Bibliography. 5. Indians of North America — Bibliography I. National Library of Canada. Resources Survey Division. II. T. III. Title: Ressources sur les études autochtones. IV. Series.
Z1209.2.C3 C6x     026/.97000497/0971 19     *ISBN* 066052676X

**Hirschfelder, Arlene B.**     5.7738
Guide to research on North American Indians / Arlene B. Hirschfelder, Mary Gloyne Byler, Michael A. Dorris. — Chicago: American Library Association, 1983. xi, 330 p.: map; 26 cm. Includes indexes. 1. Indians of North America — Bibliography I. Byler, Mary Gloyne. II. Dorris, Michael A. III. T.
Z1209.2.N67 H57 1983 E77     016.970004/97 19     *LC* 82-22787
*ISBN* 0838903533

**Mail, Patricia D.**     5.7739
Tulapai to Tokay: a bibliography of alcohol use and abuse among native Americans of North America / compiled by Patricia D. Mail and David R. McDonald; with a foreword and literature review by Joy H. Leland and indexes by Sandra Norris. — New Haven: HRAF Press, 1981 (c1980). xv, 356 p.; 23 cm. Includes indexes. 1. Indians of North America — Alcohol use — Bibliography. I. McDonald, David R. II. T.
Z1209.2.N67 M34 E98.L7     016.3622/92/08997 19     *LC* 80-81243
*ISBN* 0875362532

**Murdock, George Peter, 1897-.**     3ʳᵈ ed yes     5.7740
Ethnographic bibliography of North America / George Peter Murdock and Timothy J. O'Leary, with the assistance of John Beierle ... [et al.]. — 4th ed. — New Haven: Human Relations Area Files Press, 1975. 5 v.: maps; 29 cm. (Behavior science bibliographies.) 1. Indians of North America — Bibliography I. O'Leary, Timothy J., joint author. II. T. III. Series.
Z1209.2.N67 M87 1975 E77     016.97/0004/97     *LC* 75-17091     *ISBN*
0875362052

**Hill, Edward E.**     5.7741
Guide to records in the National Archives of the United States relating to American Indians / compiled by Edward E. Hill. — Washington, D.C.: National Archives and Records Service, General Services Administration, 1981 [i.e. 1982] xiii, 467 p., [16] p. of plates: ill.; 24 cm. Includes index. 1. United States. National Archives — Catalogs. 2. Indians of North America — Government relations — Sources — Bibliography — Catalogs. 3. Indians of

North America — History — Sources — Bibliography — Catalogs. I. United States. National Archives. II. T.
Z1209.2.U5 H54 1982 E93     016.3231/97/073 19     *LC* 81-22357

**Littlefield, Daniel F.**     5.7742
A biobibliography of native American writers, 1772–1924 / by Daniel F. Littlefield, Jr. and James W. Parins. — Metuchen, N.J.: Scarecrow Press, 1981. xvii, 343 p.; 23 cm. — (Native American bibliography series. no. 2) Includes indexes. 1. Indians of North America — Bibliography 2. American literature — Indian authors — Bibliography. 3. United States — Imprints I. Parins, James W. II. T. III. Series.
Z1209.2.U5 L57 E77     016.973/0497 19     *LC* 81-9138     *ISBN*
0810814633

**Prucha, Francis Paul.**     5.7743
A bibliographical guide to the history of Indian–white relations in the United States / Francis Paul Prucha. Chicago: University of Chicago Press, 1977. x, 454 p.; 24 cm. 'A Publication of the Center for the History of the American Indian of the Newberry Library.' Includes index. 1. Indians of North America — Government relations — Bibliography. I. T.
Z1209.2.U5 P67 E93     016.3231/19/7073     *LC* 76-16045     *ISBN*
0226684768

**Prucha, Francis Paul.**     5.7744
Indian–white relations in the United States: a bibliography of works published 1975–1980 / Francis Paul Prucha. — Lincoln, Neb.: University of Nebraska Press, c1982. viii, 179 p.; 24 cm. Supplement to: A bibliographical guide to the history of Indian-white relations in the United States / Francis Paul Prucha. Chicago: University of Chicago Press, 1977. Includes index. 1. Indians of North America — Government relations — Bibliography. I. Prucha, Francis Paul. Bibliographical guide to the history of Indian-white relations in the United States. II. T.
Z1209.2.U5 P67 Suppl E93     016.3231/197073 19     *LC* 81-14722
*ISBN* 0803236654

**Tanselle, G. Thomas (George Thomas), 1934-.**     5.7745
Guide to the study of United States imprints [by] G. Thomas Tanselle. Cambridge, Mass., Belknap Press of Harvard University Press, 1971. 2 v. (lxiv, 1050 p.) front. 26 cm. 'Appendix: A basic collection of two hundred and fifty titles on United States printing and publishing': p. 897-906. 1. Bibliography — Bibliography — United States. I. T.
Z1215.A2 T35     016.015/73     *LC* 79-143232     *ISBN* 0674367618

**Roorbach, Orville A. (Orville Augustus), 1803-1861.**     • 5.7746
Bibliotheca americana: Catalogue of American publications, including reprints and original works, from 1820 to 1852, inclusive. Together with a list of periodicals published in the United States / Compiled and arranged by O.A. Roorbach. — New York: P. Smith, 1939. xi, 652 p.; 25 cm. 'Contains the whole of the original work published in 1849, the supplement published in 1850, also some two thousand titles of books then published and not contained in either, together with such publications as have appeared since'—Introd. (dated Oct., 1852) 'Law': p. [606]-643. 1. American literature — Bibliography I. T.
Z1215.A3 1939     *LC* 39-27504

**Kelly, James, 1829-1907.**     • 5.7747
The American catalogue of books, (original and reprints,) published in the United States from Jan., 1861, to Jan. ... [1871], with date of publication, size, price, and publisher's name ... Compiled and arranged by James Kelly. New York, P. Smith, 1938. 2 v. 25.5 cm. Reprint of the edition of 1866-77. Continuation of Roorbach's 'Bibliotheca americana 1820-1860'; continued by the American catalogue 1876-1910. 1. American literature — Bibliography 2. United States — History — Civil War — Bibliography. 3. United States — Learned institutions and societies — Bibliography. I. T. II. Title: The American catalogue of books, 1861-1871.
Z1215.A4 1938     015.73     *LC* 38-29060

**The American catalogue.**     • 5.7748
New York: P. Smith, 1941. 8 v. in 13; 26 cm. Vols. 1-5 have separate author/title and subject sequences, v. 6-8 have author, title and subject entries combined, along with a separate directory of publishers. Vol. 1 compiled by Lynds E. Jones under the editorial direction of F. Leypoldt; v. 2 compiled by A.I. Appleton under the direction of R.R. Bowker; v. 3-8 under the direction of R.R. Bowker. American national trade bibliography, supplemented by the Annual American catalogue, 1886-1900; Annual American catalogue cumulated, 1900/01-1900/03; Annual American catalogue, 1905-1906; 1908-1910; and currently, by Publishers' weekly. 1. American literature — Bibliography 2. Catalogs, Booksellers' 3. Publishers and publishing — United States — Directories. 4. United States — Imprints — Catalogs. I. Appleton, Augusta Isabella, b. 1841. II. Jones, Lynds Eugene, 1853-1902. III. Bowker, Richard Rogers, 1848-1933. IV. Leypoldt, Frederick, 1835-1884. V. Publishers' weekly. VI. Title: Annual American catalog.
Z1215.A5     *LC* a 42-2938

**Books in series in the United States.**     5.7749
[1st]-2nd. ed. New York, R.R. Bowker, 1977-79. v. 29 cm. 'Original, reprinted, in-print, and out-of-print books, published or distributed in the U.S. in popular,

scholarly and professional series. First edition covers 1966-75, second ed.- has no coverage date. 1. Children's literature in series — Catalogs. 2. Monographic series — Bibliography — Catalogs. 3. Reprints (Publications) — Bibliography — Catalogs. 4. Out-of-print books — Bibliography — Catalogs. 5. United States — Imprints — Catalogs. I. R.R. Bowker Company. Z1215.B65     011     LC 79-641785

**Cooper, Gayle.**          **5.7750**
A checklist of American imprints for 1830– . — Metuchen, N.J.: Scarecrow Press, 1972-. v.; 23 cm. Continues the work by R. Shoemaker. 1. United States — Imprints I. Shoemaker, Richard H. A checklist of American imprints for 1820-1829. II. T. III. Title: American imprints.
Z1215.C66     015/.73     LC 72-187094     ISBN 0810805202

**Evans, Charles, 1850-1935.**        • **5.7751**
American bibliography. — Metuchen, N.J.: Mini-Print Corp., 1967. 13 v. in 1.; 28 cm. Vols. 1-12 first published in Chicago in 1903-34, reprinted by Peter Smith, New York, in 1941-42; v. 13, by C. K. Shipton, first published in 1955 by the American Antiquarian Society, Worcester, Mass. Vol. 14, Index, not published in this ed. Photocopy in reduced size. 1. Printing — United States — History. 2. Printers — United States. 3. United States — Imprints I. T.
Z1215.E9232 1967     015.73     LC 67-4309

**Bristol, Roger Pattrell.**        • **5.7752**
Index of printers, publishers and booksellers indicated by Charles Evans in his American bibliography. — Charlottesville, Bibliographical Society of the University of Virginia, 1961. iv, 172 p. 29 cm. 1. Book industries and trade — United States — Directories. I. Evans, Charles, 1850-1935. American bibliography. II. T.
Z1215.E9233     015.73     LC 61-64087

**Bristol, Roger Pattrell.**        • **5.7753**
Supplement to Charles Evans' American bibliography. By Roger P. Bristol. Charlottesville, Published for the Bibliographical Society of America and the Bibliographical Society of the University of Virginia [by] University Press of Virginia [1970] xix, 636 p. 29 cm. A chronological list, 1646-1800, of 'not-in-Evans' items. 1. Printing — United States — History. 2. Printers — United States. 3. United States — Imprints I. Evans, Charles, 1850-1935. American bibliography. II. Bibliographical Society of America. III. University of Virginia. Bibliographical Society. IV. T.
Z1215.E92334     015.73     LC 73-94761     ISBN 0813902878

**Howes, Wright.**        • **5.7754**
U. S. iana, 1650–1950: a selective bibliography in which are described 11,620 uncommon and significant books relating to the continental portion of the United States/ compiled by Wright Howes. — Rev. and enl. ed. — New York: Bowker for the Newberry Library, 1962. 652 p.; 26 cm. 1. United States — Bibliography I. T.
Z1215.H75 1962     015.73     LC 62-10988

**The Publishers' trade list annual.**        • **5.7755**
1874-. New York, N.Y.: R. R. Bowker Co. v.: ill.; 27 cm. Annual. An index was issued for the year 1902, with supplementary indexes for 1903 and 1904 (1904 includes 1903 material). 1. Catalogs, Publishers' — United States. 2. United States — Imprints — Catalogs. I. Leypoldt, Frederick, 1835-1884. II. R.R. Bowker Company. III. Books in print. IV. Subject guide to books in print.
Z1215.P97     015.73     LC 04-12648

**Books in print.**        **5.7756**
1948-. New York, R. R. Bowker Co. v. 28 cm. Annual. Vols. for < 1986/87-> issued in parts; e.g. 1986/87 issued in 7 v. composed of separate author, title, and publisher indexes. 1. Catalogs, Publishers' — United States. 2. United States — Imprints — Catalogs. I. Uhlendorf, Bernhard Alexander, 1893- II. Anstaett, Herbert Bulow, 1902- III. R.R. Bowker Company. IV. Publishers' trade list annual.
Z1215.P972     015.73     LC 74-643574

**Subject guide to books in print.**        **5.7757**
1957-. New York, R. R. Bowker Co. v. 29 cm. Annual. Vols. for < 1978/79 > issued in 2 or more vols. 1. Catalogs, Publishers' — United States. 2. United States — Imprints — Catalogs. I. R.R. Bowker Company. II. Publishers' trade list annual. III. Books in print.
Z1215.P973     015.73     LC 74-643573

**Shaw, Ralph R. (Ralph Robert), 1907-1972.**        • **5.7758**
American bibliography, a preliminary checklist for 1801–1819 / compiled by Ralph R. Shaw and Richard H. Shoemaker. — New York: Scarecrow Press, 1958-1963. 20 v.; 23 cm. 1. United States — Imprints I. Shoemaker, Richard H. II. T.
Z1215.S48     LC 58-7809

**Shipton, Clifford Kenyon, 1902-.**        • **5.7759**
National index of American imprints through 1800; the short–title Evans [by] Clifford K. Shipton [and] James E. Mooney. [Worcester, Mass.] American Antiquarian Society, 1969. 2 v. (xxv, 1028 p.) 26 cm. A combined alphabetical index to Evans' American bibliography, with corrections, and R. Bristol's 'not-

in-Evans' items. 1. Evans, Charles, 1850-1935. American bibliography. 2. United States — Imprints I. Mooney, James E., joint author. II. Bristol, Roger Pattrell. III. American Antiquarian Society. IV. T. V. Title: The short-title Evans
Z1215.S495     015/.73     LC 69-11248     ISBN 0827169086

**Shoemaker, Richard H.**        **5.7760**
A checklist of American imprints for 1820– / compiled by Richard H. Shoemaker. — Metuchen, N.J.: Scarecrow Press, 1964-. v.; 23 cm. Editors vary. 1. United States — Imprints I. T. II. Title: American imprints.
Z1215.S54     LC 64-11784     ISBN 0810808285

**Library of Congress. General Reference and Bibliography**        • **5.7761**
**Division.**
A guide to the study of the United States of America; representative books reflecting the development of American life and thought / Prepared under the direction of Roy P. Basler, by Donald H. Mugridge and Blanche P. McCrum. — Washington / 1960. xv, 1193 p.; 27 cm. 1. United States — Bibliography I. Mugridge, Donald Henry. II. McCrum, Blanche Prichard, 1887- III. T.
Z1215.U53     016.9173     LC 60-60009

**The United States catalog: books in print January 1, 1928 /**        • **5.7762**
**edited by Mary Burnham; managing editor, Carol Hurd.**
4th ed. — New York: Wilson, 1928. 3164 p. Supplemented by Cumulative book index. 1. American literature — Bibliography 2. United States — Bibliography I. H.W. Wilson Company.
Z1215.U6 1928     LC 28-26655

**The Book review digest: Annual cumulation. v.1– 1905–.**        • **5.7763**
New York: Wilson, 1905-. v.; 26 cm. Vol. 1 was issued as no. 12 (called no. 10 in caption) of the Cumulative book review digest. Vol. 2 was issued in addition to the 12 numbers of the Book review digest for 1906. The annual cumulation for 1907-13 are formed by the Dec. numbers of the Book review digest for 1914-23, by the Feb. number of the following year. Title varies: 1905, The Cumulative book review digest; 1906- The Book review digest. Annual cumulation. Editors: 1906-15, Clara E. Fanning (with Margaret Jackson, 1915); 1916-17, Margaret Jackson (with Mary K. Reely, 1917); 1918-20, Mary K. Reely and others; 1921-Mertice M. James (with Marion A. Knight, 1921-34, Dorothy Brown, 1931- ) and others. INDEXES: Vols. 13-17, Mar. 1917-Feb. 1922, in v.17. Vols. 18-22, Mar. 1922-Feb. 1927, v.22. Vols. 23-27, Mar. 1927-Feb. 1932, in v.27. Vols. 28-32, Mar. 1932-Feb. 1937, in v.32. Vols. 33-37, Mar. 1937-Feb. 1942, in v.37. Vols. 38-42, Mar. 1942-Feb. 1947, in v.42. Vols. 43-47, Mar. 1947-Feb. 1952, in v.47. Vols. 48-52, Mar. 1952-Feb. 1957, in v.52. 1. Books — Reviews 2. Bibliography — Periodicals. I. Fanning, Clara Elizabeth, 1878-1938, ed. II. Jackson, Margaret, ed. III. Reely, Mary Katharine, 1881- ed. IV. James, Mertice May, 1893- ed. V. H.W. Wilson Company.
Z1219.C95     LC 06-9994

**Forthcoming books.**        • **5.7764**
v. 1- Jan. 1966-. [New York, R. R. Bowker Co.] v. 22-24 cm. Bimonthly. 1. United States — Imprints I. Arny, Rose, ed. II. R.R. Bowker Company. Dept. of Bibliography. III. Books in print.
[Z1219]     Z1219.F8.     015.73     LC 67-1000

**The Cumulative book index.**        • **5.7765**
1898/99-. New York, [etc.], H. W. Wilson Company. v. 26-36 cm. Annual. Kept up to date by monthly and irregularly cumulated issues. Annual volumes for 1900-1942 called 3rd-45th. 1. American literature — Bibliography — Periodicals. 2. English literature — Bibliography — Periodicals. I. H.W. Wilson Company. II. United States catalogue; books in print. Supplement.
Z1219.M78     LC 05-33604

# Z1223 GOVERNMENT PUBLICATIONS

**United States. Superintendent of Documents.**        • **5.7766**
Checklist of United States public documents 1789–1909, congressional: to close of Sixtieth Congress; departmental: to end of calendar year 1909. 3d ed., rev. and enl. ... Comp. under direction of the superintendent of documents. Washington, Govt. print. off., 1911-. v. 24 cm. 'The compilation of this work has been in charge of Miss Mary A. Hartwell.' 1. United States — Government publications I. T.
Z1223.A113     LC 12-35731

**Larson, Donna Rae.**        **5.7767**
Guide to U.S. government directories: 1970–1980 / by Donna Rae Larson. — Phoenix, AZ: Oryx Press, c1981. 191 p.; 29 cm. Includes index. 1. United States — Government publications — Bibliography. 2. United States — Directories — Bibliography. I. T. II. Title: Guide to US government directories.
Z1223.A12 L37 J83     015.73 19     LC 81-9642     ISBN 0912700637

**United States. Superintendent of Documents.**        • **5.7768**
Catalog of the public documents of the ... Congress ... and of all departments of the government of the United States ... [being the 'Comprehensive index'

provided for by the act approved January 12, 1895]. — v. 1(1893)-v.25 (1940). — Washington: Govt. Print. Off., 1896-. 25 v.; 23-30 cm. Some vols. are reprints. 1. United States. Congress — Bibliography. 2. United States — Government publications — Bibliography. I. T. II. Title: Comprehensive index of U.S. Government publications. III. Title: Document catalogue.
Z1223 A13

**United States. Government Printing Office.**    • **5.7769**
Numerical lists and schedule of volumes of the reports and documents of Congress. 1933/34-. Washington, for sale by the Supt. of Docs., U.S. Govt. Print. Off. v. 24 cm. Annual. 'Serials 13096-1 to 13129.' Covers the 73d-Congresses. 1. United States. Congress — Bibliography — Periodicals. 2. United States — Government publications — Bibliography — Periodicals. I. T.
Z1223.A15     015.73     *LC* gp 77-10797

**United States. Superintendent of Documents.**    • **5.7770**
Monthly catalog of United States Government publications. no. [1]- Jan. 1895-. Washington, United States Government Printing Office. v. 22-24 cm. Monthly. Supplements 1941/1942-1945/1946. 1. United States — Government publications — Bibliography. I. United States. Superintendent of Documents. Catalogue of publications issued by the Government of the United States. II. United States. Superintendent of Documents. Catalogue of the United States public documents. III. United States. Superintendent of Documents. Monthly catalog, United States public documents. IV. United States. Superintendent of Documents. United States Government Publications, a monthly catalog. V. T.
Z1223.A18     *LC* 04-18088

**Bernier, Bernard A.**    **5.7771**
Popular names of U.S. Government reports: a catalog / compiled by Bernard A. Bernier, Jr., Karen A. Wood. — 4th ed. — Washington: Library of Congress: For sale by the Supt. of Docs., U.S. G.P.O., 1984. x, 272 p.; 27 cm. Includes index. S/N 030-005-00012-1 Item 818-F 1. United States — Government publications — Bibliography. I. Wood, Karen A. II. Library of Congress. Serial & Government Publications Division. III. T.
Z1223.A199 B47 1984 J83    015.73/053 19    *LC* 84-603923    *ISBN* 0844401749

**Poore, Benjamin Perley, 1820-1887.**    • **5.7772**
A descriptive catalogue of the government publications of the United States, September 5, 1774–March 4, 1881 / comp. by order of Congress by Benjamin Perley Poore. — Washington: Govt. Print. Off., 1885. iv, 1392 p.; 30 cm. ([U.S. 48th Cong., 2d sess. Senate. Misc. doc. 67]) Arranged chronologically, with general index. Continued by Ames' Comprehensive index to the publications of the United States government, 1881-1893 (2 vols., 1905) and by the Catalogue of public documents, 53d- Congress, 1893- issued by the superintendent of documents (the 'Document catalogue') 1. United States — Government publications — Bibliography. I. United States. Congress. II. T.
Z1223.A 1885     *LC* 01-9291

**United States. Superintendent of Documents.**    • **5.7773**
Tables of and annotated index to the congressional series of United States public documents / prepared in the office of the superintendent of documents, Government printing office. — Washington: Govt. print. off., 1902. 769 p.; 29 x 23 cm. Part 2 of 'A complete list of public documents' to be published in three parts ... and ... then ... consolidated and published in one volume with a general index. ' 'Contains a list of, and an index to, the documents of the Fifteenth to the Fifty-second Congress, both inclusive.' I. T.
Z1223.A 1902     *LC* 02-13262

**United States. Dept. of the Interior. Division of Documents.**    • **5.7774**
Comprehensive index to the publications of the United States government, 1881–1893 / by John G. Ames, chief of Document Division, Department of the Interior. — Washington: Govt. print. off., 1905. 2 v.; 29 cm. (58th Cong., 2d sess. House. Doc. 754) Paged continuously. A subject index, 'compiled in compliance with the provisions of a joint resolution approved March 3, 1897, which directs the preparation of an index to all publications of the government from 1881, the date at which the Descriptive catalogue of government publications by Ben: Perley Poore terminates, to 1893, the date at which the index by the superintendent of documents begins, said index to conform in its general plan to ... [Ames'] Comprehensive index of government publications from 1889 to 1893,' published in 1894.' 1. United States. Congress — Bibliography. 2. United States — Government publications — Bibliography. 3. United States — Government publications — Indexes. I. Ames, John G. (John Griffith), 1834-1910. II. T.
Z1223.A 1905     *LC* 05-32405

**Andriot, John L.**    • **5.7775**
Checklist of major U.S. Government series, edited by John L. Andriot. — McLean, Va.: Documents Index, 1972-. v. ; 28 cm. 1. United States — Government publications — Bibliography. I. T.
Z1223.Z7 A544     015/.73     *LC* 73-163950

**Andriot, John L.**    • **5.7776**
Guide to U.S. Government serials & periodicals, 1969–. McLean, Va.: Documents Index. v. in    ; 29 cm. Earlier editions cataloged separately in L.C. "Basic volumes published in March and a supplement, which updates the information through June 30 of each year, issued in September." 1. United States — Government publications — Periodicals — Bibliography. I. T. II. Title: U.S. Government serials & periodicals.
Z1223.Z7 A574     015/.73     *LC* 75-7027

**Government reference books.**    • **5.7777**
1st- ed.; 1968/69-. [Littleton, Colo.] Libraries Unlimited. v. 24 cm. Biennial. 'A biennial guide to U.S. Government publications.' 1. Reference books — Bibliography 2. United States — Government publications — Bibliography. I. Wynkoop, Sally. comp.
Z1223.Z7 G68     015/.73     *LC* 76-146307

**Leidy, W. Philip (William Philip)**    **5.7778**
A popular guide to government publications / compiled by W. Philip Leidy. — 4th ed. — New York: Columbia University Press, 1976. xx, 440 p.; 21 cm. Includes index. 1. United States — Government publications — Bibliography. I. T.
Z1223.Z7 L4 1976 J83     015/.73     *LC* 76-17803     *ISBN* 0231040199

**Morehead, Joe, 1931-.**    **5.7779**
Introduction to United States public documents / Joe Morehead. — 3rd ed. — Littleton, Colo.: Libraries Unlimited, 1983. 309 p.; 24 cm. — (Library science text series.) 1. United States. Government Printing Office. 2. United States — Government publications I. T. II. Series.
Z1223.Z7 M67 1983     015.73 19     *LC* 82-22866     *ISBN* 0872873595

**Robinson, Judith Schiek, 1947-.**    **5.7780**
Subject guide to U.S. government reference sources / Judith Schiek Robinson. — Littleton, Colo.: Libraries Unlimited, 1985. xxxi, 333 p.; 25 cm. Rev. ed. of: Subject guide to government reference books / Sally Wynkoop. 1972. Includes index. 1. Reference books — Government publications — Bibliography. 2. Bibliography — Bibliography — Government publications. 3. United States — Government publications — Bibliography. I. Wynkoop, Sally. Subject guide to government reference books. II. T.
Z1223.Z7 R63 1985 J83     015.73 19     *LC* 85-10120     *ISBN* 0872874966

**Schmeckebier, Laurence Frederick, 1877-1959.**    • **5.7781**
Government publications and their use / [by] Laurence F. Schmeckebier [and] Roy B. Eastin. — 2d rev. ed. Washington: Brookings Institution [1969] viii, 502 p.; 24 cm. 1. United States — Government publications I. Eastin, Roy B. joint author. II. Brookings Institution. III. T.
Z1223.Z7 S3 1969     025.17/3     *LC* 69-19694     *ISBN* 0815777361

**Congressional Information Service.**    **5.7782**
CIS U.S. serial set index. — Washington: Congressional Information Service, 1977. 3 v.; 29 cm. Each part consists of 3 volumes: Subject index, A-K; subject index, L-Z; Finding lists. 1. United States — Government publications — Indexes — Collected works. I. T.
Z1223.Z9 C65 1975 J74     328.73     *LC* 75-27448     *ISBN* 0912380268

**Library of Congress.**    • **5.7783**
Monthly check-list of state publications. v.1- Jan. 1910-. Washington, U.S. Govt. print. off., 1912-. At head of title: Library of Congress. 1. United States — Government publications (State governments) — Bibliography. I. T.
Z1223.5.A1 U5     *LC* 10-8924

# Z1224 BIOBIBLIOGRAPHY

**Burke, William Jeremiah, 1902-.**    • **5.7784**
American authors and books, 1640 to the present day [by] W. J. Burke and Will D. Howe. Rev. by Irving Weiss and Anne Weiss. — 3d rev. ed. — New York: Crown Publishers, [c1972] 719 p.; 25 cm. 1. American literature — Bio-bibliography. 2. American literature — Dictionaries. 3. Booksellers and bookselling — United States. 4. Publishers and publishing — United States. 5. United States — Learned institutions and societies I. Howe, Will David, 1873-1946, joint author. II. Weiss, Irving, 1921- III. Weiss, Anne. IV. T.
Z1224.B87 1972     015/.73     *LC* 75-168332     *ISBN* 0517501392

**Contemporary authors; a bio–bibliographical guide to current writers in fiction, general nonfiction, poetry, journalism, drama, motion pictures, television and other fields.**    • **5.7785**
v. 1- 1962-. Detroit, Gale Research Co. v. 26-29 cm. Three times a year. Subtitle varies slightly. 'Each year's volumes are revised about five years later.' Vols. 101- carry single volume numbers. 1. Authors, American — 20th century. 2. United States — Bio-bibliography I. Gale Research Company.
Z1224.C6     928.1     *LC* 62-52046

## Z1225–1231 AMERICAN LITERATURE

**Nilon, Charles H.**      • **5.7786**
Bibliography of bibliographies in American literature, by Charles H. Nilon. — New York: R. R. Bowker Co., 1970. xi, 483 p.; 24 cm. 1. Bibliography — Bibliography — American literature. I. T.
Z1225.A1N5    016.01681    *LC* 73-103542    *ISBN* 0835202593

**Gohdes, Clarence Louis Frank, 1901-.**      **5.7787**
Bibliographical guide to the study of the literature of the U.S.A. / Clarence Gohdes and Sanford E. Marovitz. — 5th ed., completely rev. and enl. — Durham, N.C.: Duke University Press, 1984. xv, 255 p.; 25 cm. Includes indexes. 1. American literature — Bibliography 2. Bibliography — Bibliography — American literature. 3. United States — Bibliography I. Marovitz, Sanford E. II. T.
Z1225.G6 1984 PS88    016.81 19    *LC* 84-1677    *ISBN* 0822305925

**Jones, Howard Mumford, 1892-.**      • **5.7788**
Guide to American literature and its backgrounds since 1890 [by] Howard Mumford Jones and Richard M. Ludwig. — 4th ed., rev. and enl. — Cambridge, Mass.: Harvard University Press, 1972. xii, 264 p.; 22 cm. 1. American literature — 19th century — Bibliography. 2. American literature — 20th century — Bibliography. 3. United States — Civilization — Bibliography. I. Ludwig, Richard M., 1920- joint author. II. T.
Z1225.J65 1972    016.81    *LC* 72-85143    *ISBN* 0674367537

**Jones, Steven Swann, 1949-.**      **5.7789**
Folklore and literature in the United States: an annotated bibliography of studies of folklore in American literature / Steven Swann Jones. — New York: Garland Pub., 1984. xxvii, 262 p.; 23 cm. — (Garland folklore bibliographies. v. 5) (Garland reference library of the humanities. v. 392) Includes index. 1. American literature — History and criticism — Bibliography. 2. Folklore in literature — Bibliography. 3. Folklore — United States — Bibliography. I. T. II. Series. III. Series: Garland reference library of the humanities. v. 392
Z1225.J66 1984 PS169.F64    016.81/09/3 19    *LC* 82-49182    *ISBN* 0824091868

**Leary, Lewis Gaston, 1906-.**      **5.7790**
Articles on American literature, 1900–1950. — Durham, N.C.: Duke University Press, 1954. 437 p.; 24 cm. 1. American literature — History and criticism — Bibliography. I. T.
Z1225.L49    *LC* 54-5025

**Leary, Lewis Gaston, 1906-.**      • **5.7791**
Articles on American literature, 1950–1967. Compiled by Lewis Leary, with the assistance of Carolyn Bartholet and Catharine Roth. — Durham, N.C.: Duke University Press, 1970. xxi, 751 p.; 25 cm. 1. American literature — History and criticism — Bibliography. I. Bartholet, Carolyn, joint author. II. Roth, Hans-Georg. Catharine, joint author. III. T.
Z1225.L492    016.8109    *LC* 70-132027    *ISBN* 082231239X

**Leary, Lewis Gaston, 1906-.**      **5.7792**
Articles on American literature, 1968–1975 / compiled by Lewis Leary, with John Auchard. — Durham, N.C.: Duke University Press, 1979. xxv, 745 p.; 25 cm. 1. American literature — History and criticism — Bibliography. I. Auchard, John. II. T.
Z1225.L493 PS88    016.81/09 19    *LC* 79-52535    *ISBN* 0822304325

**Rubin, Louis Decimus, 1923-.**      • **5.7793**
A bibliographical guide to the study of Southern literature, edited by Louis D. Rubin, Jr. With an appendix containing sixty–eight additional writers of the colonial South by J. A. Leo Lemay. Baton Rouge, Louisiana State University Press [1969] xxiv, 368 p. 25 cm. (Southern literary studies.) 1. American literature — Southern States — Bibliography. I. Lemay, J. A. Leo (Joseph A. Leo), 1935- II. T. III. Series.
Z1225.R8    016.81    *LC* 69-17627    *ISBN* 0807103020

**Clark, Harry Hayden, 1901-1971.**      • **5.7794**
American literature: Poe through Garland. — New York: Appleton-Century-Crofts, [1971] xii, 148 p.; 24 cm. — (Goldentree bibliographies in language and literature) 1. American literature — 19th century — Bibliography. I. T.
Z1227.C58    016.8108    *LC* 77-137641    *ISBN* 0390193232

**Gallagher, Edward Joseph, 1940-.**      **5.7795**
Early puritan writers: a reference guide: William Bradford, John Cotton, Thomas Hooker, Edward Johnson, Richard Mather, Thomas Shepard / Edward J. Gallagher, Thomas Werge. — Boston: G. K. Hall, c1976. xvi, 207 p.; 25 cm. (Reference guides in literature; no. 10) Includes index. 1. American literature — Colonial period, ca. 1600-1775 — Bibliography. 2. Puritans — New England — Bibliography. 3. American literature — Puritan authors — Bibliography. I. Werge, Thomas, joint author. II. T.
Z1227.G34 PS191    016.81/08/001    *LC* 76-2498    *ISBN* 0816111960

**Scheick, William J.**      **5.7796**
Seventeenth–century American poetry: a reference guide / William J. Scheick and JoElla Doggett. — Boston: G. K. Hall, c1977. xix, 188 p.; 25 cm. — (Reference guides in literature; no. 14) Includes indexes. 1. American poetry — Colonial period, ca. 1600-1775 — History and criticism — Bibliography. I. Doggett, JoElla, joint author. II. T.
Z1227.S3 PS312    016.811/1    *LC* 76-18756    *ISBN* 0816179832

**Afro–American poetry and drama, 1760–1975: a guide to**      **5.7797**
**information sources.**
Detroit: Gale Research Co., c1979. ix, 493 p.; 23 cm. (Gale information guide library. American literature, English literature, and world literatures in English information guide series. v. 17) Includes indexes. 1. American literature — Afro-American authors — Bibliography. 2. American poetry — Afro-American authors — Bibliography. 3. American drama — Afro-American authors — Bibliography. I. French, William P. Afro-American poetry, 1760-1975. 1979. II. Fabre, Geneviève. Afro American drama, 1850-1975. 1979. III. Series.
Z1229.N39 A37 PS153.N5    016.810/9/896073    *LC* 74-11518    *ISBN* 0810312085

**Kallenbach, Jessamine S., 1915-.**      **5.7798**
Index to Black American literary anthologies / compiled under the direction of Jessamine S. Kallenbach; sponsored by the Center of Educational Resources, Eastern Michigan University. — Boston: G. K. Hall, 1978. xvi, 219 p.; 24 cm. — (Bibliographies and guides in Black studies) 1. American literature — Afro-American authors — Indexes. I. Eastern Michigan University. Center of Educational Resources. II. T. III. Series.
Z1229.N39 K34 PS153.N5    016.8108/0896    *LC* 78-13017    *ISBN* 0816181861

**Margolies, Edward.**      **5.7799**
Afro–American fiction, 1853–1976: a guide to information sources / Edward Margolies, David Bakish. — Detroit: Gale Research Co., c1979. xviii, 161 p.; 23 cm. — (Gale information guide library. American literature, English literature, and world literatures in English information guide series. v. 25) Includes indexes. 1. American fiction — Afro-American authors — Bibliography. I. Bakish, David. joint author. II. T. III. Series.
Z1229.N39 M37 PS374.N4    016.813/008/0352    *LC* 73-16976    *ISBN* 0810312077

**Rush, Theressa Gunnels, 1945-.**      **5.7800**
Black American writers past and present: a biographical and bibliographical dictionary / by Theressa Gunnels Rush, Carol Fairbanks Myers, Esther Spring Arata. — Metuchen, N.J.: Scarecrow Press, 1975. 2 v. (865 p.): ports.; 22 cm. 1. American literature — Afro-American authors — Bio-bibliography. I. Fairbanks, Carol, 1935- joint author. II. Arata, Esther Spring, joint author. III. T.
Z1229.N39 R87    016.8108/08/96073    *LC* 74-28400    *ISBN* 0810807858

## Z1231 SPECIAL TOPICS, A–Z

**Coleman, Arthur.**      **5.7801**
Drama criticism / Arthur Coleman and Gary R. Tyler. — Denver: A. Swallow, 1966-1971. — 2 v.; 23 cm. 1. English drama — History and criticism — Bibliography 2. American drama — History and criticism — Bibliography I. Tyler, Gary R. II. T.
Z1231.D7 C6    *LC* 66-30426

**Long, E. Hudson (Eugene Hudson), 1908-.**      • **5.7802**
American drama from its beginnings to the present / compiled by E. Hudson Long. — New York: Appleton-Century-Crofts, Educational Division, c1970. xi, 78 p.; 23 cm. — (Goldentree bibliographies in language and literature) 1. American drama — Bibliography I. T.
Z1231.D7 L64    016.812    *LC* 79-79170    *ISBN* 039057130X

**Meserve, Walter J.**      **5.7803**
American drama to 1900: a guide to information sources / Walter J. Meserve. — Detroit, Mich.: Gale Research Co., c1980. xviii, 254 p.; 23 cm. — (Gale information guide library. American literature, English literature, and world literatures in English information guide series. v. 28) Includes indexes. 1. American drama — 19th century — Bibliography. 2. American drama — Bibliography. I. T. II. Series.
Z1231.D7 M45 PS345    016.812    *LC* 79-27056    *ISBN* 0810313650

**Eddleman, Floyd Eugene.**      **5.7804**
American drama criticism: interpretations, 1890–1977 / compiled by Floyd Eugene Eddleman. — 2d ed. — Hamden, Conn.: Shoe String Press, 1979. viii, 488 p.; 24 cm. First ed., by H. H. Palmer, published in 1967. Includes indexes. 1. American drama — History and criticism — Bibliography. 2. Theater — United States — Reviews — Bibliography. I. Palmer, Helen H. American drama criticism. II. T.
Z1231.D7 P3 1979 PS332    016.812/009 19    *LC* 78-31346    *ISBN* 0208017135

**Stratman, Carl Joseph, 1917-1972.**     • **5.7805**
Bibliography of the American theatre, excluding New York City [by] Carl J. Stratman. — [Chicago]: Loyola University Press, [1965] xv, 397 p.; 24 cm. 1. Theater — United States — Bibliography. I. T.
Z1231.D7 S8     016.7920973     *LC* 65-3359

**Wegelin, Oscar, 1876-1970.**     • **5.7806**
Early American plays, 1714–1830; being a compilation of the titles of plays by American authors published and performed in America previous to 1830. Edited with an introd. by John Malone. — New York: B. Franklin, [1970] xxvi, 113 p.; 19 cm. — (Burt Franklin research and source works series, 573. Theatre and drama series, 12) Reprint of the 1900 ed. 1. American drama — Bibliography. I. T.
Z1231.D7 W4 1970     016.8121     *LC* 70-130101     *ISBN* 083373721X

**Wilmeth, Don B.**     **5.7807**
The American stage to World War I: a guide to information sources / Don B. Wilmeth. — Detroit: Gale Research Co., c1978. xxi, 269 p.; 23 cm. — (Performing arts information guide series; v. 4) (Gale information guide library) Includes indexes. 1. Theater — United States — History — Bibliography. I. T.
Z1231.D7 W55 PN2221     016.792/0973     *LC* 78-53488     *ISBN* 0810313928

**Adelman, Irving.**     **5.7808**
The contemporary novel; a checklist of critical literature on the British and American novel since 1945, by Irving Adelman and Rita Dworkin. — Metuchen, N.J.: Scarecrow Press, 1972. 614 p.; 22 cm. 1. American fiction — 20th century — History and criticism — Bibliography. 2. English fiction — 20th century — History and criticism — Bibliography. I. Dworkin, Rita, joint author. II. T.
Z1231.F4 A34     016.823/03     *LC* 72-4451     *ISBN* 0810805170

**Contento, William.**     **5.7809**
Index to science fiction anthologies and collections / William Contento. — Boston: G.K. Hall, c1978. 608 p.; 29 cm. (Reference publication in science fiction.) 1. Science fiction, American — Bibliography. 2. Science fiction, English — Bibliography. 3. Science fiction — Bibliography. I. T. II. Series.
Z1231.F4 C65 PS374.S35     016.813/0876/08 19     *LC* 78-155     *ISBN* 081618092X

**Gerstenberger, Donna Lorine.**     • **5.7810**
The American novel; a checklist of twentieth–century criticism, by Donna Gerstenberger and George Hendrick. — Denver: A. Swallow, [1961-70] 2 v.; 23 cm. Vol. 2 has subtitle: a checklist of twentieth century criticism on novels written since 1789. 1. American fiction — History and criticism — Bibliography. I. Hendrick, George. joint author. II. T.
Z1231.F4 G4     016.813/03     *LC* 61-9356

**Holman, C. Hugh (Clarence Hugh), 1914- comp.**     • **5.7811**
The American novel through Henry James, compiled by C. Hugh Holman. New York, Appleton-Century-Crofts [1966] ix, 102 p. 24 cm. (Goldentree bibliographies) 1. American fiction — History and criticism — Bibliography. 2. American fiction — Bibliography. I. T.
Z1231.F4 H64     016.813     *LC* 66-24253

**Kirby, David K.**     **5.7812**
American fiction to 1900: a guide to information sources / David K. Kirby. — Detroit: Gale Research Co., [1975] xvii, 296 p.; 23 cm. — (Gale information guide library. American literature, English literature, and world literatures in English information guide series. v. 4) Includes index. 1. American fiction — 19th century — History and criticism — Bibliography. 2. American literature — 19th century — Bibliography. I. T. II. Series.
Z1231.F4 K57 PS368     016.813/008     *LC* 73-16982     *ISBN* 0810312107

**Nevius, Blake.**     • **5.7813**
The American novel: Sinclair Lewis to the present. — New York: Appleton-Century-Crofts, [1970] xii, 126 p.; 24 cm. — (Goldentree bibliographies in language and literature) Pages 109-114 blank for 'Notes.' 1. American fiction — 20th century — History and criticism — Bibliography. I. T.
Z1231.F4 N4     016.813/5/209     *LC* 76-103094     *ISBN* 0390666718

**Science fiction in America, 1870s–1930s: an annotated bibliography of primary sources / compiled by Thomas D. Clareson.**     **5.7814**
Westport, Conn.: Greenwood Press, 1984. xiv, 305 p.; 25 cm. (Bibliographies and indexes in American literature. 0742-6860; no. 1) Includes indexes. 1. Science fiction, American — Bibliography. 2. Science fiction — Bibliography. 3. Science fiction, American — Stories, plots, etc. 4. Science fiction — Stories, plots, etc. I. Clareson, Thomas D. II. Series.
Z1231.F4 S38 1984 PS374.S35     016.813/0876 19     *LC* 84-8934     *ISBN* 0313231699

**Wegelin, Oscar, 1876-1970.**     • **5.7815**
Early American fiction, 1774–1830: a compilation of the titles of works of fiction, by writers born or residing in North America, north of the Mexican

border and printed previous to 1831 / by Oscar Wegelin. — 3rd ed., corr. and enl. — New York: P. Smith, 1929. 37 p. 1. American fiction — Bibliography. I. T.
Z1231.F4 W4 1929     *LC* 29-1440

**Woodress, James Leslie.**     **5.7816**
American fiction, 1900–1950: a guide to information sources / by James Woodress. — Detroit: Gale Research Co. [1974] xxii, 260 p.; 23 cm. (Gale information guide library. American literature, English literature, and world literatures in English information guide series. v. 1) 1. American fiction — 20th century — History and criticism — Bibliography. I. T. II. Series.
Z1231.F4 W64     016.813/03     *LC* 73-17501     *ISBN* 0810312018

**Wright, Lyle Henry, 1903-.**     • **5.7817**
American fiction, 1774–1850: a contribution toward a bibliography / by Lyle H. Wright. — 2d rev. ed. San Marino, Calif.: Huntington Library, 1969. xviii, 411 p.; 24 cm. (Huntington Library publications.) 1. American fiction — Bibliography. I. T. II. Series.
Z1231.F4 W9 1969     016.813/2     *LC* 68-29777

**Wright, Lyle Henry, 1903-.**     • **5.7818**
American fiction, 1851–1875; a contribution toward a bibliography, by Lyle H. Wright. San Marino, Calif., Huntington Library, 1965. xviii, 438 p. front. 24 cm. (Huntington Library publications.) 'Additions and corrections': p. [415]-438. 1. American fiction — 19th century — Bibliography. I. T. II. Series.
Z1231F4W92 1965     016.8133     *LC* 65-20870

**Wright, Lyle H. (Lyle Henry), 1903-.**     • **5.7819**
American fiction, 1876–1900: a contribution toward a bibliography / by Lyle H. Wright. — San Marino, Calif.: Huntington Library, 1966. xix, 683 p.; 24 cm. (Huntington Library publications.) 1. American fiction — 19th century — Bibliography. I. T.
Z1231.F4 W93     *LC* 66-24112

**Gingerich, Martin E.**     **5.7820**
Contemporary poetry in America and England, 1950–1975: a guide to information sources / Martin E. Gingerich. — Detroit, Mich.: Gale Research Co., c1983. xv, 453 p.; 23 cm. — (Volume 41 in the American literature, English literature, and world literatures in English information guide series) Includes indexes. 1. American poetry — 20th century — Bibliography. 2. English poetry — 20th century — Bibliography. I. T.
Z1231.P7 G56 1983 PS303     016.811/5 19     *LC* 73-16992     *ISBN* 0810312212

**Index of American periodical verse.**     **5.7821**
1971-. Metuchen, N.J., Scarecrow Press. 22 cm. Annual. 1. Poetry — Bibliography — Periodicals. 2. American periodicals — Indexes — Periodicals. I. Zulauf, Sander W., comp. II. Weiser, Irwin H., comp.
Z1231.P7 I47     016.811/5/4     *LC* 73-3060

**Wegelin, Oscar, 1876-1970.**     • **5.7822**
Early American poetry: a compilation of the titles of volumes of verse and broadsides by writers born or residing in North America north of the Mexican border / by Oscar Wegelin. — 2d ed., rev. and enl. — New York: P. Smith, 1930. 2 v. in 1 (239 p., 4 leaves of plates): facsims.; 25 cm. 1. American poetry — Bibliography. I. T.
Z1231.P7 W4 1930     *LC* 30-17830

**Partridge, Elinore Hughes.**     **5.7823**
American prose and criticism, 1820–1900: a guide to information sources / Elinore Hughes Partridge. — Detroit, Mich.: Gale Research Co., c1983. xv, 575 p.; 23 cm. — (Gale information guide library. Volume 39 in the American literature, English literature, and world literatures in English information guide series) Includes index. 1. American prose literature — 19th century — Bibliography. 2. Criticism — United States — Bibliography. I. T.
Z1231.P8 P37 1983 PS368     016.818/08 19     *LC* 82-24241     *ISBN* 0810312131

# Z1236–1363 AMERICAN HISTORY

## Z1236 General Bibliography

**America, history and life. Part C, American history bibliography, books, articles and dissertations.**     **5.7824**
Vol. 11 (1974)-     . — Santa Barbara, Calif.: Clio Press, c1975-. v.; 28 cm. Annual. 1. United States — History — Bibliography — Periodicals. 2. Canada — History — Bibliography — Periodicals. I. American Bibliographical Center.
Z1236.A48 Pt. C     973 11     *LC* 84-640891

**Beers, Henry Putney, 1907-.**      **5.7825**
Bibliographies in American history, 1942–1978: guide to materials for research / by Henry Putney Beers. — Woodbridge, CT: Research Publications, 1982. 2 v. (xviii, 946 p.); 24 cm. Continues: Bibliographies in American history. 1942. Includes index. 1. Bibliography — Bibliography — United States. 2. United States — History — Bibliography. I. T.
Z1236.B39 1982 E178     016.016973 19     *LC* 81-68886     *ISBN* 0892350385

**Freidel, Frank Burt.**      **5.7826**
Harvard guide to American history. — Rev. ed. Frank Freidel, editor, with the assistance of Richard K. Showman. — Cambridge, Mass.: Belknap Press of Harvard University Press, 1974. 2 v. (xxx, 1290 p.); 25 cm. Editions for 1954 and 1967 by O. Handlin and others. 1. United States — History — Bibliography. I. Showman, Richard K. joint author. II. Handlin, Oscar, 1915- Harvard guide to American history. III. T.
Z1236.F77 1974     016.9173/03     *LC* 72-81272     *ISBN* 0674375602

**Gibson, Ronald.**      **5.7827**
Name and subject index to the Presidential chronology series: from George Washington to Gerald R. Ford / by Ronald Gibson. — Dobbs Ferry, N.Y.: Oceana Publications, 1977. 141 p.; 24 cm. 1. The Presidential chronology series — Indexes. 2. Presidents — United States — Biography — Indexes. 3. United States — Politics and government — Indexes. I. T.
Z1236.G5 E183     016.973     *LC* 77-21512     *ISBN* 0379120941

**Ireland, Norma Olin, 1907-.**      **5.7828**
Index to America: life and customs / compiled by Norma Olin Ireland. — Westwood, Mass.: F.W. Faxon Co., 1976. 187 p.; 22 cm. (Useful reference series; no. 108.) 1. United States — History — Indexes. I. T.
Z1236.I73 E178     016.973     *LC* 76-7196     *ISBN* 0873051084

**Writings on American History.**      • **5.7829**
1902-. Washington, D. C. [etc.]: U. S. Government Printing Office [etc.] v. 26 cm. Annual. Subtitle varies. Vols for 1900-11 reprinted from the Annual report of the American Historical Association; 1918-29 issued as supplement to the report; 1930-31, 1935- issued as v. 2 of the report; 1932, as v. 3 and 1933-34 as the complete report. Earlier information in The Literature of American history and its supplement. Vol. for 1903 issued as Publication no. 38 of the Carnegie Institution of Washington. Some vols. issued in the congressional series as House documents. No bibliographies issued for 1904-05, 1941-47. 1. United States — Bibliography 2. America — Bibliography 3. United States — History — Bibliography 4. America — History — Bibliography 5. United States — History — Periodicals — Indexes. I. Library of Congress. II. American Historical Association. III. United States. National Historical Publications Commission. IV. American Historical Association. Annual report. V. American Historical Association. Supplement.
Z1236.L331

**Marcell, David W.**      **5.7830**
American studies: a guide to information sources / David W. Marcell. — Detroit, MI: Gale Research Co., c1982. xx, 207 p.; 23 cm. — (Gale information guide library. American studies information guide series. v. 10) Includes indexes. 1. United States — Bibliography I. T. II. Series.
Z1236.M37 1982 E156     016.973 19     *LC* 73-17559     *ISBN* 0810312638

## Z1237–1245 Bibliography, 1775–

**Allen, Robert S.**      **5.7831**
Loyalist literature: an annotated bibliographic guide to the writings on the Loyalists of the American Revolution / by Robert S. Allen. — Toronto: Dundurn Press, 1982. 63 p.; 22 cm. — (Dundurn Canadian historical document series. publication no. 2) 1. American loyalists — Bibliography. 2. United Empire loyalists — Bibliography. I. T. II. Series.
Z1238.A43 1982 E277     016.9733/14 19     *LC* 83-214947     *ISBN* 091967061X

**Gephart, Ronald M.**      **5.7832**
Revolutionary America, 1763–1789: a bibliography / compiled by Ronald M. Gephart. — Washington: Library of Congress: for sale by the Supt. of Docs., U.S. G.P.O., 1984. 2 v. (xl, 1672 p.): ill.; 27 cm. Ill. on lining papers. Includes index. 1. Library of Congress — Catalogs. 2. United States — History — Revolution, 1775-1783 — Bibliography — Catalogs. 3. United States — History — Confederation, 1783-1789 — Bibliography — Catalogs. 4. United States — History — Revolution, 1775-1783 — Sources — Bibliography — Catalogs. 5. United States — History — Confederation, 1783-1789 — Sources — Bibliography — Catalogs. I. Library of Congress. II. T.
Z1238.G43 1984 E208     016.9733 19     *LC* 80-606802     *ISBN* 0844403598

**White, J. Todd.**      **5.7833**
Fighters for independence: a guide to sources of biographical information on soldiers and sailors of the American Revolution / edited by J. Todd White and Charles H. Lesser. — Chicago: University of Chicago Press, 1977. xiv, 112 p.; 24 cm. — (Clements Library Bicentennial studies) Includes index. 1. Catalogs,

Union — United States. 2. United States — History — Revolution, 1775-1783 — Biography — Bibliography — Union lists. 3. United States — History — Revolution, 1775-1783 — Sources — Bibliography — Union lists. 4. United States — Genealogy — Bibliography — Union lists. I. Lesser, Charles H., joint author. II. T. III. Series.
Z1238.W45 E206     016.9733/092/2 B     *LC* 77-78068     *ISBN* 0226894983

**Fredriksen, John C.**      **5.7834**
Free trade and sailors' rights: a bibliography of the War of 1812 / compiled by John C. Fredriksen. — Westport, Conn.: Greenwood Press, c1985. xiii, 399 p.; 24 cm. (Bibliographies and indexes in American history. 0742-6828; no. 2) Includes index. 1. United States — History — War of 1812 — Bibliography. I. T. II. Series.
Z1240.F74 1985 E354     016.9735/2 19     *LC* 84-15743     *ISBN* 0313243131

**Tutorow, Norman E.**      **5.7835**
The Mexican–American War: an annotated bibliography / compiled and edited by Norman E. Tutorow. — Westport, Conn.: Greenwood Press, 1981. xxix, 427 p.: ill.; 29 cm. Includes index. 1. United States — History — War with Mexico, 1845-1848 — Bibliography. 2. United States — History — War with Mexico, 1845-1848 — Sources — Bibliography. I. T.
Z1241.T87 E404     016.9736/2 19     *LC* 80-1789     *ISBN* 0313221812

**Dornbusch, C. E. (Charles Emil), 1907-.**      **5.7836**
[Regimental publications & personal narratives of the Civil War] Military bibliography of the Civil War / Compiled by C. E. Dornbusch. — New York: New York Public Library, [1971-. 3 v. ill. 26 cm. Vol. 1 is a reprint of the 1961-62 ed. published under title: Regimental publications & personal narratives of the Civil War. 1. United States — History — Civil War, 1861-1865 — Regimental histories — Bibliography. 2. United States — History — Civil War, 1861-1865 — Personal narratives — Bibliography. I. T.
Z1242.D612     016.9737/4     *LC* 72-137700     *ISBN* 0871045044

**Buenker, John D.**      **5.7837**
Progressive reform: a guide to information sources / John D. Buenker, Nicholas C. Burckel; pref. by Arthur Mann. — Detroit, Mich.: Gale Research Co., c1980. xiii, 366 p.; 23 cm. — (American Government and history information guide series; v. 8) (Gale information guide library) Includes indexes. 1. Progressivism (United States politics) — Bibliography. 2. United States — Politics and government — 1865-1933 — Bibliography. I. Burckel, Nicholas C. joint author. II. T. III. Series.
Z1242.8.B84 E661     016.9738 19     *LC* 80-23992     *ISBN* 0810314851

**Smith, Myron J.**      **5.7838**
Watergate: an annotated bibliography of sources in English, 1972–1982 / by Myron J. Smith, Jr. — Metuchen, N.J.: Scarecrow Press, 1983. xiii, 329 p.; 23 cm. Includes index. 1. Watergate Affair, 1972-1974 — Bibliography. I. T.
Z1245.S64 1983 E860     016.3641/32/0973 19     *LC* 83-4408     *ISBN* 0810816237

## Z1247–1249 Special Topics, A–Z

**Grim, Ronald E.**      **5.7839**
Historical geography of the United States: a guide to information sources / Ronald E. Grim. — Detroit, Mich.: Gale Research Co., 1982. xix, 291 p.; 23 cm. — (Vol. 5 in the Geography and travel information guide series) Includes indexes. 1. United States — Historical geography — Bibliography. I. T.
Z1247.G74 1982 E179.5     016.911/73 19     *LC* 82-15674     *ISBN* 0810314711

**Davis, Lenwood G.**      **5.7840**
The Ku Klux Klan: a bibliography / compiled by Lenwood G. Davis and Janet L. Sims–Wood, with the assistance of Marsha L. Moore; foreword by Earl E. Thorpe. — Westport, Conn.: Greenwood Press, 1984. xv, 643 p.; 24 cm. Includes index. 1. Ku-Klux Klan — Bibliography. 2. Ku Klux Klan (1915- ) — Bibliography. I. Sims-Wood, Janet L., 1945- II. Moore, Marsha L. III. T.
Z1249.K8 D38 1984 E668     016.322.4/2/0973 19     *LC* 83-1709
    *ISBN* 031322949X

**Davis, Lenwood G.**      **5.7841**
Blacks in the American armed forces, 1776–1983: a bibliography / compiled by Lenwood G. Davis and George Hill; forewords by Benjamin O. Davis, Jr. and Percy E. Johnston. — Westport, Conn.: Greenwood Press, 1985. xv, 198 p.; 25 cm. (Bibliographies and indexes in Afro-American and African studies. 0742-6924; no. 3) Includes index. 1. United States — Armed Forces — Afro-Americans — Bibliography. I. Hill, George H. II. T. III. Series.
Z1249.M5 D38 1985 UB418.A47     016.355/008996073 19     *LC* 84-15697     *ISBN* 0313240922

**A Guide to the sources of United States military history /**    **5.7842**
**edited by Robin Higham.**
Hamden, Conn.: Archon Books, 1975. xiii, 559 p.; 24 cm. 1. United States — History, Military — Bibliography. I. Higham, Robin D. S.
Z1249.M5 G83 1975 E181    016.355/00973    *LC* 75-14455    *ISBN* 0208014993

**Lane, Jack C., 1932-.**    **5.7843**
America's military past: a guide to information sources / Jack C. Lane. — Detroit: Gale Research Co., c1980. xi, 280 p.; 23 cm. — (American government and history information guide series; v. 7) (Gale information guide library) Includes indexes. 1. United States — History, Military — Bibliography. I. T. II. Series.
Z1249.M5 L36 E181    016.973    *LC* 74-11517    *ISBN* 0810312050

**Coletta, Paolo Enrico, 1916-.**    **5.7844**
A bibliography of American naval history / compiled by Paolo E. Coletta. — Annapolis, Md.: Naval Institute Press, c1981. xviii, 453 p.; 23 cm. Includes indexes. 1. United States. Navy — Bibliography. 2. United States — History, Naval — Bibliography. I. T.
Z1249.N3 C64 E182    016.973 19    *LC* 80-24864    *ISBN* 0870211056

**Smith, Myron J.**    **5.7845**
The United States Navy and Coast Guard, 1946–1983: a bibliography of English–language works and 16 mm films / compiled by Myron J. Smith, Jr.; foreword by E.R. Zumwalt, Jr.; historical note by John D.H. Kane, Jr. — Jefferson, N.C.: McFarland, 1984. xx, 539 p.; 24 cm. Includes indexes. 1. United States. Navy — History — 20th century — Bibliography. 2. United States. Coast Guard — History — 20th century — Bibliography. 3. United States — History, Naval — 20th century — Bibliography. I. T.
Z1249.N3 S63 1984 VA58.4    016.359/00973 19    *LC* 84-42605    *ISBN* 0899501222

**The American presidency: a historical bibliography.**    **5.7846**
Santa Barbara, Calif.: ABC-Clio Information Services, c1984. viii, 376 p.; 29 cm. — (Clio bibliography series. no. 15) Includes indexes. 1. Presidents — United States — Bibliography. 2. United States — Politics and government — Bibliography. I. ABC-Clio Information Services. II. Series.
Z1249.P7 A47 1984 E176.1    016.973/09/92 19    *LC* 83-12245    *ISBN* 0874363705

**Davison, Kenneth E.**    **5.7847**
The American presidency: a guide to information sources / Kenneth E. Davison. — Detroit, Mich.: Gale Research Co., c1983. xvi, 467 p.; 23 cm. — (Gale information guide library. American studies information guide series. v. 11) Includes indexes. 1. Presidents — United States — Bibliography. 2. United States — Politics and government — Bibliography. I. T. II. Series.
Z1249.P7 D38 1983 E176.1    016.973/09/92 19    *LC* 73-17552    *ISBN* 0810312611

**Goehlert, Robert, 1948-.**    **5.7848**
The presidency: a research guide / Robert U. Goehlert, Fenton S. Martin. — Santa Barbara, Calif.: ABC-Clio Information Services, c1985. xxv, 341 p.; 24 cm. Includes indexes. 1. Presidents — United States — Bibliography. 2. Presidents — United States — Research. I. Martin, Fenton S. II. T.
Z1249.P7 G63 1985 JK516    016.35303/1 19    *LC* 84-6425    *ISBN* 087436373X

**Dumond, Dwight Lowell, 1895-.**    • **5.7849**
A bibliography of antislavery in America / by Dwight Lowell Dumond. — Ann Arbor: University of Michigan Press, 1961. –. 119 p.; 29 cm. — 1. Slavery in the United States — Antislavery movements — Bibliography. I. T.
Z1249.S6 D8    016.326973    *LC* 61-9306

## Z1250–1357 Local Bibliography, by Region or State

**Crouch, Milton, 1937-.**    **5.7850**
Directory of state and local history periodicals / compiled by Milton Crouch and Hans Raum. Chicago: American Library Association, 1977. xi, 124 p.; 23 cm. Includes index. 1. United States — History, Local — Periodicals — Directories. I. Raum, Hans, 1940- joint author. II. T.
Z1250.C76 E180    973/.05    *LC* 77-4396    *ISBN* 0838902464

**Filby, P. William, 1911-.**    **5.7851**
A bibliography of American county histories / compiled by P. William Filby. — Baltimore: Genealogical Pub. Co., 1985. xiv, 449 p.; 24 cm. 1. United States — History, Local — Bibliography. I. T. II. Title: American county histories.
Z1250.F54 1985 E180    016.973 19    *LC* 85-80029    *ISBN* 0806311266

**Library of Congress.**    **5.7852**
United States local histories in the Library of Congress: a bibliography / edited by Marion J. Kaminkow. — Baltimore: Magna Carta Book Co., 1975. 4 v.; 29 cm. 'A Bicentennial book.' Compiled from a microfilm copy of the Library's

shelflist for LC classification Fl-975. 1. Library of Congress. 2. United States — History, Local — Bibliography — Catalogs. 3. United States — Genealogy — Bibliography — Catalogs. 4. United States — Biography — Bibliography — Catalogs. 5. United States — Description and travel — Bibliography — Catalogs. I. Kaminkow, Marion J. II. T.
Z1250.U59 1975 E180    016.973    *LC* 74-25444    *ISBN* 0910946175

**Green, Fletcher Melvin, 1895-.**    **5.7853**
The Old South / compiled by Fletcher M. Green and J. Isaac Copeland. — Arlington Heights, Ill.: AHM Pub. Corp., c1980. xvii, 173 p.; 24 cm. — (Goldentree bibliographies in American history) Includes index. 1. Southern States — History — 1775-1865 — Bibliography. I. Copeland, J. Isaac (James Isaac), 1910- II. T. III. Series.
Z1251.S7 G69 1980 F213    016.975/03 19    *LC* 79-55730    *ISBN* 088295539X

**Smith, Dwight La Vern, 1918-.**    **5.7854**
The American and Canadian West: a bibliography / Dwight L. Smith, editor; Ray A. Billington, introd. — Santa Barbara, Calif.: ABC-Clio, c1979. xi, 558 p.; 29 cm. (Clio bibliography series; no. 6) Includes indexes. 1. Northwest, Canadian — History — Abstracts. 2. West (U.S.) — History — Bibliography. 3. West (U.S.) — History — Abstracts. 4. Northwest, Canadian — History — Bibliography. I. T.
Z1251.W5 S64 F591    016.978    *LC* 78-24478    *ISBN* 0874362725

## Z1361 Special Topics, A–M

**Douglass, William A.**    **5.7855**
Basque Americans: a guide to information sources / William A. Douglass, Richard W. Etulain. — Detroit, Mich.: Gale Research Co., c1981. xiv, 169 p.; 23 cm. — (Gale Information guide library. Ethnic studies information guide series. v. 6) Includes indexes. 1. Basque Americans — Bibliography. I. Etulain, Richard W. II. T. III. Series.
Z1361.B3 D68 E184.B15    016.973/049992 19    *LC* 81-6633    *ISBN* 081031469X

**Greenwood, John, 1943-.**    **5.7856**
American defense policy since 1945: a preliminary bibliography / compiled by John Greenwood; with the advisement of Robin Higham; edited by Geoffrey Kemp, Clark Murdock [and] Frank L. Simonie. — Lawrence: Published for the National Security Education Program, by the University Press of Kansas [1973] xv, 317 p.; 23 cm. (National Security studies series) (Kansas State University Library bibliography series. no. 11) 1. United States — Defenses — Bibliography. 2. United States — Military policy — Bibliography. I. T. II. Series. III. Series: Kansas State University Library bibliography series. no. 11
Z1361.D4 G73    016.3554    *LC* 72-97468    *ISBN* 0700601058

**Buttlar, Lois, 1934-.**    **5.7857**
Building ethnic collections: an annotated guide for school media centers and public libraries / Lois Buttlar, Lubomyr R. Wynar. Littleton, Colo.: Libraries Unlimited, 1977. 434 p.; 24 cm. Includes indexes. 1. Minorities — United States — Bibliography. I. Wynar, Lubomyr Roman, 1932- joint author. II. T.
Z1361.E4 B88 E184.A1    016.973/04    *LC* 76-55398    *ISBN* 0872871304

**Miller, Wayne Charles.**    **5.7858**
A comprehensive bibliography for the study of American minorities / Wayne Charles Miller; with Faye Nell Vowell and Gary K. Crist ... [et al.]. — New York: New York University Press, 1976. 2 v.; 29 cm. 1. Minorities — United States — Bibliography. 2. United States — Foreign population — Bibliography. I. Vowell, Faye Nell. II. Crist, Gary K. III. T.
Z1361.E4 M5    Z1361E4 M5.

**Miller, Wayne Charles.**    **5.7859**
A handbook of American minorities / Wayne Charles Miller. New York: New York University Press, 1976. xi, 225 p.; 29 cm. 1. Minorities — United States — Bibliography. I. T.
Z1361.E4 M53 E184.A1    016.30145/0973    *LC* 74-21636    *ISBN* 0814753736

**Schultz, Arthur R.**    **5.7860**
German–American relations and German culture in America: a subject bibliography, 1941–1980 / Arthur R. Schultz. — Millwood, N.Y.: Kraus International Publications, c1984. 2 v. (xxiv, 1279 p.); 27 cm. Includes index. 1. German Americans — Bibliography. 2. Germans — Canada — Bibliography. 3. Germany — Relations — United States — Bibliography. 4. United States — Civilization — German influences — Bibliography. 5. United States — Relations — Germany — Bibliography. I. T.
Z1361.G37 S38 1984 E184.G3    016.3058/31/073 19    *LC* 82-48987    *ISBN* 0527715727

**Metress, Seamus P.**     **5.7861**
The Irish–American experience: a guide to the literature / Seamus P. Metress. — Washington, D.C.: University Press of America, c1981. 220 p.; 23 cm. 1. Irish Americans — Bibliography. 2. Irish — Canada — Bibliography. I. T.
Z1361.I7 M47 E184.I6     016.973/049162 19     LC 80-69050     *ISBN* 0819116947

**Cordasco, Francesco, 1920-.**     **5.7862**
Italian Americans: a guide to information sources / Francesco Cordasco. — Detroit: Gale Research Co., c1978. xix, 222 p.; 23 cm. — (Ethnic studies information guide series; v. 2) (Gale information guide library) Includes indexes. 1. Italian Americans — Bibliography. I. T.
Z1361.I8 C659 E184.I8     016.973/04/51     LC 78-4833     *ISBN* 0810313979

**Meier, Matt S.**     **5.7863**
Bibliography of Mexican American history / compiled by Matt S. Meier. — Westport, Conn.: Greenwood Press, 1984. xi, 500 p.; 25 cm. Includes indexes. 1. Mexican Americans — History — Bibliography. I. T.
Z1361.M4 M414 1984 E184.M5     016.973/046872 19     LC 83-18585     *ISBN* 031323776X

**Trejo, Arnulfo D.**     **5.7864**
Bibliografia chicana: a guide to information sources / Arnulfo D. Trejo. Detroit: Gale Research Co., c1975. xx, 193 p.; 22 cm. (Ethnic studies; v. 1) (Gale information guide library) Includes indexes. 1. Mexican Americans — Bibliography. I. T.
Z1361.M4 T73 E184.M5     016.973/04/6872     LC 74-11562     *ISBN* 0810313111

## Z1361 N–Z

**Black immigration and ethnicity in the United States: an**     **5.7865**
**annotated bibliography / Center for Afroamerican and African**
**Studies, the University of Michigan.**
Westport, Conn.: Greenwood Press, 1985. xi, 170 p.; 25 cm. (Bibliographies and indexes in Afro-American and African studies. 0742-6925; no. 2) Includes indexes. 1. Afro-Americans — Bibliography. 2. United States — Foreign population — Bibliography. 3. United States — Emigration and immigration — Bibliography. I. University of Michigan. Center for Afroamerican and African Studies. II. Series.
Z1361.N39 B553 1985 E185     016.3058/96073 19     LC 84-12886     *ISBN* 0313243662

**Brignano, Russell C. (Russell Carl), 1935-.**     **5.7866**
Black Americans in autobiography: an annotated bibliography of autobiographies and autobiographical books written since the Civil War / Russell C. Brignano. — Rev. and expanded ed. — Durham, N.C.: Duke University Press, 1984. xi, 193 p.; 25 cm. Includes indexes. 1. Afro-Americans — Biography — Bibliography — Union lists. 2. Slaves — United States — Biography — Bibliography — Union lists. 3. Autobiographies — Bibliography — Union lists. 4. Catalogs, Union — United States. I. T.
Z1361.N39 B67 1984 E185.96     016.973/0496073022 B 19     LC 83-20505     *ISBN* 0822305593

**Davis, Lenwood G.**     **5.7867**
A bibliographical guide to Black studies programs in the United States: an annotated bibliography / compiled by Lenwood G. Davis and George Hill, with the assistance of Janie Miller Harris; foreword by Bonnie J. Gillespie. — Westport, Conn.: Greenwood Press, 1985. xvii, 120 p.; 25 cm. (Bibliographies and indexes in Afro-American and African studies. 0742-6925; no. 6) Includes index. 1. Afro-Americans — Study and teaching — United States — Bibliography. 2. Afro-Americans — Bibliography. 3. Blacks — Study and teaching — United States — Bibliography. 4. Afro-Americans — Education — Bibliography. I. Hill, George H. II. Harris, Janie Miller. III. T. IV. Series.
Z1361.N39 D353 1985 E184.7     016.973/0496073 19     LC 85-12722     *ISBN* 0313233284

**Davis, Lenwood G.**     **5.7868**
The Black family in the United States: a revised, updated, selectively annotated bibliography / compiled by Lenwood G. Davis. — New York: Greenwood Press, 1986. x, 234 p.; 25 cm. — (Bibliographies and indexes in Afro-American and African studies. 0742-6925; no. 14) Includes index. 1. Afro-Americans — Families — Bibliography. I. T. II. Series.
Z1361.N39 D355 1986 E185.86     016.3068/5/08996073 19     LC 86-9926     *ISBN* 0313252378

**Davis, Lenwood G.**     **5.7869**
Black–Jewish relations in the United States, 1752–1984: a selected bibliography / compiled by Lenwood G. Davis. — Westport, Conn.: Greenwood Press, 1984. xv, 130 p.; 25 cm. (Bibliographies and indexes in Afro-American and African studies. 0742-6925; no. 1) Includes index. 1. Afro-Americans — Relations with Jews — Bibliography. I. T. II. Series.
Z1361.N39 D357 1984 E185.615     016.973/0496 19     LC 84-4685     *ISBN* 0313233292

**Davis, Nathaniel.**     **5.7870**
Afro–American reference: an annotated bibliography of selected resources / compiled and edited by Nathaniel Davis. — Westport, Conn.: Greenwood Press, 1985. xiii, 288 p.; 25 cm. (Bibliographies and indexes in Afro-American and African studies. 0742-6925; no. 9) Includes indexes. 1. Bibliography — Bibliography — Afro-Americans. 2. Afro-Americans — Bibliography. I. T. II. Series.
Z1361.N39 D37 1985 E185     016.973/0496 19     LC 85-21942     *ISBN* 031324930X

**Early Black bibliographies, 1863–1918 / [compiled by] Betty**     **5.7871**
**Kaplan Gubert.**
New York: Garland Pub., 1982. xiii, 380 p.: ill.; 23 cm. — (Critical studies on Black life and culture. v. 25) (Garland reference library of social science. v. 103) Includes index. 1. Bibliography — Bibliography — Afro-Americans. 2. Afro-Americans — Bibliography. I. Gubert, Betty Kaplan, 1934- II. Series. III. Series: Garland reference library of social science. v. 103
Z1361.N39 E25 1982 E185     016.973/0496073 19     LC 81-43340     *ISBN* 0824092902

**Glenn, Robert W., 1944-.**     **5.7872**
Black rhetoric: a guide to Afro–American communication / by Robert W. Glenn. — Metuchen, N.J.: Scarecrow Press, 1976. x, 376 p.; 23 cm. Includes indexes. 1. Afro-Americans — Bibliography. I. T.
Z1361.N39 G55 E185     016.8085     LC 75-38912     *ISBN* 0810808897

**Indiana University. Libraries.**     **5.7873**
The Black family and the Black woman: a bibliography / compiled by Phyllis Rauch Klotman with Wilmer H. Baatz. — New York: Arno Press, 1978. x, 231 p.; 24 cm. 1. Indiana University. Libraries. 2. Afro-Americans — Families — Bibliography — Catalogs. 3. Afro-American women — Bibliography — Catalogs. I. Klotman, Phyllis Rauch. II. Baatz, Wilmer H. III. T.
Z1361.N39 I45 1978 E185.86     016.9173/06/96073     LC 77-20144     *ISBN* 0405105231

**Momeni, Jamshid A., 1938-.**     **5.7874**
Demography of the Black population in the United States: an annotated bibliography with a review essay / Jamshid A. Momeni; foreword by James F. Scott; preface by Reynolds Farley. — Westport, Conn.: Greenwood Press, 1983. xxi, 354 p.; 24 cm. Includes index. 1. Afro-Americans — Population — Bibliography. I. T.
Z1361.N39 M6 1983 E185.86     016.3046/08996073 19     LC 83-5544     *ISBN* 031323812X

**Newman, Richard.**     **5.7875**
Black access: a bibliography of Afro–American bibliographies / compiled by Richard Newman. — Westport, Conn.: Greenwood Press, 1984. xxviii, 249 p.; 24 cm. Includes indexes. 1. Bibliography — Bibliography — Afro-Americans. 2. Afro-Americans — Bibliography. I. T.
Z1361.N39 N578 1984 E185     016.016973//0496073 19     LC 83-8537     *ISBN* 0313232822

**Obudho, Constance E.**     **5.7876**
Black–white racial attitudes: an annotated bibliography / Constance E. Obudho. — Westport, Conn.: Greenwood Press, 1976. xii, 180 p.; 22 cm. Includes indexes. 1. Attitude (Psychology) — Bibliography. 2. Afro-Americans — Race identity — Bibliography. 3. United States — Race question — Bibliography. I. T.
Z1361.N39 O28 1976 E185.61     016.30145/1/0420973     LC 75-35351     *ISBN* 0837185823

**Sims-Wood, Janet L., 1945-.**     **5.7877**
The progress of Afro–American women: a selected bibliography and resource guide / compiled by Janet L. Sims; foreword by Bettye Thomas. — Westport, Conn.: Greenwood Press, 1980. xvi, 378 p.; 24 cm. Includes index. 1. Afro-American women — Bibliography. I. T.
Z1361.N39 S52 E185.86     016.973/04/96073     LC 79-8948     *ISBN* 0313220832

**Spradling, Mary Mace, 1905-.**     **5.7878**
In Black and white: a guide to magazine articles, newspaper articles, and books concerning more than 15,000 Black individuals and groups / Mary Mace Spradling, editor. — 3d ed. — Detroit, Mich.: Gale Research Co., c1980. 2 v. (xiii, 1282 p.); 29 cm. 1. Afro-Americans — Biography — Indexes. I. T.
Z1361.N39 S655 1980 E185.96     920/.009296073     LC 80-15270     *ISBN* 0810304384

**Turner, Darwin T., 1931-.**     • **5.7879**
Afro–American writers, compiled by Darwin T. Turner. New York, Appleton-Century-Crofts, Educational Division [1970] xvii, 117 p. 24 cm. (Goldentree bibliographies in language and literature) 1. American literature — Afro-American authors — Bibliography. 2. Afro-Americans — History — Bibliography. I. T.
Z1361.N39 T78     016.8108//091/7496     LC 72-79171     *ISBN* 0390888729

**Welsch, Erwin K.**     • **5.7880**
The Negro in the United States: a research guide / by Erwin K. Welsch. — Bloomington: Indiana University Press, 1965. xiii, 142 p.; 21 cm. Bibliography: p. 108-138. 1. Afro-Americans — Bibliography. I. T. Z1361.N39W4 1965    016.30145196073    *LC* 65-23085

**Sourcebook of Hispanic culture in the United States** / edited by    **5.7881**
David William Foster.
Chicago: American Library Association, 1983 (c1982). x, 352 p.; 24 cm. 1. Hispanic Americans — Bibliography. I. Foster, David William. II. Title: Hispanic culture in the United States. Z1361.S7 S64 1982 E184.S75    016.306/08968073 19    *LC* 82-20688 *ISBN* 0838903541

---

# Z1365–1401 Canada

**Canadian books in print. Catalogue des livres canadiens en**    • **5.7882**
**librairie, 1970. Edited by Harald Bohne.**
[4th ed.]. — [Toronto]: Published by University of Toronto Press for the Canadian Books in Print Committee, [1970] 814 p.; 26 cm. English or French. 1. Canada — Imprints. I. Bohne, Harald, ed. II. Canadian Books in Print Committee. III. Title: Catalogue des livres canadiens en librairie. Z1365.C2197 1970    015/.71    *LC* 70-21108

**Canadiana.**    **5.7883**
Annual cumulation. 1950/51-. Ottawa: National Library of Canada. v. in v.; 28 cm. Annual. 1. Canada — Imprints. 2. Canada — Bibliography. I. National Library of Canada. Z1365.C24    015/.71    *LC* ce 76-31915

**Cariou, Mavis.**    **5.7884**
Canadian selection: books and periodicals for libraries / compiled by Mavis Cariou, Sandra J. Cox, Alvan Bregman; with the assistance of Judith M. Gummer. — 2nd ed. — Toronto: Published for the Ontario Ministry of Citizenship and Culture and the Centre for Research in Librarianship, University of Toronto [by] University of Toronto Press, c1985. xvi, 501 p.; 29 cm. Includes indexes. 1. English imprints — Canada. 2. Canada — Imprints. 3. Canada — Bibliography. I. Cox, Sandra J. II. Bregman, Alvan. III. Jarvi, Edith T., 1921- Canadian selection. IV. Ontario. Ministry of Citizenship and Culture. V. University of Toronto. Centre for Research in Librarianship. VI. T. Z1365.J38 1985    015.71/03 19    *ISBN* 0802046304

**Ryder, Dorothy E.**    **5.7885**
Canadian reference sources: a selective guide / Dorothy E. Ryder. — 2nd ed. — Ottawa, Ont.: Canadian Library Association, 1981. viii, 311 p.; 26 cm. Includes index. 1. Reference books — Canada — Bibliography. 2. Bibliography — Bibliography — Canada. 3. Canada — Bibliography. I. Canadian Library Association. II. T. Z1365.R8 1981 F1008    011/.02/0971 19    *LC* 84-106657    *ISBN* 0888021569

**Bishop, Olga Bernice.**    **5.7886**
Canadian official publications / Olga B. Bishop. — 1st ed. — Oxford; New York: Pergamon Press, 1981. ix, 297 p.; 22 cm. — (Guides to official publications; v. 9) 1. Canada — Government publications — Bibliography. I. T. II. Series. Z1373.B48 1981 J103    015.71 19    *LC* 80-41572    *ISBN* 0080246974

**The Annotated bibliography of Canada's major authors** / edited    **5.7887**
by Robert Lecker and Jack David.
Downsview, Canada: ECW Press; Boston: distributed by G.K. Hall, 1979-c1985. v. 1-6; 21 x 23 cm. Includes indexes. 1. Canadian literature — Bibliography. 2. French-Canadian literature — Bibliography. I. Lecker, Robert, 1951- II. David, Jack, 1946- Z1375.A56 PR9184.3    016.81    *LC* 80-479263    *ISBN* 0920802087

**Moyles, R. G.**    **5.7888**
English–Canadian literature to 1900: a guide to information sources / R.G. Moyles. — Detroit: Gale Research Co., c1976. xi, 346 p.; 22 cm. — (Gale information guide library. American literature, English literature, and world literatures in English information guide series. v. 6) Includes indexes. 1. Canadian literature — Bibliography. 2. Canadian literature — History and criticism. I. T. II. Series. Z1375.M68 PR9184.3    016.81/08    *LC* 73-16986    *ISBN* 0810312220

**Watters, Reginald Eyre.**    **5.7889**
A checklist of Canadian literature and background materials, 1628–1960, in two parts: first, a comprehensive list of the books which constitute Canadian literature written in English; and second, a selective list of other books by Canadian authors which reveal the backgrounds of that literature. — 2d ed., rev. and enl. — [Toronto; Buffalo]: University of Toronto Press, [1972] xxiv, 1085 p.; 24 cm. 1. Canadian literature — Bibliography. 2. Canada — Bibliography. I. T. Z1375.W3 1972    013/.971    *LC* 72-80713    *ISBN* 0802018661

**Watters, Reginald Eyre, 1912-.**    **5.7890**
On Canadian literature , 1806–1960: a check list of articles, books, and theses on English–Canadian literature, its authors, and language / compiled by Reginald Eyre Watters, Inglis Freeman Bell. — Reprinted with corrections and additions 1973. — Toronto: University of Toronto Press, 1973, c1966. ix, 165 p.; 25 cm. 1. Canadian literature (English) — History and criticism — Bibliography. I. Bell, Inglis Freeman, 1917- II. T. Z1375.W3 1973    016.81/09    *ISBN* 0802051669

**Fee, Margery, 1948-.**    **5.7891**
Canadian fiction: an annotated bibliography / Margery Fee, Ruth Cawker. — Toronto: P. Martin, c1976. xiii, 170 p.; 24 cm. 1. Canadian fiction — Bibliography. I. Cawker, Ruth, 1953- joint author. II. T. Z1377.F4 F4 PR9192.2    016.813    *LC* 77-355248    *ISBN* 0887781349

**Hoy, Helen.**    **5.7892**
Modern English–Canadian prose: a guide to information sources / Helen Hoy. — Detroit, Mich.: Gale Research Co., 1983. xxiii, 605 p.; 23 cm. (Gale information guide library. American literature, English literature, and world literatures in English; v. 38) Includes indexes. 1. Canadian fiction — 20th century — Bibliography. 2. Canadian prose literature — 20th century — Bibliography. I. T. Z1377.F4 H69 1983 PR9192.5    016.818/508 19    *LC* 73-16996 *ISBN* 081031245X

**Stevens, Peter, 1927-.**    **5.7893**
Modern English–Canadian poetry: a guide to information sources / Peter Stevens. — Detroit, Mich.: Gale Research Co., c1978. xi, 216 p.; 23 cm. — (Gale information guide library. American literature, English literature, and world literatures in English information guide series. v. 15) Includes indexes. 1. Canadian poetry — 20th century — History and criticism — Bibliography. 2. Canadian poetry — 20th century — Bibliography. I. T. II. Series. Z1377.P7 S79 PR9184.3    016.811/5    *LC* 73-16994    *ISBN* 0810312441

**Avis, Walter S.**    **5.7894**
Writings on Canadian English, 1792–1975: an annotated bibliography / Walter S. Avis; A. M. Kinloch. — Toronto: Fitzhenry & Whiteside, [1978?]. 153 p. 1. English language in Canada — Bibliography. I. Kinloch, A. Murray. II. T. Z1379.A85 1978    Z1395E5 A8 1978.    *ISBN* 088902121X

**A Reader's guide to Canadian history.**    **5.7895**
Toronto; Buffalo: University of Toronto Press, c1982. 2 v.; 22 cm. Vol. 2 previously published as: Canada since 1867. 2nd ed. 1977. 1. Canada — History — Bibliography. I. Muise, D. A. (Delphin Andrew), 1941- II. Granatstein, J. L. III. Stevens, Paul Douglas, 1938- IV. Title: Canada since 1867. Z1382.R4 1982 F1026    016.971 19    *LC* 82-219054    *ISBN* 0802064426

**Toronto Public Library.**    • **5.7896**
A bibliography of Canadiana: being items in the Public Library of Toronto, Canada, relating to the early history and development of Canada / ed. by Frances M. Staton and Marie Tremaine; with an introduction by George H. Locke. Toronto Public Library, 1934. 828 p.; 26 cm. Contains 4646 items covering the period 1534-1867. Accompanied by supplements. 1. Canada — Bibliography. 2. Canada — History — Bibliography. I. Staton, Frances Maria. II. Tremaine, Marie. III. T. Z1382.S73 B5    *LC* 35-19259

**Artibise, Alan F. J.**    **5.7897**
Western Canada since 1870: a select bibliography and guide / Alan F. J. Artibise. — Vancouver: University of British Columbia Press, c1978. xii, 294 p.: ill.; 24 cm. Includes indexes. 1. Canada, Western — History — Bibliography. 2. Canada, Western — Bibliography. I. T. Z1392.N7 A77 F1060    016.9712    *LC* 78-320314    *ISBN* 0774800909. *ISBN* 0774800917 pbk

---

# Z1411–1945 Latin America

**Raat, W. Dirk (William Dirk), 1939-.**    **5.7898**
The Mexican Revolution: an annotated guide to recent scholarship / W. Dirk Raat. — Boston, Mass.: G.K. Hall, c1982. xxxix, 275 p.; 25 cm. — (Reference publications in Latin American studies) Includes indexes. 1. Mexico — History

— 1910-1946 — Bibliography. 2. Mexico — History — 1910-1946 — Historiography. I. T.
Z1426.5.R15 1982 F1234    016.97208/2 19    *LC* 82-11783    *ISBN* 081618352X

**Woodward, Ralph Lee.**       **5.7899**
Nicaragua / Ralph Lee Woodward, Jr., compiler; edited by Sheila R. Herstein. — Oxford, England; Santa Barbara, Calif.: Clio Press, c1983. xxiii, 254 p.: map; 23 cm. — (World bibliographical series. v. 44) Includes index. 1. Nicaragua — Bibliography. I. Herstein, Sheila R. II. T. III. Series.
Z1481.W66 1983 F1523    016.97285 19    *LC* 84-109525    *ISBN* 0903450798

**Allis, Jeannette B.**       **5.7900**
West Indian literature: an index to criticism, 1930–1975 / Jeannette B. Allis. — Boston, Mass.: G.K. Hall, c1981. xxxvii, 353 p.; 25 cm. — (Reference publication in Latin American studies.) 1. West Indian literature (English) — History and criticism — Bibliography. I. T. II. Series.
Z1502.B5 A38 PR9210    016.820/9/9729 19    *LC* 80-24587    *ISBN* 0816182663

**Comitas, Lambros.**       **5.7901**
The complete Caribbeana, 1900–1975: a bibliographic guide to the scholarly literature / Lambros Comitas; under the auspices of the Research Institute for the Study of Man. — Millwood, N.Y.: KTO Press, c1977. 4 v. (1 xxiii, 2193 p.): map (on lining papers); 26 cm. 1. Caribbean Area — Bibliography. I. Research Institute for the Study of Man. II. T.
Z1595.C63 F2161    016.9729/05    *LC* 76-56709    *ISBN* 0527188204

**Bryant, Shasta M.**       **5.7902**
A selective bibliography of bibliographies of Hispanic American literature / by Shasta M. Bryant. —. 2d ed., greatly expanded and rev. — Austin: Institute of Latin American Studies, the University of Texas at Austin, 1976. x, 100 p. — (Guides and bibliographies series. 8) 1. Bibliography — Bibliography — Latin American literature 2. Bibliography — Bibliography — Latin America 3. Latin American literature — Bibliography I. T. II. Series.
Z1601 A2 B79 1976    *LC* 75-29999    *ISBN* 0292775229

**Gropp, Arthur E., 1902-.**       **5.7903**
A bibliography of Latin American bibliographies, compiled by Arthur E. Gropp. Metuchen, N.J., Scarecrow Press, 1968. ix, 515 p. 28 cm. A greatly enlarged and updated version of the work of the same title compiled by C. K. Jones and published in 1942. 1. Bibliography — Bibliography — Latin America. 2. Latin America — Bibliography. I. Jones, Cecil Knight, 1872-1945. A bibliography of Latin American bibliographies. II. T.
Z1601.A2 G76 1968    016.01698    *LC* 68-9330

**Gropp, Arthur E., 1902-.**       **5.7904**
A bibliography of Latin American bibliographies published in periodicals / by Arthur E. Gropp. — Metuchen, N.J.: Scarecrow Press, 1976. 2v. (lxxi, 1031 p.); 23 cm. Includes index. 1. Bibliography — Bibliography — Latin America. I. T.
Z1601.A2 G76 1976 F1408    Z1601A2 G76 1976.    016.01698    *LC* 75-32552    *ISBN* 0810808382

**Hartness-Kane, Ann.**       **5.7905**
Latin America in English–language reference books: a selected, annotated bibliography / Ann Hartness Graham, Richard D. Woods. — New York, N.Y.: Special Libraries Association, c1981. 49 p.; 23 cm. Includes indexes. 1. Reference books — Latin America. 2. Latin America — Bibliography. I. Woods, Richard Donovon. II. T.
Z1601.G72 F1408    016.98 19    *LC* 80-28880    *ISBN* 0871112671

**Griffin, Charles Carroll, 1902-.**       **5.7906**
Latin America: a guide to the historical literature. Charles C. Griffin, editor. J. Benedict Warren, assistant editor. — Austin: Published for the Conference on Latin American History by the University of Texas Press, [c1971] xxx, 700 p.; 27 cm. — (Conference on Latin American History. Publication no. 4) 1. Latin America — Bibliography. I. T.
Z1601.G75    016.98    *LC* 71-165916    *ISBN* 029270089X

**Libros en venta en Hispanoamérica y España.**       **5.7907**
1964- . — New York: R.R. Bowker, 1964-. v.; 29 cm. Published: San Juan, Puerto Rico: Melcher Ediciones, 1985- Vols. for 1964-<1985> called also 1. ed.-<3. ed.> Vols. for 1974-<1985> issued in 2 v. 1. Latin America — Imprints — Periodicals. 2. Catalogs, Publishers' — Spanish America — Periodicals. 3. Catalogs, Publishers' — Spain — Periodicals. 4. Catalogs, Publishers' — Spain. 5. Spanish literature — Bibliography. 6. Spanish American literature — Bibliography. 7. Spain — Imprints — Periodicals.
Z1601.L59    017/.8/0946 19    *LC* 86-656510

**Woods, Richard Donovon.**       **5.7908**
Reference materials on Latin America in English, the humanities / by Richard D. Woods. — Metuchen, N.J.: Scarecrow Press, 1980. xii, 639 p.; 23 cm.

Includes indexes. 1. Reference books — Latin America. 2. Bibliography — Bibliography — Latin America. 3. Latin America — Bibliography. I. T.
Z1601.W75 F1408    016.98    *LC* 80-11412    *ISBN* 0810812940

**Handbook of Latin American studies.**       • **5.7909**
no. [1]- 1935-. Gainesville [etc.] University of Florida Press [etc.] v. 24 cm. Annual. Beginning with v. 26, 1964, volumes alternate coverage between social sciences and humanities. 1. Latin America — Bibliography — Periodicals. I. American Council of Learned Societies. Committee on Latin American Studies. II. Joint Committee on Latin American Studies. III. Library of Congress. IV. Library of Congress. Hispanic Foundation. V. Library of Congress. Latin American, Portuguese, and Spanish Division. VI. Library of Congress. Hispanic Division.
Z1605.H23    *LC* 36-32633

**Mundo Lo, Sara de.**       **5.7910**
Index to Spanish American collective biography / Sara de Mundo Lo. — Boston, Mass.: G.K. Hall, 1981. 466 p.; 29 cm. (Reference publication in Latin American studies.) Includes bibliographies and indexes. 1. Catalogs, Union — United States. 2. Catalogs, Union — Canada. 3. Latin America — Biography — Bibliography — Union lists. I. T. II. Series.
Z1609.B6 M86 CT503    016.92/008 19    *LC* 81-4570    *ISBN* 0816181810

**Shaw, Bradley A., 1945-.**       **5.7911**
Latin American literature in English translation: an annotated bibliography / Bradley A. Shaw. New York: New York University Press, 1976. x, 144 p.; 26 cm. 'A Center for Inter-American Relations book.' Includes indexes. 1. Latin American literature — Translations into English — Bibliography. 2. English literature — Translations from Spanish — Bibliography. 3. English literature — Translations from Portuguese — Bibliography. 4. English literature — Translations from French — Bibliography. I. Center for Inter-American Relations. II. T.
Z1609.T7 S47 PQ7087.E5    016.86/008    *LC* 75-7522    *ISBN* 0814777627

# Z2001–2089 Britain. Ireland. Scotland

## Z2001–2014 ENGLISH LITERATURE

**The British national bibliography.**       • **5.7912**
1950-. [London] British Library, Bibliographic Services Division. v. 32 cm. Quarterly. 'Compiled from the entries which appeared in the weekly lists.' Vols. for 1976- issued in 2 parts: v. 1, Subject catalogue; v. 2, Indexes. 1. Great Britain — Imprints — Periodicals. I. Wells, Arthur James, 1912- ed. II. British Library. Bibliographic Services Division. III. Council of the British National Bibliography.
Z2001.B75    015.42    *LC* 51-6468

**British national bibliography cumulated subject catalogue.**       • **5.7913**
1951/54- . — London: Council of the British National Bibliography. — v in ; 28 cm. Irregular. 1. Catalogs, Subject 2. English literature — Bibliography — Catalogs 3. Great Britaiin — Bibliography — Catalogs. 4. Great Britan — Imprints. I. Council of the British National Bibliography.
Z2001.B752    *LC* 59-246    *ISBN* 090022035X

**British books in print, 1874–.**       • **5.7914**
New York, Bowker [etc.] v. in. 22-26 cm. Title varies slightly. Subtitle varies. 1. English literature — Bibliography 2. Catalogs, Publishers' — Great Britain. I. J. Whitaker & Sons.
Z2001.R33    *LC* 02-7496 rev

**Pollard, Alfred W. (Alfred William), 1859-1944.**       • **5.7915**
A short–title catalogue of books printed in England, Scotland, & Ireland and of English books printed abroad, 1475–1640, compiled by A. W. Pollard & G. R. Redgrave, with the help of G. F. Barwick and others. London, Biographical Society, 1946. xviii, 609 p. 26 cm. 82 l. 28 cm. 'Abridged entries of all 'English' books ... copies of which exist at the British Museum, the Bodleian, the Cambridge University Library, and the Henry E. Huntington Library, California, supplemented by additions from nearly one hundred and fifty other collections.'-p. xiii. ————Index of printers, publishers and booksellers, by Paul G. Morrison. Charlottsville, Biographical Society of the University of Virginia Library, 1950. Addenda & corrigenda: leaf inserted. Z2002.P77 1946 Index 1. English literature — Early modern (to 1700) — Bibliography 2. Incunabula — Bibliography 3. Rare books 4. Book industries and trade —

Great Britain 5. Great Britain — Bibliography I. Redgrave, G. R. (Gilbert Richard), b. 1844. joint author. II. Morrison, Paul Guerrant, 1896- III. T.
Z2002.P77 1946　　015.42　　*LC* 47-20884 *

**Wing, Donald Goddard, 1904-.**　　　　　• **5.7916**
Short–title catalogue of books printed in England, Scotland, Ireland, Wales, and British America, and of English books printed in other countries, 1641–1700 / Compiled by Donald Wing. 2d ed., rev. and enl. New York: Index Committee of the Modern Language Association of America, 1972. v. ; 29 cm. A continuation of A short-title catalogue of books printed in England, Scotland & Ireland and of English books printed abroad, 1475-1640, by A. W. Pollard and G. R. Redgrave, published in 1926. 1. English imprints — Union lists. 2. Bibliography — Early printed books — 17th century — Union lists. I. Pollard, Alfred W. (Alfred William), 1859-1944. comp. A short-title catalogue of books printed in England, Scotland & Ireland and of English books printed abroad, 1475-1640. II. T.
Z2002.W52　　015.42　　*LC* 70-185211　　*ISBN* 0873520440

**International books in print.**　　　　　**5.7917**
München; New York: K.G. Saur; Detroit: Distributed by Gale Research Co. v.; 31 cm. Annual. Began in 1979. 'English-language titles published outside the U.S.A. and the United Kingdom.' Description based on: 1981-1982. Issues for <1981-1982> published in two volumes. 1. English imprints — Bibliography — Periodicals.
Z2005.I57　　018/.4　　*LC* 82-645409

**Stanton, Michael N.**　　　　　**5.7918**
English literary journals, 1900–1950: a guide to information sources / Michael N. Stanton. — Detroit, Mich.: Gale Research Co., c1982. xvi, 119 p.; 23 cm. — (Gale information guide library. American literature, English literature, and world literatures in English information guide series. v. 32) Includes indexes. 1. English literature — Periodicals — Bibliography. I. T. II. Series.
Z2005.S73 1982 PR1　　016.82/08 19　　*LC* 74-32504　　*ISBN* 0810313596

**The Wellesley index to Victorian periodicals, 1824–1900: tables**　　**5.7919**
**of contents and identification of contributors, with bibliographies of their articles and stories** / Walter E. Houghton, editor, Josef L. Althoz ... [et al.], associate editors.
[Toronto]: University of Toronto Press, c1966-1979. 3v.; 26 cm. 1. English periodicals — Indexes. I. Houghton, Walter Edwards, 1904-. II. Wellesley College.
Z2005.W4　　052　　*LC* 67-79381　　*ISBN* 0802023436

**Whitaker's cumulative book list.**　　　　　• **5.7920**
1924-. London, J. Whitaker. v. 25 cm. Annual. Issued also in a quinquennial cumulation. Vol. for 1944-47 covers only 4 years. 1. Great Britain — Imprints — Periodicals. I. J. Whitaker & Sons.
Z2005.W57　　015.41　　*LC* 25-4576

**Ford, Percy, 1894-.**　　　　　**5.7921**
A guide to parliamentary papers; what they are, how to find them, how to use them [by] P. Ford and G. Ford. — 3d ed. — Totowa, N.J.: Rowman and Littlefield, 1972. xiii, 87 p.; 25 cm. — (Southampton University studies in parliamentary papers) 1. Great Britain — Government publications. I. Ford, Grace. joint author. II. T.
Z2009.A1 F6 1972　　015.42　　*LC* 72-171410　　*ISBN* 0874711002

**Butcher, David.**　　　　　**5.7922**
Official publications in Britain / David Butcher. — London: C. Bingley, 1983. 161 p.; 23 cm. 1. Great Britain — Government publications. 2. Great Britain — Government publications — Bibliography. I. T.
Z2009.B93 1983　　015.41 19　　*LC* 82-228864　　*ISBN* 0851573517

**Great Britain. Her Majesty's Stationery Office.**　　　　　**5.7923**
Cumulative index to the annual catalogues of Her Majesty's Stationery Office publications, 1922–1972 / compiled by Ruth Matteson Blackmore; with an introd. by James Gordon Ollé. — Washington: Carrollton Press, 1976. 2 v.; 29 cm. 1. Great Britain. Her Majesty's Stationery Office — Bibliography. 2. Great Britain — Government publications — Indexes. I. Blackmore, Ruth Matteson. II. T.
Z2009.G85 1976 J301　　015/.41　　*LC* 76-26730　　*ISBN* 0840801408

**Richard, Stephen.**　　　　　**5.7924**
Directory of British official publications: a guide to sources / compiled by Stephen Richard. — London: Mansell; Bronx, N.Y.: Distributed in the United States and Canada by H.W. Wilson, 1981. xxxii, 360 p.; 24 cm. Includes indexes. 1. Great Britain — Government publications — Information services — Directories. I. T.
Z2009.R533 1981 J301　　015.41/053 19　　*LC* 82-144831　　*ISBN* 0720115965

**Allibone, Samuel Austin, 1816-1889.**　　　　　• **5.7925**
A critical dictionary of English literature: and British and American authors, living and deceased, from the earliest accounts to the middle of the nineteenth century. Containing thirty thousand biographies and literary notices, with forty

indexes of subjects / By S. Austin Allibone. — Philadelphia: J. B. Lippincott & co. [etc.], 1858-71. 3 v.; 27 cm. Paged continuously. Vol. 1 has added t.-p., engraved. Vol. 1 published by Childs & Peterson, 1858; v. 2-3, by J. B. Lippincott & co., 1870-71. Title varies; v. 2: ... to the latter half of the nineteenth century. Containing over forty-three thousand articles ... v. 3: ... to the latter half of the nineteenth century. Containing over forty-six thousand articles .... Supplement by John Foster Kirk was published in 2 v., 1891. 1. English literature — Bio-bibliography 2. American literature — Bio-bibliography. 3. Authors, English — Biography 4. Authors, American — Biography. I. T.
Z2010.A44 1858　　*LC* 02-2804

**Myers, Robin, fl. 1967-.**　　　　　**5.7926**
A dictionary of literature in the English language, from Chaucer to 1940 / compiled and edited by Robin Myers, for the National Book League. — Oxford; New York: Pergamon Press, 1970-71. 2 v.: ill., facsim.; 25 cm. 1. English literature — Bio-bibliography 2. American literature — Bio-bibliography. I. National Book League (Great Britain) II. T.
Z2010.M9　　016.82　　*LC* 68-18529　　*ISBN* 0080120792

**Myers, Robin, fl. 1967-.**　　　　　**5.7927**
A dictionary of literature in the English language from 1940–1970: complete with alphabetical title–author index and a geographical–chronological index to authors being a sequel to A dictionary of literature in the English language from Chaucer to 1940, 2 vols. 1970 / compiled by Robin Myers. — Oxford; New York: Pergamon Press, 1978. xvi, 519 p.; 26 cm. Includes indexes. 1. English literature — 20th century — Bio-bibliography. 2. American literature — 20th century — Bio-bibliography. 3. English literature — Commonwealth of Nations authors — Bio-bibliography. I. T.
Z2010.M92 1978 PR471　　016.82　　*LC* 77-30534　　*ISBN* 0080180507

**Altick, Richard Daniel, 1915-.**　　　　　**5.7928**
Selective bibliography for the study of English and American literature / Richard D. Altick and Andrew Wright. — 6th ed. — New York: Macmillan, c1979. xii, 180 p.; 21 cm. Includes index. 1. English literature — History and criticism — Bibliography 2. Bibliography — Bibliography — English literature. 3. American literature — History and criticism — Bibliography. 4. Bibliography — Bibliography — American literature. 5. Literature — Research — Handbooks, manuals, etc. I. Wright, Andrew H. joint author. II. T.
Z2011.A1 A47 1979 PR83　　016.82　　*LC* 78-4130　　*ISBN* 0023021101

**Doyle, Paul A.**　　　　　**5.7929**
Guide to basic information sources in English literature / by Paul A. Doyle; with a foreword by Harrison T. Meserole. New York: Wiley; distributed by Halsted Press, c1976. xi, 143 p.; 22 cm. (Information resources series) Includes index. 1. Bibliography — Bibliography — English literature. 2. English literature — History and criticism — Bibliography 3. Reference books — English literature — Bibliography. 4. Bibliography — Bibliography — American literature. 5. American literature — History and criticism — Bibliography. 6. Reference books — American literature — Bibliography. I. T.
Z2011.A1 D68 PR83　　016.01682　　*LC* 75-43260　　*ISBN* 0470150114

**Howard-Hill, T. H. (Trevor Howard)**　　　　　**5.7930**
Index to British literary bibliography / [T. H. Howard–Hill]. — Oxford: Clarendon Press; New York: Oxford University Press, 1969- <80 >. v. <1-2, 4-6 >: 24 cm. Includes index. 1. Bibliography — Bibliography — English literature. 2. English literature — Bibliography I. T.
Z2011.A1 H68 PR83　　016.82　　*LC* 79-318524

**Mellown, Elgin W.**　　　　　**5.7931**
A descriptive catalogue of the bibliographies of 20th century British poets, novelists and dramatists / by Elgin W. Mellown. — 2d ed. rev. and enl. — Troy, N.Y.: Whitston Pub. Co., 1978. xv, 414 p.; 24 cm. Includes index. 1. Bibliography — Bibliography — Authors, English. 2. Authors, English — 20th century — Bibliography. I. T.
Z2011.A1 M43 1978　　Z2013 M45 1978.　　016.01682/08/0091　　*ISBN* 0878751378

**Annals of English literature, 1475–1950: the principal**　　• **5.7932**
**publications of each year, together with an alphabetical index of authors with their works.**
2d ed. — Oxford: Clarendon Press, 1961. vi, 380 p. The 1st ed. was compiled by J. C. Ghosh and E. G. Withycombe; the 2d ed. was revised and brought up to date by R. W. Chapman. 1. English literature — Bibliography I. Ghosh, Jyotish Chandra. II. Withycombe, Elizabeth Gidley, 1902- III. Chapman, R. W. (Robert William), 1881-1960.
Z2011.A5 1961　　*LC* 62-16029

**Bateson, Frederick Wilse, 1901-.**　　　　　**5.7933**
A guide to English and American literature / F. W. Bateson and Harrison T. Meserole, assisted by Marilyn R. Mumford ... [et al.]. — 3d ed. — New York: Gordian Press, 1976. viii, 334 p.; 22cm. Previous editions published under title: A guide to English literature. Includes index. 1. English literature —

Bibliography 2. American literature — Bibliography I. Meserole, Harrison T. joint author. II. T.
Z2011.B32 1976 PR83　　　016.82　　　*ISBN* 0977521867

**Bell, Inglis Freeman, 1917-.**　　　　　　　　　　　• **5.7934**
A reference guide to English, American and Canadian literature; an annotated checklist of bibliographical and other reference materials [by] Inglis F. Bell [and] Jennifer Gallup. Vancouver, University of British Columbia Press [1971] xii, 139 p. 24 cm. 1. English literature — History and criticism — Bibliography 2. American literature — History and criticism — Bibliography. 3. Canadian literature — History and criticism — Bibliography. I. Forbes, Jennifer, 1941- joint author. II. T.
Z2011.B42　　　016.82　　　*LC* 79-866088　　　*ISBN* 077480002X

**English literature, 1660–1800: a bibliography of modern studies**　• **5.7935**
**/ compiled for Philological quarterly by Ronald S. Crane ... [et al].**
Princeton: Princeton University Press, 1950-. v.; 24 cm. 1. English literature — Bibliography I. Crane, Ronald Salmon, 1886- II. Philological quarterly.
Z2011.E6　　　*LC* a 51-6808

**Modern Humanities Research Association.**　　　　　　• **5.7936**
Annual bibliography of English language and literature. 1920-. London [etc.] v. 22 cm. Annual. 1. English philology — Bibliography. 2. English literature — Bibliography I. Paues, Anna Carolina, 1867- ed. II. Seaton, Ethel, joint ed. III. Serjeantson, Mary Sidney, ed. IV. Broughton, Leslie Nathan, 1877-1952. ed. V. T.
Z2011.M69　　　*LC* 22-11861

**The New Cambridge bibliography of English literature, edited**　　**5.7937**
**by George Watson.**
Cambridge [Eng.]: University Press, 1969-77 [v. 1, 1974] 5 v.; 26 cm. 1940 edition edited by F. W. Bateson under title: The Cambridge bibliography of English literature. 1. English literature — Bibliography I. Watson, George, 1927- ed. II. Bateson, Frederick Wilse, 1901- The Cambridge bibliography of English literature.
Z2011.N45 PR83　　　016.82　　　*LC* 69-10199　　　*ISBN* 0521072557

**Schweik, Robert C.**　　　　　　　　　　　　　　　**5.7938**
Reference sources in English and American literature: an annotated bibliography / Robert C. Schweik, Dieter Riesner. — 1st ed. — New York: Norton, c1977. xxiv, 13-258 p.; 22 cm. Includes indexes. 1. English literature — Bibliography 2. American literature — Bibliography I. Riesner, Dieter, joint author. II. T.
Z2011.S415 PR83　　　016.82　　　*LC* 77-974　　　*ISBN* 039309104X pbk.
*ISBN* 0393044844

**The Shorter new Cambridge bibliography of English literature /**　　**5.7939**
**edited by George Watson.**
Cambridge; New York: Cambridge University Press, 1981. xiv, 1622 p.; 25 cm. Includes index. 1. English literature — Bibliography I. Watson, George, 1927- II. New Cambridge bibliography of English literature.
Z2011.S417 1981 PR83　　　016.82 19　　　*LC* 80-49948　　　*ISBN* 0521226007

**Watson, George, 1927-.**　　　　　　　　　　　　• **5.7940**
The concise Cambridge bibliography of English literature, 600–1950. 2d ed. Cambridge University Press 1965. xi, 269 p. 1. English literature — Bibliography I. T. II. Title: Cambridge bibliography of English literature 600-1950.
Z2011.W3 1965　　　*LC* 65-14341

**Brown, Carleton Fairchild, 1869-1941.**　　　　　　• **5.7941**
The index of Middle English verse / [by] Carleton Brown and Rossell Hope Robbins. — New York: Printed for the Index Society by Columbia University Press, 1943. 785 p.; 24 cm. 1. English poetry — Middle English (1100-1500) — Bibliography 2. Religious poetry, English — Bibliography 3. Didactic poetry, English — Bibliography I. Robbins, Rossell Hope, 1912- jt. author II. Brown, Carleton Fairchild, 1869-1941. A register of Middle English religious and didactic verse III. Cutler, John L, jt. comp. IV. Index Society, New York V. T.
Z2012 B86

**Greenfield, Stanley B.**　　　　　　　　　　　　　**5.7942**
A bibliography of publications on Old English literature to the end of 1972: using the collections of E.E. Ericson / Stanley B. Greenfield and Fred C. Robinson. — Toronto; Buffalo: University of Toronto Press, c1980. xxii, 437 p. 26 cm. Includes indexes. 1. English literature — Old English, ca. 450-1100 — History and criticism — Bibliography. 2. English literature — Old English, ca. 450-1100 — Bibliography. I. Robinson, Fred C. joint author. II. Ericson, Eston Everett, 1890-1964. III. T.
Z2012.G83 PR173　　　016.829　　　*LC* 78-4989　　　*ISBN* 0802022928

**Lund, Roger D., 1949-.**　　　　　　　　　　　　**5.7943**
Restoration and early eighteenth–century English literature, 1660–1740: a selected bibliography of resource materials / Roger D. Lund. — New York,

N.Y.: Modern Language Association of America, 1980. 42 p.; 21 cm. — (Selected bibliographies in language and literature. 1) Includes index. 1. English literature — Early modern, 1500-1700 — Bibliography. 2. English literature — 18th century — Bibliography. I. T. II. Series.
Z2012.L88 PR43　　　016.82　　　*LC* 79-87585　　　*ISBN* 0873529502

**Matthews, William, 1905-.**　　　　　　　　　　　• **5.7944**
Old and Middle English literature. — New York: Appleton-Century-Crofts, [1968] xvi, 112 p.; 23 cm. — (Goldentree bibliographies in language and literature) 1. English literature — Old English, ca. 450-1100 — Bibliography. 2. English literature — Middle English, 1100-1500 — Bibliography. I. T.
Z2012.M32　　　016.8209/001　　　*LC* 68-12339

**Bibliographies of studies in Victorian literature for the ten years**　　**5.7945**
**1955–1964. Edited by Robert C. Slack. Compiled by Robert A. Donovan [and others]**
Urbana, University of Illinois Press, 1967. xvi, 461 p. 24 cm. 'Collects and reproduces the annual Victorian bibliographies ... published in Modern philology (1956-57) and in Victorian studies (1958-65) ... a project of the Victorian Literature Group of the Modern Language Association of America.' 1. English literature — 19th century — Bibliography. I. Slack, Robert C., ed. II. Modern Language Association of America. Victorian Literature Group.
Z2013.B59　　　016.8209/008　　　*LC* 67-20150

**Buckley, Jerome Hamilton.**　　　　　　　　　　　• **5.7946**
Victorian poets and prose writers / Compiled by Jerome H. Buckley. — New York: Appleton-Century-Crofts, [1966] viii, 63 p.; 24 cm. (Goldentree bibliographies) 1. English literature — 19th century — History and criticism — Bibliography. I. T.
Z2013.B8　　　016.8209008　　　*LC* 66-26461

**Templeman, William Darby, 1903-.**　　　　　　　• **5.7947**
Bibliographies of studies in Victorian literature for the thirteen years 1932–1944/ edited by William D. Templeman, compiled by Samuel P. Chew...[et al.] — Urbana: University of Illinois Press, 1945. ix, 450 p.; 26 cm. 1. English literature — 19th century — Bibliography. I. Chew, Samuel Peaco, 1910- II. T.
Z2013.T4　　　PR461.Z9 B48.　　　*LC* 46-77

**Vrana, Stan A., 1916-.**　　　　　　　　　　　　**5.7948**
Interviews and conversations with 20th–century authors writing in English: an index / by Stan A. Vrana. — Metuchen, N.J.: Scarecrow Press, 1982. 237 p. 1. Authors, English — 20th century — Interviews — Indexes. 2. Authors, American — 20th century — Interviews — Indexes. 3. Interviews — Indexes. 4. Authors — Interviews — Indexes. I. T. II. Title: Interviews and conversations with twentieth-century authors writing in English. III. Title: Interviews and conversations.
Z2013.V73 1982 PR471　　　016.82/09/0091 19　　　*LC* 82-3275　　　*ISBN* 0810815427

## Z2014 Special Topics, A–Z

**Bullock, Chris, 1945-.**　　　　　　　　　　　　**5.7949**
Guide to Marxist literary criticism / compiled by Chris Bullock and David Peck. — Bloomington: Indiana University Press, c1980. xi, 176 p.; 22 cm. Includes index. 1. English literature — History and criticism — Bibliography 2. American literature — History and criticism — Bibliography. 3. Canadian literature — History and criticism — Bibliography. 4. Marxist criticism — Bibliography. I. Peck, David R. joint author. II. T.
Z2014.C8 B84 PR77　　　801/.95　　　*LC* 79-3627　　　*ISBN* 0253131448

**Bergquist, G. William, ed.**　　　　　　　　　　　• **5.7950**
Three centuries of English and American plays, a checklist: England: 1500–1800, United States: 1714–1830. — New York: Hafner Pub. Co., 1963. xii, 281 p.: facsims.; 29 cm. 1. English drama — Bibliography. 2. American drama — Bibliography. I. Wells, Henry Willis, 1895- ed. Three centuries of drama. (Indexes) II. T.
Z2014.D7 B45 1963　　　016.821

**Conolly, L. W. (Leonard W.)**　　　　　　　　　　**5.7951**
English drama and theatre, 1800–1900 / L.W. Conolly, J.P. Wearing. — Detroit: Gale Research Co., c1978. xix, 508 p.; 23 cm. — (American literature, English literature, and world literatures in English information guide series; v. 12) Includes index. 1. English drama — 19th century — Bibliography. 2. English drama — 19th century — History and criticism — Bibliography. 3. Theater — Great Britain — History — Bibliography. I. Wearing, J. P. joint author. II. T.
Z2014.D7 C72 PR721　　　016.822/7/08　　　*LC* 73-16975　　　*ISBN* 0810312255

**English drama, excluding Shakespeare: select bibliographical**    **5.7952**
**guides** / edited by Stanley Wells.
London; New York: Oxford University Press, 1975. viii, 303 p.; 21 cm.
1. English drama — Bibliography. 2. English drama — History and criticism.
I. Wells, Stanley W., 1930-
Z2014.D7 E44 PR625    822/.009    *LC* 75-332457    *ISBN*
0198710348

**Greg, Walter Wilson, 1875-.**           ● **5.7953**
A bibliography of the English printed drama to the restoration. London:
Printed for the Bibliographical Society at the University Press, Oxford,
1939-59. 4 v. (1752 p.) fronts., facsims. 29 x 23 cm. (Illustrated monographs no.
xxiv, I -) 1. English drama — Early modern
and Elizabethan — Bibliography. I. Stationers' Company (London, England)
II. T. III. Series.
Z2014.D7 G78 (Rare Bk Coll)    Z2014.D7 G7.    *LC* 40-30318

**Harbage, Alfred, 1901-.**           ● **5.7954**
Annals of English drama, 975–1700; an analytical record of all plays, extant or
lost, chronologically arranged and indexed by authors, titles, dramatic
companies, &c. Philadelphia, University of Pennsylvania Press [1964] 321 p.
1. English drama — Bibliography. 2. English literature — Chronology
3. Theater — England. I. Schoenbaum, S. (Samuel), 1927- ed. II. T.
Z2014.D7 H25x    *LC* 64-57462

**Link, Frederick M.**           **5.7955**
English drama, 1660–1800: a guide to information sources / Frederick M. Link.
— Detroit: Gale Research Co., c1976. xxii, 374 p.; 22 cm. — (Gale information
guide library. American literature, English literature, and world literatures in
English information guide series. v. 9) Includes indexes. 1. English drama —
18th century — History and criticism — Bibliography. 2. English drama —
Restoration, 1660-1700 — History and criticism — Bibliography. 3. Theater
— Great Britain — Bibliography. I. T. II. Series.
Z2014.D7 L55 PR701    016.822    *LC* 73-16984    *ISBN* 0810312247

**Mikhail, E. H.**           **5.7956**
English drama, 1900–1950: a guide to information sources / edited by E. H.
Mikhail. Detroit: Gale Research Co., 1977. 328 p. (American literature,
English literature, and world literatures in English information guide series; v.
11) (Gale information guide library) Includes index. 1. English drama — 20th
century — Bibliography. I. T.
Z2014.D7 M545 PR736    016.822/9/1    *LC* 77-76355    *ISBN*
0810312166

**Penninger, Frieda Elaine.**           **5.7957**
English drama to 1660, excluding Shakespeare: a guide to information sources /
Frieda Elaine Penninger. — Detroit: Gale Research Co., c1976. xix, 370 p.; 22
cm. — (Gale information guide library. American literature, English literature,
and world literatures in English information guide series. v. 5) Includes index.
1. English drama — Bibliography. 2. English drama — History and criticism
— Bibliography. I. T. II. Series.
Z2014.D7 P46    016.822/008    *LC* 73-16988    *ISBN* 0810312239

**Stratman, Carl Joseph, 1917-1972.**           **5.7958**
Restoration and eighteenth century theatre research: a bibliographical guide,
1900–1968 / edited by Carl J. Stratman, David G. Spencer, and Mary Elizabeth
Devine. — Carbondale: Southern Illinois University Press, [1971] ix, 811 p.; 24
cm. 1. English drama — Restoration, 1660-1700 — History and criticism —
Bibliography. 2. English drama — 18th century — History and criticism —
Bibliography. 3. Theater — England — Bibliography. I. Spencer, David
Gelvin. joint ed. II. Devine, Mary Elizabeth, joint ed. III. T.
Z2014.D7 S854    016.822/5/09    *LC* 71-112394    *ISBN* 0809304694

**Bell, Inglis Freeman, 1917-.**           ● **5.7959**
English novel, 1578–1956, Checklist of twentieth century criticism / by Inglis
F. Bell and Donald Baird. Denver: Swallow, [1959]. xii, 169 p.; 23 cm.
1. English fiction — History and criticism — Bibliography. I. Baird, Donald,
1926- II. T.
Z2014.F4 B4    016.82309    *LC* 59-8212

**Block, Andrew, 1892-.**           ● **5.7960**
The English novel, 1740–1850: a catalogue including prose romances, short
stories, and translations of foreign fiction. — [New and rev., i.e. 2d, ed.]
London: Dawsons of Pall Mall, 1961. xv, 349 p.; 25 cm. 1. English fiction —
18th century — Bibliography. 2. English fiction — 19th century —
Bibliography. 3. English fiction — Translations from foreign languages —
Bibliography. I. T.
Z2014.F4 B6 1961    *LC* 61-3325

**The English novel: twentieth century criticism.**           **5.7961**
1st ed. — Chicago: Swallow Press, c1976-. v. < 1- >; 24 cm. 1. English fiction
— History and criticism — Bibliography.
Z2014.F4 E53 PR821    016.823/91/09 19    *LC* 76-17741    *ISBN*
080400742X

**Harner, James L.**           **5.7962**
English Renaissance prose fiction, 1500–1660: an annotated bibliography of
criticism / James L. Harner. — Boston: G. K. Hall, c1978. xxiv, 556 p.; 25 cm.
(Reference publication in literature.) Includes index. 1. English fiction — Early
modern, 1500–1700 — History and criticism — Bibliography. I. T. II. Series.
Z2014.F4 H37 PR833    016.823/009 19    *LC* 78-2902    *ISBN*
0816179964

**Hubin, Allen J.**           **5.7963**
Crime fiction, 1749–1980: a comprehensive bibliography / Allen J. Hubin. —
New York: Garland Pub., 1984. xix, 712 p.; 29 cm. — (Garland reference
library of the humanities; vol. 371) Enl. ed. of: The bibliography of crime
fiction, 1749-1975. c1979. Includes indexes. 1. English fiction — Bibliography.
2. Detective and mystery stories — Bibliography. 3. American fiction —
Bibliography. 4. Crime and criminals — Fiction — Bibliography. 5. Detective
and mystery plays — Bibliography. 6. Gothic revival (Literature) —
Bibliography. I. T.
Z2014.F4 H82 1984 PR830.D4    016.823/0872 19    *LC* 82-48772
    *ISBN* 0824092198

**Mish, Charles Carroll, 1913-.**           ● **5.7964**
English prose fiction. — Charlottesville: Bibliographical Society of the
University of Virginia, 1952-. v; 28 cm. 1. English fiction — Early modern,
1500-1700 — Bibliography. I. T.
Z2014.F4 M58    *LC* 52-4458

**Sadleir, Michael, 1888-1957.**           **5.7965**
XIX century fiction; a bibliographical record based on his own collection, by
Michael Sadleir. London, Constable & co., ltd. [1951] 2 v. ill. Limited ed.
1. Bibliography — Editions 2. English fiction — 19th century — Bibliography.
I. T. II. Title: Nineteenth century fiction. III. Title: 19 century fiction.
Z2014.F4 S16    823.8    *LC* a 51-4968

**Schlobin, Roger C.**           **5.7966**
The literature of fantasy: a comprehensive, annotated bibliography of modern
fantasy fiction / Roger C. Schlobin. — New York: Garland Pub., 1979. xxxv,
425 p.; 23 cm. — (Garland reference library of the humanities; v. 176)
1. Fantastic fiction, English — Bibliography. 2. Fantastic fiction, American —
Bibliography. I. T.
Z2014.F4 S33 PR830.F3    016.823/0876    *LC* 78-68287    *ISBN*
0824097572

**Beasley, Jerry C.**           **5.7967**
English fiction, 1660–1800: a guide to information sources / Jerry C. Beasley.
— Detroit: Gale Research Co., c1978. xvi, 313 p.; 23 cm. — (Gale information
guide library. American literature, English literature, and world literatures in
English information guide series. v. 14) Includes index. 1. English fiction —
18th century — Bio-bibliography. 2. English fiction — Early modern,
1500-1700 — Bio-bibliography. 3. English fiction — 18th century — History
and criticism — Bibliography. 4. English fiction — Early modern, 1500-1700
— History and criticism — Bibliography. I. T. II. Series.
Z2014.F5 B42 PR851    016.823    *LC* 74-11526    *ISBN* 0810312263

**McNutt, Dan J.**           **5.7968**
The eighteenth–century Gothic novel: an annotated bibliography of criticism
and selected texts / by Dan J. McNutt. With a foreword by Devendra Varma
and Maurice Lévy. — New York: Garland Pub., 1975. xxii, 330 p.; 22 cm.
(Garland reference library of the humanities; v. 4) Includes index. 1. English
fiction — 18th century — Bibliography. 2. Gothic revival (Literature) —
England — Bibliography. I. T.
Z2014.F5 M3 PR858.T3    016.823/03    *LC* 74-22490    *ISBN*
0824010582

**O'Dell, Sterg.**           ● **5.7969**
A chronological list of prose fiction in English printed in England and other
countries, 1475–1640. — Cambridge, Mass.: Technology Press of M. I. T.,
1954. v, 147 p.; 30 cm. 1. English fiction — Early modern, 1500-1700 —
Bibliography. I. T.
Z2014.F5 O33    016.823    *LC* 55-1639

**English novel explication: criticisms to 1972 / compiled by**    **5.7970**
**Helen H. Palmer & Anne Jane Dyson.**
[Hamden, Conn.]: Archon, 1973. vi, 329 p.; 22 cm. Supplements The English
novel, 1578-1956, by I.F. Bell and D. Baird. 1. English fiction — History and
criticism — Bibliography. I. Palmer, Helen H. II. Dyson, Anne Jane, 1912-
joint author. III. Bell, Inglis Freeman, 1917- English novel, 1578-1956.
Z2014.F5 P26 PR821    016.823/009

**Horror literature: a core collection and reference guide / edited**    **5.7971**
**by Marshall B. Tymn.**
New York: R.R. Bowker, 1981. xviii, 559 p.; 24 cm. Includes index. 1. Horror
tales, English — Bibliography. 2. Horror tales, American — Bibliography.
3. Gothic revival (Literature) — Bibliography. 4. Supernatural in literature —

Bibliography. 5. Supernatural — Poetry — Bibliography. I. Tymn, Marshall B., 1937-
Z2014.H67 H67 PR830.T3      016.823/0872 19      *LC* 81-6176      *ISBN* 0835213412

**Kuntz, Joseph Marshall, 1911-.**                                    **5.7972**
Poetry explication: a checklist of interpretation since 1925 of British and American poems past and present / Joseph M. Kuntz, Nancy C. Martinez. — [3rd ed.]. — Boston, Mass.: G. K. Hall, c1980. xi, 570 p.; 27 cm. 1. English poetry — Explication — Bibliography. 2. American poetry — Explication — Bibliography. I. Martinez, Nancy C. (Nancy Conrad) II. T.
Z2014.P7 K8 1980 PR502      016.821/009      *LC* 80-10291      *ISBN* 0816183139

**Mell, Donald Charles.**                                    **5.7973**
English poetry, 1660–1800: a guide to information sources / Donald C. Mell, Jr. — Detroit, Mich.: Gale Research, c1982. xviii, 501 p.; 23 cm. — (American literature, English literature, and world literatures in English information guide series; v. 40) Includes index. 1. English poetry — 18th century — Bibliography. 2. English poetry — Early modern, 1500-1700 — Bibliography. I. T.
Z2014.P7 M44 1982 PR551      016.821 19      *LC* 73-16974      *ISBN* 0810312301

**Shapiro, Karl Jay, 1913-.**                                    • **5.7974**
A bibliography of modern prosody. Baltimore, Johns Hopkins Press, 1948. 36 p. 23 cm. 1. English language — Versification — Bibliography. 2. Versification — Bibliography. I. T.
Z2014.P7S5      016.426      *LC* 48-9156 *

**Brown, Christopher C.**                                    **5.7975**
English prose and criticism, 1900–1950: a guide to information sources / Christopher C. Brown, William B. Thesing. — Detroit, Mich.: Gale Research Co., c1983. xxi, 553 p.; 23 cm. — (American literature, English literature, and world literatures in English information guide series; v. 42) Includes indexes. 1. English prose literature — 20th century — Bibliography. 2. English prose literature — 20th century — History and criticism — Bibliography. I. Thesing, William B. II. T.
Z2014.P795 B76 1983 PR801      016.828/91208/09 19      *LC* 83-11581      *ISBN* 0810312360

**Heninger, S. K.**                                    **5.7976**
English prose, prose fiction, and criticism to 1660: a guide to information sources / S.K. Heninger, Jr. — Detroit: Gale Research Co., [1975] x, 255 p.; 23 cm. — (Gale information guide library. American literature, English literature, and world literatures in English information guide series. v. 2) Includes index. 1. English prose literature — Early modern, 1500-1700 — Bibliography. 2. English prose literature — Early modern, 1500-1700 — History and criticism — Bibliography. 3. English prose literature — Middle English, 1100-1500 — Bibliography. 4. English prose literature — Middle English, 1100-1500 — History and criticism — Bibliography. I. T. II. Series.
Z2014.P795 H45 PR767      016.082      *LC* 73-16980      *ISBN* 0810312751

**Sargent, Lyman Tower, 1940-.**                                    **5.7977**
British and American utopian literature, 1516–1975: an annotated bibliography / Lyman Tower Sargent. — Boston: G. K. Hall, c1979. xxvi, 324 p.; 25 cm. — (Reference publication in science fiction.) Includes indexes. 1. English literature — Bibliography 2. Utopias — Bibliography. 3. American literature — Bibliography 4. Science fiction, English — Bibliography. 5. Science fiction, American — Bibliography. I. T. II. Series.
Z2014.U84 S27 PR149.U8      016.823/008/0372      *LC* 78-11086      *ISBN* 0816182434

## Z2015 ENGLISH PHILOLOGY

**English tests and reviews: a monograph consisting of the English**                **5.7978**
**sections of the seven Mental measurements yearbooks (1938–72)**
**and Tests in print II (1974) / edited by Oscar Krisen Buros.**
Highland Park, N.J.: Gryphon Press, 1975. xxiii, 395 p.; 27 cm. (An MMY monograph) 1. English philology — Study and teaching — Bibliography. 2. English philology — Examinations, questions, etc. — Bibliography. I. Buros, Oscar Krisen, 1905- II. Buros, Oscar Krisen, 1905- ed. The mental measurements yearbook. III. Buros, Oscar Krisen, 1905- ed. Tests in print II. Selections. 1975.
Z2015.A1 E53 PE66      016.42/076      *LC* 75-8109      *ISBN* 0910674159

**An Annotated bibliography of texts on writing skills: grammar**        **5.7979**
**and usage, composition, rhetoric, and technical writing /**
**Shannon Burns ... [et al.].**
New York: Garland Pub., 1976. 259 p.; 23 cm. (Garland reference library of the humanities; v. 38) Includes index. 1. English language — Rhetoric —

Bibliography. 2. English language — Grammar — 1950- — Bibliography. 3. College readers — Bibliography. I. Burns, Shannon.
Z2015.R5 A55 PE1408      016.808/042      *LC* 75-24096      *ISBN* 0824099680

**Brogan, T. V. F. (Terry V. F.)**                                    **5.7980**
English versification, 1570–1980: a reference guide with a global appendix / T. V. F. Brogan. — Baltimore: Johns Hopkins University Press, c1981. xxix, 794 p.; 24 cm. Includes indexes. 1. English language — Versification — Bibliography. 2. English poetry — History and criticism — Bibliography. 3. Versification — Bibliography. I. T.
Z2015.V37 B76 PE1505      016.821/009 19      *LC* 80-8861      *ISBN* 0801825415

## Z2016–2027 BRITISH HISTORY

**Elton, G. R. (Geoffrey Rudolph)**                                    • **5.7981**
Modern historians on British history, 1485–1945: a critical bibliography, 1945–1969 / [by] G. R. Elton. — Ithaca, N.Y.: Cornell University Press [1971, c1970] viii, 239 p.; 22 cm. 1. Great Britain — History — Bibliography. I. T.
Z2016.E44 1970      016.942/0072      *LC* 77-137676      *ISBN* 0801406110

**Gross, Charles, 1857-1909.**                                    • **5.7982**
The sources and literature of English history from the earliest times to about 1485 by Charles Gross. 2d ed., rev. and enl. London, New York [etc] Longmans, Green, and co., 1915. xxiii, 820 p. 24 cm. More than 3234 closely classified titles (numbered to 3234, but actually more because of insertions) with general index. Appendices: A. Records of the deputy keeper of the public records. -B. The Historical mss. commission. -C. Rolls series. -D. Chronological tables of the principal sources. 1. Classification — Books — Great Britain. 2. Great Britain — History — Sources. 3. Great Britain — History — Bibliography. I. T.
Z2016.G87 1915      *LC* 15-16893

**Writings on British history.**                                    • **5.7983**
1901/1933-. London, University of London, Institute of Historical Research. v. in      24 cm. 'A bibliography of books and articles on the history of Great Britain from about 450 A.D.' 1901-1933 issued in 5 vols. with distinctive titles: 1. Auxiliary sciences and general works.—2. The Middle ages, 450-1485.—3. The Tudor and Stuart periods, 1485-1714.—4. pt. 1-2. The Eighteenth century, 1714-1815.—5. pt. 1-2. 1815-1914. 1. Great Britain — History — Bibliography. I. Milne, Alexander Taylor. II. Munro, Donald James. III. Royal Historical Society (Great Britain) IV. University of London. Institute of Historical Research.
Z2016.R88      *LC* 61-2932

**A Bibliography of English history to 1485: based on The sources**        **5.7984**
**and literature of English history from the earliest times to about**
**1485 by Charles Gross / edited by Edgar B. Graves; and issued**
**under the sponsorship of the Royal Historical Society, the**
**American Historical Association, and the Mediaeval Academy**
**of America.**
Oxford [Eng.]; New York: Clarendon Press, 1975. xxiv, 1103 p.; 24 cm. Includes index. 1. Great Britain — History — To 1485 — Sources — Bibliography. I. Graves, Edgar B. II. Gross, Charles, 1857-1909. The sources and literature of English history from the earliest times to about 1485.
Z2017.B5 DA130      016.942      *LC* 76-355448      *ISBN* 0198223919

**Bonser, Wilfrid, 1887-1972.**                                    • **5.7985**
An Anglo–Saxon and Celtic bibliography (450–1087). Oxford: Blackwell, 1957. 2 v.; 26 cm. Errata slip inserted in v. 2. 1. Great Britain — History — To 1066 — Bibliography. 2. Great Britain — History — William I, 1066-1087 — Bibliography. I. T.
Z2017.B6      *LC* a 58-1987

**Guth, DeLloyd J., 1938-.**                                    **5.7986**
Late–medieval England, 1377–1485 / DeLloyd J. Guth. — Cambridge; New York: Cambridge University Press for the Conference on British Studies, 1976. xi, 143 p.; 23 cm. — (Conference on British Studies bibliographical handbooks) Includes index. 1. Great Britain — History — Richard II, 1377-1399 — Bibliography. 2. Great Britain — History — Lancaster and York, 1399-1485 — Bibliography. I. T.
Z2017.G87 DA235      016.94204      *LC* 75-23845      *ISBN* 0521208777

**Wilkinson, Bertie, 1898-.**                                    **5.7987**
The high Middle Ages in England, 1154–1377 / Bertie Wilkinson. — Cambridge; New York: Cambridge University Press, 1978. ix, 130 p.; 22 cm. — (Conference on British Studies bibliographical handbooks) Includes index. 1. Great Britain — History — Plantagenets, 1154-1399 — Bibliography. I. T.
Z2017.W54 DA205      016.94203      *LC* 77-8490      *ISBN* 0521217326

**Davies, Godfrey, 1892-1957. ed.**                                    • **5.7988**
Bibliography of British history, Stuart period, 1603-1714. Issued under the direction of the American Historical Association and the Royal Historical

Society of Great Britain. 2nd ed. [edited by] Mary Frear Keeler. Oxford, Clarendon Press, 1970. xxxv, 734 p. 24 cm. 1. Great Britain — History — Stuarts, 1603-1714 — Bibliography. I. Keeler, Mary Frear. II. Royal Historical Society (Great Britain) III. American Historical Association. IV. T.
Z2018.D25 1970    016.9142    *LC* 77-554522    *ISBN* 0198213719

**Pargellis, Stanley McCrory, 1898-.**      • **5.7989**
Bibliography of British history; the eighteenth century, 1714–1789. Issued under the direction of the American Historical Association and the Royal Historical Society of Great Britain. Edited by Stanley Pargellis and D. J. Medley. — Oxford: Clarendon Press, 1951. xxvi, 642 p.; 25 cm. 1. Great Britain — History — 18th century — Bibliography. I. Medley, Dudley Julius, 1861- joint author. II. T.
Z2018.P37 1951 DA498    016.94207    *LC* 51-4275

**Read, Conyers, 1881-1959.**      • **5.7990**
Bibliography of British history: Tudor period, 1485 –1603; issued under the direction of the American Historical Association and the Royal Historical Society of Great Britain. — 2d ed. — Oxford: Clarendon Press, 1959. xxviii, 624 p.; 25 cm. 1. Great Britain — History — Tudors, 1485-1603 — Bibliography. I. American Historical Association. II. Royal Historical Society (Great Britain) III. T.
Z2018.R28 1959    DA315.R28 1959.    016.94205    *LC* 59-3413

**Brown, Lucy M.**      **5.7991**
Bibliography of British history, 1789–1851, issued under the direction of the American Historical Association and the Royal Historical Society of Great Britain / edited by Lucy M. Brown and Ian R. Christie. — Oxford: Clarendon Press, 1977. xxxi, 759 p.; 24 cm. Includes index. 1. Great Britain — History — 1789-1820 — Bibliography. 2. Great Britain — History — 19th century — Bibliography. I. Christie, Ian R. joint author. II. American Historical Association. III. Royal Historical Society (Great Britain) IV. T.
Z2019.B76 DA520    016.94107/3    *LC* 77-359253    *ISBN* 0198223900

**Hanham, H. J.**      **5.7992**
Bibliography of British history, 1851–1914 / compiled and edited by H. J. Hanham. — Oxford: Clarendon Press, 1976. xxvii, 1606 p.; 24 cm. 'Issued under the direction of the American Historical Association and the Royal Historical Society of Great Britain.' Includes index. 1. Great Britain — History — 19th century — Bibliography. I. American Historical Association. II. Royal Historical Society (Great Britain) III. T.
Z2019.H35 DA530    016.942    *LC* 77-350302    *ISBN* 0198223897

**Higham, Robin D. S.**      • **5.7993**
A guide to the sources of British military history. Edited by Robin Higham. — Berkeley: University of California Press, 1971. xxi, 630 p.; 25 cm. 1. Great Britain — History, Military — Bibliography. I. T.
Z2021.M5 H54    016.355/00942    *LC* 74-104108    *ISBN* 0520016742

**Matthews, William, 1905-.**      • **5.7994**
British autobiographies: an annotated bibliography of British autobiographies published or written before 1951 / compiled by William Matthews. — Berkeley: University of California Press, 1955. xiv, 376 p.; 24 cm. 1. Autobiographies — Bibliography. 2. Great Britain — Biography — Bibliography. I. T.
Z2027.A9 M3    *LC* 55-13593

## Z2031–2069 IRISH LITERATURE. SCOTTISH LITERATURE

**McKenna, Brian.**      **5.7995**
Irish literature, 1800–1875: a guide to information sources / edited by Brian McKenna. — Detroit: Gale Research Co., c1978. xvii, 388 p.; 23 cm. — (Gale information guide library. American literature, English literature, and world literatures in English information guide series. v. 13) Includes indexes. 1. English literature — Irish authors — Bibliography. 2. English literature — Irish authors — History and criticism — Bibliography. 3. English literature — 19th century — Bibliography. 4. English literature — 19th century — History and criticism — Bibliography. I. T. II. Series.
Z2037.M235 PR8750    016.82    *LC* 74-11540    *ISBN* 0810312506

**Mikhail, E. H.**      **5.7996**
An annotated bibliography of modern Anglo–Irish drama / by E.H. Mikhail. — Troy, N.Y.: Whitston Pub. Co., 1981. 300 p.; 24 cm. Includes indexes. 1. English drama — Irish authors — History and criticism — Bibliography. 2. English drama — 20th century — History and criticism — Bibliography. 3. English drama — 19th century — History and criticism — Bibliography. 4. Ireland in literature — Bibliography. 5. Theater — Ireland — Bibliography. I. T.
Z2039.D7 M528 PR8789    016.822/91/099415 19    *LC* 80-51874
   *ISBN* 0878752013

**Aitken, William Russell.**      **5.7997**
Scottish literature in English and Scots: a guide to information sources / W.R. Aitken. — Detroit, Mich.: Gale Research Co., c1982. xxiv, 421 p.; 23 cm. — (Gale information guide library. American literature, English literature, and world literatures in English information guide series. v. 37) Includes indexes. 1. Scottish literature — Bibliography. 2. English literature — Scottish authors — Bibliography. 3. Authors, Scottish — Biography — Bibliography. 4. Scotland — Bibliography. I. T. II. Series.
Z2057.A35 1982 PR8511    016.82/09/9411 19    *LC* 82-2997    *ISBN* 0810312492

## Z2161–2189 France

**Les Livres de l'année–Biblio.**      **5.7998**
1971-1979. Paris, Cercle de la librairie. 9 v. 28 cm. Annual. 'Bibliographie générale des ouvrages de langue française.' 1. French imprints I. Cercle de la librairie (France)
Z2161.L6952    011    *LC* 73-647755

**A Critical bibliography of French literature / Richard A.**      **5.7999**
**Brooks, general editor.**
Rev. [ed.] Syracuse, N.Y.: Syracuse University Press, 1985-. v. 1. French literature — Bibliography I. Brooks, Richard A., 1931-
Z2171.C74 1985 PQ103    016.84 19

**Dreher, S.**      • **5.8000**
Bibliographie de la littérature française, 1930–1939, par S. Dreher et M. Rolli.Complément à la Bibliographie de H. P. Thieme. Lille, Giard, 1948-. v. 26 cm. 'La première rédaction de cet ouvrage a été présentée à l'École de bibliothécaires de Genève pour l'obtention de son diplzome.' Includes the works of 19th and 20th century authors pub. for the most part between 1930 and 1939. Arranged alphabetically by author, with place and date of birth and death given, followed by a chronological arrangement of (1) his books, with date of publication and publisher of each (2) his periodical articles (3) reviews of the writer in book form (4) reviews in periodicals. 1. French literature — 19th cent. — Bio-bibl. 2. French literature — 20th cent. — Bio-bibl. 3. French literature — Hist. & crit. — Bibl. I. Rolli, M. joint author. II. T.
Z2171.D7    *LC* A 49-1233 *

**Drevet, Marguerite L.**      • **5.8001**
Bibliographie de la littérature française, 1940–1949 / par Marguerite L. Drevet; complément à la bibliographie de H. P. Thieme. — Genève: Droz, 1954 [i.e. 1954-1955]. xvi, 644 p.; 25 cm. 'Suite de l'œuvre de Hugo H. [sic] Thieme qui avait été continuée de 1930 à 1939 par Mesdemoiselles Dreher et Rolli.' Issued in 7 parts. 1. French literature — 19th century — Bio-bibliography. 2. French literature — 20th century — Bio-bibliography. 3. French literature — History and criticism — Bibliography. I. T.
Z2171.D73    *LC* 55-949

**French XX bibliography.**      • **5.8002**
v. 5- (no. 21- ) New York: French Institute-Alliance Française, 1969-. v.; 23 cm. Annual. 'Critical and biographical references for the study of French literature since 1885.' 1. French literature — 20th century — History and criticism — Bibliography. I. French Institute-Alliance Française de New York. II. New York (City). French Institute in the United States. III. Camargo Foundation.
Z2171.F7 PQ305    016.8409    *LC* 77-648803

**Klapp, Otto.**      **5.8003**
Bibliographie der französischen Literaturwissenschaft = Bibliographie d'histoire littéraire française / bearbeitet und herausgegeben von Otto Klopp. — Frankfürt am Main: V. Klostermann, c1960-. v.   and index. 1. French philology 2. French literature — Bibliography I. T. II. Title: Bibliographie d'histoire littéraire française.
Z2171.K55    *LC* 60-43852

**Langlois, Pierre, of Paris.**      • **5.8004**
Guide bibliographique des études littéraires / Pierre Langlois, André Mareuil. — Ed. rev. et augm d'un appendice: Contribution de la critique étrangère. — Paris: Hachette, 1960, [c1958] 254, xxxii p.; 21 cm. 1. French literature — Bibliography I. Mareuil, André. II. T.
Z2171.L17 1960    *LC* a 62-549

**Bassan, Fernande.**      **5.8005**
An annotated bibliography of French language and literature / Fernande Bassan, Paul F. Breed, Donald C. Spinelli. — New York: Garland Pub., 1976. xiv, 306 p.; 23 cm. (Garland reference library of the humanities; v. 26) Includes index. 1. French philology — Bibliography. I. Breed, Paul Francis, 1916- joint author. II. Spinelli, Donald C. joint author. III. T.
Z2175.A2 B38 PC2071    016.44    *LC* 75-24079    *ISBN* 0824099869

**Osburn, Charles B.**     **5.8006**
Research and reference guide to French studies / Charles B. Osburn. — 2nd ed. — Metuchen, N.J.: Scarecrow Press, 1981. xxxvii, 532 p.; 23 cm. Includes indexes. 1. French philology — Bibliography. I. T.
Z2175.A2 O8 1981 PC2071    016.44 19    *LC* 81-5637    *ISBN* 0810814404

## Z2221–2249 Germany

**Verzeichnis lieferbarer Bücher.**     **5.8007**
1971/72-   . — Frankfurt am Main: Verlag der Buchhändler-Vereinigung, 1972-. v.; 23 cm. Vols. for 1971/72-   issued in parts. 1. Catalogs, Publishers' — Germany. 2. Germany — Bibliography. 3. Austria — Bibliography. 4. Switzerland — Bibliography. I. Börsenverein des Deutschen Buchhandels.
Z2223.V47    018.4    *LC* sn 85-11211

**Köttelwesch, Clemens.**     **5.8008**
Bibliographisches Handbuch der deutschen Literaturwissenschaft, 1945–[1972] / hrsg. von Clemens Köttelwesch, Mitarbeit H. Hüttermann und C. Maihofer. — Frankfurt a.M.: V. Klostermann, c1973 [i.e.1971]-1979. v.; 27 cm. 1. German literature — History and criticism — Bibliography — Indexes. I. Hüttermann, H. II. Maihofer, C. III. T. IV. Title: Deutsche Literaturwissenschaft.
Z2231.K63

**Raabe, Paul.**     **5.8009**
Einführung in die Bücherkunde zur deutschen Literaturwissenschaft / Paul Raabe. — 10., unveränderte Aufl. unter Mitarbeit von Werner Arnold und Ingrid Hannich-Bode.— Stuttgart: J. B. Metzler, 1984. viii, 104 p.; 19 cm. — (Sammlung Metzler; Bd. 1: Abt. B, Literaturwissenschaftliche Methodenlehre) Two fold. tables inserted in pocket. 1. German literature — History and criticism — Bibliography. I. T.
Z2231.R24 1975 PT85    016.83/09    *LC* 78-375760    *ISBN* 3476180018

**Handbuch der Editionen: deutschsprachige Schriftsteller**     **5.8010**
**Ausgang d. 15. Jahrhunderts bis zur Gegenwart / bearb. von Waltraud Hagen (Leitung u. Gesamtred.) ... [et al.].**
München: Beck, 1979. 607 p.; 25 cm. 'Veröffentlichung des Zentralinstituts für Literaturgeschichte der Akademie der Wissenschaften der DDR.' 1. German literature — Bibliography — First editions. 2. German literature — Criticism, Textual. 3. Bibliography — Editions I. Hagen, Waltraud, Dr. II. Akademie der Wissenschaften der DDR. Zentralinstitut für Literaturgeschichte.
Z2234.F55 H36 1979b PT85    016.83 19    *LC* 80-507904    *ISBN* 3406041396

**Morgan, Bayard Quincy, 1883-.**     **5.8011**
[Bibliography of German literature in English translation] A critical bibliography of German literature in English translation, 1481–1927. 2d ed., completely rev. and greatly augm. New York, Scarecrow Press, 1965 [c1938] 690 p. 23 cm. 1. German literature — Translations into English — Bibliography. 2. English literature — Translations from German — Bibliography. I. T.
Z2234.T7 M8 1965    016.83    *LC* 65-13549

**O'Neill, Patrick, 1945-.**     **5.8012**
German literature in English translation: a select bibliography / Patrick O'Neill. — Toronto; Buffalo: University of Toronto Press, c1981. xii, 242 p.; 24 cm. Includes indexes. 1. German literature — Translations into English — Bibliography. 2. English literature — Translations from German — Bibliography. I. T.
Z2234.T7 O5 PT1113    016.83 19    *LC* 81-195851    *ISBN* 0802024092

**University of London. Institute of Germanic Studies.**     **5.8013**
German language and literature: select bibliography of reference books / by L. M. Newman. — 2nd enlarged ed. — London: Institute of Germanic Studies, University of London, 1979. x, 175 p.; 23 cm. (Publications of the Institute of Germanic Studies. 9 0076-0811) Includes index. 1. German philology — Bibliography. I. Newman, Lindsay Mary. comp. II. T. III. Series.
Z2235.A2 L6 1979 PT85    016.943    *LC* 79-318885

**Kehr, Helen.**     **5.8014**
The Nazi era, 1919–1945: a select bibliography of published works from the early roots to 1980 / compiled by Helen Kehr and Janet Langmaid. — London: Mansell Pub.; Bronx, New York: Distributed in the United States and Canada by H.W. Wilson Co., 1982. xvi, 621 p.; 24 cm. Includes index. 1. National socialism — Bibliography. 2. Germany — Politics and government — 1933-1945 — Bibliography. 3. Germany — Politics and government — 1918-1933 — Bibliography. I. Langmaid, Janet. II. T.
Z2240.K44 1982 DD256.5    016.943085 19    *LC* 83-216788    *ISBN* 072011618X

## Z2483–2537 Eastern Europe. Soviet Union

**Horak, Stephan M., 1920-.**     **5.8015**
The Soviet Union and Eastern Europe: a bibliographic guide to recommended books for small and medium-sized libraries and school media centers / Stephan M. Horak. — Littleton, Colo.: Libraries Unlimited, 1985. xiv, 373 p.; 24 cm. Includes index. 1. Bibliography — Best books — Soviet Union. 2. Bibliography — Best books — Europe, Eastern. 3. Soviet Union — Bibliography. 4. Europe, Eastern — Bibliography. I. T.
Z2491.H59 1985 DK17    016.947 19    *LC* 84-25053    *ISBN* 0872874699

**Woll, Josephine.**     **5.8016**
Soviet dissident literature, a critical guide / Josephine Woll, in collaboration with Vladimir G. Treml. — Boston, Mass.: G.K. Hall, c1983. xlviii, 241 p.; 25 cm. Rev. ed. of: Soviet unofficial literature—samizdat. 1978. Includes index. 1. Russian literature — 20th century — Bibliography. 2. Russian literature — Foreign countries — Bibliography. 3. Underground literature — Soviet Union — Bibliography. 4. Civil rights — Soviet Union — Bibliography. 5. Europe — Imprints. 6. United States — Imprints I. Treml, Vladimir G. II. T.
Z2511.U5 W64 1983 PG3026.U5    016.8917 19    *LC* 83-56    *ISBN* 081618626X

**Guide to the study of the Soviet nationalities: non–Russian**     **5.8017**
**peoples of the USSR / Stephan M. Horak, editor; contributors, Marjorie Mandelstam Balzer ... [et al.].**
Littleton, Colo.: Libraries Unlimited, 1982. 265 p.; 25 cm. Includes index. 1. Ethnology — Soviet Union — Bibliography. I. Horak, Stephan M., 1920- II. Balzer, Marjorie Mandelstam.
Z2517.E85 G84 DK33    016.947/004 19    *LC* 81-18657    *ISBN* 087287270X

**Gerould, Daniel Charles, 1928-.**     **5.8018**
Polish plays in translation. — New York: Center for Advanced Study in Theatre Arts,City University of New York, 1983. 133 p., 28 cm. I. T.
Z2528.D7 P6x

## Z2551–2650 Scandinavia

**Fry, Donald K.**     **5.8019**
Norse sagas translated into English: a bibliography / by Donald K. Fry; foreword by Paul Schach. — New York, N.Y.: AMS Press, c1980. xx, 139 p.; 24 cm. — (AMS studies in the Middle Ages. no. 3) Includes indexes. 1. Sagas — Translations into English — Bibliography. 2. English fiction — Translations from Old Norse — Bibliography. I. T. II. Series.
Z2556.F78 PT7262.E5    016.839/6/08 19    *LC* 79-8632    *ISBN* 0404180167

**Mitchell, P. M. (Phillip Marshall), 1916-.**     • **5.8020**
A bibliographical guide to Danish literature / by P.M. Mitchell. — Copenhagen: Munksgaard, 1951. 62 p.; 24 cm. 1. Danish literature — Bibliography. I. T.
Z2571.M5    *LC* 52-3783

**Bredsdorff, Elias.**     • **5.8021**
Danish literature in English translation, with a special Hans Christian Andersen supplement; a bibliography. — Copenhagen: E. Munksgaard, 1950. 198 p. 19 cm. 1. Andersen, H. C. (Hans Christian), 1805-1875 — Bibliography. 2. Danish literature — Translations into English — Bibliography. 3. English literature — Translations from Danish — Bibliography. 4. Danish literature — Bibliography. I. T.
Z2574.T7 B7    016.8398/1/08    *LC* 51-4614/r

**Schroeder, Carol L.**     **5.8022**
A bibliography of Danish literature in English translation, 1950–1980: with a selection of books about Denmark / Carol L. Schroeder; [edited by Grethe Jacobsen]. — Copenhagen: Det Danske Selskab, c1982. 197 p.; 22 cm. — (Danes of the present and past.) English and Danish. Includes index. 1. Danish literature — Translations into English — Bibliography. 2. English literature — Translations from Danish — Bibliography. 3. Denmark — Bibliography. I. Jacobsen, Grethe. II. T. III. Series.
Z2574.T7 S37 1982 PT7965    016.8398/1 19    *LC* 83-138174    *ISBN* 8774290444

## Z2681–2739 Spain. Portugal

**Foster, David William.**                                        • **5.8023**
Manual of Hispanic bibliography. Compiled by David W. Foster [and] Virginia Ramos Foster. Seattle: University of Washington Press, [1970] x, 206 p.; 24 cm. — (University of Washington publications in language and literature, v. 18) 1. Bibliography — Bibliography. 2. Bibliography — Bibliography — Spanish literature. 3. Spanish literature — Bibliography. 4. Spanish American literature — Bibliography. I. Foster, Virginia Ramos. joint author. II. T.
Z2691.A1F68    016.01686    *LC* 70-103296

**Woodbridge, Hensley Charles, 1923-.**                              **5.8024**
Spanish and Spanish–American literature: an annotated guide to selected bibliographies / Hensley C. Woodbridge. — New York, N.Y.: Modern Language Association of America, 1983. vi, 74 p.; 22 cm. — (Selected bibliographies in language and literature. 4) Includes index. 1. Bibliography — Bibliography — Spanish literature. 2. Bibliography — Bibliography — Spanish American literature. 3. Spanish literature — Bibliography. 4. Spanish American literature — Bibliography. I. T. II. Series.
Z2691.A1 W66 1983 PQ6033    016/.01686 19    *LC* 82-23958    *ISBN* 0873529545

**Simón Díaz, José.**                                             **5.8025**
Bibliografía de la literatura hispánica. Dirección y prólogo de Joaquín de Entrambasaguas. Madrid, Consejo Superior de Investigaciones Científicas, Instituto 'Miguel de Cervantes,' de Filología Hispánica, 1950-< 1984 >. v. < 1-11, 13 > facsims. 25 cm. 1. Spanish literature — Bibliography. 2. Spanish American literature — Bibliography. 3. Spain — Literatures — Bibliography. I. T.
Z2691.S5    016.86    *LC* 51-15355

**Simón Díaz, José.**                                             **5.8026**
Manual de bibliografía de la literatura española / [por] José Simón Díaz. — 3a ed. ref., corr. y aum. — Madrid: Gredos, D.L. 1980. 1156 p.; 25 cm. — (Biblioteca románica hispánica. Manuales. 47) Includes indexes. 1. Spanish literature — Bibliography. I. T. II. Series.
Z2691.S54 1980 PQ6032    016.86 19    *LC* 81-129968    *ISBN* 8424900235

**Moseley, William W.**                                           **5.8027**
Spanish literature, 1500–1700: a bibliography of Golden Age studies in Spanish and English, 1925–1980 / compiled by William W. Moseley, Glenroy Emmons, and Marilyn C. Emmons. — Westport, Conn.: Greenwood Press, 1984. lxiii, 765 p.; 24 cm. (Bibliographies and indexes in world literature. 0742-6801; no. 3) Includes indexes. 1. Spanish literature — Classical period, 1500-1700 — History and criticism — Bibliography. I. Emmons, Glenroy. II. Emmons, Marilyn C. III. T. IV. Series.
Z2692.M67 1984 PQ6064    016.86/09/003 19    *LC* 84-8965    *ISBN* 0313214913

**Modern Language Association of America. Spanish V.**            • **5.8028**
**Bibliography Committee.**
Bibliography of contemporary Spanish literature. no.1-4; 1953-56. Chapel Hill, N.C. 4 no. 1. Spanish literature — 20th century — Bibliography — Periodicals. I. T.
Z2693.3.M6    *LC* 58-2609

**Bleznick, Donald William, 1924-.**                              **5.8029**
A sourcebook for Hispanic literature and language: a selected, annotated guide to Spanish and Spanish American bibliography, literature, linguistics, journals, and other source materials / Donald W. Bleznick. — Philadelphia: Temple University Press, 1974. –. xi, 183 p.; 22 cm.-. Includes index. - 1. Reference books — Spanish philology. 2. Reference books — Spanish American literature. I. T.
Z2695.A2 B55    Z2695A2 B55.    016.86    *LC* 74-77776    *ISBN* 0877220360

## Z3001–3009 Asia: General

**Bibliography of Asian studies.**                                • **5.8030**
1969- . — Ann Arbor, Mich.: Association for Asian Studies. — Annual. 1. Asia — Bibliography — Periodicals. 2. Asia — Study and teaching — Bibliography — Periodicals. I. Association for Asian Studies.
Z3001.B49    *LC* 73-617426

**Edgar, Neal L., 1927-.**                                        **5.8031**
Travel in Asia: a guide to information sources / Neal L. Edgar, Wendy Yu Ma. — Detroit, Mich.: Gale Research Co., c1983. xvii, 413 p.; 23 cm. — (Volume 6 in the Geography and travel information guide series) Includes indexes. 1. Asia — Description and travel — Bibliography. 2. Asia — Description and travel — Audio-visual aids — Catalogs. I. Ma, Wendy Yu. II. T.
Z3001.E22 1983 DS10    016.915/0442 19    *LC* 82-24271    *ISBN* 0810314703

**Embree, John Fee, 1908-1950.**                                  • **5.8032**
Bibliography of the peoples and cultures of mainland Southeast Asia / by John F. Embree and Lillian Ota Dotson. — New York: Russell & Russell, [1972, c1950] xxxiii, 821 p., xii l.: maps; 25 cm. 1. Asia, Southeastern — Bibliography. I. Dotson, Lillian Ota, joint author. II. T.
Z3001.E5 1972    016.9159    *LC* 70-173535

**Gillin, Donald G.**                                             • **5.8033**
East Asia: a bibliography for undergraduate libraries [by] Donald Gillin, Edith Ehrman [and] Ward Morehouse. Williamsport, Pa., Bro-Dart Pub. Co., 1970. xvi, 130 p. 29 cm. (Foreign Area Materials Center, University of the State of New York. Occasional publication no. 10) 1. East Asia — Bibliography. I. Ehrman, Edith. joint author. II. Morehouse, Ward, 1929- joint author. III. T.
Z3001.G5x    016.915    *LC* 78-116140    *ISBN* 0872720101

**Nunn, Godfrey Raymond, 1918-.**                                 **5.8034**
Asia, reference works: a select annotated guide / by G. Raymond Nunn. — London: Mansell, 1980. xvi, 365 p.; 25 cm. Revised and enl. work based on the author's 1971 publication: Asia, a selected and annotated guide to reference works. Includes index. 1. Reference books — Asia. 2. Bibliography — Asia 3. Asia — Bibliography. I. T.
Z3001.N79 1980 DS35    016.95 19    *LC* 80-512146    *ISBN* 0720109213

## Z3013–3045 Middle East

**Atiyeh, George Nicholas, 1923-.**                               **5.8035**
The contemporary Middle East, 1948–1973; a selective and annotated bibliography, compiled by George N. Atiyeh. Boston, G. K. Hall [1975] xxvi, 664 p. 29 cm. 1. Middle East — Bibliography. 2. Africa, North — Bibliography. I. T.
Z3013.A85 DS44    915.6    *LC* 74-19247    *ISBN* 0816110859

**Littlefield, David W., 1940-.**                                 **5.8036**
The Islamic Near East and North Africa: an annotated guide to books in English for non–specialists / David W. Littlefield. Littleton, Colo.: Libraries Unlimited, 1977. 375 p.; 24 cm. Includes indexes. 1. Middle East — Bibliography. 2. Africa, North — Bibliography. I. T.
Z3013.L653 DS44    016.956    *LC* 76-218    *ISBN* 0872871592

**Middle East and Islam; a bibliographical introduction. Edited by**  **5.8037**
**Derek Hopwood and Diana Grimwood–Jones. Foreword by J.**
**D. Pearson.**
Zug, Switzerland, Inter Documentation Co. [c1972] vii, 368 p. 21 cm. (Bibliotheca Asiatica. 9) At head of title: Middle East Libraries Committee. 1. Islam — Bibliography. 2. Middle East — Bibliography. I. Hopwood, Derek. ed. II. Grimwood-Jones, Diana. joint author. III. Middle East Libraries Committee. IV. Series.
Z3013.M48    016.9156/03    *LC* 72-85349    *ISBN* 3857500034

**Sauvaget, Jean, 1901-1950.**                                    • **5.8038**
Introduction to the history of the Muslim East: a bibliographical guide. Berkeley: U. of California P., 1965. xxi, 252 p. Based on the 2d ed. as recast by Claude Cahen. 1. Islamic countries — Bibliography. I. T.
Z3013.S314    *LC* 64-25271

**Anderson, Margaret.**                                           **5.8039**
Arabic materials in English translation: a bibliography of works dating from the pre–Islamic period to 1977 / Margaret Anderson. — Boston: G. K. Hall, c1980. viii, 249 p.; 24 cm. — (A Reference publication in Middle Eastern studies) Includes index. 1. Arabic literature — Translations into English — Bibliography. 2. English literature — Translations from Arabic — Bibliography. I. T.
Z3014.L56 A52 PJ7692.E1    016.909/04927    *LC* 79-27708    *ISBN* 0816179549

**Bryson, Thomas A., 1931-.**                                     **5.8040**
United States/Middle East diplomatic relations, 1784–1978: an annotated bibliography / by Thomas A. Bryson. — Metuchen, N.J.: Scarecrow Press, 1979. xiv, 205 p.; 23 cm. Includes index. 1. Middle East — Foreign relations —

United States — Bibliography. 2. United States — Foreign relations — Middle East — Bibliography. I. T.
Z3014.R44 B79 DS63.2.U5     016.32756/073     *LC* 78-26754     *ISBN* 0810811979

**Olson, William J., 1947-.**        **5.8041**
Britain's elusive empire in the Middle East, 1900–1921: an annotated bibliography / William J. Olson with the assistance of Addeane S. Caelleigh. — New York: Garland Pub., 1982. xvii, 404 p.; 23 cm. — (Garland reference library of social science. v. 109) (Themes in European expansion: exploration, colonization, and the impact of empire; v. 2) Includes index. 1. Middle East — Foreign relations — Great Britain — Bibliography. 2. Great Britain — Foreign relations — Middle East — Bibliography. 3. Middle East — Politics and government — Bibliography. I. Caelleigh, Addeane S. II. T. III. Series.
Z3014.R44 O47 1982 DS63.2.G7     016.32741056 19     *LC* 81-43360
    *ISBN* 0824092732

**Kamrany, Nake M., 1934-.**        **5.8042**
Afghanistan research materials survey: bibliography of Afghanistan / Nake M. Kamrany, Leon B. Poullada. — Los Angeles, Calif.: Modeling Research Group, Dept. of Economics, University of Southern California; [Santa Monica, Calif., U.S.A.: Distributed by Fundamental Books, 1985] 5 v. (v, 1368 leaves); 29 cm. 'January 1985.' 1. Afghanistan — Bibliography. I. Poullada, Leon B., 1913- II. T.
Z3016.K35 1985 DS351.5     016.958/1 19     *LC* 85-214641

**McLachlan, K. S. (Keith Stanley)**        **5.8043**
A bibliography of Afghanistan: a working bibliography of materials on Afghanistan with special reference to economic and social change in the twentieth century / by Keith McLachlan and William Whittaker; assistant compilers, Jane Burton ... [et al.]. — Cambridge, England: Middle East & North African Studies Press,, 1983. xiii, 671 p.: ill.; 22 cm. Includes index. 1. Afghanistan — Bibliography. I. Whittaker, William. II. T.
Z3016.M4 1983 DS351.5     016.958/1 19     *LC* 83-181623     *ISBN* 090655912X

# Z3101–3109 China

**The Indiana companion to traditional Chinese literature /**        **5.8044**
**William H. Nienhauser, Jr., editor and compiler, Charles Hartman, associate editor for poetry, Y.W. Ma, associate editor for fiction, Stephen H. West, associate editor for drama.**
Bloomington: Indiana University Press, c1986. xlii, 1050 p.; 26 cm. Includes indexes. 1. Chinese literature — Bio-bibliography. 2. Chinese literature — History and criticism — Addresses, essays, lectures. I. Nienhauser, William H.
Z3108.L5 I53 1986 PL2264     895.1/09 19     *LC* 83-49511     *ISBN* 0253329833

**Yang, Winston L. Y.**        **5.8045**
Modern Chinese fiction: a guide to its study and appreciation: essays and bibliographies / edited by Winston L.Y. Yang and Nathan K. Mao; with contributions by Howard Goldblatt ... [et al.]. — Boston, Mass.: G.K. Hall, c1981. xxii, 288 p.; 24 cm. Title also in Chinese: Chung-kuo chin tai hsiao shuo. 1. Chinese fiction — 20th century — Bibliography. 2. Chinese fiction — 20th century — History and criticism — Addresses, essays, lectures. I. Mao, Nathan K. joint author. II. T. III. Title: Chung-kuo chin tai hsiao shuo.
Z3108.L5 Y293 PL2442     895.1/35/09     *LC* 80-18322     *ISBN* 0816181136

**Yang, Winston L. Y.**        **5.8046**
Classical Chinese fiction: a guide to its study and appreciation: essays and bibliographies / Winston L. Y. Yang, Peter Li, and Nathan K. Mao. — Boston: G. K. Hall, c1978. xxvi, 302 p.; 24 cm. Title also in Chinese romanized: Chung-kuo ku tien hsiao shuo. Includes index. 1. Chinese fiction — Bibliography. 2. Chinese fiction — History and criticism — Addresses, essays, lectures. I. Li, Peter, 1935- joint author. II. Mao, Nathan Kwok-kuen, 1940- III. T. IV. Title: Chung-kuo ku tien hsiao shuo.
Z3108.L5 Y29 PL2625     Z3108L5 Y39.     016.8951/3     *LC* 77-29016
    *ISBN* 0816178099

# Z3185–3220 South Asia

**Case, Margaret H.**        • **5.8047**
South Asian history, 1750–1950; a guide to periodicals, dissertations, and newspapers [by] Margaret H. Case. — Princeton, N.J.: Princeton University Press, 1968. xiii, 561 p.; 25 cm. 1. South Asia — History — Bibliography. I. T.
Z3185.C3     016.954     *LC* 67-21019

**Patterson, Maureen L. P.**        **5.8048**
South Asian civilizations: a bibliographic synthesis / Maureen L.P. Patterson, in collaboration with William J. Alspaugh. — Chicago: University of Chicago Press, 1982 (c1981). xxxvii, 853 p.: maps; 29 cm. Includes indexes. 1. South Asia — Civilization — Bibliography. I. Alspaugh, William J. II. T.
Z3185.P37 1981 DS339     016.954 19     *LC* 81-52518     *ISBN* 0226649105

**South Asian bibliography: a handbook and guide / compiled by**        **5.8049**
**the South Asia Library Group; general editor, J. D. Pearson.**
Sussex [Eng.]: Harvester Press; Atlantic Highlands, N.J.: Humanities Press, 1979. xiii, 381 p.; 24 cm. Includes index. 1. South Asia — Bibliography. I. Pearson, J. D. (James Douglas), 1911- II. South Asia Library Group.
Z3185.S65 DS335     016.954     *LC* 77-16651     *ISBN* 0391008196

**South Asia: A bibliography for undergraduate libraries [by]**        • **5.8050**
**Louis A. Jacob [and others].**
Williamsport, Pa.: Bro-Dart Pub. Co., 1970. xvi, 103 p.; 29 cm. — (University of the State of New York. Foreign Area Materials Center. Occasional publication no. 11) 1. South Asia — Bibliography. I. Jacob, Louis A.
Z3185.S6x     016.9154     *LC* 71-124578     *ISBN* 0872720160

**Sukhwal, B. L., 1929-.**        **5.8051**
South Asia; a systematic geographic bibliography, by B. L. Sukhwal. — Metuchen, N.J.: Scarecrow Press, 1974. xxii, 827 p.; 22 cm. 1. South Asia — Bibliography. I. T.
Z3185.S94     016.9159     *LC* 74-10852     *ISBN* 0810807610

**Pakistan: a comprehensive bibliography of books and**        **5.8052**
**government publications with annotations, 1947–80 / compiled by Institute's research scholars under the direction of N.A. Baloch.**
Islamabad: Institute of Islamic History, Culture, and Civilization, Islamic University, 1981. xii, 515 p.; 24 cm. (Bibliographical series; 4) 1. Pakistan — Bibliography. 2. Pakistan — Government publications — Bibliography. I. Nabī Bakhshu Khānu Balocu, 1917- II. Islamic University (Islāmābād, Pakistan). Institute of Islamic History, Culture, and Civilization.
Z3196.P33 1981 DS376.9     016.9549 19     *LC* 84-931373

**Mahar, J. Michael.**        • **5.8053**
India: a critical bibliography / by J. Michael Mahar. — Tucson: University of Arizona Press, [1964] 119 p.; 28 cm. 1. India — Bibliography. I. T.
Z3201.M3     *LC* 62-17992

**Gupta, Brijen Kishore, 1929-.**        **5.8054**
India / Brijen K. Gupta, Datta S. Kharbas, compilers; with the assistance of Judith N. Kharbas, Arthur D. Lopatin. — Oxford, England; Santa Barbara, Calif.: Clio Press, c1984. xviii, 264 p., [2] leaves of plates: ill.; 23 cm. — (World bibliographical series. v. 26) Includes index. 1. India — Bibliography. I. Kharbas, Datta Shankarrao. II. T. III. Series.
Z3206.G86 1984 DS407     016.954 19     *LC* 84-165942     *ISBN* 0903450380

**Learning about India: an annotated guide for nonspecialists /**        **5.8055**
**Barbara J. Harrison, editor.**
New Delhi: Educational Resources Center, c1977. xiii, 349 p.; 22 cm. — (Foreign Area Materials Center occasional publication; no. 24) 'Center for International Programs and Comparative Studies, New York State Education Department, in association with Educational Resources Center, New Delhi, and N.D.E.A. Center for South Asian Studies, Columbia University.' Includes index. 1. India — Bibliography. 2. India — Study and teaching — Directories. 3. India — Study and teaching — Audio-visual aids — Catalogs. I. Harrison, Barbara J.
Z3206.H3x DS407     909 s 016.954     *LC* 78-905280     Rs35.00

**Bibliography on scheduled castes and scheduled tribes:**        **5.8056**
**Occasional paper 1 of 1982.**
New Delhi: Social Studies Division, Office of the Registrar General, India, Ministry of Home Affairs, 1982. xxii, 561 p.
Z3208.E85.B5x

**Trager, Frank N.**        **5.8057**
Burma: a selected and annotated bibliography [by] Frank N. Trager, with the assistance of Janelle Wang [and others]. — New Haven: Human Relations Area Files Press, 1973. xii, 356 p.; 22 cm. — (Behavior science bibliographies.) Edition of 1956 prepared by the Burma Research Project of New York University and published under title: Annotated bibliography of Burma. 1. Burma — Bibliography. I. New York University. Burma Research Project. Annotated bibliography of Burma. II. T. III. Series.
Z3216.T7     016.91592     *LC* 72-90939     *ISBN* 0875362273

# Z3221–3299 Southeast Asia

**Jenner, Philip N.**                                                          **5.8058**
Southeast Asian literatures in translation: a preliminary bibliography, by Philip N. Jenner. — [Honolulu]: University Press of Hawaii, 1972. xvi, 198 p.; 23 cm. — (Asian studies at Hawaii. no. 9) 1. Literature, Modern — Translations from Oriental literature — Bibliography. 2. Asia, Southeastern — Literatures — Translations into foreign languages — Bibliography. I. T. II. Series.
Z3221.J4x      DS3.A2 A82 no. 9      915/.03 s 016.895      *LC* 72-619667      *ISBN* 0824802616

**Lim, Patricia Pui Huen.**                                                    **5.8059**
The Malay world of Southeast: a select cultural bibliography / compiled by P. Lim Pui Huen. — Singapore: Institute of Southeast Asian Studies, 1986. xiii, 456 p. Includes index. 1. Asia, Southeast — Bibliography. I. Institute of Southeast Asian Studies. II. T.
Z3221.L73 1986      *ISBN* 9971998364

**Sugnet, Christopher L.**                                                      **5.8060**
Vietnam War bibliography: selected from Cornell University's Echols collection / Christopher L. Sugnet, John T. Hickey, with the assistance of Robert Crispino. — Lexington, Mass.: LexingtonBooks, c1983. xiii, 572 p.; 24 cm. — (Lexington Books special series in libraries and librarianship.) Includes index. 1. Echols, John M — Library — Catalogs. 2. Cornell University. Libraries — Catalogs. 3. Vietnamese Conflict, 1961-1975 — Bibliography — Catalogs. I. Hickey, John T. II. Crispino, Robert. III. Cornell University. Libraries. IV. T. V. Series.
Z3226.S9 1983      DS557.7      016.959704/3 19      *LC* 83-16172      *ISBN* 066906680X

**Burns, Richard Dean.**                                                       **5.8061**
The wars in Vietnam, Cambodia, and Laos, 1945–1982: a bibliographic guide / Richard Dean Burns and Milton Leitenberg. — Santa Barbara, Calif.: ABC-Clio Information Services, c1984. xxxii, 290 p.: maps; 29 cm. — (War/peace bibliography series. #18) Includes index. 1. Vietnamese Conflict, 1961-1975 — Bibliography. 2. Indochina — History — 1945- — Bibliography. 3. Indochina — History, Military — Bibliography. I. Leitenberg, Milton. II. T. III. Series.
Z3228.V5 B87 1984      DS557.7      016.959704/3      *LC* 80-13246      *ISBN* 0874363101

**Cotter, Michael.**                                                           **5.8062**
Vietnam, a guide to reference sources / Michael Cotter. — Boston: G. K. Hall, c1977. xv, 272 p.; 28 cm. Includes index. 1. Reference books — Vietnam. 2. Vietnam — Bibliography. I. T.
Z3228.V5 C68      DS556.3      011/.02      *LC* 77-22448      *ISBN* 0816180504

**Watts, Michael, 1918-.**                                                     **5.8063**
Thailand / Michael Watts. — Oxford: Clio, 1986. xli, 275 p.: map; 23 cm. — (World bibliographical series. v. 65) 1. Thailand — Bibliography. I. T. II. Series.
Z3236.W3x      016.9593 19      *LC* gb85-46126      *ISBN* 1851090088

**Brown, Ian, 1947-.**                                                         **5.8064**
Malaysia / Ian Brown, Rajeswary Ampalavanar, compilers. — Oxford: Clio, c1986. xxxv, 308 p.: maps; 22 cm. — (World bibliographical series. v.12) 1. Malaysia — Bibliography. I. Ampalavanar, Rajeswary. II. T. III. Series.
Z3246.B7x      016.9595 19      *LC* gb86-3378      *ISBN* 0903450232

**Saito, Shiro.**                                                              **5.8065**
Philippine ethnography: a critically annotated and selected bibliography. Honolulu, University Press of Hawaii [c1972] xxxi, 512 p. 28 cm. (East-West bibliographic series) 1. Ethnology — Philippine Islands — Bibliography. 2. Philippines — Bibliography. I. T.
Z3296.S23      016.91599/03/4      *LC* 72-92068      *ISBN* 0824802486

# Z3301–3320 Japan. Korea

**Fukuda, Naomi.**                                                             **5.8066**
Japanese history: a guide to survey histories = [Nihon shi bunken kaidai] / edited by Naomi Fukuda. — Ann Arbor: Center for Japanese Studies, University of Michigan, 1984-1986. 2 v.; 28 cm. In English. Parallel title in Japanese. Includes indexes. 1. Japan — Bibliography. I. T. II. Title: Nihon shi bunken kaidai.
Z3306.F83 1984      DS835      016.952 19      *LC* 84-1807      *ISBN* 093951219X

**Algarin, Joanne P.**                                                         **5.8067**
Japanese folk literature: a core collection and reference guide / Joanne P. Algarin. — New York: R.R. Bowker, 1982. xiv, 226 p.; 24 cm. 1. Folk literature, Japanese — History and criticism — Bibliography. I. T.
Z3308.L5 A44 1982 PL748      016.3982/0952 19      *LC* 82-9672      *ISBN* 0835215164

**Marks, Alfred H.**                                                           **5.8068**
Guide to Japanese prose / Alfred H. Marks and Barry D. Bort. — Boston: G. K. Hall, 1975. 150 p.; 22 cm. — (Asian literature bibliography series.) Includes index. 1. Japanese prose literature — Translations into English — Bibliography. 2. English prose literature — Translations from Japanese — Bibliography. I. Bort, Barry D. joint author. II. T. III. Series.
Z3308.L5 M37 PL782.E8      016.8956/8/08 19      *LC* 74-20608      *ISBN* 0816111103

**Pronko, Leonard Cabell.**                                                    **5.8069**
Guide to Japanese drama [by] Leonard C. Pronko. — Boston: G. K. Hall, 1973. 125 p.; 22 cm. — (Asian literature bibliography series.) 1. Japanese drama — Bibliography. I. T. II. Series.
Z3308.L5 P76      016.8956/2/008      *LC* 73-8506      *ISBN* 0816111081

**Rimer, J. Thomas.**                                                          **5.8070**
Guide to Japanese poetry / J. Thomas Rimer and Robert E. Morrell. — Boston: G. K. Hall, 1975. 151 p.; 21 cm. (Asian literature bibliography series.) Includes index. 1. Japanese poetry — Translations into English — Bibliography. 2. English poetry — Translations from Japanese — Bibliography. 3. Japanese poetry — History and criticism — Bibliography. I. Morrell, Robert E. joint author. II. T. III. Series.
Z3308.L5 R54 1975 PL782.E3      016.8956/1/008      *LC* 74-20610      *ISBN* 0816111111

**Studies on Korea, a scholar's guide / edited by Han–Kyo Kim**               **5.8071**
**with the assistance of Hong Kyoo Park.**
Honolulu: University Press of Hawaii, c1980. xx, 438 p.; 25 cm. 'A study from the Center for Korean Studies, University of Hawaii.' 1. Korea — Bibliography. 2. Korea (North) — Bibliography. I. Kim, Han-Kyo, 1928- II. Park, Hong Kyoo, 1944- III. University of Hawaii at Manoa. Center for Korean Studies.
Z3316.S78 DS902      016.9519      *LC* 79-26491      *ISBN* 0824806735

# Z3366–3370 Iran

**Bibliographical guide to Iran: the Middle East Library**                    **5.8072**
**Committee guide / edited by L.P. Elwell–Sutton.**
Brighton, Sussex: Harvester Press; Totowa, N.J.: Barnes & Noble Books, 1983. xxv, 462 p.; 25 cm. Includes index. 1. Iran — Bibliography. I. Elwell-Sutton, L. P. (Laurence Paul).
Z3366.B5 1983 DS254.5      016.955 19      *LC* 82-22748      *ISBN* 0389203394

# Z3501–3999 Africa

**Scheven, Yvette.**                                                           **5.8073**
Bibliographies for African studies, 1970–1975 / compiled by Yvette Scheven. — [Los Angeles, Calif.]: Crossroads Press, c1977. xxvi, 159 p.; 28 cm. — (Archival and bibliographic series.) Includes index. 1. Bibliography — Bibliography — Africa, Sub-Saharan. 2. Bibliography — Bibliography — Humanities. 3. Humanities — Africa, Sub-Saharan — Bibliography. 4. Bibliography — Bibliography — Social sciences. 5. Social sciences — Africa, Sub-Saharan — Bibliography. 6. Africa, Sub-Saharan — Bibliography. I. T. II. Series.
Z3501.A1 S32 1977 DT351      016.967 19      *LC* 83-162616

**Duignan, Peter.**                                                           **5.8074**
Guide to research and reference works on Sub–Saharan Africa / edited by Peter Duignan; compiled by Helen F. Conover and Peter Duignan; with the assistance of Evelyn Boyce, Liselotte Hofmann [and] Karen Fung. — Stanford, Calif.: Hoover Institution Press, Stanford University [1972] xiii, 1102 p.; 29 cm. (Hoover Institution bibliographical series. 46) 1. Bibliography — Bibliography — Africa, Sub-Saharan. 2. Africa, Sub-Saharan — Bibliography. I. Conover, Helen Field. II. T. III. Series.
Z3501.D78      016.0169167/03      *LC* 76-152424      *ISBN* 0817924612

**Witherell, Julian W.**                                                       **5.8075**
The United States and Africa: guide to U.S. official documents and government–sponsored publications on Africa, 1785–1975 / compiled by Julian

W. Witherell. — Washington: Library of Congress: for sale by the Supt. of Docs., U.S. Govt. Print. Off., 1978. xix, 949 p.; 27 cm. Includes index. 1. Catalogs, Union — United States. 2. Africa — Bibliography — Union lists. 3. United States — Government publications — Bibliography — Union lists. I. T.
Z3501.W57 DT3     016.96     LC 78-1051     ISBN 0844402613

**Witherell, Julian W.**        **5.8076**
The United States and sub–Saharan Africa: guide to U.S. official documents and government–sponsored publications, 1976–1980 / compiled by Julian W. Witherell. — Washington: Library of Congress: For sale by the Supt. of Docs., U.S. G.P.O., 1984. xxiii, 721 p.; 27 cm. Includes index. 1. Catalogs, Union — United States. 2. Africa, Sub-Saharan — Bibliography — Union lists. 3. United States — Government publications — Bibliography — Union lists. I. T.
Z3501.W58 1984 DT3     016.967 19     LC 84-600009     ISBN 0844404489

**Lindfors, Bernth.**        **5.8077**
Black African literature in English: a guide to information sources / Bernth Lindfors. — Detroit: Gale Research Co., c1979. xxx, 482 p.; 23 cm. (Gale information guide library. American literature, English literature, and world literatures in English information guide series. v. 23) Includes indexes. 1. African literature (English) — Black authors — History and criticism — Bibliography. I. T. II. Series.
Z3508.L5 L56 PR9340     016.82     LC 73-16983

# Z4001–5000 Australia. New Zealand. Hawaii

**Day, A. Grove (Arthur Grove), 1904-.**        **5.8078**
Modern Australian prose, 1901–1975: a guide to information sources / A. Grove Day. — Detroit, Mich.: Gale Research Co., c1980. xix, 462 p.; 23 cm. — (Gale information guide library. American literature, English literature, and world literatures in English information guide series. v. 29) Includes index. 1. Australian literature — 20th century — Bibliography. I. T. II. Series.
Z4011.D38 PR9604.3     016.82 19     LC 80-19512     ISBN 0810312433

**Kepars, I.**        **5.8079**
Australia / I. Kepars, compiler. — Oxford, England; Santa Barbara, Calif.: Clio Press, c1984. xvii, 289 p., [2] p. of plates: map; 23 cm. (World bibliographical series. v. 46) Includes index. 1. Australia — Bibliography. I. T. II. Series.
Z4011.K46 1984 DU96     016.994 19     LC 84-232073     ISBN 0903450836

**Lock, Fred.**        **5.8080**
Australian literature: a reference guide / Fred Lock and Alan Lawson. — 2d ed. — Melbourne; New York: Oxford University Press, 1980. xiv, 120 p.; 22 cm. — (Australian bibliographies) Includes indexes. 1. Australian literature — Bibliography. 2. Reference books — Australian literature — Bibliography. 3. Bibliography — Bibliography — Australian literature. I. Lawson, Alan. joint author. II. T.
Z4011.L6 1980 PR9604.3     016.82 19     LC 80-511030     ISBN 0195542142

**Andrews, B. G.**        **5.8081**
Australian literature to 1900: a guide to information sources / Barry G. Andrews, William H. Wilde. — Detroit, Mich.: Gale Research Co., c1980. xxii, 472 p.; 22 cm. (Gale information guide library. American literature, English literature, and world literatures in English information guide series. v. 22) Includes indexes. 1. Australian literature — Bibliography. I. Wilde, W. H. (William Henry) joint author. II. T. III. Series.
Z4021.A54 PR9604.3     016.82     LC 74-11521     ISBN 0810312158

**Johnston, Grahame.**        **5.8082**
Annals of Australian literature. — Melbourne; New York: Oxford University Press, 1970. xi, 147 p.; 23 cm. 1. Australian literature — Bibliography. I. T.
Z4021.J6     016.82     LC 75-146801     ISBN 0195503155

**Miller, Edmund Morris, 1881-1964.**        **5.8083**
Australian literature from its beginnings to 1935: a descriptive and bibliographical survey of books by Australian authors in poetry, drama, fiction, criticism and anthology with subsidiary entries to 1938, by E. Morris Miller. — Facsimile ed. — Sydney: Sydney University Press, 1973. 2 v. (xi, 1074 p.); 25 cm. Initiated and commenced by the late Sir John Quick. Indices. 1. Australian literature — Bibliography. 2. Australian literature — History and criticism. 3. Australian literature — History and criticism — Bibliography. 4. Australia — Bibliography. I. T.
Z4021.M5 1940a     016.82/08     LC 73-84905     ISBN 0424069202

**Jaffa, Herbert C.**        **5.8084**
Modern Australian poetry, 1920–1970: a guide to information sources / Herbert C. Jaffa. — Detroit, Mich.: Gale Research Co., c1979. xvii, 241 p.; 23 cm. — (Gale information guide library. American literature, English literature, and world literatures in English information guide series. v. 24) Includes index. 1. Australian poetry — 20th century — Bibliography. I. T. II. Series.
Z4024.P7 J34 PR9610.5     821     LC 74-11535     ISBN 0810312425

**Bagnall, Austin Graham, 1912-.**        **5.8085**
New Zealand national bibliography to the year 1960. Editor and principal compiler: A. G. Bagnall. Wellington, A.R. Shearer, Govt. printer, 1969 [i.e. 1970]- < 80 > . < v. 1-4; in 5 > illus. 26 cm. Responsibility for bibliography assumed by the National Library Centre. 1. New Zealand — Imprints. 2. New Zealand — Bibliography. I. Wellington, N.Z. National Library Centre. II. T.
Z4101.B28     015.931     LC 71-18927

**Grover, Ray, 1931-.**        **5.8086**
New Zealand / Ray Grover, compiler. — Oxford, England; Santa Barbara, Calif.: Clio Press, c1980. xxxvii, 254 p.: maps; 22 cm. — (World bibliographical series. v. 18) Includes index. 1. New Zealand — Bibliography. I. T. II. Series.
Z4101.G76 1980 DU412     016.9931 19     LC 84-109349     ISBN 0903450313

**Thomson, J. E. P. (John Edward Palmer)**        **5.8087**
New Zealand literature to 1977: a guide to information sources / John Thomson. — Detroit: Gale Research Co., c1980. x, 272 p.; 22 cm. — (American literature, English literature, and world literature in English; 30) (Gale information guide library) Includes indexes. 1. New Zealand literature — Bibliography. I. T.
Z4111.T45 PR9624.3     016.82     LC 74-11537     ISBN 0810312468

**Burns, James Alexander Scott, 1916-.**        **5.8088**
New Zealand novels and novelists, 1861–1979: an annotated bibliography / James Burns. — Auckland; Exeter, N.H.: Heinemann, 1981. 71 p.; 25 cm. Includes indexes. 1. New Zealand fiction — Bibliography. I. T.
Z4114.F4 B83 PR9632.2     016.823/008/09931 19     LC 81-161535     ISBN 0868633720

**Kittelson, David J.**        **5.8089**
The Hawaiians: an annotated bibliography / by David J. Kittelson. — Honolulu: Social Science Research Institute, University of Hawaii, 1985. xi, 384 p.; 28 cm. (Hawaii series; no. 7) Includes index. 1. Hawaiians — Bibliography. I. T. II. Series.
Z4708.E85 K57 1985 DU624.65     016.9969 19     LC 83-51207     ISBN 082480919X

# Z5051–7999 SUBJECT BIBLIOGRAPHY, A–Z

## Z5071–5076 Agriculture

**Guide to sources for agricultural and biological research /**        **5.8090**
**edited by J. Richard Blanchard and Lois Farrell; contributors, J. Richard Blanchard ... [et al.]; consultants, Wallace Olsen, Richard Farley, Bernard Kreissman; sponsored by the United States National Agricultural Library, United States Department of Agriculture.**
Berkeley: University of California Press, c1981. xi, 735 p.; 29 cm. Includes indexes. 1. Agriculture — Bibliography 2. Biology — Bibliography 3. Agriculture — Research — Bibliography. 4. Biology — Research — Bibliography. I. Blanchard, J. Richard. II. Farrell, Lois. III. National Agricultural Library (U.S.)
Z5071.G83 S493     016.63 19     LC 76-7753     ISBN 0520032268

**Biological and agricultural index.**        • **5.8091**
Jan. 1916-. New York etc.: H. W. Wilson Co. v.; 27 cm. Monthly. 1. Agriculture — Periodicals — Indexes. 2. Agriculture — Bibliographies — Periodicals. 3. Biology — Periodicals — Indexes. 4. Biology — Bibliographies — Periodicals. I. Shimer, Neltje Marie (Tannehill) II. Arnold, Florence A.
Z5073.A46     LC 17-8906

**Bibliography of agriculture.**        **5.8092**
v. 1- July 1942-. [Phoenix, Ariz., Oryx Press] v. 28 cm. Monthly. Title varies slightly. Vols. for 1970- < 75 > have 'data provided by National Agricultural Library, U.S. Department of Agriculture.' Vols. 1-2, no. 5 issued in sections: A, Agricultual economics and rural sociology; B, Agricultural engineering; C, Entomology; D, Plant science; E, Forestry; F, Food processing and distribution. Vol. 1, Section F and all sections of June 1943 not published. 1. Agriculture — Indexes — Periodicals. 2. Agriculture — Bibliography —

Periodicals. I. National Agricultural Library (U.S.) II. United States. Dept. of Agriculture. Library.
Z5073.U572 S493     016.63     *LC 63-24851*

**Schlebecker, John T.**      **• 5.8093**
Bibliography of books and pamphlets on the history of agriculture in the United States, 1607–1967 [by] John T. Schlebecker. — Santa Barbara, Calif.: A[merican] B[ibliographical] C[enter]—Clio, 1969. vii, 183 p.; 26 cm. 'Published under contract with the Smithsonian Institution.' 1. Agriculture — U.S. — History — Bibliography. I. T.
Z5075.U5 S28     016.63/0973     *LC 69-20449*     *ISBN 0874360633*

## Z5111–5134 Anthropology. Ethnology. Archaeology

**Anthropological bibliographies: a selected guide / compiled by**     **5.8094**
**Library–Anthropology Resource Group; Margo L. Smith and**
**Yvonne M. Damien, editors.**
South Salem, N.Y.: Redgrave Pub. Co., c1981. 307 p.; 21 x 28 cm. 1. Bibliography — Bibliography — Anthropology. I. Smith, Margo L. II. Damien, Yvonne M. III. Library-Anthropology Resource Group (Chicago, Ill.)
Z5111.A58 1981     *ISBN 0913178632*

**Kanitkar, Helen A.**      **5.8095**
An anthropological bibliography of South Asia / compiled by Helen A. Kanitkar; together with a directory of anthropological field research compiled by Elizabeth von Fürer-Haimendorf. — The Hague: Mouton, 1976-. v.; 23 cm. Includes indexes. 1. Ethnology — South Asia — Bibliography. 2. Anthropology — Research — South Asia. I. Fürer-Haimendorf, Elizabeth von. An anthropological bibliography of South Asia ... II. T.
Z5115.K35 GN635.S57     016.30129/54     *LC 77-456119*     *ISBN* 9027977410

**Marshall, Mac.**      **5.8096**
Micronesia, 1944–1974: a bibliography of anthropological and related source materials / by Mac Marshall and James D. Nason. — New Haven: HRAF Press, 1975. 337 p.: ill.; 24 cm. 1. Micronesians — Bibliography. 2. Micronesia (Federated States) — Bibliography. I. Nason, James D., joint author. II. T.
Z5116.M37 GN669     016.96/5     *LC 75-28587*     *ISBN 087536215X*

**Bentley, G. Carter.**      **5.8097**
Ethnicity and nationality: a bibliographic guide / G. Carter Bentley. — Seattle: University of Washington Press, c1981. xxii, 381, [53] p.; 24 cm. — (Publications on ethnicity and nationality of the School of International Studies, University of Washington. v. 3) Includes indexes. 1. Ethnicity — Bibliography. 2. Nationalism — Bibliography. I. T. II. Series.
Z5118.E84 B46 GN495.6     016.3058 19     *LC 81-51280*     *ISBN* 0295958537

**Freedman, Robert L., 1941-.**      **5.8098**
Human food uses: a cross-cultural, comprehensive annotated bibliography / compiled by Robert L. Freedman. — Westport, Conn.: Greenwood Press, c1981. xxxvii, 552 p.; 29 cm. Includes index. 1. Food habits — Bibliography. 2. Diet — Bibliography. I. T.
Z5118.F58 F73 GT2855     016.3941 19     *LC 81-469*     *ISBN* 0313229015

**Grimes, Ronald L., 1943-.**      **5.8099**
Research in ritual studies: a programmatic essay and bibliography / by Ronald L. Grimes. — [Chicago]: American Theological Library Association; Metuchen, N.J.: Scarecrow Press, 1985. ix, 165 p.; 23 cm. (ATLA bibliography series. no. 14) Includes index. 1. Rites and ceremonies — Bibliography. 2. Ritual — Bibliography. I. T. II. Series.
Z5118.R5 G75 1985 GN473     016.392 19     *LC 84-23474*     *ISBN* 0810817624

**Heizer, Robert Fleming, 1915-.**      **5.8100**
Archaeology, a bibliographical guide to the basic literature / Robert F. Heizer, Thomas R. Hester, Carol Graves. — New York: Garland Pub., 1980. xi, 434 p.; 23 cm. — (Garland reference library of social science; v. 54) Includes index. 1. Archaeology — Bibliography. I. Hester, Thomas R. joint author. II. Graves, Carol. joint author. III. T.
Z5131.H44 1980 CC165     016.9301 19     *LC 77-83376*     *ISBN* 0824098269

## Z5151–5156 Astronomy

**Seal, Robert A.**      **5.8101**
A bibliography of astronomy, 1970–1979 / Robert A. Seal, Sarah S. Martin. — Littleton, Colo.: Libraries Unlimited, 1982. 407 p.; 24 cm. Includes indexes. 1. Astronomy — Bibliography. I. Martin, Sarah S., 1945- II. T.
Z5151.S38 1982 QB43.2     016.52 19     *LC 81-20877*     *ISBN* 0872872807

**Seal, Robert A.**      **5.8102**
A guide to the literature of astronomy / Robert A. Seal. — Littleton, Colo.: Libraries Unlimited, 1977. 306 p.; 24 cm. Includes index. 1. Astronomy — Bibliography. I. T.
Z5151.S4 QB43     016.52     *LC 77-12907*     *ISBN 0872871428*

**DeVorkin, David H., 1944-.**      **5.8103**
The history of modern astronomy and astrophysics: a selected, annotated bibliography / David H. DeVorkin. — New York: Garland, 1982. xxvii, 434 p.: ill.; 23 cm. — (Bibliographies of the history of science and technology. v. 1) (Garland reference library of the humanities. v. 304) Includes index. 1. Astronomy — History — Bibliography. 2. Astrophysics — History — Bibliography. I. T. II. Series. III. Series: Garland reference library of the humanities. v. 304
Z5154.H57 D48 1982 QB15     016.52 19     *LC 81-43349*     *ISBN* 082409283X

## Z5167 Automation

**Gomersall, Alan.**      **5.8104**
Machine intelligence: an international bibliography with abstracts of sensors in automated manufacturing / Alan Gomersall. — [Kempston, Bedford, Eng.]: IFS (Publications); Berlin: Springer-Verlag, 1984. vii, 232 p.: ill.; 30 cm. 1. Robots, Industrial — Bibliography 2. Detectors — Bibliography I. T.
Z5167 G6 1984     *ISBN 090360860X*

## Z5301–5319 Biography. Genealogy

**ARBA guide to biographical dictionaries / Bohdan S. Wynar,**     **5.8105**
**editor.**
Littleton, Colo.: Libraries Unlimited, 1986. xxiii, 444 p.; 25 cm. Includes indexes. 1. Biography — Dictionaries — Bibliography. I. Wynar, Bohdan S. II. American reference books annual.
Z5301.A82 1986 CT103     016.92 19     *LC 86-2851*     *ISBN* 0872874923

**Biography index.**      **• 5.8106**
[v.] 1- Jan. 1946/July 1949-. New York, H. W. Wilson Co. v. 27 cm. Triennial. A cumulative index to biographical material in books and magazines. 1. Biography — Indexes. 2. United States — Biography — Indexes. I. Joseph, Bea, 1899- ed. II. H.W. Wilson Company.
Z5301.B5     016.92     *LC 47-6532*

**R.R. Bowker Company.**      **5.8107**
Biographical books, 1876–1980. — New York: Bowker, c1980-1983. 2v., 1557 p.; 28 cm. Includes indexes. 1. Biography — Bibliography. I. T.
Z5301.B68 1980 CT104     016.92/002 B 19     *LC 80-149017*     *ISBN* 0835213153

**Falk, Byron A.**      **5.8108**
Personal name index to 'The New York times index,' 1851–1974 / Byron A. Falk, Jr., Valerie R. Falk. — Succasunna, N.J.: Roxbury Data Interface, c1976-<c1984 >. v. < 1-24 >; 27 cm. Vol. 23-< 24 > 1975-1979 supplement. Vols. 21-< 24 > published in: Verdi, Nev. 1. New York times — Indexes 2. Biography — Indexes. I. Falk, Valerie R. joint author. II. New York times index. III. T.
Z5301.F28 1976 CT104     071/.47/1     *LC 76-12217*     *ISBN* 089902100X

**Slocum, Robert B.**      **5.8109**
Biographical dictionaries and related works: an international bibliography of approximately 16,000 collective biographies ... / Robert B. Slocum, editor. — 2nd ed. — Detroit, Mich.: Gale Research Co., c1986. 2 v.; 29 cm. 1. Biography — Dictionaries — Bibliography. 2. Biography — Bibliography. I. T.
Z5301.S55 1986 CT104     016.92 19     *LC 85-8163*     *ISBN* 0810302438

**American autobiography, 1945–1980: a bibliography / Mary**     **5.8110**
**Louise Briscoe, editor; Barbara Tobias and Lynn Z. Bloom,**
**associate editors.**
Madison, Wis.: University of Wisconsin Press, 1983 (c1982). xiv, 365 p.; 29 cm. Includes index. 1. Autobiography — Bibliography. 2. United States — Biography — Bibliography. I. Briscoe, Mary Louise. II. Tobias, Barbara. III. Bloom, Lynn Z., 1934-
Z5305.U5 A47 1982 CT220     016.92/0073 19     *LC 82-70547*     *ISBN* 0299090906

**Arksey, Laura.**      **5.8111**
American diaries: an annotated bibliography of published American diaries and journals / Laura Arksey, Nancy Pries, and Marcia Reed. — 1st ed. — Detroit, Mich.: Gale Research, c1983. 311 p.; 29 cm. Expansion and revision of a work by William Matthews: American diaries: an annotated bibliography of American diaries written prior to the year 1861. Includes indexes. 1. American diaries — Bibliography. 2. Autobiographies — Bibliography. 3. United States

— History, Local — Sources — Bibliography. I. Pries, Nancy. II. Reed, Marcia. III. Matthews, William, 1905- American diaries. IV. T.
Z5305.U5 A74 1983 CT214    016.92/0073 19    *LC* 83-8860    *ISBN* 0810318008

**Biography and genealogy master index.**      **5.8112**
2nd ed.-    . — Detroit, Mich.: Gale Research Co., c1980-. v.; 29 cm. (Gale biographical index series.) 2nd- ed. issued in multiple vols. Supplements issued between editions. 1. Biography — Indexes. 2. United States — Biography — Indexes. 3. Canada — Biography — Indexes. I. Herbert, Miranda C. II. McNeil, Barbara. III. Gale Research Company. IV. Series.
Z5305U5B56    *LC* sn 81-6160

**Filby, P. William, 1911-.**      **5.8113**
Passenger and immigration lists bibliography, 1538–1900: being a guide to published lists of arrivals in the United States and Canada / edited by P. William Filby. — 1st ed. — Detroit, Mich.: Gale Research Co., c1981. 195 p.; 29 cm. Revision of: A bibliography of ship passenger lists, 1538-1825 / compiled by Harold Lancour. 3rd ed. / rev. and enl. by Richard J. Wolfe. 1963. Includes index. 1. Ships — Passenger lists — Bibliography. 2. Registers of births, etc — United States — Bibliography. 3. United States — Genealogy — Bibliography. 4. United States — Emigration and immigration — Bibliography. 5. United States — History — Sources — Bibliography. I. Lancour, Harold, 1908- A bibliography of ship passenger lists, 1538-1825. II. T.
Z5313.U5 F54 1981 CS47    016.929/373 19    *LC* 81-6964    *ISBN* 0810310988

## Z5320–5360 Biology. Botany

**Winton, Harry N. M.**      **5.8114**
Man and the environment: a bibliography of selected publications of the United Nations system, 1946–1971. Compiled and edited by Harry N. M. Winton. — New York: Unipub, 1972. xxi, 305 p.; 24 cm. 1. Ecology — Bibliography 2. Natural resources — Bibliography. 3. Nature conservation — Bibliography. 4. Man — Influence on nature — Bibliography. 5. Human ecology — Bibliography. I. United Nations. II. T.
Z5322.E2 W56    016.5001    *LC* 72-739    *ISBN* 0835205363

**Frodin, D. G.**      **5.8115**
Guide to standard floras of the world: an annotated, geographically arranged systematic bibliography of the principal floras, enumerations, checklists, and chorological atlases of different areas / D.G. Frodin. — Cambridge [Cambridgeshire]; New York: Cambridge University Press, 1984. xx, 619 p.; 26 cm. Includes indexes. 1. Botany — Bibliography 2. Phytogeography — Bibliography. 3. Botany — Classification — Bibliography. I. T. II. Title: Standard floras of the world. III. Title: Floras of the world.
Z5351.F76 1984 QK45.2    016.5819 19    *LC* 82-4501    *ISBN* 0521236886

**Blake, S. F. (Sidney Fay), 1892-1959.**      **5.8116**
Geographical guide to floras of the world: an annotated list with special reference to useful plants and common plant names. Washington: For sale by the Superintendent of Documents, U.S. Govt. Print. Off., 1942-1961. 2 v. 24 cm. (U.S. Dept. of Agriculture. Miscellaneous publication no. 401, 797) Running title: Floras of the world. Joint contribution from Bureau of Plant Industry and U.S. Dept. of Agriculture Library. 1. Botany — Bibliography I. Atwood, Alice C. (Alice Cary), 1876-1947. joint author. II. T. III. Title: Floras of the world.
Z5358.A12 B5    016.5819    *LC* agr42-353

## Z5521–5526 Chemistry

**American Chemical Society. Chemical Abstracts Service.**      **5.8117**
Chemical Abstracts Service source index. 1907/69-. [Columbus, Ohio] Chemical Abstracts Service. v. 29 cm. 1. Chemistry — Periodicals — Bibliography — Union lists. 2. Science — Periodicals — Bibliography — Union lists. I. American Chemical Society. Chemical Abstracts Service. Source index. II. T.
Z5523.A52 QD1    016.54/05    *LC* 73-101083

## Z5579 Civilization

**Cutcliffe, Stephen H.**      **5.8118**
Technology and values in American civilization: a guide to information sources / Stephen H. Cutcliffe, Judith A. Mistichelli, Christine M. Roysdon. — Detroit, Mich.: Gale Research Co., c1980. xviii, 704 p.; 23 cm. — (Gale information guide library. American studies information guide series. v. 9) Includes indexes. 1. Technology and civilization — Bibliography. 2. Technology — Social aspects — United States — Bibliography. 3. United States — Civilization — Bibliography. I. Mistichelli, Judith. joint author. II. Roysdon, Christine. joint author. III. T. IV. Series.
Z5579.C87 HM221    016.306/4 19    *LC* 80-23728    *ISBN* 0810314754

**Marien, Michael.**      **5.8119**
Societal directions and alternatives: a critical guide to the literature / by Michael Marien. 1st ed. — LaFayette, N.Y.: Information for Policy Design, c1976. viii, 400 p.; 23 cm. Includes indexes. 1. Civilization, Modern — 1950- — Bibliography. 2. Policy sciences — Bibliography 3. Forecasting — Bibliography. I. T.
Z5579.M36 CB428    Z5579 M36.    016.909    *LC* 76-9373    *ISBN* 0916282007

## Z5630 Communication

**Blum, Eleanor.**      **5.8120**
Basic books in the mass media: an annotated, selected booklist covering general communications, book publishing, broadcasting, editorial journalism, film, magazines, and advertising / Eleanor Blum. — 2d ed. — Urbana: University of Illinois Press, c1980. xi, 426 p.; 24 cm. Includes indexes. 1. Mass media — Bibliography. I. T.
Z5630.B55 1980 P90    016.3022/3    *LC* 80-11289    *ISBN* 0252008146

## Z5640–5703 Computer Science

**Hildebrandt, Darlene Myers.**      **5.8121**
Computing information directory: a comprehensive guide to the computing liturature [sic] / compiled and edited by Darlene Myers Hildebrandt. — 1985 ed. — Federal Way, WA: Pedaro, c1985. v, 557 p.; 28 cm. Spine title: CID, 1985. Includes index. 1. Computer science literature — Bibliography. I. T. II. Title: CID, 1985.
Z5640.H54 1985 QA76    016.004 19    *LC* 85-158092    *ISBN* 0933113005

**Best, Reba A.**      **5.8122**
Computer crime, abuse, liability, and security: a comprehensive bibliography, 1970–1984 / compiled by Reba A. Best and D. Cheryn Picquet. — Jefferson, N.C.: McFarland, c1985. iv, 155 p.; 22 cm. Spine title: Computer crime bibliography. Includes indexes. 1. Computer crimes — United States — Bibliography. 2. Electronic data processing departments — Security measures — Bibliography. I. Picquet, D. Cheryn. II. T. III. Title: Computer crime bibliography.
Z5703.4.C63 B47 1985 HV6773.2    016.3641/68 19    *LC* 84-43210    *ISBN* 0899501486

## Z5725 Death

**Miller, Albert Jay.**      **5.8123**
Death: a bibliographical guide / by Albert Jay Miller and Michael James Acri. Metuchen, N.J.: Scarecrow Press, 1977. vi, 420 p.; 23 cm. Includes indexes. 1. Death — Bibliography. I. Acri, Michael James, 1932- joint author. II. T.
Z5725.M54 BD444    016.128/5    *LC* 77-1205    *ISBN* 0810810255

## Z5781–5785 Drama. Theater. Film

**Adelman, Irving, comp.**      **• 5.8124**
Modern drama: a checklist of critical literature on 20th century plays / by Irving Adelman and Rita Dworkin. — Metuchen, N.J.: Scarecrow Press, c1967. xvii, 370 p. 1. Drama — 20th century — History and criticism — Bibliography I. Dworkin, Rita. II. T.
Z5781.A35    *LC* 67-10189

**Breed, Paul Francis, 1916-.**      **5.8125**
Dramatic criticism index: a bibliography of commentaries on playwrights from Ibsen to the avant–garde / compiled and edited by Paul F. Breed and Forence M. Sniderman. — Detroit: Gale Research Co., [1972] 1022 p.; 23 cm. 1. Drama — 20th century — History and criticism — Indexes. I. Sniderman, Florence M., joint author. II. T.
Z5781.B8    016.8092/04    *LC* 79-127598

**Chicorel, Marietta.**      **• 5.8126**
Chicorel theater index to plays in anthologies, periodicals, discs, and tapes / Marietta Chicorel, editor. — New York: Chicorel Library Pub. Co., [1970-. v.; 27 cm. — (Her [Chicorel index series, v. 1-) 1. Drama — Indexes. I. T. II. Title: Theater index to plays an anthologies, periodicals, discs, and tapes.
Z5781.C485 PN1655    016.80882    *LC* 75-330089

**Firkins, Ina Ten Eyck, 1866-1937, comp.**      **5.8127**
Index to plays, 1800–1926. New York, H. W. Wilson Co., 1927. — [New York: AMS Press, 1972] 307 p.; 27 cm. 1. Drama — 19th century — Bibliography. 2. Drama — 20th century — Bibliography. I. T.
Z5781.F57 1971    016.80882

**Keller, Dean H.**      **5.8128**
Index to plays in periodicals / by Dean H. Keller. — Rev. and expanded ed. — Metuchen, N.J.: Scarecrow Press, 1979. xi, 824 p.; 22 cm. 1. Drama — Bibliography. 2. Periodicals — Indexes I. T.
Z5781.K43 1979 PN1721    016.80882    *LC* 79-962    *ISBN* 0810812088

**Logasa, Hannah, 1879-1967.**      **5.8129**
An index to one–act plays, compiled by Hannah Logasa and Winifred Ver Nooy. Boston, W. F. Faxon Co., 1924. 327 p. 25 cm. (Useful reference series, no. 30) 'Plays written in English or translated into English ... published since 1900.'-Pref. 1. One-act plays — Bibliography. I. Ver Nooy, Winifred, 1891-1967 joint comp. II. T. III. Title: One act plays. IV. Series.
Z5781.L83    016.8082    *LC* 24-21477

**Ottemiller, John H. (John Henry), 1916-1968.**      **5.8130**
[Index to plays in collections] Ottemiller's Index to plays in collections: an author and title index to plays appearing in collections published between 1900 and early 1975 / by John M. Connor and Billie M. Connor. — 6th ed., rev. and enl. — Metuchen, N.J.: Scarecrow Press, 1976. xiii, 523 p.; 23 cm. 1. Drama — Bibliography. I. Connor, John M., 1908- II. Connor, Billie M., 1934- III. T. IV. Title: Index to plays in collections.
Z5781.O8 1976 PN1655    016.80882    *LC* 76-25610    *ISBN* 0810809192

**Palmer, Helen H.**      **5.8131**
European drama criticism, 1900–1975 / compiled by Helen H. Palmer. — 2d ed. — Hamden, Conn.: Shoe String Press, 1977. 653 p.; 24 cm. Includes index. 1. Drama — History and criticism — Bibliography. I. T.
Z5781.P2 1977 PN1721    016.809/2    *LC* 77-171    *ISBN* 0208015892

**Play index.**      • **5.8132**
1949/52-. New York, H. W. Wilson Co. v. 27 cm. I. West, Dorothy Herbert, 1901- ed. II. Peake, Dorothy Margaret, ed. III. Fidell, Estelle A. ed.
Z5781.P53    *LC* 64-1054

**Salem, James M.**      **5.8133**
A guide to critical reviews, by James M. Salem. 2d ed. Metuchen, N.J., Scarecrow Press, 1973- < 1979 >. v. < 1-3 > 22 cm. 1. Theater — New York (N.Y.) — Reviews — Indexes. 2. Motion pictures — United States — Reviews — Indexes. I. T.
Z5781.S16 1973 PN2266    016.8092 19    *LC* 73-3120    *ISBN* 0810806088

**Samples, Gordon.**      **5.8134**
The drama scholars' index to plays and filmscripts: a guide to plays and filmscripts in selected anthologies, series, and periodicals. Metuchen, N.J., Scarecrow Press [1974]- < 1980 >. v. < 1-2 >; 22 cm. 1. Drama — Indexes. I. T.
Z5781.S17    016.80882 19    *LC* 73-22165    *ISBN* 0810806991

**Stratman, Carl Joseph, 1917-1972.**      **5.8135**
Bibliography of medieval drama. — 2d ed., rev. and enl. — New York: F. Ungar, [1972] 2 v. (xv, 1035 p.); 25 cm. 1. Drama, Medieval — Bibliography. I. T.
Z5782.A2 S8 1972    016.80882/02    *LC* 78-163141    *ISBN* 0804432724

## Z5784.M9 Moving Pictures

**Bowles, Stephen E., 1943-.**      **5.8136**
Index to critical film reviews in British and American film periodicals, together with: Index to critical reviews of books about film. Compiled and edited by Stephen E. Bowles. — New York: B. Franklin, [1974-75] 3 v. in 2 (ix, 782 p.); 24 cm. 1. Motion pictures — Reviews — Indexes. 2. Motion pictures — Periodicals — Indexes. 3. Motion pictures — Book reviews — Indexes. I. Bowles, Stephen E., 1943- Index to critical reviews of books about film. 1975. II. T.
Z5784.M9 B64 PN1995    791.43/01/6    *LC* 74-12109    *ISBN* 0891020403

**Bukalski, Peter J.**      **5.8137**
Film research; a critical bibliography with annotations and essay, compiled by Peter J. Bukalski. — Boston: G. K. Hall, 1972. 215 p.; 26 cm. 1. Motion pictures — Bibliography. I. T.
Z5784.M9 B897    016.79143    *LC* 72-3794    *ISBN* 0816109710

**Ellis, Jack C., 1922-.**      **5.8138**
The film book bibliography, 1940–1975 / by Jack C. Ellis, Charles Derry, Sharon Kern; with research assistance from Stephen E. Bowles. — Metuchen, N.J.: Scarecrow Press, 1979. xii, 752 p.; 23 cm. Includes indexes. 1. Motion pictures — Bibliography I. Derry, Charles, 1951- joint author. II. Kern, Sharon. joint author. III. T.
Z5784.M9 E44 PN1994    016.79143    *LC* 78-4055    *ISBN* 0810811278

**Film literature index.**      **5.8139**
v. 1- 1973-. Albany, Filmdex, inc. 22 cm. 'Author-subject periodical index to the international literature of film.' Vol. 1, no. 1 preceded by a number dated Apr. 1973, called Prototype issue. 1. Motion pictures — Periodicals — Indexes.
Z5784.M9 F45    791.43/01/6    *LC* 74-642396

**Gerlach, John C.**      **5.8140**
The critical index: a bibliography of articles on film in English, 1946–1973, arranged by names and topics / [by] John C. Gerlach [and] Lana Gerlach. — New York: Teachers College Press, [1974] xlvi, 726 p.; 23 cm. — (New humanistic research) 1. Motion pictures — Bibliography I. Gerlach, Lana, joint author. II. T.
Z5784.M9 G47    016.79143    *LC* 74-1959

**MacCann, Richard Dyer.**      **5.8141**
The new film index; a bibliography of magazine articles in English, 1930–1970, by Richard Dyer MacCann and Edward S. Perry. With special editorial assistance by Mikki Moisio. — [1st ed.]. — New York: Dutton, 1975. xvii, 522 p.: illus.; 25 cm. 1. Motion pictures — Bibliography I. Perry, Edward S., joint author. II. T.
Z5784.M9 M29 1975    011    *LC* 74-16218    *ISBN* 0525165541

**Rehrauer, George.**      **5.8142**
Cinema booklist. — Metuchen, N.J.: Scarecrow Press, 1972. 473 p.; 22 cm. 1. Motion pictures — Bibliography I. T.
Z5784.M9 R42    016.79143    *LC* 70-188378    *ISBN* 0810805014

**Rehrauer, George.**      **5.8143**
The Macmillan film bibliography / by George Rehrauer. — New York: Macmillan, c1982. 2 v.; 29 cm. 1. Motion pictures — History — Bibliography. I. T. II. Title: Film bibliography.
Z5784.M9 R423 1982 PN1993.5.A1    016.79143/09 19    *LC* 82-20870    *ISBN* 0026964104

**Schuster, Mel.**      **5.8144**
Motion picture directors: a bibliography of magazine and periodical articles, 1900–1972. — Metuchen, N.J.: Scarecrow Press, 1973. 418 p.; 22 cm. 1. Motion picture producers and directors — Biography — Bibliography. I. T.
Z5784.M9 S34    016.79143/0233/0922    *LC* 73-780    *ISBN* 0810805901

**Sheahan, Eileen.**      **5.8145**
Moving pictures: an annotated guide to selected film literature, with suggestions for the study of film / Eileen Sheahan. — South Brunswick [N.J.]: A. S. Barnes, c1979. 146 p.; 22 cm. Includes index. 1. Motion pictures — Bibliography I. T.
Z5784.M9 S5 1979 PN1994    016.79143    *LC* 78-55576    *ISBN* 049802296X

## Z5784.S–.Z Other Special Topics

**Howard, John T.**      **5.8146**
A bibliography of theatre technology: acoustics and sound, lighting, properties, and scenery / John T. Howard, Jr. — Westport, Conn.: Greenwood Press, 1982. xii, 345 p.; 24 cm. Includes indexes. 1. Theaters — Stage-setting and scenery — Bibliography. 2. Stage lighting — Bibliography. 3. Architectural acoustics — Bibliography. 4. Theaters — Construction — Bibliography. I. T.
Z5784.S8 H68 1982 PN2091.S8    016.792/025 19    *LC* 81-7204    *ISBN* 0313228396

**Stoddard, Richard.**      **5.8147**
Stage scenery, machinery, and lighting: a guide to information sources / Richard Stoddard. Detroit: Gale Research Co., c1977. xi, 274 p.; 23 cm. (Performing arts information guide series; v. 2) (Gale information guide library) Includes indexes. 1. Theaters — Stage-setting and scenery — Bibliography. 2. Stage machinery — Bibliography. 3. Stage lighting — Bibliography. I. T.
Z5784.S8 S79 PN2091.S8    016.792/025    *LC* 76-13574    *ISBN* 081031374X

## Z5811–5819 Education

**Berry, Dorothea M.**      **5.8148**
A bibliographic guide to educational research / Dorothea M. Berry. — 2d ed. — Metuchen, N.J.: Scarecrow Press, c1980. ix, 215 p.: ill.; 23 cm. Includes indexes. 1. Education — Bibliography 2. Reference books — Education — Bibliography. I. T.
Z5811.B39 1980 LB17    016.37 19    *LC* 80-20191    *ISBN* 0810813513

**Current index to journals in education: CIJE.**      **5.8149**
Phoenix, AZ: Oryx Press, [etc.] v.; 28 cm. Monthly. Began with Jan./Feb. 1969. Description based on: Vol. 14, no. 1 (Jan. 1982). Vols. for < 198- > distributed to depository libraries in microfiche.
Z5813.C8    *LC* sc 78-1463

**Education index.**     • **5.8150**
v. 1- Jan. 1929-. New York: H. W. Wilson Co. v.; 26-29 cm. Monthly.
1. Education — Bibliography — Periodicals. 2. Education — Periodicals —
Indexes. I. H.W. Wilson Company.
Z5813.E23 L11     016.3705     LC 30-23807

**Resources in education / Educational Resources Information**     **5.8151**
**Center.**
Washington, D.C.: Dept. of Health, Education, and Welfare, National Institute
of Education: Supt. of Docs., U.S. G.P.O., [distributor. v.; 28 cm. Monthly.
Began with: Vol. 10, no. 1 (Jan. 1975). Formerly Research in education,
1966-75. Title from cover. Description based on: Vol. 14, no. 1 (Jan. 1979).
1. Education — Research — Bibliography. 2. Education — Bibliography
I. National Institute of Education (U.S.) II. Educational Resources
Information Center (U.S.)
Z5813.R4 LB1028     016.370/78     LC 75-644211

**Jones, Leon, 1936-.**     **5.8152**
From Brown to Boston: desegregation in education, 1954–1974 / by Leon
Jones. — Metuchen, N.J.: Scarecrow Press, c1979. 2 v. (xiii, 2175 p.); 23 cm.
Includes indexes. 1. School integration — United States — Bibliography.
2. School integration — Law and legislation — United States — Bibliography.
I. T.
Z5814.D5 J65 LC214.2     016.37019/342     LC 78-8312     ISBN
0810811472

**Buros, Oscar Krisen, 1905- ed.**     • **5.8153**
Tests in print: a comprehensive bibliography of tests for use in education,
psychology, and industry / Barbara A. Peace, editorial associate; William L.
Matts, editorial assistant. — Highland Park, N.J.: Gryphon Press, [1961] xxix,
479 p.: tables.; 25 cm. 1. Educational tests and measurements — Bibliography.
2. Examinations — Bibliography. I. T.
Z5814.E9 B8     016.37126     LC 61-16302

**Karnes, Frances A.**     **5.8154**
Handbook of instructional resources and references for teaching the gifted /
Frances A. Karnes, Emily C. Collins. — Boston: Allyn and Bacon, c1980. viii,
232 p.; 25 cm. 1. Gifted children — Education — Bibliography. 2. Children's
literature — Bibliography 3. Bibliography — Best books I. Collins, Emily C.
joint author. II. T.
Z5814.G5 K37 LC3993     016.3719/53     LC 79-22429     ISBN
0205068235

**Buros, Oscar Krisen, 1905-.**     • **5.8155**
The ... Mental measurements yearbook. — [1st] 1940-     . — Highland Park,
N.J.: The Mental Measurements Yearbook, 1941-. v.; 27 cm. 1. Examinations
— Bibliography. 2. Statistics — Bibliography. 3. Educational tests and
measurements — Bibliography. 4. Psychological tests — Bibliography.
I. Buros Institute of Mental Measurements. II. T.
Z5814.P8 B932     016.1512 016.159928     LC sn 85-22635

**Recent research in reading: a bibliography, 1966–1969 /**     • **5.8156**
**foreword by James L. Laffey.**
New York: CCM Information Corp., 1970. xiii, 300 p.; 24 cm. 1. Reading —
Bibliography.
Z5814.R25 R4     016.4284     LC 72-135197     ISBN 0840902751

**Altbach, Philip G.**     • **5.8157**
A select bibliography on students, politics, and higher education. With a
foreword by Seymour Martin Lipset. — [Cambridge]: Center for International
Affairs, Harvard University, 1967. vii, 54 p.; 23 cm. — (Harvard University.
Center for International Affairs. Occasional papers in international affairs no.
16) 1. Students — Political activity — Bibliography. 2. Education, Higher —
Bibliography. I. T. II. Series.
Z5814.S86 A55     016.3781/98/1     LC 67-29417

**Meyer, Manfred.**     **5.8158**
[Wirkungen und Funktionen des Fernsehens, Kinder und Jugendliche. English]
Effects and functions of television: children and adolescents: a bibliography of
selected research literature, 1970–1978 / compiled by Manfred Meyer and
Ursula Nissen. — München; New York: K. G. Saur, 1979. 172 p.; 21 cm. —
(Communication research and broadcasting. no. 2) Rev. translation of
Wirkungen und Funktionen des Fernsehens, Kinder und Jugendliche. Includes
indexes. 1. Television in education — Research — Bibliography. I. Nissen,
Ursula. joint author. II. T. III. Series.
Z5814.T45 M4913 1979 LB1044.7     016.37133/58     LC 79-248
ISBN 0896641716

**Menendez, Albert J.**     **5.8159**
School prayer and other religious issues in American public education: a
bibliography / Albert J. Menendez. — New York: Garland, 1985. x, 168 p.; 23
cm. (Garland reference library of social science; vol. 291) Includes indexes.
1. Prayer in the public schools — United States — Bibliography. 2. Religion in
the public schools — United States — Bibliography. 3. Religious education —

United States — Bibliography. 4. Prayer in the public schools — Law and
legislation — United States — Bibliography. I. T.
Z5814.U5 M46 1985 LC405     016.377/1 19     LC 84-48756     ISBN
0824087755

**Sive, Mary Robinson, 1928-.**     **5.8160**
Selecting instructional media: a guide to audiovisual and other instructional
media lists / Mary Robinson Sive. — 3rd ed. — Littleton, Colo.: Libraries
Unlimited, 1983. 330 p.; 25 cm. Includes indexes. 1. Audio-visual materials —
Catalogs — Bibliography. 2. Catalogs, Subject — Bibliography. 3. Media
programs (Education) — Bibliography. I. T.
Z5817.2.S58 1983 LB1043.Z9     016.37133 19     LC 82-21675     ISBN
0872873420

## Z5851–5853 Engineering. Energy

**A Selected annotated bibliography of professional ethics and**     **5.8161**
**social responsibility in engineering / compiled by Robert F.**
**Ladenson ... [et al.], with the assistance of Belinda K. Lewis,**
**Bettye Greene; edited by Ernest d'Anjou.**
Chicago, Ill.: Center for the Study of Ethics in the Professions, Illinois Institute
of Technology, c1980. 157 p.; 23 cm. Includes indexes. 1. Engineering ethics —
Bibliography. 2. Engineering — Social aspects — Bibliography. I. Ladenson,
Robert F. II. Center for the Study of Ethics in the Professions (U.S.)
Z5853.E8 S44 TA157     016.174/962 19     LC 80-133101

**Balachandran, Sarojini.**     **5.8162**
Energy statistics: a guide to information sources / Sarojini Balachandran. —
Detroit, Mich.: Gale Research Co., c1980. xii, 272 p.; 23 cm. — (Natural world
information guide series; v. 1) (Gale information guide library) Includes
indexes. 1. Power resources — Statistics — Bibliography. I. T. II. Series.
Z5853.P83 B25 HD9502.A2     016.33379/02/12     LC 80-13338
ISBN 0810314193

**Weber, R. David, 1941-.**     **5.8163**
Energy information guide / R. David Weber; with a foreword by Richard
Corrigan. — Santa Barbara, Calif.: ABC-Clio, 1982. 334 p.; 24 cm. Includes
indexes. 1. Power resources — Bibliography. I. T.
Z5853.P83 W38 1982 TJ163.2     016.33379 19     LC 82-8729     ISBN
0874363179

## Z5856 Entomology

**Gilbert, Pamela.**     **5.8164**
Entomology: a guide to information sources / Pamela Gilbert and Chris J.
Hamilton. — London: Mansell Pub.; Bronx, N.Y.: Distributed in the U.S. and
Canada by H.W. Wilson Co., 1983. vi, 237 p.; 24 cm. Includes index.
1. Entomology — Bibliography. 2. Entomology — Information services.
3. Information storage and retrieval systems — Entomology. I. Hamilton,
Chris J. II. T.
Z5856.G52 1983 QL463     595.7/072041 19     LC 83-239527     ISBN
0720116805

## Z5681–5863 Environment

**Sourcebook on the environment: a guide to the literature /**     **5.8165**
**edited by Kenneth A. Hammond, George Macinko, Wilma B.**
**Fairchild.**
Chicago: University of Chicago Press, 1978. x, 613 p.; 25 cm. 'The manuscript
was developed by the Association of American Geographers from original
works commissioned by the Association.' Includes indexes. 1. Human ecology
— Bibliography. 2. Environmental protection — Bibliography. I. Hammond,
Kenneth A. II. Macinko, George. III. Fairchild, Wilma B. IV. Association of
American Geographers.
Z5861.S66 GF41     016.30131     LC 77-17407     ISBN 0226315223

**EIA data index: an abstract journal.**     **5.8166**
Dec. 1980-     . — Washington, D.C.: U.S. Department of Energy, Energy
Information Administration, Office of Energy Information Services, 1980-. v.
Semiannual. I. United States. Energy Information Administration. Office of
Energy Information Services.
Z5863.E54 E34

**Buttel, Frederick H.**     **5.8167**
Labor and the environment: an analysis of and annotated bibliography on
workplace environmental quality in the United States / compiled by Frederick
H. Buttel, Charles C. Geisler, and Irving W. Wiswall. — Westport, Conn.:
Greenwood Press, c1984. viii, 148 p.; 25 cm. Includes index. 1. Environmental
policy — United States — Bibliography. 2. Environmental policy — Cost
effectiveness — Bibliography. 3. Work environment — United States —
Bibliography. 4. Industrial hygiene — United States — Bibliography.
I. Geisler, Charles C. II. Wiswall, Irving W. III. T.
Z5863.P6 B87 1984 HC110.E5     016.331 19     LC 83-22575     ISBN
0313239355

## Z5916–5918 Fiction

**Fiction index.**         **5.8168**
[1945/52]-. London, Association of Assistant Librarians. v. 1. Fiction — Bibliography — Periodicals. I. Association of Assistant Librarians. II. Title: Cumulated fiction index.
Z5916.F52    *LC* 53-7788

**Kearney, E. I.**         **• 5.8169**
The continental novel; a checklist of criticism in English, 1900–1966 [by] E. I. Kearney and L. S. Fitzgerald. Metuchen, N.J., Scarecrow Press, 1968. xiv, 460 p. 22 cm. 1. European fiction — History and criticism — Bibliography. I. Fitzgerald, L. S., joint author. II. T.
Z5916.K4    016.8093/3    *LC* 68-12626

**H.W. Wilson Company.**         **• 5.8170**
Fiction catalog. 1908-. New York [etc.] H. W. Wilson Co. v. 17-26 cm. (19 < 14-41 > : Standard catalog series) Annual. Beginning with the 9th edition, 1976, editions are cataloged separately in L.C. Issue for 1931 called 2d ed. rev., being the 2d issue under the title: Standard catalog ... fiction section. Issue for 1923 accompanied by supplement published in 1928; 1941- < 1966 > kept up to date by cumulative annual supplements. 1. Fiction — Indexes. 2. Bibliography — Best books — Fiction. I. Bacon, Corinne, 1865-1944. comp. II. Cook, Dorothy Elizabeth, 1890-1959, comp. III. Monro, Isabel Stevenson, comp. IV. T.
Z5916.W74    016.823    *LC* 09-35044

**Albert, Walter.**         **5.8171**
Detective and mystery fiction: an international bibliography of secondary sources / Walter Albert. — Madison, Ind.: Brownstone Books, 1985. xii, 781 p. 1. Detective and mystery stories — Bibliography I. T.
Z5917.D5 A4 1985x    PN3448.D4 A5x.    *ISBN* 094102802X

**Barzun, Jacques, 1907-.**         **5.8172**
A catalogue of crime [by] Jacques Barzun & Wendell Hertig Taylor. — 2d impression corr. — New York: Harper & Row, [1971] xxxi, 831 p.; 22 cm. 1. Detective and mystery stories — Bibliography. I. Taylor, Wendell Hertig, 1905- joint author. II. T.
Z5917.D5 B37 1971b    016.80883/872    *LC* 73-20705    *ISBN* 0060102667

**Queen, Ellery.**         **5.8173**
Queen's quorum; a history of the detective–crime short story as revealed in the 106 most important books published in this field since 1845. New York, Biblo and Tannen, 1969. ix, 146 p. facsim. 24 cm. Reprint of the 1951 ed., with supplements through 1967. 1. Detective and mystery stories — Bibliography. 2. Detective and mystery stories — History and criticism. I. T.
Z5917.D5 Q45 1969    016.80883/872    *LC* 68-56450

**Index to stories in thematic anthologies of science fiction /**    **5.8174**
**Marshall B. Tymn ... [et al.]; with an introd by James Gunn.**
Boston: G. K. Hall, c1978. xiii, 193 p.; 21 cm. — (Reference publication in science fiction.) Includes indexes. 1. Science fiction — Indexes. I. Tymn, Marshall B., 1937- II. Series.
Z5917.S36 I53    PN3448.S45    813/.0876/016    *LC* 78-14287    *ISBN* 081618027X

**Fletcher, Marilyn P., 1940-.**         **5.8175**
Science fiction story index, 1950–1979 / Marilyn P. Fletcher. — 2d ed. — Chicago: American Library Association, 1981. xi, 610 p.; 28 cm. 'An expanded and updated version of the Science fiction story index, 1950-1968 by Frederick Siemon.' 1. Science fiction — Bibliography. I. Siemon, Frederick, 1935- Science fiction story index, 1950-1968. II. T.
Z5917.S36 S5 1979    PN3433.5    016.823/0876 19    *LC* 80-28685    *ISBN* 0838903207

**Tuck, Donald H. (Donald Henry)**         **5.8176**
The encyclopedia of science fiction and fantasy through 1968: a bibliographic survey of the fields of science fiction, fantasy, and weird fiction through 1968. Compiled by Donald H. Tuck. [1st ed.] Chicago: Advent Publishers, 1974- < 1982 > . v. < 1-3 > ; 29 cm. Previous editions published under title: A handbook of science fiction and fantasy. 1. Science fiction — Bibliography. 2. Fantastic fiction — Bibliography. I. T.
Z5917.S36 T83    016.80883/876    *LC* 73-91828    *ISBN* 0911682201

**Smith, Myron J.**         **5.8177**
Sea fiction guide / by Myron J. Smith, Jr., and Robert C. Weller; with a foreword by Ernest M. Eller and craft notes by Edward L. Beach ... [et al.]. — Metuchen, N.J.: Scarecrow Press, 1976. xxix, 256 p.; 23 cm. Includes indexes. 1. Sea stories — Bibliography. 2. English fiction — Bibliography. 3. American fiction — Bibliography. I. Weller, Robert C., joint author. II. T.
Z5917.S4 S64    PR830.S4    016.823/008/032    *LC* 76-7590    *ISBN* 081080929X

**Cook, Dorothy Elizabeth, 1890-1959.**         **• 5.8178**
Short story index: an index to 60,000 stories in 4,320 collections / compiled by Dorothy E. Cook, Isabel S. Monro. — New York: H.W. Wilson, 1953. 1553 p. Indexes 4,320 collections containing about 60,000 stories published 1949 or earlier. 1. Short stories — Indexes I. Monro, Isabel Stevenson II. T.
Z5917.S5 C6    808.8/31/016    *LC* 53-8991

**Short story index, collections indexed 1900–1978 / edited by**    **5.8179**
**Juliette Yaakov.**
New York: H. W. Wilson Co., 1979. 349 p.; 26 cm. 1. Short stories — Bibliography. I. Yaakov, Juliette. II. Short story index.
Z5917.S5 S56    PN3451    016.808831    *LC* 79-24887    *ISBN* 0824206436

**Walker, Warren S.**         **5.8180**
Twentieth–century short story explication: interpretations, 1900–1975, of short fiction since 1800 / compiled by Warren S. Walker. 3d ed. — Hamden, Conn.: Shoe String Press, 1977. viii, 880 p.; 24 cm. Includes index. 1. Short story — Bibliography. I. T.
Z5917.S5 W33 1977    PN3373    016.8093/1    *LC* 76-30666    *ISBN* 0208015701

## Z5931–5961 Fine Arts. Architecture. City Planning

**Arntzen, Etta.**         **5.8181**
Guide to the literature of art history / Etta Arntzen, Robert Rainwater. — Chicago: American Library Association, 1981 [c1980]. xviii, 616 p.; 29 cm. Includes indexes. 1. Art — Historiography — Bibliography. I. Rainwater, Robert. joint author. II. T.
Z5931.A67 N380    016.709    *LC* 78-31711    *ISBN* 0838902634

**Ehresmann, Donald L., 1937-.**         **5.8182**
Fine arts: a bibliographic guide to basic reference works, histories, and handbooks / Donald L. Ehresmann. — 2d ed. — Littleton, Colo.: Libraries Unlimited, 1979. 349 p.; 24 cm. Includes index. 1. Art — Bibliography I. T.
Z5931.E47 1979 N7425    016.7 19    *LC* 79-9051    *ISBN* 0872872017

**Art index: a cumulative author and subject index to a selected**    **• 5.8183**
**list of fine arts periodicals and museum bulletins.**
v. 1- Jan. 1929/Sept. 1932-. New York, H. W. Wilson. v. 27 cm. Annual. *Also known as:* Art index. Quarterly with annual and biennial cumulations. 1. Art — Periodicals — Indexes. 2. Art — Bibliography I. Dougan, Alice Maria, 1876- ed. II. Furlong, Margaret, ed.
Z5937.A78    016.7    *LC* 31-7513

**Ehresmann, Donald L., 1937-.**         **5.8184**
Architecture: a bibliographic guide to basic reference works, histories, and handbooks / Donald L. Ehresmann. — Littleton, Colo.: Libraries Unlimited, 1984. xvi, 338 p.; 25 cm. Includes indexes. 1. Architecture — Bibliography. I. T.
Z5941.E38 1984 NA2520    016.72 19    *LC* 83-19600    *ISBN* 0872873943

**Buenker, John D.**         **5.8185**
Urban history: a guide to information sources / John D. Buenker, Gerald Michael Greenfield, William J. Murin; pref. by Howard P. Chudacoff. — Detroit, Mich.: Gale Research Co., c1981. xv, 448 p.; 23 cm. — (American government and history information guide series; v. 9) Includes indexes. 1. Cities and towns — United States — History — Bibliography. I. Greenfield, Gerald Michael. joint author. II. Murin, William J. joint author. III. T. IV. Series.
Z5942.B88 HT123    016.3077/6/0973 19    *LC* 80-19643    *ISBN* 0810314797

**Shearer, Barbara Smith.**         **5.8186**
Periodical literature on United States cities: a bibliography and subject guide / compiled by Barbara Smith Shearer and Benjamin F. Shearer. — Westport, Conn.: Greenwood Press, c1983. xviii, 574 p.; 25 cm. Includes indexes. 1. Cities and towns — United States — Addresses, essays, lectures — Bibliography. I. Shearer, Benjamin F. II. T.
Z5942.S464 1983 HT123    016.3077/64/0973 19    *LC* 82-24211    *ISBN* 0313235112

**Sutcliffe, Anthony, 1942-.**         **5.8187**
The history of urban and regional planning: an annotated bibliography / Anthony Sutcliffe. — New York: Facts on File, 1981. ix, 284 p.; 23 cm. Includes indexes. 1. City planning — History — Bibliography. 2. Regional planning — History — Bibliography. I. T.
Z5942.S93 HT166    016.3616/09    *LC* 80-13521    *ISBN* 0871963035

**Riggs, Timothy A., 1942-.**         **5.8188**
The Print Council index to oeuvre–catalogues of prints by European and American artists / compiled by Timothy A. Riggs under the sponsorship of the Print Council of America. — Millwood, N.Y.: Kraus International

Publications, c1983. xlv, 834 p.; 27 cm. 1. Prints — Catalogs — Indexes. I. Print Council of America. II. T.
Z5947.A3 R53 1983 NE90     769.92/2 19     *LC* 82-48986     *ISBN* 0527753467

**Davis, Lenwood G.**        **5.8189**
Black artists in the United States: an annotated bibliography of books, articles, and dissertations on Black artists, 1779–1979 / by Lenwood G. Davis and Janet L. Sims; foreword by James E. Newton. — Westport, Conn.: Greenwood Press, 1980. xiv, 138 p.; 24 cm. Includes index. 1. Afro-American art — Bibliography. 2. Afro-American artists — Bibliography. I. Sims-Wood, Janet L., 1945- joint author. II. T.
Z5956.A47 D38 N6538.N5     016.709/73 19     *LC* 79-8576     *ISBN* 0313220824

**Igoe, Lynn, 1937-.**        **5.8190**
250 years of Afro–American art: an annotated bibliography / Lynn Moody Igoe with James Igoe. — New York: Bowker, 1981. xxv, 1266 p.; 26 cm. 1. Afro-American art — Bibliography. I. Igoe, James. II. T. III. Title: Two hundred fifty years of Afro-American art.
Z5956.A47 I38 N6538.N5     016.704/0396073 19     *LC* 81-12226     *ISBN* 0835213765

**Perry, Margaret, 1933-.**        **5.8191**
The Harlem Renaissance: an annotated bibliography and commentary / Margaret Perry. — New York: Garland Pub., 1982. xxxix, 272 p. — (Critical studies on Black life and culture. v. 2) (Garland reference library of the humanities. v. 278) Includes index. 1. Afro-American arts — New York (N.Y.) — Bibliography. 2. Harlem Renaissance — Bibliography. I. T. II. Series. III. Series: Garland reference library of the humanities. v. 278
Z5956.A47 P47 1982 NX511.N4     Z5956A47 P47 1982.
    016.81/09/97471 19     *LC* 80-9048     *ISBN* 0824093208

**Yüan, T'ung-li, 1895-1965.**        **5.8192**
The T. L. Yuan bibliography of western writings on Chinese art and archaeology / Harrie A. Vanderstappen, editor; Rachel E. McClellan, principal assistant; Edward Schafer ... [et al.], assistants. — London: Mansell, 1975. xlvii, 606 p.; 29 cm. Label mounted on t.p.: Exclusive distributor in the U.S., ISBS, Beaverton, Ore. Includes indexes. 1. Art, Chinese — Bibliography. 2. China — Antiquities — Bibliography. I. Vanderstappen, Harrie A., 1921- II. T. III. Title: Bibliography of western writings on Chinese art and archaeology.
Z5961.C5 Y9 1975 N7340     016.709/51     *LC* 76-356246     *ISBN* 0720105218

## Z5981–5985 Folklore

**Brunvand, Jan Harold.**        **5.8193**
Folklore: a study and research guide / Jan Harold Brunvand; M. Thomas Inge, general editor. — New York: St. Martin's Press, c1976. vi, 144 p.; 22 cm. Includes index. 1. Folklore — Bibliography. 2. Folklore — Authorship. 3. Folklore — Methodology I. T.
Z5981.B78 GR66     016.398     *LC* 75-38016

**Eastman, Mary Huse, 1878-1963.**        **5.8194**
Index to fairy tales, myths and legends / by Mary Huse Eastman. — 2d ed. rev. and enl. — Boston: F. W. Faxon, 1926. ix, 610 p. — (Useful reference series; no. 28) 1. Fairy tales — Indexes. 2. Mythology — Indexes. I. T. II. Series.
Z5983.F17 E2 1926     398.2/01/6     *ISBN* 0873050282

**Szwed, John Francis, 1936-.**        **5.8195**
Afro–American folk culture: an annotated bibliography of materials from North, Central, and South America, and the West Indies / John F. Szwed and Roger D. Abrahams, with Robert Baron ... [et al.]. — Philadelphia: Institute for the Study of Human Issues, c1978. 2 v. — (Publications of the American Folklore Society, Bibliographical and special series; v. 31-32) Includes indexes. 1. Blacks — Folklore — America — Bibliography. 2. Blacks — America — Bibliography. I. Abrahams, Roger D. joint author. II. T.
Z5984.A44 S95 GR103     Z5984A44 S95.     016.909/04/96     *LC* 77-16567     *ISBN* 0915980800

**Fowke, Edith Fulton, 1913-.**        **5.8196**
A bibliography of Canadian folklore in English / compiled by Edith Fowke and Carole Henderson Carpenter. — Toronto; Buffalo: University of Toronto Press, c1981. xx, 272 p.; 24 cm. Includes index. 1. Folklore — Canada — Bibliography. 2. Canada — Social life and customs — Bibliography. I. Carpenter, Carole Henderson, 1944- II. T.
Z5984.C33 F68 1981 GR113     016.39/000971 19     *LC* 82-108990     *ISBN* 0802023940

**Haywood, Charles, 1904-.**        **5.8197**
A bibliography of North American folklore and folksong. — 2d rev. ed. — New York: Dover Publications, [1961] 2 v. (xxx, 1301 p.): maps (on lining papers); 25 cm. 1. Folklore — United States — Bibliography. 2. Afro-Americans — Folklore — Bibliography. 3. Indians of North America — Folklore — Bibliography. 4. Folk-songs — United States — Bibliography. 5. Afro-

Americans — Songs and music — Bibliography. 6. Indians of North America — Music — Bibliography. I. T.
Z5984.U5 H32     016.398     *LC* 62-3483

## Z5991 Forests. Forestry

**Fahl, Ronald J., 1942-.**        **5.8198**
North American forest and conservation history: a bibliography / Ronald J. Fahl. Santa Barbara, Calif.: Published under contract with the Forest History Society [by] A.B.C.—Clio Press, 1977. 408 p.; 29 cm. Includes index. 1. Forests and forestry — North America — History — Bibliography. 2. Forest conservation — North America — History — Bibliography. I. Forest History Society. II. T.
Z5991.F33 SD140     016.3337/5/0973     *LC* 76-27306     *ISBN* 0874362350

## Z6001–6028 Geography. Travel. Maps

**Wright, John Kirtland, 1891-1969.**        • **5.8199**
Aids to geographical research: bibliographies, periodicals, atlases, gazetteers and other reference books / by John Kirtland Wright and the late Elizabeth T. Platt. — 2d ed. completely rev. — New York: Columbia University Press, 1947. xii, 331 p.; 21 cm. — (Research series - American Geographical Society; no. 22) 'Classified index of American professional geographers, libraries of geographical utility, and institutions engaged in geographical research': p. [276]-294. 1. Geography — Bibliography 2. Bibliography — Bibliography — Geography. 3. Geography — Periodicals — Bibliography. I. Platt, Elizabeth T. (Elizabeth Tower), 1900-1943. II. T.
Z6001.A1 W9 1947     016.91     *LC* 47-30449

**Brewer, James Gordon.**        **5.8200**
The literature of geography: a guide to its organisation and use / by J. Gordon Brewer. — 2d ed. — London: Clive Bingley; Hamden, Conn.: Linnet Books, 1978. 264 p.: ill.; 23 cm. Includes index. 1. Geography — Bibliography. 2. Geography — Methodology I. T.
Z6001.B74 1978 G116     016.91     *LC* 78-16852     *ISBN* 0851572804

**Harris, Chauncy D.**        **5.8201**
Bibliography of geography, Part 1: Introduction to general aids / by Chauncy D. Harris. Chicago: Department of Geography, University of Chicago; Cambridge: [Distributed by] W. Heffer and Sons, Ltd, 1976. ix, 276 p.; 23 cm. (University of Chicago. Department of Geography. Research papers; no.179) 1. Geography — Bibliography. I. T. II. Series.
Z6001     Z6001.G116.     016.91     *LC* 76-1910     *ISBN* 0890650861

**A Geographical bibliography for American libraries** / edited by        **5.8202**
**Chauncy D. Harris ... [et al.]; with assistance from Susan Fifer Canby, Phillip J. Parent, Steven S. Stettes.**
Washington, D.C.: Association of American Geographers, 1985. xxiii, 437 p.; 24 cm. 'A joint project of the Association of American Geographers and the National Geographic Society.' Includes index. 1. Geography — Bibliography. I. Harris, Chauncy Dennison, 1914- II. Association of American Geographers. III. National Geographic Society (U.S.)
Z6001.G44 1985 G116     016.91 19     *LC* 85-11284     *ISBN* 089291193X

**Harris, Chauncy Dennison, 1914-.**        **5.8203**
Bibliography of geography / by Chauncy D. Harris. — Chicago: University of Chicago, Dept. of Geography, 1976-< 1984 >. pt. < 1-2, v. 1 >; 23 cm. — (Research paper - The University of Chicago, Department of Geography; no. 179, 206) Includes indexes. 1. Geography — Bibliography. 2. Bibliography — Geography. I. T.
H31.C514 no. 179, etc. Z6001.H3x     910 s 016.91

**Harris, Chauncy Dennison, 1914-.**        **5.8204**
International list of geographical serials / compiled by Chauncy D. Harris and Jerome D. Fellmann. — 3d ed., rev., expanded, and updated. — Chicago: University of Chicago, Dept. of Geography, 1980. vi, 457 p.; 23 cm. (Research paper - The University of Chicago, Department of Geography; no. 193) Includes index. 1. Geography — Periodicals — Bibliography — Union lists. I. Fellmann, Jerome Donald, 1926- joint author. II. T.
H31.C514 no. 193 Z6003.H3x     910 s 016.91/05     *LC* 80-16392     *ISBN* 0890651000

**Sanguin, André-Louis, 1945-.**        **5.8205**
Géographie politique: bibliographie internationale / A.-L. Sanguin. — Montréal: Presses de l'Université du Québec, 1976. xxi, 232 p.; 23 cm. Includes index. 1. Geography, Political — Bibliography. I. T.
Z6004.P7 S3 JC319     016.3209     *LC* 76-481053     *ISBN* 077700125X

**Bryan, M. Leonard.**        **5.8206**
Remote sensing of earth resources: a guide to information sources / M. Leonard Bryan. — Detroit: Gale Research Co., c1979. xv, 188 p.; 22 cm. — (Geography and travel information guide series. v. 1) (Gale information guide Library)

Includes indexes. 1. Remote sensing — Bibliography. 2. Remote sensing — Information services. I. T. II. Series.
Z6004.R38 B79 G70.4      016.62136/7     *LC* 79-22792      *ISBN* 0810314134

**Arctic bibliography / ed. by Maret Martna.**                                5.8207
v. 16. Montreal: McGill-Queen's University Press, 1975. 1373 p.; 24 cm.
1. Arctic regions — Bibliography. I. Martna, Maret. II. United States. Dept. of Defense. III. Arctic Institute of North America.
Z6005.P7 A72      016.9198      *LC* 53-61783

**Cox, Edward Godfrey, 1876-1963.**                                          5.8208
A reference guide to the literature of travel; including voyages, geographical descriptions, adventures, shipwrecks and expeditions. — New York: Greenwood Press, [1969] 3 v.; 27 cm. — (University of Washington publications in language and literature, v. 9-10, 12) Reprint of the 1935-49 ed. No more published. 1. Voyages and travels — Bibliography. 2. Adventure and adventurers — Bibliography. 3. Shipwrecks — Bibliography. I. T.
Z6011.C87 1969      016.91      *LC* 70-90492      *ISBN* 0837121612

**Hodgkiss, A. G.**                                                          5.8209
Keyguide to information sources in cartography / A.G. Hodgkiss and A.F. Tatham. — New York, N.Y.: Facts on File, c1986. x, 253 p.; 24 cm. Includes index. 1. Cartography — Bibliography. I. Tatham, A. F. II. T.
Z6021.H6 1986 GA105.3      016.526 19      *LC* 85-27590      *ISBN* 0816014035

**International maps and atlases in print / edited by Kenneth L.**           5.8210
**Winch.**
2d ed. — London; New York: Bowker, 1976. xvi, 866 p.: ill.; 31 cm. 'Index diagrams for multi-sheet maps': p. 595-[862] Includes index. 1. Maps — Bibliography. 2. Atlases — Bibliography. 3. Index maps I. Winch, Kenneth L., ed.
Z6021.I596 1976 GA105.3      016.912      *LC* 77-357993      *ISBN* 0859350363

**Kister, Kenneth F., 1935-.**                                              5.8211
[Atlas buying guide] Kister's Atlas buying guide: general English–language world atlases available in North America / by Kenneth F. Kister. — Phoenix, Ariz.: Oryx Press, 1984. xii, 236 p.; 24 cm. Includes index. 1. Atlases — Bibliography. I. T.
Z6021.K5 1984 GA300      912 19      *LC* 82-42920      *ISBN* 0912700629

**Ristow, Walter William, 1908-.**                                          5.8212
Guide to the history of cartography; an annotated list of references on the history of maps and mapmaking. Compiled by Walter W. Ristow. Washington, Geography and Map Division, Library of Congress [for sale by the Supt. of Docs., U.S. Govt. Print. Off.] 1973. 96 p. 24 cm. First and 2d editions issued by the Library's Map Division under title: A guide to historical cartography. 1. Cartography — History — Bibliography. I. Library of Congress. Geography and Map Division. II. Library of Congress. Map Division. A guide to historical cartography. III. T.
Z6021.R57      016.5269/8      *LC* 73-9776      *ISBN* 0844400971

**Guide to USGS geologic and hydrologic maps.**                             5.8213
5th ed. McLean, Va.: Documents Index, 1986. 1v.; 29 cm. Annual. 1. Geological Survey (U.S.) — Bibliography — Collected works. 2. Geology — United States — Maps — Bibliography — Collected works. 3. Hydrology — United States — Maps — Bibliography — Collected works. 4. Mines and mineral resources — United States — Maps — Bibliography — Collected works. 5. Geology — United States — Maps — Bibliography. 6. Hydrology — United States — Maps — Bibliography. I. Geological Survey (U.S.)
Z6026.G3 G84 QE77      016.912/5573 19      *LC* 85-650191

**Cobb, David A., 1945-.**                                                  5.8214
State atlases: an annotated bibliography / by David A. Cobb and Peter B. Ives. — Chicago, Ill.: CPL Bibliographies, c1983. 21 p.; 28 cm. — (CPL bibliography. no. 108) 'April 1983.' 1. Atlases — Bibliography — Catalogs. 2. United States — Bibliography I. Ives, Peter B. II. T. III. Series.
Z6027.U5 C643 1983 GA405      016.91273 19      *LC* 83-5231      *ISBN* 0866021086

**Wheat, James Clements.**                                                  5.8215
Maps and charts published in America before 1800: a bibliography / by James Clements Wheat and Christian F. Brun. — Rev. ed. — London: Holland Press; New York: R. B. Arkway; King of Prussia, Pa.: sole North American distributor, W. G. Arader, c1978. xxiv, 215 p.: ill.; 26 cm. — (Holland Press cartographica; 3) Includes index. 1. Cartography — United States — Bibliography. I. Brun, Christian, joint author. II. T.
Z6027.U5 W47 1978 GA405      016.912      *LC* 78-67634      *ISBN* 0900470895

**Geo Katalog (Stuttgart, Germany: 1980)**                                  5.8216
Geo Katalog. — 80-     . — Stuttgart: GeoCenter, 1980-. v.: ill.; 25 cm. Annual. Issued in 2 pts. Bd. 2 is loose-leaf for updating. 1. Maps — Bibliography — Catalogs. I. Geokartenbrief. II. T.
Z6028.G468 GA300      016.912 19      *LC* 84-647396

## Z6031–6040 Geology

**Ward, Dederick C.**                                                       5.8217
Geologic reference sources: a subject and regional bibliography of publications and maps in the geological sciences / by Dederick C. Ward, Marjorie W. Wheeler, Robert A. Bier, Jr. — 2nd ed. — Metuchen, N.J.: Scarecrow Press, 1981. 1 v. Includes indexes. 1. Geology — Bibliography I. Wheeler, Marjorie W. II. Bier, Robert A. III. T.
Z6031.W35 1981 QE26.2      016.55 19      *LC* 81-4770      *ISBN* 0810814285

**Wood, David Norris.**                                                     5.8218
Use of earth sciences literature / editor: D. N. Wood. — [Hamden, Conn.]: Archon Books, 1973. 459 p.: ill.; 23 cm. — (Information sources for research and development) 1. Earth sciences — Bibliography. I. T.
Z6031.W67      550/.7      *LC* 72-13674      *ISBN* 0208006699

**Hazen, Robert M., 1948-.**                                                5.8219
American geological literature, 1669 to 1850 / Robert M. Hazen and Margaret Hindle Hazen. — Stroudsburg, Pa.: Dowden, Hutchinson & Ross, c1980. xii, 431 p.; 26 cm. Includes index. 1. Geology — United States — Early works to 1800 — Bibliography. 2. Geology — United States — Bibliography. I. Hazen, Margaret Hindle. joint author. II. T.
Z6034.U49 H39 QE77      016.5573      *LC* 79-25898      *ISBN* 0879333715

## Z6201–6209 History: General
(see also: Z1201-5000)

**American Historical Association.**                                         5.8220
Guide to historical literature. Board of editors: George Frederick Howe, chairman [and others] assisted by section editors, a central editor and others. New York, Macmillan, 1961. xxxv, 962 p. 24 cm. 'Successor to A guide to historical literature' first published in 1931. 1. History — Bibliography. 2. Bibliography — Best books — History. I. Howe, George Frederick, ed. II. T.
Z6201.A55      016.9      *LC* 61-7602

**Havlice, Patricia Pate.**                                                 5.8221
Oral history: a reference guide and annotated bibliography / by Patricia Pate Havlice. — Jefferson, N.C.: McFarland, c1985. iv, 140 p.; 22 cm. Includes index. 1. Oral history — Bibliography. I. T.
Z6201.H38 1985 D16.14      016.907/2 19      *LC* 84-43227      *ISBN* 0899501389

**Poulton, Helen J.**                                                      • 5.8222
The historian's handbook: a descriptive guide to reference works / by Helen J. Poulton, with the assistance of Marguerite S. Howland; foreword by Wilbur S. Shepperson. — [1st ed.]. — Norman: University of Oklahoma Press, [1972] xi, 304 p.; 24 cm. 1. History — Bibliography. 2. Bibliography — Bibliography — History. I. T.
Z6201.P65      016.9      *LC* 71-165774      *ISBN* 0806109858

**Bengtson, Hermann, 1909-.**                                             • 5.8223
[Einführung in die alte Geschichte. English] Introduction to ancient history / translated from the 6th ed. by R. I. Frank and Frank D. Gilliard. — Berkeley: University of California Press, 1970. viii, 213 p.; 25 cm. Translation of Einführung in die alte Geschichte. 1. History, Ancient — Bibliography. I. T.
Z6202.B413      016.93      *LC* 78-118685      *ISBN* 0520017234

**Paetow, Louis John, 1880-1928.**                                          5.8224
A guide to the study of medieval history / by Louis John Paetow; with errata compiled by Gray C. Boyce and an addendum by Lynn Thorndike; prepared under the auspices of the Mediaeval Academy of America. — Rev. and corr. ed. — Millwood, N.Y.: Kraus Reprint, [1980] cxii, 643 p.; 24 cm. Revised ed. originally published in 1931 by F. S. Crofts, New York. Includes index. 1. Middle Ages — Bibliography. 2. Middle Ages — History — Outlines, syllabi, etc. I. Thorndike, Lynn, 1882-1965. II. Mediaeval Academy of America. III. T.
Z6203.P25 1980 D117      016.9401      *LC* 80-81364      *ISBN* 0527691011

**Boyce, Gray Cowan, 1899-.**                                               5.8225
Literature of medieval history, 1930–1975: a supplement to Louis John Paetow's A guide to the study of medieval history / compiled and edited by Gray Cowan Boyce; sponsored by the Medieval Academy of America; foreword by Paul Meyvaert. — Millwood, N.Y.: Kraus International Publications, c1981. 5 v. (civ, 2630 p.); 24 cm. Includes index. 1. Middle Ages —

Bibliography. I. Paetow, Louis John, 1880-1928. Guide to the study of medieval history II. Medieval Academy of America. III. T.
Z6203.P25 1980 Suppl D117     016./9401 19     LC 80-28773
0527691011

**Halstead, John P.**                    5.8226
Modern European imperialism: a bibliography of books and articles, 1815–1972 / [by] John P. Halstead and Serafino Porcari. — Boston: G. K. Hall, 1974. 2 v.; 29 cm. 1. History, Modern — 19th century — Bibliography. 2. History, Modern — 20th century — Bibliography. 3. Colonies — Bibliography. 4. Imperialism — Bibliography. I. Porcari, Serafino, joint author. II. T.
Z6204.H35     016.90908     LC 73-19511     ISBN 0816109893

**Roach, John, 1920-.**                 • 5.8227
A bibliography of modern history; edited by John Roach. London, Cambridge U.P., 1968. xxiv, 388 p. 24 cm. ' ... a one volume bibliography to supplement the 'New Cambridge modern history'.' 1. History, Modern — Bibliography. I. T.
Z6204.R62     016.9402     LC 67-11528     ISBN 0521071917

**Bayliss, Gwyn M.**                   5.8228
Bibliographic guide to the two world wars: an annotated survey of English–language reference materials / Gwyn M. Bayliss. — London; New York: Bowker, 1977. xv, 578 p.; 23 cm. Includes indexes. 1. World War, 1914-1918 — Bibliography. 2. World War, 1939-1945 — Bibliography. I. T.
Z6207.E8 B39 1977 D521     016.9403     LC 77-70292     ISBN 0859350134

**Schaffer, Ronald.**                   5.8229
The United States in World War I: a selected bibliography / Ronald Schaffer. — Santa Barbara, Calif.: Clio Books, c1978. xxix, 224 p.; 24 cm. (The War/peace bibliography series; #7) Includes index. 1. World War, 1914-1918 — United States — Bibliography. I. T.
Z6207.E8 S3 D570     016.940373     LC 78-18456     ISBN 0874362741

**Smith, Myron J.**                    5.8230
World War II at sea: a bibliography of sources in English / by Myron J. Smith, Jr. — Metuchen, N.J.: Scarecrow Press, 1976. 3 v.; 23 cm. Includes indexes. 1. World War, 1939-1945 — Naval operations — Bibliography. I. T.
Z6207.W8 S57 D770     016.94054/5     LC 75-34098     ISBN 0810808846

**Smith, Myron J.**                    5.8231
World War II, the European and Mediterranean theaters: an annotated bibliography / Myron J. Smith. — New York: Garland Pub., 1984. xxiii, 450 p.; 23 cm. — (Wars of the United States; vol. 2) (Garland reference library of social science; vol. 217) Includes indexes. 1. World War, 1939-1945 — Campaigns — Western — Bibliography. 2. World War, 1939-1945 — Campaigns — Mediterranean Region — Bibliography. I. T. II. Title: World War 2, the European and Mediterranean theaters.
Z6207.W8 S573 1984 D756     016.94054/21 19     LC 83-49086     ISBN 0824090136

**World War II from an American perspective: an annotated**    5.8232
**bibliography.**
Santa Barbara, Calif.: ABC-Clio, c1983. vi, 277 p.; 24 cm. Includes index. 1. World War, 1939-1945 — Bibliography. 2. World War, 1939-1945 — United States — Bibliography. 3. United States — History — 1933-1945 — Bibliography. I. Title: World War 2 from an American perspective. II. Title: World War Two from an American perspective.
Z6207.W8 W67 1983 D743     016.94053 19     LC 82-24480     ISBN 0874360358

## Z6366–6375 Jews. Judaism

**Berlin, Charles, 1936-.**                 5.8233
Index to festschriften in Jewish studies. Cambridge, Harvard College Library, 1971. xl, 319 p. 24 cm. 1. Festschriften — Jews — Indexes. 2. Jews — Bibliography. I. T.
Z6366.B45     016.909/04/924     LC 72-138460

**Brisman, Shimeon.**                  5.8234
A history and guide to Judaic bibliography / by Shimeon Brisman. — Cincinnati: Hebrew Union College Press, 1977. xix, 352 p.; 24 cm. — (Bibliographica Judaica; 7) (His Jewish research literature; v. 1 0067-6853) Includes index. 1. Bibliography — Bibliography — Jews — History. 2. Jews — Bibliography — History. 3. Jews — Bibliography — Periodicals — History. 4. Jews — Indexes — History. I. T. II. Series.
Z6366.B8 1977 vol. 1 DS102.5     016.909/04/924     LC 77-26149
ISBN 087820900X

**Cutter, Charles.**                    5.8235
Jewish reference sources: a selective, annotated bibliographic guide / Charles Cutter, Micha Falk Oppenheim. — New York: Garland, 1982. xiii, 180 p.; 23 cm. — (Garland reference library of social science. v. 126) Includes indexes.

1. Jews — Bibliography. 2. Reference books — Jews. I. Oppenheim, Micha Falk. II. T. III. Series.
Z6366.C87 1982 DS102     016.909/04924 19     LC 82-15434     ISBN 082409347X

**Kaplan, Jonathan.**                   5.8236
2000 books and more: an annotated and selected bibliography of Jewish history and thought / edited by Jonathan Kaplan. — Jerusalem: Magnes Press: Hebrew University, c1983. xviii, 483, 16 p.; 23 cm. English and Hebrew. Title on added t.p.: 2000 sefer va-sefer. At head of title: Rothberg School for Overseas Students, Hebrew University [and] Dor Hemschech Institutes, World Zionist Organization. Includes index. 1. Jews — Bibliography. 2. Judaism — Bibliography. I. Bet ha-sefer le-talmide hu. l. 'a. sh. Sh. Rotberg. II. World Zionist Organization. Dor Hemschech Institutes. III. T. IV. Title: Two thousand books and more. V. Title: 2000 sefer va-sefer. VI. Title: Alpayim sefer va-sefer.
Z6366.K33 1983 DS102.5     016.909/04924 19     LC 83-197388
ISBN 9652234443

**Shunami, Shlomo.**                   5.8237
Bibliography of Jewish bibliographies. 2d ed. enl. Jerusalem, Magnes Press, Hebrew University, 1965. xxiv, 997, xxii p. 25 cm. Added t.p. in Hebrew. Prefatory material also in Hebrew. 'Corrections': p. 993-997. 1. Bibliography — Bibliography — Jews. 2. Jews — Bibliography. I. T. II. Title: Mafteah ha-maftehot.
Z6366.S52 1965     LC he 65-1493

**Bibliographical essays in medieval Jewish studies / contributors,**    5.8238
**Lawrence V. Berman ... [et al.].**
New York: Anti-defamation League of B'nai B'rith, 1976. ix, 392 p.; 25 cm. — (The Study of Judaism; v. 2) 1. Catholic Church — Relations — Judaism — Bibliography. 2. Jews — History — 70-1789 — Bibliography. 3. Judaism — Relations — Catholic Church — Bibliography. 4. Judaism — History — Medieval and early modern period, 425-1789 — Bibliography. 5. Jews — Study and teaching — Bibliography. I. Berman, Lawrence V. (Lawrence Victor) II. B'nai B'rith. Anti-defamation League. III. Series.
Z6368.B53 DS124     016.909/04/924     LC 76-18313     ISBN 0870684868

**The Study of Judaism; bibliographical essays. Contributors:**    5.8239
**Richard Bavier [and others.**
New York, Published by Ktav Pub. House for] Anti-defamation League of B'nai B'rith [1972] 229 p. 24 cm. ([The Study of Judaism, v. 1]) 1. Judaism — Study and teaching — Bibliography. 2. Holocaust, Jewish (1939-1945) — Bibliography. I. Bavier, Richard. II. B'nai B'rith. Anti-defamation League. III. Series.
Z6370.S8 BM45     016.909/04924 19     LC 72-79129     ISBN 087068180X

**Fitzmyer, Joseph A.**                   5.8240
The Dead Sea scrolls: major publications and tools for study / Joseph A. Fitzmyer. — [s.l.]: Society of Biblical Literature; Missoula, Mont.: distributed by Scholars Press, [1975] xiv, 171 p.; 23 cm. (Sources for biblical study. 8) Includes indexes. 1. Dead Sea scrolls — Bibliography. I. T. II. Series.
Z6371.D4 F58 BM487     016.2214/4     LC 75-5987     ISBN 0884140539

**Marcus, Jacob Rader, 1896-.**             5.8241
An index to scientific articles on American Jewish history. Edited by Jacob R. Marcus. Cincinnati, American Jewish Archives; New York, KTAV Publishing House, inc., 1971. 240 p. 24 cm. (Publications of the American Jewish Archives, no. 7) 1. Jews — America — History — Periodicals — Indexes. I. T.
Z6372.M35     016.9173/06/924     LC 71-149601     ISBN 0870681397

**Hundert, Gershon David, 1946-.**           5.8242
The Jews in Poland and Russia: bibliographical essays / Gershon David Hundert and Gershon C. Bacon. — Bloomington: Indiana University Press, c1984. x, 276 p.; 25 cm. (The Modern Jewish experience) 1. Jews — Poland — Bibliography. 2. Jews — Soviet Union — Bibliography. 3. Poland — Ethnic relations — Bibliography. 4. Soviet Union — Ethnic relations — Bibliography. I. Bacon, Gershon C. (Gershon Chaim) II. T.
Z6373.P7 H86 1984 DS135.P6     016.9438/004924 19     LC 83-49285
ISBN 0253331587

**Orenstein, Sylvia.**                    5.8243
Source book on Soviet Jewry: an annotated bibliography / compiled by Sylvia Orenstein. — New York, N.Y.: American Jewish Committee, Institute of Human Relations, c1981. viii, 116 p.; 28 cm. Includes index. 1. Jews — Soviet Union — History — 1917- — Bibliography. 2. Soviet Union — Ethnic relations — Bibliography. I. T.
Z6373.S65 O73 DS135.R92     947/.004924 19     LC 81-65824     ISBN 0874950198

**Brickman, William W.**                  5.8244
The Jewish community in America: an annotated and classified bibliographical guide / by William W. Brickman. — New York: B. Franklin, c1977. xxvii,

396 p.; 24 cm. (Burt Franklin ethnic bibliographical guide; 2) Includes index. 1. Jews — United States — Bibliography. 2. United States — Bibliography I. T.
Z6373.U5 B75 E184.J5     016.973/04/924     LC 76-30284     ISBN 0891020578

**Gurock, Jeffrey S., 1949-.**           5.8245
American Jewish history: a bibliographical guide / by Jeffrey S. Gurock; [foreword by Moses Rischin]. — New York, NY: Anti-Defamation League of B'nai B'rith, c1983. xxi, 195 p.; 18 cm. Includes index. 1. Jews — United States — Bibliography. 2. United States — Ethnic relations — Bibliography. I. T.
Z6373.U5 G87 1983 E184.J5     016.973/04924 19     LC 83-71207    ISBN 088464037X

**Singerman, Robert.**           5.8246
Antisemitic propaganda: an annotated bibliography and research guide / Robert Singerman; foreword by Colin Holmes. — New York: Garland, 1982. xxxvii, 448 p.; 23 cm. — (Garland reference library of social science. v. 112) 1. Antisemitism — United States — Bibliography. 2. Antisemitism — Great Britain — Bibliography. I. T. II. Series.
Z6374.A56 S56 1982 DS141     016.3058/924 19     LC 81-43363    ISBN 0824092708

**Zubatsky, David S., 1939-.**           5.8247
Jewish genealogy: a sourcebook of family histories and genealogies / David S. Zubatsky, Irwin M. Berent. — New York: Garland Pub., 1984. xxx, 422 p.; 23 cm. — (Garland reference library of social science. v. 214) 1. Jews — Genealogy — Bibliography. I. Berent, Irwin M. II. T. III. Series.
Z6374.B5 Z79 1984 CS31     929/.1/089924 19     LC 83-16554    ISBN 0824090284

**Edelheit, Abraham J.**           5.8248
Bibliography on Holocaust literature / Abraham J. Edelheit, Hershel Edelheit. — Boulder: Westview Press, 1986. xxxvi, 842 p.; 24 cm. Includes index. 1. Holocaust, Jewish (1939-1945) — Bibliography. I. Edelheit, Hershel. II. T.
Z6374.H6 E33 1986 D810.J4     016.94053/15/03924 19     LC 86-9274    ISBN 081337233X

**The Holocaust: an annotated bibliography and resource guide /**     5.8249
**edited by David M. Szonyi.**
[Hoboken, NJ]: Ktav Pub. House for the National Jewish Resource Center, New York, c1985. xiv, 396 p.; 25 cm. 1. Holocaust, Jewish (1939-1945) — Bibliography. I. Szonyi, David M. II. National Jewish Resource Center (U.S.)
Z6374.H6 H65 1985 D810.J4     016.94053/15/03924 19     LC 84-26191    ISBN 0881250570

**Laska, Vera, 1923-.**           5.8250
Nazism, resistance & holocaust in World War II: a bibliography / by Vera Laska. — Metuchen, N.J.: Scarecrow Press, 1985. xxii, 183 p.; 23 cm. Includes index. 1. Holocaust, Jewish (1939-1945) — Bibliography. 2. World War, 1939-1945 — Underground movements, Jewish — Bibliography. 3. World War, 1939-1945 — Underground movements — Bibliography. 4. National socialism — Bibliography. 5. World War, 1939-1945 — Women — Bibliography. I. T. II. Title: Nazism, resistance and holocaust in World War II.
Z6374.H6 L37 1985 D810.J4     016.94053/15/03924 19     LC 84-23586    ISBN 0810817713

**Jones, A. Philip (Arthur Philip), 1947-.**           5.8251
Britain and Palestine, 1914-1948: archival sources for the history of the British Mandate / compiled by Philip Jones. — Oxford: Oxford University Press for the British Academy, c1979. x, 246 p.; 24 cm. 'This book constitutes the findings of the ... Anglo-Palestinian Archives Committee.' 1. Zionism — History — Archival resources. 2. Mandates — Palestine — Archival resources. 3. Palestine — History — 1929-1948 — Archival resources. I. Anglo-Palestinian Archives Committee. II. T.
Z6374.Z5 J65 DS149     016.95694/04     LC 80-454407    ISBN 0197259855

## Z6461–6485 International Law and Relations

**Detter Delupis, Ingrid, 1936-.**           5.8252
Bibliography of international law / Ingrid Delupis née Detter. — London; New York: Bowker, c1975. xxx, 670 p.; 23 cm. Includes index. 1. International law — Bibliography. I. T.
Z6461.D63 1975 JX3091     016.341     LC 75-7920    ISBN 0859350045

**The Foreign affairs 50–year bibliography; new evaluations of**     5.8253
**significant books on international relations 1920–1970. Byron**
**Dexter, editor, assisted by Elizabeth H. Bryant and Janice L.**
**Murray.**
New York: Published for the Council on Foreign Relations by R. R. Bowker Co., 1972. xxviii, 936 p.; 26 cm. 1. International relations — Bibliography

I. Dexter, Byron Vinson, 1900- ed. II. Council on Foreign Relations. III. Foreign affairs (New York)
Z6461.F62     016.327/09/04     LC 75-163904     ISBN 0835204901

**Zawodny, J. K. (Janusz Kazimierz)**           • 5.8254
Guide to the study of international relations [by] J. K. Zawodny. San Francisco: Chandler Pub. Co. [1965, c1966] xii, 151 p.; 22 cm. (Chandler publications in political science) 1. International relations — Bibliography I. T.
Z6461.Z3     016.327     LC 65-16765

**Foreign affairs bibliography.**           5.8255
1919-1932- . — New York: Published by Harper & Brothers for Council on Foreign Relations, c1933-. v.; 26 cm. Published: New York: R.R. Bowker, 1964- 1. International relations — Bibliography — Periodicals. 2. World politics — Bibliography — Periodicals. 3. Economic history — Bibliography — Periodicals. I. Council on Foreign Relations. II. Foreign affairs (Council on Foreign Relations)
Z6463.F73 JX1391     016.327 19     LC 33-7094

**Burns, Grant, 1947-.**           5.8256
The atomic papers: a citizen's guide to selected books and articles on the bomb, the arms race, nuclear power, the peace movement, and related issues / by Grant Burns. — Metuchen, N.J.: Scarecrow Press, 1984. xiv, 309 p.; 23 cm. Includes indexes. 1. Nuclear disarmament — Bibliography. 2. Nuclear warfare — Bibliography. 3. Arms race — Bibliography. 4. Nuclear energy — Bibliography. 5. Peace — Bibliography. I. T.
Z6464.D6 B85 1984 JX1974.7     016.3271/74 19     LC 84-1390    ISBN 081081692X

**Atherton, Alexine L.**           5.8257
International organizations: a guide to information sources / Alexine L. Atherton. — Detroit: Gale Research Co., c1976. xxviii, 350 p.; 22 cm. — (International relations information guide series; v. 1) (Gale information guide library) Includes indexes. 1. International agencies — Bibliography. I. T.
Z6464.I6 A74     016.06     LC 73-17502    ISBN 0810313243

**To end war: a new approach to international conflict / [edited**     5.8258
**by] Robert Woito.**
6th ed. — New York: Pilgrim Press, c1982. xx, 755 p.; 25 cm. Rev. ed. of: To end war / by Robert Pickus. 3rd ed. 1970. Includes index. 1. Peace — Bibliography. 2. International relations — Bibliography I. Woito, Robert. II. Pickus, Robert. To end war.
Z6464.Z9 T63 1982 JX1952     016.3271/.72 19     LC 81-15889    ISBN 0829804765

**Page, Donald Murray, 1939-.**           5.8259
A bibliography of works on Canadian foreign relations. Compiled by Donald M. Page. [Toronto] Canadian Institute of International Affairs [c1973-] v. 28 cm. Vol. 1-2 by Donald M. Page; vol. 3 by Jane Beaumont. 1. Canada — Foreign relations — Bibliography I. Beaumont, Jane, 1945- II. T.
Z6465C2 P3

**Aster, Sidney, 1942-.**           5.8260
British foreign policy, 1918–1945: a guide to research and research materials / compiled and edited by Sidney Aster. — Wilmington, Del.: Scholarly Resources, 1984. xi, 324 p.; 23 cm. (Guides to European diplomatic history research and research materials.) 1. Great Britain — Foreign relations — 1910-1936 — Library resources — Great Britain. 2. Great Britain — Foreign relations — 1936-1945 — Library resources — Great Britain. 3. Great Britain — Foreign relations — 1910-1936 — Archival resources — Great Britain. 4. Great Britain — Foreign relations — 1936-1945 — Archival resources — Great Britain. I. T. II. Series.
Z6465.G7 A85 1984 DA578     016.32741 19     LC 84-5339    ISBN 0842021760

**Trask, David F.**           • 5.8261
A bibliography of United States–Latin American relations since 1810; a selected list of eleven thousand published references. Compiled and edited by David F. Trask, Michael C. Meyer [and] Roger R. Trask. — Lincoln: University of Nebraska Press, [1968] xxxi, 441 p.; 26 cm. 1. Latin America — Foreign relations — United States — Bibliography. 2. United States — Foreign relations — Latin America — Bibliography. I. Meyer, Michael C. joint author. II. Trask, Roger R. joint author. III. T.
Z6465.L29 T7 F1418     016.32773/08     LC 67-14421

**Schulz, Ann.**           5.8262
International and regional politics in the Middle East and North Africa: a guide to information sources / Ann Schulz. — Detroit: Gale Research Co., c1977. xiii, 244 p.; 22 cm. — (International relations information guide series; v. 6) (Gale information guide library) 1. Middle East — Foreign relations — Bibliography. 2. Africa, North — Foreign relations — Bibliography. I. T.
Z6465.N35 S38 JX1581.N38     016.32756    LC 74-11568    ISBN 081031326X

**Bemis, Samuel Flagg, 1891-1973.** • **5.8263**
Guide to the diplomatic history of the United States, 1775–1921 / by Samuel Flagg Bemis and Grace Gardner Griffin. Washington: U.S. Govt. Print. Off., 1935; Gloucester,Mass.:bP.Smith, 1963. reprint: xvii, 979 p. At head of title: Library of Congress. 1. United States — Foreign relations — Bibliography. I. Griffin, Grace Gardner. II. Library of Congress. III. T. IV. Title: Diplomatic history of the United States, 1775-1921.
Z6465.U5B4 1963    016.32773    LC 52-6052

**Guide to American foreign relations since 1700 / edited by** **5.8264**
**Richard Dean Burns.**
Santa Barbara, Calif.: ABC-Clio, c1983. xxvi, 1311 p.: col. maps; 26 cm. 1. United States — Foreign relations — Bibliography. I. Burns, Richard Dean.
Z6465.U5 G84 1983 E183.7    016.32773 19    LC 82-13905    ISBN 0874363233

**Plischke, Elmer, 1914-.** **5.8265**
U.S. foreign relations: a guide to information sources / Elmer Plischke. — Detroit, Mich.: Gale Research Co., c1980. xvii, 715 p.; 23 cm. — (American Government and history information guide series; v. 6) (Gale information guide library) Includes index. 1. United States — Foreign relations — Bibliography. 2. United States — Foreign relations administration — Bibliography. I. T. II. Series.
Z6465.U5 P52 JX1417    026/.32773 19    LC 74-11516    ISBN 0810312042

**Dimitrov, Théodore Delchev.** **5.8266**
World bibliography of international documentation / compiled and edited by Th. D. Dimitrov. — Pleasantville, N.Y.: UNIFO Publishers, 1981. 2 v.; 26 cm. 1. United Nations — Bibliography. 2. International agencies — Bibliography. 3. International relations — Bibliography I. T.
Z6481.D57 JX1977    016.3    LC 80-5653    ISBN 0891110100

**Winton, Harry N. M.** **5.8267**
Publications of the United Nations system; a reference guide. Compiled and edited by Harry N. M. Winton. — New York: R. R. Bowker Co., 1972. xi, 202 p.; 23 cm. 1. United Nations — Bibliography. 2. International agencies — Bibliography. I. T.
Z6481.W55    011    LC 72-4923    ISBN 0835205975

**Birchfield, Mary Eva, 1909-.** **5.8268**
The complete reference guide to United Nations sales publications, 1946–1978. — Pleasantville, N.Y.: UNIFO Publishers, 1982. 2 v.; 29 cm. 1. United Nations — Bibliography — Catalogs. I. Coolman, Jacqueline, 1945- II. United Nations. III. T.
Z6485.Z9 B57 1982 JX1977    018/.4 19    LC 82-1854    ISBN 0891110119

## Z6511–6525 Literature: General
### (see also: Z1201-5000, Z5781, Z5916, Z7001-7123)

**Havlice, Patricia Pate.** **5.8269**
Index to literary biography. Metuchen, N.J., Scarecrow Press, 1975. 2 v. (viii, 1300 p.) 22 cm. 1. Literature — Bio-bibliography — Bibliography. 2. Authors — Biography — Indexes. I. T.
Z6511.H38    016.809    LC 74-8315    ISBN 0810807459

**Magill, Frank Northen, 1907-.** **5.8270**
[Bibliography of literary criticism] Magill's bibliography of literary criticism: selected sources for the study of more than 2,500 outstanding works of Western literature / edited by Frank N. Magill, associate editors, Stephen L. Hanson, Patricia King Hanson. — Englewood Cliffs, N.J.: Salem Press, c1979. 4 v. (xxx, 2380, xxxiv p.); 24 cm. Includes index. 1. Literature — History and criticism — Indexes. I. Hanson, Stephen L. joint author. II. Hanson, Patricia King. joint author. III. T. IV. Title: Bibliography of literary criticism.
Z6511.M25 PN523    016.8    LC 79-63017    ISBN 0893561886

**Patterson, Margaret C.** **5.8271**
Literary research guide / Margaret C. Patterson. — 2nd ed. — New York: Modern Language Association of America, 1983. lxxxv, 559 p.; 24 cm. Subtitle: An evaluative, annotated bibliography of important reference books and periodicals on English, Irish, Scottish, Welsh, Commonwealth, American, Afro-American, American Indian, continental, classical, and world literatures, and sixty literature-related subject areas including bibliography, biography, book collecting, film, folklore, linguistics, little magazines, prosody, reviews, teaching resources, textual criticism, women's studies. Includes index. 1. Literature — Bibliography 2. Reference books — Literature. I. Modern Language Association of America. II. T.
Z6511.P37 1983 PN43    016.8 19    LC 82-20386    ISBN 0873521285

**Thompson, George, 1941-.** **5.8272**
Key sources in comparative and world literature: an annotated guide to reference materials / George A. Thompson, Jr. with the assistance of Margaret

M. Thompson. — New York: F. Ungar Pub. Co., 1983 (c1982). xv, 383 p.; 27 cm. Includes indexes. 1. Literature — History and criticism — Bibliography. 2. Bibliography — Bibliography — Literature. 3. Reference books — Literature. I. Thompson, Margaret M. II. T.
Z6511.T47 1982 PN523    016.809 19    LC 82-40253    ISBN 0804432813

**Weiner, Alan R., 1938-.** **5.8273**
Literary criticism index / by Alan R. Weiner, Spencer Means. — Metuchen, N.J.: Scarecrow Press, 1984. xvii, 685 p.; 23 cm. 1. Literature — History and criticism — Indexes. 2. English literature — History and criticism — Indexes. 3. American literature — History and criticism — Indexes. I. Means, Spencer. II. T.
Z6511.W44 1984 PN523    016.809 19    LC 84-1371    ISBN 0810816946

**Baldensperger, Fernand, 1871-1958.** • **5.8274**
Bibliography of comparative literature / by Fernand Baldensperger and Werner P. Friederich. — New York: Russell & Russell, 1960, c1950. xxiv, 705 p. 1. Literature, Comparative — Bibliography. I. Friederich, Werner Paul, 1905- II. T.
Z6514.C7 B3 1960    016.809    LC 60-5279

**Kolar, Carol Koehmstedt, 1931-.** **5.8275**
Plot summary index / compiled by Carol Koehmstedt Kolar. — 2d ed., rev. and enl. — Metuchen, N.J.: Scarecrow Press, 1981. xviii, 526 p.; 22 cm. 1. Literature — Stories, plots, etc. — Indexes. I. T.
Z6514.P66 K64 1981 PN44    809 19    LC 80-27112    ISBN 0810813920

**The Romantic movement bibliography, 1936–1970: a master** **5.8276**
**cumulation from ELH, Philological quarterly, and English**
**language notes /edited and with a pref. by A. C. Elkins, Jr. and**
**L. J. Forstner; with a foreword by David V. Erdman.**
[Ann Arbor, Mich.]: Pierian Press, 1973. 7 v. (xiii, 3289 p.); 24 cm. — (Cumulated bibliography series. no. 3) 1. Romanticism — Bibliography. I. Elkins, Aubrey Christian, 1939- ed. II. Forstner, Lorne J., ed. III. English literary history. IV. Philological quarterly. V. English language notes. VI. Series.
Z6514.R6 R65    016.809/894    LC 77-172773    ISBN 0876500254

**Ferguson, Mary Anne.** **5.8277**
Bibliography of English translations from medieval sources, 1943–1967 / by Mary Anne Heyward Ferguson. — New York: Columbia University Press, 1974. x, 274 p.; 23 cm. — (Records of civilization, sources and studies. no. 88) Supplement to Bibliography of English translations from medieval sources, by C. P. Farrar and A. P. Evans, published in 1946. 1. Literature, Medieval — Translations into English — Bibliography. 2. English literature — Translations from foreign languages — Bibliography. I. Farrar, Clarissa Palmer. Bibliography of English translations from medieval sources. II. T. III. Series.
Z6517.F47    016.08    LC 73-7751    ISBN 0231034350

**Pownall, David E., 1925-.** **5.8278**
Articles on twentieth century literature: an annotated bibliography, 1954 to 1970, by David E. Pownall. — New York: Kraus-Thomson Organization, 1973-80. 7 v.; 27 cm. 'An expanded cumulation of 'Current bibliography' in the journal Twentieth century literature, volume one to volume sixteen, 1955 to 1970.' 1. Literature, Modern — 20th century — History and criticism — Addresses, essays, lectures — Bibliography. I. Twentieth century literature. II. T.
Z6519.P66 PN771    016.809/04 19    LC 73-6588    ISBN 0527721506

**Wortman, William A., 1940-.** **5.8279**
A guide to serial bibliographies for modern literatures / William A. Wortman. — New York, N.Y.: Modern Language Association of America, 1982. xvi, 124 p.; 22 cm. — (Selected bibliographies in language and literature. 3) Includes indexes. 1. Literature, Modern — Bibliography — Periodicals — Bibliography. 2. Bibliography — Bibliography — Literature, Modern. 3. Bibliography — Bibliography — Periodicals. I. T. II. Series.
Z6519.W67 1982 PN695    016.805 19    LC 81-18744    ISBN 0873529529

## Z6601–6625 Manuscripts

**The National union catalog of manuscript collections.** • **5.8280**
v.1(1959-61)-. Hamden, Conn.: Shoe String Press, 1962-. v. (Library of Congress catalogs) 'Based on reports from American repositories of manuscripts.' Vols. for 1959-61- compiled and edited by the Descriptive Cataloguing Division of the Library of Congress. Indexes for 1963-1974 included in vols. 4(1965)-12(1973-74). 1. Manuscripts — United States — Catalogs. 2. United States — History — Sources — Bibliography. I. Library of Congress. Descriptive Cataloging Division. II. Series.
Z6620.U5 N3.

## Z6651–6655 Mathematics

**Gaffney, Matthew P.**           5.8281
Annotated bibliography of expository writing in the mathematical sciences / Matthew P. Gaffney, Lynn Arthur Steen, with the assistance of Paul J. Campbell. — [Washington]: Mathematical Association of America, c1976. xi, 282 p.; 23 cm. 1. Mathematics — Bibliography I. Steen, Lynn Arthur, 1941- joint author. II. Campbell, Paul J. joint author. III. T.
Z6651.G33 QA36    016.51    LC 76-151289    ISBN 0883854228

## Z6658–6676 Medicine. Nursing

**Fulton, John Farquhar, 1899-1960.**     ● 5.8282
The great medical bibliographers: a study in humanism. — Philadelphia: University of Pennsylvania Press, 1951. 107 p.: ill.; 23 cm. (Publication of Historical library, Yale University, School of Medicine; no. 26) On half title page: The A. S. W. Rosenbach Fellowship in Bibliography. 1. Bibliography — Bibliography — Medicine. 2. Medicine — Bibliography 3. Bibliographers I. A. S. W. Rosenbach Fellowship in Bibliography Fund. II. Yale University. School of Medicine. Historical Library. III. T.
Z6658.A1 F8    610    LC 51-13981

**Blake, John Ballard, 1922-.**     ● 5.8283
Medical reference works, 1679–1966; a selected bibliography. John B. Blake [and] Charles Roos, editors. Chicago, Medical Library Association, 1967. viii, 343 p. 24 cm. (Medical Library Association. Publication no. 3) Supersedes the bibliographies published as part of the Medical Library Association's Handbook of medical library practice, 1943 and 1956. Prepared by the staff of the National Library of Medicine. 1. Medicine — Bibliography 2. Reference books — Medicine — Bibliography. I. Roos, Charles. joint author. II. National Library of Medicine (U.S.) III. T.
Z6658.B63 R129    016.61 19    LC 67-30664

**Garrison, Fielding H. (Fielding Hudson), 1870-1935.**     ● 5.8284
A medical bibliography (Garrison and Morton): an annotated check–list of texts illustrating the history of medicine / [by] Leslie T. Morton. — 3d ed. Philadelphia: Lippincott [1970] 872 p.; 23 cm. 1. Medicine — Bibliography 2. Medicine — History — Bibliography. I. Morton, Leslie T. (Leslie Thomas), 1907- ed. II. T.
Z6658.G243 1970    016.61    LC 76-114167

**Thornton, John Leonard.**     ● 5.8285
Medical books, libraries and collectors: a study of bibliography and the book trade in relation to the medical sciences, by John L. Thornton; with an introduction by Sir Geoffrey Keynes. — 2nd revised ed. — London: Deutsch, 1966. xvi, 445 p.: 16 plates (facsims.); 22 1/2 cm. — (A Grafton book) 1. Medicine — Bibliography 2. Medical libraries I. T.
Z6658.T5 1966    016.61    LC 67-71073

**Guerra, Francisco.**     ● 5.8286
American medical bibliography 1639–1783. A chronological catalogue, and critical and bibliographical study of books, pamphlets, broadsides, and articles in periodical publications relating to the medical sciences—medicine, surgery, pharmacy, dentistry, and veterinary medicine—printed in the present territory of the United States of America during British dominion and the Revolutionary War. Pref. by Lawrence C. Wroth. New York, L.C. Harper, 1962. 885 p. facsims. 25 cm. (Yale University. Dept. of the History of Science and Medicine. Publication no. 40) Half-title: American medical bibliography, colonial period and Revolutionary War, 1639-1783. 1. Medicine — 15th-18th centuries — Bibliography. I. T.
Z6659.G8    016.61    LC 61-17786

**Driver, Edwin D.**     5.8287
The sociology and anthropology of mental illness; a reference guide [by] Edwin D. Driver. — Rev. and enl. ed. — [Amherst]: University of Massachusetts Press, 1972. x, 487 p.; 24 cm. 1. Social psychiatry — Bibliography. 2. Mental illness — Bibliography I. T.
Z6664.N5 D7 1972    016.3622    LC 71-103476    ISBN 087023062X

**Andrews, Theodora.**     5.8288
A bibliography on herbs, herbal medicine, 'natural' foods, and unconventional medical treatment / Theodora Andrews, with the assistance of William L. Corya, Donald A. Stickel, Jr. — Littleton, Colo.: Libraries Unlimited, 1982. 339 p.; 24 cm. Includes indexes. 1. Herbs — Therapeutic use — Bibliography. 2. Herbs — Bibliography. 3. Herbals — Bibliography. 4. Food, Natural — Bibliography. 5. Folk medicine — Bibliography. I. Corya, William L. II. Stickel, Donald A., 1953- III. T.
Z6665.H47 A5 1982 RM666.H33    016.615/321 19    LC 82-128
ISBN 0872872882

**Muldoon, Maureen.**     5.8289
Abortion, an annotated indexed bibliography / by Maureen Muldoon. — New York: E. Mellen Press, c1980. ca. 150 p.; 24 cm. — (Studies in women and religion. v. 3) 1. Abortion — Bibliography. I. T. II. Series.
Z6671.2.A2 M84 RG734    016.3634/6 19    LC 79-91622    ISBN 0889469725

**Triche, Charles W.**     5.8290
The euthanasia controversy, 1812–1974: a bibliography with select annotations / by Charles W. Triche III and Diane Samson Triche. — Troy, N.Y.: Whitston Pub. Co., 1975. vii, 242 p; 24 cm. Includes index. 1. Euthanasia — Bibliography. I. Triche, Diane Samson, joint author. II. T.
Z6675.E95 T74 R726    174/.24    LC 75-8379    ISBN 0878750711

**Cumulative index to nursing & allied health literature: including**     5.8291
**a list of subject headings.**
v. 22- 1977-. Glendale, CA: Glendale Adventist Medical Center. v.; 28 cm. Bimonthly. Subject heading lists called also: Nursing & allied health (CINAHL), 1986- . 1. Nursing — Periodicals — Indexes — Periodicals. 2. Allied health personnel — Periodicals — Indexes — Periodicals. I. Glendale Adventist Medical Center. II. Seventh-Day Adventist Hospital Association. III. T.
Z6675.N7 C8 RT41    016.61/073    LC 79-642922

**Nursing studies index / Yale University School of Nursing**     5.8292
**index staff Virginia Henderson, director.**
New York: Garland Pub., 1984. 4 v.; 29 cm. (History of American nursing.) Reprint. Originally published: Philadelphia: Lippincott, c1963-1972. 1. Nursing — Indexes. 2. Nursing — Bibliography I. Henderson, Virginia. II. Yale University. School of Nursing. III. Series.
Z6675.N7 N869 1984 RT41    016.61073 19    LC 83-49133    ISBN 0824065158

**Pearman, William A., 1940-.**     5.8293
The physically handicapped: an annotated bibliography of empirical research studies, 1970–1979 / William A. Pearman, Philip Starr. — New York: Garland Pub., 1981. xxxvii, 132 p.; 23 cm. — (Garland reference library of social science. vol. 76) Includes indexes. 1. Physically handicapped — Bibliography. 2. Physically handicapped — Psychology — Bibliography. 3. Physically handicapped — Public opinion — Bibliography. I. Starr, Philip, 1935- II. T. III. Series.
Z6675.R4 P4 1981 RD797    016.3624 19    LC 80-8503    ISBN 0824094840

**Bruhn, John G., 1934-.**     5.8294
Medical sociology: an annotated bibliography, 1972–1982 / John G. Bruhn, Billy U. Philips, Paula L. Levine. — New York: Garland, 1985. xxxi, 779 p.; 23 cm. (Garland bibliographies in sociology. v. 6) (Garland reference library of social science. v. 243) Includes indexes. 1. Social medicine — Bibliography. 2. Medicine, State — Bibliography. I. Philips, Billy U., 1947- II. Levine, Paula L. III. T. IV. Series. V. Series: Garland reference library of social science. v. 243
Z6675.S53 B78 1985 RA418    016.3621 19    LC 84-48070    ISBN 0824089383

**Sternlicht, Manny.**     5.8295
Social behavior of the mentally retarded: an annotated bibliography / Manny Sternlicht, George Windholz. — New York: Garland, 1984. xxiv, 226 p.; 23 cm. (Developmental disabilities. vol. 1) (Garland reference library of social science; vol. 175) Includes index. 1. Mentally handicapped — Bibliography. 2. Mentally handicapped children — Bibliography. 3. Mentally handicapped — Abstracts. 4. Mentally handicapped children — Abstracts. 5. Social skills — Bibliography. 6. Social skills — Abstracts. I. Windholz, George. II. T. III. Series.
Z6677.S74 1984 HV3004    016.3623 19    LC 82-49140    ISBN 082409137X

## Z6721–6726 Military

**Higham, Robin D. S.**     5.8296
Official histories; essays and bibliographies from around the world. Edited by Robin Higham. — Manhattan: Kansas State University Library, 1970. xi, 644 p.; 24 cm. — (Kansas State University Library bibliography series. no. 8) 1. Military history — Bibliography. 2. Military history — Historiography. I. T. II. Series.
Z6724.H6 H5    016.355/009    LC 74-634493

**Scholar's guide to intelligence literature: bibliography of the**     5.8297
**Russell J. Bowen collection in the Joseph Mark Lavinger**
**Memorial Library, Georgetown University / edited by Marjorie**
**W. Cline, Carla E. Christiansen, and Judith M. Fontaine.**
Frederick, Md.: Published for the National Intelligence Study Center by University Publications of America, Inc., 1983. xix, 236 p. 1. Espionage — Bibliography. 2. Military intelligence — Bibliography. I. Cline, Marjorie W. II. Christiansen, Carla E. III. Fontaine, Judith M.
Z6724.I7S6x UB250 S36.    LC 83-80922    ISBN 0890935408

## Z6810 Music
(see: ML111-159)

## Z6824 Names

**Lawson, Edwin D., 1923-.**                    • 5.8298
Personal names and naming: an annotated bibliography / compiled by Edwin D. Lawson. — New York: Greenwood Press, 1987. xiii, 185 p.; 24 cm. — (Bibliographies and indexes in anthropology. 0742-6844; no. 3) Includes indexes. 1. Names, Personal — Bibliography. I. T. II. Series.
Z6824.L39 1987 CS2305      016.9294 19      LC 86-31789      *ISBN* 0313238170

**Sealock, Richard Burl, 1907-.**                    • 5.8299
Bibliography of place–name literature: United States and Canada / by Richard B. Sealock and Pauline A. Seely. — 2d ed. — Chicago: American Library Association, 1967. x, 352 p. 1. Names, Geographical — North America — Bibliography I. Seely, Pauline Augusta, 1905- II. T.
Z6824.S4 1967      *LC* 67-23000

**Smith, Elsdon Coles, 1903-.**                    5.8300
Personal names; a bibliography. New York, New York Public Library, 1952. 226 p. 26 cm. 1. Names, Personal — Bibliography. I. T.
Z6824.S55      *LC* 52-12991

## Z6831–6836 Naval Science

**Albion, Robert Greenhalgh, 1896-.**                    • 5.8301
Naval & maritime history: an annotated bibliography / Robert Greenhalph Albion. — 3d ed. re. and expanded.— Mystic, Conn.: Munson Institute of American Maritime History, 1963. viii, 230 p. 1. Naval history — Bibliography. 2. Merchant marine — History — Bibliography. I. T.
Z6834.H5 A4 1963      016.387/09      *LC* 63-25821

**Smith, Myron J.**                    5.8302
The American Navy, 1789–1860: a bibliography, by Myron J. Smith, Jr. — Metuchen, N.J.: Scarecrow Press, 1974. xiv, 489 p.; 22 cm. — (American naval bibliography, v. 2) 1. United States. Navy — Bibliography. 2. United States — History, Naval — Bibliography. I. T. II. Series.
Z6835.U5 S6      016.3593/0973      *LC* 73-18464      *ISBN* 0810806592

**Smith, Myron J.**                    5.8303
The American Navy, 1865–1918: a bibliography, by Myron J. Smith, Jr. — Metuchen, N.J.: Scarecrow Press, 1974. xiii, 372 p.; 22 cm. — (American naval bibliography, v. 4) 1. United States. Navy — Bibliography. 2. United States — History, Naval — Bibliography. I. T. II. Series.
Z6835.U5 S62      016.359/00973      *LC* 74-4230      *ISBN* 0810807203

**Smith, Myron J.**                    5.8304
The American Navy, 1918–1941: a bibliography / by Myron J. Smith, Jr. — Metuchen, N.J.: Scarecrow Press, 1974. xiv, 429 p.; 23 cm. — (American naval bibliography, v. 5) 1. United States. Navy — Bibliography. 2. United States — History, Naval — Bibliography. I. T. II. Series.
Z6835.U5 S63      016.3593/0973      *LC* 74-11077      *ISBN* 0810807564

## Z6935 Performing Arts

**The New York times directory of the theater. Introd. by Clive**                    5.8305
**Barnes.**
[New York] Arno Press [1973] 1009 p. illus. 32 cm. Contains the appendix and index to The New York times theater reviews, 1920-1970. 1. New York times — Indexes 2. Performing arts — New York (N.Y.) — Reviews — Indexes. I. New York times II. The New York times theater reviews, 1920-1970. III. Title: Directory of the theater.
Z6935.N48 1973      016.792/09747/1      *LC* 73-3054      *ISBN* 0812903641

**Performing arts resources.**                    5.8306
v. 1- 1974-. [New York] Drama Book Specialists. 22 cm. Annual. 1. Performing arts — Library resources — United States — Periodicals. I. Theatre Library Association.
Z6935.P46      016.7902/08      *LC* 75-646287

**Stratman, Carl Joseph, 1917-1972.**                    5.8307
Britain's theatrical periodicals, 1720–1967, a bibliography. — New York: New York Public Library, 1972. xxiv, 160 p.; 26 cm. First ed. published in 1962 under title: A bibliography of British dramatic periodicals, 1720-1960. 1. Performing arts — Great Britain — Periodicals — Bibliography. 2. Periodicals — Bibliography — Union lists I. T.
Z6935.S76 1972      016.792/0942      *LC* 72-134260      *ISBN* 0871040344

**Whalon, Marion K.**                    5.8308
Performing arts research: a guide to information sources / Marion K. Whalon. — Detroit: Gale Research Co., 1976. xi, 280 p.; 23 cm. — (Performing arts information guide series; v. 1) Includes index. 1. Performing arts — Bibliography. I. T.
Z6935.W5 PN1584      016.7902      *LC* 75-13828      *ISBN* 0810313642

## Z6940–6962 Periodicals. Newspapers

**McCoy, Ralph E. (Ralph Edward), 1915-.**                    5.8309
Freedom of the press; an annotated bibliography. With a foreword by Robert B. Downs. Carbondale Southern Illinois University Press [1968] [various pagings] 1. Freedom of the press — Bibliography I. T.
Z6940.M24      *LC* 67-10032

**Irregular serials & annuals; an international directory.**                    • 5.8310
1st- ed.; 1967-. New York, Bowker. v. 29 cm. Annual. 'A classified guide to current foreign and domestic serials, excepting periodicals issued more frequently than once a year.' 1. Periodicals — Directories. 2. Yearbooks — Directories. I. Koltay, Emery, ed.
Z6941.I78      016.05      *LC* 67-25026

**Katz, William A., 1924-.**                    5.8311
Magazines for libraries: for the general reader, and school, junior college, college, university, and public libraries / Bill Katz and Linda Sternberg Katz. — 5th ed. — New York: Bowker, 1986. xvii, 1057 p. Includes index. 1. Periodicals — Bibliography I. Katz, Linda Sternberg. II. T.
Z6941.K2 1986 PN4832      016.05      *ISBN* 0835222179

**National directory of newsletters and reporting services.**                    5.8312
1st- ed.; 1966-. Detroit, Gale Research Co. v. 29 cm. 'A reference guide to national and international information services, finance services, association bulletins, training and educational services' (varies). 1. Periodicals — Directories. I. Gale Research Company.
Z6941.N3      011 11      *LC* 66-15458

**Sources of serials.**                    5.8313
1st- ed.; 1977-. New York, R. R. Bowker. v. 28 cm. 'An international publisher and corporate author directory.' 'A Bowker serials bibliography.' 1. Serial publications — Directories. 2. Periodicals, Publishing of — Directories. I. Bowker (R. R.) Company. Serials Bibliography Dept.
Z6941.S74 PN4832      016.05      *LC* 77-15833

**Ulrich's international periodicals directory.**                    • 5.8314
[1st]- ed.; 1932-. New York, Bowker. v. 26-29 cm. Biennial. Vol. for 1943 called inter-American ed., with title also in Spanish; 1947 called Postwar ed. Kept up to date between editions 1972-76 by Bowker serials bibliography supplement, ISSN 0000-0094; 1977- by Ulrich's quarterly, ISSN 0000-0507. 1. Periodicals — Directories. 2. World War, 1939-1945 — Underground literature — Bibliography. I. Ulrich, Carolyn Farquhar, 1881- ed. II. Muzzy, Adrienne Florence, 1885- A list of clandestine periodicals of World War II.
Z6941.U5      011      *LC* 32-16320

**International directory of little magazines and small presses.**                    5.8315
9th- ed.; 1973/74-. [Paradise, Calif.: Dustbooks, 1964?-] v.: ill.; 24 cm. Annual. 1. Little magazines — Directories. 2. Little presses — Directories.
Z6944.L5 D5      051/.025      *LC* 73-645432

**Sader, Marion.**                    5.8316
Comprehensive index to English–language little magazines, 1890–1970, series one / edited by Marion Sader. — Millwood, N.Y.: Kraus-Thomson Organization, 1976. 8 v.; 26 cm. 1. Little magazines — Indexes. I. T.
Z6944.L5 S23 PN4836      016.051      *LC* 74-11742      *ISBN* 0527003700

**Periodical title abbreviations.**                    5.8317
Detroit, Mich.: Gale Research Co. v.; 23 cm. Began with 1969 ed. 'Covering periodical title abbreviations in science, the social sciences, the humanities, law, medicine, religion, library science, engineering, education, business, art and many other fields.' Description based on: 4th ed. Issued in two or more vols: v. 1, By abbreviation; v. 2, By title; v. 3, New periodical title abbreviations. Kept up to date by an annual supplement: New periodical title abbreviations, 3rd ed.- 1. Periodicals — Abbreviations of titles I. Wall, C. Edward. II. Alkire, Leland G. III. Gale Research Company. IV. New periodical title abbreviations.
Z6945.A2 P47 PN4832      050/.148 19      *LC* 84-640700

**American newspapers, 1821–1936; a union list of files available**                    • 5.8318
**in the United States and Canada, edited by Winifred Gregory**
**under the auspices of the Bibliographical Society of America.**
New York, H.W. Wilson Co., 1937. xvi, 791 p. 36 cm. Cover title: Union list of newspapers. Accompanied by 'An alphabetical index to the titles. Arranged by Avis G. Clarke (1036 l. 28 cm.) published: Oxford, Mass, 1958. Typescript (carbon copy). 'A bibliography of union lists of newspapers, compiled by Karl Brown and Daniel C. Haskell': p. [787]-789. 'Notes on newspapers published in foreign countries found in the libraries of the United States and Canada': p. [790]-791. 1. American newspapers — Bibliography — Union lists.

2. Canadian newspapers — Bibliography — Union lists. 3. Catalogs, Union — United States. 4. Catalogs, Union — Canada. I. Gerould, Winifred Gregory, 1885- ed. II. Clarke, Avis Gertrude, 1902- III. Title: Union list of newspapers.
Z6945.A53      LC 37-12783

**Union list of serials in libraries of the United States and Canada / Edited by Edna Brown Titus.**                    • 5.8319
3d ed. — New York: H. W. Wilson, 1965. 5 v. (4649 p.); 36 cm. 'Under the sponsorship of the Joint Committee on the Union List of Serials with the cooperation of the Library of Congress'. 1. Periodicals — Bibliography — Union lists 2. Libraries — United States 3. Libraries — Canada. 4. Bibliography — Bibliography — Periodicals. I. Titus, Edna Mae Brown, 1900- II. Joint Committee on the Union List of Serials. III. Library of Congress.
Z6945.U45 1965      016.05      LC 65-10150      ISBN 0824200551

**New serial titles: a union list of serials commencing publication**      5.8320
**after December 31, 1949: 1950–1970 cumulative.**
Washington: Library of Congress, 1974 (c1973). 4 v. Prepared under the sponsorship of the Joint Committee on the Union List of Serials. Supplements the Union list of serials. 1. Periodicals — Bibliography — Union lists I. Library of Congress. II. Joint Committee on the Union List of Serials.
Z6945.U5 S42      011.34 19      LC 53-60021      ISBN 0835205568

**The ... IMS directory of publications.**                    5.8321
118th annual ed. (1986). — Fort Washington, Pa.: IMS Press, c1986. 1 v.: maps; 28 cm. Annual. 1. American newspapers — Directories. 2. American periodicals — Directories. 3. Canadian newspapers — Directories. 4. Canadian periodicals — Directories.
Z6951.A97 PN4867      071/.025 19      071 11      LC 86-640928

**Brigham, Clarence Saunders, 1877-1963.**                    • 5.8322
History and bibliography of American newspapers, 1690–1820, by Clarence S. Brigham. Worcester, Mass., American Antiquarian Society, 1947. 2 v. 28 cm. Paged continuously. A revision of a work first issued in 18 parts in the Proceedings of the American antiquarian society, 1913 to 1927, under title: Bibliography of American newspapers, 1690-1820. 1. American newspapers — Bibliography. 2. American newspapers — History. I. T.
Z 6951 B85      LC 47-4111

**Chielens, Edward E.**                    5.8323
The literary journal in America, 1900–1950: a guide to information sources / edited by Edward E. Chielens. — Detroit: Gale Research Co., c1977. viii, 186 p.; 23 cm. — (American literature, English literature, and world literatures in English information guide series; v. 16) Vita. Includes index. 1. American periodicals — History — Bibliography. 2. American literature — Periodicals — History — Bibliography. I. T.
Z6951.C572 PN4877      016.051      LC 74-11534      ISBN 0810312409

**Smith, Myron J.**                    5.8324
U.S. television network news: a guide to sources in English / compiled by Myron J. Smith, Jr.; foreword by John Chancellor. — Jefferson, N.C.: McFarland, 1984. xx, 233 p.; 24 cm. 1. Television broadcasting of news — United States — Bibliography. 2. Documentary television programs — United States — Bibliography. I. T.
Z6951.S57 1984 PN4888.T4      016.0701/9 19      LC 82-42885      ISBN 0899500803

**The Standard periodical directory.**                    5.8325
1- ed., 1964/65-. New York, Oxbridge Pub. Co. v. 28 cm. Biennial. 1. American periodicals — Directories. 2. Canadian periodicals — Directories.
Z6951.S78      016.051      LC 64-7598

**Newspapers in microform: United States.**                    5.8326
1948/72-. Washington, Library of Congress. v. 29 cm. (Library of Congress catalogs.) 1. American newspapers — Bibliography — Union lists. 2. Newspapers in microform — Bibliography — Union lists. 3. Catalogs, Union I. Library of Congress. Catalog Publication Division. II. Newspapers on microfilm. III. Newspapers in microform. IV. Series.
Z6951.U56a PN4855      LC 79-640968

**Willing's press guide.**                    5.8327
1st- ed.;1874-. Haywards Heath, W. S.: Thomas Skinner Directories. v. Annual. 'A guide to the press of the United Kingdom and the principal publications of Europe and U.S.A.' Vol. for 1949-50 is a combined issue. 1. English newspapers — Directories. 2. English periodicals — Directories. 3. European newspapers — Directories. 4. European periodicals — Directories. 5. American newspapers — Directories. 6. American periodicals — Directories
Z6956.E5 W5      LC 53-36485

**Nunn, Godfrey Raymond, 1918-.**                    5.8328
Southeast Asian periodicals: an international union list / compiled by G. Raymond Nunn; with contributions from David Wyatt ... [et al.]. — London:

Mansell, c1977. xxiii, 456 p.; 32 cm. 1. Southeast Asian periodicals — Bibliography — Union lists. I. Wyatt, David K. II. T.
Z6958.S6 N85 PN5449.S68      016.959      LC 78-308226      ISBN 0720107253

## Z6972 Petroleum

**Chryssostomidis, Marjorie.**                    5.8329
Offshore petroleum engineering: a bibliographic guide to publications and information sources / by Marjorie Chryssostomidis. — New York: Nichols Pub. Co., 1978. 367 p.; 31 cm. (Report - M.I.T. Sea Grant Program; no. MITSG 78-5) 'Index no. 78-605-WON.' Includes indexes. 1. Petroleum in submerged lands — Bibliography. 2. Oil well drilling, Submarine — Bibliography. I. T.
Z6972.C45 1978 TN871.3      016.622/33/82      LC 78-16114      ISBN 089397045X

## Z7001–7123 Philology. Linguistics. Literature

**Abrahamsen, Adele A.**                    5.8330
Child language: an interdisciplinary guide to theory and research / by Adele A. Abrahamsen. Baltimore: University Park Press, c1977. xxiv, 381 p.; 23 cm. Includes indexes. 1. Children — Language — Bibliography. 2. Psycholinguistics — Bibliography. I. T.
Z7004.C45 A27 P118      016.3726      LC 77-5418      ISBN 0839111282

**Walford, Albert John.**                    • 5.8331
A guide to foreign language grammars and dictionaries / edited by A. J. Walford. — London: Library Association, 1964. 132 p.; 22 cm. 'An annotated list ... covering eight major languages.' 1. Language and languages — Grammars — Bibliography. 2. Encyclopedias and dictionaries — Bibliography. I. T.
Z7004.G7 W3      LC 64-57129

**Modern Language Association of America.**                    • 5.8332
MLA international bibliography of books and articles on the modern languages and literatures. [New York] Modern Language Association of America. v. 28 cm. Annual. I. Modern Language Association of America. International bibliography of books and articles on the modern languages and literatures. II. T.
Z7006.M64      LC sc 79-4878

**Gwinup, Thomas.**                    5.8333
Greek and Roman authors: a checklist of criticism / by Thomas Gwinup and Fidelia Dickinson. — 2nd ed. — Metuchen, N.J.: Scarecrow Press, 1982. xii, 280 p.; 23 cm. 1. Classical literature — History and criticism — Bibliography. I. Dickinson, Fidelia. II. T.
Z7016.G9 1982 PA3001      016.88/009 19      LC 82-690      ISBN 0810815281

**Parks, George Bruner, 1890-.**                    5.8334
The Greek and Latin literatures / editors: George B. Parks and Ruth Z. Temple. — New York: Ungar [1968] xix, 442 p.; 27 cm. (The Literatures of the world in English translation: a bibliography, v. 1) 1. Classical literature — Translations into English — Bibliography. 2. English literature — Translations from classical literature — Bibliography. I. Temple, Ruth Zabriskie. joint author. II. T. III. Series.
Z7018.T7 E85      016.88      LC 68-31454

**Parks, George Bruner, 1890-.**                    5.8335
The Romance literatures. Editors: George B. Parks and Ruth Z. Temple. — New York, F. Ungar Pub. Co. [1970] 2 v. 27 cm. — (The Literatures of the world in English translation: a bibliography, v. 3) 1. Romance literature — Translations into English — Bibliography. 2. English literature — Translations from Romance literature — Bibliography. I. Temple, Ruth Zabriskie. joint author. II. T. III. Series.
Z7033.T7 E56      016.84009      LC 70-98341      ISBN 0804432392

**Lewanski, Richard Casimir, 1918-.**                    5.8336
The Slavic literatures. Compiled by Richard C. Lewanski. Assisted by Lucia G. Lewanski and Mayo Deriugin. New York, New York Public Library, and F. Ungar Pub. Co. [1967] xiii, 630 p. 26 cm. (The Literatures of the world in English translation: a bibliography, v. 2) Prepared with the cooperation of the Slavonic Division of the New York Public Library. 1. Slavic literature — Translations into English — Bibliography. 2. English literature — Translations from Slavic languages — Bibliography. I. New York (City). Public Library. Slavonic Division. II. T.
Z7041.L59      016.8917      LC 65-23122

**Columbia College (Columbia University)**                    5.8337
A guide to Oriental classics / prepared by the staff of the Oriental Studies Program, Columbia College; and edited by Wm. Theodore De Bary and Ainslie T. Embree. — 2d ed. — New York: Columbia University Press, 1975. xi, 257 p.; 21 cm. (Companions to Asian studies.) 1. Oriental literature — Bibliography.

2. Oriental literature — Outlines, syllabi, etc. I. De Bary, William Theodore, 1918- II. Embree, Ainslie Thomas. III. T. IV. Series.
Z7046.C65 1975 PJ307     Z7046 C65 1975.     016.89     *LC* 74-14150
    *ISBN* 0231038917

**Mohanty, Jatindra Mohan, 1932-.**      **5.8338**
Indian literature in English translation: a bibliography / compiled by Jatindra Mohan Mohanty. — Mysore: Central Institute of Indian Languages, 1984. xii, 187 p.; 25 cm. (CIIL documentation series. 7) Includes index. 1. Indic literature — Translations into English — Bibliography. 2. English literature — Translations from Indic languages — Bibliography. I. Central Institute of Indian Languages. II. T. III. Series.
Z7049.I3 M63 1984 PK5461     891/3.4 19     *LC* 84-901888     Rs18.00

**Smith, H. Daniel, 1928-.**      **5.8339**
Reading the Rāmayāna: a bibliographic guide for students and college teachers: Indian variants on the Rāma–theme in English translations / by H. Daniel Smith. — Syracuse, N.Y., U.S.A.: Maxwell School of Citizenship and Public Affairs, Syracuse University, 1983. viii, 124 p.; 23 cm. — (Foreign and comparative studies. South Asian special publications; no. 4) 1. Indic literature — Translations into English — Bibliography. 2. English literature — Translations from Indic languages — Bibliography. 3. Rama (Hindu deity) in literature — Bibliography. I. T.
Z7049.I3 S6 1983 PK2978     016.2945/922 19     *LC* 83-25545     *ISBN* 0915984873

**Aggarwal, Narindar K.**      **5.8340**
A bibliography of studies on Hindi language and linguistics / compiled by Narindar K. Aggarwal. — Rev. and enl. ed. . — Gurgaon, Haryana: Indian Documentation Service, 1985. xxii, 321 p.; 23 cm. Includes index. 1. Hindi language — Bibliography. I. T.
Z7071.A34 1985 PK1931     016.491/43 19     *LC* 85-904349
    Rs195.00

**Teeuw, A.**      **5.8341**
A critical survey of studies on Malay and Bahasa Indonesia. [By] A. Teeuw with the assitance of H.W. Emanuels. 'S-Gravenhage M. Nijhoff 1961. 176p. (Bibliographical series (Koninklijk Instituut voor Taal-, Land- en Volkenkunde (Netherlands)) no. 5) 'Publication commissioned and financed by the Netherlands Institute for International Cultural Relations.' 1. Malay language — Bibliography 2. Malay language 3. Indonesian language — Bibliography 4. Indonesian language I. Emanuels, H. W., jt. author II. Nederlands Instituut voor Buitenlandse Culturele Betrekkingen III. T. IV. Series.
Z7078 T44

## Z7125–7129 Philosophy

**De George, Richard T.**      **5.8342**
The philosopher's guide to sources, research tools, professional life, and related fields / Richard T. De George. — Lawrence: Regents Press of Kansas, c1980. x, 261 p.; 24 cm. Includes index. 1. Philosophy — Bibliography. 2. Reference books — Philosophy — Bibliography. I. T.
Z7125.D445 B53     016.1 19     *LC* 79-91437     *ISBN* 0700602003

**Inada, Kenneth K.**      **5.8343**
Guide to Buddhist philosophy / Kenneth K. Inada, with contributions by Richard Chi, Shotaro Iida, and David Kalupahana. — Boston, Mass.: G.K. Hall, c1985. xxii, 226 p.; 25 cm. (Asian philosophies and religions resource guides.) Includes indexes. 1. Philosophy, Buddhist — Bibliography. 2. Buddhism — Doctrines — Bibliography. I. T. II. Series.
Z7128.B93 I53 1985 B162     016.181/043 19     *LC* 85-8530     *ISBN* 0816178992

**Kohl, Benjamin G.**      **5.8344**
Renaissance humanism, 1300–1550: a bibliography of materials in English / Benjamin G. Kohl. — New York: Garland Pub. Inc., 1985. xxii, 354 p.; 22 cm. (Garland reference library of the humanities; vol. 570) Includes indexes. 1. Humanism — Bibliography. 2. Renaissance — Bibliography. I. T.
Z7128.H9 K64 1985 B778     016.9401/9 19     *LC* 84-48760     *ISBN* 0824087739

**The Transcendentalists: a review of research and criticism /**      **5.8345**
**edited by Joel Myerson.**
New York: Modern Language Association of America, 1984. xix, 534 p.; 24 cm. — (Reviews of research / the Modern Language Association of America) Includes index. 1. Transcendentalism (New England) — Bibliography. I. Myerson, Joel. II. Modern Language Association of America.
Z7128.T7 T7 1984 B905     016.141/3/0973 19     *LC* 83-19442     *ISBN* 0873522605

**Chan, Wing-tsit, 1901-.**      **5.8346**
Chinese philosophy, 1949–1963; an annotated bibliography of Mainland China publications. — Honolulu: East-West Center Press, [c1967] xiv, 290 p.; 22 cm. 1. Philosophy, Chinese — Bibliography. I. T.
Z7129.C5 C48     016.18111     *LC* 65-20582

**Fu, Charles Wei-hsün.**      **5.8347**
Guide to Chinese philosophy / Charles Wei–hsun Fu and Wing–tsit Chan. — Boston: G. K. Hall, c1978. xxxv, 262 p.; 25 cm. (Asian philosophies and religions resource guides.) Includes index. 1. Philosophy, Chinese — Bibliography. I. Chan, Wing-tsit, 1901- joint author. II. T. III. Series.
Z7129.C5 F8 B126     016.181/11     *LC* 78-4670     *ISBN* 0816179018

**Redmond, Walter Bernard.**      **5.8348**
Bibliography of the philosophy in the Iberian colonies of America. The Hague, Nijhoff, 1972. xiv, 175 p. 24 cm. (International archives of the history of ideas, 51) 1. Philosophy, Latin American — Bibliography. 2. Philosophy — History — Latin America — Bibliography. I. T.
Z7129.L35 R43     *LC* 72-368110     *ISBN* 9024711908

## Z7141–7144 Physics

**Information sources in physics / editor, Dennis F. Shaw.**      **5.8349**
2d ed. — London; Boston: Butterworths, 1985. xii, 456 p.; 22 cm. (Butterworths guides to information sources.) Rev. enl. ed. of: Use of physics literature. 1975. Includes indexes. 1. Physics — Bibliography I. Shaw, Dennis F. II. Use of physics literature. III. Series.
Z7141.I54 1985 QC21.2     016.53 19     *LC* 84-17482     *ISBN* 0408014741

## Z7161–7163 Political and Social Sciences: General

**Li, Tze-chung, 1927-.**      **5.8350**
Social science reference sources: a practical guide / Tze–chung Li. — Westport, Conn.: Greenwood Press, 1980. xvi, 315 p.; 24 cm. — (Contributions in librarianship and information science. no. 30 0084-9243) Includes indexes. 1. Social sciences — Bibliography. 2. Reference books — Social sciences — Bibliography. 3. Bibliography — Bibliography — Social sciences. I. T. II. Series.
Z7161.A1 L5 H61     016.3     *LC* 79-54052     *ISBN* 0313214735

**McInnis, Raymond G.**      **5.8351**
Social science research handbook / Raymond G. McInnis, James W. Scott. — New York: Barnes & Noble Books, 1975, c1974. xix, 395 p.; 21 cm. (The Barnes & Noble outline series; COS 140) 1. Reference books — Social sciences — Bibliography. 2. Reference books — Area studies — Bibliography. 3. Social sciences — Bibliography. I. Scott, James William, 1925- joint author. II. T.
Z7161.A1 M3 1975 H51     016.3     *LC* 73-21854     *ISBN* 0064601404

**Goehlert, Robert, 1948-.**      **5.8352**
Policy analysis and management: a bibliography / Robert U. Goehlert and Fenton S. Martin. — Santa Barbara, Calif.: ABC-Clio Information Services, c1985. xiii, 398 p.; 29 cm. Includes indexes. 1. Policy sciences — Bibliography I. Martin, Fenton S. II. T.
Z7161.G587 1985 H97     016.3616/1 19     *LC* 84-16829     *ISBN* 087436387X

**Holler, Frederick L.**      **5.8353**
Information sources of political science / Frederick L. Holler. — 4th ed. — Santa Barbara, Calif.: ABC-Clio, c1986. xvii, 417 p.; 29 cm. Includes indexes. 1. Political science — Bibliography I. T.
Z7161.H64 1986 JA71     016.32 19     *LC* 85-11279     *ISBN* 0874363756

**Sources of information in the social sciences: a guide to the**      **5.8354**
**literature / William H. Webb ... [et al.].**
3rd ed. — Chicago: American Library Association, 1986. x, 777 p.; 27 cm. Rev. ed. of: Sources of information in the social sciences / Carl M. White and associates. 2nd ed. 1973. Includes index. 1. Social sciences — Bibliography. I. Webb, William H., 1935- II. Beals, Alan R. III. White, Carl Milton, 1903- Sources of information in the social sciences.
Z7161.S666 1986 H61     016.3 19     *LC* 84-20494     *ISBN* 083890405X

**Unity in diversity: an index to the publications of conservative**      **5.8355**
**and libertarian institutions / the New American Foundation;**
**Carol L. Birch, editor.**
Metuchen, N.J.: Scarecrow Press, 1983. xviii, 263 p.; 23 cm. Includes index. 1. Social sciences — Bibliography. I. Birch, Carol L. II. New American Foundation.
Z7161.U63 1983 H61     016.3 19     *LC* 82-20552     *ISBN* 0810815990

**Public Affairs Information Service.**      **5.8356**
Bulletin of the Public Affairs Information Service; annual cumulation. 1st-53rd; 1915-67. New York [etc.] Public Affairs Information Service. 53 v. 27 cm. Annual. 1. Social sciences — Bibliography — Periodicals. 2. Political science — Bibliography — Periodicals. 3. Legislation — Bibliography — Periodicals. 4. Economics — Bibliography — Periodicals. I. H.W. Wilson Company. II. T.
Z7163.P9     016.3     *LC* 16-920

## Z7164 Special Topics, A–Z

### Z7164 A–B

**American public administration: a bibliographical guide to the**    **5.8357**
**literature / Gerald E. Caiden ... [et al.]; preface by Warren**
**Bennis.**
New York: Garland Pub., 1983. xvii, 201 p.; 23 cm. — (Public affairs and
administration series. 3) (Garland reference library of social science; vol. 169)
Includes indexes. 1. Public administration — Bibliography. 2. Public
administration — United States — Bibliography. 3. Bibliography —
Bibliography — Public administration. 4. United States — Politics and
government — Bibliography. I. Caiden, Gerald E. II. Series.
Z7164.A2 A53 1983 JF1351    016.35/0000973 19    LC 82-49151
   ISBN 0824091523

**Czerniak, Robert J.**        **5.8358**
State atlases: a bibliography / Robert J. Czerniak and Gail Perrone. —
Monticello, Ill.: Vance Bibliographies, 1983. 19 p. — (Public administration
series—bibliography. P-1213) Cover title. 1. United States — Maps —
Bibliography. I. Perrone, Gail. II. T. III. Series.
Z7164.A2 P818 P-1213    ISBN 0880665238

### Z7164 C

**Chalfant, H. Paul, 1929-.**        **5.8359**
Sociology of poverty in the United States: an annotated bibliography / compiled
by H. Paul Chalfant. — Westport, Conn.: Greenwood Press, 1985. xxiii, 187 p.;
25 cm. (Bibliographies and indexes in sociology. 0742-6895; no. 3) Includes
index. 1. Poor — United States — Bibliography. 2. Poverty — Bibliography
I. T. II. Series.
Z7164.C4 C44 1985 HC110.P6    016.3055/69/0973 19    LC 84-25191
   ISBN 0313239290

**Social welfare in America: an annotated bibliography / edited**    **5.8360**
**by Walter I. Trattner and W. Andrew Achenbaum.**
Westport, Conn.: Greenwood Press, 1983. xxxiii, 324 p.; 25 cm. Includes
indexes. 1. Public welfare — United States — Bibliography. 2. Charities —
United States — Bibliography. 3. United States — Social conditions —
Bibliography. I. Trattner, Walter I. II. Achenbaum, W. Andrew.
Z7164.C4 S6 1983 HV91    016.361/973 19    LC 83-10855    ISBN
0313230021

**Dreyer, Sharon Spredemann.**        **5.8361**
The bookfinder: a guide to children's literature about the needs and problems of
youth aged 2–15 / by Sharon Spredemann Dreyer. — Circle Pines, Minn.:
American Guidance Service, c1977-<c1985 >. v. <[1]-3 >; 29 cm. Cover
title, v. [1]: The book finder. Vol. 2 has subtitle: Annotations of books published
1975 through 1978. Vol. 3 has subtitle: Annotations of books published 1979
through 1982: a guide to children's literature about the needs and problems of
youth aged 2 and up. Vol. 1-2 issued in a split-page format. Includes indexes.
Vol. 3 includes cumulative subject index. 1. Children — Juvenile literature —
Bibliography — Collected works. 2. Family — Juvenile literature —
Bibliography — Collected works. I. T. II. Title: Book finder.
Z7164.C5 D74 HQ767.9    011/.62 19    LC 78-105919    ISBN
0913476455

**Kemmer, Elizabeth Jane.**        **5.8362**
Violence in the family: an annotated bibliography / Elizabeth Kemmer. — New
York: Garland Pub., 1984. xii, 192 p.; 22 cm. — (Garland reference library of
social science. v. 182) Includes indexes. 1. Family violence — Bibliography.
I. T. II. Series.
Z7164.C5 K46 1984 HV741    016.3628/2 19    LC 83-48198    ISBN
082409090X

**Wells, Dorothy Pearl, 1910-.**        **5.8363**
Child abuse, an annotated bibliography / compiled by Dorothy P. Wells, in
consultation with Charles R. Carroll. — Metuchen, N.J.: Scarecrow Press,
1980. viii, 450 p.; 23 cm. Includes index. 1. Child abuse — United States —
Bibliography. 2. Child abuse — Law and legislation — United States —
Bibliography. 3. Child abuse — Services — United States. I. T.
Z7164.C5 W37 HV741    016.3627/3 19    LC 79-21641    ISBN
0810812649

**Woodbury, Marda.**        **5.8364**
Childhood information resources / Marda Woodbury. — Arlington, Va.:
Information Resources Press, 1985. xiv, 593 p.; 24 cm. Includes index.
1. Reference books — Children. 2. Children — Bibliography. I. T.
Z7164.C5 W58 1985 HQ767.9    016.3052/3 19    LC 84-80534
   ISBN 087815051X

**Bowman, James S., 1945-.**        **5.8365**
Professional dissent: an annotated bibliography and resource guide / James S.
Bowman, Frederick A. Elliston, Paula Lockhart. — New York: Garland Pub.,
1984. xii, 322 p.; 23 cm. — (Public affairs and administration series. 2) (Garland
reference library of social science. v. 128) Includes index. 1. Whistle blowing —
Bibliography. 2. Professional ethics — Bibliography. I. Elliston, Frederick.
II. Lockhart, Paula. III. T. IV. Series. V. Series: Garland reference library of
social science. v. 128
Z7164.C81 B763 1984 HD60    016.174 19    LC 82-48768    ISBN
0824092171

**Business periodicals index.**        • **5.8366**
v. 1- Jan. 1958/June 1959-. New York, H. W. Wilson Co. v. 27 cm. Annual.
Cumulation of the monthly publication. 1. Business — Periodicals — Indexes.
2. Industry — Periodicals — Indexes. I. H.W. Wilson Company.
Z7164.C81 B983    016.6505    LC 58-12645

**Business index (Quarterly).**        **5.8367**
Business index [microform]. — 01/79-12/81-    . — [Menlo Park, Calif.:
Information Access Corp.], c1983-. microfiches; 11 x 15 cm. Quarterly.
Quarterly cumulation on fiche of a monthly microfilm publication. Title from
eye-readable header. I. Information Access Corporation. II. T.
Z7164.C81B9x    LC sc 84-1316

**Daniells, Lorna M.**        **5.8368**
Business information sources / Lorna M. Daniells. — Rev. ed. — Berkeley:
University of California Press, c1985. xvi, 673 p.; 24 cm. Includes index.
1. Business — Bibliography 2. Management — Bibliography I. T.
Z7164.C81 D16 1985 HF5351    016.33 19    LC 84-2546    ISBN
0520053354

**Guide to special issues and indexes of periodicals / Miriam**    **5.8369**
**Uhlan, editor.**
3rd ed. — New York: Special Libraries Association, c1985. vi, 160 p.; 28 cm.
Includes index. 1. Business — Periodicals — Bibliography. 2. Business —
Periodicals — Indexes — Bibliography. 3. Industry — Periodicals —
Bibliography. 4. Industry — Periodicals — Indexes — Bibliography.
5. Commerce — Periodicals — Bibliography. 6. Commerce — Periodicals —
Bibliography. 7. Periodicals — Special numbers — Bibliography.
I. Uhlan, Miriam.
Z7164.C81 G85 1985 HF5351    016.051 19    LC 85-2351    ISBN
0871112639

### Z7164 D–M

**Schulze, Suzanne.**        **5.8370**
Population information in nineteenth century census volumes / by Suzanne
Schulze. — Phoenix, AZ: Oryx Press, 1983. ix, 446 p.: maps; 29 cm. Continued
by: Population information in twentieth century census volumes, 1900-1940.
1. United States — Census — Indexes. 2. United States — Population —
History — 19th century — Sources — Indexes. I. T.
Z7164.D3 S44 1983 HA214    304.6/0973 19    LC 83-17380    ISBN
0897741226

**Applegath, John.**        **5.8371**
Human economy: a bibliography / compiled and edited by John Applegath;
assisted by Vivian Applegath, Michael Marien, Jeanne Kocsis; production:
Avrum Goodblatt, Mara Loft, Gail Copen. — Amherst, Ma.: Human Economy
Center, c1981-. v. 1. Economics — Psychological aspects — Bibliography.
2. Economics — Bibliography 3. Economics — Moral and religious aspects —
Bibliography. I. Applegath, Vivian. II. Marien, Michael. III. Kocsis, Jeanne.
IV. T.
Z7164.E2A6x

**Economics selections: an international bibliography: cumulative**    **5.8372**
**bibliography, series I and II, 1963–1970.**
New York: Gordon and Breach Science Publishers, 1975 (c1974). 393 p.; 31
cm. 1. Economics — Bibliography 2. Economic history — Bibliography.
Z7164.E2 E256 HB171    Z7164E2 E326.    016.33    LC 74-78435
   ISBN 0677010702

**Index of economic journals / prepared under the auspices of the**    • **5.8373**
**American Economic Association.**
Vol. 1 (1886-1924)-v. 7 (1964-1965). — Homewood, Ill.: R.D. Irwin, Inc. v.; 27
cm. Has also supplement: Index of economic articles in collective volumes.
1. Economics — Periodicals — Indexes — Periodicals. I. American Economic
Association.
Z7164.E2 I48 HB1    016.33 19    LC 61-8020

**International bibliography of economics = Bibliographie**    **5.8374**
**internationale de science économique.**
v.1- 1952-. [Paris] UNESCO. v. Annual. Vols. for 1952-59 issued in series,
Documentation in the social sciences. 1. Economics — Bibliography
I. Fondation nationale des sciences politiques. II. International Economic
Association. III. International Committee for Social Sciences Documentation.
IV. Unesco. V. Title: Bibliographie internationale de science économique.
Z7164.E2 I 58    LC 55-2317

**Georgi, Charlotte.**                                                      **5.8375**
Fund-raising, grants, and foundations: a comprehensive bibliography /
Charlotte Georgi and Terry Fate. — Littleton, Colo.: Libraries Unlimited,
1985. x, 194 p.; 25 cm. Includes index. 1. Fund raising — United States —
Bibliography. I. Fate, Terry. II. T.
Z7164.F5 G46 1985 HG177      016.6581/522 19      *LC* 84-21821
    *ISBN* 0872874419

**Filby, P. William, 1911-.**                                              **5.8376**
Passenger and immigration lists bibliography, 1538–1900: being a guide to
published lists of arrivals in the United States and Canada / by William Filby.
— Detroit: Gale Research Co., c1981. 195 p. Includes index. 1. Ships —
Passenger lists — Bibliography. 2. Registers of births, etc — United States —
Bibliography. 3. United States — Genealogy — Bibliography. 4. United States
— Emigration and immigration — Bibliography. 5. United States — History
— Sources — Bibliography. I. Filby, P. William, 1911- Passenger and
immigration lists bibliography, 1538-1900. II. T.
Z7164.I3 F55      016.929/373 19      *LC* 84-13702      *ISBN* 0810316447

**Brooks, Alexander D.**                                                    • **5.8377**
Civil rights and liberties in the United States, an annotated bibliography. With a
selected list of fiction and audio–visual materials collected by Albert A.
Alexander and Virginia H. Ellison. New York, Civil Liberties Educational
Foundation, c1962. 151 p. 23 cm. 1. Civil rights — United States —
Bibliography. 2. United States — Race relations — Bibliography. I. T.
Z7164.L6 B7      016.32340973      *LC* 62-51084

**Human rights in Latin America, 1964–1980: a selective**                  **5.8378**
**annotated bibliography / compiled and edited by the Hispanic**
**Division.**
Washington: Library of Congress: For sale by the Supt. of Docs., U.S. G.P.O.,
1983. x, 257 p.; 27 cm. 'Compiled in cooperation with the Latin American
Studies Association'—T.p. verso. Includes index. 1. Civil rights — Latin
America — Bibliography. 2. Political rights — Latin America —
Bibliography. I. Library of Congress. Hispanic Division. II. Latin American
Studies Association.
Z7164.L6 H85 1983 JC599.L3      016.3234/098 19      *LC* 82-600339
    *ISBN* 0844404152

**History of the family and kinship: a select international**              **5.8379**
**bibliography / edited by Gerald L. Soliday, with Tamara K.**
**Hareven, Richard T. Vann, and Robert Wheaton, associate**
**editors; a project of the Journal of family history, the National**
**Council on Family Relations.**
Millwood, N.Y.: Kraus-International Publications, c1980. xxi, 410 p.; 26 cm.
Includes index. 1. Family — History — Bibliography. 2. Kinship — History
— Bibliography. I. Soliday, Gerald Lyman. II. Journal of family history.
Z7164.M2 H57 HQ503      016.3068/09      *LC* 80-11782      *ISBN*
0527844519

**August, Eugene R., 1935-.**                                              **5.8380**
Men's studies: a selected and annotated interdisciplinary bibliography / Eugene
R. August. — Littleton, Colo.: Libraries Unlimited, 1985. xvii, 215 p.; 25 cm.
Includes indexes. 1. Men — Bibliography. I. T.
Z7164.M49 A84 1985 HQ1090      016.3053/1 19      *LC* 84-28894
    *ISBN* 0872874818

## Z7164 N–R

**Andrews, Theodora.**                                                     **5.8381**
A bibliography of drug abuse, including alcohol and tobacco / Theodora
Andrews. — Littleton, Colo.: Libraries Unlimited, 1977. 306 p.; 24 cm.
Includes indexes. 1. Drug abuse — Bibliography. 2. Alcoholism —
Bibliography. 3. Tobacco habit — Bibliography. I. T.
Z7164.N17 A52 HV5801      016.3622/9      *LC* 77-22606      *ISBN*
0872871495

**Edwards, Willie M.**                                                     **5.8382**
Gerontology, a cross–national core list of significant works / Willie M.
Edwards and Frances Flynn; with M. Doreen E. Fraser and Robert Slater and
an international panel of consultants; historical perspectives by Lola Wilson,
Canada; Mark Abrams, United Kingdom; Nathan W. Shock, United States. —
New ed. — Ann Arbor, Mich.: Institute of Gerontology, The University of
Michigan c1982. xix, 365 p.; 24 cm. — Includes indexes. 1. Gerontology —
Bibliography I. Flynn, Frances. II. T. III. Title: Gerontology, a core list of
significant works.
Z7164.O4 E38 HQ1061      Z7164.O4 E38 1982.      016.3626/042
    *ISBN*

**Harris, Diana K.**                                                       **5.8383**
The sociology of aging: an annotated bibliography and sourcebook / Diana K.
Harris. — New York: Garland Pub., 1985. xiii, 283 p.; 23 cm. (Garland
bibliographies in sociology; vol. 5) (Garland reference library of social science;

vol. 206) Includes index. 1. Gerontology — Bibliography 2. Aged —
Bibliography. 3. Aging — Bibliography. I. T.
Z7164.O4 H374 1985 HQ1061      016.3052/6 19      *LC* 83-48220
    *ISBN* 0824090462

**Franklin, Jerome L.**                                                    **5.8384**
Human resource development in the organization: a guide to information
sources / Jerome L. Franklin. — Detroit: Gale Research Co., 1978, [c1977]. xi,
175 p.; 23 cm. — (Management information guide. 35) Includes indexes.
1. Organizational change — Bibliography. 2. Management — Bibliography
I. T. II. Series.
Z7164.O7 F72      016.6584/06      *LC* 76-28289      *ISBN* 0810308355

**American third parties since the Civil War: an annotated**              **5.8385**
**bibliography / D. Stephen Rockwood ... [et al.].**
New York: Garland Pub., 1985. vii, 177 p.; 23 cm. (Garland reference library of
social science; vol. 227) Includes indexes. 1. Third parties (United States
politics) — History — Bibliography. 2. United States — Politics and
government — 1865-1900 — Bibliography. 3. United States — Politics and
government — 20th century — Bibliography. I. Rockwood, D. Stephen.
Z7164.P8 A54 1985 JK2261      016.324273/09 19      *LC* 83-49298
    *ISBN* 0824089707

**The Democratic and Republican Parties in America: a historical**        **5.8386**
**bibliography.**
Santa Barbara, Calif.: ABC-Clio Information Services, c1984. xii, 290 p.; 24 cm.
(ABC-Clio research guides. 7) Includes indexes. 1. Democratic Party (U.S.) —
History — Bibliography. 2. Republican Party (U.S.: 1854- ) — History —
Bibliography. I. ABC-Clio Information Services. II. Series.
Z7164.P8 D45 1984 JK2261      016.324273 19      *LC* 83-12230      *ISBN*
0874363640

**Byerly, Greg, 1949-.**                                                   **5.8387**
Pornography, the conflict over sexually explicit materials in the United States:
an annotated bibliography / Greg Byerly, Rick Rubin. — New York: Garland
Pub., 1980. ix, 152 p.; 23 cm. — (Garland reference library of social science; v.
64) Includes indexes. 1. Pornography — Social aspects — United States —
Bibliography. 2. Pornography — United States — Psychological aspects —
Bibliography. 3. Pornography — Moral and religious aspects — Bibliography.
4. Obscenity (Law) — United States. I. Rubin, Rick, 1949- joint author. II. T.
Z7164.P84 B93 HQ471      016.3634/7      *LC* 80-14336      *ISBN*
0824095146

**Hoy, Suellen M.**                                                        **5.8388**
Public works history in the United States: a guide to the literature / by the
Public Works Historical Society; compiled and edited by Suellen M. Hoy and
Michael C. Robinson; Rita C. Lynch, research associate. — Nashville, Tenn.:
American Association for State and Local History, c1982. x, 477 p.; 24 cm. 'A
co-operative project of the Public Works Historical Society and the American
Association for State and Local History'—T.p. verso. Includes index. 1. United
States — Public works — History — Bibliography. I. Robinson, Michael C.
II. American Association for State and Local History. III. Public Works
Historical Society. IV. T.
Z7164.P97 H68 1982 HD3885      016.363/0973 19      *LC* 81-19114
    *ISBN* 0910050635

## Z7164 S–Z

**Parker, William, 1921-.**                                                **5.8389**
Homosexuality: a selective bibliography of over 3,000 items. Metuchen, N.J.,
Scarecrow Press, 1971. viii, 323 p. 22 cm. 1. Homosexuality — Bibliography.
I. T.
Z7164.S42 P35      016.30141/57      *LC* 71-163430      *ISBN* 0810804255

**Smith, John David, 1949-.**                                             **5.8390**
Black slavery in the Americas: an interdisciplinary bibliography, 1865–1980 /
compiled by John David Smith; foreword by Stanley L. Engerman. —
Westport, Conn.: Greenwood Press, 1982. 2 v. (xix, 1847 p.); 24 cm. Includes
indexes. 1. Slavery — America — Bibliography. 2. Slavery — United States —
Bibliography. I. T.
Z7164.S6 S63 1982 HT1049      016.306/362/0973 19      *LC* 82-11736
    *ISBN* 0313231184

**Filler, Louis, 1912-.**                                                  **5.8391**
Progressivism and muckraking / Louis Filler. — New York: R. R. Bowker Co.,
1976. xiv, 200 p.; 24 cm. — (Bibliographic guides for contemporary collections)
Includes index. 1. Social reformers — United States — Bibliography. 2. Social
problems — Bibliography. 3. Progressivism (United States politics) 4. United
States — Social conditions — Bibliography. I. T.
Z7164.S66 F54 HN64      016.3091/73      *LC* 76-950      *ISBN*
0835208753

**Social reform and reaction in America: an annotated**      **5.8392**
**bibliography.**
Santa Barbara, Calif.: ABC-Clio Information Services, c1984. viii, 375 p.; 29
cm. — (Clio bibliography series. no. 13) Includes indexes. 1. United States —
Social conditions — Bibliography. 2. Canada — Social conditions —
Bibliography. 3. United States — Economic conditions — Bibliography.
4. Canada — Economic conditions — Bibliography. I. ABC-Clio Information
Services. II. Series.
Z7164.S66 S543 1984 HN65      016.306/0973 19      LC 82-24294
    ISBN 087436048X

**Lakos, Amos, 1946-.**      **5.8393**
International terrorism bibliography / Amos Lakos. — Boulder: Westview
Press, 1986. p. cm. — (Westview special studies in national and international
terrorism.) Includes index. 1. Terrorism — Bibliography. 2. Terrorism —
Prevention — Bibliography. I. T. II. Series.
Z7164.T3 L34 1986 HV6431      016.3633/2 19      LC 86-1719      ISBN
0813371570

**Hoover, Dwight W., 1926-.**      **5.8394**
Cities / by Dwight W. Hoover. — New York: Bowker, 1976. x, 231 p.; 24 cm.
(Bibliographic guides for contemporary collections) Includes indexes. 1. Cities
and towns — United States — Bibliography. I. T.
Z7164.U7 H66 HT123      016.30136/3/0973      LC 76-2601      ISBN
0835207900

## Z7165 Special Countries, A–Z

### Z7165 A–T

**Canadian business and economics: a guide to sources of**      **5.8395**
**information / Barbara E. Brown, editor = Economique et**
**commerce au Canada: sources d'information / Barbara E.**
**Brown, rédactrice.**
Ottawa: Canadian Library Association, c1984. xxxiv, 469 p.; 26 cm. English
and French. Includes indexes. 1. Canada — Economic conditions —
Bibliography. 2. Canada — Commerce — Bibliography. 3. Canada —
Industries — Bibliography. I. Brown, Barbara E. II. Title: Economique et
commerce au Canada.
Z7165.C2 C225 1984 HC113      016.330971 19      LC 84-229678
    ISBN 0888021615

**Clement, Wallace.**      **5.8396**
A practical guide to Canadian political economy / Wallace Clement & Daniel
Drache. — Toronto: J. Lorimer, 1978. vi, 183 p.; 23 cm. Includes index.
1. Canada — Economic conditions — Bibliography. I. Drache, Daniel, 1941-
joint author. II. T.
Z7165.C2 C58 HC115      016.330971 19      LC 79-307248      ISBN
0888621841

**Dick, Trevor J. O.**      **5.8397**
Economic history of Canada: a guide to information sources / Trevor J. O.
Dick. — Detroit: Gale Research Co., 1978 (c1975). xiii, 174 p.; 23 cm. —
(Economics information guide series; v. 9) (Gale information guide library)
Includes indexes. 1. Canada — Economic conditions — Bibliography. I. T.
Z7165.C2 D5 HC113      016.3309/71      LC 73-17571      ISBN
0810312921

**Modern Chinese society; an analytical bibliography.**      **5.8398**
Stanford, Calif., Stanford University Press, 1973. 3 v. maps. 29 cm. Title also in
Chinese: Chin tai Chung-kuo she hui yen chiu. Sponsored by the Subcommittee
on Research on Chinese Society, Joint Committee on Contemporary China.
Vol. 1. Assisted by D.B. Honig and E.A. Wincklaer; v. 2-3. Assisted by John R.
Ziemer. 1. China — Social conditions — Bibliography. 2. China — Economic
conditions — Bibliography. 3. China — Politics and government —
Bibliography. I. Skinner, G. William (George William), 1925- ed. II. Hsieh,
Winston, ed. III. Tomita, Shigeaki, ed. IV. Joint Committee on Contemporary
China. Subcommittee on Chinese Society. V. Title: Chin tai Chung-kuo she hui
yen chiu. VI. Title: Kindai Chūgoku shakai kenkyū.
Z7165.C6 M62      016.3091/51      LC 70-130831      ISBN 0804707510

**Collester, J. Bryan.**      **5.8399**
The European communities: a guide to information sources / J. Bryan
Collester. — Detroit: Gale Research Co., c1979. xxxii, 265 p.; 23 cm. —
(International relations information guide series; v. 9) (Gale information guide
library) Includes indexes. 1. European Economic Community — Bibliography
2. European cooperation — Bibliography. 3. European Economic Community
countries — Foreign relations — Bibliography. I. T.
Z7165.E8 C58 JN94.A91      016.382/9142      LC 73-17506      ISBN
0810313227

**Jeffries, John.**      **5.8400**
A guide to the official publications of the European Communities / John
Jeffries. — 2nd ed. — London: Mansell; New York: H.W. Wilson [distributor],
1981. xiv, 318 p.; 23 cm. Includes index. 1. European communities —

Bibliography. 2. European Economic Community countries — Bibliography.
I. T.
Z7165.E8 J44 1981b JN18      015.4 19      LC 82-108954      ISBN
0720115906

**The Kibbutz: a bibliography of scientific and professional**      **5.8401**
**publications in English / by Shimon Shur ... [et al.].**
Darby, Pa.: Norwood Editions, 1981. ix, 103 p.; 26 cm. (Kibbutz, communal
society, and alternative social policy series. v. 4) Includes index. 1. Kibbutzim
— Bibliography. I. Shur, Shimon, 1921- II. Series.
Z7165.I7 K53 HX742.2.A3      016.3077 19      LC 81-16849      ISBN
0848264029

**Latin America: a guide to economic history, 1830–1930 /**      **5.8402**
[contributors, Carmen Cariola ... et al.]; Roberto Cortés Conde
& Stanley J. Stein, editors; Jiřina Rybáček-Mlýnková, editorial
assistant; sponsored by the Joint Committee on Latin American
Studies of the American Council of Learned Societies and the
Social Science Research Council and by the Consejo
Latinoamericano de Ciencias Sociales.
Berkeley: University of California Press, 1977. xviii, 685 p.; 29 cm. 'Published
in cooperation with the Latin American Center, University of California, Los
Angeles.' Spanish, English or Portuguese. Includes indexes. 1. Latin America
— Economic conditions — Bibliography. I. Cariola Sutter, Carmen. II. Cortés
Conde, Roberto. III. Stein, Stanley J. IV. Rybáček-Mlýnková, Jiřina. V. Joint
Committee on Latin American Studies. VI. Consejo Latinoamericano de
Ciencias Sociales. VII. University of California, Los Angeles. Latin American
Center.
Z7165.L3 L32 HC125      016.3309/8      LC 74-30534      ISBN
0520029569

**Sable, Martin Howard.**      **5.8403**
Latin American urbanization: a guide to the literature, organizations, and
personnel / by Martin H. Sable. — Metuchen, N.J.: Scarecrow Press, 1971.
1077 p.; 22 cm. 1. Cities and towns — Latin America — Bibliography.
2. Urbanization — Latin America — Bibliography. I. T.
Z7165.L3 S28      016.3013/6/098      LC 74-145643      ISBN 0810803542

**Kazmer, Daniel R.**      **5.8404**
Russian economic history: a guide to information sources / Daniel R. Kazmer,
and Vera Kazmer. — Detroit: Gale Research Co., c1977. x, 520 p.; 22 cm.
(Economics information guide series; v. 4) (Gale information guide library)
Includes indexes. 1. Soviet Union — Economic conditions — Bibliography.
I. Kazmer, Vera, joint author. II. T.
Z7165.R9 K34 HC333      016.3309/47      LC 73-17588      ISBN
0810313049

### Z7165 U–Z

**Buenker, John D.**      **5.8405**
Immigration and ethnicity: a guide to information sources / John D. Buenker,
Nicholas C. Burckel; pref. by Rudolph J. Vecoli. — Detroit: Gale Research Co.,
c1977. xii, 305 p.; 23 cm. — (American Government and history information
guide series; v. 1) (Gale information guide library) Includes indexes.
1. Ethnicity — United States — Bibliography. 2. United States — Emigration
and immigration — Bibliography. 3. United States — Foreign population —
Bibliography. I. Burckel, Nicholas C. joint author. II. T. III. Series.
Z7165.U5 B83 JV6465      016.32573      LC 74-11515      ISBN
0810312026

**The Great Depression: a historical bibliography.**      **5.8406**
Santa Barbara, Calif.: ABC-Clio Information Services, c1984. xii, 260 p.; 24 cm.
— (ABC-Clio research guides. 4) Includes index. 1. Depressions — 1929 —
United States — Bibliography. 2. United States — Economic conditions —
1918-1945 — Bibliography. 3. United States — Economic policy — 1933-1945
— Bibliography. 4. United States — Social conditions — 1933-1945 —
Bibliography. I. ABC-Clio Information Services. II. Series.
Z7165.U5 G73 1984 HC106.3      016.3385/42 19      LC 83-12234
    ISBN 0874363616

**Greenstein, Fred I.**      **5.8407**
Evolution of the modern presidency: a bibliographical survey / Fred I.
Greenstein, Larry Berman, Alvin S. Felzenberg, with Doris Lidtke. —
Washington: American Enterprise Institute for Public Policy Research, c1977.
xv, [369] p.; 28 cm. — (Studies in political and social processes.) (AEI studies;
153) Includes index. 1. Presidents — United States — Bibliography. 2. United
States — Politics and government — 1933-1945 — Bibliography. 3. United
States — Politics and government — 1945- — Bibliography. I. Berman, Larry.
joint author. II. Felzenberg, Alvin S. joint author. III. T. IV. Series.
Z7165.U5 G74 JK511      016.35303/13      LC 77-8022      ISBN
0844732516

**Index to current urban documents.**      **5.8408**
v. 1- July/Oct. 1972-. Westport, Conn., Greenwood Press. v. 26 cm. Quarterly.
1. Cities and towns — United States — Indexes — Periodicals.
Z7165.U5 I654      016.30136/0973      LC 73-641453

**Lovett, Robert Woodberry.**      • **5.8409**
American economic and business history information sources; an annotated bibliography of recent works pertaining to economic, business, agricultural, and labor history and the history of science and technology for the United States and Canada [by] Robert W. Lovett. — Detroit: Gale Research Co., [1971] 323 p.; 23 cm. — (Management information guide. 23) 1. U.S. — Economic conditions — Bibliography. 2. U.S. — Industries — Bibliography. I. T. II. Series.
Z7165.U5 L66     016.330973     *LC* 78-137573

**Miller, Albert Jay.**      **5.8410**
Confrontation, conflict, and dissent: a bibliography of a decade of controversy, 1960–1970. — Metuchen, N.J.: Scarecrow Press, 1972. 567 p.; 22 cm. 1. Dissenters — United States — Bibliography. 2. United States — Social conditions — 1960- — Bibliography. I. T.
Z7165.U5 M53     016.3091/73/092     *LC* 78-189440     *ISBN* 0810804905

**Tingley, Donald Fred, 1922-.**      **5.8411**
Social history of the United States: a guide to information sources / Donald F. Tingley. — Detroit: Gale Research Co., c1979. x, 260 p.; 23 cm. — (American Government and history information guide series; v. 3) (Gale information guide library) Includes indexes. 1. United States — Social conditions — Bibliography. 2. United States — Economic conditions — Bibliography. 3. United States — History — Bibliography. I. T. II. Series.
Z7165.U5 T5 HN57     016.3091/73     *LC* 78-13196     *ISBN* 0810313669

## Z7191 Proverbs

**Mieder, Wolfgang.**      **5.8412**
International proverb scholarship: an annotated bibliography / Wolfgang Mieder. — New York: Garland Pub., 1982. xviii, 613 p.; 23 cm. — (Garland folklore bibliographies. v. 3) (Garland reference library of the humanities. v. 342) Includes indexes. 1. Proverbs — History and criticism — Bibliography. I. T. II. Series. III. Series: Garland reference library of the humanities. v. 342
Z7191.M543 1982 PN6401     016.398/9 19     *LC* 82-11807     *ISBN* 0824092627

## Z7201–7205 Psychology

**McInnis, Raymond G.**      **5.8413**
Research guide for psychology / Raymond G. McInnis. — Westport, Conn.: Greenwood Press, 1982. xxvi, 604 p. — (Reference sources for the social sciences and humanities. ISSN 0730-33; no.1) Includes index. 1. Psychology — Bibliography. 2. Reference books — Psychology — Bibliography. 3. Psychology — Abstracting and indexing. I. T. II. Series.
Z7201 M35     *LC* 81-1377     *ISBN* 0313213992

**Watson, Robert Irving, 1909-.**      **5.8414**
Eminent contributors to psychology / Robert I. Watson, Sr., editor. — New York: Springer Pub. Co., 1975 (c1974) 470 p.; 26 cm. 1. Psychology — Bibliography. I. T.
Z7201.W37     016.15     *LC* 73-88108     *ISBN* 0826114504

**Watson, Robert Irving, 1909-.**      **5.8415**
The history of psychology and the behavioral sciences: a bibliographic guide / Robert I. Watson, Sr. — New York: Springer Pub. Co., c1978. ix, 241 p.; 24 cm. 1. Psychology — History — Bibliography. 2. Biology — History — Bibliography. 3. Psychiatry — History — Bibliography. 4. Social sciences — History — Bibliography. I. T.
Z7201.W373 BF81     016.15/09     *LC* 77-17371     *ISBN* 0826120806

**Butler, Francine.**      **5.8416**
Biofeedback: a survey of the literature / Francine Butler. — New York: IFI/ Plenum, c1978. xi, 340 p.; 24 cm. Includes index. 1. Biofeedback training — Bibliography. I. T.
Z7204.B56 B87 BF319.5.B5     016.1521/88     *LC* 78-6159     *ISBN* 0306651734

## Z7401–7409 Science: General

**Chen, Ching-chih, 1937-.**      **5.8417**
Scientific and technical information sources / Ching–chih Chen. — 2nd ed. — Cambridge, Mass.: MIT Press, c1986. 1 v. Includes indexes. 1. Science — Bibliography 2. Engineering — Bibliography. 3. Technology — Bibliography I. T.
Z7401.C48 1986 Q158.5     016.5 19     *LC* 86-7310     *ISBN* 0262031205

**General science index.**      **5.8418**
1- 1978/79-. New York, H. W. Wilson Co. v. 27 cm. Annual. Cumulation of the monthly publication. Period covered by index ends May 31. 1. Science — Periodicals — Indexes — Periodicals. I. H.W. Wilson Company.
Z7401.G46     016.5     *LC* 80-643165

**Malinowsky, H. Robert (Harold Robert), 1933-.**      **5.8419**
Science and engineering literature: a guide to reference sources / H. Robert Malinowsky, Jeanne M. Richardson. — 3d ed. — Littleton, Colo.: Libraries Unlimited, 1980. 342 p.; 25 cm. (Library science text series) Includes index. 1. Reference books — Science. 2. Science — Bibliography 3. Reference books — Engineering. 4. Engineering — Bibliography. I. Richardson, Jeanne M., 1951- joint author. II. T.
Z7401.M28 1980 Q158.5     016.5 19     *LC* 80-21290     *ISBN* 0872872300

**Anglemyer, Mary, 1909-.**      **5.8420**
The natural environment: an annotated bibliography on attitudes and values / compiled by Mary Anglemyer and Eleanor R. Seagraves; sponsored by Global Tomorrow Coalition. — Washington, D.C.: Smithsonian Institution Press, 1984. 268 p.; 24 cm. Includes index. 1. Nature conservation — Moral and ethical aspects — Bibliography. 2. Environmental protection — Moral and ethical aspects — Bibliography. 3. Ecology — Moral and ethical aspects — Bibliography. 4. Human ecology — Moral and ethical aspects — Bibliography. 5. Bioethics — Bibliography. I. Seagraves, Eleanor R. II. Global Tomorrow Coalition. III. T.
Z7405.N38 A52 1984 QH75     016.3042 19     *LC* 83-600232     *ISBN* 087474220X

**Anglemyer, Mary, 1909-.**      **5.8421**
A search for environmental ethics: an initial bibliography / compiled by Mary Anglemyer, Eleanor R. Seagraves, Catherine C. LeMaistre; underthe auspices of Rachel Carson Council, inc.; with an introd. by S. Dillon Ripley. — Washington, D.C.: Smithsonian Institution Press, 1980. 119 p.; 24 cm. Includes index. 1. Nature conservation — Moral and religious aspects — Bibliography. 2. Environmental protection — Moral and religious aspects — Bibliography. 3. Ecology — Moral and religious aspects — Bibliography. 4. Human ecology — Moral and ethical aspects — Bibliography. 5. Bioethics — Bibliography. I. Seagraves, Eleanor R. joint author. II. LeMaistre, Catherine C. joint author. III. T.
Z7405.N38 A53 QH75     016.3042/8     *LC* 80-15026     *ISBN* 0874742129

**Dasbach, Joseph M.**      **5.8422**
Science for society: a bibliography / prepared by Joseph M. Dasbach for the Office of Science Education, American Association for the Advancement of Science. — 6th ed. — Washington: AAAS, c1976. x, 104 p.: ill.; 28 cm. (AAAS [miscellaneous] publication; 76-2) Fourth and 5th editions by F. E. West. 1. Science — Social aspects — Bibliography. 2. Technology — Social aspects — Bibliography. I. West, Felicia E. Science for society. II. American Association for the Advancement of Science. Office of Science Education. III. T.
Z7405.S6D3x Q181.A1A68 no. 76-2 Q158.5     508/.1 s 016.30124/3     *LC* 76-259     *ISBN* 0871682419

**Behrens, Heinrich.**      **5.8423**
Datensammlungen in der Physik = Data compilations in physics / H. Behrens, G. Ebel. — Eggenstein-Leopoldshafen: Zentralstelle für Atomkernenergie-Dokumentation, 1985. 623 p. in various pagings; 30 cm. (Physik Daten. 3-5) English or German. Includes indexes. 1. Physics — Tables — Bibliography. 2. Chemistry, Physical and theoretical — Tables — Bibliography. I. Ebel, Gerhard, joint author. II. T. III. Title: Data compilations in physics. IV. Series.
Z7405.T3 B44 QC61     016.53     *LC* 77-474415

## Z7511–7516 Sports. Recreation

**Gratch, Bonnie.**      **5.8424**
Sports and physical education: a guide to the reference resources / compiled by Bonnie Gratch, Betty Chan, and Judith Lingenfelter. — Westport, Conn.: Greenwood Press, 1983. xxi, 198 p.; 24 cm. Includes indexes. 1. Sports — Bibliography 2. Physical education and training — Bibliography. 3. Reference books — Sports — Bibliography. 4. Reference books — Physical education and training — Bibliography. I. Chan, Betty. II. Lingenfelter, Judith. III. T.
Z7511.G7 1983 GV704     016.796 19     *LC* 82-24159     *ISBN* 0313234337

**Sport bibliography = Bibliographie du sport / edited by I. Draayer ... [et al.].**      **5.8425**
Ottawa: Sport Information Resource Centre, 1981-. v. < 1, 3, 5-7 > : ill.; 28 cm. English or French. Includes index. 1. Sports — Bibliography — Collected works. I. Draayer, I. (Ingrid), 1950- II. Coaching Association of Canada. Sport Information Resource Centre. III. Title: Bibliographie du sport.
Z7511.S645 GV704     016.796 19     *LC* 81-123029     *ISBN* 0920678025

**Wilmeth, Don B.**      **5.8426**
American and English popular entertainment: a guide to information sources / Don B. Wilmeth; foreword by Brooks McNamara. — Detroit: Gale Research Co., c1980. xviii, 465 p.; 22 cm. (Performing arts information guide series; v. 7) (Gale performing arts information guide library) Includes indexes. 1. Amusements — United States — Bibliography. 2. Amusements — Great Britain — Bibliography. 3. Performing arts — United States — Bibliography. 4. Performing arts —

Great Britain — Bibliography. 5. Popular culture — United States — Bibliography. 6. Popular culture — Great Britain — Bibliography. I. T. Z7511.W53 GV1815　016.79　LC 79-22869　ISBN 0810314541

### Z7514.D2 Dancing

**Forbes, Fred R., 1949-.**　　　　　5.8427
Dance: an annotated bibliography, 1965–1982 / Fred R. Forbes, Jr. — New York: Garland Pub., 1986. xii, 261 p.; 23 cm. (Garland reference library of the humanities; vol. 606) Includes indexes. 1. Dancing — Bibliography. I. T. Z7514.D2 F58 1986 GV1594　016.7933/2 19　LC 85-45150　ISBN 0824086767

**Guide to dance periodicals.**　　　　　• 5.8428
v.1-10; 1931/35-1961/62. New York [etc.] Scarecrow Press [etc.] 10 v. Biennial. 'An analytic index of articles and illustrations.' Vols. 1-4 not published in correct sequence. 1. Dancing — Periodicals — Indexes. Z7514.D2 G8　LC 60-7273

**Magriel, Paul David, 1906-.**　　　　　• 5.8429
A bibliography of dancing; a list of books and articles on the dance and related subjects. — New York: B. Blom, [1966] 229 p.: illus.; 26 cm. Reprint of the 1936 edition. 1. Dancing — Bibliography. I. T. Z7514.D2 M2 1966　016.7933　LC 65-16242

### Z7515 Sports, By Country

**Davis, Lenwood G.**　　　　　5.8430
Black athletes in the United States: a bibliography of books, articles, autobiographies, and biographies on black professional athletes in the United States, 1800–1981 / compiled by Lenwood G. Davis and Belinda S. Daniels; foreword by James E. Newton. — Westport, Conn.: Greenwood, 1981. xxvi, 265 p.; 24 cm. Includes index. 1. Afro-American athletes — Bibliography. I. Daniels, Belinda S. II. T. Z7515.U5 D38 GV697.A1　016.796/08996073 19　LC 81-6334　ISBN 0313229767

### Z7551-7556 Statistics

**Statistics sources: a subject guide to data on industrial, business,**　5.8431
**social, educational, financial, and other topics for the United States and internationally / Managing editor: Paul Wasserman. Associate editor: Joanne Paskar.**
4th ed. — Detroit: Gale Research Co., 1974. -. 892 p.; 29 cm. — 1. Statistical services 2. Statistics — Bibliography. I. Wasserman, Paul. II. Paskar, Joanne. Z7551.S84 1974　016.31　LC 74-2163　ISBN 0810303965

**Harvey, Joan M.**　　　　　5.8432
Statistics America: sources for social, economic, and market research (North, Central, & South America) / Joan M. Harvey. — 2nd ed., rev. and enl. — Beckenham, Kent, England: CBD Research; Detroit, Mich.: Gale Research, 1980. xiii, 385 p.; 31 cm. Includes indexes. 1. America — Statistics — Bibliography. 2. America — Information services — Directories. I. T. Z7554.A5 H37 1980 HA175　016.317 19　LC 81-152451　ISBN 0900246332

**Balachandran, M.**　　　　　5.8433
Regional statistics: a guide to information sources / M. Balachandran. — Detroit, Mich.: Gale Research Co., c1980. x, 257 p.; 22 cm. — (Economics information guide series; v. 13) (Gale information guide library) Includes indexes. 1. United States — Statistics — Bibliography. I. T. Z7554.U5 B34 HA217　016.3173　LC 80-14260　ISBN 0810314630

### Z7615 Suicide

**McIntosh, John L.**　　　　　5.8434
Research on suicide: a bibliography / compiled by John L. McIntosh. — Westport, Conn.: Greenwood Press, c1985. xiii, 323 p.; 25 cm. (Bibliographies and indexes in psychology. 1742-681X; no. 2) Includes index. 1. Suicide — Bibliography. 2. Suicide — United States — Bibliography. I. T. II. Series. Z7615.M38 1985 HV6545　016.3622 19　LC 84-15706　ISBN 0313239924

**Prentice, Ann E.**　　　　　5.8435
Suicide: a selective bibliography of over 2,200 items, by Ann E. Prentice. — Metuchen, N.J.: Scarecrow Press, 1974. vi, 227 p.; 22 cm. 1. Suicide — Bibliography. I. T. Z7615.P73　016.6168/5844　LC 74-19231　ISBN 0810807734

### Z7711 Television

**Cassata, Mary B., 1930-.**　　　　　5.8436
Television, a guide to the literature / by Mary Cassata and Thomas Skill. — Phoenix, Ariz.: Oryx Press, 1985. vii, 148 p.; 24 cm. Includes bibliographies and indexes. 1. Television broadcasting — Bibliography I. Skill, Thomas. II. T. Z7711.C37 1985 PN1992.5　016.38455 19　LC 83-43236　ISBN 0897741404

### Z7721 Temperance. Alcoholism

**Heath, Dwight B.**　　　　　5.8437
Alcohol use and world cultures: a comprehensive bibliography of anthropological sources / Dwight B. Heath and A.M. Cooper. — Toronto, Ont., Canada: Addiction Research Foundation, c1981. xv, 248 p.; 23 cm. — (Bibliographic series / Addiction Research Foundation, 0065-1885; no. 15) Includes indexes. 1. Alcoholism — Bibliography. 2. Drinking customs — Bibliography. I. Cooper, A. M. II. T. Z7721.H4 1981 HV5035　016.3941/3 19　LC 81-130279　ISBN 0888680457

**Milgram, Gail Gleason.**　　　　　5.8438
Alcohol education materials: an annotated bibliography / by Gail Gleason Milgram. — New Brunswick, N.J.: Publications Division, Rutgers Center of Alcohol Studies, c1975. viii, 304 p.; 22 cm. Based on a survey conducted by the Rutgers Center of Alcohol Studies. Includes indexes. 1. Alcoholism — Study and teaching — Bibliography. I. Rutgers Center of Alcohol Studies. II. T. Z7721.M54 HV5060　016.3622/92　LC 74-620158　ISBN 0911290443

### Z7751-7856 Theology. Religion

**Karpinski, Leszek M.**　　　　　5.8439
The religious life of man: guide to basic literature / compiled by Leszek M. Karpinski. — Metuchen, N.J.: Scarecrow Press, 1978. xx, 399 p.; 23 cm. Includes indexes. 1. Religion — Bibliography. I. T. Z7751.K36 BL41　016.2　LC 77-19338　ISBN 0810811103

**Thompson, Laurence G.**　　　　　5.8440
Chinese religion in Western languages: a comprehensive and classified bibliography of publications in English, French, and German through 1980 / Laurence G. Thompson. — Tucson, Ariz.: Published for the Association for Asian Studies by the University of Arizona Press, 1985, c1984. xlix, 302 p.; 27 cm. (Monographs of the Association or Asian Studies; 41) Updated ed. of: Studies of Chinese religion. c1976. Includes index. 1. China — Religion — Bibliography. I. Thompson, Laurence G. Studies of Chinese religion. II. T. Z7757.C6 T55 1985 BL1802　016.2/00951 19　LC 84-24010　ISBN 0816509263

**Yu, David C.**　　　　　5.8441
Guide to Chinese religion / David C. Yu with contributions by Laurence G. Thompson. — Boston, Mass.: G.K. Hall, c1985. xxviii, 200 p.; 25 cm. (Asian philosophies and religions resource guides.) Includes indexes. 1. China — Religion — Bibliography. I. Thompson, Laurence G. II. T. III. Series. Z7757.C6 Y8 1985 BL1802　016.299/51 19　LC 85-932　ISBN 0816179026

**Sandeen, Ernest Robert, 1931-.**　　　　　5.8442
American religion and philosophy: a guide to information sources / Ernest R. Sandeen, Frederick Hale. — Detroit: Gale Research Co., 1978. xiv, 377 p.; 23 cm. — (Gale information guide library. American studies information guide series. v. 5) Includes indexes. 1. Christianity — United States — Bibliography. 2. Philosophy, American — Bibliography. 3. United States — Religion — Bibliography. I. Hale, Frederick. joint author. II. T. III. Series. Z7757.U5 S25 BR515　016.2/00973　LC 73-17562　ISBN 081031262X

**Brown, Marshall G., 1906-.**　　　　　5.8443
Freethought in the United States: a descriptive bibliography / Marshall G. Brown and Gordon Stein. — Westport, Conn.: Greenwood Press, 1978. xi, 146 p.; 24 cm. Includes indexes. 1. Free thought — United States — Bibliography. 2. United States — Religion — Bibliography. I. Stein, Gordon. joint author. II. T. Z7765.B67 BL2710　016.211/4/0973　LC 77-91103　ISBN 031320036X

**Gorman, G. E.**　　　　　5.8444
Theological and religious reference materials: general resources and biblical studies / G.E. Gorman and Lyn Gorman; with the assistance of Donald N. Matthews and an introductory chapter by John B. Trotti. — Westport, Conn.: Greenwood Press, c1984. xvi, 526 p.; 25 cm. — (Bibliographies and indexes in

religious studies. 0742-6836; no. 1) Includes indexes. 1. Bible — Bibliography 2. Theology — Bibliography I. Gorman, Lyn. II. T. III. Series.
Z7770.G66 1984 BS511.2　　BS511.2.G67 1984.　　016.2 19　　*LC*
83-22759　　*ISBN* 0313209243

**Gottcent, John H.**　　　　　　　　　　　　　　　　　　　　　**5.8445**
The Bible as literature: a selective bibliography / John H. Gottcent. — Boston: Hall, c1979. xvii, 170 p.; 25 cm. — (Reference publication in literature.) Includes index. 1. Bible as literature — Bibliography. I. T. II. Series.
Z7770.G68 BS535　　016.2206　　*LC* 79-17450　　*ISBN* 0816181217

**Bowman, Mary Ann.**　　　　　　　　　　　　　　　　　　　　**5.8446**
Western mysticism: a guide to the basic works / compiled by Mary Ann Bowman. — Chicago, Ill.: American Library Association, c1978. vi, 113 p.; 23 cm. Includes indexes. 1. Mysticism — Bibliography. I. T.
Z7819.B68 BL625　　016.2914/2　　*LC* 78-18311　　*ISBN* 0838902669

**Bainton, Roland Herbert, 1894-.**　　　　　　　　　　　　　　**5.8447**
Bibliography of the continental reformation: materials available in English, by Roland H. Bainton and Eric W. Gritsch. — 2d ed., rev. and enl. — [Hamden, Conn.]: Archon Books, 1972. xix, 220 p.; 23 cm. 1. Reformation — Bibliography. I. Gritsch, Eric W. joint author. II. T.
Z7830.B16 1972　　016.2706　　*LC* 72-8216　　*ISBN* 0208012190

**Religion and society in North America: an annotated**　　　　　**5.8448**
**bibliography / Robert deV. Brunkow, editor.**
Santa Barbara, Calif.: ABC-Clio Information Services, c1983. xi, 515 p.; 29 cm. — (Clio bibliography series. no. 12) Includes indexes. 1. Religion and sociology — Periodicals — Indexes. 2. North America — Religion — Periodicals — Indexes. I. Brunkow, Robert deV., 1947- II. Series.
Z7831.R44 1983 BL60　　016.2/00973 19　　*LC* 82-24304　　*ISBN* 0874360420

**Adams, Charles J. ed.**　　　　　　　　　　　　　　　　　　**5.8449**
A reader's guide to the great religions / edited by Charles J. Adams. 2d ed. — New York: Free Press, c1977. xvii, 521 p.; 24 cm. Includes indexes. 1. Religions — Bibliography. I. T.
Z7833.A35 1977 BL80.2　　016.2　　*LC* 76-10496　　*ISBN* 0029002400

**Dell, David J.**　　　　　　　　　　　　　　　　　　　　　　**5.8450**
Guide to Hindu religion / David J. Dell ... [et al.]; with contributions from Bruce J. Stewart ... [et al.]. — Boston: G.K. Hall, c1981. xxvi, 461 p.; 25 cm. — (Asian philosophies and religions resource guides.) Includes index. 1. Hinduism — Bibliography. I. T. II. Series.
Z7835.B8 D44 BL1202　　016.2945　　*LC* 79-18784　　*ISBN* 0816179034

**Holland, Barron.**　　　　　　　　　　　　　　　　　　　　**5.8451**
Popular Hinduism and Hindu mythology: an annotated bibliography / compiled by Barron Holland. — Westport, Conn.: Greenwood Press, 1979. xxiv, 394 p.; 25 cm. 1. Hinduism — Bibliography. I. T.
Z7835.B8 H64 BL1202　　016.2945　　*LC* 79-7188　　*ISBN* 0313213585

**University of London. School of Oriental and African Studies.**　• **5.8452**
**Library.**
Index Islamicus, 1906–1955: a catalogue of articles on Islamic subjects in periodicals and other collective publications / compiled by J. D. Pearson, Librarian; with the assistance of Julia F. Ashton. — Cambridge, Eng.: W. Heffer, 1958. xxxvi, 897 p.; 26 cm. 1. Islam — Bibliography. 2. Civilization, Islamic — Bibliography. 3. Middle East — Bibliography. 4. Africa, North — Bibliography. I. Pearson, J. D. (James Douglas), 1911- II. Ashton, Julia F. III. T.
Z7835.M5 L6　　016.9156　　*LC* 59-23014

**Guide to Islam / David Ede ... [et al.].**　　　　　　　　　　**5.8453**
Boston, Mass.: G.K. Hall, c1983. xxiv, 261 p.; 29 cm. Includes indexes. 1. Islam — Bibliography. 2. Civilization, Islamic — Bibliography. I. Ede, David.
Z7835.M6 G84 1983 BP161.2　　016.909/097671 19　　*LC* 83-6134　　*ISBN* 0816179050

**Reynolds, Frank, 1930-.**　　　　　　　　　　　　　　　　　**5.8454**
Guide to Buddhist religion / Frank E. Reynolds, with John Holt and John Strong; arts section by Bardwell Smith, with Holly Waldo and Jonathan Clyde Glass. — Boston: Hall, c1981. xxv, 415 p.; 28 cm. (Asian philosophies and religions resource guides.) 1. Buddhism — Bibliography. I. Holt, John, 1948- joint author. II. Strong, John, 1948- joint author. III. T. IV. Series.
Z7860.R48 BQ4012　　016.2943　　*LC* 79-26809　　*ISBN* 081617900X

## Z7911–7916 Technology

**Applied science & technology index.**　　　　　　　　　　　• **5.8455**
v. 1- Feb. 1913-. New York [etc.] H. W. Wilson [etc.] v. 26 cm. Monthly. 1958- volume numbering does not appear on annual cumulations. 1. Engineering —

Periodicals — Indexes 2. Technology — Periodicals — Indexes. 3. Industrial arts — Periodicals — Indexes. I. H.W. Wilson Company.
Z7913.I7　　016.6　　*LC* 14-5408

**Multhauf, Robert P.**　　　　　　　　　　　　　　　　　　　**5.8456**
The history of chemical technology: an annotated bibliography / Robert P. Multhauf. — New York: Garland Pub., 1984. xviii, 299 p., [9] leaves of plates: ill.; 23 cm. — (Bibliographies of the history of science and technology. v. 5) (Garland reference library of the humanities. v. 348) Includes indexes. 1. Chemistry, Technical — History — Bibliography. I. T. II. Series. III. Series: Garland reference library of the humanities. v. 348
Z7914.C4 M84 1984 TP15　　016.66/09 19　　*LC* 82-48272　　*ISBN* 0824092554

**Ferguson, Eugene S.**　　　　　　　　　　　　　　　　　　• **5.8457**
Bibliography of the history of technology [by] Eugene S. Ferguson. — Cambridge, Mass.: Society for the History of Technology, [1968] xx, 347 p.; 24 cm. — (Society for the History of Technology. Monograph series, v. 5) 1. Technology — History — Bibliography. I. T. II. Series.
Z7914.H5 F4　　016.609　　*LC* 68-21559

## Z7961–7965 Women

### Z7961 General Works. History. Bibliographies

**Ballou, Patricia K.**　　　　　　　　　　　　　　　　　　　**5.8458**
Women, a bibliography of bibliographies / Patricia K. Ballou. — Boston, Mass.: G.K. Hall, c1980. xiii, 155 p.; 24 cm. — (Reference publication in women's studies.) Includes index. 1. Bibliography — Bibliography — Women. 2. Women — Bibliography. I. T. II. Series.
Z7961.A1 B34 HQ1121　　016.0163054 19　　*LC* 80-21042　　*ISBN* 0816182922

**Ritchie, Maureen.**　　　　　　　　　　　　　　　　　　　　**5.8459**
Women's studies: a checklist of bibliographies / compiled by Maureen Ritchie. — London: Mansell, 1980. xv, 107 p.; 23 cm. Includes indexes. 1. Bibliography — Bibliography — Women. 2. Women — Bibliography. I. T.
Z7961.A1 R57 HQ1121　　016.0163054 19　　*LC* 80-492457　　*ISBN* 0720109183

**Williamson, Jane, 1950-.**　　　　　　　　　　　　　　　　　**5.8460**
New feminist scholarship: a guide to bibliographies / by Jane Williamson. — Old Westbury, N.Y.: Feminist Press, c1979. 139 p.; 24 cm. Includes indexes. 1. Women's studies — United States — Bibliography. 2. Feminism — United States — Bibliography. 3. Reference books — Women. 4. Women's studies — Canada — Bibliography. 5. Feminism — Canada — Bibliography. I. T.
Z7961.A1 W54 1979 HQ1180　　016.30141/2/0973　　*LC* 79-11889　　*ISBN* 0912670541

**Jacobs, Sue-Ellen.**　　　　　　　　　　　　　　　　　　　**5.8461**
Women in perspective; a guide for cross–cultural studies. — Urbana: University of Illinois Press, [1974] xvi, 299 p.; 23 cm. 1. Women — Bibliography. I. T.
Z7961.J33　　016.30141/2　　*LC* 72-93987　　*ISBN* 0252002997

**Krichmar, Albert.**　　　　　　　　　　　　　　　　　　　　**5.8462**
The women's movement in the seventies: an international English–language bibliography / by Albert Krichmar, assisted by Virginia Carlson Smith and Ann E. Wiederrecht. — Metuchen, N.J.: Scarecrow Press, 1977. xvi, 875 p.; 22 cm. Includes indexes. 1. Feminism — Bibliography 2. Women — Social conditions — Bibliography. I. Smith, Virginia Carlson, joint author. II. Wiederrecht, Ann E., joint author. III. T.
Z7961.K74 HQ1154　　016.30141/2　　*LC* 77-21416　　*ISBN* 0810810638

**Searing, Susan E.**　　　　　　　　　　　　　　　　　　　　**5.8463**
Introduction to library research in women's studies / Susan E. Searing. — Boulder: Westview Press, 1985. xiii, 257 p.; 23 cm. (Westview guides to library research.) Includes indexes. 1. Reference books — Women — Bibliography. 2. Women — Bibliography. 3. Women — Research — Methodology. 4. Women's studies — Bibliography. I. T. II. Series.
Z7961.S42 1985 HQ1206　　016.3054 19　　*LC* 85-3162　　*ISBN* 0865312672

**Stineman, Esther, 1947-.**　　　　　　　　　　　　　　　　　**5.8464**
Women's studies: a recommended core bibliography / Esther Stineman, with the assistance of Catherine Loeb. — Littleton, Colo.: Libraries Unlimited, 1979. 670 p.; 24 cm. Includes indexes. 1. Women — Bibliography. 2. Women's studies — Bibliography. I. Loeb, Catherine. II. T.
Z7961.S75 HQ1180　　016.30141/2　　*LC* 79-13679　　*ISBN* 0872871967

**Wiesner, Merry E.**　　　　　　　　　　　　　　　　　　　　**5.8465**
Women in the sixteenth century: a bibliography / Merry E. Wiesner. — Saint Louis: Center for Reformation Research, 1983. — iii, 65 p.; 22 cm. —

(Sixteenth century bibliography. 23) 1. Women — History — Renaissance, 1450-1600 — Bibliography 2. Reformation — Bibliography. I. T. II. Series. Z7961 W5

## Z7963 Special Topics, A–Z

**First person female American: a selected and annotated**     **5.8466**
**bibliography of the autobiographies of American women living**
**after 1950** / Carolyn H. Rhodes, editor [and] Mary Louise
**Briscoe and Ernest L. Rhodes, associate editors.**
Troy, N.Y.: Whitston Publishing, 1980. xlix, 404 p. — (American notes and queries supplement (Whitston Publishing); v. 2) 1. Women — Bio-bibliography 2. Women — United States — Bibliography I. Rhodes, Carolyn H. II. Rhodes, Ernest L. III. Briscoe, Mary Louise. IV. Series.
Z7963B6 F57

**Kennedy, Susan Estabrook.**     **5.8467**
America's white working–class women: a historical bibliography / Susan Estabrook Kennedy. — New York: Garland Pub., 1981. xxv, 253 p.; 23 cm. — (Garland reference library of the humanities. v. 260) (Women's studies; v. 2) Includes indexes. 1. Working class women — United States — History — Bibliography. I. T. II. Series.
Z7963.E7 K45 1981     016.3055/6 19     *LC* 80-8593     *ISBN* 0824094549

**Leavitt, Judith A.**     **5.8468**
Women in management: an annotated bibliography and sourcelist / compiled by Judith A. Leavitt. — Phoenix, AZ: Oryx Press, 1982. xvi, 197 p.; 24 cm. Updated ed. of: Women in management, 1970-1979. 1980. Includes index. 1. Women executives — United States — Bibliography. I. T.
Z7963.E7 L43 1982 HF5500.3.U54     016.658/0088042 19     *LC* 82-2190
*ISBN* 0897740262

**McCaghy, M. Dawn.**     **5.8469**
Sexual harassment: a guide to resources / M. Dawn McCaghy. — Boston, Mass.: G.K. Hall, c1985. xvi, 181 p.; 25 cm. (G.K. Hall women's studies publications) Includes indexes. 1. Sexual harassment of women — United States — Bibliography. 2. Sexual harassment of women — Bibliography. I. T. II. Series.
Z7963.E7 M427 1985 HD6060.3     016.3054/2 19     *LC* 84-25148
*ISBN* 0816186693

**McFeely, Mary Drake.**     **5.8470**
Women's work in Britain and America: from the nineties to World War I: an annotated bibliography / Mary Drake McFeely. — Boston, Mass.: G.K. Hall, c1982. xxv, 140 p.; 25 cm. — (Reference publication in women's studies.) Includes indexes. 1. Women — Employment — Great Britain — Bibliography. 2. Women — Employment — United States — Bibliography. 3. Women volunteers in social service — Great Britain — Bibliography. 4. Women volunteers in social service — United States — Bibliography. I. T. II. Series.
Z7963.E7 M43 1982 HD6135     016.3314/0941 19     *LC* 82-9281
*ISBN* 0816185042

**Soltow, Martha Jane.**     **5.8471**
American women and the labor movement, 1825–1974: an annotated bibliography / by Martha Jane Soltow and Mary K. Wery. [2d ed.]. — Metuchen, N.J.: Scarecrow Press, 1976. viii, 247 p.; 22 cm. Includes indexes. 1. Women in trade-unions — United States — Bibliography. 2. Women — Employment — United States — Bibliography. I. Wery, Mary K., joint author. II. T.
Z7963.E7 S635 1976 HD6079.2.U5     016.3314/0973     *LC* 76-40169
*ISBN* 0810809869

## Z7964–7965 Special Topics, by Region

**Buhle, Mari Jo, 1943-.**     **5.8472**
Women and the American left: a guide to sources / Mari Jo Buhle. — Boston, Mass.: G.K. Hall, c1983. xii, 281 p.; 25 cm. (G.K. Hall women's studies publications) Includes index. 1. Feminism — United States — Bibliography. 2. Right and left (Political science) — Bibliography. 3. Radicalism — United States — Bibliography. I. T. II. Series.
Z7964.U49 B84 1983 HQ1420     016.3054/2/0973 19     *LC* 83-6158
*ISBN* 0816181950

**Krichmar, Albert.**     **5.8473**
The women's rights movement in the United States, 1848–1970; a bibliography and sourcebook, by Albert Krichmar, assisted by Barbara Case, Barbara Silver [and] Ann E. Wiederrecht. — Metuchen, N.J.: Scarecrow Press, 1972. ix, 436 p.; 22 cm. 1. Women's rights — United States — Bibliography. 2. Women's rights — United States — History — Sources. I. T.
Z7964.U49 K75     016.30141/2/0973     *LC* 72-4702     *ISBN* 0810805286

**Nelson, Barbara J., 1949-.**     **5.8474**
American women and politics: a selected bibliography and resource guide / Barbara J. Nelson. — New York: Garland Pub., 1984. xii, 255 p.; 23 cm. — (Garland reference library of social science; vol. 174) Includes indexes. 1. Women in politics — United States — Bibliography. I. T.
Z7964.U49 N38 1984 HQ1236     016.3054/2 19     *LC* 82-49142
*ISBN* 0824091396

**Sahli, Nancy Ann.**     **5.8475**
Women and sexuality in America: a bibliography / Nancy Sahli. — Boston, Mass.: G.K. Hall, 1984. xv, 404 p.; 25 cm. (G.K. Hall women's studies publications) Includes indexes. 1. Women — United States — Sexual behavior — Bibliography. 2. Women — United States — Sexual behavior — History — Bibliography. I. T. II. Series.
Z7964.U49 S26 1984 HQ29     016.3067/088042 19     *LC* 84-10751
*ISBN* 0816180997

**Schlachter, Gail A.**     **5.8476**
Minorities and women: a guide to reference literature in the social sciences / by Gail Ann Schlachter, with Donna Belli. — 1st ed. — Los Angeles: Reference Service Press, c1977. viii, 349 p.; 24 cm. Includes indexes. 1. Women — United States — Bibliography. 2. Minorities — United States — Bibliography. 3. Reference books — Women. 4. Reference books — Minorities. I. Belli, Donna, joint author. II. T.
Z7964.U49 S34 HQ1410     016.30145/1/0973     *LC* 76-53061     *ISBN* 0918276012

**Women's history sources: a guide to archives and manuscript**     **5.8477**
**collections in the United States** / edited by Andrea Hinding,
**Ames Sheldon Bower, associate editor, Clark A. Chambers,**
**consulting editor; in association with the University of**
**Minnesota.**
New York: Bowker, 1979. 2 v.; 29 cm. Vol. 2 edited by Suzanna Moody. 1. Women — United States — History — Archival resources — United States. I. Hinding, Andrea. II. Bower, Ames S.
Z7964.U49 W64 HQ1410     016.30141/2/0973     *LC* 78-15634     *ISBN* 0835211037

**Hady, Maureen E., 1952-.**     **5.8478**
Women's periodicals and newspapers from the 18th century to 1981: a union list of the holdings of Madison, Wisconsin, libraries / edited by James P. Danky; compiled by Maureen E. Hady, Barry Christopher Noonan, Neil E. Strache; in association with the State Historical Society of Wisconsin. — Boston: G.K. Hall, c1982. xxiv, 376 p.; ill.; 28 cm. — (Reference publication in women's studies.) Includes indexes. 1. Feminism — Periodicals — Bibliography — Union lists. I. Noonan, Barry Christopher. II. Strache, Neil E., 1951- III. Danky, James Philip, 1947- IV. State Historical Society of Wisconsin. V. T. VI. Series.
Z7965.H3 1982 HQ1180     016.3054/05 19     *LC* 82-11903     *ISBN* 0816181071

**McKee, Kathleen Burke.**     **5.8479**
Women's studies: a guide to reference sources / Kathleen Burke McKee; with the assistance of B. McIlvaine; with a supplement on feminist serials in the University of Connecticut Library's Alternative Press collection, by Joanne V. Akeroyd. — Storrs: University of Connecticut Library, Storrs, c1977. 112 p.; 23 cm. — (Bibliography series; no. 6) Includes indexes. 1. University of Connecticut. Library. 2. Women's studies — Bibliography — Catalogs. I. McIlvaine, B., joint author. II. Akeroyd, Joanne V. III. T.
Z7965.M33 HQ1181.U5     016.30141/2     *LC* 77-1747     *ISBN* 0917590015

## Z7991–7999 Zoology

**Animal identification: a reference guide** / edited by R.W. Sims.     **5.8480**
London: British Museum (Natural History); Chichester [Eng.]; New York: Wiley, 1980. 3 v.; 26 cm. Vol. 3: Edited by D. Hollis. Includes index. 1. Animals — Identification — Bibliography. I. Sims, R. W. (Reginald William), 1926- II. Hollis, David.
Z7994.I34 A54 QL351     016.591     *LC* 80-40006

**Munz, Lucile Thompson.**     **5.8481**
Index to illustrations of living things outside North America: where to find pictures of flora and fauna / Lucile Thompson Munz and Nedra G. Slauson. — Hamden, Conn.: Archon Books, 1981. 441 p.; 29 cm. 'A companion volume to John W. Thompson's Index to illustrations of the natural world (North America).' Includes index. 1. Zoology — Pictorial works — Indexes. 2. Botany — Pictorial works — Indexes. 3. Zoology — Indexes. 4. Botany — Indexes. I. Slauson, Nedra G. II. Thompson, John W., 1891- Index to illustrations of the natural world. III. T.
Z7998.N67 M85 QL46     016.574022/2 19     *LC* 81-8037     *ISBN* 0208018573

**Thompson, John W., 1891-.**     **5.8482**
Index to illustrations of the natural world: where to find pictures of the living things of North America / compiled by John W. Thompson; edited by Nedra

Slauson. — Syracuse, N.Y.: Gaylord Professional Publications, 1977. 265 p.; 29 cm. 1. Zoology — North America — Pictorial works — Indexes. 2. Botany — North America — Pictorial works — Indexes. 3. Zoology — North America — Indexes. 4. Botany — North America — Indexes. I. T. Z7998.N67 T45 QL151     016.57497/022/2     *LC* 77-4143     *ISBN* 0915794128